Nelson's

KidsBible.com™

This Bible Belongs to:

Elise Curit

Given By:

and ADERS

Date and Occasion:

JULY 11th 2004

LEA Present

http://www.KidsBible.com

Nelson's

KidsBible.com

The complete Bible for Today's e-kid!

with Skweek & Tagg

The Holy Bible

New Century Version

Thomas Nelson Publishers
Nashville

NELSON'S KIDSBIBLE.COM™

The preliminary research and development of the *New Century Version* was done by the World Bible Translation Center, Inc., Fort Worth, TX 76182.

Printed in the United States of America
2 3 4 5 6 7 — 06 05 04 03 02

CONTENTS

Old Testament

New Testament

CONTRIBUTORS

Our prayer is that Nelson's KidsBible.com *will launch your child on a life-long journey with God's Word.*

General Editor:
Betsy Todt Schmitt

Design & Editorial Team:
Bruce B. Barton, Christopher D. Hudson, Katie E. Gieser, David R. Veerman

Creative Development:
Vicki Wiley

Contributors:

Tim Baker, Reverend Eric Titus,	New Testament introductions
Jeanette Dall,	Livin' It pages
Katie E. Gieser,	Email from God
Carol Ochs,	Editing
Margaret Reneker, Reverend Eric Titus,	Old Testament introductions
Carol Smith,	Get the Info features
Randy Southern,	Faith Challenges and Connect 2-You features
Ashley Taylor,	Editorial assistance
Linda Washington,	Faithlinks, FAQs homepages, editorial assistance
Joan Woodhead,	Editorial assistance

Composition Team:
Kathleen Ristow, Thomas Ristow, Sarah Hanna

Proofing of Bible text and textual notes:
Peachtree Editorial & Proofreading Service

Cover Design:
Anderson Thomas Design, Inc.

Interior Design:
Mozdren and Associates

KidsBible.com™ Homepage

Welcome!

Hey, newbie, welcome to *KidsBible.com*, the Bible you can surf! We are going to have a totally awesome time together downloading all sorts of cool information that you can find in the Bible. So let's boot up and start surfing!

Whoa! Hold on a minute, Tagg, not so fast! First, before we begin we've got to introduce ourselves to our friend and explain a few things about *KidsBible.com*. And stop with all the computer lingo for a bit—we need to clear up a few things before we begin. Let's try this again.

Welcome to *KidsBible.com*. My name is Skweek, and together with my pal Tagg, we will be your hosts to the Bible. Together we'll guide you through *KidsBible.com* and help you connect to God's Word. Just look for us as you read the Bible. You'll find us just about everywhere in its pages.

Sorry about that, Skweek. I guess I got a little ahead of myself. I'm just so excited about taking our friend on through *KidsBible.com*! I can't wait to get started.

That's OK, Tagg. The Bible is exciting, and you did bring up an important feature of *KidsBible.com*. It *is* the one Bible you can surf. That means you can skip from page to page in *KidsBible.com* by following links, or connections, of related Bible verses, topics, or information. You can read as much or as little as you want about any topic just by connecting to the various links. But there are more connections to *KidsBible.com* that you can surf to, Tagg! Turn the page and I'll tell you about it.

Surfing www.kidsbible.com

You know, Skweek, the idea behind this Bible is so cool. I really feel like I'm surfing the 'net when I'm reading *KidsBible.com*. Too bad it's not really a website on the Internet.

Well, I've got a flash for you. *KidsBible.com* does have its own website on the real Internet. Kids can log on to *www.kidsbible.com* and discover a whole new way to interact with their Bible.

Wow! That is totally awesome. What exactly can they do at *www.kidsbible.com*?

Lots! There will be fun, interactive online games that match the personalities featured in *KidsBible.com*. There will be an opportunity for kids to post on the website what they have been writing in the Bible—stuff like what they did to take a faith challenge or what are some of their favorite verses. There will also be a place to collect email from yours truly, Skweek and Tagg, and a place to get a daily reading plan for the Bible, and lots more!

Kids are going to love that! Will we be there, also?

Didn't I tell you? We're the hosts, of course. Just like we help guide our friends through the Bible, we'll be on the website to lead and direct. As a matter of fact, there are a few safety rules for using the Internet that our friend should know. Before going on the Internet, our friend and a parent should read these rules together. Take a look:

- Make an agreement with your parent(s) about your own rules for using the Internet. Decide beforehand how much time you can spend on the Internet, when you can be on the Internet, and what sites have parental approval.
- Keep your last name private. If a website wants to know your last name for whatever reason, ask a parent first before giving it out.
- Keep your email address private. If possible, keep two email accounts—one that is private and is available only to family and friends and another that you use to register as a user at a web page.
- Never download a program without the permission of your parent(s).
- If you are visiting a website that has a chat room—a place where you can use your computer to "chat," or talk, to others who are connected to that same website—make sure you check with your parent(s) first.

Happy surfing, and see you at www.KidsBible.com!

That is so cool, Skweek! You can surf both *www.kidsbible.com*, the website, and *KidsBible.com*, the Bible. As Skweek mentioned before, you can surf from link to link simply by opening your Bible to any site, or Bible feature, in *KidsBible.com*. There are a number of ways for you to start surfing. Here are a few suggestions:

- The easiest place to begin is with the Table of Contents on page iii. You'll find a listing of every book in the Bible. Connect to any book of the Bible, and you'll discover the Bible book splash page. Read on!
- Log on to any Bible book splash page. That's the introduction to each book of the Bible. On the splash pages, you'll find a listing of all the different connections in each book, like cool stories to download and read, and other information sites to check out. There's also a summary of the book (what it's about) and a Jesus Watch. (That explains how God's promise for a Savior—his Son, Jesus—is mentioned in each book of the Bible.)
- Connect to a Livin' It page. These 50 sites are scattered throughout the Bible. Each one talks about a different topic that is important to you—like how to get along in your family, making new friends, or how to handle your money. By logging on to these sites, you can find out what the Bible has to say about each topic. There are more hyperlinks (related connections) called Faithlinks to help you learn more about this topic. You'll find the Livin' It pages listed according to topics in the Search Engine. (Keep going!)
- Or start with the Search Engine. You'll find the Search Engine in the back of the Bible. It has a complete listing of every site you can connect to in *KidsBible.com* according to topics. Maybe you want to learn more about following God. Check out the listings under the heading *Following God* and connect to the links that sound most interesting to you. Or maybe a friend has done something to hurt you and you want to know how to forgive them. Check out the listings under *Forgiving Others* for some straight advice right from God's Word.

Great job, Tagg. That will help our friend get started. But that's not all *KidsBible.com* has to offer. Check out these other "hotspots" that you can connect to and download all sorts of information:

Faithlinks

- There are 500 Faithlinks in *KidsBible.com*. These links discuss important faith issues, such as obeying God and your parents, learning how to be patient, how to deal with the tough times, and how to use your abilities to help others. Each Faithlink has five or six additional links listed so you can surf to as many related links as you want. Check out each Bible book splash page or the Search Engine for a listing of Faithlinks.

Get the Info

- This is the *KidsBible.com* info BBS—or bulletin board system. There are 75 different info bulletin boards where you can download facts about people in the Bible, like Moses or David; or places in the Bible, like Jerusalem or Bethlehem; or fascinating "did you know" stuff, like about King Hezekiah's amazing water tunnel or why the Israelites cast lots to make decisions. You'll find a complete listing in the Get the Info Index on page xvii.

Faith Challenges

- How are you growing in your faith? Connect to any of these 50 challenges from the Bible and put your faith to the test! There's even a place for you to write down what you learned—but more about writing in your Bible a bit later! You'll find the Faith Challenges listed in the Search Engine.

Email from God

- Everyone loves to get mail, right, Tagg? And there are a lot of important messages that God has for you in the Bible. Just look for the little envelope icon to check out what God has to say about certain topics, like Angels, Leadership, or Music. You can find an entire listing of the 500 Email from God entries in the In-Box List on page xix. Every time you "receive" an email, you can check it off in the In-Box List.

Connect 2-You

- Got a question about if it's OK to tell a little white lie, or what to do when you're feeling lonely? Then link up with Tagg and me as we talk about these kinds of issues with our online friends. You'll hear about what other kids your age are struggling with and get some suggestions for other sites to connect to for more help. Look up the Connect 2-You sites in the Search Engine.

The FAQ Homepages

- Throughout *KidsBible.com*, you'll find 16 colorful pages called FAQ homepages, which feature **F**aith **A**ction **Q**uestions about eight men and women of the Bible: Abraham, Moses, Deborah, David, Esther, Mary, Jesus, and Paul. Each of these people faced a specific faith challenge. Maybe it was being obedient to God (Abraham), or learning to handle temptations (Jesus). Connect to these sites and download how you can learn from their experiences to deal with your own faith challenges. Then if you'd like to spend more time with these faith heroes, visit www.kidsbible.com!

You know, Skweek, with all these cool connections, you can have a completely different "surfing" experience every time you open *KidsBible.com*.

Good point, Tagg. Our friend doesn't have to surf the same places over and over again. But just in case our friend wants to remember some of the cool sites to visit, we've got a place to "bookmark" those sites. Turn the page!

Favorite Places

http://www.KidsBible.com

Here it is! Your very own homepage! This is your chance to make *KidsBible.com* uniquely you! Take some time now to fill out some information. Then come back to your homepage whenever you want to write down your thoughts, discoveries, and whatever is important to you as you read the Bible.

My Personal Stuff

When I got *KidsBible.com* ______________________

Why I got this Bible ______________________

Who gave it to me ______________________

Questions I have about God, the Bible, faith, etc.

1.

2.

3.

4.

5.

6.

Hey, I've got a question! Why did God make armadillos?

Hey, this isn't your homepage!

Oops! I Forgot!

@ ________________'s dot.com!

(your name)

http://www.KidsBible.com

My Favorite Faithlinks

1.
2.
3.

My Favorite Livin' It Sites

1.
2.
3.

My Favorite Bible Books

1.
2.
3.

My Favorite Bible Heroes

1.
2.
3.

My Favorite Bible Verses

1.
2.
3.

Other Stuff to Think About...

1.
2.
3.

Wow, Skweek, you can find all that great stuff in one Bible?! Now I'm even more excited about getting into *KidsBible.com* and doing some major surfing. You might even say I'm a little "hyper"-linked! Get it? Just a little computer joke for you newbies!

Calm down, Tagg! There are a few more things our friend needs to know about *KidsBible.com*. And one is all that computer-speak you like to use so much! Our friend here may not know exactly what a hyperlink is or what you mean by a newbie. (By the way, a newbie is someone new to a website.)

Yikes! I never thought about that. What do you think we should do?

Not to worry, Tagg; it's already taken care of. All our friend has to do is surf over to p. xiii to take a look at The FACTs in Nelson's *KidsBible.com*. It's a glossary for all the computer terms a person may find in this Bible. And there's one more cool thing we need to tell any newbie to *KidsBible.com*.

Great! What's that?

You may have noticed that *KidsBible.com* has lots of places for kids to jot down their favorite Bible verses, Faithlinks, Livin' It sites, and other stuff they want to remember—right in their very own Bible. In fact, on the two pages just before this one, there is a place for you to make up your very own homepage. (That's the main starting point for your *KidsBible.com* journey.) Here are a few do's and don'ts for writing in your Bible:

- Don't use a felt-tip pen or any other kind of marker. Those kinds of pens will "bleed" through the pages and make a real mess!
- Do use a ballpoint pen or pencil for jotting down links or sites you want to remember.
- Don't stuff you Bible with extra papers, like Sunday school worksheets or other stuff. Your Bible will last longer if you don't use it as a "collect-all."
- Do use your Bible! It's not just to put on your bookshelf to look good! It's God's rulebook for living, and it's meant to be used!

THE FACTs IN NELSON'S KIDSBIBLE.COM

WHAT'S A FACT ANYWAY?

As you surf through *KidsBible.com,* you may come across a word or two that may not be so familiar to you. Don't go into panic mode, but connect here to find out what it means!

That's right, Skweek! We don't want our friend wandering out in cyberspace without a clue as to what we're talking about. That's why we've set up our own FACTs—Frequently Asked Computer Terms—that defines the most commonly asked questions about computer terms. Read on!

B

BBS—Bulletin Board System. In the real computer world, this is a computer system that you can connect to using a modem. At the BBS, you can dial in and leave messages, or play computer games, or send email. In *KidsBible.com,* our BBS is the **Get the Info** feature that gives you interesting data about people, places, and things you'll find in *KidsBible.com.*

Boot up—To start up a computer. To start up in *KidsBible.com,* try the **Table of Contents**, which tells you where to find all the great stuff!

Browser—The program, such as the Internet, that allows you to download and display sites and documents on the Web. For example, you will need a browser to connect to www.kidsbible.com.

C

Chat room—A place on the Internet where you can "talk" with other online users by typing in messages.

Crash—When a computer doesn't respond to what you ask it to do. Don't worry, *KidsBible.com* will never crash!

Cyberspace—The virtual world created where computers, the Internet, and other electronic ways of communication meet. In *KidsBible.com,* it's the place where Skweek and Tagg interact with you!

D

Data—The computer term for information. All the Bible stories, verses, and other information you will read in *KidsBible.com* is data.

Database—How data is stored and organized on a computer. The **Table of Contents** and the **Search Engine** are the two main databases for *KidsBible.com*.

Document—Any work that is created on a computer and stored as a file. In *KidsBible.com*, any feature, such as **Get the Info** or a **Faithlink**, is a form of a document.

Download—To get a file from a computer or Internet. In *KidsBible.com*, you can download information every time you read a **Faithlink**, **Livin' It** page, or any other Bible feature.

Email—Electronic mail that is sent over the Internet. In *KidsBible.com*, you can read 500 emails from God's Word that cover a wide variety of topics. Check out the **Email from God** by visiting the in-box list on page xix. When you're reading *KidsBible.com*, you'll always get mail!

Email address—This is your private address on the Internet to which your email is sent. Remember, never give out your private email address without your parent(s)' permission. It's always good to have two email addresses—one that is public, and one that is given out only to friends and family members.

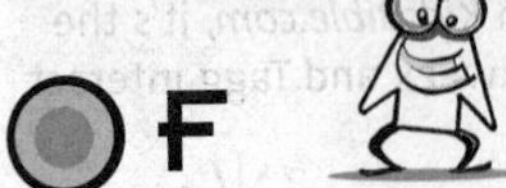

FAQs—This is short for Frequently Asked Questions. It is a report that answers the most commonly asked questions on a particular subject. In *KidsBible.com*, you'll find a different kind of **FAQs,** or **Faith Action Questions.** These **FAQs** focus on five different questions involving a Bible character's particular faith challenge. (For example, David's faith challenge was being respectful to people who wanted to do him harm.)

File—Anything stored on a computer. In *KidsBible.com*, this could be **Get the Info**, **Faithlink**, **Connect 2-You**, or other features found in the Bible.

Flash—The facts, as in "What's the flash on this story?"

Header—The top line of an information source, such as an email, which lists the sender's details and the time sent. In *KidsBible.com*, the header will let you know, among other things, the type of information packet it is (for example, a **Faithlink**, **Get the Info**, or **Livin' It** page), a title, and in some cases, where you can find more information about the topic in the Bible. Also, each page of the Bible has its own header that tells you the Bible book with chapter and verse numbers that begins or ends a page. Use these headers to locate a particular Bible story, verse, or feature in *KidsBible.com*.

Homepage—The first page loaded by a browser when you connect to that site. In *KidsBible.com*, you can create your own homepage by recording your favorite places in the Bible to read. See page x.

Host—Computer that offers some sort of services to its users. Klik and Browz are your hosts in *KidsBible.com* and on the website www.kidsbible.com. They'll serve you as they guide you through the Bible and direct you to other places to get more information.

Hypertext links—On the Web, these are the places where you can "click" that will connect you to other pages on the Web. In *KidsBible.com,* the hypertext links appear as underlined headings. To "connect" to the other pages, you'll have to do the work and turn the pages!

Internet—This is the global collection of computer networks that share a common address so you can connect to a wide variety of websites through one source.

Link—On a web page, a link is a reference to another document. When you click on a link, that document will be displayed, or played, or downloaded, depending on what kind of document it is. In *KidsBible.com,* links will take you to other Bible references that have a similar topic or theme. You can follow the links by turning to the page number and Bible verse listed for each reference.

Log on—To connect to a computer network. In *KidsBible.com,* you can log on to other Bible references by following the links listed.

MIDI—Stands for Musical Instrument Digital Interface. MIDI files contain synthesized music that can be played when the files are opened. In *KidsBible.com,* you won't find any MIDI files that will actually play music, but only ones that suggest music might be played. (For example, you may find MIDI files mentioned in the Psalms.)

The Net—Shortened form of the Internet.

Newbie—A newcomer to the Internet or to a new website. Anyone who first opens *KidsBible.com* is an official newbie!

Online—To be connected to the Internet or Web. When you log on and visit the www.kidsbible.com website, you are online through your computer. When you read *KidsBible.com,* you are online, also, but with your Bible!

Packet—A unit of data, or information, that is sent over the Internet.

Plug-in—A program that fits into another. In *KidsBible.com*, plug-ins are other Bible features that you will find in each book of the Bible. For example, one plug-in to the Book of Genesis is **The Boat That Saved the World, Genesis 7**.

Post—To send a message on the Internet or a website. In *KidsBible.com,* you can post your favorite places to visit on your homepage or on each Bible book **Splash page.** On the www.kidsbible.com website, there will be other places for you to post messages.

Search Engine—This is where you can look to see if there is information about a particular subject contained in the database for a specific web page.

KidsBible.com has its own unique **Search Engine** where you can look up topics and see what links are available on that topic.

Splash page—The introductory page to a website that has a listing of everything you'll find on that website. Each book of the Bible in *KidsBible.com* has its own **Splash page** where you will be able to see all the different **Faithlinks**, **Get the Info**, and other information available. For a complete listing of the books of the Bible, check out the **Table of Contents**.

Surf—To skip from page to page by following links. In *KidsBible.com*, there are many ways you can surf. Check it out by reading **Surfing *KidsBible.com*, page vi**.

Surfwatch—A summary of links that may be found at a particular website. You'll find **Surfwatches** on some of the Bible book **Splash pages.**

The Web—Shortened form of the World Wide Web or WWW. The Web contains all the documents and graphics that are published on the Internet and which are connected through hypertext links.

Web page—A single document.

Website—A collection of related documents.

IN-BOX LIST

EMAIL! FROM GOD

Check box when received ✔

Advice
Joshua 3:9 ☐

Angels
Genesis 32:1 ☐
2 Samuel 24:16-17 ☐
Psalm 89:6 ☐
Psalm 103:20 ☐
Psalm 148:1-2 ☐
Isaiah 6:2 ☐
Daniel 10:5-6 ☐
Matthew 22:30 ☐
Luke 20:36 ☐
1 Corinthians 6:3 ☐
2 Peter 2:4 ☐

Anger
Proverbs 15:1 ☐
Isaiah 14:5-6 ☐
John 2:13-17 ☐
Ephesians 4:26-27 ☐

Belief
Deuteronomy 27:10 ☐
1 Samuel 15:26 ☐
Ezekiel 36:36 ☐
1 Thessalonians 2:13 ☐

Bible
Joshua 23:6-7 ☐
2 Chronicles 34:31 ☐
Nehemiah 9:14 ☐
Psalm 119:99-100 ☐
Acts 17:11-12 ☐
Acts 18:28 ☐
2 Timothy 3:16 ☐

Blessings
Leviticus 26:3-5 ☐
Nehemiah 13:31 ☐
Psalm 5:12 ☐
Psalm 24:3-6 ☐
James 1:25 ☐

Caring
Exodus 23:9 ☐
Deuteronomy 7:9 ☐
Psalm 68:5 ☐
Zechariah 7:9 ☐
Luke 6:27 ☐
Luke 14:13-14 ☐

Character
1 Samuel 16:7 ☐
Jeremiah 7:5-7 ☐
Daniel 6:4-5 ☐
Amos 5:24 ☐

Comfort
2 Samuel 19:7 ☐
John 16:33 ☐
2 Corinthians 1:3-11 ☐

Correction
Job 5:17 ☐
Proverbs 4:13 ☐
Proverbs 6:20-23 ☐
Proverbs 15:10 ☐
Hebrews 12:7-11 ☐

Courage
Joshua 1:9 ☐
Isaiah 12:2 ☐
Isaiah 30:15 ☐
1 Corinthians 16:13 ☐
Hebrews 4:16 ☐
James 5:16 ☐

Death
Psalm 49:13-15 ☐
Psalm 116:1-15 ☐
John 14:19 ☐
2 Corinthians 5:6-7 ☐

Decisions
Numbers 14:1-4 ☐
1 Chronicles 13:2 ☐
Psalm 1:1-2 ☐
Psalm 119:105 ☐
Ezekiel 11:12 ☐
Matthew 7:3-5 ☐

Demons
Luke 10:17 ☐
Acts 16:16-18 ☐
Acts 19:13-16 ☐

Encouragement
Nehemiah 5:7-11 ☐
Job 4:4 ☐
Habakkuk 3:17-19 ☐
Zechariah 2:10 ☐
Acts 9:31 ☐

Enemies
Joshua 10:25 ☐
Proverbs 17:9 ☐
Proverbs 24:17-18 ☐
Proverbs 25:21-22 ☐
1 Peter 3:9 ☐

Eternal Life
Matthew 7:21 ☐
John 3:15-16 ☐
John 5:28-29 ☐
John 11:25 ☐
Titus 3:7 ☐

Faith
Luke 17:5-6 ☐

In-Box List xx

Check box when received ✔

2 Corinthians 3:18 ☐
Philippians 3:12-14 ☐
Hebrews 11:1 ☐

Family

Genesis 47:11-12 ☐
1 Kings 5:13-14 ☐
1 Chronicles 28:8 ☐
Esther 2:11 ☐
Ezekiel 18:19-20 ☐
Luke 12:51-53 ☐

Fears

Deuteronomy 20:1 ☐
Deuteronomy 31:8 ☐
Psalm 23:4 ☐
Psalm 25:15 ☐
Psalm 91:5 ☐
Psalm 112:7 ☐
Isaiah 43:1-2 ☐
Isaiah 51:12-13 ☐
Jeremiah 46:27 ☐
Micah 4:4 ☐
1 John 4:18 ☐

Feelings

Nehemiah 9:27 ☐
Psalm 34:18 ☐

Following God

Leviticus 18:3-5 ☐
Judges 5:31 ☐
1 Samuel 3:10 ☐
2 Chronicles 15:15 ☐
Psalm 27:14 ☐
Proverbs 10:24-25 ☐
Isaiah 35:10 ☐
Ezekiel 11:19 ☐
Ezekiel 36:20-21 ☐
Malachi 3:14-18 ☐
Matthew 16:24 ☐
John 8:12 ☐
John 10:25-27 ☐
John 12:26 ☐
Romans 1:20 ☐
1 Corinthians 11:17-22 ☐
1 Timothy 1:18-19 ☐
1 Timothy 6:11-12 ☐

Forgiveness

Psalm 86:5 ☐
Ezekiel 37:23 ☐
Matthew 18:21-35 ☐
Acts 13:38-39 ☐

Friendship

Samuel 18:1 ☐
1 Samuel 19:1-7 ☐
1 Samuel 20:42 ☐
2 Samuel 9:1 ☐
2 Samuel 19:33 ☐
2 Chronicles 10:1-14 ☐
Job 2:11 ☐
Psalm 55:12-14 ☐
Proverbs 17:17 ☐
Jeremiah 26:24 ☐
John 15:13-15 ☐

Future

Deuteronomy 5:29 ☐
Esther 4:14 ☐
Isaiah 65:17-25 ☐
Jeremiah 18:11 ☐
Jeremiah 31:6 ☐

Giving

Exodus 35:22 ☐
2 Kings 12:4-5 ☐
2 Chronicles 31:4 ☐
Proverbs 11:24-25 ☐
Mark 9:41 ☐
Mark 14:6-9 ☐
Acts 28:10-11 ☐
2 Corinthians 9:6-8 ☐
1 Timothy 6:18 ☐

God

Genesis 8:1 ☐
Exodus 6:7 ☐
Leviticus 11:44 ☐
Joshua 4:24 ☐
1 Samuel 2:6-7 ☐
1 Samuel 6:20 ☐
2 Samuel 7:22 ☐
2 Samuel 23:5 ☐
1 Kings 8:27 ☐
2 Kings 5:15 ☐
2 Kings 20:6 ☐
Job 11:11 ☐
Job 21:22 ☐
Job 40:2 ☐
Psalm 27:1 ☐
Psalm 33:13-18 ☐
Isaiah 41:4 ☐
Ezekiel 38:23 ☐
Hosea 11:1 ☐
Romans 12:2 ☐

God's Family

Deuteronomy 8:5 ☐
Deuteronomy 26:18 ☐
Matthew 12:50 ☐

God's Promises

Psalm 37:23-24 ☐
Jeremiah 32:40-41 ☐
John 5:24 ☐
2 Timothy 1:12 ☐

God's Will

Psalm 16:7 ☐
Psalm 48:14 ☐
Acts 16:6-7 ☐

Good News

Luke 24:46-47 ☐
1 Thessalonians 1:4-5 ☐

Gossip

Proverbs 4:24 ☐
Proverbs 16:28 ☐
Proverbs 26:20 ☐

Greed

Isaiah 5:8 ☐
Jeremiah 8:10 ☐

Check box when received ☑

Guilt
Psalm 19:12-13 ☐
Psalm 32:5 ☐
Zechariah 13:1 ☐
Romans 3:9-12 ☐

Hate
Ezekiel 35:11-12 ☐
Romans 12:9 ☐

Heaven
Isaiah 25:8 ☐
Philippians 1:23 ☐
Revelation 4:8 ☐
Revelation 7:17 ☐
Revelation 21:4 ☐
Revelation 22:8-9 ☐

Hell
Psalm 86:13 ☐
Matthew 8:12 ☐
Jude 6 ☐

Help
Genesis 49:25 ☐
Judges 3:9 ☐
Psalm 121 ☐
Hebrews 1:14 ☐

Honesty
Exodus 20:16 ☐
Exodus 23:2 ☐
Isaiah 33:15-16 ☐
Ezekiel 45:9-11 ☐
Matthew 15:18 ☐

Honoring God
Isaiah 29:13 ☐
Isaiah 58:5-7 ☐

Hope
Ezra 10:2 ☐
Psalm 9:18 ☐
Psalm 42:5-6 ☐
Psalm 130:5-6 ☐
Ecclesiastes 5:18-20 ☐
Jeremiah 23:16 ☐
Lamentations 3:21-22 ☐

Humbleness
Job 25:6 ☐
Proverbs 22:4 ☐
Isaiah 57:15 ☐
Zephaniah 2:3 ☐
Philippians 2:3 ☐

Idols
Deuteronomy 4:23 ☐
1 Kings 14:21-23 ☐

Jealousy
Acts7:9 ☐
Galatians 2:6 ☐

Jesus
Mark 14:61-62 ☐
Luke 1:35 ☐
Luke 19:10 ☐
John 1:1-5 ☐
John 4:21-26 ☐
Acts 3:15 ☐
Colossians 1:15-16 ☐
1 Timothy 1:2 ☐
1 Timothy 3:16 ☐
Hebrews 8:6 ☐

Joy
Nehemiah 12:43 ☐
Isaiah 55:12 ☐
Isaiah 61:10 ☐

Judgment
Psalm 9:7-8 ☐
Jeremiah 20:12 ☐
Ezekiel 7:3-4 ☐
Ezekiel 12:17-25 ☐
Obadiah 15 ☐
Malachi 3:5 ☐
Matthew 12:36 ☐
John 7:24 ☐

Kindness
Joshua 2:12 ☐
1 Kings 2:7 ☐
Proverbs 3:3-4 ☐
Proverbs 14:31 ☐
Isaiah 63:7 ☐
Romans 2:4 ☐
Romans 15:14 ☐

Laziness
Proverbs 19:15 ☐
1 Thessalonians 5:12-14 ☐

Leadership
Exodus 18:21 ☐
Numbers 27:16-17 ☐
1 Samuel 24:1-6 ☐
2 Kings 15:3-5 ☐
2 Kings 23:3 ☐
2 Chronicles 19:5-7 ☐
Esther 10:3 ☐
Psalm 78:72 ☐
Matthew 20:25-28 ☐

Learning
Proverbs 18:2 ☐
Ephesians 4:13-14 ☐

Life
Joshua 14:10-11 ☐
2 Samuel 4:9-11 ☐
Luke 9:24 ☐
John 10:10 ☐
Philippians 4:8-9 ☐
Colossians 3:8-9 ☐
1 Thessalonians 4:11 ☐
3 John 11 ☐

Love
Ezra 3:11 ☐

Check box when received ✔

Matthew 5:43-44 ☐
Mark 12:29-30 ☐
John 13:34-35 ☐
1 Corinthians 13:4-8 ☐
Ephesians 4:2 ☐
2 John 5 ☐

Money

1 Chronicles 26:27 ☐
Isaiah 17:10 ☐
Isaiah 31:6-7 ☐
Matthew 6:19-20 ☐
Matthew 19:21-22 ☐
Matthew 22:21 ☐
Mark 8:34-36 ☐
Luke 16:13 ☐
Acts 2:42-45 ☐
Revelation 3:17-18 ☐

Music

Exodus 15:1 ☐
Psalm 81:1-5 ☐
Colossians 3:16 ☐

Obedience

Deuteronomy 12:28 ☐
Deuteronomy 13:17-18 ☐
Deuteronomy 28:1 ☐
1 Samuel 12:14 ☐
1 Samuel 15:22 ☐
1 Kings 6:12-13 ☐
1 Chronicles 6:49 ☐
2 Chronicles 26:4 ☐
Proverbs 5:1 ☐
Jeremiah 11:7-8 ☐
Jeremiah 42:6 ☐
Luke 11:28 ☐
John 14:15-23 ☐
Acts 5:29 ☐
Acts 11:2-18 ☐
Romans 13:1 ☐
Romans 16:19 ☐
Ephesians 6:1-3 ☐
1 Peter 1:2 ☐
1 John 2:3 ☐
1 John 5:1-3 ☐

Pain

Psalm 12:5 ☐
1 Thessalonians 4:18 ☐

Peace

Numbers 6:24-26 ☐
Romans 14:19 ☐
Ephesians 2:14 ☐

Perseverance

Job 17:9 ☐
Matthew 10:22 ☐
Romans 5:3 ☐
1 Corinthians 1:8 ☐
Ephesians 6:13 ☐
Colossians 2:7 ☐
James 5:7-8 ☐
2 Peter 1:5-8 ☐

Prayer

1 Samuel 1:17 ☐
2 Chronicles 1:9-10 ☐
Nehemiah 2:4 ☐
Psalm 17:1-2 ☐
Psalm 40:13 ☐
Isaiah 38:1-6 ☐
Jeremiah 29:7 ☐
Jonah 2:1 ☐
John 16:23-24 ☐
Colossians 4:2 ☐
1 John 5:13-15 ☐
Jude 20 ☐

Pride

Deuteronomy 17:18-20 ☐
2 Kings 19:27-28 ☐
Psalm 131:1 ☐
Proverbs 16:18 ☐
Proverbs 29:23 ☐
Isaiah 10:15-16 ☐
Luke 22:27 ☐
1 Corinthians 1:28 ☐
2 Corinthians 10:12-13 ☐

Protection

Genesis 15:1 ☐

Numbers 18:20 ☐
Psalm 73:24-26 ☐
Psalm 82:3-4 ☐

Purity

Psalm 101:3-8 ☐
Psalm 119:1-20 ☐
Matthew 23:27-28 ☐

Repentance

Luke 3:7-8 ☐
Luke 13:3-5 ☐
Luke 15:7 ☐

Reputation

Deuteronomy 4:6-9 ☐
Malachi 1:11 ☐
2 Corinthians 12:6 ☐

Respect

Exodus 3:5 ☐
Leviticus 19:3 ☐
Job 31:13-14 ☐
Proverbs 31:30 ☐
Acts 10:28 ☐
Galatians 3:28-29 ☐
1 Peter 2:15 ☐

Responsibility

Deuteronomy 11:1 ☐
Joshua 22:5 ☐
Psalm 31:23 ☐
Proverbs 23:26 ☐
Ezekiel 33:1-6 ☐
Matthew 4:10 ☐
Matthew 25:14-30 ☐
Acts 4:19-20 ☐

Resurrection

John 6:38-40 ☐
1 Corinthians 15:12-21 ☐

Revenge

1 Peter 2:21-23 ☐

Check box when received ☑

Salvation
- 2 Samuel 22:2 ☐
- 2 Samuel 22:47-48 ☐
- Joel 2:32 ☐
- Luke 15:32 ☐
- John 17:23 ☐
- Acts 2:37-38 ☐
- Romans 10:8-10 ☐
- Hebrews 9:27-28 ☐
- 1 Peter 1:18-19 ☐

Satan
- John 8:44 ☐
- 2 Corinthians 11:14 ☐
- 1 Timothy 4:1 ☐
- 1 Peter 5:8 ☐
- 1 John 3:7-8 ☐

Sickness
- Psalm 41 ☐
- Matthew 25:34-40 ☐

Sin
- Exodus 32:34 ☐
- 2 Chronicles 6:24-25 ☐
- Ezra 9:6 ☐
- Proverbs 21:23 ☐
- Isaiah 53:6 ☐
- Isaiah 59:12-13 ☐
- Isaiah 64:6 ☐
- Jeremiah 16:17 ☐
- Daniel 9:4-8 ☐
- Hosea 7:13 ☐
- Romans 3:23 ☐

Success
- Joshua 6:27 ☐
- 1 Chronicles 11:14 ☐
- 2 Chronicles 7:14 ☐
- 2 Chronicles 12:1 ☐
- Psalm 18:32-50 ☐

Talents
- Ezekiel 28:5 ☐
- Daniel 1:17 ☐

Temptation
- 2 Kings 21:8-9 ☐
- Proverbs 2:10-14 ☐
- 2 Timothy 2:22 ☐
- 1 John 2:16 ☐

Thankfulness
- 1 Chronicles 16:4-36 ☐
- Psalm 100 ☐
- Psalm 107:1-3 ☐
- Psalm 138 ☐
- Isaiah 62:5 ☐
- Acts 27:35 ☐
- Ephesians 1:15-16 ☐
- Ephesians 5:20 ☐
- Hebrews 13:15 ☐

Troubles
- Joshua 8:1 ☐
- 1 Samuel 17:37 ☐
- Job 14:1 ☐
- Psalm 22:19-24 ☐
- Psalm 46:1-2 ☐
- Psalm 142 ☐
- Isaiah 37:20 ☐
- Lamentations 5:16 ☐
- Matthew 11:30 ☐
- Romans 8:17-18 ☐
- 1 Peter 4:12-19 ☐

Trust
- 1 Chronicles 14:10 ☐
- 1 Chronicles 17:26-27 ☐
- Psalm 11:1 ☐
- Psalm 20:7 ☐
- Psalm 52:5-9 ☐
- Psalm 56:11 ☐
- Psalm 62:8 ☐
- Psalm 146:3 ☐
- Proverbs 16:3 ☐
- Proverbs 28:25-26 ☐
- Isaiah 26:4 ☐
- Isaiah 40:25-28 ☐
- Isaiah 50:10 ☐
- Romans 4:5 ☐

Truth
- 1 Samuel 7:3 ☐
- 1 Samuel 12:24 ☐
- Psalm 51:6 ☐
- Jeremiah 9:3 ☐
- Jeremiah 22:3-5 ☐
- John 17:17 ☐
- Hebrews 6:18 ☐

Wisdom
- Genesis 41:16 ☐
- Psalm 90:12 ☐
- Proverbs 1:7 ☐
- Proverbs 8:12-14 ☐
- Proverbs 24:3-4 ☐
- Proverbs 24:13-14 ☐
- Ecclesiastes 9:13-18 ☐
- 1 Corinthians 2:6-8 ☐
- 1 Corinthians 8:1-3 ☐

Witnessing
- Matthew 13:23 ☐
- Matthew 28:19-20 ☐
- John 4:34-38 ☐
- Acts 1:8 ☐
- Acts 18:9 ☐
- Romans 10:14-15 ☐
- 1 Corinthians 3:5-9 ☐
- 2 Corinthians 5:18-21 ☐
- Colossians 4:6 ☐
- 2 Timothy 4:1-2 ☐

Worry
- 1 Chronicles 29:12 ☐
- Psalm 69 ☐
- Proverbs 12:25 ☐
- 2 Corinthians 4:8-12 ☐

Worship
- Exodus 34:14 ☐
- Judges 5:3 ☐
- 2 Samuel 6:21 ☐
- Nehemiah 8:6 ☐
- Psalm 29:1-2 ☐
- Psalm 107:31-32 ☐
- Psalm 150 ☐
- Isaiah 66:2 ☐
- James 4:8 ☐
- Revelation 15:3-4 ☐

Preface to the *New Century Version*

God intended for everyone to be able to understand his Word. Earliest Scriptures were in Hebrew, ideally suited for a barely literate society because of its economy of words, acrostic literary form and poetic parallelism. The New Testament was first written in the simple Greek of everyday life, not in the Latin of Roman courts or the classical Greek of the academies. Even Jesus, the Master Teacher, taught spiritual principles by comparing them to such familiar terms as pearls, seeds, rocks, trees, and sheep. Likewise, the *New Century Version* translates the Scriptures in familiar, everyday words of our times.

The *New Century Version* is a translation of God's Word from the original Hebrew and Greek languages. Several previous editions of the complete *New Century Version* have been published, such as the *International Children's Bible* (1986); *Time with God* (1991); *The Odyssey Bible* (1994); *The Answer* (1993); and *The Inspirational Study Bible* (1995), among others.

A Trustworthy Translation

Two basic premises guided the translation process of the *New Century Version.* The first concern was that the translation be faithful to the manuscripts in the original languages. A team composed of the World Bible Translation Center and fifty additional, highly qualified and experienced Bible scholars and translators was assembled. The team included people with translation experience on such accepted versions as the *New International Version,* the *New American Standard Bible,* and the *New King James Version.* The most recent scholarship and the best available Hebrew and Greek texts were used, principally the third edition of the United Bible Societies' Greek text and the latest edition of the Bible Hebraica, along with the Septuagint.

A Clear Translation

The second concern was to make the language clear enough for anyone to read the Bible and understand it for himself. In maintaining clear language, several guidelines were followed. Vocabulary choice has been based upon *The Living Word Vocabulary* by Dr. Edgar Dale and Dr. Joseph O'Rourke (Worldbook-Childcraft International), which is the standard used by the editors of *The World Book Encyclopedia* to determine appropriate vocabulary. For difficult words which have no simpler synonyms, footnotes are provided. Footnotes appear at the bottom of the page and are indicated in the text by an ⁿ (for "note").

The *New Century Version* aids understanding by putting concepts into natural terms. Modern measurements and geographical locations have been used as much as possible. For instance, terms such as "shekels," cubits," "omer," and "hin" have been converted to modern equivalents of weights and measures. Where geographical references are identical, the modern name has been used, such as the "Mediterranean Sea" instead of "Great Sea" or "Western Sea." Also, to minimize confusion, the most familiar name for a place is used consistently, instead of using variant names for the same place. "Lake Galilee" is used throughout rather than its variant forms, "Sea of Kinnereth," "Lake Gennesaret," and "Sea of Tiberias."

Ancient customs are often unfamiliar to modern readers. Customs such as shaving a man's beard to shame him or walking between the halves of a dead animal to seal an agreement are meaningless to most people. So these are clarified either in the text or in a footnote.

Since *meanings* of words change with time, care has been taken to avoid potential misunderstandings. Frequently in the Old Testament God tells his people to "devote" something to him, as when he tells the Israelites to devote Jericho and everything in it to him. While we might understand this to mean he is telling them to keep it safe and holy, the exact opposite is true. He is telling them to destroy it totally as an offering to him. The *New Century Version* communicates the idea clearly by translating "devoted," in these situations, as "destroyed as an offering to the Lord."

Rhetorical questions have been stated according to their implied answers. The psalmist's question, "What god is so great as our God?" has been stated more directly as, "No god is as great as our God."

Figures of speech have been translated according to their meanings. For instance, the expression, "The Virgin Daughter of Zion," which is frequently used in the Old Testament, is simply translated "the people of Jerusalem."

Idiomatic expressions of the biblical languages are translated to communicate the same meaning to today's reader that would have been understood by the original audience. For example, the Hebrew idiom "he rested with his fathers" is translated by its corresponding meaning—"he died."

Obscure terms have been clarified. In the Old Testament God frequently condemns the people for their "high places" and "Asherah poles." The *New Century Version* translates these according to their meanings, which would have been understood by the Hebrews. "High places" is translated "places where gods were worshiped," and "Asherah poles" is translated "Asherah idols."

Gender language has also been translated with a concern for clarity. To avoid the misconception that "man" and "mankind" and "he" are exclusively masculine when they are being used in a generic sense, this translation has chosen to use less ambiguous language, such as "people" and "humans" and "human beings," and has prayerfully attempted throughout to choose gender language that would accurately convey the intent of the original writers. Specifically and exclusively masculine and feminine references in the text have been retained.

Following in the tradition of other English versions, the *New Century Version* indicates the divine name YHWH, the Tetragrammaton, by putting LORD, and sometimes GOD, in capital letters. This is to distinguish it from Adonai, another Hebrew word that is translated Lord.

Every attempt has been made to maintain proper English style, while clarifying concepts and communication. The beauty of the Hebrew parallelism in poetry and the word plays have been retained, and the images of the ancient languages have been captured in equivalent English images wherever possible.

Our Prayer

It is with great humility and prayerfulness that this Bible is presented. We acknowledge the infallibility of God's Word and yet our own human frailty. We pray that God has worked through us as his vessels so that we all might better learn his truth for ourselves and that it might richly grow in our lives. It is to his glory that this Bible is given.

THE PUBLISHER

THE OLD TESTAMENT

HOW DID IT ALL BEGIN?

Hi, there! My name is Moses. Does my name sound familiar? I'm the one God chose to lead his people out of Egypt, but you'll have to surf on over to the Book of Exodus for that story. The events in this book, Genesis, happened hundreds of years before I was born, so God told me what to write. Some of the coolest stories in the Bible are in this book. Be sure to check them out.

I wrote this book to tell everyone about the beginning of all things. I described how God created the sky and the earth, the plants and the animals, and finally, the best part of his creation, human beings. I told about the beginning of sin: how Adam and Eve did not obey God and had to leave the Garden of Eden. People have been sinning ever since! Most important, I wrote about the beginning of the special friendship God has with his people, starting with Abraham, and of his plan to save his people.

JESUS WATCH

Many people in Genesis remind us of Jesus. Abel, Adam's son, brought the best parts of his firstborn animals as a sacrifice to God. This sacrifice points to Jesus, the firstborn Son of God, who offered himself as a sacrifice for our sins. Melchizedek, the king of Salem and a priest of God Most High, brought out bread and wine when he blessed Abraham. This reminds us of the Last Supper when Jesus, our high priest, took bread and wine to bless the disciples the night before He died on the cross. In many ways Joseph's life points to the life of Jesus. Both were beloved sons of their fathers, but were hated by many. His own brothers sold Joseph into slavery, and Jesus was betrayed for money by one of his disciples. Both were accused of crimes they did not commit and both were raised to high positions. Joseph was in prison many years before he was freed and made a ruler of Egypt. Jesus died on the cross to take the punishment for our sins. He rose from the dead and later was bought up to heaven to be with God.

my FAVORITE links

__________ __________

__________ __________

__________ __________

__________ __________

OTHER CONNECTIONS

Livin' it

Ever been hurt badly by a friend? What was your first reaction—to get mad and then get even, or to forgive that friend? Connect to You Want Me to Do What?, Genesis 50:15–21, to find out how God wants you to react when. You can follow the Faithlinks for more on this topic.

Stop at any of these bulletin boards to find out cool facts about people, places, and things mentioned in the Book of Genesis. Here are just a few of the places you can visit:

- The Garden of Delight, Genesis 2:8–10, the first home of Adam And Eve before they were kicked out for disobeying God. No one knows exactly where Eden was located, but check here to find out how many rivers flowed out of the garden.
- Find out what happened when the first rain fell on earth when you visit The Boat That Saved the World, Genesis 7. You'll quickly discover that this was no ordinary boat, but more like a floating zoo!
- Take a trip back in time, tracing the path that Abraham traveled thousands of years ago when you connect to A New Home for Abraham, Genesis 16. Then stop by From Deceiver to Wrestler, Genesis 28:1, to read about Abraham's grandson Jacob and see where his adventures took him.

"Hey, Tagg—what's the flash on Noah's boat?"

"I think he thought it was going to rain—a lot! Surf on over to Genesis 6 and check it out."

did YOU know?

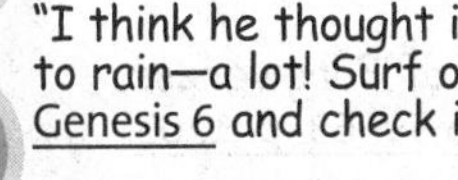

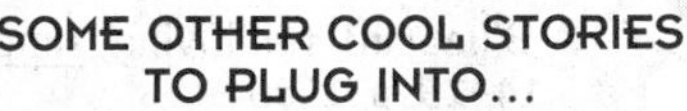

SOME OTHER COOL STORIES TO PLUG INTO...

The Tower of Babel, Genesis 11:1–9
God's agreement with Abraham, Genesis 15
Pillar of salt, Genesis 19:23–29
Esau's bowl of soup, Genesis 25:27–34
Jacob's wrestling match with God, Genesis 32:22–32
Joseph's special robe, Genesis 37:1–11

FAITH links

- Out of Control?, **Genesis 4**
- The Trouble with Sin, **Genesis 6—8**
- Just Kidding?, **Genesis 21:8–10**
- Family Feud, **Genesis 27**
- The Best Policy, **Genesis 29:16–29**
- When You're Afraid, **Genesis 32:9–12**
- The Trouble with Jealousy, **Genesis 37**
- Alone and Forgotten?, **Genesis 40:23**
- Good Plans, **Genesis 45:7–8**
- More Powerful Than Revenge, **Genesis 50:14–21**

The Beginning of the World

1 In the beginning God created the sky
and the earth. 2The earth was empty
and had no form. Darkness covered the
ocean, and God's Spirit was moving over
the water.
3Then God said, "Let there be light,"
and there was light. 4God saw that the
light was good, so he divided the light
from the darkness. 5God named the light
"day" and the darkness "night." Evening
passed, and morning came. This was the
first day.
6Then God said, "Let there be something to divide the water in two." 7So
God made the air and placed some of the
water above the air and some below it.
8God named the air "sky." Evening
passed, and morning came. This was the
second day.
9Then God said, "Let the water under
the sky be gathered together so the dry
land will appear." And it happened. 10God
named the dry land "earth" and the water
that was gathered together "seas." God
saw that this was good.
11Then God said, "Let the earth produce plants—some to make grain for
seeds and others to make fruits with
seeds in them. Every seed will produce
more of its own kind of plant." And it happened. 12The earth produced plants with
grain for seeds and trees that made fruits
with seeds in them. Each seed grew its
own kind of plant. God saw that all this
was good. 13Evening passed, and morning came. This was the third day.
14Then God said, "Let there be lights
in the sky to separate day from night.
These lights will be used for signs, seasons, days, and years. 15They will be in
the sky to give light to the earth." And it
happened.
16So God made the two large lights.
He made the brighter light to rule the day
and made the smaller light to rule the
night. He also made the stars. 17God put
all these in the sky to shine on the earth,
18to rule over the day and over the night,
and to separate the light from the darkness. God saw that all these things were
good. 19Evening passed, and morning
came. This was the fourth day.
20Then God said, "Let the water be
filled with living things, and let birds fly
in the air above the earth."
21So God created the large sea animals
and every living thing that moves in the

FAITH links

MADE IN HIS IMAGE

GENESIS 1:26-27

Ever have a woe-is-me day, a day when you've wondered, *What's so great about being me?* Here's what's so great: you are one of God's greatest creations. After creating the world and all of the animals and plants, God created people in his own image. News flash: We didn't evolve from apes! Being made in God's image means you have some of his characteristics. Does this mean you have God's nose or chin? No. God doesn't have a body. Instead it means you can love, be forgiving, and creative—just like God.

Hey, want to know more about God and how to love like him? Connect to these:

Count on His Mercy, Judges 2:16–17; 3, p. 313

A Model of Forgiveness, Ezekiel 16:59–63, p. 1103

A Blueprint for Living, Amos 5:14–15, p. 1200

Go! No!, Jonah 1, p. 1213

Love for Free, Romans 5:8, p. 1524

The Best Choice, 1 Corinthians 13, p. 1560

GET THE INFO

GARDEN OF DELIGHT

Genesis 2:8–10

We don't know exactly where God created the garden of Eden. We think it was near the place that we call Arabia today. We do know that four rivers flowed out of the garden. One was called the Tigris and another was called the Euphrates. We may not know exactly where the garden was, but we do know what it was for—it was the home God created for Adam and Eve, the first people on earth. (Check out Genesis 2:4—3:24.) It was a wonderful place to live. *Eden* means "delight," and the garden of Eden was a place of delightful things. When Adam and Eve had to leave such a wonderful place because of their sin, it was a sad day for all of us.

sea. The sea is filled with these living
things, with each one producing more of
its own kind. He also made every bird
that flies, and each bird produced more of
its own kind. God saw that this was good.
22God blessed them and said, "Have
many young ones so that you may grow
in number. Fill the water of the seas, and
let the birds grow in number on the
earth." **23**Evening passed, and morning
came. This was the fifth day.

24Then God said, "Let the earth be
filled with animals, each producing more
of its own kind. Let there be tame animals and small crawling animals and wild
animals, and let each produce more of its
kind." And it happened.

25So God made the wild animals, the
tame animals, and all the small crawling
animals to produce more of their own
kind. God saw that this was good.

26Then God said, "Let us make human beings in our image and likeness.
And let them rule over the fish in the sea
and the birds in the sky, over the tame
animals, over all the earth, and over all
the small crawling animals on the earth."

27So God created human beings in his
image. In the image of God he created
them. He created them male and female.
28God blessed them and said, "Have
many children and grow in number. Fill
the earth and be its master. Rule over the
fish in the sea and over the birds in the
sky and over every living thing that
moves on the earth."

29God said, "Look, I have given you
all the plants that have grain for seeds
and all the trees whose fruits have seeds
in them. They will be food for you. **30**I
have given all the green plants as food for
every wild animal, every bird of the air,
and every small crawling animal." And it
happened. **31**God looked at everything he
had made, and it was very good. Evening
passed, and morning came. This was the
sixth day.

The Seventh Day—Rest

2 So the sky, the earth, and all that
filled them were finished. **2**By the
seventh day God finished the work he
had been doing, so he rested from all his
work. **3**God blessed the seventh day and
made it a holy day, because on that day he
rested from all the work he had done in
creating the world.

The First People

4This is the story of the creation of
the sky and the earth. When the LORD
God first made the earth and the sky,

5there were still no plants on the earth.
Nothing was growing in the fields because the LORD God had not yet made it
rain on the land. And there was no person
to care for the ground, 6but a mist would
rise up from the earth and water all the
ground.

7Then the LORD God took dust from
the ground and formed a man from it. He
breathed the breath of life into the man's
nose, and the man became a living person. 8Then the LORD God planted a garden in the east, in a place called Eden,
and put the man he had formed into it.
9The LORD God caused every beautiful
tree and every tree that was good for food
to grow out of the ground. In the middle
of the garden, God put the tree that gives
life and also the tree that gives the
knowledge of good and evil.

10A river flowed through Eden and
watered the garden. From there the river
branched out to become four rivers.
11The first river, named Pishon, flows
around the whole land of Havilah, where
there is gold. 12The gold of that land is
excellent. Bdellium and onyx[n] are also
found there. 13The second river, named
Gihon, flows around the whole land of
Cush. 14The third river, named Tigris,
flows out of Assyria toward the east. The
fourth river is the Euphrates.

15The LORD God put the man in the
garden of Eden to care for it and work it.
16The LORD God commanded him, "You
may eat the fruit from any tree in the garden, 17but you must not eat the fruit
from the tree which gives the knowledge
of good and evil. If you ever eat fruit from
that tree, you will die!"

The First Woman

18Then the LORD God said, "It is not
good for the man to be alone. I will make
a helper who is right for him."

19From the ground God formed every
wild animal and every bird in the sky, and
he brought them to the man so the man
could name them. Whatever the man
called each living thing, that became its
name. 20The man gave names to all the
tame animals, to the birds in the sky, and
to all the wild animals. But Adam[n] did not
find a helper that was right for him. 21So
the LORD God caused the man to sleep
very deeply, and while he was asleep,
God removed one of the man's ribs. Then
God closed up the man's skin at the place
where he took the rib. 22The LORD God
used the rib from the man to make a
woman, and then he brought the woman
to the man.

23And the man said,

"Now, this is someone whose bones
came from my bones,
whose body came from my body.
I will call her 'woman,'
because she was taken out of
man."

24So a man will leave his father and
mother and be united with his wife, and
the two will become one body.

25The man and his wife were naked,
but they were not ashamed.

The Beginning of Sin

3 Now the snake was the most clever of
all the wild animals the LORD God had
made. One day the snake said to the
woman, "Did God really say that you
must not eat fruit from any tree in the
garden?"

2The woman answered the snake,
"We may eat fruit from the trees in the
garden. 3But God told us, 'You must not
eat fruit from the tree that is in the middle of the garden. You must not even
touch it, or you will die.' "

4But the snake said to the woman,
"You will not die. 5God knows that if
you eat the fruit from that tree, you will
learn about good and evil and you will be
like God!"

6The woman saw that the tree was
beautiful, that its fruit was good to eat,
and that it would make her wise. So she
took some of its fruit and ate it. She also
gave some of the fruit to her husband,
and he ate it.

7Then, it was as if their eyes were

2:12 bdellium and onyx Bdellium is an expensive, sweet-smelling resin like myrrh, and onyx is a gem.

2:20 Adam This is the name of the first man. It also means "humans," including men and women.

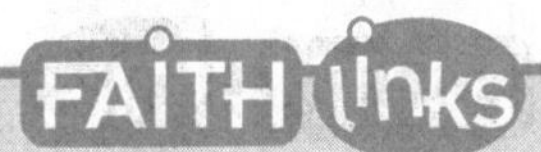

CAN'T LIVE WITHOUT IT?

GENESIS 3

Is there anything you want that you would do *anything* to get, even something wrong? The snake tempted Eve to eat fruit from the tree in the middle of the garden that God told Adam and Eve not to eat from. (See Genesis 2:16–17.) The snake made the fruit sound wonderful. So Adam and Eve reached for the one thing they felt they didn't have and couldn't live without.

Sometimes we're tempted by the things we think we can't live without. At those times, we also might doubt that God knows what's best for our lives. When that happens, don't give in to temptation and doubt. Instead, ask God for help.

Complaints, Complaints!, Exodus 16:1–3, p. 97

A Hidden Sin, Joshua 7, p. 285

Learning to Trust, Psalm 25:4–5, p. 727

Obeying God or Man?, Daniel 3:8–30, p. 1154

The Temptation Fighter, Matthew 4:1–11, p. 1278

Faith God Notices, Luke 18:35–43, p. 1406

opened. They realized they were naked, so they sewed fig leaves together and made something to cover themselves.

8Then they heard the LORD God walk-
ing in the garden during the cool part of the day, and the man and his wife hid from the LORD God among the trees in the garden. 9But the LORD God called to the
man and said, "Where are you?"

10The man answered, "I heard you walking in the garden, and I was afraid because I was naked, so I hid."

11God asked, "Who told you that you were naked? Did you eat fruit from the tree from which I commanded you not to eat?"

12The man said, "You gave this woman to me and she gave me fruit from the tree, so I ate it."

13Then the LORD God said to the woman, "How could you have done such a thing?"

She answered, "The snake tricked me, so I ate the fruit."

14The LORD God said to the snake,
"Because you did this,
a curse will be put on you.
You will be cursed as no other
animal, tame or wild, will ever be.
You will crawl on your stomach,
and you will eat dust all the days of
your life.
15I will make you and the woman
enemies to each other.
Your descendants and her
descendants
will be enemies.
One of her descendants will crush
your head,
and you will bite his heel."

16Then God said to the woman,
"I will cause you to have much
trouble
when you are pregnant,
and when you give birth to
children,
you will have great pain.
You will greatly desire your
husband,
but he will rule over you."

17Then God said to the man, "You listened to what your wife said, and you ate fruit from the tree from which I commanded you not to eat.

"So I will put a curse on the ground,

and you will have to work very
hard for your food.
In pain you will eat its food
all the days of your life.
18 The ground will produce thorns and
weeds for you,
and you will eat the plants of the
field.
19 You will sweat and work hard
for your food.
Later you will return to the ground,
because you were taken from it.
You are dust,
and when you die, you will return
to the dust."

20 The man named his wife Eve,* because she is the mother of everyone who
has ever lived.

21 The LORD God made clothes from
animal skins for the man and his wife and
dressed them. 22 Then the LORD God
said, "The man has become like one of
us; he knows good and evil. We must
keep him from eating some of the fruit
from the tree of life, or he will live forever." 23 So the LORD God forced the man
out of the garden of Eden to work the
ground from which he was taken. 24 After
God forced the man out of the garden, he
placed angels and a sword of fire that
flashed around in every direction on its
eastern border. This kept people from
getting to the tree of life.

The First Family

4 Adam had sexual relations with his
wife Eve, and she became pregnant
and gave birth to Cain.* Eve said, "With
the LORD's help, I have given birth to a
man." 2 After that, Eve gave birth to
Cain's brother Abel. Abel took care of
flocks, and Cain became a farmer.

3 Later, Cain brought some food from
the ground as a gift to God. 4 Abel
brought the best parts from some of the
firstborn of his flock. The LORD accepted
Abel and his gift, 5 but he did not accept
Cain and his gift. So Cain became very
angry and felt rejected.

3:20 Eve This name sounds like the Hebrew word meaning "alive."

4:1 Cain This name sounds like the Hebrew word for "I have given birth."

FAITH links

OUT OF CONTROL?

GENESIS 4

Ever been so mad at someone that you were ready to explode? When God did not accept Cain's sacrifice, Cain became angry—angry enough to kill his own brother. Earlier, God had warned Cain to "rule over" his anger. By this, God meant that Cain needed to control his anger. But Cain wouldn't listen.

Feeling angry? Anger itself is not sinful. Sin happens when anger gets out of control. God has tools you can use to master anger before it masters you. One of those tools is a fruit of the Spirit: self-control. (Read about it in Galatians 5:22–23, p. 1593.) Another tool is prayer. Use them when needed!

Need to cool off some more? Surf over to these Faithlinks!

What God "Hates," Proverbs 6:16–19, p. 835

Justice Served, Isaiah 35:3–4, p. 940

The "Ruler" of Our Lives, Amos 7:7–9, p. 1202

Don't Get Mad; Get Even?, Matthew 26:57–63; 27:11–14, p. 1323

Fear-Fighters, 2 Timothy 1:7, p. 1652

The "Quality" of Life, 2 Peter 1:5–8, p. 1708

6The LORD asked Cain, "Why are you
angry? Why do you look so unhappy? 7If
you do things well, I will accept you, but
if you do not do them well, sin is ready to
attack you. Sin wants you, but you must
rule over it."
8Cain said to his brother Abel, "Let's
go out into the field." While they were
out in the field, Cain attacked his brother
Abel and killed him.
9Later, the LORD said to Cain, "Where
is your brother Abel?"
Cain answered, "I don't know. Is it my
job to take care of my brother?"
10Then the LORD said, "What have
you done? Your brother's blood is crying
out to me from the ground. 11And now
you will be cursed in your work with the
ground, the same ground where your
brother's blood fell and where your hands
killed him. 12You will work the ground,
but it will not grow good crops for you anymore, and you will wander
around on the earth."
13Then Cain said to
the LORD, "This punish-
ment is more than I can
stand! 14Today you have
forced me to stop work-
ing the ground, and now
I must hide from you. I
must wander around on
the earth, and anyone who
meets me can kill me."
15The LORD said to Cain, "No! If anyone kills you, I will punish that person
seven times more." Then the LORD put a
mark on Cain warning anyone who met
him not to kill him.

He created them male and female, and on that day he blessed them and named them human beings.
—Genesis 5:2

Cain's Family

16So Cain went away from the LORD
and lived in the land of Nod,[n] east of
Eden. 17He had sexual relations with his
wife, and she became pregnant and gave
birth to Enoch. At that time Cain was
building a city, which he named after his
son Enoch. 18Enoch had a son named
Irad, Irad had a son named Mehujael,
Mehujael had a son named Methushael,
and Methushael had a son named Lamech.
19Lamech married two women, Adah
and Zillah. 20Adah gave birth to Jabal,
who became the first person to live in
tents and raise cattle. 21Jabal's brother
was Jubal, the first person to play the
harp and flute. 22Zillah gave birth to
Tubal-Cain, who made tools out of bronze
and iron. The sister of Tubal-Cain was
Naamah.
23Lamech said to his wives:
"Adah and Zillah, hear my voice!
You wives of Lamech, listen to
what I say.
I killed a man for wounding me,
a young man for hitting me.
24If Cain's killer is punished seven
times,
then Lamech's killer will be
punished seventy-seven times."

Adam and Eve Have a New Son

25Adam had sexual relations with his
wife Eve again, and she gave birth to a
son. She named him
Seth[n] and said, "God has
given me another child.
He will take the place of
Abel, who was killed by
Cain." 26Seth also had a
son, and they named him
Enosh. At that time peo-
ple began to pray to the
LORD.

Adam's Family History

5 This is the family history of Adam.
When God created human beings, he
made them in his own likeness. 2He created them male and female, and on that
day he blessed them and named them human beings.
3When Adam was 130 years old, he
became the father of another son in his
likeness and image, and Adam named him
Seth. 4After Seth was born, Adam lived
800 years and had other sons and daughters. 5So Adam lived a total of 930 years,
and then he died.

4:16 Nod This name sounds like the Hebrew word for "wander."

4:25 Seth This name sounds like the Hebrew word for "to give."

6When Seth was 105 years old, he had
a son named Enosh. 7After Enosh was
born, Seth lived 807 years and had other
sons and daughters. 8So Seth lived a total
of 912 years, and then he died.

9When Enosh was 90 years old, he
had a son named Kenan. 10After Kenan
was born, Enosh lived 815 years and had
other sons and daughters. 11So Enosh
lived a total of 905 years, and then he
died.

12When Kenan was 70 years old, he
had a son named Mahalalel. 13After Mahalalel was born, Kenan lived 840 years
and had other sons and daughters. 14So
Kenan lived a total of 910 years, and then
he died.

15When Mahalalel was 65 years old,
he had a son named Jared. 16After Jared
was born, Mahalalel lived 830 years
and had other sons and daughters. 17So
Mahalalel lived a total of 895 years, and
then he died.

18When Jared was 162 years old, he had
a son named Enoch. 19After Enoch was
born, Jared lived 800 years and had other
sons and daughters. 20So Jared lived a total of 962 years, and then he died.

21When Enoch was 65 years old, he
had a son named Methuselah. 22After
Methuselah was born, Enoch walked with
God 300 years more and had other sons
and daughters. 23So Enoch lived a total of
365 years. 24Enoch walked with God; one
day Enoch could not be found, because
God took him.

25When Methuselah was 187 years
old, he had a son named Lamech. 26After
Lamech was born, Methuselah lived 782
years and had other sons and daughters.
27So Methuselah lived a total of 969
years, and then he died.

28When Lamech was 182, he had a
son. 29Lamech named his son Noah[n] and
said, "He will comfort us in our work,
which comes from the ground the LORD
has cursed." 30After Noah was born, Lamech lived 595 years and had other sons
and daughters. 31So Lamech lived a total
of 777 years, and then he died.

32After Noah was 500 years old, he
became the father of Shem, Ham, and
Japheth.

The Human Race Becomes Evil

6 The number of people on earth began
to grow, and daughters were born to
them. 2When the sons of God saw that
these girls were beautiful, they married
any of them they chose. 3The LORD said,
"My Spirit will not remain in human beings forever, because they are flesh.
They will live only 120 years."

4The Nephilim were on the earth in
those days and also later. That was when
the sons of God had sexual relations with
the daughters of human beings. These
women gave birth to children, who became famous and were the mighty warriors of long ago.

5The LORD saw that the human beings on the earth were very wicked and
that everything they thought about was
evil. 6He was sorry he had made human
beings on the earth, and his heart was
filled with pain. 7So the LORD said, "I will
destroy all human beings that I made on
the earth. And I will destroy every animal
and everything that crawls on the earth
and the birds of the air, because I am
sorry I have made them." 8But Noah
pleased the LORD.

Noah and the Great Flood

9This is the family history of Noah.
Noah was a good man, the most innocent
man of his time, and he walked with God.
10He had three sons: Shem, Ham, and Japheth.

11People on earth did what God said
was evil, and violence was everywhere.
12When God saw that everyone on the
earth did only evil, 13he said to Noah,
"Because people have made the earth full
of violence, I will destroy all of them from
the earth. 14Build a boat of cypress wood
for yourself. Make rooms in it and cover
it inside and outside with tar. 15This is
how big I want you to build the boat: four
hundred fifty feet long, seventy-five feet
wide, and forty-five feet high. 16Make an
opening around the top of the boat that is
eighteen inches high from the edge of the
roof down. Put a door in the side of the

5:29 Noah This name sounds like the Hebrew word for "rest."

FAITH links

THE TROUBLE WITH SIN

GENESIS 6–8

Have you ever heard your mom or dad say, "I've had it up to here"? That usually means, "I'm fed up!" It also means, "You're in trouble." God had "had it up to here" with just about everyone on earth. No one thought about obeying him—no one except Noah. So God decided to destroy almost all human and animal life on earth. Because of Noah's obedience, his whole family was saved from the flood.

Sin has consequences. Those consequences may not involve a flood in your life. But they can mean trouble. That's why God gives us ways to obey. He's given us the Bible, which tells us how to please him.

Connect to these Faithlinks to find out what else God has to say about sin.

The Perfect Sacrifice, Leviticus 1–7, p. 135

Real Repentance, Jeremiah 4:1–4, p. 993

A Fake Apology, Hosea 6:1–7, p. 1177

Hope That Doesn't Fail, Acts 26:4–7, p. 1510

The Sin Habit, Romans 7:15–20, p. 1527

The Finished Product, Philippians 1:6, p. 1609

boat. Make an upper, middle, and lower
deck in it. 17I will bring a flood of water
on the earth to destroy all living things
that live under the sky, including everything that has the breath of life. Everything on the earth will die. 18But I will
make an agreement with you—you, your
sons, your wife, and your sons' wives will
all go into the boat. 19Also, you must
bring into the boat two of every living
thing, male and female. Keep them alive
with you. 20Two of every kind of bird, animal, and crawling thing will come to you
to be kept alive. 21Also gather some of
every kind of food and store it on the boat
as food for you and the animals."

22Noah did everything that God commanded him.

The Flood Begins

7 Then the LORD said to Noah, "I have
seen that you are the best person
among the people of this time, so you and
your family can go into the boat. 2Take
with you seven pairs, each male with its
female, of every kind of clean animal, and
take one pair, each male with its female,
of every kind of unclean animal. 3Take
seven pairs of all the birds of the sky,
each male with its female. This will allow
all these animals to continue living on the
earth after the flood. 4Seven days from
now I will send rain on the earth. It will
rain forty days and forty nights, and I will
wipe off from the earth every living thing
that I have made."

5Noah did everything the LORD commanded him.

6Noah was six hundred years old when
the flood came. 7He and his wife and his
sons and their wives went into the boat to
escape the waters of the flood. 8The clean
animals, the unclean animals, the birds,
and everything that crawls on the ground
9came to Noah. They went into the boat in
groups of two, male and female, just as
God had commanded Noah. 10Seven days
later the flood started.

11When Noah was six hundred years
old, the flood started. On the seventeenth day of the second month of that
year the underground springs split open,
and the clouds in the sky poured out rain.

THE BOAT THAT SAVED THE WORLD Genesis 7

Noah built the boat to save himself, his family, and animals from a flood that covered the whole earth. (Read about it in Genesis 6:14—9:19.) The boat was about 450 feet long, 75 feet wide, and 45 feet high, with three decks. Experts say the boat could hold more than 43,000 tons.

Noah and his family lived in the boat for almost a year as it floated on the floodwaters. The boat finally landed on Mount Ararat in what is now Turkey. No one has ever found the boat if it is still there.

The story of Noah's boat teaches us about God's judgment and his mercy. In the New Testament, Jesus compared the days before the flood to the days before he comes back to earth. (See Matthew 24:37–38, p. 1316; Luke 17:26–27, p. 1404.) Other references to the flood include Hebrews 11:7; 1 Peter 3:20; and 2 Peter 2:5.

12The rain fell on the earth for forty days
and forty nights.
13On that same day Noah and his
wife, his sons Shem, Ham, and Japheth,
and their wives went into the boat.
14They had every kind of wild and tame
animal, every kind of animal that crawls
on the earth, and every kind of bird.
15Every creature that had the breath of
life came to Noah in the boat in groups of
two. **16**One male and one female of every
living thing came, just as God had commanded Noah. Then the LORD closed the
door behind them.
17Water flooded the earth for forty
days, and as it rose it lifted the boat off
the ground. **18**The water continued to
rise, and the boat floated on it above the
earth. **19**The water rose so much that
even the highest mountains under the
sky were covered by it. **20**It continued to
rise until it was more than twenty feet
above the mountains.
21All living things that moved on the
earth died. This included all the birds,
tame animals, wild animals, and creatures that swarm on the earth, as well as
all human beings. **22**So everything on dry
land that had the breath of life in it died.
23God destroyed from the earth every
living thing that was on the land—every
man, animal, crawling thing, and bird of
the sky. All that was left was Noah and
what was with him in the boat. **24**And the
waters continued to cover the earth for
one hundred fifty days.

The Flood Ends

8 But God remembered Noah and all
the wild and tame animals with him
in the boat. He made a wind blow over the
earth, and the water went down. **2**The
underground springs stopped flowing,
and the clouds in the sky stopped pouring
down rain. **3-4**The water that covered
the earth began to
go down. After one
hundred fifty days it
had gone down so
much that the boat
touched land again. It
came to rest on one
of the mountains of Ararat[n] on the seventeenth day of the seventh month. **5**The

8:1 **God**
Check out how much God cares for his creation.

8:3-4 Ararat The ancient land of Urartu, an area in Eastern Turkey.

water continued to go down so that by
the first day of the tenth month the tops
of the mountains could be seen.
6Forty days later Noah opened the
window he had made in the boat, and **7**he
sent out a raven. It flew here and there
until the water had dried up from the
earth. **8**Then Noah sent out a dove to find
out if the water had dried up from the
ground. **9**The dove could not find a place
to land because water still covered the
earth, so it came back to the boat. Noah
reached out his hand and took the bird
and brought it back into the boat.
10After seven days Noah again sent
out the dove from the boat, **11**and that
evening it came back to him with a fresh
olive leaf in its mouth. Then Noah knew
that the ground was almost dry. **12**Seven
days later he sent the dove out again, but
this time it did not come back.
13When Noah was six hundred and
one years old, in the first day of the first
month of that year, the water was dried
up from the land. Noah removed the
covering of the boat and saw that the
land was dry. **14**By the twenty-seventh
day of the second month the land was
completely dry.
15Then God said to Noah, **16**"You and
your wife, your sons, and their wives
should go out of the boat. **17**Bring every
animal out of the boat with you—the
birds, animals, and everything that crawls
on the earth. Let them have many young
ones so that they might grow in number."
18So Noah went out with his sons, his
wife, and his sons' wives. **19**Every animal, everything that crawls on the earth,
and every bird went out of the boat by
families.
20Then Noah built an altar to the
LORD. He took some of all the clean birds
and animals, and he burned them on the
altar as offerings to God. **21**The LORD
was pleased with these sacrifices and
said to himself, "I will never again curse
the ground because of human beings.
Their thoughts are evil even when they
are young, but I will never again destroy
every living thing on the earth as I did
this time.

22"As long as the earth continues,
planting and harvest,
cold and hot,
summer and winter,
day and night
will not stop."

The New Beginning

9 Then God blessed Noah and his sons
and said to them, "Have many children; grow in number and fill the earth.
2Every animal on earth, every bird in
the sky, every animal that crawls on
the ground, and every fish in the sea will
respect and fear you. I have given them
to you.
3"Everything that moves, everything
that is alive, is yours for food. Earlier I
gave you the green plants, but now I give
you everything for food. **4**But you must
not eat meat that still has blood in it, because blood gives life. **5**I will demand
blood for life. I will demand the life of any
animal that kills a person, and I will demand the life of anyone who takes another person's life.

6"Whoever kills a human being
will be killed by a human being,
because God made humans
in his own image.

7"As for you, Noah, I want you and
your family to have many children, to
grow in number on the earth, and to become many."
8Then God said to Noah and his sons,
9"Now I am making my agreement with
you and your people who will live after
you, **10**and with every living thing that is
with you—the birds, the tame and the
wild animals, and with everything that
came out of the boat with you—with
every living thing on earth. **11**I make this
agreement with you: I will never again
destroy all living things by a flood. A flood
will never again destroy the earth."
12And God said, "This is the sign of
the agreement between me and you and
every living creature that is with you. **13**I
am putting my rainbow in the clouds as
the sign of the agreement between me
and the earth. **14**When I bring clouds
over the earth and a rainbow appears in

them, 15I will remember my agreement
between me and you and every living
thing. Floods will never again destroy all
life on the earth. 16When the rainbow appears in the clouds, I will see it and I will
remember the agreement that continues forever between me and every living thing on the earth."
17So God said to Noah, "The rainbow is a sign of the agreement that I made with all living things on earth."

FAITH links

THE RAINBOW PROMISE

GENESIS 9:1-17

Think about the last time you saw a rainbow fill the sky. Some of us may take rainbows for granted. Sure they're nice and colorful. After all, they're the result of the bending and reflecting of sunlight through the moisture in the air. But that rainbow, as routine as it may seem after a spring rain, is the sign of an ancient promise. God promised that he would never again destroy all living creatures by a flood. The rainbow is a sign of his faithfulness. Next time you see a rainbow, let it remind you that God keeps his promises.

Check out God's great love for you by linking up here:

Your Heavenly Parent, Exodus 2:1–10, p. 77

The God of Big Things, Joshua 10, p. 289

How Big Is God?, Job 38—41, p. 703

Hope That Doesn't Fail, Acts 26:4–7, p. 1510

But I Want It?, Philippians 4:19, p. 1615

His Best Qualities, 2 Peter 3:9, p. 1711

Noah and His Sons

18The sons of Noah who came out of
the boat with him were Shem, Ham, and
Japheth. (Ham was the father of Canaan.)
19These three men were Noah's sons,
and all the people on earth came from
these three sons.
20Noah became a farmer and planted
a vineyard. 21When he drank wine made
from his grapes, he became drunk and lay
naked in his tent. 22Ham, the father of
Canaan, looked at his naked father and
told his brothers outside. 23Then Shem
and Japheth got a coat and, carrying it on
both their shoulders, they walked back-
wards into the tent and covered their father. They turned their faces away so
that they did not see their father's nakedness.
24Noah was sleeping because of the
wine. When he woke up and learned what
his youngest son, Ham, had done to him,
25he said,

"May there be a curse on Canaan!
May he be the lowest slave to his brothers."

26Noah also said,

"May the LORD, the God of Shem, be praised!
May Canaan be Shem's slave.
27May God give more land to Japheth.
May Japheth live in Shem's tents,
and may Canaan be their slave."

28After the flood Noah lived 350
years. 29He lived a total of 950 years, and
then he died.

Nations Grow and Spread

10 This is the family history of Shem,
Ham, and Japheth, the sons of
Noah. After the flood these three men
had sons.

Japheth's Sons

2The sons of Japheth were Gomer, Magog, Madai, Javan, Tubal, Meshech, and Tiras.

3The sons of Gomer were Ashkenaz, Riphath, and Togarmah.

4The sons of Javan were Elishah, Tarshish, Kittim,[n] and Rodanim. **5**Those who lived in the lands around the Mediterranean Sea came from these sons of Japheth. All the families grew and became different nations, each nation with its own land and its own language.

Ham's Sons

6The sons of Ham were Cush, Mizraim,[n] Put, and Canaan.

7The sons of Cush were Seba, Havilah, Sabtah, Raamah, and Sabteca.

The sons of Raamah were Sheba and Dedan.

8Cush also had a descendant named Nimrod, who became a very powerful man on earth. **9**He was a great hunter before the LORD, which is why people say someone is "like Nimrod, a great hunter before the LORD." **10**At first Nimrod's kingdom covered Babylon, Erech, Akkad, and Calneh in the land of Babylonia. **11**From there he went to Assyria, where he built the cities of Nineveh, Rehoboth Ir, and Calah. **12**He also built Resen, the great city between Nineveh and Calah.

13Mizraim was the father of the Ludites, Anamites, Lehabites, Naphtuhites, **14**Pathrusites, Casluhites, and the people of Crete. (The Philistines came from the Casluhites.)

15Canaan was the father of Sidon, his first son, and of Heth. **16**He was also the father of the Jebusites, Amorites, Girgashites, **17**Hivites, Arkites, Sinites, **18**Arvadites, Zemarites, and Hamathites. The families of the Canaanites scattered. **19**Their land reached from Sidon to Gerar as far as Gaza, and then to Sodom, Gomorrah, Admah, and Zeboiim, as far as Lasha.

20All these people were the sons of Ham, and all these families had their own languages, their own lands, and their own nations.

Shem's Sons

21Shem, Japheth's older brother, also had sons. One of his descendants was the father of all the sons of Eber.

22The sons of Shem were Elam, Ashur, Arphaxad, Lud, and Aram.

23The sons of Aram were Uz, Hul, Gether, and Meshech.

24Arphaxad was the father of Shelah, who was the father of Eber. **25**Eber was the father of two sons—one named Peleg,[n] because the earth was divided during his life, and the other was named Joktan.

26Joktan was the father of Almodad, Sheleph, Hazarmaveth, Jerah, **27**Hadoram, Uzal, Diklah, **28**Obal, Abimael, Sheba, **29**Ophir, Havilah, and Jobab. All these people were the sons of Joktan. **30**They lived in the area between Mesha and Sephar in the hill country in the East.

31These are the people from the family of Shem, arranged by families, languages, countries, and nations.

32This is the list of the families from the sons of Noah, arranged according to their nations. From these families came all the nations who spread across the earth after the flood.

This is the list of the families from the sons of Noah, arranged according to their nations. From these families came all the nations who spread across the earth after the flood.
—Genesis 10:32

10:4 Kittim His descendants were the people of Cyprus.

10:6 Mizraim This is another name for Egypt.

10:25 Peleg This name sounds like the Hebrew word for "divided."

TOWER OF PRIDE **Genesis 11:3–9**

The tower of Babel was built like a pyramid. The tower was made of bricks and mortar instead of stone. It was built after the great flood. (Remember Noah and his boat?)

The problem with the tower was that the people built it out of their own pride. They weren't humbly reaching out to God. They were trying to build their own tower to heaven. God did something that got the people's attention as they were building the tower. He confused their languages. That means that all of a sudden different people were talking different languages. Can you imagine talking to your friend, who suddenly starts speaking in Spanish or French? It would be pretty hard to get anything done. That's what happened to the builders of the tower. They got frustrated because they couldn't communicate and finally stopped building altogether. (Look at Genesis 11:3–9.)

The Languages Confused

11 At this time the whole world spoke one language, and everyone used the same words. **2**As people moved from the east, they found a plain in the land of Babylonia and settled there.

3They said to each other, "Let's make bricks and bake them to make them hard." So they used bricks instead of stones, and tar instead of mortar. **4**Then they said to each other, "Let's build a city and a tower for ourselves, whose top will reach high into the sky. We will become famous. Then we will not be scattered over all the earth."

5The LORD came down to see the city and the tower that the people had built. **6**The LORD said, "Now, these people are united, all speaking the same language. This is only the beginning of what they will do. They will be able to do anything they want. **7**Come, let us go down and confuse their language so they will not be able to understand each other."

8So the LORD scattered them from there over all the earth, and they stopped building the city. **9**The place is called Babel[n] since that is where the LORD confused the language of the whole world. So the LORD caused them to spread out from there over the whole world.

The Story of Shem's Family

10This is the family history of Shem. Two years after the flood, when Shem was 100 years old, his son Arphaxad was born. **11**After that, Shem lived 500 years and had other sons and daughters.

12When Arphaxad was 35 years old, his son Shelah was born. **13**After that, Arphaxad lived 403 years and had other sons and daughters.

14When Shelah was 30 years old, his son Eber was born. **15**After that, Shelah lived 403 years and had other sons and daughters.

16When Eber was 34 years old, his son Peleg was born. **17**After that, Eber lived 430 years and had other sons and daughters.

18When Peleg was 30 years old, his

11:9 Babel This name sounds like the Hebrew word for "confused."

son Reu was born. **19**After that, Peleg
lived 209 years and had other sons and
daughters.
20When Reu was 32 years old, his son
Serug was born. **21**After that, Reu lived
207 years and had other sons and daughters.
22When Serug was 30 years old, his
son Nahor was born. **23**After that, Serug
lived 200 years and had other sons and
daughters.
24When Nahor was 29 years old, his
son Terah was born. **25**After that, Nahor
lived 119 years and had other sons and
daughters.
26After Terah was 70 years old, his
sons Abram, Nahor, and Haran were
born.

The Story of Terah's Family

27This is the family history of Terah.
Terah was the father of Abram, Nahor,
and Haran. Haran was the father of Lot.
28While his father, Terah, was still alive,
Haran died in Ur in Babylonia, where he
was born. **29**Abram and Nahor both married. Abram's wife was named Sarai, and
Nahor's wife was named Milcah. She was
the daughter of Haran, who was the father of both Milcah and Iscah. **30**Sarai
was not able to have children.
31Terah took his son Abram, his grandson Lot (Haran's son), and his daughter-
in-law Sarai (Abram's wife) and moved
out of Ur of Babylonia. They had planned
to go to the land of Canaan, but when
they reached the city of Haran, they settled there.
32Terah lived to be 205 years old, and
then he died in Haran.

God Calls Abram

12 The LORD said to Abram, "Leave
your country, your relatives, and
your father's family, and go to the land I
will show you.

2I will make you a great nation,
and I will bless you.
I will make you famous,
and you will be a blessing to
others.
3I will bless those who bless you,
and I will place a curse on those
who harm you.
And all the people on earth
will be blessed through you."

4So Abram left Haran as the LORD
had told him, and Lot went with him. At
this time Abram was 75 years old. **5**He
took his wife Sarai, his nephew Lot, and

FAITH links

LIGHTS, CAMERA,...ACTIONS!

GENESIS 12:1-3

Imagine being asked to pack your things and move to a foreign country—one you know nothing about. Would you go? You would if you were Abraham (called Abram in these verses). Abraham was told to leave his home and relatives in Ur and go to a new land. Abraham showed faith in God by his actions.

Faith in God involves action, not just words. One action is obedience. Many people say that they trust God. Yet their actions tell a different story. What do your actions reveal?

Moses' Champion, Numbers 12, p. 192

Trailblazers of Faith, 2 Kings 22:1–2, p. 510

In the Lions' Den, Daniel 6, p. 1160

Ask, Search, Knock, Matthew 7:7–10, p. 1286

Prove It!, Matthew 16:1–4, p. 1302

Our Gift to God, Romans 12:1–2, p. 1536

everything they owned, as well as all the
servants they had gotten in Haran. They
set out from Haran, planning to go to the
land of Canaan, and in time they arrived
there.
6Abram traveled through that land as
far as the great tree of Moreh at Shechem. The Canaanites were living in the
land at that time. 7The LORD appeared to
Abram and said, "I will give this land to
your descendants." So Abram built an altar there to the LORD, who had appeared
to him. 8Then he traveled from Shechem
to the mountain east of Bethel and set up
his tent there. Bethel was to the west,
and Ai was to the east. There Abram built
another altar to the LORD and worshiped
him. 9After this, he traveled on toward
southern Canaan.

Abram Goes to Egypt

10At this time there was not much
food in the land, so Abram went down to
Egypt to live because there was so little
food. 11Just before they arrived in Egypt,
he said to his wife Sarai, "I know you are
a very beautiful woman. 12When the
Egyptians see you, they will say, 'This
woman is his wife.' Then they will kill me
but let you live. 13Tell them you are my
sister so that things will go well with me
and I may be allowed to live because of
you."
14When Abram came to Egypt, the
Egyptians saw that Sarai was very beautiful. 15The Egyptian officers saw her
and told the king of Egypt how beautiful
she was. They took her to the king's palace, and 16the king was kind to Abram
because he thought Abram was her
brother. He gave Abram sheep, cattle,
male and female donkeys, male and female servants, and camels.
17But the LORD sent terrible diseases
on the king and all the people in his house
because of Abram's wife Sarai. 18So the
king sent for Abram and said, "What have
you done to me? Why didn't you tell me
Sarai was your wife? 19Why did you say,
'She is my sister' so that I made her my
wife? Now, here is your wife. Take her
and leave!" 20Then the king commanded
his men to make Abram leave Egypt; so
Abram and his wife left with everything
they owned.

Abram and Lot Separate

13 So Abram, his wife, and Lot left
Egypt, taking everything they
owned, and traveled to southern Canaan.
2Abram was very rich in cattle, silver,
and gold.
3He left southern Canaan and went
back to Bethel where he had camped before, between Bethel and Ai, 4and where
he had built an altar. So he worshiped the
LORD there.
5During this time Lot was traveling
with Abram, and Lot also had flocks,
herds, and tents. 6Abram and Lot had so
many animals that the land could not support both of them together, 7so Abram's
herdsmen and Lot's herdsmen began to
argue. The Canaanites and the Perizzites
were living in the land at this time.
8Abram said to Lot, "There should be
no arguing between you and me, or between your herdsmen and mine, because
we are brothers. 9We should separate.
The whole land is there in front of you.
If you go to the left, I will go to the
right. If you go to the right, I will go to
the left."
10Lot looked all around and saw the
whole Jordan Valley and that there was
much water there. It was like the LORD's
garden, like the land of Egypt in the direction of Zoar. (This was before the
LORD destroyed Sodom and Gomorrah.)
11So Lot chose to move east and live in
the Jordan Valley. In this way Abram and
Lot separated. 12Abram lived in the land
of Canaan, but Lot lived among the cities
in the Jordan Valley, very near to Sodom.
13Now the people of Sodom were very
evil and were always sinning against the
LORD.
14After Lot left, the LORD said to
Abram, "Look all around you—to the
north and south and east and west. 15All
this land that you see I will give to you
and your descendants forever. 16I will
make your descendants as many as the
dust of the earth. If anyone could count
the dust on the earth, he could count
your people. 17Get up! Walk through all

this land because I am now giving it
to you."
18So Abram moved his tents and went
to live near the great trees
of Mamre at the city of Hebron. There he built an altar to the LORD.

> Get up! Walk through all this land because I am now giving it to you.
> —Genesis 13:17

Lot Is Captured

14 Now Amraphel was
king of Babylonia,
Arioch was king of Ellasar,
Kedorlaomer was king of
Elam, and Tidal was king of
Goiim. 2All these kings went to war
against several other kings: Bera king of
Sodom, Birsha king of Gomorrah, Shinab
king of Admah, Shemeber king of Zeboiim, and the king of Bela. (Bela is also
called Zoar.)
3These kings who were attacked
united their armies in the Valley of Siddim (now the Dead Sea). 4They had
served Kedorlaomer for twelve years,
but in the thirteenth year, they all turned
against him. 5Then in the fourteenth
year, Kedorlaomer and the kings with
him came and defeated the Rephaites in
Ashteroth Karnaim, the Zuzites in Ham,
and the Emites in Shaveh Kiriathaim.
6They also defeated the Horites in the
mountains of Edom to El Paran (near the
desert). 7Then they turned back and
went to En Mishpat (that is, Kadesh).
They defeated all the Amalekites, as well
as the Amorites who lived in Hazazon
Tamar.
8At that time the kings of Sodom, Gomorrah, Admah, Zeboiim, and Bela went
out to fight in the Valley of Siddim. (Bela
is called Zoar.) 9They fought against
Kedorlaomer king of Elam, Tidal king of
Goiim, Amraphel king of Babylonia, and
Arioch king of Ellasar—four kings fighting against five. 10There were many tar
pits in the Valley of Siddim. When the
kings of Sodom and Gomorrah and their
armies ran away, some of the soldiers fell
into the tar pits, but the others ran away
to the mountains.
11Now Kedorlaomer and his armies
took everything the people of Sodom and
Gomorrah owned, including their food.
12They took Lot, Abram's nephew who
was living in Sodom, and everything he
owned. Then they left. 13One of the men
who was not captured went
to Abram, the Hebrew, and
told him what had hap-
pened. At that time Abram
was camped near the great
trees of Mamre the Amo-
rite. Mamre was a brother
of Eshcol and Aner, and
they had all made an agreement to help Abram.

Abram Rescues Lot

14When Abram learned that Lot had
been captured, he called out his 318
trained men who had been born in his
camp. He led the men and chased the enemy all the way to the town of Dan.
15That night he divided his men into
groups, and they made a surprise attack
against the enemy. They chased them all
the way to Hobah, north of Damascus.
16Then Abram brought back everything
the enemy had stolen, the women and
the other people, and Lot, and everything
Lot owned.
17After defeating Kedorlaomer and
the kings who were with him, Abram
went home. As he was returning, the
king of Sodom came out to meet him in
the Valley of Shaveh (now called King's
Valley).
18Melchizedek king of Salem brought
out bread and wine. He was a priest for
God Most High 19and blessed Abram,
saying,
"Abram, may you be blessed by God
Most High,
the God who made heaven and
earth.
20And we praise God Most High,
who has helped you to defeat your
enemies."
Then Abram gave Melchizedek a tenth of
everything he had brought back from the
battle.
21The king of Sodom said to Abram,
"You may keep all these things for yourself. Just give me my people who were
captured."

22But Abram said to the king of
Sodom, "I make a promise to the LORD,
the God Most High, who made heaven
and earth. 23I promise that I will not keep
anything that is yours. I will not keep
even a thread or a sandal strap so that
you cannot say, 'I made Abram rich.' 24I
will keep nothing but the food my young
men have eaten. But give Aner, Eshcol,
and Mamre their share of what we won,
because they went with me into battle."

God's Agreement with Abram

15 After these things happened, the
LORD spoke his word to Abram in
a vision: "Abram, don't be
afraid. I will defend
you, and I will give
you a great reward."
2But Abram said,
"Lord GOD, what can
you give me? I have
no son, so my slave Eliezer from Damascus will get everything I own after I die."
3Abram said, "Look, you have given me
no son, so a slave born in my house will
inherit everything I have."
4Then the LORD spoke his word to
Abram: "He will not be the one to inherit
what you have. You will have a son of
your own who will inherit what you
have."
5Then God led Abram outside and
said, "Look at the sky. There are so many
stars you cannot count them. Your descendants also will be too many to
count."
6Abram believed the LORD. And the
LORD accepted Abram's faith, and that
faith made him right with God.
7God said to Abram, "I am the LORD
who led you out of Ur of Babylonia so that
I could give you this land to own."
8But Abram said, "Lord GOD, how can
I be sure that I will own this land?"
9The LORD said to Abram, "Bring me
a three-year-old cow, a three-year-old
goat, a three-year-old male sheep, a dove,
and a young pigeon."
10Abram brought them all to God.
Then Abram killed the animals and cut
each of them into two pieces, laying each
half opposite the other half. But he did
not cut the birds in half. 11Later, large
birds flew down to eat the animals, but
Abram chased them away.

eMAIL! FROM GOD 15:1

Protection

Who will protect you? Check it out here!

FAITH links

A MAJOR PROBLEM

GENESIS 15:6

What is the most impossible problem you've ever faced? Abraham had a major one: his wife Sarah could not have children. Both Abraham and Sarah (called Abram and Sarai in Genesis 15 and 16) were old enough to be grandparents, not parents. But God told Abraham that he would have a son one day. Abraham believed God, even though his situation seemed impossible.

A major problem calls for major faith in God—faith that he can do the impossible. Got a major problem? Talk to God about it. He's always there to help, and all things are possible with God. (Read Luke 18:27, p. 1405.)

The Green Light, 2 Samuel 2:1, p. 401

A Given, 1 Chronicles 5:18–20, p. 526

God's Sure Protection, Psalm 18, p. 721

Rock Solid, Habakkuk 1:12, p. 1236

Perfectly Pleasing?, Matthew 5:1–12, p. 1280

Prayer Anywhere, Mark 1:35, p. 1331

GET THE INFO

A NEW HOME FOR ABRAHAM

Genesis 16

1. God called Abram to leave his father's family in Haran and go to a land that God promised to his people. So at age 75, Abram left with his wife Sarai and his nephew Lot and moved to Canaan. (Read Genesis 12:4–5.)

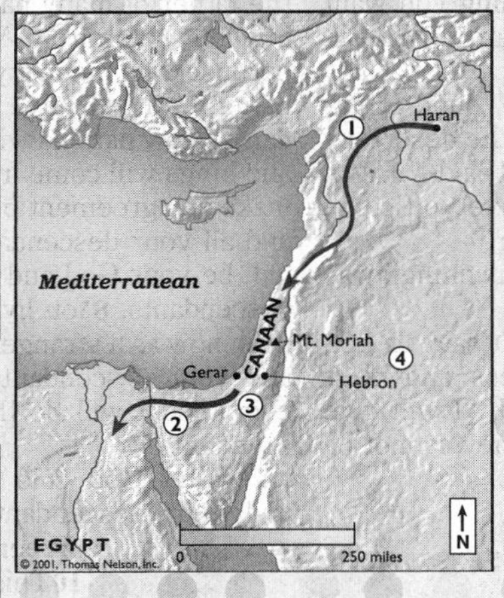

2. Abram and his family went to live in Egypt because there wasn't enough food in Canaan. (Look at Genesis 12:10.)

3. Abram returned to Canaan and settled near Hebron. It was here that the Lord promised Abram that he would be the father of a great nation, changing his name to Abraham, which means "honored father." God also promised Abraham a son, even though he and Sarai (whose name God changed to Sarah) were very old. (See Genesis 17.)

4. God tested Abraham at Mount Moriah in northern Canaan, when he asked Abraham to sacrifice his only son, Isaac. At the last moment, God provided a ram. Because of his obedience, God promised to bless Abraham with descendants—"as many as the stars in the sky and the sand on the seashore." (Look up Genesis 22:1–18.)

12As the sun was going down, Abram
fell into a deep sleep. While he was
asleep, a very terrible darkness came.
13Then the LORD said to Abram, "You
can be sure that your descendants will be
strangers and travel in a land they don't
own. The people there will make them
slaves and be cruel to them for four hundred years. 14But I will punish the nation
where they are slaves. Then your descendants will leave that land, taking
great wealth with them. 15And you,
Abram, will die in peace and will be
buried at an old age. 16After your great-
great-grandchildren are born, your people will come to this land again. It will
take that long, because I am not yet going
to punish the Amorites for their evil behavior."

17After the sun went down, it was
very dark. Suddenly a smoking firepot
and a blazing torch passed between the
halves of the dead animals.* 18So on that
day the LORD made an agreement with
Abram and said, "I will give to your descendants the land between the river of
Egypt and the great river Euphrates.
19This is the land of the Kenites, Keniz-
zites, Kadmonites, 20Hittites, Perizzites,
Rephaites, 21Amorites, Canaanites, Girgashites, and Jebusites."

Ishmael Is Born

16 Sarai, Abram's wife, had no children, but she had a slave girl from
Egypt named Hagar. 2Sarai said to Abram,
"Look, the LORD has not allowed me to
have children, so have sexual relations
with my slave girl. If she has a child, maybe I can have my own family through her."

Abram did what Sarai said. 3It was af-
ter he had lived ten years in Canaan that
Sarai gave Hagar to her husband Abram.
(Hagar was her slave girl from Egypt.)

4Abram had sexual relations with
Hagar, and she became pregnant. When
Hagar learned she was pregnant, she

15:17 passed . . . animals This showed that God sealed the agreement between himself and Abram.

began to treat her mistress Sarai badly.
5Then Sarai said to Abram, "This is your
fault. I gave my slave girl to you, and
when she became pregnant, she began to
treat me badly. Let the LORD decide who
is right—you or me."
6But Abram said to Sarai, "You are
Hagar's mistress. Do anything you want
to her." Then Sarai was hard on Hagar,
and Hagar ran away.
7The angel of the LORD found Hagar
beside a spring of water in the desert, by
the road to Shur. 8The angel said, "Hagar,
Sarai's slave girl, where have you come
from? Where are you going?"
Hagar answered, "I am running away
from my mistress Sarai."
9The angel of the LORD said to her,
"Go home to your mistress and obey
her." 10The angel also said, "I will give
you so many descendants they cannot be
counted."
11The angel added,

"You are now pregnant,
and you will have a son.
You will name him Ishmael,[n]
because the LORD has heard your cries.
12 Ishmael will be like a wild donkey.
He will be against everyone,
and everyone will be against him.
He will attack all his brothers."

13The slave girl gave a name to the
LORD who spoke to her: "You are 'God
who sees me,'" because she said to herself, "Have I really seen God who sees
me?" 14So the well there, between Kadesh and Bered, was called Beer Lahai
Roi.[n]
15Hagar gave birth to a son for
Abram, and Abram named him Ishmael.
16Abram was eighty-six years old when
Hagar gave birth to Ishmael.

Proof of the Agreement

17 When Abram was ninety-nine years
old, the LORD appeared to him and
said, "I am God Almighty. Obey me and
do what is right. 2I will make an agreement between us, and I will make you the
ancestor of many people."
3Then Abram bowed facedown on the
ground. God said to him, 4"I am making
my agreement with you: I will make you
the father of many nations. 5I am changing your name from Abram[n] to Abraham[n]
because I am making you a father of many
nations. 6I will give you many descendants. New nations will be born from you,
and kings will come from you. 7And I will
make an agreement between me and you
and all your descendants from now on: I
will be your God and the God of all your
descendants. 8You live in the land of Canaan now as a stranger, but I will give you
and your descendants all this land forever. And I will be the God of your descendants."
9Then God said to Abraham, "You
and your descendants must keep this
agreement from now on.
10This is my agreement
with you and all your de-
scendants, which you must
obey: Every male among
you must be circumcised.
11Cut away your foreskin
to show that you are pre-
pared to follow the agreement between me and
you. 12From now on when
a baby boy is eight days
old, you will circumcise him. This includes
any boy born among your people or any
who is your slave, who is not one of your
descendants. 13Circumcise every baby
boy whether he is born in your family or
bought as a slave. Your bodies will be
marked to show that you are part of my
agreement that lasts forever. 14Any male
who is not circumcised will be cut off from

I am changing your name from Abram to Abraham because I am making you a father of many nations.
—Genesis 17:5

16:11 Ishmael The Hebrew words for "Ishmael" and "has heard" sound similar.

16:14 Beer Lahai Roi This means "the well of the Living One who sees me."

17:5 Abram This name means "honored father."

17:5 Abraham The end of the Hebrew word for "Abraham" sounds like the beginning of the Hebrew word for "many."

his people, because he has broken my
agreement."

Isaac—the Promised Son

15God said to Abraham, "I will change
the name of Sarai,[n] your wife, to Sarah.[n]
16I will bless her and give her a son, and
you will be the father. She will be the
mother of many nations. Kings of nations
will come from her."
17Abraham bowed facedown on the
ground and laughed. He said to himself,
"Can a man have a child when he is a hundred years old? Can Sarah give birth to a
child when she is ninety?" 18Then Abraham said to God, "Please let Ishmael be
the son you promised."
19God said, "No, Sarah your wife will
have a son, and you will name him Isaac.[n]
I will make my agreement with him to be
an agreement that continues forever with
all his descendants.
20"As for Ishmael, I have heard you. I
will bless him and give him many descendants. And I will cause their numbers to grow greatly. He will be the father
of twelve great leaders, and I will make
him into a great nation. 21But I will make
my agreement with Isaac, the son whom
Sarah will have at this same time next
year." 22After God finished talking with
Abraham, God rose and left him.
23Then Abraham gathered Ishmael,
all the males born in his camp, and the
slaves he had bought. So that day Abraham circumcised every man and boy in his
camp as God had told him to do. 24Abra-
ham was ninety-nine years old when he
was circumcised. 25And Ishmael, his son,
was thirteen years old when he was circumcised. 26Abraham and his son were
circumcised on the same day. 27Also on
that day all the men in Abraham's camp
were circumcised, including all those
born in his camp and all the slaves he had
bought from other nations.

The Three Visitors

18 Later, the LORD again appeared to
Abraham near the great trees of
Mamre. Abraham was sitting at the entrance of his tent during the hottest part
of the day. 2He looked up and saw three
men standing near him. When Abraham
saw them, he ran from his tent to meet
them. He bowed facedown on the ground
before them 3and said, "Sir, if you think
well of me, please stay awhile with me,
your servant. 4I will bring some water so
all of you can wash your feet. You may
rest under the tree, 5and I will get some
bread for you so you can regain your
strength. Then you may continue your
journey."
The three men said, "That is fine. Do
as you said."
6Abraham hurried to the tent where
Sarah was and said to her, "Hurry, prepare twenty quarts of fine flour, and make
it into loaves of bread." 7Then Abraham
ran to his herd and took one of his best
calves. He gave it to a servant, who hurried to kill it and to prepare it for food.
8Abraham gave the three men the calf
that had been cooked and milk curds and
milk. While they ate, he stood under the
tree near them.
9The men asked Abraham, "Where is
your wife Sarah?"
"There, in the tent," said Abraham.
10Then the LORD said, "I will certainly return to you about this time a year
from now. At that time your wife Sarah
will have a son."
Sarah was listening at the entrance of
the tent which was behind him. 11Abra-
ham and Sarah were very old. Since
Sarah was past the age when women normally have children, 12she laughed to
herself, "My husband and I are too old to
have a baby."
13Then the LORD said to Abraham,
"Why did Sarah laugh? Why did she say, 'I
am too old to have a baby'? 14Is anything
too hard for the LORD? No! I will return
to you at the right time a year from now,
and Sarah will have a son."
15Sarah was afraid, so she lied and
said, "I didn't laugh."

17:15 Sarai An Aramaic name meaning "princess."
17:15 Sarah A Hebrew name meaning "princess."
17:19 Isaac The Hebrew words for "he laughed" (v. 17) and "Isaac" sound the same.

FAITH links

ROLL OUT THE WELCOME WAGON

GENESIS 18:2-8

If three strangers showed up at your door, would you invite them in for a meal? In these days of "Stranger Danger," we're sometimes afraid to be hospitable, even to people we know. When three strangers came to visit, Abraham did everything possible to make his guests feel welcome. These weren't just ordinary visitors. One of them happened to be the Lord himself. The other two were angels.

You can make people feel welcome, just as Abraham did—anywhere, anytime. How? Give a smile, a kind word, or an offer to share your stuff. When you welcome others, you welcome God, too.

Connect to these Faithlinks to find out how else you can care for others like God does.

Care for the Lost, Deuteronomy 22:1–3, p. 255

Help for the Outsiders, Nehemiah 5:9–10, p. 630

Helpful Advice, Job 12:4–5, p. 673

Welcome!, Matthew 19:13–15, p. 1307

Kindness Counts, Acts 14:3, p. 1489

Come On In!, 1 Peter 4:9–10, p. 1705

But the LORD said, "No. You did laugh."

16Then the men got up to leave and started out toward Sodom. Abraham walked along with them a short time to send them on their way.

Abraham's Bargain with God

17The LORD said, "Should I tell Abraham what I am going to do now?
18Abraham's children will certainly become a great and powerful nation, and all nations on earth will be blessed through
him. 19I have chosen him so he would command his children and his descendants to live the way the LORD wants them to, to live right and be fair. Then I, the LORD, will give Abraham what I promised him."

20Then the LORD said, "I have heard many complaints against the people of Sodom and Gomorrah. They are very
evil. 21I will go down and see if they are as bad as I have heard. If not, I will know."

22So the men turned and went toward Sodom, but Abraham stood there before
the LORD. 23Then Abraham approached him and asked, "Do you plan to destroy the good people along with the evil ones?
24What if there are fifty good people in that city? Will you still destroy it? Surely you will save the city for the fifty good
people living there. 25Surely you will not destroy the good people along with the evil ones; then they would be treated the same. You are the judge of all the earth. Won't you do what is right?"

26The LORD said, "If I find fifty good people in the city of Sodom, I will save the whole city because of them."

27Then Abraham said, "Though I am only dust and ashes, I have been brave to
speak to the Lord. 28What if there are only forty-five good people in the city? Will you destroy the whole city for the lack of five good people?"

The LORD said, "If I find forty-five there, I will not destroy the city."

29Again Abraham said to him, "If you find only forty good people there, will you destroy the city?"

The LORD said, "If I find forty, I will not destroy it."

30Then Abraham said, "Lord, please
don't be angry with me, but let me ask
you this. If you find only thirty good people in the city, will you destroy it?"
He said, "If I find thirty good people
there, I will not destroy the city."
31Then Abraham said, "I have been
brave to speak to the Lord. But what if
there are twenty good people in the city?"
He answered, "If I find twenty there, I
will not destroy the city."
32Then Abraham said, "Lord, please
don't be angry with me, but let me bother
you this one last time. What if you find
ten there?"
He said, "If I find ten there, I will not
destroy it."
33When the LORD finished speaking
to Abraham, he left, and Abraham returned home.

Lot Leaves Sodom

19 The two angels came to Sodom in
the evening as Lot was sitting
near the city gate. When he saw them, he
got up and went to them and bowed facedown on the ground. **2**Lot said, "Sirs,
please come to my house and spend the
night. There you can wash your feet, and
then tomorrow you may continue your
journey."
The angels answered, "No, we will
spend the night in the city's public
square."
3But Lot begged them to come, so
they agreed and went to his house. Then
Lot prepared a meal for them. He baked
bread without yeast, and they ate it.
4Before bedtime, men both young and
old and from every part of Sodom surrounded Lot's house. **5**They called to
Lot, "Where are the two men who came
to you tonight? Bring them out to us so
we can have sexual relations with them."
6Lot went outside to them, closing
the door behind him. **7**He said, "No, my
brothers! Do not do this evil thing.
8Look! I have two daughters who have
never slept with a man. I will give them
to you, and you may do anything you
want with them. But please don't do anything to these men. They have come to
my house, and I must protect them."
9The men around the house answered, "Move out of the way!" Then
they said to each other, "This man Lot
came to our city as a stranger, and now he
wants to tell us what to do!" They said to
Lot, "We will do worse things to you than
to them." They started pushing him back
and were ready to break down the door.
10But the two men staying with Lot
opened the door, pulled him back inside
the house, and then closed the door.
11They struck those outside the door
with blindness, so the men, both young
and old, could not find the door.
12The two men said to Lot, "Do you
have any other relatives in this city? Do
you have any sons-in-law, sons, daughters, or any other relatives? If you do, tell
them to leave now, **13**because we are
about to destroy this city. The LORD has
heard of all the evil that is here, so he has
sent us to destroy it."
14So Lot went out and said to his future sons-in-law who were pledged to
marry his daughters, "Hurry and leave
this city! The LORD is about to destroy
it!" But they thought Lot was joking.
15At dawn the next morning, the angels begged Lot to hurry. They said, "Go!
Take your wife and your two daughters
with you so you will not be destroyed
when the city is punished."
16But Lot delayed. So the two men
took the hands of Lot, his wife, and his
two daughters and led them safely out of
the city. So the LORD was merciful to Lot
and his family. **17**After they brought them
out of the city, one of the men said, "Run
for your lives! Don't look back or stop
anywhere in the valley. Run to the mountains, or you will be destroyed."
18But Lot said to one of them, "Sir,
please don't force me to go so far! **19**You
have been merciful and kind to me and
have saved my life. But I can't run to the
mountains. The disaster will catch me,
and I will die. **20**Look, that little town
over there is not too far away. Let me run
there. It's really just a little town, and I'll
be safe there."
21The angel said to Lot, "Very well, I
will allow you to do this also. I will not
destroy that town. **22**But run there fast,

because I cannot destroy Sodom until
you are safely in that town." (That town
is named Zoar,* because it is little.)

Sodom and Gomorrah Are Destroyed

23The sun had already come up when
Lot entered Zoar. **24**The LORD sent a rain
of burning sulfur down from the sky on
Sodom and Gomorrah **25**and destroyed
those cities. He also destroyed the whole
Jordan Valley, everyone living in the cities, and even all the plants.
26At that point Lot's wife looked back.
When she did, she became a pillar of salt.
27Early the next morning, Abraham
got up and went to the place where he
had stood before the LORD. **28**He looked
down toward Sodom and Gomorrah and
all the Jordan Valley and saw smoke rising from the land, like smoke from a furnace.
29God destroyed the cities in the valley, but he remembered what Abraham
had asked. So God saved Lot's life, but he
destroyed the city where Lot had lived.

Lot and His Daughters

30Lot was afraid to
continue living in Zoar,
so he and his two daugh-
ters went to live in the
mountains in a cave.
31One day the older
daughter said to the
younger, "Our father is
old. Everywhere on the
earth women and men
marry, but there are no
men around here for us
to marry. **32**Let's get our
father drunk and have
sexual relations with him. We can use him
to have children and continue our family."
33That night the two girls got their father drunk, and the older daughter went
and had sexual relations with him. But
Lot did not know when she lay down or
when she got up.
34The next day the older daughter
said to the younger, "Last night I had
sexual relations with my father. Let's get
him drunk again tonight so you can go
and have sexual relations with him, too.
In this way we can use our father to have
children to continue our family." **35**So
that night they got their father drunk
again, and the younger daughter went
and had sexual relations with him. Again,
Lot did not know when she lay down or
when she got up.
36So both of Lot's daughters became
pregnant by their father. **37**The older
daughter gave birth to a son and named
him Moab. He is the ancestor of all the
Moabite people who are still living today.
38The younger daughter also gave birth
to a son and named him Ben-Ammi. He is
the father of all the Ammonite people
who are still living today.

> God destroyed the cities in the valley, but he remembered what Abraham had asked. So God saved Lot's life, but he destroyed the city where Lot had lived.
>
> —Genesis 19:29

Abraham Tricks Abimelech

20 Abraham left Hebron and traveled to southern Canaan where
he stayed awhile between Kadesh and
Shur. When he moved to Gerar, **2**he told
people that his wife Sarah was his sister.
Abimelech king of Gerar
heard this, so he sent
some servants to take
her. **3**But one night God
spoke to Abimelech in a
dream and said, "You will
die. The woman you took
is married."
4But Abimelech had
not gone near Sarah, so
he said, "Lord, would
you destroy an innocent
nation? **5**Abraham him-
self told me, 'This wom-
an is my sister,' and she
also said, 'He is my
brother.' I am innocent.
I did not know I was doing anything
wrong."
6Then God said to Abimelech in the
dream, "Yes, I know you did not realize
what you were doing. So I did not allow
you to sin against me and touch her.
7Give Abraham his wife back. He is a

19:22 Zoar This name sounds like the Hebrew word for "little."

prophet. He will pray for you, and you will
not die. But if you do not give Sarah back,
you and all your family will surely die."
8So early the next morning, Abimelech called all his officers and told them
everything that had happened in the
dream. They were very afraid. **9**Then
Abimelech called Abraham to him and
said, "What have you done to us? What
wrong did I do against you? Why did you
bring this trouble to my kingdom? You
should not have done these things to me.
10What were you thinking that caused
you to do this?"
11Then Abraham answered, "I thought
no one in this place respected God and
that someone would kill me to get Sarah.
12And it is true that she is my sister. She
is the daughter of my father, but she is
not the daughter of my mother. **13**When
God told me to leave my father's house
and wander in many different places, I
told Sarah, 'You must do a special favor
for me. Everywhere we go tell people I
am your brother.' "
14Then Abimelech gave Abraham
some sheep, cattle, and male and female
slaves. He also gave Sarah, Abraham's
wife, back to him **15**and said, "Look
around you at my land. You may live anywhere you want."
16Abimelech said to Sarah, "I gave
your brother Abraham twenty-five
pounds of silver to make up for any wrong
that people may think
about you. I want every-
one to know that you are
innocent."
17Then Abraham
prayed to God, and God
healed Abimelech, his
wife, and his servant
girls so they could have
children. **18**The LORD
had kept all the women
in Abimelech's house
from having children as
a punishment on Abimelech for taking
Abraham's wife Sarah.

Then Abraham prayed to God, and God healed Abimelech, his wife, and his servant girls so they could have children.
—Genesis 20:17

A Baby for Sarah

21 The LORD cared for Sarah as he
had said and did for her what he
had promised. **2**Sarah became pregnant
and gave birth to a son for Abraham in his
old age. Everything happened at the time
God had said it would. **3**Abraham named
his son Isaac, the son Sarah gave birth to.
4He circumcised Isaac when he was
eight days old as God had commanded.
5Abraham was one hundred years old
when his son Isaac was born. **6**And Sarah
said, "God has made me laugh." Everyone who hears about this will laugh with
me. **7**No one thought that I would be able
to have Abraham's child, but even though
Abraham is old I have given him a son."

Hagar and Ishmael Leave

8Isaac grew, and when he became old
enough to eat food, Abraham gave a great
feast. **9**But Sarah saw Ishmael making
fun of Isaac. (Ishmael was the son of
Abraham by Hagar, Sarah's Egyptian
slave.) **10**So Sarah said to Abraham,
"Throw out this slave woman and her
son. Her son should not inherit anything;
my son Isaac should receive it all."
11This troubled Abraham very much
because Ishmael was also his son. **12**But
God said to Abraham, "Don't be troubled
about the boy and the slave woman. Do
whatever Sarah tells you. The descendants I promised you will be from Isaac.
13I will also make the descendants of Ishmael into a great nation because he is
your son, too."
14Early the next
morning Abraham took
some food and a leather
bag full of water. He
gave them to Hagar and
sent her away. Carrying
these things and her
son, Hagar went and
wandered in the desert
of Beersheba.
15Later, when all the
water was gone from the
bag, Hagar put her son under a bush.
16Then she went away a short distance
and sat down. She thought, "My son will

21:6 laugh The Hebrew words for "he laughed" and "Isaac" sound the same.

FAITH links

JUST KIDDING?

GENESIS 21:8-10

Has anyone ever said something hurtful to you, then added, "I'm just kidding"? "Just kidding" around can lead to trouble sometimes. Take Ishmael for instance. After hearing Ishmael making fun of Isaac, Sarah had Ishmael and his mother Hagar sent away. Although there were other circumstances involved in the decision, Ishmael's behavior didn't make things better.

There is nothing wrong with a little teasing, if it is done in love. When teasing turns into a put-down, that means trouble. Telling a person "I'm just playing!" does little to heal the pain of a careless remark. Treat others the way you want to be treated.

Just a Little Respect, 1 Chronicles 11:10–19, p. 534

The Problem with Gossip, Proverbs 11:12–13, p. 840

What's Wrong About Rumors, Jeremiah 29:24–32, p. 1032

Say What?!, Ephesians 4:22–29, p. 1603

Trouble with the Tongue, James 3:3–12, p. 1692

Who's on First?, 3 John 9–10, p. 1723

die, and I cannot watch this happen." She
sat there and began to cry.
17God heard the boy crying, and
God's angel called to Hagar from heaven.
He said, "What is wrong, Hagar? Don't
be afraid! God has heard the boy crying
there. **18**Help him up and take him by the
hand. I will make his descendants into a
great nation."
19Then God showed Hagar a well of
water. So she went to the well and filled
her bag with water and gave the boy a
drink.
20God was with the boy as he grew
up. Ishmael lived in the desert and became an archer. **21**He lived in the Desert
of Paran, and his mother found a wife for
him in Egypt.

Abraham's Bargain with Abimelech

22Then Abimelech came with Phicol,
the commander of his army, and said to
Abraham, "God is with you in everything
you do. **23**So make a promise to me here
before God that you will be fair with me
and my children and my descendants. Be
kind to me and to this land where you
have lived as a stranger—as kind as I
have been to you."
24And Abraham said, "I promise."
25Then Abraham complained to Abimelech about Abimelech's servants who had
seized a well of water.
26But Abimelech said, "I don't know
who did this. You never told me about
this before today."
27Then Abraham gave Abimelech
some sheep and cattle, and they made an
agreement. **28**Abraham also put seven
female lambs in front of Abimelech.
29Abimelech asked Abraham, "Why
did you put these seven female lambs by
themselves?"
30Abraham answered, "Accept these
lambs from me to prove that you believe I
dug this well."
31So that place was called Beersheba[n]
because they made a promise to each
other there.
32After Abraham and Abimelech
made the agreement at Beersheba, Abimelech and Phicol, the commander of his

21:31 Beersheba This name means "well of the promise" or "well of seven."

army, went back to the land of the Philistines.
33Abraham planted a tamarisk tree at
Beersheba and prayed to the LORD, the
God who lives forever. 34And Abraham
lived as a stranger in the land of the Philistines for a long time.

God Tests Abraham

22 After these things God tested
Abraham's faith. God said to him,
"Abraham!"
And he answered, "Here I am."
2Then God said, "Take your only son,
Isaac, the son you love, and go to the land
of Moriah. Kill him there and offer him as
a whole burnt offering on one of the
mountains I will tell you about."
3Abraham got up early in the morning
and saddled his donkey. He took Isaac
and two servants with him. After he cut
the wood for the sacrifice, they went
to the place God had told them to go. 4On
the third day Abraham looked up and saw
the place in the distance. 5He said to his
servants, "Stay here with the donkey. My
son and I will go over there and worship,
and then we will come back to you."
6Abraham took the wood for the sacrifice and gave it to his son to carry, but he
himself took the knife and the fire. So he
and his son went on together.
7Isaac said to his father Abraham,
"Father!"
Abraham answered, "Yes, my son."
Isaac said, "We have the fire and the
wood, but where is the lamb we will burn
as a sacrifice?"
8Abraham answered, "God will give
us the lamb for the sacrifice, my son."
So Abraham and his son went on together 9and came to the place God had
told him about. Abraham built an altar
there. He laid the wood on it and then
tied up his son Isaac and laid him on the
wood on the altar. 10Then Abraham took
his knife and was about to kill his son.
11But the angel of the LORD called to
him from heaven and said, "Abraham!
Abraham!"
Abraham answered, "Yes."
12The angel said, "Don't kill your son
or hurt him in any way. Now I can see that
you trust God and that you have not kept
your son, your only son, from me."
13Then Abraham looked up and saw a
male sheep caught in a bush by its horns.

FAITH links

THE SACRIFICE 

GENESIS 22

If God told you to give up the thing you love most, would you do it? Abraham was obedient to God, no matter what the cost. He was willing to sacrifice his son, the one he had waited *decades* for. God was pleased by his obedience and provided a ram for Abraham to use as a sacrifice.

God may not call you to sacrifice your most-loved possession. But he does call you to obedience. He wants you to put him above anyone or anything else. What are you willing to sacrifice to be obedient to God?

Link here to find out more about how God wants us to obey him.

What You Value, Genesis 25:21–34, p. 34

Remembering What He Said, Deuteronomy 6:4–9, p. 236

I Insist!, 1 Samuel 8; 9, p. 363

When God Says No, 2 Samuel 7, p. 407

A Reminder to Do What Is Right and True, Zechariah 7:8–10, p. 1257

Believe It or Not, Luke 1:20, 38, p. 1366

So Abraham went and took the sheep and
killed it. He offered it as a whole burnt
offering to God, and his son was saved.
14So Abraham named that place The
LORD Provides. Even today people say,
"On the mountain of the LORD it will be
provided."
15The angel of the LORD called to
Abraham from heaven a second time
16and said, "The LORD says, 'Because
you did not keep back your son, your only
son, from me, I make you this promise by
my own name: **17**I will surely bless you
and give you many descendants. They
will be as many as the stars in the sky and
the sand on the seashore, and they will
capture the cities of their enemies.
18Through your descendants all the nations on the earth will be blessed, because you obeyed me.' "
19Then Abraham returned to his servants. They all traveled back to Beersheba, and Abraham stayed there.
20After these things
happened, someone told
Abraham: "Your brother
Nahor and his wife Mil-
cah have children now.
21The first son is Uz,
and the second is Buz.
The third son is Kem-
uel (the father of Aram).
22Then there are Ke-
sed, Hazo, Pildash,
Jidlaph, and Bethuel."
23Bethuel became the
father of Rebekah. Mil-
cah was the mother of these eight sons,
and Nahor, Abraham's brother, was the
father. **24**Also Nahor had four other sons
by his slave woman Reumah. Their
names were Tebah, Gaham, Tahash, and
Maacah.

> The Hittites answered Abraham, "Sir, you are a great leader among us. You may have the best place we have to bury your dead."
> —Genesis 23:5–6a

Sarah Dies

23 Sarah lived to be one hundred
twenty-seven years old. **2**She died
in Kiriath Arba (that is, Hebron) in the
land of Canaan. Abraham was very sad
and cried because of her. **3**After a while
he got up from the side of his wife's body
and went to talk to the Hittites. He said,
4"I am only a stranger and a foreigner
here. Sell me some of your land so that I
can bury my dead wife."
5The Hittites answered Abraham,
6"Sir, you are a great leader among us.
You may have the best place we have to
bury your dead. You may have any of our
burying places that you want, and none of
us will stop you from burying your dead
wife."
7Abraham rose and bowed to the people of the land, the Hittites. **8**He said to
them, "If you truly want to help me bury
my dead wife here, speak to Ephron, the
son of Zohar for me. **9**Ask him to sell me
the cave of Machpelah at the edge of his
field. I will pay him the full price. You can
be the witnesses that I am buying it as a
burial place."
10Ephron was sitting among the Hittites at the city gate. He answered Abraham, **11**"No, sir. I will give you the land
and the cave that is in it, with these people as witnesses. Bury your dead wife."
12Then Abraham
bowed down before the
Hittites. **13**He said to
Ephron before all the
people, "Please let me
pay you the full price
for the field. Accept my
money, and I will bury
my dead there."
14Ephron answered
Abraham, **15**"Sir, the land
is worth ten pounds of
silver, but I won't argue
with you over the price.
Take the land, and bury your dead wife."
16Abraham agreed and paid Ephron
in front of the Hittite witnesses. He
weighed out the full price, ten pounds of
silver, and they counted the weight as the
traders normally did.
17-18 So Ephron's field in Machpelah,
east of Mamre, was sold. Abraham became the owner of the field, the cave in it,
and all the trees that were in the field.
The sale was made at the city gate, with
the Hittites as witnesses. **19**After this,
Abraham buried his wife Sarah in the
cave in the field of Machpelah, near
Mamre. (Mamre was later called Hebron
in the land of Canaan.) **20**So Abraham

bought the field and the cave in it from
the Hittites to use as a burying place.

A Wife for Isaac

24 Abraham was now very old, and
the LORD had blessed him in
every way. 2Abraham said to his oldest
servant, who was in charge of everything
he owned, "Put your hand under my leg."
3Make a promise to me before the LORD,
the God of heaven and earth. Don't get a
wife for my son from the Canaanite girls
who live around here. 4Instead, go back
to my country, to the land of my relatives,
and get a wife for my son Isaac."
5The servant said to him, "What if
this woman does not want to return with
me to this land? Then, should I take your
son with me back to your homeland?"
6Abraham said to him, "No! Don't
take my son back there. 7The LORD, the
God of heaven, brought me from the
home of my father and the land of my relatives. And he promised me, 'I will give
this land to your descendants.' The LORD
will send his angel before you to help you
get a wife for my son there. 8If the girl
won't come back with you, you will be
free from this promise. But you must not
take my son back there." 9So the servant
put his hand under his master's leg and
made a promise to Abraham about this.
10The servant took ten of Abraham's
camels and left, carrying with him many
different kinds of beautiful gifts. He went
to Northwest Mesopotamia to Nahor's
city. 11In the evening, when the women
come out to get water, he made the camels kneel down at the well outside the
city.
12The servant said, "LORD, God of my
master Abraham, allow me to find a wife
for his son today. Please show this kindness to my master Abraham. 13Here I
am, standing by the spring, and the girls
from the city are coming out to get water.
14I will say to one of them, 'Please put
your jar down so I can drink.' Then let
her say, 'Drink, and I will also give water
to your camels.' If that happens, I will
know she is the right one for your servant Isaac and that you have shown kindness to my master."
15Before the servant had finished
praying, Rebekah, the daughter of Bethuel, came out of the city. (Bethuel was
the son of Milcah and Nahor, Abraham's
brother.) Rebekah was carrying her
water jar on her shoulder. 16She was
very pretty, a virgin; she had never had
sexual relations with a man. She went
down to the spring and filled her jar, then
came back up. 17The servant ran to her
and said, "Please give me a little water
from your jar."

24:2 Put . . . leg This showed that a person would keep the promise.

FAITH CHALLENGE

Here's one for you. Read 24:17-19 to see how one woman responded to a simple request from a servant. How do you usually respond when someone asks you for a favor?

TESTING IT

Genesis 24:17–19

The servant ran to her and said, "Please give me a little water from your jar." Rebekah said, "Drink, sir." She quickly lowered the jar from her shoulder and gave him a drink. After he finished drinking, Rebekah said, "I will also pour some water for your camels."

____

____

____

____

____

____

____

18Rebekah said, "Drink, sir." She quickly lowered the jar from her shoulder and gave him a drink. **19**After he finished drinking, Rebekah said, "I will also pour some water for your camels." **20**So she quickly poured all the water from her jar into the drinking trough for the camels. Then she kept running to the well until she had given all the camels enough to drink.

21The servant quietly watched her. He wanted to be sure the LORD had made his trip successful. **22**After the camels had finished drinking, he gave Rebekah a gold ring weighing one-fifth of an ounce and two gold arm bracelets weighing about four ounces each. **23**He asked, "Who is your father? Is there a place in his house for me and my men to spend the night?"

24Rebekah answered, "My father is Bethuel, the son of Milcah and Nahor." **25**Then she said, "And, yes, we have straw for your camels and a place for you to spend the night."

26The servant bowed and worshiped the LORD **27**and said, "Blessed is the LORD, the God of my master Abraham. The LORD has been kind and truthful to him and has led me to my master's relatives."

28Then Rebekah ran and told her mother's family about all these things. **29**She had a brother named Laban, who ran out to Abraham's servant, who was still at the spring. **30**Laban had heard what she had said and had seen the ring and the bracelets on his sister's arms. So he ran out to the well, and there was the man standing by the camels at the spring. **31**Laban said, "Sir, you are welcome to come in; you don't have to stand outside. I have prepared the house for you and also a place for your camels."

32So Abraham's servant went into the house. After Laban unloaded the camels and gave them straw and food, he gave water to Abraham's servant so he and the men with him could wash their feet. **33**Then Laban gave the servant food, but the servant said, "I will not eat until I have told you why I came."

So Laban said, "Then tell us."

34He said, "I am Abraham's servant. **35**The LORD has greatly blessed my master in everything, and he has become a rich man. The LORD has given him many flocks of sheep, herds of cattle, silver and gold, male and female servants, camels, and horses. **36**Sarah, my master's wife, gave birth to a son when she was old, and my master has given everything he owns to that son. **37**My master had me make a promise to him and said, 'Don't get a wife for my son from the Canaanite girls who live around here. **38**Instead, you must go to my father's people and to my family. There you must get a wife for my son.' **39**I said to my master, 'What if the woman will not come back with me?' **40**But he said, 'I serve the LORD, who will send his angel with you and will help you. You will get a wife for my son from my family and my father's people. **41**Then you will be free from the promise. But if they will not give you a wife for my son, you will be free from this promise.'

42"Today I came to this spring. I said, 'LORD, God of my master Abraham, please make my trip successful. **43**I am standing by this spring. I will wait for a young woman to come out to get water, and I will say, "Please give me water from your jar to drink." **44**Then let her say, "Drink this water, and I will also get water for your camels." By this I will know the LORD has chosen her for my master's son.'

45"Before I finished my silent prayer, Rebekah came out of the city with her water jar on her shoulder. She went down to the spring and got water. I said to her, 'Please give me a drink.' **46**She quickly lowered the jar from her shoulder and said, 'Drink this. I will also get water for your camels.' So I drank, and she gave water to my camels too. **47**When I asked her, 'Who is your father?' she answered, 'My father is Bethuel son of Milcah and Nahor.' Then I put the ring in her nose and the bracelets on her arms, **48**and I bowed my head and thanked the LORD. I praised the LORD, the God of my master Abraham, because he led me on the right road to get the granddaughter of my master's brother for his son. **49**Now, tell

me, will you be kind and truthful to my
master? And if not, tell me so. Then I will
know what I should do."
50Laban and Bethuel answered, "This
is clearly from the LORD, and we cannot
change what must happen. **51**Rebekah is
yours. Take her and go. Let her marry
your master's son as the LORD has commanded."
52When Abraham's servant heard
these words, he bowed facedown on the
ground before the LORD. **53**Then he gave
Rebekah gold and silver jewelry and
clothes. He also gave expensive gifts to
her brother and mother. **54**The servant
and the men with him ate and drank and
spent the night there. When they got up
the next morning, the servant said, "Now
let me go back to my master."
55Rebekah's mother and her brother
said, "Let Rebekah stay with us at least
ten days. After that she may go."
56But the servant said to them, "Do
not make me wait, because the LORD has
made my trip successful. Now let me go
back to my master."
57Rebekah's brother and mother said,
"We will call Rebekah and ask her what
she wants to do." **58**They called her and
asked her, "Do you want to go with this
man now?"
She said, "Yes, I do."
59So they allowed Rebekah and her
nurse to go with Abraham's servant and
his men. **60**They blessed Rebekah and
said,

"Our sister, may you be the mother
of thousands of people,
and may your descendants capture
the cities of their enemies."

61Then Rebekah and her servant girls
got on the camels and followed the servant and his men. So the servant took
Rebekah and left.
62At this time Isaac had left Beer Lahai Roi and was living in southern Canaan. **63**One evening when he went out
to the field to think, he looked up and saw
camels coming. **64**Rebekah also looked
and saw Isaac. Then she jumped down
from the camel **65**and asked the servant,
"Who is that man walking in the field to
meet us?"
The servant answered, "That is my
master." So Rebekah covered her face
with her veil.
66The servant told Isaac everything
that had happened. **67**Then Isaac brought
Rebekah into the tent of Sarah, his
mother, and she became his wife. Isaac
loved her very much, and so he was comforted after his mother's death.

Abraham's Family

25 Abraham married again, and his
new wife was Keturah. **2**She gave
birth to Zimran, Jokshan, Medan, Midian,
Ishbak, and Shuah. **3**Jokshan was the father of Sheba and Dedan. Dedan's descendants were the people of Assyria,
Letush, and Leum. **4**The sons of Midian
were Ephah, Epher, Hanoch, Abida, and
Eldaah. All these were descendants of
Keturah. **5**Abraham left everything he
owned to Isaac. **6**But before Abraham
died, he did give gifts to the sons of his
other wives, then sent them to the East
to be away from Isaac.
7Abraham lived to be one hundred
seventy-five years old. **8**He breathed his
last breath and died at an old age, after a
long and satisfying life. **9**His sons Isaac
and Ishmael buried him in the cave of
Machpelah in the field of Ephron east of
Mamre. (Ephron was the son of Zohar the
Hittite.) **10**So Abraham was buried with
his wife Sarah in the same field that he
had bought from the Hittites. **11**After
Abraham died, God blessed his son Isaac.
Isaac was now living at Beer Lahai Roi.
12This is the family history of Ishmael, Abraham's son. (Hagar, Sarah's
Egyptian servant, was Ishmael's mother.)
13These are the names of Ishmael's sons
in the order they were born: Nebaioth,
the first son, then Kedar, Adbeel, Mibsam, **14**Mishma, Dumah, Massa, **15**Hadad, Tema, Jetur, Naphish, and Kedemah.
16These were Ishmael's sons, and these
are the names of the tribal leaders listed
according to their settlements and camps.
17Ishmael lived one hundred thirty-
seven years and then breathed his last
breath and died. **18**His descendants lived
from Havilah to Shur, which is east of
Egypt stretching toward Assyria. They

often attacked the descendants of his
brothers.

Isaac's Family

19This is the family history of Isaac.
Abraham had a son named Isaac. 20When
Isaac was forty years old, he married
Rebekah, who came from Northwest
Mesopotamia. She was Bethuel's daugh-
ter and the sister of Laban the Aramean.
21Isaac's wife could not have children, so
Isaac prayed to the LORD for her. The
LORD heard Isaac's prayer, and Rebekah
became pregnant.

22While she was pregnant, the babies
struggled inside her. She asked, "Why is
this happening to me?" Then she went to
get an answer from the LORD.
23The LORD said to her,

"Two nations are in your body,
and two groups of people will be
taken from you.
One group will be stronger than the
other,
and the older will serve the
younger."

24When the time came, Rebekah gave
birth to twins. 25The first baby was born
red. Since his skin was like a hairy robe,
he was named Esau.ⁿ 26When the second
baby was born, he was holding on to
Esau's heel, so that baby was named
Jacob.ⁿ Isaac was sixty years old when
they were born.

27When the boys grew up, Esau became a skilled hunter. He loved to be out
in the fields. But Jacob was a quiet man
and stayed among the tents. 28Isaac
loved Esau because he hunted the wild
animals that Isaac enjoyed eating. But
Rebekah loved Jacob.

29One day Jacob was boiling a pot of
vegetable soup. Esau came in from hunting in the fields, weak from hunger. 30So
Esau said to Jacob, "Let me eat some of
that red soup, because I am weak with
hunger." (That is why people call him
Edom.ⁿ)

31But Jacob said, "You must sell me
your rights as the firstborn son."ⁿ

25:25 Esau This name may mean "hairy."
25:26 Jacob This name sounds like the Hebrew word for "heel." "Grabbing someone's heel" is a Hebrew saying for tricking someone.
25:30 Edom This name sounds like the Hebrew word for "red."
25:31 rights . . . son Usually the firstborn son had a high rank in the family. The firstborn son usually became the new head of the family.

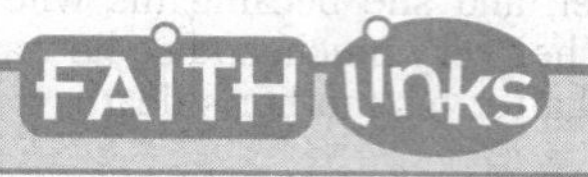

WHAT YOU VALUE

GENESIS 25:21-34

What's the most valuable thing you have? How much is it worth to you? Esau traded away his rights as the firstborn son for a bowl of soup. Although Esau and his brother Jacob were twins, Esau was still the firstborn. That meant he had more privileges than Jacob did. Unfortunately, Esau didn't value what he had. He also didn't consider what would happen in the long run.

A good reputation is one of the most valuable treasures that anyone can have. If you're a Christian, your relationship with Jesus is also beyond price. In the long run, they're worth hanging on to.

Fatherly Advice, Exodus 18, p. 99

The Fence Riders, 1 Kings 18, p. 464

Mind Guard, Proverbs 4:23, p. 831

A Useless Thing, Isaiah 44:9, 18–20, p. 954

Put God First, Acts 5:27–32, p. 1472

That's False!, 2 John 7–11, p. 1722

32Esau said, "I am almost dead from
hunger. If I die, all of my father's wealth
will not help me."
33But Jacob said, "First, promise me
that you will give it to me." So Esau made
a promise to Jacob and sold his part of
their father's wealth to Jacob. 34Then
Jacob gave Esau bread and vegetable
soup, and he ate and drank, and then left.
So Esau showed how little he cared about
his rights as the firstborn son.

Isaac Lies to Abimelech

26 Now there was a time of hunger in
the land, besides the time of hunger that happened during Abraham's life.
So Isaac went to the town of Gerar to see
Abimelech king of the Philistines. 2The
LORD appeared to Isaac and said, "Don't
go down to Egypt, but live in the land
where I tell you to live. 3Stay in this land,
and I will be with you and bless you. I will
give you and your descendants all these
lands, and I will keep the oath I made to
Abraham your father. 4I will give you
many descendants, as hard to count as
the stars in the sky, and I will give them
all these lands. Through your descendants all the nations on the earth will be
blessed. 5I will do this because your
father Abraham obeyed me. He did what
I said and obeyed my commands, my
teachings, and my rules."
6So Isaac stayed in Gerar. 7His wife
Rebekah was very beautiful, and the men
of that place asked Isaac about her. Isaac
said, "She is my sister," because he was
afraid to tell them she was his wife. He
thought they might kill him so they could
have her.
8Isaac lived there a long time. One
day as Abimelech king of the Philistines
looked out his window, he saw Isaac holding his wife Rebekah tenderly. 9Abime-
lech called for Isaac and said, "This
woman is your wife. Why did you say she
was your sister?"
Isaac said to him, "I was afraid you
would kill me so you could have her."
10Abimelech said, "What have you
done to us? One of our men might have
had sexual relations with your wife. Then
we would have been guilty of a great sin."
11So Abimelech warned everyone,
"Anyone who touches this man or his
wife will be put to death."

Isaac Becomes Rich

12Isaac planted seed in that land, and
that year he gathered a great harvest.
The LORD blessed him very much, 13and
he became rich. He gathered more
wealth until he became a very rich man.
14He had so many slaves and flocks and
herds that the Philistines envied him.
15So they stopped up all the wells the
servants of Isaac's father Abraham had
dug. (They had dug them when Abraham
was alive.) The Philistines filled those
wells with dirt. 16And Abimelech said to
Isaac, "Leave our country because you
have become much more powerful than
we are."
17So Isaac left that place and camped
in the Valley of Gerar and lived there.
18Long before this time Abraham had
dug many wells, but after he died, the
Philistines filled them with dirt. So Isaac
dug those wells again and gave them the
same names his father had given them.
19Isaac's servants dug a well in the valley, from which a spring of water flowed.
20But the herdsmen of Gerar argued
with them and said, "This water is ours."
So Isaac named that well Argue because
they argued with him. 21Then his servants dug another well. When the people
also argued about it, Isaac named that
well Fight. 22He moved from there and
dug another well. No one argued about
this one, so he named it Room Enough.
Isaac said, "Now the LORD has made
room for us, and we will be successful in
this land."
23From there Isaac went to Beersheba. 24The LORD appeared to him that
night and said, "I am the God of your father Abraham. Don't be afraid, because I
am with you. I will bless you and give you
many descendants because of my servant
Abraham." 25So Isaac built an altar and
worshiped the LORD there. He also made
a camp there, and his servants dug a well.
26Abimelech came from Gerar to
see Isaac. He brought with him Ahuz-
zath, who advised him, and Phicol, the

commander of his army. 27Isaac asked
them, "Why have you come to see me?
You were my enemy and forced me to
leave your country."

28They answered, "Now we know
that the LORD is with you. Let us swear
an oath to each other.
Let us make an
agreement with you
29that since we did
not hurt you, you will
not hurt us. We were
good to you and sent
you away in peace.
Now the LORD has
blessed you."

30So Isaac pre-
pared food for them,
and they all ate and
drank. 31Early the
next morning the
men swore an oath
to each other. Then Isaac sent them away,
and they left in peace.

32That day Isaac's servants came and
told him about the well they had dug, saying, "We found water in that well." 33So
Isaac named it Shibah[n] and that city is
called Beersheba even now.

34When Esau was forty years old, he
married two Hittite women—Judith
daughter of Beeri and Basemath daughter of Elon. 35These women brought
much sorrow to Isaac and Rebekah.

> The LORD appeared to him that night and said, "I am the God of your father Abraham. Don't be afraid, because I am with you. I will bless you and give you many descendants because of my servant Abraham."
> —Genesis 26:24

Jacob Tricks Isaac

27 When Isaac was old, his eyesight
was poor, so he could not see
clearly. One day he called his older son
Esau to him and said, "Son."

Esau answered, "Here I am."

2Isaac said, "I am old and don't know
when I might die. 3So take your bow and
arrows and go hunting in the field for an
animal for me to eat. 4When you prepare
the tasty food that I love, bring it to me,
and I will eat. Then I will bless you before
I die." 5So Esau went out in the field to
hunt.

Rebekah was listening as Isaac said
this to his son Esau. 6She said to her son
Jacob, "Listen, I heard your father saying
to your brother Esau, 7'Kill an animal and
prepare some tasty food for me to eat.
Then I will bless you in the presence of
the LORD before I die.' 8So obey me,
my son, and do what I tell you. 9Go out to
our goats and bring me two of the best
young ones. I will prepare them just
the way your father
likes them. 10Then
you will take the
food to your father,
and he will bless you
before he dies."

11But Jacob said
to his mother Re-
bekah, "My brother
Esau is a hairy man,
and I am smooth! 12If
my father touches
me, he will know I
am not Esau. Then
he will not bless me
but will place a curse
on me because I tried to trick him."

13So Rebekah said to him, "If your father puts a curse on you, I will accept the
blame. Just do what I said and go, get the
goats for me."

14So Jacob went out and got two goats
and brought them to his mother, and she
cooked them in the special way Isaac enjoyed. 15She took the best clothes of her
older son Esau that were in the house
and put them on the younger son Jacob.
16She also took the skins of the goats and
put them on Jacob's hands and neck.
17Then she gave Jacob the tasty food and
the bread she had made.

18Jacob went in to his father and said,
"Father."

And his father said, "Yes, my son.
Who are you?"

19Jacob said to him, "I am Esau, your
first son. I have done what you told me.
Now sit up and eat some meat of the animal I hunted for you. Then bless me."

20But Isaac asked his son, "How did
you find and kill the animal so quickly?"

Jacob answered, "Because the LORD
your God helped me to find it."

21Then Isaac said to Jacob, "Come

26:33 Shibah This name sounds like the Hebrew words for "seven" and "promise."

near so I can touch you, my son. Then
I will know if you are really my son
Esau."
22So Jacob came near to Isaac his father. Isaac touched him and said, "Your
voice sounds like Jacob's voice, but your
hands are hairy like the hands of Esau."
23Isaac did not know it was Jacob, because his hands were hairy like Esau's
hands, so Isaac blessed him. 24Isaac
asked, "Are you really my son Esau?"
Jacob answered, "Yes, I am."
25Then Isaac said, "Bring me the
food, and I will eat it and bless you." So
Jacob gave him the food, and he ate. Jacob
gave him wine, and he drank. 26Then
Isaac said to him, "My son, come near
and kiss me." 27So Jacob went to his father and kissed him. When Isaac smelled
Esau's clothes, he blessed him and said,

"The smell of my son
  is like the smell of the field
  that the LORD has blessed.
28 May God give you plenty of rain
  and good soil
  so that you will have plenty of
    grain and new wine.
29 May nations serve you
  and peoples bow down to you.
May you be master over your
    brothers,
  and may your mother's sons bow
    down to you.
May everyone who curses you be
    cursed,
  and may everyone who blesses
    you be blessed."

30Isaac finished blessing Jacob. Then,
just as Jacob left his father Isaac, Esau
came in from hunting. 31He also prepared some tasty food and brought it to
his father. He said, "Father, rise and eat
the food that your son killed for you and
then bless me."
32Isaac asked, "Who are you?"
He answered, "I am your son—your
firstborn son—Esau."
33Then Isaac trembled greatly and
said, "Then who was it that hunted the
animals and brought me food before you
came? I ate it, and I blessed him, and it is
too late now to take back my blessing."
34When Esau heard the words of his

FAMILY FEUD

GENESIS 27

Most of us have moments when someone in our family bugs us. You do, too, right? But have you ever deliberately set out to make someone in your family angry? Jacob did, when he tricked his father into giving him the blessing Esau would have received. A blessing was very important. A blessing was the official "giving" of the firstborn's privileges and rights. After the blessing, these rights could not be taken away. As a result of stealing his brother's blessing, Jacob had to run for his life.

What causes a family feud? Selfish thinking usually does. How can a feud be avoided? Instead of thinking *Me first*, consider *You first*. That means putting someone else's needs ahead of your own. It beats fussin' and feudin'.

Need more help in learning to live with your family? Surf over to these links!

Peace in the Family, Psalm 133, p. 811

Some Friendly Advice, Proverbs 17:9, 14, 17, p. 851

The Gentle Way, Titus 3:1–5, p. 1661

Family Time, Hebrews 10:25, p. 1678

father, he let out a loud and bitter cry. He said to his father, "Bless me—me, too, my father!"

35But Isaac said, "Your brother came and tricked me. He has taken your blessing."

36Esau said, "Jacob" is the right name for him. He has tricked me these two times. He took away my share of everything you own, and now he has taken away my blessing." Then Esau asked, "Haven't you saved a blessing for me?"

37Isaac answered, "I gave Jacob the power to be master over you, and all his brothers will be his servants. And I kept him strong with grain and new wine. There is nothing left to give you, my son."

38But Esau continued, "Do you have only one blessing, Father? Bless me, too, Father!" Then Esau began to cry out loud.

39Isaac said to him,

"You will live far away from the best
land,
far from the rain.

40 You will live by using your sword,
and you will be a slave to your
brother.
But when you struggle,
you will break free from him."

41After that Esau hated Jacob because of the blessing from Isaac. He thought to himself, "My father will soon die, and I will be sad for him. Then I will kill Jacob."

42Rebekah heard about Esau's plan to kill Jacob. So she sent for Jacob and said to him, "Listen, your brother Esau is comforting himself by planning to kill you. **43**So, my son, do what I say. My brother Laban is living in Haran. Go to him at once! **44**Stay with him for a while, until your brother is not so angry. **45**In time, your brother will not be angry, and he will forget what you did to him. Then I will send a servant to bring you back. I don't want to lose both of my sons on the same day."

46Then Rebekah said to Isaac, "I am tired of Hittite women. If Jacob marries one of these Hittite women here in this land, I want to die."

Jacob Searches for a Wife

28 Isaac called Jacob and blessed him and commanded him, "You must not marry a Canaanite woman. **2**Go to the house of Bethuel, your mother's father, in Northwest Mesopotamia. Laban, your mother's brother, lives there. Marry one of his daughters. **3**May God Almighty bless you and give you many children, and may you become a group of many peoples. **4**May he give you and your descendants the blessing of Abraham so that you may own the land where you are now living as a stranger, the land God gave to Abraham." **5**So Isaac sent Jacob to Northwest Mesopotamia, to Laban the brother of Rebekah. Bethuel the Aramean was the father of Laban and Rebekah, and Rebekah was the mother of Jacob and Esau.

6Esau learned that Isaac had blessed Jacob and sent him to Northwest Mesopotamia to find a wife there. He also learned that Isaac had commanded Jacob not to marry a Canaanite woman **7**and that Jacob had obeyed his father and mother and had gone to Northwest Mesopotamia. **8**So Esau saw that his father Isaac did not want his sons to marry Canaanite women. **9**Now Esau already had wives, but he went to Ishmael son of Abraham, and he married Mahalath, Ishmael's daughter. Mahalath was the sister of Nebaioth.

Jacob's Dream at Bethel

10Jacob left Beersheba and set out for Haran. **11**When he came to a place, he spent the night there because the sun had set. He found a stone and laid his head on it to go to sleep. **12**Jacob dreamed that there was a ladder resting on the earth and reaching up into heaven, and he saw angels of God going up and coming down the ladder. **13**Then Jacob saw the LORD standing above the ladder, and he said, "I am the LORD, the God of Abraham your grandfather, and the God of Isaac. I will give you and your descendants the land

---

27:36 Jacob This name sounds like the Hebrew word for "heel." "Grabbing someone's heel" is a Hebrew saying for tricking someone.

FROM DECEIVER TO WRESTLER Genesis 28:1–19

1. Jacob was one of the twin boys born to Rebekah and Isaac in the town of Beersheba. As a young man, Jacob convinced his older twin, Esau, to trade his rights as the firstborn son (which meant a bigger portion of the family wealth) for some vegetable soup! Jacob later tricked his dad into giving him the family blessing instead of giving it to Esau. (See Genesis 25:24–34.)

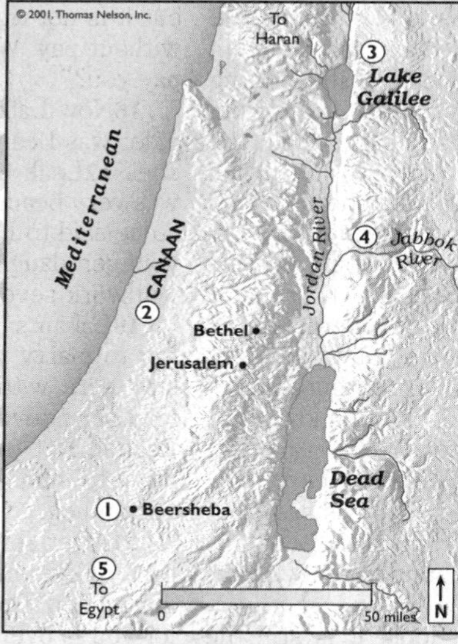

3. Jacob worked for his Uncle Laban for 14 years. He married two of Laban's daughters, first Leah, then her younger sister Rachel. Having two wives is a big enough problem. On top of that, Jacob loved Rachel much more than Leah. This caused even more problems in his family. (Check out Genesis 29:15–28.)

2. Jacob left home after he tricked his brother and his dad. He traveled to a place where his ancestors came from called Haran to live with his Uncle Laban and find a wife. On his way, he spent the night and dreamed about a ladder with angels coming up and down from heaven. It was at Bethel where God promised Jacob that his descendants would fill the land. (Read Genesis 28:1–19.)

4. Jacob returned home to face his brother Esau. On his way home, Jacob had an amazing wrestling match with God. After this, God changed Jacob's name to Israel. (Look at Genesis 32:22–32.) Jacob's sons and their families formed the 12 tribes of Israel.

5. Jacob moved to Egypt with his sons and their families because there was no food in Canaan where he lived. Jacob died in Egypt, but was buried back in Canaan. (See Genesis 49:1–33; 50:13–14.)

on which you are now sleeping. **14**Your
descendants will be as many as the dust of the earth. They will spread west and east, north and south, and all the families of the earth will be blessed through you and your descendants. **15**I am with you
and will protect you everywhere you go and will bring you back to this land. I will not leave you until I have done what I have promised you."

16Then Jacob woke from his sleep and
said, "Surely the LORD is in this place, but I did not know it." **17**He was afraid and
said, "This place frightens me! It is surely the house of God and the gate of heaven."

18Jacob rose early in the morning and
took the stone he had slept on and set it up on its end. Then he poured olive oil on the top of it. **19**At first, the name of that
city was Luz, but Jacob named it Bethel.*

20Then Jacob made a promise. He
said, "I want God to be with me and to protect me on this journey. I want him to give me food to eat and clothes to wear
21so I will be able to return in peace to
my father's house. If the LORD does

28:19 Bethel This name means "house of God."

these things, he will be my God. **22**This
stone which I have set up on its end will
be the house of God. And I will give God
one-tenth of all he gives me."

Jacob Arrives in Northwest Mesopotamia

29 Then Jacob continued his journey
and came to the land of the people
of the East. **2**He looked and saw a well in
the field and three flocks of sheep lying
nearby, because they drank water from
this well. A large stone covered the
mouth of the well. **3**When all the flocks
would gather there, the shepherds would
roll the stone away from the well and water the sheep. Then they would put the
stone back in its place.
4Jacob said to the shepherds there,
"My brothers, where are you from?"
They answered, "We are from Haran."
5Then Jacob asked, "Do you know Laban, grandson of Nahor?"
They answered, "We know him."
6Then Jacob asked, "How is he?"
They answered, "He is well. Look, his
daughter Rachel is coming now with his
sheep."
7Jacob said, "But look, it is still the
middle of the day. It is not time for the
sheep to be gathered for the night, so
give them water and let them go back
into the pasture."
8But they said, "We cannot do that
until all the flocks are gathered. Then we
will roll away the stone from the mouth of
the well and water the sheep."
9While Jacob was talking with the
shepherds, Rachel came with her father's
sheep, because it was her job to care for
the sheep. **10**When Jacob saw Laban's
daughter Rachel and Laban's sheep, he
went to the well and rolled the stone
from its mouth and watered Laban's
sheep. Now Laban was the brother of
Rebekah, Jacob's mother. **11**Then Jacob
kissed Rachel and cried. **12**He told her
that he was from her father's family
and that he was the son of Rebekah. So
Rachel ran home and told her father.
13When Laban heard the news about
his sister's son Jacob, he ran to meet him.
Laban hugged him and kissed him and
brought him to his house, where Jacob
told Laban everything that had happened.
14Then Laban said, "You are my own
flesh and blood."

Jacob Is Tricked

Jacob stayed there a month. **15**Then
Laban said to Jacob, "You are my relative,
but it is not right for you to work for me
without pay. What would you like me to
pay you?"
16Now Laban had two daughters. The
older was Leah, and the younger was Rachel. **17**Leah had weak eyes, but Rachel
was very beautiful. **18**Jacob loved Rachel,
so he said to Laban, "Let me marry your
younger daughter Rachel. If you will, I
will work seven years for you."
19Laban said, "It would be better for
her to marry you than someone else, so
stay here with me." **20**So Jacob worked
for Laban seven years so he could marry
Rachel. But they seemed like just a few
days to him because he loved Rachel
very much.
21After seven years Jacob said to Laban, "Give me Rachel so that I may
marry her. The time I promised to work
for you is over."
22So Laban gave a feast for all the
people there. **23**That evening he brought
his daughter Leah to Jacob, and they had
sexual relations. **24**(Laban gave his slave
girl Zilpah to his daughter to be her
servant.) **25**In the morning when Jacob
saw that he had had sexual relations with
Leah, he said to Laban, "What have you
done to me? I worked hard for you so
that I could marry Rachel! Why did you
trick me?"
26Laban said, "In our country we do
not allow the younger daughter to marry
before the older daughter. **27**But complete the full week of the marriage ceremony with Leah, and I will give you
Rachel to marry also. But you must serve
me another seven years."
28So Jacob did this, and when he had
completed the week with Leah, Laban
gave him his daughter Rachel as a wife.
29(Laban gave his slave girl Bilhah to his
daughter Rachel to be her servant.) **30**So
Jacob had sexual relations with Rachel

THE BEST POLICY

GENESIS 29:16-29

Know what Jacob's name means? It is a word that means to trick someone. Boy, did he ever. He conned his father into giving him the blessing meant for Esau. Yet the trickster found himself tricked by his uncle—Laban. Jacob had worked several years for Laban in order to marry Laban's daughter Rachel. But Laban tricked him by giving Rachel's sister Leah to Jacob instead.

Think deceiving others is cool? Think again. When you try to deceive others, you might find yourself deceived one day. That's why God instructs us to be honest. As the old saying goes, honesty is always the best policy. Honest!

Surf on to find out what else God has to say about honesty!

A Special Promise, Numbers 30:1–2, p. 217

An Honest Reputation, Nehemiah 13:13, p. 644

Who Do You Prefer?, Proverbs 3:32, p. 830

Down on the Ant Farm, Proverbs 6:6–11, p. 833

The Whole Truth, John 8:31–32, 45, p. 1438

The Deadliest Lie, Acts 5:1–11, p. 1471

also, and Jacob loved Rachel more than
Leah. Jacob worked for Laban for another
seven years.

Jacob's Family Grows

31When the LORD saw that Jacob
loved Rachel more than Leah, he made it
possible for Leah to have children, but
not Rachel. 32Leah became pregnant
and gave birth to a son. She named him
Reuben,* because she said, "The LORD
has seen my troubles. Surely now my
husband will love me."
33Leah became pregnant again and
gave birth to another son. She named him
Simeon* and said, "The LORD has heard
that I am not loved, so he has given me
this son."
34Leah became pregnant again and
gave birth to another son. She named him
Levi* and said, "Now, surely my husband
will be close to me, because I have given
him three sons."
35Then Leah gave birth to another
son. She named him Judah,* because she
said, "Now I will praise the LORD." Then
Leah stopped having children.

30 When Rachel saw that she was not
having children for Jacob, she envied her sister Leah. She said to Jacob,
"Give me children, or I'll die!" 2Jacob
became angry with her and said, "Can I
do what only God can do? He is the one
who has kept you from having children."
3Then Rachel said, "Here is my slave
girl Bilhah. Have sexual relations with
her so she can give birth to a child for
me. Then I can have my own family
through her."
4So Rachel gave Bilhah, her slave girl,
to Jacob as a wife, and he had sexual relations with her. 5She became pregnant
and gave Jacob a son. 6Rachel said, "God
has judged me innocent. He has listened

29:32 Reuben This name sounds like the Hebrew word for "he has seen my troubles."
29:33 Simeon This name sounds like the Hebrew word for "has heard."
29:34 Levi This name sounds like the Hebrew word for "be close to."
29:35 Judah This name sounds like the Hebrew word for "praise."

to my prayer and has given me a son," so
she named him Dan.[n]

7Bilhah became pregnant again and
gave Jacob a second son. 8Rachel said, "I
have struggled hard with my sister, and I
have won." So she named
that son Naphtali.[n]

9Leah saw that she
had stopped having chil-
dren, so she gave her slave
girl Zilpah to Jacob as a
wife. 10When Zilpah had a
son, 11Leah said, "I am
lucky," so she named him
Gad.[n] 12Zilpah gave birth
to another son, 13and Leah
said, "I am very happy!
Now women will call me
happy," so she named him Asher.[n]

14During the wheat harvest Reuben
went into the field and found some
mandrake[n] plants and brought them to
his mother Leah. But Rachel said to
Leah, "Please give me some of your
son's mandrakes."

15Leah answered, "You have already
taken away my husband, and now you are
trying to take away my son's mandrakes."

But Rachel answered, "If you will give
me your son's mandrakes, you may sleep
with Jacob tonight."

16When Jacob came in from the field
that night, Leah went out to meet him.
She said, "You will have sexual relations
with me tonight because I have paid for
you with my son's mandrakes." So Jacob
slept with her that night.

17Then God answered Leah's prayer,
and she became pregnant again. She gave
birth to a fifth son 18and said, "God has
given me what I paid for, because I gave
my slave girl to my husband." So Leah
named her son Issachar.[n]

19Leah became pregnant again and
gave birth to a sixth son. 20She said,
"God has given me a fine gift. Now surely
Jacob will honor me, because I have given
him six sons," so she named him Zebulun.[n] 21Later Leah gave birth to a
daughter and named her Dinah.

22Then God remembered Rachel and
answered her prayer, making it possible
for her to have children. 23When she became pregnant and gave birth to a son,
she said, "God has taken away my
shame," 24and she named him Joseph.[n]
Rachel said, "I wish the LORD would give
me another son."

Then God remembered Rachel and answered her prayer, making it possible for her to have children.
—Genesis 30:22

Jacob Tricks Laban

25After the birth of
Joseph, Jacob said to La-
ban, "Now let me go to
my own home and coun-
try. 26Give me my wives
and my children and let
me go. I have earned
them by working for you,
and you know that I have
served you well."

27Laban said to him, "If I have
pleased you, please stay. I know the LORD
has blessed me because of you. 28Tell me
what I should pay you, and I will give it
to you."

29Jacob answered, "You know that I
have worked hard for you, and your
flocks have grown while I cared for them.
30When I came, you had little, but now
you have much. Every time I did something for you, the LORD blessed you. But
when will I be able to do something for
my own family?"

31Laban asked, "Then what should I
give you?"

Jacob answered, "I don't want you to
give me anything. Just do this one thing,
and I will come back and take care of your
flocks. 32Today let me go through all
your flocks. I will take every speckled
or spotted sheep, every black lamb, and

30:6 Dan This name means "he has judged."

30:8 Naphtali This name sounds like the Hebrew word for "my struggle."

30:11 Gad This name may mean "lucky."

30:13 Asher This name may mean "happy."

30:14 mandrake A plant which was believed to cause a woman to become pregnant.

30:18 Issachar This name sounds like the Hebrew word for "paid for."

30:20 Zebulun This name sounds like the Hebrew word for "honor."

30:24 Joseph This name sounds like the Hebrew word for "he adds."

every spotted or speckled goat. That will
be my pay. **33**In the future you can easily
see if I am honest. When you come to
look at my flocks, if I have any goat that
isn't speckled or spotted or any lamb that
isn't black, you will know I stole it."

34Laban answered, "Agreed! We will
do what you ask." **35**But that day Laban
took away all the male goats that had
streaks or spots, all the speckled and
spotted female goats (all those that had
white on them), and all the black sheep.
He told his sons to watch over them.
36Then he took these animals to a place
that was three days' journey away from
Jacob. Jacob took care of all the flocks
that were left.

37So Jacob cut green branches from
poplar, almond, and plane trees and
peeled off some of the bark so that the
branches had white stripes on them.
38He put the branches in front of the
flocks at the watering places. When the
animals came to drink, they also mated
there, **39**so the flocks mated in front of
the branches. Then the young that were
born were streaked, speckled, or spotted.
40Jacob separated the young animals
from the others, and he made them face
the streaked and dark animals in Laban's
flock. Jacob kept his animals separate
from Laban's. **41**When the stronger animals in the flock were mating, Jacob put
the branches before their eyes so they
would mate near the branches. **42**But
when the weaker animals mated, Jacob
did not put the branches there. So the animals born from the weaker animals were
Laban's, and those born from the stronger animals were Jacob's. **43**In this way
Jacob became very rich. He had large
flocks, many male and female servants,
camels, and donkeys.

Jacob Runs Away

31 One day Jacob heard Laban's sons
talking. They said, "Jacob has
taken everything our father owned, and
in this way he has become rich." **2**Then
Jacob noticed that Laban was not as
friendly as he had been before. **3**The
LORD said to Jacob, "Go back to the land
where your ancestors lived, and I will be
with you."

4So Jacob told Rachel and Leah to
meet him in the field where he kept his
flocks. **5**He said to them, "I have seen
that your father is not as friendly with me
as he used to be, but the God of my father
has been with me. **6**You both know that I
have worked as hard as I could for your
father, **7**but he cheated me and changed
my pay ten times. But God has not allowed your father to harm me. **8**When
Laban said, 'You can have all the speckled
animals as your pay,' all the animals gave
birth to speckled young ones. But when
he said, 'You can have all the streaked animals as your pay,' all the flocks gave
birth to streaked babies. **9**So God has tak-
en the animals away from your father and
has given them to me.

10"I had a dream during the season
when the flocks were mating. I saw that
the only male goats who were mating
were streaked, speckled, or spotted. **11**The
angel of God spoke to me in that dream
and said, 'Jacob!' I answered, 'Yes!' **12**The
angel said, 'Look! Only the streaked,
speckled, or spotted male goats are mating. I have seen all the wrong things Laban has been doing to you. **13**I am the
God who appeared to you at Bethel,
where you poured olive oil on the stone
you set up on end and where you made a
promise to me. Now I want you to leave
here and go back to the land where you
were born.' "

14Rachel and Leah answered Jacob,
"Our father has nothing to give us when
he dies. **15**He has treated us like strangers. He sold us to you, and then he spent
all of the money you paid for us. **16**God
took all this wealth from our father, and
now it belongs to us and our children. So
do whatever God has told you to do."

17So Jacob put his children and his
wives on camels, **18**and they began their
journey back to Isaac, his father, in the
land of Canaan. All the flocks of animals
that Jacob owned walked ahead of them.
He carried everything with him that he
had gotten while he lived in Northwest
Mesopotamia.

19While Laban was gone to cut the

wool from his sheep, Rachel stole the
idols that belonged to him. **20**And Jacob
tricked Laban the Aramean by not telling
him he was leaving. **21**Jacob and his family left quickly, crossed the Euphrates
River, and traveled toward the mountains
of Gilead.

22Three days later Laban learned that
Jacob had run away, **23**so he gathered his
relatives and began to chase him. After
seven days Laban found him in the mountains of Gilead. **24**That night God came to
Laban the Aramean in a dream and said,
"Be careful! Do not say anything to Jacob, good or bad."

The Search for the Stolen Idols

25So Laban caught up with Jacob.
Now Jacob had made his camp in the
mountains, so Laban and his relatives set
up their camp in the mountains of Gilead.
26Laban said to Jacob, "What have you
done? You cheated me and took my
daughters as if you had captured them in
a war. **27**Why did you run away secretly
and trick me? Why didn't you tell me?
Then I could have sent you away with joy
and singing and with the music of tambourines and harps. **28**You did not even
let me kiss my grandchildren and my
daughters good-bye. You were very foolish to do this! **29**I have the power to harm
you, but last night the God of your father
spoke to me and warned me not to say
anything to you, good or bad. **30**I know
you want to go back to your home, but
why did you steal my idols?"

31Jacob answered Laban, "I left without telling you, because I was afraid you
would take your daughters away from
me. **32**If you find anyone here who has
taken your idols, that person will be
killed! Your relatives will be my witnesses. You may look for anything that
belongs to you and take anything that is
yours." (Now Jacob did not know that Rachel had stolen Laban's idols.)

33So Laban looked in Jacob's tent, in
Leah's tent, and in the tent where the
two slave women stayed, but he did not
find his idols. When he left Leah's tent,
he went into Rachel's tent. **34**Rachel had
hidden the idols inside her camel's saddle
and was sitting on them. Although Laban
looked through the whole tent, he did not
find them.

35Rachel said to her father, "Father,
don't be angry with me. I am not able to
stand up before you because I am having
my monthly period." So Laban looked
through the camp, but he did not find his
idols.

36Then Jacob became very angry and
said, "What wrong have I done? What law
have I broken to cause you to chase me?
37You have looked through everything I
own, but you have found nothing that belongs to you. If you have found anything,
show it to everyone. Put it in front of
your relatives and my relatives, and let
them decide which one of us is right. **38**I
have worked for you now for twenty
years. During all that time none of the
lambs and kids died during birth, and I
have not eaten any of the male sheep
from your flocks. **39**Any time an animal
was killed by wild beasts, I did not bring
it to you, but made up for the loss myself.
You made me pay for any animal that was
stolen during the day or night. **40**In the
daytime the sun took away my strength,
and at night I was cold and could not
sleep. **41**I worked like a slave for you for
twenty years—the first fourteen to get
your two daughters and the last six to
earn your flocks. During that time you
changed my pay ten times. **42**But the
God of my father, the God of Abraham
and the God of Isaac, was with me. Otherwise, you would have sent me away with
nothing. But he saw the trouble I had and
the hard work I did, and last night he corrected you."

Jacob and Laban's Agreement

43Laban said to Jacob, "These girls
are my daughters. Their children belong
to me, and these flocks are mine. Everything you see here belongs to me, but I
can do nothing to keep my daughters and
their children. **44**Let us make an agreement, and let us set up a pile of stones to
remind us of it."

45So Jacob took a large rock and set it
up on its end. **46**He told his relatives to
gather rocks, so they took the rocks and

piled them up; then they ate beside the
pile. 47Laban named that place in his language A Pile to Remind Us, and Jacob
gave the place the same name in Hebrew.
48Laban said to Jacob, "This pile of
rocks will remind us of the agreement
between us." That is why the place was
called A Pile to Remind Us. 49It was also
called Mizpah,ⁿ because Laban said, "Let
the LORD watch over us while we are
separated from each other. 50Remember
that God is our witness even if no one
else is around us. He will know if you
harm my daughters or marry other wom-
en. 51Here is the pile of rocks that I have
put between us and here is the rock I set
up on end. 52This pile of rocks and this
rock set on end will remind us of our
agreement. I will never go past this pile
to hurt you, and you must never come to
my side of them to hurt me. 53Let the
God of Abraham, who is the God of Nahor
and the God of their fathers, punish either of us if we break this agreement."
So Jacob made a promise in the name
of the God whom his father Isaac worshiped. 54Then Jacob killed an animal
and offered it as a sacrifice on the mountain, and he invited his relatives to share
in the meal. After they finished eating,
they spent the night on the mountain.
55Early the next morning Laban kissed
his grandchildren and his daughters and
blessed them, and then he left to return
home.

Jacob Meets Esau

32 When Jacob also went his way, the
angels of God met him. 2When he
saw them, he said, "This is the
camp of God!" So he
named that place
Mahanaim.ⁿ
3Jacob's brother
Esau was living in
the area called Seir
in the country of Edom. Jacob sent messengers to Esau, 4telling them, "Give
this message to my master Esau: 'This is
what Jacob, your servant, says: I have
lived with Laban and have remained
there until now. 5I have cattle, donkeys,
flocks, and male and female servants. I
send this message to you and ask you to
accept us.' "

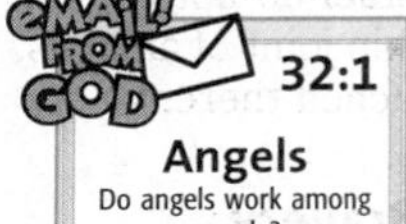

Angels
Do angels work among people?

FAITH links

WHEN YOU'RE AFRAID

GENESIS 32:9-12

Think of a time when you were really afraid. Jacob knew that kind of knock-kneed fear as he thought about returning to his homeland. He had not seen his brother Esau for many years. He was afraid that Esau still had a grudge against him and would cause him harm. But Jacob didn't waste time worrying. Instead, he asked God for help.

When you're afraid, think about handling your fear the way that Jacob did. Give it to God. He'll gladly trade some of his courage for your fear.

Here's some more advice on dealing with things that go bump in the night.

Real Faith or Really Scared?, Judges 4, p. 315
A Message of Courage and Hope, 2 Kings 19:4–10, p. 505
In Deep Water, Psalm 69, p. 760
Future Hope, Joel 3:17–21, p. 1191
A Safe Place, Nahum 1:7, p. 1231
An Energy Boost, Acts 4:31, p. 1469

31:49 Mizpah This name sounds like the Hebrew word for "watch."
32:2 Mahanaim This name means "two camps."

6The messengers returned to Jacob
and said, "We went to your brother Esau.
He is coming to meet you and has four
hundred men with him."
7Then Jacob was very afraid and worried. He divided the people who were
with him and all the flocks, herds, and
camels into two camps. 8Jacob thought,
"Esau might come and destroy one camp,
but the other camp can run away and be
saved."
9Then Jacob said, "God of my father
Abraham! God of my father Isaac! LORD,
you told me to return to my country and
my family. You said that you would treat
me well. 10I am not worthy of the kindness and continual goodness you have
shown me. The first time I traveled
across the Jordan River, I had only my
walking stick, but now I own enough to
have two camps. 11Please save me from
my brother Esau. I am afraid he will come
and kill all of us, even the mothers with
the children. 12You said to me, 'I will
treat you well and will make your children as many as the sand of the seashore.
There will be too many to count.' "
13Jacob stayed there for the night and
prepared a gift for Esau from what he had
with him: 14two hundred female goats
and twenty male goats, two hundred female sheep and twenty male sheep,
15thirty female camels and their young,
forty cows and ten bulls, twenty female
donkeys, and ten male donkeys. 16Jacob
gave each separate flock of animals to
one of his servants and said to them, "Go
ahead of me and keep some space between each herd." 17Jacob gave them
their orders. To the servant with the first
group of animals he said, "My brother
Esau will come to you and ask, 'Whose
servant are you? Where are you going
and whose animals are these?' 18Then
you will answer, 'They belong to your
servant Jacob. He sent them as a gift to
you, my master Esau, and he also is coming behind us.' "
19Jacob ordered the second servant,
the third servant, and all the other servants to do the same thing. He said, "Say
the same thing to Esau when you meet
him. 20Say, 'Your servant Jacob is coming
behind us.' " Jacob thought, "If I send
these gifts ahead of me, maybe Esau will
forgive me. Then when I see him, perhaps he will accept me." 21So Jacob sent
the gifts to Esau, but he himself stayed
that night in the camp.

Jacob Wrestles with God

22During the night Jacob rose and
crossed the Jabbok River at the crossing,
taking with him his two wives, his two
slave girls, and his eleven sons. 23He
sent his family and everything he had
across the river. 24So Jacob was alone,
and a man came and wrestled with
him until the sun came up. 25When the
man saw he could not defeat Jacob, he
struck Jacob's hip and put it out of joint.
26Then he said to Jacob, "Let me go. The
sun is coming up."
But Jacob said, "I will let you go if you
will bless me."
27The man said to him, "What is your
name?"
And he answered, "Jacob."
28Then the man said, "Your name will
no longer be Jacob. Your name will
now be Israel,[n] because you have wrestled with God and with people, and you
have won."
29Then Jacob asked him, "Please tell
me your name."
But the man said, "Why do you ask my
name?" Then he blessed Jacob there.
30So Jacob named that place Peniel,[n]
saying, "I have seen God face to face, but
my life was saved." 31Then the sun rose
as he was leaving that place, and Jacob
was limping because of his leg. 32So even
today the people of Israel do not eat the
muscle that is on the hip joint of animals,
because Jacob was touched there.

Jacob Shows His Bravery

33 Jacob looked up and saw Esau
coming, and with him were four
hundred men. So Jacob divided his children among Leah, Rachel, and the two

---

32:28 Israel This name means "he wrestles with God."

32:30 Peniel This name means "the face of God."

FAITH links

FORGIVE INSTEAD

GENESIS 33

What's the worst thing anyone has ever done to you? Maybe someone told a lie about you or made fun of you in some way. Jacob tricked Esau out of an important blessing from their father Isaac. Esau was really mad at the time. Several years later, however, Esau's focus changed. Missing out on the blessing didn't seem as important to him anymore. Esau was glad to have his brother back. He gladly forgave Jacob.

Instead of holding a grudge, think about forgiving those who hurt you. Forgiveness doesn't mean that what the person did wasn't wrong. It just means you're willing to do what God did for us: forgive.

Here's some more help on how to handle those hard-to-forgive people in your life.

Mercy for an Enemy, Jonah 4, p. 1216

The Peril of Poisonous Plans, Micah 2:1–3, p. 1221

Quick to Forgive?, Mark 11:25, p. 1349

Forgive and Forget, Ephesians 4:32, p. 1604

A Peacemaker or a Peacebreaker?, James 3:18, p. 1693

The Way to Get Along, 1 Peter 3:8–9, p. 1703

slave girls. 2Jacob put the slave girls with
their children first, then Leah and her
children behind them, and Rachel and Joseph last. 3Jacob himself went out in
front of them and bowed down flat on the
ground seven times as he was walking
toward his brother.

4But Esau ran to meet Jacob and put
his arms around him and hugged him.
Then Esau kissed him, and they both
cried. 5When Esau looked up and saw the
women and children, he asked, "Who are
these people with you?"

Jacob answered, "These are the children God has given me. God has been
good to me, your servant."

6Then the two slave girls and their
children came up to Esau and bowed
down flat on the earth before him. 7Leah
and her children also came up to Esau
and also bowed down flat on the earth.
Last of all, Joseph and Rachel came up to
Esau, and they, too, bowed down flat before him.

8Esau said, "I saw many herds as I
was coming here. Why did you bring
them?"

Jacob answered, "They were to please
you, my master."

9But Esau said, "I already have
enough, my brother. Keep what you
have."

10Jacob said, "No! Please! If I have
pleased you, then accept the gift I give
you. I am very happy to see your face
again. It is like seeing the face of God, because you have accepted me. 11So I beg
you to accept the gift I give you. God has
been very good to me, and I have more
than I need." And because Jacob begged,
Esau accepted the gift.

12Then Esau said, "Let us be going. I
will travel with you."

13But Jacob said to him, "My master,
you know that the children are weak. And
I must be careful with my flocks and their
young ones. If I force them to go too far in
one day, all the animals will die. 14So, my
master, you go on ahead of me, your servant. I will follow you slowly and let the
animals and the children set the speed at
which we travel. I will meet you, my master, in Edom."

15So Esau said, "Then let me leave some of my people with you."

"No, thank you," said Jacob. "I only want to please you, my master." **16**So that day Esau started back to Edom. **17**But Jacob went to Succoth, where he built a house for himself and shelters for his animals. That is why the place was named Succoth.ⁿ

18Jacob left Northwest Mesopotamia and arrived safely at the city of Shechem in the land of Canaan. There he camped east of the city. **19**He bought a part of the field where he had camped from the sons of Hamor father of Shechem for one hundred pieces of silver. **20**He built an altar there and named it after God, the God of Israel.

Dinah Is Attacked

34 At this time Dinah, the daughter of Leah and Jacob, went out to visit the women of the land. **2**When Shechem son of Hamor the Hivite, the ruler of the land, saw her, he took her and forced her to have sexual relations with him. **3**Shechem fell in love with Dinah, and he spoke kindly to her. **4**He told his father, Hamor, "Please get this girl for me so I can marry her."

5Jacob learned how Shechem had disgraced his daughter, but since his sons were out in the field with the cattle, Jacob said nothing until they came home. **6**While he waited, Hamor father of Shechem went to talk with Jacob.

7When Jacob's sons heard what had happened, they came in from the field. They were very angry that Shechem had done such a wicked thing to Israel. It was wrong for him to have sexual relations with Jacob's daughter; a thing like this should not be done.

8But Hamor talked to Dinah's brothers and said, "My son Shechem is deeply in love with Dinah. Please let him marry her. **9**Marry our people. Give your women to our men as wives and take our women for your men as wives. **10**You can live in the same land with us. You will be free to own land and to trade here."

11Shechem also talked to Jacob and to Dinah's brothers and said, "Please accept my offer. I will give anything you ask. **12**Ask as much as you want for the payment for the bride, and I will give it to you. Just let me marry Dinah."

13Jacob's sons answered Shechem and his father with lies, because Shechem had disgraced their sister Dinah. **14**The brothers said to them, "We cannot allow you to marry our sister, because you are not circumcised. That would be a disgrace to us. **15**But we will allow you to marry her if you do this one thing: Every man in your town must be circumcised like us. **16**Then your men can marry our women, and our men can marry your women, and we will live in your land and become one people. **17**If you refuse to be circumcised, we will take Dinah and leave."

18What they asked seemed fair to Hamor and Shechem. **19**So Shechem quickly went to be circumcised because he loved Jacob's daughter.

Now Shechem was the most respected man in his family. **20**So Hamor and Shechem went to the gate of their city and spoke to the men of their city, saying, **21**"These people want to be friends with us. So let them live in our land and trade here. There is enough land for all of us. Let us marry their women, and we can let them marry our women. **22**But we must agree to one thing: All our men must be circumcised as they are. Then they will agree to live in our land, and we will be one people. **23**If we do this, their cattle and their animals will belong to us. Let us do what they say, and they will stay in our land." **24**All the people who had come to the city gate heard this. They agreed with Hamor and Shechem, and every man was circumcised.

25Three days later the men who were circumcised were still in pain. Two of Jacob's sons, Simeon and Levi (Dinah's brothers), took their swords and made a surprise attack on the city, killing all the men there. **26**They killed Hamor and his son Shechem and then took Dinah out of Shechem's house and left. **27**Jacob's sons came upon the dead bodies and stole

---

33:17 Succoth This name means "shelters."

everything that was in the city, to pay
them back for what Shechem had done to
their sister. **28**So the brothers took the
flocks, herds, and donkeys, and everything in the city and in the fields. **29**They
took every valuable thing the people
owned, even their wives and children and
everything in the houses.

30Then Jacob said to Simeon and
Levi, "You have caused me a lot of trouble. Now the Canaanites and the Perizzites who live in the land will hate me.
Since there are only a few of us, if they
join together to attack us, my people and
I will be destroyed."

31But the brothers said, "We will not
allow our sister to be treated like a prostitute."

Jacob in Bethel

35 God said to Jacob, "Go to the city
of Bethel and live there. Make an
altar to the God who appeared to you
there when you were running away from
your brother Esau."

2So Jacob said to his family and to all
who were with him, "Put away the foreign gods you have, and make yourselves
clean, and change your clothes. **3**We will
leave here and go to Bethel. There I will
build an altar to God, who has helped me
during my time of trouble. He has been
with me everywhere I have gone." **4**So
they gave Jacob all the foreign gods they
had, and the earrings they were wearing,
and he hid them under the great tree near
the town of Shechem. **5**Then Jacob and
his sons left there. But God caused the
people in the nearby cities to be afraid, so
they did not follow them. **6**And Jacob and
all the people who were with him went to
Luz, which is now called Bethel, in the
land of Canaan. **7**There Jacob built an
altar and named the place Bethel, after
God, because God had appeared to him
there when he was running from his
brother.

8Deborah, Rebekah's nurse, died and
was buried under the oak tree at Bethel,
so they named that place Oak of Crying.

Jacob's New Name

9When Jacob came back from Northwest Mesopotamia, God appeared to him
again and blessed him. **10**God said to him,
"Your name is Jacob, but you will not be
called Jacob any longer. Your new name
will be Israel." So he called him Israel.
11God said to him, "I am God Almighty.
Have many children and grow in number
as a nation. You will be the ancestor of

FAITH links

MY WORSHIP PLACE

GENESIS 35:1-14

Where do you worship God? Jacob built two altars at Bethel to worship God. He wanted to show how thankful he was for God's presence and his help. Each altar was set up in a special place where God had revealed himself to Jacob.

Think about where you meet with God or sense his presence. You can worship God in the shower, on the playground—anywhere. You don't need a rock to mark the place, however. All you need is a heart full of praise. That's where worship really begins.

Serious About the Sabbath, Exodus 31:15, p. 117

A Song of Thanks, 1 Samuel 2, p. 356

Gratitude Attitude, Ezra 3, p. 611

Your Heavenly Dad, Psalm 103:13, p. 786

The Gift of Worship, Matthew 2:10–12, p. 1275

Our Good Shepherd, John 10:11–15, p. 1441

many nations and kings. **12**The same
land I gave to Abraham and Isaac I will
give to you and your descendants."
13Then God left him. **14**Jacob set up a
stone on edge in that place where God
had talked to him, and he poured a drink
offering and olive oil on it to make it special for God. **15**And Jacob named the
place Bethel.

Rachel Dies Giving Birth

16Jacob and his group left Bethel. Before they came to Ephrath, Rachel began
giving birth to her baby, **17**but she was
having much trouble. When Rachel's
nurse saw this, she said, "Don't be afraid,
Rachel. You are giving birth to another
son." **18**Rachel gave birth to the son, but
she herself died. As
she lay dying, she
named the boy Son of
My Suffering, but Ja-
cob called him Ben-
jamin.[n]

19Rachel was bur-
ied on the road to
Ephrath, a district of
Bethlehem, **20**and Ja-
cob set up a rock on
her grave to honor
her. That rock is still
there. **21**Then Israel[n]
continued his jour-
ney and camped just
south of Migdal Eder.

22While Israel was
there, Reuben had
sexual relations with
Israel's slave woman
Bilhah, and Israel heard about it.

The Family of Israel

Jacob had twelve sons. **23**He had six
sons by his wife Leah: Reuben, his first
son, then Simeon, Levi, Judah, Issachar,
and Zebulun.

24He had two sons by his wife Rachel:
Joseph and Benjamin.

25He had two sons by Rachel's slave
girl Bilhah: Dan and Naphtali.

26And he had two sons by Leah's
slave girl Zilpah: Gad and Asher.

These are Jacob's sons who were born
in Northwest Mesopotamia.

27Jacob went to his father Isaac at
Mamre near Hebron, where Abraham
and Isaac had lived. **28**Isaac lived one
hundred eighty years. **29**So Isaac
breathed his last breath and died when he
was very old, and his sons Esau and Jacob
buried him.

Esau's Family

36 This is the family history of Esau
(also called Edom). **2**Esau married
women from the land of Canaan: Adah
daughter of Elon the Hittite; and Oholibamah daughter of Anah, the son of Zibeon the Hivite; **3**and Basemath, Ishmael's
daughter, the sister of Nebaioth.

4Adah gave birth
to Eliphaz for Esau.
Basemath gave him
Reuel, **5**and Oholi-
bamah gave him Je-
ush, Jalam, and Korah.
These were Esau's
sons who were born in
the land of Canaan.

6Esau took his
wives, his sons, his
daughters, and all the
people who lived with
him, his herds and
other animals, and all
the belongings he had
gotten in Canaan, and
he went to a land away
from his brother Jacob.
7Esau's and Jacob's belongings were becom-
ing too many for them to live in the same
land. The land where they had lived could
not support both of them, because they
had too many herds. **8**So Esau lived in the
mountains of Edom. (Esau is also named
Edom.)

9This is the family history of Esau. He
is the ancestor of the Edomites, who live
in the mountains of Edom.

10Esau's sons were Eliphaz, son of

Esau's and Jacob's belongings were becoming too many for them to live in the same land. The land where they had lived could not support both of them, because they had too many herds. So Esau lived in the mountains of Edom. (Esau is also named Edom.)
—Genesis 36:7–8

35:18 Benjamin This name means "right-hand son" or "favorite son."
35:21 Israel Also called Jacob.

Adah and Esau, and Reuel, son of Basemath and Esau.
11Eliphaz had five sons: Teman,
Omar, Zepho, Gatam, and Kenaz. **12**Eliphaz also had a slave woman named Timna, and Timna and Eliphaz gave birth to
Amalek. These were Esau's grandsons
by his wife Adah.
13Reuel had four sons: Nahath, Zerah,
Shammah, and Mizzah. These were
Esau's grandsons by his wife Basemath.
14Esau's third wife was Oholibamah
the daughter of Anah. (Anah was the son
of Zibeon.) Esau and Oholibamah gave
birth to Jeush, Jalam, and Korah.
15These were the leaders that came
from Esau: Esau's first son was Eliphaz.
From him came these leaders: Teman,
Omar, Zepho, Kenaz, **16**Korah, Gatam,
and Amalek. These were the leaders that
came from Eliphaz in the land of Edom.
They were the grandsons of Adah.
17Esau's son Reuel was the father of
these leaders: Nahath, Zerah, Shammah,
and Mizzah. These were the leaders that
came from Reuel in the land of Edom.
They were the grandsons of Esau's wife
Basemath.
18Esau's wife Oholibamah gave birth
to these leaders: Jeush, Jalam, and Korah.
These are the leaders that came from
Esau's wife Oholibamah the daughter of
Anah. **19**These were the sons of Esau
(also called Edom), and these were their
leaders.
20These were the sons of Seir the
Horite, who were living in the land:
Lotan, Shobal, Zibeon, Anah, **21**Dishon, Ezer, and Dishan. These sons of
Seir were the leaders of the Horites in
Edom.
22The sons of Lotan were Hori and
Homam. (Timna was Lotan's sister.)
23The sons of Shobal were Alvan,
Manahath, Ebal, Shepho, and Onam.
24The sons of Zibeon were Aiah and
Anah. Anah is the man who found the hot
springs in the desert while he was caring
for his father's donkeys.
25The children of Anah were Dishon
and Oholibamah daughter of Anah.
26The sons of Dishon were Hemdan,
Eshban, Ithran, and Keran.
27The sons of Ezer were Bilhan, Zaavan, and Akan.
28The sons of Dishan were Uz and
Aran.
29These were the names of the Horite leaders: Lotan, Shobal, Zibeon, Anah,
30Dishon, Ezer, and Dishan.
These men were the leaders of the
Horite families who lived in the land of
Edom.
31These are the kings who ruled in
the land of Edom before the Israelites
ever had a king:
32Bela son of Beor was the king of
Edom. He came from the city of Dinhabah.
33When Bela died, Jobab son of Zerah
became king. Jobab was from Bozrah.
34When Jobab died, Husham became
king. He was from the land of the Temanites.
35When Husham died, Hadad son of
Bedad, who had defeated Midian in the
country of Moab, became king. Hadad
was from the city of Avith.
36When Hadad died, Samlah became
king. He was from Masrekah.
37When Samlah died, Shaul became
king. He was from Rehoboth on the Euphrates River.
38When Shaul died, Baal-Hanan son
of Acbor became king.
39When Baal-Hanan son of Acbor
died, Hadad became king. He was from
the city of Pau. His wife's name was Mehetabel daughter of Matred, who was the
daughter of Me-Zahab.
40These Edomite leaders, listed by
their families and regions, came from
Esau. Their names were Timna, Alvah,
Jetheth, **41**Oholibamah, Elah, Pinon,
42Kenaz, Teman, Mibzar, **43**Magdiel, and
Iram. They were the leaders of Edom.
(Esau was the father of the Edomites.)
The area where each of these families
lived was named after that family.

Joseph the Dreamer

37 Jacob lived in the land of Canaan,
where his father had lived. **2**This
is the family history of Jacob:
Joseph was a young man, seventeen
years old. He and his brothers, the sons

of Bilhah and Zilpah, his father's wives,
cared for the flocks. Joseph gave his father bad reports about his brothers.
3Since Joseph was born when his father
Israel[n] was old, Israel loved him more
than his other sons. He made Joseph a
special robe with long sleeves. 4When
Joseph's brothers saw that their father
loved him more than he loved them, they
hated their brother and could not speak
to him politely.

5One time Joseph had a dream, and
when he told his brothers about it, they
hated him even more. 6Joseph said, "Listen to the dream I had. 7We were in the
field tying bundles of wheat together. My
bundle stood up, and your bundles of
wheat gathered around it and bowed
down to it."

8His brothers said, "Do you really
think you will be king over us? Do you
truly think you will rule over us?" His
brothers hated him even more because of
his dreams and what he had said.

9Then Joseph had another dream, and
he told his brothers about it also. He said,
"Listen, I had another dream. I saw the
sun, moon, and eleven stars bowing
down to me."

10Joseph also told his father about
this dream, but his father scolded him,
saying, "What kind of dream is this? Do
you really believe that your mother, your
brothers, and I will bow down to you?"
11Joseph's brothers were jealous of him,
but his father thought about what all
these things could mean.

12One day Joseph's brothers went to
Shechem to graze their father's flocks.
13Israel said to Joseph, "Go to Shechem
where your brothers are grazing the
flocks."

Joseph answered, "I will go."

14His father said, "Go and see if your
brothers and the flocks are all right. Then
come back and tell me." So Joseph's father sent him from the Valley of Hebron.

When Joseph came to Shechem, 15a
man found him wandering in the field and
asked him, "What are you looking for?"

16Joseph answered, "I am looking for
my brothers. Can you tell me where they
are grazing the flocks?"

17The man said, "They have already
gone. I heard them say they were going
to Dothan." So Joseph went to look for
his brothers and found them in Dothan.

Joseph Sold into Slavery

18Joseph's brothers saw him coming
from far away. Before he reached them,
they made a plan to kill him. 19They said
to each other, "Here comes that dreamer.
20Let's kill him and throw his body into
one of the wells. We can tell our father
that a wild animal killed him. Then we
will see what will become of his dreams."

21But Reuben heard their plan and
saved Joseph, saying, "Let's not kill him.
22Don't spill any blood. Throw him into
this well here in the desert, but don't
hurt him!" Reuben planned to save Joseph later and send him back to his father. 23So when Joseph came to his
brothers, they pulled off his robe with
long sleeves 24and threw him into the
well. It was empty, and there was no water in it.

25While Joseph was in the well, the
brothers sat down to eat. When they
looked up, they saw a group of Ishmaelites traveling from Gilead to Egypt. Their
camels were carrying spices, balm, and
myrrh.

26Then Judah said to his brothers,
"What will we gain if we kill our brother
and hide his death? 27Let's sell him to
these Ishmaelites. Then we will not be
guilty of killing our own brother. After all,
he is our brother, our own flesh and
blood." And the other brothers agreed.
28So when the Midianite traders came
by, the brothers took Joseph out of the
well and sold him to the Ishmaelites for
eight ounces of silver. And the Ishmaelites took him to Egypt.

29When Reuben came back to the
well and Joseph was not there, he tore his
clothes to show he was upset. 30Then he
went back to his brothers and said, "The
boy is not there! What shall I do?" 31The
brothers killed a goat and dipped Joseph's
robe in its blood. 32Then they brought
the long-sleeved robe to their father and

37:3 Israel Also called Jacob.

said, “We found this robe. Look it over
carefully and see if it is your son’s robe.”
33Jacob looked it over and said, “It is
my son’s robe! Some savage animal has
eaten him. My son Joseph has been torn
to pieces!” 34Then Jacob tore his clothes
and put on rough cloth to show that he
was upset, and he continued to be sad
about his son for a long time. 35All of his
sons and daughters tried to comfort him,
but he could not be comforted. He said, “I
will be sad about my son until the day I
die.” So Jacob cried for his son Joseph.
36Meanwhile the Midianites who had
bought Joseph had taken him to Egypt.
There they sold him to Potiphar, an officer to the king of Egypt and captain of the
palace guard.

Judah and Tamar

38 About that time, Judah left his
brothers and went to stay with a
man named Hirah in the town of Adullam.
2There Judah met a Canaanite girl, the
daughter of a man named Shua, and married her. Judah had sexual relations with
her, 3and she became pregnant and gave
birth to a son, whom Judah named Er.
4Later she gave birth to another son and
named him Onan. 5Still later she had
another son and named him Shelah. She
was at Kezib when this third son was
born.
6Judah chose a girl named Tamar to be
the wife of his first son Er. 7But Er,
Judah’s oldest son, did what the LORD
said was evil, so the LORD killed him.
8Then Judah said to Er’s brother Onan,
“Go and have sexual relations with your
dead brother’s wife.” It is your duty to
provide children for your brother in this
way.”
9But Onan knew that the children
would not belong to him, so when he was
supposed to have sexual relations with
Tamar he did not complete the sex act.
This made it impossible for Tamar to
become pregnant and for Er to have

38:8 Go . . . wife It was a custom in Israel that if a man died without children, one of his brothers would marry the widow. If a child was born, it would be considered the dead man’s child.

THE TROUBLE WITH JEALOUSY

GENESIS 37

Did you ever argue with a brother or sister over who the favorite one is in your family? Joseph’s brothers were jealous of him because he was the favorite. In fact, Joseph’s brothers hated him. Joseph didn’t help matters when he bragged about seeing his brothers bowing down to him in his dreams. The fancy coat that Jacob gave to Joseph added more fuel to the fire. The brothers became so jealous that they sold Joseph into slavery.

Jealousy and envy can lead to trouble if you allow them to control you. When you’re tempted to be jealous or envious of what someone else has, run—don’t walk—to God for help!

Need more advice on dealing with jealousy? Connect to these Faithlinks:

Forgive Instead, Genesis 33, p. 47

Facing the Consequences, Deuteronomy 3:21–29, p. 232

A Right to Get Even?, 1 Samuel 24, p. 388

I’ll Be the Judge!, 1 Corinthians 4:4–5, p. 1549

Winning a Friend, 2 Timothy 2:23–24, p. 1654

The Sin “Braker,” Jude 24–25, p. 1727

descendants. 10The LORD was displeased by this wicked thing Onan had
done, so the LORD killed Onan also.
11Then Judah said to his daughter-in-law
Tamar, "Go back to live in your father's
house, and don't marry until my young
son Shelah grows up." Judah was afraid
that Shelah also would die like his brothers. So Tamar returned to her father's
home.
12After a long time Judah's wife, the
daughter of Shua, died. After Judah had
gotten over his sorrow, he went to Timnah to his men who were cutting the
wool from his sheep. His friend Hirah
from Adullam went with him. 13Tamar
learned that Judah, her father-in-law, was
going to Timnah to cut the wool from his
sheep. 14So she took off the clothes that
showed she was a widow and covered her
face with a veil to hide who she was.
Then she sat down by the gate of Enaim
on the road to Timnah. She did this because Judah's younger son Shelah had
grown up, but Judah had not made plans
for her to marry him.
15When Judah saw her, he thought
she was a prostitute, because she had
covered her face with a veil. 16So Judah
went to her and said, "Let me have sexual relations with you." He did not know
that she was Tamar, his daughter-in-law.

CONNECT 2-YOU

THE TRUTH HURTS

Hey, everybody. Tagg and I are talking about being honest with each other. I think Charli, age 9, has something to add to our conversation. Let's welcome Charli to Connect 2-You.

Hi, Charli. What is it that you want to add?

Charli

Well, yesterday I got in trouble for being honest with someone. A bunch of us were walking home from school together. One of the kids in the group was this guy who always smells bad. Everyone notices it. So I told him he needs to use deodorant. Some of the other kids started laughing, and he got real embarrassed, but he didn't say anything. Anyhow, my mom found out about it and grounded me for two days. Can you believe it? Just for telling the truth!

I can see why you're confused, Charli. You may have thought you were doing your friend a favor by telling him the truth. But Jesus wants us to be compassionate and kind to others. Take a look at the Livin' It page on gentleness, Colossians 3:1–14, p. 1624, to see how you can be honest and kind at the same time.

Here's another idea that might help you, Charli. Try putting yourself in other people's shoes before you say something to them. Think about whether you would be offended or upset if someone said the same thing to you. If you think you would be, try coming up with a different way of saying it! I think you'll find some very different results.

She asked, "What will you give me if I
let you have sexual relations with me?"
17Judah answered, "I will send you a
young goat from my flock."
She answered, "First give me something to keep as a deposit until you send
the goat."
18Judah asked, "What do you want me
to give you as a deposit?"
Tamar answered, "Give me your seal
and its cord,[n] and give me your walking
stick." So Judah gave these things to her.
Then Judah and Tamar had sexual relations, and Tamar became pregnant.
19When Tamar went home, she took off
the veil that covered her face and put on
the clothes that showed she was a widow.
20Judah sent his friend Hirah with the
young goat to find the woman and get
back his seal and the walking stick he had
given her, but Hirah could not find her.
21He asked some of the people at the
town of Enaim, "Where is the prostitute
who was here by the road?"
They answered, "There has never
been a prostitute here."
22So he went back
to Judah and said, "I
could not find the wom-
an, and the people who
lived there said, 'There
has never been a prosti-
tute here.' "
23Judah said, "Let
her keep the things. I
don't want people to
laugh at us. I sent her
the goat as I promised,
but you could not find
her."
24About three months later someone
told Judah, "Tamar, your daughter-in-law,
is guilty of acting like a prostitute, and
now she is pregnant."
Then Judah said, "Bring her out and
let her be burned to death."
25When the people went to bring
Tamar out, she sent a message to her
father-in-law that said, "The man who
owns these things has made me pregnant. Look at this seal and its cord and
this walking stick, and tell me whose
they are."
26Judah recognized them and said,
"She is more in the right than I. She did
this because I did not give her to my son
Shelah as I promised." And Judah did not
have sexual relations with her again.
27When the time came for Tamar to
give birth, there were twins in her body.
28While she was giving birth, one baby
put his hand out. The nurse tied a red
string on his hand and said, "This baby
came out first." **29**But he pulled his hand
back in, so the other baby was born first.
The nurse said, "So you are able to break
out first," and they named him Perez.[n]
30After this, the baby with the red string
on his hand was born, and they named
him Zerah.

Joseph Is Sold to Potiphar

39 Now Joseph had been taken down
to Egypt. An Egyptian named Potiphar was an officer to the king of Egypt
and the captain of the palace guard. He
bought Joseph from the Ishmaelites who
had brought him down there. **2**The LORD
was with Joseph, and he became a successful man. He lived in
the house of his master,
Potiphar the Egyptian.
3Potiphar saw that
the LORD was with Jo-
seph and that the LORD
made Joseph successful
in everything he did.
4So Potiphar was very
happy with Joseph and
allowed him to be his
personal servant. He
put Joseph in charge of
the house, trusting him
with everything he owned. **5**When Joseph was put in charge of the house and
everything Potiphar owned, the LORD
blessed the people in Potiphar's house
because of Joseph. And the LORD blessed
everything that belonged to Potiphar,
both in the house and in the field. **6**So

> The LORD was with Joseph, and he became a successful man. He lived in the house of his master, Potiphar the Egyptian.
> —Genesis 39:2

38:18 seal . . . cord A seal was used like a rubber stamp, and people ran a string through it to tie around the neck. They wrote a contract, folded it, put wax or clay on the contract, and pressed the seal onto it as a signature.

38:29 Perez This name means "breaking out."

Potiphar left Joseph in charge of everything he owned and was not concerned about anything except the food he ate.

Joseph Is Put into Prison

Now Joseph was well built and handsome. **7**After some time the wife of Joseph's master began to desire Joseph, and one day she said to him, "Have sexual relations with me."

8But Joseph refused and said to her, "My master trusts me with everything in his house. He has put me in charge of everything he owns. **9**There is no one in his house greater than I. He has not kept anything from me except you, because you are his wife. How can I do such an evil thing? It is a sin against God."

10The woman talked to Joseph every day, but he refused to have sexual relations with her or even spend time with her.

11One day Joseph went into the house to do his work as usual and was the only man in the house at that time. **12**His master's wife grabbed his coat and said to him, "Come and have sexual relations with me." But Joseph left his coat in her hand and ran out of the house.

13When she saw that Joseph had left his coat in her hands and had run outside, **14**she called to the servants in her house and said, "Look! This Hebrew slave was brought here to shame us. He came in and tried to have sexual relations with me, but I screamed. **15**My scream scared him and he ran away, but he left his coat with me." **16**She kept his coat until her husband came home, **17**and she told him the same story. She said, "This Hebrew slave you brought here came in to shame me! **18**When he came near me, I screamed. He ran away, but he left his coat."

19When Joseph's master heard what his wife said Joseph had done, he became very angry. **20**So Potiphar arrested Joseph and put him into the prison where the king's prisoners were put. And Joseph stayed there in the prison.

21But the LORD was with Joseph and showed him kindness and caused the prison warden to like Joseph. **22**The prison warden chose Joseph to take care of all the prisoners, and he was responsible for whatever was done in the prison. **23**The warden paid no attention to anything that was in Joseph's care because the LORD was with Joseph and made him successful in everything he did.

Joseph Interprets Two Dreams

40 After these things happened, two of the king's officers displeased the king—the man who served wine to the king and the king's baker. **2**The king became angry with his officer who served him wine and his baker, **3**so he put them in the prison of the captain of the guard, the same prison where Joseph was kept. **4**The captain of the guard put the two prisoners in Joseph's care, and they stayed in prison for some time.

5One night both the king's officer who served him wine and the baker had a dream. Each had his own dream with its own meaning. **6**When Joseph came to them the next morning, he saw they were worried. **7**He asked the king's officers who were with him, "Why do you look so unhappy today?"

8The two men answered, "We both had dreams last night, but no one can explain their meaning to us."

Joseph said to them, "God is the only One who can explain the meaning of dreams. Tell me your dreams."

9So the man who served wine to the king told Joseph his dream. He said, "I dreamed I saw a vine, and **10**on the vine were three branches. I watched the branches bud and blossom, and then the grapes ripened. **11**I was holding the king's cup, so I took the grapes and squeezed the juice into the cup. Then I gave it to the king."

12Then Joseph said, "I will explain the dream to you. The three branches stand for three days. **13**Before the end of three days the king will free you, and he will allow you to return to your work. You will serve the king his wine just as you did before. **14**But when you are free, remember me. Be kind to me, and tell the king about me so I can get out of this pris-

ALONE AND FORGOTTEN?

GENESIS 40:23

Ever feel as if everyone in the whole world has forgotten you? Maybe someone forgot your birthday or disappointed you in some way. Joseph could relate to those feelings. While in prison, he did a favor for the chief officer who served the king his wine, and he asked for one in return. But the officer forgot about Joseph for two whole years. God never forgot about him, however.

During times of waiting or disappointment, you can trust that God will never forget you. He promises never to leave you or forget about you. (See Hebrews 13:5–6, p. 1684.)

Here are some more Faithlinks on trusting God:

Good and Bad Times, 1 Kings 17, p. 462

Depend on Him!, 2 Chronicles 16:1–9, p. 579

Like a Tree, Jeremiah 17:5–8, p. 1016

Flex Your Faith, Acts 3:1–16, p. 1467

It's Under Control, Romans 8:28, p. 1529

Hard Times, 2 Corinthians 1:8–10, p. 1570

on. **15**I was taken by force from the land
of the Hebrews, and I have done nothing
here to deserve being put in prison."

16The baker saw that Joseph's explanation of the dream was good, so he said
to him, "I also had a dream. I dreamed
there were three bread baskets on my
head. **17**In the top basket were all kinds
of baked food for the king, but the birds
were eating this food out of the basket on
my head."

18Joseph answered, "I will tell you
what the dream means. The three baskets stand for three days. **19**Before the
end of three days, the king will cut off
your head! He will hang your body on a
pole, and the birds will eat your flesh."

20Three days later, on his birthday,
the king gave a feast for all his officers. In
front of his officers, he released from
prison the chief officer who served his
wine and the chief baker. **21**The king
gave his chief officer who served wine his
old position, and once again he put the
king's cup of wine into the king's hand.
22But the king hanged the baker on a
pole. Everything happened just as Joseph
had said it would, **23**but the officer who
served wine did not remember Joseph.
He forgot all about him.

The King's Dreams

41 Two years later the king dreamed
he was standing on the bank of the
Nile River. **2**He saw seven fat and beautiful cows come up out of the river, and
they stood there, eating the grass. **3**Then
seven more cows came up out of the
river, but they were thin and ugly. They
stood beside the seven beautiful cows on
the bank of the Nile. **4**The seven thin and
ugly cows ate the seven beautiful fat
cows. Then the king woke up. **5**The king
slept again and dreamed a second time. In
his dream he saw seven full and good
heads of grain growing on one stalk. **6**After that, seven more heads of grain
sprang up, but they were thin and burned
by the hot east wind. **7**The thin heads of
grain ate the seven full and good heads.
Then the king woke up again, and he realized it was only a dream. **8**The next
morning the king was troubled about
these dreams, so he sent for all the magicians and wise men of Egypt. The king

told them his dreams, but no one could
explain their meaning to him.
9Then the chief officer who served
wine to the king said to him, “Now I remember something I promised to do, but
I forgot about it. **10**There was a time
when you were angry with the baker and
me, and you put us in prison in the house
of the captain of the guard. **11**In prison
we each had a dream on the same night,
and each dream had a different meaning.
12A young Hebrew man, a servant of the
captain of the guard, was in the prison
with us. When we told him our dreams,
he explained their meanings to us. He
told each man the meaning of his dream,
and **13**things happened exactly as he said
they would: I was given back my old position, and the baker was hanged.”
14So the king called for Joseph. The
guards quickly brought him out of the
prison, and he shaved, put on clean
clothes, and went before the king.
15The king said to Joseph, “I have had
a dream, but no one can explain its meaning to me. I have heard that you can
explain a dream when someone tells it
to you.”
16Joseph answered the king, “I am
not able to explain the meaning of
dreams, but God will do this
for the king.”
17Then the king
said to Joseph, “In
my dream I was
standing on the
bank of the Nile
River. **18**I saw seven fat and beautiful
cows that came up out of the river and ate
the grass. **19**Then I saw seven more cows
come out of the river that were thin and
lean and ugly—the worst looking cows I
have seen in all the land of Egypt. **20**And
these thin and ugly cows ate the first
seven fat cows, **21**but after they had eaten
the seven cows, no one could tell they had
eaten them. They looked just as thin and
ugly as they did in the beginning. Then I
woke up.
22“I had another dream. I saw seven
full and good heads of grain growing on
one stalk. **23**Then seven more heads of
grain sprang up after them, but these
heads were thin and ugly and were
burned by the hot east wind. **24**Then the
thin heads ate the seven good heads. I
told this dream to the magicians, but no
one could explain its meaning to me.”

EMAIL FROM GOD
41:16
Wisdom
Where can you find wisdom?

Joseph Tells the Dreams' Meaning

25Then Joseph said to the king, “Both
of these dreams mean the same thing.
God is telling you what he is about to do.
26The seven good cows stand for seven
years, and the seven good heads of grain
stand for seven years. Both dreams mean
the same thing. **27**The seven thin and
ugly cows stand for seven years, and the
seven thin heads of grain burned by the
hot east wind stand for seven years of
hunger. **28**This will happen as I told you.
God is showing the king what he is about
to do. **29**You will have seven years of
good crops and plenty to eat in all the
land of Egypt. **30**But after those seven
years, there will come seven years of
hunger, and all the food that grew in the
land of Egypt will be forgotten. The time
of hunger will eat up the land. **31**People
will forget what it was like to have plenty
of food, because the hunger that follows
will be so great. **32**You had two dreams
which mean the same thing. This shows
that God has firmly decided that this will
happen, and he will make it happen soon.
33“So let the king choose a man who
is very wise and understanding and set
him over the land of Egypt. **34**And let the
king also appoint officers over the land,
who should take one-fifth of all the food
that is grown during the seven good
years. **35**They should gather all the food
that is produced during the good years
that are coming, and under the king's authority they should store the grain in the
cities and guard it. **36**That food should be
saved to use during the seven years of
hunger that will come on the land of
Egypt. Then the people in Egypt will not
die during the seven years of hunger.”

Joseph Is Made Ruler over Egypt

37This seemed like a very good idea
to the king, and all his officers agreed.
38And the king asked them, “Can we find

FAITH links

A USE FOR YOUR ABILITIES

GENESIS 41

Joseph was a man of many talents. He had the ability to organize and lead others. This was proved during his time as a slave in Potiphar's house and while in prison. He was also wise. But his ability to explain the meaning of dreams was the one that got him noticed by the king of Egypt. Joseph used all of his abilities to bring honor to God.

Everyone has an ability to do something. Some of us have more than one. With these abilities comes a choice: to use them only to win fame and honor for ourselves or to bring honor to God. Which will you choose?

A Serious Promise, Deuteronomy 23:21–23, p. 257

Too Young to Serve, Jeremiah 1:4–9, p. 988

Empty Words, Ezekiel 33:30–33, p. 1127

Just Say Yes!, Matthew 9:9–13, p. 1289

One of the Faithful, Acts 10:1–34, p. 1482

Your Faith Example, 1 Timothy 4:12, p. 1646

a better man than Joseph to take this job?
God's spirit is truly in him!"
39So the king said to Joseph, "God has
shown you all this. There is no one as
wise and understanding as you are, so **40**I
will put you in charge of my palace. All
the people will obey your orders, and
only I will be greater than you."
41Then the king said to Joseph,
"Look! I have put you in charge of all the
land of Egypt." **42**Then the king took off
from his own finger his ring with the
royal seal on it, and he put it on Joseph's
finger. He gave Joseph fine linen clothes
to wear, and he put a gold chain around
Joseph's neck. **43**The king had Joseph
ride in the second royal chariot, and people walked ahead of his chariot calling,
"Bow down!" By doing these things, the
king put Joseph in charge of all of Egypt.
44The king said to him, "I am the
king, and I say that no one in all the land
of Egypt may lift a hand or a foot without
your permission." **45**The king gave
Joseph the name Zaphenath-Paneah. He
also gave Joseph a wife named Asenath,
who was the daughter of Potiphera,
priest of On. So Joseph traveled through
all the land of Egypt.
46Joseph was thirty years old when
he began serving the king of Egypt. And
he left the king's court and traveled
through all the land of Egypt. **47**During
the seven good years, the crops in the
land grew well. **48**And Joseph gathered
all the food which was produced in Egypt
during those seven years of good crops
and stored the food in the cities. In every
city he stored grain that had been grown
in the fields around that city. **49**Joseph
stored much grain, as much as the sand of
the seashore—so much that he could not
measure it.
50Joseph's wife was Asenath daughter of Potiphera, the priest of On. Before
the years of hunger came, Joseph and Asenath had two sons. **51**Joseph named the
first son Manasseh[n] and said, "God has
made me forget all the troubles I have
had and all my father's family." **52**Joseph
named the second son Ephraim[n] and said,

41:51 Manasseh This name sounds like the Hebrew word for "made me forget."
41:52 Ephraim This name sounds like the Hebrew word for "given me children."

"God has given me children in the land of
my troubles."
53The seven years of good crops
came to an end in the land of Egypt.
54Then the seven years of hunger began,
just as Joseph had said. In all the lands
people had nothing to eat, but in Egypt
there was food. **55**The time of hunger became terrible in all of Egypt, and the people cried to the king for food. He said to
all the Egyptians, "Go to Joseph and do
whatever he tells you."
56The hunger was everywhere in that
part of the world. And Joseph opened the
storehouses and sold grain to the people
of Egypt, because the time of hunger became terrible in Egypt. **57**And all the
people in that part of the world came to
Joseph in Egypt to buy grain because the
hunger was terrible everywhere in that
part of the world.

The Dreams Come True

42 Jacob learned that there was grain
in Egypt, so he said to his sons,
"Why are you just
sitting here looking
at one another? **2**I
have heard that there
is grain in Egypt. Go
down there and buy
grain for us to eat, so
that we will live and
not die."
3So ten of Jo-
seph's brothers went
down to buy grain
from Egypt. **4**But Ja-
cob did not send
Benjamin, Joseph's
brother, with them,
because he was afraid that something terrible might happen to him. **5**Along with
many other people, the sons of Israel[n]
went to Egypt to buy grain, because the
people in the land of Canaan were also
hungry.
6Now Joseph was governor over
Egypt. He was the one who sold the grain
to people who came to buy it. So Joseph's
brothers came to him and bowed facedown on the ground before him. **7**When
Joseph saw his brothers, he knew who
they were, but he acted as if he didn't
know them. He asked unkindly, "Where
do you come from?"
They answered, "We have come from
the land of Canaan to buy food."
8Joseph knew they were his brothers,
but they did not know who he was. **9**And
Joseph remembered his dreams about his
brothers bowing to him. He said to them,
"You are spies! You came to learn where
the nation is weak!"
10But his brothers said to him, "No,
my master. We come as your servants
just to buy food. **11**We are all sons of the
same father. We are honest men, not
spies."
12Then Joseph said to them, "No! You
have come to learn where this nation is
weak!"
13And they said, "We are ten of
twelve brothers, sons of the same father,
and we live in the land of Canaan. Our
youngest brother is there with our father
right now, and our other brother is gone."
14But Joseph said to them, "I can see
I was right! You are
spies! **15**But I will
give you a way to
prove you are telling
the truth. As surely
as the king lives,
you will not leave
this place until your
youngest brother
comes here. **16**One
of you must go and
get your brother.
The rest of you will
stay here in prison.
We will see if you
are telling the truth.
If not, as surely as the king lives, you are
spies." **17**Then Joseph put them all in
prison for three days.
18On the third day Joseph said to
them, "I am a God-fearing man. Do this
and I will let you live: **19**If you are honest
men, let one of your brothers stay here in
prison while the rest of you go and carry
grain back to feed your hungry families.
20Then bring your youngest brother back

> They said to each other, "We are being punished for what we did to our brother. We saw his trouble, and he begged us to save him, but we refused to listen. That is why we are in this trouble now."
>
> —Genesis 42:21

42:5 Israel Also called Jacob.

here to me. If you do this, I will know
you are telling the truth, and you will
not die."

The brothers agreed to this. 21They
said to each other, "We are being punished for what we did to our brother. We
saw his trouble, and he begged us to save
him, but we refused to listen. That is why
we are in this trouble now."

22Then Reuben said to them, "I told
you not to harm the boy, but you refused
to listen to me. So now we are being punished for what we did to him."

23When Joseph talked to his brothers,
he used an interpreter, so they did not
know that Joseph understood what they
were saying. 24Then Joseph left them
and cried. After a short time he went back
and spoke to them. He took Simeon and
tied him up while the other brothers
watched. 25Joseph told his servants to fill
his brothers' bags with grain and to put
the money the brothers had paid for the
grain back in their bags. The servants
were also to give them what they would
need for their trip back home. And the
servants did this.

26So the brothers put the grain on
their donkeys and left. 27When they
stopped for the night, one of the brothers
opened his sack to get food for his donkey. Then he saw his money in the top of
the sack. 28He said to the other brothers,
"The money I paid for the grain has been
put back. Here it is in my sack!"

The brothers were very frightened.
They said to each other, "What has God
done to us?"

The Brothers Return to Jacob

29The brothers went to their father
Jacob in the land of Canaan and told him
everything that had happened. 30They
said, "The master of that land spoke unkindly to us. He accused us of spying on
his country, 31but we told him that we
were honest men, not spies. 32We told
him that we were ten of twelve brothers—sons of one father. We said that one
of our brothers was gone and that our
youngest brother was with our father in
Canaan.

33"Then the master of the land said to
us, 'Here is a way I can know you are
honest men: Leave one of your brothers
with me, and take grain to feed your hungry families, and go. 34And bring your
youngest brother to me so I will know
you are not spies but honest men. Then I
will give you back your brother whom
you leave with me, and you can move
about freely in our land.' "

35As the brothers emptied their
sacks, each of them found his money in
his sack. When they and their father saw
it, they were afraid.

36Their father Jacob said to them,
"You are robbing me of all my children.
Joseph is gone, Simeon is gone, and now
you want to take Benjamin away, too.
Everything is against me."

37Then Reuben said to his father,
"You may put my two sons to death if I
don't bring Benjamin back to you. Trust
him to my care, and I will bring him back
to you."

38But Jacob said, "I will not allow
Benjamin to go with you. His brother is
dead, and he is the only son left from my
wife Rachel. I am afraid something terrible might happen to him during the trip
to Egypt. Then I would be sad until the
day I die."

The Brothers Go Back to Egypt

43 Still no food grew in the land of
Canaan. 2When Jacob's family had
eaten all the grain they had brought from
Egypt, Jacob said to them, "Go to Egypt
again and buy a little more grain for us
to eat."

3But Judah said to Jacob, "The governor of that country strongly warned us,
'If you don't bring your brother back with
you, you will not be allowed to see me.'
4If you will send Benjamin with us, we
will go down and buy food for you. 5But if
you refuse to send Benjamin, we will not
go. The governor of that country warned
us that we would not see him if we didn't
bring Benjamin with us."

6Israel[n] said, "Why did you tell the
man you had another brother? You have
caused me a lot of trouble."

43:6 Israel Also called Jacob.

7The brothers answered, "He questioned us carefully about ourselves and
our family. He asked us, 'Is your father
still alive? Do you have another brother?'
We just answered his questions. How
could we know he would ask us to bring
our other brother to him?"

8Then Judah said to his father Jacob,
"Send Benjamin with me, and we will go
at once so that we, you, and our children
may live and not die. **9**I will guarantee
you that he will be safe, and I will be personally responsible for him. If I don't
bring him back to you, you can blame me
all my life. **10**If we had not wasted all this
time, we could have already made two
trips."

11Then their father Jacob said to
them, "If it has to be that way, then do
this: Take some of the best foods in our
land in your packs. Give them to the man
as a gift: some balm, some honey, spices,
myrrh, pistachio nuts, and almonds.
12Take twice as much money with you
this time, and take back the money that
was returned to you in your sacks last
time. Maybe it was a mistake. **13**And take
Benjamin with you. Now leave and go to
the man. **14**I pray that God Almighty will
cause the governor to be merciful to you
and that he will allow Simeon and Benjamin to come back with you. If I am robbed
of my children, then I am robbed of
them!"

15So the brothers took the gifts. They
also took twice as much money as they
had taken the first
time, and they took
Benjamin. They hur-
ried down to Egypt and
stood before Joseph.

16When Joseph saw
Benjamin with them,
he said to the servant
in charge of his house,
"Bring those men into
my house. Kill an ani-
mal and prepare a
meal. Those men will
eat with me today at
noon." **17**The servant
did as Joseph told him and brought the
men to Joseph's house.

Then Joseph hurried off because he had to hold back the tears when he saw his brother Benjamin. So Joseph went into his room and cried there.
—Genesis 43:30

18The brothers were afraid when
they were brought to Joseph's house and
thought, "We were brought here because
of the money that was put in our sacks on
the first trip. He wants to attack us, make
us slaves, and take our donkeys." **19**So
the brothers went to the servant in
charge of Joseph's house and spoke to
him at the door of the house. **20**They
said, "Master, we came here once before
to buy food. **21**While we were going
home, we stopped for the night and when
we opened our sacks each of us found all
his money in his sack. We brought that
money with us to give it back to you.
22And we have brought more money to
pay for the food we want to buy this time.
We don't know who put that money in our
sacks."

23But the servant answered, "It's all
right. Don't be afraid. Your God, the God
of your father, must have put the money
in your sacks. I got the money you paid
me for the grain last time." Then the servant brought Simeon out to them.

24The servant led the men into
Joseph's house and gave them water, and
they washed their feet. Then he gave
their donkeys food to eat. **25**The men
prepared their gift to give to Joseph when
he arrived at noon, because they had
heard they were going to eat with him
there.

26When Joseph came home, the
brothers gave him the gift they had
brought into the house and bowed down to
the ground in front of
him. **27**Joseph asked
them how they were
doing. He said, "How
is your aged father you
told me about?. Is he
still alive?"

28The brothers an-
swered, "Your servant,
our father, is well. He
is still alive." And they
bowed low before Jo-
seph to show him re-
spect.

29When Joseph saw
his brother Benjamin, who had the same
mother as he, Joseph asked, "Is this your

youngest brother you told me about?"
Then he said to Benjamin, "God be good
to you, my son!" **30**Then Joseph hurried
off because he had to hold back the tears
when he saw his brother Benjamin. So
Joseph went into his room and cried
there. **31**Then he washed his face and
came out. He controlled himself and said,
"Serve the meal."

32So they served Joseph at one table,
his brothers at another table, and the
Egyptians who ate with him at another
table. This was because Egyptians did
not like Hebrews and never ate with
them. **33**Joseph's brothers were seated
in front of him in order of their ages, from
oldest to youngest. They looked at each
other because they were so amazed.
34Food from Joseph's table was taken to
them, but Benjamin was given five times
more food than the others. Joseph's
brothers ate and drank freely with him.

Joseph Sets a Trap

44 Then Joseph gave a command to
the servant in charge of his house.
He said, "Fill the men's sacks with as
much grain as they can carry, and put
each man's money into his sack with the
grain. **2**Put my silver cup in the sack of
the youngest brother,
along with his money
for the grain." The
servant did what Jo-
seph told him.

3At dawn the
brothers were sent
away with their don-
keys. **4**They were not
far from the city when
Joseph said to the
servant in charge of
his house, "Go after
the men. When you
catch up with them,
say, 'Why have you paid back evil for
good? **5**The cup you have stolen is the one
my master uses for drinking and for explaining dreams. You have done a very
wicked thing!' "

6So the servant caught up with the
brothers and said to them what Joseph
had told him to say.

7But the brothers said to the servant,
"Why do you say these things? We would
not do anything like that! **8**We brought
back to you from the land of Canaan the
money we found in our sacks. So surely
we would not steal silver or gold from
your master's house. **9**If you find that silver cup in the sack of one of us, then let
him die, and we will be your slaves."

10The servant said, "We will do as
you say, but only the man who has taken
the cup will become my slave. The rest of
you may go free."

11Then every brother quickly lowered his sack to the ground and opened it.
12The servant searched the sacks, going
from the oldest brother to the youngest,
and found the cup in Benjamin's sack.
13The brothers tore their clothes to
show they were afraid. Then they put
their sacks back on the donkeys and returned to the city.

14When Judah and his brothers went
back to Joseph's house, Joseph was still
there, so the brothers bowed facedown
on the ground before him. **15**Joseph said
to them, "What have you done? Didn't
you know that a man like me can learn
things by signs and dreams?"

16Judah said, "Master, what can we
say? And how can we
show we are not
guilty? God has un-
covered our guilt, so
all of us will be your
slaves, not just Ben-
jamin."

17But Joseph said,
"I will not make you
all slaves! Only the
man who stole the
cup will be my slave.
The rest of you may
go back safely to
your father."

18Then Judah went to Joseph and
said, "Master, please let me speak plainly
to you, and please don't be angry with
me. I know that you are as powerful as
the king of Egypt himself. **19**When we
were here before, you asked us, 'Do you
have a father or a brother?' **20**And we answered you, 'We have an old father. And

Judah said, "Master, what can we say? And how can we show we are not guilty? God has uncovered our guilt, so all of us will be your slaves, not just Benjamin."
—Genesis 44:16

we have a younger brother, who was born
when our father was old. This youngest
son's brother is dead, so he is the only
one of his mother's children left alive,
and our father loves him very much.'
21Then you said to us, 'Bring that
brother to me. I want to see him.' **22**And
we said to you, 'That young boy cannot
leave his father, because if he leaves him,
his father would die.' **23**But you said to
us, 'If you don't bring your youngest
brother, you will not be allowed to see me
again.' **24**So we went back to our father
and told him what you had said.

25"Later, our father said, 'Go again
and buy us a little more food.' **26**We said
to our father, 'We cannot go without our
youngest brother. Without our youngest
brother, we will not be allowed to see the
governor.' **27**Then my father said to us,
'You know that my wife Rachel gave me
two sons. **28**When one son left me, I
thought, "Surely he has been torn apart
by a wild animal," and I haven't seen him
since. **29**Now you want to take this son
away from me also. But something terrible might happen to him, and I would be
miserable until the day I die.' **30**Now
what will happen if we go home to our father without our youngest brother? He is
so important in our father's life that
31when our father sees the young boy is
not with us, he will die. And it will be our
fault. We will cause the great sorrow that
kills our father.

32"I gave my father a guarantee that
the young boy would be safe. I said to my
father, 'If I don't bring him back to you,
you can blame me all my life.' **33**So now,
please allow me to stay here and be your
slave, and let the young boy go back
home with his brothers. **34**I cannot go
back to my father if the boy is not with
me. I couldn't stand to see my father
that sad."

Joseph Reveals Who He Is

45 Joseph could not control himself in
front of his servants any longer, so
he cried out, "Have everyone leave me."
When only the brothers were left with Joseph, he told them who he was. **2**Joseph
cried so loudly that the Egyptians heard

FAITH links

GOOD PLANS

GENESIS 45:7-8

Think about how you'd feel if your brother or sister sold you into slavery in a foreign country. Could you honestly see the good in such an action? Most of us would say no. Yet after that happened to Joseph, he realized that God had a greater plan beyond his brothers' evil one. God's plan was to save their lives during the great famine that later occurred.

God has good plans for his people—including you! When something bad happens and you're tempted to doubt God's love, think about what Joseph learned. Some people make evil plans. But God's plans are always good.

Thinking about your future? Surf on to see what plans God has in store for you!

The Sign of His Presence, Exodus 40:34–38, p. 130

Full Circle, Job 42, p. 706

Love That Will Last, Psalm 136, p. 813

When the Going Gets Tough, Lamentations 3:22–27, p. 1079

A Soldier's Story, 2 Timothy 2:3, p. 1653

Never Alone, Hebrews 13:5–6, p. 1684

him, and the people in the king's palace
heard about it. **3**He said to his brothers,
"I am Joseph. Is my father still alive?"
But the brothers could not answer him,
because they were very afraid of him.

4So Joseph said to them, "Come close
to me." When the brothers came close to
him, he said to them, "I am your brother
Joseph, whom you sold as a slave to go to
Egypt. **5**Now don't be worried or angry
with yourselves because you sold me
here. God sent me here ahead of you to
save people's lives. **6**No food has grown
on the land for two years now, and there
will be five more years without planting
or harvest. **7**So God sent me here ahead
of you to make sure you have some descendants left on earth and to keep you
alive in an amazing way. **8**So it was not
you who sent me here, but God. God has
made me the highest officer of the king of
Egypt. I am in charge of his palace, and I
am the master of all the land of Egypt.

9"So leave quickly and go to my father. Tell him, 'Your son Joseph says: God
has made me master over all Egypt.
Come down to me quickly. **10**Live in the
land of Goshen where you will be near
me. Your children, your grandchildren,
your flocks and herds, and all that you
have will also be near me. **11**I will care
for you during the next five years of hunger so that you and your family and all
that you have will not starve.'

12"Now you can see for yourselves,
and so can my brother Benjamin, that the
one speaking to you is really Joseph.
13So tell my father about how powerful I
have become in Egypt. Tell him about
everything you have seen. Now hurry
and bring him back to me." **14**Then Joseph hugged his brother Benjamin and
cried, and Benjamin cried also. **15**And Joseph kissed all his brothers and cried as
he hugged them. After this, his brothers
talked with him.

16When the king of Egypt and his officers learned that Joseph's brothers had
come, they were very happy. **17**So the
king said to Joseph, "Tell your brothers
to load their animals and go back to the
land of Canaan **18**and bring their father
and their families back here to me. I will
give them the best land in Egypt, and
they will eat the best food we have here.
19Tell them to take some wagons from
Egypt for their children and their wives
and to bring their father back also. **20**Tell
them not to worry about bringing any of
their things with them, because we will
give them the best of what we have in
Egypt."

21So the sons of Israel did this. Joseph
gave them wagons as the king had ordered and food for their trip. **22**He gave
each brother a change of clothes, but he
gave Benjamin five changes of clothes
and about seven and one-half pounds of
silver. **23**Joseph also sent his father ten
donkeys loaded with the best things from
Egypt and ten female donkeys loaded
with grain, bread, and other food for his
father on his trip back. **24**Then Joseph
told his brothers to go. As they were
leaving, he said to them, "Don't quarrel
on the way home."

25So the brothers left Egypt and went
to their father Jacob in the land of Canaan. **26**They told him, "Joseph is still
alive and is the ruler over all the land of
Egypt." Their father was shocked and did
not believe them. **27**But when the brothers told him everything Joseph had said,
and when Jacob saw the wagons Joseph
had sent to carry him back to Egypt, he
felt better. **28**Israel[n] said, "Now I believe
you. My son Joseph is still alive, and I will
go and see him before I die."

Jacob Goes to Egypt

46 So Israel[n] took all he had and
started his trip. He went to Beer-
sheba, where he offered sacrifices to the
God of his father Isaac. **2**During the night
God spoke to Israel in a vision and said,
"Jacob, Jacob."

And Jacob answered, "Here I am."

3Then God said, "I am God, the God
of your father. Don't be afraid to go to
Egypt, because I will make your descendants a great nation there. **4**I will go to
Egypt with you, and I will bring you out of
Egypt again. Joseph's own hands will
close your eyes when you die."

45:28; 46:1 Israel Also called Jacob.

5Then Jacob left Beersheba. The sons of Israel loaded their father, their children, and their wives in the wagons the king of Egypt had sent. **6**They also took their farm animals and everything they had gotten in Canaan. So Jacob went to Egypt with all his descendants— **7**his sons and grandsons, his daughters and granddaughters. He took all his family to Egypt with him.

> Then God said, "I am God, the God of your father. Don't be afraid to go to Egypt, because I will make your descendants a great nation there."
> —Genesis 46:3

Jacob's Family

8Now these are the names of the children of Israel who went into Egypt (Jacob and his descendants).

Reuben was Jacob's first son. **9**Reuben's sons were Hanoch, Pallu, Hezron, and Carmi.

10Simeon's sons were Jemuel, Jamin, Ohad, Jakin, Zohar, and Shaul (Simeon's son by a Canaanite woman).

11Levi's sons were Gershon, Kohath, and Merari.

12Judah's sons were Er, Onan, Shelah, Perez, and Zerah (but Er and Onan had died in the land of Canaan). Perez's sons were Hezron and Hamul.

13Issachar's sons were Tola, Puah, Jashub, and Shimron.

14Zebulun's sons were Sered, Elon, and Jahleel.

15These are the sons of Leah and Jacob born in Northwest Mesopotamia, in addition to his daughter Dinah. There were thirty-three persons in this part of Jacob's family.

16Gad's sons were Zephon, Haggi, Shuni, Ezbon, Eri, Arodi, and Areli.

17Asher's sons were Imnah, Ishvah, Ishvi, and Beriah, and their sister was Serah. Beriah's sons were Heber and Malkiel.

18These are Jacob's sons by Zilpah, the slave girl whom Laban gave to his daughter Leah. There were sixteen persons in this part of Jacob's family.

19The sons of Jacob's wife Rachel were Joseph and Benjamin. **20**In Egypt, Joseph became the father of Manasseh and Ephraim by his wife Asenath, the daughter of Potiphera, priest of On.

21Benjamin's sons were Bela, Beker, Ashbel, Gera, Naaman, Ehi, Rosh, Muppim, Huppim, and Ard.

22These are the sons of Jacob by his wife Rachel. There were fourteen persons in this part of Jacob's family.

23Dan's son was Hushim.

24Naphtali's sons were Jahziel, Guni, Jezer, and Shillem.

25These are Jacob's sons by Bilhah, the slave girl whom Laban gave to his daughter Rachel. There were seven persons in this part of Jacob's family.

26So the total number of Jacob's direct descendants who went to Egypt was sixty-six, not counting the wives of Jacob's sons. **27**Joseph had two sons born in Egypt, so the total number in the family of Jacob in Egypt was seventy.

Jacob Arrives in Egypt

28Jacob sent Judah ahead of him to see Joseph in Goshen. When Jacob and his people came into the land of Goshen, **29**Joseph prepared his chariot and went to meet his father Israel in Goshen. As soon as Joseph saw his father, he hugged him, and cried there for a long time.

30Then Israel said to Joseph, "Now I am ready to die, because I have seen your face and I know you are still alive."

31Joseph said to his brothers and his father's family, "I will go and tell the king you are here. I will say, 'My brothers and my father's family have left the land of Canaan and have come here to me. **32**They are shepherds and take care of farm animals, and they have brought their flocks and their herds and everything they own with them.' **33**When the king calls you, he will ask, 'What work do you do?' **34**This is what you should tell

him: 'We, your servants, have taken care
of farm animals all our lives. Our ancestors did the same thing.' Then the king
will allow you to settle in the land of Goshen, away from the Egyptians, because
they don't like to be near shepherds."

Jacob Settles in Goshen

47 Joseph went in to the king and
said, "My father and my brothers
have arrived from Canaan with their
flocks and herds and everything they
own. They are now in the land of Goshen." **2**Joseph chose five of his brothers
to introduce to the king.

3The king said to the brothers, "What
work do you do?"

And they said to him, "We, your servants, are shepherds, just as our ancestors were." **4**They said to the king, "We
have come to live in this land, because
there is no grass in the land of Canaan for
our animals to eat, and the hunger is terrible there. So please allow us to live in
the land of Goshen."

5Then the king said to Joseph, "Your
father and your brothers have come to
you, **6**and you may choose any place in
Egypt for them to live. Give your father
and your brothers the best land; let them
live in the land of Goshen. And if any of
them are skilled shepherds, put them in
charge of my sheep and cattle."

7Then Joseph brought in his father Jacob and introduced him to the king, and
Jacob blessed the king.

8Then the king said to Jacob, "How
old are you?"

9Jacob said to him, "My life has been
spent wandering from place to place. It
has been short and filled with trouble—
only one hundred thirty years. My ancestors lived much longer than I." **10**Then
Jacob blessed the king and left.

11Joseph obeyed the king and gave
his father and brothers the best land in
Egypt, near the city of
Rameses. **12**And Jo-
seph gave his father,
his brothers, and
everyone who lived
with them the food
they needed.

EMAIL FROM GOD
47:11–12
Family
Check out this example of caring for family.

Joseph Buys Land for the King

13The hunger became worse, and
since there was no food anywhere in the
land, Egypt and Canaan became very
poor. **14**Joseph collected all the money
that was to be found in Egypt and Canaan.
People paid for the grain they were buying, and he brought that money to the
king's palace. **15**After some time, when
the people in Egypt and Canaan had no
money left, they went to Joseph and said,
"Please give us food. Our money is gone,
and if we don't eat, we will die here in
front of you."

16Joseph answered, "Since you have
no money, give me your farm animals,
and I will give you food in return." **17**So
people brought their farm animals to Joseph, and he gave them food in exchange
for their horses, sheep, goats, cattle, and
donkeys. And he kept them alive by trading food for their farm animals that year.

18The next year the people came to
Joseph and said, "You know we have no
money left, and all our animals belong to
you. We have nothing left except our bodies and our land. **19**Surely both we and
our land will die here in front of you. Buy
us and our land in exchange for food, and
we will be slaves to the king, together
with our land. Give us seed to plant so
that we will live and not die, and the land
will not become a desert."

20So Joseph bought all the land in
Egypt for the king. Every Egyptian sold
Joseph his field, because the hunger was
very great. So the land became the
king's, **21**and Joseph made the people
slaves from one end of Egypt to the other.
22The only land he did not buy was the
land the priests owned. They did not
need to sell their land because the king
paid them for their work. So they had
money to buy food.

23Joseph said to the people, "Now I
have bought you and your land for the king,
so I will give you seed and you can plant
your fields. **24**At harvest time you must
give one-fifth to the king. You may keep
four-fifths for yourselves to use as seed
for the field and as food for yourselves,
your families, and your children."

25The people said, "You have saved

our lives. If you like, we will become
slaves of the king."
26So Joseph made a law in Egypt,
which continues today: One-fifth of
everything from the land belongs to the
king. The only land the king did not get
was the priests' land.

"Don't Bury Me in Egypt"

27The Israelites continued to live in
the land of Goshen in Egypt. There they
got possessions and had many children
and grew in number.
28Jacob[n] lived in Egypt seventeen
years, so he lived to be one hundred
forty-seven years old. **29**When Israel
knew he soon would die, he called his son
Joseph to him and said to him, "If you
love me, put your hand under my leg.[n]
Promise me you will not bury me in
Egypt. **30**When I die, carry me out of
Egypt, and bury me where my ancestors
are buried."

Joseph answered, "I will do as you
say."
31Then Jacob said, "Promise me."
And Joseph promised him that he would
do this. Then Israel worshiped as he
leaned on the top of his walking stick.

Blessings for Manasseh and Ephraim

48 Some time later Joseph learned
that his father was very sick, so he
took his two sons Manasseh and Ephraim
and went to his father. **2**When Joseph arrived, someone told Jacob,[n] "Your son Joseph has come to see you." Jacob was
weak, so he used all his strength and sat
up on his bed.
3Then Jacob said to Joseph, "God Almighty appeared to me at Luz in the land
of Canaan and blessed me there. **4**He said
to me, 'I will give you many children. I
will make you the father of many peoples,
and I will give your descendants this land
forever.' **5**Your two sons, who were born
here in Egypt before I came, will be
counted as my own sons. Ephraim and
Manasseh will be my sons just as Reuben
and Simeon are my sons. **6**But if you have
other children, they will be your own, and
their land will be part of the land given to
Ephraim and Manasseh. **7**When I came
from Northwest Mesopotamia, Rachel
died in the land of Canaan, as we were
traveling toward Ephrath. This made me
very sad, and I buried her there beside
the road to Ephrath." (Today Ephrath is
Bethlehem.)
8Then Israel saw Joseph's sons and
said, "Who are these boys?"
9Joseph said to his father, "They are

47:28; 48:2 Jacob Also called Israel.
47:29 put . . . leg This showed that a person would keep a promise.

FAITH CHALLENGE

Hey there! Read 48:1 to see what one famous Bible character did when he heard that his father was very ill. What would you do if you found out that someone you loved was too sick to get out of bed?

TESTING IT

Genesis 48:1
Some time later Joseph learned that his father was very sick, so he took his two sons Manasseh and Ephraim and went to his father.

my sons that God has given me here in
Egypt."

Israel said, "Bring your sons to me so
I may bless them."

10At this time Israel's eyesight was
bad because he was old. So Joseph
brought the boys close to him, and Israel
kissed the boys and put his arms around
them. **11**He said to Joseph, "I thought I
would never see you alive again, and now
God has let me see you and also your
children." **12**Then Joseph moved his
sons off Israel's lap and bowed facedown
to the ground. **13**He put Ephraim on his
right side and Manasseh on his left. (So
Ephraim was near Israel's left hand, and
Manasseh was near Israel's right hand.)
Joseph brought the boys close to Israel.
14But Israel crossed his arms and put
his right hand on the head of Ephraim,
who was younger. He put his left hand on
the head of Manasseh, the firstborn son.
15And Israel blessed Joseph and said,

"My ancestors Abraham and Isaac
served our God,
and like a shepherd God has led
me all my life.
16 He was the Angel who saved me
from all my troubles.
Now I pray that he will bless these
boys.
May my name be known through
these boys,
and may the names of my
ancestors Abraham and Isaac be
known through them.
May they have many descendants
on the earth."

17When Joseph saw that his father put
his right hand on Ephraim's head, he
didn't like it. So he took hold of his
father's hand, wanting to move it from
Ephraim's head to Manasseh's head.
18Joseph said to his father, "You are doing it wrong, Father. Manasseh is the
firstborn son. Put your right hand on his
head."

19But his father refused and said, "I
know, my son, I know. Manasseh will be
great and have many descendants. But
his younger brother will be greater, and
his descendants will be enough to make a
nation."

20So Israel blessed them that day and
said,

"When a blessing is given in Israel,
they will say:
'May God make you like Ephraim
and Manasseh.' "

In this way he made Ephraim greater
than Manasseh.

21Then Israel said to Joseph, "Look at
me; I am about to die. But God will be
with you and will take you back to the
land of your fathers. **22**I have given you
something that I did not give your brothers—the land of Shechem that I took
from the Amorite people with my sword
and my bow."

Jacob Blesses His Sons

49 Then Jacob called his sons to him.
He said, "Come here to me, and I
will tell you what will happen to you in
the future.

2 "Come together and listen, sons of
Jacob.
Listen to Israel, your father."

3 "Reuben, my first son, you are my
strength.
Your birth showed I could be a
father.
You have the highest position among
my sons,
and you are the most powerful.
4 But you are uncontrolled like water,
so you will no longer lead your
brothers.
This is because you got into your
father's bed
and shamed me by having sexual
relations with my slave girl.

5 "Simeon and Levi are brothers
who used their swords to do
violence.
6 I will not join their secret talks,
and I will not meet with them to
plan evil.
They killed men because they were
angry,
and they crippled oxen just for fun.
7 May their anger be cursed, because it
is too violent.

May their violence be cursed,
because it is too cruel.
I will divide them up among the tribes of Jacob
and scatter them through all the tribes of Israel.

8 "Judah, your brothers will praise you.
You will grab your enemies by the neck,
and your brothers will bow down to you.
9 Judah is like a young lion.
You have returned from killing, my son.
Like a lion, he stretches out and lies down to rest,
and no one is brave enough to wake him.
10 Kings will come from Judah's family;
someone from Judah will always be on the throne.
Judah will rule until Shiloh comes,
and the nations will obey him.
11 He ties his donkey to a grapevine,
his young donkey to the best branch.
He can afford to use wine to wash his clothes
and the best wine to wash his robes.
12 His eyes are dark like the color of wine,
and his teeth are as white as the color of milk.

13 "Zebulun will live near the sea.
His shore will be a safe place for ships,
and his land will reach as far as Sidon.

14 "Issachar is like a strong donkey
who lies down while carrying his load.
15 When he sees his resting place is good
and how pleasant his land is,
he will put his back to the load
and become a slave.

16 "Dan will rule his own people
like the other tribes in Israel.
17 Dan will be like a snake by the side of the road,
a dangerous snake lying near the path.
That snake bites a horse's leg,
and the rider is thrown off backward.

18 "LORD, I wait for your salvation.

19 "Robbers will attack Gad,
but he will defeat them and drive them away.

20 "Asher's land will grow much good food;
he will grow food fit for a king.

21 "Naphtali is like a female deer that runs free,
that has beautiful fawns.

22 "Joseph is like a grapevine that produces much fruit,
a healthy vine watered by a spring,
whose branches grow over the wall.
23 Archers attack him violently
and shoot at him angrily,
24 but he aims his bow well.
His arms are made strong.
He gets his power from the Mighty God of Jacob
and his strength from the Shepherd, the Rock of Israel.
25 Your father's God helps you.
God Almighty
blesses you.
He blesses you
with rain
from above,
with water
from
springs below,
with many babies born to your wives,
and many young ones born to your animals.
26 The blessings of your father are greater
than the blessings of the oldest mountains,
greater than the good things of the long-lasting hills.

eMAIL! FROM GOD
49:25
Help
Where can you find dependable help?

May these blessings rest on the head
of Joseph,
on the forehead of the one who
was separated from his brothers.

27 "Benjamin is like a hungry wolf.
In the morning he eats what he has
caught,
and in the evening he divides what
he has taken."

28 These are the twelve tribes of Israel, and this is what their father said to
them. He gave each son the blessing that
was right for him. 29 Then Israel gave
them a command and said, "I am about to
die. Bury me with my ancestors in the
cave in the field of Ephron the Hittite.
30 That cave is in the field of Machpelah
east of Mamre in the land of Canaan.
Abraham bought the field and cave from
Ephron the Hittite for a burying place.
31 Abraham and Sarah his wife are buried
there. Isaac and Rebekah his wife are
buried there, and I buried my wife Leah
there. 32 The field and the cave in it were
bought from the Hittite people." 33 After
Jacob finished talking to his sons, he lay
down. He put his feet back on the bed,
took his last breath, and died.

Jacob's Burial

50 When Jacob died, Joseph hugged
his father and cried over him and
kissed him. 2 He commanded the doctors
who served him to prepare his father's
body, so the doctors prepared Jacob's body
to be buried. 3 It took the doctors forty
days to prepare his body (the usual time it
took). And the Egyptians had a time of
sorrow for Jacob that lasted seventy days.
4 When this time of sorrow had ended,
Joseph spoke to the king's officers and
said, "If you think well of me, please tell
this to the king: 5 'When my father was
near death, I made a promise to him that I
would bury him in a cave in the land of
Canaan, in a burial place that he cut out
for himself. So please let me go and bury
my father, and then I will return.' "
6 The king answered, "Keep your
promise. Go and bury your father."
7 So Joseph went to bury his father. All
the king's officers, the older leaders,
and all the leading men of Egypt went
with Joseph. 8 Everyone who lived with
Joseph and his brothers went with him,
as well as everyone who lived with his

FAITH links

MORE POWERFUL THAN REVENGE

GENESIS 50:14-21

Imagine being in a position where you could get even with someone who treated you badly. Joseph's brothers had treated him very badly. As the second in command of Egypt, Joseph had the power to do anything he wanted to his brothers. He could have had them thrown into prison or even killed. Instead, when they came to him for forgiveness, he gladly gave it to them. Not only that, he promised to take care of them.

Forgiving others can be hard sometimes. But God wants you to forgive, rather than think about getting even. Forgiveness is more powerful than revenge!

Give Revenge a Rest, Leviticus 19:18, p. 160

Kind or Fair?, 1 Samuel 30, p. 395

Putting an Enemy in Check, 2 Kings 6:8–23, p. 486

Wronged for What's Right, Ezra 4:4–5, p. 612

The Best Protection Plan, Matthew 2:13–18, p. 1276

A Friend in Need, Acts 9:27, p. 1480

Livin' it

FORGIVENESS

Genesis 50:15–21

You Want Me to Do What? What would you do if your friend told a lie about you? Some kids would think of ways to get even. Or they might even stop being friends. But what if your friend is sorry for what he did and asks you to forgive him?

Joseph had ten older brothers who treated him very badly. Joseph had the power to do anything he wanted to his brothers. But when they said they were sorry, Joseph gladly forgave them. (Check out Genesis 50:14–21.)

Sometimes it's hard to forgive others—we would rather get even. But God is always willing to forgive us when we sin against him. God models forgiveness for us so we can forgive others. (See Ezekiel 16:59–63, p. 1102.) How will you react to someone who has hurt you—get even or follow God's example of forgiveness?

MORE FAITH links

"Hey, Skweek, I'm really sorry about the other day when I got a little crazy when you were trying to explain that Bible verse to me."

"That's OK, Tagg. You know, God wants us to forgive each other. You can learn more by surfing these links."

A Change of Heart, Matthew 3:1–12, p. 1277

- When you do something wrong, are you quick to say, "I'm sorry," but slow to really mean it?
- John told the people to *repent*. To repent means to be sorry for what you did wrong and then to stop doing it. When you want to change, ask God. He's always glad to help!

Quick to Forgive?, Mark 11:25, p. 1349

- How quick are you to forgive someone who has hurt you? Are you cheetah-quick or turtle-slow? God wants you to forgive no matter what—not just when you feel like it. Are you in a cheetah-quick mode of forgiveness?

Forgive Again?, Luke 17:3–4, p. 1402

- How many times do you think someone should be forgiven for the same thing?
- Could you forgive a friend if she said the same mean thing to you over and over again? How many times does God forgive you for the same thing?

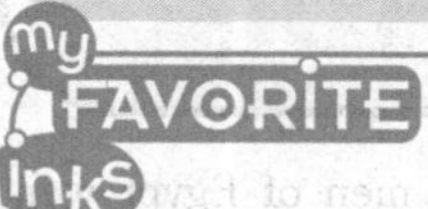

father. They left only their children, their
flocks, and their herds in the land of Goshen. **9**They went with Joseph in chariots
and on horses. It was a very large group.
10When they came to the threshing
floor of Atad, near the Jordan River, they
cried loudly and bitterly for his father.
Joseph's time of sorrow continued for
seven days. **11**The people that lived in
Canaan saw the sadness at the threshing
floor of Atad and said, "Those Egyptians
are showing great sorrow!" So now that
place is named Sorrow of the Egyptians.
12So Jacob's sons did as their father
commanded. **13**They carried his body to
the land of Canaan and buried it in the
cave in the field of Machpelah near Mamre. Abraham had bought this cave and
field from Ephron the Hittite to use as a
burial place. **14**After Joseph buried his father, he returned to Egypt, along with his
brothers and everyone who had gone
with him to bury his father.

The Brothers Fear Joseph

15After Jacob died, Joseph's brothers
said, "What if Joseph is still angry with
us? We did many wrong things to him.
What if he plans to pay us back?" **16**So
they sent a message to Joseph that said,
"Your father gave this command before
he died. **17**He said to us, 'You have done
wrong and have sinned and done evil to
Joseph. Tell Joseph to forgive you, his
brothers.' So now, Joseph, we beg you to
forgive our wrong. We are the servants of
the God of your father." When Joseph received the message, he cried.
18And his brothers went to him and
bowed low before him and said, "We are
your slaves."
19Then Joseph said to them, "Don't
be afraid. Can I do what only God can do?
20You meant to hurt me, but God turned
your evil into good to save the lives of
many people, which is being done. **21**So
don't be afraid. I will take care of you and
your children." So Joseph comforted his
brothers and spoke kind words to them.
22Joseph continued to live in Egypt
with all his father's family. He died when
he was one hundred ten years old.
23During Joseph's life Ephraim had children and grandchildren, and Joseph's son
Manasseh had a son named Makir. Joseph
accepted Makir's children as his own.

The Death of Joseph

24Joseph said to his brothers, "I am
about to die, but God will take care of
you. He will lead you out of this land to
the land he promised to Abraham, Isaac,
and Jacob." **25**Then Joseph had the sons
of Israel make a promise. He said,
"Promise me that you will carry my
bones with you out of Egypt."
26Joseph died when he was one hundred ten years old. Doctors prepared his
body for burial, and then they put him in a
coffin in Egypt.

MOSES, GET US OUT OF HERE!

Hi; it's Moses again. You may already know that I was born a slave and raised a prince, but did you also know that I killed a man and had to flee from the law? (Check out Exodus 2:11–15 for the details.) I still can't figure out why God chose me to be the leader of his people. I had just spent the last 40 years being a shepherd, not a diplomat. Still, when God spoke to me from the burning bush, I knew I had to obey. "Go! Bring my people, the Israelites, out of Egypt!" God said (Exodus 3:10). He promised that he would always be with me.

I wrote this book so that everyone would know how God rescued his people from slavery in Egypt. The king wanted to keep us as slaves, so God sent ten plagues to convince him to let us go. (Read about it in Exodus 7—11.) When the Egyptian soldiers came after us, God sent a great wind to part the water of the Red Sea, so we could escape to the other side (Exodus 14:21–31). Be sure to check out all these awesome stories.

JESUS WATCH

The last, most terrible plague of all that God sent to Egypt was the death of the firstborn. All firstborn sons of the land were going to die, from the sons of the slaves to the son of the king. However, God provided a way for the Israelites to escape this plague. All the Israelite households were to sacrifice a lamb and put its blood on the sides and tops of the doorframes of their houses. Those houses protected by the blood of the sacrificed lamb would be spared. Death would "pass over" their houses. Jesus is like the lamb of Passover. He is the perfect sacrifice for our sins. The punishment for our sins is death, but if we believe in Jesus, the blood of his sacrifice on the cross protects us from the punishment we deserve. Death "passes over" us and we have eternal life.

my FAVORITE links

OTHER CONNECTIONS

Livin' it

Living with your family sometimes can be tough—especially since we all are so different from each other. Find out some good advice on how to live together by visiting Give Me Space!, Exodus 20:12. Then follow the Faithlinks for more help.

GET THE INFO

Exodus is (literally) a moving story about the journey of God's people from captivity as slaves in Egypt to the border of the land that God promised to them. You can learn more by stopping at these sites:

- Church on the Road, Exodus 27:9–19. You've probably heard about mobile phones and mobile homes, but how about a mobile church? Find out how the Israelites carried their church with them as they wandered through the wilderness.
- Or stop by the Ten Curses, Exodus 9, to get the facts on how God convinced the king of Egypt to finally free the Israelites. (The king was a slow learner, but by the tenth curse, he finally got it! Do you remember which curse finally convinced the king?)

"Why do you suppose the Israelites made a gold calf?"

"Sounds crazy to me. We'd better connect to Exodus 32 and check it out."

SURFWATCH FOR THESE STORIES:

Who's the baby in the basket?, Exodus 2:1–10
Pass over that house, Exodus 12:1–30
Manna—what's this stuff?, Exodus 16:31
The Ten Commandments, Exodus 20:1–17
The Ark of the Agreement, Exodus 25:10–22
Levites don't wear blue jeans, Exodus 28

FAITH links

- Obey? No Way!, **Exodus 1:15–21**
- Fearful Service?, **Exodus 4:1–17**
- When Bad Turns to Worse, **Exodus 5:6–12**
- Your Worst Enemy, **Exodus 7—11**
- Time to Celebrate, **Exodus 15:1–21**
- Complaints, Complaints!, **Exodus 16:1–3**
- Serious About the Sabbath, **Exodus 31:15**
- Share What You Have, **Exodus 35:5–18**
- The Sign of His Presence, **Exodus 40:34–38**

Jacob's Family Grows Strong

1 When Jacob[a] went to Egypt, he took
his sons, and each son took his own
family with him. These are the names of
the sons of Israel: 2Reuben, Simeon,
Levi, Judah, 3Issachar, Zebulun, Benjamin, 4Dan, Naphtali, Gad, and Asher.
5There was a total of seventy people who
were descendants of Jacob. Jacob's son
Joseph was already in Egypt.
6Some time later, Joseph and his
brothers died, along with all the people
who had lived at that same time. 7But the
people of Israel had many children, and
their number grew greatly. They became
very strong, and the country of Egypt
was filled with them.

Trouble for the People of Israel

8Then a new king began to rule
Egypt, who did not know who Joseph
was. 9This king said to his people,
"Look! The people of Israel are too many
and too strong for us to handle! 10If we
don't make plans against them, the number of their people will grow even more.
Then if there is a war, they might join our
enemies and fight us and escape from the
country!"
11So the Egyptians made life hard for
the Israelites. They put slave masters
over them, who forced the Israelites to
build the cities Pithom and Rameses as
supply centers for the king. 12But the
harder the Egyptians forced the Israelites to work, the more the Israelites grew
in number and spread out. So the Egyptians became very afraid of them 13and
demanded even more of them. 14They
made their lives bitter. They forced the
Israelites to work hard to make bricks
and mortar and to do all kinds of work in
the fields. The Egyptians were not merciful to them in all their painful work.
15Two Hebrew nurses, named Shiph-
rah and Puah, helped the Israelite women
give birth to their babies. The king of
Egypt said to the nurses, 16"When you
are helping the Hebrew women give
birth to their babies, watch! If the baby is
a girl, let her live, but if it is a boy, kill

[a] **1:1 Jacob** Also called Israel.

FAITH links

OBEY? NO WAY!

EXODUS 1:15-21

Suppose you knew that the principal of your school disliked a certain group of kids. Now let's say she asked you to think of a way to get these kids expelled. If you don't, *you'll* be expelled. Would you do what you were told?

The king of Egypt didn't like the fact that the Hebrew population had grown. To decrease the population, he told two Hebrew midwives to kill all Hebrew boy babies. (A midwife is a woman who helps women give birth.) Yet Shiprah and Puah chose to obey God by refusing to kill these babies. God rewarded them by giving them children of their own. Although God wants you to obey people in authority, he would not expect you to obey an order that would cause you to sin.

Take Me to Your Leader, Numbers 27:12–23, p. 214

A Choice to Make, Deuteronomy 30:15–20, p. 265

The Right Thing to Do, 1 Samuel 26, p. 391

When I Need Advice, 1 Kings 12:1–17, p. 455

Going My Way?, Hosea 8:1–6, p. 1179

Obey or Disobey?, Luke 20:20–26, p. 1409

him!" 17But the nurses feared God, so
they did not do as the king told them;
they let all the boy babies live. 18Then
the king of Egypt sent for the nurses and
said, "Why did you do this? Why did you
let the boys live?"
19The nurses said to him, "The Hebrew women are much stronger than the
Egyptian women. They give birth to their
babies before we can get there." 20God
was good to the nurses. And the Hebrew
people continued to grow in number, so
they became even stronger. 21Because
the nurses feared God, he gave them
families of their own.
22So the king commanded all his people, "Every time a boy is born to the Hebrews, you must throw him into the Nile
River, but let all the girl babies live."

Baby Moses

2 Now a man from the family of Levi
married a woman who was also from
the family of Levi. 2She became pregnant
and gave birth to a son. When she saw
how wonderful the baby was, she hid him
for three months. 3But after three
months she was not able to hide the baby
any longer, so she got a basket made of
reeds and covered it with tar so that it
would float. She put the baby in the basket. Then she put the basket among the
tall stalks of grass at the edge of the Nile
River. 4The baby's sister stood a short
distance away to see what would happen
to him.
5Then the daughter of the king of
Egypt came to the river to take a bath,
and her servant girls were walking beside the river. When she saw the basket
in the tall grass, she sent her slave girl to
get it. 6The king's daughter opened the
basket and saw the baby boy. He was crying, so she felt sorry for him and said,
"This is one of the Hebrew babies."
7Then the baby's sister asked the
king's daughter, "Would you like me to go
and find a Hebrew woman to nurse the
baby for you?"
8The king's daughter said, "Go!" So
the girl went and got the baby's own
mother.
9The king's daughter said to the

FAITH links

YOUR HEAVENLY PARENT

EXODUS 2:1-10

You know your parents would do anything to protect you, right? They love you and wouldn't want anything to happen to you. Moses' mother felt the same way about her child. The king of Egypt made a cruel law. All of the Hebrew boy babies were to be killed. Moses' mother kept her son hidden. But after a while, she could hide him no longer. She placed him in the river, trusting that God would keep little Moses safe.

That's the kind of trust that God wants you to have. He's a heavenly parent who wants to take care of his earthly kid. If your parents are followers of Jesus, they're also trusting that God will take care of you.

Connect to these Faithlinks on how much God cares for you:

A Major Problem, Genesis 15:6, p. 20

Good Plans, Genesis 45:7–8, p. 64

Lower Than Low, Job 19:13–25, p. 680

Who Ya' Gonna Call?, Psalm 3:4, p. 711

When Bad Things Happen, Ecclesiastes 3:16–17, p. 876

Facing Your Fears, Matthew 8:23–27, p. 1288

woman, "Take this baby and nurse him
for me, and I will pay you." So the woman
took her baby and nursed him. **10**When
the child grew older, the woman took him
to the king's daughter, and she adopted
the baby as her own son. The king's
daughter named him Moses,[n] because
she had pulled him out of the water.

Moses Tries to Help

11Moses grew and became a man.
One day he visited his people and saw
that they were forced to work very hard.
He saw an Egyptian beating a Hebrew
man, one of Moses' own people. **12**Moses
looked all around and saw that no one was
watching, so he killed the Egyptian and
hid his body in the sand.

13The next day Moses returned and
saw two Hebrew men fighting each other.
He said to the one that was in the wrong,
"Why are you hitting one of your own
people?"

14The man answered, "Who made
you our ruler and judge? Are you going to
kill me as you killed the Egyptian?"

Moses was afraid and thought, "Now
everyone knows what I did."

15When the king heard what Moses
had done, he tried to kill him. But Moses
ran away from the king and went to live in
the land of Midian. There he sat down
near a well.

Moses in Midian

16There was a priest in Midian who
had seven daughters. His daughters went
to that well to get water to fill the water
troughs for their father's flock. **17**Some
shepherds came and chased the girls
away, but Moses defended the girls and
watered their flock.

18When they went back to their father Reuel,[n] he asked them, "Why have
you come home early today?"

19The girls answered, "The shepherds chased us away, but an Egyptian
defended us. He got water for us and watered our flock."

20He asked his daughters, "Where is
this man? Why did you leave him? Invite
him to eat with us."

21Moses agreed to stay with Jethro,
and he gave his daughter Zipporah to
Moses to be his wife. **22**Zipporah gave
birth to a son. Moses named him Ger-

PUT PRIDE ASIDE

EXODUS 2:11-15

Ever come up with a plan you thought was good, but it failed? Moses tried to help the Hebrew people in his own strength and timing. His plan was a complete disaster. Because of it, he had to run for his life.

Pride causes us to trust in our own ideas and plans. But sometimes our plans can lead us in the wrong direction. God wants us to put pride aside and give our plans to him for his approval.

Struggle with pride sometimes? Here are some thoughts on how to deal with that:

The Sacrifice, Genesis 22, p. 29

The Weak Link, Judges 16, p. 334

Your Full Trust, Jeremiah 22:20–22, p. 1023

Eating Humble Pie, Daniel 4, p. 1156

Brag on Him!, 1 Corinthians 3:18–23, p. 1548

The Way to Be Wise, James 1:5, p. 1689

2:10 Moses The name "Moses" sounds like the Hebrew word for "to pull out."

2:18 Reuel He was also called Jethro.

shom,[*] because Moses was a stranger in
a land that was not his own.
23After a long time, the king of Egypt
died. The people of Israel groaned, because they were forced to work very
hard. When they cried for help, God
heard them. 24God heard their cries, and
he remembered the agreement he had
made with Abraham, Isaac, and Jacob.
25He saw the troubles of the people of
Israel, and he was concerned about them.

The Burning Bush

3 One day Moses was taking care of
Jethro's flock. (Jethro was the priest
of Midian and also Moses' father-in-law.)
When Moses led the flock to the west
side of the desert, he came to Sinai, the
mountain of God. 2There the angel of
the LORD appeared to him in flames of
fire coming out of a bush. Moses saw that
the bush was on fire, but it was not burning up. 3So he said, "I will go closer to
this strange thing. How can a bush continue burning without burning up?"
4When the LORD saw Moses was
coming to look at the bush, God called to
him from the bush, "Moses, Moses!"
And Moses said, "Here I am."
5Then God said, "Do not
come any closer.
Take off your san-
dals, because you
are standing on holy
ground. 6I am the
God of your ances-
tors—the God of Abraham, the God of
Isaac, and the God of Jacob." Moses covered his face because he was afraid to
look at God.

EMAIL FROM GOD
3:5
Respect
Who is worthy of your respect?

7The LORD said, "I have seen the
troubles my people have suffered in
Egypt, and I have heard their cries when
the Egyptian slave masters hurt them. I
am concerned about their pain, 8and I
have come down to save them from the
Egyptians. I will bring them out of that
land and lead them to a good land with
lots of room—a fertile land. It is the land
of the Canaanites, Hittites, Amorites,
Perizzites, Hivites, and Jebusites. 9I
have heard the cries of the people of Israel, and I have seen the way the Egyptians have made life hard for them. 10So
now I am sending you to the king of
Egypt. Go! Bring my people, the Israelites, out of Egypt!"
11But Moses said to God, "I am not a
great man! How can I go to the king and
lead the Israelites out of Egypt?"
12God said, "I will be with you. This
will be the proof that I am sending you:
After you lead the people out of Egypt, all
of you will worship me on this mountain."
13Moses said to God, "When I go to
the Israelites, I will say to them, 'The
God of your fathers sent me to you.' What
if the people say, 'What is his name?'
What should I tell them?"
14Then God said to Moses, "I AM WHO
I AM.[*] When you go to the people of Israel, tell them, 'I AM sent me to you.' "
15God also said to Moses, "This is
what you should tell the people: 'The
LORD is the God of your ancestors—the
God of Abraham, the God of Isaac, and
the God of Jacob. He sent me to you.'
This will always be my name, by which
people from now on will know me.
16"Go and gather the older leaders
and tell them this: 'The LORD, the God of
your ancestors Abraham, Isaac, and Jacob, has appeared to me. He said, I care
about you, and I have seen what has happened to you in Egypt. 17I promised I
would take you out of your troubles in
Egypt. I will lead you to the land of the
Canaanites, Hittites, Amorites, Perizzites, Hivites, and Jebusites—a fertile
land.'
18"The older leaders will listen to
you. And then you and the older leaders
of Israel will go to the king of Egypt and
tell him, 'The LORD, the God of the Hebrews, appeared to us. Let us travel
three days into the desert to offer sacrifices to the LORD our God.'
19"But I know that the king of Egypt
will not let you go. Only a great power

2:22 Gershom This name sounds like the Hebrew word meaning "a stranger there."

3:14 I . . . I AM The Hebrew words are like the name "Yahweh." This Hebrew name for God, usually called "LORD," shows that God always lives and is always with his people.

will force him to let you go, 20so I will use my great power against Egypt. I will strike Egypt with all the miracles that will happen in that land. After I do that, he will let you go. 21I will cause the Egyptians to think well of the Israelites. So when you leave, they will give gifts to your people. 22Each woman should ask her Egyptian neighbor and any Egyptian woman living in her house for gifts—silver, gold, and clothing. You should put those gifts on your children when you leave Egypt. In this way you will take with you the riches of the Egyptians."

Proof for Moses

4 Then Moses answered, "What if the people of Israel do not believe me or listen to me? What if they say, 'The LORD did not appear to you'?"

2The LORD said to him, "What is that in your hand?"

Moses answered, "It is my walking stick."

3The LORD said, "Throw it on the ground."

So Moses threw it on the ground, and it became a snake. Moses ran from the snake, 4but the LORD said to him, "Reach out and grab the snake by its tail." When Moses reached out and took hold of the snake, it again became a stick in his hand. 5The LORD said, "This is so that the Israelites will believe that the LORD appeared to you. I am the God of their ancestors, the God of Abraham, the God of Isaac, and the God of Jacob."

6Then the LORD said to Moses, "Put your hand inside your coat." So Moses put his hand inside his coat. When he took it out, it was white with a skin disease.

7Then he said, "Now put your hand inside your coat again." So Moses put his hand inside his coat again. When he took it out, his hand was healthy again, like the rest of his skin.

8Then the LORD said, "If the people do not believe you or pay attention to the first miracle, they may believe you when you show them this second miracle. 9After these two miracles, if they still do not believe or listen to you, take some water from the Nile River and pour it on the dry ground. The water will become blood when it touches the ground."

10But Moses said to the LORD, "Please, Lord, I have never been a skilled speaker. Even now, after talking to you, I cannot speak well. I speak slowly and can't find the best words."

FAITH links

FEARFUL SERVICE?

EXODUS 4:1-17

What's the biggest fear you have about serving God? Many people fear that God will force them to do something they don't want to do. God wanted Moses to return to Egypt and lead the people out of slavery. The very thought of that terrified Moses. He came up with excuse after excuse. For every excuse, God explained how he would help Moses.

When it comes to serving him, God doesn't want his people to fall back on excuses. God will always give you the resources you need when he calls you to a task. Your part is to be obedient.

What God Wants, Deuteronomy 10:12–13, p. 242

From Zero to Hero, Judges 6; 7, p. 319

The Big Risk, Esther 4:11–5:2, p. 652

Be Brave!, Haggai 2:4, p. 1249

Our Gift to God, Romans 12:1–2, p. 1536

Blessed Are the Weak?, 2 Corinthians 12:7–10, p. 1582

11Then the LORD said to him, "Who
made a person's mouth? And who makes
someone deaf or not able to speak? Or
who gives a person sight or blindness? It
is I, the LORD. **12**Now go! I will help you
speak, and I will teach you what to say."

13But Moses said, "Please, Lord,
send someone else."

14The LORD became angry with Moses and said, "Your brother Aaron, from
the family of Levi, is a skilled speaker. He
is already coming to meet you, and he
will be happy when he sees you. **15**You
will speak to Aaron and tell him what
to say. I will help both of you to speak and
will teach you what to do. **16**Aaron will
speak to the people for you. You will tell
him what God says, and he will speak for
you. **17**Take your walking stick with you,
and use it to do the miracles."

Moses Returns to Egypt

18Moses went back to Jethro, his
father-in-law, and said to him, "Let me go
back to my people in Egypt. I want to see
if they are still alive."

Jethro said to Moses, "Go! I wish you well."

19While Moses was still in Midian,
the LORD said to him, "Go back to Egypt,
because the men who wanted to kill you
are dead now."

20So Moses took his wife and his
sons, put them on a donkey, and started
back to Egypt. He took with him the
walking stick of God.

21The LORD said to Moses, "When
you get back to Egypt, do all the miracles
I have given you the power to do. Show
them to the king of Egypt. But I will
make the king very stubborn, and he will
not let the people go. **22**Then say to the
king, 'This is what the LORD says: Israel
is my firstborn son. **23**I told you to let my
son go so he may worship me. But you
refused to let Israel go, so I will kill your
firstborn son.' "

24As Moses was on his way to Egypt,
he stopped at a resting place for the
night. The LORD met him there and tried
to kill him. **25**But Zipporah took a flint
knife and circumcised her son. Taking
the skin, she touched Moses' feet with it
and said to him, "You are a bridegroom of
blood to me." **26**She said, "You are a
bridegroom of blood," because she had to
circumcise her son. So the LORD let Moses alone.

27Meanwhile the LORD said to Aaron,
"Go out into the desert to meet Moses."
When Aaron went, he met Moses at Sinai, the mountain of God, and kissed him.
28Moses told Aaron everything the LORD
had said to him when he sent him to
Egypt. He also told him about the miracles which the LORD had commanded him
to do.

29Moses and Aaron gathered all the
older leaders of the Israelites, **30**and
Aaron told them everything that the
LORD had told Moses. Then Moses did
the miracles for all the people to see,
31and the Israelites believed. When they
heard that the LORD was concerned
about them and had seen their troubles,
they bowed down and worshiped him.

Moses and Aaron Before the King

5 After Moses and Aaron talked to the
people, they went to the king of
Egypt and said, "This is what the LORD,
the God of Israel, says: 'Let my people go
so they may hold a feast for me in the
desert.' "

2But the king of Egypt said, "Who is
the LORD? Why should I obey him and let
Israel go? I do not know the LORD, and I
will not let Israel go."

3Then Aaron and Moses said, "The
God of the Hebrews has met with us.
Now let us travel three days into the
desert to offer sacrifices to the LORD our
God. If we don't do this, he may kill us
with a disease or in war."

4But the king said to them, "Moses
and Aaron, why are you taking the people
away from their work? Go back to your
jobs! **5**There are very many Hebrews,
and now you want them to quit working!"

6That same day the king gave a command to the slave masters and foremen.
7He said, "Don't give the people straw to
make bricks as you used to do. Let them
gather their own straw. **8**But they must
still make the same number of bricks as
they did before. Do not accept fewer.

They have become lazy, and that is why
they are asking me, 'Let us go to offer
sacrifices to our God.' 9Make these people work harder and keep them busy;
then they will not have time to listen to
the lies of Moses."
10So the slave masters and foremen
went to the Israelites and said, "This is
what the king says: I will no longer give
you straw. 11Go and get your own straw
wherever you can find it. But you must
make as many bricks as you made before." 12So the people went everywhere
in Egypt looking for dry stalks to use for
straw. 13The slave masters kept forcing
the people to work harder. They said,
"You must make just as many bricks as
you did when you were given straw."
14The king's slave masters had made the
Israelite foremen responsible for the
work the people did. The Egyptian slave
masters beat these men and asked them,
"Why aren't you making as many bricks
as you made in the past?"
15Then the Israelite foremen went to
the king and complained, "Why are you
treating us, your servants, this way?
16You give us no straw, but we are commanded to make bricks. Our slave masters beat us, but it is your own people's
fault."
17The king answered, "You are lazy!
You don't want to work! That is why you
ask to leave here and make sacrifices to
the LORD. 18Now, go back to work! We
will not give you any straw, but you must
make just as many bricks as you did before."
19The Israelite foremen knew they
were in trouble, because the king had told
them, "You must make just as many
bricks each day as you did before." 20As
they were leaving the meeting with the
king, they met Moses and Aaron, who
were waiting for them. 21So they said to
Moses and Aaron, "May the LORD punish
you. You caused the king and his officers
to hate us. You have given them an excuse to kill us."

Moses Complains to God

22Then Moses returned to the LORD
and said, "Lord, why have you brought

FAITH links

WHEN BAD TURNS TO WORSE

EXODUS 5:6-12

Ever have an already bad day that suddenly took a turn for the worse? Moses didn't want to be the chosen leader of the Israelites. Yet he obeyed God by going to Egypt to tell the king to let the Israelites go. After Moses and Aaron gave the king God's message, the king made the people work harder than ever! Who was blamed for this? Moses!

Sometimes things seem to get worse when we follow God. Has that been your experience? Even when that happens, God still wants you to be obedient. He wants you to trust that he'll see you through the hard times.

How do you handle tough times? Surf over to these links for some help:

Alone and Forgotten?, Genesis 40:23, p. 57

Your Worst Enemy, Exodus 7—11, p. 85

A Pity Party, Job 10, p. 671

A Promise from the Heart, Jeremiah 31:31–33, p. 1037

Our Good Shepherd, John 10:11–15, p. 1441

As Strong as Superman?, Philippians 4:13, p. 1615

this trouble on your people? Is this why
you sent me here? 23I went to the king
and said what you told me to say, but ever
since that time he has made the people
suffer. And you have done nothing to save
them."
6 Then the LORD said to Moses, "Now
you will see what I will do to the king
of Egypt. I will use my great power
against him, and he will let my people go.
Because of my power, he will force them
out of his country."
2Then God said to Moses, "I am the
LORD. 3I appeared to Abraham, Isaac, and
Jacob by the name God Almighty, but
they did not know me by my name, the
LORD. 4I also made my agreement with
them to give them the land of Canaan.
They lived in that land, but it was not
their own. 5Now I have heard the cries of
the Israelites, whom the Egyptians are
treating as slaves, and I remember my
agreement. 6So tell the people of Israel
that I say to them, 'I am the LORD. I will
save you from the hard work the Egyptians force you to do. I will make you free,
so you will not be slaves to the Egyptians. I will free you by my great power,
and I will punish the Egyptians terribly.
7I will make you my own people, and I
will be your God. You will know that I am
the LORD your God, the One who
saves you from the
hard work the Egyp-
tians force you to
do. 8I will lead you
to the land that I
promised to Abra-
ham, Isaac, and Jacob, and I will give you
that land to own. I am the LORD.' "
9So Moses told this to the Israelites,
but they would not listen to him. They
were discouraged, and their slavery was
hard.
10Then the LORD said to Moses,
11"Go tell the king of Egypt that he must
let the Israelites leave his land."
12But Moses answered, "The Israelites will not listen to me, so surely the
king will not listen to me either. I am not
a good speaker."
13But the LORD spoke to Moses and
Aaron and gave them orders about the

EMAIL FROM GOD 6:7

God

Does God promise to take care of you?

FAITH links

FROM HOPELESS TO HOPEFUL

EXODUS 6:9

Have you ever felt hopeless? Imagine feeling like that for months or even years. The Israelites felt hopeless. They had been stuck in slavery for many years. When God sent them a leader, the king increased their work duties out of spite. As a result, they could hardly believe the message of hope that Moses gave them.

When things aren't going very well, you may feel discouraged. You may even doubt that God loves you. God still wants to help you, even if you find that hard to believe. The best thing to do is to not give up on prayer. When you pray, ask God to give you hope.

Here are some more Faithlinks on prayer:

Our Thorough God, Leviticus 13, p. 149

Keep On Praying, 1 Samuel 1, p. 354

Your Best Defense, 2 Chronicles 20:1–12, p. 584

Go for the Gold, Job 23:10, p. 685

Uprooted by Change, Amos 9:15, p. 1205

Keep On Keepin' On, Revelation 13:10, p. 1744

Israelites and the king of Egypt. He commanded them to lead the Israelites out of
Egypt.

Families of Israel

14These are the leaders of the families of Israel:

Israel's first son, Reuben, had four
sons: Hanoch, Pallu, Hezron, and Carmi.
These are the family groups of Reuben.
15Simeon's sons were Jemuel, Jamin,
Ohad, Jakin, Zohar, and Shaul, the son of a
Canaanite woman. These are the family
groups of Simeon.
16Levi lived one hundred thirty-
seven years. These are the names of his
sons according to their family history:
Gershon, Kohath, and Merari.
17Gershon had two sons, Libni and
Shimei, with their families.
18Kohath lived one hundred thirty-
three years. The sons of Kohath were
Amram, Izhar, Hebron, and Uzziel.
19The sons of Merari were Mahli and
Mushi.
These are the family groups of Levi,
according to their family history.
20Amram married his father's sister
Jochebed, who gave birth to Aaron and
Moses. Amram lived one hundred thirty-
seven years.
21Izhar's sons were Korah, Nepheg,
and Zicri.
22Uzziel's sons were Mishael, Elzaphan, and Sithri.
23Aaron married Elisheba, the daughter of Amminadab and the sister of Nahshon. Elisheba gave birth to Nadab,
Abihu, Eleazar, and Ithamar.
24The sons of Korah were Assir, Elkanah, and Abiasaph. These are the family groups of the Korahites.
25Eleazar son of Aaron married a
daughter of Putiel, and she gave birth to
Phinehas.
These are the leaders of the family
groups of the Levites.
26This was the Aaron and Moses to
whom the LORD said, "Lead the people of
Israel out of Egypt by their divisions."
27Aaron and Moses are the ones who
talked to the king of Egypt and told him
to let the Israelites leave Egypt.

God Repeats His Call to Moses

28The LORD spoke to Moses in the
land of Egypt 29and said, "I am the LORD.
Tell the king of Egypt everything I tell
you."
30But Moses answered, "I am not
a good speaker. The king will not listen
to me."
7 The LORD said to Moses, "I have
made you like God to the king of
Egypt, and your brother Aaron will be
like a prophet for you. 2Tell Aaron your
brother everything that I command you,
and let him tell the king of Egypt to let
the Israelites leave his country. 3But I
will make the king stubborn. I will do
many miracles in Egypt, 4but he will still
refuse to listen. So then I will punish
Egypt terribly, and I will lead my divisions, my people the Israelites, out of
that land. 5I will punish Egypt with my
power, and I will bring the Israelites out
of that land. Then they will know I am the
LORD."
6Moses and Aaron did just as the
LORD had commanded them. 7Moses was
eighty years old and Aaron was eighty-
three when they spoke to the king.

Aaron's Walking Stick Becomes a Snake

8The LORD said to Moses and Aaron,
9"Moses, when the king asks you to do a
miracle, tell Aaron to throw his walking
stick down in front of the king, and it will
become a snake."
10So Moses and Aaron went to the
king as the LORD had commanded. Aaron
threw his walking stick down in front of
the king and his officers, and it became a
snake.
11So the king called in his wise men
and his magicians, and with their tricks
the Egyptian magicians were able to do
the same thing. 12They threw their
walking sticks on the ground, and their
sticks became snakes. But Aaron's stick
swallowed theirs. 13Still the king was
stubborn and refused to listen to Moses
and Aaron, just as the LORD had said.

YOUR WORST ENEMY

EXODUS 7–11

You've heard the saying, "You're your own worst enemy," haven't you? That means you've done something to cause pain and suffering in your own life. In the king's case, that was certainly true. He thought he had successfully gotten even with Moses for daring to ask that the Israelites be freed from slavery. The king's stubbornness led to ten awful plagues that ruined Egypt; and in the last one, his firstborn son also died.

Sometimes we *are* our own worst enemy. What's the cure for that? Trusting that God—not we—knows what's best for our lives.

Who Do You Trust?, Joshua 9, p. 287

Big Lack Attack, 2 Kings 4:1–7, p. 480

A Direct Path, Proverbs 3:5–6, p. 829

The Love Magnet, James 4:7–8, p. 1694

Ya' Gotta Love It?, 1 John 2:15, p. 1715

Love and Obey, 2 John 6, p. 1721

The Water Becomes Blood

14Then the LORD said to Moses, "The king is being stubborn and refuses to let the people go. **15**In the morning the king will go out to the Nile River. Go meet him by the edge of the river, and take with you the walking stick that became a snake. **16**Tell him: The LORD, the God of the Hebrews, sent me to you. He said, 'Let my people go worship me in the desert.' Until now you have not listened. **17**This is what the LORD says: 'This is how you will know that I am the LORD. I will strike the water of the Nile River with this stick in my hand, and the water will change into blood. **18**Then the fish in the Nile will die, and the river will begin to stink. The Egyptians will not be able to drink the water from the Nile.' "

19The LORD said to Moses, "Tell Aaron: 'Take the walking stick in your hand and stretch your hand over the rivers, canals, ponds, and pools in Egypt.' The water will become blood everywhere in Egypt, both in wooden buckets and in stone jars."

20So Moses and Aaron did just as the LORD had commanded. In front of the king and his officers, Aaron raised his walking stick and struck the water in the Nile River. So all the water in the Nile changed into blood. **21**The fish in the Nile died, and the river began to stink, so the Egyptians could not drink water from it. Blood was everywhere in the land of Egypt.

22Using their tricks, the magicians of Egypt did the same thing. So the king was stubborn and refused to listen to Moses and Aaron, just as the LORD had said. **23**The king turned and went into his palace and ignored what Moses and Aaron had done. **24**The Egyptians could not drink the water from the Nile, so all of them dug along the bank of the river, looking for water to drink.

The Frogs

25Seven days passed after the LORD changed the Nile River.

8 Then the LORD told Moses, "Go to the king of Egypt and tell him, 'This is what the LORD says: Let my people go to worship me. **2**If you refuse, I will punish Egypt with frogs. **3**The Nile River will be filled with frogs. They will come up into your palace, into your bedroom, on your bed, into the houses of your officers, and onto your people. They will come

into your ovens and into your baking
pans. 4The frogs will jump all over you,
your people, and your officers.' "
5Then the LORD said to Moses, "Tell
Aaron to hold his walking stick in his
hand over the rivers, canals, and ponds. Make
frogs come up out of the
water onto the land of
Egypt."
6So Aaron held his
hand over all the waters
of Egypt, and the frogs
came up out of the water
and covered the land of
Egypt. 7The magicians
used their tricks to do the
same thing, so even more frogs came up
onto the land of Egypt.

> Then the LORD told Moses, "Go to the king of Egypt and tell him, 'This is what the LORD says: Let my people go to worship me.' "
>
> —Exodus 8:1

8The king called for Moses and Aaron
and said, "Pray to the LORD to take the
frogs away from me and my people. I will
let your people go to offer sacrifices to
the LORD."
9Moses said to the king, "Please set
the time when I should pray for you, your
people, and your officers. Then the frogs
will leave you and your houses and will
remain only in the Nile."
10The king answered, "Tomorrow."
Moses said, "What you want will happen. By this you will know that there is
no one like the LORD our God. 11The
frogs will leave you, your houses, your
officers, and your people. They will remain only in the Nile."
12After Moses and Aaron left the
king, Moses asked the LORD about the
frogs he had sent to the king. 13And the
LORD did as Moses asked. The frogs died
in the houses, in the yards, and in the
fields. 14The Egyptians put them in
piles, and the whole country began to
stink. 15But when the king saw that they
were free of the frogs, he became stubborn again. He did not listen to Moses
and Aaron, just as the LORD had said.

The Gnats

16Then the LORD said to Moses, "Tell
Aaron to raise his walking stick and
strike the dust on the ground. Then
everywhere in Egypt the dust will
change into gnats." 17They did this, and
when Aaron raised the walking stick that
was in his hand and struck the dust on
the ground, everywhere in Egypt the
dust changed into gnats. The gnats got on
the people and animals.
18Using their tricks, the
magicians tried to do the
same thing, but they
could not make the dust
change into gnats. The
gnats remained on the
people and animals. 19So
the magicians told the
king that the power of
God had done this. But
the king was stubborn
and refused to listen to them, just as the
LORD had said.

The Flies

20The LORD told Moses, "Get up
early in the morning, and meet the king
of Egypt as he goes out to the river. Tell
him, 'This is what the LORD says: Let my
people go so they can worship me. 21If
you don't let them go, I will send swarms
of flies into your houses. The flies will be
on you, your officers, and your people.
The houses of Egypt will be full of flies,
and they will be all over the ground, too.
22But I will not treat the Israelites the
same as the Egyptian people. There will
not be any flies in the land of Goshen,
where my people live. By this you will
know that I, the LORD, am in this land.
23I will treat my people differently from
your people. This miracle will happen tomorrow.' "
24So the LORD did as he had said, and
great swarms of flies came into the king's
palace and his officers' houses. All over
Egypt flies were ruining the land. 25The
king called for Moses and Aaron and told
them, "Offer sacrifices to your God here
in this country."
26But Moses said, "It wouldn't be
right to do that, because the Egyptians
hate the sacrifices we offer to the LORD
our God. If they see us offering sacrifices
they hate, they will throw stones at us
and kill us. 27Let us make a three-day
journey into the desert. We must offer

TEN CURSES

Exodus 9

The Israelites had been slaves in Egypt for a long time. Moses went to the king of Egypt and asked him to let the Israelites leave and go back to their homeland. The king said a big "No!" So God sent ten plagues to convince the king to let the Israelites leave. Here's what he did:

1. The water of the Nile River turned to blood (Exodus 7:14–25).
2. Frogs overran the country (Exodus 8:1–15).
3. People and animals were infested with gnats (Exodus 8:16–19).
4. Swarms of flies covered the land and got into Egyptian homes (Exodus 8:20–32).
5. Disease killed the farm animals (Exodus 9:1–7).
6. Boils and sores infected the Egyptians and their animals (Exodus 9:8–12).
7. Hail destroyed crops and vegetation (Exodus 9:13–35).
8. Swarms of locusts covered the land (Exodus 10:1–20).
9. Thick darkness covered Egypt for three days (Exodus 10:21–29).
10. The oldest Egyptian child and animal from each household died (Exodus 11:1—12:30).

Finally, after this last plague, the king of Egypt let Moses and the Israelites leave Egypt.

sacrifices to the LORD our God there, as
the LORD told us to do."
28The king said, "I will let you go so
that you may offer sacrifices to the LORD
your God in the desert, but you must
not go very far away. Now go and pray
for me."
29Moses said, "I will leave and pray to
the LORD, and he will take the flies away
from you, your officers, and your people
tomorrow. But do not try to trick us
again. Do not stop the people from going
to offer sacrifices to the LORD."
30So Moses left the king and prayed
to the LORD, **31**and the LORD did as he
asked. He removed the flies from the
king, his officers, and his people so that
not one fly was left. **32**But the king became stubborn again and did not let the
people go.

The Disease on the Farm Animals

9 Then the LORD told Moses, "Go to
the king of Egypt and tell him, 'This
is what the LORD, the God of the Hebrews, says: Let my people go to worship
me. **2**If you refuse to let them go and continue to hold them, **3**the LORD will punish
you. He will send a terrible disease on
your farm animals that are in the fields.
He will cause your horses, donkeys, camels, cattle, goats, and sheep to become
sick. **4**But the LORD will treat Israel's animals differently from the animals of
Egypt. None of the animals that belong to
the Israelites will die. **5**The LORD has set
tomorrow as the time he will do this in
the land.' " **6**The next day the LORD did
as he promised. All the farm animals in
Egypt died, but none of the animals belonging to Israelites died. **7**The king sent

people to see what had happened to the
animals of Israel, and they found that
not one of them had died. But the king
was still stubborn and did not let the people go.

The Boils

8The LORD said to Moses and Aaron,
"Fill your hands with ashes from a furnace. Moses, throw the ashes into the air
in front of the king of Egypt. 9The ashes
will spread like dust through all the land
of Egypt. They will cause boils to break
out and become sores on the skin of people and animals everywhere in the land."

10So Moses and Aaron took ashes
from a furnace and went and stood before
the king. Moses threw ashes into the air,
which caused boils to break out and become sores on people and animals. 11The
magicians could not stand before Moses,
because all the Egyptians had boils, even
the magicians. 12But the LORD made the
king stubborn, so he refused to listen to
Moses and Aaron, just as the LORD had
said.

The Hail

13Then the LORD said to Moses, "Get
up early in the morning and go to the king
of Egypt. Tell him, 'This is what the
LORD, the God of the Hebrews, says: Let
my people go to worship me. 14If you
don't, this time I will punish you, your officers, and your people, with all my
power. Then you will know there is no
one in the whole land like me. 15By now I
could have used my power and caused a
terrible disease that would have destroyed you and your people from the
earth. 16But I have let you live for this
reason: to show you my power so that my
name will be talked about in all the earth.
17You are still against my people and do
not want to let them go. 18So at this time
tomorrow, I will send a terrible hailstorm, the worst in Egypt since it became a nation. 19Now send for your
animals and whatever you have in the
fields, and bring them into a safe place.
The hail will fall on every person or animal that is still in the fields. If they have
not been brought in, they will die.'"
20Some of the king's officers respected
the word of the LORD and hurried to bring
their slaves and animals inside. 21But
others ignored the LORD's message and
left their slaves and animals in the fields.

22The LORD told Moses, "Raise your
hand toward the sky. Then the hail will
start falling in all the land of Egypt. It will
fall on people, animals, and on everything
that grows in the fields of Egypt."
23When Moses raised his walking stick
toward the sky, the LORD sent thunder
and hail, and lightning flashed down to
the earth. So he caused hail to fall upon
the land of Egypt. 24There was hail, and
lightning flashed as it hailed—the worst
hailstorm in Egypt since it had become a
nation. 25The hail destroyed all the people and animals that were in the fields in
all the land of Egypt. It also destroyed everything that grew in the fields and broke
all the trees in the fields. 26The only
place it did not hail was in the land of Goshen, where the Israelites lived.

27The king sent for Moses and Aaron
and told them, "This time I have sinned.
The LORD is in the right, and I and my
people are in the wrong. 28Pray to the
LORD. We have had enough of God's
thunder and hail. I will let you go; you do
not have to stay here any longer."

29Moses told the king, "When I leave
the city, I will raise my hands to the LORD
in prayer, and the thunder and hail will
stop. Then you will know that the earth
belongs to the LORD. 30But I know that
you and your officers do not yet fear the
LORD God."

31The flax was in bloom, and the barley had ripened, so these crops were destroyed. 32But both wheat crops ripen
later, so they were not destroyed.

33Moses left the king and went outside the city. He raised his hands to the
LORD, and the thunder and hail stopped.
The rain also stopped falling to the
ground. 34When the king saw that the
rain, hail, and thunder had stopped, he
sinned again, and he and his officers became stubborn. 35So the king became
stubborn and refused to let the Israelites
go, just as the LORD had said through
Moses.

The Locusts

10 The LORD said to Moses, "Go to
the king of Egypt. I have made him
and his officers stubborn so I could show
them my powerful miracles. **2**I also did
this so you could tell your children and
your grandchildren how I was hard on the
Egyptians. Tell them about the miracles I
did among them so that all of you will
know that I am the LORD."
3So Moses and Aaron went to the
king and told him, "This is what the
LORD, the God of the Hebrews, says:
'How long will you refuse to be sorry for
what you have done? Let my people go to
worship me. **4**If you refuse to let my people go, tomorrow I will bring locusts into
your country. **5**They will cover the land
so that no one will be able to see the
ground. They will eat anything that was
left from the hailstorm and the leaves
from every tree growing in the field.
6They will fill your palaces and all your
officers' houses, as well as the houses of
all the Egyptians. There will be more locusts than your fathers or ancestors have
ever seen—more than there have been
since people began living in Egypt.' "
Then Moses turned and walked away
from the king.
7The king's officers asked him, "How
long will this man make trouble for us?
Let the Israelites go to worship the LORD
their God. Don't you know that Egypt is
ruined?"
8So Moses and Aaron were brought
back to the king. He said to them, "Go
and worship the LORD your God. But tell
me, just who is going?"
9Moses answered, "We will go with
our young and old people, our sons and
daughters, and our flocks and herds, because we are going to have a feast to
honor the LORD."
10The king said to them, "The LORD
will really have to be with you if ever I let
you and all of your children leave Egypt.
See, you are planning something evil!
11No! Only the men may go and worship
the LORD, which is what you have been
asking for." Then the king forced Moses
and Aaron out of his palace.
12The LORD told Moses, "Raise your
hand over the land of Egypt, and the locusts will come. They will spread all over
the land of Egypt and will eat all the
plants the hail did not destroy."
13So Moses raised his walking stick
over the land of Egypt, and the LORD
caused a strong wind to blow from the
east. It blew across the land all that day
and night, and when morning came, the
east wind had brought the locusts.
14Swarms of locusts covered all the land
of Egypt and settled everywhere. There
were more locusts than ever before or
after, **15**and they covered the whole land
so that it was black. They ate everything
that was left after the hail—every plant
in the field and all the fruit on the trees.
Nothing green was left on any tree or
plant anywhere in Egypt.
16The king quickly called for Moses
and Aaron. He said, "I have sinned
against the LORD your God and against
you. **17**Now forgive my sin this time.
Pray to the LORD your God, and ask him
to stop this punishment that kills."
18Moses left the king and prayed to
the LORD. **19**So the LORD changed the
wind. He made a very strong wind blow
from the west, and it blew the locusts
away into the Red Sea. Not one locust
was left anywhere in Egypt. **20**But the
LORD caused the king to be stubborn
again, and he did not let the Israelites go.

The Darkness

21Then the LORD told Moses, "Raise
your hand toward the sky, and darkness
will cover the land of Egypt. It will be so
dark you will be able to feel it." **22**Moses
raised his hand toward the sky, and total
darkness was everywhere in Egypt for
three days. **23**No one could see anyone
else, and no one could go anywhere for
three days. But the Israelites had light
where they lived.
24Again the king of Egypt called for
Moses. He said, "All of you may go and
worship the LORD. You may take your
women and children with you, but you
must leave your flocks and herds here."
25Moses said, "You must let us have
animals to use as sacrifices and burnt offerings, because we have to offer them to

the LORD our God. 26So we must take
our animals with us; not a hoof will be left
behind. We have to use some of the animals to worship the LORD our God. We
won't know exactly what we will need to
worship the LORD until we get there."

27But the LORD made the king stubborn again, so he refused to let them go.
28Then he told Moses, "Get out of here,
and don't come again! The next time you
see me, you will die."

29Then Moses told the king, "I'll do
what you say. I will not come to see you
again."

The Death of the Firstborn

11 Now the LORD had told Moses, "I
have one more way to punish the
king and the people of Egypt. After this,
the king will send all of you away from
Egypt. When he does, he will force you to
leave completely. 2Tell the men and
women of Israel to ask their neighbors
for things made of silver and gold." 3The
LORD had caused the Egyptians to respect the Israelites, and both the king's
officers and the Egyptian people considered Moses to be a great man.

4So Moses said to the king, "This is
what the LORD says: 'About midnight tonight I will go through all
Egypt. 5Every firstborn
son in the land of Egypt
will die—from the first-
born son of the king, who
sits on his throne, to the
firstborn of the slave girl
grinding grain. Also the
firstborn farm animals
will die. 6There will be
loud outcries everywhere
in Egypt, worse than any
time before or after this. 7But not even a
dog will bark at the Israelites or their animals.' Then you will know that the LORD
treats Israel differently from Egypt. 8All
your officers will come to me. They will
bow facedown to the ground before me
and say, 'Leave and take all your people
with you.' After that, I will leave." Then
Moses very angrily left the king.

9The LORD had told Moses, "The king
will not listen to you and Aaron so that I
may do many miracles in the land of
Egypt." 10Moses and Aaron did all these
great miracles in front of the king. But
the LORD made him stubborn, and the
king would not let the Israelites leave his
country.

> Every firstborn son in the land of Egypt will die—from the firstborn son of the king, . . . to the firstborn of the slave girl.
>
> —Exodus 11:5

The First Passover

12 The LORD spoke to Moses and
Aaron in the land of Egypt: 2"This
month will be the beginning of months,
the first month of the year for you.
3Tell the whole community of Israel that
on the tenth day of this month each man
must get one lamb for the people in his
house. 4If there are not enough people in
his house to eat a whole lamb, he must
share it with his closest neighbor, considering the number of people. There must
be enough lamb for everyone to eat.
5The lamb must be a one-year-old male
that has nothing wrong with it. This animal can be either a young sheep or a
young goat. 6Take care of the animals until the fourteenth day of the month. On
that day all the people of the community
of Israel will kill them in the evening before dark. 7The people must take some of
the blood and put it on the sides and tops
of the doorframes of the houses where
they eat the lambs. 8On
this night they must roast
the lamb over a fire. They
must eat it with bitter
herbs and bread made
without yeast. 9Do not
eat the lamb raw or boiled
in water. Roast the whole
lamb over a fire—with its
head, legs, and inner or-
gans. 10You must not
leave any of it until morn-
ing, but if any of it is left over until morning, you must burn it with fire.

11"This is the way you must eat it:
You must be fully dressed as if you were
going on a trip. You must have your sandals on and your walking stick in your
hand. You must eat it in a hurry; this is
the LORD's Passover.

12"That night I will go through the
land of Egypt and kill all the firstborn
animals and people in the land of Egypt. I

A THANKSGIVING REMINDER

EXODUS 12

When are you most thankful? When you've received a gift? When things are going well in your life? Holidays or celebrations are times that remind us to be thankful. God instructed the Israelites to establish a holiday to remember how he had saved them from slavery in Egypt. This holiday was known as Passover. For centuries, the Israelites have celebrated the Passover as a way of saying thanks to God.

Holidays like Easter, Thanksgiving, and Christmas remind us that we have a lot to be thankful for. God sent his Son, Jesus, to be our deliverer. He deserves our thanks.

Link here for some more ways to tell God thank-you:

A Life of Thanksgiving, 1 Kings 1:47–48, p. 435

A Holiday Letter, Esther 9:20–23, p. 657

The One Who Suffered, Isaiah 53, p. 966

How Do I Love You?, Malachi 1:1–5, p. 1267

Too Busy to Worship, Luke 2:8–20, p. 1368

One Big, Happy Family, John 1:12, p. 1422

will also punish all the gods of Egypt.
I am the LORD. **13**But the blood will be a
sign on the houses where you are. When
I see the blood, I will pass over you.
Nothing terrible will hurt you when I
punish the land of Egypt.

14"You are always to remember this
day and celebrate it with a feast to the
LORD. Your descendants are to honor the
LORD with this feast from now on. **15**For
this feast you must eat bread made without yeast for seven days. On the first day,
you are to remove all the yeast from your
houses. No one should eat any yeast for
the full seven days of the feast, or that
person will be cut off from Israel. **16**You
are to have holy meetings on the first and
last days of the feast. You must not do any
work on these days; the only work you
may do is to prepare your meals. **17**You
must celebrate the Feast of Unleavened
Bread, because on this very day I brought
your divisions of people out of Egypt. So
all of your descendants must celebrate
this day. This is a law that will last from
now on. **18**In the first month of the year
you are to eat bread made without yeast,
from the evening of the fourteenth day
until the evening of the twenty-first day.
19For seven days there must not be any
yeast in your houses. Anybody who eats
yeast during this time, either an Israelite
or non-Israelite, must be cut off from the
community of Israel. **20**During this feast
you must not eat anything made with
yeast. You must eat only bread made
without yeast wherever you live."

21Then Moses called all the older
leaders of Israel together and told them,
"Get the animals for your families and
kill the lamb for the Passover. **22**Take a
branch of the hyssop plant, dip it into the
bowl filled with blood, and then wipe the
blood on the sides and tops of the doorframes. No one may leave that house until morning. **23**When the LORD goes
through Egypt to kill the Egyptians, he
will see the blood on the sides and tops of
the doorframes, and he will pass over
that house. He will not let the one who
brings death come into your houses and
kill you.

24"You must keep this command as a

law for you and your descendants from
now on. **25**Do this when you go to the
land the LORD has promised to give you.
26When your children ask you, 'Why are
we doing these things?' **27**you will say,
'This is the Passover sacrifice to honor
the LORD. When we were in Egypt, the
LORD passed over the houses of Israel,
and when he killed the Egyptians, he
saved our homes.' " Then the people
bowed down and worshiped the LORD.
28They did just as the LORD commanded
Moses and Aaron.

29At midnight the LORD killed all the
firstborn sons in the land of Egypt—from
the firstborn of the king who sat on the
throne to the firstborn of the prisoner in
jail. Also, all the firstborn farm animals
died. **30**The king, his officers, and all the
Egyptians got up during the night because someone had died in every house.
So there was a loud outcry everywhere in
Egypt.

Israel Leaves Egypt

31During the night the king called for
Moses and Aaron and said, "Get up and
leave my people. You and your people
may do as you have asked; go and worship the LORD. **32**Take all of your flocks
and herds as you have asked, and go.
And also bless me." **33**The Egyptians
also asked the Israelites to hurry and
leave, saying, "If you don't leave, we will
all die!"

34So the people took their dough before the yeast was added. They wrapped
the bowls for making dough in clothing
and carried them on their shoulders.
35The Israelites did what Moses told
them to do and asked their Egyptian
neighbors for things made of silver and
gold and for clothing. **36**The LORD caused
the Egyptians to think well of them, and
the Egyptians gave the people everything they asked for. So the Israelites
took rich gifts from them.

37The Israelites traveled from Rameses to Succoth. There were about six
hundred thousand men walking, not including the women and children. **38**Many
other people who were not Israelites
went with them, as well as a large number of sheep, goats, and cattle. **39**The Israelites used the dough they had brought
out of Egypt to bake loaves of bread without yeast. The dough had no yeast in it,
because they had been rushed out of
Egypt and had no time to get food ready
for their trip.

40The people of Israel had lived in
Egypt for four hundred thirty years; **41**on
the very day the four hundred thirty
years ended, the LORD's divisions of people left Egypt. **42**That night the LORD
kept watch to bring them out of Egypt,
and so on this same night the Israelites
are to keep watch to honor the LORD from
now on.

43The LORD told Moses and Aaron,
"Here are the rules for Passover: No foreigner is to eat the Passover. **44**If someone buys a slave and circumcises him,
the slave may eat the Passover. **45**But
neither a person who lives for a short
time in your country nor a hired worker
may eat it.

46"The meal must be eaten inside a
house; take none of the meat outside the
house. Don't break any of the bones.
47The whole community of Israel must
take part in this feast. **48**A foreigner who
lives with you may share in the LORD's
Passover if all the males in his house become circumcised. Then, since he will be
like a citizen of Israel, he may share in
the meal. But a man who is not circumcised may not eat the Passover meal.
49The same rules apply to an Israelite
born in the country or to a foreigner living there."

50So all the Israelites did just as the
LORD had commanded Moses and Aaron.
51On that same day the LORD led the Israelites out of Egypt by their divisions.

The Law of the Firstborn

13 Then the LORD said to Moses,
2"Give every firstborn male to
me. Every firstborn male among the Israelites belongs to me, whether human or
animal."

3Moses said to the people, "Remember this day, the day you left Egypt. You
were slaves in that land, but the LORD
with his great power brought you out of

it. You must not eat bread made with
yeast. **4**Today, in the month of Abib, you
are leaving Egypt. **5**The LORD will lead
you to the land of the Canaanites, Hittites, Amorites, Hivites, and Jebusites.
This is the land he promised your ancestors he would give you, a fertile land.
There you must celebrate this feast during the first month of every year. **6**For
seven days you must eat bread made
without yeast, and on the seventh day
there will be a feast to honor the LORD.
7So for seven days you must not eat any
bread made with yeast. There must be no
bread made with yeast anywhere in your
land. **8**On that day you should tell your
son: 'We are having this feast because of
what the LORD did for me when I came
out of Egypt.' **9**This feast will help you
remember, like a mark on your hand or a
reminder on your forehead. This feast
will remind you to speak the LORD's
teachings, because the LORD used his
great power to bring you out of Egypt.
10So celebrate this feast every year at
the right time.

11"And when the LORD takes you into
the land of the Canaanites, the land he
promised to give you and your ancestors,
12you must give him every firstborn
male. Also every firstborn male animal
must be given to the LORD. **13**Buy back
every firstborn donkey by offering a
lamb. But if you don't want to buy the
donkey back, then break its neck. You
must buy back from the LORD every firstborn of your sons.

14"From now on when your son asks
you, 'What does this mean?' you will answer, 'With his great power, the LORD
brought us out from Egypt, the land
where we were slaves. **15**The king of
Egypt was stubborn and refused to let us
leave. But the LORD killed every firstborn male in Egypt, both human and animal. That is why I sacrifice every
firstborn male animal to the LORD, and
that is why I buy back each of my firstborn sons from the LORD.' **16**This feast is
like a mark on your hand and a reminder
on your forehead to help you remember
that the LORD brought us out of Egypt
with his great power."

The Way Out of Egypt

17When the king sent the people out
of Egypt, God did not lead them on the
road through the Philistine country,
though that was the shortest way. God
said, "If they have to fight, they might
change their minds and go back to
Egypt." **18**So God led them through the
desert toward the Red Sea. The Israelites were dressed for fighting when they
left the land of Egypt.

19Moses carried the bones of Joseph
with him, because before Joseph died, he
had made the Israelites promise to do
this. He had said, "When God saves you,
remember to carry my bones with you
out of Egypt."

20The Israelites left Succoth and
camped at Etham, on the edge of the
desert. **21**The LORD showed them the
way; during the day he went ahead of
them in a pillar of cloud, and during the
night he was in a pillar of fire to give them
light. In this way they could travel during
the day or night. **22**The pillar of cloud
was always with them during the day, and
the pillar of fire was always with them at
night.

14 Then the LORD said to Moses,
2"Tell the Israelites to turn back
to Pi Hahiroth and to camp between Migdol and the Red Sea. Camp across from
Baal Zephon, on the shore of the sea.
3The king will think, 'The Israelites are
lost, trapped by the desert.' **4**I will make
the king stubborn again so he will chase
after them, but I will defeat the king and
his army. This will bring honor to me, and
the Egyptians will know that I am the
LORD." The Israelites did just as they
were told.

The King Chases the Israelites

5When the king of Egypt was told that
the Israelites had left, he and his officers
changed their minds about them. They
said, "What have we done? We have let
the Israelites leave. We have lost our
slaves!" **6**So the king prepared his war
chariot and took his army with him. **7**He
took six hundred of his best chariots,
together with all the other chariots of
Egypt, each with an officer in it. **8**The

LORD made the king of Egypt stubborn,
so he chased the Israelites, who were
leaving victoriously. 9The Egyptians—
with all the king's horses, chariot drivers, and army—chased the Israelites.
They caught up with them while they
were camped by the Red Sea, near Pi Hahiroth and Baal Zephon.
10When the Israelites saw the king
and his army coming after them, they
were very frightened
and cried to the LORD
for help. 11They said to
Moses, "What have you
done to us? Why did
you bring us out of
Egypt to die in the
desert? There were
plenty of graves for us
in Egypt. 12We told you
in Egypt, 'Let us alone;
we will stay and serve
the Egyptians.' Now we
will die in the desert."
13But Moses answered, "Don't be
afraid! Stand still and you will see the
LORD save you today. You will never see
these Egyptians again after today. 14You
only need to remain calm; the LORD will
fight for you."
15Then the LORD said to Moses,
"Why are you crying out to me? Command the Israelites to start moving.
16Raise your walking stick and hold it
over the sea so that the sea will split and
the people can cross it on dry land. 17I
will make the Egyptians stubborn so they
will chase the Israelites, but I will be honored when I defeat the king and all of his
chariot drivers and chariots. 18When I
defeat the king, his chariot drivers, and
chariots, the Egyptians will know that I
am the LORD."
19Now the angel of God that usually
traveled in front of Israel's army moved
behind them. Also, the pillar of cloud
moved from in front of the people and
stood behind them. 20So the cloud came
between the Egyptians and the Israelites. This made it dark for the Egyptians
but gave light to the Israelites. So the
cloud kept the two armies apart all night.
21Then Moses held his hand over the
sea. All that night the LORD drove back
the sea with a strong east wind, making
the sea become dry ground. The water
was split, 22and the Israelites went
through the sea on dry land, with a wall of
water on their right and on their left.
23Then all the king's horses, chariots,
and chariot drivers followed them into
the sea. 24When morning came, the
LORD looked down from the pillar of
cloud and fire at the
Egyptian army and
made them panic. 25He
kept the wheels of the
chariots from turning,
making it hard to drive
the chariots. The Egyp-
tians shouted, "Let's
get away from the Isra-
elites! The LORD is
fighting for them and
against Egypt."
26Then the LORD
told Moses, "Hold your
hand over the sea so that the water will
come back over the Egyptians, their chariots, and chariot drivers." 27So Moses
raised his hand over the sea, and at dawn
the sea returned to its place. The Egyptians tried to run from it, but the LORD
swept them away into the sea. 28The water returned, covering the chariots, chariot drivers, and all the king's army that had
followed the Israelites into the sea. Not
one of them survived.
29But the Israelites crossed the sea
on dry land, with a wall of water on their
right and on their left. 30So that day the
LORD saved the Israelites from the Egyptians, and the Israelites saw the Egyptians lying dead on the seashore. 31When
the Israelites saw the great power the
LORD had used against the Egyptians,
they feared the LORD, and they trusted
him and his servant Moses.

But Moses answered, "Don't be afraid! Stand still and you will see the LORD save you today. You will never see these Egyptians again after today."
—Exodus 14:13

The Song of Moses

15 Then Moses
and the Isra-
elites sang this song
to the LORD:
"I will sing to the
LORD,

15:1
Music
Check out what you should sing to.

because he is worthy of great
honor.
He has thrown the horse and its rider
into the sea.
2 The LORD gives me strength and
makes me sing;
he has saved me.
He is my God,
and I will praise him.

TIME TO CELEBRATE

EXODUS 15:1-21

How do you celebrate a great victory? When a favorite sports team wins, some towns throw parades in honor of the team. When a person graduates from school, family members take him or her out to dinner or throw a party. Moses and the Israelites sang of God's deliverance at the Red Sea. This was their way of celebrating the great victory God had brought about. He had saved them from the wrath of the Egyptians after they left Egypt. Think about what God has done for you. How will you celebrate?

Approaching God, Numbers 3:10, p. 180

A Cause for Celebration, 1 Kings 8:62–66, p. 449

No Thanksgiving?, 2 Kings 23:21–23, p. 512

A Love Song, Zephaniah 3:17, p. 1246

The Gift, John 3:16–18, p. 1427

Always Do This!, 1 Thessalonians 5:16–18, p. 1636

He is the God of my fathers,
and I will honor him.
3 The LORD is a warrior;
the LORD is his name.
4 The chariots and soldiers of the king
of Egypt
he has thrown into the sea.
The king's best officers
are drowned in the Red Sea.
5 The deep waters covered them,
and they sank to the bottom like a
rock.
6 Your right hand, LORD,
is amazingly strong.
LORD, your right hand
broke the enemy to pieces.
7 In your great victory
you destroyed those who were
against you.
Your anger destroyed them,
like fire burning straw.
8 Just a blast of your breath,
and the waters piled up.
The moving water stood like a wall;
the deep waters became solid in
the middle of the sea.

9 "The enemy bragged,
'I'll chase them and catch them.
I'll take all their riches;
I'll take all I want.
I'll pull out my sword,
and my hand will destroy them.'
10 But you blew on them with your
breath
and covered them with the sea.
They sank like lead
in the raging water.

11 "Are there any gods like you, LORD?
There are no gods like you.
You are wonderfully holy,
amazingly powerful,
a worker of miracles.
12 You reached out with your right hand,
and the earth swallowed our
enemies.
13 You keep your loving promise
and lead the people you have
saved.
With your strength you will guide
them
to your holy place.

14 "The other nations will hear this and
tremble with fear;
terror will take hold of the
Philistines.
15 The leaders of the tribes of Edom
will be very frightened;
the powerful men of Moab will shake
with fear;
the people of Canaan will lose all
their courage.
16 Terror and horror will fall on them.
When they see your strength,
they will be as still as a rock.
They will be still until your people
pass by, LORD.
They will be still until the people
you have taken as your own
pass by.
17 You will lead your people and place
them
on your very own mountain,
the place that you, LORD, made for
yourself to live,
the temple, Lord, that your hands
have made.
18 The LORD will be king forever!"

19The horses, chariot drivers, and
chariots of the king of Egypt went into
the sea, and the LORD covered them with
water from the sea. But the Israelites
walked through the sea on dry land.
20Then Aaron's sister Miriam, a prophetess, took a tambourine in her hand. All
the women followed her, playing tambourines and dancing. 21Miriam told them:

"Sing to the LORD,
because he is worthy of great
honor;
he has thrown the horse and its rider
into the sea."

Bitter Water Becomes Good

22Moses led the Israelites away from
the Red Sea into the Desert of Shur.
They traveled for three days in the
desert but found no water. 23Then they
came to Marah, where there was water,
but they could not drink it because it was
too bitter. (That is why the place was
named Marah.") 24The people grumbled
to Moses and asked, "What will we
drink?"

25So Moses cried out to the LORD,
and the LORD showed him a tree. When
Moses threw the tree into the water, the
water became good to drink.

There the LORD gave the people a
rule and a law to live by, and there he
tested their loyalty to him. 26He said,
"You must obey the LORD your God and
do what he says is right. If you obey all
his commands and keep his rules, I will
not bring on you any of the sicknesses I
brought on the Egyptians. I am the LORD
who heals you."

27Then the people traveled to Elim,
where there were twelve springs of water and seventy palm trees. So the people
camped there near the water.

The People Demand Food

16 The whole Israelite community
left Elim and came to the Desert
of Sin, which was between Elim and Sinai; they arrived there on the fifteenth
day of the second month after they had
left Egypt. 2Then the whole Israelite
community grumbled to Moses and
Aaron in the desert. 3They said to them,
"It would have been better if the LORD
had killed us in the land of Egypt. There
we had meat to eat and all the food we
wanted. But you have brought us into
this desert to starve us to death."

4Then the LORD said to Moses, "I will
cause food to fall like rain from the sky
for all of you. Every day the people must
go out and gather what they need for that
day. I want to see if the people will do
what I teach them. 5On the sixth day of
each week, they are to gather twice as
much as they gather on other days. Then
they are to prepare it."

6So Moses and Aaron said to all the
Israelites: "This evening you will know
that the LORD is the one who brought you
out of Egypt. 7Tomorrow morning you
will see the glory of the LORD, because
he has heard you grumble against him.
We are nothing, so you are not grumbling
against us, but against the LORD." 8And
Moses said, "Each evening the LORD will
give you meat to eat, and every morning

15:23 Marah This name means "bitter."

FAITH links

COMPLAINTS, COMPLAINTS!

EXODUS 16:1-3

Suppose you helped someone with a big project. Instead of thanking you, suppose that person complained to you about something that he felt you *didn't* do. How would you feel? God had delivered the Israelites from slavery. He guided them with a cloud by day and fire by night. Instead of being thankful, the people complained. They felt that God had treated them badly by bringing them out of Egypt. Why? Because they were hungry and wanted food *right now!*

When something isn't going your way, are you tempted to complain? Being thankful is one antidote for having a pity party.

Feeling sorry for yourself? Link here for help:

My Worship Place, Genesis 35:1–14, p. 49

Take My Advice, 1 Kings 2:2–4, p. 436

You're Invited!, Psalm 100, p. 784

A Need to Change, Ecclesiastes 1:1–11, p. 873

His Valentine, Jeremiah 31:3, p. 1035

The Power of *If*, Mark 9:14–24, p. 1344

he will give you all the bread you want,
because he has heard you grumble against
him. You are not grumbling against Aaron
and me, because we are nothing; you are
grumbling against the LORD."
9Then Moses said to Aaron, "Speak to
the whole community of the Israelites,
and say to them, 'Meet together in the
presence of the LORD, because he has
heard your grumblings.' "
10While Aaron was speaking to the
whole community of the Israelites, they
looked toward the desert. There the
glory of the LORD appeared in a cloud.
11The LORD said to Moses, **12**"I have
heard the grumblings of the people of Israel. So tell them, 'At twilight you will eat
meat, and every morning you will eat all
the bread you want. Then you will know I
am the LORD your God.' "
13That evening quail came and covered the camp, and in the morning dew lay
around the camp. **14**When the dew was
gone, thin flakes like frost were on the
desert ground. **15**When the Israelites saw
it, they asked each other, "What is it?" because they did not know what it was.
So Moses told them, "This is the bread
the LORD has given you to eat. **16**The
LORD has commanded, 'Each one of you
must gather what he needs, about two
quarts for every person in your family.' "
17So the people of Israel did this;
some people gathered much, and some
gathered little. **18**Then they measured it.
The person who gathered more did not
have too much, nor did the person who
gathered less have too little. Each person
gathered just as much as he needed.
19Moses said to them, "Don't keep
any of it to eat the next day." **20**But some
of the people did not listen to Moses and
kept part of it to eat the next morning. It
became full of worms and began to stink,
so Moses was angry with those people.
21Every morning each person gathered as much food as he needed, but
when the sun became hot, it melted away.
22On the sixth day the people gathered twice as much food—four quarts for
every person. When all the leaders of the
community came and told this to Moses,
23he said to them, "This is what the

LORD commanded, because tomorrow is
the Sabbath, the LORD's holy day of rest.
Bake what you want to bake, and boil
what you want to boil today. Save the rest
of the food until tomorrow morning."

24So the people saved it until the next
morning, as Moses had commanded, and
none of it began to stink or have worms
in it. **25**Moses told the people, "Eat the
food you gathered yesterday. Today is a
Sabbath, the LORD's day of rest; you will
not find any out in the field today. **26**You
should gather the food for six days, but
the seventh day is a Sabbath day. On that
day there will not be any food on the
ground."

27On the seventh day some of the
people went out to gather food, but they
couldn't find any. **28**Then the LORD said
to Moses, "How long will you people refuse to obey my commands and teachings? **29**Look, the LORD has made the
Sabbath a day of rest for you. So on the
sixth day he will give you enough food for
two days, but on the seventh day each of
you must stay where you are. Do not go
anywhere." **30**So the people rested on
the seventh day.

31The people of Israel called the food
manna. It was like small white seeds and
tasted like wafers made with honey.

32Then Moses said, "The LORD said,
'Save two quarts of this food for your descendants. Then they can see the food I
gave you to eat in the desert when I
brought you out of Egypt.' "

33Moses told Aaron, "Take a jar and
fill it with two quarts of manna. Then
place it before the LORD, and save it for
your descendants." **34**So Aaron did what
the LORD had commanded Moses. He put
the jar of manna in front of the Agreement to keep it safe. **35**The Israelites ate
manna for forty years, until they came to
the land where they settled—the edge of
the land of Canaan. **36**The measure they
used for the manna was two quarts, or
one-tenth of an ephah.[n]"

Water from a Rock

17 The whole Israelite community
left the Desert of Sin and traveled
from place to place, as the LORD commanded. They camped at Rephidim, but
there was no water there for the people
to drink. **2**So they quarreled with Moses
and said, "Give us water to drink."

Moses said to them, "Why do you
quarrel with me? Why are you testing the
LORD?"

3But the people were very thirsty for
water, so they grumbled against Moses.
They said, "Why did you bring us out of
Egypt? Was it to kill us, our children, and
our farm animals with thirst?"

4So Moses cried to the LORD, "What
can I do with these people? They are almost ready to stone me to death."

5The LORD said to Moses, "Go ahead
of the people, and take some of the older
leaders of Israel with you. Carry with you
the walking stick that you used to strike
the Nile River. Now go! **6**I will stand in
front of you on a rock at Mount Sinai. Hit
that rock with the stick, and water will
come out of it so that the people can
drink." Moses did these things as the
older leaders of Israel watched. **7**He
named that place Massah,[n]" because the
Israelites tested the LORD when they
asked, "Is the LORD with us or not?" He
also named it Meribah,[n]" because they
quarreled.

The Amalekites Fight Israel

8At Rephidim the Amalekites came
and fought the Israelites. **9**So Moses said
to Joshua, "Choose some men and go and
fight the Amalekites. Tomorrow I will
stand on the top of the hill, holding the
walking stick of God in my hands."

10Joshua obeyed Moses and went to
fight the Amalekites, while Moses,
Aaron, and Hur went to the top of the hill.
11As long as Moses held his hands up,
the Israelites would win the fight, but
when Moses put his hands down, the
Amalekites would win. **12**Later, when
Moses' arms became tired, the men put a

16:36 ephah An ephah was a measure that equaled twenty quarts.

17:7 Massah This name is the Hebrew word for "testing."

17:7 Meribah This name is the Hebrew word for "quarrel."

FAITH links

FATHERLY ADVICE

EXODUS 18

When you need help, who do you go to for advice? Moses worked too hard making decisions for the people of Israel. His father-in-law Jethro came up with a plan to help Moses with his workload. Moses accepted his father-in-law's advice. He appointed leaders from every tribe to help do some of the work.

God puts people in our lives who care about us. Like Moses, we can learn to listen to the advice of caring family members and trusted adults.

Here is some other good advice to follow:

- In Your Best Interests, Ruth 3, p. 349
- Choosing Sides, 1 Samuel 20, p. 382
- A Wise Wish, 1 Kings 3:5–9, p. 439
- A Parent's Advice, Proverbs 1:8–9, p. 825
- The Way to Be Wise, James 1:5, p. 1689
- What Any Parent Wants, 3 John 3–4, p. 1723

large rock under him, and he sat on it.
Then Aaron and Hur held up Moses'
hands—Aaron on one side and Hur on
the other. They kept his hands steady until the sun went down. **13**So Joshua defeated the Amalekites in this battle.
14Then the LORD said to Moses,
"Write about this battle in a book so people will remember. And be sure to tell
Joshua, because I will completely destroy
the Amalekites from the earth."
15Then Moses built an altar and
named it The LORD is my Banner. **16**Moses said, "I lifted my hands toward the
LORD's throne. The LORD will fight
against the Amalekites forever."

Jethro Visits Moses

18 Jethro, Moses' father-in-law, was
the priest of Midian. He heard
about everything that God had done for
Moses and his people, the Israelites, and
how the LORD had led the Israelites out
of Egypt. **2**Now Moses had sent his wife
Zipporah to Jethro, his father-in-law,
3along with his two sons. The first son
was named Gershom,[n] because when he
was born, Moses said, "I am a stranger in
a foreign country." **4**The other son was
named Eliezer,[n] because when he was
born, Moses said, "The God of my father
is my help. He saved me from the king of
Egypt."
5So Jethro, Moses' father-in-law, took
Moses' wife and his two sons and went to
Moses. He was camped in the desert
near the mountain of God. **6**Jethro had
sent a message ahead to Moses that said,
"I, Jethro, your father-in-law, am coming
to you with your wife and her two sons."
7So Moses went out to meet his
father-in-law and bowed down and kissed
him. After the two men asked about each
other's health, they went into Moses'
tent. **8**Moses told his father-in-law
everything the LORD had done to the
king and the Egyptians to help Israel. He
told about all the problems they had faced
along the way and how the LORD had
saved them.
9Jethro was very happy to hear all the
good things the LORD had done for Israel
when he had saved them from the Egyptians. **10**He said, "Praise the LORD. He
has saved you from the Egyptians and
their king, and he has saved the people

18:3 Gershom This name sounds like the Hebrew word for "a stranger there."

18:4 Eliezer This name sounds like the Hebrew words "My God is my help."

from the power of the Egyptians. 11Now
I know the LORD is greater than all gods,
because he did this to those who looked
down on Israel." 12Then Jethro, Moses'
father-in-law, gave a whole burnt offering
and other sacrifices to God. Aaron and
all the older leaders of Israel came to
Moses' father-in-law to eat the holy meal
together before God.

13The next day Moses solved disagreements among the people, and the
people stood around him from morning
until night. 14When Moses' father-in-law
saw all that Moses was doing for the people, he asked, "What is all this you are
doing for the people? Why are you the
only one to solve disagreements? All the
people are standing around you from
morning until night!"

15Then Moses said to his father-in-
law, "It is because the people come to me
for God's help in solving their disagreements. 16When people have a disagreement, they come to me, and I decide who
is right. I tell them God's laws and teachings."

17Moses' father-in-law said to him,
"You are not doing this right. 18You and
the people who come to
you will get too tired.
This is too much work for
you; you can't do it by
yourself. 19Now listen
to me, and I will give you
some advice. I want God
to be with you. You must
speak to God for the peo-
ple and tell him about their
disagreements. 20Warn
them about the laws and
teachings, and teach them the right way
to live and what they should do. 21But
choose some capable men from among
the people—men who respect God, who
can be trusted, and
who will not change
their decisions for
money. Make these
men officers over
the people, to rule
over groups of thou-
sands, hundreds, fifties, and tens. 22Let
these officers solve the disagreements
among the people all the time. They can
bring the hard cases to you, but they can
decide the simple cases themselves.
That will make it easier for you, because
they will share the work with you. 23If
you do this as God commands you, then
you will be able to do your job, and all the
people will go home with their disagreements solved."

24So Moses listened to his father-in-
law and did everything he said. 25He
chose capable men from all the Israelites
and made them leaders over the people;
they were officers over groups of thousands, hundreds, fifties, and tens.
26These officers solved disagreements
among the people all the time. They
brought the hard cases to Moses, but
they decided the simple cases themselves.

27So Moses sent his father-in-law on
his way, and Jethro went back to his own
home.

eMAIL FROM GOD
18:21
Leadership
What makes a good leader?

Israel Camps at Sinai

19 Exactly three months after the
Israelites had left Egypt, they
reached the Desert of Sinai. 2When they
left Rephidim, they came
to the Desert of Sinai and
camped in the desert in
front of the mountain.
3Then Moses went up on
the mountain to God. The
LORD called to him from
the mountain and said,
"Say this to the family of
Jacob, and tell the people
of Israel: 4'Every one of
you has seen what I did to
the people of Egypt. You saw how I carried you out of Egypt, as if on eagle's
wings. And I brought you here to me. 5So
now if you obey me and keep my agreement, you will be my own possession,
chosen from all nations. Even though the
whole earth is mine, 6you will be my
kingdom of priests and a holy nation.' You
must tell the Israelites these words."

7So Moses went down and called the
older leaders of the people together. He
told them all the words the LORD had
commanded him to say. 8All the people

Every one of you has seen what I did to the people of Egypt. You saw how I carried you out of Egypt, as if on eagle's wings.
—Exodus 19:4

answered together, "We will do everything he has said." Then Moses took
their answer back to the LORD.
9And the LORD said to Moses, "I will
come to you in a thick cloud and speak to
you. The people will hear me speaking
with you and will always trust you." Then
Moses told the LORD what the people had
said.
10The LORD said to Moses, "Go to the
people and have them spend today and
tomorrow preparing themselves. They
must wash their clothes **11**and be ready
by the day after tomorrow. On that day I,
the LORD, will come down on Mount
Sinai, and all the people will see me.
12But you must set a limit around the
mountain that the people are not to cross.
Tell them not to go up on the mountain
and not to touch the foot of it. Anyone
who touches the mountain must be put to
death **13**with stones or shot with arrows.
No one is allowed to touch him. Whether
it is a person or an animal, he will not
live. But the trumpet will make a long
blast, and only then may the people go up
on the mountain."
14After Moses went down from the
mountain to the people, he made them
prepare themselves for service to God,
and they washed their clothes. **15**Then
Moses said to the people, "Be ready in
three days. Do not have sexual relations
during this time."
16On the morning of the third day,
there was thunder and lightning with a
thick cloud on the mountain. There was a
very loud blast from a trumpet, and all
the people in the camp trembled. **17**Then
Moses led the people out of the camp to
meet God, and they stood at the foot of
the mountain. **18**Mount Sinai was covered with smoke, because the LORD
came down on it in fire. The smoke rose
from the mountain like smoke from a furnace, and the whole mountain shook
wildly. **19**The sound from the trumpet became louder. Then Moses spoke, and the
voice of God answered him.
20When the LORD came down on top
of Mount Sinai, he called Moses to come
up to the top of the mountain, and Moses
went up. **21**The LORD said to Moses, "Go
down and warn the people that they must
not force their way through to see me. If
they do, many of them will die. **22**Even
the priests, who may come near me,
must first prepare themselves. If they
don't, I, the LORD, will punish them."
23Moses told the LORD, "The people
cannot come up on Mount Sinai, because
you yourself told us, 'Set a limit around
the mountain, and set it apart as holy.' "
24The LORD said to him, "Go down
and bring Aaron up with you, but don't allow the priests or the people to force
their way through. They must not come
up to the LORD, or I will punish them."
25So Moses went down to the people
and told them these things.

The Ten Commandments

20 Then God spoke all these words:
2"I am the LORD your God, who
brought you out of the land of Egypt
where you were slaves.
3"You must not have any other gods
except me.
4"You must not make for yourselves
an idol that looks like anything in the sky
above or on the earth below or in the water below the land. **5**You must not worship
or serve any idol, because I, the LORD
your God, am a jealous God. If you hate
me, I will punish your children, and even
your grandchildren and great-grandchildren. **6**But I show kindness to thousands
who love me and obey my commands.
7"You must not use the name of the
LORD your God thoughtlessly; the LORD
will punish anyone who misuses his
name.
8"Remember to keep the Sabbath
holy. **9**Work and get everything done during six days each week, **10**but the seventh day is a day of rest to honor the
LORD your God. On that day no one may
do any work: not you, your son or daughter, your male or female slaves, your animals, or the foreigners living in your
cities. **11**The reason is that in six days
the LORD made everything—the sky, the
earth, the sea, and everything in them.
On the seventh day he rested. So the
LORD blessed the Sabbath day and made
it holy.

LIVING WITH MY FAMILY
Exodus 20:12

Livin' it

Give Me Space! Living with other people isn't always easy—especially in families. Even though you are all part of the same family, you aren't alike in everything. Actually, that would be sort of boring! How do you handle disagreements that come up in your family?

From the time that God created the first people, Adam and Eve, he told them to live together in love and have children. (Read Genesis 1:27–28, p. 5.) God wants families to be committed to each other in love. That means living together peacefully, helping each other, and being loyal to each other.

MORE FAITH links

Family Feud, p. 37

Fatherly Advice, p. 99

Peace in the Family, p. 811

How to Worship God, p. 972

What Any Parent Wants, p. 1723

"Sometimes my family really bugs me. What do you do when that happens, Skweek?"

"Well, I try to remember how important families are to God. These other Faithlinks might help you, Tagg."

God's Valuable Gift: You, Psalm 127:3–5, p. 809
- What's the best gift you've been given recently? Why is it so valuable to you? Want to know a great gift that God gave your parents or guardians? Look in the mirror! God considers families with children blessed—like yours.

The Way to Get Along, 1 Peter 3:8–9, p. 1703
- What was the last thing you argued about with your brother or sister? How did you feel afterwards? How do you feel when you get along? Link here to discover God's formula for getting along with each other.

The True Test, 1 John 3:18, p. 1718
- If someone said that he loved you, but acted like he didn't want to be around you, would you believe him? You would want proof that he loved you. This Faithlink tells you what love really involves. Use the suggestion with your family!

my FAVORITE links

______ ______

______ ______

______ ______

FAITH links

TEN WAYS TO OBEY

EXODUS 20

Who makes the rules at home or at school? These rules help you know the behavior that is expected of you. They also remind you of the consequences of bad behavior. God came up with the Ten Commandments to help the people of Israel—and us—know how to obey him and get along with each other. These weren't suggestions that the people could take or leave. These were specific rules God expected them to follow. That goes for you, too!

Think rules aren't important? Surf on!

Do What You Want?, Judges 21:25, p. 341

A Traveling Bible Study, 2 Chronicles 17:9, p. 580

The Writing's on the Wall, Daniel 5, p. 1159

The Best Advice, Zechariah 10:2, p. 1261

Attention, Please!, Luke 8:11–15, p. 1383

Cut to the Quick, Hebrews 4:12, p. 1670

12"Honor your father and your mother
so that you will live a long time in the
land that the LORD your God is going to
give you.
13"You must not murder anyone.
14"You must not be guilty of adultery.
15"You must not steal.
16"You must not tell lies about your
neighbor.

EMAIL FROM GOD

20:16 Honesty

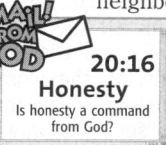

Is honesty a command from God?

17"You must not
want to take your
neighbor's house.
You must not want
his wife or his male
or female slaves, or
his ox or his donkey, or anything that belongs to your neighbor."
18When the people heard the thunder
and the trumpet, and when they saw the
lightning and the smoke rising from the
mountain, they shook with fear and stood
far away from the mountain. **19**Then they
said to Moses, "Speak to us yourself, and
we will listen. But don't let God speak to
us, or we will die."
20Then Moses said to the people,
"Don't be afraid, because God has come
to test you. He wants you to respect him
so you will not sin."
21The people stood far away from the
mountain while Moses went near the
dark cloud where God was. **22**Then the
LORD told Moses to say these things to
the Israelites: "You yourselves have seen
that I talked with you from heaven. **23**You
must not use gold or silver to make idols
for yourselves; do not worship these
gods in addition to me.
24"Make an altar of dirt for me, and
sacrifice on it your whole burnt offerings
and fellowship offerings, your sheep and
your cattle. Worship me in every place
that I choose, and I will come and bless
you. **25**If you use stones to make an altar
for me, don't use stones that you have
shaped with tools. When you use any
tools on them, you make them unsuitable
for use in worship. **26**And you must not
go up to my altar on steps, or people will
be able to see under your clothes."

Laws for Living

21 Then God said to Moses, "These
are the laws for living that you will
give to the Israelites:
2"If you buy a Hebrew slave, he will
serve you for six years. In the seventh
year you are to set him free, and he will
have to pay nothing. **3**If he is not married
when he becomes your slave, he must

leave without a wife. But if he is married
when he becomes your slave, he may
take his wife with him. **4**If the slave's
master gives him a wife, and she gives
birth to sons or daughters, the woman
and her children will belong to the master. When the slave is set free, only he
may leave.
5"But if the slave says, 'I love my
master, my wife and my children, and I
don't want to go free,' **6**then the slave's
master must take him to God. The master is to take him to a door or doorframe
and punch a hole through the slave's ear
using a sharp tool. Then the slave will
serve that master all his life.
7"If a man sells his daughter as a
slave, the rules for setting her free are
different from the rules for setting the
male slaves free. **8**If the master wanted
to marry her but then decided he was not
pleased with her, he must let one of her
close relatives buy her back. He has no
right to sell her to foreigners, because he
has treated her unfairly. **9**If the man who
bought her promises to let the woman
marry his son, he must treat her as a
daughter. **10**If the man who bought her
marries another woman, he must not
keep his first wife from having food or
clothing or sexual relations. **11**If he does
not give her these three things, she may
go free, and she owes him no money.

Laws About Injuries

12"Anyone who hits a person and kills
him must be put to death. **13**But if a person kills someone accidentally, God allowed that to happen, so the person must
go to a place I will choose. **14**But if someone plans and murders another person on
purpose, put him to death, even if he has
run to my altar for safety.
15"Anyone who hits his father or his
mother must be put to death.
16"Anyone who kidnaps someone and
either sells him as a slave or still has him
when he is caught must be put to death.
17"Anyone who says cruel things to
his father or mother must be put to
death.
18"If two men argue, and one hits the
other with a rock or with his fist, the one
who is hurt but not killed might have to
stay in bed. **19**Later if he is able to get up
and walk around outside with his walking
stick, the one who hit him is not to be
punished. But he must pay the injured
man for the loss of his time, and he must
support the injured man until he is completely healed.
20"If a man beats his male or female
slave with a stick, and the slave dies on
the spot, the owner must be punished.
21But if the slave gets well after a day or
two, the owner will not be punished since
the slave belongs to him.
22"Suppose two men are fighting
and hit a pregnant woman, causing the
baby to come out. If there is no further
injury, the man who caused the accident
must pay money—whatever amount the
woman's husband says and the court allows. **23**But if there is further injury, then
the punishment that must be paid is life
for life, **24**eye for eye, tooth for tooth,
hand for hand, foot for foot, **25**burn for
burn, wound for wound, and bruise for
bruise.
26"If a man hits his male or female
slave in the eye, and the eye is blinded,
the man is to free the slave to pay for the
eye. **27**If a master knocks out a tooth of
his male or female slave, the man is to
free the slave to pay for the tooth.
28"If a man's bull kills a man or
woman, you must kill that bull by throwing stones at it, and you should not eat
the bull. But the owner of the bull is not
guilty. **29**However, suppose the bull has
hurt people in the past and the owner,
though warned, did not keep it in a pen.
Then if it kills a man or woman, the bull
must be stoned to death, and the owner
must also be put to death. **30**But if the
family of the dead person accepts money,
the one who owned the bull may buy back
his life, but he must pay whatever is demanded. **31**Use this same law if the bull
kills a person's son or daughter. **32**If the
bull kills a male or female slave, the
owner must pay the master the price for
a new slave, or twelve ounces of silver,
and the bull must also be stoned to death.
33"If a man takes the cover off a pit, or
digs a pit and does not cover it, and an-

other man's ox or donkey comes and falls
into it, **34**the owner of the pit must pay
the owner of the animal for the loss. The
dead animal will belong to the one who
pays.
35"If a man's bull kills another man's
bull, they must sell the bull that is alive.
Both men will get half of the money and
half of the bull that was killed. **36**But if a
person's bull has hurt other animals in
the past and the owner did not keep it in a
pen, that owner must pay bull for bull,
and the dead animal is his.

Property Laws

22 "If a man steals a bull or a sheep
and kills or sells it, he must pay
back five bulls for the one bull he stole
and four sheep for the one sheep he stole.
2-4"The robber who is caught must
pay back what he stole. If he owns nothing, he must be sold as a slave to pay for
what he stole. If the stolen animal is
found alive with the robber, he must give
the owner two animals for every animal
he stole, whether it was a bull, donkey, or
sheep.
"If a thief is killed while breaking into
a house at night, the one who killed
him is not guilty of murder. But if this
happens during the day, he is guilty of
murder.
5"If a man lets his farm animal graze
in his field or vineyard, and it wanders
into another man's field or vineyard, the
owner of the animal must pay back the
loss from the best of his crop.
6"Suppose a man starts a fire that
spreads through the thornbushes to his
neighbor's field. If the fire burns his
neighbor's growing grain or grain that
has been stacked, or if it burns his whole
field, the person who started the fire
must pay for what was burned.
7"Suppose a man gives his neighbor
money or other things to keep for him
and those things are stolen from the
neighbor's house. If the thief is caught,
he must pay back twice as much as he
stole. **8**But if the thief is never found, the
owner of the house must make a promise
before God that he has not stolen his
neighbor's things.
9"Suppose two men disagree about
who owns something—whether ox, donkey, sheep, clothing, or something else
that is lost. If each says, 'This is mine,'
each man must bring his case to God.
God's judges will decide who is guilty,
and that person must pay the other man
twice as much as the object is worth.
10"Suppose a man asks his neighbor
to keep his donkey, ox, sheep, or some
other animal for him, and that animal
dies, gets hurt, or is taken away, without
anyone seeing what happened. **11**That
neighbor must promise before the LORD
that he did not harm or kill the other
man's animal, and the owner of the animal must accept his promise made before
God. The neighbor does not have to pay
the owner for the animal. **12**But if the animal was stolen from the neighbor, he
must pay the owner for it. **13**If wild animals killed it, the neighbor must bring
the body as proof, and he will not have to
pay for the animal that was killed.
14"If a man borrows an animal from
his neighbor, and it gets hurt or dies
while the owner is not there, the one who
borrowed it must pay the owner for the
animal. **15**But if the owner is with the animal, the one who borrowed it does not
have to pay. If the animal was rented, the
rental price covers the loss.

Laws and Relationships

16"Suppose a man finds a woman who
is not pledged to be married and has
never had sexual relations with a man. If
he tricks her into having sexual relations
with him, he must give her family the
payment to marry her, and she will become his wife. **17**But if her father refuses
to allow his daughter to marry him, the
man must still give the usual payment for
a bride who has never had sexual relations.
18"Put to death any woman who does
evil magic.
19"Put to death anyone who has sexual relations with an animal.
20"Destroy completely any person
who makes a sacrifice to any god except
the LORD.
21"Do not cheat or hurt a foreigner,

because you were foreigners in the land
of Egypt.
22"Do not cheat a widow or an orphan. 23If you do, and they cry out to me
for help, I certainly will hear their cry.
24And I will be very angry and kill you
in war. Then your wives will become
widows, and your children will become
orphans.
25"If you lend money to one of my
people who is poor, do not treat him as a
moneylender would. Charge him nothing
for using your money. 26If your neighbor
gives you his coat as a promise for the
money he owes you, you must give it
back to him by sunset, 27because it is the
only cover to keep his body warm. He has
nothing else to sleep in. If he cries out to
me for help, I will listen, because I am
merciful.
28"You must not speak against God or
curse a leader of your people.
29"Do not hold back your offering
from the first of your harvest and the first
wine that you make. Also, you must give
me your firstborn sons. 30You must do
the same with your bulls and your sheep.
Let the firstborn males stay with their
mothers for seven days, and on the
eighth day you must give them to me.
31"You are to be my holy people. You
must not eat the meat of any animal that
has been killed by wild animals. Instead,
give it to the dogs.

Laws About Fairness

23 "You must not tell lies. If you are a
witness in court, don't help a
wicked person by telling lies.
2"You must not do wrong
just because every-
one else is doing it.

EMAIL! FROM GOD
23:2
Honesty
Don't follow the crowd.

If you are a witness
in court, you must
not ruin a fair trial.
You must not tell
lies just because everyone else is. 3If a
poor person is in court, you must not take
his side just because he is poor.
4"If you see your enemy's ox or donkey wandering away, you must return it
to him. 5If you see that your enemy's
donkey has fallen because its load is too
heavy, do not leave it there. You must
help your enemy get the donkey back on
its feet.
6"You must not be unfair to a poor
person when he is in court. 7You must
not lie when you accuse someone in
court. Never allow an innocent or honest
person to be put to death as punishment,
because I will not treat guilty people as if
they were innocent.
8"You must not accept money from a
person who wants you to lie in court, because such money will not let you see
what is right. Such money makes good
people tell lies.

FAITH CHALLENGE

Got another challenge for you. Read 22:28 to find out what God says about respecting people in authority. What would you say to someone who was talking bad about the president?

TESTING IT

Exodus 22:28
You must not speak against God or curse a leader of your people.

______

______

______

______

______

______

EMAIL FROM GOD
23:9
Caring
Do you have to be nice to everyone?

9"You must not mistreat a
foreigner. You know
how it feels to be a
foreigner, because
you were foreigners
in Egypt.

Laws for the Sabbath

10"For six years you are to plant and
harvest crops on your land. 11Then during the seventh year, do not plow or plant
your land. If any food grows there, allow
the poor people to have it, and let the
wild animals eat what is left. You should
do the same with your vineyards and
your orchards of olive trees.
12"You should work six days a week,
but on the seventh day you must rest.
This lets your ox and your donkey rest,
and it also lets the slave born in your
house and the foreigner be refreshed.
13"Be sure to do all that I have said to
you. You must not even say the names of
other gods; those names must not come
out of your mouth.

Three Yearly Feasts

14"Three times each year you must
hold a feast to honor me. 15You must celebrate the Feast of Unleavened Bread in
the way I commanded you. For seven
days you must eat bread that is made
without yeast at the set time during the
month of Abib, the month when you came
out of Egypt. No one is to come to worship me without bringing an offering.
16"You must celebrate the Feast of
Weeks. Offer to God the first things you
harvest from the crops you planted in
your fields.

"You must celebrate the Feast of Shelters in the fall, when you gather all the
crops from your fields.
17"So three times during every year
all your males must come to worship the
LORD God.
18"You must not offer animal blood
along with anything that has yeast in it.

"You must not save any of the fat from
the sacrifice for the next day.
19"You must bring the best of the
firstfruits of your land to the Holy Tent[n]
of the LORD your God.

"You must not cook a young goat in its
mother's milk.

God Will Help Israel

20"I am sending an angel ahead of
you, who will protect you as you travel.
He will lead you to the place I have prepared. 21Pay attention to the angel and
obey him. Do not turn against him; he
will not forgive such turning against him
because my power is in him. 22If you listen carefully to all he says and do everything that I tell you, I will be an enemy to
your enemies. I will fight all who fight
against you. 23My angel will go ahead of
you and take you into the land of the Amorites, Hittites, Perizzites, Canaanites,
Hivites, and Jebusites, and I will destroy
them.
24"You must not bow down to their
gods or worship them. You must not live
the way those people live. You must destroy their idols, breaking into pieces the
stone pillars they use in worship. 25If
you worship the LORD your God, I will
bless your bread and your water. I will
take away sickness from you. 26None of
your women will have her baby die before it is born, and all women will have
children. I will allow you to live long
lives.
27"I will make your enemies afraid of
me. I will confuse any people you fight
against, and I will make all your enemies
run away from you. 28I will send terror
ahead of you that will force the Hivites,
Canaanites, and Hittites out of your way.
29But I will not force all those people out
in only one year. If I did, the land would
become a desert and the wild animals
would become too many for you. 30In-
stead, I will force those people out slowly,
until there are enough of you to take over
the land.
31"I will give you the land from the
Red Sea to the Mediterranean Sea, and
from the desert to the Euphrates River. I
will give you power over the people who
now live in the land, and you will force
them out ahead of you. 32You must not

23:19 Holy Tent Literally, "house of the LORD your God." See Exodus 25:9.

make an agreement with those people or
with their gods. **33**You must not let them
live in your land, or they will make you
sin against me. If you worship their gods,
you will be caught in a trap."

God and Israel Make Their Agreement

24 The LORD told Moses, "You,
Aaron, Nadab, Abihu, and seventy
of the older leaders of Israel must come
up to me and worship me from a distance.
2Then Moses alone must
come near me; the others
must not come near. The
rest of the people must
not come up the moun-
tain with Moses."

3Moses told the peo-
ple all the LORD's words
and laws for living. Then
all of the people answered
out loud together, "We
will do all the things the
LORD has said." **4**So Moses wrote down
all the words of the LORD. And he got up
early the next morning and built an altar
near the bottom of the mountain. He set
up twelve stones, one stone for each of
the twelve tribes of Israel. **5**Then Moses
sent young Israelite men to offer whole
burnt offerings and to sacrifice young
bulls as fellowship offerings to the LORD.
6Moses put half of the blood of these animals in bowls, and he sprinkled the other
half of the blood on the altar. **7**Then he
took the Book of the Agreement and read
it so the people could hear him. And they
said, "We will do everything that the
LORD has said; we will obey."

8Then Moses took the blood from the
bowls and sprinkled it on the people, saying, "This is the blood that begins the
Agreement, the Agreement which the
LORD has made with you about all these
words."

9Moses, Aaron, Nadab, Abihu, and
seventy of the older leaders of Israel
went up the mountain **10**and saw the God
of Israel. Under his feet was a surface
that looked as if it were paved with blue
sapphire stones, and it was as clear as the
sky! **11**These leaders of the Israelites
saw God, but God did not destroy them.
Then they ate and drank together.

God Promises Moses the Stone Tablets

12The LORD said to Moses, "Come up
the mountain to me. Wait there, and I will
give you two stone tablets. On these are
the teachings and the commands I have
written to instruct the people."

13So Moses and his helper Joshua set
out, and Moses went up to Sinai, the
mountain of God. **14**Mo-
ses said to the older leaders, "Wait here for us
until we come back to
you. Aaron and Hur are
with you, and anyone
who has a disagreement
with others can take it to
them."

The LORD said to Moses, "Come up the mountain to me. Wait there, and I will give you two stone tablets."
—Exodus 24:12

Moses Meets with God

15When Moses went up on the mountain, the cloud covered it. **16**The glory of
the LORD came down on Mount Sinai, and
the cloud covered it for six days. On the
seventh day the LORD called to Moses
from inside the cloud. **17**To the Israelites
the glory of the LORD looked like a fire
burning on top of the mountain. **18**Then
Moses went into the cloud and went
higher up the mountain. He was on the
mountain for forty days and forty nights.

Gifts for the Lord

25 The LORD said to Moses, **2**"Tell
the Israelites to bring me gifts.
Receive for me the gifts each person
wants to give. **3**These are the gifts that
you should receive from them: gold,
silver, bronze; **4**blue, purple, and red
thread; fine linen, goat hair, **5**sheepskins
that are dyed red; fine leather; acacia
wood; **6**olive oil to burn in the lamps;
spices for sweet-smelling incense, and
the special olive oil poured on a person's
head to make him a priest; **7**onyx stones,
and other jewels to be put on the holy
vest and the chest covering.

8"The people must build a holy place
for me so that I can live among them.

9Build this Holy Tent and everything in it
by the plan I will show you.

The Ark of the Agreement

10"Use acacia wood and build an Ark
forty-five inches long, twenty-seven
inches wide, and twenty-seven inches
high. 11Cover the Ark inside and out
with pure gold, and put a gold strip all
around it. 12Make four gold rings for the
Ark and attach them to its four feet, two
rings on each side. 13Then make poles
from acacia wood and cover them with
gold. 14Put the poles through the rings
on the sides of the Ark, and use these
poles to carry it. 15These poles must always stay in the rings of the Ark. Do not
take them out. 16Then put in the Ark the
Agreement which I will make with you.
17"Then make a lid of pure gold for
the Ark; this is the mercy seat. Make it
forty-five inches long and
twenty-seven inches
wide. 18Then hammer
gold to make two crea-
tures with wings, and put
one on each end of the lid.
19Attach one creature on
one end of the lid and the
other creature on the
other end. Make them to
be one piece with the lid
at the ends. 20The crea-
tures' wings should be
spread upward, covering the lid, and the
creatures are to face each other across
the lid. 21Put this lid on top of the Ark,
and put in the Ark the Agreement which I
will make with you. 22I will meet with
you there, above the lid between the two
winged creatures on the Ark of the
Agreement. There I will give you all my
commands for the Israelites.

> "The people must build a holy place for me so that I can live among them."
> —Exodus 25:8

The Table

23"Make a table out of acacia wood,
thirty-six inches long, eighteen inches
wide, and twenty-seven inches high.
24Cover it with pure gold, and put a
gold strip around it. 25Make a frame
three inches high that stands up all
around the edge, and put a gold strip
around it. 26Then make four gold rings.
Attach them to the four corners of the
table where the four legs are. 27Put the
rings close to the frame around the top
of the table, because they will hold the
poles for carrying it. 28Make the poles
out of acacia wood, cover them with
gold, and carry the table with these
poles. 29Make the plates and bowls for
the table, as well as the jars and cups,
out of pure gold. They will be used for
pouring out the drink offerings. 30On
this table put the bread that shows you
are in my presence so that it is always
there in front of me.

The Lampstand

31"Hammer pure gold to make a
lampstand. Its base, stand, flower-like
cups, buds, and petals must all be joined
together in one piece. 32The lampstand
must have six branches
going out from its sides—
three on one side and
three on the other.
33Each branch must have
three cups shaped like almond flowers on it. Each
cup must have a bud and a
petal. Each of the six
branches going out from
the lampstand must be
the same. 34And there
must be four more cups
made like almond flowers on the lampstand itself. These cups must also have
buds and petals. 35Put a bud under each
pair of branches that goes out from the
lampstand. Each of the six branches going out from the lampstand must be the
same. 36The branches, buds, and lampstand must be made of one piece, hammered out of pure gold.
37"Then make seven small oil lamps
and put them on the lampstand so that
they give light to the area in front of it.
38The wick trimmers and trays must be
made of pure gold. 39Use seventy-five
pounds of pure gold to make the lampstand and everything with it. 40Be very
careful to make them by the plan I
showed you on the mountain.

The Holy Tent

26 "Make for the Holy Tent ten curtains of fine linen and blue, purple,
and red thread. Have a skilled craftsman
sew designs of creatures with wings on
the pieces of cloth. **2**Make each curtain
the same size—forty-two feet long and
six feet wide. **3**Sew five curtains together
for one set, and sew the other curtains
together for the second set. **4**Make loops
of blue cloth on the edge of the end curtain of one set, and do the same for the
end curtain of the other set. **5**Make fifty
loops on the end curtain of the first set
and fifty loops on the end curtain of the
second set. These loops must be opposite each other. **6**And make fifty gold
hooks to join the two sets of curtains so
that the Holy Tent is one piece.

7"Then make another tent that will
cover the Holy Tent, using eleven curtains made from goat hair. **8**All these curtains must be the same size—forty-five
feet long and six feet wide. **9**Sew five of
the curtains together into one set. Then
sew the other six curtains together into
the second set. Fold the sixth curtain
double over the front of the Tent. **10**Make
fifty loops down the edge of the end curtain of one set, and do the same for the
end curtain of the other set. **11**Then
make fifty bronze hooks
and put them in the loops
to join the tent together
so that the covering is
one piece. **12**Let the extra half piece of cloth
hang over the back of the
Holy Tent. **13**There will
be eighteen inches hang-
ing over the sides of the
Holy Tent, to protect it.
14Make a covering for
the Holy Tent from sheepskins colored
red, and over that make a covering from
fine leather.

> Set up the Holy Tent by the plan shown to you on the mountain.
> —Exodus 26:30

15"Use acacia wood to make upright
frames for the Holy Tent. **16**Each frame
must be fifteen feet long and twenty-sev-
en inches wide, **17**with two pegs side by
side. Every frame must be made the
same way. **18**Make twenty frames for the
south side of the Holy Tent. **19**Each
frame must have two silver bases to go
under it, a peg fitting into each base. You
must make forty silver bases for the
frames. **20**Make twenty more frames for
the north side of the Holy Tent **21**and
forty silver bases for them—two bases for
each frame. **22**You must make six frames
for the rear or west end of the Holy Tent
23and two frames for each corner at the
rear. **24**The two frames are to be doubled
at the bottom and joined at the top with a
metal ring. Both corner frames must be
made this way. **25**So there will be a total
of eight frames at the rear of the Tent,
and there will be sixteen silver bases—
two bases under each frame.

26"Make crossbars of acacia wood to
connect the upright frames of the Holy
Tent. Make five crossbars to hold the
frames together on one side **27**and five to
hold the frames together on the other
side. Also make five crossbars to hold the
frames together on the west end, at the
rear. **28**The middle crossbar is to be set
halfway up the frames, and it is to run
along the entire length of each side and
rear. **29**Make gold rings on the sides of
the frames to hold the crossbars, and
cover the frames and the crossbars with
gold. **30**Set up the Holy Tent by the plan
shown to you on the mountain.

31"Make a curtain of
fine linen and blue, pur-
ple, and red thread, and
have a skilled craftsman
sew designs of creatures
with wings on it. **32**Hang
the curtain by gold hooks
on four posts of acacia
wood that are covered
with gold, and set them in
four silver bases. **33**Hang
the curtain from the
hooks in the roof, and put the Ark of the
Agreement containing the two stone tablets behind it. This curtain will separate
the Holy Place from the Most Holy Place.
34Put the lid on the Ark of the Agreement in the Most Holy Place.

35"Outside the curtain, put the table
on the north side of the Holy Tent. Put
the lampstand on the south side of the
Holy Tent across from the table.

CHURCH ON THE ROAD

Exodus 27:9–19

The Meeting Tent was a moveable church tent. The Israelites used the Meeting Tent as their church when they were wandering through the wilderness on their way back home from Egypt. Sometimes it is called the "Holy Tent." Wherever they stopped to camp, they put up the Meeting Tent in the center of the camp. God himself taught the Israelites how to build the Meeting Tent and how to take care of it.

The Meeting Tent measured 15 by 45 feet and had two main sections: the outer room, known as the Holy Place, and the inner room called the Most Holy Place. (See Exodus 26:33.) The only person who went into the Most Holy Place was the high priest. He only went in there once a year to offer a sacrifice for his sins and the sins of all the people. There was only one thing in this place: the Ark of the Agreement.

The Israelites used the Meeting Tent for their place of worship until Solomon built the Temple in Jerusalem.

The Entrance of the Holy Tent

36"Then, for the entrance of the Tent,
make a curtain with fine linen and blue,
purple, and red thread. Someone who can
sew well is to sew designs on it. **37**Make
five posts of acacia wood covered with
gold. Make gold hooks for them on which
to hang the curtain, and make five bronze
bases for them.

The Altar for Burnt Offerings

27 "Make an altar of acacia wood,
four and one-half feet high. It
should be square—seven and one-half
feet long and seven and one-half feet
wide. **2**Make each of the four corners of
the altar stick out like a horn, in such a
way that the corners with their horns are
all one piece. Then cover the whole altar
with bronze.

3"Use bronze to make all the tools and
dishes that will be used on the altar: the
pots to remove the ashes, the shovels,
the bowls for sprinkling blood, the meat
forks, and the pans for carrying the burning wood.

4"Make a large bronze screen to hold
the burning wood, and put a bronze ring
at each of the four corners of it. **5**Put the
screen inside the altar, under its rim,
halfway up from the bottom.

6"Make poles of acacia wood for the
altar, and cover them with bronze. **7**Put
the poles through the rings on both sides
of the altar to carry it. **8**Make the altar
out of boards and leave the inside hollow.
Make it as you were shown on the mountain.

The Courtyard of the Holy Tent

9"Make a wall of curtains to form a
courtyard around the Holy Tent. The
south side should have a wall of fine linen
curtains one hundred fifty feet long.
10Hang the curtains with silver hooks and
bands on twenty bronze posts with twenty
bronze bases. **11**The north side must also
be one hundred fifty feet long. Hang its
curtains on silver hooks and bands on
twenty bronze posts with twenty bronze
bases.

12"The west end of the courtyard

must have a wall of curtains seventy-five feet long, with ten posts and ten bases on that wall. **13**The east end of the courtyard must also be seventy-five feet long. **14**On one side of the entry, there is to be a wall of curtains twenty-two and one-half feet long, held up by three posts on three bases. **15**On the other side of the entry, there is also to be a wall of curtains twenty-two and one-half feet long, held up by three posts on three bases.

16"The entry to the courtyard is to be a curtain thirty feet wide, made of fine linen with blue, purple, and red thread. Someone who can sew well is to sew designs on it. It is to be held up by four posts on four bases. **17**All the posts around the courtyard must have silver bands and hooks and bronze bases. **18**The courtyard must be one hundred fifty feet long and seventy-five feet wide, with a wall of curtains around it seven and one-half feet high, made of fine linen. The bases in which the posts are set must be bronze. **19**All the things used in the Holy Tent and all the tent pegs for the Holy Tent and the wall around the courtyard must be made of bronze.

Oil for the Lamp

20"Command the people of Israel to bring you pure olive oil, made from pressed olives, to keep the lamps on the lampstand burning. **21**Aaron and his sons must keep the lamps burning before the LORD from evening till morning. This will be in the Meeting Tent, outside the curtain which is in front of the Ark. The Israelites and their descendants must obey this rule from now on.

Clothes for the Priests

28 "Tell your brother Aaron to come to you, along with his sons Nadab, Abihu, Eleazar, and Ithamar. Separate them from the other Israelites to serve me as priests. **2**Make holy clothes for your brother Aaron to give him honor and beauty. **3**Tell all the skilled craftsmen to whom I have given wisdom to make special clothes for Aaron—clothes to show that he belongs to me so that he may serve me as a priest. **4**These are the clothes they must make: a chest covering, a holy vest, an outer robe, a woven inner robe, a turban, and a cloth belt. The craftsmen must make these holy clothes for your brother Aaron and his sons. Then they may serve me as priests. **5**The craftsmen must use gold and blue, purple and red thread, and fine linen.

The Holy Vest

6"Use gold and blue, purple and red thread, and fine linen to make the holy vest; skilled craftsmen are to make it. **7**At each top corner of this holy vest there will be a pair of shoulder straps tied together over each shoulder.

8"The craftsmen will very carefully weave a belt on the holy vest that is made with the same materials—gold and blue, purple and red thread, and fine linen.

9"Take two onyx stones and write the names of the twelve sons of Israel on them, **10**six on one stone and six on the other. Write the names in order, from the oldest son to the youngest. **11**Carve the names of the sons of Israel on these stones in the same way a person carves words and designs on a seal. Put gold around the stones to hold them on the holy vest. **12**Then put the two stones on the two straps of the holy vest as reminders of the twelve sons of Israel. Aaron is to wear their names on his shoulders in the presence of the LORD as reminders of the sons of Israel. **13**Make two gold pieces to hold the stones **14**and two chains of pure gold, twisted together like a rope. Attach the chains to the two gold pieces that hold the stones.

The Chest Covering

15"Make a chest covering to help in making decisions. The craftsmen should make it as they made the holy vest, using gold and blue, purple and red thread, and fine linen. **16**The chest covering must be square—nine inches long and nine inches wide—and folded double to make a pocket. **17**Put four rows of beautiful gems on the chest covering: The first row must have a ruby, topaz, and yellow quartz; **18**the second must have turquoise, a sapphire, and an emerald; **19**the third must have a jacinth, an agate, and an amethyst; **20**the fourth must have a chrysolite, an onyx, and a jasper. Put gold around these jewels to attach them to the chest covering. **21**There must be twelve jewels on the chest covering—one jewel for each of the names of the sons of Israel. Carve the name of one of the twelve tribes on each of the stones as you would carve a seal.

22"Make chains of pure gold, twisted together like rope, for the chest covering. **23**Make two gold rings and put them on the two upper corners of the chest covering. **24**Attach the two gold chains to the two rings at the upper corners of the chest covering. **25**Attach the other ends of the two chains to the two gold pieces on the shoulder straps in the front of the holy vest.

> Make a strip of pure gold and carve these words on it as you would carve a seal: "Holy to the LORD."
> —Exodus 28:36

26"Make two gold rings and put them at the two lower corners of the chest covering, on the inside edge next to the holy vest. **27**Make two more gold rings and attach them to the bottom of the shoulder straps in the front of the holy vest. Put them close to the seam above the woven belt of the holy vest. **28**Join the rings of the chest covering to the rings of the holy vest with blue ribbon, connecting it to the woven belt so the chest covering will not swing out from the holy vest.

29"When Aaron enters the Holy Place, he will wear the names of the sons of Israel over his heart, on the chest covering that helps in making decisions. This will be a continual reminder before the LORD. **30**And put the Urim and Thummim inside the chest covering so that they will be on Aaron's heart when he goes before the LORD. They will help in making decisions for the Israelites. So Aaron will always carry them with him when he is before the LORD.

31"Make the outer robe to be worn under the holy vest, using only blue cloth. **32**Make a hole in the center for Aaron's head, with a woven collar around the hole so it will not tear. **33**Make balls like pomegranates of blue, purple, and red thread, and hang them around the bottom of the outer robe with gold bells between them. **34**All around the bottom of the outer robe there should be a gold bell and a pomegranate ball, a gold bell and a pomegranate ball. **35**Aaron must wear this robe when he serves as priest. The ringing of the bells will be heard when he enters and leaves the Holy Place before the LORD so that Aaron will not die.

36"Make a strip of pure gold and carve these words on it as you would carve a seal: 'Holy to the LORD.' **37**Use blue ribbon to tie it to the turban; put it on the front of the turban. **38**Aaron must wear this on his forehead. In this way, he will be blamed if anything is wrong with the gifts of the Israelites. Aaron must always wear this on his head so the LORD will accept the gifts of the people.

39"Make the woven inner robe of fine linen, and make the turban of fine linen also. Make the cloth belt with designs sewn on it. **40**Also make woven inner robes, cloth belts, and headbands for Aaron's sons, to give them honor and beauty. **41**Put these clothes on your brother Aaron and his sons, and pour olive oil on their heads to appoint them as priests. Make them belong to me so they may serve me as priests.

42"Make for them linen underclothes to cover them from the waist to the upper parts of the legs. **43**Aaron and his sons must wear these underclothes when they enter the Meeting Tent and anytime they come near the altar to serve as priests in the Holy Place. If they do not wear these clothes, they will be guilty of wrong, and they will die. This will be a law that will last from now on for Aaron and all his descendants.

Appointing the Priests

29 "This is what you must do to appoint Aaron and his sons to serve

me as priests. Take one young bull and
two male sheep that have nothing wrong
with them. 2Use fine wheat flour without
yeast to make bread, cakes mixed with
olive oil, and wafers brushed with olive
oil. 3Put these in one basket, and bring
them along with the bull and two male
sheep. 4Bring Aaron and his sons to the
entrance of the Meeting Tent and wash
them with water. 5Take the clothes and
dress Aaron in the inner robe and the
outer robe of the holy vest. Then put on
him the holy vest and the chest covering,
and tie the holy vest on him with its skillfully woven belt. 6Put the turban on his
head, and put the holy crown on the turban. 7Take the special olive oil and pour it
on his head to make him a priest.

8"Then bring his sons and put the inner robes on them. 9Put the headbands
on their heads, and tie cloth belts around
their waists. Aaron and his descendants
will be priests in Israel, according to a
rule that will continue from now on. This
is how you will appoint Aaron and his
sons as priests.

10"Bring the bull to the front of the
Meeting Tent, and Aaron and his sons
must put their hands on the bull's head.
11Then kill the bull before the LORD at
the entrance to the Meeting Tent. 12Use
your finger to put some of the bull's blood
on the corners of the altar, and then pour
the blood that is left at the bottom of the
altar. 13Take all the fat that covers the inner organs, as well as the best part of the
liver, both kidneys, and the fat around
them, and burn them on the altar. 14Take
the bull's meat, skin, and intestines, and
burn them outside the camp. This is an
offering to take away sin.

15"Take one of the male sheep, and
have Aaron and his sons put their hands
on its head. 16Kill it, and take its blood
and sprinkle it on all four sides of the altar. 17Then cut it into pieces and wash its
inner organs and its legs, putting them
with its head and its other pieces. 18Burn
the whole sheep on the altar; it is a burnt
offering made by fire to the LORD. Its
smell is pleasing to the LORD.

19"Take the other male sheep, and
have Aaron and his sons put their hands
on its head. 20Kill it and take some of its
blood. Put the blood on the bottom of the
right ears of Aaron and his sons and on
the thumbs of their right hands and on
the big toes of their right feet. Then
sprinkle the rest of the blood against all
four sides of the altar. 21Take some of the
blood from the altar, and mix it with the
special oil used in appointing priests.
Sprinkle this on Aaron and his clothes
and on his sons and their clothes. This
will show that Aaron and his sons and
their clothes are given to my service.

22"Then take the fat from the male
sheep, the fat tail, and the fat that covers
the inner organs. In addition, take the
best part of the liver, both kidneys, and
the fat around them, and the right thigh.
(This is the male sheep to be used in appointing priests.)

23"Then take the basket of bread that
you made without yeast, which you put
before the LORD. From it take a loaf of
bread, a cake made with olive oil, and a
wafer. 24Put all of these in the hands of
Aaron and his sons, and tell them to present them as an offering to the LORD.
25Then take them from their hands and
burn them on the altar with the whole
burnt offering. This is an offering made
by fire to the LORD; its smell is pleasing
to the LORD. 26Then take the breast of
the male sheep used to appoint Aaron as
priest, and present it before the LORD as
an offering. This part of the animal will be
your share. 27Set aside the breast and
the thigh of the sheep that were used to
appoint Aaron and his sons as priests.
These parts belong to them. 28They are
to be the regular share which the Israelites will always give to Aaron and his
sons. It is the gift the Israelites must give
to the LORD from their fellowship offerings.

29"The holy clothes made for Aaron
will belong to his descendants so that
they can wear these clothes when they
are appointed as priests. 30Aaron's son,
who will become high priest after Aaron,
will come to the Meeting Tent to serve in
the Holy Place. He is to wear these
clothes for seven days.

31"Take the male sheep used to appoint priests and boil its meat in a place that is holy. 32Then at the entrance of the Meeting Tent, Aaron and his sons must eat the meat of the sheep and the bread that is in the basket. 33They should eat these offerings that were used to remove their sins and to make them holy when they were made priests. But no one else is to eat them, because they are holy things. 34If any of the meat from that sheep or any of the bread is left the next morning, it must be burned. It must not be eaten, because it is holy.

> I will live with the people of Israel and be their God.
> —Exodus 29:45

35"Do all these things that I commanded you to do to Aaron and his sons, and spend seven days appointing them. 36Each day you are to offer a bull to remove the sins of Aaron and his sons so they will be given for service to the LORD. Make the altar ready for service to the LORD, and pour oil on it to make it holy. 37Spend seven days making the altar ready for service to God and making it holy. Then the altar will become very holy, and anything that touches it must be holy.

The Daily Sacrifices

38"Every day from now on, offer on the altar two lambs that are one year old. 39Offer one lamb in the morning and the other in the evening before dark. 40In the morning, when you offer the first lamb, offer also two quarts of fine flour mixed with one quart of oil from pressed olives. Pour out a quart of wine as a drink offering. 41Offer the second lamb in the evening with the same grain offering and drink offering as you did in the morning. This is an offering made by fire to the LORD, and its smell is pleasing to him.

42"You must burn these things as an offering to the LORD every day, from now on, at the entrance of the Meeting Tent before the LORD. When you make the offering, I, the LORD, will meet you there and speak to you. 43I will meet with the people of Israel there, and that place will be holy because of my glory.

44"So I will make the Meeting Tent and the altar holy; I will also make Aaron and his sons holy so they may serve me as priests. 45I will live with the people of Israel and be their God. 46And they will know that I am the LORD their God who led them out of Egypt so that I could live with them. I am the LORD their God.

The Altar for Burning Incense

30 "Make an altar out of acacia wood for burning incense. 2Make it square—eighteen inches long and eighteen inches wide—and make it thirty-six inches high. The corners that stick out like horns must be one piece with the altar. 3Cover its top, its sides, and its corners with pure gold, and put a gold strip all around the altar. 4Make two gold rings beneath the gold strip on opposite sides of the altar, and slide poles through them to carry the altar. 5Make the poles from acacia wood and cover them with gold. 6Put the altar of incense in front of the curtain that is near the Ark of the Agreement, in front of the lid that covers that Ark. There I will meet with you.

7"Aaron must burn sweet-smelling incense on the altar every morning when he comes to take care of the oil lamps. 8He must burn incense again in the evening when he lights the lamps, so incense will burn before the LORD every day from now on. 9Do not use this altar for offering any other incense, or burnt offering, or any kind of grain offering, or drink offering. 10Once a year Aaron must make the altar ready for service to God by putting blood on its corners—the blood of the animal offered to remove sins. He is to do this once a year from now on. This altar belongs completely to the LORD's service."

The Tax for the Meeting Tent

11The LORD said to Moses, 12"When you count the people of Israel, every

person must buy back his life from the
LORD so that no terrible things will happen to the people when you number
them. **13**Every person who is counted
must pay one-fifth of an ounce of silver.
(This is set by using one-half of the Holy
Place measure, which weighs two-fifths
of an ounce.) This amount is a gift to the
LORD. **14**Every person who is counted
and is twenty years old or older must
give this amount to the LORD. **15**A rich
person must not give more than one-fifth
of an ounce, and a poor person must not
give less. You are paying this to the LORD
to buy back your lives. **16**Gather from the
people of Israel this money paid to buy
back their lives, and spend it on things for
the service in the Meeting Tent. This
payment will remind the LORD that the
Israelites' lives have been bought back."

The Bronze Bowl

17The LORD said to Moses, **18**"Make
a bronze bowl, on a bronze stand, for
washing. Put the bowl and stand between
the Meeting Tent and the altar, and put
water in the bowl. **19**Aaron and his sons
must wash their hands and feet with the
water from this bowl. **20**Each time they
enter the Meeting Tent they must wash
with water so they will not die. Whenever they approach the altar to serve as
priests and offer a sacrifice to the LORD
by fire, **21**they must wash their hands and
their feet so they will not die. This is a
rule which Aaron and his descendants are
to keep from now on."

Oil for Appointing

22Then the LORD said to Moses,
23"Take the finest spices: twelve pounds
of liquid myrrh, half that amount (that is,
six pounds) of sweet-smelling cinnamon,
six pounds of sweet-smelling cane, **24**and
twelve pounds of cassia. Weigh all these
by the Holy Place measure. Also take
four quarts of olive oil, **25**and mix all
these things like a perfume to make a
holy olive oil. This special oil must be put
on people and things to make them ready
for service to God. **26**Put this oil on the
Meeting Tent and the Ark of the Agreement, **27**on the table and all its dishes, on
the lampstand and all its tools, and on the
incense altar. **28**Also, put the oil on the
altar for burnt offerings and on all its
tools, as well as on the bowl and the stand
under the bowl. **29**You will prepare all
these things for service to God, and they
will be very holy. Anything that touches
these things must be holy.

30"Put the oil on Aaron and his sons
to give them for service to me, that they
may serve me as priests. **31**Tell the Israelites, 'This is to be my holy olive oil
from now on. It is to be put on people and
things to make them ready for service to
God. **32**Do not pour it on the bodies of
ordinary people, and do not make perfume the same way you make this oil.
It is holy, and you must treat it as holy.
33If anyone makes perfume like it or puts
it on someone who is not a priest, that
person must be cut off from his people.' "

Incense

34Then the LORD said to Moses,
"Take these sweet-smelling spices: resin,
onycha, galbanum, and pure frankincense. Be sure that you have equal
amounts of each. **35**Make incense as a
person who makes perfume would do.
Add salt to it to keep it pure and holy.
36Beat some of the incense into a fine
powder, and put it in front of the Ark of
the Agreement in the Meeting Tent,
where I will meet with you. You must use
this incense powder only for its very special purpose. **37**Do not make incense for
yourselves the same way you make this
incense. Treat it as holy to the LORD.
38Whoever makes incense like this to
use as perfume must be cut off from his
people."

Bezalel and Oholiab Help

31 Then the LORD said to Moses,
2"See, I have chosen Bezalel son
of Uri from the tribe of Judah. (Uri was
the son of Hur.) **3**I have filled Bezalel
with the Spirit of God and have given
him the skill, ability, and knowledge to
do all kinds of work. **4**He is able to
design pieces to be made from gold, silver, and bronze, **5**to cut jewels and put
them in metal, to carve wood, and to do

SERIOUS ABOUT THE SABBATH

EXODUS 31:15

What's the best day of the week for you? Friday? Saturday? Any day that you don't have to go to school? God has a special day, too—the Sabbath day. God set this as a day for the people to rest and think about him. How serious was God about keeping the Sabbath? Serious enough to slap the death penalty on anyone who broke the Sabbath. That's why keeping the Sabbath is mentioned a number of times in Exodus (16:23; 20:8; 23:12; 35:2) and other places. (Look up Leviticus 19:30, p. 161.)

For Christians, the Sabbath day is Sunday. Most Christians attend a worship service as their way of keeping the Sabbath. How do you show how special this day is for you?

Time to Celebrate, Exodus 15:1–21, p. 95

A Holiday Every Week, Leviticus 23:1–3, p. 166

Plans for a Son, 1 Chronicles 22:5–19, p. 548

The Number One Rule, Mark 12:28–31, p. 1351

A Christian's Responsibility, Acts 11:26, p. 1484

Meeting Together, 1 Corinthians 16:19, p. 1567

all kinds of work. **6**I have also chosen
Oholiab son of Ahisamach from the tribe
of Dan to work with Bezalel. I have given
skills to all the craftsmen, and they will
be able to make all these things I have
commanded you: **7**the Meeting Tent, the
Ark of the Agreement, the lid that covers
the Ark, and everything in the Tent.
8This includes the table and everything
on it, the pure gold lampstand and everything with it, the altar of incense, **9**the
altar for burnt offerings and everything
used with it, and the bowl and the stand
under it. **10**They will make the woven
clothes and the holy clothes for Aaron
and the clothes for his sons to wear when
they serve as priests. **11**They will also
make the special olive oil used in appointing people and things to the service of
the LORD, and the sweet-smelling incense for the Holy Place.

"These workers will make all these
things just as I have commanded you."

The Day of Rest

12Then the LORD said to Moses,
13"Tell the Israelites, 'You must keep the
rules about my Sabbaths, because they
will be a sign between you and me from
now on. In this way you will know that I,
the LORD, make you holy.

14" 'Make the Sabbath a holy day. If
anyone treats the Sabbath like any other
day, that person must be put to death;
anyone who works on the Sabbath day
must be cut off from his people. **15**There
are six days for working, but the seventh
day is a day of rest, a day holy for the
LORD. Anyone who works during the Sabbath day must be put to death. **16**The Israelites must remember the Sabbath day
as an agreement between them and me
that will continue from now on. **17**The
Sabbath day will be a sign between me
and the Israelites forever, because in six
days I, the LORD, made the sky and the
earth. On the seventh day I did not work;
I rested.' "

18When the LORD finished speaking
to Moses on Mount Sinai, he gave him
the two stone tablets with the Agreement written on them, written by the finger of God.

The People Make a Gold Calf

32 The people saw that a long time
had passed and Moses had not
come down from the mountain. So they
gathered around Aaron and said, "Moses
led us out of Egypt, but we don't know
what has happened to him. Make us gods
who will lead us."
2Aaron said to the people, "Take off
the gold earrings that your wives, sons,
and daughters are wearing, and bring
them to me." **3**So all the people took
their gold earrings and brought them to
Aaron. **4**He took the gold from the people
and formed it with a tool and made a
statue of a calf. Then the people said, "Israel, these are your gods who brought
you out of the land of Egypt!"
5When Aaron saw all this, he built an
altar before the calf and announced, "Tomorrow there will be a special feast to
honor the LORD." **6**The people got up
early the next morning and offered whole
burnt offerings and fellowship offerings.
They sat down to eat and drink, and then
they got up and sinned sexually.
7Then the LORD said to Moses, "Go
down from this mountain, because your
people, the people you brought out of the
land of Egypt, have ruined themselves.
8They have quickly turned away from
the things I commanded them to do.
They have made for themselves a calf
covered with gold, and they have worshiped it and offered sacrifices to it. They
have said, 'Israel, these are your gods
who brought you out of Egypt.' "
9The LORD said to Moses, "I have
seen these people, and I know that they
are very stubborn. **10**So now do not stop
me. I am so angry with them that I am
going to destroy them. Then I will make
you and your descendants a great nation."
11But Moses begged the LORD his
God and said, "LORD, don't let your anger
destroy your people, whom you brought
out of Egypt with your great power and
strength. **12**Don't let the people of Egypt
say, 'The LORD brought the Israelites out
of Egypt for an evil purpose. He planned
to kill them in the mountains and destroy
them from the earth.' So stop being angry,
and don't destroy your people. **13**Remember the men who served you—Abraham,
Isaac, and Israel. You promised with an
oath to them and said, 'I will make your
descendants as many as the stars in the

FAITH links

IDOL TALK 

EXODUS 32

What is an idol? It is anyone or anything that takes the place of God in your life. The Israelites sinned by worshiping a gold calf that Aaron made. When God gave the Ten Commandments, he told the people of Israel never to worship anyone or anything besides him. The consequences of disobedience were high for the people of Israel. Many died that day.

Some people "worship" money, other people, or fame. That's all they can think about. Got any idols in your life? Give 'em the heave-ho! God wants first place in your life. He won't share that place with anyone or anything!

What He's Really Like, Deuteronomy 4:15–20, p. 233

No Middle Ground, Joshua 24:14–15, p. 307

What I've Got, 2 Kings 20:12–17, p. 508

The Foundation of Our Hope, Isaiah 31:1–8, p. 934

Faith That Pleases God, Luke 7:1–9, p. 1380

Your Heart's Desire, Luke 16:13–15, p. 1401

sky. I will give your descendants all
this land that I have promised them, and
it will be theirs forever.' " **14**So the LORD
changed his mind and did not destroy the
people as he had said he might.

15Then Moses went down the mountain, and in his hands he had the two
stone tablets with the Agreement on
them. The commands were written on
both sides of each stone, front and back.
16God himself had made the tablets, and
God himself had written the commands
on the tablets.

17When Joshua heard the sound of the
people shouting, he said to Moses, "It
sounds like war down in the camp."

18Moses answered:

"It is not a shout of victory;
it is not a cry of defeat.
It is the sound of singing that I
hear."

19When Moses came close to the
camp, he saw the gold calf and the dancing, and he became very angry. He threw
down the stone tablets that he was carrying and broke them at the bottom of the
mountain. **20**Then he took the calf that
the people had made and melted it in the
fire. He ground it into powder. Then he
threw the powder into the water and
forced the Israelites to drink it.

21Moses said to Aaron, "What did
these people do to you? Why did you
cause them to do such a terrible sin?"

22Aaron answered, "Don't be angry,
master. You know that these people are
always ready to do wrong. **23**The people
said to me, 'Moses led us out of Egypt,
but we don't know what has happened to
him. Make us gods who will lead us.'
24So I told the people, 'Take off your gold
jewelry.' When they gave me the gold, I
threw it into the fire and out came this
calf!"

25Moses saw that the people were
acting wildly. Aaron had let them get out
of control and become fools in front of
their enemies. **26**So Moses stood at the
entrance to the camp and said, "Let anyone who wants to follow the LORD come
to me." And all the people from the family of Levi gathered around Moses.

27Then Moses said to them, "The
LORD, the God of Israel, says this: 'Every
man must put on his sword and go
through the camp from one end to the
other. Each man must kill his brother, his
friend, and his neighbor.' " **28**The people
from the family of Levi obeyed Moses,
and that day about three thousand of the
Israelites died. **29**Then Moses said, "Today you have been given for service to
the LORD. You were willing to kill your
own sons and brothers, and God has
blessed you for this."

30The next day Moses told the people, "You have done a terrible sin. But
now I will go up to the LORD. Maybe I can
do something so your sins will be removed." **31**So Moses went back to the
LORD and said, "How terribly these people have sinned! They have made for
themselves gods from gold. **32**Now,
please forgive them of this sin. If you will
not, then erase my name from the book in
which you have written the names of
your people."

33But the LORD told Moses, "I will
erase from my book the names of the
people who sin against me. **34**So now,
go. Lead the people where I
have told you, and
my angel will lead
you. When the time
comes to punish, I
will punish them for
their sin."

eMAIL! FROM GOD
32:34
Sin
Is there punishment for your sin?

35So the LORD caused terrible things
to happen to the people because of what
they did with the calf Aaron had made.

33 Then the LORD said to Moses,
"You and the people you brought
out of Egypt must leave this place. Go to
the land that I promised with an oath to
give to Abraham, Isaac, and Jacob when I
said, 'I will give that land to your descendants.' **2**I will send an angel to lead
you, and I will force these people out of
the land: the Canaanites, Amorites, Hittites, Perizzites, Hivites, and Jebusites.
3Go up to a fertile land. But I will not go
with you, because I might destroy you on
the way, since you are such a stubborn
people."

4When the people heard this bad
news, they became very sad, and none of

them put on jewelry. 5This was because
the LORD had said to Moses, "Tell the Israelites, 'You are a stubborn people. If
I were to go with you even for a moment,
I would destroy you. So take off all your
jewelry, and I will decide what to do with
you.' " 6So the people of Israel took off
their jewelry at Mount Sinai.

The Meeting Tent

7Moses used to take a tent and set
it up a long way outside the camp; he
called it the "Meeting Tent." Anyone
who wanted to ask the LORD about something would go to the Meeting Tent outside the camp. 8Whenever Moses went
out to the Tent, all the people would rise
and stand at the entrances of their tents,
watching him until he entered the Meeting Tent. 9When Moses went into the
Tent, the pillar of cloud would always
come down and stay at the entrance of
the Tent while the LORD spoke with Moses. 10Whenever the people saw the pillar of cloud at the entrance of the Tent,
they stood and worshiped, each person at
the entrance of his own tent.

11The LORD spoke to Moses face to
face as a man speaks with his friend.
Then Moses would return to the camp,
but Moses' young helper, Joshua son of
Nun, did not leave the Tent.

12Moses said to the LORD, "You have
told me to lead these people, but you did
not say whom you would send with me.
You have said to me, 'I know you very
well, and I am pleased with you.' 13If I
have truly pleased you, show me your
plans so that I may know you and continue to please you. Remember that this
nation is your people."

14The LORD answered, "I myself will
go with you, and I will give you victory."

15Then Moses said to him, "If you
yourself don't go with us, then don't send
us away from this place. 16If you don't go
with us, no one will know that you are
pleased with me and with your people.
These people and I will be no different
from any other people on earth."

17Then the LORD said to Moses, "I
will do what you ask, because I know you
very well, and I am pleased with you."

FAITH links

THE NAME OF THE LORD

EXODUS 33:19-23; 34:5-8

Ever wish you could see God face-to-face? Although he could hear God speak to him, Moses wanted to "see" God. He wanted to know that God was around. God allowed him to understand the richness of his love in a special way. He passed by Moses calling out his own name. God's character is wrapped up in his name. His name describes what he does.

We can understand the richness of God's love through one name: *Jesus*. His name describes what he did. The name *Jesus* means "salvation." He saved us from sin. When we pray, we go to God in Jesus' name. One day, we will see Jesus face-to-face!

What's in a Name?, Isaiah 9:6, p. 908

God's New Temple, Ezekiel 40–44, p. 1135

Concern for All, Daniel 9, p. 1165

Name with a Purpose, Matthew 1:21, p. 1274

Remembering Jesus, Matthew 26:26–29, p. 1321

MVFM?, Galatians 3:26–27, p. 1589

Moses Sees God's Glory

18Then Moses said, "Now, please
show me your glory."

19The LORD answered, "I will cause
all my goodness to pass in front of you,
and I will announce my name, the LORD,
so you can hear it. I will show kindness to
anyone to whom I want to show kindness, and I will show mercy to anyone to
whom I want to show mercy. 20But you
cannot see my face, because no one can
see me and live.

21"There is a place near me where
you may stand on a rock. 22When my
glory passes that place, I will put you in a
large crack in the rock and cover you
with my hand until I have passed by.
23Then I will take away my hand, and you
will see my back. But my face must not
be seen."

Moses Gets New Stone Tablets

34 The LORD said to Moses, "Cut two
more stone tablets like the first
two, and I will write the same words on
them that were on the first two stones
which you broke. 2Be ready tomorrow
morning, and then come up on Mount
Sinai. Stand before me there on the top
of the mountain. 3No one may come
with you or even be seen any place on
the mountain. Not even the flocks or
herds may eat grass near that mountain."

4So Moses cut two stone tablets like
the first ones. Then early the next morning he went up Mount Sinai, just as the
LORD had commanded him, carrying
the two stone tablets with him. 5Then
the LORD came down in the cloud and
stood there with Moses, and the LORD
called out his name: the LORD.

6The LORD passed in front of Moses
and said, "I am the LORD. The LORD is a
God who shows mercy, who is kind, who
doesn't become angry quickly, who has
great love and faithfulness 7and is kind to
thousands of people. The LORD forgives
people for evil, for sin, and for turning
against him, but he does not forget to
punish guilty people. He will punish
not only the guilty people, but also their
children, their grandchildren, their great-
grandchildren, and their great-great-
grandchildren."

8Then Moses quickly bowed to the
ground and worshiped. 9He said, "Lord,
if you are pleased with me, please go with
us. I know that these are stubborn people, but forgive our evil and our sin. Take
us as your own people."

10Then the LORD said, "I am making
this agreement with you. I will do miracles in front of all your people—things
that have never before been done for any
other nation on earth—and the people
with you will see my work. I, the LORD,
will do wonderful things for you. 11Obey
the things I command you today, and I
will force out the Amorites, Canaanites,
Hittites, Perizzites, Hivites, and Jebusites ahead of you. 12Be careful that you
don't make an agreement with the people
who live in the land where you
are going, because it
will bring you trou-
ble. 13Destroy their
altars, break their
stone pillars, and cut
down their Asherah
idols. 14Don't worship any other god, because I, the LORD, the Jealous One, am a
jealous God.

eMAIL! FROM GOD
34:14
Worship
Is worship meant for anyone besides God?

15"Be careful that you don't make an
agreement with the people who live in
that land. When they worship their gods,
they will invite you to join them. Then
you will eat their sacrifices. 16If you
choose some of their daughters as wives
for your sons and those daughters worship gods, they will lead your sons to do
the same thing.

17"Do not make gods of melted
metal.

18"Celebrate the Feast of Unleavened
Bread. For seven days you must eat
bread made without yeast as I commanded you. Do this during the month I
have chosen, the month of Abib, because
in that month you came out of Egypt.

19"The firstborn of every mother belongs to me, including every firstborn
male animal that is born in your flocks
and herds. 20You may buy back a donkey
by paying for it with a lamb, but if you
don't want to buy back a donkey, you

must break its neck. You must buy back
all your firstborn sons.
"No one is to come before me without
a gift.
21"You must work for six days, but on
the seventh day you must rest—even
during the planting season and the harvest season.
22"Celebrate the Feast of Weeks
when you gather the first grain of the
wheat harvest. And celebrate the Feast
of Shelters in the fall.
23"Three times each year all your
males must come before the Lord GOD,
the God of Israel. 24I will force out nations ahead of you and expand the borders of your land. You will go before the
LORD your God three times each year,
and at that time no one will try to take
your land from you.
25"Do not offer the blood of a sacrifice
to me with anything containing yeast, and
do not leave any of the sacrifice of the
Feast of Passover until the next morning.
26"Bring the best first crops that you
harvest from your ground to the Tent of
the LORD your God.
"You must not cook a young goat in its
mother's milk."
27Then the LORD said to Moses,
"Write down these words, because with
these words I have made an agreement
with you and Israel."
28Moses stayed there with the LORD
forty days and forty nights, and during
that time he did not eat food or drink water. And Moses wrote the words of the
Agreement—the Ten Commandments—
on the stone tablets.

The Face of Moses Shines

29Then Moses came down from
Mount Sinai, carrying the two stone tablets of the Agreement in his hands. But
he did not know that his face was shining
because he had talked with the LORD.
30When Aaron and all the people of Israel
saw that Moses' face was shining, they
were afraid to go near him. 31But Moses
called to them, so Aaron and all the leaders of the people returned to Moses, and
he talked with them. 32After that, all the
people of Israel came near him, and he
gave them all the commands that the
LORD had given him on Mount Sinai.
33When Moses finished speaking to
the people, he put a covering over his
face. 34Anytime Moses went before the
LORD to speak with him, Moses took off
the covering until he came out. Then
Moses would come out and tell the Israelites what the LORD had commanded.
35They would see that Moses' face was
shining. So he would cover his face again
until the next time he went in to speak
with the LORD.

Rules About the Sabbath

35 Moses gathered all the Israelite
community together and said to
them, "These are the things the LORD
has commanded you to do. 2You are to
work for six days, but the seventh day
will be a holy day, a Sabbath of rest to
honor the LORD. Anyone who works on
that day must be put to death. 3On the
Sabbath day you must not light a fire in
any of your houses."
4Moses said to all the Israelites,
"This is what the LORD has commanded:
5From what you have, take an offering for
the LORD. Let everyone who is willing
bring this offering to the LORD: gold, silver, bronze, 6blue, purple and red thread,
and fine linen, goat hair 7and male sheepskins that are colored red. They may also
bring fine leather, acacia wood, 8olive oil
for the lamps, spices for the special olive
oil used for appointing priests and for the
sweet-smelling incense, 9onyx stones,
and other jewels to be put on the holy
vest and chest covering of the priests.
10"Let all the skilled workers come
and make everything the LORD commanded: 11the Holy Tent, its outer tent and its
covering, the hooks, frames, crossbars,
posts, and bases; 12the Ark of the Agreement, its poles, lid, and the curtain in front
of it; 13the table, and its poles, all the
things that go with the table, and the
bread that shows we are in God's presence; 14the lampstand for the light and all
the things that go with it, the lamps, and
olive oil for the light; 15the altar of incense and its poles, the special oil and the
sweet-smelling incense, the curtain for

FAITH links

SHARE WHAT YOU HAVE

EXODUS 35:5-18

Moses and the Israelites wanted to build a place where God could be worshiped. God told them to build the Meeting Tent. This was to be a portable "house" for God. The Israelites gave generously to help with the building. Moses also asked them to share their skills and talents to build it.

God wants us to share what we have with others. We can share our money, time, and talents to do the work of God.

When we share what we have, everyone is helped.

Here are some more Faithlinks on sharing:

Help for the Poor, Leviticus 5:7, p. 138

Give What You Can, Numbers 7:1–11, p. 186

A Robbery in Progress, Malachi 3:8–10, p. 1270

Give from the Heart, Luke 21:1–4, p. 1410

Share and Share Alike?, Acts 2:43–47, p. 1466

Help for the Body, Romans 12:3–8, p. 1536

the entrance of the Meeting Tent; **16**the
altar of burnt offering and its bronze
screen, its poles and all its tools, the
bronze bowl and its base; **17**the curtains
around the courtyard, their posts and bases, and the curtain at the entry to the
courtyard; **18**the pegs of the Holy Tent
and of the courtyard and their ropes;
19the special clothes that the priest will
wear in the Holy Place. These are the
holy clothes for Aaron the priest and his
sons to wear when they serve as priests."

20Then all the people of Israel went
away from Moses. **21**Everyone who
wanted to give came and brought a gift to
the LORD for making the Meeting Tent,
all the things in the Tent, and
the special clothes.
22All the men and
women who wanted
to give brought gold
jewelry of all kinds—
pins, earrings, rings,
and bracelets. They all presented their
gold to the LORD. **23**Everyone who had
blue, purple, and red thread, and fine
linen, and anyone who had goat hair or
male sheepskins colored red or fine
leather brought them to the LORD.
24Everyone who could give silver or
bronze brought that as a gift to the LORD,
and everyone who had acacia wood to be
used in the work brought it. **25**Every
skilled woman used her hands to make
the blue, purple, and red thread, and fine
linen, and they brought what they had
made. **26**All the women who were skilled
and wanted to help made thread of the
goat hair. **27**The leaders brought onyx
stones and other jewels to put on the
holy vest and chest covering for the
priest. **28**They also brought spices and
olive oil for the sweet-smelling incense,
the special oil, and the oil to burn in the
lamps. **29**All the men and women of Israel who wanted to help brought gifts to
the LORD for all the work the LORD had
commanded Moses and the people to do.

30Then Moses said to the Israelites,
"Look, the LORD has chosen Bezalel son
of Uri the son of Hur, from the tribe of
Judah. **31**The LORD has filled Bezalel
with the Spirit of God and has given him
the skill, ability, and knowledge to do all
kinds of work. **32**He is able to design
pieces to be made of gold, silver, and
bronze, **33**to cut stones and jewels and
put them in metal, to carve wood, and to
do all kinds of work. **34**Also, the LORD
has given Bezalel and Oholiab, the son of
Ahisamach from the tribe of Dan, the

EMAIL FROM GOD **35:22**
Giving
Check out this attitude of giving.

ability to teach others. **35**The LORD has
given them the skill to do all kinds of
work. They are able to cut designs in
metal and stone. They can plan and sew
designs in the fine linen with the blue,
purple, and red thread. And they are also
36 able to weave things. **1**So Bezalel,
Oholiab, and every skilled person
will do the work the LORD has commanded, because he gave them the
wisdom and understanding to do all the
skilled work needed to
build the Holy Tent."

> So Bezalel, Oholiab, and every skilled person will do the work the LORD has commanded.
> —Exodus 36:1

2Then Moses called
Bezalel, Oholiab, and all
the other skilled people
to whom the LORD had
given skills, and they
came because they want-
ed to help with the work.
3They received from Moses everything the peo-
ple of Israel had brought
as gifts to build the Holy
Tent. The people continued to bring gifts
each morning because they wanted to.
4So all the skilled workers left the work
they were doing on the Holy Tent, **5**and
they said to Moses, "The people are
bringing more than we need to do the
work the LORD commanded."

6Then Moses sent this command
throughout the camp: "No man or woman
should make anything else as a gift for
the Holy Tent." So the people were kept
from giving more, **7**because what they
had was already more than enough to do
all the work.

The Holy Tent

8Then the skilled workers made the
Holy Tent. They made the ten curtains of
blue, purple, and red cloth, and they
sewed designs of creatures with wings on
the curtains. **9**Each curtain was the same
size—forty-two feet long and six feet
wide. **10**Five of the curtains were fastened together to make one set, and the
other five were fastened together to
make another set. **11**Then they made
loops of blue cloth along the edge of the
end curtain on the first set of five, and
they did the same thing with the other
set of five. **12**There were fifty loops on
one curtain and fifty loops on the other
curtain, with the loops opposite each
other. **13**They made fifty gold hooks to
join the two curtains together so that the
Holy Tent was joined together as one
piece.

14Then the workers made another
tent of eleven curtains made of goat hair,
to put over the Holy Tent. **15**All eleven
curtains were the same size—forty-five
feet long and six feet
wide. **16**The workers
sewed five curtains to-
gether into one set and
six together into another
set. **17**They made fifty
loops along the edge of
the outside curtain of one
set and fifty loops along
the edge of the outside
curtain of the other set.
18Then they made fifty
bronze rings to join the
two sets of cloth together and make the
tent one piece. **19**They made two more
coverings for the outer tent—one made
of male sheepskins colored red and the
other made of fine leather.

20Then they made upright frames of
acacia wood for the Holy Tent. **21**Each
frame was fifteen feet tall and twenty-
seven inches wide, **22**and there were two
pegs side by side on each one. Every
frame of the Holy Tent was made this
same way. **23**They made twenty frames
for the south side of the Tent, **24**and they
made forty silver bases that went under
the twenty frames. There were two bases
for every frame—one for each peg of each
frame. **25**They also made twenty frames
for the north side of the Holy Tent **26**and
forty silver bases—two to go under each
frame. **27**They made six frames for the
rear or west end of the Holy Tent **28**and
two frames for the corners at the rear of
the Holy Tent. **29**These two frames were
doubled at the bottom and joined at the
top with a metal ring. They did this for
each of these corners. **30**So there were
eight frames and sixteen silver bases—
two bases under each frame.

31Then they made crossbars of acacia

wood to connect the upright frames of the Holy Tent. Five crossbars held the frames together on one side of the Tent, **32**and five held the frames together on the other side. Also, five crossbars held the frames together on the west end, at the rear of the Tent. **33**They made the middle crossbar run along the entire length of each side and rear of the Tent. It was set halfway up the frames. **34**They made gold rings on the sides of the frames to hold the crossbars, and they covered the frames and the crossbars with gold.

35Then they made the curtain of blue, purple, and red thread, and fine linen. A skilled craftsman sewed designs of creatures with wings on it. **36**They made four posts of acacia wood for it and covered them with gold. Then they made gold hooks for the posts, as well as four silver bases in which to set the posts. **37**For the entrance to the Tent, they made a curtain of blue, purple, and red thread, and fine linen. A person who sewed well sewed designs on it. **38**Then they made five posts and hooks for it. They covered the tops of the posts and their bands with gold, and they made five bronze bases for the posts.

The Ark of the Agreement

37 Bezalel made the Ark of acacia wood; it was forty-five inches long, twenty-seven inches wide, and twenty-seven inches high. **2**He covered it, both inside and out, with pure gold, and he put a gold strip around it. **3**He made four gold rings for it and attached them to its four feet, with two rings on each side. **4**Then he made poles of acacia wood and covered them with gold. **5**He put the poles through the rings on each side of the Ark to carry it. **6**Then he made a lid of pure gold that was forty-five inches long and twenty-seven inches wide. **7**Then Bezalel hammered gold to make two creatures with wings and attached them to each end of the lid. **8**He made one creature on one end of the lid and the other creature on the other end. He attached them to the lid so that it would be one piece. **9**The creatures' wings were spread upward, covering the lid, and the creatures faced each other across the lid.

The Table

10Then he made the table of acacia wood; it was thirty-six inches long, eighteen inches wide, and twenty-seven inches high. **11**He covered it with pure gold and put a gold strip around it. **12**He made a frame three inches high that stood up all around the edge, and he put a gold strip around it. **13**Then he made four gold rings for the table and attached them to the four corners of the table where the four legs were. **14**The rings were put close to the frame around the top of the table, because they held the poles for carrying it. **15**The poles for carrying the table were made of acacia wood and were covered with gold. **16**He made of pure gold all the things that were used on the table: the plates, bowls, cups, and jars used for pouring the drink offerings.

The Lampstand

17Then he made the lampstand of pure gold, hammering out its base and stand. Its flower-like cups, buds, and petals were joined together in one piece with the base and stand. **18**Six branches went out from the sides of the lampstand—three on one side and three on the other. **19**Each branch had three cups shaped like almond flowers, and each cup had a bud and a petal. Each of the six branches going out from the lampstand was the same. **20**There were four more cups shaped like almond flowers on the lampstand itself, each with its buds and petals. **21**Three pairs of branches went out from the lampstand. A bud was under the place where each pair was attached to the lampstand. Each of the six branches going out from the lampstand was the same. **22**The buds, branches, and lampstand were all one piece of pure, hammered gold. **23**He made seven pure gold lamps for this lampstand, and he made pure gold wick trimmers and trays. **24**He used about seventy-five pounds of pure gold to make the lampstand and all the things that go with it.

The Altar for Burning Incense

25Then he made the altar of incense
out of acacia wood. It was square—eighteen inches long and eighteen inches
wide—and it was thirty-six inches high.
Each corner that stuck out like a horn
was joined into one piece with the altar.
26He covered the top and all the sides
and the corners with pure gold, and he
put gold trim around the altar. 27He made
two gold rings and put them below the
trim on opposite sides of the altar; these
rings held the poles for carrying it. 28He
made the poles of acacia wood and covered them with gold.
29Then he made the holy olive oil for
appointing the priests and the pure,
sweet-smelling incense. He made them
like a person who mixes perfumes.

The Altar for Burnt Offerings

38 Then he built the altar for burnt
offerings out of acacia wood. The
altar was square—seven and one-half
feet long and seven and one-half feet
wide—and it was four and one-half feet
high. 2He made each corner stick out like
a horn so that the horns and the altar
were joined together in one piece. Then
he covered the altar with bronze. 3He
made all the tools of bronze to use on
the altar: the pots, shovels, bowls for

YOU'RE NOT ALONE

Hey, kids. Skweek and I were just talking about what it's like to be lonely. We have a friend who also knows the feeling. Let's welcome Lindsay, age 10, to Connect 2-You.

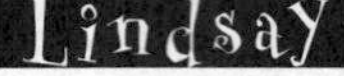

Hi, Lindsay. Tell us what's going on in your life.

Well, my best friend moved away a few weeks ago. The two of us used to do everything together. Now that she's gone, I feel like I'm all alone. I have other people that I hang out with sometimes, but it just isn't the same. I feel so lonely. What can I do?

Boy, I know how you feel, Lindsay. Losing your best friend can hurt a lot. God created us with a desire to connect with other people. Friendships are some of the best gifts he gives us. Take a look at the Livin' It page on friendship, 1 Samuel 18:1, p. 378, to see what else the Bible says about friends.

It's okay to be sad about losing your friend, Lindsay, but that shouldn't keep you from looking for new ones. You never know where your new best friend is going to come from. The key is to be patient. God promises to give us what we need when we need it—and that includes friends!

sprinkling blood, meat forks, and pans for
carrying the fire. 4He made a large
bronze screen to hold the burning wood
for the altar and put it inside the altar,
under its rim, halfway up from the bottom. 5He made bronze rings to hold the
poles for carrying the altar, and he put
them at the four corners of the screen.
6Then he made poles of acacia wood and
covered them with bronze. 7He put the
poles through the rings on both sides of
the altar, to carry it. He made the altar of
boards and left the inside hollow.

The Bronze Bowl

8He made the bronze bowl for washing, and he built it on a bronze stand. He
used the bronze from mirrors that belonged to the women who served at the
entrance to the Meeting Tent.

The Courtyard of the Holy Tent

9Then he made a wall of curtains to
form a courtyard around the Holy Tent.
On the south side the curtains were one
hundred fifty feet long and were made of
fine linen. 10The curtains hung on silver
hooks and bands, placed on twenty
bronze posts with twenty bronze bases.
11On the north side the wall of curtains
was also one hundred fifty feet long, and
it hung on silver hooks and bands on
twenty posts with twenty bronze bases.

12On the west side of the courtyard,
the wall of curtains was seventy-five feet
long. It was held up by silver hooks and
bands on ten posts with ten bases. 13The
east side was also seventy-five feet long.
14On one side of the entry there was a
wall of curtains twenty-two and one-half
feet long, held up by three posts and
three bases. 15On the other side of the
entry there was also a wall of curtains
twenty-two and one-half feet long, held
up by three posts and three bases. 16All
the curtains around the courtyard were
made of fine linen. 17The bases for the
posts were made of bronze. The hooks
and the bands on the posts were made of
silver, and the tops of the posts were covered with silver also. All the posts in the
courtyard had silver bands.

18The curtain for the entry of the
courtyard was made of blue, purple, and
red thread, and fine linen, sewn by a person who could sew well. The curtain was
thirty feet long and seven and one-half
feet high, the same height as the curtains
around the courtyard. 19It was held up by
four posts and four bronze bases. The
hooks and bands on the posts were made
of silver, and the tops on the posts were
covered with silver. 20All the tent pegs
for the Holy Tent and for the curtains
around the courtyard were made of
bronze.

21This is a list of the materials used to
make the Holy Tent, where the Agreement was kept. Moses ordered the Levites to make this list, and Ithamar son
of Aaron was in charge of keeping it.
22Bezalel son of Uri, the son of Hur of
the tribe of Judah, made everything the
LORD commanded Moses. 23Oholiab son
of Ahisamach of the tribe of Dan helped
him. He could cut designs into metal
and stone; he was a designer and also
skilled at sewing the blue, purple, and red
thread, and fine linen.

24The total amount of gold used to
build the Holy Tent was presented to the
LORD. It weighed over 2,000 pounds, as
set by the Holy Place measure.

25The silver was given by the
members of the community who were
counted. It weighed 7,550 pounds, as set
by the Holy Place measure. 26All the
men twenty years old or older were
counted. There were 603,550 men, and
each man had to pay one-fifth of an ounce
of silver, as set by the Holy Place measure. 27Of this silver, 7,500 pounds were
used to make the one hundred bases for
the Holy Tent and for the curtain—75
pounds of silver in each base. 28They
used 50 pounds of silver to make the
hooks for the posts and to cover the tops
of the posts and to make the bands on
them.

29The bronze which was presented to
the LORD weighed about 5,000 pounds.
30They used the bronze to make the bases at the entrance of the Meeting Tent, to
make the altar and the bronze screen, and
to make all the tools for the altar. 31This
bronze was also used to make bases for

the wall of curtains around the courtyard
and bases for curtains at the entry to the
courtyard, as well as to make the tent
pegs for the Holy Tent and the curtains
that surrounded the courtyard.

Clothes for the Priests

39 They used blue, purple, and red
thread to make woven clothes for
the priests to wear when they served in
the Holy Place. They made the holy
clothes for Aaron as the LORD had commanded Moses.

2They made the holy vest of gold, and
blue, purple, and red thread, and fine lin-
en. **3**They hammered the gold into
sheets and then cut it into long, thin
strips. They worked the gold into the
blue, purple, and red thread, and fine
linen. This was done by skilled craftsmen. **4**They made the shoulder straps for
the holy vest, which were attached to the
top corners of the vest and tied together
over each shoulder. **5**The skillfully woven belt was made in the same way; it
was joined to the holy vest as one piece.
It was made of gold, and blue, purple, and
red thread, and fine linen, the way the
LORD commanded Moses.

6They put gold around the onyx
stones and then wrote the names of the
sons of Israel on these gems, as a person carves words and designs on a seal.
7Then they attached the gems on the
shoulder straps of the holy vest, as reminders of the twelve sons of Israel.
This was done just as the LORD had
commanded Moses.

8The skilled craftsmen made the
chest covering like the holy vest; it was
made of gold, and blue, purple, and red
thread, and fine linen. **9**The chest covering was square—nine inches long and
nine inches wide—and it was folded double to make a pocket. **10**Then they put
four rows of beautiful jewels on it: In the
first row there was a ruby, a topaz, and a
yellow quartz; **11**in the second there was
a turquoise, a sapphire, and an emerald;
12in the third there was a jacinth, an agate, and an amethyst; **13**in the fourth
there was a chrysolite, an onyx, and a jasper. Gold was put around these jewels to
attach them to the chest covering, **14**and
the names of the sons of Israel were
carved on these twelve jewels as a person carves a seal. Each jewel had the
name of one of the twelve tribes of Israel.

15They made chains of pure gold,
twisted together like a rope, for the chest
covering. **16**The workers made two gold
pieces and two gold rings. They put the
two gold rings on the two upper corners
of the chest covering. **17**Then they put
two gold chains in the two rings at the
ends of the chest covering, **18**and they
fastened the other two ends of the chains
to the two gold pieces. They attached
these gold pieces to the two shoulder
straps in the front of the holy vest.
19They made two gold rings and put
them at the lower corners of the chest
covering on the inside edge next to the
holy vest. **20**They made two more gold
rings on the bottom of the shoulder
straps in front of the holy vest, near the
seam, just above the woven belt of the
holy vest. **21**They used a blue ribbon and
tied the rings of the chest covering to the
rings of the holy vest, connecting it to the
woven belt. In this way the chest covering would not swing out from the holy
vest. They did all these things the way
the LORD commanded.

22Then they made the outer robe to
be worn under the holy vest. It was woven only of blue cloth. **23**They made a
hole in the center of the outer robe,
with a woven collar sewn around it so it
would not tear. **24**Then they made balls
like pomegranates of blue, purple, and
red thread, and fine linen and hung
them around the bottom of the outer
robe. **25**They also made bells of pure
gold and hung these around the bottom
of the outer robe between the balls.
26So around the bottom of the outer
robe there was a bell and a pomegranate ball, a bell and a pomegranate ball.
The priest wore this outer robe when
he served as priest, just as the LORD
had commanded Moses.

27They wove inner robes of fine linen
for Aaron and his sons, **28**and they made
turbans, headbands, and underclothes of
fine linen. **29**Then they made the cloth

belt of fine linen, and blue, purple, and red thread, and designs were sewn onto it, just as the LORD had commanded Moses.

30They made a strip of pure gold, which is the holy crown, and carved these words in the gold, as one might carve on a seal: "Holy to the LORD." **31**Then they tied this flat piece to the turban with a blue ribbon, as the LORD had commanded Moses.

32So all the work on the Meeting Tent was finished. The Israelites did everything just as the LORD had commanded Moses. **33**Then they brought the Holy Tent to Moses: the Tent and all its furniture, hooks, frames, crossbars, posts, and bases; **34**the covering made of male sheepskins colored red, the covering made of fine leather, and the curtain that covered the entrance to the Most Holy Place; **35**the Ark of the Agreement, its poles and lid; **36**the table, all its containers, and the bread that showed they were in God's presence; **37**the pure gold lampstand with its lamps in a row, all its tools, and the olive oil for the light; **38**the gold altar, the special olive oil used for appointing priests, the sweet-smelling incense, and the curtain that covered the entrance to the Tent; **39**the bronze altar and its screen, its poles and all its tools, the bowl and its stand; **40**the curtains for the courtyard with their posts and bases, the curtain that covered the entry to the courtyard, the cords, pegs, and all the things in the Meeting Tent. **41**They brought the clothes for the priests to wear when they served in the Holy Tent—the holy clothes for Aaron the priest and the clothes for his sons, which they wore when they served as priests.

42The Israelites had done all this work just as the LORD had commanded Moses. **43**Moses looked closely at all the work and saw they had done it just as the LORD had commanded. So Moses blessed them.

The Israelites had done all this work just as the LORD had commanded Moses.
—Exodus 39:42

Setting Up the Holy Tent

40 Then the LORD said to Moses: **2**"On the first day of the first month, set up the Holy Tent, which is the Meeting Tent. **3**Put the Ark of the Agreement in it and hang the curtain in front of the Ark. **4**Bring in the table and arrange everything on the table that should be there. Then bring in the lampstand and set up its lamps. **5**Put the gold altar for burning incense in front of the Ark of the Agreement, and put the curtain at the entrance to the Holy Tent.

6"Put the altar of burnt offerings in front of the entrance of the Holy Tent, the Meeting Tent. **7**Put the bowl between the Meeting Tent and the altar, and put water in it. **8**Set up the courtyard around the Holy Tent, and put the curtain at the entry to the courtyard.

9"Use the special olive oil and pour it on the Holy Tent and everything in it, in order to give the Tent and all that is in it for service to the LORD. They will be holy. **10**Pour the special oil on the altar for burnt offerings and on all its tools. Give the altar for service to God, and it will be very holy. **11**Then pour the special olive oil on the bowl and the base under it so that they will be given for service to God.

12"Bring Aaron and his sons to the entrance of the Meeting Tent, and wash them with water. **13**Then put the holy clothes on Aaron. Pour the special oil on him, and give him for service to God so that he may serve me as a priest. **14**Bring Aaron's sons and put the inner robes on them. **15**Pour the special oil on them in the same way that you appointed their father as priest so that they may also serve me as priests. Pouring oil on them will make them a family of priests, they and their descendants from now on." **16**Moses did everything that the LORD commanded him.

17So the Holy Tent was set up on the first day of the first month during the second year after they left Egypt. **18**When

Moses set up the Holy Tent, he put the
bases in place, and he put the frames on
the bases. Next he put the crossbars
through the rings of the frames and set
up the posts. **19**After that, Moses spread
the cloth over the Holy Tent and put the
covering over it, just as the LORD commanded.
20Moses put the stone tablets that
had the Agreement written on them into
the Ark. He put the poles through the
rings of the Ark and put the lid on it.
21Next he brought the Ark into the Tent
and hung the curtain to cover the Ark,
just as the LORD commanded him.
22Moses put the table in the Meeting
Tent on the north side of the Holy Tent in
front of the curtain. **23**Then he put the
bread on the table before the LORD, just
as the LORD commanded him. **24**Moses
put the lampstand in the Meeting Tent on
the south side of the Holy Tent across
from the table. **25**Then he put the lamps
on the lampstand before the LORD, just as
the LORD commanded him.
26Moses put the gold altar for burning
incense in the Meeting Tent in front of
the curtain. **27**Then he burned sweet-
smelling incense on it, just as the LORD
commanded him. **28**Then he hung the
curtain at the entrance to the Holy Tent.
29He put the altar for burnt offerings
at the entrance to the Holy Tent, the
Meeting Tent, and offered a whole burnt
offering and grain offerings on it, just
as the LORD commanded him. **30**Moses
put the bowl between the Meeting Tent
and the altar for burnt offerings, and he
put water in it for washing. **31**Moses,
Aaron, and Aaron's sons used this water
to wash their hands and feet. **32**They
washed themselves every time they entered the Meeting Tent and every time
they went near the altar for burnt offerings, just as the LORD commanded Moses.
33Then Moses set up the courtyard
around the Holy Tent and the altar, and he
put up the curtain at the entry to the
courtyard. So Moses finished the work.

The Cloud over the Holy Tent

34Then the cloud covered the Meeting Tent, and the glory of the LORD filled
the Holy Tent. **35**Moses could not enter
the Meeting Tent, because the cloud had
settled on it, and the glory of the LORD
filled the Holy Tent.
36When the cloud rose from the Holy
Tent, the Israelites would begin to travel,
37but as long as the cloud stayed on
the Holy Tent, they did not travel. They

FAITH links

THE SIGN OF HIS PRESENCE

EXODUS 40:34-38

God appeared to the Israelites in the form of a cloud. When the people of Israel saw the cloud hovering over the Meeting Tent, they knew that God was with them. The Holy Spirit is the sign of God's presence today. Before leaving the earth, Jesus promised that the Holy Spirit would come. He came at Pentecost. Jesus promised that the Holy Spirit would come and live within anyone who believes in Jesus. Although we can't see him, we can trust that he's there.

A Priest Without Sin, Leviticus 4:3–7, p. 136

The Cloud Guide, Numbers 9:15–23, p. 188

God's New Home, 2 Chronicles 7:11–22, p. 570

The Dead End of Occult, Ezekiel 13:17–23, p. 1098

Fully God, Fully Human, John 11:35, p. 1444

Just for the Asking, Romans 3:23–28, p. 1522

stayed in that place until the cloud rose.
38So the cloud of the LORD was over the
Holy Tent during the day, and there was
a fire in the cloud at night. So all the Israelites could see the cloud while they traveled.

RULE, RULES, RULES

It's me, Moses, the leader of God's people. Perhaps you've read my previous book, Exodus? I wrote the Book of Leviticus shortly after we escaped Egypt and were camped in the desert near Mount Sinai. (For the incredible story of how God appeared on the mountain and spoke to me, be sure to plug into Exodus 19:16–25, p. 101.) Leviticus is a rulebook for the nation of Israel. You may not like rules, but they are important. God gave us rules so we could be healthy (In Leviticus 11, God even told the people what to eat!) and rules for special holidays, like Passover.

I wrote this book so that the people of Israel would know how to please God. As you probably already figured out from the title, Leviticus has many rules for the Levites, the family God chose to be our priests. Because God is holy, the people could not come into his presence without a sacrifice for their sins. This book tells the priests how to make sacrifices, so sins will be forgiven.

JESUS WATCH

God is holy and wants us to be holy, too. Because of our sins we could never be holy enough to be with God. In Leviticus, God gave rules for offerings so the people could atone or "pay" for their sins with the sacrifice of an animal. The animal was to be young and have nothing wrong with it. When the animal was sacrificed on the altar, it took the place of the person who sinned and deserved punishment. Because people sin more than once, sacrifices had to be offered again and again. All of these sacrifices point to the perfect sacrifice, Jesus, who died one time to take away all our sins. Like the sacrificed animals, he took the punishment we deserve for our sins. When our sins are forgiven, we are made holy by the sacrifice Jesus made for us.

my FAVORITE links

_______________ _______________

_______________ _______________

_______________ _______________

_______________ _______________

OTHER CONNECTIONS

How important is it to you to be one of the crowd? Will you do *anything* just to fit in with your friends, or are you willing to stand against those things you think are wrong? It's not easy to go against the crowd. That's why God has a lot to say about it. Check it out by connecting to Totally "Uncool"?, Leviticus 18:1–5.

Do you know what was the most important possession the Israelites had? Find out more about this most holy item by checking into:

- God's Presence with the Israelites, Leviticus 16:1–15. The Israelites believed they had God's presence with them at all times because they carried around the Ark of the Agreement. How do you know God is with you?

MORE STUFF . . .

Rules to Eat By Check out what God said to the Israelites about what they could and could not eat. You can read about it in Leviticus 11.

- The people could eat cows, but not camels, rabbits, or pigs.
- They could not eat eagles, vultures, owls, storks, or bats.
- They could eat locusts, grasshoppers, and crickets.

"Boy, Skweek, there sure are a lot of rules in Leviticus."

"You're right, Tagg. But the rules are there to help God's people live healthy and happy lives. Connect to these sites to find out more."

did YOU know?

OTHER SITES TO VISIT:

Bugs you can eat, Leviticus 11:21–25
The goat that removes sin, Leviticus 16:7–10
Don't go to fortune-tellers, Leviticus 20:6
One day to rest, Leviticus 23:3
The year of Jubilee, Leviticus 25:8–22

FAITH links

- A Priest Without Sin, **Leviticus 4:3–7**
- Help for the Poor, **Leviticus 5:7**
- A Different Kind of People, **Leviticus 11**
- An Example Not to Follow, **Leviticus 18:1–3**
- Show Some Respect, **Leviticus 19:32**
- A Holiday Every Week, **Leviticus 23:1–3**
- Reward for Obedience, **Leviticus 26:3–13**
- Giving Your Part, **Leviticus 27:30**

The Burnt Offering

1 The LORD called to Moses and spoke
to him from the Meeting Tent, saying,
2"Tell the people of Israel: 'When you
bring an offering to the LORD, bring as
your offering an animal from the herd or
flock.

3" 'If the offering is a whole burnt offering from the herd, it must be a male
that has nothing wrong with it. The person must take the animal to the entrance
of the Meeting Tent so that the LORD will
accept the offering. 4He must put his
hand on the animal's head, and the LORD
will accept it to remove the person's sin
so he will belong to God. 5He must kill
the young bull before the LORD, and
Aaron's sons, the priests, must bring its
blood and sprinkle it on all sides of the
altar at the entrance to the Meeting Tent.
6After that he will skin the animal and
cut it into pieces. 7The priests, when
they have put wood and fire on the altar,
8are to lay the head, the fat, and other
pieces on the wood that is on the fire of
the altar. 9The animal's inner organs and
legs must be washed with water. Then
the priest must burn all the animal's
parts on the altar. It is a whole burnt offering, an offering made by fire, and its
smell is pleasing to the LORD.

10" 'If the burnt offering is a sheep or
a goat from the flock, it must be a male
that has nothing wrong with it. 11The
person must kill the animal on the north
side of the altar before the LORD, and
Aaron's sons, the priests, must sprinkle
its blood on all sides of the altar. 12The
person must cut the animal into pieces,
and the priest must lay them, with the
head and fat, on the wood that is on the
fire of the altar. 13The person must wash
the animal's inner organs and legs with
water, and then the priest must burn all
its parts on the altar. It is a whole burnt
offering, an offering made by fire, and its
smell is pleasing to the LORD.

14" 'If the whole burnt offering for the
LORD is a bird, it must be a dove or a
young pigeon. 15The priest will bring it
to the altar and pull off its head, which he
will burn on the altar; the bird's blood
must be drained out on the side of the altar. 16The priest must remove the bird's
crop[n] and its contents and throw them on
the east side of the altar, where the ashes
are. 17Then he must tear the bird open
by its wings without dividing it into two
parts. He must burn the bird on the altar,
on the wood which is on the fire. It is a
whole burnt offering, an offering made by
fire, and its smell is pleasing to the LORD.

The Grain Offering

2 " 'When anyone offers a grain offering to the LORD, it must be made from
fine flour. The person must pour oil on it,
put incense on it, 2and then take it to
Aaron's sons, the priests. The priest
must take a handful of the fine flour and
oil and all the incense, and burn it on the
altar as a memorial portion. It is an offering made by fire, and its smell is pleasing
to the LORD. 3The rest of the grain offering will belong to Aaron and the priests;
it is a most holy part of the offerings
made by fire to the LORD.

4" 'If you bring a grain offering that
was baked in the oven, it must be made
from fine flour. It may be loaves made
without yeast and mixed with oil, or it
may be wafers made without yeast that
have oil poured over them. 5If your grain
offering is cooked on a griddle, it must be
made, without yeast, of fine flour mixed
with oil. 6Crumble it and pour oil over it;
it is a grain offering. 7If your grain offering is cooked in a pan, it must be made
from fine flour and oil. 8Bring the grain
offering made of these things to the
LORD. Give it to the priest, and he will
take it to the altar. 9He will take out the
memorial portion from the grain offering
and burn it on the altar, as an offering
made by fire. Its smell is pleasing to the
LORD. 10The rest of the grain offering
belongs to Aaron and the priests. It is a
most holy part of the offerings made to
the LORD by fire.

11" 'Every grain offering you bring to
the LORD must be made without yeast,

1:16 crop A small bag inside a bird's throat. When a bird eats, its food goes into this part first. There, the food is made soft before it goes into the stomach.

FAITH links

THE PERFECT SACRIFICE

LEVITICUS 1–7

During Old Testament times, the Israelites were required to offer many different kinds of sacrifices. Each sacrifice had very specific instructions. Sacrifices were the only way that sins could be forgiven. An animal or grain sacrifice was offered on the altar at the Meeting Tent. The animal or crops had to be perfect—no flaws.

Today we do not need to offer sacrifices to God. Why? Because Jesus has already been sacrificed for us. He is the only one perfect enough to be offered for the sins of the whole world. No other sacrifice will ever be needed. Anyone who accepts that sacrifice on his or her behalf will be forgiven.

Can't Live Without It, Genesis 3, p. 7

Count on His Mercy, Judges 2:16–17; 3, p. 313

The Cover-up, Psalm 32:1–2, p. 733

The Watchman, Ezekiel 3:16–22, p. 1088

A Change of Heart, Matthew 3:1–12, p. 1277

The Sin Habit, Romans 7:15–20, p. 1527

because you must not burn any yeast or
honey in an offering made by fire to the
LORD. **12**You may bring yeast and honey
to the LORD as an offering from the first
harvest, but they must not be burned on
the altar as a pleasing smell. **13**You must
also put salt on all your grain offerings.
Salt stands for your agreement with God
that will last forever; do not leave it out of
your grain offering. You must add salt to
all your offerings.

14" 'If you bring a grain offering from
the first harvest to the LORD, bring
crushed heads of new grain roasted in the
fire. **15**Put oil and incense on it; it is a
grain offering. **16**The priest will burn the
memorial portion of the crushed grain
and oil, with the incense on it. It is an offering by fire to the LORD.

The Fellowship Offering

3 " 'If a person's fellowship offering to
the LORD is from the herd, it may be a
male or female, but it must have nothing
wrong with it. **2**The person must put his
hand on the animal's head and kill it at
the entrance to the Meeting Tent. Then
Aaron's sons, the priests, must sprinkle
the blood on all sides of the altar. **3**From
the fellowship offering he must make a
sacrifice by fire to the LORD. He must offer the fat of the animal's inner organs
(both the fat that is in them and that covers them), **4**both kidneys with the fat that
is on them near the lower back muscle,
and the best part of the liver, which he
will remove with the kidneys. **5**Then the
priests will burn these parts on the altar,
on the whole burnt offering that is on the
wood of the fire. It is an offering made by
fire, and its smell is pleasing to the LORD.

6" 'If a person's fellowship offering to
the LORD is a lamb or a goat, it may be a
male or female, but it must have nothing
wrong with it. **7**If he offers a lamb, he
must bring it before the LORD **8**and put
his hand on its head. Then he must kill
the animal in front of the Meeting Tent,
and the priests must sprinkle its blood on
all sides of the altar. **9**From the fellowship
offering the person must make a sacrifice
by fire to the LORD. He must bring the
fat, the whole fat tail cut off close to the
backbone, the fat of the inner organs
(both the fat that is in them and that covers them), **10**both kidneys with the fat

that is on them, near the lower back
muscle, and the best part of the liver,
which he will remove with the kidneys.
11Then the priest will burn these parts
on the altar as food; it will be an offering
made by fire to the LORD.

12" 'If a person's offering is a goat, he
must offer it before the LORD **13**and put
his hand on its head. Then he must kill it
in front of the Meeting Tent, and the
priests must sprinkle its blood on all
sides of the altar. **14**From this offering
the person must make a sacrifice by fire
to the LORD. He must offer all the fat of
the goat's inner organs (both the fat that
is in them and that covers them), **15**both
kidneys with the fat that is on them near
the lower back muscle, and the best part
of the liver, which he will remove with
the kidneys. **16**The priest will burn these
parts on the altar as food. It is an offering
made by fire, and its smell is pleasing to
the LORD. All the fat belongs to the LORD.

17" 'This law will continue for people
from now on, wherever you live: You
must not eat any fat or blood.' "

The Sin Offering

4 The LORD said to Moses, **2**"Tell the
people of Israel this: 'When a person
sins by accident and does some things
the LORD has commanded not to be done,
that person must do these things:

3" 'If the appointed priest sins so that
he brings guilt on the people, then he
must offer a young bull to the LORD, one
that has nothing wrong with it, as a sin
offering for the sin he has done. **4**He will
bring the bull to the entrance of the
Meeting Tent in front of the LORD, put his
hand on its head, and kill it before the
LORD. **5**Then the appointed priest must
bring some of the bull's blood into the
Meeting Tent. **6**The priest is to dip his
finger into the blood and sprinkle it seven
times before the LORD in front of the curtain of the Most Holy Place. **7**The priest
must also put some of the blood on the
corners of the altar of incense that stands
before the LORD in the Meeting Tent.
The rest of the blood he must pour out at
the bottom of the altar of burnt offering,
which is at the entrance of the Meeting
Tent. **8**He must remove all the fat from
the bull of the sin offering—the fat on and
around the inner organs, **9**both kidneys
with the fat that is on them near the

FAITH links

A PRIEST WITHOUT SIN

LEVITICUS 4:3-7

Even people of God sin. God required a certain sacrifice to be made when the appointed priest (the high priest) sinned. When this priest sinned, however, his sin brought guilt on everyone. After all, he was the one who usually offered the sacrifices. He had to offer a special sacrifice to cleanse all of their sin.

Jesus is called our "great high priest." (Check out Hebrews 4:14, p. 1671.) Jesus is the only sinless high priest. When God looks at your sin, he sees only the sacrifice that Jesus made for you.

Check out these other Faithlinks on how God forgives us:

Own Up to It, 2 Samuel 12:1–3, p. 412

Dirty Inside, Isaiah 6:1–7, p. 904

Believe the Impossible?, Ezekiel 37, p. 1131

Inside the Heart of God, Micah 7:18–20, p. 1228

Clean Inside and Out, Luke 11:39–40, p. 1392

That's Much Better!, Ephesians 2:4–5, p. 1599

lower back muscle, and the best part of
the liver which he will remove with the
kidneys. **10**(He must do this in the same
way the fat is removed from the bull of
the fellowship offering.) Then the priest
must burn the animal parts on the altar of
burnt offering. **11**But the priest must
carry off the skin of the bull and all its
meat, along with the rest of the bull—its
head, legs, intestines, and other inner
organs. **12**He must take it outside the
camp to the special clean place where the
ashes are poured out. He must burn it on
a wood fire on the pile of ashes.

13" 'If the whole nation of Israel sins
accidentally without knowing it and does
something the LORD has commanded not
to be done, they are guilty. **14**When they
learn about the sin they have done, they
must offer a young bull as a sin offering
and bring it before the Meeting Tent.
15The older leaders of the group of people must put their hands on the bull's
head before the LORD, and it must be
killed before the LORD. **16**Then the appointed priest must bring some of the
bull's blood into the Meeting Tent.
17Dipping his finger in the blood, he
must sprinkle it seven times before the
LORD in front of the curtain. **18**Then he
must put some of the blood on the corners of the altar that is before the LORD
in the Meeting Tent. The priest must
pour out the rest of the blood at the bottom of the altar of burnt offering, which is
at the entrance to the Meeting Tent.
19He must remove all the fat from the
animal and burn it on the altar; **20**he will
do the same thing with this bull that he
did with the first bull of the sin offering.
In this way the priest removes the sins of
the people so they will belong to the
LORD and be forgiven. **21**Then the priest
must carry the bull outside the camp and
burn it, just as he did with the first bull.
This is the sin offering for the whole
community.

22" 'If a ruler sins by accident and
does something the LORD his God has
commanded must not be done, he is
guilty. **23**When he learns about his sin, he
must bring a male goat that has nothing
wrong with it as his offering. **24**The ruler
must put his hand on the goat's head and
kill it in the place where they kill the
whole burnt offering before the LORD; it
is a sin offering. **25**The priest must take
some of the blood of the sin offering on
his finger and put it on the corners of the
altar of burnt offering. He must pour out
the rest of the blood at the bottom of the
altar of burnt offering. **26**He must burn
all the goat's fat on the altar in the same
way he burns the fat of the fellowship offerings. In this way the priest removes
the ruler's sin so he belongs to the LORD,
and the LORD will forgive him.

27" 'If any person in the community
sins by accident and does something
which the LORD has commanded must
not be done, he is guilty. **28**When the person learns about his sin, he must bring a
female goat that has nothing wrong with
it as an offering for his sin. **29**He must
put his hand on the animal's head and kill
it at the place of the whole burnt offering.
30Then the priest must take some of the
goat's blood on his finger and put it on the
corners of the altar of burnt offering. He
must pour out the rest of the goat's blood
at the bottom of the altar. **31**Then the
priest must remove all the goat's fat in
the same way the fat is removed from the
fellowship offerings. He must burn it on
the altar as a smell pleasing to the LORD.
In this way the priest will remove that
person's sin so he will belong to the
LORD, and the LORD will forgive him.

32" 'If this person brings a lamb as his
offering for sin, he must bring a female
that has nothing wrong with it. **33**He
must put his hand on the animal's head
and kill it as a sin offering in the place
where the whole burnt offering is killed.
34The priest must take some of the blood
from the sin offering on his finger and put
it on the corners of the altar of burnt offering. He must pour out the rest of the
lamb's blood at the bottom of the altar.
35Then the priest must remove all the
lamb's fat in the same way that the lamb's
fat is removed from the fellowship offerings. He must burn the pieces on the
altar on top of the offerings made by fire
for the LORD. In this way the priest will
remove that person's sins so he will

belong to the LORD, and the LORD will
forgive him.

Special Types of Accidental Sins

5 " 'If a person is ordered to tell in
court what he has seen or what he
knows and he does not tell the court, he
is guilty of sin.
2" 'Or someone might touch something unclean, such as the dead body of
an unclean wild animal or an unclean
farm animal or an unclean crawling animal. Even if he does not know that he
touched it, he will still be unclean and
guilty of sin.
3" 'Someone might touch human uncleanness—anything that makes someone unclean—and not know it. But when
he learns about it, he will be guilty.
4" 'Or someone might make a promise before the LORD without thinking. It
might be a promise to do something bad
or something good; it might be about anything. Even if he forgets about it, when
he remembers, he will be guilty.
5" 'When anyone is guilty of any of
these things, he must tell how he sinned.
6He must bring an offering to the LORD
as a penalty for sin; it must be a female
lamb or goat from the flock. The priest
will perform the acts to remove that
person's sin so he will belong to the
LORD.
7" 'But if the person cannot afford a
lamb, he must bring two doves or two
young pigeons to the LORD as the penalty
for his sin. One bird must be for a sin offering, and the other must be for a whole
burnt offering. 8He must bring them to
the priest, who will first offer the one for
the sin offering. He will pull the bird's
head from its neck, but he will not pull it
completely off. 9He must sprinkle the
blood from the sin offering on the side of
the altar, and then he must pour the rest
of the blood at the bottom of the altar; it
is a sin offering. 10Then the priest must
offer the second bird as a whole burnt offering, as the law says. In this way the
priest will remove the person's sin so he
will belong to the LORD, and the LORD
will forgive him.
11" 'If the person cannot afford two
doves or two pigeons, he must bring
about two quarts of fine flour as an offering for sin. He must not put oil or incense
on the flour, because it is a sin offering.
12He must bring the flour to the priest.
The priest will take a handful of the flour

FAITH links

HELP FOR THE POOR

LEVITICUS 5:7

Throughout the Old Testament are laws written with the poor in mind. God had great concern for the poor. He even came up with a sin offering that the poor could afford. They could sacrifice two doves or two pigeons. This is the offering Mary brought to the temple when Jesus was presented. (See Luke 2:22–24, p. 1369.)

God still looks out for those who are poor or suffering in some way. Sometimes he shows his kindness through people. How will you show God's kindness to those who are poor or suffering?

Yours, Mine, and Ours?, 1 Samuel 25, p. 389

Your Best Work, 1 Kings 6, p. 443

You Are What You Do, Proverbs 20:11, p. 854

Love Him? Show It!, Amos 2:6–7, p. 1196

The Greatest Commandment, Matthew 22:36–40, p. 1313

The Person Most Likely to Give?, Acts 9:36–42, p. 1481

as a memorial offering and burn it on the
altar on top of the offerings made by fire
to the LORD; it is a sin offering. **13**In this
way the priest will remove the person's
sins so he will belong to
the LORD, and the LORD
will forgive him. What is
left of the sin offering belongs to the priest, like
the grain offering.' "

> If he does any of these things, he is guilty of sin.
> —Leviticus 6:4

The Penalty Offering

14The LORD said to
Moses, **15**"If a person accidentally sins and does
something against the
holy things of the LORD, he must bring
from the flock a male sheep that has
nothing wrong with it. This will be his
penalty offering to the LORD. Its value in
silver must be correct as set by the Holy
Place measure. It is a penalty offering.
16That person must pay for the sin he did
against the holy thing, adding one-fifth to
its value. Then he must give it all to the
priest. In this way the priest will remove
the person's sin so he will belong to the
LORD, by using the male sheep as the
penalty offering. And the LORD will forgive the person.

17"If a person sins and does something the LORD has commanded not to be
done, even if he does not know it, he is
still guilty. He is responsible for his sin.
18He must bring the priest a male sheep
from the flock, one that has nothing
wrong with it and that is worth the correct amount. It will be a penalty offering.
Though the person sinned without knowing it, with this offering the priest will remove the sin so the person will belong to
the LORD, and the LORD will forgive him.
19The person is guilty of doing wrong, so
he must give the penalty offering to the
LORD."

6 The LORD said to Moses, **2**"A person
might sin against the LORD by doing
one of these sins: He might lie about
what happened to something he was taking care of for someone else, or he might
lie about a promise he made. He might
steal something or cheat someone. **3**He
might find something that had been lost
and then lie about it. He might make a
promise before the LORD about something and not mean it, or he might do
some other sin. **4**If he does any of these
things, he is guilty of sin.
He must bring back what-
ever he stole or whatever
he took by cheating. He
must bring back the thing
he took care of for some-
one else. He must bring
back what he found and
lied about **5**or what he
made a false promise
about. He must pay the
full price plus an extra
one-fifth of the value of what he took. He
must give the money to the true owner
on the day he brings his penalty offering.
6He must bring his penalty to the
priest—a male sheep from the flock, one
that does not have anything wrong with it
and that is worth the correct amount. It
will be a penalty offering to the LORD.
7Then the priest will perform the acts to
remove that person's sin so he will belong to the LORD, and the LORD will forgive him for the sins that made him
guilty."

The Whole Burnt Offering

8The LORD said to Moses, **9**"Give this
command to Aaron and the priests:
'These are the teachings about the whole
burnt offering: The burnt offering must
stay on the altar all night until morning,
and the altar's fire must be kept burning.
10The priest must put on his linen robe
and linen underclothes next to his body.
Then he will remove the ashes from the
burnt offering on the altar and put them
beside the altar. **11**Then he must take off
those clothes and put on others and carry
the ashes outside the camp to a special
clean place. **12**But the fire must be kept
burning on the altar; it must not be allowed to go out. The priest must put
more firewood on the altar every morning, place the whole burnt offering on the
fire, and burn the fat of the fellowship
offerings. **13**The fire must be kept burning on the altar all the time; it must not
go out.

The Grain Offering

14" 'These are the teachings about
the grain offering: The priests must bring
it to the LORD in front of the altar. 15The
priest must take a handful of fine flour,
with the oil and all of the incense on it,
and burn the grain offering on the altar as
a memorial offering to the LORD. Its
smell is pleasing to him. 16Aaron and the
priests may eat what is left, but it must
be eaten without yeast in a holy place.
They must eat it in the courtyard of the
Meeting Tent. 17It must not be cooked
with yeast. I have given it as their share
of the offerings made to me by fire; it is
most holy, like the sin offering and the
penalty offering. 18Any male descendant
of Aaron may eat it as his share of the offerings made to the LORD by fire, and this
will continue from now on. Whatever
touches these offerings shall become
holy.' "

19The LORD said to Moses, 20"This is
the offering Aaron and the priests must
bring to the LORD on the day they appoint
Aaron as high priest: They must bring
two quarts of fine flour for a continual
grain offering, half of it in the morning
and half in the evening. 21The fine flour
must be mixed with oil and cooked on a
griddle. Bring it when it is well mixed.
Present the grain offering that is broken
into pieces, and it will be a smell that
is pleasing to the LORD. 22One of the
priests appointed to take Aaron's place as
high priest must make the grain offering.
It is a rule forever that the grain offering
must be completely burned to the LORD.
23Every grain offering made by a priest
must be completely burned; it must not
be eaten."

The Sin Offering

24The LORD said to Moses, 25"Tell
Aaron and the priests: 'These are the
teachings about the sin offering: The sin
offering must be killed in front of the
LORD in the same place the whole burnt
offering is killed; it is most holy. 26The
priest who offers the sin offering must
eat it in a holy place, in the courtyard of
the Meeting Tent. 27Whatever touches
the meat of the sin offering must be holy,
and if the blood is sprinkled on any
clothes, you must wash them in a holy
place. 28The clay pot the meat is cooked
in must be broken, or if a bronze pot is
used, it must be scrubbed and rinsed with
water. 29Any male in a priest's family
may eat the offering; it is most holy.
30But if the blood of the sin offering is
taken into the Meeting Tent and used to
remove sin in the Holy Place, that sin offering must be burned with fire. It must
not be eaten.

The Penalty Offering

7 " 'These are the teachings about the
penalty offering, which is most holy:
2The penalty offering must be killed
where the whole burnt offering is killed.
Then the priest must sprinkle its blood
on all sides of the altar. 3He must offer all
the fat from the penalty offering—the fat
tail, the fat that covers the inner organs,
4both kidneys with the fat that is on them
near the lower back muscle, and the best
part of the liver, which is to be removed
with the kidneys. 5The priest must burn
all these things on the altar as an offering
made by fire to the LORD. It is a penalty
offering. 6Any male in a priest's family
may eat it. It is most holy, so it must be
eaten in a holy place.

7" 'The penalty offering is like the sin
offering in that the teachings are the
same for both. The priest who offers the
sacrifice to remove sins will get the meat
for food. 8The priest who offers the burnt
offering may also have the skin from it.
9Every grain offering that is baked in an
oven, cooked on a griddle, or baked in a
dish belongs to the priest who offers it.
10Every grain offering, either dry or
mixed with oil, belongs to the priests,
and all priests will share alike.

The Fellowship Offering

11" 'These are the teachings about
the fellowship offering a person may offer
to the LORD: 12If he brings the fellowship
offering to show his thanks, he should
also bring loaves of bread made without
yeast that are mixed with oil, wafers
made without yeast that have oil poured
over them, and loaves of fine flour that

are mixed with oil. **13**He must also offer
loaves of bread made with yeast along
with his fellowship offering, which he
gives to show thanks. **14**One of each kind
of offering will be for the LORD; it will be
given to the priest who sprinkles the
blood of the fellowship offering. **15**When
the fellowship offering is given to thank
the LORD, the meat from it must be eaten
the same day it is offered; none of it must
be left until morning.

16" 'If a person brings a fellowship offering just to give a gift to God or because
of a special promise to him, the sacrifice
should be eaten the same day he offers it.
If there is any left, it may be eaten the
next day. **17**If any meat from this sacrifice
is left on the third day, it must be burned
up. **18**Any meat of the fellowship offering
eaten on the third day will not be accepted, nor will the sacrifice count for the
person who offered it. It will become unclean, and anyone who eats the meat will
be guilty of sin.

19" 'People must not eat meat that
touches anything unclean; they must
burn this meat with fire. Anyone who is
clean may eat other meat. **20**But if anyone is unclean and eats the meat from the
fellowship offering that belongs to the
LORD, he must be cut off from his people.

21" 'If anyone touches something

CHEEK TO CHEEK

Hi, everybody! Tagg and I are talking about dealing with people who are hard to get along with. Scott, age 10, knows someone who fits that exact description!

Welcome, Scott. Who do you want to tell us about?

Scott

It's my older brother. He picks on me all the time. Sometimes he pushes me around, but most of the time he just makes fun of me. It seems like I can't say or do anything without him laughing at me or telling me how dumb I am. Sometimes I get so mad that I try to hit him. Other times I just tell my mom what he's doing. But nothing seems to stop him.

Scott, Jesus set the example we should follow when someone hurts us. When people made fun of him, he did nothing. When people lied about him, he said nothing. When people hit him on one cheek, he gave them the other cheek to hit. "Turning the other cheek" is a tough thing to do, but it's the best way to handle people like your brother.

That's right, Scott. You can't control what your brother does, but you can make sure that *you* do everything possible to keep things peaceful between the two of you. Check out the Livin' It page on being a peacemaker, Romans 14:19, p. 1539. You may find some more tips on dealing with people who are hard to get along with.

unclean—uncleanness that comes from
people, from an animal, or from some
hated thing—touching it will make him
unclean. If he then eats meat from the fellowship offering that belongs to the LORD,
he must be cut off from his people.' "

22The LORD said to Moses, **23**"Tell
the people of Israel: 'You must not eat
any of the fat from cattle, sheep, or goats.
24If an animal is found dead or torn by
wild animals, you may use its fat for other
things, but you must not eat it. **25**If
someone eats fat from an animal offering
made by fire to the LORD, he must be cut
off from his people. **26**No matter where
you live, you must not eat blood from any
bird or animal. **27**Anyone who eats blood
must be cut off from his people.' "

The Priests' Share

28The LORD said to Moses, **29**"Tell
the people of Israel: 'If someone brings a
fellowship offering to the LORD, he must
give part of it as his sacrifice to the LORD.
30He must carry that part of the gift in
his own hands as an offering made by fire
to the LORD. He must bring the fat and
the breast of the animal to the priest, to
be presented to the LORD as the priests'
share. **31**Then the priest must burn the
fat on the altar, but the breast of the animal will belong to Aaron and the priests.
32You must also give the right thigh from
the fellowship offering to the priest as a
gift; **33**it will belong to the priest who offers the blood and fat of the fellowship offering. **34**I have taken the breast and the
thigh from the fellowship offerings of the
Israelites, and I have given these parts to
Aaron and the priests as their share for
all time from the Israelites.' "

35This is the portion that belongs to
Aaron and his sons from the offerings
made by fire to the LORD. They were
given this share on the day they were
presented to the LORD as priests. **36**On
the day the LORD appointed the priests,
he commanded Israel to give this share
to them, and it is to be given to the
priests as their share from now on.

37These are the teachings about the
whole burnt offering, the grain offering,
the sin offering, the penalty offering, the
offering for the appointment of priests,
and the fellowship offering. **38**The LORD
gave these teachings to Moses on Mount
Sinai on the day he commanded the Israelites to bring their offerings to the LORD
in the Sinai Desert.

Aaron and His Sons Appointed

8 The LORD said to Moses, **2**"Bring
Aaron and his sons and their clothes,
the special olive oil used in appointing
people and things to the service of the
LORD, the bull of the sin offering and the
two male sheep, and the basket of bread
made without yeast. **3**Then gather the
people together at the entrance to the
Meeting Tent." **4**Moses did as the LORD
commanded him, and the people met together at the entrance to the Meeting
Tent.

5Then Moses spoke to the people and
said, "This is what the LORD has commanded to be done." **6**Bringing Aaron
and his sons forward, Moses washed
them with water. **7**He put the inner robe
on Aaron and tied the cloth belt around
him. Then Moses put the outer robe on
him and placed the holy vest on him. He
tied the skillfully woven belt around him
so that the holy vest was tied to Aaron.
8Then Moses put the chest covering on
him and put the Urim and the Thummim
in the chest covering. **9**He also put the
turban on Aaron's head. He put the strip
of gold, the holy crown, on the front of
the turban, as the LORD commanded him
to do.

10Then Moses put the special oil on
the Holy Tent and everything in it, making them holy for the LORD. **11**He sprinkled some oil on the altar seven times,
sprinkling the altar and all its tools and
the large bowl and its base. In this way he
made them holy for the LORD. **12**He
poured some of the special oil on Aaron's
head to make Aaron holy for the LORD.
13Then Moses brought Aaron's sons forward. He put the inner robes on them,
tied cloth belts around them, and put
headbands on them, as the LORD had
commanded him.

14Then Moses brought the bull for
the sin offering, and Aaron and his sons

put their hands on its head. **15**Moses
killed the bull, took the blood, and with
his finger put some of it on all the corners
of the altar, to make it pure. Then he
poured out the rest of the blood at the
bottom of the altar. In this way he made it
holy and ready for service to God. **16**Moses took all the fat from the inner organs
of the bull, the best part of the liver, and
both kidneys with the fat that is on them,
and he burned them on the altar. **17**But
he took the bull's skin, its meat, and its
intestines and burned them in a fire outside the camp, as the LORD had commanded him.

18Next Moses brought the male
sheep of the burnt offering, and Aaron
and his sons put their hands on its head.
19Then Moses killed it and sprinkled the
blood on all sides of the altar. **20**He cut
the male sheep into pieces and burned
the head, the pieces, and the fat. **21**He
washed the inner organs and legs with
water and burned the whole sheep on the
altar as a burnt offering made by fire to
the LORD; its smell was pleasing to the
LORD. Moses did these things as the
LORD had commanded him.

22Then Moses brought the other
male sheep, the one used in appointing
Aaron and his sons as priests, and Aaron
and his sons put their hands on its head.
23Then Moses killed the sheep and put
some of its blood on the bottom of
Aaron's right ear, some on the thumb of
Aaron's right hand, and
some on the big toe of his
right foot. **24**Then Moses
brought Aaron's sons
close to the altar. He put
some of the blood on the
bottom of their right ears,
some on the thumbs of
their right hands, and
some on the big toes of
their right feet. Then he
sprinkled blood on all
sides of the altar. **25**He took the fat, the
fat tail, all the fat on the inner organs, the
best part of the liver, both kidneys with
their fat, and the right thigh. **26**From the
basket of bread made without yeast that
is put before the LORD each day, Moses
took a loaf of bread, a loaf made with oil,
and a wafer. He put these pieces of bread
on the fat and right thigh of the male
sheep. **27**All these things he put in the
hands of Aaron and his sons and presented them as an offering before the
LORD. **28**Then Moses took them from
their hands and burned them on the altar
on top of the burnt offering. So this was
the offering for appointing Aaron and his
sons as priests. It was an offering made
by fire to the LORD, and its smell was
pleasing to him. **29**Moses also took the
breast and presented it as an offering
before the LORD. It was Moses' share
of the male sheep used in appointing
the priests, as the LORD had commanded
him.

30Moses took some of the special oil
and some of the blood which was on the
altar, and he sprinkled them on Aaron and
Aaron's clothes and on Aaron's sons and
their clothes. In this way Moses made
Aaron, his clothes, his sons, and their
clothes holy for the LORD.

31Then Moses said to Aaron and his
sons, "I gave you a command, saying,
'Aaron and his sons will eat these things.'
So take the meat and basket of bread from
the offering for appointing priests. Boil
the meat at the door of the Meeting Tent,
and eat it there with the bread. **32**If any of
the meat or bread is left, burn it. **33**The
time of appointing will last seven days;
you must not go outside the entrance
of the Meeting Tent until
that time is up. Stay there
until the time of your appointing is finished. **34**The
LORD commanded the
things that were done to-
day to remove your sins
so you will belong to him.
35You must stay at the
entrance of the Meeting
Tent day and night for
seven days. If you don't
obey the LORD's commands, you will die.
The LORD has given me these commands."

36So Aaron and his sons did everything the LORD had commanded through
Moses.

So Aaron and his sons did everything the LORD had commanded through Moses.
—Leviticus 8:36

Aaron and His Sons Offer Sacrifices

9 On the eighth day after the time of
appointing, Moses called for Aaron
and his sons and for the older leaders of
Israel. 2He said to Aaron, "Take a bull
calf and a male sheep that have nothing
wrong with them, and offer them to the
LORD. The calf will be a sin offering, and
the male sheep will be a whole burnt offering. 3Tell the people of Israel, 'Take a
male goat for a sin offering and a calf and
a lamb for a whole burnt offering; each
must be one year old, and it must have
nothing wrong with it. 4Also take a bull
and a male sheep for fellowship offerings,
along with a grain offering mixed with oil.
Offer all these things to the LORD, because the LORD will appear to you today.' "

5So all the people came to the front of
the Meeting Tent, bringing the things
Moses had commanded them to bring,
and they stood before the LORD. 6Moses
said, "You have done what the LORD commanded, so you will see the LORD's
glory."

7Then Moses told Aaron, "Go to the
altar and offer sin offerings and whole
burnt offerings. Do this to remove your
sins and the people's sins so you will belong to God. Offer the sacrifices for the
people and perform the
acts to remove their sins
for them so they will be-
long to the LORD, as the
LORD has commanded."

8So Aaron went to the
altar and killed the bull
calf as a sin offering for
himself. 9Then his sons
brought the blood to him,
and he dipped his finger
in the blood and put it on
the corners of the altar. He poured out
the rest of the blood at the bottom of the
altar. 10Aaron took the fat, the kidneys,
and the best part of the liver from the sin
offering and burned them on the altar, in
the way the LORD had commanded Moses. 11The meat and skin he burned outside the camp.

12Then Aaron killed the animal for
the whole burnt offering. His sons
brought the blood to him, and he sprinkled it on all sides of the altar. 13As they
gave him the pieces and head of the burnt
offering, Aaron burned them on the altar.
14He also washed the inner organs and
the legs of the burnt offering and burned
them on top of the burnt offering on the
altar.

15Then Aaron brought the offering
that was for the people. He took the goat
of the people's sin offering and killed it
and offered it for the sin offering, just as
he had done the first sin offering.

16Then Aaron brought the whole
burnt offering and offered it in the way
that the LORD had commanded. 17He
also brought the grain offering to the altar. He took a handful of the grain and
burned it on the altar, in addition to the
morning's burnt offering.

18Aaron also killed the bull and the
male sheep as the fellowship offerings for
the people. His sons brought him the
blood, and he sprinkled it on all sides of
the altar. 19Aaron's sons also brought to
Aaron the fat of the bull and the male
sheep—the fat tail, the fat covering the
inner organs, the kidneys, and the best
part of the liver. 20Aaron's sons put them
on the breasts of the bull and the sheep.
Then Aaron burned these fat parts on the
altar. 21He presented the
breasts and the right thigh
before the LORD as the
priests' share of the offering, as Moses had com-
manded.

22Then Aaron lifted
his hands toward the peo-
ple and blessed them.
When he had finished of-
fering the sin offering,
the burnt offering, and
the fellowship offering, he stepped down
from the altar.

23Moses and Aaron went into the
Meeting Tent. Then they came out and
blessed the people, and the LORD's glory
came to all the people. 24Fire came out
from the LORD and burned up the burnt
offering and fat on the altar. When the
people saw this, they shouted with joy
and bowed facedown on the ground.

> Then Aaron lifted his hands toward the people and blessed them.
>
> —Leviticus 9:22

God Destroys Nadab and Abihu

10 Aaron's sons Nadab and Abihu
took their pans for burning incense,
put fire in them, and added incense;
but they did not use the special fire Moses
had commanded them to use in the presence of the LORD. 2So fire came down
from the LORD and destroyed Nadab and
Abihu, and they died in front of the LORD.
3Then Moses said to Aaron, "This is
what the LORD was speaking about when
he said,

'I must be respected as holy
by those who come near me;
before all the people
I must be given honor.' "

So Aaron did not say anything about the
death of his sons.
4Aaron's uncle Uzziel had two sons
named Mishael and Elzaphan. Moses said
to them, "Come here and pick up your
cousins' bodies. Carry them outside the
camp away from the front of the Holy
Place." 5So Mishael and Elzaphan obeyed
Moses and carried the bodies of Nadab
and Abihu, still clothed in the special
priest's inner robes, outside the camp.
6Then Moses said to Aaron and his
other sons, Eleazar and Ithamar, "Don't
show sadness by tearing your clothes or
leaving your hair uncombed. If you do,
you will die, and the LORD will be angry
with all the people. All the people of Israel, your relatives, may cry loudly about
the LORD burning Nadab and Abihu, 7but
you must not even leave the Meeting
Tent. If you go out of the entrance, you
will die, because the LORD has appointed
you to his service." So Aaron, Eleazar,
and Ithamar obeyed Moses.
8Then the LORD said to Aaron, 9"You
and your sons must not drink wine or
beer when you go into the Meeting Tent.
If you do, you will die. This law will continue from now on. 10You must keep
what is holy separate from what is not
holy; you must keep what is clean separate from what is unclean. 11You must
teach the people all the laws that the
LORD gave to them through Moses."
12Moses said to Aaron and his remaining sons, Eleazar and Ithamar, "Eat
the part of the grain offering that is left

FAITH CHALLENGE

Here's another one for you. Read 10:3 to find out how God wants us to treat him. How do you show respect and honor to God when you are with your friends?

TESTING IT

Leviticus 10:3
This is what the LORD was speaking about when he said, "I must be respected as holy by those who come near me; before all the people I must be given honor."

from the sacrifices offered by fire to the
LORD, but do not add yeast to it. Eat it near
the altar because it is most holy. 13You
must eat it in a holy place, because this
part of the offerings made by fire to the
LORD belongs to you and your sons. I
have been commanded to tell you this.
14"Also, you and your sons and
daughters may eat the breast and thigh of
the fellowship offering that was presented to the LORD. You must eat them in
a clean place; they are your share of the
fellowship offerings given by the Israelites. 15The people must bring the fat

from their animals that was part of the offering made by fire, and they must present it to the LORD along with the thigh
and the breast of the fellowship offering.
They will be the regular share of the offerings for you and your children, as the
LORD has commanded."

16Moses looked for the goat of the sin
offering, but it had already been burned
up. So he became very angry with Eleazar and Ithamar, Aaron's remaining sons.
He said, **17**"Why didn't you eat that goat
in a holy place? It is most holy, and the
LORD gave it to you to take away the guilt
of the people, to remove their sins so
they will belong to the LORD. **18**You
didn't bring the goat's blood inside the
Holy Place. You were supposed to eat the
goat in a holy place, as I commanded!"

19But Aaron said to Moses, "Today
they brought their sin offering and burnt
offering before the LORD, but these terrible things have still happened to me! Do
you think the LORD would be any happier
if I ate the sin offering today?" **20**When
Moses heard this, he was satisfied.

Rules About What May Be Eaten

11 The LORD said to Moses and
Aaron, **2**"Tell the Israelites this:
'These are the land animals you may eat:
3You may eat any animal that has split
hoofs completely divided and that chews
the cud.

4" 'Some animals only chew the cud
or only have split hoofs, and you must not
eat them. The camel chews the cud but
does not have a split hoof; it is unclean
for you. **5**The rock badger chews the cud
but does not have a split hoof; it is unclean for you. **6**The rabbit chews the cud
but does not have a split hoof; it is unclean for you. **7**Now the pig has a split
hoof that is completely divided, but it
does not chew the cud; it is unclean for
you. **8**You must not eat the meat from
these animals or even touch their dead
bodies; they are unclean for you.

9" 'Of the animals that live in the sea
or in a river, if the animal has fins and
scales, you may eat it. **10**But whatever
lives in the sea or in a river and does not
have fins and scales—including the

FAITH links

A DIFFERENT KIND OF PEOPLE

LEVITICUS 11

God wanted the Israelites to be different from other nations. That's why he gave them a lot of rules to follow. Some of these rules had to do with food. The Israelites were told which types of animals they could eat and which ones they could not eat. The ones they could eat were known as "clean" animals.

We don't have strict laws about the foods we eat today. But God still expects our behavior as Christians to be different from that of non-believers. Knowing Jesus makes all the difference.

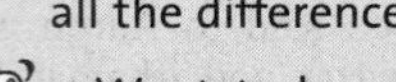

Want to know what else the Bible has to say about following God? Check out these Faithlinks:

Lights, Camera, . . . Actions!, Genesis 12:1–3, p. 17

The Wisdom of Obeying God, 1 Kings 11:1–13, p. 453

The Bible: Good for Your Faith, Psalm 119, p. 802

Your Spiritual Roots, Zechariah 1:1–6, p. 1253

When We Agree, Matthew 18:19–20, p. 1306

Faith That Pleases God, Luke 7:1–9, p. 1380

things that fill the water and all other
things that live in it—you should hate.
11You must not eat any meat from them
or even touch their dead bodies, because
you should hate them. **12**You must hate
any animal in the water that does not
have fins and scales.

13“ ‘Also, these are the birds you are
to hate. They are hateful and should not
be eaten. You must not eat eagles, vultures, black vultures, **14**kites, any kind of
falcon, **15**any kind of raven, **16**horned
owls, screech owls, sea gulls, any kind of
hawk, **17**little owls, cormorants, great
owls, **18**white owls, desert owls, ospreys,
19storks, any kind of heron, hoopoes, or
bats.

20“ ‘Don’t eat insects that have wings
and walk on all four feet; they also are to
be hated.

21“ ‘But you may eat certain insects
that have wings and walk on four feet.
You may eat those that have legs with
joints above their feet so they can jump.
22These are the insects you may eat: all
kinds of locusts, winged locusts, crickets,
and grasshoppers. **23**But all other insects
that have wings and walk on four feet you
are to hate. **24**Those insects will make
you unclean, and anyone who touches the
dead body of one of these insects will become unclean until evening. **25**Anyone
who picks up one of these dead insects
must wash his clothes and be unclean until evening.

26“ ‘Some animals have split hoofs,
but the hoofs are not completely divided;
others do not chew the cud. They are unclean for you, and anyone who touches
the dead body of one of these animals will
become unclean. **27**Of all the animals that
walk on four feet, the animals that walk
on their paws are unclean for you. Anyone who touches the dead body of one of
these animals will become unclean until
evening. **28**Anyone who picks up their
dead bodies must wash his clothes and be
unclean until evening; these animals are
unclean for you.

29“ ‘These crawling animals are unclean for you: moles, rats, all kinds of
great lizards, **30**geckos, crocodiles, lizards,
sand reptiles, and chameleons. **31**These
crawling animals are unclean for you;
anyone who touches their dead bodies
will be unclean until evening.

32“ ‘If an unclean animal dies and falls
on something, that item will also become
unclean. This includes anything made
from wood, cloth, leather, or rough cloth,
regardless of its use. Whatever the animal falls on must be washed with water
and be unclean until evening; then it will
become clean again. **33**If the dead, unclean animal falls into a clay bowl, anything in the bowl will become unclean,
and you must break the bowl. **34**If water
from the unclean clay bowl gets on any
food, that food will become unclean. **35**If
any dead, unclean animal falls on something, it becomes unclean. If it is a clay
oven or a clay baking pan, it must be
broken into pieces. These things will be
unclean; they are unclean for you.

36“ ‘A spring or well that collects
water will stay clean, but anyone who
touches the dead body of any unclean
animal will become unclean. **37**If a dead,
unclean animal falls on a seed to be planted, that seed is still clean. **38**But if you
put water on some seeds and a dead, unclean animal falls on them, they are unclean for you.

39“ ‘Also, if an animal which you use
for food dies, anyone who touches its body
will be unclean until evening. **40**Anyone
who eats meat from this animal’s dead
body must wash his clothes and be unclean until evening. Anyone who picks up
the animal’s dead body must wash his
clothes and be unclean until evening.

41“ ‘Every animal that crawls on the
ground is to be hated; it must not be
eaten. **42**You must not eat any of the animals that crawl on the ground, including
those that crawl on their stomachs, that
walk on all four feet, or on
many feet. They are
to be hated. **43**Do
not make yourself
unclean by these an-
imals; you must not
become unclean by
them. **44**I am the LORD your God. Keep
yourselves holy for me because I am holy.
Don’t make yourselves unclean with any

of these crawling animals. **45**I am the
LORD who brought you out of Egypt to be
your God; you must be holy because I am
holy.
46" 'These are the teachings about all
of the cattle, birds, and other animals on
earth, as well as the animals in the sea
and those that crawl on the ground.
47These teachings help people know the
difference between unclean animals and
clean animals; they help people know
which animals may be eaten and which
ones must not be eaten.' "

Rules for New Mothers

12 The LORD said to Moses, **2**"Tell
the people of Israel this: 'If a woman
gives birth to a son, she will become unclean for seven days, as she is unclean
during her monthly period. **3**On the
eighth day the boy must be circumcised.
4Then it will be thirty-three days before
she becomes clean from her loss of blood.
She must not touch anything that is holy
or enter the Holy Tent until her time of
cleansing is finished. **5**But
if she gives birth to a
daughter, the mother will
be unclean for two weeks,
as she is unclean during
her monthly period. It will
be sixty-six days before
she becomes clean from
her loss of blood.
6" 'After she has a son
or daughter and her days
of cleansing are over, the
new mother must bring certain sacrifices
to the Meeting Tent. She must give the
priest at the entrance a year-old lamb for
a burnt offering and a dove or young pigeon for a sin offering. **7**He will offer
them before the LORD to make her clean
so she will belong to the LORD again;
then she will be clean from her loss of
blood. These are the teachings for a
woman who gives birth to a boy or girl.
8" 'If she cannot afford a lamb, she is
to bring two doves or two young pigeons,
one for a burnt offering and one for a sin
offering. In this way the priest will make
her clean so she will belong to the LORD
again, and she will be clean.' "

> In this way the priest will make her clean so she will belong to the LORD again, and she will be clean.
>
> —Leviticus 12:8

Rules About Skin Diseases

13 The LORD said to Moses and
Aaron, **2**"Someone might have on
his skin a swelling or a rash or a bright
spot. If the sore looks like a harmful skin
disease, the person must be brought to
Aaron the priest or to one of Aaron's
sons, the priests. **3**The priest must look
at the sore on the person's skin. If the
hair in the sore has become white, and
the sore seems deeper than the person's
skin, it is a harmful skin disease. When
he has finished looking at the person, the
priest must announce that the person is
unclean.
4"If there is a white spot on a person's
skin, but the spot does not seem deeper
than the skin, and if the hair from the spot
has not turned white, the priest must separate that person from other people for
seven days. **5**On the seventh day the
priest must look at the person again. If he
sees that the sore has not changed and
it has not spread on the skin, the priest
must keep the person
separated for seven more
days. **6**On the seventh day
the priest must look at
the person again. If the
sore has faded and has
not spread on the skin,
the priest must announce
that the person is clean.
The sore is only a rash.
The person must wash
his clothes, and he will become clean again.
7"But if the rash spreads again after
the priest has announced him clean, the
person must come again to the priest.
8The priest must look at him, and if the
rash has spread on the skin, the priest
must announce that the person is unclean; it is a harmful skin disease.
9"If a person has a harmful skin disease, he must be brought to the priest,
10and the priest must look at him. If
there is a white swelling in the skin, and
the hair has become white, and the skin
looks raw in the swelling, **11**it is a harmful skin disease. It is one he has had for a
long time. The priest must announce that

FAITH links

OUR THOROUGH GOD

LEVITICUS 13

Do you think your town has a law about fungus? What about a law about mildew? The people of Israel had laws about both, plus several other laws about contagious diseases like harmful skin diseases. (This skin disease was often referred to as leprosy. Today it's known as Hansen's disease.) Obeying these laws kept infections from spreading.

Reading this chapter reminds us that God cares about every part of our lives. God is pretty thorough! He makes rules for our protection and to protect others. Don't be afraid to take any concern you have to him. He cares about everything you care about.

The Name of the Lord, Exodus 33:19–23; 34:5–8, p. 120

Problem Solved, 2 Kings 20:1–11, p. 507

Our Heavenly Shepherd, Psalm 23, p. 726

Our Awesome God, Ezekiel 1:26–28, p. 1087

Faith God Notices, Luke 18:35–43, p. 1406

You've Got the Power!, Acts 1:1–8; 2:1–4, p. 1463

the person is unclean. He will not need to
separate that person from other people,
because everyone already knows that the
person is unclean.

12"If the skin disease spreads all over
a person's body, covering his skin from
his head to his feet, as far as the priest
can see, the priest must look at the
person's whole body. **13**If the priest sees
that the disease covers the whole body
and has turned all of the person's skin
white, he must announce that the person
is clean.

14"But when the person has an open
sore, he is unclean. **15**When the priest
sees the open sore, he must announce
that the person is unclean. The open sore
is not clean; it is a harmful skin disease.
16If the open sore becomes white again,
the person must come to the priest.
17The priest must look at him, and if the
sores have become white, the priest
must announce that the person with the
sores is clean. Then he will be clean.

18"Someone may have a boil on his
skin that is healed. **19**If in the place
where the boil was, there is a white
swelling or a bright red spot, this place on
the skin must be shown to the priest.
20And the priest must look at it. If the
spot seems deeper than the skin and the
hair on it has become white, the priest
must announce that the person is unclean. The spot is a harmful skin disease
that has broken out from inside the boil.
21But if the priest looks at the spot and
there are no white hairs in it and the spot
is not deeper than the skin and it has
faded, the priest must separate the person from other people for seven days.
22If the spot spreads on the skin, the
priest must announce that the person is
unclean; it is a disease that will spread.
23But if the bright spot does not spread
or change, it is only the scar from the old
boil. Then the priest must announce that
the person is clean.

24"When a person gets a burn on his
skin, if the open sore becomes white or
red, **25**the priest must look at it. If the
white spot seems deeper than the skin
and the hair at that spot has become
white, it is a harmful skin disease. The
disease has broken out in the burn, and
the priest must announce that the person
is unclean. It is a harmful skin disease.
26But if the priest looks at the spot and

there is no white hair in the bright spot, and the spot is no deeper than the skin and has faded, the priest must separate the person from other people for seven days. **27**On the seventh day the priest must look at him again. If the spot has spread on the skin, the priest must announce that the person is unclean. It is a harmful skin disease. **28**But if the bright spot has not spread on the skin but has faded, it is the swelling from the burn. The priest must announce that the person is clean, because the spot is only a scar from the burn.

29"When a man or a woman gets a sore on the scalp or on the chin, **30**a priest must look at the sore. If it seems deeper than the skin and the hair around it is thin and yellow, the priest must announce that the person is unclean. It is an itch, a harmful skin disease of the head or chin. **31**But if the priest looks at it and it does not seem deeper than the skin and there is no black hair in it, the priest must separate the person from other people for seven days. **32**On the seventh day the priest must look at the sore. If it has not spread, and there are no yellow hairs growing in it, and the sore does not seem deeper than the skin, **33**the person must shave himself, but he must not shave the sore place. The priest must separate that person from other people for seven more days. **34**On the seventh day the priest must look at the sore. If it has not spread on the skin and it does not seem deeper than the skin, the priest must announce that the person is clean. So the person must wash his clothes and become clean. **35**But if the sore spreads on the skin after the person has become clean, **36**the priest must look at him again. If the sore has spread on the skin, the priest doesn't need to look for the yellowish hair; the person is unclean. **37**But if the priest thinks the sore has stopped spreading, and black hair is growing in it, the sore has healed. The person is clean, and the priest must announce that he is clean.

38"When a man or a woman has white spots on the skin, **39**a priest must look at them. If the spots on the skin are dull white, the disease is only a harmless rash. That person is clean.

40"When anyone loses hair from his head and is bald, he is clean. **41**If he loses hair from the front of his head and has a bald forehead, he is clean. **42**But if there is a red-white sore on his bald head or forehead, it is a skin disease breaking out in those places. **43**A priest must look at that person. If the swelling of the sore on his bald head or forehead is red-white, like a skin disease that spreads, **44**that person has a skin disease. He is unclean. The priest must announce that the person is unclean because of the sore on his head.

45"If a person has a skin disease that spreads, he must warn other people by shouting, 'Unclean, unclean!' His clothes must be torn at the seams, he must let his hair stay uncombed, and he must cover his mouth. **46**That person will be unclean the whole time he has the disease; he is unclean. He must live alone outside the camp.

Rules About Mildew

47"Clothing might have mildew on it. It might be clothing made of linen or wool **48**(either woven or knitted), or of leather, or something made from leather. **49**If the mildew in the clothing, leather, or woven or knitted material is green or red, it is a spreading mildew. It must be shown to the priest. **50**The priest must look at the mildew, and he must put that piece of clothing in a separate place for seven days. **51**On the seventh day he must look at the mildew again. If the mildew has spread on the cloth (either woven or knitted) or the leather, no matter what the leather was used for, it is a mildew that destroys; it is unclean. **52**The priest must burn the clothing. It does not matter if it is woven or knitted, wool or linen, or made of leather, because the mildew is spreading. It must be burned.

53"If the priest sees that the mildew has not spread in the cloth (either knitted or woven) or leather, **54**he must order the people to wash that piece of leather or cloth. Then he must separate the clothing for seven more days. **55**After the

piece with the mildew has been washed,
the priest must look at it again. If the mildew still looks the same, the piece is unclean, even if the mildew has not spread.
You must burn it in fire; it does not matter if the mildew is on one side or the
other.

56"But when the priest looks at that
piece of leather or cloth, the mildew might
have faded after the piece has been
washed. Then the priest must tear the
mildew out of the piece of leather or cloth
(either woven or knitted). **57**But if the
mildew comes back to that piece of
leather or cloth (either woven or knitted),
the mildew is spreading. And whatever
has the mildew must be burned with fire.
58When the cloth (either woven or knitted) or the leather is washed and the mildew is gone, it must be washed again;
then it will be clean.

59"These are the teachings about mildew on pieces of cloth (either woven or
knitted) or leather, to decide if they are
clean or unclean."

Rules for Cleansing from Skin Diseases

14 The LORD said to Moses, **2**"These
are the teachings for the time at
which people who had a harmful skin disease are made clean.

"The person shall be brought to the
priest, **3**and the priest must go outside
the camp and look at the one who had the
skin disease. If the skin disease is healed,
4the priest will command that two living,
clean birds, a piece of cedar wood, a piece
of red string, and a hyssop plant be
brought for cleansing the person with the
skin disease.

5"The priest must order one bird to be
killed in a clay bowl containing fresh water. **6**Then he will take the living bird, the
piece of cedar wood, the red string, and
the hyssop; all these he will dip into the
blood of the bird that was killed over
the fresh water. **7**The priest will sprinkle
the blood seven times on the person being
cleansed from the skin disease. He must
announce that the person is clean and
then go to an open field and let the living
bird go free.

8"The person to be cleansed must
wash his clothes, shave off all his hair,
and bathe in water. Then he will be clean
and may go into the camp, though he
must stay outside his tent for the first
seven days. **9**On the seventh day he must
shave off all his hair—the hair from his
head, his beard, his eyebrows, and the
rest of his hair. He must wash his clothes
and bathe his body in water, and he will
be clean.

10"On the eighth day the person who
had the skin disease must take two male
lambs that have nothing wrong with them
and a year-old female lamb that has nothing wrong with it. He must also take six
quarts of fine flour mixed with oil for a
grain offering and two-thirds of a pint of
olive oil. **11**The priest who is to announce that the person is clean must
bring him and his sacrifices before the
LORD at the entrance of the Meeting
Tent. **12**The priest will take one of the
male lambs and offer it with the olive oil
as a penalty offering; he will present
them before the LORD as an offering.
13Then he will kill the male lamb in the
holy place, where the sin offering and the
whole burnt offering are killed. The penalty offering is like the sin offering—it
belongs to the priest and it is most holy.

14"The priest will take some of the
blood of the penalty offering and put it on
the bottom of the right ear of the person
to be made clean. He will also put some
of it on the thumb of the person's right
hand and on the big toe of the person's
right foot. **15**Then the priest will take
some of the oil and pour it into his own
left hand. **16**He will dip a finger of his
right hand into the oil that is in his left
hand, and with his finger he will sprinkle
some of the oil seven times before the
LORD. **17**The priest will put some oil
from his hand on the bottom of the right
ear of the person to be made clean, some
on the thumb of the person's right hand,
and some on the big toe of the person's
right foot. The oil will go on these places
on top of the blood for the penalty offering. **18**He will put the rest of the oil that
is in his left hand on the head of the person to be made clean. In this way the priest

will make that person clean so he can belong to the LORD again.
19"Next the priest will offer the sin
offering to make that person clean so he
can belong to the LORD again. After this
the priest will kill the animal for the
whole burnt offering,
20and he will offer the
burnt offering and grain
offering on the altar. In
this way he will make that
person clean so he can
belong to the LORD again.
21"But if the person is
poor and unable to afford
these offerings, he must
take one male lamb for a
penalty offering. It will be
presented to the LORD to
make him clean so he can belong to the
LORD again. The person must also take
two quarts of fine flour mixed with oil for
a grain offering. He must also take two-
thirds of a pint of olive oil **22**and two
doves or two young pigeons, which he
can afford. One bird is for a sin offering
and the other for a whole burnt offering.
23On the eighth day the person will bring
them for his cleansing to the priest at the
entrance of the Meeting Tent, before the
LORD. **24**The priest will take the lamb for
the penalty offering and the oil, and he
will present them as an offering before
the LORD. **25**Then he will kill the lamb of
the penalty offering, take some of its
blood, and put it on the bottom of the
right ear of the person to be made clean.
The priest will put some of this blood on
the thumb of the person's right hand and
some on the big toe of the person's right
foot. **26**He will also pour some of the oil
into his own left hand. **27**Then with a finger of his right hand, he will sprinkle
some of the oil from his left hand seven
times before the LORD. **28**The priest will
take some of the oil from his hand and put
it on the bottom of the right ear of the
person to be made clean. He will also put
some of it on the thumb of the person's
right hand and some on the big toe of the
person's right foot. The oil will go on
these places on top of the blood from the
penalty offering. **29**The priest must put
the rest of the oil that is in his hand on
the head of the person to be made clean,
to make him clean so he can belong to the
LORD again. **30**Then the priest will offer
one of the doves or young pigeons, which
the person can afford. **31**He must offer
one of the birds for a sin
offering and the other for
a whole burnt offering,
along with the grain of-
fering. In this way the
priest will make the per-
son clean so he can be-
long to the LORD again;
he will become clean.
32"These are the
teachings for making a
person clean after he has
had a skin disease, if he
cannot afford the regular sacrifices for
becoming clean."

The priest must put the rest of the oil that is in his hand on the head of the person to be made clean, to make him clean so he can belong to the LORD again.—Leviticus 14:29

Rules for Cleaning Mildew

33The LORD also said to Moses and
Aaron, **34**"I am giving the land of Canaan
to your people. When they enter that
land, if I cause mildew to grow in
someone's house in that land, **35**the owner of that house must come and tell the
priest. He should say, 'I have seen something like mildew in my house.' **36**Then
the priest must order the people to
empty the house before he goes in to
look at the mildew. This is so he will not
have to say that everything in the house
is unclean. After this, the priest will go in
to look at it. **37**He will look at the mildew,
and if the mildew on the walls of the
house is green or red and goes into the
wall's surface, **38**he must go out and
close up the house for seven days. **39**On
the seventh day the priest must come
back and check the house. If the mildew
has spread on the walls of the house,
40the priest must order the people to
tear out the stones with the mildew on
them. They should throw them away, at a
certain unclean place outside the city.
41Then the priest must have all the inside
of the house scraped. The people must
throw away the plaster they scraped off
the walls, at a certain unclean place outside the city. **42**Then the owner must put

new stones in the walls, and he must
cover the walls with new clay plaster.
43"Suppose a person has taken away
the old stones and plaster and put in new
stones and plaster. If mildew again appears in his house, **44**the priest must
come back and check the house again. If
the mildew has spread in the house, it is a
mildew that destroys things; the house is
unclean. **45**Then the owner must tear
down the house, remove all its stones,
plaster, and wood, and take them to the
unclean place outside the city. **46**Anyone
who goes into that house while it is
closed up will be unclean until evening.
47Anyone who eats in that house or lies
down there must wash his clothes.
48"Suppose after new stones and
plaster have been put in a house, the
priest checks it again and the mildew has
not spread. Then the priest will announce that the house is clean, because
the mildew is gone.
49"Then, to make the house clean,
the priest must take two birds, a piece of
cedar wood, a piece of red string, and a
hyssop plant. **50**He will kill one bird in a
clay bowl containing fresh water. **51**Then
he will take the bird that is still alive, the
cedar wood, the hyssop, and the red
string, and he will dip them into the blood
of the bird that was killed over the fresh
water. The priest will sprinkle the blood
on the house seven times. **52**He will use
the bird's blood, the fresh water, the live
bird, the cedar wood, the hyssop, and the
red string to make the house clean. **53**He
will then go to an open field outside the
city and let the living bird go free. This is
how the priest makes the house clean and
ready for service to the LORD."
54These are the teachings about any
kind of skin disease, **55**mildew on pieces
of cloth or in a house, **56**swellings,
rashes, or bright spots on the skin;
57they help people decide when things
are unclean and when they are clean.
These are the teachings about all these
kinds of diseases.

Rules About a Person's Body

15 The LORD also said to Moses and
Aaron, **2**"Say to the people of Israel: 'When a fluid comes from a person's
body, the fluid is unclean. **3**It doesn't matter if the fluid flows freely or if it is
blocked from flowing; the fluid will make
him unclean. This is the way the fluid
makes him unclean:
4" 'If the person who discharges the
body fluid lies on a bed, that bed becomes
unclean, and everything he sits on becomes unclean. **5**Anyone who touches
his bed must wash his clothes and bathe
in water, and the person will be unclean
until evening. **6**Whoever sits on something that the person who discharges the
fluid sat on must wash his clothes and
bathe in water; he will be unclean until
evening. **7**Anyone who touches the person who discharges the body fluid must
wash his clothes and bathe in water; he
will be unclean until evening.
8" 'If the person who discharges the
body fluid spits on someone who is clean,
that person must wash his clothes and
bathe in water; he will be unclean until
evening. **9**Everything on which the person who is unclean sits when riding will
become unclean. **10**Anyone who touches
something that was under him will be unclean until evening. And anyone who carries these things must wash his clothes
and bathe in water; he will be unclean
until evening.
11" 'If the person who discharges a
body fluid has not washed his hands in
water and touches another person, that
person must wash his clothes and bathe
in water; he will be unclean until evening.
12" 'If a person who discharges a body
fluid touches a clay bowl, that bowl must
be broken. If he touches a wooden bowl,
that bowl must be washed in water.
13" 'When a person who discharges a
body fluid is made clean, he must count
seven days for himself for his cleansing.
He must wash his clothes and bathe his
body in fresh water, and he will be clean.
14On the eighth day he must take two
doves or two young pigeons before the
LORD at the entrance of the Meeting
Tent. He will give the two birds to the
priest. **15**The priest will offer the birds,
one for a sin offering and the other for a

burnt offering. And the priest will make
that person clean so he can belong to the
LORD again.
16" 'If semen[n] goes out from a man,
he must bathe in water; he will be unclean until evening. **17**If the fluid gets on
any clothing or leather, it must be washed
with water; it will be unclean until evening.
18" 'If a man has sexual relations with
a woman and semen comes out, both people must bathe in water; they will be unclean until evening.

Rules About a Woman's Body

19" 'When a woman has her monthly
period, she is unclean for seven days;
anyone who touches her will be unclean
until evening. **20**Anything she lies on
during this time will be unclean, and
everything she sits on during this time
will be unclean. **21**Anyone who touches
her bed must wash his clothes and bathe
in water; that person will be unclean until
evening. **22**Anyone who touches something she has sat on must wash his
clothes and bathe in water; that person
will be unclean until evening. **23**It does
not matter if the person touched the
woman's bed or something she sat on; he
will be unclean until evening.
24" 'If a man has sexual relations with
a woman and her monthly period touches
him, he will be unclean for seven days;
every bed he lies on will be unclean.
25" 'If a woman has a loss of blood for
many days and it is not during her regular
monthly period, or if she continues to
have a loss of blood after her regular period, she will be unclean, as she is during
her monthly period. She will be unclean
for as long as she continues to bleed.
26Any bed she lies on during all the time
of her bleeding will be like her bed during
her regular monthly period. Everything
she sits on will be unclean, as during her
regular monthly period.
27" 'Whoever touches those things
will be unclean and must wash his
clothes and bathe in water; he will be unclean until evening. **28**When the woman
becomes clean from her bleeding, she
must wait seven days, and after this she
will be clean. **29**Then on the eighth day
she must take two doves or two young
pigeons and bring them to the priest at
the entrance of the Meeting Tent. **30**The
priest must offer one bird for a sin offering and the other for a whole burnt offering. In this way the priest will make her
clean so she can belong to the LORD
again.
31" 'So you must warn the people of
Israel to stay separated from things that
make them unclean. If you don't warn the
people, they might make my Holy Tent
unclean, and then they would have to
die!' "
32These are the teachings for the
person who discharges a body fluid and
for the man who becomes unclean from
semen[n] coming out of his body. **33**These
are the teachings for the woman who becomes unclean from her monthly period,
for a man or woman who has a discharge,
and for a man who becomes unclean by
having sexual relations with a woman
who is unclean.

The Day of Cleansing

16 Now two of Aaron's sons had died
while offering incense to the
LORD, and after that time the LORD spoke
to Moses. **2**The LORD said to him, "Tell
your brother Aaron that there are times
when he cannot go behind the curtain
into the Most Holy Place where the Ark
is. If he goes in when I appear in a cloud
over the lid on the Ark, he will die.
3"This is how Aaron may enter the
Most Holy Place: Before he enters, he
must offer a bull for a sin offering and a
male sheep for a whole burnt offering.
4He must put on the holy linen inner
robe, with the linen underclothes next to
his body. His belt will be the cloth belt,
and he will wear the linen turban. These
are holy clothes, so he must bathe his
body in water before he puts them on.
5"Aaron must take from the people of
Israel two male goats for a sin offering
and one male sheep for a burnt offering.
6Then he will offer the bull for the sin of-

15:16, 32 semen A man's body fluid by which he can make a woman pregnant.

GOD'S PRESENCE WITH THE ISRAELITES

Leviticus 16:1–15

The Ark of the Agreement was like a box. It was almost four feet long and a little over two feet wide and high. It was made from acacia wood. There were two rings on each side so that poles could be slipped through them. This way men could carry the Ark without touching it. Why would they want to do that? Because this Ark was the most holy thing that the Israelites had. They believed that God's presence was with the Ark. That's why they kept it in a special place in the Meeting Tent. This was a holy place the Israelites had built, so God could live among them. They also carried it to some battles because they wanted God to be with them.

Inside of the Ark, the Israelites kept the Ten Commandments (Check out Exodus 20, p. 101.), a golden jar of manna (the food that God sent them while they were wandering in the desert), and Aaron's miraculous rod—reminders that God provided for them in the wilderness. (Read Hebrews 9:4, p. 1676.)

fering for himself to remove sins from
him and his family so they will belong to
the LORD.
7"Next Aaron will take the two goats
and bring them before the LORD at the entrance to the Meeting Tent. 8He will
throw lots for the two goats—one will be
for the LORD and the other for the goat
that removes sin. 9Then Aaron will take
the goat that was chosen for the LORD by
throwing the lot, and he will offer it as a
sin offering. 10The other goat, which was
chosen by lot to remove the sin, must be
brought alive before the LORD. The priest
will use it to perform the acts that remove
Israel's sin so they will belong to the
LORD. Then this goat will be sent out into
the desert as a goat that removes sin.
11"Then Aaron will offer the bull as a
sin offering for himself, to remove the
sins from him and his family so they will
belong to the LORD; he will kill the bull
for the sin offering for himself. 12Then
he must take a pan full of burning coals
from the altar before the LORD and two
handfuls of sweet incense that has been
ground into powder. He must bring it into
the room behind the curtain. 13He must
put the incense on the fire before the
LORD so that the cloud of incense will
cover the lid on the Ark. Then when Aaron
comes in, he will not die. 14Also, he must
take some of the blood from the bull and
sprinkle it with his finger on the front of the
lid; with his finger he will sprinkle the
blood seven times in front of the lid.
15"Then Aaron must kill the goat of
the sin offering for the people and bring
its blood into the room behind the curtain. He must do with the goat's blood as
he did with the bull's blood, sprinkling it
on the lid and in front of the lid. 16Be-
cause the people of Israel have been unclean, Aaron will perform the acts to
make the Most Holy Place ready for service to the LORD. Then it will be clean
from the sins and crimes of the Israelites.
He must also do this for the Meeting

Tent, because it stays in the middle of
unclean people. **17**When Aaron makes
the Most Holy Place ready for service to
the LORD, no one is allowed in the Meeting Tent until he comes out. So Aaron
will perform the acts to remove sins from
himself, his family, and all the people of
Israel, so they will belong to the LORD.
18Afterward he will go out to the altar
that is before the LORD and will make it
ready for service to the LORD. Aaron will
take some of the bull's blood and some of
the goat's blood and put it on the corners
of the altar on all sides. **19**Then, with his
finger, he will sprinkle some of the blood
on the altar seven times to make the altar
holy for the LORD and clean from all the
sins of the Israelites.

20"When Aaron has finished making
the Most Holy Place, the Meeting Tent,
and the altar ready for service to the
LORD, he will offer the living goat. **21**He
will put both his hands on the head of the
living goat, and he will confess over it all
the sins and crimes of Israel. In this way
Aaron will put the people's sins on the
goat's head. Then he will send the goat
away into the desert, and a man who has
been appointed will lead the goat away.
22So the goat will carry on itself all the
people's sins to a lonely place in the
desert. The man who leads the goat will
let it loose there.

23"Then Aaron will enter the Meeting Tent and take off the linen clothes he
had put on before he went into the Most
Holy Place; he must leave these clothes
there. **24**He will bathe his body in water
in a holy place and put on his regular
clothes. Then he will come out and offer
the whole burnt offering for himself and
for the people, to remove sins from himself and the people so they will belong to
the LORD. **25**Then he will burn the fat of
the sin offering on the altar.

26"The person who led the goat, the
goat to remove sins, into the desert must
wash his clothes and bathe his body in water. After that, he may come back into the
camp.

27"The bull and the goat for the sin
offerings, whose blood was brought into
the Most Holy Place to make it ready for
service to the LORD, must be taken outside the camp; the animals' skins, bodies,
and intestines will be burned in the fire.
28Then the one who burns them must
wash his clothes and bathe his body in
water. After that, he may come back into
the camp.

29"This law will always continue for
you: On the tenth day of the seventh
month, you must not eat and you must
not do any work. The travelers or foreigners living with you must not work either. **30**It is on this day that the priests
will make you clean so you will belong to
the LORD again. All your sins will be removed. **31**This is a very important day of
rest for you, and you must not eat. This
law will continue forever.

32"The priest appointed to take his
father's place, on whom the oil was
poured, will perform the acts for making
things ready for service to the LORD. He
must put on the holy linen clothes **33**and
make the Most Holy Place, the Meeting
Tent, and the altar ready for service to
the LORD. He must also remove the sins
of the priests and all the people of Israel
so they will belong to the LORD. **34**That
law for removing the sins of the Israelites
so they will belong to the LORD will continue forever. You will do these things
once a year."

So they did the things the LORD had
commanded Moses.

Offering Sacrifices

17 The LORD said to Moses, **2**"Speak
to Aaron, his sons, and all the people of Israel. Tell them: 'This is what the
LORD has commanded. **3**If an Israelite
kills an ox, a lamb, or a goat either inside
the camp or outside it, **4**when he should
have brought the animal to the entrance
of the Meeting Tent as a gift to the LORD
in front of the LORD's Holy Tent, he is
guilty of killing. He has killed, and he
must be cut off from the people. **5**This
rule is so people will bring their sacrifices, which they have been sacrificing in
the open fields, to the LORD. They must
bring those animals to the LORD at the
entrance of the Meeting Tent; they must
bring them to the priest and offer them as

fellowship offerings. 6Then the priest
will sprinkle the blood from those animals on the LORD's altar near the entrance of the Meeting Tent. And he will
burn the fat from those animals on the altar, as a smell pleasing to the LORD.
7They must not offer any more sacrifices
to their goat idols, which they have
chased like prostitutes. These rules will
continue for people from now on.'
8"Tell the people this: 'If any citizen
of Israel or foreigner living with you offers a burnt offering or sacrifice, 9that
person must take his sacrifice to the entrance of the Meeting Tent to offer it to
the LORD. If he does not do this, he must
be cut off from the people.
10" 'I will be against any citizen of Israel or foreigner living with you who eats
blood. I will cut off that person from the
people. 11This is because the life of the
body is in the blood, and I have given you
rules for pouring that blood on the altar
to remove your sins so you will belong to
the LORD. It is the blood that removes
the sins, because it is life. 12So I tell the
people of Israel this: "None of you may
eat blood, and no foreigner living among
you may eat blood."
13" 'If any citizen of Israel or foreigner living among you catches a wild animal
or bird that can be eaten, that person
must pour the blood on the ground and
cover it with dirt. 14If blood is still in the
meat, the animal's life is still in it. So I
give this command to the people of Israel: "Don't eat meat that still has blood
in it, because the animal's life is in its
blood. Anyone who eats blood must be
cut off."
15" 'If a person, either a citizen or a
foreigner, eats an animal that died by itself or was killed by another animal, he
must wash his clothes and bathe in water.
He will be unclean until evening; then he
will be clean. 16If he does not wash his
clothes and bathe his body, he will be
guilty of sin.' "

Rules About Sexual Relations

18 The LORD said to Moses, 2"Tell the
people of Israel: 'I am the LORD
your God. 3In the past you lived in Egypt,

FAITH links

AN EXAMPLE NOT TO FOLLOW

LEVITICUS 18:1-3

Did your mom or dad ever tell you not to act like someone you know? Maybe this person behaves in a way that would cause you to break a rule your parents made. God warned the Israelites not to follow the ways of the people of Canaan. The Canaanites did many things that God did not like. He expected his people to obey his rules.

God doesn't want you to imitate those who do wrong. When someone tries to pressure you to do wrong, think about what God tells you to do in the Bible. Don't follow the crowd if the crowd leads you the wrong way.

Surf on to these Faithlinks for some other good advice:

Good Advice?, Leviticus 20:6, p. 162

Following the Crowd, Numbers 13; 14, p. 193

Learning to Listen, 1 Samuel 3, p. 358

Wisdom in Store, Proverbs 2:6–7, p. 828

Get Ready!, Mark 13:26–27, p. 1354

How Do You Grow?, Titus 1:1, p. 1659

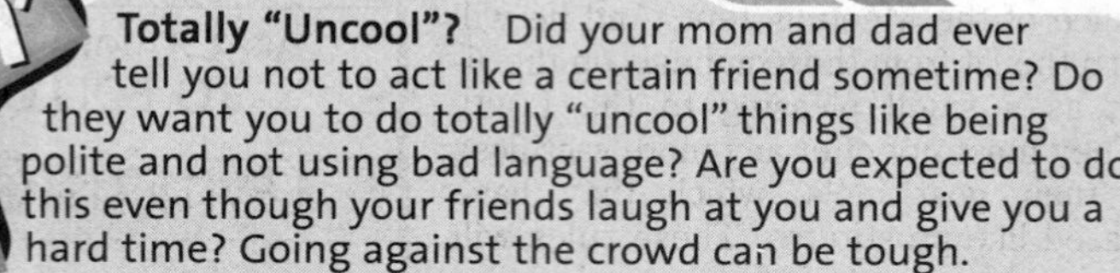

PEER PRESSURE
Leviticus 18:1–5

Livin' it

Totally "Uncool"? Did your mom and dad ever tell you not to act like a certain friend sometime? Do they want you to do totally "uncool" things like being polite and not using bad language? Are you expected to do this even though your friends laugh at you and give you a hard time? Going against the crowd can be tough.

But God warns us not to follow the crowd, especially when the crowd is going in the opposite direction of what God wants us to do. Following those who are doing the wrong things goes against what God says. (Check out Leviticus 18:1–3.)

Some people like to follow the crowd and it can get them in big trouble! (Read Numbers 13; 14.) Are you a crowd-follower, or are you willing to take a stand for God?

MORE FAITH links

An Example Not to Follow, p. 157
Following the Crowd, p. 193
Fear God or People?, p. 1047
A Real Crowd-pleaser?, p. 1222

"Hey, Skweek, I've got some friends who think it's cool to make fun of other kids. I'm not too sure about that."

"Good idea, Tagg, to stop and think before you follow what the crowd thinks is 'cool.' That could get you into lots of trouble. Better check out these Faithlinks, too, for some more good advice."

Give In or Take a Stand?, 1 Kings 22:13–14, p. 472
- "C'mon and try it. Everybody's doin' it." Ever heard words like that before? What do you do when you feel pressured to do something "everybody else" is doing?
- Have you ever been the only one to stand up for what's right? How did you feel? Whenever you stand for what's right, remember God stands with you.

Two Kinds of People, Psalm 1, p. 710
- Link here to find out how to choose between the two different kinds of people you meet.

The Unpopular Choice, Mark 15:42–43, p. 1360
- How important is popularity to you? Would you be willing to admit you believed in something if doing so made you unpopular?
- It often takes courage to follow Jesus. Are you courageous enough to make an unpopular choice and take the risk of being thought of as "uncool"?

my FAVORITE links

but you must not do what was done in
that country. And you must not do as they
do in the land of Canaan, where I am
bringing you. Do not follow their customs. 4You must obey my rules
and follow them. I
am the LORD your
God. 5Obey my laws
and rules; a person
who obeys them will
live because of them.
I am the LORD.

EMAIL FROM GOD
18:3–5
Following God
Should you follow other people?

6" 'You must never have sexual relations with your close relatives. I am the
LORD.
7" 'You must not shame your father by
having sexual relations with your mother.
She is your mother; do not have sexual
relations with her. 8You must not have
sexual relations with your father's wife;
that would shame your father.
9" 'You must not have sexual relations
with your sister, either the daughter of
your father or your mother. It doesn't
matter if she was born in your house or
somewhere else.
10" 'You must not have sexual relations with your son's daughter or your
daughter's daughter; that would bring
shame on you.
11" 'If your father and his wife have a
daughter, she is your sister. You must not
have sexual relations with her.
12" 'You must not have sexual relations with your father's sister; she is your
father's close relative. 13You must not
have sexual relations with your mother's
sister; she is your mother's close relative.
14You must not have sexual relations with
the wife of your father's brother, because
this would shame him. She is your aunt.
15" 'You must not have sexual relations with your daughter-in-law; she is
your son's wife. Do not have sexual relations with her.
16" 'You must not have sexual relations with your brother's wife. That
would shame your brother.
17" 'You must not have sexual relations with both a woman and her daughter.
And do not have sexual relations with
this woman's granddaughter, either the
daughter of her son or her daughter; they
are her close relatives. It is evil to do this.
18" 'While your wife is still living, you
must not take her sister as another wife. Do
not have sexual relations with her.
19" 'You must not go near a woman to
have sexual relations with her during her
monthly period, when she is unclean.
20" 'You must not have sexual relations with your neighbor's wife and make
yourself unclean with her.
21" 'You must not give any of your
children to be sacrificed to Molech, because this would show that you do not
respect your God. I am the LORD.
22" 'You must not have sexual relations with a man as you would a woman.
That is a hateful sin.
23" 'You must not have sexual relations with an animal and make yourself
unclean with it. Also a woman must not
have sexual relations with an animal; it is
not natural.
24" 'Don't make yourself unclean by
any of these wrong things. I am forcing
nations out of their countries because
they did these sins, and I am giving their
land to you. 25The land has become unclean, and I punished it for its sins, so the
land is throwing out those people who
live there.
26" 'You must obey my laws and
rules, and you must not do any of these
hateful sins. These rules are for the citizens of Israel and for the people who live
with you. 27The people who lived in the
land before you did all these hateful
things and made the land unclean. 28If
you do these things, you will also make
the land unclean, and it will throw you
out as it threw out the nations before you.
29Anyone who does these hateful sins
must be cut off from the people. 30Keep
my command not to do these hateful sins
that were done by the people who lived in
the land before you. Don't make yourself
unclean by doing them. I am the LORD
your God.' "

Other Laws

19 The LORD said to Moses, 2"Tell
all the people of Israel: 'I am the
LORD your God. You must be holy because I am holy.

3" 'You must respect your mother and
father, and you must keep my
Sabbaths. I am the
LORD your God.
4" 'Do not wor-
ship idols or make
statues or gods for
yourselves. I am the
LORD your God.

EMAIL FROM GOD
19:3
Respect
Respect your parents.

5" 'When you sacrifice a fellowship offering to the LORD, offer it in such a way
that will be accepted. 6You may eat it the
same day you offer it or on the next day.
But if any is left on the third day, you must
burn it up. 7If any of it is eaten on the
third day, it is unclean, and it will not
be accepted. 8Anyone who eats it then
will be guilty of sin, because he did not
respect the holy things that belong to
the LORD. He must be cut off from the
people.

9" 'When you harvest your crops on
your land, do not harvest all the way to
the corners of your fields. If grain falls
onto the ground, don't gather it up.
10Don't pick all the grapes in your vineyards, and don't pick up the grapes that
fall to the ground. You must leave those
things for poor people and for people
traveling through your country. I am the
LORD your God.

11" 'You must not steal. You must not
cheat people, and you must not lie to
each other. 12You must not make a false
promise by my name, or you will show
that you don't respect your God. I am the
LORD.

13" 'You must not cheat your neighbor or rob him. You must not keep a hired
worker's salary all night until morning.
14You must not curse a deaf person or
put something in front of a blind person
to make him fall. But you must respect
your God. I am the LORD.

15" 'Be fair in your judging. You must
not show special favor to poor people or
great people, but be fair when you judge
your neighbor. 16You must not spread
false stories against other people, and
you must not do anything that would put
your neighbor's life in danger. I am the
LORD.

17" 'You must not hate your fellow

FAITH links

GIVE REVENGE A REST

LEVITICUS 19:18

More than likely, you've heard someone talk about getting even with someone for what that person did. Maybe the person talking *was* you. A special law was given to the people of Israel about getting even with others. That law is also for us today. God told the people to avoid getting even with someone or holding a grudge. Instead, they were to love their neighbors.

Thoughts of revenge are natural for humans. But God doesn't want us to do what comes naturally. When we're angry, we easily sin. That's why God commands us to give revenge a rest. Instead, we're to love our neighbors.

Want to know more about loving your enemies? Check out these links:

More Powerful Than Revenge, Genesis 50:14–21, p. 71

Play Fair or Play Favorites?, Deuteronomy 1:16–18, p. 227

Mourning for an Enemy, 2 Samuel 1, p. 399

Anger: Quick or Slow?, Psalm 86:15, p. 776

Get Hot or Keep Cool?, Proverbs 12:16, p. 842

Forgive Again?, Luke 17:3–4, p. 1402

FAITH links

SHOW SOME RESPECT

LEVITICUS 19:32

Ever feel like grown-ups put you down or ignore you because you're a kid? Guess what. Many elderly people feel the same way. They often find themselves forgotten or disrespected by those who are younger.

God commanded the people of Israel to show respect to the elderly. That command is for you as well. Elderly people have a lot of wisdom and experience to offer. If you can, take time to get to know someone older. He or she will be pleased with the respect you offer.

Roll Out the Welcome Wagon, Genesis 18:2–8, p. 24

Obey? No Way!, Exodus 1:15–21, p. 76

Play Fair or Play Favorites?, Deuteronomy 1:16–18, p. 227

A Blueprint for Living, Amos 5:14–15, p. 1200

The Right Ingredients, Micah 6:8, p. 1227

Full of Faith, 1 Thessalonians 4:1, p. 1633

citizen in your heart. If your neighbor
does something wrong, tell him about it,
or you will be partly to blame. **18**Forget
about the wrong things people do to you,
and do not try to get even. Love your
neighbor as you love yourself. I am the
LORD.

19" 'Obey my laws. You must not mate
two different kinds of cattle or sow your
field with two different kinds of seed. You
must not wear clothing made from two different kinds of material mixed together.

20" 'If a man has sexual relations with
a slave girl of another man, but this slave
girl has not been bought or given her freedom, there must be punishment. But they
are not to be put to death, because the
woman was not free. **21**The man must
bring a male sheep as his penalty offering
to the LORD at the entrance to the Meeting Tent. **22**The priest will offer the sheep
as a penalty offering before the LORD for
the man's sin, to remove the sins of the
man so he will belong to the LORD. Then
he will be forgiven for his sin.

23" 'In the future, when you enter
your country, you will plant many kinds
of trees for food. After planting a tree,
wait three years before using its fruit.
24In the fourth year the fruit from the
tree will be the LORD's, a holy offering of
praise to him. **25**Then in the fifth year,
you may eat the fruit from the tree. The
tree will then produce more fruit for you.
I am the LORD your God.

26" 'You must not eat anything with
the blood in it.

" 'You must not try to tell the future
by signs or black magic.

27" 'You must not cut the hair on the
sides of your heads or cut the edges of
your beard. **28**You must not cut your body
to show sadness for someone who died or
put tattoo marks on yourselves. I am the
LORD.

29" 'Do not dishonor your daughter
by making her become a prostitute. If you
do this, the country will be filled with all
kinds of sin.

30" 'Obey the laws about Sabbaths,
and respect my Most Holy Place. I am
the LORD.

31" 'Do not go to mediums or fortune-
tellers for advice, or you will become unclean. I am the LORD your God.

32" 'Show respect to old people; stand
up in their presence. Show respect also
to your God. I am the LORD.

33" 'Do not mistreat foreigners living
in your country, **34**but treat them just as
you treat your own citizens. Love foreigners as you love yourselves, because

you were foreigners one time in Egypt. I
am the LORD your God.
35“ ‘Do not cheat when you measure
the length or weight or amount of something. **36**Your weights and balances
should weigh correctly, with your weighing baskets the right size and your jars
holding the right amount of liquid. I am
the LORD your God. I brought you out of
the land of Egypt.
37“ ‘Remember all my laws and rules,
and obey them. I am the LORD.’ ”

Warnings About Various Sins

20 The LORD said to Moses, **2**“You
must also tell the people of Israel
these things: ‘If a person in your country
gives one of his children to Molech, that
person must be killed. It doesn’t matter if
he is a citizen or a foreigner living in Israel; you must throw stones at him and
kill him. **3**I will be against him and cut
him off from his people, because he gave
his children to Molech. He showed that
he did not respect my holy name, and he
made my Holy Place unclean. **4**The people of the community might ignore that
person and not kill the one who gave his
children to Molech. **5**But I will be against
him and his family, and I will cut him off
from his people. I will do this to anyone
who follows him in being unfaithful to me
by worshiping Molech.
6“ ‘I will be against anyone who goes
to mediums and fortune-tellers for advice,
because that person is being unfaithful to
me. So I will cut him off from his people.
7“ ‘Be my holy people. Be holy because I am the LORD your God. **8**Remember and obey my laws. I am the LORD, and
I have made you holy.
9“ ‘Anyone who curses his father or
mother must be put to death. He has
cursed his father or mother, so he has
brought his own death on himself.

Punishments for Sexual Sins

10“ ‘If a man has sexual relations with
his neighbor’s wife, both the man and the
woman are guilty of adultery and must be
put to death. **11**If a man has sexual relations with his father’s wife, he has
shamed his father, and both the man and
his father’s wife must be put to death.
They have brought it on themselves.
12“ ‘If a man has sexual relations with
his daughter-in-law, both of them must be
put to death. What they have done is not

GOOD ADVICE?

LEVITICUS 20:6

What do you depend on for answers when you need direction? Some people call up the psychic hotline. Others don’t make a move without checking their horoscope in the newspaper or online. Still others think that Magic 8 balls or Ouija boards are fun ways to find out information.

God told the Israelites to avoid asking fortune-tellers or mediums for advice. He knew that these individuals offered “quick-fix” information that did not come from him. God wanted the people to trust him for answers. That’s what he wants you to do, too.

An Example Not to Follow, Leviticus 18:1–3, p. 157

The Cloud Guide, Numbers 9:15–23, p. 188

Facts About Following, Joshua 6, p. 283

Help to Understand, 2 Samuel 14, p. 416

What God Thinks, Isaiah 55:8–9, p. 969

One Thing to Do, Romans 4:1–5, p. 1523

natural. They have brought their own
deaths on themselves.
13" 'If a man has sexual relations with
another man as a man does with a woman,
these two men have done a hateful sin.
They must be put to death. They have
brought it on themselves.
14" 'If a man has sexual relations with
both a woman and her mother, this is evil.
The people must burn that man and the
two women in fire so that your people
will not be evil.
15" 'If a man has sexual relations with
an animal, he must be put to death. You
must also kill the animal. **16**If a woman
approaches an animal and has sexual
relations with it, you must kill the woman
and the animal. They must be put to
death. They have brought it on themselves.
17" 'It is shameful for a brother to
marry his sister, the daughter of either
his father or his mother, and to have sexual relations with her. In front of everyone they must both be cut off from their
people. The man has shamed his sister,
and he is guilty of sin.
18" 'If a man has sexual relations with
a woman during her monthly period, both
the woman and the man must be cut off
from their people. They sinned because
they showed the source of her blood.
19" 'Do not have sexual relations with
your mother's sister or your father's sister, because that would shame a close relative. Both of you are guilty of this sin.
20" 'If a man has sexual relations with
his uncle's wife, he has shamed his uncle.
That man and his uncle's wife will die
without children; they are guilty of sin.
21" 'It is unclean for a man to marry
his brother's wife. That man has shamed
his brother, and they will have no children.
22" 'Remember all my laws and rules,
and obey them. I am leading you to your
own land, and if you obey my laws and
rules, that land will not throw you out.
23I am forcing out ahead of you the people who live there. Because they did all
these sins, I have hated them. Do not live
the way those people lived.
24" 'I have told you that you will get
their land, which I will give to you as your
very own; it is a fertile land. I am the
LORD your God, and I have set you apart
from other people and made you my own.
25So you must treat clean animals and
birds differently from unclean animals
and birds. Do not make yourselves unclean by any of these unclean birds or animals or things that crawl on the ground,
which I have made unclean for you. **26**So
you must be holy to me because I, the
LORD, am holy, and I have set you apart
from other people to be my own.
27" 'A man or woman who is a medium or a fortune-teller must be put to
death. You must stone them to death;
they have brought it on themselves.' "

How Priests Must Behave

21 The LORD said to Moses, "Tell
these things to Aaron's sons, the
priests: 'A priest must not make himself
unclean by touching a dead person. **2**But
if the dead person was one of his close
relatives, he may touch him. The priest
may make himself unclean if the dead
person is his mother or father, son or
daughter, brother or **3**unmarried sister
who is close to him because she has no
husband. The priest may make himself
unclean for her if she dies. **4**But a priest
must not make himself unclean if the
dead person was only related to him by
marriage.
5" 'Priests must not shave their
heads, or shave off the edges of their
beards, or cut their bodies. **6**They must
be holy to their God and show respect for
God's name, because they present the offerings made by fire to the LORD, which is
the food of their God. So they must
be holy.
7" 'A priest must not marry an unclean prostitute or a divorced woman, because he is holy to his God. **8**Treat him as
holy, because he offers up the food of
your God. Think of him as holy; I am the
LORD who makes you holy, and I am holy.
9" 'If a priest's daughter makes herself unclean by becoming a prostitute,
she shames her father. She must be
burned with fire.
10" 'The high priest, who was chosen

from among his brothers, had the special
olive oil poured on his head. He was also
appointed to wear the priestly clothes. So
he must not show his sadness by letting
his hair go uncombed or tearing his
clothes. **11**He must not go into a house
where there is a dead body. He must not
make himself unclean, even if it is for his
own father or mother. **12**The high priest
must not go out of the Holy Place, because if he does and becomes unclean, he
will make God's Holy Place unclean. The
special oil used in appointing priests was
poured on his head to separate him from
the rest of the people. I am the LORD.

13" 'The high priest must marry a
woman who is a virgin. **14**He must not
marry a widow, a divorced woman, or a
prostitute. He must marry a virgin from
his own people **15**so the people will respect his children as his own. I am the
LORD. I have set the high priest apart for
his special job.' "

16The LORD said to Moses, **17**"Tell
Aaron: 'If any of your descendants have
something wrong with them, they must
never come near to offer the special food
of their God. **18**Anyone who has something wrong with him must not come
near: blind men, crippled men, men with
damaged faces, deformed men, **19**men
with a crippled foot or hand, **20**hunchbacks,
dwarfs, men who have something wrong
with their eyes, men who have an itching
disease or a skin disease,
or men who have dam-
aged sex glands.

21" 'If one of Aaron's
descendants has some-
thing wrong with him, he
cannot come near to make
the offerings made by fire
to the LORD. He has some-
thing wrong with him; he
cannot offer the food of
his God. **22**He may eat
the most holy food and also the holy food.
23But he may not go through the curtain
into the Most Holy Place, and he may not
go near the altar, because he has something wrong with him. He must not make
my Holy Place unfit. I am the LORD who
makes these places holy.' "

> These offerings are holy, and they are mine, so you must respect them to show that you respect my holy name.
> —Leviticus 22:2

24So Moses told these things to
Aaron, Aaron's sons, and all the people of
Israel.

22 The LORD said to Moses, **2**"Tell
Aaron and his sons: 'The people of
Israel will give offerings to me. These offerings are holy, and they are mine, so
you must respect them to show that you
respect my holy name. I am the LORD.'
3Say to them: 'If any one of your descendants from now on is unclean and comes
near the offerings that the Israelites
made holy for me, that person must be
cut off from appearing before me. I am
the LORD.

4" 'If one of Aaron's descendants has
a harmful skin disease, or if he discharges a body fluid, he cannot eat the
holy offerings until he becomes clean. He
could also become unclean from touching
a dead body, from his own semen,[n] **5**from
touching any unclean crawling animal, or
from touching an unclean person (no
matter what made the person unclean).
6Anyone who touches those things will
become unclean until evening. That person must not eat the holy offerings unless he washes with water. **7**He will be
clean only after the sun goes down. Then
he may eat the holy offerings; the offerings are his food.

8" 'If a priest finds an animal that died
by itself or that was killed by some other
animal, he must not eat it. If he does, he
will become unclean. I am
the LORD.

9" 'If the priests keep
all the rules I have given,
they will not become
guilty; if they are careful,
they will not die. I am the
LORD who has made them
holy. **10**Only people in a
priest's family may eat the
holy offering. A visitor
staying with the priest or
a hired worker must not eat it. **11**But if the
priest buys a slave with his own money,
that slave may eat the holy offerings;
slaves who were born in his house may

22:4 semen A man's body fluid by which he can make a woman pregnant.

also eat his food. **12**If a priest's daughter marries a person who is not a priest, she must not eat any of the holy offerings. **13**But if the priest's daughter becomes widowed or divorced, with no children to support her, and if she goes back to her father's house where she lived as a child, she may eat some of her father's food. But only people from a priest's family may eat this food.

14" 'If someone eats some of the holy offering by mistake, that person must pay back the priest for that holy food, adding another one-fifth of the price of that food.

15" 'When the Israelites give their holy offerings to the LORD, the priest must not treat these holy things as though they were not holy. **16**The priests must not allow those who are not priests to eat the holy offerings. If they do, they cause the ones who eat the holy offerings to become guilty, and they will have to pay for it. I am the LORD, who makes them holy.' "

17The LORD said to Moses, **18**"Tell Aaron and his sons and all the people of Israel: 'A citizen of Israel or a foreigner living in Israel might want to bring a whole burnt offering, either for some special promise he has made or for a special gift he wants to give to the LORD. **19**If he does, he must bring a male animal that has nothing wrong with it—a bull, a sheep, or a goat—so it might be accepted for him. **20**He must not bring an animal that has something wrong with it, or it will not be accepted for him.

21" 'If someone brings a fellowship offering to the LORD, either as payment for a special promise the person has made or as a special gift the person wants to give the LORD, it might be from the herd or from the flock. But it must be healthy, with nothing wrong with it, so that it will be accepted. **22**You must not offer to the LORD any animal that is blind, that has broken bones or is crippled, that has running sores or any sort of skin disease. You must not offer any animals like these on the altar as an offering by fire to the LORD.

23" 'If an ox or lamb is smaller than normal or is not perfectly formed, you may give it as a special gift to the LORD; it will be accepted. But it will not be accepted as payment for a special promise you have made.

24" 'If an animal has bruised, crushed, torn, or cut sex glands, you must not offer it to the LORD. You must not do this in your own land, **25**and you must not take such animals from foreigners as sacrifices to the LORD. Because the animals have been hurt in some way and have something wrong with them, they will not be accepted for you.' "

26The LORD said to Moses, **27**"When an ox, a sheep, or a goat is born, it must stay seven days with its mother. But from the eighth day on, this animal will be accepted as a sacrifice by fire to the LORD. **28**But you must not kill the animal and its mother on the same day, either an ox or a sheep.

29"If you want to offer some special offering of thanks to the LORD, you must do it in a way that pleases him. **30**You must eat the whole animal that same day and not leave any of the meat for the next morning. I am the LORD.

31"Remember my commands and obey them; I am the LORD. **32**Show respect for my holy name. You Israelites must remember that I am holy; I am the LORD, who has made you holy. **33**I brought you out of Egypt to be your God. I am the LORD."

Special Holidays

23 The LORD said to Moses, **2**"Tell the people of Israel: 'You will announce the LORD's appointed feasts as holy meetings. These are my special feasts.

The Sabbath

3" 'There are six days for you to work, but the seventh day will be a special day of rest. It is a day for a holy meeting; you must not do any work. It is a Sabbath to the LORD in all your homes.

The Passover and Unleavened Bread

4" 'These are the LORD's appointed feasts, the holy meetings, which you will

A HOLIDAY EVERY WEEK

LEVITICUS 23:1-3

Wouldn't it be great to have a holiday every week? Well, guess what. God took care of that! There *is* a special day each week that is considered a holiday. That day is Sunday. God set aside the Sabbath day for his people to rest and worship him. That makes Sunday a mini-holiday every week.

Many people spend time preparing for holidays in special ways. You can prepare for Sunday, too. How? One way to prepare is to get your heart ready to worship God. You can do this by reminding yourself of what God has done for you. You can also tell him you're sorry for anything you did wrong.

Here are some more Faithlinks about the importance of spending time with God:

A Thanksgiving Reminder, Exodus 12, p. 91

Idol Talk, Exodus 32, p. 118

You're Invited!, Psalm 100, p. 784

The One Who Suffered, Isaiah 53, p. 966

First Place, Haggai 1:7–11, p. 1248

From Useless to Useful, Philemon 11, p. 1663

announce at the times set for them. **5**The
LORD's Passover is on the fourteenth day
of the first month, beginning at twilight.
6The Feast of Unleavened Bread begins
on the fifteenth day of the same month.
You will eat bread made without yeast for
seven days. **7**On the first day of this feast
you will have a holy meeting, and you
must not do any work. **8**For seven days
you will bring an offering made by fire to
the LORD. There will be a holy meeting
on the seventh day, and on that day you
must not do any regular work.' "

The First of the Harvest

9The LORD said to Moses, **10**"Tell the
people of Israel: 'You will enter the land I
will give you and gather its harvest. At
that time you must bring the first bundle
of grain from your harvest to the priest.
11The priest will present the bundle before the LORD, and it will be accepted for
you; he will present the bundle on the
day after the Sabbath.
12" 'On the day when you present the
bundle of grain, offer a male lamb, one
year old, that has nothing wrong with it,
as a burnt offering to the LORD. **13**You
must also offer a grain offering—four
quarts of fine flour mixed with olive oil as
an offering made by fire to the LORD; its
smell will be pleasing to him. You must
also offer a quart of wine as a drink offering. **14**Until the day you bring your offering to your God, do not eat any new grain,
roasted grain, or bread made from new
grain. This law will always continue for
people from now on, wherever you live.

The Feast of Weeks

15" 'Count seven full weeks from the
morning after the Sabbath. (This is the
Sabbath that you bring the bundle of
grain to present as an offering.) **16**On the
fiftieth day, the first day after the seventh
week, you will bring a new grain offering
to the LORD. **17**On that day bring two
loaves of bread from your homes to be
presented as an offering. Use yeast and
four quarts of flour to make those loaves
of bread; they will be your gift to the
LORD from the first wheat of your harvest.

18" 'Offer with the bread one young
bull, two male sheep, and seven male
lambs that are one year old and have
nothing wrong with them. Offer them
with their grain offerings and drink offerings, as a burnt offering to the LORD.
They will be an offering made by fire, and
the smell will be pleasing to the LORD.
19You must also offer one male goat for a
sin offering and two male, one-year-old
lambs as a fellowship offering.

20" 'The priest will present the two
lambs as an offering before the LORD,
along with the bread from the first wheat
of the harvest. They are holy to the
LORD, and they will belong to the priest.
21On that same day you will call a holy
meeting; you must not do any work that
day. This law will continue for you from
now on, wherever you live.

22" 'When you harvest your crops on
your land, do not harvest all the way to
the corners of your field. If grain falls
onto the ground, don't gather it up. Leave
it for poor people and foreigners in your
country. I am the LORD your God.' "

The Feast of Trumpets

23Again the LORD said to Moses,
24"Tell the people of Israel: 'On the first
day of the seventh month you must have
a special day of rest, a holy meeting,
when you blow the trumpet for a special
time of remembering. **25**Do not do any
work, and bring an offering made by fire
to the LORD.' "

The Day of Cleansing

26The LORD said to Moses, **27**"The
Day of Cleansing will be on the tenth day
of the seventh month. There will be a
holy meeting, and you will give up eating
and bring an offering made by fire to the
LORD. **28**Do not do any work on that day,
because it is the Day of Cleansing. On
that day the priests will go before the
LORD and perform the acts to make you
clean so you will belong to the LORD.

29"Anyone who refuses to give up
food on this day must be cut off from the
people. **30**If anyone works on this day, I
will destroy that person from among the
people. **31**You must not do any work at
all; this law will continue for people from
now on wherever you live. **32**It will be a
special day of rest for you, and you must
not eat. You will start this special day of
rest on the evening after the ninth day of
the month, and it will continue from that
evening until the next evening."

The Feast of Shelters

33Again the LORD said to Moses,
34"Tell the people of Israel: 'On the fifteenth day of the seventh month is the
Feast of Shelters. This feast to the LORD
will continue for seven days. **35**There
will be a holy meeting on the first day; do
not do any work. **36**You will bring an offering made by fire to the LORD each day
for seven days. On the eighth day you
will have another holy meeting, and you
will bring an offering made by fire to the
LORD. This will be a holy meeting; do not
do any work.

37(" 'These are the LORD's special
feasts, when there will be holy meetings
and when you bring offerings made by
fire to the LORD. You will bring whole
burnt offerings, grain offerings, sacrifices, and drink offerings—each at the
right time. **38**These offerings are in addition to those for the LORD's Sabbath
days, in addition to offerings you give as
payment for special promises, and in addition to special offerings you want to
give to the LORD.)

39" 'So on the fifteenth day of the seventh month, after you have gathered in
the crops of the land, celebrate the
LORD's festival for seven days. You must
rest on the first day and the eighth day.
40On the first day you will take good fruit
from the fruit trees, as well as branches
from palm trees, poplars, and other leafy
trees. You will celebrate before the LORD
your God for seven days. **41**Celebrate
this festival to the LORD for seven days
each year. This law will continue from
now on; you will celebrate it in the seventh month. **42**Live in shelters for seven
days. All the people born in Israel must
live in shelters **43**so that all your descendants will know I made Israel live in shelters during the time I brought them out
of Egypt. I am the LORD your God.' "

44So Moses told the people of Israel
about all of the LORD's appointed feast
days.

The Lampstand and the Holy Bread

24 The LORD said to Moses, **2**"Command the people of Israel to bring
you pure oil from crushed olives. That oil
is for the lamps so that these lamps may
never go out. **3**Aaron will keep the lamps
burning in the Meeting Tent from evening until morning before the LORD; this
is in front of the curtain of the Ark of the
Agreement. This law will continue from
now on. **4**Aaron must always keep the
lamps burning on the lampstands of pure
gold before the LORD.
5"Take fine flour and bake twelve
loaves of bread with it, using four quarts
of flour for each loaf. **6**Put them in two
rows on the golden table before the
LORD, six loaves in each row. **7**Put pure
incense on each row as the memorial portion to take the place of the bread. It is an
offering made by fire to the LORD.
8Every Sabbath day Aaron will put the
bread in order before the LORD, as an
agreement with the people of Israel that
will continue forever. **9**That bread will
belong to Aaron and his
sons. They will eat it in a
holy place, because it is a
most holy part of the of-
ferings made by fire to
the LORD. That bread is
their share forever."

The Man Who Cursed God

10Now there was a
son of an Israelite woman
and an Egyptian father who was walking
among the Israelites. A fight broke out in
the camp between him and an Israelite.
11The son of the Israelite woman began
cursing and speaking against the LORD,
so the people took him to Moses. (The
mother's name was Shelomith, the
daughter of Dibri from the family of Dan.)
12The people held him as a prisoner
while they waited for the LORD's command to be made clear to them.
13Then the LORD said to Moses,
14"Take the one who spoke against me
outside the camp. Then all the people
who heard him must put their hands on
his head, and all the people must throw
stones at him and kill him. **15**Tell the people of Israel this: 'If anyone curses his
God, he is guilty of sin. **16**Anyone who
speaks against the LORD must be put to
death; all the people must kill him by
throwing stones at him. Foreigners must
be punished just like the people born in
Israel; if they speak against the LORD,
they must be put to death.
17" 'Whoever kills another person
must be put to death. **18**Whoever kills an
animal that belongs to another person
must give that person another animal to
take its place. **19**And whoever causes an
injury to a neighbor must receive the
same kind of injury in return: **20**Broken
bone for broken bone, eye for eye, tooth
for tooth. Anyone who injures another
person must be injured in the same way in
return. **21**Whoever kills another person's
animal must give that person another animal to take its place. But whoever kills another person must be put to death.
22" 'The law will be the same for the
foreigner as for those from your own
country. I am the LORD
your God.' "
23Then Moses spoke
to the people of Israel,
and they took the person
who had cursed outside
the camp and killed him
by throwing stones at
him. So the people of Is-
rael did as the LORD had
commanded Moses.

> The law will be the same for the foreigner as for those from your own country. I am the LORD your God.
> —Leviticus 24:22

The Time of Rest for the Land

25 The LORD said to Moses at Mount
Sinai, **2**"Tell the people of Israel
this: 'When you enter the land I will give
you, let it have a special time of rest, to
honor the LORD. **3**You may plant seed in
your field for six years, and you may trim
your vineyards for six years and bring in
their fruits. **4**But during the seventh
year, you must let the land rest. This will
be a special time to honor the LORD. You

must not plant seed in your field or trim
your vineyards. **5**You must not cut the
crops that grow by themselves after harvest, or gather the grapes from your
vines that are not trimmed. The land will
have a year of rest.

6" 'You may eat whatever the land
produces during that year of rest. It will
be food for your men and women servants, for your hired workers, and for the
foreigners living in your country. **7**It will
also be food for your cattle and the wild
animals of your land. Whatever the land
produces may be eaten.

The Year of Jubilee

8" 'Count off seven groups of seven
years, or forty-nine years. During that
time there will be seven years of rest for
the land. **9**On the Day of Cleansing, you
must blow the horn of a male sheep; this
will be on the tenth day of the seventh
month. You must blow the horn through
the whole country. **10**Make the fiftieth
year a special year, and announce freedom for all the people living in your country. This time will be called Jubilee.* You
will each go back to your own property,
each to your own family and family group.
11The fiftieth year will be a special time
for you to celebrate. Don't plant seeds, or
harvest the crops that grow by themselves, or gather grapes from the vines
that are not trimmed. **12**That year is Jubilee; it will be a holy time for you. You may
eat only the crops that come from the
field. **13**In the year of Jubilee you each
must go back to your own property.

14" 'If you sell your land to your
neighbor, or if you buy land from your
neighbor, don't cheat each other. **15**If you
want to buy your neighbor's land, count
the number of years since the last Jubilee, and use that number to decide the
right price. If your neighbor sells the land
to you, count the number of years left for
harvesting crops, and use that number to
decide the right price. **16**If there are
many years, the price will be high. But
if there are only a few years, lower the
price, because your neighbor is really
selling only a few crops to you. **17**You
must not cheat each other, but you must
respect your God. I am the LORD your
God.

18" 'Remember my laws and rules,
and obey them so that you will live safely
in the land. **19**The land will give good
crops to you, and you will eat as much as
you want and live safely in the land.

20" 'But you might ask, "If we don't
plant seeds or gather crops, what will we
eat the seventh year?" **21**I will send you
such a great blessing during the sixth
year that the land will produce enough
crops for three years. **22**When you plant
in the eighth year, you will still be eating
from the old crop; you will eat the old
crop until the harvest of the ninth year.

Property Laws

23" 'The land really belongs to me, so
you can't sell it for all time. You are only
foreigners and travelers living for a while
on my land. **24**People might sell their
land, but it must always be possible for
the family to get its land back. **25**If a person in your country becomes very poor
and sells some land, then close relatives
must come and buy it back. **26**If there is
not a close relative to buy the land back,
but if the person makes enough money to
be able to buy it back, **27**the years must
be counted since the land was sold. That
number must be used to decide how
much the first owner should pay back the
one who bought it. Then the land will belong to the first owner again. **28**But if
there is not enough money to buy it back,
the one who bought it will keep it until
the year of Jubilee. During that celebration, the land will go back to the first
owner's family.

29" 'If someone sells a home in a
walled city, for a full year after it is sold,
the person has the right to buy it back.
30But if the owner does not buy back the
house before a full year is over, it will belong to the one who bought it and to his
future sons. The house will not go back
to the first owner at Jubilee. **31**But
houses in small towns without walls are
like open country; they can be bought

25:10 Jubilee This word comes from the Hebrew word for a horn of a male sheep.

back, and they must be returned to their
first owner at Jubilee.
32" 'The Levites may always buy
back their houses in the cities that belong to them. **33**If someone buys a house
from a Levite, that house in the Levites'
city will again belong to the Levites in
the Jubilee. This is because houses in
Levite cities belong to the people of Levi;
the Israelites gave these cities to them.
34Also the fields and pastures around the
Levites' cities cannot be sold, because
those fields belong to the Levites forever.

Rules for Slave Owners

35" 'If anyone from your country becomes too poor to support himself, help
him to live among you as you would a
stranger or foreigner. **36**Do not charge
him any interest on money you loan to
him, but respect your God; let the poor
live among you. **37**Don't lend him money
for interest, and don't try to make a profit
from the food he buys. **38**I am the LORD
your God, who brought you out of the
land of Egypt to give the land of Canaan
to you and to become your God.
39" 'If anyone from your country becomes very poor and sells himself as a
slave to you, you must not make him
work like a slave. **40**He will be like a
hired worker and a visitor with you until
the year of Jubilee. **41**Then he may leave
you, take his children, and go back to his
family and the land of his ancestors.
42This is because the Israelites are my
servants, and I brought them out of slavery in Egypt. They must not become
slaves again. **43**You must not rule this
person cruelly, but you must respect
your God.
44" 'Your men and women slaves
must come from other nations around
you; from them you may buy slaves.
45Also you may buy as slaves children
from the families of foreigners living in
your land. These child slaves will belong
to you, **46**and you may even pass them on
to your children after you die; you can
make them slaves forever. But you must
not rule cruelly over your own people,
the Israelites.
47" 'Suppose a foreigner or visitor
among you becomes rich. If someone in
your country becomes so poor that he has
to sell himself as a slave to the foreigner
living among you or to a member of the
foreigner's family, **48**the poor person has
the right to be bought back and become
free. One of his relatives may buy him
back: **49**His uncle, his uncle's son, or any
one of his close relatives may buy him
back. Or, if he gets enough money, he may
pay the money to free himself.
50" 'He and the one who bought him
must count the time from when he sold
himself up to the next year of Jubilee.
Use that number to decide the price, because the person really only hired himself out for a certain number of years.
51If there are still many years before the
year of Jubilee, the person must pay back
a large part of the price. **52**If there are
only a few years left until Jubilee, the
person must pay a small part of the first
price. **53**But he will live like a hired person with the foreigner every year; don't
let the foreigner rule cruelly over him.
54" 'Even if no one buys him back, at
the year of Jubilee, he and his children
will become free. **55**This is because the
people of Israel are servants to me. They
are my servants, whom I brought out of
Egypt. I am the LORD your God.

Rewards for Obeying God

26 " 'Don't make idols for yourselves
or set up statues or memorials.
Don't put stone statues in your land to
bow down to, because I am the LORD
your God.
2" 'Remember my Sabbaths, and respect my Holy Place. I am the
LORD.

eMAiL! FROM GOD
26:3–5
Blessings
Find out the key to God's blessings.

3" 'If you remem-
ber my laws and
commands and obey
them, **4**I will give
you rains at the right
season; the land will produce crops, and
the trees of the field will produce their
fruit. **5**Your threshing will continue until
the grape harvest, and your grape harvest will continue until it is time to plant.
Then you will have plenty to eat and live

FAITH links

REWARD FOR OBEDIENCE

LEVITICUS 26:3-13

Have you ever been rewarded for doing the right thing? God told the people of Israel that he would reward them for obeying him. He would give them children and they would have a good harvest. Best of all, he promised not to turn away from them.

God does not always reward us with material things in this life. But he does promise to supply what we need. He also promises never to leave us. As a Christian, you can look forward to the biggest reward of all—living forever with Jesus.

A Special Promise, Numbers 30:1–2, p. 217

Your Stats, 1 Kings 15; 16, p. 460

All Talk, No Action, Jeremiah 5:1–2, p. 996

The God of Second Chances, Jonah 3, p. 1215

Perfectly Pleasing?, Matthew 5:1–12, p. 1280

The Way to Heaven, John 14:1–6, p. 1448

safely in your land. **6**I will give peace to
your country; you will lie down in peace,
and no one will make you afraid. I will
keep harmful animals out of your country,
and armies will not pass through it.
7" 'You will chase your enemies and
defeat them, killing them with your
sword. **8**Five of you will chase a hundred
men; a hundred of you will chase ten
thousand men. You will defeat your enemies and kill them with your sword.
9" 'Then I will show kindness to you
and let you have many children; I will
keep my agreement with you. **10**You will
have enough crops to last for more than a
year. When you harvest the new crops,
you will have to throw out the old ones to
make room for them. **11**Also I will place
my Holy Tent among you, and I will not
turn away from you. **12**I will walk with
you and be your God, and you will be my
people. **13**I am the LORD your God, who
brought you out of Egypt, where you
were slaves. I broke the heavy weights
that were on your shoulders and let you
walk proudly again.

Punishment for Not Obeying God

14" 'But if you do not obey me and
keep all my commands, **15**and if you turn
away from my rules and hate my laws,
refusing to obey all my commands, you
have broken our agreement. **16**As a result, I will do this to you: I will cause terrible things to happen to you. I will cause
you to have disease and fever that will
destroy your eyes and slowly kill you.
You will not have success when you plant
your seed, and your enemy will eat your
crops. **17**I will be against you, and your
enemies will defeat you. These people
who hate you will rule over you, and you
will run away even when no one is chasing you.
18" 'If after all this you still do not
obey me, I will punish you seven times
more for your sins. **19**I will break your
great pride, and I will make the sky like
iron and the earth like bronze.ⁿ **20**You will
work hard, but it will not help. Your land
will not grow any crops, and your trees
will not give their fruit.
21" 'If you still turn against me and
refuse to obey me, I will beat you seven
times harder. The more you sin, the more
you will be punished. **22**I will send wild

26:19 sky . . . bronze This means the sky will give no rain and the earth will produce no crops.

animals to attack you, and they will take your children away from you and destroy your cattle. They will make you so few in number the roads will be empty.

23" 'If you don't learn your lesson after all these things, and if you still turn against me, **24**I will also turn against you. I will punish you seven more times for your sins. **25**You broke my agreement, and I will punish you. I will bring armies against you, and if you go into your cities for safety, I will cause diseases to spread among you so that your enemy will defeat you. **26**There will be very little bread to eat; ten women will be able to cook all your bread in one oven. They will measure each piece of bread, and you will eat, but you will still be hungry.

27" 'If you still refuse to listen to me and still turn against me, **28**I will show my great anger; I will punish you seven more times for your sins. **29**You will eat the bodies of your sons and daughters. **30**I will destroy your places where gods are worshiped and cut down your incense altars. I will pile your dead bodies on the lifeless forms of your idols. I will hate you. **31**I will destroy your cities and make your holy places empty, and I will not smell the pleasing smell of your offerings. **32**I will make the land empty so that your enemies who come to live in it will be shocked at it. **33**I will scatter you among the nations, and I will pull out my sword and destroy you. Your land will become empty, your cities a waste. **34**When you are taken to your enemy's country, your land will finally get its rest. It will enjoy its time of rest all the time it lies empty. **35**During the time the land is empty, it will have the rest you should have given it while you lived in it.

36" 'Those of you who are left alive will lose their courage in the land of their enemies. They will be frightened by the sound of a leaf being blown by the wind. They will run as if someone were chasing them with a sword, and they will fall even when no one is chasing them. **37**They will fall over each other, as if someone were chasing them with a sword, even though no one is chasing them. You will not be strong enough to stand up against your enemies. **38**You will die among other nations and disappear in your enemies' countries. **39**So those who are left alive will rot away in their enemies' countries because of their sins. They will also rot away because of their ancestors' sins.

There Is Always Hope

40" 'But maybe the people will confess their sins and the sins of their ancestors; maybe they will admit they turned against me and sinned against me, **41**which made me turn against them and send them into the land of their enemies. If these disobedient people are sorry for what they did and accept punishment for their sin, **42**I will remember my agreement with Jacob, my agreement with Isaac, and my agreement with Abraham, and I will remember the land. **43**The land will be left empty by its people, and it will enjoy its time of rest as it lies bare without them. Then those who are left alive will accept the punishment for their sins. They will learn that they were punished because they hated my laws and refused to obey my rules. **44**But even though this is true, I will not turn away from them when they are in the land of their enemies. I will not hate them so much that I completely destroy them and break my agreement with them, because I am the LORD their God. **45**For their good I will remember the agreement with their ancestors, whom I brought out of the land of Egypt so I could become their God; the other nations saw these things. I am the LORD.' "

46These are the laws, rules, and teachings the LORD made between himself and the Israelites through Moses at Mount Sinai.

Promises Are Important

27 The LORD said to Moses, **2**"Speak to the people of Israel and tell them: 'If someone makes a special promise to give a person as a servant to the LORD by paying a price that is the same value as that person, **3**the price for a man twenty to sixty years old is about one and one-fourth pounds of silver. (You must

use the measure as set by the Holy
Place.) 4The price for a woman twenty to
sixty years old is about twelve ounces of
silver. 5The price for a man five to twenty
years old is about eight ounces of silver;
for a woman it is about four ounces of silver.
6The price for a baby boy one month
to five years old is about two ounces of
silver; for a baby girl the price is about
one and one-half ounces of silver. 7The
price for a man sixty years old or older is
about six ounces of silver; for a woman it
is about four ounces of silver.
8" 'If anyone is too poor to pay the
price, bring him to the priest, and the
priest will set the price. The priest will
decide how much money the person
making the vow can afford to pay.

Gifts to the Lord

9" 'Some animals may be used as sacrifices to the LORD. If someone promises
to bring one of these to the LORD, it will
become holy. 10That person must not try
to put another animal in its place or exchange it, a good animal for a bad one, or
a bad animal for a good one. If this happens, both animals will become holy.
11" 'Unclean animals cannot be offered as sacrifices to the LORD, and if
someone brings one of them to the LORD,
that animal must be brought to the priest.
12The priest will decide a price for the
animal, according to whether it is good or
bad; as the priest decides, that is the price
for the animal. 13If the person wants to
buy back the animal, an additional one-fifth must be added to the price.

Value of a House

14" 'If a person gives a house as holy
to the LORD, the priest must decide its
value, according to whether the house is
good or bad; as the priest decides, that is
the price for the house. 15But if the person who gives the house wants to buy it
back, an additional one-fifth must be added to the price. Then the house will belong to that person again.

Value of Land

16" 'If a person gives some family
property to the LORD, the value of the
fields will depend on how much seed is
needed to plant them. It will cost about
one and one-fourth pounds of silver for
each six bushels of barley seed needed.
17If the person gives a field at the year of
Jubilee, its value will stay at what the
priest has decided. 18But if the person

FAITH links

GIVING YOUR PART

LEVITICUS 27:30

Through Moses, God told the Israelites to give one-tenth or ten percent of their harvest to him. The offerings given to God were given to the priests and Levites who served at the Meeting Tent. Many Christians today give a tithe or ten percent of the money they earn to God. This money goes to support the work of the church.

God wants you to give from the heart, not out of obligation. He wants you to be willing to share what you have with others. How will you do your part to share with others?

Share What You Have, Exodus 35:5–18, p. 123

Gifts from the Heart, 1 Chronicles 29, p. 557

Operation Cooperation, Ezra 1:5, p. 609

Seeing the Needs, Nehemiah 1, p. 625

A Halfhearted Offering, Malachi 1:6–14, p. 1268

One of the Faithful, Acts 10:1–34, p. 1482

gives the field after the Jubilee, the priest must decide the exact price by counting the number of years to the next year of Jubilee. Then he will subtract that number from its value. **19**If the person who gave the field wants to buy it back, one-fifth must be added to that price, and the field will belong to the first owner again.

20" 'If the person does not buy back the field, or if it is sold to someone else, the first person cannot ever buy it back. **21**When the land is released at the year of Jubilee, it will become holy to the LORD, like land specially given to him. It will become the property of the priests.

22" 'If someone gives to the LORD a field he has bought, which is not a part of his family land, **23**the priest must count the years to the next Jubilee. He must decide the price for the land, and the price must be paid on that day. Then that land will be holy to the LORD. **24**At the year of Jubilee, the land will go back to its first owner, to the family who sold the land.

25" 'You must use the measure as set by the Holy Place in paying these prices; it weighs two-fifths of an ounce.

Value of Animals

26" 'If an animal is the first one born to its parent, it already belongs to the LORD, so people may not give it again. If it is a cow or a sheep, it is the LORD's. **27**If the animal is unclean, the person must buy it back for the price set by the priest, and the person must add one-fifth to that price. If it is not bought back, the priest must sell it for the price he had decided.

28" 'There is a special kind of gift that people set apart to give to the LORD; it may be a person, animal, or field from the family property. That gift cannot be bought back or sold. Every special kind of gift is most holy to the LORD.

29" 'If anyone is given for the purpose of being destroyed, he cannot be bought back; he must be put to death.

30" 'One-tenth of all crops belongs to the LORD, including the crops from fields and the fruit from trees. That one-tenth is holy to the LORD. **31**If a person wants to get back that tenth, one-fifth must be added to its price.

32" 'The priest will take every tenth animal from a person's herd or flock, and it will be holy to the LORD. **33**The owner should not pick out the good animals from the bad or exchange one animal for another. If that happens, both animals will become holy; they cannot be bought back.' "

34These are the commands the LORD gave to Moses at Mount Sinai for the people of Israel.

LET'S COUNT

Hi; Moses here. Remember me from Exodus, leading God's people out of Egypt? In Numbers I tell the next part of the story. You probably think Numbers sounds like a math book, but the title actually refers to the number of Israelites in our army. With over 600,000 soldiers, we were ready to conquer the land God promised to us, but the people were afraid to go. Some actually thought we should go back to Egypt and be slaves again! Surf on over to the story of the 12 spies in Numbers 13:26–33 to find out why they were so afraid.

I wrote this book to remind people how important it is to obey God. Because Israel disobeyed, we had to wander the desert for nearly 40 more years. Life was hard, and the people complained all the time. You may not think complaining is that big a deal, but God punished us severely. One time God sent poisonous snakes when the people complained about the food. Check out that story in Numbers 21:4–9.

JESUS WATCH

Many things in Numbers make us think of Jesus. Moses made a bronze snake and put it on a pole. When he lifted the pole up, people who looked at the snake were saved from snakebites. This is like the cross, on which Jesus was lifted up to die. The people who believed in him were saved. Many times Moses struck a rock and life-saving water came out for the people. This points to Jesus who gives us living water, the Holy Spirit, so that we will enjoy eternal life with God. (See the story of the woman at the well in John 4:1–26, p. 1428.) God fed the Israelites with manna every day when they were in the desert. This reminds us of Jesus who is the bread that gives life. (Read about Jesus as the bread of life in John 6:25–58, p. 1432.) Just as the manna was the food that kept the Israelites alive in the desert, Jesus is the bread who gives us eternal life with God.

my FAVORITE links

______________ ______________

______________ ______________

______________ ______________

______________ ______________

OTHER CONNECTIONS

GET THE INFO

Check out these amazing facts and places mentioned in the Book of Numbers by connecting to:

- Time for Breakfast, Numbers 11:4–9. Can you imagine being hungry and having bags of potato chips falling from the sky? Well, it was almost like that for the Israelites when they were wandering in the wilderness and God provided them with miracle food. Check it out!
- Ever have trouble making a decision? The Israelites had an unique way of finding out what God wanting them to do. Read all about it in One Potato, Two Potato . . ., Numbers 26:55–56.
- True or false: The Dead Sea is really a lake. Find out the answer by linking to Let's Visit the Dead Sea, Numbers 34:12. You also will learn how the Dead Sea got its name.

"Why did Moses hit the rock twice with a stick?"

"Not sure. But you can download that information by reading Numbers 20:1-13."

did you know?

OTHER COOL STORIES:

Follow that cloud!, Numbers 9:15–23
Knee-deep in quail, Numbers 11:31–35
Are there really giants in the land?, Numbers 13
The angel and the talking donkey, Numbers 22

FAITH links

- **Approaching God, Numbers 3:10**
- **Give What You Can, Numbers 7:1–11**
- **The Cloud Guide, Numbers 9:15–23**
- **Following the Crowd, Numbers 13; 14**
- **The Perfect Leader?, Numbers 20:1–13**
- **An Attention-Getter, Numbers 22**
- **Take Me to Your Leader, Numbers 27:12–23**
- **A Special Promise, Numbers 30:1–2**

The People of Israel Are Counted

1 The LORD spoke to Moses in the
Meeting Tent in the Desert of Sinai.
This was on the first day of the second
month in the second year after the Israelites left Egypt. He said to Moses: 2"You
and Aaron must count all the people of
Israel by families and family groups, listing the name of each man. 3You and
Aaron must count every man twenty
years old or older who will serve in the
army of Israel, and list them by their divisions. 4One man from each tribe, the
leader of his family, will help you. 5These
are the names of the men who will help
you:

from the tribe of Reuben—Elizur son of Shedeur;
6 from the tribe of Simeon—Shelumiel son of Zurishaddai;
7 from the tribe of Judah—Nahshon son of Amminadab;
8 from the tribe of Issachar—Nethanel son of Zuar;
9 from the tribe of Zebulun—Eliab son of Helon;
10 from the tribe of Ephraim son of
Joseph—Elishama son of
Ammihud;
from the tribe of Manasseh son
of Joseph—Gamaliel son of
Pedahzur;
11 from the tribe of Benjamin—
Abidan son of Gideoni;
12 from the tribe of Dan—Ahiezer
son of Ammishaddai;
13 from the tribe of Asher—Pagiel
son of Ocran;
14 from the tribe of Gad—Eliasaph
son of Deuel;
15 from the tribe of Naphtali—
Ahira son of Enan."

16These were the men chosen from
the people to be leaders of their tribes,
the heads of Israel's family groups.

17Moses and Aaron took these men
who had been picked 18and called all the
people of Israel together on the first day
of the second month. Then the people
were listed by their families and family
groups, and all the men who were twenty
years old or older were listed by name.
19Moses did exactly what the LORD had
commanded and listed the people while
they were in the Desert of Sinai.

20The tribe of Reuben, the first son
born to Israel, was counted; all the men
twenty years old or older who were able
to serve in the army were listed by name
with their families and family groups.
21The tribe of Reuben totaled 46,500
men.

22The tribe of Simeon was counted; all
the men twenty years old or older who
were able to serve in the army were listed
by name with their families and family
groups. 23The tribe of Simeon totaled
59,300 men.

24The tribe of Gad was counted; all the
men twenty years old or older who were
able to serve in the army were listed by
name with their families and family
groups. 25The tribe of Gad totaled 45,650
men.

26The tribe of Judah was counted; all
the men twenty years old or older who
were able to serve in the army were listed
by name with their families and family
groups. 27The tribe of Judah totaled
74,600 men.

28The tribe of Issachar was counted;
all the men twenty years old or older who
were able to serve in the army were listed
by name with their families and family
groups. 29The tribe of Issachar totaled
54,400 men.

30The tribe of Zebulun was counted;
all the men twenty years old or older who
were able to serve in the army were listed
by name with their families and family
groups. 31The tribe of Zebulun totaled
57,400 men.

32The tribe of Ephraim, a son of Joseph, was counted; all the men twenty
years old or older who were able to serve
in the army were listed by name with
their families and family groups. 33The
tribe of Ephraim totaled 40,500 men.

34The tribe of Manasseh, also a son of
Joseph, was counted; all the men twenty
years old or older who were able to serve
in the army were listed by name with
their families and family groups. 35The
tribe of Manasseh totaled 32,200 men.

36The tribe of Benjamin was counted;
all the men twenty years old or older who

were able to serve in the army were listed by name with their families and family groups. **37**The tribe of Benjamin totaled 35,400 men.

38The tribe of Dan was counted; all the men twenty years old or older who were able to serve in the army were listed by name with their families and family groups. **39**The tribe of Dan totaled 62,700 men.

40The tribe of Asher was counted; all the men twenty years old or older who were able to serve in the army were listed by name with their families and family groups. **41**The tribe of Asher totaled 41,500 men.

42The tribe of Naphtali was counted; all the men twenty years old or older who were able to serve in the army were listed by name with their families and family groups. **43**The tribe of Naphtali totaled 53,400 men.

44Moses, Aaron, and the twelve leaders of Israel, one from each of the families, counted these men. **45**Every man of Israel twenty years old or older who was able to serve in the army was counted and listed with his family. **46**The total number of men was 603,550.

47The families from the tribe of Levi were not listed with the others, because **48**the LORD had told Moses: **49**"Do not count the tribe of Levi or include them with the other Israelites. **50**Instead put the Levites in charge of the Holy Tent of the Agreement and everything that is with it. They must carry the Holy Tent and everything in it, and they must take care of it and make their camp around it. **51**Any time the Holy Tent is moved, the Levites must take it down, and any time it is set up, the Levites must do it. Anyone else who goes near the Holy Tent will be put to death. **52**The Israelites will make their camps in separate divisions, each family near its flag. **53**But the Levites must make their camp around the Holy Tent of the Agreement so that I will not be angry with the Israelites. The Levites will take care of the Holy Tent of the Agreement."

54So the Israelites did everything just as the LORD commanded Moses.

The Camp Arrangement

2 The LORD said to Moses and Aaron: **2**"The Israelites should make their camps around the Meeting Tent, but they should not camp too close to it. They should camp under their family flag and banners."

3The camp of Judah will be on the east side, where the sun rises, and they will camp by divisions there under their flag. The leader of the people of Judah is Nahshon son of Amminadab. **4**There are 74,600 men in his division.

5Next to them the tribe of Issachar will camp. The leader of the people of Issachar is Nethanel son of Zuar. **6**There are 54,400 men in his division.

7Next is the tribe of Zebulun. The leader of the people of Zebulun is Eliab son of Helon. **8**There are 57,400 men in his division.

9There are a total of 186,400 men in the camps of Judah and its neighbors, in all their divisions. They will be the first to march out of camp.

10The divisions of the camp of Reuben will be on the south side, where they will camp under their flag. The leader of the people of Reuben is Elizur son of Shedeur. **11**There are 46,500 men in his division.

12Next to them the tribe of Simeon will camp. The leader of the people of Simeon is Shelumiel son of Zurishaddai. **13**There are 59,300 men in his division.

14Next is the tribe of Gad. The leader of the people of Gad is Eliasaph son of Deuel. **15**There are 45,650 men in his division.

16There are a total of 151,450 men in the camps of Reuben and its neighbors, in all their divisions. They will be the second group to march out of camp.

17When the Levites march out with the Meeting Tent, they will be in the middle of the other camps. The tribes will march out in the same order as they camp, each in its place under its flag.

18The divisions of the camp of Ephraim will be on the west side, where they will camp under their flag. The leader of the people of Ephraim is Elishama son of

Ammihud. **19**There are 40,500 men in his
division.

20Next to them the tribe of Manasseh
will camp. The leader of the people of
Manasseh is Gamaliel son of Pedahzur.
21There are 32,200 men in his division.

22Next is the tribe of Benjamin. The
leader of the people of Benjamin is Abidan son of Gideoni. **23**There are 35,400
men in his division.

24There are a total of 108,100 men in
the camps of Ephraim and its neighbors,
in all their divisions. They will be the
third group to march out of camp.

25The divisions of the camp of Dan
will be on the north side, where they will
camp under their flag. The leader of the
people of Dan is Ahiezer son of Ammishaddai. **26**There are 62,700 men in his
division.

27Next to them the tribe of Asher will
camp. The leader of the people of Asher
is Pagiel son of Ocran. **28**There are 41,500
men in his division.

29Next is the tribe of Naphtali. The
leader of the people of Naphtali is Ahira
son of Enan. **30**There are 53,400 men in
his division.

31There are 157,600 men in the
camps of Dan and its neighbors. They
will be the last to march out of camp, and
they will travel under their own flag.

32These are the Isra-
elites who were counted
by families. The total number of Israelites in the
camps, counted by divi-
sions, is 603,550. **33**Moses
obeyed the LORD and did
not count the Levites
among the other people of
Israel.

34So the Israelites
obeyed everything the
LORD commanded Moses. They camped
under their flags and marched out by families and family groups.

> They camped under their flags and marched out by families and family groups.
> —Numbers 2:34

Aaron's Family, the Priests

3 This is the family history of Aaron
and Moses at the time the LORD
talked to Moses on Mount Sinai.

2Aaron had four sons: Nadab, the oldest, Abihu, Eleazar, and Ithamar. **3**These
were the names of Aaron's sons, who
were appointed to serve as priests. **4**But
Nadab and Abihu died in the presence of
the LORD when they offered the wrong
kind of fire before the LORD in the Desert
of Sinai. They had no sons. So Eleazar
and Ithamar served as priests during the
lifetime of their father Aaron.

5The LORD said to Moses, **6**"Bring
the tribe of Levi and present them to
Aaron the priest to help him. **7**They will
help him and all the Israelites at the
Meeting Tent, doing the work in the Holy
Tent. **8**The Levites must take care of everything in the Meeting Tent and serve
the people of Israel by doing the work in
the Holy Tent. **9**Give the Levites to
Aaron and his sons; of all the Israelites,
the Levites are given completely to him.
10Appoint Aaron and his sons to serve as
priests, but anyone else who comes near
the holy things must be put to death."

11The LORD also said to Moses, **12**"I
am choosing the Levites from all the Israelites to take the place of all the firstborn children of Israel. The Levites will
be mine, **13**because the firstborn are
mine. When you were in Egypt, I killed
all the firstborn children of the Egyptians
and took all the firstborn of Israel to be
mine, both animals and children. They are
mine. I am the LORD."

14The LORD again
said to Moses in the
Desert of Sinai, **15**"Count
the Levites by families
and family groups. Count
every male one month
old or older." **16**So Moses
obeyed the LORD and
counted them all.

17Levi had three sons,
whose names were Ger-
shon, Kohath, and Merari.

18The Gershonite family groups were
Libni and Shimei.

19The Kohathite family groups were
Amram, Izhar, Hebron, and Uzziel.

20The Merarite family groups were
Mahli and Mushi.

These were the family groups of the
Levites.

FAITH links

APPROACHING GOD

NUMBERS 3:10

How would you react if your pastor one Sunday suddenly announced, "Anyone but me who touches the altar or puts anything on it will instantly be put to death"? In Moses' day, that statement was true. Certain items and areas of the Meeting Tent were considered off-limits to everyone except Aaron and his sons, who served as priests. These items and areas were symbols of God's holiness. Only appointed priests could handle these items and enter these special areas.

Jesus' death makes it possible for anyone to approach him, without the fear of death. You don't have to go through a minister. All you have to do is pray.

Check out these other Faithlinks on prayer:

The Rainbow Promise, Genesis 9:1–17, p. 14

The Name of the Lord, Exodus 33:19–23; 34:5–8, p. 120

A Friend in Deed, Job 2:13, p. 662

The Prayer Habit, Psalm 5:1–3, p. 712

A Hopeful Name, Hosea 1:3–11, p. 1172

Praise Him!, Revelation 5:12, p. 1736

21The family groups of Libni and
Shimei belonged to Gershon; they were
the Gershonite family groups. **22**The
number that was counted was 7,500 males
one month old or older. **23**The Gershonite
family groups camped on the west side,
behind the Holy Tent. **24**The leader of
the families of Gershon was Eliasaph son
of Lael. **25**In the Meeting Tent the Gershonites were in charge of the Holy Tent,
its covering, the curtain at the entrance
to the Meeting Tent, **26**the curtains in the
courtyard, the curtain at the entry to
the courtyard around the Holy Tent and
the altar, the ropes, and all the work connected with these items.

27The family groups of Amram, Izhar,
Hebron, and Uzziel belonged to Kohath;
they were the Kohathite family groups.
28They had 8,600 males one month old
or older, and they were responsible for
taking care of the Holy Place. **29**The Kohathite family groups camped south of
the Holy Tent. **30**The leader of the Kohathite families was Elizaphan son of Uzziel. **31**They were responsible for the
Ark, the table, the lampstand, the altars,
the tools of the Holy Place which they
were to use, the curtain, and all the work
connected with these items. **32**The main
leader of the Levites was Eleazar son of
Aaron, the priest, who was in charge of all
those responsible for the Holy Place.

33The family groups of Mahli and Mushi belonged to Merari; they were the
Merarite family groups. **34**The number
that was counted was 6,200 males one
month old or older. **35**The leader of the
Merari families was Zuriel son of Abihail,
and they were to camp north of the Holy
Tent. **36**The Merarites were responsible
for the frames of the Holy Tent, the
braces, the posts, the bases, and all the
work connected with these items. **37**They
were also responsible for the posts in the
courtyard around the Holy Tent and their
bases, tent pegs, and ropes.

38Moses, Aaron, and his sons camped
east of the Holy Tent, toward the sunrise,
in front of the Meeting Tent. They were
responsible for the Holy Place for the Israelites. Anyone else who came near the
Holy Place was to be put to death.

39Moses and Aaron counted the Levite men by their families, as the LORD
commanded, and there were 22,000
males one month old or older.

Levites Take the Place of the Firstborn Sons

40The LORD said to Moses, "Count all
the firstborn sons in Israel one month old
or older, and list their names. 41Take the
Levites for me instead of the firstborn
sons of Israel; take the animals of the Levites instead of the firstborn animals
from the rest of Israel. I am the LORD."
42So Moses did what the LORD commanded and counted all the firstborn
sons of the Israelites. 43When he listed
all the firstborn sons one month old or
older, there were 22,273 names.
44The LORD also said to Moses,
45"Take the Levites instead of all the
firstborn sons of the Israelites, and take
the animals of the Levites instead of the
animals of the other people. The Levites
are mine. I am the LORD. 46Since there
are 273 more firstborn sons than Levites,
47collect two ounces of silver for each of
the 273 sons. Use the measure as set by
the Holy Place, which is two-fifths of an
ounce. 48Give the silver to Aaron and his
sons as the payment for the 273 Israelites."
49So Moses collected the money for
the people the Levites could not replace.
50From the firstborn of the Israelites, he
collected thirty-five pounds of silver, using the measure set by the Holy Place.
51Moses obeyed the command of the
LORD and gave the silver to Aaron and his
sons.

The Jobs of the Kohath Family

4 The LORD said to Moses and Aaron,
2"Count the Kohathites among the
Levites by family groups and families.
3Count the men from thirty to fifty years
old, all who come to serve in the Meeting
Tent.
4"The Kohathites are responsible for
the most holy things in the Meeting Tent.
5When the Israelites are ready to move,
Aaron and his sons must go into the Holy
Tent, take down the curtain, and cover
the Ark of the Agreement with it. 6Over
this they must put a covering made from
fine leather, then spread the solid blue
cloth over that, and put the poles in place.
7"Then they must spread a blue cloth
over the table for the bread that shows a

FAITH links

EVERYONE CAN HELP

NUMBERS 4

Does your pastor preach the sermon, collect the offering, teach Sunday school, lead the choir, clean the church, and pass out the bulletins each Sunday? No way, right? One person couldn't do all that needs to be done. That's the way it was in Moses' day. Everyone had specific duties within the Meeting Tent. Certain families were responsible for certain jobs.

Everyone has specific duties within the church today. We all work together as a body to worship God. This allows everyone the opportunity to serve. How will you serve?

A Use for Your Abilities, Genesis 41, p. 59

His OK to Obey, Deuteronomy 2:24–36, p. 230

Your Response to Responsibility, Ruth 2:1–7, p. 346

The Way to Serve God, 1 Kings 9:4, p. 450

My Best Serve, Acts 6:1–6, p. 1473

Glad to Help!, Romans 15:17–20, p. 1541

person is in God's presence. They must put the plates, pans, bowls, and the jars for drink offerings on the table; they must leave the bread that is always there on the table. **8**Then they must put a red cloth over all of these things, cover everything with fine leather, and put the poles in place.

9"With a blue cloth they must cover the lampstand, its lamps, its wick trimmers, its trays, and all the jars for the oil used in the lamps. **10**Then they must wrap everything in fine leather and put all these things on a frame for carrying them.

11"They must spread a blue cloth over the gold altar, cover it with fine leather, and put the poles in place.

12"They must gather all the things used for serving in the Holy Place and wrap them in a blue cloth. Then they must cover that with fine leather and put these things on a frame for carrying them.

13"They must clean the ashes off the bronze altar and spread a purple cloth over it. **14**They must gather all the things used for serving at the altar—the pans for carrying the fire, the meat forks, the shovels, and the bowls—and put them on the bronze altar. Then they must spread a covering of fine leather over it and put the poles in place.

15"When the Israelites are ready to move, and when Aaron and his sons have covered the holy furniture and all the holy things, the Kohathites may go in and carry them away. In this way they won't touch the holy things and die. It is the Kohathites' job to carry the things that are in the Meeting Tent.

16"Eleazar son of Aaron, the priest, will be responsible for the Holy Tent and for everything in it, for all the holy things it has: the oil for the lamp, the sweet-smelling incense, the continual grain offering, and the oil used to appoint priests and things to the LORD's service."

17The LORD said to Moses and Aaron, **18**"Don't let the Kohathites be cut off from the Levites. **19**Do this for the Kohathites so that they may go near the Most Holy Place and not die: Aaron and his sons must go in and show each Kohathite what to do and what to carry. **20**The Kohathites must not enter and look at the holy things, even for a second, or they will die."

The Jobs of the Gershon Family

21The LORD said to Moses, **22**"Count the Gershonites by families and family groups. **23**Count the men from thirty to fifty years old, all who have a job to do in the Meeting Tent.

24"This is what the Gershonite family groups must do and what they must carry. **25**They must carry the curtains of the Holy Tent, the Meeting Tent, its covering, and its outer covering made from fine leather. They must also carry the curtains for the entrance to the Meeting Tent, **26**the curtains of the courtyard that go around the Holy Tent and the altar, the curtain for the entry to the courtyard, the ropes, and all the things used with the curtains. They must do everything connected with these things. **27**Aaron and his sons are in charge of what the Gershonites do or carry; you tell them what they are responsible for carrying. **28**This is the work of the Gershonite family group at the Meeting Tent. Ithamar son of Aaron, the priest, will direct their work.

The Jobs of the Merari Family

29"Count the Merarite families and family groups. **30**Count the men from thirty to fifty years old, all who work at the Meeting Tent. **31**It is their job to carry the following as they serve in the Meeting Tent: the frames of the Holy Tent, the crossbars, the posts, and bases, **32**in addition to the posts that go around the courtyard, their bases, tent pegs, ropes, and everything that is used with the poles around the courtyard. Tell each man exactly what to carry. **33**This is the work the Merarite family group will do for the Meeting Tent. Ithamar son of Aaron, the priest, will direct their work."

The Levite Families

34Moses, Aaron, and the leaders of Israel counted the Kohathites by families and family groups, **35**the men from thirty to fifty years old who were to work at the Meeting Tent. **36**There were 2,750 men in the family groups. **37**This was the total of the Kohath family groups who worked at the Meeting Tent, whom Moses and Aaron counted as the LORD had commanded Moses.

38Also, the Gershonites were counted by families and family groups, **39**the men from thirty to fifty years old who were given work at the Meeting Tent. **40**The families and family groups had 2,630 men. **41**This was the total of the Gershon family groups who worked at the Meeting Tent, whom Moses and Aaron counted as the LORD had commanded.

42Also, the men in the families and family groups of the Merari family were counted, **43**the men from thirty to fifty years old who were to work at the Meeting Tent. **44**The family groups had 3,200 men. **45**This was the total of the Merari family groups, whom Moses and Aaron counted as the LORD had commanded Moses.

46So Moses, Aaron, and the leaders of Israel counted all the Levites by families and family groups. **47**They counted the men from thirty to fifty who were given work at the Meeting Tent and who carried the Tent. **48**The total number of these men was 8,580. **49**Each man was counted as the LORD had commanded Moses; each man was given his work and told what to carry as the LORD had commanded Moses.

Rules About Cleanliness

5 The LORD said to Moses, **2**"Command the Israelites to send away from camp anyone with a harmful skin disease. Send away anyone who gives off body fluid or who has become unclean by touching a dead body. **3**Send both men and women outside the camp so that they won't spread the disease there, where I am living among you." **4**So Israel obeyed the LORD's command and sent those people outside the camp. They did just as the LORD had told Moses.

Paying for Doing Wrong

5The LORD said to Moses, **6**"Tell the Israelites: 'When a man or woman does something wrong to another person, that is really sinning against the LORD. That person is guilty **7**and must admit the wrong that has been done. The person must fully pay for the wrong that has been done, adding one-fifth to it, and giving it to the person who was wronged. **8**But if that person is dead and does not have any close relatives to receive the payment, the one who did wrong owes the LORD and must pay the priest. In addition, the priest must sacrifice a male sheep to remove the wrong so that the person will belong to the LORD. **9**When an Israelite brings a holy gift, it should be given to the priest. **10**No one has to give these holy gifts, but if someone does give them, they belong to the priest.' "

> The person must fully pay for the wrong that has been done, adding one-fifth to it.
> —Numbers 5:7

Suspicious Husbands

11Then the LORD said to Moses, **12**"Tell the Israelites: 'A man's wife might be unfaithful to him **13**and have sexual relations with another man. Her sin might be kept hidden from her husband so that he does not know about the wrong she did. Perhaps no one saw it, and she wasn't caught. **14**But if her husband has feelings of jealousy and suspects she has sinned—whether she has or not—**15**he should take her to the priest. The husband must also take an offering for her of two quarts of barley flour. He must not pour oil or incense on it, because this is a grain offering for jealousy, an offering of remembrance. It is to find out if she is guilty.

16" 'The priest will bring in the woman and make her stand before the LORD. **17**He will take some holy water in a clay jar, and he will put some dirt from the floor of the Holy Tent into the water.

18The priest will make the woman stand before the LORD, and he will loosen her hair. He will hand her the offering of remembrance, the grain offering for jealousy; he will hold the bitter water that brings a curse. **19**The priest will make her take an oath and ask her, "Has another man had sexual relations with you? Have you been unfaithful to your husband? If you haven't, this bitter water that brings a curse won't hurt you. **20**But if you have been unfaithful to your husband and have had sexual relations with a man besides him"— **21**the priest will then put on her the curse that the oath will bring—"the LORD will make the people curse and reject you. He will make your stomach get big, and he will make your body unable to give birth to another baby. **22**This water that brings a curse will go inside you and make your body unable to give birth to another baby."

" 'The woman must say, "I agree."

23" 'The priest should write these curses on a scroll, wash the words off into the bitter water, **24**and make the woman drink the bitter water that brings a curse. If she is guilty, the water will make her sick. **25**Then the priest will take the grain offering for jealousy from her. He will present it before the LORD and bring it to the altar. **26**He will take a handful of the grain, which is a memorial offering, and burn it on the altar. After that he will make the woman drink the water **27**to see if she is not pure and if she has sinned against her husband. When it goes into her, if her stomach gets big so that she is not able to have another baby, her people will reject her. **28**But if the woman has not sinned, she is pure. She is not guilty, and she will be able to have babies.

29" 'So this is the teaching about jealousy. This is what to do when a woman does wrong and is unfaithful while she is married to her husband. **30**It also should be done if the man gets jealous because he suspects his wife. The priest will have her stand before the LORD, and he will do all these things, just as the teaching commands. **31**In this way the husband can be proven correct, and the woman will suffer if she has done wrong.' "

Rules for the Nazirites

6 The LORD said to Moses, **2**"Tell the Israelites: 'If men or women want to promise to belong to the LORD in a special way, they will be called Nazirites. **3**During this time, they must not drink wine or beer, or vinegar made from wine or beer. They must not even drink grape juice or eat grapes or raisins. **4**While they are Nazirites, they must not eat anything that comes from the grapevine, even the seeds or the skin.

5" 'During the time they have promised to belong to the LORD, they must not cut their hair. They must be holy until this special time is over. They must let their hair grow long. **6**During their special time of belonging to the LORD, Nazirites must not go near a dead body. **7**Even if their own father, mother, brother, or sister dies, they must not touch them, or they will become unclean. They must still keep their promise to belong to God in a special way. **8**While they are Nazirites, they belong to the LORD in a special way.

9" 'If they are next to someone who dies suddenly, their hair, which was part of their promise, has been made unclean. So they must shave their head seven days later to be clean. **10**Then on the eighth day, they must bring two doves or two young pigeons to the priest at the entrance to the Meeting Tent. **11**The priest will offer one as a sin offering and the other as a burnt offering. This removes sin so they will belong to the LORD. (They had sinned because they were near a dead body.) That same day they will again promise to let their hair grow **12**and give themselves to the LORD for another special time. They must bring a male lamb a year old as a penalty offering. The days of the special time before don't count, because they became unclean during their first special time.

13" 'This is the teaching for the Nazirites. When the promised time is over, they must go the entrance of the Meeting Tent **14**and give their offerings to the LORD. They must offer a year-old male lamb that has nothing wrong with it, as a burnt offering, a year-old female lamb

that has nothing wrong with it, as a sin
offering, and a male sheep that has nothing wrong with it, for a fellowship offering. **15**They must also bring the grain
offerings and drink offerings that go with
them. And they must bring a basket of
bread made without yeast, loaves made
with fine flour mixed with oil, and wafers
made without yeast spread with oil.

16" 'The priest will give these offerings to the LORD and make the sin offering and the burnt offering. **17**Then he will
kill the male sheep as a fellowship offering to the LORD; along with it, he will
present the basket of bread made without
yeast, the grain offering, and the drink
offering.

18" 'The Nazirites must go to the entrance of the Meeting Tent and shave off
their hair that they grew for their promise. The hair will be put in the fire that is
under the sacrifice of the fellowship offering.

19" 'After the Nazirites cut off their
hair, the priest will give them a boiled
shoulder from the male sheep. From the
basket he will also give a loaf and a wafer,
both made without yeast. **20**Then the
priest will present them to the LORD.
They are holy and belong to the priest.
Also, he is to present the breast and the
thigh from the male sheep. After that, the
Nazirites may drink wine.

21" 'This is the teaching for the Nazirites who make a promise. Everyone
who makes the Nazirite promise must
give all of these gifts to the LORD. If they
promised to do more, they must keep
their promise, according to the teaching
of the Nazirites.' "

The Priests' Blessings

22The LORD said to Moses, **23**"Tell
Aaron and his sons, 'This is how you
should bless the Israelites. Say to them:

24 "May the LORD bless you
and keep
you.
25 May the LORD
show you his
kindness
and have mercy
on you.

eMail! FROM GOD
6:24–26
Peace
What does God
give you?

26 May the LORD watch over you
and give you peace." '

27"So Aaron and his sons will bless
the Israelites with my name, and I will
bless them."

The Holy Tent

7 When Moses finished setting up the
Holy Tent, he gave it for service to
the LORD by pouring olive oil on the Tent
and on everything used in it. He also
poured oil on the altar and all its tools to
prepare them for service to the LORD.
2Then the leaders of Israel made offerings. These were the heads of the families, the leaders of each tribe who counted
the people. **3**They brought to the LORD
six covered carts and twelve oxen—each
leader giving an ox, and every two leaders
giving a cart. They brought these to the
Holy Tent.

4The LORD said to Moses, **5**"Accept
these gifts from the leaders and use them
in the work of the Meeting Tent. Give
them to the Levites as they need them."

6So Moses accepted the carts and the
oxen and gave them to the Levites. **7**He
gave two carts and four oxen to the Gershonites, which they needed for their
work. **8**Then Moses gave four carts and
eight oxen to the Merarites, which they
needed for their work. Ithamar son of
Aaron, the priest, directed the work of all
of them. **9**Moses did not give any oxen or
carts to the Kohathites, because their job
was to carry the holy things on their
shoulders.

10When the oil was poured on the altar, the leaders brought their offerings to
it to give it to the LORD's service; they
presented them in front of the altar.
11The LORD told Moses, "Each day one
leader must bring his gift to make the altar ready for service to me."

12-83 Each of the twelve leaders
brought these gifts. Each leader brought
one silver plate that weighed about three
and one-fourth pounds, and one silver
bowl that weighed about one and three-
fourths pounds. These weights were set
by the Holy Place measure. The bowl and
the plate were filled with fine flour mixed
with oil for a grain offering. Each leader

GIVE WHAT YOU CAN

NUMBERS 7:1-11

If you've ever watched public television, you know the station sometimes asks for donations. In order for viewers to continue enjoying the programs, money must be given to help support the station. "After all, this is your station," viewers are sometimes reminded.

When the Meeting Tent was finished, the leaders of the twelve tribes gave gifts to the priests. The offerings were given to support the work. This way everyone shared in supplying the needs of the priests. Our offerings today help to support the activities of the church. We all have the responsibility to give what we can, whether it's money, time, or help.

Giving Your Part, Leviticus 27:30, p. 173

What's the Use?, 2 Kings 12:6–12, p. 495

Service with a Smile, 1 Chronicles 6:31–49, p. 527

A Reminder to Be Fair, 2 Chronicles 19:5–11, p. 583

The Way to Greatness, Matthew 20:20–28, p. 1309

The Most Fun, Acts 20:35, p. 1502

also brought a large gold dish that weighed about four ounces and was filled with incense.

In addition, each of the leaders brought one young bull, one male sheep, and one male lamb a year old for a burnt offering; one male goat for a sin offering; and two oxen, five male sheep, five male goats, and five male lambs a year old for a fellowship offering.

On the first day Nahshon son of Amminadab brought his gifts. He was the leader of the tribe of Judah.

On the second day Nethanel son of Zuar brought his gifts. He was the leader of the tribe of Issachar.

On the third day Eliab son of Helon brought his gifts. He was the leader of the tribe of Zebulun.

On the fourth day Elizur son of Shedeur brought his gifts. He was the leader of the tribe of Reuben.

On the fifth day Shelumiel son of Zurishaddai brought his gifts. He was the leader of the tribe of Simeon.

On the sixth day Eliasaph son of Deuel brought his gifts. He was the leader of the tribe of Gad.

On the seventh day Elishama son of Ammihud brought his gifts. He was the leader of the tribe of Ephraim.

On the eighth day Gamaliel son of Pedahzur brought his gifts. He was the leader of the tribe of Manasseh.

On the ninth day Abidan son of Gideoni brought his gifts. He was the leader of the tribe of Benjamin.

On the tenth day Ahiezer son of Ammishaddai brought his gifts. He was the leader of the tribe of Dan.

On the eleventh day Pagiel son of Ocran brought his gifts. He was the leader of the tribe of Asher.

On the twelfth day Ahira son of Enan brought his gifts. He was the leader of the tribe of Naphtali.

84So these were the gifts from the Israelite leaders when oil was poured on the
altar and it was given for service to the
LORD: twelve silver plates, twelve silver
bowls, and twelve gold dishes. **85**Each silver plate weighed about three and one-
fourth pounds, and each bowl weighed
about one and three-fourths pounds. All
the silver plates and silver bowls together
weighed about sixty pounds according to

a weight set by the Holy Place measure.
86The twelve gold dishes filled with
incense weighed four ounces each, according to the weight set by the Holy
Place measure. Together the gold dishes
weighed about three pounds. **87**The total
number of animals for the burnt offering
was twelve bulls, twelve male sheep, and
twelve male lambs a year
old. There was also a
grain offering, and there
were twelve male goats
for a sin offering. **88**The
total number of animals
for the fellowship offering
was twenty-four bulls,
sixty male sheep, sixty
male goats, and sixty male
lambs a year old. All these
offerings were for giving
the altar to the service of the LORD after
the oil had been poured on it.

89When Moses went into the Meeting
Tent to speak with the LORD, he heard
the LORD speaking to him. The voice was
coming from between the two gold creatures with wings that were above the lid
of the Ark of the Agreement. In this way
the LORD spoke with him.

In this way you must set apart the Levites from the other Israelites; the Levites will be mine.
—Numbers 8:14

The Lampstand

8 The LORD said to Moses, **2**"Speak to
Aaron and tell him, 'Put the seven
lamps where they can light the area in
front of the lampstand.' "

3Aaron did this, putting the lamps so
they lighted the area in front of the lampstand; he obeyed the command the LORD
gave Moses. **4**The lampstand was made
from hammered gold, from its base to the
flowers. It was made exactly the way the
LORD had showed Moses.

The Levites Are Given to God

5The LORD said to Moses, **6**"Take the
Levites away from the other Israelites
and make them clean. **7**This is what you
should do to make them clean: Sprinkle
the cleansing water on them, and have
them shave their bodies and wash their
clothes so they will be clean. **8**They must
take a young bull and the grain offering of
flour mixed with oil that goes with it.
Then take a second young bull for a sin
offering. **9**Bring the Levites to the front
of the Meeting Tent, and gather all the Israelites around. **10**When you bring the
Levites before the LORD, the Israelites
should put their hands on them.ⁿ **11**Aaron
will present the Levites before the LORD
as an offering presented from the Israelites. Then the Levites
will be ready to do the
work of the LORD.

12"The Levites will
put their hands on the
bulls' heads—one bull will
be a sin offering to the
LORD, and the other will
be a burnt offering, to remove the sins of the Le-
vites so they will belong
to the LORD. **13**Make the
Levites stand in front of Aaron and his
sons and present the Levites as an offering to the LORD. **14**In this way you must
set apart the Levites from the other Israelites; the Levites will be mine.

15"Make the Levites pure, and present them as an offering so that they may
come to work at the Meeting Tent.
16They will be given completely to me
from the Israelites; I have taken them for
myself instead of the firstborn of every
Israelite woman. **17**All the firstborn in
Israel—people or animals—are mine.
When I killed all the firstborn in Egypt, I
set the firstborn in Israel aside for myself. **18**But I have taken the Levites instead of all the firstborn in Israel. **19**From
all the Israelites I have given the Levites
to Aaron and his sons so that they may
serve the Israelites at the Meeting Tent.
They will help remove the Israelites' sins
so they will belong to the LORD and so
that no disaster will strike the Israelites
when they approach the Holy Place."

20So Moses, Aaron, and all the Israelites obeyed and did with the Levites what
the LORD commanded Moses. **21**The
Levites made themselves clean and
washed their clothes. Then Aaron presented them as an offering to the LORD.

8:10 put . . . them This showed that the people had a part in giving the Levites their special work.

He also removed their sins so they would be pure. **22**After that, the Levites came to the Meeting Tent to work, and Aaron and his sons told them what to do. They did with the Levites what the LORD commanded Moses.

23The LORD said to Moses, **24**"This command is for the Levites. Everyone twenty-five years old or older must come to the Meeting Tent, because they all have jobs to do there. **25**At the age of fifty, they must retire from their jobs and not work again. **26**They may help their fellow Levites with their work at the Meeting Tent, but they must not do the work themselves. This is the way you are to give the Levites their jobs."

The Passover Is Celebrated

9 The LORD spoke to Moses in the Desert of Sinai in the first month of the second year after the Israelites left Egypt. He said, **2**"Tell the Israelites to celebrate the Passover at the appointed time. **3**That appointed time is the fourteenth day of this month at twilight; they must obey all the rules about it."

4So Moses told the Israelites to celebrate the Passover, **5**and they did; it was in the Desert of Sinai at twilight on the fourteenth day of the first month. The Israelites did everything just as the LORD commanded Moses.

6But some of the people could not celebrate the Passover on that day because they were unclean from touching a dead body. So they went to Moses and Aaron that day and **7**said to Moses, "We are unclean because of touching a dead body. But why should we be kept from offering gifts to the LORD at this appointed time? Why can't we join the other Israelites?"

8Moses said to them, "Wait, and I will find out what the LORD says about you."

9Then the LORD said to Moses, **10**"Tell the Israelites this: 'If you or your descendants become unclean because of a dead body, or if you are away on a trip during the Passover, you must still celebrate the LORD's Passover. **11**But celebrate it at twilight on the fourteenth day of the second month. Eat the lamb with bitter herbs and bread made without yeast. **12**Don't leave any of it until the next morning or break any of its bones. When you celebrate the Passover, follow all the rules. **13**Anyone who is clean and is not away on a trip but does not eat the Passover must be cut off from the people. That person did not give an offering to the LORD at the appointed time and must be punished for the sin.

FAITH links

THE CLOUD GUIDE

NUMBERS 9:15-23

Certain clouds are a sign of changing weather conditions. Black clouds are the sign of a thunderstorm. For the Israelites, a cloud was the sign of change. God's presence took the form of a cloud over the Meeting Tent. When the cloud moved, the people knew that the time had come to break camp and move out.

Today, God doesn't use a cloud to guide his people. God is present with us through the Holy Spirit. He has also given us the Bible and wise advice from fellow Christians.

Try to Remember, Deuteronomy 11:18–21, p. 243

Learning to Listen, 1 Samuel 3, p. 358

Deciding Wisely, 1 Kings 3:16–28, p. 440

Like Silver, Psalm 12:6–8, p. 717

A Hopeful Future, Jeremiah 29:11, p. 1031

Out of Your Mind?, 1 Corinthians 2:16, p. 1547

14" 'Foreigners among you may celebrate the LORD's Passover, but they must follow all the rules. You must have the same rules for foreigners as you have for yourselves.' "

The Cloud Above the Tent

15On the day the Holy Tent, the Tent of the Agreement, was set up, a cloud covered it. From dusk until dawn the cloud above the Tent looked like fire. **16**The cloud stayed above the Tent, and at night it looked like fire. **17**When the cloud moved from its place over the Tent, the Israelites moved, and wherever the cloud stopped, the Israelites camped. **18**So the Israelites moved at the LORD's command, and they camped at his command. While the cloud stayed over the Tent, they remained camped. **19**Sometimes the cloud stayed over the Tent for a long time, but the Israelites obeyed the LORD and did not move. **20**Sometimes the cloud was over it only a few days. At the LORD's command the people camped, and at his command they moved. **21**Sometimes the cloud stayed only from dusk until dawn; when the cloud lifted the next morning, the people moved. When the cloud lifted, day or night, the people moved. **22**The cloud might stay over the Tent for two days, a month, or a year. As long as it stayed, the people camped, but when it lifted, they moved. **23**At the LORD's command the people camped, and at his command they moved. They obeyed the LORD's order that he commanded through Moses.

The Silver Trumpets

10 The LORD said to Moses, **2**"Make two trumpets of hammered silver, and use them to call the people together and to march out of camp. **3**When both trumpets are blown, the people should gather before you at the entrance to the Meeting Tent. **4**If you blow only one trumpet, the leaders, the heads of the family groups of Israel, should meet before you. **5**When you loudly blow the trumpets, the tribes camping on the east should move. **6**When you loudly blow them again, the tribes camping on the south should move; the loud sound will tell them to move. **7**When you want to gather the people, blow the trumpets, but don't blow them as loudly.

8"Aaron's sons, the priests, should blow the trumpets. This is a law for you and your descendants from now on. **9**When you are fighting an enemy who attacks you in your own land, blow the trumpets loudly. The LORD your God will take notice of you and will save you from your enemies. **10**Also blow your trumpets at happy times and during your feasts and at New Moon festivals. Blow them over your burnt offerings and fellowship offerings, because they will help you remember your God. I am the LORD your God."

The Israelites Move Camp

11The cloud lifted from the Tent of the Agreement on the twentieth day of the second month of the second year. **12**So the Israelites moved from the Desert of Sinai and continued until the cloud stopped in the Desert of Paran. **13**This was their first time to move, and they did it as the LORD had commanded Moses.

14The divisions from the camp of Judah moved first under their flag. Nahshon son of Amminadab was the commander. **15**Nethanel son of Zuar was over the division of the tribe of Issachar. **16**Eliab son of Helon was over the division of the tribe of Zebulun. **17**Then the Holy Tent was taken down, and the Gershonites and Merarites, who carried it, moved next.

18Then came the divisions from the camp of Reuben under their flag, and Elizur son of Shedeur was the commander. **19**Shelumiel son of Zurishaddai was over the division of the tribe of Simeon. **20**Eliasaph son of Deuel was over the division of the tribe of Gad. **21**Then came the Kohathites, who carried the holy things; the Holy Tent was to be set up before they arrived.

22Next came the divisions from the camp of Ephraim under their flag, and Elishama son of Ammihud was the commander. **23**Gamaliel son of Pedahzur was over the division of the tribe of Manasseh,

24and Abidan son of Gideoni was over the
division of the tribe of Benjamin.
25The last ones were the rear guard
for all the tribes. These were the divisions from the camp of Dan under their
flag, and Ahiezer son of Ammishaddai
was the commander. 26Pagiel son of Ocran was over the division of the tribe of
Asher; 27Ahira son of Enan was over the
division of the tribe of Naphtali. 28This
was the order the Israelite divisions
marched in when they moved.
29Hobab was the son of Reuel the
Midianite,[n] who was Moses' father-in-
law. Moses said to Hobab, "We are moving to the land the LORD promised to give
us. Come with us and we will be good to
you, because the LORD has promised
good things to Israel."
30But Hobab answered, "No, I will
not go. I will go back to my own land
where I was born."
31But Moses said, "Please don't leave
us. You know where we
can camp in the desert,
and you can be our guide.
32Come with us. We will
share with you all the
good things the LORD
gives us." 33So they left
the mountain of the LORD
and traveled for three
days. The Ark of the
LORD's Agreement went
in front of the people for
those three days, as they looked for a
place to camp. 34The LORD's cloud was
over them during the day when they left
their camp.

The LORD's cloud was over them during the day when they left their camp.
—Numbers 10:34

35When the Ark left the camp, Moses
said,
"Rise up, LORD!
Scatter your enemies:
make those who hate you run from
you."
36And when the Ark was set down,
Moses said,
"Return, LORD,
to the thousands of people of Israel."

Fire from the Lord

11 Now the people complained to the
LORD about their troubles, and
when he heard them, he became angry.
Then fire from the LORD burned among
the people at the edge of the camp. 2The
people cried out to Moses, and when he
prayed to the LORD, the fire stopped burning. 3So that place was called Taberah,[n]
because the LORD's fire had burned
among them.

Seventy Older Leaders Help Moses

4Some troublemakers among them
wanted better food, and soon all the Israelites began complaining. They said, "We
want meat! 5We remember the fish we
ate for free in Egypt. We also had cucum-
bers, melons, leeks, onions, and garlic.
6But now we have lost our appetite; we
never see anything but this manna!"
7The manna was like small white
seeds. 8The people would go to gather it,
and then grind it in handmills, or crush
it between stones. After they cooked it
in a pot or made cakes
with it, it tasted like bread
baked with olive oil.
9When the dew fell on the
camp each night, so did
the manna.
10Moses heard every
family crying as they
stood in the entrances of
their tents. Then the
LORD became very angry,
and Moses got upset.
11He asked the LORD, "Why have you
brought me, your servant, this trouble?
What have I done wrong that you made
me responsible for all these people? 12I
am not the father of all these people, and
I didn't give birth to them. So why do you
make me carry them to the land you
promised to our ancestors? Must I carry
them in my arms as a nurse carries a
baby? 13Where can I get meat for all
these people? They keep crying to me,
'We want meat!' 14I can't take care of all
these people alone. It is too much for me.
15If you are going to continue doing this
to me, then kill me now. If you care about

10:29 Reuel the Midianite Also called Jethro.
11:3 Taberah This name means "burning."

TIME FOR BREAKFAST

Numbers 11:4–9

Manna was a food. You can't find it anywhere in the world today. It was a miracle food God supplied to the Israelites. During the years that the Israelites wandered through the wilderness, God made "food fall like rain from the sky." (Read Exodus 16:4, p. 96.) Each morning when the people woke up, there was manna on the ground. It looked like thin flakes of frost. (See Exodus 16:14, p. 97.)

The Israelites gathered the manna every day except on the Sabbath. The leftover manna would melt in the sun. No one was supposed to gather more than they needed. If they did, it would become infested with worms. (Look at Exodus 16:16–18, 20–21, p. 97.) When manna appeared on the ground, it was sticky. Later when it dried it became solid and could be ground up like flour and baked into wafers or cakes. It tasted a little like wafers made with honey. (Check out Exodus 16:31, p. 98.)

me, put me to death, and then I won't
have any more troubles."
16The LORD said to Moses, "Bring
me seventy of Israel's older leaders, men
that you know are leaders among the
people. Bring them to the Meeting Tent,
and have them stand there with you. **17**I
will come down and speak with you
there. I will take some of the Spirit that is
in you, and I will give it to them. They
will help you care for the people so that
you will not have to care for them alone.
18"Tell the people this: 'Make yourselves holy for tomorrow, and you will eat
meat. You cried to the LORD, "We want
meat! We were better off in Egypt!" So
now the LORD will give you meat to eat.
19You will eat it not for just one, two,
five, ten, or even twenty days, **20**but you
will eat that meat for a whole month. You
will eat it until it comes out your nose,
and you will grow to hate it. This is because you have rejected the LORD, who is
with you. You have cried to him, saying,
"Why did we ever leave Egypt?"' "
21Moses said, "LORD, here are six
hundred thousand people standing around
me, and you say, 'I will give them enough
meat to eat for a month!' **22**If we killed all
the flocks and herds, that would not be
enough. If we caught all the fish in the
sea, that would not be enough."
23But the LORD said to Moses, "Do
you think I'm weak? Now you will see if I
can do what I say."
24So Moses went out to the people
and told them what the LORD had said.
He gathered seventy of the older leaders
together and had them stand around the
Tent. **25**Then the LORD came down in the
cloud and spoke to Moses. The LORD
took some of the Spirit Moses had, and
he gave it to the seventy leaders. With
the Spirit in them, they prophesied, but
just that one time.
26Two men named Eldad and Medad
were also listed as leaders, but they did
not go to the Tent. They stayed in the
camp, but the Spirit was also given to
them, and they prophesied in the camp.
27A young man ran to Moses and said,
"Eldad and Medad are prophesying in the
camp."
28Joshua son of Nun said, "Moses, my

master, stop them!" (Ever since he was a
young boy, Joshua had been Moses' assistant.)

29But Moses answered, "Are you jealous for me? I wish all the LORD's people
could prophesy. I wish the LORD would
give his Spirit to all of them!" 30Then
Moses and the leaders of Israel went
back to the camp.

The Lord Sends Quail

31The LORD sent a strong wind from
the sea, and it blew quail into the area all
around the camp. The quail were about
three feet deep on the ground, and there
were quail a day's walk in any direction.
32The people went out and gathered quail
all that day, that night, and the next day.
Everyone gathered at least sixty bushels,
and they spread them around the camp.
33But the LORD became very angry, and
he gave the people a terrible sickness that
came while the meat was still in their
mouths. 34So the people named that place
Kibroth Hattaavah,[n] because there they
buried those who wanted other food.

35From Kibroth Hattaavah the people
went to stay at Hazeroth.

Miriam and Aaron Speak Against Moses

12 Miriam and Aaron began to talk
against Moses because of his Cushite wife (he had married a Cushite). 2They
said, "Is Moses the only one the LORD
speaks through? Doesn't he also speak
through us?" And the LORD heard this.

3(Now Moses was very humble. He
was the least proud person on earth.)

4So the LORD suddenly spoke to Moses, Aaron, and Miriam and said, "All
three of you come to the Meeting Tent."
So they went. 5The LORD came down in a
pillar of cloud and stood at the entrance
to the Tent. He called to Aaron and Miriam, and they both came near. 6He said,
"Listen to my words:

When a prophet is among you,
I, the LORD, will show myself to
him in visions;

11:34 Kibroth Hattaavah This name in Hebrew means "graves of wanting."

FAITH links

MOSES' CHAMPION

NUMBERS 12

If you've ever been picked on by a brother or sister, you can understand how Moses felt. He was criticized by his brother Aaron and his sister Miriam. But Moses did not try to get even with them or criticize them in return for their harsh words. When they put him down, God stuck up for him in a powerful way.

When you're criticized by others, it's easy to think you have to defend yourself or strike back in some way. Consider the Moses way of dealing with criticism. Let God handle it. Although he may not use a skin disease to correct the person who wronged you, he does have a way of protecting his people.

Here's some more advice on forgiving others:

Forgive Instead, Genesis 33, p. 47

An Attention-Getter, Numbers 22, p. 207

What's Out Becomes In, Judges 11, p. 327

A Tight Spot, Jonah 2, p. 1215

Justice Desserts, Habakkuk 2:4–8, p. 1237

Two Birthdays, John 3:1–7, p. 1426

I will speak to him in dreams.
7 But this is not true with my servant
Moses.
I trust him to lead all my people.
8 I speak face to face with him—
clearly, not with hidden meanings.
He has even seen the form of the
LORD.
You should be afraid
to speak against my servant
Moses."

9 The LORD was very angry with
them, and he left.
10 When the cloud lifted from the Tent
and Aaron turned toward Miriam, she
was as white as snow; she had a skin disease. 11 Aaron said to Moses, "Please,
my master, forgive us for our foolish sin.
12 Don't let her be like a baby who is born
dead. (Sometimes a baby is born with half
of its flesh eaten away.)"
13 So Moses cried out to the LORD,
"God, please heal her!"
14 The LORD answered Moses, "If her
father had spit in her face, she would
have been shamed for seven days, so put
her outside the camp for seven days. After that, she may come back." 15 So Miriam was put outside of the camp for
seven days, and the people did not move
on until she came back.
16 After that, the people left Hazeroth
and camped in the Desert of Paran.

The Spies Explore Canaan

13 The LORD said to Moses, 2 "Send
men to explore the land of Canaan,
which I will give to the Israelites. Send
one leader from each tribe."
3 So Moses obeyed the LORD's command and sent the Israelite leaders out
from the Desert of Paran. 4 These are
their names: from the tribe of Reuben,
Shammua son of Zaccur; 5 from the tribe
of Simeon, Shaphat son of Hori; 6 from
the tribe of Judah, Caleb son of Jephunneh; 7 from the tribe of Issachar, Igal son
of Joseph; 8 from the tribe of Ephraim,
Hoshea son of Nun; 9 from the tribe of
Benjamin, Palti son of Raphu; 10 from the
tribe of Zebulun, Gaddiel son of Sodi;
11 from the tribe of Manasseh (a tribe of
Joseph), Gaddi son of Susi; 12 from the
tribe of Dan, Ammiel son of Gemalli;
13 from the tribe of Asher, Sethur son of
Michael; 14 from the tribe of Naphtali,

FAITH links

FOLLOWING THE CROWD

NUMBERS 13; 14

Some people like to follow the crowd. Whatever the group thinks is right is fine with them. Is that your belief? The people of Israel would agree. Joshua, Caleb, and ten others went to explore the land of Canaan. Ten returned with a fearful story of giants in the land. But Joshua and Caleb believed that God would help them take possession of the land. Because the Israelites chose not to trust God, they were forced to wander in the wilderness for 40 years.

Following the crowd can get you into trouble at times. If the crowd decides to disobey God, are you willing to take a stand for God?

An Example Not to Follow, Leviticus 18:1–3, p. 157

I'll Never Forget What's-His-Name, Deuteronomy 8, p. 239

The Green Light, 2 Samuel 2:1, p. 401

Give In or Take a Stand?, 1 Kings 22:13–14, p. 472

Choosing a Friend, Proverbs 28:7, p. 865

Heavenly Treasure, Luke 12:32–34, p. 1394

Nahbi son of Vophsi; **15**from the tribe of
Gad, Geuel son of Maki.
16These are the names of the men
Moses sent to explore the land. (Moses
gave Hoshea son of Nun the new name
Joshua.)
17Moses sent them to explore Canaan
and said, "Go through southern Canaan
and then into the mountains. **18**See what
the land looks like. Are the people who
live there strong or weak? Are there a
few or many? **19**What kind of land do they
live in? Is it good or bad? What about the
towns they live in—are they open like
camps, or do they have walls? **20**What
about the soil? Is it fertile or poor? Are
there trees there? Try to bring back some
of the fruit from that land." (It was the
season for the first grapes.)
21So they went up and explored the
land, from the Desert of Zin all the way to
Rehob by Lebo Hamath. **22**They went
through the southern area to Hebron,
where Ahiman, Sheshai, and Talmai, the
descendants of Anak lived. (The city of
Hebron had been built seven years before Zoan in Egypt.) **23**In the Valley of
Eshcol, they cut off a branch of a grapevine that had one bunch of grapes on it
and carried that branch on a pole between two of them. They also got some
pomegranates and figs. **24**That place was
called the Valley of Eshcol,[n] because the
Israelites cut off the bunch of grapes
there. **25**After forty days of exploring the
land, the men returned to the camp.
26They came back to Moses and
Aaron and all the Israelites at Kadesh, in
the Desert of Paran. The men reported to
them and showed everybody the fruit
from the land. **27**They told Moses, "We
went to the land where you sent us, and it
is a fertile land! Here is some of its fruit.
28But the people who live there are
strong. Their cities are walled and very
large. We even saw some Anakites there.
29The Amalekites live in the southern
area; the Hittites, Jebusites, and Amorites live in the mountains; and the Canaanites live near the sea and along the
Jordan River."
30Then Caleb told the people near
Moses to be quiet, and he said, "We
should certainly go up and take the land
for ourselves. We can certainly do it."
31But the men who had gone with him
said, "We can't attack those people; they
are stronger than we are." **32**And those
men gave the Israelites a bad report
about the land they explored, saying,
"The land that we explored is too large to
conquer. All the people we saw are very
tall. **33**We saw the Nephilim people
there. (The Anakites come from the
Nephilim people.) We felt like grasshoppers, and we looked like grasshoppers to
them."

The People Complain Again

14 That night all the people in the
camp began crying loudly. **2**All the
Israelites complained against Moses and
Aaron, and all the people said to them,
"We wish we had died in Egypt or
in this desert. **3**Why
is the LORD bringing
us to this land to be
killed with swords?
Our wives and chil-
dren will be taken
away. We would be
better off going back to Egypt." **4**They
said to each other, "Let's choose a leader
and go back to Egypt."

EMAIL! FROM GOD
14:1–4
Decisions
Find out what poor decisions the Israelites want to make.

5Then Moses and Aaron bowed facedown in front of all the Israelites gathered there. **6**Joshua son of Nun and Caleb
son of Jephunneh, who had explored the
land, tore their clothes. **7**They said to all
of the Israelites, "The land we explored
is very good. **8**If the LORD is pleased with
us, he will lead us into that land and give
us that fertile land. **9**Don't turn against
the LORD! Don't be afraid of the people in
that land! We will chew them up. They
have no protection, but the LORD is with
us. So don't be afraid of them."
10Then all the people talked about
killing them with stones. But the glory of
the LORD appeared at the Meeting Tent
to all the Israelites. **11**The LORD said to
Moses, "How long will these people ig-

13:24 Eshcol This name in Hebrew means "bunch."

nore me? How long will they not believe
me in spite of the miracles I have done
among them? **12**I will give them a terrible sickness and get rid of them. But I
will make you into a great nation that will
be stronger than they are."

13Then Moses said to the LORD, "The
Egyptians will hear about it! You brought
these people from there by your great
power, **14**and the Egyptians will tell this
to those who live in this land. They have
already heard about you, LORD. They
know that you are with your people and
that you were seen face to face. They
know that your cloud stays over your
people and that you lead your people with
that cloud during the day and with fire at
night. **15**If you put these people to death
all at once, the nations who have heard
about your power will say, **16**'The LORD
was not able to bring them into the land
he promised them. So he killed them in
the desert.'

17"So show your strength now, Lord.
Do what you said: **18**'The LORD doesn't
become angry quickly, but he has great
love. He forgives sin and law breaking.
But the LORD never forgets to punish
guilty people. When parents sin, he will
also punish their children, their grandchildren, their great-grandchildren, and
their great-great-grandchildren.' **19**By
your great love, forgive these people's
sin, just as you have forgiven them from
the time they left Egypt until now."

20The LORD answered, "I have forgiven them as you asked. **21**But, as surely
as I live and as surely as my glory fills
the whole earth, I make this promise:
22All these men saw my glory and the
miracles I did in Egypt and in the desert,
but they disobeyed me and tested me ten
times. **23**So not one of them will see the
land I promised to their ancestors. No
one who rejected me will see that land.
24But my servant Caleb thinks differently and follows me completely. So I will
bring him into the land he has already
seen, and his children will own that land.
25Since the Amalekites and the Canaanites are living in the valleys, leave tomorrow and follow the desert road toward the
Red Sea."

The Lord Punishes the People

26The LORD said to Moses and Aaron,
27"How long will these evil people complain about me? I have heard the grumbling and complaining of these Israelites.
28So tell them, 'This is what the LORD
says. I heard what you said, and as surely
as I live, I will do those very things to
you: **29**You will die in this desert. Every
one of you who is twenty years old or
older and who was counted with the people—all of you who complained against
me—will die. **30**Not one of you will enter
the land where I promised you would
live; only Caleb son of Jephunneh and
Joshua son of Nun will go in. **31**You said
that your children would be taken away,
but I will bring them into the land to enjoy what you refused. **32**As for you, you
will die in this desert. **33**Your children
will be shepherds here for forty years.
Because you were not loyal, they will suffer until you lie dead in the desert. **34**For
forty years you will suffer for your sins—
a year for each of the forty days you explored the land. You will know me as your
enemy.' **35**I, the LORD, have spoken, and I
will certainly do these things to all these
evil people who have come together
against me. So they will all die here in
this desert."

36The men Moses had sent to explore
the land had returned and spread complaints among all the people. They had
given a bad report about the land. **37**The
men who gave a very bad report died; the
LORD killed them with a terrible sickness. **38**Only two of the men who explored the land did not die—Joshua son of
Nun and Caleb son of Jephunneh.

39When Moses told these things to
all the Israelites, they were very sad.
40Early the next morning they started to
go toward the top of the mountains, saying, "We have sinned. We will go where
the LORD told us."

41But Moses said, "Why are you disobeying the LORD's command? You will
not win! **42**Don't go, because the LORD is
not with you and you will be beaten by
your enemies. **43**You will run into the
Amalekites and Canaanites, who will kill
you with swords. You have turned away

from the LORD, so the LORD will not be
with you."
44But they were proud. They went
toward the top of the mountains, but Moses and the Ark of the Agreement with
the LORD did not leave the camp. 45The
Amalekites and the Canaanites who lived
in those mountains came down and attacked the Israelites and beat them back
all the way to Hormah.

Rules About Sacrifices

15 The LORD said to Moses, 2"Speak
to the Israelites and say to them,
'When you enter the land that I am giving
you as a home, 3give the LORD offerings
made by fire. These may be from your
herds or flocks, as a smell pleasing to the
LORD. These may be burnt offerings or
sacrifices for special promises, or as gifts
to him, or as festival offerings. 4The one
who brings the offering shall also give the
LORD a grain offering. It should be two
quarts of fine flour mixed with one quart
of olive oil. 5Each time you offer a lamb
as a burnt offering or sacrifice, also prepare a quart of wine as a drink offering.
6" 'If you are giving a male sheep, also
prepare a grain offering of four quarts of
fine flour mixed with one and one-fourth
quarts of olive oil. 7Also prepare one and
one-fourth quarts of wine as a drink offering. Its smell will be pleasing to the
LORD.
8" 'If you prepare a young bull as a
burnt offering or sacrifice, whether it is
for a special promise or a fellowship offering to the LORD, 9bring a grain offering
with the bull. It should be six quarts of
fine flour mixed with two quarts of olive
oil. 10Also bring two quarts of wine as a
drink offering. This offering is made by
fire, and its smell will be pleasing to the
LORD. 11Prepare each bull or male
sheep, lamb or young goat this way. 12Do
this for every one of the animals you
bring.
13" 'All citizens must do these things
in this way, and the smell of their offerings by fire will be pleasing to the LORD.
14From now on if foreigners who live
among you want to make offerings by fire
so the smell will be pleasing to the LORD,
they must offer them the same way you
do. 15The law is the same for you and for
foreigners, and it will be from now on;
you and the foreigners are alike before
the LORD. 16The teachings and rules are
the same for you and for the foreigners
among you.' "
17The LORD said to Moses, 18"Tell
the Israelites: 'You are going to another
land, where I am taking you. 19When you
eat the food there, offer part of it to the
LORD. 20Offer a loaf of bread from the
first of your grain, which will be your offering from the threshing floor. 21From
now on offer to the LORD the first part of
your grain.
22" 'Now what if you forget to obey
any of these commands the LORD gave
Moses? 23These are the LORD's commands given to you through Moses,
which began the day the LORD gave them
to you and will continue from now on.
24If the people forget to obey one of
these commands, all the people must offer a young bull as a burnt offering, a
smell pleasing to the LORD. By law you
must also give the grain offering and the
drink offering with it, and you must bring
a male goat as a sin offering.
25" 'The priest will remove that sin
for all the Israelites so they will belong to
the LORD. They are forgiven, because
they didn't know they were sinning. For
the wrong they did they brought offerings to the LORD, an offering by fire and a
sin offering. 26So all of the people of Israel and the foreigners living among
them will be forgiven. No one meant to
do wrong.
27" 'If just one person sins without
meaning to, a year-old female goat must
be brought for a sin offering. 28The
priest will remove the sin of the person
who sinned accidentally. He will remove
it before the LORD, and the person will be
forgiven. 29The same teaching is for
everyone who sins accidentally—for
those born Israelites and for foreigners
living among you.
30" 'But anyone who sins on purpose
is against the LORD and must be cut off
from the people, whether it is someone
born among you or a foreigner. 31That

person has turned against the LORD's
word and has not obeyed his commands.
Such a person must surely be cut off from
the others. He is guilty.' "

A Man Worked on the Sabbath

32When the Israelites were still in the
desert, they found a man gathering wood
on the Sabbath day. **33**Those who found
him gathering wood brought him to Moses and Aaron and all the people. **34**They
held the man under guard, because they
did not know what to do with him.
35Then the LORD said to Moses, "The
man must surely die. All the people must
kill him by throwing stones at him outside the camp." **36**So all the people took
him outside the camp and
stoned him to death, as
the LORD commanded
Moses.

The Tassels

37The LORD said to
Moses, **38**"Speak to the
Israelites and tell them
this: 'Tie several pieces
of thread together and attach them to the corners
of your clothes. Put a blue thread in each
one of these tassels. Wear them from
now on. **39**You will have these tassels to
look at to remind you of all the LORD's
commands. Then you will obey them and
not be disloyal by following what your
bodies and eyes want. **40**Then you will
remember to obey all my commands, and
you will be God's holy people. **41**I am the
LORD your God, who brought you out of
Egypt to be your God. I am the LORD
your God.' "

Korah, Dathan, Abiram, and On

16 Korah, Dathan, Abiram, and On
turned against Moses. (Korah was
the son of Izhar, the son of Kohath, the
son of Levi; Dathan and Abiram were
brothers, the sons of Eliab; and On was
the son of Peleth; Dathan, Abiram, and
On were from the tribe of Reuben.)
2These men gathered two hundred fifty
other Israelite men, well-known leaders
chosen by the community, and challenged
Moses. **3**They came as a group to speak
to Moses and Aaron and said, "You have
gone too far. All the people are holy,
every one of them, and the LORD is
among them. So why do you put yourselves above all the people of the LORD?"

4When Moses heard this, he bowed
facedown. **5**Then he said to Korah and all
his followers: "Tomorrow morning the
LORD will show who belongs to him. He
will bring the one who is holy near to
him; he will bring to himself the person
he chooses. **6**So Korah, you and all your
followers do this: Get some pans for
burning incense. **7**Tomorrow put fire and
incense in them and take them before the
LORD. He will choose the man who is
holy. You Levites have
gone too far."

8Moses also said to
Korah, "Listen, you Le-
vites. **9**The God of Israel
has separated you from
the rest of the Israelites.
He brought you near to
himself to do the work in
the LORD's Holy Tent and
to stand before all the Israelites and serve them.
Isn't that enough? **10**He has brought you
and all your fellow Levites near to himself, yet now you want to be priests.
11You and your followers have joined together against the LORD. Your complaint
is not against Aaron."

12Then Moses called Dathan and Abiram, the sons of Eliab, but they said, "We
will not come! **13**You have brought us out
of a fertile land to this desert to kill us,
and now you want to order us around.
14You haven't brought us into a fertile
land; you haven't given us any land with
fields and vineyards. Will you put out the
eyes of these men? No! We will not
come!"

15Then Moses became very angry
and said to the LORD, "Don't accept their
gifts. I have not taken anything from
them, not even a donkey, and I have not
done wrong to any of them."

16Then Moses said to Korah, "You
and all your followers must stand before
the LORD tomorrow. And Aaron will stand

> The God of Israel has separated you from the rest of the Israelites.
> —Numbers 16:9

there with you and them. **17**Each of you must take your pan and put incense in it; present these two hundred fifty pans before the LORD. You and Aaron must also present your pans." **18**So each man got his pan and put burning incense in it and stood with Moses and Aaron at the entrance to the Meeting Tent. **19**Korah gathered all his followers who were against Moses and Aaron, and they stood at the entrance to the Meeting Tent. Then the glory of the LORD appeared to everyone.

20The LORD said to Moses and Aaron, **21**"Move away from these men so I can destroy them quickly."

22But Moses and Aaron bowed facedown and cried out, "God, you are the God over the spirits of all people. Please don't be angry with this whole group. Only one man has really sinned."

23Then the LORD said to Moses, **24**"Tell everyone to move away from the tents of Korah, Dathan, and Abiram."

25Moses stood and went to Dathan and Abiram; the older leaders of Israel followed him. **26**Moses warned the people, "Move away from the tents of these evil men! Don't touch anything of theirs, or you will be destroyed because of their sins." **27**So they moved away from the tents of Korah, Dathan, and Abiram. Dathan and Abiram were standing outside their tents with their wives, children, and little babies.

28Then Moses said, "Now you will know that the LORD has sent me to do all these things; it was not my idea. **29**If these men die a normal death—the way men usually die—then the LORD did not really send me. **30**But if the LORD does something new, you will know they have insulted the LORD. The ground will open and swallow them. They will be buried alive and will go to the place of the dead, and everything that belongs to them will go with them."

31When Moses finished saying these things, the ground under the men split open. **32**The earth opened and swallowed them and all their families. All Korah's men and everything they owned went down. **33**They were buried alive, going to the place of the dead, and everything they owned went with them. Then the earth covered them. They died and were gone from the community. **34**The people of Israel around them heard their screams and ran away, saying, "The earth will swallow us, too!"

35Then a fire came down from the LORD and destroyed the two hundred fifty men who had presented the incense.

36The LORD said to Moses, **37**"Tell Eleazar son of Aaron, the priest, to take all the incense pans out of the fire. Have him scatter the coals a long distance away. But the incense pans are still holy. **38**Take the pans of these men who sinned and lost their lives, and hammer them into flat sheets that will be used to cover the altar. They are holy, because they were presented to the LORD, and they will be a sign to the Israelites."

39So Eleazar the priest gathered all the bronze pans that had been brought by the men who were burned up. He had the pans hammered into flat sheets to put on the altar, **40**as the LORD had commanded him through Moses. These sheets were to remind the Israelites that only descendants of Aaron should burn incense before the LORD. Anyone else would die like Korah and his followers.

Aaron Saves the People

41The next day all the Israelites complained against Moses and Aaron and said, "You have killed the LORD's people."

42When the people gathered to complain against Moses and Aaron, they turned toward the Meeting Tent, and the cloud covered it. The glory of the LORD appeared. **43**Then Moses and Aaron went in front of the Meeting Tent.

44The LORD said to Moses, **45**"Move away from these people so I can destroy them quickly." So Moses and Aaron bowed facedown.

46Then Moses said to Aaron, "Get your pan, and put fire from the altar and incense in it. Hurry to the people and remove their sin. The LORD is angry with them; the sickness has already started." **47**So Aaron did as Moses said. He ran to the middle of the people, where the sickness had already started among them. So

Aaron offered the incense to remove
their sin. 48He stood between the dead
and the living, and the sickness stopped
there. 49But 14,700 people died from
that sickness, in addition to those who
died because of Korah. 50Then Aaron
went back to Moses at the entrance to
the Meeting Tent. The terrible sickness
had been stopped.

Aaron's Walking Stick Buds

17 The LORD said to Moses, 2"Speak
to the people of Israel and get
twelve walking sticks from them—one
from the leader of each tribe. Write the
name of each man on his stick, and 3on
the stick from Levi, write Aaron's name.
There must be one stick for the head of
each tribe. 4Put them in the Meeting
Tent in front of the Ark of the Agreement, where I meet with you. 5I will
choose one man whose walking stick
will begin to grow leaves; in this way I
will stop the Israelites from always complaining against you."

6So Moses spoke to the Israelites.
Each of the twelve leaders gave him a
walking stick—one from each tribe—and
Aaron's walking stick was among them.
7Moses put them before the LORD in the
Tent of the Agreement.

8The next day, when Moses entered

SHARING WITH A FRIEND

Tagg and I are talking about telling our friends about Jesus. We have a friend who has a problem in this area. Welcome Kelly, age 12, to Connect 2-You.

Howdy, Kelly. Tell us about your problem.

Well, my best friend knows I go to church, but we've never really talked about spiritual things. I'm pretty sure she's not a Christian, but I don't know what to do. I really want to tell her about Jesus, but I'm afraid she'll think I'm weird or something. I want her to know about Jesus, but I don't want her to feel uncomfortable around me.

I understand how you feel, Kelly. It takes a lot of courage to share your faith with a friend. But the Bible tells us that before someone can become a Christian, she has to hear about Jesus. If your best friend doesn't hear about Jesus from you, can you be sure that she'll hear about him from someone else? Check out the Livin' It page on sharing your faith, Romans 10:14–17, p. 1532, for some tips on how to talk to your friend about Jesus.

You may be surprised, Kelly. Your best friend may be more interested in talking about spiritual things than you think. Ask her what she thinks happens to us after we die or how she thinks the world began. After she gives you her answer, she may ask what you think. Then you'll have a chance to tell her why you believe what you do.

the Tent, he saw that Aaron's stick
(which stood for the family of Levi) had
grown leaves. It had even budded, blos-
somed, and produced almonds. 9So Moses brought out to the Israelites all the
walking sticks from the LORD's presence.
They all looked, and each man took back
his stick.

10Then the LORD said to Moses, "Put
Aaron's walking stick back in front of the
Ark of the Agreement. It will remind these
people who are always turning against me
to stop their complaining against me so
they won't die." 11So Moses obeyed what
the LORD commanded him.

12The people of Israel said to Moses,
"We are going to die! We are destroyed.
We are all destroyed! 13Anyone who
even comes near the Holy Tent of the
LORD will die. Will we all die?"

The Work of the Priests and Levites

18 The LORD said to Aaron, "You,
your sons, and your family are now
responsible for any wrongs done against
the Holy Place; you and your sons are responsible for any wrongs done against
the priests. 2Bring with you your fellow
Levites from your tribe, and they will
help you and your sons serve in the Tent
of the Agreement. 3They are under your
control, to do all the work that needs to
be done in the Tent. But they must not go
near the things in the Holy Place or near
the altar. If they do, both you and they
will die. 4They will join you in taking care
of the Meeting Tent. They must do the
work at the Tent, and no one else may
come near you.

5"You must take care of the Holy
Place and the altar so that I won't become
angry with the Israelites again. 6I myself
chose your fellow Levites from among
the Israelites as a gift given for you to the
LORD, to work at the Meeting Tent. 7But
only you and your sons may serve as
priests. Only you may serve at the altar
or go behind the curtain. I am giving you
this gift of serving as a priest, and anyone
else who comes near the Holy Place will
be put to death."

8Then the LORD said to Aaron, "I myself make you responsible for the offerings given to me. All the holy offerings
that the Israelites give to me, I give to
you and your sons as your share, your
continual portion. 9Your share of the holy
offerings is that part which is not burned.
When the people bring me gifts as most
holy offerings, whether they are grain or
sin or penalty offerings, they will be set
apart for you and your sons. 10You must
eat the offering in a most holy place. Any
male may eat it, but you must respect it
as holy.

11"I also give you the offerings the Israelites present to me. I give these to you
and your sons and daughters as your continual share. Anyone in your family who
is clean may eat it.

12"And I give you all the best olive oil
and all the best new wine and grain. This
is what the Israelites give to me, the
LORD, from the first crops they harvest.
13When they bring to the LORD all the
first things they harvest, they will be
yours. Anyone in your family who is
clean may eat these things.

14"Everything in Israel that is given
to the LORD is yours. 15The first one
born to any family, whether people or animals, will be offered to the LORD. And
that will be yours. But you must make a
payment for every firstborn child and
every firstborn animal that is unclean.
16When they are one month old, you
must make a payment for them of two
ounces of silver, as set by the Holy Place
measure.

17"But you must not make a payment
for the firstborn ox or sheep or goat.
Those animals are holy. Sprinkle their
blood on the altar and burn their fat as an
offering made by fire. The smell is pleasing to the LORD. 18But the meat will be
yours, just as the breast that is presented
and the right thigh will be yours. 19Any-
thing the Israelites present as holy gifts
I, the LORD, give to you, your sons and
daughters as your continual portion. This
is a lasting agreement of salt[*] before the

18:19 agreement of salt The meaning is not clear, but Leviticus 2:13 says, "Salt stands for your agreement with God that will last forever."

LORD for you and your children
forever."

eMail! FROM GOD
18:20
Protection
Who provides for you?

20The LORD also
said to Aaron, "You
will not inherit any
of the land, and you
will not own any
land among the other people. I will be
yours. Out of all the Israelites, only you
will inherit me.
21"When the people of Israel give me
a tenth of what they make, I will give that
tenth to the Levites. This is their payment for the work they do serving at the
Meeting Tent. 22But the other Israelites
must never go near the Meeting Tent, or
they will die for their sin. 23Only the Levites should work in the Meeting Tent
and be responsible for any sins against it.
This is a rule from now on. The Levites
will not inherit any land among the other
Israelites, 24but when the Israelites give
a tenth of everything they make to me, I
will give that tenth to the Levites as a reward. That is why I said about the Levites: 'They will not inherit any land
among the Israelites.' "
25The LORD said to Moses, 26"Speak
to the Levites and tell them: 'You will receive a tenth of everything the Israelites
make, which I will give to you. But you
must give a tenth of that back to the
LORD. 27I will accept your offering just as
much as I accept the offerings from others, who give new grain or new wine.
28In this way you will present an offering
to the LORD as the other Israelites do.
When you receive a tenth from the Israelites, you will give a tenth of that to
Aaron, the priest, as the LORD's share.
29Choose the best and holiest part from
what you are given as the portion you
must give to the LORD.'
30"Say to the Levites: 'When you
present the best, it will be accepted as
much as the grain and wine from the other
people. 31You and your families may eat
all that is left anywhere, because it is your
pay for your work in the Meeting Tent.
32And if you always give the best part to
the LORD, you will never be guilty. If you
do not sin against the holy offerings of the
Israelites, you will not die.' "

FAITH CHALLENGE

Try this one. Read 18:25–26 to find out what God says we should do with everything we own. How can you give one-tenth of everything you have back to the Lord?

TESTING IT

Numbers 18:25–26
The LORD said to Moses, "Speak to the Levites and tell them: 'You will receive a tenth of everything the Israelites make, which I will give to you. But you must give a tenth of that back to the LORD.' "

The Offering for Cleansing

19 The LORD said to Moses and Aaron,
2"These are the teachings that
the LORD commanded. Tell the Israelites
to get a young red cow that does not have
anything wrong with it and that has never
been worked. 3Give the cow to Eleazar
the priest; he will take it outside the
camp and kill it. 4Then Eleazar the priest
must put some of its blood on his finger
and sprinkle it seven times toward the
front of the Meeting Tent. 5The whole
cow must be burned while he watches;
the skin, the meat, the blood, and the intestines must all be burned. 6Then the

priest must take a cedar stick, a hyssop branch, and a red string and throw them onto the burning cow. **7**After the priest has washed himself and his clothes with water, he may come back into the camp, but he will be unclean until evening. **8**The man who burns the cow must wash himself and his clothes in water; he will be unclean until evening.

> Tell the Israelites to get a young red cow that does not have anything wrong with it and that has never been worked.
> —Numbers 19:2

9"Then someone who is clean will collect the ashes from the cow and put them in a clean place outside the camp. The Israelites will keep these ashes to use in the cleansing water, in a special ceremony to cleanse away sin. **10**The man who collected the cow's ashes must wash his clothes and be unclean until evening. This is a lasting rule for the Israelites and for the foreigners among them.

11"Those who touch a dead person's body will be unclean for seven days. **12**They must wash themselves with the cleansing water on the third day and on the seventh day; then they will be clean. But if they do not wash themselves on the third day and the seventh day, they cannot be clean. **13**If those who touch a dead person's body stay unclean and go to the LORD's Holy Tent, it becomes unclean; they must be cut off from Israel. If the cleansing water is not sprinkled on them, they are unclean and will stay unclean.

14"This is the teaching about someone who dies in a tent: Anyone in the tent or anyone who enters it will be unclean for seven days. **15**And every open jar or pot without a cover becomes unclean. **16**If anyone is outside and touches someone who was killed by a sword or who died a natural death, or if anyone touches a human bone or a grave, that person will be unclean for seven days.

17"So you must use the ashes from the burnt offering to make that person clean again. Pour fresh water over the ashes into a jar. **18**A clean person must take a hyssop branch and dip it into the water, and then he must sprinkle it over the tent and all its objects. He must also sprinkle the people who were there, as well as anyone who touched a bone, or the body of someone who was killed, or a dead person, or a grave. **19**The person who is clean must sprinkle this water on the unclean people on the third day and on the seventh day. On the seventh day they will become clean. They must wash their clothes and take a bath, and they will be clean that evening. **20**If any who are unclean do not become clean, they must be cut off from the community. Since they were not sprinkled with the cleansing water, they stay unclean, and they could make the LORD's Holy Tent unclean. **21**This is a lasting rule. Those who sprinkle the cleansing water must also wash their clothes, and anyone who touches the water will be unclean until evening. **22**Anything an unclean person touches becomes unclean, and whoever touches it will be unclean until evening."

Moses Disobeys God

20 In the first month all the people of Israel arrived at the Desert of Zin, and they stayed at Kadesh. There Miriam died and was buried. **2**There was no water for the people, so they came together against Moses and Aaron. **3**They argued with Moses and said, "We should have died in front of the LORD as our brothers did. **4**Why did you bring the LORD's people into this desert? Are we and our animals to die here? **5**Why did you bring us from Egypt to this terrible place? It has no grain, figs, grapevines, or pomegranates, and there's no water to drink!"

6So Moses and Aaron left the people and went to the entrance of the Meeting Tent. There they bowed facedown, and the glory of the LORD appeared to them. **7**The LORD said to Moses, **8**"Take your walking stick, and you and your brother Aaron should gather the people. Speak to that rock in front of them so that its water

FAITH links

THE PERFECT LEADER?

NUMBERS 20:1-13

Quick! Think of someone you know right now who has never sinned. (Someone besides Jesus.) Can't think of anyone? What about someone in history, someone like . . . Moses? There was a time when Moses blew his cool. The people of Israel made him angry. Moses reacted in sin. Because of his disobedience, God told him that he would not enter the Promised Land.

As humans, we sometimes "worship" our leaders. We think they can do no wrong. But sometimes they disappoint us by being all too human. None of us is without sin. That's why all of us—including leaders—need Jesus.

Surf over to these Faithlinks for the 411 on sin.

The Trouble with Sin, Genesis 6—8, p. 11

The Weak Link, Judges 16, p. 334

Plan for Success, 1 Chronicles 14:8–17, p. 538

Dirty Inside, Isaiah 6:1–7, p. 904

A Model of Forgiveness, Ezekiel 16:59–63, p. 1103

It's Free!, Ephesians 2:8–9, p. 1600

will flow from it. When you bring the
water out from that rock, give it to the
people and their animals."
9So Moses took the stick from in front
of the LORD, as he had said. **10**Moses and
Aaron gathered the people in front of the
rock, and Moses said, "Now listen to me,
you who turn against God! Do you want
us to bring water out of this rock?"
11Then Moses lifted his hand and hit the
rock twice with his stick. Water began
pouring out, and the people and their animals drank it.
12But the LORD said to Moses and
Aaron, "Because you did not believe me,
and because you did not honor me as holy
before the people, you will not lead them
into the land I will give them."
13These are the waters of Meribah,ⁿ
where the Israelites argued with the
LORD and where he showed them he was
holy.

Edom Will Not Let Israel Pass

14From Kadesh, Moses sent messengers to the king of Edom. He said, "Your
brothers, the Israelites, say to you: You
know about all the troubles we have had,
15how our ancestors went down into
Egypt and we lived there for many years.
The people of Egypt were cruel to us and
our ancestors, **16**but when we cried out
to the LORD, he heard us and sent us an
angel to bring us out of Egypt.

"Now we are here at Kadesh, a town
on the edge of your land. **17**Please let us
pass through your country. We will not
touch any fields of grain or vineyards, and
will not drink water from the wells. We
will travel only along the king's road, not
turning right or left until we have passed
through your country."
18But the king of Edom answered:
"You may not pass through here. If you
try, I will come and meet you with
swords."
19The Israelites answered: "We will
go along the main road, and if we or our
animals drink any of your water, we will

20:13 Meribah This name in Hebrew means "argument."

pay for it. We only want to walk through.
That's all."

20But he answered: "You may not
pass through here."

Then the Edomites went out to meet
the Israelites with a large and powerful
army. 21The Edomites refused to let
them pass through their country, so the
Israelites turned back.

Aaron Dies

22All the Israelites moved from Kadesh to Mount Hor, 23near the border of
Edom. There the LORD said to Moses and
Aaron, 24"Aaron will die. He will not enter the land that I'm giving to the Israelites, because you both acted against my
command at the waters of Meribah.
25Take Aaron and his son Eleazar up on
Mount Hor, 26and take off Aaron's special clothes and put them on his son Eleazar. Aaron will die there; he will join his
ancestors."

27Moses obeyed the LORD's command. They climbed up Mount Hor, and
all the people saw them go. 28Moses
took off Aaron's clothes and put them on
Aaron's son Eleazar. Then Aaron died
there on top of the mountain. Moses and
Eleazar came back down the mountain,
29and when all the people learned that
Aaron was dead, everyone in Israel cried
for him for thirty days.

War with the Canaanites

21 The Canaanite king of Arad lived
in the southern area. When he
heard that the Israelites were coming on
the road to Atharim, he attacked them
and captured some of them. 2Then the
Israelites made this promise to the LORD:
"If you will help us defeat these people,
we will completely destroy their cities."
3The LORD listened to the Israelites, and
he let them defeat the Canaanites. The
Israelites completely destroyed the Canaanites and their cities, so the place was
named Hormah."

The Bronze Snake

4The Israelites left Mount Hor and
went on the road toward the Red Sea, in
order to go around the country of Edom.
But the people became impatient on the
way 5and grumbled at God and Moses.
They said, "Why did you bring us out of
Egypt to die in this desert? There is no
bread and no water, and we hate this terrible food!"

6So the LORD sent them poisonous
snakes; they bit the people, and many of
the Israelites died. 7The people came to
Moses and said, "We sinned when we
grumbled at you and the LORD. Pray that
the LORD will take away these snakes."
So Moses prayed for the people.

8The LORD said to Moses, "Make a
bronze snake, and put it on a pole. When
anyone who is bitten looks at it, that person will live." 9So Moses made a bronze
snake and put it on a pole. Then when a
snake bit anyone, that person looked at
the bronze snake and lived.

The Journey to Moab

10The Israelites went and camped at
Oboth. 11They went from Oboth to Iye
Abarim, in the desert east of Moab.
12From there they went and camped in
the Zered Valley. 13From there they went
and camped across the Arnon, in the
desert just inside the Amorite country.
The Arnon is the border between the Moabites and the Amorites. 14That is why
the Book of the Wars of the LORD says:

". . . and Waheb in Suphah, and the
ravines,
the Arnon, 15and the slopes of the
ravines
that lead to the settlement of Ar.
These places are at the border of
Moab."

16The Israelites went from there to
Beer; a well is there where the LORD said
to Moses, "Gather the people and I will
give them water."

17Then the Israelites sang this song:
"Pour out water, well!
Sing about it.
18Princes dug this well.
Important men made it.
With their scepters and poles, they
dug it."

21:3 Hormah This name in Hebrew means "completely destroyed."

The people went from the desert to
Mattanah. 19From Mattanah they went
to Nahaliel and on to Bamoth. 20From
Bamoth they went to the valley of Moab
where the top of Mount Pisgah looks
over the desert.

Israel Kills Sihon and Og

21The Israelites sent messengers to
Sihon, king of the Amorites, saying,
22"Let us pass through
your country. We will not
go through any fields of
grain or vineyards, or drink
water from the wells. We
will travel only along the
king's road until we have
passed through your coun-
try."
23But King Sihon
would not let the Israel-
ites pass through his
country. He gathered his whole army together, and they marched out to meet Israel in the desert. At Jahaz they fought
the Israelites. 24Israel killed the king and
captured his land from the Arnon River to
the Jabbok River. They took the land as
far as the Ammonite border, which was
strongly defended. 25Israel captured all
the Amorite cities and lived in them, taking Heshbon and all the towns around it.
26Heshbon was the city where Sihon, the
Amorite king, lived. In the past he had
fought with the king of Moab and had
taken all the land as far as the Arnon.
27That is why the poets say:

"Come to Heshbon
and rebuild it;
rebuild Sihon's city.
28 A fire began in Heshbon;
flames came from Sihon's city.
It destroyed Ar in Moab,
and it burned the Arnon highlands.
29 How terrible for you, Moab!
The people of Chemosh are
ruined.
His sons ran away
and his daughters were captured
by Sihon, king of the Amorites.
30 But we defeated those Amorites.
We ruined their towns from
Heshbon to Dibon,
and we destroyed them as far as
Nophah, near Medeba."

31So Israel lived in the land of the
Amorites.
32After Moses sent spies to the town
of Jazer, they captured the towns around
it, forcing out the Amorites who lived
there.
33Then the Israelites went up the
road toward Bashan. Og king of Bashan and
his whole army marched
out to meet the Israelites,
and they fought at Edrei.
34The LORD said to
Moses, "Don't be afraid
of him. I will hand him,
his whole army, and his
land over to you. Do to
him what you did to Si-
hon, the Amorite king
who lived in Heshbon."
35So the Israelites
killed Og and his sons and all his army;
no one was left alive. And they took his
land.

> The LORD said to Moses, "Don't be afraid of him. I will hand him, his whole army, and his land over to you."
> —Numbers 21:34

Balak Sends for Balaam

22 Then the people of Israel went
to the plains of Moab, and they
camped near the Jordan River across from
Jericho.
2Balak son of Zippor saw everything
the Israelites had done to the Amorites.
3And Moab was scared of so many Israelites; truly, Moab was terrified by them.
4The Moabites said to the older leaders of Midian, "These people will take
everything around us like an ox eating
grass."
Balak son of Zippor was the king of
Moab at this time. 5He sent messengers
to Balaam son of Beor at Pethor, near the
Euphrates River in his native land. Balak
said, "A nation has come out of Egypt that
covers the land. They have camped next
to me, 6and they are too powerful for me.
So come and put a curse on them. Maybe
then I can defeat them and make them
leave the area. I know that if you bless
someone, the blessings happen, and if
you put a curse on someone, it happens."
7The older leaders of Moab and Midian went with payment in their hands.

When they found Balaam, they told him
what Balak had said.
8Balaam said to them, "Stay here for
the night, and I will tell you what the
LORD tells me." So the Moabite leaders
stayed with him.
9God came to Balaam and asked,
"Who are these men with you?"
10Balaam said to God, "The king of
Moab, Balak son of Zippor, sent them to
me with this message: **11**'A nation has
come out of Egypt that covers the land.
So come and put a curse on them, and
maybe I can fight them and force them
out of my land.' "
12But God said to Balaam, "Do not go
with them. Don't put a curse on those
people, because I have blessed them."
13The next morning Balaam awoke
and said to Balak's leaders, "Go back to
your own country; the LORD has refused
to let me go with you."
14So the Moabite leaders went back
to Balak and said, "Balaam refused to
come with us."
15So Balak sent other leaders—this
time there were more of them, and they
were more important. **16**They went to Balaam and said, "Balak son of Zippor says
this: Please don't let anything stop you
from coming to me. **17**I will pay you very
well, and I will do what you say. Come and
put a curse on these people for me."
18But Balaam answered Balak's servants, "King Balak could give me his palace full of silver and gold, but I cannot
disobey the LORD my God in anything,
great or small. **19**You stay here tonight as
the other men did, and I will find out what
more the LORD tells me."
20That night God came to Balaam and
said, "These men have come to ask you
to go with them. Go, but only do what I
tell you."

Balaam's Donkey Speaks

21Balaam got up the next morning
and put a saddle on his donkey. Then he
went with the Moabite leaders. **22**But
God became angry because Balaam went,
so the angel of the LORD stood in the road
to stop Balaam. Balaam was riding his
donkey, and he had two servants with
him. **23**When the donkey saw the angel of
the LORD standing in the road with a
sword in his hand, the donkey left the
road and went into the field. Balaam hit
the donkey to force her back on the road.
24Later, the angel of the LORD stood
on a narrow path between two vineyards,
with walls on both sides. **25**Again the
donkey saw the angel of the LORD, and
she walked close to one wall, crushing
Balaam's foot against it. So he hit her
again.
26The angel of the LORD went ahead
again and stood at a narrow place, too
narrow to turn left or right. **27**When the
donkey saw the angel of the LORD, she
lay down under Balaam. This made him
so angry that he hit her with his stick.
28Then the LORD made the donkey talk,
and she said to Balaam, "What have I
done to make you hit me three times?"
29Balaam answered the donkey, "You
have made me look foolish! I wish I had a
sword in my hand! I would kill you right
now!"
30But the donkey said to Balaam, "I
am your very own donkey, which you
have ridden for years. Have I ever done
this to you before?"
"No," Balaam said.
31Then the LORD let Balaam see the
angel of the LORD, who was standing in
the road with his sword drawn. Then Balaam bowed facedown on the ground.
32The angel of the LORD asked Balaam, "Why have you hit your donkey
three times? I have stood here to stop
you, because what you are doing is
wrong. **33**The donkey saw me and turned
away from me three times. If she had not
turned away, I would have killed you by
now, but I would have let her live."
34Then Balaam said to the angel of
the LORD, "I have sinned; I did not know
you were standing in the road to stop me.
If I am wrong, I will go back."
35The angel of the LORD said to Balaam, "Go with these men, but say only
what I tell you." So Balaam went with
Balak's leaders.
36When Balak heard that Balaam was
coming, he went out to meet him at Ar in
Moab, which was beside the Arnon, at

FAITH links

AN ATTENTION-GETTER

NUMBERS 22

Do you have a pet? What would you do if your pet suddenly talked to you one morning, instead of barking or meowing? That would certainly get your attention, wouldn't it? Balaam was a prophet who was determined to curse the people of Israel, all because a king told him to do so. But God told him not to do it. Since Balaam resisted God, God used a talking donkey to get his attention.

God will do whatever it takes to protect his people from harm and to keep people from harming others. He knows how to get someone's attention. Does he have yours?

Ten Ways to Obey, Exodus 20, p. 103

Our Thorough God, Leviticus 13, p. 149

Reward for Obedience, Leviticus 26:3–13, p. 171

A Shortcut, 1 Samuel 13:1–14, p. 369

Listen Up!, 1 Kings 19:11–13, p. 467

The Doubt Remover, Romans 10:8–10, p. 1533

the edge of his country. **37**Balak said to
Balaam, "I had asked you before to come
quickly. Why didn't you come to me? I am
able to reward you well."
38But Balaam answered, "I have come
to you now, but I can't say just anything. I
can only say what God tells me to say."
39Then Balaam went with Balak to
Kiriath Huzoth. **40**Balak offered cattle
and sheep as a sacrifice and gave some
meat to Balaam and the leaders with him.
41The next morning Balak took Balaam to Bamoth Baal; from there he could
see the edge of the Israelite camp.

Balaam's First Message

23 Balaam said to Balak, "Build me
seven altars here, and prepare
seven bulls and seven male sheep for
me." **2**Balak did what Balaam asked, and
they offered a bull and a male sheep on
each of the altars.
3Then Balaam said to Balak, "Stay
here beside your burnt offering and I will
go. If the LORD comes to me, I will tell
you whatever he shows me." Then Balaam went to a higher place.
4God came to Balaam there, and Balaam said to him, "I have prepared seven
altars, and I have offered a bull and a male
sheep on each altar."
5The LORD told Balaam what he
should say. Then the LORD said, "Go back
to Balak and give him this message."
6So Balaam went back to Balak. Balak
and all the leaders of Moab were still
standing beside his burnt offering **7**when
Balaam gave them this message:

"Balak brought me here from Aram;
the king of Moab brought me from the eastern mountains.
Balak said, 'Come, put a curse on the people of Jacob for me.
Come, call down evil on the people of Israel.'
8But God has not cursed them,
so I cannot curse them.
The LORD has not called down evil on them,
so I cannot call down evil on them.
9I see them from the top of the mountains;
I see them from the hills.
I see a people who live alone,
who think they are different from other nations.
10No one can number the many people of Jacob,

and no one can count a fourth of
Israel.
Let me die like good men,
and let me end up like them!"
11Balak said to Balaam, "What have
you done to me? I brought you here to
curse my enemies, but you have only
blessed them!"
12But Balaam answered, "I must say
what the LORD tells me to say."

Balaam's Second Message

13Then Balak said to him, "Come
with me to another place, where you can
also see the people. But you can only see
part of them, not all of them. Curse them
for me from there." 14So Balak took Balaam to the field of Zophim, on top of
Mount Pisgah. There Balak built seven
altars and offered a bull and a male sheep
on each altar.
15So Balaam said to Balak, "Stay here
by your burnt offering, and I will meet
with God over there."
16So the LORD came to Balaam and
told him what to say. Then he said, "Go
back to Balak and say such and such."
17So Balaam went to Balak, where he
and the leaders of Moab were standing
beside his burnt offering. Balak asked
him, "What did the LORD say?"
18Then Balaam gave this message:
"Stand up, Balak, and listen.
Hear me, son of Zippor.
19 God is not a human being, and he will
not lie.
He is not a human, and he does not
change his mind.
What he says he will do, he does.
What he promises, he makes come
true.
20 He told me to bless them,
so I cannot change the blessing.
21 He has found no wrong in the people
of Jacob;
he saw no fault in Israel.
The LORD their God is with them,
and they praise their King.
22 God brought them out of Egypt;
they are as strong as a wild ox.
23 No tricks will work on the people of
Jacob,
and no magic will work against
Israel.
People now say about them,
'Look what God has done for
Israel!'
24 The people rise up like a lioness;
they get up like a lion.
Lions don't rest until they have
eaten,

FAITH links

ALWAYS TRUTHFUL

NUMBERS 23:19

Is there anyone you know who has never lied? Some people think that George Washington never told a lie because of a popular story about a cherry tree. That story may or may not be true. One thing is true, though: God never lies. He always does what he says he will do. He won't suddenly change his mind or say, "Whoops! I made a mistake!" When he makes a promise, you can be sure that he will keep it.

Find out what else God has to say about keeping your word.

A Long Wait, Joshua 14:6–15, p. 294

An Unsung Hero, Ruth 2:12, 15–16, p. 347

A Given, 1 Chronicles 5:18–20, p. 526

All Talk, No Action, Jeremiah 5:1–2, p. 996

The Whole Truth, John 8:31–32, 45, p. 1438

The Finished Product, Philippians 1:6, p. 1609

until they have drunk their
enemies' blood."
25Then Balak said to Balaam, "You
haven't cursed these people, so at least,
don't bless them!"
26Balaam answered Balak, "I told you
before that I can only do what the LORD
tells me."

Balaam's Third Message

27Then Balak said to Balaam, "Come,
I will take you to another place. Maybe
God will be pleased to let you curse them
from there." 28So Balak took Balaam to
the top of Peor, the mountain that looks
over the desert.
29Balaam told Balak, "Build me seven
altars here and prepare for me seven
bulls and seven male sheep." 30Balak did
what Balaam asked, and he offered a bull
and a male sheep on each altar.
24 Balaam saw that the LORD wanted
to bless Israel, so he did not try to
use any magic but looked toward the
desert. 2When Balaam saw the Israelites
camped in their tribes, the Spirit of God
took control of him, 3and he gave this
message:

"This is the message of Balaam son
of Beor,
the message of a man who sees
clearly;
4 this is the message of a man who
hears the words of God.
I see a vision from the Almighty,
and my eyes are open as I fall
before him.
5 Your tents are beautiful, people of
Jacob!
So are your homes, Israel!
6 Your tents spread out like valleys,
like gardens beside a river.
They are like spices planted by the
LORD,
like cedar trees growing by the
water.
7 Israel's water buckets will always be
full,
and their crops will have plenty of
water.
Their king will be greater than Agag;
their kingdom will be very great.
8 God brought them out of Egypt;
they are as strong as a wild ox.
They will defeat their enemies
and break their enemies' bones;
they will shoot them with arrows.
9 Like a lion, they lie waiting to
attack;
like a lioness, no one would be
brave enough to wake them.
Anyone who blesses you will be
blessed,
and anyone who curses you will be
cursed."

10Then Balak was angry with Balaam,
and he pounded his fist. He said to Balaam, "I called you here to curse my enemies, but you have continued to bless
them three times. 11Now go home! I said
I would pay you well, but the LORD has
made you lose your reward."
12Balaam said to Balak, "When you
sent messengers to me, I told them,
13'Balak could give me his palace filled
with silver and gold, but I still cannot go
against the LORD's commands. I could
not do anything, good or bad, on my own,
but I must say what the LORD says.'
14Now I am going back to my own people, but I will tell you what these people
will do to your people in the future."

Balaam's Final Message

15Then Balaam gave this message:
"This is the message of Balaam son
of Beor,
the message of a man who sees
clearly;
16 this is the message of a man who
hears the words of God.
I know well the Most High God.
I see a vision from the Almighty,
and my eyes are open as I fall
before him.
17 I see someone who will come some
day,
someone who will come, but not
soon.
A star will come from Jacob;
a ruler will rise from Israel.
He will crush the heads of the
Moabites
and smash the skulls of the sons of
Sheth.
18 Edom will be conquered;

his enemy Edom will be
conquered,
but Israel will grow wealthy.
19 A ruler will come from the
descendants of Jacob
and will destroy those left in the
city."

20Then Balaam saw Amalek and gave
this message:
"Amalek was the most important
nation,
but Amalek will be destroyed at
last."

21Then Balaam saw
the Kenites and gave this
message:
"Your home is safe,
like a nest on a
cliff.
22 But you Kenites will
be burned up;
Assyria will keep
you captive."

So the Israelites began to worship Baal of Peor, and the LORD was very angry with them.
—Numbers 25:3

23Then Balaam gave this message:
"No one can live when God does this.
24 Ships will sail from the shores of
Cyprus
and defeat Assyria and Eber,
but they will also be destroyed."

25Then Balaam got up and returned
home, and Balak also went on his way.

Israel Worships Baal at Peor

25 While the people of Israel were
still camped at Acacia, the men
began sinning sexually with Moabite
women. **2**The women invited them to
their sacrifices to their gods, and the Israelites ate food there and worshiped
these gods. **3**So the Israelites began to
worship Baal of Peor, and the LORD was
very angry with them.
4The LORD said to Moses, "Get all the
leaders of the people and kill them in
open daylight in the presence of the
LORD. Then the LORD will not be angry
with the people of Israel."
5So Moses said to Israel's judges,
"Each of you must put to death your people who have become worshipers of Baal
of Peor."
6Moses and the Israelites were gathered at the entrance to the Meeting Tent,
crying there. Then an Israelite man
brought a Midianite woman to his brothers in plain sight of Moses and all the
people. **7**Phinehas son of Eleazar, the son
of Aaron, the priest, saw this, so he left
the meeting and got his spear. **8**He followed the Israelite into his tent and
drove his spear through both the Israelite
man and the Midianite woman. Then the
terrible sickness among the Israelites
stopped.
9This sickness had
killed twenty-four thou-
sand people.
10The LORD said to
Moses, **11**"Phinehas son of
Eleazar, the son of Aaron,
the priest, has saved the
Israelites from my anger.
He hates sin as much as I
do. Since he tried to save
my honor among them, I
will not kill them. **12**So tell Phinehas that
I am making my peace agreement with
him. **13**He and his descendants will always be priests, because he had great
concern for the honor of his God. He removed the sins of the Israelites so they
would belong to God."
14The Israelite man who was killed
with the Midianite woman was named
Zimri son of Salu. He was the leader of a
family in the tribe of Simeon. **15**And the
name of the Midianite woman who was
put to death was Cozbi daughter of Zur,
who was the chief of a Midianite family.
16The LORD said to Moses, **17**"The
Midianites are your enemies, and you
should kill them. **18**They have already
made you their enemies, because they
tricked you at Peor and because of their
sister Cozbi, the daughter of a Midianite
leader. She was the woman who was
killed when the sickness came because
the people sinned at Peor."

The People Are Counted

26 After the great sickness, the LORD
said to Moses and Eleazar son of

Aaron, the priest, **2**"Count all the people of Israel by families. Count all the men who are twenty years old or older who will serve in the army of Israel." **3**Moses and Eleazar the priest spoke to the people on the plains of Moab near the Jordan River, across from Jericho. They said, **4**"Count the men twenty years old or older, as the LORD commanded Moses."

Here are the Israelites who came out of Egypt:

5The tribe of Reuben, the first son born to Israel, was counted. From Hanoch came the Hanochite family group; from Pallu came the Palluite family group; **6**from Hezron came the Hezronite family group; from Carmi came the Carmite family group. **7**These were the family groups of Reuben, and the total number of men was 43,730.

8The son of Pallu was Eliab, **9**and Eliab's sons were Nemuel, Dathan, and Abiram. Dathan and Abiram were the leaders who turned against Moses and Aaron and followed Korah when he turned against the LORD. **10**The earth opened up and swallowed them and Korah; they died at the same time the fire burned up the 250 men. This was a warning, **11**but the children of Korah did not die.

12These were the family groups in the tribe of Simeon: From Nemuel came the Nemuelite family group; from Jamin came the Jaminite family group; from Jakin came the Jakinite family group; **13**from Zerah came the Zerahite family group; from Shaul came the Shaulite family group. **14**These were the family groups of Simeon, and the total number of men was 22,200.

15These were the family groups in the tribe of Gad: From Zephon came the Zephonite family group; from Haggi came the Haggite family group; from Shuni came the Shunite family group; **16**from Ozni came the Oznite family group; from Eri came the Erite family group; **17**from Arodi came the Arodite family group; from Areli came the Arelite family group. **18**These were the family groups of Gad, and the total number of men was 40,500.

19Two of Judah's sons, Er and Onan, died in Canaan.

20These were the family groups in the tribe of Judah: From Shelah came the Shelanite family group; from Perez came the Perezite family group; from Zerah came the Zerahite family group. **21**These were the family groups from Perez: From Hezron came the Hezronite family group; from Hamul came the Hamulite family group. **22**These were the family groups of Judah, and the total number of men was 76,500.

23These were the family groups in the tribe of Issachar: From Tola came the Tolaite family group; from Puah came the Puite family group; **24**from Jashub came the Jashubite family group; from Shimron came the Shimronite family group. **25**These were the family groups of Issachar, and the total number of men was 64,300.

26These were the family groups in the tribe of Zebulun: From Sered came the Seredite family group; from Elon came the Elonite family group; from Jahleel came the Jahleelite family group. **27**These were the family groups of Zebulun, and the total number of men was 60,500.

28These were the family groups of Joseph through Manasseh and Ephraim.

29These were the family groups of Manasseh: From Makir came the Makirite family group (Makir was the father of Gilead); from Gilead came the Gileadite family group. **30**These were the family groups that came from Gilead: From Iezer came the Iezerite family group; from Helek came the Helekite family group; **31**from Asriel came the Asrielite family group; from Shechem came the Shechemite family group; **32**from Shemida came the Shemidaite family group; from Hepher came the Hepherite family group. **33**(Zelophehad son of Hepher had no sons; he had only daughters, and their names were Mahlah, Noah, Hoglah, Milcah, and Tirzah.) **34**These were the family groups of Manasseh, and the total number of men was 52,700.

35These were the family groups in the tribe of Ephraim: From Shuthelah came the Shuthelahite family group; from Beker came the Bekerite family group;

ONE POTATO, TWO POTATO . . . Numbers 26:55–56

Have you ever made a decision by counting off, "One-potato, two-potato, three-potato, four"? It's an easy way to get a quick answer to who should be "it." Throwing lots was a little like that. It was kind of like drawing straws (to see who gets the short straw) or flipping a coin (heads or tails). We don't know what the lots were made of or exactly how they were thrown. We just know they were used to make big and important decisions. Throwing lots was the way that people in biblical times gave God some room to help them make their decisions, like:

Choosing the goat to remove sins on the Day of Cleansing. (Read Leviticus 16:8–10, p. 155.)

Dividing the land after the Israelites moved back into it. (Check out Numbers 26:55–56, p. 213; Joshua 14:2, p. 294.)

Dividing Jesus' garments among the soldiers. (Look at Matthew 27:35, p. 1325.)

Even choosing the new disciple to take the place of Judas. (Check out Acts 1:24–26, p. 1464.)

from Tahan came the Tahanite family
group. **36**This was the family group from
Shuthelah: From Eran came the Eranite
family group. **37**These were the family
groups of Ephraim, and the total number
of men was 32,500. These are the family
groups that came from Joseph.

38These were the family groups in
the tribe of Benjamin: From Bela came
the Belaite family group; from Ashbel
came the Ashbelite family group; from
Ahiram came the Ahiramite family group;
39from Shupham came the Shuphamite
family group; from Hupham came the
Huphamite family group. **40**These were
the family groups from Bela through Ard
and Naaman: From Ard came the Ardite
family group; from Naaman came the
Naamite family group. **41**These were the
family groups of Benjamin, and the total
number of men was 45,600.

42This was the family group in the
tribe of Dan: From Shuham came the Shuhamite family group. That was the family
of Dan, **43**and the total number of men in
the Shuhamite family group of Dan was
64,400.

44These were the family groups in
the tribe of Asher: From Imnah came the
Imnite family group; from Ishvi came the
Ishvite family group; from Beriah came
the Beriite family group. **45**These were
the family groups that came from Beriah:
From Heber came the Heberite family
group; from Malkiel came the Malkielite
family group. **46**(Asher also had a daughter named Serah.) **47**These were the
family groups of Asher, and the total
number of men was 53,400.

48These were the family groups in
the tribe of Naphtali: From Jahzeel came
the Jahzeelite family group; from Guni
came the Gunite family group; **49**from Jezer came the Jezerite family group; from
Shillem came the Shillemite family
group. **50**These were the family groups
of Naphtali, and the total number of men
was 45,400.

51So the total number of the men of
Israel was 601,730.
52The LORD said to Moses, 53"Divide
the land among these people by the number of names. 54A large tribe will get
more land, and a small tribe will get less
land; the amount of land each tribe gets
will depend on the number of its people.
55Divide the land by drawing lots, and
the land each tribe gets will be named for
that tribe. 56Divide the land between
large and small groups by drawing lots."
57The tribe of Levi was also counted.
These were the family groups of Levi:
From Gershon came the Gershonite family group; from Kohath came the Kohathite family group; from Merari came the
Merarite family group. 58These also
were Levite family groups: the Libnite
family group, the Hebronite family group,
the Mahlite family group, the Mushite
family group, and the Korahite family
group. (Kohath was the ancestor of Amram, 59whose wife was named Jochebed.
She was from the tribe of Levi and she
was born in Egypt. She and Amram had
two sons, Aaron and Moses, and their
sister Miriam. 60Aaron was the father of
Nadab, Abihu, Eleazar, and Ithamar.
61But Nadab and Abihu died because
they made an offering before the LORD
with the wrong kind of fire.)
62The total number of male Levites
one month old or older was 23,000. But
these men were not counted with the
other Israelites, because they were not
given any of the land among the other Israelites.
63Moses and Eleazar the priest counted all these people. They counted the Israelites on the plains of Moab across the
Jordan River from Jericho. 64Moses and
Aaron the priest had counted the Israelites in the Desert of Sinai, but no one Moses counted on the plains of Moab was in
the first counting. 65The LORD had told
the Israelites they would all die in the
desert, and the only two left were Caleb
son of Jephunneh and Joshua son of Nun.

Zelophehad's Daughters

27 Then the daughters of Zelophehad
came near. Zelophehad was the
son of Hepher, the son of Gilead, the son
of Makir, the son of Manasseh. Zelophehad's daughters belonged to the family
groups of Manasseh son of Joseph. The
daughters' names were Mahlah, Noah,
Hoglah, Milcah, and Tirzah. 2They went
to the entrance of the Meeting Tent and
stood before Moses, Eleazar the priest,
the leaders, and all the people. They said,
3"Our father died in the desert. He was
not one of Korah's followers who came
together against the LORD, but he died
because of his own sin, and he had no
sons. 4Our father's name will die out because he had no sons. Give us property
among our father's relatives."
5So Moses brought their case to the
LORD, 6and the LORD said to him, 7"The
daughters of Zelophehad are right; they
should certainly get what their father
owned. Give them property among their
father's relatives.
8"Tell the Israelites, 'If a man dies and
has no son, then everything he owned
should go to his daughter. 9If he has no
daughter, then everything he owned
should go to his brothers. 10If he has no
brothers, then everything he owned
should go to his father's brothers. 11And
if his father had no brothers, then everything he owned should go to the nearest
relative in his family group. This should
be a rule among the people of Israel, as
the LORD has given this command to
Moses.' "

Joshua Is the New Leader

12Then the LORD said to Moses,
"Climb this mountain in the Abarim
Mountains, and look at the land I have
given to the Israelites. 13After you have
seen it, you will die and join your ancestors as your brother Aaron did, 14because
you both acted against my command in
the Desert of Zin. You did not
honor me as holy be-
fore the people at
the waters of Meri-
bah." (This was at
Meribah in Kadesh
in the Desert of Zin.)
15Moses said to
the LORD, 16"The LORD is the God of the

EMAIL FROM GOD
27:16–17
Leadership
The leader is a shepherd.

FAITH links

TAKE ME TO YOUR LEADER

NUMBERS 27:12-23

God told the Israelites that their leader, Moses, would not enter the land God promised to them. God knew that the people would need another leader. So he chose Joshua to lead the Israelites. He told the Israelites to give Joshua the same respect that they had given to Moses.

God gives us leaders in the church, in our communities, and in the government. Those in authority over us deserve our respect and obedience. How do you show your respect for your leaders?

Family Feud, Genesis 27, p. 37

Fatherly Advice, Exodus 18, p. 99

Show Some Respect, Leviticus 19:32, p. 161

The Heart of the Matter, 1 Samuel 16, p. 375

Help to Understand, 2 Samuel 14, p. 416

The Verdict Is In?, Matthew 7:1–2, p. 1285

spirits of all people. May he choose a
leader for these people, **17**who will go in
and out before them. He must lead them
out like sheep and bring them in; the
LORD's people must not be like sheep
without a shepherd."
18So the LORD said to Moses, "Take
Joshua son of Nun, because my Spirit is
in him. Put your hand on him, **19**and have
him stand before Eleazar the priest and
all the people. Then give him his orders
as they watch. **20**Let him share your
honor so that all the Israelites will obey
him. **21**He must stand before Eleazar the
priest, and Eleazar will get advice from
the LORD by using the Urim. At his command all the Israelites will go out, and at
his command they will all come in."
22Moses did what the LORD told him.
He took Joshua and had him stand before
Eleazar the priest and all the people,
23and he put his hands on him and gave
him orders, just as the LORD had told
him.

Daily Offerings

28 The LORD said to Moses, **2**"Give
this command to the Israelites.
Tell them: 'Bring me food offerings made
by fire, for a smell that is pleasing to me,
and be sure to bring them at the right
time.' **3**Say to them, 'These are the offerings you must bring to the LORD: two
male lambs, a year old, as a burnt offering
each day. They must have nothing wrong
with them. **4**Offer one lamb in the morning and the other lamb at twilight. **5**Also
bring a grain offering of two quarts of fine
flour, mixed with one quart of oil from
pressed olives. **6**This is the daily burnt
offering which began at Mount Sinai; its
smell is pleasing to the LORD. **7**Offer one
quart of wine with each lamb as a drink
offering; pour it out to the LORD at the
Holy Place. **8**Offer the second lamb at
twilight. As in the morning, also give a
grain offering and a drink offering. This
offering is made by fire, and its smell is
pleasing to the LORD.

Sabbath Offerings

9" 'On the Sabbath day you must give
two male lambs, a year old, that have
nothing wrong with them. Also give a
drink offering and a grain offering; the
grain offering must be four quarts of fine
flour mixed with olive oil. **10**This is the
burnt offering for every Sabbath, in addition to the daily burnt offering and drink
offering.

Monthly Offerings

11" 'On the first day of each month bring a burnt offering to the LORD. This will be two young bulls, one male sheep, and seven male lambs a year old, and they must have nothing wrong with them. **12**Give a grain offering with each bull of six quarts of fine flour mixed with olive oil. Also give a grain offering with the male sheep. It must be four quarts of fine flour mixed with olive oil. **13**And give a grain offering with each lamb of two quarts of fine flour mixed with olive oil. This is a burnt offering, and its smell is pleasing to the LORD. **14**The drink offering with each bull will be two quarts of wine, with the male sheep it will be one and one-third quarts, and with each lamb it will be one quart of wine. This is the burnt offering that must be offered each month of the year. **15**Besides the daily burnt offerings and drink offerings, bring a sin offering of one goat to the LORD.

> The LORD's Passover will be on the fourteenth day of the first month.
> —Numbers 28:16

The Passover

16" 'The LORD's Passover will be on the fourteenth day of the first month. **17**The Feast of Unleavened Bread begins on the fifteenth day of that month. For seven days, you may eat only bread made without yeast. **18**Have a holy meeting on the first day of the festival, and don't work that day. **19**Bring to the LORD an offering made by fire, a burnt offering of two young bulls, one male sheep, and seven male lambs a year old. They must have nothing wrong with them. **20**With each bull give a grain offering of six quarts of fine flour mixed with olive oil. With the male sheep it must be four quarts of fine flour mixed with oil. **21**With each of the seven lambs, it must be two quarts of fine flour mixed with oil. **22**Bring one goat as a sin offering, to remove your sins so you will belong to God. **23**Bring these offerings in addition to the burnt offerings you give every morning. **24**So bring food for the offering made by fire each day for seven days, for a smell that is pleasing to the LORD. Do it in addition to the daily burnt offering and its drink offering. **25**On the seventh day have a holy meeting, and don't work that day.

The Feast of Weeks

26" 'On the day of firstfruits when you bring new grain to the LORD during the Feast of Weeks, have a holy meeting. Don't work that day. **27**Bring this burnt offering to the LORD: two young bulls, one male sheep, and seven male lambs a year old. This smell is pleasing to the LORD. **28**Also, with each bull give a grain offering of six quarts of fine flour mixed with oil. With the male sheep, it must be four quarts of flour, **29**and with each of the seven lambs offer two quarts of flour. **30**Offer one male goat to remove your sins so you will belong to God. **31**Bring these offerings and their drink offerings in addition to the daily burnt offering and its grain offering. The animals must have nothing wrong with them.

The Feast of Trumpets

29 " 'Have a holy meeting on the first day of the seventh month, and don't work on that day. That is the day you blow the trumpets. **2**Bring these burnt offerings as a smell pleasing to the LORD: one young bull, one male sheep, and seven male lambs a year old. They must have nothing wrong with them. **3**With the bull give a grain offering of six quarts of fine flour mixed with oil. With the male sheep offer four quarts, **4**and with each of the seven lambs offer two quarts. **5**Offer one male goat for a sin offering to remove your sins so you will belong to God. **6**These offerings are in addition to the monthly and daily burnt offerings. Their grain offerings and drink offerings must be done as you have been told. These offerings are made by fire to the LORD, and their smell is pleasing to him.

The Day of Cleansing

7" 'Have a holy meeting on the tenth day of the seventh month. On that day do not eat and do not work. **8**Bring these burnt offerings as a smell pleasing to the LORD: one young bull, one male sheep, and seven male lambs a year old. They must have nothing wrong with them. **9**With the bull give a grain offering of six quarts of fine flour mixed with oil. With the male sheep it must be four quarts, **10**and with each of the seven lambs it must be two quarts. **11**Offer one male goat as a sin offering. This will be in addition to the sin offering which removes your sins, the daily burnt offering with its grain offering, and the drink offerings.

The Feast of Shelters

12" 'Have a holy meeting on the fifteenth day of the seventh month, and do not work on that day. Celebrate a festival to the LORD for seven days. **13**Bring these burnt offerings, made by fire, as a smell pleasing to the LORD: thirteen young bulls, two male sheep, and fourteen male lambs a year old. They must have nothing wrong with them. **14**With each of the thirteen bulls offer a grain offering of six quarts of fine flour mixed with oil. With each of the two male sheep it must be four quarts, **15**and with each of the fourteen lambs it must be two quarts. **16**Offer one male goat as a sin offering in addition to the daily burnt offering with its grain and drink offerings.

17" 'On the second day of this festival give an offering of twelve bulls, two male sheep, and fourteen male lambs a year old. They must have nothing wrong with them. **18**Bring the grain and drink offerings for the bulls, sheep, and lambs, according to the number required. **19**Offer one male goat as a sin offering, in addition to the daily burnt offering with its grain and drink offerings.

20" 'On the third day offer eleven bulls, two male sheep, and fourteen male lambs a year old. They must have nothing wrong with them. **21**Bring the grain and drink offerings for the bulls, sheep, and lambs, according to the number required. **22**Offer one male goat as a sin offering, in addition to the daily burnt offering with its grain and drink offerings.

23" 'On the fourth day offer ten bulls, two male sheep, and fourteen male lambs a year old. They must have nothing wrong with them. **24**Bring the grain and drink offerings for the bulls, sheep, and lambs, according to the number required. **25**Offer one male goat as a sin offering, in addition to the daily burnt offering with its grain and drink offerings.

26" 'On the fifth day offer nine bulls, two male sheep, and fourteen male lambs a year old. They must have nothing wrong with them. **27**Bring the grain and drink offerings for the bulls, sheep, and lambs, according to the number required. **28**Offer one male goat as a sin offering, in addition to the daily burnt offering with its grain and drink offerings.

29" 'On the sixth day offer eight bulls, two male sheep, and fourteen male lambs a year old. They must have nothing wrong with them. **30**Bring the grain and drink offerings for the bulls, sheep, and lambs, according to the number required. **31**Offer one male goat as a sin offering, in addition to the daily burnt offering with its grain and drink offerings.

32" 'On the seventh day offer seven bulls, two male sheep, and fourteen male lambs a year old. They must have nothing wrong with them. **33**Bring the grain and drink offerings for the bulls, sheep, and lambs, according to the number required. **34**Offer one male goat as a sin offering, in addition to the daily burnt offering with its grain and drink offerings.

35" 'On the eighth day have a closing meeting, and do not work on that day. **36**Bring an offering made by fire, a burnt offering, as a smell pleasing to the LORD. Offer one bull, one male sheep, and seven male lambs a year old. They must have nothing wrong with them. **37**Bring the grain and drink offerings for the bull, the male sheep, and the lambs, according to the number required. **38**Offer one male goat as a sin offering, in addition to the daily burnt offering with its grain and drink offerings.

39" 'At your festivals you should bring these to the LORD: your burnt offerings,

grain offerings, drink offerings and fellowship offerings. These are in addition
to other promised offerings and special
gifts you want to give to the LORD.' "
40Moses told the Israelites everything the LORD had commanded him.

Rules About Special Promises

30 Moses spoke with the leaders of
the Israelite tribes. He told them
these commands from the LORD.
2"If a man makes a promise to the
LORD or says he will do something special, he must keep his promise. He must
do what he said. 3If a young woman still
living at home makes a promise to the
LORD or pledges to do something special,
4and if her father hears about the promise or pledge and says nothing, she must
do what she promised. She must keep
her pledge. 5But if her father hears about
the promise or pledge and does not allow
it, then the promise or pledge does not
have to be kept. Her father would not allow it, so the LORD will free her from her
promise.
6"If a woman makes a pledge or a
careless promise and then gets married,
7and if her husband hears about it and
says nothing, she must keep her promise
or the pledge she made. 8But if her husband hears about it and does not allow it,
he cancels her pledge or the careless
promise she made. The LORD will free
her from keeping it.
9"If a widow or divorced woman
makes a promise, she must do whatever
she promised.
10"If a woman makes a promise or
pledge while she is married, 11and if her
husband hears about it but says nothing
and does not stop her, she must keep her
promise or pledge. 12But if her husband
hears about it and cancels it, she does not
have to do what she said. Her husband
has canceled it, so the LORD will free her
from it. 13A woman's husband may make
her keep or cancel any promise or pledge
she has made. 14If he says nothing to her
about it for several days, she must keep
her promises. If he hears about them and
says nothing, she must keep her promises. 15But if he cancels them long after
he heard about them, he is responsible if
she breaks her promise."
16These are commands that the LORD

FAITH links

A SPECIAL PROMISE

NUMBERS 30:1-2

Do you believe in keeping your word? During Bible times, people often made vows to God or to someone else. A vow was a special promise. For example, Hannah made a promise to God that if he gave her a son, she would give her son back to him. (See 1 Samuel 1, p. 354.) Moses told the people of Israel that anyone who made this kind of promise to God had to keep it. That's why Jesus later warned against making rash promises. (Read Matthew 5:33–37, p. 1281.)

God wants you to avoid making promises that you don't intend to keep. When you give your word about something, make sure you keep it.

Just Kidding?, Genesis 21:8–10, p. 28

Promises, Promises, Judges 2:1–3, p. 312

Who Do You Prefer?, Proverbs 3:32, p. 830

The Problem with Gossip, Proverbs 11:12–13, p. 840

A Gentle Answer, Proverbs 15:1, p. 847

Your Choice of Fruit, Matthew 12:33–35, p. 1295

gave to Moses for husbands and wives,
and for fathers with daughters living at
home.

Israel Attacks the Midianites

31 The LORD spoke to Moses and
said, **2**"Pay back the Midianites for
what they did to the Israelites; after that
you will die."

3So Moses said to the people, "Get
some men ready for war. The LORD will
use them to pay back the Midianites.
4Send to war a thousand men from each
of the tribes of Israel." **5**So twelve thousand men got ready for war, a thousand
men from each tribe. **6**Moses sent those
men to war; Phinehas son of Eleazar the
priest was with them. He took with him
the holy things and the trumpets for giving the alarm. **7**They fought the Midianites as the LORD had commanded Moses,
and they killed every Midianite man.
8Among those they killed were Evi, Rekem, Zur, Hur, and Reba, who were the
five kings of Midian. They also killed Balaam son of Beor with a sword.

9The Israelites captured the Midianite women and children, and they took all
their flocks, herds, and goods. **10**They
burned all the Midianite towns where
they had settled and all their camps,
11but they took all the people and animals and goods. **12**Then they brought the
captives, the animals, and the goods back
to Moses and Eleazar the priest and all
the Israelites. Their camp was on the
plains of Moab near the Jordan River,
across from Jericho.

13Moses, Eleazar the priest, and all
the leaders of the people went outside
the camp to meet them. **14**Moses was
angry with the army officers, the commanders over a thousand men, and those
over a hundred men, who returned from
war.

15He asked them, "Why did you let the
women live? **16**They were the ones who
followed Balaam's advice and turned the
Israelites from the LORD at Peor. Then a
terrible sickness struck the LORD's people. **17**Kill all the Midianite boys, and kill
all the Midianite women who have had
sexual relations. **18**But save for yourselves the girls who have not had sexual
relations with a man.

19"All you men who killed anyone or
touched a dead body must stay outside
the camp for seven days. On the third and
seventh days you and your captives must
make yourselves clean. **20**You must clean
all your clothes and anything made of
leather, goat hair, or wood."

21Then Eleazar the priest said to the
soldiers who had gone to war, "These are
the teachings that the LORD gave to Moses: **22**Put any gold, silver, bronze, iron,
tin, or lead— **23**anything that will not
burn—into the fire, and then it will be
clean. But also purify those things with
the cleansing water. Then they will be
clean. If something cannot stand the fire,
wash it with the water. **24**On the seventh
day wash your clothes, and you will be
clean. After that you may come into the
camp."

Dividing the Goods

25The LORD said to Moses, **26**"You,
Eleazar the priest, and the leaders of the
family groups should take a count of the
goods, the men, and the animals that
were taken. **27**Then divide those possessions between the soldiers who went to
war and the rest of the people. **28**From
the soldiers who went to war, take a tax
for the LORD of one item out of every five
hundred. This includes people, cattle,
donkeys, or sheep. **29**Take it from the
soldiers' half, and give it to Eleazar the
priest as the LORD's share. **30**And from
the people's half, take one item out of
every fifty. This includes people, cattle,
donkeys, sheep, or other animals. Give
that to the Levites, who take care of the
LORD's Holy Tent." **31**So Moses and Eleazar did as the LORD commanded Moses.

32There remained from what the soldiers had taken 675,000 sheep, **33**72,000
cattle, **34**61,000 donkeys, **35**and 32,000
women who had not had sexual relations
with a man. **36**The soldiers who went to
war got 337,000 sheep, **37**and they gave
675 of them to the LORD. **38**They got
36,000 cattle, and they gave 72 of them to
the LORD. **39**They got 30,500 donkeys,
and they gave 61 of them to the LORD.

40They got 16,000 people, and they gave
32 of them to the LORD. **41**Moses gave
the LORD's share to Eleazar the priest, as
the LORD had commanded him.

42Moses separated the people's half
from the soldiers' half. **43**The people got
337,500 sheep, **44**36,000 cattle, **45**30,500
donkeys, **46**and 16,000 people. **47**From
the people's half Moses took one item out
of every fifty for the LORD. This included
the animals and the people. Then he gave
them to the Levites, who took care of the
LORD's Holy Tent. This was what the
LORD had commanded Moses.

48Then the officers of the army, the
commanders of a thousand men and commanders of a hundred men, came to
Moses. **49**They told Moses, "We, your
servants, have counted our soldiers under
our command, and not one of them is
missing. **50**So we have brought the LORD
a gift of the gold things that each of us
found: arm bands, bracelets, signet rings,
earrings, and necklaces. These are to remove our sins so we will belong to the
LORD."

51So Moses and Eleazar the priest
took the gold from them, which had been
made into all kinds of objects. **52**The commanders of a thousand
men and the commanders
of a hundred men gave the
LORD the gold, and all of it
together weighed about
420 pounds; **53**each soldier had taken something
for himself. **54**Moses and
Eleazar the priest took
the gold from the com-
manders of a thousand
men and the commanders
of a hundred men. Then they put it in the
Meeting Tent as a memorial before the
LORD for the people of Israel.

> We, your servants, have counted our soldiers under our command, and not one of them is missing.
> —Numbers 31:49

The Tribes East of the Jordan

32 The people of Reuben and Gad had
large flocks and herds. When they
saw that the lands of Jazer and Gilead
were good for the animals, **2**they came to
Moses, Eleazar the priest, and the leaders of the people. **3-4**They said, "We,
your servants, have flocks and herds.
The LORD has captured for the Israelites
a land that is good for animals—the land
around Ataroth, Dibon, Jazer, Nimrah,
Heshbon, Elealeh, Sebam, Nebo, and
Beon. **5**If it pleases you, we would like
this land to be given to us. Don't make us
cross the Jordan River."

6Moses told the people of Gad and
Reuben, "Shall your brothers go to war
while you stay behind? **7**You will discourage the Israelites from going over to the
land the LORD has given them. **8**Your ancestors did the same thing. I sent them
from Kadesh Barnea to look at the land.
9They went as far as the Valley of Eshcol,
and when they saw the land, they discouraged the Israelites from going into
the land the LORD had given them. **10**The
LORD became very angry that day and
made this promise: **11**'None of the people
who came from Egypt and who are twenty
years old or older will see the land that I
promised to Abraham, Isaac, and Jacob.
These people have not followed me completely. **12**Only Caleb son of Jephunneh
the Kenizzite and Joshua son of Nun followed the LORD completely.'

13"The LORD was angry with Israel, so
he made them wander in the desert for
forty years. Finally all the
people who had sinned
against the LORD died,
14and now you are acting
just like your ancestors!
You sinful people are making the LORD even more
angry with Israel. **15**If you
quit following him, it will
add to their stay in the
desert, and you will de-
stroy all these people."

16Then the Reubenites and Gadites
came up to Moses and said, "We will
build pens for our animals and cities for
our children here. **17**Then our children
will be in strong, walled cities, safe from
the people who live in this land. Then we
will prepare for war. We will help the
other Israelites get their land, **18**and we
will not return home until every Israelite
has received his land. **19**We won't take
any of the land west of the Jordan River;
our part of the land is east of the Jordan."

20So Moses told them, "You must do
these things. You must go before the
LORD into battle 21and cross the Jordan
River armed, until the LORD forces out
the enemy. 22After the LORD helps us
take the land, you may return home. You
will have done your duty to the LORD and
Israel, and you may have this land as your
own.

23"But if you don't do these things,
you will be sinning against the LORD;
know for sure that you will be punished
for your sin. 24Build cities for your children and pens for your animals, but then
you must do what you promised."

25The Gadites and Reubenites said to
Moses, "We are your servants, and we
will do what you, our master, command.
26Our children, wives, and all our cattle
will stay in the cities of Gilead, 27but we,
your servants, will prepare for battle. We
will go over and fight for the LORD, as
you, our master, have said."

28So Moses gave orders about them
to Eleazar the priest, to
Joshua son of Nun, and to
the leaders of the tribes
of Israel. 29Moses said to
them, "If the Gadites and
Reubenites prepare for
battle and cross the Jor-
dan River with you, to go
before the LORD and help
you take the land, give
them the land of Gilead
for their own. 30But if
they do not go over armed, they will not
receive it; their land will be in Canaan
with you."

> These are the places the Israelites went as Moses and Aaron led them out of Egypt in divisions.
>
> —Numbers 33:1

31The Gadites and Reubenites answered, "We are your servants, and we
will do as the LORD said. 32We will cross
over into Canaan and go before the LORD
ready for battle. But our land will be east
of the Jordan River."

33So Moses gave that land to the
tribes of Gad, Reuben, and East Manasseh. (Manasseh was Joseph's son.) That
land had been the kingdom of Sihon, king
of the Amorites, and the kingdom of Og,
king of Bashan, as well as all the cities
and the land around them.

34The Gadites rebuilt the cities of Dibon, Ataroth, Aroer, 35Atroth Shophan,
Jazer, Jogbehah, 36Beth Nimrah, and
Beth Haran. These were strong, walled
cities. And they built sheep pens.

37The Reubenites rebuilt Heshbon,
Elealeh, Kiriathaim, 38Nebo, Baal Meon,
and Sibmah. They renamed Nebo and
Baal Meon when they rebuilt them.

39The descendants of Makir son of
Manasseh went and captured Gilead and
forced out the Amorites who were there.
40So Moses gave Gilead to the family of
Makir son of Manasseh, and they settled
there. 41Jair son of Manasseh went out
and captured the small towns there, and
he called them the Towns of Jair. 42No-
bah went and captured Kenath and the
small towns around it; then he named it
Nobah after himself.

Israel's Journey from Egypt

33 These are the places the Israelites
went as Moses and Aaron led them
out of Egypt in divisions. 2At the LORD's
command Moses record-
ed the places they went,
and these are the places
they went.

3On the fifteenth day
of the first month, the day
after the Passover, the Israelites left Rameses and
marched out boldly in
front of all the Egyptians.
4The Egyptians were
burying their firstborn
sons, whom the LORD had killed; the
LORD showed that the gods of Egypt
were false.

5The Israelites left Rameses and
camped at Succoth.

6They left Succoth and camped at
Etham, at the edge of the desert.

7They left Etham and went back to Pi
Hahiroth, to the east of Baal Zephon, and
camped near Migdol.

8They left Pi Hahiroth and walked
through the sea into the desert. After going three days through the Desert of
Etham, they camped at Marah.

9They left Marah and went to Elim;
there were twelve springs of water and
seventy palm trees where they camped.

10They left Elim and camped near the
Red Sea.
11They left the Red Sea and camped
in the Desert of Sin.
12They left the Desert of Sin and
camped at Dophkah.
13They left Dophkah and camped at
Alush.
14They left Alush and camped at
Rephidim, where the people had no water
to drink.
15They left Rephidim and camped in
the Desert of Sinai.
16They left the Desert of Sinai and
camped at Kibroth Hattaavah.
17They left Kibroth Hattaavah and
camped at Hazeroth.
18They left Hazeroth and camped at
Rithmah.
19They left Rithmah and camped at
Rimmon Perez.
20They left Rimmon Perez and
camped at Libnah.
21They left Libnah and camped at
Rissah.
22They left Rissah and camped at Kehelathah.
23They left Kehelathah and camped
at Mount Shepher.
24They left Mount Shepher and
camped at Haradah.
25They left Haradah and camped at
Makheloth.
26They left Makheloth and camped at
Tahath.
27They left Tahath and camped at Terah.
28They left Terah and camped at
Mithcah.
29They left Mithcah and camped at
Hashmonah.
30They left Hashmonah and camped
at Moseroth.
31They left Moseroth and camped at
Bene Jaakan.
32They left Bene Jaakan and camped
at Hor Haggidgad.
33They left Hor Haggidgad and
camped at Jotbathah.
34They left Jotbathah and camped at
Abronah.
35They left Abronah and camped at
Ezion Geber.
36They left Ezion Geber and camped
at Kadesh in the Desert of Zin.
37They left Kadesh and camped at
Mount Hor, on the border of Edom.
38Aaron the priest obeyed the LORD and
went up Mount Hor. There he died on the
first day of the fifth month in the fortieth
year after the Israelites left Egypt.
39Aaron was 123 years old when he died
on Mount Hor.
40The Canaanite king of Arad, who
lived in the southern area of Canaan,
heard that the Israelites were coming.
41The people left Mount Hor and
camped at Zalmonah.
42They left Zalmonah and camped at
Punon.
43They left Punon and camped at
Oboth.
44They left Oboth and camped at Iye
Abarim, on the border of Moab.
45They left Iye Abarim and camped at
Dibon Gad.
46They left Dibon Gad and camped at
Almon Diblathaim.
47They left Almon Diblathaim and
camped in the mountains of Abarim, near
Nebo.
48They left the mountains of Abarim
and camped on the plains of Moab near
the Jordan River across from Jericho.
49They camped along the Jordan on the
plains of Moab, and their camp went from
Beth Jeshimoth to Abel Acacia.
50On the plains of Moab by the Jordan
River across from Jericho, the LORD
spoke to Moses. He said, 51"Speak to the
Israelites and tell them, 'When you cross
the Jordan River and go into Canaan,
52force out all the people who live there.
Destroy all of their carved statues and
metal idols. Wreck all of their places of
worship. 53Take over the land and settle
there, because I have given this land to
you to own. 54Throw lots to divide up the
land by family groups, giving larger portions to larger family groups and smaller
portions to smaller family groups. The
land will be given as the lots decide; each
tribe will get its own land.
55" 'But if you don't force those people out of the land, they will bring you
trouble. They will be like sharp hooks in

LET'S VISIT THE DEAD SEA Numbers 34:12

Check this out: the Dead Sea is really a lake, not a sea. While the Jordan and some other waters run *into* it, nothing runs *out* of it. The water slowly evaporates but the salt and other minerals stay in the lake. The water is so full of these minerals that no water creatures can live in it. That's why it's called the Dead Sea. (It's also sometimes called the Salt Sea.)

Some famous Bible events happened nearby. God used fire to totally destroy Sodom and Gomorrah because they were so evil. (Check out Genesis 19:23–29, p. 26.) King David hid from King Saul in some caves. (See 1 Samuel 24:1, p. 387.) More recently, someone found some old, old copies of parts of the Bible. We call these copies the "Dead Sea Scrolls."

your eyes and thorns in your sides. They
will bring trouble to the land where you
live. **56**Then I will punish you as I had
planned to punish them.' "

The Borders of Canaan

34 The LORD said to Moses, **2**"Give
this command to the people of Israel: 'You will soon enter Canaan and it
will be yours. These shall be the borders:
3On the south you will get part of the
Desert of Zin near the border of Edom.
On the east side your southern border
will start at the south end of the Dead
Sea, **4**cross south of Scorpion Pass, and
go through the Desert of Zin and south of
Kadesh Barnea. Then it will go to Hazar
Addar and over to Azmon. **5**From Azmon
it will go to the brook of Egypt, and it will
end at the Mediterranean Sea.

6" 'Your western border will be the
Mediterranean Sea.

7" 'Your northern border will begin at
the Mediterranean Sea and go to Mount
Hor. **8**From Mount Hor it will go to Lebo
Hamath, and on to Zedad. **9**Then the border will go to Ziphron, and it will end at
Hazar Enan. This will be your northern
border.

10" 'Your eastern border will begin at
Hazar Enan and go to Shepham. **11**From
Shepham the border will go east of Ain to
Riblah and along the hills east of Lake
Galilee. **12**Then the border will go down
along the Jordan River and end at the
Dead Sea.

" 'These are the borders around your
country.' "

13So Moses gave this command to the
Israelites: "This is the land you will receive. Throw lots to divide it among the
nine and one-half tribes, because the
LORD commanded that it should be theirs.
14The tribes of Reuben, Gad, and East
Manasseh have already received their
land. **15**These two and one-half tribes received land east of the Jordan River,
across from Jericho."

16Then the LORD said to Moses,
17"These are the men who will divide
the land: Eleazar the priest and Joshua
son of Nun. **18**Also take one leader from
each tribe to help divide the land.
19These are the names of the leaders:
from the tribe of Judah, Caleb son of Jephunneh; **20**from the tribe of Simeon,
Shemuel son of Ammihud; **21**from the
tribe of Benjamin, Elidad son of Kislon;

22from the tribe of Dan, Bukki son of Jogli; **23**from the tribe of Manasseh son of Joseph, Hanniel son of Ephod; **24**from the tribe of Ephraim son of Joseph, Kemuel son of Shiphtan; **25**from the tribe of Zebulun, Elizaphan son of Parnach; **26**from the tribe of Issachar, Paltiel son of Azzan; **27**from the tribe of Asher, Ahihud son of Shelomi; **28**from the tribe of Naphtali, Pedahel son of Ammihud."

29The LORD commanded these men to divide the land of Canaan among the Israelites.

The Levites' Towns

35 The LORD spoke to Moses on the plains of Moab across from Jericho by the Jordan River. He said, **2**"Command the Israelites to give the Levites cities to live in from the land they receive. Also give the Levites the pastureland around these cities. **3**Then the Levites will have cities where they may live and pastureland for their cattle, flocks, and other animals. **4**The pastureland you give the Levites will extend fifteen hundred feet from the city wall. **5**Also measure three thousand feet in each direction outside the city wall—three thousand feet east of the city, three thousand feet south of the city, three thousand feet west of the city, and three thousand feet north of the city, with the city in the center. This will be pastureland for the Levites' cities.

> You must choose . . . cities of safety, so that a person who accidentally kills someone may run to them for safety.
> —Numbers 35:11

Cities of Safety

6"Six of the cities you give the Levites will be cities of safety. A person who accidentally kills someone may run to one of those cities for safety. You must also give forty-two other cities to the Levites; **7**give the Levites a total of forty-eight cities and their pastures. **8**The larger tribes of Israel must give more cities, and the smaller tribes must give fewer cities. Each tribe must give some of its cities to the Levites, but the number of cities they give will depend on the size of their land."

9Then the LORD said to Moses, **10**"Tell the Israelites these things: 'When you cross the Jordan River and go into Canaan, **11**you must choose cities to be cities of safety, so that a person who accidentally kills someone may run to them for safety. **12**There the person will be safe from the dead person's relative who has the duty of punishing the killer. He will not die before he receives a fair trial in court. **13**The six cities you give will be cities of safety. **14**Give three cities east of the Jordan River and three cities in Canaan as cities of safety. **15**These six cities will be places of safety for citizens of Israel, as well as for foreigners and other people living with you. Any of these people who accidentally kills someone may run to one of these cities.

16" 'Anyone who uses an iron weapon to kill someone is a murderer. He must be put to death. **17**Anyone who takes a rock and kills a person with it is a murderer. He must be put to death. **18**Anyone who picks up a piece of wood and kills someone with it is a murderer. He must be put to death. **19**A relative of the dead person must put the murderer to death; when they meet, the relative must kill the murderer. **20**A person might shove someone or throw something at someone and cause death. **21**Or a person might hit someone with his hand and cause death. If it were done from hate, the person is a murderer and must be put to death. A relative of the dead person must kill the murderer when they meet.

22" 'But a person might suddenly shove someone, and not from hatred. Or a person might accidentally throw something and hit someone. **23**Or a person might drop a rock on someone he couldn't see and kill that person. There was no plan to hurt anyone and no hatred for the one who was killed. **24**If that happens, the community must judge between the relative of the dead person and the killer, according to these rules. **25**They must

protect the killer from the dead person's
relative, sending the killer back to the
original city of safety, to stay there until
the high priest dies (the high priest had
the holy oil poured on him).
26" 'Such a person must never go outside the limits of the city of safety. **27**If a
relative of the dead person finds the
killer outside the city, the relative may
kill that person and not be guilty of murder. **28**The killer must stay in the city of
safety until the high priest dies. After the
high priest dies, the killer may go home.
29" 'These laws are for you from now
on, wherever you live.
30" 'If anyone kills a person, the murderer may be put to death only if there
are witnesses. No one may be put to
death with only one witness.
31" 'Don't take money to spare the
life of a murderer who should be put to
death. A murderer must be put to death.
32" 'If someone has run to a city of
safety, don't take money to let the person
go back home before the high priest dies.
33" 'Don't let murder spoil your land.
The only way to remove the sin of killing
an innocent person is for the murderer to
be put to death. **34**I am the LORD, and
I live among the Israelites. I live in that
land with you, so do not spoil it with
murder.' "

Land for Zelophehad's Daughters

36 The leaders of Gilead's family
group went to talk to Moses and
the leaders of the families of Israel. (Gilead was the son of Makir, the son of Manasseh, the son of Joseph.) **2**They said,
"The LORD commanded you, our master,
to give the land to the Israelites by
throwing lots, and the LORD commanded
you to give the land of Zelophehad, our
brother, to his daughters. **3**But if his
daughters marry men from other tribes
of Israel, then that land will leave our
family, and the people of the other tribes
will get that land. So we will lose some of
our land. **4**When the time of Jubilee
comes for the Israelites, their land will go
to the tribes of the people they marry;
their land will be taken away from us, the
land we received from our fathers."
5Then Moses gave the Israelites this
command from the LORD: "These men
from the tribe of Joseph are right. **6**This
is the LORD's command to Zelophehad's
daughters: You may marry anyone you
wish, as long as the person is from your
own tribe. **7**In this way the Israelites'
land will not pass from tribe to tribe, and
each Israelite will keep the land in the
tribe that belonged to his ancestors. **8**A
woman who inherits her father's land
may marry, but she must marry someone
from her own tribe. In this way every Israelite will keep the land that belonged to
his ancestors. **9**The land must not pass
from tribe to tribe, and each Israelite
tribe will keep the land it received from
its ancestors."
10Zelophehad's daughters obeyed the
LORD's command to Moses.
11So Zelophehad's daughters—Mahlah, Tirzah, Hoglah, Milcah, and Noah—
married their cousins, their father's
relatives. **12**Their husbands were from
the tribe of Manasseh son of Joseph, so
their land stayed in their father's family
group and tribe.
13These were the laws and commands that the LORD gave to the Israelites through Moses on the plains of Moab
by the Jordan River, across from Jericho.

Deuteronomy

TELL US AGAIN, MOSES

Remember me? I'm Moses and this is my last book. By the time I wrote Deuteronomy, I was a very old man, and this book was my farewell speech. I remembered all the awesome things God did for us when he brought us out of Egypt (Read about it in Deuteronomy 4:32–38), and I looked forward to the day when Israel would live in the Promised Land. I warned the people that they must not worship the false gods of the land but only the Lord our God.

I wrote this book to remind people to follow God's laws. So that people would understand how important the laws were, I wrote them down a second time. (The word *Deuteronomy* means "second law.") In fact, the laws were so important, I told the people to write them down and tie them to their foreheads! (See Deuteronomy 6:4–9 for other ways to remember God's law.) God promises great blessings for those who obey his laws.

JESUS WATCH

In many ways Moses was very much like Jesus. Just like Jesus, Moses was chosen by God to serve his people as prophet, priest, and king. As a prophet, Moses performed miracles so that everyone would know that he spoke for God. He gave the people the Law so that they could honor God and get along with each other. Jesus also performed many miracles that proved he was from God and he explained the laws of God. Moses warned the people not to sin and spoke of their future in the land God promised to them. Today Jesus is our high priest, asking God to forgive our sins and blot them out forever. Because of him, our future is in heaven. Like a priest, Moses prayed many times that God would forgive the Israelites and that their punishment would not be too harsh. (See Deuteronomy 9:7–29.) Although Moses was not a king, he served as ruler of Israel, just as Jesus is king of all who believe in him.

my FAVORITE links

OTHER CONNECTIONS

Livin' it It's easy to become proud when you've accomplished something, or you love something you have, but God warns us over and over again about being proud. Check it out by linking to Struttin' Our Stuff, Deuteronomy 8:11–18, to find out what God has to say about pride.

Making good choices is tough. Something may appear to be a good choice, but later turn out to be a bad choice. How can you know you're making the right decision? Connect to This or That?, Deuteronomy 30:15–20, for help on making good choices.

Learn more cool facts about events and places mentioned in the Book of Deuteronomy by connecting here:

- A Feast for Remembering, Deuteronomy 16:1–8. You and your family probably remember special days in different ways—with parades, celebrations, festivals, family traditions. The Israelites had a special feast to help them remember an important event in their history. Check it out by linking here.
- Follow Moses' life by tracking his many journeys—from Egypt to the wilderness and back, when you visit The Deliverer, Deuteronomy 34.

"Hey, Tagg, what's the data on a 'safe city'?"

"I don't know. Try connecting to Deuteronomy 19:1-7, and see if we can find out."

did you know?

The Ten Commandments, Deuteronomy 5:1–22
Burn the idols, Deuteronomy 7:1–6
One-tenth of all we have, Deuteronomy 14:22–29
Follow the new leader: Joshua, Deuteronomy 31:1–8
Moses dies, Deuteronomy 34

- Play Fair or Play Favorites?, **Deuteronomy 1:16–18**
- His OK to Obey, **Deuteronomy 2:24–36**
- Facing the Consequences, **Deuteronomy 3:21–29**
- I'll Never Forget What's-His-Name, **Deuteronomy 8**
- What God Wants, **Deuteronomy 10:12–13**
- Care for the Lost, **Deuteronomy 22:1–3**
- A Serious Promise, **Deuteronomy 23:21–23**
- Read My Lips?, **Deuteronomy 26:16–19**
- A Choice to Make, **Deuteronomy 30:15–20**

Moses Talks to the Israelites

1 This is the message Moses gave to all
the people of Israel in the desert east
of the Jordan River. They were in the
desert area near Suph, between Paran and
the towns of Tophel, Laban, Hazeroth, and
Dizahab.
2(The trip from Mount Sinai to Kadesh Barnea on the Mount Seir road
takes eleven days.) 3Forty years after the
Israelites had left Egypt, on the first day
of the eleventh month, Moses told the
people of Israel everything the LORD had
commanded him to tell them. 4This was
after the LORD had defeated Sihon and
Og. Sihon was king of the Amorite people
and lived in Heshbon. Og was king of Bashan and lived in Ashteroth and Edrei.
5Now the Israelites were east of the
Jordan River in the land of Moab, and
there Moses began to explain what God
had commanded. He said:
6The LORD our God spoke to us at
Mount Sinai and said, "You have stayed
long enough at this mountain. 7Get ready,
and go to the mountain country of the Amorites, and to all the places around there—
the Jordan Valley, the mountains, the
western hills, the southern area, the seacoast, the land of Canaan, and Lebanon.
Go as far as the great river, the Euphrates.
8See, I have given you this land, so go in
and take it for yourselves. The LORD
promised it to your ancestors—Abraham,
Isaac, and Jacob and their descendants."

Moses Appoints Leaders

9At that time I said, "I am not able to
take care of you by myself. 10The LORD
your God has made you grow in number
so that there are as many of you as there
are stars in the sky. 11I pray that the
LORD, the God of your ancestors, will
give you a thousand times more people
and do all the wonderful things he promised. 12But I cannot take care of your
problems, your troubles, and your arguments by myself. 13So choose some men
from each tribe—wise men who have understanding and experience—and I will
make them leaders over you."
14And you said, "That's a good thing
to do."
15So I took the wise and experienced
leaders of your tribes, and I made them
your leaders. I appointed commanders

FAITH links

PLAY FAIR OR PLAY FAVORITES?

DEUTERONOMY 1:16-18

"That's not fair!" Have you said that statement within the last week? Many of us hope to be treated fairly, especially by people in authority. Moses talked to the leaders of the Israelites about being fair. God commanded them to be fair. When these leaders ruled on arguments between two people, they were to decide with fairness. They were not to play favorites.

Many times we act with more fairness toward the people we like than we do toward those people we don't like. Is that true for you? God doesn't want us to be fair to some and not to others. He has one rule for all: be fair!

Made in His Image, Genesis 1:26–27, p. 4

Moses' Champion, Numbers 12, p. 192

The Right Thing to Do, 1 Samuel 26, p. 391

Mercy for an Enemy, Jonah 4, p. 1216

The Way to Greatness, Matthew 20:20–28, p. 1309

Who Needs Love?, Luke 6:27–36, p. 1379

over a thousand people, over a hundred
people, over fifty people, and over ten
people and made them officers over your
tribes. **16**Then I told your leaders, "Listen to the arguments between your people. Judge fairly between two Israelites
or between an Israelite and a foreigner.
17When you judge, be fair to everyone;
don't act as if one person is more important than another, and don't be afraid of
anyone, because your decision comes
from God. Bring the hard cases to me,
and I will judge them." **18**At that time I
told you everything you must do.

Spies Enter the Land

19Then, as the LORD our God commanded us, we left Mount Sinai and went
toward the mountain country of the Amorite people. We went through that large
and terrible desert you saw, and then we
came to Kadesh Barnea. **20**I said to you,
"You have now come to the mountain
country of the Amorites, to the land the
LORD our God will give us. **21**Look, here
it is! Go up and take it. The LORD, the
God of your ancestors, told you to do this,
so don't be afraid and don't worry."

22Then all of you came to me and said,
"Let's send men before us to spy out the
land. They can come back and tell us
about the way we should go and the cities
we will find."

23I thought that was a good idea, so I
chose twelve of your men, one for each
tribe. **24**They left and went up to the
mountains, and when they came to the
Valley of Eshcol they explored it. **25**They
took some of the fruit from that land and
brought it down to us, saying, "It is a good
land that the LORD our God is giving us."

Israel Refuses to Enter

26But you refused to go. You would
not obey the command of the LORD your
God, **27**but grumbled in your tents, saying, "The LORD hates us. He brought us
out of Egypt just to give us to the Amorites, who will destroy us. **28**Where can
we go now? The spies we sent have made
us afraid, because they said, 'The people
there are stronger and taller than we are.
The cities are big, with walls up to the
sky. And we saw the Anakites there!' "

29Then I said to you, "Don't be frightened; don't be afraid of those people.
30The LORD your God will go ahead of
you and fight for you as he did in Egypt;
you saw him do it. **31**And in the desert you
saw how the LORD your God carried you,
like one carries a child. And he has
brought you safely all the way to this
place."

32But you still did not trust the LORD
your God, even though **33**he had always
gone before you to find places for you to
camp. In a fire at night and in a cloud
during the day, he showed you which way
to go.

34When the LORD heard what you
said, he was angry and made an oath, saying, **35**"I promised a good land to your
ancestors, but none of you evil people
will see it. **36**Only Caleb son of Jephunneh will see it. I will give him and his descendants the land he walked on, because
he followed the LORD completely."

37Because of you, the LORD was also
angry with me and said, "You won't enter
the land either, **38**but your assistant,
Joshua son of Nun, will enter it. Encourage him, because he will lead Israel to
take the land for their own.

39"Your little children that you said
would be captured, who do not know
right from wrong at this time, will go into
the land. I will give the land to them, and
they will take it for their own. **40**But you
must turn around and follow the desert
road toward the Red Sea."

41Then you said to me, "We have
sinned against the LORD, but now we will
go up and fight, as the LORD our God
commanded us." Then all of you put on
weapons, thinking it would be easy to go
into the mountains.

42But the LORD said to me, "Tell the
people, 'You must not go up there and
fight. I will not be with you, and your enemies will defeat you.' "

43So I told you, but you would not listen. You would not obey the LORD's command. You were proud, so you went on up
into the mountains, **44**and the Amorites
who lived in those mountains came out
and fought you. They chased you like

FAITH links

YOUR TOTAL TRUST

DEUTERONOMY 1:32

During their journey to the land God promised them, God helped the Israelites many times. While they wandered through the wilderness, he kept them safe, gave them food, and took care of them. Still, they had a hard time trusting him, as Moses reminded them. Do you trust God all of the time or only when you really need help? God wants your total trust always.

Link here for some more thoughts on trusting God:

Lights, Camera, . . . Actions!, Genesis 12:1–3, p. 17

Always Truthful, Numbers 23:19, p. 208

Love for a Lifetime, Song of Solomon 6:8–9, p. 891

A Broken Promise, Jeremiah 2:1–8, p. 989

Exercising Patience, Luke 2:25–28, 36–37, p. 1369

Keeping Clean, 2 Corinthians 7:1, p. 1576

bees and defeated you from Edom to
Hormah. 45So you came back and cried
before the LORD, but the LORD did not listen to you; he refused to pay attention to
you. 46So you stayed in Kadesh a long
time.

Israel Wanders in the Desert

2 Then we turned around, and we traveled on the desert road toward the Red
Sea, as the LORD had told me to do. We
traveled through the mountains of Edom
for many days.
2Then the LORD said to me, 3"You
have traveled through these mountains
long enough. Turn north 4and give the
people this command: 'You will soon go
through the land that belongs to your relatives, the descendants of Esau who live
in Edom. They will be afraid of you, but
be very careful. 5Do not go to war against
them. I will not give you any of their
land—not even a foot of it, because I have
given the mountains of Edom to Esau as
his own. 6You must pay them in silver for
any food you eat or water you drink.' "
7The LORD your God has blessed
everything you have done; he has protected you while you traveled through
this great desert. The LORD your God has
been with you for the past forty years,
and you have had everything you needed.
8So we passed by our relatives, the
descendants of Esau who lived in Edom.
We turned off the Jordan Valley road that
comes from the towns of Elath and Ezion
Geber and traveled along the desert road
to Moab.

The Land of Ar

9Then the LORD said to me, "Don't
bother the people of Moab. Don't go to
war against them, because I will not give
you any of their land as your own; I have
given Ar to the descendants of Lot as
their own." 10(The Emites, who lived in
Ar before, were strong people, and there
were many of them. They were very tall,
like the Anakites. 11The Emites were
thought to be Rephaites, like the Anakites, but the Moabite people called them
Emites. 12The Horites also lived in Edom
before, but the descendants of Esau
forced them out and destroyed them, taking their place as Israel did in the land the
LORD gave them as their own.)
13And the LORD said to me, "Now get
up and cross the Zered Valley." So we
crossed the valley. 14It had been thirty-
eight years from the time we left Kadesh
Barnea until we crossed the Zered Valley.
By then, all the fighting men from that
time had died, as the LORD had promised

would happen. **15**The LORD continued to
work against them to remove them from
the camp until they were all dead.

16When the last of those fighting men
had died, **17**the LORD said to me, **18**"Today you will pass by Ar, on the border of
Moab. **19**When you come near the people
of Ammon, don't bother them or go to
war against them, because I will not give
you any of their land as your own. I have
given it to the descendants of Lot for
their own."

20(That land was also thought to be a
land of the Rephaites, because those people used to live there, but the Ammonites
called them Zamzummites. **21**They were
strong people, and there were many of
them; they were very tall, like the Anakites. The LORD destroyed the Zamzummites, and the Ammonites forced them
out of the land and took their place.
22The LORD did the same thing for the
descendants of Esau, who lived in Edom,
when he destroyed the Horites. The
Edomites forced them out of the land and
took their place, and they live there to
this day. **23**The Cretan people came from
Crete and destroyed the Avvites, who
lived in towns all the way to Gaza; the
Cretans destroyed them and took their
place.)

Fighting the Amorites

24The LORD said, "Get up and cross
the Arnon Ravine. See, I am giving you
the power to defeat Sihon the Amorite,
king of Heshbon, and I am giving you his
land. So fight against him and begin taking his land. **25**Today I will begin to make
all the people in the world afraid of you.
When they hear reports about you, they
will shake with fear, and they will be terrified of you."

26I sent messengers from the desert
of Kedemoth to Sihon king of Heshbon.
They offered him peace, saying, **27**"If you
let us pass through your country, we will
stay on the road and not turn right or left.
28We will pay you in silver for any food
we eat or water we drink. We only want
to walk through your country. **29**The descendants of Esau in Edom let us go
through their land, and so did the Moabites in Ar. We want to cross the Jordan
River into the land the LORD our God has
given us." **30**But Sihon king of Heshbon
would not let us pass, because the LORD

FAITH links

HIS OK TO OBEY

DEUTERONOMY 2:24-36

Think of the biggest kid at your school. Suppose God told you that he would give you something that kid owns. All you have to do is tell him of God's plans. Would you do it? How do you think that kid would react?

God told the Israelites many times that he would give them land. To begin taking possession of that land, they had to fight an enemy nation. But the Lord kept them safe because they were obedient.

When God wants you to do something, he gives you the resources and the ability to do it. He'll never tell you to do something that you can't do with his help.

Fearful Service?, Exodus 4:1–17, p. 80

God's Pep Talk, Joshua 1:5–9, p. 276

Building Together, Nehemiah 3, p. 627

Standing for What's Right, Esther 3:2–4, p. 651

Stand!, Jeremiah 19:14—20:6, p. 1019

Your Civic Duty, Matthew 17:24–27, p. 1304

your God had made him stubborn. The
LORD wanted you to defeat Sihon, and
now this has happened.
31The LORD said to me, "See, I have
begun to give Sihon and his country to
you. Begin taking the land as your own."
32Then Sihon and all his army came
out and fought us at Jahaz, 33but the
LORD our God gave Sihon to us. We defeated him, his sons, and all his army.
34We captured all his cities at that time
and completely destroyed them, as well
as the men, women, and children. We left
no one alive. 35But we kept the cattle and
valuable things from the cities for ourselves. 36We defeated Aroer on the edge
of the Arnon Ravine, and we defeated the
town in the ravine, and even as far as Gilead. No town was too strong for us; the
LORD our God gave us all of them. 37But
you did not go near the land of the Ammonites, on the shores of the Jabbok
River, or the towns in the mountains, as
the LORD our God had commanded.

The Battle at Bashan

3 When we turned and went up the
road toward Bashan, Og king of Bashan and all his army came out to fight us
at Edrei. 2The LORD said to me, "Don't
be afraid of Og, because I will hand him,
his whole army, and his land over to you.
Do to him what you did to Sihon king of
the Amorites, who ruled in Heshbon."
3So the LORD our GOD gave us Og
king of Bashan and all his army; we defeated them and left no one alive. 4Then
we captured all of Og's cities, all sixty of
them, and took the whole area of Argob,
Og's kingdom in Bashan. 5All these were
strong cities, with high walls and gates
with bars. And there were also many
small towns with no walls. 6We completely destroyed them, just like the cities of Sihon king of Heshbon. We killed
all the men, women, and children, 7but
we kept all the cattle and valuable things
from the cities for ourselves.
8So at that time we took the land east
of the Jordan River, from the Arnon Ravine to Mount Hermon, from these two
Amorite kings. 9(Hermon is called Sirion
by the Sidonian people, but the Amorites
call it Senir.) 10We captured all the cities
on the high plain and all of Gilead, and we
took all of Bashan as far as Salecah and
Edrei, towns in Og's kingdom of Bashan.
11(Only Og king of Bashan was left of the
few Rephaites. His bed was made of iron,
and it was more than thirteen feet long
and six feet wide! It is still in the Ammonite city of Rabbah.)

The Land Is Divided

12At that time we took this land to be
our own. I gave the people of Reuben and
Gad the land from Aroer by the Arnon
Ravine, as well as half of the mountain
country of Gilead and the cities in it. 13To
the people of East Manasseh I gave the
rest of Gilead and all of Bashan, the kingdom of Og. (The area of Argob in Bashan
was called the land of the Rephaites.
14Jair, a descendant of Manasseh, took
the whole area of Argob, all the way to
the border of the Geshurites and Maaca-
thites. So that land was named for Jair,
and even today Bashan is called the
Towns of Jair.) 15I gave Gilead to Makir.
16I gave the Reubenites and the Gadites
the land that begins at Gilead and goes
from the Arnon Ravine (the middle of the
Arnon is the border) to the Jabbok River,
which is the Ammonite border. 17The
border on the west was the Jordan River
in the Jordan Valley, and it goes from Lake
Galilee to the Dead Sea west of Mount
Pisgah.
18At that time I gave you this command: "The LORD your God has given
you this land as your own. Now your
fighting men must take their weapons,
and you must lead the other Israelites
across the river. 19Your wives, your
young children, and your cattle may stay
here. I know you have many cattle, and
they may stay here in the cities I have
given you, 20until the LORD also gives
your Israelite relatives a place to rest.
They will receive the land the LORD your
God has given them on the other side of
the Jordan River. After that, you may
each return to the land I have given you."
21Then I gave this command to
Joshua: "You have seen for yourself all
that the LORD your God has done to these

FACING THE CONSEQUENCES

DEUTERONOMY 3:21-29

Think about the last time that you did something wrong. Did you get in trouble for it? Wrong behavior has consequences. When Moses sinned, the consequence was that he would not be allowed to enter the land God promised to the Israelites. Even though Moses pleaded with God, God did not change his mind.

Although God forgives us when we sin, we still have to face the consequences of our actions. A consequence is when a parent grounds you for doing something wrong. Before you take a step in the wrong direction, consider this: can you afford to pay the consequences?

Can't Live Without It, Genesis 3, p. 7

A Hidden Sin, Joshua 7, p. 285

Above the Law, 1 Kings 21, p. 470

A Life-Saving Message, Esther 2:19–22, p. 650

Just a Test, Luke 4:1–13, p. 1373

Just Say No!, Titus 2:11–12, p. 1660

two kings. The LORD will do the same thing to all the kingdoms where you are going. 22Don't be afraid of them, because the LORD your God will fight for you."

Moses Cannot Enter the Land

23Then I begged the LORD: 24"Lord
GOD, you have begun to show me, your servant, how great you are. You have great strength, and no other god in heaven or on earth can do the powerful things you do. There is no other god like you.
25Please let me cross the Jordan River so that I may see the good land by the Jordan. I want to see the beautiful mountains and Lebanon."

26But the LORD was angry with me because of you, and he would not listen to me. The LORD said to me, "That's enough. Don't talk to me anymore about it.
27Climb to the top of Mount Pisgah and look west, north, south, and east. You can look at the land, but you will not cross the Jordan River.
28Appoint Joshua and help him be brave and strong. He will lead the people across the river and give them the land that they are to inherit, but you can only look at it."
29So we stayed in the valley opposite Beth Peor.

Moses Tells Israel to Obey

4 Now, Israel, listen to the laws and commands I will teach you. Obey them so that you will live and so that you will go over and take the land the LORD, the God of your ancestors, is giving to you.
2Don't add to these commands, and don't leave anything out, but obey the commands of the LORD your God that I give you.

3You have seen for yourselves what the LORD did at Baal Peor, how the LORD your God destroyed everyone among you who followed Baal in Peor.
4But all of you who continued following the LORD your God are still alive today.

5Look, I have taught you the laws and rules the LORD my God commanded me. Now you can obey the laws in the land you are entering, in the land you will take.
6Obey these laws carefully, in order to show the other nations that you have wisdom and understanding. When they hear about these laws, they will say, "This great nation of Israel is wise and understanding."
7No other nation is as great as we are. Their gods do not come near them, but the LORD our God comes

near when we pray to him. 8And no other
nation has such good teachings and commands as those I am giving to you today.
9But be careful! Watch out and don't
forget the things you have seen.
Don't forget them as
long as you live, but
teach them to your
children and grand-
children. 10Remem-
ber the day you stood
before the LORD your God at Mount Sinai.
He said to me, "Bring the people together
so I can tell them what I have to say. Then
they will respect me as long as they live
in the land, and they will teach these
things to their children." 11When you
came and stood at the bottom of the
mountain, it blazed with fire that reached
to the sky, and black clouds made it very
dark. 12The LORD spoke to you from the
fire. You heard the sound of words, but
you did not see him; there was only a
voice. 13The LORD told you about his
Agreement, the Ten Commandments. He
told you to obey them, and he wrote them
on two stone tablets. 14Then the LORD
commanded me to teach you the laws and
rules that you must obey in the land you
will take when you cross the Jordan
River.

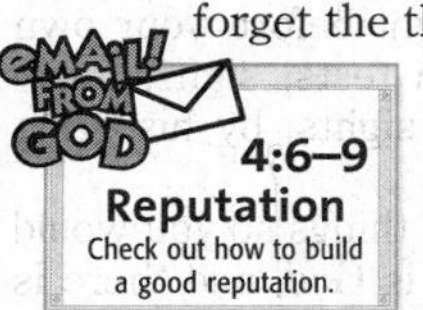

EMAIL FROM GOD
4:6–9
Reputation
Check out how to build a good reputation.

Laws About Idols

15Since the LORD spoke to you from
the fire at Mount Sinai, but you did not
see him, watch yourselves carefully!
16Don't sin by making idols of any kind,
and don't make statues—of men or wom-
en, 17of animals on earth or birds that fly
in the air, 18of anything that crawls on
the ground, or of fish in the water below.
19When you look up at the sky, you see
the sun, moon, and stars, and everything
in the sky. But don't bow down and worship them, because the LORD your God
has made these things for all people
everywhere. 20But the LORD brought you
out of Egypt, which tested you like a furnace for melting iron, and he made you his
very own people, as you are now.
21The LORD was angry with me because of you, and he swore that I would
not cross the Jordan River to go into the

FAITH links

WHAT HE'S REALLY LIKE

DEUTERONOMY 4:15-20

Ever wonder what God looks like? Moses reminded the people of Israel that God did not physically appear to them when he talked to them at Mount Sinai. God is spirit. (See John 4:24, p. 1428.) He has no physical shape. God warned the people not to make statues of what they thought he looked like. These statues were called idols. God did not want the people to worship a man-made image. A statue could not represent what God was like.

Although we may not worship statues of God, we can have ideas about him that are just as wrong. We sometimes try to limit God by what we think he's like. If you want to know what he's really like, just ask him, or read his Book!

Want to know more about the danger of having false gods in our lives? Read on!

Idol Talk, Exodus 32, p. 118

A Look for the Book, 2 Chronicles 34:14–18, p. 603

Remember Your Creator, Ecclesiastes 12:1, 13, p. 885

What God Thinks, Isaiah 55:8–9, p. 969

Two Ways to Grow, Luke 2:46–52, p. 1370

Life's Rule Book, 2 Timothy 3:15–17, p. 1655

good land the LORD your God is giving
you as your own. **22**I will die here in this
land and not cross the Jordan, but you will
soon go across and take that good land.
23Be careful. Don't forget the Agreement of the LORD your God
that he made with
you, and don't make
any idols for your-
selves, as the LORD
your God has com-
manded you not to
do. **24**The LORD your God is a jealous
God, like a fire that burns things up.

EMAIL FROM GOD
4:23
Idols
Is it okay to love something more than God?

25Even after you have lived in the
land a long time and have had children
and grandchildren, don't do evil things.
Don't make any kind of idol, and don't do
what the LORD your God says is evil, because that will make him angry. **26**If you
do, I ask heaven and earth to speak
against you this day that you will quickly
be removed from this land that you are
crossing the Jordan River to take. You
will not live there long after that, but you
will be completely destroyed. **27**The
LORD will scatter you among the other
nations. Only a few of you will be left
alive, and those few will be in other nations where the LORD will send you.
28There you will worship gods made by
people, gods made of wood and stone,
that cannot see, hear, eat, or smell. **29**But
even there you can look for the LORD
your God, and you will find him if you
look for him with your whole being. **30**It
will be hard when all these things happen
to you. But after that you will come back
to the LORD your God and obey him,
31because the LORD your God is a merciful God. He will not leave you or destroy
you. He will not forget the Agreement
with your ancestors, which he swore to
them.

The Lord Is Great

32Nothing like this has ever happened
before! Look at the past, long before you
were even born. Go all the way back to
when God made humans on the earth,
and look from one end of heaven to the
other. Nothing like this has ever been
heard of! **33**No other people have ever
heard God speak from a fire and have still
lived. But you have. **34**No other god has
ever taken for himself one nation out of
another. But the LORD your God did this
for you in Egypt, right before your own
eyes. He did it with tests, signs, miracles, war, and great sights, by his great
power and strength.

35He showed you things so you would
know that the LORD is God, and there is
no other God besides him. **36**He spoke to
you from heaven to teach you. He showed
you his great fire on earth, and you heard
him speak from the fire. **37**Because the
LORD loved your ancestors, he chose you,
their descendants, and he brought you out
of Egypt himself by his great strength.
38He forced nations out of their land
ahead of you, nations that were bigger and
stronger than you were. The LORD did
this so he could bring you into their land
and give it to you as your own, and this
land is yours today.

39Know and believe today that the
LORD is God. He is God in heaven above
and on the earth below. There is no other
god! **40**Obey his laws and commands that
I am giving you today so that things will go
well for you and your children. Then you
will live a long time in the land that the
LORD your God is giving to you forever.

Cities of Safety

41Moses chose three cities east of the
Jordan River, **42**where a person who accidentally killed someone could go. If the
person was not killed because of hatred,
the murderer's life could be saved by
running to one of these cities. **43**These
were the cities: Bezer in the desert high
plain was for the Reubenites; Ramoth in
Gilead was for the Gadites; and Golan in
Bashan was for the Manassites.

The Laws Moses Gave

44These are the teachings Moses gave
to the people of Israel. **45**They are the
rules, commands, and laws he gave them
when they came out of Egypt. **46**They
were in the valley near Beth Peor, east of
the Jordan River, in the land of Sihon. Sihon king of the Amorites ruled in Heshbon and was defeated by Moses and the

Israelites as they came out of Egypt.
47The Israelites took his land and the land
of Og king of Bashan, the two Amorite
kings east of the Jordan River. **48**This land
went from Aroer, on the edge of the Arnon
Ravine, to Mount Hermon. **49**It included
all the Jordan Valley east of the Jordan
River, and it went as far as the Dead Sea
below Mount Pisgah.

The Ten Commandments

5 Moses called all the people of Israel
together and said: Listen, Israel, to
the commands and laws I am giving you
today. Learn them and obey them carefully. **2**The LORD our God made an Agreement with us at Mount Sinai. **3**He did not
make this Agreement with our ancestors,
but he made it with us, with all of us who
are alive here today. **4**The LORD spoke to
you face to face from the fire on the
mountain. **5**(At that time I stood between
you and the LORD in order to tell you
what the LORD said; you were afraid of
the fire, so you would not go up on the
mountain.) The LORD said:

6"I am the LORD your God; I brought
you out of the land of Egypt where you
were slaves.

7"You must not have any other gods
except me.

8"You must not make for yourselves
any idols or anything to worship that
looks like something in the sky above or
on the earth below or in the water below
the land. **9**You must not worship or serve
any idol, because I, the LORD your God,
am a jealous God. If people sin against me
and hate me, I will punish their children,
even their grandchildren and great-
grandchildren. **10**But I will be very kind
for a thousand lifetimes to those who
love me and obey my commands.

11"You must not use the name of the
LORD your God thoughtlessly, because
the LORD will punish anyone who uses
his name in this way.

12"Keep the Sabbath as a holy day, as
the LORD your God has commanded you.
13You may work and get everything done
during six days each week, **14**but the
seventh day is a day of rest to honor the
LORD your God. On that day no one may
do any work: not you, your son or daughter, your male or female slaves, your ox,
your donkey, or any of your animals, or
the foreigners living in your cities. That
way your servants may rest as you do.
15Remember that you were slaves in
Egypt and that the LORD your God
brought you out of there by his great
power and strength. So the LORD your
God has commanded you to rest on the
Sabbath day.

16"Honor your father and your mother
as the LORD your God has commanded
you. Then you will live a long time, and
things will go well for you in the land that
the LORD your God is going to give you.

17"You must not murder anyone.

18"You must not be guilty of adultery.

19"You must not steal.

20"You must not tell lies about your
neighbor.

21"You must not want to take your
neighbor's wife. You must not want to
take your neighbor's house or land, his
male or female slaves, his ox or his donkey, or anything that belongs to your
neighbor."

22The LORD spoke these commands
to all of you on the mountain in a loud
voice out of the fire, the cloud, and the
deep darkness; he did not say anything
else. Then he wrote them on two stone
tablets, and he gave them to me.

23When you heard the voice from the
darkness, as the mountain was blazing
with fire, all your older leaders and leaders of your tribes came to me. **24**And you
said, "The LORD our God has shown us
his glory and majesty, and we have heard
his voice from the fire. Today we have
seen that a person can live even if God
speaks to him. **25**But now, we will die!
This great fire will burn us up, and we
will die if we hear the LORD our God
speak anymore. **26**No human being has
ever heard the living God speaking from
a fire and still lived, but we have. **27**Moses, you go near and listen to everything
the LORD our God says. Then you tell us
what the LORD our God tells you, and we
will listen and obey."

28The LORD heard what you said to
me, and he said to me, "I have heard what

the people said to you. Everything they
said was good. **29**I wish their hearts would
always respect me and that they would
always obey my commands so that things
would go well for them and their
children forever!

EMAIL! FROM GOD
5:29
Future
How can your future be blessed?

30"Go and tell
the people to return
to their tents, **31**but
you stay here with
me so that I may
give you all the commands, rules, and
laws that you must teach the people to
obey in the land I am giving them as their
own."

32So be careful to do what the LORD
your God has commanded you, and follow
the commands exactly. **33**Live the way
the LORD your God has commanded you
so that you may live and have what is
good and have a long life in the land you
will take.

The Command to Love God

6 These are the commands, rules, and
laws that the LORD your God told me
to teach you to obey in the land you are
crossing the Jordan River to take. **2**You,
your children, and your grandchildren
must respect the LORD your God as long
as you live. Obey all his rules and commands I give you so that you will live a
long time. **3**Listen, Israel, and carefully
obey these laws. Then all will go well for
you, and you will become a great nation
in a fertile land, just as the LORD, the God
of your ancestors, has promised you.

4Listen, people of Israel! The LORD
our God is the only LORD. **5**Love the
LORD your God with all your heart, all
your soul, and all your strength. **6**Always
remember these commands I give you
today. **7**Teach them to your children, and
talk about them when you sit at home and
walk along the road, when you lie down
and when you get up. **8**Write them down
and tie them to your hands as a sign. Tie
them on your forehead to remind you,
9and write them on your doors and gates.

10The LORD your God will bring you
into the land he promised to your ancestors, to Abraham, Isaac, and Jacob, and
he will give it to you. The land has large,
growing cities you did not build, **11**houses
full of good things you did not buy, wells
you did not dig, and vineyards and olive

FAITH links

REMEMBERING WHAT HE SAID

DEUTERONOMY 6:4-9

Think of something your parents have spent a lot of time teaching you. Perhaps they taught you how to read or play a sport. They probably helped you remember what they taught by telling you the same thing over and over again. God wanted the parents of Israel to spend a lot of time teaching their children how to obey God. That was the most important lesson they could teach their children. They weren't to say these things once and never again. They were to tell their children over and over again. How have your parents helped you learn about God? What will you do to remember what they said?

Good Advice?, Leviticus 20:6, p. 162

An Attention-Getter, Numbers 22, p. 207

A Wise Wish, 1 Kings 3:5–9, p. 439

Teaching Others, Ezra 7:8–10, p. 617

God's Instructions, Ezekiel 4:1–15, p. 1089

Want to Know? Ask!, Luke 9:45, p. 1386

trees you did not plant. You will eat as
much as you want. 12But be careful! Do
not forget the LORD, who brought you out
of the land of Egypt where you were
slaves.
13Respect the LORD your God. You
must worship him and make your promises only in his name. 14Do not worship
other gods as the people around you do,
15because the LORD your God is a jealous God. He is present with you, and if
you worship other gods, he will become
angry with you and destroy you from the
earth. 16Do not test the LORD your God
as you did at Massah. 17Be sure to obey
the commands of the LORD your God and
the rules and laws he has given you.
18Do what the LORD says is good and
right so that things will go well for you.
Then you may go in and take the good
land the LORD promised to your ancestors. 19He will force all your enemies out
as you go in, as the LORD has said.
20In the future when your children
ask you, "What is the meaning of the
laws, commands, and rules the LORD our
God gave us?" 21tell them, "We were
slaves to the king of Egypt, but the LORD
brought us out of Egypt by his great power. 22The LORD showed us great and terrible signs and miracles, which he did to
Egypt, the king, and his whole family.
23The LORD brought us out of Egypt to
lead us here and to give us the land he
promised our ancestors. 24The LORD ordered us to obey all these commands and
to respect the LORD our God so that we
will always do well and stay alive, as we
are today. 25The right thing for us to do is
this: Obey all these rules in the presence
of the LORD our God, as he has commanded."

You Are God's People

7The LORD your God will bring you
into the land that you are entering
and that you will have as your own. As
you go in, he will force out these nations:
the Hittites, Girgashites, Amorites, Canaanites, Perizzites, Hivites, and Jebusites—seven nations that are stronger
than you. 2The LORD your God will hand
these nations over to you, and when you
defeat them, you must destroy them
completely. Do not make a peace treaty
with them or show them any mercy. 3Do
not marry any of them, or let your daughters marry their sons, or let your sons
marry their daughters. 4If you do, those
people will turn your children away from
me, to begin serving other gods. Then
the LORD will be very angry with you,
and he will quickly destroy you. 5This is
what you must do to those people: Tear
down their altars, smash their holy stone
pillars, cut down their Asherah idols, and
burn their idols in the fire. 6You are holy
people who belong to the LORD your God.
He has chosen you from all the people on
earth to be his very own.
7The LORD did not care for you and
choose you because there were many of
you—you are the smallest nation of all.
8But the LORD chose you because he
loved you, and he kept his promise to
your ancestors. So he brought you out
of Egypt by his great power and freed you
from the land of slavery, from
the power of the
king of Egypt. 9So
know that the LORD
your God is God,
the faithful God. He
will keep his agree-
ment of love for a thousand lifetimes for
people who love him and obey his commands. 10But he will pay back those people who hate him. He will destroy them,
and he will not be slow to pay back those
who hate him. 11So be careful to obey the
commands, rules, and laws I give you today.
12If you pay attention to these laws
and obey them carefully, the LORD your
God will keep his agreement and show his
love to you, as he promised your ancestors. 13He will love and bless you. He will
make the number of your people grow; he
will bless you with children. He will bless
your fields with good crops and will give
you grain, new wine, and oil. He will
bless your herds with calves and your
flocks with lambs in the land he promised
your ancestors he would give you. 14You
will be blessed more than any other
people. Every husband and wife will have

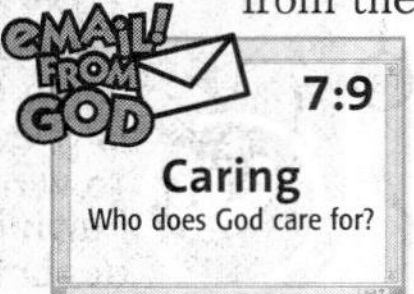
eMAIL! FROM GOD
7:9
Caring
Who does God care for?

PRIDE

Deuteronomy 8:11–18

Livin' it

Struttin' Our Stuff How do you feel when a classmate gets a blue ribbon for a science project? Or a teammate hits a grand-slam homerun? You're probably OK with those things *unless* they keep bragging about how good they are. Sometimes braggers are said to be "proud as peacocks." Got any peacock feathers on your back?

Pride in what we have or can do makes us trust in our own ideas or plans. But God wants us to put our pride aside and give our plans to him for his OK. (Look at Exodus 2:11–15, p. 78.)

Samson was a real-life superman—but he had a weakness. Samson was proud of his strength and believed it could get him out of anything. This led to total disaster. (Read Judges 16, p. 334.) Want to be a "proud peacock" or the world's most powerful Christian? Faith in God makes the difference!

MORE FAITH links

"Hey, Skweek, how do you like my new super-fast computer? It's the best and latest model out there. I bet no one else has one like it. Boy, wait until I tell everyone about it!"

"Whoa! Am I hearing a little bit of braggin' going on here, Tagg? I think your computer is great, but your style is not exactly going to win you friends. Better connect to these Faithlinks for some advice in the pride department."

The Problem with Pride, Isaiah 2:11, p. 898
- What do you think when someone "rolls her eyes"? Or raises his eyebrows? Or wrinkles up her nose? What would make you do one of those things? How about a nose-in-the-air look? That usually means someone thinks he or she is better than everyone else is—it's called being proud. Where is your nose pointed?

Eating Humble Pie, Daniel 4, p. 1156
- Link here to discover the best "food" for someone who has an appetite for being proud.

Better Than Some?, Luke 18:9–14, p. 1405
- Do you feel you're pretty good—or at least better than some people are? Does your pride make you feel superior? Surf over here to find out how God feels about a proud attitude.

Brag on Him!, 1 Corinthians 3:18–23, p. 1548
- Link here to discover something God wants us to brag about.

my FAVORITE links

_______________ _______________

_______________ _______________

_______________ _______________

children, and all your cattle will have
calves. **15**The LORD will take away all disease from you; you will not have the terrible diseases that were in Egypt, but he
will give them to all the people who hate
you. **16**You must destroy all the people the
LORD your God hands over to you. Do not
feel sorry for them, and do not worship
their gods, or they will trap you.

17You might say to yourselves, "Because these nations are stronger than we
are, we can't force them out." **18**But
don't be afraid of them. Remember what
the LORD your God did to all of Egypt and
its king. **19**You saw for yourselves the
troubles, signs, and miracles he did, how
the LORD's great power and strength
brought you out of Egypt. The LORD your
God will do the same thing to all the nations you now fear. **20**The LORD your
God will also send terror among them so
that even those who are alive and hiding
from you will die. **21**Don't be afraid of
them, because the LORD your God is with
you; he is a great God and people are
afraid of him. **22**When the LORD your God
forces those nations out of the land, he
will do it little by little ahead of you. You
won't be able to destroy them all at once;
otherwise, the wild animals will grow too
many in number. **23**But the LORD your
God will hand those nations over to you,
confusing them until they are destroyed.
24The LORD will help you defeat their
kings, and the world will forget who they
were. No one will be able to stop you; you
will destroy them all. **25**Burn up their
idols in the fire. Do not wish for the silver
and gold they have, and don't take it for
yourselves, or you will be trapped by it.
The LORD your God hates it. **26**Do not
bring one of those hateful things into
your house, or you will be completely destroyed along with it. Hate and reject
those things; they must be completely
destroyed.

FAITH links

I'LL NEVER FORGET WHAT'S-HIS-NAME

DEUTERONOMY 8

Did you ever forget someone's name? That's easy to do if you've only met the person once or haven't spent much time with that person. God reminded the people of Israel to make an effort to remember him and his commands. He didn't want them to forget all that he had done for them. That reminder is for you, too. One way to remember God is to spend time with him each day. If you make time with God a priority, you won't easily forget him.

Here's some more advice on taking time to be with God:

Try to Remember, Deuteronomy 11:18–21, p. 243

I Insist!, 1 Samuel 8; 9, p. 363

When God Says No, 2 Samuel 7, p. 407

More Precious Than Gold, Psalm 19:7–10, p. 723

My Favorite!, Mark 10:17–23, p. 1347

Faith Workout, Acts 16:4–5, p. 1493

Remember the Lord

8 Carefully obey every command I give
you today. Then you will live and
grow in number, and you will enter and
take the land the LORD promised your ancestors. **2**Remember how the LORD your
God has led you in the desert for these
forty years, taking away your pride and
testing you, because he wanted to know
what was in your heart. He wanted to
know if you would obey his commands.
3He took away your pride when he let

you get hungry, and then he fed you with
manna, which neither you nor your ancestors had ever seen. This was to teach
you that a person does not live by eating
only bread, but by everything the LORD
says. 4During these forty years, your
clothes did not wear out, and your feet
did not swell. 5Know in your heart that
the LORD your God cor-
rects you as a parent
corrects a child.

EMAIL FROM GOD 8:5
God's Family
Find out how God helps his children to grow.

6Obey the com-
mands of the LORD
your God, living as
he has commanded
you and respecting him. 7The LORD your
God is bringing you into a good land, a
land with rivers and pools of water, with
springs that flow in the valleys and hills,
8a land that has wheat and barley, vines,
fig trees, pomegranates, olive oil, and
honey. 9It is a land where you will have
plenty of food, where you will have
everything you need, where the rocks
are iron, and where you can dig copper
out of the hills.

10When you have all you want to eat,
then praise the LORD your God for giving
you a good land. 11Be careful not to forget the LORD your God so that you fail to
obey his commands, laws, and rules that I
am giving to you today. 12When you eat
all you want and build nice houses and
live in them, 13when your herds and
flocks grow large and your silver and gold
increase, when you have more of everything, 14then your heart will become
proud. You will forget the LORD your
God, who brought you out of the land of
Egypt, where you were slaves. 15He led
you through the large and terrible desert
that was dry and had no water, and that
had poisonous snakes and stinging insects. He gave you water from a solid
rock 16and manna to eat in the desert.
Manna was something your ancestors
had never seen. He did this to take away
your pride and to test you, so things
would go well for you in the end. 17You
might say to yourself, "I am rich because
of my own power and strength," 18but
remember the LORD your God! It is he
who gives you the power to become rich,
keeping the agreement he promised to
your ancestors, as it is today.

19If you ever forget the LORD your
God and follow other gods and worship
them and bow down to them, I warn you
today that you will be destroyed. 20Just
as the LORD destroyed the other nations
for you, you can be destroyed if you do
not obey the LORD your God.

The Lord Will Be with Israel

9 Listen, Israel. You will soon cross the
Jordan River to go in and force out nations that are bigger and stronger than
you. They have large cities with walls up
to the sky. 2The people there are Anakites, who are strong and tall. You know
about them, and you have heard it said:
"No one can stop the Anakites." 3But today remember that the LORD your God
goes in before you to destroy them like a
fire that burns things up. He will defeat
them ahead of you, and you will force
them out and destroy them quickly, just
as the LORD has said.

4After the LORD your God has forced
those nations out ahead of you, don't say
to yourself, "The LORD brought me here
to take this land because I am so good."
No! It is because these nations are evil
that the LORD will force them out ahead
of you. 5You are going in to take the land,
not because you are good and honest, but
because these nations are evil. That is
why the LORD your God will force them
out ahead of you, to keep his promise to
your ancestors, to Abraham, Isaac, and
Jacob. 6The LORD your God is giving you
this good land to take as your own. But
know this: It is not because you are good;
you are a stubborn people.

Remember the Lord's Anger

7Remember this and do not forget it:
You made the LORD your God angry in
the desert. You would not obey the LORD
from the day you left Egypt until you arrived here. 8At Mount Sinai you made
the LORD angry—angry enough to destroy you. 9When I went up on the mountain to receive the stone tablets, the
tablets with the Agreement the LORD had
made with you, I stayed on the mountain

for forty days and forty nights; I did not eat bread or drink water. **10**The LORD gave me two stone tablets, which God had written on with his own finger. On them were all the commands that the LORD gave to you on the mountain out of the fire, on the day you were gathered there.

11When the forty days and forty nights were over, the LORD gave me the two stone tablets, the tablets with the Agreement on them. **12**Then the LORD told me, "Get up and go down quickly from here, because the people you brought out from Egypt are ruining themselves. They have quickly turned away from what I commanded and have made an idol for themselves."

13The LORD said to me, "I have watched these people, and they are very stubborn! **14**Get away so that I may destroy them and make the whole world forget who they are. Then I will make another nation from you that will be bigger and stronger than they are."

> But today remember that the LORD your God goes in before you to destroy them like a fire that burns things up.
> —Deuteronomy 9:3

15So I turned and came down the mountain that was burning with fire, and the two stone tablets with the Agreement were in my hands. **16**When I looked, I saw you had sinned against the LORD your God and had made an idol in the shape of a calf. You had quickly turned away from what the LORD had told you to do. **17**So I took the two stone tablets and threw them down, breaking them into pieces right in front of you.

18Then I again bowed facedown on the ground before the LORD for forty days and forty nights; I did not eat bread or drink water. You had sinned by doing what the LORD said was evil, and you made him angry. **19**I was afraid of the LORD's anger and rage, because he was angry enough with you to destroy you, but the LORD listened to me again. **20**And the LORD was angry enough with Aaron to destroy him, but then I prayed for Aaron, too. **21**I took that sinful calf idol you had made and burned it in the fire. I crushed it into a powder like dust and threw the dust into a stream that flowed down the mountain.

22You also made the LORD angry at Taberah, Massah, and Kibroth Hattaavah.

23Then the LORD sent you away from Kadesh Barnea and said, "Go up and take the land I have given you." But you rejected the command of the LORD your God. You did not trust him or obey him. **24**You have refused to obey the LORD as long as I have known you.

25The LORD had said he would destroy you, so I threw myself down in front of him for those forty days and forty nights. **26**I prayed to the LORD and said, "Lord GOD, do not destroy your people, your own people, whom you freed and brought out of Egypt by your great power and strength. **27**Remember your servants Abraham, Isaac, and Jacob. Don't look at how stubborn these people are, and don't look at their sin and evil. **28**Otherwise, Egypt will say, 'It was because the LORD was not able to take his people into the land he promised them, and it was because he hated them that he took them into the desert to kill them.' **29**But they are your people, LORD, your own people, whom you brought out of Egypt with your great power and strength."

New Stone Tablets

10 At that time the LORD said to me, "Cut two stone tablets like the first ones and come up to me on the mountain. Also make a wooden Ark. **2**I will write on the tablets the same words that were on the first tablets, which you broke, and you will put the new tablets in the Ark."

3So I made the Ark out of acacia wood, and I cut out two stone tablets like the first ones. Then I went up on the mountain with the two tablets in my hands. **4**The LORD wrote the same things on these tablets he had written before—the Ten Commandments that he had told you

on the mountain from the fire, on the day
you were gathered there. And the LORD
gave them to me. 5Then I turned and
came down the mountain; I put the tablets in the Ark I had made, as the LORD
had commanded, and they are still there.
6(The people of Israel went from the
wells of the Jaakanites to Moserah.
Aaron died there and was buried; his son
Eleazar became priest in his place.
7From Moserah they went to Gudgodah,
and from Gudgodah they went to Jotbathah, a place with streams of water. 8At
that time the LORD chose the tribe of
Levi to carry the Ark of the Agreement
with the LORD. They were to serve the
LORD and to bless the people in his name,
which they still do today. 9That is why
the Levites did not receive any land of
their own; instead, they received the
LORD himself as their gift, as the LORD
your God told them.)
10I stayed on the mountain forty days
and forty nights just like the first time,
and the LORD listened to me this time
also. He did not want to destroy you.
11The LORD said to me, "Go and lead the
people so that they will go in and take the
land I promised their ancestors."

What the Lord Wants You to Do

12Now, Israel, this is what the LORD
your God wants you to do: Respect the
LORD your God, and do what he has told
you to do. Love him. Serve the LORD
your God with your whole being, 13and
obey the LORD's commands and laws that
I am giving you today for your own good.
14The LORD owns the world and
everything in it—the heavens, even the
highest heavens, are his. 15But the LORD
cared for and loved your ancestors, and
he chose you, their descendants, over all
the other nations, just as it is today.
16Give yourselves completely to serving
him, and do not be stubborn any longer.
17The LORD your God is God of all gods
and Lord of all lords. He is the great God,
who is strong and wonderful. He does not
take sides, and he will not be talked into
doing evil. 18He helps orphans and widows, and he loves foreigners and gives
them food and clothes. 19You also must
love foreigners, because you were foreigners in Egypt. 20Respect the LORD
your God and serve him. Be loyal to him
and make your promises in his name.
21He is the one you should praise; he is

FAITH links

WHAT GOD WANTS

DEUTERONOMY 10:12-13

Ever wonder what God wants from you? Wonder no more. God wants you to love him and others. He also wants your obedience. That's what he told the people of Israel through Moses. That doesn't sound so hard, does it? Yet, we sometimes allow fear to keep us from giving God what he wants. Many times we worry that God has some horrible, icky task just waiting to assign us. So we spend our lives trying to avoid doing what he wants. God doesn't want fear to keep you from obeying him. That's why he promises to help you respect, love, and obey him.

Fearful Service?, Exodus 4:1–17, p. 80

Everyone Can Help, Numbers 4, p. 181

The Gift of Friendship, 1 Samuel 18:1–3; 19, p. 381

The Fence Riders, 1 Kings 18, p. 464

A Reminder to Do What Is Right and True, Zechariah 7:8–10, p. 1257

The Unpopular Choice, Mark 15:42–43, p. 1360

your God, who has done great and wonderful things for you, which you have
seen with your own eyes. 22There were
only seventy of your ancestors when
they went down to Egypt, and now the
LORD your God has made you as many as
the stars in the sky.

Great Things Israel Saw

11 Love the LORD your God and always
obey his orders, rules, laws, and
commands. 2Remember today it was not
your children who saw and felt the correction of the LORD your God.

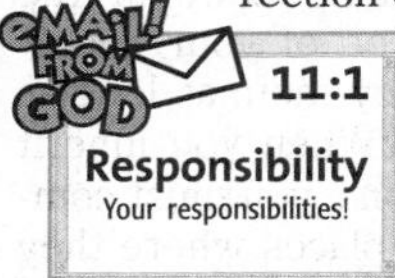

Responsibility
Your responsibilities!

They did not see his
majesty, his power,
his strength, 3or his
signs and the things
he did in Egypt to the
king and his whole
country. 4They did not see what he did to
the Egyptian army, its horses and chariots, when he drowned them in the Red
Sea as they were chasing you. The LORD
ruined them forever. 5They did not see
what he did for you in the desert until you
arrived here. 6They did not see what he
did to Dathan and Abiram, the sons of Eliab the Reubenite, when the ground
opened up and swallowed them, their
families, their tents, and everyone who
stood with them in Israel. 7It was you
who saw all these great things the LORD
has done.

8So obey all the commands I am giving you today so that you will be strong
and can go in and take the land you are
going to take as your own. 9Then you will
live a long time in the land that the LORD
promised to give to your ancestors and
their descendants, a fertile land. 10The
land you are going to take is not like
Egypt, where you were. There you had to
plant your seed and water it, like a vegetable garden, by using your feet. 11But
the land that you will soon cross the Jordan River to take is a land of hills and valleys, a land that drinks rain from heaven.
12It is a land the LORD your God cares
for. His eyes are on it continually, and he
watches it from the beginning of the year
to the end.

13If you carefully obey the commands
I am giving you today and love the LORD
your God and serve him with your whole
being, 14then he will send rain on your

FAITH links

TRY TO REMEMBER

DEUTERONOMY 11:18-21

What do you do to remember what you need to remember? Some people use memory tools like making up a song, tying a string around their finger, or sticking a self-adhesive note on a backpack or a bathroom mirror. God gave Moses different ways that the people of Israel could use to remember his commands. They could write them down and tie them to their hands or foreheads. They were to remember these words wherever they went. God wants you to remember his words, too. What is your favorite way to memorize God's Word?

Surf over here to find out more about learning God's Word:

When I Need Advice, 1 Kings 12:1–17, p. 455

Comfort from the Word, Job 26:3–4, p. 688

Our Thirst Quencher, Psalm 42:1–3, p. 741

If You Want My Advice . . . , Proverbs 13:1, p. 843

Long-lasting Hope, Hosea 14 , p. 1184

Our Heavenly Connection, Matthew 6:9–13, p. 1283

land at the right time, in the fall and
spring, and you will be able to gather
your grain, new wine, and oil. **15**He will
put grass in the fields for your cattle, and
you will have plenty to eat.

16Be careful, or you will be fooled and
will turn away to serve and worship other
gods. **17**If you do, the LORD will become
angry with you and will shut the heavens
so it will not rain. Then the land will not
grow crops, and you will soon die in the
good land the LORD is giving you. **18**Remember my words with your whole
being. Write them down and tie them to
your hands as a sign; tie them on your
foreheads to remind you. **19**Teach them
well to your children, talking about them
when you sit at home and walk along the
road, when you lie down and when you
get up. **20**Write them on your doors and
gates **21**so that both you and your children will live a long time in the land the
LORD promised your ancestors, as long
as the skies are above the earth.

22If you are careful to obey every
command I am giving you to follow, and
love the LORD your God, and do what he
has told you to do, and are loyal to him,
23then the LORD will force all those nations out of the land ahead of you, and you
will take the land from nations that are
bigger and stronger than you. **24**Everywhere you step will be yours. Your land
will go from the desert to Lebanon and
from the Euphrates River to the Mediterranean Sea. **25**No one will be able to stop
you. The LORD your God will do what he
promised and will make the people afraid
everywhere you go.

26See, today I am letting you choose a
blessing or a curse. **27**You will be blessed
if you obey the commands of the LORD
your God that I am giving you today.
28But you will be cursed if you disobey
the commands of the LORD your God. So
do not disobey the commands I am giving
you today, and do not worship other gods
you do not know. **29**When the LORD your
God brings you into the land you will take
as your own, you are to announce the
blessings from Mount Gerizim and the
curses from Mount Ebal. **30**(These
mountains are on the other side of the
Jordan River, to the west, toward the
sunset. They are near the great trees of
Moreh in the land of the Canaanites who
live in the Jordan Valley opposite Gilgal.)
31You will soon cross the Jordan River to
enter and take the land the LORD your
God is giving you. When you take it over
and live there, **32**be careful to obey all
the commands and laws I am giving you
today.

The Place for Worship

12 These are the commands and laws
you must carefully obey in the
land the LORD, the God of your ancestors, is giving you. Obey them as long as
you live in the land. **2**When you inherit
the lands of these nations, you must completely destroy all the places where they
serve their gods, on high mountains and
hills and under every green tree. **3**Tear
down their altars, smash their holy stone
pillars, and burn their Asherah idols in
the fire. Cut down their idols and destroy
their names from those places.

4Don't worship the LORD your God
that way, **5**but look for the place the LORD
your God will choose—a place among
your tribes where he is to be worshiped.
Go there, **6**and bring to that place your
burnt offerings and sacrifices; bring a
tenth of what you gain and your special
gifts; bring what you have promised and
the special gifts you want to give the
LORD, and bring the first animals born to
your herds and flocks.

7There you will be together with the
LORD your God. There you and your families will eat, and you will enjoy all the
good things for which you have worked,
because the LORD your God has blessed
you.

8Do not worship the way we have
been doing today, each person doing what
he thinks is right. **9**You have not yet
come to a resting place, to the land the
LORD your God will give you as your
own. **10**But soon you will cross the Jordan River to live in the land the LORD
your God is giving you as your own,
where he will give you rest from all your
enemies and you will live in safety.
11Then the LORD your God will choose a

place where he is to be worshiped. To
that place you must bring everything I
tell you: your burnt offerings and sacrifices, your offerings of a tenth of what
you gain, your special gifts, and all your
best things you promised to the LORD.
12There rejoice before the LORD your
God. Everyone should rejoice: you, your
sons and daughters, your male and female servants, and the Levites from your
towns who have no land of their own.
13Be careful that you don't sacrifice your
burnt offerings just anywhere you please.
14Offer them only in the place the LORD
will choose. He will choose a place in one
of your tribes, and there you must do
everything I am commanding you.

15But you may kill your animals in
any of your towns and eat as much of the
meat as you want, as if it were a deer or a
gazelle; this is the blessing the LORD
your God is giving you. Anyone, clean or
unclean, may eat this meat, 16but do not
eat the blood. Pour it out on the ground
like water. 17Do not eat in your own
towns what belongs to the LORD: one-
tenth of your grain, new wine, or oil; the
first animals born to your herds or flocks;
whatever you have promised to give; the
special gifts you want to give to the LORD,
or any other gifts. 18Eat these things
when you are together with the LORD
your God, in the place the LORD your God
chooses to be worshiped. Everyone must
do this: you, your sons and daughters,
your male and female servants, and the
Levites from your towns. Rejoice in
the LORD your God's presence about the
things you have worked for. 19Be careful
not to forget the Levites as long as you
live in the land.

20When the LORD your God enlarges
your country as he has promised, and you
want some meat so you say, "I want some
meat," you may eat as much meat as you
want. 21If the LORD your God chooses a
place where he is to be worshiped that is
too far away from you, you may kill animals from your herds and flocks, which
the LORD has given to you. I have commanded that you may do this. You may
eat as much of them as you want in your
own towns, 22as you would eat gazelle or
deer meat. Both clean and unclean people may eat this meat, 23but be sure you
don't eat the blood, because the life is in
the blood. Don't eat the life with the
meat. 24Don't eat the blood, but pour it
out on the ground like water. 25If you
don't eat it, things will go well for you and
your children, because you will be doing
what the LORD says is right.

26Take your holy things and the
things you have promised to give, and go
to the place the LORD will choose. 27Pre-
sent your burnt offerings on the altar of
the LORD your God, both the meat and
the blood. The blood of your sacrifices
should be poured beside the altar
of the LORD your
God, but you may
eat the meat. 28Be
careful to obey all
the rules I am giving
you so that things
will always go well for you and your children, and you will be doing what the
LORD your God says is good and right.

EMAIL FROM GOD
12:28
Obedience
Check out what happens when you obey.

29You will enter the land and take it
away from the nations that the LORD your
God will destroy ahead of you. When you
force them out and live in their land,
30they will be destroyed for you, but be
careful not to be trapped by asking about
their gods. Don't say, "How do these nations worship? I will do the same."
31Don't worship the LORD your God that
way, because the LORD hates the evil
ways they worship their gods. They even
burn their sons and daughters as sacrifices to their gods!

32Be sure to do everything I have
commanded you. Do not add anything to
it, and do not take anything away from it.

False Prophets

13 Prophets or those who tell the future with dreams might come to
you and say they will show you a miracle
or a sign. 2The miracle or sign might
even happen, and then they might say,
"Let's serve other gods" (gods you have
not known) "and let's worship them."
3But you must not listen to those prophets or dreamers. The LORD your God is
testing you, to find out if you love him

with your whole being. **4**Serve only the
LORD your God. Respect him, keep his
commands, and obey him. Serve him and
be loyal to him. **5**The prophets or dreamers must be killed, because they said you
should turn against the LORD your God,
who brought you out of Egypt and saved
you from the land where you were slaves.
They tried to turn you from doing what
the LORD your God commanded you to
do. You must get rid of the evil among
you.

6Someone might try to lead you to
serve other gods—it might be your
brother, your son or daughter, the wife
you love, or a close friend. The person
might say, "Let's go and worship other
gods." (These are gods that neither you
nor your ancestors have known, **7**gods of
the people who live around you, either
nearby or far away, from one end of the
land to the other.) **8**Do not give in to such
people. Do not listen or feel sorry for
them, and do not let them go free or protect them. **9**You must put them to death.
You must be the first one to start to kill
them, and then everyone else must join
in. **10**You must throw stones at them until they die, because they tried to turn
you away from the LORD your God, who
brought you out of the land of Egypt,
where you were slaves. **11**Then everyone in Israel will hear about this and be
afraid, and no one among you will ever do
such an evil thing again.

Cities to Destroy

12The LORD your God is giving you
cities in which to live, and you might hear
something about one of them. Someone
might say **13**that evil people have moved
in among you. And they might lead the
people of that city away from God, saying,
"Let's go and worship other gods."
(These are gods you have not known.)
14Then you must ask about it, looking
into the matter and checking carefully
whether it is true. If it is proved that a
hateful thing has happened among you,
15you must kill with a sword everyone
who lives in that city. Destroy the city
completely and kill everyone in it, as well
as the animals, with a sword. **16**Gather
up everything those people owned, and
put it in the middle of the city square.
Then completely burn the city and
everything they owned as a burnt offering to the LORD your God. That city
should never be rebuilt; let it be ruined
forever. **17**Don't keep for yourselves any
of the things found in that city, so the
LORD will not be angry anymore. He will
give you mercy and feel sorry for you,
and he will make your nation grow larger,
as he promised to your ancestors. **18**You
will have obeyed the LORD your
God by keeping all
his commands that I
am giving to you to-
day, and you will be
doing what the LORD
says is right.

> eMAIL! FROM GOD
> **13:17–18**
> **Obedience**
> Is it important to listen to God?

God's Special People

14 You are the children of the LORD
your God. When someone dies, do
not cut yourselves or shave your heads
to show your sadness. **2**You are holy people, who belong to the LORD your God.
He has chosen you from all the people on
earth to be his very own.

3Do not eat anything the LORD hates.
4These are the animals you may eat:
oxen, sheep, goats, **5**deer, gazelle, roe
deer, wild goats, ibex, antelope, and
mountain sheep. **6**You may eat any animal that has a split hoof and chews the
cud, **7**but you may not eat camels, rabbits, or rock badgers. These animals
chew the cud, but they do not have split
hoofs, so they are unclean for you. **8**Pigs
are also unclean for you; they have split
hoofs, but they do not chew the cud. Do
not eat their meat or touch their dead
bodies.

9There are many things that live in
the water. You may eat anything that has
fins and scales, **10**but do not eat anything
that does not have fins and scales. It is
unclean for you.

11You may eat any clean bird. **12**But
do not eat these birds: eagles, vultures,
black vultures, **13**red kites, falcons, any
kind of kite, **14**any kind of raven,
15horned owls, screech owls, sea gulls,
any kind of hawk, **16**little owls, great

FAITH links

A SMALL PERCENT

DEUTERONOMY 14:22-23

Do you receive an allowance? Suppose God told you, "I want ten percent of your allowance each month." Would you give it? God commanded the people of Israel to give him one-tenth of their crops. Giving it was a sign of their respect for him. These crops went to provide for the priests who served in the Meeting Tent.

God wants us to be willing givers. He doesn't force us to give. How much are you willing to give to God?

Giving Your Part, Leviticus 27:30, p. 173

Yours, Mine, and Ours?, 1 Samuel 25, p. 389

Wisdom About Wealth, Ecclesiastes 5:10–12, p. 878

The Gift of Worship, Matthew 2:10–12, p. 1275

Give to Give, 1 Corinthians 16:1–4, p. 1566

More Money?, 1 Timothy 6:10, p. 1649

owls, white owls, **17**desert owls, ospreys,
cormorants, **18**storks, any kind of heron,
the hoopoes, or bats.
19All insects with wings are unclean
for you; do not eat them. **20**Other things
with wings are clean, and you may eat
them.
21Do not eat anything you find that is
already dead. You may give it to a foreigner living in your town, and he may
eat it, or you may sell it to a foreigner.
But you are holy people, who belong to
the LORD your God.

Do not cook a baby goat in its mother's milk.

Giving One-Tenth

22Be sure to save one-tenth of all
your crops each year. **23**Take it to the
place the LORD your God will choose
where he is to be worshiped. There,
where you will be together with the
LORD, eat the tenth of your grain, new
wine, and oil, and eat the animals born
first to your herds and flocks. Do this so
that you will learn to respect the LORD
your God always. **24**But if the place the
LORD will choose to be worshiped is too
far away and he has blessed you so much
you cannot carry a tenth, **25**exchange
your one-tenth for silver. Then take the
silver with you to the place the LORD
your God shall choose. **26**Use the silver
to buy anything you wish—cattle, sheep,
wine, beer, or anything you wish. Then
you and your family will eat and celebrate
there before the LORD your God. **27**Do
not forget the Levites in your town, because they have no land of their own
among you.
28At the end of every third year,
everyone should bring one-tenth of that
year's crop and store it in your towns.
29This is for the Levites so they may eat
and be full. (They have no land of their
own among you.) It is also for strangers,
orphans, and widows who live in your
towns so that all of them may eat and be
full. Then the LORD your God will bless
you and all the work you do.

The Special Seventh Year

15 At the end of every seven years,
you must tell those who owe you
anything that they do not have to pay you
back. **2**This is how you must do it: Everyone who has loaned money must cancel
the loan and not make a neighbor or relative pay it back. This is the LORD's time
for canceling what people owe. **3**You may
make a foreigner pay what is owed to you,

but you must not collect what another Israelite owes you. 4But there should be no poor people among you, because the LORD your God will richly bless you in the land he is giving you as your own. 5He will bless you if you obey the LORD your God completely, but you must be careful to obey all the commands I am giving you today. 6The LORD your God will bless you as he promised, and you will lend to other nations, but you will not need to borrow from them. You will rule over many nations, but none will rule over you.

7If there are poor among you, in one of the towns of the land the LORD your God is giving you, do not be selfish or greedy toward them. 8But give freely to them, and freely lend them whatever they need. 9Beware of evil thoughts. Don't think, "The seventh year is near, the year to cancel what people owe." You might be mean to the needy and not give them anything. Then they will complain to the LORD about you, and he will find you guilty of sin. 10Give freely to the poor person, and do not wish that you didn't have to give. The LORD your God will bless your work and everything you touch. 11There will always be poor people in the land, so I command you to give freely to your neighbors and to the poor and needy in your land.

Letting Slaves Go Free

12If one of your own people sells himself to you as a slave, whether it is a Hebrew man or woman, that person will serve you for six years. But in the seventh year you must let the slave go free. 13When you let slaves go, don't send them away without anything. 14Give them some of your flock, your grain, and your wine, giving to them as the LORD has given to you. 15Remember that you were slaves in Egypt, and the LORD your God saved you. That is why I am commanding this to you today.

16But if your slave says to you, "I don't want to leave you," because he loves you and your family and has a good life with you, 17stick an awl[*] through his ear into the door; he will be your slave for life. Also do this to a female slave.

18Do not think of it as a hard thing when you let your slaves go free. After all, they served you six years and did twice the work of a hired person. The LORD your God will bless you in everything you do.

Rules About Firstborn Animals

19Save all the first male animals born to your herds and flocks. They are for the LORD your God. Do not work the first calf

FAITH CHALLENGE

Here's one for you. Read 15:6 to find out what God said about taking care of His people. How do you respond when your brother, sister, or one of your friends asks to borrow something from you?

TESTING IT

Deuteronomy 15:6
The LORD your God will bless you as he promised, and you will lend to other nations, but you will not need to borrow from them.

15:17 awl A tool like a big needle with a handle at one end.

A FEAST FOR REMEMBERING

Deuteronomy 16:1–8

God sent ten plagues to convince the king of Egypt to let the Israelites leave his country. The last plague was a plague of death. One night God passed through the city. If a house was not protected by lamb's blood on the doorframe, then the firstborn child and animal of that household died. If there was lamb's blood on the doorframe, then God would "pass over" that house. It was a sad and horrible night. But it was a night the Israelites would never forget. (Check out Exodus 12:1—13:16, p. 90.)

So that they would remember how God protected and delivered them, every year they had a feast to celebrate his "passing over." They called it the Passover Feast. Each year for the feast they would eat the same meal that they ate that sad night. They also kept certain customs to remind them that God had performed a miracle and that he would always take care of them.

born to your oxen, and do not cut off the
wool from the first lamb born to your
sheep. **20**Each year you and your family
are to eat these animals in the presence of
the LORD your God, in the place he will
choose to be worshiped. **21**If an animal is
crippled or blind or has something else
wrong, do not sacrifice it to the LORD your
God. **22**But you may eat that animal in
your own town. Both clean and unclean
people may eat it, as they would eat a
gazelle or a deer. **23**But don't eat its blood;
pour it out on the ground like water.

The Passover

16 Celebrate the Passover of the
LORD your God during the month
of Abib, because it was during Abib that
he brought you out of Egypt at night. **2**As
the sacrifice for the Passover to the LORD
your God, offer an animal from your flock
or herd at the place the LORD will choose
to be worshiped. **3**Do not eat it with
bread made with yeast. But for seven
days eat bread made without yeast, the
bread of suffering, because you left Egypt
in a hurry. So all your life you will remember the time you left Egypt. **4**There
must be no yeast anywhere in your land
for seven days. Offer the sacrifice on the
evening of the first day, and eat all the
meat before morning; do not leave it
overnight.

5Do not offer the Passover sacrifice in
just any town the LORD your God gives
you, **6**but offer it in the place he will
choose to be worshiped. Offer it in the
evening as the sun goes down, which is
when you left Egypt. **7**Roast the meat
and eat it at the place the LORD your God
will choose. The next morning go back to
your tents. **8**Eat bread made without
yeast for six days. On the seventh day
have a special meeting for the LORD your
God, and do not work that day.

The Feast of Weeks

9Count seven weeks from the time
you begin to harvest the grain, **10**and then
celebrate the Feast of Weeks for the LORD
your God. Bring an offering as a special
gift to him, giving to him just as he has
blessed you. **11**Rejoice before the LORD
your God at the place he will choose to be
worshiped. Everybody should rejoice:
you, your sons and daughters, your male
and female servants, the Levites in your
town, the strangers, orphans, and widows

living among you. **12**Remember that you
were slaves in Egypt, and carefully obey
all these laws.

The Feast of Shelters

13Celebrate the Feast of Shelters for
seven days, after you have gathered your
harvest from the threshing floor and
winepress. **14**Everybody should rejoice
at your Feast: you, your sons and daughters, your male and female servants, the
Levites, strangers, orphans, and widows
who live in your towns. **15**Celebrate the
Feast to the LORD your God for seven
days at the place he will choose, because
the LORD your God will
bless all your harvest and
all the work you do, and
you will be completely
happy.

16All your men must
come before the LORD
three times a year to the
place he will choose.
They must come at these
times: the Feast of Un-
leavened Bread, the Feast
of Weeks, and the Feast of Shelters. No
man should come before the LORD without a gift. **17**Each of you must bring a gift
that will show how much the LORD your
God has blessed you.

Judges for the People

18Appoint judges and officers for your
tribes in every town the LORD your God
is giving you; they must judge the people
fairly. **19**Do not judge unfairly or take
sides. Do not let people pay you to make
wrong decisions, because that kind of
payment makes wise people seem blind,
and it changes the words of good people.
20Always do what is right so that you will
live and always have the land the LORD
your God is giving you.

God Hates Idols

21Do not set up a wooden Asherah
idol next to the altar you build for the
LORD your God, **22**and do not set up holy
stone pillars. The LORD your God hates
them.

> You must follow the decision they give you at the place the LORD your God will choose.
> —Deuteronomy 17:10

17 If an ox or sheep has something
wrong with it, do not offer it as a
sacrifice to the LORD your God. He would
hate that.

2A man or woman in one of the towns
the LORD gave you might be found
doing something evil and breaking the
Agreement. **3**That person may have
served other gods and bowed down to
them or to the sun or moon or stars of the
sky, which I have commanded should not
be done. **4**If someone has told you about
it, you must look into the matter carefully. If it is true that such a hateful thing
has happened in Israel, **5**take the man or
woman who has done the
evil thing to the city gates
and throw stones at that
person until he dies.
6There must be two or
three witnesses that it
is true before the person
is put to death; if there is
only one witness, the person should not be put to
death. **7**The witnesses
must be the first to throw
stones at the person, and then everyone
else will follow. You must get rid of the
evil among you.

Courts of Law

8Some cases that come before you,
such as murder, quarreling, or attack,
may be too difficult to judge. Take these
cases to the place the LORD your God will
choose. **9**Go to the priests who are Levites and to the judge who is on duty at
that time. Ask them about the case, and
they will decide. **10**You must follow the
decision they give you at the place the
LORD your God will choose. Be careful to
do everything they tell you. **11**Follow the
teachings they give you, and do whatever
they decide, exactly as they tell you.
12The person who does not show respect
for the judge or priest who is there serving the LORD your God must be put to
death. You must get rid of that evil from
Israel. **13**Then everyone will hear about
this and will be afraid, and they will not
show disrespect anymore.

Choosing a King

14When you enter the land the LORD your God is giving you, taking it as your own and living in it, you will say, "Let's appoint a king over us like the nations all around us." **15**Be sure to appoint over you the king the LORD your God chooses. He must be one of your own people. Do not appoint as your king a foreigner who is not a fellow Israelite. **16**The king must not have too many horses for himself, and he must not send people to Egypt to get more horses, because the LORD has told you, "Don't return that way again." **17**The king must not have many wives, or his heart will be led away from God. He must not have too much silver and gold.

18When he becomes king, he should write a copy of the teachings on a scroll for himself, a copy taken from the priests and Levites. **19**He should keep it with him all the time and read from it every day of his life. Then he will learn to respect the LORD his God, and he will obey all the teachings and commands. **20**He should not think he is better than his fellow Israelites, and he must not stop obeying the law in any way so that he and his descendants may rule the kingdom for a long time.

EMAIL FROM GOD
17:18–20
Pride
Find out how to keep from being proud.

Shares for Priests and Levites

18 The priests are from the tribe of Levi, and that tribe will not receive a share of the land with the Israelites. They will eat the offerings made to the LORD by fire, which is their share. **2**They will not inherit any of the land like their brothers, but they will inherit the LORD himself, as he has promised them.

3When you offer a bull or sheep as a sacrifice, you must share with the priests, giving them the shoulder, the cheeks, and the inner organs. **4**Give them the first of your grain, new wine, and oil, as well as the first wool you cut from your sheep. **5**The LORD your God has chosen the priests and their descendants out of all your tribes to stand and serve the LORD always.

6If a Levite moves from one of your towns anywhere in Israel where he lives and comes to the place the LORD will choose, because he wants to serve the LORD there, **7**he may serve the LORD his God. He will be like his fellow Levites who serve there before the LORD. **8**They all will have an equal share of the food. That is separate from what he has received from the sale of family possessions.

Do Not Follow Other Nations

9When you enter the land the LORD your God is giving you, don't learn to do the hateful things the other nations do. **10**Don't let anyone among you offer a son or daughter as a sacrifice in the fire. Don't let anyone use magic or witchcraft, or try to explain the meaning of signs. **11**Don't let anyone try to control others with magic, and don't let them be mediums or try to talk with the spirits of dead people. **12**The LORD hates anyone who does these things. Because the other nations do these things, the LORD your God will force them out of the land ahead of you. **13**But you must be innocent in the presence of the LORD your God.

The Lord's Special Prophet

14The nations you will force out listen to people who use magic and witchcraft, but the LORD your God will not let you do those things. **15**The LORD your God will give you a prophet like me, who is one of your own people. Listen to him. **16**This is what you asked the LORD your God to do when you were gathered at Mount Sinai. You said, "Don't make us listen to the voice of the LORD our God again, and don't make us look at this terrible fire anymore, or we will die."

17So the LORD said to me, "What they have said is good. **18**So I will give them a prophet like you, who is one of their own people. I will tell him what to say, and he will tell them everything I command. **19**This prophet will speak for me; anyone who does not listen when he speaks will answer to me. **20**But if a prophet says

something I did not tell him to say as
though he were speaking for me, or if a
prophet speaks in the name of other
gods, that prophet must be killed."
21You might be thinking, "How can
we know if a message is not from the
LORD?" **22**If what a prophet says in the
name of the LORD does not happen, it is
not the LORD's message. That prophet
was speaking his own ideas. Don't be
afraid of him.

Cities of Safety

19 When the LORD your God gives
you land that belongs to the other
nations, nations that he will destroy, you
will force them out and live in their cities
and houses. **2**Then choose three cities in
the middle of the land the LORD your God
is giving you as your own. **3**Build roads to
these cities, and divide the land the LORD
is giving you into three parts so that
someone who kills another person may
run to these cities.
4This is the rule for someone who
kills another person and runs to one of
these cities in order to save his life. But
the person must have killed a neighbor
without meaning to, not out of hatred.
5For example, suppose someone goes
into the forest with a neighbor to cut
wood and swings an ax to cut down a tree.
If the ax head flies off the handle, hitting
and killing the neighbor, the one who
killed him may run to one of these cities
to save his life. **6**Otherwise, the dead
person's relative who has the duty of
punishing a murderer might be angry and
chase him. If the city is far away, the relative might catch and kill the person, even
though he should not be killed because
there was no intent to kill his neighbor.
7This is why I command you to choose
these three cities.
8-9 Carefully obey all these laws I'm
giving you today. Love the LORD your
God, and always do what he wants you to
do. Then the LORD your God will enlarge
your land as he promised your ancestors,
giving you the whole land he promised to
them. After that, choose three more cities of safety **10**so that innocent people
will not be killed in your land, the land
that the LORD your God is giving you as
your own. By doing this you will not be
guilty of allowing the death of innocent
people.
11But if a person hates his neighbor
and, after hiding and waiting, attacks and
kills him and then runs to one of these
cities for safety, **12**the older leaders of his
own city should send for the murderer.
They should bring the person back from
the city of safety and hand him over to
the relative who has the duty of punishing the murderer. **13**Show no mercy. You
must remove from Israel the guilt of murdering innocent people so that things will
go well for you.
14Do not move the stone that marks
the border of your neighbor's land, which
people long ago set in place. It marks
what you inherit in the land the LORD
your God is giving you as your own.

Rules About Witnesses

15One witness is not enough to accuse a person of a crime or sin. A case
must be proved by two or three witnesses.
16If a witness lies and accuses a person of a crime, **17**the two people who are
arguing must stand in the presence of the
LORD before the priests and judges who
are on duty. **18**The judges must check the
matter carefully. The witness who is a
liar, lying about a fellow Israelite, **19**must
be punished. He must be punished in the
same way the other person would have
been punished. You must get rid of the
evil among you. **20**The rest of the people
will hear about this and be afraid, and no
one among you will ever do such an evil
thing again. **21**Show no mercy. A life
must be paid for a life, an eye for an eye, a
tooth for a tooth, a hand for a hand, a foot
for a foot.

Laws for War

20 When you go to war against your
enemies and
you see horses and
chariots and an army
that is bigger than
yours, don't be afraid
of them. The LORD

EMAIL FROM GOD 20:1
Fears
When is God with you?

your God, who brought you out of Egypt, will be with you. **2**The priest must come and speak to the army before you go into battle. **3**He will say, "Listen, Israel! Today you are going into battle against your enemies. Don't lose your courage or be afraid. Don't panic or be frightened, **4**because the LORD your God goes with you, to fight for you against your enemies and to save you."

5The officers should say to the army, "Has anyone built a new house but not given it to God? He may go home, because he might die in battle and someone else would get to give his house to God. **6**Has anyone planted a vineyard and not begun to enjoy it? He may go home, because he might die in battle and someone else would enjoy his vineyard. **7**Is any man engaged to a woman and not yet married to her? He may go home, because he might die in battle and someone else would marry her." **8**Then the officers should also say, "Is anyone here afraid? Has anyone lost his courage? He may go home so that he will not cause others to lose their courage, too." **9**When the officers finish speaking to the army, they should appoint commanders to lead it.

10When you march up to attack a city, first make them an offer of peace. **11**If they accept your offer and open their gates to you, all the people of that city will become your slaves and work for you. **12**But if they do not make peace with you and fight you in battle, you should surround that city. **13**The LORD your God will give it to you. Then kill all the men with your swords, **14**and you may take everything else in the city for yourselves. Take the women, children, and animals, and you may use these things the LORD your God gives you from your enemies. **15**Do this to all the cities that are far away, that do not belong to the nations nearby.

> But if they do not make peace with you and fight you in battle, you should surround that city.
> —Deuteronomy 20:12

16But leave nothing alive in the cities of the land the LORD your God is giving you. **17**Completely destroy these people: the Hittites, Amorites, Canaanites, Perizzites, Hivites, and Jebusites, as the LORD your God has commanded. **18**Otherwise, they will teach you what they do for their gods, and if you do these hateful things, you will sin against the LORD your God.

19If you surround and attack a city for a long time, trying to capture it, do not destroy its trees with an ax. You can eat the fruit from the trees, but do not cut them down. These trees are not the enemy, so don't make war against them. **20**But you may cut down trees that you know are not fruit trees and use them to build devices to attack the city walls, until the city is captured.

A Person Found Murdered

21 Suppose someone is found murdered, lying in a field in the land the LORD your God is giving you as your own, and no one knows who killed the person. **2**Your older leaders and judges should go to where the body was found, and they should measure how far it is to the nearby cities. **3**The older leaders of the city nearest the body must take a young cow that has never worked or worn a yoke, **4**and they must lead her down to a valley that has never been plowed or planted, with a stream flowing through it. There they must break the young cow's neck. **5**The priests, the sons of Levi, should come forward, because they have been chosen by the LORD your God to serve him and to give blessings in the LORD's name. They are the ones who decide cases of quarreling and attacks. **6**Then all the older leaders of the city nearest the murdered person should wash their hands over the young cow whose neck was broken in the valley. **7**They should declare: "We did not kill this person, and we did not see it happen. **8**LORD, remove this sin from your people Israel, whom you have saved. Don't blame your people, the Israelites, for the murder of this innocent person." And so the murder will be paid for. **9**Then you will have removed from yourselves the guilt of murdering an innocent person, because you will be doing what the LORD says is right.

Captive Women as Wives

10When you go to war against your enemies, the LORD will help you defeat them so that you will take them captive. **11**If you see a beautiful woman among the captives and are attracted to her, you may take her as your wife. **12**Bring her into your home, where she must shave her head and cut her nails **13**and change the clothes she was wearing when you captured her. After she has lived in your house and cried for her parents for a month, you may marry her. You will be her husband, and she will be your wife. **14**But if you are not pleased with her, you must let her go anywhere she wants. You must not sell her for money or make her a slave, because you have taken away her honor.

The Oldest Son

15A man might have two wives, one he loves and one he doesn't. Both wives might have sons by him. If the older son belongs to the wife he does not love, **16**when that man wills his property to his sons he must not give the son of the wife he loves what belongs to the older son, the son of the wife he does not love. **17**He must agree to give the older son two shares of everything he owns, even though the older son is from the wife he does not love. That son was the first to prove his father could have children, so he has the rights that belong to the older son.

Sons Who Refuse to Obey

18If someone has a son who is stubborn, who turns against his father and mother and doesn't obey them or listen when they correct him, **19**his parents must take him to the older leaders at the city gate. **20**They will say to the leaders, "Our son is stubborn and turns against us. He will not obey us. He eats too much, and he is always drunk." **21**Then all the men in his town must throw stones at him until he dies. Get rid of the evil among you, because then all the people of Israel will hear about this and be afraid.

Other Laws

22If someone is guilty of a sin worthy of death, he must be put to death and his body displayed on a tree. **23**But don't leave his body hanging on the tree overnight; be sure to bury him that same day, because anyone whose body is displayed on a tree is cursed by God. You must not ruin the land the LORD your God is giving you as your own.

22 If you see your fellow Israelite's ox or sheep wandering away, don't ignore it. Take it back to its owner. **2**If the owner does not live close to you, or if you do not know who the owner is, take the animal home with you. Keep it until the owner comes looking for it; then give it back. **3**Do the same thing if you find a donkey or coat or anything someone lost. Don't just ignore it.

4If you see your fellow Israelite's donkey or ox fallen on the road, don't ignore it. Help the owner get it up.

5A woman must not wear men's clothes, and a man must not wear women's clothes. The LORD your God hates anyone who does that.

6If you find a bird's nest by the road, either in a tree or on the ground, and the mother bird is sitting on the young birds or eggs, do not take the mother bird with the young birds. **7**You may take the young birds, but you must let the mother bird go free. Then things will go well for you, and you will live a long time.

8When you build a new house, build a low wall around the edge of the roof[n] so you will not be guilty if someone falls off the roof.

9Don't plant two different kinds of seeds in your vineyard. Otherwise, both crops will be ruined.

10Don't plow with an ox and a donkey tied together.

22:8 roof In Bible times houses were built with flat roofs. The roof was used for drying things such as flax and fruit. And it was used as an extra room, as a place for worship, and as a cool place to sleep in the summer.

FAITH links

CARE FOR THE LOST

DEUTERONOMY 22:1-3

Have you ever found a lost dog or cat? Even if you wanted to keep it, you knew that finding the owner was the right thing to do. God made a rule for the people of Israel about lost animals. Animals were very important to them. Having livestock was a sign of God's blessing. If a poor person lost a sheep, many times he couldn't afford to get another one. That's why God commanded the people to return lost animals.

After God created Adam, he was given the job of caring for and naming the animals. We're still caretakers of the earth. Being a caretaker includes caring for animals.

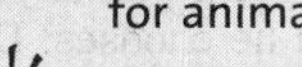

God really wants us to care for others. Read on!

Help for the Poor, Leviticus 5:7, p. 138

Help for the Hurting, Job 6:29–30, p. 666

You Are What You Do, Proverbs 20:11, p. 854

Let's Make a Deal, Daniel 1:8–21, p. 1150

The Greatest Commandment, Matthew 22:36–40, p. 1313

The Worst Chore, John 13:3–17, p. 1447

11Don't wear clothes made of wool
and linen woven together.
12Tie several pieces of thread together; then put these tassels on the four
corners of your coat.

Marriage Laws

13If a man marries a girl and has sexual relations with her but then decides he
does not like her, **14**he might talk badly
about her and give her a bad name. He
might say, "I married this woman, but
when I had sexual relations with her, I did
not find that she was a virgin." **15**Then
the girl's parents must bring proof that
she was a virgin to the older leaders at
the city gate. **16**The girl's father will say
to the leaders, "I gave my daughter to
this man to be his wife, but now he does
not want her. **17**This man has told lies
about my daughter. He has said, 'I did not
find your daughter to be a virgin,' but
here is the proof that my daughter was a
virgin." Then her parents are to show the
sheet to the city leaders, **18**and the leaders must take the man and punish him.
19They must make him pay about two
and one-half pounds of silver to the girl's
father, because the man has given an Israelite virgin a bad name. The girl will
continue to be the man's wife, and he
may not divorce her as long as he lives.
20But if the things the husband said
about his wife are true, and there is no
proof that she was a virgin, **21**the girl
must be brought to the door of her
father's house. Then the men of the town
must put her to death by throwing stones
at her. She has done a disgraceful thing in
Israel by having sexual relations before
she was married. You must get rid of the
evil among you.
22If a man is found having sexual relations with another man's wife, both the
woman and the man who had sexual relations with her must die. Get rid of this
evil from Israel.
23If a man meets a virgin in a city and
has sexual relations with her, but she is
engaged to another man, **24**you must
take both of them to the city gate and put
them to death by throwing stones at
them. Kill the girl, because she was in a

city and did not scream for help. And kill
the man for having sexual relations with
another man's wife. You must get rid of
the evil among you.

25But if a man meets an engaged girl
out in the country and forces her to have
sexual relations with him, only the man
who had sexual relations with her must
be put to death. **26**Don't do anything to
the girl, because she has not done a sin
worthy of death. This is like the person
who attacks and murders a neighbor;
27the man found the engaged girl in the
country and she screamed, but no one
was there to save her.

28If a man meets a virgin who is not
engaged to be married and forces her to
have sexual relations with him and people find out about it, **29**the man must pay
the girl's father about one and one-fourth
pounds of silver. He must also marry the
girl, because he has dishonored her, and
he may never divorce her for as long as
he lives.

30A man must not marry his father's
wife; he must not dishonor his father in
this way.

The Lord's People

23 No man who has had part of his
sex organ cut off may come into
the meeting to worship the LORD.

2No one born to parents who were
forbidden by law to marry may come into
the meeting to worship the LORD. The
descendants for ten generations may not
come in either.

3No Ammonite or Moabite may come
into the meeting to worship the LORD,
and none of their descendants for ten
generations may come in. **4**This is because the Ammonites and Moabites did
not give you bread and water when you
came out of Egypt. And they hired Balaam son of Beor, from Pethor in Northwest Mesopotamia, to put a curse on you.
5But the LORD your God would not listen
to Balaam. He turned the curse into a
blessing for you, because the LORD your
God loves you. **6**Don't wish for their
peace or success as long as you live.

7Don't hate Edomites; they are your
close relatives. Don't hate Egyptians, because you were foreigners in their country. **8**The great-grandchildren of these
two peoples may come into the meeting
to worship the LORD.

Keeping the Camp Clean

9When you are camped in time of war,
keep away from unclean things. **10**If a
man becomes unclean during the night,
he must go outside the camp and not
come back. **11**But when evening comes,
he must wash himself, and at sunset he
may come back into the camp.

12Choose a place outside the camp
where people may go to relieve themselves. **13**Carry a tent peg with you, and
when you relieve yourself, dig a hole and
cover up your dung. **14**The LORD your
God moves around through your camp to
protect you and to defeat your enemies
for you, so the camp must be holy. He
must not see anything unclean among
you so that he will not leave you.

Other Laws

15If an escaped slave comes to you, do
not hand over the slave to his master.
16Let the slave live with you anywhere
he likes, in any town he chooses. Do not
mistreat him.

17No Israelite man or woman must
ever become a temple prostitute. **18**Do
not bring a male or female prostitute's
pay to the Temple of the LORD your God
to pay what you have promised to the
LORD, because the LORD your God hates
prostitution.

19If you loan your fellow Israelites
money or food or anything else, don't
make them pay back more than you
loaned them. **20**You may charge foreigners, but not fellow Israelites. Then the
LORD your God will bless everything you
do in the land you are entering to take as
your own.

21If you make a promise to give something to the LORD your God, do not be
slow to pay it, because the LORD your
God demands it from you. Do not be
guilty of sin. **22**But if you do not make the
promise, you will not be guilty. **23**You
must do whatever you say you will do,

FAITH links

A SERIOUS PROMISE

DEUTERONOMY 23:21-23

Has someone ever borrowed money from you and promised to pay it back but didn't? When that person did not keep his or her word, how did that make you feel? God takes promises made to him just as seriously as you do. He told Moses to tell the Israelites to always keep their promises to him. If a person promised to give an offering to the Meeting Tent, God expected him to do it. When you make a promise to God, keep it!

A Different Kind of People, Leviticus 11, p. 146

Loyal to a Friend, 2 Samuel 9, p. 409

"Handle" Your Responsibilities, 2 Kings 6:5–7, p. 485

The Salt Promise, 2 Chronicles 13:5, p. 576

Fear God or People?, Jeremiah 38:14–21, p. 1047

A Christian's Responsibility, Acts 11:26, p. 1484

because you chose to make the promise
to the LORD your God.
24If you go into your neighbor's vineyard, you may eat as many grapes as you
wish, but do not put any grapes into your
basket. **25**If you go into your neighbor's
grainfield, you may pick grain with your
hands, but you must not cut down your
neighbor's grain with your sickle.

24 A man might marry a woman but
later decide she doesn't please
him because he has found something bad
about her. He writes out divorce papers
for her, gives them to her, and sends her
away from his house. **2**After she leaves
his house, she goes and marries another
man, **3**but her second husband does not
like her either. So he writes out divorce
papers for her, gives them to her, and
sends her away from his house. Or the
second husband might die. **4**In either
case, her first husband who divorced her
must not marry her again, because she
has become unclean. The LORD would
hate this. Don't bring this sin into the
land the LORD your God is giving you as
your own.
5A man who has just married must
not be sent to war or be given any other
duty. He should be free to stay home for a
year to make his new wife happy.
6If someone owes you something, do
not take his two stones for grinding
grain—not even the upper one—in place
of what he owes, because this is how the
person makes a living.
7If someone kidnaps a fellow Israelite, either to make him a slave or sell
him, the kidnapper must be killed. You
must get rid of the evil among you.
8Be careful when someone has a skin
disease. Do exactly what the priests, the
Levites, teach you, being careful to do
what I have commanded them. **9**Remember what the LORD your God did to Miriam on your way out of Egypt.
10When you make a loan to your
neighbors, don't go into their homes to
get something in place of it. **11**Stay outside and let them go in and get what they
promised you. **12**If a poor person gives
you a coat to show he will pay the loan
back, don't keep it overnight. **13**Give the
coat back at sunset, because your neighbor needs that coat to sleep in, and he
will be grateful to you. And the LORD
your God will see that you have done a
good thing.
14Don't cheat hired servants who are
poor and needy, whether they are fellow
Israelites or foreigners living in one of
your towns. **15**Pay them each day before

sunset, because they are poor and need the money. Otherwise, they may complain to the LORD about you, and you will be guilty of sin.

FAITH links

FAIRNESS FOR ALL

DEUTERONOMY 24:17

How would you react if someone passed out cookies to you and your friends, but gave you less than everyone else had? Everyone likes to be treated fairly. God commanded the Israelites to treat widows, orphans, and people from other nations fairly. Why them? They were the people who had the least of all the people in Israel. Sometimes they were treated unfairly. Others tried to ignore them. God did not want the Israelites to treat them unkindly. God wants us to treat everyone fairly, especially those whom we feel do not deserve fairness.

Link here for some more thoughts on fairness:

Just Kidding?, Genesis 21:8–10, p. 28

Care to Be Fair?, Joshua 18:1–8, p. 299

Fair All the Time?, 2 Samuel 8:15, p. 408

Meaningless Words, Job 21:34, p. 684

My Favorite!, Mark 10:17–23, p. 1347

I'll Be the Judge!, 1 Corinthians 4:4–5, p. 1549

16Parents must not be put to death if
their children do wrong, and children
must not be put to death if their parents
do wrong. Each person must die for his
own sin.

17Do not be unfair to a foreigner or an
orphan. Don't take a widow's coat to
make sure she pays you back. **18**Remember that you were slaves in Egypt, and
the LORD your God saved you from there.
That is why I am commanding you to do
this.

19When you are gathering your harvest in the field and leave behind a bundle
of grain, don't go back and get it. Leave it
there for foreigners, orphans, and widows so that the LORD your God can bless
everything you do. **20**When you beat
your olive trees to knock the olives off,
don't beat the trees a second time. Leave
what is left for foreigners, orphans, and
widows. **21**When you harvest the grapes
in your vineyard, don't pick the vines a
second time. Leave what is left for foreigners, orphans, and widows. **22**Remember that you were slaves in Egypt;
that is why I am commanding you to do
this.

25 If two people have an argument
and go to court, the judges will
decide the case. They will declare one
person right and the other guilty. **2**If the
guilty person has to be punished with a
beating, the judge will make that person
lie down and be beaten in front of him.
The number of lashes should match the
crime. **3**But don't hit a person more than
forty times, because more than that
would disgrace him before others.

4When an ox is working in the grain,
do not cover its mouth to keep it from
eating.

5If two brothers are living together,
and one of them dies without having a
son, his widow must not marry someone
outside her husband's family. Her husband's brother must marry her, which is
his duty to her as a brother-in-law. **6**The
first son she has counts as the son of
the dead brother so that his name will not
be forgotten in Israel.

7But if a man does not want to marry

his brother's widow, she should go to the older leaders at the town gate. She should say, "My brother-in-law will not carry on his brother's name in Israel. He refuses to do his duty for me."

8Then the older leaders of the town must call for the man and talk to him. But if he is stubborn and says, "I don't want to marry her," 9the woman must go up to him in front of the leaders. She must take off one of his sandals and spit in his face and say, "This is for the man who won't continue his brother's family!" 10Then that man's family shall be known in Israel as the Family of the Unsandaled.

11If two men are fighting and one man's wife comes to save her husband from his attacker, grabbing the attacker by his sex organs, 12you must cut off her hand. Show her no mercy.

13Don't carry two sets of weights with you, one heavy and one light. 14Don't have two different sets of measures in your house, one large and one small. 15You must have true and honest weights and measures so that you will live a long time in the land the LORD your God is giving you. 16The LORD your God hates anyone who is dishonest and uses dishonest measures.

> You must have true and honest weights and measures.
> —Deuteronomy 25:15

17Remember what the Amalekites did to you when you came out of Egypt. 18When you were tired and worn out, they met you on the road and attacked all those lagging behind. They were not afraid of God. 19When the LORD your God gives you rest from all the enemies around you in the land he is giving you as your own, you shall destroy any memory of the Amalekites on the earth. Do not forget!

The First Harvest

26 When you go into the land the LORD your God is giving you as your own, to take it over and live in it, 2you must take some of the first harvest of crops that grow from the land the LORD your God is giving you. Put the food in a basket and go to the place where the LORD your God will choose to be worshiped. 3Say to the priest on duty at that time, "Today I declare before the LORD your God that I have come into the land the LORD promised our ancestors that he would give us." 4The priest will take your basket and set it down in front of the altar of the LORD your God. 5Then you shall announce before the LORD your God: "My father was a wandering Aramean. He went down to Egypt with only a few people, but they became a great, powerful, and large nation there. 6But the Egyptians were cruel to us, making us suffer and work very hard. 7So we prayed to the LORD, the God of our ancestors, and he heard us. When he saw our trouble, hard work, and suffering, 8the LORD brought us out of Egypt with his great power and strength, using great terrors, signs, and miracles. 9Then he brought us to this place and gave us this fertile land. 10Now I bring part of the first harvest from this land that you, LORD, have given me." Place the basket before the LORD your God and bow down before him. 11Then you and the Levites and foreigners among you should rejoice, because the LORD your God has given good things to you and your family.

12Bring a tenth of all your harvest the third year (the year to give a tenth of your harvest). Give it to the Levites, foreigners, orphans, and widows so that they may eat in your towns and be full. 13Then say to the LORD your God, "I have taken out of my house the part of my harvest that belongs to God, and I have given it to the Levites, foreigners, orphans, and widows. I have done everything you commanded me; I have not broken your commands, and I have not forgotten any of them. 14I have not eaten any of the holy part while I was in sorrow. I have not removed any of it while I was unclean, and I have not offered it for dead people. I have obeyed you, the LORD my

God, and have done everything you commanded me. 15So look down from
heaven, your holy home. Bless your people Israel and bless the land you have
given us, which you promised to our
ancestors—a fertile land."

Obey the Lord's Commands

16Today the LORD your God commands you to obey all these rules and
laws; be careful to obey them with your

READ MY LIPS?

DEUTERONOMY 26:16-19

Suppose you told your mother you would take out the garbage, but didn't do it. Do you think she would believe that you really meant what you said? Nope!

The Israelites told the Lord that they would follow his commands. Through Moses, God called the people to do what they said they would do. God still calls people to action, not lip service. Do you mean what you say? Then act like you mean it by doing it!

Always Truthful, Numbers 23:19, p. 208

A Special Promise, Numbers 30:1–2, p. 217

A Broken Promise, Jeremiah 2:1–8, p. 989

The Verdict Is In?, Matthew 7:1–2, p. 1285

Calling Anyone!, Acts 23:12–22, p. 1506

Say What?!, Ephesians 4:22–29, p. 1603

whole being. 17Today you have said that
the LORD is your God, and you have promised to do what he wants you to do—to
keep his rules, commands, and laws. You
have said you will
obey him. 18And to-
day the LORD has
said that you are his
very own people, as
he has promised you.
But you must obey
his commands. 19He will make you greater than all the other nations he made. He
will give you praise, fame, and honor, and
you will be a holy people to the LORD your
God, as he has said.

26:18
God's Family
What are God's people supposed to do?

The Law Written on Stones

27 Then Moses, along with the older
leaders of Israel, commanded the
people, saying, "Keep all the commands I
have given you today. 2Soon you will
cross the Jordan River to go into the land
the LORD your God is giving you. On that
day set up some large stones and cover
them with plaster. 3When you cross over,
write all the words of these teachings on
them. Then you may enter the land the
LORD your God is giving you, a fertile
land, just as the LORD, the God of your
ancestors, promised. 4After you have
crossed the Jordan River, set up these
stones on Mount Ebal, as I command you
today, and cover them with plaster.
5Build an altar of stones there to the
LORD your God, but don't use any iron
tool to cut the stones; 6build the altar of
the LORD your God with stones from the
field. Offer burnt offerings on it to the
LORD your God, 7and offer fellowship offerings there, and eat them and rejoice
before the LORD your God. 8Then write
clearly all the words of these teachings
on the stones."

Curses of the Law

9Then Moses and the Levites
who were priests
spoke to all Israel and
said, "Be quiet, Is-
rael. Listen! Today
you have become the
people of the LORD

eMAIL! FROM GOD
27:10
Belief
What else should go with belief in God?

your God. 10Obey the LORD your God,
and keep his commands and laws that I
give you today."
11That day Moses also gave the people this command:
12When you cross the Jordan River,
these tribes must stand on Mount Gerizim to bless the people: Simeon, Levi, Judah, Issachar, Joseph and Benjamin.
13And these tribes must stand on Mount
Ebal to announce the curses: Reuben,
Gad, Asher, Zebulun, Dan, and Naphtali.
14The Levites will say to all the people
of Israel in a loud voice:
15"Anyone will be cursed who makes
an idol or statue and secretly sets it up,
because the LORD hates the idols people
make."
Then all the people will say, "Amen!"
16"Anyone will be cursed who dis-
honors his father or mother."
Then all the people will say, "Amen!"
17"Anyone will be cursed who moves
the stone that marks a neighbor's border."
Then all the people will say, "Amen!"
18"Anyone will be cursed who sends a
blind person down the wrong road."
Then all the people will say, "Amen!"
19"Anyone will be cursed who is unfair to foreigners, orphans, or widows."
Then all the people will say, "Amen!"
20"A man will be cursed who has
sexual relations with his father's wife,
because it is a dishonor to his father."
Then all the people will say, "Amen!"
21"Anyone will be cursed who has
sexual relations with an animal."
Then all the people will say, "Amen!"
22"A man will be cursed who has sexual relations with his sister, whether she
is his father's daughter or his mother's
daughter."
Then all the people will say, "Amen!"
23"A man will be cursed who has sexual relations with his mother-in-law."
Then all the people will say, "Amen!"
24"Anyone will be cursed who kills a
neighbor secretly."
Then all the people will say, "Amen!"
25"Anyone will be cursed who takes
money to murder an innocent person."
Then all the people will say, "Amen!"
26"Anyone will be cursed who does
not agree with the words of these teachings and does not obey them."
Then all the people will say, "Amen!"

Blessings for Obeying

28 You must completely obey the
LORD your God, and you must
carefully follow all his com-

EMAIL FROM GOD
28:1
Obedience
How does God reward obedience?

mands I am giving
you today. Then the
LORD your God will
make you greater
than any other na-
tion on earth. 2Obey
the LORD your God so that all these
blessings will come and stay with you:
3You will be blessed in the city and
blessed in the country.
4Your children will be blessed, as well
as your crops; your herds will be blessed
with calves and your flocks with lambs.
5Your basket and your kitchen will be
blessed.
6You will be blessed when you come
in and when you go out.
7The LORD will help you defeat the
enemies that come to fight you. They will
attack you from one direction, but they
will run from you in seven directions.
8The LORD your God will bless you
with full barns, and he will bless everything you do. He will bless the land he is
giving you.
9The LORD will make you his holy
people, as he promised. But you must
obey his commands and do what he wants
you to do. 10Then everyone on earth will
see that you are the LORD's people, and
they will be afraid of you. 11The LORD
will make you rich: You will have many
children, your animals will have many
young, and your land will give good
crops. It is the land that the LORD promised your ancestors he would give to you.
12The LORD will open up his heavenly
storehouse so that the skies send rain on
your land at the right time, and he will
bless everything you do. You will lend to
other nations, but you will not need to
borrow from them. 13The LORD will
make you like the head and not like the
tail; you will be on top and not on bottom.
But you must obey the commands of the

LORD your God that I am giving you today, being careful to keep them. **14**Do not
disobey anything I com-
mand you today. Do ex-
actly as I command, and
do not follow other gods
or serve them.

> Obey the LORD your God so that all these blessings will come and stay with you.
> —Deuteronomy 28:2

Curses for Disobeying

15But if you do not
obey the LORD your God
and carefully follow all his
commands and laws I am
giving you today, all these curses will
come upon you and stay:

16You will be cursed in the city and
cursed in the country.

17Your basket and your kitchen will
be cursed.

18Your children will be cursed, as well
as your crops; the calves of your herds and
the lambs of your flocks will be cursed.

19You will be cursed when you go in
and when you go out.

20The LORD will send you curses,
confusion, and punishment in everything
you do. You will be destroyed and suddenly ruined because you did wrong
when you left him. **21**The LORD will give
you terrible diseases and destroy you
from the land you are going to take.
22The LORD will punish you with disease, fever, swelling, heat, lack of rain,
plant diseases, and mildew until you die.
23The sky above will be like bronze,[n] and
the ground below will be like iron. **24**The
LORD will turn the rain into dust and
sand, which will fall from the skies until
you are destroyed.

25The LORD will help your enemies
defeat you. You will attack them from one
direction, but you will run from them in
seven directions. And you will become a
thing of horror among all the kingdoms
on earth. **26**Your dead bodies will be food
for all the birds and wild animals, and
there will be no one to scare them away.
27The LORD will punish you with boils
like those the Egyptians had. You will
have bad growths, sores, and itches that
can't be cured. **28**The LORD will give
you madness, blindness, and a confused
mind. **29**You will have to feel around in
the daylight like a blind person. You will
fail in everything you do.
People will hurt you and
steal from you every day,
and no one will save you.

30You will be engaged
to a woman, but another
man will force her to have
sexual relations with him.
You will build a house, but
you will not live in it. You
will plant a vineyard, but
you will not get its grapes.
31Your ox will be killed before your eyes,
but you will not eat any of it. Your donkey
will be taken away from you, and it will
not be brought back. Your sheep will be
given to your enemies, and no one will
save you. **32**Your sons and daughters
will be given to another nation, and you
will grow tired looking for them every
day, but there will be nothing you can do.
33People you don't know will eat the
crops your land and hard work have produced. You will be mistreated and abused
all your life. **34**The things you see will
cause you to go mad. **35**The LORD will
give you sore boils on your knees and
legs that cannot be cured, and they will
go from the soles of your feet to the tops
of your heads.

36The LORD will send you and your
king away to a nation neither you nor
your ancestors know, where you will
serve other gods made of wood and
stone. **37**You will become a hated thing to
the nations where the LORD sends you;
they will laugh at you and make fun of
you.

38You will plant much seed in your
field, but your harvest will be small, because locusts will eat the crop. **39**You will
plant vineyards and work hard in them,
but you will not pick the grapes or drink
the wine, because the worms will eat
them. **40**You will have olive trees in all
your land, but you will not get any olive
oil, because the olives will drop off the
trees. **41**You will have sons and daugh-

28:23 sky . . . bronze This means the sky will give no rain and the earth will produce no crops.

ters, but you will not be able to keep
them, because they will be taken captive.
42Locusts will destroy all your trees and
crops.

43The foreigners who live among
you will get stronger and stronger, and
you will get weaker and weaker. **44**Foreigners will lend money to you, but you
will not be able to lend to them. They will
be like the head, and you will be like the
tail.

45All these curses will come upon
you. They will chase you and catch you
and destroy you, because you did not
obey the LORD your God and keep the
commands and laws he gave you. **46**The
curses will be signs and miracles to you
and your descendants forever. **47**You had
plenty of everything, but you did not
serve the LORD your God with joy and a
pure heart, **48**so you will serve the enemies the LORD sends against you. You
will be hungry, thirsty, naked, and poor,
and the LORD will put a load on you until
he has destroyed you.

The Curse of an Enemy Nation

49The LORD will bring a nation
against you from far away, from the end of
the world, and it will swoop down like an
eagle. You won't understand their language, **50**and they will look mean. They
will not respect old people or feel sorry
for the young. **51**They will eat the calves
from your herds and the harvest of your
field, and you will be destroyed. They will
not leave you any grain, new wine or oil,
or any calves from your herds or lambs
from your flocks. You will be ruined.
52That nation will surround and attack
all your cities. You trust in your high,
strong walls, but they will fall down. That
nation will surround all your cities everywhere in the land the LORD your God is
giving you.

53Your enemy will surround you.
Those people will make you starve so that
you will eat your own babies, the bodies of
the sons and daughters the LORD your
God gave you. **54**Even the most gentle
and kind man among you will become
cruel to his brother, his wife whom he
loves, and his children who are still alive.
55He will not even give them any of the
flesh of his children he is eating, because
it will be all he has left. Your enemy will
surround you and make you starve in all
your cities. **56**The most gentle and kind
woman among you, so gentle and kind she
would hardly even walk on the ground,
will be cruel to her husband whom she
loves and to her son and daughter. **57**She
will give birth to a baby, but she will plan
to eat the baby and what comes after the
birth itself. She will eat them secretly
while the enemy surrounds the city.
Those people will make you starve in all
your cities.

58Be careful to obey everything in
these teachings that are written in this
book. You must respect the glorious and
wonderful name of the LORD your God,
59or the LORD will give terrible diseases
to you and your descendants. You will
have long and serious diseases, and long
and miserable sicknesses. **60**He will give
you all the diseases of Egypt that you
dread, and the diseases will stay with
you. **61**The LORD will also give you every
disease and sickness not written in this
Book of the Teachings, until you are
destroyed. **62**You people may have out-
numbered the stars, but only a few of you
will be left, because you did not obey the
LORD your God. **63**Just as the LORD was
once happy with you and gave you good
things and made you grow in number, so
then the LORD will be happy to ruin and
destroy you, and you will be removed
from the land you are entering to take as
your own.

64Then the LORD will scatter you
among the nations—from one end of the
earth to the other. There you will serve
other gods of wood and stone, gods that
neither you nor your ancestors have
known. **65**You will have no rest among
those nations and no place that is yours.
The LORD will make your mind worried,
your sight weak, and your soul sad.
66You will live with danger and be afraid
night and day. You will not be sure that
you will live. **67**In the morning you will
say, "I wish it were evening," and in the
evening you will say, "I wish it were
morning." Terror will be in your heart,

and the things you have seen will scare
you. **68**The LORD will send you back to
Egypt in ships, even though I, Moses,
said you would never go back to Egypt.
And there you will try to sell yourselves
as slaves to your enemies, but no one will
buy you.

The Agreement in Moab

29 The LORD commanded Moses to
make an agreement with the Israelites in Moab in addition to the agreement he had made with them at Mount
Sinai. These are the words of that agreement.

2Moses called all the Israelites together and said to them:

You have seen every-
thing the LORD did before
your own eyes to the king
of Egypt and to the king's
leaders and to the whole
country. **3**With your own
eyes you saw the great
troubles, signs, and miracles. **4**But to this day the
LORD has not given you a
mind that understands;
you don't really understand what you see
with your eyes or hear with your ears. **5**I
led you through the desert for forty
years, and during that time neither your
clothes nor sandals wore out. **6**You ate no
bread and drank no wine or beer. This
was so you would understand that I am
the LORD your God.

7When you came to this place, Sihon
king of Heshbon and Og king of Bashan
came out to fight us, but we defeated
them. **8**We captured their land and gave it
to the tribes of Reuben, Gad, and East
Manasseh to be their own.

9You must carefully obey everything
in this agreement so that you will succeed in everything you do. **10**Today you
are all standing here before the LORD
your God—your leaders and important
men, your older leaders, officers, and all
the other men of Israel, **11**your wives and
children and the foreigners who live
among you, who chop your wood and
carry your water. **12**You are all here to
enter into an agreement and a promise
with the LORD your God, an agreement
the LORD your God is making with you
today. **13**This will make you today his
own people. He will be your God, as he
told you and as he promised your ancestors Abraham, Isaac, and Jacob. **14**But I
am not just making this agreement and
its promises with you **15**who are standing
here before the LORD your God today, but
also with those who are not here today.

16You know how we lived in Egypt
and how we passed through the countries
when we came here. **17**You saw their
hateful idols made of wood, stone, silver,
and gold. **18**Make sure no man, woman,
family group, or tribe among you leaves
the LORD our God to go
and serve the gods of those
nations. They would be to
you like a plant that grows
bitter, poisonous fruit.

19These are the kind
of people who hear these
curses but bless them-
selves, thinking, "We will
be safe even though we
continue doing what we
want to do." Those peo-
ple may destroy all of your land, both wet
and dry. **20**The LORD will not forgive
them. His anger will be like a burning fire
against those people, and all the curses
written in this book will come on them.
The LORD will destroy any memory of
them on the earth. **21**He will separate
them from all the tribes of Israel for punishment. All the curses of the Agreement
that are written in this Book of the
Teachings will happen to them.

22Your children who will come after
you, as well as foreigners from faraway
lands, will see the disasters that come to
this land and the diseases the LORD will
send on it. They will say, **23**"The land is
nothing but burning cinders and salt.
Nothing is planted, nothing grows, and
nothing blooms. It is like Sodom and Gomorrah, and Admah and Zeboiim, which
the LORD destroyed because he was very
angry." **24**All the other nations will ask,
"Why has the LORD done this to the land?
Why is he so angry?"

25And the answer will be, "It is be-

> There are some things the LORD our God has kept secret, but there are some things he has let us know.
> —Deuteronomy 29:29

cause the people broke the Agreement of the LORD, the God of their ancestors, which he made with them when he brought them out of Egypt.
26They went and served other gods and bowed down to gods they did not even know. The LORD did not allow that,
27so he became very angry at the land and brought all the curses on it that are written in this book.
28Since the LORD became angry and furious with them, he took them out of their land and put them in another land where they are today."

29There are some things the LORD our God has kept secret, but there are some things he has let us know. These things belong to us and our children forever so that we will do everything in these teachings.

The Israelites Will Return

30 When all these blessings and curses I have described happen to you, and the LORD your God has sent you away to other nations, think about these things.
2Then you and your children will return to the LORD your God, and you will obey him with your whole being in everything I am commanding you today.
3Then the LORD your God will give you back your freedom. He will feel sorry for you, and he will bring you back again from the nations where he scattered you.
4He may send you to the ends of the earth, but he will gather you and bring you back from there,
5back to the land that belonged to your ancestors. It will be yours. He will give you success, and there will be more of you than there were of your ancestors.
6The LORD your God will prepare you and your descendants to love him with your whole being so that you will live.
7The LORD your God will put all these curses on your enemies, who hate you and are cruel to you.
8And you will again obey the LORD, keeping all his commands that I give you today.
9The LORD your God will make you successful in everything you do. You will have many children, your cattle will have many calves, and your fields will produce good crops, because the LORD will again be happy with you, just as he was with your

FAITH links

A CHOICE TO MAKE

DEUTERONOMY 30:15-20

If someone offered you a choice between eating a nice, juicy apple and eating a poisoned one, which would you choose? That's an easy one, right? Life is full of choices, some of which seem like no-brainers. God offered the people of Israel a choice between doing what was right and what was wrong. That was an easy choice for those who truly wanted to obey God. For those who weren't sure, well . . . the choice was a lot harder.

God gives you the same choice. He can help you make right choices. But you have to *want* his help first.

Connect to these links to find out what else God has to say about making the right choice:

What You Value, Genesis 25:21–34, p. 34

I Want It *Now!*, Judges 14:1–3, p. 332

A Memorial for Two Thieves, 1 Chronicles 7:21, p. 530

Two Kinds of People, Psalm 1, p. 710

Love Him? Show It!, Amos 2:6–7, p. 1196

That Thing You Do, Matthew 25:14–30, p. 1319

ancestors. **10**But you must obey the
LORD your God by keeping all his commands and rules that are written in this
Book of the Teachings. You must return
to the LORD your God with your whole
being.

Choose Life or Death

11This command I give you today is
not too hard for you; it is not beyond what
you can do. **12**It is not up in heaven. You
do not have to ask, "Who will go up to
heaven and get it for us so we can obey it
and keep it?" **13**It is not on the other side
of the sea. You do not have to ask, "Who
will go across the sea and get it? Who will
tell it to us so we can keep it?" **14**No, the
word is very near you. It is in your mouth
and in your heart so you may obey it.

15Look, today I offer you life and success, death and destruction. **16**I command you today to love the LORD your
God, to do what he wants you to do, and
to keep his commands, his rules, and his
laws. Then you will live and grow in number, and the LORD your God will bless you
in the land you are entering to take as
your own.

17But if you turn away from the LORD
and do not obey him, if you are led to bow
and serve other gods, **18**I tell you today
that you will surely be destroyed. And
you will not live long in the land you are
crossing the Jordan River to enter and
take as your own.

19Today I ask heaven and earth to be
witnesses. I am offering you life or death,
blessings or curses. Now, choose life!
Then you and your children may live.
20To choose life is to love the LORD your
God, obey him, and stay close to him. He
is your life, and he will let you live many
years in the land, the land he promised to
give your ancestors Abraham, Isaac, and
Jacob.

Joshua Takes Moses' Place

31 Then Moses went and spoke
these words to all the Israelites:
2"I am now one hundred twenty years
old, and I cannot lead you anymore. The
LORD told me I would not cross the Jordan River; **3**the LORD your God will lead
you across himself. He will destroy those
nations for you, and you will take over
their land. Joshua will also lead you
across, as the LORD has said. **4**The LORD
will do to those nations what he did to Sihon and Og, the kings of the Amorites,
when he destroyed them and their land.
5The LORD will give those nations to
you; do to them everything I told you.
6Be strong and brave. Don't be afraid of
them and don't be frightened, because
the LORD your God will go with you. He
will not leave you or forget you."

7Then Moses called Joshua and said
to him in front of the people, "Be strong
and brave, because you will lead these
people into the land the LORD promised
to give their ancestors,
and help them take
it as their own. **8**The
LORD himself will go
before you. He will
be with you; he will
not leave you or for-
get you. Don't be afraid and don't worry."

> eMail FROM GOD **31:8**
> **Fears**
> Where is God when you are afraid?

Moses Writes the Teachings

9So Moses wrote down these teachings and gave them to the priests and all
the older leaders of Israel. (The priests
are the sons of Levi, who carry the Ark of
the Agreement with the LORD.) **10-11**Then
Moses commanded them: "Read these
teachings for all Israel to hear at the end
of every seven years, which is the year to
cancel what people owe. Do it during the
Feast of Shelters, when all the Israelites
will come to appear before the LORD your
God and stand at the place he will choose.
12Gather all the people: the men, women,
children, and foreigners living in your
towns so that they can listen and learn to
respect the LORD your God and carefully
obey everything in this law. **13**Since their
children do not know this law, they must
hear it. They must learn to respect the
LORD your God for as long as they live in
the land you are crossing the Jordan River
to take for your own."

The Lord Calls Moses and Joshua

14The LORD said to Moses, "Soon you
will die. Get Joshua and come to the

MAKING GOOD CHOICES

Deuteronomy 30:15–20

Livin' it

This or That? Which would you rather do, stay home and do chores or go to an amusement park for the day? No-brainer, right? Some choices are like that—easy to make. Others, though, are tougher. How about doing what you know is right even if your friends make fun of you? Is that a harder choice for you to make? How would you decide what to do?

God offered the people of Israel a choice between doing what was right and what was wrong. That was an easy choice for those who truly wanted to obey God. For some of the others the choice was a lot harder. (Read Deuteronomy 30:15–20.) God gives you the same choice. He can help you make the right choices. How badly do you want his help?

MORE FAITH links

What You Value, p. 34
A Choice to Make, p. 265
The Fence Riders, p. 464
Mind Guard, p. 831
The Choices of a Choice, p. 1375

"Skweek! I need some help! I can't decide what I want to do when I get older. What do you think?"

"That's a pretty important decision, Tagg. Maybe you ought to check out these links for some help in making good choices!"

Choosing Sides, 1 Samuel 20, p. 382
- In an argument between two people, do you find yourself taking sides? How do you decide whose side you're on? Link here to learn about being on the side of what's right.

Let's Make a Deal, Daniel 1:8–21, p. 1150
- Suppose your teacher involved your class in an activity that you and your parents agreed was wrong for you. Should you go along with it in order to obey your teacher? Or should you refuse to go along with it in order to obey your parents? What could help you make that choice? This Faithlink explains how Daniel resolved a similar situation.

Keeping Clean, 2 Corinthians 7:1, p. 1576
- Suppose you just put on some cool new clothes. Would you immediately leap into the nearest mud puddle? Probably not. You would want to keep them clean and looking good. God wants Christians to be clean on the *inside*. What are some things that can make you have bad or wrong ideas and do wrong things (so that you become *dirty* on the inside)? How can you get clean inside? God can help with the cleanup—just ask!

my FAVORITE links

Meeting Tent so that I may command
him." So Moses and Joshua went to the
Meeting Tent.
15The LORD appeared at the Meeting
Tent in a cloud; the cloud stood over the
entrance of the Tent. 16And the LORD
said to Moses, "You will soon die. Then
these people will not be loyal to me but
will worship the foreign gods of the land
they are entering. They will leave me,
breaking the Agreement I made with
them. 17Then I will become very angry at
them, and I will leave them. I will turn
away from them, and they will be destroyed. Many terrible things will happen
to them. Then they will say, 'It is because
God is not with us that these terrible
things are happening.' 18I will surely turn
away from them then, because they have
done wrong and have turned to other
gods.
19"Now write down this song and
teach it to the Israelites. Then have them
sing it, because it will be my witness
against them. 20When I bring them into
the land I promised to their ancestors, a
fertile land, they will eat as much as they
want and get fat. Then they will turn to
other gods and serve them. They will reject me and break my Agreement. 21Then
when many troubles and terrible things
happen to them, this song will testify
against them, because the song will not be
forgotten by their descendants. I know
what they plan to do, even before I take
them into the land I promised them."
22So Moses wrote down the song that
day, and he taught it to the Israelites.
23Then the LORD gave this command
to Joshua son of Nun: "Be strong and
brave, because you will lead the people of
Israel to the land I promised them, and I
will be with you."
24After Moses finished writing all the
words of the teachings in a book, 25he
gave a command to the Levites, who carried the Ark of the Agreement with the
LORD. 26He said, "Take this Book of the
Teachings and put it beside the Ark of the
Agreement with the LORD your God. It
must stay there as a witness against you.
27I know how stubborn and disobedient
you are. You have disobeyed the LORD
while I am alive and with you, and you will
disobey even more after I die! 28Gather
all the older leaders of your tribes and all
your officers to me so that I may say these
things for them to hear, and so that I may
ask heaven and earth to testify against
them. 29I know that after I die you will
become completely evil. You will turn
away from the commands I have given
you. Terrible things will happen to you in
the future when you do what the LORD
says is evil, and you will make him angry
with the idols you have made."

Moses' Song

30And Moses spoke this whole song
for all the people of Israel to hear:

32 Hear, heavens, and I will speak.
Listen, earth, to what I say.
2 My teaching will drop like rain;
my words will fall like dew.
They will be like showers on the grass;
they will pour down like rain on young plants.
3 I will announce the name of the LORD.
Praise God because he is great!
4 He is like a rock; what he does is perfect,
and he is always fair.
He is a faithful God who does no wrong,
who is right and fair.

5 They have done evil against him.
To their shame they are no longer his children;
they are an evil and lying people.
6 This is not the way to repay the LORD,
you foolish and unwise people.
He is your Father and Maker,
who made you and formed you.

7 Remember the old days.
Think of the years already passed.
Ask your father and he will tell you;
ask your older leaders and they will inform you.
8 God Most High gave the nations their lands,

dividing up the human race.
He set up borders for the people
and even numbered the Israelites.
9 The LORD took his people as his share,
the people of Jacob as his very own.

10 He found them in a desert,
a windy, empty land.
He surrounded them and brought them up,
guarding them as those he loved very much.
11 He was like an eagle building its nest
that flutters over its young.
It spreads its wings to catch them
and carries them on its feathers.
12 The LORD alone led them,
and there was no foreign god helping him.

13 The LORD brought them to the heights of the land
and fed them the fruit of the fields.
He gave them honey from the rocks,
bringing oil from the solid rock.
14 There were milk curds from the cows and milk from the flock;
there were fat sheep and goats.
There were sheep and goats from Bashan
and the best of the wheat.
You drank the juice of grapes.

15 Israel grew fat and kicked;
they were fat and full and firm.
They left the God who made them
and rejected the Rock who saved them.
16 They made God jealous with foreign gods
and angry with hateful idols.
17 They made sacrifices to demons, not God,
to gods they had never known,
new gods from nearby,
gods your ancestors did not fear.
18 You left God who is the Rock, your Father,
and you forgot the God who gave you birth.

19 The LORD saw this and rejected them;
his sons and daughters had made him angry.
20 He said, "I will turn away from them
and see what will happen to them.
They are evil people,
unfaithful children.
21 They used things that are not gods to make me jealous
and worthless idols to make me angry.
So I will use those who are not a nation to make them jealous;
I will use a nation that does not understand to make them angry.
22 My anger has started a fire
that burns down to the place of the dead.
It will burn up the ground and its crops,
and it will set fire to the base of the mountains.

23 "I will pile troubles upon them
and shoot my arrows at them.
24 They will be starved and sick,
destroyed by terrible diseases.
I will send them vicious animals
and gliding, poisonous snakes.
25 In the streets the sword will kill;
in their homes there will be terror.
Young men and women will die,
and so will babies and gray-haired men.
26 I will scatter them as I said,
and no one will remember them.
27 But I didn't want their enemy to brag;
their enemy might misunderstand
and say, 'We have won!
The LORD has done none of this.' "

28 Israel has no sense;
they do not understand.
29 I wish they were wise and understood this;
I wish they could see what will happen to them.
30 One person cannot chase a thousand people,
and two people cannot fight ten thousand

unless their Rock has sold them,
unless the LORD has given them
up.
31 The rock of these people is not like
our Rock;
our enemies agree to that.
32 Their vine comes from Sodom,
and their fields are like Gomorrah.
Their grapes are full of poison;
their bunches of grapes are bitter.
33 Their wine is like snake poison,
like the deadly poison of cobras.

34 "I have been saving this,
and I have it locked in my
storehouses.
35 I will punish those who do wrong; I
will repay them.
Soon their foot will slip,
because their day of trouble is near,
and their punishment will come
quickly."

36 The LORD will defend his people
and have mercy on his servants.
He will see that their strength is
gone,
that nobody is left, slaves or free.
37 Then he will say, "Where are their
gods?
Where is the rock they trusted?
38 Who ate the fat from their sacrifices,
and who drank the wine of their
drink offerings?
Let those gods come to help you!
Let them protect you!

39 "Now you will see that I am the one
God!
There is no god but me.
I send life and death;
I can hurt, and I can heal.
No one can escape from me.
40 I raise my hand toward heaven and
make this promise:
As surely as I live forever,
41 I will sharpen my flashing sword,
and I will take it in my hand to
judge.
I will punish my enemies
and pay back those who hate me.
42 My arrows will be covered with their
blood;
my sword will eat their flesh.
The blood will flow from those who
are killed and the captives.
The heads of the enemy leaders
will be cut off."

43 Be happy, nations, with his people,
because he will repay you for the
blood of his servants.
He will punish his enemies,
and he will remove the sin of his
land and people.

44 Moses came with Joshua son of
Nun, and they spoke all the words of this
song for the people to hear. 45 When Moses finished speaking these words to all
Israel, 46 he said to them: "Pay careful attention to all the words I have said to you
today, and command your children to
obey carefully everything in these teachings. 47 These should not be unimportant
words for you, but rather they mean life
for you! By these words you will live a
long time in the land you are crossing the
Jordan River to take as your own."

Moses Goes Up to Mount Nebo

48 The LORD spoke to Moses again
that same day and said, 49 "Go up the Abarim Mountains, to Mount Nebo in the
country of Moab, across from Jericho.
Look at the land of Canaan that I am giving to the Israelites as their own. 50 On
that mountain that you climb, you will die
and join your ancestors, just as your
brother Aaron died on Mount Hor and
joined his ancestors. 51 You both sinned
against me at the waters of Meribah Kadesh in the Desert of Zin, and you did not
honor me as holy there among the Israelites. 52 So now you will only look at the
land from far away. You will not enter the
land I am giving the people of Israel."

Moses Blesses the People

33 Moses, the man of God, gave this
blessing to the Israelites before he
died. 2 He said:

"The LORD came from Mount Sinai
and rose like the sun from
Edom;

he showed his greatness from
Mount Paran.
He came with thousands of angels
from the southern mountains.
3 The LORD surely loves his people
and takes care of all those who
belong to him.
They bow down at his feet,
and they are taught by him.
4 Moses gave us the teachings
that belong to the
people of Jacob.
5 The LORD became
king of Israel
when the leaders of
the people
gathered,
when the tribes of
Israel came
together.

The LORD's loved ones will lie down in safety, because he protects them all day long.
—Deuteronomy 33:12

6 "Let the people of Reuben live and
not die,
but let the people be few."

7 Moses said this about the people of
Judah:
"LORD, listen to Judah's prayer;
bring them back to their people.
They defend themselves with their
hands.
Help them fight their enemies!"

8 Moses said this about the people of
Levi:
"LORD, your Thummim and Urim
belong
to Levi, whom you love.
LORD, you tested him at Massah
and argued with him at the waters
of Meribah.
9 He said about his father and mother,
'I don't care about them.'
He did not treat his brothers as
favorites
or give special favors to his
children,
but he protected your word
and guarded your agreement.
10 He teaches your laws to the people
of Jacob
and your teachings to the people of
Israel.
He burns incense before you
and makes whole burnt offerings
on your altar.
11 LORD, make them strong;
be pleased with the work they do.
Defeat those who attack them,
and don't let their enemies rise up
again."

12 Moses said this about the people of
Benjamin:
"The LORD's loved ones
will lie down in
safety,
because he protects
them all day long.
The ones he loves
rest with him."

13 Moses said this about
the people of Joseph:
"May the LORD bless their land with
wonderful dew from heaven,
with water from the springs below,
14 with the best fruits that the sun
brings,
and with the best fruits that the
moon brings.
15 Let the old mountains give the finest
crops,
and let the everlasting hills give
the best fruits.
16 Let the full earth give the best fruits,
and let the LORD who lived in the
burning bush be pleased.
May these blessings rest on the head
of Joseph,
on the forehead of the one who
was blessed among his brothers.
17 Joseph has the majesty of a firstborn
bull;
he is as strong as a wild ox.
He will stab other nations,
even those nations far away.
These are the ten thousands of
Ephraim,
and these are the thousands of
Manasseh."

18 Moses said this about the people of
Zebulun:
"Be happy when you go out,
Zebulun,

THE DELIVERER

Deuteronomy 34

1. Moses was born in Egypt to Israelite slaves. But Moses got to grow up in the king's palace when the king's daughter rescued him from a basket floating down the Nile River. Later, as a young man, he ran away to Midian because he killed an Egyptian guard to protect the Hebrew slaves. (Check out Exodus 2:1–15, p. 77.)

2. Moses worked for 40 years as a shepherd in Midian. He stayed with a man named Jethro and married one of his daughters, Zipporah. While he lived there, God talked to him from a burning bush and instructed Moses to return to Egypt and lead the Israelites out of Egypt. (Read Exodus 2:16—3:22, p. 78.)

3. Moses returned to Egypt. It took a series of 10 plagues—the final one where the firstborn son of every Egyptian died—to convince the king of Egypt to let the Israelites go free. (Look at Exodus 4:18—12:50, p. 81.)

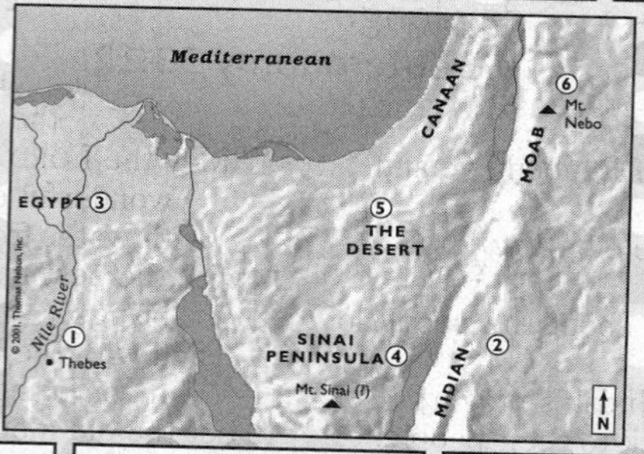

4. Moses and the Israelites traveled through the Sinai Peninsula. At Mount Sinai, God gave the Ten Commandments. (See Exodus 19 and 20, p. 100.)

5. Moses led the Israelites through the desert for 40 years while God prepared them to reenter their homeland of Canaan. (Look up Numbers 14:20–34, p. 195.)

6. Joshua was appointed the new leader and the one to lead the people into the land God promised them. Moses died near Mount Nebo, overlooking the land of Canaan. (Check out Numbers 27:12–23, p. 213; Deuteronomy 34:1–9.)

and be happy in your tents,
Issachar.
19 They will call the people to the
mountain,
and there they will offer the right
sacrifices.
They will do well from all that is in
the sea,
and they will do well from the
treasures hidden in the sand on
the shore."

20 Moses said this about the people of
Gad:
"Praise God who gives Gad more
land!
Gad lives there like a lion,
who tears off arms and heads.
21 They chose the best land for
themselves.
They received a large share, like
that given to an officer.
When the leaders of the people
gathered,
the people of Gad did what the
LORD said was right,
and they judged Israel fairly."

22 Moses said this about the people of
Dan:
"Dan is like a lion's cub,
who jumps out of Bashan."

23Moses said this about the people of Naphtali:

"Naphtali enjoys special kindnesses,
and they are full of the LORD's
blessings.
Take as your own the west and
south."

24Moses said this about the people of Asher:

"Asher is the most blessed of the
sons;
let him be his brothers' favorite.
Let him bathe his feet in olive oil.
25 Your gates will have locks of iron and
bronze,
and you will be strong as long as
you live.

26 "There is no one like the God of
Israel,
who rides through the skies to
help you,
who rides on the clouds in his
majesty.
27 The everlasting God is your place of
safety,
and his arms will hold you up
forever.
He will force your enemy out ahead
of you,
saying, 'Destroy the enemy!'
28 The people of Israel will lie down in
safety.
Jacob's spring is theirs alone.
Theirs is a land full of grain and new
wine,
where the skies drop their dew.
29 Israel, you are blessed!
No one else is like you,
because you are a people saved by
the LORD.
He is your shield and helper,
your glorious sword.
Your enemies will be afraid of you,
and you will walk all over their
holy places."

Moses Dies

34 Then Moses climbed Mount Nebo
from the plains of Moab to the top
of Mount Pisgah, across from Jericho.
From there the LORD showed him all the
land from Gilead to Dan, 2all of Naphtali
and the lands of Ephraim and Manasseh,
all the land of Judah as far as the Mediterranean Sea, 3as well as the southern
desert and the whole Valley of Jericho up
to Zoar. (Jericho is called the city of palm
trees.) 4Then the LORD said to Moses,
"This is the land I promised to Abraham,
Isaac, and Jacob when I said to them, 'I
will give this land to your descendants.'
I have let you look at it, Moses, but you
will not cross over there."

5Then Moses, the servant of the
LORD, died there in Moab, as the LORD
had said. 6He buried Moses in Moab in
the valley opposite Beth Peor, but even
today no one knows where his grave is.
7Moses was one hundred twenty years
old when he died. His eyes were not
weak, and he was still strong. 8The Israelites cried for Moses for thirty days,
staying in the plains of Moab until the
time of sadness was over.

9Joshua son of Nun was then filled
with wisdom, because Moses had put his
hands on him. So the Israelites listened
to Joshua, and they did what the LORD
had commanded Moses.

10There has never been another
prophet in Israel like Moses. The LORD
knew Moses face to face 11and sent him
to do signs and miracles in Egypt—to the
king, to all his officers, and to the whole
land of Egypt. 12Moses had great power,
and he did great and wonderful things for
all the Israelites to see.

CONQUER THE LAND!

Hello! My name is Joshua. You may remember me as one of the 12 spies sent out by Moses to check out the land God promised to the Israelites. (Surf on over to Numbers 13, p. 193, for that story.) After Moses died, God made me the leader of his people. In this book, I describe how Israel conquered the land God promised them. Because the people already living in the land worshiped false gods and did many evil things, God wanted us to defeat these people completely. Don't miss any of the exciting stories of our many battles.

I wrote this book so everyone would know that God gave us victory in conquering the land he promised to us. When we followed his commands, he was with us in battle. You have probably already heard of our most famous victory: how we marched around the city of Jericho seven times, blew some trumpets, and the city walls fell down. (See Joshua 6 for the whole story. Also visit the plug-in about the town of Jericho, Let's Visit Jericho, Joshua 5.) When we were unfaithful, God allowed us to be defeated. (See the details of our most stunning defeat, when one man, Achan, sinned against God in Joshua 7.) After most of the country had been defeated, we divided the land among the tribes, or families, of God's people.

JESUS WATCH

Many people believe that the commander of the Lord's army mentioned in Joshua 5 is really Jesus. Notice that Joshua takes off his sandals in respect and calls the commander "master." In many ways, Joshua himself reminds us of Jesus. In fact, in Hebrew their names are the same and mean "the LORD saves." As a young man, Joshua was with Moses when Moses wrote down the laws of God. When he was a boy, Jesus studied these same laws. As a leader, Joshua urged the people to follow God and obey his laws. Jesus taught that the law pointed out our need for a savior. Joshua led the people into a new land where God had promised to bless them richly. Jesus leads us to heaven where we will live forever.

my FAVORITE links

OTHER CONNECTIONS

Livin' it

Has anyone ever called you "brave" or "courageous"? What do you think it takes to be brave? Connect to Captain Courageous?, Joshua 1:6–9, for some thoughts from God on being brave. Follow the Faithlinks for more information.

The Book of Joshua has some incredible stories of adventures, battles, and victories as the Israelites entered the land that God promised them. Connect to these sites for more information about:

- The stunning defeat of the town of Jericho at the hands—or should we say sounds—of the Israelites. Check it out and the other historical significance of this old Bible city by linking to Let's Visit Jericho, Joshua 5.
- Joshua's Victories, Joshua 11. Surf here for the highlights of Joshua and the Israelites' battle plan against the kings and people who occupied Canaan.
- After the Israelites had conquered the land, Joshua and the leaders had to fairly divide up the land among the 12 tribes. Find out how they did it by visiting Dividing the Land, Joshua 21.

"Tagg, here's a puzzle for you. Why did the Gibeonites wear old clothes and carry old sacks?"

"I'm not sure, but I think it was a trick. Log on to Joshua 9 for that answer."

OTHER COOL STORIES:

Spies in Jericho, Joshua 2
Rocks to remind us, Joshua 4:1–7
The commander of the Lord's army, Joshua 5:13–15
The sun stands still, Joshua 10:12–14

- **God's Pep Talk, Joshua 1:5–9**
- **What Will You Risk?, Joshua 2**
- **Facts About Following, Joshua 6**
- **Who Do You Trust?, Joshua 9**
- **The God of Big Things, Joshua 10**
- **A Long Wait, Joshua 14:6–15**
- **No Middle Ground, Joshua 24:14–15**

God's Command to Joshua

1 After Moses, the servant of the LORD,
died, the LORD spoke to Joshua son of
Nun, Moses' assistant. 2The LORD said,
"My servant Moses is dead. Now you and
all these people go across the Jordan
River into the land I am giving to the Israelites. 3I promised Moses I would give
you this land, so I will give you every
place you go in the land. 4All the land
from the desert in the south to Lebanon
in the north will be yours. All the land
from the great river, the Euphrates, in
the east, to the Mediterranean Sea in the
west will be yours, too, including the land
of the Hittites. 5No one will be able to
defeat you all your life. Just as I was with
Moses, so I will be with you. I will not
leave you or forget you.

6"Joshua, be strong and brave! You
must lead these people so they can take
the land that I promised their fathers I
would give them. 7Be strong and brave.
Be sure to obey all the teachings my servant Moses gave you. If you follow them
exactly, you will be successful in everything you do. 8Always remember what is
written in the Book of the Teachings.
Study it day and night to be sure to obey
everything that is
written there. If you
do this, you will be
wise and successful
in everything. 9Re-
member that I com-
manded you to be strong and brave. Don't
be afraid, because the LORD your God
will be with you everywhere you go."

1:9
Courage
How can you be brave?

Joshua's Orders to the People

10Then Joshua gave orders to the officers of the people: 11"Go through the
camp and tell the people, 'Get your supplies ready. Three days from now you will
cross the Jordan River and take the land
the LORD your God is giving you.'"

12Then Joshua said to the people of
Reuben, Gad, and East Manasseh, 13"Remember what Moses, the servant of the
LORD, told you. He said the LORD your
God would give you rest and would give
you this land. 14Now the LORD has given
you this land east of the Jordan River. Your

FAITH links

GOD'S PEP TALK

JOSHUA 1:5-9

How do you usually face the big challenges of your life? Many sports team coaches give their teams a pep talk when they're about to go into the big game. That pep talk helps them to be strong and brave. Joshua and the Israelites were about to face one of the biggest challenges of their lives. They were about to move into the land that God promised them. They would have to fight many battles. That was scary! So God gave Joshua "the pep talk." After all, Joshua was the one who would lead them into battle. God's command to be strong and brave is one to remember when you're afraid.

Check out these other Faithlinks on being brave!

When You're Afraid, Genesis 32:9–12, p. 45

Listen Up!, 1 Kings 19:11–13, p. 467

A Life-Saving Message, Esther 2:19–22, p. 650

Who Ya' Gonna Call?, Psalm 3:4, p. 711

A Word About Worry, Matthew 6:25–34, p. 1284

Thoughts on Thoughts, Philippians 4:8–9, p. 1614

COURAGE

Joshua 1:6–9

Livin' it

Captain Courageous? What do you think of when someone tells you to "be brave" and have courage?

Does it mean acting like the comic book character, Captain Courageous, and rushing into danger to save the world? Or does it mean not crying when you bust open your knee and the blood is puddling in your socks? And then again, courage could mean walking away from an argument instead of fighting.

Sometimes coaches give their teams pep talks to help them be strong and courageous. God gave Joshua a pep talk, too, before Joshua was about to lead the Israelites into enemy territory. (Check Joshua 1:5–9.) How can God's pep talk help you when you are not feeling especially courageous?

The king of Assyria made fun of King Hezekiah because of his faith in God. But God gave Hezekiah a message of courage and hope. (Read 2 Kings 19:4–10, p. 505.)

MORE FAITH links

What Will You Risk?, p. 278
Give In or Take a Stand?, p. 472
Standing for What's Right, p. 651
Who Ya' Gonna Call?, p. 711
Stand!, p. 1019

"Tagg, what's with the long, blue cape and the black mask?"

"Don't you know who I am? I'm Super Tagg—ready to stomp out any computer viruses that come my way!"

"That sounds pretty courageous, Tagg, but if you want to know about real courage, why don't you connect to these links?"

The Big Risk, Esther 4:11—5:2, p. 652

- What's the biggest risk you've ever taken? What happened when you took this risk?
- What are some risks you may have to take in life? Where will you find the courage to deal with them? Surf here to find out where Esther got her courage.

Your Feet on High Places, Habakkuk 3:18–19, p. 1239

- Are you like a mountain goat, unafraid and skipping along, no matter what? Link here to discover how to deal with the good and bad times in your life.

Be Brave!, Haggai 2:4, p. 1249

- What fears, if any, stop you from serving God? How do you handle fear of failure and discouragement? Find out how to trust God to help you be courageous and do whatever he has called you to do.

As Strong as Superman?, Philippians 4:13, p. 1615

- Do you ever worry about what you can't do? Find out how you can "do all things" by linking here.

my FAVORITE links

wives, children, and animals may stay
here, but your fighting men must dress for
war and cross the Jordan River ahead of
your brothers to help them. **15**The LORD
has given you a place to rest and will do
the same for your brothers. But you must
help them until they take the land the
LORD their God is giving them. Then you
may return to your own land east of the
Jordan River, the land that Moses, the servant of the LORD, gave you."

16Then the people answered Joshua,
"Anything you command us to do, we will
do. Any place you send us, we will go.
17Just as we fully obeyed Moses, we will
obey you. We ask only that the LORD your
God be with you just as he was with Moses. **18**Whoever refuses to obey your
commands or turns against you will be
put to death. Just be strong and brave!"

Spies Sent to Jericho

2 Joshua son of Nun secretly sent out
two spies from Acacia and said to
them, "Go and look at the land, particularly at the city of Jericho."

So the men went to Jericho and stayed
at the house of a prostitute named Rahab.

2Someone told the king of Jericho,
"Some men from Israel have come here
tonight to spy out the land."

3So the king of Jericho sent this message to Rahab: "Bring out the men who
came to you and entered your house.
They have come to spy out our whole
land."

4But the woman had hidden the two
men. She said, "They did come here, but I
didn't know where they came from. **5**In
the evening, when it was time to close the
city gate, they left. I don't know where
they went, but if you go quickly, maybe
you can catch them." **6**(The woman had
taken the men up to the roof* and had
hidden them there under stalks of flax
that she had spread out.) **7**So the king's
men went out looking for the spies on the
road that leads to the crossings of the Jordan River. The city gate was closed just
after the king's men left the city.

8Before the spies went to sleep for
the night, Rahab went up to the roof.
9She said to them, "I know the LORD has
given this land to your people. You fright-
en us very much. Everyone living in this
land is terribly afraid of you **10**because

FAITH links

WHAT WILL YOU RISK?

JOSHUA 2

Would you willingly risk going to jail or some other punishment in order to obey God? Rahab chose to hide two spies from Israel. The king of her city found out about the spies and wanted to capture them. But Rahab knew that God was with them. She disobeyed a command of the king in order to save the two men from Israel. Had she been caught, she would have been punished.

Obeying God takes courage. It takes a willingness to face the risks that come your way. What are you willing to risk to serve God?

Give In or Take a Stand?, 1 Kings 22:13–14, p. 472

A Message of Courage and Hope, 2 Kings 19:4–10, p. 505

Fear God or People?, Jeremiah 38:14–21, p. 1047

A Real Crowd-pleaser?, Micah 2:6–11, p. 1222

Be Brave!, Haggai 2:4, p. 1249

Facing Your Fears, Matthew 8:23–27, p. 1288

2:6 roof In Bible times houses were built with flat roofs. The roof was used for drying things such as flax and fruit. And it was used as an extra room, as a place for worship, and as a cool place to sleep in the summer.

we have heard how the LORD dried up the Red Sea when you came out of Egypt. We have heard how you destroyed Sihon and Og, two Amorite kings who lived east of the Jordan. **11**When we heard this, we were very frightened. Now our men are afraid to fight you because the LORD your God rules the heavens above and the earth below! **12**So now, promise me before the LORD that you will show kindness to my family just as I showed kindness to you. Give me some proof that you will do this. **13**Allow my father, mother, brothers, sisters, and all of their families to live. Save us from death."

eMAIL! FROM GOD **2:12**
Kindness
Show kindness to others.

14The men agreed and said, "It will be our lives for your lives if you don't tell anyone what we are doing. When the LORD gives us the land, we will be kind and true to you."

15The house Rahab lived in was built on the city wall, so she used a rope to let the men down through a window. **16**She said to them, "Go into the hills so the king's men will not find you. Hide there for three days. After the king's men return, you may go on your way."

17The men said to her, "You must do as we say. If not, we cannot be responsible for keeping this oath you have made us swear. **18**When we return to this land, you must tie this red rope in the window through which you let us down. Bring your father, mother, brothers, and all your family into your house. **19**If anyone leaves your house and is killed, it is his own fault. We cannot be responsible for him. If anyone in your house is hurt, we will be responsible. **20**But if you tell anyone about this, we will be free from the oath you made us swear."

21Rahab answered, "I agree to this." So she sent them away, and they left. Then she tied the red rope in the window.

22The men left and went into the hills where they stayed for three days. The king's men looked for them all along the road, but after three days, they returned to the city without finding them. **23**Then the two men started back. They left the hills and crossed the river and came to Joshua son of Nun and told him everything that had happened to them. **24**They said, "The LORD surely has given us all of the land. All the people in that land are terribly afraid of us."

Crossing the Jordan

3 Early the next morning Joshua and all the Israelites left Acacia. They traveled to the Jordan River and camped there before crossing it. **2**After three days the officers went through the camp **3**and gave orders to the people: "When you see the priests and Levites carrying the Ark of the Agreement with the LORD your God, leave where you are and follow it. **4**That way you will know which way to go since you have never been here before. But do not follow too closely. Stay about a thousand yards behind the Ark."

5Then Joshua told the people, "Make yourselves holy, because tomorrow the LORD will do amazing things among you."

6Joshua said to the priests, "Take the Ark of the Agreement and go ahead of the people." So the priests lifted the Ark and carried it ahead of the people.

7Then the LORD said to Joshua, "Today I will begin to make you great in the opinion of all the Israelites so the people will know I am with you just as I was with Moses. **8**Tell the priests who carry the Ark of the Agreement to go to the edge of the Jordan River and stand in the water."

9Then Joshua said to the Israelites, "Come here and listen to the words of the LORD your God. **10**Here is proof that the living God is with you and that he will force out the Canaanites, Hittites, Hivites, Perizzites, Girgashites, Amorites, and Jebusites. **11**The Ark of the Agreement with the Lord of the whole world will go ahead of you into the Jordan River. **12**Now choose twelve men from among you, one from each of the twelve tribes of Israel. **13**The priests will carry the Ark of the LORD, the Master of the whole world, into the

eMAIL! FROM GOD
3:9
Advice
Need advice? Here's the place to start.

Jordan ahead of you. When they step into
the water, it will stop. The river will stop
flowing and will stand up in a heap."
14So the people left the place where
they had camped, and they followed the
priests who carried the Ark of the Agreement across the Jordan River. 15During
harvest the Jordan overflows its banks.
When the priests carrying the Ark came
to the edge of the river and stepped into
the water, 16the water upstream stopped
flowing. It stood up in a heap a great distance away at Adam, a town near Zarethan. The water flowing down to the Sea
of Arabah (the Dead Sea) was completely
cut off. So the people crossed the river
near Jericho. 17The priests carried the
Ark of the Agreement with the LORD to
the middle of the river and stood there on
dry ground. They waited there while all
the people of Israel walked across the
Jordan River on dry land.

Rocks to Remind the People

4 After all the people had finished
crossing the Jordan, the LORD said to
Joshua, 2"Choose twelve men from
among the people, one from each tribe.
3Tell them to get twelve rocks from the
middle of the river, from where the priests
stood. Carry the rocks and put them down
where you stay tonight."
4So Joshua chose one man from each
tribe. Then he called the twelve men together 5and said to them, "Go out into
the river where the Ark of the LORD your
God is. Each of you bring back one rock,
one for each tribe of Israel, and carry it on
your shoulder. 6They will be a sign among
you. In the future your children will ask
you, 'What do these rocks mean?' 7Tell
them the water stopped flowing in the Jordan when the Ark of the Agreement with
the LORD crossed the river. These rocks
will always remind the Israelites of this."
8So the Israelites obeyed Joshua and
carried twelve rocks from the middle of
the Jordan River, one rock for each of the
twelve tribes of Israel, just as the LORD
had commanded Joshua. They carried the
rocks with them and put them down
where they made their camp. 9Joshua
also put twelve rocks in the middle of the

FAITH links

FAITH OF OUR FATHERS

JOSHUA 4:4-9

Whenever something special happens to a people, the story of that event is usually passed on from one generation to another. We know about the American Revolution because that story was passed down. The Israelites were about to cross the Jordan River and enter the land God promised to them. Joshua had them build a memorial out of stones. He knew how important it was to pass on the story of their journey to the children yet to come.

Stories of faith are important to pass on. They remind us of the ways that God helps people. If you think about it, ask your parents to tell you their faith story. They'll be glad that you asked.

Link here for other thoughts on sharing your faith:

Learning from Mistakes, Psalm 51:12–13, p. 748

A Picture of the Past, Psalm 105, p. 789

A Bad Reaction, Jeremiah 36, p. 1043

Pass It On!, Joel 1:2–3, p. 1187

Flex Your Faith, Acts 3:1–16, p. 1467

The Doubt Remover, Romans 10:8–10, p. 1533

Jordan River where the priests had stood while carrying the Ark of the Agreement. These rocks are still there today.

10The priests carrying the Ark continued standing in the middle of the river until everything was done that the LORD had commanded Joshua to tell the people, just as Moses had told Joshua. The people hurried across the river. **11**After they finished crossing the river, the priests carried the Ark of the LORD to the other side as the people watched. **12**The men from the tribes of Reuben, Gad, and East Manasseh obeyed what Moses had told them. They were dressed for war, and they crossed the river ahead of the other people. **13**About forty thousand soldiers prepared for war passed before the LORD as they marched across the river, going toward the plains of Jericho.

14That day the LORD made Joshua great in the opinion of all the Israelites. They respected Joshua all his life, just as they had respected Moses.

15Then the LORD said to Joshua, **16**"Command the priests to bring the Ark of the Agreement out of the river."

17So Joshua commanded the priests, "Come up out of the Jordan."

18Then the priests carried the Ark of the Agreement with the LORD out of the river. As soon as their feet touched dry land, the water began flowing again. The river again overflowed its banks, just as it had before they crossed.

19The people crossed the Jordan on the tenth day of the first month and camped at Gilgal, east of Jericho. **20**They carried with them the twelve rocks taken from the Jordan, and Joshua set them up at Gilgal. **21**Then he spoke to the Israelites: "In the future your children will ask you, 'What do these rocks mean?' **22**Tell them, 'Israel crossed the Jordan River on dry land. **23**The LORD your God caused the water to stop flowing until you finished crossing it, just as the LORD did to the Red Sea. He stopped the water until we crossed it. **24**The LORD did this so all people would know he has great power and so you would always respect the LORD your God.' "

eMAIL FROM GOD 4:24
God
Is God powerful?

5 All the kings of the Amorites west of the Jordan and the Canaanite kings living by the Mediterranean Sea heard that the LORD dried up the Jordan River until the Israelites had crossed it. After that they were scared and too afraid to face the Israelites.

The Israelites Are Circumcised

2At that time the LORD said to Joshua, "Make knives from flint stones and circumcise the Israelites." **3**So Joshua made knives from flint stones and circumcised the Israelites at Gibeath Haaraloth.

4This is why Joshua circumcised the men: After the Israelites left Egypt, all the men old enough to serve in the army died in the desert on the way out of Egypt. **5**The men who had come out of Egypt had been circumcised, but none of those who were born in the desert on the trip from Egypt had been circumcised. **6**The Israelites had moved about in the desert for forty years. During that time all the fighting men who had left Egypt had died because they had not obeyed the LORD. So the LORD swore they would not see the land he had promised their ancestors to give them, a fertile land. **7**Their sons took their places. But none of the sons born on the trip from Egypt had been circumcised, so Joshua circumcised them. **8**After all the Israelites had been circumcised, they stayed in camp until they were healed.

9Then the LORD said to Joshua, "As slaves in Egypt you were ashamed, but today I have removed that shame." So Joshua named that place Gilgal, which it is still named today.

10The people of Israel were camped at Gilgal on the plains of Jericho. It was there, on the evening of the fourteenth day of the month, they celebrated the Passover Feast. **11**The day after the Passover, the people ate food grown on that land: bread made without yeast and roasted grain. **12**The day they ate this food, the manna stopped coming. The Israelites no longer got the manna from

LET'S VISIT JERICHO

Joshua 5

The city of Jericho is an old, old city that was built just north of the Dead Sea. In the Old Testament when the Hebrews entered the Promised Land, Jericho was the first city they captured. They marched around the walls of Jericho for six days. On the seventh day, the walls of the city miraculously fell down when the priests blew their trumpets and the people shouted, and the Israelites took over the city. (Check out Joshua 6.)

In the New Testament, Jesus spent time in Jericho. This is where he told the story of the Good Samaritan. (Check out Luke 10:30–37, p. 1388.) It's also where he met blind Bartimaeus (Read Mark 10:46–52, p. 1348.) and Zacchaeus. (Look at Luke 19:1–10, p. 1406.)

Today Jericho is called er-Riha. It sits at the bottom of a deep gorge, like a canyon, and is a hot, tropical place.

heaven. They ate the food grown in the land of Canaan that year.

13Joshua was near Jericho when he looked up and saw a man standing in front of him with a sword in his hand. Joshua went to him and asked, "Are you a friend or an enemy?"

14The man answered, "I am neither. I have come as the commander of the LORD's army."

Then Joshua bowed facedown on the ground and asked, "Does my master have a command for me, his servant?"

15The commander of the LORD's army answered, "Take off your sandals, because the place where you are standing is holy." So Joshua did.

The Fall of Jericho

6 The people of Jericho were afraid because the Israelites were near. They closed the city gates and guarded them. No one went into the city, and no one came out.

2Then the LORD said to Joshua, "Look, I have given you Jericho, its king, and all its fighting men. **3**March around the city with your army once a day for six days. **4**Have seven priests carry trumpets made from horns of male sheep and have them march in front of the Ark. On the seventh day march around the city seven times and have the priests blow the trumpets as they march. **5**They will make one long blast on the trumpets. When you hear that sound, have all the people give a loud shout. Then the walls of the city will fall so the people can go straight into the city."

6So Joshua son of Nun called the priests together and said to them, "Carry the Ark of the Agreement. Tell seven priests to carry trumpets and march in front of it." **7**Then Joshua ordered the people, "Now go! March around the city. The soldiers with weapons should march in front of the Ark of the Agreement with the LORD."

8When Joshua finished speaking to the people, the seven priests began marching before the LORD. They carried the seven trumpets and blew them as they marched. The priests carrying the Ark of the Agreement with the LORD followed them. **9**Soldiers with weapons marched in front of the priests, and armed men walked behind the Ark. The priests were blowing their trumpets. **10**But Joshua had told the people not to give a war cry. He said, "Don't shout. Don't say a word until the day I tell you. Then shout." **11**So Joshua had the Ark of the LORD carried around the city one time. Then they went back to camp for the night.

FAITH links

FACTS ABOUT FOLLOWING

JOSHUA 6

What are the weirdest instructions you ever had to follow? More than likely those instructions didn't involve walking around a city once a day for six days and seven times on the seventh day. Yet those were the instructions the people of Israel had to follow for taking over the city of Jericho! They had to listen carefully and do exactly what God told them. Otherwise, nothing would happen. Because of their obedience, the wall around the city of Jericho fell.

God expects you to listen carefully to his instructions. Listening is the first step to obedience.

Help to Understand, 2 Samuel 14, p. 416

A Look for the Book, 2 Chronicles 34:14–18, p. 603

If You Want My Advice . . . , Proverbs 13:1, p. 843

Like a Tree, Jeremiah 17:5–8, p. 1016

Going My Way?, Hosea 8:1–6, p. 1179

Two Ways to Grow, Luke 2:46–52, p. 1370

12Early the next morning Joshua got up, and the priests carried the Ark of the LORD again. **13**The seven priests carried the seven trumpets and marched in front of the Ark of the LORD, blowing their trumpets. Soldiers with weapons marched in front of them, and other soldiers walked behind the Ark of the LORD. All this time the priests were blowing their trumpets. **14**So on the second day they marched around the city one time and then went back to camp. They did this every day for six days.

15On the seventh day they got up at dawn and marched around the city, just as they had on the days before. But on that day they marched around the city seven times. **16**The seventh time around the priests blew their trumpets. Then Joshua gave the command: "Now, shout! The LORD has given you this city! **17**The city and everything in it are to be destroyed as an offering to the LORD. Only Rahab the prostitute and everyone in her house should remain alive. They must not be killed, because Rahab hid the two spies we sent out. **18**Don't take any of the things that are to be destroyed as an offering to the LORD. If you take them and bring them into our camp, you yourselves will be destroyed, and you will bring trouble to all of Israel. **19**All the silver and gold and things made from bronze and iron belong to the LORD and must be saved for him."

20When the priests blew the trumpets, the people shouted. At the sound of the trumpets and the people's shout, the walls fell, and everyone ran straight into the city. So the Israelites defeated that city. **21**They completely destroyed with the sword every living thing in the city—men and women, young and old, cattle, sheep, and donkeys.

22Joshua said to the two men who had spied out the land, "Go into the prostitute's house. Bring her out and bring out those who are with her, because of the promise you made to her." **23**So the two men went into the house and brought out Rahab, her father, mother, brothers, and all those with her. They put all of her family in a safe place outside the camp of Israel.

24Then Israel burned the whole city and everything in it, but they did not burn the things made from silver, gold, bronze,

and iron. These were saved for the LORD.
25Joshua saved Rahab the prostitute, her
family, and all who were with her, because Rahab had helped the men he had
sent to spy out Jericho. Rahab still lives
among the Israelites today.
26Then Joshua made this oath:

"Anyone who tries to rebuild this city
of Jericho
will be cursed by the LORD.
The one who lays the foundation of
this city
will lose his oldest son,
and the one who sets up the gates
will lose his youngest son."

eMAIL! FROM GOD
6:27
Success
Who gives you success?

27So the LORD
was with Joshua,
and Joshua became
famous through all
the land.

The Sin of Achan

7 But the Israelites did not obey the
LORD. There was a man from the tribe
of Judah named Achan. (He was the son of
Carmi and grandson of Zabdi, who was
the son of Zerah.) Because Achan kept
some of the things that were to be given
to the LORD, the LORD became very angry at the Israelites.
2Joshua sent some men from Jericho
to Ai, which was near Beth Aven, east
of Bethel. He told them, "Go to Ai and
spy out the area." So the men went to spy
on Ai.
3Later they came back to Joshua and
said, "There are only a few people in Ai,
so we will not need all our people to defeat them. Send only two or three thousand men to fight. There is no need to
send all of our people." 4So about three
thousand men went up to Ai, but the people of Ai beat them badly. 5The people of
Ai killed about thirty-six Israelites and
then chased the rest from the city gate all
the way down to the canyon, killing them
as they went down the hill. When the Israelites saw this, they lost their courage.
6Then Joshua tore his clothes in sorrow. He bowed facedown on the ground
before the Ark of the LORD and stayed
there until evening. The leaders of Israel
did the same thing. They also threw dirt
on their heads to show their sorrow.
7Then Joshua said, "Lord GOD, you
brought our people across the Jordan
River. Why did you bring us this far and
then let the Amorites destroy us? We
would have been happy to stay on the
other side of the Jordan. 8Lord, there is
nothing I can say now. Israel has been
beaten by the enemy. 9The Canaanites
and all the other people in this country
will hear about this and will surround and
kill us all! Then what will you do for your
own great name?"
10The LORD said to Joshua, "Stand
up! Why are you down on your face?
11The Israelites have sinned; they have
broken the agreement I commanded
them to obey. They took some of the
things I commanded them to destroy.
They have stolen and lied and have taken
those things for themselves. 12That is
why the Israelites cannot face their enemies. They turn away from the fight and
run, because I have commanded that
they be destroyed. I will not help you
anymore unless you destroy everything
as I commanded you.
13"Now go! Make the people holy.
Tell them, 'Set yourselves apart to the
LORD for tomorrow. The LORD, the God
of Israel, says some of you are keeping
things he commanded you to destroy. You
will never defeat your enemies until you
throw away those things.
14" 'Tomorrow morning you must be
present with your tribes. The LORD will
choose one tribe to stand alone before
him. Then the LORD will choose one family group from that tribe to stand before
him. Then the LORD will choose one family from that family group to stand before
him, person by person. 15The one who is
keeping what should have been destroyed will himself be destroyed by fire.
Everything he owns will be destroyed
with him. He has broken the agreement
with the LORD and has done a disgraceful
thing among the people of Israel!' "
16Early the next morning Joshua led
all of Israel to present themselves in their
tribes, and the LORD chose the tribe of Judah. 17So the family groups of Judah pre-

A HIDDEN SIN

JOSHUA 7

Ever hear the expression, "You can run, but you can't hide"? That means you'll be found out, no matter what you do. Many people think they can do something wrong and never be found out. That's what Achan believed. He stole some items from the ruins of the city of Jericho despite strict instructions from God not to take anything. He tried to hide what he did, but God found out anyway.

Sin can never be hidden from God. He sees everything, because he is everywhere. We may fool others, but we can never fool God. Don't be an Achan or you'll be achin' spiritually. You can run, but you can't hide.

Here's some more advice on what to do with your sin.

A Priest Without Sin, Leviticus 4:3–7, p. 136

When the Green-eyed Monster Strikes, 1 Samuel 18:6–9, p. 379

This Hurts Me More?, 2 Chronicles 36:17–22, p. 606

A Swarm of Trouble, Joel 2:25–27, p. 1190

The Choices of a Choice, Luke 5:1–11, p. 1375

The Sin "Braker," Jude 24–25, p. 1727

sented themselves, and the LORD then
chose the family group of Zerah. When all
the families of Zerah presented themselves, the family of Zabdi was chosen.
18And Joshua told all the men in that
family to present themselves. The LORD
chose Achan son of Carmi. (Carmi was the
son of Zabdi, who was the son of Zerah.)
19Then Joshua said to Achan, "My
son, tell the truth. Confess to the LORD,
the God of Israel. Tell me what you did,
and don't try to hide anything from me."
20Achan answered, "It is true! I have
sinned against the LORD, the God of Israel. This is what I did: 21Among the
things I saw was a beautiful coat from
Babylonia and about five pounds of silver
and more than one and one-fourth pounds
of gold. I wanted these things very much
for myself, so I took them. You will find
them buried in the ground under my tent,
with the silver underneath."
22So Joshua sent men who ran to the
tent and found the things hidden there,
with the silver. 23The men brought them
out of the tent, took them to Joshua and
all the Israelites, and spread them out on
the ground before the LORD. 24Then
Joshua and all the people led Achan son of
Zerah to the Valley of Trouble. They also
took the silver, the coat, the gold,
Achan's sons, daughters, cattle, donkeys,
sheep, tent, and everything he owned.
25Joshua said, "I don't know why you
caused so much trouble for us, but now
the LORD will bring trouble to you." Then
all the people threw stones at Achan and
his family until they died. Then the people burned them. 26They piled rocks
over Achan's body, and they are still
there today. That is why it is called the
Valley of Trouble. After this the LORD
was no longer angry.

Ai Is Destroyed

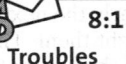

EMAIL! FROM GOD **8:1 Troubles** Who cheers you on to win victories?

8 Then the LORD
said to Joshua,
"Don't be afraid or
give up. Lead all your
fighting men to Ai. I will help you defeat
the king of Ai, his people, his city, and his
land. 2You will do to Ai and its king what
you did to Jericho and its king. Only this

time you may take all the wealth and
keep it for yourselves. Now tell some of
your soldiers to set up an ambush behind
the city."

3So Joshua led his whole army toward
Ai. Then he chose thirty thousand of his
best fighting men and sent them out at
night. **4**Joshua gave them these orders:
"Listen carefully. You must set up an ambush behind the city. Don't go far from it,
but continue to watch and be ready. **5**I and
the men who are with me will march toward the city, and the men in the city will
come out to fight us, just as they did
before. Then we will turn and run away
from them. **6**They will chase us away
from the city, thinking we are running
away from them as we did before. When
we run away, **7**come out from your ambush and take the city. The LORD your
God will give you the power to win. **8**After you take the city, burn it. See to it!
You have your orders."

9Then Joshua sent them to wait in
ambush between Bethel and Ai, to the
west of Ai. But Joshua stayed the night
with his people.

10Early the next morning Joshua
gathered his men together. He and the
older leaders of Israel led them up to Ai.
11All of the soldiers who were with
Joshua marched up to Ai and stopped in
front of the city and made camp north of
it. There was a valley between them and
the city. **12**Then Joshua chose about five
thousand men and set them in ambush in
the area west of the city between Bethel
and Ai. **13**So the people took their positions; the main camp was north of the
city, and the other men were hiding to the
west. That night Joshua went down into
the valley.

14Now when the king of Ai saw the
army of Israel, he and his people got up
early the next morning and hurried out to
fight them. They went out to a place east
of the city, but the king did not know soldiers were waiting in ambush behind the
city. **15**Joshua and all the men of Israel let
the army of Ai push them back. Then
they ran toward the desert. **16**The men in
Ai were called to chase Joshua and his
men, so they left the city and went after
them. **17**All the men of Ai and Bethel
chased the army of Israel. The city was
left open; not a man stayed to protect it.

18Then the LORD said to Joshua,
"Hold your spear toward Ai, because I
will give you that city." So Joshua held his
spear toward the city of Ai. **19**When the
Israelites who were in ambush saw this,
they quickly came out of their hiding
place and hurried toward the city. They
entered the city, took control of it, and
quickly set it on fire.

20When the men of Ai looked back,
they saw smoke rising from their city. At
the same time the Israelites stopped running and turned against the men of Ai,
who could not escape in any direction.
21When Joshua and all his men saw that
the army had taken control of the city and
saw the smoke rising from it, they
stopped running and turned to fight the
men of Ai. **22**The men who were in ambush also came out of the city to help
with the fight. So the men of Ai were
caught between the armies of Israel.
None of the enemy escaped. The Israelites fought until not one of the men of Ai
was left alive, except **23**the king of Ai,
and they brought him to Joshua.

A Review of the Fighting

24During the fighting the army of
Israel chased the men of Ai into the fields
and desert and killed all of them. Then
they went back to Ai and killed everyone
there. **25**All the people of Ai died that
day, twelve thousand men and women.
26Joshua had held his spear toward Ai, as
a sign to destroy the city, and did not draw
it back until all the people of Ai were destroyed. **27**The people of Israel kept for
themselves the animals and the other
things the people of Ai had owned, as the
LORD had commanded Joshua to do.

28Then Joshua burned the city of Ai
and made it a pile of ruins. And it is still
like that today. **29**Joshua hanged the king
of Ai on a tree and left him there until
evening. At sunset Joshua told his men to
take the king's body down from the tree
and to throw it down at the city gate.
Then they covered it with a pile of rocks,
which is still there today.

30Joshua built an altar for the LORD,
the God of Israel, on Mount Ebal, as
31Moses, the LORD's servant, had commanded. Joshua built the altar as it was
explained in the Book of the Teachings of
Moses. It was made from uncut stones;
no tool was ever used on them. On that
altar the Israelites offered burnt offerings
to the LORD and fellowship offerings.
32There Joshua wrote the teachings of
Moses on stones for all the people of Israel to see. 33The older leaders, officers,
judges, and all the Israelites were there;
Israelites and non-Israelites were all
standing around the Ark of the Agreement
with the LORD in front of the priests, the
Levites who had carried the Ark. Half of
the people stood in front of Mount Ebal,
and half stood in front of Mount Gerizim.
This was the way the LORD's servant Moses had earlier commanded the people to
be blessed.
34Then Joshua read all the words of
the teachings, the blessings and the
curses, exactly as they were written in
the Book of the Teachings. 35All the Israelites were gathered together—men,
women, and children—along with the
non-Israelites who lived among them.
Joshua read every command that Moses
had given.

The Gibeonite Trickery

9 All the kings west of the Jordan River
heard about these things: the kings of
the Hittites, Amorites, Canaanites, Perizzites, Hivites, and Jebusites. They lived
in the mountains and on the western hills
and along the whole Mediterranean Sea
coast. 2So all these kings gathered to
fight Joshua and the Israelites.
3When the people of Gibeon heard
how Joshua had defeated Jericho and Ai,
4they decided to trick the Israelites.
They gathered old sacks and old leather
wine bags that were cracked and mended,
and they put them on the backs of their
donkeys. 5They put old sandals on their
feet and wore old clothes, and they took
some dry, moldy bread. 6Then they went
to Joshua in the camp near Gilgal.
The men said to Joshua and the

FAITH links

WHO DO YOU TRUST? 

JOSHUA 9

Do you know when someone is trying to trick you? The Israelites would have to answer no to that question. The people of Gibeon tricked them into believing that they lived far away. But they really lived nearby. God had told Israel not to make a treaty with the people in Canaan. But the Israelites made an agreement with the people of Gibeon before they realized that they had been tricked.

We need God's wisdom to know when to trust and when not to. When in doubt about who to trust, here's a simple rule to remember. *Always* trust God. When you do that, you've already begun to be wise.

Surf here for some more thoughts on being a wise guy—or girl!

From Zero to Hero, Judges 6; 7, p. 319

An Admirable Quality, 1 Kings 10:1–13, p. 451

Wisdom in Store, Proverbs 2:6–7, p. 828

Down on Discipline?, Proverbs 29:15, p. 867

Small Beginnings, Zechariah 4:10, p. 1255

The Winner's Crown, 1 Corinthians 9:24–27, p. 1555

Israelites, "We have traveled from a faraway country. Make a peace agreement
with us."
7The Israelites said to these Hivites,
"Maybe you live near us. How can we
make a peace agreement with you?"
8The Hivites said to Joshua, "We are
your servants."
But Joshua asked, "Who are you?
Where do you come from?"
9The men answered, "We are your
servants who have come from a far country, because we heard of the fame of the
LORD your God. We heard about what he
has done and everything he did in Egypt.
10We heard that he defeated the two
kings of the Amorites from the east side
of the Jordan River—Sihon king of Heshbon and Og king of Bashan who ruled in
Ashtaroth. **11**So our older leaders and
our people said to us, 'Take food for your
journey and go and meet the Israelites.
Tell them, "We are your servants. Make a
peace agreement with us."'
12"Look at our bread. On the day we
left home to come to you it was warm and
fresh, but now it is dry and moldy. **13**Look
at our leather wine bags. They were new
and filled with wine, but now they are
cracked and old. Our clothes and sandals
are worn out from the long journey."
14The men of Israel tasted the bread,
but they did not ask the LORD what to do.
15So Joshua agreed to make peace with
the Gibeonites and to let them live. And
the leaders of the Israelites swore an
oath to keep the agreement.
16Three days after they had made the
agreement, the Israelites learned that
the Gibeonites lived nearby. **17**So the Israelites went to where they lived and on
the third day came to their cities: Gibeon,
Kephirah, Beeroth, and Kiriath Jearim.
18But the Israelites did not attack those
cities, because they had made a promise
to them before the LORD, the God of Israel.
All the Israelites grumbled against
the leaders. **19**But the leaders answered,
"We have given our promise before the
LORD, the God of Israel, so we cannot attack them now. **20**This is what we must
do. We must let them live. Otherwise,
God's anger will be against us for breaking the oath we swore to them. **21**So let
them live, but they will cut wood and
carry water for our people." So the leaders kept their promise to them.
22Joshua called for the Gibeonites and
asked, "Why did you lie to us? Your land
was near our camp, but you told us you
were from a far country. **23**Now, you will
be placed under a curse to be our slaves.
You will have to cut wood and carry water
for the house of my God."
24The Gibeonites answered Joshua,
"We lied to you because we were afraid
you would kill us. We heard that the
LORD your God commanded his servant
Moses to give you all of this land and to
kill all the people who lived in it. That is
why we did this. **25**Now you can decide
what to do with us, whatever you think is
right."
26So Joshua saved their lives by not
allowing the Israelites to kill them, **27**but
he made the Gibeonites slaves. They cut
wood and carried water for the Israelites,
and they did it for the altar of the LORD—
wherever he chose it to be. They are still
doing this today.

The Sun Stands Still

10 At this time Adoni-Zedek king of
Jerusalem heard that Joshua had
defeated Ai and completely destroyed it,
as he had also done to Jericho and its king.
The king also learned that the Gibeonites
had made a peace agreement with Israel
and that they lived nearby. **2**Adoni-Zedek
and his people were very afraid because of
this. Gibeon was not a little town like Ai; it
was a large city, as big as a city that had a
king, and all its men were good fighters.
3So Adoni-Zedek king of Jerusalem sent a
message to Hoham king of Hebron, Piram
king of Jarmuth, Japhia king of Lachish,
and Debir king of Eglon. He begged them,
4"Come with me and help me attack Gibeon, which has made a peace agreement
with Joshua and the Israelites."
5Then these five Amorite kings—the
kings of Jerusalem, Hebron, Jarmuth, Lachish, and Eglon—gathered their armies,
went to Gibeon, surrounded it, and attacked it.

THE GOD OF BIG THINGS

JOSHUA 10

Have you ever read a tall tale? Tall tales are fiction stories about people who did amazing things. The stories of Pecos Bill and Johnny Appleseed are tall tales. Sometimes they were able to control the weather. We know that story isn't true! One of the most amazing things that ever happened did not take place in a fiction story. It happened in real life! God made the sun stand still during one of Israel's battles. Only God can control the forces of nature. Since he can do that, we can trust that God can do anything.

From Hopeless to Hopeful, Exodus 6:9, p. 83

How God Speaks, Job 33:14–17, p. 696

In Deep Water, Psalm 69, p. 760

Believe the Impossible?, Ezekiel 37, p. 1131

A Safe Place, Nahum 1:7, p. 1231

Go for It!, Hebrews 12:1–4, p. 1682

6The Gibeonites sent this message to
Joshua in his camp at Gilgal: "Don't let
us, your servants, be destroyed. Come
quickly and help us! Save us! All the Amorite kings from the mountains have
joined their armies and are fighting
against us."
7So Joshua marched out of Gilgal with
his whole army, including his best fighting men. **8**The LORD said to Joshua,
"Don't be afraid of those armies, because
I will hand them over to you. None of
them will be able to stand against you."
9Joshua and his army marched all
night from Gilgal for a surprise attack.
10The LORD confused those armies
when Israel attacked, so Israel defeated
them in a great victory at Gibeon. They
chased them along the road going up to
Beth Horon and killed men all the way to
Azekah and Makkedah. **11**As they chased
the enemy down the Beth Horon Pass to
Azekah, the LORD threw large hailstones
on them from the sky and killed them.
More people were killed by the hailstones than by the Israelites' swords.
12On the day that the LORD gave up
the Amorites to the Israelites, Joshua
stood before all the people of Israel and
said to the LORD:

"Sun, stand still over Gibeon.
Moon, stand still over the Valley of
Aijalon."
13So the sun stood still,
and the moon stopped
until the people defeated their
enemies.

These words are written in the Book of
Jashar.
The sun stopped in the middle of the
sky and waited to go down for a full day.
14That has never happened at any time
before that day or since. That was the day
the LORD listened to a human being.
Truly the LORD was fighting for Israel!
15After this, Joshua and his army
went back to the camp at Gilgal.
16During the fight the five kings ran
away and hid in a cave near Makkedah,
17but someone found them hiding in the
cave at Makkedah and told Joshua. **18**So
he said, "Cover the opening of the cave
with large rocks. Put some men there to
guard it, **19**but don't stay there yourselves. Continue chasing the enemy and
attacking them from behind. Don't let
them get to their cities, because the LORD
your God will hand them over to you."
20So Joshua and the Israelites killed
the enemy, but a few were able to get back
to their strong, walled cities. **21**After the

fighting, Joshua's men came back safely
to him at Makkedah. No one was brave
enough to say a word against the Israelites.

22Joshua said, "Move the rocks that
are covering the opening of the cave and
bring those five kings out to me." **23**So
Joshua's men brought the five kings out
of the cave—the kings of Jerusalem, Hebron, Jarmuth, Lachish, and Eglon.
24When they brought the five kings out
to Joshua, he called for all his men. He
said to the commanders of his army,
"Come here! Put your feet on the necks
of these kings." So
they came close and
put their feet on
their necks.

EMAIL FROM GOD
10:25
Enemies
Who can defeat your enemies?

25Joshua said to
his men, "Be strong
and brave! Don't be
afraid, because I will show you what the
LORD will do to the enemies you will fight
in the future." **26**Then Joshua killed the
five kings and hung their bodies on five
trees, where he left them until evening.

27At sunset Joshua told his men to
take the bodies down from the trees.
Then they threw them into the same
cave where they had been hiding and covered the opening of the cave with large
rocks, which are still there today.

28That day Joshua defeated Makkedah. He killed the king and completely
destroyed all the people in that city as an
offering to the LORD; no one was left
alive. He did the same thing to the king of
Makkedah that he had done to the king of
Jericho.

Defeating Southern Cities

29Joshua and all the Israelites traveled from Makkedah to Libnah and attacked it. **30**The LORD handed over the
city and its king. They killed every person in the city; no one was left alive. And
they did the same thing to that king that
they had done to the king of Jericho.

31Then Joshua and all the Israelites
left Libnah and went to Lachish, which
they surrounded and attacked. **32**The
LORD handed over Lachish on the second
day. The Israelites killed everyone in that
city just as they had done to Libnah.
33During this same time Horam king of
Gezer came to help Lachish, but Joshua
also defeated him and his army; no one
was left alive.

34Then Joshua and all the Israelites
went from Lachish to Eglon. They surrounded Eglon, attacked it, and **35**captured it the same day. They killed all its
people and completely destroyed everything in it as an offering to the LORD, just
as they had done to Lachish.

36Then Joshua and the Israelites
went from Eglon to Hebron and attacked
it, **37**capturing it and all the little towns
near it. The Israelites killed everyone in
Hebron; no one was left alive there. Just
as they had done to Eglon, they completely destroyed the city and all its people as an offering to the LORD.

38Then Joshua and the Israelites
went back to Debir and attacked it.
39They captured that city, its king, and all
the little towns near it, completely destroying everyone in Debir as an offering
to the LORD; no one was left alive there.
Israel did to Debir and its king just as
they had done to Libnah and its king, just
as they had done to Hebron.

40So Joshua defeated all the kings of
the cities of these areas: the mountains,
southern Canaan, the western hills, and
the slopes. The LORD, the God of Israel,
had told Joshua to completely destroy all
the people as an offering to the LORD, so
he left no one alive in those places.
41Joshua captured all the cities from Kadesh Barnea to Gaza, and from Goshen to
Gibeon. **42**He captured all these cities
and their kings on one trip, because the
LORD, the God of Israel, was fighting for
Israel.

43Then Joshua and all the Israelites
returned to their camp at Gilgal.

Defeating Northern Kings

11 When Jabin king of Hazor heard
about all that had happened, he
sent messages to Jobab king of Madon, to
the king of Shimron, and to the king of
Acshaph. **2**He sent messages to the kings
in the northern mountains and also to the

CLAIMING THE PROMISED LAND

Joshua 11

Under Joshua's leadership, the Israelites were able to enter Canaan and defeat the people living there. It took Joshua and the Israelites about seven years to conquer the many kings and armies in the land. Here are some highlights of those important battles:

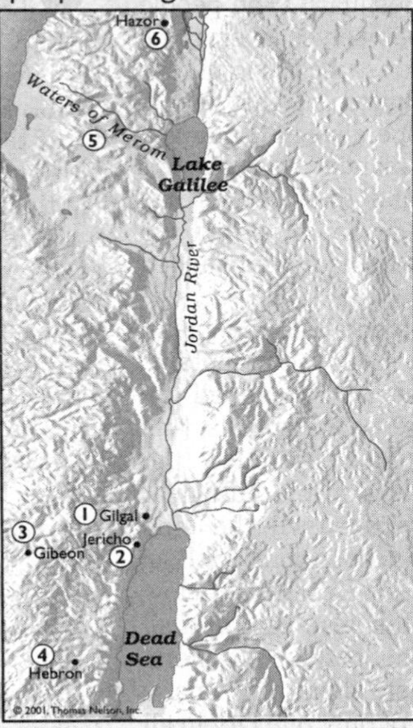

1. Under Joshua's military plan, the Israelites set up their main camp in the central part of Canaan at Gilgal. Joshua launched all his battles from there. (Read Joshua 4:19.)

2. In his first victory, Joshua and the Israelites conquered Jericho. The city walls toppled over when the Israelites shouted and blew their trumpets. (Check out Joshua 6.)

3. At Gibeon, the Israelites completed their conquest of the central part of Canaan when they defeated five Canaanite kings. God made the sun stand still until all Israel's enemies were defeated. (Look up Joshua 10:1–14.)

4. Joshua then turned south. He defeated and destroyed the cities of Lachish, Eglon, Hebron, and Debir. (Read Joshua 10:29–43.)

5. Next Joshua headed north. He defeated three northern kings and their armies at the waters of Merom. (See Joshua 11:11–9.)

6. Joshua's last battle was an important one. His army destroyed and burned Hazor, a strong Canaanite fort. With that victory, Joshua and his army controlled all the area of Canaan. (Look up Joshua 11:10–16.)

kings in the Jordan Valley south of Lake
Galilee and in the western hills. He sent
a message to the king of Naphoth Dor in
the west 3and to the kings of the Canaanites in the east and in the west. He sent
messages to the Amorites, Hittites, Perizzites, and Jebusites in the mountains.
Jabin also sent one to the Hivites, who
lived below Mount Hermon in the area of
Mizpah. 4So the armies of all these kings
came together with their horses and
chariots. There were as many soldiers as
grains of sand on the seashore.

5All of these kings met together at
the waters of Merom, joined their armies
together into one camp, and made plans
to fight against the Israelites.

6Then the LORD said to Joshua, "Don't
be afraid of them, because at this time tomorrow I will give them to you. You will
cripple their horses and burn all their
chariots."

7So Joshua and his whole army surprised the enemy by attacking them at
the waters of Merom. 8The LORD handed
them over to Israel. They chased them to
Greater Sidon, Misrephoth Maim, and
the Valley of Mizpah in the east. Israel
fought until none of the enemy was left
alive. 9Joshua did what the LORD said to
do; he crippled their horses and burned
their chariots.

10Then Joshua went back and captured the city of Hazor and killed its king.
(Hazor had been the leader of all the kingdoms that fought against Israel.) 11Israel

killed everyone in Hazor, completely destroying them; no one was left alive. Then
they burned Hazor itself.
12Joshua captured all of these cities,
killed all of their kings, and completely
destroyed everything in these cities. He
did this just as Moses, the servant of the
LORD, had commanded. **13**But the Israelites did not burn any cities that were built
on their mounds, except Hazor; only that
city was burned by Joshua. **14**The people
of Israel kept for themselves everything
they found in the cities, including all the
animals. But they killed all the people
there; they left no one alive. **15**Long ago
the LORD had commanded his servant
Moses to do this, and then Moses had
commanded Joshua to do it. Joshua did
everything the LORD had commanded
Moses.
16So Joshua defeated all the people in
the land. He had control of the mountains
and the area of southern Canaan, all the
areas of Goshen, the western hills, and
the Jordan Valley. He controlled the
mountains of Israel and all the hills near
them. **17**Joshua controlled all the land
from Mount Halak near Edom to Baal
Gad in the Valley of Lebanon, below
Mount Hermon. Joshua also captured all
the kings in the land and killed them.
18He fought against them for many
years. **19**The people of only one city in all
the land had made a peace agreement
with Israel—the Hivites living in Gibeon.
All the other cities were defeated in war.
20The LORD made those people stubborn
so they would fight against Israel and he
could completely destroy them without
mercy. This is what the LORD had commanded Moses to do.
21Now Joshua fought the Anakites
who lived in the mountains of Hebron,
Debir, Anab, Judah, and Israel, and he
completely destroyed them and their
towns. **22**There were no Anakites left
living in the land of the Israelites and
only a few were left in Gaza, Gath, and
Ashdod. **23**Joshua took control of all the
land of Israel as the LORD had told Moses
to do long ago. He gave the land to Israel,
because he had promised it to them.
Then Joshua divided the land among the
tribes of Israel, and there was peace in
the land.

Kings Defeated by Israel

12 The Israelites took control of the
land east of the Jordan River from
the Arnon Ravine to Mount Hermon and
all the land along the eastern side of the
Jordan Valley. These lands belonged to
the kings whom the Israelites defeated.
2Sihon king of the Amorites lived in
the city of Heshbon and ruled the land
from Aroer at the Arnon Ravine to the
Jabbok River. His land started in the middle of the ravine, which was their border
with the Ammonites. Sihon ruled over
half the land of Gilead **3**and over the eastern side of the Jordan Valley from Lake
Galilee to the Dead Sea. And he ruled
from Beth Jeshimoth south to the slopes
of Pisgah.
4Og king of Bashan was one of the last
of the Rephaites. He ruled the land in
Ashtaroth and Edrei. **5**He ruled over
Mount Hermon, Salecah, and all the area
of Bashan up to where the people of Geshur and Maacah lived. Og also ruled half
the land of Gilead up to the border of Sihon king of Heshbon.
6The LORD's servant Moses and the
Israelites defeated all these kings, and
Moses gave that land to the tribes of
Reuben and Gad and to East Manasseh as
their own.
7Joshua and the Israelites also defeated kings in the land west of the Jordan River. He gave the people the land
and divided it among the twelve tribes to
be their own. It was between Baal Gad in
the Valley of Lebanon and Mount Halak
near Edom. **8**This included the mountains, the western hills, the Jordan Valley,
the slopes, the desert, and southern Canaan. This was the land where the Hittites, Amorites, Canaanites, Perizzites,
Hivites, and Jebusites had lived. The Israelites defeated the king of each of the following cities: **9**Jericho, Ai (near Bethel),
10Jerusalem, Hebron, **11**Jarmuth, Lachish, **12**Eglon, Gezer, **13**Debir, Geder,
14Hormah, Arad, **15**Libnah, Adullam,
16Makkedah, Bethel, **17**Tappuah, Hepher,
18Aphek, Lasharon, **19**Madon, Hazor,

20Shimron Meron, Acshaph, **21**Taanach,
Megiddo, **22**Kedesh, Jokneam in Carmel,
23Dor (in Naphoth Dor), Goyim in Gilgal,
and **24**Tirzah.

The total number of kings was thirty-
one.

Land Still to Be Taken

13 When Joshua was very old, the
LORD said to him, "Joshua, you
have grown old, but there is still much
land for you to take. **2**This is what is left:
the regions of Geshur and of the Philistines; **3**the area from the Shihor River at
the border of Egypt to Ekron in the north,
which belongs to the Canaanites; the five
Philistine leaders at Gaza, Ashdod, Ashkelon, Gath, and Ekron; the Avvites, **4**who
live south of the Canaan-
ite land; **5**the Gebalites,
and the area of Lebanon
east of Baal Gad below
Mount Hermon to Lebo
Hamath.

6"The Sidonians are
living in the hill country
from Lebanon to Misre-
photh Maim, but I will
force all of them out ahead
of the Israelites. Be sure
to remember this land when you divide
the land among the Israelites, as I told
you.

7"Now divide the land among the nine
tribes and West Manasseh."

Now divide the land among the nine tribes and West Manasseh.
—Joshua 13:7

Dividing the Land

8East Manasseh and the tribes of
Reuben and Gad had received their land.
The LORD's servant Moses had given
them the land east of the Jordan River.
9Their land started at Aroer at the Arnon
Ravine and continued to the town in the
middle of the ravine, and it included the
whole plain from Medeba to Dibon. **10**All
the towns ruled by Sihon king of the Amorites, who ruled in the city of Heshbon,
were in that land. The land continued to
the area where the Ammonites lived.
11Gilead was also there, as well as the
area where the people of Geshur and Maacah lived, and all of Mount Hermon and
Bashan as far as Salecah. **12**All the kingdom of Og king of Bashan was in the land.
Og was one of the last of the Rephaites,
and in the past he ruled in Ashtaroth and
Edrei. Moses had defeated them and had
taken their land. **13**Because the Israelites did not force out the people of Geshur and Maacah, they still live among
the Israelites today.

14The tribe of Levi was the only one
that did not get any land. Instead, they
were given all the burned sacrifices made
to the LORD, the God of Israel, as he had
promised them.

15Moses had given each family group
from the tribe of Reuben some land:
16Theirs was the land from Aroer near
the Arnon Ravine to the town of Medeba,
including the whole plain and the town in
the middle of the ravine;
17Heshbon and all the
towns on the plain: Dibon,
Bamoth Baal, and Beth
Baal Meon, **18**Jahaz, Kedemoth, Mephaath, **19**Kiriathaim, Sibmah, Zereth
Shahar on the hill in the
valley, **20**Beth Peor, the
hills of Pisgah, and Beth
Jeshimoth. **21**So that land
included all the towns on
the plain and all the area that Sihon king of
the Amorites had ruled from the town of
Heshbon. Moses had defeated him along
with the leaders of the Midianites, including Evi, Rekem, Zur, Hur, and Reba. All
these leaders fought together with Sihon
and lived in that country. **22**The Israelites
killed many people during the fighting, including Balaam of Beor, who tried to use
magic to tell the future. **23**The land given
to Reuben stopped at the shore of the Jordan River. So the land given to the family
groups of Reuben included all these towns
and their villages that were listed.

24This is the land Moses gave to the
tribe of Gad, to all its family groups:
25the land of Jazer and all the towns of
Gilead; half the land of the Ammonites
that went as far as Aroer near Rabbah;
26the area from Heshbon to Ramath Mizpah and Betonim; the area from Mahanaim to the land of Debir; **27**in the valley,
Beth Haram, Beth Nimrah, Succoth, and

Zaphon, the other land Sihon king of
Heshbon had ruled east of the Jordan
River and continuing to the end of Lake
Galilee. **28**All this land went to the family
groups of Gad, including all these towns
and their villages.

29This is the land Moses had given to
East Manasseh. Half of all the family
groups in the tribe of Manasseh were
given this land: **30**The land started at
Mahanaim and included all of Bashan and
the land ruled by Og king of Bashan; all
the towns of Jair in Bashan, sixty cities in
all; **31**half of Gilead, Ashtaroth, and Edrei, the cities where Og king of Bashan
had ruled. All this went to the family of
Makir son of Manasseh, and half of all his
sons were given this land.

32Moses had given this land to these
tribes on the plains of Moab across the
Jordan River east of Jericho. **33**But Moses had given no land to the tribe of Levi
because the LORD, the God of Israel,
promised that he himself would be the
gift for the Levites.

14 Eleazar the priest, Joshua son of
Nun, and the leaders of all the
tribes of Israel decided what land to give
to the people in the land of Canaan. **2**The
LORD had commanded Moses long ago
how he wanted the people to choose their
land. The people of the nine-and-a-half
tribes threw lots to decide which land
they would receive. **3**Moses had already
given the two-and-a-half tribes their land
east of the Jordan River. But the tribe of
Levi was not given any land like the others. **4**The sons of Joseph had divided into
two tribes—Manasseh and Ephraim. The
tribe of Levi was not given any land. It
was given only some towns in which to
live and pastures for its animals. **5**The
LORD had told Moses how to give the
land to the tribes of Israel, and the Israelites divided the land.

Caleb's Land

6One day some men from the tribe of
Judah went to Joshua at Gilgal. Among
them was Caleb son of Jephunneh the
Kenizzite. He said to Joshua, "You remember what the LORD said at Kadesh
Barnea when he was speaking to the
prophet Moses about you and me. **7**Moses, the LORD's servant, sent me to look

FAITH links

A LONG WAIT

JOSHUA 14:6-15

Could you imagine having to wait 40 years to get something you were promised? Caleb was one of ten spies whom Moses sent to look over the land. Because of Israel's sin, both Caleb and Joshua had to wait 40 years to receive their inheritance. Caleb was 85 years old when he finally received his land!

God keeps his promises, although his timing might seem long in your understanding. God may not have you wait until you're 85 to give you something you've always wanted. He just wants you to trust his timing.

Don't like to wait? Connect to these Faithlinks to find out what God wants you to do:

I Want It *Now!*, Judges 14:1–3, p. 332

Learning to Trust, Psalm 25:4–5, p. 727

Patience, Please, Psalm 145:8–9, p. 819

Think About Him, Isaiah 26:3, p. 926

Ask, Search, Knock, Matthew 7:7–10, p. 1286

At the Right Time, Galatians 4:4, p. 1590

1

Have you ever moved to another house or to another state? If your family had to move to a place you knew nothing about, how would you feel? What would you do?

2

Suppose your parent promised to give you something you've always wanted, like a dog or your very own computer. The only condition is that you have to be obedient. And you would have to wait—a very long time. Would you be willing to be obedient even if you had to wait years to receive what you wanted?

ABRAHAM

Open to Obedience

How quick are you to obey? When told to do something, would you rather whine or would you rather say "Okay"? Being obedient to God takes faith and persistence. Sometimes it means following God even when you don't know where he is taking you! Don't believe it? Read the story of Abram, who God later renamed Abraham. Check out how Abraham responded when God told him to do something by turning the page to

HERE'S THE SCOOP

You'll find the number matches the question number on this page. Then decide for yourself: how open are you to obedience?

3

Dependability is part of obedience. Would your friends and others around you consider you a dependable friend? Abram, who was now called Abraham, was considered a good friend. Find out what he did to earn that reputation.

4

If someone told you to change your first name, would you? Would you still do it if that person chose the name? Abram got a new name that changed his life.

5

Would you give up your most valued possession, immediately and willingly, if God told you to do so? Or would you try to "make a deal" with God and give up something of less value to you?

Here's the Scoop

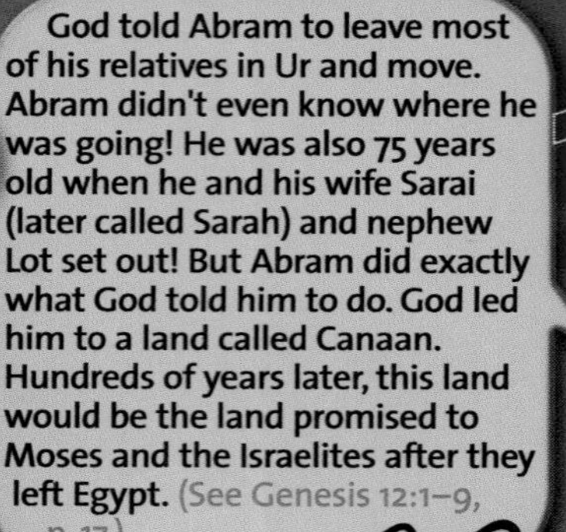

1

God told Abram to leave most of his relatives in Ur and move. Abram didn't even know where he was going! He was also 75 years old when he and his wife Sarai (later called Sarah) and nephew Lot set out! But Abram did exactly what God told him to do. God led him to a land called Canaan. Hundreds of years later, this land would be the land promised to Moses and the Israelites after they left Egypt. (See Genesis 12:1–9, p. 17.)

2

Imagine being able to have what you've always wanted. Abraham and his wife Sarah were unable to have children. But God had promised that one day they would have a son. During the wait, Abraham wasn't always obedient. But God kept his promise anyway. Finally, the promised son arrived. Abraham obediently named him Isaac, a name that God had given him (Genesis 17:19). (Read about it in Genesis 21:1–3, p. 27.)

3

Abraham was a friend of God. That's why God didn't keep his plans hidden from Abraham. He knew that Abraham would "command his children and his descendants to live the way the LORD wants them to, to live right and be fair" (Genesis 18:19). Obedience is the mark of friendship with God. That's why Jesus later told his disciples, "You are my friends if you do what I command you" (John 15:14). Are you a friend of God? (Check it out in Genesis 18:17–19, p. 24. See also 2 Chronicles 20:7, p. 583.)

4

God had a good reason for telling Abram to change his name. His new name, *Abraham*, was like a promise from God. Abraham would be a "father of nations" and Abraham would have many descendants. But God also told him to "obey me and do what is right" (Genesis 17:1). Abraham was to continue following God. His change in name would be a constant reminder of God's special agreement between Abraham and his descendants. (Look up Genesis 17:1–9, p. 22.)

5

This was the ultimate test of obedience. Abraham was told to take the one thing he loved the most—his beloved and long-awaited son—and sacrifice him on a mountain. Abraham didn't ask questions. He didn't try to make a deal with God. He didn't whine or complain. He simply obeyed. Would you have made the same choice? God did not really want Abraham to sacrifice his son. But he was pleased that Abraham was obedient. (Read about it in Genesis 22:1–19, p. 29.)

answers page

MOSES

Faith to Grow On

What do you know about Moses? That he was a Hebrew raised in an Egyptian palace? That he took on Pharaoh and won, thanks to God and the ten plagues? That he led the Israelites out of Egypt? Do you think that Moses instantly became mature in the faith or grew into it? Like you, Moses had to grow in faith. It didn't come overnight. God had a lot to teach the man who would become Israel's greatest prophet. Discover more about the lessons Moses had to learn by checking out

HERE'S THE SCOOP

on the following page. The numbers match the numbered questions on this page. As you see how Moses' faith developed, ask yourself: How is my faith growing?

1 Have you ever tried, but failed to do something good? When you failed, did you want to give up or get going again? Everyone knows about Moses' successes. But did you also know about Moses' failures? Find out how Moses handled his failures and how God was able to take those failures and use them to help Moses grow in his faith.

2 When someone hands you a difficult task, is your first response to make excuses about why you can't do it? Or do you look for the possible ways to tackle the assignment?

3 What do you think helps your faith to grow? Is it learning from your parents or Sunday school teacher? Is it reading the Bible or being with other Christians? Or is it seeing how God works in your life and in the lives of others?

4 When you've had a victory, what do you do first? Do you immediately celebrate, or do you say thanks to those people who helped you win? Do you stop to thank God?

5 When you haven't seen someone in a long time, what do they typically say to you? "My, how you've grown," right? What do you think someone would say about your faith? Has your faith grown, too?

Here's the Scoop

1 Moses was the deliverer God planned to use to lead Israel out of slavery. After all, God had rescued him when other Hebrew baby boys were put to death. But when Moses became a man, he tried to do things his own way. Doing so caused him to have to run for his life. He had not yet learned what God could do. Many years would pass before he saw Egypt again. (Check it out in Exodus 2:11–15, p. 78.)

2 Moses spent 40 years as a shepherd in the desert of Midian. Watching sheep and goats was good training for being a leader of people! (Don't believe it? Try it sometime!) But when God called him through a burning bush to return to Egypt, Moses didn't want to go. He gave every excuse in the book to get out of going. Although Moses said, "No," God said, "Go!" (Read about it in Exodus 3:1—4:17, p. 79.)

3 Through the ten plagues, Moses and his brother Aaron delivered God's message to Pharaoh. That wasn't always easy! Moses and Aaron had to be persistent. Pharaoh's hard heart and God's strong hand helped Moses learn to rely on God. Finally, Pharaoh agreed to do what God had said all along that he would do. He let the people go. Seeing God at work was a real faith-builder for Moses! (See Exodus 6—14, p. 83.)

4 The Israelites had not gotten very far when they encountered their first test of faith. With their backs to the Red Sea, they watched the approaching Egyptian army coming to capture them and take them back into slavery. Yet Moses remained confident in his faith that God would deliver them—and God did! Moses and the people responded by showing their gratitude and faith with this song of praise. (Read Exodus 15:1–18, p. 94.)

5 The closing sentences in the Book of Deuteronomy are a glowing tribute to a man who learned to be a great leader. Moses didn't do everything perfectly. In fact, one mistake cost him a home in the Promised Land. (For that story, read Numbers 20:2–13, p. 202, and Deuteronomy 3:23–28, p. 232.) Yet, despite the hardships, the failures, and the setbacks, Moses' life is an example of how anyone can grow in faith. All it takes is a willingness to trust God. (Look up Deuteronomy 34:10–12, p. 273.)

answers page

at the land where we were going. I was forty years old then. When I came back, I told Moses what I thought about the land. **8**The other men who went with me frightened the people, but I fully believed the LORD would allow us to take the land. **9**So that day Moses promised me, 'The land where you went will become your land, and your children will own it forever. I will give you that land because you fully believed in the LORD, my God.'

10"Now then, the LORD has kept his promise. He has kept me alive for forty-five years from the time he said this to Moses during the time we all wandered in the desert. Now here I am, eighty-five years old. **11**I am still as strong today as I was the day Moses sent me out, and I am just as ready to fight now as I was then. **12**So give me the mountain country the LORD promised me that day long ago. Back then you heard that the Anakite people lived there and the cities were large and well protected. But now with the LORD helping me, I will force them out, just as the LORD said."

eMAIL! FROM GOD
14:10–11
Life
Where do you get your strength?

13Joshua blessed Caleb son of Jephunneh and gave him the city of Hebron as his own. **14**Hebron still belongs to the family of Caleb son of Jephunneh the Kenizzite because he had faith and obeyed the LORD, the God of Israel. **15**(In the past it was called Kiriath Arba, named for Arba, the greatest man among the Anakites.)

After this there was peace in the land.

Land for Judah

15 The land that was given to the tribe of Judah was divided among all the family groups. It went all the way to the Desert of Zin in the far south, at the border of Edom.

2The southern border of Judah's land started at the south end of the Dead Sea **3**and went south of Scorpion Pass to Zin. From there it passed to the south of Kadesh Barnea and continued past Hezron to Addar. From Addar it turned and went to Karka. **4**It continued to Azmon, the brook of Egypt, and then to the Mediterranean Sea. This was the southern border.

5The eastern border was the shore of the Dead Sea, as far as the mouth of the Jordan River.

The northern border started at the bay of the sea at the mouth of the Jordan River. **6**Then it went to Beth Hoglah and continued north of Beth Arabah to the stone of Bohan son of Reuben. **7**Then the northern border went through the Valley of Achor to Debir where it turned toward the north and went to Gilgal. Gilgal is across from the road that goes through Adummim Pass, on the south side of the ravine. The border continued to the waters of En Shemesh and stopped at En Rogel. **8**Then it went through the Valley of Ben Hinnom, next to the southern side of the Jebusite city (which is called Jerusalem). There the border went to the top of the hill on the west side of Hinnom Valley, at the northern end of the Valley of Giants. **9**From there it went to the spring of the waters of Nephtoah and then it went to the cities near Mount Ephron. There it turned and went toward Baalah, which is called Kiriath Jearim. **10**At Baalah the border turned west and went toward Mount Seir. It continued along the north side of Mount Jearim (also called Kesalon) and came to Beth Shemesh. From there it went past Timnah **11**to the hill north of Ekron. Then it turned toward Shikkeron and went past Mount Baalah and continued on to Jabneel, ending at the sea.

12The Mediterranean Sea was the western border. Inside these borders lived the family groups of Judah.

13The LORD had commanded Joshua to give Caleb son of Jephunneh part of the land in Judah, so he gave Caleb the town of Kiriath Arba, also called Hebron. (Arba was the father of Anak.) **14**Caleb forced out the three Anakite families living in Hebron: Sheshai, Ahiman, and Talmai, the descendants of Anak. **15**Then he left there and went to fight against the people living in Debir. (In the past Debir had been called Kiriath Sepher.) **16**Caleb said, "I will give Acsah, my daughter, as a

wife to the man who attacks and captures
the city of Kiriath Sepher." 17Othniel son
of Kenaz, Caleb's brother, captured the
city, so Caleb gave his daughter Acsah to
Othniel to be his wife. 18When Acsah
came to Othniel, she told him to ask her
father for a field.
So Acsah went to her father. When
she got down from her donkey, Caleb
asked her, "What do you want?"
19Acsah answered, "Do me a special
favor. Since you have given me land in
southern Canaan, also give me springs of
water." So Caleb gave her the upper and
lower springs.

20The tribe of Judah got the land God
had promised them. Each family group
got part of the land.
21The tribe of Judah got all these
towns in the southern part of Canaan
near the border of Edom: Kabzeel, Eder,
Jagur, 22Kinah, Dimonah, Adadah, 23Ke-
desh, Hazor, Ithnan, 24Ziph, Telem, Bea-
loth, 25Hazor Hadattah, Kerioth Hezron
(also called Hazor), 26Amam, Shema,
Moladah, 27Hazar Gaddah, Heshmon,
Beth Pelet, 28Hazar Shual, Beersheba,
Biziothiah, 29Baalah, Iim, Ezem, 30Elto-
lad, Kesil, Hormah, 31Ziklag, Madmannah, Sansannah, 32Lebaoth, Shilhim, Ain,

A CHANCE TO BE POPULAR

Hey, kids! Tagg and I are having fun arguing about which one of us is more popular with our Connect 2-You friends. But we know someone who is struggling with a serious popularity problem. Let's welcome Amy, age 12, to Connect 2-You.

Hi, Amy. What's the problem?

Amy

Well, lately, one of the most popular girls in school and I have been talking to each other before and after class. Last week she even asked me to eat lunch with her and her cheerleader friends. To top it all off, yesterday she invited me to her birthday party. The only problem is, I know what kind of a party it's going to be. All the popular kids will be there—but her parents won't. She told me some of the things she has planned, and my parents would have heart attacks if they knew. But this is my big chance to be part of the popular crowd! What should I do?

It sounds pretty tempting, Amy. But is popularity worth more than your relationship with Jesus, your bond with your parents, and your reputation? No way. Popularity fades as fast as it comes. Your relationship with Jesus, your bond with your parents, and your reputation are things to hold on to. Check out the Livin' It page on peer pressure, Leviticus 18:1-5, p. 158, for some other ways to handle tempting situations.

Think of it this way, Amy. If you have to change who you are to become popular, then it's not really *you* who's popular.

and Rimmon. There were twenty-nine
towns and their villages.
33The tribe of Judah got these towns
in the western hills: Eshtaol, Zorah, Ashnah, **34**Zanoah, En Gannim, Tappuah,
Enam, **35**Jarmuth, Adullam, Socoh, Azekah, **36**Shaaraim, Adithaim, and Gederah
(also called Gederothaim). There were
fourteen towns and their villages.
37Judah was also given these towns in
the western hills: Zenan, Hadashah, Migdal Gad, **38**Dilean, Mizpah, Joktheel,
39Lachish, Bozkath, Eglon, **40**Cabbon,
Lahmas, Kitlish, **41**Gederoth, Beth Dagon, Naamah, and Makkedah. There were
sixteen towns and their villages.
42Judah was also given these towns in
the western hills: Libnah, Ether, Ashan,
43Iphtah, Ashnah, Nezib, **44**Keilah, Aczib,
and Mareshah. There were nine towns
and their villages.
45The tribe of Judah was also given
these towns: Ekron and all the small
towns and villages near it; **46**the area
west of Ekron and all the villages and
small towns near Ashdod; **47**Ashdod and
the small towns and villages around it;
the villages and small towns around Gaza
as far as the brook of Egypt and along the
coast of the Mediterranean Sea.
48The tribe of Judah was also given
these towns in the mountains: Shamir,
Jattir, Socoh, **49**Dannah, Kiriath Sannah
(also called Debir), **50**Anab, Eshtemoh,
Anim, **51**Goshen, Holon, and Giloh.
There were eleven towns and their villages.
52They were also given these towns
in the mountains: Arab, Dumah, Eshan,
53Janim, Beth Tappuah, Aphekah, **54**Hum-
tah, Kiriath Arba (also called Hebron), and
Zior. There were nine towns and their villages.
55Judah was also given these towns in
the mountains: Maon, Carmel, Ziph, Juttah, **56**Jezreel, Jokdeam, Zanoah, **57**Kain,
Gibeah, and Timnah. There were ten
towns and their villages.
58They were also given these towns
in the mountains: Halhul, Beth Zur, Gedor, **59**Maarath, Beth Anoth, and Eltekon.
There were six towns and their villages.
60The people of Judah were also
given the two towns of Rabbah and Kiriath Baal (also called Kiriath Jearim) and
their villages.
61Judah was given these towns in the
desert: Beth Arabah, Middin, Secacah,
62Nibshan, the City of Salt, and En Gedi.
There were six towns and all their villages.
63The army of Judah was not able to
force out the Jebusites living in Jerusalem, so the Jebusites still live among the
people of Judah to this day.

Land for Ephraim and Manasseh

16 This is the land the tribe of Joseph
received. It started at the Jordan
River near Jericho and continued to the
waters of Jericho, just east of the city.
The border went up from Jericho to the
mountains of Bethel. **2**Then it continued
from Bethel (also called Luz) to the Arkite border at Ataroth. **3**From there it
went west to the border of the Japhletites
and continued to the area of the Lower
Beth Horon. Then it went to Gezer and
ended at the sea.
4So Manasseh and Ephraim, sons of
Joseph, received their land.
5This is the land that was given to the
family groups of Ephraim: Their border
started at Ataroth Addar in the east, went
to Upper Beth Horon, **6**and then to the
sea. From Micmethath it turned eastward toward Taanath Shiloh and continued eastward to Janoah. **7**Then it went
down from Janoah to Ataroth and to Naarah. It continued until it touched Jericho
and stopped at the Jordan River. **8**The
border went from Tappuah west to Kanah
Ravine and ended at the sea. This is all
the land that was given to each family
group in the tribe of the Ephraimites.
9Many of the towns were actually within
Manasseh's borders, but the people of
Ephraim got those towns and their villages. **10**The Ephraimites could not force
the Canaanites to leave Gezer, so the Canaanites still live among the Ephraimites
today, but they became slaves of the
Ephraimites.

17 Then land was given to the tribe of
Manasseh, Joseph's first son. Manasseh's first son was Makir, the father of

Gilead. Makir was a great soldier, so the
lands of Gilead and Bashan were given to
his family. 2Land was also given to the
other family groups of Manasseh—Abiezer, Helek, Asriel, Shechem, Hepher,
and Shemida. These were all the other
sons of Manasseh son of Joseph.

3Zelophehad was the son of Hepher,
who was the son of Gilead, who was the
son of Makir, who was the son of Manasseh. Zelophehad had no sons, but he had
five daughters, named Mahlah, Noah,
Hoglah, Milcah, and Tirzah. 4They went
to Eleazar the priest and to Joshua son
of Nun and all the leaders. They said,
"The LORD told Moses to give us land
like the men received." So Eleazar
obeyed the LORD and
gave the daughters some
land, just like the brothers of their father. 5So the
tribe of Manasseh had ten
sections of land west of
the Jordan River and two
more sections, Gilead and
Bashan, on the east side
of the Jordan River. 6The
daughters of Manasseh
received land just as the
sons did. Gilead was given to the rest of
the families of Manasseh.

> So Eleazar obeyed the LORD and gave the daughters some land, just like the brothers of their father.
>
> —Joshua 17:4

7The lands of Manasseh were in the
area between Asher and Micmethath,
near Shechem. The border went south to
the En Tappuah area, 8which belonged to
Manasseh, except for the town of Tappuah. It was along the border of Manasseh's
land and belonged to the sons of Ephraim. 9The border of Manasseh continued
south to Kanah Ravine. The cities in this
area of Manasseh belonged to Ephraim.
Manasseh's border was on the north side
of the ravine and went to the sea. 10The
land to the south belonged to Ephraim,
and the land to the north belonged to Manasseh. The Mediterranean Sea was the
western border. The border touched
Asher's land on the north and Issachar's
land on the east.

11In the areas of Issachar and Asher,
the people of Manasseh owned these
towns: Beth Shan and its small towns; Ibleam and its small towns; the people who
lived in Dor and its small towns; the people in Naphoth Dor and its small towns;
the people who lived in Taanach and its
small towns; the people in Megiddo and
its small towns. 12Manasseh was not
able to defeat those cities, so the Canaanites continued to live there. 13When the
Israelites grew strong, they forced the
Canaanites to work for them, although
they did not force them to leave the land.

14The people from the tribes of Joseph said to Joshua, "You gave us only
one area of land, but we are many people.
Why did you give us only one part of all
the land the LORD gave his people?"

15And Joshua answered them, "If you
have too many people, go up to the forest
and make a place for your-
selves to live there in the
land of the Perizzites and
the Rephaites. The moun-
tain country of Ephraim is
too small for you."

16The people of Jo-
seph said, "It is true. The
mountain country of Eph-
raim is not enough for us,
but the land where the
Canaanites live is danger-
ous. They are skilled fighters. They have
powerful weapons in Beth Shan and all the
small towns in that area, and they are also
in the Valley of Jezreel."

17Then Joshua said to the people of
Joseph—to Ephraim and Manasseh,
"There are many of you, and you have
great power. You should be given more
than one share of land. 18You also will
have the mountain country. It is a forest,
but you can cut down the trees and make
it a good place to live. You will own all of
it because you will force the Canaanites
to leave the land even though they have
powerful weapons and are strong."

The Rest of the Land Divided

18 All of the Israelites gathered together at Shiloh where they set up
the Meeting Tent. The land was now under their control. 2But there were still
seven tribes of Israel that had not yet received their land.

3So Joshua said to the Israelites:

CARE TO BE FAIR?

JOSHUA 18:1-8

When you need to share with someone, what do you do to be fair? The Israelites chose a fair way to divide up the land. They cast lots and let God do the choosing. Using the lots was a special way of choosing. When Joshua had been chosen to be the leader, God told him to use the lots. (See Numbers 27:21, p. 214.) In this way, no one had to argue over who received what.

God wants his people to care about being fair. We can learn fair ways to share with others. What is one way you've come up with to share what God gives you with others?

Link here to find out some ways to share with others:

A Small Percent, Deuteronomy 14:22–23, p. 247

Kind or Fair?, 1 Samuel 30, p. 395

A Reminder to Be Fair, 2 Chronicles 19:5–11, p. 583

The Person Most Likely to Give?, Acts 9:36–42, p. 1481

You're Welcomed!, Acts 16:14–15, p. 1494

Give Till It Hurts?, 2 Corinthians 8:6–9; 9:6–9, p. 1578

"Why do you wait so long to take your land? The LORD, the God of your ancestors, has given this land to you.
4Choose three men from each tribe, and I will send them out to study the land. They will describe in writing the land their tribe wants as its share, and then they will come back to me.
5They will divide the land into seven parts. The people of Judah will keep their land in the south, and the people of Joseph will keep their land in the north.
6You should describe the seven parts of land in writing and bring what you have written to me. Then I will throw lots in the presence of the LORD our God.
7But the Levites do not get any part of these lands, because they are priests, and their work is to serve the LORD. Gad, Reuben, and East Manasseh have received the land promised to them, which is east of the Jordan River. Moses, the servant of the LORD, gave it to them."

8So the men who were chosen to map the land started out. Joshua told them, "Go and study the land and describe it in writing. Then come back to me, and I will throw lots in the presence of the LORD here in Shiloh."
9So the men left and went into the land. They described in a scroll each town in the seven parts of the land. Then they came back to Joshua, who was still at the camp at Shiloh.
10There Joshua threw lots in the presence of the LORD to choose the lands that should be given to each tribe.

Land for Benjamin

11The first part of the land was given to the tribe of Benjamin. Each family group received some land between the land of Judah and the land of Joseph. This is the land chosen for Benjamin:
12The northern border started at the Jordan River and went along the northern edge of Jericho, and then it went west into the mountains. That boundary continued until it was just east of Beth Aven.
13From there it went south to Luz (also called Bethel) and then down to Ataroth Addar, which is on the hill south of Lower Beth Horon.

14At the hill to the south of Beth Horon, the border turned and went south

near the western side of the hill. It went
to Kiriath Baal (also called Kiriath Jearim), a town where people of Judah lived.
This was the western border.
15The southern border started near
Kiriath Jearim and went west to the waters of Nephtoah. **16**Then it went down to
the bottom of the hill, which was near the
Valley of Ben Hinnom, on the north side of
the Valley of Rephaim. The border continued down the Hinnom Valley just south of
the Jebusite city to En Rogel. **17**There it
turned north and went to En Shemesh. It
continued to Geliloth near the Adummim
Pass. Then it went down to the great
Stone of Bohan son of Reuben. **18**The border continued to the northern part of Beth
Arabah and went down into the Jordan
Valley. **19**From there it went to the northern part of Beth Hoglah and ended at the
north shore of the Dead Sea, where the
Jordan River flows into the sea. This was
the southern border.
20The Jordan River was the border on
the eastern side. So this was the land
given to the family groups of Benjamin
with the borders on all sides.
21The family groups of Benjamin received these cities: Jericho, Beth Hoglah,
Emek Keziz, **22**Beth Arabah, Zemaraim,
Bethel, **23**Avvim, Parah, Ophrah, **24**Ke-
phar Ammoni, Ophni, and Geba. There
were twelve towns and all their villages.
25The tribe of Benjamin also received
Gibeon, Ramah, Beeroth, **26**Mizpah, Kephirah, Mozah, **27**Rekem, Irpeel, Taralah,
28Zelah, Haeleph, the Jebusite city (Jerusalem), Gibeah, and Kiriath. There
were fourteen towns and their villages.
All these areas are the lands the family
groups of Benjamin were given.

Land for Simeon

19 The second part of the land was
given to the tribe of Simeon. Each
family group received some of the land
inside the area of Judah. **2**They received
Beersheba (also called Sheba), Moladah,
3Hazar Shual, Balah, Ezem, **4**Eltolad,
Bethul, Hormah, **5**Ziklag, Beth Marcaboth, Hazar Susah, **6**Beth Lebaoth, and
Sharuhen. There were thirteen towns
and their villages.
7They received the towns of Ain,
Rimmon, Ether, and Ashan, four towns
and their villages. **8**They also received all
the very small areas with people living in
them as far as Baalath Beer (this is the
same as Ramah in southern Canaan). So
these were the lands given to the family
groups in the tribe of Simeon. **9**The land
of the Simeonites was taken from part of
the land of Judah. Since Judah had much
more land than they needed, the Simeonites received part of their land.

Land for Zebulun

10The third part of the land was given
to the tribe of Zebulun. Each family group
of Zebulun received some of the land.
The border of Zebulun went as far as Sarid. **11**Then it went west to Maralah and
came near Dabbesheth and then near
Jokneam. **12**Then it turned to the east. It
went from Sarid to the area of Kisloth Tabor and on to Daberath and to Japhia. **13**It
continued eastward to Gath Hepher and
Eth Kazin, ending at Rimmon. There the
border turned and went toward Neah.
14At Neah it turned again and went to the
north to Hannathon and continued to the
Valley of Iphtah El. **15**Inside this border
were the cities of Kattath, Nahalal, Shimron, Idalah, and Bethlehem. There were
twelve towns and their villages.
16So these are the towns and the villages that were given to the family groups
of Zebulun.

Land for Issachar

17The fourth part of the land was
given to the tribe of Issachar. Each family
group of Issachar received some of the
land. **18**Their land included Jezreel, Ke-
sulloth, Shunem, **19**Hapharaim, Shion,
Anaharath, **20**Rabbith, Kishion, Ebez,
21Remeth, En Gannim, En Haddah, and
Beth Pazzez.
22The border of their land touched
the area called Tabor, Shahazumah, and
Beth Shemesh and stopped at the Jordan
River. There were sixteen towns and
their villages.
23These cities and towns were part of
the land that was given to the family
groups of Issachar.

Land for Asher

24The fifth part of the land was given to the tribe of Asher. Each family group of Asher received some of the land. 25Their land included Helkath, Hali, Beten, Acshaph, 26Allammelech, Amad, and Mishal.

The western border touched Mount Carmel and Shihor Libnath. 27Then it turned east and went to Beth Dagon, touching Zebulun and the Valley of Iphtah El. Then it went north of Beth Emek and Neiel and passed north to Cabul. 28From there it went to Abdon, Rehob, Hammon, and Kanah and continued to Greater Sidon. 29Then the border went back south toward Ramah and continued to the strong, walled city of Tyre. There it turned and went toward Hosah, ending at the sea. This was in the area of Aczib, 30Ummah, Aphek, and Rehob. There were twenty-two towns and their villages.

31These cities and their villages were part of the land that was given to the family groups of Asher.

Land for Naphtali

32The sixth part of the land was given to the tribe of Naphtali. Each family group of Naphtali received some of the land. 33The border of their land started at the large tree in Zaanannim, which is near Heleph. Then it went through Adami Nekeb and Jabneel, as far as Lakkum, and ended at the Jordan River. 34Then it went to the west through Aznoth Tabor and stopped at Hukkok. It went to the area of Zebulun on the south, Asher on the west, and Judah, at the Jordan River, on the east. 35The strong, walled cities inside these borders were called Ziddim, Zer, Hammath, Rakkath, Kinnereth, 36Adamah, Ramah, Hazor, 37Kedesh, Edrei, En Hazor, 38Iron, Migdal El, Horem, Beth Anath, and Beth Shemesh. There were nineteen towns and all their villages.

39The towns and the villages around them were in the land that was given to the family groups of Naphtali.

> Eleazar the priest, Joshua son of Nun, and the leaders of each tribe divided up the land by lots at Shiloh.
>
> —Joshua 19:51

Land for Dan

40The seventh part of the land was given to the tribe of Dan. Each family group of Dan received some of the land. 41Their land included Zorah, Eshtaol, Ir Shemesh, 42Shaalabbin, Aijalon, Ithlah, 43Elon, Timnah, Ekron, 44Eltekeh, Gibbethon, Baalath, 45Jehud, Bene Berak, Gath Rimmon, 46Me Jarkon, Rakkon, and the area near Joppa.

47(But the Danites had trouble taking their land. They went and fought against Leshem, defeated it, and killed the people who lived there. So the Danites moved into the town of Leshem and changed its name to Dan, because he was the father of their tribe.) 48All of these towns and villages were given to the family groups of Dan.

Land for Joshua

49After the leaders finished dividing the land and giving it to the different tribes, the Israelites gave Joshua son of Nun his land also. 50They gave Joshua the town he asked for, Timnath Serah in the mountains of Ephraim, just as the LORD commanded. He built up the town and lived there.

51So these lands were given to the different tribes of Israel. Eleazar the priest, Joshua son of Nun, and the leaders of each tribe divided up the land by lots at Shiloh. They met in the presence of the LORD at the entrance to the Meeting Tent. Now they were finished dividing the land.

Cities of Safety

20 Then the LORD said to Joshua: 2"Tell the Israelites to choose the special cities of safety, as I had Moses command you to do. 3If a person kills someone accidentally and without meaning to kill him, that person may go to a city of safety to hide. There the killer will be safe from the relative who has the duty of punishing a murderer.

4"When the killer runs to one of those

DIVIDING THE LAND

Joshua 21

The land of Israel is called that because the land was divided among the 12 sons of a man named Israel. (He was born with the name Jacob, but God later changed it to Israel.) The land of Israel stretched from the Jordan River on the east to the Mediterranean Sea on the west. From the north to the south it covered the land between the Sinai Peninsula and the boundary of Phoenicia.

Israel's sons were: Reuben, Simeon, Levi, Judah, Zebulun, Issachar, Dan, Gad, Asher, Naphtali, Joseph, and Benjamin.

The only son of Israel whose descendants didn't get a tract of land was Levi. (Check out Joshua 13:33.) That's because Levi's descendants (the Levites) were selected to be priests. (Read Numbers 18:20, p. 201.) They would work and live from the Temple, so they didn't need any land. The land that would have gone to the Levites was divided between the two sons of Joseph—Manasseh and Ephraim.

cities, he must stop at the entrance gate,
stand there, and tell the leaders of the
people what happened. Then that person
will be allowed to enter the city and will
be given a place to live among them. **5**But
if the one who is chasing him follows him
to that city, the leaders of the city must
not hand over the killer. It was an accident. He did not hate him beforehand or
kill him on purpose. **6**The killer must
stay in the city until a court comes to a
decision and until the high priest dies.
Then he may go back home to the town
from which he ran away."

7So the Israelites chose these cities to
be cities of safety: Kedesh in Galilee in
the mountains of Naphtali; Shechem in
the mountains of Ephraim; Kiriath Arba
(also called Hebron) in the mountains of
Judah; **8**Bezer on the east side of the Jordan River near Jericho in the desert in the
land of Reuben; Ramoth in Gilead in
the land of Gad; and Golan in Bashan in
the land of Manasseh. **9**Any Israelite or
anyone living among them who killed
someone accidentally was to be allowed to
run to one of these cities of safety. There
he would not be killed, before he was
judged, by the relative who had the duty of
punishing a murderer.

Towns for the Levites

21 The heads of the Levite families
went to talk to Eleazar the priest,
to Joshua son of Nun, and to the heads of
the families of all the tribes of Israel. **2**At
Shiloh in the land of Canaan, the heads of
the Levite families said to them, "The
LORD commanded Moses that you give
us towns where we may live and pastures
for our animals." **3**So the Israelites
obeyed this command of the LORD and
gave the Levite people these towns and
pastures for their own land: **4**The Kohath
family groups were part of the tribe of
Levi. Some of the Levites in the Kohath
family groups were from the family of
Aaron the priest. To these Levites were
given thirteen towns in the areas of Judah, Simeon, and Benjamin. **5**The other
family groups of Kohath were given ten

towns in the areas of Ephraim, Dan, and
West Manasseh.

6The people from the Gershon family
groups were given thirteen towns in the
land of Issachar, Asher, Naphtali, and the
East Manasseh in Bashan.

7The family groups of Merari were
given twelve towns in the areas of Reuben, Gad, and Zebulun.

8So the Israelites gave the Levites
these towns and the pastures around
them, just as the LORD had commanded
Moses.

9These are the names of the towns
that came from the lands of Judah and
Simeon. **10**The first choice of towns was
given to the Kohath family groups of the
Levites. **11**They gave them Kiriath Arba,
also called Hebron, and all its pastures in
the mountains of Judah. (Arba was the father of Anak.) **12**But the fields and the
villages around Kiriath Arba had been
given to Caleb son of Jephunneh.

13So they gave the city of Hebron to
the descendants of Aaron (Hebron was a
city of safety). They also gave them the
towns of Libnah, **14**Jattir, Eshtemoa,
15Holon, Debir, **16**Ain, Juttah, and Beth
Shemesh, and all the pastures around
them. Nine towns were given from these
two tribes.

17They also gave the people of Aaron
these cities that belonged to the tribe of
Benjamin: Gibeon, Geba, **18**Anathoth,
and Almon. They gave them these four
towns and the pastures around them.

19So these thirteen towns with their
pastures were given to the priests, who
were from the family of Aaron.

20The other Kohathite family groups
of the Levites were given these towns
from the tribe of Ephraim: **21**Shechem in
the mountains of Ephraim (which was a
city of safety), Gezer, **22**Kibzaim, and
Beth Horon. There were four towns and
their pastures.

23The tribe of Dan gave them Elte-
keh, Gibbethon, **24**Aijalon, and Gath
Rimmon. There were four towns and
their pastures.

25West Manasseh gave them Taanach
and Gath Rimmon and the pastures
around these two towns.

26So these ten towns and the pastures around them were given to the rest
of the Kohathite family groups.

27The Gershonite family groups of
the Levite tribe were given these towns:
East Manasseh gave them Golan in Bashan, which was a city of safety, and Be
Eshtarah, and the pastures around these
two towns.

28The tribe of Issachar gave them
Kishion, Daberath, **29**Jarmuth, and En
Gannim, and the pastures around these
four towns.

30The tribe of Asher gave them Mishal, Abdon, **31**Helkath, and Rehob, and
the pastures around these four towns.

32The tribe of Naphtali gave them
Kedesh in Galilee (a city of safety), Ham-
moth Dor, and Kartan, and the pastures
around these three towns.

33So the Gershonite family groups received thirteen towns and the pastures
around them.

34The Merarite family groups (the
rest of the Levites) were given these
towns: The tribe of Zebulun gave them
Jokneam, Kartah, **35**Dimnah, and Nahalal, and the pastures around these four
towns.

36The tribe of Reuben gave them Bezer, Jahaz, **37**Kedemoth, and Mephaath,
along with the pastures around these four
towns.

38The tribe of Gad gave them Ramoth
in Gilead (a city of safety), Mahanaim,
39Heshbon, and Jazer, and the pastures
around these four towns.

40So the total number of towns given
to the Merarite family groups was
twelve.

41A total of forty-eight towns with
their pastures in the land of Israel were
given to the Levites. **42**Each town had
pastures around it.

43So the LORD gave the people all the
land he had promised their ancestors. The
people took the land and lived there.
44The LORD gave them peace on all sides,
as he had promised their ancestors. None
of their enemies defeated them; the LORD
handed all their enemies over to them.
45He kept every promise he had made to
the Israelites; each one came true.

Three Tribes Go Home

22 Then Joshua called a meeting of all the people from the tribes of Reuben, Gad, and East Manasseh. **2**He said to them, "You have done everything Moses, the LORD's servant, told you to do. You have also obeyed all my commands. **3**For a long time you have supported the other Israelites. You have been careful to obey the commands the LORD your God gave you. **4**The LORD your God promised to give the Israelites peace, and he has kept his promise. Now you may go back to your homes, to the land that Moses, the LORD's servant, gave you, on the east side of the Jordan River. **5**But be careful to obey the teachings and laws Moses, the LORD's servant, gave you: to love the LORD your God and obey his commands, to continue to follow him and serve him the very best you can."

> **EMAIL FROM GOD**
> **22:5**
> **Responsibility**
> Be careful to do this!

6Then Joshua said good-bye to them, and they left and went away to their homes. **7**Moses had given the land of Bashan to East Manasseh. Joshua gave land on the west side of the Jordan River to West Manasseh. And he sent them to their homes and he blessed them. **8**He said, "Go back to your homes and your riches. You have many animals, silver, gold, bronze, and iron, and many beautiful clothes. Also, you have taken many things from your enemies that you should divide among yourselves."

9So the people from the tribes of Reuben, Gad, and East Manasseh left the other Israelites at Shiloh in Canaan and went back to Gilead. It was their own land, given to them by Moses as the LORD had commanded.

10The people of Reuben, Gad, and East Manasseh went to Geliloth, near the Jordan River in the land of Canaan. There they built a beautiful altar. **11**The other Israelites still at Shiloh heard about the altar these three tribes built at the border of Canaan at Geliloth, near the Jordan River on Israel's side. **12**All the Israelites became very angry at these three tribes, so they met together and decided to fight them.

13The Israelites sent Phinehas son of Eleazar the priest to Gilead to talk to the people of Reuben, Gad, and East Manasseh. **14**They also sent one leader from each of the ten tribes at Shiloh. Each of them was a leader of his family group of Israelites.

15These leaders went to Gilead to talk to the people of Reuben, Gad, and East Manasseh. They said: **16**"All the Israelites ask you: 'Why did you turn against the God of Israel by building an altar for yourselves? You know that this

FAITH CHALLENGE

Got another challenge for you. Read 22:18 to find out what warning the Israelites received from God. How can you make sure that the Lord does not get angry with you?

TESTING IT

Joshua 22:18
And now are you turning against the LORD and refusing to follow him? If you don't stop what you're doing today, the LORD will be angry with everyone in Israel tomorrow.

____

____

____

____

____

____

____

is against God's law. **17**Remember what
happened at Peor? We still suffer today
because of that sin, for which God made
many Israelites very sick. **18**And now are
you turning against the LORD and refusing to follow him?
" 'If you don't stop what you're doing
today, the LORD will be angry with everyone in Israel tomorrow. **19**If your land is
unclean, come over into our land where
the LORD's Tent is. Share it with us. But
don't turn against the LORD and us by
building another altar for the LORD our
God. **20**Remember how Achan son of Zerah refused to obey the command about
what must be completely destroyed.
That one man broke God's law, but all the
Israelites were punished. Achan died because of his sin, but others also died.' "
21The people from Reuben, Gad, and
East Manasseh answered, **22**"The LORD
is God of gods! The LORD is God of gods!
God knows, and we want you to know
also. If we have done something wrong,
you may kill us. **23**If we broke God's law,
we ask the LORD himself to punish us.
We did not build this altar to offer burnt
offerings or grain and fellowship offerings.
24"We did not build it for that reason.
We feared that some day your people
would not accept us as part of your nation. Then they might say, 'You cannot
worship the LORD, the God of Israel.
25The LORD made the Jordan River a
border between us and you people of
Reuben and Gad. You cannot worship the
LORD.' So we feared that your children
might make our children stop worshiping
the LORD.
26"That is why we decided to build
this altar. But it is not for burnt offerings
and sacrifices. **27**This altar is proof to you
and us and to all our children who will
come after us that we worship the LORD
with our whole burnt offerings, grain, and
fellowship offerings. This was so your
children would not say to our children,
'You are not the LORD's.'
28"In the future if your children say
that, our children can say, 'See the altar
made by our ancestors. It is exactly like
the LORD's altar, but we do not use it for
sacrifices. It shows that we are part of
Israel.'
29"Truly, we don't want to be against
the LORD or to stop following him by
building an altar for burnt offerings, grain
offerings, or sacrifices. We know the only
true altar to the LORD our God is in front
of the Holy Tent."
30When Phinehas the priest and the
ten leaders heard the people of Reuben,
Gad, and East Manasseh, they were
pleased. **31**So Phinehas, son of Eleazar
the priest, said, "Now we know the LORD
is with us and that you didn't turn against
him. Now the Israelites will not be punished by the LORD."
32Then Phinehas and the leaders left
the people of Reuben and Gad in Gilead
and went back to Canaan where they told
the Israelites what had happened. **33**They
were pleased and thanked God. So they
decided not to fight the people of Reuben
and Gad and destroy those lands.
34And the people of Reuben and Gad
named the altar Proof That We Believe
the LORD Is God.

The Last Words of Joshua

23 The LORD gave Israel peace from
their enemies around them. Many
years passed, and Joshua grew very old.
2He called a meeting of all the older leaders, heads of families, judges, and officers
of Israel. He said, "I am now very old.
3You have seen what the LORD has done
to our enemies to help us. The LORD
your God fought for you. **4**Remember
that your people have been given their
land between the Jordan River and the
Mediterranean Sea in the west, the land I
promised to give you. **5**The LORD your
God will force out the people living there.
The LORD will push them out ahead of
you. And you will own the land,
as he has promised
you.
6"Be strong. You
must be careful to
obey everything com-
manded in the Book
of the Teachings of
Moses. Do exactly as it says. **7**Don't become friends with the people living

eMAIL FROM GOD
23:6–7
Bible
Read this to see what God's teachings tell you to do.

among us who are not Israelites. Don't
say the names of their gods or make anyone swear by them. Don't serve or worship them. **8**You must continue to follow
the LORD your God, as you have done in
the past.

9"The LORD has forced many great
and powerful nations to leave ahead of
you. No nation has been able to defeat
you. **10**With his help, one Israelite could
defeat a thousand, because the LORD
your God fights for you, as he promised
to do. **11**So you must be careful to love
the LORD your God.

12"If you turn away from the way of
the LORD and become friends with these
people who are not part of Israel and
marry them, **13**the LORD your God will
not help you defeat your enemies. They
will be like traps for you, like whips on
your back and thorns in your eyes, and
none of you will be left in this good land
the LORD your God has given you.

14"It's almost time for me to die. You
know and fully believe that the LORD has
done great things for you. You know that
he has not failed to keep any of his promises. **15**Every good promise that the LORD
your God made has come true, and in the
same way, his other promises will come
true. He promised that evil will come to
you and that he will destroy you from this
good land that he gave you. **16**This will
happen if you don't keep your agreement
with the LORD your God. If you go and
serve other gods and worship them, the
LORD will become very angry with you.
Then none of you will be left in this good
land he has given you."

24 Joshua gathered all the tribes of
Israel together at Shechem. He
called the older leaders, heads of families, judges, and officers of Israel to stand
before God.

2Then Joshua said to all the people,
"Here's what the LORD, the God of Israel, says to you: 'A long time ago your
ancestors lived on the other side of the
Euphrates River. Terah, the father of
Abraham and Nahor, worshiped other
gods. **3**But I, the LORD, took your ancestor Abraham from the other side of the
river and led him through the land of Canaan. And I gave him many children, including his son Isaac. **4**I gave Isaac two
sons named Jacob and Esau. I gave the
land around the mountains of Edom to
Esau, but Jacob and his sons went down
to Egypt. **5**Then I sent Moses and Aaron
to Egypt, where I brought many disasters
on the Egyptians. Afterwards I brought
you out. **6**When I brought your ancestors
out of Egypt, they came to the Red Sea,
and the Egyptians chased them with
chariots and men on horses. **7**So the people called out to the LORD. And I brought
darkness between you and the Egyptians
and made the sea to cover them. You
yourselves saw what I did to the army of
Egypt. After that, you lived in the desert
for a long time.

8" 'Then I brought you to the land of
the Amorites, east of the Jordan River.
They fought against you, but I handed
them over to you. I destroyed them before you, and you took control of that
land. **9**But the king of Moab, Balak son of
Zippor, prepared to fight against the Israelites. The king sent for Balaam son of
Beor to curse you, **10**but I refused to listen to Balaam. So he asked for good
things to happen to you! I saved you and
brought you out of his power.

11" 'Then you crossed the Jordan
River and came to Jericho, where the
people of Jericho fought against you.
Also, the Amorites, Perizzites, Canaanites, Hittites, Girgashites, Hivites, and
Jebusites fought against you. But I handed them over to you. **12**I sent terror
ahead of you to force out two Amorite
kings. You took the land without using
swords and bows. **13**I gave you that land
where you did not have to work. I gave
you cities that you did not have to build.
And now you live in that land and in those
cities, and you eat from vineyards and
olive trees that you did not plant.' "

14Then Joshua said to the people,
"Now respect the LORD and serve him
fully and sincerely. Throw away the gods
that your ancestors worshiped on the
other side of the Euphrates River and in
Egypt. Serve the LORD. **15**But if you
don't want to serve the LORD, you must

FAITH links

NO MIDDLE GROUND

JOSHUA 24:14-15

Some choices we have to make are cut and dried—either this or that. Joshua told the people of Israel to choose either to worship God or to worship idols made by people. There was no choice in between.

God offers you the same choice. An idol is someone or something you value more than God. You can either choose him or choose someone or something else you value more. You decide.

The Wisdom of Obeying God, 1 Kings 11:1–13, p. 453

A Useless Thing, Isaiah 44:9, 18–20, p. 954

How to Worship God, Isaiah 58, p. 972

Obeying God or Man?, Daniel 3:8–30, p. 1154

First Place, Haggai 1:7–11, p. 1248

Heavenly Treasure, Luke 12:32–34, p. 1394

choose for yourselves today whom you
will serve. You may serve the gods that
your ancestors worshiped when they
lived on the other side of the Euphrates
River, or you may serve the gods of the
Amorites who lived in this land. As for
me and my family, we will serve the
LORD."
16Then the people answered, "We
will never stop following the LORD to
serve other gods! **17**It was the LORD our
God who brought our ancestors out of
Egypt. We were slaves in that land, but
the LORD did great things for us there.
He brought us out and protected us while
we traveled through other lands. **18**Then
he forced out all the people living in these
lands, even the Amorites. So we will
serve the LORD, because he is our God."
19Then Joshua said, "You are not able
to serve the LORD, because he is a holy
God and a jealous God. If you turn against
him and sin, he will not forgive you. **20**If
you leave the LORD and serve other gods,
he will send you great trouble. The LORD
may have been good to you, but if you
turn against him, he will destroy you."
21But the people said to Joshua, "No!
We will serve the LORD."
22Then Joshua said, "You are your
own witnesses that you have chosen to
serve the LORD."
The people said, "Yes, we are."
23Then Joshua said, "Now throw
away the gods that you have. Love the
LORD, the God of Israel, with all your
heart."
24Then the people said to Joshua,
"We will serve the LORD our God, and we
will obey him."
25On that day at Shechem Joshua
made an agreement for the people. He
made rules and laws for them to follow.
26Joshua wrote these things in the Book
of the Teachings of God. Then he took a
large stone and set it up under the oak
tree near the LORD's Holy Tent.
27Joshua said to all the people, "See
this stone! It will remind you of what
we did today. It was here the LORD spoke
to us today. It will remind you of what
happened so you will not turn against
your God."

Joshua Dies

28Then Joshua sent the people back
to their land.
29After that, Joshua son of Nun died
at the age of one hundred ten. **30**They
buried him in his own land at Timnath
Serah, in the mountains of Ephraim,
north of Mount Gaash.
31The Israelites served the LORD
during the lifetime of Joshua and during

the lifetimes of the older leaders who
lived after Joshua who had seen what the
LORD had done for Israel.

Joseph Comes Home

32When the Israelites left Egypt, they
carried the bones of Joseph with them.
They buried them at Shechem, in the
land Jacob had bought for a hundred
pieces of silver from the sons of Hamor
(Hamor was the father of Shechem). This
land now belonged to Joseph's children.
33And Eleazar son of Aaron died and
was buried at Gibeah in the mountains of
Ephraim, which had been given to
Eleazar's son Phinehas.

SAVE US FROM OUR ENEMIES!

Greetings! My name is Samuel, and I was the last judge of Israel. (Although I wrote the Book of Judges, my story is in 1 Samuel. Link with 1 Samuel 1:1–20, p. 354, for the story of my birth.) Seeing a title like Judges, you might think that this would be a boring book about court cases, but Judges has some of the most interesting and strangest stories in the Bible. You'll need to do some surfing through this book!

I wrote the Book of Judges to remind people to be faithful to God. "At that time Israel did not have a king, so everyone did what seemed right" (Judges 17:6). Unfortunately, for most people it did not "seem right" to follow God, so God allowed them to be conquered by their enemies. It was not until the people were sorry for their sins and called out to God that God sent a judge, or leader, to save them.

JESUS WATCH

In the Book of Judges, we see many people who point to Jesus. Each judge was a ruler and a savior of the nation of Israel as Jesus is the ruler and savior for those who believe in him. The judges in this book were imperfect, and the effects of their actions were only temporary. Jesus is perfect, and his salvation is forever. Several judges ruled Israel. Some, like Gideon, were warrior-rulers who defeated Israel's enemies. Jesus defeated Satan and rules his kingdom from heaven. Other judges, like Deborah and Samuel, were prophets who urged the people to follow God's laws. Jesus was the ultimate prophet who showed us God's love. Some judges were priests who prayed and sacrificed for the people. Jesus is our high priest who sacrificed himself for our sins and is always asking God to forgive us.

my FAVORITE links

______________ ______________

______________ ______________

______________ ______________

______________ ______________

OTHER CONNECTIONS

GET THE INFO

Surf these connections to find out more about what some consider to be Israel's "dark ages," a time when people strayed from God and began to worship other gods.

- The Judges, Judges 9, will introduce you to some of the main leaders of the young nation of Israel as they began to settle in the land God had promised to them.
- Check out the earliest religious capital for the Israelites when you connect to Let's Visit Shiloh, Judges 18:31. This ancient Canaan city was where the Israelites kept the Holy Tent of God. It's also where a young woman named Hannah prayed for God to give her a son.

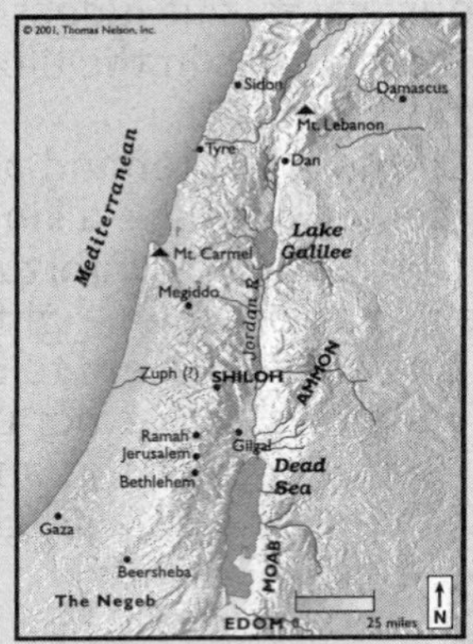

- Promises, Promises, Judges 2:1–3
- Count on His Mercy, Judges 2:16–17; 3
- From Zero to Hero, Judges 6; 7
- What's Out Becomes In, Judges 11
- I Want it *Now!*, Judges 14:1–3
- The Weak Link, Judges 16
- Do What You Want?, Judges 21:25

"Do you know what was Ehud's secret message for the king of Moab?"

"No, but if we connect to Judges 3:12-28, I'm sure we can find out."

CHECK OUT THESE STRANGE STORIES:

A stake through the head?, Judges 4:14–24
Gideon's fleece, Judges 6:36–40
Samson eats honey from a dead lion, Judges 14:5–9
Samson's seven braids, Judges 16:15–22

Judah Fights the Canaanites

1 After Joshua died, the Israelites
asked the LORD, "Who will be first to
go and fight for us against the Canaanites?"
2The LORD said to them, "The tribe of
Judah will go. I have handed the land over
to them."
3The men of Judah said to the men of
Simeon, their relatives, "Come and help
us fight the Canaanites for our land. If
you do, we will go and help you fight for
your land." So the men of Simeon went
with them.
4When Judah attacked, the LORD
handed over the Canaanites and the Perizzites to them, and they defeated ten
thousand men at the city of Bezek.
5There they found Adoni-Bezek, the ruler of the city, and fought him. The men of
Judah defeated the Canaanites and the
Perizzites, 6but Adoni-
Bezek ran away. The men
of Judah chased him, and
when they caught him,
they cut off his thumbs
and big toes.
7Adoni-Bezek said,
"Seventy kings whose
thumbs and big toes had
been cut off used to eat
scraps that fell from my
table. Now God has paid
me back for what I did to them." The men
of Judah took Adoni-Bezek to Jerusalem,
and he died there.
8Then the men of Judah fought
against Jerusalem and captured it. They
attacked with their swords and burned
the city.
9Later, they went down to fight the
Canaanites who lived in the mountains,
in the dry country to the south, and in the
western hills. 10The men of Judah went
to fight against the Canaanites in the city
of Hebron (which used to be called Kiriath Arba). And they defeated Sheshai,
Ahiman, and Talmai.

After Joshua died, the Israelites asked the LORD, "Who will be first to go and fight for us against the Canaanites?"
—Judges 1:1

Caleb and His Daughter

11Then they left there and went to
fight against the people living in Debir.
(In the past Debir had been called Kiriath
Sepher.) 12Before attacking the city, Caleb said, "I will give Acsah, my daughter,
as a wife to the man who attacks and captures the city of Kiriath Sepher." 13Oth-
niel son of Kenaz, Caleb's younger
brother, captured the city, so Caleb gave
his daughter Acsah to Othniel to be his
wife. 14When Acsah came to Othniel, she
told him to ask her father for a field.
When she got down from her donkey, Caleb asked her, "What do you want?"
15Acsah answered him, "Do me a special favor. Since you have given me land
in southern Canaan, also give me springs
of water." So Caleb gave her the upper
and lower springs.

Fights with the Canaanites

16The Kenite people, who were from
the family of Moses' father-in-law, left
Jericho, the city of palm trees. They went
with the men of Judah to
the Desert of Judah to
live with them there in
southern Judah near the
city of Arad.
17The men of Judah
and the men of Simeon,
their relatives, defeated
the Canaanites who lived
in Zephath. They com-
pletely destroyed the city,
so they called it Hormah.
18The men of Judah captured Gaza, Ashkelon, Ekron, and the lands around them.
19The LORD was with the men of Judah. They took the land in the mountains,
but they could not force out the people
living on the plain, because they had iron
chariots. 20As Moses had promised, Hebron was given to Caleb, and Caleb forced
out the three sons of Anak. 21But the
people of Benjamin could not make the
Jebusite people leave Jerusalem. Since
that time the Jebusites have lived with
the Benjaminites in Jerusalem.
22The men of Joseph went to fight
against the city of Bethel, and the LORD
was with them. 23They sent some spies
to Bethel (which used to be called Luz).

1:17 Hormah Hormah sounds like the Hebrew word meaning "to destroy completely."

24The spies saw a man coming out of the
city and said to him, "Show us a way into
the city, and we will be kind to you." 25So
the man showed them the way into the
city. The men of Joseph attacked with
swords the people in Bethel, but they let
the man and his family go free. 26He
went to the land where the Hittites lived
and built a city. He named it Luz, which it
is called even today.

27There were Canaanites living in the
cities of Beth Shan, Taanach, Dor, Ibleam,
Megiddo, and the small towns around
them. The people of Manasseh did not
force those people out of their towns, because the Canaanites were determined to
stay there. 28Later, the Israelites grew
strong and forced the Canaanites to work
as slaves, but they did not make all the
Canaanites leave their land. 29The people of Ephraim did not force out all of the
Canaanites living in Gezer. So the Canaanites continued to live in Gezer with
the people of Ephraim. 30The people of
Zebulun did not force out the Canaanites
living in the cities of Kitron and Nahalol.
They stayed and lived with the people of
Zebulun, but Zebulun made them work as
slaves.

31The people of Asher did not force
the Canaanites from the cities of Acco,
Sidon, Ahlab, Aczib, Helbah, Aphek, and
Rehob. 32Since the people of Asher did
not force them out, the Canaanites continued to live with them. 33The people of
Naphtali did not force out the people of
the cities of Beth Shemesh and Beth
Anath. So they continued to live with the
Canaanites in those cities, and the Canaanites worked as slaves. 34The Amorites forced the Danites back into the
mountains and would not let them come
down to live in the plain. 35The Amorites
were determined to stay in Mount Heres,
Aijalon, and Shaalbim. But when the Israelites grew stronger, they made the Amorites work as slaves. 36The land of the
Amorites was from Scorpion Pass to Sela
and beyond.

The Angel of the Lord at Bokim

2 The angel of the LORD went up from
Gilgal to Bokim and said, "I brought
you up from Egypt and led you to the land
I promised to give your ancestors. I said, 'I
will never break my agreement with you.
2But you must not make an agreement
with the people who live in this land. You
must destroy their altars.' But you did not
obey me. How could you do this? 3Now I

FAITH links

PROMISES, PROMISES

JUDGES 2:1-3

Have you ever made a promise that you did not keep? The Israelites broke a promise to God. They promised not to make peace treaties with other nations. They also promised to get rid of the idols in the land. Because the Israelites broke their promise, God said he would not help them to conquer the land.

Sometimes people break promises because they don't want to go through the trouble of keeping them. Being a person of your word means keeping the promises you make, even if you face difficulty in doing so.

A Serious Promise, Deuteronomy 23:21–23, p. 257

A Big Responsibility, 2 Kings 11, p. 494

Said It? Do It!, Lamentations 2:17, p. 1077

Your Choice of Fruit, Matthew 12:33–35, p. 1295

Your Civic Duty, Matthew 17:24–27, p. 1304

Another Lazy Day?, 2 Thessalonians 3:6–13, p. 1640

tell you, 'I will not force out the people in
this land. They will be your enemies, and
their gods will be a trap for you.' "
4After the angel gave Israel this message from the LORD, they cried loudly.
5So they named the place Bokim.[a] There
they offered sacrifices to the LORD.

Joshua Dies

6Then Joshua sent the people back to
their land. 7The people served the LORD
during the lifetime of Joshua and during
the lifetimes of the older leaders who
lived after Joshua and who had seen what
great things the LORD had done for Israel.
8Joshua son of Nun, the servant of the
LORD, died at the age of one hundred ten.
9They buried him in his own land at Timnath Serah in the mountains of Ephraim,
north of Mount Gaash.

The People Disobey

10After those people had died, their
children grew up and did not know the
LORD or what he had done for Israel.
11So they did what the LORD said was
wrong, and they worshiped the Baal
idols. 12They quit following the LORD,
the God of their ancestors who had
brought them out of Egypt. They began
to worship the gods of the people who
lived around them, and that made the
LORD angry. 13The Israelites quit following the LORD and worshiped Baal and
Ashtoreth. 14The LORD was angry with
the people of Israel, so he handed them
over to robbers who took their possessions. He let their enemies who lived
around them defeat them; they could not
protect themselves. 15When the Israelites went out to fight, they always lost,
because the LORD was not with them.
The LORD had sworn to them this would
happen. So the Israelites suffered very
much.

God Chooses Judges

16Then the LORD chose leaders called
judges,[a] who saved the Israelites from

FAITH links

COUNT ON HIS MERCY

JUDGES 2:16-17; 3

Time and time again, the Israelites sinned. You'd think that God would be done with them, wouldn't you? Nope. God showed them love and forgiveness by raising up judges to lead them against their enemies. You've seen the superheroes in comic books or on video games, right? Well, meet the real superheroes. Judges were the leaders God equipped to help his people. They didn't have X-ray vision or cool costumes. But they did have access to God's power and wisdom.

When we blow it, we can count on God's love and forgiveness, just as the people of Israel did. We don't deserve it. But it sure helps when we're in trouble.

Think you've messed up big time? Link here to see what God can do for you!

Own Up to It, 2 Samuel 12:1–13, p. 412

The Cover-up, Psalm 32:1–2, p. 733

Red to White, Isaiah 1:18, p. 896

A Hard Place, Ezekiel 28:25–26, p. 1120

Clean Inside and Out, Luke 11:39–40, p. 1392

A Friendly Welcome, Philemon 18, p. 1664

2:5 Bokim This name means "crying."
2:16 judges They were not judges in courts of law, but leaders of the people in times of emergency.

the robbers. **17**But the Israelites did not listen to their judges. They were not faithful to God but worshiped other gods instead. Their ancestors had obeyed the LORD's commands, but they quickly turned away and did not obey. **18**When their enemies hurt them, the Israelites cried for help. So the LORD felt sorry for them and sent judges to save them from their enemies. The LORD was with those judges all their lives. **19**But when the judges died, the Israelites again sinned and worshiped other gods. They became worse than their ancestors. The Israelites were very stubborn and refused to change their evil ways.

20So the LORD became angry with the Israelites. He said, "These people have broken the agreement I made with their ancestors. They have not listened to me. **21**I will no longer defeat the nations who were left when Joshua died. **22**I will use them to test Israel, to see if Israel will keep the LORD's commands as their ancestors did." **23**In the past the LORD had permitted those nations to stay in the land. He did not quickly force them out or help Joshua's army defeat them.

3 These are the nations the LORD did not force to leave. He wanted to test the Israelites who had not fought in the wars of Canaan. **2**(The only reason the LORD left those nations in the land was to teach the descendants of the Israelites who had not fought in those wars how to fight.) **3**These are the nations: the five rulers of the Philistines, all the Canaanites, the people of Sidon, and the Hivites who lived in the Lebanon mountains from Mount Baal Hermon to Lebo Hamath. **4**Those nations were in the land to test the Israelites—to see if they would obey the commands the LORD had given to their ancestors by Moses.

5The people of Israel lived with the Canaanites, Hittites, Amorites, Perizzites, Hivites, and Jebusites. **6**The Israelites began to marry the daughters of those people, and they allowed their daughters to marry the sons of those people. Israel also served their gods.

Othniel, the First Judge

7The Israelites did what the LORD said was wrong. They forgot about the LORD their God and served the idols of Baal and Asherah. **8**So the LORD was angry with Israel and allowed Cushan-Rishathaim king of Northwest Mesopotamia to rule over the Israelites for eight years. **9**When Israel cried to the LORD, the LORD sent someone to save them. Othniel son of Kenaz, Caleb's younger brother, saved the Israelites. **10**The Spirit of the LORD entered Othniel, and he became Israel's judge. When he went to war, the LORD handed over to him Cushan-Rishathaim king of Northwest Mesopotamia. **11**So the land was at peace for forty years. Then Othniel son of Kenaz died.

EMAIL! FROM GOD
3:9
Help
Who should you call for help?

Ehud, the Judge

12Again the people of Israel did what the LORD said was wrong. So the LORD gave Eglon king of Moab power to defeat Israel because of the evil Israel did. **13**Eglon got the Ammonites and the Amalekites to join him. Then he attacked Israel and took Jericho, the city of palm trees. **14**So the people of Israel were ruled by Eglon king of Moab for eighteen years.

15When the people cried to the LORD, he sent someone to save them. He was Ehud, son of Gera from the people of Benjamin, who was left-handed. Israel sent Ehud to give Eglon king of Moab the payment he demanded. **16**Ehud made himself a sword with two edges, about eighteen inches long, and he tied it to his right hip under his clothes. **17**Ehud gave Eglon king of Moab the payment he demanded. Now Eglon was a very fat man. **18**After he had given Eglon the payment, Ehud sent away the people who had carried it. **19**When he passed the statues near Gilgal, he turned around and said to Eglon, "I have a secret message for you, King Eglon."

The king said, "Be quiet!" Then he sent all of his servants out of the room.

20Ehud went to King Eglon, as he was
sitting alone in the room above his summer palace.
Ehud said, "I have a message from God
for you." As the king stood up from his
chair, 21Ehud reached with his left hand
and took out the sword that was tied to his
right hip. Then he stabbed the sword deep
into the king's belly! 22Even the handle
sank in, and the blade came out his back.
The king's fat covered the whole sword,
so Ehud left the sword in Eglon. 23Then
he went out of the room and closed and
locked the doors behind him.
24When the servants returned just after Ehud left, they found the doors to the
room locked. So they thought the king
was relieving himself. 25They waited for a
long time. Finally they became worried
because he still had not opened the doors.
So they got the key and unlocked them
and saw their king lying dead on the floor!
26While the servants were waiting,
Ehud had escaped. He passed by the statues and went to Seirah. 27When he
reached the mountains of Ephraim he
blew the trumpet. The people of Israel
heard it and went down from the hills
with Ehud leading them.
28He said to them, "Follow me! The
LORD has helped you to defeat your enemies, the Moabites." So Israel followed
Ehud and captured the crossings of the
Jordan River. They did not allow the Moabites to cross the Jordan River. 29Israel
killed about ten thousand strong and able
men from Moab; not one escaped. 30So
that day Moab was forced to be under the
rule of Israel, and there was peace in the
land for eighty years.

Shamgar, the Judge

31After Ehud, Shamgar son of Anath
saved Israel. Shamgar killed six hundred
Philistines with a sharp stick used to
guide oxen.

Deborah, the Woman Judge

4 After Ehud died, the Israelites again
did what the LORD said was wrong.
2So he let Jabin, a king of Canaan who
ruled in the city of Hazor, defeat Israel.
Sisera, who lived in Harosheth Haggoyim, was the commander of Jabin's
army. 3Because he had nine hundred iron
chariots and was very cruel to the people
of Israel for twenty years, they cried to
the LORD for help.

FAITH links

REAL FAITH OR REALLY SCARED?

JUDGES 4

When you think about facing something scary, are you a Barak or a Deborah? Deborah told Barak that he had been chosen by God to fight Sisera and his army. Sisera, with his 900 chariots, seemed impossible to beat. Barak said he wouldn't go unless Deborah went with him. Deborah agreed to go with him into battle. As a leader of Israel, Deborah had faith in God. She trusted that God would do the fighting.

God wants you to have faith in him when you're scared. That means focusing on him, rather than on your fear. Trust him to handle what you're afraid of.

Alone and Forgotten? Genesis 40:23, p. 57

How Big Is God?, Job 38—41, p. 703

911, Psalm 28:6, p. 730

Long-lasting Hope, Hosea 14, p. 1184

Our Heavenly Connection, Matthew 6:9–13, p. 1283

A Word About Worry, Matthew 6:25–34, p. 1284

4A prophetess named Deborah, the
wife of Lappidoth, was judge of Israel at
that time. 5Deborah would sit under the
Palm Tree of Deborah, which was between the cities of Ramah and Bethel, in
the mountains of Ephraim. And the people of Israel would come to her to settle
their arguments.
6Deborah sent a message to Barak
son of Abinoam. Barak lived in the city of
Kedesh, which is in the area of Naphtali.
Deborah said to Barak, "The LORD, the
God of Israel, commands you: 'Go and
gather ten thousand men of Naphtali and
Zebulun and lead them to Mount Tabor.
7I will make Sisera, the commander of
Jabin's army, and his chariots, and his
army meet you at the Kishon River. I will
hand Sisera over to you.'"
8Then Barak said to Deborah, "I will
go if you will go with me, but if you won't
go with me, I won't go."
9"Of course I will go with you," Deborah answered, "but you will not get credit
for the victory. The LORD will let a woman defeat Sisera." So Deborah went with
Barak to Kedesh. 10At Kedesh, Barak
called the people of Zebulun and Naphtali
together. From them, he gathered ten
thousand men to follow him, and Deborah
went with him also.
11Now Heber the Kenite had left the
other Kenites, the descendants of Hobab,
Moses' brother-in-law. Heber had put up
his tent by the great tree in Zaanannim,
near Kedesh.
12When Sisera was told that Barak
son of Abinoam had gone to Mount Tabor,
13Sisera gathered his nine hundred iron
chariots and all the men with him, from
Harosheth Haggoyim to the Kishon
River.
14Then Deborah said to Barak, "Get
up! Today is the day the LORD will hand
over Sisera. The LORD has already cleared
the way for you." So Barak led ten thousand men down Mount Tabor. 15As Barak
approached, the LORD confused Sisera
and his army and chariots. The LORD defeated them with the sword, but Sisera
left his chariot and ran away on foot.
16Barak and his men chased Sisera's
chariots and army to Harosheth Haggoyim. With their swords they killed all of
Sisera's men; not one of them was left
alive.
17But Sisera himself ran away to the
tent where Jael lived. She was the wife of
Heber, one of the Kenite family groups.
Heber's family was at peace with Jabin
king of Hazor. 18Jael went out to meet
Sisera and said to him, "Come into my
tent, master! Come in. Don't be afraid."
So Sisera went into Jael's tent, and she
covered him with a rug.
19Sisera said to Jael, "I am thirsty.
Please give me some water to drink." So
she opened a leather bag of milk and gave
him a drink. Then she covered him up.
20He said to her, "Go stand at the entrance to the tent. If anyone comes and
asks you, 'Is anyone here?' say, 'No.'"
21But Jael, the wife of Heber, took a
tent peg and a hammer and quietly went
to Sisera. Since he was very tired, he was
in a deep sleep. She hammered the tent
peg through the side of Sisera's head and
into the ground. And so Sisera died.
22At that very moment Barak came
by Jael's tent, chasing Sisera. Jael went
out to meet him and said, "Come. I will
show you the man you are looking for."
So Barak entered her tent, and there Sisera lay dead, with the tent peg in his
head.
23On that day God defeated Jabin king
of Canaan in the sight of Israel.
24Israel became stronger and stronger against Jabin king of Canaan until finally they destroyed him.

The Song of Deborah

5 On that day Deborah and Barak son of
Abinoam sang this song:
2"The leaders led Israel.
The people
volunteered
to go to
battle.
Praise the
LORD!
3Listen, kings.
Pay attention,
rulers!
I myself will sing to the LORD.

EMAIL FROM GOD 5:3
Worship
Who should you worship?

I will make music to the LORD, the
God of Israel.

4 "LORD, when you came from Edom,
when you marched from the land of
Edom,
the earth shook,
the skies rained,
and the clouds dropped water.
5 The mountains shook before the
LORD, the God of Mount Sinai,
before the LORD, the God of Israel!

6 "In the days of Shamgar son of
Anath,
in the days of Jael, the main roads
were empty.
Travelers went on the back roads.
7 There were no warriors in Israel
until I, Deborah, arose,
until I arose to be a mother to
Israel.
8 At that time they chose to follow new
gods.
Because of this, enemies fought us
at our city gates.
No one could find a shield or a spear
among the forty thousand people
of Israel.
9 My heart is with the commanders of
Israel.
They volunteered freely from
among the people.
Praise the LORD!

10 "You who ride on white donkeys
and sit on saddle blankets,
and you who walk along the road,
listen!
11 Listen to the sound of the singers
at the watering holes.
There they tell about the victories of
the LORD,
the victories of the LORD's
warriors in Israel.
Then the LORD's people went down
to the city gates.

12 "Wake up, wake up, Deborah!
Wake up, wake up, sing a song!
Get up, Barak!
Go capture your enemies, son of
Abinoam!

13 "Then those who were left came
down to the important leaders.
The LORD's people came down to
me with strong men.
14 They came from Ephraim in the
mountains of Amalek.
Benjamin was among the people
who followed you.
From the family group of Makir, the
commanders came down.
And from Zebulun came those who
lead.
15 The princes of Issachar were with
Deborah.
The people of Issachar were loyal
to Barak
and followed him into the valley.
The Reubenites thought hard
about what they would do.
16 Why did you stay by the
sheepfold?
Was it to hear the music played for
your sheep?
The Reubenites thought hard
about what they would do.
17 The people of Gilead stayed east of
the Jordan River.
People of Dan, why did you stay by
the ships?
The people of Asher stayed at the
seashore,
at their safe harbors.
18 But the people of Zebulun risked
their lives,
as did the people of Naphtali on the
battlefield.

19 "The kings came, and they fought.
At that time the kings of Canaan
fought
at Taanach, by the waters of
Megiddo.
But they took away no silver or
possessions of Israel.
20 The stars fought from heaven;
from their paths, they fought
Sisera.
21 The Kishon River swept Sisera's
men away,
that old river, the Kishon River.
March on, my soul, with strength!
22 Then the horses' hoofs beat the
ground.

Galloping, galloping go Sisera's
mighty horses.
23 'May the town of Meroz be cursed,'
said the angel of the LORD.
'Bitterly curse its people,
because they did not come to help
the LORD.
They did not fight the strong
enemy.'

24 "May Jael, the wife of Heber the
Kenite,
be blessed above all women who
live in tents.
25 Sisera asked for water,
but Jael gave him milk.
In a bowl fit for a ruler,
she brought him cream.
26 Jael reached out and took the tent
peg.
Her right hand reached for the
workman's hammer.
She hit Sisera! She smashed his
head!
She crushed and pierced the side
of his head!
27 At Jael's feet he sank.
He fell, and he lay there.
At her feet he sank. He fell.
Where Sisera sank, there he fell,
dead!

28 "Sisera's mother looked out through
the window.
She looked through the curtains
and cried out,
'Why is Sisera's chariot so late in
coming?
Why are sounds of his chariots'
horses delayed?'
29 The wisest of her servant ladies
answer her,
and Sisera's mother says to
herself,
30 'Surely they are robbing the people
they defeated!
Surely they are dividing those
things among themselves!
Each soldier is given a girl or two.
Maybe Sisera is taking pieces of
dyed cloth.
Maybe they are even taking
pieces of dyed, embroidered cloth
for the necks of the victors!'

31 "Let all your enemies die this way,
LORD!
But let all the
people who
love you
be as strong as
the rising
sun!"
Then there was
peace in the land for forty years.

EMAIL FROM GOD
5:31
Following God
Check to see what God's people are like.

The Midianites Attack Israel

6 Again the Israelites did what the
LORD said was wrong. So for seven
years the LORD handed them over to
Midian. 2 Because the Midianites were
very powerful and were cruel to Israel,
the Israelites made hiding places in the
mountains, in caves, and in safe places.
3 Whenever the Israelites planted crops,
the Midianites, Amalekites, and other
peoples from the east would come and attack them. 4 They camped in the land and
destroyed the crops that the Israelites
had planted as far away as Gaza. They left
nothing for Israel to eat, and no sheep,
cattle, or donkeys. 5 The Midianites came
with their tents and their animals like
swarms of locusts to ruin the land. There
were so many people and camels they
could not be counted. 6 Israel became
very poor because of the Midianites, so
they cried out to the LORD.
7 When the Israelites cried out to the
LORD against the Midianites, 8 the LORD
sent a prophet to them. He said, "This is
what the LORD, the God of Israel, says: I
brought you out of Egypt, the land of
slavery. 9 I saved you from the Egyptians
and from all those who were against you.
I forced the Canaanites out of their land
and gave it to you. 10 Then I said to you, 'I
am the LORD your God. Live in the land
of the Amorites, but do not worship their
gods.' But you did not obey me."

The Angel of the Lord Visits Gideon

11 The angel of the LORD came and sat
down under the oak tree at Ophrah that

FAITH links

FROM ZERO TO HERO

JUDGES 6; 7

Would you get up and conquer an army of people if God said that you could? Or, would you head for the hills? When Gideon learned that he had been chosen to lead the people of Israel against the Midianites, he was ready to head for the hills. He could hardly believe that God had chosen him for the job. After all, he was a nobody! He was the youngest in his family. He was no hero! But God proved him wrong.

Faith in God makes anyone go from being a zero to being a hero. With God on your side, you are a conqueror!

Want to be a real hero? Connect to these Faithlinks:

The Way to Serve God, 1 Kings 9:4, p. 450

Building Together, Nehemiah 3, p. 627

The Foundation of Our Hope, Isaiah 31:1–8, p. 934

Jesus' Mission and Yours, Isaiah 61:1–2, p. 978

Go! No!, Jonah 1, p. 1213

Just a Test, Luke 4:1–13, p. 1373

belonged to Joash, one of the Abiezrite people. Gideon, Joash's son, was separating some wheat from the chaff in a winepress to keep the wheat from the
Midianites. 12The angel of the LORD ap-
peared to Gideon and said, "The LORD is
with you, mighty warrior!"
13Then Gideon said, "Sir, if the LORD
is with us, why are we having so much
trouble? Where are the miracles our ancestors told us he did when the LORD
brought them out of Egypt? But now he
has left us and has handed us over to the
Midianites."
14The LORD turned to Gideon and
said, "Go with your strength and save Israel from the Midianites. I am the one
who is sending you."
15But Gideon answered, "Lord, how
can I save Israel? My family group is the
weakest in Manasseh, and I am the least
important member of my family."
16The LORD answered him, "I will be
with you. It will seem as if the Midianites
you are fighting are only one man."
17Then Gideon said to the LORD, "If
you are pleased with me, give me proof
that it is really you talking with me.
18Please wait here until I come back to
you. Let me bring my offering and set it
in front of you."
And the LORD said, "I will wait until
you return."
19So Gideon went in and cooked a
young goat, and with twenty quarts of
flour, made bread without yeast. Then he
put the meat into a basket and the broth
into a pot. He brought them out and gave
them to the angel under the oak tree.
20The angel of God said to Gideon,
"Put the meat and the bread without
yeast on that rock over there. Then pour
the broth on them." And Gideon did as he
was told. 21The angel of the LORD
touched the meat and the bread with the
end of the stick that was in his hand.
Then fire jumped up from the rock and
completely burned up the meat and the
bread! And the angel of the LORD disappeared! 22Then Gideon understood he
had been talking to the angel of the LORD.
So Gideon cried out, "Lord GOD! I have
seen the angel of the LORD face to face!"
23But the LORD said to Gideon, "Calm
down! Don't be afraid! You will not die!"
24So Gideon built an altar there to
worship the LORD and named it The

LORD Is Peace. It still stands at Ophrah,
where the Abiezrites live.

Gideon Tears Down the Altar of Baal

25That same night the LORD said to
Gideon, "Take the bull that belongs to
your father and a second bull seven years
old. Pull down your father's altar to Baal,
and cut down the Asherah idol beside it.
26Then build an altar to the LORD your
God with its stones in the right order on
this high ground. Kill and burn a second
bull on this altar, using the wood from the
Asherah idol."

27So Gideon got ten of his servants
and did what the LORD had told him to do.
But Gideon was afraid that his family and
the men of the city might see him, so he
did it at night, not in the daytime.

28When the men of the city got up the
next morning, they saw that the altar for
Baal had been destroyed and that the
Asherah idol beside it had been cut
down! They also saw the altar Gideon
had built and the second bull that had
been sacrificed on it. 29The men of the
city asked each other, "Who did this?"

After they asked many questions,
someone told them, "Gideon son of Joash
did this."

30So they said to Joash, "Bring your
son out. He has pulled down the altar of
Baal and cut down the Asherah idol beside it. He must die!"

31But Joash said to the angry crowd
around him, "Are you going to take Baal's
side? Are you going to defend him? Anyone who takes Baal's side will be killed
by morning! If Baal is a god, let him fight
for himself. It's his altar that has been
pulled down." 32So on that day Gideon
got the name Jerub-Baal, which means
"let Baal fight against him," because Gideon pulled down Baal's altar.

Gideon Defeats Midian

33All the Midianites, the Amalekites,
and other peoples from the east joined together and came across the Jordan River
and camped in the Valley of Jezreel. 34But
the Spirit of the LORD entered Gideon,
and he blew a trumpet to call the Abiezrites to follow him. 35He sent messengers to all of Manasseh, calling them to
follow him. He also sent messengers to
the people of Asher, Zebulun, and Naphtali. So they also went up to meet Gideon
and his men.

36Then Gideon said to God, "You said
you would help me save Israel. 37I will
put some wool on the threshing floor. If
there is dew only on the wool but all of
the ground is dry, then I will know that
you will use me to save Israel, as you
said." 38And that is just what happened.
When Gideon got up early the next morning and squeezed the wool, he got a full
bowl of water from it.

39Then Gideon said to God, "Don't be
angry with me if I ask just one more
thing. Please let me make one more test.
Let only the wool be dry while the
ground around it gets wet with dew."
40That night God did that very thing.
Just the wool was dry, but the ground
around it was wet with dew.

7 Early in the morning Jerub-Baal (also
called Gideon) and all his men set up
their camp at the spring of Harod. The
Midianites were camped north of them in
the valley at the bottom of the hill called
Moreh. 2Then the LORD said to Gideon,
"You have too many men to defeat the
Midianites. I don't want the Israelites to
brag that they saved themselves. 3So
now, announce to the people, 'Anyone
who is afraid may leave Mount Gilead and
go back home.' " So twenty-two thousand men returned home, but ten thousand remained.

4Then the LORD said to Gideon,
"There are still too many men. Take the
men down to the water, and I will test
them for you there. If I say, 'This man will
go with you,' he will go. But if I say, 'That
one will not go with you,' he will not go."

5So Gideon led the men down to the
water. There the LORD said to him, "Separate them into those who drink water by
lapping it up like a dog and those who
bend down to drink." 6There were three
hundred men who used their hands to
bring water to their mouths, lapping it as
a dog does. All the rest got down on their
knees to drink.

7Then the LORD said to Gideon, "Using the three hundred men who lapped
the water, I will save you and hand Midian over to you. Let all the others go
home." 8So Gideon sent the rest of Israel
to their homes. But he kept three hundred men and took the jars and the trumpets of those who left.

Now the camp of Midian was in the
valley below Gideon. 9That night the
LORD said to Gideon, "Get up. Go down
and attack the camp of the Midianites,
because I will give them to you. 10But if
you are afraid to go down, take your servant Purah with you. 11When you come
to the camp of Midian, you will hear what
they are saying. Then you will not be
afraid to attack the camp."

Gideon Is Encouraged

So Gideon and his servant Purah went
down to the edge of the enemy camp.
12The Midianites, the Amalekites, and
all the peoples from the east were
camped in that valley. There were so
many of them they seemed like locusts.
Their camels could not be counted because they were as many as the grains of
sand on the seashore!

13When Gideon came to the enemy
camp, he heard a man telling his friend
about a dream. He was saying, "I dreamed
that a loaf of barley bread rolled into the
camp of Midian. It hit the tent so hard that
the tent turned over and fell flat!"

14The man's friend said, "Your dream
is about the sword of Gideon son of Joash,
a man of Israel. God will hand Midian and
the whole army over to him!"

15When Gideon heard about the
dream and what it meant, he worshiped
God. Then Gideon went back to the camp
of Israel and called out to them, "Get up!
The LORD has handed the army of Midian
over to you!" 16Gideon divided the three
hundred men into three groups. He gave
each man a trumpet and an empty jar
with a burning torch inside.

17Gideon told the men, "Watch me
and do what I do. When I get to the edge
of the camp, do what I do. 18Surround the
enemy camp. When I and everyone with
me blow our trumpets, you blow your
trumpets, too. Then shout, 'For the LORD
and for Gideon!'"

Midian Is Defeated

19So Gideon and the one hundred
men with him came to the edge of the
enemy camp just after they had changed
guards. It was during the middle watch of
the night. Then Gideon and his men blew
their trumpets and smashed their jars.
20All three groups of Gideon's men blew
their trumpets and smashed their jars.
They held the torches in their left hands
and the trumpets in their right hands.
Then they shouted, "A sword for the
LORD and for Gideon!" 21Each of Gideon's men stayed in his place around the
camp, but the Midianites began shouting
and running to escape.

22When Gideon's three hundred men
blew their trumpets, the LORD made all
the Midianites fight each other with their
swords! The enemy army ran away to the
city of Beth Shittah toward Zererah.
They ran as far as the border of Abel Meholah, near the city of Tabbath. 23Then
men of Israel from Naphtali, Asher, and
all of Manasseh were called out to chase
the Midianites. 24Gideon sent messengers through all the mountains of Ephraim, saying, "Come down and attack the
Midianites. Take control of the Jordan
River as far as Beth Barah before the
Midianites can get to it."

So they called out all the men of
Ephraim, who took control of the Jordan
River as far as Beth Barah. 25The men of
Ephraim captured two princes of Midian
named Oreb and Zeeb. They killed Oreb
at the rock of Oreb and Zeeb at the winepress of Zeeb, and they continued chasing the Midianites. They brought the
heads of Oreb and Zeeb to Gideon, who
was east of the Jordan River.

8 The men of Ephraim asked Gideon,
"Why did you treat us this way? Why
didn't you call us when you went to fight
against Midian?" They argued angrily
with Gideon.

2But he answered them, "I have not
done as well as you! The small part you
did was better than all that my people of
Abiezer did. 3God let you capture Oreb

and Zeeb, the princes of Midian. How can
I compare what I did with what you did?"
When the men of Ephraim heard
Gideon's answer, they were not as angry
anymore.

Gideon Captures Two Kings

4When Gideon and his three hundred
men came to the Jordan River, they were
tired, but they chased the enemy across
to the other side. **5**Gideon said to the
men of Succoth, "Please give my soldiers
some bread because they are very tired. I
am chasing Zebah and Zalmunna, the
kings of Midian."

6But the leaders of Succoth said,
"Why should we give your soldiers
bread? You haven't caught Zebah and Zalmunna yet."

7Then Gideon said, "The LORD will
surrender Zebah and Zalmunna to me.
After that, I will whip your skin with
thorns and briers from the desert."

8Gideon left Succoth and went to the
city of Peniel and asked them for food.
But the people of Peniel gave him the
same answer as the people of Succoth.
9So Gideon said to the men of Peniel, "After I win the victory, I will return and pull
down this tower."

10Zebah and Zalmunna and their army
were in the city of Karkor. About fifteen
thousand men were left of the armies of
the peoples of the east. Already one hundred twenty thousand soldiers had been
killed. **11**Gideon went up the road of those
who live in tents east of Nobah and Jogbehah, and he attacked the enemy army
when they did not expect it. **12**Zebah and
Zalmunna, the kings of Midian, ran away,
but Gideon chased and captured them and
frightened away their army.

13Then Gideon son of Joash returned
from the battle by the Pass of Heres.
14Gideon captured a young man from
Succoth and asked him some questions.
So the young man wrote down for Gideon
the names of seventy-seven officers and
older leaders of Succoth.

Gideon Punishes Succoth

15When Gideon came to Succoth, he
said to the people of that city, "Here are
Zebah and Zalmunna. You made fun of me
by saying, 'Why should we give bread to
your tired men? You have not caught Zebah and Zalmunna yet.' " **16**So Gideon
took the older leaders of the city and punished them with thorns and briers from
the desert. **17**He also pulled down the
tower of Peniel and killed the people in
that city.

18Gideon asked Zebah and Zalmunna,
"What were the men like that you killed
on Mount Tabor?"

They answered, "They were like you.
Each one of them looked like a prince."

19Gideon said, "Those were my
brothers, my mother's sons. As surely as
the LORD lives, I would not kill you if you
had spared them." **20**Then Gideon said to
Jether, his oldest son, "Kill them." But
Jether was only a boy and was afraid, so
he did not take out his sword.

21Then Zebah and Zalmunna said to
Gideon, "Come on. Kill us yourself. As
the saying goes, 'It takes a man to do a
man's job.' " So Gideon got up and killed
Zebah and Zalmunna and took the decorations off their camels' necks.

Gideon Makes an Idol

22The people of Israel said to Gideon,
"You saved us from the Midianites. Now,
we want you and your son and your
grandson to rule over us."

23But Gideon told them, "The LORD
will be your ruler. I will not rule over you,
nor will my son rule over you." **24**He
said, "I want you to do this one thing for
me. I want each of you to give me a gold
earring from the things you took in the
fighting." (The Ishmaelites[n] wore gold
earrings.)

25They said, "We will gladly give you
what you want." So they spread out a
coat, and everyone threw down an earring from what he had taken. **26**The gold
earrings weighed about forty-three
pounds. This did not count the decorations, necklaces, and purple robes worn
by the kings of Midian, nor the chains
from the camels' necks. **27**Gideon used

8:24 Ishmaelites Another name for the
Midianites. See Genesis 37:25-28.

FAITH CHALLENGE

Here's a challenge for you. Read 8:23 to find out what a famous Israelite leader told his people about their government. What could you do to let your friends know that the Lord is ruler of your life?

TESTING IT

Judges 8:23
But Gideon told them, "The LORD will be your ruler. I will not rule over you, nor will my son rule over you."

the gold to make a holy vest, which he put in his hometown of Ophrah. But all the Israelites were unfaithful to God and worshiped it, so it became a trap for Gideon and his family.

The Death of Gideon

28So Midian was under the rule of Israel; they did not cause trouble anymore. And the land had peace for forty years, as long as Gideon was alive.

29Gideon[n] son of Joash went to his home to live. **30**He had seventy sons of his own, because he had many wives. **31**He had a slave woman who lived in Shechem, and he had a son by her, whom he named Abimelech. **32**So Gideon son of Joash died at a good old age. He was buried in the tomb of Joash, his father, in Ophrah, where the Abiezrites live.

33As soon as Gideon died, the people of Israel were again unfaithful to God and followed the Baals. They made Baal-Berith their god. **34**The Israelites did not remember the LORD their God, who had saved them from all their enemies living all around them. **35**And they were not kind to the family of Jerub-Baal, also called Gideon, for all the good he had done for Israel.

Abimelech Becomes King

9 Abimelech son of Gideon went to his uncles in the city of Shechem. He said to his uncles and all of his mother's family group, **2**"Ask the leaders of Shechem, 'Is it better for the seventy sons of Gideon to rule over you or for one man to rule?' Remember, I am your relative."

3Abimelech's uncles spoke to all the leaders of Shechem about this. And they decided to follow Abimelech, because they said, "He is our relative." **4**So the leaders of Shechem gave Abimelech about one and three-quarter pounds of silver from the temple of the god Baal-Berith. Abimelech used the silver to hire some worthless, reckless men, who followed him wherever he went. **5**He went to Ophrah, the hometown of his father, and murdered his seventy brothers, the sons of Gideon. He killed them all on one stone. But Gideon's youngest son, Jotham, hid from Abimelech and escaped. **6**Then all of the leaders of Shechem and Beth Millo gathered beside the great tree standing in Shechem. There they made Abimelech their king.

Jotham's Story

7When Jotham heard this, he went and stood on the top of Mount Gerizim. He shouted to the people: "Listen to me, you leaders of Shechem, so that God will listen to you! **8**One day the trees decided to appoint a king to rule over them.

8:29 Gideon Also called Jerub-Baal.

THE JUDGES

Judges 9

After the death of Joshua, the Israelites were ruled by judges, or leaders, for about 300 years. This was a dark time in Israel's history because "everyone did what seemed right" and did not obey God. The judges tried to steer the people back to God, but many of them also were disobedient. Here are some of the judges from that time:

1. Othniel was the first judge of Israel. He delivered the Israelites from the king of Northwest Mesopotamia. (Check out Judges 3:7–11.)

© 2001, Thomas Nelson, Inc.

Mediterranean
River Kishon
Lake Galilee
Jordan River
AMMON
Jerusalem
Debir
Gaza
Dead Sea
MOAB
0 25 miles
N

2. Shamgar was famous for killing 600 men with a sharp stick used to guide oxen. He delivered Israel from the Philistines. (Look up Judges 3:31.)

3. Deborah was the only woman judge of Israel. She and her military commander, Barak, fought against Jabin, king of Canaan, and his commander, Sisera. (See Judges 4:1–24.)

4. Gideon wasn't a judge or a soldier. Still God used him to be a judge of Israel and to lead a small army of 300 men to defeat the much greater forces of Midian. (Look up Judges 6—8.)

5. Samson was a judge in Israel. He ruled for 20 years. His body was strong, but his character was weak. Because of that, the Philistines captured him and made him a slave. Samson died when he destroyed a pagan temple, but he killed many Philistine enemies at the same time. (See Judges 13—16.)

They said to the olive tree, 'You be king over us!'

9"But the olive tree said, 'Men and gods are honored by my oil. Should I stop making it and go and sway over the other trees?'

10"Then the trees said to the fig tree, 'Come and be king over us!'

11"But the fig tree answered, 'Should I stop making my sweet and good fruit and go and sway over the other trees?'

12"Then the trees said to the vine, 'Come and be king over us!'

13"But the vine answered, 'My new wine makes men and gods happy. Should I stop making it and go and sway over the trees?'

14"Then all the trees said to the thornbush, 'Come and be king over us.'

15"But the thornbush said to the trees, 'If you really want to appoint me king over you, come and find shelter in my shade! But if not, let fire come out of the thornbush and burn up the cedars of Lebanon!'

16"Now, were you completely honest

and sincere when you made Abimelech
king? Have you been fair to Gideon[n] and
his family? Have you treated Gideon as
you should? **17**Remember, my father
fought for you and risked his life to save
you from the power of the Midianites.
18But now you have turned against my
father's family and have killed his seventy sons on one stone. You have made
Abimelech, the son of my father's slave
girl, king over the leaders of Shechem
just because he is your relative! **19**So
then, if you have been honest and sincere
to Gideon and his family today, be happy
with Abimelech as your king. And may he
be happy with you! **20**But if not, may fire
come out of Abimelech and completely
burn you leaders of Shechem and Beth
Millo! Also may fire come out of the leaders of Shechem and Beth Millo and burn
up Abimelech!"

21Then Jotham ran away and escaped
to the city of Beer. He lived there because he was afraid of his brother Abimelech.

Abimelech Fights Against Shechem

22Abimelech ruled Israel for three
years. **23**Then God sent an evil spirit to
make trouble between Abimelech and
the leaders of Shechem so that the leaders of Shechem turned against him.
24Abimelech had killed Gideon's[n] seventy sons, his own brothers, and the
leaders of Shechem had helped him. So
God sent the evil spirit to punish them.
25The leaders of Shechem were against
Abimelech then. They put men on the
hilltops in ambush who robbed everyone
going by. And Abimelech was told.

26A man named Gaal son of Ebed and
his brothers moved into Shechem, and
the leaders of Shechem trusted him.
27They went out to the vineyards to pick
grapes, and they squeezed the grapes.
Then they had a feast in the temple of
their god, where they ate and drank and
cursed Abimelech. **28**Gaal son of Ebed
said, "We are the men of Shechem. Who
is Abimelech that we should serve him?
Isn't he one of Gideon's sons, and isn't
Zebul his officer? We should serve the
men of Hamor, Shechem's father. Why
should we serve Abimelech? **29**If you
made me commander of these people, I
would get rid of Abimelech. I would say
to him, 'Get your army ready and come
out to battle.' "

30Now when Zebul, the ruler of Shechem, heard what Gaal son of Ebed said,
he was very angry. **31**He sent secret
messengers to Abimelech, saying, "Gaal
son of Ebed and Gaal's brothers have
come to Shechem, and they are turning
the city against you! **32**You and your men
should get up during the night and hide
in the fields outside the city. **33**As soon as
the sun comes up in the morning, attack
the city. When Gaal and his men come out
to fight you, do what you can to them."

34So Abimelech and all his soldiers
got up during the night and hid near Shechem in four groups. **35**Gaal son of Ebed
went out and was standing at the entrance to the city gate. As he was standing there, Abimelech and his soldiers
came out of their hiding places.

36When Gaal saw the soldiers, he said
to Zebul, "Look! There are people coming down from the mountains!"

But Zebul said, "You are seeing the
shadows of the mountains. The shadows
just look like people."

37But again Gaal said, "Look, there
are people coming down from the center
of the land, and there is a group coming
from the fortune-tellers' tree!"

38Zebul said to Gaal, "Where is your
bragging now? You said, 'Who is Abimelech that we should serve him?' You
made fun of these men. Now go out and
fight them."

39So Gaal led the men of Shechem out
to fight Abimelech. **40**Abimelech and his
men chased them, and many of Gaal's
men were killed before they could get
back to the city gate. **41**While Abimelech
stayed at Arumah, Zebul forced Gaal and
his brothers to leave Shechem.

42The next day the people of Shechem went out to the fields. When Abimelech was told about it, **43**he separated
his men into three groups and hid them in

9:16, 24 Gideon Also called Jerub-Baal.

the fields. When he saw the people coming out of the city, he jumped up and attacked them. 44Abimelech and his group
ran to the entrance gate to the city. The
other two groups ran out to the people in
the fields and struck them down. 45Abim-
elech and his men fought the city of Shechem all day until they captured it and
killed its people. Then he tore it down and
threw salt[n] over the ruins.

The Tower of Shechem Burns

46When the leaders who were in the
Tower of Shechem heard what had happened to Shechem, they gathered in the
safest room of the temple of El Berith.
47Abimelech heard that all the leaders of
the Tower of Shechem had gathered
there. 48So he and all his men went up
Mount Zalmon, near Shechem. Abimelech took an ax and cut some branches
and put them on his shoulders. He said to
all those with him, "Hurry! Do what I
have done!" 49So all those men cut
branches and followed Abimelech and
piled them against the safest room of the
temple. Then they set them on fire and
burned the people inside. So all the people who were at the Tower of Shechem
also died—about a thou-
sand men and women.

Abimelech's Death

50Then Abimelech
went to the city of The-
bez. He surrounded the
city, attacked it, and captured it. 51But inside the
city was a strong tower,
so all the men, women,
and leaders of that city
ran to the tower. When they got inside,
they locked the door behind them. Then
they climbed up to the roof of the tower.
52Abimelech came to the tower to attack
it. He approached the door of the tower
to set it on fire, 53but as he came near, a
woman dropped a grinding stone on his
head, crushing his skull.
54He quickly called to the officer who
carried his armor and said, "Take out your
sword and kill me. I don't want people to
say, 'A woman killed Abimelech.' " So the
officer stabbed Abimelech, and he died.
55When the people of Israel saw Abimelech was dead, they all returned home.
56In that way God punished Abimelech for all the evil he had done to his father by killing his seventy brothers.
57God also punished the men of Shechem for the evil they had done. So the
curse spoken by Jotham, the youngest
son of Gideon,[n] came true.

Tola, the Judge

10 After Abimelech died, another
judge came to save Israel. He was
Tola son of Puah, the son of Dodo. Tola
was from the people of Issachar and lived
in the city of Shamir in the mountains of
Ephraim. 2Tola was a judge for Israel for
twenty-three years. Then he died and
was buried in Shamir.

Jair, the Judge

3After Tola died, Jair from the region
of Gilead became judge. He was a judge
for Israel for twenty-two years. 4Jair had
thirty sons, who rode thirty donkeys.
These thirty sons controlled thirty towns
in Gilead, which are called the Towns of
Jair to this day. 5Jair died and was buried
in the city of Kamon.

So the LORD was angry with them and handed them over to the Philistines and the Ammonites.
—Judges 10:7

The Ammonites Trouble Israel

6Again the Israelites
did what the LORD said
was wrong. They wor-
shiped Baal and Ashto-
reth, the gods of Aram,
Sidon, Moab, and Ammon,
and the gods of the Philistines. The Israelites left
the LORD and stopped serving him. 7So
the LORD was angry with them and handed them over to the Philistines and the
Ammonites. 8In the same year those people destroyed the Israelites who lived east
of the Jordan River in the region of Gilead,
where the Amorites lived. So the Israelites suffered for eighteen years. 9The

9:45 salt The salt would keep crops from growing there.

9:57 Gideon Also called Jerub-Baal.

Ammonites then crossed the Jordan River
to fight the people of Judah, Benjamin, and
Ephraim, causing much trouble to the
people of Israel. 10So the Israelites cried
out to the LORD, "We have sinned against
you. We left our God and worshiped the
Baal idols."
11The LORD answered the Israelites,
"When the Egyptians, Amorites, Ammonites, Philistines, 12Sidonians, Amalekites, and Maonites were cruel to you,
you cried out to me, and I saved you.
13But now you have left me again and
have worshiped other gods. So I refuse to
save you again. 14You have chosen those
gods. So go call to them for help. Let
them save you when you are in trouble."
15But the people of Israel said to the
LORD, "We have sinned. Do to us whatever you want, but please save us today!"
16Then the Israelites threw away the
foreign gods among them, and they worshiped the LORD again. So he felt sorry
for them when he saw their suffering.
17The Ammonites gathered for war
and camped in Gilead. The Israelites
gathered and camped at Mizpah. 18The
leaders of the people of Gilead said, "Who
will lead us to attack the Ammonites? He
will become the head of all those who live
in Gilead."

Jephthah Is Chosen as Leader

11 Jephthah was a strong soldier from
Gilead. His father was named Gilead, and his mother was a prostitute.
2Gilead's wife had several sons. When
they grew up, they forced Jephthah to
leave his home, saying to him, "You will
not get any of our father's property, because you are the son of another woman." 3So Jephthah ran away from his
brothers and lived in the land of Tob.
There some worthless men began to follow him.
4After a time the Ammonites fought
against Israel. 5When the Ammonites
made war against Israel, the older leaders of Gilead went to Jephthah to bring
him back from Tob. 6They said to him,
"Come and lead our army so we can fight
the Ammonites."
7But Jephthah said to them, "Didn't

FAITH links

WHAT'S OUT BECOMES IN

JUDGES 11

If someone called you a loser, then turned around and asked you for help, what would you do? That was the situation Jephthah found himself in. His own family told him they didn't want him around. But when the Ammonites attacked, they begged Jephthah for help. Suddenly, Jephthah the outcast was in. Jephthah didn't let their first opinion of him affect his behavior. He agreed to help them because he knew that God would help him.

If someone treats you unkindly, you don't have to respond with unkindness. You also don't have to accept someone else's bad opinion as the truth. Instead, trust God to help you see the truth and do what's right.

When Bad Turns to Worse, Exodus 5:6–12, p. 82

Play Fair or Play Favorites?, Deuteronomy 1:16–18, p. 227

Wronged for What's Right, Ezra 4:4–5, p. 612

Does Crime Pay?, Psalm 37:1–7, p. 736

In the Lions' Den, Daniel 6, p. 1160

Who Needs Love?, Luke 6:27–36, p. 1379

you hate me? You forced me to leave my
father's house. Why are you coming to
me now that you are in trouble?"

8The older leaders of Gilead said to
Jephthah, "It is because of those troubles
that we come to you now. Please come
with us and fight against the Ammonites.
You will be the ruler over everyone who
lives in Gilead."

9Then Jephthah answered, "If you
take me back to Gilead to fight the Ammonites and the LORD helps me win, I
will be your ruler."

10The older leaders of Gilead said to
him, "The LORD is listening to everything we are saying. We promise to do all
that you tell us to do." **11**So Jephthah
went with the older leaders of Gilead, and
the people made him their leader and
commander of their army. Jephthah repeated all of his words in front of the
LORD at Mizpah.

Jephthah Sends Messengers to the Ammonite King

12Jephthah sent messengers to the
king of the Ammonites, asking, "What
have you got against Israel? Why have
you come to attack our land?"

13The king of the Ammonites answered the messengers of Jephthah, "We
are fighting Israel because you took our
land when you came up from Egypt. You
took our land from the Arnon River to the
Jabbok River to the Jordan River. Now
give our land back to us peacefully."

14Jephthah sent the messengers to
the Ammonite king again. **15**They said:

"This is what Jephthah says: Israel did
not take the land of the people of Moab or
Ammon. **16**When the Israelites came out
of Egypt, they went into the desert to the
Red Sea and then to Kadesh. **17**Israel
sent messengers to the king of Edom,
saying, 'Let the people of Israel go across
your land.' But the king of Edom refused.
We sent the same message to the king of
Moab, but he also refused. So the Israelites stayed at Kadesh.

18"Then the Israelites went into the
desert around the borders of the lands of
Edom and Moab. Israel went east of the
land of Moab and camped on the other
side of the Arnon River, the border of
Moab. They did not cross it to go into the
land of Moab.

19"Then Israel sent messengers to
Sihon king of the Amorites, king of the
city of Heshbon, asking, 'Let the people
of Israel pass through your land to go to
our land.' **20**But Sihon did not trust the
Israelites to cross his land. So he gathered all of his people and camped at Jahaz
and fought with Israel.

21"But the LORD, the God of Israel,
handed Sihon and his army over to Israel.
All the land of the Amorites became the
property of Israel. **22**So Israel took all the
land of the Amorites from the Arnon
River to the Jabbok River, from the
desert to the Jordan River.

23"It was the LORD, the God of Israel,
who forced out the Amorites ahead of the
people of Israel. So do you think you can
make them leave? **24**Take the land that
your god Chemosh has given you. We will
live in the land the LORD our God has
given us!

25"Are you any better than Balak son
of Zippor, king of Moab? Did he ever
quarrel or fight with the people of Israel?
26For three hundred years the Israelites
have lived in Heshbon and Aroer and the
towns around them and in all the cities
along the Arnon River. Why have you not
taken these cities back in all that time?
27I have not sinned against you, but you
are sinning against me by making war on
me. May the LORD, the Judge, decide
whether the Israelites or the Ammonites
are right."

28But the king of the Ammonites ignored this message from Jephthah.

Jephthah's Promise

29Then the Spirit of the LORD entered
Jephthah. Jephthah passed through Gilead and Manasseh and the city of Mizpah
in Gilead to the land of the Ammonites.
30Jephthah made a promise to the LORD,
saying, "If you will hand over the Ammonites to me, **31**I will give you as a
burnt offering the first thing that comes
out of my house to meet me when I return from the victory. It will be the
LORD's."

32Then Jephthah went over to fight
the Ammonites, and the LORD handed
them over to him. **33**In a great defeat
Jephthah struck them down from the city
of Aroer to the area of Minnith, and
twenty cities as far as the city of Abel
Keramim. So the Ammonites were defeated by the Israelites.

34When Jephthah returned to his
home in Mizpah, his daughter was the
first one to come out to meet him, playing
a tambourine and dancing. She was his
only child; he had no other sons or daughters. **35**When Jephthah saw his daughter,
he tore his clothes to show his sorrow.
He said, "My daughter! You have made
me so sad because I made a promise to
the LORD, and I cannot break it!"

36Then his daughter said, "Father,
you made a promise to the LORD. So do to
me just what you promised, because the
LORD helped you defeat your enemies,
the Ammonites." **37**She also said, "But
let me do one thing. Let me be alone for
two months to go to the mountains. Since
I will never marry, let me and my friends
go and cry together."

38Jephthah said, "Go." So he sent her
away for two months. She and her friends
stayed in the mountains and cried for her
because she would never marry. **39**After
two months she returned to her father,
and Jephthah did to her what he had
promised. Jephthah's daughter never had
a husband.

From this came a custom in Israel that
40every year the young women of Israel
would go out for four days to remember
the daughter of Jephthah from Gilead.

Jephthah and Ephraim

12 The men of Ephraim called all their
soldiers together and crossed the
river to the town of Zaphon. They said to
Jephthah, "Why didn't you call us to help
you fight the Ammonites? We will burn
your house down with you in it."

2Jephthah answered them, "My people and I fought a great battle against the
Ammonites. I called you, but you didn't
come to help me. **3**When I saw that you
would not help me, I risked my own life
and went against the Ammonites. The
LORD handed them over to me. So
why have you come to fight against me
today?"

4Then Jephthah called the men of Gilead together and fought the men of Ephraim. The men of Gilead struck them down
because the Ephraimites had said, "You
men of Gilead are nothing but deserters
from Ephraim—living between Ephraim
and Manasseh." **5**The men of Gilead captured the crossings of the Jordan River
that led to the country of Ephraim. A person from Ephraim trying to escape would
say, "Let me cross the river." Then the
men of Gilead would ask him, "Are you
from Ephraim?" If he replied no, **6**they
would say to him, "Say the word 'Shibbo-
leth.' " The men of Ephraim could not say
that word correctly. So if the person from
Ephraim said, "Sibboleth," the men of
Gilead would kill him at the crossing. So
forty-two thousand people from Ephraim
were killed at that time.

7Jephthah was a judge for Israel for
six years. Then Jephthah, the man from
Gilead, died and was buried in a town in
Gilead.

Ibzan, the Judge

8After Jephthah died, Ibzan from
Bethlehem was a judge for Israel. **9**He
had thirty sons and thirty daughters. He
let his daughters marry men who were
not in his family group, and he brought
thirty women who were not in his tribe to
be wives for his sons. Ibzan judged Israel
for seven years. **10**Then he died and was
buried in Bethlehem.

Elon, the Judge

11After Ibzan died, Elon from the
tribe of Zebulun was a judge for Israel.
He judged Israel for ten years. **12**Then
Elon, the man of Zebulun, died and was
buried in the city of Aijalon in the land of
Zebulun.

Abdon, the Judge

13After Elon died, Abdon son of Hillel
from the city of Pirathon was a judge for
Israel. **14**He had forty sons and thirty
grandsons, who rode on seventy donkeys. He judged Israel for eight years.

15Then Abdon son of Hillel died and was
buried in Pirathon in the land of Ephraim,
in the mountains where the Amalekites
lived.

The Birth of Samson

13 Again the people of Israel did what
the LORD said was wrong. So he
handed them over to the Philistines for
forty years.

2There was a man named Manoah
from the tribe of Dan, who lived in the
city of Zorah. He had a wife, but she could
not have children. 3The angel of the
LORD appeared to Manoah's wife and
said, "You have not been able to have
children, but you will become pregnant
and give birth to a son. 4Be careful not to
drink wine or beer or eat anything that is
unclean, 5because you will become pregnant and have a son. You must never cut
his hair, because he will be a Nazirite,
given to God from birth. He will begin to
save Israel from the power of the Philistines."

6Then Manoah's wife went to him and
told him what had happened. She said, "A
man from God came to me. He looked
like an angel from God; his appearance
was frightening. I didn't ask him where
he was from, and he didn't tell me his
name. 7But he said to me, 'You will be-

CONNECT 2-YOU

ME AND MY PARENTS

Hi, everybody. Tagg and I are talking about getting along with parents. A friend of ours is having a problem with his parents that he would like to share with us. Let's welcome Erik, age 10, to Connect 2-You.

Erik

My problem is that my parents are way stricter than all my friends' parents! My friends can play whatever video games, movies, and music they want. But my parents ruin my fun with, like, a billion rules about that stuff. They say it's for my own good, but sometimes I feel like just doing what I want and not listening to what they say.

Welcome, Erik.
What's your problem?

I know how you feel, Erik. It's tough to do what other people tell us to do—but God tells us that obeying Mom and Dad is always best. God gives us parents to help "light our path." Their job is to steer us away from danger areas—no matter how badly we may want to explore those areas. It's not an easy job. That's why God wants us to honor our parents. Honoring means more than obeying. It means treating them with respect, love, and appreciation.

A funny thing happens when you honor your parents, Erik. They start to honor you back. When you show them that you're responsible enough to follow their rules, you may find that your parents give you more freedom and trust. For some tips on how to obey your parents, take a look at the Livin' It page on obeying your mom and dad, Proverbs 6:20-23, p. 834. It may encourage you!

come pregnant and will have a son. Don't
drink wine or beer or eat anything that is
unclean, because the boy will be a Nazirite to God from his birth until the day of
his death.' "

8Then Manoah prayed to the LORD:
"Lord, I beg you to let the man of God
come to us again. Let him teach us what
we should do for the boy who will be born
to us."

9God heard Manoah's prayer, and the
angel of God came to Manoah's wife
again while she was sitting in the field.
But her husband Manoah was not with
her. **10**So she ran to tell him, "He is here!
The man who appeared to me the other
day is here!"

11Manoah got up and followed his
wife. When he came to the man, he said,
"Are you the man who spoke to my
wife?"

The man said, "I am."

12So Manoah asked, "When what you
say happens, what kind of life should the
boy live? What should he do?"

13The angel of the LORD said, "Your
wife must be careful to do everything I
told her to do. **14**She must not eat anything that grows on a grapevine, or drink
any wine or beer, or eat anything that is
unclean. She must do everything I have
commanded her."

15Manoah said to the angel of the
LORD, "We would like you to stay awhile
so we can cook a young goat for you."

16The angel of the LORD answered,
"Even if I stay awhile, I would not eat
your food. But if you want to prepare
something, offer a burnt offering to the
LORD." (Manoah did not understand that
the man was really the angel of the
LORD.)

17Then Manoah asked the angel of
the LORD, "What is your name? Then we
will honor you when what you have said
really happens."

18The angel of the LORD said, "Why do
you ask my name? It is too amazing for
you to understand." **19**So Manoah sacrificed a young goat on a rock and offered
some grain as a gift to the LORD. Then an
amazing thing happened as Manoah and
his wife watched. **20**The flames went up
to the sky from the altar. As the fire
burned, the angel of the LORD went up to
heaven in the flame. When Manoah and
his wife saw that, they bowed facedown
on the ground. **21**The angel of the LORD
did not appear to them again. Then Manoah understood that the man was really the
angel of the LORD. **22**Manoah said, "We
have seen God, so we will surely die."

23But his wife said to him, "If the
LORD wanted to kill us, he would not
have accepted our burnt offering or grain
offering. He would not have shown us all
these things or told us all this."

24So the woman gave birth to a boy
and named him Samson. He grew, and the
LORD blessed him. **25**The Spirit of the
LORD began to work in Samson while he
was in the city of Mahaneh Dan, between
the cities of Zorah and Eshtaol.

Samson's First Marriage

14 Samson went down to the city of
Timnah where he saw a Philistine
woman. **2**When he returned home, he
said to his father and mother, "I saw a
Philistine woman in Timnah. I want you
to get her for me so I can marry her."

3His father and mother answered,
"Surely there is a woman from Israel you
can marry. Do you have to marry a woman from the Philistines, who are not circumcised?"

But Samson said, "Get that woman for
me! She is the one I want!" **4**(Samson's
parents did not know that the LORD
wanted this to happen because he was
looking for a way to challenge the Philistines, who were ruling over Israel at this
time.) **5**Samson went down with his father and mother to Timnah, as far as the
vineyard near there. Suddenly, a young
lion came roaring toward Samson! **6**The
Spirit of the LORD entered Samson with
great power, and he tore the lion apart
with his bare hands. For him it was as
easy as tearing apart a young goat. But
Samson did not tell his father or mother
what he had done. **7**Then he went down
to the city and talked to the Philistine
woman, and he liked her.

8Several days later Samson went back
to marry her. On his way he went over to

FAITH links

I WANT IT *NOW!*

JUDGES 14:1-3

Samson wanted what he wanted when he wanted it. He demanded that his parents get him the wife he wanted, even though they knew his choice was not good. His lack of self-control and his failure to make good choices led him into trouble.

Part of self-control means learning to control your need to have everything *right now!* It means learning the value of waiting. Self-control is a fruit of the Spirit. (Read about it in Galatians 5:22–23, p. 1593.) A person with self-control takes the time to make wise choices about his or her wants. One way to make wise choices is to seek wise advice.

Connect here to find out more about self-control:

Obey? No Way!, Exodus 1:15–21, p. 76

Choosing Sides, 1 Samuel 20, p. 382

Mind Guard, Proverbs 4:23, p. 831

The Right Ingredients, Micah 6:8, p. 1227

Exercising Patience, Luke 2:25–28, 36–37, p. 1369

Best Seat in the House, Luke 14:7–11, p. 1398

look at the body of the dead lion and
found a swarm of bees and honey in it.
9Samson got some of the honey with his
hands and walked along eating it. When
he came to his parents, he gave some to
them. They ate it, too, but Samson did
not tell them he had taken the honey
from the body of the dead lion.
10Samson's father went down to see
the Philistine woman. And Samson gave
a feast, as was the custom for the bridegroom. **11**When the people saw him, they
sent thirty friends to be with him.

Samson's Riddle

12Samson said to them, "Let me tell
you a riddle. Try to find the answer during the seven days of the feast. If you can,
I will give you thirty linen shirts and thirty changes of clothes. **13**But if you can't,
you must give me thirty linen shirts and
thirty changes of clothes."

So they said, "Tell us your riddle so
we can hear it."
14Samson said,

"Out of the eater comes something
to eat.
Out of the strong comes something
sweet."

After three days, they had not found the
answer.
15On the fourth[n] day they said to
Samson's wife, "Did you invite us here to
make us poor? Trick your husband into
telling us the answer to the riddle. If you
don't, we will burn you and everyone in
your father's house."
16So Samson's wife went to him, crying, and said, "You hate me! You don't
really love me! You told my people a riddle, but you won't tell me the answer."

Samson said, "I haven't even told my
father or mother. Why should I tell you?"
17Samson's wife cried for the rest of
the seven days of the feast. So he finally
gave her the answer on the seventh day,
because she kept bothering him. Then
she told her people the answer to the
riddle.

14:15 fourth The Hebrew word is "seventh." Some old translations say "fourth," which fits the order of events better.

18Before sunset on the seventh day of
the feast, the Philistine men had the answer. They came to Samson and said,

"What is sweeter than honey?
What is stronger than a lion?"

Then Samson said to them,

"If you had not plowed with my
young cow,
you would not have solved my
riddle!"

19Then the Spirit of the LORD entered
Samson and gave him great power. Samson went down to the city of Ashkelon
and killed thirty of its men and took all
that they had and gave the clothes to the
men who had answered his riddle. Then
he went to his father's house very angry.
20And Samson's wife was given to his
best man.

Samson Troubles the Philistines

15 At the time of the wheat harvest,
Samson went to visit his wife, taking a young goat with him. He said, "I'm
going to my wife's room,"
but her father would not
let him go in.
2He said to Samson, "I
thought you really hated
your wife, so I gave her to
your best man. Her youn-
ger sister is more beautiful. Take her instead."
3But Samson said to
them, "This time no one
will blame me for hurting
you Philistines!" 4So Samson went out
and caught three hundred foxes. He took
two foxes at a time, tied their tails together, and then tied a torch to the tails of each
pair of foxes. 5After he lit the torches, he
let the foxes loose in the grainfields of the
Philistines so that he burned up their
standing grain, the piles of grain, their
vineyards, and their olive trees.
6The Philistines asked, "Who did this?"
Someone told them, "Samson, the
son-in-law of the man from Timnah, did
because his father-in-law gave his wife to
his best man."
So the Philistines burned Samson's
wife and her father to death. 7Then Samson said to the Philistines, "Since you
did this, I won't stop until I pay you back!"
8Samson attacked the Philistines and
killed many of them. Then he went down
and stayed in a cave in the rock of Etam.
9The Philistines went up and camped
in the land of Judah, near a place named
Lehi. 10The men of Judah asked them,
"Why have you come here to fight us?"
They answered, "We have come to
make Samson our prisoner, to pay him
back for what he did to our people."
11Then three thousand men of Judah
went to the cave in the rock of Etam and
said to Samson, "What have you done to
us? Don't you know that the Philistines
rule over us?"
Samson answered, "I only paid them
back for what they did to me."
12Then they said to him, "We have
come to tie you up and to hand you over
to the Philistines."
Samson said to them, "Promise me
you will not hurt me yourselves."
13The men from Judah said, "We
agree. We will just tie you
up and give you to the
Philistines. We will not kill
you." So they tied Sam-
son with two new ropes
and led him up from the
cave in the rock. 14When
Samson came to the place
named Lehi, the Philis-
tines came to meet him,
shouting for joy. Then the
Spirit of the LORD en-
tered Samson and gave him great power.
The ropes on him weakened like burned
strings and fell off his hands! 15Samson
found the jawbone of a dead donkey, took
it, and killed a thousand men with it!
16Then Samson said,

"With a donkey's jawbone
I made donkeys out of them.
With a donkey's jawbone
I killed a thousand men!"

17When he finished speaking, he threw
away the jawbone. So that place was
named Ramath Lehi.*
18Samson was very thirsty, so he

> Then Samson said, "With a donkey's jawbone . . . I killed a thousand men!"
> —Judges 15:16

15:17 Ramath Lehi This name means "Jawbone Hill."

cried out to the LORD, "You gave me, your servant, this great victory. Do I have to die of thirst now? Do I have to be captured by people who are not circumcised?"
19Then God opened up a hole in the ground at Lehi, and water came out. When Samson drank, he felt better; he felt strong again. So he named that spring Caller's Spring, which is still in Lehi.
20Samson judged Israel for twenty years in the days of the Philistines.

Samson Goes to the City of Gaza

16 One day Samson went to Gaza and saw a prostitute there. He went in to spend the night with her.
2When the people of Gaza heard, "Samson has come here!" they surrounded the place and waited for him near the city gate all night. They whispered to each other, "When dawn comes, we will kill Samson!"
3But Samson only stayed with the prostitute until midnight. Then he got up and took hold of the doors and the two posts of the city gate and tore them loose, along with the bar. He put them on his shoulders and carried them to the top of the hill that faces the city of Hebron.

Samson and Delilah

4After this, Samson fell in love with a woman named Delilah, who lived in the Valley of Sorek.
5The Philistine rulers went to Delilah and said, "Find out what makes Samson so strong. Trick him into telling you how we can overpower him and capture him and tie him up. If you do this, each one of us will give you twenty-eight pounds of silver."
6So Delilah said to Samson, "Tell me why you are so strong. How can someone tie you up and capture you?"
7Samson answered, "Someone would have to tie me up with seven new bowstrings that have not been dried. Then I would be as weak as any other man."
8The Philistine rulers brought Delilah seven new bowstrings that had not been dried, and she tied Samson with them.
9Some men were hiding in another room. Delilah said to him, "Samson, the Philistines are here!" But Samson broke the bowstrings like pieces of burned string.

FAITH links

THE WEAK LINK

JUDGES 16

You've heard of Hercules, right? Well, he's just a myth. Samson, however, was the real thing. God gave Samson super strength to use in defeating Israel's enemies, the Philistines. But the world's strongest man had a weakness—he relied on himself and his super strength, rather than on God. He was soon led into a trap that cost him his strength.

God gives each of us the ability to serve him. But he expects us to rely on him—not on our abilities. Want to be the world's most powerful Christian? Then take time to see the God behind your abilities. Faith in God gives you the power to serve him.

Complaints, Complaints!, Exodus 16:1–3, p. 97

Weak? Great!, 2 Chronicles 14:11, p. 577

Remember Your Creator, Ecclesiastes 12:1, 13, p. 885

Your Feet on High Places, Habakkuk 3:18–19, p. 1239

Small Beginnings, Zechariah 4:10, p. 1255

The Way to Greatness, Matthew 20:20–28, p. 1309

So the Philistines did not find out the secret of Samson's strength.
10Then Delilah said to Samson, "You

made a fool of me. You lied to me. Now
tell me how someone can tie you up."
11Samson said, "They would have to
tie me with new ropes that have not been
used before. Then I would become as
weak as any other man."
12So Delilah took new ropes and tied
Samson. Some men were hiding in another room. She called out to him, "Samson, the Philistines are here!" But he
broke the ropes as easily as if they were
threads.
13Then Delilah said to Samson,
"Again you have made a fool of me. You
lied to me. Tell me how someone can tie
you up."

He said, "Using the loom,[n] weave the
seven braids of my hair into the cloth, and
tighten it with a pin. Then I will be as
weak as any other man."

While Samson slept, Delilah wove the
seven braids of his hair into the cloth.
14Then she fastened it with a pin.

Again she said to him, "Samson, the
Philistines are here!" Samson woke up
and pulled out the pin and the loom with
the cloth.
15Then Delilah said to him, "How can
you say, 'I love you,' when you don't even
trust me? This is the third time you have
made a fool of me. You haven't told me
the secret of your great strength." **16**She
kept bothering Samson about his secret
day after day until he felt he was going
to die!
17So he told her everything. He said,
"I have never had my hair cut, because I
have been set apart to God as a Nazirite
since I was born. If someone shaved my
head, I would lose my strength and be as
weak as any other man."
18When Delilah saw that he had told
her everything sincerely, she sent a message to the Philistine rulers. She said,
"Come back one more time, because he
has told me everything." So the Philistine rulers came back to Delilah and
brought the silver with them. **19**Delilah
got Samson to sleep, lying in her lap.
Then she called in a man to shave off the
seven braids of Samson's hair. In this way
she began to make him weak, and his
strength left him.
20Then she said, "Samson, the Philistines are here!"

He woke up and thought, "I'll leave as
I did before and shake myself free." But
he did not know that the LORD had left
him.
21Then the Philistines captured Samson and tore out his eyes. They took him
down to Gaza, where they put bronze
chains on him and made him grind grain
in the prison. **22**But his hair began to
grow again.

Samson Dies

23The Philistine rulers gathered to
celebrate and to offer a great sacrifice to
their god Dagon. They said, "Our god has
handed Samson our enemy over to us."
24When the people saw him, they
praised their god, saying,

"This man destroyed our country.
He killed many of us!
But our god handed over
our enemy to us."

25While the people were enjoying the
celebration, they said, "Bring Samson
out to perform for us." So they brought
Samson from the prison, and he performed for them. They made him stand
between the pillars. **26**Samson said to the
servant holding his hand, "Let me feel
the pillars that hold up the temple so I
can lean against them." **27**Now the temple was full of men and women. All the
Philistine rulers were there, and about
three thousand men and women were
on the roof[n] watching Samson perform.
28Then Samson prayed to the LORD,
"Lord GOD, remember me. God, please
give me strength one more time so I can
pay these Philistines back for putting out
my two eyes!" **29**Then Samson turned to
the two center pillars that supported the
whole temple. He braced himself between the two pillars, with his right hand
on one and his left hand on the other.

16:13 loom A machine for making cloth from thread.

16:27 roof In Bible times houses were built with flat roofs. The roof was used for drying things such as flax and fruit. And it was used as an extra room, as a place for worship, and as a cool place to sleep in the summer.

30Samson said, "Let me die with these
Philistines!" Then he pushed as hard as
he could, causing the temple to fall on the
rulers and all the people in it. So Samson
killed more of the Philistines when he
died than when he was alive.
31Samson's brothers and his whole
family went down to get his body. They
brought him back and buried him in the
tomb of Manoah, his father, between the
cities of Zorah and Eshtaol. Samson was a
judge for the people of Israel for twenty
years.

Micah's Idols

17 There was a man named Micah
who lived in the mountains of
Ephraim. 2He said to his
mother, "I heard you
speak a curse about the
twenty-eight pounds of
silver that were taken
from you. I have the silver
with me; I took it."
His mother said, "The
LORD bless you, my son!"
3Micah gave the
twenty-eight pounds of
silver to his mother. Then
she said, "I will give this
silver to the LORD. I will have my son
make an idol and a statue. So I will give
the silver back to you."
4When he gave the silver back to his
mother, she took about five pounds and
gave it to a silversmith. With it he made
an idol and a statue, which stood in
Micah's house. 5Micah had a special holy
place, and he made a holy vest and some
household idols. Then Micah chose one
of his sons to be his priest. 6At that time
Israel did not have a king, so everyone
did what seemed right.
7There was a young man who was a
Levite[n] from the city of Bethlehem in Judah who was from the people of Judah.
8He left Bethlehem to look for another
place to live, and on his way he came to
Micah's house in the mountains of
Ephraim. 9Micah asked him, "Where are
you from?"
He answered, "I'm a Levite from
Bethlehem in Judah. I'm looking for a
place to live."
10Micah said to him, "Live with me
and be my father and my priest. I will give
you four ounces of silver each year and
clothes and food." So the Levite went in.
11He agreed to live with Micah and became like one of Micah's own sons. 12Mi-
cah made him a priest, and he lived in
Micah's house. 13Then Micah said,
"Now I know the LORD will be good to
me, because I have a Levite as my
priest."

> At that time Israel did not have a king, so everyone did what seemed right.
> —Judges 17:6

Dan's Family Captures Laish

18 At that time Israel did not have a
king. And at that time the tribe of
Dan was still looking for a
land where they could
live, a land of their own.
The Danites had not yet
been given their own land
among the tribes of Isra-
el. 2So, from their family
groups, they chose five
soldiers from the cities of
Zorah and Eshtaol to spy
out and explore the land.
They were told, "Go, ex-
plore the land."
They came to the mountains of
Ephraim, to Micah's house, where they
spent the night. 3When they came near
Micah's house, they recognized the voice
of the young Levite.[n] So they stopped
there and asked him, "Who brought you
here? What are you doing here? Why are
you here?"
4He told them what Micah had done
for him, saying, "He hired me. I am his
priest."
5They said to him, "Please ask God if
our journey will be successful."
6The priest said to them, "Go in
peace. The LORD is pleased with your
journey."
7So the five men left. When they
came to the city of Laish, they saw that
the people there lived in safety, like the

17:7; 18:3 Levite The Levites were the only ones God had appointed as priests.

LET'S VISIT SHILOH

Judges 18:31

At one time, Shiloh was the religious capital for the Hebrews. This was because they kept the Holy Tent of God there. (See Judges 18:31.) Shiloh also is where a woman named Hannah prayed to God to give her a son. That little boy, Samuel, grew up at the Lord's house at Shiloh. You might remember that while Samuel lived there, God woke him up and actually talked to him. When Samuel grew up, he became the priest in the Lord's house. (Look at 1 Samuel 1:9, p. 354.)

Later, Solomon built the Temple in Jerusalem, the capital of Israel. When that happened, Shiloh was not as important to the Israelites. For a while it was like a ghost town, but hundreds of years later the Greeks and Romans moved in and rebuilt the city.

people of Sidon. They thought they were
safe and had plenty of everything. They
lived a long way from the Sidonians and
had no dealings with anyone else.

8When the five men returned to Zorah and Eshtaol, their relatives asked
them, "What did you find?"

9They answered, "We have seen the
land, and it is very good. We should attack them. Aren't you going to do something? Don't wait! Let's go and take that
land! **10**When you go, you will see there
is plenty of land—plenty of everything!
The people are not expecting an attack.
Surely God has handed that land over
to us!"

11So six hundred Danites left Zorah
and Eshtaol ready for war. **12**On their
way they set up camp near the city of Kiriath Jearim in Judah. That is why the
place west of Kiriath Jearim is named
Mahaneh Dan[n] to this day. **13**From there
they traveled on to the mountains of
Ephraim. Then they came to Micah's
house.

14The five men who had explored the
land around Laish said to their relatives,
"Do you know in one of these houses
there are a holy vest, household gods, an
idol, and a statue? You know what to do."
15So they stopped at the Levite's house,
which was also Micah's house, and
greeted the Levite. **16**The six hundred
Danites stood at the entrance gate, wearing their weapons of war. **17**The five
spies went into the house and took the
idol, the holy vest, the household idols,
and the statue. The priest and the six
hundred men armed for war stood by the
entrance gate.

18When the spies went into Micah's
house and took the image, the holy vest,
the household idols, and the statue, the
priest asked them, "What are you doing?"

19They answered, "Be quiet! Don't
say a word. Come with us and be our father and priest. Is it better for you to be a
priest for one man's house or for a tribe
and family group in Israel?" **20**This made
the priest happy. So he took the holy vest,
the household idols, and the idol and went
with the Danites. **21**They left Micah's
house, putting their little children, their

18:12 Mahaneh Dan This name means "the camp of Dan."

animals, and everything they owned in
front of them.

22When they had gone a little way
from Micah's house, the men who lived
near Micah were called out and caught up
with them. **23**The men with Micah shouted at the Danites, who turned around and
said to Micah, "What's the matter with
you? Why have you been called out to
fight?"

24Micah answered, "You took my
gods that I made and my priest. What do I
have left? How can you ask me, 'What's
the matter?' "

25The Danites answered, "You should
not argue with us. Some of our angry
men might attack you, killing you and
your family." **26**Then the Danites went
on their way. Micah knew they were too
strong for him, so he turned and went
back home.

27Then the Danites took what Micah
had made and his priest and went on to
Laish. They attacked those peaceful people and killed them with their swords and
then burned the city. **28**There was no one
to save the people of Laish. They lived
too far from Sidon, and they had no dealings with anyone else. Laish was in a valley near Beth Rehob.

The people of Dan rebuilt the city and
lived there. **29**They changed the name of
Laish to Dan, naming it for their ancestor
Dan, one of the sons of Israel.

30The people of Dan set up the idols
in the city of Dan. Jonathan son of Gershom, Moses' son, and his sons served as
priests for the tribe of Dan until the land
was captured. **31**The people of Dan set
up the idols Micah had made as long as
the Holy Tent of God was in Shiloh.

A Levite and His Servant

19 At that time Israel did not have a
king.

There was a Levite who lived in the
faraway mountains of Ephraim. He had
taken a slave woman from the city of
Bethlehem in the land of Judah to live
with him, **2**but she was unfaithful to him.
She left him and went back to her father's
house in Bethlehem in Judah and stayed
there for four months. **3**Then her husband went to ask her to come back to
him, taking with him his servant and two
donkeys. When the Levite came to her
father's house, she invited him to come
in, and her father was happy to see him.
4The father-in-law, the young woman's
father, asked him to stay. So he stayed for
three days and ate, drank, and slept
there.

5On the fourth day they got up early
in the morning. The Levite was getting
ready to leave, but the woman's father
said to his son-in-law, "Refresh yourself
by eating something. Then go." **6**So the
two men sat down to eat and drink together. After that, the father said to him,
"Please stay tonight. Relax and enjoy
yourself." **7**When the man got up to go,
his father-in-law asked him to stay. So he
stayed again that night. **8**On the fifth day
the man got up early in the morning to
leave. The woman's father said, "Refresh
yourself. Wait until this afternoon." So
the two men ate together.

9When the Levite, his slave woman,
and his servant got up to leave, the father-in-law, the young woman's father,
said, "It's almost night. The day is almost
gone. Spend the night here and enjoy
yourself. Tomorrow morning you can get
up early and go home." **10**But the Levite
did not want to stay another night. So he
took his two saddled donkeys and his
slave woman and traveled toward the city
of Jebus (also called Jerusalem).

11As the day was almost over, they
came near Jebus. So the servant said to
his master, "Let's stop at this city of the
Jebusites, and spend the night here."

12But his master said, "No. We won't
go inside a foreign city. Those people are
not Israelites. We will go on to the city of
Gibeah." **13**He said, "Come on. Let's try
to make it to Gibeah or Ramah so we can
spend the night in one of those cities."
14So they went on. The sun went down
as they came near Gibeah, which belongs
to the tribe of Benjamin. **15**They stopped
there to spend the night. They came to
the public square of the city and sat
down, but no one invited them home to
spend the night.

16Finally, in the evening an old man

came in from his work in the fields. His
home was in the mountains of Ephraim,
but now he was living in Gibeah. (The
people of Gibeah were from the tribe of
Benjamin.) **17**He saw the traveler in the
public square and asked, "Where are you
going? Where did you come from?"

18The Levite answered, "We are traveling from Bethlehem in Judah to my
home in the mountains of Ephraim. I
have been to Bethlehem in Judah, but
now I am going to the Holy Tent of the
LORD. No one has invited me to stay in
his house. **19**We already have straw and
food for our donkeys and bread and wine
for me, the young woman, and my servant. We don't need anything."

20The old man said, "You are welcome to stay at my house. Let me give
you anything you need, but don't spend
the night in the public square." **21**So the
old man took the Levite into his house,
and he fed their donkeys. They washed
their feet and had something to eat and
drink.

22While they were enjoying themselves, some wicked men of the city surrounded the house and beat on the door.
They shouted to the old man who owned
the house, "Bring out the man who came
to your house. We want to have sexual
relations with him."

23The owner of the house went outside and said to them, "No, my friends.
Don't be so evil. This man is a guest in
my house. Don't do this terrible thing!
24Look, here are my daughter, who has
never had sexual relations before, and
the man's slave woman. I will bring them
out to you now. Do anything you want
with them, but don't do such a terrible
thing to this man."

25But the men would not listen to
him. So the Levite took his slave woman
and sent her outside to them. They
forced her to have sexual relations with
them, and they abused her all night long.
Then, at dawn, they let her go. **26**She
came back to the house where her master was staying and fell down at the door
and lay there until daylight.

27In the morning when the Levite got
up, he opened the door of the house and
went outside to go on his way. But his
slave woman was lying at the doorway of
the house, with her hands on the doorsill.
28The Levite said to her, "Get up; let's
go." But she did not answer. So he put
her on his donkey and went home.

29When the Levite got home, he took
a knife and cut his slave woman into
twelve parts, limb by limb. Then he sent
a part to each area of Israel. **30**Everyone
who saw this said, "Nothing like this has
ever happened before, not since the people of Israel came out of Egypt. Think
about it. Tell us what to do."

The War Between Israel and Benjamin

20 So all the Israelites from Dan to
Beersheba,[n] including the land of
Gilead, joined together before the LORD
in the city of Mizpah. **2**The leaders of all
the tribes of Israel took their places in
the meeting of the people of God. There
were 400,000 soldiers with swords. **3**(The
people of Benjamin heard that the Israelites had gone up to Mizpah.) Then the Israelites said to the Levite, "Tell us how
this evil thing happened."

4So the husband of the murdered
woman answered, "My slave woman and
I came to Gibeah in Benjamin to spend
the night. **5**During the night the men of
Gibeah came after me. They surrounded
the house and wanted to kill me. They
forced my slave woman to have sexual
relations and she died. **6**I took her and cut
her into parts and sent one part to each
area of Israel because the people of Benjamin did this wicked and terrible thing in
Israel. **7**Now, all you Israelites, speak up.
What is your decision?"

8Then all the people stood up at the
same time, saying, "None of us will go
home. Not one of us will go back to his
house! **9**Now this is what we will do to
Gibeah. We will throw lots. **10**That way
we will choose ten men from every hundred men from all the tribes of Israel, and

---

20:1 Dan . . . Beersheba Dan was the city farthest north in Israel. Beersheba was the city farthest south. So this means all the people of Israel.

we will choose a hundred men from every
thousand, and a thousand men from every
ten thousand. These will find supplies for
the army. Then the army will go to the city
of Gibeah of Benjamin to repay them for
the terrible thing they have done in Israel." **11**So all the men of Israel were united and gathered against the city.

12The tribes of Israel sent men
throughout the tribe of Benjamin demanding, "What is this evil thing some of
your men have done? **13**Hand over the
wicked men in Gibeah so that we can put
them to death. We must remove this evil
from Israel."

But the Benjaminites would not listen
to their fellow Israelites. **14**The Benjaminites left their own cities and met at
Gibeah to fight the Israelites. **15**In only
one day the Benjaminites got 26,000 soldiers together who were trained with
swords. They also had 700 chosen men
from Gibeah. **16**Seven hundred of these
trained soldiers were left-handed, each of
whom could sling a stone at a hair and not
miss!

17The Israelites, except for the Benjaminites, gathered 400,000 soldiers with
swords.

18The Israelites went up to the city of
Bethel and asked God, "Which tribe shall
be first to attack the Benjaminites?"

The LORD answered, "Judah shall go
first."

19The next morning the Israelites got
up and made a camp near Gibeah. **20**The
men of Israel went out to fight the Benjaminites and took their battle position at
Gibeah. **21**Then the Benjaminites came
out of Gibeah and killed 22,000 Israelites
during the battle that day. **22-23**The Israelites went before the LORD and cried until evening. They asked the LORD, "Shall
we go to fight our relatives, the Benjaminites, again?"

The LORD answered, "Go up and fight
them." The men of Israel encouraged
each other. So they took the same battle
positions they had taken the first day.

24The Israelites came to fight the
Benjaminites the second day. **25**The
Benjaminites came out of Gibeah to attack
the Israelites. This time, the Benjaminites killed 18,000 Israelites, all of whom
carried swords.

26Then the Israelites went up to
Bethel. There they sat down and cried to
the LORD and went without food all day
until evening. They also brought burnt
offerings and fellowship offerings to the
LORD. **27**The Israelites asked the LORD a
question. (In those days the Ark of the
Agreement with God was there at
Bethel. **28**A priest named Phinehas son
of Eleazar, the son of Aaron, served before the Ark of the Agreement.) They
asked, "Shall we go to fight our relatives,
the Benjaminites, again, or shall we stop
fighting?"

The LORD answered, "Go, because tomorrow I will hand them over to you."

29Then the Israelites set up ambushes all around Gibeah. **30**They went
to fight against the Benjaminites at Gibeah on the third day, getting into position for battle as they had done before.
31When the Benjaminites came out to
fight them, the Israelites backed up and
led the Benjaminites away from the city.
The Benjaminites began to kill some of
the Israelites as they had done before.
About thirty Israelites were killed—
some in the fields and some on the roads
leading to Bethel and to Gibeah.

32The Benjaminites said, "We are winning as before!"

But the Israelites said, "Let's run.
Let's trick them into going farther away
from their city and onto the roads."

33All the Israelites moved from their
places and got into battle positions at a
place named Baal Tamar. Then the Israelites ran out from their hiding places west
of Gibeah. **34**Ten thousand of the best
trained soldiers from all of Israel attacked
Gibeah. The battle was very hard. The
Benjaminites did not know disaster was
about to come to them. **35**The LORD used
the Israelites to defeat the Benjaminites.
On that day the Israelites killed 25,100
Benjaminites, all armed with swords.
36Then the Benjaminites saw that they
were defeated.

The Israelites had moved back because they were depending on the surprise attack they had set up near Gibeah.

37The men in hiding rushed into Gibeah,
spread out, and killed everyone in the
city with their swords. 38Now the Israelites had set up a signal with the men in
hiding. The men in the surprise attack
were to send up a cloud of smoke from
the city. 39Then the army of Israel
turned around in the battle.
The Benjaminites had killed about
thirty Israelites. They were saying, "We
are winning, as in the first battle!" 40But
then a cloud of smoke began to rise from
the city. The Benjaminites turned around
and saw that the whole city was going up
in smoke. 41Then the Israelites turned
and began to fight. The Benjaminites
were terrified because they knew that disaster was coming to them. 42So the
Benjaminites ran away from the Israelites
toward the desert, but they could not escape the battle. And the Israelites who
came out of the cities killed them. 43They
surrounded the Benjaminites and chased
them and caught them in the area east of
Gibeah. 44So 18,000 brave Benjaminite
fighters were killed. 45The Benjaminites
ran toward the desert to the rock of Rimmon, but the Israelites killed 5,000 Benjaminites along the roads. They chased
them as far as Gidom and killed 2,000
more Benjaminites there.
46On that day 25,000 Benjaminites
were killed, all of whom had fought
bravely with swords. 47But 600 Benjaminites ran to the rock of Rimmon in the
desert, where they stayed for four
months. 48Then the Israelites went back
to the land of Benjamin and killed the
people in every city and also the animals
and everything they could find. And they
burned every city they found.

Wives for the Men of Benjamin

21 At Mizpah the men of Israel had
sworn, "Not one of us will let his
daughter marry a man from the tribe of
Benjamin."
2The people went to the city of Bethel
and sat before God until evening, crying
loudly. 3They said, "LORD, God of Israel,
why has this terrible thing happened to
us so that one tribe of Israel is missing
today?"

FAITH links

DO WHAT YOU WANT?

JUDGES 21:25

Ever hear the same message over and over again? The same message occurs in the Book of Judges over and over again. You can find it in the last verse of the book. "Everyone did what seemed right." (Check out Judges 17:6.) The Israelites did what *they* thought was right, rather than what God taught them. This is the pattern throughout the Book of Judges. Does that sound familiar to you? It should. People do the same thing today.

God wants us to be obedient to him. He doesn't want us to follow our own opinions of what's right or wrong. Do you want what he wants?

Take My Advice, 1 Kings 2:2–4, p. 436

See the Heart Behind It, Nehemiah 8; 9, p. 636

More Precious Than Gold, Psalm 19:7–10, p. 723

Said It? Do It!, Lamentations 2:17, p. 1077

Get Ready!, Mark 13:26–27, p. 1354

Hold On!, 2 Thessalonians 2:15–17, p. 1639

4Early the next day the people built
an altar and put burnt offerings and fellowship offerings to God on it.
5Then the Israelites asked, "Did any
tribe of Israel not come here to meet with

us in the presence of the LORD?" They
asked this question because they had
sworn that anyone who did not meet with
them at Mizpah would be killed.
6The Israelites felt sorry for their relatives, the Benjaminites. They said, "Today one tribe has been cut off from Israel.
7We swore before the LORD that we
would not allow our daughters to marry a
Benjaminite. How can we make sure that
the remaining men of Benjamin will have
wives?" **8**Then they asked, "Which one
of the tribes of Israel did not come here
to Mizpah?" They found that no one from
the city of Jabesh Gilead had come. **9**The
people of Israel counted everyone, but
there was no one from Jabesh Gilead.
10So the whole group of Israelites
sent twelve thousand soldiers to Jabesh
Gilead to kill the people with their
swords, even the women and children.
11"This is what you must do: Kill
every man in Jabesh Gilead and every
married woman." **12**The soldiers found
four hundred young unmarried women in
Jabesh Gilead, so they brought them to
the camp at Shiloh in Canaan.
13Then the whole group of Israelites
sent a message to the men of Benjamin,
who were at the rock of Rimmon, offering
to make peace with them. **14**So the men
of Benjamin came back at that time. The
Israelites gave them the women from Jabesh Gilead who had not been killed, but
there were not enough women.
15The people of Israel felt sorry for
the Benjaminites because the LORD had
separated the tribes of Israel. **16**The
older leaders of the Israelites said, "The
women of Benjamin have been killed.
Where can we get wives for the men of
Benjamin who are still alive? **17**These
men must have children to continue their
families so a tribe in Israel will not die
out. **18**But we cannot allow our daughters to marry them, because we swore,
'Anyone who gives a wife to a man of
Benjamin is cursed.' **19**We have an idea!
There is a yearly festival of the LORD
at Shiloh, which is north of the city of
Bethel, east of the road that goes from
Bethel to Shechem, and south of the city
of Lebonah."
20So the older leaders told the men of
Benjamin, "Go and hide in the vineyards.
21Watch for the young women from Shiloh to come out to join the dancing. Then
run out from the vineyards and take one
of the young Shiloh women and return to
the land of Benjamin. **22**If their fathers or
brothers come to us and complain, we
will say: 'Be kind to the men of Benjamin.
We did not get wives for Benjamin during
the war, and you did not give the women
to the men from Benjamin. So you are not
guilty.' "
23So that is what the Benjaminites
did. While the young women were dancing, each man caught one of them, took
her away, and married her. Then they
went back to the land God had given
them and rebuilt their cities and lived
there.
24Then the Israelites went home to
their own tribes and family groups, to
their own land that God had given them.
25In those days Israel did not have a
king. Everyone did what seemed right.

ALWAYS FAITHFUL

Hello! My name is Ruth. No one is sure who wrote this book, but I can tell you that it is the true story of my life. You may have heard the famous quote: "Where you go, I will go. Where you live, I will live. Your people will be my people, and your God will be my God" (Ruth 1:16). Did you know that I was speaking to my mother-in-law when I said that? With no husband or sons to care for her, Naomi had decided to back to Israel to be with other relatives. I could not bear to be separated from my mother-in-law, so I went with her. Most importantly, I decided to follow the true God of Israel.

This book was written to tell about the love and devotion my family had for God and for each other. God rewarded me for my devotion to Naomi by giving me a husband and a son in my new land. I was especially honored to be the great-grandmother of King David and an ancestor of Jesus. (You can see my name listed in Jesus' family history in Matthew 1:5, p. 1274.)

JESUS WATCH

In Israel a near relative or "kinsman" had the right to buy or "redeem" the property of a poor person to keep the property in the family. Naomi's closest relative chose not to buy her land, so Boaz willingly bought her land and took on the responsibility of her family. In his sacrifice for others, Boaz points to Jesus, who promises to take care of us. Jesus became a man, so he could be our kinsman; and he willingly paid the price for our lives. Because Jesus died on the cross and took the punishment for our sins, we have eternal life.

my FAVORITE links

___________________ ___________________

___________________ ___________________

___________________ ___________________

___________________ ___________________

OTHER CONNECTIONS

GET THE INFO

- Women Who Made a Difference, Ruth 4. Connect here to learn more about some amazing and faithful women whose stories can be found in the Old Testament—women such as Ruth, Naomi, Hannah, and Esther.

MORE STUFF...

It's the Custom! There are many Israelite customs found in the Book of Ruth that are important to the story. Here are a couple:

- Gathering the leftover grain in the field (Ruth 2:2) was a practice called gleaning. According to the law, any grain that was dropped during the harvest was to be left for the poor people to pick up and use for food. (See Leviticus 19:9, p. 160.) For Ruth and Naomi, this was the only way for them to get food.
- The "one who should take care of us" (Ruth 2:20) refers to the closest relative, or the kinsman-redeemer. According to social customs, the closest relative was responsible for helping a person if a catastrophe struck, like a death in the family.

FAITH links

The MLP, Ruth 1:16–17

Your Response to Responsibility, Ruth 2:1–7

An Unsung Hero, Ruth 2:12, 15–16

In Your Best Interests, Ruth 3

"What's the flash on Boaz's relative taking off his sandal?"

"You've got me. Maybe he had sore feet. Let's connect to Ruth 4:7-8 to find out."

TAKE A LOOK AT THESE:

Ruth follows Naomi, Ruth 1:16–22
Boaz first notices Ruth, Ruth 2:5–13
Ruth uncovers Boaz's feet, Ruth 3:5–14
Naomi's grandson, Ruth 4:13–17

1 Long ago when the judges[a] ruled Israel, there was a shortage of food in
the land. 2So a man named Elimelech left
the town of Bethlehem in Judah to live
in the country of Moab with his wife and
his two sons. His wife was named Naomi,
and his two sons were named Mahlon and
Kilion. They were Ephrathahites from
Bethlehem in Judah. When they came to
Moab, they settled there.
3Then Naomi's husband, Elimelech,
died, and she was left with her two sons.
4These sons married women from Moab.
One was named Orpah, and the other was
named Ruth. Naomi and her sons had
lived in Moab about ten years 5when
Mahlon and Kilion also died. So Naomi
was left alone without her husband or her
two sons.
6While Naomi was in Moab, she heard
that the LORD had come to help his people and had given them food again. So she
and her daughters-in-law got ready to
leave Moab and return home. 7Naomi
and her daughters-in-law left the place
where they had lived and started back to
the land of Judah. 8But Naomi said to her
two daughters-in-law, "Go back home,
each of you to your own mother's house.
May the LORD be as kind to you as you
have been to me and my sons who are
now dead. 9May the LORD give you another happy home and a new husband."
When Naomi kissed the women good-
bye, they began to cry out loud. 10They
said to her, "No, we want to go with you
to your people."
11But Naomi said, "My daughters, return to your own homes. Why do you
want to go with me? I cannot give birth to
more sons to give you new husbands;
12go back, my daughters, to your own
homes. I am too old to have another husband. Even if I told myself, 'I still have
hope' and had another husband tonight,
and even if I had more sons, 13should you
wait until they were grown into men?
Should you live for so many years without husbands? Don't do that, my daughters. My life is much too sad for you to

1:1 judges They were not judges in courts of law, but leaders of the people in times of emergency.

FAITH links

THE MLP

RUTH 1:16-17

Who is the most loyal person you know? In the Bible, one candidate for the MLP (Most Loyal Person) award is Ruth. Ruth showed loyalty to her mother-in-law Naomi by refusing to leave her. Naomi tried to convince Ruth to stay in Moab. But instead of staying put, Ruth chose to stay loyal and leave her homeland to be with Naomi.

Loyalty is more than just admitting you're someone's friend. It involves sticking with that friend even through tough times. It also means offering your friendship without a thought of what you might get out of it. Would someone consider you an MLP? How do you show your loyalty for friends or family?

Want to be a good friend? Connect here:

A Use for Your Abilities, Genesis 41, p. 59

What God Wants, Deuteronomy 10:12–13, p. 242

Loyal to a Friend, 2 Samuel 9, p. 409

A Friend in Deed, Job 2:13, p. 662

Two Are Better, Ecclesiastes 4:9–12, p. 877

Kindness First, Matthew 9:35–36, p. 1290

share, because the LORD has been
against me!"
14The women cried together out loud
again. Then Orpah kissed her mother-in-law Naomi good-bye, but Ruth held on to
her tightly.
15Naomi said to Ruth, "Look, your
sister-in-law is going back to her own people and her own gods. Go back with her."

Ruth Stays with Naomi

16But Ruth said, "Don't beg me to
leave you or to stop following you. Where you go, I will go. Where you live, I will live. Your people will be my people, and
your God will be my God. 17And where
you die, I will die, and there I will be buried. I ask the LORD to punish me terribly if I do not keep this promise: Not even death will separate us."
18When Naomi saw that Ruth had
firmly made up her mind to go with her,
she stopped arguing with her. 19So Naomi
and Ruth went on until they came to the town of Bethlehem. When they entered Bethlehem, all the people became very excited. The women of the town said, "Is this really Naomi?"
20Naomi answered the people, "Don't
call me Naomi.[n] Call me Mara,[n] because the Almighty has made my life very sad.
21When I left, I had all I wanted, but now, the LORD has brought me home with nothing. Why should you call me Naomi when the LORD has spoken against me and the Almighty has given me so much trouble?"
22So Naomi and her daughter-in-law
Ruth, the Moabite, returned from Moab and arrived at Bethlehem at the beginning of the barley harvest.

Ruth Meets Boaz

2 Now Naomi had a rich relative named
Boaz, from Elimelech's family.
2One day Ruth, the Moabite, said to
Naomi, "I am going to the fields. Maybe someone will be kind enough to let me gather the grain he leaves behind."

1:20 Naomi This name means "happy" or "pleasant."
1:20 Mara This name means "bitter" or "sad."

FAITH links

YOUR RESPONSE TO RESPONSIBILITY

RUTH 2:1-7

Of all the qualities others notice about you, is being *responsible* one of them? Ruth not only was loyal, but she also was responsible. She had a "What can I do to help others?" attitude rather than an attitude of "What can others do for me?" Since Ruth and Naomi were poor when they returned to Bethlehem, Ruth volunteered to gather grain left in the fields by the harvesters. That was hard work! But Ruth's hard work provided food for herself and for Naomi.

Showing responsibility for others means taking an active role to care for others. Part of learning to be responsible is being willing to work hard if necessary. What is your response to responsibility?

Roll Out the Welcome Wagon, Genesis 18:2–8, p. 24

Loyal to a Friend, 2 Samuel 9, p. 409

On the Wrong Foot, 2 Kings 21:1–2, 16, p. 509

You Are What You Do, Proverbs 20:11, p. 854

A Halfhearted Offering, Malachi 1:6–14, p. 1268

The Worst Chore, John 13:3–17, p. 1447

FAITH links

AN UNSUNG HERO

RUTH 2:12, 15-16

Have you ever felt unappreciated in what you do to help others? Or maybe you're convinced that the hard work you do is totally unnoticed by anyone. Ruth worked hard to support herself and her mother-in-law Naomi. God caused the servant in charge of the land to notice how faithful and responsible she was. Boaz, the owner of the field, rewarded Ruth for her faithfulness to her mother-in-law.

Feeling unnoticed? Don't forget that God sees everything. He wants you to be faithful in doing what's right even if no one else notices.

Here are some more thoughts on doing the right thing:

Your Total Trust, Deuteronomy 1:32, p. 229

Care for the Lost, Deuteronomy 22:1–3, p. 255

Trailblazers of Faith, 2 Kings 22:1–2, p. 510

Good Enough?, Ezekiel 8, p. 1093

Just Say Yes!, Matthew 9:9–13, p. 1289

Another Lazy Day?, 2 Thessalonians 3:6–13, p. 1640

Naomi said, "Go, my daughter."
3So Ruth went to the fields and gathered the grain that the workers cutting
the grain had left behind. It just so happened that the field belonged to Boaz,
from Elimelech's family.
4Soon Boaz came from Bethlehem
and greeted his workers, "The LORD be
with you!"
And the workers answered, "May the
LORD bless you!"
5Then Boaz asked his servant in
charge of the workers, "Whose girl is
that?"
6The servant answered, "She is the
young Moabite woman who came back
with Naomi from the country of Moab.
7She said, 'Please let me follow the
workers cutting grain and gather what
they leave behind.' She came and has remained here, from morning until just
now. She has stopped only a few moments to rest in the shelter."
8Then Boaz said to Ruth, "Listen, my
daughter. Don't go to gather grain for
yourself in another field. Don't even
leave this field at all, but continue following closely behind my women workers.
9Watch to see into which fields they go to
cut grain and follow them. I have warned
the young men not to bother you. When
you are thirsty, you may go and drink
from the water jugs that the young men
have filled."
10Then Ruth bowed low with her face
to the ground and said to him, "I am not
an Israelite. Why have you been so kind
to notice me?"
11Boaz answered her, "I know about
all the help you have given your mother-
in-law after your husband died. You left
your father and mother and your own
country to come to a nation where you
did not know anyone. 12May the LORD
reward you for all you have done. May
your wages be paid in full by the LORD,
the God of Israel, under whose wings you
have come for shelter."
13Then Ruth said, "I hope I can continue to please you, sir. You have said
kind and encouraging words to me, your
servant, though I am not one of your servants."
14At mealtime Boaz told Ruth, "Come
here. Eat some of our bread and dip it in
our sauce."

So Ruth sat down beside the workers.
Boaz handed her some roasted grain, and
she ate until she was full; she even had
some food left over. **15**When Ruth rose
and went back to work, Boaz commanded
his workers, "Let her gather even around
the piles of cut grain. Don't tell her to go
away. **16**In fact, drop some full heads of
grain for her from what you have in your
hands, and let her gather them. Don't tell
her to stop."

17So Ruth gathered grain in the field
until evening. Then she separated the
grain from the chaff, and there was about
one-half bushel of barley. **18**Ruth carried
the grain into town, and her mother-in-
law saw how much she had gathered.
Ruth also took out the food that was left
over from lunch and gave it to Naomi.

19Naomi asked her, "Where did you
gather all this grain today? Where did you
work? Blessed be whoever noticed you!"

Ruth told her mother-in-law whose
field she had worked in. She said, "The
man I worked with today is named Boaz."

20Naomi told her daughter-in-law,
"The LORD bless him! He continues to be
kind to us—both the living and the
dead!" Then Naomi told Ruth, "Boaz is
one of our close relatives,[n] one who
should take care of us."

21Then Ruth, the Moabite, said,
"Boaz also told me, 'Keep close to my
workers until they have finished my
whole harvest.' "

22But Naomi said to her daughter-in-
law Ruth, "It is better for you to continue
working with his women workers. If you
work in another field, someone might hurt
you." **23**So Ruth continued working closely with the workers of Boaz, gathering
grain until the barley harvest and the
wheat harvest were finished. And she
continued to live with Naomi, her mother-
in-law.

Naomi's Plan

3 Then Naomi, Ruth's mother-in-law,
said to her, "My daughter, I must find
a suitable home for you, one that will be
good for you. **2**Now Boaz, whose young
women you worked with, is our close
relative.[n] Tonight he will be working at
the threshing floor. **3**Wash yourself, put
on perfume, change your clothes, and go
down to the threshing floor. But don't let
him know you're there until he has finished his dinner. **4**Watch him so you will
know where he lies down to sleep. When
he lies down, go and lift the cover off his
feet[n] and lie down. He will tell you what
you should do."

5Then Ruth answered, "I will do
everything you say."

6So Ruth went down to the threshing
floor and did all her mother-in-law told
her to do. **7**After his evening meal, Boaz
felt good and went to sleep lying beside
the pile of grain. Ruth went to him quietly
and lifted the cover from his feet and lay
down.

8About midnight Boaz was startled
and rolled over. There was a woman lying
near his feet! **9**Boaz asked, "Who are
you?"

She said, "I am Ruth, your servant
girl. Spread your cover over me, because
you are a relative who is supposed to take
care of me."[n]

10Then Boaz said, "The LORD bless
you, my daughter. This act of kindness is
greater than the kindness you showed to
Naomi in the beginning. You didn't look
for a young man to marry, either rich or
poor. **11**Now, my daughter, don't be
afraid. I will do everything you ask, because all the people in our town know
you are a good woman. **12**It is true that I
am a relative who is to take care of you,
but you have a closer relative than I.
13Stay here tonight, and in the morning
we will see if he will take care of you. If
he decides to take care of you, that is fine.
But if he refuses, I will take care of you
myself, as surely as the LORD lives. So
stay here until morning."

2:20; 3:2 close relatives In Bible times the closest relative could marry a widow without children so she could have children. He would care for this family, but they and their property would not belong to him. They would belong to the dead husband.

3:4 lift . . . feet This showed Ruth was asking him to be her husband.

3:9 Spread . . . me By this, Ruth was asking Boaz to marry her.

FAITH links

IN YOUR BEST INTERESTS

RUTH 3

When your parents offer you advice, how do you usually respond? Choose one of the following or come up with your own. (Be honest.) (1) The advice goes in one ear and out the other. (2) I usually take their advice. (3) I listen, then offer my advice about their advice. (4) I complain about being given advice. (5) Other. When Ruth's mother-in-law Naomi offered Ruth advice, Ruth's response was No. 2. She respected Naomi's wisdom. She also knew that Naomi had her best interests at heart.

Unwanted advice can seem annoying at times. But when you know that a person has your best interests at heart, advice is easier to take.

Take Me to Your Leader, Numbers 27:12–23, p. 214

See the Heart Behind It, Nehemiah 8; 9, p. 636

Peace in the Family, Psalm 133, p. 811

A Parent's Advice, Proverbs 1:8–9, p. 825

Sow It and Reap, Lamentations 1:18, p. 1075

How to Make God Glad, Ephesians 6:1–2, p. 1605

14So Ruth stayed near his feet until
morning but got up while it was still too
dark to recognize anyone. Boaz thought,
"People in town must not know that the
woman came here to the threshing floor."
15So Boaz said to Ruth, "Bring me your
shawl and hold it open."

So Ruth held her shawl open, and
Boaz poured six portions of barley into it.
Boaz then put it on her head and went
back to the city.

16When Ruth went back to her
mother-in-law, Naomi asked, "How did
you do, my daughter?"

Ruth told Naomi everything that Boaz
did for her. 17She said, "Boaz gave me
these six portions of barley, saying, 'You
must not go home without a gift for your
mother-in-law.'"

18Naomi answered, "Ruth, my daughter, wait here until you see what happens.
Boaz will not rest until he has finished
doing what he should do today."

Boaz Marries Ruth

4 Boaz went to the city gate and sat
there until the close relative he had
mentioned passed by. Boaz called to him,
"Come here, friend, and sit down." So the
man came over and sat down. 2Boaz
gathered ten of the older leaders of the
city and told them, "Sit down here!" So
they sat down.

3Then Boaz said to the close relative,
"Naomi, who has come back from the
country of Moab, wants to sell the piece
of land that belonged to our relative
Elimelech. 4So I decided to tell you about
it: If you want to buy back the land, then
buy it in front of the people who are sitting here and in front of the older leaders
of my people. But if you don't want to buy
it, tell me, because you are the only one
who can buy it, and I am next after you."

The close relative answered, "I will
buy back the land."

5Then Boaz explained, "When you
buy the land from Naomi, you must also
marry Ruth, the Moabite, the dead man's
wife. That way, the land will stay in the
dead man's name."

6The close relative answered, "I can't
buy back the land. If I did, I might harm

WOMEN WHO MADE A DIFFERENCE — Ruth 4

One of the outstanding women of the Old Testament was Hannah, who prayed for a son and dedicated him to the Lord even before he was born. Hannah's faithfulness was rewarded. Her son, Samuel, became a great prophet, priest, and judge. He led Israel to be a great nation. (Read 1 Samuel 1—7, p. 354.)

Other outstanding women you'll read about in the Old Testament include:

Deborah	Hebrew judge who defeated the Canaanites under Sisera	Judges 4:4, p. 316
Esther	Jewish queen who saved her people from destruction	Esther 7:3–4, p. 655
Eve	First woman	Genesis 3:20, p. 8
Miriam	Aaron's sister; a prophetess	Exodus 15:20, p. 96
Naomi	Ruth's mother-in-law	Ruth 1:2, 4, p. 345
Rachel	Wife of Jacob	Genesis 29:28, p. 40
Rahab	Cared for Israel's spies; ancestor of Jesus	Joshua 2:3–21, p. 278; Matthew 1:5, p. 1274
Ruth	Boaz's wife; ancestor of Jesus	Ruth 4:13–17, p. 351; Matthew 1:5, p. 1274
Sarah (Sarai)	Abraham's wife; Isaac's mom	Genesis 11:29, p. 17; 21:2–3, p. 27
Zipporah	Wife of Moses	Exodus 2:21, p. 78

what I can pass on to my own sons. I cannot buy the land back, so buy it yourself."

7Long ago in Israel when people traded or bought back something, one person took off his sandal and gave it to the other person. This was the proof of ownership in Israel.

8So the close relative said to Boaz, "Buy the land yourself," and he took off his sandal.

9Then Boaz said to the older leaders and to all the people, "You are witnesses today. I am buying from Naomi everything that belonged to Elimelech and Kilion and Mahlon.
10I am also taking Ruth, the Moabite who was the wife of Mahlon, as my wife. I am doing this so her dead husband's property will stay in his name and his name will not be separated from his family and his hometown. You are witnesses today."

11So all the people and older leaders

who were at the city gate said, "We are
witnesses. May the LORD make this
woman, who is coming into your home,
like Rachel and Leah, who had many children and built up the people of Israel.
May you become powerful in the district
of Ephrathah and famous in Bethlehem.
12As Tamar gave birth to Judah's son
Perez,* may the LORD give you many
children through Ruth. May your family
be great like his."

13So Boaz took Ruth home as his wife
and had sexual relations with her. The
LORD let her become pregnant, and she
gave birth to a son. **14**The women told
Naomi, "Praise the LORD who gave you
this grandson. May he become famous in
Israel. **15**He will give you new life and
will take care of you in your old age because of your daughter-in-law who loves
you. She is better for you than seven
sons, because she has given birth to your
grandson."

16Naomi took the boy, held him in her
arms, and cared for him. **17**The neighbors gave the boy his name, saying, "This
boy was born for Naomi." They named
him Obed. Obed was the father of Jesse,
and Jesse was the father of David.

18This is the family history of Perez,
the father of Hezron. **19**Hezron was the
father of Ram, who was the father of Amminadab. **20**Amminadab was the father of
Nahshon, who was the father of Salmon.
21Salmon was the father of Boaz, who
was the father of Obed. **22**Obed was the
father of Jesse, and Jesse was the father
of David.

4:12 Perez One of Boaz's ancestors.

WAITING TO BE KING

Hi, there! My name is David. You may remember me, the shepherd boy who defeated the terrible giant Goliath? The stories in this book are true, but no one is sure who wrote them. It may have been the prophet Samuel. I was only a boy when God chose me to be the next king of Israel. (For that surprising story, link to 1 Samuel 16:1–13.) For many years I faithfully served Saul, the first king of Israel. His son Jonathan was my best friend. I never could understand why Saul was so angry with me. He even tried to kill me! (See 1 Samuel 19:9–10.)

This book was written to tell the story of how Israel became a nation ruled by kings. Soon after Saul became our first king, he disobeyed God and turned away from him. God rejected Saul and chose me to be the next king. I always respected Saul because he was appointed by God to be king. When Saul and his soldiers tried to kill me, I relied on God to protect me. Check out the MIDI file on Psalm 18, p. 721, for the words to a song I wrote after God saved me from my enemies.

JESUS WATCH

David reminds us of Jesus. David and Jesus were both born in Bethlehem and were from the family of Judah. David spent many years watching sheep in his father's fields, risking his life to defend them from lions and bears. Jesus is our good shepherd. He knows us by name and loves us so much that he laid down his life for us. When David was anointed by Samuel, the Spirit of God came to him and set him apart to be king of Israel. The Spirit of God came to Jesus when he was baptized by John, equipping him to be our savior and king. David suffered at the hands of his enemies before becoming king. Jesus, too, suffered before God exalted him in heaven.

my FAVORITE links

OTHER CONNECTIONS

One of the best examples of true friendship can be found between David and his friend Jonathan, the son of King Saul. Despite many obstacles, these two remained loyal to one another. Connect to The Perfect Friend, 1 Samuel 18:1, to learn more about the qualities that make up a good friend.

GET THE INFO

Find out more about the transition from Samuel, the last judge of Israel, to when Saul became Israel's first king and other interesting facts found in the first Book of Samuel by linking here:

- Samuel, the Prophet, 1 Samuel 4. Follow the life of Samuel, Israel's last judge before God granted the people's request for a king.
- King Saul, the Soldier, 1 Samuel 14. As long as King Saul obeyed God, he achieved many successes on the battlefield. Check out the highlights of his battles here.
- God to the Rescue!, 1 Samuel 23. Link here to learn more about some pretty amazing rescues found throughout the Old Testament that only God could make happen.
- Israel was surrounded by enemies, but the biggest bullies in the neighborhood were a people called the Philistines. Learn more about Israel's archenemies by linking to Some Bad Guys, 1 Samuel 31:1–4.

DOWNLOAD THESE EXCITING STORIES:

Wake up; God is calling, 1 Samuel 3
The idol that bowed down to God, 1 Samuel 5
The shepherd and the giant, 1 Samuel 17
David escapes out a window, 1 Samuel 19:9–17
Best friends, 1 Samuel 20:41–42
The corner of Saul's robe, 1 Samuel 24
Nabal insults David, 1 Samuel 25

- **Learning to Listen, 1 Samuel 3**
- **I Insist!, 1 Samuel 8; 9**
- **A Shortcut, 1 Samuel 13:1–14**
- **A Giant Problem, 1 Samuel 17:32–51**
- **When the Green-eyed Monster Strikes, 1 Samuel 18:6–9**
- **The Gift of Friendship, 1 Samuel 18:1–3; 19**
- **A Right to Get Even?, 1 Samuel 24**
- **The Right Thing to Do, 1 Samuel 26**
- **Kind or Fair?, 1 Samuel 30**

Samuel's Birth

1 There was a man named Elkanah son
of Jeroham from Ramathaim in the
mountains of Ephraim. Elkanah was from
the family of Zuph. (Jeroham was Elihu's
son. Elihu was Tohu's son, and Tohu was
the son of Zuph from the family group of
Ephraim.) **2**Elkanah had two wives named
Hannah and Peninnah. Peninnah had children, but Hannah had none.
3Every year Elkanah left his town of
Ramah and went up to Shiloh to worship
the LORD All-Powerful and to offer sacrifices to him. Shiloh was where Hophni
and Phinehas, the sons of Eli, served as
priests of the LORD. **4**When Elkanah offered sacrifices, he always gave a share of
the meat to his wife Peninnah and to her
sons and daughters. **5**But Elkanah always
gave a special share of the meat to Hannah, because he loved Hannah and because the LORD had kept her from having
children. **6**Peninnah would tease Hannah
and upset her, because the LORD had
made her unable to have children. **7**This
happened every year when they went up
to the house of the LORD at Shiloh. Peninnah would upset Hannah until Hannah
would cry and not eat anything. **8**Her
husband Elkanah would say to her, "Hannah, why are you crying and why won't
you eat? Why are you sad? Don't I mean
more to you than ten sons?"
9Once, after they had eaten their meal
in Shiloh, Hannah got up. Now Eli the
priest was sitting on a chair near the entrance to the LORD's house. **10**Hannah
was so sad that she cried and prayed to
the LORD. **11**She made a promise, saying,
"LORD All-Powerful, see how sad I am.
Remember me and don't forget me. If
you will give me a son, I will give him
back to you all his life, and no one will
ever cut his hair with a razor."[n]
12While Hannah kept praying, Eli
watched her mouth. **13**She was praying
in her heart so her lips moved, but her
voice was not heard. Eli thought she was
drunk **14**and said to her, "Stop getting
drunk! Throw away your wine!"
15Hannah answered, "No, sir, I have
not drunk any wine or beer. I am a deeply
troubled woman, and I was telling the
LORD about all my problems. **16**Don't
think I am an evil woman. I have been

FAITH links

KEEP ON PRAYING

1 SAMUEL 1

When it comes to prayer, how persistent are you? Many times, we might pray about something once. If God doesn't answer right away, we give up. Hannah was persistent in asking God for a son. She desperately wanted one! She didn't just ask once. She kept on asking. God wants you to have this kind of perseverance about prayer. You won't annoy God if you keep on asking him about something. So . . . keep on asking!

Link here for some more encouraging words on prayer:

From Hopeless to Hopeful, Exodus 6:9, p. 83

What He's Really Like, Deuteronomy 4:15–20, p. 233

Two Enemies, Nehemiah 6, p. 631

The Prayer Habit, Psalm 5:1–3, p. 712

Ask, Search, Knock, Matthew 7:7–10, p. 1286

While You Wait, Jude 21, p. 1726

1:11 cut . . . razor People who made special promises not to cut their hair or to drink wine or beer were called Nazirites. These people gave a specific time in their lives, or sometimes their entire lives, to the Lord. See Numbers 6:1-5.

praying because I have many troubles
and am very sad."

eMAIL! FROM GOD
1:17
Prayer
Who answers prayer?

17Eli answered,
"Go! I wish you well.
May the God of Is-
rael give you what
you asked of him."
18Hannah said,
"May I always please you." When she left
and ate something, she was not sad anymore.
19Early the next morning Elkanah's
family got up and worshiped the LORD.
Then they went back home to Ramah.
Elkanah had sexual relations with his
wife Hannah, and the LORD remembered
her. 20So Hannah became pregnant, and
in time she gave birth to a son. She
named him Samuel,[n] saying, "His name
is Samuel because I asked the LORD
for him."

Hannah Gives Samuel to God

21Every year Elkanah went with his
whole family to Shiloh to offer sacrifices
and to keep the promise he had made to
God. 22But one time Hannah did not go
with him. She told him, "When the boy is
old enough to eat solid food, I will take
him to Shiloh. Then I will give him to the
LORD, and he will always live there."
23Elkanah, Hannah's husband, said to
her, "Do what you think is best. You may
stay home until the boy is old enough to
eat. May the LORD do what you have
said." So Hannah stayed at home to nurse
her son until he was old enough to eat.
24When Samuel was old enough to
eat, Hannah took him to the house of the
LORD at Shiloh, along with a three-year-
old bull, one-half bushel of flour, and a
leather bag filled with wine. 25After they
had killed the bull for the sacrifice, Hannah brought Samuel to Eli. 26She said
to Eli, "As surely as you live, sir, I am
the same woman who stood near you
praying to the LORD. 27I prayed for this
child, and the LORD answered my prayer
and gave him to me. 28Now I give him
back to the LORD. He will belong to the
LORD all his life." And he worshiped the
LORD there.

Hannah Gives Thanks

2 Hannah prayed:
"The LORD has filled my heart with
joy;
I feel very strong in the LORD.
I can laugh at my enemies;
I am glad because you have helped
me!

2"There is no one holy like the LORD.
There is no God but you;
there is no Rock like our God.

3"Don't continue bragging,
don't speak proud words.
The LORD is a God who knows
everything,
and he judges what people do.

4"The bows of warriors break,
but weak people become strong.
5Those who once had plenty of food
now must work for food,
but people who were hungry are
hungry no more.
The woman who could not have
children now has seven,
but the woman who had many
children now is sad.

6"The LORD sends death,
and he brings to
life.
He sends people
to the grave,
and he raises
them to life
again.

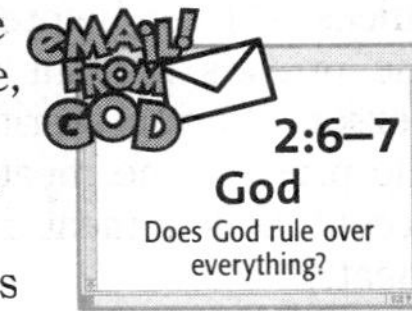
eMAIL! FROM GOD
2:6–7
God
Does God rule over everything?

7The LORD makes
some people
poor,
and others he makes rich.
He makes some people humble,
and others he makes great.
8The LORD raises the poor up from
the dust,
and he lifts the needy from the
ashes.
He lets the poor sit with princes
and receive a throne of honor.

1:20 Samuel This name sounds like the Hebrew word for "God heard."

"The foundations of the earth belong
to the LORD,
and the LORD set the world upon
them.
9 He protects those who are loyal to
him,
but evil people will be silenced in
darkness.
Power is not the key to success.
10 The LORD destroys his enemies;
he will thunder in heaven against
them.
The LORD will judge all the earth.
He will give power to his king
and make his appointed king
strong."

Eli's Evil Sons

11 Then Elkanah went home to Ramah, but the boy continued to serve the LORD under Eli the priest.

12 Now Eli's sons were evil men; they did not care about the LORD. 13 This is what the priests would normally do to the people: Every time someone brought a sacrifice, the meat would be cooked in a pot. The priest's servant would then come carrying a fork that had three prongs. 14 He would plunge the fork into the pot or the kettle. Whatever the fork brought out of the pot belonged to the priest. But this is how they treated all the Israelites who came to Shiloh to offer sacrifices. 15 Even before the fat was burned, the priest's servant would come to the person offering sacrifices and say, "Give the priest some meat to roast. He won't accept boiled meat from you, only raw meat."

16 If the one who offered the sacrifice said, "Let the fat be burned up first as usual, and then take anything you want," the priest's servant would answer, "No, give me the meat now. If you don't, I'll take it by force."

17 The LORD saw that the sin of the servants was very great because they did not show respect for the offerings made to the LORD.

Samuel Grows Up

18 But Samuel obeyed the LORD. As a boy he wore a linen holy vest. 19 Every year Samuel's mother made a little coat for him and took it to him when she went with her husband to Shiloh for the sacrifice. 20 When Eli blessed Elkanah and his

FAITH links

A SONG OF THANKS

1 SAMUEL 2

When you're feeling thankful, how do you show it? Hannah was thankful that God answered her prayer. She showed thanks to God with song. Other people in the Bible also sang songs to thank God: Moses and Miriam (Check out Exodus 15, p. 94); Deborah and Barak (Read Judges 5, p. 316); David (Look up 2 Samuel 22, p. 427; Psalm 18, p. 721, and Psalms 23—25, p. 726, just to name a few); Mary (Read Luke 1:46–55, p. 1366); Zechariah (See Luke 1:68–79, p. 1367); and Simeon (Check out Luke 2:29–32, p. 1369). What are you thankful to God for? How will you show your thanks?

A Thanksgiving Reminder, Exodus 12, p. 91

No Thanksgiving?, 2 Kings 23:21–23, p. 512

Love That Will Last, Psalm 136, p. 813

Braggin' Rights, Jeremiah 9:23–24, p. 1005

Your Spiritual Roots, Zechariah 1:1–6, p. 1253

A Family Meal, Mark 14:23–26, p. 1356

wife, he would say, "May the LORD repay
you with children through Hannah to take
the place of the boy Hannah prayed for
and gave back to the LORD." Then Elkanah and Hannah would go home. 21The
LORD was kind to Hannah, so she became
the mother of three sons and two daughters. And the boy Samuel grew up serving the LORD.

22Now Eli was very old. He heard
about everything his sons were doing to
all the Israelites and how his sons had
sexual relations with the women who
served at the entrance to the Meeting
Tent. 23Eli said to his sons, "Why do you
do these evil things that the people tell
me about? 24No, my sons. The LORD's
people are spreading a bad report about
you. 25If you sin against someone, God
can help you. But if you sin against the
LORD himself, no one can help you!" But
Eli's sons would not listen to him, because the LORD had decided to put them
to death.

26The boy Samuel grew physically.
He pleased the LORD and the people.

27A man of God came to Eli and said,
"This is what the LORD says: 'I clearly
showed myself to the family of your ancestor Aaron when they were slaves to
the king of Egypt. 28I chose them from all
the tribes of Israel to be my priests. I
wanted them to go up to my altar, to burn
incense, and to wear the holy vest. I also
let the family of your ancestor have part of
all the offerings sacrificed by the Israelites. 29So why don't you respect the sacrifices and gifts? You honor your sons more
than me. You grow fat on the best parts of
the meat the Israelites bring to me.'

30"So the LORD, the God of Israel,
says: 'I promised that your family and
your ancestor's family would serve me
always.' But now the LORD says: 'This
must stop! I will honor those who honor
me, but I will dishonor those who ignore
me. 31The time is coming when I will destroy the descendants of both you and
your ancestors. No man will grow old in
your family. 32You will see trouble in my
house. No matter what good things happen to Israel, there will never be an old
man in your family. 33I will not totally cut
off your family from my altar. But your
eyes will cry and your heart be sad, because all your descendants will die.

34" 'I will give you a sign. Both your
sons, Hophni and Phinehas, will die on
the same day. 35I will choose a loyal
priest for myself who will listen to me
and do what I want. I will make his family
continue, and he will always serve before
my appointed king. 36Then everyone left
in your family will come and bow down
before him. They will beg for a little money or a little food and say, "Please give
me a job as priest so I can have food to
eat." ' "

God Calls Samuel

3 The boy Samuel served the LORD under Eli. In those days the LORD did
not speak directly to people very often;
there were very few visions.

2Eli's eyes were so weak he was almost blind. One night he was lying in bed.
3Samuel was also in bed in the LORD's
house, where the Ark of the Agreement
was. God's lamp was still burning.

4Then the LORD called Samuel, and
Samuel answered, "I am here!" 5He ran
to Eli and said, "I am here. You called me."

But Eli said, "I didn't call you. Go back
to bed." So Samuel went back to bed.

6The LORD called again, "Samuel!"

Samuel again went to Eli and said, "I
am here. You called me."

Again Eli said, "I didn't call you. Go
back to bed."

7Samuel did not yet know the LORD,
and the LORD had not spoken directly to
him yet.

8The LORD called Samuel for the third
time. Samuel got up and went to Eli and
said, "I am here. You called me."

Then Eli realized the LORD was calling the boy. 9So he told Samuel, "Go to
bed. If he calls you again, say, 'Speak,
LORD. I am your servant and I am listening.' " So Samuel went and lay
down in bed.

10The LORD came
and stood there and
called as he had be-
fore, "Samuel, Sam-
uel!"

EMAIL FROM GOD 3:10
Following God
Who should you listen to?

LEARNING TO LISTEN

1 SAMUEL 3

When you were a baby, your parents probably spoke your name to you often. They wanted you to learn your name. They also wanted you to learn to listen to them.

Hundreds of years had passed since the Israelites had heard from God directly. That all changed one night when Samuel heard someone call his name. At first, he didn't know who had called him. He had to learn how to listen and respond to God. God wants you to learn to listen to him, too. There are many ways that God can speak to you. He uses the Bible, prayer, and the wise advice of Christians. Are you ready to listen?

The Cloud Guide, Numbers 9:15–23, p. 188

Plan for Success, 1 Chronicles 14:8–17, p. 538

How God Speaks, Job 33:14–17, p. 696

The Bible: Good for Your Faith, Psalm 119, p. 802

A Word to the Wise, Proverbs 10:1, p. 838

That's False!, 2 John 7–11, p. 1722

Samuel said, "Speak, LORD. I am your
servant and I am listening."
11The LORD said to Samuel, "Watch, I
am going to do something in Israel that
will shock those who hear about it. 12At
that time I will do to Eli and his family
everything I promised, from beginning
to end. 13I told Eli I would punish his
family always, because he knew his sons
were evil. They acted without honor, but
he did not stop them. 14So I swore to
Eli's family, 'Your guilt will never be removed by sacrifice or offering.' "
15Samuel lay down until morning.
Then he opened the doors of the house of
the LORD. He was afraid to tell Eli about
the vision, 16but Eli called to him, "Samuel, my son!"
Samuel answered, "I am here."
17Eli asked, "What did the LORD say
to you? Don't hide it from me. May God
punish you terribly if you hide from me
anything he said to you." 18So Samuel
told Eli everything and did not hide anything from him. Then Eli said, "He is the
LORD. Let him do what he thinks is best."
19The LORD was with Samuel as he
grew up; he did not let any of Samuel's
messages fail to come true. 20Then all
Israel, from Dan to Beersheba,[n] knew
Samuel was a true prophet of the LORD.
21And the LORD continued to show himself at Shiloh, and he showed himself to
Samuel through his word.

4 So, news about Samuel spread through
all of Israel.

The Philistines Capture the Ark of the Agreement

At that time the Israelites went out
to fight the Philistines. The Israelites
camped at Ebenezer and the Philistines
at Aphek. 2The Philistines went to meet
the Israelites in battle. And as the battle
spread, they defeated the Israelites, killing about four thousand soldiers on the
battlefield. 3When some Israelite soldiers went back to their camp, the older
leaders of Israel asked, "Why did the
LORD let the Philistines defeat us? Let's
bring the Ark of the Agreement with the
LORD here from Shiloh and take it with us
into battle. Then God will save us from
our enemies."

3:20 Dan to Beersheba Dan was the city farthest north in Israel, and Beersheba was the city farthest south. So this means all the people of Israel.

GET THE INFO

SAMUEL, THE PROPHET

1 Samuel 4

1. Hannah prayed for a son at the Lord's house near Shiloh. She promised if God would give her a son that she would dedicate him to the Lord's service. (Read 1 Samuel 1:10–17.)

2. Samuel was born to Hannah and Elkanah at Ramah. (Look up 1 Samuel 1:19–20.)

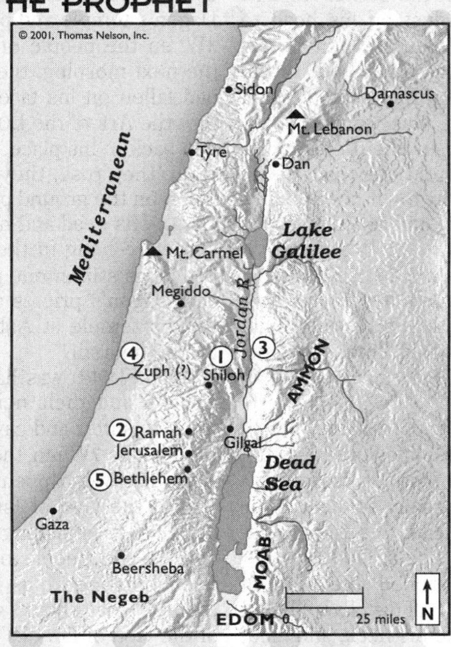

3. Hannah brought Samuel to live at the Lord's house at Shiloh when he was "old enough to eat solid food." Samuel became a helper to Eli, a priest at the Lord's house. While Samuel was there, God called him to do a special job. (See 1 Samuel 2:18—3:21.)

4. As a grown-up, Samuel served as a prophet and a judge. In the district of Zuph, Samuel secretly appointed Saul to be the first king of Israel. (Check out 1 Samuel 9:1—10:1.)

5. After Saul failed to obey God, Samuel appointed David, the youngest son of Jesse, to become the second king of Israel. (Read 1 Samuel 16:1–13.)

4So the people sent men to Shiloh.
They brought back the Ark of the Agreement with the LORD All-Powerful, who sits between the gold creatures with wings. Eli's two sons, Hophni and Phinehas, were there with the Ark.
5When the Ark of the Agreement with
the LORD came into the camp, all the Israelites gave a great shout of joy that made
the ground shake. 6When the Philistines
heard Israel's shout, they asked, "What's all this shouting in the Hebrew camp?"

Then the Philistines found out that the Ark of the LORD had come into the Hebrew camp. 7They were afraid and said, "A
god has come into the Hebrew camp! We're in trouble! This has never happened before! 8How terrible it will be for
us! Who can save us from these powerful gods? They are the ones who struck the Egyptians with all kinds of disasters in the desert. 9Be brave, Philistines! Fight like
men! In the past they were our slaves. So fight like men, or we will become their slaves."
10So the Philistines fought hard and
defeated the Israelites, and every Israelite soldier ran away to his own home. It

was a great defeat for Israel, because
thirty thousand Israelite soldiers were
killed. **11**The Ark of God was taken by
the Philistines, and Eli's two sons, Hophni and Phinehas, died.

12That same day a man from the tribe
of Benjamin ran from the battle. He tore
his clothes and put dust on his head to
show his great sadness. **13**When he arrived in Shiloh, Eli was by the side of the
road. He was sitting there in a chair,
watching, because he was worried about
the Ark of God. When the Benjaminite
entered Shiloh, he told the bad news.
Then all the people in town cried loudly.
14Eli heard the crying and asked, "What's
all this noise?"

The Benjaminite ran to Eli and told
him what had happened. **15**Eli was now
ninety-eight years old, and he was blind.
16The Benjaminite told him, "I have
come from the battle. I ran all the way
here today."

Eli asked, "What happened, my son?"

17The Benjaminite answered, "Israel
ran away from the Philistines, and the Israelite army has lost many soldiers. Your
two sons are both dead, and the Philistines have taken the Ark of God."

18When he mentioned the Ark of
God, Eli fell backward off his chair. He fell
beside the gate, broke his neck, and died,
because he was old and fat. He had led
Israel for forty years.

The Glory Is Gone

19Eli's daughter-in-law, the wife of
Phinehas, was pregnant and was about to
give birth. When she heard the news that
the Ark of God had been taken and that
Eli, her father-in-law, and Phinehas, her
husband, were both dead, she began to
give birth to her child. The child was
born, but the mother had much trouble in
giving birth. **20**As she was dying, the
women who helped her said, "Don't
worry! You've given birth to a son!" But
she did not answer or pay attention.
21She named the baby Ichabod,[n] saying,
"Israel's glory is gone." She said this because the Ark of God had been taken and
her father-in-law and husband were dead.
22She said, "Israel's glory is gone, because the Ark of God has been taken
away."

Trouble for the Philistines

5 After the Philistines had captured the
Ark of God, they took it from Ebenezer to Ashdod. **2**They carried it into
Dagon's temple and put it next to Dagon.
3When the people of Ashdod rose early
the next morning, they found that Dagon
had fallen on his face on the ground before the Ark of the LORD. So they put Dagon back in his place. **4**The next morning
when they rose, they again found Dagon
fallen on the ground before the Ark of the
LORD. His head and hands had broken off
and were lying in the doorway. Only his
body was still in one piece. **5**So, even today, Dagon's priests and others who enter his temple at Ashdod refuse to step
on the doorsill.

6The LORD was hard on the people of
Ashdod and their neighbors. He caused
them to suffer and gave them growths on
their skin. **7**When the people of Ashdod
saw what was happening, they said, "The
Ark of the God of Israel can't stay with
us. God is punishing us and Dagon our
god." **8**The people of Ashdod called all
five Philistine kings together and asked
them, "What should we do with the Ark
of the God of Israel?"

The rulers answered, "Move the Ark
of the God of Israel to Gath." So the Philistines moved it to Gath.

9But after they moved it to Gath,
there was a great panic. The LORD was
hard on that city also, and he gave both
old and young people in Gath growths on
their skin. **10**Then the Philistines sent
the Ark of God to Ekron.

But when it came into Ekron, the people of Ekron yelled, "Why are you bringing the Ark of the God of Israel to our
city? Do you want to kill us and our people?" **11**So they called all the kings of the
Philistines together and said, "Send the
Ark of the God of Israel back to its place
before it kills us and our people!" All the
people in the city were struck with terror
because God was so hard on them there.

4:21 Ichabod This name means "no glory."

12The people who did not die were troubled with growths on their skin. So the
people of Ekron cried loudly to heaven.

The Ark of God Is Sent Home

6 The Philistines kept the Ark of God
in their land seven months. **2**Then
they called for their priests and magicians and said, "What should we do with
the Ark of the LORD? Tell us how to send
it back home!"
3The priests and magicians answered,
"If you send back the Ark of the God of
Israel, don't send it back empty. You must
give a penalty offering. If you are then
healed, you will know that it was because
of the Ark that you had such trouble."
4The Philistines asked, "What kind of
penalty offering should we send to
Israel's God?"

They answered, "Make five gold models of the growths on your skin and five
gold models of rats. The number of models must match the number of Philistine
kings, because the same sickness has
come on you and your kings. **5**Make models of the growths and the rats that are
ruining the country, and give honor to
Israel's God. Then maybe he will stop
being so hard on you, your gods, and your
land. **6**Don't be stubborn like the king of
Egypt and the Egyptians. After God punished them terribly, they let the Israelites leave Egypt.
7"You must build a new cart and get
two cows that have just had calves. These
must be cows that have never had yokes
on their necks. Hitch the cows to the
cart, and take the calves home, away
from their mothers. **8**Put the Ark of the
LORD on the cart and the gold models for
the penalty offering in a box beside the
Ark. Then send the cart straight on its
way. **9**Watch the cart. If it goes toward
Beth Shemesh in Israel's own land, the
LORD has given us this great sickness.
But if it doesn't, we will know that
Israel's God has not punished us. Our
sickness just happened by chance."
10The Philistines did what the priests
and magicians said. They took two cows
that had just had calves and hitched them
to the cart, but they kept their calves at
home. **11**They put the Ark of the LORD
and the box with the gold rats and models
of growths on the cart. **12**Then the cows
went straight toward Beth Shemesh.
They stayed on the road, mooing all the
way, and did not turn right or left. The
Philistine kings followed the cows as far
as the border of Beth Shemesh.
13Now the people of Beth Shemesh
were harvesting their wheat in the valley.
When they looked up and saw the Ark of
the LORD, they were very happy. **14**The
cart came to the field belonging to Joshua
of Beth Shemesh and stopped near a
large rock. The people of Beth Shemesh
chopped up the wood of the cart. Then
they sacrificed the cows as burnt offerings to the LORD. **15**The Levites took
down the Ark of the LORD and the box
that had the gold models, and they put
both on the large rock. That day the people of Beth Shemesh offered whole burnt
offerings and made sacrifices to the
LORD. **16**After the five Philistine kings
saw this, they went back to Ekron the
same day.
17The Philistines had sent these gold
models of the growths as penalty offerings to the LORD. They sent one model
for each Philistine town: Ashdod, Gaza,
Ashkelon, Gath, and Ekron. **18**And the
Philistines also sent gold models of rats.
The number of rats matched the number
of towns belonging to the Philistine
kings, including both strong, walled cities
and country villages. The large rock on
which they put the Ark of the LORD is
still there in the field of Joshua of Beth
Shemesh.
19But some of the men of Beth Shemesh looked into the Ark of the LORD.
So God killed seventy of them.

EMAIL FROM GOD
6:20
God
Who can stand before God?

The people of Beth
Shemesh cried be-
cause the LORD had
struck them down.
20They said, "Who
can stand before the
LORD, this holy God? Whom will he strike
next?"
21Then they sent messengers to the
people of Kiriath Jearim, saying, "The
Philistines have brought back the Ark of

the LORD. Come down and take it to your
city."

7 The men of Kiriath Jearim came and
took the Ark of the LORD to Abinadab's house on a hill. There they made
Abinadab's son Eleazar holy for the LORD
so he could guard the Ark of the LORD.

The Lord Saves the Israelites

2The Ark stayed at Kiriath Jearim a
long time—twenty years in all. And the
people of Israel began to follow the LORD
again. **3**Samuel spoke to the whole group
of Israel, saying, "If you're turning back to
the LORD with all your hearts, you must
remove your foreign gods and
your idols of Ashto-
reth. You must give
yourselves fully to
the LORD and serve
only him. Then he
will save you from
the Philistines."

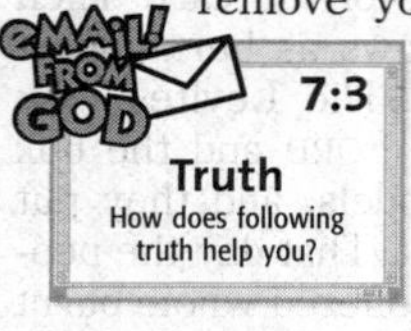

EMAIL! FROM GOD
7:3
Truth
How does following truth help you?

4So the Israelites put away their idols
of Baal and Ashtoreth, and they served
only the LORD.

5Samuel said, "All Israel must meet at
Mizpah, and I will pray to the LORD for
you." **6**So the Israelites met together
at Mizpah. They drew water from the
ground and poured it out before the LORD
and did not eat that day. They confessed,
"We have sinned against the LORD."
And Samuel served as judge of Israel at
Mizpah.

7The Philistines heard the Israelites
were meeting at Mizpah, so the Philistine kings came up to attack them. When
the Israelites heard they were coming,
they were afraid. **8**They said to Samuel,
"Don't stop praying to the LORD our God
for us! Ask him to save us from the
Philistines!" **9**Then Samuel took a baby
lamb and offered it to the LORD as a
whole burnt offering. He called to the
LORD for Israel's sake, and the LORD answered him.

10While Samuel was burning the offering, the Philistines came near to attack Israel. But the LORD thundered
against them with loud thunder. They
were so frightened they became confused. So the Israelites defeated the Philistines in battle. **11**The men of Israel ran
out of Mizpah and chased the Philistines
almost to Beth Car, killing the Philistines
along the way.

Peace Comes to Israel

12After this happened Samuel took a
stone and set it up between Mizpah and
Shen. He named the stone Ebenezer,[n]
saying, "The LORD has helped us to this
point." **13**So the Philistines were defeated and did not enter the Israelites'
land again.

The LORD was against the Philistines
all Samuel's life. **14**Earlier the Philistines
had taken towns from the Israelites, but
the Israelites won them back, from Ekron to Gath. They also took back from the
Philistines the lands near these towns.
There was peace also between Israel and
the Amorites.

15Samuel continued as judge of Israel
all his life. **16**Every year he went from
Bethel to Gilgal to Mizpah and judged the
Israelites in all these towns. **17**But Samuel always went back to Ramah, where
his home was. There he judged Israel and
built an altar to the LORD.

Israel Asks for a King

8 When Samuel was old, he made his
sons judges for Israel. **2**His first son
was named Joel, and his second son was
named Abijah. Joel and Abijah were judges
in Beersheba. **3**But Samuel's sons did not
live as he did. They tried to get money
dishonestly, and they accepted money secretly to make wrong judgments.

4So all the older leaders came together and met Samuel at Ramah. **5**They
said to him, "You're old, and your sons
don't live as you do. Give us a king to rule
over us like all the other nations."

6When the older leaders said that,
Samuel was not pleased. He prayed to
the LORD, **7**and the LORD told Samuel,
"Listen to whatever the people say to
you. They have not rejected you. They
have rejected me from being their king.
8They are doing as they have always
done. When I took them out of Egypt,

7:12 Ebenezer This name means "stone of help."

I INSIST!

1 SAMUEL 8; 9

Have you ever begged your parents for something that you later regretted having? Maybe this was something your parents insisted was not good for you. The people did not want Samuel's sons to rule over them. God knew that the people really did not want *him* to rule over them. He also knew they would later regret having a king. He told Samuel to warn the people not to insist on having a king. But they wouldn't listen.

Have you ever insisted on having your own way? If your way is God's way, there's no problem. But if your way involves disobeying God, there is one way to avoid having regrets. Follow God his way!

Here are some more Faithlinks on obeying God:

An Attention-Getter, Numbers 22, p. 207

Try to Remember, Deuteronomy 11:18–21, p. 243

Your Stats, 1 Kings 15; 16, p. 460

God's Instructions, Ezekiel 4:1–15, p. 1089

The Writing's on the Wall, Daniel 5, p. 1159

The Choices of a Choice, Luke 5:1–11, p. 1375

they left me and served other gods. They
are doing the same to you. **9**Now listen to
the people, but warn them what the king
who rules over them will do."

10So Samuel told those who had
asked him for a king what the LORD had
said. **11**Samuel said, "If you have a king
ruling over you, this is what he will do:
He will take your sons and make them
serve with his chariots and his horses,
and they will run in front of the king's
chariot. **12**The king will make some of
your sons commanders over thousands
or over fifties. He will make some of your
other sons plow his ground and reap his
harvest. He will take others to make
weapons of war and equipment for his
chariots. **13**He will take your daughters
to make perfume and cook and bake for
him. **14**He will take your best fields, vineyards, and olive groves and give them to
his servants. **15**He will take one-tenth of
your grain and grapes and give it to his
officers and servants. **16**He will take your
male and female servants, your best cattle, and your donkeys and use them all for
his own work. **17**He will take one-tenth
of your flocks, and you yourselves will
become his slaves. **18**When that time
comes, you will cry out because of the
king you chose. But the LORD will not answer you then."

19But the people would not listen to
Samuel. They said, "No! We want a king
to rule over us. **20**Then we will be the
same as all the other nations. Our king
will judge for us and go with us and fight
our battles."

21After Samuel heard all that the people said, he repeated their words to the
LORD. **22**The LORD answered, "You must
listen to them. Give them a king."

Then Samuel told the people of Israel,
"Go back to your towns."

Saul Looks for His Father's Donkeys

9 Kish, son of Abiel from the tribe of
Benjamin, was an important man.
(Abiel was the son of Zeror, who was the
son of Becorath, who was the son of
Aphiah of Benjamin.) **2**Kish had a son
named Saul, who was a fine young man.

There was no Israelite better than he.
Saul stood a head taller than any other
man in Israel.
3Now the donkeys of Saul's father,
Kish, were lost. So Kish said to Saul, his
son, "Take one of the servants, and go
and look for the donkeys." **4**Saul went
through the mountains of Ephraim and
the land of Shalisha, but he and the servant could not find the donkeys. They
went into the land of Shaalim, but the
donkeys were not there. They went
through the land of Benjamin, but they
still did not find them. **5**When they arrived in the area of Zuph, Saul said to his
servant, "Let's go back or my father will
stop thinking about the donkeys and will
start worrying about us."
6But the servant answered, "A man of
God is in this town. People respect him
because everything he says comes true.
Let's go into the town now. Maybe he can
tell us something about the journey we
have taken."
7Saul said to his servant, "If we go
into the town, what can we give him? The
food in our bags is gone. We have no gift
to give him. Do we have anything?"
8Again the servant answered Saul.
"Look, I have one-tenth of an ounce of
silver. Give it to the man of God. Then he
will tell us about our journey." **9**(In the
past, if someone in Israel wanted to ask
something from God, he would say,
"Let's go to the seer." We call the person
a prophet today, but in the past he was
called a seer.)
10Saul said to his servant, "That's a
good idea. Come, let's
go." So they went toward
the town where the man
of God was.
11As Saul and the servant were going up the
hill to the town, they met
some young women com-
ing out to get water. Saul
and the servant asked
them, "Is the seer here?"
12The young women
answered, "Yes, he's here. He's ahead of
you. Hurry now. He has just come to our
town today, because the people will offer
a sacrifice at the place of worship. **13**As
soon as you enter the town, you will find
him before he goes up to the place of worship to eat. The people will not begin eating until the seer comes, because he
must bless the sacrifice. After that, the
guests will eat. Go now, and you should
find him."

Saul Meets Samuel

14Saul and the servant went up to the
town. Just as they entered it, they saw
Samuel coming toward them on his way
up to the place of worship.
15The day before Saul came, the LORD
had told Samuel: **16**"About this time tomorrow I will send you a man from the
land of Benjamin. Appoint him to lead my
people Israel. He will save my people
from the Philistines. I have seen the suffering of my people, and I have listened to
their cry."
17When Samuel first saw Saul, the
LORD said to Samuel, "This is the man
I told you about. He will organize my
people."
18Saul approached Samuel at the gate
and said, "Please tell me where the
seer's house is."
19Samuel answered, "I am the seer.
Go with me to the place of worship. Today
you and your servant are to eat with me.
Tomorrow morning I will answer all your
questions and send you home. **20**Don't
worry about the donkeys you lost three
days ago, because they have been found.
Soon all the wealth of Israel will belong to
you and your family."
21Saul answered, "But
I am from the tribe of
Benjamin, the smallest
tribe in Israel. And my
family group is the smallest in the tribe of Benjamin. Why are you saying
such things?"
22Then Samuel took
Saul and his servant into a
large room and gave them
a choice place at the table.
About thirty guests were there. **23**Samuel
said to the cook, "Bring the meat I gave
you, the portion I told you to set aside."

When Samuel first saw Saul, the LORD said to Samuel, "This is the man I told you about. He will organize my people."
—1 Samuel 9:17

24So the cook took the thigh and put it on the table in front of Saul. Samuel said, "This is the meat saved for you. Eat it, because it was set aside for you for this special time. As I said, 'I had invited the people.' " So Saul ate with Samuel that day.

25After they finished eating, they came down from the place of worship and went to the town. Then Samuel talked with Saul on the roof[n] of his house. **26**At dawn they got up, and Samuel called to Saul on the roof. He said, "Get up, and I will send you on your way." So Saul got up and went out of the house with Samuel. **27**As Saul, his servant, and Samuel were getting near the edge of the city, Samuel said to Saul, "Tell the servant to go on ahead of us, but you stay, because I have a message from God for you."

Samuel Appoints Saul

10 Samuel took a jar of olive oil and poured it on Saul's head. He kissed Saul and said, "The LORD has appointed you to lead his people. **2**After you leave me today, you will meet two men near Rachel's tomb on the border of Benjamin at Zelzah. They will say to you, 'The donkeys you were looking for have been found. But now your father has stopped thinking about his donkeys and is worrying about you. He is asking, "What will I do about my son?" '

3"Then you will go on until you reach the big tree at Tabor. Three men on their way to worship God at Bethel will meet you there. One man will be carrying three goats. Another will be carrying three loaves of bread. And the third will have a leather bag full of wine. **4**They will greet you and offer you two loaves of bread, which you must accept. **5**Then you will go to Gibeah of God, where a Philistine camp is. When you approach this town, a group of prophets will come down from the place of worship. They will be playing harps, tambourines, flutes, and lyres, and they will be prophesying. **6**Then the Spirit of the LORD will rush upon you with power. You will prophesy with these prophets, and you will be changed into a different man. **7**After these signs happen, do whatever you find to do, because God will help you.

8"Go ahead of me to Gilgal. I will come down to you to offer whole burnt offerings and fellowship offerings. But you must wait seven days. Then I will come and tell you what to do."

Saul Made King

9When Saul turned to leave Samuel, God changed Saul's heart. All these signs came true that day. **10**When Saul and his servant arrived at Gibeah, Saul met a group of prophets. The Spirit of God rushed upon him, and he prophesied with the prophets. **11**When people who had known Saul before saw him prophesying with the prophets, they asked each other, "What has happened to Kish's son? Is even Saul one of the prophets?"

12A man who lived there said, "Who is the father of these prophets?" So this became a famous saying: "Is even Saul one of the prophets?" **13**When Saul finished prophesying, he entered the place of worship.

14Saul's uncle asked him and his servant, "Where have you been?"

Saul said, "We were looking for the donkeys. When we couldn't find them, we went to talk to Samuel."

15Saul's uncle asked, "Please tell me. What did Samuel say to you?"

16Saul answered, "He told us the donkeys had already been found." But Saul did not tell his uncle what Samuel had said about his becoming king.

17Samuel called all the people of Israel to meet with the LORD at Mizpah. **18**He said, "This is what the LORD, the God of Israel, says: 'I led Israel out of Egypt. I saved you from Egypt's control and from other kingdoms that were troubling you.' **19**But now you have rejected your God. He saves you from all your troubles and problems, but you said, 'No! We want a king to rule over us.' Now

9:25 roof In Bible times houses were built with flat roofs. The roof was used for drying things such as flax and fruit. And it was used as an extra room, as a place for worship, and as a cool place to sleep in the summer. See Deuteronomy 22:8.

come, stand before the LORD in your
tribes and family groups."
20When Samuel gathered all the
tribes of Israel, the tribe of Benjamin was
picked. 21Samuel had them pass by in
family groups, and Matri's family was
picked. Then he had each man of Matri's
family pass by, and Saul son of Kish was
picked. But when they looked for Saul,
they could not find him. 22They asked
the LORD, "Has Saul come here yet?"
The LORD said, "Yes. He's hiding behind the baggage."
23So they ran and brought him out.
When Saul stood among the people, he
was a head taller than anyone else.
24Then Samuel said to the people, "See
the man the LORD has chosen. There is
no one like him among all the people."
Then the people shouted, "Long live
the king!"
25Samuel explained
the rights and duties of
the king and then wrote
them in a book and put it
before the LORD. Then he
told the people to go to
their homes.
26Saul also went to
his home in Gibeah. God
touched the hearts of certain brave men who went
along with him. 27But some troublemakers said, "How can this man save us?"
They disapproved of Saul and refused to
bring gifts to him. But Saul kept quiet.

Then Samuel said to the people, "See the man the LORD has chosen. There is no one like him among all the people."
—1 Samuel 10:24

Nahash Troubles Jabesh Gilead

11 About a month later Nahash the
Ammonite and his army sur-
rounded the city of Jabesh in Gilead. All
the people of Jabesh said to Nahash,
"Make a treaty with us, and we will serve
you."
2But he answered, "I will make a
treaty with you only if I'm allowed to
poke out the right eye of each of you.
Then all Israel will be ashamed!"
3The older leaders of Jabesh said to
Nahash, "Give us seven days to send
messengers through all Israel. If no one
comes to help us, we will give ourselves
up to you."
4When the messengers came to Gibeah where Saul lived and told the people
the news, they cried loudly. 5Saul was
coming home from plowing the fields
with his oxen when he heard the people
crying. He asked, "What's wrong with
the people that they are crying?" Then
they told Saul what the messengers from
Jabesh had said. 6When Saul heard their
words, God's Spirit rushed upon him
with power, and he became very angry.
7So he took a pair of oxen and cut them
into pieces. Then he gave the pieces of
the oxen to messengers and ordered
them to carry them through all the land of
Israel.
The messengers said, "This is what
will happen to the oxen of anyone who
does not follow Saul and Samuel." So the
people became very afraid of the LORD.
They all came together as
if they were one person.
8Saul gathered the peo-
ple together at Bezek.
There were three hun-
dred thousand men from
Israel and thirty thousand
men from Judah.
9They said to the mes-
sengers who had come,
"Tell the people at Jabesh
Gilead this: 'Before the
day warms up tomorrow, you will be
saved.' " So the messengers went and reported this to the people at Jabesh, and
they were very happy. 10The people said
to Nahash the Ammonite, "Tomorrow we
will come out to meet you. Then you can
do anything you want to us."
11The next morning Saul divided his
soldiers into three groups. At dawn they
entered the Ammonite camp and defeated them before the heat of the day.
The Ammonites who escaped were scattered; no two of them were still together.
12Then the people said to Samuel,
"Who didn't want Saul as king? Bring
them here and we will kill them!"
13But Saul said, "No! No one will be
put to death today. Today the LORD has
saved Israel!"
14Then Samuel said to the people,
"Come, let's go to Gilgal. There we will

again promise to obey the king." 15So all
the people went to Gilgal, and there, before the LORD, the people made Saul
king. They offered fellowship offerings to
the LORD, and Saul and all the Israelites
had a great celebration.

Samuel's Farewell Speech

12 Samuel said to all Israel, "I have
done everything you wanted me
to do and have put a king over you. 2Now
you have a king to lead you. I am old and
gray, and my sons are here with you. I
have been your leader since I was young.
3Here I am. If I have done anything
wrong, you must testify against me before the LORD and his appointed king. Did
I steal anyone's ox or donkey? Did I hurt
or cheat anyone? Did I ever secretly accept money to pretend not to see something wrong? If I did any of these things, I
will make it right."

4The Israelites answered, "You have
not cheated us, or hurt us, or taken anything unfairly from anyone."

5Samuel said to them, "The LORD is a
witness to what you have said. His appointed king is also a witness today that
you did not find anything wrong in me."

"He is our witness," they said.

6Then Samuel said to the people, "It
is the LORD who chose Moses and Aaron

LOOK AT ME!

What are some things you're proud of? Everyone has something they do well and can be proud of what they do. But sometimes pride can cause problems. Let's listen in as Danielle, age 11, tells us about her problem with pride.

Hi, Danielle, welcome to Connect 2-You. What's your story?

My sister says I'm a conceited show-off because I told her friends about all the medals I've won in gymnastics. I say she's just jealous. I've been competing for seven years now, and my coach says I'm one of the best students she's ever had. If I'm that good, what's wrong with telling people about it?

It sounds like you're quite a gymnast, Danielle. The question you need to ask yourself is why you want to tell other people how good you are. The Bible tells us that pride makes us forget about God because we're too busy focusing on ourselves. Ask yourself this: How good of a gymnast would you be if God hadn't given you a healthy body?

Also, don't forget about other people's feelings. Maybe your sister is jealous. Maybe she wishes she had your talent. The Bible instructs us to build each other up, not make each other feel miserable. Think of something your sister is good at. Instead of talking about your own skills, talk about hers. For more tips on how to keep pride under control, check out the Livin' It page on pride, Deuteronomy 8:11–18, p. 238.

and brought your ancestors out of Egypt.
7Now, stand there, and I will remind you
of all the good things the LORD did for
you and your ancestors.

8"After Jacob entered Egypt, his descendants cried to the LORD for help. So
the LORD sent Moses and Aaron, who
took your ancestors out of Egypt and
brought them to live in this place.

9"But they forgot the LORD their God.
So he handed them over as slaves to Sisera, the commander of the army of Hazor,
and as slaves to the Philistines and the
king of Moab. They all fought against
your ancestors. **10**Then your ancestors
cried to the LORD and said, 'We have
sinned. We have left the LORD and served
the Baals and the Ashtoreths. But now
save us from our enemies, and we will
serve you.' **11**So the LORD sent Gideon,[n]
Barak, Jephthah, and Samuel. He saved
you from your enemies around you, and
you lived in safety. **12**But when you saw
Nahash king of the Ammonites coming
against you, you said, 'No! We want a king
to rule over us!'—even though the LORD
your God was your king. **13**Now here is
the king you chose, the one you asked for.
The LORD has put him over you.

eMAIL! FROM GOD
12:14
Obedience
How do you follow God?

14You must honor
the LORD and serve
him. You must obey
his word and not
turn against his com-
mands. Both you and
the king ruling over you must follow the
LORD your God. If you do, it will be well
with you. **15**But if you don't obey the
LORD, and if you turn against his commands, he will be against you. He will do
to you what he did to your ancestors.

16"Now stand still and see the great
thing the LORD will do before your eyes.
17It is now the time of the wheat harvest.[n] I will pray for the LORD to send
thunder and rain. Then you will know
what an evil thing you did against the
LORD when you asked for a king."

18Then Samuel prayed to the LORD,
and that same day the LORD sent thunder
and rain. So the people were very afraid
of the LORD and Samuel. **19**They said to
Samuel, "Pray to the LORD your God for
us, your servants! Don't let us die! We've
added to all our sins the evil of asking for
a king."

20Samuel answered, "Don't be afraid.
It's true that you did wrong, but don't turn
away from the LORD. Serve the LORD with
all your heart. **21**Idols are of no use, so
don't worship them. They can't help you
or save you. They are useless! **22**For his
own sake, the LORD won't leave his people. Instead, he was pleased to make you
his own people. **23**I will surely not stop
praying for you, because that would be
sinning against the LORD. I will teach you
what is good and right. **24**You

eMAIL! FROM GOD
12:24
Truth
Find out how to serve God.

must honor the LORD
and truly serve him
with all your heart.
Remember the won-
derful things he did
for you! **25**But if you
are stubborn and do evil, he will sweep you
and your king away."

13 Saul was thirty years old when he
became king, and he was king
over Israel forty-two years.[n] **2**Saul chose
three thousand men from Israel. Two
thousand men stayed with him at Micmash in the mountains of Bethel, and one
thousand men stayed with Jonathan at
Gibeah in Benjamin. Saul sent the other
men in the army back home.

3Jonathan attacked the Philistine camp
in Geba, and the other Philistines heard
about it. Saul said, "Let the Hebrews hear
what happened." So he told the men to
blow trumpets through all the land of Israel. **4**All the Israelites heard the news.
The men said, "Saul has defeated the Philistine camp. Now the Philistines will
really hate us!" Then the Israelites were
called to join Saul at Gilgal.

5The Philistines gathered to fight Israel with three thousand[n] chariots and six

---

12:11 Gideon Also called Jerub-Baal.

12:17 time . . . harvest This was a dry time in the summer when no rains fell.

13:1 Saul . . . years This is how the verse is worded in some early Greek copies. The Hebrew is not clear here.

13:5 three thousand Some Greek copies say three thousand. The Hebrew copies say thirty thousand.

FAITH links

A SHORTCUT

1 SAMUEL 13:1-14

Ever take a shortcut? They can save you time sometimes. But there are some instances where taking shortcuts can get you into trouble. Obeying God is one of those instances. Instead of doing what Samuel told him to do, Saul couldn't wait. He wanted to take a shortcut instead. His impatience cost him the kingdom.

God wants you to obey him fully, not just when or how you might feel like doing it. After all, when it comes to loving you, God never takes shortcuts. Why should you?

Your Worst Enemy, Exodus 7—11, p. 85

A Long Wait, Joshua 14:6–15, p. 294

Hurry Up and Wait, 2 Samuel 5, p. 405

Fly Like an Eagle, Isaiah 40:28–31, p. 947

A Hopeful Future, Jeremiah 29:11, p. 1031

Faith That Pleases God, Luke 7:1–9, p. 1380

thousand men to ride in them. Their soldiers were as many as the grains of sand
on the seashore. The Philistines went
and camped at Micmash, which is east of
Beth Aven. 6When the Israelites saw that
they were in trouble, they went to hide in
caves and bushes, among the rocks, and
in pits and wells. 7Some Hebrews even
went across the Jordan River to the land
of Gad and Gilead.

But Saul stayed at Gilgal, and all the
men in his army were shaking with fear.
8Saul waited seven days, because Samuel had said he would meet him then. But
Samuel did not come to Gilgal, and the
soldiers began to leave.

9So Saul said, "Bring me the whole
burnt offering and the fellowship offerings." Then Saul offered the whole burnt
offering. 10Just as he finished, Samuel arrived, and Saul went to greet him.

11Samuel asked, "What have you
done?"

Saul answered, "I saw the soldiers
leaving me, and you were not here when
you said you would be. The Philistines
were gathering at Micmash. 12Then I
thought, 'The Philistines will come against
me at Gilgal, and I haven't asked for the
LORD's approval.' So I forced myself to
offer the whole burnt offering."

13Samuel said, "You acted foolishly!
You haven't obeyed the command of the
LORD your GOD. If you had obeyed him,
the LORD would have made your kingdom continue in Israel always, 14but now
your kingdom will not continue. The
LORD has looked for the kind of man he
wants. He has appointed him to rule his
people, because you haven't obeyed his
command."

15Then Samuel left Gilgal and went to
Gibeah in Benjamin. Saul counted the
men who were still with him, and there
were about six hundred.

Hard Times for Israel

16Saul and his son Jonathan and the
soldiers with him stayed in Gibeah in the
land of Benjamin. The Philistines made
their camp at Micmash. 17Three groups
went out from the Philistine camp to
make raids. One group went on the Ophrah road in the land of Shual. 18The second group went on the Beth Horon road.
The third group went on the border road
that overlooks the Valley of Zeboim toward the desert.

19The whole land of Israel had no
blacksmith because the Philistines had
said, "The Hebrews might make swords

and spears." **20**So all the Israelites had to
go down to the Philistines to have their
plows, hoes, axes, and sickles sharpened.
21The Philistine blacksmiths charged
about one-fourth of an ounce of silver for
sharpening plows and hoes. And they
charged one-eighth of an ounce of silver
for sharpening picks, axes, and the sticks
used to guide oxen.

22So when the battle came, the soldiers with Saul and Jonathan had no
swords or spears. Only Saul and his son
Jonathan had them.

Israel Defeats the Philistines

23A group from the Philistine army
had gone out to the pass at Micmash.

14 One day Jonathan, Saul's son, said
to the officer who carried his armor, "Come, let's go over to the Philistine
camp on the other side." But Jonathan did
not tell his father.

2Saul was sitting under a pomegranate tree at the threshing floor near Gibeah. He had about six hundred men with
him. **3**One man was Ahijah who was
wearing the holy vest. (Ahijah was a son
of Ichabod's brother Ahitub. Ichabod was
the son of Phinehas, the son of Eli, the
LORD's priest in Shiloh.) No one knew
Jonathan had left.

4There was a steep slope on each side
of the pass that Jonathan planned to go
through to reach the Philistine camp.
The cliff on one side was named Bozez,
and the cliff on the other side was named
Seneh. **5**One cliff faced north toward
Micmash. The other faced south toward
Geba.

6Jonathan said to his officer who carried his armor, "Come. Let's go to the
camp of those men who are not circumcised. Maybe the LORD will help us. The
LORD can give us victory if we have many
people, or just a few."

7The officer who carried Jonathan's
armor said to him, "Do whatever you
think is best. Go ahead. I'm with you."

8Jonathan said, "Then come. We will
cross over to the Philistines and let them
see us. **9**If they say to us, 'Stay there until we come to you,' we will stay where
we are. We won't go up to them. **10**But if
they say, 'Come up to us,' we will climb
up, and the LORD will let us defeat them.
This will be the sign for us."

11When both Jonathan and his officer
let the Philistines see them, the Philistines said, "Look! The Hebrews are
crawling out of the holes they were hiding
in!" **12**The Philistines in the camp shouted to Jonathan and his officer, "Come up to
us. We'll teach you a lesson!"

Jonathan said to his officer, "Climb up
behind me, because the LORD has given
the Philistines to Israel!" **13**So Jonathan
climbed up, using his hands and feet, and
his officer climbed just behind him. Jonathan struck down the Philistines as he
went, and his officer killed them as he followed behind him. **14**In that first fight
Jonathan and his officer killed about
twenty Philistines over a half acre of
ground.

15All the Philistine soldiers pan-
icked—those in the camp and those in
the raiding party. The ground itself
shook! God had caused the panic.

16Saul's guards were at Gibeah in the
land of Benjamin when they saw the Philistine soldiers running in every direction. **17**Saul said to his army, "Check to
see who has left our camp." When they
checked, they learned that Jonathan and
his officer were gone.

18So Saul said to Ahijah the priest,
"Bring the Ark of God." (At that time it
was with the Israelites.) **19**While Saul
was talking to the priest, the confusion
in the Philistine camp was growing.
Then Saul said to Ahijah, "Put your hand
down!"

20Then Saul gathered his army and
entered the battle. They found the Philistines confused, striking each other with
their swords! **21**Earlier, there were Hebrews who had served the Philistines and
had stayed in their camp, but now they
joined the Israelites with Saul and Jonathan. **22**When all the Israelites hidden in
the mountains of Ephraim heard that the
Philistine soldiers were running away,
they also joined the battle and chased the
Philistines. **23**So the LORD saved the Israelites that day, and the battle moved on
past Beth Aven.

KING SAUL, THE SOLDIER 1 Samuel 14

As the first king of a united Israel, Saul's first priority was to conquer his enemies. At first, Saul won many important battles. But as he became more concerned about chasing and capturing David, his armies began to lose. Ultimately, Saul and his sons were killed by the Philistines. Here are some important highlights from Saul's battles:

1. King Saul won his first battle against the Philistines at Geba. (See 1 Samuel 13 and 14.)

2. Saul's army also won battles against the Moabites, Ammonites, and Edomites. (Look up 1 Samuel 14:47.)

© 2001, Thomas Nelson, Inc.
Lake Galilee
Mediterranean
Mt. Gilboa
Jordan R.
AMMON
Geba
Jerusalem
Dead Sea
MOAB
EDOM
0 25 miles
N

3. Saul and his armies defeated the Amalekites, but Saul disobeyed God by sparing the life of King Agag and not destroying some of the best Amalekite possessions. (Check out 1 Samuel 15:1–9.)

4. Saul took his own life after being seriously wounded at the end of a losing battle with the Philistines. (Read 1 Samuel 31.)

Saul Makes Another Mistake

24The men of Israel were miserable
that day because Saul had made an oath
for all of them. He had said, "No one
should eat food before evening and before I finish defeating my enemies. If he
does, he will be cursed!" So no Israelite
soldier ate food.

25Now the army went into the woods,
where there was some honey on the
ground. **26**They came upon some honey,
but no one took any because they were
afraid of the oath. **27**Jonathan had not
heard the oath Saul had put on the army,
so he dipped the end of his stick into the
honey and lifted some out and ate it.
Then he felt better. **28**Then one of the
soldiers told Jonathan, "Your father
made an oath for all the soldiers. He said
any man who eats today will be cursed!
That's why they are so weak."

29Jonathan said, "My father has
made trouble for the land! See how
much better I feel after just tasting a little of this honey! **30**It would have been
much better for the men to eat the food
they took from their enemies today. We
could have killed many more Philistines!"

31That day the Israelites defeated

the Philistines from Micmash to Aijalon.
After that, they were very tired. **32**They
had taken sheep, cattle, and calves from
the Philistines. Now they were so hungry
they killed the animals on the ground and
ate them, without draining the blood
from them! **33**Someone said to Saul,
"Look! The men are sinning against the
LORD. They're eating meat without
draining the blood from it!"

Saul said, "You have sinned! Roll a
large stone over here now!" **34**Then he
said, "Go to the men and tell them that
each person must bring his ox and sheep
to me and kill it here and eat it. Don't sin
against the LORD by eating meat without
draining the blood from it."

That night everyone brought his animals and killed them there. **35**Then Saul
built an altar to the LORD. It was the first
altar he had built to the LORD.

36Saul said, "Let's go after the Philistines tonight and rob them. We won't let
any of them live!"

The men answered, "Do whatever
you think is best."

But the priest said, "Let's ask God."

37So Saul asked God, "Should I chase
the Philistines? Will you let us defeat
them?" But God did not answer Saul at
that time. **38**Then Saul said to all the
leaders of his army, "Come here. Let's
find out what sin has been done today.
39As surely as the LORD lives who has
saved Israel, even if my son Jonathan did
the sin, he must die." But no one in the
army spoke.

40Then Saul said to all the Israelites,
"You stand on this side. I and my son Jonathan will stand on the other side."

The men answered, "Do whatever
you think is best."

41Then Saul prayed to the LORD, the
God of Israel, "Give me the right answer."

And Saul and Jonathan were picked;
the other men went free. **42**Saul said,
"Now let us discover if it is I or Jonathan
my son who is guilty." And Jonathan was
picked.

43Saul said to Jonathan, "Tell me what
you have done."

So Jonathan told Saul, "I only tasted a
little honey from the end of my stick. And
must I die now?"

44Saul said, "Jonathan, if you don't
die, may God punish me terribly."

45But the soldiers said to Saul, "Must
Jonathan die? Never! He is responsible
for saving Israel today! As surely as the
LORD lives, not even a hair of his head
will fall to the ground! Today Jonathan
fought against the Philistines with God's
help!" So the army saved Jonathan, and
he did not die.

46Then Saul stopped chasing the Philistines, and they went back to their own
land.

Saul Fights Israel's Enemies

47When Saul became king over Israel,
he fought against Israel's enemies all
around. He fought Moab, the Ammonites,
Edom, the king of Zobah, and the Philistines. Everywhere Saul went he defeated
Israel's enemies. **48**He fought bravely
and defeated the Amalekites. He saved
the Israelites from their enemies who
had robbed them.

49Saul's sons were Jonathan, Ishvi,
and Malki-Shua. His older daughter was
named Merab, and his younger daughter
was named Michal. **50**Saul's wife was
Ahinoam daughter of Ahimaaz. The commander of his army was Abner son of
Ner, Saul's uncle. **51**Saul's father Kish
and Abner's father Ner were sons of
Abiel.

52All Saul's life he fought hard against
the Philistines. When he saw strong or
brave men, he took them into his army.

Saul Rejected as King

15 Samuel said to Saul, "The LORD
sent me to appoint you king over
Israel. Now listen to his message. **2**This
is what the LORD All-Powerful says:
'When the Israelites came out of Egypt,
the Amalekites tried to stop them from
going to Canaan. So I will punish them.
3Now go, attack the Amalekites and destroy everything they own as an offering
to the LORD. Don't let anything live. Put
to death men and women, children and
small babies, cattle and sheep, camels
and donkeys.' "

4So Saul called the army together at
Telaim. There were two hundred thousand foot soldiers and ten thousand men
from Judah. 5Then Saul went to the city of
Amalek and set up an ambush in the ravine. 6He said to the Kenites, "Go away.
Leave the Amalekites so that I won't destroy you with them, because you showed
kindness to the Israelites when they came
out of Egypt." So the Kenites moved away
from the Amalekites.
7Then Saul defeated the Amalekites.
He fought them all the way from Havilah
to Shur, at the border of Egypt. 8He took
King Agag of the Amalekites alive, but he
killed all of Agag's army with the sword.
9Saul and the army let Agag live, along
with the best sheep, fat cattle, and lambs.
They let every good animal live, because
they did not want to destroy them. But
when they found an animal that was weak
or useless, they killed it.
10Then the LORD spoke his word to
Samuel: 11"I am sorry I made Saul king,
because he has stopped following me and
has not obeyed my commands." Samuel
was upset, and he cried out to the LORD
all night long.
12Early the next morning Samuel got
up and went to meet Saul. But the people
told Samuel, "Saul has gone to Carmel,
where he has put up a monument in
his own honor. Now he has gone down to
Gilgal."
13When Samuel came to Saul, Saul
said, "May the LORD bless you! I have
obeyed the LORD's commands."
14But Samuel said, "Then why do I
hear cattle mooing and sheep bleating?"
15Saul answered, "The soldiers took
them from the Amalekites. They saved
the best sheep and cattle to offer as sacrifices to the LORD your God, but we destroyed all the other animals."
16Samuel said to Saul, "Stop! Let me
tell you what the LORD said to me last
night."
Saul answered, "Tell me."
17Samuel said, "Once you didn't think
much of yourself, but now you have become the leader of the tribes of Israel.
The LORD appointed you to be king over
Israel. 18And he sent you on a mission.
He said, 'Go and destroy those evil people, the Amalekites. Make war on them
until all of them are dead.' 19Why didn't
you obey the LORD? Why did you take the
best things? Why did you do what the
LORD said was wrong?"
20Saul said, "But I did obey the LORD.
I did what the LORD told me to do. I destroyed all the Amalekites, and I brought
back Agag their king. 21The soldiers
took the best sheep and cattle to sacrifice
to the LORD your God at Gilgal."
22But Samuel answered,
"What pleases the LORD more:
burnt offerings and sacrifices
or obedience to his voice?
It is better to
obey than to
sacrifice.
It is better to
listen to God
than to offer
the fat of
sheep.

eMAIL FROM GOD
15:22
Obedience
Find out what pleases God the most.

23 Disobedience is as bad as the sin of
sorcery.
Pride is as bad as the sin of
worshiping idols.
You have rejected the LORD's
command.
Now he rejects you as king."
24Then Saul said to Samuel, "I have
sinned. I didn't obey the LORD's commands and your words. I was afraid of the
people, and I did what they said. 25Now, I
beg you, forgive my sin. Come back with
me so I may worship the LORD."
26But Samuel said to
Saul, "I won't go
back with you. You
rejected the LORD's
command, and now
he rejects you as
king of Israel."

15:26
Belief
What happens if you reject God?

27As Samuel turned to leave, Saul
caught his robe, and it tore. 28Samuel
said to him, "The LORD has torn the kingdom of Israel from you today and has
given it to one of your neighbors who is
better than you. 29The LORD is the Eternal One of Israel. He does not lie or
change his mind. He is not a human being, so he does not change his mind.

30Saul answered, "I have sinned. But
please honor me in front of the older
leaders of my people and in front of the
Israelites. Come back with me so that I
can worship the LORD your GOD." 31So
Samuel went back with Saul, and Saul
worshiped the LORD.
32Then Samuel said, "Bring me King
Agag of the Amalekites."
Agag came to Samuel in chains, but
Agag thought, "Surely the threat of death
has passed."
33Samuel said to him, "Your sword
made other mothers lose their children.
Now your mother will have no children."
And Samuel cut Agag to pieces before the
LORD at Gilgal.
34Then Samuel left and went to Ramah, but Saul went up to his home in Gibeah. 35And Samuel never saw Saul again
the rest of his life, but he was sad for
Saul. And the LORD was very sorry he
had made Saul king of Israel.

Samuel Goes to Bethlehem

16 The LORD said to Samuel, "How
long will you continue to feel sorry for Saul? I have rejected him as king of
Israel. Fill your container with olive oil
and go. I am sending you to Jesse who
lives in Bethlehem, because I have chosen one of his sons to be king."
2But Samuel said, "If I go, Saul will
hear the news and will try to kill me."
The LORD said, "Take a young calf
with you. Say, 'I have come to offer a sacrifice to the LORD.' 3Invite Jesse to the
sacrifice. Then I will tell you what to do.
You must appoint the one I show you."
4Samuel did what the LORD told him
to do. When he arrived at Bethlehem, the
older leaders of Bethlehem shook with
fear. They met him and asked, "Are you
coming in peace?"
5Samuel answered, "Yes, I come in
peace. I have come to make a sacrifice to
the LORD. Set yourselves apart to the
LORD and come to the sacrifice with me."
Then he set Jesse and his sons apart to
the LORD, and he invited them to come to
the sacrifice.
6When they arrived, Samuel saw Eliab, and he thought, "Surely the LORD has
appointed this person standing here before him."
7But the LORD said to Samuel, "Don't
look at how handsome Eliab is or
how tall he is, be-
cause I have not cho-
sen him. God does
not see the same
way people see. Peo-
ple look at the out-
side of a person, but the LORD looks at the
heart."

EMAIL FROM GOD
16:7
Character
God cares most about what's on the inside.

8Then Jesse called Abinadab and told
him to pass by Samuel. But Samuel said,
"The LORD has not chosen this man either." 9Then Jesse had Shammah pass by.
But Samuel said, "No, the LORD has not
chosen this one." 10Jesse had seven of
his sons pass by Samuel. But Samuel said
to him, "The LORD has not chosen any of
these."
11Then he asked Jesse, "Are these all
the sons you have?"
Jesse answered, "I still have the
youngest son. He is out taking care of the
sheep."
Samuel said, "Send for him. We will
not sit down to eat until he arrives."
12So Jesse sent and had his youngest
son brought in. He was a fine boy, tanned,
and handsome.
The LORD said to Samuel, "Go, appoint him, because he is the one."
13So Samuel took the container of olive oil and poured it on Jesse's youngest
son to appoint him in front of his brothers.
From that day on, the LORD's Spirit
worked in David. Samuel then went back
to Ramah.

David Serves Saul

14But the LORD's Spirit had left Saul,
and an evil spirit from the LORD troubled
him.
15Saul's servants said to him, "See,
an evil spirit from God is troubling you.
16Give us the command to look for someone who can play the harp. When the evil
spirit from God troubles you, he will play,
and you will feel better."
17So Saul said to his servants, "Find
someone who can play well and bring him
to me."

FAITH links

THE HEART OF THE MATTER

1 SAMUEL 16

How do you choose someone to hang around with? Many of us make choices based on how a person looks or acts. God has a different way of choosing people to serve him. When God was ready to anoint a king to take Saul's place, Samuel assumed that God wanted the biggest and best looking of Jesse's sons. Instead, God chose David, the youngest in his family, to be king. God didn't consider how David looked on the outside. How David was on the inside was more important.

When you meet someone new, remember to look not just at the outside of a person's appearance, but look at the inside. That's what counts!

Want to fit in with God? Link here:

Following the Crowd, Numbers 13; 14, p. 193

Facts About Following, Joshua 6, p. 283

Choosing a Friend, Proverbs 28:7, p. 865

Going My Way?, Hosea 8:1–6, p. 1179

That Thing You Do, Matthew 25:14–30, p. 1319

Help for a Friend, Mark 2:1–5, p. 1332

18One of the servants said, "I have
seen a son of Jesse of Bethlehem play the
harp. He is brave and courageous. He is a
good speaker and handsome, and the
LORD is with him."
19Then Saul sent messengers to Jesse, saying, "Send me your son David,
who is with the sheep." **20**So Jesse loaded a donkey with bread, a leather bag full
of wine, and a young goat, and he sent
them with his son David to Saul.
21When David came to Saul, he began
to serve him. Saul liked David and made
him the officer who carried his armor.
22Saul sent a message to Jesse, saying,
"Let David stay and serve me because I
like him."
23When the evil spirit from God troubled Saul, David would take his harp and
play. Then the evil spirit would leave him,
and Saul would feel better.

David and Goliath

17 The Philistines gathered their
armies for war. They met at Socoh
in Judah and camped at Ephes Dammim
between Socoh and Azekah. **2**Saul and
the Israelites gathered in the Valley of
Elah and camped there and took their positions to fight the Philistines. **3**The Philistines controlled one hill while the
Israelites controlled another. The valley
was between them.
4The Philistines had a champion
fighter from Gath named Goliath. He was
about nine feet, four inches tall. He came
out of the Philistine camp **5**with a bronze
helmet on his head and a coat of bronze
armor that weighed about one hundred
twenty-five pounds. **6**He wore bronze
protectors on his legs, and he had a bronze
spear on his back. **7**The wooden part of
his larger spear was like a weaver's rod,
and its blade weighed about fifteen
pounds. The officer who carried his shield
walked in front of him.
8Goliath stood and shouted to the Israelite soldiers, "Why have you taken positions for battle? I am a Philistine, and
you are Saul's servants! Choose a man
and send him to fight me. **9**If he can fight
and kill me, we will be your servants. But
if I can kill him, you will be our servants."

10Then he said, "Today I stand and dare the army of Israel! Send one of your men to fight me!" **11**When Saul and the Israelites heard the Philistine's words, they were very scared.

12Now David was the son of Jesse, an Ephrathite from Bethlehem in Judah. Jesse had eight sons. In Saul's time Jesse was an old man. **13**His three oldest sons followed Saul to the war. The first son was Eliab, the second was Abinadab, and the third was Shammah. **14**David was the youngest. Jesse's three oldest sons followed Saul, **15**but David went back and forth from Saul to Bethlehem, where he took care of his father's sheep.

16For forty days the Philistine came out every morning and evening and stood before the Israelite army.

17Jesse said to his son David, "Take this half bushel of cooked grain and ten loaves of bread to your brothers in the camp. **18**Also take ten pieces of cheese to the commander and to your brothers. See how your brothers are and bring back some proof to show me that they are all right. **19**Your brothers are with Saul and the army in the Valley of Elah, fighting against the Philistines."

20Early in the morning David left the sheep with another shepherd. He took the food and left as Jesse had told him. When David arrived at the camp, the army was going out to their battle positions, shouting their war cry. **21**The Israelites and Philistines were lining up their men to face each other in battle.

22David left the food with the man who kept the supplies and ran to the battle line to talk to his brothers. **23**While he was talking with them, Goliath, the Philistine champion from Gath, came out. He shouted things against Israel as usual, and David heard him. **24**When the Israelites saw Goliath, they were very much afraid and ran away.

25They said, "Look at this man! He keeps coming out to challenge Israel. The king will give much money to whoever kills him. He will also let whoever kills him marry his daughter. And his father's family will not have to pay taxes in Israel."

26David asked the men who stood near him, "What will be done to reward the man who kills this Philistine and takes away the shame from Israel? Who does this uncircumcised Philistine think he is? Does he think he can speak against the armies of the living God?"

27The Israelites told David what would be done for the man who would kill Goliath.

28When David's oldest brother Eliab heard David talking with the soldiers, he was angry with David. He asked David, "Why did you come here? Who's taking care of those few sheep of yours in the desert? I know you are proud and wicked at heart. You came down here just to watch the battle."

29David asked, "Now what have I done wrong? Can't I even talk?" **30**When he turned to other people and asked the same questions, they gave him the same answer as before. **31**Yet what David said was told to Saul, and he sent for David.

32David said to Saul, "Don't let anyone be discouraged. I, your servant, will go and fight this Philistine!"

33Saul answered, "You can't go out against this Philistine and fight him. You're only a boy. Goliath has been a warrior since he was a young man."

34But David said to Saul, "I, your servant, have been keeping my father's sheep. When a lion or bear came and took a sheep from the flock, **35**I would chase it. I would attack it and save the sheep from its mouth. When it attacked me, I caught it by its fur and hit

eMAIL! FROM GOD
17:37
Troubles
Where can you find strength?

it and killed it. **36**I, your servant, have killed both a lion and a bear! This uncircumcised Philistine will be like them, because he has spoken against the armies of the living God. **37**The LORD who saved me from a lion and a bear will save me from this Philistine."

Saul said to David, "Go, and may the LORD be with you." **38**Saul put his own clothes on David. He put a bronze helmet on his head and dressed him in armor. **39**David put on Saul's sword and tried to

FAITH links

A GIANT PROBLEM

1 SAMUEL 17:32-51

If you've ever seen a sumo wrestler, you know how huge these wrestlers can be. Now compare your size to that of a sumo wrestler. Feeling puny? Imagine how David felt when he saw Goliath. But David had something that Goliath didn't have: faith in God. His faith led to Goliath's downfall. He succeeded where stronger and older men had failed.

Some problems in life can seem as big as Goliath. But faith in God makes you the giant. Got a giant problem? Talk to God about it. He'll soon cut that problem down to size.

A Major Problem, Genesis 15:6, p. 20

God's Pep Talk, Joshua 1:5–9, p. 276

Good Times and Bad, 1 Kings 17, p. 462

A Hometown Hurt, Jeremiah 11:8—12:6, p. 1008

Prayer Anywhere, Mark 1:35, p. 1331

Mission Impossible?, Mark 5:21–24, 35–43, p. 1337

walk around, but he was not used to all
the armor Saul had put on him.
He said to Saul, "I can't go in this, because I'm not used to it." Then David
took it all off. **40**He took his stick in his
hand and chose five smooth stones from a
stream. He put them in his shepherd's
bag and grabbed his sling. Then he went
to meet the Philistine.
41At the same time, the Philistine
was coming closer to David. The man
who held his shield walked in front of
him. **42**When Goliath looked at David and
saw that he was only a boy, tanned and
handsome, he looked down on David with
disgust. **43**He said, "Do you think I am a
dog, that you come at me with a stick?"
He used his gods' names to curse David.
44He said to David, "Come here. I'll feed
your body to the birds of the air and the
wild animals!"
45But David said to him, "You come to
me using a sword and two spears. But I
come to you in the name of the LORD All-
Powerful, the God of the armies of Israel!
You have spoken against him. **46**Today
the LORD will hand you over to me, and
I'll kill you and cut off your head. Today
I'll feed the bodies of the Philistine soldiers to the birds of the air and the wild
animals. Then all the world will know
there is a God in Israel! **47**Everyone
gathered here will know the LORD does
not need swords or spears to save people. The battle belongs to him, and he will
hand you over to us."
48As Goliath came near to attack him,
David ran quickly to meet him. **49**He
took a stone from his bag, put it into his
sling, and slung it. The stone hit the Philistine and went deep into his forehead,
and Goliath fell facedown on the ground.
50So David defeated the Philistine
with only a sling and a stone. He hit him
and killed him. He did not even have a
sword in his hand. **51**Then David ran and
stood beside him. He took Goliath's
sword out of its holder and killed him by
cutting off his head.
When the Philistines saw that their
champion was dead, they turned and ran.
52The men of Israel and Judah shouted
and chased the Philistines all the way to
the entrance of the city of Gath and to the
gates of Ekron.
The Philistines' bodies lay on the Shaaraim road as far as Gath and Ekron.
53The Israelites returned after chasing
the Philistines and robbed their camp.

Livin' it

FRIENDSHIP

1 Samuel 18:1

The Perfect Friend If you advertised for a friend in the newspaper or on the Internet, what would you look for? What kind of person would be the perfect friend for you? Would you ask for a super jock, or a rich kid, or maybe someone who is a genius? What if you could find all of these things in one kid—would that be the perfect friend?

If God advertised for a special friend, he wouldn't choose someone by how he looks or what he can do. God looks at the inside—what's in a person's heart. (Look at 1 Samuel 16.)

One the best things in the world is having a friend you can count on. But being a good friend takes a lot of work. One person can't do it alone—friendship means sharing. (Check out 1 Samuel 18:1–3; 20.) How do you show your friend that he or she is special to you?

MORE FAITH links

The Heart of the Matter, p. 375
The Gift of Friendship, p. 381
Choosing a Friend, p. 865
A Fair-weather Friend, p. 1209
An Encouraging Word, p. 1545

"Hey, Tagg, what do you think makes up a good friend?"

"I would have to say it would be someone like you, Skweek! After all, you're my very best friend. Surf on to find out what the Bible has to say about being a good friend."

The MLP (Most Loyal Person), Ruth 1:16–17, p. 345
- Who is the most loyal person you know? How does he or she show loyalty to you?
- Would someone consider you an MLP? How do you show loyalty for friends or family?

Two Are Better, Ecclesiastes 4:9–12, p. 877
- God made us to need each other. What are the things you do to help your family or friends?
- To earn a friend, you have to be a friend. What can you do to be the best friend possible?

Help for a Friend, Mark 2:1–5, p. 1332
- Would you go out of your way to help a friend? Link up here to find out about some people who became "house wreckers" to help a friend!

Thanks for a Friend, 1 Thessalonians 1:1–3, p. 1630
- Do you ever tell your friend thanks for being a friend? Stop and do it right now!

my FAVORITE links

54David took Goliath's head to Jerusalem
and put Goliath's weapons in his own
tent.
55When Saul saw David go out to
meet Goliath, Saul asked Abner, commander of the army, "Abner, who is that
young man's father?"

Abner answered, "As surely as you
live, my king, I don't know."
56The king said, "Find out whose son
he is."
57When David came back from killing
Goliath, Abner brought him to Saul. David was still holding Goliath's head.
58Saul asked him, "Young man, who is
your father?"

David answered, "I am the son of your
servant Jesse of Bethlehem."

Saul Fears David

18 When David finished talking with
Saul, Jonathan felt very close to
David. He loved David as much
as he loved himself.
2Saul kept David
with him from that
day on and did not
let him go home to
his father's house.
3Jonathan made an agreement with David, because he loved David as much as
himself. 4He took off his coat and gave it
to David, along with his armor, including
his sword, bow, and belt.
5Saul sent David to fight in different
battles, and David was very successful.
Then Saul put David over the soldiers,
which pleased Saul's officers and all the
other people.
6After David had killed the Philistine,
he and the men returned home. Women
came out from all the towns of Israel to
meet King Saul. They sang songs of joy,
danced, and played tambourines and
stringed instruments. 7As they played,
they sang,

"Saul has killed thousands of his
enemies,
but David has killed tens of
thousands."

8The women's song upset Saul, and
he became very angry. He thought, "The

eMAIL FROM GOD **18:1**
Friendship
Check out this great friend.

FAITH links

WHEN THE GREEN-EYED MONSTER STRIKES

1 SAMUEL 18:6-9

Has someone ever compared you with someone else? If we're thought to be better than others are, that can be easier to take. When we're compared unfavorably with someone, trouble can be the result. Saul grew jealous of David when the Israelite women cheered louder for David than for him. Saul wanted the people to praise only him. So, he tried to get rid of David.

We call jealousy the "green-eyed monster." That's because it can lead us to act like one. When jealousy strikes, you don't have to give in to it. Instead, talk to God about how you feel.

Here are some more hints on battling that green-eyed monster:

The Trouble with Jealousy, Genesis 37, p. 53

Complaints, Complaints!, Exodus 16:1–3, p. 97

A Life of Thanksgiving, 1 Kings 1:47–48, p. 435

Weak? Great!, 2 Chronicles 14:11, p. 577

A Need to Change, Ecclesiastes 1:1–11, p. 873

Eating Humble Pie, Daniel 4, p. 1156

women say David has killed tens of thousands, but they say I have killed only thousands. The only thing left for him to have is the kingdom!" **9**So Saul watched David closely from then on, because he was jealous.

10The next day an evil spirit from God rushed upon Saul, and he prophesied in his house. David was playing the harp as he usually did, but Saul had a spear in his hand. **11**He threw the spear, thinking, "I'll pin David to the wall." But David escaped from him twice.

12The LORD was with David but had left Saul. So Saul was afraid of David. **13**He sent David away and made him commander of a thousand soldiers. So David led them in battle. **14**He had great success in everything he did because the LORD was with him. **15**When Saul saw that David was very successful, he feared David even more. **16**But all the people of Israel and Judah loved David because he led them well in battle.

Saul's Daughter Marries David

17Saul said to David, "Here is my older daughter Merab. I will let you marry her. All I ask is that you remain brave and fight the LORD's battles." Saul thought, "I won't have to kill David. The Philistines will do that."

18But David answered Saul, saying, "Who am I? My family is not important enough for me to become the king's son-in-law." **19**So, when the time came for Saul's daughter Merab to marry David, Saul gave her instead to Adriel of Meholah.

20Now Saul's other daughter, Michal, loved David. When they told Saul, he was pleased. **21**He thought, "I will let her marry David. Then she will be a trap for him, and the Philistines will defeat him." So Saul said to David a second time, "You may become my son-in-law."

22And Saul ordered his servants to talk with David in private and say, "Look, the king likes you. His servants love you. You should be his son-in-law."

23Saul's servants said these words to David, but David answered, "Do you think it is easy to become the king's son-in-law? I am poor and unimportant."

24When Saul's servants told him what David had said, **25**Saul said, "Tell David, 'The king doesn't want money for the bride. All he wants is a hundred Philistine foreskins to get even with his enemies.' " Saul planned to let the Philistines kill David.

26When Saul's servants told this to David, he was pleased to become the king's son-in-law. **27**So he and his men went out and killed two hundred Philistines. David brought all their foreskins to Saul so he could be the king's son-in-law. Then Saul gave him his daughter Michal for his wife. **28**Saul saw that the LORD was with David and that his daughter Michal loved David. **29**So he grew even more afraid of David, and he was David's enemy all his life.

30The Philistine commanders continued to go out to fight the Israelites, but every time, David was more skillful than Saul's officers. So he became famous.

Saul Tries to Kill David

19 Saul told his son Jonathan and all his servants to kill David, but Jonathan liked David very much. **2**So he warned David, "My father Saul is looking for a chance to kill you. Watch out in the morning. Hide in a secret place. **3**I will go out and stand with my father in the field where you are hiding, and I'll talk to him about you. Then I'll let you know what I find out."

4When Jonathan talked to Saul his father, he said good things about David. Jonathan said, "The king should do no wrong to your servant David since he has done nothing wrong to you. What he has done has helped you greatly. **5**David risked his life when he killed Goliath the Philistine, and the LORD won a great victory for all Israel. You saw it and were happy. Why would you do wrong against David? He's innocent. There's no reason to kill him!"

EMAIL FROM GOD
19:1–7
Friendship
How can you be a good friend?

THE GIFT OF FRIENDSHIP

1 SAMUEL 18:1-3; 19

Do you have a best friend? One of life's blessings is having a friend you can count on. David and Jonathan were best friends. Jonathan showed his friendship by sharing what he had with David. David and Jonathan promised to be loyal to each other.

Friendship is a gift that's meant to be shared. Being a friend takes effort. One person can't do it alone. How do you show your friend that he or she is special to you?

Link here to find out how to be a good friend:

Family Feud, Genesis 27, p. 37

Show Some Respect, Leviticus 19:32, p. 161

The MLP, Ruth 1:16–17, p. 345

The Salt Promise, 2 Chronicles 13:5, p. 576

A Fair-weather Friend, Obadiah 7, p. 1209

Help for a Friend, Mark 2:1–5, p. 1332

6Saul listened to Jonathan and then
made this promise: "As surely as the
LORD lives, David won't be put to death."
7So Jonathan called to David and told
him everything that had been said. He
brought David to Saul, and David was
with Saul as before.

8When war broke out again, David
went out to fight the Philistines. He defeated them, and they ran away from him.
9But once again an evil spirit from the
LORD rushed upon Saul as he was sitting
in his house with his spear in his hand.
David was playing the harp. 10Saul tried
to pin David to the wall with his spear, but
David jumped out of the way. So Saul's
spear went into the wall, and David ran
away that night.
11Saul sent messengers to David's
house to watch it and to kill him in the
morning. But Michal, David's wife,
warned him, saying, "Tonight you must
run for your life. If you don't, you will be
dead in the morning." 12So she let David
down out of a window, and he ran away
and escaped. 13Then Michal took an idol,
laid it on the bed, covered it with clothes,
and put goats' hair at its head.
14Saul sent messengers to take David
prisoner, but Michal said, "He is sick."
15Saul sent them back to see David,
saying, "Bring him to me on his bed so I
can kill him."
16When the messengers entered
David's house, they found just an idol on
the bed with goats' hair on its head.
17Saul said to Michal, "Why did you
trick me this way? You let my enemy go
so he could run away!"
Michal answered Saul, "David told
me if I did not help him escape, he would
kill me."
18After David had escaped from Saul,
he went to Samuel at Ramah and told him
everything Saul had done to him. Then
David and Samuel went to Naioth and
stayed there. 19Saul heard that David
was in Naioth at Ramah. 20So he sent
messengers to capture him. But they met
a group of prophets prophesying, with
Samuel standing there leading them. So
the Spirit of God entered Saul's men, and
they also prophesied.
21When Saul heard the news, he sent
more messengers, but they also prophesied. Then he sent messengers a third
time, but they also prophesied. 22Finally,
Saul himself went to Ramah, to the well
at Secu. He asked, "Where are Samuel
and David?"

The people answered, "In Naioth at
Ramah."
23When Saul went to Naioth at Ramah, the Spirit of God also rushed upon
him. And he walked on, prophesying until
he came to Naioth at Ramah. 24He took
off his robes and prophesied in front of
Samuel. He lay that way all day and all
night. That is why people ask, "Is even
Saul one of the prophets?"

Jonathan Helps David

20 Then David ran away from Naioth
in Ramah. He went to Jonathan
and asked, "What have I done? What is
my crime? How did I sin against your father? Why is he trying to kill me?"
2Jonathan answered, "No! You won't
die! See, my father doesn't do anything
great or small without first telling me.
Why would he keep this from me? It's not
true!"
3But David took an oath, saying,
"Your father knows very well that you
like me. He says to himself, 'Jonathan
must not know about it, or he will tell
David.' As surely as the LORD lives and
as you live, I am only a step away from
death!"
4Jonathan said to David, "I'll do anything you want me to do."
5So David said, "Look, tomorrow is
the New Moon festival. I am supposed to
eat with the king, but let me hide in the
field until the third evening. 6If your father notices I am gone, tell him, 'David
begged me to let him go to his hometown
of Bethlehem. Every year at this time his
family group offers a sacrifice.' 7If your
father says, 'Fine,' I am safe. But if he
becomes angry, you will know that he
wants to hurt me. 8Jonathan, be loyal to
me, your servant. You have made an
agreement with me before the LORD. If I
am guilty, you may kill me yourself! Why
hand me over to your father?"
9Jonathan answered, "No, never! If I
learn that my father plans to hurt you, I
will warn you!"
10David asked, "Who will let me
know if your father answers you unkindly?"
11Then Jonathan said, "Come, let's go
out into the field." So the two of them
went out into the field.
12Jonathan said to David, "I promise
this before the LORD, the God of Israel:
At this same time the day after tomorrow,

FAITH links

CHOOSING SIDES

1 SAMUEL 20

In an argument between two people, do you ever find yourself taking sides? How do you decide whose side you're on? Jonathan was caught in the middle when his father, King Saul, declared David to be his enemy. When Jonathan chose to do what was right, his father became angry with him. He could not stop being loyal to David, even though his father demanded that he do so.

God wants you to do the right thing, even if choosing to do so makes someone angry with you. The side of right is always the best side to choose to be on.

An Example Not to Follow, Leviticus 18:1–3, p. 157

Remembering What He Said, Deuteronomy 6:4–9, p. 236

Sow It and Reap, Lamentations 1:18, p. 1075

A Blueprint for Living, Amos 5:14–15, p. 1200

The "Eyes" Have It?, 1 Corinthians 12, p. 1559

Keeping Clean, 2 Corinthians 7:1, p. 1576

I will find out how my father feels. If he
feels good toward you, I will send word to
you and let you know. **13**But if my father
plans to hurt you, I will let you know and
send you away safely. May the LORD punish me terribly if I don't do this. And may
the LORD be with you as he has been with
my father. **14**But show me the kindness
of the LORD as long as I live so that I may
not die. **15**You must never stop showing
your kindness to my family, even when
the LORD has destroyed all your enemies
from the earth."

16So Jonathan made an agreement
with David. He said, "May the LORD hold
David's enemies responsible." **17**And
Jonathan asked David to repeat his promise of love for him, because he loved David as much as he loved himself.

18Jonathan said to David, "Tomorrow
is the New Moon festival. Your seat will
be empty, so my father will miss you.
19On the third day go to the place where
you hid when this trouble began. Wait by
the rock Ezel. **20**On the third day I will
shoot three arrows to the side of the rock
as if I am shooting at a target. **21**Then I
will send a boy to find the arrows. If I say
to him, 'The arrows are near you; bring
them here,' you may come out of hiding.
You are safe. As the LORD lives, there is
no danger. **22**But if I say to the boy, 'Look,
the arrows are beyond you,' you must go,
because the LORD is sending you away.
23Remember what we talked about. The
LORD is a witness between you and me
forever."

24So David hid in the field. When the
New Moon festival came, the king sat
down to eat. **25**He sat where he always
sat, near the wall. Jonathan sat across
from him, and Abner sat next to Saul, but
David's place was empty. **26**That day Saul
said nothing. He thought, "Maybe something has happened to David so that he is
unclean." **27**But the next day was the
second day of the month, and David's
place was still empty. So Saul said to Jonathan, "Why hasn't the son of Jesse come
to the feast yesterday or today?"

28Jonathan answered, "David begged
me to let him go to Bethlehem. **29**He
said, 'Let me go, because our family has a
sacrifice in the town, and my brother has
ordered me to be there. Now if I am your
friend, please let me go to see my brothers.' That is why he has not come to the
king's table."

30Then Saul became very angry with
Jonathan. He said, "You son of a wicked,
worthless woman! I know you are on the
side of David son of Jesse! You bring
shame on yourself and on your mother
who gave birth to you. **31**As long as
Jesse's son lives, you will never be king
or have a kingdom. Now send for David
and bring him to me. He must die!"

32Jonathan asked his father, "Why
should David be killed? What wrong has
he done?" **33**Then Saul threw his spear at
Jonathan, trying to kill him. So Jonathan
knew that his father really wanted to kill
David. **34**Jonathan was very angry and left
the table. That second day of the month
he refused to eat. He was ashamed of his
father and upset over David.

35The next morning Jonathan went
out to the field to meet David as they had
agreed. He had a young boy with him.
36Jonathan said to the boy, "Run and find
the arrows I shoot." When he ran, Jonathan shot an arrow beyond him. **37**The
boy ran to the place where Jonathan's arrow fell, but Jonathan called, "The arrow
is beyond you!" **38**Then he shouted,
"Hurry! Go quickly! Don't stop!" The
boy picked up the arrow and brought it
back to his master. **39**(The boy knew
nothing about what this meant; only Jonathan and David knew.) **40**Then Jonathan
gave his weapons to the boy and told him,
"Go back to town."

41When the boy left, David came out
from the south side of the rock. He
bowed facedown on the ground before
Jonathan three times. Then David and
Jonathan kissed each other and cried together, but David cried the most.

42Jonathan said
to David, "Go in
peace. We have prom-
ised by the LORD that
we will be friends.
We said, 'The LORD
will be a witness between you and me,
and between our descendants always.' "

eMAIL! FROM GOD
20:42
Friendship
See what bonds friends together.

Then David left, and Jonathan went back
to town.

David Goes to See Ahimelech

21 David went to Nob to see Ahimelech the priest. Ahimelech shook
with fear when he saw David, and he
asked, "Why are you alone? Why is no
one with you?"
2David answered him,
"The king gave me a spe-
cial order. He told me, 'No
one must know what I am
sending you to do or what I
told you to do.' I told my
men where to meet me.
3Now, what food do you
have with you? Give me
five loaves of bread or anything you find."

> Saul has killed thousands of his enemies, but David has killed tens of thousands.
> —1 Samuel 21:11

4The priest said to David, "I don't have
any plain bread here, but I do have some
holy bread.[n] You may eat it if your men
have kept themselves from women."
5David answered, "No women have
been near us for days. My men always
keep themselves holy, even when we do
ordinary work. And this is especially true
when the work is holy."
6So the priest gave David the holy
bread from the presence of God because
there was no other. Each day the holy
bread was replaced with hot bread.
7One of Saul's servants happened to
be there that day. He had been held there
before the LORD. He was Doeg the
Edomite, the chief of Saul's shepherds.
8David asked Ahimelech, "Do you
have a spear or sword here? The king's
business was very important, so I left
without my sword or any other weapon."
9The priest answered, "The sword of
Goliath the Philistine, the one you killed
in the Valley of Elah, is here. It is
wrapped in a cloth behind the holy vest. If
you want it, you may take it. There's no
other sword here but that one."

David said, "There is no other sword
like it. Give it to me."

David Goes to Gath

10That day David ran away from Saul
and went to Achish king of Gath. 11But
the servants of Achish said to him, "This
is David, the king of the Israelites. He's
the man they dance and sing about, saying:

'Saul has killed thousands of his
enemies,
but David has killed tens of
thousands.' "

12David paid attention
to these words and was
very much afraid of Achish
king of Gath. 13So he pretended to be crazy in front
of Achish and his servants.
While he was with them,
he acted like a madman
and clawed on the doors of
the gate and let spit run
down his beard.
14Achish said to his servants, "Look
at the man! He's crazy! Why do you bring
him to me? 15I have enough madmen. I
don't need you to bring him here to act
like this in front of me! Don't let him in
my house!"

David at Adullam and Mizpah

22 David left Gath and escaped to the
cave of Adullam. When his brothers and other relatives heard that he was
there, they went to see him. 2Everyone
who was in trouble, or who owed money,
or who was unsatisfied gathered around
David, and he became their leader. About
four hundred men were with him.
3From there David went to Mizpah in
Moab and spoke to the king of Moab. He
said, "Please let my father and mother
come and stay with you until I learn what
God is going to do for me." 4So he left
them with the king of Moab, and they
stayed with him as long as David was hiding in the stronghold.
5But the prophet Gad said to David,
"Don't stay in the stronghold. Go to the
land of Judah." So David left and went to
the forest of Hereth.

21:4 holy bread This was the bread that showed the people were in the presence of God. Normally only the priests ate this bread.

Saul Destroys Ahimelech's Family

6Saul heard that David and his men had been seen. Saul was sitting under the tamarisk tree on the hill at Gibeah, and all his officers were standing around him. He had a spear in his hand. 7Saul said to them, "Listen, men of Benjamin! Do you think the son of Jesse will give all of you fields and vineyards? Will David make you commanders over thousands of men or hundreds of men? 8You have all made plans against me! No one tells me when my son makes an agreement with the son of Jesse! No one cares about me! No one tells me when my son has encouraged my servant to ambush me this very day!"

9Doeg the Edomite, who was standing there with Saul's officers, said, "I saw the son of Jesse. He came to see Ahimelech son of Ahitub at Nob. 10Ahimelech prayed to the LORD for David and gave him food and gave him the sword of Goliath the Philistine."

> Everyone who was in trouble, or who owed money, or who was unsatisfied gathered around David, and he became their leader.
> —1 Samuel 22:2

11Then the king sent for the priest Ahimelech son of Ahitub and for all of Ahimelech's relatives who were priests at Nob. And they all came to the king. 12Saul said to Ahimelech, "Listen now, son of Ahitub."

Ahimelech answered, "Yes, master."

13Saul said, "Why are you and Jesse's son against me? You gave him bread and a sword! You prayed to God for him. David has turned against me and is waiting to attack me even now!"

14Ahimelech answered, "You have no other servant who is as loyal as David, your own son-in-law and captain of your bodyguards. Everyone in your house respects him. 15That was not the first time I prayed to God for David. Don't blame me or any of my relatives. I, your servant, know nothing about what is going on."

16But the king said, "Ahimelech, you and all your relatives must die!" 17Then he told the guards at his side, "Go and kill the priests of the LORD, because they are on David's side. They knew he was running away, but they didn't tell me."

But the king's officers refused to kill the priests of the LORD.

18Then the king ordered Doeg, "Go and kill the priests." So Doeg the Edomite went and killed the priests. That day he killed eighty-five men who wore the linen holy vest. 19He also killed the people of Nob, the city of the priests. With the sword he killed men, women, children, babies, cattle, donkeys, and sheep.

20But Abiathar, a son of Ahimelech, who was the son of Ahitub, escaped. He ran away and joined David. 21He told David that Saul had killed the LORD's priests. 22Then David told him, "Doeg the Edomite was there at Nob that day. I knew he would surely tell Saul. So I am responsible for the death of all your father's family. 23Stay with me. Don't be afraid. The man who wants to kill you also wants to kill me. You will be safe with me."

David Saves the People of Keilah

23 Someone told David, "Look, the Philistines are fighting against Keilah and stealing grain from the threshing floors."

2David asked the LORD, "Should I go and fight these Philistines?"

The LORD answered him, "Go. Attack them, and save Keilah."

3But David's men said to him, "We're afraid here in Judah. We will be more afraid if we go to Keilah where the Philistine army is."

4David again asked the LORD, and the LORD answered, "Go down to Keilah. I will help you defeat the Philistines." 5So David and his men went to Keilah and fought the Philistines and took their cattle. David killed many Philistines and saved the people of Keilah. 6(Now Abiathar son of Ahimelech had brought the holy vest with him when he came to David at Keilah.)

GOD TO THE RESCUE!

1 Samuel 23

In the Old Testament, God helped his people over and over again. Sometimes he helped them through the miracles he sent. Once the angel of the Lord went through an enemy camp outside of Jerusalem and killed nearly *two hundred thousand* soldiers. In the morning, the Israelites woke up to discover that God already had saved them from their enemies. (Look at 2 Kings 19:35, p. 507.)

God delivered these people too:

Noah and his family were delivered from the flood.	Genesis 6—8, p. 10
Lot and his family were saved from Sodom and Gomorrah.	Genesis 19:29, p. 26
The Israelites were delivered from slavery and cared for on their journey.	Exodus 12:1—17:7, p. 90
David and his army were saved from Saul's army more than once.	1 Samuel 23:7–29, p. 386
Birds fed Elijah when he was in the wilderness.	1 Kings 17:2–6, p. 462
Daniel's friends were delivered from a fiery furnace.	Daniel 3:19–30, p. 1155
Daniel was saved from a den of hungry lions.	Daniel 6:1–24, p. 1160

Saul Chases David

7Someone told Saul that David was
now at Keilah. Saul said, "God has handed David over to me! He has trapped
himself, because he has entered a town
with gates and bars." 8Saul called all his
army together for battle, and they prepared to go down to Keilah to attack David and his men.

9David learned Saul was making evil
plans against him. So he said to Abiathar
the priest, "Bring the holy vest." 10Da-
vid prayed, "LORD, God of Israel, I have
heard that Saul plans to come to Keilah to
destroy the town because of me. 11Will
the leaders of Keilah hand me over to
Saul? Will Saul come down to Keilah, as I
heard? LORD, God of Israel, tell me, your
servant!"

The LORD answered, "Saul will come down."

12Again David asked, "Will the leaders of Keilah hand me and my men over
to Saul?"

The LORD answered, "They will."

13So David and his six hundred men
left Keilah and kept moving from place to
place. When Saul found out that David

had escaped from Keilah, he did not go
there.
14David stayed in the desert hideouts
and in the hills of the Desert of Ziph.
Every day Saul looked for David, but the
LORD did not surrender David to him.
15While David was at Horesh in the
Desert of Ziph, he learned that Saul was
coming to kill him. 16But Saul's son Jonathan went to David at Horesh and
strengthened his faith in God. 17Jonathan
told him, "Don't be afraid, because my father won't touch you. You will be king of
Israel, and I will be second to you. Even
my father Saul knows this." 18The two of
them made an agreement before the
LORD. Then Jonathan went home, but
David stayed at Horesh.
19The people from Ziph went to Saul
at Gibeah and told him, "David is hiding
in our land. He's at the hideouts of Horesh, on the hill of Hakilah, south of Jeshimon. 20Now, our king, come down
anytime you want. It's our duty to hand
David over to you."
21Saul answered, "The LORD bless
you for helping me. 22Go and learn more
about him. Find out where he is staying
and who has seen him there. I have heard
that he is clever. 23Find all the hiding
places he uses, and come back and tell
me everything. Then I'll go with you. If
David is in the area, I will track him down
among all the families in Judah."
24So they went back to Ziph ahead of
Saul. Now David and his men were in the
Desert of Maon[n] in the desert area south
of Jeshimon. 25Saul and his men went to
look for David, but David heard about it
and went down to a rock and stayed in the
Desert of Maon. When Saul heard that,
he followed David into the Desert of
Maon.
26Saul was going along one side of the
mountain, and David and his men were
on the other side. They were hurrying to
get away from Saul, because Saul and his
men were closing in on them. 27But a
messenger came to Saul, saying, "Come
quickly! The Philistines are attacking our
land!" 28So Saul stopped chasing David
and went to challenge the Philistines.
That is why people call this place Rock of
Parting. 29David also left the Desert of
Maon and stayed in the hideouts of En
Gedi.

David Shames Saul

24 After Saul returned from chasing
the Philistines, he was told, "David is in the Desert of En Gedi." 2So he
took three thousand chosen men from all
Israel and began looking for David and
his men near the Rocks of the
Wild Goats.
3Saul came to
the sheep pens be-
side the road. A
cave was there, and
he went in to relieve
himself. Now David and his men were
hiding far back in the cave. 4The men
said to David, "Today is the day the LORD
spoke of when he said, 'I will give your
enemy over to you. Do anything you
want with him.' "
Then David crept up to Saul and
quietly cut off a corner of Saul's robe.
5Later David felt guilty because he had
cut off a corner of Saul's robe. 6He said to
his men, "May the LORD keep me from
doing such a thing to my master! Saul is
the LORD's appointed king. I should not
do anything against him, because he is
the LORD's appointed king!" 7David used
these words to stop his men; he did not
let them attack Saul. Then Saul left the
cave and went his way.
8When David came out of the cave, he
shouted to Saul, "My master and king!"
Saul looked back, and David bowed facedown on the ground. 9He said to Saul,
"Why do you listen when people say, 'David wants to harm you'? 10You have seen
something with your own eyes today.
The LORD put you in my power in the
cave. They said I should kill you, but I
was merciful. I said, 'I won't harm my
master, because he is the LORD's appointed king.' 11My father, look at this
piece of your robe in my hand! I cut off
the corner of your robe, but I didn't kill
you. Now understand and know I am not

EMAIL FROM GOD
24:1–6
Leadership
Why should you respect your leaders?

23:24 Maon Some early Greek copies say "Maon." The Hebrew copies say "Paran."

FAITH links

A RIGHT TO GET EVEN?

1 SAMUEL 24

If you've ever felt like getting even with someone, consider David's story. David had an opportunity to kill Saul and stop Saul from trying to kill him. Instead, David showed respect for Saul and for God by not harming Saul. David knew that God had placed Saul in his position. He knew that he did not have the right to judge Saul, even though Saul had treated him disrespectfully.

A person's disrespectful actions do not give you the right to respond to him or her in the same way. Not getting even with someone shows your respect for that person and for God.

It's not easy to turn away from an "enemy." Here's some more advice on how to do that:

The Trouble with Jealousy, Genesis 37, p. 53

Mourning for an Enemy, 2 Samuel 1, p. 399

God's Sure Protection, Psalm 18, p. 721

Justice Served, Isaiah 35:3–4, p. 940

Don't Get Mad; Get Even?, Matthew 26:57–63; 27:11–14, p. 1323

Full of Faith, 1 Thessalonians 4:1, p. 1633

planning any evil against you. I did nothing wrong to you, but you are hunting me
to kill me. 12May the LORD judge between us, and may he punish you for the
wrong you have done to me! But I am not
against you. 13There is an old saying:
'Evil things come from evil people.' But I
am not against you. 14Whom is the king
of Israel coming out against? Whom are
you chasing? It's as if you are chasing a
dead dog or a flea. 15May the LORD be
our judge and decide between you and
me. May he support me and show that I
am right. May he save me from you!"

16When David finished saying these
words, Saul asked, "Is that your voice,
David my son?" And he cried loudly.
17He said, "You are a better man than I
am. You have been good to me, but I have
done wrong to you. 18You told me what
good things you did. The LORD handed
me over to you, but you did not kill me.
19If a person finds his enemy, he doesn't
just send him on his way, does he? May
the LORD reward you because you were
good to me today. 20I know you will surely be king, and you will rule the kingdom
of Israel. 21Now swear to me by the
LORD that you will not kill my descendants and that you won't wipe out my
name from my father's family."

22So David made the promise to Saul.
Then Saul went back home, and David
and his men went up to their hideout.

Nabal Insults David

25 Now Samuel died, and all the Israelites met and had a time of sadness for him. Then they buried him at his
home in Ramah.

David moved to the Desert of Maon.[n]
2A man in Maon who had land at Carmel
was very rich. He had three thousand
sheep and a thousand goats. He was cutting the wool off his sheep at Carmel.
3His name was Nabal, and he was a descendant of Caleb. His wife was named
Abigail. She was wise and beautiful, but
Nabal was cruel and mean.

4While David was in the desert, he

25:1 Maon Some early Greek copies say "Maon." The Hebrew copies say "Paran."

FAITH links

YOURS, MINE, AND OURS?

1 SAMUEL 25

Has someone ever refused to share something with you? Nabal didn't want to share when David asked him for food for himself and his men. David's men had protected Nabal's flocks. But Nabal wanted to keep all that he had for himself.

God wants his people to be generous toward others. Since he graciously gives us all that we have and need, he wants us to share that grace with others.

A Small Percent, Deuteronomy 14:22–23, p. 247

Fairness for All, Deuteronomy 24:17, p. 258

Two Are Better, Ecclesiastes 4:9–12, p. 877

The Right Ingredients, Micah 6:8, p. 1227

Give from the Heart, Luke 21:1–4, p. 1410

The Most Fun, Acts 20:35, p. 1502

heard that Nabal was cutting the wool
from his sheep. **5**So he sent ten young
men and told them, "Go to Nabal at Carmel, and greet him for me. **6**Say to Nabal,
'May you and your family and all who belong to you have good health! **7**I have
heard that you are cutting the wool from
your sheep. When your shepherds were
with us, we did not harm them. All the
time your shepherds were at Carmel, we
stole nothing from them. **8**Ask your servants, and they will tell you. We come at a
happy time, so be kind to my young men.
Please give anything you can find for
them and for your son David.' "

9When David's men arrived, they
gave the message to Nabal, but Nabal insulted them. **10**He answered them, "Who
is David? Who is this son of Jesse? Many
slaves are running away from their masters today! **11**I have bread and water, and
I have meat that I killed for my servants
who cut the wool. But I won't give it to
men I don't know."

12David's men went back and told
him all Nabal had said. **13**Then David said
to them, "Put on your swords!" So they
put on their swords, and David put on his
also. About four hundred men went with
David, but two hundred men stayed with
the supplies.

14One of Nabal's servants said to Abigail, Nabal's wife, "David sent messengers from the desert to greet our master,
but Nabal insulted them. **15**These men
were very good to us. They did not harm
us. They stole nothing from us during all
the time we were out in the field with
them. **16**Night and day they protected us.
They were like a wall around us while we
were with them caring for the sheep.
17Now think about it, and decide what
you can do. Terrible trouble is coming to
our master and all his family. Nabal is
such a wicked man that no one can even
talk to him."

18Abigail hurried. She took two hundred loaves of bread, two leather bags full
of wine, five cooked sheep, a bushel of
cooked grain, a hundred cakes of raisins,
and two hundred cakes of pressed figs
and put all these on donkeys. **19**Then she
told her servants, "Go on. I'll follow
you." But she did not tell her husband.

20Abigail rode her donkey and came
down toward the mountain hideout.
There she met David and his men coming
down toward her.

21David had just said, "It's been useless! I watched over Nabal's property in
the desert. I made sure none of his sheep
was missing. I did good to him, but he
has paid me back with evil. **22**May God

punish my enemies even more. I will not
leave one of Nabal's men alive until
morning."
23When Abigail saw David, she
quickly got off her donkey and bowed
facedown on the ground before him.
24She fell at David's feet and said, "My
master, let the blame be on me! Please let
me talk to you. Listen to what I say. **25**My
master, don't pay attention to this worthless man Nabal. He is like his name. His
name means 'fool,' and he is truly a fool.
But I, your servant, didn't see the men
you sent. **26**The LORD has kept you from
killing and punishing anyone. As surely as
the LORD lives and as surely as you live,
may your enemies become like Nabal! **27**I
have brought a gift to you for the men who
follow you.**28**Please forgive my wrong.
The LORD will certainly let your family
have many kings, because you fight his
battles. As long as you live, may you do
nothing bad. **29**Someone might chase you
to kill you, but the LORD your God will
keep you alive. He will throw away your
enemies' lives as he would throw a stone
from a sling. **30**The LORD will keep all his
promises of good things for you. He will
make you leader over Israel. **31**Then you
won't feel guilty or troubled because you
killed innocent people and punished them.
Please remember me when the LORD
brings you success."
32David answered Abigail, "Praise
the LORD, the God of Israel, who sent you
to meet me. **33**May you be blessed for
your wisdom. You have kept me from killing or punishing people today. **34**As
surely as the LORD, the God of Israel,
lives, he has kept me from hurting you. If
you hadn't come quickly to meet me, not
one of Nabal's men would have lived until
morning."
35Then David accepted Abigail's
gifts. He told her, "Go home in peace. I
have heard your words, and I will do what
you have asked."

Nabal's Death

36When Abigail went back to Nabal,
he was in the house, eating like a king.
He was very drunk and in a good mood.
So she told him nothing until the next
morning. **37**In the morning when he was
not drunk, his wife told him everything.
His heart stopped, and he became like
stone. **38**About ten days later the LORD
struck Nabal and he died.
39When David heard that Nabal was
dead, he said, "Praise the LORD! Nabal
insulted me, but the LORD has supported
me! He has kept me from doing wrong.
The LORD has punished Nabal for his
wrong."
Then David sent a message to Abigail,
asking her to be his wife. **40**His servants
went to Carmel and said to Abigail, "David sent us to take you so you can become
his wife."
41Abigail bowed facedown on the
ground and said, "I am your servant. I'm
ready to serve you and to wash the feet of
my master's servants." **42**Abigail quickly
got on a donkey and went with David's
messengers, with her five maids following her. And she became David's wife.
43David also had married Ahinoam of
Jezreel. So they were both David's wives.
44Saul's daughter Michal was also
David's wife, but Saul had given her to
Paltiel son of Laish, who was from Gallim.

David Shames Saul Again

26 The people of Ziph went to Saul at
Gibeah and said to him, "David is
hiding on the hill of Hakilah opposite Jeshimon."
2So Saul went down to the Desert of
Ziph with three thousand chosen men of
Israel to look for David there. **3**Saul made
his camp beside the road on the hill of
Hakilah opposite Jeshimon, but David
stayed in the desert. When he heard Saul
had followed him, **4**he sent out spies and
learned for certain that Saul had come to
Hakilah.
5Then David went to the place where
Saul had camped. He saw where Saul and
Abner son of Ner, the commander of
Saul's army, were sleeping. Saul was
sleeping in the middle of the camp with
all the army around him.
6David asked Ahimelech the Hittite
and Abishai son of Zeruiah, Joab's
brother, "Who will go down into Saul's
camp with me?"

FAITH links

THE RIGHT THING TO DO

1 SAMUEL 26

What if a friend tried to convince you to do something by telling you God wanted you to do it? What would you do? One of David's men, Abishai, tried to get David to kill Saul. He told David that God had created the opportunity for him to do so. But David chose not to harm Saul, even though Saul had wronged him. David knew that God would not allow him to get even with Saul.

God will never tell you to do something wrong. If you're not sure about what God wants you to do, you can always ask him to help you know what to do. He'll be glad to do it!

Here are some more Faithlinks on doing the right thing:

What's Out Becomes In, Judges 11, p. 327

Fair All the Time?, 2 Samuel 8:15, p. 408

On the Wrong Foot, 2 Kings 21:1–2, 16, p. 509

Just a Little Respect, 1 Chronicles 11:10–19, p. 534

Forgive and Forget, Ephesians 4:32, p. 1604

The Leaders in Your Life, 1 Timothy 2:1–4, p. 1645

Abishai answered, "I'll go with you."
7So that night David and Abishai went
into Saul's camp. Saul was asleep in the
middle of the camp with his spear stuck
in the ground near his head. Abner and
the army were sleeping around Saul.
8Abishai said to David, "Today God has
handed your enemy over to you. Let me
pin Saul to the ground with my spear. I'll
only have to do it once. I won't need to hit
him twice."
9But David said to Abishai, "Don't kill
Saul! No one can harm the LORD's appointed king and still be innocent! **10**As
surely as the LORD lives, the LORD himself will punish Saul. Maybe Saul will die
naturally, or maybe he will go into battle
and be killed. **11**But may the LORD keep
me from harming his appointed king!
Take the spear and water jug that are
near Saul's head. Then let's go."
12So David took the spear and water
jug that were near Saul's head, and they
left. No one saw them or knew about it or
woke up, because the LORD had put them
sound asleep.
13David crossed over to the other
side of the hill and stood on top of the
mountain far from Saul's camp. They
were a long way away from each other.
14David shouted to the army and to Abner son of Ner, "Won't you answer me,
Abner?"
Abner answered, "Who is calling for
the king? Who are you?"
15David said, "You're the greatest man
in Israel. Isn't that true? Why didn't you
guard your master the king? Someone
came into your camp to kill your master
the king! **16**You have not done well. As
surely as the LORD lives, you and your
men should die. You haven't guarded your
master, the LORD's appointed king. Look!
Where are the king's spear and water jug
that were near his head?"
17Saul knew David's voice. He said,
"Is that your voice, David my son?"
David answered, "Yes, it is, my master and king." **18**David also said, "Why
are you chasing me, my master? What
wrong have I done? What evil am I guilty
of? **19**My master and king, listen to me.
If the LORD made you angry with me, let

him accept an offering. But if people did
it, may the LORD curse them! They have
made me leave the land the LORD gave
me. They have told me, 'Go and serve
other gods.' 20Now don't let me die far
away from the LORD's presence. The
king of Israel has come out looking for a
flea! You're just hunting a bird in the
mountains!"

21Then Saul said, "I have sinned.
Come back, David my son. Today you respected my life, so I will not try to hurt
you. I have been very stupid and foolish."

22David answered, "Here is your
spear. Let one of your young men come
here and get it. 23The LORD rewards us
for the things we do right and for our loyalty to him. The LORD handed you over to
me today, but I wouldn't harm the LORD's
appointed king. 24As I respected your
life today, may the LORD also respect my
life and save me from all trouble."

25Then Saul said to David, "You are
blessed, my son David. You will do great
things and succeed."

So David went on his way, and Saul
went back home.

David Lives with the Philistines

27 But David thought to himself, "Saul
will catch me someday. The best
thing I can do is escape to the land of the
Philistines. Then he will give up looking
for me in Israel, and I can get away from
him."

2So David and his six hundred men
left Israel and went to Achish son of Ma-
och, king of Gath. 3David, his men, and
their families made their home in Gath
with Achish. David had his two wives
with him—Ahinoam of Jezreel and Abigail of Carmel, the widow of Nabal.
4When Saul heard that David had run
away to Gath, he stopped looking for him.

5Then David said to Achish, "If you are
pleased with me, give me a place in one of
the country towns where I can live. I don't
need to live in the royal city with you."

6That day Achish gave David the
town of Ziklag, and Ziklag has belonged
to the kings of Judah ever since. 7David
lived in the Philistine land a year and four
months.

8David and his men raided the people
of Geshur, Girzi, and Amalek. (These
people had lived for a long time in the
land that reached to Shur and Egypt.)
9When David fought them, he killed all
the men and women and took their
sheep, cattle, donkeys, camels, and
clothes. Then he returned to Achish.

10Achish would ask David, "Where
did you go raiding today?" And David
would tell him that he had gone to the
southern part of Judah, or Jerahmeel, or
to the land of the Kenites. 11David never
brought a man or woman alive to Gath.
He thought, "If we bring people alive,
they may tell Achish, 'This is what David
really did.' " David did this all the time he
lived in the Philistine land. 12So Achish
trusted David and said to himself,
"David's own people, the Israelites, now
hate him very much. He will serve me
forever."

Saul and the Witch of Endor

28 Later, the Philistines gathered their
armies to fight against Israel.
Achish said to David, "You understand
that you and your men must join my
army."

2David answered, "You will see for
yourself what I, your servant, can do!"

Achish said, "Fine, I'll make you my
permanent bodyguard."

3Now Samuel was dead, and all the Israelites had shown their sadness for him.
They had buried Samuel in his hometown
of Ramah.

And Saul had forced out the mediums
and fortune-tellers from the land.

4The Philistines came together and
made camp at Shunem. Saul gathered all
the Israelites and made camp at Gilboa.
5When he saw the Philistine army, he
was afraid, and his heart pounded with
fear. 6He prayed to the LORD, but the
LORD did not answer him through
dreams, Urim, or prophets. 7Then Saul
said to his servants, "Find me a woman
who is a medium so I may go and ask her
what will happen."

His servants answered, "There is a
medium in Endor."

8Then Saul put on other clothes to

disguise himself, and at night he and two
of his men went to see the woman. Saul
said to her, "Talk to a spirit for me. Bring
up the person I name."
9But the woman said to him, "Surely
you know what Saul has done. He has
forced the mediums and fortune-tellers
from the land. You are trying to trap me
and get me killed."
10Saul made a promise to the woman
in the name of the LORD. He said, "As
surely as the LORD lives, you won't be
punished for this."
11The woman asked, "Whom do you
want me to bring up?"

FAITH CHALLENGE

Here's another challenge for you. Read 28:7 to discover the terrible mistake King Saul made when he tried to learn about his future. What would you say to a friend who reads and depends on horoscopes for advice?

TESTING IT

1 Samuel 28:7
Then Saul said to his servants, "Find me a woman who is a medium so I may go and ask her what will happen."

He answered, "Bring up Samuel."
12When the woman saw Samuel, she
screamed. She said, "Why have you
tricked me? You are Saul!"
13The king said to the woman, "Don't
be afraid! What do you see?"
The woman said, "I see a spirit coming up out of the ground."
14Saul asked, "What does he look
like?"
The woman answered, "An old man
wearing a coat is coming up."
Then Saul knew it was Samuel, and he
bowed facedown on the ground.
15Samuel asked Saul, "Why have you
disturbed me by bringing me up?"
Saul said, "I am greatly troubled. The
Philistines are fighting against me, and
God has left me. He won't answer me
anymore, either by prophets or in
dreams. That's why I called for you. Tell
me what to do."
16Samuel said, "The LORD has left
you and has become your enemy. So why
do you call on me? **17**He has done what
he said he would do—the things he said
through me. He has torn the kingdom out
of your hands and given it to one of your
neighbors, David. **18**You did not obey the
LORD; you did not show the Amalekites
how angry he was with them. That's why
he has done this to you today. **19**The
LORD will hand over both Israel and you
to the Philistines. Tomorrow you and
your sons will be with me. The LORD will
hand over the army of Israel to the Philistines."
20Saul quickly fell flat on the ground
and was afraid of what Samuel had said.
He was also very weak because he had
eaten nothing all that day and night.
21Then the woman came to Saul and
saw that he was really frightened. She
said, "Look, I, your servant, have obeyed
you. I have risked my life and done what
you told me to do. **22**Now please listen
to me. Let me give you some food so you
may eat and have enough strength to go
on your way."
23But Saul refused, saying, "I won't
eat."
His servants joined the woman in asking him to eat, and he listened to them.

So he got up from the ground and sat on
the bed.
24At the house the woman had a fat
calf, which she quickly killed. She took
some flour and mixed dough with her
hands. Then she baked some bread without yeast. 25She put the food before
them, and they ate. That same night they
got up and left.

David Goes Back to Ziklag

29 The Philistines gathered all their
soldiers at Aphek. Israel camped
by the spring at Jezreel. 2The Philistine
kings were marching with their groups of
a hundred and a thousand men. David and
his men were marching behind Achish.
3The Philistine commanders asked,
"What are these Hebrews doing here?"
Achish told them, "This is David. He
served Saul king of Israel, but he has
been with me for over a
year now. I have found
nothing wrong in David
since the time he left
Saul."
4But the Philistine
commanders were angry
with Achish and said,
"Send David back to the
city you gave him. He
cannot go with us into
battle. If he does, we'll
have an enemy in our own camp. He could
please his king by killing our own men.
5David is the one the Israelites dance and
sing about, saying:
'Saul has killed thousands of his
enemies,
but David has killed tens of
thousands.'"
6So Achish called David and said to
him, "As surely as the LORD lives, you
are loyal. I would be pleased to have you
serve in my army. Since the day you
came to me, I have found no wrong in
you. But the other kings don't trust you.
7Go back in peace. Don't do anything to
displease the Philistine kings."
8David asked, "What wrong have I
done? What evil have you found in me
from the day I came to you until now?

As surely as the LORD lives, you are loyal. I would be pleased to have you serve in my army.
—1 Samuel 29:6

Why can't I go fight your enemies, my
lord and king?"
9Achish answered, "I know you are as
good as an angel from God. But the Philistine commanders have said, 'David
must not go with us into battle.' 10Early
in the morning you and your master's
servants should leave. Get up as soon as
it is light and go."
11So David and his men got up early
in the morning and went back to the
country of the Philistines. And the Philistines went up to Jezreel.

David's War with the Amalekites

30 On the third day, when David and
his men arrived at Ziklag, he found
that the Amalekites had raided southern
Judah and Ziklag, attacking Ziklag and
burning it. 2They captured the women
and everyone, young and old, but they
had not killed anyone.
They had only taken them
away.
3When David and his
men came to Ziklag, they
found the town had been
burned and their wives,
sons, and daughters had
been taken as prisoners.
4Then David and his
army cried loudly until
they were too weak to cry
anymore. 5David's two wives had also
been taken—Ahinoam of Jezreel and Abigail the widow of Nabal from Carmel.
6The men in the army were threatening
to kill David with stones, which greatly
upset David. Each man was sad and angry
because his sons and daughters had been
captured, but David found strength in the
LORD his God. 7David said to Abiathar
the priest, "Bring me the holy vest."
8Then David asked the LORD, "Should
I chase the people who took our families?
Will I catch them?"
The LORD answered, "Chase them.
You will catch them, and you will succeed
in saving your families."
9David and the six hundred men with
him came to the Besor Ravine, where
some of the men stayed. 10David and

KIND OR FAIR?

1 SAMUEL 30

Suppose you and a friend did a project together to win a prize, but a third friend chose not to help you. Would it be fair to let the third friend share in the prize? When a group of enemy soldiers burned down their village and stole their possessions, David and 400 of his men went after them. But 200 of David's 600 men were too tired to go. Some of the men who fought the enemy didn't want to share with the men who didn't go. They felt that sharing with them wasn't fair. But David agreed to share and share alike. Sometimes, you might have to choose between kindness and your idea of fairness. Which will you choose?

Forgive Instead, Genesis 33, p. 47

Share What You Have, Exodus 35:5–18, p. 123

Play Fair or Play Favorites?, Deuteronomy 1:16–18, p. 227

Fairness for All, Deuteronomy 24:17, p. 258

Wronged for What's Right, Ezra 4:4–5, p. 612

The Way to Get Along, 1 Peter 3:8–9, p. 1703

four hundred men kept up the chase. The other two hundred men stayed behind because they were too tired to cross the ravine.

11They found an Egyptian in a field
and brought him to David. They gave the
Egyptian some water to drink and some
food to eat. **12**And they gave him a piece
of a fig cake and two clusters of raisins.
Then he felt better, because he had not
eaten any food or drunk any water for
three days and nights.

13David asked him, "Who is your
master? Where do you come from?"

He answered, "I'm an Egyptian, the
slave of an Amalekite. Three days ago my
master left me, because I was sick. **14**We
had raided the southern area of the Kerethites, the land of Judah, and the southern area of Caleb. We burned Ziklag, as
well."

15David asked him, "Can you lead me
to the people who took our families?"

He answered, "Yes, if you promise me
before God that you won't kill me or give
me back to my master. Then I will take
you to them."

16So the Egyptian led David to the
Amalekites. They were lying around on
the ground, eating and drinking and celebrating with the things they had taken
from the land of the Philistines and from
Judah. **17**David fought them from sunset
until the evening of the next day. None of
them escaped, except four hundred young
men who rode off on their camels. **18**David got his two wives back and everything
the Amalekites had taken. **19**Nothing was
missing. David brought back everyone,
young and old, sons and daughters. He recovered the valuable things and everything the Amalekites had taken. **20**David
took all the sheep and cattle, and his men
made these animals go in front, saying,
"They are David's prize."

21Then David came to the two hundred men who had been too tired to follow
him, who had stayed at the Besor Ravine.
They came out to meet David and the people with him. When he came near, David
greeted the men at the ravine.

22But the evil men and troublemakers
among those who followed David said,
"Since these two hundred men didn't go
with us, we shouldn't give them any of
the things we recovered. Just let each
man take his wife and children and go."

SOME BAD GUYS

1 Samuel 31:1–4

The Philistines were a fierce tribe of people. They were called the "sea people" because they probably came from an island in the Mediterranean Sea. (See Genesis 10:14, p. 15, and Amos 9:7, p. 1204.) The land that they lived in was called Philistia. Maybe the most famous Philistine was Goliath, the giant that David killed with a slingshot and five stones.

The Philistines are mostly mentioned in the Bible at two different times. First, they were mentioned in the stories about Abraham. These Philistines were peaceful and were ruled by King Abimelech. Later on, the Philistines were mentioned when the Israelites were just about to get their first two kings: Saul and David. These Philistines were made up of a confederation of five different Philistine states ruled by five different leaders. They were dangerous, and the Israelites were afraid of them. In fact, one of the main reasons that the Israelites wanted a king was for protection against the Philistines. King David was the king who finally broke the power of the great Philistines.

23David answered, "No, my brothers.
Don't do that after what the LORD has
given us. He has protected us and given
us the enemy who attacked us. 24Who
will listen to what you say? The share will
be the same for the one who stayed with
the supplies as for the one who went into
battle. All will share alike." 25David made
this an order and rule for Israel, which
continues even today.

26When David arrived in Ziklag, he
sent some of the things he had taken
from the Amalekites to his friends, the
leaders of Judah. He said, "Here is a present for you from the things we took from
the LORD's enemies."

27David also sent some things to the
leaders in Bethel, Ramoth in the southern
part of Judah, Jattir, 28Aroer, Siphmoth,
Eshtemoa, 29Racal, the cities of the Je-
rahmeelites and the Kenites, 30Hormah,
Bor Ashan, Athach, 31Hebron, and to the
people in all the other places where he
and his men had been.

The Death of Saul

31 The Philistines fought against Israel, and the Israelites ran away
from them. Many Israelites were killed
on Mount Gilboa. 2The Philistines fought
hard against Saul and his sons, killing his
sons Jonathan, Abinadab, and Malki-
Shua. 3The fighting was heavy around
Saul. The archers shot him, and he was
badly wounded. 4He said to the officer
who carried his armor, "Pull out your
sword and kill me. Then those uncircumcised men won't make fun of me and kill
me." But Saul's officer refused, because
he was afraid. So Saul took his own sword
and threw himself on it. 5When the officer saw that Saul was dead, he threw
himself on his own sword, and he died
with Saul. 6So Saul, his three sons, and
the officer who carried his armor died together that day.

7When the Israelites who lived across
the Jezreel Valley and those who lived
across the Jordan River saw how the Is-

raelite army had run away, and that Saul
and his sons were dead, they left their
cities and ran away. Then the Philistines
came and lived there.
8The next day when the Philistines
came to take all the valuable things from
the dead soldiers, they found Saul and his
three sons dead on Mount Gilboa. 9They
cut off Saul's head and took off his armor.
Then they sent messengers through all
the land of the Philistines to tell the news
in the temple of their idols and to their
people. 10They put Saul's armor in the
temple of the Ashtoreths and hung his
body on the wall of Beth Shan.
11When the people living in Jabesh
Gilead heard what the Philistines had
done to Saul, 12the brave men of Jabesh
marched all night and came to Beth Shan.
They removed the bodies of Saul and his
sons from the wall of Beth Shan and
brought them to Jabesh. There they
burned the bodies. 13They took their
bones and buried them under the tamarisk tree in Jabesh. Then the people of
Jabesh gave up eating for seven days.

2 Samuel

KING AT LAST

Greetings! I am King David. You may remember me, the shepherd boy who played the harp for King Saul? This book tells how I was made king over all of Israel. No one is sure who wrote these stories, but I know they are true. These were exciting days for God's people. We defeated our enemies, and Israel became a great nation. I danced for joy when we brought the Ark of God to Jerusalem. Check out 2 Samuel 6 for the big celebration.

This book was written to tell the story of my rule. God was good to me and gave me many victories. Sadly, I did not always obey God, and I had times of trouble, too. When the prophet Nathan pointed out my sin, I asked God to forgive me. Check out the MIDI in Psalm 51, p. 748, for the words of the song I wrote telling God I was sorry.

JESUS WATCH

David had a close relationship with God and a desire to bring him glory, just as Jesus did. Even though David sinned, he remained close to God because he was willing to ask God for forgiveness. David wrote many psalms praising God and made worship the most important part of his kingdom. His rule was known for justice and compassion. God made a special promise to David that his family would rule forever. Israel and the prophets looked forward to the Son of David, the Messiah, who would bring people to God and make Israel a great nation again. The angel Gabriel told Mary that Jesus would reign on the throne of King David and that his kingdom would never end. People were looking for a military hero who would defeat Israel's enemies, but Jesus rules forever from heaven. When we believe in Jesus, he becomes our king. His justice and mercy never end.

"Tagg, do you know why King David's son, Absalom, was hanging by his hair in a tree?"

"Sounds like trouble to me. Maybe we should surf over to 2 Samuel 18 to find out more."

FAITH links

- **The Green Light, 2 Samuel 2:1**
- **When God Says No, 2 Samuel 7**
- **Loyal to a Friend, 2 Samuel 9**
- **Help to Understand, 2 Samuel 14**

David Learns About Saul's Death

1 Now Saul was dead. After David had
defeated the Amalekites, he returned
to Ziklag and stayed there two days. 2On
the third day a young man from Saul's
camp came to Ziklag. To show his sadness, his clothes were torn and he had
dirt on his head. He came and bowed
facedown on the ground before David.
3David asked him, "Where did you
come from?"
The man answered, "I escaped from
the Israelite camp."
4David asked him, "What happened?
Please tell me!"
The man answered, "The people have
run away from the battle, and many of
them have fallen and are dead. Saul and
his son Jonathan are dead also."
5David asked him, "How do you know
Saul and his son Jonathan are dead?"
6The young man answered, "I happened to be on Mount Gilboa. There I
saw Saul leaning on his spear. The Philistine chariots and the men riding in them
were coming closer to Saul. 7When he
looked back and saw me, he called to me.
I answered him, 'Here I am!'
8"Then Saul asked me, 'Who are
you?'
"I told him, 'I am an Amalekite.'
9"Then Saul said to me, 'Please come
here and kill me. I am badly hurt and am
almost dead already.'
10"So I went over and killed him. He
had been hurt so badly I knew he couldn't
live. Then I took the crown from his head
and the bracelet from his arm, and I have
brought them here to you, my master."
11Then David tore his clothes to
show his sorrow, and all the men with
him did also. 12They were very sad and
cried and did not eat until evening. They
cried for Saul and his son Jonathan and
for all the people of the LORD and for all
the Israelites who had died in the battle.

FAITH links

MOURNING FOR AN ENEMY

2 SAMUEL 1

If you had an enemy, would you feel glad if that enemy fell into trouble? Even though Saul had been his enemy for several years, David remained respectful to Saul. He did not celebrate when his enemy was killed. Instead he mourned the loss of Saul. He even sang a song in honor of his fallen enemy.

Are you tempted to laugh when your enemy gets hit with trouble? Taking pleasure in your enemy's misfortune or causing it doesn't make you a hero. Showing respect for an enemy does. When you're respectful even to an enemy, God is pleased.

Give Revenge a Rest, Leviticus 19:18, p. 160

A Right to Get Even?, 1 Samuel 24, p. 388

The Problem with Pride, Isaiah 2:11, p. 898

A Hometown Hurt, Jeremiah 11:8—12:6, p. 1008

Quick to Forgive?, Mark 11:25, p. 1349

Better Than Some?, Luke 18:9–14, p. 1405

David Orders the Amalekite Killed

13David asked the young man who
brought the report, "Where are you from?"
The young man answered, "I am the
son of a foreigner, an Amalekite."
14David asked him, "Why were you
not afraid to kill the LORD's appointed
king?"
15Then David called one of his men

and told him, "Go! Kill the Amalekite!" So
the Israelite killed him. 16David had said
to the Amalekite, "You are responsible
for your own death. You confessed by saying, 'I have killed the LORD's appointed
king.' "

David's Song About Saul and Jonathan

17David sang a funeral song about
Saul and his son Jonathan, 18and he ordered that the people of Judah be taught
this song. It is called "The Bow," and it is
written in the Book of Jashar:

19 "Israel, your leaders have been killed
on the hills.
How the mighty have fallen in
battle!
20 Don't tell it in Gath.
Don't announce it in the streets of
Ashkelon.
If you do, the Philistine women will
be happy.
The daughters of the Philistines
will rejoice.

21 "May there be no dew or rain on the
mountains of Gilboa,
and may their fields produce no
grain,
because there the mighty warrior's
shield was dishonored.
Saul's shield will no longer be
rubbed with oil.
22 Jonathan's bow did not fail
to kill many soldiers.
Saul's sword did not fail
to wound many strong men.

23 "We loved Saul and Jonathan
and enjoyed them while they
lived.
They are together even in death.
They were faster than eagles.
They were stronger than lions.

24 "You daughters of Israel, cry for Saul.
Saul clothed you with red dresses
and put gold decorations on them.

25 "How the mighty have fallen in
battle!
Jonathan is dead on Gilboa's hills.
26 I cry for you, my brother Jonathan.
I enjoyed your friendship so much.
Your love to me was wonderful,
better than the love of women.

27 "How the mighty have fallen!
The weapons of war are gone."

David Is Made King of Judah

2 Later, David prayed to the LORD, saying, "Should I go up to any of the cities of Judah?"

The LORD said to David, "Go."
David asked, "Where should I go?"
The LORD answered, "To Hebron."
2So David went up to Hebron with his
two wives: Ahinoam from Jezreel and Abigail, the widow of Nabal from Carmel.
3David also brought his men and their
families, and they all made their homes in
the cities of Hebron. 4Then the men of
Judah came to Hebron and appointed David king over Judah.

They told David that the men of Jabesh Gilead had buried Saul. 5So David
sent messengers to the men of Jabesh
Gilead and said to them, "The LORD bless
you. You have shown loyalty to your master Saul by burying him. 6May the LORD
now be loyal and true to you. I will also
treat you well because you have done
this. 7Now be strong and brave. Saul your
master is dead, and the people of Judah
have appointed me their king."

War Between Judah and Israel

8Abner son of Ner was the commander of Saul's army. Abner took Saul's
son Ish-Bosheth to Mahanaim 9and made
him king of Gilead, Ashuri, Jezreel,
Ephraim, Benjamin, and all Israel.
10Saul's son Ish-Bosheth was forty years
old when he became king over Israel, and
he ruled two years. But the people of Judah followed David. 11David was king in
Hebron for seven years and six months.

12Abner son of Ner and the servants of
Ish-Bosheth son of Saul left Mahanaim
and went to Gibeon. 13Joab son of Zeruiah
and David's men also went there and met
Abner and Ish-Bosheth's men at the pool
of Gibeon. Abner's group sat on one side
of the pool; Joab's group sat on the other.

FAITH links

THE GREEN LIGHT

2 SAMUEL 2:1

When a producer in Hollywood is given permission to make a movie, the project is said to be "green-lighted." That means he or she can go ahead with it. God gave David "the green light" to move to Hebron. David didn't make a move before checking with God. He trusted God's timing.

When you're about to make plans, do you ever think about checking with God for his approval? Although you may not want to stop and ask God about things like whether you should wear orange socks or red, consider talking over the major decisions of your life. God cares about you. Commit your plans to God. Wait for him to give you the green light.

Here are some more Faithlinks on making good plans:

A Giant Problem, 1 Samuel 17:32–51, p. 377

When God Says No, 2 Samuel 7, p. 407

A Need to Change, Ecclesiastes 1:1–11, p. 873

First Place, Haggai 1:7–11, p. 1248

The Best Advice, Zechariah 10:2, p. 1261

Prayer Priority, Luke 5:15–16, p. 1376

14Abner said to Joab, "Let the young
men have a contest here."

Joab said, "Yes, let them have a contest."

15Then the men got up and were
counted—twelve from the people of Benjamin for Ish-Bosheth son of Saul, and
twelve from David's men. **16**Each man
grabbed the one opposite him by the head
and stabbed him in the side with a knife.
So the men fell down together. For that
reason, that place in Gibeon is called the
Field of Knives. **17**That day there was a
terrible battle, and David's men defeated
Abner and the Israelites.

Abner Kills Asahel

18Zeruiah's three sons, Joab, Abishai,
and Asahel, were there. Now Asahel was
a fast runner, as fast as a deer in the field.
19Asahel chased Abner, going straight
toward him. **20**Abner looked back and
asked, "Is that you, Asahel?"

Asahel said, "Yes, it is."

21Then Abner said to Asahel, "Turn
to your right or left and catch one of the
young men and take his armor." But Asahel refused to stop chasing him.

22Abner again said to Asahel, "Stop
chasing me! If you don't stop, I'll have to
kill you! Then I won't be able to face your
brother Joab again!"

23But Asahel refused to stop chasing
Abner. So using the back end of his spear,
Abner stabbed Asahel in the stomach, and
the spear came out of his back. Asahel
died right there, and everyone stopped
when they came to the place where
Asahel's body lay.

24But Joab and Abishai continued
chasing Abner. As the sun was going
down, they arrived at the hill of Ammah,
near Giah on the way to the desert near
Gibeon. **25**The men of Benjamin came to
Abner, and all stood together at the top of
the hill.

26Abner shouted to Joab, "Must the
sword kill forever? Surely you must
know this will only end in sadness! Tell
the people to stop chasing their own
brothers!"

27Then Joab said, "As surely as God
lives, if you had not said anything, the

people would have chased their brothers
until morning." **28**Then Joab blew a
trumpet, and his people stopped chasing
the Israelites. They did not fight them
anymore.
29Abner and his men marched all
night through the Jordan Valley. They
crossed the Jordan River, and after
marching all day, arrived at Mahanaim.
30After he had stopped chasing Abner,
Joab came back and gathered the people
together. Asahel and nineteen of David's
men were missing. **31**But David's men
had killed three hundred sixty Benjaminites who had followed Abner.
32David's men took Asahel and buried
him in the tomb of his father at Bethlehem. Then Joab and his men marched all
night. The sun came up as they reached
Hebron.
3 There was a long war between the
people who supported Saul's family
and those who supported David's family.
The supporters of David's family became
stronger and stronger, but the supporters
of Saul's family became weaker and
weaker.

David's Sons

2Sons were born to David at Hebron.
The first was Amnon, whose mother was
Ahinoam from Jezreel. **3**The second son
was Kileab, whose mother was Abigail,
the widow of Nabal from Carmel. The
third son was Absalom, whose mother
was Maacah daughter of Talmai, the king
of Geshur. **4**The fourth son was Adonijah,
whose mother was Haggith. The fifth son
was Shephatiah, whose mother was Abital. **5**The sixth son was Ithream, whose
mother was Eglah, David's wife. These
sons were born to David at Hebron.

Abner Joins David

6During the war between the supporters of Saul's family and the supporters of David's family, Abner made himself
a main leader among the supporters of
Saul.
7Saul once had a slave woman named
Rizpah, who was the daughter of Aiah.
Ish-Bosheth said to Abner, "Why did you
have sexual relations with my father's
slave woman?"
8Abner was very angry because of
what Ish-Bosheth said, and he replied, "I
have been loyal to Saul and his family and
friends! I didn't hand you over to David. I
am not a traitor working for Judah! But
now you are saying I did something
wrong with this woman! **9**May God help
me if I don't join David! I will make sure
that what the LORD promised does happen! **10**I will take the kingdom from the
family of Saul and make David king of Israel and Judah, from Dan to Beersheba!'"
11Ish-Bosheth couldn't say anything
to Abner, because he was afraid of him.
12Then Abner sent messengers to
ask David, "Who is going to rule the
land? Make an agreement with me, and I
will help you unite all Israel."
13David answered, "Good! I will
make an agreement with you, but I ask
you one thing. I will not meet with you
unless you bring Saul's daughter Michal
to me." **14**Then David sent messengers
to Saul's son Ish-Bosheth, saying, "Give
me my wife Michal. She was promised to
me, and I killed a hundred Philistines to
get her."
15So Ish-Bosheth sent men to take
Michal from her husband Paltiel son of
Laish. **16**Michal's husband went with her,
crying as he followed her to Bahurim.
But Abner said to Paltiel, "Go back
home." So he went home.
17Abner sent this message to the
older leaders of Israel: "You have been
wanting to make David your king. **18**Now
do it! The LORD said of David, 'Through
my servant David, I will save my people
Israel from the Philistines and all their
enemies.' "
19Abner also said these things to the
people of Benjamin. He then went to Hebron to tell David what the Benjaminites
and Israel wanted to do. **20**Abner came
with twenty men to David at Hebron.
There David prepared a feast for them.
21Abner said to David, "My master and

3:10 Dan to Beersheba Dan was the city farthest north in Israel, and Beersheba was the city farthest south. So this means all the people of Israel.

king, I will go and bring all the Israelites
to you. Then they will make an agreement with you so you will rule over all
Israel as you wanted." So David let Abner
go, and he left in peace.

Abner's Death

22Just then Joab and David's men
came from a battle, bringing many valuable things they had taken from the
enemy. David had let Abner leave in
peace, so he was not with David at Hebron. **23**When Joab and all his army arrived at Hebron, the army said to Joab,
"Abner son of Ner came to King David,
and David let him leave in peace."

24Joab came to the king and said,
"What have you done? Abner came to you.
Why did you let him go? Now he's gone.
25You know Abner son of Ner! He came
to trick you! He came to
learn about everything
you are doing!"

26After Joab left Da-
vid, he sent messengers
after Abner, and they
brought him back from
the well of Sirah. But David did not know this.
27When Abner arrived at
Hebron, Joab took him
aside into the gateway.
He acted as though he wanted to talk
with Abner in private, but Joab stabbed
him in the stomach, and Abner died. Abner had killed Joab's brother Asahel, so
Joab killed Abner to pay him back.

28Later when David heard the news,
he said, "My kingdom and I are innocent
forever of the death of Abner son of Ner.
The LORD knows this. **29**Joab and his
family are responsible for this. May his
family always have someone with sores
or with a skin disease. May they always
have someone who must lean on a
crutch. May some of his family be killed
in war. May they always have someone
without food to eat."

30(Joab and his brother Abishai killed
Abner, because he had killed their
brother Asahel in the battle at Gibeon.)

31Then David said to Joab and to all
the people with Joab, "Tear your clothes
and put on rough cloth to show how sad
you are. Cry for Abner." King David himself followed the body of Abner. **32**They
buried Abner in Hebron, and David and
all the people cried at Abner's grave.

33King David sang this funeral song
for Abner.

"Did Abner die like a fool?
34 His hands were not tied.
His feet were not in chains.
He fell at the hands of evil men."

Then all the people cried again for Abner. **35**They came to encourage David to
eat while it was still day. But he made a
promise, saying, "May God punish me
terribly if I eat bread or anything else before the sun sets!"

36All the people saw what happened,
and they agreed with what the king was
doing, just as they agreed with everything
he did. **37**That day all the
people of Judah and Israel
understood that David did
not order the killing of
Abner son of Ner.

38David said to his officers, "You know that a
great man died today in
Israel. **39**Even though I
am the appointed king, I
feel empty. These sons of
Zeruiah are too much for
me. May the LORD give them the punishment they should have."

> Tear your clothes and put on rough cloth to show how sad you are. Cry for Abner.
> —2 Samuel 3:31

Ish-Bosheth's Death

4 When Ish-Bosheth son of Saul heard
that Abner had died at Hebron, he
was shocked and all Israel became frightened. **2**Two men who were captains in
Saul's army came to Ish-Bosheth. One
was named Baanah, and the other was
named Recab. They were the sons of
Rimmon of Beeroth, who was a Benjaminite. (The town Beeroth belonged to
the tribe of Benjamin. **3**The people of Beeroth ran away to Gittaim, and they still
live there as foreigners today.)

4(Saul's son Jonathan had a son
named Mephibosheth, who was crippled
in both feet. He was five years old when
the news came from Jezreel that Saul and
Jonathan were dead. Mephibosheth's

nurse had picked him up and run away.
But as she hurried to leave, she dropped
him, and now he was lame.)
5Recab and Baanah, sons of Rimmon
from Beeroth, went to Ish-Bosheth's
house in the afternoon while he was taking a nap. **6-7**They went into the middle
of the house as if to get some wheat. Ish-
Bosheth was lying on his bed in his bedroom. Then Recab and Baanah stabbed
him in the stomach, killed him, cut off his
head, and took it with them. They escaped and traveled all night through the
Jordan Valley. **8**When they arrived at Hebron, they gave his head to David and
said to the king, "Here is the head of Ish-
Bosheth son of Saul, your enemy. He
tried to kill you! Today the LORD has paid
back Saul and his family for what they did
to you!"
9David answered Recab and his
brother Baanah, the sons of Rimmon of
Beeroth, "As surely as the LORD lives, he
has saved me from all trouble! **10**Once a
man thought he was bringing me
good news. When he
told me, 'Saul is
dead!' I seized him
and killed him at
Ziklag. That was the
reward I gave him
for his news! **11**So even more I must put
you evil men to death because you have
killed an innocent man on his own bed in
his own house!"
12So David commanded his men to
kill Recab and Baanah. They cut off the
hands and feet of Recab and Baanah and
hung them over the pool of Hebron. Then
they took Ish-Bosheth's head and buried
it in Abner's tomb at Hebron.

EMAIL! FROM GOD
4:9–11
Life
Is life sacred?

David Is Made King of Israel

5 Then all the tribes of Israel came to
David at Hebron and said to him,
"Look, we are your own family. **2**Even
when Saul was king, you were the one
who led Israel in battle. The LORD said to
you, 'You will be a shepherd for my people Israel. You will be their leader.' "
3So all the older leaders of Israel
came to King David at Hebron, and he
made an agreement with them in Hebron
in the presence of the LORD. Then they
poured oil on David to make him king
over Israel.
4David was thirty years old when he
became king, and he ruled forty years.
5He was king over Judah in Hebron for
seven years and six months, and he was
king over all Israel and Judah in Jerusalem for thirty-three years.
6When the king and his men went to
Jerusalem to attack the Jebusites who
lived there, the Jebusites said to David,
"You can't get inside our city. Even the
blind and the crippled can stop you."
They thought David could not enter their
city. **7**But David did take the city of Jerusalem with its strong walls, and it became
the City of David.
8That day David said to his men, "To
defeat the Jebusites you must go through
the water tunnel. Then you can reach
those 'crippled' and 'blind' enemies. This
is why people say, 'The blind and the crippled may not enter the palace.' "
9So David lived in the strong, walled
city and called it the City of David. David
built more buildings around it, beginning
where the land was filled in. He also built
more buildings inside the city. **10**He became stronger and stronger, because the
LORD God All-Powerful was with him.
11Hiram king of the city of Tyre sent
messengers to David, along with cedar
logs, carpenters, and stonecutters. They
built a palace for David. **12**Then David
knew that the LORD really had made him
king of Israel and that the LORD had made
his kingdom great because the LORD
loved his people Israel.
13After he came from Hebron, David
took for himself more slave women and
wives in Jerusalem. More sons and
daughters were born to David. **14**These
are the names of the sons born to David
in Jerusalem: Shammua, Shobab, Nathan,
Solomon, **15**Ibhar, Elishua, Nepheg, Japhia, **16**Elishama, Eliada, and Eliphelet.

David Defeats the Philistines

17When the Philistines heard that David had been made king over Israel, all the

HURRY UP AND WAIT

2 SAMUEL 5

When it comes to waiting for something, how would you rate yourself on a scale of 1 to 10 (1 = not at all patient; 10 = very patient)? Several years passed between David's anointing as king and his taking the throne. He had several opportunities to force his way onto the throne. But he chose to be patient and wait for God to bring him to the throne.

Patience doesn't come overnight. One step to take on the path to patience is to let go of your expectations about when something should take place.

Another step is to trust in God's timing.

Want to know how to trust God? Link here:

A Long Wait, Joshua 14:6–15, p. 294

A Shortcut, 1 Samuel 13:1–14, p. 369

Does Crime Pay?, Psalm 37:1–7, p. 736

Think About Him, Isaiah 26:3, p. 926

Faith God Notices, Luke 18:35–43, p. 1406

A Different Kind of Fruit, Galatians 5:22–23, p. 1592

Philistines went to look for him. But when
David heard the news, he went down to
the stronghold. **18**The Philistines came
and camped in the Valley of Rephaim.
19David asked the LORD, "Should I attack
the Philistines? Will you hand them over
to me?"

The LORD said to David, "Go! I will
certainly hand them over to you."

20So David went to Baal Perazim and
defeated the Philistines there. David
said, "Like a flood of water, the LORD has
broken through my enemies in front of
me." So David named the place Baal
Perazim.ⁿ **21**The Philistines left their
idols behind at Baal Perazim, so David
and his men carried them away.

22Once again the Philistines came and
camped at the Valley of Rephaim. **23**When
David prayed to the LORD, he answered,
"Don't attack the Philistines from the
front. Instead, go around and attack them
in front of the balsam trees. **24**When you
hear the sound of marching in the tops of
the balsam trees, act quickly. I, the LORD,
will have gone ahead of you to defeat the
Philistine army." **25**So David did what the
LORD commanded. He defeated the Philistines and chased them all the way from
Gibeon to Gezer.

The Ark Is Brought to Jerusalem

6 David again gathered all the chosen
men of Israel—thirty thousand of
them. **2**Then he and all his people went
to Baalah in Judahⁿ to bring back the Ark
of God. The Ark is called by the Name,
the name of the LORD All-Powerful,
whose throne is between the gold creatures with wings. **3**They put the Ark of
God on a new cart and brought it out of
Abinadab's house on the hill. Uzzah and
Ahio, sons of Abinadab, led the new cart
4which had the Ark of God on it. Ahio
was walking in front of it. **5**David and all
the Israelites were celebrating in the
presence of the LORD. They were playing
wooden instruments: lyres, harps, tambourines, rattles, and cymbals.

6When David's men came to the
threshing floor of Nacon, the oxen stumbled. So Uzzah reached out to steady the
Ark of God. **7**The LORD was angry with

5:20 Baal Perazim This name means "the Lord breaks through."

6:2 Baalah in Judah Another name for Kiriath Jearim.

Uzzah and killed him because of what he
did. So Uzzah died there beside the Ark
of God. 8David was angry because the
LORD had killed Uzzah. Now that place is
called the Punishment of Uzzah.
9David was afraid of the LORD that
day, and he said, "How can the Ark of the
LORD come to me now?" 10So David
would not move the Ark of the LORD to
be with him in Jerusalem. Instead, he
took it to the house of Obed-Edom, a man
from Gath. 11The Ark of the LORD stayed
in Obed-Edom's house for three months,
and the LORD blessed Obed-Edom and all
his family.
12The people told David, "The LORD
has blessed the family of Obed-Edom and
all that belongs to him, because the Ark
of God is there." So David went and
brought it up from Obed-Edom's house to
Jerusalem with joy. 13When the men
carrying the Ark of the LORD had walked
six steps, David sacrificed a bull and a fat
calf. 14Then David danced with all his
might before the LORD. He had on a holy
linen vest. 15David and all the Israelites
shouted with joy and blew the trumpets
as they brought the Ark of the LORD to
the city.
16As the Ark of the LORD came into
the city, Saul's daughter Michal looked
out the window. When she saw David
jumping and dancing in the presence of
the LORD, she hated him.
17David put up a tent for the Ark of
the LORD, and then the Israelites put it in
its place inside the tent. David offered
whole burnt offerings and fellowship offerings before the LORD. 18When David
finished offering the whole burnt offerings and the fellowship offerings, he
blessed the people in the name of the
LORD All-Powerful. 19David gave a loaf
of bread, a cake of dates, and a cake of raisins to every Israelite, both men and
women. Then all the people went home.
20David went back to bless the people
in his home, but Saul's daughter Michal
came out to meet him. She said, "With
what honor the king of Israel acted today!
You took off your clothes in front of the
servant girls of your officers like one who
takes off his clothes without shame!"
21Then David said to Michal, "I did it
in the presence of the LORD. The LORD
chose me, not your father or anyone from
Saul's family. The LORD appointed me to
be over Israel. So I will celebrate in the pres-
ence of the LORD.
22Maybe I will lose
even more honor,
and maybe I will be
brought down in my
own opinion, but the girls you talk about
will honor me!"
23And Saul's daughter Michal had no
children to the day she died.

EMAIL FROM GOD
6:21
Worship
How should you worship God?

David Wants to Build a Temple

7 King David was living in his palace,
and the LORD had given him peace
from all his enemies around him. 2Then
David said to Nathan the prophet, "Look,
I am living in a palace made of cedar
wood, but the Ark of God is in a tent!"
3Nathan said to the king, "Go and do
what you really want to do, because the
LORD is with you."
4But that night the LORD spoke his
word to Nathan, 5"Go and tell my servant
David, 'This is what the LORD says: Will
you build a house for me to live in? 6From
the time I brought the Israelites out of
Egypt until now I have not lived in a
house. I have been moving around all this
time with a tent as my home. 7As I have
moved with the Israelites, I have never
said to the tribes, whom I commanded to
take care of my people Israel, "Why
haven't you built me a house of cedar?" '
8"You must tell my servant David,
'This is what the LORD All-Powerful says:
I took you from the pasture and from tending the sheep and made you leader of
my people Israel. 9I have been with you
everywhere you have gone and have defeated your enemies for you. I will make
you as famous as any of the great people
on the earth. 10Also I will choose a place
for my people Israel, and I will plant them
so they can live in their own homes. They
will not be bothered anymore. Wicked
people will no longer bother them as they
have in the past 11when I chose judges for
my people Israel. But I will give you peace

FAITH links

WHEN GOD SAYS NO

2 SAMUEL 7

The Constitution gives the president the authority to veto a proposed law made by Congress. That's a fancy way of saying that the president has the power to say no to something. David wanted to build a temple for God, but God vetoed his plan. Even though David's desire to build was good, God knew that he wasn't the right man for the job. (Plug in to this same story by reading 1 Chronicles 17, p. 541.)

If we say that God is the president of lives, that gives him veto power. He has the right to say no to our plans. Are you willing to trust that he knows what's best?

The Sacrifice, Genesis 22, p. 29

I'll Never Forget What's-His-Name, Deuteronomy 8, p. 239

The Fence Riders, 1 Kings 18, p. 464

The Foundation of Our Hope, Isaiah 31:1–8, p. 934

Prayer Priority, Luke 5:15–16, p. 1376

The "Quality" of Life, 2 Peter 1:5–8, p. 1708

from all your enemies. I also tell you that I
will make your descendants kings of Israel after you.
12" 'When you die and join your ancestors, I will make one of your sons the
next king, and I will set up his kingdom.
13He will build a house for me, and I will
let his kingdom rule always. **14**I will be
his father, and he will be my son. When
he sins, I will use other people to punish
him. They will be my whips. **15**I took
away my love from Saul, whom I removed before you, but I will never stop
loving your son. **16**But your family and
your kingdom will continue always before me. Your throne will last forever.' "
17Nathan told David everything God
had said in this vision.

David Prays to God

18Then King David went in and sat in
front of the LORD. David said, "Lord GOD,
who am I? What is my family? Why did
you bring me to this point? **19**But even
this is not enough for you, Lord GOD. You
have also made promises about my future
family. This is not normal, Lord GOD.
20"What more can I say to you, Lord
GOD, since you know me, your servant,
so well! **21**You have done this great thing
because you said you would and because
you wanted to, and you have let me know
about it. **22**This is
why you are great,
Lord GOD! There is
no one like you. There
is no God except you.
We have heard all this
ourselves! **23**There is
no nation like your people Israel. They are
the only people on earth that God chose
to be his own. You made your name well
known. You did great and wonderful miracles for them. You went ahead of them
and forced other nations and their gods
out of the land. You freed your people
from slavery in Egypt. **24**You made the
people of Israel your very own people
forever, and, LORD, you are their God.
25"Now, LORD God, keep the promise
forever that you made about my family
and me, your servant. Do what you
have said. **26**Then you will be honored always, and people will say, 'The LORD All-
Powerful is God over Israel!' And the
family of your servant David will continue before you.

EMAIL FROM GOD
7:22
God
Is there anyone like God?

27"LORD All-Powerful, the God of Israel, you have said to me, 'I will make
your family great.' So I, your servant, am
brave enough to pray to you. 28Lord
GOD, you are God, and your words are
true. And you have promised these good
things to me, your servant. 29Please,
bless my family. Let it continue before
you always. Lord GOD, you have said so.
With your blessing let my family always
be blessed."

David Wins Many Wars

8 Later, David defeated the Philistines,
conquered them, and took the city of
Metheg Ammah.

2He also defeated the people of Moab.
He made them lie on the ground, and
then he used a rope to measure them.
Those who were measured within two
rope lengths were killed, but those who
were within the next rope length were allowed to live. So the people of Moab became servants of David and gave him the
payment he demanded.

3David also defeated Hadadezer son
of Rehob, king of Zobah, as he went to
take control again at the Euphrates River.
4David captured one thousand chariots,
seven thousand men who rode in chariots, and twenty thousand foot soldiers.
He crippled all but a hundred of the chariot horses.

5Arameans from Damascus came to
help Hadadezer king of Zobah, but David
killed twenty-two thousand of them.
6Then David put groups of soldiers in
Damascus in Aram. The Arameans became David's servants and gave him the
payment he demanded. The LORD gave
David victory everywhere he went.

7David took the shields of gold that
had belonged to Hadadezer's officers and
brought them to Jerusalem. 8David also
took many things made of bronze from
Tebah and Berothai, which had been cities under Hadadezer's control.

9Toi king of Hamath heard that David
had defeated all the army of Hadadezer.
10So Toi sent his son Joram to greet and
congratulate King David for defeating
Hadadezer. (Hadadezer had been at war
with Toi.) Joram brought items made of
silver, gold, and bronze. 11King David
gave them to the LORD, along with the
silver and gold he had taken from the
other nations he had defeated. 12These
nations were Edom, Moab, Ammon, Philistia, and Amalek. David also gave the
LORD what he had taken from Hadadezer
son of Rehob, king of Zobah.

13David was famous after he returned
from defeating eighteen thousand Arameans in the Valley of Salt. 14He put groups
of soldiers all over Edom, and all the
Edomites became his servants. The LORD
gave David victory everywhere he went.

FAITH links

FAIR ALL THE TIME?

2 SAMUEL 8:15

Do you treat everyone the same way? As a king, David was known to be fair to everyone. That meant he made good laws and was merciful toward those who were punished. He was able to do this because he trusted God to help him. Respecting God and others helps you to be fair not some of the time, but all of the time.

Show Some Respect, Leviticus 19:32, p. 161

Fairness for All, Deuteronomy 24:17, p. 258

Kind or Fair?, 1 Samuel 30, p. 395

Service with a Smile, 1 Chronicles 6:31–49, p. 527

Seeing the Needs, Nehemiah 1, p. 625

I'll Be the Judge!, 1 Corinthians 4:4–5, p. 1549

15David was king over all Israel, and he did what was fair and right for all his people. 16Joab son of Zeruiah was commander over the army. Jehoshaphat son of Ahilud was the recorder. 17Zadok son of Ahitub and Abiathar son of Ahimelech were priests. Seraiah was the royal secretary. 18Benaiah son of Jehoiada was over the Kerethites and Pelethites.[n] And David's sons were priests.

David Helps Saul's Family

9 David asked, "Is anyone still left in Saul's family? I want to show kindness to that person for Jonathan's sake!"

> EMAIL! FROM GOD **9:1**
> **Friendship**
> Check out a friendship that outlasted death.

2Now there was a servant named Ziba from Saul's family. So David's servants called Ziba to him. King David said to him, "Are you Ziba?"

He answered, "Yes, I am your servant."

3The king asked, "Is anyone left in Saul's family? I want to show God's kindness to that person."

Ziba answered the king, "Jonathan has a son still living who is crippled in both feet."

4The king asked Ziba, "Where is this son?"

Ziba answered, "He is at the house of Makir son of Ammiel in Lo Debar."

5Then King David had servants bring Jonathan's son from the house of Makir son of Ammiel in Lo Debar. 6Mephibosheth, Jonathan's son, came before David and bowed facedown on the floor.

David said, "Mephibosheth!"

Mephibosheth said, "I am your servant."

7David said to him, "Don't be afraid. I will be kind to you for your father Jonathan's sake. I will give you back all the land of your grandfather Saul, and you will always eat at my table."

8Mephibosheth bowed to David again

8:18 Kerethites and Pelethites These were probably special units of the army that were responsible for the king's safety, a kind of palace guard.

FAITH links

LOYAL TO A FRIEND

2 SAMUEL 9

How long should you be loyal to a friend? Does loyalty end when a friend dies? David's best friend Jonathan had died. But David was kind to Jonathan's son, Mephibosheth, because of his loyalty to Jonathan. Long before, David and Jonathan made a promise of loyalty to each other and to each other's family. David faithfully kept that promise.

Loyalty is like a promise two people make to each other. You both promise to be faithful to each other and to care for one another. Loyalty doesn't have a time limit. Aren't you glad that it doesn't?

Are you good at keeping promises? Connect here for some hints:

A Special Promise, Numbers 30:1–2, p. 217

Read My Lips?, Deuteronomy 26:16–19, p. 260

The Gift of Friendship, 1 Samuel 18:1–3; 19, p. 381

A Fair-weather Friend, Obadiah 7, p. 1209

The Right Ingredients, Micah 6:8, p. 1227

The Number One Rule, Mark 12:28–31, p. 1351

and said, "You are being very kind to me,
your servant! And I am no better than a
dead dog!"
9Then King David called Saul's servant Ziba. David said to him, "I have
given your master's grandson everything
that belonged to Saul and his family.
10You, your sons, and your servants will
farm the land and harvest the crops.
Then your family will have food to eat.
But Mephibosheth, your master's grandson, will always eat at my table."
(Now Ziba had fifteen sons and twenty
servants.) 11Ziba said to King David, "I,
your servant, will do everything my master, the king, commands me."
So Mephibosheth ate at David's table
as if he were one of the king's sons.
12Mephibosheth had a young son named
Mica. Everyone in Ziba's family became
Mephibosheth's servants. 13Mephibo-
sheth lived in Jerusalem, because he always ate at the king's table. And he was
crippled in both feet.

War with the Ammonites and Arameans

10 When Nahash king of the Ammonites died, his son Hanun became
king after him. 2David said, "Nahash was
loyal to me, so I will be loyal to his son
Hanun." So David sent his messengers to
comfort Hanun about his father's death.
David's officers went to the land of the
Ammonites. 3But the Ammonite leaders
said to Hanun, their master, "Do you think
David wants to honor
your father by sending
men to comfort you? No!
David sent them to study
the city and spy it out and
capture it!" 4So Hanun arrested David's officers. To
shame them he shaved off
half their beards and cut
off their clothes at the
hips. Then he sent them
away.
5When the people told David, he sent
messengers to meet his officers because
they were very ashamed. King David
said, "Stay in Jericho until your beards
have grown back. Then come home."

David said, "Nahash was loyal to me, so I will be loyal to his son Hanun."
—2 Samuel 10:2

6The Ammonites knew that they had
insulted David. So they hired twenty
thousand Aramean foot soldiers from
Beth Rehob and Zobah. They also hired
the king of Maacah with a thousand men
and twelve thousand men from Tob.
7When David heard about this, he
sent Joab with the whole army. 8The Ammonites came out and prepared for battle
at the city gate. The Arameans from Zobah and Rehob and the men from Tob and
Maacah were out in the field by themselves.
9Joab saw that there were enemies
both in front of him and behind him. So he
chose some of the best soldiers of Israel
and sent them out to fight the Arameans.
10Joab put the rest of the army under the
command of Abishai, his brother. Then
he sent them out to fight the Ammonites.
11Joab said to Abishai, "If the Arameans
are too strong for me, you must help me.
Or, if the Ammonites are too strong for
you, I will help you. 12Be strong. We
must fight bravely for our people and the
cities of our God. The LORD will do what
he thinks is right."
13Then Joab and the army with him
went to attack the Arameans, and the Arameans ran away. 14When the Ammonites saw that the Arameans were running
away, they also ran away from Abishai
and went back to their city. So Joab returned from the battle with the Ammonites and came to Jerusalem.
15When the Arameans saw that Israel
had defeated them, they
came together into one
big army. 16Hadadezer
sent messengers to bring
the Arameans from east
of the Euphrates River,
and they went to Helam.
Their leader was Sho-
bach, the commander of
Hadadezer's army.
17When David heard
about this, he gathered all
the Israelites together. They crossed
over the Jordan River and went to Helam.
There the Arameans prepared for battle
and attacked him. 18But the Arameans
ran away from the Israelites. David killed

seven hundred Aramean chariot drivers
and forty thousand Aramean horsemen.
He also killed Shobach, the commander
of the Aramean army.
19When the kings who served Hadadezer saw that the Israelites had defeated
them, they made peace with the Israelites and served them. And the Arameans
were afraid to help the Ammonites again.

David Sins with Bathsheba

11 In the spring, when the kings normally went out to war, David sent
out Joab, his servants, and all the Israelites. They destroyed the Ammonites and
attacked the city of Rabbah. But David
stayed in Jerusalem. **2**One evening David
got up from his bed and walked around on
the roof[n] of his palace. While he was on
the roof, he saw a woman bathing. She
was very beautiful. **3**So David sent his
servants to find out who she was. A servant answered, "That woman is Bathsheba daughter of Eliam. She is the wife
of Uriah the Hittite." **4**So David sent
messengers to bring Bathsheba to him.
When she came to him, he had sexual relations with her. (Now Bathsheba had purified herself from her monthly period.)
Then she went back to her house. **5**But
Bathsheba became pregnant and sent
word to David, saying, "I am pregnant."
6So David sent a message to Joab:
"Send Uriah the Hittite to me." And Joab
sent Uriah to David. **7**When Uriah came
to him, David asked him how Joab was,
how the soldiers were, and how the war
was going. **8**Then David said to Uriah,
"Go home and rest."
So Uriah left the palace, and the king
sent a gift to him. **9**But Uriah did not go
home. Instead, he slept outside the door
of the palace as all the king's officers did.
10The officers told David, "Uriah did
not go home."
Then David said to Uriah, "You came
from a long trip. Why didn't you go
home?"
11Uriah said to him, "The Ark and the
soldiers of Israel and Judah are staying in
tents. My master Joab and his officers are
camping out in the fields. It isn't right for
me to go home to eat and drink and have
sexual relations with my wife!"
12David said to Uriah, "Stay here today. Tomorrow I'll send you back to the
battle." So Uriah stayed in Jerusalem that
day and the next. **13**Then David called
Uriah to come to see him, so Uriah ate
and drank with David. David made Uriah
drunk, but he still did not go home. That
evening Uriah again slept with the king's
officers.
14The next morning David wrote a
letter to Joab and sent it by Uriah. **15**In
the letter David wrote, "Put Uriah on the
front lines where the fighting is worst
and leave him there alone. Let him be
killed in battle."
16Joab watched the city and saw
where its strongest defenders were and
put Uriah there. **17**When the men of the
city came out to fight against Joab, some
of David's men were killed. And Uriah
the Hittite was one of them.
18Then Joab sent David a complete
account of the war. **19**Joab told the messenger, "Tell King David what happened
in the war. **20**After you finish, the king
may be angry and ask, 'Why did you go so
near the city to fight? Didn't you know
they would shoot arrows from the city
wall? **21**Do you remember who killed
Abimelech son of Jerub-Besheth?[n] It was
a woman on the city wall. She threw a
large stone for grinding grain on Abimelech and killed him there in Thebez. Why
did you go so near the wall?' If King David asks that, tell him, 'Your servant
Uriah the Hittite also died.' "
22The messenger left and went to
David and told him everything Joab had
told him to say. **23**The messenger told
David, "The men of Ammon were winning. They came out and attacked us in
the field, but we fought them back to the
city gate. **24**The archers on the city wall
shot at your servants, and some of your

11:2 roof In Bible times houses were built with flat roofs. The roof was used for drying things such as flax and fruit. And it was used as an extra room, as a place for worship, and as a cool place to sleep in the summer.

11:21 Jerub-Besheth Another name for Gideon.

men were killed. Your servant Uriah the
Hittite also died."
25David said to the messenger, "Say
this to Joab: 'Don't be upset about this.
The sword kills everyone the same.
Make a stronger attack against the city
and capture it.' Encourage Joab with
these words."
26When Bathsheba heard that her
husband was dead, she cried for him.
27After she finished her time of sadness,
David sent servants to bring her to his
house. She became David's wife and gave
birth to his son, but the LORD did not like
what David had done.

David's Son Dies

12 The LORD sent Nathan to David.
When he came to David, he said,
"There were two men in a city. One was
rich, but the other was poor. 2The rich
man had many sheep and cattle. 3But the
poor man had nothing except one little
female lamb he had bought. The poor
man fed the lamb, and it grew up with him
and his children. It shared his food and
drank from his cup and slept in his arms.
The lamb was like a daughter to him.
4"Then a traveler stopped to visit the
rich man. The rich man wanted to feed
the traveler, but he didn't want to take
one of his own sheep or cattle. Instead,
he took the lamb from the poor man and
cooked it for his visitor."
5David became very angry at the rich
man. He said to Nathan, "As surely as the
LORD lives, the man who did this should
die! 6He must pay for the lamb four times
for doing such a thing. He had no mercy!"
7Then Nathan said to David, "You are
the man! This is what the LORD, the God
of Israel, says: 'I appointed you king of
Israel and saved you from Saul. 8I gave
you his kingdom and his wives. And I
made you king of Israel and Judah. And if
that had not been enough, I would have
given you even more. 9So why did you ignore the LORD's command? Why did you
do what he says is wrong? You killed
Uriah the Hittite with the sword of the
Ammonites and took his wife to be your
wife! 10Now there will always be people
in your family who will die by a sword,

FAITH links

OWN UP TO IT

2 SAMUEL 12:1-13

When someone tells you about something you've done wrong, do you usually own up to it? Or do you make excuses or try to find someone else to take the blame? We call that "playing the blame game." When David did wrong, he didn't play the blame game or excuse his way out of it. Instead, he owned up to it. God forgave him for his disobedience.

When God confronts us about something we've done wrong, he doesn't want excuses. He just wants us to admit that we were wrong. No matter what you do, God will forgive you. Just ask him.

A Priest Without Sin, Leviticus 4:3–7, p. 136

You're Out!, 2 Kings 17:5–7, p. 501

Red to White, Isaiah 1:18, p. 896

Real Repentance, Jeremiah 4:1–4, p. 993

Just for the Asking, Romans 3:23–28, p. 1522

It's Guaranteed!, 1 John 1:9–10, p. 1714

because you did not respect me; you took
the wife of Uriah the Hittite for yourself!'
11"This is what the LORD says: 'I am
bringing trouble to you from your own
family. While you watch, I will take your
wives from you and give them to someone

who is very close to you. He will have
sexual relations with your wives, and
everyone will know it. **12**You had sexual
relations with Bathsheba in secret, but I
will do this so all the people of Israel can
see it.' "

13Then David said to Nathan, "I have
sinned against the LORD."

Nathan answered, "The LORD has
taken away your sin. You will not die.
14But what you did caused the LORD's
enemies to lose all respect for him. For
this reason the son who was born to you
will die."

15Then Nathan went home. And the
LORD caused the son of David and Bathsheba, Uriah's widow, to be very sick.
16David prayed to God for the baby. David refused to eat or drink. He went into
his house and stayed there, lying on the
ground all night. **17**The older leaders of
David's family came to him and tried to
pull him up from the ground, but he refused to get up or to eat food with them.

18On the seventh day the baby died.
David's servants were afraid to tell him
that the baby was dead. They said,
"Look, we tried to talk to David while the
baby was alive, but he refused to listen to
us. If we tell him the baby is dead, he may
do something awful."

19When David saw his servants whispering, he knew that the baby was dead.
So he asked them, "Is the baby dead?"

They answered, "Yes, he is dead."

20Then David got up from the floor,
washed himself, put lotions on, and
changed his clothes. Then he went into
the LORD's house to worship. After that,
he went home and asked for something to
eat. His servants gave him some food,
and he ate.

21David's servants said to him, "Why
are you doing this? When the baby was
still alive, you refused to eat and you
cried. Now that the baby is dead, you get
up and eat food."

22David said, "While the baby was
still alive, I refused to eat, and I cried. I
thought, 'Who knows? Maybe the LORD
will feel sorry for me and let the baby
live.' **23**But now that the baby is dead,
why should I go without food? I can't
bring him back to life. Some day I will go
to him, but he cannot come back to me."

24Then David comforted Bathsheba
his wife. He slept with her and had sexual
relations with her. She became pregnant
again and had another son, whom David
named Solomon. The LORD loved Solomon. **25**The LORD sent word through
Nathan the prophet to name the baby
Jedidiah,* because the LORD loved the
child.

David Captures Rabbah

26Joab fought against Rabbah, a royal
city of the Ammonites, and he was about
to capture it. **27**Joab sent messengers to
David and said, "I have fought against
Rabbah and have captured its water supply. **28**Now bring the other soldiers together and attack this city. Capture it
before I capture it myself and it is called
by my name!"

29So David gathered all the army and
went to Rabbah and fought against it and
captured it. **30**David took the crown off
their king's head and had it placed on his
own head. That gold crown weighed
about seventy-five pounds, and it had
valuable gems in it. And David took many
valuable things from the city. **31**He also
brought out the people of the city and
forced them to work with saws, iron
picks, and axes. He also made them build
with bricks. David did this to all the Ammonite cities. Then David and all his
army returned to Jerusalem.

Amnon and Tamar

13 David had a son named Absalom
and a son named Amnon. Absalom
had a beautiful sister named Tamar, and
Amnon loved her. **2**Tamar was a virgin.
Amnon made himself sick just thinking
about her, because he could not find any
chance to be alone with her.

3Amnon had a friend named Jonadab
son of Shimeah, David's brother. Jonadab
was a very clever man. **4**He asked Amnon,
"Son of the king, why do you look so sad
day after day? Tell me what's wrong!"

12:25 Jedidiah This name means "loved by the LORD."

Amnon told him, "I love Tamar, the
sister of my half-brother Absalom."
5Jonadab said to Amnon, "Go to bed
and act as if you are sick. Then your father will come to see you. Tell him,
'Please let my sister Tamar come in and
give me food to eat. Let her make the
food in front of me so I can watch and eat
it from her hand.' "
6So Amnon went to bed and acted
sick. When King David came in to see
him, Amnon said to him, "Please let my
sister Tamar come in. Let her make two
of her special cakes for me while I watch.
Then I will eat them from her hands."
7David sent for Tamar in the palace,
saying, "Go to your brother Amnon's
house and make some food for him." **8**So
Tamar went to her brother Amnon's
house, and he was in bed. Tamar took
some dough and pressed it together with
her hands. She made some special cakes
while Amnon watched. Then she baked
them. **9**Next she took the pan and served
him, but he refused to eat.

He said to his servants, "All of you,
leave me alone!" So they all left him
alone. **10**Amnon said to Tamar, "Bring
the food into the bedroom so I may eat
from your hand."

Tamar took the cakes she had made
and brought them to her brother Amnon
in the bedroom. **11**She went to him so he
could eat from her hands, but Amnon
grabbed her. He said, "Sister, come and
have sexual relations with me."
12Tamar said to him, "No, brother!
Don't force me! This should never be
done in Israel! Don't do this shameful
thing! **13**I could never get rid of my
shame! And you will be like the shameful
fools in Israel! Please talk with the king,
and he will let you marry me."
14But Amnon refused to listen to her.
He was stronger than she was, so he
forced her to have sexual relations with
him. **15**After that, Amnon hated Tamar.
He hated her more than he had loved her
before. Amnon said to her, "Get up and
leave!"
16Tamar said to him, "No! Sending
me away would be worse than what
you've already done!"

But he refused to listen to her. **17**He
called his young servant back in and said,
"Get this woman out of here and away
from me! Lock the door after her." **18**So
his servant led her out of the room and
bolted the door after her.

Tamar was wearing a special robe
with long sleeves, because the king's virgin daughters wore this kind of robe.
19To show how upset she was, Tamar put
ashes on her head and tore her special
robe and put her hand on her head. Then
she went away, crying loudly.
20Absalom, Tamar's brother, said to
her, "Has Amnon, your brother, forced
you to have sexual relations with him?
For now, sister, be quiet. He is your half-
brother. Don't let this upset you so
much!" So Tamar lived in her brother
Absalom's house and was sad and lonely.
21When King David heard the news,
he was very angry. **22**Absalom did not say
a word, good or bad, to Amnon. But he
hated Amnon for disgracing his sister
Tamar.

Absalom's Revenge

23Two years later Absalom had some
men come to Baal Hazor, near Ephraim,
to cut the wool from his sheep. Absalom
invited all the king's sons to come also.
24Absalom went to the king and said, "I
have men coming to cut the wool. Please
come with your officers and join me."
25King David said to Absalom, "No,
my son. We won't all go, because it would
be too much trouble for you." Although
Absalom begged David, he would not go,
but he did give his blessing.
26Absalom said, "If you don't want to
come, then please let my brother Amnon
come with us."

King David asked, "Why should he go
with you?"
27Absalom kept begging David until
he let Amnon and all the king's sons go
with Absalom.
28Then Absalom instructed his servants, "Watch Amnon. When he is drunk,
I will tell you, 'Kill Amnon.' Right then,
kill him! Don't be afraid, because I have
commanded you! Be strong and brave!"
29So Absalom's young men killed Amnon

as Absalom commanded, but all of
David's other sons got on their mules and
escaped.
30While the king's sons were on their
way, the news came to David, "Absalom
has killed all of the king's sons! Not one
of them is left alive!" **31**King David tore
his clothes and lay on the ground to show
his sadness. All his servants standing
nearby tore their clothes also.
32Jonadab son of Shimeah, David's
brother, said to David, "Don't think all the
young men, your sons, are killed. No, only
Amnon is dead! Absalom has planned this
ever since Amnon forced his sister Tamar
to have sexual relations with him. **33**My
master and king, don't think that all of
the king's sons are dead. Only Amnon is
dead!"
34In the meantime Absalom had run
away.
A guard standing on the city wall saw
many people coming from the other side
of the hill. **35**So Jonadab said to King David, "Look, I was right! The king's sons
are coming!"
36As soon as Jonadab had said this,
the king's sons arrived, crying loudly.
David and all his servants
began crying also. **37**David cried for his son every
day.
But Absalom ran away
to Talmai[n] son of Am-
mihud, the king of Ge-
shur. **38**After Absalom
ran away to Geshur, he
stayed there for three
years. **39**When King David got over Amnon's
death, he missed Absalom greatly.

David cried for his son every day.
—2 Samuel 13:37

Joab Sends a Wise Woman to David

14 Joab son of Zeruiah knew that King
David missed Absalom very much.
2So Joab sent messengers to Tekoa to
bring a wise woman from there. He said
to her, "Pretend to be very sad. Put on
funeral clothes and don't put lotion on
yourself. Act like a woman who has been
crying many days for someone who died.
3Then go to the king and say these
words." Then Joab told her what to say.
4So the woman from Tekoa spoke to
the king. She bowed facedown on the
ground to show respect and said, "My
king, help me!"
5King David asked her, "What is the
matter?"
The woman said, "I am a widow; my
husband is dead. **6**I had two sons. They
were out in the field fighting, and no one
was there to stop them. So one son killed
the other son. **7**Now all the family group
is against me. They said to me, 'Bring the
son who killed his brother so we may kill
him for killing his brother. That way we
will also get rid of the one who would receive what belonged to his father.' My
son is like the last spark of a fire. He is all
I have left. If they kill him, my husband's
name and property will be gone from the
earth."
8Then the king said to the woman, "Go
home. I will take care of this for you."
9The woman of Tekoa said to him,
"Let the blame be on me and my father's
family. My master and king, you and your
throne are innocent."
10King David said, "Bring me anyone
who says anything bad
to you. Then he won't
bother you again."
11The woman said,
"Please promise in the
name of the LORD your
God. Then my relative
who has the duty of pun-
ishing a murderer won't
add to the destruction by
killing my son."
David said, "As surely
as the LORD lives, no one will hurt your
son. Not one hair from his head will fall to
the ground."
12The woman said, "Let me say
something to you, my master and king."
The king said, "Speak."
13Then the woman said, "Why have
you decided this way against the people
of God? When you judge this way, you
show that you are guilty for not bringing
back your son who was forced to leave

13:37 Talmai He was Absalom's grandfather.

FAITH links

HELP TO UNDERSTAND

2 SAMUEL 14

Have you ever heard the phrase, "You can't see the forest for the trees"? That means you're so close to something you can't see it for what it is. Sometimes we can't see the forest for the trees about situations in life. King David couldn't understand the problems within his own family. A wise woman went to David with helpful advice.

Part of learning to listen to God is learning to listen to people who provide wise advice. God brings these people into your life to help you understand his truths. As you pay attention to what you hear, your faith will grow.

Surf these links to see how your faith can grow:

The Cloud Guide, Numbers 9:15–23, p. 188

Facts About Following, Joshua 6, p. 283

The Right Thing to Do, 1 Samuel 26, p. 391

Plan for Success, 1 Chronicles 14:8–17, p. 538

Like Silver, Psalm 12:6–8, p. 717

Just Like a Tree, Colossians 1:23, p. 1621

home. 14We will all die some day. We're
like water spilled on the ground; no one
can gather it back. But God doesn't take
away life. Instead, he plans ways that
those who have been sent away will not
have to stay away from him! 15My master and king, I came to say this to you because the people have made me afraid! I
thought, 'Let me talk to the king. Maybe
he will do what I ask. 16Maybe he will listen. Perhaps he will save me from those
who want to keep both me and my son
from getting what God gave us.'
17"Now I say, 'May the words of my
master the king give me rest. Like an angel of God, you know what is good and
what is bad. May the LORD your God be
with you!' "
18Then King David said, "Do not hide
the truth. Answer me one question."

The woman said, "My master the king, please ask your question."

19The king said, "Did Joab tell you to
say all these things?"

The woman answered, "As you live,
my master the king, no one could avoid
that question. You are right. Your servant
Joab did tell me to say these things.
20Joab did it so you would see things differently. My master, you are wise like an
angel of God who knows everything that
happens on earth."

Absalom Returns to Jerusalem

21The king said to Joab, "Look, I will
do what I promised. Bring back the young
man Absalom."
22Joab bowed facedown on the ground
and blessed the king. Then he said, "Today I know you are pleased with me, because you have done what I asked."
23Then Joab got up and went to Geshur and brought Absalom back to Jerusalem. 24But King David said, "Absalom
must go to his own house. He may not
come to see me." So Absalom went to his
own house and did not go to see the king.
25Absalom was greatly praised for his
handsome appearance. No man in Israel
was as handsome as he. No blemish was
on him from his head to his foot. 26At the
end of every year, Absalom would cut his
hair, because it became too heavy. When

he weighed it, it would weigh about five pounds by the royal measure.

27Absalom had three sons and one daughter. His daughter's name was also Tamar, and she was a beautiful woman.

28Absalom lived in Jerusalem for two full years without seeing King David. **29**Then Absalom sent for Joab so he could send him to the king, but Joab would not come. Absalom sent a message a second time, but Joab still refused to come. **30**Then Absalom said to his servants, "Look, Joab's field is next to mine, and he has barley growing there. Go burn it." So Absalom's servants set fire to Joab's field.

31Then Joab went to Absalom's house and said to him, "Why did your servants burn my field?"

32Absalom said to Joab, "I sent a message to you, asking you to come here. I wanted to send you to the king to ask him why he brought me home from Geshur. It would have been better for me to stay there! Now let me see the king. If I have sinned, he can put me to death!"

33So Joab went to the king and told him Absalom's words. Then the king called for Absalom. Absalom came and bowed facedown on the ground before the king, and the king kissed him.

Absalom Plans to Take David's Kingdom

15 After this, Absalom got a chariot and horses for himself and fifty men to run before him. **2**Absalom would get up early and stand near the city gate.[n] Anyone who had a problem for the king to settle would come here. When someone came, Absalom would call out and say, "What city are you from?"

The person would answer, "I'm from one of the tribes of Israel."

3Then Absalom would say, "Look, your claims are right, but the king has no one to listen to you." **4**Absalom would also say, "I wish someone would make me judge in this land! Then people with problems could come to me, and I could help them get justice."

5People would come near Absalom to bow to him. When they did, Absalom would reach out his hand and take hold of them and kiss them. **6**Absalom did that to all the Israelites who came to King David for decisions. In this way, Absalom stole the hearts of all Israel.

7After four years Absalom said to King David, "Please let me go to Hebron. I want to carry out my promise that I made to the LORD **8**while I was living in Geshur in Aram. I said, 'If the LORD takes me back to Jerusalem, I will worship him in Hebron.' "

9The king said, "Go in peace."

So Absalom went to Hebron. **10**But he sent secret messengers through all the tribes of Israel. They told the people, "When you hear the trumpets, say this: 'Absalom is the king at Hebron!' "

11Absalom had invited two hundred men to go with him. So they went from Jerusalem with him, but they didn't know what he was planning. **12**While Absalom was offering sacrifices, he sent for Ahithophel, one of the people who advised David, to come from his hometown of Giloh. So Absalom's plans were working very well. More and more people began to support him.

13A messenger came to David, saying, "The Israelites are giving their loyalty to Absalom."

14Then David said to all his officers who were with him in Jerusalem, "We must leave quickly! If we don't, we won't be able to get away from Absalom. We must hurry before he catches us and destroys us and kills the people of Jerusalem."

15The king's officers said to him, "We will do anything you say."

16The king set out with everyone in his house, but he left ten slave women to take care of the palace. **17**The king left with all his people following him, and they stopped at a house far away. **18**All the king's servants passed by him—the Kerethites and Pelethites,[n] all those from

---

15:2 city gate People came here to conduct business. Public meetings and court cases were also held here.

15:18 Kerethites and Pelethites These were probably special units of the army that were responsible for the king's safety, a kind of palace guard.

Gath, and the six hundred men who had followed him.

19The king said to Ittai, a man from Gath, "Why are you also going with us? Turn back and stay with King Absalom because you are a foreigner. This is not your homeland. **20**You joined me only a short time ago. Should I make you wander with us when I don't even know where I'm going? Turn back and take your brothers with you. May kindness and loyalty be shown to you."

21But Ittai said to the king, "As surely as the LORD lives and as you live, I will stay with you, whether it means life or death."

22David said to Ittai, "Go, march on." So Ittai from Gath and all his people with their children marched on. **23**All the people cried loudly as everyone passed by. King David crossed the Kidron Valley, and then all the people went on to the desert. **24**Zadok and all the Levites with him carried the Ark of the Agreement with God. They set it down, and Abiathar offered sacrifices until all the people had left the city.

25The king said to Zadok, "Take the Ark of God back into the city. If the LORD is pleased with me, he will bring me back and will let me see both it and Jerusalem again. **26**But if the LORD says he is not pleased with me, I am ready. He can do what he wants with me."

27The king also said to Zadok the priest, "Aren't you a seer? Go back to the city in peace and take your son Ahimaaz and Abiathar's son Jonathan with you. **28**I will wait near the crossings into the desert until I hear from you." **29**So Zadok and Abiathar took the Ark of God back to Jerusalem and stayed there.

30David went up the Mount of Olives, crying as he went. He covered his head and went barefoot. All the people with David covered their heads also and cried as they went. **31**Someone told David, "Ahithophel is one of the people with Absalom who made secret plans against you."

So David prayed, "LORD, please make Ahithophel's advice foolish."

32When David reached the top of the mountain where people used to worship God, Hushai the Arkite came to meet him. Hushai's coat was torn, and there was dirt on his head to show how sad he was. **33**David said to Hushai, "If you go with me, you will be just one more person for me to take care of. **34**But if you return to the city, you can make Ahithophel's advice useless. Tell Absalom, 'I am your servant, my king. In the past I served your father, but now I will serve you.' **35**The priests Zadok and Abiathar will be with you. Tell them everything you hear in the royal palace. **36**Zadok's son Ahimaaz and Abiathar's son Jonathan are with them. Send them to tell me everything you hear." **37**So David's friend Hushai entered Jerusalem just as Absalom arrived.

Ziba Meets David

16 When David had passed a short way over the top of the Mount of Olives, Ziba, Mephibosheth's servant, met him. Ziba had a row of donkeys loaded with two hundred loaves of bread, one hundred cakes of raisins, one hundred cakes of figs, and leather bags full of wine. **2**The king asked Ziba, "What are these things for?"

Ziba answered, "The donkeys are for your family to ride. The bread and cakes of figs are for the servants to eat. And the wine is for anyone to drink who might become weak in the desert."

3The king asked, "Where is Mephibosheth?"

Ziba answered him, "Mephibosheth is staying in Jerusalem because he thinks, 'Today the Israelites will give my father's kingdom back to me!'"

4Then the king said to Ziba, "All right. Everything that belonged to Mephibosheth, I now give to you!"

Ziba said, "I bow to you. I hope I will always be able to please you."

Shimei Curses David

5As King David came to Bahurim, a man came out and cursed him. He was from Saul's family group, and his name was Shimei son of Gera. **6**He threw stones at David and his officers, but the people and soldiers gathered all around

David. 7Shimei cursed David, saying,
"Get out, get out, you murderer, you
troublemaker. 8The LORD is punishing
you for the people in Saul's family you
killed! You took Saul's place as king, but
now the LORD has given the kingdom to
your son Absalom! Now
you are ruined because
you are a murderer!"
9Abishai son of Zeru-
iah said to the king, "Why
should this dead dog
curse you, the king? Let
me go over and cut off his
head!"
10But the king an-
swered, "This does not
concern you, sons of Zer-
uiah! If he is cursing me because the
LORD told him to, who can question him?"
11David also said to Abishai and all his
officers, "My own son is trying to kill me!
This man is a Benjaminite and has more
right to kill me! Leave him alone, and let
him curse me because the LORD told him
to do this. 12Maybe the LORD will see my
misery and repay me with something
good for Shimei's curses today!"
13So David and his men went on down
the road, but Shimei followed on the
nearby hillside. He kept cursing David
and throwing stones and dirt at him.
14When the king and all his people arrived at the Jordan, they were very tired,
so they rested there.
15Meanwhile, Absalom, Ahithophel,
and all the Israelites arrived at Jerusalem. 16David's friend Hushai the Arkite
came to Absalom and said to him, "Long
live the king! Long live the king!"
17Absalom asked, "Why are you not
loyal to your friend David? Why didn't
you leave Jerusalem with your friend?"
18Hushai said, "I belong to the one
chosen by the LORD and by these people
and everyone in Israel. I will stay with
you. 19In the past I served your father. So
whom should I serve now? David's son! I
will serve you as I served him."

> If he is cursing me because the LORD told him to, who can question him?
> —2 Samuel 16:10

Ahithophel's Advice

20Absalom said to Ahithophel, "Tell
us what we should do."
21Ahithophel said, "Your father left
behind some of his slave women to take
care of the palace. Have sexual relations
with them. Then all Israel will hear that
your father is your enemy, and all your
people will be encouraged to give you
more support." 22So they
put up a tent for Absalom
on the roof[n] of the palace
where everyone in Israel
could see it. And Absalom
had sexual relations with
his father's slave women.
23At that time people
thought Ahithophel's ad-
vice was as reliable as
God's own word. Both Da-
vid and Absalom thought
it was that reliable.

17 Ahithophel said to Absalom, "Let
me choose twelve thousand men
and chase David tonight. 2I'll catch him
while he is tired and weak, and I'll fright-
en him so all his people will run away. But
I'll kill only King David. 3Then I'll bring
everyone back to you. If the man you are
looking for is dead, everyone else will return safely." 4This plan seemed good to
Absalom and to all the leaders of Israel.
5But Absalom said, "Now call Hushai
the Arkite, so I can hear what he says."
6When Hushai came to Absalom, Absalom said to him, "This is the plan
Ahithophel gave. Should we follow it? If
not, tell us."
7Hushai said to Absalom, "Ahithophel's advice is not good this time."
8Hushai added, "You know your father
and his men are strong. They are as angry as a bear that is robbed of its cubs.
Your father is a skilled fighter. He won't
stay all night with the army. 9He is probably already hiding in a cave or some
other place. If the first attack fails, people
will hear the news and think, 'Absalom's
followers are losing!' 10Then even the
men who are as brave as lions will be
frightened, because all the Israelites

16:22 roof In Bible times houses were built with flat roofs. The roof was used for drying things such as flax and fruit. And it was used as an extra room, as a place for worship, and as a cool place to sleep in the summer.

know your father is a fighter. They know
his men are brave!
11"This is what I suggest: Gather all
the Israelites from Dan to Beersheba.ⁿ
There will be as many people as grains of
sand by the sea. Then you yourself must
go into the battle. 12We will go to David
wherever he is hiding. We will fall on him
as dew falls on the ground. We will kill
him and all of his men so that no one will
be left alive. 13If David escapes into a
city, all the Israelites will bring ropes to
that city and pull it into the valley. Not a
stone will be left!"
14Absalom and all the Israelites said,
"The advice of Hushai the Arkite is better than that of Ahithophel." (The LORD
had planned to destroy the good advice of
Ahithophel so the LORD could bring disaster on Absalom.)
15Hushai told Zadok and Abiathar, the
priests, what Ahithophel had suggested to
Absalom and the older leaders of Israel.
He also reported to them what he himself
had suggested. Hushai said, 16"Quickly!
Send a message to David. Tell him not
to stay tonight at the crossings into the

17:11 Dan to Beersheba Dan was the city farthest north in Israel, and Beersheba was the city farthest south. So this means all the people of Israel.

I CAN'T DO IT!

Hi, kids. Do you avoid trying something new because you're afraid it will be too hard? We've got a friend, Devon, age 9, who's having a problem just like that. Devon is struggling to develop a new skill, and it's not going very well. But let's let him tell you about it.

Piano lessons. I've been taking them for over a year now. My mom thinks I'm going to be a great musician someday, but I'm not. I'm terrible. Every other note I play is wrong. The piano is just too hard. I want to quit, but I don't know what to tell my mom. I guess I'll just tell her that I'll never be any good.

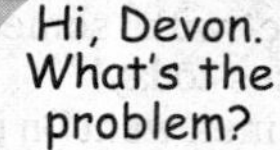

Hi, Devon. What's the problem?

Sounds like you're having a tough time, Devon. I wish I could tell you that your lessons will get easier, but I can't. What I can tell you is that your reward for sticking with them will be worth the work. Check out what Proverbs 13:4, p. 843, says about those who continue to work hard. Then take a look at the tips in the Livin' It page on the need to keep going when the going gets tough! (Check out Job 17:9, p. 679.)

Sticking with something is called perseverance. God likes it when we persevere. As a result, he makes all kinds of good things happen if we refuse to give up when things get tough.

desert but to cross over the Jordan River at once. If he crosses the river, he and all his people won't be destroyed."

17Jonathan and Ahimaaz were waiting at En Rogel. They did not want to be seen going into the city, so a servant girl would go out to them and give them messages. Then Jonathan and Ahimaaz would go and tell King David.

18But a boy saw Jonathan and Ahimaaz and told Absalom. So Jonathan and Ahimaaz left quickly and went to a man's house in Bahurim. He had a well in his courtyard, and they climbed down into it. 19The man's wife spread a sheet over the opening of the well and covered it with grain. No one could tell that anyone was hiding there.

20Absalom's servants came to the woman at the house and asked, "Where are Ahimaaz and Jonathan?"

She said to them, "They have already crossed the brook."

Absalom's servants then went to look for Jonathan and Ahimaaz, but they could not find them. So they went back to Jerusalem.

21After Absalom's servants left, Jonathan and Ahimaaz climbed out of the well and went to tell King David. They said, "Hurry, cross over the river! Ahithophel has said these things against you!" 22So David and all his people crossed the Jordan River. By dawn, everyone had crossed the Jordan.

23When Ahithophel saw that the Israelites did not accept his advice, he saddled his donkey and went to his hometown. He left orders for his family and property, and then he hanged himself. He died and was buried in his father's tomb.

War Between David and Absalom

24David arrived at Mahanaim. And Absalom and all his Israelites crossed over the Jordan River. 25Absalom had made Amasa captain of the army instead of Joab. Amasa was the son of a man named Jether the Ishmaelite. Amasa's mother was Abigail daughter of Nahash and sister of Zeruiah, Joab's mother. 26Absalom and the Israelites camped in the land of Gilead.

27Shobi, Makir, and Barzillai were at Mahanaim when David arrived. Shobi son of Nahash was from the Ammonite town of Rabbah. Makir son of Ammiel was from Lo Debar, and Barzillai was from Rogelim in Gilead. 28They brought beds, bowls, clay pots, wheat, barley, flour, roasted grain, beans, small peas, 29honey, milk curds, sheep, and cheese made from cows' milk for David and his people. They said, "The people are hungry and tired and thirsty in the desert."

18 David counted his men and placed over them commanders of thousands and commanders of hundreds. 2He sent the troops out in three groups. Joab commanded one-third of the men. Joab's brother Abishai son of Zeruiah commanded another third. And Ittai from Gath commanded the last third. King David said to them, "I will also go with you."

3But the men said, "You must not go with us! If we run away in the battle, Absalom's men won't care. Even if half of us are killed, Absalom's men won't care. But you're worth ten thousand of us! You can help us most by staying in the city."

4The king said to his people, "I will do what you think is best." So the king stood at the side of the gate as the army went out in groups of a hundred and a thousand.

5The king commanded Joab, Abishai, and Ittai, "Be gentle with young Absalom for my sake." Everyone heard the king's orders to the commanders about Absalom.

6David's army went out into the field against Absalom's Israelites, and they fought in the forest of Ephraim. 7There David's army defeated the Israelites. Many died that day—twenty thousand men. 8The battle spread through all the country, but that day more men died in the forest than in the fighting.

Absalom Dies

9Then Absalom happened to meet David's troops. As Absalom was riding his mule, it went under the thick branches of a large oak tree. Absalom's head got caught in the tree, and his mule

ran out from under him. So Absalom was
left hanging above the ground.
10When one of the men saw it happen,
he told Joab, "I saw Absalom hanging in
an oak tree!"
11Joab said to him, "You saw him?
Why didn't you kill him and let him fall to
the ground? I would have given you a belt
and four ounces of silver!"
12The man answered, "I wouldn't
touch the king's son even if you gave me
twenty-five pounds of silver. We heard
the king command you, Abishai, and Ittai,
'Be careful not to hurt young Absalom.'
13If I had killed him, the king would have
found out, and you would not have protected me!"
14Joab said, "I won't waste time here
with you!" Absalom was still alive in the
oak tree, so Joab took three spears and
stabbed him in the heart. **15**Ten young
men who carried Joab's armor also gathered around Absalom and struck him and
killed him.
16Then Joab blew the trumpet, so the
troops stopped chasing the Israelites.
17Then Joab's men took Absalom's body
and threw it into a large pit in the forest
and filled the pit with many stones. All
the Israelites ran away to their homes.
18When Absalom was alive, he had
set up a pillar for himself in the King's
Valley. He said, "I have no son to keep my
name alive." So he named the pillar after
himself, and it is called Absalom's Monument even today.
19Ahimaaz son of Zadok said to Joab,
"Let me run and take the news to King
David. I'll tell him the LORD has saved
him from his enemies."
20Joab answered Ahimaaz, "No, you
are not the one to take the news today.
You may do it another time, but do not
take it today, because the king's son is
dead."
21Then Joab said to a man from Cush,
"Go, tell the king what you have seen."
The Cushite bowed to Joab and ran to tell
David.
22But Ahimaaz son of Zadok begged
Joab again, "No matter what happens,
please let me go along with the Cushite!"
Joab said, "Son, why do you want to
carry the news? You won't get any reward."
23Ahimaaz answered, "No matter
what happens, I will run."
So Joab said to Ahimaaz, "Run!" Then
Ahimaaz ran by way of the Jordan Valley
and passed the Cushite.
24David was sitting between the inner and outer gates of the city. The
watchman went up to the roof of the gate
by the walls, and as he looked up, he saw
a man running alone. **25**He shouted the
news to the king.
The king said, "If he is alone, he is
bringing good news!"
The man came nearer and nearer to
the city. **26**Then the watchman saw another man running, and he called to the
gatekeeper, "Look! Another man is running alone!"
The king said, "He is also bringing
good news!"
27The watchman said, "I think the
first man runs like Ahimaaz son of Zadok."
The king said, "Ahimaaz is a good
man. He must be bringing good news!"
28Then Ahimaaz called a greeting to
the king. He bowed facedown on the
ground before the king and said, "Praise
the LORD your God! The LORD has defeated those who were against you, my
king."
29The king asked, "Is young Absalom
all right?"
Ahimaaz answered, "When Joab sent
me, I saw some great excitement, but I
don't know what it was."
30The king said, "Step over here and
wait." So Ahimaaz stepped aside and
stood there.
31Then the Cushite arrived. He said,
"Master and king, hear the good news!
Today the LORD has punished those who
were against you!"
32The king asked the Cushite, "Is
young Absalom all right?"
The Cushite answered, "May your
enemies and all who come to hurt you be
like that young man!"
33Then the king was very upset, and
he went to the room over the city gate
and cried. As he went, he cried out, "My
son Absalom, my son Absalom! I wish I

had died and not you. Absalom, my son,
my son!"

Joab Scolds David

19 People told Joab, "Look, the king
is sad and crying because of Absalom." 2David's army had won the battle
that day. But it became a very sad day for
all the people, because they heard that
the king was very sad for his son. 3The
people came into the city quietly that day.
They were like an army that had been
defeated in battle and had run away. 4The
king covered his face and cried loudly,
"My son Absalom! Absalom, my son, my
son!"

5Joab went into the king's house and
said, "Today you have shamed all your
men. They saved your life and the lives of
your sons, daughters, wives, and slave
women. 6You have shamed them because
you love those who hate you, and you
hate those who love you. Today you have
made it clear that your commanders and
men mean nothing to you. What if Absalom had lived and all of us were dead?
I can see you would be pleased.
7Now go out and en-
courage your ser-
vants. I swear by
the LORD that if you
don't go out, no man
will be left with you
by tonight! That will
be worse than all the troubles you have
had from your youth until today."

EMAIL FROM GOD 19:7
Comfort
Does God want you to comfort others?

8So the king went to the city gate.[n]
When the news spread that the king was
at the gate, everyone came to see him.

David Goes Back to Jerusalem

All the Israelites who had followed
Absalom had run away to their homes.
9People in all the tribes of Israel began to
argue, saying, "The king saved us from
the Philistines and our other enemies,
but he left the country because of Absalom. 10We appointed Absalom to rule us,
but now he has died in battle. We should
make David the king again."

11King David sent a message to Zadok and Abiathar, the priests, that said,
"Speak to the older leaders of Judah. Say,
'Even in my house I have heard what all
the Israelites are saying. So why are you
the last tribe to bring the king back to his
palace? 12You are my brothers, my own
family. Why are you the last tribe to bring
back the king?' 13And say to Amasa, 'You
are part of my own family. May God punish me terribly if I don't make you commander of the army in Joab's place!' "

14David touched the hearts of all the
people of Judah at once. They sent a message to the king that said, "Return with
all your men." 15Then the king returned
as far as the Jordan River. The men of Judah came to Gilgal to meet him and to
bring him across the Jordan.

16Shimei son of Gera, a Benjaminite
who lived in Bahurim, hurried down with
the men of Judah to meet King David.
17With Shimei came a thousand Benjaminites. Ziba, the servant from Saul's
family, also came, bringing his fifteen
sons and twenty servants with him. They
all hurried to the Jordan River to meet
the king. 18The people went across the
Jordan to help bring the king's family
back to Judah and to do whatever the king
wanted. As the king was crossing the
river, Shimei son of Gera came to him and
bowed facedown on the ground in front of
the king. 19He said to the king, "My master, don't hold me guilty. Don't remember
the wrong I did when you left Jerusalem!
Don't hold it against me. 20I know I have
sinned. That is why I am the first person
from Joseph's family to come down and
meet you today, my master and king!"

21But Abishai son of Zeruiah said,
"Shimei should die because he cursed
you, the LORD's appointed king!"

22David said, "This does not concern
you, sons of Zeruiah! Today you're against
me! No one will be put to death in Israel
today. Today I know I am king over Israel!" 23Then the king promised Shimei,
"You won't die."

24Mephibosheth, Saul's grandson,
also went down to meet King David. Mephibosheth had not cared for his feet, cut

19:8 city gate People came here to conduct business. Public meetings and court cases were also held here.

his beard, or washed his clothes from the
time the king had left Jerusalem until he
returned safely. 25When Mephibosheth
came from Jerusalem to meet the king,
the king asked him, "Mephibosheth, why
didn't you go with me?"

26He answered, "My master, my servant Ziba tricked me! I said to Ziba, 'I am
crippled, so saddle a donkey. Then I will
ride it so I can go with the king.' 27But he
lied about me to you. You, my master and
king, are like an angel from God. Do what
you think is good. 28You could have
killed all my grandfather's family. Instead, you put me with those people who
eat at your own table. So I don't have a
right to ask anything more from the
king!"

29The king said to him, "Don't say
anything more. I have decided that you
and Ziba will divide the land."

30Mephibosheth said to the king,
"Let Ziba take all the land now that my
master the king has arrived safely
home."

31Barzillai of Gilead came down from
Rogelim to cross the Jordan River with
the king. 32Barzillai was a very old man,
eighty years old. He had taken care of the
king when David was staying at Mahanaim, because Barzillai was a very rich
man. 33David said to
Barzillai, "Cross the
river with me. Come
with me to Jerusa-
lem, and I will take
care of you."

EMAIL FROM GOD
19:33
Friendship
How should you care for your friends?

34But Barzillai
answered the king, "Do you know how
old I am? Do you think I can go with you
to Jerusalem? 35I am eighty years old! I
am too old to taste what I eat or drink. I
am too old to hear the voices of men and
women singers. Why should you be bothered with me? 36I am not worthy of a reward from you, but I will cross the Jordan
River with you. 37Then let me go back so
I may die in my own city near the grave of
my father and mother. But here is Kimham, your servant. Let him go with you,
my master and king. Do with him whatever you want."

38The king answered, "Kimham will
go with me. I will do for him anything you
wish, and I will do anything for you that
you wish." 39The king kissed Barzillai
and blessed him. Then Barzillai returned
home, and the king and all the people
crossed the Jordan.

40When the king crossed over to Gilgal, Kimham went with him. All the
troops of Judah and half the troops of Israel led David across the river.

41Soon all the Israelites came to the
king and said to him, "Why did our relatives, the people of Judah, steal you
away? Why did they bring you and your
family across the Jordan River with your
men?"

42All the people of Judah answered
the Israelites, "We did this because the
king is our close relative. Why are you
angry about it? We have not eaten food at
the king's expense or taken anything for
ourselves!"

43The Israelites answered the people
of Judah, "We have ten tribes in the kingdom, so we have more right to David than
you do! But you ignored us! We were the
first ones to talk about bringing our king
back!"

But the people of Judah spoke even
more unkindly than the people of Israel.

Sheba Leads Israel Away from David

20 It happened that a troublemaker
named Sheba son of Bicri from the
tribe of Benjamin was there. He blew the
trumpet and said:

"We have no share in David!
We have no part in the son of
Jesse!
People of Israel, let's go home!"

2So all the Israelites left David and
followed Sheba son of Bicri. But the people of Judah stayed with their king all the
way from the Jordan River to Jerusalem.

3David came back to his palace in Jerusalem. He had left ten of his slave
women there to take care of the palace.
Now he put them in a locked house. He
gave them food, but he did not have sexual relations with them. So they lived like
widows until they died.

4The king said to Amasa, "Tell the

men of Judah to meet with me in three
days, and you must also be here." 5So
Amasa went to call the men of Judah together, but he took more time than the
king had said.
6David said to Abishai, "Sheba son of
Bicri is more dangerous to us than Absalom was. Take my men and chase him before he finds walled cities and escapes
from us." 7So Joab's men, the Kerethites
and the Pelethites,[n] and all the soldiers
went with Abishai. They went out from
Jerusalem to chase Sheba son of Bicri.
8When Joab and the army came to the
great rock at Gibeon, Amasa came out to
meet them. Joab was wearing his uniform, and at his waist he wore a belt that
held his sword in its case. As Joab
stepped forward, his sword fell out of its
case. 9Joab asked Amasa, "Brother, is
everything all right with you?" Then with
his right hand he took Amasa by the
beard to kiss him. 10Amasa was not
watching the sword in Joab's hand. So
Joab pushed the sword into Amasa's
stomach, causing Amasa's insides to spill
onto the ground. Joab did not have to stab
Amasa again; he was already dead. Then
Joab and his brother Abishai continued to
chase Sheba son of Bicri.
11One of Joab's young men stood by
Amasa's body and said, "Everyone who is
for Joab and David should follow Joab!"
12Amasa lay in the middle of the road,
covered with his own blood. When the
young man saw that everyone was stopping to look at the body, he dragged it
from the road, laid it in a field, and put a
cloth over it. 13After Amasa's body was
taken off the road, all the men followed
Joab to chase Sheba son of Bicri.
14Sheba went through all the tribes of
Israel to Abel Beth Maacah. All the Be-
rites also came together and followed him.
15So Joab and his men came to Abel Beth
Maacah and surrounded it. They piled dirt
up against the city wall, and they began
hacking at the walls to bring them down.
16But a wise woman shouted out from
the city, "Listen! Listen! Tell Joab to
come here. I want to talk to him!"
17So Joab came near her. She asked
him, "Are you Joab?"
He answered, "Yes, I am."
Then she said, "Listen to what I say."
Joab said, "I'm listening."
18Then the woman said, "In the past
people would say, 'Ask for advice at Abel,'
and the problem would be solved. 19I am
one of the peaceful, loyal people of Israel.
You are trying to destroy an important
city of Israel. Why must you destroy what
belongs to the LORD?"
20Joab answered, "I would prefer not
to destroy or ruin anything! 21That is not
what I want. But there is a man here from
the mountains of Ephraim, who is named
Sheba son of Bicri. He has turned against
King David. If you bring him to me, I will
leave the city alone."
The woman said to Joab, "His head
will be thrown over the wall to you."
22Then the woman spoke very wisely
to all the people of the city. They cut off
the head of Sheba son of Bicri and threw
it over the wall to Joab. So he blew the
trumpet, and the army left the city. Every
man returned home, and Joab went back
to the king in Jerusalem.
23Joab was commander of all the army
of Israel. Benaiah son of Jehoiada led the
Kerethites and Pelethites. 24Adoniram
was in charge of the men who were
forced to do hard work. Jehoshaphat son
of Ahilud was the recorder. 25Sheba was
the royal secretary. Zadok and Abiathar
were the priests, 26and Ira the Jairite
was David's priest.

The Gibeonites Punish Saul's Family

21 During the time David was king,
there was a shortage of food that
lasted for three years. So David prayed to
the LORD.
The LORD answered, "Saul and his
family of murderers are the reason for
this shortage, because he killed the Gibeonites." 2(Now the Gibeonites were not
Israelites; they were a group of Amorites
who were left alive. The Israelites had

20:7 Kerethites and Pelethites These were probably special units of the army that were responsible for the king's safety, a kind of palace guard.

promised not to hurt the Gibeonites, but
Saul had tried to kill them, because he
was eager to help the people of Israel and
Judah.)

King David called the Gibeonites together and spoke to them. 3He asked,
"What can I do for you? How can I make
up for the harm done so you can bless the
LORD's people?"

4The Gibeonites said to David, "We
cannot demand silver or gold from Saul
or his family. And we don't have the right
to kill anyone in Israel."

Then David asked, "What do you want
me to do for you?"

FAITH CHALLENGE

Try this one. Read 21:7 to find out how David kept a promise to his friend. How far would you be willing to go to keep a promise to one of your friends?

TESTING IT

2 Samuel 21:7
But the king protected Mephibosheth, the son of Jonathan, the son of Saul, because of the promise he had made to Jonathan in the LORD's name.

5The Gibeonites said, "Saul made
plans against us and tried to destroy all
our people who are left in the land of Israel. 6So bring seven of his sons to us.
Then we will kill them and hang them on
stakes in the presence of the LORD at
Gibeah, the hometown of Saul, the
LORD's chosen king."

The king said, "I will give them to
you." 7But the king protected Mephibosheth, the son of Jonathan, the son of
Saul, because of the promise he had made
to Jonathan in the LORD's name. 8The
king did take Armoni and Mephibosheth,*
sons of Rizpah and Saul. (Rizpah was the
daughter of Aiah.) And the king took the
five sons of Saul's daughter Merab.
(Adriel son of Barzillai the Meholathite
was the father of Merab's five sons.) 9Da-
vid gave these seven sons to the Gibeonites. Then the Gibeonites killed them and
hung them on stakes on a hill in the presence of the LORD. All seven sons died together. They were put to death during
the first days of the harvest season at the
beginning of barley harvest.

10Aiah's daughter Rizpah took the
rough cloth that was worn to show sadness and put it on a rock for herself. She
stayed there from the beginning of the
harvest until the rain fell on her sons'
bodies. During the day she did not let the
birds of the sky touch her sons' bodies,
and during the night she did not let the
wild animals touch them.

11People told David what Aiah's
daughter Rizpah, Saul's slave woman, was
doing. 12Then David took the bones of
Saul and Jonathan from the men of Jabesh
Gilead. (The Philistines had hung the bodies of Saul and Jonathan in the public
square of Beth Shan after they had killed
Saul at Gilboa. Later the men of Jabesh
Gilead had secretly taken them from
there.) 13David brought the bones of Saul
and his son Jonathan from Gilead. Then
the people gathered the bodies of Saul's
seven sons who were hanged on stakes.
14The people buried the bones of Saul and
his son Jonathan at Zela in Benjamin in the

21:8 Mephibosheth This is not Jonathan's son but another man with the same name.

tomb of Saul's father Kish. The people did everything the king commanded.

Then God answered the prayers for the land.

Wars with the Philistines

15Again there was war between the
Philistines and Israel. David and his men
went out to fight the Philistines, but David became tired. **16**Ishbi-Benob, one of
the sons of Rapha, had a bronze spear-
head weighing about seven and one-half
pounds and a new sword. He planned to
kill David, **17**but Abishai son of Zeruiah
killed the Philistine and saved David's
life.

Then David's men made a promise to him, saying, "Never again will you go out with us to battle. If you were killed, Israel would lose its greatest leader."

18Later, at Gob, there was another battle with the Philistines. Sibbecai the Hushathite killed Saph, another one of the sons of Rapha.

19Later, there was another battle at Gob with the Philistines. Elhanan son of Jaare-Oregim from Bethlehem killed Goliath[n] from Gath. His spear was as large as a weaver's rod.

20At Gath another battle took place. A
huge man was there; he had six fingers
on each hand and six toes on each foot—
twenty-four fingers and toes in all. This
man also was one of the sons of Rapha.
21When he challenged Israel, Jonathan
son of Shimeah, David's brother, killed
him.

22These four sons of Rapha from Gath were killed by David and his men.

David's Song of Praise

22 David sang this song to the LORD when the LORD saved him from Saul and all his other enemies. **2**He said:

"The LORD is my
rock, my
protection,
my Savior.

EMAIL! FROM GOD
22:2
Salvation
Who will save you?

3My God is my
rock.
I can run to
him for safety.
He is my shield and my saving
strength,
my defender and my place of
safety.
The LORD saves me from those
who want to harm me.
4I will call to the LORD, who is worthy
of praise,
and I will be saved from my
enemies.

5"The waves of death came around me;
the deadly rivers overwhelmed me.
6The ropes of death wrapped around
me.
The traps of death were before me.
7In my trouble I called to the LORD;
I cried out to my God.
From his temple he heard my voice;
my call for help reached his ears.

8"The earth trembled and shook.
The foundations of heaven began
to shake.
They trembled because the LORD
was angry.
9Smoke came out of his nose,
and burning fire came out of his
mouth.
Burning coals went before him.
10He tore open the sky and came down
with dark clouds under his feet.
11He rode a creature with wings and
flew.
He raced on the wings of the wind.
12He made darkness his shelter,
surrounded by fog and clouds.
13Out of the brightness of his presence
came flashes of lightning.
14The LORD thundered from heaven;
the Most High raised his voice.
15He shot his arrows and scattered his
enemies.
His bolts of lightning confused
them with fear.
16The LORD spoke strongly.
The wind blew from his nose.
Then the valleys of the sea appeared,
and the foundations of the earth
were seen.

21:19 Goliath In 1 Chronicles 20:5 he is called Lahmi, brother of Goliath.

17 "The LORD reached down from above
and took me;
he pulled me from the deep water.
18 He saved me from my powerful
enemies,
from those who hated me, because
they were too strong for me.
19 They attacked me at my time of
trouble,
but the LORD supported me.
20 He took me to a safe place.
Because he delights in me, he
saved me.

21 "The LORD spared me because I did
what was right.
Because I have not done evil, he
has rewarded me.
22 I have followed the ways of the
LORD;
I have not done evil by turning
from my God.
23 I remember all his laws
and have not broken his rules.
24 I am innocent before him;
I have kept myself from doing evil.
25 The LORD rewarded me because I did
what was right,
because I did what the LORD said
was right.

26 "LORD, you are loyal to those who
are loyal,
and you are good to those who are
good.
27 You are pure to those who are pure,
but you are against those who are
evil.
28 You save the humble,
but you bring down those who are
proud.
29 LORD, you give light to my lamp.
The LORD brightens the darkness
around me.
30 With your help I can attack an army.
With God's help I can jump over a
wall.

31 "The ways of God are without fault;
the LORD's words are pure.
He is a shield to those who trust him.
32 Who is God? Only the LORD.
Who is the Rock? Only our God.
33 God is my protection.
He makes my way free from fault.
34 He makes me like a deer that does
not stumble;
he helps me stand on the steep
mountains.
35 He trains my hands for battle
so my arms can bend a bronze bow.
36 You protect me with your saving
shield.
You have stooped to make me
great.
37 You give me a better way to live,
so I live as you want me to.
38 I chased my enemies and destroyed
them.
I did not quit till they were
destroyed.
39 I destroyed and crushed them
so they couldn't rise up again.
They fell beneath my feet.
40 You gave me strength in battle.
You made my enemies bow before
me.
41 You made my enemies turn back,
and I destroyed those who hated
me.
42 They called for help,
but no one came to save them.
They called to the LORD,
but he did not answer them.
43 I beat my enemies into pieces,
like dust on the ground.
I poured them out and walked on
them
like mud in the streets.

44 "You saved me when my people
attacked me.
You kept me as the leader of
nations.
People I never knew serve me.
45 Foreigners obey me.
As soon as they hear me, they
obey me.
46 They all become
afraid
and tremble in
their hiding
places.

EMAIL FROM GOD

22:47–48
Salvation
Why should you praise God?

47 "The LORD lives!
May my Rock be praised!

Praise God, the Rock, who saves me!
48 God gives me victory over my enemies
and brings people under my rule.
49 He frees me from my enemies.

"You set me over those who hate me.
You saved me from cruel men.
50 So I will praise you, LORD, among the nations.
I will sing praises to your name.
51 The LORD gives great victories to his king.
He is loyal to his appointed king,
to David and his descendants forever."

David's Last Words

23 These are the last words of David.

This is the message of David son of Jesse.
The man made great by the Most High God speaks.
He is the appointed king of the God of Jacob;
he is the sweet singer of Israel:

Whoever rules fairly over people, who rules with respect for God, is like the morning light at dawn.
—2 Samuel 23:3–4

2 "The LORD's Spirit spoke through me,
and his word was on my tongue.
3 The God of Israel spoke;
the Rock of Israel said to me:
'Whoever rules fairly over people,
who rules with respect for God,
4 is like the morning light at dawn,
like a morning without clouds.
He is like sunshine after a rain
that makes the grass sprout from the ground.'

EMAIL FROM GOD 23:5
God
Does God keep his promises?

5 "This is how God has cared for my family.
God made a lasting agreement with me,
right and sure in every way.
He will accomplish my salvation
and satisfy all my desires.

6 "But all evil people will be thrown away like thorns
that cannot be held in a hand.
7 No one can touch them
except with a tool of iron or wood.
They will be thrown in the fire and burned where they lie."

David's Army

8 These are the names of David's warriors:
Josheb-Basshebeth, the Tahkemonite,
was head of the Three.* He killed eight
hundred men at one time.
9 Next was Eleazar son of Dodai the
Ahohite. Eleazar was one of the three soldiers who were with David when they
challenged the Philistines. The Philistines were gathered for battle, and the Israelites drew back. 10 But
Eleazar stayed where he
was and fought the Philistines until he was so tired
his hand stuck to his
sword. The LORD gave a
great victory for the Israelites that day. The troops
came back after Eleazar
had won the battle, but
only to take weapons and
armor from the enemy.
11 Next there was Shammah son of
Agee the Hararite. The Philistines came
together to fight in a vegetable field.
Israel's troops ran away from the Philistines, 12 but Shammah stood in the middle
of the field and fought for it and killed the
Philistines. And the LORD gave a great
victory.
13 Once, three of the Thirty, David's
chief soldiers, came down to him at the
cave of Adullam during harvest. The Philistine army had camped in the Valley of
Rephaim. 14 At that time David was in the
stronghold, and some of the Philistines
were in Bethlehem.

23:8 Three These were David's most powerful soldiers. See 1 Chronicles 11:11.

15David had a strong desire for some
water. He said, "Oh, I wish someone
would get me water from the well near
the city gate of Bethlehem!" 16So the
three warriors broke through the Philistine army and took water from the well
near the city gate of Bethlehem. Then
they brought it to David, but he refused
to drink it. He poured it out before the
LORD, 17saying, "May the LORD keep me
from drinking this water! It would be like
drinking the blood of the men who risked
their lives!" So David refused to drink it.
These were the brave things that the
three warriors did.

18Abishai, brother of Joab son of Zeruiah, was captain of the Three. Abishai
fought three hundred soldiers with his
spear and killed them. He became as famous as the Three 19and was more honored than the Three. He became their
commander even though he was not one
of them.

20Benaiah son of Jehoiada was a brave
fighter from Kabzeel who did mighty
things. He killed two of the best warriors
from Moab. He also went down into a pit
and killed a lion on a snowy day. 21Bena-
iah killed a large Egyptian who had a
spear in his hand. Benaiah had a club, but
he grabbed the spear from the Egyptian's
hand and killed him with his own spear.
22These were the things Benaiah son of
Jehoiada did. He was as famous as the
Three. 23He received more honor than
the Thirty, but he did not become a member of the Three. David made him leader
of his bodyguards.

The Thirty Chief Soldiers

24The following men were among the
Thirty:

Asahel brother of Joab;
Elhanan son of Dodo from Bethlehem;
25 Shammah the Harodite;
Elika the Harodite;
26 Helez the Paltite;
Ira son of Ikkesh from Tekoa;
27 Abiezer the Anathothite;
Mebunnai the Hushathite;
28 Zalmon the Ahohite;
Maharai the Netophathite;
29 Heled son of Baanah the Netophathite;
Ithai son of Ribai from Gibeah in Benjamin;
30 Benaiah the Pirathonite;
Hiddai from the ravines of Gaash;
31 Abi-Albon the Arbathite;
Azmaveth the Barhumite;
32 Eliahba the Shaalbonite;
the sons of Jashen;
Jonathan 33son of Shammah the Hararite;
Ahiam son of Sharar the Hararite;
34 Eliphelet son of Ahasbai the Maacathite;
Eliam son of Ahithophel the Gilonite;
35 Hezro the Carmelite;
Paarai the Arbite;
36 Igal son of Nathan of Zobah;
the son of Hagri;
37 Zelek the Ammonite;
Naharai the Beerothite, who carried the armor of Joab son of Zeruiah;
38 Ira the Ithrite;
Gareb the Ithrite,
39 and Uriah the Hittite.

There were thirty-seven in all.

David Counts His Army

24 The LORD was angry with Israel
again, and he caused David to turn
against the Israelites. He said, "Go,
count the people of Israel and Judah."

2So King David said to Joab, the commander of the army, "Go through all the
tribes of Israel, from Dan to Beersheba,"
and count the people. Then I will know
how many there are."

3But Joab said to the king, "May the
LORD your God give you a hundred times
more people, and may my master the
king live to see this happen. Why do you
want to do this?"

24:2 Dan to Beersheba Dan was the city farthest north in Israel, and Beersheba was the city farthest south. So this means all the people of Israel.

4But the king commanded Joab and
the commanders of the army, so they left
the king to count the Israelites.
5After crossing the Jordan River, they
camped near Aroer on the south side of
the city in the ravine. They went through
Gad and on to Jazer. 6Then they went to
Gilead and the land of Tahtim Hodshi and
to Dan Jaan and around to Sidon. 7They
went to the strong, walled city of Tyre
and to all the cities of the Hivites and Canaanites. Finally, they went to southern
Judah, to Beersheba. 8After nine months
and twenty days, they had gone through
all the land. Then they came back to Jerusalem.
9Joab gave the list of the people to the
king. There were eight hundred thousand men in Israel who could use the
sword and five hundred thousand men in
Judah.
10David felt ashamed after he had
counted the people. He said to the LORD,
"I have sinned greatly by what I have
done. LORD, I beg you to forgive me, your
servant, because I have been very foolish."
11When David got up in the morning,
the LORD spoke his word to Gad, who
was a prophet and David's seer. 12The
LORD told Gad, "Go and tell David, 'This
is what the LORD says: I offer you three
choices. Choose one of them and I will do
it to you.' "
13So Gad went to David and said to
him, "Should three years of hunger come
to you and your land? Or should your enemies chase you for three months? Or
should there be three days of disease in
your land? Think about it. Then decide
which of these things I should tell the
LORD who sent me."
14David said to Gad, "I am in great
trouble. Let the LORD punish us, because
the LORD is very merciful. Don't let my
punishment come from human beings!"
15So the LORD sent a terrible disease
on Israel. It began in the morning and
continued until the chosen time to stop.
From Dan to Beersheba seventy thousand people died. 16When the angel
raised his arm toward Jerusalem to destroy it, the LORD felt very sorry about
the terrible things that had happened. He
said to the angel who was destroying the
people, "That is enough! Put down your
arm!" The angel of the LORD was
then by the threshing
floor of Araunah the
Jebusite.

EMAIL FROM GOD
24:16–17
Angels
This angel has a terrible job.

17When David saw
the angel that killed
the people, he said to
the LORD, "I am the
one who sinned and did wrong. These
people only followed me like sheep. They
did nothing wrong. Please punish me and
my family."
18That day Gad came to David and
said, "Go and build an altar to the LORD
on the threshing floor of Araunah the Jebusite." 19So David did what Gad told him
to do, just as the LORD commanded.
20Araunah looked and saw the king
and his servants coming to him. So he
went out and bowed facedown on the
ground before the king. 21He said, "Why
has my master the king come to me?"
David answered, "To buy the threshing floor from you so I can build an altar
to the LORD. Then the terrible disease
will stop."
22Araunah said to David, "My master
and king, you may take anything you
want for a sacrifice. Here are some oxen
for the whole burnt offering and the
threshing boards and the yokes for the
wood. 23My king, I give everything to
you." Araunah also said to the king, "May
the LORD your God be pleased with you."
24But the king answered Araunah,
"No, I will pay you for the land. I won't
offer to the LORD my God burnt offerings
that cost me nothing."
So David bought the threshing floor
and the oxen for one and one-fourth
pounds of silver. 25He built an altar to the
LORD there and offered whole burnt offerings and fellowship offerings. Then
the LORD answered his prayer for the
country, and the disease in Israel
stopped.

GIVE ME WISDOM

Hello. My name is Jeremiah, and I am a prophet of God. Have you ever heard of King Solomon, the one who asked God for wisdom? God was so pleased with his request that he made Solomon wiser than anyone else on earth and gave him fabulous riches as well. In gratitude, Solomon built the Temple of the Lord, which was the center of worship for the whole nation of Israel. Check out the details of the Temple in 1 Kings 6. Even the floors were covered with gold!

I wrote this book to tell the history of King Solomon and the kings who came after him. When Solomon died, his kingdom was split into two nations, Israel and Judah. The kings of both nations led the people into worshiping false gods, so God sent prophets to tell people about the true God. Don't miss the story of the famous contest on Mount Carmel between Elijah, the prophet of God, and 450 prophets of Baal. Log onto 1 Kings 18 for the awesome way God answered Elijah's prayer.

JESUS WATCH

In many ways Solomon reminds us of Jesus. Solomon was well known for his wisdom. People came from all over to hear him speak. Jesus, too, was known for wisdom. People followed Jesus all over the country, listening to him talk about God. Solomon, however, was not always wise. He married many foreign women and toward the end of his life, he started to follow their false gods. Jesus is always wise, pointing the way to the true God. Solomon's reign was a time of peace because Israel was strong and Solomon was skillful in diplomacy. When Solomon died, the peaceful time ended, and the kingdom split into two countries. Because Jesus took our punishment for the sin that separates us from God, our peace with God will never end. The magnificence of the Temple is a picture of the splendor of heaven where we will worship God forever.

my FAVORITE links

OTHER CONNECTIONS

Find out more about the many adventures and struggles Elijah encountered during his ministry in the Northern Kingdom of Israel by connecting to Elijah, the Prophet, 1 Kings 18.

MORE STUFF...

What a miracle! The story of Elijah, one of the most famous prophets in the Old Testament, is filled with miracles. Here are just a few you can read about:

- Elijah predicted there would be a drought in the land (1 Kings 17:1).
- Elijah helped a widow and her son survive the drought by providing through God's power a never-ending supply of flour and oil (1 Kings 17:10–16).
- Elijah was used by God to bring the widow's son back to life after he had died from an illness (1 Kings 17:17–24).
- Elijah was God's representative in a battle between him and the prophets of the idols Baal and Asherah (1 Kings 18:18–40).

"Here's one for you, Tagg. Why did Solomon tell his servants to cut the baby in two?"

"Yikes! That doesn't sound very wise to me. We'd better surf over to 1 Kings 3:16-28 to find out."

DON'T MISS THESE HOT SITES:

Give me wisdom!, 1 Kings 3:4–15
The queen of Sheba, 1 Kings 10:1–13
Air-express food, 1 Kings 17:1–6
The boy who came back to life, 1 Kings 17:17–24
Running on God's power, 1 Kings 18:41–46
God's whisper, 1 Kings 19:9–13

FAITH links

- Take My Advice, 1 Kings 2:2–4
- A Wise Wish, 1 Kings 3:5–9
- Your Best Work, 1 Kings 6
- The Way to Serve God, 1 Kings 9:4
- An Admirable Quality, 1 Kings 10:1–13
- Your Stats, 1 Kings 15; 16
- Good Times and Bad, 1 Kings 17
- The Fence Riders, 1 Kings 18
- Listen Up!, 1 Kings 19: 11–13
- Give In or Take a Stand?, 1 Kings 22:13–14

Adonijah Tries to Become King

1 At this time King David was very old,
and although his servants covered
him with blankets, he could not keep
warm. **2**They said to him, "We will look
for a young woman to care for you. She
will lie close to you and keep you warm."
3After searching everywhere in Israel for
a beautiful young woman, they found a
girl named Abishag from Shunam and
brought her to the king. **4**The girl was
very beautiful, and she cared for the king
and served him. But the king did not have
sexual relations with her.

5Adonijah was the son of King David
and Haggith, and he was very proud. "I
will be the king," he said. So he got chariots and horses for himself and fifty men
for his personal bodyguard. **6**Now David
had never interfered with Adonijah by
questioning what he did. Born next after
Absalom, Adonijah was a very handsome
man.

7Adonijah spoke with Joab son of Zeruiah and Abiathar the priest, and they
agreed to help him. **8**But Zadok the priest,
Benaiah son of Jehoiada, Nathan the
prophet, Shimei, Rei, and King David's
special guard did not join Adonijah.

9Then Adonijah killed some sheep,
cows, and fat calves for sacrifices at the
Stone of Zoheleth near the spring of Rogel. He invited all his brothers, the other
sons of King David, to come, as well as all
the men of Judah. **10**But Adonijah did not
invite Nathan the prophet, Benaiah, his
father's special guard, or his brother Solomon.

11When Nathan heard about this, he
went to Bathsheba, Solomon's mother.
"Have you heard that Adonijah, Haggith's
son, has made himself king?" Nathan
asked. "Our real king, David, does not
know it. **12**I strongly advise you to save
yourself and your sons. **13**Go to King David and tell him, 'My master and king, you
promised that my son Solomon would be
king and would rule on your throne after
you. Why then has Adonijah become
king?' **14**While you are still talking to the
king, I will come in and tell him that what
you have said about Adonijah is true."

15So Bathsheba went in to see the
aged king in his bedroom, where Abishag, the girl from Shunam, was caring
for him. **16**Bathsheba bowed and knelt
before the king. He asked, "What do you
want?"

17She answered, "My master, you
made a promise to me in the name of the
LORD your God. You said, 'Your son Solomon will become king after me, and he
will rule on my throne.' **18**But now, unknown to you, Adonijah has become king.
19He has killed many cows, fat calves,
and sheep for sacrifices. And he has invited all your sons, as well as Abiathar
the priest and Joab the commander of the
army, but he did not invite Solomon, who
serves you. **20**My master and king, all
the Israelites are watching you, waiting
for you to decide who will be king after
you. **21**As soon as you die, Solomon and I
will be treated as criminals."

22While Bathsheba was still talking
with the king, Nathan the prophet arrived. **23**The servants told the king, "Nathan the prophet is here." So Nathan
went to the king and bowed facedown on
the ground before him.

24Nathan said, "My master and king,
have you said that Adonijah will be the
king after you and that he will rule on
your throne? **25**Today he has sacrificed
many cows, fat calves, and sheep, and he
has invited all your other sons, the commanders of the army, and Abiathar the
priest. Right now they are eating and
drinking with him. They are saying,
'Long live King Adonijah!' **26**But he did
not invite me, your own servant, or Zadok the priest, or Benaiah son of Jehoiada, or your son Solomon. **27**Did you do
this? Since we are your servants, why
didn't you tell us who should be king after you?"

David Makes Solomon King

28Then the king said, "Tell Bathsheba
to come in!" So she came in and stood
before the king.

29Then the king made this promise,
"The LORD has saved me from all trouble. As surely as he lives, **30**I will do today what I have promised you in the
name of the LORD, the God of Israel. I

promised that your son Solomon would
be king after me and rule on my throne in
my place."
31Then Bathsheba bowed facedown on
the ground and knelt before the king and
said, "Long live my master King David!"
32Then King David said, "Tell Zadok
the priest, Nathan the prophet, and Benaiah son of Jehoiada to come in." When
they came before the king, 33he said to
them, "Take my servants with you and
put my son Solomon on my own mule.
Take him down to the spring called Gihon. 34There Zadok the priest and Nathan the prophet should pour olive oil on
him and make him king over Israel. Blow
the trumpet and shout, 'Long live King
Solomon!' 35Then come back up here
with him. He will sit on my throne and
rule in my place, because he is the one I
have chosen to be the ruler over Israel
and Judah."
36Benaiah son of Jehoiada answered
the king, "Amen! This is what the LORD,
the God of my master, has declared!
37The LORD has always helped you, our
king. May he also help Solomon and
make King Solomon's throne an even
greater throne than yours."
38So Zadok the priest, Nathan the
prophet, and Benaiah son of Jehoiada left
with the Kerethites and Pelethites.*
They put Solomon on King David's mule
and took him to the spring called Gihon.
39Zadok the priest took the container of
olive oil from the Holy Tent and poured
the oil on Solomon's head to show he was
the king. Then they blew the trumpet,
and all the people shouted, "Long live
King Solomon!" 40All the people followed Solomon into the city. Playing
flutes and shouting for joy, they made so
much noise the ground shook.
41At this time Adonijah and all the
guests with him were finishing their
meal. When he heard the sound from the
trumpet, Joab asked, "What does all that
noise from the city mean?"

1:38 Kerethites and Pelethites These were probably special units of the army that were responsible for the king's safety, a kind of palace guard.

FAITH links

A LIFE OF THANKSGIVING

1 KINGS 1:47-48

Your parents may tell you to make the most of your life. That means they want you to have a full life. Think about the activities you do the most. What would you say that your life is full of right now? Fun? Boring activities? Complaints? David's life was full of thankfulness to God. Just before he died, David thanked God for making his son Solomon king.

Want to have a life full of thankfulness? Instead of always asking God for things, every once in awhile you can tell God "thanks" for who he is and for what he does. When you do that, you're building a life of thanksgiving like David's.

Check out these links on being thankful:

Serious About the Sabbath, Exodus 31:15, p. 117

The Name of the Lord, Exodus 33:19–23; 34:5–8, p. 120

When the Green-eyed Monster Strikes, 1 Samuel 18:6–9, p. 379

Gratitude Attitude, Ezra 3, p. 611

Happiness or Joy?, Job 29:18–19, p. 691

Thanks for a Friend, 1 Thessalonians 1:1–3, p. 1630

42While Joab was speaking, Jonathan
son of Abiathar the priest arrived. Adonijah said, "Come in! You are an important
man, so you must be bringing good news."
43But Jonathan answered, "No! Our
master King David has made Solomon
the new king. 44King David sent Zadok
the priest, Nathan the prophet, Benaiah
son of Jehoiada, and all the king's bodyguards with him, and they have put Solomon on the king's own mule. 45Then
Zadok the priest and Nathan the prophet
poured olive oil on Solomon at Gihon to
make him king. After that they went into
the city, shouting with joy. Now the whole
city is excited, and that is the noise you
hear. 46Solomon has now become the
king. 47All the king's officers have come
to tell King David that he has done a good
thing. They are saying, 'May your God
make Solomon even more famous than
you and an even greater king than you.' "
Jonathan continued, "And King David
bowed down on his bed to worship God,
48saying, 'Bless the LORD, the God of Israel. Today he has made one of my sons
the king and allowed me to see it.' "
49Then all of Adonijah's guests were
afraid, and they left quickly and scattered. 50Adonijah was also afraid of Solomon, so he went and took hold of the
corners of the altar.* 51Then someone
told Solomon, "Adonijah is afraid of you, so
he is at the altar, holding on to its corners.
He says, 'Tell King Solomon to promise
me today that he will not kill me.' "
52So Solomon answered, "Adonijah
must show that he is a man of honor. If he
does that, I promise he will not lose even
a single hair from his head. But if he does
anything wrong, he will die." 53Then
King Solomon sent some men to get Adonijah. When he was brought from the altar, he came before King Solomon and
bowed down. Solomon told him, "Go
home."

The Death of David

2 Since it was almost time for David to
die, he gave his son Solomon his last
commands. 2David said, "My time to die
is near. Be a good and strong leader.
3Obey the LORD your God. Follow him by
obeying his demands, his commands, his
laws, and his rules that are written in
the teachings of Moses. If you do these

FAITH links

TAKE MY ADVICE

1 KINGS 2:2-4

What is the most important advice your parents have passed on to you? Think about that for a moment as you consider this. King David was about to die. He had one last chance to talk to his son Solomon. David did not teach him how to fight a battle or how to make the people of Israel happy. He told Solomon that the most important thing he could do in life was to obey the Lord. Is that your goal, too? How do your actions show that you've taken this advice to heart?

A Use for Your Abilities, Genesis 41, p. 59

Prayer + Action = Success, Nehemiah 2:4–9, p. 626

Our Thirst Quencher, Psalm 42:1–3, p. 741

Think About Him, Isaiah 26:3, p. 926

Empty Words, Ezekiel 33:30–33, p. 1127

That Thing You Do, Matthew 25:14–30, p. 1319

1:50 corners of the altar If a person were innocent of a crime, he could run into the Holy Place where the altar was. If he held on to the corners of the altar, which looked like horns, he would be safe.

things, you will be successful in all you do
and wherever you go. 4And if you obey
the LORD, he will keep the promise he
made to me. He said: 'If your descendants live as I tell them and have complete faith in me, a man from your family
will always be king over the people of Israel.'
5"Also, you remember what Joab son
of Zeruiah did to me. He killed the two
commanders of Israel's armies: Abner
son of Ner and Amasa son of Jether. He
did this as if he and they were at war, although it was a time of peace. He put
their blood on the belt around his waist
and on his sandals on his feet. 6Punish
him in the way you think is wisest, but do
not let him die peacefully of old age.
7"Be kind to the children of Barzillai
of Gilead, and allow them to eat
at your table. They
welcomed me when
I ran away from
your brother Absa-
lom.
8"And remember,
Shimei son of Gera,
the Benjaminite, is here with you. He
cursed me the day I went to Mahanaim.
But when he came down to meet me at
the Jordan River, I promised him before
the Lord, 'Shimei, I will not kill you.'
9But you should not leave him unpunished. You are a wise man, and you will
know what to do to him, but you must be
sure he is killed."
10Then David died and was buried
with his ancestors in Jerusalem. 11He
had ruled over Israel forty years—seven
years in Hebron and thirty-three years in
Jerusalem.

EMAIL FROM GOD 2:7
Kindness
How should you treat those who have been kind to you?

Solomon Takes Control as King

12Solomon became king after David,
his father, and he was in firm control of
his kingdom.
13At this time Adonijah son of Haggith
went to Bathsheba, Solomon's mother.
"Do you come in peace?" Bathsheba
asked.
"Yes. This is a peaceful visit," Adonijah answered. 14"I have something to say
to you."
"You may speak," she said.
15"You remember that at one time the
kingdom was mine," Adonijah said. "All
the people of Israel recognized me as
their king, but things have changed. Now
my brother is the king, because the LORD
chose him. 16Now I have one thing to ask
you; please do not refuse me."
Bathsheba answered, "What do you
want?"
17"I know King Solomon will do anything you ask him," Adonijah continued.
"Please ask him to give me Abishag the
Shunammite to be my wife."
18"Very well," she answered. "I will
speak to the king for you."
19So Bathsheba went to King Solomon to speak to him for Adonijah. When
Solomon saw her, he stood up to meet
her, then bowed down, and sat on the
throne. He told some servants to bring
another throne for his mother. Then she
sat down at his right side.
20Bathsheba said, "I have one small
thing to ask you. Please do not refuse
me."
"Ask, mother," the king answered. "I
will not refuse you."
21So she said, "Allow Abishag the
Shunammite to marry your brother Adonijah."
22King Solomon answered his mother,
"Why do you ask me to give him Abishag?
Why don't you also ask for him to become
the king since he is my older brother?
Abiathar the priest and Joab son of Zeruiah would support him!"
23Then King Solomon swore by the
name of the LORD, saying, "May God
punish me terribly if this doesn't cost
Adonijah his life! 24By the LORD who has
given me the throne that belonged to my
father David and who has kept his promise and given the kingdom to me and my
people, Adonijah will die today!" 25Then
King Solomon gave orders to Benaiah
son of Jehoiada, and he went and killed
Adonijah.
26King Solomon said to Abiathar the
priest, "I should kill you too, but I will allow you to go back to your fields in Anathoth. I will not kill you at this time,
because you helped carry the Ark of the

Lord GOD while marching with my father
David. And I know you shared in all the
hard times with him." **27**Then Solomon
removed Abiathar from being the LORD's
priest. This happened as the LORD had
said it would, when he was speaking in
Shiloh about the priest Eli and his descendants.

28When Joab heard about what had
happened, he was afraid. He had supported Adonijah but not Absalom. So Joab ran
to the Tent of the LORD and took hold of
the corners of the altar.ⁿ **29**Someone told
King Solomon that Joab had run to the
Tent of the LORD and was beside the altar.
Then Solomon ordered Benaiah to go and
kill him.

30Benaiah went into the Tent of the
LORD and said to Joab, "The king says,
'Come out!' "

But Joab answered, "No, I will die
here."

So Benaiah went back to the king and
told him what Joab had said. **31**Then the
king ordered Benaiah, "Do as he says!
Kill him there and bury him. Then my
family and I will be free of the guilt of
Joab, who has killed innocent people.
32Without my father knowing it, he killed
two men who were much better than he
was—Abner son of Ner, the commander
of Israel's army, and Amasa son of Jether,
the commander of Judah's army. So the
LORD will pay him back for those deaths.
33Joab and his family will be forever
guilty for their deaths, but there will be
peace from the LORD for David, his descendants, his family, and his throne forever."

34So Benaiah son of Jehoiada killed
Joab, and he was buried near his home in
the desert. **35**The king then made Benaiah son of Jehoiada commander of the
army in Joab's place. He also made Zadok
the new high priest in Abiathar's place.

36Next the king sent for Shimei. Solomon said to him, "Build a house for yourself in Jerusalem and live there. Don't
leave the city. **37**The very day you leave
and cross the Kidron Valley, someone will
kill you, and it will be your own fault."

38So Shimei answered the king, "I
agree with what you say. I will do what
you say, my master and king." So Shimei
lived in Jerusalem for a long time.

39But three years later two of
Shimei's slaves ran away to Achish king
of Gath, who was the son of Maacah.
Shimei heard that his slaves were in
Gath, **40**so he put his saddle on his don-
key and went to Achish at Gath to find
them. Then he brought them back from
Gath.

41Someone told Solomon that Shimei
had gone from Jerusalem to Gath and had
returned. **42**So Solomon sent for Shimei
and said, "I made you promise in the
name of the LORD not to leave Jerusalem.
I warned you if you went out anywhere
you would die, and you agreed to what I
said. **43**Why did you break your promise
to the LORD and disobey my command?"
44The king also said, "You know the
many wrong things you did to my father
David, so now the LORD will punish you
for those wrongs. **45**But the LORD will
bless me and make the rule of David safe
before the LORD forever."

46Then the king ordered Benaiah to
kill Shimei, and he did. Now Solomon was
in full control of his kingdom.

Solomon Asks for Wisdom

3 Solomon made an agreement with the
king of Egypt by marrying his daughter and bringing her to Jerusalem. At this
time Solomon was still building his palace and the Temple of the LORD, as well
as a wall around Jerusalem. **2**The Temple
for the worship of the LORD had not yet
been finished, so people were still sacrificing at altars in many places of worship.
3Solomon showed he loved the LORD by
following the commands his father David
had given him, except many other places
of worship were still used to offer sacrifices and to burn incense.

4King Solomon went to Gibeon to offer a sacrifice, because it was the most
important place of worship. He offered a

2:28 corners of the altar If a person were innocent of a crime, he could run into the Holy Place where the altar was. If he held on to the corners of the altar, which looked like horns, he would be safe.

thousand burnt offerings on that altar.
5While he was at Gibeon, the LORD appeared to him in a dream during the
night. God said, "Ask for whatever you
want me to give you."
6Solomon answered, "You were very
kind to your servant, my father David.

A WISE WISH

1 KINGS 3:5-9

If you could have one wish, what would you ask for? That is what happened to Solomon. God told him that he would give him whatever he asked for. Solomon did not ask for money or a huge palace. Solomon took a step of faith and asked for wisdom. He became wiser than anyone who ever lived. (Link to 2 Chronicles 1:7–13, p. 563, for another version of this story.)

Want to be like Solomon? When you pray, ask God for wisdom. He will give it to you. (Download James 1:5, p. 1688, for more on getting God's wisdom.)

Remembering What He Said, Deuteronomy 6:4–9, p. 236

The Green Light, 2 Samuel 2:1, p. 401

Learning to Trust, Psalm 25:4–5, p. 727

A Need to Change, Ecclesiastes 1:1–11, p. 873

A Hopeful Future, Jeremiah 29:11, p. 1031

The Power of Prayer, Acts 12:5, p. 1485

He obeyed you, and he was honest and
lived right. You showed great kindness to
him when you allowed his son to be king
after him. 7LORD my God, now you have
made me, your servant, king in my
father's place. But I am like a little child; I
don't know how to do what must be done.
8I, your servant, am here among your
chosen people, and there are too many of
them to count. 9I ask that you give me an
obedient heart so I can rule the people in
the right way and will know the difference between right and wrong. Otherwise, it is impossible to rule this great
people of yours."
10The Lord was pleased that Solomon
had asked this. 11So God said to him,
"You did not ask for a long life, or riches
for yourself, or the death of your enemies. Since you asked for wisdom to
make the right decisions, 12I will do what
you asked. I will give you wisdom and
understanding that is greater than anyone has had in the past or will have in the
future. 13I will also give you what you did
not ask for: riches and honor. During
your life no other king will be as great as
you. 14If you follow me and obey my laws
and commands, as your father David did,
I will also give you a long life."
15After Solomon woke up from the
dream, he went to Jerusalem. He stood
before the Ark of the Agreement with the
LORD, where he made burnt offerings and
fellowship offerings. After that, he gave a
feast for all his leaders and officers.

Solomon Makes a Wise Decision

16One day two women who were
prostitutes came to Solomon. As they
stood before him, 17one of the women
said, "My master, this woman and I live in
the same house. I gave birth to a baby
while she was there with me. 18Three
days later this woman also gave birth to a
baby. No one else was in the house with
us; it was just the two of us. 19One night
this woman rolled over on her baby, and
he died. 20So she took my son from my
bed during the night while I was asleep,
and she carried him to her bed. Then she
put the dead baby in my bed. 21The next
morning when I got up to feed my baby, I

FAITH links

DECIDING WISELY

1 KINGS 3:16-28

Ever have a tough decision to make? What helped you make the decision? Solomon made a good decision by asking God for wisdom. That wisdom was put to the test when he was asked to decide a very difficult case. But Solomon was able to make a fair decision because he had great wisdom from God. Everyone respected Solomon for his wisdom.

When you have a hard decision to make, you can use God's wisdom, too. The wise person knows when to ask for help to make a decision. God has given us the Bible, which is full of wise advice. God also gives us godly people who can help us make good choices.

Wise up by linking on to these notes:

Learning to Listen, 1 Samuel 3, p. 358

A Traveling Bible Study, 2 Chronicles 17:9, p. 580

Let's Make a Deal, Daniel 1:8–21, p. 1150

Want to Know? Ask!, Luke 9:45, p. 1386

Faith Workout, Acts 16:4–5, p. 1493

How Do You Grow?, Titus 1:1, p. 1659

saw that he was dead! When I looked at
him more closely, I realized he was not
my son."
22"No!" the other woman cried. "The
living baby is my son, and the dead baby
is yours!"
But the first woman said, "No! The
dead baby is yours, and the living one is
mine!" So the two women argued before
the king.
23Then King Solomon said, "One of
you says, 'My son is alive and your son is
dead.' Then the other one says, 'No! Your
son is dead and my son is alive.' "
24The king sent his servants to get a
sword. When they brought it to him, 25he
said, "Cut the living baby into two pieces,
and give each woman half."
26The real mother of the living child
was full of love for her son. So she said to
the king, "Please, my master, don't kill
him! Give the baby to her!"
But the other woman said, "Neither of
us will have him. Cut him into two
pieces!"
27Then King Solomon said, "Don't kill
him. Give the baby to the first woman,
because she is the real mother."
28When the people of Israel heard
about King Solomon's decision, they respected him very much. They saw he had
wisdom from God to make the right decisions.

Solomon's Officers

4 King Solomon ruled over all Israel.
2These are the names of his leading
officers:
Azariah son of Zadok was the priest;
3Elihoreph and Ahijah, sons of Shisha,
recorded what happened in the courts;
Jehoshaphat son of Ahilud recorded
the history of the people;
4Benaiah son of Jehoiada was commander of the army;
Zadok and Abiathar were priests;
5Azariah son of Nathan was in charge
of the district governors;
Zabud son of Nathan was a priest and
adviser to the king;
6Ahishar was responsible for everything in the palace;

Adoniram son of Abda was in charge
of the labor force.
7Solomon placed twelve governors
over the districts of Israel, who gathered
food from their districts for the king and
his family. Each governor was responsible
for bringing food to the king one month of
each year. **8**These are the names of the
twelve governors:

Ben-Hur was governor of the mountain country of Ephraim.

9Ben-Deker was governor of Makaz,
Shaalbim, Beth Shemesh, and Elon Beth-
hanan.

10Ben-Hesed was governor of Arub-
both, Socoh, and all the land of Hepher.

11Ben-Abinadab was governor of Naphoth Dor. (He was married to Taphath,
Solomon's daughter.)

12Baana son of Ahilud was governor
of Taanach, Megiddo, and all of Beth Shan
next to Zarethan. This was below Jezreel
from Beth Shan to Abel Meholah across
from Jokmeam.

13Ben-Geber was governor of Ramoth in Gilead. (He was governor of all
the towns of Jair in Gilead. Jair was the
son of Manasseh. Ben-Geber was also
over the district of Argob in Bashan,
which had sixty large, walled cities with
bronze bars on their gates.)

14Ahinadab son of Iddo was governor
of Mahanaim.

15Ahimaaz was governor of Naphtali.
(He was married to Basemath, Solomon's daughter.)

16Baana son of Hushai was governor
of Asher and Aloth.

17Jehoshaphat son of Paruah was governor of Issachar.

18Shimei son of Ela was governor of
Benjamin.

19Geber son of Uri was governor of
Gilead. Gilead had been the country of
Sihon king of the Amorites and Og king
of Bashan. But Geber was the only governor over this district.

Solomon's Kingdom

20There were as many people in Judah
and Israel as grains of sand on the seashore. The people ate, drank, and were
happy. **21**Solomon ruled over all the kingdoms from the Euphrates River to the
land of the Philistines, as far as the border
of Egypt. These countries brought Solomon the payments he demanded, and
they were under his control all his life.
22Solomon needed much food each
day to feed himself and all the people who
ate at his table: one hundred ninety-five
bushels of fine flour, three hundred ninety bushels of grain, **23**ten cows that were
fed on good grain, twenty cows that were
raised in the fields, one hundred sheep,
three kinds of deer, and fattened birds.
24Solomon controlled all the countries west of the Euphrates River—the
land from Tiphsah to Gaza. And he had
peace on all sides of his kingdom. **25**During Solomon's life Judah and Israel, from
Dan to Beersheba,[n] also lived in peace; all
of his people were able to sit under their
own fig trees and grapevines.
26Solomon had four thousand stalls
for his chariot horses and twelve thousand horses. **27**Each month one of the
district governors gave King Solomon all
the food he needed—enough for every
person who ate at the king's table. The
governors made sure he had everything
he needed. **28**They also brought enough
barley and straw for Solomon's chariot
and work horses; each person brought
this grain to the right place.

Solomon's Wisdom

29God gave Solomon great wisdom so
he could understand many things. His
wisdom was as hard to measure as the
grains of sand on the seashore. **30**His
wisdom was greater than any wisdom of
the East, or any wisdom in Egypt. **31**He
was wiser than anyone on earth. He was
even wiser than Ethan the Ezrahite, as
well as Heman, Calcol, and Darda—the
three sons of Mahol. King Solomon became famous in all the surrounding countries. **32**During his life he spoke three
thousand wise sayings and also wrote
one thousand five songs. **33**He taught
about many kinds of plants—everything

4:25 Dan to Beersheba Dan was the city farthest north in Israel, and Beersheba was the city farthest south. So this means all the people of Israel.

from the great cedar trees of Lebanon to
the weeds that grow out of the walls. He
also taught about animals, birds, crawling
things, and fish. 34People from all nations
came to listen to King Solomon's wisdom. The kings of all nations sent them
to him, because they had heard of
Solomon's wisdom.

Preparing to Build the Temple

5 Hiram, the king of Tyre, had always
been David's friend. When Hiram
heard that Solomon had been made king
in David's place, he sent his messengers
to Solomon. 2Solomon sent this message
back to King Hiram: 3"You remember my
father David had to fight many wars with
the countries around him, so he was
never able to build a temple for worshiping the LORD his God. David was waiting
until the LORD allowed him to defeat all
his enemies. 4But now the LORD my God
has given me peace on all sides of my
country. I have no enemies now, and no
danger threatens my people.

5"The LORD promised my father David, 'I will make your son king after you,
and he will build a temple
for worshiping me.' Now,
I plan to build that temple
for worshiping the LORD
my God. 6So send your
men to cut down cedar
trees for me from Leba-
non. My servants will
work with yours, and I
will pay them whatever
wages you decide. We
don't have anyone who
can cut down trees as
well as the people of Sidon."

Praise the LORD today! He has given David a wise son to rule over this great nation!
—1 Kings 5:7

7When Hiram heard what Solomon
asked, he was very happy. He said,
"Praise the LORD today! He has given
David a wise son to rule over this great
nation!" 8Then Hiram sent back this
message to Solomon: "I received the
message you sent, and I will give you all
the cedar and pine trees you want. 9My
servants will bring them down from Lebanon to the sea. There I will tie them together and float them along the shore to
the place you choose. Then I will separate the logs there, and you can take
them away. In return it is my wish that
you give food to all those who live with
me." 10So Hiram gave Solomon as much
cedar and pine as he wanted. 11And Solomon gave Hiram about one hundred
twenty-five thousand bushels of wheat
each year to feed the people who lived
with him. Solomon also gave him about
one hundred fifteen thousand gallons of
pure olive oil every year.

12The LORD gave Solomon wisdom as
he had promised. And there was peace between Hiram and Solomon; these two
kings made a treaty between themselves.

eMAIL FROM GOD
5:13–14
Family
What's more important: family or work?

13King Solomon
forced thirty thou-
sand men of Israel to
help in this work.
14He sent a group of
ten thousand men
each month to Leba-
non. Each group worked in Lebanon one
month, then went home for two months.
A man named Adoniram was in charge.
15Solomon forced eighty thousand men to
work in the hill country, cutting stone, and
he had seventy thousand
men to carry the stones.
16There were also thirty-
three hundred men who
directed the workers.
17King Solomon com-
manded them to cut large
blocks of fine stone to be
used for the foundation of
the Temple. 18Solomon's
and Hiram's builders and
the men from Byblos
carved the stones and
prepared the stones and the logs for building the Temple.

Solomon Builds the Temple

6 Solomon began to build the Temple
four hundred eighty years after the
people of Israel had left Egypt. This was
during the fourth year of King Solomon's
rule over Israel. It was the second
month, the month of Ziv.

2The Temple was ninety feet long,
thirty feet wide, and forty-five feet high.
3The porch in front of the main room of

the Temple was fifteen feet deep and
thirty feet wide. This room ran along the
front of the Temple itself. Its width was
equal to that of the Temple. **4**The Temple
also had windows that opened and closed.
5Solomon also built some side rooms
against the walls of the main room and
the inner room of the Temple. He built
rooms all around. **6**The rooms on the bottom floor were seven and one-half feet
wide. Those on the middle floor were
nine feet wide, and the rooms above
them were ten and one-half feet wide.
The Temple wall that formed the side of
each room was thinner than the wall in
the room below. These rooms were
pushed against the Temple wall, but they
did not have their main beams built into
this wall.

7The stones were prepared at the
same place where they were cut from the
ground. Since these stones were the only
ones used to build the Temple, there was
no noise of hammers, axes, or any other
iron tools at the Temple.

8The entrance to the lower rooms beside the Temple was on the south side.
From there, stairs went up to the second-
floor rooms. And from there, stairs went
on to the third-floor rooms. **9**Solomon put
a roof made from beams and cedar boards
on the Temple. So he finished building
the Temple **10**as well as the bottom floor
that was beside the Temple. This bottom
floor was seven and one-half feet high
and was attached to the Temple by cedar
beams.

11The LORD said to Solomon: **12**"If
you obey all my laws and commands,
I will do for you what I
promised your fa-
ther David. **13**I will
live among the Isra-
elites in this Tem-
ple, and I will never
leave my people Is-
rael."

EMAIL FROM GOD
6:12–13
Obedience
Read this to see God's promises.

14So Solomon finished building the
Temple. **15**The inside walls were covered
from floor to ceiling with cedar boards.
The floor was made from pine boards.
16A room thirty feet long was built in the
back part of the Temple. This room,
called the Most Holy Place, was separated from the rest of the Temple by cedar boards which reached from floor to
ceiling. **17**The main room, the one in
front of the Most Holy Place, was sixty
feet long. **18**Everything inside the Temple

FAITH links

YOUR BEST WORK

1 KINGS 6

What are the activities you put the most effort in? Only the things you like to do? Everything you do? You know what doing your best is like. Solomon used the best laborers and the best material to work on God's Temple. He knew that God's house deserved the very best materials he could find. The people he hired worked very hard to complete the Temple.

Part of learning to do your best means putting effort into whatever you do. When you do your best, your efforts show.

Check out these links on giving it your all:

Everyone Can Help, Numbers 4, p. 181

An Unsung Hero, Ruth 2:12, 15–16, p. 347

Operation Cooperation, Ezra 1:5, p. 609

Said It? Do It!, Lamentations 2:17, p. 1077

A Halfhearted Offering, Malachi 1:6–14, p. 1268

With All Your Heart, Colossians 3:23, p. 1626

was covered with cedar, which was
carved with pictures of flowers and
plants. A person could not see the stones
of the wall, only the cedar.
19Solomon prepared the inner room
at the back of the Temple to keep the Ark
of the Agreement with the LORD. **20**This
inner room was thirty feet long, thirty
feet wide, and thirty feet high. He covered this room with pure gold, and he
also covered the altar of cedar. **21**He covered the inside of the Temple with pure
gold, placing gold chains across the front
of the inner room, which was also covered with gold. **22**So all the inside of the
Temple, as well as the altar of the Most
Holy Place, was covered with gold.
23Solomon made two creatures from
olive wood and placed them in the Most
Holy Place. Each creature was fifteen
feet tall **24**and had two wings. Each wing
was seven and one-half feet long, so it
was fifteen feet from the end of one wing
to the end of the other. **25**The creatures
were the same size and shape; **26**each
was fifteen feet tall. **27**These creatures
were put beside each other in the Most
Holy Place with their wings spread out.
One creature's wing touched one wall,
and the other creature's wing touched
the other wall with their wings touching
each other in the middle of the room.
28These two creatures were covered
with gold.
29All the walls around the Temple
were carved with pictures of creatures
with wings, as well as palm trees and
flowers. This was true for both the main
room and the inner room. **30**The floors of
both rooms were covered with gold.
31Doors made from olive wood were
placed at the entrance to the Most Holy
Place. These doors had five-sided frames.
32Creatures with wings, as well as palm
trees and flowers, were also carved on the
two olive wood doors that were covered
with gold. The creatures and the palm
trees on the doors were covered with
gold as well. **33**At the entrance to the
main room there was a square door frame
made of olive wood. **34**Two doors were
made from pine. Each door had two parts
so the doors folded. **35**The doors were
covered with pictures of creatures with
wings, as well as palm trees and flowers.
All of the carvings were covered with
gold, which was evenly spread over
them.
36The inner courtyard was enclosed
by walls, which were made of three rows
of cut stones and one row of cedar boards.
37Work began on the Temple in Ziv,
the second month, during the fourth year
Solomon was king over Israel. **38**The
Temple was finished during the eleventh
year he was king, in the eighth month,
the month of Bul. It was built exactly as it
was planned. Solomon had spent seven
years building it.

Solomon's Palace

7 King Solomon also built a palace for
himself; it took him thirteen years to
finish it. **2**Built of cedars from the Forest
of Lebanon, it was one hundred fifty feet
long, seventy-five feet wide, and forty-
five feet high. It had four rows of cedar
columns which supported the cedar
beams. **3**There were forty-five beams on
the roof, with fifteen beams in each row,
and the ceiling was covered with cedar
above the beams. **4**Windows were placed
in three rows facing each other. **5**All the
doors were square, and the three doors at
each end faced each other.
6Solomon also built the porch that had
pillars. This porch was seventy-five feet
long and forty-five feet wide. Along the
front of the porch was a roof supported by
pillars.
7Solomon also built a throne room
where he judged people, called the Hall
of Justice. This room was covered with
cedar from the floor to the ceiling. **8**The
palace where Solomon lived was built
like the Hall of Justice, and it was behind
this hall. Solomon also built the same
kind of palace for his wife, who was the
daughter of the king of Egypt.
9All these buildings were made with
blocks of fine stone. First they were carefully cut. Then they were trimmed with a
saw in the front and back. These fine
stones went from the foundations of the
buildings to the top of the walls. Even the
courtyard was made with blocks of stone.

10The foundations were made with large
blocks of fine stone, some as long as fifteen feet. Others were twelve feet long.
11On top of these foundation stones
were other blocks of fine stone and cedar
beams. 12The palace courtyard, the
courtyard inside the Temple, and the
porch of the Temple were surrounded
by walls. All of these walls had three
rows of stone blocks and one row of cedar
beams.

The Temple Is Completed Inside

13King Solomon sent to Tyre and had
Huram brought to him. 14Huram's mother was a widow from the tribe of Naphtali.
His father was from Tyre and had been
skilled in making things from bronze.
Huram was also very skilled and experienced in bronze work. So he came to
King Solomon and did all the bronze
work.

15He made two bronze pillars, each
one twenty-seven feet tall and eighteen
feet around. 16He also made two bronze
capitals that were seven and one-half feet
tall, and he put them on top of the pillars.
17Then he made a net of seven chains for
each capital, which covered the capitals
on top of the two pillars. 18He made two
rows of bronze pomegranates to go on
the nets. These covered the capitals at
the top of the pillars. 19The capitals on
top of the pillars in the porch were
shaped like lilies, and they were six feet
tall. 20The capitals were on top of both
pillars, above the bowl-shaped section
and next to the nets. At that place there
were two hundred pomegranates in rows
all around the capitals. 21Huram put
these two bronze pillars at the porch of
the Temple. He named the south pillar
He Establishes and the north pillar In
Him Is Strength. 22The capitals on top of
the pillars were shaped like lilies. So the
work on the pillars was finished.

23Then Huram made from bronze a
large round bowl, which was called the
Sea. It was forty-five feet around, fifteen
feet across, and seven and one-half feet
deep. 24Around the outer edge of the
bowl was a rim. Under this rim were two
rows of bronze plants which surrounded
the bowl. There were ten plants every
eighteen inches, and these plants were
made in one piece with the bowl. 25The
bowl rested on the backs of twelve
bronze bulls that faced outward from the
center of the bowl. Three bulls faced
north, three faced west, three faced
south, and three faced east. 26The sides
of the bowl were four inches thick, and it
held about eleven thousand gallons. The
rim of the bowl was like the rim of a cup
or like a lily blossom.

27Then Huram made ten bronze
stands, each one six feet long, six feet
wide, and four and one-half feet high.
28The stands were made from square
sides, which were put on frames. 29On
the sides were bronze lions, bulls, and
creatures with wings. On the frames
above and below the lions and bulls were
designs of flowers hammered into the
bronze. 30Each stand had four bronze
wheels with bronze axles. At the corners
there were bronze supports for a large
bowl, and the supports had designs of
flowers. 31There was a frame on top of
the bowls, eighteen inches high above
the bowls. The opening of the bowl was
round, twenty-seven inches deep. Designs were carved into the bronze on the
frame, which was square, not round.
32The four wheels, placed under the
frame, were twenty-seven inches high.
The axles between the wheels were
made as one piece with the stand. 33The
wheels were like a chariot's wheels.
Everything on the wheels—the axles,
rims, spokes, and hubs—were made of
bronze.

34The four supports were on the four
corners of each stand. They were made
as one piece with the stand. 35A strip of
bronze around the top of each stand was
nine inches deep. It was also made as one
piece with the stand. 36The sides of the
stand and the frames were covered with
carvings of creatures with wings, as well
as lions, palm trees, and flowers. 37This
is the way Huram made the ten stands.
The bronze for each stand was melted
and poured into a mold, so all the stands
were the same size and shape.

38Huram also made ten bronze bowls,

one bowl for each of the ten stands. Each
bowl was six feet across and could hold
about two hundred thirty gallons. **39**Huram put five stands on the south side of
the Temple and five on the north side. He
put the large bowl in the southeast corner of the Temple. **40**Huram also made
bowls, shovels, and small bowls.

So Huram finished all his work for
King Solomon on the
Temple of the LORD:

41 two pillars;
two large bowls for the capitals on top of the pillars;
two nets to cover the two large bowls for the capitals on top of the pillars;
42 four hundred pomegranates for the two nets (there were two rows of pomegranates for each net covering the bowls for the capitals on top of the pillars);
43 ten stands with a bowl on each stand;
44 the large bowl with twelve bulls under it;
45 the pots, shovels, small bowls, and all the utensils for the Temple of the LORD.

Huram made everything King Solomon wanted from polished bronze.
46The king had these things poured into
clay molds that were made in the plain of
the Jordan River between Succoth and
Zarethan. **47**Solomon never weighed the
bronze used to make these things, because there was too much to weigh. So
the total weight of all the bronze was
never known.
48Solomon also made all the items for
the Temple of the LORD:

the golden altar;
the golden table which held the bread that shows God's people are in his presence;
49 the lampstands of pure gold (five on the right side and five on the left side in front of the Most Holy Place);
the flowers, lamps, and tongs of gold;
50 the pure gold bowls, wick trimmers, small bowls, pans, and dishes used to carry coals;
the gold hinges for the doors of the Most Holy Place and the main room of the Temple.

Finally the work King Solomon did for the Temple of the LORD was finished.
—1 Kings 7:51

51Finally the work
King Solomon did for the
Temple of the LORD was
finished. Solomon brought
in everything his father
David had set apart for
the Temple—silver, gold,
and other articles. He put
everything in the trea-
suries of the Temple of
the LORD.

The Ark Is Brought into the Temple

8 King Solomon called for the older
leaders of Israel, the heads of the
tribes, and the leaders of the families to
come to him in Jerusalem. He wanted
them to bring the Ark of the Agreement
with the LORD from the older part of the
city. **2**So all the Israelites came together
with King Solomon during the festival in
the month of Ethanim, the seventh
month.
3When all the older leaders of Israel
arrived, the priests lifted up the Ark.
4They carried the Ark of the LORD, the
Meeting Tent, and the holy utensils; the
priests and the Levites brought them up.
5King Solomon and all the Israelites
gathered before the Ark and sacrificed so
many sheep and cattle no one could count
them all. **6**Then the priests put the Ark of
the Agreement with the LORD in its place
inside the Most Holy Place in the Temple, under the wings of the golden creatures. **7**The wings of these creatures
were spread out over the place for the
Ark, covering it and its carrying poles.
8The carrying poles were so long that
anyone standing in the Holy Place in
front of the Most Holy Place could see
the ends of the poles, but no one could

see them from outside the Holy Place.
The poles are still there today. 9The only
things inside the Ark were two stone
tablets[n] that Moses had put in the Ark at
Mount Sinai. That was where the LORD
made his agreement with the Israelites
after they came out of Egypt.
10When the priests left the Holy
Place, a cloud filled the Temple of the
LORD. 11The priests could not continue
their work, because the Temple was
filled with the glory of the LORD.

Solomon Speaks to the People

12Then Solomon said, "The LORD said
he would live in a dark cloud. 13LORD, I
have truly built a wonderful Temple for
you—a place for you to live forever."
14While all the Israelites were standing there, King Solomon turned to them
and blessed them.
15Then he said, "Praise the LORD, the
God of Israel. He has done what he promised to my father David. The LORD said,
16'Since the time I brought my people Israel out of Egypt, I have not chosen a city
in any tribe of Israel where a temple will
be built for me. But I have chosen David
to lead my people Israel.'
17"My father David wanted to build a
temple for the LORD, the God of Israel.
18But the LORD said to my father David,
'It was good that you wanted to build a
temple for me. 19But you are not the one
to build it. Your son, who comes from
your own body, is the one who will build
my temple.'
20"Now the LORD has kept his promise. I am the king now in place of David
my father. Now I rule Israel as the LORD
promised, and I have built the Temple for
the LORD, the God of Israel. 21I have
made a place there for the Ark, in which
is the Agreement the LORD made with
our ancestors when he brought them out
of Egypt."

Solomon's Prayer

22Then Solomon stood facing the
LORD's altar, and all the Israelites were
standing behind him. He spread out his
hands toward the sky 23and said:
"LORD, God of Israel, there is no god
like you in heaven above or on earth below. You keep your agreement of love
with your servants who truly follow you.
24You have kept the promise you made to
your servant David, my father. You spoke
it with your own mouth and finished it
with your hands today. 25Now LORD, God
of Israel, keep the promise you made to
your servant David, my father. You said,
'If your sons are careful to obey me as
you have obeyed me, there will always be
someone from your family ruling Israel.'
26Now, God of Israel, please continue to
keep that promise you made to your servant David, my father.
27"But, God, can you really live here
on the earth? The sky and the highest
place in heaven cannot contain

you. Surely this
house which I have
built cannot contain
you. 28But please
listen to my prayer
and my request, be-
cause I am your servant. LORD my God,
hear this prayer your servant prays to you
today. 29Night and day please watch over
this Temple where you have said, 'I will be
worshiped there.' Hear the prayer I pray
facing this Temple. 30Hear my prayers
and the prayers of your people Israel
when we pray facing this place. Hear from
your home in heaven, and when you hear,
forgive us.
31"If someone wrongs another per-
son, he will be brought to the altar in this
Temple. If he swears an oath that he is
not guilty, 32then hear in heaven. Judge
the case, punish the guilty, but declare
that the innocent person is not guilty.
33"When your people, the Israelites,
sin against you, their enemies will defeat
them. But if they come back to you and
praise you and pray to you in this Temple,
34then hear them in heaven. Forgive the
sins of your people Israel, and bring them
back to the land you gave to their ancestors.
35"When they sin against you, you
will stop the rain from falling on their

8:9 stone tablets They were the two tablets on which God wrote the Ten Commandments.

land. Then they will pray, facing this
place and praising you; they will stop sinning when you make them suffer.
36When this happens, please hear their
prayer in heaven, and forgive the sins of
your servants, the Israelites. Teach them
to do what is right. Then please send rain
to this land you have given particularly to
them.

37"At times the land will become so
dry that no food will grow, or a great sickness will spread among the people. Sometimes all the crops will be destroyed by
locusts or grasshoppers. Your people will
be attacked in their cities by their enemy
or will become sick. 38When any of these
things happen, the people will become
truly sorry. If your people spread their
hands in prayer toward this Temple,
39then hear their prayers from your home
in heaven. Forgive and treat each person
as he should be treated because you know
what is in a person's heart. Only you know
what is in everyone's heart. 40Then your
people will respect you as long as they
live in this land you gave to our ancestors.

41-42"People who are not Israelites,
foreigners from other lands, will hear
about your greatness and power. They
will come from far away to pray at this
Temple. 43Then hear from your home in
heaven, and do whatever they ask you.
Then people everywhere will know you
and respect you, just as your people in
Israel do. Then everyone will know I
built this Temple as a place to worship
you.

44"When your people go out to fight
their enemies along some road on which
you send them, your people will pray to
you, facing the city which you have chosen and the Temple I have built for you.
45Then hear in heaven their prayers, and
do what is right.

46"Everyone sins, so your people will
also sin against you. You will become angry with them and hand them over to
their enemies. Their enemies will capture them and take them away to their
countries far or near. 47Your people will
be sorry for their sins when they are held
as prisoners in another country. They
will be sorry and pray to you in the land
where they are held as prisoners, saying,
'We have sinned. We have done wrong
and acted wickedly.' 48They will truly
turn back to you in the land of their enemies. They will pray to you, facing this
land you gave their ancestors, this city
you have chosen, and the Temple I have
built for you. 49Then hear their prayers
from your home in heaven, and do what is
right. 50Forgive your people of all their
sins and for turning against you. Make
those who have captured them show
them mercy. 51Remember, they are your
special people. You brought them out of
Egypt, as if you were pulling them out of
a blazing furnace.

52"Give your attention to my prayers
and the prayers of your people Israel.
Listen to them anytime they ask you for
help. 53You chose them from all the nations on earth to be your very own people. This is what you promised through
Moses your servant when you brought
our ancestors out of Egypt, Lord GOD."

54Solomon prayed this prayer to the
LORD, kneeling in front of the altar with
his arms raised toward heaven. When he
finished praying, he got up. 55Then, in a
loud voice, he stood and blessed all the
people of Israel, saying: 56"Praise the
LORD! He promised he would give rest to
his people Israel, and he has given us
rest. The LORD has kept all the good
promises he gave through his servant
Moses. 57May the LORD our God be with
us as he was with our ancestors. May he
never leave us, 58and may he turn us to
himself so we will follow him. Let us
obey all the laws and commands he gave
our ancestors. 59May the LORD our God
remember this prayer day and night and
do what is right for his servant and his
people Israel day by day. 60Then all the
people of the world will know the LORD is
the only true God. 61You must fully obey
the LORD our God and follow all his laws
and commands. Continue to obey in the
future as you do now."

Sacrifices Are Offered

62Then King Solomon and all Israel
with him offered sacrifices to the LORD.
63Solomon killed twenty-two thousand

FAITH links

A CAUSE FOR CELEBRATION

1 KINGS 8:62-66

What are some occasions you like to celebrate? Birthdays? Anniversaries? Many churches hold a celebration when the church anniversary rolls around. Church anniversaries are a reminder of how a church has grown together as a family. They're also a way to thank God for what he has done. The people of Israel celebrated after the completion of the Temple. A lot of hard work went into building the Temple. The people showed their thankfulness to God for blessing them.

You don't have to wait for a church anniversary to express your thanks to God. You can do it right now. In fact, why not make a habit out of it? That's how holiday celebrations get their start.

My Worship Place, Genesis 35:1–14, p. 49

A Holiday Every Week, Leviticus 23:1–3, p. 166

A Song of Thanks, 1 Samuel 2, p. 356

The Gift of Worship, Matthew 2:10–12, p. 1275

Ten Things I Like About You, 2 Thessalonians 1:3–4, p. 1638

Touched by an Angel?, Hebrews 1:3–4, p. 1667

cattle and one hundred twenty thousand
sheep as fellowship offerings. So the king
and all the people gave the Temple to the
LORD.
64On that day King Solomon made
holy the middle part of the courtyard
which is in front of the Temple of the
LORD. There he offered whole burnt offerings, grain offerings, and the fat of the
fellowship offerings. He offered them in
the courtyard, because the bronze altar
before the LORD was too small to hold all
the burnt offerings, the grain offerings,
and the fat of the fellowship offerings.
65Solomon and all the Israelites celebrated the other festival that came at that
time. People came from as far away as
Lebo Hamath and the brook of Egypt. A
great many people celebrated before the
LORD for seven days, then seven more
days, for a total of fourteen days. **66**On
the following day Solomon sent the people home. They blessed the king as they
went, happy because of all the good
things the LORD had done for his servant
David and his people Israel.

The Lord Appears to Solomon Again

9 Solomon finished building the Temple
of the LORD and his royal palace and
everything he wanted to build. **2**Then the
LORD appeared to him again just as he
had done before, in Gibeon. **3**The LORD
said to him: "I have heard your prayer
and what you have asked me to do. You
built this Temple, and I have made it a
holy place. I will be worshiped there forever and will watch over it and protect it
always.
4"But you must serve me as your father David did; he was fair and sincere.
You must obey all I have commanded and
keep my laws and rules. **5**If you do, I will
make your kingdom strong. This is the
promise I made to your father David—
that someone from his family would always rule Israel.
6"But you and your children must follow me and obey the laws and commands
I have given you. You must not serve or
worship other gods. **7**If you do, I will
force Israel to leave the land I have given

THE WAY TO SERVE GOD

1 KINGS 9:4

If God were to describe your character to someone else, what do you think he would say? What would you want him to say? When God talked to Solomon about his father David, he described David as "fair and sincere." God wanted Solomon to be like that when he served God. God has that in mind for you as well. Are you like that?

What words come to mind to describe how you serve God? Connect here to see how God wants us to serve:

Share What You Have, Exodus 35:5–18, p. 123

Your Response to Responsibility, Ruth 2:1–7, p. 346

A Reminder to Be Fair, 2 Chronicles 19:5–11, p. 583

Let's Make a Deal, Daniel 1:8–21, p. 1150

Perfectly Pleasing?, Matthew 5:1–12, p. 1280

Our Gift to God, Romans 12:1–2, p. 1536

them, and I will leave this Temple that I have made holy. All the nations will make fun of Israel and speak evil about them.
8If the Temple is destroyed, everyone who passes by will be shocked. They will make fun of you and ask, 'Why did the LORD do this terrible thing to this land and this Temple?' **9**People will answer, 'This happened because they left the LORD their God. This was the God who brought their ancestors out of Egypt, but they decided to follow other gods. They worshiped and served those gods, so the LORD brought all this disaster on them.' "

Solomon's Other Achievements

10By the end of twenty years, King Solomon had built two buildings—the Temple of the LORD and the royal palace.
11At that time King Solomon gave twenty towns in Galilee to Hiram king of Tyre, because Hiram had helped with the buildings. Hiram had given Solomon all the cedar, pine, and gold he wanted. **12**So Hiram traveled from Tyre to see the towns Solomon had given him, but when he saw them, he was not pleased. **13**He asked, "What good are these towns you have given me, my brother?" So he named them the Land of Cabul,* and they are still called that today. **14**Hiram had sent Solomon about nine thousand pounds of gold.

15This is the account of the forced labor Solomon used to build the Temple and the palace. He had them fill in the land and build the wall around Jerusalem. He also had them rebuild the cities of Hazor, Megiddo, and Gezer. **16**(In the past the king of Egypt had attacked and captured Gezer. After burning it, he killed the Canaanites who lived there. Then he gave it as a wedding present to his daughter, who married Solomon.
17So Solomon rebuilt it.) He also built the cities of Lower Beth Horon **18**and Baalath, as well as Tadmor, which is in the desert. **19**King Solomon also built cities for storing grain and supplies and cities for his chariots and horses. He built whatever he wanted in Jerusalem, Lebanon, and everywhere he ruled.

20There were other people in the land who were not Israelites—Amorites, Hittites, Perizzites, Hivites, and Jebusites.
21They were descendants of people that the Israelites had not destroyed. Solomon forced them to work for him as slaves, as is still true today. **22**But Solomon did not make slaves of the Israelites. They were his soldiers, government

9:13 Cabul This name sounds like the Hebrew word for "worthless."

leaders, officers, captains, chariot commanders, and drivers.
23These were his most important officers over the work. There were five
hundred fifty supervisors over the people
who did the work on Solomon's projects.
24The daughter of the king of Egypt
moved from the old part of Jerusalem to
the palace that Solomon had built for her.
Then Solomon filled in the surrounding
land.
25Three times each year Solomon offered whole burnt offerings and fellowship offerings on the altar he had built for
the LORD. He also burned incense before
the LORD. So he finished the work on the
Temple.
26King Solomon also built ships at
Ezion Geber, a town near Elath on the
shore of the Red Sea, in the land of Edom.
27Hiram had skilled sailors, so he sent
them to serve in these ships with Solomon's men. 28The ships sailed to Ophir
and brought back about thirty-two thousand pounds of gold to King Solomon.

The Queen of Sheba Visits Solomon

10 When the queen of Sheba heard
about Solomon, she came to test
him with hard questions. 2She traveled
to Jerusalem with a large group of servants and camels carrying spices, jewels,
and much gold. When she came to Solomon, she talked with him about all she
had in mind, 3and Solomon answered all
her questions. Nothing was too hard for
him to explain to her. 4The queen of Sheba learned that Solomon was very wise.
She saw the palace he had built, 5the food
on his table, his many officers, the palace
servants, and their good clothes. She saw
the servants who served him at feasts
and the whole burnt offerings he made in
the Temple of the LORD. All these things
amazed her.
6So she said to King Solomon, "What
I heard in my own country about your
achievements and wisdom is true. 7I
could not believe it then, but now I have
come and seen it with my own eyes. I
was not told even half of it! Your wisdom
and wealth are much greater than I had
heard. 8Your men and officers are very
lucky, because in always serving you,
they are able to hear your wisdom.
9Praise the LORD your God, who was
pleased to make you king of Israel. The
LORD has constant love for Israel, so he

FAITH links

AN ADMIRABLE QUALITY

1 KINGS 10:1-13

Who is the person you most admire? What qualities make this person worth admiring? The queen of Sheba admired Solomon's wisdom. Even though there were no newspapers or TV, people all over the world had heard about Solomon's wisdom. The queen traveled a long way to ask Solomon questions and bring him gifts.

In today's society wisdom isn't prized as much as wealth or power. Still, God wants you to value having wisdom. Why? Because it comes from him. (Check out 2 Chronicles 9, p. 571, which also tells this story.)

A Different Kind of People, Leviticus 11, p. 146

Who Do You Trust?, Joshua 9, p. 287

Our Thirst Quencher, Psalm 42:1–3, p. 741

The Best Advice, Zechariah 10:2, p. 1261

Put God First, Acts 5:27–32, p. 1472

Out of Your Mind?, 1 Corinthians 2:16, p. 1547

made you king to keep justice and to rule
fairly."
10Then she gave the king about nine
thousand pounds of gold and many spices
and jewels. No one since that time has
brought more spices than the queen of
Sheba gave to King Solomon.
11(Hiram's ships brought gold from
Ophir, as well as much juniper wood and
jewels. 12Solomon used the juniper wood
to build supports for the Temple of the
LORD and the palace, and to make harps
and lyres for the musicians. Such fine juniper wood has not been brought in or
been seen since that time.)
13King Solomon gave the queen of
Sheba everything she wanted and asked
for, in addition to what he had already
given her of his wealth. Then she and her
servants returned to her own country.

Solomon's Wealth

14Every year King Solomon received
about fifty thousand pounds of gold.
15Besides that, he also received gold
from the traders and merchants, as well
as from the kings of Arabia and governors
of the land.
16King Solomon made two hundred
large shields of hammered gold, each of
which contained about seven and one-
half pounds of gold. 17He also made three
hundred smaller shields of hammered
gold, each of which contained about four
pounds of gold. The king put them in the
Palace of the Forest of Lebanon.
18The king built a large throne of ivory and covered it with fine gold. 19The
throne had six steps on it, and its back
was round at the top. There were armrests on both sides of the chair, and each
armrest had a lion beside it. 20Twelve lions stood on the six steps, one lion at
each end of each step. Nothing like this
had ever been made for any other kingdom. 21All of Solomon's drinking cups,
as well as the dishes in the Palace of the
Forest of Lebanon, were made of pure
gold. Nothing was made from silver, because silver was not valuable in Solomon's time.
22King Solomon also had many trading ships at sea, along with Hiram's
ships. Every three years the ships returned, bringing back gold, silver, ivory,
apes, and baboons.
23So Solomon had more riches and
wisdom than all the other kings on earth.
24People everywhere wanted to see
King Solomon and listen to the wisdom
God had given him. 25Every year those
who came brought gifts of silver and gold,
clothes, weapons, spices, horses, and
mules.
26Solomon had fourteen hundred
chariots and twelve thousand horses. He
kept some in special cities for the chariots, and others he kept with him in Jerusalem. 27In Jerusalem Solomon made
silver as common as stones and cedar
trees as common as the fig trees on the
western hills. 28He imported horses
from Egypt and Kue. His traders bought
them in Kue. 29A chariot from Egypt cost
about fifteen pounds of silver, and a horse
cost nearly four pounds of silver. Solomon's traders also sold horses and chariots to all the kings of the Hittites and the
Arameans.

Solomon's Many Wives

11 King Solomon loved many women
who were not from Israel. He
loved the daughter of the king of Egypt,
as well as women of the Moabites, Ammonites, Edomites, Sidonians, and Hittites. 2The LORD had told the Israelites,
"You must not marry people of other nations. If you do, they will cause you to follow their gods." But Solomon fell in love
with these women. 3He had seven hundred wives who were from royal families
and three hundred slave women who
gave birth to his children. His wives
caused him to turn away from God. 4As
Solomon grew old, his wives caused him
to follow other gods. He did not follow
the LORD completely as his father David
had done. 5Solomon worshiped Ashtoreth, the goddess of the people of Sidon,
and Molech, the hated god of the Ammonites. 6So Solomon did what the LORD
said was wrong and did not follow the
LORD completely as his father David had
done.
7On a hill east of Jerusalem, Solomon

built two places for worship. One was a
place to worship Chemosh, the hated god
of the Moabites, and the other was a
place to worship Molech, the hated god of
the Ammonites. **8**Solomon did the same
thing for all his foreign wives so they
could burn incense and offer sacrifices to
their gods.
9The LORD had appeared to Solomon
twice, but the king turned away from following the LORD, the God of Israel. The
LORD was angry with Solomon, **10**because he had commanded Solomon not to
follow other gods. But Solomon did not
obey the LORD's command. **11**So the
LORD said to Solomon, "Because you
have chosen to break your agreement
with me and have not obeyed my commands, I will tear your kingdom away
from you and give it to one of your officers. **12**But I will not take it away while
you are alive because of my love for your
father David. I will tear it away from your
son when he becomes king. **13**I will not
tear away all the kingdom from him, but I
will leave him one tribe to rule. I will do
this because of David, my servant, and
because of Jerusalem, the city I have chosen."

THE WISDOM OF OBEYING GOD

1 KINGS 11:1-13

On his deathbed, David told his son Solomon to always obey God. Solomon obeyed God for a while. But later he disobeyed God's law by marrying foreign women and by worshiping other gods. Solomon had forgotten his father's wise advice.

Want to be wise? Don't forget the wise advice you've been given. If you have trouble remembering anything else, remember David's advice to Solomon: always obey God.

The Best Policy, Genesis 29:16–19, p. 41

Ten Ways to Obey, Exodus 20, p. 103

A Word to the Wise, Proverbs 10:1, p. 838

A Useless Thing, Isaiah 44:9, 18–20, p. 954

A Hometown Hurt, Jeremiah 11:8—12:6, p. 1008

Faith God Notices, Luke 18:35–43, p. 1406

Solomon's Enemies

14The LORD caused Hadad the Edomite, a member of the family of the king of
Edom, to become Solomon's enemy.
15Earlier, David had defeated Edom.
When Joab, the commander of David's
army, went into Edom to bury the dead,
he killed all the males. **16**Joab and all the
Israelites stayed in Edom for six months
and killed every male in Edom. **17**At that
time Hadad was only a young boy, so he
ran away to Egypt with some of his
father's officers. **18**They left Midian and
went to Paran, where they were joined by
other men. Then they all went to Egypt
to see the king, who gave Hadad a house,
some food, and some land.
19The king liked Hadad so much he
gave Hadad a wife—the sister of Tahpenes,
the king's wife. **20**They had a son named
Genubath. Queen Tahpenes brought him
up in the royal palace with the king's own
children.
21While he was in Egypt, Hadad
heard that David had died and that Joab,
the commander of the army, was dead
also. So Hadad said to the king, "Let me
go; I will return to my own country."
22"Why do you want to go back to
your own country?" the king asked.
"What haven't I given you here?"
"Nothing," Hadad answered, "but
please, let me go."

23God also caused another man to be
Solomon's enemy—Rezon son of Eliada.
Rezon had run away from his master,
Hadadezer king of Zobah. 24After David
defeated the army of Zobah, Rezon gathered some men and became the leader of
a small army. They went to Damascus
and settled there, and Rezon became
king of Damascus. 25Rezon ruled Aram,
and he hated Israel. So he was an enemy
of Israel all the time Solomon was alive.
Both Rezon and Hadad made trouble for
Israel.

26Jeroboam son of Nebat was one of
Solomon's officers. He was an Ephraim-
ite from the town of Zeredah, and he was
the son of a widow named Zeruah. Jeroboam turned against the king.

27This is the story of how Jeroboam
turned against the king. Solomon was filling in the land and repairing the wall of
Jerusalem, the city of David, his father.
28Jeroboam was a capable man, and Solomon saw that this young man was a
good worker. So Solomon put him over all
the workers from the tribes of Ephraim
and Manasseh.

29One day as Jeroboam was leaving
Jerusalem, Ahijah, the prophet from Shiloh, who was wearing a new coat, met
him on the road. The two men were alone
out in the country. 30Ahijah took his new
coat and tore it into twelve pieces.
31Then he said to Jeroboam, "Take ten
pieces of this coat for yourself. The
LORD, the God of Israel, says: 'I will tear
the kingdom away from Solomon and
give you ten tribes. 32But I will allow him
to control one tribe. I will do this for the
sake of my servant David and for Jerusalem, the city I have chosen from all the
tribes of Israel. 33I will do this because
Solomon has stopped following me and
has worshiped the Sidonian god Ashtoreth, the Moabite god Chemosh, and the
Ammonite god Molech. Solomon has not
obeyed me by doing what I said is right
and obeying my laws and commands, as
his father David did.

34" 'But I will not take all the kingdom away from Solomon. I will let him
rule all his life because of my servant David, whom I chose, who obeyed all my
commands and laws. 35But I will take the
kingdom away from his son, and I will allow you to rule over the ten tribes. 36I
will allow Solomon's son to continue to
rule over one tribe so that there will always be a descendant of David, my servant, in Jerusalem, the city where I chose
to be worshiped. 37But I will make you
rule over everything you want. You will
rule over all of Israel, 38and I will always
be with you if you do what I say is right.
You must obey all my commands. If you
obey my laws and commands as David
did, I will be with you. I will make your
family a lasting family of kings, as I did for
David, and give Israel to you. 39I will
punish David's children because of this,
but I will not punish them forever.' "

Solomon's Death

40Solomon tried to kill Jeroboam, but
he ran away to Egypt, to Shishak king of
Egypt, where he stayed until Solomon
died.

41Everything else King Solomon did,
and the wisdom he showed, is written in
the book of the history of Solomon.
42Solomon ruled in Jerusalem over all Israel for forty years. 43Then he died and
was buried in Jerusalem, the city of David, his father. And his son Rehoboam became king in his place.

Israel Turns Against Rehoboam

12 Rehoboam went to Shechem,
where all the Israelites had gone
to make him king. 2Jeroboam son of Nebat was still in Egypt, where he had gone
to escape from Solomon. When Jeroboam
heard about Rehoboam being made king,
he was living in Egypt. 3After the people
sent for him, he and the people went to
Rehoboam and said to him, 4"Your father
forced us to work very hard. Now, make it
easier for us, and don't make us work as
hard as he did. Then we will serve you."

5Rehoboam answered, "Go away for
three days, and then come back to me."
So the people left.

6King Rehoboam asked the older
leaders who had advised Solomon during
his lifetime, "How do you think I should
answer these people?"

7They said, "You should be like a servant to them today. If you serve them and
give them a kind answer, they will serve
you always."
8But Rehoboam rejected this advice.
Instead, he asked the young men who had
grown up with him and who served as his
advisers. 9Rehoboam asked them, "What
is your advice? How should we answer
these people who said, 'Don't make us
work as hard as your father did'?"
10The young men who had grown up
with him answered, "Those people said
to you, 'Your father forced us to work
very hard. Now make our work easier.'
You should tell them, 'My little finger is
bigger than my father's legs. 11He forced
you to work hard, but I will make you
work even harder. My father beat you
with whips, but I will beat you with whips
that have sharp points.' "
12Rehoboam had told the people,
"Come back to me in three days." So after three days Jeroboam and all the people returned to Rehoboam. 13King
Rehoboam spoke cruel words to them,
because he had rejected the advice the
older leaders had given him. 14He followed the advice of the young men and
said to the people, "My father forced you
to work hard, but I will make you work
even harder. My father beat you with
whips, but I will beat you with whips that
have sharp points." 15So the king did not
listen to the people. The LORD caused
this to happen to keep the promise he had
made to Jeroboam son of Nebat through
Ahijah, a prophet from Shiloh.
16When all the Israelites saw that the
new king refused to listen to them, they
said to the king,

"We have no share in David!
We have no part in the son of Jesse!
People of Israel, let's go to our own homes!
Let David's son rule his own people!"

So the Israelites went home. 17But Rehoboam still ruled over the Israelites
who lived in the towns of Judah.
18Adoniram was in charge of the
forced labor. When Rehoboam sent him

FAITH links

WHEN I NEED ADVICE

1 KINGS 12:1-17

What is your favorite source of advice: your friends or adults? After Solomon died, his son Rehoboam became king of Israel. Two groups of people came to him with advice on running the kingdom: a group of older leaders and a group of his friends. The older leaders told him to be kind to the people. The friends told him to be hard on the people. Rehoboam took his friends' advice. When he did, most of the kingdom rebelled against him.

There's nothing wrong with asking your friends for advice. But take time to consider the advice of godly adults as well. Their wisdom and experience might be just what you need.

Who do you ask for advice? Connect here to find out some good sources:

Good Advice?, Leviticus 20:6, p. 162

I Want It *Now!*, Judges 14:1–3, p. 332

Teaching Others, Ezra 7:8–10, p. 617

The Dead End of the Occult, Ezekiel 13:17–23, p. 1098

Going My Way?, Hosea 8:1–6, p. 1179

Two Ways to Grow, Luke 2:46–52, p. 1370

to the people of Israel, they threw stones
at him until he died. But King Rehoboam
ran to his chariot and escaped to Jerusalem. **19**Since then, Israel has been
against the family of David.

20When all the Israelites heard that
Jeroboam had returned, they called him
to a meeting and made him king over all
Israel. Only the tribe of Judah continued
to follow the family of David.

21When Rehoboam arrived in Jerusalem, he gathered one hundred eighty
thousand of the best soldiers from the
tribes of Judah and Benjamin. As son of
Solomon, Rehoboam wanted to fight the
people of Israel to take back his kingdom.

22But God spoke his word to Shemaiah, a man of God, saying, **23**"Speak to
Solomon's son Rehoboam, the king of Judah, and to all the people of Judah and
Benjamin and the rest of the people. Say
to them, **24**'The LORD says you must not
go to war against your brothers, the Israelites. Every one of you should go home,
because I made all these things happen.' " So they obeyed the LORD's command and went home as the LORD had
commanded.

25Then Jeroboam made Shechem in
the mountains of Ephraim a very strong
city, and he lived there. He also went to
the city of Peniel and made it stronger.

Jeroboam Builds Golden Calves

26Jeroboam said to himself, "The
kingdom will probably go back to David's
family. **27**If the people continue going to
the Temple of the LORD in Jerusalem to
offer sacrifices, they will want to be ruled
again by Rehoboam. Then they will kill
me and follow Rehoboam king of Judah."

28King Jeroboam asked for advice.
Then he made two golden calves. "It is
too long a journey for you to go to Jerusalem to worship," he said to the people.
"Israel, here are your gods who brought
you out of Egypt." **29**Jeroboam put one
golden calf in the city of Bethel and the
other in the city of Dan. **30**This became a
very great sin, because the people traveled as far as Dan to worship the calf
there.

31Jeroboam built temples on the
places of worship. He also chose priests
from all the people, not just from the
tribe of Levi. **32**And he started a new festival on the fifteenth day of the eighth
month, just like the festival in Judah.
During that time the king offered sacrifices on the altar, along with sacrifices to
the calves in Bethel he had made. He also
chose priests in Bethel to serve at the
places of worship he had made. **33**So Jeroboam chose his own time for a festival
for the Israelites—the fifteenth day of
the eighth month. During that time he offered sacrifices on the altar he had built
in Bethel. He set up a festival for the Israelites and offered sacrifices on the altar.

The Man of God Speaks Against Bethel

13 The LORD commanded a man of
God from Judah to go to Bethel.
When he arrived, Jeroboam was standing
by the altar to offer a sacrifice. **2**The
LORD had commanded the man of God to
speak against the altar. The man said,
"Altar, altar, the LORD says to you:
'David's family will have a son named Josiah. The priests for the places of worship now make their sacrifices on you,
but Josiah will sacrifice those priests on
you. Human bones will be burned on
you.' " **3**That same day the man of God
gave proof that these things would happen. "This is the LORD's sign that this
will happen," he said. "This altar will
break apart, and the ashes on it will fall to
the ground."

4When King Jeroboam heard what the
man of God said about the altar in Bethel,
the king raised his hand from the altar
and pointed at the man. "Take him!" he
said. But when the king said this, his arm
was paralyzed, and he could not move it.
5The altar also broke into pieces, and its
ashes fell to the ground. This was the
sign the LORD had told the man of God to
give.

6Then the king said to the man of
God, "Please pray to the LORD your God
for me, and ask him to heal my arm."

So the man of God prayed to the
LORD, and the king's arm was healed, becoming as it was before.

7Then the king said to the man of
God, "Please come home and eat with
me, and I will give you a gift."
8But the man of God answered the
king, "Even if you gave me half of your
kingdom, I would not go with you. I will
not eat or drink anything in this place.
9The LORD commanded me not to eat or
drink anything nor to return on the same
road by which I came." **10**So he took a different road and did not return on the same
road by which he had come to Bethel.
11Now an old prophet was living in
Bethel. His sons came and told him what
the man of God had done there that day.
They also told their father what he had
said to King Jeroboam. **12**The father
asked, "Which road did he use when he
left?" So his sons showed him the road
the man of God from Judah had taken.
13Then the prophet told his sons to put a
saddle on his donkey. So they saddled the
donkey, and he left.
14He went after the man of God and
found him sitting under an oak tree. The
prophet asked, "Are you the man of God
who came from Judah?"
The man answered, "Yes, I am."
15The prophet said, "Please come
home and eat with me."
16"I can't go home with you," the man
of God answered. "I can't eat or drink
with you in this place. **17**The LORD said
to me, 'Don't eat or drink anything there
or return on the same road by which you
came.' "
18Then the old prophet said, "But I
also am a prophet like you." Then he told
a lie. He said, "An angel from the LORD
came to me and told me to bring you to
my home. He said you should eat and
drink with me." **19**So the man of God
went to the old prophet's house, and he
ate and drank with him there.
20While they were sitting at the table,
the LORD spoke his word to the old
prophet. **21**The old prophet cried out to
the man of God from Judah, "The LORD
said you did not obey him! He said you
did not do what the LORD your God commanded you. **22**The LORD commanded
you not to eat or drink anything in this
place, but you came back and ate and
drank. So your body will not be buried in
your family grave."
23After the man of God finished eating and drinking, the prophet put a saddle
on his donkey for him, and the man left.
24As he was traveling home, a lion attacked and killed him. His body lay on the
road, with the donkey and the lion standing nearby. **25**Some men who were traveling on that road saw the body and the
lion standing nearby. So they went to the
city where the old prophet lived and told
what they had seen.
26The old prophet who had brought
back the man of God heard what had happened. "It is the man of God who did not
obey the LORD's command," he said. "So
the LORD sent a lion to kill him, just as he
said he would."
27Then the prophet said to his sons,
"Put a saddle on my donkey," which they
did. **28**The old prophet went out and
found the body lying on the road, with the
donkey and the lion still standing nearby.
The lion had not eaten the body or hurt
the donkey. **29**The prophet put the body
on his donkey and carried it back to the
city to have a time of sadness for him and
to bury him. **30**The prophet buried the
body in his own family grave, and they
were sad for the man of God and said,
"Oh, my brother."
31After the prophet buried the body,
he said to his sons, "When I die, bury me
in this same grave. Put my bones next to
his. **32**Through him the LORD spoke
against the altar at Bethel and against the
places of worship in the towns of Samaria. What the LORD spoke through him
will certainly come true."
33After this incident King Jeroboam
did not stop doing evil. He continued to
choose priests for the places of worship
from among all the people. Anyone who
wanted to be a priest for the places of
worship was allowed to be one. **34**In this
way the family of Jeroboam sinned, and
this sin caused its ruin and destruction
from the earth.

Jeroboam's Son Dies

14 At that time Jeroboam's son Abijah
became very sick. **2**So Jeroboam

said to his wife, “Go to Shiloh to see the
prophet Ahijah. He is the one who said I
would become king of Israel. But dress
yourself so people won’t know you are
my wife. 3Take the prophet ten loaves of
bread, some cakes, and a jar of honey.
Then ask him what will happen to our
son, and he will tell you.” 4So the king’s
wife did as he said and went to Ahijah’s
home in Shiloh.
Now Ahijah was very old and blind.
5The LORD said to him, “Jeroboam’s son
is sick, and Jeroboam’s wife is coming to
ask you about him. When she arrives, she
will pretend to be someone else.” Then
the LORD told Ahijah what to say.
6When Ahijah heard her walking to
the door, he said, “Come in, wife of Jeroboam. Why are you pretending to be
someone else? I have bad news for you.
7Go back and tell Jeroboam that this is
what the LORD, the God of Israel, says:
‘Jeroboam, I chose you from among all
the people and made you the leader of my
people Israel. 8I tore the kingdom away
from David’s family, and I gave it to you.
But you are not like my servant David,
who always obeyed my
commands and followed
me with all his heart. He
did only what I said was
right. 9But you have done
more evil than anyone
who ruled before you.
You have quit following
me and have made other
gods and idols of metal.
This has made me very
angry, 10so I will soon
bring disaster to your family. I will kill all
the men in your family, both slaves and
free men. I will destroy your family as
completely as fire burns up manure.
11Anyone from your family who dies in
the city will be eaten by dogs, and those
who die in the fields will be eaten by the
birds. The LORD has spoken.’ ”
12Then Ahijah said to Jeroboam’s
wife, “Go home now. As soon as you enter your city, your son will die, 13and all
Israel will be sad for him and bury him.
He is the only one of Jeroboam’s family
who will be buried, because he is the only
one in the king’s family who pleased the
LORD, the God of Israel.
14“The LORD will put a new king over
Israel, who will destroy Jeroboam’s family, and this will happen soon. 15Then the
LORD will punish Israel, which will be
like grass moving in the water. The LORD
will pull up Israel from this good land, the
land he gave their ancestors. He will
scatter Israel beyond the Euphrates
River, because he is angry with the people. They made the LORD angry when
they set up idols to worship Asherah.
16Jeroboam sinned, and then he made
the people of Israel sin. So the LORD will
let the people of Israel be defeated.”
17Then Jeroboam’s wife left and returned to Tirzah. As soon as she entered
her home, the boy died. 18After they buried him, all Israel had a time of sadness for
him, just as the LORD had said through his
servant, the prophet Ahijah.
19Everything else Jeroboam did is
written in the book of the history of the
kings of Israel. He fought wars and continued to rule the people, 20serving as
king for twenty-two years. Then he died,
and his son Nadab be-
came king in his place.

> But you are not like my servant David, who always obeyed my commands and followed me with all his heart.
> —1 Kings 14:8

The Death of Rehoboam

21Solomon’s son Re-
hoboam was forty-one
years old when he be-
came king of Judah. His
mother was Naamah from
Ammon. Rehoboam ruled
in Jerusalem for seven-
teen years. (The LORD had chosen that
city from all the land of Israel as the place
where he would be worshiped.)
22The people of Judah did what the
LORD said was wrong. Their sins made
the LORD very angry, even more angry
than he had been at their ancestors.
23The people built
stone pillars and
places to worship
gods and Asherah
idols on every high
hill and under every
green tree. 24There

> eMAIL FROM GOD
> **14:21–23**
> **Idols**
> What does God think of worshiping other things?

were even male prostitutes in the land. They acted like the people who had lived in the land before the Israelites. They had done many evil things, and God had taken the land away from them.

25During the fifth year Rehoboam was king, Shishak king of Egypt attacked Jerusalem. **26**He took the treasures from the Temple of the LORD and the king's palace. He took everything, even the gold shields Solomon had made. **27**So King Rehoboam made bronze shields to put in their place and gave them to the commanders of the guards for the palace gates. **28**Whenever the king went to the Temple of the LORD, the guards carried the shields. Later, they would put them back in the guardroom.

29Everything else King Rehoboam did is written in the book of the history of the kings of Judah. **30**There was war between Rehoboam and Jeroboam the whole time. **31**Rehoboam, son of Naamah from Ammon, died and was buried with his ancestors in Jerusalem, and his son Abijah became king in his place.

Abijah King of Judah

15 Abijah became king of Judah during the eighteenth year Jeroboam son of Nebat was king of Israel. **2**Abijah ruled in Jerusalem for three years. His mother was Maacah daughter of Abishalom. **3**He did all the same sins his father before him had done. Abijah was not faithful to the LORD his God as David, his great-grandfather, had been. **4**Because the LORD loved David, the LORD gave him a kingdom in Jerusalem and allowed him to have a son to be king after him. The LORD also kept Jerusalem safe. **5**David always did what the LORD said was right and obeyed his commands all his life, except the one time when David sinned against Uriah the Hittite.

6There was war between Abijah and Jeroboam during Abijah's lifetime. **7**Everything else Abijah did is written in the book of the history of the kings of Judah. During the time Abijah ruled, there was war between Abijah and Jeroboam. **8**Abijah died and was buried in Jerusalem, and his son Asa became king in his place.

Asa King of Judah

9During the twentieth year Jeroboam was king of Israel, Asa became king of Judah. **10**His grandmother's name was Maacah, the daughter of Abishalom. Asa ruled in Jerusalem for forty-one years.

11Asa did what the LORD said was right, as his ancestor David had done. **12**He forced the male prostitutes at the worship places to leave the country. He also took away the idols that his ancestors had made. **13**His grandmother Maacah had made a terrible Asherah idol, so Asa removed her from being queen mother. He cut down that idol and burned it in the Kidron Valley. **14**The places of worship to gods were not removed. Even so, Asa was faithful to the LORD all his life. **15**Asa brought into the Temple of the LORD the gifts he and his father had given: gold, silver, and utensils.

16There was war between Asa and Baasha king of Israel all the time they were kings. **17**Baasha attacked Judah, and he made the town of Ramah strong so he could keep people from leaving or entering Judah, Asa's country.

18Asa took the rest of the silver and gold from the treasuries of the Temple of the LORD and his own palace and gave it to his officers. Then he sent them to Ben-Hadad son of Tabrimmon, who was the son of Hezion. Ben-Hadad was the king of Aram and ruled in the city of Damascus. Asa said, **19**"Let there be a treaty between you and me as there was between my father and your father. I am sending you a gift of silver and gold. Break your treaty with Baasha king of Israel so he will leave my land."

20Ben-Hadad agreed with King Asa, so he sent the commanders of his armies to attack the towns of Israel. They defeated the towns of Ijon, Dan, and Abel Beth Maacah, as well as all Galilee and the area of Naphtali. **21**When Baasha heard about these attacks, he stopped building up Ramah and returned to Tirzah. **22**Then King Asa gave an order to all the people of Judah; everyone had to help. They carried away all the stones and wood Baasha had been using in Ramah, and they used them to build

FAITH links

YOUR STATS

1 KINGS 15; 16

You can look at a sport player's stats (statistics) to know whether he or she is good at what he/she does. Any bubble-gum card, poster, or scorecard will tell you. The listings or "stats" of the kings of Israel in 1 Kings reveal only one important item: whether or not they were obedient to God.

Your life is one big scorecard. Although you're in the early innings right now, people still can tell by your life whether or not obeying God is important to you. Is it?

Obey? No Way!, Exodus 1:15–21, p. 76

Remembering What He Said, Deuteronomy 6:4–9, p. 236

Braggin' Rights, Jeremiah 9:23–24, p. 1005

Obeying God or Man?, Daniel 3:8–30, p. 1154

Perfectly Pleasing?, Matthew 5:1–12, p. 1280

Out with the Old!, Colossians 3:1–14, p. 1625

up Geba and Mizpah in the land of Benjamin.
23Everything else Asa did—his victories and the cities he built—is written in
the book of the history of the kings of Judah. When he became old, he got a disease in his feet. 24After Asa died, he was
buried with his ancestors in Jerusalem,
the city of David, his ancestor. Then Jehoshaphat, Asa's son, became king in his
place.

Nadab King of Israel

25Nadab son of Jeroboam became
king of Israel during the second year Asa
was king of Judah. Nadab was king of Israel for two years, 26and he did what the
LORD said was wrong. Jeroboam had led
the people of Israel to sin, and Nadab
sinned in the same way as his father Jeroboam.
27Baasha son of Ahijah, from the tribe
of Issachar, made plans to kill Nadab. Nadab and all Israel were attacking the Philistine town of Gibbethon, so Baasha
killed Nadab there. 28This happened during Asa's third year as king of Judah, and
Baasha became the next king of Israel.

Baasha King of Israel

29As soon as Baasha became king, he
killed all of Jeroboam's family, leaving no
one in Jeroboam's family alive. He destroyed them all as the LORD had said
would happen through his servant Ahijah
from Shiloh. 30King Jeroboam had sinned
very much and had led the people of Israel to sin, so he made the LORD, the God of
Israel, very angry.
31Everything else Nadab did is written in the book of the history of the kings
of Israel. 32There was war between Asa
king of Judah and Baasha king of Israel all
the time they ruled.
33Baasha son of Ahijah became king
of Israel during Asa's third year as king of
Judah. Baasha ruled in Tirzah for twenty-
four years, 34and he did what the LORD
said was wrong. Jeroboam had led the
people of Israel to sin, and Baasha sinned
in the same way as Jeroboam.
16 Jehu son of Hanani spoke the word
of the LORD against King Baasha.
2The LORD said, "You were nothing, but I
took you and made you a leader over my
people Israel. But you have followed the
ways of Jeroboam and have led my people
Israel to sin. Their sins have made me
angry, 3so, Baasha, I will soon destroy
you and your family. I will do to you what
I did to the family of Jeroboam son of Nebat. 4Anyone from your family who dies

in the city will be eaten by dogs, and anyone from your family who dies in the
fields will be eaten by birds."
5Everything else Baasha did and all
his victories are written down in the book
of the history of the kings of Israel. **6**So
Baasha died and was buried in Tirzah, and
his son Elah became king in his place.
7The LORD spoke his word against
Baasha and his family through the prophet Jehu son of Hanani. Baasha had done
many things the LORD said were wrong,
which made the LORD very angry. He did
the same evil deeds that Jeroboam's family had done before him. The LORD also
spoke against Baasha because he killed
all of Jeroboam's family.

Elah King of Israel

8Elah son of Baasha became king of
Israel during Asa's twenty-sixth year as
king of Judah, and Elah ruled in Tirzah for
two years.
9Zimri, one of Elah's officers, commanded half of Elah's chariots. Zimri
made plans against Elah while the king
was in Tirzah, getting drunk at Arza's
home. (Arza was in charge of the palace
at Tirzah.) **10**Zimri went into Arza's
house and killed Elah during Asa's twenty-seventh year as king of Judah. Then
Zimri became king of Israel in Elah's
place.

Zimri King of Israel

11As soon as Zimri became king, he
killed all of Baasha's family, not allowing
any of Baasha's family or friends to live.
12So Zimri destroyed all of Baasha's family just as the LORD had said it would happen through the prophet Jehu. **13**Baasha
and his son Elah sinned and led the people of Israel to sin, and they made the
LORD, the God of Israel, angry because of
their worthless idols.
14Everything else Elah did is written
in the book of the history of the kings of
Israel.
15So during Asa's twenty-seventh
year as king of Judah, Zimri became king
of Israel and ruled in Tirzah seven days.
The army of Israel was camped near
Gibbethon, a Philistine town. **16**The men
in the camp heard that Zimri had made
secret plans against King Elah and had
killed him. So that day in the camp they
made Omri, the commander of the army,
king over Israel. **17**So Omri and all the
Israelite army left Gibbethon and attacked Tirzah. **18**When Zimri saw that
the city had been captured, he went into
the palace and set it on fire, burning the
palace and himself with it. **19**So Zimri
died because he had sinned by doing what
the LORD said was wrong. Jeroboam had
led the people of Israel to sin, and Zimri
sinned in the same way as Jeroboam.
20Everything else Zimri did and the
story of how he turned against King Elah
are written down in the book of the history of the kings of Israel.

Omri King of Israel

21The people of Israel were divided
into two groups. Half of the people wanted Tibni son of Ginath to be king, while
the other half wanted Omri. **22**Omri's followers were stronger than the followers
of Tibni son of Ginath, so Tibni died, and
Omri became king.
23Omri became king of Israel during
the thirty-first year Asa was king of Judah. Omri ruled Israel for twelve years,
six of those years in the city of Tirzah.
24He bought the hill of Samaria from
Shemer for about one hundred fifty
pounds of silver. Omri built a city on that
hill and called it Samaria after the name
of its earlier owner, Shemer.
25But Omri did what the LORD said
was wrong; he did more evil than all the
kings who came before him. **26**Jeroboam
son of Nebat had led the people of Israel
to sin, and Omri sinned in the same way
as Jeroboam. The Israelites made the
LORD, the God of Israel, very angry because they worshiped worthless idols.
27Everything else Omri did and all his
successes are written in the book of the
history of the kings of Israel. **28**So Omri
died and was buried in Samaria, and his
son Ahab became king in his place.

Ahab King of Israel

29Ahab son of Omri became king of
Israel during Asa's thirty-eighth year as

king of Judah, and Ahab ruled Israel in
the city of Samaria for twenty-two years.
30More than any king before him, Ahab
son of Omri did many things the LORD
said were wrong. 31He sinned in the
same ways as Jeroboam son of Nebat, but
he did even worse things. He married
Jezebel daughter of Ethbaal, the king of
Sidon. Then Ahab began to serve Baal
and worship him. 32He built a temple in
Samaria for worshiping Baal and put an
altar there for Baal. 33Ahab also made an
idol for worshiping Asherah. He did more
things to make the LORD, the God of
Israel, angry than all the other kings before him.

34During the time of Ahab, Hiel from
Bethel rebuilt the city of Jericho. It cost
Hiel the life of Abiram, his oldest son, to
begin work on the city, and it cost the life
of Segub, his youngest son, to build the
city gates. This happened just as the
LORD, speaking through Joshua son of
Nun, said it would happen.ⁿ

Elijah Stops the Rain

17 Now Elijah the Tishbite was a
prophet from the settlers in Gilead.
"I serve the LORD, the God of Israel,"
Elijah said to Ahab. "As surely as
the LORD lives, no rain or dew will fall
during the next few years unless I command it."

2Then the LORD spoke his word to
Elijah: 3"Leave this place and go east and
hide near Kerith Ravine east of the Jordan River.
4You may drink from the
stream, and I have commanded ravens to
bring you food there." 5So Elijah did what
the LORD said; he went to Kerith Ravine,
east of the Jordan, and lived there. 6The
birds brought Elijah bread and meat
every morning and evening, and he drank
water from the stream.

7After a while the stream dried up because there was no rain.
8Then the LORD
spoke his word to Elijah, 9"Go to Zarephath in Sidon and live there. I have commanded a widow there to take care of
you."

10So Elijah went to Zarephath. When
he reached the town gate, he saw a widow gathering wood for a fire. Elijah asked

FAITH links

GOOD TIMES AND BAD

1 KINGS 17

Did you ever think that serving God means you'd never have problems? During the prophet Elijah's time, there was no rain for three years. Without rain, food became scarce. But God took care of Elijah and a poor widow during the drought.

Jesus once said that God causes the rain to fall on "those who do right and . . . those who do wrong" (Matthew 5:45). Good times and hard times fall in the lives of Christians as well as people who don't believe in Jesus. God wants his people to have faith that he'll take care of them and bring them through the hard times.

Find out how your faith can get you through the tough times:

Good Plans, Genesis 45:7–8, p. 64

Your Best Defense, 2 Chronicles 20:1–12, p. 584

A Really Bad Day, Job 1:20–22; 2:10, p. 661

Facing Your Fears, Matthew 8:23–27, p. 1288

Hard Times, 2 Corinthians 1:8–10, p. 1570

A Good Habit, Ephesians 6:18, p. 1606

16:34 the LORD . . . happen When Joshua destroyed Jericho, he said whoever rebuilt the city would lose his oldest and youngest sons. See Joshua 6:26.

her, "Would you bring me a little water in
a cup so I may have a drink?" **11**As she
was going to get his water, Elijah said,
"Please bring me a piece of bread, too."
12The woman answered, "As surely
as the LORD your God lives, I have no
bread. I have only a handful of flour in a
jar and only a little olive oil in a jug. I
came here to gather some wood so I
could go home and cook our last meal.
My son and I will eat it and then die from
hunger."
13"Don't worry," Elijah said to her.
"Go home and cook your food as you
have said. But first make a small loaf of
bread from the flour you have, and bring
it to me. Then cook something for yourself and your son. **14**The LORD, the God
of Israel, says, 'That jar of flour will never
be empty, and the jug will always have oil
in it, until the day the LORD sends rain to
the land.' "
15So the woman went home and did
what Elijah told her to do. And the woman and her son and Elijah had enough
food every day. **16**The jar of flour and the
jug of oil were never empty, just as the
LORD, through Elijah, had promised.

Elijah Brings a Boy Back to Life

17Some time later the son of the
woman who owned the house became
sick. He grew worse and worse and finally stopped breathing. **18**The woman said
to Elijah, "Man of God, what have you
done to me? Did you come here to remind me of my sin and to kill my son?"
19Elijah said to her, "Give me your
son." Elijah took the boy from her, carried him upstairs, and laid him on the
bed in the room where he was staying.
20Then he prayed to the LORD: "LORD
my God, this widow is letting me stay in
her house. Why have you done this terrible thing to her and caused her son to
die?" **21**Then Elijah lay on top of the boy
three times. He prayed to the LORD,
"LORD my God, let this boy live again!"
22The LORD answered Elijah's
prayer; the boy began breathing again
and was alive. **23**Elijah carried the boy
downstairs and gave him to his mother
and said, "See! Your son is alive!"
24"Now I know you really are a man
from God," the woman said to Elijah. "I
know that the LORD truly speaks through
you!"

Elijah Kills the Prophets of Baal

18 During the third year without rain,
the LORD spoke his word to Elijah:
"Go and meet King Ahab, and I will soon
send rain." **2**So Elijah went to meet Ahab.
By this time there was no food in Samaria. **3**King Ahab sent for Obadiah, who
was in charge of the king's palace. (Obadiah was a true follower of the LORD.
4When Jezebel was killing all the LORD's
prophets, Obadiah hid a hundred of them
in two caves, fifty in one cave and fifty in
another. He also brought them food and
water.) **5**Ahab said to Obadiah, "Let's
check every spring and valley in the land.
Maybe we can find enough grass to keep
our horses and mules alive and not have
to kill our animals." **6**So each one chose a
part of the country to search; Ahab went
in one direction and Obadiah in another.
7While Obadiah was on his way, Elijah
met him. Obadiah recognized Elijah, so
he bowed down to the ground and said,
"Elijah? Is it really you, master?"
8"Yes," Elijah answered. "Go tell your
master that I am here."
9Then Obadiah said, "What wrong
have I done for you to hand me over to
Ahab like this? He will put me to death.
10As surely as the LORD your God lives,
the king has sent people to every country
to search for you. If the ruler said you
were not there, Ahab forced the ruler to
swear you could not be found in his country. **11**Now you want me to go to my master and tell him, 'Elijah is here'? **12**The
Spirit of the LORD may carry you to some
other place after I leave. If I go tell King
Ahab you are here, and he comes and
doesn't find you, he will kill me! I have
followed the LORD since I was a boy.
13Haven't you been told what I did?
When Jezebel was killing the LORD's
prophets, I hid a hundred of them, fifty in
one cave and fifty in another. I brought
them food and water. **14**Now you want
me to go and tell my master you are
here? He will kill me!"

FAITH links

THE FENCE RIDERS

1 KINGS 18

Ever hear someone say, "You're riding the fence"? That means, "You're not on one side or the other." Elijah knew that the Israelites rode the fence about God. Sometimes they wanted to serve God. Other times, they wanted to worship Baal, a false god the people of Canaan worshiped. Elijah told the people to get off the fence and choose between God and Baal once and for all. Once they saw how amazing God was, they chose God.

Are you riding the fence about God? Maybe you're not sure about being a Christian. Or, maybe you're not sure how much of your life you want God to have. Want to stop riding the fence? It's up to you to choose a side, pardner.

The Perfect Leader?, Numbers 20:1–13, p. 203

Remember Your Creator, Ecclesiastes 12:1, 13, p. 885

How to Worship God, Isaiah 58, p. 972

A Fake Apology, Hosea 6:1–7, p. 1177

Prove It!, Matthew 16:1–4, p. 1302

Keeping Clean, 2 Corinthians 7:1, p. 1576

15Elijah answered, "As surely as the
LORD All-Powerful lives, whom I serve, I
will be seen by Ahab today."

16So Obadiah went to Ahab and told
him where Elijah was. Then Ahab went
to meet Elijah.

17When he saw Elijah, he asked, "Is
it you—the biggest troublemaker in
Israel?"

18Elijah answered, "I have not made
trouble in Israel. You and your father's
family have made all this trouble by not
obeying the LORD's commands. You have
gone after the Baals. **19**Now tell all Israel
to meet me at Mount Carmel. Also bring
the four hundred fifty prophets of Baal
and the four hundred prophets of Asherah, who eat at Jezebel's table."

20So Ahab called all the Israelites and
those prophets to Mount Carmel. **21**Elijah approached the people and said, "How
long will you not decide between two
choices? If the LORD is the true God, follow him, but if Baal is the true God, follow him!" But the people said nothing.

22Elijah said, "I am the only prophet
of the LORD here, but there are four hundred fifty prophets of Baal. **23**Bring two
bulls. Let the prophets of Baal choose
one bull and kill it and cut it into pieces.
Then let them put the meat on the wood,
but they are not to set fire to it. I will prepare the other bull, putting the meat on
the wood but not setting fire to it. **24**You
prophets of Baal, pray to your god, and I
will pray to the LORD. The god who answers by setting fire to his wood is the
true God."

All the people agreed that this was a good idea.

25Then Elijah said to the prophets of
Baal, "There are many of you, so you go
first. Choose a bull and prepare it. Pray to
your god, but don't start the fire."

26So they took the bull that was given
to them and prepared it. They prayed to
Baal from morning until noon, shouting
"Baal, answer us!" But there was no
sound, and no one answered. They
danced around the altar they had built.

27At noon Elijah began to make fun of
them. "Pray louder!" he said. "If Baal
really is a god, maybe he is thinking, or

GET THE INFO

ELIJAH, THE PROPHET

1 Kings 18

1. Elijah was known as a Tishbite, which probably means he was from a town called Tishbe. (Read 1 Kings 17:1.)

2. As God's prophet, Elijah predicted a drought (a water shortage) as a punishment against the wicked kings of Samaria, Ahab and Ahaziah.

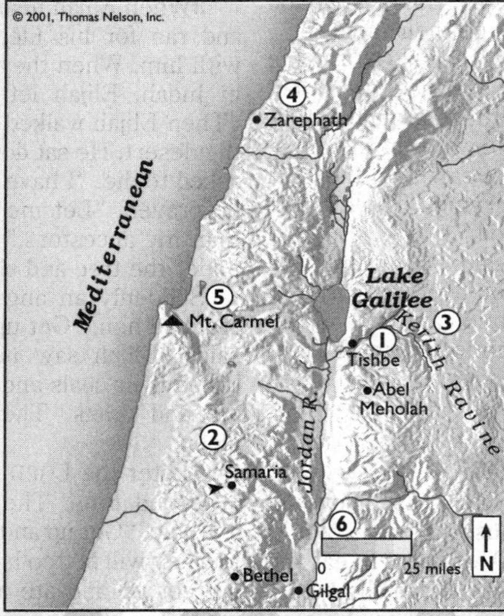

4. Elijah helped a widow and her son in a town called Zarephath. Through a miracle, her oil and flour never ran out until the drought was over. (See 1 Kings 17:8–24.)

5. Elijah had a big showdown with 450 prophets of Baal on Mount Carmel. God sent fire from heaven to burn the altar and proved his power. (Look up 1 Kings 18:20–40.)

3. During the drought, Elijah hid by a brook near the Kerith Ravine. He drank the water there and was miraculously fed by ravens.

6. Elijah was taken up into heaven in a chariot of fire. (Look at 2 Kings 2:1–12, p. 476.)

busy, or traveling! Maybe he is sleeping
so you will have to wake him!" **28**The
prophets prayed louder, cutting themselves with swords and spears until their
blood flowed, which was the way they
worshiped. **29**The afternoon passed, and
the prophets continued to act like this
until it was time for the evening sacrifice.
But no voice was heard; Baal did not answer, and no one paid attention.

30Then Elijah said to all the people,
"Now come to me." So they gathered
around him, and Elijah rebuilt the altar of
the LORD, which had been torn down.
31He took twelve stones, one stone for
each of the twelve tribes, the number of
Jacob's sons. (The LORD changed Jacob's
name to Israel.) **32**Elijah used these
stones to rebuild the altar in honor of the
LORD. Then he dug a ditch around the altar that was big enough to hold about thirteen quarts of seed. **33**Elijah put the wood
on the altar, cut the bull into pieces, and
laid the pieces on the wood. **34**Then he
said, "Fill four jars with water, and pour it
on the meat and on the wood." Then Elijah said, "Do it again," and they did it
again. Then he said, "Do it a third time,"
and they did it the third time. **35**So the
water ran off the altar and filled the ditch.

36At the time for the evening sacrifice, the prophet Elijah went near the altar. "LORD, you are the God of Abraham,
Isaac, and Israel," he prayed. "Prove that
you are the God of Israel and that I am
your servant. Show these people that you
commanded me to do all these things.
37LORD, answer my prayer so these people will know that you, LORD, are God
and that you will change their minds."
38Then fire from the LORD came
down and burned the sacrifice, the wood,
the stones, and the ground around the altar. It also dried up the water in the ditch.
39When all the people saw this, they fell
down to the ground, crying, "The LORD is
God! The LORD is God!"
40Then Elijah said, "Capture the
prophets of Baal! Don't let any of them
run away!" The people captured all the
prophets. Then Elijah led them down to
the Kishon Valley, where he killed
them.

The Rain Comes Again

41Then Elijah said to Ahab, "Now, go,
eat, and drink, because a heavy rain is
coming." **42**So King Ahab went to eat and
drink. At the same time Elijah climbed to
the top of Mount Carmel, where he bent
down to the ground with his head between his knees.
43Then Elijah said to his servant, "Go
and look toward the sea."
The servant went and looked. "I see
nothing," he said.
Elijah told him to go and look again.
This happened seven times. **44**The seventh time, the servant said, "I see a small
cloud, the size of a human fist, coming
from the sea."
Elijah told the servant, "Go to Ahab
and tell him to get his chariot ready and
go home now. Otherwise, the rain will
stop him."
45After a short time the sky was covered with dark clouds. The wind began to
blow, and soon a heavy rain began to fall.
Ahab got in his chariot and started back
to Jezreel. **46**The LORD gave his power to
Elijah, who tightened his clothes around
him and ran ahead of King Ahab all the
way to Jezreel.

Elijah Runs Away

19 King Ahab told Jezebel everything
Elijah had done and how Elijah had
killed all the prophets with a sword. **2**So
Jezebel sent a messenger to Elijah, saying, "May the gods punish me terribly if
by this time tomorrow I don't kill you just
as you killed those prophets."
3When Elijah heard this, he was afraid
and ran for his life, taking his servant
with him. When they came to Beersheba
in Judah, Elijah left his servant there.
4Then Elijah walked for a whole day into
the desert. He sat down under a bush and
asked to die. "I have had enough, LORD,"
he prayed. "Let me die. I am no better
than my ancestors." **5**Then he lay down
under the tree and slept.
Suddenly an angel came to him and
touched him. "Get up and eat," the angel
said. **6**Elijah saw near his head a loaf
baked over coals and a jar of water, so he
ate and drank. Then he went back to
sleep.
7Later the LORD's angel came to him
a second time. The angel touched him
and said, "Get up and eat. If you don't, the
journey will be too hard for you." **8**So Elijah got up and ate and drank. The food
made him strong enough to walk for forty
days and nights to Mount Sinai, the
mountain of God. **9**There Elijah went into
a cave and stayed all night.
Then the LORD spoke his word to him:
"Elijah! Why are you here?"
10He answered, "LORD God All-Powerful, I have always served you as well as I
could. But the people of Israel have broken their agreement with you, destroyed
your altars, and killed your prophets with
swords. I am the only prophet left, and
now they are trying to kill me, too."
11The LORD said to Elijah, "Go, stand
in front of me on the mountain, and I will
pass by you." Then a very strong wind
blew until it caused the mountains to fall
apart and large rocks to break in front of
the LORD. But the LORD was not in the
wind. After the wind, there was an earthquake, but the LORD was not in the earthquake. **12**After the earthquake, there was
a fire, but the LORD was not in the fire.
After the fire, there was a quiet, gentle

FAITH links

LISTEN UP!

1 KINGS 19:11-13

When you're feeling discouraged, what cheers you up? Elijah needed some encouragement. Queen Jezebel, the wife of Ahab, wanted to give him a new address—six feet under. So he ran for his life. During that time, God taught him how to listen for his voice. God's voice was a "quiet, gentle sound." Elijah had not expected God to come to him in that way!

In what ways do you expect God to speak to you? Some might want God to speak in a noticeable way. (Like dropping a note to earth from heaven.) But God wants you to be ready to listen in whatever way he speaks. Are you ready?

Here are some other Faithlinks on listening to God's word:

Comfort from the Word, Job 26:3–4, p. 688

Our Heavenly Shepherd, Psalm 23, p. 726

Learning from Mistakes, Psalm 51:12–13, p. 748

How Do I Love You?, Malachi 1:1–5, p. 1267

Flex Your Faith, Acts 3:1–16, p. 1467

One Thing to Do, Romans 4:1–5, p. 1523

sound. 13When Elijah heard it, he covered his face with his coat and went out
and stood at the entrance to the cave.
Then a voice said to him, "Elijah! Why
are you here?"
14He answered, "LORD God All-Powerful, I have always served you as well as
I could. But the people of Israel have broken their agreement with you, destroyed
your altars, and killed your prophets with
swords. I am the only prophet left, and
now they are trying to kill me, too."
15The LORD said to him, "Go back on
the road that leads to the desert around
Damascus. Enter that city, and pour olive
oil on Hazael to make him king over
Aram. 16Then pour oil on Jehu son of
Nimshi to make him king over Israel.
Next, pour oil on Elisha son of Shaphat
from Abel Meholah to make him a prophet
in your place. 17Jehu will kill anyone who
escapes from Hazael's sword, and Elisha
will kill anyone who escapes from Jehu's
sword. 18I have seven thousand people
left in Israel who have never bowed down
before Baal and whose mouths have
never kissed his idol."

Elisha Becomes a Prophet

19So Elijah left that place and found
Elisha son of Shaphat plowing a field with
a team of oxen. He owned twelve teams
of oxen and was plowing with the twelfth
team. Elijah came up to Elisha, took off
his coat, and put it on Elisha. 20Then Elisha left his oxen and ran to follow Elijah.
"Let me kiss my father and my mother
good-bye," Elisha said. "Then I will go
with you."
Elijah answered, "Go back. It does not
matter to me."
21So Elisha went back and took his
pair of oxen and killed them. He used
their wooden yoke for a fire. Then he
cooked the meat and gave it to the people. After they ate it, Elisha left and followed Elijah and became his helper.

Ben-Hadad and Ahab Go to War

20 Ben-Hadad king of Aram gathered
together all his army. There
were thirty-two kings with their horses
and chariots who went with him and

surrounded Samaria and attacked it.
2The king sent messengers into the city
to Ahab king of Israel.
This was his message: "Ben-Hadad
says, **3**'Your silver and gold belong to me,
as well as the best of your wives and children.' "
4Ahab king of Israel answered, "My
master and king, I agree to what you say.
I and everything I have belong to you."
5Then the messengers came to Ahab
again. They said, "Ben-Hadad says, 'I
told you before that you must give me
your silver and gold, your wives and your
children. **6**About this time tomorrow I
will send my men, who will search everywhere in your palace and in the homes of
your officers. Whatever they want they
will take and carry off.' "
7Then Ahab called a meeting of all the
older leaders of his country. He said,
"Ben-Hadad is looking for trouble. First
he said I had to give him my wives, my
children, my silver, and my gold, and I
have not refused him."
8The older leaders and all the people
said, "Don't listen to him or agree to
this."
9So Ahab said to Ben-Hadad's messengers, "Tell my master the king: 'I will
do what you said at first, but I cannot allow this second command.' " And King
Ben-Hadad's men carried the message
back to him.
10Then Ben-Hadad sent another
message to Ahab: "May the gods punish
me terribly if I don't completely destroy
Samaria. There won't be enough left for
each of my men to get a handful of dust!"
11Ahab answered, "Tell Ben-Hadad,
'The man who puts on his armor should
not brag. It's the man who lives to take it
off who has the right to brag.' "
12Ben-Hadad was drinking in his tent
with the other rulers when the message
came from Ahab. Ben-Hadad commanded
his men to prepare to attack the city, and
they moved into place for battle.
13At the same time a prophet came to
Ahab king of Israel. The prophet said,
"Ahab, the LORD says to you, 'Do you see
that big army? I will hand it over to you
today so you will know I am the LORD.' "
14Ahab asked, "Who will you use to
defeat them?"
The prophet answered, "The LORD
says, 'The young officers of the district
governors will defeat them.' "
Then the king asked, "Who will command the main army?"
The prophet answered, "You will."
15So Ahab gathered the young officers of the district governors, two hundred thirty-two of them. Then he called
together the army of Israel, about seven
thousand people in all.
16They marched out at noon, while
Ben-Hadad and the thirty-two rulers
helping him were getting drunk in their
tents. **17**The young officers of the district
governors attacked first. Ben-Hadad sent
out scouts who told him that soldiers
were coming from Samaria. **18**Ben-Hadad
said, "They may be coming to fight, or
they may be coming to ask for peace. In
either case capture them alive."
19The young officers of the district
governors led the attack, followed by the
army of Israel. **20**Each officer of Israel
killed the man who came against him.
The men from Aram ran away as Israel
chased them, but Ben-Hadad king of
Aram escaped on a horse with some of
his horsemen. **21**Ahab king of Israel led
the army and destroyed the Arameans'
horses and chariots. King Ahab thoroughly defeated the Aramean army.
22Then the prophet went to Ahab
king of Israel and said, "The king of Aram
will attack you again next spring. So go
home now and strengthen your army and
see what you need to do."
23Meanwhile the officers of Ben-
Hadad king of Aram said to him, "The
gods of Israel are mountain gods. Since
we fought in a mountain area, Israel won.
Let's fight them on the flat land, and then
we will win. **24**This is what you should do.
Don't allow the thirty-two rulers to command the armies, but put other commanders in their places. **25**Gather an army like
the one that was destroyed and as many
horses and chariots as before. We will
fight the Israelites on flat land, and then
we will win." Ben-Hadad agreed with
their advice and did what they said.

26The next spring Ben-Hadad gathered the army of Aram and went up to
Aphek to fight against Israel.
27The Israelites also had prepared for
war. They marched out to meet the Arameans and camped opposite them. The Israelites looked like two small flocks of
goats, but the Arameans covered the area.
28A man of God came to the king of
Israel with this message: "The LORD
says, 'The people of Aram say that I, the
LORD, am a god of the mountains, not a
god of the valleys. So I will allow you to
defeat this huge army, and then you will
know I am the LORD.' "
29The armies were camped across
from each other for seven days. On the
seventh day the battle began. The Israelites killed one hundred thousand Aramean soldiers in one day. 30The rest of them
ran away to the city of Aphek, where a
city wall fell on twenty-seven thousand of
them. Ben-Hadad also ran away to the
city and hid in a room.
31His officers said to him, "We have
heard that the kings of Israel are trustworthy. Let's dress in rough cloth to
show our sadness, and wear ropes on our
heads. Then we will go to the king of Israel, and perhaps he will let you live."
32So they dressed in rough cloth and
wore ropes on their heads and went to
the king of Israel. They said, "Your servant Ben-Hadad says, 'Please let me
live.' "

Ahab answered, "Is he still alive? He
is my brother."
33Ben-Hadad's men had wanted a
sign from Ahab. So when Ahab called
Ben-Hadad his brother, they quickly said,
"Yes! Ben-Hadad is your brother."

Ahab said, "Bring him to me." When
Ben-Hadad came, Ahab asked him to join
him in the chariot.
34Ben-Hadad said to him, "Ahab, I will
give you back the cities my father took
from your father. And you may put shops
in Damascus, as my father did in Samaria."

Ahab said, "If you agree to this, I will
allow you to go free." So the two kings
made a peace agreement. Then Ahab let
Ben-Hadad go free.

A Prophet Speaks Against Ahab

35One prophet from one of the
groups of prophets told another, "Hit
me!" He said this because the LORD
had commanded it, but the other man
refused. 36The prophet said, "You did
not obey the LORD's command, so a lion
will kill you as soon as you leave me."
When the man left, a lion found him and
killed him.
37The prophet went to another man
and said, "Hit me, please!" So the man
hit him and hurt him. 38The prophet
wrapped his face in a cloth so no one
could tell who he was. Then he went and
waited by the road for the king. 39As
Ahab king of Israel passed by, the prophet
called out to him. "I went to fight in the
battle," the prophet said. "One of our
men brought an enemy soldier to me.
Our man said, 'Guard this man. If he runs
away, you will have to give your life in his
place. Or, you will have to pay a fine of
seventy-five pounds of silver.' 40But I
was busy doing other things, so the man
ran away."

The king of Israel answered, "You
have already said what the punishment
is. You must do what the man said."
41Then the prophet quickly took the
cloth from his face. When the king of Israel saw him, he knew he was one of the
prophets. 42The prophet said to the king,
"This is what the LORD says: 'You freed
the man I said should die, so your life will
be taken instead of his. The lives of your
people will also be taken instead of the
lives of his people.' "
43Then King Ahab went back to his
palace in Samaria, angry and upset.

Ahab Takes Naboth's Vineyard

21 After these things had happened,
this is what followed. A man
named Naboth owned a vineyard in Jezreel, near the palace of Ahab king of Israel.
2One day Ahab said to Naboth, "Give me
your vineyard. It is near my palace, and I
want to make it into a vegetable garden. I
will give you a better vineyard in its
place, or, if you prefer, I will pay you what
it is worth."
3Naboth answered, "May the LORD

keep me from ever giving my land to you.
It belongs to my family."
4Ahab went home angry and upset,
because he did not like what Naboth from
Jezreel had said. (Naboth had said, "I will
not give you my family's land.") Ahab lay
down on his bed, turned his face to the
wall, and refused to eat.
5His wife, Jezebel, came in and asked
him, "Why are you so upset that you refuse to eat?"
6Ahab answered, "I talked to Naboth,
the man from Jezreel. I said, 'Sell me
your vineyard, or, if you prefer, I will give
you another vineyard for it.' But Naboth
refused."
7Jezebel answered, "Is this how you
rule as king over Israel? Get up, eat
something, and cheer up. I will get
Naboth's vineyard for you."
8So Jezebel wrote some letters,
signed Ahab's name to them, and used
his own seal to seal them. Then she sent
them to the older leaders and important
men who lived in Naboth's town. 9The
letter she wrote said: "Declare a day during which the people are to give up eating. Call the people together, and give
Naboth a place of honor among them.
10Seat two troublemakers across from
him, and have them say they heard Naboth speak against God and the king.
Then take Naboth out of the city and kill
him with stones."
11The older leaders and important
men of Jezreel obeyed Jezebel's command, just as she wrote in the letters.
12They declared a special day on which
the people were to give up eating. And
they put Naboth in a place of honor before
the people. 13Two troublemakers sat
across from Naboth and said in front of
everybody that they had heard him speak
against God and the king. So the people
carried Naboth out of the city and killed
him with stones. 14Then the leaders sent
a message to Jezebel, saying, "Naboth
has been killed."
15When Jezebel heard that Naboth
had been killed, she told Ahab, "Naboth
of Jezreel is dead. Now you may go and
take for yourself the vineyard he would
not sell to you." 16When Ahab heard that
Naboth of Jezreel was dead, he got up and
went to the vineyard to take it for his
own.
17At this time the LORD spoke his

FAITH links

ABOVE THE LAW

1 KINGS 21

Ahab, the king of the northern kingdom of Israel, was considered one of the worst kings ever. With his wife Jezebel, he did whatever he had to do to get what he wanted. When he disobeyed God's laws (don't steal; don't kill) by taking a vineyard that didn't belong to him, he thought he was above the law. After all, he *was* the king. But God had one law about sin for all people.

When it comes to sin, a person's name, rank, and serial number don't matter to God. Fame or influence won't get you out of the consequences of sin. What can make a difference in your life is who you know: Jesus.

The Trouble with Sin, Genesis 6—8, p. 11

Facing the Consequences, Deuteronomy 3:21–29, p. 232

What God "Hates," Proverbs 6:16–19, p. 835

Believe the Impossible?, Ezekiel 37, p. 1131

A High Price, Romans 6:23, p. 1526

The Winner's Crown, 1 Corinthians 9:24–27, p. 1555

word to the prophet Elijah the Tishbite.
The LORD said, **18**"Go to Ahab king of Israel in Samaria. He is at Naboth's vineyard, where he has gone to take it as his
own. **19**Tell Ahab that I, the LORD, say to
him, 'You have murdered Naboth and tak-
en his land. So I tell you this: In the same
place the dogs licked up Naboth's blood,
they will also lick up your blood!' "
20When Ahab saw Elijah, he said, "So
you have found me, my enemy!"

Elijah answered, "Yes, I have found
you. You have always chosen to do what
the LORD says is wrong. **21**So the LORD
says to you, 'I will soon destroy you. I will
kill you and every male in your family,
both slave and free. **22**Your family will be
like the family of King Jeroboam son of
Nebat and like the family of King Baasha
son of Ahijah. I will destroy you, because
you have made me angry and have led the
people of Israel to sin.'

23"And the LORD also says, 'Dogs will
eat the body of Jezebel in the city of Jezreel.'

24"Anyone in your family who dies in
the city will be eaten by dogs, and anyone
who dies in the fields will be eaten by
birds."

25There was no one like Ahab who
had chosen so often to do what the LORD
said was wrong, because his wife Jezebel
influenced him to do evil. **26**Ahab sinned
terribly by worshiping idols, just as the
Amorite people did. And the LORD had
taken away their land and given it to the
people of Israel.

27After Elijah finished speaking,
Ahab tore his clothes. He put on rough
cloth, refused to eat, and even slept in
the rough cloth to show how sad and upset he was.

28The LORD spoke his word to Elijah
the Tishbite: **29**"I see that Ahab is now
sorry for what he has done. So I will not
cause the trouble to come to him during
his life, but I will wait until his son is
king. Then I will bring this trouble to
Ahab's family."

The Death of Ahab

22 For three years there was peace
between Israel and Aram. **2**During
the third year Jehoshaphat king of Judah
went to visit Ahab king of Israel.

3At that time Ahab asked his officers,
"Do you remember that the king of Aram
took Ramoth in Gilead from us? Why
have we done nothing to get it back?"
4So Ahab asked King Jehoshaphat, "Will
you go with me to fight at Ramoth in Gilead?"

"I will go with you," Jehoshaphat answered. "My soldiers are yours, and my
horses are yours." **5**Jehoshaphat also
said to Ahab, "But first we should ask if
this is the LORD's will."

6Ahab called about four hundred
prophets together and asked them,
"Should I go to war against Ramoth in
Gilead or not?"

They answered, "Go, because the
Lord will hand them over to you."

7But Jehoshaphat asked, "Isn't there
a prophet of the LORD here? Let's ask
him what we should do."

8Then King Ahab said to Jehoshaphat,
"There is one other prophet. We could
ask the LORD through him, but I hate
him. He never prophesies anything good
about me, but something bad. He is Micaiah son of Imlah."

Jehoshaphat said, "King Ahab, you
shouldn't say that!"

9So Ahab king of Israel told one of his
officers to bring Micaiah to him at once.

10Ahab king of Israel and Jehoshaphat
king of Judah had on their royal robes and
were sitting on their thrones at the
threshing floor, near the entrance to the
gate of Samaria. All the prophets were
standing before them, speaking their
messages. **11**Zedekiah son of Kenaanah
had made some iron horns. He said to
Ahab, "This is what the LORD says, 'You
will use these horns to fight the Arameans until they are destroyed.' "

12All the other prophets said the
same thing. "Attack Ramoth in Gilead and
win, because the LORD will hand the Arameans over to you."

13The messenger who had gone to
get Micaiah said to him, "All the other
prophets are saying King Ahab will succeed. You should agree with them and
give the king a good answer."

FAITH links

GIVE IN OR TAKE A STAND?

1 KINGS 22:13-14

"C'mon and try it. Everybody's doin' it." Have you heard words like that before? You feel pressured to do something that "everyone else" is doing. Even Old Testament prophets know what being pressured is like. King Ahab tried to pressure Micaiah into siding with him about going to war. Four hundred other prophets told the king what he wanted to hear. Micaiah was the only one who spoke for the Lord. (Surf over to 2 Chronicles 18, p. 581, for another version of this story.)

There may be times when you'll have to stand alone in order to do what's right. That can seem pretty scary. But whenever you stand for what's right, God stands with you.

Who do you stand for? Connect here for some links on that:

His OK to Obey, Deuteronomy 2:24–36, p. 230

No Middle Ground, Joshua 24:14–15, p. 307

The Big Risk, Esther 4:11—5:2, p. 652

When Bad Things Happen, Ecclesiastes 3:16–17, p. 876

Stand!, Jeremiah 19:14—20:6, p. 1019

The Unpopular Choice, Mark 15:42–43, p. 1360

14But Micaiah answered, "As surely
as the LORD lives, I can tell him only what
the LORD tells me."
15When Micaiah came to Ahab, the
king asked him, "Micaiah, should we attack Ramoth in Gilead or not?"

Micaiah answered, "Attack and win! The LORD will hand them over to you."
16But Ahab said to Micaiah, "How
many times do I have to tell you to speak only the truth to me in the name of the LORD?"
17So Micaiah answered, "I saw the
army of Israel scattered over the hills like sheep without a shepherd. The LORD said, 'They have no leaders. They should go home and not fight.' "
18Then Ahab king of Israel said to Jehoshaphat, "I told you! He never prophesies anything good about me, but only bad."
19But Micaiah said, "Hear the message from the LORD: I saw the LORD sitting on his throne with his heavenly army standing near him on his right and on his
left. 20The LORD said, 'Who will trick
Ahab into attacking Ramoth in Gilead where he will be killed?'

"Some said one thing; some said another. 21Then one spirit came and stood
before the LORD and said, 'I will trick him.'
22"The LORD asked, 'How will you do
it?'

"The spirit answered, 'I will go to Ahab's prophets and make them tell lies.'

"So the LORD said, 'You will succeed in tricking him. Go and do it.' "
23Micaiah said, "Ahab, the LORD has
made your prophets lie to you, and the LORD has decided that disaster should come to you."
24Then Zedekiah son of Kenaanah
went up to Micaiah and slapped him in the face. Zedekiah said, "Has the LORD's spirit left me to speak through you?"
25Micaiah answered, "You will find
out on the day you go to hide in an inside room."
26Then Ahab king of Israel ordered,
"Take Micaiah and send him to Amon, the governor of the city, and to Joash, the
king's son. 27Tell them I said to put this

man in prison and give him only bread
and water until I return safely from the
battle."
28Micaiah said, "Ahab, if you come
back safely from battle, the LORD has not
spoken through me. Remember my
words, all you people!"
29So Ahab king of Israel and Jehoshaphat king of Judah went to Ramoth in Gilead. **30**King Ahab said to Jehoshaphat, "I
will go into battle, but I will wear other
clothes so no one will recognize me. But
you wear your royal clothes." So Ahab
wore other clothes and went into battle.
31The king of Aram had ordered his
thirty-two chariot commanders, "Don't
fight with anyone—important or unimportant—except the king of Israel."
32When these commanders saw Jehoshaphat, they thought he was certainly the
king of Israel, so they turned to attack
him. But Jehoshaphat began shouting.
33When they saw he was not King Ahab,
they stopped chasing him.
34By chance, a soldier shot an arrow,
but he hit Ahab king of Israel between
the pieces of his armor. King Ahab said to
his chariot driver, "Turn around and get
me out of the battle, because I am hurt!"
35The battle continued all day. King Ahab
was held up in his chariot and faced the
Arameans. His blood flowed down to the
bottom of the chariot. That evening he
died. **36**Near sunset a cry went out
through the army of Israel: "Each man go
back to his own city and land."
37In that way King Ahab died. His
body was carried to Samaria and buried
there. **38**The men cleaned Ahab's chariot
at a pool in Samaria where prostitutes
bathed, and the dogs licked his blood
from the chariot. These things happened
as the LORD had said they would.
39Everything else Ahab did is written
in the book of the history of the kings of
Israel. It tells about the palace Ahab built
and decorated with ivory and the cities
he built. **40**So Ahab died, and his son Ahaziah became king in his place.

Jehoshaphat King of Judah

41Jehoshaphat son of Asa became king
of Judah during Ahab's fourth year as king
of Israel. **42**Jehoshaphat was thirty-five
years old when he became king, and he
ruled in Jerusalem for twenty-five years.
His mother's name was Azubah daughter
of Shilhi. **43**Jehoshaphat was good, like his
father Asa, and he did what the LORD said
was right. But Jehoshaphat did not destroy the places where gods were worshiped, so the people continued offering
sacrifices and burning incense there.
44Jehoshaphat was at peace with the king
of Israel. **45**Jehoshaphat fought many
wars, and these wars and his successes
are written in the book of the history of
the kings of Judah. **46**There were male
prostitutes still in the places of worship
from the days of his father, Asa. So Jehoshaphat forced them to leave.
47During this time the land of Edom
had no king; it was ruled by a governor.
48King Jehoshaphat built trading
ships to sail to Ophir for gold. But the
ships were wrecked at Ezion Geber, so
they never set sail. **49**Ahaziah son of
Ahab went to help Jehoshaphat, offering
to give Jehoshaphat some men to sail
with his men, but Jehoshaphat refused.
50Jehoshaphat died and was buried
with his ancestors in Jerusalem, the city
of David, his ancestor. Then his son Jehoram became king in his place.

Ahaziah King of Israel

51Ahaziah son of Ahab became king of
Israel in Samaria during Jehoshaphat's
seventeenth year as king over Judah.
Ahaziah ruled Israel for two years, **52**and
he did what the LORD said was wrong. He
did the same evil his father Ahab, his
mother Jezebel, and Jeroboam son of Nebat had done. All these rulers led the
people of Israel into more sin. **53**Ahaziah
worshiped and served the god Baal, and
this made the LORD, the God of Israel,
very angry. In these ways Ahaziah did
what his father had done.

A SAD STORY

Welcome, newbie! Jeremiah, the prophet, here. Have you ever tried to go up the stairs when *everyone* else is going down? That's what it was like to be a prophet during the time I wrote about in this book. The prophets were sent by God to tell the people to obey his commands, but few people listened. Because of their unwillingness to worship God and obey him, God allowed his people to be conquered by their enemies and driven away from the land he had given them. The saddest day of all was the day Jerusalem was destroyed. You can find out more about that terrible day by surfing over to 2 Kings 25:8–21.

I wrote this book to remind people to be faithful to the true God and to worship only him. By the time Josiah was king (did you know that Josiah was only eight years old when he became king?), people were worshiping all sorts of false idols and had forgotten about God. Imagine Josiah's surprise when the book of God's laws (called the Book of the Teachings) was found! Check out 2 Kings 23 to see how Josiah obeyed God.

JESUS WATCH

The many miracles Elisha performed show God's concern for the people and point to the miracles of Jesus. Elisha cared for the family of a poor widow by multiplying her supply of oil so that she could pay off debts and save her sons from being sold into slavery. This reminds us of how Jesus showed his concern for family friends at the wedding in Cana. (Surf over to John 2:1–11, p. 1424, for the story.) Elisha healed the Aramean army's commander of leprosy to show that he was God's prophet. Jesus showed his power and love by healing people of leprosy, blindness, and other physical problems. A family in Shunem showed their love for Elisha by preparing a room for him to use whenever he needed it. When their son died, Elisha prayed to the Lord and the boy came back to life. This reminds us of the special compassion Jesus had for his friends Mary and Martha when he raised their brother Lazarus from the dead. (Check out that miracle in John 11:37–44, p. 1443.)

my FAVORITE links

OTHER CONNECTIONS

Stop at these information bulletin boards to find out more about some of the key people and places found in the second Book of Kings:

- Let's Visit the Jordan River, 2 Kings 2:13–15. The Jordan is frequently mentioned in both Old and New Testament stories. It's where the Israelites had to cross in order to enter the land God promised them, and it's where Jesus was baptized. For more about this famous body of water, connect here!

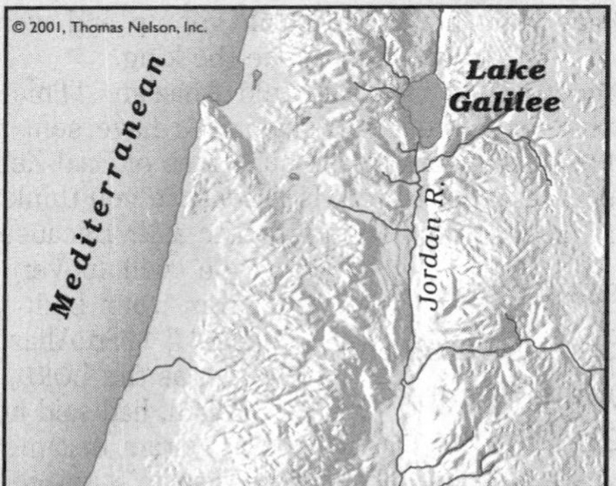

- Link to Elisha's Ministry, 2 Kings 4, to find out more about this handpicked successor to Elijah.

"Here's a FAQ for you—who went to heaven in a chariot of fire?"

"Got me. But if we link to 2 Kings 2:7-12, I think we'll find the answer."

CHECK OUT THESE STORIES:

A dip in the Jordan, 2 Kings 5:1–15
The floating axhead, 2 Kings 6:1–7
Elisha and the army of angels, 2 Kings 6:8–23
Joash repairs the Temple, 2 Kings 12:4–16

FAITH links

- Big Lack Attack, 2 Kings 4:1–7
- Advice from a Kid, 2 Kings 5
- Putting an Enemy in Check, 2 Kings 6:8–23
- A Big Responsibility, 2 Kings 11
- You're Out!, 2 Kings 17:5–7
- A Message of Courage and Hope, 2 Kings 19:4–10
- Problem Solved, 2 Kings 20:1–11
- On the Wrong Foot, 2 Kings 21:1–2, 16
- Trailblazers of Faith, 2 Kings 22:1–2
- No Thanksgiving?, 2 Kings 23:21–23

Elijah and King Ahaziah

1 After Ahab died, Moab broke away from Israel's rule. 2Ahaziah fell down through the wooden bars in his upstairs room in Samaria and was badly hurt. He sent messengers and told them, "Go, ask Baal-Zebub, god of Ekron, if I will recover from my injuries."

3But the LORD's angel said to Elijah the Tishbite, "Go up and meet the messengers sent by the king of Samaria. Ask them, 'Why are you going to ask questions of Baal-Zebub, god of Ekron? Is it because you think there is no God in Israel?' 4This is what the LORD says: 'You will never get up from the bed you are lying on; you will die.' " Then Elijah left.

5When the messengers returned to Ahaziah, he asked them, "Why have you returned?"

6They said, "A man came to meet us. He said, 'Go back to the king who sent you and tell him what the LORD says: "Why do you send messengers to ask questions of Baal-Zebub, god of Ekron? Is it because you think there is no God in Israel? You will never get up from the bed you are lying on; you will die." ' "

7Ahaziah asked them, "What did the man look like who met you and told you this?"

8They answered, "He was a hairy man and wore a leather belt around his waist."

Ahaziah said, "It was Elijah the Tishbite."

9Then he sent a captain with his fifty men to Elijah. The captain went to Elijah, who was sitting on top of the hill, and said to him, "Man of God, the king says, 'Come down!' "

10Elijah answered the captain, "If I am a man of God, let fire come down from heaven and burn up you and your fifty men." Then fire came down from heaven and burned up the captain and his fifty men.

11Ahaziah sent another captain and fifty men to Elijah. The captain said to him, "Man of God, this is what the king says: 'Come down quickly!' "

12Elijah answered, "If I am a man of God, let fire come down from heaven and burn up you and your fifty men!" Then fire came down from heaven and burned up the captain and his fifty men.

13Ahaziah then sent a third captain with his fifty men. The third captain came and fell down on his knees before Elijah and begged, "Man of God, please respect my life and the lives of your fifty servants. 14See, fire came down from heaven and burned up the first two captains of fifty with all their men. But now, respect my life."

15The LORD's angel said to Elijah, "Go down with him and don't be afraid of him." So Elijah got up and went down with him to see the king.

16Elijah told Ahaziah, "This is what the LORD says: 'You have sent messengers to ask questions of Baal-Zebub, god of Ekron. Is it because you think there is no God in Israel to ask? Because of this, you will never get up from your bed; you will die.' " 17So Ahaziah died, just as the LORD, through Elijah, had said he would.

Joram became king in Ahaziah's place during the second year Jehoram son of Jehoshaphat was king of Judah. Joram ruled because Ahaziah had no son to take his place. 18The other things Ahaziah did are written in the book of the history of the kings of Israel.

> Elijah answered the captain, "If I am a man of God, let fire come down from heaven and burn up you and your fifty men."
> —2 Kings 1:10

Elijah Is Taken to Heaven

2 It was almost time for the LORD to take Elijah by a whirlwind up into heaven. While Elijah and Elisha were leaving Gilgal, 2Elijah said to Elisha, "Please stay here. The LORD has told me to go to Bethel."

But Elisha said, "As the LORD lives, and as you live, I won't leave you." So they went down to Bethel. 3The groups of prophets at Bethel came out to Elisha and said to him, "Do you know the LORD

LET'S VISIT THE JORDAN RIVER 2 Kings 2:13–15

The Jordan River is a famous river that starts near Mount Hermon, passes through the Sea of Galilee, and empties out into the Dead Sea. That means it starts at the top of a mountain and ends at the lowest point on earth. Its name is thought to mean "the river that rushes down."

In the Old Testament, Abraham let Lot choose his own land, and he chose land by the Jordan River. (See Genesis 13:10–11, p. 18.) The Jordan was also the place where the Israelites crossed into the land of Canaan with Joshua. (Look at Deuteronomy 3:20, 25, 27, p. 231.) A man named Naaman once washed in the river to be healed of leprosy. (Look up 2 Kings 5:10–12.) In the New Testament, John the Baptist baptized Jesus in the Jordan. Because of that, a lot of people who visit Israel ask to be baptized in these waters. (Read Matthew 3:13, p. 1278.)

will take your master away from you today?"
Elisha said, "Yes, I know, but don't
talk about it."
4Elijah said to him, "Stay here, Elisha,
because the LORD has sent me to Jericho."
But Elisha said, "As the LORD lives,
and as you live, I won't leave you."
So they went to Jericho. **5**The groups
of prophets at Jericho came to Elisha and
said, "Do you know that the LORD will
take your master away from you today?"
Elisha answered, "Yes, I know, but
don't talk about it."
6Elijah said to Elisha, "Stay here. The
LORD has sent me to the Jordan River."
Elisha answered, "As the LORD lives,
and as you live, I won't leave you."
So the two of them went on. **7**Fifty
men of the groups of prophets came and
stood far from where Elijah and Elisha
were by the Jordan. **8**Elijah took off his
coat, rolled it up, and hit the water. The
water divided to the right and to the left,
and Elijah and Elisha crossed over on dry
ground.
9After they had crossed over, Elijah
said to Elisha, "What can I do for you before I am taken from you?"
Elisha said, "Leave me a double share
of your spirit."[n]
10Elijah said, "You have asked a hard
thing. But if you see me when I am taken
from you, it will be yours. If you don't, it
won't happen."
11As they were walking and talking, a
chariot and horses of fire appeared and
separated Elijah from Elisha. Then Elijah
went up to heaven in a whirlwind. **12**Elisha saw it and shouted, "My father! My
father! The chariots of Israel and their
horsemen!" And Elisha did not see him
anymore. Then Elisha grabbed his own
clothes and tore them to show how sad
he was.
13He picked up Elijah's coat that had
fallen from him. Then he returned and
stood on the bank of the Jordan. **14**Elisha
hit the water with Elijah's coat and said,

2:9 Leave . . . spirit By law, the first son in a family would inherit a double share of his father's possessions. Elisha is asking to inherit a share of his master's power as his follower. He is not asking for twice as much power as Elijah had.

"Where is the LORD, the God of Elijah?"
When he hit the water, it divided to the
right and to the left, and Elisha crossed
over.
15The groups of prophets at Jericho
were watching and said, "Elisha now has
the spirit Elijah had." And they came to
meet him, bowing down to the ground
before him. 16They said to him, "There
are fifty strong men with us. Please let
them go and look for your master. Maybe
the Spirit of the LORD has taken Elijah up
and set him down on some mountain or in
some valley."
But Elisha answered, "No, don't send
them."
17When the groups of prophets had
begged Elisha until he couldn't refuse
them anymore, he said, "Send them." So
they sent fifty men who looked for three
days, but they could not find him. 18Then
they came back to Elisha at Jericho
where he was staying. He said to them, "I
told you not to go, didn't I?"

Elisha Makes the Water Pure

19The people of the city said to Elisha, "Look, master, this city is a nice
place to live as you can see. But the water is so bad the land cannot grow crops."
20Elisha said, "Bring me a new bowl
and put salt in it." So they brought it to
him.
21Then he went out to the spring and
threw the salt in it. He said, "This is what
the LORD says: 'I have healed this water.
From now on it won't cause death, and it
won't keep the land from growing
crops.' " 22So the water has been healed
to this day just as Elisha had said.

Boys Make Fun of Elisha

23From there Elisha went up to
Bethel. On the way some boys came out
of the city and made fun of him. They said
to him, "Go up too, you baldhead! Go up
too, you baldhead!" 24Elisha turned
around, looked at them, and put a curse
on them in the name of the LORD. Then
two mother bears came out of the woods
and tore forty-two of the boys to pieces.
25Elisha went to Mount Carmel and from
there he returned to Samaria.

War Between Israel and Moab

3 Joram son of Ahab became king over
Israel at Samaria in Jehoshaphat's
eighteenth year as king of Judah. And Joram ruled twelve years. 2He did what the
LORD said was wrong, but he was not like
his father and mother; he removed the
stone pillars his father had made for Baal.
3But he continued to sin like Jeroboam
son of Nebat who had led Israel to sin.
Joram did not stop doing these same sins.
4Mesha king of Moab raised sheep.
He paid the king of Israel one hundred
thousand lambs and the wool of one hundred thousand sheep. 5But when Ahab
died, the king of Moab turned against the
king of Israel. 6So King Joram went out
from Samaria and gathered Israel's army.
7He also sent messengers to Jehoshaphat king of Judah. "The king of Moab has
turned against me," he said. "Will you go
with me to fight Moab?"
Jehoshaphat replied, "I will go with
you. My soldiers and my horses are
yours."
8Jehoshaphat asked, "Which way should
we attack?"
Joram answered, "Through the Desert
of Edom."
9So the king of Israel went with the
king of Judah and the king of Edom. After
they had marched seven days, there was
no more water for the army or for their
animals that were with them. 10The king
of Israel said, "This is terrible! The LORD
has called us three kings together to
hand us over to the Moabites!"
11But Jehoshaphat asked, "Is there a
prophet of the LORD here? We can ask
the LORD through him."
An officer of the king of Israel answered, "Elisha son of Shaphat is here.
He was Elijah's servant."
12Jehoshaphat said, "He speaks the
LORD's truth." So the king of Israel and
Jehoshaphat and the king of Edom went
down to see Elisha.
13Elisha said to the king of Israel, "I
have nothing to do with you. Go to the
prophets of your father and to the prophets of your mother!"
The king of Israel said to Elisha, "No,
the LORD has called us three kings to-

gether to hand us over to the Moabites."

14Elisha said, "As surely as the LORD All-Powerful lives, whom I serve, I tell you the truth. I wouldn't even look at you or notice you if Jehoshaphat king of Judah were not here. I respect him. **15**Now bring me someone who plays the harp."

While the harp was being played, the LORD gave Elisha power. **16**Then Elisha said, "The LORD says to dig holes in the valley. **17**The LORD says you won't see wind or rain, but the valley will be filled with water. Then you, your cattle, and your other animals can drink. **18**This is easy for the LORD to do; he will also hand Moab over to you. **19**You will destroy every strong, walled city and every important town. You will cut down every good tree and stop up all springs. You will ruin every good field with rocks."

20The next morning, about the time the sacrifice was offered, water came from the direction of Edom and filled the valley.

21All the Moabites heard that the kings had come up to fight against them. So they gathered everyone old enough to put on armor and waited at the border. **22**But when the Moabites got up early in the morning, the sun was shining on the water. They saw the water across from them, and it looked as red as blood. **23**Then they said, "This is blood! The kings must have fought and killed each other! Come, Moabites, let's take the valuables from the dead bodies!"

24When the Moabites came to the camp of Israel, the Israelites came out and fought them until they ran away. Then the Israelites went on into the land, killing the Moabites. **25**They tore down the cities and threw rocks all over every good field. They stopped up all the springs and cut down all the good trees. Kir Hareseth was the only city with its stones still in place, but the men with slingshots surrounded it and conquered it, too.

26When the king of Moab saw that the battle was too much for him, he took seven hundred men with swords to try to break through to the king of Edom. But they could not break through. **27**Then the king of Moab took his oldest son, who would have been king after him, and offered him as a burnt offering on the wall. So there was great anger against the Israelites, who left and went back to their own land.

While the harp was being played, the LORD gave Elisha power.
—2 Kings 3:15

A Widow Asks Elisha for Help

4 The wife of a man from the groups of prophets said to Elisha, "Your servant, my husband, is dead. You know he honored the LORD. But now the man he owes money to is coming to take my two boys as his slaves!"

2Elisha answered, "How can I help you? Tell me, what do you have in your house?"

The woman said, "I don't have anything there except a pot of oil."

3Then Elisha said, "Go and get empty jars from all your neighbors. Don't ask for just a few. **4**Then go into your house and shut the door behind you and your sons. Pour oil into all the jars, and set the full ones aside."

5So she left Elisha and shut the door behind her and her sons. As they brought the jars to her, she poured out the oil. **6**When the jars were all full, she said to her son, "Bring me another jar."

But he said, "There are no more jars." Then the oil stopped flowing.

7She went and told Elisha. And the prophet said to her, "Go, sell the oil and pay what you owe. You and your sons can live on what is left."

The Shunammite Woman

8One day Elisha went to Shunem, where an important woman lived. She begged Elisha to stay and eat. So every time Elisha passed by, he stopped there to eat. **9**The woman said to her husband, "I know that this is a holy man of God who passes by our house all the time. **10**Let's

make a small room on the roof[a] and put a
bed in the room for him. We can put a table, a chair, and a lampstand there. Then
when he comes by, he can stay there."
11One day Elisha came to the woman's house. After he went to his room and
rested, **12**he said to his servant Gehazi,
"Call the Shunammite woman."
When the servant had called her, she
stood in front of him. **13**Elisha had told
his servant, "Now say to her, 'You have
gone to all this trouble for us. What can I
do for you? Do you want me to speak to
the king or the commander of the army
for you?' "
She answered, "I live among my own
people."
14Elisha said to Gehazi, "But what
can we do for her?"
He answered, "She has no son, and
her husband is old."
15Then Elisha said to Gehazi, "Call
her." When he called her, she stood in the
doorway. **16**Then Elisha said, "About this
time next year, you will hold a son in your
arms."
The woman said, "No, master, man of
God, don't lie to me, your servant!"
17But the woman became pregnant
and gave birth to a son at that time the
next year, just as Elisha had told her.
18The boy grew up and one day went
out to his father, who was with the grain
harvesters. **19**The boy said to his father,
"My head! My head!"
The father said to his servant, "Take
him to his mother!" **20**The servant took
him to his mother, and he lay on his
mother's lap until noon. Then he died.
21So she took him up and laid him on
Elisha's bed. Then she shut the door and
left.
22She called to her husband, "Send
me one of the servants and one of the
donkeys. Then I can go quickly to the
man of God and return."
23The husband said, "Why do you
want to go to him today? It isn't the New
Moon or the Sabbath day."
She said, "It will be all right."
24Then she saddled the donkey and
said to her servant, "Lead on. Don't slow
down for me unless I tell you." **25**So she
went to Elisha, the man of God, at Mount
Carmel.

BIG LACK ATTACK

2 KINGS 4:1-7

Ever worry that you'll run out of what you need? An Old Testament widow faced that problem. Because she lacked money, her sons would be sold as slaves to pay her debts. She asked Elisha for help. God miraculously provided for her by multiplying the oil that she had. During New Testament times, Jesus did something similar with loaves and fish. (Download Matthew 14:13–21, p. 1299, for that story.) Both stories show how God took care of his people. He can do the same for you.

The Rainbow Promise, Genesis 9:1–17, p. 14

From Hopeless to Hopeful, Exodus 6:9, p. 83

His Valentine, Jeremiah 31:3, p. 1035

Rock Solid, Habakkuk 1:12, p. 1236

When We Agree, Matthew 18:19–20, p. 1306

Two Birthdays, John 3:1–7, p. 1426

4:10 roof In Bible times houses were built with flat roofs. The roof was used for drying things such as flax and fruit. And it was used as an extra room, as a place for worship, and as a cool place to sleep in the summer.

SHOW YOU CARE

2 KINGS 4:10

How do you show others that you care? Some people show their love by opening their homes to others. An important woman in Shunem went out of her way to welcome Elisha. What are some ways you can show you care for others? Make someone feel welcome in your home, give someone a hug, or make a card. You don't have to do anything major. Sometimes a warm smile can say "I care" better than anything else.

Check out these Faithlinks to see how you can show others you care:

Give What You Can, Numbers 7:1–11, p. 186

Care to Be Fair?, Joshua 18:1–8, p. 299

Help for the Hurting, Job 6:29–30, p. 666

Mercy for an Enemy, Jonah 4, p. 1216

Kindness First, Matthew 9:35–36, p. 1290

Come On In!, 1 Peter 4:9–10, p. 1705

When he saw her coming from far
away, he said to his servant Gehazi,
"Look, there's the Shunammite woman!
26Run to meet her and ask, 'Are you all
right? Is your husband all right? Is the
boy all right?' "

She answered, "Everything is all
right."

27Then she came to Elisha at the hill
and grabbed his feet. Gehazi came near to
pull her away, but Elisha said to him,
"Leave her alone. She's very upset, and
the LORD has not told me about it. He has
hidden it from me."

28She said, "Master, did I ask you for
a son? Didn't I tell you not to lie to me?"

29Then Elisha said to Gehazi, "Get
ready. Take my walking stick in your
hand and go quickly. If you meet anyone,
don't say hello. If anyone greets you,
don't respond. Lay my walking stick on
the boy's face."

30The boy's mother said, "As surely
as the LORD lives and as you live, I won't
leave you!" So Elisha got up and followed
her.

31Gehazi went on ahead and laid the
walking stick on the boy's face, but the
boy did not talk or move. Then Gehazi
went back to meet Elisha. "The boy has
not awakened," he said.

32When Elisha came into the house,
the boy was lying dead on his bed. **33**Elisha entered the room and shut the door,
so only he and the boy were in the room.
Then he prayed to the LORD. **34**He went
to the bed and lay on the boy, putting his
mouth on the boy's mouth, his eyes on
the boy's eyes, and his hands on the boy's
hands. He stretched himself out on top of
the boy. Soon the boy's skin became
warm. **35**Elisha turned away and walked
around the room. Then he went back and
put himself on the boy again. The boy
sneezed seven times and opened his
eyes.

36Elisha called Gehazi and said, "Call
the Shunammite!" So he did. When she
came, Elisha said, "Pick up your son."
37She came in and fell at Elisha's feet,
bowing facedown to the floor. Then she
picked up her son and went out.

Elisha and the Stew

38When Elisha returned to Gilgal,
there was a shortage of food in the land.
While the groups of prophets were sitting
in front of him, he said to his servant,
"Put the large pot on the fire, and boil
some stew for these men."

GET THE INFO

ELISHA'S MINISTRY

2 Kings 4

1. Elijah chose Elisha to carry on his ministry in the northern kingdom of Israel. (See 1 Kings 19:16–21, p. 467.)

2. At Shunem, an important woman offered Elisha a place to stay. Elisha repaid the woman's hospitality by promising her a son. (Read about what happens later by looking up 2 Kings 4:8–37.)

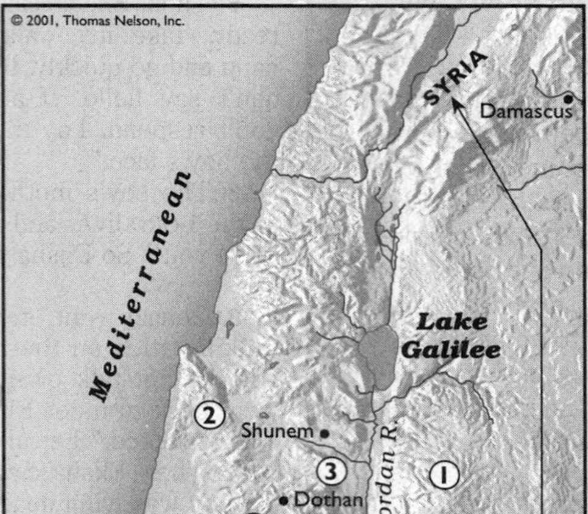

3. Elisha healed Naaman, commander of the army of Aram, of a terrible skin disease by ordering him to wash himself seven times in the Jordan River. (Check out this amazing story in 2 Kings 5:1–15.)

4. Elisha helped defeat the Aramean army at Dothan by blinding them and leading them into the city of Samaria. (To learn more about Elisha's battle plan, read 2 Kings 6:8–23.)

39One of them went out into the field
to gather plants. Finding a wild vine, he
picked fruit from the vine and filled his
robe with it. Then he came and cut up the
fruit into the pot. But they didn't know
what kind of fruit it was. **40**They poured
out the stew for the others to eat. When
they began to eat it, they shouted, "Man
of God, there's death in the pot!" And
they could not eat it.

41Elisha told them to bring some
flour. He threw it into the pot and said,
"Pour it out for the people to eat." Then
there was nothing harmful in the pot.

Elisha Feeds the People

42A man from Baal Shalishah came to
Elisha, bringing him twenty loaves of
barley bread from the first harvest. He
also brought fresh grain in his sack. Elisha said, "Give it to the people to eat."
43Elisha's servant asked, "How can I
feed a hundred people with so little?"
"Give the bread to the people to eat,"
Elisha said. "This is what the LORD says:
'They will eat and will have food left
over.' " 44After he gave it to them, the
people ate and had food left over, as the
LORD had said.

Naaman Is Healed

5 Naaman was commander of the army
of the king of Aram. He was honored
by his master, and he had much respect
because the LORD used him to give victory to Aram. He was a mighty and brave
man, but he had a skin disease.
2The Arameans had gone out to raid
the Israelites and had taken a little girl
as a captive. This little girl served
Naaman's wife. 3She said to her mistress, "I wish my master would meet the
prophet who lives in Samaria. He would
cure him of his disease."
4Naaman went to the king and told
him what the girl from Israel had said.
5The king of Aram said, "Go ahead, and I
will send a letter to the king of Israel." So
Naaman left and took with him about
seven hundred fifty pounds of silver, as
well as one hundred fifty pounds of gold
and ten changes of clothes. 6He brought
the letter to the king of Israel, which
read, "I am sending my servant Naaman
to you so you can heal him of his skin disease."
7When the king of Israel read the letter, he tore his clothes to show how upset
he was. He said, "I'm not God! I can't kill
and make alive again! Why does this man
send someone with a skin disease for me
to heal? You can see that the king of Aram
is trying to start trouble with me."
8When Elisha, the man of God, heard
that the king of Israel had torn his clothes,
he sent the king this message: "Why have
you torn your clothes? Let Naaman come
to me. Then he will know there is a prophet in Israel." 9So Naaman went with his
horses and chariots to Elisha's house and
stood outside the door.
10Elisha sent Naaman a messenger
who said, "Go and wash in the Jordan
River seven times. Then your skin will
be healed, and you will be clean."
11Naaman became angry and left. He
said, "I thought Elisha would surely
come out and stand before me and call on
the name of the LORD his God. I thought
he would wave his hand over the place
and heal the disease. 12The Abana and
the Pharpar, the rivers of Damascus, are
better than all the waters of Israel. Why
can't I wash in them and become clean?"
So Naaman went away very angry.
13Naaman's servants came near and
said to him, "My father, if the prophet had
told you to do some great thing, wouldn't
you have done it? Doesn't it make more
sense just to do it? After all, he only told
you, 'Wash, and you will be clean.' " 14So
Naaman went down and dipped in the Jordan seven times, just as Elisha had said.
Then his skin became new again, like the
skin of a child. And he was clean.
15Naaman and all his group returned
to Elisha. He stood before Elisha and said,
"Look, I now know there is no
God in all the earth
except in Israel. Now
please accept a gift
from me."
16But Elisha said,
"As surely as the
LORD lives whom I
serve, I won't accept anything." Naaman
urged him to take the gift, but he refused.
17Then Naaman said, "If you won't
take the gift, then please give me some
soil—as much as two of my mules can
carry. From now on I'll not offer any
burnt offering or sacrifice to any other
gods but the LORD. 18But let the LORD
pardon me for this: When my master
goes into the temple of Rimmon[n] to worship, he leans on my arm. Then I must
bow in that temple. May the LORD pardon
me when I do that."

eMAIL! FROM GOD 5:15
God
Read to see how to honor God.

5:18 temple of Rimmon The place where the Aramean people worshiped the god Rimmon.

FAITH links

ADVICE FROM A KID

2 KINGS 5

Do you think you have to be older before you can do anything for God? Think again. Naaman was a great army commander with a terrible skin disease. He never would have been cured if he had not listened to the advice of a servant girl. She told Naaman's wife about a prophet who could cure him. Naaman's wife then told him about this prophet. Elisha was that prophet. That little piece of advice changed Naaman's life forever.

You never know what great things you can do for God. Yes, you! You'll never know unless you make yourself available.

Think you're too young to serve God? Surf on to these links:

The Heart of the Matter, 1 Samuel 16, p. 375

The Way to Serve God, 1 Kings 9:4, p. 450

Too Young to Serve, Jeremiah 1:4–9, p. 988

Love Him? Show It!, Amos 2:6–7, p. 1196

A Friend of Jesus, John 15:9–17, p. 1450

Helpful Hints, 3 John 11, p. 1724

19Elisha said to him, "Go in peace."
Naaman left Elisha and went a short
way. 20Gehazi, the servant of Elisha the
man of God, thought, "My master has not
accepted what Naaman the Aramean
brought. As surely as the LORD lives, I'll
run after him and get something from
him." 21So Gehazi went after Naaman.
When Naaman saw someone running
after him, he got off the chariot to meet
Gehazi. He asked, "Is everything all
right?"
22Gehazi said, "Everything is all
right. My master has sent me. He said,
'Two young men from the groups of
prophets in the mountains of Ephraim
just came to me. Please give them
seventy-five pounds of silver and two
changes of clothes.' "
23Naaman said, "Please take one hundred fifty pounds," and he urged Gehazi
to take it. He tied one hundred fifty
pounds of silver in two bags with two
changes of clothes. Then he gave them to
two of his servants to carry for Gehazi.
24When they came to the hill, Gehazi
took these things from Naaman's servants and put them in the house. Then he
let Naaman's servants go, and they left.
25When he came in and stood before
his master, Elisha said to him, "Where
have you been, Gehazi?"
"I didn't go anywhere," he answered.
26But Elisha said to him, "My spirit
was with you. I knew when the man
turned from his chariot to meet you. This
isn't a time to take money, clothes, olives, grapes, sheep, oxen, male servants,
or female servants. 27So Naaman's skin
disease will come on you and your children forever." When Gehazi left Elisha,
he had the disease and was as white as
snow.

An Axhead Floats

6 The groups of prophets said to Elisha,
"The place where we meet with you
is too small for us. 2Let's go to the Jordan
River. There everyone can get a log, and
let's build a place there to live."
Elisha said, "Go."
3One of them said, "Please go
with us."

FAITH links

"HANDLE" YOUR RESPONSIBILITIES

2 KINGS 6:5-7

Have you ever borrowed something from one of your friends but then lost it? It isn't a good feeling, is it? An unnamed Old Testament man could relate! He had borrowed an ax, and the axhead fell into the water. There he was, left with the handle! That axhead was too expensive to lose. Yet, he showed responsibility by going to the one person he felt could do something about it—Elisha. The prophet made the heavy iron axhead float so the man could grab it!

The things we have are meant to be taken care of. The things we borrow should receive the same care.

The Sacrifice, Genesis 22, p. 29

A Serious Promise, Deuteronomy 23:21–23, p. 257

Promises, Promises, Judges 2:1–3, p. 312

Wisdom About Wealth, Ecclesiastes 5:10–12, p. 878

Obeying God or Man?, Daniel 3:8–30, p. 1154

That Thing You Do, Matthew 25:14–30, p. 1319

Elisha answered, "I will go," 4so he
went with them. When they arrived at
the Jordan, they cut down some trees.
5As one man was cutting down a tree, the
head of his ax fell into the water. He
yelled, "Oh, my master! I borrowed that
ax!"
6Elisha asked, "Where did it fall?"
The man showed him the place. Then
Elisha cut down a stick and threw it into
the water, and it made the iron head float.
7Elisha said, "Pick up the axhead." Then
the man reached out and took it.

Elisha and the Blinded Arameans

8The king of Aram was at war with Israel. He had a council meeting with his officers and said, "I will set up my camp in this place."
9Elisha, the man of God, sent a message to the king of Israel, saying, "Be careful! Don't pass that place, because the Arameans are going down there!"
10The king of Israel checked the place about which Elisha had warned him. Elisha warned him several times, so the king protected himself there.
11The king of Aram was angry about this. He called his officers together and demanded, "Tell me who of us is working for the king of Israel."
12One of the officers said, "None, my master and king. It's Elisha, the prophet from Israel. He can tell you what you speak in your bedroom."
13The king said, "Go and find him so I can send men and catch him."

The servants came back and reported, "He is in Dothan."
14Then the king sent horses, chariots, and many troops to Dothan. They arrived at night and surrounded the city.
15Elisha's servant got up early, and when he went out, he saw an army with horses and chariots all around the city. The servant said to Elisha, "Oh, my master, what can we do?"
16Elisha said, "Don't be afraid. The army that fights for us is larger than the one against us."
17Then Elisha prayed, "LORD, open my servant's eyes, and let him see."

The LORD opened the eyes of the young man, and he saw that the mountain was full of horses and chariots of fire all around Elisha.
18As the enemy came down toward

FAITH links

PUTTING AN ENEMY IN CHECK

2 KINGS 6:8-23

In the game of chess the object is to capture your opponent's king. You do this by putting the king in "check." That means making sure the king cannot be moved without being captured. During Elisha's day, an enemy king tried to put Elisha in "check" by sending his army after him. They surrounded the city where Elisha stayed. But God put *them* in "check" by having them captured instead. But this game had a surprise ending. Instead of calling "checkmate" and destroying the enemy, Elisha showed mercy.

Mercy for an enemy won't win you any chess games. But it makes you a winner in God's eyes.

Connect here to find out how you can be a winner!

Forgive Instead, Genesis 33, p. 47

The Right Thing to Do, 1 Samuel 26, p. 391

Anger: Quick or Slow?, Psalm 86:15, p. 776

Mercy for an Enemy, Jonah 4, p. 1216

Forgive Again?, Luke 17:3–4, p. 1402

Forgive and Forget?, Ephesians 4:32, p. 1604

Elisha, he prayed to the LORD, "Make
these people blind." So he made the Aramean army blind, as Elisha had asked.
19Elisha said to them, "This is not the
right road or the right city. Follow me and
I'll take you to the man you are looking
for." Then Elisha led them to Samaria.
20After they entered Samaria, Elisha
said, "LORD, open these men's eyes so
they can see." So the LORD opened their
eyes, and the Aramean army saw that
they were inside the city of Samaria!
21When the king of Israel saw the Aramean army, he said to Elisha, "My father, should I kill them? Should I kill
them?"
22Elisha answered, "Don't kill them.
You wouldn't kill people whom you captured with your sword and bow. Give
them food and water, and let them eat and
drink and then go home to their master."
23So he prepared a great feast for the Aramean army. After they ate and drank,
the king sent them away, and they went
home to their master. The soldiers of
Aram did not come anymore into the land
of Israel.

A Shortage of Food

24Later, Ben-Hadad king of Aram
gathered his whole army and surrounded
and attacked Samaria. 25There was a
shortage of food in Samaria. It was so bad
that a donkey's head sold for about two
pounds of silver, and half of a pint of
dove's dung sold for about two ounces of
silver.
26As the king of Israel was passing by
on the wall, a woman yelled out to him,
"Help me, my master and king!"
27The king said, "If the LORD doesn't
help you, how can I? Can I get help from
the threshing floor or from the winepress?" 28Then the king said to her,
"What is your trouble?"

She answered, "This woman said to
me, 'Give up your son so we can eat him
today. Then we will eat my son tomorrow.' 29So we boiled my son and ate him.
Then the next day I said to her, 'Give up
your son so we can eat him.' But she had
hidden him."
30When the king heard the woman's

words, he tore his clothes in grief. As he
walked along the wall, the people looked
and saw he had on rough cloth under his
clothes to show his sadness. **31**He said,
"May God punish me terribly if the head
of Elisha son of Shaphat isn't cut off from
his body today!"

32The king sent a messenger to Elisha, who was sitting in his house with the
older leaders. But before the messenger
arrived, Elisha said to them, "See, this
murderer is sending men to cut off my
head. When the messenger arrives, shut
the door and hold it; don't let him in. The
sound of his master's feet is behind him."

33Elisha was still talking with the
leaders when the messenger arrived.
The king said, "This trouble has come
from the LORD. Why should I wait for the
LORD any longer?"

7 Elisha said, "Listen to the LORD's
word. This is what the LORD says:
'About this time tomorrow seven quarts
of fine flour will be sold for two-fifths of
an ounce of silver, and thirteen quarts of
barley will be sold for two-fifths of an
ounce of silver. This will happen at the
gate of Samaria.' "

2Then the officer who was close to
the king answered Elisha, "Even if the
LORD opened windows in the sky, that
couldn't happen."

Elisha said, "You will see it with your
eyes, but you will not eat any of it."

3There were four men with a skin disease at the entrance to the city gate.
They said to each other, "Why do we sit
here until we die? **4**There is no food in
the city. So if we go into the city, we will
die there. If we stay here, we will die. So
let's go to the Aramean camp. If they let
us live, we will live. If they kill us, we
die."

5So they got up at twilight and went to
the Aramean camp, but when they arrived, no one was there. **6**The Lord had
caused the Aramean army to hear the
sound of chariots, horses, and a large
army. They had said to each other, "The
king of Israel has hired the Hittite and
Egyptian kings to attack us!" **7**So they
got up and ran away in the twilight, leaving their tents, horses, and donkeys.
They left the camp standing and ran for
their lives.

8When the men with the skin disease
came to the edge of the camp, they went
into one of the tents and ate and drank.
They carried silver, gold, and clothes out
of the camp and hid them. Then they
came back and entered another tent.
They carried things from this tent and
hid them, also. **9**Then they said to each
other, "We're doing wrong. Today we
have good news, but we are silent. If we
wait until the sun comes up, we'll be discovered. Let's go right now and tell the
people in the king's palace."

10So they went and called to the gatekeepers of the city. They said, "We went
to the Aramean camp, but no one is
there; we didn't hear anyone. The horses
and donkeys were still tied up, and the
tents were still standing." **11**Then the
gatekeepers shouted out and told the
people in the palace.

12The king got up in the night and
said to his officers, "I'll tell you what the
Arameans are doing to us. They know we
are starving. They have gone out of the
camp to hide in the field. They're saying,
'When the Israelites come out of the city,
we'll capture them alive. Then we'll enter the city.' "

13One of his officers answered, "Let
some men take five of the horses that are
still left in the city. These men are like all
the Israelites who are left; they are also
about to die. Let's send them to see what
has happened."

14So the men took two chariots with
horses. The king sent them after the Aramean army, saying, "Go and see what
has happened." **15**The men followed the
Aramean army as far as the Jordan River.
The road was full of clothes and equipment that the Arameans had thrown
away as they had hurriedly left. So the
messengers returned and told the king.
16Then the people went out and took
valuables from the Aramean camp. So
seven quarts of fine flour were sold for
two-fifths of an ounce of silver, and thirteen quarts of barley were sold for two-
fifths of an ounce of silver, just as the
LORD had said.

17The king chose the officer who was
close to him to guard the gate, but the
people trampled the officer to death. This
happened just as Elisha had told the king
when the king came to his house. **18**He
had said, "Thirteen quarts of barley and
seven quarts of fine flour will each sell for
two-fifths of an ounce of silver about this
time tomorrow at the gate of Samaria."
19But the officer had answered,
"Even if the LORD opened windows in the
sky, that couldn't happen." And Elisha
had told him, "You will see it with your
eyes, but you won't eat any of it." **20**It
happened to the officer just that way. The
people trampled him in the gateway, and
he died.

The Shunammite Regains Her Land

8 Elisha spoke to the woman whose
son he had brought back to life. He
said, "Get up and go with your family.
Stay any place you can, because the LORD
has called for a time without food that will
last seven years." **2**So the woman got up
and did as the man of God had said. She
left with her family, and they stayed in
the land of the Philistines for seven
years. **3**After seven years she returned
from the land of the Philistines and went
to beg the king for her house and land.
4The king was talking with Gehazi, the
servant of the man of God. The king had
said, "Please tell me all the great things
Elisha has done." **5**Gehazi was telling the
king how Elisha had brought a dead boy
back to life. Just then the woman whose
son Elisha had brought back to life came
and begged the king for her house and
land.
Gehazi said, "My master and king,
this is the woman, and this is the son Elisha brought back to life."
6The king asked the woman, and she
told him about it. Then the king chose an
officer to help her. "Give the woman
everything that is hers," the king said.
"Give her all the money made from her
land from the day she left until now."

Ben-Hadad Is Killed

7Then Elisha went to Damascus,
where Ben-Hadad king of Aram was sick.
Someone told him, "The man of God has
arrived."
8The king said to Hazael, "Take a gift
in your hand and go meet him. Ask the
LORD through him if I will recover from
my sickness."
9So Hazael went to meet Elisha, taking with him a gift of forty camels loaded
with every good thing in Damascus. He
came and stood before Elisha and said,
"Your son Ben-Hadad king of Aram sent
me to you. He asks if he will recover from
his sickness."
10Elisha said to Hazael, "Go and tell
Ben-Hadad, 'You will surely recover,' but
the LORD has told me he will really die."
11Hazael stared at Elisha until he felt
ashamed. Then Elisha cried.
12Hazael asked, "Why are you crying,
master?"
Elisha answered, "Because I know
what evil you will do to the Israelites. You
will burn their strong, walled cities with
fire and kill their young men with swords.
You will throw their babies to the ground
and split open their pregnant women."
13Hazael said, "Am I a dog? How
could I do such things?"
Elisha answered, "The LORD has
shown me that you will be king over
Aram."
14Then Hazael left Elisha and came to
his master. Ben-Hadad said to him,
"What did Elisha say to you?"
Hazael answered, "He told me that
you will surely recover." **15**But the next
day Hazael took a blanket and dipped it in
water. Then he put it over Ben-Hadad's
face, and he died. So Hazael became king
in Ben-Hadad's place.

Jehoram King of Judah

16While Jehoshaphat was king in Judah, Jehoram son of Jehoshaphat became
king of Judah. This was during the fifth
year Joram son of Ahab was king of Israel. **17**Jehoram was thirty-two years old
when he began to rule, and he ruled eight
years in Jerusalem. **18**He followed the
ways of the kings of Israel, just as the
family of Ahab had done, because he married Ahab's daughter. Jehoram did what
the LORD said was wrong. **19**But the

LORD would not destroy Judah because of his servant David. The LORD had promised that one of David's descendants would always rule.

20In Jehoram's time Edom broke away from Judah's rule and chose their own king. 21So Jehoram and all his chariots went to Zair. The Edomites surrounded him and his chariot commanders. Jehoram got up and attacked the Edomites at night, but his army ran away to their tents. 22From then until now the country of Edom has fought against the rule of Judah. At the same time Libnah also broke away from Judah's rule.

> The LORD had promised that one of David's descendants would always rule.
> —2 Kings 8:19

23The other acts of Jehoram and all the things he did are written in the book of the history of the kings of Judah. 24Jehoram died and was buried with his ancestors in Jerusalem, and Jehoram's son Ahaziah ruled in his place.

25Ahaziah son of Jehoram became king of Judah during the twelfth year Joram son of Ahab was king of Israel. 26Ahaziah was twenty-two years old when he became king, and he ruled one year in Jerusalem. His mother's name was Athaliah, a granddaughter of Omri king of Israel. 27Ahaziah followed the ways of Ahab's family. He did what the LORD said was wrong, as Ahab's family had done, because he was a son-in-law to Ahab.

28Ahaziah went with Joram son of Ahab to Ramoth in Gilead, where they fought against Hazael king of Aram. The Arameans wounded Joram. 29So King Joram returned to Jezreel to heal from the wound he had received from the Arameans at Ramoth when he fought Hazael king of Aram. Ahaziah son of Jehoram king of Judah went down to visit Joram son of Ahab at Jezreel, because he had been wounded.

Jehu Is Chosen King

9 At the same time, Elisha the prophet called a man from the groups of prophets. Elisha said, "Get ready, and take this small bottle of olive oil in your hand. Go to Ramoth in Gilead. 2When you arrive, find Jehu son of Jehoshaphat, the son of Nimshi. Go in and make Jehu get up from among his brothers, and take him to an inner room. 3Then take the bottle and pour the oil on Jehu's head and say, 'This is what the LORD says: I have appointed you king over Israel.' Then open the door and run away. Don't wait!"

4So the young man, the prophet, went to Ramoth in Gilead. 5When he arrived, he saw the officers of the army sitting together. He said, "Commander, I have a message for you."

Jehu asked, "For which one of us?"

The young man said, "For you, commander."

6Jehu got up and went into the house. Then the young prophet poured the olive oil on Jehu's head and said to him, "This is what the LORD, the God of Israel says: 'I have appointed you king over the LORD's people Israel. 7You must destroy the family of Ahab your master. I will punish Jezebel for the deaths of my servants the prophets and for all the LORD's servants who were murdered. 8All of Ahab's family must die. I will not let any male child in Ahab's family live in Israel, whether slave or free. 9I will make Ahab's family like the family of Jeroboam son of Nebat and like the family of Baasha son of Ahijah. 10The dogs will eat Jezebel at Jezreel, and no one will bury her.' "

Then the young prophet opened the door and ran away.

11When Jehu went back to his master's officers, one of them said to Jehu, "Is everything all right? Why did this crazy man come to you?"

Jehu answered, "You know the man and how he talks."

12They answered, "That's not true. Tell us."

Jehu said, "He said to me, 'This is what the LORD says: I have appointed you to be king over Israel.' "

13Then the officers hurried, and each
man took off his own coat and put it on
the stairs for Jehu. They blew the trumpet and shouted, "Jehu is king!"

Joram and Ahaziah Are Killed

14So Jehu son of Jehoshaphat, the son
of Nimshi, made plans against Joram.
Now Joram and all Israel had been defending Ramoth in Gilead from Hazael
king of Aram. 15But King Joram had to
return to Jezreel to heal from the injuries
the Arameans had given him when he
fought against Hazael king of Aram.

Jehu said, "If you agree with this,
don't let anyone leave the city. They
might tell the news in Jezreel." 16Then
he got into his chariot and set out for Jezreel, where Joram was resting. Ahaziah
king of Judah had gone down to see him.

17The lookout was standing on the
watchtower in Jezreel when he saw
Jehu's troops coming. He said, "I see
some soldiers!"

Joram said, "Take a horseman and send him to meet them. Tell him to ask, 'Is all in order?' "

18The horseman rode out to meet
Jehu, and he said, "This is what the king
says: 'Is all in order?' "

Jehu said, "Why bother yourself with order? Come along behind me."

TV OR NOT TV: THAT IS THE QUESTION

Tagg and I are talking about our favorite ways to spend our time. Let's hear what a friend of ours has to say. Welcome Justin, age 11, to Connect 2-You.

I love TV. I'd have it on 24 hours a day if I could. Of course, there's no way my mom would ever let that happen. She says I spend way too much time in front of the tube as it is. She says that TV is too much of a "priority" to me, and that it's interfering with what's really important in life. I don't know what she's talking about. What's wrong with TV?

Hey, Justin. How do you like to spend your time?

Good question, Justin. Let's go back to what your mom said about it being a priority in your life. God warns us not to have any other gods except him. A "god" could be anything that is more important to you than your relationship with Jesus. That includes TV. Maybe you've never bowed down and worshiped your television, but if watching TV is a higher priority in your life than things like praying, reading the Bible, or writing in your journal, you may have a new god in your life.

Think of it this way. Someday we'll all stand before God, and he'll ask us to explain how we spent our time on earth—and why. How pleased do you think he'll be if you tell him you spent most of it in front of a TV? For tips on how to spend your time wisely, take a look at the Livin' It page on making good choices, Deuteronomy 30:15-20, p. 267.

The lookout reported, "The messenger reached them, but he is not coming
back."
19Then Joram sent out a second
horseman. This rider came to Jehu's
group and said, "This is what the king
says: 'Is all in order?' "
Jehu answered, "Why bother yourself
with order? Come along behind me."
20The lookout reported, "The second
man reached them, but he is not coming
back. The man in the chariot is driving
like Jehu son of Nimshi. He drives as if he
were crazy!"
21Joram said, "Get my chariot ready."
Then the servant got Joram's chariot
ready. Joram king of Israel and Ahaziah
king of Judah went out, each in his own
chariot, to meet Jehu at the property of
Naboth the Jezreelite.
22When Joram saw Jehu, he said, "Is
all in order, Jehu?"
Jehu answered, "There will never be
any order as long as your mother Jezebel
worships idols and uses witchcraft."
23Joram turned the horses to run
away and yelled to Ahaziah, "It's a trick,
Ahaziah!"
24Then Jehu drew his bow and shot
Joram between his shoulders. The arrow
went through Joram's heart, and he fell
down in his chariot.
25Jehu ordered Bidkar, his chariot officer, "Pick up Joram's body, and throw it
into the field of Naboth the Jezreelite.
Remember when you and I rode together
with Joram's father Ahab. The LORD
made this prophecy against him: 26'Yesterday I saw the blood of Naboth and his
sons, says the LORD, so I will punish
Ahab in his field, says the LORD.' Take
Joram's body and throw it into the field,
as the LORD has said."
27When Ahaziah king of Judah saw
this, he ran away toward Beth Haggan.
Jehu chased him, saying, "Shoot Ahaziah,
too!" Ahaziah was wounded in his chariot
on the way up to Gur near Ibleam. He got
as far as Megiddo but died there.
28Ahaziah's servants carried his body in
a chariot to Jerusalem and buried him
with his ancestors in his tomb in Jerusalem. 29(Ahaziah had become king over
Judah in the eleventh year Joram son of
Ahab was king.)

Death of Jezebel

30When Jehu came to Jezreel, Jezebel
heard about it. She put on her eye
makeup and fixed her hair. Then she
looked out the window. 31When Jehu entered the city gate, Jezebel said, "Have
you come in peace, you Zimri,[n] you who
killed your master?"
32Jehu looked up at the window and
said, "Who is on my side? Who?" Two or
three servants looked out the window at
Jehu. 33He said to them, "Throw her
down." So they threw Jezebel down, and
the horses ran over her. Some of her
blood splashed on the wall and on the
horses.
34Jehu went into the house and ate
and drank. Then he said, "Now see about
this cursed woman. Bury her, because
she is a king's daughter."
35The men went to bury Jezebel, but
they could not find her. They found only
her skull, feet, and the palms of her
hands. 36When they came back and told
Jehu, he said, "The LORD said this
through his servant Elijah the Tishbite:
'The dogs will eat Jezebel at Jezreel.
37Her body will be like manure on the
field in the land at Jezreel. No one will be
able to say that this is Jezebel.' "

Families of Ahab and Ahaziah Killed

10 Ahab had seventy sons in Samaria.
Jehu wrote letters and sent them
to Samaria to the officers and older leaders of Jezreel and to the guardians of the
sons of Ahab. Jehu said, 2"You have your
master's sons with you, and you have
chariots, horses, a city with strong walls,
and weapons. When you get this letter,
3choose the best and most worthy person among your master's sons, and make
him king. Then fight for your master's
family."
4But the officers and leaders of Jezreel were frightened. They said, "Two

9:31 Zimri He was the man who killed Elah and the family of Baasha. Read 1 Kings 16:8-12.

kings could not stand up to Jehu, so how
can we?"
5The palace manager, the city governor, the leaders, and the guardians sent a
message to Jehu. "We are your servants," they said. "We will do everything
you tell us to do. We won't make any man
king, so do whatever you think is best."
6Then Jehu wrote a second letter,
saying, "If you are on my side and will
obey me, cut off the heads of your
master's sons and come to me at Jezreel
tomorrow about this time."
Now the seventy sons of the king's
family were with the leading men of the
city who were their guardians. **7**When
the leaders received the letter, they took
the king's sons and killed all seventy of
them. They put their heads in baskets
and sent them to Jehu at Jezreel. **8**The
messenger came to Jehu and told him,
"They have brought the heads of the
king's sons."
Then Jehu said, "Lay the heads in two
piles at the city gate until morning."
9In the morning, Jehu went out and
stood before the people
and said to them, "You are
innocent. Look, I made
plans against my master
and killed him. But who
killed all these? **10**You
should know that every-
thing the LORD said about
Ahab's family will come
true. The LORD has spo-
ken through his servant
Elijah, and the LORD has
done what he said." **11**So Jehu killed everyone of Ahab's family in Jezreel who
was still alive. He also killed all Ahab's
leading men, close friends, and priests.
No one who had helped Ahab was left
alive.
12Then Jehu left and went to Samaria
by way of the road to Beth Eked of the
Shepherds. **13**There Jehu met some relatives of Ahaziah king of Judah. Jehu
asked, "Who are you?"
They answered, "We are relatives of
Ahaziah. We have come down to get revenge for the families of the king and the
king's mother."

> You should know that everything the LORD said about Ahab's family will come true.
> —2 Kings 10:10

14Then Jehu said, "Take them alive!"
So they captured Ahaziah's relatives
alive and killed them at the well near
Beth Eked—forty-two of them. Jehu did
not leave anyone alive.
15After Jehu left there, he met Jehonadab son of Recab, who was also on his
way to meet Jehu. Jehu greeted him and
said, "Are you as good a friend to me as I
am to you?"
Jehonadab answered, "Yes, I am."
Jehu said, "If you are, then give me
your hand." So Jehonadab gave him his
hand, and Jehu pulled him into the chariot. **16**"Come with me," Jehu said. "You
can see how strong my feelings are for
the LORD." So Jehu had Jehonadab ride in
his chariot.
17When Jehu came to Samaria, he
killed all of Ahab's family in Samaria. He
destroyed all those who were left, just as
the LORD had told Elijah it would happen.

Baal Worshipers Killed

18Then Jehu gathered all the people
together and said to them, "Ahab served
Baal a little, but Jehu will
serve Baal much. **19**Now
call for me all Baal's
prophets and priests and
all the people who wor-
ship Baal. Don't let any-
one miss this meeting,
because I have a great
sacrifice for Baal. Anyone
who is not there will not
live." But Jehu was tricking them so he could de-
stroy the worshipers of Baal. **20**He said,
"Prepare a holy meeting for Baal." So
they announced the meeting. **21**Then
Jehu sent word through all Israel, and all
the worshipers of Baal came; not one
stayed home. They came into the temple
of Baal, and the temple was filled from
one side to the other.
22Jehu said to the man who kept the
robes, "Bring out robes for all the worshipers of Baal." After he brought out
robes for them, **23**Jehu and Jehonadab
son of Recab went into the temple of
Baal. Jehu said to the worshipers of Baal,
"Look around, and make sure there are

no servants of the LORD with you. Be
sure there are only worshipers of Baal."
24Then the worshipers of Baal went in to
offer sacrifices and burnt offerings.

Jehu had eighty men waiting outside.
He had told them, "Don't let anyone escape. If you do, you must pay with your
own life."

25As soon as Jehu finished offering
the burnt offering, he ordered the guards
and the captains, "Go in and kill the worshipers of Baal. Don't let anyone come
out." So the guards and captains killed
the worshipers of Baal with the sword
and threw their bodies out. Then they
went to the inner rooms of the temple
26and brought out the pillars of the temple of Baal and burned them. **27**They tore
down the stone pillar of Baal, as well as
the temple of Baal. And they made it into
a sewage pit, as it is today.

28So Jehu destroyed Baal worship in
Israel, **29**but he did not stop doing the
sins Jeroboam son of Nebat had done.
Jeroboam had led Israel to sin by wor-
shiping the golden calves in Bethel and
Dan.

30The LORD said to Jehu, "You have
done well in obeying what I said was
right. You have done to the family of Ahab
as I wanted. Because of this, your descendants as far as your great-great-
grandchildren will be kings of Israel."
31But Jehu was not careful to follow the
teachings of the LORD, the God of Israel,
with all his heart. He did not stop doing
the same sins Jeroboam had done, by
which he had led Israel to sin.

32At that time the LORD began to
make Israel smaller. Hazael defeated the
Israelites in all the land of Israel, **33**taking all the land of the Jordan known as the
land of Gilead. (It was the region of Gad,
Reuben, and Manasseh.) He took land
from Aroer by the Arnon Ravine through
Gilead to Bashan.

34The other things Jehu did—everything he did and all his victories—are
recorded in the book of the history of the
kings of Israel. **35**Jehu died and was buried
in Samaria, and his son Jehoahaz became
king in his place. **36**Jehu was king over Israel in Samaria for twenty-eight years.

Athaliah and Joash

11 When Ahaziah's mother, Athaliah,
saw that her son was dead, she
killed all the royal family. **2**But Jehosheba,
King Jehoram's daughter and Ahaziah's
sister, took Joash, Ahaziah's son. She
stole him from among the other sons of
the king who were about to be murdered.
She put Joash and his nurse in a bedroom
to hide him from Athaliah, so he was not
killed. **3**He hid with her in the Temple of
the LORD for six years. During that time
Athaliah ruled the land.

4In the seventh year Jehoiada sent for
the commanders of groups of a hundred
men, as well as the Carites.[n] He brought
them together in the Temple of the LORD
and made an agreement with them.
There, in the Temple of the LORD, he
made them promise loyalty, and then he
showed them the king's son. **5**He commanded them, "This is what you must do.
A third of you who go on duty on the Sabbath will guard the king's palace. **6**A third
of you will be at the Sur Gate, and another third will be at the gate behind the
guard. This way you will guard the Temple. **7**The two groups who go off duty on
the Sabbath must protect the Temple of
the LORD for the king. **8**All of you must
stand around the king, each man with his
weapons in his hand. If anyone comes
near, kill him. Stay close to the king when
he goes out and when he comes in."

9The commanders over a hundred
men obeyed everything Jehoiada the
priest had commanded. Each one took his
men who came on duty on the Sabbath
and those who went off duty on the Sabbath, and they came to Jehoiada the
priest. **10**He gave the commanders the
spears and shields that had belonged to
King David and that were kept in the
Temple of the LORD.

Joash Becomes King

11Then each guard took his place with
his weapons in his hand. There were

11:4 Carites This was probably a special unit of the army that was responsible for the king's safety, a kind of palace guard similar to the Kerethites and the Pelethites.

FAITH links

A BIG RESPONSIBILITY

2 KINGS 11

Think back to the time when you were seven. (Waaaaayyyy back then.) Imagine being told that you were the new president of the United States. How would you react? Joash was only seven when he became king of Judah. Although he had people to help him run the country, he still had to learn how to be responsible. (You can also read this story in 2 Chronicles 24, p. 588.)

You may not have a country to run, but you can still learn to be responsible. One of the first steps is to take your responsibilities seriously whatever they may be—chores, homework, going to school. That means doing what's expected of you.

A Use for Your Abilities, Genesis 41, p. 59

Read My Lips?, Deuteronomy 26:16–19, p. 260

Your Best Work, 1 Kings 6, p. 443

Down on the Ant Farm, Proverbs 6:6–11, p. 833

Calling Anyone!, Acts 23:12–22, p. 1506

Help for the Body, Romans 12:3–8, p. 1536

guards from the south side of the Temple
to the north side. They stood by the altar
and the Temple and around the king.
12Jehoiada brought out the king's son
and put the crown on him and gave him a
copy of the agreement. They appointed
him king and poured olive oil on him.
Then they clapped their hands and said,
"Long live the king!"
13When Athaliah heard the noise of
the guards and the people, she went to
them at the Temple of the LORD. **14**She
looked, and there was the king, standing
by the pillar, as the custom was. The officers and trumpeters were standing beside him, and all the people of the land
were very happy and were blowing trumpets. Then Athaliah tore her clothes and
screamed, "Traitors! Traitors!"
15Jehoiada the priest gave orders to
the commanders of a hundred men, who
led the army. He said, "Surround her
with soldiers and kill with a sword anyone who follows her." He commanded this
because he had said, "Don't put Athaliah
to death in the Temple of the LORD." **16**So
they caught her when she came to the
horses' entrance near the palace. There
she was put to death.
17Then Jehoiada made an agreement
between the LORD and the king and the
people that they would be the LORD's
special people. He also made an agreement between the king and the people.
18All the people of the land went to the
temple of Baal and tore it down, smashing the altars and idols. They also killed
Mattan, the priest of Baal, in front of the
altars.
Then Jehoiada the priest placed
guards at the Temple of the LORD. **19**He
took with him the commanders of a hundred men and the Carites, the royal bodyguards, as well as the guards and all the
people of the land. Together they took
the king out of the Temple of the LORD
and went into the palace through the gate
of the guards. Then the king sat on the
royal throne. **20**So all the people of the
land were very happy, and Jerusalem had
peace, because Athaliah had been put to
death with the sword at the palace.
21Joash was seven years old when he
became king.

12 Joash became king of Judah in
Jehu's seventh year as king of Israel, and he ruled for forty years in Jeru-

salem. His mother's name was Zibiah,
and she was from Beersheba. 2Joash did
what the LORD said was right as long as
Jehoiada the priest taught him. 3But the
places where gods were worshiped were
not removed; the people still made sacrifices and burned incense there.

Joash Repairs the Temple

4Joash said to the priests, "Take all the
money brought as offerings to the Temple
of the LORD. This includes the
money each person
owes in taxes and
the money each per-
son promises or
brings freely to the
LORD. 5Each priest
will take the money
from the people he serves. Then the
priests must repair any damage they find
in the Temple."

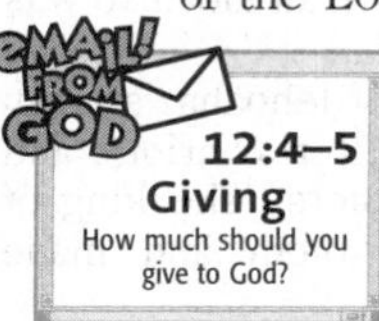

eMAIL! FROM GOD
12:4–5
Giving
How much should you give to God?

6But by the twenty-third year Joash
was king, the priests still had not repaired the Temple. 7So King Joash called
for Jehoiada the priest and the other
priests and said to them, "Why aren't you
repairing the damage of the Temple?
Don't take any more money from the
people you serve, but hand over the
money for the repair of the Temple."
8The priests agreed not to take any more
money from the people and not to repair
the Temple themselves.
9Jehoiada the priest took a box and
made a hole in the top of it. Then he put it
by the altar, on the right side as the people came into the Temple of the LORD.
The priests guarding the doorway put all
the money brought to the Temple of the
LORD into the box.
10Each time the priests saw that the
box was full of money, the king's royal
secretary and the high priest came. They
counted the money that had been
brought to the Temple of the LORD, and
they put it into bags. 11Next they
weighed the money and gave it to the
people in charge of the work on the Temple. With it they paid the carpenters and
the builders who worked on the Temple
of the LORD, 12as well as the bricklayers
and stonecutters. They also used the

FAITH links

WHAT'S THE USE?

2 KINGS 12:6-12

What's your first thought when you see the offering plate go by? Do you think *I have to give?* or *I want to give?* Many people grumble about giving because they're not sure what their money is used for. During Old Testament times, the Temple was in need of repair. Instead of demanding money from the people to repair the Temple, King Joash had a wooden box placed at the entrance to the Temple. All of the money in the box was used to repair the Temple. When the people saw how the money was used, they gave more.

If you're not sure what your offerings are used for, ask your pastor or church secretary. Knowing where your money goes can help you be more generous.

Connect here for the 411 on being generous:

A Small Percent, Deuteronomy 14:22–23, p. 247

Gifts from the Heart, 1 Chronicles 29, p. 557

Wisdom About Wealth, Ecclesiastes 5:10–12, p. 878

Set for Life?, Obadiah 2–4, p. 1208

One of the Faithful, Acts 10:1–34, p. 1482

Give to Give, 1 Corinthians 16:1–4, p. 1566

money to buy timber and cut stone to repair the damage of the Temple of the
LORD. It paid for everything.
13The money brought into the Temple
of the LORD was not used to make silver
cups, wick trimmers, bowls, trumpets, or
gold or silver vessels. **14**They paid the
money to the workers, who used it to repair the Temple of the LORD. **15**They did
not demand to know how the money was
spent, because the workers were honest.
16The money from the penalty offerings
and sin offerings was not brought into the
Temple of the LORD, because it belonged
to the priests.

Joash Saves Jerusalem

17About this time Hazael king of
Aram attacked Gath and captured it.
Then he went to attack Jerusalem. **18**Joash king of Judah took all the holy things
given by his ancestors, the kings of Judah—Jehoshaphat, Jehoram, and Ahaziah. He also took his own holy things as
well as the gold that was found in the
treasuries of the Temple of the LORD and
the gold from the palace. Joash sent all
this treasure to Hazael king of Aram, who
turned away from Jerusalem.
19Everything else Joash did is written
in the book of the history of the kings of
Judah. **20**His officers made plans against
him and killed him at Beth Millo on the
road down to Silla. **21**The officers who
killed him were Jozabad son of Shimeath
and Jehozabad son of Shomer. Joash was
buried with his ancestors in Jerusalem,
and Amaziah, his son, became king in his
place.

Jehoahaz King of Israel

13 Jehoahaz son of Jehu became king
over Israel in Samaria during the
twenty-third year Joash son of Ahaziah
was king of Judah. Jehoahaz ruled seventeen years, **2**and he did what the LORD
said was wrong. Jehoahaz did the same
sins Jeroboam son of Nebat had done.
Jeroboam had led Israel to sin, and Jehoahaz did not stop doing these same sins.
3So the LORD was angry with Israel and
handed them over to Hazael king of Aram
and his son Ben-Hadad for a long time.
4Then Jehoahaz begged the LORD,
and the LORD listened to him. The LORD
had seen the troubles of Israel; he saw
how terribly the king of Aram was treating them. **5**He gave Israel a man to save
them, and they escaped from the Arameans. The Israelites then lived in their
own homes as they had before, **6**but they
still did not stop doing the same sins that
the family of Jeroboam had done. He had
led Israel to sin, and they continued doing those sins. The Asherah idol also was
left standing in Samaria.
7Nothing was left of Jehoahaz's army
except fifty horsemen, ten chariots, and
ten thousand foot soldiers. The king of
Aram had destroyed them and made
them like chaff.
8Everything else Jehoahaz did and all
his victories are written in the book of
the history of the kings of Israel. **9**Jehoahaz died and was buried in Samaria, and
his son Jehoash became king in his place.

Jehoash King of Israel

10Jehoash son of Jehoahaz became
king of Israel in Samaria during Joash's
thirty-seventh year as king of Judah. Jehoash ruled sixteen years, **11**and he did
what the LORD said was wrong. He did
not stop doing the same sins Jeroboam
son of Nebat had done. Jeroboam had led
Israel to sin, and Jehoash continued to do
the same thing. **12**Everything else he did
and all his victories, including his war
against Amaziah king of Judah, are written in the book of the history of the kings
of Israel. **13**Jehoash died, and Jeroboam
took his place on the throne. Jehoash was
buried in Samaria with the kings of Israel.

The Death of Elisha

14At this time Elisha became sick.
Before he died, Jehoash king of Israel
went to Elisha and cried for him. Jehoash
said, "My father, my father! The chariots
of Israel and their horsemen!"
15Elisha said to Jehoash, "Take a bow
and arrows." So he took a bow and arrows. **16**Then Elisha said to him, "Put
your hand on the bow." So Jehoash put
his hand on the bow. Then Elisha put his
hands on the king's hands. **17**Elisha said,

"Open the east window." So Jehoash
opened the window. Then Elisha said,
"Shoot," and Jehoash shot. Elisha said,
"The LORD's arrow of victory over Aram!
You will defeat the Arameans at Aphek
until you destroy them."
18Elisha said, "Take the arrows." So
Jehoash took them. Then Elisha said to
him, "Strike the ground." So Jehoash
struck the ground three times and
stopped. 19The man of God was angry
with him. "You should have struck five or
six times!" Elisha said. "Then you would
have struck Aram until you had completely destroyed it. But now you will defeat it only three times."
20Then Elisha died and was buried.
At that time groups of Moabites would
rob the land in the springtime. 21Once as
some Israelites were burying a man, suddenly they saw a group of Moabites coming. The Israelites threw the dead man
into Elisha's grave. When the man
touched Elisha's bones, the man came
back to life and stood on his feet.

War with Aram

22During all the days Jehoahaz was
king, Hazael king of Aram troubled Israel. 23But the LORD was kind to the Israelites; he had mercy on them and
helped them because of his agreement
with Abraham, Isaac, and Jacob. To this
day he has never wanted to destroy them
or reject them.
24When Hazael king of Aram died, his
son Ben-Hadad became king in his place.
25During a war Hazael had taken some
cities from Jehoahaz, Jehoash's father.
Now Jehoash took back those cities from
Hazael's son Ben-Hadad. He defeated
Ben-Hadad three times and took back the
cities of Israel.

Amaziah King of Judah

14 Amaziah son of Joash became king
of Judah during the second year
Jehoash son of Jehoahaz was king of Israel. 2Amaziah was twenty-five years old
when he became king, and he ruled
twenty-nine years in Jerusalem. His
mother was named Jehoaddin, and she
was from Jerusalem. 3Amaziah did what
the LORD said was right. He did everything his father Joash had done, but he
did not do as his ancestor David had
done. 4The places where gods were worshiped were not removed, so the people
still sacrificed and burned incense there.
5As soon as Amaziah took control of
the kingdom, he executed the officers
who had murdered his father the king.
6But he did not put to death the children
of the murderers because of the rule
written in the Book of the Teachings of
Moses. The LORD had commanded: "Parents must not be put to death when their
children do wrong, and children must not
be put to death when their parents do
wrong. Each must die for his own sins."[n]
7In battle Amaziah killed ten thousand Edomites in the Valley of Salt. He
also took the city of Sela. He called it Joktheel, as it is still called today.
8Amaziah sent messengers to Jehoash son of Jehoahaz, the son of Jehu, king
of Israel. They said, "Come, let's meet
face to face."
9Then Jehoash king of Israel answered Amaziah king of Judah, "A thornbush in Lebanon sent a message to a
cedar tree in Lebanon. It said, 'Let your
daughter marry my son.' But then a wild
animal from Lebanon came by, walking
on and crushing the thornbush. 10You
have defeated Edom, but you have become proud. Stay at home and brag.
Don't ask for trouble, or you and Judah
will be defeated."
11But Amaziah would not listen, so
Jehoash king of Israel went to attack. He
and Amaziah king of Judah faced each
other in battle at Beth Shemesh in Judah.
12Israel defeated Judah, and every man
of Judah ran away to his home. 13At Beth
Shemesh Jehoash king of Israel captured
Amaziah king of Judah. (Amaziah was the
son of Joash, who was the son of Ahaziah.) Jehoash went up to Jerusalem and
broke down the wall of Jerusalem from
the Gate of Ephraim to the Corner Gate,
which was about six hundred feet. 14He
took all the gold and silver and all the

14:6 "Parents . . . sins." See Deuteronomy 24:16.

utensils in the Temple of the LORD, and he took the treasuries of the palace and some hostages. Then he returned to Samaria.

15The other acts of Jehoash and his victories, including his war against Amaziah king of Judah, are written in the book of the history of the kings of Israel. **16**Jehoash died and was buried in Samaria with the kings of Israel, and his son Jeroboam became king in his place.

17Amaziah son of Joash, the king of Judah, lived fifteen years after the death of Jehoash son of Jehoahaz, the king of Israel. **18**The other things Amaziah did are written in the book of the history of the kings of Judah. **19**The people in Jerusalem made plans against him. So he ran away to the town of Lachish, but they sent men after him to Lachish and killed him. **20**They brought his body back on horses, and he was buried with his ancestors in Jerusalem, in the city of David.

21Then all the people of Judah made Uzziah[n] king in place of his father Amaziah. Uzziah was sixteen years old. **22**He rebuilt the town of Elath and made it part of Judah again after Amaziah died.

Jeroboam King of Israel

23Jeroboam son of Jehoash became king of Israel in Samaria during the fifteenth year Amaziah was king of Judah. (Amaziah was the son of Joash.) Jeroboam ruled forty-one years, **24**and he did what the LORD said was wrong. Jeroboam son of Nebat had led Israel to sin, and Jeroboam son of Jehoash did not stop doing the same sins. **25**Jeroboam won back Israel's border from Lebo Hamath to the Dead Sea. This happened as the LORD, the God of Israel, had said through his servant Jonah son of Amittai, the prophet from Gath Hepher. **26**The LORD had seen how the Israelites, both slave and free, were suffering terribly. No one was left who could help Israel. **27**The LORD had not said he would completely destroy Israel from the world, so he saved the Israelites through Jeroboam son of Jehoash.

> The LORD had seen how the Israelites, both slave and free, were suffering terribly.
> —2 Kings 14:26

28Everything else Jeroboam did is written down—all his victories and how he won back from Judah the towns of Damascus and Hamath for Israel. All this is written in the book of the history of the kings of Israel. **29**Jeroboam died and was buried with his ancestors, the kings of Israel. Jeroboam's son Zechariah became king in his place.

Uzziah King of Judah

15 Uzziah son of Amaziah became king of Judah during Jeroboam's twenty-seventh year as king of Israel. **2**Uzziah was sixteen years old when he became king, and he ruled fifty-two years in Jerusalem. His mother was named Jecoliah, and she was from Jerusalem. **3**He did what the LORD said was right, just as his father Amaziah had done. **4**But the places where gods were worshiped were not removed, so the people still made sacrifices and burned incense there.

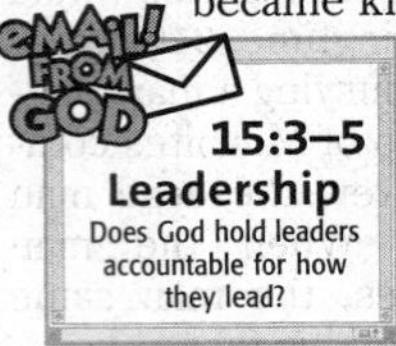

eMAIL! FROM GOD
15:3–5
Leadership
Does God hold leaders accountable for how they lead?

5The LORD struck Uzziah with a skin disease, which he had until the day he died. So he had to live in a separate house. Jotham, the king's son, was in charge of the palace, and he governed the people of the land.

6All the other things Uzziah did are written in the book of the history of the kings of Judah. **7**Uzziah died and was buried near his ancestors in Jerusalem, and his son Jotham became king in his place.

Zechariah King of Israel

8Zechariah son of Jeroboam was king over Israel in Samaria. He ruled for six months during Uzziah's[n] thirty-eighth

---

14:21; 15:8 Uzziah Also called Azariah.

year as king of Judah. **9**Zechariah did
what the LORD said was wrong, just as his
ancestors had done. Jeroboam son of Nebat had led the people of Israel to sin, and
Zechariah did not stop doing the same
sins.

10Shallum son of Jabesh made plans
against Zechariah and killed him in front
of the people. Then Shallum became king
in his place. **11**The other acts of Zechariah are written in the book of the history
of the kings of Israel. **12**The LORD had
told Jehu: "Your sons down to your great-
great-grandchildren will be kings of Israel," and the LORD's word came true.

Shallum King of Israel

13Shallum son of Jabesh became king
during Uzziah's thirty-ninth year as king
of Judah. Shallum ruled for a month in
Samaria. **14**Then Menahem son of Gadi
came up from Tirzah to Samaria and attacked Shallum son of Jabesh in Samaria.
He killed him and became king in
Shallum's place.

15The other acts of Shallum and his
secret plans are written in the book of the
history of the kings of Israel.

Menahem King of Israel

16Menahem started out from Tirzah
and attacked Tiphsah, destroying the city
and the area nearby. This was because
the people had refused to open the city
gate for him. He defeated them and
ripped open all their pregnant women.

17Menahem son of Gadi became king
over Israel during Uzziah's thirty-ninth
year as king of Judah. Menahem ruled ten
years in Samaria, **18**and he did what the
LORD said was wrong. Jeroboam son of
Nebat had led Israel to sin, and all the
time Menahem was king, he did not stop
doing the same sins.

19Pul king of Assyria came to attack
the land. Menahem gave him about
seventy-four thousand pounds of silver
so Pul would support him and make his
hold on the kingdom stronger. **20**Menahem taxed Israel to pay about one and
one-fourth pounds of silver to each soldier of the king of Assyria. So the king
left and did not stay in the land.

21Everything else Menahem did is
written in the book of the history of the
kings of Israel. **22**Then Menahem died,
and his son Pekahiah became king in his
place.

Pekahiah King of Israel

23Pekahiah son of Menahem became
king over Israel in Samaria during
Uzziah's[n] fiftieth year as king of Judah.
Pekahiah ruled two years, **24**and he did
what the LORD said was wrong. Jeroboam
son of Nebat had led Israel to sin, and
Pekahiah did not stop doing the same
sins.

25Pekah son of Remaliah was one of
Pekahiah's captains, and he made plans
against Pekahiah. He took fifty men of
Gilead with him and killed Pekahiah, as
well as Argob and Arieh, in the palace at
Samaria. Then Pekah became king in
Pekahiah's place.

26Everything else Pekahiah did is
written in the book of the history of the
kings of Israel.

Pekah King of Israel

27Pekah son of Remaliah became king
over Israel in Samaria during Uzziah's[n]
fifty-second year as king of Judah. Pekah
ruled twenty years, **28**and he did what
the LORD said was wrong. Jeroboam son
of Nebat had led Israel to sin, and Pekah
did not stop doing the same sins.

29Tiglath-Pileser[n] was king of Assyria. He attacked while Pekah was king
of Israel, capturing the cities of Ijon, Abel
Beth Maacah, Janoah, Kedesh, and Hazor.
He also captured Gilead and Galilee and
all the land of Naphtali and carried the
people away to Assyria. **30**Then Hoshea
son of Elah made plans against Pekah son
of Remaliah and attacked and killed him.
Then Hoshea became king in Pekah's
place during the twentieth year Jotham
son of Uzziah was king.

31Everything else Pekah did is written in the book of the history of the kings
of Israel.

15:23, 27 Uzziah Also called Azariah.
15:29 Tiglath-Pileser Also called Pul.

Jotham King of Judah

32Jotham son of Uzziah became king
of Judah during the second year Pekah
son of Remaliah was king of Israel. 33Jo-
tham was twenty-five years old when he
became king, and he ruled sixteen years
in Jerusalem. His mother's name was Jerusha daughter of Zadok. 34Jotham did
what the LORD said was right, just as his
father Uzziah had done. 35But the places
where gods were worshiped were not removed, and the people still made sacrifices and burned incense there. Jotham
rebuilt the Upper Gate of the Temple of
the LORD.

36The other things Jotham did while
he was king are written in the book of the
history of the kings of Judah. 37At that
time the LORD began to send Rezin king
of Aram and Pekah son of Remaliah
against Judah. 38Jotham died and was
buried with his ancestors in Jerusalem,
the city of David, his ancestor. Then
Jotham's son Ahaz became king in his
place.

Ahaz King of Judah

16 Ahaz was the son of Jotham king
of Judah. Ahaz became king of Judah in the seventeenth year Pekah son of
Remaliah was king of Israel. 2Ahaz was
twenty years old when he became king,
and he ruled sixteen years in Jerusalem.
Unlike his ancestor David, he did not do
what the LORD his God said was right.
3Ahaz did the same things the kings of
Israel had done. He even made his son
pass through fire. He did the same hateful sins as the nations had done whom the
LORD had forced out of the land ahead of
the Israelites. 4Ahaz offered sacrifices
and burned incense at the places where
gods were worshiped, on the hills, and
under every green tree.

5Rezin king of Aram and Pekah son of
Remaliah, the king of Israel, came up to
attack Jerusalem. They surrounded Ahaz
but could not defeat him. 6At that time
Rezin king of Aram took back the city of
Elath for Aram, and he forced out all the
people of Judah. Then Edomites moved
into Elath, and they still live there today.

7Ahaz sent messengers to Tiglath-
Pileser king of Assyria, saying, "I am
your servant and your friend. Come and
save me from the king of Aram and the
king of Israel, who are attacking me."
8Ahaz took the silver and gold that was in
the Temple of the LORD and in the treasuries of the palace, and he sent these as
a gift to the king of Assyria. 9So the king
of Assyria listened to Ahaz. He attacked
Damascus and captured it and sent all its
people away to Kir. And he killed Rezin.

10Then King Ahaz went to Damascus
to meet Tiglath-Pileser king of Assyria.
Ahaz saw an altar at Damascus, and he
sent plans and a pattern of this altar to
Uriah the priest. 11So Uriah the priest
built an altar, just like the plans King
Ahaz had sent him from Damascus. Uriah
finished the altar before King Ahaz came
back from Damascus. 12When the king
arrived from Damascus, he saw the altar
and went near and offered sacrifices on it.
13He burned his burnt offerings and
grain offerings and poured out his drink
offering. He also sprinkled the blood of
his fellowship offerings on the altar.

14Ahaz moved the bronze altar that
was before the LORD at the front of the
Temple. It was between Ahaz's altar and
the Temple of the LORD, but he put it on
the north side of his altar. 15King Ahaz
commanded Uriah the priest, "On the
large altar burn the morning burnt offering, the evening grain offering, the king's
burnt offering and grain offering, and the
whole burnt offering, the grain offering,
and the drink offering for all the people of
the land. Sprinkle on the altar all the
blood of the burnt offering and of the sacrifice. But I will use the bronze altar to
ask questions of God." 16So Uriah the
priest did everything as King Ahaz commanded him.

17Then King Ahaz took off the side
panels from the bases and removed the
washing bowls from the top of the bases.
He also took the large bowl, which was
called the Sea, off the bronze bulls that
held it up, and he put it on a stone base.
18Ahaz took away the platform for the
royal throne, which had been built at the
Temple of the LORD. He also took away
the outside entrance for the king. He did

these things because of the king of Assyria.
19The other things Ahaz did as king
are written in the book of the history of
the kings of Judah. **20**Ahaz died and was
buried with his ancestors in Jerusalem,
and Ahaz's son Hezekiah became king in
his place.

Hoshea, Last King of Israel

17 Hoshea son of Elah became king
over Israel during Ahaz's twelfth
year as king of Judah. Hoshea ruled in
Samaria nine years. **2**He did what the
LORD said was wrong, but he was not as
bad as the kings of Israel who had ruled
before him.
3Shalmaneser king of Assyria came to
attack Hoshea. Hoshea had been Shalmaneser's servant and had made the payments to Shalmaneser that he had
demanded. **4**But the king of Assyria
found out that Hoshea had made plans
against him by sending messengers to
So, the king of Egypt. Hoshea had also
stopped giving Shalmaneser the payments, which he had paid every year in
the past. For that, the king put Hoshea in
prison. **5**Then the king of Assyria came
and attacked all the land of Israel. He surrounded Samaria and attacked it for three
years. **6**He defeated Samaria in the ninth
year Hoshea was king, and he took the
Israelites away to Assyria. He settled
them in Halah, in Gozan on the Habor
River, and in the cities of the Medes.

Israelites Punished for Sin

7All these things happened because
the Israelites had sinned against the
LORD their God. He had brought them
out of Egypt and had rescued them from
the power of the king of Egypt, but the
Israelites had honored other gods. **8**They
lived like the nations the LORD had forced
out of the land ahead of them. They lived
as their evil kings had shown them, **9**secretly sinning against the LORD their
God. They built places to worship gods in
all their cities, from the watchtower to
the strong, walled city. **10**They put up
stone pillars to gods and Asherah idols on
every high hill and under every green

FAITH links

YOU'RE OUT!

2 KINGS 17:5-7

The old saying "three strikes and you're out" applies to the Israelites. Time and time again they had sinned. God allowed an enemy nation—the Assyrians—to invade the land three times. This was a warning for the Israelites to stop worshiping false gods and worship him instead. But they kept on doing what they wanted to do. So the third time, God didn't rescue them. The king of Assyria sent his army to carry them away to another land.

Sin puts you on the "outs" with God. When you sin, God wants you to confess it and ask for his forgiveness.

Are you on the "outs" with God? Link here to find out how to get back "in."

Count on His Mercy, Judges 2:16–17; 3, p. 313

Dirty Inside, Isaiah 6:1–7, p. 904

World News, Isaiah 13—19, p. 913

The Watchman, Ezekiel 3:16–22, p. 1088

Just for the Asking, Romans 3:23–28, p. 1522

Lost Love?, Revelation 2:4, p. 1733

tree. **11**The Israelites burned incense
everywhere gods were worshiped, just
as the nations who lived there before
them had done, whom the LORD had
forced out of the land. The Israelites did
wicked things that made the LORD angry.
12They served idols when the LORD had
said, "You must not do this." **13**The LORD
used every prophet and seer to warn Israel and Judah. He said, "Stop your evil
ways and obey my commands and laws.
Follow all the teachings that I commanded your ancestors, the teachings that I
gave you through my servants the prophets."

14But the people would not listen.
They were stubborn, just as their ancestors had been who did not believe in the
LORD their God. **15**They rejected the
LORD's laws and the agreement he had
made with their ancestors. And they refused to listen to his warnings. They
worshiped useless idols and became useless themselves. They did what the nations around them did, which the LORD
had warned them not to do.

16The people rejected all the commands of the LORD their God. They
molded statues of two calves, and they
made an Asherah idol. They worshiped
all the stars of the sky and served Baal.
17They made their sons and daughters
pass through fire and tried to find out the
future by magic and witchcraft. They always chose to do what the LORD said was
wrong, which made him angry. **18**Because he was very angry with the people
of Israel, he removed them from his presence. Only the tribe of Judah was left.

Judah Is Also Guilty

19But even Judah did not obey the
commands of the LORD their God. They
did what the Israelites had done, **20**so the
LORD rejected all the people of Israel. He
punished them and let others destroy
them; he threw them out of his presence.
21When the LORD separated them from
the family of David, the Israelites made
Jeroboam son of Nebat their king. Jeroboam led the Israelites away from the
LORD and led them to sin greatly. **22**So
they continued to do all the sins Jeroboam did. They did not stop doing these
sins **23**until the LORD removed the Israelites from his presence, just as he had
said through all his servants the prophets. So the Israelites were taken out of
their land to Assyria, and they have been
there to this day.

The Beginning of the Samaritan People

24The king of Assyria brought people
from Babylon, Cuthah, Avva, Hamath,
and Sepharvaim and put them in the cities of Samaria to replace the Israelites.
These people took over Samaria and
lived in the cities. **25**At first they did not
worship the LORD, so he sent lions
among them which killed some of them.
26The king of Assyria was told, "You sent
foreigners into the cities of Samaria who
do not know the law of the god of the
land. This is why he has sent lions among
them. The lions are killing them because
they don't know what the god wants."

27Then the king of Assyria commanded, "Send back one of the priests
you took away. Let him live there and
teach the people what the god wants."
28So one of the priests who had been carried away from Samaria returned to live
in Bethel. And he taught the people how
to honor the LORD.

29But each nation made gods of its
own and put them in the cities where
they lived and in the temples where gods
were worshiped. These temples had
been built by the Samaritans. **30**The people from Babylon made Succoth Benoth
their god. The people from Cuthah worshiped Nergal. The people of Hamath
worshiped Ashima. **31**The Avvites worshiped Nibhaz and Tartak. The Sephar-
vites burned their children in the fire,
sacrificing them to Adrammelech and
Anammelech, the gods of Sepharvaim.
32They also honored the LORD, but they
chose priests for the places where gods
were worshiped. The priests were chosen from among themselves, and they
made sacrifices for the people. **33**The
people honored the LORD but also served
their own gods, just as the nations did
from which they had been brought.

34Even today they do as they did in the
past. They do not worship the LORD nor
obey his rules and commands. They do
not obey the teachings or the commands
of the LORD, which he gave to the children of Jacob, whom he had named Israel.
35The LORD had made an agreement
with them and had commanded them,
"Do not honor other gods. Do not bow
down to them or worship them or offer
sacrifices to them. **36**Worship the LORD
who brought you up out of the land of
Egypt with great power and strength.
Bow down to him and offer sacrifices to
him. **37**Always obey the rules, orders,
teachings, and commands he wrote for
you. Do not honor other gods. **38**Do not
forget the agreement I made with you,
and do not honor other gods. **39**Instead
worship the LORD your God, who will
save you from all your enemies."

40But the Israelites did not listen.
They kept on doing the same things they
had done before. **41**So these nations honored the LORD but also worshiped their
idols, and their children and grandchildren still do as their ancestors did.

Hezekiah King of Judah

18 Hezekiah son of Ahaz king of Judah became king during the third
year Hoshea son of Elah was king of Israel. **2**Hezekiah was twenty-five years
old when he became king, and he ruled
twenty-nine years in Je-
rusalem. His mother's
name was Abijah daugh-
ter of Zechariah. **3**Hezekiah did what the LORD
said was right, just as his
ancestor David had done.
4He removed the places
where gods were wor-
shiped. He smashed the
stone pillars and cut
down the Asherah idols.
Also the Israelites had been burning incense to Nehushtan, the bronze snake
Moses had made. But Hezekiah broke it
into pieces.

5Hezekiah trusted in the LORD, the
God of Israel. There was no one like him
among all the kings of Judah, either before him or after him. **6**Hezekiah was
loyal to the LORD and did not stop following him; he obeyed the commands the
LORD had given Moses. **7**And the LORD
was with Hezekiah, so he had success in
everything he did. He turned against the
king of Assyria and stopped serving him.
8Hezekiah defeated the Philistines all
the way to Gaza and its borders, including the watchtowers and the strong,
walled cities.

The Assyrians Capture Samaria

9Shalmaneser king of Assyria surrounded Samaria and attacked it in the
fourth year Hezekiah was king. This was
the seventh year Hoshea son of Elah was
king of Israel. **10**After three years the
Assyrians captured Samaria. This was in
the sixth year Hezekiah was king, which
was Hoshea's ninth year as king of Israel.
11The king of Assyria took the Israelites
away to Assyria and settled them in Halah, in Gozan on the Habor River, and in
the cities of the Medes. **12**This happened
because they did not obey the LORD their
God. They broke his agreement and did
not obey all that Moses, the LORD's servant, had commanded. They would not
listen to the commands or do them.

Assyria Attacks Judah

13During Hezekiah's fourteenth year
as king, Sennacherib king of Assyria
attacked all the strong,
walled cities of Judah and
captured them. **14**Then
Hezekiah king of Judah
sent a message to the
king of Assyria at La-
chish. He said, "I have
done wrong. Leave me
alone, and I will pay anything you ask." So the
king of Assyria made Hez-
ekiah pay about twenty-
two thousand pounds of silver and two
thousand pounds of gold. **15**Hezekiah gave
him all the silver that was in the Temple
of the LORD and in the palace treasuries.
16Hezekiah stripped all the gold that
covered the doors and doorposts of the
Temple of the LORD. Hezekiah had put

> Hezekiah did what the LORD said was right, just as his ancestor David had done.
>
> —2 Kings 18:3

gold on these doors himself, but he gave
it all to the king of Assyria.

17The king of Assyria sent out his supreme commander, his chief officer, and
his field commander. They went with a
large army from Lachish to King Hezekiah in Jerusalem. When they came near
the waterway from the upper pool on the
road where people do their laundry, they
stopped. 18They called for the king, so
the king sent Eliakim, Shebna, and Joah
out to meet them. Eliakim son of Hilkiah
was the palace manager, Shebna was the
royal secretary, and Joah son of Asaph
was the recorder.

19The field commander said to them,
"Tell Hezekiah this:

" 'The great king, the king of Assyria,
says: What can you trust in now? 20You
say you have battle plans and power for
war, but your words mean nothing. Whom
are you trusting for help so that you turn
against me? 21Look, you are depending
on Egypt to help you, but Egypt is like a
splintered walking stick. If you lean on it
for help, it will stab your hand and hurt
you. The king of Egypt will hurt all those
who depend on him. 22You might say, "We
are depending on the LORD our God," but
Hezekiah destroyed the LORD's altars and
the places of worship. Hezekiah told Judah and Jerusalem, "You must worship
only at this one altar in Jerusalem."

23" 'Now make an agreement with my
master, the king of Assyria: I will give
you two thousand horses if you can find
enough men to ride them. 24You cannot
defeat one of my master's least important
officers, so why do you depend on Egypt
to give you chariots and horsemen? 25I
have not come to attack and destroy this
place without an order from the LORD.
The LORD himself told me to come to this
country and destroy it.' "

26Then Eliakim son of Hilkiah,
Shebna, and Joah said to the field commander, "Please speak to us in the Aramaic language. We understand it. Don't
speak to us in Hebrew, because the people on the city wall can hear you."

27"No," the commander said, "my
master did not send me to tell these
things only to you and your king. He sent
me to speak also to those people sitting
on the wall who will have to eat their own
dung and drink their own urine like you."

28Then the commander stood and
shouted loudly in the Hebrew language,
"Listen to what the great king, the king
of Assyria, says! 29The king says you
should not let Hezekiah fool you, because
he can't save you from my power.
30Don't let Hezekiah talk you into trusting the LORD by saying, 'The LORD will
surely save us. This city won't be handed
over to the king of Assyria.'

31"Don't listen to Hezekiah. The king
of Assyria says, 'Make peace with me,
and come out of the city to me. Then
everyone will be free to eat the fruit from
his own grapevine and fig tree and to
drink water from his own well. 32After
that I will come and take you to a land like
your own—a land with grain and new
wine, bread and vineyards, olives, and
honey. Choose to live and not to die!'

"Don't listen to Hezekiah. He is fooling you when he says, 'The LORD will
save us.' 33Has a god of any other nation
saved his people from the power of the
king of Assyria? 34Where are the gods of
Hamath and Arpad? Where are the gods
of Sepharvaim, Hena, and Ivvah? They
did not save Samaria from my power.
35Not one of all the gods of these countries has saved his people from me. Neither can the LORD save Jerusalem from
my power."

36The people were silent. They didn't
answer the commander at all, because
King Hezekiah had ordered, "Don't answer him."

37Then Eliakim, Shebna, and Joah
tore their clothes to show how upset they
were. (Eliakim son of Hilkiah was the
palace manager, Shebna was the royal
secretary, and Joah son of Asaph was the
recorder.) The three men went to Hezekiah and told him what the field commander had said.

Jerusalem Will Be Saved

19 When King Hezekiah heard the
message, he tore his clothes and
put on rough cloth to show how sad he
was. Then he went into the Temple of the

LORD. 2Hezekiah sent Eliakim, the palace
manager, and Shebna, the royal secretary,
and the older priests to Isaiah. They were
all wearing rough cloth when they came to
Isaiah the prophet, the son of Amoz.
3They told Isaiah, "This is what Hezekiah
says: Today is a day of sorrow and punishment and disgrace, as when a child should
be born, but the mother is not strong
enough to give birth to it. 4The king of
Assyria sent his field commander to make
fun of the living God. Maybe the LORD
your God will hear what the commander
said and will punish him for it. So pray for
the few of us who are left alive."

5When Hezekiah's officers came to
Isaiah, 6he said to them, "Tell your master this: The LORD says, 'Don't be afraid
of what you have heard. Don't be frightened by the words the servants of the
king of Assyria have spoken against me.
7Listen! I am going to put a spirit in the
king of Assyria. He will hear a report that
will make him return to his own country,
and I will cause him to die by the sword
there.' "

8The field commander heard that the
king of Assyria had left Lachish. When he
went back, he found the king fighting
against the city of Libnah.

9The king received a report that Tir-
hakah, the Cushite king of Egypt, was
coming to attack him. When the king of
Assyria heard this, he sent messengers
to Hezekiah, saying, 10"Tell Hezekiah
king of Judah: Don't be fooled by the god
you trust. Don't believe him when he
says Jerusalem will not be handed over to
the king of Assyria. 11You have heard
what the kings of Assyria have done.
They have completely defeated every
country, so do not think you will be
saved. 12Did the gods of those people
save them? My ancestors destroyed
them, defeating the cities of Gozan, Haran, and Rezeph, and the people of Eden
living in Tel Assar. 13Where are the kings
of Hamath and Arpad? Where are the
kings of Sepharvaim, Hena, and Ivvah?"

Hezekiah Prays to the Lord

14When Hezekiah received the letter
from the messengers and read it, he went
up to the Temple of the LORD. He spread
the letter out before the LORD 15and
prayed to the LORD: "LORD, God of Israel, whose throne is between the gold
creatures with wings, only you are God of
all the kingdoms of the earth. You made
the heavens and the earth. 16Hear, LORD,

FAITH links

A MESSAGE OF COURAGE AND HOPE

2 KINGS 19:4-10

Has anyone ever made fun of you because of your faith? The king of Assyria made fun of King Hezekiah because of his faith in God. But God gave Hezekiah a message of hope. He told Hezekiah not to be afraid. He would help Hezekiah and his people.

People who don't believe in God may call you names or think you're weird for believing in a God you can't see. When that happens, the same message of hope that God gave to Hezekiah is there for you, too.

When You're Afraid, Genesis 32:9–12, p. 45

Moses' Champion, Numbers 12, p. 192

God's Sure Protection, Psalm 18, p. 721

Uprooted by Change, Amos 9:15, p. 1205

A Real Crowd-pleaser?, Micah 2:6–11, p. 1222

Hope That Doesn't Fail, Acts 26:4–7, p. 1510

and listen. Open your eyes, LORD, and
see. Listen to the words Sennacherib has
said to insult the living God. 17It is true,
LORD, that the kings of Assyria have destroyed these countries and their lands.
18They have thrown the gods of these
nations into the fire, but they were only
wood and rock statues that people made.
So the kings have destroyed them.
19Now, LORD our God, save us from the
king's power so that all the kingdoms of
the earth will know that you, LORD, are
the only God."

God Answers Hezekiah

20Then Isaiah son of Amoz sent a
message to Hezekiah that said, "This is
what the LORD, the God of Israel, says: I
have heard your prayer to me about Sennacherib king of Assyria. 21This is what
the LORD has said against Sennacherib:

'The people of Jerusalem
hate you and make fun of you.
The people of Jerusalem
laugh at you as you run away.
22 You have insulted me and spoken
against me;
you have raised your voice against
me.
You have a proud look on your face,
which is against me, the Holy One
of Israel.
23 You have sent your messengers to
insult the Lord.
You have said, "With my many
chariots
I have gone to the tops of the
mountains,
to the highest mountains of
Lebanon.
I have cut down its tallest cedars
and its best pine trees.
I have gone to its farthest places
and to its best forests.
24 I have dug wells in foreign
countries
and drunk water there.
By the soles of my feet,
I have dried up all the rivers of
Egypt."

25 " 'King of Assyria, surely you have
heard.
Long ago I, the LORD, planned
these things.
Long ago I designed them,
and now I have made them happen.
I allowed you to turn those strong,
walled cities
into piles of rocks.
26 The people in those cities were
weak;
they were frightened and put to
shame.
They were like grass in the field,
like tender, young grass,
like grass on the housetop
that is burned by the wind before it
can grow.

27 " 'I know when you rest,
when you come and go,
and how you rage against me.
28 Because you rage against me,
and because I have heard your
proud words,
I will put my hook in your nose
and my bit in
your mouth.
Then I will force
you to leave
my country
the same way
you came.'

19:27–28
Pride
Read to see how God views pride.

29"Then the LORD said, 'Hezekiah, I
will give you this sign:
This year you will eat the grain that
grows wild,
and the second year you will eat
what grows wild from that.
But in the third year, plant grain and
harvest it.
Plant vineyards and eat their fruit.
30 Some of the people in the family of
Judah
will escape.
Like plants that take root,
they will grow strong and have
many children.
31 A few people will come out of
Jerusalem alive;
a few from Mount Zion will live.
The strong love of the LORD All-
Powerful
will make this happen.'

32"So this is what the LORD says
about the king of Assyria:
'He will not enter this city
or even shoot an arrow here.
He will not fight against it with
shields
or build a ramp to attack the city
walls.
33 He will return to his country the
same way he came,
and he will not enter this city,'
says the LORD.
34 'I will defend and save this city
for my sake and for the sake of
David, my servant.' "
35That night the angel of the LORD
went out and killed one hundred eighty-
five thousand men in the Assyrian camp.
When the people got up early the next
morning, they saw all the dead bodies.
36So Sennacherib king of Assyria left and
went back to Nineveh and stayed there.
37One day as Sennacherib was worshiping in the temple of his god Nisroch,
his sons Adrammelech and Sharezer
killed him with a sword. Then they escaped to the land of Ararat. So Sennacherib's son Esarhaddon became king
of Assyria.

Hezekiah's Illness

20 At that time Hezekiah became so
sick he almost died. The prophet
Isaiah son of Amoz went to see him and
told him, "This is what the LORD says:
Make arrangements because you are not
going to live, but die."
2Hezekiah turned toward the wall and
prayed to the LORD, 3"LORD, please remember that I have always obeyed you. I
have given myself completely to you and
have done what you said was right."
Then Hezekiah cried loudly.
4Before Isaiah had left the middle
courtyard, the LORD spoke his word to
Isaiah: 5"Go back and tell Hezekiah, the
leader of my people: 'This is what the
LORD, the God of your ancestor David,
says: I have heard your prayer and seen
your tears, so I will heal you. Three days
from now you will go up to the Temple of
the LORD. 6I will add fifteen years to your
life. I will save you
and this city from
the king of Assyria;
I will protect the
city for my sake and
for the sake of my
servant David.' "
7Then Isaiah said, "Make a paste from

FAITH links

PROBLEM SOLVED

2 KINGS 20:1-11

Who do you turn to when you're worried about a problem? Some problems can only be solved by God. Hezekiah was dying of an illness. No one could help him. He prayed to God. God heard his prayer and let him live 15 more years. When the king asked for proof of God's answer, God made the sun go backward!

When you're worried, pray. God may not always answer yes or make the sun go backward. But he will answer.

Got a problem? Link here for help:

When You're Afraid, Genesis 32:9–12, p. 45

God's Pep Talk, Joshua 1:5–9, p. 276

A Really Bad Day, Job 1:20–22; 2:10, p. 661

Who Ya' Gonna Call?, Psalm 3:4, p. 711

The Best Protection Plan, Matthew 2:13–18, p. 1276

You've Got the Power!, Acts 1:1–8; 2:1–4, p. 1463

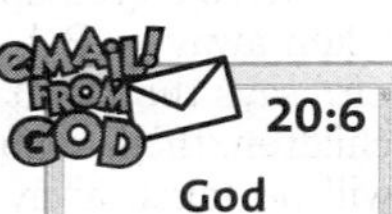

20:6

God

How does God fight for his people?

figs." So they made it and put it on Hezekiah's boil, and he got well.
8Hezekiah had asked Isaiah, "What
will be the sign that the LORD will heal
me and that I will go up to the Temple of
the LORD on the third day?"
9Isaiah said, "The LORD will do what
he says. This is the sign from the LORD to
show you: Do you want the shadow to go
forward ten steps or back ten steps?"
10Hezekiah answered, "It's easy for
the shadow to go forward ten steps. Instead, let it go back ten steps."
11Then Isaiah the prophet called to
the LORD, and the LORD brought the
shadow ten steps back up the stairway of
Ahaz that it had gone down.

Messengers from Babylon

12At that time Merodach-Baladan
son of Baladan was king of Babylon. He
sent letters and a gift to Hezekiah, because he had heard that Hezekiah was
sick. 13Hezekiah listened to the messengers, so he showed them what was in
his storehouses: the silver, gold, spices,
expensive perfumes, his swords and
shields, and all his wealth. He showed
them everything in his palace and his
kingdom.
14Then Isaiah the prophet went to
King Hezekiah and asked him, "What did
these men say? Where did they come
from?"
Hezekiah said, "They came from a faraway country—from Babylon."
15So Isaiah asked him, "What did they
see in your palace?"
Hezekiah said, "They saw everything
in my palace. I showed them all my
wealth."
16Then Isaiah said to Hezekiah, "Listen to the words of the LORD: 17'In the future everything in your palace and
everything your ancestors have stored up
until this day will be taken away to Babylon. Nothing will be left,' says the LORD.
18'Some of your own children, those who
will be born to you, will be taken away.
And they will become servants in the palace of the king of Babylon.' "
19Hezekiah told Isaiah, "These words
from the LORD are good." He said this
because he thought, "There will be peace
and security in my lifetime."
20Everything else Hezekiah did—all
his victories, his work on the pool, his
work on the tunnel to bring water into

FAITH links

WHAT I'VE GOT

2 KINGS 20:12-17

Are you ever tempted to brag about the cool stuff you have? Maybe you think that what you have makes you cool. What would you do if one day you no longer had those things? King Hezekiah showed some messengers from Babylon all of his treasures. The prophet Isaiah warned him that these valuable things would one day be taken away.

There is nothing wrong with having nice things. But your possessions are not what make you special. If you want to brag, brag about someone who made it possible for you to have what you have: God.

Put Pride Aside, Exodus 2:11–15, p. 78

Uniquely You, Psalm 139:13–14, p. 815

The Problem with Pride, Isaiah 2:11, p. 898

Braggin' Rights, Jeremiah 9:23–24, p. 1005

Set for Life?, Obadiah 2–4, p. 1208

Better Than Some?, Luke 18:9–14, p. 1405

the city—is written in the book of the
history of the kings of Judah. 21Then
Hezekiah died, and his son Manasseh became king in his place.

Manasseh King of Judah

21 Manasseh was twelve years old
when he became king, and he was
king fifty-five years in Jerusalem. His
mother's name was Hephzibah. 2He did
what the LORD said was wrong. He did
the hateful things the other nations had
done—the nations that the LORD had
forced out of the land ahead of the Israelites. 3Manasseh's father, Hezekiah, had
destroyed the places where gods were
worshiped, but Manasseh rebuilt them.
He built altars for Baal, and he made an
Asherah idol as Ahab king of Israel had
done. Manasseh also worshiped all the
stars of the sky and served them. 4The
LORD had said about the Temple, "I will
be worshiped in Jerusalem," but Manasseh built altars in the Temple of the
LORD. 5He built altars to worship the
stars in the two courtyards of the Temple
of the LORD. 6He made his own son pass
through fire. He practiced magic and told
the future by explaining signs and
dreams, and he got advice from mediums
and fortune-tellers. He did many things
the LORD said were wrong, which made
the LORD angry.
7Manasseh carved an Asherah idol
and put it in the Temple. The LORD had
said to David and his son Solomon about
the Temple, "I will be worshiped forever
in this Temple and in Jerusalem, which I
have chosen from all the tribes of Israel.
8I will never again make the Israelites
wander out of the
land I gave their an-
cestors. But they
must obey every-
thing I have com-
manded them and
all the teachings my
servant Moses gave them." 9But the
people did not listen. Manasseh led them
to do more evil than the nations the LORD
had destroyed ahead of the Israelites.
10The LORD said through his servants the prophets, 11"Manasseh king
of Judah has done these hateful things.
He has done more evil than the Amorites before him. He also has led Judah
to sin with his idols. 12So this is what
the LORD, the God of Israel, says: 'I will
bring so much trouble on Jerusalem and

EMAIL FROM GOD

21:8–9
Temptation
What can you do to avoid temptation?

FAITH links

ON THE WRONG FOOT

2 KINGS 21:1-2, 16

Ever have your parents warn you about someone's bad influence? Israel had a number of kings who were a bad influence. One was Manasseh, who became king at age 12. Unlike Joash, Manasseh started off on the wrong foot. He did things and influenced others to do things that God considered evil.

Believe it or not, you can influence people for good or evil. Being a Christian starts you off on the right foot for influencing people for good.

Connect here to see how you can be a good influence on others:

A Choice to Make, Deuteronomy 30:15–20, p. 265

The Right Thing to Do, 1 Samuel 26, p. 391

A Useless Thing, Isaiah 44:9, 18–20, p. 954

The Dead End of the Occult, Ezekiel 13:17–23, p. 1098

Kindness Counts, Acts 14:3, p. 1489

Love for Free, Romans 5:8, p. 1524

Judah that anyone who hears about it will
be shocked. 13I will stretch the measuring line of Samaria over Jerusalem, and
the plumb line used against Ahab's family
will be used on Jerusalem. I will wipe out
Jerusalem as a person wipes a dish and
turns it upside down. 14I will throw away
the rest of my people who are left. I will
give them to their enemies, and they will
be robbed by all their enemies, 15be-
cause my people did what I said was
wrong. They have made me angry from
the day their ancestors left Egypt until
now.' "

16Manasseh also killed many innocent people, filling Jerusalem from one
end to the other with their blood. This
was besides the sin he led Judah to do; he
led Judah to do what the LORD said was
wrong.

17The other things Manasseh did as
king, even the sin he did, are written in
the book of the history of the kings of Judah. 18Manasseh died and was buried in
the garden of his own palace, the garden
of Uzza. Then Manasseh's son Amon became king in his place.

Amon King of Judah

19Amon was twenty-two years old
when he became king, and he was king
for two years in Jerusalem. His mother's
name was Meshullemeth daughter of Ha-
ruz, who was from Jotbah. 20Amon did
what the LORD said was wrong, as his father Manasseh had done. 21He lived in
the same way his father had lived: he
worshiped the idols his father had worshiped, and he bowed down before them.
22Amon rejected the LORD, the God of
his ancestors, and did not follow the ways
of the LORD.

23Amon's officers made plans against
him and killed him in his palace. 24Then
the people of the land killed all those who
had made plans to kill King Amon, and
they made his son Josiah king in his
place.

25Everything else Amon did is written in the book of the history of the kings
of Judah. 26He was buried in his grave in
the garden of Uzza, and his son Josiah became king in his place.

Josiah King of Judah

22 Josiah was eight years old when he
became king, and he ruled thirty-
one years in Jerusalem. His mother's
name was Jedidah daughter of Adaiah,
who was from Bozkath. 2Josiah did what

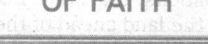

TRAILBLAZERS OF FAITH

2 KINGS 22:1-2

Did you ever walk in someone else's footprints in sand or snow? If you were lost, following someone else's steps could lead you in the right direction. Josiah was only eight years old when he became king of Judah. He followed in David's footsteps. That means he did the right things that David did.

If you have parents or grandparents who are Christians, they've blazed a path of faith for you to follow. Although they've shown you the way to go, you need to have your own relationship with God in order to follow in those faith-steps.

Lights, Camera, . . . Actions!, Genesis 12:1–3, p. 17

An Unsung Hero, Ruth 2:12, 15–16, p. 347

A Memorial for Two Thieves, 1 Chronicles 7:21, p. 530

Jesus' Mission and Yours, Isaiah 61:1–2, p. 978

Pass It On!, Joel 1:2–3, p. 1187

Our Good Shepherd, John 10:11–15, p. 1441

the LORD said was right. He lived as his ancestor David had lived, and he did not stop doing what was right.

3In Josiah's eighteenth year as king, he sent Shaphan to the Temple of the LORD. Shaphan son of Azaliah, the son of Meshullam, was the royal secretary. Josiah said, 4"Go up to Hilkiah the high priest, and have him empty out the money the gatekeepers have gathered from the people. This is the money they have brought into the Temple of the LORD. 5Have him give the money to the supervisors of the work on the Temple of the LORD. They must pay the workers who repair the Temple of the LORD— 6the carpenters, builders, and bricklayers. Also use the money to buy timber and cut stone to repair the Temple. 7They do not need to report how they use the money given to them, because they are working honestly."

The Book of the Teachings Is Found

8Hilkiah the high priest said to Shaphan the royal secretary, "I've found the Book of the Teachings in the Temple of the LORD." He gave it to Shaphan, who read it.

9Then Shaphan the royal secretary went to the king and reported to Josiah, "Your officers have paid out the money that was in the Temple of the LORD. They have given it to the workers and supervisors at the Temple." 10Then Shaphan the royal secretary told the king, "Hilkiah the priest has given me a book." And Shaphan read from the book to the king.

11When the king heard the words of the Book of the Teachings, he tore his clothes to show how upset he was. 12He gave orders to Hilkiah the priest, Ahikam son of Shaphan, Acbor son of Micaiah, Shaphan the royal secretary, and Asaiah the king's servant. These were the orders: 13"Go and ask the LORD about the words in the book that was found. Ask for me, for all the people, and for all Judah. The LORD's anger is burning against us, because our ancestors did not obey the words of this book; they did not do all the things written for us to do."

14So Hilkiah the priest, Ahikam, Acbor, Shaphan, and Asaiah went to talk to Huldah the prophetess. She was the wife of Shallum son of Tikvah, the son of Harhas, who took care of the king's clothes. Huldah lived in Jerusalem, in the new area of the city.

15She said to them, "This is what the LORD, the God of Israel, says: Tell the man who sent you to me, 16'This is what the LORD says: I will bring trouble to this place and to the people living here, as it is written in the book which the king of Judah has read. 17The people of Judah have left me and have burned incense to other gods. They have made me angry by all that they have done. My anger burns against this place like a fire, and it will not be put out.' 18Tell the king of Judah, who sent you to ask the LORD, 'This is what the LORD, the God of Israel, says about the words you heard: 19When you heard my words against this place and its people, you became sorry for what you had done and humbled yourself before me. I said they would be cursed and would be destroyed. You tore your clothes to show how upset you were, and you cried in my presence. This is why I have heard you, says the LORD. 20So I will let you die, and you will be buried in peace. You won't see all the trouble I will bring to this place.' "

So they took her message back to the king.

The People Hear the Agreement

23 Then the king gathered all the older leaders of Judah and Jerusalem together. 2He went up to the Temple of the LORD, and all the people from Judah and Jerusalem went with him. The priests, prophets, and all the people—from the least important to the most important—went with him. He read to them all the words of the Book of the Agreement that was found in the Temple of the LORD. 3The king stood by the pillar and made an agreement in the presence of the LORD to follow the LORD and obey his commands,

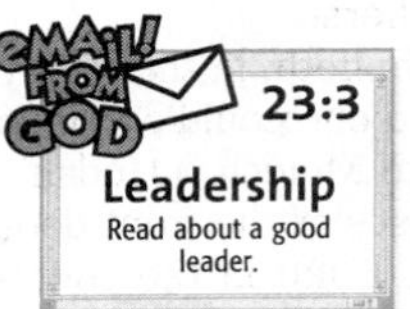
eMAIL! FROM GOD
23:3
Leadership
Read about a good leader.

rules, and laws with his whole being, and
to obey the words of the agreement written in this book. Then all the people
promised to obey the agreement.

Josiah Destroys the Places for Idol Worship

4The king commanded Hilkiah the
high priest and the priests of the next
rank and the gatekeepers to bring out of
the Temple of the LORD everything made
for Baal, Asherah, and all the stars of the
sky. Then Josiah burned them outside Jerusalem in the open country of the Kidron Valley and carried their ashes to
Bethel. 5The kings of Judah had chosen
priests for these gods. These priests
burned incense in the places where gods
were worshiped in the cities of Judah
and the towns around Jerusalem. They
burned incense to Baal, the sun, the
moon, the planets, and all the stars of the
sky. But Josiah took those priests away.
6He removed the Asherah idol from the
Temple of the LORD and took it outside
Jerusalem to the Kidron Valley, where he
burned it and beat it into dust. Then he
threw the dust on the graves of the common people. 7He also tore down the
houses of the male prostitutes who were
in the Temple of the LORD, where the
women did weaving for Asherah.

8King Josiah brought all the false
priests from the cities of Judah. He ruined the places where gods were worshiped, where the priests had burned
incense, from Geba to Beersheba. He destroyed the places of worship at the entrance to the Gate of Joshua, the ruler of
the city, on the left side of the city gate.
9The priests at the places where gods
were worshiped were not allowed to
serve at the LORD's altar in Jerusalem.
But they could eat bread made without
yeast with their brothers.

10Josiah ruined Topheth, in the Valley
of Ben Hinnom, so no one could sacrifice
his son or daughter to Molech. 11Judah's
kings had placed horses at the front door
of the Temple of the LORD in the courtyard near the room of Nathan-Melech, an
officer. These horses were for the worship of the sun. So Josiah removed them

FAITH links

NO THANKSGIVING? 

2 KINGS 23:21-23

Can you imagine what it would be like if the whole country stopped celebrating Thanksgiving Day? For the Israelites, Passover was like Thanksgiving. When they celebrated Passover they remembered how thankful they were to God. He had rescued them from slavery in Egypt and had taken care of them. Yet, for many years, the Israelites did not celebrate Passover. King Josiah wanted them to start celebrating once more.

We don't have to wait until Thanksgiving to be thankful. Each time we go to church, take communion, talk with someone about God, or read the Bible we are reminded about what God has done for us.

Want to tell God thank-you? Click here:

Time to Celebrate, Exodus 15:1–21, p. 95

A Cause for Celebration, 1 Kings 8:62–66, p. 449

Like Silver, Psalm 12:6–8, p. 717

Uniquely You, Psalm 139:13–14, p. 815

Too Busy to Worship?, Luke 2:8–20, p. 1368

Always Do This!, 1 Thessalonians 5:16–18, p. 1636

and burned the chariots that were for sun worship also.

12The kings of Judah had built altars on the roof[n] of the upstairs room of Ahaz. Josiah broke down these altars and the altars Manasseh had made in the two courtyards of the Temple of the LORD. Josiah smashed them to pieces and threw their dust into the Kidron Valley. **13**King Josiah ruined the places where gods were worshiped east of Jerusalem, south of the Mount of Olives.[n] Solomon king of Israel had built these places. One was for Ashtoreth, the hated goddess of the Sidonians. One was for Chemosh, the hated god of Moab. And one was for Molech, the hated god of the Ammonites. **14**Josiah smashed to pieces the stone pillars they worshiped, and he cut down the Asherah idols. Then he covered the places with human bones.

15Josiah also broke down the altar at Bethel—the place of worship made by Jeroboam son of Nebat, who had led Israel to sin. Josiah burned that place, broke the stones of the altar into pieces, then beat them into dust. He also burned the Asherah idol. **16**When he turned around, he saw the graves on the mountain. He had the bones taken from the graves, and he burned them on the altar to ruin it. This happened as the LORD had said it would through the man of God.

17Josiah asked, "What is that monument I see?"

The people of the city answered, "It's the grave of the man of God who came from Judah. This prophet announced the things you have done against the altar of Bethel."

18Josiah said, "Leave the grave alone. No one may move this man's bones." So they left his bones and the bones of the prophet who had come from Samaria.

19The kings of Israel had built temples for worshiping gods in the cities of Samaria, which had caused the LORD to be angry. Josiah removed all those temples and did the same things as he had done at Bethel. **20**He killed all the priests of those places of worship; he killed them on the altars and burned human bones on the altars. Then he went back to Jerusalem.

Josiah Celebrates the Passover

21The king commanded all the people, "Celebrate the Passover to the LORD your God as it is written in this Book of the Agreement." **22**The Passover had not been celebrated like this since the judges led Israel. Nor had one like it happened while there were kings of Israel and kings of Judah. **23**This Passover was celebrated to the LORD in Jerusalem in the eighteenth year of King Josiah's rule.

24Josiah destroyed the mediums, fortune-tellers, house gods, and idols. He also destroyed all the hated gods seen in the land of Judah and Jerusalem. This was to obey the words of the teachings written in the book Hilkiah the priest had found in the Temple of the LORD.

25There was no king like Josiah before or after him. He obeyed the LORD with all his heart, soul, and strength, following all the Teachings of Moses.

26Even so, the LORD did not stop his strong and terrible anger. His anger burned against Judah because of all Manasseh had done to make him angry. **27**The LORD said, "I will send Judah out of my sight, as I have sent Israel away. I will reject Jerusalem, which I chose. And I will take away the Temple about which I said, 'I will be worshiped there.' "

28Everything else Josiah did is written in the book of the history of the kings of Judah.

29While Josiah was king, Neco king of Egypt went to help the king of Assyria at the Euphrates River. King Josiah marched out to fight against Neco, but at Megiddo, Neco faced him and killed him. **30**Josiah's servants carried his body in a chariot from Megiddo to Jerusalem and buried him in his own grave. Then the people of Judah chose Josiah's son Jehoahaz and poured olive oil on him to make him king in his father's place.

23:12 roof In Bible times houses were built with flat roofs. The roof was used for drying things such as flax and fruit. And it was used as an extra room, as a place for worship, and as a cool place to sleep in the summer.

23:13 Mount of Olives Literally, "The Mountain of Ruin."

Jehoahaz King of Judah

31Jehoahaz was twenty-three years
old when he became king, and he was
king in Jerusalem for three months. His
mother's name was Hamutal, who was
the daughter of Jeremiah from Libnah.
32Jehoahaz did what the LORD said was
wrong, just as his ancestors had done.

33King Neco took Jehoahaz prisoner
at Riblah in the land of Hamath so that
Jehoahaz could not rule in Jerusalem.
Neco made the people of Judah pay about
seventy-five hundred pounds of silver
and about seventy-five pounds of gold.

34King Neco made Josiah's son Eliakim the king in place of Josiah his father.
Then Neco changed Eliakim's name to
Jehoiakim. But Neco took Jehoahaz to
Egypt, where he died. 35Jehoiakim gave
King Neco the silver and gold he demanded. Jehoiakim taxed the land and
took silver and gold from the people of
the land to give to King Neco. Each person had to pay his share.

Jehoiakim King of Judah

36Jehoiakim was twenty-five years
old when he became king, and he was
king in Jerusalem for eleven years. His
mother's name was Zebidah daughter of
Pedaiah, who was from Rumah. 37Jehoia-
kim did what the LORD said was wrong,
just as his ancestors had done.

24 While Jehoiakim was king, Nebuchadnezzar king of Babylon attacked the land of Judah. So Jehoiakim
became Nebuchadnezzar's servant for
three years. Then he
turned against Nebuchad-
nezzar and broke away
from his rule. 2The LORD
sent raiding parties from
Babylon, Aram, Moab,
and Ammon against Je-
hoiakim to destroy Judah.
This happened as the
LORD had said it would
through his servants the
prophets.

3The LORD commanded this to happen to the people of Judah, to remove
them from his presence, because of all
the sins of Manasseh. 4He had killed
many innocent people and had filled Jerusalem with their blood. And the LORD
would not forgive these sins.

5The other things that happened
while Jehoiakim was king and all he did
are written in the book of the history of
the kings of Judah. 6Jehoiakim died, and
his son Jehoiachin became king in his
place.

7The king of Egypt did not leave his
land again, because the king of Babylon
had captured all that belonged to the king
of Egypt, from the brook of Egypt to the
Euphrates River.

Jehoiachin King of Judah

8Jehoiachin was eighteen years old
when he became king, and he was king
three months in Jerusalem. His mother's
name was Nehushta daughter of Elnathan from Jerusalem. 9Jehoiachin did
what the LORD said was wrong, just as his
father had done.

10At that time the officers of Nebuchadnezzar king of Babylon came up to
Jerusalem. When they reached the city,
they attacked it. 11Nebuchadnezzar himself came to the city while his officers
were attacking it. 12Jehoiachin king of
Judah surrendered to the king of Babylon, along with Jehoiachin's mother, servants, older leaders, and officers. So
Nebuchadnezzar made Jehoiachin a prisoner in the eighth year he was king of
Babylon. 13Nebuchadnezzar took all the
treasures from the Temple of the LORD
and from the palace. He cut up all the
gold objects Solomon
king of Israel had made
for the Temple of the
LORD. This happened as
the LORD had said it
would. 14Nebuchadnez-
zar took away all the
people of Jerusalem, in-
cluding all the leaders, all
the wealthy people, and
all the craftsmen and
metal workers. There
were ten thousand prisoners in all. Only
the poorest people in the land were left.
15Nebuchadnezzar carried away Jehoiachin to Babylon, as well as the king's

Nebuchadnezzar took all the treasures from the Temple of the LORD and from the palace.
—2 Kings 24:13

mother and his wives, the officers, and
the leading men of the land. They were
taken captive from Jerusalem to Babylon.
16The king of Babylon also took all seven
thousand soldiers, who were strong and
able to fight in war, and about a thousand
craftsmen and metal workers. Nebuchadnezzar took them as prisoners to
Babylon. 17Then he made Mattaniah,
Jehoiachin's uncle, king in Jehoiachin's
place. He also changed Mattaniah's name
to Zedekiah.

Zedekiah King of Judah

18Zedekiah was twenty-one years old
when he became king,
and he was king in Jeru-
salem for eleven years.
His mother's name was
Hamutal daughter of Jer-
emiah[n] from Libnah.
19Zedekiah did what the
LORD said was wrong,
just as Jehoiakim had
done. 20All this happened
in Jerusalem and Judah
because the LORD was an-
gry with them. Finally, he threw them out
of his presence.

Nebuzaradan set fire to the Temple of the LORD and the palace and all the houses of Jerusalem.
—2 Kings 25:9

The Fall of Jerusalem

Zedekiah turned against the king of
Babylon.

25 Nebuchadnezzar king of Babylon
marched against Jerusalem with
his whole army during Zedekiah's ninth
year as king, on the tenth day of the tenth
month. He made a camp around the city
and piled dirt against the city walls to attack it. 2The city was under attack until
Zedekiah's eleventh year as king. 3By
the ninth day of the fourth month, the
hunger was terrible in the city. There
was no food for the people to eat. 4Then
the city was broken into, and the whole
army ran away at night through the gate
between the two walls by the king's garden. While the Babylonians were still
surrounding the city, Zedekiah and his
men ran away toward the Jordan Valley.
5But the Babylonian army chased King
Zedekiah and caught up with him in the
plains of Jericho. All of his army was scattered from him, 6so they captured Zedekiah and took him to the king of Babylon
at Riblah. There he passed sentence on
Zedekiah. 7They killed Zedekiah's sons
as he watched. Then they put out his
eyes and put bronze chains on him and
took him to Babylon.

8Nebuzaradan was the commander of
the king's special guards. This officer of
the king of Babylon came to Jerusalem on
the seventh day of the fifth month, in
Nebuchadnezzar's nineteenth year as
king of Babylon. 9Nebuzaradan set fire to
the Temple of the LORD and the palace
and all the houses of Jerusalem. Every
important building was
burned.

10The whole Babylo-
nian army, led by the commander of the king's spe-
cial guards, broke down
the walls around Jerusa-
lem. 11Nebuzaradan, the
commander of the guards,
captured the people left in
Jerusalem, those who had
surrendered to the king of
Babylon, and the rest of the people. 12But
the commander left behind some of the
poorest people of the land to take care of
the vineyards and fields.

13The Babylonians broke up the
bronze pillars, the bronze stands, and the
large bronze bowl, which was called the
Sea, in the Temple of the LORD. Then
they carried the bronze to Babylon.
14They also took the pots, shovels, wick
trimmers, dishes, and all the bronze objects used to serve in the Temple. 15The
commander of the king's special guards
took away the pans for carrying hot coals,
the bowls, and everything made of pure
gold or silver. 16There were two pillars
and the large bronze bowl and the movable stands which Solomon had made for
the Temple of the LORD. There was so
much bronze that it could not be weighed.
17Each pillar was about twenty-seven
feet high. The bronze capital on top of the
pillar was about four and one-half feet

24:18 Jeremiah This is not the prophet Jeremiah, but a different man with the same name.

high. It was decorated with a net design and bronze pomegranates all around it. The other pillar also had a net design and was like the first pillar.

Judah Is Taken Prisoner

18The commander of the guards took some prisoners—Seraiah the chief priest, Zephaniah the priest next in rank, and the three doorkeepers. **19**Of the people who were still in the city, he took the officer in charge of the fighting men, as well as five people who advised the king. He took the royal secretary who selected people for the army and sixty other men who were in the city. **20**Nebuzaradan, the commander, took all these people and brought them to the king of Babylon at Riblah. **21**There at Riblah, in the land of Hamath, the king had them killed. So the people of Judah were led away from their country as captives.

Gedaliah Becomes Governor

22Nebuchadnezzar king of Babylon left some people in the land of Judah. He appointed Gedaliah son of Ahikam, the son of Shaphan, as governor.

23The army captains and their men heard that the king of Babylon had made Gedaliah governor, so they came to Gedaliah at Mizpah. They were Ishmael son of Nethaniah, Johanan son of Kareah, Seraiah son of Tanhumeth the Netophathite, Jaazaniah son of the Maacathite, and their men. **24**Then Gedaliah promised these army captains and their men, "Don't be afraid of the Babylonian officers. Live in the land and serve the king of Babylon, and everything will go well for you."

25In the seventh month Ishmael son of Nethaniah, son of Elishama from the king's family, came with ten men and killed Gedaliah. They also killed the men of Judah and Babylon who were with Gedaliah at Mizpah. **26**Then all the people, from the least important to the most important, along with the army leaders, ran away to Egypt, because they were afraid of the Babylonians.

Jehoiachin Is Set Free

27Jehoiachin king of Judah was held in Babylon for thirty-seven years. In the thirty-seventh year Evil-Merodach became king of Babylon, and he let Jehoiachin out of prison on the twenty-seventh day of the twelfth month. **28**Evil-Merodach spoke kindly to Jehoiachin and gave him a seat of honor above the seats of the other kings who were with him in Babylon. **29**So Jehoiachin put away his prison clothes. For the rest of his life, he ate at the king's table. **30**Every day, for as long as Jehoiachin lived, the king gave him an allowance.

GOD MAKES A LIST

Hello. My name is Ezra, and I am a teacher and priest. Have you ever asked your parents and grandparents about the history of your family? First Chronicles is a history book of God's family, starting with the first man Adam and ending with our great King David. Israel became a strong nation under David's rule because David loved God and obeyed his commands. Download 1 Chronicles 17 to read about God's promise to David that his family would rule forever.

I wrote this book so that people would know that God is faithful through all generations. The people of God were returning to Israel from exile in a foreign land and needed to be reminded of God's blessing for those who love and obey him. Don't miss the MIDI file on David's song of praise celebrating God's love for the people of Israel at 1 Chronicles 16:8–36.

JESUS WATCH

At first glance, 1 Chronicles seems packed with boring lists, but take a second look. All the people on the lists were important to God and to his plan for salvation. Jesus often called himself the Son of Man; and his family history can be traced all the way back to Adam, the first man. Jesus was also called the Son of David. Notice the special emphasis placed on the genealogy of the tribe of Judah, David's family. God promised David that his son would rule forever. David's descendants did rule as kings until Judah was conquered and the people were exiled to Babylon. The list of family generations continues in Matthew 1 and ends with Jesus, the promised Son of David. Jesus is our king, but his rule lasts forever!

my FAVORITE links

______________ ______________

______________ ______________

______________ ______________

______________ ______________

OTHER CONNECTIONS

GET THE INFO

Connect to these info bulletin boards for more fascinating facts about David and God's special messengers, angels:

- A Man After God's Own Heart, 1 Chronicles 17. David—shepherd boy, warrior, musician, poet, king—answered to all these descriptions, but he perhaps is best known for being called "a man after God's own heart." Discover more about this man by following key events in his life.
- A Special Angel, 1 Chronicles 21:6–22. Learn about the angel of the Lord, who appeared to numerous people throughout the Old Testament, performing special jobs for God. Consider what you would do if you had a visit from God's special messenger.

MORE STUFF...

David's Mighty Men David had a strong and loyal following of soldiers. Read about them and their adventures in 1 Chronicles 11; 12. Here are a few facts about them:

- Joab defeated the Jebusites living in Jerusalem and became commander of David's army.
- Jashobeam was commander of the Three, David's most powerful soldiers. He once used his spear to fight 300 men, and he killed all of them.
- Benaiah killed an Egyptian who was over seven feet tall.

"Hey, Tagg, do you know who was the commander of David's army?"

"No clue. How about we download 1 Chronicles 11:4-9 to find out?"

SOME OTHER PLACES TO SURF IN 1 CHRONICLES:

David's mighty warriors, 1 Chronicles 11:15–25
Don't touch—or else!, 1 Chronicles 13
The "how-to" on carrying the Ark, 1 Chronicles 15
David tells Solomon to build the Temple, 1 Chronicles 28

FAITH links

- A Given, 1 Chronicles 5:18–20
- Service with a Smile, 1 Chronicles 6:31–49
- A Memorial for Two Thieves, 1 Chronicles 7:21
- Just a Little Respect, 1 Chronicles 11:10–19
- Plan for Success, 1 Chronicles 14:8–17
- Plans for a Son, 1 Chronicles 22:5–19
- Gifts from the Heart, 1 Chronicles 29

From Adam to Abraham

1 Adam was the father of Seth. Seth
was the father of Enosh. Enosh was
the father of Kenan. 2Kenan was the father of Mahalalel. Mahalalel was the father of Jared. Jared was the father of
Enoch. 3Enoch was the father of Methuselah. Methuselah was the father of Lamech, and Lamech was the father of
Noah.

4The sons of Noah were Shem, Ham,
and Japheth.

5Japheth's sons were Gomer, Magog,
Madai, Javan, Tubal, Meshech, and Tiras.

6Gomer's sons were Ashkenaz, Riphath, and Togarmah.

7Javan's sons were Elishah, Tarshish,
Kittim,* and Rodanim.

8Ham's sons were Cush, Mizraim,*
Put, and Canaan.

9Cush's sons were Seba, Havilah,
Sabta, Raamah, and Sab-
teca.

Raamah's sons were
Sheba and Dedan.

10Cush was the father
of Nimrod, who grew up
to become a mighty war-
rior on the earth.

11Mizraim was the
father of the Ludites,
Anamites, Lehabites, and
Naphtuhites,

12Pathrusites, Casluhites, and Caph-
torites. (The Philistines came from the
Casluhites.)

13Canaan's first child was Sidon. He
was also the father of the Hittites, 14Jeb-
usites, Amorites, Girgashites, 15Hivites,
Arkites, Sinites, 16Arvadites, Zemarites,
and Hamathites.

17Shem's sons were Elam, Asshur,
Arphaxad, Lud, and Aram.

Aram's sons were Uz, Hul, Gether,
and Meshech.

18Arphaxad was the father of Shelah,
who was the father of Eber.

19Eber had two sons. One son was
named Peleg,* because the people on the
earth were divided into different languages during his life. Peleg's brother
was named Joktan.

20Joktan was the father of Almodad,
Sheleph, Hazarmaveth, Jerah, 21Hado-
ram, Uzal, Diklah, 22Obal, Abimael, Sheba, 23Ophir, Havilah, and Jobab. All these
were Joktan's sons. 24The family line included Shem, Arphaxad, Shelah, 25Eber,
Peleg, Reu, 26Serug, Nahor, Terah, 27and
Abram, who was called Abraham.

> Cush was the father of Nimrod, who grew up to become a mighty warrior on the earth.
> —1 Chronicles 1:10

Abraham's Family

28Abraham's sons were Isaac and Ishmael.

29These were the sons of Isaac and
Ishmael. Ishmael's first son was Nebaioth. His other sons were Kedar, Adbeel,
Mibsam, 30Mishma, Dumah, Massa, Hadad, Tema, 31Jetur, Naphish, and Kedemah. These were Ishmael's sons.
32Keturah, Abraham's slave woman,
gave birth to Zimran, Jokshan, Medan,
Midian, Ishbak, and Shuah.

Jokshan's sons were Sheba and Dedan.

33Midian's sons were
Ephah, Epher, Hanoch,
Abida, and Eldaah. All
these were descendants
of Keturah.

34Abraham was the
father of Isaac, and
Isaac's sons were Esau
and Israel.

35Esau's sons were
Eliphaz, Reuel, Jeush, Jalam, and Korah.

36Eliphaz's sons were Teman, Omar,
Zepho, Gatam, Kenaz, Timna, and Amalek.

37Reuel's sons were Nahath, Zerah,
Shammah, and Mizzah.

The Edomites from Seir

38Seir's sons were Lotan, Shobal, Zibeon, Anah, Dishon, Ezer, and Dishan.

39Lotan's sons were Hori and Homam, and his sister was Timna.

40Shobal's sons were Alvan, Manahath, Ebal, Shepho, and Onam.

1:7 Kittim His descendants were the people of Cyprus.

1:8 Mizraim This is another name for Egypt.

1:19 Peleg This name sounds like the Hebrew word for "divided."

Zibeon's sons were Aiah and Anah.
41Anah's son was Dishon.
Dishon's sons were Hemdan, Eshban,
Ithran, and Keran.
42Ezer's sons were Bilhan, Zaavan,
and Akan.
Dishan's sons were Uz and Aran.

The Kings of Edom

43These kings ruled in Edom before
there were kings in Israel. Bela son of
Beor was king of Edom, and his city was
named Dinhabah.
44When Bela died, Jobab son of Zerah
became king. He was from Bozrah.
45When Jobab died,
Husham became king. He
was from the land of the
Temanites.
46When Husham died,
Hadad son of Bedad be-
came king, and his city
was named Avith. Hadad
defeated Midian in the
country of Moab.
47When Hadad died,
Samlah became king. He
was from Masrekah.
48When Samlah died, Shaul became
king. He was from Rehoboth by the river.
49When Shaul died, Baal-Hanan son
of Acbor became king.
50When Baal-Hanan died, Hadad became king, and his city was named Pau.
Hadad's wife was named Mehetabel, and
she was the daughter of Matred, who was
the daughter of Me-Zahab. **51**Then Hadad died.
The leaders of the family groups of
Edom were Timna, Alvah, Jetheth,
52Oholibamah, Elah, Pinon, **53**Kenaz, Teman, Mibzar, **54**Magdiel, and Iram. These
were the leaders of Edom.

Israel's Family

2 The sons of Israel[n] were Reuben,
Simeon, Levi, Judah, Issachar, Zebu-
lun, **2**Dan, Joseph, Benjamin, Naphtali,
Gad, and Asher.

Judah's Family

3Judah's sons were Er, Onan, and
Shelah. A Canaanite woman, the daughter of Shua, was their mother. Judah's
first son, Er, did what the LORD said was
wicked, so the LORD put him to death.
4Judah's daughter-in-law Tamar gave
birth to Perez and Zerah. Judah was the
father, so Judah had five sons.
5Perez's sons were Hezron and Hamul.
6Zerah had five sons: Zimri, Ethan,
Heman, Calcol, and Darda.
7Carmi's son was Achan, who caused
trouble for Israel because he took things
that had been given to the LORD to be destroyed.
8Ethan's son was Azariah.

> Carmi's son was Achan, who . . . took things that had been given to the LORD to be destroyed.
> —1 Chronicles 2:7

9Hezron's sons were
Jerahmeel, Ram, and Ca-
leb.
10Ram was Ammina-
dab's father, and Ammina-
dab was Nahshon's father.
Nahshon was the leader
of the people of Judah.
11Nahshon was the father
of Salmon, who was the
father of Boaz. **12**Boaz
was the father of Obed,
and Obed was the father of Jesse.
13Jesse's first son was Eliab. His second son was Abinadab, his third was
Shimea, **14**his fourth was Nethanel, his
fifth was Raddai, **15**his sixth was Ozem,
and his seventh son was David. **16**Their
sisters were Zeruiah and Abigail.
Zeruiah's three sons were Abishai, Joab,
and Asahel. **17**Abigail was the mother of
Amasa, and his father was Jether, an Ishmaelite.

Caleb's Family

18Caleb son of Hezron had children by
his wife Azubah and by Jerioth. Caleb and
Azubah's sons were Jesher, Shobab, and
Ardon. **19**When Azubah died, Caleb married Ephrath. They had a son named Hur,
20who was the father of Uri, who was the
father of Bezalel.
21Later, when Hezron was sixty years
old, he married the daughter of Makir,
Gilead's father. Hezron had sexual rela-

2:1 Israel Another name for Jacob.

tions with Makir's daughter, and she had
a son named Segub. **22**Segub was the father of Jair. Jair controlled twenty-three
cities in the country of Gilead. **23**(But
Geshur and Aram captured the Towns of
Jair, as well as Kenath and the small
towns around it—sixty towns in all.) All
these were descendants of Makir, the father of Gilead.

24After Hezron died in Caleb Ephra-
thah, his wife Abijah had his son, named
Ashhur. Ashhur became the father of
Tekoa.

Jerahmeel's Family

25Hezron's first son was Jerahmeel.
Jerahmeel's sons were Ram, Bunah,
Oren, Ozem, and Ahijah. Ram was Jerahmeel's first son. **26**Jerahmeel had another wife, named Atarah. She was the
mother of Onam.

27Jerahmeel's first son, Ram, had
sons. They were Maaz, Jamin, and Eker.

28Onam's sons were Shammai and
Jada.

Shammai's sons were Nadab and Abishur.

29Abishur's wife was named Abihail,
and their sons were Ahban and Molid.

30Nadab's sons were Seled and Appaim. Seled died without having children.

31Appaim's son was Ishi, who became
the father of Sheshan.

Sheshan was the father of Ahlai.

32Jada was Shammai's brother, and
Jada's sons were Jether and Jonathan. Jether died without having children.

33Jonathan's sons were Peleth and
Zaza.

These were Jerahmeel's descendants.

34Sheshan did not have any sons, only
daughters. He had a servant from Egypt
named Jarha. **35**Sheshan let his daughter
marry his servant Jarha, and she had a
son named Attai.

36Attai was the father of Nathan. Nathan was the father of Zabad. **37**Zabad
was the father of Ephlal. Ephlal was the
father of Obed. **38**Obed was the father of
Jehu. Jehu was the father of Azariah.
39Azariah was the father of Helez. Helez
was the father of Eleasah. **40**Eleasah was
the father of Sismai. Sismai was the father of Shallum. **41**Shallum was the father of Jekamiah, and Jekamiah was the
father of Elishama.

Caleb's Family

42Caleb was Jerahmeel's brother.
Caleb's first son was Mesha. Mesha was
the father of Ziph, and his son Mareshah
was the father of Hebron.

43Hebron's sons were Korah, Tappuah, Rekem, and Shema. **44**Shema was
the father of Raham, who was the father of Jorkeam. Rekem was the father
of Shammai. **45**Shammai was the father
of Maon, and Maon was the father of
Beth Zur.

46Caleb's slave woman was named
Ephah, and she was the mother of Haran,
Moza, and Gazez. Haran was the father of
Gazez.

47Jahdai's sons were Regem, Jotham,
Geshan, Pelet, Ephah, and Shaaph.

48Caleb had another slave woman
named Maacah. She was the mother of
Sheber, Tirhanah, **49**Shaaph, and Sheva.
Shaaph was the father of Madmannah.
Sheva was the father of Macbenah and
Gibea. Caleb's daughter was Acsah.

50-51 These were Caleb's descendants: Caleb's son Hur was the first son
of his mother Ephrathah. Hur's sons
were Shobal, Salma, and Hareph. Shobal
was the father of Kiriath Jearim. Salma
was the father of Bethlehem. And Hareph was the father of Beth Gader.

52Shobal was the father of Kiriath Jearim. Shobal's descendants were Haroeh,
half the Manahathites, **53**and the family
groups of Kiriath Jearim: the Ithrites, Pu-
thites, Shumathites, and Mishraites. The
Zorathites and the Eshtaolites came from
the Mishraite people.

54Salma's descendants were Bethlehem, the Netophathites, Atroth Beth
Joab, half the Manahathites, and the Zo-
rites. **55**His descendants included the families who lived at Jabez, who wrote and
copied important papers. They were
called the Tirathites, Shimeathites, and
Sucathites and were from the Kenite
family group who came from Hammath.
He was the father of the people living in
Recab.

David's Family

3 These are David's sons who were
born in Hebron. The first was Amnon, whose mother was Ahinoam from
Jezreel. The second son was Daniel,
whose mother was Abigail from Carmel.
2The third son was Absalom, whose
mother was Maacah daughter of Talmai,
the king of Geshur. The fourth son was
Adonijah, whose mother was Haggith.
3The fifth son was Shephatiah, whose
mother was Abital. The sixth son was
Ithream, whose mother was Eglah.
4These six sons of David were born to
him in Hebron, where David ruled for
seven and one-half years.

David ruled in Jerusalem thirty-three
years. 5These were his children who
were born in Jerusalem: Shammua, Shobab, Nathan, and Solomon—the four children of David and Bathsheba, Ammiel's
daughter. 6-8David's other nine children
were Ibhar, Elishua, Eliphelet, Nogah,
Nepheg, Japhia, Elishama, Eliada, and
Eliphelet. 9These were all of David's
sons, except for those born to his slave
women. David also had a daughter named
Tamar.

The Kings of Judah

10Solomon's son was Rehoboam.
Rehoboam's son was Abijah. Abijah's son

FOR BETTER OR WORSHIP

Hey, kids. We were just chatting about what it means to worship God. And we've got a friend who has something to say. Please welcome Maria, age 10, to Connect 2-You.

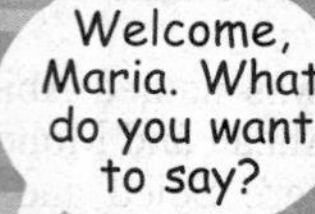

Welcome, Maria. What do you want to say?

Maria

I want to know why kids have to go to Sunday school and church. Everything is so boring—especially at my church. We never talk about anything interesting in Sunday school, the hymns in church are old and slow, and I can't understand a word of the pastor's sermon. Church is for grown-ups. I think kids should be allowed to stay home.

I know what you're saying, Maria. Many church services and many kids' Sunday school classes aren't very "kid-friendly." But the reason we go to church is not to have a good time or be entertained, but to give worship to God. It gives us a chance to let God know how we feel about him—through the things we talk about, the things we think about, the songs we sing, and the way we act. Think of it as "paying him back" once a week for everything he does for you.

If there are things that would make your Sunday school class or church service better for you, tell your teacher or pastor. They will probably be glad to hear your ideas. For some tips on how to make worship meaningful to you, check out the Livin' It page on worshiping God, Nehemiah 8:6, p. 634.

was Asa. Asa's son was Jehoshaphat.
11Jehoshaphat's son was Jehoram. Jehoram's son was Ahaziah. Ahaziah's son was
Joash. 12Joash's son was Amaziah. Amaziah's son was Azariah. Azariah's son was
Jotham. 13Jotham's son was Ahaz. Ahaz's
son was Hezekiah. Hezekiah's son was
Manasseh. 14Manasseh's son was Amon,
and Amon's son was Josiah.

15These were Josiah's sons: His first
son was Johanan, his second was Jehoiakim, his third was Zedekiah, and his
fourth was Shallum.

16Jehoiakim was followed by Jehoiachin, and he was followed by Zedekiah.

David's Descendants After the Babylonian Captivity

17Jehoiachin was taken as a prisoner.
His sons were Shealtiel, 18Malkiram,
Pedaiah, Shenazzar, Jeka-
miah, Hoshama, and Ned-
abiah.

19Pedaiah's sons were
Zerubbabel and Shimei.

Zerubbabel's sons were
Meshullam and Hananiah,
and their sister was Shelomith. 20Zerubbabel also
had five other sons: Ha-
shubah, Ohel, Berekiah,
Hasadiah, and Jushab-
Hesed.

21Hananiah's descendants were Pelatiah and Jeshaiah, and the sons of Rephaiah, Arnan, Obadiah, and Shecaniah.

22Shecaniah's son was Shemaiah.
Shemaiah's sons were Hattush, Igal, Ba-
riah, Neariah, and Shaphat. There were
six in all.

23Neariah had three sons: Elioenai,
Hizkiah, and Azrikam.

24Elioenai had seven sons: Hodaviah,
Eliashib, Pelaiah, Akkub, Johanan, Delaiah, and Anani.

Other Family Groups of Judah

4 Judah's descendants were Perez, Hezron, Carmi, Hur, and Shobal.

2Reaiah was Shobal's son. Reaiah was
the father of Jahath, and Jahath was the father of Ahumai and Lahad. They were the
family groups of the Zorathite people.

3-4Hur was the oldest son of Caleb
and his wife Ephrathah. Hur was the
leader of Bethlehem. His three sons
were Etam, Penuel, and Ezer. Etam's
sons were Jezreel, Ishma, and Idbash.
They had a sister named Hazzelelponi.
Penuel was the father of Gedor, and Ezer
was the father of Hushah.

5Tekoa's father was Ashhur. Ashhur
had two wives named Helah and Naarah.

6The sons of Ashhur and Naarah were
Ahuzzam, Hepher, Temeni, and Haahash-
tari. These were the descendants of Naarah.

7Helah's sons were Zereth, Zohar,
Ethnan, 8and Koz. Koz was the father
of Anub, Hazzobebah, and the Aharhel
family group. Aharhel was the son of
Harum.

9There was a man named Jabez, who
was respected more than
his brothers. His mother
named him Jabez* be-
cause she said, "I was in
much pain when I gave
birth to him." 10Jabez
prayed to the God of Israel, "Please do good things
for me and give me more
land. Stay with me, and
don't let anyone hurt me.
Then I won't have any
pain." And God did what Jabez had asked.

> Please do good things for me and give me more land. Stay with me, and don't let anyone hurt me.
> —1 Chronicles 4:10

11Kelub, Shuhah's brother, was the
father of Mehir. Mehir was the father of
Eshton. 12Eshton was the father of Beth
Rapha, Paseah, and Tehinnah. Tehinnah
was the father of the people from the
town of Nahash. These people were from
Recah.

13The sons of Kenaz were Othniel
and Seraiah.

Othniel's sons were Hathath and Me-
onothai. 14Meonothai was the father of
Ophrah.

Seraiah was the father of Joab. Joab
was the ancestor of the people from
Craftsmen's Valley, named that because
the people living there were craftsmen.

15Caleb was Jephunneh's son. Caleb's

4:9 Jabez This name in Hebrew sounds like the word for "pain."

sons were Iru, Elah, and Naam. Elah's son was Kenaz.

16Jehallelel's sons were Ziph, Ziphah, Tiria, and Asarel.

17-18 Ezrah's sons were Jether, Mered, Epher, and Jalon. Mered married Bithiah, the daughter of the king of Egypt. The children of Mered and Bithiah were Miriam, Shammai, and Ishbah. Ishbah was the father of Eshtemoa. Mered also had a wife from Judah, who gave birth to Jered, Heber, and Jekuthiel. Jered became the father of Gedor. Heber became the father of Soco. And Jekuthiel became the father of Zanoah.

19Hodiah's wife was Naham's sister. The sons of Hodiah's wife were Eshtemoa and the father of Keilah. Keilah was from the Garmite people, and Eshtemoa was from the Maacathite people.

20Shimon's sons were Amnon, Rinnah, Ben-Hanan, and Tilon.

Ishi's sons were Zoheth and Ben-Zoheth.

21-22 Shelah was Judah's son. Shelah's sons were Er, Laadah, Jokim, the men from Cozeba, Joash, and Saraph. Er was the father of Lecah. Laadah was the father of Mareshah and the family groups of linen workers at Beth Ashbea. Joash and Saraph ruled in Moab and Jashubi Lehem. The writings about this family are very old. **23**These sons of Shelah were potters. They lived in Netaim and Gederah and worked for the king.

Simeon's Children

24Simeon's sons were Nemuel, Jamin, Jarib, Zerah, and Shaul. **25**Shaul's son was Shallum. Shallum's son was Mibsam. Mibsam's son was Mishma.

26Mishma's son was Hammuel. Hammuel's son was Zaccur. Zaccur's son was Shimei. **27**Shimei had sixteen sons and six daughters, but his brothers did not have many children, so there were not as many people in their family group as there were in Judah.

28Shimei's children lived in Beersheba, Moladah, Hazar Shual, **29**Bilhah, Ezem, Tolad, **30**Bethuel, Hormah, Ziklag, **31**Beth Marcaboth, Hazar Susim, Beth Biri, and Shaaraim. They lived in these cities until David became king. **32**The five villages near these cities were Etam, Ain, Rimmon, Token, and Ashan. **33**There were also other villages as far away as Baalath. This is where they lived. And they wrote the history of their family.

34-38 The men in this list were leaders of their family groups: Meshobab, Jamlech, Joshah son of Amaziah, Joel, Jehu son of Joshibiah (Joshibiah was the son of Seraiah, who was the son of Asiel), Elioenai, Jaakobah, Jeshohaiah, Asaiah, Adiel, Jesimiel, Benaiah, and Ziza. (Ziza was the son of Shiphi, who was the son of Allon. Allon was the son of Jedaiah, who was the son of Shimri. And Shimri was the son of Shemaiah.)

These families grew very large. **39**They went outside the city of Gedor to the east side of the valley to look for pasture for their flocks. **40**They found good pastures with plenty of grass, and the land was open country and peaceful and quiet. Ham's descendants had lived there in the past.

41These men who were listed came to Gedor while Hezekiah was king of Judah. They fought against the Hamites, destroying their tents, and also against the Meunites who lived there, and completely destroyed them. So there are no Meunites there even today. Then these men began to live there, because there was pasture for their flocks. **42**Ishi's sons, Pelatiah, Neariah, Rephaiah, and Uzziel, led five hundred of the Simeonites and attacked the people living in the mountains of Edom. **43**They killed the few Amalekites who were still alive. From that time until now these Simeonites have lived in Edom.

Reuben's Children

5 Reuben was Israel's first son. Reuben should have received the special privileges of the oldest son, but he had sexual relations with his father's slave woman. So those special privileges were given to Joseph's sons. (Joseph was a son of Israel.) In the family history Reuben's name is not listed as the first son. **2**Judah became stronger than his brothers, and a leader came from his family. But Joseph's family received the privileges that belonged to the oldest son. **3**Reuben was Israel's first son. Reuben's sons were Hanoch, Pallu, Hezron, and Carmi.

4These were the children of Joel: Shemaiah was Joel's son. Gog was Shemaiah's son. Shimei was Gog's son. **5**Micah was Shimei's son. Reaiah was Micah's son. Baal was Reaiah's son. **6**Beerah was Baal's son. Beerah was a leader of the tribe of Reuben. Tiglath-Pileser king of Assyria captured him and took him away.

7Joel's brothers and all his family groups are listed just as they are written in their family histories: Jeiel was the first, then Zechariah, **8**and Bela. (Bela was the son of Azaz. Azaz was the son of Shema, and Shema was the son of Joel.) They lived in the area of Aroer all the way to Nebo and Baal Meon. **9**Bela's people lived to the east—as far as the edge of the desert, which is beside the Euphrates River—because they had too many cattle for the land of Gilead.

10When Saul was king, Bela's people fought a war against the Hagrite people and defeated them. Then Bela's people lived in the tents that had belonged to the Hagrites in all the area east of Gilead.

Gad's Children

11The people from the tribe of Gad lived near the Reubenites. The Gadites lived in the area of Bashan all the way to Salecah. **12**Joel was the main leader, Shapham was second, and then Janai and Shaphat were leaders in Bashan.

13The seven relatives in their families were Michael, Meshullam, Sheba, Jorai, Jacan, Zia, and Eber. **14**They were the descendants of Abihail. Abihail was Huri's son. Huri was Jaroah's son. Jaroah was Gilead's son. Gilead was Michael's son. Michael was Jeshishai's son. Jeshishai was Jahdo's son, and Jahdo was the son of Buz. **15**Ahi was Abdiel's son, and Abdiel was Guni's son. Ahi was the leader of their family.

16The Gadites lived in Gilead, Bashan and the small towns around it, and on all the pasturelands in the Plain of Sharon all the way to the borders.

17All these names were written in the family history of Gad during the time Jotham was king of Judah and Jeroboam was king of Israel.

Soldiers Skilled in War

18There were forty-four thousand seven hundred sixty soldiers from the tribes of Reuben and Gad and East Manasseh who carried shields and swords and bows. They were skilled in war. **19**They started a war against the Hagrites and the people of Jetur, Naphish, and Nodab. **20**The men from the tribes of Manasseh, Reuben, and Gad prayed to God during the war, asking him to help them. So he helped them because they trusted him. He handed over to them the Hagrites and all those who were with them. **21**They took the animals that belonged to the Hagrites: fifty thousand camels, two hundred fifty thousand sheep, and two thousand donkeys. They also captured one hundred thousand people. **22**Many Hagrites were killed because God helped the people of Reuben, Gad, and Manasseh. Then they lived there until Babylon captured them and took them away.

East Manasseh

23There were many people in East Manasseh, and they lived in the area of Bashan all the way to Baal Hermon, Senir, and Mount Hermon.

24These were the family leaders: Epher, Ishi, Eliel, Azriel, Jeremiah, Hodaviah, and Jahdiel. They were all strong, brave, and famous men, and leaders in their families. **25**But they sinned against the God that their ancestors had worshiped. They began worshiping the gods of the people in that land, and those were the people God was destroying. **26**So the God of Israel made Pul king of Assyria want to go to war. (Pul was also called Tiglath-Pileser.) He captured the people of Reuben, Gad, and East Manasseh, and he took them away to Halah, Habor, Hara, and near the Gozan River. They have lived there from that time until this day.

A GIVEN

1 CHRONICLES 5:18-20

Certain things in life are givens. That means you can count on them to happen. You expect the sun to come up. Even if it rains, you know the sun is still there somewhere. Certain things about faith are givens, too. In 1 Chronicles 5:20, eight little words explain one of the "givens." Some men of Israel prayed to God for help. "So he [God] helped them because they trusted him" (5:20). Read those eight words again. That means he'll help you if you trust him. The key word is *trust*. Do you trust him?

Here are some more Faithlinks on trust:

From Hopeless to Hopeful, Exodus 6:9, p. 83

God's New Home, 2 Chronicles 7:11–22, p. 570

A Mother's Love, Isaiah 49:13–16, p. 961

A Safe Place, Nahum 1:7, p. 1231

Jesus' Prayer, John 17, p. 1453

The Finished Product, Philippians 1:6, p. 1609

Levi's Children

6 Levi's sons were Gershon, Kohath,
and Merari.
2Kohath's sons were Amram, Izhar,
Hebron, and Uzziel.
3Amram's children were Aaron, Moses, and Miriam.
Aaron's sons were Nadab, Abihu, Eleazar, and Ithamar. 4Eleazar was the father
of Phinehas. Phinehas was the father of
Abishua. 5Abishua was the father of
Bukki. Bukki was the father of Uzzi.
6Uzzi was the father of Zerahiah. Zerahiah was the father of Meraioth. 7Meraioth was the father of Amariah. Amariah
was the father of Ahitub. 8Ahitub was the
father of Zadok. Zadok was the father of
Ahimaaz. 9Ahimaaz was the father of Azariah. Azariah was the father of Johanan.
10Johanan was the father of Azariah. (Azariah was a priest in the Temple Solomon
built in Jerusalem.) 11Azariah was the father of Amariah. Amariah was the father
of Ahitub. 12Ahitub was the father of Zadok. Zadok was the father of Shallum.
13Shallum was the father of Hilkiah. Hilkiah was the father of Azariah. 14Azariah
was the father of Seraiah, and Seraiah
was the father of Jehozadak.
15Jehozadak was forced to leave his
home when the LORD sent Judah and Jerusalem into captivity under the control
of Nebuchadnezzar.
16Levi's sons were Gershon, Kohath,
and Merari.
17The names of Gershon's sons were
Libni and Shimei.
18Kohath's sons were Amram, Izhar,
Hebron, and Uzziel.
19Merari's sons were Mahli and Mushi.
This is a list of the family groups of Levi, listed by the name of the father of each group.
20Gershon's son was Libni. Libni's
son was Jehath. Jehath's son was Zimmah. 21Zimmah's son was Joah. Joah's
son was Iddo. Iddo's son was Zerah. And
Zerah's son was Jeatherai.
22Kohath's son was Amminadab. Amminadab's son was Korah. Korah's son
was Assir. 23Assir's son was Elkanah.
Elkanah's son was Ebiasaph. Ebiasaph's
son was Assir. 24Assir's son was Tahath.
Tahath's son was Uriel. Uriel's son was
Uzziah, and Uzziah's son was Shaul.
25Elkanah's sons were Amasai and
Ahimoth. 26Ahimoth's son was Elkanah.

Elkanah's son was Zophai. Zophai's son
was Nahath. **27**Nahath's son was Eliab.
Eliab's son was Jeroham. Jeroham's son
was Elkanah, and Elkanah's son was
Samuel.
28Samuel's sons were Joel, the first
son, and Abijah, the second son.
29Merari's son was Mahli. Mahli's
son was Libni. Libni's son was Shimei.
Shimei's son was Uzzah. **30**Uzzah's son
was Shimea. Shimea's son was Haggiah,
and Haggiah's son was Asaiah.

The Temple Musicians

31David chose some people to be in
charge of the music in the house of the
LORD. They began their work after the
Ark of the Agreement was put there.
32They served by making music at the
Holy Tent (also called the Meeting Tent),
and they served until Solomon built the
Temple of the LORD in Jerusalem. They
followed the rules for their work.
33These are the musicians and their
sons:
From Kohath's family there was Heman the singer. Heman was Joel's son.
Joel was Samuel's son. **34**Samuel was
Elkanah's son. Elkanah was Jeroham's
son. Jeroham was Eliel's son. Eliel was
Toah's son. **35**Toah was Zuph's son. Zuph
was Elkanah's son. Elkanah was Mahath's son. Mahath was Amasai's son.
36Amasai was Elkanah's son. Elkanah
was Joel's son. Joel was Azariah's son.
Azariah was Zephaniah's son. **37**Zephaniah was Tahath's son. Tahath was Assir's
son. Assir was Ebiasaph's son. Ebiasaph
was Korah's son. **38**Korah was Izhar's
son. Izhar was Kohath's son. Kohath was
Levi's son. Levi was Israel's son.
39There was Heman's helper Asaph,
whose group stood by Heman's right side.
Asaph was Berekiah's son. Berekiah was
Shimea's son. **40**Shimea was Michael's
son. Michael was Baaseiah's son. Baaseiah was Malkijah's son. **41**Malkijah was
Ethni's son. Ethni was Zerah's son. Zerah
was Adaiah's son. **42**Adaiah was Ethan's
son. Ethan was Zimmah's son. Zimmah
was Shimei's son. **43**Shimei was Jahath's
son. Jahath was Gershon's son, and
Gershon was Levi's son.

FAITH links

SERVICE WITH A SMILE

1 CHRONICLES 6:31-49

Think about something you do well that brings a smile to your face when you do it. Maybe you like to paint or sing. Music brought a smile to David's face. He used his musical ability to serve God. He played the harp and wrote many of the psalms. David wanted others to please God with their talents, too. As king, David chose certain people who were good musicians to be in charge of the music in the Temple. Other groups had different roles.

You can serve God with what you enjoy doing, too. God is pleased when you serve him with a smile.

How do you serve? Connect to these links for thoughts on serving:

Share What You Have, Exodus 35:5–18, p. 123

Help for the Poor, Leviticus 5:7, p. 138

What God Wants, Deuteronomy 10:12–13, p. 242

Advice from a Kid, 2 Kings 5, p. 484

The Way to Greatness, Matthew 20:20–28, p. 1309

My Best Serve, Acts 6:1–6, p. 1473

44Merari's family were the helpers of
Heman and Asaph, and they stood by
Heman's left side. In this group was
Ethan son of Kishi. Kishi was Abdi's son.
Abdi was Malluch's son. **45**Malluch was
Hashabiah's son. Hashabiah was Ama-
ziah's son. Amaziah was Hilkiah's son.
46Hilkiah was Amzi's son. Amzi was
Bani's son. Bani was Shemer's son.
47Shemer was Mahli's son. Mahli was
Mushi's son. Mushi was Merari's son,
and Merari was Levi's son.

48The other Levites served by doing
their own special work in the Holy Tent,
the house of God. **49**Aaron and his descendants offered the sacrifices on the altar
of burnt offering and burned the
incense on the altar
of incense. They of-
fered the sacrifices
that removed the Is-
raelites' sins so they
could belong to God.
They did all the
work in the Most Holy Place and followed all the laws that Moses, God's servant, had commanded.

EMAIL FROM GOD 6:49
Obedience
How did the Israelites obey God?

50These were Aaron's sons: Eleazar
was Aaron's son. Phinehas was Eleazar's
son. Abishua was Phinehas' son. **51**Bukki
was Abishua's son. Uzzi was Bukki's son.
Zerahiah was Uzzi's son. **52**Meraioth was
Zerahiah's son. Amariah was Meraioth's
son. Ahitub was Amariah's son. **53**Zadok
was Ahitub's son, and Ahimaaz was
Zadok's son.

Land for the Levites

54These are the places where Aaron's
descendants lived. His descendants from
the Kohath family group received the
first share of the land.

55They were given the city of Hebron
in Judah and the pastures around it, **56**but
the fields farther from the city and the
villages near Hebron were given to Caleb
son of Jephunneh. **57**So the descendants
of Aaron were given Hebron, one of the
cities of safety. They also received the
towns and pastures of Libnah, Jattir, Eshtemoa, **58**Hilen, Debir, **59**Ashan, Juttah,
and Beth Shemesh. **60**They also received
these towns and pastures from the tribe
of Benjamin: Gibeon, Geba, Alemeth, and
Anathoth.

The Kohath family groups received a
total of thirteen towns.

61The rest of the Kohath family group
was given ten towns from the family
groups of West Manasseh. The towns
were chosen by throwing lots.

62The Gershon family group received
thirteen towns from the tribes of Issachar, Asher, Naphtali, and the part of Manasseh living in Bashan.

63The Merari family group received
twelve towns from the tribes of Reuben,
Gad, and Zebulun. Those towns were
chosen by throwing lots.

64So the Israelites gave these towns
and their pastures to the Levites. **65**The
towns from the tribes of Judah, Simeon,
and Benjamin, which were named, were
chosen by throwing lots.

66Some of the Kohath family groups
received towns and pastures from the
tribe of Ephraim. **67**They received Shechem, one of the cities of safety,[n] with its
pastures in the mountains of Ephraim.
They also received the towns and pastures of Gezer, **68**Jokmeam, Beth Horon,
69Aijalon, and Gath Rimmon.

70The rest of the people in the Ko-
hath family group received the towns of
Aner and Bileam and their pastures from
West Manasseh.

71From East Manasseh, the Gershon
family received the towns and pastures of
Golan in Bashan and Ashtaroth.

72-73 From the tribe of Issachar, the
Gershon family received the towns and
pastures of Kedesh, Daberath, Ramoth,
and Anem.

74-75 From the tribe of Asher, the
Gershon family received the towns and
pastures of Mashal, Abdon, Hukok, and
Rehob.

76From the tribe of Naphtali, the Gershon family received the towns and pastures of Kedesh in Galilee, Hammon, and
Kiriathaim.

6:67 cities of safety A person who had accidentally killed someone could go to one of the six cities of safety to receive protection and a fair trial.

77The rest of the Levites, the people
from the Merari family, received from
the tribe of Zebulun the towns and pastures of Jokneam, Kartah, Rimmono, and
Tabor.
78-79From the tribe of Reuben, the
Merari family received the towns and
pastures of Bezer in the desert, Jahzah,
Kedemoth, and Mephaath. (The tribe of
Reuben lived east of the Jordan River,
across from Jericho.)
80-81From the tribe of Gad, the Merari family received the towns and pastures of Ramoth in Gilead, Mahanaim,
Heshbon, and Jazer.

Issachar's Children

7 Issachar had four sons: Tola, Puah, Jashub, and Shimron.
2Tola's sons were Uzzi, Rephaiah, Je-
riel, Jahmai, Ibsam, and Samuel, and they
were leaders of their families. In the family history of Tola's descendants, twenty-
two thousand six hundred men were
listed as fighting men during the time
David was king.
3Uzzi's son was Izrahiah.
Izrahiah's sons were Michael, Obadiah, Joel, and Isshiah. All five of them
were leaders. 4Their family history
shows they had thirty-six thousand men
ready to serve in the army, because they
had many wives and children.
5The records of the family groups of
Issachar show there were eighty-seven
thousand fighting men.

Benjamin's Children

6Benjamin had three sons: Bela, Beker, and Jediael.
7Bela had five sons: Ezbon, Uzzi, Uzziel, Jerimoth, and Iri, and they were
leaders of their families. Their family history shows they had twenty-two thousand thirty-four fighting men.
8Beker's sons were Zemirah, Joash,
Eliezer, Elioenai, Omri, Jeremoth, Abijah, Anathoth, and Alemeth. They all
were Beker's sons. 9Their family history
listed the family leaders and twenty thousand two hundred fighting men.
10Jediael's son was Bilhan.
Bilhan's sons were Jeush, Benjamin,
Ehud, Kenaanah, Zethan, Tarshish, and
Ahishahar. 11All these sons of Jediael
were leaders of their families. They had
seventeen thousand two hundred fighting men ready to serve in the army.
12The Shuppites and Huppites were
descendants of Ir, and the Hushites were
descendants of Aher.

Naphtali's Children

13Naphtali's sons were Jahziel, Guni,
Jezer, and Shillem. They were Bilhah's
grandsons.

Manasseh's Children

14These are Manasseh's descendants. Manasseh had an Aramean slave
woman, who was the mother of Asriel
and Makir. Makir was Gilead's father.
15Makir took a wife from the Huppites
and Shuppites. His sister was named Maacah. His second son was named Zelophehad, and he had only daughters.
16Makir's wife Maacah had a son whom
she named Peresh. Peresh's brother was
named Sheresh. Sheresh's sons were
Ulam and Rakem.
17Ulam's son was Bedan.
These were the sons of Gilead, who
was the son of Makir. Makir was Manasseh's son. 18Makir's sister Hammole-
keth gave birth to Ishhod, Abiezer, and
Mahlah.
19The sons of Shemida were Ahian,
Shechem, Likhi, and Aniam.

Ephraim's Children

20These are the names of Ephraim's
descendants. Ephraim's son was Shuthelah. Shuthelah's son was Bered. Bered's
son was Tahath. Tahath's son was Eleadah. Eleadah's son was Tahath. 21Ta-
hath's son was Zabad. Zabad's son was
Shuthelah.
Ezer and Elead went to Gath to steal
cows and sheep and were killed by some
men who grew up in that city. 22Their father Ephraim cried for them many days,
and his family came to comfort him.
23Then he had sexual relations with his
wife again. She became pregnant and
gave birth to a son whom Ephraim named

A MEMORIAL FOR TWO THIEVES

1 CHRONICLES 7:21

Genealogies, or family histories, are records of people's lives. You'll find many of them in the Bible. They tell what people did, both good and bad. Two men, Ezer and Elead, had only one deed listed: they stole some cows and sheep! Would you want to be remembered for that?

If someone wrote about your life, what would your actions say about you? Each day, you're adding to the record of your life. Following Jesus can guarantee you a better memorial than the one for two thieves.

Show Some Respect, Leviticus 19:32, p. 161

I'll Never Forget What's-His-Name, Deuteronomy 8, p. 239

What's Out Becomes In, Judges 11, p. 327

Trailblazers of Faith, 2 Kings 22:1–2, p. 510

Good Enough?, Ezekiel 8, p. 1093

The Worst Chore, John 13:3–17, p. 1447

Beriah" because of the trouble that had
happened to his family. 24Ephraim's
daughter was Sheerah. She built Lower
Beth Horon, Upper Beth Horon, and Uz-
zen Sheerah.
25Rephah was Ephraim's son. Resheph was Rephah's son. Telah was
Resheph's son. Tahan was Telah's son.
26Ladan was Tahan's son. Ammihud was
Ladan's son. Elishama was Ammihud's
son. 27Nun was Elishama's son, and
Joshua was the son of Nun.
28Ephraim's descendants lived in
these lands and towns: Bethel and the
villages near it, Naaran on the east, Gezer and the villages near it on the west,
and Shechem and the villages near it.
These villages went all the way to Ayyah
and its villages. 29Along the borders of
Manasseh's land were the towns of Beth
Shan, Taanach, Megiddo, and Dor, and
the villages near them. The descendants
of Joseph son of Israel lived in these
towns.

Asher's Children

30Asher's sons were Imnah, Ishvah,
Ishvi, and Beriah. Their sister was Serah.
31Beriah's sons were Heber and Malkiel. Malkiel was Birzaith's father.
32Heber was the father of Japhlet,
Shomer, Hotham, and their sister Shua.
33Japhlet's sons were Pasach, Bimhal,
and Ashvath. They were Japhlet's children.
34Japhlet's brother was Shomer.
Shomer's sons were Rohgah, Hubbah,
and Aram.
35Shomer's brother was Hotham.
Hotham's sons were Zophah, Imna, She-
lesh, and Amal.
36Zophah's sons were Suah, Harne-
pher, Shual, Beri, Imrah, 37Bezer, Hod,
Shamma, Shilshah, Ithran, and Beera.
38Jether's sons were Jephunneh, Pis-
pah, and Ara.
39Ulla's sons were Arah, Hanniel, and
Rizia.
40All these men were descendants of
Asher and leaders of their families. They
were powerful warriors and outstanding
leaders. Their family history lists that
they had twenty-six thousand soldiers
ready to serve in the army.

The Family History of King Saul

8 Benjamin was the father of Bela, his
first son. Ashbel was his second son,

7:23 Beriah This name sounds like the Hebrew word for "trouble."

Aharah was his third, 2Nohah was his fourth, and Rapha was his fifth son.

3Bela's sons were Addar, Gera, Abihud, 4Abishua, Naaman, Ahoah, 5Gera, Shephuphan, and Huram.

6These were the descendants of Ehud and leaders of their families in Geba. They were forced to move to Manahath. 7Ehud's descendants were Naaman, Ahijah, and Gera. Gera forced them to leave. He was the father of Uzza and Ahihud.

8-11Shaharaim and his wife Hushim had sons named Abitub and Elpaal. In Moab, Shaharaim divorced his wives Hushim and Baara. Shaharaim and his wife Hodesh had these sons: Jobab, Zibia, Mesha, Malcam, Jeuz, Sakia, and Mirmah. They were leaders of their families.

12-13Elpaal's sons were Eber, Misham, Shemed, Beriah, and Shema. Shemed built the towns of Ono and Lod and the villages around them. Beriah and Shema were leaders of the families living in Aijalon, and they forced out the people who lived in Gath.

14Beriah's sons were Ahio, Shashak, Jeremoth, 15Zebadiah, Arad, Eder, 16Michael, Ishpah, and Joha.

17Elpaal's sons were Zebadiah, Meshullam, Hizki, Heber, 18Ishmerai, Izliah, and Jobab.

19Shimei's sons were Jakim, Zicri, Zabdi, 20Elienai, Zillethai, Eliel, 21Adaiah, Beraiah, and Shimrath.

22Shashak's sons were Ishpan, Eber, Eliel, 23Abdon, Zicri, Hanan, 24Hananiah, Elam, Anthothijah, 25Iphdeiah, and Penuel.

26Jeroham's sons were Shamsherai, Shehariah, Athaliah, 27Jaareshiah, Elijah, and Zicri.

28The family histories show that all these men were leaders of their families and lived in Jerusalem.

> The names of all the people of Israel were listed in their family histories.
> —1 Chronicles 9:1

29Jeiel lived in the town of Gibeon, where he was the leader. His wife was named Maacah. 30Jeiel's first son was Abdon. His other sons were Zur, Kish, Baal, Ner, Nadab, 31Gedor, Ahio, Zeker, 32and Mikloth. Mikloth was the father of Shimeah. These sons also lived near their relatives in Jerusalem.

33Ner was the father of Kish. Kish was the father of Saul, and Saul was the father of Jonathan, Malki-Shua, Abinadab, and Esh-Baal.

34Jonathan's son was Merib-Baal, who was the father of Micah.

35Micah's sons were Pithon, Melech, Tarea, and Ahaz. 36Ahaz was the father of Jehoaddah. Jehoaddah was the father of Alemeth, Azmaveth, and Zimri. Zimri was the father of Moza. 37Moza was the father of Binea. Raphah was Binea's son. Eleasah was Raphah's son, and Azel was Eleasah's son.

38Azel had six sons: Azrikam, Bokeru, Ishmael, Sheariah, Obadiah, and Hanan. All these were Azel's sons.

39Azel's brother was Eshek. Eshek's first son was Ulam, his second was Jeush, and Eliphelet was his third. 40Ulam's sons were mighty warriors and good archers. They had many sons and grandsons—one hundred fifty of them in all.

All these men were Benjamin's descendants.

9 The names of all the people of Israel were listed in their family histories, and those family histories were put in the book of the kings of Israel.

The People in Jerusalem

The people of Judah were captured and forced to go to Babylon, because they were not faithful to God.

2The first people to come back and live in their own lands and towns were some Israelites, priests, Levites, and Temple servants.

3People from the tribes of Judah, Benjamin, Ephraim, and Manasseh lived in Jerusalem. This is a list of those people.

4There was Uthai son of Ammihud. (Ammihud was Omri's son. Omri was Imri's son. Imri was Bani's son. Bani was

a descendant of Perez, and Perez was
Judah's son.)
5Of the Shilonite people there were
Asaiah and his sons. Asaiah was the oldest son in his family.
6Of the Zerahite people there were
Jeuel and other relatives of Zerah. There
were six hundred ninety of them in all.
7From the tribe of Benjamin there
was Sallu son of Meshullam. (Meshullam
was Hodaviah's son, and Hodaviah was
Hassenuah's son.) 8There was also Ibne-
iah son of Jeroham and Elah son of Uzzi.
(Uzzi was Micri's son.) And there was
Meshullam son of Shephatiah. (Shephatiah was Reuel's son, and Reuel was
Ibnijah's son.) 9The family history of
Benjamin lists nine hundred fifty-six people living in Jerusalem, and all these
were leaders of their families.
10Of the priests there were Jedaiah,
Jehoiarib, Jakin, and 11Azariah son of Hilkiah. (Hilkiah was Meshullam's son. Meshullam was Zadok's son. Zadok was
Meraioth's son. Meraioth was Ahitub's
son. Ahitub was the officer responsible
for the Temple of God.) 12Also there was
Adaiah son of Jeroham. (Jeroham was
Pashhur's son, and Pashhur was Malkijah's son.) And there was Maasai son of
Adiel. (Adiel was Jahzerah's son. Jahzerah was Meshullam's son. Meshullam
was Meshillemith's son, and Meshillemith was Immer's son.) 13There were
one thousand seven hundred sixty
priests. They were leaders of their families, and they were responsible for serving in the Temple of God.
14Of the Levites there was Shemaiah
son of Hasshub. (Hasshub was Azrikam's
son, and Azrikam was Hashabiah's son.
Hashabiah was from the family of Merari.) 15There were also Bakbakkar, He-
resh, Galal, and Mattaniah son of Mica.
(Mica was Zicri's son, and Zicri was
Asaph's son.) 16There was also Obadiah
son of Shemaiah. (Shemaiah was Galal's
son, and Galal was Jeduthun's son.) And
there was Berekiah son of Asa. (Asa was
the son of Elkanah, who lived in the villages of the Netophathites.)
17Of the gatekeepers there were
Shallum, Akkub, Talmon, Ahiman, and
their relatives. Shallum was their leader.
18These gatekeepers from the tribe of
Levi still stand next to the King's Gate on
the east side of the city. 19Shallum was
Kore's son. Kore was Ebiasaph's son, and
Ebiasaph was Korah's son. Shallum and
his relatives from the family of Korah
were gatekeepers and were responsible
for guarding the gates of the Temple.
Their ancestors had also been responsible for guarding the entrance to the Temple of the LORD. 20In the past Phinehas,
Eleazar's son, was in charge of the gatekeepers, and the LORD was with Phinehas. 21Zechariah son of Meshelemiah
was the gatekeeper at the entrance to the
Temple.
22In all, two hundred twelve men
were chosen to guard the gates, and their
names were written in their family histories in their villages. David and Samuel
the seer chose these men because they
were dependable. 23The gatekeepers
and their descendants had to guard the
gates of the Temple of the LORD. (The
Temple took the place of the Holy Tent.)
24There were gatekeepers on all four
sides of the Temple: east, west, north,
and south. 25The gatekeepers' relatives
who lived in the villages had to come and
help them at times. Each time they came
they helped the gatekeepers for seven
days. 26Because they were dependable,
four gatekeepers were made the leaders
of all the gatekeepers. They were Levites, and they were responsible for the
rooms and treasures in the Temple of
God. 27They stayed up all night guarding
the Temple of God, and they opened it
every morning.
28Some of the gatekeepers were responsible for the utensils used in the
Temple services. They counted these
utensils when people took them out and
when they brought them back. 29Other
gatekeepers were chosen to take care of
the furniture and utensils in the Holy
Place. They also took care of the flour,
wine, oil, incense, and spices, 30but
some of the priests took care of mixing
the spices. 31There was a Levite named
Mattithiah who was dependable and had
the job of baking the bread used for the

offerings. He was the first son of Shallum, who was from the family of Korah.
32Some of the gatekeepers from the Kohath family had the job of preparing the
special bread that was put on the table
every Sabbath day.
33Some of the Levites were musicians in the Temple. The leaders of these
families stayed in the rooms of the Temple. Since they were on duty day and
night, they did not do other work in the
Temple.
34These are the leaders of the Levite
families. Their names were listed in their
family histories, and they lived in Jerusalem.

The Family History of King Saul

35Jeiel lived in the town of Gibeon,
where he was the leader. His wife was
named Maacah. **36**Jeiel's first son was
Abdon. His other sons were Zur, Kish,
Baal, Ner, Nadab, **37**Gedor, Ahio, Zechariah, and Mikloth. **38**Mikloth was Shime-
am's father. Jeiel's family lived near their
relatives in Jerusalem.
39Ner was Kish's father. Kish was
Saul's father. Saul was the father of Jonathan, Malki-Shua, Abinadab, and Esh-
Baal.
40Jonathan's son was Merib-Baal,
who was the father of Mi-
cah.
41Micah's sons were
Pithon, Melech, Tahrea,
and Ahaz. **42**Ahaz was
Jadah's father. Jadah was
the father of Alemeth,
Azmaveth, and Zimri.
Zimri was Moza's father.
43Moza was Binea's
father. Rephaiah was
Binea's son. Eleasah was
Rephaiah's son, and Azel was Eleasah's
son.
44Azel had six sons: Azrikam, Bokeru, Ishmael, Sheariah, Obadiah, and
Hanan. They were Azel's sons.

The Death of King Saul

10 The Philistines fought against Israel, and the Israelites ran away
from them. Many Israelites were killed
on Mount Gilboa. **2**The Philistines fought
hard against Saul and his sons, killing his
sons Jonathan, Abinadab, and Malki-
Shua. **3**The fighting was heavy around
Saul, and the archers shot him with their
arrows and wounded him.
4Then Saul said to the officer who carried his armor, "Pull out your sword and
stab me. If you don't, these Philistines
who are not circumcised will come and
hurt me." But Saul's officer refused, because he was afraid. So Saul took his own
sword and threw himself on it. **5**When
the officer saw that Saul was dead, he
threw himself on his own sword and died.
6So Saul and three of his sons died; all his
family died together.
7When the Israelites living in the valley saw that their army had run away and
that Saul and his sons were dead, they
left their towns and ran away. Then the
Philistines came and settled in them.
8The next day when the Philistines
came to strip the dead soldiers, they
found Saul and his sons dead on Mount
Gilboa. **9**The Philistines stripped Saul's
body and took his head and his armor.
Then they sent messengers through all
their country to tell the news to their
idols and to their people. **10**The Philistines put Saul's armor in
the temple of their idols
and hung his head in the
temple of Dagon.
11All the people in Jabesh Gilead heard what
the Philistines had done
to Saul. **12**So the brave
men of Jabesh went and
got the bodies of Saul and
his sons and brought them
to Jabesh. They buried
their bones under the large tree in Jabesh. Then the people of Jabesh gave up
eating for seven days.
13Saul died because he was not faithful to the LORD and did not obey the
LORD. He even went to a medium and
asked her for advice **14**instead of asking
the LORD. This is why the LORD put Saul
to death and gave the kingdom to Jesse's
son David.

Saul died because he was not faithful to the LORD and did not obey the LORD.
—1 Chronicles 10:13

David Becomes King

11 Then the people of Israel came to
David at the town of Hebron and
said, "Look, we are your own family.
2Even when Saul was king, you were the
one who led Israel in battle. The LORD
your God said to you, 'You will be the
shepherd for my people Israel. You will
be their leader.' "
3So all the older leaders of Israel
came to King David at Hebron. He made
an agreement with them in Hebron in the
presence of the LORD. Then they poured
oil on David to make him king over Israel.
The LORD had promised through Samuel
that this would happen.

David Captures Jerusalem

4David and all the Israelites went to
the city of Jerusalem. At that time Jerusalem was called Jebus, and the people living there were named Jebusites. 5They
said to David, "You can't get inside our
city." But David did take the city of Jerusalem with its strong walls, and it became
the City of David.
6David had said, "The person who
leads the attack against the Jebusites will
become the commander over all my
army." Joab son of Zeruiah led the attack,
so he became the commander of the
army.
7Then David made his home in the
strong, walled city, which is why it was
named the City of David. 8David rebuilt
the city, beginning where the land was
filled in and going to the wall that was
around the city. Joab repaired the other
parts of the city. 9David became stronger
and stronger, and the LORD All-Powerful
was with him.

David's Mighty Warriors

10This is a list of the leaders over
David's warriors who helped make
David's kingdom strong. All the people of
Israel also supported David's kingdom.
These heroes and all the people of Israel
made David king, just as the LORD had
promised.
11This is a list of David's warriors:
Jashobeam was from the Hacmonite
people. He was the head of the Three,[n]

FAITH links

JUST A LITTLE RESPECT

1 CHRONICLES 11:10-19

Think about the leaders in your life: teachers, scout masters, pastors, and so on. What would you do to show your respect for them? David's men once risked their lives to cross enemy lines just to bring him some water. Their actions showed his value as a leader. David was touched by their act. Instead of drinking the water, he offered it to God.

You can offer the leaders in your life a gift. You don't have to cross enemy lines to acquire it, either. You can offer them your respect and encouragement. You can also offer to pray for them. That's the best gift you can give.

Link here for more tips on helping the leaders in your life:

Play Fair or Play Favorites?, Deuteronomy 1:16–18, p. 227

The MLP, Ruth 1:16–17, p. 345

Seeing the Needs, Nehemiah 1, p. 625

Help for a Friend, Mark 2:1–5, p. 1332

Best Seat in the House, Luke 14:7–11, p. 1398

The True Test, 1 John 3:18, p. 1718

11:11 Three Or maybe "Thirty." These were David's most powerful soldiers. See 2 Samuel 23:8.

David's most powerful soldiers. He used
his spear to fight three hundred men at
one time, and he killed them all.
12Next was Eleazar, one of the Three.
Eleazar was Dodai's son from the Ahohite people. 13Eleazar was with David at
Pas Dammim when the Philis-
tines came there to
fight. There was a
field of barley at
that place. The Isra-
elites ran away from
the Philistines, 14but
they stopped in the
middle of that field and fought for it and
killed the Philistines. The LORD gave
them a great victory.

11:14
Success
Can you trust God for your success?

15Once, three of the Thirty, David's
chief soldiers, came down to him at the
rock by the cave near Adullam. At the
same time the Philistine army had
camped in the Valley of Rephaim.
16At that time David was in a stronghold, and some of the Philistines were in
Bethlehem. 17David had a strong desire
for some water. He said, "Oh, I wish
someone would get me water from the
well near the city gate of Bethlehem!"
18So the Three broke through the Philistine army and took water from the well
near the city gate in Bethlehem. Then
they brought it to David, but he refused
to drink it. He poured it out before the
LORD, 19saying, "May God keep me from
drinking this water! It would be like
drinking the blood of the men who risked
their lives to bring it to me!" So David
refused to drink it.

These were the brave things that the three warriors did.

20Abishai brother of Joab was the captain of the Three. Abishai fought three
hundred soldiers with his spear and
killed them. He became as famous as the
Three 21and was more honored than the
Three. He became their commander
even though he was not one of them.
22Benaiah son of Jehoiada was a brave
fighter from Kabzeel who did mighty
things. He killed two of the best warriors
from Moab. He also went down into a pit
and killed a lion on a snowy day. 23Bena-
iah killed an Egyptian who was about
seven and one-half feet tall and had a
spear as large as a weaver's rod. Benaiah
had a club, but he grabbed the spear from
the Egyptian's hand and killed him with
his own spear. 24These were the things
Benaiah son of Jehoiada did. He was as
famous as the Three. 25He received
more honor than the Thirty, but he did
not become a member of the Three. David made him leader of his bodyguards.

The Thirty Chief Soldiers

26 These were also mighty warriors: Asahel brother of Joab; Elhanan son of Dodo from Bethlehem;
27 Shammoth the Harorite; Helez the Pelonite;
28 Ira son of Ikkesh from Tekoa; Abiezer the Anathothite;
29 Sibbecai the Hushathite; Ilai the Ahohite;
30 Maharai the Netophathite; Heled son of Baanah the Netophathite;
31 Ithai son of Ribai from Gibeah in Benjamin; Benaiah the Pirathonite;
32 Hurai from the ravines of Gaash; Abiel the Arbathite;
33 Azmaveth the Baharumite; Eliahba the Shaalbonite;
34 the sons of Hashem the Gizonite; Jonathan son of Shagee the Hararite;
35 Ahiam son of Sacar the Hararite; Eliphal son of Ur;
36 Hepher the Mekerathite; Ahijah the Pelonite;
37 Hezro the Carmelite; Naarai son of Ezbai;
38 Joel brother of Nathan; Mibhar son of Hagri;
39 Zelek the Ammonite; Naharai the Berothite, the officer who carried the armor for Joab son of Zeruiah;
40 Ira the Ithrite;
Gareb the Ithrite;
41 Uriah the Hittite;
Zabad son of Ahlai;
42 Adina son of Shiza the Reubenite, who was the

leader of the Reubenites,
and his thirty soldiers;
43 Hanan son of Maacah;
Joshaphat the Mithnite;
44 Uzzia the Ashterathite;
Shama and Jeiel sons of
Hotham the Aroerite;
45 Jediael son of Shimri;
Joha, Jediael's brother, the
Tizite;
46 Eliel the Mahavite;
Jeribai and Joshaviah, Elnaam's
sons;
Ithmah the Moabite;
47 Eliel, Obed, and Jaasiel the
Mezobaites.

Warriors Join David

12 These were the men who came to
David at Ziklag when David was
hiding from Saul son of Kish. They were
among the warriors who helped David in
battle. 2They came with bows for weapons and could use either their right or left
hands to shoot arrows or to sling rocks.
They were Saul's relatives from the tribe
of Benjamin. 3Ahiezer was their leader,
and there was Joash. (Ahiezer and Joash
were sons of Shemaah, who was from the
town of Gibeah.) There were also Jeziel
and Pelet, the sons of Azmaveth. There
were Beracah and Jehu from the town of
Anathoth. 4And there was Ishmaiah from
the town of Gibeon; he was one of the
Thirty. In fact, he was the leader of the
Thirty. There were Jeremiah, Jahaziel,
Johanan, and Jozabad from Gederah.
5There were Eluzai, Jerimoth, Bealiah,
and Shemariah. There was Shephatiah
from Haruph. 6There were Elkanah, Isshiah, Azarel, Joezer, and Jashobeam
from the family group of Korah. 7And
there were Joelah and Zebadiah, the sons
of Jeroham, from the town of Gedor.

8Part of the people of Gad joined David at his stronghold in the desert. They
were brave warriors trained for war and
skilled with shields and spears. They
were as fierce as lions and as fast as gazelles over the hills.

9Ezer was the leader of Gad's army,
and Obadiah was second in command.
Eliab was third, 10Mishmannah was
fourth, Jeremiah was fifth, 11Attai was
sixth, Eliel was seventh, 12Johanan was
eighth, Elzabad was ninth, 13Jeremiah
was tenth, and Macbannai was eleventh
in command.

14They were the commanders of the
army from Gad. The least of these leaders was in charge of a hundred soldiers,
and the greatest was in charge of a thousand. 15They crossed the Jordan River
and chased away the people living in the
valleys, to the east and to the west. This
happened in the first month of the year
when the Jordan floods the valley.

16Other people from the tribes of
Benjamin and Judah also came to David at
his stronghold. 17David went out to meet
them and said to them, "If you have come
peacefully to help me, I welcome you.
Join me. But if you have come to turn me
over to my enemies, even though I have
done nothing wrong, the God of our fathers will see this and punish you."

18Then the Spirit entered Amasai,
the leader of the Thirty, and he said:
"We belong to you, David.
We are with you, son of Jesse.
Success, success to you.
Success to those who help you,
because your God helps you."
So David welcomed these men and
made them leaders of his army.

19Some of the men from Manasseh
also joined David when he went with the
Philistines to fight Saul. But David and
his men did not really help the Philistines. After talking about it, the Philistine
leaders decided to send David away.
They said, "If David goes back to his
master Saul, we will be killed." 20These
are the men from Manasseh who joined
David when he went to Ziklag: Adnah,
Jozabad, Jediael, Michael, Jozabad, Elihu,
and Zillethai. Each of them was a leader
of a thousand men from Manasseh.
21All these men of Manasseh were brave
soldiers, and they helped David fight
against groups of men who went around
the country robbing people. These soldiers became commanders in David's
army. 22Every day more men joined David, and his army became large, like the
army of God.

Others Join David at Hebron

23These are the numbers of the soldiers ready for battle who joined David at
Hebron. They came to help turn the
kingdom of Saul over to David, just as the
LORD had said.

24There were sixty-eight hundred
men with their weapons from Judah.
They carried shields and spears.

25There were seventy-one hundred
men from Simeon. They were warriors
ready for war.

26There were forty-six hundred men
from Levi. **27**Jehoiada, a leader from
Aaron's family, was in that group. There
were thirty-seven hundred with him.
28Zadok was also in that group. He was a
strong young warrior, and with him came
twenty-two leaders from his family.

29There were three thousand men
from Benjamin, who were Saul's relatives. Most of them had remained loyal to
Saul's family until then.

30There were twenty thousand eight
hundred men from Ephraim. They were
brave warriors and were famous men in
their own family groups.

31There were eighteen thousand men
from West Manasseh. Each one was especially chosen to make David king.

32There were two hundred leaders
from Issachar. They knew what Israel
should do, and they knew the right time
to do it. Their relatives were with them
and under their command.

33There were fifty thousand men
from Zebulun. They were trained soldiers and knew how to use every kind of
weapon of war. They followed David completely.

34There were one thousand officers
from Naphtali. They had thirty-seven
thousand soldiers with them who carried
shields and spears.

35There were twenty-eight thousand
six hundred men from Dan, who were
ready for war.

36There were forty thousand trained
soldiers from Asher, who were ready
for war.

37There were one hundred twenty
thousand soldiers from the east side of
the Jordan River from the people of Reuben, Gad, and East Manasseh. They had
every kind of weapon.

38All these fighting men were ready
to go to war. They came to Hebron fully
agreed to make David king of all Israel.
All the other Israelites also agreed to
make David king. **39**They spent three
days there with David, eating and drinking, because their relatives had prepared
food for them. **40**Also, their neighbors
came from as far away as Issachar, Zebulun, and Naphtali, bringing food on donkeys, camels, mules, and oxen. They
brought much flour, fig cakes, raisins,
wine, oil, cows, and sheep, because the
people of Israel were very happy.

Bringing Back the Ark

13 David talked with all the officers of
his army, the commanders of a
hundred men and the commanders of a
thousand men. **2**Then David called the
people of Israel together and said, "If you
think it is a good idea, and if it is what the
LORD our God wants, let's send a message. Let's tell our fellow Israelites in all the areas
of Israel and the
priests and Levites
living with them in
their towns and pas-
tures to come and
join us. **3**Let's bring the Ark of our God
back to us. We did not use it to ask God
for help while Saul was king." **4**All the
people agreed with David, because they
all thought it was the right thing to do.

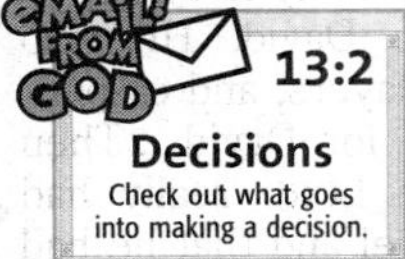

eMAIL! FROM GOD
13:2
Decisions
Check out what goes into making a decision.

5So David gathered all the Israelites,
from the Shihor River in Egypt to Lebo
Hamath, to bring the Ark of God back
from the town of Kiriath Jearim. **6**David
and all the Israelites with him went to
Baalah of Judah, which is Kiriath Jearim,
to get the Ark of God the LORD. God's
throne is between the golden, winged
creatures on the Ark, and the Ark is
called by his name.

7The people carried the Ark of God
from Abinadab's house on a new cart, and
Uzzah and Ahio guided it. **8**David and all
the Israelites were celebrating in the
presence of God. With all their strength
they were singing and playing lyres,

harps, tambourines, cymbals, and trumpets.
9When David's men came to the
threshing floor of Kidon, the oxen stumbled, and Uzzah reached out his hand to
steady the Ark. 10The LORD was angry
with Uzzah and killed him, because he
had touched the Ark. So Uzzah died there
in the presence of God.
11David was angry because the LORD
had punished Uzzah in his anger. Now
that place is called The Punishment of
Uzzah.
12David was afraid of God that day
and asked, "How can I bring the Ark of
God home to me?" 13So David did not
take the Ark with him to Jerusalem. Instead, he took it to the house of Obed-
Edom who was from Gath. 14The Ark of
God stayed with Obed-Edom's family in
his house for three months, and the LORD
blessed Obed-Edom's family and everything he owned.

David's Kingdom Grows

14 Hiram king of the city of Tyre sent
messengers to David. He also
sent cedar logs, bricklayers, and carpenters to build a palace for David. 2Then
David knew that the LORD really had
made him king of Israel and that he had
made his kingdom great. The LORD did
this because he loved his people Israel.
3David married more women in Jerusalem and had more sons and daughters.
4These are the names of David's children
born in Jerusalem: Shammua, Shobab,
Nathan, Solomon, 5Ibhar, Elishua, Elpe-
let, 6Nogah, Nepheg, Japhia, 7Elishama,
Beeliada, and Eliphelet.

FAITH links

PLAN FOR SUCCESS

1 CHRONICLES 14:8-17

Many successful business people write books or make videos about their success strategies. People buy these books to copy the success of these individuals. David, the king who defeated the Philistines, had a strategy for success. He didn't write a book about it, but you can still know his strategy. Here it is: seek God's wisdom; then do what he says. In other words, have faith in God. That's a strategy you can follow, too.

Choosing Sides, 1 Samuel 20, p. 382

A Wise Wish, 1 Kings 3:5–9, p. 439

The Wisdom of Obeying God, 1 Kings 11:1–13, p. 453

911, Psalm 28:6, p. 730

What God Thinks, Isaiah 55:8–9, p. 969

When We Agree, Matthew 18:19–20, p. 1306

David Defeats the Philistines

8When the Philistines heard that David had been made king of all Israel, they went to
look for him. But
David heard about it
and went out to fight
them. 9The Philis-
tines had attacked
and robbed the people in the Valley of
Rephaim. 10David asked God, "Should I
go and attack the Philistines? Will you
hand them over to me?"
The LORD answered him, "Go, I will
hand them over to you."
11So David and his men went up to
the town of Baal Perazim and defeated
the Philistines. David said, "Like a flood
of water, God has broken through my enemies by using me." So that place was

14:10
Trust
You can trust God to lead you.

named Baal Perazim." 12The Philistines
had left their idols there, so David ordered his men to burn them.

13Soon the Philistines attacked the
people in the valley again. 14David
prayed to God again, and God answered
him, saying, "Don't attack the Philistines
from the front. Instead, go around them
and attack them in front of the balsam
trees. 15When you hear the sound of
marching in the tops of the balsam trees,
then attack. I, God, will have gone out before you to defeat the Philistine army."
16David did as God commanded, and he
and his men defeated the Philistine army
all the way from Gibeon to Gezer.

17So David became famous in all the
countries, and the LORD made all nations
afraid of him.

The Ark Is Brought to Jerusalem

15 David built houses for himself in
Jerusalem. Then he prepared a
place for the Ark of God, and he set up a
tent for it. 2David said,
"Only the Levites may
carry the Ark of God. The
LORD chose them to carry
the Ark of the LORD and
to serve him forever."

3David called all the
people of Israel to come
to Jerusalem. He wanted
to bring the Ark of the
LORD to the place he had
made for it. 4David called
together the descendants of Aaron and
the Levites. 5There were one hundred
twenty people from Kohath's family
group, with Uriel as their leader. 6There
were two hundred twenty people from
Merari's family group, with Asaiah as
their leader. 7There were one hundred
thirty people from Gershon's family
group, with Joel as their leader. 8There
were two hundred people from Elizaphan's family group, with Shemaiah as
their leader. 9There were eighty people
from Hebron's family group, with Eliel as
their leader. 10And there were one hundred twelve people from Uzziel's family
group, with Amminadab as their leader.

11Then David asked the priests Zadok and Abiathar and these Levites to
come to him: Uriel, Asaiah, Joel, Shemaiah, Eliel, and Amminadab. 12David said
to them, "You are the leaders of the families of Levi. You and the other Levites
must give yourselves for service to the
LORD. Bring up the Ark of the LORD, the
God of Israel, to the place I have made
for it. 13The last time we did not ask
the LORD how to carry it. You Levites
didn't carry it, so the LORD our God punished us."

14Then the priests and Levites prepared themselves for service to the LORD
so they could carry the Ark of the LORD,
the God of Israel. 15The Levites used
special poles to carry the Ark of God on
their shoulders, as Moses had commanded, just as the LORD had said they
should.

16David told the leaders of the Levites to appoint their brothers as singers
to play their lyres, harps, and cymbals
and to sing happy songs.

17So the Levites ap-
pointed Heman and his
relatives Asaph and
Ethan. Heman was Joel's
son. Asaph was Bere-
kiah's son. And Ethan,
from the Merari family
group, was Kushaiah's
son. 18There was also a
second group of Levites:
Zechariah, Jaaziel, She-
miramoth, Jehiel, Unni,
Eliab, Benaiah, Maaseiah, Mattithiah,
Eliphelehu, Mikneiah, Obed-Edom, and
Jeiel. They were the Levite guards.

19The singers Heman, Asaph, and
Ethan played bronze cymbals. 20Zecha-
riah, Jaaziel, Shemiramoth, Jehiel, Unni,
Eliab, Maaseiah, and Benaiah played the
lyres. 21Mattithiah, Eliphelehu, Mikneiah, Obed-Edom, Jeiel, and Azaziah
played the harps. 22The Levite leader
Kenaniah was in charge of the singing,
because he was very good at it.

23Berekiah and Elkanah were two of
the guards for the Ark of the Agreement.

> David said, "Only the Levites may carry the Ark of God. The LORD chose them to carry the Ark of the LORD and to serve him forever."
> —1 Chronicles 15:2

14:11 Baal Perazim This name means "the Lord breaks through."

24The priests Shebaniah, Joshaphat, Nethanel, Amasai, Zechariah, Benaiah,
and Eliezer had the job of blowing trumpets in front of the Ark of God. Obed-
Edom and Jehiah were also guards for
the Ark.
25David, the leaders of Israel, and the
commanders of a thousand soldiers went
to get the Ark of the Agreement with the
LORD. They all went to bring the Ark
from Obed-Edom's house with great joy.
26Because God helped the Levites who
carried the Ark of the Agreement with
the LORD, they sacrificed seven bulls and
seven male sheep. 27All the Levites who
carried the Ark, and Kenaniah, the man
in charge of the singing, and all the singers wore robes of fine linen. David also
wore a robe of fine linen and a holy vest of
fine linen. 28So all the people of Israel
brought up the Ark of the Agreement
with the LORD. They shouted, blew
horns and trumpets, and played cymbals,
lyres, and harps.
29As the Ark of the Agreement with
the LORD entered Jerusalem, Saul's
daughter Michal watched from a window.
When she saw King David dancing and
celebrating, she hated him.

16 They brought the Ark of God and
put it inside the tent that David
had set up for it. Then they offered burnt
offerings and fellowship offerings to God.
2When David had finished giving the
burnt offerings and fellowship offerings,
he blessed the people in the name of the
LORD. 3He gave a loaf of bread, some
dates, and raisins to every
Israelite man and
woman.
4Then David ap-
pointed some of the
Levites to serve be-
fore the Ark of the
LORD. They had the job of leading the
worship and giving thanks and praising
the LORD, the God of Israel. 5Asaph, who
played the cymbals, was the leader. Zechariah was second to him. The other Levites were Jaaziel, Shemiramoth, Jehiel,
Mattithiah, Eliab, Benaiah, Obed-Edom,
and Jeiel. They played the lyres and harps.
6Benaiah and Jahaziel were priests who
blew the trumpets regularly before the
Ark of the Agreement with God. 7That
day David first gave Asaph and his relatives the job of singing praises to the
LORD.

EMAIL FROM GOD
16:4–36
Thankfulness
A song of thanks!

David's Song of Thanks

8 Give thanks to the LORD and pray to
him.
Tell the nations what he has done.
9 Sing to him; sing praises to him.
Tell about all his miracles.
10 Be glad that you are his;
let those who seek the LORD be
happy.
11 Depend on the LORD and his
strength;
always go to him for help.
12 Remember the miracles he has done,
his wonders, and his decisions.
13 You are the descendants of his
servant, Israel;
you are the children of Jacob, his
chosen people.

14 He is the LORD our God.
His laws are for all the world.
15 He will keep his agreement forever;
he will keep his promises always.
16 He will keep the agreement he made
with Abraham
and the promise he made to Isaac.
17 He made it a law for the people of
Jacob;
he made it an agreement with
Israel to last forever.
18 He said, "I will give the land of
Canaan to you,
to belong to you."

19 Then God's people were few in
number,
and they were strangers in the
land.
20 They went from one nation to
another,
from one kingdom to another.
21 But he did not let anyone hurt them;
he warned kings not to harm
them.
22 He said, "Don't touch my chosen
people,
and don't harm my prophets."

23 Sing to the LORD, all the earth.
Every day tell how he saves us.
24 Tell the nations about his glory;
tell all peoples the miracles he
does.
25 The LORD is great; he should be
praised.
He should be respected more than
all the gods.
26 All the gods of the nations are only
idols,
but the LORD made the skies.
27 He has glory and majesty;
he has power and joy in his
Temple.

28 Praise the LORD, all nations on earth.
Praise the LORD's glory and
power;
29 praise the glory of the LORD's
name.
Bring an offering and come to him.
Worship the LORD because he is
holy.
30 Tremble before him, everyone on
earth.
The earth is set, and it cannot be
moved.
31 Let the skies rejoice and the earth be
glad.
Let people everywhere say, "The
LORD is king!"
32 Let the sea and everything in it
shout;
let the fields and everything in
them rejoice.
33 Then the trees of the forest will sing
for joy before the LORD.
They will sing because he is
coming to judge the world.

34 Thank the LORD because he is good.
His love continues forever.
35 Say to him, "Save us, God our Savior,
and bring us back and save us from
other nations.
Then we will thank you
and will gladly praise you."
36 Praise the LORD, the God of Israel.
He always was and always will be.
All the people said "Amen" and praised
the LORD.

37Then David left Asaph and the other
Levites there in front of the Ark of the
Agreement with the LORD. They were to
serve there every day. **38**David also left
Obed-Edom and sixty-eight other Levites
to serve with them. Hosah and Obed-
Edom son of Jeduthun were guards.

39David left Zadok the priest and the
other priests who served with him in
front of the Tent of the LORD at the place
of worship in Gibeon. **40**Every morning
and evening they offered burnt offerings
on the altar of burnt offerings, following
the rules written in the Teachings of the
LORD, which he had given Israel. **41**With
them were Heman and Jeduthun and
other Levites. They were chosen by
name to sing praises to the LORD because
his love continues forever. **42**Heman and
Jeduthun also had the job of playing the
trumpets and cymbals and other musical
instruments when songs were sung to
God. Jeduthun's sons guarded the gates.

43Then all the people left. Each person went home, and David also went
home to bless the people in his home.

God's Promise to David

17 When David moved into his palace, he said to Nathan the prophet,
"Look, I am living in a palace made of cedar, but the Ark of the Agreement with
the LORD sits in a tent."

2Nathan said to David, "Do what you
want to do, because God is with you."

3But that night God spoke his word to
Nathan, saying, **4**"Go and tell David my
servant, 'This is what the LORD says: You
are not the person to build a house for me
to live in. **5**From the time I brought Israel
out of Egypt until now I have not lived in
a house. I have moved from one tent site
to another and from one place to another.
6As I have moved with the Israelites to
different places, I have never said to the
leaders, whom I commanded to take care
of my people, "Why haven't you built me
a house of cedar?" '

7"Now, tell my servant David: 'This is
what the LORD All-Powerful says: I took
you from the pasture and from tending
the sheep and made you king of my people Israel. **8**I have been with you everywhere you have gone. I have defeated

A MAN AFTER GOD'S OWN HEART

1 Chronicles 17

1. David was born in Bethlehem, the youngest of Jesse's eight sons. David was given the job of caring for the family sheep. (Look at 1 Samuel 17:12–15, p. 376.)

2. As a boy, David helped the army of Israel defeat the Philistines when he killed the giant Goliath with a slingshot in the Valley of Elah. (Catch all the details of this familiar story in 1 Samuel 17:19–50, p. 376.)

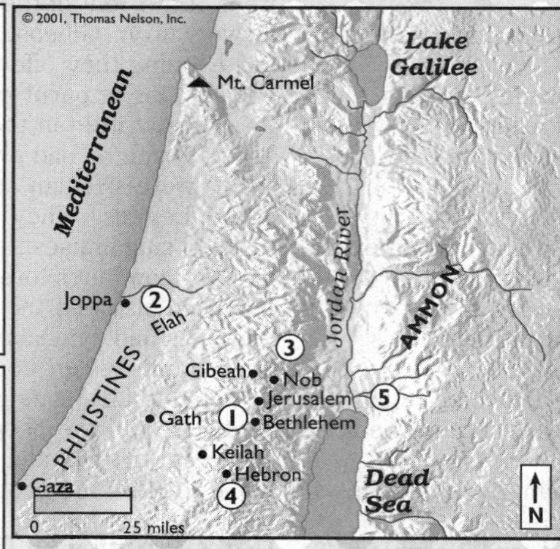

3. David became a popular and successful warrior for King Saul. Saul, though, was jealous of David's success and began a campaign to have David killed. David was forced to run and hide in the hill country from his enemy, Saul. (Follow David's chase in 1 Samuel 19:1—23:29, p. 380.)

4. After Saul's death, David became the king of Judah. He made his first capital at Hebron. (Read 2 Samuel 2:1–4, p. 400.)

5. After defeating his enemies, David united the tribes of Israel and Judah and made Jerusalem his capital. (See 2 Samuel 5:1–5, p. 404.)

your enemies for you. I will make you as
famous as any of the great people on the
earth. **9**I will choose a place for my people Israel, and I will plant them so they
can live in their own homes. They will
not be bothered anymore. Wicked people
will no longer hurt them as they have in
the past **10**when I chose judges for my
people Israel. I will defeat all your enemies.

"'I tell you that the LORD will make
your descendants kings of Israel after
you. **11**When you die and join your ancestors, I will make one of your sons the new
king, and I will set up his kingdom. **12**He
will build a house for me, and I will let his
kingdom rule always. **13**I will be his father, and he will be my son. I took away
my love from Saul, who ruled before you,
but I will never stop loving your son. **14**I
will put him in charge of my house and
kingdom forever. His family will rule forever.'"

15Nathan told David everything God
had said in this vision.

David Prays to God

16Then King David went in and sat in
front of the LORD. David said, "LORD
God, who am I? What is my family? Why
did you bring me to this point? **17**But that
was not enough for you, God. You have

also made promises about my future family. LORD God, you have treated me like a
very important person.
18"What more can I say to you for
honoring me, your servant? You know
me so well. 19LORD, you have done this
wonderful thing for my sake and because
you wanted to. You have made known all
these great things.
20"There is no one like you, LORD.
There is no God except you. We have
heard all this ourselves! 21There is no
nation like your people Israel. They are
the only people on earth that God chose
to be his own. You made your name well
known by the great and wonderful things
you did for them. You went ahead of them
and forced other nations out of the land.
You freed your people from slavery in
Egypt. 22You made the people of Israel
your very own people forever, and, LORD,
you are their God.
23"LORD, keep the promise forever
that you made about my family and me,
your servant. Do what you have said.
24Then you will be honored always, and
people will say, 'The LORD All-Powerful,
the God over Israel, is Israel's God!' And
the family of your servant David will continue before you.
25"My God, you have told me that you
would make my family great. So I, your
servant, am brave enough to pray to you.
26LORD, you are God, and you have
promised these
good things to me,
your servant. 27You
have chosen to bless
my family. Let it
continue before you
always. LORD, you
have blessed my family, so it will always
be blessed."

eMAIL FROM GOD
17:26–27
Trust
You can count on this!

David Defeats Nations

18 Later, David defeated the Philistines, conquered them, and took
the city of Gath and the small towns
around it.
2He also defeated the people of Moab.
So the people of Moab became servants
of David and gave him the payment he
demanded.
3David also defeated Hadadezer king
of Zobah all the way to the town of Hamath as he tried to spread his kingdom to
the Euphrates River. 4David captured
one thousand of his chariots, seven thousand men who rode in chariots, and twenty thousand foot soldiers. He crippled all
but a hundred of the chariot horses.
5Arameans from Damascus came to
help Hadadezer king of Zobah, but David
killed twenty-two thousand of them.
6Then David put groups of soldiers in
Damascus in Aram. The Arameans became David's servants and gave him the
payments he demanded. So the LORD
gave David victory everywhere he went.
7David took the shields of gold that
had belonged to Hadadezer's officers and
brought them to Jerusalem. 8David also
took many things made of bronze from
Tebah and Cun, which had been cities under Hadadezer's control. Later, Solomon
used this bronze to make things for the
Temple: the large bronze bowl, which
was called the Sea, the pillars, and other
bronze utensils.
9Toi king of Hamath heard that David
had defeated all the army of Hadadezer
king of Zobah. 10So Toi sent his son Hadoram to greet and congratulate King
David for defeating Hadadezer. (Hadadezer had been at war with Toi.) Hadoram
brought items made of gold, silver, and
bronze. 11King David gave them to the
LORD, along with the silver and gold he
had taken from these nations: Edom,
Moab, the Ammonites, the Philistines,
and Amalek.
12Abishai son of Zeruiah killed eighteen thousand Edomites in the Valley of
Salt. 13David put groups of soldiers in
Edom, and all the Edomites became his
servants. The LORD gave David victory
everywhere he went.

David's Important Officers

14David was king over all of Israel,
and he did what was fair and right for all
his people. 15Joab son of Zeruiah was
commander over the army. Jehoshaphat
son of Ahilud was the recorder. 16Zadok
son of Ahitub and Abiathar son of Ahimelech were priests. Shavsha was the royal

secretary. 17Benaiah son of Jehoiada was over the Kerethites and Pelethites.* And David's sons were important officers who served at his side.

War with the Ammonites and Arameans

19 When Nahash king of the Ammonites died, his son became king after him. 2David said, "Nahash was loyal to me, so I will be loyal to his son Hanun." So David sent messengers to comfort Hanun about his father's death.

David's officers went to the land of the Ammonites to comfort Hanun. 3But the Ammonite leaders said to Hanun, "Do you think David wants to honor your father by sending men to comfort you? No! David sent them to study the land and capture it and spy it out." 4So Hanun arrested David's officers. To shame them he shaved their beards and cut off their clothes at the hips. Then he sent them away.

5When the people told David what had happened to his officers, he sent messengers to meet them, because they were very ashamed. King David said, "Stay in Jericho until your beards have grown back. Then come home."

6The Ammonites knew that they had insulted David. So Hanun and the Ammonites sent about seventy-four thousand pounds of silver to hire chariots and chariot drivers from Northwest Mesopotamia, Aram Maacah, and Zobah. 7The Ammonites hired thirty-two thousand chariots and the king of Maacah and his army. So they came and set up camp near the town of Medeba. The Ammonites themselves came out of their towns and got ready for battle.

8When David heard about this, he sent Joab with the whole army. 9The Ammonites came out and prepared for battle at the city gate. The kings who had come to help were out in the field by themselves.

10Joab saw that there were enemies both in front of him and behind him. So he chose some of the best soldiers of Israel and sent them out to fight the Arameans. 11Joab put the rest of the army under the command of Abishai, his brother. Then they went out to fight the Ammonites. 12Joab said to Abishai, "If the Arameans are too strong for me, you must help me. Or, if the Ammonites are too strong for you, I will help you. 13Be strong. We must fight bravely for our people and the cities of our God. The LORD will do what he thinks is right."

Be strong. We must fight bravely for our people and the cities of our God. The LORD will do what he thinks is right.
—1 Chronicles 19:13

14Then Joab and the army with him went to attack the Arameans, and the Arameans ran away. 15When the Ammonites saw that the Arameans were running away, they also ran away from Joab's brother Abishai and went back to their city. So Joab went back to Jerusalem.

16When the Arameans saw that Israel had defeated them, they sent messengers to bring other Arameans from east of the Euphrates River. Their leader was Shophach, the commander of Hadadezer's army.

17When David heard about this, he gathered all the Israelites, and they crossed over the Jordan River. He prepared them for battle, facing the Arameans. The Arameans fought with him, 18but they ran away from the Israelites. David killed seven thousand Aramean chariot drivers and forty thousand Aramean foot soldiers. He also killed Shophach, the commander of the Aramean army.

19When those who served Hadadezer saw that the Israelites had defeated them, they made peace with David and served him. So the Arameans refused to help the Ammonites again.

18:17 Kerethites and Pelethites These were probably special units of the army that were responsible for the king's safety, a kind of palace guard.

Joab Destroys the Ammonites

20 In the spring, the time of year when
kings normally went out to battle,
Joab led out the army of Israel. But David
stayed in Jerusalem. The army of Israel
destroyed the land of Ammon and went
to the city of Rabbah and attacked it. 2Da-
vid took the crown off the head of their
king,* and had it placed on his own head.
That gold crown weighed about seventy-
five pounds, and it had valuable gems in
it. And David took many valuable things
from the city. 3He also brought out the
people of the city and forced them to
work with saws, iron picks, and axes. David did this to all the Ammonite cities.
Then David and all his army returned to
Jerusalem.

Philistine Giants Are Killed

4Later, at Gezer, war broke out with
the Philistines. Sibbecai the Hushathite
killed Sippai, who was one of the descendants of the Rephaites. So those Philistines were defeated.

5Later, there was another battle with
the Philistines. Elhanan son of Jair killed
Lahmi, the brother of Goliath, who was
from the town of Gath. His spear was as
large as a weaver's rod.

6At Gath another battle took place. A
huge man was there; he had six fingers
on each hand and six toes on each foot—
twenty-four fingers and toes in all. This
man also was one of the sons of Rapha.
7When he spoke against Israel, Jonathan
son of Shimea, David's brother, killed
him.

8These descendants of Rapha from
Gath were killed by David and his men.

David Counts the Israelites

21 Satan was against Israel, and he
caused David to count the people
of Israel. 2So David said to Joab and the
commanders of the troops, "Go and count
all the Israelites from Beersheba to Dan.*
Then tell me so I will know how many
there are."

3But Joab said, "May the LORD give
the nation a hundred times more people.
My master the king, all the Israelites are
your servants. Why do you want to do
this, my master? You will make Israel
guilty of sin."

4But the king commanded Joab, so
Joab left and went through all Israel. Then
he returned to Jerusalem. 5Joab gave the
list of the people to David. There were
one million one hundred thousand men
in all of Israel who could use the sword,
and there were four hundred seventy

FAITH CHALLENGE

Hey there! Read 21:8 to find out what King David did after he disobeyed God. What do you do after you know you've done something wrong—either to your brother or sister, your parents, or God?

TESTING IT

1 Chronicles 21:8
Then David said to God, "I have sinned greatly by what I have done! Now, I beg you to forgive me, your servant, because I have been very foolish."

20:2 their king Or, "Milcom," the god of the Ammonite people.

21:2 Beersheba to Dan Beersheba was the city farthest south in Israel. Dan was the city farthest north. So this means all the people of Israel.

thousand men in Judah who could use the sword. **6**But Joab did not count the tribes of Levi and Benjamin, because he didn't like King David's order. **7**David had done something God had said was wrong, so God punished Israel.

8Then David said to God, "I have sinned greatly by what I have done! Now, I beg you to forgive me, your servant, because I have been very foolish."

9The LORD said to Gad, who was David's seer, **10**"Go and tell David, 'This is what the LORD says: I offer you three choices. Choose one of them and I will do it.' "

11So Gad went to David and said to him, "This is what the LORD says: 'Choose for yourself **12**three years of hunger. Or choose three months of running from your enemies as they chase you with their swords. Or choose three days of punishment from the LORD, in which a terrible disease will spread through the country. The angel of the LORD will go through Israel destroying the people.' Now, David, decide which of these things I should tell the LORD who sent me."

13David said to Gad, "I am in great trouble. Let the LORD punish me, because the LORD is very merciful. Don't let my punishment come from human beings."

14So the LORD sent a terrible disease on Israel, and seventy thousand people died. **15**God sent an angel to destroy Jerusalem, but when the angel started to destroy it, the LORD saw it and felt very sorry about the terrible things that had happened. So he said to the angel who was destroying, "That is enough! Put down your arm!" The angel of the LORD was then standing at the threshing floor of Araunah the Jebusite.

16David looked up and saw the angel of the LORD in the sky, holding his sword drawn and pointed at Jerusalem. Then David and the older leaders bowed facedown on the ground. They were wearing rough cloth to show their grief. **17**David said to God, "I am the one who sinned and did wrong. I gave the order for the people to be counted. These people only followed me like sheep. They did nothing wrong. LORD my God, please punish me and my family, but stop the terrible disease that is killing your people."

18Then the angel of the LORD told Gad to tell David that he should build an altar to the LORD on the threshing floor of Araunah the Jebusite. **19**So David did what Gad told him to do, in the name of the LORD.

20Araunah was separating the wheat from the straw. When he turned around, he saw the angel. Araunah's four sons who were with him hid. **21**David came to Araunah, and when Araunah saw him, he left the threshing floor and bowed facedown on the ground before David.

22David said to him, "Sell me your threshing floor so I can build an altar to the LORD here. Then the terrible disease will stop. Sell it to me for the full price."

23Araunah said to David, "Take this threshing floor. My master the king, do anything you want. Look, I will also give you oxen for the whole burnt offerings, the threshing boards for the wood, and wheat for the grain offering. I give everything to you."

24But King David answered Araunah, "No, I will pay the full price for the land. I won't take anything that is yours and give it to the LORD. I won't offer a burnt offering that costs me nothing."

25So David paid Araunah about fifteen pounds of gold for the place. **26**David built an altar to the LORD there and offered whole burnt offerings and fellowship offerings. David prayed to the LORD, and he answered him by sending down fire from heaven on the altar of burnt offering. **27**Then the LORD commanded the angel to put his sword back into its holder.

28When David saw that the LORD had answered him on the threshing floor of Araunah, he offered sacrifices there. **29**The Holy Tent that Moses made while the Israelites were in the desert and the altar of burnt offerings were in Gibeon at the place of worship. **30**But David could not go to the Holy Tent to speak with God, because he was afraid of the angel of the LORD and his sword.

A SPECIAL ANGEL 1 CHRONICLES 21:6–22

In the Old Testament, the angel of the Lord is a mysterious messenger of God. God used this angel to appear to human beings who would not be able to see him and live. The angel of the Lord accomplished God's work. Sometimes that work was revelation (giving a message), or deliverance, or even judgment. The angel of the Lord was a special angel, like the other angels, but responsible for more.

In the Old Testament, the angel of the Lord appeared to many people. Check out the chart below for some special sightings of how the angel of the Lord helped different people in the Bible:

Abraham	Prevented Abraham from sacrificing his son Isaac	Genesis 22:11–13, p. 29
Jacob	Wrestled with Jacob through the night and blessed him at daybreak	Genesis 32:24–30, p. 46
Moses	Spoke to Moses from the burning bush, promising to deliver the Israelites from enslavement	Exodus 3:1–8, p. 79
Israelites	Protected them from the pursuing Egyptian army	Exodus 14:19–20, p. 94
Balaam	Blocked Balaam's path, then sent him to deliver a message to Balak	Numbers 22:22–35, p. 206
Joshua	Reassured Joshua in his role as commander of the Lord's people	Joshua 5:13—6:5, p. 282
Gideon	Commissioned Gideon to fight against the Midianites	Judges 6:11–24, p. 318
Elijah	Provided food for Elijah in the wilderness	1 Kings 19:4–8, p. 466
David	Appeared to David at the threshing floor of Araunah, where David built an altar	1 Chronicles 21:16–27, p. 546
Three Hebrew Men	Protected them in Nebuchadnezzar's fiery furnace	Daniel 3:25, p. 1155

22 David said, "The Temple of the
LORD God and the altar for Israel's
burnt offerings will be built here."

David Makes Plans for the Temple

2So David ordered all foreigners living in Israel to gather together. From that
group David chose stonecutters to cut
stones to be used in building the Temple
of God. 3David supplied a large amount of
iron to be used for making nails and
hinges for the gate doors. He also supplied more bronze than could be weighed,
4and he supplied more cedar logs than
could be counted. Much of the cedar had
been brought to David by the people from
Sidon and Tyre.
5David said, "We should build a great
Temple for the LORD, which will be famous everywhere for its greatness and
beauty. But my son Solomon is young. He
hasn't yet learned what he needs to
know, so I will prepare for the building of
it." So David got many of the materials
ready before he died.
6Then David called for his son Solomon and told him to build the Temple for
the LORD, the God of Israel. 7David said
to him, "My son, I wanted to build a temple for worshiping the LORD my God.
8But the LORD spoke his word to me,
'David, you have killed many people. You
have fought many wars. You cannot build
a temple for worship to me, because you
have killed many people. 9But, you will
have a son, a man of peace and rest. I will
give him rest from all his enemies around
him. His name will be Solomon," and I
will give Israel peace and quiet while he
is king. 10Solomon will build a temple for
worship to me. He will be my son, and I
will be his father. I will make his kingdom
strong; someone from his family will rule
Israel forever.' "
11David said, "Now, my son, may the
LORD be with you. May you build a temple for the LORD your God, as he said you
would. 12He will make you the king of Israel. May the LORD give you wisdom and
understanding so you will be able to obey
the teachings of the LORD your God.
13Be careful to obey the rules and laws

FAITH links

PLANS FOR A SON

1 CHRONICLES 22:5-19

David wanted to help his son honor God by building a Temple. He gathered the materials necessary and told the Israelite leaders to be ready to help Solomon.

Have you noticed lately what your mom or dad does to help you follow God? Maybe he yanks the covers off of your head on Sundays to encourage you to get ready for church. Maybe she insists that you say your memory verse in front of Aunt Martha. They do things like this to make sure you live a life that honors God. That makes your mom or dad pretty special, huh?

Check out these other Faithlinks on obeying your parents:

Reward for Obedience, Leviticus 26:3–13, p. 171

A Look for the Book, 2 Chronicles 34:14–18, p. 603

All Talk, No Action, Jeremiah 5:1–2, p. 996

Just Say Yes!, Matthew 9:9–13, p. 1289

The Number One Rule, Mark 12:28–31, p. 1351

Glad to Help!, Romans 15:17–20, p. 1541

22:9 Solomon This name sounds like the Hebrew word for "peace."

the LORD gave Moses for Israel. If you
obey them, you will have success. Be
strong and brave. Don't be afraid or discouraged.
14"Solomon, I have worked hard getting many of the materials for building
the Temple of the LORD. I have supplied
about seven and one-half million pounds
of gold, about seventy-five million
pounds of silver, so much bronze and iron
it cannot be weighed, and wood and
stone. You may add to them. 15You have
many workmen—stonecutters, bricklayers, carpenters, and people skilled in
every kind of work. 16They are skilled in
working with gold, silver, bronze, and
iron. You have more craftsmen than can
be counted. Now begin the work, and
may the LORD be with you."
17Then David ordered all the leaders
of Israel to help his son Solomon. 18Da-
vid said to them, "The LORD your God is
with you. He has given you rest from our
enemies. He has handed over to me the
people living around us. The LORD and
his people are in control of this land.
19Now give yourselves completely to
obeying the LORD your God. Build the
holy place of the LORD God; build the
Temple for worship to the LORD. Then
bring the Ark of the Agreement with the
LORD and the holy items that belong to
God into the Temple."

The Levites

23 After David had lived long and was
old, he made his son Solomon the
new king of Israel. 2David
gathered all the leaders of
Israel, along with the
priests and Levites. 3He
counted the Levites who
were thirty years old and
older. In all, there were
thirty-eight thousand Le-
vites. 4David said, "Of
these, twenty-four thou-
sand Levites will direct
the work of the Temple of
the LORD, six thousand Levites will be officers and judges, 5four thousand Levites
will be gatekeepers, and four thousand
Levites will praise the LORD with musical
instruments I made for giving praise."
6David separated the Levites into
three groups that were led by Levi's three
sons: Gershon, Kohath, and Merari.

> After David had lived long and was old, he made his son Solomon the new king of Israel.
> —1 Chronicles 23:1

The People of Gershon

7From the people of Gershon, there
were Ladan and Shimei.
8Ladan had three sons. His first son
was Jehiel, and his other sons were Zetham and Joel.
9Shimei's sons were Shelomoth, Haziel, and Haran. These three sons were
leaders of Ladan's families. 10Shimei had
four sons: Jahath, Ziza, Jeush, and Beriah.
11Jahath was the first son, and Ziza was
the second son. But Jeush and Beriah did
not have many children, so they were
counted as if they were one family.

The People of Kohath

12Kohath had four sons: Amram, Izhar, Hebron, and Uzziel.
13Amram's sons were Aaron and Moses. Aaron and his descendants were
chosen to be special forever. They were
chosen to prepare the holy things for the
LORD's service, to offer sacrifices before
the LORD, and to serve him as priests.
They were to give blessings in his name
forever.
14Moses was the man of God, and his
sons were counted as part of the tribe of
Levi. 15Moses' sons were Gershom and
Eliezer. 16Gershom's first son was Shubael. 17Eliezer's first son was Rehabiah.
Eliezer had no other sons, but Rehabiah
had many sons.
18Izhar's first son was
Shelomith.
19Hebron's first son
was Jeriah, his second was
Amariah, his third was Jahaziel, and his fourth was
Jekameam.
20Uzziel's first son
was Micah and his second
was Isshiah.

The People of Merari

21Merari's sons were Mahli and Mushi. Mahli's sons were Eleazar and Kish.
22Eleazar died without sons; he had only

daughters. Eleazar's daughters married
their cousins, the sons of Kish. 23Mushi's
three sons were Mahli, Eder, and Jerimoth.

The Levites' Work

24These were Levi's descendants
listed by their families. They were the
leaders of families. Each person who was
twenty years old or older was listed.
They served in the LORD's Temple.

25David had said, "The LORD, the God
of Israel, has given rest to his people. He
has come to live in Jerusalem forever.
26So the Levites don't need to carry the
Holy Tent or any of the things used in its
services anymore." 27David's last instructions were to count the Levites who
were twenty years old and older.

28The Levites had the job of helping
Aaron's descendants in the service of the
Temple of the LORD. They cared for the
Temple courtyard and side rooms, and
they made all the holy things pure. Their
job was to serve in the Temple of God.
29They were responsible for putting the
holy bread on the table, for the flour in
the grain offerings, for the bread made
without yeast, for the baking and mixing,
and for the measuring. 30The Levites
also stood every morning and gave
thanks and praise to the LORD. They also

CONNECT 2-YOU
LIFE AFTER LIFE
Tagg and I have a friend who has a question that at one time or another we've all probably wondered about. Please welcome Joel, age 9, to Connect 2-You.
Joel
Hi, Joel. What's your question?
My grandmother died last month, and I miss her a lot. She was the first person who ever told me about Jesus. She was also the nicest person in the world. I don't understand why God let her die. Can you tell me?
It's natural for you to have these questions, Joel. Your grandmother sounds like a very special person. We can't tell you why God let her die, but we can tell you that you won't be separated from her forever. Death is just the beginning for people who believe in Christ. We will be resurrected (raised up) to live forever with God.
That doesn't mean you won't miss your grandmother here on earth. It's natural to feel grief. But if you know that you will see her again someday, the grief isn't quite as bad. If you'd like to learn more about dealing with the death of a loved one, check out the Livin' It page on death, 1 Corinthians 15:50-57, p. 1564.

did this every evening. 31The Levites offered all the burnt offerings to the LORD
on the special days of rest, at the New
Moon festivals, and at all appointed
feasts. They served before the LORD
every day. They were to follow the rules
for how many Levites should serve each
time. 32So the Levites took care of the
Meeting Tent and the Holy Place. And
they helped their relatives, Aaron's descendants, with the services at the Temple of the LORD.

The Groups of the Priests

24 These were the groups of Aaron's
sons: Aaron's sons were Nadab,
Abihu, Eleazar, and Ithamar. 2But Nadab
and Abihu died before their father did,
and they had no sons. So Eleazar and Ithamar served as the priests. 3David, with
the help of Zadok, a descendant of Eleazar, and Ahimelech, a descendant of Ithamar, separated their family groups into
two different groups. Each group had certain duties. 4There were more leaders
from Eleazar's family than from Ithamar's—sixteen leaders from Eleazar's
family and eight leaders from Ithamar's
family. 5Men were chosen from Eleazar's
and Ithamar's families by throwing lots.
Some men from each family were chosen
to be in charge of the Holy Place, and
some were chosen to serve as priests.

6Shemaiah son of Nethanel, from the
tribe of Levi, was the secretary. He recorded the names of those descendants
in front of King David, the officers, Zadok
the priest, Ahimelech son of Abiathar,
and the leaders of the families of the
priests and Levites. The work was divided by lots among the families of Eleazar
and Ithamar. The following men with
their groups were chosen.

7The first one chosen was Jehoiarib.
The second was Jedaiah. 8The third was
Harim. The fourth was Seorim. 9The
fifth was Malkijah. The sixth was Mijamin. 10The seventh was Hakkoz. The
eighth was Abijah. 11The ninth was Jeshua. The tenth was Shecaniah. 12The
eleventh was Eliashib. The twelfth was
Jakim. 13The thirteenth was Huppah.
The fourteenth was Jeshebeab. 14The fifteenth was Bilgah. The sixteenth was
Immer. 15The seventeenth was Hezir.
The eighteenth was Happizzez. 16The
nineteenth was Pethahiah. The twentieth
was Jehezkel. 17The twenty-first was Jakin. The twenty-second was Gamul.
18The twenty-third was Delaiah. The
twenty-fourth was Maaziah.

19These were the groups chosen to
serve in the Temple of the LORD. They
obeyed the rules given them by Aaron,
just as the LORD, the God of Israel, had
commanded him.

The Other Levites

20These are the names of the rest of
Levi's descendants:

Shubael was a descendant of Amram,
and Jehdeiah was a descendant of Shubael.

21Isshiah was the first son of Rehabiah.

22From the Izhar family group, there
was Shelomoth, and Jahath was a descendant of Shelomoth.

23Hebron's first son was Jeriah, Amariah was his second, Jahaziel was his
third, and Jekameam was his fourth.

24Uzziel's son was Micah. Micah's
son was Shamir. 25Micah's brother was
Isshiah, and Isshiah's son was Zechariah.

26Merari's descendants were Mahli
and Mushi. Merari's son was Jaaziah.
27Jaaziah son of Merari had sons named
Shoham, Zaccur, and Ibri. 28Mahli's son
was Eleazar, but Eleazar did not have any
sons.

29Kish's son was Jerahmeel.

30Mushi's sons were Mahli, Eder, and
Jerimoth.

These are the Levites, listed by their
families. 31They were chosen for special
jobs by throwing lots in front of King David, Zadok, Ahimelech, the leaders of the
families of the priests, and the Levites.
They did this just as their relatives, the
priests, Aaron's descendants, had done.
The families of the oldest brother and the
youngest brother were treated the same.

The Music Groups

25 David and the commanders of the
army chose some of the sons of

Asaph, Heman, and Jeduthun to preach
and play harps, lyres, and cymbals. Here
is a list of the men who served in this
way:
2Asaph's sons who served were Zaccur, Joseph, Nethaniah, and Asarelah.
King David chose Asaph to preach, and
Asaph directed his sons.
3Jeduthun's sons who served were
Gedaliah, Zeri, Jeshaiah, Shimei, Hashabiah, and Mattithiah. There were six of
them, and Jeduthun directed them. He
preached and used a harp to give thanks
and praise to the LORD.
4Heman's sons who served were
Bukkiah, Mattaniah, Uzziel, Shubael, Jerimoth, Hananiah, Hanani, Eliathah, Giddalti, Romamti-Ezer, Joshbekashah, Mallothi, Hothir, and Mahazioth. 5All these
were sons of Heman, David's seer. God
promised to make Heman strong, so Heman had many sons. God gave him fourteen sons and three daughters. 6Heman
directed all his sons in making music for
the Temple of the LORD with cymbals,
lyres, and harps; that was their way of
serving in the Temple of
God. King David was in
charge of Asaph, Jedu-
thun, and Heman. 7These
men and their relatives
were trained and skilled
in making music for the
LORD. There were two
hundred eighty-eight of
them. 8Everyone threw
lots to choose the time his
family was to serve at the
Temple. The young and
the old, the teacher and the student, had
to throw lots.

> These men and their relatives were trained and skilled in making music for the LORD.
> —1 Chronicles 25:7

9First, the lot fell to Joseph, from the
family of Asaph.
Second, twelve men were chosen
from Gedaliah, his sons and relatives.
10Third, twelve men were chosen
from Zaccur, his sons and relatives.
11Fourth, twelve men were chosen
from Izri, his sons and relatives.
12Fifth, twelve men were chosen
from Nethaniah, his sons and relatives.
13Sixth, twelve men were chosen
from Bukkiah, his sons and relatives.
14Seventh, twelve men were chosen
from Jesarelah, his sons and relatives.
15Eighth, twelve men were chosen
from Jeshaiah, his sons and relatives.
16Ninth, twelve men were chosen
from Mattaniah, his sons and relatives.
17Tenth, twelve men were chosen
from Shimei, his sons and relatives.
18Eleventh, twelve men were chosen
from Azarel, his sons and relatives.
19Twelfth, twelve men were chosen
from Hashabiah, his sons and relatives.
20Thirteenth, twelve men were chosen from Shubael, his sons and relatives.
21Fourteenth, twelve men were chosen from Mattithiah, his sons and relatives.
22Fifteenth, twelve men were chosen
from Jerimoth, his sons and relatives.
23Sixteenth, twelve men were chosen
from Hananiah, his sons and relatives.
24Seventeenth, twelve men were
chosen from Joshbekashah, his sons and
relatives.
25Eighteenth, twelve men were chosen from Hanani, his sons and relatives.
26Nineteenth, twelve
men were chosen from
Mallothi, his sons and relatives.
27Twentieth, twelve
men were chosen from
Eliathah, his sons and relatives.
28Twenty-first,
twelve men were chosen
from Hothir, his sons and
relatives.
29Twenty-second,
twelve men were chosen from Giddalti,
his sons and relatives.
30Twenty-third, twelve men were
chosen from Mahazioth, his sons and relatives.
31Twenty-fourth, twelve men were
chosen from Romamti-Ezer, his sons and
relatives.

The Gatekeepers

26 These are the groups of the gatekeepers. From the family of Korah, there was Meshelemiah son of Kore,
who was from Asaph's family. 2Meshele-

miah had sons. Zechariah was his first
son, Jediael was second, Zebadiah was
third, Jathniel was fourth, 3Elam was
fifth, Jehohanan was sixth, and Eliehoenai was seventh.
4Obed-Edom had sons. Shemaiah was
his first son, Jehozabad was second, Joah
was third, Sacar was fourth, Nethanel was
fifth, 5Ammiel was sixth, Issachar was
seventh, and Peullethai
was eighth. God blessed
Obed-Edom with chil-
dren.
6Obed-Edom's son
Shemaiah also had sons.
They were leaders in
their father's family be-
cause they were capable
men. 7Shemaiah's sons
were Othni, Rephael,
Obed, Elzabad, Elihu, and
Semakiah. Elihu, and Semakiah were
skilled workers. 8All these were Obed-
Edom's descendants. They and their
sons and relatives were capable men and
strong workers. Obed-Edom had sixty-
two descendants in all.
9Meshelemiah had sons and relatives
who were skilled workers. In all, there
were eighteen.
10From the Merari family, Hosah had
sons. Shimri was chosen to be in charge.
Although he was not the oldest son, his
father chose him to be in charge. 11Hil-
kiah was his second son, Tabaliah was
third, and Zechariah was fourth. In all,
Hosah had thirteen sons and relatives.
12These were the leaders of the
groups of gatekeepers, and they served
in the Temple of the LORD. Their relatives also worked in the Temple. 13By
throwing lots, each family chose a gate to
guard. Young and old threw lots.
14Meshelemiah was chosen by lot to
guard the East Gate. Then lots were
thrown for Meshelemiah's son Zechariah. He was a wise counselor and was chosen for the North Gate. 15Obed-Edom
was chosen for the South Gate, and
Obed-Edom's sons were chosen to guard
the storehouse. 16Shuppim and Hosah
were chosen for the West Gate and the
Shalleketh Gate on the upper road.
Guards stood side by side with
guards. 17Six Levites stood guard every
day at the East Gate; four Levites stood
guard every day at the North Gate; four
Levites stood guard every day at the
South Gate; and two Levites at a time
guarded the storehouse. 18There were
two guards at the western court and four
guards on the road to the court.
19These were the
groups of the gatekeep-
ers from the families of
Korah and Merari.

> Other Levites were responsible for guarding the treasuries of the Temple of God.
> —1 Chronicles 26:20

Other Leaders

20Other Levites were
responsible for guarding
the treasuries of the
Temple of God and for the
places where the holy
items were kept.
21Ladan was Gershon's son and the
ancestor of several family groups. Jehiel
was a leader of one of the family groups.
22His sons were Zetham and Joel his
brother, and they were responsible for
the treasuries of the Temple of the LORD.
23Other leaders were chosen from
the family groups of Amram, Izhar, Hebron, and Uzziel. 24Shubael, the descendant of Gershom, who was Moses'
son, was the leader responsible for the
treasuries. 25These were Shubael's relatives from Eliezer: Eliezer's son Rehabiah, Rehabiah's son Jeshaiah, Jeshaiah's
son Joram, Joram's son Zicri, and Zicri's
son Shelomith. 26Shelomith and his relatives were responsible for everything
that had been collected for the Temple by
King David, by the heads of families, by
the commanders of a thousand men
and of a hundred
men, and by other
army commanders.
27They also gave
some of the things
they had taken in
wars to be used in
repairing the Temple of the LORD. 28She-
lomith and his relatives took care of all
the holy items. Some had been given by
Samuel the seer, Saul son of Kish, Abner
son of Ner, and Joab son of Zeruiah.

eMAIL FROM GOD
26:27
Money
What's a good way to spend some of the money you earn?

29Kenaniah was from the Izhar family.
He and his sons worked outside the Temple as officers and judges in different
places in Israel.
30Hashabiah was from the Hebron
family. He and his relatives were responsible for the LORD's work and the king's
business in Israel west of the Jordan
River. There were seventeen hundred
skilled men in Hashabiah's group. **31**The
history of the Hebron family shows that
Jeriah was their leader. In David's fortieth year as king, the records were
searched, and some capable men of the
Hebron family were found living at Jazer
in Gilead. **32**Jeriah had twenty-seven
hundred relatives who were skilled men
and leaders of families. King David gave
them the responsibility of directing the
tribes of Reuben, Gad, and East Manasseh in God's work and the king's business.

Army Divisions

27 This is the list of the Israelites
who served the king in the army.
Each division was on duty one month
each year. There were leaders of families,
commanders of a hundred men, commanders of a thousand men, and other officers. Each division had twenty-four
thousand men.
2Jashobeam son of Zabdiel was in
charge of the first division for the first
month. There were twenty-four thousand men in his division. **3**Jashobeam,
one of the descendants of Perez, was
leader of all the army officers for the first
month.
4Dodai, from the Ahohites, was in
charge of the division for the second
month. Mikloth was a leader in the division. There were twenty-four thousand
men in Dodai's division.
5The third commander, for the third
month, was Benaiah son of Jehoiada the
priest. There were twenty-four thousand
men in his division. **6**He was the Benaiah
who was one of the Thirty[n] soldiers. Benaiah was a brave warrior who led those
men. Benaiah's son Ammizabad was in
charge of Benaiah's division.
7The fourth commander, for the
fourth month, was Asahel, the brother of
Joab. Later, Asahel's son Zebadiah took
his place as commander. There were
twenty-four thousand men in his division.
8The fifth commander, for the fifth
month, was Shamhuth, from Izrah's family. There were twenty-four thousand
men in his division.
9The sixth commander, for the sixth
month, was Ira son of Ikkesh from the
town of Tekoa. There were twenty-four
thousand men in his division.
10The seventh commander, for the
seventh month, was Helez. He was from
the Pelonites and a descendant of Ephraim.
There were twenty-four thousand men in
his division.
11The eighth commander, for the
eighth month, was Sibbecai. He was from
Hushah and was from Zerah's family.
There were twenty-four thousand men in
his division.
12The ninth commander, for the ninth
month, was Abiezer. He was from Anathoth in Benjamin. There were twenty-
four thousand men in his division.
13The tenth commander, for the tenth
month, was Maharai. He was from Netophah and was from Zerah's family. There
were twenty-four thousand men in his division.
14The eleventh commander, for the
eleventh month, was Benaiah. He was
from Pirathon in Ephraim. There were
twenty-four thousand men in his division.
15The twelfth commander, for the
twelfth month, was Heldai. He was from
Netophah and was from Othniel's family.
There were twenty-four thousand men in
his division.

Leaders of the Tribes

16These were the leaders of the
tribes of Israel. Eliezer son of Zicri was
over the tribe of Reuben. Shephatiah son
of Maacah was over the tribe of Simeon.
17Hashabiah son of Kemuel was over the
tribe of Levi. Zadok was over the people

27:6 Thirty These were David's most powerful soldiers. See 2 Samuel 23:24.

of Aaron. **18**Elihu, one of David's brothers, was over the tribe of Judah. Omri son of Michael was over the tribe of Issachar. **19**Ishmaiah son of Obadiah was over the tribe of Zebulun. Jerimoth son of Azriel was over the tribe of Naphtali. **20**Hoshea son of Azaziah was over the tribe of Ephraim. Joel son of Pedaiah was over West Manasseh. **21**Iddo son of Zechariah was over East Manasseh. Jaasiel son of Abner was over the tribe of Benjamin. **22**Azarel son of Jeroham was over the tribe of Dan.

These were the leaders of the tribes of Israel.

23The LORD had promised to make the Israelites as many as the stars in the sky. So David only counted the men who were twenty years old and older. **24**Joab son of Zeruiah began to count the people, but he did not finish. God became angry with Israel for counting the people, so the number of the people was not put in the history book about King David's rule.

> The LORD had promised to make the Israelites as many as the stars in the sky.
> —1 Chronicles 27:23

The King's Directors

25Azmaveth son of Adiel was in charge of the royal storehouses.

Jonathan son of Uzziah was in charge of the storehouses in the country, towns, villages, and towers.

26Ezri son of Kelub was in charge of the field workers who farmed the land.

27Shimei, from the town of Ramah, was in charge of the vineyards.

Zabdi, from Shapham, was in charge of storing the wine that came from the vineyards.

28Baal-Hanan, from Geder, was in charge of the olive trees and sycamore trees in the western hills.

Joash was in charge of storing the olive oil.

29Shitrai, from Sharon, was in charge of the herds that fed in the Plain of Sharon.

Shaphat son of Adlai was in charge of the herds in the valleys.

30Obil, an Ishmaelite, was in charge of the camels.

Jehdeiah, from Meronoth, was in charge of the donkeys.

31Jaziz, from the Hagrites, was in charge of the flocks.

All these men were the officers who took care of King David's property.

32Jonathan was David's uncle, and he advised David. Jonathan was a wise man and a teacher of the law. Jehiel son of Hacmoni took care of the king's sons. **33**Ahithophel advised the king. Hushai, from the Arkite people, was the king's friend. **34**Jehoiada and Abiathar later took Ahithophel's place in advising the king. Jehoiada was Benaiah's son. Joab was the commander of the king's army.

David's Plans for the Temple

28 David commanded all the leaders of Israel to come to Jerusalem. There were the leaders of the tribes, commanders of the divisions serving the king, commanders of a thousand men and of a hundred men, leaders who took care of the property and animals that belonged to the king and his sons, men over the palace, the powerful men, and all the brave warriors.

2King David stood up and said, "Listen to me, my relatives and my people. I wanted to build a place to keep the Ark of the Agreement with the LORD. I wanted it to be God's footstool. So I made plans to build a temple. **3**But God said to me, 'You must not build a temple for worshiping me, because you are a soldier and have killed many people.'

4"But the LORD, the God of Israel, chose me from my whole family to be king of Israel forever. He chose the tribe of Judah to lead, and from the people of Judah, he chose my father's family. From that family God was pleased to make me king of Israel. **5**The LORD has given me many sons, and from those sons he has chosen Solomon to be the new king of Israel. Israel is the LORD's kingdom.

6The LORD said to me, 'Your son Solomon

FAITH CHALLENGE

Here's one for you. Read 28:6–7 to find out what God said to King David about David's son. What do you think God would say to your parents about you?

TESTING IT

1 Chronicles 28:6–7
I have chosen Solomon to be my son, and I will be his father. He is obeying my laws and commands now. If he continues to obey them, I will make his kingdom strong forever.

will build my Temple and its courtyards. I
have chosen Solomon to be my son, and I
will be his father. **7**He is obeying my laws
and commands now. If he continues to
obey them, I will make his kingdom
strong forever.' "
8David said, "Now, in front of all Israel, the assembly of the LORD, and in the
hearing of God, I tell
you these things:
Be careful to obey
all the commands of
the LORD your God.
Then you will keep
this good land and

EMAIL FROM GOD 28:8
Family
Check out David's advice to his children.

pass it on to your descendants forever.
9"And you, my son Solomon, accept
the God of your father. Serve him completely and willingly, because the LORD
knows what is in everyone's mind. He
understands everything you think. If you
go to him for help, you will get an answer.
But if you turn away from him, he will
leave you forever. **10**Solomon, you must
understand this. The LORD has chosen
you to build the Temple as his holy place.
Be strong and finish the job."
11Then David gave his son Solomon
the plans for building the Temple and the
courtyard around the Temple. They included its buildings, its storerooms, its
upper rooms, its inside rooms, and the
place where the people's sins were removed. **12**David gave him plans for
everything he had in mind: the courtyards around the LORD's Temple and all
the rooms around it, the Temple treasuries, and the treasuries of the holy items
used in the Temple. **13**David gave Solomon directions for the groups of the
priests and Levites. David told him about
all the work of serving in the Temple of
the LORD and about the items to be used
in the Temple service **14**that were made
of gold or silver. David told Solomon how
much gold or silver should be used to
make each thing. **15**David told him how
much gold to use for each gold lampstand
and its lamps and how much silver to use
for each silver lampstand and its lamps.
The different lampstands were to be used
where needed. **16**David told how much
gold should be used for each table that
held the holy bread and how much silver
should be used for the silver tables. **17**He
told how much pure gold should be used
to make the forks, bowls, and pitchers
and how much gold should be used to
make each gold dish. He told how much
silver should be used to make each silver
dish **18**and how much pure gold should be
used for the altar of incense. He also gave
Solomon the plans for the chariot of the
golden creatures that spread their wings
over the Ark of the Agreement with the
LORD.
19David said, "All these plans were
written with the LORD guiding me. He

helped me understand everything in the
plans."
20David also said to his son Solomon,
"Be strong and brave, and do the work.
Don't be afraid or discouraged, because
the LORD God, my God, is with you. He
will not fail you or leave you until all the
work for the Temple of the LORD is finished. **21**The groups of the priests and
Levites are ready for all the work on the
Temple of God. Every skilled worker is
ready to help you with all the work. The
leaders and all the people will obey every
command you give."

Gifts for Building the Temple

29 King David said to all the Israelites who were gathered, "God
chose my son Solomon, who is young and
hasn't yet learned what he needs to
know, but the work is important. This
palace is not for people; it is for the LORD
God. **2**I have done my best to prepare for
building the Temple of God. I have given
gold for the things made of gold and silver for the things made of silver. I have
given bronze for the things made of
bronze and iron for the things made of
iron. I have given wood for the things
made of wood and onyx for the settings. I
have given turquoise gems of many different colors, valuable stones, and white
marble. I have given much of all these
things. **3**I have already given this for the
Temple, but now I am also giving my own
treasures of gold and silver, because I
really want the Temple of my God to be
built. **4**I have given about two hundred
twenty thousand pounds of pure gold
from Ophir and about five hundred twenty thousand pounds of pure silver. They
will be used to cover the walls of the
buildings **5**and for all the gold and silver
work. Skilled men may use the gold and
silver to make things for the Temple.
Now, who is ready to give himself to the
service of the LORD today?"
6The family leaders and the leaders of
the tribes of Israel, the commanders of a
thousand men and of a hundred men, and
the leaders responsible for the king's
work gave their valuable things. **7**They
donated about three hundred eighty
thousand pounds of gold, about seven
hundred fifty thousand pounds of silver,
about one million three hundred fifty
thousand pounds of bronze, and about
seven million five hundred thousand
pounds of iron to the Temple of God.
8People who had valuable gems gave
them to the treasury of the Temple of the
LORD, and Jehiel, from the Gershon family, took care of the valuable gems. **9**The
leaders gave willingly and completely to

FAITH links

GIFTS FROM THE HEART

1 CHRONICLES 29

Have you ever participated in a fundraising drive? Meeting your goal can be pretty exciting! King David asked the Israelites to give to the building fund for the Temple. They gave generously and cheerfully. They celebrated because so much was given!

Giving that takes place from the heart is always exciting. Whatever is given—whether money, time, or a smile—it's all good! Search your heart. What would you like to give?

Giving Your Part, Leviticus 27:30, p. 173

Wisdom About Wealth, Ecclesiastes 5:10–12, p. 878

The Foundation of Our Hope, Isaiah 31:1–8, p. 934

Your Feet on High Places, Habakkuk 3:18–19, p. 1239

Your Heart's Desire, Luke 16:13–15, p. 1401

More Money?, 1 Timothy 6:10, p. 1649

the LORD. The people rejoiced to see their leaders give so gladly, and King David was also very happy.

David's Prayer

10David praised the LORD in front of
all the people who were gathered. He
said:

"We praise you, LORD,
God of our father Israel.
We praise you forever and ever.
11 LORD, you are great and powerful.
You have glory, victory, and honor.
Everything in heaven and on earth belongs to you.
The kingdom belongs to you, LORD;
you are the ruler over everything.
12 Riches and honor come from you.
You rule everything.
You have the power and strength
to make anyone great and strong.
13 Now, our God, we thank you
and praise your glorious name.

EMAIL FROM GOD
29:12
Worry
Where do you find confidence?

14 "These things did not really come from me and my people.
Everything comes from you;
we have given you back what you gave us.
15 We are like foreigners and strangers,
as our ancestors were.
Our time on earth is like a shadow.
There is no hope.
16 LORD our God, we have gathered all this
to build your Temple for worship to you.
But everything has come from you;
everything belongs to you.
17 I know, my God, that you test people's hearts.
You are happy when people do what is right.
I was happy to give all these things,
and I gave with an honest heart.
Your people gathered here are happy to give to you,
and I rejoice to see their giving.
18 LORD, you are the God of our ancestors,
the God of Abraham, Isaac, and Jacob.
Make your people want to serve you always,
and make them want to obey you.
19 Give my son Solomon a desire to serve you.
Help him always obey your commands, laws, and rules.
Help him build the Temple
for which I have prepared."

20Then David said to all the people
who were gathered, "Praise the LORD
your God." So they all praised the LORD,
the God of their ancestors, and they
bowed to the ground to give honor to the
LORD and the king.

Solomon Becomes King

21The next day the people sacrificed
to the LORD. They offered burnt offerings
to him of a thousand bulls, a thousand
male sheep, and a thousand male lambs.
They also brought drink offerings. Many
sacrifices were made for all the people of
Israel. 22That day the people ate and
drank with much joy, and the LORD was
with them.

And they made David's son Solomon
king for the second time. They poured olive oil on Solomon to appoint him king in
the presence of the LORD. And they
poured oil on Zadok to appoint him as
priest. 23Then Solomon sat on the
LORD's throne as king and took his father
David's place. Solomon was very successful, and all the people of Israel
obeyed him. 24All the leaders and soldiers and King David's sons accepted
Solomon as king and promised to obey
him. 25The LORD made Solomon great
before all the Israelites and gave Solomon much honor. No king of Israel before Solomon had such honor.

David's Death

26David son of Jesse was king over all
Israel. 27He had ruled over Israel forty
years—seven years in Hebron and
thirty-three years in Jerusalem. 28David
died when he was old. He had lived a

good, long life and had received many
riches and honors. His son Solomon became king after him.
29Everything David did as king, from
beginning to end, is recorded in the
records of Samuel the seer, the records of
Nathan the prophet, and the records of
Gad the seer. **30**Those writings tell what
David did as king of Israel. They tell
about his power and what happened to
him and to Israel and to all the kingdoms
around them.

2 Chronicles

THE GLORIOUS TEMPLE

Hello, there! I'm Ezra, teacher and historian. Step back in time with me to the day Solomon dedicated the Temple to the Lord. Imagine as you walk up the hill, the Temple of stone glitters in the sun. In the courtyard stands the huge bronze altar where the priests make sacrifices to the Lord. To the side is an enormous basin of water resting on 12 bronze bulls. Walk up the steps and through the doors. Every surface is coated with gold and is encrusted with jewels. Admire the golden lampstands, tables, and bowls. What a day! God was pleased with the Temple that Solomon built. Link to 2 Chronicles 7:1–3 to read about the awesome way his presence filled the Temple. (You can also plug in to The Temple in Jerusalem, p. 564.)

I wrote this book to remind people to be faithful to God and to worship only him. After Solomon died, many people turned away from God and started to worship idols. They did not take care of the Temple and even gave away some of its treasures. King Hezekiah remembered God and restored the Temple. He united the whole nation to worship the true God. Be sure to check out how God saved Jerusalem from the Assyrians in 2 Chronicles 32:1–23.

JESUS WATCH

The Temple had two rooms that were divided by a thick curtain: the Holy Place and the Most Holy Place. Bread offerings from the 12 tribes were placed on gold tables in the Holy Place. Behind the curtain, shielded from sight, the Ark of God was placed in the Most Holy Place. This was God's throne room in Israel. Only the high priest was allowed access. Once a year, on the Day of Cleansing, the high priest entered into the Most Holy Place with the sacrifice for the people's sins. In a similar, but more permanent way, Jesus is our high priest. When he died on the cross, Jesus became our perfect sacrifice, giving up his life for our sins. Unlike the Old Testament high priests, though, Jesus does not need to make this sacrifice every year; his one sacrifice is enough for all our sins. When Jesus died, the curtain shielding the Most Holy Place was torn. (Check out Matthew 27:45–51, p. 1325, for that story.)

my FAVORITE links

OTHER CONNECTIONS

Livin' it

Want to know a secret for success? Surf over to Eyes on the Prize, 2 Chronicles 1:7–12, to learn the importance of setting goals for yourself and of learning the goals God has set for you! Your life will never be the same!

GET THE INFO

Visit these information bulletin boards for some interesting facts that you will read about in 2 Chronicles:

- Israel's Glory Years, 2 Chronicles 9. Stop here for some cool facts about one of Israel's most famous builders, Solomon. Under King Solomon, Israel stretched its empire to its limits and built the Temple and a breathtaking palace.
- Skin diseases are mentioned frequently in the Bible. Check out the facts behind these skin diseases by connecting to Disease or Curse?, 2 Chronicles 26:20–23.
- King Hezekiah had a secret weapon to defend Jerusalem when their enemies surrounded the city and attempted to stop food and water supplies from coming in. Find out what his secret was by linking to A Secret Water Supply, 2 Chronicles 32.

"Tagg, what's the flash on Josiah? I heard he was only a kid when he became king."

"Let's link to 2 Chronicles 34:1-2 to find out."

did YOU know?

CHECK OUT THESE COOL STORIES:

Solomon builds the Temple, 2 Chronicles 3
Joash restores the Temple, 2 Chronicles 24
Hezekiah's water supply, 2 Chronicles 32:1–5, 30
God's Temple on fire, 2 Chronicles 36:15–21

FAITH links

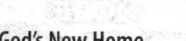

- God's New Home, 2 Chronicles 7:11–22
- The Salt Promise, 2 Chronicles 13:5
- Weak? Great!, 2 Chronicles 14:11
- Depend on Him!, 2 Chronicles 16:1–9
- A Traveling Bible Study, 2 Chronicles 17:9
- A Reminder to Be Fair, 2 Chronicles 19:5–11
- Your Best Defense, 2 Chronicles 20:1–12
- A Look for the Book, 2 Chronicles 34:14–18
- This Hurts Me More?, 2 Chronicles 36:17–22

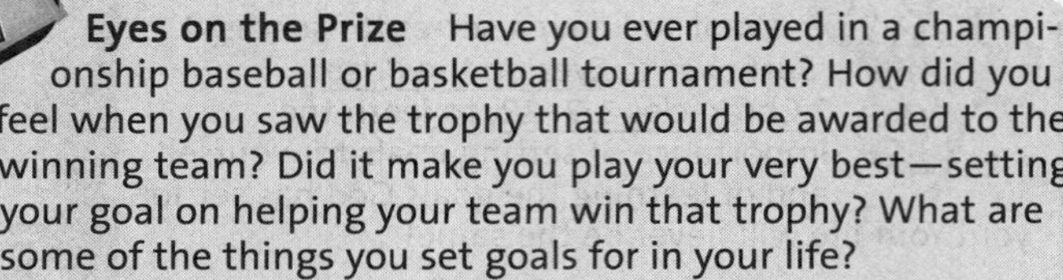

SETTING GOALS

2 Chronicles 1:7–12

Livin' it

Eyes on the Prize Have you ever played in a championship baseball or basketball tournament? How did you feel when you saw the trophy that would be awarded to the winning team? Did it make you play your very best—setting your goal on helping your team win that trophy? What are some of the things you set goals for in your life?

Sometimes it's difficult to reach the goals we set for ourselves. Bad things happen and we face hard times. But just like Paul, we can trust God to help us no matter what. (Read 2 Corinthians 1:8–10, p. 1570.) Set your goals and then trust God to help you reach them.

MORE FAITH links

I'll Never Forget What's-His-Name, p. 239

A Need to Change, p. 873

My Favorite!, p. 1347

Heavenly Treasure, p. 1394

Put God First, p. 1472

"Tagg, do you have any goals for the future?"

"Sure I do! I want to grow up so I can stay up as late as I want and eat all the snack foods I want."

"Hmmmm, those are *interesting* goals, Tagg. Maybe you ought to log on to these Faithlinks for more info on setting goals."

A Hopeful Future, Jeremiah 29:11, p. 1031

- What are some of the plans you and your parents have made concerning your future? What will you need to do to carry out those plans and reach your goals? Why were the plans made? Link here to learn about God's plans for your future.

First Place, Haggai 1:7–11, p. 1248

- Suppose your parents' goal was to remodel every room in the house—except yours. How would that make you feel? What would you think of the goal they had set?
- How many goals have you set concerning God and serving him? God wants his work to be important to us. How important is it to you?

The Choices of a Choice, Luke 5:1–11, p. 1375

- You have plans and goals for your life, right? Now suppose you met someone who could do amazing things. Would you give up your life plans to work with that person? Link here to discover some people who made life-changing choices.

my FAVORITE links

Solomon Asks for Wisdom

1 Solomon, David's son, became a powerful king, because the LORD his God
was with him and made him very great.
2Solomon spoke to all the people of
Israel—the commanders of a hundred
men and of a thousand men, the judges,
every leader in all Israel, and the leaders
of the families. **3**Then Solomon and all
the people with him went to the place of
worship at the town of Gibeon. God's
Meeting Tent, which Moses the LORD's
servant had made in the desert, was
there. **4**David had brought the Ark of God
from Kiriath Jearim to Jerusalem, where
he had made a place for it and had set up a
tent for it. **5**The bronze altar that Bezalel
son of Uri, who was the son of Hur, had
made was in Gibeon in front of the Holy
Tent. So Solomon and the people worshiped there. **6**Solomon went up to the
bronze altar in the presence of the LORD
at the Meeting Tent and offered a thousand burnt offerings on it.
7That night God appeared to Solomon
and said to him, "Ask for whatever you
want me to give you."
8Solomon answered, "You have been
very kind to my father David, and you
have made me king
in his place. **9**Now,
LORD God, may your
promise to my father
David come true. You
have made me king
of a people who are
as many as the dust of the
earth. **10**Now give me
wisdom and knowledge so
I can lead these people in
the right way, because no
one can rule them without
your help."
11God said to Sol-
omon, "You have not
asked for wealth or riches
or honor, or for the death
of your enemies, or for a
long life. But since you have asked for
wisdom and knowledge to lead my people, over whom I have made you king, **12**I
will give you wisdom and knowledge. I
will also give you more wealth, riches,
and honor than any king who has lived
before you or any who will live after
you."
13Then Solomon left the place of worship, the Meeting Tent, at Gibeon and
went back to Jerusalem. There King Solomon ruled over Israel.

EMAIL FROM GOD
1:9–10
Prayer
What can you pray for?

Solomon's Wealth

14Solomon had fourteen hundred
chariots and twelve thousand horses. He
kept some in special cities for the chariots, and others he kept with him in Jerusalem. **15**In Jerusalem Solomon made
silver and gold as plentiful as stones and
cedar trees as plentiful as the fig trees on
the western hills. **16**He imported horses
from Egypt and Kue; his traders bought
them in Kue. **17**They imported chariots
from Egypt for about fifteen pounds of
silver apiece, and horses cost nearly four
pounds of silver apiece. Then they sold
the horses and chariots to all the kings of
the Hittites and the Arameans.

Solomon Prepares for the Temple

2 Solomon decided to build a temple as
a place to worship the LORD and also
a palace for himself. **2**He chose seventy
thousand men to carry loads, eighty
thousand men to cut stone in the hill
country, and thirty-six hundred men to
direct the workers.
3Solomon sent this message to Hiram
king of the city of Tyre: "Help me as you
helped my father David by sending him
cedar logs so he could
build himself a palace to
live in. **4**I will build a temple for worshiping the
LORD my God, and I will
give this temple to him.
There we will burn
sweet-smelling spices in
his presence. We will
continually set out the
holy bread in God's pres-
ence. And we will burn
sacrifices every morning and evening, on
Sabbath days and New Moons, and on the
other feast days commanded by the LORD
our God. This is a rule for Israel to obey
forever.

Solomon decided to build a temple as a place to worship the LORD and also a palace for himself.
—2 Chronicles 2:1

5"The temple I build will be great, because our God is greater than all gods.
6But no one can really build a house for
our God. Not even the highest of heavens
can hold him. How then can I build a temple for him except as a place to burn sacrifices to him?
7"Now send me a man skilled in
working with gold, silver, bronze, and
iron, and with purple, red, and blue
thread. He must also know how to make
engravings. He will work with my skilled
craftsmen in Judah and Jerusalem, whom
my father David chose.
8"Also send me cedar, pine, and juniper logs from Lebanon. I know your servants are experienced at cutting down
the trees in Lebanon, and my servants
will help them. **9**Send me a lot of wood,
because the temple I am going to build
will be large and wonderful. **10**I will give
your servants who cut the wood one hundred twenty-five thousand bushels of
wheat, one hundred twenty-five thousand
bushels of barley, one hundred fifteen thousand gallons of wine, and one hundred fifteen thousand gallons of oil."
11Then Hiram king of Tyre answered
Solomon with this letter:
"Solomon, because the
LORD loves his people, he
chose you to be their
king." **12**Hiram also said:
"Praise the LORD, the
God of Israel, who made
heaven and earth! He has
given King David a wise
son, one with wisdom and
understanding, who will
build a temple for the
LORD and a palace for himself.
13"I will send you a skilled and wise
man named Huram-Abi. **14**His mother
was from the people of Dan, and his father was from Tyre. Huram-Abi is skilled
in working with gold, silver, bronze, iron,
stone, and wood, and with purple, blue,
and red thread, and expensive linen. He
is skilled in making engravings and can
make any design you show him. He will
help your craftsmen and the craftsmen of
your father David.
15"Now send my servants the wheat,
barley, oil, and wine you promised. **16**We
will cut as much wood from Lebanon as
you need and will bring it on rafts by sea
to Joppa. Then you may carry it to Jerusalem."
17Solomon counted all the foreigners
living in Israel. (This was after the time
his father David had counted the people.)
There were one hundred fifty-three
thousand six hundred foreigners in the
country. **18**Solomon chose seventy thousand of them to carry loads, eighty thousand of them to cut stone in the
mountains, and thirty-six hundred of
them to direct the workers and to keep
the people working.

Solomon Builds the Temple

3 Then Solomon began to build the
Temple of the LORD in Jerusalem on
Mount Moriah. This was where the LORD
had appeared to David, Solomon's father.
Solomon built the Temple on the place
David had prepared on the threshing
floor of Araunah the Jebusite. **2**Solomon
began building in the second month of
the fourth year he ruled Israel.
3Solomon used these measurements
for building the Temple of
God. It was ninety feet
long and thirty feet wide,
using the old measure-
ment. **4**The porch in front
of the main room of the
Temple was thirty feet
long and thirty feet high.
He covered the inside
of the porch with pure
gold. **5**He put panels of
pine on the walls of the
main room and covered them with pure
gold. Then he put designs of palm trees
and chains in the gold. **6**He decorated the
Temple with gems and gold from
Parvaim.* **7**He put gold on the Temple's
ceiling beams, doorposts, walls, and
doors, and he carved creatures with
wings on the walls.
8Then he made the Most Holy Place.
It was thirty feet long and thirty feet

> Solomon built the Temple on the place David had prepared on the threshing floor of Araunah the Jebusite.
> —2 Chronicles 3:1

3:6 Parvaim There was much gold there. It may have been in the country of Ophir.

wide, as wide as the Temple. He covered
its walls with about forty-six thousand
pounds of pure gold. **9**The gold nails
weighed over a pound. He also covered
the upper rooms with gold.
10He made two creatures with wings
for the Most Holy Place and covered
them with gold. **11**The wings of the gold
creatures were thirty feet across. One
wing of one creature was seven and one-
half feet long and touched the Temple
wall. The creature's other wing was also
seven and one-half feet long, and it
touched a wing of the second creature.
12One wing of the second creature
touched the other side of the room and
was also seven and one-half feet long. The
second creature's other wing touched the
first creature's wing, and it was also
seven and one-half feet long. **13**Together,
the creatures' wings were thirty feet
across. The creatures stood on their feet,
facing the main room.
14He made the curtain of blue, purple,
and red thread, and expensive linen, and
he put designs of creatures with wings
in it.
15He made two pillars to stand in
front of the Temple. They were about
fifty-two feet tall, and the capital of each
pillar was over seven feet tall. **16**He
made a net of chains and put them on the
tops of the pillars. He made a hundred
pomegranates and put them on the
chains. **17**Then he put the pillars up in
front of the Temple. One pillar stood on
the south side, the other on the north. He
named the south pillar He Establishes
and the north pillar In Him Is Strength.

Things for the Temple

4 He made a bronze altar thirty feet
long, thirty feet wide, and fifteen feet
tall. **2**Then he made from bronze a large
round bowl, which was called the Sea. It
was forty-five feet around, fifteen feet
across, and seven and one-half feet deep.
3There were carvings of bulls under the
rim of the bowl—ten bulls every eighteen inches. They were in two rows and
were made in one piece with the bowl.
4The bowl rested on the backs of
twelve bronze bulls that faced outward
from the center of the bowl. Three bulls
faced north, three faced west, three faced
south, and three faced east. **5**The sides of
the bowl were four inches thick, and it
held about seventeen thousand five hundred gallons. The rim of the bowl was like
the rim of a cup or like a lily blossom.
6He made ten smaller bowls and put
five on the south side and five on the
north. They were for washing the animals for the burnt offerings, but the large
bowl was for the priests to wash in.
7He made ten lampstands of gold, following the plans. He put them in the
Temple, five on the south side and five on
the north.
8He made ten tables and put them in
the Temple, five on the south side and
five on the north. And he used gold to
make a hundred other bowls.
9He also made the priests' courtyard
and the large courtyard. He made the
doors that opened to the courtyard and
covered them with bronze. **10**Then he
put the large bowl in the southeast corner of the Temple.
11Huram also made bowls, shovels,
and small bowls. So he finished his work
for King Solomon on the Temple of God:
12two pillars;
two large bowls for the capitals
on top of the pillars;
two nets to cover the two large
bowls for the capitals on top
of the pillars;
13four hundred pomegranates for
the two nets (there were
two rows of pomegranates
for each net covering the
bowls for the capitals on top
of the pillars);
14the stands with a bowl on each
stand;
15the large bowl with twelve bulls
under it;
16the pots, shovels, forks, and all
the things to go with them.
All the things that Huram-Abi made
for King Solomon for the Temple of the
LORD were made of polished bronze.
17The king had these things poured into
clay molds that were made in the plain of

the Jordan River between Succoth and
Zarethan. **18**Solomon had so many things
made that the total weight of all the
bronze was never known.

19Solomon also made all the things
for God's Temple: the golden altar; tables
which held the bread that shows God's
people are in his presence; **20**the lampstands and their lamps of pure gold, to
burn in front of the Most Holy Place as
planned; **21**the flowers, lamps, and tongs
of pure gold; **22**the pure gold wick trimmers, small bowls, pans, and dishes used
to carry coals, the gold doors for the
Temple, and the inside doors of the Most
Holy Place and of the main room.

5 Finally all the work Solomon did for
the Temple of the LORD was finished.
He brought in everything his father David had set apart for the Temple—all the
silver and gold and other articles. And he
put everything in the treasuries of God's
Temple.

The Ark Is Brought into the Temple

2Solomon called for the older leaders
of Israel, the heads of the tribes, and the
leaders of the families to come to him in
Jerusalem. He wanted them to bring the
Ark of the Agreement with the LORD
from the older part of the city. **3**So all the

THE HAVES AND HAVE NOTS

Ever wish you had all the money in the world to buy whatever you wanted? Tagg and I have a friend who has something to share about what it's like to be rich. Let's welcome Geoff, age 11, to Connect 2-You.

Geoff

I have this friend who has everything. And if there's ever anything he doesn't have, his parents will go buy it for him. Whenever I hang around with him, I feel like a total loser. My parents want me to invite him over, but there's no way. I'd freak if he ever saw how old and rundown our house is. I always wonder what it would be like if I could trade places with him.

Hi, Geoff. What can you add?

I understand how you feel, Geoff. Don't forget, though, God's Word makes it clear that money does not equal happiness. If you could trade places with your friend, you might find that you got the worst part of the deal. Think about everything God has given you—not just money or possessions, but loving relationships, health, unique talents, and everything else that makes your life valuable.

That's right, Geoff. I'll bet there are people you know who are jealous of you. They see what you have and wish that they could trade places with you. The key to happiness is to learn to be content with what God has given us. If you're interested in learning how to do that, check out the tips in the Livin' It page on being content, Philippians 4:10-13, p. 1616.

Israelites came together with the king
during the festival in the seventh month.
4When all the older leaders of Israel
arrived, the Levites lifted up the Ark.
5They carried the Ark of the Agreement,
the Meeting Tent, and the holy utensils
in it; the priests and the Levites brought
them up. 6King Solomon and all the Israelites gathered before the Ark of the
Agreement and sacrificed so many sheep
and bulls no one could count them.
7Then the priests put the Ark of the
Agreement with the LORD in its place inside the Most Holy Place in the Temple,
under the wings of the golden creatures.
8The wings of these creatures were
spread out over the place for the Ark,
covering it and its carrying poles. 9The
carrying poles were so long that anyone
standing in the Holy Place in front of the
Most Holy Place could see the ends of
the poles. But no one could see them
from outside the Holy Place. The poles
are still there today. 10The only things
inside the Ark were two stone tablets[n]
that Moses had put in the Ark at Mount
Sinai. That was where the LORD made his
agreement with the Israelites after they
came out of Egypt.
11Then all the priests left the Holy
Place. (All the priests from each group
had made themselves ready to serve the
LORD.) 12All the Levite musicians—
Asaph, Heman, Jeduthun, and all their
sons and relatives—stood on the east
side of the altar. They were dressed in
white linen and played
cymbals, harps, and lyres.
With them were one hun-
dred twenty priests who
blew trumpets. 13Those
who blew the trumpets
and those who sang to-
gether sounded like one
person as they praised
and thanked the LORD.
They sang as others
played their trumpets,
cymbals, and other instruments. They
praised the LORD with this song:

"He is good;
his love continues forever."

Then the Temple of the LORD was
filled with a cloud. 14The priests could
not continue their work because of the
cloud, because the LORD's glory filled the
Temple of God.

> They praised the LORD with this song: "He is good; his love continues forever."
> —2 Chronicles 5:13

Solomon Speaks to the People

6 Then Solomon said, "The LORD said
he would live in the dark cloud.
2LORD, I have built a wonderful Temple
for you—a place for you to live forever."
3While all the Israelites were standing there, King Solomon turned to them
and blessed them. 4Then he said, "Praise
the LORD, the God of Israel. He has done
what he promised to my father David.
The LORD said, 5'Since the time I
brought my people out of Egypt, I have
not chosen a city in any tribe of Israel
where a temple will be built for me. I did
not choose a man to lead my people Israel. 6But now I have chosen Jerusalem as
the place I am to be worshiped, and I have
chosen David to lead my people Israel.'
7"My father David wanted to build a
temple for the LORD, the God of Israel.
8But the LORD said to my father David,
'It was good that you wanted to build a
temple for me. 9But you are not the one
to build it. Your son, who comes from
your own body, is the one who will build
my temple.'
10"Now the LORD has kept his promise. I am the king now in place of David
my father. Now I rule Israel as the LORD
promised, and I have built the Temple for
the LORD, the God of Israel. 11There I
have put the Ark, in
which is the Agreement
the LORD made with the
Israelites."

Solomon's Prayer

12Then Solomon stood
facing the LORD's altar,
and all the Israelites were
standing behind him. He
spread out his hands.
13He had made a bronze
platform seven and one-half feet long,

5:10 stone tablets They were the two stone tablets on which God wrote the Ten Commandments.

seven and one-half feet wide, and seven
and one-half feet high, and he had placed
it in the middle of the outer courtyard.
Solomon stood on the platform. Then he
kneeled in front of all the people of Israel
gathered there, and he spread out his
hands toward the sky. **14**He said, "LORD,
God of Israel, there is no god like you
in heaven or on earth. You keep your
agreement of love with your servants
who truly follow you. **15**You have kept
the promise you made to your servant
David, my father. You spoke it with your
own mouth and finished it with your
hands today.

16"Now, LORD, God of Israel, keep the
promise you made to your servant David,
my father. You said, 'If your sons are careful to obey my teachings as you have
obeyed, there will always be someone
from your family ruling Israel.' **17**Now,
LORD, God of Israel, please continue to
keep that promise you made to your servant.

18"But, God, can you really live here
on the earth with people? The sky and
the highest place in heaven cannot contain you. Surely this house which I have
built cannot contain you. **19**But please
listen to my prayer and my request, because I am your servant. LORD my God,
hear this prayer your servant prays to
you. **20**Day and night please watch over
this Temple where you have said you
would be worshiped. Hear the prayer I
pray facing this Temple. **21**Hear my
prayers and the prayers of your people
Israel when we pray facing this place.
Hear from your home in heaven, and
when you hear, forgive us.

22"If someone wrongs another person, he will be brought to the altar in this
Temple. If he swears an oath that he is
not guilty, **23**then hear in heaven. Judge
the case, punish the guilty, but declare
that the innocent person is not guilty.

24"When your people, the Israelites, sin against
you, their enemies
will defeat them.
But if they come
back to you and
praise you and pray
to you in this Temple, **25**then listen from
heaven. Forgive the sin of your people Israel, and bring them back to the land you
gave to them and their ancestors.

EMAIL FROM GOD
6:24–25
Sin
Do you need to confess your sins?

26"When they sin against you, you
will stop the rain from falling on their
land. Then they will pray, facing this
place and praising you; they will stop
sinning when you make them suffer.
27When this happens, hear their prayer
in heaven, and forgive the sins of your
servants, the Israelites. Teach them to do
what is right. Then please send rain to
this land you have given particularly to
them.

28"At times the land will get so dry
that no food will grow, or a great sickness
will spread among the people. Sometimes the crops will be destroyed by locusts or grasshoppers. Your people will
be attacked in their cities by their enemies, or will become sick. **29**When any of
these things happens, the people will become truly sorry. If your people spread
their hands in prayer toward this Temple,
30then hear their prayers from your
home in heaven. Forgive and treat each
person as he should be treated because
you know what is in a person's heart.
Only you know what is in people's
hearts. **31**Then the people will respect
and obey you as long as they live in this
land you gave our ancestors.

32"People who are not Israelites, foreigners from other lands, will hear about
your greatness and power. They will
come from far away to pray at this Temple. **33**Then hear from your home in
heaven, and do whatever they ask you.
Then people everywhere will know you
and respect you, just as your people Israel do. Then everyone will know that I
built this Temple as a place to worship
you.

34"When your people go out to fight
their enemies along some road on which
you send them, your people will pray to
you, facing this city which you have chosen and the Temple I have built for you.
35Then hear in heaven their prayers, and
do what is right.

36"Everyone sins, so your people will
also sin against you. You will become an-

gry with them and will hand them over to
their enemies. Their enemies will capture them and take them away to a country far or near. **37**Your people will be
sorry for their sins when they are held as
prisoners in another country. They will
be sorry and pray to you in the land
where they are held as prisoners, saying,
'We have sinned. We have done wrong
and acted wickedly.' **38**They will truly
turn back to you in the land where they
are captives. They will pray, facing this
land you gave their ancestors, this city
you have chosen, and the Temple I have
built for you. **39**Then hear their prayers
from your home in heaven and do what is
right. Forgive your people who have
sinned against you.
40"Now, my God, look at us. Listen to
the prayers we pray in this place.
41 Now, rise, LORD God, and come to
your resting place.
Come with the Ark of the
Agreement that shows your
strength.
Let your priests receive your
salvation, LORD God,
and may your holy people be happy
because of your goodness.
42 LORD God, do not reject your
appointed one.
Remember your love for your
servant David."

The Temple Is Given to the Lord

7 When Solomon finished praying, fire
came down from the sky and burned
up the burnt offering and the sacrifices.
The LORD's glory filled the Temple. **2**The
priests could not enter the Temple of the
LORD, because the LORD's glory filled it.
3When all the people of Israel saw the
fire come down from heaven and the
LORD's glory on the Temple, they bowed
down on the pavement with their faces to
the ground. They worshiped and thanked
the LORD, saying,
"He is good;
his love continues forever."
4Then King Solomon and all the people
offered sacrifices to the LORD. **5**King
Solomon offered a sacrifice of twenty-
two thousand cattle and one hundred
twenty thousand sheep. So the king and
all the people gave the Temple to God.
6The priests stood ready to do their
work. The Levites also stood with the instruments of the LORD's music that King
David had made for praising the LORD.
The priests and Levites were saying,
"His love continues forever." The
priests, who stood across from the Levites, blew their trumpets, and all the Israelites were standing.
7Solomon made holy the middle part
of the courtyard, which is in front of the
Temple of the LORD. There he offered
whole burnt offerings and the fat of the
fellowship offerings. He offered them in
the courtyard, because the bronze altar
he had made could not hold the burnt offerings, grain offerings, and fat.
8Solomon and all the Israelites celebrated the festival for seven days. There
were many people, and they came from
as far away as Lebo Hamath and the
brook of Egypt. **9**For seven days they celebrated giving the altar for the worship of
God. Then they celebrated the festival
for seven days. On the eighth day they
had a meeting. **10**On the twenty-third day
of the seventh month Solomon sent the
people home, full of joy. They were happy
because the LORD had been so good to
David, Solomon, and his people Israel.

The Lord Appears to Solomon

11Solomon finished the Temple of the
LORD and his royal palace. He had success in doing everything he planned in
the Temple of the LORD and his own palace. **12**Then the LORD appeared to Solomon at night and said to him, "I have
heard your prayer and have chosen this
place for myself to be a Temple for sacrifices.
13"I may stop the sky from sending
rain. I may command the locusts to destroy the land. I may send sicknesses to
my people. **14**Then if my people,
who are called by
my name, are sorry
for what they have
done, if they pray
and obey me and
stop their evil ways,

EMAIL FROM GOD 7:14
Success
Check out what will bring success.

FAITH links

GOD'S NEW HOME

2 CHRONICLES 7:11-22

Have you ever moved to a new home? New homeowners like to inspect the homes they've bought before moving in. Once everything checks out, they feel comfortable enough to move in. After Solomon had the Temple built, God appeared to him to give him advice. He also wanted Solomon to know how pleased he was with his new house. God told him that he would always love it. These days, however, God has a different sort of house on earth. If you're a Christian, he's made his home in you. He will always love this new house, too!

Ever think of yourself as a temple? God does! Surf on:

Good Plans, Genesis 45:7–8, p. 64

The God of Big Things, Joshua 10, p. 289

Your Heavenly Dad, Psalm 103:13, p. 786

God's New Temple, Ezekiel 40—44, p. 1135

One Big, Happy Family, John 1:12, p. 1422

Life After Death?, 1 Corinthians 15:12–13, p. 1563

I will hear them from heaven. I will forgive their sin, and I will heal their land.
15Now I will see them, and I will listen to
the prayers prayed in this place. **16**I have
chosen this Temple and made it holy. So I
will be worshiped there forever. Yes, I
will always watch over it and love it.

17"But you must serve me as your father David did. You must obey all I have
commanded and keep my laws and rules.
18If you do, I will make your kingdom
strong. This is the agreement I made with
your father David, saying, 'Someone from
your family will always rule in Israel.'

19"But you must follow me and obey
the laws and commands I have given you.
You must not serve or worship other
gods. **20**If you do, I will take the Israelites
out of my land, the land I have given
them, and I will leave this Temple that I
have made holy. All the nations will make
fun of it and speak evil about it. **21**This
Temple is honored now, but then, everyone who passes by will be shocked. They
will ask, 'Why did the LORD do this terrible thing to this land and this Temple?'
22People will answer, 'This happened because they left the LORD, the God of their
ancestors, the God who brought them out
of Egypt. They decided to follow other
gods and worshiped and served them, so
he brought all this disaster on them.' "

Solomon's Other Achievements

8 By the end of twenty years, Solomon
had built the Temple of the LORD and
the royal palace. **2**Solomon rebuilt the
towns that Hiram had given him, and Solomon sent Israelites to live in them.
3Then he went to Hamath Zobah and captured it. **4**Solomon also built the town of
Tadmor in the desert, and he built all the
towns in Hamath as towns for storing
grain and supplies. **5**He rebuilt the towns
of Upper Beth Horon and Lower Beth
Horon, protecting them with strong
walls, gates, and bars in the gates. **6**He
also rebuilt the town of Baalath. And he
built all the other towns for storage and
all the cities for his chariots and horses.
He built all he wanted in Jerusalem, Lebanon, and everywhere he ruled.

7There were other people in the land
who were not Israelites—the Hittites,
Amorites, Perizzites, Hivites, and Jebusites. **8**They were descendants of the

people that the Israelites had not destroyed. Solomon forced them to be slave
workers, as is still true today. 9But Solomon did not make slaves of the Israelites.
They were his soldiers, chief captains,
commanders of his chariots, and his chariot drivers. 10These were his most important officers. There were
two hundred fifty of them
to direct the people.
11Solomon brought the
daughter of the king of
Egypt from the older part
of Jerusalem to the palace
he had built for her. Solomon said, "My wife must
not live in King David's
palace, because the places
where the Ark of the
Agreement has been are holy."
12Then Solomon offered burnt offerings to the LORD on the altar he had built
for the LORD in front of the Temple porch.
13He offered sacrifices every day as Moses had commanded. They were offered
on the Sabbath days, New Moons, and
the three yearly feasts—the Feast of Unleavened Bread, the Feast of Weeks, and
the Feast of Shelters. 14Solomon followed his father David's instructions and
chose the groups of priests for their service and the Levites to lead the praise
and to help the priests do their daily
work. And he chose the gatekeepers by
their groups to serve at each gate, as David, the man of God, had commanded.
15They obeyed all of Solomon's commands to the priests and Levites, as well
as his commands about the treasuries.
16All Solomon's work was done as he
had said from the day the foundation of
the Temple of the LORD was begun, until
it was finished. So the Temple was finished.
17Then Solomon went to the towns of
Ezion Geber and Elath near the Red Sea
in the land of Edom. 18Hiram sent ships
to Solomon that were commanded by his
own men, who were skilled sailors.
Hiram's men went with Solomon's men
to Ophir and brought back about thirty-
four thousand pounds of gold to King Solomon.

But Solomon did not make slaves of the Israelites.
—2 Chronicles 8:9

The Queen of Sheba Visits

9 When the queen of Sheba heard about
Solomon's fame, she came to Jerusalem to test him with hard questions. She
had a large group of servants with her and
camels carrying spices, jewels, and much
gold. When she came to Solomon, she
talked with him about all
she had in mind, 2and
Solomon answered all
her questions. Nothing
was too hard for him to
explain to her. 3The
queen of Sheba saw that
Solomon was very wise.
She saw the palace he
had built, 4the food on his
table, his many officers,
the palace servants and
their good clothes, the servants who
served Solomon his wine and their good
clothes. She saw the whole burnt offerings he made in the Temple of the LORD.
All these things amazed her.
5So she said to King Solomon, "What
I heard in my own country about your
achievements and wisdom is true. 6I did
not believe it then, but now I have come
and seen it with my own eyes. I was not
told even half of your great wisdom! You
are much greater than I had heard. 7Your
men and officers are very lucky, because
in always serving you, they are able to
hear your wisdom. 8Praise the LORD
your God who was pleased to make you
king. He has put you on his throne to rule
for the LORD your God, because your God
loves the people of Israel and supports
them forever. He has made you king over
them to keep justice and to rule fairly."
9Then she gave the king about nine
thousand pounds of gold and many spices
and jewels. No one had ever given such
spices as the queen of Sheba gave to King
Solomon.
10Hiram's men and Solomon's men
brought gold from Ophir, juniper wood,
and jewels. 11King Solomon used the juniper wood to build steps for the Temple
of the LORD and the palace and to make
lyres and harps for the musicians. No one
in Judah had ever seen such beautiful
things as these.

GET THE INFO

ISRAEL'S GLORY YEARS

2 Chronicles 9

1. It took thousands of men 7 years to build the Temple at Jerusalem and another 13 years to finish King Solomon's royal palace. (Check it out in 1 Kings 5—7, p. 442.)

2. The Euphrates River marked the possible northern limits of King Solomon's empire. It was said all Israel and Judah lived at peace "from Dan to Beersheba." (Read about it in 1 Kings 4:24–25, p. 441.)

3. The area around Gaza probably was the southern border of King Solomon's kingdom. (Look up 1 Kings 4:21, p. 441.)

4. Solomon built a tremendous shipping fleet at Ezion Geber, a town near Elath on the shore of the Red Sea. (Read 1 Kings 9:26–28, p. 451.)

5. Solomon also rebuilt the cities of Hazor, Megiddo, Gezer, and others as important outposts to defend his empire. (Check it out in 1 Kings 9:15–19, p. 450.)

12King Solomon gave the queen of
Sheba everything she wanted and asked
for, even more than she had brought to
him. Then she and her servants returned
to her own country.

Solomon's Wealth

13Every year King Solomon received
about fifty thousand pounds of gold.
14Besides that, he also received gold
from traders and merchants. All the
kings of Arabia and the governors of the
land also brought gold and silver.

15King Solomon made two hundred
large shields of hammered gold, each of
which contained about seven and one-
half pounds of hammered gold. **16**He also
made three hundred smaller shields of
hammered gold, each of which contained
about four pounds of gold. The king put

them in the Palace of the Forest of Lebanon.

17The king built a large throne of ivory and covered it with pure gold.
18The throne had six steps on it and a gold footstool. There were armrests on both sides of the chair, and each armrest had a lion beside it.
19Twelve lions stood on the six steps, one lion at each end of each step. Nothing like this had ever been made for any other kingdom.
20All of Solomon's drinking cups, as well as the dishes in the Palace of the Forest of Lebanon, were made of pure gold. In Solomon's time people did not think silver was valuable.

21King Solomon had many ships that he sent out to trade, with Hiram's men as the crews. Every three years the ships returned, bringing back gold, silver, ivory, apes, and baboons.

22King Solomon had more riches and wisdom than all the other kings on earth.
23All the kings of the earth wanted to see Solomon and listen to the wisdom God had given him.
24Year after year everyone who came brought gifts of silver and gold, clothes, weapons, spices, horses, and mules.

25Solomon had four thousand stalls for horses and chariots, and he had twelve thousand horses. He kept some in special cities for the chariots, and others he kept with him in Jerusalem.
26Solomon ruled over all the kingdoms from the Euphrates River to the land of the Philistines, as far as the border of Egypt.
27In Jerusalem the king made silver as common as stones and cedar trees as plentiful as the fig trees on the western hills.
28Solomon imported horses from Egypt and all other countries.

Solomon's Death

29Everything else Solomon did, from the beginning to the end, is written in the records of Nathan the prophet, and in the prophecy of Ahijah the Shilonite, and in the visions of Iddo the seer, who wrote about Jeroboam, Nebat's son.
30Solomon ruled in Jerusalem over all Israel for forty years.
31Then Solomon died and was buried in Jerusalem, the city of David, his father. And Solomon's son Rehoboam became king in his place.

Israel Turns Against Rehoboam

10 Rehoboam went to Shechem, where all the Israelites had gone to make him king.
2Jeroboam son of Nebat was in Egypt, where he had gone to escape from King Solomon. When Jeroboam heard about Rehoboam being made king, he returned from Egypt.
3After the people sent for him, he and the people went to Rehoboam and said to him,
4"Your father forced us to work very hard. Now, make it easier for us, and don't make us work as he did. Then we will serve you."

EMAIL FROM GOD
10:1–14
Friendship
How can friends pull you down?

5Rehoboam answered, "Come back to me in three days." So the people left.

6King Rehoboam asked the older leaders who had advised Solomon during his lifetime, "How do you think I should answer these people?"

7They answered, "Be kind to these people. If you please them and give them a kind answer, they will serve you always."

8But Rehoboam rejected this advice. Instead, he asked the young men who had grown up with him and who served as his advisers.
9Rehoboam asked them, "What is your advice? How should we answer these people who said, 'Don't make us work as hard as your father did'?"

10The young men who had grown up with him answered, "The people said to you, 'Your father forced us to work very hard. Now make our work easier.' You should tell them, 'My little finger is bigger than my father's legs.
11He forced you to work hard, but I will make you work even harder. My father beat you with whips, but I will beat you with whips that have sharp points.' "

12Rehoboam had told the people, "Come back to me in three days." So after three days Jeroboam and all the people returned to Rehoboam.
13King Rehoboam spoke cruel words to them,

because he had rejected the advice of the
older leaders. 14He followed the advice
of the young men and said, "My father
forced you to work hard, but I will make
you work even harder. My father beat
you with whips, but I will beat you with
whips that have sharp points." 15So the
king did not listen to the people. God
caused this to happen so that the LORD
could keep the promise he had made to
Jeroboam son of Nebat through Ahijah, a
prophet from Shiloh.

16When all the Israelites saw that the
king refused to listen to them, they said
to the king,

"We have no share in David!
We have no part in the son of
Jesse!
People of Israel, let's go to our own
homes!
Let David's son rule his own
people."

So all the Israelites went home. 17But
Rehoboam still ruled over the Israelites
who lived in the towns of Judah.

18Adoniram was in charge of the
forced labor. When Rehoboam sent him
to the people, they threw stones at him
until he died. But King Rehoboam ran to
his chariot and escaped to Jerusalem.
19Since then, Israel has been against the
family of David.

11 When Rehoboam arrived in Jerusalem, he gathered one hundred
eighty thousand of the best soldiers from
Judah and Benjamin. He wanted to fight
Israel to take back his kingdom. 2But the
LORD spoke his word to
Shemaiah, a man of God,
saying, 3"Speak to Sol-
omon's son Rehoboam,
the king of Judah, and to
all the Israelites living in
Judah and Benjamin. Say
to them, 4'The LORD says
you must not go to war
against your brothers.
Every one of you should
go home, because I made
all these things hap-
pen.' " So they obeyed the LORD's command and turned back and did not attack
Jeroboam.

These people made the kingdom of Judah strong, and they supported Solomon's son Rehoboam for three years.
—2 Chronicles 11:17

Rehoboam Makes Judah Strong

5Rehoboam lived in Jerusalem and
built strong cities in Judah to defend it.
6He built up the cities of Bethlehem,
Etam, Tekoa, 7Beth Zur, Soco, Adullam,
8Gath, Mareshah, Ziph, 9Adoraim, Lachish, Azekah, 10Zorah, Aijalon, and Hebron. These were strong, walled cities in
Judah and Benjamin. 11When Rehoboam
made those cities strong, he put commanders and supplies of food, oil, and
wine in them. 12Also, Rehoboam put
shields and spears in all the cities and
made them very strong. Rehoboam kept
the people of Judah and Benjamin under
his control.

13The priests and the Levites from all
over Israel joined Rehoboam. 14The Levites even left their pasturelands and
property and came to Judah and Jerusalem, because Jeroboam and his sons refused to let them serve as priests to the
LORD. 15Jeroboam chose his own priests
for the places of worship and for the goat
and calf idols he had made. 16There were
people from all the tribes of Israel who
wanted to obey the LORD, the God of Israel. So they went to Jerusalem with the
Levites to sacrifice to the LORD, the God
of their fathers. 17These people made
the kingdom of Judah strong, and they
supported Solomon's son Rehoboam for
three years. During this time they lived
the way David and Solomon had lived.

Rehoboam's Family

18Rehoboam married Mahalath, the
daughter of Jerimoth and
Abihail. Jerimoth was Da-
vid's son, and Abihail was
the daughter of Eliab,
Jesse's son. 19Mahalath
gave Rehoboam these
sons: Jeush, Shemariah,
and Zaham. 20Then Reho-
boam married Absalom's
daughter Maacah, and she
gave Rehoboam these chil-
dren: Abijah, Attai, Ziza,
and Shelomith. 21Reho-
boam loved Maacah more than his other
wives and slave women. Rehoboam had
eighteen wives and sixty slave women

and was the father of twenty-eight sons and sixty daughters.

22Rehoboam chose Abijah son of Maacah to be the leader of his own brothers, because he planned to make Abijah king. 23Rehoboam acted wisely. He spread his sons through all the areas of Judah and Benjamin, sending them to every strong, walled city. He gave plenty of supplies to his sons, and he also found wives for them.

Shishak Attacks Jerusalem

12 After Rehoboam's kingdom was set up and he became strong, he and the people of Judah stopped obeying the teachings of the LORD. 2During the fifth year Rehoboam was king, Shishak king of Egypt attacked Jerusalem, because Rehoboam and the people were unfaithful to the LORD. 3Shishak had twelve hundred chariots and sixty thousand horsemen. He brought troops of Libyans, Sukkites, and Cushites from Egypt with him, so many they couldn't be counted. 4Shishak captured the strong, walled cities of Judah and came as far as Jerusalem.

EMAIL FROM GOD 12:1
Success
Find out when success is bad.

5Then Shemaiah the prophet came to Rehoboam and the leaders of Judah who had gathered in Jerusalem because they were afraid of Shishak. Shemaiah said to them, "This is what the LORD says: 'You have left me, so now I will leave you to face Shishak alone.' "

6Then the leaders of Judah and King Rehoboam were sorry for what they had done. They said, "The LORD does what is right."

7When the LORD saw they were sorry for what they had done, the LORD spoke his word to Shemaiah, saying, "The king and the leaders are sorry. So I will not destroy them but will save them soon. I will not use Shishak to punish Jerusalem in my anger. 8But the people of Jerusalem will become Shishak's servants so they may learn that serving me is different than serving the kings of other nations."

9Shishak king of Egypt attacked Jerusalem and took the treasures from the Temple of the LORD and the king's palace. He took everything, even the gold shields Solomon had made. 10So King Rehoboam made bronze shields to take their place and gave them to the commanders of the guards for the palace gates. 11Whenever the king went to the Temple of the LORD, the guards went with him, carrying the shields. Later, they would put them back in the guardroom.

12When Rehoboam was sorry for what he had done, the LORD held his anger back and did not fully destroy Rehoboam. There was some good in Judah.

13King Rehoboam made himself a strong king in Jerusalem. He was forty-one years old when he became king, and he was king in Jerusalem for seventeen years. Jerusalem is the city that the LORD chose from all the tribes of Israel in which he was to be worshiped. Rehoboam's mother was Naamah from the country of Ammon. 14Rehoboam did evil because he did not want to obey the LORD.

15The things Rehoboam did as king, from the beginning to the end, are written in the records of Shemaiah the prophet and Iddo the seer, in the family histories. There were wars between Rehoboam and Jeroboam all the time they ruled. 16Rehoboam died and was buried in Jerusalem, and his son Abijah became king in his place.

Abijah King of Judah

13 Abijah became the king of Judah during the eighteenth year Jeroboam was king of Israel. 2Abijah ruled in Jerusalem for three years. His mother was Maacah daughter of Uriel from the town of Gibeah.

And there was war between Abijah and Jeroboam. 3Abijah led an army of four hundred thousand capable soldiers into battle, and Jeroboam prepared to fight him with eight hundred thousand capable soldiers.

4Abijah stood on Mount Zemaraim in the mountains of Ephraim and said, "Jeroboam and all Israel, listen to me!

FAITH links

THE SALT PROMISE

2 CHRONICLES 13:5

Salt has many uses, but did you ever think of it as a symbol of loyalty? King Abijah of Judah recalled God's promise to David that his family would rule over Israel forever. Salt was the sign that God would keep this promise.

Loyalty is a gift we give to each other. It is a promise of faithfulness. What do you do to show *your* loyalty? How do your friends show their loyalty to you?

A Special Promise, Numbers 30:1–2, p. 217

Promises, Promises, Judges 2:1–3, p. 312

The Heart of the Matter, 1 Samuel 16, p. 375

A Big Responsibility, 2 Kings 11, p. 494

A Promise from the Heart, Jeremiah 31:31–33, p. 1037

A Friend of Jesus, John 15:9–17, p. 1450

5You should know that the LORD, the God
of Israel, gave David and his sons the
right to rule Israel forever by an agreement of salt. 6But Jeroboam son of Nebat,
one of the officers of Solomon, David's
son, turned against his master. 7Then
worthless, evil men joined Jeroboam
against Rehoboam, Solomon's son. He
was young and didn't know what to do, so
he could not stop them.

8"Now you people are making plans
against the LORD's kingdom, which belongs to David's sons. There are many of
you, and you have the gold calves Jeroboam made for you as gods. 9You have
thrown out the Levites and the LORD's
priests, Aaron's sons. You have chosen
your own priests as people in other countries do. Anyone who comes with a young
bull and seven male sheep can become a
priest of idols that are not gods.

10"But as for us, the LORD is our God;
we have not left him. The priests who
serve the LORD are Aaron's sons, and the
Levites help them. 11They offer burnt offerings and sweet-smelling incense to
the LORD every morning and evening.
They put the bread on the special table in
the Temple. And they light the lamps on
the gold lampstand every evening. We
obey the command of the LORD our God,
but you have left him. 12God himself is
with us as our ruler. His priests blow the
trumpet to call us to war against you.
Men of Israel, don't fight against the
LORD, the God of your ancestors, because you won't succeed."

13But Jeroboam had sent some troops
to sneak behind Judah's army. So while
Jeroboam was in front of Judah's army,
Jeroboam's soldiers were behind them.
14When the soldiers of Judah turned
around, they saw Jeroboam's army attacking both in front and back. So they
cried out to the LORD, and the priests
blew the trumpets. 15Then the men of
Judah gave a battle cry. When they shouted, God caused Jeroboam and the army of
Israel to run away from Abijah and the
army of Judah. 16When the army of Israel
ran away from the men of Judah, God
handed them over to Judah. 17Abijah's
army struck Israel so that five hundred
thousand of Israel's best men were
killed. 18So at that time the people of Israel were defeated. And the people of Judah won, because they depended on the
LORD, the God of their ancestors.

19Abijah's army chased Jeroboam's
army and captured from him the towns of
Bethel, Jeshanah, and Ephron, and the
small villages near them. 20Jeroboam
never became strong again while Abijah
was alive. The LORD struck Jeroboam,
and he died.

21But Abijah became strong. He married fourteen women and was the father of twenty-two sons and sixteen daughters. 22Everything else Abijah did—what he said and what he did—is recorded in the writings of the prophet Iddo.

14 Abijah died and was buried in Jerusalem. His son Asa became king in his place, and there was peace in the country for ten years during Asa's time.

Asa King of Judah

2Asa did what the LORD his God said
was good and right. 3He removed the foreign altars and the places where gods
were worshiped. He smashed the stone
pillars that honored other gods, and he
tore down the Asherah idols. 4Asa commanded the people of Judah to follow the
LORD, the God of their ancestors, and to
obey his teachings and commandments.
5He also removed the places where gods
were worshiped and the incense altars
from every town in Judah. So the kingdom had peace while Asa was king. 6Asa
built strong, walled cities in Judah during
the time of peace. He had no war in these
years, because the LORD gave him peace.
7Asa said to the people of Judah,
"Let's build up these towns and put walls
around them. Let's make towers, gates,
and bars in the gates. This country is
ours, because we have obeyed the LORD
our God. We have followed him, and he
has given us peace all around." So they
built and had success.
8Asa had an army of three hundred
thousand men from Judah and two hundred eighty thousand men from Benjamin. The men from Judah carried large
shields and spears. The men from Benjamin carried small shields and bows and
arrows. All of them were brave fighting
men.
9Then Zerah from Cush came out to
fight them with an enormous army and
three hundred chariots. They came as far
as the town of Mareshah. 10So Asa went
out to fight Zerah and prepared for battle
in the Valley of Zephathah at Mareshah.
11Asa called out to the LORD his God,
saying, "LORD, only you can help weak

FAITH links

WEAK? GREAT!

2 CHRONICLES 14:11

What's so great about being weak? If you asked five or six of your friends that question, how would they respond? Most of us, if we're honest, would not have an answer. In our society, weakness is not considered a good thing.

When an enemy nation threatened Judah, King Asa asked God for help. He admitted how weak his people were. The enemy nation was much stronger. God, however, was much stronger still. He had the power to defeat the enemy.

When we're weak, God is strong. What's so great about being weak? We can rely on God's strength to help us.

Check out these Faithlinks on being strong—in God:

Out of Control?, Genesis 4, p. 8

Put Pride Aside, Exodus 2:11–15, p. 78

The Perfect Leader?, Numbers 20:1–13, p. 203

When the Green-eyed Monster Strikes, 1 Samuel 18:6–9, p. 379

An Energy Boost, Acts 4:31, p. 1469

Thoughts on Thoughts, Philippians 4:8–9, p. 1614

people against the strong. Help us, LORD
our God, because we depend on you. We
fight against this enormous army in your
name. LORD, you are our God. Don't let
anyone win against you."
12So the LORD defeated the Cushites
when Asa's army from Judah attacked
them, and the Cushites ran away. **13**Asa's
army chased them as far as the town of
Gerar. So many Cushites were killed that
the army could not fight again; they were
crushed by the LORD and his army. Asa
and his army carried many valuable
things away from the enemy. **14**They destroyed all the towns near Gerar, because
the people living in these towns were
afraid of the LORD. Since these towns had
many valuable things, Asa's army took
them away. **15**Asa's army also attacked
the camps where the shepherds lived and
took many sheep and camels. Then they
returned to Jerusalem.

Asa's Changes

15 The Spirit of God entered Azariah
son of Oded. **2**Azariah went to
meet Asa and said, "Listen to me, Asa
and all you people of Judah and Benjamin.
The LORD is with you when you are with
him. If you obey him, you will find him,
but if you leave him, he will leave you.
3For a long time Israel was without the
true God and without a priest to teach
them and without the teachings. **4**But
when they were in trouble, they turned
to the LORD, the God of Israel. They
looked for him and found him. **5**In those
days no one could travel safely. There
was much trouble in all the nations. **6**One
nation would destroy another nation, and
one city would destroy another city, because God troubled them with all kinds of
distress. **7**But you should be strong.
Don't give up, because you will get a reward for your good work."
8Asa felt brave when he heard these
words and the message from Azariah son
of Oded the prophet. So he removed the
hateful idols from all of Judah and Benjamin and from the towns he had captured
in the hills of Ephraim. He repaired the
LORD's altar that was in front of the porch
of the Temple of the LORD.
9Then Asa gathered all the people
from Judah and Benjamin and from the
tribes of Ephraim, Manasseh, and Simeon who were living in Judah. Many people
came to Asa even from Israel, because
they saw that the LORD, Asa's God, was
with him.
10Asa and these people gathered in
Jerusalem in the third month of the fifteenth year of Asa's rule. **11**At that time
they sacrificed to the LORD seven hundred bulls and seven thousand sheep and
goats from the valuable things Asa's
army had taken from their enemies.
12Then they made an agreement to obey
the LORD, the God of their ancestors,
with their whole being. **13**Anyone who
refused to obey the LORD, the God of Israel, was to be killed. It did not matter if
that person was important or unimportant, a man or woman. **14**Then Asa and
the people made a promise before the
LORD, shouting with a loud voice and blowing trumpets and sheep's horns. **15**All the
people of Judah were happy about the
promise, because they had promised with
all their heart. They looked for
God and found him.
So the LORD gave
them peace in all the
country.

> EMAIL FROM GOD
> **15:15**
> **Following God**
> How should you follow God?

16King Asa also
removed Maacah, his
grandmother, from
being queen mother, because she had made
a terrible Asherah idol. Asa cut down that
idol, smashed it into pieces, and burned it in
the Kidron Valley. **17**But the places of worship to gods were not removed from Judah. Even so, Asa was faithful all his life.
18Asa brought into the Temple of God
the gifts he and his father had given: silver, gold, and utensils.
19There was no more war until the
thirty-fifth year of Asa's rule.

Asa's Last Years

16 In the thirty-sixth year of Asa's
rule, Baasha king of Israel attacked Judah. He made the town of Ramah strong so he could keep people from
leaving or entering Judah, Asa's country.
2Asa took silver and gold from the

FAITH links

DEPEND ON HIM!

2 CHRONICLES 16:1-9

When you fall into trouble, who do you depend on for help? King Asa of Judah needed help. Instead of asking God for help, he depended on the help of the king of Aram and his army. A prophet predicted disaster for King Asa.

God wants us to ask him for help, but many times, he's the last one we go to. Whenever you have a problem, even if you think you can find a solution by yourself, ask God to help you. Getting help from a parent is fine, too. God wants you to depend on trusted adults. He also wants you to learn to depend on him.

Need someone to depend on? Link here:

Two Enemies, Nehemiah 6, p. 631

A Pity Party, Job 10, p. 671

Uprooted by Change, Amos 9:15, p. 1205

Our Heavenly Connection, Matthew 6:9–13, p. 1283

At the Right Time, Galatians 4:4, p. 1590

Keep Going!, James 1:2–3, p. 1688

treasuries of the Temple of the LORD and
out of his own palace. Then he sent it
with messengers to Ben-Hadad king of
Aram, who lived in Damascus. Asa said,
3"Let there be a treaty between you and
me as there was between my father and
your father. I am sending you silver and
gold. Break your treaty with Baasha king
of Israel so he will leave my land."

4Ben-Hadad agreed with King Asa
and sent the commanders of his armies
to attack the towns of Israel. They defeated the towns of Ijon, Dan, and Abel
Beth Maacah, and all the towns in Naphtali where treasures were stored. 5When
Baasha heard about this, he stopped
building up Ramah and left his work.
6Then King Asa brought all the people of
Judah to Ramah, and they carried away
the rocks and wood that Baasha had used.
And they used them to build up Geba and
Mizpah.

7At that time Hanani the seer came to
Asa king of Judah and said to him, "You
depended on the king of Aram to help you
and not on the LORD your God. So the
king of Aram's army escaped from you.
8The Cushites and Libyans had a large
and powerful army and many chariots and
horsemen. But you depended on the
LORD to help you, so he handed them over
to you. 9The LORD searches all the earth
for people who have given themselves
completely to him. He wants to make
them strong. Asa, you did a foolish thing,
so from now on you will have wars."

10Asa was angry with Hanani the seer
because of what he had said; he was so
angry that he put Hanani in prison. And
Asa was cruel to some of the people at
the same time.

11Everything Asa did as king, from the
beginning to the end, is written in the book
of the kings of Judah and Israel. 12In the
thirty-ninth year of his rule, Asa got a disease in his feet. Though his disease was
very bad, he did not ask for help from the
LORD, but only from the doctors. 13Then
Asa died in the forty-first year of his rule.
14The people buried Asa in the tomb he
had made for himself in Jerusalem. They
laid him on a bed filled with spices and different kinds of mixed perfumes, and they
made a large fire to honor him.

Jehoshaphat King of Judah

17 Jehoshaphat, Asa's son, became
king of Judah in his place. Jehoshaphat made Judah strong so they could

fight against Israel. **2**He put troops in all
the strong, walled cities of Judah, in the
land of Judah, and in the towns of Ephraim that his father Asa had captured.
3The LORD was with Jehoshaphat, because he lived as his ancestor David had
lived when he first became king. Jehoshaphat did not ask for help from the Baal
idols, **4**but from the God of his father. He
obeyed God's commands and did not live
as the people of Israel lived. **5**The LORD
made Jehoshaphat a strong king over Judah. All the people of Judah brought gifts
to Jehoshaphat, so he had much wealth
and honor. **6**He wanted very much to
obey the LORD. He also removed the
places for worshiping gods and the Asherah idols from Judah.
7During the third year of his rule, Jehoshaphat sent his officers to teach in the
towns of Judah. These officers were Ben-
Hail, Obadiah, Zechariah, Nethanel, and
Micaiah. **8**Jehoshaphat sent with them
these Levites: Shemaiah, Nethaniah,
Zebadiah, Asahel, Shemiramoth, Jehona-
than, Adonijah, Tobijah, and Tob-Adonijah.
He also sent the priests Elishama and Jehoram. **9**These leaders, Levites, and
priests taught the people in Judah. They
took the Book of the Teachings of the
LORD and went through all the towns of
Judah and taught the people.
10The nations near Judah were afraid
of the LORD, so they did not start a war
against Jehoshaphat. **11**Some of the Philistines brought gifts and silver to Jehoshaphat as he demanded. Some Arabs
brought him flocks: seventy-seven hundred sheep and seventy-seven hundred
goats.
12Jehoshaphat grew more and more
powerful. He built strong, walled cities
and towns for storing supplies in Judah.
13He kept many supplies in the towns of
Judah, and he kept trained soldiers in Jerusalem. **14**These soldiers were listed by
families. From the families of Judah,
these were the commanders of groups of
a thousand men: Adnah was the commander of three hundred thousand soldiers; **15**Jehohanan was the commander
of two hundred eighty thousand soldiers;
16Amasiah was the commander of two

FAITH links

A TRAVELING BIBLE STUDY

2 CHRONICLES 17:9

King Jehoshaphat of Judah knew the importance of obeying God. One of the ways to obey God was to study God's law. He had two priests carry God's law, called the Book of the Teachings of the Lord, throughout Judah and teach the people about God. At that time, the people did not have the whole Bible. They only had the Book of the Teachings.

You don't have to wait for a teacher to travel to your town to teach you about God. God has provided teachers in your church to teach you about the Bible. You also have the Bible itself to read and study. And Bible reference books like a concordance, a dictionary, and Bible study guides can help you understand what you read.

Check out these links on reading the Bible:

The Cloud Guide, Numbers 9:15–23, p. 188

Facts About Following, Joshua 6, p. 283

Do What You Want?, Judges 21:25, p. 341

The "Ruler" of Our Lives, Amos 7:7–9, p. 1202

The Power of *If*, Mark 9:14–24, p. 1344

Just Like a Tree, Colossians 1:23, p. 1621

hundred thousand soldiers. Amasiah son
of Zicri had volunteered to serve the
LORD.
17These were the commanders from
the families of Benjamin: Eliada, a brave
soldier, had two hundred thousand soldiers who used bows and shields. 18And
Jehozabad had one hundred eighty thousand men armed for war.
19All these soldiers served King Jehoshaphat. The king also put other men
in the strong, walled cities through all of
Judah.

Micaiah Warns King Ahab

18 Jehoshaphat had much wealth and
honor, and he made an agreement
with King Ahab through marriage.[n] 2A
few years later Jehoshaphat went to visit
Ahab in Samaria. Ahab sacrificed many
sheep and cattle as a great feast to honor
Jehoshaphat and the people with him. He
encouraged Jehoshaphat to attack Ramoth in Gilead. 3Ahab king of Israel
asked Jehoshaphat king of Judah, "Will
you go with me to attack Ramoth in Gilead?"
Jehoshaphat answered, "I will go with
you, and my soldiers are yours. We will
join you in the battle." 4Jehoshaphat also
said to Ahab, "But first
we should ask if this is
the LORD's will."
5So King Ahab called
four hundred prophets to-
gether and asked them,
"Should we go to war
against Ramoth in Gilead
or not?"
They answered, "Go,
because God will hand
them over to you."
6But Jehoshaphat asked, "Isn't there
a prophet of the LORD here? Let's ask
him what we should do."
7Then King Ahab said to Jehoshaphat,
"There is one other prophet. We could
ask the LORD through him, but I hate
him. He never prophesies anything good
about me, but always something bad. He
is Micaiah son of Imlah."
Jehoshaphat said, "King Ahab, you
shouldn't say that!"

> He never prophesies anything good about me, but always something bad.
> —2 Chronicles 18:7

8So Ahab king of Israel told one of his
officers to bring Micaiah to him at once.
9Ahab king of Israel and Jehoshaphat
king of Judah had on their royal robes and
were sitting on their thrones at the
threshing floor, near the entrance to the
gate of Samaria. All the prophets were
standing before them speaking their
messages. 10Zedekiah son of Kenaanah
had made some iron horns. He said to
Ahab, "This is what the LORD says: 'You
will use these horns to fight the Arameans until they are destroyed.' "
11All the other prophets said the
same thing, "Attack Ramoth in Gilead and
win, because the LORD will hand the Arameans over to you."
12The messenger who had gone to
get Micaiah said to him, "All the other
prophets are saying King Ahab will win.
You should agree with them and give the
king a good answer."
13But Micaiah answered, "As surely
as the LORD lives, I can tell him only what
my God says."
14When Micaiah came to Ahab, the
king asked him, "Micaiah, should we attack Ramoth in Gilead or not?"
Micaiah answered, "Attack and win!
They will be handed over to you."
15But Ahab said to
Micaiah, "How many
times do I have to tell you
to speak only the truth to
me in the name of the
LORD?"
16So Micaiah an-
swered, "I saw the army
of Israel scattered over
the hills like sheep without a shepherd. The
LORD said, 'They have no
leaders. They should go home and not
fight.' "
17Then Ahab king of Israel said to Jehoshaphat, "I told you! He never prophesies anything good about me, but only
bad."
18But Micaiah said, "Hear the message

18:1 agreement . . . through marriage Jehoshaphat's son Jehoram married Athaliah, Ahab's daughter. See 2 Chronicles 21:6.

from the LORD: I saw the LORD sitting on
his throne with his heavenly army standing on his right and on his left. **19**The
LORD said, 'Who will trick King Ahab of
Israel into attacking Ramoth in Gilead
where he will be killed?'

"Some said one thing; some said another. **20**Then one spirit came and stood
before the LORD and said, 'I will trick
him.'

"The LORD asked, 'How will you do it?'

21"The spirit answered, 'I will go to
Ahab's prophets and make them tell lies.'

"So the LORD said, 'You will succeed
in tricking him. Go and do it.' "

22Micaiah said, "Ahab, the LORD has
made your prophets lie to you, and the
LORD has decided that disaster should
come to you."

23Then Zedekiah son of Kenaanah
went up to Micaiah and slapped him in
the face. Zedekiah said, "Has the LORD's
Spirit left me to speak through you?"

24Micaiah answered, "You will find
out on the day you go to hide in an inside
room."

25Then Ahab king of Israel ordered,
"Take Micaiah and send him to Amon,
the governor of the city, and to Joash, the
king's son. **26**Tell them I said to put this
man in prison and give him only bread
and water until I return safely from the
battle."

27Micaiah said, "Ahab, if you come
back safely from the battle, the LORD has
not spoken through me. Remember my
words, all you people!"

Ahab Is Killed

28So Ahab king of Israel and Jehoshaphat king of Judah went to Ramoth in Gilead. **29**King Ahab said to Jehoshaphat, "I
will go into battle, but I will wear other
clothes so no one will recognize me. But
you wear your royal clothes." So Ahab
wore other clothes, and they went into
battle.

30The king of Aram ordered his chariot commanders, "Don't fight with anyone—important or unimportant—except
the king of Israel." **31**When these commanders saw Jehoshaphat, they thought
he was the king of Israel, so they turned
to attack him. But Jehoshaphat began
shouting, and the LORD helped him. God
made the chariot commanders turn away
from Jehoshaphat. **32**When they saw he
was not King Ahab, they stopped chasing
him.

33By chance, a soldier shot an arrow
which hit Ahab king of Israel between the
pieces of his armor. King Ahab said to his
chariot driver, "Turn around and get me
out of the battle, because I am hurt!"
34The battle continued all day. King Ahab
held himself up in his chariot and faced
the Arameans until evening. Then he
died at sunset.

19 Jehoshaphat king of Judah came
back safely to his palace in Jerusalem. **2**Jehu son of Hanani, a seer, went
out to meet him and said to the king,
"Why did you help evil people? Why do
you love those who hate the LORD? That
is the reason the LORD is angry with you.
3But there is some good in you. You took
the Asherah idols out of this country, and
you have tried to obey God."

Jehoshaphat Chooses Judges

4Jehoshaphat lived in Jerusalem. He
went out again to be with the people,
from Beersheba to the mountains of
Ephraim, and he turned them back to the
LORD, the God of their ancestors. **5**Jehoshaphat appointed judges in all the
land, in each of the strong, walled cities of
Judah. **6**Jehoshaphat said to them,
"Watch what you do, because you are
not judging for peo-
ple but for the
LORD. He will be
with you when you
make a decision.
7Now let each of
you fear the LORD.
Watch what you do, because the LORD
our God wants people to be fair. He wants
all people to be treated the same, and he
doesn't want decisions influenced by
money."

> EMAIL FROM GOD
> **19:5–7**
> **Leadership**
> Check out how to make good decisions.

8And in Jerusalem Jehoshaphat appointed some of the Levites, priests, and
leaders of Israelite families to be judges.
They were to decide cases about the law
of the LORD and settle problems between

the people who lived in Jerusalem. 9Je-
hoshaphat commanded them, "You must
always serve the LORD completely, and
you must fear him. 10Your people living
in the cities will bring you cases about
killing, about the teachings, commands,
rules, or some other law. In all these cases you must warn the people not to sin against the LORD. If you don't, he will be angry with you and your people. But if you warn them, you won't be guilty.
11"Amariah, the leading priest, will be
over you in all cases about the LORD. Zebadiah son of Ishmael, a leader in the tribe of Judah, will be over you in all cases about the king. Also, the Levites will serve as officers for you. Have courage. May the LORD be with those who do what is right."

FAITH links

A REMINDER TO BE FAIR

2 CHRONICLES 19:5-11

Have you ever had to be reminded to be fair? King Jehoshaphat of Judah wanted to rule his people wisely. But he couldn't be everywhere at the same time. So, he assigned judges to make fair decisions over the people they governed. He also reminded them to be obedient to the Lord while they did their jobs. Obedience to God would help them be fair.

Remembering to do what God says can help you be fair to others, too. One of God's rules that can help you be fair is called the Golden Rule: "Do to others what you would want them to do to you" (Luke 6:31).

Fairness for All, Deuteronomy 24:17, p. 258

Fair All the Time?, 2 Samuel 8:15, p. 408

Help for the Outsiders, Nehemiah 5:9–10, p. 630

A Bad Reaction, Jeremiah 36, p. 1043

One of the Faithful, Acts 10:1–34, p. 1482

The Sacrifice of Service, Philippians 2:17, 25–30, p. 1612

Jehoshaphat Faces War

20 Later the Moabites, Ammonites,
and some Meunites came to start
a war with Jehoshaphat. 2Messengers
came and told Jehoshaphat, "A large army is coming against you from Edom, from the other side of the Dead Sea. They are already in Hazazon Tamar!" (Hazazon Tamar is also called En Gedi.) 3Jehoshaphat
was afraid, so he decided to ask the LORD what to do. He announced that no one in Judah should eat during this special time of prayer to God. 4The people of Judah
came together to ask the LORD for help; they came from every town in Judah.
5The people of Judah and Jerusalem
met in front of the new courtyard in the Temple of the LORD. Then Jehoshaphat
stood up, 6and he said, "LORD, God of our
ancestors, you are the God in heaven. You rule over all the kingdoms of the nations. You have power and strength, so no
one can stand against you. 7Our God, you
forced out the people who lived in this land as your people Israel moved in. And you gave this land forever to the descendants of your friend Abraham. 8They
lived in this land and built a Temple for
you. They said, 9'If trouble comes upon
us, or war, punishment, sickness, or hunger, we will stand before you and before this Temple where you have chosen to be worshiped. We will cry out to you when we are in trouble. Then you will hear and save us.'
10"But now here are men from Am-
mon, Moab, and Edom. You wouldn't let the Israelites enter their lands when the Israelites came from Egypt. So the

FAITH links

YOUR BEST DEFENSE

2 CHRONICLES 20:1-12

In video or computer games, you're often faced with an overwhelming problem. The game gives you several defense resources you can use to overcome the problem. If you run out of resources, you can shut the game off. Ta-da! You're no longer facing that problem. In life, though, when you're facing an overwhelming problem, you can't push a button to shut it off. King Jehoshaphat of Judah felt overwhelmed when an enemy army marched to attack his people. He faced certain defeat until he used the best resource a person can have when trouble comes: prayer. When an overwhelming problem comes your way, remember God is your best defense.

Need a good defense against problems? Check out these links:

Your Heavenly Parent, Exodus 2:1–10, p. 77

Keep On Praying, 1 Samuel 1, p. 354

No Doubt About It, Job 36:5, p. 699

A Tight Spot, Jonah 2, p. 1215

Our Heavenly Connection, Matthew 6:9–13, p. 1283

Hold On!, 2 Thessalonians 2:15–17, p. 1639

Israelites turned away and did not destroy them. 11But see how they repay us
for not destroying them! They have come
to force us out of your land, which you
gave us as our own. 12Our God, punish
those people. We have no power against
this large army that is attacking us. We
don't know what to do, so we look to you
for help."

13All the men of Judah stood before
the LORD with their babies, wives, and
children. 14Then the Spirit of the LORD
entered Jahaziel. (Jahaziel was Zechariah's son. Zechariah was Benaiah's son.
Benaiah was Jeiel's son, and Jeiel was
Mattaniah's son.) Jahaziel, a Levite and a
descendant of Asaph, stood up in the
meeting. 15He said, "Listen to me, King
Jehoshaphat and all you people living in
Judah and Jerusalem. The LORD says this
to you: 'Don't be afraid or discouraged
because of this large army. The battle is
not your battle, it is God's. 16Tomorrow
go down there and fight those people.
They will come up through the Pass of
Ziz. You will find them at the end of the
ravine that leads to the Desert of Jeruel.
17You won't need to fight in this battle.
Just stand strong in your places, and you
will see the LORD save you. Judah and Jerusalem, don't be afraid or discouraged,
because the LORD is with you. So go out
against those people tomorrow.' "

18Jehoshaphat bowed facedown on
the ground. All the people of Judah and
Jerusalem bowed down before the LORD
and worshiped him. 19Then some Levites from the Kohathite and Korahite
people stood up and praised the LORD,
the God of Israel, with very loud voices.

20Jehoshaphat's army went out into
the Desert of Tekoa early in the morning.
As they were starting out, Jehoshaphat
stood and said, "Listen to me, people of
Judah and Jerusalem. Have faith in the
LORD your God, and you will stand
strong. Have faith in his prophets, and
you will succeed." 21Jehoshaphat listened to the people's advice. Then he
chose men to be singers to the LORD, to
praise him because he is holy and wonderful. As they marched in front of the
army, they said,

"Thank the LORD,
because his love continues
forever."
22As they began to sing and praise
God, the LORD set ambushes for the people of Ammon, Moab, and Edom who had
come to attack Judah. And they were defeated. 23The Ammonites and Moabites
attacked the Edomites, destroying them
completely. After they had killed the
Edomites, they killed each other.
24When the men from Judah came to a
place where they could see the desert,
they looked at the enemy's large army.
But they only saw dead bodies lying on
the ground; no one had escaped. 25When
Jehoshaphat and his army came to take
their valuables, they found many supplies, much clothing, and other valuable
things. There was more than they could
carry away; there was so much it took
three days to gather it all. 26On the
fourth day Jehoshaphat and his army met
in the Valley of Beracah and praised the
LORD. That is why that place has been
called the Valley of Beracah[n] to this day.
27Then Jehoshaphat led all the men
from Judah and Jerusalem back to Jerusalem. The LORD had made them happy because their enemies were defeated.
28They entered Jerusalem with harps,
lyres, and trumpets and went to the Temple of the LORD.
29When all the kingdoms of the lands
around them heard how the LORD had
fought Israel's enemies, they feared God.
30So Jehoshaphat's kingdom was not at
war. His God gave him peace from all the
countries around him.

Jehoshaphat's Rule Ends

31Jehoshaphat ruled over the country
of Judah. He was thirty-five years old
when he became king, and he ruled in Jerusalem for twenty-five years. His
mother's name was Azubah daughter of
Shilhi. 32Jehoshaphat was good like his
father Asa, and he did what the LORD said
was right. 33But the places where gods
were worshiped were not removed, and
the people did not really want to follow
the God of their ancestors.
34The other things Jehoshaphat did
as king, from the beginning to the end,
are written in the records of Jehu son of
Hanani, which are in the book of the
kings of Israel.
35Later, Jehoshaphat king of Judah
made a treaty with Ahaziah king of Israel,
which was a wrong thing to do. 36Jehosh-
aphat agreed with Ahaziah to build trading ships, which they built in the town of
Ezion Geber. 37Then Eliezer son of Do-
davahu from the town of Mareshah spoke
against Jehoshaphat. He said, "Jehoshaphat, because you joined with Ahaziah,
the LORD will destroy what you have
made." The ships were wrecked so they
could not sail out to trade.

21 Jehoshaphat died and was buried
with his ancestors in Jerusalem,
the city of David. Then his son Jehoram
became king in his place. 2Jehoram's
brothers were Azariah, Jehiel, Zechariah,
Azariahu, Michael, and Shephatiah. They
were the sons of Jehoshaphat king of Judah. 3Jehoshaphat gave his sons many
gifts of silver, gold, and valuable things,
and he gave them strong, walled cities in
Judah. But Jehoshaphat gave the kingdom to Jehoram, because he was the first
son.

Jehoram King of Judah

4When Jehoram took control of his
father's kingdom, he killed all his brothers with a sword and also killed some of
the leaders of Judah. 5He was thirty-two
years old when he began to rule, and he
ruled eight years in Jerusalem. 6He followed in the ways of the kings of Israel,
just as the family of Ahab had done, because he married Ahab's daughter. Jehoram did what the LORD said was wrong.
7But the LORD would not destroy David's
family because of the agreement he had
made with David. He had promised that
one of David's descendants would always
rule.
8In Jehoram's time, Edom broke away
from Judah's rule and chose their own
king. 9So Jehoram went to Edom with
all his commanders and chariots. The

20:26 Beracah This name means "blessing" or "praise."

Edomites surrounded him and his chariot
commanders, but Jehoram got up and attacked the Edomites at night. **10**From
then until now the country of Edom has
fought against the rule of Judah. At the
same time the people of Libnah also
broke away from Jehoram because Jehoram left the LORD, the God of his ancestors.

11Jehoram also built places to worship gods on the hills in Judah. He led the
people of Jerusalem to sin, and he led the
people of Judah away from the LORD.
12Then Jehoram received this letter
from Elijah the prophet:

> This is what the LORD, the God
> of your ancestor David, says, "Je-
> horam, you have not
> lived as your father Je-
> hoshaphat lived and as
> Asa king of Judah
> lived. **13**But you have
> lived as the kings of
> Israel lived, leading
> the people of Judah
> and Jerusalem to sin
> against God, as Ahab
> and his family did. You
> have killed your broth-
> ers, and they were better than you.
> **14**So now the LORD is about to pun-
> ish your people, your children,
> wives, and everything you own.
> **15**You will have a terrible disease in
> your intestines that will become
> worse every day. Finally it will
> cause your intestines to come out."

16The LORD caused the Philistines
and the Arabs who lived near the Cushites to be angry with Jehoram. **17**So the
Philistines and Arabs attacked Judah and
carried away all the wealth of Jehoram's
palace, as well as his sons and wives.
Only Jehoram's youngest son, Ahaziah,
was left.

18After these things happened, the
LORD gave Jehoram a disease in his intestines that could not be cured. **19**After
he was sick for two years, Jehoram's intestines came out because of the disease,
and he died in terrible pain. The people
did not make a fire to honor Jehoram as
they had done for his ancestors.

20Jehoram was thirty-two years old
when he became king, and he ruled eight
years in Jerusalem. No one was sad when
he died. He was buried in Jerusalem, but
not in the graves for the kings.

Ahaziah King of Judah

22 The people of Jerusalem chose
Ahaziah, Jehoram's youngest son,
to be king in his place. The robbers who
had come with the Arabs to attack
Jehoram's camp had killed all of Jehoram's
older sons. So Ahaziah began to rule Judah. **2**Ahaziah was twenty-two years old
when he became king, and he ruled one
year in Jerusalem. His
mother's name was Atha-
liah, a granddaughter of
Omri. **3**Ahaziah followed
the ways of Ahab's family,
because his mother en-
couraged him to do wrong.
4Ahaziah did what the
LORD said was wrong, as
Ahab's family had done.
They gave advice to Aha-
ziah after his father died,
and their bad advice led to his death. **5**Following their advice, Ahaziah went with Joram son of Ahab to Ramoth in Gilead,
where they fought against Hazael king of
Aram. The Arameans wounded Joram.
6So Joram returned to Jezreel to heal from
the wounds he received at Ramoth when
he fought Hazael king of Aram.

Ahaziah son of Jehoram and king of
Judah went down to visit Joram son of
Ahab at Jezreel because he had been
wounded.

7God caused Ahaziah's death when he
went to visit Joram. Ahaziah arrived and
went out with Joram to meet Jehu son of
Nimshi, whom the LORD had appointed to
destroy Ahab's family. **8**While Jehu was
punishing Ahab's family, he found the
leaders of Judah and the sons of
Ahaziah's relatives who served Ahaziah,
and Jehu killed them all. **9**Then Jehu
looked for Ahaziah. Jehu's men caught
him hiding in Samaria, so they brought

> Ahaziah followed the ways of Ahab's family, because his mother encouraged him to do wrong.
> —2 Chronicles 22:3

him to Jehu. Then they killed and buried
him. They said, "Ahaziah is a descendant
of Jehoshaphat, and Jehoshaphat obeyed
the LORD with all his heart." No one in
Ahaziah's family had the power to take
control of the kingdom of Judah.

Athaliah and Joash

10When Ahaziah's mother, Athaliah,
saw that her son was dead, she killed all
the royal family in Judah. **11**But Jehosheba, King Jehoram's daughter, took Joash,
Ahaziah's son. She stole him from among
the other sons of the king who were going to be murdered and put him and his
nurse in a bedroom. So Jehosheba, who
was King Jehoram's daughter and
Ahaziah's sister and the wife of Jehoiada
the priest, hid Joash so Athaliah could not
kill him. **12**He hid with them in the Temple of God for six years. During that time
Athaliah ruled the land.

23 In the seventh year Jehoiada decided to do something. He made
an agreement with the commanders of
the groups of a hundred men: Azariah son
of Jeroham, Ishmael son of Jehohanan,
Azariah son of Obed, Maaseiah son of
Adaiah, and Elishaphat son of Zicri.
2They went around in Judah and gathered the Levites from all the towns, and
they gathered the leaders of the families

MY FAULT

Tagg and I are talking about the most embarrassing mistakes we've ever made. We have a friend who's still trying to recover from one of his mistakes. Let's welcome Brady, age 10, to Connect 2-You.

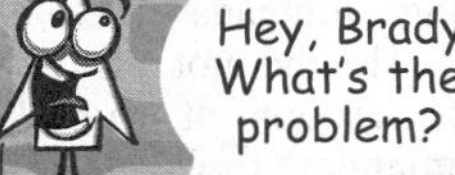

Hey, Brady. What's the problem?

Brady

The problem is, I did something really stupid at church camp last week. I don't really want to go into all the details about it, so I'll just say it was bad enough to get me sent home from camp and grounded by my parents for a month. I've never done anything like it before, and I don't even know why I did it. What do you think is wrong with me?

You're human, Brady. We all make mistakes—some just seem worse than others. The good news is that no matter how bad your mistake is, God will forgive you for it—if you sincerely ask him to. The Bible tells us that nothing, not even the worst mistake in the world, can separate us from God. You can read about that in Romans 8:38–39, p. 1530. For more tips on how to deal with mistakes, check out the Livin' It page on failures and weaknesses, Luke 22:54–62, p. 1414.

Look at the men Jesus chose for his disciples, Brady. They were always making mistakes—especially Peter, one of Jesus' closest friends. But Peter didn't let his mistakes ruin his life. He learned from them and became a stronger person in the process. With God's help, you can, too!

of Judah. Then they went to Jerusalem.
3All the people together made an agreement with the king in the Temple of God.
Jehoiada said to them, "The king's son
will rule, as the LORD promised about
David's descendants. **4**Now this is what
you must do: You priests and Levites go
on duty on the Sabbath. A third of you will
guard the doors. **5**A third of you will be at
the king's palace, and a third of you will
be at the Foundation Gate. All the other
people will stay in the courtyards of the
Temple of the LORD. **6**Don't let anyone
come into the Temple of the LORD except
the priests and Levites who serve. They
may come because they have been made
ready to serve the LORD, but all the others must do the job the LORD has given
them. **7**The Levites must stay near the
king, each man with his weapon in his
hand. If anyone tries to enter the Temple,
kill him. Stay close to the king when he
goes in and when he goes out."

Joash Becomes King

8The Levites and all the people of Judah obeyed everything Jehoiada the
priest had commanded. He did not excuse anyone from the groups of the
priests. So each commander took his
men who came on duty on the Sabbath
with those who went off duty on the Sabbath. **9**Jehoiada gave the commanders of
a hundred men the spears and the large
and small shields that had belonged to
King David and that were kept in the
Temple of God. **10**Then Jehoiada told the
men where to stand, each man with his
weapon in his hand. There were guards
from the south side of the Temple to the
north side. They stood by the altar and
the Temple and around the king.
11Jehoiada and his sons brought out
the king's son and put the crown on him
and gave him a copy of the agreement.
Then they appointed him king and
poured olive oil on him and shouted,
"Long live the king!"
12When Athaliah heard the noise of
the people running and praising the king,
she went to them at the Temple of the
LORD. **13**She looked, and there was the
king standing by his pillar at the entrance. The officers and the trumpeters
were standing beside him, and all the
people of the land were happy and blowing trumpets. The singers were playing
musical instruments and leading praises.
Then Athaliah tore her clothes and
screamed, "Traitors! Traitors!"
14Jehoiada the priest sent out the
commanders of a hundred men, who led
the army. He said, "Surround her with
soldiers and take her out of the Temple
area. Kill with a sword anyone who follows her." He had said, "Don't put Athaliah to death in the Temple of the LORD."
15So they caught her when she came to
the entrance of the Horse Gate near the
palace. There they put her to death.
16Then Jehoiada made an agreement
with the people and the king that they
would be the LORD's special people.
17All the people went to the temple of
Baal and tore it down, smashing the altars and idols. They killed Mattan, the
priest of Baal, in front of the altars.
18Then Jehoiada chose the priests,
who were Levites, to be responsible for
the Temple of the LORD. David had given
them duties in the Temple of the LORD.
They were to offer the burnt offerings to
the LORD as the Teachings of Moses
commanded, and they were to offer them
with much joy and singing as David had
commanded. **19**Jehoiada put guards at the
gates of the Temple of the LORD so that
anyone who was unclean in any way
could not enter.
20Jehoiada took with him the commanders of a hundred men, the important
men, the rulers of the people, and all the
people of the land to take the king out of
the Temple of the LORD. They went
through the Upper Gate into the palace,
and then they seated the king on the
throne. **21**So all the people of the land
were very happy, and Jerusalem had
peace, because Athaliah had been put to
death with the sword.

Joash Repairs the Temple

24 Joash was seven years old when
he became king, and he ruled forty
years in Jerusalem. His mother's name
was Zibiah, and she was from Beersheba.

2Joash did what the LORD said was right as long as Jehoiada the priest was alive. **3**Jehoiada chose two wives for Joash, and Joash had sons and daughters.

4Later, Joash decided to repair the Temple of the LORD. **5**He called the priests and the Levites together and said to them, "Go to the towns of Judah and gather the money all the Israelites have to pay every year. Use it to repair the Temple of your God. Do this now." But the Levites did not hurry.

> Joash was seven years old when he became king, and he ruled forty years in Jerusalem.
> —2 Chronicles 24:1

6So King Joash called for Jehoiada the leading priest and said to him, "Why haven't you made the Levites bring in from Judah and Jerusalem the tax money that Moses, the LORD's servant, and the people of Israel used for the Holy Tent?"

7In the past the sons of wicked Athaliah had broken into the Temple of God and used its holy things for worshiping the Baal idols.

8King Joash commanded that a box for contributions be made. They put it outside, at the gate of the Temple of the LORD. **9**Then the Levites made an announcement in Judah and Jerusalem, telling people to bring to the LORD the tax money Moses, the servant of God, had made the Israelites give while they were in the desert. **10**All the officers and people were happy to bring their money, and they put it in the box until the box was full. **11**When the Levites would take the box to the king's officers, they would see that it was full of money. Then the king's royal secretary and the leading priest's officer would come and take out the money and return the box to its place. They did this often and gathered much money. **12**King Joash and Jehoiada gave the money to the people who worked on the Temple of the LORD. And they hired stoneworkers and carpenters to repair the Temple of the LORD. They also hired people to work with iron and bronze to repair the Temple.

13The people worked hard, and the work to repair the Temple went well. They rebuilt the Temple of God to be as it was before, but even stronger. **14**When the workers finished, they brought the money that was left to King Joash and Jehoiada. They used that money to make utensils for the Temple of the LORD, utensils for the service in the Temple and for the burnt offerings, and bowls and other utensils from gold and silver. Burnt offerings were given every day in the Temple of the LORD while Jehoiada was alive.

15Jehoiada grew old and lived many years. Then he died when he was one hundred thirty years old. **16**Jehoiada was buried in Jerusalem with the kings, because he had done much good in Judah for God and his Temple.

Joash Does Evil

17After Jehoiada died, the officers of Judah came and bowed down to King Joash, and he listened to them. **18**The king and these leaders stopped worshiping in the Temple of the LORD, the God of their ancestors. Instead, they began to worship the Asherah idols and other idols. Because they did wrong, God was angry with the people of Judah and Jerusalem. **19**Even though the LORD sent prophets to the people to turn them back to him and even though the prophets warned them, they refused to listen.

20Then the Spirit of God entered Zechariah son of Jehoiada the priest. Zechariah stood before the people and said, "This is what God says: 'Why do you disobey the LORD's commands? You will not be successful. Because you have left the LORD, he has also left you.' "

21But the king and his officers made plans against Zechariah. At the king's command they threw stones at him in the courtyard of the Temple of the LORD until he died. **22**King Joash did not remember Jehoiada's kindness to him, so Joash killed Zechariah, Jehoiada's son. Before Zechariah died, he said, "May the LORD

see what you are doing and punish you."
23At the end of the year, the Aramean
army came against Joash. They attacked
Judah and Jerusalem, killed all the leaders of the people, and sent all the valuable things to their king in Damascus.
24The Aramean army came with only a
small group of men, but the LORD handed
over to them a very large army from Judah, because the people of Judah had left
the LORD, the God of their ancestors. So
Joash was punished. 25When the Arameans left, Joash was badly wounded. His
own officers made plans against him because he had killed Zechariah son of Jehoiada the priest. So they killed Joash in
his own bed. He died and was buried in
Jerusalem but not in the graves of the
kings.
26The officers who made plans
against Joash were Jozabad and Jehozabad. Jozabad was the son of Shimeath, a
woman from Ammon. And Jehozabad was
the son of Shimrith, a woman from Moab.
27The story of Joash's sons, the great
prophecies against him, and how he repaired the Temple of God are written in
the book of the kings. Joash's son Amaziah became king in his place.

Amaziah King of Judah

25 Amaziah was twenty-five years
old when he became king, and he
ruled for twenty-nine years in Jerusalem.
His mother's name was Jehoaddin, and
she was from Jerusalem. 2Amaziah did
what the LORD said was right, but he did
not really want to obey him. 3As soon as
Amaziah took strong control of the kingdom, he executed the officers who had
murdered his father the king. 4But Amaziah did not put to death their children.
He obeyed what was written in the Book
of Moses, where the LORD commanded,
"Parents must not be put to death when
their children do wrong, and children
must not be put to death when their parents do wrong. Each must die for his own
sins."*
5Amaziah gathered the people of Judah together. He grouped all the people
of Judah and Benjamin by families, and he
put commanders over groups of a thou-

FAITH CHALLENGE
Hey there! Read 25:2 to see how one king responded to God's rules. How do you respond when you're faced with something you really don't want to do—like watching your baby brother while your mom runs errands or doing your homework before going out with your friends?
TESTING IT
2 Chronicles 25:2
Amaziah did what the LORD said was right, but he did not really want to obey him.

sand and over groups of a hundred. He
counted the men who were twenty years
old and older. In all there were three hundred thousand soldiers ready to fight and
skilled with spears and shields. 6Amazi-
ah also hired one hundred thousand soldiers from Israel for about seventy-five
hundred pounds of silver. 7But a man of
God came to Amaziah and said, "My king,
don't let the army of Israel go with you.
The LORD is not with Israel or the people
from the tribe of Ephraim. 8You can make

25:4 "Parents . . . sins." See Deuteronomy 24:16.

yourself strong for war, but God will defeat you. He has the power to help you or
to defeat you."
9Amaziah said to the man of God,
"But what about the seventy-five hundred pounds of silver I paid to the Israelite army?"
The man of God answered, "The
LORD can give you much more than that."
10So Amaziah sent the Israelite army
back home to Ephraim. They were very
angry with the people of Judah and went
home angry.
11Then Amaziah became very brave
and led his army to the Valley of Salt in
the country of Edom. There Amaziah's
army killed ten thousand Edomites.
12The army of Judah also captured ten
thousand and took them to the top of a
cliff and threw them off so that they split
open.
13At the same time the Israelite
troops that Amaziah had not let fight in
the war were robbing towns in Judah.
From Samaria to Beth Horon they killed
three thousand people and took many
valuable things.
14When Amaziah came home after
defeating the Edomites, he brought back
the idols they worshiped and started to
worship them himself. He bowed down to
them and offered sacrifices to them.
15The LORD was very angry with Amaziah, so he sent a prophet to him who
said, "Why have you asked their gods for
help? They could not even save their own
people from you!"
16As the prophet spoke, Amaziah said
to him, "We never gave you the job of advising the king. Stop, or you will be
killed."
The prophet stopped speaking except
to say, "I know that God has decided to
destroy you because you have done this.
You did not listen to my advice."
17Amaziah king of Judah talked with
those who advised him. Then he sent a
message to Jehoash son of Jehoahaz, who
was the son of Jehu king of Israel. Amaziah said to Jehoash, "Come, let's meet
face to face."
18Then Jehoash king of Israel answered Amaziah king of Judah, "A thornbush in Lebanon sent a message to a cedar tree in Lebanon. It said, 'Let your
daughter marry my son.' But then a wild
animal from Lebanon came by, walking
on and crushing the thornbush. 19You
say to yourself that you have defeated
Edom, but you have become proud, and
you brag. But you stay at home! Don't
ask for trouble, or you and Judah will be
defeated."
20But Amaziah would not listen. God
caused this to happen so that Jehoash
would defeat Judah, because Judah asked
for help from the gods of Edom. 21So Jehoash king of Israel went to attack. He
and Amaziah king of Judah faced each
other in battle at Beth Shemesh in Judah.
22Israel defeated Judah, and every man
of Judah ran away to his home. 23At Beth
Shemesh Jehoash king of Israel captured
Amaziah king of Judah. (Amaziah was the
son of Joash, who was the son of Ahaziah.) Then Jehoash brought him to Jerusalem. Jehoash broke down the wall of
Jerusalem, from the Gate of Ephraim to
the Corner Gate, about six hundred feet.
24He took all the gold and silver and all
the utensils from the Temple of God that
Obed-Edom had taken care of. He also
took the treasures from the palace and
some hostages. Then he returned to Samaria.
25Amaziah son of Joash, the king of
Judah, lived fifteen years after the death
of Jehoash son of Jehoahaz, the king of
Israel. 26The other things Amaziah did
as king, from the beginning to the end,
are written in the book of the kings of Judah and Israel. 27When Amaziah stopped
obeying the LORD, the people in Jerusalem made plans against him. So he ran
away to the town of Lachish, but they
sent men after him to Lachish and killed
him. 28They brought his body back on
horses, and he was buried with his ancestors in Jerusalem, the city of David.

Uzziah King of Judah

26 Then all the people of Judah made
Uzziah[n] king in place of his father
Amaziah. Uzziah was sixteen years old.

26:1 Uzziah Also called Azariah.

2He rebuilt the town of Elath and made it
part of Judah again after Amaziah died.
3Uzziah was sixteen years old when
he became king, and he ruled fifty-two
years in Jerusalem. His mother's name
was Jecoliah, and she was from

EMAIL FROM GOD
26:4
Obedience
What's an example of obedience?

Jerusalem. 4He did
what the LORD said
was right, just as
his father Amaziah
had done. 5Uzziah
obeyed God while
Zechariah was alive, because he taught
Uzziah how to respect and obey God. And
as long as Uzziah obeyed the LORD, God
gave him success.
6Uzziah fought a war against the Philistines. He tore down the walls around
their towns of Gath, Jabneh, and Ashdod
and built new towns near Ashdod and in
other places among the Philistines. 7God
helped Uzziah fight the Philistines, the
Arabs living in Gur Baal, and the Meunites. 8Also, the Ammonites made the
payments Uzziah demanded. He was
very powerful, so his name became famous all the way to the border of Egypt.
9Uzziah built towers in Jerusalem at
the Corner Gate, the Valley Gate, and
where the wall turned, and he made them
strong. 10He also built towers in the
desert and dug many wells, because he
had many cattle on the western hills and
in the plains. He had people who worked
his fields and vineyards in the hills and in
the fertile lands, because he loved the
land.
11Uzziah had an army of trained soldiers. They were counted and put in
groups by Jeiel the royal secretary and
Maaseiah the officer. Hananiah, one of
the king's commanders, was their leader.
12There were twenty-six hundred leaders over the soldiers. 13They were in
charge of an army of three hundred seven
thousand five hundred men who fought
with great power to help the king against
the enemy. 14Uzziah gave his army
shields, spears, helmets, armor, bows,
and stones for their slings. 15In Jerusalem Uzziah made devices that were invented by clever men. These devices on
the towers and corners of the city walls
were used to shoot arrows and large
rocks. So Uzziah became famous in faraway places, because he had much help
until he became powerful.
16But when Uzziah became powerful,
his pride led to his ruin. He was unfaithful to the LORD his God; he went into the
Temple of the LORD to burn incense on
the altar for incense. 17Azariah and
eighty other brave priests who served
the LORD followed Uzziah into the Temple. 18They told him he was wrong and
said to him, "You don't have the right to
burn incense to the LORD. Only the
priests, Aaron's descendants, should
burn the incense, because they have
been made holy. Leave this holy place.
You have been unfaithful, and the LORD
God will not honor you for this."
19Uzziah was standing beside the altar for incense in the Temple of the LORD,
and in his hand was a pan for burning incense. He was very angry with the
priests. As he was standing in front of the
priests, a skin disease broke out on his
forehead. 20Azariah, the leading priest,
and all the other priests looked at him
and saw the skin disease on his forehead.
So they hurried him out of the Temple.
Uzziah also rushed out, because the
LORD was punishing him. 21So King Uzziah had the skin disease until the day he
died. He had to live in a separate house
and could not enter the Temple of the
LORD. His son Jotham was in charge of
the palace, and he governed the people of
the land.
22The other things Uzziah did as
king, from beginning to end, were written down by the prophet Isaiah son of
Amoz. 23Uzziah died and was buried near
his ancestors in a graveyard that belonged to the kings. This was because
people said, "He had a skin disease." And
his son Jotham became king in his place.

Jotham King of Judah

27 Jotham was twenty-five years old
when he became king, and he
ruled sixteen years in Jerusalem. His
mother's name was Jerusha daughter of
Zadok. 2Jotham did what the LORD said
was right, just as his father Uzziah had

GET THE INFO

DISEASE OR CURSE? 2 Chronicles 26:20–23

The Bible mentions skin diseases in many places. In Bible times, there was no cure for these skin diseases, so when a person got the disease they had to move away from their home and family. It was like a curse. It was such a big deal that one book of the Bible, Leviticus, gave detailed instruction about how to spot skin diseases and how to keep from getting them. One of the symptoms of a particular skin disease, sometimes called leprosy, was shiny white spots under the skin. (See Leviticus 13:3–4, p. 148.)

The Bible tells about several times when skin diseases were cured miraculously. Both Moses (Exodus 4:6–7, p. 80) and Miriam (Numbers 12:10–15, p. 193) were cured of skin diseases. God used the prophet Elisha to heal Naaman, a Syrian military officer, of his skin disease. (Read 2 Kings 5:1–14, p. 483.) Once, Jesus even healed ten people suffering from skin diseases at the same time. (See Luke 17:11–19, p. 1402.) After a person was cured from skin disease, they had to show themselves to the priests to prove they were healed. (Look at Luke 17:14, p. 1402.)

Today, we know there are many different kinds of skin diseases, and we know what to do to take care of most of them. The skin disease often described in the Bible is sometimes called Hansen's disease today.

done. But Jotham did not enter the Temple of the LORD to burn incense as his father had. But the people continued doing
wrong. 3Jotham rebuilt the Upper Gate of
the Temple of the LORD, and he added
greatly to the wall at Ophel. 4He also built
towns in the hill country of Judah, as well
as walled cities and towers in the forests.
5Jotham also fought the king of the
Ammonites and defeated them. So each
year for three years they gave Jotham
about seventy-five hundred pounds of silver, about sixty-two thousand bushels of
wheat, and about sixty-two thousand
bushels of barley. 6Jotham became powerful, because he always obeyed the
LORD his God.
7The other things Jotham did while he
was king and all his wars are written in
the book of the kings of Israel and Judah.
8Jotham was twenty-five years old when
he became king, and he ruled sixteen
years in Jerusalem. 9Jotham died and was
buried in Jerusalem, the city of David.
Then Jotham's son Ahaz became king in
his place.

Ahaz King of Judah

28 Ahaz was twenty years old when
he became king, and he ruled sixteen years in Jerusalem. Unlike his ancestor David, he did not do what the
LORD said was right. 2Ahaz did the same
things the kings of Israel had done. He
made metal idols to worship Baal. 3He
burned incense in the Valley of Ben Hinnom and made his children pass through
the fire. He did the same hateful sins as
the nations had done whom the LORD had
forced out of the land ahead of the Israelites. 4Ahaz offered sacrifices and burned
incense at the places where gods were
worshiped, and on the hills, and under
every green tree.

5So the LORD his God handed over
Ahaz to the king of Aram. The Arameans
defeated Ahaz and took many people of
Judah as prisoners to Damascus.

He also handed over Ahaz to Pekah
king of Israel, and Pekah's army killed
many soldiers of Ahaz. **6**The army of Pekah son of Remaliah killed one hundred
twenty thousand brave soldiers from Judah in one day. Pekah defeated them because they had left the LORD, the God of
their ancestors. **7**Zicri, a warrior from
Ephraim, killed King Ahaz's son Maaseiah. He also killed Azrikam, the officer in
charge of the palace, and Elkanah, who
was second in command to the king.
8The Israelite army captured two hundred thousand of their own relatives.
They took women, sons and daughters,
and many valuable things from Judah and
carried them back to Samaria. **9**But a
prophet of the LORD named Oded was
there. He met the Israelite army when it
returned to Samaria and said to them,
"The LORD, the God of your ancestors,
handed Judah over to you, because he
was angry with those people. But God
has seen the cruel way you killed them.
10Now you plan to make the people of
Judah and Jerusalem your slaves, but you
also have sinned against the LORD your
God. **11**Now listen to me. Send back your
brothers and sisters whom you captured,
because the LORD is very angry with
you."

12Then some of the leaders in Ephraim—Azariah son of Jehohanan, Berekiah
son of Meshillemoth, Jehizkiah son of
Shallum, and Amasa son of Hadlai—met
the Israelite soldiers coming home from
war. **13**They warned the soldiers, "Don't
bring the prisoners from Judah here. If
you do, we will be guilty of sin against the
LORD, and that will make our sin and guilt
even worse. Our guilt is already so great
that he is angry with Israel."

14So the soldiers left the prisoners
and valuable things in front of the officers
and people there. **15**The leaders who
were named took the prisoners and gave
those who were naked the clothes that
the Israelite army had taken. They gave
the prisoners clothes, sandals, food,
drink, and medicine. They put the weak
prisoners on donkeys and took them back
to their families in Jericho, the city of
palm trees. Then they returned home to
Samaria.

16-17 At that time the Edomites came
again and attacked Judah and carried
away prisoners. So King Ahaz sent to the
king of Assyria for help. **18**The Philistines also robbed the towns in the western hills and in southern Judah. They
captured the towns of Beth Shemesh, Aijalon, Gederoth, Soco, Timnah, and Gim-
zo, and the villages around them. Then
the Philistines lived in those towns.
19The LORD brought trouble on Judah
because Ahaz their king led the people of
Judah to sin, and he was unfaithful to the
LORD. **20**Tiglath-Pileser king of Assyria
came to Ahaz, but he gave Ahaz trouble
instead of help. **21**Ahaz took some valuable things from the Temple of the LORD,
from the palace, and from the princes,
and he gave them to the king of Assyria,
but it did not help.

22During Ahaz's troubles he was
even more unfaithful to the LORD. **23**He
offered sacrifices to the gods of the people of Damascus, who had defeated him.
He thought, "The gods of the kings of
Aram helped them. If I offer sacrifices to
them, they will help me also." But this
brought ruin to Ahaz and all Israel.

24Ahaz gathered the things from the
Temple of God and broke them into
pieces. Then he closed the doors of the
Temple of the LORD. He made altars and
put them on every street corner in Jerusalem. **25**In every town in Judah, Ahaz made
places for burning sacrifices to worship
other gods. So he made the LORD, the God
of his ancestors, very angry.

26The other things Ahaz did as king,
from beginning to end, are written in the
book of the kings of Judah and Israel.
27Ahaz died and was buried in the city of
Jerusalem, but not in the graves of the
kings of Israel. Ahaz's son Hezekiah became king in his place.

Hezekiah Purifies the Temple

29 Hezekiah was twenty-five years
old when he became king, and he

ruled twenty-nine years in Jerusalem.
His mother's name was Abijah daughter
of Zechariah. 2Hezekiah did what the
LORD said was right, just as his ancestor
David had done.
3Hezekiah opened the doors of the
Temple of the LORD and repaired them in
the first month of the first year he was
king. 4Hezekiah brought in the priests
and Levites and gathered them in the
courtyard on the east side of the Temple.
5Hezekiah said, "Listen to me, Levites.
Make yourselves ready for the LORD's
service, and make holy the Temple of the
LORD, the God of your ancestors. Remove from the Temple everything that
makes it impure. 6Our ancestors were
unfaithful to God and did what the LORD
said was wrong. They left the LORD and
stopped worshiping at the Temple where
he lives. They rejected him. 7They shut
the doors of the porch of the Temple, and
they let the fire go out in the lamps. They
stopped burning incense and offering
burnt offerings in the holy place to the
God of Israel. 8So the LORD became very
angry with the people of
Judah and Jerusalem, and
he punished them. Other
people are frightened and
shocked by what he did to
them. So they insult the
people of Judah. You know
these things are true.
9That is why our ances-
tors were killed in battle
and our sons, daughters,
and wives were taken
captive. 10Now I, Hezekiah, have decided to make an agreement with the LORD,
the God of Israel, so he will not be angry
with us anymore. 11My sons, don't waste
any more time. The LORD chose you to
stand before him, to serve him, to be his
servants, and to burn incense to him."
12These are the Levites who started
to work. From the Kohathite family there
were Mahath son of Amasai and Joel son
of Azariah. From the Merarite family
there were Kish son of Abdi and Azariah
son of Jehallelel. From the Gershonite
family there were Joah son of Zimmah
and Eden son of Joah. 13From Elizaphan's family there were Shimri and
Jeiel. From Asaph's family there were
Zechariah and Mattaniah. 14From Heman's family there were Jehiel and Shimei. From Jeduthun's family there were
Shemaiah and Uzziel.
15These Levites gathered their
brothers together and made themselves
holy for service in the Temple. Then they
went into the Temple of the LORD to purify it. They obeyed the king's command
that had come from the LORD. 16When
the priests went into the Temple of the
LORD to purify it, they took out all the
unclean things they found in the Temple
of the LORD and put them in the Temple
courtyard. Then the Levites took these
things out to the Kidron Valley. 17Begin-
ning on the first day of the first month,
they made the Temple holy for the LORD's
service. On the eighth day of the month,
they came to the porch of the Temple,
and for eight more days they made the
Temple of the LORD holy. So they finished
on the sixteenth day of the first month.
18Then they went to King Hezekiah
and said, "We have puri-
fied the entire Temple of
the LORD, the altar for
burnt offerings and its
utensils, and the table for
the holy bread and all its
utensils. 19When Ahaz
was king, he was unfaith-
ful to God and removed
some things from the
Temple. But we have put
them back and made
them holy for the LORD. They are now in
front of the LORD's altar."
20Early the next morning King Hezekiah gathered the leaders of the city and
went up to the Temple of the LORD.
21They brought seven bulls, seven male
sheep, seven lambs, and seven male
goats. These animals were an offering
to remove the sin of the people and the
kingdom of Judah and to make the
Temple ready for service to God. King
Hezekiah commanded the priests, the
descendants of Aaron, to offer these animals on the LORD's altar. 22So the priests
killed the bulls and sprinkled their blood

> Now I, Hezekiah, have decided to make an agreement with the LORD.
> —2 Chronicles 29:10

on the altar. They killed the sheep and sprinkled their blood on the altar. Then they killed the lambs and sprinkled their blood on the altar. 23Then the priests brought the male goats for the sin offering before the king and the people there. After the king and the people put their hands on the goats, 24the priests killed them. With the goats' blood they made an offering on the altar to remove the sins of the Israelites so they would belong to God. The king had said that the burnt offering and sin offering should be made for all Israel.

25King Hezekiah put the Levites in the Temple of the LORD with cymbals, harps, and lyres, as David, Gad, and Nathan had commanded. (Gad was the king's seer, and Nathan was a prophet.) This command came from the LORD through his prophets. 26So the Levites stood ready with David's instruments of music, and the priests stood ready with their trumpets.

27Then Hezekiah gave the order to sacrifice the burnt offering on the altar. When the burnt offering began, the singing to the LORD also began. The trumpets were blown, and the musical instruments of David king of Israel were played. 28All the people worshiped, the singers sang, and the trumpeters blew their trumpets until the burnt offering was finished.

29When the sacrifices were completed, King Hezekiah and everyone with him bowed down and worshiped. 30King Hezekiah and his officers ordered the Levites to praise the LORD, using the words David and Asaph the seer had used. So they praised God with joy and bowed down and worshiped.

31Then Hezekiah said, "Now that you people of Judah have given yourselves to the LORD, come near to the Temple of the LORD. Bring sacrifices and offerings, to show thanks to him." So the people brought sacrifices and thank offerings, and anyone who was willing also brought burnt offerings. 32For burnt offerings they brought a total of seventy bulls, one hundred male sheep, and two hundred lambs; all these animals were sacrificed as burnt offerings to the LORD. 33The holy offerings totaled six hundred bulls and three thousand sheep and goats. 34There were not enough priests to skin all the animals for the burnt offerings. So their relatives the Levites helped them until the work was finished and other priests could be made holy. The Levites had been more careful to make themselves holy for the LORD's service than the priests. 35There were many burnt offerings along with the fat of fellowship offerings and drink offerings. So the service in the Temple of the LORD began again. 36And Hezekiah and the people were very happy that God had made it happen so quickly for his people.

The Passover Celebration

30 King Hezekiah sent messages to all the people of Israel and Judah, and he wrote letters to the people of Ephraim and Manasseh. Hezekiah invited all these people to come to the Temple of the LORD in Jerusalem to celebrate the Passover for the LORD, the God of Israel. 2King Hezekiah, his officers, and all the people in Jerusalem agreed to celebrate the Passover in the second month. 3They could not celebrate it at the normal time, because not enough priests had made themselves ready to serve the LORD, and the people had not yet gathered in Jerusalem. 4This plan satisfied King Hezekiah and all the people. 5So they made an announcement everywhere in Israel, from Beersheba to Dan,[n] telling the people to come to Jerusalem to celebrate the Passover for the LORD, the God of Israel. For a long time most of the people had not celebrated the Passover as the law commanded. 6At the king's command, the messengers took letters from him and his officers all through Israel and Judah. This is what the letters said:

People of Israel, return to the
LORD, the God of Abraham, Isaac,

30:5 Beersheba to Dan Dan was the city farthest north in Israel, and Beersheba was the city farthest south. So this means all the people of Israel.

and Israel. Then God will return to
you who are still alive, who have
escaped from the kings of Assyria.
7Don't be like your ancestors or
your relatives. They turned against
the LORD, the God of their ancestors, so he caused other people to
be disgusted with them. You know
this is true. **8**Don't be stubborn as
your ancestors were, but obey the
LORD willingly. Come to the Temple, which he has made holy forever. Serve the LORD your God so
he will not be angry with you.
9Come back to the LORD. Then
the people who captured your relatives and children will be kind
to them and will let them return to
this land. The LORD your God is
kind and merciful. He
will not turn away
from you if you return
to him.

> Don't be stubborn as
> your ancestors were,
> but obey the LORD
> willingly.
> —2 Chronicles 30:8

10The messengers
went to every town in
Ephraim and Manasseh,
and all the way to Zeb-
ulun, but the people
laughed at them and made
fun of them. **11**But some
men from Asher, Manas-
seh, and Zebulun were sorry for what they
had done and went to Jerusalem. **12**And
God united all the people of Judah in obeying King Hezekiah and his officers, because their command had come from the
LORD.

13In the second month a large crowd
came together in Jerusalem to celebrate
the Feast of Unleavened Bread. **14**The
people removed the altars and incense altars to gods in Jerusalem and threw them
into the Kidron Valley.

15They killed the Passover lamb on
the fourteenth day of the second month.
The priests and the Levites were
ashamed, so they made themselves holy
and brought burnt offerings into the Temple of the LORD. **16**They took their regular places in the Temple as the Teachings
of Moses, the man of God, commanded.
The Levites gave the blood of the sacrifices to the priests, who sprinkled it on
the altar. **17**Since many people in the
crowd had not made themselves holy, the
Levites killed the Passover lambs for
everyone who was not clean. The Levites made each lamb holy for the LORD.
18-19 Although many people from Ephraim, Manasseh, Issachar, and Zebulun
had not purified themselves for the feast,
they ate the Passover even though it was
against the law. So Hezekiah prayed for
them, saying, "LORD, you are good. You
are the LORD, the God of our ancestors.
Please forgive all those who try to
obey you even if they did not make themselves clean as the rules of the Temple
command." **20**The LORD listened to
Hezekiah's prayer, and he healed the
people. **21**The Israelites in Jerusalem
celebrated the Feast of
Unleavened Bread for
seven days with great joy
to the LORD. The Levites
and priests praised the
LORD every day with loud
music. **22**Hezekiah en-
couraged all the Levites
who showed they under-
stood well how to do their
service for the LORD. The
people ate the feast for
seven days, offered fel-
lowship offerings, and praised the LORD,
the God of their ancestors.

23Then all the people agreed to stay
seven more days, so they celebrated with
joy for seven more days. **24**Hezekiah
king of Judah gave one thousand bulls and
seven thousand sheep to the people. The
officers gave one thousand bulls and ten
thousand sheep to the people. Many
priests made themselves holy. **25**All the
people of Judah, the priests, the Levites,
those who came from Israel, the foreigners from Israel, and the foreigners living
in Judah were very happy. **26**There was
much joy in Jerusalem, because there had
not been a celebration like this since the
time of Solomon son of David and king of
Israel. **27**The priests and Levites stood
up and blessed the people, and God heard
them because their prayer reached
heaven, his holy home.

The Collection for the Priests

31 When the Passover celebration was finished, all the Israelites in Jerusalem went out to the towns of Judah. There they smashed the stone pillars used to worship gods. They cut down the Asherah idols and destroyed the altars and places for worshiping gods in all of Judah, Benjamin, Ephraim, and Manasseh. After they had destroyed all of them, the Israelites returned to their own towns and homes.

2King Hezekiah appointed groups of priests and Levites for their special duties. They were to offer burnt offerings and fellowship offerings, to worship, and to give thanks and praise at the gates of the LORD's house. **3**Hezekiah gave some of his own animals for the burnt offerings, which were given every morning and evening, on Sabbath days, during New Moons, and at other feasts commanded in the LORD's Teachings.

eMAIL! FROM GOD
31:4
Giving
How can you help your church?

4Hezekiah commanded the people living in Jerusalem to give the priests and Levites the portion that belonged to them. Then the priests and Levites could give all their time to the LORD's Teachings. **5**As soon as the king's command went out to the Israelites, they gave freely of the first portion of their grain, new wine, oil, honey, and everything they grew in their fields. They brought a large amount, one-tenth of everything. **6**The people of Israel and Judah who lived in Judah also brought one-tenth of their cattle and sheep and one-tenth of the holy things that were given to the LORD their God, and they put all of them in piles. **7**The people began the piles in the third month and finished in the seventh month. **8**When Hezekiah and his officers came and saw the piles, they praised the LORD and his people, the people of Israel. **9**Hezekiah asked the priests and Levites about the piles. **10**Azariah, the leading priest from Zadok's family, answered Hezekiah, "Since the people began to bring their offerings to the Temple of the LORD, we have had plenty to eat and plenty left over, because the LORD has blessed his people. So we have all this left over."

11Then Hezekiah commanded the priests to prepare the storerooms in the Temple of the LORD. So this was done. **12**Then the priests brought in the offerings and the things given to the LORD and one-tenth of everything the people had given. Conaniah the Levite was in charge of these things, and his brother Shimei was second to him. **13**Conaniah and his brother Shimei were over these supervisors: Jehiel, Azaziah, Nahath, Asahel, Jerimoth, Jozabad, Eliel, Ismakiah, Mahath, and Benaiah. King Hezekiah and Azariah the officer in charge of the Temple of God had chosen them.

14Kore son of Imnah the Levite was in charge of the special gifts the people wanted to give to God. He was responsible for giving out the contributions made to the LORD and the holy gifts. Kore was the guard at the East Gate. **15**Eden, Miniamin, Jeshua, Shemaiah, Amariah, and Shecaniah helped Kore in the towns where the priests lived. They gave from what was collected to the other groups of priests, both young and old.

16From what was collected, these men also gave to the males three years old and older who had their names in the Levite family histories. They were to enter the Temple of the LORD for their daily service, each group having its own responsibilities. **17**The priests were given their part of the collection, by families, as listed in the family histories. The Levites twenty years old and older were given their part of the collection, based on their responsibilities and their groups. **18**The Levites' babies, wives, sons, and daughters also got part of the collection. This was done for all the Levites who were listed in the family histories, because they always kept themselves ready to serve the LORD.

19Some of Aaron's descendants, the priests, lived on the farmlands near the towns or in the towns. Men were chosen by name to give part of the collection to these priests. All the males and those named in the family histories of the Levites received part of the collection.

A SECRET WATER SUPPLY

2 Chronicles 32

A tunnel built by King Hezekiah runs under the city wall of Jerusalem. One crew of men started digging at the Gihon Spring, outside the city walls. Another crew started digging at the Pool of Siloam, inside the city walls. They dug and dug until they met in the middle of the tunnel. This was a difficult job because the tunnel had to be dug through solid rock.

Can you figure out why King Hezekiah built the tunnel? When an enemy attacked a city like Jerusalem, the army surrounded the city. That meant that no one from inside the city could go outside of the wall without being captured or killed. Once a city started running out of food and water, they *had* to try and sneak out to find some. (Check out 2 Kings 6:25–29, p. 486.) But with King Hezekiah's tunnel, Jerusalem never ran out of water no matter how long an enemy camped around them.

King Hezekiah's tunnel was 1,750 feet long. At some places it was 60 feet below ground. Today water doesn't run through the tunnel. In fact, these days, tourists can walk through what is left of the tunnel when they visit Jerusalem.

20This is what King Hezekiah did in
Judah. He did what was good and right
and obedient before the LORD his God.
21Hezekiah tried to obey God in his service of the Temple of God, and he tried to
obey God's teachings and commands. He
gave himself fully to his work for God. So
he had success.

Assyria Attacks Judah

32 After Hezekiah did all these
things to serve the LORD, Sennacherib king of Assyria came and
attacked Judah. He and his army surrounded and attacked the strong, walled
cities, hoping to take them for himself.
2Hezekiah knew that Sennacherib had
come to Jerusalem to attack it. **3**So Hezekiah and his officers and army commanders decided to cut off the water from the
springs outside the city. So the officers
and commanders helped Hezekiah.
4Many people came and cut off all the
springs and the stream that flowed
through the land. They said, "The king of
Assyria will not find much water when he
comes here." **5**Then Hezekiah made Jerusalem stronger. He rebuilt all the broken parts of the wall and put towers on it.
He also built another wall outside the
first one and strengthened the area that
was filled in on the east side of the old
part of Jerusalem. He also made many
weapons and shields.

6Hezekiah put army commanders
over the people and met with them at the
open place near the city gate. Hezekiah
encouraged them, saying, **7**"Be strong
and brave. Don't be afraid or worried because of the king of Assyria or his large
army. There is a greater power with us
than with him. **8**He only has men, but we
have the LORD our God to help us and to
fight our battles." The people were encouraged by the words of Hezekiah king
of Judah.

9After this King Sennacherib of Assyria and all his army surrounded and
attacked Lachish. Then he sent his officers to Jerusalem with this message for

King Hezekiah of Judah and all the people
of Judah in Jerusalem:

> **10**Sennacherib king of Assyria
> says this: "You have nothing to
> trust in to help you. It is no use for
> you to stay in Jerusalem under at-
> tack. **11**Hezekiah says to you, 'The
> LORD our God will save us from
> the king of Assyria,' but he is fool-
> ing you. If you stay in Jerusalem,
> you will die from hunger and thirst.
> **12**Hezekiah himself removed your
> LORD's places of worship and al-
> tars. He told you people of Judah
> and Jerusalem that you must wor-
> ship and burn incense on only one
> altar.
> **13**"You know what my ances-
> tors and I have done to all the peo-
> ple in other nations. The gods of
> those nations could not save their
> people from my power. **14**My an-
> cestors destroyed those nations;
> none of their gods could save them
> from me. So your god cannot save
> you from my power. **15**Do not let
> Hezekiah fool you or trick you, and
> do not believe him. No god of any
> nation or kingdom has been able to
> save his people from me or my an-
> cestors. Your god is even less able
> to save you from me."

16Sennacherib's officers said worse
things against the LORD God and his servant Hezekiah. **17**King Sennacherib also
wrote letters insulting the LORD, the God
of Israel. They spoke against him, saying,
"The gods of the other nations could not
save their people from me. In the same
way Hezekiah's god won't be able to save
his people from me." **18**Then the king's
officers shouted in Hebrew, calling out to
the people of Jerusalem who were on the
city wall. The officers wanted to scare
the people away so they could capture Jerusalem. **19**They spoke about the God of
Jerusalem as though he were like the
gods the people of the world worshiped,
which are made by human hands.
20King Hezekiah and the prophet Isaiah son of Amoz prayed to heaven about
this. **21**Then the LORD sent an angel who
killed all the soldiers, leaders, and officers in the camp of the king of Assyria.
So the king went back to his own country
in disgrace. When he went into the temple of his god, some of his own sons killed
him with a sword.
22So the LORD saved Hezekiah and
the people in Jerusalem from Sennacherib king of Assyria and from all other
people. He took care of them on every
side. **23**Many people brought gifts for the
LORD to Jerusalem, and they also brought
valuable gifts to King Heze-kiah of Judah.
From then on all the nations respected
Hezekiah.

Hezekiah Dies

24At that time Hezekiah became so
sick he almost died. When he prayed to
the LORD, the LORD spoke to him and
gave him a sign.* **25**But Hezekiah did
not thank God for his kindness, because he was so proud. So the LORD
was angry with him and the people of Judah and Jerusalem. **26**But later Hezekiah
and the people of Jerusalem were sorry
and stopped being proud, so the LORD did
not punish them while Hezekiah was
alive.
27Hezekiah had many riches and
much honor. He made treasuries for his
silver, gold, gems, spices, shields, and
other valuable things. **28**He built storage
buildings for grain, new wine, and oil and
stalls for all the cattle and pens for the
sheep. **29**He also built many towns. He
had many flocks and herds, because God
had given Hezekiah much wealth.
30It was Hezekiah who cut off the upper pool of the Gihon spring and made
those waters flow straight down to the
west side of the older part of Jerusalem.
And Hezekiah was successful in everything he did. **31**But one time the leaders
of Babylon sent messengers to Hezekiah, asking him about a strange sign that
had happened in the land. When they
came, God left Hezekiah alone to test

32:24 sign See Isaiah 38:1-8. It tells the story about the sign and how the Lord gave Hezekiah fifteen more years to live.

him so he could know everything that
was in Hezekiah's heart."
32Hezekiah's love for God and the
other things he did as king are written in
the vision of the prophet Isaiah son of
Amoz. This is in the book of the kings of
Judah and Israel. 33Hezekiah died and
was buried on a hill, where the graves of
David's ancestors are. All the people of
Judah and Jerusalem honored Hezekiah
when he died, and his son Manasseh became king in his place.

Manasseh King of Judah

33 Manasseh was twelve years old
when he became king, and he was
king for fifty-five years in Jerusalem. 2He
did what the LORD said was wrong. He
did the hateful things the nations had
done—the nations that
the LORD had forced out
of the land ahead of the Israelites. 3Manasseh's fa-
ther, Hezekiah, had torn
down the places where
gods were worshiped, but
Manasseh rebuilt them.
He also built altars for the
Baal gods, and he made
Asherah idols and wor-
shiped all the stars of the
sky and served them. 4The LORD had
said about the Temple, "I will be worshiped in Jerusalem forever," but Manasseh built altars in the Temple of the
LORD. 5He built altars to worship the
stars in the two courtyards of the Temple
of the LORD. 6He made his children pass
through fire in the Valley of Ben Hinnom.
He practiced magic and witchcraft and
told the future by explaining signs and
dreams. He got advice from mediums and
fortune-tellers. He did many things the
LORD said were wrong, which made the
LORD angry.
7Manasseh carved an idol and put it in
the Temple of God. God had said to David
and his son Solomon about the Temple, "I
will be worshiped forever in this Temple
and in Jerusalem, which I have chosen
from all the tribes of Israel. 8I will never
again make the Israelites leave the land I
gave to their ancestors. But they must
obey everything I have commanded them
in all the teachings, rules, and commands
I gave them through Moses." 9But Manasseh led the people of Judah and Jerusalem to do wrong. They did more evil
than the nations the LORD had destroyed
ahead of the Israelites.
10The LORD spoke to Manasseh and
his people, but they did not listen. 11So
the LORD brought the king of Assyria's
army commanders to attack Judah. They
captured Manasseh, put hooks in him,
placed bronze chains on his hands, and
took him to Babylon. 12As Manasseh suffered, he begged the LORD his God for
help and humbled himself before the God
of his ancestors. 13When Manasseh
prayed, the LORD heard him and had pity
on him. So the LORD let him return to Jerusalem and to his king-
dom. Then Manasseh
knew that the LORD is
the true God.
14After that hap-
pened, Manasseh rebuilt
the outer wall of Jerusa-
lem and made it higher. It
was in the valley on the
west side of the Gihon
spring and went to the
entrance of the Fish Gate
and around the hill of Ophel. Then he put
commanders in all the strong, walled cities in Judah.
15Manasseh removed the idols of
other nations, including the idol in the
Temple of the LORD. He removed all the
altars he had built on the Temple hill and
in Jerusalem and threw them out of the
city. 16Then he set up the LORD's altar
and sacrificed on it fellowship offerings
and offerings to show thanks to God. Manasseh commanded all the people of Judah to serve the LORD, the God of Israel.
17The people continued to offer sacrifices at the places of worship, but their
sacrifices were only to the LORD their
God. 18The other things Manasseh did as
king, his prayer to his God, and what the
seers said to him in the name of the
LORD, the God of Israel—all are recorded

> As Manasseh suffered, he begged the LORD his God for help and humbled himself before the God of his ancestors.
> —2 Chronicles 33:12

32:31 God . . . heart See 2 Kings 20:12-19.

in the book of the history of the kings of
Israel. **19**Manasseh's prayer and God's
pity for him, his sins, his unfaithfulness,
the places he built for worshiping gods
and the Asherah idols before he humbled
himself—all are written in the book of
the seers. **20**Manasseh died and was buried in his palace. Then Manasseh's son
Amon became king in his place.

Amon King of Judah

21Amon was twenty-two years old
when he became king, and he was king
for two years in Jerusalem. **22**He did
what the LORD said was wrong, as his father Manasseh had done. Amon worshiped and offered sacrifices to all the
carved idols Manasseh had made.
23Amon did not humble himself before
the LORD as his father Manasseh had
done. Instead, Amon sinned even more.

24King Amon's officers made plans
against him and killed him in his palace.
25Then the people of the land killed all
those who had made plans to kill King
Amon, and they made his son Josiah king
in his place.

Josiah King of Judah

34 Josiah was eight years old when
he became king, and he ruled
thirty-one years in Jerusalem. **2**He did
what the LORD said was right. He lived as
his ancestor David had lived, and he did
not stop doing what was right.

3In his eighth year as king while he
was still young, Josiah began to obey the
God of his ancestor David. In his twelfth
year as king, Josiah began to remove
from Judah and Jerusalem the gods, the
places for worshiping gods, the Asherah
idols, and the wooden and metal idols.
4The people tore down the altars for the
Baal gods as Josiah directed. Then Josiah
cut down the incense altars that were
above them. He broke up the Asherah
idols and the wooden and metal idols and
beat them into powder. Then he sprinkled the powder on the graves of the people who had offered sacrifices to these
gods. **5**He burned the bones of their
priests on their own altars. So Josiah removed idol worship from Judah and Jerusalem, **6**and from the towns in the areas
of Manasseh, Ephraim, and Simeon all
the way to Naphtali, and in the ruins near
these towns. **7**Josiah broke down the altars and Asherah idols and beat the idols
into powder. He cut down all the incense
altars in all of Israel. Then he went back
to Jerusalem.

8In Josiah's eighteenth year as king,
he made Judah and the Temple pure
again. He sent Shaphan son of Azaliah,
Maaseiah the city leader, and Joah son of
Joahaz the recorder to repair the Temple
of the LORD, the God of Josiah. **9**These
men went to Hilkiah the high priest and
gave him the money the Levite gatekeepers had gathered from the people of
Manasseh, Ephraim, and all the Israelites
who were left alive, and also from all the
people of Judah, Benjamin, and Jerusalem. This is the money they had brought
into the Temple of God. **10**Then the Levites gave it to the supervisors of the
work on the Temple of the LORD, and
they paid the workers who rebuilt and repaired the Temple. **11**They gave money
to carpenters and builders to buy cut
stone and wood. The wood was used to
rebuild the buildings and to make beams
for them, because the kings of Judah had
let the buildings fall into ruin. **12**The men
did their work well. Their supervisors
were Jahath and Obadiah, who were Levites from the family of Merari, and Zechariah and Meshullam, who were from the
family of Kohath. These Levites were all
skilled musicians. **13**They were also in
charge of the workers who carried loads
and all the other workers. Some Levites
worked as secretaries, officers, and gatekeepers.

The Book of the Teachings Is Found

14The Levites brought out the money
that was in the Temple of the LORD. As
they were doing this, Hilkiah the priest
found the Book of the LORD's Teachings
that had been given through Moses.
15Hilkiah said to Shaphan the royal secretary, "I've found the Book of the Teachings in the Temple of the LORD!" Then he
gave it to Shaphan.

FAITH links

A LOOK FOR THE BOOK

2 CHRONICLES 34:14-18

Imagine living in a world where there was only one copy of the Bible—and only part of one at that. Now imagine what would happen if that copy became lost. In King Josiah's day, the book of the law was lost. A priest, Hilkiah, discovered it buried in the Temple. When King Josiah heard that the book had been found, he wanted to read it to find out what God wanted his people to do.

Making a habit of reading the Bible can help you remember what God wants you to do. So don't bury your Bible somewhere under your bed. Be a discoverer of the hidden treasures inside it.

Learning to Listen, 1 Samuel 3, p. 358

Your Stats, 1 Kings 15; 16, p. 460

The Best Advice, Zechariah 10:2, p. 1261

Believe It or Not, Luke 1:20, 38, p. 1366

Pay Attention!, Hebrews 2:1, p. 1668

You're a Fake!, 2 Peter 2:1, p. 1709

16Shaphan took the book to the king
and reported to Josiah, "Your officers are
doing everything you told them to do.
17They have paid out the money that was
in the Temple of the LORD and have given
it to the supervisors and the workers."
18Then Shaphan the royal secretary told
the king, "Hilkiah the priest has given
me a book." And Shaphan read from the
book to the king.

19When the king heard the words of
the Teachings, he tore his clothes to
show how upset he was. **20**He gave orders to Hilkiah, Ahikam son of Shaphan,
Acbor son of Micaiah, Shaphan the royal
secretary, and Asaiah, the king's servant.
These were the orders: **21**"Go and ask
the LORD about the words in the book
that was found. Ask for me and for the
people who are left alive in Israel and Judah. The LORD is very angry with us, because our ancestors did not obey the
LORD's word; they did not do everything
this book says to do."

22So Hilkiah and those the king sent
with him went to talk to Huldah the
prophetess. She was the wife of Shallum
son of Tikvah, the son of Harhas, who
took care of the king's clothes. Huldah
lived in Jerusalem, in the new area of the
city.

23She said to them, "This is what the
LORD, the God of Israel, says: Tell the
man who sent you to me, **24**'This is what
the LORD says: I will bring trouble to this
place and to the people living here. I will
bring all the curses that are written in the
book that was read to the king of Judah.
25The people of Judah have left me and
have burned incense to other gods. They
have made me angry by all the evil things
they have made. So I will punish them in
my anger, which will not be put out.'
26Tell the king of Judah, who sent you to
ask the LORD, 'This is what the LORD, the
God of Israel, says about the words you
heard: **27**When you heard my words
against this place and its people, you became sorry for what you had done and you
humbled yourself before me. You tore
your clothes to show how upset you were,
and you cried in my presence. This is why
I have heard you, says the LORD. **28**So I
will let you die and be buried in peace. You
won't see all the trouble I will bring to this
place and the people living here.'"

So they took her message back to the
king.

29Then the king gathered all the older
leaders of Judah and Jerusalem together.
30He went up to the Temple of the LORD,
and all the people from Judah and from Jerusalem went with him. The priests, the
Levites, and all the people—from the
most important to the least important—
went with him. He read to them all the
words in the Book of the Agreement that
was found in the Temple of the LORD.
31The king stood by his pillar and made
an agreement in the presence of the
LORD to follow the LORD and obey his
commands, rules, and laws with
his whole being and
to obey the words of
the agreement writ-
ten in this book.
32Then Josiah made
all the people in Je-
rusalem and Benjamin promise to accept
the agreement. So the people of Jerusalem obeyed the agreement of God, the
God of their ancestors.

EMAIL FROM GOD
34:31
Bible
How hard should you try to obey the Bible?

33And Josiah threw out the hateful
idols from all the land that belonged to
the Israelites. He led everyone in Israel
to serve the LORD their God. While Josiah lived, the people obeyed the LORD,
the God of their ancestors.

Josiah Celebrates the Passover

35 King Josiah celebrated the Passover to the LORD in Jerusalem.
The Passover lamb was killed on the
fourteenth day of the first month. 2Josiah
chose the priests to do their duties, and
he encouraged them as they served in
the Temple of the LORD. 3The Levites
taught the Israelites and were made holy
for service to the LORD. Josiah said to
them, "Put the Holy Ark in the Temple
that David's son Solomon, the king of Israel, built. Do not carry it from place to
place on your shoulders anymore. Now
serve the LORD your God and his people
Israel. 4Prepare yourselves by your family groups for service, and do the jobs that
King David and his son Solomon gave
you to do.

5"Stand in the holy place with a group
of the Levites for each family group of the
people. 6Kill the Passover lambs, and
make yourselves holy to the LORD. Prepare the lambs for your relatives, the
people of Israel, as the LORD through
Moses commanded us to do."

7Josiah gave the Israelites thirty
thousand sheep and goats to kill for the
Passover sacrifices, and he gave them
three thousand cattle. They were all his
own animals.

8Josiah's officers also gave willingly
to the people, the priests, and the Levites. Hilkiah, Zechariah, and Jehiel, the
officers in charge of the Temple, gave the
priests twenty-six hundred lambs and
goats and three hundred cattle for Passover sacrifices. 9Conaniah, his brothers
Shemaiah and Nethanel, and Hashabiah,
Jeiel, and Jozabad gave the Levites five
thousand sheep and goats and five hundred cattle for Passover sacrifices. These
men were leaders of the Levites.

10When everything was ready for the
Passover service, the priests and Levites
went to their places, as the king had commanded. 11The Passover lambs were
killed. Then the Levites skinned the animals and gave the blood to the priests,
who sprinkled it on the altar. 12Then
they gave the animals for the burnt offerings to the different family groups so the
burnt offerings could be offered to the
LORD as was written in the book of Moses. They also did this with the cattle.
13The Levites roasted the Passover sacrifices over the fire as they were commanded, and they boiled the holy
offerings in pots, kettles, and pans. Then
they quickly gave the meat to the people.
14After this was finished, the Levites
prepared meat for themselves and for the
priests, the descendants of Aaron. The
priests worked until night, offering the
burnt offerings and burning the fat of
the sacrifices.

15The Levite singers from Asaph's
family stood in the places chosen for
them by King David, Asaph, Heman, and
Jeduthun, the king's seer. The gatekeepers at each gate did not have to leave
their places, because their fellow Levites
had prepared everything for them for the
Passover.

16So everything was done that day for

the worship of the LORD, as King Josiah
commanded. The Passover was celebrated, and the burnt offerings were offered
on the LORD's altar. 17The Israelites who
were there celebrated the Passover and
the Feast of Unleavened Bread for seven
days. 18The Passover had not been celebrated like this in Israel since the prophet Samuel was alive. None of the kings of
Israel had ever celebrated
a Passover like it was celebrated by King Josiah,
the priests, the Levites,
the people of Judah and
Israel who were there,
and the people of Jerusa-
lem. 19This Passover was
celebrated in the eigh-
teenth year Josiah was
king.

> The Passover had not been celebrated like this in Israel since the prophet Samuel was alive.
> —2 Chronicles 35:18

The Death of Josiah

20After Josiah did all this for the Temple, Neco king of Egypt led an army to
attack Carchemish, a town on the Euphrates River. And Josiah marched out to
fight against Neco. 21But Neco sent messengers to Josiah, saying, "King Josiah,
there should not be war between us. I did
not come to fight you, but my enemies.
God told me to hurry, and he is on my
side. So don't fight God, or he will destroy you."

22But Josiah did not go away. He wore
different clothes so no one would know
who he was. Refusing to listen to what
Neco said at God's command, Josiah went
to fight on the plain of Megiddo. 23In the
battle King Josiah was shot by archers.
He told his servants, "Take me away because I am badly wounded." 24So they
took him out of his chariot and put him in
another chariot and carried him to Jerusalem. There he died and was buried in
the graves where his ancestors were buried. All the people of Judah and Jerusalem
were very sad because he was dead.

25Jeremiah wrote some sad songs
about Josiah. Even to this day all the men
and women singers remember and honor
Josiah with these songs. It became a custom in Israel to sing these songs that are
written in the collection of sad songs.

26-27The other things Josiah did as
king, from beginning to end, are written
in the book of the kings of Israel and Judah. It tells how he loved what was written in the LORD's teachings.

Jehoahaz King of Judah

36 The people of Judah chose Josiah's
son Jehoahaz and made him king
in Jerusalem in his fa-
ther's place.

2Jehoahaz was twenty-
three years old when he
became king, and he was
king in Jerusalem for
three months. 3Then
King Neco of Egypt re-
moved Jehoahaz from be-
ing king in Jerusalem.
Neco made the people of
Judah pay about seventy-
five hundred pounds of
silver and about seventy-five pounds of
gold. 4The king of Egypt made Jehoahaz's brother Eliakim the king of Judah
and Jerusalem and changed his name to
Jehoiakim. But Neco took his brother Jehoahaz to Egypt.

Jehoiakim King of Judah

5Jehoiakim was twenty-five years old
when he became king, and he was king in
Jerusalem for eleven years. He did what
the LORD his God said was wrong. 6King
Nebuchadnezzar of Babylon attacked
Judah, captured Jehoiakim, put bronze
chains on him, and took him to Babylon.
7Nebuchadnezzar removed some of the
things from the Temple of the LORD, took
them to Babylon, and put them in his own
palace.

8The other things Jehoiakim did as
king, the hateful things he did, and everything he was guilty of doing, are written
in the book of the kings of Israel and Judah. And Jehoiakim's son Jehoiachin became king in his place.

Jehoiachin King of Judah

9Jehoiachin was eighteen years old
when he became king of Judah, and he was
king in Jerusalem for three months and
ten days. He did what the LORD said was

wrong. 10In the spring King Nebuchad-
nezzar sent for Jehoiachin and brought
him and some valuable treasures from the
Temple of the LORD to Babylon. Then
Nebuchadnezzar made Jehoiachin's uncle
Zedekiah the king of Judah and Jerusalem.

Zedekiah King of Judah

11Zedekiah was twenty-one years old
when he became king of Judah, and he
was king in Jerusalem for eleven years.
12Zedekiah did what the LORD his God
said was wrong. The prophet Jeremiah
spoke messages from the LORD, but Zedekiah did not obey. 13Zedekiah turned
against King Nebuchadnezzar, who had
forced him to swear in God's name to be
loyal to him. But Zedekiah became stubborn and refused to obey the LORD, the
God of Israel. 14Also, all the leaders of
the priests and the people of Judah became more wicked, following the evil example of the other nations. The LORD had
made the Temple in Jerusalem holy, but
the leaders made it unholy.

The Fall of Jerusalem

15The LORD, the God of their ancestors, sent prophets again and again to
warn his people, because he had pity on
them and on his Temple. 16But they made
fun of God's prophets and hated God's
messages. They refused to listen to the
prophets until, finally, the LORD became
so angry with his people that he could not
be stopped. 17So God brought the king of
Babylon to attack them. The king killed
the young men even when they were in
the Temple. He had no mercy on the
young men or women, the old men or
those who were sick. God handed all of
them over to Nebuchadnezzar. 18Nebu-
chadnezzar carried away to Babylon all
the things from the Temple of God, both
large and small, and all the treasures from
the Temple of the LORD and from the king
and his officers. 19Nebuchadnezzar and
his army set fire to God's Temple and
broke down Jerusalem's wall and burned
all the palaces. They took or destroyed
every valuable thing in Jerusalem.
20Nebuchadnezzar took captive to
Babylon the people who were left alive,

FAITH links

THIS HURTS ME MORE?

2 CHRONICLES 36:17-22

"This hurts me more than it hurts you." Ever hear your mom or dad say that after punishing you for breaking a rule? When a rule is broken, a punishment typically follows. God had warned his people of the consequences for their disobedience. The Israelites were not obedient to him, so God allowed an enemy army to destroy the Temple and take the Israelites to another land.

God established his rules to show his people that he knew what was best for them. He never enjoyed seeing his people suffer the consequences of their behavior. Your parents don't like to see you suffer either. So, why make them, God, or yourself miserable? You know what you have to do. Do it!

Fatherly Advice, Exodus 18, p. 99

Above the Law, 1 Kings 21, p. 470

If You Want My Advice . . . , Proverbs 13:1, p. 843

Sow It and Reap, Lamentations 1:18, p. 1075

A Reminder to Do What Is Right and True, Zechariah 7:8–10, p. 1257

A Change of Heart, Matthew 3:1–12, p. 1277

and he forced them to be slaves for him
and his descendants. They remained
there as slaves until the Persian kingdom
defeated Babylon. **21**And so what the
LORD had told Israel through the prophet
Jeremiah happened: The country was an
empty wasteland for seventy years to
make up for the years of Sabbath rest[n]
that the people had not kept.

22In the first year Cyrus was king of
Persia, the LORD had Cyrus send an announcement to his whole kingdom. This
happened so the LORD's message spoken
by Jeremiah would come true. He wrote:

23This is what Cyrus king of Persia says:

The LORD, the God of heaven,
has given me all the kingdoms of
the earth, and he has appointed me
to build a Temple for him at Jerusalem in Judah. Now may the LORD
your God be with all of you who are
his people. You are free to go to Jerusalem.

36:21 Sabbath rest The law said that every seventh year the land was not to be farmed. See Leviticus 25:1-7.

GOING HOME

Hi! My name is Ezra, and I am a teacher of God's Law. Imagine returning "home" to a place you have never been. Think about leaving your house, your friends, your school, and starting over again in the land where your grandparents once lived a short time ago. Many years ago God's people were conquered by their enemies and forced to live in foreign lands as punishment for their disobedience. As I wrote this book, the long time of exile was over, and the people were allowed to return to Israel. Download Ezra 1:5–11 to find out what treasure they brought with them.

I wrote this book to remind people of God's faithfulness to them. The people were discouraged when their enemies prevented them from rebuilding the Temple of the Lord. To our surprise, the new king of Persia ordered the Temple to be rebuilt at government expense. He even asked us to pray for his family. When the Temple was finished, I urged the people to confess their sins and ask God to forgive them.

JESUS WATCH

When Judah was conquered by Babylon, all of God's people were forced to leave the land that God had given them. The Temple was destroyed, and the people had no central place of worship. While they were held captive in Babylon, God sent prophets to assure the people that he loved them and that he would bring them back to their homeland. In Ezra we see the first people return to rebuild their nation. God promised that a Messiah, a Son of David, would come to save his people and rule forever. The ancestors of Jesus came back to the land God had promised them, so Jesus would be born in the land where David ruled, not in Babylon. Zerubbabel, one of the men who rebuilt the Temple, was an ancestor of Jesus. (Surf over to Matthew 1, p. 1274, to see Zerubbabel's name listed in Jesus' family history.)

DON'T MISS THESE EXCITING STORIES:

- Cyrus sends the captives home, Ezra 1
- Letters from enemies, Ezra 4
- The Temple is completed, Ezra 6:13–18
- Why Ezra pulled his hair, Ezra 9

FAITH links

- Operation Cooperation, **Ezra 1:5**
- Gratitude Attitude, **Ezra 3**
- Wronged for What's Right, **Ezra 4:4–5**
- Building Tools, **Ezra 6:15**
- Teaching Others, **Ezra 7:8–10**

Cyrus Helps the Captives Return

1 In the first year Cyrus was king of
Persia, the LORD caused Cyrus to
send an announcement to his whole kingdom and to put it in writing. This happened so the LORD's message spoken by
Jeremiah would come true. He wrote:

2This is what Cyrus king of Persia
says:

The LORD, the God of heaven,
has given all the kingdoms of the
earth to me, and he has appointed
me to build a Temple for him at Jerusalem in Judah. 3May God be
with all of you who are his people.
You are free to go to Jerusalem in
Judah and build the Temple of the
LORD, the God of Israel, who is in
Jerusalem. 4Those who stay behind, wherever they live, should
support those who want to go.
Give them silver and gold, supplies
and cattle, and special gifts for the
Temple of God in Jerusalem.

5Then the family leaders of Judah and
Benjamin and the priests and Levites got
ready to go to Jerusalem—everyone God
had caused to want to go to Jerusalem to
build the Temple of the LORD. 6All their
neighbors helped them, giving them
things made of silver and gold, along with
supplies, cattle, valuable gifts, and special gifts for the Temple. 7Also, King Cyrus brought out the bowls and pans that
belonged in the Temple of the LORD,
which Nebuchadnezzar had taken from
Jerusalem and put in the temple of his
own god. 8Cyrus king of Persia had Mithredath the treasurer bring them and
count them out for Sheshbazzar, the
prince of Judah.
9He listed thirty gold dishes, one
thousand silver dishes, twenty-nine
pans, 10thirty gold bowls, four hundred
ten matching silver bowls, and one thousand other pieces.
11There was a total of fifty-four hundred pieces of gold and silver. Sheshbazzar brought all these things along when
the captives went from Babylon to Jerusalem.

FAITH links

OPERATION COOPERATION

EZRA 1:5

When you have a big project to do, isn't it great to have help? In Ezra's day, the Israelites had lived in Babylon for a long while. They wanted to return to their own land to rebuild the Temple. The plan was to work together to get things done. Some would do the actual work of rebuilding. Others gave valuable items to pay for the work.

Learning to cooperate with others is one way to serve God. No one can do everything by himself. We all need to work together.

Connect here for tips on working with others:

A Use for Your Abilities, Genesis 41, p. 59

Building Together, Nehemiah 3, p. 627

A Halfhearted Offering, Malachi 1:6–14, p. 1268

With All Your Heart, Colossians 3:23, p. 1626

From Useless to Useful, Philemon 11, p. 1663

Come On In!, 1 Peter 4:9–10, p. 1705

The Captives Who Returned

2 These are the people of the area who
returned from captivity, whom Nebuchadnezzar king of Babylon had taken

away to Babylon. They returned to Jerusalem and Judah, each going back to his
own town. **2**These people returned with
Zerubbabel, Jeshua, Nehemiah, Seraiah,
Reelaiah, Mordecai, Bilshan, Mispar, Bigvai, Rehum, and Baanah.

These are the people from Israel: **3**the
descendants of Parosh—2,172; **4**the descendants of Shephatiah—372; **5**the descendants of Arah—775; **6**the descendants
of Pahath-Moab (through the family of
Jeshua and Joab)—2,812; **7**the descendants
of Elam—1,254; **8**the descendants of
Zattu—945; **9**the descendants of Zaccai—
760; **10**the descendants of Bani—642;
11the descendants of Bebai—623; **12**the
descendants of Azgad—1,222; **13**the descendants of Adonikam—666; **14**the
descendants of Bigvai—2,056; **15**the descendants of Adin—454; **16**the descendants of Ater (through the family of
Hezekiah)—98; **17**the descendants of Bezai—323; **18**the descendants of Jorah—
112; **19**the descendants of Hashum—223;
20the descendants of Gibbar—95.

21These are the people from the
towns: of Bethlehem—123; **22**of Netophah—56; **23**of Anathoth—128; **24**of Azmaveth—42; **25**of Kiriath Jearim, Kephirah, and Beeroth—743; **26**of Ramah
and Geba—621; **27**of Micmash—122;
28of Bethel and Ai—223; **29**of Nebo—52;
30of Magbish—156; **31**of the other town
of Elam—1,254; **32**of Harim—320; **33**of
Lod, Hadid and Ono—
725; **34**of Jericho—345;
35of Senaah—3,630.

36These are the priests:
the descendants of Jeda-
iah (through the family
of Jeshua)—973; **37**the
descendants of Immer—
1,052; **38**the descendants
of Pashhur—1,247; **39**the
descendants of Harim—
1,017.

40These are the Levites: the descendants of Jeshua and Kadmiel (through the
family of Hodaviah)—74.

41These are the singers: the descendants of Asaph—128.

42These are the gatekeepers of the
Temple: the descendants of Shallum,
Ater, Talmon, Akkub, Hatita, and Sho-
bai—139.

43These are the Temple servants: the
descendants of Ziha, Hasupha, Tabbaoth,
44Keros, Siaha, Padon, **45**Lebanah, Haga-
bah, Akkub, **46**Hagab, Shalmai, Hanan,
47Giddel, Gahar, Reaiah, **48**Rezin, Nekoda, Gazzam, **49**Uzza, Paseah, Besai,
50Asnah, Meunim, Nephussim, **51**Bakbuk, Hakupha, Harhur, **52**Bazluth, Mehida, Harsha, **53**Barkos, Sisera, Temah,
54Neziah, and Hatipha.

55These are the descendants of the
servants of Solomon: the descendants of
Sotai, Hassophereth, Peruda, **56**Jaala,
Darkon, Giddel, **57**Shephatiah, Hattil,
Pokereth-Hazzebaim, and Ami.

58The Temple servants and the descendants of the servants of Solomon
numbered 392.

59Some people came to Jerusalem
from the towns of Tel Melah, Tel Harsha,
Kerub, Addon, and Immer, but they could
not prove that their ancestors came from
Israel. **60**They were the descendants of
Delaiah, Tobiah, and Nekoda—652.

61Also these priests: the descendants
of Hobaiah, Hakkoz, and Barzillai, who
had married a daughter of Barzillai from
Gilead and was called by her family name.

62These people searched for their
family records but could not find them. So
they could not be priests, because they
were thought to be unclean. **63**The governor ordered them not
to eat any of the food offered to God until a priest
had settled this matter by
using the Urim and
Thummim.

64The total number of
those who returned was
42,360. **65**This is not
counting their 7,337 male
and female servants and
the 200 male and female
singers they had with them. **66**They had
736 horses, 245 mules, **67**435 camels,
and 6,720 donkeys.

68When they arrived at the Temple of
the LORD in Jerusalem, some of the leaders of families gave offerings to rebuild
the Temple of God on the same site as

> Some of the leaders of families gave offerings to rebuild the Temple of God on the same site as before.
>
> —Ezra 2:68

before. 69They gave as much as they
could to the treasury to rebuild the Temple—about 1,100 pounds of gold, about
6,000 pounds of silver, and 100 pieces of
clothing for the priests.
70All the Israelites settled in their
hometowns. The priests, Levites, singers, gatekeepers, and Temple servants,
along with some of the other people, settled in their own towns as well.

Rebuilding the Altar

3 In the seventh month, after the Israelites were settled in their hometowns, they met together in Jerusalem.
2Then Jeshua son of Jozadak and his fellow priests joined Zerubbabel son of Shealtiel and began to build the altar of the
God of Israel where they could offer
burnt offerings, just as it is written in the
Teachings of Moses, the man of God.
3Even though they were afraid of the
people living around them, they built the
altar where it had been before. And they
offered burnt offerings on it to the LORD
morning and evening. 4Then, to obey
what was written, they celebrated the
Feast of Shelters. They offered the right
number of sacrifices for each day of the
festival. 5After the Feast of Shelters,
they had regular sacrifices every day, as
well as sacrifices for the New Moon and
all the festivals commanded by the LORD.
Also there were special offerings brought
as gifts to the LORD. 6On the first day of
the seventh month they began to bring
burnt offerings to the LORD, but the foundation of the LORD's Temple had not yet
been laid.

Rebuilding the Temple

7Then they gave money to the bricklayers and carpenters. They also gave
food, wine, and oil to the cities of Sidon
and Tyre so they would float cedar logs
from Lebanon to the seacoast town of
Joppa. Cyrus king of Persia had given
permission for this.
8In the second month of the second
year after their arrival at the Temple of
God in Jerusalem, Zerubbabel son of
Shealtiel, Jeshua son of Jozadak, their fellow priests and Levites, and all who had

FAITH links

GRATITUDE ATTITUDE 

EZRA 3

What is the most exciting project you've ever worked on? This could be something you've wanted to do for a long time. The Israelites were happy about rebuilding the Temple. For years they had lived in a foreign land. Now that they were back home, they could repair the damage done to God's house. They gave thanks to God at every step of the building process to show how happy they were to work.

Next time you're working on an exciting project, think about giving God thanks each step of the way. It helps to build an attitude of gratitude that will make the work even more fun!

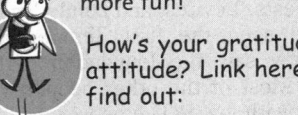

How's your gratitude attitude? Link here to find out:

My Worship Place, Genesis 35:1–14, p. 49

The Name of the Lord, Exodus 33:19–23; 34:5–8, p. 120

Everyone Can Help, Numbers 4, p. 181

You're Invited!, Psalm 100, p. 784

Small Beginnings, Zechariah 4:10, p. 1255

Glad to Help!, Romans 15:17–20, p. 1541

returned from captivity to Jerusalem began to work. They chose Levites twenty
years old and older to be in charge of the
building of the Temple of the LORD.
9These men were in charge of the work
of building the Temple of God: Jeshua and
his sons and brothers; Kadmiel and his
sons who were the descendants of Hodaviah; and the sons of Henadad and their
sons and brothers. They were all Levites.
10The builders finished laying the
foundation of the Temple of
the LORD. Then the
priests, dressed in
their robes, stood
with their trumpets,
and the Levites, the
sons of Asaph, stood
with their cymbals. They all took their
places and praised the LORD just as David
king of Israel had said to do. **11**With
praise and thanksgiving, they sang to the
LORD:

"He is good;
his love for Israel continues
forever."

And then all the people shouted loudly,
"Praise the LORD! The foundation of his
Temple has been laid." **12**But many of the
older priests, Levites, and family leaders
who had seen the first Temple cried
when they saw the foundation of this
Temple. Most of the other people were
shouting with joy. **13**The people made so
much noise it could be heard far away,
and no one could tell the difference between the joyful shouting and the sad
crying.

Enemies of the Rebuilding

4 When the enemies of the people of
Judah and Benjamin heard that the
returned captives were building a Temple
for the LORD, the God of Israel, **2**they
came to Zerubbabel and the leaders of
the families. The enemies said, "Let us
help you build, because we are like you
and want to worship your God. We have
been offering sacrifices to him since the
time of Esarhaddon king of Assyria, who
brought us here."
3But Zerubbabel, Jeshua, and the
leaders of Israel answered, "You will not
help us build a Temple to our God. We
will build it ourselves for the LORD, the
God of Israel, as King Cyrus, the king of
Persia, commanded us to do."

WRONGED FOR WHAT'S RIGHT

EZRA 4:4-5

Ever have someone try to stop you from doing something you knew was right? The Israelites faced trouble for rebuilding the Temple. A group of people who lived in the area tried to stop the Israelites from working. As a Christian, you can expect trouble whenever you do anything for the Lord. Jesus told his followers that trouble would find them. Why? Christians have an enemy—Satan. He doesn't want to see the good results God's work brings about. But Jesus said, "Be brave! I have defeated the world" (John 16:33). That means your enemy has already lost. So be brave!

Family Feud, Genesis 27, p. 37

What Will You Risk?, Joshua 2, p. 278

A Right to Get Even?, 1 Samuel 24, p. 388

Quick to Forgive?, Mark 11:25, p. 1349

A Peacemaker or a Peacebreaker?, James 3:18, p. 1693

Who's on First?, 3 John 9–10, p. 1723

4Then the people around them tried
to discourage the people of Judah by making them afraid to build. 5Their enemies
hired others to delay the building plans
during the time Cyrus was king of Persia.
And it continued to the time Darius was
king of Persia.

More Problems for the Builders

6When Xerxes first became king,
those enemies wrote a letter against the
people of Judah and Jerusalem.

7When Artaxerxes became king of
Persia, Bishlam, Mithredath, Tabeel, and
those with them wrote a letter to Artaxerxes. It was written in the Aramaic language and translated.

8Rehum the governor and Shimshai
the governor's secretary wrote a letter
against Jerusalem to Artaxerxes the
king. It said:

9This letter is from Rehum the
governor, Shimshai the secretary,
and their fellow workers—the
judges and important officers over
the men who came from Tripolis,
Persia, Erech, and Babylon, the
Elamite people of Susa, 10and
those whom the great and honorable Ashurbanipal forced out of
their countries and settled in the
city of Samaria and in other places
of the Trans-Euphrates.

11(This is a copy of the letter they
sent to Artaxerxes.)

To King Artaxerxes.
From your servants who live in
Trans-Euphrates.

12King Artaxerxes, you should
know that the Jewish people who
came to us from you have gone to
Jerusalem to rebuild that evil city
that refuses to obey. They are fix-
ing the walls and repairing the
foundations of the buildings.

13Now, King Artaxerxes, you
should know that if Jerusalem is
built and its walls are fixed, Jerusalem will not pay taxes of any kind.
Then the amount of money your
government collects will be less.
14Since we must be loyal to the
government, we don't want to see
the king dishonored. So we are
writing to let the king know. 15We
suggest you search the records of
the kings who ruled before you.
You will find out that the city of Jerusalem refuses to obey and makes
trouble for kings and areas controlled by Persia. Since long ago it
has been a place where disobedience has started. That is why it
was destroyed. 16We want you to
know, King Artaxerxes, that if this
city is rebuilt and its walls fixed,
you will be left with nothing in
Trans-Euphrates.

17King Artaxerxes sent this answer:

To Rehum the governor and Shimshai the secretary, to all their fellow workers living in Samaria, and
to those in other places in Trans-
Euphrates.

Greetings.

18The letter you sent to us has
been translated and read to me. 19I
ordered the records to be searched,
and it was done. We found that Jerusalem has a history of disobedience to kings and has been a place
of problems and trouble. 20Jerusa-
lem has had powerful kings who
have ruled over the whole area of
Trans-Euphrates, and taxes of all
kinds have been paid to them.
21Now, give an order for those men
to stop work. The city of Jerusalem
will not be rebuilt until I say so.
22Make sure you do this, because if
they continue, it will hurt the government.

23A copy of the letter that King Artaxerxes sent was read to Rehum and
Shimshai the secretary and the others.
Then they quickly went to the Jewish
people in Jerusalem and forced them to
stop building.

24So the work on the Temple of God
in Jerusalem stopped until the second
year Darius was king of Persia.

Tattenai's Letter to Darius

5 The prophets Haggai and Zechariah, a
descendant of Iddo, prophesied to the
Jewish people in Judah and Jerusalem in
the name of the God of Israel, who was
over them. **2**Then Zerubbabel son of Shealtiel and
Jeshua son of Jozadak
started working again to
rebuild the Temple of
God in Jerusalem. And
the prophets of God were
there, helping them.

> We are rebuilding the Temple that a great king of Israel built and finished many years ago.
> —Ezra 5:11

3At that time Tattenai,
the governor of Trans-
Euphrates, and Shethar-
Bozenai, and their fellow
workers went to the Jewish people and
asked, "Who gave you permission to rebuild this Temple and fix these walls?"
4They also asked, "What are the names of
the men working on this building?" **5**But
their God was watching over the older
leaders of the Jewish people. The builders
were not stopped until a report could go to
King Darius and his written answer could
be received.

6This is a copy of the letter that was
sent to King Darius by Tattenai, the governor of Trans-Euphrates, Shethar-Bozenai, and the other important officers of
Trans-Euphrates. **7**This is what was said
in the report they sent to him:

To King Darius.

Greetings. May you have peace.

8King Darius, you should know
that we went to the district of Judah where the Temple of the great
God is. The people are building
that Temple with large stones, and
they are putting timbers in the
walls. They are working very hard
and are building very fast.

9We asked their older leaders,
"Who gave you permission to rebuild this Temple and these walls?"
10We also asked for their names,
and we wrote down the names of
their leaders so you would know
who they are.

11This is the answer they gave
to us: "We are the servants of the
God of heaven and earth. We are
rebuilding the Temple that a great
king of Israel built and finished
many years ago. **12**But our ancestors made the God of
heaven angry, so he
handed them over to
Nebuchadnezzar king
of Babylon, who de-
stroyed this Temple
and took the people to
Babylon as captives.

13"Later, in the
first year Cyrus was
king of Babylon, he
gave a special order for
this Temple to be rebuilt. **14**Cyrus
brought out from the temple in
Babylon the gold and silver bowls
and pans that came from the Temple of God. Nebuchadnezzar had
taken them from the Temple in Jerusalem and had put them in the
temple in Babylon.

"Then King Cyrus gave them
to Sheshbazzar, his appointed governor. **15**Cyrus said to him, 'Take
these gold and silver bowls and
pans, and put them back in the
Temple in Jerusalem and rebuild
the Temple of God where it was.'
16So Sheshbazzar came and laid
the foundations of the Temple of
God in Jerusalem. From that day
until now the work has been going
on, but it is not yet finished."

17Now, if the king wishes, let a
search be made in the royal
records of Babylon. See if King Cyrus gave an order to rebuild this
Temple in Jerusalem. Then let the
king write us and tell us what he
has decided.

The Order of Darius

6 So King Darius gave an order to
search the records kept in the treasury in Babylon. **2**A scroll was found in

Ecbatana, the capital city of Media. This is what was written on it:

Note:

3King Cyrus gave an order about the Temple of God in Jerusalem in the first year he was king. This was the order:

"Let the Temple be rebuilt as a place to present sacrifices. Let its foundations be laid; it should be ninety feet high and ninety feet wide.
4It must have three layers of large stones and then one layer of timbers. The costs should be paid from the king's treasury.
5The gold and silver utensils from the Temple of God should be put back in their places. Nebuchadnezzar took them from the Temple in Jerusalem and brought them to Babylon, but they are to be put back in the Temple of God in Jerusalem."

6Now then, Tattenai, governor of Trans-Euphrates, Shethar-Bozenai, and all the officers of that area, stay away from there.
7Do not bother the work on that Temple of God. Let the governor of the Jewish people and the older Jewish leaders rebuild this Temple where it was before.

8Also, I order you to do this for those older leaders of the Jewish people who are building this Temple: The cost of the building is to be fully paid from the royal treasury, from taxes collected from Trans-Euphrates. Do this so the work will not stop.
9Give those people anything they need—young bulls, male sheep, or lambs for burnt offerings to the God of heaven, or wheat, salt, wine, or olive oil. Give the priests in Jerusalem anything they ask for every day without fail.
10Then they may offer sacrifices pleasing to the God of heaven, and they may pray for the life of the king and his sons.

11Also, I give this order: If anyone changes this order, a wood beam is to be pulled from his house and driven through his body. Because of his crime, make his house

FAITH links

BUILDING TOOLS

EZRA 6:15

What gets you through a project that takes a long time to finish? Plenty of pepperoni pizza and soda? The promise of a reward? How about hard work and perseverance (another way to say not quitting)? Both helped the Israelites to rebuild the Temple. Without these "tools," they would not have completed such a long, hard project.

Hard work and perseverance may not seem as appetizing or fun as pizza. But they can help you do all sorts of things that a pepperoni pizza can't do.

Stuck someplace? Connect to these links for help in getting back on track:

Keep On Praying, 1 Samuel 1, p. 354

The Green Light, 2 Samuel 2:1, p. 401

Plan for Success, 1 Chronicles 14:8–17, p. 538

Two Enemies, Nehemiah 6, p. 631

Fly Like an Eagle, Isaiah 40:28–31, p. 947

Exercising Patience, Luke 2:25–28, 36–37, p. 1369

a pile of ruins. 12God has chosen
Jerusalem as the place he is to
be worshiped. May he punish
any king or person who tries to
change this order and destroy this
Temple.

I, Darius, have given this order.
Let it be obeyed quickly and carefully.

Completion of the Temple

13So, Tattenai, the governor of Trans-
Euphrates, Shethar-Bozenai, and their
fellow workers carried out King Darius'
order quickly and carefully. 14The older
Jewish leaders continued to build and
were successful because of the preaching
of Haggai the prophet and Zechariah, a
descendant of Iddo. They finished building the Temple as the God of Israel had
commanded and as kings Cyrus, Darius,
and Artaxerxes of Persia had ordered.
15The Temple was finished on the third
day of the month of Adar in the sixth year
Darius was king.

16Then the people of Israel celebrated and gave the Temple to God to honor
him. Everybody was happy: the priests,
the Levites, and the rest of the Jewish
people who had returned from captivity.
17They gave the Temple to God by offering a hundred bulls, two hundred male
sheep, and four hundred lambs as sacrifices. And as an offering to forgive the
sins of all Israel, they offered twelve male
goats, one goat for each tribe in Israel.
18Then they put the priests and the Levites into their separate groups. Each
group had a certain time to serve God in
the Temple at Jerusalem as it is written
in the Book of Moses.

The Passover Is Celebrated

19The Jewish people who returned
from captivity celebrated the Passover on
the fourteenth day of the first month.
20The priests and Levites had made
themselves clean. Then the Levites
killed the Passover lambs for all the people who had returned from captivity, for
their relatives the priests, and for themselves. 21So all the people of Israel who
returned from captivity ate the Passover
lamb. So did the people who had given up
the unclean ways of their non-Jewish
neighbors in order to worship the LORD,
the God of Israel. 22For seven days they
celebrated the Feast of Unleavened
Bread in a very joyful way. The LORD had
made them happy by changing the mind
of the king of Assyria so that he helped
them in the work on the Temple of the
God of Israel.

Ezra Comes to Jerusalem

7 After these things[n] during the rule of
Artaxerxes king of Persia, Ezra came
up from Babylon. Ezra was the son of Seraiah, the son of Azariah, the son of Hilkiah, 2the son of Shallum, the son of
Zadok, the son of Ahitub, 3the son of Amariah, the son of Azariah, the son of Meraioth, 4the son of Zerahiah, the son of Uzzi,
the son of Bukki, 5the son of Abishua, the
son of Phinehas, the son of Eleazar, the
son of Aaron the high priest. 6This Ezra
came to Jerusalem from Babylon. He was
a teacher and knew well the Teachings of
Moses that had been given by the LORD,
the God of Israel. Ezra received everything he asked for from the king, because
the LORD his God was helping him. 7In
the seventh year of King Artaxerxes
more Israelites came to Jerusalem.
Among them were priests, Levites, singers, gatekeepers, and Temple servants.

8Ezra arrived in Jerusalem in the fifth
month of Artaxerxes' seventh year as
king. 9Ezra had left Babylon on the first
day of the first month, and he arrived in
Jerusalem on the first day of the fifth
month, because God was helping him.
10Ezra had worked hard to know and
obey the Teachings of the LORD and to
teach his rules and commands to the Israelites.

Artaxerxes' Letter to Ezra

11King Artaxerxes had given a letter
to Ezra, a priest and teacher who taught
about the commands and laws the LORD
gave Israel. This is a copy of the letter:

7:1 After these things There is a time period of about sixty years between chapters six and seven.

TEACHING OTHERS

EZRA 7:8-10

Have you ever taught someone a sport or helped someone with a school subject? If so, you know how important it is for you to know the sport or subject well before teaching someone else. Ezra worked hard to know the Teachings of the Lord in order to teach others about God's laws.

Your Sunday school teacher, youth leader, or youth pastor also worked hard to learn what they know in order to teach you about God. They do it to encourage you to study the Bible for yourself. Who knows? Maybe *you'll* teach someone about the Bible someday!

An Example Not to Follow, Leviticus 18:1–3, p. 157

The Prayer Habit, Psalm 5:1–3, p. 712

Your Full Trust, Jeremiah 22:20–22, p. 1023

God's Instructions, Ezekiel 4:1–15, p. 1089

Attention, Please!, Luke 8:11–15, p. 1383

How to Make God Glad, Ephesians 6:1–2, p. 1605

12From Artaxerxes, king of kings,
to Ezra the priest, a teacher of the
Law of the God of heaven.

Greetings.
13Now I give this order: Any
Israelite in my kingdom who
wishes may go with you to Jerusalem, including priests and Levites.
14Ezra, you are sent by the king
and the seven people who advise
him to ask how Judah and Jerusalem are obeying the Law of your
God, which you are carrying with
you. **15**Also take with you the
silver and gold that the king and
those who advise him have given
freely to the God of Israel, whose
Temple is in Jerusalem. **16**Also
take the silver and gold you receive from the area of Babylon.
Take the offerings the Israelites
and their priests have given as
gifts for the Temple of your God in
Jerusalem. **17**With this money buy
bulls, male sheep, and lambs, and
the grain offerings and drink offerings that go with those sacrifices.
Then sacrifice them on the altar in
the Temple of your God in Jerusalem.

18You and your fellow Jews may
spend the silver and gold left over
as you want and as God wishes.
19Take to the God of Jerusalem all
the utensils for worship in the Temple of your God, **20**which we have
given you. Use the royal treasury to
pay for anything else you need for
the Temple of your God.

21Now I, King Artaxerxes, give
this order to all the men in charge
of the treasury of Trans-Euphrates: Give Ezra, a priest and a
teacher of the Law of the God of
heaven, whatever he asks for.
22Give him up to seventy-five
hundred pounds of silver, six hundred bushels of wheat, six hundred
gallons of wine, and six hundred
gallons of olive oil. And give him as
much salt as he wants. **23**Carefully
give him whatever the God of
heaven wants for the Temple of the
God of heaven. We do not want
God to be angry with the king and
his sons. **24**Remember, you must
not make these people pay taxes of
any kind: priests, Levites, singers,

gatekeepers, Temple servants, and other workers in this Temple of God.
25And you, Ezra, use the wisdom you have from your God to choose judges and lawmakers to rule the Jewish people of Trans-Euphrates. They know the laws of your God, and you may teach anyone who does not know them.
26Whoever does not obey the law of your God or of the king must be punished. He will be killed, or sent away, or have his property taken away, or be put in jail.

27Praise the LORD, the God of our ancestors. He caused the king to want to honor the Temple of the LORD in Jerusalem.
28The LORD has shown me, Ezra, his love in the presence of the king, those who advise the king, and the royal officers. Because the LORD my God was helping me, I had courage, and I gathered the leaders of Israel to return with me.

Leaders Who Returned with Ezra

8 These are the leaders of the family groups and those who were listed with them who came back with me from Babylon during the rule of King Artaxerxes.

2From the descendants of Phinehas: Gershom.

From the descendants of Ithamar: Daniel.

From the descendants of David: Hattush
3of the descendants of Shecaniah.

From the descendants of Parosh: Zechariah, with one hundred fifty men.

4From the descendants of Pahath-Moab: Eliehoenai son of Zerahiah, with two hundred men.

5From the descendants of Zattu: Shecaniah son of Jahaziel, with three hundred men.

6From the descendants of Adin: Ebed son of Jonathan, with fifty men.

7From the descendants of Elam: Jeshaiah son of Athaliah, with seventy men.

8From the descendants of Shephatiah: Zebadiah son of Michael, with eighty men.

9From the descendants of Joab: Obadiah son of Jehiel, with two hundred eighteen men.

10From the descendants of Bani: Shelomith son of Josiphiah, with one hundred sixty men.

11From the descendants of Bebai: Zechariah son of Bebai, with twenty-eight men.

12From the descendants of Azgad: Johanan son of Hakkatan, with one hundred ten men.

13From the descendants of Adonikam, these were the last ones: Eliphelet, Jeuel, and Shemaiah, with sixty men.

14From the descendants of Bigvai: Uthai and Zaccur, with seventy men.

The Return to Jerusalem

15I called all those people together at the canal that flows toward Ahava, where we camped for three days. I checked all the people and the priests, but I did not find any Levites.
16So I called these leaders: Eliezer, Ariel, Shemaiah, Elnathan, Jarib, Elnathan, Nathan, Zechariah, and Meshullam. And I called Joiarib and Elnathan, who were teachers.
17I sent these men to Iddo, the leader at Casiphia, and told them what to say to Iddo and his relatives, who are the Temple servants in Casiphia. I sent them to bring servants to us for the Temple of our God.
18Our God was helping us, so Iddo's relatives gave us Sherebiah, a wise man from the descendants of Mahli son of Levi, who was the son of Israel. And they brought Sherebiah's sons and brothers, for a total of eighteen men.
19And they brought to us Hashabiah and Jeshaiah from the descendants of Merari, and his brothers and nephews. In all there were twenty men.
20They also brought two hundred twenty of the Temple servants, a group David and the officers had set up to help the Levites. All of those men were listed by name.

21There by the Ahava Canal, I announced we would all give up eating and humble ourselves before our God. We would ask God for a safe trip for ourselves, our children, and all our possessions.
22I was ashamed to ask the king

for soldiers and horsemen to protect us
from enemies on the road. We had said to
the king, "Our God helps everyone who
obeys him, but he is very angry with all
who reject him." **23**So we gave up eating
and prayed to our God about our trip, and
he answered our prayers.

24Then I chose twelve of the priests
who were leaders, Sherebiah, Hashabiah,
and ten of their relatives. **25**I weighed
the offering of silver and gold and the
utensils given for the Temple of our God,
and I gave them to the twelve priests I
had chosen. The king, the people who advised him, his officers, and all the Israelites there with us had given these things
for the Temple. **26**I weighed out and gave
them about fifty thousand pounds of silver, about seventy-five hundred pounds
of silver objects, and about seventy-five
hundred pounds of gold. **27**I gave them
twenty gold bowls that weighed about
nineteen pounds and two fine pieces of
polished bronze that were as valuable as
gold.

28Then I said to the priests, "You and
these utensils belong to the LORD for his
service. The silver and gold are gifts to
the LORD, the God of your ancestors.
29Guard these things carefully. In Jerusalem, weigh them in front of the leading
priests, Levites, and the leaders of the
family groups of Israel in the rooms of the
Temple of the LORD." **30**So the priests
and Levites accepted the silver, the gold,
and the utensils that had been weighed to
take them to the Temple of our God in
Jerusalem.

31On the twelfth day of the first month
we left the Ahava Canal and started toward Jerusalem. Our God helped us and
protected us from enemies and robbers
along the way. **32**Finally we arrived in Jerusalem where we rested three days.

33On the fourth day we weighed out
the silver, the gold, and the utensils in
the Temple of our God. We handed them
to the priest Meremoth son of Uriah. Eleazar son of Phinehas was with him, as
were the Levites Jozabad son of Jeshua
and Noadiah son of Binnui. **34**We checked
everything by number and by weight, and
the total weight was written down.

35Then the captives who returned
made burnt offerings to the God of Israel.
They sacrificed twelve bulls for all Israel,
ninety-six male sheep, and seventy-seven
lambs. For a sin offering there were
twelve male goats. All this was a burnt
offering to the LORD. **36**They took King
Artaxerxes' orders to the royal officers
and to the governors of Trans-Euphrates.
Then these men gave help to the people
and the Temple of God.

Ezra's Prayer

9 After these things had been done, the
leaders came to me and said, "Ezra,

FAITH CHALLENGE

Here's a challenge for you. Read 8:36 to discover how the leaders of Babylon helped the Israelites who were rebuilding their temple. How could you and your friends help the people who work at your church?

TESTING IT

Ezra 8:36

They took King Artaxerxes' orders to the royal officers and to the governors of Trans-Euphrates. Then these men gave help to the people and the Temple of God.

the Israelites, including the priests and
Levites, have not kept themselves separate from the people around us. Those
neighbors do evil things, as the Canaanites, Hittites, Perizzites, Jebusites, Ammonites, Moabites, Egyptians, and Amorites did. 2The Israelite men and their
sons have married these women. They
have mixed the people who belong to
God with the people around them. The
leaders and officers of Israel have led the
rest of the Israelites to do this unfaithful
thing."

3When I heard this, I angrily tore my
robe and coat, pulled hair from my head
and beard, and sat down in shock.
4Everyone who trembled in fear at the
word of the God of Israel gathered around
me because of the unfaithfulness of the
captives who had returned. I sat there in
shock until the evening sacrifice.

eMAIL! FROM GOD
9:6
Sin
How to deal with your sins.

5At the evening
sacrifice I got up
from where I had
shown my shame.
My robe and coat
were torn, and I fell
on my knees with
my hands spread out to the LORD my
God. 6I prayed,

"My God, I am too ashamed and embarrassed to lift up my face to you, my
God, because our sins are so many. They
are higher than our heads. Our guilt even
reaches up to the sky. 7From the days of
our ancestors until now, our guilt has
been great. Because of our sins, we, our
kings, and our priests have been punished by the sword and captivity. Foreign
kings have taken away our things and
shamed us, even as it is today.

8"But now, for a short time, the LORD
our God has been kind to us. He has let
some of us come back from captivity and
has let us live in safety in his holy place.
And so our God gives us hope and a little
relief from our slavery. 9Even though we
are slaves, our God has not left us. He
caused the kings of Persia to be kind to
us and has given us new life. We can rebuild the Temple and repair its ruins. And
he has given us a wall to protect us in Judah and Jerusalem.

10"But now, our God, what can we say
after you have done all this? We have disobeyed your commands 11that you gave
through your servants the prophets. You
said, 'The land you are entering to own is
ruined; the people living there have
spoiled it by the evil they do. Their evil
filled the land with uncleanness from one
end to the other. 12So do not let your
daughters marry their sons, and do not
let their daughters marry your sons. Do
not wish for their peace or success. Then
you will be strong and eat the good things
of the land. Then you can leave this land
to your descendants forever.'

13"What has happened to us is our
own fault. We have done evil things, and
our guilt is great. But you, our God, have
punished us less than we deserve; you
have left a few of us alive. 14We should
not again break your commands by allowing marriages with these wicked people. If
we did, you would get angry enough to
destroy us, and none of us would be left
alive. 15LORD, God of Israel, by your
goodness a few of us are left alive today.
We admit that we are guilty and none of us
should be allowed to stand before you."

The People Confess Sin

10 As Ezra was praying and confessing and crying and throwing himself down in front of the Temple, a large
group of Israelite men, women, and children gathered around him who were also
crying loudly. 2Then Shecaniah son of Jehiel the Elamite said to Ezra, "We have
been unfaithful to
our God by marry-
ing women from the
peoples around us.
But even so, there is
still hope for Israel.
3Now let us make an
agreement before our
God. We will send away all these women
and their children as you and those who
respect the commands of our God advise.
Let it be done to obey God's Teachings.
4Get up, Ezra. You are in charge, and we
will support you. Have courage and do
it."

eMAIL! FROM GOD
10:2
Hope
Will God still love you even if you sin?

5So Ezra got up and made the priests,

Levites, and all the people of Israel promise to do what was suggested; and they
promised. 6Then Ezra left the Temple
and went to the room of Jehohanan son of
Eliashib. While Ezra was there, he did
not eat or drink, because he was still sad
about the unfaithfulness of the captives
who had returned.

7They sent an order in Judah and Jerusalem for all the captives who had returned to meet together in Jerusalem.
8Whoever did not come to Jerusalem
within three days would lose his property
and would no longer be a member of the
community of the returned captives.
That was the decision of the officers and
older leaders.

9So within three days all the people of
Judah and Benjamin gathered in Jerusalem. It was the twentieth day of the ninth
month. All the people were sitting in the
open place in front of the Temple and
were upset because of the meeting and
because it was raining. 10Ezra the priest
stood up and said to them, "You have
been unfaithful and have married non-
Jewish women. You have made Israel
more guilty. 11Now, confess it to the
LORD, the God of your ancestors. Do his
will and separate yourselves from the
people living around you and from your
non-Jewish wives."

12Then the whole group answered
Ezra with a loud voice, "Ezra, you're
right! We must do what you say. 13But
there are many people here, and it's the
rainy season. We can't stand outside, and
this problem can't be solved in a day or
two, because we have sinned badly. 14Let
our officers make a decision for the whole
group. Then let everyone in our towns
who has married a non-Jewish woman
meet with the older leaders and judges of
each town at a planned time, until the hot
anger of our God turns away from us."
15Only Jonathan son of Asahel, Jahzeiah
son of Tikvah, Meshullam, and Shabbethai the Levite were against the plan.

16So the returned captives did what
was suggested. Ezra the priest chose
men who were leaders of the family
groups and named one from each family
division. On the first day of the tenth
month they sat down to study each case.
17By the first day of the first month, they
had finished with all the men who had
married non-Jewish women.

Those Guilty of Marrying Non-Jewish Women

18These are the descendants of the
priests who had married foreign women:

From the descendants of Jeshua son
of Jozadak and Jeshua's brothers: Maaseiah, Eliezer, Jarib, and Gedaliah. 19(They
all promised to divorce their wives, and
each one brought a male sheep from the
flock as a penalty offering.)

20From the descendants of Immer:
Hanani and Zebadiah.

21From the descendants of Harim:
Maaseiah, Elijah, Shemaiah, Jehiel, and
Uzziah.

22From the descendants of Pashhur:
Elioenai, Maaseiah, Ishmael, Nethanel,
Jozabad, and Elasah.

23Among the Levites: Jozabad, Shimei, Kelaiah (also called Kelita), Pethahiah,
Judah, and Eliezer.

24Among the singers: Eliashib.

Among the gatekeepers: Shallum, Telem, and Uri.

25And among the other Israelites,
these married non-Jewish women:

From the descendants of Parosh: Ra-
miah, Izziah, Malkijah, Mijamin, Eleazar,
Malkijah, and Benaiah.

26From the descendants of Elam:
Mattaniah, Zechariah, Jehiel, Abdi, Jeremoth, and Elijah.

27From the descendants of Zattu: Elioenai, Eliashib, Mattaniah, Jeremoth, Zabad, and Aziza.

28From the descendants of Bebai: Jehohanan, Hananiah, Zabbai, and Athlai.

29From the descendants of Bani: Meshullam, Malluch, Adaiah, Jashub, Sheal,
and Jeremoth.

30From the descendants of Pahath-
Moab: Adna, Kelal, Benaiah, Maaseiah,
Mattaniah, Bezalel, Binnui, and Manas-
seh.

31From the descendants of Harim:
Eliezer, Ishijah, Malkijah, Shemaiah,
Shimeon, 32Benjamin, Malluch, and
Shemariah.

33From the descendants of Hashum:
Mattenai, Mattattah, Zabad, Eliphelet,
Jeremai, Manasseh, and Shimei.
34From the descendants of Bani: Ma-
adai, Amram, Uel, 35Benaiah, Bedeiah,
Keluhi, 36Vaniah, Meremoth, Eliashib,
37Mattaniah, Mattenai, and Jaasu.
38From the descendants of Binnui:
Shimei, 39Shelemiah, Nathan, Adaiah,
40Macnadebai, Shashai, Sharai, 41Azarel,
Shelemiah, Shemariah, 42Shallum, Amariah, and Joseph.
43From the descendants of Nebo:
Jeiel, Mattithiah, Zabad, Zebina, Jaddai,
Joel, and Benaiah.
44All these men had married non-
Jewish women, and some of them had
children by these wives.

Nehemiah

BUILD THE WALL

Hi! My name is Nehemiah. I was the one who served wine to the king of Persia when I heard about the poor conditions in Israel, the land of my parents and grandparents. The city of Jerusalem had no wall and the people were not following God's laws. The king noticed how sad I was; and when he asked me why, I told him about my homeland. He gave me permission to go to Jerusalem and rebuild the walls.

Have you ever run an obstacle course? Rebuilding the wall of Jerusalem was like running an obstacle course, but in this case the obstacles were people! Foreigners living in our land tried to stop our work and even threatened to kill us. Half of our workers had to stand guard while the other half built the wall. Link to Nehemiah 4:7–23 to see how we prepared for attack.

I wrote this book to tell people to be faithful to God. When the wall was finished, Ezra the teacher read God's laws to the people. The people cried when they understood what God's law said and how disobedient they were. But I told them, "Today is a holy day to the Lord. Don't be sad, because the joy of the LORD will make you strong" (Nehemiah 8:10). We offered the wall of Jerusalem as a gift to God. Check out Nehemiah 12:27–43 for the big party we had after the work was done.

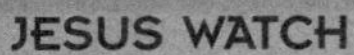

JESUS WATCH

Nehemiah had the privilege of selecting and serving the finest wine to the king, as well as the responsibility of tasting it to make sure it was not poisoned. He earned the respect of the king and was a trusted advisor. Nehemiah gave up his high-ranking job so that he could help his people in Jerusalem. This reminds us of Jesus, the Son of God, who left his place in heaven so that he could become our savior.

Like Jesus, Nehemiah showed great compassion for the poor. As governor of Jerusalem, Nehemiah did not demand all that was owed to him, because he knew the people were already working very hard. Nehemiah also spent a lot of time in prayer. He asked God to make him strong. Jesus often went to a quiet place to pray to his Father in heaven.

OTHER CONNECTIONS

What are some ways that you worship God? Can God only be worshiped at church on Sundays, or when you are with other Christians? Find out more about worshiping God by connecting to An Awesome God, Nehemiah 8:6.

It was a sad day for Israel when the city of Jerusalem finally was captured and destroyed and its people taken as captives to a foreign land. But, just as God had promised, the day came when the people were allowed to return to their homeland. Read about it at The Homecoming, Nehemiah 8:1–12.

my FAVORITE links

____

____

____

____

"Tagg, do you know how the people decided who should live in Jerusalem?"

"Not really. But if we access Nehemiah 11:1-2, I think we can find out."

THE NEHEMIAH SURFWATCH:

Nehemiah's sad face, Nehemiah 2:1–10
Nehemiah shakes his robe, Nehemiah 5:1–13
The people build shelters, Nehemiah 8:13–18
Let's celebrate, Nehemiah 12:27–43

FAITH links

- Seeing the Needs, **Nehemiah 1**
- Prayer + Action = Success, **Nehemiah 2:4–9**
- Building Together, **Nehemiah 3**
- Help for the Outsiders, **Nehemiah 5:9–10**
- Two Enemies, **Nehemiah 6**
- See the Heart Behind It, **Nehemiah 8; 9**
- An Honest Reputation, **Nehemiah 13:13**

Nehemiah's Prayer

1 These are the words of Nehemiah son
of Hacaliah.
In the month of Kislev in the twentieth year,[a] I, Nehemiah, was in the capital
city of Susa. **2**One of my brothers named
Hanani came with some other men from
Judah. I asked them about Jerusalem and
the Jewish people who lived through the
captivity.
3They answered me, "Those who are
left from the captivity are back in Judah,
but they are in much trouble and are full
of shame. The wall around Jerusalem is
broken down, and its gates have been
burned."
4When I heard these things, I sat
down and cried for several days. I was sad
and ate nothing. I prayed to the God of
heaven, **5**"LORD, God of heaven, you are
the great God who is to be respected. You
are loyal, and you keep your agreement
with those who love you and obey your
commands. **6**Look and listen carefully.
Hear the prayer that I, your servant, am
praying to you day and night for your servants, the Israelites. I confess the sins
we Israelites have done against you. My
father's family and I have sinned against
you. **7**We have been wicked toward you
and have not obeyed the commands,
rules, and laws you gave your servant
Moses.
8"Remember what you taught your
servant Moses, saying, 'If you are unfaithful, I will scatter you among the nations. **9**But if you return to me and obey
my commands, I will gather your people
from the far ends of the earth. And I will
bring them from captivity to where I have
chosen to be worshiped.'
10"They are your servants and your
people, whom you have saved with your
great strength and power. **11**Lord, listen
carefully to the prayer of your servant
and the prayers of your servants who
love to honor you. Give me, your servant,
success today; allow this king to show
kindness to me."
I was the one who served wine to the
king.

SEEING THE NEEDS

NEHEMIAH 1

What's the first thing you need to do in order to help someone? If your answer is pray, you're half right. You first need to know what kind of help is needed. Nehemiah saw a need and wanted to do something about it. He heard how the Israelites had returned to their land. The wall around Jerusalem had been destroyed. So the people were defenseless. Nehemiah then talked to God about that need.

God wants us to notice the needs of the people around us. Seeing the needs of others reminds us to care for them.

Your Response to Responsibility, Ruth 2:1–7, p. 346

Just a Little Respect, 1 Chronicles 11:10–19, p. 534

Meaningless Words, Job 21:34, p. 684

You Are What You Do, Proverbs 20:11, p. 854

Your Choice of Fruit, Matthew 12:33–35, p. 1295

An Encouraging Word, 1 Corinthians 1:3–5, p. 1545

Nehemiah Is Sent to Jerusalem

2 It was the month of Nisan in the twentieth year Artaxerxes was king. He
wanted some wine, so I took some and
gave it to the king. I had not been sad in
his presence before. **2**So the king said,

1:1 twentieth year This is probably referring to the twentieth year King Artaxerxes I ruled Persia.

"Why does your face look sad even
though you are not sick? Your heart must
be sad."

Then I was very afraid. 3I said to the
king, "May the king live forever! My face
is sad because the city where my ancestors are buried lies in ruins,
and its gates have
been destroyed by
fire."

EMAIL! FROM GOD
2:4
Prayer
Do you need to kneel to pray?

4Then the king
said to me, "What do
you want?"

First I prayed to the God of heaven.
5Then I answered the king, "If you are
willing and if I have pleased you, send me
to the city in Judah where my ancestors
are buried so I can rebuild it."

6The queen was sitting next to the
king. He asked me, "How long will your
trip take, and when will you get back?" It
pleased the king to send me, so I set a
time.

7I also said to him, "If you are willing,
give me letters for the governors of
Trans-Euphrates. Tell them to let me
pass safely through their lands on my
way to Judah. 8And may I have a letter for
Asaph, the keeper of the king's forest,
telling him to give me timber? I will need
it to make boards for the gates of the palace, which is by the Temple, and for the
city wall, and for the house in which I will
live." So the king gave me the letters, because God was showing kindness to me.
9Then I went to the governors of Trans-
Euphrates and gave them the king's letters. The king had also sent army officers
and soldiers on horses with me.

10When Sanballat the Horonite and
Tobiah the Ammonite officer heard about
this, they were upset that someone had
come to help the Israelites.

Nehemiah Inspects Jerusalem

11I went to Jerusalem and stayed
there three days. 12Then at night I
started out with a few men. I had not told
anyone what God had caused me to do for
Jerusalem. There were no animals with
me except the one I was riding.

13I went out at night through the Valley Gate. I rode toward the Dragon Well

FAITH links

PRAYER + ACTION = SUCCESS

NEHEMIAH 2:4-9

Suppose you had a big homework assignment to do. Would just thinking about it get the assignment done? Nope. You've also got to do it. Nehemiah knew that the wall around Jerusalem needed to be repaired. But just thinking about it wouldn't move a brick. First, he prayed about the problem. Second, he acted. God gave Nehemiah the wisdom to know what to do next. Nehemiah didn't expect God to do all the work. But he knew that God would help *him* do the work.

Prayer and action make a winning combination. It's one you can use often to get things done.

Link here to find out more about that winning combination:

The Right Thing to Do, 1 Samuel 26, p. 391

A Wise Wish, 1 Kings 3:5–9, p. 439

Mind Guard, Proverbs 4:23, p. 831

Your Civic Duty, Matthew 17:24–27, p. 1304

You've Got the Power!, Acts 1:1–8; 2:1–4, p. 1463

Keep Up the Good Work!, Galatians 6:9–10, p. 1593

and the Trash Gate, inspecting the walls of Jerusalem that had been broken down and the gates that had been destroyed by fire. **14**Then I rode on toward the Fountain Gate and the King's Pool, but there was not enough room for the animal I was riding to pass through. **15**So I went up the valley at night, inspecting the wall. Finally, I turned and went back in through the Valley Gate. **16**The guards did not know where I had gone or what I was doing. I had not yet said anything to the Jewish people, the priests, the important men, the officers, or any of the others who would do the work.

17Then I said to them, "You can see the trouble we have here. Jerusalem is a pile of ruins, and its gates have been burned. Come, let's rebuild the wall of Jerusalem so we won't be full of shame any longer." **18**I also told them how God had been kind to me and what the king had said to me.

Then they answered, "Let's start rebuilding." So they began to work hard.

19But when Sanballat the Horonite, Tobiah the Ammonite officer, and Geshem the Arab heard about it, they made fun of us and laughed at us. They said, "What are you doing? Are you turning against the king?"

20But I answered them, "The God of heaven will give us success. We, his servants, will start rebuilding, but you have no share, claim, or memorial in Jerusalem."

Builders of the Wall

3 Eliashib the high priest and his fellow priests went to work and rebuilt the Sheep Gate. They gave it to the Lord's service and set its doors in place. They worked as far as the Tower of the Hundred and gave it to the Lord's service. Then they went on to the Tower of Hananel. **2**Next to them, the men of Jericho built part of the wall, and Zaccur son of Imri built next to them.

3The sons of Hassenaah rebuilt the Fish Gate, laying its boards and setting its doors, bolts, and bars in place. **4**Meremoth son of Uriah, the son of Hakkoz, made repairs next to them. Meshullam son of Berekiah, the son of Meshezabel, made repairs next to Meremoth. And Zadok son of Baana made repairs next to Meshullam. **5**The men from Tekoa made

FAITH links

BUILDING TOGETHER

NEHEMIAH 3

Ever pay attention to the credits at the end of a movie? They remind you that the actors weren't the only ones involved in making the movie. Many people with different skills work together to make a film. In Nehemiah's day, many people with different skills helped to rebuild the wall around Jerusalem.

God gave you the skills you have. You can use those skills to serve God. When God's people work together using the skills God provided each person, much is accomplished.

Connect here to discover how God wants you to use your skills:

Kind or Fair?, 1 Samuel 30, p. 395

Your Best Work, 1 Kings 6, p. 443

A Big Responsibility, 2 Kings 11, p. 494

Operation Cooperation, Ezra 1:5, p. 609

Get Ready!, Mark 13:26–27, p. 1354

The Worst Chore, John 13:3–17, p. 1447

repairs next to them, but the leading men
of Tekoa would not work under their
supervisors.

6Joiada son of Paseah and Meshullam
son of Besodeiah repaired the Old Gate.
They laid its boards and set its doors,
bolts, and bars in place. **7**Next to them,
Melatiah from Gibeon, other men from
Gibeon and Mizpah, and Jadon from
Meronoth made repairs. These places
were ruled by the governor of Trans-
Euphrates. **8**Next to them, Uzziel son of
Harhaiah, a goldsmith, made repairs. And
next to him, Hananiah, a perfume maker,
made repairs. These men rebuilt Jerusalem as far as the Broad Wall. **9**The next
part of the wall was repaired by Rephaiah
son of Hur, the ruler of half of the district
of Jerusalem. **10**Next to him, Jedaiah son
of Harumaph made repairs opposite his
own house. And next to him, Hattush son
of Hashabneiah made repairs. **11**Malkijah
son of Harim and Hasshub son of Pahath-
Moab repaired another part of the wall and
the Tower of the Ovens. **12**Next to them
Shallum son of Hallohesh, the ruler of half
of the district of Jerusalem, and his daughters made repairs.

13Hanun and the people of Zanoah repaired the Valley Gate, rebuilding it and
setting its doors, bolts, and bars in place.
They also repaired the five hundred
yards of the wall to the Trash Gate.

14Malkijah son of Recab, the ruler of
the district of Beth Hakkerem, repaired
the Trash Gate. He rebuilt that gate and
set its doors, bolts, and bars in place.

15Shallun son of Col-Hozeh, the ruler
of the district of Mizpah, repaired the
Fountain Gate. He rebuilt it, put a roof
over it, and set its doors, bolts, and bars
in place. He also repaired the wall of the
Pool of Siloam next to the King's Garden
all the way to the steps that went down
from the older part of the city. **16**Next to
Shallun was Nehemiah[n] son of Azbuk, the
ruler of half of the district of Beth Zur. He
made repairs opposite the tombs of David
and as far as the man-made pool and the
House of the Heroes.

17Next to him, the Levites made repairs, working under Rehum son of Bani.
Next to him, Hashabiah, the ruler of half
of the district of Keilah, for his district.
18Next to him, Binnui son of Henadad
and his Levites made repairs. Binnui was
the ruler of the other half of the district of
Keilah. **19**Next to them, Ezer son of
Jeshua, the ruler of Mizpah, repaired another part of the wall. He worked across
from the way up to the armory, as far as
the bend. **20**Next to him, Baruch son of
Zabbai worked hard on the wall that went
from the bend to the entrance to the
house of Eliashib, the high priest. **21**Next
to him, Meremoth son of Uriah, the son
of Hakkoz, repaired the wall that went
from the entrance to Eliashib's house to
the far end of it.

22Next to him worked the priests
from the surrounding area. **23**Next to
them, Benjamin and Hasshub made repairs in front of their own house. Next to
them, Azariah son of Maaseiah, the son of
Ananiah, made repairs beside his own
house. **24**Next to him, Binnui son of Henadad repaired the wall that went from
Azariah's house to the bend and on to the
corner. **25**Palal son of Uzai worked across
from the bend and by the tower on the
upper palace, which is near the courtyard
of the king's guard. Next to Palal, Pedaiah
son of Parosh made repairs. **26**The Temple servants who lived on the hill of
Ophel made repairs as far as a point opposite the Water Gate. They worked toward
the east and the tower that extends from
the palace. **27**Next to them, the people of
Tekoa repaired the wall from the great
tower that extends from the palace to the
wall of Ophel.

28The priests made repairs above the
Horse Gate, each working in front of his
own house. **29**Next to them, Zadok son of
Immer made repairs across from his own
house. Next to him, Shemaiah son of
Shecaniah, the guard of the East Gate,
made repairs. **30**Next to him, Hananiah
son of Shelemiah, and Hanun, the sixth
son of Zalaph, made repairs on another
part of the wall. Next to them, Meshullam son of Berekiah made repairs across
from where he lived. **31**Next to him, Mal-

3:16 Nehemiah This is a different Nehemiah than the one who wrote this book.

kijah, one of the goldsmiths, made repairs. He worked as far as the house of
the Temple servants and the traders,
which is across from the Inspection Gate,
and as far as the room above the corner of
the wall. **32**The goldsmiths and the traders made repairs between the room
above the corner of the wall and the
Sheep Gate.

Those Against the Rebuilding

4 When Sanballat heard we were rebuilding the wall, he was very angry,
even furious. He made fun of the Jewish
people. **2**He said to his friends and those
with power in Samaria, "What are these
weak Jews doing? Will they rebuild the
wall? Will they offer sacrifices? Can they
finish it in one day? Can they bring stones
back to life from piles of trash and ashes?"

3Tobiah the Ammonite, who was next
to Sanballat, said, "If a fox climbed up on
the stone wall they are building, it would
break it down."

4I prayed, "Hear us, our God. We are
hated. Turn the insults of Sanballat and
Tobiah back on their own heads. Let
them be captured and stolen like valuables. **5**Do not hide their
guilt or take away their
sins so that you can't see
them, because they have
insulted the builders."

6So we rebuilt the
wall to half its height, because the people were
willing to work.

7But Sanballat, Tobiah,
the Arabs, the Ammon-
ites, and the people from
Ashdod were very angry when they
heard that the repairs to Jerusalem's
walls were continuing and that the holes
in the wall were being closed. **8**So they
all made plans to come to Jerusalem and
fight and stir up trouble. **9**But we prayed
to our God and appointed guards to watch
for them day and night.

10The people of Judah said, "The
workers are getting tired. There is so
much trash we cannot rebuild the wall."

11And our enemies said, "The Jews
won't know or see anything until we
come among them and kill them and stop
the work."

12Then the Jewish people who lived
near our enemies came and told us ten
times, "Everywhere you turn, the enemy
will attack us." **13**So I put people behind
the lowest places along the wall—the
open places—and I put families together
with their swords, spears, and bows.
14Then I looked around and stood up and
said to the important men, the leaders,
and the rest of the people: "Don't be
afraid of them. Remember the Lord, who
is great and powerful. Fight for your
brothers, your sons and daughters, your
wives, and your homes."

15Then our enemies heard that we
knew about their plans and that God had
ruined their plans. So we all went back to
the wall, each to his own work.

16From that day on, half my people
worked on the wall. The other half was
ready with spears, shields, bows, and armor. The officers stood in back of the
people of Judah **17**who were building the
wall. Those who carried materials did
their work with one hand and carried a
weapon with the other. **18**Each builder
wore his sword at his side
as he worked. The man
who blew the trumpet to
warn the people stayed
next to me.

19Then I said to the
important men, the lead-
ers, and the rest of the
people, "This is a very big
job. We are spreading out
along the wall so that we
are far apart. **20**Wherever
you hear the sound of the trumpet, assemble there. Our God will fight for us."

21So we continued to work with half
the men holding spears from sunrise till
the stars came out. **22**At that time I also
said to the people, "Let every man and
his helper stay inside Jerusalem at night.
They can be our guards at night and
workmen during the day." **23**Neither I,
my brothers, my workers, nor the guards
with me ever took off our clothes. Each
person carried his weapon even when he
went for water.

Don't be afraid of them. Remember the Lord, who is great and powerful.
—Nehemiah 4:14

Nehemiah Helps Poor People

5 The men and their wives complained
loudly against their fellow Jews.
2Some of them were saying, "We have
many sons and daughters in our families.
To eat and stay alive, we need grain."
3Others were saying, "We are borrowing money against our fields, vineyards, and homes to get grain because
there is not much food."
4And still others were saying, "We are
borrowing money to pay the king's tax on
our fields and vineyards. 5We are just like
our fellow Jews, and our sons are like
their sons. But we have to sell our sons
and daughters as slaves. Some of our
daughters have already been sold. But
there is nothing we can do, because our
fields and vineyards already belong to
other people."
6When I heard their complaints about
these things, I was very angry. 7After I
thought about it, I accused the important
people and the leaders, "You are charging
your own brothers too much interest."
So I called a large meeting to deal with
them. 8I said to them, "As much
as possible, we have
bought freedom for
our fellow Jews who
had been sold to for-
eigners. Now you
are selling your fel-
low Jews to us!" The
leaders were quiet and had nothing to say.
9Then I said, "What you are doing is
not right. Don't you fear God? Don't let
our foreign enemies shame us. 10I, my
brothers, and my men are also lending
money and grain to the people. But stop
charging them so much for this. 11Give
back their fields, vineyards, olive trees,
and houses right now. Also give back the
extra amount you charged—the hun-
dredth part of the money, grain, new
wine, and oil."
12They said, "We will give it back and
not demand anything more from them.
We will do as you say."
Then I called for the priests, and I
made the important men and leaders take
an oath to do what they had said. 13Also I
shook out the folds of my robe and said,
"In this way may God shake out everyone who does not keep his promise. May
God shake him out of his house and out of
the things that are his. Let that person be
shaken out and emptied!"

eMail FROM GOD

5:7–11
Encouragement
How should you stand up for those who need help?

FAITH links

HELP FOR THE OUTSIDERS

NEHEMIAH 5:9-10

Think of a kid at your school or in your neighborhood whom everyone seems to ignore or make fun of. In Nehemiah's day, the poor were like that kid in your neighborhood. Nehemiah wanted to do something to help them. When he saw how people who had more treated the poor, he put a stop to it.

It is easy to forget how important it is to treat all people kindly. God wants you to be kind to other people. What could you do to help those whom others ignore or treat badly?

How do you treat those on the "outside" at school? Link here for some good advice:

Help for the Poor, Leviticus 5:7, p. 138

Fairness for All, Deuteronomy 24:17, p. 258

I Want It *Now!*, Judges 14:1–3, p. 332

A Friend in Deed, Job 2:13, p. 662

Two Are Better, Ecclesiastes 4:9–12, p. 877

You're Correct!, Hebrews 12:5–7, p. 1683

Then the whole group said, "Amen,"
and they praised the LORD. So the people
did what they had promised.
14I was appointed governor in the
land of Judah in the twentieth year of
King Artaxerxes' rule. I was governor of
Judah for twelve years, until his thirty-
second year. During that time neither my
brothers nor I ate the food that was allowed for a governor. 15But the governors before me had placed a heavy load
on the people. They took about one
pound of silver from each person, along
with food and wine. The governors' helpers before me also controlled the people,
but I did not do that, because I feared
God. 16I worked on the wall, as did all my
men who were gathered there. We did
not buy any fields.
17Also, I fed one hundred fifty Jewish
people and officers at my table, as well as
those who came from the nations around
us. 18This is what was prepared every
day: one ox, six good sheep, and birds.
And every ten days there were all kinds
of wine. But I never demanded the food
that was due a governor, because the
people were already working very hard.
19Remember to be kind to me, my
God, for all the good I have done for these
people.

More Problems for Nehemiah

6 Then Sanballat, Tobiah, Geshem the
Arab, and our other enemies heard
that I had rebuilt the wall and that there
was not one gap in it. But I had not yet set
the doors in the gates. 2So Sanballat and
Geshem sent me this message: "Come,
Nehemiah, let's meet together in Kephi-
rim on the plain of Ono."
But they were planning to harm me.
3So I sent messengers to them with this
answer: "I am doing a great work, and I
can't come down. I don't want the work
to stop while I leave to meet you." 4San-
ballat and Geshem sent the same message to me four times, and each time I
sent back the same answer.
5The fifth time Sanballat sent his
helper to me with the message, and in his
hand was an unsealed letter. 6This is
what was written:

FAITH links

TWO ENEMIES

NEHEMIAH 6

When you're faced with a long project, are you ever tempted to put off doing the work? Enemies led by two men, Sanballat and Tobiah, tried to get Nehemiah and the Israelites to put off working on the wall.

There are two other enemies that can keep you from doing your work: procrastination and worry. *Procrastination* is a long word that means to keep putting off doing something. It can become a habit after awhile. Worried thoughts like *I'll never get this done* also can zap your energy. One way to fight both can be found in one word: *perseverance*. Don't give up! Ask God to give you the desire to get to work and keep on doing it.

When Bad Turns to Worse, Exodus 5:6–12, p. 82

Building Tools, Ezra 6:15, p. 615

When the Going Gets Tough, Lamentations 3:22–27, p. 1079

Small Beginnings, Zechariah 4:10, p. 1255

Faith God Notices, Luke 18:35–43, p. 1406

Just Like a Tree, Colossians 1:23, p. 1621

A report is going around to all
the nations, and Geshem says it is
true, that you and the Jewish people are planning to turn against the

king and that you are rebuilding
the wall. They say you are going to
be their king **7**and that you have
appointed prophets to announce in
Jerusalem: "There is a king of Judah!" The king will hear about
this. So come, let's discuss this together.

8So I sent him back this answer:
"Nothing you are saying is really happening. You are just making it up in your own
mind."
9Our enemies were trying to scare us,
thinking, "They will get too weak to
work. Then the wall will not be finished."
But I prayed, "God, make me strong."
10One day I went to the house of Shemaiah son of Delaiah, the son of Mehetabel. Shemaiah had to stay at home. He
said, "Nehemiah, let's meet in the Temple of God. Let's go inside the Temple
and close the doors, because men are
coming at night to kill you."
11But I said, "Should a man like me
run away? Should I run for my life into
the Temple? I will not go." **12**I knew that
God had not sent him but that Tobiah and
Sanballat had paid him to prophesy
against me. **13**They paid
him to frighten me so I
would do this and sin.
Then they could give me
a bad name to shame me.
14I prayed, "My God,
remember Tobiah and
Sanballat and what they
have done. Also remem-
ber the prophetess Noa-
diah and the other
prophets who have been
trying to frighten me."

> Then my God caused me to gather the important men, the leaders, and the common people so I could register them.
> —Nehemiah 7:5

The Wall Is Finished

15The wall of Jerusalem was completed on the twenty-fifth day of the month of
Elul. It took fifty-two days to rebuild.
16When all our enemies heard about it
and all the nations around us saw it, they
were shamed. They then understood that
the work had been done with the help of
our God.
17Also in those days the important
men of Judah sent many letters to Tobiah,
and he answered them. **18**Many Jewish
people had promised to be faithful to Tobiah, because he was the son-in-law of
Shecaniah son of Arah. And Tobiah's son
Jehohanan had married the daughter of
Meshullam son of Berekiah. **19**These important men kept telling me about the
good things Tobiah was doing, and then
they would tell Tobiah what I said about
him. So Tobiah sent letters to frighten me.

7 After the wall had been rebuilt and I
had set the doors in place, the gatekeepers, singers, and Levites were chosen. **2**I put my brother Hanani, along with
Hananiah, the commander of the palace,
in charge of Jerusalem. Hananiah was
honest and feared God more than most
people. **3**I said to them, "The gates of Jerusalem should not be opened until the
sun is hot. While the gatekeepers are still
on duty, have them shut and bolt the
doors. Appoint people who live in Jerusalem as guards, and put some at guard
posts and some near their own houses."

The Captives Who Returned

4The city was large and roomy, but
there were few people in it, and the
houses had not yet been
rebuilt. **5**Then my God
caused me to gather the
important men, the lead-
ers, and the common peo-
ple so I could register
them by families. I found
the family history of
those who had returned
first. This is what I found
written there:
6These are the people
of the area who returned from captivity,
whom Nebuchadnezzar king of Babylon
had taken away. They returned to Jerusalem and Judah, each going back to his
own town. **7**These people returned with
Zerubbabel, Jeshua, Nehemiah, Azariah,
Raamiah, Nahamani, Mordecai, Bilshan,
Mispereth, Bigvai, Nehum, and Baanah.
These are the people from Israel: **8**the
descendants of Parosh—2,172; **9**the descendants of Shephatiah—372; **10**the descendants of Arah—652; **11**the descen-

dants of Pahath-Moab (through the family
of Jeshua and Joab)—2,818; **12**the descendants of Elam—1,254; **13**the descendants of Zattu—845; **14**the descendants
of Zaccai—760; **15**the descendants of
Binnui—648; **16**the descendants of Bebai—628; **17**the descendants of Azgad—
2,322; **18**the descendants of Adonikam—
667; **19**the descendants of Bigvai—
2,067; **20**the descendants of Adin—655;
21the descendants of Ater (through
Hezekiah)—98; **22**the descendants of
Hashum—328; **23**the descendants of
Bezai—324; **24**the descendants of Hariph—112; **25**the descendants of Gibeon—95.
26These are the people from the
towns of Bethlehem and Netophah—188;
27of Anathoth—128; **28**of Beth Azmaveth—42; **29**of Kiriath Jearim, Kephirah,
and Beeroth—743; **30**of Ramah and
Geba—621; **31**of Micmash—122; **32**of
Bethel and Ai—123; **33**of the other
Nebo—52; **34**of the other Elam—1,254;
35of Harim—320; **36**of Jericho—345; **37**of
Lod, Hadid, and Ono—721; **38**of Senaah—
3,930.
39These are the priests: the descendants of Jedaiah (through the family of
Jeshua)—973; **40**the descendants of Immer—1,052; **41**the descendants of Pashhur—1,247; **42**the descendants of
Harim—1,017.
43These are the Levites: the descendants of Jeshua (through Kadmiel
through the family of Hodaviah)—74.
44These are the singers: the descendants of Asaph—148.
45These are the gatekeepers: the descendants of Shallum, Ater, Talmon, Akkub, Hatita, and Shobai—138.
46These are the Temple servants: the
descendants of Ziha, Hasupha, Tabbaoth,
47Keros, Sia, Padon, **48**Lebana, Hagaba,
Shalmai, **49**Hanan, Giddel, Gahar, **50**Reaiah, Rezin, Nekoda, **51**Gazzam, Uzza, Paseah, **52**Besai, Meunim, Nephussim,
53Bakbuk, Hakupha, Harhur, **54**Bazluth,
Mehida, Harsha, **55**Barkos, Sisera, Temah, **56**Neziah, and Hatipha.
57These are the descendants of the
servants of Solomon: the descendants of
Sotai, Sophereth, Perida, **58**Jaala, Darkon,
Giddel, **59**Shephatiah, Hattil, Pokereth-
Hazzebaim, and Amon.
60The Temple servants and the descendants of the servants of Solomon totaled 392 people.
61Some people came to Jerusalem
from the towns of Tel Melah, Tel Harsha,
Kerub, Addon, and Immer, but they could
not prove that their ancestors came from
Israel. Here are their names and their
number: **62**the descendants of Delaiah,
Tobiah, and Nekoda—642.
63And these priests could not prove
that their ancestors came from Israel: the
descendants of Hobaiah, Hakkoz, and
Barzillai. (He had married a daughter of
Barzillai from Gilead and was called by
her family name.)
64These people searched for their
family records, but they could not find
them. So they could not be priests, because they were thought to be unclean.
65The governor ordered them not to eat
any of the holy food until a priest settled
this matter by using the Urim and Thummim.
66The total number of those who returned was 42,360. **67**This is not counting their 7,337 male and female servants
and the 245 male and female singers with
them. **68**They had 736 horses, 245
mules, **69**435 camels, and 6,720 donkeys.
70Some of the family leaders gave to
the work. The governor gave to the treasury about 19 pounds of gold, 50 bowls,
and 530 pieces of clothing for the priests.
71Some of the family leaders gave about
375 pounds of gold and about 2,660
pounds of silver to the treasury for the
work. **72**The total of what the other people gave was about 375 pounds of gold,
about 2,250 pounds of silver, and 67
pieces of clothing for the priests. **73**So
these people all settled in their own
towns: the priests, the Levites, the gatekeepers, the singers, the Temple servants, and all the other people of Israel.

Ezra Reads the Teachings

By the seventh month the Israelites
were settled in their own towns.
8 All the people of Israel gathered together in the square by the Water

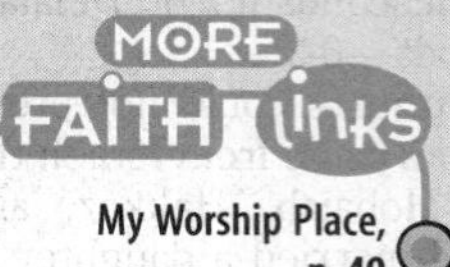

WORSHIPING GOD

Nehemiah 8:6

An Awesome God How would you explain the word *worship* to someone? Would you talk about going to church? Or maybe singing? Maybe you'd mention prayers. Good answers, but that's only the beginning. You can worship God anytime, anywhere, and in many ways.

When God answered Job's prayer for understanding, God told Job how big he was. God is big, yet loving. God is in control of everything. When we begin to understand how awesome God is, we can't help but worship him in our everyday life. (Check out Job 38—41, p. 701.) How do you worship God when you're alone? When you're with others?

MORE FAITH links

My Worship Place, p. 49

Time to Celebrate, p. 95

How to Worship God, p. 972

The Gift of Worship, p. 1275

Meeting Together, p. 1567

Praise Him!, p. 1736

"You know, Skweek, I love to sing really loud when I worship."

"I know; I've heard you! But did you know that worship can be very quiet, too—you know, like a mouse? Read on to find out what the Bible has to say about worship."

You're Invited!, Psalm 100, p. 784

- When someone invites you to a special event, how do you feel? Excited? Glad to be invited? You probably would go and have a good time. Link here for a special invitation. Feel free to invite a friend to join in!

God's New Temple, Ezekiel 40—44, p. 1135

- Where do you meet with other believers to worship God? In a church? A school? A house or maybe outdoors? Does it matter where you worship? Why or why not?
- If you're a Christian, you provide a temple for God within your own body. That's where the Holy Spirit lives. How do you worship God in your "body" temple?

Too Busy to Worship?, Luke 2:8–20, p. 1368

- Too busy to worship God? Take time to make worship an important part of your life. Link here to meet some very busy people who dropped everything to worship.

my FAVORITE links

THE HOMECOMING

Nehemiah 8:1–12

Because the Israelites didn't stay obedient to God, they became a weak nation. Eventually the city of Jerusalem (the capital city) was destroyed by the Babylonians, and many Israelites were carried away to Babylon to live. Later, Babylon was taken over by the Persians, and the Israelites finally were allowed to return home.

Not all of the Israelites wanted to go back home. They had lived in Babylon a long time. It felt like home. The ones who did make the trip went back in three groups. Each of these groups had a specific job to do.

1. The first group, led by Zerubbabel, returned home to rebuild the Temple. (Check out Ezra 6:3–22, p. 615.)
2. Ezra's group helped the people relearn how to follow God's laws. (Read Nehemiah 8:1–12.)
3. The last group, led by Nehemiah, rebuilt the wall around Jerusalem in just 52 days. (See Nehemiah 6:15.)

There were three prophets God sent to encourage and teach the people as they returned—Haggai, Zechariah, and Malachi.

Gate. They asked Ezra the teacher to
bring out the Book of the Teachings of
Moses, which the LORD had given to Israel.
2So on the first day of the seventh
month, Ezra the priest brought out the
Teachings for the crowd. Men, women,
and all who could listen and understand
had gathered. 3At the square by the Water
Gate Ezra read the Teachings out loud
from early morning until noon to the men,
women, and everyone who could listen
and understand. All the people listened
carefully to the Book of the Teachings.
4Ezra the teacher stood on a high
wooden platform that had been built just
for this time. On his right were Mattithiah, Shema, Anaiah, Uriah, Hilkiah, and
Maaseiah. And on his left were Pedaiah,
Mishael, Malkijah, Hashum, Hashbaddanah, Zechariah, and Meshullam.
5Ezra opened the book in full view of
everyone, because he was above them.
As he opened it, all the people stood up.
6Ezra praised the LORD, the great God,
and all the people held up their hands and
said, "Amen! Amen!" Then they bowed
down and worshiped
the LORD with their
faces to the ground.
7These Levites
explained the Teachings to the people as
they stood there:
Jeshua, Bani, Sherebiah, Jamin, Akkub,
Shabbethai, Hodiah, Maaseiah, Kelita,
Azariah, Jozabad, Hanan, and Pelaiah.
8They read from the Book of the Teachings of God and explained what it meant
so the people understood what was being
read.

EMAIL FROM GOD **8:6**
Worship
What should your attitude be toward God?

9Then Nehemiah the governor, Ezra
the priest and teacher, and the Levites
who were teaching said to all the people,
"This is a holy day to the LORD your God.
Don't be sad or cry." All the people had
been crying as they listened to the words
of the Teachings.

FAITH links

SEE THE HEART BEHIND IT

NEHEMIAH 8; 9

Picture your mom or dad in full lecture mode. He or she is telling you about the kind of behavior he/she expects from you. Picture your own expression as you're listening to this. What does it show? Boredom? Restlessness? When the Temple was completed, Ezra read the Book of the Teachings to the people. Everyone stood there for hours listening. In response, they confessed their sins. What made them do it? They could see the heart behind the words. They understood how much God loved them.

Your parents and God want you to have the best life possible. When your mom or dad goes into lecture mode, look for the heart behind it.

Check out these other Faithlinks on listening:

Faith of Our Fathers, Joshua 4:4–9, p. 280

In Your Best Interests, Ruth 3, p. 349

Deciding Wisely, 1 Kings 3:16–28, p. 440

A Word to the Wise, Proverbs 10:1, p . 838

Cut to the Quick, Hebrews 4:12, p. 1670

The Way to Be Wise, James 1:5, p. 1689

10Nehemiah said, "Go and enjoy good
food and sweet drinks. Send some to people who have none, because today is a
holy day to the Lord. Don't be sad, because the joy of the LORD will make you
strong."

11The Levites helped calm the people, saying, "Be quiet, because this is a
holy day. Don't be sad."

12Then all the people went away to
eat and drink, to send some of their food
to others, and to celebrate with great joy.
They finally understood what they had
been taught.

13On the second day of the month, the
leaders of all the families, the priests, and
the Levites met with Ezra the teacher.
They gathered to study the words of the
Teachings. **14**This is what they found
written in the Teachings: The LORD commanded through Moses that the people of
Israel were to live in shelters during the
feast of the seventh month. **15**The people
were supposed to preach this message
and spread it through all their towns and
in Jerusalem: "Go out into the mountains,
and bring back branches from olive and
wild olive trees, myrtle trees, palms, and
shade trees. Make shelters with them, as
it is written."

16So the people went out and got tree
branches. They built shelters on their
roofs,[n] in their courtyards, in the courtyards of the Temple, in the square by the
Water Gate, and in the square next to the
Gate of Ephraim. **17**The whole group that
had come back from captivity built shelters and lived in them. The Israelites had
not done this since the time of Joshua son
of Nun. And they were very happy.

18Ezra read to them every day from
the Book of the Teachings, from the first
day to the last. The people of Israel celebrated the feast for seven days, and then
on the eighth day the people gathered as
the law said.

8:16 roofs In Bible times houses were built with flat roofs. The roof was used for drying things such as flax and fruit. And it was used as an extra room, as a place for worship, and as a cool place to sleep in the summer.

Israel Confesses Sins

9 On the twenty-fourth day of that same
month, the people of Israel gathered.
They did not eat, and they wore rough
cloth and put dust on their heads to show
their sadness. 2Those people whose ancestors were from Israel had separated
themselves from all foreigners. They
stood and confessed their sins and their
ancestors' sins. 3For a fourth of the day
they stood where they were and read
from the Book of the Teachings of the
LORD their God. For another fourth of the
day they confessed their sins and worshiped the LORD their God. 4These Levites were standing on the stairs: Jeshua,
Bani, Kadmiel, Shebaniah, Bunni, Sherebiah, Bani, and Kenani. They called out to
the LORD their God with loud voices.
5Then these Levites spoke: Jeshua, Kadmiel, Bani, Hashabneiah, Sherebiah, Hodiah, Shebaniah, and Pethahiah. They
said, "Stand up and praise the LORD your
God, who lives forever and ever."

The People's Prayer

"Blessed be your wonderful name.
It is more wonderful than all
blessing and praise.
6 You are the only LORD.
You made the heavens, even the
highest heavens,
with all the stars.
You made the earth and everything
on it,
the seas and everything in them;
you give life to everything.
The heavenly army worships you.

7 "You are the LORD,
the God who chose Abram
and brought him out of Ur in
Babylonia
and named him Abraham.
8 You found him faithful to you,
so you made an agreement with
him
to give his descendants the land of
the Canaanites,
Hittites, Amorites,
Perizzites, Jebusites, and
Girgashites.
You have kept your promise,
because you do what is right.

9 "You saw our ancestors suffering in
Egypt
and heard them cry out at the Red
Sea.
10 You did signs and miracles against
the king of Egypt,
and against all his officers and all
his people,
because you knew how proud they
were.
You became as famous as you are
today.
11 You divided the sea in front of our
ancestors;
they walked through on dry
ground.
But you threw the people chasing
them into the deep water,
like a stone thrown into mighty
waters.
12 You led our ancestors with a pillar of
cloud by day
and with a pillar of fire at night.
It lit the way
they were supposed to go.
13 You came down to Mount Sinai
and spoke from heaven to our
ancestors.
You gave them fair rules and true
teachings,
good orders and commands.
14 You told them
about your
holy Sabbath
and gave them
commands,
orders, and
teachings
through your servant Moses.

EMAIL FROM GOD 9:14
Bible
Where did the Bible come from?

15 When they were hungry, you gave
them bread from heaven.
When they were thirsty, you
brought them water from the
rock.
You told them to enter and take over
the land you had promised to give
them.

16 "But our ancestors were proud and
stubborn

and did not obey your commands.
17 They refused to listen;
they forgot the miracles you did for them.
So they became stubborn and turned against you,
choosing a leader to take them back to slavery.
But you are a forgiving God.
You are kind and full of mercy.
You do not become angry quickly, and you have great love.
So you did not leave them.
18 Our ancestors even made an idol of a calf for themselves.
They said, 'This is your god, Israel,
who brought you up out of Egypt.'
They spoke against you.

19 "You have great mercy,
so you did not leave them in the desert.
The pillar of cloud guided them by day,
and the pillar of fire led them at night,
lighting the way they were to go.
20 You gave your good Spirit to teach them.
You gave them manna to eat
and water when they were thirsty.
21 You took care of them for forty years in the desert;
they needed nothing.
Their clothes did not wear out,
and their feet did not swell.

22 "You gave them kingdoms and nations;
you gave them more land.
They took over the country of Sihon king of Heshbon
and the country of Og king of Bashan.
23 You made their children as many as the stars in the sky,
and you brought them into the land
that you told their fathers to enter and take over.
24 So their children went into the land and took over.
The Canaanites lived there, but you defeated them for our ancestors.
You handed over to them the Canaanites, their kings, and the people of the land.
Our ancestors could do what they wanted with them.
25 They captured strong, walled cities and fertile land.
They took over houses full of good things,
wells that were already dug,
vineyards, olive trees, and many fruit trees.
They ate until they were full and grew fat;
they enjoyed your great goodness.

26 "But they were disobedient and turned against you
and ignored your teachings.
Your prophets warned them to come back to you,
but they killed those prophets
and spoke against you.
27 So you handed them over to their enemies,
and their enemies treated them badly.

EMAIL FROM GOD 9:27
Feelings
Does God care when you hurt?

But in this time of trouble our ancestors cried out to you,
and you heard from heaven.
You had great mercy
and gave them saviors who saved them from the power of their enemies.
28 But as soon as they had rest,
they again did what was evil.
So you left them to their enemies who ruled over them.
When they cried out to you again,
you heard from heaven.
Because of your mercy, you saved them again and again.
29 You warned them to return to your teachings,
but they were proud and did not obey your commands.

If someone obeys your laws, he will
live,
but they sinned against your laws.
They were stubborn, unwilling, and
disobedient.
30 You were patient with them for many
years
and warned them by your Spirit
through the prophets,
but they did not pay attention.
So you handed them over to other
countries.
31 But because your mercy is great, you
did not kill them all or leave
them.
You are a kind and merciful God.

32 "And so, our God, you are the great
and mighty and wonderful God.
You keep your agreement of love.
Do not let all our trouble seem
unimportant to you.
This trouble has come to us, to our
kings and our leaders,
to our priests and prophets,
to our ancestors and all your
people
from the days of the kings of Assyria
until today.
33 You have been fair in everything that
has happened to us;
you have been loyal, but we have
been wicked.
34 Our kings, leaders, priests, and
ancestors did not obey your
teachings;
they did not pay attention to the
commands and warnings you
gave them.
35 Even when our ancestors were living
in their kingdom,
enjoying all the good things you
had given them,
enjoying the land that was fertile
and full of room,
they did not stop their evil ways.

36 "Look, we are slaves today
in the land you gave our
ancestors.
They were to enjoy its fruit and its
good things,
but look, we are slaves here.
37 The land's great harvest belongs to
the kings you have put over us
because of our sins.
Those kings rule over us and our
cattle as they please,
so we are in much trouble.

The People's Agreement

38 "Because of all this, we are making
an agreement in writing, and our leaders,
Levites, and priests are putting their
seals on it."

10 These are the men who sealed the
agreement:
Nehemiah the governor, son of Hacaliah.
Zedekiah, 2 Seraiah, Azariah, Jeremiah, 3 Pashhur, Amariah, Malkijah,
4 Hattush, Shebaniah, Malluch, 5 Harim,
Meremoth, Obadiah, 6 Daniel, Ginnethon,
Baruch, 7 Meshullam, Abijah, Mijamin,
8 Maaziah, Bilgai, and Shemaiah. These
are the priests.
9 These are the Levites who sealed it:
Jeshua son of Azaniah, Binnui of the sons
of Henadad, Kadmiel, 10 and their fellow
Levites: Shebaniah, Hodiah, Kelita, Pelaiah, Hanan, 11 Mica, Rehob, Hashabiah,
12 Zaccur, Sherebiah, Shebaniah, 13 Hodiah, Bani, and Beninu.
14 These are the leaders of the people
who sealed the agreement: Parosh, Pahath-
Moab, Elam, Zattu, Bani, 15 Bunni, Azgad,
Bebai, 16 Adonijah, Bigvai, Adin, 17 Ater,
Hezekiah, Azzur, 18 Hodiah, Hashum, Bezai, 19 Hariph, Anathoth, Nebai, 20 Mag-
piash, Meshullam, Hezir, 21 Meshezabel,
Zadok, Jaddua, 22 Pelatiah, Hanan, Anaiah,
23 Hoshea, Hananiah, Hasshub, 24 Hallohesh, Pilha, Shobek, 25 Rehum, Hashab-
nah, Maaseiah, 26 Ahiah, Hanan, Anan,
27 Malluch, Harim, and Baanah.
28 The rest of the people took an oath.
They were the priests, Levites, gatekeepers, singers, Temple servants, all
those who separated themselves from
foreigners to keep the Teachings of God,
and also their wives and their sons and
daughters who could understand. 29 They
joined their fellow Israelites and their
leading men in taking an oath, which was
tied to a curse in case they broke the

oath. They promised to follow the Teachings of God, which they had been given
through Moses the servant of God, and to
obey all the commands, rules, and laws of
the LORD our God.
30They said:

We promise not to let our
daughters marry foreigners nor to
let our sons marry their daughters.
31Foreigners may bring goods or
grain to sell on the Sabbath, but we
will not buy on the Sabbath or any
holy day. Every seventh year we
will not plant, and that year we will
forget all that people owe us.
32We will be responsible for the
commands to pay for the service of
the Temple of our God. We will
give an eighth of an ounce of silver
each year. **33**It is for the bread that
is set out on the table; the regular
grain offerings and burnt offerings;
the offerings on the Sabbaths, New
Moon festivals, and special feasts;
the holy offerings; the offerings to
remove the sins of the Israelites so
they will belong to God; and for the
work of the Temple of our God.
34We, the priests, the Levites,
and the people, have thrown lots to
decide at what time of
year each family must
bring wood to the
Temple. The wood is
for burning on the al-
tar of the LORD our
God, and we will do
this as it is written in
the Teachings.
35We also will
bring the first fruits
from our crops and the
first fruits of every tree to the
Temple each year.
36We will bring to the Temple
our firstborn sons and cattle and
the firstborn of our herds and
flocks, as it is written in the Teachings. We will bring them to the
priests who are serving in the
Temple.
37We will bring to the priests at
the storerooms of the Temple the
first of our ground meal, our offerings, the fruit from all our trees,
and our new wine and oil. And we
will bring a tenth of our crops to the
Levites, who will collect these
things in all the towns where we
work. **38**A priest of Aaron's family
must be with the Levites when
they receive the tenth of the
people's crops. The Levites must
bring a tenth of all they receive to
the Temple of our God to put in the
storerooms of the treasury. **39**The
people of Israel and the Levites are
to bring to the storerooms the gifts
of grain, new wine, and oil. That is
where the utensils for the Temple
are kept and where the priests who
are serving, the gatekeepers, and
singers stay.
We will not ignore the Temple
of our God.

We also will bring the first fruits from our crops and the first fruits of every tree to the Temple each year.
—Nehemiah 10:35

New People Move into Jerusalem

11 The leaders of Israel lived in
Jerusalem. But the rest of the people threw lots to choose one person out
of every ten to come and live in Jerusalem, the holy city. The other nine could
stay in their own cities. **2**The people
blessed those who volun-
teered to live in Jerusa-
lem.
3These are the area
leaders who lived in Jerusalem. (Some people lived
on their own land in the
cities of Judah. These included Israelites, priests,
Levites, Temple servants,
and descendants of Sol-
omon's servants. **4**Others
from the families of Judah and Benjamin
lived in Jerusalem.)
These are the descendants of Judah
who moved into Jerusalem. There was
Athaiah son of Uzziah. (Uzziah was the
son of Zechariah, the son of Amariah.
Amariah was the son of Shephatiah, the
son of Mahalalel. Mahalalel was a descendant of Perez.) **5**There was also Masseiah
son of Baruch. (Baruch was the son of

Col-Hozeh, the son of Hazaiah. Hazaiah was the son of Adaiah, the son of Joiarib. Joiarib was the son of Zechariah, a descendant of Shelah.) **6**All the descendants of Perez who lived in Jerusalem totaled 468 men. They were soldiers.

7These are descendants of Benjamin who moved into Jerusalem. There was Sallu son of Meshullam. (Meshullam was the son of Joed, the son of Pedaiah. Pedaiah was the son of Kolaiah, the son of Maaseiah. Maaseiah was the son of Ithiel, the son of Jeshaiah.) **8**Following him were Gabbai and Sallai, for a total of 928 men. **9**Joel son of Zicri was appointed over them, and Judah son of Hassenuah was second in charge of the new area of the city.

10These are the priests who moved into Jerusalem. There was Jedaiah son of Joiarib, Jakin, **11**and Seraiah son of Hilkiah, the supervisor in the Temple. (Hilkiah was the son of Meshullam, the son of Zadok. Zadok was the son of Meraioth, the son of Ahitub.) **12**And there were others with them who did the work for the Temple. All together there were 822 men. Also there was Adaiah son of Jeroham. (Jeroham was the son of Pelaliah, the son of Amzi. Amzi was the son of Zechariah, the son of Pashhur. Pashhur was the son of Malkijah.) **13**And there were family heads with him. All together there were 242 men. Also there was Amashsai son of Azarel. (Azarel was the son of Ahzai, the son of Meshillemoth. Meshillemoth was the son of Immer.) **14**And there were brave men with Amashsai. All together there were 128 men. Zabdiel son of Haggedolim was appointed over them.

The people blessed those who volunteered to live in Jerusalem.
—Nehemiah 11:2

15These are the Levites who moved into Jerusalem. There was Shemaiah son of Hasshub. (Hasshub was the son of Azrikam, the son of Hashabiah. Hashabiah was the son of Bunni.) **16**And there were Shabbethai and Jozabad, two of the leaders of the Levites who were in charge of the work outside the Temple. **17**There was Mattaniah son of Mica. (Mica was the son of Zabdi, the son of Asaph.) Mattaniah was the director who led the people in thanksgiving and prayer. There was Bakbukiah, who was second in charge over his fellow Levites. And there was Abda son of Shammua. (Shammua was the son of Galal, the son of Jeduthun.) **18**All together 284 Levites lived in the holy city of Jerusalem.

19The gatekeepers who moved into Jerusalem were Akkub, Talmon, and others with them. There was a total of 172 men who guarded the city gates.

20The other Israelites, priests, and Levites lived on their own land in all the cities of Judah.

21The Temple servants lived on the hill of Ophel, and Ziha and Gishpa were in charge of them.

22Uzzi son of Bani was appointed over the Levites in Jerusalem. (Bani was the son of Hashabiah, the son of Mattaniah. Mattaniah was the son of Mica.) Uzzi was one of Asaph's descendants, who were the singers responsible for the service of the Temple. **23**The singers were under the king's orders, which regulated them day by day.

24Pethahiah son of Meshezabel was the king's spokesman. (Meshezabel was a descendant of Zerah, the son of Judah.)

25Some of the people of Judah lived in villages with their surrounding fields. They lived in Kiriath Arba and its surroundings, in Dibon and its surroundings, in Jekabzeel and its surroundings, **26**in Jeshua, Moladah, Beth Pelet, **27**Hazar Shual, Beersheba and its surroundings, **28**in Ziklag and Meconah and its surroundings, **29**in En Rimmon, Zorah, Jarmuth, **30**Zanoah, Adullam and their villages, in Lachish and the fields around it, and in Azekah and its surroundings. So they settled from Beersheba all the way to the Valley of Hinnom.

31The descendants of the Benjaminites

from Geba lived in Micmash, Aija, Bethel
and its surroundings, **32**in Anathoth, Nob,
Ananiah, **33**Hazor, Ramah, Gittaim, **34**Hadid, Zeboim, Neballat, **35**Lod, Ono, and in
the Valley of the Craftsmen.
36Some groups of the Levites from
Judah settled in the land of Benjamin.

Priests and Levites

12 These are the priests and Levites
who returned with Zerubbabel
son of Shealtiel and with Jeshua. There
were Seraiah, Jeremiah, Ezra, **2**Amariah,
Malluch, Hattush, **3**Shecaniah, Rehum,
Meremoth, **4**Iddo, Ginnethon, Abijah,
5Mijamin, Moadiah, Bilgah, **6**Shemaiah,
Joiarib, Jedaiah, **7**Sallu, Amok, Hilkiah,
and Jedaiah. They were the leaders of the
priests and their relatives in the days of
Jeshua.
8The Levites were Jeshua, Binnui,
Kadmiel, Sherebiah, Judah, and Mattaniah. Mattaniah and his relatives were in
charge of the songs of thanksgiving.
9Bakbukiah and Unni, their relatives,
stood across from them in the services.
10Jeshua was the father of Joiakim.
Joiakim was the father of Eliashib. Eliashib was the father of Joiada. **11**Joiada
was the father of Jonathan, and Jonathan
was the father of Jaddua.
12In the days of Joiakim, these priests
were the leaders of the families of
priests: Meraiah, from Seraiah's family;
Hananiah, from Jeremiah's family; **13**Meshullam, from Ezra's family; Jehohanan,
from Amariah's family; **14**Jonathan, from
Malluch's family; Joseph, from Shecaniah's family; **15**Adna, from Harim's
family; Helkai, from Meremoth's family;
16Zechariah, from Iddo's family; Meshullam, from Ginnethon's family; **17**Zicri,
from Abijah's family; Piltai, from
Miniamin's and Moadiah's families;
18Shammua, from Bilgah's family; Jehon-
athan, from Shemaiah's family; **19**Mattenai, from Joiarib's family; Uzzi, from
Jedaiah's family; **20**Kallai, from Sallu's
family; Eber, from Amok's family;
21Hashabiah, from Hilkiah's family; and
Nethanel, from Jedaiah's family.
22The leaders of the families of the
Levites and the priests were written
down in the days of Eliashib, Joiada, Johanan, and Jaddua, while Darius the Persian
was king. **23**The family leaders among
the Levites were written down in the history book, but only up to the time of Johanan son of Eliashib. **24**The leaders of the
Levites were Hashabiah, Sherebiah,
Jeshua son of Kadmiel, and their relatives. Their relatives stood across from
them and gave praise and thanksgiving to
God. One group answered the other
group, as David, the man of God, had
commanded.
25These were the gatekeepers who
guarded the storerooms next to the

FAITH CHALLENGE

I've got one for you. Read 12:27 to discover how the people of Israel gave thanks to God for everything he had done for them. What are your favorite and least favorite ways to worship God?

TESTING IT

Nehemiah 12:27

When the wall of Jerusalem was offered as a gift to God, they asked the Levites to come from wherever they lived to Jerusalem to celebrate with joy the gift of the wall. They were to celebrate with songs of thanksgiving and with the music of cymbals, harps, and lyres.

gates: Mattaniah, Bakbukiah, Obadiah,
Meshullam, Talmon, and Akkub. **26**They
served in the days of Joiakim son of Jeshua, the son of Jozadak. They also served
in the days of Nehemiah the governor
and Ezra the priest and teacher.

The Wall of Jerusalem

27When the wall of Jerusalem was offered as a gift to God, they asked the Levites to come from wherever they lived
to Jerusalem to celebrate with joy the gift
of the wall. They were to celebrate with
songs of thanksgiving and with the music
of cymbals, harps, and lyres. **28**They also
brought together singers from all around
Jerusalem, from the Netophathite villages, **29**from Beth Gilgal, and from the
areas of Geba and Azmaveth. The singers
had built villages for themselves around
Jerusalem. **30**The priests and Levites
made themselves pure, and they also
made the people, the gates, and the wall
of Jerusalem pure.

31I had the leaders of Judah go up on
top of the wall, and I appointed two large
choruses to give thanks. One chorus
went to the right on top of the wall, toward the Trash Gate. **32**Behind them
went Hoshaiah and half the leaders of Judah. **33**Azariah, Ezra, Meshullam, **34**Judah, Benjamin, Shemaiah, and Jeremiah
also went. **35**Some priests with trumpets
also went, along with Zechariah son of
Jonathan. (Jonathan was the son of Shemaiah, the son of Mattaniah. Mattaniah
was the son of Micaiah, the son of Zaccur.
Zaccur was the son of Asaph.) **36**Zechariah's relatives also went. They were
Shemaiah, Azarel, Milalai, Gilalai, Maai,
Nethanel, Judah, and Hanani. These men
played the musical instruments of David,
the man of God, and Ezra the teacher
walked in front of them. **37**They went
from the Fountain Gate straight up the
steps to the highest part of the wall by
the older part of the city. They went on
above the house of David to the Water
Gate on the east.

38The second chorus went to the left,
while I followed them on top of the wall
with half the people. We went from the
Tower of the Ovens to the Broad Wall,
39over the Gate of Ephraim to the Old
Gate and the Fish Gate, to the Tower of
Hananel and the Tower of the Hundred.
We went as far as the Sheep Gate and
stopped at the Gate of the Guard.

40The two choruses took their places
at the Temple. Half of the leaders and I
did also. **41**These priests were there with
their trumpets: Eliakim, Maaseiah, Miniamin, Micaiah, Elioenai, Zechariah, and
Hananiah. **42**These people were also
there: Maaseiah, Shemaiah, Eleazar,
Uzzi, Jehohanan, Malkijah, Elam, and
Ezer. The choruses sang, led
by Jezrahiah. **43**The
people offered many
sacrifices that day
and were happy be-
cause God had given
them great joy. The
women and children were happy. The
sound of happiness in Jerusalem could be
heard far away.

eMAIL! FROM GOD
12:43
Joy
Who gives you joy?

44At that time the leaders appointed
men to be in charge of the storerooms.
These rooms were for the gifts, the first
fruits, and the ten percent that the people
brought. The Teachings said they should
bring a share for the priests and Levites
from the fields around the towns. The
people of Judah were happy to do this for
the priests and Levites who served.
45They performed the service of their
God in making things pure. The singers
and gatekeepers also did their jobs, as
David had commanded his son Solomon.
46Earlier, in the time of David and Asaph,
there was a leader of the singers and of
the songs of praise and thanksgiving to
God. **47**So it was in the days of Zerubbabel and Nehemiah. All the people of Israel gave something to the singers and
gatekeepers, and they also set aside part
for the Levites. Then the Levites set
aside part for the descendants of Aaron.

Foreign People Are Sent Away

13 On that day they read the Book of
Moses to the people, and they
found that it said no Ammonite or Moabite should ever be allowed in the meeting
to worship. **2**The Ammonites and Moabites had not welcomed the Israelites with

food and water. Instead, they had hired
Balaam to put a curse on Israel. (But our
God turned the curse into a blessing.)
3When the people heard this teaching,
they separated all foreigners from Israel.

Nehemiah Returns to Jerusalem

4Before that happened, Eliashib the
priest, who was in charge of the Temple
storerooms, was friendly with Tobiah.
5Eliashib let Tobiah use one of the large
storerooms. Earlier it had been used for
grain offerings, incense, the utensils, and
the tenth offerings of grain, new wine,
and olive oil that belonged to the Levites,
singers, and gatekeepers. It had also
been used for gifts for the priests.
6I was not in Jerusalem when this
happened. I had gone back to Artaxerxes
king of Babylon in the thirty-second year
he was king. Finally I asked the king to
let me leave. **7**When I returned to Jerusalem, I found out the evil Eliashib had
done by letting Tobiah have a room in the
Temple courtyard. **8**I was very upset at
this, so I threw all of Tobiah's goods out
of the room. **9**I ordered the rooms to be
purified, and I brought back the utensils
for God's Temple, the grain offerings, and
the incense.
10Then I found out the people were
not giving the Levites their shares. So
the Levites and singers who served had
gone back to their own farms. **11**I argued
with the officers, saying, "Why haven't
you taken care of the Temple?" Then I
gathered the Levites and singers and put
them back at their places.
12All the people of Judah then brought
to the storerooms a tenth of their crops,
new wine, and olive oil. **13**I put these
men in charge of the storerooms: Shelemiah the priest, Zadok the teacher, and
Pedaiah a Levite. I made Hanan son of
Zaccur, the son of Mattaniah, their helper.
Everyone knew they were honest men.
They gave out the portions that went to
their relatives.
14Remember me, my God, for this.
Do not ignore my love for the Temple and
its service.
15In those days I saw people in Judah
working in the winepresses on the Sabbath day. They were bringing in grain and
loading it on donkeys. And they were
bringing loads of wine, grapes, and figs
into Jerusalem on the Sabbath day. So I
warned them about selling food on that

FAITH links

AN HONEST REPUTATION

NEHEMIAH 13:13

If you needed someone to watch your wallet for a while, would you hand it to someone who has the reputation for being a thief? Not likely! When Nehemiah looked for people to put in charge of the Temple storerooms, he looked for people he could count on. That was a position of great responsibility! So he found three men who had a reputation for honesty.

What's your reputation at home? At school? You're known by how you act. Are you known for honesty? Dependability? If you want a good rep, you've got to earn it by consistent behavior.

The Best Policy, Genesis 29:16–19, p. 41

Always Truthful, Numbers 23:19, p. 208

Down on the Ant Farm, Proverbs 6:6–11, p. 833

A Broken Promise, Jeremiah 2:1–8, p. 989

The Deadliest Lie, Acts 5:1–11, p. 1471

Say What?!, Ephesians 4:22–29, p. 1603

day. **16**People from the city of Tyre who
were living in Jerusalem brought in fish
and other things and sold them there on
the Sabbath day to the people of Judah.
17I argued with the important men of Judah and said to them, "What is this evil
thing you are doing? You are ruining the
Sabbath day. **18**This is just what your ancestors did. So our God did terrible
things to us and this city. Now you are
making him even more angry at Israel by
ruining the Sabbath day."

19So I ordered that the doors be shut
at sunset before the Sabbath and not be
opened until the Sabbath was over. I put
my servants at the gates so no load could
come in on the Sabbath. **20**Once or twice
traders and sellers of all kinds of goods
spent the night outside Jerusalem. **21**So I
warned them, "Why are you spending the
night by the wall? If you do it again, I will
force you away." After that, they did not
come back on the Sabbath. **22**Then I ordered the Levites to purify themselves
and to guard the city gates to make sure
the Sabbath remained holy.

Remember me, my God, for this.
Have mercy on me because of your great
love.

23In those days I saw men of Judah
who had married women from Ashdod,
Ammon, and Moab. **24**Half their children
were speaking the language of Ashdod or
some other place, and they couldn't
speak the language of Judah. **25**I argued
with those people, put curses on them,
hit some of them, and pulled out their
hair. I forced them to make a promise to
God, saying, "Do not let your daughters
marry the sons of foreigners, and do not
take the daughters of foreigners as wives
for your sons or yourselves. **26**Foreign
women made King Solomon of Israel sin.
There was never a king like him in any of
the nations. God loved Solomon and
made him king over all Israel, but foreign
women made him sin. **27**And now you are
not obedient when you do this evil thing.
You are unfaithful to our God when you
marry foreign wives."

28Joiada was the son of Eliashib the
high priest. One of Joiada's sons married
a daughter of Sanballat the Horonite, so I
sent him away from me.

29Remember them, my God, because
they made the priesthood unclean and
the agreement of the priests and Levites
unclean.

30So I purified them of everything that
was foreign. I appointed duties
for the priests and
Levites, giving each
man his own job. **31**I
also made sure wood
was brought for the
altar at regular times
and that the first
fruits were brought.

eMAIL! FROM GOD
13:31
Blessings
See what Nehemiah asks for from God.

Remember me, my God; be kind
to me.

IN THE RIGHT PLACE

Greetings! I am Esther, queen of Persia. I did not write this book, but the author was mostly likely a fellow Jew living in Persia. Have you ever heard the expression "being in the right place at the right time"? I was very young when I was brought to the royal palace; but after a year of beauty treatments and training, I was ready to meet the king. Imagine my surprise when the king chose me to be his queen! Little did I know that my position was part of God's plan to save his people. Haman, one of the king's trusted servants, plotted to have all the Jews in the kingdom put to death. My cousin Mordecai urged me to beg the king for mercy: "Who knows, you may have been chosen queen for just such a time as this" (Esther 4:14).

This book was written to show how God takes care of his people. Sometimes he uses ordinary people like you and me as part of his plan. God placed me in a high position so I would be able to influence the king. Has God placed you in a position to serve him in a special way?

JESUS WATCH

Esther may have been queen, but she risked her life by attempting to see the king when he had not sent for her. She prepared for her meeting by fasting and praying for three days and asking other people to do the same. She was willing to give up her own life in hope of saving God's people. Jesus not only was willing, but he did give up his life to save God's people. Jesus became a man, knowing that he would die as punishment for our wrongdoings. Jesus was willing to die on the cross so that we can be saved from a life of sin.

my FAVORITE links

OTHER CONNECTIONS

GET THE INFO

Imagine—a foreign-born woman becoming the queen of England. Not possible? God made something similar to that happen when Esther, an Israelite woman, became queen of Persia! Read more about it by linking to A Foreign Queen, Esther 6.

MORE STUFF...

Behind the Scenes God's name is never mentioned in the Book of Esther. Yet, he makes himself known in many different ways throughout the book.

Consider one way God is at work in Esther. Esther was part of the Jewish community that had been taken captive from Jerusalem by Nebuchadnezzar to Babylon and that worshiped God. She was taken to the royal palace and later made queen (Esther 2:5–18). (See also Mordecai's comment in Esther 4:13–14.)

"Hey, Skweek, what happened to that plan Haman had for the king to honor him?"

"Well, the king used Haman's ideas, but not exactly the way Haman had planned! Connect to Esther 6:6-12 to see what happened!"

did YOU know?

DON'T MISS THESE OTHER COOL STORIES:

Esther's beauty plan, Esther 2:8–18
Haman's evil plan, Esther 3
A robe and a horse for Mordecai, Esther 6
Haman begs for his life, Esther 7

FAITH links

A Life-Saving Message, Esther 2:19–22

Standing for What's Right, Esther 3:2–4

The Big Risk, Esther 4:11—5:2

A Holiday Letter, Esther 9:20–23

Queen Vashti Disobeys the King

1 This is what happened during the time
of King Xerxes, the king who ruled
the one hundred twenty-seven states
from India to Cush. 2In those days King
Xerxes ruled from his capital city of Susa.
3In the third year of his rule, he gave a
banquet for all his important men and
royal officers. The army leaders from the
countries of Persia and Media and the important men from all Xer-
xes' empire were there.
4The banquet lasted
one hundred eighty days.
All during that time King
Xerxes was showing off
the great wealth of his
kingdom and his own
great riches and glory.
5When the one hundred
eighty days were over,
the king gave another
banquet. It was held in the courtyard of
the palace garden for seven days, and it
was for everybody in the palace at Susa,
from the greatest to the least. 6The
courtyard had fine white curtains and
purple drapes that were tied to silver
rings on marble pillars by white and purple cords. And there were gold and silver
couches on a floor set with tiles of white
marble, shells, and gems. 7Wine was
served in gold cups of various kinds. And
there was plenty of the king's wine, because he was very generous. 8The king
commanded that the guests be permitted
to drink as much as they wished. He told
the wine servers to serve each person
what he wanted.
9Queen Vashti also gave a banquet for
the women in the royal palace of King
Xerxes.
10On the seventh day of the banquet,
King Xerxes was very happy, because he
had been drinking much wine. He gave a
command to the seven eunuchs who
served him—Mehuman, Biztha, Harbo-
na, Bigtha, Abagtha, Zethar, and Carcas.
11He commanded them to bring him
Queen Vashti, wearing her royal crown.
She was to come to show her beauty to
the people and important men, because
she was very beautiful. 12The eunuchs
told Queen Vashti about the king's command, but she refused to come. Then the
king became very angry; his anger was
like a burning fire.
13It was a custom for the king to ask
advice from experts about law and order.
So King Xerxes spoke with the wise men
who would know the right thing to do.
14The wise men the king usually talked
to were Carshena, Shethar, Admatha,
Tarshish, Meres, Marse-
na, and Memucan, seven
of the important men of
Persia and Media. These
seven had special privi-
leges to see the king and
had the highest rank in
the kingdom. 15The king
asked them, "What does
the law say must be done
to Queen Vashti? She has
not obeyed the command
of King Xerxes, which the eunuchs took
to her."
16Then Memucan said to the king and
the other important men, "Queen Vashti
has not done wrong to the king alone.
She has also done wrong to all the important men and all the people in all the empire of King Xerxes. 17All the wives of
the important men of Persia and Media
will hear about the queen's actions. Then
they will no longer honor their husbands.
They will say, 'King Xerxes commanded
Queen Vashti to be brought to him, but
she refused to come.' 18Today the wives
of the important men of Persia and Media
have heard about the queen's actions. So
they will speak in the same way to their
husbands, and there will be no end to disrespect and anger.
19"So, our king, if it pleases you, give
a royal order, and let it be written in the
laws of Persia and Media, which cannot
be changed. The law should say Vashti is
never again to enter the presence of King
Xerxes. Also let the king give her place
as queen to someone who is better than
she is. 20And let the king's order be announced everywhere in his enormous
kingdom. Then all the women will respect their husbands, from the greatest
to the least."

Also let the king give her place as queen to someone who is better than she is.
—Esther 1:19

21The king and his important men
were happy with this advice, so King Xerxes did as Memucan suggested. 22He
sent letters to all the states of the kingdom in the writing of each state and in
the language of each group of people.
These letters announced that each man
was to be the ruler of his own family.

Esther Is Made Queen

2 Later, when King Xerxes was not so
angry, he remembered Vashti and
what she had done and his order about
her. 2Then the king's personal servants
suggested, "Let a search be made for
beautiful young girls for the king. 3Let
the king choose supervisors in every
state of his kingdom to bring every beautiful young girl to the palace at Susa.
They should be taken to the women's
quarters and put under the care of Hegai,
the king's eunuch in charge of the wom-
en. And let beauty treatments be given to
them. 4Then let the girl who most
pleases the king become queen in place
of Vashti." The king liked this idea, so he
did as they said.

5Now there was a Jewish man in the
palace of Susa whose name was Mordecai
son of Jair. Jair was the son of Shimei, the
son of Kish. Mordecai was from the tribe
of Benjamin, 6which had been taken captive from Jerusalem by Nebuchadnezzar
king of Babylon. They were part of the
group taken into captivity with Jehoiachin king of Judah. 7Mordecai had a cousin named Hadassah, who had no father or
mother, so Mordecai took care of her. Hadassah was also called Esther, and she
had a very pretty figure and face. Mordecai had adopted her as his own daughter
when her father and mother died.

8When the king's command and order
had been heard, many girls had been
brought to the palace in Susa and put under the care of Hegai. Esther was also
taken to the king's palace and put under
the care of Hegai, who was in charge of
the women. 9Esther pleased Hegai, and
he liked her. So Hegai quickly began giving Esther her beauty treatments and
special food. He gave her seven servant
girls chosen from the king's palace. Then
he moved her and her seven servant girls
to the best part of the women's quarters.

10Esther did not tell anyone about her
family or who her people were, because
Mordecai had told her not to. 11Every
day Mordecai walked back and forth
near the courtyard
where the king's
women lived to find
out how Esther was
and what was hap-
pening to her.

eMAIL! FROM GOD 2:11
Family
Here's a good example of love for family.

12Before a girl
could take her turn with King Xerxes,
she had to complete twelve months of
beauty treatments that were ordered for
the women. For six months she was
treated with oil and myrrh and for six
months with perfumes and cosmetics.
13Then she was ready to go to the king.
Anything she asked for was given to her
to take with her from the women's quarters to the king's palace. 14In the evening she would go to the king's palace,
and in the morning she would return to
another part of the women's quarters.
There she would be placed under the
care of Shaashgaz, the king's eunuch in
charge of the slave women. The girl
would not go back to the king again unless he was pleased with her and asked
for her by name.

15The time came for Esther daughter
of Abihail, Mordecai's uncle, who had
been adopted by Mordecai, to go to the
king. She asked for only what Hegai suggested she should take. (Hegai was the
king's eunuch who was in charge of the
women.) Everyone who saw Esther liked
her. 16So Esther was taken to King Xerxes in the royal palace in the tenth
month, the month of Tebeth, during Xerxes' seventh year as king.

17And the king was pleased with Esther more than with any of the other girls.
He liked her more than any of the other
girls, so he put a royal crown on her head
and made her queen in place of Vashti.
18Then the king gave a great banquet for
Esther and invited all his important men
and royal officers. He announced a holiday
for all the empire and had the government
give away gifts.

FAITH links

A LIFE-SAVING MESSAGE

ESTHER 2:19-22

Some things in life take courage, even if they're the right thing to do. Mordecai had the courage to tell the king of an assassination attempt on his life. By doing what was right Mordecai risked his own safety and risked looking foolish had the king not chosen to believe him.

Even though you may not hear about an assassination attempt against someone, you do have important news to share. The gospel message reminds us that because of sin, we're all under a penalty of death. But Jesus saved our lives by dying for us. Do you have the courage to share that news with someone?

His OK to Obey, Deuteronomy 2:24–36, p. 230

Faith of Our Fathers, Joshua 4:4–9, p. 280

The One Who Suffered, Isaiah 53, p. 966

A Friend in Need, Acts 9:27, p. 1480

Blessed Are the Weak?, 2 Corinthians 12:7–10, p. 1582

Keep Up the Good Work!, Galatians 6:9–10, p. 1593

Mordecai Discovers an Evil Plan

19Now Mordecai was sitting at the king's gate when the girls were gathered the second time. 20Esther still had not told anyone about her family or who her people were, just as Mordecai had commanded her. She obeyed Mordecai just as she had done when she was under his care.

21Now Bigthana and Teresh were two of the king's officers who guarded the doorway. While Mordecai was sitting at the king's gate, they became angry and began to make plans to kill King Xerxes. 22But Mordecai found out about their plans and told Queen Esther. Then Esther told the king how Mordecai had discovered the evil plan. 23When the report was investigated, it was found to be true, and the two officers who had planned to kill the king were hanged. All this was written down in the daily court record in the king's presence.

Haman Plans to Destroy the Jewish People

3 After these things happened, King Xerxes honored Haman son of Hammedatha the Agagite. He gave him a new rank that was higher than all the important men. 2All the royal officers at the king's gate would bow down and kneel before Haman, as the king had ordered. But Mordecai would not bow down or show him honor.

3Then the royal officers at the king's gate asked Mordecai, "Why don't you obey the king's command?" 4And they said this to him every day. When he did not listen to them, they told Haman about it. They wanted to see if Haman would accept Mordecai's behavior because Mordecai had told them he was Jewish.

5When Haman saw that Mordecai would not bow down to him or honor him, he became very angry. 6He thought of himself as too important to try to kill only Mordecai. He had been told who the people of Mordecai were, so he looked for a way to destroy all of Mordecai's people, the Jews, in all of Xerxes' kingdom.

7It was in the first month of the twelfth year of King Xerxes' rule—the month of Nisan. Pur (that is, the lot) was thrown before Haman to choose a day and a month. So the twelfth month, the month of Adar, was chosen.

8Then Haman said to King Xerxes,

FAITH links

STANDING FOR WHAT'S RIGHT

ESTHER 3:2-4

Suppose the principal of your school told you to stand up whenever he or she entered your classroom. No problem, right? He or she deserves respect because of his/her position as the head of your school. Now suppose the principal told you to do something you know is against God's laws. Suddenly there's a problem, right? Mordecai refused to bow down to Haman, a Persian official. Bowing to Haman was a law the king made. Mordecai felt that bowing to Haman was not what God wanted him to do. Even though Haman tried to get even with Mordecai, Mordecai stood firm. Are you willing to stand for what's right, even if no one else does?

Check out these Faithlinks on standing up for what you believe:

A Choice to Make, Deuteronomy 30:15–20, p. 265

Learning to Listen, 1 Samuel 3, p. 358

Give In or Take a Stand?, 1 Kings 22:13–14, p. 472

Wronged for What's Right, Ezra 4:4–5, p. 612

Facing Your Fears, Matthew 8:23–27, p. 1288

Don't Play Favorites, James 2:1–7, p. 1691

"There is a certain group of people scattered among the other people in all the states of your kingdom. Their customs are different from those of all the other people, and they do not obey the king's laws. It is not right for you to allow them
to continue living in your kingdom. **9**If it
pleases the king, let an order be given to destroy those people. Then I will pay seven hundred fifty thousand pounds of silver to those who do the king's business, and they will put it into the royal treasury."

10So the king took his signet ring off
and gave it to Haman son of Hammedatha, the Agagite, the enemy of the Jewish
people. **11**Then the king said to Haman,
"The money and the people are yours. Do with them as you please."

12On the thirteenth day of the first
month, the royal secretaries were called, and they wrote out all of Haman's orders. They wrote to the king's governors and to the captains of the soldiers in each state and to the important men of each group of people. The orders were written in the writing of each state and in the language of each people. They were written in the name of King Xerxes and sealed
with his signet ring. **13**Letters were sent
by messengers to all the king's empire ordering them to destroy, kill, and completely wipe out all the Jewish people. That meant young and old, women and little children, too. It was to happen on a single day—the thirteenth day of the twelfth month, which was Adar. And they could take everything the Jewish people
owned. **14**A copy of the order was given
out as a law in every state so all the people would be ready for that day.

15The messengers set out, hurried by
the king's command, as soon as the order was given in the palace at Susa. The king and Haman sat down to drink, but the city of Susa was in confusion.

Mordecai Asks Esther to Help

4 When Mordecai heard about all that had been done, he tore his clothes, put on rough cloth and ashes, and went out into the city crying loudly and painfully. **2**But Mordecai went only as far as

the king's gate, because no one was allowed to enter that gate dressed in rough
cloth. 3As the king's order reached every
area, there was great sadness and loud
crying among the Jewish people. They
gave up eating and cried out loud, and
many of them lay down on rough cloth
and ashes to show how sad they were.
4When Esther's servant girls and eunuchs came to her and told her about
Mordecai, she was very upset and afraid.
She sent clothes for Mordecai to put on
instead of the rough cloth, but he would
not wear them. 5Then Esther called for
Hathach, one of the king's eunuchs chosen by the king to serve her. Esther ordered him to find out what was bothering
Mordecai and why.
6So Hathach went to Mordecai, who
was in the city square in front of the king's
gate. 7Mordecai told Hathach everything
that had happened to him, and he told
Hathach about the amount of money Haman had promised to pay into the king's
treasury for the killing of the Jewish people. 8Mordecai also gave him a copy of
the order to kill the Jewish people, which
had been given in Susa. He wanted Hathach to show it to Esther and to tell her
about it. And Mordecai told him to order
Esther to go into the king's presence to
beg for mercy and to plead with him for
her people.
9Hathach went back and reported to
Esther everything Mordecai had said.
10Then Esther told Hathach to tell Mordecai, 11"All the royal officers and people
of the royal states know that no man or
woman may go to the king in the inner
courtyard without being called. There is
only one law about this: Anyone who enters must be put to death unless the king
holds out his gold scepter. Then
that person may live.
And I have not been
called to go to the
king for thirty days."
12Esther's mes-
sage was given to
Mordecai. 13Then
Mordecai sent back word to Esther: "Just
because you live in the king's palace,
don't think that out of all the Jewish people you alone will escape. 14If you keep
quiet at this time, someone else will help
and save the Jewish people, but you and
your father's family will all die. And who
knows, you may have been chosen queen
for just such a time as this."

eMAIL! FROM GOD

4:14

Future

Does God put you in situations to make a difference?

THE BIG RISK

ESTHER 4:11–5:2

Think about the biggest risk you've ever taken. What made you decide to take the risk? Taking a risk can be very scary. Esther faced a big risk when Mordecai told her about Haman's plot to have the Jewish people killed. He knew that she needed to tell the king. But to go to the king without his permission meant death! Esther had to take that risk in order to save lives—including her own.

There are certain risks you'll have to take in life. God will give you the courage to take any risk you face on his behalf.

How brave are you? Link here to find out:

Fearful Service?, Exodus 4:1–17, p. 80

Everyone Can Help, Numbers 4, p. 181

When Bad Things Happen, Ecclesiastes 3:16–17, p. 876

A Bad Reaction, Jeremiah 36, p. 1043

The Unpopular Choice, Mark 15:42–43, p. 1360

Obey or Disobey?, Luke 20:20–26, p. 1409

15Then Esther sent this answer to
Mordecai: 16"Go and get all the Jewish
people in Susa together. For my sake,
give up eating; do not eat or drink for
three days, night and day. I and my servant girls will also give up eating. Then I
will go to the king, even though it is
against the law, and if I die, I die."

17So Mordecai went away and did
everything Esther had told him to do.

Esther Speaks to the King

5 On the third day Esther put on her
royal robes and stood in the inner
courtyard of the king's palace, facing the
king's hall. The king was
sitting on his royal throne
in the hall, facing the
doorway. 2When the king
saw Queen Esther stand-
ing in the courtyard, he
was pleased. He held out
to her the gold scepter
that was in his hand, so
Esther went forward and
touched the end of it.

3The king asked,
"What is it, Queen Esther? What do you
want to ask me? I will give you as much
as half of my kingdom."

The king asked, "What is it, Queen Esther? What do you want to ask me? I will give you as much as half of my kingdom."
—Esther 5:3

4Esther answered, "My king, if it
pleases you, come today with Haman to a
banquet that I have prepared for him."

5Then the king said, "Bring Haman
quickly so we may do what Esther asks."

So the king and Haman went to the
banquet Esther had prepared for them.
6As they were drinking wine, the king
said to Esther, "Now, what are you asking
for? I will give it to you. What is it you
want? I will give you as much as half of
my kingdom."

7Esther answered, "This is what I
want and what I ask for. 8My king, if you
are pleased with me and if it pleases you,
give me what I ask for and do what I want.
Come with Haman tomorrow to the banquet I will prepare for you. Then I will answer your question about what I want."

Haman's Plans Against Mordecai

9Haman left the king's palace that day
happy and content. But when he saw
Mordecai at the king's gate and saw that
Mordecai did not stand up or tremble
with fear before him, Haman became
very angry with Mordecai. 10But he controlled his anger and went home.

Then Haman called together his
friends and his wife, Zeresh. 11He told
them how wealthy he was and how many
sons he had. He also told them all the
ways the king had honored him and how
the king had placed him higher than his
important men and his royal officers.
12He also said, "I'm the only person
Queen Esther invited to come with the
king to the banquet she gave. And tomorrow also the queen has
asked me to be her guest
with the king. 13But all
this does not really make
me happy when I see that
Jew Mordecai sitting at
the king's gate."

14Then Haman's wife,
Zeresh, and all his friends
said, "Have a seventy-
five foot platform built,
and in the morning ask
the king to have Mordecai hanged on it.
Then go to the banquet with the king and
be happy." Haman liked this suggestion,
so he ordered the platform to be built.

Mordecai Is Honored

6 That same night the king could not
sleep. So he gave an order for the daily
court record to be brought in and read to
him. 2It was found recorded that Mordecai
had warned the king about Bigthana and
Teresh, two of the king's officers who
guarded the doorway and who had
planned to kill the king.

3The king asked, "What honor and reward have been given to Mordecai for
this?"

The king's personal servants answered, "Nothing has been done for Mordecai."

4The king said, "Who is in the courtyard?" Now Haman had just entered the
outer court of the king's palace. He had
come to ask the king about hanging Mordecai on the platform he had prepared.

A FOREIGN QUEEN

Esther 6

Esther was an Israelite woman who became a queen of Persia. That was an amazing thing! Esther's people were captives in Persia, and yet she became queen. While she was the queen, Esther helped save the life of her uncle and the lives of all her people. She also gave us some insight into how the Persians lived.

Royal Persian feasts were fancy, fancy, fancy. The guests ate while lying back on a bed or couch, sort of like when you lie back in a recliner. All the cups were made of gold, and each was different from the others. (Check out Esther 1:7.)

Special laws protected the Persian king. There were only seven important men who could meet with the king. (Read Esther 1:14.) Nobody else could come to see the king unless he called them in. (See Esther 4:11.) That's why Esther took such a risk when she went to the king to ask for his help.

5The king's personal servants said,
"Haman is standing in the courtyard."
The king said, "Bring him in."
6So Haman came in. And the king
asked him, "What should be done for a
man whom the king wants very much to
honor?"
And Haman thought to himself,
"Whom would the king want to honor
more than me?" 7So he answered the
king, "This is what you could do for the
man you want very much to honor. 8Have
the servants bring a royal robe that the
king himself has worn. And also bring a
horse with a royal crown on its head, a
horse that the king himself has ridden.
9Let the robe and the horse be given to
one of the king's most important men.
Let the servants put the robe on the man
the king wants to honor, and let them
lead him on the horse through the city
streets. As they are leading him, let them
announce: 'This is what is done for the
man whom the king wants to honor!' "
10The king commanded Haman, "Go
quickly. Take the robe and the horse just
as you have said, and do all this for Mordecai the Jew who sits at the king's gate.
Do not leave out anything you have suggested."
11So Haman took the robe and the
horse, and he put the robe on Mordecai.
Then he led him on horseback through
the city streets, announcing before Mordecai: "This is what is done for the man
whom the king wants to honor!"
12Then Mordecai returned to the
king's gate, but Haman hurried home
with his head covered, because he was
embarrassed and ashamed. 13He told his
wife, Zeresh, and all his friends everything that had happened to him.
Haman's wife and the men who gave
him advice said, "You are starting to lose
power to Mordecai. Since he is a Jew, you
cannot win against him. You will surely
be ruined." 14While they were still talking, the king's eunuchs came to Haman's
house and made him hurry to the banquet
Esther had prepared.

Haman Is Hanged

7 So the king and Haman went in to eat
with Queen Esther. 2As they were
drinking wine on the second day, the king
asked Esther again, "What are you asking

for? I will give it to you. What is it you
want? I will give you as much as half of
my kingdom."
3Then Queen Esther answered, "My
king, if you are pleased with me, and if it
pleases you, let me live. This is what I
ask. And let my people live, too. This is
what I want. 4My people and I have been
sold to be destroyed, to be killed and
completely wiped out. If we had been
sold as male and female slaves, I would
have kept quiet, because that would not
be enough of a problem to bother the
king."
5Then King Xerxes asked Queen Esther, "Who is he, and
where is he? Who has
done such a thing?"
6Esther said, "Our en-
emy and foe is this wicked
Haman!"
Then Haman was
filled with terror before
the king and queen. 7The
king was very angry, so
he got up, left his wine,
and went out into the pal-
ace garden. But Haman stayed inside to
beg Queen Esther to save his life. He
could see that the king had already decided to kill him.
8When the king returned from the
palace garden to the banquet hall, he saw
Haman falling on the couch where Esther
was lying. The king said, "Will he even
attack the queen while I am in the
house?"
As soon as the king said that, servants
came in and covered Haman's face. 9Har-
bona, one of the eunuchs there serving
the king, said, "Look, a seventy-five foot
platform stands near Haman's house.
This is the one Haman had prepared for
Mordecai, who gave the warning that
saved the king."
The king said, "Hang Haman on it!"
10So they hanged Haman on the platform
he had prepared for Mordecai. Then the
king was not so angry anymore.

Esther said, "Our enemy and foe is this wicked Haman!" Then Haman was filled with terror before the king and queen.
—Esther 7:6

The King Helps the Jewish People

8 That same day King Xerxes gave
Queen Esther everything Haman,
the enemy of the Jewish people, had left
when he died. And Mordecai came in to
see the king, because Esther had told the
king how he was related to her. 2Then
the king took off his signet ring that he
had taken back from Haman, and he gave
it to Mordecai. Esther put Mordecai in
charge of everything Haman left when he
died.
3Once again Esther spoke to the king.
She fell at the king's feet and cried and
begged him to stop the evil plan that Haman the Agagite had planned against the
Jews. 4The king held out the gold scepter
to Esther. So Esther got up and stood in
front of him.
5She said, "My king, if
you are pleased with me,
and if it pleases you to do
this, if you think it is the
right thing to do, and if
you are happy with me,
let an order be written to
cancel the letters Haman
wrote. Haman the Agag-
ite sent messages to de-
stroy all the Jewish
people in all of your kingdom. 6I could
not stand to see that terrible thing happen to my people. I could not stand to see
my family killed."
7King Xerxes answered Queen Esther and Mordecai the Jew, "Because Haman was against the Jewish people, I
have given his things to Esther, and my
soldiers have hanged him. 8Now, in the
king's name, write another order to the
Jewish people as it seems best to you.
Then seal the order with the king's signet ring, because no letter written in the
king's name and sealed with his signet
ring can be canceled."
9At that time the king's secretaries
were called. This was the twenty-third
day of the third month, which is Sivan.
The secretaries wrote out all of
Mordecai's orders to the Jews, to the
governors, to the captains of the soldiers
in each state, and to the important men of
the one hundred twenty-seven states
that reached from India to Cush. They
wrote in the writing of each state and in
the language of each people. They also

wrote to the Jewish people in their own
writing and language. 10Mordecai wrote
orders in the name of King Xerxes and
sealed the letters with the king's signet
ring. Then he sent the king's orders by
messengers on fast horses, horses that
were raised just for the king.

11These were the king's orders: The
Jewish people in every city have the right
to gather together to protect themselves.
They may destroy, kill, and completely
wipe out the army of any state or people
who attack them. And they are to do the
same to the women and children of that
army. They may also take by force the
property of their enemies. 12The one day
set for the Jewish people to do this in all
the empire of King Xerxes was the thirteenth day of the twelfth month, the
month of Adar. 13A copy of the king's order was to be sent out as a law in every
state. It was to be made known to the people of every nation living in the kingdom
so the Jewish people
would be ready on that set
day to strike back at their
enemies.

14The messengers hur-
ried out, riding on the
royal horses, because the
king commanded those
messengers to hurry. And
the order was also given
in the palace at Susa.

15Mordecai left the
king's presence wearing royal clothes of
blue and white and a large gold crown. He
also had a purple robe made of the best
linen. And the people of Susa shouted for
joy. 16It was a time of happiness, joy,
gladness, and honor for the Jewish people. 17As the king's order went to every
state and city, there was joy and gladness
among the Jewish people. In every state
and city to which the king's order went,
they were having feasts and celebrating.
And many people through all the empire
became Jews, because they were afraid of
the Jewish people.

> She fell at the king's feet and cried and begged him to stop the evil plan that Haman . . . had planned against the Jews.
>
> —Esther 8:3

Victory for the Jewish People

9The order the king had commanded
was to be done on the thirteenth day
of the twelfth month, the month of Adar.
That was the day the enemies of the Jewish people had hoped to defeat them, but
that was changed. So the Jewish people
themselves defeated those who hated
them. 2The Jews met in their cities in all
the empire of King Xerxes in order to attack those who wanted to harm them. No
one was strong enough to fight against
them, because all the other people living
in the empire were afraid of them. 3All
the important men of the states, the governors, captains of the soldiers, and the
king's officers helped the Jewish people,
because they were afraid of Mordecai.
4Mordecai was very important in the
king's palace. He was famous in all the
empire, because he was becoming a
leader of more and more people.

5And, with their swords, the Jewish
people defeated all their enemies, killing
and destroying them. And they did what
they wanted with those people who hated
them. 6In the palace at
Susa, they killed and de-
stroyed five hundred
men. 7They also killed:
Parshandatha, Dalphon,
Aspatha, 8Poratha, Ada-
lia, Aridatha, 9Parmashta,
Arisai, Aridai, and Vaiza-
tha, 10the ten sons of Haman, son of Hammedatha,
the enemy of the Jewish
people. But the Jewish
people did not take their belongings.

11On that day the number killed in the
palace at Susa was reported to the king.
12The king said to Queen Esther, "The
Jewish people have killed and destroyed
five hundred people in the palace at Susa,
and they have also killed Haman's ten
sons. What have they done in the rest of
the king's empire! Now what else are you
asking? I will do it! What else do you
want? It will be done!"

13Esther answered, "If it pleases the
king, give the Jewish people who are in
Susa permission to do again tomorrow
what the king ordered for today. And let
the bodies of Haman's ten sons be
hanged on the platform."

14So the king ordered that it be done.

A law was given in Susa, and the bodies
of the ten sons of Haman were hanged.
15The Jewish people in Susa came together on the fourteenth day of the
month of Adar. They killed three hundred
people in Susa, but they did not take their
belongings.
16At that same time, all the Jewish
people in the king's empire also met to
protect themselves and get rid of their
enemies. They killed seventy-five thousand of those who hated them, but they
did not take their belongings. 17This happened on the thirteenth day of the month
of Adar. On the fourteenth day they rested and made it a day of joyful feasting.

The Feast of Purim

18But the Jewish people in Susa met
on the thirteenth and fourteenth days of
the month of Adar. Then they rested on
the fifteenth day and made it a day of joyful feasting.
19This is why the Jewish people who
live in the country and small villages celebrate on the fourteenth day of the
month of Adar. It is a day of joyful feasting
and a day for exchanging gifts.
20Mordecai wrote down everything
that had happened. Then he sent letters
to all the Jewish people in all the empire
of King Xerxes, far and near. 21He told
them to celebrate every year on the fourteenth and fifteenth days of the month of
Adar, 22because that was when the Jewish people got rid of their enemies. They
were also to celebrate it as the month
their sadness was turned to joy and their
crying for the dead was turned into celebration. He told them to celebrate those
days as days of joyful feasting and as a
time for giving food to each other and
presents to the poor.
23So the Jewish people agreed to do
what Mordecai had written to them, and
they agreed to hold the celebration every
year. 24Haman son of Hammedatha, the
Agagite, was the enemy of all the Jewish
people. He had made an evil plan against
the Jewish people to destroy them, and
he had thrown the Pur (that is, the lot) to
choose a day to ruin and destroy them.
25But when the king learned of the evil

FAITH links

A HOLIDAY LETTER

ESTHER 9:20-23

Many people write letters at Christmas. They tell friends and relatives about the events that happened to them during the year. Many times, they mention their thankfulness to God. Esther and Mordecai started a holiday called Purim to remember how God protected the Jewish people. Mordecai wrote letters to remind people to celebrate this festival. He recorded the main reason to celebrate: God had saved their lives.

We celebrate Christmas and Easter for the same reason. Both holidays remind us of God's love and grace. Jesus came to earth to save us from the penalty of death. Because of Jesus, we have eternal life.

Here are some more links on celebrating our great God:

Approaching God, Numbers 3:10, p. 180

Love That Will Last, Psalm 136, p. 813

A Need to Change, Ecclesiastes 1:1–11, p. 873

Inside the Heart of God, Micah 7:18–20, p. 1228

A Love Song, Zephaniah 3:17, p. 1246

Life After Death?, 1 Corinthians 15:12–13, p. 1563

plan, he sent out written orders that the
evil plans Haman had made against the
Jewish people would be used against him.
And those orders said that Haman and his
sons should be hanged on the platform.
26So these days were called Purim,
which comes from the word "Pur" (the
lot). Because of everything written in
this letter and what they had seen and
what happened to them, **27**the Jewish
people set up this custom. They and their
descendants and all those who join them
are always to celebrate these two days
every year. They should do it in the right
way and at the time Mordecai had ordered them in the letter. **28**These two
days should be remembered and celebrated from now on in every family, in
every state, and in every city. These days
of Purim should always be celebrated by
the Jewish people, and their descendants
should always remember to celebrate
them, too.

29So Queen Esther daughter of Abihail, along with Mordecai the Jew, wrote
this second letter about Purim. Using the
power they had, they wrote to prove the
first letter was true. **30**And Mordecai
sent letters to all the Jewish people in the
one hundred twenty-seven states of the
kingdom of Xerxes, writing them a message of peace and truth. **31**He wrote to
set up these days of Purim at the chosen
times. Mordecai the Jew and Queen Esther had sent out the order for the Jewish
people, just as they had set up things for
themselves and their descendants: On
these two days the people should give up
eating and cry loudly. **32**Esther's letter
set up the rules for Purim, and they were
written down in the records.

The Greatness of Mordecai

10 King Xerxes demanded taxes
everywhere, even from the cities
on the seacoast. **2**And all the great things
Xerxes did by his power and strength are
written in the record books of the kings
of Media and Persia. Also written in
those record books are all the things
done by Mordecai, whom the king made
great. **3**Mordecai the Jew was
second in impor-
tance to King Xer-
xes, and he was the
most important man
among the Jewish
people. His fellow
Jews respected him
very much, because he worked for the
good of his people and spoke up for the
safety of all the Jewish people.

E-MAIL FROM GOD **10:3**

Leadership

What's a good way to get your followers to like you?

WHY ME, GOD?

Hi, there! My name is Job, and I lived a very long time ago. Today no one remembers who wrote this book, but I can tell you that it is the true story of my life. Do you think you have bad days? I hope you never have a day like *this:* One day enemies stole all my oxen, donkeys, and camels; lightning struck and killed all my servants and all my sheep; and then a great wind collapsed the house my sons and daughters were in and killed them all. The next day I was covered head to toe with painful sores. My wife thought I should curse God and die, but I said, "Should we take only good things from God and not trouble?" (Job 2:10). You'll have to read my book to see how things turned out for me.

This book was written to tell people to be faithful to God even when life is difficult. My friends thought I was being punished for a great sin, but I knew that this was not true. I didn't understand why God allowed me to suffer, but can anyone understand God? He is *always* worthy of our worship, no matter what he chooses to do. You won't want to miss the awesome way God spoke to me from a storm in Job 38—41.

JESUS WATCH

At the beginning of the story, we learn that Job was an honest and innocent man. He honored God and stayed away from evil. Yet, God allowed Satan to destroy Job's health, his possessions, and all of his children. Job suffered greatly, but not because he had sinned against God. Job is a picture of innocent suffering that reminds us of Jesus. Jesus had no sin. He lived a perfect life and did not deserve to suffer in any way. Jesus chose to become a man so that he could take the punishment we deserve for our sins. The punishment for sin is death, and Jesus willingly died in our place. Because Jesus suffered for us, we can have eternal life with him in heaven.

my FAVORITE links

OTHER CONNECTIONS

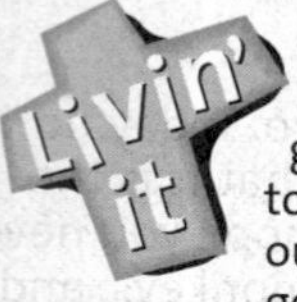

Sometimes the hardest part of getting a difficult assignment done is to keep going. It's tempting to throw in the towel when things get difficult. Check out a few thoughts on the value of getting the job done by visiting Hang in There!, Job 17:9. How do you show respect to others? Is that important to you? Is it important that other people respect you? Find out what God has to say about this topic by surfing over to Just a Little Respect, Job 31:13–14.

MORE STUFF . . .

Take the Challenge! Job went through a lot. He lost his children, his home, his possessions, and his wealth. Throughout it all, what Job really wanted was a chance to tell God that he was innocent and not deserving of these terrible things. Instead of answering his questions, God had a few questions of his own for Job. Take a look and see how you would answer:

- "Where were you when I made the earth's foundation? Tell me, if you understand?" Job 38:4
- "Have you ever ordered the morning to begin, or shown the dawn where its place was?" Job 38:12
- "Job, are you the one who gives the horse its strength or puts a flowing mane on its neck?" Job 39:20
- "Are you as strong as God? Can your voice thunder like his?" Job 40:9

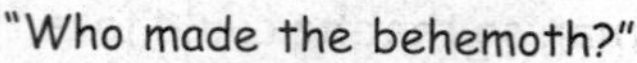

"Who made the behemoth?"

"I don't know—what's a behemoth? Better connect to Job 40:15-24 to find out."

MORE THINGS TO LOOK FOR IN JOB:

Satan makes trouble, Job 1:6–11
More trouble for Job, Job 2
Job cries out to God, Job 10
Job confesses; God blesses Job 42

FAITH links

A Really Bad Day, Job 1:20–22; 2:10

A Friend in Deed, Job 2:13

A Pity Party, Job 10

Helpful Advice., Job 12:4–5

Meaningless Words, Job 21:34

Go for the Gold, Job 23:10

Happiness or Joy?, Job 29:18–19

No Doubt About It, Job 36:5

How Big Is God?, Job 38—41

Full Circle, Job 42

Job, the Good Man

1 A man named Job lived in the land of
Uz. He was an honest and innocent
man; he honored God and stayed away
from evil. 2Job had seven sons and three
daughters. 3He owned seven thousand
sheep, three thousand camels, five hundred teams of oxen, and five hundred
female donkeys. He also had a large number of servants. He was the greatest man
among all the people of the East.
4Job's sons took turns holding feasts
in their homes and invited their sisters to
eat and drink with them. 5After a feast
was over, Job would send and have them
made clean. Early in the morning Job
would offer a burnt offering for each of
them, because he thought, "My children
may have sinned and cursed God in their
hearts." Job did this every time.

Satan Appears Before the Lord

6One day the angels came to show
themselves before the LORD, and Satan
was with them. 7The LORD said to Satan,
"Where have you come from?"
Satan answered the LORD, "I have
been wandering around the earth, going
back and forth in it."
8Then the LORD said to Satan, "Have
you noticed my servant Job? No one else
on earth is like him. He is an honest and
innocent man, honoring God and staying
away from evil."
9But Satan answered the LORD, "Job
honors God for a good reason. 10You
have put a wall around him, his family,
and everything he owns. You have
blessed the things he has done. His
flocks and herds are so large they almost
cover the land. 11But reach out your
hand and destroy everything he has, and
he will curse you to your face."
12The LORD said to Satan, "All right,
then. Everything Job has is in your power, but you must not touch Job himself."
Then Satan left the LORD's presence.
13One day Job's sons and daughters
were eating and drinking wine together
at the oldest brother's house. 14A messenger came to Job and said, "The oxen
were plowing and the donkeys were eating grass nearby, 15when the Sabeans attacked and carried them away. They
killed the servants with swords, and I am
the only one who escaped to tell you!"
16The messenger was still speaking

FAITH links

A REALLY BAD DAY

JOB 1:20-22; 2:10

There are good days and there are bad days. But some days are worse than anything you can imagine. One day, Job had everything going for him. The next day, his family and wealth were wiped out. How would you respond to a disaster like that? Job didn't blame or yell at God. He gave a faithful response, even in the worst times imaginable!

Hard times are hard. That's how they get their name. Like Job, you can seek God's help when life gets rough. Don't let hard times turn you away from God. Instead, turn toward God.

What do you do when you have a bad day? Check out these links:

A Major Problem, Genesis 15:6, p. 20

From Hopeless to Hopeful, Exodus 6:9, p. 83

Our Heavenly Shepherd, Psalm 23, p. 726

A Swarm of Trouble, Joel 2:25–27, p. 1190

A Word About Worry, Matthew 6:25–34, p. 1284

Our Interpreter, Romans 8:26, p. 1528

when another messenger arrived and
said, "Lightning from God fell from the
sky. It burned up the sheep and the servants, and I am the only one who escaped
to tell you!"
17The second messenger was still
speaking when another messenger arrived and said, "The Babylonians sent
three groups of attackers that swept
down and stole your camels and killed
the servants. I am the only one who escaped to tell you!"
18The third messenger was still
speaking when another messenger arrived and said, "Your sons and daughters
were eating and drinking wine together
at the oldest brother's house. 19Sudden-
ly a great wind came from the desert, hitting all four corners of the house at once.
The house fell in on the young people,
and they are all dead. I am the only one
who escaped to tell you!"
20When Job heard this, he got up and
tore his robe and shaved his head to show
how sad he was. Then he bowed down to
the ground to worship God. 21He said:

"I was naked when I was born,
and I will be naked when I die.
The LORD gave these things to me,
and he has taken them away.
Praise the name of the LORD."

22In all this Job did not sin or blame
God.

Satan Appears Before the Lord Again

2 On another day the angels came to
show themselves before the LORD,
and Satan was with them again. 2The
LORD said to Satan, "Where have you
come from?"
Satan answered the LORD, "I have
been wandering around the earth, going
back and forth in it."
3Then the LORD said to Satan, "Have
you noticed my servant Job? No one else
on earth is like him. He is an honest and
innocent man, honoring God and staying
away from evil. You caused me to ruin
him for no good reason, but he continues
to be without blame."
4"One skin for another!" Satan answered. "A man will give all he has to

FAITH links

A FRIEND IN DEED

JOB 2:13

The test of friendship is when you go through hard times. A friend who sticks with you through hard times is a true friend. Three of Job's friends stayed with him during the first week of his terrible loss. They mourned with him.

When you have a friend who is going through a hard time, don't be afraid to be around him, even if you don't know what to say. Just be available, ready to listen. You don't have to say a word. If you're going through hard times, what friend can you count on? If you can't think of one, here is a name to call: Jesus. He can "be more loyal than a brother" (Proverbs 18:24).

Connect here to find out how to help a friend:

God's Pep Talk, Joshua 1:5–9, p. 276

Loyal to a Friend, 2 Samuel 9, p. 409

A Direct Path, Proverbs 3:5–6, p. 829

The Right Ingredients, Micah 6:8, p. 1227

A Friend in Need, Acts 9:27, p. 1480

Toss Those Troubles!, 1 Peter 5:7, p. 1706

save his own life. 5But reach out your
hand and destroy his flesh and bones, and
he will curse you to your face."
6The LORD said to Satan, "All right,
then. Job is in your power, but you may
not take his life."
7So Satan left the LORD's presence.
He put painful sores on Job's body, from
the top of his head to the soles of his feet.
8Job took a piece of broken pottery to
scrape himself, and he sat in ashes in
misery.
9Job's wife said to him, "Why are you
trying to stay innocent? Curse God and
die!"
10Job answered, "You are talking like
a foolish woman. Should we take only
good things from God and not trouble?"
In spite of all this Job did not sin in what
he said.

Job's Three Friends Come to Help

11Now Job had three friends: Eliphaz
the Temanite, Bildad the Shuhite, and
Zophar the Naamathite. When these
friends heard about Job's troubles, they agreed to
meet and visit him.
They wanted to
show their concern
and to comfort him.
12They saw Job from
far away, but he looked so different they
almost didn't recognize him. They began
to cry loudly and tore their robes and put
dirt on their heads to show how sad they
were. 13Then they sat on the ground
with Job seven days and seven nights. No
one said a word to him because they saw
how much he was suffering.

EMAIL FROM GOD 2:11
Friendship
How can you help hurting friends?

Job Curses His Birth

3 After seven days Job cried out and
cursed the day he had been born,
2saying:

3 "Let the day I was born be
destroyed,
and the night it was said, 'A boy is
born!'
4 Let that day turn to darkness.
Don't let God care about it.
Don't let light shine on it.
5 Let darkness and gloom have that
day.
Let a cloud hide it.
Let thick darkness cover its
light.
6 Let thick darkness capture that
night.
Don't count it among the days of
the year
or put it in any of the months.
7 Let that night be empty,
with no shout of joy to be heard.
8 Let those who curse days curse that
day.
Let them prepare to wake up the
sea monster Leviathan.
9 Let that day's morning stars never
appear;
let it wait for daylight that never
comes.
Don't let it see the first light of
dawn,
10 because it allowed me to be born
and did not hide trouble from my
eyes.

11 "Why didn't I die as soon as I was
born?
Why didn't I die when I came out
of the womb?
12 Why did my mother's knees receive
me,
and my mother's breasts feed me?
13 If they had not been there,
I would be lying dead in peace;
I would be asleep and at rest
14 with kings and wise men of the earth
who built places for themselves
that are now ruined.
15 I would be asleep with rulers
who filled their houses with gold
and silver.
16 Why was I not buried like a child
born dead,
like a baby who never saw the light
of day?
17 In the grave the wicked stop making
trouble,
and the weary workers are at rest.
18 In the grave there is rest for the
captives
who no longer hear the shout of
the slave driver.

19 People great and small are in the grave,
and the slave is freed from his master.

20 "Why is light given to those in misery?
Why is life given to those who are so unhappy?
21 They want to die, but death does not come.
They search for death more than for hidden treasure.
22 They are very happy
when they get to the grave.
23 They cannot see where they are going.
God has hidden the road ahead.
24 I make sad sounds as I eat;
my groans pour out like water.
25 Everything I feared and dreaded
has happened to me.
26 I have no peace or quietness.
I have no rest, only trouble."

Eliphaz Speaks

4 Then Eliphaz the Temanite answered:
2 "If someone tried to speak with you,
would you be upset?
I cannot keep from speaking.
3 Think about the many people you have taught
and the weak hands you have made strong.
4 Your words have comforted those who fell,
and you have strengthened those who could not stand.

EMAIL FROM GOD 4:4
Encouragement
How can you encourage others?

5 But now trouble comes to you, and you are discouraged;
trouble hits you, and you are terrified.
6 You should have confidence because you respect God;
you should have hope because you are innocent.

7 "Remember that the innocent will not die;
honest people will never be destroyed.
8 I have noticed that people who plow evil
and plant trouble, harvest it.
9 God's breath destroys them,
and a blast of his anger kills them.
10 Lions may roar and growl,
but when the teeth of a strong lion are broken,
11 that lion dies of hunger.
The cubs of the mother lion are scattered.

12 "A word was brought to me in secret,
and my ears heard a whisper of it.
13 It was during a nightmare
when people are in deep sleep.
14 I was trembling with fear;
all my bones were shaking.
15 A spirit glided past my face,
and the hair on my body stood on end.
16 The spirit stopped,
but I could not see what it was.
A shape stood before my eyes,
and I heard a quiet voice.
17 It said, 'Can a human be more right than God?
Can a person be pure before his maker?
18 God does not trust his angels;
he blames them for mistakes.
19 So he puts even more blame on
people who live in clay houses,[n]
whose foundations are made of dust,
who can be crushed like a moth.
20 Between dawn and sunset many people are broken to pieces;
without being noticed, they die and are gone forever.
21 The ropes of their tents are pulled up,
and they die without wisdom.'

5 "Call if you want to, Job, but no one will answer you.
You can't turn to any of the holy ones.

4:19 clay houses This is probably talking about people's bodies.

2 Anger kills the fool,
and jealousy slays the stupid.
3 I have seen a fool succeed,
but I cursed his home immediately.
4 His children are far from safety
and are crushed in court with no
defense.
5 The hungry eat his harvest,
even taking what grew among the
thorns,
and thirsty people want his wealth.
6 Hard times do not come up from the
ground,
and trouble does not grow from the
earth.
7 People produce trouble
as surely as sparks fly upward.

8 "But if I were you, I would call on
God
and bring my problem before him.
9 God does wonders that cannot be
understood;
he does so many miracles they
cannot be counted.
10 He gives rain to the earth
and sends water on the fields.
11 He makes the humble person
important
and lifts the sad to places of safety.
12 He ruins the plans of those who trick
others
so they have no success.
13 He catches the wise in their own
clever traps
and sweeps away the plans of
those who try to trick others.
14 Darkness covers them up in the
daytime;
even at noon they feel around in
the dark.
15 God saves the needy from their lies
and from the harm done by
powerful people.
16 So the poor have hope,
while those
who are
unfair are
silenced.

eMAIL! FROM GOD
5:17
Correction
Is God's correction
good?

17 "The one whom
God corrects
is happy,
so do not hate being corrected by
the Almighty.
18 God hurts, but he also bandages up;
he injures, but his hands also heal.
19 He will save you from six troubles;
even seven troubles will not harm
you.
20 God will buy you back from death in
times of hunger,
and in battle he will save you from
the sword.
21 You will be protected from the tongue
that strikes like a whip,
and you will not be afraid when
destruction comes.
22 You will laugh at destruction and
hunger,
and you will not fear the wild
animals,
23 because you will have an agreement
with the stones in the field,
and the wild animals will be at
peace with you.
24 You will know that your tent is safe,
because you will check the things
you own and find nothing
missing.
25 You will know that you will have
many children,
and your descendants will be like
the grass on the earth.
26 You will come to the grave with all
your strength,
like bundles of grain gathered at
the right time.

27 "We have checked this, and it is true,
so hear it and decide what it means
to you."

Job Answers Eliphaz

6 Then Job answered:

2 "I wish my suffering could be
weighed
and my misery put on scales.
3 My sadness would be heavier than
the sand of the seas.
No wonder my words seem
careless.
4 The arrows of the Almighty are in
me;
my spirit drinks in their poison;

God's terrors are gathered against
me.
5 A wild donkey does not bray when it
has grass to eat,
and an ox is quiet when it has feed.
6 Tasteless food is not eaten without
salt,
and there is no flavor in the white
of an egg.
7 I refuse to touch it;
such food makes me sick.

8 "How I wish that I might have what I
ask for
and that God would give me what I
hope for.
9 How I wish God would crush me
and reach out his hand to destroy
me.
10 Then I would have this comfort
and be glad even in this unending
pain,
because I would know I did not
reject the words of the Holy One.

11 "I do not have the strength to wait.
There is nothing to hope for,
so why should I be patient?
12 I do not have the strength of stone;
my flesh is not bronze.
13 I have no power to help myself,
because success has been taken
away from me.

14 "They say, 'A man's friends should be
kind to him when he is in
trouble,
even if he stops fearing the
Almighty.'
15 But my brothers cannot be counted
on.
They are like streams that do not
always flow,
streams that sometimes run over.
16 They are made dark by melting ice
and rise with melting snow.
17 But they stop flowing in the dry
season;
they disappear when it is hot.
18 Travelers turn away from their paths
and go into the desert and die.
19 The groups of travelers from Tema
look for water,
and the traders of Sheba look
hopefully.
20 They are upset because they had
been sure;

FAITH links

HELP FOR THE HURTING

JOB 6:29-30

Have you ever been tempted to judge someone by the way he reacted to a problem? Maybe you thought a friend overreacted when you made a comment that seemed to hurt her. Or maybe you wondered why a friend didn't just snap out of a bad mood. We tend to judge people by how we would react. Job's friends didn't know how to help Job. Their judgments about his behavior made him feel worse.

God warns us not to judge others, especially not those who are going through hard times. Since we really don't know how others *should* feel, the best thing to do for a person who's hurting is to pray for that person.

Care for the Lost, Deuteronomy 22:1–3, p. 255

Show You Care, 2 Kings 4:10, p. 481

Depend on Him!, 2 Chronicles 16:1–9, p. 579

A Gentle Answer, Proverbs 15:1, p. 847

Concern for All, Daniel 9, p. 1165

An Encouraging Word, 1 Corinthians 1:3–5, p. 1545

when they arrive, they are
disappointed.
21 You also have been no help.
You see something terrible, and
you are afraid.
22 I have never said, 'Give me a gift.
Use your wealth to pay my debt.
23 Save me from the enemy's power.
Buy me back from the clutches of
cruel people.'

24 "Teach me, and I will be quiet.
Show me where I have been
wrong.
25 Honest words are painful,
but your arguments prove nothing.
26 Do you mean to correct what I say?
Will you treat the words of a
troubled man as if they were
only wind?
27 You would even gamble for orphans
and would trade away your friend.

28 "But now please look at me.
I would not lie to your face.
29 Change your mind; do not be unfair;
think again, because my innocence
is being questioned.
30 What I am saying is not wicked;
I can tell the difference between
right and wrong.

7 "People have a hard task on earth,
and their days are like those of a
laborer.
2 They are like a slave wishing for the
evening shadows,
like a laborer waiting to be paid.
3 But I am given
months that are
empty,
and nights of
misery have
been given to
me.
4 When I lie down, I
think, 'How long
until I get up?'
The night is long,
and I toss until
dawn.
5 My body is covered with worms and
scabs,
and my skin is broken and full of
sores.

6 "My days go by faster than a
weaver's tool,
and they come to an end without
hope.
7 Remember, God, that my life is only a
breath.
My eyes will never see happy
times again.
8 Those who see me now will see me
no more;
you will look for me, but I will be
gone.
9 As a cloud disappears and is gone,
people go to the grave and never
return.
10 They will never come back to their
houses again,
and their places will not know
them anymore.

11 "So I will not stay quiet;
I will speak out in the suffering of
my spirit.
I will complain because I am so
unhappy.
12 I am not the sea or the sea monster.
So why have you set a guard over
me?
13 Sometimes I think my bed will
comfort me
or that my couch will stop my
complaint.
14 Then you frighten me with dreams
and terrify me with visions.
15 My throat prefers to be choked;
my bones welcome
death.
16 I hate my life; I don't
want to live
forever.
Leave me alone,
because my days
have no meaning.

17 "Why do you make
people so
important
and give them so
much attention?
18 You examine them every morning

My days go by faster than a weaver's tool, and they come to an end without hope.
—Job 7:6

and test them every moment.
19 Will you never look away from me
or leave me alone even long
enough to swallow?
20 If I have sinned, what have I done to
you,
you watcher of humans?
Why have you made me your target?
Have I become a heavy load for
you?
21 Why don't you pardon my wrongs
and forgive my sins?
I will soon lie down in the dust of
death.
Then you will search for me, but I
will be no more."

Bildad Speaks to Job

8 Then Bildad the Shuhite answered:
2 "How long will you say such things?
Your words are no more than
wind.
3 God does not twist justice;
the Almighty does not make wrong
what is right.
4 Your children sinned against God,
and he punished them for their
sins.
5 But you should ask God for help
and pray to the Almighty for
mercy.
6 If you are good and honest,
he will stand up for you
and bring you back where you
belong.
7 Where you began will seem
unimportant,
because your future will be so
successful.

8 "Ask old people;
find out what their ancestors
learned,
9 because we were only born
yesterday and know nothing.
Our days on earth are only a
shadow.
10 Those people will teach you and tell
you
and speak about what they know.
11 Papyrus plants cannot grow where
there is no swamp,
and reeds cannot grow tall without
water.
12 While they are still growing and not
yet cut,
they will dry up quicker than grass.
13 That is what will happen to those
who forget God;
the hope of the wicked will be
gone.
14 What they hope in is easily broken;
what they trust is like a spider's
web.
15 They lean on the spider's web, but it
breaks.
They grab it, but it does not hold
up.

FAITH CHALLENGE

Here's one for you. Read 8:20 to find out what God does to make sure that evil does not overcome good in this world. How can you tell the difference between an innocent person and an evil person?

TESTING IT

Job 8:20
Surely God does not reject the innocent or give strength to those who do evil.

16 They are like well-watered plants in the sunshine
that spread their roots all through the garden.
17 They wrap their roots around a pile of rocks
and look for a place among the stones.
18 But if a plant is torn from its place,
then that place rejects it and says, 'I never saw you.'
19 Now joy has gone away;
other plants grow up from the same dirt.

20 "Surely God does not reject the innocent
or give strength to those who do evil.
21 God will yet fill your mouth with laughter
and your lips with shouts of joy.
22 Your enemies will be covered with shame,
and the tents of the wicked will be gone."

Job Answers Bildad

9 Then Job answered:

2 "Yes, I know that this is true,
but how can anyone be right in the presence of God?
3 Someone might want to argue with God,
but no one could answer God,
not one time out of a thousand.
4 God's wisdom is deep, and his power is great;
no one can fight him without getting hurt.
5 God moves mountains without anyone knowing it
and turns them over when he is angry.
6 He shakes the earth out of its place
and makes its foundations tremble.
7 He commands the sun not to shine
and shuts off the light of the stars.
8 He alone stretches out the skies
and walks on the waves of the sea.
9 It is God who made the Bear, Orion, and the Pleiades*
and the groups of stars in the southern sky.
10 He does wonders that cannot be understood;
he does so many miracles they cannot be counted.
11 When he passes me, I cannot see him;
when he goes by me, I do not recognize him.
12 If he snatches something away, no one can stop him
or say to him, 'What are you doing?'
13 God will not hold back his anger.
Even the helpers of the monster Rahab lie at his feet in fear.
14 So how can I argue with God,
or even find words to argue with him?
15 Even if I were right, I could not answer him;
I could only beg God, my Judge, for mercy.
16 If I called to him and he answered,
I still don't believe he would listen to me.
17 He would crush me with a storm
and multiply my wounds for no reason.
18 He would not let me catch my breath
but would overwhelm me with misery.
19 When it comes to strength, God is stronger than I;
when it comes to justice, no one can accuse him.
20 Even if I were right, my own mouth would say I was wrong;
if I were innocent, my mouth would say I was guilty.

God's wisdom is deep, and his power is great; no one can fight him without getting hurt.
—Job 9:4

9:9 Bear . . . Pleiades Names of well-known groups of stars.

21 "I am innocent,
but I don't care about myself.
I hate my own life.
22 It is all the same. That is why I say,
'God destroys both the innocent
and the guilty.'
23 If the whip brings sudden death,
God will laugh at the suffering of
the innocent.
24 When the land falls into the hands of
evil people,
he covers the judges' faces so they
can't see it.
If it is not God who does this, then
who is it?

25 "My days go by faster than a runner;
they fly away without my seeing
any joy.
26 They glide past like paper boats.
They attack like eagles swooping
down to feed.
27 Even though I say, 'I will forget my
complaint;
I will change the look on my face
and smile,'
28 I still dread all my suffering.
I know you will hold me guilty.
29 I have already been found guilty,
so why should I struggle for no
reason?
30 I might wash myself with soap
and scrub my hands with strong
soap,
31 but you would push me into a dirty
pit,
and even my clothes would hate
me.

32 "God is not a man like me, so I
cannot answer him.
We cannot meet each other in
court.
33 I wish there were someone to make
peace between us,
someone to decide our case.
34 Maybe he could remove God's
punishment
so his terror would no longer
frighten me.
35 Then I could speak without being
afraid,
but I am not able to do that.

10 "I hate my life,
so I will complain without holding
back;
I will speak because I am so
unhappy.
2 I will say to God: Do not hold me
guilty,
but tell me what you have against
me.
3 Does it make you happy to trouble
me?
Don't you care about me, the work
of your hands?
Are you happy with the plans of
evil people?
4 Do you have human eyes
that see as we see?
5 Are your days like the days of
humans,
and your years like our years?
6 You look for the evil I have done
and search for my sin.
7 You know I am not guilty,
but no one can save me from your
power.

8 "Your hands shaped and made me.
Do you now turn around and
destroy me?
9 Remember that you molded me like a
piece of clay.
Will you now turn me back into
dust?
10 You formed me inside my mother
like cheese formed from milk.
11 You dressed me with skin and flesh;
you sewed me together with bones
and muscles.
12 You gave me life and showed me
kindness,
and in your care you watched over
my life.

13 "But in your heart you hid other
plans.
I know this was in your mind.
14 If I sinned, you would watch me
and would not let my sin go
unpunished.
15 How terrible it will be for me if I am
guilty!
Even if I am right, I cannot lift my
head.

I am full of shame
and experience only pain.
16 If I hold up my head, you hunt me like a lion
and again show your terrible power against me.
17 You bring new witnesses against me
and increase your anger against me.
Your armies come against me.

18 "So why did you allow me to be born?
I wish I had died before anyone saw me.
19 I wish I had never lived,
but had been carried straight from birth to the grave.
20 The few days of my life are almost over.
Leave me alone so I can have a moment of joy.
21 Soon I will leave; I will not return
from the land of darkness and gloom,
22 the land of darkest night,
from the land of gloom and confusion,
where even the light is darkness."

Zophar Speaks to Job

11 Then Zophar the Naamathite answered:

2 "Should these words go unanswered?
Is this talker in the right?
3 Your lies do not make people quiet;
people should correct you when you make fun of God.
4 You say, 'My teachings are right,
and I am clean in God's sight.'
5 I wish God would speak
and open his lips against you
6 and tell you the secrets of wisdom,
because wisdom has two sides.
Know this: God has even forgotten some of your sin.

7 "Can you understand the secrets of God?
Can you search the limits of the Almighty?

FAITH links

A PITY PARTY

JOB 10

Ever feel sorry for yourself? Usually that feeling comes when hard times hit. During times like those, many people question God. Job had a hard time understanding why God allowed such trouble in his life. He began to feel sorry for himself. When things were going well, Job could easily sense God's love for him. Now when things were not going well, he had a hard time sensing God's concern.

It's natural to feel sorry for yourself when you're having a hard time. That's what's known as a "pity party." But that feeling only makes matters worse, not better. Remembering God's love for you, even when things seem rotten, can help.

Feeling sorry for yourself? Surf on to these links:

A Giant Problem, 1 Samuel 17:32–51, p. 377

A Hometown Hurt, Jeremiah 11:8—12:6, p. 1008

A Hard Place, Ezekiel 28:25–26, p. 1120

Your Feet on High Places, Habakkuk 3:18–19, p. 1239

Sad Times, Matthew 14:13–14, p. 1299

Hard Times, 2 Corinthians 1:8–10, p. 1570

8 His limits are higher than the heavens;
you cannot reach them!
They are deeper than the grave;
you cannot understand them!
9 His limits are longer than the earth
and wider than the sea.

10 "If God comes along and puts you in prison
or calls you into court, no one can stop him.
11 God knows who is evil,
and when he sees evil, he takes note of it.
12 A fool cannot become wise
any more than a wild donkey
can be born tame.

EMAIL FROM GOD 11:11
God
Does God know when you do wrong?

13 "You must give your whole heart to him
and hold out your hands to him for help.
14 Put away the sin that is in your hand;
let no evil remain in your tent.
15 Then you can lift up your face without shame,
and you can stand strong without fear.
16 You will forget your trouble
and darkness will seem like morning.
17 Your life will be as bright as the noonday sun,
and darkness will seem like morning.
18 You will feel safe because there is hope;
you will look around and rest in safety.
19 You will lie down, and no one will scare you.
Many people will want favors from you.
20 But the wicked will not be able to see,
so they will not escape.
Their only hope will be to die."

Job Answers Zophar

12 Then Job answered:

2 "You really think you are the only wise people
and that when you die, wisdom will die with you!
3 But my mind is as good as yours;
you are not better than I am.
Everyone knows all these things.
4 My friends all laugh at me
when I call on God and expect him to answer me;
they laugh at me even though I am right and innocent!
5 Those who are comfortable don't care that others have trouble;
they think it right that those people should have troubles.
6 The tents of robbers are not bothered,
and those who make God angry are safe.
They have their god in their pocket.

7 "But ask the animals, and they will teach you,
or ask the birds of the air, and they will tell you.
8 Speak to the earth, and it will teach you,
or let the fish of the sea tell you.
9 Every one of these knows
that the hand of the LORD has done this.
10 The life of every creature
and the breath of all people are in God's hand.
11 The ear tests words
as the tongue tastes food.
12 Older people are wise,
and long life brings understanding.

13 "But only God has wisdom and power,
good advice and understanding.
14 What he tears down cannot be rebuilt;
anyone he puts in prison cannot be let out.
15 If God holds back the waters, there is no rain;

FAITH links

HELPFUL ADVICE

JOB 12:4-5

When life goes well with you, it's easy to forget about those who don't have it as good. We might pass someone homeless and think *Why couldn't he just get a job?* Or we might see a kid who isn't wearing the latest clothes and think *Why couldn't he dress better?*

Job was angry with his friends for the way they judged him. He felt that others made fun of him for the trouble in his life. Like Job's friends did, it's far easier to judge someone than to offer a helping hand. Next time you're tempted to offer an opinion about someone in need, offer your help instead.

The MLP, Ruth 1:16–17, p. 345

Some Friendly Advice, Proverbs 17:9, 14, 17, p. 851

Love for a Lifetime, Song of Solomon 6:8–9, p. 891

A Safe Place, Nahum 1:7, p. 1231

Welcome!, Matthew 19:13–15, p. 1307

Most Wanted?, 2 Corinthians 10:1, p. 1580

if he lets the waters go, they flood
the land.
16 He is strong and victorious;
both the one who fools others and
the one who is fooled belong to
him.
17 God leads the wise away as captives
and turns judges into fools.
18 He takes off chains that kings put on
and puts a garment on their bodies.
19 He leads priests away naked
and destroys the powerful.
20 He makes trusted people be silent
and takes away the wisdom of
older leaders.
21 He brings disgrace on important
people
and takes away the weapons of the
strong.
22 He uncovers the deep things of
darkness
and brings dark shadows into the
light.
23 He makes nations great and then
destroys them;
he makes nations large and then
scatters them.
24 He takes understanding away from
the leaders of the earth
and makes them wander through a
pathless desert.
25 They feel around in darkness with no
light;
he makes them stumble like
drunks.

13 "Now my eyes have seen all this;
my ears have heard and
understood it.
2 What you know, I also know.
You are not better than I am.
3 But I want to speak to the Almighty
and to argue my case with God.
4 But you smear me with lies.
You are worthless doctors, all of
you!
5 I wish you would just stop talking;
then you would really be wise!
6 Listen to my argument,
and hear the pleading of my lips.
7 You should not speak evil in the
name of God;
you cannot speak God's truth by
telling lies.
8 You should not unfairly choose his
side against mine;
you should not argue the case for
God.
9 You will not do well if he examines
you;

you cannot fool God as you might
fool humans.
10 God would surely scold you
if you unfairly took one person's
side.
11 His bright glory would scare you,
and you would be very much afraid
of him.
12 Your wise sayings are worth no more
than ashes,
and your arguments are as weak as
clay.

13 "Be quiet and let me speak.
Let things happen to me as they
will.
14 Why should I put myself in danger
and take my life in my own hands?
15 Even if God kills me, I have hope in
him;
I will still defend my ways to his
face.
16 This is my salvation.
The wicked cannot come before
him.
17 Listen carefully to my words;
let your ears hear what I say.
18 See, I have prepared my case,
and I know I will be proved right.
19 No one can accuse me of doing
wrong.
If someone can, I will be quiet and
die.

20 "God, please just give me these two
things,
and then I will not hide from you:
21 Take your punishment away from
me,
and stop frightening me with your
terrors.
22 Then call me, and I will answer,
or let me speak, and you answer.
23 How many evil things and sins have I
done?
Show me my wrong and my sin.
24 Don't hide your face from me;
don't think of me as your enemy.
25 Don't punish a leaf that is blown by
the wind;
don't chase after straw.
26 You write down cruel things against
me
and make me suffer for my
boyhood sins.
27 You put my feet in chains
and keep close watch wherever I
go.
You even mark the soles of my
feet.

28 "Everyone wears out like something
rotten,
like clothing eaten by moths.

14 "All of us born to women
live only a few days and
have lots
of trouble.
2 We grow up like
flowers and
then dry up
and die.
We are like a
passing shadow that does not
last.
3 Lord, do you need to watch me like
this?
Must you bring me before you to
be judged?
4 No one can bring something clean
from something dirty.
5 Our time is limited.
You have given us only so many
months to live
and have set limits we cannot go
beyond.
6 So look away from us and leave us
alone
until we put in our time like a
laborer.

7 "If a tree is cut down,
there is hope that it will grow
again
and will send out new branches.
8 Even if its roots grow old in the
ground,
and its stump dies in the dirt,
9 at the smell of water it will bud
and put out new shoots like a plant.
10 But we die, and our bodies are laid in
the ground;
we take our last breath and are
gone.
11 Water disappears from a lake,

EMAIL FROM GOD 14:1
Troubles
Troubles ahead!

and a river loses its water and
dries up.
12 In the same way, we lie down and do
not rise again;
we will not get up or be awakened
until the heavens disappear.

13 "I wish you would hide me in the
grave;
hide me until your anger is gone.
I wish you would set a time
and then remember me!
14 If a person dies, will he live again?
All my days are a struggle;
I will wait until my change comes.
15 You will call, and I will answer you;
you will desire the creature your
hands have made.
16 Then you will count my steps,
but you will not keep track of my
sin.
17 My wrongs will be closed up in a bag,
and you will cover up my sin.

18 "A mountain washes away and
crumbles;
and a rock can be moved from its
place.
19 Water washes over stones and wears
them down,
and rushing waters wash away the
dirt.
In the same way, you destroy my
hope.
20 You defeat a person forever, and he is
gone;
you change his appearance and
send him away.
21 His sons are honored, but he does
not know it;
his sons are disgraced, but he does
not see it.
22 He only feels the pain of his body
and feels sorry for himself."

Eliphaz Answers Job

15 Then Eliphaz the Temanite answered:

2 "A wise person would not answer
with empty words
or fill his stomach with the hot
east wind.
3 He would not argue with useless
words
or make speeches that have no
value.
4 But you even destroy respect for God
and limit the worship of him.
5 Your sin teaches your mouth what to
say;
you use words to trick others.
6 It is your own mouth, not mine, that
shows you are wicked;
your own lips testify against you.

7 "You are not the first man ever born;
you are not older than the hills.
8 You did not listen in on God's secret
council.
But you limit wisdom to yourself.
9 You don't know any more than we
know.
You don't understand any more
than we understand.
10 Old people with gray hair are on our
side;
they are even older than your
father.
11 Is the comfort God gives you not
enough for you,
even when words are spoken
gently to you?
12 Has your heart carried you away
from God?
Why do your eyes flash with
anger?
13 Why do you speak out your anger
against God?
Why do these words pour out of
your mouth?

14 "How can anyone be pure?
How can someone born to a
woman be good?
15 God places no trust in his holy ones,
and even the heavens are not pure
in his eyes.
16 How much less pure is one who is
terrible and rotten
and drinks up evil as if it were
water!

17 "Listen to me, and I will tell you
about it;
I will tell you what I have seen.

18 These are things wise men have told;
their fathers told them, and they have hidden nothing.
19 (The land was given to their fathers only,
and no foreigner lived among them.)
20 The wicked suffer pain all their lives;
the cruel suffer during all the years saved up for them.
21 Terrible sounds fill their ears,
and when things seem to be going well, robbers attack them.
22 Evil people give up trying to escape from the darkness;
it has been decided that they will die by the sword.
23 They wander around and will become food for vultures.
They know darkness will soon come.
24 Worry and suffering terrify them;
they overwhelm them, like a king ready to attack,
25 because they shake their fists at God
and try to get their own way against the Almighty.
26 They stubbornly charge at God
with thick, strong shields.

CONNECT 2-YOU

NO FEAR

Are there some things that make you really nervous? Like speaking in front of a large group, or maybe a bad thunderstorm? Tagg and I have a friend who's facing a nervous time right now. We'll let her tell you about it. Please welcome Kristi, age 10, to Connect 2-You.

Welcome, Kristi. What are you nervous about?

Kristi

Well, my family moved to a new city this summer. That means I'm starting the school year in a new building, with new teachers, and nobody around that I know. I'm really scared. What if I don't make any new friends? Who will I eat lunch with? Who's going to make sure that I get to where I need to be?

It's normal to be nervous, Kristi. Being the new kid is never easy. But don't let your fears get the best of you. The Bible tells us that God is with us no matter where we go. He will not abandon you. Trust him—he will take care of everything you need.

If you look at the Livin' It page on fear, Isaiah 43:1-2, p. 951, you'll find some tips on what the Bible has to say about overcoming your fears.

When you walk down the hall on your first day of school, remind yourself that you're not walking alone. God is right beside you. And he'll stay there every minute of the day.

27 "Although the faces of the wicked are
thick with fat,
and their bellies are fat with flesh,
28 they will live in towns that are
ruined,
in houses where no one lives,
which are crumbling into ruins.
29 The wicked will no longer get rich,
and the riches they have will not
last;
the things they own will no longer
spread over the land.
30 They will not escape the darkness.
A flame will dry up their branches;
God's breath will carry the wicked
away.
31 The wicked should not fool
themselves by
trusting what is
useless.
If they do, they will
get nothing in
return.
32 Their branches will
dry up before
they finish
growing
and will never turn
green.
33 They will be like a vine whose grapes
are pulled off before they are
ripe,
like an olive tree that loses its
blossoms.
34 People without God can produce
nothing.
Fire will destroy the tents of those
who take money to do evil,
35 who plan trouble and give birth to
evil,
whose hearts plan ways to trick
others."

I have heard many things like these. You are all painful comforters!
—Job 16:2

Job Answers Eliphaz

16 Then Job answered:

2 "I have heard many things like these.
You are all painful comforters!
3 Will your long-winded speeches
never end?
What makes you keep on arguing?
4 I also could speak as you do
if you were in my place.
I could make great speeches against
you
and shake my head at you.
5 But, instead, I would encourage you,
and my words would bring you
relief.

6 "Even if I speak, my pain is not less,
and if I don't speak, it still does not
go away.
7 God, you have surely taken away my
strength
and destroyed my whole family.
8 You have made me thin and weak,
and this shows I have done wrong.
9 God attacks me and tears me with
anger;
he grinds his teeth
at me;
my enemy stares
at me with his
angry eyes.
10 People open their
mouths to make
fun of me
and hit my cheeks
to insult me.
They join together
against me.
11 God has turned me over to evil
people
and has handed me over to the
wicked.
12 Everything was fine with me,
but God broke me into pieces;
he held me by the neck and
crushed me.
He has made me his target;
13 his archers surround me.
He stabs my kidneys without
mercy;
he spills my blood on the
ground.
14 Again and again God attacks me;
he runs at me like a soldier.

15 "I have sewed rough cloth over my
skin to show my sadness
and have buried my face in the
dust.
16 My face is red from crying;
I have dark circles around my
eyes.

17 Yet my hands have never done
anything cruel,
and my prayer is pure.

18 "Earth, please do not cover up my
blood.
Don't let my cry ever stop being
heard!
19 Even now I have one who speaks for
me in heaven;
the one who is on my side is high
above.
20 The one who speaks for me is my
friend.
My eyes pour out tears to God.
21 He begs God on behalf of a human
as a person begs for his friend.

22 "Only a few years will pass
before I go on the journey of no
return.

17 My spirit is broken;
the days of my life are almost
gone.
The grave is waiting for me.
2 Those who laugh at me surround me;
I watch them insult me.

3 "God, make me a promise.
No one will make a pledge for me.
4 You have closed their minds to
understanding.
Do not let them win over me.
5 A person might speak against his
friends for money,
but if he does, the eyes of his
children go blind.

6 "God has made my name a curse
word;
people spit in my face.
7 My sight has grown weak because of
my sadness,
and my body is as thin as a
shadow.
8 Honest people are upset about this;
innocent people are upset with
those who
do wrong.
9 But those who do
right will
continue to
do right,

17:9
Perseverance
Why should you keep doing right?

and those whose hands are not
dirty with sin will grow stronger.

10 "But, all of you, come and try again!
I do not find a wise person among
you.
11 My days are gone, and my plans have
been destroyed,
along with the desires of my heart.
12 These men think night is day;
when it is dark, they say, 'Light is
near.'
13 If the only home I hope for is the
grave,
if I spread out my bed in darkness,
14 if I say to the grave, 'You are my
father,'
and to the worm, 'You are my
mother' or 'You are my sister,'
15 where, then, is my hope?
Who can see any hope for me?
16 Will hope go down to the gates of
death?
Will we go down together into the
dust?"

Bildad Answers Job

18 Then Bildad the Shuhite answered:

2 "When will you stop these speeches?
Be sensible, and then we can talk.
3 You think of us as cattle,
as if we are stupid.
4 You tear yourself to pieces in your
anger.
Should the earth be vacant just for
you?
Should the rocks move from their
places?

5 "The lamp of the wicked will be put
out,
and the flame in their lamps will
stop burning.
6 The light in their tents will grow
dark,
and the lamps by their sides will go
out.
7 Their strong steps will grow weak;
they will fall into their own evil
traps.
8 Their feet will be caught in a net

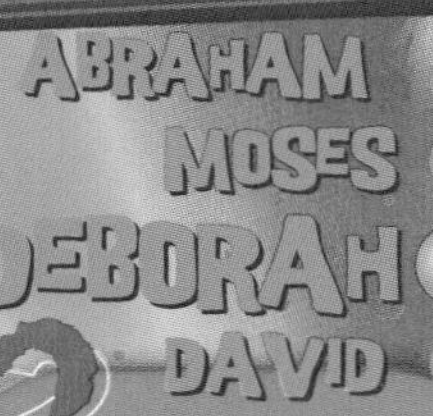

1 Are you always careful in what you say? Or do you think your words don't matter? Words mattered a lot to Deborah because of her job. She had to set a good example through her words for the people.

2 Ever have good news and bad news to tell someone? Maybe the good news is that you found your missing library book, but the bad news is that you now have an enormous fine! If you had bad news to give, would you be tempted to avoid delivering the message? Deborah had both good and bad news to give to someone else.

DEBORAH

Ready for Responsibility

When it comes to being responsible in word or deed, how would you rate on a scale of 1 to 10 (1 being not responsible at all)? Don't worry if you're not a perfect 10. For most people being responsible is challenging. As a judge in Israel, Deborah was faced with this challenge. Deborah's responsibilities included giving the people wise counsel and settling their arguments, providing rest and stability for the people, and providing leadership in times of war and turmoil. How did she rate? You can "judge" how she did by checking out

Here's the Scoop

on the following page. The numbers match numbered questions on this page.

3 What does it take to be a good leader? Do you think a good leader tells everyone else what to do? Or do you think a good leader shows everyone what to do? Part of Deborah's responsibilities included providing leadership for the Israelites.

4 Are you quick to take all of the credit when you accomplish something, or look for some congratulations? Deborah was part of a great victory. Did she take all of the credit?

5 If a friend needed help to face a bully at school or in the neighborhood, would you take up this responsibility? Would you have to consider the situation first? Would it depend on whether you thought you could win? Deborah had to make this decision.

Here's the Scoop

1

As a prophet of God, Deborah had to always watch what she said. Why? Because she told God's words to the people of Israel. She was also the only woman called to be a judge in Israel. A judge was a leader who ruled on legal cases. Deborah helped people to decide what was right. This was a position of great responsibility. But Deborah was responsible and wise. (Check out Judges 4:4–5, p. 316.)

2

Imagine having to tell someone to go to war against an army that is impossible to beat! That was the news Deborah had for Barak. He was called to lead an army against Sisera, the general of the powerful army of Canaan. But Deborah also had good news: God would help Barak and Israel to defeat their enemy. Deborah didn't worry about how Barak *might* respond to the news. She just did what God told her to do. (Read about it in Judges 4:6–7, p. 316.)

3

Deborah was the kind of leader people wanted to follow. Deborah didn't just tell the people what to do; she showed them. She took the responsibility of being a good leader very seriously. When Deborah gave the order to Barak to fight Sisera, she didn't sit safely behind the battlelines. She went with Barak to rally the troops and then she marched with the army into battle. Deborah demonstrated that her confidence was in God, not herself, and that inspired others to follow her. (Read Judges 4:6–10, p. 316.)

4

Part of being responsible means giving credit where credit is due. Deborah could have claimed the victory for defeating the Canaanites. After all, she was the leader of the Israelites; she gave the order to attack Sisera; and she agreed to accompany Barak to the battlefield, or he would not have gone. Yet Deborah didn't take the credit for winning the battle. She knew who was really behind the Israelites' victory—God! Look at her praise song to God following the battle in Judges 5, p. 316.

5

When Barak heard that God wanted him to fight the fierce Canaanite army, he did what he thought was the only sensible thing—he refused to go without Deborah! Instead of clucking like a chicken, Deborah risked being responsible and agreed to go with him. Because Barak passed the buck, a woman would give the victory "crow" later on! (Read Judges 4:15–22, p. 316.) Deborah showed that being a responsible leader means standing up for what's right, even when doing so is risky. (Look up Judges 4:8–10, p. 316.)

answers page

ABRAHAM
MOSES
DEBORAH
DAVID

DAVID

Willing to Respect

Would you say that respecting others comes easily for you? Why or why not? Sometimes the behavior of others can make respecting them a challenge! David, who was considered a man after God's own heart, understood that truth. As David learned, respect for others often requires an act of will and the help of God. Check out the challenges David faced; then turn the page to

Here's the Scoop

to discover how David earned that reputation of being a godly man. The numbers match the question numbers on this page.

1 Quick—is it easier to respect someone who treats you well or to respect someone who is not so nice to you? Do you think respecting someone depends on how that person treats you? Think about a classmate who won't let you join the kickball game at recess. How do you show that person respect? David had to show respect to a very difficult person in his life, and it wasn't always easy.

2 In what ways do you show respect for friends or family members? Do you go out of your way to show kindness to a brother or sister? Are you willing to help your friends?

3 Ever hear the phrase *Kick a man when he's down*? That means to cause further injury to someone who has already been defeated. How do you react when an "enemy" is defeated? Do you think it is OK to talk badly about an enemy?

4 When someone does something to hurt you, how do you respond? What if you were given a chance to get even with that person? David was given that opportunity.

5 Would you go out of your way to help someone whose family has been mean to you? Imagine that the family next door is mean to you. Then one day you are walking by when the youngest child of that family is hurt in a bike accident. What would you do?

Here's the Scoop

1

King Saul was jealous of David. Saul even tried to kill David. But David still showed respect for Saul. He knew that God made Saul king of Israel. By respecting Saul, David also showed respect for God. He knew that he could please God by respecting others. (Check out 1 Samuel 18:18; 19:1, 9–11, p. 380.)

2

David showed respect and love for Jonathan, Saul's son. Because they were friends, they made a promise to be loyal to each other. Part of that loyalty involved being kind to the members of each others' families. David remembered this promise throughout his life. (Read about it in 1 Samuel 18:1–4; 19:1–2; 20:14–17, 42, p. 379.)

3

It was the perfect opportunity for David to take revenge on Saul. King Saul fell asleep in the very cave where David and his men were hiding. David's own men begged him to kill Saul. After all, Saul had tried several times to kill David. But David showed respect for Saul by refusing to harm him when he had the chance. David said no to revenge and yes to respect. Would you have made the same choice? (Look up 1 Samuel 24, p. 387.)

4

David had a second chance to harm his enemy, Saul. David and one of his soldiers sneaked into Saul's camp while the king was sleeping. David's soldier volunteered to kill Saul right then and there. But David refused. David knew that he was going to the next king of Israel. (See 1 Samuel 16:1–13, p. 374.) But David did not want to push himself onto a throne that Saul still occupied. He wanted to wait for God's timing. (Read 1 Samuel 26, p. 390.)

5

In Bible times, it was a common practice for the new king to kill off the surviving members of rival families. They wanted to make sure that no one tried to take the throne away from them. But as the new king of Israel, David showed respect and love for his friend Jonathan by choosing to be kind to Jonathan's son Mephibosheth. He made sure that Mephibosheth ate at his table and was given the land that belonged to his grandfather Saul. (See 2 Samuel 9, p. 409.)

answers page

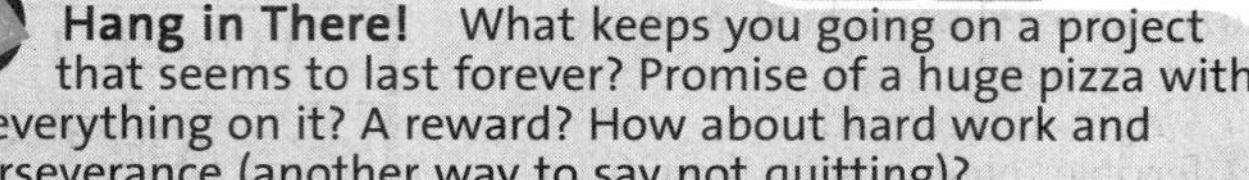

Perseverance

Job 17:9

Livin' it

Hang in There! What keeps you going on a project that seems to last forever? Promise of a huge pizza with everything on it? A reward? How about hard work and perseverance (another way to say not quitting)?

Hard work and perseverance don't seem as tasty and fun as pizza but they can help you do all sorts of things a giant pizza could never do! Both helped the Israelites rebuild the Temple. Without perseverance they wouldn't have completed such a hard, long project. (Read Ezra 6:15, p. 616.)

Two things can keep you from persevering—putting off doing something and worry. Nehemiah and the Israelites faced these things as they were rebuilding the wall, but they didn't give up. (Check Nehemiah 6, p. 631.) What project needs your perseverance? Pray for God's help, and hang in there to the end!

MORE FAITH links

Two Enemies, p. 631
Fly Like an Eagle, p. 947
Small Beginnings, p. 1255
Keep Going!, p. 1688

"I can't believe it! I worked hard all day, and I still haven't finished this huge project yet. I quit!"

"Wait a sec, Tagg. Before you quit, why don't you download some of these Faithlinks about keepin' on keepin' on! They may help you get the work done."

A Soldier's Story, 2 Timothy 2:3, p. 1653
- Think a soldier's life is easy? No way! A soldier's life is one of long marches and difficulties. It's a job that requires lots of perseverance. Sometimes Christians are called soldiers of the Lord. In what ways do you think Christians are like soldiers? How can you persevere at the Christian life?

Go for It!, Hebrews 12:1–4, p. 1682
- Do you have what it takes to be a marathon runner? Could you go the distance and do all 26 miles? Link here to see how the Christian life can be compared to a race.

While You Wait, Jude 21, p. 1726
- What events do you find the hardest to wait for? Your birthday? Christmas? Vacation? Many believers have a hard time waiting for Jesus' return to earth. How can you persevere and stick with God while you are waiting?

Keep On Keepin' On, Revelation 13:10, p. 1744
- Everyone has hard times in life. Hard times help develop perseverance. Find out about the most wonderful reward for hanging in there by linking here.

my FAVORITE links

______________ ______________

______________ ______________

______________ ______________

when they walk into its web.
9 A trap will catch them by the heel
and hold them tight.
10 A trap for them is hidden on the ground,
right in their path.
11 Terrible things startle them from every side
and chase them at every step.
12 Hunger takes away their strength,
and disaster is at their side.
13 Disease eats away parts of their skin;
death gnaws at their arms and legs.
14 They are torn from the safety of their tents
and dragged off to Death, the King of Terrors.
15 Their tents are set on fire,
and sulfur is scattered over their homes.
16 Their roots dry up below ground,
and their branches die above ground.
17 People on earth will not remember them;
their names will be forgotten in the land.
18 They will be driven from light into darkness
and chased out of the world.
19 They have no children or descendants among their people,
and no one will be left alive where they once lived.
20 People of the west will be shocked at what has happened to them,
and people of the east will be very frightened.
21 Surely this is what will happen to the wicked;
such is the place of one who does not know God."

FAITH links

LOWER THAN LOW

JOB 19:13-25

Some problems in life don't have easy answers. Job's problems made him feel miserable. All of his children had died. His livestock had been taken. Everyone made fun of him. Now his health was bad. Job was lower than low. Yet, even through the lowest times a person could face, Job still had hope in God.

We call the place where Job was "rock bottom." That means life can't get any worse than this. When you're at rock bottom, do what Job did. Look up. Remember that Jesus still cares about you.

Listen Up!, 1 Kings 19:11–13, p. 467

A Message of Courage and Hope, 2 Kings 19:4–10, p. 505

911, Psalm 28:6, p. 730

Your Full Trust, Jeremiah 22:20–22, p. 1023

Our Heavenly Connection, Matthew 6:9–13, p. 1283

Toss Those Troubles!, 1 Peter 5:7, p. 1706

Job Answers Bildad

19 Then Job answered:

2 "How long will you hurt me
and crush me with your words?
3 You have insulted me ten times now
and attacked me without shame.
4 Even if I have sinned,
it is my worry alone.
5 If you want to make yourselves look better than I,
you can blame me for my suffering.
6 Then know that God has wronged me
and pulled his net around me.

7 "I shout, 'I have been wronged!'
But I get no answer.

I scream for help
but I get no justice.
8 God has blocked my way so I cannot pass;
he has covered my paths with darkness.
9 He has taken away my honor
and removed the crown from my head.
10 He beats me down on every side
until I am gone;
he destroys my hope like a fallen tree.
11 His anger burns against me,
and he treats me like an enemy.
12 His armies gather;
they prepare to attack me.
They camp around my tent.

13 "God has made my brothers my enemies,
and my friends have become strangers.
14 My relatives have gone away,
and my friends have forgotten me.
15 My guests and my female servants
treat me like a stranger;
they look at me as if I were a foreigner.
16 I call for my servant, but he does not answer,
even when I beg him with my own mouth.
17 My wife can't stand my breath,
and my own family dislikes me.
18 Even the little boys hate me
and talk about me when I leave.
19 All my close friends hate me;
even those I love have turned against me.
20 I am nothing but skin and bones;
I have escaped by the skin of my teeth.
21 Pity me, my friends, pity me,
because the hand of God has hit me.
22 Why do you chase me as God does?
Haven't you hurt me enough?

23 "How I wish my words were written down,
written on a scroll.
24 I wish they were carved with an iron pen into lead,
or carved into stone forever.
25 I know that my Defender lives,
and in the end he will stand upon the earth.
26 Even after my skin has been destroyed,
in my flesh I will see God.
27 I will see him myself;
I will see him with my very own eyes.
How my heart wants that to happen!

28 "If you say, 'We will continue to trouble Job,
because the problem lies with him,'
29 you should be afraid of the sword yourselves.
God's anger will bring punishment by the sword.
Then you will know there is judgment."

Zophar Answers

20 Then Zophar the Naamathite answered:

2 "My troubled thoughts cause me to answer,
because I am very upset.
3 You correct me and I am insulted,
but I understand how to answer you.

4 "You know how it has been for a long time,
ever since people were first put on the earth.
5 The happiness of evil people is brief,
and the joy of the wicked lasts only a moment.
6 Their pride may be as high as the heavens,

The happiness of evil people is brief, and the joy of the wicked lasts only a moment. —Job 20:5

and their heads may touch the
clouds,
7 but they will be gone forever, like
their own dung.
People who knew them will say,
'Where are they?'
8 They will fly away like a dream
and not be found again;
they will be chased away like a
vision in the night.
9 Those who saw them will not see
them again;
the places where they lived will
see them no more.
10 Their children will have to pay back
the poor,
and they will have to give up their
wealth.
11 They had the strength of their youth
in their bones,
but it will lie with them in the dust
of death.

12 "Evil may taste sweet in their
mouths,
and they may hide it under their
tongues.
13 They cannot stand to let go of it;
they keep it in their mouths.
14 But their food will turn sour in their
stomachs,
like the poison of a snake inside
them.
15 They have swallowed riches, but
they will spit them out;
God will make them vomit their
riches up.
16 They will suck the poison of
snakes,
and the snake's fangs will kill
them.
17 They will not admire the sparkling
streams
or the rivers flowing with honey
and cream.
18 They must give back what they
worked for without eating it;
they will not enjoy the money they
made from their trading,
19 because they troubled the poor and
left them with nothing.
They have taken houses they did
not build.

20 "Evil people never lack an appetite,
and nothing escapes their
selfishness.
21 But nothing will be left for them to
eat;
their riches will not continue.
22 When they still have plenty, trouble
will catch up to them,
and great misery will come down
on them.
23 When the wicked fill their stomachs,
God will send his burning anger
against them,
and blows of punishment will fall
on them like rain.
24 The wicked may run away from an
iron weapon,
but a bronze arrow will stab them.
25 They will pull the arrows out of their
backs
and pull the points out of their
livers.
Terrors will come over them;
26 total darkness waits for their
treasure.
A fire not fanned by people will
destroy them
and burn up what is left of their
tents.
27 The heavens will show their guilt,
and the earth will rise up against
them.
28 A flood will carry their houses away,
swept away on the day of God's
anger.
29 This is what God plans for evil
people;
this is what he has decided they
will receive."

Job Answers Zophar

21 Then Job answered:

2 "Listen carefully to my words,
and let this be the way you comfort
me.
3 Be patient while I speak.
After I have finished, you may
continue to make fun of me.

4 "My complaint is not just against
people;
I have reason to be impatient.

5 Look at me and be shocked;
put your hand over your mouth in shock.
6 When I think about this, I am terribly afraid
and my body shakes.
7 Why do evil people live a long time?
They grow old and become more powerful.
8 They see their children around them;
they watch them grow up.
9 Their homes are safe and without fear;
God does not punish them.
10 Their bulls never fail to mate;
their cows have healthy calves.
11 They send out their children like a flock;
their little ones dance about.
12 They sing to the music of tambourines and harps,
and the sound of the flute makes them happy.
13 Evil people enjoy successful lives
and then go peacefully to the grave.
14 They say to God, 'Leave us alone!
We don't want to know your ways.
15 Who is the Almighty that we should serve him?
What would we gain by praying to him?'
16 The success of the wicked is not their own doing.
Their way of thinking is different from mine.
17 Yet how often are the lamps of evil people turned off?
How often does trouble come to them?
How often do they suffer God's angry punishment?
18 How often are they like straw in the wind
or like chaff that is blown away by a storm?
19 It is said, 'God saves up a person's punishment for his children.'
But God should punish the wicked themselves so they will know it.
20 Their eyes should see their own destruction,
and they should suffer the anger of the Almighty.
21 They do not care about the families they leave behind
when their lives have come to an end.

22 "No one can teach knowledge to God;
he is the one who judges
even the most important people.

eMAIL! FROM GOD 21:22
God
Is God above all others?

23 One person dies while he still has all his strength,
feeling completely safe and comfortable.
24 His body was well fed,
and his bones were strong and healthy.
25 But another person dies with an unhappy heart,
never enjoying any happiness.
26 They are buried next to each other,
and worms cover them both.

27 "I know very well your thoughts
and your plans to wrong me.
28 You ask about me, 'Where is this great man's house?
Where are the tents where the wicked live?'
29 Have you never asked those who travel?
Have you never listened to their stories?
30 On the day of God's anger and punishment,
it is the wicked who are spared.
31 Who will accuse them to their faces?
Who will pay them back for the evil they have done?
32 They are carried to their graves,
and someone keeps watch over their tombs.
33 The dirt in the valley seems sweet to them.
Everybody follows after them,
and many people go before them.

34 "So how can you comfort me with this nonsense?
Your answers are only lies!"

FAITH links

MEANINGLESS WORDS

JOB 21:34

Have you ever listened to someone talking in a foreign language? If you don't know the language, the words spoken have little meaning to you. Sometimes when we try to comfort someone who is hurting, our words may seem as meaningless as if we were speaking in a foreign language. That's the way Job felt when his friends tried to comfort him. He could find no comfort in their words.

One of the best ways to help someone who is suffering is to listen. A true listening ear is often more valuable than words.

Know how to be a good listener? Link here to find out:

Problem Solved, 2 Kings 20:1–11, p. 507

A Gentle Answer, Proverbs 15:1, p. 847

How to Worship God, Isaiah 58, p. 972

Love Him? Show It!, Amos 2:6–7, p. 1196

Help for a Friend, Mark 2:1–5, p. 1332

Kindness Counts, Acts 14:3, p. 1489

Eliphaz Answers

22 Then Eliphaz the Temanite answered:

2 "Can anyone be of real use to God?
Can even a wise person do him good?
3 Does it help the Almighty for you to be good?
Does he gain anything if you are innocent?
4 Does God punish you for respecting him?
Does he bring you into court for this?
5 No! It is because your evil is without limits
and your sins have no end.
6 You took your brothers' things for a debt they didn't owe;
you took clothes from people and left them naked.
7 You did not give water to tired people,
and you kept food from the hungry.
8 You were a powerful man who owned land;
you were honored and lived in the land.
9 But you sent widows away empty-handed,
and you mistreated orphans.
10 That is why traps are all around you
and sudden danger frightens you.
11 That is why it is so dark you cannot see
and a flood of water covers you.

12 "God is in the highest part of heaven.
See how high the highest stars are!
13 But you ask, 'What does God know?
Can he judge us through the dark clouds?
14 Thick clouds cover him so he cannot see us
as he walks around high up in the sky.'
15 Are you going to stay on the old path
where evil people walk?
16 They were carried away before their time was up,
and their foundations were washed away by a flood.
17 They said to God, 'Leave us alone!
The Almighty can do nothing to us.'

18 But it was God who filled their
houses with good things.
Their way of thinking is different
from mine.
19 "Good people can watch and be glad;
the innocent can laugh at them and
say,
20 'Surely our enemies are destroyed,
and fire burns up their wealth.'

21 "Obey God and be at peace with him;
this is the way to happiness.
22 Accept teaching from his mouth,
and keep his words in your heart.
23 If you return to the Almighty, you
will be blessed again.
So remove evil from your house.
24 Throw your gold nuggets into the
dust
and your fine gold among the rocks
in the ravines.
25 Then the Almighty will be your gold
and the best silver for you.
26 You will find pleasure in the
Almighty,
and you will look up to him.
27 You will pray to him, and he will hear
you,
and you will keep your promises to
him.
28 Anything you decide will be done,
and light will shine on your ways.
29 When people are made humble and
you say, 'Have courage,'
then the humble will be saved.
30 Even a guilty person will escape
and be saved because your hands
are clean."

Job Answers

23 Then Job answered:

2 "My complaint is still bitter today.
I groan because God's heavy hand
is on me.
3 I wish I knew where to find God
so I could go to where he lives.
4 I would present my case before him
and fill my mouth with arguments.
5 I would learn how he would answer me
and would think about what he
would say.

FAITH links

GO FOR THE GOLD

JOB 23:10

Job was confident that once God had finished testing him, he would "come out like gold." Do you know what happens to gold when it is refined? To refine something means to purify it. The impurities have to be removed from gold to make it useful. Nowadays, electrolysis or acid are two methods used to refine gold.

You're like gold to God. Throughout your life he works on you to remove the things that aren't pure in your life. Sometimes, you'll go through hard times as part of the refining process. Although this is not always easy, God promises to be with you all the way.

Check out how valuable you are to God:

Alone and Forgotten?, Genesis 40:23, p. 57

Moses' Champion, Numbers 12, p. 192

In Deep Water, Psalm 69, p. 760

Believe the Impossible?, Ezekiel 37, p. 1131

Prayer Anywhere, Mark 1:35, p. 1331

Thoughts on Thoughts, Philippians 4:8–9, p. 1614

6 Would he not argue strongly against
me?
No, he would really listen to me.

7 Then an honest person could present
his case to God,
and I would be saved forever by
my judge.

8 "If I go to the east, God is not there;
if I go to the west, I do not see
him.
9 When he is at work in the north, I
catch no sight of him;
when he turns to the south, I
cannot see him.
10 But God knows the way that I take,
and when he has tested me, I will
come out like gold.
11 My feet have closely followed his
steps;
I have stayed in his way;
I did not turn aside.
12 I have never left the commands he
has spoken;
I have treasured his words more
than my own.

13 "But he is the only God.
Who can come against him?
He does anything he wants.
14 He will do to me what he said he
would do,
and he has many plans like this.
15 That is why I am frightened of him;
when I think of this, I am afraid of
him.
16 God has made me
afraid;
the Almighty
terrifies me.
17 But I am not hidden
by the darkness,
by the thick
darkness that
covers my face.

24 "I wish the
Almighty would
set a time for
judging.
Those who know God do not see
such a day.
2 Wicked people take other people's
land;
they steal flocks and take them to
new pastures.
3 They chase away the orphan's
donkey
and take the widow's ox when she
has no money.
4 They push needy people off the path;
all the poor of the land hide from
them.
5 The poor become like wild donkeys
in the desert
who go about their job of finding
food.
The desert gives them food for
their children.
6 They gather hay and straw in the
fields
and pick up leftover grapes from
the vineyard of the wicked.
7 They spend the night naked, because
they have no clothes,
nothing to cover themselves in the
cold.
8 They are soaked from mountain rains
and stay near the large rocks
because they have no shelter.
9 The fatherless child is grabbed from
its mother's breast;
they take a poor mother's baby to
pay for what she owes.
10 So the poor go around naked without
any clothes;
they carry bundles of grain but still
go hungry;
11 they crush olives to get oil
and grapes to get
wine, but they
still go thirsty.
12 Dying people groan in
the city,
and the injured cry
out for help,
but God accuses no
one of doing
wrong.

Those who fight against the light do not know God's ways or stay in his paths.

—Job 24:13

13 "Those who fight
against the light
do not know God's ways
or stay in his paths.
14 When the day is over, the murderers
get up
to kill the poor and needy.
At night they go about like
thieves.

15 Those who are guilty of adultery
watch for the night,
thinking, 'No one will see us,'
and they keep their faces
covered.
16 In the dark, evil people break into
houses.
In the daytime they shut
themselves up in their own
houses,
because they want nothing to do
with the light.
17 Darkness is like morning to all these
evil people
who make friends with the terrors
of darkness.

18 "They are like foam floating on the
water.
Their part of the land is cursed;
no one uses the road that goes by
their vineyards.
19 As heat and dryness quickly melt the
snow,
so the grave quickly takes away
the sinners.
20 Their mothers forget them,
and worms will eat their bodies.
They will not be remembered,
so wickedness is broken in pieces
like a stick.
21 These evil people abuse women who
cannot have children
and show no kindness to
widows.
22 But God drags away the strong by his
power.
Even though they seem strong,
they do not know how long they
will live.
23 God may let these evil people feel
safe,
but he is watching their ways.
24 For a little while they are important,
and then they die;
they are laid low and buried like
everyone else;
they are cut off like the heads of
grain.
25 If this is not true, who can prove I am
wrong?
Who can show that my words are
worth nothing?"

Bildad Answers

25 Then Bildad the Shuhite answered:

2 "God rules and he must be honored;
he set up order in his high heaven.
3 No one can count God's armies.
His light shines on all people.
4 So no one can be good in the
presence of God,
and no one born to a woman can be
pure.
5 Even the moon is not bright
and the stars are not pure in his
eyes.
6 People are much
less! They
are like
insects.
They are only
worms!"

EMAIL FROM GOD 25:6
Humbleness
How do people compare to God?

Job Answers Bildad

26 Then Job answered:

2 "You are no help to the helpless!
You have not aided the weak!
3 Your advice lacks wisdom!
You have shown little
understanding!
4 Who has helped you say these
words?
And where did you get these
ideas?

5 "The spirits of the dead tremble,
those who are beneath and in the
waters.
6 Death is naked before God;
destruction is uncovered before
him.
7 God stretches the northern sky out
over empty space
and hangs the earth on nothing.
8 He wraps up the waters in his thick
clouds,
but the clouds do not break under
their weight.
9 He covers the face of the moon,
spreading his clouds over it.
10 He draws the horizon like a circle on
the water

FAITH links

COMFORT FROM THE WORD

JOB 26:3-4

Have you experienced someone trying but failing to cheer you up during a tough time? Job could relate. His friends offered him words of advice that really didn't hit the spot. When we experience tough times, true comfort often comes from God's Word. The Bible can offer comfort and refreshment to you like water does when you're thirsty. It's the ultimate thirst quencher!

The God of Big Things, Joshua 10, p. 289

God's Sure Protection, Psalm 18, p. 721

Learning to Trust, Psalm 25:4–5, p. 727

Like a Tree, Jeremiah 17:5–8, p. 1016

The Best Advice, Zechariah 10:2, p. 1261

Flex Your Faith, Acts 3:1–16, p. 1467

at the place where light and
darkness meet.
11 Heaven's foundations shake
when he thunders at them.
12 With his power he quiets the sea;
by his wisdom he destroys Rahab,
the sea monster.
13 He breathes, and the sky clears.
His hand stabs the fleeing snake.
14 And these are only a small part of
God's works.
We only hear a small whisper of
him.
Who could understand God's
thundering power?"

27 And Job continued speaking:

2 "As surely as God lives, who has
taken away my rights,
the Almighty, who has made me
unhappy,
3 as long as I am alive
and God's breath of life is in my
nose,
4 my lips will not speak evil,
and my tongue will not tell a lie.
5 I will never agree you are right;
until I die, I will never stop saying
I am innocent.
6 I will insist that I am right; I will not
back down.
My conscience will never bother
me.

7 "Let my enemies be like evil people,
my foes like those who are
wrong.
8 What hope do the wicked have when
they die,
when God takes their life away?
9 God will not listen to their cries
when trouble comes to them.
10 They will not find joy in the
Almighty,
even though they call out to God
all the time.

11 "I will teach you about the power of
God
and will not hide the ways of the
Almighty.
12 You have all seen this yourselves.
So why are we having all this talk
that means nothing?

13 "Here is what God has planned for
evil people,
and what the Almighty will give to
cruel people:
14 They may have many children, but
the sword will kill them.
Their children who are left will
never have enough to eat.

15 Then they will die of disease and be
buried,
and the widows will not even cry
for them.
16 The wicked may heap up silver like
piles of dirt
and have so many clothes they are
like piles of clay.
17 But good people will wear what evil
people have gathered,
and the innocent will divide up
their silver.
18 The houses the wicked build are like
a spider's web,
like a hut that a guard builds.
19 The wicked are rich when they go to
bed,
but they are rich for the last time;
when they open their eyes,
everything is gone.
20 Fears come over them like a flood,
and a storm snatches them away in
the night.
21 The east wind will carry them away,
and then they are gone,
because it sweeps them out of
their place.
22 The wind will hit them without
mercy
as they try to run away from its
power.
23 It will be as if the wind is clapping its
hands;
it will whistle at them as they run
from their place.

28 "There are mines where people
dig silver
and places where gold is made
pure.
2 Iron is taken from the ground,
and copper is melted out of rocks.
3 Miners bring lights
and search deep into the mines
for ore in thick darkness.
4 Miners dig a tunnel far from where
people live,
where no one has ever walked;
they work far from people,
swinging and swaying from
ropes.
5 Food grows on top of the earth,
but below ground things are
changed as if by fire.
6 Sapphires are found in rocks,
and gold dust is also found there.
7 No hawk knows that path;
the falcon has not seen it.
8 Proud animals have not walked
there,
and no lions cross over it.
9 Miners hit the rocks of flint
and dig away at the bottom of the
mountains.
10 They cut tunnels through the rock
and see all the treasures there.
11 They search for places where rivers
begin
and bring things hidden out into
the light.

12 "But where can wisdom be found,
and where does understanding
live?
13 People do not understand the value
of wisdom;
it cannot be found among those
who are alive.
14 The deep ocean says, 'It's not in me;'
the sea says, 'It's not in me.'
15 Wisdom cannot be bought with gold,
and its cost cannot be weighed in
silver.
16 Wisdom cannot be bought with fine
gold
or with valuable onyx or sapphire
gems.
17 Gold and crystal are not as valuable
as wisdom,
and you cannot buy it with jewels
of gold.
18 Coral and jasper are not worth
talking about,
and the price of wisdom is much
greater than rubies.
19 The topaz from Cush cannot compare
to wisdom;
it cannot be bought with the purest
gold.

20 "So where does wisdom come from,
and where does understanding
live?
21 It is hidden from the eyes of every
living thing,
even from the birds of the air.

22 The places of destruction and death
say,
'We have heard reports about it.'
23 Only God understands the way to
wisdom,
and he alone knows where it lives,
24 because he looks to the farthest parts
of the earth
and sees everything under the sky.
25 When God gave power to the wind
and measured the
water,
26 when he made rules
for the rain
and set a path for a
thunderstorm to
follow,
27 then he looked at
wisdom and
decided its
worth;
he set wisdom up
and tested it.
28 Then he said to humans,
'The fear of the Lord is wisdom;
to stay away from evil is
understanding.' "

Then he said to humans, "The fear of the Lord is wisdom; to stay away from evil is understanding."
—Job 28:28

Job Continues

29 Job continued to speak:
2 "How I wish for the months that
have passed
and the days when God watched
over me.
3 God's lamp shined on my head,
and I walked through darkness by
his light.
4 I wish for the days when I was
strong,
when God's close friendship
blessed my house.
5 The Almighty was still with me,
and my children were all around
me.
6 It was as if my path were covered
with cream
and the rocks poured out olive oil
for me.
7 I would go to the city gate
and sit in the public square.
8 When the young men saw me, they
would step aside,
and the old men would stand up in
respect.
9 The leading men stopped speaking
and covered their mouths with
their hands.
10 The voices of the important men
were quiet,
as if their tongues stuck to the roof
of their mouths.
11 Anyone who heard me spoke well of
me,
and those who saw
me praised me,
12 because I saved the
poor who called
out
and the orphan who
had no one to
help.
13 The dying person
blessed me,
and I made the
widow's heart
sing.
14 I put on right living as if it were
clothing;
I wore fairness like a robe and a
turban.
15 I was eyes for the blind
and feet for the lame.
16 I was like a father to needy people,
and I took the side of strangers
who were in trouble.
17 I broke the fangs of evil people
and snatched the captives from
their teeth.

18 "I thought, 'I will live for as many
days as there are grains of sand,
and I will die in my own house.
19 My roots will reach down to the water.
The dew will lie on the branches
all night.
20 New honors will come to me
continually,
and I will always have great strength.'

21 "People listened to me carefully
and waited quietly for my advice.
22 After I finished speaking, they spoke
no more.
My words fell very gently on their
ears.

HAPPINESS OR JOY?

JOB 29:18-19

Have you ever wished that everything in life would just freeze during a happy moment? That's how Job felt. Before trouble came, he had everything that he wanted. Job wished that he still felt that happiness.

Do you know the difference between happiness and joy? Happiness depends on circumstances. If everything is going great, you feel happy. But happiness doesn't last forever. Joy, on the other hand, doesn't depend on what you have. Joy comes from God. You can be joyful even when things aren't going great. Joy is more long lasting than happiness. Which would you prefer: joy or happiness?

Are you happy? Or do you have joy? Check it out at these links:

A Life of Thanksgiving, 1 Kings 1:47–48, p. 435

When Bad Things Happen, Ecclesiastes 3:16–17, p. 876

The Foundation of Our Hope, Isaiah 31:1–8, p. 934

Mission Impossible?, Mark 5:21–24, 35–43, p. 1337

Always Do This!, 1 Thessalonians 5:16–18, p. 1636

The "Quality" of Life, 2 Peter 1:5–8, p. 1708

23 They waited for me as they would for
rain
and drank in my words like spring
rain.
24 I smiled at them when they doubted,
and my approval was important to
them.
25 I chose the way for them and was
their leader.
I lived like a king among his army,
like a person who comforts sad
people.

30 "But now men who are younger
than I
make fun of me.
I would not have even let their
fathers
sit with my sheep dogs.
2 What use did I have for their
strength
since they had lost their strength
to work?
3 They were thin from hunger
and wandered the dry and ruined
land at night.
4 They gathered desert plants among
the brush
and ate the root of the broom tree.
5 They were forced to live away from
people;
people shouted at them as if they
were thieves.
6 They lived in dried up streambeds,
in caves, and among the rocks.
7 They howled like animals among the
bushes
and huddled together in the brush.
8 They are worthless people without
names
and were forced to leave the land.

9 "Now they make fun of me with
songs;
my name is a joke among them.
10 They hate me and stay far away from
me,
but they do not mind spitting in my
face.
11 God has taken away my strength and
made me suffer,
so they attack me with all their
anger.

12 On my right side they rise up like a
mob.
They lay traps for my feet
and prepare to attack me.
13 They break up my
road
and work to
destroy me,
and no one helps
me.
14 They come at me as if
through a hole in
the wall,
and they roll in
among the ruins.
15 Great fears
overwhelm me.
They blow my honor away as if by
a great wind,
and my safety disappears like a
cloud.

16 "Now my life is almost over;
my days are full of suffering.
17 At night my bones ache;
gnawing pains never stop.
18 In his great power God grabs hold of
my clothing
and chokes me with the collar of
my coat.
19 He throws me into the mud,
and I become like dirt and ashes.

20 "I cry out to you, God, but you do not
answer;
I stand up, but you just look at me.
21 You have turned on me without
mercy;
with your powerful hand you
attacked me.
22 You snatched me up and threw me
into the wind
and tossed me about in the storm.
23 I know you will bring me down to
death,
to the place where all living people
must go.

24 "Surely no one would hurt a ruined
man
when he cries for help in his time
of trouble.
25 I cried for those who were in trouble;
I have been very sad for poor
people.
26 But when I hoped for good, only evil
came to me;
when I looked for
light, darkness
came.
27 I never stop being
upset;
days of suffering
are ahead of me.
28 I have turned black,
but not by the
sun.
I stand up in public
and cry for help.
29 I have become a brother to wild
dogs
and a friend to ostriches.
30 My skin has become black and peels
off,
as my body burns with fever.
31 My harp is tuned to sing a sad song,
and my flute is tuned to moaning.

I cried for those who were in trouble; I have been very sad for poor people.
—Job 30:25

31 "But I made an agreement with
my eyes
not to look with desire at a girl.
2 What has God above promised for
people?
What has the Almighty planned
from on high?
3 It is ruin for evil people
and disaster for those who do
wrong.
4 God sees my ways
and counts every step I take.

5 "If I have been dishonest
or lied to others,
6 then let God weigh me on honest
scales.
Then he will know I have done
nothing wrong.
7 If I have turned away from doing
what is right,
or my heart has been led by my
eyes to do wrong,
or my hands have been made
unclean,
8 then let other people eat what I have
planted,
and let my crops be plowed up.

9 "If I have desired another woman
or have waited at my neighbor's
door for his wife,
10 then let my wife grind another man's
grain,
and let other men have sexual
relations with her.
11 That would be shameful,
a sin to be punished.
12 It is like a fire that burns and
destroys;
all I have done would be plowed up.

13 "If I have been unfair to my male and
female slaves
when they had a complaint against
me,
14 how could I tell
God what I
did?
What will I
answer when
he asks me
to explain what I've done?
15 God made me in my mother's womb,
and he also made them;
the same God formed both of us in
our mothers' wombs.

EMAIL! FROM GOD
31:13–14
Respect
Treat others with
respect.

16 "I have never refused the appeals of
the poor
or let widows give up hope while
looking for help.
17 I have not kept my food to myself
but have given it to the orphans.
18 Since I was young, I have been like a
father to the orphans.
From my birth I guided the
widows.
19 I have not let anyone die for lack of
clothes
or let a needy person go without a
coat.
20 That person's heart blessed me,
because I warmed him with the
wool of my sheep.
21 I have never hurt an orphan
even when I knew I could win in
court.
22 If I have, then let my arm fall off my
shoulder
and be broken at the joint.
23 I fear destruction from God,
and I fear his majesty, so I could
not do such things.

24 "I have not put my trust in gold
or said to pure gold, 'You are my
security.'
25 I have not celebrated my great
wealth
or the riches my hands had gained.
26 I have not thought about worshiping
the sun in its brightness
nor admired the moon moving in
glory
27 so that my heart was pulled away
from God.
My hand has never offered the sun
and moon a kiss of worship.
28 If I had, these also would have been
sins to be punished,
because I would have been
unfaithful to God.

29 "I have not been happy when my
enemy fell
or laughed when he had trouble.
30 I have not let my mouth sin
by cursing my enemy's life.
31 The men of my house have always
said,
'Everyone has eaten all he wants
of Job's food.'
32 No stranger ever had to spend the
night in the street,
because I always let travelers stay
in my home.
33 I have not hidden my sin as others
do,
secretly keeping my guilt to
myself.
34 I was not so afraid of the crowd
that I kept quiet and stayed inside
because I feared being hated by
other families.

35 ("How I wish a court would hear my
case!
Here I sign my name to show I
have told the truth.
Now let the Almighty answer me;
let the one who accuses me write
it down.
36 I would wear the writing on my
shoulder;

RESPECTING OTHERS

Job 31:13–14

Just a Little Respect Do you bow or give a snappy salute when you meet your family members or friends? Probably not. But if you were in the army, you would do a lot of saluting. And if you were presented to the queen of England, you would bow or curtsy. These are special ways of showing respect. But there are other ways of showing respect to people. How do you show respect to your family? To older people?

God wants us to respect him and the people he places in our life. David's soldiers risked their lives out of respect for him. (Read 1 Chronicles 11:10–19, p. 534.) You may never have to risk your life for someone to show them respect, but think of the leaders in your life: teachers, scout masters, pastors, and so on. Do you listen to them when they speak? Do you answer them politely? What would you do to show respect for them?

MORE FAITH links

Show Some Respect, p. 161

Take Me to Your Leader, p. 214

In Your Best Interests, p. 349

Just a Little Respect, p. 534

Who's on First?, p. 1723

"Tagg! What's with the trumpet and the confetti?"

"I wanted to give our newbies a little fanfare when they arrive!"

"I guess that's one way to show our friends respect. Why don't you log on to these Faithlinks for some other ways to show respect?"

Fairness for All, Deuteronomy 24:17, p. 258

- What if someone passed out treats to you and your friends, but gave you the least? Would you feel the person had respect for you? Treating people fairly is one way to show respect for others. Link here to find out more.

Fair All the Time?, 2 Samuel 8:15, p. 408

- Do you show the same respect to everyone and treat everyone the same way? Check out this link to find out about King David's treatment of others.

The Verdict Is In?, Matthew 7:1–2, p. 1285

- Do you make judgments about others? Are you always right in your opinion? This Faithlink tells you what Jesus taught about judging others.

Best Seat in the House, Luke 14:7–11, p. 1398

- Suppose you and a friend were invited to a party for a famous person. There is only one seat next to this person. Would you sit there or let your friend have the seat? Jesus teaches us to be humble—not try to make ourselves important. How does being humble show respect for others?

my FAVORITE links

______ ______

______ ______

______ ______

I would put it on like a crown.
37 I would explain to God every step I took,
and I would come near to him like a prince.)

38 "If my land cries out against me
and its plowed rows are not wet with tears,
39 if I have taken the land's harvest without paying
or have broken the spirit of those who worked the land,
40 then let thorns come up instead of wheat,
and let weeds come up instead of barley."

The words of Job are finished.

Elihu Speaks

32 These three men stopped trying to
answer Job, because he was so
sure he was right. 2 But Elihu son of Bar-
akel the Buzite, from the family of Ram,
became very angry with Job, because Job
claimed he was right instead of God. 3 Elihu was also angry with Job's three
friends who had no an-
swer to show that Job
was wrong, yet continued
to blame him. 4 Elihu had
waited before speaking to
Job, because the three
friends were older than
he was. 5 But when Elihu
saw that the three men
had nothing more to say,
he became very angry.
6 So Elihu son of Bara-
kel the Buzite said this:

> But it is the spirit in a person, the breath of the Almighty, that gives understanding.
> —Job 32:8

"I am young,
and you are old.
That is why I was afraid
to tell you what I know.
7 I thought, 'Older people should speak,
and those who have lived many years should teach wisdom.'
8 But it is the spirit in a person,
the breath of the Almighty, that gives understanding.
9 It is not just older people who are wise;
they are not the only ones who understand what is right.
10 So I say, listen to me.
I too will tell you what I know.
11 I waited while you three spoke,
and listened to your explanations.
While you looked for words to use,
12 I paid close attention to you.
But not one of you has proved Job wrong;
none of you has answered his arguments.
13 Don't say, 'We have found wisdom;
only God will show Job to be wrong, not people.'
14 Job has not spoken his words against me,
so I will not use your arguments to answer Job.

15 "These three friends are defeated
and have no more to say;
words have failed them.
16 Now they are standing there with no answers for Job.
Now that they are quiet, must I wait to speak?
17 No, I too will speak and tell what I know.
18 I am full of words,
and the spirit in me causes me to speak.
19 I am like wine that has been bottled up;
I am ready to burst like a new leather wine bag.
20 I must speak so I will feel relief;
I must open my mouth and answer.
21 I will be fair to everyone
and not flatter anyone.
22 I don't know how to flatter,
and if I did, my Maker would quickly take me away.

33 "Now, Job, listen to my words.
Pay attention to everything I say.
2 I open my mouth

and am ready to speak.
3 My words come from an honest heart,
and I am sincere in saying what I know.
4 The Spirit of God created me,
and the breath of the Almighty gave me life.
5 Answer me if you can;
get yourself ready and stand before me.
6 I am just like you before God;
I too am made out of clay.

FAITH links

HOW GOD SPEAKS

JOB 33:14-17

Ever wonder how God speaks to a person? Elihu, one of Job's friends, told Job about the different ways God used to speak to people. God still speaks to people today, although we don't always recognize his voice. He speaks to you through the Bible, through the Holy Spirit, and through the people he puts in your life. You have to learn to listen for his voice.

Help to Understand, 2 Samuel 14, p. 416

Deciding Wisely, 1 Kings 3:16–28, p. 440

Teaching Others, Ezra 7:8–10, p. 617

The Bible: Good for Your Faith, Psalm 119, p. 802

Heavenly Treasure, Luke 12:32–34, p. 1394

Pay Attention!, Hebrews 2:1, p. 1668

7 Don't be afraid of me;
I will not be hard on you.

8 "But I heard what you have said;
I heard every word.
9 You said, 'I am pure and without sin;
I am innocent and free from guilt.
10 But God has found fault with me;
he considers me his enemy.
11 He locks my feet in chains
and closely watches everywhere I go.'

12 "But I tell you, you are not right in saying this,
because God is greater than we are.
13 Why do you accuse God
of not answering anyone?
14 God does speak—sometimes one way and sometimes another—
even though people may not understand it.
15 He speaks in a dream or a vision of the night
when people are in a deep sleep,
lying on their beds.
16 He speaks in their ears
and frightens them with warnings
17 to turn them away from doing wrong
and to keep them from being proud.
18 God does this to save a person from death,
to keep him from dying.
19 A person may be corrected while in bed in great pain;
he may have continual pain in his very bones.
20 He may be in such pain that he even hates food,
even the very best meal.
21 His body becomes so thin there is almost nothing left of it,
and his bones that were hidden now stick out.
22 He is near death,
and his life is almost over.

23 "But there may be an angel to speak for him,
one out of a thousand, who will tell him what to do.

24 The angel will beg for mercy and say:
'Save him from death.
I have found a way to pay for his life.'
25 Then his body is made new like a child's.
It will return to the way it was when he was young.
26 That person will pray to God, and God will listen to him.
He will see God's face and will shout with happiness.
And God will set things right for him again.
27 Then he will say to others,
'I sinned and twisted what was right,
but I did not receive the punishment I should have received.
28 God bought my life back from death,
and I will continue to enjoy life.'

29 "God does all these things to a person
two or even three times
30 so he won't die as punishment for his sins
and so he may still enjoy life.

31 "Job, pay attention and listen to me;
be quiet, and I will speak.
32 If you have anything to say, answer me;
speak up, because I want to prove you right.
33 But if you have nothing to say, then listen to me;
be quiet, and I will teach you wisdom."

34

Then Elihu said:

2 "Hear my words, you wise men;
listen to me, you who know a lot.
3 The ear tests words
as the tongue tastes food.
4 Let's decide for ourselves what is right,
and let's learn together what is good.

5 "Job says, 'I am not guilty,
and God has refused me a fair trial.
6 Instead of getting a fair trial,
I am called a liar.
I have been seriously hurt,
even though I have not sinned.'
7 There is no other man like Job;
he takes insults as if he were drinking water.
8 He keeps company with those who do evil
and spends time with wicked men,
9 because he says, 'It is no use
to try to please God.'

10 "So listen to me, you who can understand.
God can never do wrong!
It is impossible for the Almighty to do evil.
11 God pays a person back for what he has done
and gives him what his actions deserve.
12 Truly God will never do wrong;
the Almighty will never twist what is right.
13 No one chose God to rule over the earth
or put him in charge of the whole world.
14 If God should decide
to take away life and breath,
15 then everyone would die together
and turn back into dust.

16 "If you can understand, hear this;
listen to what I have to say.
17 Can anyone govern who hates what is right?
How can you blame God who is both fair and powerful?
18 God is the one who says to kings,
'You are worthless,'
or to important people, 'You are evil.'
19 He is not nicer to princes than other people,
nor kinder to rich people than poor people,
because he made them all with his own hands.
20 They can die in a moment, in the middle of the night.

They are struck down, and then
they pass away;
powerful people die without help.

21 "God watches where people go;
he sees every step
they take.
22 There is no dark place
or deep shadow
where those who
do evil can hide
from him.
23 He does not set a
time
for people to come
before him for
judging.
24 Without asking questions, God
breaks powerful people into
pieces
and puts others in their place.
25 Because God knows what people do,
he defeats them in the night, and
they are crushed.
26 He punishes them for the evil they
do
so that everyone else can watch,
27 because they stopped following God
and did not care about any of his
ways.
28 The cry of the poor comes to God;
he hears the cry of the needy.
29 But if God keeps quiet, who can
blame him?
If he hides his face, who can see
him?
God still rules over both nations and
persons alike.
30 He keeps the wicked from ruling
and from trapping others.

31 "But suppose someone says to
God,
'I am guilty, but I will not sin
anymore.
32 Teach me what I cannot see.
If I have done wrong, I will not do
it again.'
33 So, Job, should God reward you as
you want
when you refuse to change?
You must decide, not I,
so tell me what you know.

God watches where people go; he sees every step they take.
—Job 34:21

34 "Those who understand speak,
and the wise who hear me say,
35 'Job speaks without knowing what is
true;
his words show he does not
understand.'
36 I wish Job would be
tested completely,
because he
answered like an
evil man!
37 Job now adds to his
sin by turning
against God.
He claps his hands
in protest,
speaking more and
more against God."

35 Then Elihu said:

2 "Do you think this is fair?
You say, 'God will show that I am
right,'
3 but you also ask, 'What's the use?
I don't gain anything by not
sinning.'

4 "I will answer you
and your friends who are with you.
5 Look up at the sky
and see the clouds so high above
you.
6 If you sin, it does nothing to God;
even if your sins are many, they do
nothing to him.
7 If you are good, you give nothing to
God;
he receives nothing from your hand.
8 Your evil ways only hurt a man like
yourself,
and the good you do only helps
other human beings.

9 "People cry out when they are in
trouble;
they beg for relief from powerful
people.
10 But no one asks, 'Where is God, my
Maker,
who gives us songs in the night,
11 who makes us smarter than the
animals of the earth

and wiser than the birds of the
air?'
12 God does not answer evil people
when they cry out,
because the wicked are proud.
13 God does not listen to their useless
begging;
the Almighty pays no attention to
them.
14 He will listen to you even less
when you say that you do not see
him,
that your case is before him,
that you must wait for him,
15 that his anger never punishes,
and that he doesn't notice evil.
16 So Job is only speaking nonsense,
saying many words without
knowing what is true."

Elihu's Speech Continues

36 Elihu continued:

2 "Listen to me a little longer, and I
will show you
that there is more to be said for
God.
3 What I know comes from far away.
I will show that my Maker is
right.
4 You can be sure that my words are
not false;
one who really knows is with you.

5 "God is powerful, but he does not
hate people;
he is powerful and sure of what he
wants to do.
6 He will not keep evil people alive,
but he gives the poor their rights.
7 He always watches over those who
do right;
he sets them on thrones with
kings
and they are honored forever.
8 If people are bound in chains,
or if trouble, like ropes, ties them
up,
9 God tells them what they have done,
that they have sinned in their
pride.
10 God makes them listen to his
warning
and commands them to change
from doing evil.
11 If they obey and serve him,

FAITH links

NO DOUBT ABOUT IT

JOB 36:5

Think about the things you're certain that you know—no doubts cross your mind at all. You're certain about what your name is and where you live. (You *are* sure of that, right?) You're sure that your parents love you. You can be sure of something else: God cares. One of Job's friends talked to Job about God. He told Job that God was all-powerful, but still cared about everyone. No matter what happens in your life, you can be sure that God cares about you. Since he's all-powerful, he can help you through the toughest problems you will ever face. No doubt about it.

Here are some more Faithlinks on God's care for you:

Good Plans, Genesis 45:7–8, p. 64

What God Thinks, Isaiah 55:8–9, p. 969

A Tight Spot, Jonah 2, p. 1215

Your Feet on High Places, Habakkuk 3:18–19, p. 1239

But I Want It?, Philippians 4:19, p. 1615

A Happy Ending, Revelation 22:16–21, p. 1754

the rest of their lives will be
successful,
and the rest of their years will be
happy.
12 But if they do not listen,
they will die by the sword,
and they will die without knowing
why.

13 "Those who have wicked hearts hold
on to anger.
Even when God punishes them,
they do not cry for help.
14 They die while they are still young,
and their lives end in disgrace.
15 But God saves those who suffer
through their suffering;
he gets them to listen through
their pain.

16 "God is gently calling you from the
jaws of trouble
to an open place of freedom
where he has set your table full of
the best food.
17 But now you are being punished like
the wicked;
you are getting justice.
18 Be careful! Don't be led away from
God by riches;
don't let much money turn you away.
19 Neither your wealth nor all your
great strength
will keep you out of trouble.
20 Don't wish for the night
when people are taken from their
homes.
21 Be careful not to turn to evil,
which you seem to want more than
suffering.

22 "God is great and powerful;
no other teacher is like him.
23 No one has planned his ways for him;
no one can say to God, 'You have
done wrong.'
24 Remember to praise his work,
about which people have sung.
25 Everybody has seen it;
people look at it from far off.
26 God is so great, greater than we can
understand!
No one knows how old he is.

27 "He evaporates the drops of water
from the earth
and turns them into rain.
28 The rain then pours down from the
clouds,
and showers fall on people.
29 No one understands how God
spreads out the clouds
or how he sends thunder from
where he lives.
30 Watch how God scatters his lightning
around him,
lighting up the deepest parts of the
sea.
31 This is the way God governs the
nations;
this is how he gives us enough
food.
32 God fills his hands with lightning
and commands it to strike its
target.
33 His thunder announces the coming
storm,
and even the cattle know it is near.

37 "At the sound of his thunder, my
heart pounds
as if it will jump out of my chest.
2 Listen! Listen to the thunder of
God's voice
and to the rumbling that comes
from his mouth.
3 He turns his lightning loose under
the whole sky
and sends it to the farthest parts of
the earth.
4 After that you can hear the roar
when he thunders with a great
sound.
He does not hold back the flashing
when his voice is heard.
5 God's voice thunders in wonderful
ways;
he does great things we cannot
understand.
6 He says to the snow, 'Fall on the
earth,'
and to the shower, 'Be a heavy
rain.'
7 With it, he stops everyone from
working
so everyone knows it is the work
of God.

8 The animals take cover from the rain
and stay in their dens.
9 The storm comes from where it was
stored;
the cold comes with the strong
winds.
10 The breath of God makes ice,
and the wide waters become
frozen.
11 He fills the clouds with water
and scatters his lightning through
them.
12 At his command they swirl around
over the whole earth,
doing whatever he commands.

FAITH CHALLENGE

Got another challenge for you. Read 37:14 to discover the good advice Job got from one of his friends. What's the most amazing thing you've ever seen God do in your life or in the life of someone you know?

TESTING IT

Job 37:14
Job, listen to this: Stop and notice God's miracles.

13 He uses the clouds to punish people
or to water his earth and show his
love.

14 "Job, listen to this:
Stop and notice God's miracles.
15 Do you know how God controls the
clouds
and makes his lightning flash?
16 Do you know how the clouds hang in
the sky?
Do you know the miracles of God,
who knows everything?
17 You suffer in your clothes
when the land is silenced by the
hot, south wind.
18 You cannot stretch out the sky like
God
and make it look as hard as
polished bronze.
19 Tell us what we should say to him;
we cannot get our arguments
ready because we do not have
enough understanding.
20 Should God be told that I want to
speak?
Would a person ask to be
swallowed up?
21 No one can look at the sun
when it is bright in the sky
after the wind has blown all the
clouds away.
22 God comes out of the north in golden
light,
in overwhelming greatness.
23 The Almighty is too high for us to
reach.
He has great strength;
he is always right and never
punishes unfairly.
24 That is why people honor him;
he does not respect those who say
they are wise."

The Lord Questions Job

38 Then the LORD answered Job from
the storm. He said:
2 "Who is this that makes my purpose
unclear
by saying things that are not true?
3 Be strong like a man!
I will ask you questions,
and you must answer me.

4 Where were you when I made the earth's foundation?
Tell me, if you understand.
5 Who marked off how big it should be?
Surely you know!
Who stretched a ruler across it?
6 What were the earth's foundations set on,
or who put its cornerstone in place
7 while the morning stars sang together
and all the angels shouted with joy?

8 "Who shut the doors to keep the sea in
when it broke through and was born,
9 when I made the clouds like a coat for the sea
and wrapped it in dark clouds,
10 when I put limits on the sea
and put its doors and bars in place,
11 when I said to the sea, 'You may come this far, but no farther;
this is where your proud waves must stop'?

12 "Have you ever ordered the morning to begin,
or shown the dawn where its place was
13 in order to take hold of the earth by its edges
and shake evil people out of it?
14 At dawn the earth changes like clay being pressed by a seal;
the hills and valleys stand out like folds in a coat.
15 Light is not given to evil people;
their arm is raised to do harm, but it is broken.

16 "Have you ever gone to where the sea begins
or walked in the valleys under the sea?
17 Have the gates of death been opened to you?
Have you seen the gates of the deep darkness?
18 Do you understand how wide the earth is?
Tell me, if you know all these things.

19 "What is the path to light's home,
and where does darkness live?
20 Can you take them to their places?
Do you know the way to their homes?
21 Surely you know, if you were already born when all this happened!
Have you lived that many years?

22 "Have you ever gone into the storehouse of the snow
or seen the storehouses for hail,
23 which I save for times of trouble,
for days of war and battle?
24 Where is the place from which light comes?
Where is the place from which the east winds blow over the earth?
25 Who cuts a waterway for the heavy rains
and sets a path for the thunderstorm?
26 Who waters the land where no one lives,
the desert that has no one in it?
27 Who sends rain to satisfy the empty land
so the grass begins to grow?
28 Does the rain have a father?
Who is father to the drops of dew?
29 Who is the mother of the ice?
Who gives birth to the frost from the sky
30 when the water becomes hard as stone,
and even the surface of the ocean is frozen?

31 "Can you tie up the stars of the Pleiades
or loosen the ropes of the stars in Orion?
32 Can you bring out the stars on time
or lead out the stars of the Bear with its cubs?
33 Do you know the laws of the sky
and understand their rule over the earth?

HOW BIG IS GOD?

JOB 38–41

Want to know how big God is? When God answered Job's prayer for understanding about his situation, God told him how big he was. God was big enough to create the world and everything in it and big enough to order the stars in the sky. That information made Job feel small.

God is in control of everything. He's big, yet loving. When we begin to understand how much we don't know about God, we begin to understand how awesome he is.

Think God can't handle your problems? Check it out again at these links:

Your Heavenly Dad, Psalm 103:13, p. 786

Our Awesome God, Ezekiel 1:26–28, p. 1087

A Love Song, Zephaniah 3:17, p. 1246

The Best Protection Plan, Matthew 2:13–18, p. 1276

Who Needs Love?, Luke 6:27–36, p. 1379

Hope That Doesn't Fail, Acts 26:4–7, p. 1510

34 "Can you shout an order to the clouds
and cover yourself with a flood of water?
35 Can you send lightning bolts on their way?
Do they come to you and say, 'Here we are'?
36 Who put wisdom inside the mind
or understanding in the heart?
37 Who has the wisdom to count the clouds?
Who can pour water from the jars of the sky
38 when the dust becomes hard
and the clumps of dirt stick together?

39 "Do you hunt food for the female lion
to satisfy the hunger of the young lions
40 while they lie in their dens
or hide in the bushes waiting to attack?
41 Who gives food to the birds
when their young cry out to God
and wander about without food?

39 "Do you know when the mountain goats give birth?
Do you watch when the deer gives birth to her fawn?
2 Do you count the months until they give birth
and know the right time for them to give birth?
3 They lie down, their young are born,
and then the pain of giving birth is over.
4 Their young ones grow big and strong in the wild country.
Then they leave their homes and do not return.

5 "Who let the wild donkey go free?
Who untied its ropes?
6 I am the one who gave the donkey the desert as its home;
I gave it the desert lands as a place to live.
7 The wild donkey laughs at the confusion in the city,
and it does not hear the drivers shout.
8 It roams the hills looking for pasture,
looking for anything green to eat.

9 "Will the wild ox agree to serve you
and stay by your feeding box at
night?
10 Can you hold it to the plowed row
with a harness
so it will plow the valleys for you?
11 Will you depend on the wild ox for its
great strength
and leave your heavy work for it to
do?
12 Can you trust the ox to bring in your
grain
and gather it to your threshing
floor?

13 "The wings of the ostrich flap
happily,
but they are not like the feathers of
the stork.
14 The ostrich lays its
eggs on the
ground
and lets them warm
in the sand.
15 It does not stop to
think that a foot
might step on
them and crush
them;
it does not care that
some animal
might walk on
them.
16 The ostrich is cruel to its young, as if
they were not even its own.
It does not care that its work is for
nothing,
17 because God did not give the ostrich
wisdom;
God did not give it a share of good
sense.
18 But when the ostrich gets up to run,
it is so fast
that it laughs at the horse and its
rider.

19 "Job, are you the one who gives the
horse its strength
or puts a flowing mane on its neck?
20 Do you make the horse jump like a
locust?
It scares people with its proud
snorting.
21 It paws wildly, enjoying its strength,
and charges into battle.
22 It laughs at fear and is afraid of
nothing;
it does not run away from the
sword.
23 The bag of arrows rattles against the
horse's side,
along with the flashing spears and
swords.
24 With great excitement, the horse
races over the ground;
and it cannot stand still when it
hears the trumpet.
25 When the trumpet blows, the horse
snorts, 'Aha!'
It smells the battle from far away;
it hears the shouts of commanders
and the battle cry.

Is it through your wisdom that the hawk flies and spreads its wings toward the south?
—Job 39:26

26 "Is it through your
wisdom that the
hawk flies
and spreads its
wings toward the
south?
27 Are you the one that
commands the
eagle to fly
and build its nest
so high?
28 It lives on a high cliff and stays there
at night;
the rocky peak is its protected
place.
29 From there it looks for its food;
its eyes can see it from far away.
30 Its young eat blood,
and where there is something
dead, the eagle is there."

40 The LORD said to Job:
2 "Will the person who argues
with the Almighty correct him?
Let the person
who accuses
God answer
him."

eMAIL! FROM GOD 40:2
God
Can you correct God?

3 Then Job an-
swered the LORD:
4 "I am not worthy; I cannot answer
you anything,

so I will put my hand over my
mouth.
5 I spoke one time, but I will not
answer again;
I even spoke two times, but I will
say nothing more."

6 Then the LORD spoke to Job from the
storm:
7 "Be strong, like a man!
I will ask you questions,
and you must answer me.
8 Would you say that I am unfair?
Would you blame me to make
yourself look right?
9 Are you as strong as God?
Can your voice thunder like his?
10 If so, then decorate yourself with
glory and beauty;
dress in honor and greatness as if
they were clothing.
11 Let your great anger punish;
look at the proud and bring them
down.
12 Look at the proud and make them
humble.
Crush the wicked
wherever they
are.
13 Bury them all in the
dirt together;
cover their faces in
the grave.
14 If you can do that,
then I myself will
praise you,
because you are
strong enough to
save yourself.

15 "Look at the behemoth,[n]
which I made just as I made you.
It eats grass like an ox.
16 Look at the strength it has in its
body;
the muscles of its stomach are
powerful.
17 Its tail is like a cedar tree;
the muscles of its thighs are
woven together.
18 Its bones are like tubes of bronze;
its legs are like bars of iron.
19 It is one of the first of God's works,
but its Maker can destroy it.
20 The hills, where the wild animals
play,
provide food for it.
21 It lies under the lotus plants,
hidden by the tall grass in the
swamp.
22 The lotus plants hide it in their
shadow;
the poplar trees by the streams
surround it.
23 If the river floods, it will not be
afraid;
it is safe even if the Jordan River
rushes to its mouth.
24 Can anyone blind its eyes and
capture it?
Can anyone put hooks in its nose?

41 "Can you catch the leviathan[n] on
a fish hook
or tie its tongue down with a rope?
2 Can you put a cord through its nose
or a hook in its jaw?
3 Will it keep begging you for mercy
and speak to you with gentle
words?
4 Will it make an
agreement with
you
and let you take it as
your slave for life?
5 Can you make a pet of
the leviathan as
you would a bird
or put it on a leash
for your girls?
6 Will traders try to
bargain with you
for it?
Will they divide it up among the
merchants?
7 Can you stick darts all over its skin
or fill its head with fishing spears?
8 If you put one hand on it,
you will never forget the battle,
and you will never do it again!
9 There is no hope of defeating it;

Can you catch the leviathan on a fish hook or tie its tongue down with a rope?
—Job 41:1

40:15 behemoth A large land animal. It could refer to the hippopotamus, the elephant, or a monster.

41:1 leviathan Possibly a crocodile or a sea monster.

just seeing it overwhelms people.
10 No one is brave enough to make it angry,
so who would be able to stand up against me?
11 No one has ever given me anything that I must pay back,
because everything under the sky belongs to me.

12 "I will speak about Leviathan's arms and legs,
its great strength and well-formed body.
13 No one can tear off its outer hide
or poke through its double armor.
14 No one can force open its great jaws;
they are filled with frightening teeth.
15 It has rows of shields on its back
that are tightly sealed together.
16 Each shield is so close to the next one
that no air can go between them.
17 They are joined strongly to one another;
they hold on to each other and cannot be separated.
18 When it snorts, flashes of light are thrown out,
and its eyes look like the light at dawn.
19 Flames blaze from its mouth;
sparks of fire shoot out.
20 Smoke pours out of its nose,
as if coming from a large pot over a hot fire.
21 Its breath sets coals on fire,
and flames come out of its mouth.
22 There is great strength in its neck.
People are afraid and run away.
23 The folds of its skin are tightly joined;
they are set and cannot be moved.
24 Its chest is as hard as a rock,
even as hard as a grinding stone.
25 The powerful fear its terrible looks
and draw back in fear as it moves.
26 The sword that hits it does not hurt it,
nor the arrows, darts, and spears.
27 It treats iron as if it were straw
and bronze metal as if it were rotten wood.
28 It does not run away from arrows;

FAITH links

FULL CIRCLE

JOB 42

Picture in your mind a skater gracefully spinning in a circle. When someone is said to do a 360, that means she has turned around in a complete circle. She's right back where she started from. That's also known as "coming full circle." Job did a 360 after having a talk with God. He realized that since God knew everything, he could put his whole trust in God. After that, God gave him a new family and restored his wealth. Job had come full circle.

If you're having a hard time right now, you might wonder when you'll ever "come to full circle." God waits for you to put your full trust in him, just as Job did.

Our Thorough God, Leviticus 13, p. 149

A Long Wait, Joshua 14:6–15, p. 294

Fly Like an Eagle, Isaiah 40:28–31, p. 947

Future Hope, Joel 3:17–21, p. 1191

It's Under Control, Romans 8:28, p. 1529

Keep On Keepin' On, Revelation 13:10, p. 1744

stones from slings are like chaff
to it.
29 Clubs feel like pieces of straw to it,
and it laughs when they shake a
spear at it.
30 The underside of its body is like
broken pieces of pottery.
It leaves a trail in the mud like a
threshing board.
31 It makes the deep sea bubble like a
boiling pot;
it stirs up the sea like a pot of oil.
32 When it swims, it leaves a shining
path in the water
that makes the sea look as if it had
white hair.
33 Nothing else on earth is equal to it;
it is a creature without fear.
34 It looks down on all those who are
too proud;
it is king over all proud
creatures."

Job Answers the Lord

42 Then Job answered the LORD:
2"I know that you can do all
things
and that no plan of yours can be
ruined.
3 You asked, 'Who is this that made my
purpose unclear by saying things
that are not true?'
Surely I spoke of things I did not
understand;
I talked of things too wonderful for
me to know.
4 You said, 'Listen now, and I will
speak.
I will ask you questions,
and you must answer me.'
5 My ears had heard of you before,
but now my eyes have seen you.
6 So now I hate myself;
I will change my heart and life.
I will sit in the dust and ashes."

End of the Story

7After the LORD had said these things
to Job, he said to Eliphaz the Temanite, "I
am angry with you and your two friends,
because you have not said what is right
about me, as my servant Job did. 8Now
take seven bulls and seven male sheep,
and go to my servant Job, and offer a
burnt offering for yourselves. My servant
Job will pray for you, and I will listen to
his prayer. Then I will not punish you for
being foolish. You have not said what is
right about me, as my servant Job did."
9So Eliphaz the Temanite, Bildad the
Shuhite, and Zophar the Naamathite did
as the LORD said, and the LORD listened
to Job's prayer.

10After Job had prayed for his friends,
the LORD gave him success again. The
LORD gave Job twice as much as he had
owned before. 11Job's brothers and sisters came to his house, along with everyone who had known him before, and they
all ate with him there. They comforted
him and made him feel better about the
trouble the LORD had brought on him,
and each one gave Job a piece of silver
and a gold ring.

12The LORD blessed the last part of
Job's life even more than the first part. Job
had fourteen thousand sheep, six thousand camels, a thousand teams of oxen,
and a thousand female donkeys. 13Job also
had seven sons and three daughters.
14He named the first daughter Jemimah,
the second daughter Keziah, and the third
daughter Keren-Happuch. 15There were
no other women in all the land as beautiful
as Job's daughters. And their father Job
gave them land to own along with their
brothers.

16After this, Job lived one hundred
forty years. He lived to see his children,
grandchildren, great-grandchildren, and
great-great-grandchildren. 17Then Job
died; he was old and had lived many years.

SONGS OF PRAISE

Hello! Do you remember me, David, the shepherd boy who became the king of the great nation of Israel? My days of watching sheep inspired me to write my most famous song—The Lord is my shepherd, Psalm 23. Maybe you've heard of it? Over the years I wrote many songs. Check out the MIDI on Psalm 19 for my song praising God for his wonderful creation and his perfect law. Do you want to worship God in a special way? Try writing your own song of praise!

The Book of Psalms is a book of songs written to praise God. I was not the only author of Psalms. Asaph and the sons of Korah, our chief musicians, also wrote many psalms to use in the Temple. Check out Psalm 136. The leader praises God in the first part of each verse; and the people sing, "His love continues forever." Try reading this psalm out loud with your family or friends. You can be the leader!

JESUS WATCH

We can see Jesus, the promised Messiah, in many of the psalms. In some psalms the words are true for the writer, but are truer of the life of Jesus. David wrote Psalm 22 when he was hiding from his enemies. The words that describe David's trouble also give us a picture of Jesus' death on the cross. Evil people made fun of David and took his clothes. Like dogs, they trapped him and bit his arms and legs. Compare this psalm to Matthew 27, p. 1324. The soldiers who arrested Jesus made fun of him and gambled for his clothes. They nailed his hands and feet to the cross and put him in a public place so people could stare at him. Jesus knew that this psalm was written about him. He quoted the first verse just before he died: "My God, my God, why have you rejected me?" (Psalm 22:1). Other psalms, like Psalms 96—99, describe Jesus as our king who will rule forever in heaven. Worship him because he is holy! Sing praise to him for he rules in glory and majesty! Turn to these psalms for other reasons to praise Jesus.

my FAVORITE links

OTHER CONNECTIONS

Livin' it

Think it's OK to tell a little fib now and then? Find out what God has to say about being honest by connecting to Hangin' with God, Psalm 15.

Who is it in your life that you totally trust with your deepest secrets? Your parents? Maybe your best friend? Discover who you can entrust everything to by checking out Trustometer, Psalm 56.

What's the first thing you do when you're feeling down, or you've just aced the history final, or your mom is sick in the hospital? Does prayer come to mind? Learn more about this important lifeline to God by checking out No Answering Machine, Psalm 86:1–7.

Quick! What's the most precious thing you own? While you're thinking, surf over to A Burning Lamp, Psalm 119:12–18, to discover what the psalmist has to say about it.

Check out these information bulletin boards:

- Jerusalem was the center of Israel's worship life and its government. It was an important center for Jesus' ministry and today is a holy city for three different religions. Find out more by linking to Let's Visit Jerusalem, Psalm 68:29.
- God's Glory, Psalm 115. What does the Bible means when it refers to "the glory of the Lord"? Is it something people actually saw? Check it out here.
- The Temple in Jerusalem, Psalm 122. Nothing was more important to the Israelite people in terms of worship than the Temple. Find out more about it here.

"Whose voice makes the lightning flash?"

"Sounds pretty electrifying to me! Let's check out Psalm 29 to find out."

did YOU know?

THE PSALMS SURFWATCH:

Lower than angels, Psalm 8
A thirsty deer, Psalm 42
Why do the bad guys get rich?, Psalm 73
Before I was born, Psalm 139
A musical tribute, Psalm 150

- Who Ya' Gonna Call?, Psalm 3:4
- Like Silver, Psalm 12:6-8
- Our Heavenly Shepherd, Psalm 23
- 911, Psalm 28:6
- Does Crime Pay?, Psalm 37:1–7
- Learning from Mistakes, Psalm 51:12–13
- In Deep Water, Psalm 69
- A Picture of the Past, Psalm 105
- God's Valuable Gift: You, Psalm 127:3–5
- Love That Will Last, Psalm 136

Book 1

Two Ways to Live

1 Happy are those who don't listen to
the wicked,
who don't go where sinners go,
who don't do what evil people do.
2 They love the LORD's teachings,
and they think
about those
teachings day
and night.
3 They are strong,
like a tree
planted by a
river.
The tree produces fruit in season,
and its leaves don't die.
Everything they do will succeed.

4 But wicked people are not like that.
They are like chaff that the wind
blows away.
5 So the wicked will not escape God's
punishment.
Sinners will not worship with
God's people.
6 This is because the LORD takes care
of his people,
but the wicked will be destroyed.

The Lord's Chosen King

2 Why are the nations so angry?
Why are the people making useless
plans?
2 The kings of the earth prepare to
fight,
and their leaders make plans
together
against the LORD
and his appointed one.
3 They say, "Let's break the chains
that hold us back
and throw off the ropes that tie us
down."

4 But the one who sits in heaven
laughs;
the LORD makes fun of them.
5 Then the LORD warns them
and frightens them with his anger.
6 He says, "I have appointed my own
king
to rule in Jerusalem on my holy
mountain, Zion."

7 Now I will tell you what the LORD
has declared:
He said to me, "You are my son.

eMAIL FROM GOD

1:1–2

Decisions

What's the best way to spend your time? Check it out!

TWO KINDS OF PEOPLE

PSALM 1

You've been at your school long enough to observe the different groups of kids there are. The popular kids. The smart kids. The athletic kids. Every school has similar groups. Some kids try to fit in one group or another, depending on what's important to them. This psalm describes two kinds of people. One group of people follows those who do evil things. The other group follows those who do good things. Those who do good things are happier than those who do evil things.

The people you hang with can influence you to do good or to do evil. Which will you choose?

What You Value, Genesis 25:21–34, p. 34

An Example Not to Follow, Leviticus 18:1–3, p. 157

The Gift of Friendship, 1 Samuel 18:1–3; 19, p. 381

Deciding Wisely, 1 Kings 3:16–28, p. 440

The Verdict Is In?, Matthew 7:1–2, p. 1285

Don't Play Favorites, James 2:1–7, p. 1691

Today I have become your father.
8 If you ask me, I will give you the nations;
all the people on earth will be yours.
9 You will rule over them with an iron rod.
You will break them into pieces like pottery."

10 So, kings, be wise;
rulers, learn this lesson.
11 Obey the LORD with great fear.
Be happy, but tremble.
12 Show that you are loyal to his son,
or you will be destroyed by his anger,
because he can quickly become angry.
But happy are those who trust him for protection.

A Morning Prayer

David sang this when he ran away from his son Absalom.

3 LORD, I have many enemies!
Many people have turned against me.
2 Many are saying about me,
"God won't rescue him." *Selah*

3 But, LORD, you are my shield,
my wonderful God who gives me courage.
4 I will pray to the LORD,
and he will answer me from his holy mountain. *Selah*

5 I can lie down and go to sleep,
and I will wake up again,
because the LORD gives me strength.
6 Thousands of troops may surround me,
but I am not afraid.

7 LORD, rise up!
My God, come save me!
You have struck my enemies on the cheek;
you have broken the teeth of the wicked.

8 The LORD can save his people.
LORD, bless your people. *Selah*

An Evening Prayer

For the director of music. With stringed instruments. A psalm of David.

4 Answer me when I pray to you,
my God who does what is right.
Make things easier for me when I am in trouble.

WHO YA' GONNA CALL?

PSALM 3:4

What is the most scared you've ever been? At one point, King David's son Absalom was his enemy. He was on the run from Absalom's army when he wrote this psalm. He told God that he was afraid and needed help. Even while he was afraid, he knew that God would answer his prayer.

David's psalm provides good advice to use when you're scared. For those heart-pounding times, call on God.

Need help? Call God!

A Major Problem, Genesis 15:6, p. 20

A Given, 1 Chronicles 5:18–20, p. 526

A Really Bad Day, Job 1:20–22; 2:10, p. 661

When the Going Gets Tough, Lamentations 3:22–27, p. 1079

The Best Protection Plan, Matthew 2:13–18, p. 1276

Prayer for a Friend, Colossians 1:9–12, p. 1620

Have mercy on me and hear my
prayer.

2 People, how long will you turn my
honor into shame?
How long will you love what is
false and look for new lies? *Selah*
3 You know that the LORD has chosen
for himself those who are loyal
to him.
The LORD listens when I pray to
him.
4 When you are angry, do not sin.
Think about these things quietly
as you go to bed. *Selah*
5 Do what is right as a sacrifice to the
LORD
and trust the LORD.

6 Many people ask,
"Who will give us anything good?"
LORD, be kind to us.
7 But you have made me very happy,
happier than they are,
even with all their grain and new
wine.
8 I go to bed and sleep in peace,
because, LORD, only you keep me
safe.

A Morning Prayer for Protection

For the director of music. For flutes.
A psalm of David.

5 LORD, listen to my words.
Understand my sadness.
2 Listen to my cry for help, my King
and my God,
because I pray to you.
3 LORD, every morning you hear my
voice.
Every morning, I tell you what I
need,
and I wait for your answer.

4 You are not a God who is pleased
with the wicked;
you do not live with those who do
evil.
5 Those people who make fun of you
cannot stand before you.
You hate all those who do evil.
6 You destroy liars;

FAITH links

THE PRAYER HABIT

PSALM 5:1-3

There are certain things you can do regularly to make your life better in the long run. Taking vitamins, studying, and spending time with friends are important habits to get into. Prayer is another habit to develop. David, the writer of this psalm, prayed every morning.

Do you have a special time to pray? Whenever or wherever you pray, God will hear you. Make prayer a part of your daily routine.

Approaching God, Numbers 3:10, p. 180

Good Times and Bad, 1 Kings 17, p. 462

Your Best Defense, 2 Chronicles 20:1–12, p. 584

Wisdom in Store, Proverbs 2:6–7, p. 828

Prayer Priority, Luke 5:15–16, p. 1376

Go for It!, Hebrews 12:1–4, p. 1682

the LORD hates those who kill and
trick others.

7 Because of your great love,
I can come into your Temple.
Because I fear and respect you,
I can worship in your holy Temple.
8 LORD, since I have many enemies,
show me the right thing to do.
Show me clearly how you want me
to live.

9 My enemies' mouths do not tell the truth;
in their hearts they want to destroy others.
Their throats are like open graves;
they use their tongues for telling lies.
10 God, declare them guilty!
Let them fall into their own traps.
Send them away because their sins are many;
they have turned against you.

11 But let everyone who trusts you be happy;
let them sing glad songs forever.
Protect those who love you
and who are happy because of you.
12 LORD, you bless those who do what is right;
you protect them like a soldier's shield.

EMAIL FROM GOD 5:12
Blessings
What kind of people does God bless?

A Prayer for Mercy in Troubled Times

For the director of music. With stringed instruments. Upon the sheminith. A psalm of David.

6 LORD, don't correct me when you are angry;
don't punish me when you are very angry.
2 LORD, have mercy on me because I am weak.
Heal me, LORD, because my bones ache.
3 I am very upset.
LORD, how long will it be?

4 LORD, return and save me;
save me because of your kindness.
5 Dead people don't remember you;
those in the grave don't praise you.

6 I am tired of crying to you.
Every night my bed is wet with tears;
my bed is soaked from my crying.
7 My eyes are weak from so much crying;
they are weak from crying about my enemies.

8 Get away from me, all you who do evil,
because the LORD has heard my crying.
9 The LORD has heard my cry for help;
the LORD will answer my prayer.
10 All my enemies will be ashamed and troubled.
They will turn and suddenly leave in shame.

A Prayer for Fairness

A shiggaion of David which he sang to the LORD about Cush, from the tribe of Benjamin.

7 LORD my God, I trust in you for protection.
Save me and rescue me
from those who are chasing me.
2 Otherwise, like a lion they will tear me apart.
They will rip me to pieces, and no one can save me.

LORD, have mercy on me because I am weak.
—Psalm 6:2

3 LORD my God, what have I done?
Have my hands done something wrong?
4 Have I done wrong to my friend
or stolen without reason from my enemy?
5 If I have, let my enemy chase me and capture me.
Let him trample me into the dust
and bury me in the ground. *Selah*

6 LORD, rise up in your anger;
stand up against my enemies' anger.
Get up and demand fairness.

FAITH CHALLENGE

Here's one for you. Read the first part of 7:4 to learn how David, the writer of the psalm, felt about his friends. How can you make sure that you don't do wrong to any of your friends?

TESTING IT

Psalm 7:4
Have I done wrong to my friend?

7 Gather the nations around you
and rule them from above.
8 LORD, judge the people.
LORD, defend me because I am right,
because I have done no wrong,
God Most High.
9 God, you do what is right.
You know our thoughts and feelings.
Stop those wicked actions done by evil people,
and help those who do what is right.
10 God protects me like a shield;
he saves those whose hearts are right.
11 God judges by what is right,
and God is always ready to punish the wicked.
12 If they do not change their lives,
God will sharpen his sword;
he will string his bow and take aim.
13 He has prepared his deadly weapons;
he has made his flaming arrows.

14 There are people who think up evil
and plan trouble and tell lies.
15 They dig a hole to trap others,
but they will fall into it themselves.
16 They will get themselves into trouble;
the violence they cause will hurt only themselves.

17 I praise the LORD because he does what is right.
I sing praises to the LORD Most High.

The Lord's Greatness

For the director of music. On the gittith.
A psalm of David.

8 LORD our Lord,
your name is the most wonderful name in all the earth!
It brings you praise in heaven above.
2 You have taught children and babies
to sing praises to you
because of your enemies.
And so you silence your enemies
and destroy those who try to get even.

3 I look at your heavens,
which you made with your fingers.
I see the moon and stars,
which you created.
4 But why are people important to you?
Why do you take care of human beings?
5 You made them a little lower than the angels

and crowned them with glory and
honor.
6 You put them in charge of everything
you made.
You put all things under their
control:
7 all the sheep, the cattle,
and the wild animals,
8 the birds in the sky,
the fish in the sea,
and everything that
lives under
water.

9 LORD our Lord,
your name is the
most wonderful
name in all the
earth!

LORD our Lord,
your name is the
most wonderful
name in all the
earth!
—Psalm 8:9

Thanksgiving for Victory

For the director of music. To the tune
of "The Death of the Son."
A psalm of David.

9 I will praise you, LORD, with all my
heart.
I will tell all the miracles you have
done.
2 I will be happy because of you;
God Most High, I will sing praises
to your name.

3 My enemies turn back;
they are overwhelmed and die
because of you.
4 You have heard my complaint;
you sat on your throne and judged
by what was right.
5 You spoke strongly against the
foreign nations
and destroyed the wicked;
you wiped out their names forever
and ever.
6 The enemy is gone forever.
You destroyed their cities;
no one even
remembers
them.

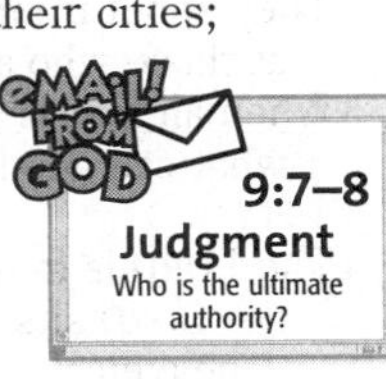
eMAIL! FROM GOD
9:7–8
Judgment
Who is the ultimate authority?

7 But the LORD
rules
forever.
He sits on his throne to judge,
8 and he will judge the world in
fairness;
he will decide what is fair for the
nations.
9 The LORD defends those who suffer;
he defends them in times of
trouble.
10 Those who know the
LORD trust him,
because he will not
leave those who
come to him.

11 Sing praises to the
LORD who is king
on Mount Zion.
Tell the nations
what he has done.
12 He remembers who
the murderers are;
he will not forget the cries of those
who suffer.
13 LORD, have mercy on me.
See how my enemies hurt me.
Do not let me go through the gates
of death.
14 Then, at the gates of Jerusalem, I will
praise you;
I will rejoice because you saved me.

15 The nations have fallen into the pit
they dug.
Their feet are caught in the nets
they laid.
16 The LORD has made himself known
by his fair decisions;
the wicked get trapped by what
they do. *Higgaion. Selah*
17 Wicked people will go to the grave,
and so will all those who forget
God.
18 But those who have troubles will not
be forgotten.
The hopes of
the poor will
never die.

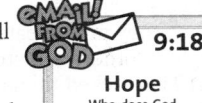

eMAIL! FROM GOD
9:18
Hope
Who does God give hope?

19 LORD, rise up and
judge the
nations.
Don't let people think they are
strong.

20 Teach them to fear you, LORD.
The nations must learn that they are only human. *Selah*

A Complaint About Evil People

10 LORD, why are you so far away?
Why do you hide when there is trouble?
2 Proudly the wicked chase down those who suffer.
Let them be caught in their own traps.
3 They brag about the things they want.
They bless the greedy but hate the LORD.
4 The wicked people are too proud.
They do not look for God;
there is no room for God in their thoughts.
5 They always succeed.
They are far from keeping your laws;
they make fun of their enemies.
6 They say to themselves, "Nothing bad will ever happen to me;
I will never be ruined."
7 Their mouths are full of curses, lies, and threats;
they use their tongues for sin and evil.
8 They hide near the villages.
They look for innocent people to kill;
they watch in secret for the helpless.
9 They wait in hiding like a lion.
They wait to catch poor people;
they catch the poor in nets.
10 The poor are thrown down and crushed;
they are defeated because the others are stronger.
11 The wicked think, "God has forgotten us.
He doesn't see what is happening."

12 LORD, rise up and punish the wicked.
Don't forget those who need help.
13 Why do wicked people hate God?
They say to themselves, "God won't punish us."
14 LORD, surely you see these cruel and evil things;
look at them and do something.
People in trouble look to you for help.
You are the one who helps the orphans.

> LORD, you have heard what the poor people want. Do what they ask, and listen to them.
> —Psalm 10:17

15 Break the power of wicked people.
Punish them for the evil they have done.
16 The LORD is King forever and ever.
Destroy from your land those nations that do not worship you.
17 LORD, you have heard what the poor people want.
Do what they ask, and listen to them.
18 Protect the orphans and put an end to suffering
so they will no longer be afraid of evil people.

Trust in the Lord

For the director of music. Of David.

11 I trust in the LORD for protection.
So why do you say to me,
"Fly like a bird to your mountain.
2 Like hunters, the wicked string their bows;
they set their arrows on the bowstrings.
They shoot from dark places at those who are honest.
3 When all that is good falls apart,
what can good people do?"

EMAIL! FROM GOD 11:1
Trust
Where is your trust?

4 The LORD is in his holy temple;
the LORD sits on his throne in heaven.

He sees what people do;
he keeps his eye on them.
5 The LORD tests those who do right,
but he hates the wicked and those
who love to hurt others.
6 He will send hot coals and burning
sulfur on the wicked.
A whirlwind is what they will get.
7 The LORD does what is right, and he
loves justice,
so honest people will see his face.

A Prayer Against Liars

For the director of music. Upon the sheminith. A psalm of David.

12 Save me, LORD, because the good
people are all gone;
no true believers are left on earth.
2 Everyone lies to his neighbors;
they say one thing and mean
another.

3 The LORD will stop those flattering
lips
and cut off those bragging tongues.
4 They say, "Our tongues will help us
win.
We can say what we wish; no one
is our master."

5 But the LORD says,
"I will now rise up,
because the poor are being hurt.
Because of the moans of the
helpless,
I will give
them the
help they
want."
6 The LORD's
words are
pure,
like silver purified by fire,
like silver purified seven times
over.

7 LORD, you will keep us safe;
you will always protect us from
such people.
8 But the wicked are all around us;
everyone loves what is wrong.

12:5
Pain
Who does God watch over?

FAITH links

LIKE SILVER

PSALM 12:6-8

Do you own anything silver? Silver is valuable to many people. That's why David compared God's word (the Bible) to silver. Like gold, the impurities in silver have to be removed in order for the silver to be useful. When silver is heated in a fiery furnace, it becomes more pure. When you test the truth of the Bible against some of what you hear at school or read in the newspaper or on the Internet, it will seem more pure to you. The more you read it, the more valuable it will become.

What do you value? Is one of those items the Bible? Connect here to find out what God values:

Lights, Camera, . . . Actions!, Genesis 12:1–3, p. 17

Comfort from the Word, Job 26:3–4, p. 688

The Foundation of Our Hope, Isaiah 31:1–8, p. 934

Your Full Trust, Jeremiah 22:20–22, p. 1023

Faith Workout, Acts 16:4–5, p. 1493

Pay Attention!, Hebrews 2:1, p. 1668

A Prayer for God to Be Near

For the director of music.
A psalm of David.

13 How long will you forget me,
LORD? Forever?
How long will you
hide from me?
2 How long must I
worry
and feel sad in my
heart all day?
How long will my
enemy win over
me?

3 LORD, look at me.
Answer me, my
God;
tell me, or I will die.
4 Otherwise my enemy will say, "I
have won!"
Those against me will rejoice that
I've been defeated.

5 I trust in your love.
My heart is happy because you
saved me.
6 I sing to the LORD
because he has taken care of me.

I trust in your love. My heart is happy because you saved me.
—Psalm 13:5

The Unbelieving Fool

For the director of music. Of David.

14 Fools say to themselves,
"There is no God."
Fools are evil and do terrible
things;
there is no one who does anything
good.

2 The LORD looked down from heaven
on all people
to see if anyone understood,
if anyone was looking to God for
help.
3 But all have turned away.
Together, everyone has become
evil.
There is no one who does anything
good,
not even one.

4 Don't the wicked understand?
They destroy my people as if they
were eating bread.
They do not ask the LORD for help.
5 But the wicked are filled with terror,
because God is with those who do
what is right.
6 The wicked upset the
plans of the poor,
but the LORD will
protect them.

7 I pray that victory will
come to Israel
from Mount Zion!
May the LORD
bring them back.
Then the people of
Jacob will rejoice,
and the people of Israel will be
glad.

What the Lord Demands

A psalm of David.

15 LORD, who may enter your Holy
Tent?
Who may live on your holy
mountain?

2 Only those who are innocent
and who do what is right.
Such people speak the truth from
their hearts
3 and do not tell lies about others.
They do no wrong to their
neighbors
and do not gossip.
4 They do not respect hateful
people
but honor those who honor the
LORD.
They keep their promises to their
neighbors,
even when it hurts.
5 They do not charge interest on
money they lend
and do not take money to hurt
innocent people.

Whoever does all these things will
never be destroyed.

Livin' it

HONESTY

Psalm 15

Hangin' with God Who do you like to hang with? The cool kids or the jocks? Kids who are smart? Or maybe the kids that you hang with like to get into trouble. There's an old saying that goes: "Birds of a feather flock together." What kind of "birds" are you flying with?

Nehemiah needed people to look after the Temple storerooms, which was a lot of responsibility. What kind of people did he look for? (Check out Nehemiah 13:13, p. 644, to see.)

God tells us he is a friend of those who are honest. (Look at Proverbs 3:32, p. 829.) That means God values honesty. A person usually hangs with others who have the same interests and values that he or she has. Is being honest important to you? If you want to hang with God, your answer had better be yes.

MORE FAITH links

Always Truthful, p. 208
An Honest Reputation, p. 644
Who Do You Prefer?, p. 830
All Talk, No Action, p. 996
What's Wrong About Rumors, p. 1032

"Skweek, you know, sometimes I tell little fibs. Not big lies. Do you think that's OK?"

"If I were you, I'd link up with what God has to say about telling the truth. Check it out below!"

The Best Policy, Genesis 29:16–29, p. 41
- Do you think tricking someone is cool? Think again! When you try to trick others, you might find yourself on the other end of a trick someday. How cool would that be?

A Serious Promise, Deuteronomy 23:21–23, p. 257
- Has someone ever borrowed money from you and promised to pay it back, but didn't? How did that make you feel?
- God expects us to keep our promises to him and to others. How well do you keep the promises you make?

The Whole Truth, John 8:31–32, 45, p. 1438
- It's hard to believe someone who has lied to you in the past, isn't it? Find out what Jesus said about the truth by linking here.

The Deadliest Lie, Acts 5:1–11, p. 1471
- Link here to read a very scary story about lying!

my FAVORITE links

The Lord Takes Care of His People

A miktam of David.

16 Protect me, God,
because I trust in you.
2 I said to the LORD, "You are my Lord.
Every good thing I have comes
from you."
3 As for the godly people in the world,
they are the wonderful ones I
enjoy.
4 But those who turn to idols
will have much pain.
I will not offer blood to those idols
or even speak their names.

5 No, the LORD is all I need.
He takes care of me.
6 My share in life has been pleasant;
my part has been beautiful.

7 I praise the LORD because he advises
me.
Even at night,
I feel his
leading.
8 I keep the LORD
before me
always.
Because he is close by my side,
I will not be hurt.
9 So I rejoice and am glad.
Even my body has hope,
10 because you will not leave me in the
grave.
You will not let your holy one rot.
11 You will teach me how to live a holy
life.
Being with you will fill me with
joy;
at your right hand I will find
pleasure forever.

eMAIL! FROM GOD 16:7
God's Will
Who can you trust in decisions?

A Prayer for Protection

A prayer of David.

17 LORD, hear me
begging for
fairness;
listen to my cry
for help.
Pay attention to
my prayer,
because I speak the truth.
2 You will judge that I am right;
your eyes can see what is true.
3 You have examined my heart;
you have tested me all night.
You questioned me without finding
anything wrong;
I have not sinned with my mouth.
4 I have obeyed your commands,
so I have not done what evil people
do.
5 I have done what you told me;
I have not failed.

6 I call to you, God,
and you answer me.
Listen to me now,
and hear what I say.
7 Your love is wonderful.
By your power you save those who
trust you
from their enemies.
8 Protect me as you would protect
your own eye.
Hide me under the shadow of your
wings.
9 Keep me from the wicked who attack
me,
from my enemies who surround
me.
10 They are selfish
and brag about themselves.
11 They have chased me until they have
surrounded me.
They plan to throw me to the
ground.
12 They are like lions ready to kill;
like lions, they sit in hiding.

13 LORD, rise up, face the enemy, and
throw them down.
Save me from the wicked with
your sword.
14 LORD, save me by your power
from those whose reward is in this
life.
They have plenty of food.
They have many sons
and leave much money to their
children.

15 Because I have lived right, I will see
your face.

eMAIL! FROM GOD 17:1–2
Prayer
Does God hear your prayers?

When I wake up, I will see your
likeness and be satisfied.

A Song of Victory

For the director of music. By the LORD's servant, David. David sang this song to the LORD when the LORD had saved him from Saul and all his other enemies.

18 I love you, LORD. You are my
strength.

2 The LORD is my rock, my protection,
my Savior.
My God is my rock.
I can run to him for safety.
He is my shield and my saving
strength, my defender.
3 I will call to the LORD, who is worthy
of praise,
and I will be saved from my
enemies.

4 The ropes of death came around me;
the deadly rivers overwhelmed
me.
5 The ropes of death wrapped around
me.
The traps of death were before me.
6 In my trouble I called to the LORD.
I cried out to my God for help.
From his temple he heard my voice;
my call for help reached his ears.

7 The earth trembled and shook.
The foundations of the mountains
began to shake.
They trembled because the LORD
was angry.
8 Smoke came out of his nose,
and burning fire came out of his
mouth.
Burning coals went before him.
9 He tore open the sky and came down
with dark clouds under his feet.
10 He rode a creature with wings and
flew.
He raced on the wings of the wind.
11 He made darkness his covering, his
shelter around him,
surrounded by fog and clouds.
12 Out of the brightness of his presence
came clouds

FAITH links

GOD'S SURE PROTECTION

PSALM 18

What is the largest rock or stone you have ever seen? If you live in an area with mountains, you're face-to-face with the biggest rocks of all! A large rock is tough to move. A mountain is impossible to move. That's why David, the writer of this psalm, called God his "rock." David was constantly on the run from his enemies. He often needed God's protection. Like David, we can count on God's protection. It's a sure thing!

When You're Afraid, Genesis 32:9–12, p. 45

Real Faith or Really Scared?, Judges 4, p. 315

Fly Like an Eagle, Isaiah 40:28–31, p. 947

The Best Protection Plan, Matthew 2:13–18, p. 1276

Prayer Anywhere, Mark 1:35, p. 1331

Fully God, Fully Human, John 11:35, p. 1444

with hail and lightning.
13 The LORD thundered from heaven;
the Most High raised his voice,
and there was hail and lightning.
14 He shot his arrows and scattered his
enemies.
His many bolts of lightning
confused them with fear.
15 LORD, you spoke strongly.

The wind blew from your nose.
Then the valleys of the sea appeared,
and the foundations of the earth
were seen.

16 The LORD reached down from above
and took me;
he pulled me from the deep water.
17 He saved me from my powerful
enemies,
from those who hated me, because
they were too strong for me.
18 They attacked me at my time of
trouble,
but the LORD supported me.
19 He took me to a safe place.
Because he delights in me, he
saved me.

20 The LORD spared me because I did
what was right.
Because I have not done evil, he
has rewarded me.
21 I have followed the ways of the
LORD;
I have not done evil by turning
away from my God.
22 I remember all his laws
and have not broken his rules.
23 I am innocent before him;
I have kept myself from doing
evil.
24 The LORD rewarded me because I did
what was right,
because I did what the LORD said
was right.

25 LORD, you are loyal to those who are
loyal,
and you are good to those who are
good.
26 You are pure to those who are pure,
but you are against those who are
bad.
27 You save the humble,
but you bring down those who are
proud.
28 LORD, you give light to my lamp.
My God brightens the darkness
around me.
29 With your help I can attack an army.
With God's help I can jump over a
wall.

30 The ways of God are without fault.
The LORD's words are pure.
He is a shield to those who trust him.
31 Who is God? Only the LORD.
Who is the Rock? Only our God.
32 God is my
protection.
He makes my
way free
from fault.
33 He makes me like
a deer that
does not stumble;
he helps me stand on the steep
mountains.
34 He trains my hands for battle
so my arms can bend a bronze bow.
35 You protect me with your saving
shield.
You support me with your right
hand.
You have stooped to make me
great.
36 You give me a better way to live,
so I live as you want me to.
37 I chased my enemies and caught
them.
I did not quit until they were
destroyed.
38 I crushed them so they couldn't rise
up again.
They fell beneath my feet.
39 You gave me strength in battle.
You made my enemies bow before
me.
40 You made my enemies turn back,
and I destroyed those who hated
me.
41 They called for help,
but no one came to save them.
They called to the LORD,
but he did not answer them.
42 I beat my enemies into pieces, like
dust in the wind.
I poured them out like mud in the
streets.

43 You saved me when the people
attacked me.
You made me the leader of nations.
People I never knew serve me.
44 As soon as they hear me, they obey
me.

EMAIL FROM GOD
18:32–50
Success
Where do you turn for success?

Foreigners obey me.
45 They all become afraid
and tremble in their hiding places.

46 The LORD lives!
May my Rock be praised.
Praise the God who saves me!
47 God gives me victory over my enemies
and brings people under my rule.
48 He saves me from my enemies.

You set me over those who hate me.
You saved me from cruel men.
49 So I will praise you, LORD, among the nations.
I will sing praises to your name.
50 The LORD gives great victories to his king.
He is loyal to his appointed king,
to David and his descendants forever.

God's Works and Word

For the director of music.
A psalm of David.

19 The heavens tell the glory of God,
and the skies announce what his hands have made.
2 Day after day they tell the story;
night after night they tell it again.
3 They have no speech or words;
they have no voice to be heard.
4 But their message goes out through all the world;
their words go everywhere on earth.
The sky is like a home for the sun.
5 The sun comes out like a bridegroom from his bedroom.
It rejoices like an athlete eager to run a race.
6 The sun rises at one end of the sky
and follows its path to the other end.
Nothing hides from its heat.

7 The teachings of the LORD are perfect;
they give new strength.
The rules of the LORD can be trusted;
they make plain people wise.
8 The orders of the LORD are right;
they make people happy.
The commands of the LORD are pure;
they light up the way.
9 Respect for the LORD is good;
it will last forever.

FAITH links

MORE PRECIOUS THAN GOLD

PSALM 19:7-10

Name something you own that's worth more than anything else you have. Your CD collection? Your favorite sweatshirt? The psalm writer described God's commands and promises as "worth more than gold." That's pretty valuable! They're not only priceless, they're perfect. Many people value gold more than they value what God said. Yet gold is here today and gone tomorrow. Only God's word will last forever.

Ten Ways to Obey, Exodus 20, p. 103

When I Need Advice, 1 Kings 12:1–17, p. 455

Plan for Success, 1 Chronicles 14:8–17, p. 538

Said It? Do It!, Lamentations 2:17, p. 1077

Want to Know? Ask!, Luke 9:45, p. 1386

Life's Rule Book, 2 Timothy 3:15–17, p. 1655

The judgments of the LORD are true;
they are completely right.
10 They are worth more than gold,
even the purest gold.
They are sweeter than honey,
even the finest honey.
11 By them your servant is warned.
Keeping them brings great reward.

12 People cannot see their own
mistakes.
Forgive me for
my secret
sins.
13 Keep me from the
sins of pride;
don't let them
rule me.
Then I can be
pure
and innocent of the greatest of
sins.

eMAIL! FROM GOD
19:12–13
Guilt
Can you hide sins from God?

14 I hope my words and thoughts please
you.
LORD, you are my Rock, the one
who saves me.

A Prayer for the King

For the director of music.
A psalm of David.

20 May the LORD answer you in
times of trouble.
May the God of Jacob protect you.
2 May he send you help from his
Temple
and support you from Mount Zion.
3 May he remember all your offerings
and accept all your sacrifices. *Selah*
4 May he give you what you want
and make all your plans succeed,
5 and we will shout for joy when you
succeed,
and we will raise a flag in the name
of our God.
May the LORD give you all that you
ask for.

6 Now I know the LORD helps his
appointed king.
He answers him from his holy
heaven
and saves him with his strong right
hand.
7 Some trust in
chariots,
others in
horses,
but we trust
the LORD our
God.

eMAIL! FROM GOD
20:7
Trust
What do some people trust in?

8 They are overwhelmed and defeated,
but we march forward and win.
9 LORD, save the king!
Answer us when we call for help.

Thanksgiving for the King

For the director of music.
A psalm of David.

21 LORD, the king rejoices because
of your strength;
he is so happy when you save him!
2 You gave the king what he wanted
and did not refuse what he asked
for. *Selah*
3 You put good things before him
and placed a gold crown on his
head.
4 He asked you for life,
and you gave it to him,
so his years go on and on.
5 He has great glory because you gave
him victories;
you gave him honor and praise.
6 You always gave him blessings;
you made him glad because you
were with him.
7 The king truly trusts the LORD.
Because God Most High always
loves him,
he will not be overwhelmed.
8 Your hand is against all your
enemies;
those who hate you will feel your
power.
9 When you appear,
you will burn them as in a furnace.
In your anger you will swallow them
up,
and fire will burn them up.
10 You will destroy their families from
the earth;
their children will not live.
11 They made evil plans against you,

but their traps won't work.
12 You will make them
turn their backs
when you aim your
arrows at them.
13 Be supreme, LORD, in
your power.
We sing and praise
your greatness.

Be supreme, LORD, in your power. We sing and praise your greatness.
—Psalm 21:13

The Prayer of a Suffering Man

For the director of music. To the tune of "The Doe of Dawn." A psalm of David.

22 My God, my God, why have you
rejected me?
You seem far from saving me,
far from the words of my groaning.
2 My God, I call to you during the day,
but you do not answer.
I call at night;
I am not silent.

3 You sit as the Holy One.
The praises of Israel are your
throne.
4 Our ancestors trusted you;
they trusted, and you saved them.
5 They called to you for help
and were rescued.
They trusted you
and were not disappointed.

6 But I am like a worm instead of a
man.
People make fun of me and hate
me.
7 Those who look at me laugh.
They stick out their tongues and
shake their heads.
8 They say, "Turn to the LORD for help.
Maybe he will save you.
If he likes you,
maybe he will rescue you."

9 You had my mother give birth to me.
You made me trust you
while I was just a baby.
10 I have leaned on you since the day I
was born;
you have been my God since my
mother gave me birth.
11 So don't be far away from me.
Now trouble is
near,
and there is no one
to help.
12 People have
surrounded me
like angry bulls.
Like the strong
bulls of Bashan,
they are on
every side.
13 Like hungry, roaring
lions
they open their mouths at me.
14 My strength is gone,
like water poured out onto the
ground,
and my bones are out of joint.
My heart is like wax;
it has melted inside me.
15 My strength has dried up like a clay
pot,
and my tongue sticks to the top of
my mouth.
You laid me in the dust of death.
16 Evil people have surrounded me;
like dogs they have trapped me.
They have bitten my arms and
legs.
17 I can count all my bones;
people look and stare at me.
18 They divided my clothes among
them,
and they threw lots for my
clothing.

19 But, LORD, don't be far away.
You are my strength; hurry to help
me.
20 Save me from the sword;
save my life from the dogs.
21 Rescue me from
the lion's
mouth;
save me from
the horns of
the bulls.

eMAIL! FROM GOD 22:19–24
Troubles
Does God care if you have problems?

22 Then I will tell
my fellow Israelites about you;
I will praise you in the public
meeting.

23 Praise the LORD, all you who respect him.
All you descendants of Jacob, honor him;
fear him, all you Israelites.
24 He does not ignore those in trouble.
He doesn't hide from them
but listens when they call out to him.
25 LORD, I praise you in the great meeting of your people;
these worshipers will see me do what I promised.
26 Poor people will eat until they are full;
those who look to the LORD will praise him.
May your hearts live forever!
27 People everywhere will remember and will turn to the LORD.
All the families of the nations will worship him
28 because the LORD is King,
and he rules the nations.

29 All the powerful people on earth will eat and worship.
Everyone will bow down to him,
all who will one day die.
30 The people in the future will serve him;
they will always be told about the Lord.
31 They will tell that he does what is right.
People who are not yet born
will hear what God has done.

The Lord the Shepherd

A psalm of David.

23 The LORD is my shepherd;
I have everything I need.
2 He lets me rest in green pastures.
He leads me to calm water.
3 He gives me new strength.
He leads me on paths that are right
for the good
of his name.
4 Even if I walk
through a
very dark
valley,

23:4
Fears
Who is your comforter?

I will not be afraid,
because you are with me.
Your rod and your walking stick"
comfort me.

FAITH links

OUR HEAVENLY SHEPHERD

PSALM 23

One of the most well-known psalms in the Bible is Psalm 23. This psalm may be familiar, but its message never gets old. God watches over us as a shepherd watches over sheep. David wrote this psalm based on his own experiences as a shepherd. He knew the kind of care sheep needed. The best shepherds took good care of their sheep. That's the kind of care God provides you.

Here are some more Faithlinks on how much God cares for you:

A Thanksgiving Reminder, Exodus 12, p. 91

See the Heart Behind It, Nehemiah 8; 9, p. 636

How Big Is God?, Job 38—41, p. 703

Your Heavenly Dad, Psalm 103:13, p. 786

Justice Desserts, Habakkuk 2:4–8, p. 1237

Two Birthdays, John 3:1–7, p. 1426

23:4 walking stick The stick a shepherd uses to guide and protect his sheep.

5 You prepare a meal for me
in front of my enemies.
You pour oil on my head;[n]
you fill my cup to overflowing.
6 Surely your goodness and love will
be with me
all my life,
and I will live in the house of the
LORD forever.

A Welcome for God into the Temple

A psalm of David.

24 The earth belongs to the LORD,
and everything in it—
the world and all its people.
2 He built it on the waters
and set it on the rivers.

3 Who may go up on the mountain of
the LORD?
Who may stand in his holy
Temple?
4 Only those with
clean hands
and pure
hearts,
who have not
worshiped
idols,
who have not made promises in
the name of a false god.
5 They will receive a blessing from the
LORD;
the God who saves them will
declare them right.
6 They try to follow God;
they look to the God of Jacob for
help. *Selah*

eMAIL! FROM GOD
24:3–6
Blessings
Who can get a blessing from God?

7 Gates, open all the way.
Open wide, aged doors
so the glorious King will come in.
8 Who is this glorious King?
The LORD, strong and mighty.
The LORD, the powerful warrior.
9 Gates, open all the way.
Open wide, aged doors
so the glorious King will come in.
10 Who is this glorious King?
The LORD All-Powerful—
he is the glorious King. *Selah*

A Prayer for God to Guide

Of David.

25 LORD, I give myself to you;
2 my God, I trust you.
Do not let me be disgraced;

23:5 pour oil . . . head This can mean that God gave him great wealth and blessed him.

FAITH links

LEARNING TO TRUST

PSALM 25:4-5

When you were a little kid, you had to be taught everything. All you knew how to do was drool. As you grew older, you learned more and more new things. (Hopefully, you stopped drooling.) If you're a Christian, there are also new things to learn. Trusting God is one of them.

David wrote this psalm as a prayer for help to learn how to live a life that honored God. He wanted God to teach him his ways. Is this your prayer, too? You can learn God's ways by reading the Bible and getting involved at your church.

The Name of the Lord, Exodus 33:19–23; 34:5–8, p. 120

What He's Really Like, Deuteronomy 4:15–20, p. 233

Listen Up!, 1 Kings 19:11–13, p. 467

The Writing's on the Wall, Daniel 5, p. 1159

Ask, Search, Knock, Matthew 7:7–10, p. 1286

Faith God Notices, Luke 18:35–43, p. 1406

do not let my enemies laugh at me.
3 No one who trusts you will be disgraced,
but those who sin without excuse will be disgraced.

4 LORD, tell me your ways.
Show me how to live.
5 Guide me in your truth,
and teach me, my God, my Savior.
I trust you all day long.
6 LORD, remember your mercy and love
that you have shown since long ago.
7 Do not remember the sins
and wrong things I did when I was young.
But remember to love me always
because you are good, LORD.

8 The LORD is good and right;
he points sinners to the right way.
9 He shows those who are humble how to do right,
and he teaches them his ways.
10 All the LORD's ways are loving and true
for those who follow the demands of his agreement.
11 For the sake of your name, LORD,
forgive my many sins.
12 Are there those who respect the LORD?
He will point them to the best way.
13 They will enjoy a good life,
and their children will inherit the land.
14 The LORD tells his secrets to those who respect him;
he tells them about his agreement.
15 My eyes are always looking to the LORD for help.

EMAIL! FROM GOD
25:15
Fears
Who should you look to for help?

He will keep me from any traps.
16 Turn to me and have mercy on me,
because I am lonely and hurting.
17 My troubles have grown larger;
free me from my problems.
18 Look at my suffering and troubles,
and take away all my sins.
19 Look at how many enemies I have!
See how much they hate me!
20 Protect me and save me.
I trust you, so do not let me be disgraced.
21 My hope is in you,
so may goodness and honesty guard me.
22 God, save Israel from all their troubles!

The Prayer of an Innocent Believer

Of David.

26 LORD, defend me because I have lived an innocent life.
I have trusted the LORD and never doubted.
2 LORD, try me and test me;
look closely into my heart and mind.
3 I see your love,
and I live by your truth.
4 I do not spend time with liars,
nor do I make friends with those who hide their sin.
5 I hate the company of evil people,
and I won't sit with the wicked.
6 I wash my hands to show I am innocent,
and I come to your altar, LORD.
7 I raise my voice in praise
and tell of all the miracles you have done.
8 LORD, I love the Temple where you live,
where your glory is.
9 Do not kill me with those sinners
or take my life with those murderers.
10 Evil is in their hands,

> LORD, try me and test me; look closely into my heart and mind.
> —Psalm 26:2

and they do wrong for money.
11 But I have lived an innocent life,
so save me and have mercy on me.
12 I stand in a safe place.
LORD, I praise you in the great
meeting.

A Song of Trust in God

Of David.

27 The LORD is my light and the one
who saves me.
I fear no one.
The LORD
protects my
life;
I am afraid of
no one.

eMAIL FROM GOD 27:1
God
Check out who is your light.

2 Evil people may
try to destroy my body.
My enemies and those who hate
me attack me,
but they are overwhelmed and
defeated.
3 If an army surrounds me,
I will not be afraid.
If war breaks out,
I will trust the LORD.

4 I ask only one thing from the LORD.
This is what I want:
Let me live in the LORD's house
all my life.
Let me see the LORD's beauty
and look with my own eyes at his
Temple.
5 During danger he will keep me safe
in his shelter.
He will hide me in his Holy Tent,
or he will keep me safe on a high
mountain.
6 My head is higher than my enemies
around me.
I will offer joyful sacrifices in his
Holy Tent.
I will sing and praise the LORD.

7 LORD, hear me when I call;
have mercy and answer me.
8 My heart said of you, "Go, worship
him."
So I come to worship you, LORD.
9 Do not turn away from me.
Do not turn your servant away in
anger;
you have helped me.
Do not push me away or leave me
alone,
God, my Savior.
10 If my father and mother leave me,
the LORD will take me in.
11 LORD, teach me your ways,
and guide me to do what is right
because I have enemies.
12 Do not hand me over to my enemies,
because they tell lies about me
and say they will hurt me.

13 I truly believe
I will live to see the LORD's
goodness.
14 Wait for the
LORD's help.
Be strong and
brave,
and wait for the
LORD's help.

eMAIL FROM GOD 27:14
Following God
What will come from waiting on the Lord?

A Prayer in Troubled Times

Of David.

28 LORD, my Rock, I call out to you
for help.
Do not be deaf to me.
If you are silent,
I will be like those in the grave.
2 Hear the sound of my prayer,
when I cry out to you for help.
I raise my hands
toward your Most Holy Place.
3 Don't drag me away with the wicked,
with those who do evil.
They say "Peace" to their neighbors,
but evil is in their hearts.
4 Pay them back for what they have
done,
for their evil deeds.
Pay them back for what they have
done;
give them their reward.
5 They don't understand what the
LORD has done
or what he has made.
So he will knock them down
and not lift them up.

911

PSALM 28:6

Whenever a person dials 911, he or she expects a quick answer. After all, the situation is usually a life-or-death emergency! For many years, David was surrounded by trouble. He often prayed for relief from life-threatening situations. He begged God not to ignore him.

Do you ever wish that God would respond as quickly as the 911 operators do? He doesn't always answer quickly. When you pray, just know that God *will* answer you, even if you have to wait awhile for the answer.

Got an emergency? Link here for quick help:

Problem Solved, 2 Kings 20:1–11, p. 507

Full Circle, Job 42, p. 706

When the Going Gets Tough, Lamentations 3:22–27, p. 1079

Long-lasting Hope, Hosea 14, p. 1184

Prayer Anywhere, Mark 1:35, p. 1331

Hold On!, 2 Thessalonians 2:15–17, p. 1639

6 Praise the LORD,
because he heard my prayer for help.
7 The LORD is my strength and shield.
I trust him, and he helps me.
I am very happy,
and I praise him with my song.
8 The LORD is powerful;
he gives victory to his chosen one.
9 Save your people
and bless those who are your own.
Be their shepherd and carry them forever.

God in the Thunderstorm

A psalm of David.

29 Praise the LORD, you angels;
praise the LORD's glory and power.
2 Praise the LORD for the glory of his name;
worship the LORD
because he is holy.

EMAIL FROM GOD
29:1–2
Worship
What should you give to the Lord during worship?

3 The LORD's voice
is heard over the sea.
The glorious God thunders;
the LORD thunders over the ocean.
4 The LORD's voice is powerful;
the LORD's voice is majestic.
5 The LORD's voice breaks the trees;
the LORD breaks the cedars of Lebanon.
6 He makes the land of Lebanon dance like a calf
and Mount Hermon jump like a baby bull.
7 The LORD's voice makes the lightning flash.
8 The LORD's voice shakes the desert;
the LORD shakes the Desert of Kadesh.
9 The LORD's voice shakes the oaks
and strips the leaves off the trees.
In his Temple everyone says, "Glory to God!"

10 The LORD controls the flood.
The LORD will be King forever.
11 The LORD gives strength to his people;
the LORD blesses his people with peace.

Thanksgiving for Escaping Death

A psalm of David. A song for giving the Temple to the LORD.

30 I will praise you, LORD,
because you rescued me.
You did not let my enemies laugh at me.
2 LORD, my God, I prayed to you,
and you healed me.
3 You lifted me out of the grave;
you spared me from going down to the place of the dead.

4 Sing praises to the LORD, you who belong to him;
praise his holy name.
5 His anger lasts only a moment,
but his kindness lasts for a lifetime.
Crying may last for a night,
but joy comes in the morning.

6 When I felt safe, I said,
"I will never fear."
7 LORD, in your kindness you made my mountain safe.
But when you turned away, I was frightened.

8 I called to you, LORD,
and asked you to have mercy on me.
9 I said, "What good will it do if I die
or if I go down to the grave?
Dust cannot praise you;
it cannot speak about your truth.
10 LORD, hear me and have mercy on me.
LORD, help me."

11 You changed my sorrow into dancing.
You took away my clothes of sadness,
and clothed me in happiness.
12 I will sing to you and not be silent.
LORD, my God, I will praise you forever.

His anger lasts only a moment, but his kindness lasts for a lifetime.
—Psalm 30:5

A Prayer of Faith in Troubled Times

For the director of music.
A psalm of David.

31 LORD, I trust in you;
let me never be disgraced.
Save me because you do what is right.
2 Listen to me
and save me quickly.
Be my rock of protection,
a strong city to save me.
3 You are my rock and my protection.
For the good of your name, lead me and guide me.
4 Set me free from the trap they set for me,
because you are my protection.
5 I give you my life.
Save me, LORD, God of truth.

6 I hate those who worship false gods.
I trust only in the LORD.
7 I will be glad and rejoice in your love,
because you saw my suffering;
you knew my troubles.
8 You have not handed me over to my enemies
but have set me in a safe place.

9 LORD, have mercy, because I am in misery.
My eyes are weak from so much crying,
and my whole being is tired from grief.
10 My life is ending in sadness,
and my years are spent in crying.
My troubles are using up my strength,
and my bones are getting weaker.
11 Because of all my troubles, my enemies hate me,

and even my neighbors look down
on me.
When my friends see me,
they are afraid and run.
12 I am like a piece of a broken pot.
I am forgotten as if I were dead.
13 I have heard many insults.
Terror is all around me.
They make plans against me
and want to kill me.

14 LORD, I trust you.
I have said, "You are my God."
15 My life is in your hands.
Save me from my enemies
and from those who are chasing
me.
16 Show your kindness to me, your
servant.
Save me because of your love.
17 LORD, I called to you,
so do not let me be disgraced.
Let the wicked be disgraced
and lie silent in the grave.
18 With pride and hatred
they speak against those who do
right.
So silence their lying lips.

19 How great is your goodness
that you have stored up for those
who fear you,
that you have given to those who
trust you.
You do this for all to see.
20 You protect them by your presence
from what people plan against
them.
You shelter them from evil words.
21 Praise the LORD.
His love to me was wonderful
when my city was attacked.
22 In my distress, I said,
"God cannot see me!"
But you heard my prayer
when I cried out to you for help.
23 Love the LORD, all you
who belong
to him.
The LORD
protects those
who truly
believe,

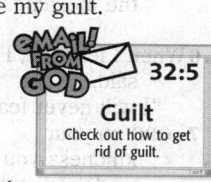

31:23
Responsibility
God is responsible for you.

but he punishes the proud as much
as they have sinned.
24 All you who put your hope in the
LORD
be strong and brave.

It Is Better to Confess Sin

A maskil of David.

32 Happy is the person
whose sins are forgiven,
whose wrongs are pardoned.
2 Happy is the person
whom the LORD does not consider
guilty
and in whom there is nothing false.

3 When I kept things to myself,
I felt weak deep inside me.
I moaned all day long.
4 Day and night you punished me.
My strength was gone as in the
summer heat. *Selah*
5 Then I confessed my sins to you
and didn't hide my guilt.
I said, "I will
confess my
sins to the
LORD,"
and you
forgave my
guilt. *Selah*

eMAIL! FROM GOD
32:5
Guilt
Check out how to get rid of guilt.

6 For this reason, all who obey you
should pray to you while they still
can.
When troubles rise like a flood,
they will not reach them.
7 You are my hiding place.
You protect me from my troubles
and fill me with songs of salvation.
Selah

8 The LORD says, "I will make you
wise and show you where to go.
I will guide you and watch over
you.
9 So don't be like a horse or donkey,
that doesn't understand.
They must be led with bits and reins,
or they will not come near you."

10 Wicked people have many troubles,

FAITH links

THE COVER-UP

PSALM 32:1-2

How long do you think you could hide a bag of smelly garbage—old food, that sort of thing—in your room? Not very long, right? The smell would give it away. Sin is like that bag of garbage. When we try to cover it up, God sniffs it out. Confessing it is the only way to really "cover up" sin. God's forgiveness completely covers it and takes it away. David knew great joy because of this. You can, too!

Made in His Image, Genesis 1:26–27, p. 4

Think About Him, Isaiah 26:3, p. 926

A Hard Place, Ezekiel 28:25–26, p. 1120

A Swarm of Trouble, Joel 2:25–27, p. 1190

Inside the Heart of God, Micah 7:18–20, p. 1228

Just for the Asking, Romans 3:23–28, p. 1522

but the LORD's love surrounds
those who trust him.
11 Good people, rejoice and be happy in
the LORD.
Sing all you whose hearts are
right.

Praise God Who Creates and Saves

33 Sing to the LORD, you who do
what is right;
honest people should praise him.
2 Praise the LORD on the harp;
make music for him on a ten-
stringed lyre.
3 Sing a new song to him;
play well and joyfully.

4 God's word is true,
and everything he does is right.
5 He loves what is right and fair;
the LORD's love fills the earth.

6 The sky was made at the LORD's
command.
By the breath from his mouth, he
made all the stars.
7 He gathered the water of the sea into
a heap.
He made the great ocean stay in
its place.
8 All the earth should worship the
LORD;
the whole world should fear him.
9 He spoke, and it happened.
He commanded, and it appeared.
10 The LORD upsets the plans of
nations;
he ruins all their plans.
11 But the LORD's plans will stand
forever;
his ideas will last from now on.
12 Happy is the nation whose God is the
LORD,
the people he chose for his very
own.
13 The LORD looks down from heaven
and sees every person.
14 From his throne he watches
all who live on earth.
15 He made their hearts
and understands everything they
do.
16 No king is saved by his great army.
No warrior escapes by his great
strength.
17 Horses can't bring victory;
they can't save
by their
strength.
18 But the LORD
looks after
those who
fear him,

33:13–18
God
Does God see you?

those who put their hope in his
love.
19 He saves them from death
and spares their lives in times of
hunger.
20 So our hope is in the LORD.
He is our help, our shield to
protect us.
21 We rejoice in him,
because we trust his holy name.
22 LORD, show your love to us
as we put our hope in you.

Praise God Who Judges and Saves

David's song from the time he acted
crazy so Abimelech would send him away,
and David did leave.

34 I will praise the LORD at all times;
his praise is always on my lips.
2 My whole being praises the LORD.
The poor will hear and be glad.
3 Glorify the LORD with me,
and let us praise his name
together.

4 I asked the LORD for help, and he
answered me.
He saved me from all that I feared.
5 Those who go to him for help are
happy,
and they are never disgraced.
6 This poor man called, and the LORD
heard him
and saved him from all his
troubles.
7 The angel of the LORD camps around
those who fear God,
and he saves them.

8 Examine and see how good the LORD
is.
Happy is the person who trusts
him.
9 You who belong to the LORD, fear
him!
Those who fear him will have
everything they need.
10 Even lions may get weak and
hungry,
but those who look to the LORD
will have every good thing.

11 Children, come and listen to me.
I will teach you to worship the
LORD.
12 You must do these things
to enjoy life and have many happy
days.
13 You must not say evil things,
and you must not tell lies.
14 Stop doing evil and do good.
Look for peace and work for it.

15 The LORD sees the good people
and listens to their prayers.
16 But the LORD is against those who do
evil;
he makes the world forget them.
17 The LORD hears good people when
they cry out to him,
and he saves them from all their
troubles.
18 The LORD is close to the
brokenhearted,
and he saves
those whose
spirits have
been
crushed.

EMAIL! FROM GOD
34:18
Feelings
Who heals a broken heart?

19 People who do
what is right may have many
problems,
but the LORD will solve them all.
20 He will protect their very bones;
not one of them will be broken.
21 Evil will kill the wicked;
those who hate good people will be
judged guilty.
22 But the LORD saves his servants'
lives;
no one who trusts him will be
judged guilty.

A Prayer for Help

Of David.

35 LORD, battle with those who
battle with me.
Fight against those who fight
against me.
2 Pick up the shield and armor.
Rise up and help me.
3 Lift up your spears, both large and
small,

against those who chase me.
Tell me, "I will save you."

4 Make those who want to kill me
be ashamed and disgraced.
Make those who plan to harm me
turn back and run away.
5 Make them like chaff blown by the
wind
as the angel of the LORD forces
them away.
6 Let their road be dark and slippery
as the angel of the LORD chases
them.
7 For no reason they spread out their
net to trap me;
for no reason they dug a pit for me.
8 So let ruin strike them suddenly.
Let them be caught in their own
nets;
let them fall into the pit and die.
9 Then I will rejoice in the LORD;
I will be happy when he saves me.
10 Even my bones will say,
"LORD, who is like you?
You save the weak from the strong,
the weak and poor from robbers."

11 Men without mercy stand up to
testify.
They ask me things I do not know.
12 They repay me with evil for the good
I have done,
and they make me
very sad.
13 Yet when they were
sick, I put on
clothes of
sadness
and showed my
sorrow by going
without food.
But my prayers were
not answered.
14 I acted as if they
were my friends
or brothers.
I bowed in sadness as if I were crying
for my mother.
15 But when I was in trouble, they
gathered and laughed;
they gathered to attack before I
knew it.
They insulted me without
stopping.
16 They made fun of me and were cruel
to me
and ground their teeth at me in
anger.

17 Lord, how long will you watch this
happen?
Save my life from their attacks;
save me from these people who
are like lions.
18 I will praise you in the great meeting.
I will praise you among crowds of
people.
19 Do not let my enemies laugh at me;
they hate me for no reason.
Do not let them make fun of me;
they have no cause to hate me.
20 Their words are not friendly
but are lies about peace-loving
people.
21 They speak against me
and say, "Aha! We saw what you
did!"

22 LORD, you have been watching. Do
not keep quiet.
Lord, do not leave me alone.
23 Wake up! Come and defend me!
My God and Lord, fight for me!
24 LORD my God, defend me with your
justice.
Don't let them
laugh at me.
25 Don't let them think,
"Aha! We got
what we
wanted!"
Don't let them say,
"We destroyed
him."
26 Let them be ashamed
and embarrassed,
because they were
happy when I
hurt.
Cover them with shame and
disgrace,
because they thought they were
better than I was.
27 May my friends sing and shout for
joy.

LORD, you have been watching. Do not keep quiet. Lord, do not leave me alone.
—Psalm 34:22

May they always say, "Praise the
greatness of the LORD,
who loves to see his servants do
well."
28 I will tell of your goodness
and will praise you every day.

Wicked People and a Good God

For the director of music. Of David,
the servant of the LORD.

36 Sin speaks to the wicked in their
hearts.
They have no fear of God.
2 They think too much of themselves
so they don't see their sin and hate
it.
3 Their words are wicked lies;
they are no longer wise or good.
4 At night they make evil plans;
what they do leads to nothing
good.
They don't refuse things that are
evil.

5 LORD, your love reaches to the
heavens,
your loyalty to the skies.
6 Your goodness is as high as the
mountains.
Your justice is as deep as the great
ocean.
LORD, you protect both people and
animals.
7 God, your love is so precious!
You protect people in the shadow
of your wings.
8 They eat the rich food in your house,
and you let them drink from your
river of pleasure.
9 You are the giver of life.
Your light lets us enjoy life.

10 Continue to love those who know
you
and to do good to those who are
good.
11 Don't let proud people attack me
and the wicked force me away.
12 Those who do evil have been
defeated.
They are overwhelmed;
they cannot do evil any longer.

God Will Reward Fairly

Of David.

37 Don't be upset because of evil
people.
Don't be jealous of those who do
wrong,
2 because like the grass, they will soon
dry up.
Like green plants, they will soon
die away.

FAITH links

DOES CRIME PAY?

PSALM 37:1-7

Did you ever wonder whether people who do evil things are ever punished? Maybe you know of a kid who bullies others at school and never gets in trouble. If so, David offers this advice to you from his psalm: Don't worry when those who do evil seem to get ahead. Instead, trust God. Wait for him to even things out.

Connect here to find out how to get God—not get even:

More Powerful Than Revenge, Genesis 50:14–21, p. 71

Learning from Mistakes, Psalm 51:12–13, p. 748

A Change of Heart, Matthew 3:1–12, p. 1277

Forgive Again?, Luke 17:3–4, p. 1402

A Friend in Need, Acts 9:27, p. 1480

His Best Qualities, 2 Peter 3:9, p. 1711

3 Trust the LORD and do good.
Live in the land and feed on truth.
4 Enjoy serving the LORD,
and he will give you what you want.
5 Depend on the LORD;
trust him, and he will take care of you.
6 Then your goodness will shine like the sun,
and your fairness like the noonday sun.

7 Wait and trust the LORD.
Don't be upset when others get rich
or when someone else's plans succeed.
8 Don't get angry.
Don't be upset; it only leads to trouble.
9 Evil people will be sent away,
but those who trust the LORD will inherit the land.
10 In a little while the wicked will be no more.
You may look for them, but they will be gone.
11 People who are not proud will inherit the land
and will enjoy complete peace.

12 The wicked make evil plans against good people.
They grind their teeth at them in anger.
13 But the Lord laughs at the wicked,
because he sees that their day is coming.
14 The wicked draw their swords
and bend their bows
to kill the poor and helpless,
to kill those who are honest.
15 But their swords will stab their own hearts,
and their bows will break.

16 It is better to have little and be right
than to have much and be wrong.
17 The power of the wicked will be broken,
but the LORD supports those who do right.
18 The LORD watches over the lives of the innocent,
and their reward will last forever.
19 They will not be ashamed when trouble comes.
They will be full in times of hunger.
20 But the wicked will die.
The LORD's enemies will be like the flowers of the fields;
they will disappear like smoke.
21 The wicked borrow and don't pay back,
but those who do right give freely to others.
22 Those whom the LORD blesses will inherit the land,
but those he curses will be sent away.

eMAIL! FROM GOD
37:23–24
God's Promises
Find out how God cares for his children.

23 When a person's steps follow the LORD,
God is pleased with his ways.
24 If he stumbles, he will not fall,
because the LORD holds his hand.

25 I was young, and now I am old,
but I have never seen good people left helpless
or their children begging for food.
26 Good people always lend freely to others,
and their children are a blessing.

27 Stop doing evil and do good,
so you will live forever.
28 The LORD loves justice
and will not leave those who worship him.
He will always protect them,
but the children of the wicked will die.
29 Good people will inherit the land
and will live in it forever.

30 A good person speaks with wisdom,
and he says what is fair.
31 The teachings of his God are in his heart,
so he does not fail to keep them.

32 The wicked watch for good people
so that they may kill them.
33 But the LORD will not take away his protection
or let good people be judged guilty.

34 Wait for the LORD's help
and follow him.
He will honor you and give you the land,
and you will see the wicked sent away.

35 I saw a wicked and cruel man
who looked strong like a healthy tree in good soil.
36 But he died and was gone;
I looked for him,
but he couldn't be found.

37 Think of the innocent person,
and watch the honest one.
The man who has peace
will have children to live after him.
38 But sinners will be destroyed;
in the end the wicked will die.

39 The LORD saves good people;
he is their strength in times of trouble.
40 The LORD helps them and saves them;
he saves them from the wicked,
because they trust in him for protection.

A Prayer in Time of Sickness

A psalm of David to remember.

38 LORD, don't correct me when you are angry.
Don't punish me when you are furious.
2 Your arrows have wounded me,
and your hand has come down on me.
3 My body is sick from your punishment.
Even my bones are not healthy
because of my sin.
4 My guilt has overwhelmed me;
like a load it weighs me down.

5 My sores stink and become infected
because I was foolish.
6 I am bent over and bowed down;
I am sad all day long.
7 I am burning with fever,
and my whole body is sore.
8 I am weak and faint.
I moan from the pain I feel.

9 Lord, you know everything I want;
my cries are not hidden from you.

Lord, you know everything I want; my cries are not hidden from you.
—Psalm 38:9

10 My heart pounds, and my strength is gone.
I am losing my sight.
11 Because of my wounds, my friends and neighbors avoid me,
and my relatives stay far away.
12 Some people set traps to kill me.
Those who want to hurt me plan trouble;
all day long they think up lies.

13 I am like a deaf man; I cannot hear.
Like a mute, I cannot speak.
14 I am like a person who does not hear,
who has no answer to give.
15 I trust you, LORD.
You will answer, my LORD and God.
16 I said, "Don't let them laugh at me
or brag when I am defeated."
17 I am about to die,
and I cannot forget my pain.
18 I confess my guilt;
I am troubled by my sin.
19 My enemies are strong and healthy,
and many hate me for no reason.
20 They repay me with evil for the good I did.
They lie about me because I try to do good.

21 LORD, don't leave me;
my God, don't go away.
22 Quickly come and help me,
my Lord and Savior.

Life Is Short

For the director of music. For Jeduthun.
A psalm of David.

39 I said, "I will be careful how I act
and will not sin by what I say.
I will be careful what I say
around wicked people."
2 So I kept very quiet.
I didn't even say anything good,
but I became even more upset.
3 I became very angry inside,
and as I thought about it, my anger
burned.
So I spoke:
4 "LORD, tell me when the end will
come
and how long I will live.
Let me know how long I have.
5 You have given me only a short life;
my lifetime is like nothing to you.
Everyone's life is only a breath.
Selah
6 People are like shadows moving
about.
All their work is for nothing;
they collect things
but don't know
who will get
them.

7 "So, Lord, what hope
do I have?
You are my hope.
8 Save me from all my
sins.
Don't let wicked
fools make fun of
me.
9 I am quiet; I do not open my mouth,
because you are the one who has
done this.
10 Quit punishing me;
your beating is about to kill me.
11 You correct and punish people for
their sins;
like a moth, you destroy what they
love.
Everyone's life is only a breath.
Selah

12 "LORD, hear my prayer,
and listen to my cry.
Do not ignore my tears.
I am like a visitor with you.
Like my ancestors, I'm only here a
short time.
13 Leave me alone so I can be happy
before I leave and am no more."

Praise and Prayer for Help

For the director of music.
A psalm of David.

40 I waited patiently for the LORD.
He turned to me and heard my
cry.
2 He lifted me out of the pit of
destruction,
out of the sticky mud.
He stood me on a rock
and made my feet steady.
3 He put a new song in my mouth,
a song of praise to our God.
Many people will see this and
worship him.
Then they will trust the LORD.

4 Happy is the person
who trusts the
LORD,
who doesn't turn to
those who are
proud
or to those who
worship false
gods.
5 LORD my God, you
have done many
miracles.
Your plans for us are
many.
If I tried to tell them all,
there would be too many to count.

6 You do not want sacrifices and
offerings.
But you have made a hole in my
ear
to show that my body and life are
yours.

Save me from all my sins. Don't let wicked fools make fun of me.
—Psalm 39:8

You do not ask for burnt offerings
and sacrifices to take away sins.
7 Then I said, "Look, I have come.
It is written about me in the book.
8 My God, I want to do what you want.
Your teachings are in my heart."

9 I will tell about your goodness in the
great meeting of your people.
LORD, you know my lips are not
silent.
10 I do not hide your goodness in my
heart;
I speak about your loyalty and
salvation.
I do not hide your love and truth
from the people in the great
meeting.

11 LORD, do not hold back your mercy
from me;
let your love and truth always
protect me.
12 Troubles have surrounded me;
there are too many to count.
My sins have caught me
so that I cannot see a way to
escape.
I have more sins than hairs on my
head,
and I have lost my courage.
13 Please, LORD,
save me.
Hurry, LORD, to
help me.

eMAIL! FROM GOD
40:13
Prayer
Who should you go to for help?

14 People are trying
to kill me.
Shame them and disgrace them.
People want to hurt me.
Let them run away in disgrace.
15 People are making fun of me.
Let them be shamed into silence.
16 But let those who follow you
be happy and glad.
They love you for saving them.
May they always say, "Praise the
LORD!"

17 Lord, because I am poor and
helpless,
please remember me.
You are my helper and savior.
My God, do not wait.

A Prayer in Time of Sickness

For the director of music.
A psalm of David.

41 Happy is the person who thinks
about the poor.
When trouble comes, the LORD
will save him.
2 The LORD will protect him and spare
his life
and will bless
him in the
land.
He will not let
his enemies
take him.

eMAIL! FROM GOD
41
Sickness
Check out how God cares for the sick.

3 The LORD will
give him
strength when he is sick,
and he will make him well again.

4 I said, "LORD, have mercy on me.
Heal me, because I have sinned
against you."
5 My enemies are saying evil things
about me.
They say, "When will he die and be
forgotten?"
6 Some people come to see me,
but they lie.
They just come to get bad news.
Then they go and gossip.
7 All my enemies whisper about me
and think the worst about me.
8 They say, "He has a terrible disease.
He will never get out of bed
again."
9 My best and truest friend, who ate at
my table,
has even turned against me.

10 LORD, have mercy on me.
Give me strength so I can pay
them back.
11 Because my enemies do not defeat
me,
I know you are pleased with me.
12 Because I am innocent, you support
me
and will let me be with you forever.

13 Praise the LORD, the God of Israel.
He has always been,

and he will always be.
Amen and amen.

Book 2

Wishing to Be Near God

For the director of music.
A maskil of the sons of Korah.

42 As a deer thirsts for streams of water,
so I thirst for you, God.
2 I thirst for the living God.
When can I go to meet with him?
3 Day and night, my tears have been my food.
People are always saying,
"Where is your God?"
4 When I remember these things,
I speak with a broken heart.
I used to walk with the crowd
and lead them to God's Temple
with songs of praise.

5 Why am I so sad?
Why am I so upset?
I should put my hope in God
and keep praising him,
my Savior and 6 my God.

EMAIL FROM GOD 42:5–6
Hope
How can you chase away the blues?

I am very sad.
So I remember you where the Jordan River begins,
near the peaks of Hermon and Mount Mizar.
7 Troubles have come again and again,
sounding like waterfalls.
Your waves are crashing all around me.
8 The LORD shows his true love every day.
At night I have a song,
and I pray to my living God.
9 I say to God, my Rock,
"Why have you forgotten me?
Why am I sad
and troubled by my enemies?"
10 My enemies' insults make me feel
as if my bones were broken.

FAITH links

OUR THIRST QUENCHER

PSALM 42:1-3

Think of a time when you were really thirsty. If someone had handed you a juice drink or a glass of milk, would that have quenched your thirst? Only partially. Water is the only liquid that can fully quench someone's thirst. Both animals and humans need water to live. That's why David compared our need for God to a deer's need for water. Our hearts "thirst" for God. Only God can satisfy the need we have. The more you get to know about God, the more you will "thirst" for him.

I'll Never Forget What's-His-Name, Deuteronomy 8, p. 239

Help to Understand, 2 Samuel 14, p. 416

Choosing a Friend, Proverbs 28:7, p. 865

A Need to Change, Ecclesiastes 1:1–11, p. 873

Two Ways to Grow, Luke 2:46–52, p. 1370

That's False!, 2 John 7–11, p. 1722

They are always saying,
"Where is your God?"

11 Why am I so sad?
Why am I so upset?

I should put my hope in God
and keep praising him,
my Savior and my God.

A Prayer for Protection

43 God, defend me.
Argue my case against those who don't follow you.
Save me from liars and those who do evil.
2 God, you are my strength.
Why have you rejected me?
Why am I sad
and troubled by my enemies?
3 Send me your light and truth
to guide me.
Let them lead me to your holy mountain,
to where you live.
4 Then I will go to the altar of God,
to God who is my joy and happiness.
I will praise you with a harp,
God, my God.

5 Why am I so sad?
Why am I so upset?
I should put my hope in God
and keep praising him,
my Savior and my God.

CONNECT 2-YOU

TEMPER, TEMPER

Ever get so mad you could hardly see straight? Well, Tagg and I have a friend who has a problem with his temper. Let's welcome David, age 11, to Connect 2-You.

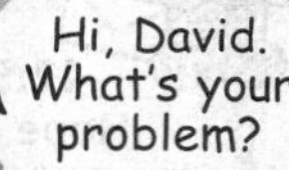
Hi, David.
What's your problem?

David

My mom says I have a "quick fuse," and I have to admit she's right. When something makes me mad, I just explode. I get so angry at my brother sometimes that I feel like hitting him—or worse. Does that make me a bad person?

We all get mad sometimes, David. There's nothing wrong with feeling angry. But the way we handle our anger says a lot about us, whether we like it or not. God wants us to turn our anger over to him, admit what we're feeling, and let him deal with it. If you'd like to find out more about this process, check out the Livin' It page on anger, James 1:19-21, p. 1690.

One of the best ways to keep your temper under control is to pray before you do anything out of anger. Praying gives you the chance to ask God for help and it gives you time to cool down. Why not give it a try the next time you feel your temperature rising?

A Prayer for Help

For the director of music.
A maskil of the sons of Korah.

44 God, we have heard about you.
Our ancestors told us
what you did in their days,
in days long ago.
2 With your power you forced the nations out of the land
and placed our ancestors here.
You destroyed those other nations,
but you made our ancestors grow strong.
3 It wasn't their swords that took the land.
It wasn't their power that gave them victory.
But it was your great power and strength.
You were with them because you loved them.

4 My God, you are my King.
Your commands led Jacob's people to victory.
5 With your help we pushed back our enemies.
In your name we trampled those who came against us.
6 I don't trust my bow to help me,
and my sword can't save me.
7 You saved us from our foes,
and you made our enemies ashamed.
8 We will praise God every day;
we will praise your name forever. *Selah*

I don't trust my bow to help me, and my sword can't save me.
—Psalm 44:6

9 But you have rejected us and shamed us.
You don't march with our armies anymore.
10 You let our enemies push us back,
and those who hate us have taken our wealth.
11 You gave us away like sheep to be eaten
and have scattered us among the nations.
12 You sold your people for nothing
and made no profit on the sale.

13 You made us a joke to our neighbors;
those around us laugh and make fun of us.
14 You made us a joke to the other nations;
people shake their heads.
15 I am always in disgrace,
and I am covered with shame.
16 My enemy is getting even
with insults and curses.

17 All these things have happened to us,
but we have not forgotten you
or failed to keep our agreement with you.
18 Our hearts haven't turned away from you,
and we haven't stopped following you.
19 But you crushed us in this place where wild dogs live,
and you covered us with deep darkness.

20 If we had forgotten our God
or lifted our hands in prayer to foreign gods,
21 God would have known,
because he knows what is in our hearts.
22 But for you we are in danger of death all the time.
People think we are worth no more than sheep to be killed.

23 Wake up, Lord! Why are you sleeping?
Get up! Don't reject us forever.
24 Why do you hide from us?
Have you forgotten our pain and troubles?

25 We have been pushed down into the
dirt;
we are flat on the ground.
26 Get up and help us.
Because of your love, save us.

A Song for the King's Wedding

For the director of music. To the tune of "Lilies." A maskil. A love song of the sons of Korah.

45 Beautiful words fill my mind.
I am speaking of royal things.
My tongue is like the pen of a
skilled writer.

2 You are more
handsome than
anyone,
and you are an
excellent
speaker,
so God has blessed
you forever.
3 Put on your sword,
powerful warrior.
Show your glory and majesty.
4 In your majesty win the victory
for what is true and right.
Your power will do amazing things.
5 Your sharp arrows will enter
the hearts of the king's enemies.
Nations will be defeated before
you.
6 God, your throne will last forever and
ever.
You will rule your kingdom with
fairness.
7 You love right and hate evil,
so God has chosen you from
among your friends;
he has set you apart with much joy.
8 Your clothes smell like myrrh, aloes,
and cassia.
From palaces of ivory
music comes to make you happy.
9 Kings' daughters are among your
honored women.
Your bride stands at your right side
wearing gold from Ophir.

10 Listen to me, daughter; look and pay
attention.
Forget your people and your
father's family.
11 The king loves your beauty.
Because he is your master, you
should obey him.
12 People from the city of Tyre have
brought a gift.
Wealthy people will want to meet
you.

13 The princess is very beautiful.
Her gown is woven with gold.
14 In her beautiful clothes she is
brought to the king.
Her bridesmaids
follow behind
her,
and they are also
brought to him.
15 They come with
happiness and
joy;
they enter the
king's palace.

16 You will have sons to
replace your
fathers.
You will make them rulers through
all the land.
17 I will make your name famous from
now on,
so people will praise you forever
and ever.

God, your throne will last forever and ever. You will rule your kingdom with fairness.
—Psalm 45:6

God Protects His People

For the director of music. By alamoth. A psalm of the sons of Korah.

46 God is our protection and our
strength.
He always helps in times of
trouble.
2 So we will not
be afraid
even if the
earth
shakes,
or the
mountains fall into the sea,
3 even if the oceans roar and foam,
or the mountains shake at the
raging sea. *Selah*

EMAIL FROM GOD
46:1–2
Troubles
Who is your help in bad times?

4 There is a river that brings joy to the
city of God,
the holy place where God Most
High lives.
5 God is in that city, and so it will not
be shaken.
God will help her at dawn.
6 Nations tremble and kingdoms shake.
God shouts and the earth
crumbles.

7 The LORD All-Powerful is with us;
the God of Jacob is our defender.
Selah

8 Come and see what the LORD has
done,
the amazing things he has done on
the earth.
9 He stops wars everywhere on the
earth.
He breaks all bows and spears
and burns up the chariots with fire.
10 God says, "Be quiet and know that I
am God.
I will be supreme over all the
nations;
I will be supreme in the earth."

11 The LORD All-Powerful is with us;
the God of Jacob is our defender.
Selah

God, the King of the World

For the director of music.
A psalm of the sons of Korah.

47 Clap your hands, all you people.
Shout to God with joy.
2 The LORD Most High
is wonderful.
He is the great
King over all the
earth!
3 He defeated nations
for us
and put them under
our control.
4 He chose the land we
would inherit.
We are the children
of Jacob, whom he loved. *Selah*

Clap your hands,
all you people.
Shout to God
with joy.
—Psalm 47:1

5 God has risen with a shout of joy;
the LORD has risen as the
trumpets sounded.
6 Sing praises to God. Sing praises.
Sing praises to our King. Sing
praises.
7 God is King of all the earth,
so sing a song of praise to him.
8 God is King over the nations.
God sits on his holy throne.
9 The leaders of the nations meet
with the people of the God of
Abraham,
because the leaders of the earth
belong to God.
He is supreme.

Jerusalem, the City of God

A psalm of the sons of Korah.

48 The LORD is great; he should be
praised
in the city of our God, on his holy
mountain.
2 It is high and beautiful
and brings joy to the whole world.
Mount Zion is like the high
mountains of the north;
it is the city of the Great King.
3 God is within its palaces;
he is known as its defender.
4 Kings joined together
and came to attack the city.
5 But when they saw it, they were
amazed.
They ran away in fear.
6 Fear took hold of them;
they hurt like a woman having a
baby.
7 You destroyed the large trading ships
with an east wind.

8 First we heard
and now we have
seen
that God will always
keep his city
safe.
It is the city of
the LORD
All-Powerful,
the city of our God
Selah

9 God, we come into your Temple
to think about your love.
10 God, your name is known
everywhere;
all over the earth people praise
you.
Your right hand is full of goodness.
11 Mount Zion is happy
and all the towns of Judah rejoice,
because your decisions are fair.

12 Walk around Jerusalem
and count its towers.
13 Notice how strong they are.
Look at the palaces.

FAITH CHALLENGE

Here's another one for you. Read 48:9 to discover what the writer of the psalm thought about when he worshiped God. What can you do to make sure that you think about the right things when you're in church?

TESTING IT

Psalm 48:9
God, we come into your Temple to think about your love.

Then you can tell your children
about them.
14 This God is our
God forever
and ever.
He will guide us
from now on.

EMAIL FROM GOD 48:14
God's Will
Why can you be hopeful about the future?

Trusting Money Is Foolish

For the director of music.
A psalm of the sons of Korah.

49 Listen to this, all you nations;
listen, all you who live on earth.
2 Listen, both great and small,
rich and poor together.
3 What I say is wise,
and my heart speaks with
understanding.
4 I will pay attention to a wise saying;
I will explain my riddle on the
harp.

5 Why should I be afraid of bad days?
Why should I fear when evil men
surround me?
6 They trust in their money
and brag about their riches.
7 No one can buy back the life of
another.
No one can pay God for his own
life,
8 because the price of a life is high.
No payment is ever enough.
9 Do people live forever?
Don't they all face death?

10 See, even wise people die.
Fools and stupid people also die
and leave their wealth to others.
11 Their graves will always be their
homes.
They will live there from now on,
even though they named places
after themselves.
12 Even rich people do not live forever;
like the animals, people die.

13 This is what will happen to those
who trust in themselves
and to their followers who believe
them. *Selah*

14 Like sheep, they must die,
and death will be their shepherd.
Honest people will rule over them in the morning,
and their bodies will rot in a grave far from home.
15 But God will save my life
and will take me from the grave. *Selah*

EMAIL FROM GOD
49:13–15
Death
Who will God save from death?

16 Don't be afraid of rich people
because their houses are more beautiful.
17 They don't take anything to the grave;
their wealth won't go down with them.
18 Even though they were praised when they were alive—
and people may praise you when you succeed—
19 they will go to where their ancestors are.
They will never see light again.
20 Rich people with no understanding
are just like animals that die.

God Wants True Worship

A psalm of Asaph.

50 The God of gods, the LORD, speaks.
He calls the earth from the rising to the setting sun.
2 God shines from Jerusalem,
whose beauty is perfect.
3 Our God comes, and he will not be silent.
A fire burns in front of him,
and a powerful storm surrounds him.
4 He calls to the sky above and to the earth
that he might judge his people.
5 He says, "Gather around, you who worship me,
who have made an agreement with me, using a sacrifice."
6 God is the judge,
and even the skies say he is right. *Selah*

7 God says, "My people, listen to me;
Israel, I will testify against you.
I am God, your God.
8 I do not scold you for your sacrifices.
You always bring me your burnt offerings.
9 But I do not need bulls from your stalls
or goats from your pens,
10 because every animal of the forest is already mine.
The cattle on a thousand hills are mine.
11 I know every bird on the mountains,
and every living thing in the fields is mine.
12 If I were hungry, I would not tell you,
because the earth and everything in it are mine.
13 I don't eat the meat of bulls
or drink the blood of goats.
14 Give an offering to show thanks to God.
Give God Most High what you have promised.
15 Call to me in times of trouble.
I will save you, and you will honor me."

16 But God says to the wicked,
"Why do you talk about my laws?
Why do you mention my agreement?
17 You hate my teachings
and turn your back on what I say.
18 When you see a thief, you join him.
You take part in adultery.
19 You don't stop your mouth from speaking evil,
and your tongue makes up lies.
20 You speak against your brother
and lie about your mother's son.
21 I have kept quiet while you did these things,
so you thought I was just like you.
But I will scold you
and accuse you to your face.

22 "Think about this, you who forget God.

Otherwise, I will tear you apart,
and no one will save you.
23 Those people honor me
who bring me offerings to show thanks.
And I, God, will save those who do that."

A Prayer for Forgiveness

For the director of music. A psalm of David when the prophet Nathan came to David after David's sin with Bathsheba.

51 God, be merciful to me
because you are loving.
Because you are always ready to be merciful,
wipe out all my wrongs.
2 Wash away all my guilt
and make me clean again.

3 I know about my wrongs,
and I can't forget my sin.
4 You are the only one I have sinned against;
I have done what you say is wrong.
You are right when you speak
and fair when you judge.
5 I was brought into this world in sin.
In sin my mother gave birth to me.

6 You want me
to be completely truthful,
so teach me wisdom.

51:6
Truth
How does God want you to live?

7 Take away my sin, and I will be clean.
Wash me, and I will be whiter than snow.
8 Make me hear sounds of joy and gladness;
let the bones you crushed be happy again.
9 Turn your face from my sins
and wipe out all my guilt.

10 Create in me a pure heart, God,
and make my spirit right again.
11 Do not send me away from you
or take your Holy Spirit away from me.

FAITH links

LEARNING FROM MISTAKES

PSALM 51:12-13

Suppose you were punished for something you did wrong. If you saw a friend about to do the same thing that got you in trouble, you would try to stop him, wouldn't you? That's what is known as learning from your mistakes.

David wrote this psalm after God sent a prophet to tell David about a sin that David tried to cover up. Once God forgave him, David wanted to encourage others to ask God for forgiveness. Telling others about God—and even about the mistakes for which you've received forgiveness—helps you and others grow in faith.

How can you help others learn from your mistakes? Link here to find out:

An Attention-Getter, Numbers 22, p. 207

On the Wrong Foot, 2 Kings 21:1–2, 16, p. 509

A Useless Thing, Isaiah 44:9, 18–20, p. 954

Real Repentance, Jeremiah 4:1–4, p. 993

Prayer for a Friend, Colossians 1:9–12, p. 1620

You're a Fake!, 2 Peter 2:1, p. 1709

12 Give me back the joy of your
salvation.
Keep me strong by giving me a
willing spirit.
13 Then I will teach your ways to those
who do wrong,
and sinners will turn back to you.

14 God, save me from the guilt of
murder,
God of my salvation,
and I will sing about your
goodness.
15 Lord, let me speak
so I may praise you.
16 You are not pleased by sacrifices, or I
would give them.
You don't want burnt offerings.
17 The sacrifice God wants is a broken
spirit.
God, you will not reject a heart
that is broken and sorry for sin.

18 Do whatever good you wish for
Jerusalem.
Rebuild the walls of Jerusalem.
19 Then you will be pleased with right
sacrifices and whole burnt
offerings,
and bulls will be offered on your
altar.

God Will Punish the Proud

For the director of music. A maskil of David. When Doeg the Edomite came to Saul and said to him, "David is in Ahimelech's house."

52 Mighty warrior, why do you brag
about the evil you do?
God's love will continue forever.
2 You think up evil plans.
Your tongue is like a sharp razor,
making up lies.
3 You love wrong more than right
and lies more than truth. *Selah*
4 You love words that bite
and tongues that lie.

5 But God will ruin you forever.
He will grab you and throw you out
of your tent;
he will tear you away from the land
of the living. *Selah*
6 Those who do right will see this and
fear God.
They will laugh at you and say,
7 "Look what happened to the man
who did not depend on God
but depended on his money.
He grew strong by his evil plans."

8 But I am like an
olive tree
growing in
God's
Temple.
I trust God's love
forever and ever.
9 God, I will thank you forever for what
you have done.
With those who worship you, I will
trust you because you are good.

EMAIL! FROM GOD
52:5–9
Trust
Trusting in God makes a difference.

The Unbelieving Fool

For the director of music. By mahalath. A maskil of David.

53 Fools say to themselves,
"There is no God."
Fools are evil and do terrible things;
none of them does anything good.

2 God looked down from heaven on all
people
to see if anyone was wise,
if anyone was looking to God for
help.
3 But all have turned away.
Together, everyone has become
evil;
none of them does anything good.
Not a single person.

4 Don't the wicked understand?
They destroy my people as if they
were eating bread.
They do not ask God for help.
5 The wicked are filled with terror
where there had been nothing to
fear.
God will scatter the bones of your
enemies.
You will defeat them,
because God has rejected them.

6 I pray that victory will come to Israel
from Mount Zion!
May God bring them back.
Then the people of Jacob will
rejoice,
and the people of Israel will be
glad.

A Prayer for Help

For the director of music. With stringed instruments. A maskil of David when the Ziphites went to Saul and said, "We think David is hiding among our people."

54 God, save me because of who you
are.
By your strength show that I am
innocent.
2 Hear my prayer, God;
listen to what I say.
3 Strangers turn against me,
and cruel men want to kill me.
They do not care about God. *Selah*

4 See, God will help me;
the Lord will support me.
5 Let my enemies be punished with
their own evil.
Destroy them because you are
loyal to me.

6 I will offer a sacrifice as a special gift
to you.
I will thank you, LORD, because
you are good.
7 You have saved me from all my
troubles,
and I have seen my enemies
defeated.

A Prayer About a False Friend

For the director of music. With stringed instruments. A maskil of David.

55 God, listen to my prayer
and do not ignore my cry for help.
2 Pay attention to me and answer me.
I am troubled and upset
3 by what the enemy says
and how the wicked look at me.
They bring troubles down on me,
and in anger they attack me.
4 I am frightened inside;
the terror of death has attacked
me.
5 I am scared and shaking,
and terror grips me.
6 I said, "I wish I had wings like a
dove.
Then I would fly away and rest.
7 I would wander far away
and stay in the desert. *Selah*
8 I would hurry to my place of escape,
far away from the wind and storm."

9 Lord, destroy and confuse their
words,
because I see violence and fighting
in the city.
10 Day and night they are all around its
walls,
and evil and trouble are
everywhere inside.
11 Destruction is everywhere in the
city;
trouble and lying never leave its
streets.

12 It was not an
enemy
insulting me.
I could stand
that.
It was not
someone who hated me.
I could hide from him.
13 But it is you, a person like me,
my companion and good friend.
14 We had a good friendship
and walked together to God's
Temple.

EMAIL FROM GOD
55:12–14
Friendship
Can friends cause you pain?

15 Let death take away my enemies.
Let them die while they are still
young
because evil lives with them.
16 But I will call to God for help,
and the LORD will save me.
17 Morning, noon, and night I am
troubled and upset,
but he will listen to me.
18 Many are against me,
but he keeps me safe in battle.
19 God who lives forever
will hear me and punish them. *Selah*

But they will not change;
they do not fear God.

20 The one who was my friend attacks his friends
and breaks his promises.
21 His words are slippery like butter,
but war is in his heart.
His words are smoother than oil,
but they cut like knives.

22 Give your worries to the LORD,
and he will take care of you.
He will never let good people down.
23 But, God, you will bring down
the wicked to the grave.
Murderers and liars will live
only half a lifetime.
But I will trust in you.

Trusting God for Help

For the director of music. To the tune of "The Dove in the Distant Oak." A miktam of David when the Philistines captured him in Gath.

56 God, be merciful to me because people are chasing me;
the battle has pressed me all day long.
2 My enemies have chased me all day;
there are many proud people fighting me.
3 When I am afraid,
I will trust you.
4 I praise God for his word.
I trust God, so I am not afraid.
What can human beings do to me?

5 All day long they twist my words;
all their evil plans are against me.
6 They wait. They hide.
They watch my steps,
hoping to kill me.
7 God, do not let them escape;
punish the foreign nations in your anger.
8 You have recorded my troubles.
You have kept a list of my tears.
Aren't they in your records?

9 On the day I call for help, my enemies will be defeated.
I know that God is on my side.
10 I praise God for his word to me;
I praise the LORD for his word.
11 I trust in God.
I will not be afraid.
What can people do to me?

eMAIL FROM GOD
56:11
Trust
Why you should not fear

12 God, I must keep my promises to you.
I will give you my offerings to thank you,
13 because you have saved me from death.
You have kept me from being defeated.
So I will walk with God
in light among the living.

A Prayer in Troubled Times

For the director of music. To the tune of "Do Not Destroy." A miktam of David when he escaped from Saul in the cave.

57 Be merciful to me, God; be merciful to me
because I come to you for protection.
Let me hide under the shadow of your wings
until the trouble has passed.

2 I cry out to God Most High,
to the God who does everything for me.
3 He sends help from heaven and saves me.
He punishes those who chase me. *Selah*
God sends me his love and truth.

4 Enemies, like lions, are all around me;
I must lie down among them.
Their teeth are like spears and arrows,
their tongues as sharp as swords.

5 God is supreme over the skies;
his majesty covers the earth.

6 They set a trap for me.
I am very worried.

Livin' it

TRUSTING IN GOD

Psalm 56

Trustometer Who can you count on to always stick with you—someone you can trust completely? Imagine having a "trustometer" marked off from 1 to 10. Who would send the pointer up to 10? Is there anyone who wouldn't even move the pointer to 1?

Sometimes it's hard to know who you can trust. And sometimes people we trust let us down. But we can always trust God in everything, no matter what comes up. (Check it out in Psalm 18.)

You can count on certain things to happen. You know everyone will get older, the sun is always in the sky, and God will help those who trust him. (Read 1 Chronicles 5:18–20, p. 525.) God always rates a 10+ on the trustometer!

MORE FAITH links

Your Total Trust, p. 229

Learning to Trust, p. 727

A Direct Path, p. 829

When Bad Things Happen, p. 876

The Power of *If*, p. 1344

Toss Those Troubles!, p. 1706

"Hey, Tagg, where would you rate on the trustometer?"

"I'm not sure. Some days, I think I would be up there, but others, I might rate pretty low. I'm glad that God's not like that! Download some of these Faithlinks about trusting God."

From Zero to Hero, Judges 6; 7, p. 319

- Would you stand up to all the toughest kids in school if God said you could? Or would you hide in your room for a month?
- Gideon faced a tough situation—and he was scared. But faith in God made him go from zero to hero. Where do you fit in—zero or hero—or somewhere in between?

The Foundation of Our Hope, Isaiah 31:1–8, p. 934

- Some people trust money or power. But those things can disappear overnight. What should your hope be based on? This Faithlink will give you the answer.

Our Good Shepherd, John 10:11–15, p. 1441

- Sheep are pretty helpless by themselves. They trust the shepherd for everything. How are you like a sheep? What do you trust Jesus, the good shepherd, to do for you?

my FAVORITE links

They dug a pit in my path,
but they fell into it themselves. *Selah*

7 My heart is steady, God; my heart is steady.
I will sing and praise you.
8 Wake up, my soul.
Wake up, harp and lyre!
I will wake up the dawn.
9 Lord, I will praise you among the nations;
I will sing songs of praise about you to all the nations.
10 Your great love reaches to the skies,
your truth to the clouds.
11 God, you are supreme above the skies.
Let your glory be over all the earth.

Unfair Judges

For the director of music. To the tune of "Do Not Destroy." A miktam of David.

58 Do you rulers really say what is right?
Do you judge people fairly?
2 No, in your heart you plan evil;
you think up violent crimes in the land.
3 From birth, evil people turn away from God;
they wander off and tell lies as soon as they are born.
4 They are like poisonous snakes,
like deaf cobras that stop up their ears
5 so they cannot hear the music of the snake charmer
no matter how well he plays.

6 God, break the teeth in their mouths!
Tear out the fangs of those lions, LORD!
7 Let them disappear like water that flows away.
Let them be cut short like a broken arrow.

From birth, evil people turn away from God; they wander off and tell lies as soon as they are born.
—Psalm 58:3

8 Let them be like snails that melt as they move.
Let them be like a child born dead who never saw the sun.
9 His anger will blow them away alive faster than burning thorns can heat a pot.
10 Good people will be glad when they see him get even.
They will wash their feet in the blood of the wicked.
11 Then people will say,
"There really are rewards for doing what is right.
There really is a God who judges the world."

A Prayer for Protection

For the director of music. To the tune of "Do Not Destroy." A miktam of David when Saul sent men to watch David's house to kill him.

59 God, save me from my enemies.
Protect me from those who come against me.
2 Save me from those who do evil
and from murderers.

3 Look, men are waiting to ambush me.
Cruel men attack me,
but I have not sinned or done wrong, LORD.
4 I have done nothing wrong, but they are ready to attack me.
Wake up to help me, and look.
5 You are the LORD God All-Powerful, the God of Israel.
Arise and punish those people.
Do not give those traitors any mercy. *Selah*

6 They come back at night.
Like dogs they growl and roam around the city.
7 Notice what comes from their mouths.

Insults come from their lips,
because they say, "Who's listening?"
8 But, LORD, you laugh at them;
you make fun of all of them.

9 God, my strength, I am looking to you,
because God is my defender.
10 My God loves me, and he goes in front of me.
He will help me defeat my enemies.
11 Lord, our protector, do not kill them,
or my people will forget.
With your power scatter them and defeat them.
12 They sin by what they say;
they sin with their words.
They curse and tell lies,
so let their pride trap them.
13 Destroy them in your anger;
destroy them completely!
Then they will know
that God rules over Israel
and to the ends of the earth. *Selah*

14 They come back at night.
Like dogs they growl
and roam around the city.
15 They wander about looking for food,
and they howl if they do not find enough.
16 But I will sing about your strength.
In the morning I will sing about your love.
You are my defender,
my place of safety in times of trouble.
17 God, my strength, I will sing praises to you.
God, my defender, you are the God who loves me.

A Prayer After a Defeat

For the director of music. To the tune of "Lily of the Agreement." A miktam of David. For teaching. When David fought the Arameans of Northwest Mesopotamia and Zobah, and when Joab returned and defeated twelve thousand Edomites at the Valley of Salt.

60 God, you have rejected us and scattered us.
You have been angry, but please come back to us.
2 You made the earth shake and crack.
Heal its breaks because it is shaking.
3 You have given your people trouble.
You made us unable to walk straight, like people drunk with wine.
4 You have raised a banner to gather those who fear you.
Now they can stand up against the enemy. *Selah*

5 Answer us and save us by your power
so the people you love will be rescued.

6 God has said from his Temple,
"When I win, I will divide Shechem
and measure off the Valley of Succoth.
7 Gilead and Manasseh are mine.
Ephraim is like my helmet.
Judah holds my royal scepter.
8 Moab is like my washbowl.
I throw my sandals at Edom.
I shout at Philistia."

9 Who will bring me to the strong, walled city?
Who will lead me to Edom?
10 God, surely you have rejected us;
you do not go out with our armies.
11 Help us fight the enemy.
Human help is useless,
12 but we can win with God's help.
He will defeat our enemies.

A Prayer for Protection

For the director of music. With stringed instruments. Of David.

61 God, hear my cry;
listen to my prayer.
2 I call to you from the ends of the earth
when I am afraid.
Carry me away to a high mountain.
3 You have been my protection,
like a strong tower against my enemies.

4 Let me live in your Holy Tent
forever.
Let me find safety in the shelter of
your wings. *Selah*

5 God, you have heard my promises.
You have given me what belongs to
those who fear you.

6 Give the king a long life;
let him live many
years.
7 Let him rule in the
presence of God
forever.
Protect him with
your love and
truth.
8 Then I will praise
your name
forever,
and every day I will
keep my promises.

You have been my protection.
—Psalm 61:3

Trust Only in God

For the director of music. For Jeduthun.
A psalm of David.

62 I find rest in God;
only he can save me.
2 He is my rock and my salvation.
He is my defender;
I will not be defeated.

3 How long will you attack someone?
Will all of you kill that person?
Who is like a leaning wall, like a
fence ready to fall?
4 They are planning to make that
person fall.
They enjoy telling lies.
With their mouths they bless,
but in their hearts they curse. *Selah*

5 I find rest in God;
only he gives me hope.
6 He is my rock and my salvation.
He is my defender;
I will not be defeated.
7 My honor and salvation come from
God.
He is my mighty rock and my
protection.

8 People, trust God
all the time.
Tell him all
your
problems,
because God is
our
protection. *Selah*

Trust
Who do you trust with your problems?

9 The least of people are only a breath,
and even the
greatest are just
a lie.
On the scales, they
weigh nothing;
together they are
only a breath.
10 Do not trust in force.
Stealing is of no
use.
Even if you gain more
riches,
don't put your trust in them.

11 God has said this,
and I have heard it over and over:
God is strong.
12 The Lord is loving.
You reward people for what they
have done.

Wishing to Be Near God

A psalm of David when he was
in the desert of Judah.

63 God, you are my God.
I search for you.
I thirst for you
like someone in a dry, empty land
where there is no water.
2 I have seen you in the Temple
and have seen your strength and
glory.
3 Because your love is better than
life,
I will praise you.
4 I will praise you as long as I live.
I will lift up my hands in prayer to
your name.
5 I will be content as if I had eaten the
best foods.
My lips will sing, and my mouth
will praise you.

6 I remember you while I'm lying in
bed;
I think about you through the
night.
7 You are my help.
Because of your
protection, I
sing.
8 I stay close to you;
you support me
with your right
hand.

9 Some people are
trying to kill me,
but they will go down to the grave.
10 They will be killed with swords
and eaten by wild dogs.
11 But the king will rejoice in his God.
All who make promises in his
name will praise him,
but the mouths of liars will be
shut.

I remember you while I'm lying in bed; I think about you through the night.
—Psalm 63:6

A Prayer Against Enemies

For the director of music.
A psalm of David.

64 God, listen to my complaint.
I am afraid of my enemies;
protect my life from them.
2 Hide me from those who plan wicked
things,
from that gang who does evil.
3 They sharpen their tongues like
swords
and shoot bitter words like arrows.
4 From their hiding places they shoot
at innocent people;
they shoot suddenly and are not
afraid.
5 They encourage each other to do
wrong.
They talk about setting traps,
thinking no one will see them.
6 They plan wicked things and say,
"We have a perfect plan."
The mind of human beings is hard
to understand.

7 But God will shoot them with
arrows;
they will suddenly be struck down.
8 Their own words will be used against
them.
All who see them will shake their
heads.
9 Then everyone will
fear God.
They will tell what
God has done,
and they will learn
from what he
has done.
10 Good people will be
happy in the
LORD
and will find
protection in him.
Let everyone who is honest praise
the LORD.

A Hymn of Thanksgiving

For the director of music. A psalm of
David. A song.

65 God, you will be praised in
Jerusalem.
We will keep our promises to you.
2 You hear our prayers.
All people will come to you.
3 Our guilt overwhelms us,
but you forgive our sins.
4 Happy are the people you choose
and invite to stay in your court.
We are filled with good things in your
house,
your holy Temple.

5 You answer us in amazing ways,
God our Savior.
People everywhere on the earth
and beyond the sea trust you.
6 You made the mountains by your
strength;
you are dressed in power.
7 You stopped the roaring seas,
the roaring waves,
and the uproar of the nations.
8 Even those people at the ends of the
earth fear your miracles.
You are praised from where the
sun rises to where it sets.

9 You take care of the land and water
it;

you make it very fertile.
The rivers of God are full of water.
Grain grows because you make it
grow.
10 You send rain to the plowed fields;
you fill the rows with water.
You soften the ground with rain,
and then you bless it with crops.
11 You give the year a good harvest,
and you load the wagons with
many crops.
12 The desert is covered with grass
and the hills with happiness.
13 The pastures are full of flocks,
and the valleys are covered with
grain.
Everything shouts and sings for
joy.

Praise God for What He Has Done

For the director of music.
A song. A psalm.

66 Everything on earth, shout with
joy to God!
2 Sing about his glory!
Make his praise glorious!
3 Say to God, "Your
works are
amazing!
Because your
power is great,
your enemies fall
before you.
4 All the earth worships
you
and sings praises to
you.
They sing praises
to your name." *Selah*

5 Come and see what God has done,
the amazing things he has done for
people.
6 He turned the sea into dry land.
The people crossed the river on
foot.
So let us rejoice because of what
he did.
7 He rules forever with his power.
He keeps his eye on the nations,
so people should not turn against
him. *Selah*

8 You people, praise our God;
loudly sing his praise.
9 He protects our lives
and does not let us be defeated.
10 God, you have tested us;
you have purified us like silver.
11 You let us be trapped
and put a heavy load on us.
12 You let our enemies walk on our
heads.
We went through fire and flood,
but you brought us to a place with
good things.

13 I will come to your Temple with
burnt offerings.
I will give you what I promised,
14 things I promised when I was in
trouble.
15 I will bring you offerings of fat
animals,
and I will offer sheep, bulls, and
goats. *Selah*

16 All of you who fear God, come and
listen,
and I will tell you what he has done
for me.
17 I cried out to him
with my mouth
and praised him
with my
tongue.
18 If I had known of any
sin in my
heart,
the Lord would not
have listened
to me.
19 But God has listened;
he has heard my prayer.
20 Praise God,
who did not ignore my prayer
or hold back his love from me.

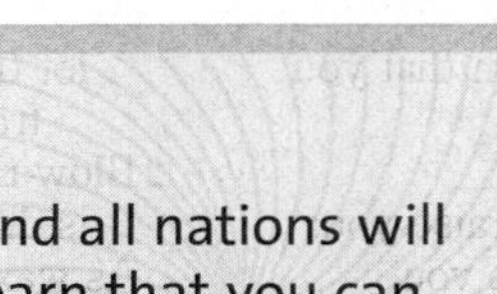
And all nations will
learn that you can
save.
—Psalm 67:2

Everyone Should Praise God

For the director of music. With stringed
instruments. A psalm. A song.

67 God, have mercy on us and
bless us
and show us your kindness *Selah*
2 so the world will learn your ways,

LET'S VISIT JERUSALEM **Psalm 68:29**

The city of Jerusalem was on top of a hill. That was a great thing for a city in those days because the city guards could see any enemies that might come to attack them. When David was king, one of the first things he did was make Jerusalem the capital of Israel. (Check out 2 Samuel 5:6–10, p. 404; 1 Chronicles 11:4–9, p. 534.) This made Jerusalem the most important city for the people of Israel. It was important to their religion and their politics. When Solomon (David's son) became king, he built an amazing Temple in Jerusalem. (Read 1 Kings 6; 7, p. 442; 2 Chronicles 3; 4, p. 564.) Jerusalem became the most beautiful city in the country.

Later, Jerusalem played an important role in Jesus' life and ministry. Jesus went to Temple in Jerusalem. It was also in Jerusalem that Jesus was crucified and buried, and it was there that God brought him back to life.

Today, Jerusalem is a holy city for three world religions: Christianity, Judaism, and Islam.

and all nations will learn that you
can save.

3 God, the people should praise you;
all people should praise you.
4 The nations should be glad and sing
because you judge people fairly.
You guide all the nations on earth.
Selah
5 God, the people should praise you;
all people should praise you.

6 The land has given its crops.
God, our God, blesses us.
7 God blesses us
so people all over the earth will
fear him.

Praise God Who Saved the Nation

For the director of music. A psalm of David. A song.

68 Let God rise up and scatter his
enemies;
let those who hate him run away
from him.
2 Blow them away as smoke
is driven away by the wind.
As wax melts before a fire,
let the wicked be destroyed before
God.
3 But those who do right should be
glad
and should rejoice before God;
they should be happy and glad.

4 Sing to God; sing praises to his
name.
Prepare the way for him
who rides
through the
desert,
whose name is
the LORD.
Rejoice before
him.
5 God is in his holy Temple.
He is a father to orphans,
and he defends the widows.

EMAIL! FROM GOD **68:5**
Caring
Check out if God cares for needy people.

6 God gives the lonely a home.
He leads prisoners out with joy,
but those who turn against God
will live in a dry land.

7 God, you led your people out
when you marched through the
desert. *Selah*

8 The ground shook
and the sky poured down rain
before God, the God of Mount Sinai,
before God, the God of Israel.
9 God, you sent much rain;
you refreshed your tired land.
10 Your people settled there.
God, in your goodness
you took care of the poor.

11 The Lord gave the command,
and a great army told the news:
12 "Kings and their armies run away.
In camp they divide the wealth
taken in war.
13 Those who stayed by the campfires
will share the riches taken in
battle."
14 The Almighty scattered kings
like snow on Mount Zalmon.

15 The mountains of Bashan are high;
the mountains of Bashan have
many peaks.
16 Why do you mountains with many
peaks look with envy
on the mountain that God chose
for his home?
The LORD will live there forever.
17 God comes with millions of chariots;
the Lord comes from Mount Sinai
to his holy place.
18 When you went up to the heights,
you led a parade of captives.
You received gifts from the people,
even from those who turned against
you.
And the LORD God will live there.

19 Praise the Lord, God our Savior,
who helps us every day. *Selah*
20 Our God is a God who saves us;
the LORD God saves us from
death.
21 God will crush his enemies' heads,
the hairy skulls of those who
continue to sin.
22 The Lord said, "I will bring the
enemy back from Bashan;
I will bring them back from the
depths of the sea.
23 Then you can stick your feet in their
blood,
and your dogs can lick their
share."

24 God, people have seen your victory
march;
God my King marched into the
holy place.
25 The singers are in front and the
instruments are behind.
In the middle are the girls with the
tambourines.
26 Praise God in the meeting place;
praise the LORD in the gathering of
Israel.
27 There is the smallest tribe,
Benjamin, leading them.
And there are the leaders of Judah
with their group.
There also are the leaders of
Zebulun and of Naphtali.

28 God, order up your power;
show the mighty power you have
used for us before.
29 Kings will bring their wealth to you,
to your Temple in Jerusalem.
30 Punish Egypt, the beast in the tall
grass along the river.
Punish the leaders of nations,
those bulls among the cows.
Defeated, they will bring you their
silver.
Scatter those nations that love war.
31 Messengers will come from Egypt;
the people of Cush will pray to
God.

32 Kingdoms of the earth, sing to God;
sing praises to the Lord. *Selah*
33 Sing to the one who rides through
the skies, which are from long
ago.
He speaks with a thundering voice.
34 Announce that God is powerful.

He rules over Israel,
and his power is in the skies.
35 God, you are wonderful in your Temple.
The God of Israel gives his people strength and power.

Praise God!

A Cry for Help

For the director of music. To the tune of "Lilies." A psalm of David.

69 God, save me,
because the water has risen to my neck.
2 I'm sinking down into the mud,
and there is nothing to stand on.
I am in deep water,
and the flood covers me.
3 I am tired from calling for help;
my throat is sore.
My eyes are tired from waiting
for God to help me.
4 There are more people who hate me
for no reason than hairs on my head;
powerful enemies want to destroy
me for no reason.
They make me pay back
what I did not steal.

5 God, you know what I have done wrong;
I cannot hide my guilt from you.
6 Lord GOD All-Powerful,
do not let those who hope in you
be ashamed because of me.
God of Israel,
do not let your worshipers be
disgraced because of me.
7 For you, I carry this shame,
and my face is covered with disgrace.
8 I am like a stranger to my closest relatives
and a foreigner to my mother's children.
9 My strong love for your Temple
completely controls me.
When people insult you, it hurts me.
10 When I cry and go without food,
they make fun of me.
11 When I wear clothes of sadness,
they joke about me.
12 They make fun of me in public places,
and the drunkards make up songs about me.

IN DEEP WATER

PSALM 69

If you've ever been in an ocean or in the deep end of a swimming pool, you know what water up to the neck feels like. The conflicts in life can make you feel like you're in deep water or even mud. David wrote psalms like this one to express his feelings of distress. These psalms were prayers to God for help to handle the conflicts in his life.

You can't go through life without having some conflict. But you can follow David's example and rely on God. He offers wisdom and other tools to help you handle the conflicts in life.

More Powerful Than Revenge, Genesis 50:14–21, p. 71

Approaching God, Numbers 3:10, p. 180

Real Faith or Really Scared?, Judges 4, p. 315

Learning to Trust, Psalm 25:4–5, p. 727

Sad Times, Matthew 14:13–14, p. 1299

How Do You Grow?, Titus 1:1, p. 1659

13 But I pray to you, LORD, for favor.
God, because of your great love,
answer me.
You are truly able to save.
14 Pull me from the mud,
and do not let me sink.
Save me from those who hate me
and from the deep water.
15 Do not let the flood drown me
or the deep water swallow me
or the grave close its mouth over
me.
16 LORD, answer me because your love
is so good.
Because of your great kindness,
turn to me.
17 Do not hide from me, your servant.
I am in trouble. Hurry to help me!
18 Come near and save me;
rescue me from my enemies.

19 You see my shame and disgrace.
You know all
my enemies
and what
they have
said.

EMAIL! FROM GOD 69
Worry
How do you handle stress?

20 Insults have
broken my
heart
and left me weak.
I looked for sympathy, but there was
none;
I found no one to comfort me.
21 They put poison in my food
and gave me vinegar to drink.

22 Let their own feasts cause their ruin;
let their feasts trap them and pay
them back.
23 Let their eyes be closed so they
cannot see
and their backs be forever weak
from troubles.
24 Pour your anger out on them;
let your anger catch up with them.
25 May their place be empty;
leave no one to live in their tents.
26 They chase after those you have
hurt,
and they talk about the pain of
those you have wounded.
27 Charge them with crime after crime,
and do not let them have anything
good.
28 Wipe their names from the book of
life,
and do not list them with those
who do what is right.

29 I am sad and hurting.
God, save me and protect me.

30 I will praise God in a song
and will honor him by giving
thanks.
31 That will please the LORD more than
offering him cattle,
more than sacrificing a bull with
horns and hoofs.
32 Poor people will see this and be glad.
Be encouraged, you who worship
God.
33 The LORD listens to those in need
and does not look down on
captives.

34 Heaven and earth should praise him,
the seas and everything in them.
35 God will save Jerusalem
and rebuild the cities of Judah.
Then people will live there and own
the land.
36 The descendants of his servants
will inherit that land,
and those who love him will live
there.

A Cry for God to Help Quickly

For the director of music.
A psalm of David. To help
people remember.

70 God, come quickly and save me.
LORD, hurry to help me.
2 Let those who are trying to kill me
be ashamed and disgraced.
Let those who want to hurt me
run away in disgrace.
3 Let those who make fun of me
stop because of their shame.
4 But let all those who worship you
rejoice and be glad.
Let those who love your salvation
always say, "Praise the greatness
of God."

5 I am poor and helpless;
God, hurry to me.
You help me and save me.
LORD, do not wait.

An Old Person's Prayer

71 In you, LORD, is my protection.
Never let me be ashamed.
2 Because you do what is right, save
and rescue me;
listen to me and save me.
3 Be my place of safety
where I can always come.
Give the command to save me,
because you are my rock and my
strong, walled city.
4 My God, save me from the power of
the wicked
and from the hold of evil and cruel
people.
5 LORD, you are my
hope.
LORD, I have
trusted you since
I was young.
6 I have depended on
you since I was
born;
you helped me
even on the day
of my birth.
I will always praise
you.

God, your justice reaches to the skies. You have done great things; God, there is no one like you.
—Psalm 71:19

7 I am an example to many people,
because you are my strong
protection.
8 I am always praising you;
all day long I honor you.
9 Do not reject me when I am old;
do not leave me when my strength
is gone.
10 My enemies make plans against me,
and they meet together to kill me.
11 They say, "God has left him.
Go after him and take him,
because no one will save him."

12 God, don't be far off.
My God, hurry to help me.
13 Let those who accuse me
be ashamed and destroyed.
Let those who are trying to hurt me
be covered with shame and
disgrace.
14 But I will always have hope
and will praise you more and more.
15 I will tell how you do what is right.
I will tell about your salvation all
day long,
even though it is more than I can
tell.
16 I will come and tell about your
powerful works, Lord GOD.
I will remind people that only you
do what is right.

17 God, you have taught me since I was
young.
To this day I tell about the miracles
you do.
18 Even though I am old and gray,
do not leave me, God.
I will tell the children
about your
power;
I will tell those who
live after me
about your
might.

19 God, your justice
reaches to the
skies.
You have done
great things;
God, there is no one like you.
20 You have given me many troubles
and bad times,
but you will give me life again.
When I am almost dead,
you will keep me alive.
21 You will make me greater than ever,
and you will comfort me again.

22 I will praise you with the harp.
I trust you, my God.
I will sing to you with the lyre,
Holy One of Israel.
23 I will shout for joy when I sing
praises to you.
You have saved me.
24 I will tell about your justice all day
long.
And those who want to hurt me
will be ashamed and disgraced.

A Prayer for the King

Of Solomon.

72 God, give the king your good judgment
and the king's son your goodness.
2 Help him judge your people fairly
and decide what is right for the poor.
3 Let there be peace on the mountains
and goodness on the hills for the people.
4 Help him be fair to the poor
and save the needy
and punish those who hurt them.

5 May they respect you as long as the sun shines
and as long as the moon glows.
6 Let him be like rain on the grass,
like showers that water the earth.
7 Let goodness be plentiful while he lives.
Let peace continue as long as there is a moon.

8 Let his kingdom go from sea to sea,
and from the Euphrates River to the ends of the earth.
9 Let the people of the desert bow down to him,
and make his enemies lick the dust.
10 Let the kings of Tarshish and the faraway lands
bring him gifts.
Let the kings of Sheba and Seba
bring their presents to him.
11 Let all kings bow down to him
and all nations serve him.

12 He will help the poor when they cry out
and will save the needy when no one else will help.
13 He will be kind to the weak and poor,
and he will save their lives.
14 He will save them from cruel people who try to hurt them,
because their lives are precious to him.

15 Long live the king!
Let him receive gold from Sheba.
Let people always pray for him
and bless him all day long.
16 Let the fields grow plenty of grain
and the hills be covered with crops.
Let the land be as fertile as Lebanon,
and let the cities grow like the grass in a field.
17 Let the king be famous forever;
let him be remembered as long as the sun shines.
Let the nations be blessed because of him,
and may they all bless him.

18 Praise the LORD God, the God of Israel,
who alone does such miracles.
19 Praise his glorious name forever.
Let his glory fill the whole world.
Amen and amen.

20 This ends the prayers of David son of Jesse.

Book 3

Should the Wicked Be Rich?

A psalm of Asaph.

73 God is truly good to Israel,
to those who have pure hearts.
2 But I had almost stopped believing;
I had almost lost my faith
3 because I was jealous of proud people.
I saw wicked people doing well.

4 They are not suffering;
they are healthy and strong.
5 They don't have troubles like the rest of us;
they don't have problems like other people.
6 They wear pride like a necklace
and put on violence as their clothing.
7 They are looking for profits
and do not control their selfish desires.
8 They make fun of others and speak evil;

proudly they speak of hurting
others.
9 They brag to the sky.
They say that they own the earth.
10 So their people turn to them
and give them whatever they want.
11 They say, "How can God know?
What does God Most High know?"
12 These people are wicked,
always at ease, and getting richer.
13 So why have I kept my heart pure?
Why have I kept my hands from
doing wrong?
14 I have suffered all day long;
I have been punished every
morning.

15 God, if I had decided to talk like this,
I would have let your people down.
16 I tried to understand all this,
but it was too hard for me to see
17 until I went to the Temple of God.
Then I understood what will
happen to them.
18 You have put them in danger;
you cause them to be destroyed.
19 They are destroyed in a moment;
they are swept away by terrors.
20 It will be like waking from a dream.
Lord, when you rise up, they will
disappear.

21 When my heart was sad
and I was angry,
22 I was senseless and stupid.
I acted like an animal toward you.
23 But I am always with you;
you have held my hand.
24 You guide me with your advice,
and later you
will receive
me in honor.
25 I have no one in
heaven but
you;
I want nothing
on earth besides you.
26 My body and my mind may become
weak,
but God is my strength.
He is mine forever.

27 Those who are far from God will die;
you destroy those who are
unfaithful.
28 But I am close to God, and that is
good.
The Lord GOD is my protection.
I will tell all that you have done.

EMAIL FROM GOD
73:24–26
Protection
Who is your strength?

A Nation in Trouble Prays

A maskil of Asaph.

74 God, why have you rejected us
for so long?
Why are you angry with us, the
sheep of your pasture?
2 Remember the people you bought
long ago.
You saved us, and we are your very
own.
After all, you live on Mount Zion.
3 Make your way through these old
ruins;
the enemy wrecked everything in
the Temple.

4 Those who were against you shouted
in your meeting place
and raised their flags there.
5 They came with axes raised
as if to cut down a forest of trees.
6 They smashed the carved panels
with their axes and hatchets.
7 They burned your Temple to the
ground;
they have made the place where
you live unclean.
8 They thought, "We will completely
crush them!"
They burned every place where
God was worshiped in the land.
9 We do not see any signs.
There are no more prophets,
and no one knows how long this
will last.
10 God, how much longer will the
enemy make fun of you?
Will they insult you forever?
11 Why do you hold back your power?
Bring your power out in the open
and destroy them!

12 God, you have been our king for a
long time.
You bring salvation to the earth.

13 You split open the sea by your power
and broke the heads of the sea
monster.
14 You smashed the heads of the
monster Leviathan
and gave him to the desert
creatures as food.
15 You opened up the springs and
streams
and made the flowing rivers run
dry.
16 Both the day and the night are yours;
you made the sun and the moon.
17 You set all the limits on the earth;
you created summer and winter.

18 LORD, remember how
the enemy
insulted you.
Remember how
those foolish
people made fun
of you.
19 Do not give us, your
doves, to those
wild animals.
Never forget your
poor people.

You set all the limits on the earth; you created summer and winter.
—Psalm 74:17

20 Remember the agreement you made
with us,
because violence fills every dark
corner of this land.
21 Do not let your suffering people be
disgraced.
Let the poor and helpless praise you.

22 God, arise and defend yourself.
Remember the insults that come
from those foolish people all day
long.
23 Don't forget what your enemies said;
don't forget their roar as they rise
against you always.

God the Judge

For the director of music. To the tune of "Do Not Destroy." A psalm of Asaph. A song.

75 God, we thank you;
we thank you because you are
near.
We tell about the miracles you do.

2 You say, "I set the time for trial,
and I will judge fairly.
3 The earth with all its people may
shake,
but I am the one who holds it
steady. *Selah*
4 I say to those who are proud, 'Don't
brag,'
and to the wicked, 'Don't show
your power.
5 Don't try to use your power against
heaven.
Don't be stubborn.' "

6 No one from the east or the west
or the desert
can judge you.
7 God is the judge;
he judges one
person as guilty
and another as
innocent.
8 The LORD holds a cup
of anger in his
hand;
it is full of wine
mixed with
spices.
He pours it out even to the last drop,
and the wicked drink it all.

9 I will tell about this forever;
I will sing praise to the God of
Jacob.
10 He will take all power away from the
wicked,
but the power of good people will
grow.

The God Who Always Wins

For the director of music.
With stringed instruments.
A psalm of Asaph. A song.

76 People in Judah know God;
his fame is great in Israel.
2 His Tent is in Jerusalem;
his home is on Mount Zion.
3 There God broke the flaming arrows,
the shields, the swords, and the
weapons of war. *Selah*

4 God, how wonderful you are!

You are more splendid than the
hills full of animals.
5 The brave soldiers were stripped
as they lay asleep in death.
Not one warrior
had the strength to stop it.
6 God of Jacob, when you spoke
strongly,
horses and riders
fell dead.
7 You are feared;
no one can stand
against you when
you are angry.
8 From heaven you
gave the
decision,
and the earth was
afraid and silent.
9 God, you stood up to
judge
and to save the needy people of
the earth. *Selah*
10 People praise you for your anger
against evil.
Those who live through your anger
are stopped from doing more
evil.
11 Make and keep your promises to the
LORD your God.
From all around, gifts should come
to the God we worship.
12 God breaks the spirits of great
leaders;
the kings on earth fear him.

Make and keep your promises to the LORD your God.
—Psalm 76:11

Remembering God's Help

For the director of music. For Jeduthun.
A psalm of Asaph.

77 I cry out to God;
I call to God, and he will hear me.
2 I look for the Lord on the day of
trouble.
All night long I reach out my
hands,
but I cannot be comforted.
3 When I remember God, I become
upset;
when I think, I become afraid. *Selah*

4 You keep my eyes from closing.
I am too upset to say anything.
5 I keep thinking about the old days,
the years of long ago.
6 At night I remember my songs.
I think and I ask myself:
7 "Will the Lord reject us forever?
Will he never be kind to us again?
8 Is his love gone forever?
Has he stopped speaking
for all time?
9 Has God forgotten
mercy?
Is he too angry to
pity us?" *Selah*
10 Then I say "This is
what makes
me sad:
For years the
power of God
Most High was
with us."

11 I remember what the LORD did;
I remember the miracles you did
long ago.
12 I think about all the things you did
and consider your deeds.

13 God, your ways are holy.
No god is as great as our God.
14 You are the God who does miracles;
you have shown people your power.
15 By your power you have saved your
people,
the descendants of Jacob and
Joseph. *Selah*

16 God, the waters saw you;
they saw you and became afraid;
the deep waters shook with fear.
17 The clouds poured down their rain.
The sky thundered.
Your lightning flashed back and
forth like arrows.
18 Your thunder sounded in the
whirlwind.
Lightning lit up the world.
The earth trembled and shook.
19 You made a way through the sea
and paths through the deep waters,
but your footprints were not seen.
20 You led your people like a flock
by using Moses and Aaron.

God Saved Israel from Egypt

A maskil of Asaph.

78 My people, listen to my teaching;
listen to what I say.
2 I will speak using stories;
I will tell secret things from long ago.
3 We have heard them and known them
by what our ancestors have told us.
4 We will not keep them from our children;
we will tell those who come later
about the praises of the LORD.
We will tell about his power
and the miracles he has done.

5 The LORD made an agreement with Jacob
and gave the teachings to Israel,
which he commanded our ancestors
to teach to their children.
6 Then their children would know them,
even their children not yet born.
And they would tell their children.
7 So they would all trust God
and would not forget what he had done

CONNECT 2-YOU

ASK AND YOU SHALL RECEIVE

Tagg and I are talking about why prayer is such a cool thing. We have a friend who has some questions about prayer. Let's welcome Michael, age 9, to Connect 2-You.

Hey, Michael. What do you want to know?

Michael

I don't understand prayer. I always hear people in church talk about how God answered their prayers. But when I ask God for the things that I want, I never get them. Does that mean he's not listening to me—or that he doesn't like me?

Michael, it sounds like you're thinking of prayer as a Christmas list. It's much, much more than that. Prayer gives us the chance to talk personally with the Creator of the universe. We can thank God for the things he does for us every day. We can ask him to forgive us for the bad things we've done. We can ask him to guide our lives. He will listen to everything we say and then answer us. He may say "Yes," he may say "No," or he may say, "Not yet"—but he hears and will answer every prayer. For tips on talking to God, check out the Livin' It page on prayer, Psalm 86:1-7, p. 775.

Remember, Michael, prayer is a two-way conversation. You talk to God and then let him talk to you. He may speak through a Bible verse or through some events in your life, but he will speak. And if you keep your eyes and ears open, you'll know when he does.

but would obey his commands.
8 They would not be like their ancestors
who were stubborn and disobedient.
Their hearts were not loyal to God,
and they were not true to him.

9 The men of Ephraim had bows for weapons,
but they ran away on the day of battle.
10 They didn't keep their agreement with God
and refused to live by his teachings.
11 They forgot what he had done
and the miracles he had shown them.
12 He did miracles while their ancestors watched,
in the fields of Zoan in Egypt.
13 He divided the Red Sea and led them through.
He made the water stand up like a wall.
14 He led them with a cloud by day
and by the light of a fire by night.
15 He split the rocks in the desert
and gave them more than enough water, as if from the deep ocean.
16 He brought streams out of the rock
and caused water to flow down like rivers.

17 But the people continued to sin against him;
in the desert they turned against God Most High.
18 They decided to test God
by asking for the food they wanted.
19 Then they spoke against God,
saying, "Can God prepare food in the desert?
20 When he hit the rock, water poured out
and rivers flowed down.
But can he give us bread also?
Will he provide his people with meat?"
21 When the LORD heard them, he was very angry.
His anger was like fire to the people of Jacob;
his anger grew against the people of Israel.
22 They had not believed God
and had not trusted him to save them.
23 But he gave a command to the clouds above
and opened the doors of heaven.
24 He rained manna down on them to eat;
he gave them grain from heaven.
25 So they ate the bread of angels.
He sent them all the food they could eat.
26 He sent the east wind from heaven
and led the south wind by his power.
27 He rained meat on them like dust.
The birds were as many as the sand of the sea.
28 He made the birds fall inside the camp,
all around the tents.
29 So the people ate and became very full.
God had given them what they wanted.
30 While they were still eating,
and while the food was still in their mouths,
31 God became angry with them.
He killed some of the healthiest of them;
he struck down the best young men of Israel.

32 But they kept on sinning;
they did not believe even with the miracles.
33 So he ended their days without meaning
and their years in terror.
34 Anytime he killed them, they would look to him for help;
they would come back to God and follow him.
35 They would remember that God was their Rock,
that God Most High had saved them.
36 But their words were false,

and their tongues lied to him.
37 Their hearts were not really loyal to God;
they did not keep his agreement.
38 Still God was merciful.
He forgave their sins
and did not destroy them.
Many times he held back his anger
and did not stir up all his anger.
39 He remembered that they were only human,
like a wind that blows and does not come back.

40 They turned against God so often in the desert
and grieved him there.
41 Again and again they tested God
and brought pain to the Holy One of Israel.
42 They did not remember his power
or the time he saved them from the enemy.
43 They forgot the signs he did in Egypt
and his wonders in the fields of Zoan.
44 He turned their rivers to blood
so no one could drink the water.
45 He sent flies that bit the people.
He sent frogs that destroyed them.
46 He gave their crops to grasshoppers
and what they worked for to locusts.
47 He destroyed their vines with hail
and their sycamore trees with sleet.
48 He killed their animals with hail
and their cattle with lightning.
49 He showed them his hot anger.
He sent his strong anger against them,
his destroying angels.
50 He found a way to show his anger.
He did not keep them from dying
but let them die by a terrible disease.
51 God killed all the firstborn sons in Egypt,
the oldest son of each family of Ham.[n]
52 But God led his people out like sheep
and he guided them like a flock through the desert.
53 He led them to safety so they had nothing to fear,
but their enemies drowned in the sea.
54 So God brought them to his holy land,
to the mountain country he took with his own power.
55 He forced out the other nations,
and he had his people inherit the land.
He let the tribes of Israel settle there in tents.

56 But they tested God
and turned against God Most High;
they did not keep his rules.
57 They turned away and were disloyal just like their ancestors.
They were like a crooked bow that does not shoot straight.
58 They made God angry by building places to worship gods;
they made him jealous with their idols.
59 When God heard them, he became very angry
and rejected the people of Israel completely.
60 He left his dwelling at Shiloh,
the Tent where he lived among the people.
61 He let the Ark, his power, be captured;
he let the Ark, his glory, be taken by enemies.
62 He let his people be killed;
he was very angry with his children.
63 The young men died by fire,
and the young women had no one to marry.
64 Their priests fell by the sword,
but their widows were not allowed to cry.

65 Then the Lord got up as if he had been asleep;

78:51 Ham The people in Egypt were descendants of Ham, one of Noah's sons. See Genesis 10:6.

he awoke like a man who had been
drunk with wine.
66 He struck down his enemies
and disgraced them forever.
67 But God rejected the family of
Joseph;
he did not choose the tribe of
Ephraim.
68 Instead, he chose the tribe of Judah
and Mount Zion, which he loves.
69 And he built his Temple high like the
mountains.
Like the earth, he built it to last
forever.
70 He chose David to be his servant
and took him from the sheep pens.
71 He brought him from tending the
sheep
so he could lead the flock, the
people of Jacob,
his own people, the people of
Israel.
72 And David led
them with
an innocent
heart
and guided them
with skillful
hands.

EMAIL! FROM GOD
78:72
Leaderships
Is it important for leaders to have integrity?

The Nation Cries for Jerusalem

A psalm of Asaph.

79 God, nations have come against
your chosen people.
They have ruined your holy
Temple.
They have turned Jerusalem into
ruins.
2 They have given the bodies of your
servants as food to the wild
birds.
They have given the bodies of those
who worship you to the wild
animals.
3 They have spilled blood like water all
around Jerusalem.
No one was left to bury the dead.
4 We are a joke to the other nations;
they laugh and make fun of us.

5 LORD, how long will this last?
Will you be angry forever?
How long will your jealousy burn
like a fire?
6 Be angry with the nations that do not
know you
and with the kingdoms that do not
honor you.
7 They have gobbled up the people of
Jacob
and destroyed their land.
8 Don't punish us for our past sins.
Show your mercy to us soon,
because we are helpless!
9 God our Savior, help us
so people will praise you.
Save us and forgive our sins
so people will honor you.
10 Why should the nations say,
"Where is their God?"
Tell the other nations in our presence
that you punish those who kill
your servants.
11 Hear the moans of the prisoners.
Use your great power
to save those sentenced to die.

12 Repay those around us seven times
over
for their insults to you, Lord.
13 We are your people, the sheep of
your flock.
We will thank you always;
forever and ever we will praise
you.

A Prayer to Bring Israel Back

For the director of music. To the tune of "Lilies of the Agreement." A psalm of Asaph.

80 Shepherd of Israel, listen to us.
You lead the people of Joseph like
a flock.
You sit on your throne between the
gold creatures with wings.
Show your greatness 2 to the
people of Ephraim, Benjamin,
and Manasseh.
Use your strength,
and come to save us.

3 God, take us back.
Show us your kindness so we can
be saved.

4 LORD God All-Powerful,
how long will you be angry
at the prayers of your people?
5 You have fed your people with tears;
you have made them drink many tears.
6 You made those around us fight over us,
and our enemies make fun of us.

7 God All-Powerful, take us back.
Show us your kindness so we can be saved.

8 You brought us out of Egypt as if we were a vine.
You forced out other nations and planted us in the land.
9 You cleared the ground for us.
Like a vine, we took root and filled the land.
10 We covered the mountains with our shade.
We had limbs like the mighty cedar tree.
11 Our branches reached the Mediterranean Sea,
and our shoots went to the Euphrates River.

12 So why did you pull down our walls?
Now everyone who passes by steals from us.
13 Like wild pigs they walk over us;
like wild animals they feed on us.

14 God All-Powerful, come back.
Look down from heaven and see.
Take care of us, your vine.
15 You planted this shoot with your own hands
and strengthened this child.
16 Now it is cut down and burned with fire;
you destroyed us by your angry looks.
17 With your hand,
strengthen the one you have chosen for yourself.
18 Then we will not turn away from you.
Give us life again, and we will call to you for help.

19 LORD God All-Powerful, take us back.
Show us your kindness so we can be saved.

A Song for a Holiday

For the director of music. By the gittith.
A psalm of Asaph.

81 Sing for joy to God, our strength;
shout out loud to the God of Jacob.
2 Begin the music. Play the tambourines.
Play pleasant music on the harps and lyres.
3 Blow the trumpet at the time of the New Moon,
when the moon is full, when our feast begins.
4 This is the law for Israel;
it is the command of the God of Jacob.
5 He gave this rule to the people of Joseph
when they went out of the land of Egypt.

EMAIL FROM GOD
81:1–5
Music
How is music useful?

I heard a language I did not know, saying:
6 "I took the load off their shoulders;
I let them put down their baskets.
7 When you were in trouble, you called, and I saved you.
I answered you with thunder.
I tested you at the waters of Meribah. *Selah*
8 My people, listen. I am warning you.
Israel, please listen to me!
9 You must not have foreign gods;
you must not worship any false god.
10 I, the LORD, am your God,
who brought you out of Egypt.
Open your mouth and I will feed you.

11 "But my people did not listen to me;
Israel did not want me.
12 So I let them go their stubborn way
and follow their own advice.

FAITH CHALLENGE

Hey there! Read 81:8-9 to find out the serious warning the writer had for his fellow Israelites. Let's say a false god is anything that has a higher priority in your life than God. How can you keep false gods out of your life?

TESTING IT

Psalm 81:8–9
My people, listen. I am warning you. Israel, please listen to me! You must not have foreign gods; you must not worship any false god.

13 I wish my people would listen to
me;
I wish Israel would live my way.
14 Then I would quickly defeat their
enemies
and turn my hand against their
foes.
15 Those who hate the LORD would bow
before him.
Their punishment would continue
forever.
16 But I would give you the finest
wheat
and fill you with honey from the
rocks."

A Cry for Justice

A psalm of Asaph.

82 God is in charge of the great
meeting;
he judges among the "gods."
2 He says, "How long will you defend
evil people?
How long will you show greater
kindness to the wicked? *Selah*
3 Defend the weak and the orphans;
defend the
rights of the
poor and
suffering.
4 Save the weak
and helpless;
free them from
the power of the wicked.

EMAIL! FROM GOD
82:3–4
Protection
Protect the helpless!

5 "You know nothing. You don't
understand.
You walk in the dark,
while the world is falling apart.
6 I said, 'You are "gods."
You are all sons of God Most High.'
7 But you will die like any other
person;
you will fall like all the leaders."

8 God, come and judge the earth,
because you own all the nations.

A Prayer Against the Enemies

A song. A psalm of Asaph.

83 God, do not keep quiet;
God, do not be silent or still.
2 Your enemies are making noises;
those who hate you are getting
ready to attack.
3 They are making secret plans against
your people;
they plot against those you love.
4 They say, "Come, let's destroy them
as a nation.
Then no one will ever remember
the name 'Israel.'"
5 They are united in their plan.
These have made an agreement
against you:
6 the families of Edom and the
Ishmaelites,

Moab and the Hagrites,
7 the people of Byblos, Ammon, Amalek,
Philistia, and Tyre.
8 Even Assyria has joined them
to help Ammon and Moab, the descendants of Lot. *Selah*

9 God, do to them what you did to Midian,
what you did to Sisera and Jabin at the Kishon River.
10 They died at Endor,
and their bodies rotted on the ground.
11 Do to their important leaders what you did to Oreb and Zeeb.
Do to their princes what you did to Zebah and Zalmunna.
12 They said, "Let's take for ourselves
the pasturelands that belong to God."
13 My God, make them like tumbleweed,
like chaff blown away by the wind.
14 Be like a fire that burns a forest
or like flames that blaze through the hills.
15 Chase them with your storm,
and frighten them with your wind.
16 Cover them with shame.
Then people will look for you, LORD.
17 Make them afraid and ashamed forever.
Disgrace them and destroy them.
18 Then they will know that you are the LORD,
that only you are God Most High over all the earth.

Wishing to Be in the Temple

For the director of music. On the gittith. A psalm of the sons of Korah.

84 LORD All-Powerful,
how lovely is your Temple!
2 I want more than anything
to be in the courtyards of the LORD's Temple.
My whole being wants
to be with the living God.
3 The sparrows have found a home,
and the swallows have nests.
They raise their young near your altars,
LORD All-Powerful, my King and my God.
4 Happy are the people who live at your Temple;
they are always praising you. *Selah*

5 Happy are those whose strength comes from you,
who want to travel to Jerusalem.
6 As they pass through the Valley of Baca,
they make it like a spring.
The autumn rains fill it with pools of water.
7 The people get stronger as they go,
and everyone meets with God in Jerusalem.

8 LORD God All-Powerful, hear my prayer;
God of Jacob, listen to me. *Selah*
9 God, look at our shield;
be kind to your appointed king.

10 One day in the courtyards of your Temple is better
than a thousand days anywhere else.
I would rather be a doorkeeper in the Temple of my God
than live in the homes of the wicked.
11 The LORD God is like a sun and shield;
the LORD gives us kindness and honor.
He does not hold back anything good
from those whose lives are innocent.

> One day in the courtyards of your Temple is better than a thousand days anywhere else.
> —Psalm 84:10

12 LORD All-Powerful,
happy are the people who trust
you!

A Prayer for the Nation

For the director of music.
A psalm of the sons of Korah.

85 LORD, you have been kind to your
land;
you brought back the people of
Jacob.
2 You forgave the guilt of the people
and covered all their sins. *Selah*
3 You stopped all your anger;
you turned back from your strong
anger.

4 God our Savior, bring us back again.
Stop being angry
with us.
5 Will you be angry
with us forever?
Will you stay angry
from now on?
6 Won't you give us life
again?
Your people would
rejoice in you.
7 LORD, show us your
love,
and save us.

Goodness will go before God and prepare the way for him.
—Psalm 85:13

8 I will listen to God the LORD.
He has ordered peace for those
who worship him.
Don't let them go back to
foolishness.
9 God will soon save those who
respect him,
and his glory will be seen in our
land.
10 Love and truth belong to God's
people;
goodness and peace will be
theirs.
11 On earth people will be loyal to God,
and God's goodness will shine
down from heaven.
12 The LORD will give his goodness,
and the land will give its crops.
13 Goodness will go before God
and prepare the way for him.

A Cry for Help

A prayer of David.

86 LORD, listen to me and answer
me.
I am poor and helpless.
2 Protect me, because I worship you.
My God, save me, your servant
who trusts in you.
3 Lord, have mercy on me,
because I have called to you all day.
4 Give happiness to
me, your
servant,
because I give
my life to you,
Lord.

eMAIL! FROM GOD 86:5
Forgiveness
Check out why God forgives you.

5 Lord, you are kind
and forgiving
and have great love
for those who
call to you.
6 LORD, hear my prayer,
and listen when I
ask for mercy.
7 I call to you in times
of trouble,
because you will
answer me.

8 Lord, there is no god
like you
and no works like yours.
9 Lord, all the nations you have made
will come and worship you.
They will honor you.
10 You are great and you do miracles.
Only you are God.
11 LORD, teach me what you want me to
do,
and I will live by your truth.
Teach me to respect you completely.
12 Lord, my God, I will praise you with
all my heart,
and I will honor your name forever.
13 You have great
love for me.
You have saved
me from
death.

eMAIL! FROM GOD 86:13
Hell
Who will be saved from hell?

14 God, proud men
are attacking me;

PRAYER

Psalm 86:1–7

Livin' it

No Answering Machine How do you feel when you really want to talk to someone or ask him or her a question and all you get is an answering machine? Or a busy signal? Or someone saying, "Tell me later"? That's a real bummer, isn't it?

God always hears our prayers—no answering machines and no busy signals. God doesn't always answer prayers immediately, but he *will* answer. (Read Psalm 28:6, p. 730.) How do you wait for God's answer?

Don't give up if God doesn't answer right away. Just keep on praying! (Check out 1 Samuel 1, p. 354.) You won't annoy God if you keep on asking him about something. So . . . keep on asking!

MORE FAITH links

Your Best Defense, p. 584
Prayer + Action = Success, p. 626
Our Heavenly Connection, p. 1283
Prayer Anywhere, p. 1331
Prayer Priority, p. 1376
The Power of Prayer, p. 1485

"What do you think, Skweek? If I pray every day at the same time, do you think God will save that time slot for me so my prayers will get heard?"

"God hears all our prayers—no matter what time we pray or how often we pray. Maybe these Faithlinks will help you understand more about prayer."

The Prayer Habit, Psalm 5:1–3, p. 712
- When you do the same thing every day, you develop a habit. What are some good habits you've developed? How do these habits help you? Do you have a special time to pray? What can you do to make prayer a daily habit?

Concern for All, Daniel 9, p. 1165
- How would you show concern for a large group of people? Would you buy everyone ice cream, if you could? Link here to discover a super way to show concern for others.

Ask, Search, Knock, Matthew 7:7–10, p. 1286
- Have you ever wanted to ask for something, but weren't sure what to ask? Jesus said to just keep asking for what you need.
- Do you think this means that God will automatically give you what you ask for if you keep asking him? God knows what we need, and the final decision is up to him.

Our Interpreter, Romans 8:26, p. 1528
- An interpreter translates for two people who can't understand each other. Did you know you have an interpreter? Link here to find out about him.

my FAVORITE links

FAITH links

ANGER: QUICK OR SLOW?

PSALM 86:15

Which do you do the quickest: become angry or show mercy and forgiveness? When someone does something to annoy you, getting angry is usually the easiest, right? Now, which do you think God does the quickest: become angry or show mercy and forgiveness? Many people believe that God is angry all the time, but that's not true. God is slow to anger, but quick on the draw as far as mercy and forgiveness are concerned. He wants you to be the same way.

Here are some more Faithlinks on anger:

Out of Control?, Genesis 4, p. 8

Get Hot or Keep Cool?, Proverbs 12:16, p. 842

Justice Served, Isaiah 35:3–4, p. 940

The Peril of Poisonous Plans, Micah 2:1–3, p. 1221

Don't Get Mad; Get Even?, Matthew 26:57–63; 27:11–14, p. 1323

The Best Choice, 1 Corinthians 13, p. 1560

a gang of cruel men is trying to kill
me.
They do not respect you.
15 But Lord, you are a God who shows
mercy and is kind.
You don't become angry quickly.
You have great love and
faithfulness.
16 Turn to me and have mercy.
Give me, your servant, strength.
Save me, the son of your female
servant.
17 Show me a sign of your goodness.
When my enemies look, they will
be ashamed.
You, LORD, have helped me and
comforted me.

God Loves Jerusalem

A song. A psalm of the sons of Korah.

87 The LORD built Jerusalem on the
holy mountain.
2 He loves its gates more than any
other place in Israel.
3 City of God,
wonderful things are said about
you. *Selah*
4 God says, "I will put Egypt and
Babylonia
on the list of nations that know
me.
People from Philistia, Tyre, and Cush
will be born there."

5 They will say about Jerusalem,
"This one and that one were born
there.
God Most High will strengthen
her."
6 The LORD will keep a list of the
nations.
He will note, "This person was
born there." *Selah*
7 They will dance and sing,
"All good things come from
Jerusalem."

A Sad Complaint

A song. A psalm of the sons of Korah.
For the director of music.
By the mahalath leannoth.
A maskil of Heman the Ezrahite.

88 LORD, you are the God who saves
me.
I cry out to you day and night.

2 Receive my prayer,
and listen to my cry.

3 My life is full of troubles,
and I am nearly dead.
4 They think I am on the way to my grave.
I am like a man with no strength.
5 I have been left as dead,
like a body lying in a grave
whom you don't remember anymore,
cut off from your care.
6 You have brought me close to death;
I am almost in the dark place of the dead.
7 You have been very angry with me;
all your waves crush me. *Selah*
8 You have taken my friends away from me
and have made them hate me.
I am trapped and cannot escape.
9 My eyes are weak from crying.
LORD, I have prayed to you every day;
I have lifted my hands in prayer to you.

10 Do you show your miracles for the dead?
Do their spirits rise up and praise you? *Selah*

11 Will your love be told in the grave?
Will your loyalty be told in the place of death?
12 Will your miracles be known in the dark grave?
Will your goodness be known in the land of forgetfulness?

13 But, LORD, I have called out to you for help;
every morning I pray to you.
14 LORD, why do you reject me?
Why do you hide from me?
15 I have been weak and dying since I was young.
I suffer from your terrors, and I am helpless.
16 You have been angry with me,
and your terrors have destroyed me.
17 They surround me daily like a flood;
they are all around me.
18 You have taken away my loved ones and friends.
Darkness is my only friend.

A Song About God's Loyalty

A maskil of Ethan the Ezrahite.

89 I will always sing about the LORD's love;
I will tell of his loyalty from now on.
2 I will say, "Your love continues forever;
your loyalty goes on and on like the sky."
3 You said, "I made an agreement with the man of my choice;
I made a promise to my servant David.
4 I told him, 'I will make your family continue forever.
Your kingdom will go on and on.' " *Selah*

5 LORD, the heavens praise you for your miracles
and for your loyalty in the meeting of your holy ones.
6 Who in heaven is equal to the LORD?
None of the angels is like the LORD.
7 When the holy ones meet, it is God they fear.
He is more frightening than all who surround him.
8 LORD God All-Powerful, who is like you?
LORD, you are powerful and completely trustworthy.
9 You rule the mighty sea
and calm the stormy waves.
10 You crushed the sea monster Rahab;
by your power you scattered your enemies.

11 The skies and the earth belong to you.
You made the world and everything in it.

EMAIL FROM GOD 89:6
Angels
Are angels equal to God?

12 You created the north and the south.
Mount Tabor and Mount Hermon
sing for joy at your name.
13 Your arm has great power.
Your hand is strong; your right
hand is lifted up.
14 Your kingdom is built on what is right
and fair.
Love and truth are in all you do.

15 Happy are the people who know how
to praise you.
LORD, let them live in the light of
your presence.
16 In your name they rejoice
and continually praise your
goodness.
17 You are their glorious strength,
and in your kindness you honor
our king.
18 Our king, our shield, belongs to the
LORD,
to the Holy One of Israel.

19 Once, in a vision, you spoke
to those who worship you.
You said, "I have given strength to a
warrior;
I have raised up a young man from
my people.
20 I have found my servant David;
I appointed him by pouring holy oil
on him.
21 I will steady him with my hand
and strengthen him with my arm.
22 No enemy will make him give forced
payments,
and wicked people will not defeat
him.
23 I will crush his enemies in front of
him;
I will defeat those who hate him.
24 My loyalty and love will be with him.
Through me he will be strong.
25 I will give him power over the sea
and control over the rivers.
26 He will say to me, 'You are my father,
my God, the Rock, my Savior.'
27 I will make him my firstborn son,
the greatest king on earth.
28 My love will watch over him forever,
and my agreement with him will
never end.
29 I will make his family continue,
and his kingdom will last as long as
the skies.

30 "If his descendants reject my
teachings
and do not follow my laws,
31 if they ignore my demands
and disobey my commands,
32 then I will punish their sins with a
rod
and their wrongs with a whip.
33 But I will not hold back my love from
David,
nor will I stop being loyal.
34 I will not break my agreement
nor change what I have said.
35 I have promised by my holiness,
I will not lie to David.
36 His family will go on forever.
His kingdom will last before me
like the sun.
37 It will continue forever, like the
moon,
like a dependable witness in the
sky." *Selah*

38 But now you have refused and
rejected your appointed king.
You have been angry with him.
39 You have abandoned the agreement
with your servant
and thrown his crown to the
ground.
40 You have torn down all his city walls;
you have turned his strong cities
into ruins.
41 Everyone who passes by steals from
him.
His neighbors insult him.
42 You have given strength to his
enemies
and have made them all happy.
43 You have made his sword useless;
you did not help him stand in
battle.
44 You have kept him from winning
and have thrown his throne to the
ground.
45 You have cut his life short
and covered him with shame. *Selah*

46 LORD, how long will this go on?

Will you ignore us forever?
How long will your anger burn like a fire?
47 Remember how short my life is.
Why did you create us? For nothing?
48 What person alive will not die?
Who can escape the grave? *Selah*

49 Lord, where is your love from times past,
which in your loyalty you promised to David?
50 Lord, remember how they insulted your servant;
remember how I have suffered the insults of the nations.
51 LORD, remember how your enemies insulted you
and how they insulted your appointed king wherever he went.

52 Praise the LORD forever!
Amen and amen.

Book 4

God Is Eternal, and We Are Not

A prayer of Moses, the man of God.

90 Lord, you have been our home since the beginning.
2 Before the mountains were born
and before you created the earth and the world,
you are God.
You have always been, and you will always be.

3 You turn people back into dust.
You say, "Go back into dust, human beings."
4 To you, a thousand years
is like the passing of a day,
or like a few hours in the night.
5 While people sleep, you take their lives.
They are like grass that grows up in the morning.
6 In the morning they are fresh and new,
but by evening they dry up and die.

7 We are destroyed by your anger;
we are terrified by your hot anger.
8 You have put the evil we have done right in front of you;
you clearly see our secret sins.
9 All our days pass while you are angry.
Our years end with a moan.
10 Our lifetime is seventy years
or, if we are strong, eighty years.
But the years are full of hard work and pain.
They pass quickly, and then we are gone.

11 Who knows the full power of your anger?
Your anger is as great as our fear of you should be.
12 Teach us how short our lives really are
so that we may be wise.

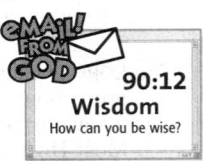

EMAIL! FROM GOD
90:12
Wisdom
How can you be wise?

13 LORD, how long before you return
and show kindness to your servants?
14 Fill us with your love every morning.
Then we will sing and rejoice all our lives.
15 We have seen years of trouble.
Now give us as much joy as you gave us sorrow.
16 Show your servants the wonderful things you do;
show your greatness to their children.
17 Lord our God, treat us well.
Give us success in what we do;
yes, give us success in what we do.

Safe in the Lord

91 Those who go to God Most High for safety
will be protected by the Almighty.
2 I will say to the LORD, "You are my place of safety and protection.
You are my God and I trust you."

3 God will save you from hidden traps

and from deadly diseases.
4 He will cover you with his feathers,
and under his wings you can hide.
His truth will be your shield and protection.
5 You will not fear any danger by night
or an arrow during the day.

EMAIL! FROM GOD
91:5
Fears
Don't fear these things!

6 You will not be afraid of diseases that come in the dark
or sickness that strikes at noon.
7 At your side one thousand people may die,
or even ten thousand right beside you,
but you will not be hurt.
8 You will only watch
and see the wicked punished.

9 The LORD is your protection;
you have made God Most High your place of safety.
10 Nothing bad will happen to you;
no disaster will come to your home.
11 He has put his angels in charge of you
to watch over you wherever you go.
12 They will catch you in their hands
so that you will not hit your foot on a rock.
13 You will walk on lions and cobras;
you will step on strong lions and snakes.

14 The LORD says, "Whoever loves me, I will save.
I will protect those who know me.
15 They will call to me, and I will answer them.
I will be with them in trouble;
I will rescue them and honor them.
16 I will give them a long, full life,
and they will see how I can save."

Thanksgiving for God's Goodness

A psalm. A song for the Sabbath day.

92 It is good to praise you, LORD,
to sing praises to God Most High.
2 It is good to tell of your love in the morning
and of your loyalty at night.
3 It is good to praise you with the ten-stringed lyre
and with the soft-sounding harp.

4 LORD, you have made me happy by what you have done;
I will sing for joy about what your hands have done.
5 LORD, you have done such great things!
How deep are your thoughts!
6 Stupid people don't know these things,
and fools don't understand.

> It is good to tell of your love in the morning and of your loyalty at night.
> —Psalm 92:2

7 Wicked people grow like the grass.
Evil people seem to do well,
but they will be destroyed forever.
8 But, LORD, you will be honored forever.

9 LORD, surely your enemies,
surely your enemies will be destroyed,
and all who do evil will be scattered.
10 But you have made me as strong as an ox.
You have poured fine oils on me.
11 When I looked, I saw my enemies;
I heard the cries of those who are against me.

12 But good people will grow like palm trees;
they will be tall like the cedars of Lebanon.
13 Like trees planted in the Temple of the LORD,
they will grow strong in the courtyards of our God.

14 When they are old, they will still
produce fruit;
they will be healthy and fresh.
15 They will say that the LORD is good.
He is my Rock, and there is no
wrong in him.

The Majesty of the Lord

93 The LORD is king. He is clothed
in majesty.
The LORD is clothed in majesty
and armed with strength.
The world is set,
and it cannot be moved.
2 LORD, your kingdom was set up long
ago;
you are everlasting.

3 LORD, the seas raise,
the seas raise their
voice.
The seas raise up
their pounding
waves.
4 The sound of the
water is loud;
the ocean waves
are powerful,
but the LORD above
is much greater.

5 LORD, your laws will stand forever.
Your Temple will be holy
forevermore.

God Will Pay Back His Enemies

94 The LORD is a God who punishes.
God, show your greatness and
punish!
2 Rise up, Judge of the earth,
and give the proud what they
deserve.
3 How long will the wicked be happy?
How long, LORD?

4 They are full of proud words;
those who do evil brag about what
they have done.
5 LORD, they crush your people
and make your children suffer.
6 They kill widows and foreigners
and murder orphans.
7 They say, "The LORD doesn't see;
the God of Jacob doesn't notice."
8 You stupid ones among the people,
pay attention.
You fools, when will you
understand?
9 Can't the creator of ears hear?
Can't the maker of eyes see?
10 Won't the one who corrects nations
punish you?
Doesn't the teacher of people
know everything?
11 The LORD knows what people think.
He knows their thoughts are just a
puff of wind.

12 LORD, those you correct are happy;
you teach them from your law.
13 You give them rest
from times of
trouble
until a pit is dug for
the wicked.
14 The LORD won't leave
his people
nor give up his
children.
15 Judgment will again
be fair,
and all who are
honest will
follow it.

> LORD, those you correct are happy; you teach them from your law.
> —Psalm 94:12

16 Who will help me fight against the
wicked?
Who will stand with me against
those who do evil?
17 If the LORD had not helped me,
I would have died in a minute.
18 I said, "I am about to fall,"
but, LORD, your love kept me safe.
19 I was very worried,
but you comforted me and made
me happy.

20 Crooked leaders cannot be your
friends.
They use the law to cause
suffering.
21 They join forces against people who
do right
and sentence to death the
innocent.

22 But the LORD is my defender;
my God is the rock of my protection.
23 God will pay them back for their sins
and will destroy them for their evil.
The LORD our God will destroy them.

A Call to Praise and Obedience

95 Come, let's sing for joy to the LORD.
Let's shout praises to the Rock who saves us.
2 Let's come to him with thanksgiving.
Let's sing songs to him,
3 because the LORD is the great God,
the great King over all gods.
4 The deepest places on earth are his,
and the highest mountains belong to him.
5 The sea is his because he made it,
and he created the land with his own hands.

Come, let's worship him and bow down. Let's kneel before the LORD who made us.
—Psalm 95:6

6 Come, let's worship him and bow down.
Let's kneel before the LORD who made us,
7 because he is our God
and we are the people he takes care of
and the sheep that he tends.

Today listen to what he says:
8 "Do not be stubborn, as your ancestors were at Meribah,
as they were that day at Massah in the desert.
9 There your ancestors tested me
and tried me even though they saw what I did.
10 I was angry with those people for forty years.
I said, 'They are not loyal to me
and have not understood my ways.'
11 I was angry and made a promise,
'They will never enter my rest.' "

Praise for the Lord's Glory

96 Sing to the LORD a new song;
sing to the LORD, all the earth.
2 Sing to the LORD and praise his name;
every day tell how he saves us.
3 Tell the nations of his glory;
tell all peoples the miracles he does,

4 because the LORD is great; he should be praised at all times.
He should be honored more than all the gods,
5 because all the gods of the nations are only idols,
but the LORD made the heavens.
6 The LORD has glory and majesty;
he has power and beauty in his Temple.

7 Praise the LORD, all nations on earth;
praise the LORD's glory and power.
8 Praise the glory of the LORD's name.
Bring an offering and come into his Temple courtyards.
9 Worship the LORD because he is holy.
Tremble before him, everyone on earth.
10 Tell the nations, "The LORD is king."
The earth is set, and it cannot be moved.
He will judge the people fairly.
11 Let the skies rejoice and the earth be glad;
let the sea and everything in it shout.
12 Let the fields and everything in them rejoice.
Then all the trees of the forest will sing for joy
13 before the LORD, because he is coming.
He is coming to judge the world;

he will judge the world with fairness
and the peoples with truth.

A Hymn About the Lord's Power

97 The LORD is king. Let the earth rejoice;
faraway lands should be glad.
2 Thick, dark clouds surround him.
His kingdom is built on what is right and fair.
3 A fire goes before him
and burns up his enemies all around.
4 His lightning lights up the world;
when the people see it, they tremble.
5 The mountains melt like wax before the LORD,
before the Lord of all the earth.
6 The heavens tell about his goodness,
and all the people see his glory.

7 Those who worship idols should be ashamed;
they brag about their gods.
All the gods should worship the LORD.
8 When Jerusalem hears this, she is glad,
and the towns of Judah rejoice.
They are happy because of your judgments, LORD.
9 You are the LORD Most High over all the earth;
you are supreme over all gods.

10 People who love the LORD hate evil.
The LORD watches over those who follow him
and frees them from the power of the wicked.
11 Light shines on those who do right;
joy belongs to those who are honest.
12 Rejoice in the LORD, you who do right.
Praise his holy name.

The Lord of Power and Justice

A psalm.

98 Sing to the LORD a new song,
because he has done miracles.
By his right hand and holy arm
he has won the victory.
2 The LORD has made known his power to save;
he has shown the other nations his victory for his people.
3 He has remembered his love
and his loyalty to the people of Israel.
All the ends of the earth have seen
God's power to save.

4 Shout with joy to the LORD, all the earth;
burst into songs and make music.
5 Make music to the LORD with harps,
with harps and the sound of singing.
6 Blow the trumpets and the sheep's horns;
shout for joy to the LORD the King.

7 Let the sea and everything in it shout;
let the world and everyone in it sing.
8 Let the rivers clap their hands;
let the mountains sing together for joy.
9 Let them sing before the LORD,
because he is coming to judge the world.
He will judge the world fairly;
he will judge the peoples with fairness.

> He will judge the world fairly;
> he will judge the peoples with fairness.
> —Psalm 98:9

The Lord, the Fair and Holy King

99 The LORD is king.
Let the peoples shake with fear.
He sits between the gold creatures with wings.
Let the earth shake.
2 The LORD in Jerusalem is great;
he is supreme over all the peoples.

3 Let them praise your name;
it is great, holy and to be feared.

4 The King is powerful and loves justice.
LORD, you made things fair;
you have done what is fair and right for the people of Jacob.
5 Praise the LORD our God,
and worship at the Temple, his footstool.
He is holy.

6 Moses and Aaron were among his priests,
and Samuel was among his worshipers.
They called to the LORD,
and he answered them.
7 He spoke to them from the pillar of cloud.
They kept the rules and laws he gave them.

8 LORD our God, you answered them.
You showed them that you are a forgiving God,
but you punished them for their wrongs.
9 Praise the LORD our God,
and worship at his holy mountain,
because the LORD our God is holy.

A Call to Praise the Lord

A psalm of thanks.

100 Shout to the LORD, all the earth.
2 Serve the LORD with joy;
come before him with singing.
3 Know that the LORD is God.
He made us, and we belong to him;
we are his people, the sheep he tends.

EMAIL! FROM GOD 100
Thankfulness
How can you express thankfulness?

4 Come into his city with songs of thanksgiving
and into his courtyards with songs of praise.
Thank him and praise his name.
5 The LORD is good. His love is forever,
and his loyalty goes on and on.

YOU'RE INVITED!

PSALM 100

When someone hands you a special invitation to a party or some other gathering, how do you feel? Excited? Glad to be invited? More than likely you wouldn't grumble about it. You would go and have a good time. This psalm is a special invitation to praise God. You're invited to come and tell him how awesome he is. You're also encouraged to thank him for all that he does. Feel free to invite a friend to join in!

A Holiday Every Week, Leviticus 23:1–3, p. 166

Gratitude Attitude, Ezra 3, p. 611

Uniquely You, Psalm 139:13–14, p. 815

Jesus' Mission and Yours, Isaiah 61:1–2, p. 978

A Family Meal, Mark 14:23–26, p. 1356

Your Faith Story, 2 Timothy 1:5, p. 1650

A Promise to Rule Well

A psalm of David.

101 I will sing of your love and fairness;

LORD, I will sing praises to you.
2 I will be careful to live an innocent life.
When will you come to me?

I will live an innocent life in my house.

EMAIL FROM GOD
101:3–8
Being pure
Find out why we should stay away from evil.

3 I will not look at anything wicked.
I hate those who turn against you;
they will not be found near me.
4 Let those who want to do wrong stay away from me;
I will have nothing to do with evil.
5 If anyone secretly says things against his neighbor,
I will stop him.
I will not allow people
to be proud and look down on others.

6 I will look for trustworthy people
so I can live with them in the land.
Only those who live innocent lives
will be my servants.
7 No one who is dishonest will live in my house;
no liars will stay around me.
8 Every morning I will destroy the wicked in the land.
I will rid the LORD's city of people who do evil.

A Cry for Help

A prayer of a person who is suffering when he is discouraged and tells the LORD his complaints.

102 LORD, listen to my prayer;
let my cry for help come to you.
2 Do not hide from me
in my time of trouble.
Pay attention to me.
When I cry for help, answer me quickly.

3 My life is passing away like smoke,
and my bones are burned up with fire.
4 My heart is like grass
that has been cut and dried.
I forget to eat.
5 Because of my grief,
my skin hangs on my bones.
6 I am like a desert owl,
like an owl living among the ruins.
7 I lie awake.
I am like a lonely bird on a housetop.
8 All day long enemies insult me;
those who make fun of me use my name as a curse.
9 I eat ashes for food,
and my tears fall into my drinks.
10 Because of your great anger,
you have picked me up and thrown me away.
11 My days are like a passing shadow;
I am like dried grass.

12 But, LORD, you rule forever,
and your fame goes on and on.
13 You will come and have mercy on Jerusalem,
because the time has now come to be kind to her;
the right time has come.
14 Your servants love even her stones;
they even care about her dust.
15 Nations will fear the name of the LORD,
and all the kings on earth will honor you.
16 The LORD will rebuild Jerusalem;
there his glory will be seen.
17 He will answer the prayers of the needy;
he will not reject their prayers.

18 Write these things for the future
so that people who are not yet born will praise the LORD.
19 The LORD looked down from his holy place above;
from heaven he looked down at the earth.
20 He heard the moans of the prisoners,
and he freed those sentenced to die.
21 The name of the LORD will be heard in Jerusalem;
his praise will be heard there.

22 People will come together,
and kingdoms will serve the LORD.

23 God has made me tired of living;
he has cut short my life.
24 So I said, "My God, do not take me in
the middle of my life.
Your years go on and on.
25 In the beginning you made the earth,
and your hands made the skies.
26 They will be destroyed, but you will
remain.
They will all wear out like clothes.
And, like clothes, you will change
them
and throw them away.
27 But you never change,
and your life will never end.
28 Our children will live in your
presence,
and their children will remain with
you."

Praise to the Lord of Love

Of David.

103 My whole being, praise the
LORD;
all my being, praise his holy name.
2 My whole being, praise the LORD
and do not forget all his kindnesses.
3 He forgives all my sins
and heals all my diseases.
4 He saves my life from the grave
and loads me with love and mercy.
5 He satisfies me with good things
and makes me young again, like
the eagle.

6 The LORD does what is right and fair
for all who are wronged by others.
7 He showed his ways to Moses
and his deeds to the people of
Israel.
8 The LORD shows mercy and is kind.
He does not become angry quickly,
and he has great love.
9 He will not always accuse us,
and he will not be angry forever.
10 He has not punished us as our sins
should be punished;
he has not repaid us for the evil we
have done.
11 As high as the sky is above the earth,
so great is his love for those who
respect him.
12 He has taken our sins away from us
as far as the east is from west.
13 The LORD has mercy on those who
respect him,
as a father has mercy on his
children.
14 He knows how we were made;
he remembers that we are dust.

FAITH links

YOUR HEAVENLY DAD

PSALM 103:13

Pause a minute to think about your father or someone who is like a father to you. Think about what he does to show his love for you. Would you hesitate to talk to him or ask him for anything, knowing how much he cares about you? God cares for us, just as a father cares for his children. That means you can talk to him like you talk to your dad.

Need to talk to God? He's available any time! Read on:

My Worship Place, Genesis 35:1–14, p. 49

Your Heavenly Parent, Exodus 2:1–10, p. 77

A Holiday Letter, Esther 9:20–23, p. 657

How God Speaks, Job 33:14–17, p. 696

What's in a Name?, Isaiah 9:6, p. 908

Jesus' Prayer, John 17, p. 1453

15 Human life is like grass;
we grow like a flower in the field.
16 After the wind blows, the flower is gone,
and there is no sign of where it was.
17 But the LORD's love for those who respect him
continues forever and ever,
and his goodness continues to their grandchildren
18 and to those who keep his agreement
and who remember to obey his orders.

19 The LORD has set his throne in heaven,
and his kingdom rules over everything.
20 You who are his angels, praise the LORD.
You are the mighty warriors who do what he says
and who obey his voice.
21 You, his armies, praise the LORD;
you are his servants who do what he wants.
22 Everything the LORD has made
should praise him in all the places he rules.
My whole being, praise the LORD.

EMAIL! FROM GOD
103:20
Angels
Find out who are God's mighty warriors.

Praise to God Who Made the World

104 My whole being, praise the LORD.
LORD my God, you are very great.
You are clothed with glory and majesty;
2 you wear light like a robe.
You stretch out the skies like a tent.
3 You build your room above the clouds.
You make the clouds your chariot,
and you ride on the wings of the wind.
4 You make the winds your messengers,
and flames of fire are your servants.
5 You built the earth on its foundations
so it can never be moved.
6 You covered the earth with oceans;
the water was above the mountains.
7 But at your command, the water rushed away.
When you thundered your orders, it hurried away.
8 The mountains rose; the valleys sank.
The water went to the places you made for it.
9 You set borders for the seas that they cannot cross,
so water will never cover the earth again.

10 You make springs pour into the ravines;
they flow between the mountains.
11 They water all the wild animals;
the wild donkeys come there to drink.
12 Wild birds make nests by the water;
they sing among the tree branches.
13 You water the mountains from above.
The earth is full of the things you made.
14 You make the grass for cattle
and vegetables for the people.
You make food grow from the earth.
15 You give us wine that makes happy hearts
and olive oil that makes our faces shine.
You give us bread that gives us strength.
16 The LORD's trees have plenty of water;
they are the cedars of Lebanon, which he planted.
17 The birds make their nests there;
the stork's home is in the fir trees.
18 The high mountains belong to the wild goats.
The rocks are hiding places for the badgers.

19 You made the moon to mark the seasons,

and the sun always knows when to
set.
20 You make it dark, and it becomes
night.
Then all the wild animals creep
around.
21 The lions roar as they attack.
They look to God for food.
22 When the sun rises, they leave
and go back to their dens to lie
down.
23 Then people go to work
and work until evening.

24 LORD, you have made many things;
with your wisdom you made them
all.
The earth is full of your riches.
25 Look at the sea, so big and wide,
with creatures large and small that
cannot be counted.
26 Ships travel over the ocean,
and there is the sea monster
Leviathan,
which you made to play there.

27 All these things depend on you
to give them their food at the right
time.
28 When you give it to them,
they gather it up.
When you open your hand,
they are filled with good food.
29 When you turn away from them,
they become frightened.
When you take away their breath,
they die and turn to dust.
30 When you breathe on
them,
they are created,
and you make the
land new again.

31 May the glory of the
LORD be forever.
May the LORD
enjoy what he
has made.
32 He just looks at the
earth, and it
shakes.
He touches the mountains, and
they smoke.

May my thoughts
please him;
I am happy in
the LORD.
—Psalm 104:34

33 I will sing to the LORD all my life;
I will sing praises to my God as
long as I live.
34 May my thoughts please him;
I am happy in the LORD.
35 Let sinners be destroyed from the
earth,
and let the wicked live no longer.

My whole being, praise the LORD.
Praise the LORD.

God's Love for Israel

105 Give thanks to the LORD and
pray to him.
Tell the nations what he has done.
2 Sing to him; sing praises to him.
Tell about all his miracles.
3 Be glad that you are his;
let those who seek the LORD be
happy.
4 Depend on the LORD and his
strength;
always go to him for help.
5 Remember the miracles he has done;
remember his wonders and his
decisions.
6 You are descendants of his servant
Abraham,
the children of Jacob, his chosen
people.
7 He is the LORD our God.
His laws are for all the world.

8 He will keep his agreement
forever;
he will keep his promises always.
9 He will keep the
agreement he
made with
Abraham
and the promise he
made to Isaac.
10 He made it a law for
the people of
Jacob;
he made it an
agreement with
Israel to last
forever.
11 The LORD said, "I will give you the
land of Canaan,
and it will belong to you."

FAITH links

A PICTURE OF THE PAST

PSALM 105

Your family photo album or videos tell the story of the past. When you look at old pictures, you can see the events of your family's life. Reading this psalm is like looking at a photo album of Israel's history. How many of these stories do you remember? Throughout Israel's history, leaders like Joseph and Moses reminded people to pass on the stories of what God did for their people.

Maybe your family never crossed the Red Sea or followed a cloud through a wilderness. But the message of this psalm is still for you: Remember what God has done for you, and pass it on!

Here's some more advice on telling others about God:

Care for the Lost, Deuteronomy 22:1–3, p. 255

Faith of Our Fathers, Joshua 4:4–9, p. 280

Remember Your Creator, Ecclesiastes 12:1, 13, p. 885

A Bad Reaction, Jeremiah 36, p. 1043

Pass It On!, Joel 1:2–3, p. 1187

Tell All About Him!, Matthew 28:19, p. 1326

12 Then God's people were few in
number.
They were strangers in the land.
13 They went from one nation to
another,
from one kingdom to another.
14 But the LORD did not let anyone hurt
them;
he warned kings not to harm them.
15 He said, "Don't touch my chosen
people,
and don't harm my prophets."

16 God ordered a time of hunger in the
land,
and he destroyed all the food.
17 Then he sent a man ahead of them—
Joseph, who was sold as a slave.
18 They put chains around his feet
and an iron ring around his neck.
19 Then the time he had spoken of
came,
and the LORD's words proved that
Joseph was right.
20 The king of Egypt sent for Joseph
and freed him;
the ruler of the people set him
free.
21 He made him the master of his
house;
Joseph was in charge of his riches.
22 He could order the princes as he
wished.
He taught the older men to be wise.
23 Then his father Israel came to Egypt;
Jacob[n] lived in Egypt.[n]
24 The LORD made his people grow in
number,
and he made them stronger than
their enemies.
25 He caused the Egyptians to hate his
people
and to make plans against his
servants.
26 Then he sent his servant Moses,
and Aaron, whom he had chosen.
27 They did many signs among the
Egyptians
and worked wonders in Egypt.
28 The LORD sent darkness and made
the land dark,

105:23 Jacob Also called Israel.
105:23 Egypt Literally, "the land of Ham." Also in verse 27. The people in Egypt were descendants of Ham, one of Noah's sons. See Genesis 10:6.

but the Egyptians turned against
what he said.
29 So he changed their water into blood
and made their fish die.
30 Then their country was filled with
frogs,
even in the bedrooms of their
rulers.
31 The LORD spoke and flies came,
and gnats were everywhere in the
country.
32 He made hail fall like rain
and sent lightning through their
land.
33 He struck down their grapevines and
fig trees,
and he destroyed every tree in the
country.
34 He spoke and grasshoppers came;
the locusts were too many to
count.
35 They ate all the plants in the land
and everything the earth produced.
36 The LORD also killed all the firstborn
sons in the land,
the oldest son of each family.

37 Then he brought his people out,
and they carried with them silver
and gold.
Not one of his people stumbled.
38 The Egyptians were glad when they
left,
because the Egyptians were afraid
of them.
39 The LORD covered them with a cloud
and lit up the night with fire.
40 When they asked, he brought them
quail
and filled them with bread from
heaven.
41 God split the rock, and water flowed
out;
it ran like a river through the
desert.
42 He remembered his holy promise
to his servant Abraham.

43 So God brought his people out with
joy,
his chosen ones with singing.
44 He gave them lands of other
nations,
so they received what others had
worked for.
45 This was so they would keep his
orders
and obey his teachings.

Praise the LORD!

Israel's Failure to Trust God

106 Praise the LORD!
Thank the LORD because he is good.
His love continues forever.
2 No one can tell all the mighty things
the LORD has done;
no one can speak all his praise.

FAITH CHALLENGE

I've got another one for you. Read 106:3 to find out what kind of people are most likely to be happy. How do you respond when you see people cheating or not doing what they're supposed to do?

TESTING IT

Psalm 106:3
Happy are those who do right, who do what is fair at all times.

3 Happy are those who do right,
who do what is fair at all times.

4 LORD, remember me when you are
kind to your people;
help me when you save them.
5 Let me see the good things you do
for your chosen people.
Let me be happy along with your
happy nation;
let me join your own people in
praising you.

6 We have sinned just as our ancestors
did.
We have done wrong; we have
done evil.
7 Our ancestors in Egypt
did not learn from your
miracles.
They did not remember all your
kindnesses,
so they turned against you at the
Red Sea.
8 But the LORD saved them for his own
sake,
to show his great power.
9 He commanded the Red Sea, and it
dried up.
He led them through the deep sea
as if it were a desert.
10 He saved them from those who hated
them.
He saved them from their
enemies,
11 and the water covered their foes.
Not one of them escaped.
12 Then the people believed what the
LORD said,
and they sang praises to him.

13 But they quickly forgot what he had
done;
they did not wait for his advice.
14 They became greedy for food in the
desert,
and they tested God there.
15 So he gave them what they wanted,
but he also sent a terrible disease
among them.

16 The people in the camp were jealous
of Moses
and of Aaron, the holy priest of the
LORD.
17 Then the ground opened up and
swallowed Dathan
and closed over Abiram's group.
18 A fire burned among their followers,
and flames burned up the wicked.

19 The people made a gold calf at Mount
Sinai
and worshiped a metal statue.
20 They exchanged their glorious God
for a statue of a bull that eats
grass.
21 They forgot the God who saved
them,
who had done great things in
Egypt,
22 who had done miracles in Egypt[n]
and amazing things by the Red
Sea.
23 So God said he would destroy them.
But Moses, his chosen one, stood
before him
and stopped God's anger from
destroying them.

24 Then they refused to go into the
beautiful land of Canaan;
they did not believe what God
promised.
25 They grumbled in their tents
and did not obey the LORD.
26 So he swore to them
that they would die in the desert.
27 He said their children would be killed
by other nations
and that they would be scattered
among other countries.

28 They joined in worshiping Baal at
Peor
and ate meat that had been
sacrificed to lifeless statues.
29 They made the LORD angry by what
they did,
so many people became sick with a
terrible disease.
30 But Phinehas prayed to the LORD,

106:22 Egypt Literally, "the land of Ham." The people in Egypt were descendants of Ham, one of Noah's sons. See Genesis 10:6.

and the disease stopped.
31 Phinehas did what was right,
and it will be remembered from now on.

32 The people also made the LORD angry at Meribah,
and Moses was in trouble because of them.
33 The people turned against the Spirit of God,
so Moses spoke without stopping to think.

34 The people did not destroy the other nations
as the LORD had told them to do.
35 Instead, they mixed with the other nations
and learned their customs.
36 They worshiped other nations' idols
and were trapped by them.
37 They even killed their sons and daughters
as sacrifices to demons.
38 They killed innocent people,
their own sons and daughters,
as sacrifices to the idols of Canaan.
So the land was made unholy by their blood.
39 The people became unholy by their sins;
they were unfaithful to God in what they did.

40 So the LORD became angry with his people
and hated his own children.
41 He handed them over to other nations
and let their enemies rule over them.
42 Their enemies were cruel to them
and kept them under their power.
43 The LORD saved his people many times,
but they continued to turn against him.
So they became even more wicked.

44 But God saw their misery
when he heard their cry.
45 He remembered his agreement with them,
and he felt sorry for them because of his great love.
46 He caused them to be pitied
by those who held them captive.

47 LORD our God, save us
and bring us back from other nations.
Then we will thank you
and will gladly praise you.

48 Praise the LORD, the God of Israel.
He always was and always will be.
Let all the people say, "Amen!"

Praise the LORD!

Book 5

God Saves from Many Dangers

107 Thank the LORD because he is good.
His love continues forever.
2 That is what those whom the LORD has saved should say.
He has saved them from the enemy
3 and has gathered them from other lands,
from east and west, north and south.

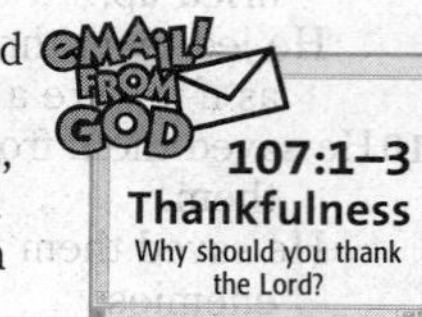

eMAIL! FROM GOD
107:1–3
Thankfulness
Why should you thank the Lord?

4 Some people had wandered in the desert lands.
They found no city in which to live.
5 They were hungry and thirsty,
and they were discouraged.
6 In their misery they cried out to the LORD,
and he saved them from their troubles.
7 He led them on a straight road
to a city where they could live.
8 Let them give thanks to the LORD for his love
and for the miracles he does for people.
9 He satisfies the thirsty
and fills up the hungry.

10 Some sat in gloom and darkness;
they were prisoners suffering in chains.
11 They had turned against the words of God
and had refused the advice of God Most High.
12 So he broke their pride by hard work.
They stumbled, and no one helped.
13 In their misery they cried out to the LORD,
and he saved them from their troubles.
14 He brought them out of their gloom and darkness
and broke their chains.
15 Let them give thanks to the LORD for his love
and for the miracles he does for people.
16 He breaks down bronze gates
and cuts apart iron bars.

17 Some fools turned against God
and suffered for the evil they did.
18 They refused to eat anything,
so they almost died.
19 In their misery they cried out to the LORD,
and he saved them from their troubles.
20 God gave the command and healed them,
so they were saved from dying.
21 Let them give thanks to the LORD for his love
and for the miracles he does for people.
22 Let them offer sacrifices to thank him.
With joy they should tell what he has done.

23 Others went out to sea in ships
and did business on the great oceans.
24 They saw what the LORD could do,
the miracles he did in the deep oceans.
25 He spoke, and a storm came up,
which blew up high waves.
26 The ships were tossed as high as the sky and fell low to the depths.
The storm was so bad that they lost their courage.
27 They stumbled and fell like people who were drunk.
They did not know what to do.
28 In their misery they cried out to the LORD,
and he saved them from their troubles.
29 He stilled the storm
and calmed the waves.
30 They were happy that it was quiet,
and God guided them to the port they wanted.
31 Let them give thanks to the LORD for his love
and for the miracles he does for people.
32 Let them praise his greatness in the meeting of the people;
let them praise him in the meeting of the older leaders.

eMAIL! FROM GOD
107:31–32
Worship
A call to worship.

33 He changed rivers into a desert
and springs of water into dry ground.
34 He made fertile land salty,
because the people there did evil.
35 He changed the desert into pools of water
and dry ground into springs of water.
36 He had the hungry settle there
so they could build a city in which to live.
37 They planted seeds in the fields and vineyards,
and they had a good harvest.
38 God blessed them, and they grew in number.
Their cattle did not become fewer.

39 Because of disaster, troubles, and sadness,
their families grew smaller and weaker.
40 He showed he was displeased with their leaders

and made them wander in a pathless desert.
41 But he lifted the poor out of their suffering
and made their families grow like flocks of sheep.
42 Good people see this and are happy,
but the wicked say nothing.

43 Whoever is wise will remember these things
and will think about the love of the LORD.

A Prayer for Victory

A song. A psalm of David.

108 God, my heart is steady.
I will sing and praise you with all my being.
2 Wake up, harp and lyre!
I will wake up the dawn.
3 LORD, I will praise you among the nations;
I will sing songs of praise about you to all the nations.
4 Your great love reaches to the skies,
your truth to the heavens.
5 God, you are supreme above the skies.
Let your glory be over all the earth.

6 Answer us and save us by your power
so the people you love will be rescued.
7 God has said from his Temple,
"When I win, I will divide Shechem
and measure off the Valley of Succoth.
8 Gilead and Manasseh are mine.
Ephraim is like my helmet.
Judah holds my royal scepter.
9 Moab is like my washbowl.
I throw my sandals at Edom.
I shout at Philistia."

10 Who will bring me to the strong, walled city?
Who will lead me to Edom?
11 God, surely you have rejected us;
you do not go out with our armies.
12 Help us fight the enemy.
Human help is useless,
13 but we can win with God's help.
He will defeat our enemies.

A Prayer Against an Enemy

For the director of music.
A psalm of David.

109 God, I praise you.
Do not be silent.
2 Wicked people and liars have spoken against me;
they have told lies about me.
3 They have said hateful things about me
and attack me for no reason.
4 They attacked me, even though I loved them
and prayed for them.
5 I was good to them, but they repay me with evil.
I loved them, but they hate me in return.

6 They say about me, "Have an evil person work against him,
and let an accuser stand against him.
7 When he is judged, let him be found guilty,
and let even his prayers show his guilt.
8 Let his life be cut short,
and let another man replace him as leader.
9 Let his children become orphans
and his wife a widow.
10 Make his children wander around, begging for food.
Let them be forced out of the ruins in which they live.
11 Let the people to whom he owes money take everything he owns,
and let strangers steal everything he has worked for.
12 Let no one show him love
or have mercy on his orphaned children.
13 Let all his descendants die
and be forgotten by those who live after him.

14 LORD, remember how wicked his
ancestors were,
and don't let the sins of his mother
be wiped out.
15 LORD, always remember their sins.
Then make people forget about
them completely.

16 "He did not remember to be loving.
He hurt the poor, the needy, and
those who were sad
until they were
nearly dead.
17 He loved to put
curses on others,
so let those same
curses fall on
him.
He did not like to
bless others,
so do not let good
things happen to
him.
18 He cursed others as often as he wore
clothes.
Cursing others filled his body and
his life,
like drinking water and using olive
oil.
19 So let curses cover him like clothes
and wrap around him like a belt."
20 May the LORD do these things to
those who accuse me,
to those who speak evil against
me.

21 But you, Lord GOD,
be kind to me so others will know
you are good.
Because your love is good, save
me.
22 I am poor and helpless
and very sad.
23 I am dying like an evening shadow;
I am shaken off like a locust.
24 My knees are weak from hunger,
and I have grown thin.
25 My enemies insult me;
they look at me and shake their
heads.

26 LORD my God, help me;
because you are loving, save me.

I will thank the LORD very much; I will praise him in front of many people.
—Psalm 109:30

27 Then they will know that your power
has done this;
they will know that you have done
it, LORD.
28 They may curse me, but you bless
me.
They may attack me, but they will
be disgraced.
Then I, your servant, will be glad.
29 Let those who accuse me be
disgraced
and covered with
shame like a
coat.

30 I will thank the LORD
very much;
I will praise him in
front of many
people.
31 He defends the
helpless
and saves them
from those who
accuse them.

The Lord Appoints a King

A psalm of David.

110 The LORD said to my Lord,
"Sit by me at my right side
until I put your enemies under
your control."
2 The LORD will enlarge your kingdom
beyond Jerusalem,
and you will rule over your
enemies.
3 Your people will join you on your day
of battle.
You have been dressed in holiness
from birth;
you have the freshness of a child.

4 The LORD has made a promise
and will not change his mind.
He said, "You are a priest forever,
a priest like Melchizedek."

5 The Lord is beside you to help you.
When he becomes angry, he will
crush kings.
6 He will judge those nations, filling
them with dead bodies;

he will defeat rulers all over the
world.
7 The king will drink from the brook on
the way.
Then he will be strengthened.

Praise the Lord's Goodness

111 Praise the LORD!

I will thank the LORD with all my
heart
in the meeting of his good people.
2 The LORD does great things;
those who enjoy them seek them.
3 What he does is glorious and
splendid,
and his goodness continues
forever.
4 His miracles are unforgettable.
The LORD is kind and merciful.
5 He gives food to those who fear him.
He remembers his agreement
forever.
6 He has shown his people his power
when he gave them the lands of
other nations.

7 Everything he does is good and fair;
all his orders can be trusted.
8 They will continue forever.
They were made true and right.
9 He sets his people free.
He made his agreement
everlasting.
He is holy and wonderful.

10 Wisdom begins with respect for the
LORD;
those who obey his orders have
good understanding.
He should be praised forever.

Honest People Are Blessed

112 Praise the LORD!

Happy are those who respect the
LORD,
who want what he commands.
2 Their descendants will be powerful
in the land;
the children of honest people will
be blessed.
3 Their houses will be full of wealth
and riches,
and their goodness will continue
forever.
4 A light shines in the dark for honest
people,
for those who are merciful and
kind and good.
5 It is good to be merciful and
generous.
Those who are fair in their
business
6 will never be defeated.
Good people will always be
remembered.
7 They won't be
afraid of bad
news;
their hearts
are steady
because they
trust the
LORD.

eMAIL! FROM GOD
112:7
Fears
Should we fear
bad news?

8 They are confident and will not be
afraid;
they will look down on their
enemies.
9 They give freely to the poor.
The things they do are right and
will continue forever.
They will be given great honor.

10 The wicked will see this and become
angry;
they will grind their teeth in anger
and then disappear.
The wishes of the wicked will
come to nothing.

Praise for the Lord's Kindness

113 Praise the LORD!

Praise him, you servants of the
LORD;
praise the name of the LORD.
2 The LORD's name should be praised
now and forever.
3 The LORD's name should be praised
from where the sun rises to where
it sets.
4 The LORD is supreme over all the
nations;
his glory reaches to the skies.

GOD'S GLORY

Psalm 115

The "glory of the Lord" is the appearance of God's presence. God doesn't have a body with a face, like you. He is a spirit. When people catch a glimpse of him, they see his "glory." Moses saw God's glory in a bush that was on fire but never burned up. (Look at Exodus 3:1–6, p. 79.) Moses also saw God's glory in a cloud on Mount Sinai. (Check out Exodus 24:9–17, p. 108.) Aaron and all the Israelites saw God's glory when Aaron made his first sacrifice in the wilderness as a priest. (Read Leviticus 9:23, p. 144.) God showed his glory the most through his Son, Jesus Christ. (See John 1:14, p. 1422.)

God has revealed himself to people in some amazing ways. He has spoken through dreams. (Look at Genesis 37:5–10, p. 52, and Matthew 1:20–21, p. 1275.) He has also shown himself through nature. (Check out Romans 1:20, p. 1519.) He has shown himself through his Son and then through giving us the Holy Spirit to lead us. (Read John 3:16, p. 1426; 14:16–17, p. 1449.)

God shows himself to us so that we can know him and worship him for who he really is.

5 No one is like the LORD our God,
who rules from heaven,
6 who bends down to look
at the skies and the earth.
7 The LORD lifts the poor from the dirt
and takes the helpless from the
ashes.
8 He seats them with princes,
the princes of his people.
9 He gives children to the woman who
has none
and makes her a happy mother.

Praise the LORD!

God Brought Israel from Egypt

114 When the Israelites went out
of Egypt,
the people of Jacob left that foreign
country.
2 Then Judah became God's holy place;
Israel became the land he ruled.

3 The Red Sea looked and ran away;
the Jordan River turned back.
4 The mountains danced like sheep
and the hills like little lambs.
5 Sea, why did you run away?
Jordan, why did you turn back?
6 Mountains, why did you dance like
sheep?
Hills, why did you dance like little
lambs?

7 Earth, shake with fear before the
Lord,
before the God of Jacob.
8 He turned a rock into a pool of water,
a hard rock into a spring of water.

The One True God

115 It does not belong to us,
LORD.
The glory belongs to you
because of your love and loyalty.

2 Why do the nations ask,
"Where is their God?"

3 Our God is in heaven.
He does what he pleases.
4 Their idols are made of silver and gold,
the work of human hands.
5 They have mouths, but they cannot speak.
They have eyes, but they cannot see.
6 They have ears, but they cannot hear.
They have noses, but they cannot smell.
7 They have hands, but they cannot feel.
They have feet, but they cannot walk.
No sounds come from their throats.
8 People who make idols will be like them,
and so will those who trust them.

9 Family of Israel, trust the LORD;
he is your helper and your protection.
10 Family of Aaron, trust the LORD;
he is your helper and your protection.
11 You who respect the LORD should trust him;
he is your helper and your protection.

12 The LORD remembers us and will bless us.
He will bless the family of Israel;
he will bless the family of Aaron.
13 The LORD will bless those who respect him,
from the smallest to the greatest.

14 May the LORD give you success,
and may he give you and your children success.
15 May you be blessed by the LORD,
who made heaven and earth.

16 Heaven belongs to the LORD,
but he gave the earth to people.
17 Dead people do not praise the LORD;
those in the grave are silent.
18 But we will praise the LORD
now and forever.

Praise the LORD!

Thanksgiving for Escaping Death

116 I love the LORD,
because he listens to my prayers for help.
2 He paid attention to me,
so I will call to him for help as long as I live.
3 The ropes of death bound me,
and the fear of the grave took hold of me.
I was troubled and sad.
4 Then I called out the name of the LORD.
I said, "Please, LORD, save me!"

EMAIL! FROM GOD
116:1–15
Death
Should Christians be afraid of death?

5 The LORD is kind and does what is right;
our God is merciful.
6 The LORD watches over the foolish;
when I was helpless, he saved me.
7 I said to myself, "Relax,
because the LORD takes care of you."
8 LORD, you saved me from death.
You stopped my eyes from crying;
you kept me from being defeated.
9 So I will walk with the LORD
in the land of the living.
10 I believed, so I said,
"I am completely ruined."
11 In my distress I said,
"All people are liars."

12 What can I give the LORD
for all the good things he has given to me?
13 I will lift up the cup of salvation,
and I will pray to the LORD.
14 I will give the LORD what I promised
in front of all his people.

15 The death of one that belongs to the LORD
is precious in his sight.
16 LORD, I am your servant;

I am your servant and the son of
your female servant.
You have freed me from my chains.
17 I will give you an offering to show
thanks to you,
and I will pray to the LORD.
18 I will give the LORD what I promised
in front of all his people,
19 in the Temple courtyards
in Jerusalem.

Praise the LORD!

A Hymn of Praise

117 All you nations, praise the
LORD.
All you people, praise him
2 because the LORD loves us very
much,
and his truth is everlasting.

Praise the LORD!

Thanksgiving for Victory

118 Thank the LORD because he is
good.
His love continues forever.
2 Let the people of Israel say,
"His love continues forever."
3 Let the family of Aaron say,
"His love continues forever."
4 Let those who respect the LORD say,
"His love continues forever."

5 I was in trouble, so I called to the
LORD.
The LORD answered me and set
me free.
6 I will not be afraid, because the LORD
is with me.
People can't do anything to me.
7 The LORD is with me to help me,
so I will see my enemies defeated.
8 It is better to trust the LORD
than to trust people.
9 It is better to trust the LORD
than to trust princes.

10 All the nations surrounded me,
but I defeated them in the name of
the LORD.
11 They surrounded me on every side,
but with the LORD's power I
defeated them.
12 They surrounded me like a swarm of
bees,
but they died as quickly as thorns
burn.
By the LORD's power, I defeated
them.
13 They chased me until I was almost
defeated,
but the LORD helped me.
14 The LORD gives me strength and a
song.
He has saved me.

FAITH CHALLENGE

Got another challenge for you. Read 118:18 to discover the bright side of learning hard lessons. What's the hardest lesson you've ever had to learn? What made it so hard?

TESTING IT

Psalm 118:18
The LORD has taught me a hard lesson, but he did not let me die.

15 Shouts of joy and victory
come from the tents of those who do right:
"The LORD has done powerful things."
16 The power of the LORD has won the victory;
with his power the LORD has done mighty things.

17 I will not die, but live,
and I will tell what the LORD has done.
18 The LORD has taught me a hard lesson,
but he did not let me die.

19 Open for me the Temple gates.
Then I will come in and thank the LORD.
20 This is the LORD's gate;
only those who are good may enter through it.
21 LORD, I thank you for answering me.
You have saved me.

22 The stone that the builders rejected
became the cornerstone.
23 The LORD did this,
and it is wonderful to us.
24 This is the day that the LORD has made.
Let us rejoice and be glad today!

25 Please, LORD, save us;
please, LORD, give us success.
26 God bless the one who comes in the name of the LORD.
We bless all of you from the Temple of the LORD.
27 The LORD is God,
and he has shown kindness to us.
With branches in your hands, join the feast.
Come to the corners of the altar.

28 You are my God, and I will thank you;
you are my God, and I will praise your greatness.

29 Thank the LORD because he is good.
His love continues forever.

The Word of God

119 Happy are those who live pure lives,
who follow the LORD's teachings.
2 Happy are those who keep his rules,
who try to obey him with their whole heart.
3 They don't do what is wrong;
they follow his ways.
4 LORD, you gave your orders
to be obeyed completely.
5 I wish I were more loyal
in obeying your demands.
6 Then I would not be ashamed
when I study your commands.
7 When I learned that your laws are fair,
I praised you with an honest heart.
8 I will obey your demands,
so please don't ever leave me.

9 How can a young person live a pure life?
By obeying your word.
10 With all my heart I try to obey you.
Don't let me break your commands.
11 I have taken your words to heart
so I would not sin against you.
12 LORD, you should be praised.
Teach me your demands.
13 My lips will tell about
all the laws you have spoken.
14 I enjoy living by your rules
as people enjoy great riches.
15 I think about your orders
and study your ways.
16 I enjoy obeying your demands,
and I will not forget your word.

EMAIL! FROM GOD
119:1–20
Being Pure
How can you live a pure life?

17 Do good to me, your servant, so I can live,
so I can obey your word.
18 Open my eyes to see
the miracles in your teachings.
19 I am a stranger on earth.
Do not hide your commands from me.
20 I wear myself out with desire

GOD'S WORD

Psalm 119:12–18

Livin' it

A Burning Lamp What's one thing you would need and want if you were camping overnight in the woods? A computer? A TV? Pizza? Probably more than anything else you would need a good flashlight—or something to light the way. Computers and TVs won't help you find your way in the dark, and they certainly won't scare off any beasts that may be lurking about! A trusty light can show you where to go and keep you from tripping.

God's Word is like a strong light showing you how to live. God's Word tells you how much he loves you and how to please him. (Check out Psalm 119:105.) Do you have God's burning lamp to use in the dark world?

MORE FAITH links

More Precious Than Gold, p. 723
The Bible: Good for Your Faith, p. 802
Said It? Do It!, p. 1077
The "Ruler" of Our Lives, p. 1202
Cut to the Quick, p. 1670

"OK, I'm ready for anything. I've got my map, my compass, my flashlight, my first aid kit, six bottles of water, and a dozen candy bars!"

"You do look really prepared, Tagg. But do you know what is the best thing to have to prepare you for life in the real world? Take a look at these Faithlinks to find out what it is!"

A Look for the Book, 2 Chronicles 34:14–18, p. 603

- How many Bibles are in your house? In your church? Imagine that there was only one copy of the Bible in the world—and only part of one at that. And then it was lost! King Josiah was eager to read God's teachings when the Book of the Teachings was found. Do you read the Bible to learn about God? Discover hidden treasures inside it!

Life's Rule Book, 2 Timothy 3:15–17, p. 1655

- Have you ever tried to learn a new sport? What did you do to learn the rules? Link here to learn about the "rule book" for life.

Pay Attention!, Hebrews 2:1, p. 1668

- What are the things that grab your attention? A favorite TV show or video? A computer game? We usually pay attention to things that interest us. The writer of Hebrews wanted to remind Christians to pay attention to God's Word. Link here to find out why that's so important.

my FAVORITE links

THE BIBLE: GOOD FOR YOUR FAITH

PSALM 119

When a subject is important enough for the public to know about, you'll find the information splashed across billboards and ads. You've seen ads about drinking milk, not smoking, and eating healthy. Although the subject discussed in Psalm 119 can't be found on a billboard, it's also important. That subject is God's word. Through God's word you can learn how much God loves you and how you can please him. What you learn about God helps your faith in God to grow. Reading the Bible won't give you a cool milk moustache, but it will keep you spiritually healthy.

Want to grow spiritually? Link here to find out how:

Try to Remember, Deuteronomy 11:18–21, p. 243

Learning to Listen, 1 Samuel 3, p. 358

A Traveling Bible Study, 2 Chronicles 17:9, p. 580

Future Hope, Joel 3:17–21, p. 1191

Heavenly Treasure, Luke 12:32–34, p. 1394

Life's Rule Book, 2 Timothy 3:15–17, p. 1655

for your laws all the time.
21 You scold proud people;
those who ignore your commands are cursed.
22 Don't let me be insulted and hated
because I keep your rules.
23 Even if princes speak against me,
I, your servant, will think about your demands.
24 Your rules give me pleasure;
they give me good advice.

25 I am about to die.
Give me life, as you have promised.
26 I told you about my life, and you answered me.
Teach me your demands.
27 Help me understand your orders.
Then I will think about your miracles.
28 I am sad and tired.
Make me strong again as you have promised.
29 Don't let me be dishonest;
have mercy on me by helping me obey your teachings.
30 I have chosen the way of truth;
I have obeyed your laws.
31 I hold on to your rules.
LORD, do not let me be disgraced.
32 I will quickly obey your commands,
because you have made me happy.

33 LORD, teach me your demands,
and I will keep them until the end.
34 Help me understand, so I can keep your teachings,
obeying them with all my heart.
35 Lead me in the path of your commands,
because that makes me happy.
36 Make me want to keep your rules
instead of wishing for riches.
37 Keep me from looking at worthless things.
Let me live by your word.
38 Keep your promise to me, your servant,
so you will be respected.
39 Take away the shame I fear,
because your laws are good.
40 How I want to follow your orders.

Give me life because of your
goodness.

41 LORD, show me your love,
and save me as you have promised.
42 I have an answer for people who
insult me,
because I trust what you say.
43 Never keep me from speaking your
truth,
because I depend on your fair laws.
44 I will obey your teachings
forever and ever.
45 So I will live in freedom,
because I want to follow your
orders.
46 I will discuss your rules with kings
and will not be ashamed.
47 I enjoy obeying your commands,
which I love.
48 I praise your commands, which I
love,
and I think about your demands.

49 Remember your promise to me, your
servant;
it gives me hope.
50 When I suffer, this comforts me:
Your promise gives me life.
51 Proud people always make fun of me,
but I do not reject your teachings.
52 I remember your laws from long ago,
and they comfort me, LORD.
53 I become angry with wicked people
who do not keep your teachings.
54 I sing about your demands
wherever I live.
55 LORD, I remember you at night,
and I will obey your teachings.
56 This is what I do:
I follow your orders.

57 LORD, you are my share in life;
I have promised to obey your
words.
58 I prayed to you with all my heart.
Have mercy on me as you have
promised.
59 I thought about my life,
and I decided to follow your rules.
60 I hurried and did not wait
to obey your commands.
61 Wicked people have tied me up,
but I have not forgotten your
teachings.
62 In the middle of the night, I get up to
thank you
because your laws are right.
63 I am a friend to everyone who fears
you,
to anyone who obeys your orders.
64 LORD, your love fills the earth.
Teach me your demands.

65 You have done good things for your
servant,
as you have promised, LORD.
66 Teach me wisdom and knowledge
because I trust your commands.
67 Before I suffered, I did wrong,
but now I obey your word.
68 You are good, and you do what is
good.
Teach me your demands.
69 Proud people have made up lies
about me,
but I will follow your orders with
all my heart.
70 Those people have no feelings,
but I love your teachings.
71 It was good for me to suffer
so I would learn your demands.
72 Your teachings are worth more to me
than thousands of pieces of gold
and silver.

73 You made me and formed me with
your hands.
Give me understanding so I can
learn your commands.
74 Let those who respect you rejoice
when they see me,
because I put my hope in your
word.
75 LORD, I know that your laws are right
and that it was right for you to
punish me.
76 Comfort me with your love,
as you promised me, your servant.
77 Have mercy on me so that I may live.
I love your teachings.
78 Make proud people ashamed because
they lied about me.
But I will think about your orders.
79 Let those who respect you return to
me,

those who know your rules.
80 Let me obey your demands perfectly
so I will not be ashamed.

81 I am weak from waiting for you to
save me,
but I hope in your word.
82 My eyes are tired from looking for
your promise.
When will you comfort me?
83 Even though I am like a wine bag
going up in smoke,
I do not forget your demands.
84 How long will I live?
When will you judge those who are
hurting me?
85 Proud people have dug pits to trap
me.
They have nothing to do with your
teachings.
86 All of your commands can be trusted.
Liars are hurting me. Help me!
87 They have almost put me in the
grave,
but I have not rejected your
orders.
88 Give me life by your love
so I can obey your rules.

89 LORD, your word is everlasting;
it continues forever in heaven.
90 Your loyalty will go on and on;
you made the earth, and it still
stands.
91 All things continue to this day
because of your laws,
because all things serve you.
92 If I had not loved your teachings,
I would have died from my
sufferings.
93 I will never forget your orders,
because you have given me life by
them.
94 I am yours. Save me.
I want to obey your orders.
95 Wicked people are waiting to destroy
me,
but I will think about your rules.
96 Everything I see has its limits,
but your commands have none.

97 How I love your teachings!
I think about them all day long.
98 Your commands make me wiser than
my enemies,
because they are mine forever.
99 I am wiser than all my teachers,
because I think
about your
rules.
100 I have more
understanding
than the older
leaders,
because I follow
your orders.

EMAIL FROM GOD
119:99–100
Bible
What does the Bible give you?

101 I have avoided every evil way
so I could obey your word.
102 I haven't walked away from your
laws,
because you yourself are my
teacher.
103 Your promises are sweet to me,
sweeter than honey in my mouth!
104 Your orders give me understanding,
so I hate lying ways.

105 Your word is like
a lamp for
my feet
and a light for
my path.

EMAIL FROM GOD
119:105
Decisions
What helps you make decisions?

106 I will do what I
have promised
and obey your fair laws.
107 I have suffered for a long time.
LORD, give me life by your word.
108 LORD, accept my willing praise
and teach me your laws.
109 My life is always in danger,
but I haven't forgotten your
teachings.
110 Wicked people have set a trap for
me,
but I haven't strayed from your
orders.
111 I will follow your rules forever,
because they make me happy.
112 I will try to do what you demand
forever, until the end.
113 I hate disloyal people,
but I love your teachings.
114 You are my hiding place and my
shield;
I hope in your word.
115 Get away from me, you who do evil,

so I can keep my God's commands.
116 Support me as you promised so I can live.
Don't let me be embarrassed because of my hopes.
117 Help me, and I will be saved.
I will always respect your demands.
118 You reject those who ignore your demands,
because their lies mislead them.
119 You throw away the wicked of the world like trash.
So I will love your rules.
120 I shake in fear of you;
I respect your laws.

121 I have done what is fair and right.
Don't leave me to those who wrong me.
122 Promise that you will help me, your servant.
Don't let proud people wrong me.
123 My eyes are tired from looking for your salvation
and for your good promise.
124 Show your love to me, your servant,
and teach me your demands.
125 I am your servant. Give me wisdom
so I can understand your rules.
126 LORD, it is time for you to do something,
because people have disobeyed your teachings.
127 I love your commands
more than the purest gold.
128 I respect all your orders,
so I hate lying ways.

129 Your rules are wonderful.
That is why I keep them.
130 Learning your words gives wisdom
and understanding for the foolish.
131 I am nearly out of breath.
I really want to learn your commands.
132 Look at me and have mercy on me
as you do for those who love you.
133 Guide my steps as you promised;
don't let any sin control me.
134 Save me from harmful people
so I can obey your orders.
135 Show your kindness to me, your servant.
Teach me your demands.
136 Tears stream from my eyes,
because people do not obey your teachings.

137 LORD, you do what is right,
and your laws are fair.
138 The rules you commanded are right
and completely trustworthy.
139 I am so upset I am worn out,
because my enemies have forgotten your words.
140 Your promises are proven,
so I, your servant, love them.
141 I am unimportant and hated,
but I have not forgotten your orders.
142 Your goodness continues forever,
and your teachings are true.
143 I have had troubles and misery,
but I love your commands.
144 Your rules are always good.
Help me understand so I can live.

145 LORD, I call to you with all my heart.
Answer me, and I will keep your demands.
146 I call to you.
Save me so I can obey your rules.
147 I wake up early in the morning and cry out.
I hope in your word.
148 I stay awake all night
so I can think about your promises.
149 Listen to me because of your love;
LORD, give me life by your laws.
150 Those who love evil are near.
but they are far from your teachings.
151 But, LORD, you are also near,
and all your commands are true.
152 Long ago I learned from your rules
that you made them to continue forever.

153 See my suffering and rescue me,
because I have not forgotten your teachings.
154 Argue my case and save me.
Let me live by your promises.

155 Wicked people are far from being saved,
because they do not want your demands.
156 LORD, you are very kind;
give me life by your laws.
157 Many enemies are after me,
but I have not rejected your rules.
158 I see those traitors, and I hate them,
because they do not obey what you say.
159 See how I love your orders.
LORD, give me life by your love.
160 Your words are true from the start,
and all your laws will be fair forever.

161 Leaders attack me for no reason,
but I fear your law in my heart.
162 I am as happy over your promises
as if I had found a great treasure.
163 I hate and despise lies,
but I love your teachings.
164 Seven times a day I praise you
for your fair laws.
165 Those who love your teachings will find true peace,
and nothing will defeat them.
166 I am waiting for you to save me, LORD.
I will obey your commands.
167 I obey your rules,
and I love them very much.
168 I obey your orders and rules,
because you know everything I do.

169 Hear my cry to you, LORD.
Let your word help me understand.
170 Listen to my prayer;
save me as you promised.
171 Let me speak your praise,
because you have taught me your demands.
172 Let me sing about your promises,
because all your commands are fair.
173 Give me your helping hand,
because I have chosen your commands.
174 I want you to save me, LORD.
I love your teachings.
175 Let me live so I can praise you,
and let your laws help me.
176 I have wandered like a lost sheep.
Look for your servant, because I have not forgotten your commands.

A Prayer of Someone Far from Home

A psalm for going up to worship.

120 When I was in trouble, I called to the LORD,
and he answered me.
2 LORD, save me from liars
and from those who plan evil.

3 You who plan evil, what will God do to you?
How will he punish you?
4 He will punish you with the sharp arrows of a warrior
and with burning coals of wood.

5 How terrible it is for me to live in the land of Meshech,
to live among the people of Kedar.
6 I have lived too long
with people who hate peace.
7 When I talk peace,
they want war.

The Lord Guards His People

A song for going up to worship.

121 I look up to the hills,
but where does my help come from?
2 My help comes from the LORD,
who made heaven and earth.

3 He will not let you be defeated.
He who guards you never sleeps.
4 He who guards Israel
never rests or sleeps.
5 The LORD guards you.
The LORD is the shade that protects you from the sun.
6 The sun cannot
hurt you during the day,

EMAIL! FROM GOD 121
Help
Where does your help come from?

THE TEMPLE IN JERUSALEM

Psalm 122

The Temple in Jerusalem was a very important place for the Israelite people. Through Temple services, the Israelite people pledged their lives to follow the laws and teachings of their creator. They worshiped God there, and they offered sacrifices for their sins.

Three different Temples were actually built in Jerusalem. All three were built on the same site on a hill called Mount Moriah. (See 2 Chronicles 3:1, p. 564.)

The first Temple, built by King Solomon, stood on a platform about ten feet high. Thousands of laborers and craftsmen built this Temple. (Read 1 Kings 6 and 7, p. 442; 2 Chronicles 3 and 4, p. 564.) This building was destroyed by the Babylonians when they captured Jerusalem. Then Cyrus, king of Persia, had the Temple rebuilt on the same site when he allowed the Israelite people to return to Jerusalem. (Check out Ezra 1, p. 609.) This Temple was known as Zerubbabel's Temple. (Look at Ezra 6:13–15, p. 616.) Several centuries later, Herod the Great, Roman ruler of Palestine, ordered construction of the third Temple—a cream-colored building of stone and gold. The Romans destroyed this Temple about 40 years after Jesus' resurrection and ascension.

and the moon cannot hurt you at
night.
7 The LORD will protect you from all
dangers;
he will guard your life.
8 The LORD will guard you as you
come and go,
both now and forever.

Happy People in Jerusalem

A song for going up to worship.
Of David.

122 I was happy when they said to
me,
"Let's go to the Temple of the
LORD."
2 Jerusalem, we are standing
at your gates.

3 Jerusalem is built as a city
with the buildings close together.
4 The tribes go up there,
the tribes who belong to the
LORD.
It is the rule in Israel
to praise the LORD at Jerusalem.
5 There the descendants of David
set their thrones to judge the
people.

6 Pray for peace in Jerusalem:
"May those who love her be safe.
7 May there be peace within her walls
and safety within her strong
towers."
8 To help my relatives and friends,
I say, "Let Jerusalem have
peace."
9 For the sake of the Temple of the
LORD our God,
I wish good for her.

A Prayer for Mercy

A song for going up to worship.

123 LORD, I look upward to you,
you who live in heaven.
2 Slaves depend on their masters,
and a female servant depends on
her mistress.
In the same way, we depend on the
LORD our God;
we wait for him to show us mercy.

3 Have mercy on us, LORD. Have
mercy on us,
because we have been insulted.

FAITH CHALLENGE

Here's another challenge for you. Read 123:3–4 to find out why it's sometimes tough to follow the Lord. What do you do when someone insults you or calls you a name?

TESTING IT

Psalm 123:3–4
Have mercy on us, LORD. Have mercy on us, because we have been insulted. We have suffered many insults from lazy people and much cruelty from the proud.

4 We have suffered many insults from
lazy people
and much cruelty from the proud.

The Lord Saves His People

A song for going up to worship.
Of David.

124 What if the LORD had not been
on our side?
(Let Israel repeat this.)
2 What if the LORD had not been on our
side
when we were attacked?
3 When they were angry with us,
they would have swallowed us
alive.
4 They would have been like a flood
drowning us;
they would have poured over us
like a river.
5 They would have swept us away
like a mighty stream.

6 Praise the LORD,
who did not let them chew us up.
7 We escaped like a bird
from the hunter's trap.
The trap broke,
and we escaped.
8 Our help comes from the LORD,
who made heaven and earth.

God Protects Those Who Trust Him

A song for going up to worship.

125 Those who trust the LORD are
like Mount Zion,
which sits unmoved forever.
2 As the mountains surround
Jerusalem,
the LORD surrounds his people
now and forever.

3 The wicked will not rule
over those who do right.
If they did, the people who do right
might use their power to do evil.

4 LORD, be good to those who are
good,
whose hearts are honest.

5 But, LORD, when you remove those
who do evil,
also remove those who stop
following you.

Let there be peace in Israel.

Lord, Bring Your People Back

A song for going up to worship.

126 When the LORD brought the
prisoners back to
Jerusalem,
it seemed as if we were dreaming.
2 Then we were filled with laughter,
and we sang happy songs.
Then the other nations said,
"The LORD has done great things
for them."
3 The LORD has done great things for
us,
and we are very glad.

4 LORD, return our prisoners again,
as you bring streams to the desert.
5 Those who cry as they plant crops
will sing at harvest time.
6 Those who cry
as they carry out the seeds
will return singing
and carrying bundles of grain.

All Good Things Come from God

A song for going up to worship.
Of Solomon.

127 If the LORD doesn't build the
house,
the builders are working for
nothing.
If the LORD doesn't guard the city,
the guards are watching for
nothing.
2 It is no use for you to get up early
and stay up late,
working for a living.
The LORD gives sleep to those he
loves.
3 Children are a gift from the LORD;
babies are a reward.
4 Children who are born to a young man
are like arrows in the hand of a
warrior.

FAITH links

GOD'S VALUABLE GIFT: YOU

PSALM 127:3-5

What's the best gift you've been given recently? What makes that gift so valuable to you? Want to know a great gift that God gave your parents or guardians? Take a look in the mirror. One of the main points of this psalm by Solomon is how much God values children. The families with children are considered blessed. Like yours.

Check out these Faithlinks to see how God loves his creations:

Made in His Image, Genesis 1:26–27, p. 4
The MLP, Ruth 1:16–17, p. 345
Love for a Lifetime, Song of Solomon 6:8–9, p. 891
Rock Solid, Habakkuk 1:12, p. 1236
One Big, Happy Family, John 1:12, p. 1422
A Family Celebration, 1 Corinthians 11:23–29, p. 1558

5 Happy is the man
who has his bag full of arrows.
They will not be defeated
when they fight their enemies at
the city gate.

The Happy Home

A song for going up to worship.

128 Happy are those who respect
the LORD and obey him.

2 You will enjoy what you work for,
and you will be blessed with good things.
3 Your wife will give you many children,
like a vine that produces much fruit.
Your children will bring you much good,
like olive branches that produce many olives.
4 This is how the man who respects the LORD
will be blessed.
5 May the LORD bless you from Mount Zion;
may you enjoy the good things of Jerusalem all your life.
6 May you see your grandchildren.

Let there be peace in Israel.

A Prayer Against the Enemies

A song for going up to worship.

129 They have treated me badly all my life.
(Let Israel repeat this.)
2 They have treated me badly all my life,
but they have not defeated me.
3 Like farmers plowing, they plowed over my back,
making long wounds.
4 But the LORD does what is right;
he has set me free from those wicked people.

5 Let those who hate Jerusalem
be turned back in shame.
6 Let them be like the grass on the roof
that dries up before it has grown.
7 There is not enough of it to fill a hand
or to make into a bundle to fill one's arms.
8 Let those who pass by them not say,
"May the LORD bless you.
We bless you by the power of the LORD."

A Prayer for Mercy

A song for going up to worship.

130 LORD, I am in great trouble,
so I call out to you.
2 Lord, hear my voice;
listen to my prayer for help.
3 LORD, if you punished people for all their sins,
no one would be left, Lord.
4 But you forgive us,
so you are respected.

5 I wait for the LORD to help me,
and I trust his word.
6 I wait for the Lord to help me
more than night watchmen wait for the dawn,
more than night watchmen wait for the dawn.

EMAIL! FROM GOD
130:5–6
Hope
Wait for the Lord.

7 People of Israel, put your hope in the LORD
because he is loving
and able to save.
8 He will save Israel
from all their sins.

Childlike Trust in the Lord

A song for going up to worship.
Of David.

131 LORD, my heart is not proud;
I don't look down on others.
I don't do great things,
and I can't do miracles.
2 But I am calm and quiet,
like a baby with its mother.
I am at peace, like a baby with its mother.

EMAIL! FROM GOD
131:1
Pride
What should your attitude be like?

3 People of Israel, put your hope in the LORD
now and forever.

In Praise of the Temple

A song for going up to worship.

132 LORD, remember David
and all his suffering.
2 He made an oath to the LORD,
a promise to the Mighty God of Jacob.
3 He said, "I will not go home to my house,
or lie down on my bed,
4 or close my eyes,
or let myself sleep
5 until I find a place for the LORD.
I want to provide a home for the Mighty God of Jacob."

6 We heard about the Ark in Bethlehem.
We found it at Kiriath Jearim.
7 Let's go to the LORD's house.
Let's worship at his footstool.
8 Rise, LORD, and come to your resting place;
come with the Ark that shows your strength.
9 May your priests do what is right.
May your people sing for joy.

10 For the sake of your servant David,
do not reject your appointed king.
11 The LORD made a promise to David,
a sure promise that he will not take back.
He promised, "I will make one of your descendants
rule as king after you.
12 If your sons keep my agreement
and the rules that I teach them,
then their sons after them will rule
on your throne forever and ever."

13 The LORD has chosen Jerusalem;
he wants it for his home.
14 He says, "This is my resting place forever.
Here is where I want to stay.
15 I will bless her with plenty;
I will fill her poor with food.
16 I will cover her priests with salvation,
and those who worship me will really sing for joy.

17 "I will make a king come from the family of David.
I will provide my appointed one descendants to rule after him.
18 I will cover his enemies with shame,
but his crown will shine."

FAITH links

PEACE IN THE FAMILY

PSALM 133

"He started it!" "No she did!" Sound familiar? Maybe you've said something similar in an argument with a sister or brother. Ever wish you and your siblings could get along all the time? Maybe you also wish that for your brothers and sisters in Christ. That is the hope expressed in this psalm. Getting along with siblings is not an impossible dream. God's love makes it possible for people to "live together in peace." Even siblings.

Link here to find out how to live with your brothers and sisters:

Family Feud, Genesis 27, p. 37

Fair All the Time?, 2 Samuel 8:15, p. 408

In Deep Water, Psalm 69, p. 760

Better Than Some?, Luke 18:9–14, p. 1405

The Gentle Way, Titus 3:1–5, p. 1661

Who's on First?, 3 John 9–10, p. 1723

The Love of God's People

A song for going up to worship.
Of David.

133 It is good and pleasant
when God's people live
together in peace!
2 It is like perfumed oil poured on the
priest's head
and running down his beard.
It ran down Aaron's beard
and on to the collar of his robes.
3 It is like the dew of Mount Hermon
falling on the hills of Jerusalem.
There the LORD gives his blessing
of life forever.

Temple Guards, Praise the Lord

A song for going up to worship.

134 Praise the LORD, all you
servants of the LORD,
you who serve at night in the
Temple of the LORD.
2 Raise your hands in the Temple
and praise the LORD.

3 May the LORD bless you from Mount
Zion,
he who made heaven and earth.

The Lord Saves, Idols Do Not

135 Praise the LORD!
Praise the name of the LORD;
praise him, you servants of the
LORD,
2 you who stand in the
LORD's Temple
and in the Temple
courtyards.
3 Praise the LORD,
because he is
good;
sing praises to him,
because it is
pleasant.

4 The LORD has chosen
the people of Jacob for himself;
he has chosen the people of Israel
for his very own.
5 I know that the LORD is great.
Our Lord is greater than all the
gods.
6 The LORD does what he pleases,
in heaven and on earth,
in the seas and the deep oceans.
7 He brings the clouds from the ends
of the earth.
He sends the lightning with the
rain.
He brings out the wind from his
storehouses.

8 He destroyed the firstborn sons in
Egypt
the firstborn of both people and
animals.
9 He did many signs and miracles in
Egypt
against the king and his servants.
10 He defeated many nations
and killed powerful kings:
11 Sihon king of the Amorites,
Og king of Bashan,
and all the kings of Canaan.
12 Then he gave their land as a gift,
a gift to his people, the Israelites.

13 LORD, your name is everlasting;
LORD, you will be remembered
forever.
14 The LORD defends his people
and has mercy on his servants.

15 The idols of other nations are made
of silver and gold,
the work of human hands.
16 They have mouths, but they cannot
speak.
They have eyes,
but they cannot
see.
17 They have ears, but
they cannot hear.
They have no
breath in their
mouths.
18 People who make
idols will be like
them,
and so will those who trust them.

19 Family of Israel, praise the LORD.

> Our Lord is greater than all the gods.
> —Psalm 135:5

Family of Aaron, praise the LORD.
20 Family of Levi, praise the LORD.
You who respect the LORD should praise him.
21 You people of Jerusalem, praise the LORD on Mount Zion.
Praise the LORD!

God's Love Continues Forever

136 Give thanks to the LORD because he is good.
His love continues forever.
2 Give thanks to the God of gods.
His love continues forever.
3 Give thanks to the Lord of lords.
His love continues forever.

4 Only he can do great miracles.
His love continues forever.
5 With his wisdom he made the skies.
His love continues forever.
6 He spread out the earth on the seas.
His love continues forever.
7 He made the sun and the moon.
His love continues forever.
8 He made the sun to rule the day.
His love continues forever.
9 He made the moon and stars to rule the night.
His love continues forever.

10 He killed the firstborn sons of the Egyptians.
His love continues forever.
11 He brought the people of Israel out of Egypt.
His love continues forever.
12 He did it with his great power and strength.
His love continues forever.
13 He parted the water of the Red Sea.
His love continues forever.
14 He brought the Israelites through the middle of it.
His love continues forever.
15 But the king of Egypt and his army drowned in the Red Sea.
His love continues forever.

16 He led his people through the desert.
His love continues forever.
17 He defeated great kings.
His love continues forever.
18 He killed powerful kings.
His love continues forever.
19 He defeated Sihon king of the Amorites.
His love continues forever.
20 He defeated Og king of Bashan.

FAITH links

LOVE THAT WILL LAST

PSALM 136

Is there anything you know of that lasts forever? Some things like poison ivy or Aunt Myrtle's bean salad may seem to last forever, but eventually they disappear. Even some friendships don't seem to last. Maybe you had a friend you thought you'd have forever. Throughout this psalm of praise, one statement stands out: "His love continues forever." God's love will never end. Even though others may disappoint you, you can count on God.

Surf over to these Faithlinks to find out about the One who will never disappoint you:

Your Worst Enemy, Exodus 7—11, p. 85

God's New Home, 2 Chronicles 7:11–22, p. 570

Lower Than Low, Job 19:13–25, p. 680

The One Who Suffered, Isaiah 53, p. 966

His Valentine, Jeremiah 31:3, p. 1035

A Heavenly Sight, Revelation 21:1–4, p. 1753

His love continues forever.
21 He gave their land as a gift.
His love continues forever.
22 It was a gift to his servants, the Israelites.
His love continues forever.

23 He remembered us when we were in trouble.
His love continues forever.
24 He freed us from our enemies.
His love continues forever.
25 He gives food to every living creature.
His love continues forever.

26 Give thanks to the God of heaven.
His love continues forever.

Israelites in Captivity

137 By the rivers in Babylon we sat and cried
when we remembered Jerusalem.
2 On the poplar trees nearby
we hung our harps.
3 Those who captured us asked us to sing;
our enemies wanted happy songs.
They said, "Sing us a song about Jerusalem!"

4 But we cannot sing songs about the LORD
while we are in this foreign country!
5 Jerusalem, if I forget you,
let my right hand lose its skill.
6 Let my tongue stick to the roof of my mouth
if I do not remember you,
if I do not think about Jerusalem
as my greatest joy.

7 LORD, remember what the Edomites did
on the day Jerusalem fell.
They said, "Tear it down!
Tear it down to its foundations!"

8 People of Babylon, you will be destroyed.
The people who pay you back for what you did to us will be happy.
9 They will grab your babies
and throw them against the rocks.

A Hymn of Thanksgiving

A psalm of David.

138 LORD, I will thank you with all my heart;
I will sing to you before the gods.
2 I will bow down facing your holy Temple,
and I will thank you for your love and loyalty.
You have made your name and your word
greater than anything.
3 On the day I called to you, you answered me.
You made me strong and brave.

4 LORD, let all the kings of the earth praise you
when they hear the words you speak.
5 They will sing about what the LORD has done,
because the LORD's glory is great.

EMAIL FROM GOD 138
Thankfulness
What should you be thankful for?

6 Though the LORD is supreme,
he takes care of those who are humble,
but he stays away from the proud.
7 LORD, even when I have trouble all around me,
you will keep me alive.
When my enemies are angry,
you will reach down and save me by your power.
8 LORD, you do everything for me.
LORD, your love continues forever.
Do not leave us, whom you made.

God Knows Everything

For the director of music.
A psalm of David.

139 LORD, you have examined me
and know all about me.

2 You know when I sit down and when
I get up.
You know my thoughts before I
think them.
3 You know where I go and where I lie
down.
You know thoroughly everything I
do.
4 LORD, even before I say a word,
you already know it.
5 You are all around me—in front and
in back—
and have put your hand on me.
6 Your knowledge is amazing to me;
it is more than I can understand.

7 Where can I go to get away from your
Spirit?
Where can I run from you?
8 If I go up to the heavens, you are
there.
If I lie down in the grave, you are
there.
9 If I rise with the sun in the east
and settle in the west beyond the
sea,
10 even there you would guide me.
With your right hand you would
hold me.

11 I could say, "The darkness will hide
me.
Let the light around me turn into
night."
12 But even the darkness is not dark to
you.
The night is as light as the day;
darkness and light are the same to
you.

13 You made my whole being;
you formed me in my mother's
body.
14 I praise you because you made me in
an amazing and wonderful way.
What you have done is wonderful.
I know this very well.
15 You saw my bones being formed
as I took shape in my mother's
body.
When I was put together there,
16 you saw my body as it was formed.
All the days planned for me
were written in your book
before I was one day old.

17 God, your thoughts are precious to
me.
They are so many!
18 If I could count them,
they would be more than all the
grains of sand.
When I wake up,
I am still with you.

FAITH links

UNIQUELY YOU

PSALM 139:13-14

Take a good look at yourself in the mirror. You've probably heard relatives tell you how much you look like various family members. Maybe you have your mother's eyebrows or your grandfather's left ear. Maybe there are some features you like and some you wish you could change. But guess what? God made you exactly the way he wanted you to be. You are unique. That means there is only one of you. And that makes you pretty cool.

Complaints, Complaints!, Exodus 16:1–3, p. 97

The Perfect Sacrifice, Leviticus 1—7, p. 135

How to Worship God, Isaiah 58, p. 972

The Way to Heaven, John 14:1–6, p. 1448

The "Eyes" Have It?, 1 Corinthians 12, p. 1559

It's Free!, Ephesians 2:8–9, p. 1600

19 God, I wish you would kill the
wicked!
Get away from me, you murderers!
20 They say evil things about you.
Your enemies use your name
thoughtlessly.
21 LORD, I hate those who hate you;
I hate those who rise up against
you.
22 I feel only hate for them;
they are my enemies.

23 God, examine me and know my
heart;
test me and know my nervous
thoughts.
24 See if there is any bad thing in me.
Lead me on the road to everlasting
life.

A Prayer for Protection

For the director of music.
A psalm of David.

140 LORD, rescue me from evil
people;
protect me from cruel people
2 who make evil plans,
who always start fights.
3 They make their tongues sharp as a
snake's;
their words are like snake poison.
Selah

4 LORD, guard me from the power of
wicked people;
protect me from
cruel people
who plan to trip me
up.
5 The proud hid a trap
for me.
They spread out a
net beside the
road;
they set traps for
me. *Selah*

6 I said to the LORD, "You are my
God."
LORD, listen to my prayer for help.
7 LORD God, my mighty savior,
you protect me in battle.
8 LORD, do not give the wicked what
they want.
Don't let their plans succeed,
or they will become proud. *Selah*

9 Those around me have planned
trouble.
Now let it come to them.
10 Let burning coals fall on them.
Throw them into the fire
or into pits from which they cannot
escape.
11 Don't let liars settle in the land.
Let evil quickly hunt down cruel
people.

12 I know the LORD will get justice for
the poor
and will defend the needy in court.
13 Good people will praise his name;
honest people will live in his
presence.

A Prayer Not to Sin

A psalm of David.

141 LORD, I call to you. Come
quickly.
Listen to me when I call to you.
2 Let my prayer be like incense placed
before you,
and my praise like the evening
sacrifice.

3 LORD, help me control my tongue;
help me be careful about what I
say.
4 Take away my desire to
do evil
or to join others in
doing wrong.
Don't let me eat tasty
food
with those who do
evil.

LORD, help me control my tongue; help me be careful about what I say.
—Psalm 141:3

5 If a good person
punished me, that
would be kind.
If he corrected me, that would be
like perfumed oil on my head.
I shouldn't refuse it.
But I pray against those who do evil.

6 Let their leaders be thrown down
the cliffs.
Then people will know that I have
spoken correctly:
7 "The ground is plowed and broken
up.
In the same way, our bones have
been scattered at the grave."

8 GOD, I look to you for help.
I trust in you, LORD. Don't let me
die.
9 Protect me from the traps they set
for me
and from the net that evil people
have spread.
10 Let the wicked fall into their own
nets,
but let me pass by safely.

A Prayer for Safety

A maskil of David when he was
in the cave. A prayer.

142 I cry out to the LORD;
I pray to the LORD for mercy.
2 I pour out my problems to him;
I tell him my troubles.
3 When I am afraid,
you, LORD, know the way out.
In the path where I walk,
a trap is hidden for me.
4 Look around me
and see.
No one cares
about me.
I have no place of
safety;
no one cares if
I live.

EMAIL FROM GOD 142
Troubles
Who do you bring your troubles to?

5 LORD, I cry out to you.
I say, "You are my protection.
You are all I want in this life."
6 Listen to my cry,
because I am helpless.
Save me from those who are chasing
me,
because they are too strong for
me.
7 Free me from my prison,
and then I will praise your name.
Then good people will surround me,
because you have taken care of
me.

A Prayer Not to Be Killed

A psalm of David.

143 LORD, hear my prayer;
listen to my cry for mercy.
Answer me
because you are loyal and good.
2 Don't judge me, your servant,
because no one alive is right
before you.
3 My enemies are chasing me;
they crushed me to the ground.
They made me live in darkness
like those long dead.
4 I am afraid;
my courage is gone.

5 I remember what happened long ago;
I consider everything you have
done.
I think about all you have made.
6 I lift my hands to you in prayer.
As a dry land needs rain, I thirst
for you. *Selah*

7 LORD, answer me quickly,
because I am getting weak.
Don't turn away from me,
or I will be like those who are
dead.
8 Tell me in the morning about your
love,
because I trust you.
Show me what I should do,
because my prayers go up to you.
9 LORD, save me from my enemies;
I hide in you.
10 Teach me to do what you want,
because you are my God.
Let your good Spirit
lead me on level ground.

11 LORD, let me live
so people will praise you.
In your goodness
save me from my troubles.
12 In your love defeat my enemies.
Destroy all those who trouble me,
because I am your servant.

A Prayer for Victory

Of David.

144 Praise the LORD, my Rock,
who trains me for war,
who trains me for battle.
2 He protects me like a strong, walled
city, and he loves me.
He is my defender and my Savior,
my shield and my protection.
He helps me keep my people
under control.

3 LORD, why are people important to
you?
Why do you even think about
human beings?
4 People are like a breath;
their lives are like passing
shadows.

5 LORD, tear open the sky and come
down.
Touch the mountains so they will
smoke.
6 Send the lightning and scatter my
enemies.
Shoot your arrows
and force them
away.
7 Reach down from
above.
Save me and
rescue me out of
this sea of
enemies,
from these
foreigners.
8 They are liars;
they are dishonest.

9 God, I will sing a new song to you;
I will play to you on the ten-
stringed harp.
10 You give victory to kings.
You save your servant David from
cruel swords.
11 Save me, rescue me from these
foreigners.
They are liars; they are dishonest.

12 Let our sons in their youth
grow like plants.
Let our daughters be
like the decorated stones in the
Temple.
13 Let our barns be filled
with crops of all kinds.
Let our sheep in the fields have
thousands and tens of thousands of
lambs.
14 Let our cattle be strong.
Let no one break in.
Let there be no war,
no screams in our streets.

15 Happy are those who are like this;
happy are the people whose God is
the LORD.

Praise to God the King

A psalm of praise. Of David.

145 I praise your greatness, my
God the King;
I will praise you forever and ever.
2 I will praise you every day;
I will praise you forever and ever.
3 The LORD is great and worthy of our
praise;
no one can
understand how
great he is.

4 Parents will tell their
children what you
have done.
They will retell your
mighty acts,
5 wonderful majesty, and
glory.
And I will think
about your
miracles.

6 They will tell about the amazing
things you do,
and I will tell how great you are.
7 They will remember your great
goodness
and will sing about your fairness.

8 The LORD is kind and shows mercy.
He does not become angry quickly
but is full of love.
9 The LORD is good to everyone;
he is merciful to all he has made.

> The LORD is kind and shows mercy. He does not become angry quickly but is full of love.
> —Psalm 145:8

PATIENCE, PLEASE

PSALM 145:8-9

Who among your family has the most patience? Have you ever noticed how this person acts toward others? Maybe he doesn't seem to mind when others go ahead of him. Or maybe she takes time to answer your questions or explain things. A patient person never seems to do things in a hurry.

That's a description of God. This psalm mentions one thing that God doesn't do in a hurry: become angry. That means he's always patient with us. He never demands that we "hurry up" and do something. He wants his people to be just as patient with each other as he is with us.

Here are some more Faithlinks on patience:

Just Kidding?, Genesis 21:8–10, p. 28

Give Revenge a Rest, Leviticus 19:18, p. 160

Putting an Enemy in Check, 2 Kings 6:8–23, p. 486

Helpful Advice, Job 12:4–5, p. 673

Ask, Search, Knock, Matthew 7:7–10, p. 1286

Your Civic Duty, Matthew 17:24–27, p. 1304

10 LORD, everything you have made will
praise you;
those who belong to you will bless
you.
11 They will tell about the glory of your
kingdom
and will speak about your power.
12 Then everyone will know the mighty
things you do
and the glory and majesty of your
kingdom.
13 Your kingdom will go on and on,
and you will rule forever.

The LORD will keep all his promises;
he is loyal to all he has made.
14 The LORD helps those who have
been defeated
and takes care of those who are in
trouble.
15 All living things look to you for food,
and you give it to them at the right
time.
16 You open your hand,
and you satisfy all living things.

17 Everything the LORD does is right.
He is loyal to all he has made.
18 The LORD is close to everyone who
prays to him,
to all who truly pray to him.
19 He gives those who respect him
what they want.
He listens when they cry, and he
saves them.
20 The LORD protects everyone who
loves him,
but he will destroy the wicked.

21 I will praise the LORD.
Let everyone praise his holy name
forever.

Praise God Who Helps the Weak

146 Praise the LORD!

My whole being, praise the LORD.
2 I will praise the LORD all my life;
I will sing praises to my God as
long as I live.

3 Do not put your trust in princes

or other people, who cannot save
you.
4 When people die,
they are
buried.
Then all of
their plans
come to an
end.

EMAIL! FROM GOD
146:3
Trust
Don't put your
trust here.

5 Happy are those who are helped by
the God of Jacob.
Their hope is in the LORD their
God.
6 He made heaven and earth,
the sea and everything in it.
He remains loyal forever.
7 He does what is fair for those who
have been wronged.

FAITH CHALLENGE

Try this one. Read 146:8 to find out how God helps people who have special needs. When you find yourself in trouble, what's the first thing you usually do?

TESTING IT

Psalm 146:8
The LORD gives sight to the blind. The LORD lifts up people who are in trouble. The LORD loves those who do right.

He gives food to the hungry.
The LORD sets the prisoners free.
8 The LORD gives sight to the blind.
The LORD lifts up people who are in
trouble.
The LORD loves those who do
right.
9 The LORD protects the foreigners.
He defends the orphans and
widows,
but he blocks the way of the
wicked.

10 The LORD will be King forever.
Jerusalem, your God is
everlasting.

Praise the LORD!

Praise God Who Helps His People

147 Praise the LORD!

It is good to sing praises to our God;
it is good and pleasant to praise
him.
2 The LORD rebuilds Jerusalem;
he brings back the captured
Israelites.
3 He heals the brokenhearted
and bandages their wounds.

4 He counts the stars
and names each one.
5 Our Lord is great and very
powerful.
There is no limit to what he
knows.
6 The LORD defends the humble,
but he throws the wicked to the
ground.

7 Sing praises to the LORD;
praise our God with harps.
8 He fills the sky with clouds
and sends rain to the earth
and makes grass grow on the
hills.
9 He gives food to cattle
and to the little birds that call.

10 He does not enjoy the strength of a
horse
or the strength of a man.

11 The LORD is pleased with those who
respect him,
with those who trust his love.

12 Jerusalem, praise the LORD;
Jerusalem, praise
your God.
13 He makes your city
gates strong
and blesses your
children inside.
14 He brings peace to
your country
and fills you with
the finest grain.

He counts the stars and names each one.
—Psalm 147:4

15 He gives a command
to the earth,
and it quickly obeys him.
16 He spreads the snow like wool
and scatters the frost like ashes.
17 He throws down hail like rocks.
No one can stand the cold he
sends.
18 Then he gives a command, and it
melts.
He sends the breezes, and the
waters flow.

19 He gave his word to Jacob,
his laws and demands to Israel.
20 He didn't do this for any other nation.
They don't know his laws.

Praise the LORD!

The World Should Praise the Lord

148 Praise the LORD!

Praise the LORD from the skies.
Praise him high above the earth.
2 Praise him, all
you angels.
Praise him, all
you armies
of heaven.
3 Praise him, sun
and moon.
Praise him, all
you shining stars.
4 Praise him, highest heavens
and you waters above the sky.
5 Let them praise the LORD,
because they were created by his
command.
6 He put them in place forever and
ever;
he made a law that will never
change.

EMAIL FROM GOD
148:1–2
Angels
Who do angels praise?

7 Praise the LORD from
the earth,
you large sea
animals and all the
oceans,
8 lightning and hail,
snow and mist,
and stormy winds
that obey him,
9 mountains and all hills,
fruit trees and all cedars,
10 wild animals and all cattle,
crawling animals and birds,
11 kings of the earth and all nations,
princes and all rulers of the earth,
12 young men and women,
old people and children.

13 Praise the LORD,
because he alone is great.
He is more wonderful than heaven
and earth.
14 God has given his people a king.
He should be praised by all who
belong to him;
he should be praised by the
Israelites, the people closest to
his heart.

Praise the LORD!

Praise the God of Israel

149 Praise the LORD!

Sing a new song to the LORD;
sing his praise in the meeting of
his people.

2 Let the Israelites be happy because
of God, their Maker.
Let the people of Jerusalem rejoice
because of their King.
3 They should praise him with dancing.
They should sing praises to him
with tambourines and harps.
4 The LORD is pleased with his people;

he saves the humble.
5 Let those who worship him rejoice in
his glory.
Let them sing for joy even in bed!

6 Let them shout his praise
with their two-edged swords in
their hands.
7 They will punish the nations
and defeat the people.
8 They will put those kings in chains
and those important men in iron
bands.
9 They will punish them as God has
written.
God is honored by all who worship
him.

Praise the LORD!

Praise the Lord with Music

150 Praise the LORD!

Praise God in his Temple;
praise him in his mighty heaven.
2 Praise him for his strength;
praise him for his greatness.
3 Praise him with trumpet blasts;
praise him with harps and lyres.
4 Praise him with tambourines and
dancing;
praise him with stringed
instruments and flutes.
5 Praise him with loud cymbals;
praise him with crashing cymbals.
6 Let everything that breathes praise
the LORD.

Praise the LORD!

EMAIL! FROM GOD 150
Worship
Check out ways to worship God.

BE WISE!

Greetings! I am Solomon, the king of Israel and the builder of the Lord's Temple. One night, shortly after I became king, God appeared to me in a dream and said he would give me whatever I wanted. Whatever I wanted! Can you imagine? What would you ask for? Toys? Money? Popularity? I could have asked for a long life or money or victory over my enemies, but I asked for wisdom so that I could rule my kingdom well. God granted my request, and I became famous for my wisdom. People said that I was the wisest man who had ever lived!

I wrote Proverbs to share God's wisdom. This book is a collection of proverbs, or wise sayings, that help us make good decisions in daily life. Many proverbs show a choice between two paths: the way of the wise and the way of the fool. Here's an example: "Wise people are careful and stay out of trouble, but fools are careless and quick to act" (Proverbs 14:16). Do you want to be wise? Read some proverbs today!

JESUS WATCH

Solomon describes wisdom as a woman who has set up her house on the highest hill. She calls out for all to come and learn the ways of God. Her teachings are more precious than gold and silver and rubies. Those who follow her teachings will make good decisions and will be richly rewarded. Those who find wisdom will find life with God. Those who hate wisdom will find death. In 1 Corinthians 1:30, Paul says that Jesus has become wisdom for us. Jesus invites everyone to believe in him and obey his teachings. It is wise to follow Jesus because the reward is more precious than gold. It is eternal life with God.

my FAVORITE links

______________________ ______________________

______________________ ______________________

______________________ ______________________

______________________ ______________________

OTHER CONNECTIONS

Livin' it

The Book of Proverbs is all about gaining wisdom—not just the kind that comes from reading books and studying hard, but wisdom that comes from God. Find out what the difference is by linking to Wise or Wise Guy?, Proverbs 2.

- It may not be the easiest thing to do, but listening and obeying your parents is the wisest thing you can do! Surf over to How to Be a Real Wise Guy!, Proverbs 6:20–23, and find out all about what it takes to have true wisdom. Really!

- It may be one of the hardest things to do—to walk away from a fight or a kid who has just insulted you—but that's what the Bible tells you to do. Check it out by downloading Now You're Asking for It!, Proverbs 25:21–22.

"Can you name seven things the Lord hates?"

"That's a tough one! We'd better surf over to Proverbs 6:16-19."

did YOU know?

SOME MORE COOL STUFF FROM PROVERBS:

Who do you trust?, Proverbs 3:5–6
Be like an ant?, Proverbs 6:6–8
Like a gold ring in a pig's snout, Proverbs 11:22
Reward this woman!, Proverbs 31:10–31

FAITH links

- A Parent's Advice, Proverbs 1:8–9
- A Direct Path, Proverbs 3:5–6
- Down on the Ant Farm, Proverbs 6:6–11
- What God "Hates," Proverbs 6:16–19
- The Problem with Gossip, Proverbs 11:12–13
- If You Want My Advice . . ., Proverbs 13:1
- A Gentle Answer, Proverbs 15:1
- Choosing a Friend, Proverbs 28:7
- Down on Discipline?, Proverbs 29:15

The Importance of Proverbs

1 These are the wise words of Solomon
son of David, king of Israel.
2 They teach wisdom and self-control;
they will help you understand wise words.
3 They will teach you how to be wise and self-controlled
and will teach you to do what is honest and fair and right.
4 They make the uneducated smarter
and give knowledge and sense to the young.
5 Wise people can also listen and learn;
even smart people can find good advice in these words.
6 Then anyone can understand wise words and stories,
the words of the wise and their riddles.

EMAIL! FROM GOD 1:7
Wisdom
Where does wisdom begin?

7 Knowledge begins with respect for the LORD,
but fools hate wisdom and self-control.

Warnings Against Evil

8 My child, listen to your father's teaching
and do not forget your mother's advice.
9 Their teaching will be like flowers in your hair
or a necklace around your neck.

FAITH links

A PARENT'S ADVICE

PROVERBS 1:8-9

You can find advice all over the place: the newspaper, the Internet, magazines, billboards, and your friends. But there is only one source of advice that this proverb tells you to listen to: your parents. Listening to them is one way to show your respect for them. If you really want to be wise, lend your parents your ear.

His OK to Obey, Deuteronomy 2:24–36, p. 230

In Your Best Interests, Ruth 3, p. 349

God's Valuable Gift: You, Psalm 127:3–5, p. 809

Sow It and Reap, Lamentations 1:18, p. 1075

Obey or Disobey?, Luke 20:20–26, p. 1409

The Best Choice, 1 Corinthians 13, p. 1560

10 My child, if sinners try to lead you into sin,
do not follow them.
11 They will say, "Come with us.
Let's ambush and kill someone;
let's attack some innocent people just for fun.
12 Let's swallow them alive, as death does;
let's swallow them whole, as the grave does.
13 We will take all kinds of valuable things
and fill our houses with stolen goods.
14 Come join us,
and we will share with you stolen goods."
15 My child, do not go along with them;
do not do what they do.
16 They are eager to do evil
and are quick to kill.
17 It is useless to spread out a net
right where the birds can see it.
18 But sinners will fall into their own traps;
they will only catch themselves!
19 All greedy people end up this way;
greed kills selfish people.

Wisdom Speaks

20 Wisdom is like a woman shouting in
the street;
she raises her voice in the city
squares.
21 She cries out in the noisy street
and shouts at the city gates:
22 "You fools, how long will you be
foolish?
How long will you make fun of
wisdom
and hate knowledge?
23 If only you had listened when I
corrected you,
I would have told you what's in my
heart;
I would have told you what I am
thinking.
24 I called, but you refused to listen;
I held out my hand, but you paid no
attention.
25 You did not follow my advice
and did not listen when I corrected
you.
26 So I will laugh when you are in
trouble.
I will make fun when disaster
strikes you,
27 when disaster comes over you like a
storm,
when trouble strikes you like a
whirlwind,
when pain and trouble overwhelm
you.

28 "Then you will call to me,
but I will not answer.
You will look for me,
but you will not find me.
29 It is because you rejected knowledge
and did not choose to respect the
LORD.
30 You did not accept my advice,
and you rejected my correction.
31 So you will get what you deserve;
you will get what you planned for
others.
32 Fools will die because they refuse to
listen;
they will be destroyed because
they do not care.
33 But those who listen to me will live
in safety
and be at peace, without fear of
injury."

Rewards of Wisdom

2 My child, listen to what I say
and remember what I command
you.
2 Listen carefully to wisdom;
set your mind on understanding.
3 Cry out for wisdom,
and beg for understanding.
4 Search for it like silver,
and hunt for it like hidden treasure.
5 Then you will understand respect for
the LORD,
and you will find that you know
God.
6 Only the LORD gives wisdom;
he gives knowledge and
understanding.
7 He stores up wisdom for those who
are honest.
Like a shield he protects the
innocent.
8 He makes sure that justice is done,
and he protects those who are
loyal to him.

9 Then you will understand what is
honest and fair
and what is the good and right
thing to do.
10 Wisdom will
come into
your mind,
and knowledge
will be
pleasing to
you.

eMAIL! FROM GOD
2:10–14
Temptation
Check out how to guard against temptation.

11 Good sense will protect you;
understanding will guard you.
12 It will keep you from the wicked,
from those whose words are bad,
13 who don't do what is right
but what is evil.
14 They enjoy doing wrong
and are happy to do what is
crooked and evil.
15 What they do is wrong,
and their ways are dishonest.

16 It will save you from the unfaithful
wife

Livin' it

GROWING IN WISDOM

Proverbs 2

Wise or Wise Guy? Which of the above titles fits you? You probably wouldn't want to be called a wise guy—someone who thinks he knows everything about everything. But being called *wise* is a compliment. It means you really think about things and make good decisions. What is the difference between being smart and being wise? How can someone be smart and not wise?

Where does true wisdom come from? The Bible tells us it comes from God because he is the source of all wisdom. (Check out Proverbs 2:6–7.) God has plenty of wisdom for everyone. When you need it, be wise—just ask.

MORE FAITH links

Deciding Wisely, p. 440
Plan for Success, p. 538
Like Silver, p. 717
Wisdom in Store, p. 828
Want to Know? Ask!, p. 1386

"Hey, Skweek, are you a wise guy?"

"Well, I know a lot about computers. But I don't think that makes me wise. Better read up on it!"

Fatherly Advice, Exodus 18, p. 99

- When you need help, who do you go to for advice? Why do you go to them? Do you accept their advice and follow through on what they suggest? God puts people in your life who care about you and can give you good advice. Be wise—learn to listen to them.

Take My Advice, 1 Kings 2:2–4, p. 436

- What is the most important advice your parents have passed on to you? Link here to find out the advice King David gave his son, Solomon.

The Way to Be Wise, James 1:5, p. 1689

- What do you think is the secret to being wise? What does having wisdom mean to you? Where do you get this wisdom?
- When you are looking for some wisdom, remember God is the source of all wisdom. The best thing about having wisdom is this: God helps you to use it.

my FAVORITE links

who tries to lead you into adultery
with pleasing words.
17 She leaves the husband she married
when she was young.
She ignores the promise she made
before God.
18 Her house is on the way to death;
those who took that path are now
all dead.
19 No one who goes to her comes back
or walks the path of life again.

FAITH links

WISDOM IN STORE

PROVERBS 2:6-7

Do you have a savings account? If you do, you know that you collect interest every three months. The more you store in the bank, the more interest you receive. God is a "storehouse" of wisdom. That means he is the source of wisdom. It also means he has plenty in reserve for those who might need it. When you need it, just ask. (See James 1:5, p. 1688.)

Looking for some good advice? Check out these Faithlinks:

Good Advice?, Leviticus 20:6, p. 162

Who Do You Trust?, Joshua 9, p. 287

A Promise from the Heart, Jeremiah 31:31–33, p. 1037

How Do You Grow?, Titus 1:1, p. 1659

The Way to Be Wise, James 1:5, p. 1689

That's False!, 2 John 7–11, p. 1722

20 But wisdom will help you be good
and do what is right.
21 Those who are honest will live in the
land,
and those who are innocent will
remain in it.
22 But the wicked will be removed from
the land,
and the unfaithful will be thrown
out of it.

Advice to Children

3 My child, do not forget my teaching,
but keep my commands in mind.
2 Then you will live a long time,
and your life will be successful.

3 Don't ever forget kindness and truth.
Wear them like a necklace.
Write them on your heart as if on a
tablet.
4 Then you will
be respected
and will please
both God and
people.

3:3–4
Kindness
Remember kindness and truth.

5 Trust the LORD with all your heart,
and don't depend on your own
understanding.
6 Remember the LORD in all you do,
and he will give you success.

7 Don't depend on your own wisdom.
Respect the LORD and refuse to do
wrong.
8 Then your body will be healthy,
and your bones will be strong.

9 Honor the LORD with your wealth
and the firstfruits from all your
crops.
10 Then your barns will be full,
and your wine barrels will
overflow with new wine.

11 My child, do not reject the LORD's
discipline,
and don't get angry when he
corrects you.
12 The LORD corrects those he loves,
just as parents correct the child
they delight in.

13 Happy is the person who finds
wisdom,
the one who gets understanding.
14 Wisdom is worth more than silver;
it brings more profit than gold.
15 Wisdom is more precious than rubies;
nothing you could want is equal
to it.
16 With her right hand wisdom offers
you a long life,
and with her left hand she gives
you riches and honor.
17 Wisdom will make your life pleasant
and will bring you peace.

A DIRECT PATH

PROVERBS 3:5-6

If you were a tourist in a city, would you depend on your own thoughts or guesses about how to get around? You wouldn't, would you? You would ask someone knowledgeable to give you directions. You would also look at a map. Trusting God is like looking at a map. He promises to direct your steps and "give you success" (3:6).

The Wisdom of Obeying God, 1 Kings 11:1–13, p. 453

A Picture of the Past, Psalm 105, p. 789

What God Thinks, Isaiah 55:8–9, p. 969

Obeying God or Man?, Daniel 3:8–30, p. 1154

The Writing's on the Wall, Daniel 5, p. 1159

Perfectly Pleasing?, Matthew 5:1–12, p. 1280

18 As a tree produces fruit, wisdom
gives life to those who use it,
and everyone who uses it will be
happy.

19 The LORD made the earth, using his
wisdom.
He set the sky in place, using his
understanding.
20 With his knowledge, he made springs
flow into rivers
and the clouds drop rain on the
earth.

21 My child, hold on to wisdom and
good sense.
Don't let them out of your sight.
22 They will give you life
and beauty like a necklace around
your neck.
23 Then you will go your way in safety,
and you will not get hurt.
24 When you lie down, you won't be
afraid;
when you lie down, you will sleep
in peace.
25 You won't be afraid of sudden trouble;
you won't fear the ruin that comes
to the wicked,
26 because the LORD will keep you safe.
He will keep you from being
trapped.

27 Whenever you are able,
do good to people who need help.
28 If you have what your neighbor asks
for,
don't say, "Come back later.
I will give it to you tomorrow."
29 Don't make plans to hurt your
neighbor
who lives nearby and trusts you.
30 Don't accuse a person for no good
reason;
don't accuse someone who has not
harmed you.

31 Don't be jealous of those who use
violence,
and don't choose to be like them.
32 The LORD hates those who do wrong,
but he is a friend to those who are
honest.

FAITH links

WHO DO YOU PREFER?

PROVERBS 3:32

Who do you like to hang around the most? The popular kids? Cool kids? Kids who know a lot about computers? Kids who get into trouble? A person usually hangs with those who value the same things he or she values. This proverb describes God as a friend to those who are honest. That means he values honesty. Is being honest important to you? If you want to hang with God, that means yes, right?

Here are some more Faithlinks on being honest:

The Best Policy, Genesis 29:16–29, p. 41

Read My Lips?, Deuteronomy 26:16–19, p. 260

The Salt Promise, 2 Chronicles 13:5, p. 576

The Problem with Gossip, Proverbs 11:12–13, p. 840

What's Wrong About Rumors, Jeremiah 29:24–32, p. 1032

The Verdict Is In?, Matthew 7:1–2, p. 1285

33 The LORD will curse the evil
person's house,
but he will bless the home of those
who do right.
34 The LORD laughs at those who laugh
at him,
but he gives grace to those who
are not proud.
35 Wise people will receive honor,
but fools will be disgraced.

Wisdom Is Important

4 My children, listen to your father's
teaching;
pay attention so you will
understand.
2 What I am telling you is good,
so do not forget what I teach you.
3 When I was a young boy in my
father's house
and like an only child to my
mother,
4 my father taught me and said,
"Hold on to my words with all your
heart.
Keep my commands and you will
live.
5 Get wisdom and understanding.
Don't forget or ignore my words.
6 Hold on to wisdom, and it will take
care of you.
Love it, and it will keep you safe.
7 Wisdom is the most important thing;
so get wisdom.
If it costs everything you have, get
understanding.
8 Treasure wisdom, and it will make
you great;
hold on to it, and it will bring you
honor.
9 It will be like flowers in your hair
and like a beautiful crown on your
head."

10 My child, listen and accept what I
say.
Then you will have a long life.
11 I am guiding you in the way of
wisdom,
and I am leading you on the right
path.
12 Nothing will hold you back;
you will not be overwhelmed.
13 Always remember what you have
been taught,
and don't let
go of it.
Keep all that you
have learned;
it is the most
important
thing in life.
14 Don't follow the ways of the wicked;
don't do what evil people do.

EMAIL! FROM GOD 4:13
Correction
What is important to remember?

15 Avoid their ways, and don't follow
them.
Stay away from them and keep on
going,
16 because they cannot sleep until they
do evil.
They cannot rest until they harm
someone.
17 They feast on wickedness and
cruelty
as if they were eating bread and
drinking wine.

18 The way of the good person is like
the light of dawn,
growing brighter and brighter until
full daylight.
19 But the wicked walk around in the
dark;
they can't even see what makes
them stumble.

20 My child, pay attention to my words;
listen closely to what I say.
21 Don't ever forget my words;
keep them always in mind.
22 They are the key to life for those
who find them;
they bring health to the whole
body.
23 Be careful what you think,
because your thoughts run your
life.
24 Don't use your
mouth to tell
lies;
don't ever say
things that
are not true.

eMAIL! FROM GOD 4:24
Gossip
Should you repeat gossip?

25 Keep your eyes focused on what is
right,
and look straight ahead to what is
good.
26 Be careful what you do,
and always do what is right.
27 Don't turn off the road of goodness;
keep away from evil paths.

Warning About Adultery

5 My son, pay
attention to
my wisdom;

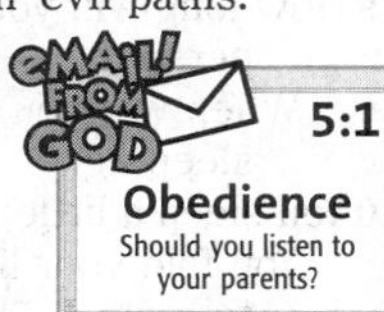
eMAIL! FROM GOD
5:1
Obedience
Should you listen to your parents?

listen to my words of
understanding.
2 Be careful to use good sense,
and watch what you say.
3 The words of another man's wife may
seem sweet as honey;

FAITH links

MIND GUARD

PROVERBS 4:23

What are you thinking of right now? Did you ever see or hear something that you had a hard time getting off your mind? Some images and songs stay with you a long time. That's why this proverb advises you to be careful about what you think. Thoughts are what lead a person to do good or evil. The more you think about something, the more it influences your actions. Memorizing Bible verses can help you guard your thoughts. Think about it.

Here are some more thoughts on thinking!

An Example Not to Follow, Leviticus 18:1–3, p. 157

The Right Thing to Do, 1 Samuel 26, p. 391

Take My Advice, 1 Kings 2:2–4, p. 436

A Reminder to Do What Is Right and True, Zechariah 7:8–10, p. 1257

Just Say No!, Titus 2:11–12, p. 1660

The "Quality" of Life, 2 Peter 1:5–8, p. 1708

they may be as smooth as olive oil.
4 But in the end she will bring you sorrow,
causing you pain like a two-edged sword.
5 She is on the way to death;
her steps are headed straight to the grave.
6 She gives little thought to life.
She doesn't even know that her ways are wrong.

7 Now, my sons, listen to me,
and don't ignore what I say.
8 Stay away from such a woman.
Don't even go near the door of her house,
9 or you will give your riches to others,
and the best years of your life will be given to someone cruel.
10 Strangers will enjoy your wealth,
and what you worked so hard for will go to someone else.
11 You will groan at the end of your life
when your health is gone.
12 Then you will say, "I hated being told what to do!
I would not listen to correction!
13 I would not listen to my teachers
or pay attention to my instructors.
14 I came close to being completely ruined
in front of a whole group of people."

15 Be faithful to your own wife,
just as you drink water from your own well.
16 Don't pour your water in the streets;
don't give your love to just any woman.
17 These things are yours alone
and shouldn't be shared with strangers.
18 Be happy with the wife you married when you were young.
She gives you joy, as your fountain gives you water.
19 She is as lovely and graceful as a deer.
Let her love always make you happy;
let her love always hold you captive.
20 My son, don't be held captive by a woman who takes part in adultery.
Don't hug another man's wife.
21 The LORD sees everything you do,
and he watches where you go.
22 An evil man will be caught in his wicked ways;
the ropes of his sins will tie him up.
23 He will die because he does not control himself,
and he will be held captive by his foolishness.

Dangers of Being Foolish

6 My child, be careful about giving a guarantee for somebody else's loan,
about promising to pay what someone else owes.
2 You might get trapped by what you say;
you might be caught by your own words.
3 My child, if you have done this and are under your neighbor's control,
here is how to get free.
Don't be proud. Go to your neighbor
and beg to be free from your promise.
4 Don't go to sleep
or even rest your eyes,
5 but free yourself like a deer running from a hunter,
like a bird flying away from a trapper.

6 Go watch the ants, you lazy person.
Watch what they do and be wise.
7 Ants have no commander,
no leader or ruler,
8 but they store up food in the summer
and gather their supplies at harvest.
9 How long will you lie there, you lazy person?
When will you get up from sleeping?
10 You sleep a little; you take a nap.
You fold your hands and lie down to rest.

FAITH links

DOWN ON THE ANT FARM

PROVERBS 6:6-11

Have you ever watched ants working away on an anthill or in an ant farm? Ants work very hard to store up food before they need it. No one has to tell them to do it. The wise person follows the ants' example by working hard and getting things done ahead of time. The unwise person prefers every day to be a lazy, sleep-in sort of day.

Sleeping-in can be fun sometimes. However, you can't get much done if you do it all the time. Think about the things you have to do right now. If you're a do-it-at-the-last-minute kind of person, take a lesson from the ants.

Your Response to Responsibility, Ruth 2:1–7, p. 346

Listen Up!, 1 Kings 19:11–13, p. 467

Operation Cooperation, Ezra 1:5, p. 609

Our Thirst Quencher, Psalm 42:1–3, p. 741

A Gentle Answer, Proverbs 15:1, p. 847

That Thing You Do, Matthew 25:14–30, p. 1319

11 So you will be as poor as if you had
been robbed;
you will have as little as if you had
been held up.

12 Some people are wicked and no good.
They go around telling lies,
13 winking with their eyes, tapping with
their feet,
and making signs with their
fingers.
14 They make evil plans in their hearts
and are always starting
arguments.
15 So trouble will strike them in an
instant;
suddenly they will be so hurt no
one can help them.

16 There are six things the LORD hates.
There are seven things he cannot
stand:
17 a proud look,
a lying tongue,
hands that kill innocent people,
18 a mind that thinks up evil plans,
feet that are quick to do evil,
19 a witness who lies,
and someone who starts
arguments among families.

Warning About Adultery

20 My son, keep your father's
commands,
and don't forget your mother's
teaching.
21 Keep their
words in
mind forever
as though you
had them
tied around
your neck.

> **EMAIL! FROM GOD**
> **6:20–23**
> **Correction**
> What are the benefits of listening to instructions?

22 They will guide you when you walk.
They will guard you when you
sleep.
They will speak to you when you
are awake.
23 These commands are like a lamp;
this teaching is like a light.
And the correction that comes from
them
will help you have life.
24 They will keep you from sinful
women
and from the pleasing words of
another man's unfaithful wife.

HONORING MOM AND DAD

Proverbs 6:20–23

Livin' it

How to Be a Real Wise Guy! Got a big problem? Where do you go to find help? There are lots of places to go for advice: your friends, magazines, newspapers, the Internet, TV. But the best place to go is to your parents. You may not always like what they say, but listening to them is a way of showing them respect. (Check out Proverbs 1:8–9.)

Being a wise son or daughter or a foolish one has to do with how willingly you obey your parents. A foolish child makes her parents sad, but a wise one makes his parents happy. (Read about it in Proverbs 10:1.) How can you be a wise kid and make your parents happy?

MORE FAITH links

A Parent's Advice, p. 825
A Word to the Wise, p. 838
If You Want My Advice . . ., p. 843
Down on Discipline?, p. 867
Sow It and Reap, p. 1075
What Any Parent Wants, p. 1723

"Sometimes I don't feel like obeying my parents. Especially when I've got something better to do—like play on the computer!"

"Better wise up, Tagg! God doesn't say obey your parents when you want to—he says *always* obey your parents. Read on to see how you can really be wise!"

Plans for a Son, 1 Chronicles 22:5–19, p. 548

- Have you noticed what your mom or dad does to help you follow and obey God? Why do you think they do these things? How do you react to the things they do?

See the Heart Behind It, Nehemiah 8; 9, p. 636

- What expression is usually on your face when your mom or dad tells you exactly what kind of behavior he/she expects from you? Do you look bored? Off in space somewhere? Or restless?
- Your parents and God want the best life possible for you. How can your response to their advice change?

How to Make God Glad, Ephesians 6:1–2, p. 1605

- Link here to find out how to really please God—and your parents.

my FAVORITE links

__________ __________
__________ __________
__________ __________

WHAT GOD "HATES"

PROVERBS 6:16-19

So much is said about God's love. But did you know there are things that God hates? They all have to do with sin: pride; lying; murder; evil thoughts; feet that hurry to commit crimes; lying about others; causing others to fight among themselves. This kind of hatred isn't like the hatred people sometimes feel for each other. After all, God cannot sin. He doesn't hate the people who do wrong. He hates sin. He wants you to hate it even more than he does. But don't just talk about hating it. Do something about it.

Take a look at some other sins that God hates:

Out of Control?, Genesis 4, p. 8

Patience, Please, Psalm 145:8–9, p. 819

God's Instructions, Ezekiel 4:1–15, p. 1089

Good Enough?, Ezekiel 8, p. 1093

Want to Know? Ask!, Luke 9:45, p. 1386

The Deadliest Lie, Acts 5:1–11, p. 1471

25 Don't desire her because she is
beautiful.
Don't let her capture you by the
way she looks at you.
26 A prostitute will treat you like a loaf
of bread,
and a woman who takes part in
adultery may cost you your life.
27 You cannot carry hot coals against
your chest
without burning your clothes,
28 and you cannot walk on hot coals
without burning your feet.
29 The same is true if you have sexual
relations with another man's
wife.
Anyone who does so will be
punished.

30 People don't hate a thief
when he steals because he is
hungry.
31 But if he is caught, he must pay back
seven times what he stole,
and it may cost him everything he
owns.
32 A man who takes part in adultery has
no sense;
he will destroy himself.
33 He will be beaten up and disgraced,
and his shame will never go away.
34 Jealousy makes a husband very
angry,
and he will have no pity when he
gets revenge.
35 He will accept no payment for the
wrong;
he will take no amount of money.

The Woman of Adultery

7 My son, remember what I say, and
treasure my commands.
2 Obey my commands, and you will
live.
Guard my teachings as you would
your own eyes.
3 Remind yourself of them;
write them on your heart as if on a
tablet.
4 Treat wisdom as a sister,
and make understanding your
closest friend.
5 Wisdom and understanding will keep
you away from adultery,
away from the unfaithful wife and
her pleasing words.

6 Once while I was at the window of
my house
I looked out through the shutters
7 and saw some foolish, young men.
I noticed one of them had no
wisdom.
8 He was walking down the street near
the corner
on the road leading to her house.
9 It was the twilight of the evening;
the darkness of the night was just
beginning.
10 Then the woman approached him,
dressed like a prostitute
and planning to trick him.
11 She was loud and stubborn
and never stayed at home.
12 She was always out in the streets or
in the city squares,
waiting around on the corners of
the streets.
13 She grabbed him and kissed him.
Without shame she said to him,
14 "I made my fellowship offering and
took some of the meat home.
Today I have kept my special
promises.
15 So I have come out to meet you;
I have been looking for you and
have found you.
16 I have covered my bed
with colored sheets from Egypt.
17 I have made my bed smell sweet
with myrrh, aloes, and cinnamon.
18 Come, let's make love until
morning.
Let's enjoy each other's love.
19 My husband is not home;
he has gone on a long trip.
20 He took a lot of money with him
and won't be home for weeks."
21 By her clever words she made him
give in;
by her pleasing words she led him
into doing wrong.
22 All at once he followed her,
like an ox led to the butcher,
like a deer caught in a trap
23 and shot through the liver with an
arrow.
Like a bird caught in a trap,
he didn't know what he did would
kill him.
24 Now, my sons, listen to me;
pay attention to what I say.
25 Don't let yourself be tricked by such
a woman;
don't go where she leads you.
26 She has ruined many good men,
and many have died because of her.
27 Her house is on the road to death,
the road that leads down to the
grave.

Listen to Wisdom

8 Wisdom calls to you like someone
shouting;
understanding raises her voice.
2 On the hilltops along the road
and at the crossroads, she stands
calling.
3 Beside the city gates,
at the entrances into the city, she
calls out:
4 "Listen, everyone, I'm calling out to
you;
I am shouting to all people.
5 You who are uneducated, be smarter.
You who are foolish, get
understanding.
6 Listen, because I have important
things to say,
and what I tell you is right.
7 What I say is true,
I refuse to speak evil.
8 Everything I say is honest;
nothing I say is crooked or false.
9 People with good sense know what I
say is true;
and those with knowledge know
my words are right.
10 Choose my teachings instead of
silver,
and knowledge rather than the
finest gold.
11 Wisdom is more precious than
rubies.
Nothing you could want is equal
to it.

12 "I am wisdom,
and I am
smart.
I also have
knowledge
and good sense.

eMAIL! FROM GOD
8:12–14
Wisdom
What comes with wisdom?

13 If you respect the LORD, you will also
hate evil.
I hate pride and bragging,
evil ways and lies.
14 I have good sense and advice,
and I have understanding and
power.
15 I help kings to govern
and rulers to make fair laws.
16 Princes use me to lead,
and so do all important people who
judge fairly.
17 I love those who love me,
and those who seek me find me.
18 Riches and honor are mine to give.
So are wealth and lasting success.
19 What I give is better than the finest
gold,
better than the purest silver.
20 I do what is right
and follow the path of justice.
21 I give wealth to those who love me,
filling their houses with treasures.

22 "I, wisdom, was with the LORD when
he began his work,
long before he made anything else.
23 I was created in the very beginning,
even before the world began.
24 I was born before there were oceans,
or springs overflowing with water,
25 before the hills were there,
before the mountains were put in
place.
26 God had not made the
earth or fields,
not even the first
dust of the earth.
27 I was there when God
put the skies in
place,
when he stretched
the horizon over
the oceans,
28 when he made the
clouds above
and put the deep underground
springs in place.
29 I was there when he ordered the sea
not to go beyond the borders he
had set.
I was there when he laid the earth's
foundation.
30 I was like a child by his side.
I was delighted every day,
enjoying his presence all the time,
31 enjoying the whole world,
and delighted with all its people.

32 "Now, my children, listen to me,
because those who follow my ways
are happy.
33 Listen to my teaching, and you will
be wise;
do not ignore it.
34 Happy are those who listen to me,
watching at my door every day,
waiting at my open doorway.
35 Those who find me find life,
and the LORD will be pleased with
them.
36 Those who do not find me hurt
themselves.
Those who hate me love death."

Being Wise or Foolish

9 Wisdom has built her house; she has
made its seven columns.
2 She has prepared her food and wine;
she has set her table.
3 She has sent out her servant girls,
and she calls out from the highest
place in the city.
4 She says to those who are
uneducated,
"Come in here, you foolish people!
5 Come and eat my food
and drink the wine I
have prepared.
6 Stop your foolish
ways, and you will
live;
take the road of
understanding.

Stop your foolish ways, and you will live; take the road of understanding.
—Proverbs 9:6

7 "If you correct
someone who
makes fun of
wisdom, you
will be insulted.
If you correct an evil person, you
will get hurt.
8 Do not correct those who make fun
of wisdom, or they will hate you.
But correct the wise, and they will
love you.

9 Teach the wise, and they will become
even wiser;
teach good people, and they will
learn even more.

10 "Wisdom begins with respect for the
LORD,
and understanding begins with
knowing the Holy One.
11 If you live wisely, you will live a long
time;
wisdom will add years to your life.
12 The wise person is rewarded by
wisdom,
but whoever makes fun of wisdom
will suffer for it."

13 Foolishness is like a loud woman;
she does not have wisdom or
knowledge.
14 She sits at the door of her house
at the highest place in the city.
15 She calls out to those who are
passing by,
who are going along, minding their
own business.
16 She says to those who are
uneducated,
"Come in here, you foolish people!
17 Stolen water is sweeter,
and food eaten in secret tastes
better."
18 But these people don't know that
everyone who goes there dies,
that her guests end up deep in the
grave.

The Wise Words of Solomon

10 These are the wise words of Solomon:
A wise son makes his father happy,
but a foolish son makes his mother
sad.

2 Riches gotten by doing wrong have
no value,
but right living will save you from
death.

3 The LORD does not let good people
go hungry,
but he keeps evil people from
getting what they want.

FAITH links

A WORD TO THE WISE

PROVERBS 10:1

Want to know how you can make your parents joyful? Be a wise kid. Being a wise son or daughter or a foolish one has to do with how much you listen to your parents. Solomon mentioned that a foolish child makes his parent sad. A wise child makes her parent happy. So, how can you be wise? Do what your parents tell you to do. It's as simple as that!

Fatherly Advice, Exodus 18, p. 99

What God Wants, Deuteronomy 10:12–13, p. 242

Advice from a Kid, 2 Kings 5, p. 484

A Reminder to Do What Is Right and True, Zechariah 7:8–10, p. 1257

How to Make God Glad, Ephesians 6:1–2, p. 1605

Full of Faith, 1 Thessalonians 4:1, p. 1633

4 A lazy person will end up poor,
but a hard worker will become
rich.

5 Those who gather crops on time are
wise,
but those who sleep through the
harvest are a disgrace.

6 Good people will have rich blessings,
but the wicked will be
overwhelmed by violence.

7 Good people will be remembered as a
blessing,
but evil people will soon be
forgotten.

8 The wise do what they are told,
but a talkative fool will be ruined.

9 The honest person will live in
safety,
but the dishonest will be caught.

10 A wink may get you into trouble,
and foolish talk will lead to your
ruin.

11 The words of a good person give life,
like a fountain of water,
but the words of the wicked
contain nothing but violence.

12 Hatred stirs up trouble,
but love forgives all wrongs.

13 Smart people speak wisely,
but people without wisdom should
be punished.

14 The wise don't tell everything they
know,
but the foolish talk too much and
are ruined.

15 Having lots of money protects the
rich,
but having no money destroys the
poor.

16 Good people are rewarded with life,
but evil people are paid with
punishment.

17 Whoever accepts correction is on the
way to life,
but whoever ignores correction
will lead others away from life.

18 Whoever hides hate is a liar.
Whoever tells lies is a fool.

19 If you talk a lot, you are sure to sin;
if you are wise, you will keep quiet.

20 The words of a good person are like
pure silver,
but an evil person's thoughts are
worth very little.
21 Good people's words will help many
others,
but fools will die because they
don't have wisdom.

22 The LORD's blessing brings wealth,
and no sorrow comes with it.

23 A foolish person enjoys doing wrong,
but a person with understanding
enjoys doing what is wise.

24 Evil people will get what they fear
most,
but good people will get what they
want most.

25 A storm will
blow the evil
person away,
but a good
person will
always be
safe.

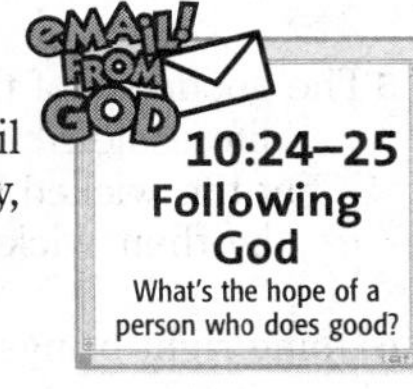

eMAIL! FROM GOD
10:24–25
Following God
What's the hope of a person who does good?

26 A lazy person affects the one he
works for
like vinegar on the teeth or smoke
in the eyes.

27 Whoever respects the LORD will
have a long life,
but the life of an evil person will be
cut short.

28 A good person can look forward to
happiness,
but an evil person can expect
nothing.

29 The LORD will protect good people
but will ruin those who do evil.

30 Good people will always be safe,
but evil people will not remain in
the land.

31 A good person says wise things,
but a liar's tongue will be stopped.

32 Good people know the right thing to say,
but evil people only tell lies.

11 The LORD hates dishonest scales,
but he is pleased with honest weights.

2 Pride leads only to shame;
it is wise to be humble.

3 Good people will be guided by honesty;
dishonesty will destroy those who are not trustworthy.

4 Riches will not help when it's time to die,
but right living will save you from death.

5 The goodness of the innocent makes life easier,
but the wicked will be destroyed by their wickedness.

6 Doing right brings freedom to honest people,
but those who are not trustworthy will be caught by their own desires.

7 When the wicked die, hope dies with them;
their hope in riches will come to nothing.

8 The good person is saved from trouble;
it comes to the wicked instead.

9 With words an evil person can destroy a neighbor,
but a good person will escape by being smart.

10 When good people succeed, the city is happy.
When evil people die, there are shouts of joy.

FAITH links

THE PROBLEM WITH GOSSIP

PROVERBS 11:12-13

Let's say a friend told you a secret and made you promise not to tell. Now suppose you came upon another friend of yours. Let's say that person asked you about your other friend. Would you tell the secret anyway?

Gossip doesn't always mean passing on a rumor about someone. It can also mean repeating to someone else something told in confidence to you. Know what else gossip is? Trouble. Gossip and rumors have never been known to strengthen friendships. Trustworthiness and faithfulness do, however. Want to be a trustworthy friend? Learn to keep a secret.

How do you rate in the friendship department? Link here to find out:

The MLP, Ruth 1:16–17, p. 345

Loyal to a Friend, 2 Samuel 9, p. 409

An Honest Reputation, Nehemiah 13:13, p. 644

Fear God or People?, Jeremiah 38:14–21, p. 1047

Your Civic Duty, Matthew 17:24–27, p. 1304

The Whole Truth, John 8:31–32, 45, p. 1438

11 Good people bless and build up their city,
but the wicked can destroy it with their words.

12 People without good sense find fault with their neighbors,
but those with understanding keep quiet.

13 Gossips can't keep secrets,
but a trustworthy person can.

14 Without leadership a nation falls,
but lots of good advice will save it.

15 Whoever guarantees to pay somebody else's loan will suffer.
It is safer to avoid such promises.

16 A kind woman gets respect,
but cruel men get only wealth.

17 Kind people do themselves a favor,
but cruel people bring trouble on themselves.

18 An evil person really earns nothing,
but a good person will surely be rewarded.

19 Those who are truly good will live,
but those who chase after evil will die.

20 The LORD hates those with evil hearts
but is pleased with those who are innocent.

21 Evil people will certainly be punished,
but those who do right will be set free.

22 A beautiful woman without good sense
is like a gold ring in a pig's snout.

23 Those who do right only wish for good,
but the wicked can expect to be defeated by God's anger.

24 Some people give much but get back even more.
Others don't give what they should and end up poor.

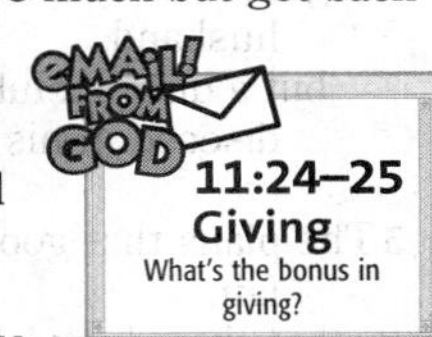

11:24–25
Giving
What's the bonus in giving?

25 Whoever gives to others will get richer;
those who help others will themselves be helped.

26 People curse those who keep all the grain,
but they bless the one who is willing to sell it.

27 Whoever looks for good will find kindness,
but whoever looks for evil will find trouble.

28 Those who trust in riches will be ruined,
but a good person will be healthy like a green leaf.

29 Whoever brings trouble to his family will be left with nothing but the wind.
A fool will be a servant to the wise.

30 A good person gives life to others;
the wise person teaches others how to live.

31 Good people will be rewarded on earth,
and the wicked and the sinners will be punished.

12 Anyone who loves learning accepts correction,
but a person who hates being corrected is stupid.

2 The LORD is pleased with a good person,
but he will punish anyone who plans evil.

3 Doing evil brings no safety at all,
but a good person has safety and security.

4 A good wife is like a crown for her
husband,
but a disgraceful wife is like a
disease in his bones.

5 The plans that good people make are
fair,
but the advice of the wicked will
trick you.

6 The wicked talk about killing people,
but the words of good people will
save them.

7 Wicked people die and they are no
more,
but a good person's family
continues.

8 The wisdom of the wise wins praise,
but there is no respect for the
stupid.

9 A person who is not important but
has a servant is better off
than someone who acts important
but has no food.

10 Good people take care of their animals,
but even the kindest acts of the
wicked are cruel.

11 Those who work their land will have
plenty of food,
but the one who chases empty
dreams is not wise.

12 The wicked want what other evil
people have stolen,
but good people want to give what
they have to others.

13 Evil people are trapped by their evil
talk,
but good people stay out of trouble.

14 People will be rewarded for what
they say,
and they will also be rewarded for
what they do.

15 Fools think they are doing right,
but the wise listen to advice.

FAITH links

GET HOT OR KEEP COOL?

PROVERBS 12:16

If someone called you a name, what would you do? Get mad and call that person the same name? Sulk about it? Keep your cool and ignore it? Some people might tell you that ignoring an insult makes you a wimp. But God's way is to be self-controlled. When someone insults you, remember Jesus' example. When he was insulted, he didn't try to get even. Thanks to him, we have the power to do likewise.

I Want It *Now!*, Judges 14:1–3, p. 332

Anger: Quick or Slow?, Psalm 86:15, p. 776

Peace in the Family, Psalm 133, p. 811

Kindness First, Matthew 9:35–36, p. 1290

Don't Get Mad; Get Even?, Matthew 26:57–63; 27:11–14, p. 1323

Out with the Old!, Colossians 3:1–14, p. 1625

16 Fools quickly show that they are
upset,
but the wise ignore insults.

17 An honest witness tells the truth,
but a dishonest witness tells lies.

18 Careless words stab like a sword,
but wise words bring healing.

19 Truth will continue forever,
but lies are only for a moment.

20 Those who plan evil are full of lies,
but those who plan peace are happy.

21 No harm comes to a good person,
but an evil person's life is full of trouble.

22 The LORD hates those who tell lies
but is pleased with those who keep their promises.

23 Wise people keep what they know to themselves,
but fools can't keep from showing how foolish they are.

24 Hard workers will become leaders,
but those who are lazy will be slaves.

25 Worry is a heavy load,
but a kind word cheers you up.

EMAIL FROM GOD 12:25
Worry
What's the cure for worry?

26 Good people take advice from their friends,
but an evil person is easily led to do wrong.

27 The lazy catch no food to cook,
but a hard worker will have great wealth.

28 Doing what is right is the way to life,
but there is another way that leads to death.

13 Wise children take their parents' advice,
but whoever makes fun of wisdom won't listen to correction.

2 People will be rewarded for what they say,
but those who can't be trusted want only violence.

3 Those who are careful about what they say protect their lives,
but whoever speaks without thinking will be ruined.

4 The lazy will not get what they want,
but those who work hard will.

5 Good people hate what is false,
but the wicked do shameful and disgraceful things.

FAITH links

IF YOU WANT MY ADVICE . . .

PROVERBS 13:1

When your parents give you advice or discipline you, do you get angry or do you accept what they say? Solomon, the writer of this proverb, mentioned that wise children accept their parents' advice. But don't think of it as yet one more adult telling you what to do. Think of it as God showing you the way to be wise.

Check out these Faithlinks on learning to be wise:

Your Stats, 1 Kings 15; 16, p. 460

This Hurts Me More?, 2 Chronicles 36:17–22, p. 606

Help for the Outsiders, Nehemiah 5:9–10, p. 630

The Problem with Pride, Isaiah 2:11, p. 898

A Friend of Jesus, John 15:9–17, p. 1450

You're a Fake!, 2 Peter 2:1, p. 1709

6 Doing what is right protects the honest person,
but doing evil ruins the sinner.

7 Some people pretend to be rich but really have nothing.
Others pretend to be poor but really are wealthy.

8 The rich may have to pay a ransom for their lives,
but the poor will face no such danger.

9 Good people can look forward to a bright future,
but the future of the wicked is like a flame going out.

10 Pride only leads to arguments,
but those who take advice are wise.

11 Money that comes easily disappears quickly,
but money that is gathered little by little will grow.

12 It is sad not to get what you hoped for.
But wishes that come true are like eating fruit from the tree of life.

13 Those who reject what they are taught will pay for it,
but those who obey what they are told will be rewarded.

14 The teaching of a wise person gives life.
It is like a fountain that can save people from death.

15 People with good understanding will be well liked,
but the lives of those who are not trustworthy are hard.

16 Every wise person acts with good sense,
but fools show how foolish they are.

17 A wicked messenger brings nothing but trouble,
but a trustworthy one makes everything right.

18 A person who refuses correction will end up poor and disgraced,
but the one who accepts correction will be honored.

19 It is so good when wishes come true,
but fools hate to stop doing evil.

20 Spend time with the wise and you will become wise,
but the friends of fools will suffer.

21 Trouble always comes to sinners,
but good people enjoy success.

22 Good people leave their wealth to their grandchildren,
but a sinner's wealth is stored up for good people.

23 A poor person's field might produce plenty of food,
but others often steal it away.

24 If you do not punish your children, you don't love them,
but if you love your children, you will correct them.

25 Good people have enough to eat,
but the wicked will go hungry.

14 A wise woman strengthens her family,
but a foolish woman destroys hers by what she does.

2 People who live good lives respect the LORD,
but those who live evil lives don't.

3 Fools will be punished for their proud words,
but the words of the wise will protect them.

4 When there are no oxen, no food is in
the barn.
But with a strong ox, much grain
can be grown.

5 A truthful witness does not lie,
but a false witness tells nothing
but lies.

6 Those who make fun of wisdom look
for it and do not find it,
but knowledge comes easily to
those with understanding.

7 Stay away from fools,
because they can't teach you
anything.

8 A wise person will understand what
to do,
but a foolish person is dishonest.

9 Fools don't care if they sin,
but honest people work at being
right.

10 No one else can know your sadness,
and strangers cannot share your joy.

11 The wicked person's house will be
destroyed,
but a good person's tent will still
be standing.

12 Some people think they are doing
right,
but in the end it leads to death.

13 Someone who is laughing may be sad
inside,
and joy may end in sadness.

14 Evil people will be paid back for their
evil ways,
and good people will be rewarded
for their good ones.

15 Fools will believe anything,
but the wise think about what they
do.

16 Wise people are careful and stay out
of trouble,
but fools are careless and quick to
act.

17 Someone with a quick temper does
foolish things,
but someone with understanding
remains calm.

18 Fools are rewarded with nothing but
more foolishness,
but the wise are rewarded with
knowledge.

19 Evil people will bow down to those
who are good;
the wicked will bow down at the
door of those who do right.

20 The poor are rejected, even by their
neighbors,
but the rich have many friends.

21 It is a sin to hate your neighbor,
but being kind to the needy brings
happiness.

22 Those who make evil plans will be
ruined,
but those who plan to do good will
be loved and trusted.

23 Those who work hard make a profit,
but those who only talk will be poor.

24 Wise people are rewarded with
wealth,
but fools only get more
foolishness.

25 A truthful witness saves lives,
but a false witness is a traitor.

26 Those who respect the LORD will
have security,
and their children will be
protected.

27 Respect for the LORD gives life.
It is like a fountain that can save
people from death.

28 A king is honored when he has many
people to rule,

FAITH CHALLENGE

Hey there! Read 14:21 to discover what God says about helping people in need. What can you and your friends do to help needy people in your community?

TESTING IT

Proverbs 14:21
It is a sin to hate your neighbor, but being kind to the needy brings happiness.

____

____

____

____

____

____

but a prince is ruined if he has none.

29 Patient people have great
understanding,
but people with quick tempers
show their foolishness.

30 Peace of mind means a healthy body,
but jealousy will rot
your bones.

31 Whoever mistreats
the poor
insults their
Maker,

14:31
Kindness
Be kind to the poor.

but whoever is kind to the needy
honors God.

32 The wicked are ruined by their own
evil,
but those who do right are
protected even in death.

33 Wisdom lives in those with
understanding,
and even fools recognize it.

34 Doing what is right makes a nation
great,
but sin will bring disgrace to any
people.

35 A king is pleased with a wise
servant,
but he will become angry with one
who causes him shame.

15 A gentle
answer
will
calm a
person's
anger,
but an unkind
answer will cause more anger.

15:1
Anger
Check out a cure for anger.

2 Wise people use knowledge when
they speak,
but fools pour out foolishness.

3 The LORD's eyes see everything;
he watches both evil and good
people.

4 As a tree gives fruit, healing words
give life,
but dishonest words crush the
spirit.

5 Fools reject their parents'
correction,
but anyone who accepts correction
is wise.

6 Much wealth is in the houses of good
people,
but evil people get nothing but
trouble.

FAITH links

A GENTLE ANSWER

PROVERBS 15:1

Have you ever noticed that when someone makes you mad and you say something mean back to that person, you both feel angrier? That's why Solomon advised giving a gentle answer to a person, even someone who has made you angry. A gentle answer has a calming effect. A mean or sarcastic answer just fans the flames of anger. Giving a gentle answer isn't always easy. It takes self-control—a gift from the Holy Spirit. (Surf over to Galatians 5:22–23, p. 1593, to read more about this special gift.)

Just Kidding?, Genesis 21:8–10, p. 28

A Friend in Deed, Job 2:13, p. 662

Patience, Please, Psalm 145:8–9, p. 819

World News, Isaiah 13—19, p. 913

Kindness Counts, Acts 14:3, p. 1489

A Different Kind of Fruit, Galatians 5:22–23, p. 1592

7 Wise people use their words to
spread knowledge,
but there is no knowledge in the
thoughts of fools.

8 The LORD hates the sacrifice that the
wicked offer,
but he likes the prayers of honest
people.

9 The LORD hates what evil people do,
but he loves those who do what is
right.

10 The person who
quits doing
what is right
will be
punished,
and the one who hates to be
corrected will die.

EMAIL FROM GOD
15:10
Correction
What happens if you hate correction?

11 The LORD knows what is happening
in the world of the dead,
so he surely knows the thoughts of
the living.

12 Those who make fun of wisdom don't
like to be corrected;
they will not ask the wise for
advice.

13 Happiness makes a person smile,
but sadness can break a person's
spirit.

14 People with understanding want
more knowledge,
but fools just want more
foolishness.

15 Every day is hard for those who
suffer,
but a happy heart is like a
continual feast.

16 It is better to be poor and respect the
LORD
than to be wealthy and have much
trouble.

17 It is better to eat vegetables with
those who love you
than to eat meat with those who
hate you.

18 People with quick tempers cause
trouble,
but those who control their
tempers stop a quarrel.

19 A lazy person's life is like a patch of thorns,
but an honest person's life is like a smooth highway.

20 A wise son makes his father happy,
but a foolish son disrespects his mother.

21 A person without wisdom enjoys being foolish,
but someone with understanding does what is right.

22 Plans fail without good advice,
but they succeed with the advice of many others.

23 People enjoy giving good advice.
Saying the right word at the right time is so pleasing.

24 Wise people's lives get better and better.
They avoid whatever would cause their death.

25 The LORD will tear down the proud person's house,
but he will protect the widow's property.

26 The LORD hates evil thoughts
but is pleased with kind words.

27 Greedy people bring trouble to their families,
but the person who can't be paid to do wrong will live.

28 Good people think before they answer,
but the wicked simply pour out evil.

29 The LORD does not listen to the wicked,
but he hears the prayers of those who do right.

30 Good news makes you feel better.
Your happiness will show in your eyes.

31 If you listen to correction to improve your life,
you will live among the wise.

32 Those who refuse correction hate themselves,
but those who accept correction gain understanding.

33 Respect for the LORD will teach you wisdom.
If you want to be honored, you must be humble.

16 People may make plans in their minds,
but only the LORD can make them come true.

2 You may believe you are doing right,
but the LORD will judge your reasons.

3 Depend on the LORD in whatever you do,
and your plans will succeed.

4 The LORD makes everything go as he pleases.
He has even prepared a day of disaster for evil people.

5 The LORD hates those who are proud.
They will surely be punished.

6 Love and truth bring forgiveness of sin.
By respecting the LORD you will avoid evil.

7 When people live so that they please the LORD,
even their enemies will make peace with them.

8 It is better to be poor and right
than to be wealthy and dishonest.

9 People may make plans in their minds,

but the LORD decides what they will do.

10 The words of a king are like a message from God, so his decisions should be fair.

11 The LORD wants honest balances and scales; all the weights are his work.

12 Kings hate those who do wrong, because governments only continue if they are fair.

13 Kings like honest people; they value someone who speaks the truth.

14 An angry king can put someone to death, so a wise person will try to make him happy.

15 A smiling king can give people life; his kindness is like a spring shower.

16 It is better to get wisdom than gold, and to choose understanding rather than silver!

17 Good people stay away from evil. By watching what they do, they protect their lives.

18 Pride will destroy a person; a proud attitude leads to ruin.

16:18
Pride
What can pride do?

19 It is better to be humble and be with those who suffer than to share stolen property with the proud.

20 Whoever listens to what is taught will succeed, and whoever trusts the LORD will be happy.

21 The wise are known for their understanding. Their pleasant words make them better teachers.

22 Understanding is like a fountain which gives life to those who use it, but foolishness brings punishment to fools.

23 Wise people's minds tell them what to say, and that helps them be better teachers.

24 Pleasant words are like a honeycomb, making people happy and healthy.

25 Some people think they are doing right, but in the end it leads to death.

26 The workers' hunger helps them, because their desire to eat makes them work.

27 Useless people make evil plans, and their words are like a burning fire.

28 A useless person causes trouble, and a gossip ruins friendships.

16:28
Gossip
Check out the bad results of gossip.

29 Cruel people trick their neighbors and lead them to do wrong.

30 Someone who winks is planning evil, and the one who grins is planning something wrong.

31 Gray hair is like a crown of honor; it is earned by living a good life.

32 Patience is better than strength. Controlling your temper is better than capturing a city.

33 People throw lots to make a decision, but the answer comes from the LORD.

17 It is better to eat a dry crust of bread in peace
than to have a feast where there is quarreling.

2 A wise servant will rule over the master's disgraceful child
and will even inherit a share of what the master leaves his children.

3 A hot furnace tests silver and gold,
but the LORD tests hearts.

4 Evil people listen to evil words.
Liars pay attention to cruel words.

5 Whoever mistreats the poor insults their Maker;
whoever enjoys someone's trouble will be punished.

6 Old people are proud of their grandchildren,
and children are proud of their parents.

7 Fools should not be proud,
and rulers should not be liars.

8 Some people think they can pay others to do anything they ask.
They think it will work every time.

9 Whoever forgives someone's sin makes a friend,
but gossiping about the sin breaks up friendships.

eMAIL! FROM GOD 17:9
Enemies
How can you avoid making enemies?

10 A wise person will learn more from a warning
than a fool will learn from a hundred lashings.

11 Disobedient people look only for trouble,
so a cruel messenger will be sent against them.

12 It is better to meet a bear robbed of her cubs
than to meet a fool doing foolish things.

13 Whoever gives evil in return for good
will always have trouble at home.

14 Starting a quarrel is like a leak in a dam,
so stop it before a fight breaks out.

15 The LORD hates both of these things:
freeing the guilty and punishing the innocent.

16 It won't do a fool any good to try to buy wisdom,
because he doesn't have the ability to be wise.

17 A friend loves you all the time,
and a brother helps in time of trouble.

eMAIL! FROM GOD 17:17
Friendship
Why are friends special?

18 It is not wise to promise
to pay what your neighbor owes.

19 Whoever loves to argue loves to sin.
Whoever brags a lot is asking for trouble.

20 A person with an evil heart will find no success,
and the person whose words are evil will get into trouble.

21 It is sad to have a foolish child;
there is no joy in being the parent of a fool.

22 A happy heart is like good medicine,
but a broken spirit drains your strength.

23 When the wicked accept money to do wrong
there can be no justice.

SOME FRIENDLY ADVICE

PROVERBS 17:9, 14, 17

What can two people share that one person can't own and that also lasts a lifetime? Give up? Friendship. Solomon offers some friendly advice about friendship. Everyone wants to have friends. Being a friend takes effort. It takes forgiveness and love. It also takes a willingness to stop quarrels before they start. Both people in a friendship need to be willing to do whatever is necessary to be a good friend.

How willing are you to be a good friend?

Want to be a good friend? Check out these Faithlinks:

Yours, Mine, and Ours?, 1 Samuel 25, p. 389

Peace in the Family, Psalm 133, p. 811

Two Are Better, Ecclesiastes 4:9–12, p. 877

Concern for All, Daniel 9, p. 1165

The Right Ingredients, Micah 6:8, p. 1227

I'll Be the Judge!, 1 Corinthians 4:4–5, p. 1549

24 The person with understanding is
always looking for wisdom,
but the mind of a fool wanders
everywhere.

25 A foolish son makes his father sad
and causes his mother great
sorrow.

26 It is not good to punish the innocent
or to beat leaders for being honest.

27 The smart person says very little,
and one with understanding stays
calm.

28 Even fools seem to be wise if they
keep quiet;
if they don't speak, they appear to
understand.

18 Unfriendly people are selfish
and hate all good sense.

2 Fools do not
want to
understand
anything.
They only want
to tell others
what they think.

EMAIL! FROM GOD 18:2
Learning
Check out what makes some people foolish.

3 Do something evil, and people won't
like you.
Do something shameful, and they
will make fun of you.

4 Spoken words can be like deep water,
but wisdom is like a flowing
stream.

5 It is not good to honor the wicked
or to be unfair to the innocent.

6 The words of fools start quarrels.
They make people want to beat
them.

7 The words of fools will ruin them;
their own words will trap them.

8 The words of a gossip are like tasty
bits of food.
People like to gobble them up.

9 A person who doesn't work hard
is just like someone who destroys
things.

10 The LORD is like a strong tower;
those who do right can run to him
for safety.

11 Rich people trust their wealth to
protect them.
They think it is like the high walls
of a city.

12 Proud people will be ruined,
but the humble will be honored.

13 Anyone who answers without
listening
is foolish and confused.

14 The will to live can get you through
sickness,
but no one can live with a broken
spirit.

15 The mind of a person with
understanding gets knowledge;
the wise person listens to learn
more.

16 Taking a gift to an important man
will help get you in to see him.

17 The person who tells one side of a
story seems right,
until someone else comes and asks
questions.

18 Throwing lots can settle arguments
and keep the two sides from
fighting.

19 A brother who has been insulted is
harder to win back than a walled
city,
and arguments separate people
like the barred gates of a palace.

20 People will be rewarded for what
they say;
they will be rewarded by how they
speak.

21 What you say can mean life or death.
Those who speak with care will be
rewarded.

22 When a man finds a wife, he finds
something good.
It shows that the LORD is pleased
with him.

23 The poor beg for mercy,
but the rich give rude answers.

24 Some friends may ruin you,
but a real friend will be more loyal
than a brother.

19 It is better to be poor and honest
than to be foolish and tell lies.

2 Enthusiasm without knowledge is
not good.
If you act too quickly, you might
make a mistake.

3 People's own foolishness ruins their
lives,
but in their minds they blame the
LORD.

4 Wealthy people are always finding
more friends,
but the poor lose all theirs.

5 A witness who lies will not go free;
liars will never escape.

6 Many people want to please a leader,
and everyone is friends with those
who give gifts.

7 Poor people's relatives avoid them;
even their friends stay far away.
They run after them, begging,
but they are gone.

8 Those who get wisdom do
themselves a favor,
and those who love learning will
succeed.

9 A witness who lies will not go free,
liars will die.

10 A fool should not live in luxury.
A slave should not rule over
princes.

11 Smart people are patient;
they will be honored if they ignore
insults.

12 An angry king is like a roaring lion,

but his kindness is like the dew on
the grass.

13 A foolish son will ruin his father,
and a quarreling wife is like
dripping water.

14 Houses and wealth are inherited
from parents,
but a wise wife is a gift from the
LORD.

15 Lazy people sleep
a lot,
and idle people
will go
hungry.

EMAIL FROM GOD
19:15
Laziness
What the lazy can expect

16 Those who obey the commands
protect themselves,
but those who are careless will die.

17 Being kind to the poor is like lending
to the LORD;
he will reward you for what you
have done.

18 Correct your children while there is
still hope;
do not let them destroy
themselves.

19 People with quick tempers will have
to pay for it.
If you help them out once, you will
have to do it again.

20 Listen to advice and accept
correction,
and in the end you will be wise.

21 People can make all kinds of plans,
but only the LORD's plan will
happen.

22 People want others to be loyal,
so it is better to be poor than to be
a liar.

23 Those who respect the LORD will
live
and be satisfied, unbothered by
trouble.

24 Though the lazy person puts his hand
in the dish,
he won't lift the food to his mouth.

25 Whip those who make fun of wisdom,
and perhaps foolish people will
gain some wisdom.
Correct those with understanding,
and they will gain knowledge.

26 A son who robs his father and sends
away his mother
brings shame and disgrace on
himself.

27 Don't stop listening to correction, my
child,
or you will forget what you have
already learned.

28 An evil witness makes fun of
fairness,
and wicked people love what is
evil.

29 People who make fun of wisdom will
be punished,
and the backs of foolish people will
be beaten.

20 Wine and beer make people loud
and uncontrolled;
it is not wise to get drunk on them.

2 An angry king is like a roaring lion.
Making him angry may cost you
your life.

3 Foolish people are always fighting,
but avoiding quarrels will bring
you honor.

4 Lazy farmers don't plow when they
should;
they expect a harvest, but there is
none.

5 People's thoughts can be like a deep
well,
but someone with understanding
can find the wisdom there.

6 Many people claim to be loyal,

but it is hard to find a trustworthy
person.

7 The good people who live honest
lives
will be a blessing to their children.

8 When a king sits on his throne to
judge,
he knows evil when he sees it.

9 No one can say, "I am innocent;
I have never done anything
wrong."

10 The LORD hates both these things:
dishonest weights and dishonest
measures.

11 Even children are known by their
behavior;
their actions show if they are
innocent and good.

12 The LORD has made both these
things:
ears to hear and eyes to see.

13 If you love to sleep, you will be poor.
If you stay awake, you will have
plenty of food.

14 Buyers say, "This is bad. It's no
good."
Then they go away and brag about
what they bought.

15 There is gold and plenty of rubies,
but only a few people speak with
knowledge.

16 Take the coat of someone who
promises to pay a stranger's
debts,
and keep it until he pays what the
stranger owes.

17 Stolen food may taste sweet at first,
but later it will feel like a mouth
full of gravel.

18 Get advice if you want your plans to
work.

FAITH links

YOU ARE WHAT YOU DO

PROVERBS 20:11

Have you heard the old saying "You are what you eat"? That means the foods you eat make you healthy or unhealthy. Now what about the expression "Actions speak louder than words"? You've heard that before, right? This proverb suggests that your character is shown by your actions. In other words, you are what you do. What do your actions show? If you claim to love others, your actions should be loving. You are known by what you do. Let Jesus be the model for the things you do and say.

Looking for a good role model? Connect here:

A Different Kind of People, Leviticus 11, p. 146

Your Response to Responsibility, Ruth 2:1–7, p. 346

Choosing Sides, 1 Samuel 20, p. 382

"Handle" Your Responsibilities, 2 Kings 6:5–7, p. 485

Calling Anyone!, Acts 23:12–22, p. 1506

An Unselfish Example, Philippians 2:5–8, p. 1611

If you go to war, get the advice of
others.

19 Gossips can't keep secrets,
so avoid people who talk too much.

20 Those who curse their father or
mother
will be like a light going out in
darkness.

21 Wealth inherited quickly in the
beginning
will do you no good in the end.

22 Don't say, "I'll pay you back for the
wrong you did."
Wait for the LORD, and he will
make things right.

23 The LORD hates dishonest weights,
and dishonest scales do not please
him.

24 The LORD decides what a person will
do;
no one understands what his life is
all about.

25 It's dangerous to promise something
to God too quickly.
After you've thought about it, it
may be too late.

26 A wise king sorts out the evil people,
and he punishes them as they
deserve.

27 The LORD looks deep inside people
and searches through their
thoughts.

28 Loyalty and truth keep a king in power;
he continues to rule if he is loyal.

29 Young men glory in their strength,
and old men are honored for their
gray hair.

30 Hard punishment will get rid of evil,
and whippings can change an evil
heart.

21 The LORD can control a king's
mind as he controls a river;
he can direct it as he pleases.

2 You may believe you are doing right,
but the LORD judges your reasons.

3 Doing what is right and fair
is more important to the LORD
than sacrifices.

4 Proud looks, proud thoughts,
and evil actions are sin.

5 The plans of hard-working people
earn a profit,
but those who act too quickly
become poor.

6 Wealth that comes from telling lies
vanishes like a mist and leads to
death.

7 The violence of the wicked will
destroy them,
because they refuse to do what is
right.

8 Guilty people live dishonest lives,
but honest people do right.

9 It is better to live in a corner on the
roof[*]
than inside the house with a
quarreling wife.

10 Evil people only want to harm others.
Their neighbors get no mercy from
them.

11 If you punish those who make fun of
wisdom, a foolish person may
gain some wisdom.
But if you teach the wise, they will
get knowledge.

12 God, who is always right, watches
the house of the wicked
and brings ruin on every evil
person.

13 Whoever ignores the poor when they
cry for help
will also cry for help and not be
answered.

21:9 roof In Bible times houses were built with flat roofs. The roof was used for drying things such as flax and fruit. And it was used as an extra room, as a place for worship, and as a cool place to sleep in the summer.

14 A secret gift will calm an angry
person;
a present given in secrecy will
quiet great anger.

15 When justice is done, good people
are happy,
but evil people are ruined.

16 Whoever does not use good sense
will end up among the dead.

17 Whoever loves pleasure will become
poor;
whoever loves wine and perfume
will never be rich.

18 Wicked people will suffer instead of
good people,
and those who cannot be trusted
will suffer instead of those who
do right.

19 It is better to live alone in the desert
than with a quarreling and
complaining wife.

20 Wise people's houses are full of the
best foods and olive oil,
but fools waste everything they
have.

21 Whoever tries to live right and be
loyal
finds life, success, and honor.

22 A wise person can defeat a city full of
warriors
and tear down the defenses they
trust in.

23 Those who are
careful about
what they say
keep themselves
out of trouble.

eMAIL! FROM GOD 21:23
Sin
Why is it important to watch what you say?

24 People who act with stubborn pride
are called "proud," "bragger," and
"mocker."

25 Lazy people's desire for sleep will
kill them,
because they refuse to work.

26 All day long they wish for more,
but good people give without
holding back.

27 The LORD hates sacrifices brought by
evil people,
particularly when they offer them
for the wrong reasons.

28 A lying witness will be forgotten,
but a truthful witness will
speak on.

29 Wicked people are stubborn,
but good people think carefully
about what they do.

30 There is no wisdom, understanding,
or advice
that can succeed against the
LORD.

31 You can get the horses ready for
battle,
but it is the LORD who gives the
victory.

22 Being respected is more
important than having great
riches.
To be well thought of is better than
silver or gold.

2 The rich and the poor are alike
in that the LORD made them all.

3 The wise see danger ahead and
avoid it,
but fools keep going and get into
trouble.

4 Respecting the
LORD and
not being
proud
will bring you
wealth,
honor, and
life.

eMAIL! FROM GOD 22:4
Humbleness
Don't be proud.

5 Evil people's lives are like paths
covered with thorns and traps.

FAITH CHALLENGE

Here's one for you. Read 22:6 to find out what happens to children with good parents. What is the most important thing your parents have taught you—the one thing you will remember for the rest of your life?

TESTING IT

Proverbs 22:6
Train children how to live right, and when they are old, they will not change.

People who guard themselves
don't have such problems.

6 Train children how to live right,
and when they are old, they will
not change.

7 The rich rule over the poor,
and borrowers are servants to
lenders.

8 Those who plan evil will receive
trouble.
Their cruel anger will come to an
end.

9 Generous people will be blessed,
because they share their food with
the poor.

10 Get rid of the one who makes fun of
wisdom.
Then fighting, quarrels, and insults
will stop.

11 Whoever loves pure thoughts and
kind words
will have even the king as a friend.

12 The LORD guards knowledge,
but he destroys false words.

13 The lazy person says, "There's a lion
outside!
I might get killed out in the
street!"

14 The words of an unfaithful wife are
like a deep trap.
Those who make the LORD angry
will get caught by them.

15 Every child is full of foolishness,
but punishment can get rid of it.

16 Whoever gets rich by mistreating the
poor,
and gives presents to the wealthy,
will become poor.

Other Wise Sayings

17 Listen carefully to what wise people
say;
pay attention to what I am teaching
you.
18 It will be good to keep these things in
mind
so that you are ready to repeat
them.
19 I am teaching them to you now
so that you will put your trust in
the LORD.
20 I have written thirty sayings for you,
which give knowledge and good
advice.
21 I am teaching you true and reliable
words
so that you can give true answers
to anyone who asks.

22 Do not abuse poor people because
they are poor,
and do not take away the rights of
the needy in court.
23 The LORD will defend them in court
and will take the life of those who
take away their rights.

24 Don't make friends with quick-
tempered people
or spend time with those who have
bad tempers.
25 If you do, you will be like them.
Then you will be in real danger.

26 Don't promise to pay what someone
else owes,
and don't guarantee anyone's loan.
27 If you cannot pay the loan,
your own bed may be taken right
out from under you.

28 Don't move an old stone that marks a
border,
because those stones were set up
by your ancestors.

29 Do you see people skilled in their
work?
They will work for kings, not for
ordinary people.

23 If you sit down to eat with a ruler,
notice the food that is in front of
you.
2 Control yourself
if you have a big appetite.
3 Don't be greedy for his fine foods,
because that food might be a trick.

4 Don't wear yourself out trying to get
rich;
be wise enough to control yourself.
5 Wealth can vanish in the wink of an
eye.
It can seem to grow wings
and fly away like an eagle.

6 Don't eat the food of selfish people;
don't be greedy for their fine foods.
7 Selfish people are always worrying
about how much the food costs.
They tell you, "Eat and drink,"
but they don't really mean it.
8 You will throw up the little you have
eaten,
and you will have wasted your kind
words.

9 Don't speak to fools;
they will only ignore your wise
words.

10 Don't move an old stone that marks a
border,
and don't take fields that belong to
orphans.
11 God, their defender, is strong;
he will take their side against you.

12 Remember what you are taught,
and listen carefully to words of
knowledge.

13 Don't fail to punish children.
If you spank them, they won't die.
14 If you spank them,
you will save them from death.

15 My child, if you are wise,
then I will be happy.
16 I will be so pleased
if you speak what is right.

17 Don't envy sinners,
but always respect the LORD.
18 Then you will have hope for the
future,
and your wishes will come true.

19 Listen, my child, and be wise.
Keep your mind on what is right.
20 Don't drink too much wine
or eat too much food.
21 Those who drink and eat too much
become poor.
They sleep too much and end up
wearing rags.

22 Listen to your father, who gave you
life,
and do not forget your mother
when she is old.
23 Learn the truth and never reject it.
Get wisdom, self-control, and
understanding.

24 The father of a good child is very
happy;
parents who have wise children are
glad because of them.
25 Make your father and mother happy;
give your mother a reason to be
glad.

26 My son, pay
attention to
me,
and watch closely
what I do.

eMAiL! FROM GOD
23:26
Responsibility
How can you learn to be responsible?

27 A prostitute is as dangerous as a
deep pit,
and an unfaithful wife is like a
narrow well.
28 They ambush you like robbers
and cause many men to be
unfaithful to their wives.

29 Who has trouble? Who has pain?
Who fights? Who complains?
Who has unnecessary bruises?
Who has bloodshot eyes?
30 It is people who drink too much
wine,
who try out all different kinds of
strong drinks.
31 Don't stare at the wine when it is
red,
when it sparkles in the cup,
when it goes down smoothly.
32 Later it bites like a snake
with poison in its fangs.
33 Your eyes will see strange sights,
and your mind will be confused.
34 You will feel dizzy as if you're in a
storm on the ocean,
as if you're on top of a ship's sails.
35 You will think, "They hit me, but I'm
not hurt.
They beat me up, but I don't
remember it.
I wish I could wake up.
Then I would get another drink."

24 Don't envy evil people
or try to be friends with them.
2 Their minds are always planning
violence,
and they always talk about making
trouble.

3 It takes wisdom
to have a
good family,
and it takes
understanding
to make it
strong.

eMAiL! FROM GOD
24:3–4
Wisdom
Why is wisdom important?

4 It takes knowledge to fill a home
with rare and beautiful treasures.

5 Wise people have great power,
and those with knowledge have
great strength.
6 So you need advice when you go to
war.
If you have lots of good advice, you
will win.

7 Foolish people cannot understand
wisdom.
They have nothing to say in a
discussion.

8 Whoever makes evil plans
will be known as a troublemaker.
9 Making foolish plans is sinful,
and making fun of wisdom is
hateful.

10 If you give up when trouble comes,
it shows that you are weak.

11 Save those who are being led to their
death;
rescue those who are about to be
killed.
12 If you say, "We don't know anything
about this,"
God, who knows what's in your
mind, will notice.
He is watching you, and he will know.
He will reward each person for
what he has done.

13 My child, eat honey because it is
good.
Honey from the
honeycomb
tastes sweet.
14 In the same way,
wisdom is
pleasing to
you.

eMAiL! FROM GOD
24:13–14
Wisdom
Check out what wisdom is like.

If you find it, you have hope for the future,
and your wishes will come true.

15 Don't be wicked and attack a good family's house;
don't rob the place where they live.
16 Even though good people may be bothered by trouble seven times, they are never defeated,
but the wicked are overwhelmed by trouble.

17 Don't be happy when your enemy is defeated;
don't be glad when he is overwhelmed.

24:17–18
Enemies
Should you be glad when your enemy gets hurt?

18 The LORD will notice and be displeased.
He may not be angry with them anymore.

19 Don't envy evil people,
and don't be jealous of the wicked.
20 An evil person has nothing to hope for;
the wicked will die like a flame that is put out.

21 My child, respect the LORD and the king.
Don't join those people who refuse to obey them.
22 The LORD and the king will quickly destroy such people.
Those two can cause great disaster!

More Words of Wisdom

23 These are also sayings of the wise:
It is not good to take sides when you are the judge.
24 Don't tell the wicked that they are innocent;
people will curse you, and nations will hate you.
25 But things will go well if you punish the guilty,
and you will receive rich blessings.
26 An honest answer is as pleasing as a kiss on the lips.

27 First, finish your outside work
and prepare your fields.
After that, you can build your house.

28 Don't testify against your neighbor for no good reason.
Don't say things that are false.
29 Don't say, "I'll get even;
I'll do to him what he did to me."

30 I passed by a lazy person's field
and by the vineyard of someone with no sense.
31 Thorns had grown up everywhere.
The ground was covered with weeds,
and the stone walls had fallen down.
32 I thought about what I had seen;
I learned this lesson from what I saw.
33 You sleep a little; you take a nap.
You fold your hands and lie down to rest.
34 Soon you will be as poor as if you had been robbed;
you will have as little as if you had been held up.

More Wise Sayings of Solomon

25 These are more wise sayings of Solomon, copied by the men of Hezekiah king of Judah.
2 God is honored for what he keeps secret.
Kings are honored for what they can discover.

3 No one can measure the height of the skies or the depth of the earth.
So also no one can understand the mind of a king.

4 Remove the scum from the silver,
so the silver can be used by the silversmith.
5 Remove wicked people from the king's presence;
then his government will be honest and last a long time.

6 Don't brag to the king
and act as if you are great.
7 It is better for him to give you a
higher position
than to bring you down in front of
the prince.

Because of something you have
seen,
8 do not quickly take someone to
court.
What will you do later
when your neighbor proves you
wrong?

9 If you have an argument with your
neighbor,
don't tell other people what was
said.
10 Whoever hears it might shame you,
and you might not ever be
respected again.

11 The right word spoken at the right
time
is as beautiful as gold apples in a
silver bowl.

12 A wise warning to someone who will
listen
is as valuable as gold earrings or
fine gold jewelry.

13 Trustworthy messengers refresh
those who send them,
like the coolness of snow in the
summertime.

14 People who brag about gifts they
never give
are like clouds and wind that give
no rain.

15 With patience you can convince a
ruler,
and a gentle word can get through
to the hard-headed.

16 If you find honey, don't eat too
much,
or it will make you throw up.
17 Don't go to your neighbor's house
too often;
too much of you will make him
hate you.

18 When you lie about your neighbors,
it hurts them as much as a club, a
sword, or a sharp arrow.

19 Trusting unfaithful people when you
are in trouble
is like eating with a broken tooth
or walking with a crippled foot.

20 Singing songs to someone who is sad
is like taking away his coat on a
cold day
or pouring vinegar on soda.

21 If your enemy is
hungry, feed
him.
If he is thirsty,
give him a
drink.
22 Doing this will be
like pouring burning coals on his
head,
and the LORD will reward you.

EMAIL FROM GOD
25:21–22
Enemies
How should you treat your enemies?

23 As the north wind brings rain,
telling gossip brings angry looks.

24 It is better to live in a corner on the
roof[n]
than inside the house with a
quarreling wife.

25 Good news from a faraway place
is like a cool drink when you are
tired.

26 A good person who gives in to evil
is like a muddy spring or a dirty
well.

27 It is not good to eat too much honey,
nor does it bring you honor to brag
about yourself.

25:24 roof In Bible times houses were built with flat roofs. The roof was used for drying things such as flax and fruit. And it was used as an extra room, as a place for worship, and as a cool place to sleep in the summer.

HANDLING MY ENEMIES

Proverbs 25:21–22

Livin' it

Now You're Asking for It! In TV shows and movies, we feel like cheering when the "bad guy" gets what he deserves. What do you do when someone makes you angry or does something rotten to you? Do you feel like getting even? Or do you forgive and forget?

God has a different idea about justice. He claims revenge as part of his territory. (Look at Isaiah 35:3–4, p. 940.) When someone acts like an enemy, tell God about it. Let him take care of it. In Israel, a special law was given to the people about getting even with others. (Check out Leviticus 19:18, p. 161.) When we are angry, we easily sin. What are some things you can do instead of getting even?

MORE FAITH links

Give Revenge a Rest, p. 160
What's Out Becomes In, p. 327
Putting an Enemy in Check, p. 486
Mercy for an Enemy, p. 1216
Who Needs Love?, p. 1379

"Tagg, what are you going to do with that water balloon?"

"You know that mean virobug, Crash? Well, he tripped me up the other day and then laughed at me. This is for him if he dares to come this way."

"Why don't you put that down and log on to these Faithlinks? I think there's a better way to handle your enemies."

A Right to Get Even?, 1 Samuel 24, p. 388

- If you've ever felt like getting even with someone, think of David's story. King Saul was David's enemy, determined to kill David. Link here to discover how David reacted when he had a chance to get even.

Justice Desserts, Habakkuk 2:4–8, p. 1237

- Have you ever heard someone say, "There's no justice in the world!"? Have *you* ever said that? How do you feel when you see people get away with doing wrong things? What would you like to see happen to them? This Faithlink points out God's faithfulness in serving justice.

Don't Get Mad; Get Even?, Matthew 26:57–63; 27:11–14, p. 1323

- When someone treats you terribly, what do you do? Do you get mad or think about getting even? When we are mistreated, many of us are tempted to get even. Would that solve the problem? How could getting even make things worse? Next time you feel like getting even ask yourself, "What would Jesus do?" and try to follow his example.

my FAVORITE links

28 Those who do not control
themselves
are like a city whose walls are
broken down.

26 It shouldn't snow in summer or
rain at harvest.
Neither should a foolish person
ever be honored.

2 Curses will not harm someone who
is innocent;
they are like sparrows or swallows
that fly around and never land.

3 Whips are for horses, and harnesses
are for donkeys,
so paddles are good for fools.

4 Don't give fools a foolish answer,
or you will be just like them.

5 But answer fools as they should be
answered,
or they will think they are really
wise.

6 Sending a message by a foolish person
is like cutting off your feet or
drinking poison.

7 A wise saying spoken by a fool
is as useless as the legs of a
crippled person.

8 Giving honor to a foolish person
is like tying a stone in a slingshot.

9 A wise saying spoken by a fool
is like a thorn stuck in the hand of
a drunk.

10 Hiring a foolish person or anyone
just passing by
is like an archer shooting at just
anything.

11 A fool who repeats his foolishness
is like a dog that goes back to what
it has thrown up.

12 There is more hope for a foolish
person
than for those who think they are
wise.

13 The lazy person says, "There's a lion
in the road!
There's a lion in the streets!"

14 Like a door turning back and forth on
its hinges,
the lazy person turns over and
over in bed.

15 Lazy people may put their hands in
the dish,
but they are too tired to lift the
food to their mouths.

16 The lazy person thinks he is wiser
than seven people who give
sensible answers.

17 Interfering in someone else's quarrel
as you pass by
is like grabbing a dog by the ears.

18 Like a madman shooting
deadly, burning arrows
19 is the one who tricks a neighbor
and then says, "I was just joking."

20 Without wood, a
fire will go
out,
and without
gossip,
quarreling
will stop.

EMAIL FROM GOD
26:20
Gossip
What happens when
gossip is stopped?

21 Just as charcoal and wood keep a fire
going,
a quarrelsome person keeps an
argument going.

22 The words of a gossip are like tasty
bits of food;
people like to gobble them up.

23 Kind words from a wicked mind
are like a shiny coating on a clay
pot.

24 Those who hate you may try to fool
you with their words,

but in their minds they are
planning evil.
25 People's words may be kind, but
don't believe them,
because their minds are full of evil
thoughts.
26 Lies can hide hate,
but the evil will be plain to
everyone.

27 Whoever digs a pit for others will fall
into it.
Whoever tries to roll a boulder
down on others will be crushed
by it.

28 Liars hate the people they hurt,
and false praise can ruin others.

27 Don't brag about tomorrow;
you don't know what may
happen then.

2 Don't praise yourself.
Let someone
else do it.
Let the praise
come from a
stranger and not
from your own
mouth.

3 Stone is heavy, and
sand is weighty,
but a complaining fool is worse
than either.

4 Anger is cruel and destroys like a
flood,
but no one can put up with
jealousy!

5 It is better to correct someone
openly
than to have love and not show it.

6 The slap of a friend can be trusted to
help you,
but the kisses of an enemy are
nothing but lies.

7 When you are full, not even honey
tastes good,
but when you are hungry, even
something bitter tastes sweet.

8 A person who leaves his home
is like a bird that leaves its nest.

9 The sweet smell of perfume and oils
is pleasant,
and so is good advice from a friend.

10 Don't forget your friend or your
parent's friend.
Don't always go to your family for
help when trouble comes.
A neighbor close by is better than
a family far away.

11 Be wise, my child, and make me
happy.
Then I can respond to any insult.

12 The wise see danger
ahead and
avoid it,
but fools keep
going and get
into trouble.

The wise see danger ahead and avoid it.
—Proverbs 27:12

13 Take the coat of
someone who
promises to pay a
stranger's loan,
and keep it until he
pays what the
stranger owes.

14 If you loudly greet your neighbor
early in the morning,
he will think of it as a curse.

15 A quarreling wife is as bothersome
as a continual dripping on a rainy
day.
16 Stopping her is like stopping the wind
or trying to grab oil in your hand.

17 As iron sharpens iron,
so people can improve each other.

18 Whoever tends a fig tree gets to eat
its fruit,
and whoever takes care of his
master will receive honor.

19 As water reflects your face,
so your mind shows what kind of
person you are.

20 People will never stop dying and
being destroyed,
and they will never stop wanting
more than they have.

21 A hot furnace tests silver and gold,
and people are tested by the praise
they receive.

22 Even if you ground up a foolish
person like grain in a bowl,
you couldn't remove the
foolishness.

23 Be sure you know how your sheep
are doing,
and pay attention to the condition
of your cattle.
24 Riches will not go on forever,
nor do governments go on forever.
25 Bring in the hay, and let the new
grass appear.
Gather the grass from the hills.
26 Make clothes from the lambs' wool,
and sell some goats to buy a field.
27 There will be plenty of goat's milk
to feed you and your family
and to make your servant girls
healthy.

28 Evil people run even though no
one is chasing them,
but good people are as brave as a
lion.

2 When a country is lawless, it has one
ruler after another;
but when it is led by a man with
understanding and knowledge, it
continues strong.

3 Rulers who mistreat the poor
are like a hard rain that destroys
the crops.

4 Those who disobey what they have
been taught praise the wicked,
but those who obey what they have
been taught are against them.

5 Evil people do not understand
justice,
but those who follow the LORD
understand it completely.

6 It is better to be poor and innocent
than to be rich and wicked.

7 Children who obey what they have
been taught are smart,
but friends of troublemakers
disgrace their parents.

FAITH links

CHOOSING A FRIEND 

PROVERBS 28:7

Have you ever taken a magazine quiz on choosing a friend? Those same magazines usually offer advice on making friends. The friends you choose are not only important to you; they're important to your parents as well. As this proverb mentions, those who have troublemakers for friends wind up embarrassing their parents. If that's not your goal, choose your friends wisely.

An Admirable Quality, 1 Kings 10:1–13, p. 451

Two Kinds of People, Psalm 1, p. 710

A Hopeful Future, Jeremiah 29:11, p. 1031

A Blueprint for Living, Amos 5:14–15, p. 1200

A Real Crowd-pleaser?, Micah 2:6–11, p. 1222

My Favorite!, Mark 10:17–23, p. 1347

8 Some people get rich by
overcharging others,
but their wealth will be given to
those who are kind to the poor.

9 If you refuse to obey what you have
been taught,
your prayers will not be heard.

10 Those who lead good people to do
wrong
will be ruined by their own evil,
but the innocent will be rewarded
with good things.

11 Rich people may think they are wise,
but the poor with understanding
will prove them wrong.

12 When good people triumph, there is
great happiness,
but when the wicked get control,
everybody hides.

13 If you hide your sins, you will not
succeed.
If you confess and reject them, you
will receive mercy.

14 Those who are always respectful will
be happy,
but those who are stubborn will
get into trouble.

15 A wicked ruler is as dangerous to
poor people
as a roaring lion or a charging bear.

16 A ruler without wisdom will be cruel,
but the one who refuses to take
dishonest money will rule a long
time.

17 Don't help those who are guilty of
murder;
let them run until they die.

18 Innocent people will be kept safe,
but those who are dishonest will
suddenly be ruined.

19 Those who work their land will have
plenty of food,
but the ones who chase empty
dreams instead will end up poor.

20 A truthful person will have many
blessings,
but those eager to get rich will be
punished.

21 It is not good for a judge to take sides,
but some will sin for only a piece
of bread.

22 Selfish people are in a hurry to get rich
and do not realize they soon will be
poor.

23 Those who correct others will later
be liked
more than those who give false
praise.

24 Whoever robs his father or mother
and says, "It's not wrong,"
is just like someone who destroys
things.

25 A greedy person causes trouble,
but the one who trusts the LORD
will succeed.

EMAIL! FROM GOD
28:25–26
Trust
How successful
will you be?

26 Those who
trust in
themselves
are foolish,
but those who
live wisely will be kept safe.

27 Whoever gives to the poor will have
everything he needs,
but the one who ignores the poor
will receive many curses.

28 When the wicked get control,
everybody hides,
but when they die, good people do
well.

29 Whoever is stubborn after being
corrected many times
will suddenly be hurt beyond cure.

2 When good people do well, everyone
is happy,

but when evil people rule,
everyone groans.

3 Those who love wisdom make their
parents happy,
but friends of prostitutes waste
their money.

4 If a king is fair, he makes his country
strong,
but if he takes gifts dishonestly, he
tears his country down.

5 Those who give false praise to their
neighbors
are setting a trap for them.

6 Evil people are trapped by their own
sin,
but good people can sing and be
happy.

7 Good people care about justice for
the poor,
but the wicked are not concerned.

8 People who make fun of wisdom
cause trouble in a city,
but wise people calm anger down.

9 When a wise person takes a foolish
person to court,
the fool only shouts or laughs, and
there is no peace.

10 Murderers hate an honest person
and try to kill those who do right.

11 Foolish people lose their tempers,
but wise people control theirs.

12 If a ruler pays attention to lies,
all his officers will become
wicked.

13 The poor person and the cruel
person are alike
in that the LORD gave eyes to both
of them.

14 If a king judges poor people fairly,
his government will continue
forever.

15 Correction and punishment make
children wise,
but those left alone will disgrace
their mother.

FAITH links

DOWN ON DISCIPLINE?

PROVERBS 29:15

If you wish your parents would never nag about something you've done wrong, raise your hand. Is your hand up? Thought so. Now, if you would like to be wise, raise your hand. Is your hand up? If so, consider this: A parent's discipline provides wisdom for each child. You've probably seen or heard enough news stories about kids who were "left alone" as this proverb states. The result is usually trouble. So . . . want to change your answer to the first question?

No one likes to be disciplined, but connect here to see why it's important:

In Your Best Interests, Ruth 3, p. 349

This Hurts Me More?, 2 Chronicles 36:17–22, p. 606

See the Heart Behind It, Nehemiah 8; 9, p. 636

A Word to the Wise, Proverbs 10:1, p. 838

Remember Your Creator, Ecclesiastes 12:1, 13, p. 885

Just Say No!, Titus 2:11–12, p. 1660

16 When there are many wicked people,
there is much sin,
but those who do right will see
them destroyed.

17 Correct your children, and you will
be proud;
they will give you satisfaction.

18 Where there is no word from God,
people are uncontrolled,
but those who obey what they
have been taught are happy.

19 Words alone cannot correct a
servant,
because even if he understands, he
won't respond.

20 Do you see people
who speak too
quickly?
There is more hope
for a foolish
person than for
them.

21 If you spoil your
servants when
they are young,
they will bring you
grief later on.

22 An angry person causes trouble;
a person with a quick temper sins
a lot.

23 Pride will ruin
people,
but those who
are humble
will be
honored.

29:23
Pride
Check out who will be honored.

24 Partners of thieves are their own
worst enemies.
If they have to testify in court,
they are afraid to say anything.

25 Being afraid of people can get you
into trouble,
but if you trust the LORD, you will
be safe.

26 Many people want to speak to a ruler,
but justice comes only from the
LORD.

27 Good people hate those who are
dishonest,
and the wicked hate those who are
honest.

Wise Words from Agur

30 These are the words of Agur son
of Jakeh.
This is his message to Ithiel and
Ucal:

2 "I am the most stupid person there
is,
and I have no understanding.
3 I have not learned to
be wise,
and I don't know
much about God,
the Holy One.
4 Who has gone up to
heaven and come
back down?
Who can hold the
wind in his
hand?
Who can gather up
the waters in his
coat?
Who has set in place the ends of
the earth?
What is his name or his son's name?
Tell me, if you know!

> Every word of God is true.
> —Proverbs 30:5

5 "Every word of God is true.
He guards those who come to him
for safety.
6 Do not add to his words,
or he will correct you and prove
you are a liar.

7 "I ask two things from you, LORD.
Don't refuse me before I die.
8 Keep me from lying and being
dishonest.
And don't make me either rich or
poor;
just give me enough food for each
day.

9 If I have too much, I might reject you
and say, 'I don't know the LORD.'
If I am poor, I might steal
and disgrace the name of my God.

10 "Do not say bad things about
servants to their masters,
or they will curse you, and you will
suffer for it.

11 "Some people curse their fathers
and do not bless their mothers.
12 Some people think they are pure,
but they are not really free from
evil.
13 Some people have such a proud
look!
They look down on others.
14 Some people have teeth like swords;
their jaws seem full of knives.
They want to remove the poor from
the earth
and the needy from the land.

15 "Greed has two daughters
named 'Give' and 'Give.'
There are three things that are never
satisfied,
really four that never say, 'I've had
enough!':
16 the cemetery, the childless mother,
the land that never gets enough
rain,
and fire that never says, 'I've had
enough!'

17 "If you make fun of your father
and refuse to obey your mother,
the birds of the valley will peck out
your eyes,
and the vultures will eat them.

18 "There are three things that are too
hard for me,
really four I don't understand:
19 the way an eagle flies in the sky,
the way a snake slides over a rock,
the way a ship sails on the sea,
and the way a man and a woman
fall in love.

20 "This is the way of a woman who
takes part in adultery:
She acts as if she had eaten and
washed her face;
she says, 'I haven't done anything
wrong.'

21 "There are three things that make
the earth tremble,
really four it cannot stand:
22 a servant who becomes a king,
a foolish person who has plenty to
eat,
23 a hated woman who gets married,
and a maid who replaces her
mistress.

24 "There are four things on earth that
are small,
but they are very wise:
25 Ants are not very strong,
but they store up food in the
summer.
26 Rock badgers are not very powerful,
but they can live among the rocks.
27 Locusts have no king,
but they all go forward in formation.
28 Lizards can be caught in the hand,
but they are found even in kings'
palaces.

29 "There are three things that strut
proudly,
really four that walk as if they
were important:
30 a lion, the proudest animal,
which is strong and runs from
nothing,
31 a rooster, a male goat,
and a king when his army is around
him.

32 "If you have been foolish and proud,
or if you have planned evil, shut
your mouth.
33 Just as stirring milk makes butter,
and twisting noses makes them
bleed,
so stirring up anger causes
trouble."

Wise Words of King Lemuel

31 These are the words of King
Lemuel, the message his mother
taught him:

2 "My son, I gave birth to you.
You are the son I prayed for.
3 Don't waste your strength on women
or your time on those who ruin kings.

4 "Kings should not drink wine, Lemuel,
and rulers should not desire beer.
5 If they drink, they might forget the law
and keep the needy from getting their rights.
6 Give beer to people who are dying
and wine to those who are sad.
7 Let them drink and forget their need
and remember their misery no more.

8 "Speak up for those who cannot speak for themselves;
defend the rights of all those who have nothing.
9 Speak up and judge fairly,
and defend the rights of the poor and needy."

The Good Wife

10 It is hard to find a good wife,
because she is worth more than rubies.
11 Her husband trusts her completely.
With her, he has everything he needs.
12 She does him good and not harm
for as long as she lives.
13 She looks for wool and flax
and likes to work with her hands.
14 She is like a trader's ship,
bringing food from far away.
15 She gets up while it is still dark
and prepares food for her family
and feeds her servant girls.
16 She inspects a field and buys it.
With money she earned, she plants a vineyard.
17 She does her work with energy,
and her arms are strong.
18 She knows that what she makes is good.
Her lamp burns late into the night.
19 She makes thread with her hands
and weaves her own cloth.
20 She welcomes the poor
and helps the needy.
21 She does not worry about her family when it snows,
because they all have fine clothes to keep them warm.
22 She makes coverings for herself;
her clothes are made of linen and other expensive material.
23 Her husband is known at the city meetings,
where he makes decisions as one of the leaders of the land.
24 She makes linen clothes and sells them
and provides belts to the merchants.
25 She is strong and is respected by the people.
She looks forward to the future with joy.
26 She speaks wise words
and teaches others to be kind.
27 She watches over her family
and never wastes her time.
28 Her children speak well of her.
Her husband also praises her,
29 saying, "There are many fine women,
but you are better than all of them."
30 Charm can fool you, and beauty can trick you,
but a woman who respects the LORD should be praised.
31 Give her the reward she has earned;
she should be praised in public for what she has done.

EMAIL! FROM GOD
31:30
Respect
Check out how to gain respect.

USELESS! USELESS!

Hi! Solomon, here. You probably have heard of me, the king who asked God for wisdom. (I also wrote Proverbs.) Not only did God grant my request for wisdom, but he also blessed me with fabulous riches and power. I did great things with my wealth. I built houses and vineyards, bought large herds of animals, and gathered gold and silver treasure for myself. Anything I wanted, I got. But something was missing. Have you ever put together a puzzle and discovered a piece in the middle was missing? The missing piece of my life was God.

I wrote this book to tell others that life without God is useless. Don't think you can find meaning in your life by collecting treasure or gaining a high position. It's like chasing the wind. The best advice I can give is to obey God and enjoy the life he gives you.

JESUS WATCH

How empty is life without God! The pleasures of this life will never satisfy us. We always want more. The need for Jesus is clearly seen in this book. When we believe in Jesus, our lives are full of his love and care for us. The work we do is not useless, but is pleasing to God. Jesus takes care of us like a good shepherd. He knows each one of us by name, and he protects us from our enemies. Jesus is not only our shepherd; he is also our friend. How rich and full our lives are when Jesus is our friend! Without Jesus, our life, like Solomon said, is useless.

my FAVORITE links

______ ______

______ ______

______ ______

______ ______

OTHER CONNECTIONS

Want to find out what real wisdom is all about? Connect to Wise Books, Ecclesiastes 7, and you can learn more about what books in the Bible are considered the "Wisdom Literature" and in what forms you will discover wisdom in the Bible.

MORE STUFF...

Some Good Advice King Solomon had a lot of questions in the Book of Ecclesiastes. But he also had some good advice to share. Take a look at some advice that Solomon had to offer:

- Two people are better than one because they can help each other, can get more done, and can protect one another (Ecclesiastes 4:9–12).
- Think before you speak and be careful about what you promise God (Ecclesiastes 5:1–7).
- Enjoy the things that God has given you to do (Ecclesiastes 5:18–20).
- Don't get angry quickly (Ecclesiastes 7:9).
- Don't make fun of others because your words may get back to them (Ecclesiastes 10:20).
- Honor and obey all God's commands (Ecclesiastes 12:13–14).

"What is Solomon's final advice?"

"Let's be wise and look it up in Ecclesiastes 12:13-14."

did you know?

IT'S NOT USELESS TO LOOK THESE UP:

A time for everything, Ecclesiastes 3:1–8
Two are better than one, Ecclesiastes 4:9–12
Never enough, Ecclesiastes 5:10–12
Enjoy every day, Ecclesiastes 11:7–10

FAITH links

A Need to Change, Ecclesiastes 1:1–11

When Bad Things Happen, Ecclesiastes 3:16–17

Two Are Better, Ecclesiastes 4:9–12

Wisdom About Wealth, Ecclesiastes 5:10–12

Remember Your Creator, Ecclesiastes 12:1, 13

1 These are the words of the Teacher, a son of David, king in Jerusalem.
2 The Teacher says,
"Useless! Useless!
Completely useless!
Everything is useless."

3 What do people really gain
from all the hard work they do
here on earth?

Things Never Change

4 People live, and people die,
but the earth continues forever.
5 The sun rises, the sun sets,
and then it hurries back to where it
rises again.
6 The wind blows to the south;
it blows to the north.
It blows from one direction and then
another.
Then it turns around and repeats
the same pattern, going
nowhere.
7 All the rivers flow to the sea,
but the sea never becomes full.
8 Everything is boring,
so boring that you don't even want
to talk about it.
Words come again and again to our
ears,
but we never hear enough,
nor can we ever really see all we
want to see.
9 All things continue the way they
have been since the beginning.
What has happened will happen
again;
there is nothing new here on
earth.
10 Someone might say,
"Look, this is new,"
but really it has always been here.
It was here before we were.
11 People don't remember what
happened long ago,
and in the future people will not
remember what happens now.
Even later, other people will not
remember what was done before
them.

FAITH links

A NEED TO CHANGE

ECCLESIASTES 1:1-11

Booooorrrring! Have you uttered that word lately? Solomon was very wise and rich, but he was not satisfied in his life. Nothing seemed new or exciting to him. Solomon could already have anything he wanted. Yet he felt that he needed something else.

Boredom is sometimes a sign of a lack of contentment or a need to change. When you're stuck in the "everything is boring" (v. 8) mode, think about what you could do to change your situation.

Bored? Connect here:

Complaints, Complaints!, Exodus 16:1–3, p. 97

A Life of Thanksgiving, 1 Kings 1:47–48, p. 435

Our Thirst Quencher, Psalm 42:1–3, p. 741

First Place, Haggai 1:7–11, p. 1248

My Favorite!, Mark 10:17–23, p. 1347

A Different Kind of Fruit, Galatians 5:22–23, p. 1592

Does Wisdom Bring Happiness?

12 I, the Teacher, was king over Israel
in Jerusalem. 13 I decided to use my wisdom to learn about everything that happens on earth. I learned that God has
given us terrible things to face. 14 I
looked at everything done on earth and

saw that it is all useless, like chasing the
wind.
15 If something is crooked,
you can't make it straight.
If something is missing,
you can't say it is there.
16I said to myself, "I have become
very wise and am now wiser than anyone
who ruled Jerusalem before me. I know
what wisdom and knowledge really are."
17So I decided to find out about wisdom
and knowledge and also about foolish
thinking, but this turned out to be like
chasing the wind.
18 With much wisdom comes much
disappointment;
the person who gains more
knowledge also gains more
sorrow.

Does "Having Fun" Bring Happiness?

2 I said to myself, "I will try having fun.
I will enjoy myself." But I found that
this is also useless. 2It is foolish to laugh
all the time, and having fun doesn't accomplish anything. 3I decided to cheer
myself up with wine while my mind was
still thinking wisely. I wanted to find a
way to enjoy myself and see what was
good for people to do during their few
days of life.

Does Hard Work Bring Happiness?

4Then I did great things: I built houses
and planted vineyards for myself. 5I made
gardens and parks, and I planted all kinds
of fruit trees in them. 6I made pools of
water for myself and used them to water
my growing trees. 7I bought male and female slaves, and slaves were also born in
my house. I had large herds and flocks,
more than anyone in Jerusalem had ever
had before. 8I also gathered silver and
gold for myself, treasures from kings and
other areas. I had male and female singers
and all the women a man could ever want.
9I became very famous, even greater than
anyone who had lived in Jerusalem before
me. My wisdom helped me in all this.
10 Anything I saw and wanted, I got for
myself;
I did not miss any pleasure I
desired.
I was pleased with everything I did,
and this pleasure was the reward
for all my hard work.
11 But then I looked at what I had done,
and I thought about all the hard
work.
Suddenly I realized it was useless,
like chasing the wind.
There is nothing to gain from
anything we do here on earth.

Maybe Wisdom Is the Answer

12 Then I began to think again about
being wise,
and also about being foolish and
doing crazy things.
But after all, what more can anyone
do?
He can't do more than what the
other king has already done.
13 I saw that being wise is certainly
better than being foolish,
just as light is better than
darkness.
14 Wise people see where they are
going,
but fools walk around in the dark.
Yet I saw that
both wise and foolish people end
the same way.

15 I thought to myself,
"What happens to a fool will happen
to me, too,
so what is the reward for being
wise?"
I said to myself,
"Being wise is also useless."
16 The wise person and the fool
will both die,
and no one will remember either one
for long.
In the future, both will be
forgotten.

Is There Real Happiness in Life?

17So I hated life. It made me sad to
think that everything here on earth is
useless, like chasing the wind. 18I hated

all the things I had worked for here on
earth, because I must leave them to
someone who will live after me. **19**Someone else will control everything for
which I worked so hard here on earth,
and I don't know if he will be wise or foolish. This is also useless. **20**So I became
sad about all the hard work I had done
here on earth. **21**People can work hard
using all their wisdom, knowledge, and
skill, but they will die, and other people
will get the things for which they worked.
They did not do the work, but they will
get everything. This is also unfair and
useless. **22**What do people get for all
their work and struggling here on earth?
23All of their lives their work is full of
pain and sorrow, and even at night their
minds don't rest. This is also useless.

24The best that peo-
ple can do is eat, drink,
and enjoy their work. I
saw that even this comes
from God, **25**because no
one can eat or enjoy life
without him. **26**If people
please God, God will give
them wisdom, knowl-
edge, and joy. But sinners
will get only the work of
gathering and storing
wealth that they will have to give to the
ones who please God. So all their work is
useless, like chasing the wind.

The best that people can do is eat, drink, and enjoy their work.
—Ecclesiastes 2:24

There Is a Time for Everything

3 There is a time for everything,
and everything on earth has its
special season.
2There is a time to be born
and a time to die.
There is a time to plant
and a time to pull up plants.
3There is a time to kill
and a time to heal.
There is a time to destroy
and a time to build.
4There is a time to cry
and a time to laugh.
There is a time to be sad
and a time to dance.
5There is a time to throw away stones
and a time to gather them.
There is a time to hug
and a time not to hug.
6There is a time to look for something
and a time to stop looking for it.
There is a time to keep things
and a time to throw things away.
7There is a time to tear apart
and a time to sew together.
There is a time to be silent
and a time to speak.
8There is a time to love
and a time to hate.
There is a time for war
and a time for peace.

God Controls His World

9Do people really gain anything from
their work? **10**I saw the hard work God
has given people to do.
11God has given them a
desire to know the fu-
ture. He does everything
just right and on time, but
people can never com-
pletely understand what
he is doing. **12**So I realize
that the best thing for
them is to be happy and
enjoy themselves as long
as they live. **13**God wants
all people to eat and drink and be happy in
their work, which are gifts from God. **14**I
know that everything God does will continue forever. People cannot add anything
to what God has done, and they cannot
take anything away from it. God does it
this way to make people respect him.
15What happens now has happened in
the past,
and what will happen in the future
has happened before.
God makes the same things
happen again and again.

Unfairness on Earth

16I also saw this here on earth:
Where there should have been
justice, there was evil;
where there should have been
right, there was wrong.
17I said to myself,

FAITH links

WHEN BAD THINGS HAPPEN

ECCLESIASTES 3:16-17

You can't go through life without hearing about something bad happening to someone. Sometimes bad things happen even to people who trust God. When that happens, we call it an injustice. Often people use the evil in the world as an excuse not to believe in God. "Why would a good God allow evil?" they might ask.

God wants you to trust him, even when bad things happen. He wants you to trust that he's still in control of everything.

When You're Afraid, Genesis 32:9–12, p. 45

A Giant Problem, 1 Samuel 17:32–51, p. 377

Fly Like an Eagle, Isaiah 40:28–31, p. 947

Small Beginnings, Zechariah 4:10, p. 1255

An Energy Boost, Acts 4:31, p. 1469

It's Under Control, Romans 8:28, p. 1529

God has planned a time for every
thing and every action,
so he will judge both good people
and bad.

18I decided that God leaves it the way
it is to test people and to show them they
are just like animals. 19The same thing
happens to animals and to people; they
both have the same breath, so they both
die. People are no better off than the animals, because everything is useless.
20Both end up the same way; both came
from dust and both will go back to dust.
21Who can be sure that the human spirit
goes up to God and that the spirit of an
animal goes down into the ground? 22So I
saw that the best thing people can do is to
enjoy their work, because that is all they
have. No one can help another person
see what will happen in the future.

Is It Better to Be Dead?

4 Again I saw all the people who were
mistreated here on earth.
I saw their tears
and that they had no one to
comfort them.
Cruel people had all the power,
and there was no one to comfort
those they hurt.
2I decided that the dead
are better off than the living.
3But those who have never been
born
are better off still;
they have not seen the evil
that is done here on earth.

Why Work So Hard?

4I realized the reason people work
hard and try to succeed: They are jealous
of each other. This, too, is useless, like
chasing the wind.

5Some say it is foolish to fold your
hands and do nothing,
because you will starve to death.
6Maybe so, but I say it is better to be
content
with what little you have.
Otherwise, you will always be
struggling for more,
and that is like chasing the wind.

7Again I saw something here on earth
that was useless:
8I saw a man who had no family,
no son or brother.
He always worked hard
but was never satisfied with what
he had.

He never asked himself, "For whom
am I working so hard?
Why don't I let myself enjoy life?"
This also is very sad and useless.

Friends and Family Give Strength

9 Two people are better than one,
because they get more done by
working together.
10 If one falls down,
the other can help him up.
But it is bad for the person who is
alone and falls,
because no one is there to help.
11 If two lie down together, they will be
warm,
but a person alone will not be warm.
12 An enemy might defeat one person,
but two people together can defend
themselves;
a rope that is woven of three strings
is hard to break.

Fame and Power Are Useless

13 A poor but wise boy is better than a
foolish but old king who doesn't listen to
advice. 14 A boy became king. He had
been born poor in the kingdom and had
even gone to prison before becoming
king. 15 I watched all the people who live
on earth follow him and make him their
king. 16 Many followed him at first, but
later, they did not like him, either. So
fame and power are useless, like chasing
the wind.

Be Careful About Making Promises

5 Be careful when you go to worship at the Temple. It is better to listen than to offer foolish sacrifices without even knowing you are doing wrong.

2 Think before you speak,
and be careful about what you say
to God.
God is in heaven,
and you are on the earth,
so say only a few words to God.
3 The saying is true: Bad dreams come
from too much worrying,
and too many words come from
foolish people.

FAITH links

TWO ARE BETTER

ECCLESIASTES 4:9-12

What are the things you do to help your family or friends? God made us to need each other. Friends and family support each other by being there for each other. If your friends and family love God like you do, they can encourage you in your faith.

To earn a friend, you have to be a friend. You can do that by sharing with someone, helping that person, and offering words of encouragement.

Want a recipe for being a good friend? Link here:

Help for the Poor, Leviticus 5:7, p. 138

An Unsung Hero, Ruth 2:12, 15–16, p. 347

Show You Care, 2 Kings 4:10, p. 481

Some Friendly Advice, Proverbs 17:9, 14, 17, p. 851

How to Worship God, Isaiah 58, p. 972

An Encouraging Word, 1 Corinthians 1:3–5, p. 1545

4 If you make a promise to God, don't
be slow to keep it. God is not happy with
fools, so give God what you promised. 5 It
is better not to promise anything than to
promise something and not do it. 6 Don't
let your words cause you to sin, and don't
say to the priest at the Temple, "I didn't
mean what I promised." If you do, God
will become angry with your words and

will destroy everything you have worked
for. 7Many useless promises are like so
many dreams; they mean nothing. You
should respect God.

Officers Cheat Each Other

8In some places you will see poor
people mistreated. Don't be surprised
when they are not treated fairly or given
their rights. One officer is cheated by a
higher officer who in turn is cheated by
even higher officers. 9The wealth of the
country is divided up among them all.
Even the king makes sure he gets his
share of the profits.

Wealth Cannot Buy Happiness

10 Whoever loves money
will never have enough money;
Whoever loves wealth
will not be satisfied with it.
This is also useless.
11 The more wealth people have,
the more friends they have to help
spend it.
So what do people really gain?
They gain nothing except to look
at their riches.
12 Those who work hard sleep in peace;
it is not important if they eat little
or much.
But rich people worry about their
wealth
and cannot sleep.

13 I have seen real misery here on
earth:
Money saved is a curse to its owners.
14 They lose it all in a bad deal
and have nothing to give to their
children.
15 People come into this world with
nothing,
and when they die they leave with
nothing.
In spite of all their hard work,
they leave just as they came.
16 This, too, is real misery:
They leave just as they came.
So what do they gain from chasing
the wind?
17 All they get are days full of sadness
and sorrow,

FAITH links

WISDOM ABOUT WEALTH

ECCLESIASTES 5:10-12

Did you ever believe that all of your problems would be solved if your family just had a little more money? Maybe you believe that right now. Solomon was the wisest man in the world. He was also the richest at one time. Even though he had money, it didn't satisfy him.

The more money a person has, the more he or she wants. Want to be wise about money? Don't make it the center of your life.

Here are some more Faithlinks on handling your money:

Idol Talk, Exodus 32, p. 118

What I've Got, 2 Kings 20:12–17, p. 508

Gifts from the Heart, 1 Chronicles 29, p. 557

A Robbery in Progress, Malachi 3:8–10, p. 1270

Your Heart's Desire, Luke 16:13–15, p. 1401

More Money?, 1 Timothy 6:10, p. 1649

and they end up sick, defeated, and
angry.

Enjoy Your Life's Work

18I have seen what is best for people
here on earth. They should eat and drink
and enjoy their work, because the life

God has given them on earth is short.
19God gives some people the
ability to enjoy the
wealth and property
he gives them, as
well as the ability to
accept their state in
life and enjoy their
work. 20They do not worry about how
short life is, because God keeps them
busy with what they love to do.

eMAIL! FROM GOD
5:18–20
Hope
God says not to worry.

6 I have seen something else wrong
here on earth that causes serious
problems for people. 2God gives great
wealth, riches, and honor to some people; they have everything they want. But
God does not let them enjoy such things;
a stranger enjoys them instead. This is
useless and very wrong. 3A man might
have a hundred children and live a long
time, but what good is it if he can't enjoy
the good God gives him or have a proper
burial? I say a baby born dead is better off
than he is. 4A baby born dead is useless.
It returns to darkness without even a
name. 5That baby never saw the sun and
never knew anything, but it finds more
rest than that man. 6Even if he lives two
thousand years, he doesn't enjoy the
good God gives him. Everyone is going to
the same place.

7 People work just to feed themselves,
but they never seem to get enough
to eat.
8 In this way a wise person
is no better off than a fool.
Then, too, it does a poor person little
good
to know how to get along in life.
9 It is better to see what you have
than to want more.
Wanting more is useless–
like chasing the wind.

Who Can Understand God's Plan?

10 Whatever happens was planned long
ago.
Everyone knows what people are
like.
No one can argue with God,
who is stronger than anyone.
11 The more you say,
the more useless it is.
What good does it do?

12People have only a few useless days
of life on the earth; their short life passes
like a shadow. Who knows what is best
for them while they live? Who can tell
them what the future will bring?

Some Benefits of Serious Thinking

7 It is better to have respect than good
perfume.
The day of death is better than the
day of birth.
2 It is better to go to a funeral
than to a party.
We all must die,
and everyone living should think
about this.
3 Sorrow is better than laughter,
and sadness has a good influence
on you.
4 A wise person thinks about death,
but a fool thinks only about having
a good time.
5 It is better to be criticized by a wise
person
than to be praised by a fool.
6 The laughter of fools
is like the crackling of thorns in a
cooking fire.
Both are useless.

7 Even wise people are fools
if they let money change their
thinking.

8 It is better to finish something
than to start it.
It is better to be patient
than to be proud.
9 Don't become angry quickly,
because getting angry is foolish.

10 Don't ask, "Why was life better in
the 'good old days'?"
It is not wise to ask such
questions.

11 Wisdom is better when it comes with
money.
They both help those who are
alive.

WISE BOOKS

Ecclesiastes 7

The Israelite word for "wisdom" means "skill for living." There are a few books in the Bible that are all about wisdom: Job, Proverbs, Ecclesiastes, and some of the Psalms. In these books, we will find helpful advice on how to live our lives. We call these books the Wisdom Literature. The wisdom you'll find in these books is in three different forms:

1. proverbs, or short, little nuggets of truth;
2. riddles or stories with a spiritual meaning; and
3. discussions about the problems of life.

The Book of Proverbs is a book filled with nuggets of truth about attitudes and behaviors. Ecclesiastes is a discussion about how empty life is without God. (Check out Ecclesiastes 1:2, 14.) Job is a story about evil and suffering. (Read Job 28:20–28, p. 689.) Many of the Psalms talk about how to face the problems of life. (See Psalm 37:9, p. 737.)

12 Wisdom is like money:
they both help.
But wisdom is better,
because it can save whoever has it.

13 Look at what God has done:
No one can straighten what he has bent.
14 When life is good, enjoy it.
But when life is hard, remember:
God gives good times and hard times,
and no one knows what tomorrow will bring.

It Is Impossible to Be Truly Good

15 In my useless life I have seen both of these:
I have seen good people die in spite of their goodness
and evil people live a long time in spite of their evil.
16 Don't be too right,
and don't be too wise.
Why destroy yourself?
17 Don't be too wicked,
and don't be foolish.
Why die before your time?
18 It is good to grab the one and not let go of the other;
those who honor God will hold them both.

19 Wisdom makes a person stronger
than ten leaders in a city.

20 Surely there is not a good person on earth
who always does good and never sins.

21 Don't listen to everything people say,
or you might hear your servant insulting you.
22 You know that many times
you have insulted others.

23 I used wisdom to test all these things.
I wanted to be wise,
but it was too hard for me.
24 I cannot understand why things are as they are.

It is too hard for anyone to
understand.
25 I studied and tried very hard to find
wisdom,
to find some meaning for
everything.
I learned that it is foolish to be evil,
and it is crazy to act like a fool.

26 I found that some women are worse
than death
and are as dangerous as traps.
Their love is like a net,
and their arms hold men like
chains.
A man who pleases God will be saved
from them,
but a sinner will be caught by
them.

27 The Teacher says, "This is what I
learned:
I added all these things together
to find some meaning for
everything.
28 While I was searching,
I did not find one man among the
thousands I found.
Nor did I find a woman among all
these.
29 One thing I have learned:
God made people good,
but they have found all kinds of
ways to be bad."

Obey the King

8 No one is like the
wise person
who can understand
what things
mean.
Wisdom brings
happiness;
it makes sad faces
happy.

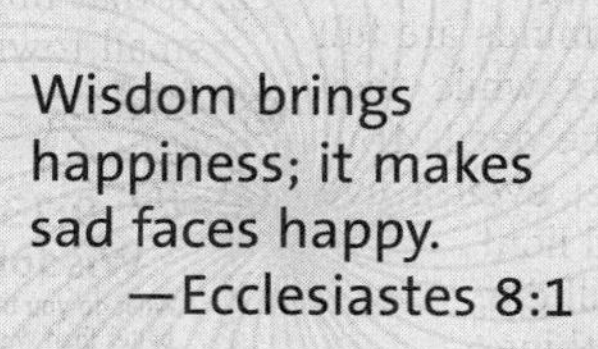
Wisdom brings
happiness; it makes
sad faces happy.
—Ecclesiastes 8:1

2Obey the king's com-
mand, because you made
a promise to God. 3Don't be too quick
to leave the king. Don't support something that is wrong, because the king
does whatever he pleases. 4What the
king says is law; no one tells him what
to do.
5 Whoever obeys the king's command
will be safe.
A wise person does the right thing
at the right time.
6 There is a right time and a right way
for everything,
yet people often have many
troubles.
7 They do not know what the future
holds,
and no one can tell them what will
happen.
8 No one can control the wind
or stop his own death.
No soldier is released in times of war,
and evil does not set free those
who do evil.

Justice, Rewards, and Punishment

9I saw all of this as I considered all
that is done here on earth. Sometimes
men harm those they control. 10I saw the
funerals of evil people who used to go in
and out of the holy place. They were honored in the same towns where they had
done evil. This is useless, too.
11When evil people are not punished
right away, it makes others want to do
evil, too. 12Though a sinner might do a
hundred evil things and might live a long
time, I know it will be better for those who
honor God. 13I also know it will not go
well for evil people, be-
cause they do not honor
God. Like a shadow, they
will not last. 14Some-
times something useless
happens on earth. Bad
things happen to good
people, and good things
happen to bad people. I
say that this is also useless. 15So I decided it was
more important to enjoy
life. The best that people
can do here on earth is to eat, drink, and
enjoy life, because these joys will help
them do the hard work God gives them
here on earth.

We Cannot Understand All God Does

16I tried to understand all that happens on earth. I saw how busy people are, working day and night and hardly ever sleeping. **17**I also saw all that God has done. Nobody can understand what God does here on earth. No matter how hard people try to understand it, they cannot. Even if wise people say they understand, they cannot; no one can really understand it.

Is Death Fair?

9 I thought about all this and tried to understand it. I saw that God controls good people and wise people and what they do, but no one knows if they will experience love or hate.

2 Good and bad people end up the same—
those who are right and those who are wrong,
those who are good and those who are evil,
those who are clean and those who are unclean,
those who sacrifice and those who do not.
The same things happen to a good person
as happen to a sinner,
to a person who makes promises to God
and to one who does not.

3This is something wrong that happens here on earth: What happens to one happens to all. So people's minds are full of evil and foolish thoughts while they live. After that, they join the dead. **4**But anyone still alive has hope; even a live dog is better off than a dead lion!

5 The living know they will die,
but the dead know nothing.
Dead people have no more reward,
and people forget them.
6 After people are dead,
they can no longer love or hate or envy.
They will never again share
in what happens here on earth.

Enjoy Life While You Can

7 So go eat your food and enjoy it;
drink your wine and be happy,
because that is what God wants you to do.
8 Put on nice clothes
and make yourself look good.

9Enjoy life with the wife you love. Enjoy all the useless days of this useless life God has given you here on earth, because it is all you have. So enjoy the work you do here on earth. **10**Whatever work you do, do your best, because you are going to the grave, where there is no working, no planning, no knowledge, and no wisdom.

Time and Chance

11 I also saw something else here on earth:
The fastest runner does not always win the race,
the strongest soldier does not always win the battle,
the wisest does not always have food,
the smartest does not always become wealthy,
and the talented one does not always receive praise.
Time and chance happen to everyone.
12 No one knows what will happen next.
Like a fish caught in a net,
or a bird caught in a trap,
people are trapped by evil
when it suddenly falls on them.

Wisdom Does Not Always Win

13I also saw something wise here on earth that impressed me. **14**There was a small town with only a few people in it. A great king fought against it and put his armies all around it. **15**Now there was a poor but wise man in the town who used his wisdom to save his town. But later on, everyone forgot about him. **16**I still think wisdom is better than strength. But those people forgot about the poor man's wisdom and stopped listening to what he said.

EMAIL! FROM GOD
9:13–18
Wisdom
What do you think is better than wisdom?

17 The quiet words of a wise person are better
than the shouts of a foolish ruler.
18 Wisdom is better than weapons of war,
but one sinner can destroy much good.

10 Dead flies can make even perfume stink.
In the same way, a little foolishness can spoil wisdom.
2 The heart of the wise leads to right,
but the heart of a fool leads to wrong.
3 Even in the way fools walk along the road,
they show they are not wise;
they show everyone how stupid they are.
4 Don't leave your job
just because your boss is angry with you.
Remaining calm solves great problems.

5 There is something else wrong that happens here on earth.
It is the kind of mistake rulers make:
6 Fools are given important positions
while gifted people are given lower ones;
7 I have seen servants ride horses
while princes walk like servants on foot.
8 Anyone who digs a pit might fall into it;
anyone who knocks down a wall
might be bitten by a snake;
9 anyone who moves boulders might be hurt by them;
and anyone who cuts logs might be harmed by them.
10 A dull ax means
harder work.
Being wise will make it easier.
11 If a snake bites the tamer before it is tamed,
what good is the tamer?

12 The words of the wise bring them praise,
but the words of a fool will destroy them.
13 A fool begins by saying foolish things
and ends by saying crazy and wicked things.
14 A fool talks too much.
No one knows the future,
and no one can tell what will happen after death.
15 Work wears fools out;
they don't even know how to get home.

The Value of Work

16 How terrible it is for a country
whose king is a child

FAITH CHALLENGE

Hey there! Read 10:20 to see what can happen when people talk about others behind their back. What would you do if you heard that someone was making fun of you behind your back? Why is it important to watch your words?

TESTING IT

Ecclesiastes 10:20
Don't make fun of the king, and don't make fun of rich people, even in your bedroom. A little bird might carry your words; a bird might fly and tell what you said.

and whose leaders eat all morning.
17 How lucky a country is whose king
comes from a good family,
whose leaders eat only at
mealtime
and for strength, not to get drunk.

18 If someone is lazy, the
roof will begin to
fall.
If he doesn't fix it,
the house will
leak.

19 A party makes you
feel good,
wine makes you
feel happy,
and money buys
anything.

20 Don't make fun of the king,
and don't make fun of rich people,
even in your bedroom.
A little bird might carry your words;
a bird might fly and tell what you
said.

Boldly Face the Future

11 Invest what you have,
because after a while you will get
a return.
2 Invest what you have in several
different businesses,
because you don't know what
disasters might happen.

3 If clouds are full of rain,
they will shower on the earth.
A tree can fall to the north or south,
but it will stay where it falls.
4 Those who wait for perfect weather
will never plant seeds;
those who look at every cloud
will never harvest crops.

5 You don't know where the wind will
blow,
and you don't know how a baby
grows inside the mother.
In the same way, you don't know
what God is doing,
or how he created everything.

Sunshine is sweet;
it is good to see the
light of day.
—Ecclesiastes 11:7

6 Plant early in the morning,
and work until evening,
because you don't know if this or that
will succeed.
They might both do well.

Serve God While You Are Young

7 Sunshine is sweet;
it is good to see the
light of day.
8 People ought to enjoy
every day of their
lives,
no matter how long
they live.
But they should also
remember this:
You will be dead a
long time.
Everything that
happens then is
useless.
9 Young people, enjoy yourselves while
you are young;
be happy while you are young.
Do whatever your heart desires,
whatever you want to do.
But remember that God will judge you
for everything you do.
10 Don't worry,
and forget the troubles of your
body,
because youth and childhood are
useless.

The Problems of Old Age

12 Remember your Creator
while you are young,
before the days of trouble come
and the years when you say,
"I find no pleasure in them."
2 When you get old,
the light from the sun, moon, and
stars will grow dark;
the rain clouds will never seem to
go away.
3 At that time your arms will shake
and your legs will become weak.
Your teeth will fall out so you cannot
chew,
and your eyes will not see clearly.
4 Your ears will be deaf to the noise in
the streets,

FAITH links

REMEMBER YOUR CREATOR

ECCLESIASTES 12:1, 13

If you learn a musical instrument or a foreign language when you're young, you'll have a better chance of being good at it and remembering it later. Why? Your brain is like a sponge. It soaks information up quickly. As you get older, learning new things gets harder. That's why Solomon advises you to remember your Creator while you are young. If you get to know God now, your faith will grow with you.

Listen Up!, 1 Kings 19:11–13, p. 467

More Precious Than Gold, Psalm 19:7–10, p. 723

Jesus' Mission and Yours, Isaiah 61:1–2, p. 978

The Writing's on the Wall, Daniel 5, p. 1159

The Best Advice, Zechariah 10:2, p. 1261

Prove It!, Matthew 16:1–4, p. 1302

and you will barely hear the
millstone grinding grain.
You'll wake up when a bird starts
singing,
but you will barely hear singing.

5 You will fear high places
and will be afraid to go for a walk.
Your hair will become white like the
flowers on an almond tree.
You will limp along like a
grasshopper when you walk.
Your appetite will be gone.
Then you will go to your everlasting
home,
and people will go to your funeral.

6 Soon your life will snap like a silver
chain
or break like a golden bowl.
You will be like a broken pitcher at a
spring,
or a broken wheel at a well.
7 You will turn back into the dust of the
earth again,
but your spirit will return to God
who gave it.

8 Everything is useless!
The Teacher says that everything
is useless.

Conclusion: Honor God

9 The Teacher was very wise and
taught the people what he knew. He very
carefully thought about, studied, and set
in order many wise teachings. 10 The
Teacher looked for just the right words to
write what is dependable and true.
11 Words from wise people are like
sharp sticks used to guide animals. They
are like nails that have been driven in
firmly. Altogether they are wise teachings that come from one Shepherd. 12 So
be careful, my son, about other teachings. People are always writing books,
and too much study will make you tired.
13 Now, everything has been heard,
so I give my final advice:
Honor God and obey his commands,
because this is all people must do.
14 God will judge everything,
even what is done in secret,
the good and the evil.

A SONG OF LOVE

Hi! I'm Solomon, king of the great nation of Israel. You probably already know that I asked God for wisdom and that he not only made me wise but fantastically wealthy as well. You may also know that I built the Temple of the Lord, a splendid building that was the center of worship for all of Israel. I was a powerful king, but I also had a private life. One day as I was traveling in the northern part of my kingdom, I met a beautiful young woman who was tending her vineyard. I loved her so much that I made her my bride. This book is a song describing the love we had for each other.

I wrote this book to let people know that marriage is a wonderful gift from God. God wants husbands and wives to share the joys—and the sorrows—of life together. They are to be faithful in their love for each other for the rest of their lives. Maybe one day you will be married and enjoy life with a special person.

JESUS WATCH

The Song of Solomon tells about the love that Solomon had for his bride, which is also a picture of the love that Jesus has for his church. In Ephesians 5, the church is described as the bride of Christ. Jesus is the head of the church and the savior of all who believe. Jesus loved the church so much that he gave up his life to make it holy and pure, like a bride. The church is to be faithful to Jesus and love only him. Someday all the members of the church will live forever with Jesus in heaven.

"Where did the bride work?"

Love for a Lifetime, Song of Solomon 6:8–9

"Not sure. Let's connect to Song of Solomon 1:5–7 to find out."

OTHER STUFF TO LOOK UP:

Apple (tree) of my eye, Song of Solomon 2:3–6
Springtime!, Song of Solomon 2:8–13
Moonstruck, Song of Solomon 6:10

1 Solomon's Greatest Song.

The Woman Speaks to the Man She Loves

2 Kiss me with the kisses of your mouth,
because your love is better than wine.
3 The smell of your perfume is pleasant,
and your name is pleasant like expensive perfume.
That's why the young women love you.
4 Take me with you; let's run together.
The king takes me into his rooms.

Friends Speak to the Man

We will rejoice and be happy with you;
we praise your love more than wine.
With good reason, the young women love you.

The Woman Speaks

5 I'm dark but lovely,
women of Jerusalem,
dark like the tents of Kedar,
like the curtains of Solomon.
6 Don't look at how dark I am,
at how dark the sun has made me.
My brothers were angry with me
and made me tend the vineyards,
so I haven't tended my own vineyard!
7 Tell me, you whom I love,
where do you feed your sheep?
Where do you let them rest at noon?
Why should I look for you near your friend's sheep,
like a woman who wears a veil?"

The Man Speaks to the Woman

8 You are the most beautiful of women.
Surely you know to follow the sheep
and feed your young goats
near the shepherds' tents.
9 My darling, you are like a mare
among the king's stallions.
10 Your cheeks are beautiful with ornaments,
and your neck with jewels.
11 We will make for you gold earrings
with silver hooks.

The Woman Speaks

12 The smell of my perfume spreads out
to the king on his couch.
13 My lover is like a bag of myrrh
that lies all night between my breasts.
14 My lover is like a bunch of flowers
from the vineyards at En Gedi.

The Man Speaks

15 My darling, you are beautiful!
Oh, you are beautiful,
and your eyes are like doves.

The Woman Answers the Man

16 You are so handsome, my lover,
and so pleasant!
Our bed is the grass.
17 Cedar trees form our roof;
our ceiling is made of juniper wood.

The Woman Speaks Again

2 I am a rose in the Plain of Sharon,
a lily in the valleys.

The Man Speaks Again

2 Among the young women, my darling
is like a lily among thorns!

The Woman Answers

3 Among the young men, my lover
is like an apple tree in the woods!
I enjoy sitting in his shadow;
his fruit is sweet to my taste.
4 He brought me to the banquet room,
and his banner over me is love.
5 Strengthen me with raisins,
and refresh me with apples,
because I am weak with love.
6 My lover's left hand is under my head,
and his right arm holds me tight.

1:7 veil This was the way a prostitute usually dressed.

The Woman Speaks to the Friends

7 Women of Jerusalem, promise me
by the gazelles and the deer
not to awaken
or excite my feelings of love
until it is ready.

The Woman Speaks Again

8 I hear my lover's voice.
Here he comes jumping across the mountains,
skipping over the hills.
9 My lover is like a gazelle or a young deer.
Look, he stands behind our wall
peeking through the windows,
looking through the blinds.
10 My lover spoke and said to me,
"Get up, my darling;
let's go away, my beautiful one.
11 Look, the winter is past;
the rains are over and gone.
12 Blossoms appear through all the land.
The time has come to sing;
the cooing of doves is heard in our land.
13 There are young figs on the fig trees,
and the blossoms on the vines smell sweet.
Get up, my darling;
let's go away, my beautiful one."

Blossoms appear
through all the land.
The time has come
to sing.
—Song of Solomon
2:12

The Man Speaks

14 My beloved is like a dove hiding in the cracks of the rock,
in the secret places of the cliff.
Show me your face,
and let me hear your voice.
Your voice is sweet,
and your face is lovely.
15 Catch the foxes for us—
the little foxes that ruin the vineyards
while they are in blossom.

The Woman Speaks

16 My lover is mine, and I am his.
He feeds among the lilies
17 until the day dawns
and the shadows disappear.
Turn, my lover.
Be like a gazelle or a young deer
on the mountain valleys.

The Woman Dreams

3 At night on my bed,
I looked for the one I love;
I looked for him, but I could not find him.
2 I got up and went around the city,
in the streets and squares,
looking for the one I love.
I looked for him, but I could not find him.
3 The watchmen found me as they patrolled the city,
so I asked, "Have you seen the one I love?"
4 As soon as I had left them,
I found the one I love.
I held him and would not let him go
until I brought him to my mother's house,
to the room where I was born.

The Woman Speaks to the Friends

5 Women of Jerusalem, promise me
by the gazelles and the deer
not to awaken
or excite my feelings of love
until it is ready.
6 Who is this coming out of the desert
like a cloud of smoke?
Who is this that smells like myrrh, incense,
and other spices?
7 Look, it's Solomon's couch[n]
with sixty soldiers around it,
the finest soldiers of Israel.

3:7 couch Something like a bed carried by slaves on which the king lay or sat while traveling.

8 These soldiers all carry swords
and have been trained in war.
Every man wears a sword at his side
and is ready for the dangers of the night.
9 King Solomon had a couch made for himself
of wood from Lebanon.
10 He made its posts of silver
and its braces of gold.
The seat was covered with purple cloth
that the women of Jerusalem wove with love.
11 Women of Jerusalem, go out and see King Solomon.
He is wearing the crown his mother put on his head
on his wedding day,
when his heart was happy!

The Man Speaks to the Woman

4 How beautiful you are, my darling!
Oh, you are beautiful!
Your eyes behind your veil are like doves.
Your hair is like a flock of goats
streaming down Mount Gilead.
2 Your teeth are white like newly sheared sheep
just coming from their bath.
Each one has a twin,
and none of them is missing.
3 Your lips are like red silk thread,
and your mouth is lovely.
Your cheeks behind your veil
are like slices of a pomegranate.
4 Your neck is like David's tower,
built with rows of stones.
A thousand shields hang on its walls;
each shield belongs to a strong soldier.
5 Your breasts are like two fawns,
like twins of a gazelle,
feeding among the lilies.
6 Until the day dawns
and the shadows disappear,
I will go to that mountain of myrrh
and to that hill of incense.
7 My darling, everything about you is beautiful,
and there is nothing at all wrong with you.
8 Come with me from Lebanon, my bride.
Come with me from Lebanon,
from the top of Mount Amana,
from the tops of Mount Senir and Mount Hermon.
Come from the lions' dens
and from the leopards' hills.
9 My sister, my bride,
you have thrilled my heart;
you have thrilled my heart
with a glance of your eyes,
with one sparkle from your necklace.
10 Your love is so sweet, my sister, my bride.
Your love is better than wine,
and your perfume smells better than any spice.
11 My bride, your lips drip honey;
honey and milk are under your tongue.
Your clothes smell like the cedars of Lebanon.
12 My sister, my bride, you are like a garden locked up,
like a walled-in spring, a closed-up fountain.
13 Your limbs are like an orchard
of pomegranates with all the best fruit,
filled with flowers and nard,
14 nard and saffron, calamus, and cinnamon,
with trees of incense, myrrh, and aloes—
all the best spices.
15 You are like a garden fountain—
a well of fresh water
flowing down from the mountains of Lebanon.

The Woman Speaks

16 Awake, north wind.
Come, south wind.
Blow on my garden,
and let its sweet smells flow out.
Let my lover enter the garden
and eat its best fruits.

The Man Speaks

5 I have entered my garden, my sister, my bride.

I have gathered my myrrh with my
spice.
I have eaten my honeycomb and my
honey.
I have drunk my wine and my milk.

The Friends Speak

Eat, friends, and drink;
yes, drink deeply, lovers.

The Woman Dreams

2 I sleep, but my heart is awake.
I hear my lover knocking.
"Open to me, my sister, my darling,
my dove, my perfect one.
My head is wet with dew,
and my hair with the dampness of
the night."
3 I have taken off my garment
and don't want to put it on again.
I have washed my feet
and don't want to get them dirty
again.
4 My lover put his hand through the
opening,
and I felt excited inside.
5 I got up to open the door for my
lover.
Myrrh was dripping from my hands
and flowing from my fingers,
onto the handles of the lock.
6 I opened the door for my lover,
but my lover had left and was
gone.
When he spoke, he took my breath
away.
I looked for him, but I could not find
him;
I called for him, but he did not
answer.
7 The watchmen found me
as they patrolled the city.
They hit me and hurt me;
the guards on the wall took away
my veil.
8 Promise me, women of Jerusalem,
if you find my lover,
tell him I am weak with love.

The Friends Answer the Woman

9 How is your lover better than other
lovers,
most beautiful of women?
How is your lover better than other
lovers?
Why do you want us to promise
this?

The Woman Answers the Friends

10 My lover is healthy and tan,
the best of ten thousand men.
11 His head is like the finest gold;
his hair is wavy and black like a
raven.
12 His eyes are like doves
by springs of water.
They seem to be bathed in cream
and are set like jewels.
13 His cheeks are like beds of spices;
they smell like mounds of
perfume.
His lips are like lilies
flowing with myrrh.
14 His hands are like gold hinges,
filled with jewels.
His body is like shiny ivory
covered with sapphires.
15 His legs are like large marble posts,
standing on bases of fine gold.
He is like a cedar of Lebanon,
like the finest of the trees.
16 His mouth is sweet to kiss,
and I desire him very much.
Yes, daughters of Jerusalem,
this is my lover
and my friend.

The Friends Speak to the Woman

6 Where has your lover gone,
most beautiful of women?
Which way did your lover turn?
We will look for him with you.

The Woman Answers the Friends

2 My lover has gone down to his
garden,
to the beds of spices,
to feed in the gardens
and to gather lilies.
3 I belong to my lover,
and my lover belongs to me.
He feeds among the lilies.

The Man Speaks to the Woman

4 My darling, you are as beautiful as
the city of Tirzah,

LOVE FOR A LIFETIME

SONG OF SOLOMON 6:8-9

Who in your family has been married the longest? Part of loving someone involves making a commitment to that person. When two people decide to marry, they agree to be faithful to each other. The vows they say at their wedding are a public sign of their commitment to each other.

God helps a person to make a commitment and stick to it, even through hard times. Maybe you can't imagine being married right now. But you've certainly seen the results of a committed marriage. You can begin learning to make commitments to others by the way you treat your friends and family.

Connect to these Faithlinks for more thoughts on being a part of a family:

Fatherly Advice, Exodus 18, p. 99

Yours, Mine, and Ours?, 1 Samuel 25, p. 389

A Parent's Advice, Proverbs 1:8–9, p. 825

A Broken Promise, Jeremiah 2:1–8, p. 989

A Friend of Jesus, John 15:9–17, p. 1450

MVFM?, Galatians 3:26–27, p. 1589

as lovely as the city of Jerusalem,
like an army flying flags.
5 Turn your eyes from me,
because they excite me too much.
Your hair is like a flock of goats
streaming down Mount Gilead.
6 Your teeth are white like sheep
just coming from their bath;
each one has a twin,
and none of them is missing.
7 Your cheeks behind your veil
are like slices of a pomegranate.
8 There may be sixty queens and eighty slave women
and so many girls you cannot count them,
9 but there is only one like my dove,
my perfect one.
She is her mother's only daughter,
the brightest of the one who gave her birth.
The young women saw her and called her happy;
the queens and the slave women also praised her.

The Young Women Praise the Woman

10 Who is that young woman
that shines out like the dawn?
She is as pretty as the moon,
as bright as the sun,
as wonderful as an army flying flags.

The Man Speaks

11 I went down into the orchard of nut trees
to see the blossoms of the valley,
to look for buds on the vines,
to see if the pomegranate trees had bloomed.
12 Before I realized it, my desire for you made me feel
like a prince in a chariot.

The Friends Call to the Woman

13 Come back, come back, woman of Shulam.
Come back, come back,
so we may look at you!

The Woman Answers the Friends

Why do you want to look at the
woman of Shulam
as you would at the dance of two
armies?

The Man Speaks to the Woman

7 Your feet are beautiful in sandals,
you daughter of a prince.
Your round thighs are like jewels
shaped by an artist.
2 Your navel is like a round drinking
cup
always filled with wine.
Your stomach is like a pile of wheat
surrounded with lilies.
3 Your breasts are like two fawns,
like twins of a gazelle.
4 Your neck is like an ivory tower.
Your eyes are like the pools in
Heshbon
near the gate of Bath Rabbim.
Your nose is like the mountain of
Lebanon
that looks down on Damascus.
5 Your head is like Mount Carmel,
and your hair is like purple cloth;
the king is captured in its folds.
6 You are beautiful and pleasant;
my love, you are full of delights.
7 You are tall like a palm tree,
and your breasts are like its
bunches of fruit.
8 I said, "I will climb up the palm tree
and take hold of its fruit."
Let your breasts be like bunches of
grapes,
the smell of your breath like apples,
9 and your mouth like the best wine.

The Woman Speaks to the Man

Let this wine go down sweetly for
my lover;
may it flow gently past the lips and
teeth.
10 I belong to my lover,
and he desires only me.
11 Come, my lover,
let's go out into the country
and spend the night in the fields.
12 Let's go early to the vineyards
and see if the buds are on the
vines.
Let's see if the blossoms have
already opened
and if the pomegranates have
bloomed.
There I will give you my love.
13 The mandrake flowers give their
sweet smell,
and all the best fruits are at our
gates.
I have saved them for you, my lover,
the old delights and the new.

8 I wish you were like my brother
who fed at my mother's breasts.
If I found you outside,
I would kiss you,
and no one would look down on
me.
2 I would lead you and bring you
to my mother's house;
she is the one who taught me.
I would give you a drink of spiced
wine
from my pomegranates.

The Woman Speaks to the Friends

3 My lover's left hand is under my
head,
and his right arm holds me tight.
4 Women of Jerusalem,
promise not to awaken
or excite my feelings of love
until it is ready.

The Friends Speak

5 Who is this coming out of the desert,
leaning on her lover?

The Man Speaks to the Woman

I woke you under the apple tree
where you were born;
there your mother gave birth to
you.
6 Put me like a seal on your heart,
like a seal on your arm.
Love is as strong as death;
jealousy is as strong as the grave.
Love bursts into flames
and burns like a hot fire.
7 Even much water cannot put out the
flame of love;
floods cannot drown love.

If a man offered everything in his
house for love,
people would totally reject it.

The Woman's Brothers Speak

8 We have a little sister,
and her breasts are not yet grown.
What should we do for our sister
on the day she becomes engaged?
9 If she is a wall,
we will put silver
towers on her.
If she is a door,
we will protect her
with cedar boards.

The Woman Speaks

10 I am a wall,
and my breasts are
like towers.
So I was to him,
as one who brings happiness.
11 Solomon had a vineyard at Baal
Hamon.
He rented the vineyards for others
to tend,
and everyone who rented had to pay
twenty-five pounds of silver for the
fruit.
12 But my own vineyard is mine to
give.
Solomon, the twenty-five pounds
of silver are for you,
and five pounds are for those who
tend the fruit.

Put me like a seal on your heart, like a seal on your arm.
—Song of Solomon 8:6

The Man Speaks to the Woman

13 You who live in the
gardens,
my friends are
listening for your
voice;
let me hear it.

The Woman Speaks to the Man

14 Hurry, my lover,
be like a gazelle
or a young deer
on the mountains where spices
grow.

BURNING COALS ON THE LIPS

Hello! I am Isaiah, prophet of God. Would you like to see a picture of heaven? God gave me this picture of heaven when he called me to be his messenger. I saw the Lord sitting on a very high throne with heavenly creatures of fire all around him. The creatures had six wings and they called "Holy, holy, holy." One of the creatures touched my mouth with a hot coal. Why? You better surf on over to Isaiah 6 to find out.

I wrote this book to tell people to stop worshiping idols and turn back to God. I urged them to trust in the power of God, not in friendships with other nations. The people of Israel did not follow God's laws, so God allowed the king of Assyria to conquer them. The southern kingdom of Judah would have been conquered, too, but good King Hezekiah wisely asked God for help. Check out Isaiah 37:14–20 for this important prayer.

JESUS WATCH

Even though he lived 700 years before Jesus was born, Isaiah told us many things about Jesus, the promised Messiah. In Isaiah 9, we learn the Messiah will be born into the family of David and that he will rule as king on David's throne. His kingdom will be strong for he will rule with justice and goodness. The Messiah will be a great leader and will have the following names: Wonderful Counselor, Powerful God, Father Who Lives Forever, Prince of Peace. Jesus is not only our king; but he also is our savior. In Isaiah 53, we find a picture of Jesus as the sacrifice for our sins. He was willing to die so that we can have eternal life in heaven. Jesus knew that much of the Book of Isaiah was about him. During his ministry, Jesus quoted passages from Isaiah to announce that he was the long-awaited Messiah.

my FAVORITE links

_______________ _______________

_______________ _______________

_______________ _______________

_______________ _______________

OTHER CONNECTIONS

Livin' it Try it, you'll like it! Sounds pretty harmless, but temptation often starts with something small and then grows into something big. Check out how to handle those trying times by linking to Go Ahead; Try It, Isaiah 33:15–16.

What frightens you? You can find some practical advice on what to do when your fears try to get the better of you by connecting to Scared to Death!, Isaiah 43:1–2.

Do you think your sin problem is not so bad? It only takes a little sin to separate us from God. But God has the best sin-cleaner in the world. Discover what it is by logging onto Covered with Mud!, Isaiah 59:12–13.

GET THE INFO

The Egyptians play an important role in Bible history. Check out some cool facts about these amazing ancient people by connecting to Who Are the Egyptians?, Isaiah 30:2–5.

"Here's one for you, Tagg. What good are false gods?"

"Well, Skweek, they seem pretty useless to me. Let's plug into Isaiah 44:9–20 to find out what God had to say about this."

did you know?

HAVE YOU HEARD ABOUT . . .

Whispering fortune-tellers, Isaiah 8:19–20
God's greatest gift, Isaiah 9:6–7
Party time!, Isaiah 25:6–12
A happy desert, Isaiah 35
Get ready!, Isaiah 40

FAITH links

- The Problem with Pride, Isaiah 2:11
- Dirty Inside, Isaiah 6:1–7
- What's in a Name?, Isaiah 9:6
- World News, Isaiah 13—19
- The Foundation of Our Hope, Isaiah 31:1–8
- Fly Like an Eagle, Isaiah 40:28–31
- A Useless Thing, Isaiah 44:9, 18–20
- The One Who Suffered, Isaiah 53
- What God Thinks, Isaiah 55:8–9
- Jesus' Mission and Yours, Isaiah 61:1–2

1 This is the vision Isaiah son of Amoz saw about what would happen to Judah and Jerusalem. Isaiah saw these things while Uzziah, Jotham, Ahaz, and Hezekiah were kings of Judah.

God's Case Against His Children

2 Heaven and earth, listen,
because the LORD is speaking:
"I raised my children and helped them grow up,
but they have turned against me.
3 An ox knows its master,
and a donkey knows where its owner feeds it,
but the people of Israel do not know me;
my people do not understand."

4 How terrible! Israel is a nation of sin,
a people loaded down with guilt,
a group of children doing evil,
children who are full of evil.
They have left the LORD;
they hate God, the Holy One of Israel,
and have turned away from him as if he were a stranger.

5 Why should you continue to be punished?
Why do you continue to turn against him?
Your whole head is hurt,
and your whole heart is sick.
6 There is no healthy spot
from the bottom of your foot to the top of your head;
you are covered with wounds, hurts, and open sores
that are not cleaned and covered,
and no medicine takes away the pain.

7 Your land is ruined;
your cities have been burned with fire.
While you watch,
your enemies are stealing everything from your land;
it is ruined like a country destroyed by enemies.
8 Jerusalem is left alone

FAITH links

RED TO WHITE 

ISAIAH 1:18

Think about the color red. If you've ever spilled red paint or tomato sauce on your clothes, you know that kind of stain is difficult to wash out. Now picture a blanket of newly fallen snow. If you've never seen actual snow before because you live in a warm climate, know this: snow covers everything. It can turn a brown and green world into a soft, cottony white one. When you do something wrong, your sin is like the tomato sauce stain—very noticeable. God's forgiveness can make it the color of newly fallen snow. In other words, he can make it disappear. All you have to do is ask for his forgiveness.

Link here for other thoughts on our sin problem:

A Priest Without Sin, Leviticus 4:3–7, p. 136

The Cover-up, Psalm 32:1–2, p. 733

Our Awesome God, Ezekiel 1:26–28, p. 1087

The God of Second Chances, Jonah 3, p. 1215

A High Price, Romans 6:23, p. 1526

The Sin "Braker," Jude 24–25, p. 1727

like an empty shelter in a vineyard,
like a hut left in a field of melons,
like a city surrounded by enemies.
9 The LORD All-Powerful
allowed a few of our people to live.
Otherwise we would have been completely destroyed
like the cities of Sodom and Gomorrah.

10 Jerusalem, your rulers are like those of Sodom,
and your people are like those of Gomorrah.
Hear the word of the LORD;
listen to the teaching of our God!
11 The LORD says,
"I do not want all these sacrifices.
I have had enough of your burnt sacrifices
of male sheep and fat from fine animals.
I am not pleased
by the blood of bulls, lambs, and goats.
12 You come to meet with me,
but who asked you to do
all this running in and out of my Temple's rooms?
13 Don't continue bringing me worthless sacrifices!
I hate the incense you burn.
I can't stand your New Moons,
Sabbaths, and other feast days;
I can't stand the evil you do in your holy meetings.
14 I hate your New Moon feasts
and your other yearly feasts.
They have become a heavy weight on me,
and I am tired of carrying it.
15 When you raise your arms to me in prayer,
I will refuse to look at you.
Even if you say many prayers,
I will not listen to you,
because your hands are full of blood.
16 Wash yourselves and make yourselves clean.
Stop doing the evil things I see you do.
Stop doing wrong.
17 Learn to do good.
Seek justice.
Punish those who hurt others.
Help the orphans.
Stand up for the rights of widows."

18 The LORD says,
"Come, let us talk about these things.
Though your sins are like scarlet,
they can be as white as snow.
Though your sins are deep red,
they can be white like wool.
19 If you become willing and obey me,
you will eat good crops from the land.
20 But if you refuse to obey and if you turn against me,
you will be destroyed by your enemies' swords."
The LORD himself said these things.

Jerusalem Is Not Loyal to God

21 The city of Jerusalem once followed the LORD,
but she is no longer loyal to him.
She used to be filled with fairness;
people there lived the way God wanted.
But now, murderers live there.
22 Jerusalem, you have become like the scum left when silver is purified;
you are like wine mixed with water.
23 Your rulers are rebels
and friends of thieves.
They all accept money for doing wrong,
and they are paid to cheat people.
They don't seek justice for the orphans
or listen to the widows' needs.
24 So the Lord GOD All-Powerful,
the Mighty One of Israel, says:
"You, my enemies, will not cause me any more trouble.
I will pay you back for what you did.
25 I will turn against you
and clean away all your wrongs as if with soap;
I will take all the worthless things out of you.
26 I will bring back judges as you had long ago;

your counselors will be like those
you had in the beginning.
Then you will be called the City That
Is Right with God,
the Loyal City."

27 By doing what is fair,
Jerusalem will be free again.
By doing what is right,
her people who come back to the
LORD will have freedom.
28 But sinners and those who turn
against him will be destroyed;
those who have left the LORD will
die.

29 "You will be ashamed,
because you have worshiped gods
under the oak trees.
You will be disgraced,
because you have worshiped idols
in your gardens.
30 You will be like an oak whose leaves
are dying
or like a garden without water.
31 Powerful people will be like small,
dry pieces of wood,
and their works will be like sparks.
They will burn together,
and no one will be able to put out
that fire."

The Message About Jerusalem

2 Isaiah son of Amoz saw this message
about Judah and Jerusalem:
2 In the last days
the mountain on which the LORD's
Temple stands
will become the most important of
all mountains.
It will be raised above the hills,
and people from all nations will
come streaming to it.
3 Many nations will come and say,
"Come, let us go up to the
mountain of the LORD,
to the Temple of the God of Jacob.
Then God will teach us his ways,
and we will obey his teachings."
His teachings will go out from
Jerusalem;
the message of the LORD will go
out from Jerusalem.
4 He will settle arguments among the
nations
and will make decisions for many
nations.
Then they will make their swords
into plows

FAITH links

THE PROBLEM WITH PRIDE

ISAIAH 2:11

A look can mean a lot. When someone rolls her eyes, that can mean, "Get real." You may have even flashed one of your parents a look that inspired him to say, "Don't give me that look."

There's a certain look that the prophet Isaiah wrote about: a proud look. A proud look isn't always a kind of nose-in-the-air look. A person could have no expression at all and still be proud. Pride starts in the heart. It's when you feel that no one is better than you. The opposite of pride is humility. God plans to humble those who are proud.

The Weak Link, Judges 16, p. 334

Mourning for an Enemy, 2 Samuel 1, p. 399

Help for the Outsiders, Nehemiah 5:9–10, p. 630

Fear God or People?, Jeremiah 38:14–21, p. 1047

The "Eyes" Have It?, 1 Corinthians 12, p. 1559

The Sacrifice of Service, Philippians 2:17, 25–30, p. 1612

and their spears into hooks for
trimming trees.
Nations will no longer fight other
nations,
nor will they train for war
anymore.

5 Come, family of Jacob,
and let us follow the way of the
LORD.

A Terrible Day Is Coming

6 LORD, you have left your people,
the family of Jacob,
because they have become filled with
wrong ideas from people in the
East.
They try to tell the future like the
Philistines,
and they have completely accepted
those foreign ideas.
7 Their land has been filled with silver
and gold;
there are a great many treasures
there.
Their land has been filled with
horses;
there are many chariots there.
8 Their land is full of idols.
The people worship these idols
they made with their own hands
and shaped with their own fingers.
9 People will not be proud any longer
but will bow low with shame.
God, do not forgive them.

10 Go into the caves of the cliffs;
dig holes and hide in the ground
from the anger of the LORD
and from his great power!
11 Proud people will be made humble,
and they will bow low with shame.
At that time only the LORD will still
be praised.

12 The LORD All-Powerful has a certain
day planned
when he will punish the proud and
those who brag,
and they will no longer be
important.
13 He will bring down the tall cedar
trees from Lebanon
and the great oak trees of Bashan,
14 all the tall mountains
and the high hills,
15 every tall tower
and every high, strong wall,
16 all the trading ships
and the beautiful ships.
17 At that time proud people will be
made humble,
and they will bow low with shame.
At that time only the LORD will be
praised,
18 but all the idols will be gone.

19 People will run to caves in the rocky
cliffs
and will dig holes and hide in the
ground
from the anger of the LORD
and his great power,
when he stands to shake the
earth.
20 At that time people will throw away
their gold and silver idols,
which they made for themselves to
worship;
they will throw them away to the
bats and moles.
21 Then the people will hide in caves
and cracks in the rocks
from the anger of the LORD
and his great power,
when he stands to shake the earth.

22 You should stop trusting in people to
save you,
because people are only human;
they aren't able to help you.

God Will Punish Judah and Jerusalem

3 Understand this:
The Lord GOD All-Powerful
will take away everything Judah and
Jerusalem need—
all the food and water,
2 the heroes and great soldiers,
the judges and prophets,
people who do magic and older
leaders,
3 the military leaders and government
leaders,
the counselors, the skilled

craftsmen, and those who try to
tell the future.
4 The LORD says, "I will cause young
boys to be your leaders,
and foolish children will rule over
you.
5 People will be against each other;
everyone will be against his
neighbor.
Young people will not respect older
people,
and common people will not
respect important people."
6 At that time a man will grab one of
his brothers
from his own family and say,
"You have a coat, so you will be our
leader.
These ruins will be under your
control."
7 But that brother will stand up and
say,
"I cannot help you,
because I do not have food or clothes
in my house.
You will not make me your leader."
8 This will happen because Jerusalem
has stumbled,
and Judah has fallen.
The things they say
and do are
against the
LORD;
they turn against
him.
9 The look on their
faces shows they
are guilty;
like the people of
Sodom, they are
proud of their
sin.
They don't care who sees it.
How terrible it will be for them,
because they have brought much
trouble on themselves.
10 Tell those who do what is right that
things will go well for them,
because they will receive a reward
for what they do.
11 But how terrible it will be for the
wicked!
They will be punished for all the
wrong they have done.
12 Children treat my people cruelly,
and women rule over them.
My people, your guides lead you in
the wrong way
and turn you away from what is
right.

13 The LORD takes his place in court
and stands to judge the people.
14 The LORD presents his case
against the older leaders and other
leaders of his people:
"You have burned the vineyard.
Your houses are full of what you
took from the poor.
15 What gives you the right to crush my
people
and grind the faces of the poor into
the dirt?"
The Lord GOD All-Powerful says
this.

> Tell those who do what is right that things will go well for them.
> —Isaiah 3:10

A Warning to Women of Jerusalem

16 The LORD says,
"The women of Jerusalem are
proud.
They walk around
with their heads
held high,
and they flirt with
their eyes.
They take quick,
short steps,
making noise with
their ankle
bracelets."
17 So the Lord will put
sores on the
heads of those
women in
Jerusalem,
and he will make them lose their
hair.
18 At that time the Lord will take away
everything that makes them proud: their
beautiful ankle bracelets, their headbands, their necklaces shaped like the
moon, 19 their earrings, bracelets, and
veils, 20 their scarves, ankle chains, the
cloth belts worn around their waists,

their bottles of perfume, and charms,
21their signet rings, nose rings, 22their
fine robes, capes, shawls, and purses,
23their mirrors, linen dresses, turbans,
and long shawls.

24 Instead of wearing sweet-smelling
perfume, they will stink.
Instead of fine cloth belts, they will
wear the ropes of captives.
Instead of having their hair fixed in
fancy ways, they will be bald.
Instead of fine clothes, they will
wear clothes of sadness.
Instead of being beautiful, they will
wear the brand of a captive.

25 At that time your men will be killed
with swords,
and your heroes will die in war.
26 There will be crying and sadness
near the city gates.
Jerusalem will be like a woman
who has lost everything and sits
on the ground.

4 At that time seven women
will grab one man
and say, "We will eat our own bread
and make our own clothes,
but please marry us!
Please, take away our shame."

CONNECT 2-YOU

THE B-I-B-L-E

Tagg and I are talking about our favorite verses from God's Word. A friend of ours has something different to say about the Bible. Let's welcome Brian, age 11, to Connect 2-You.

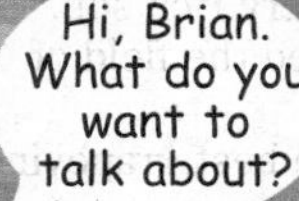

Hi, Brian. What do you want to talk about?

Brian

Well, I'm kind of embarrassed to admit it, but I really don't understand the Bible. It's okay when someone tells a story from it, but when I read it on my own, nothing really makes sense. Do you think the Bible is written for kids?

Some Bibles, like the one you're holding in your hands, are. That's why it's important to find a version of the Bible that works for you. It's also important to pray before you read the Bible and ask God to help you understand what you're reading. For some other tips on understanding the Bible, check out the Livin' It page on studying God's Word, Psalm 119:12–18, p. 801.

Nothing brings us closer to God than reading and understanding his Word. If you try to read a version of the Bible that you can't understand, you don't know what you're missing.

The Branch of the Lord

2At that time the LORD's branch will
be very beautiful and great. The people
still living in Israel will be proud of what
the land grows. 3Those who are still living in Jerusalem will be called holy; their
names are recorded among the living in
Jerusalem. 4The Lord will wash away the
filth from the women of Jerusalem. He
will wash the bloodstains out of Jerusalem and clean the city with the spirit of
fairness and the spirit of fire. 5Then the
LORD will cover Mount Zion and the people who meet there with a cloud of smoke
during the day and with a bright, flaming
fire at night. There will be a covering
over every person. 6This covering will
protect the people from the heat of the
sun and will provide a safe place to hide
from the storm and rain.

Israel, the Lord's Vineyard

5 Now I will sing for my friend a song
about his vineyard.
My friend had a vineyard
on a hill with very rich soil.
2 He dug and cleared the field of
stones
and planted the best grapevines
there.
He built a tower in the middle of it
and cut out a winepress as well.
He hoped good grapes would grow
there,
but only bad ones grew.

3 My friend says, "You people living in
Jerusalem,
and you people of Judah,
judge between me and my
vineyard.
4 What more could I have done for my
vineyard
than I have already done?
Although I expected good grapes to
grow,
why were there only bad ones?
5 Now I will tell you
what I will do to my vineyard:
I will remove the hedge,
and it will be burned.
I will break down the stone wall,
and it will be walked on.
6 I will ruin my field.
It will not be trimmed or hoed,
and weeds and thorns will grow
there.
I will command the clouds
not to rain on it."

7 The vineyard belonging to the LORD
All-Powerful
is the nation of Israel;
the garden that he loves
is the people of Judah.
He looked for justice, but there was
only killing.
He hoped for right living, but there
were only cries of pain.

8 How terrible it will be for you who
add more houses to your
houses
and more
fields to
your fields
until there is no
room left for
other people.
Then you are
left alone in the land.

EMAIL FROM GOD 5:8
Greed
What's wrong with greed?

9The LORD All-Powerful said this to
me:
"The fine houses will be destroyed;
the large and beautiful houses will
be left empty.
10 At that time a ten-acre vineyard will
make only six gallons of wine,
and ten bushels of seed will grow
only half a bushel of grain."

11 How terrible it will be for people who
rise early in the morning
to look for strong drink,
who stay awake late at night,
becoming drunk with wine.
12 At their parties they have lyres,
harps,
tambourines, flutes, and wine.
They don't see what the LORD has
done
or notice the work of his hands.
13 So my people will be captured and
taken away,
because they don't really
know me.

All the great people will die of hunger,
and the common people will die of thirst.
14 So the place of the dead wants more and more people,
and it opens wide its mouth.
Jerusalem's important people and common people will go down into it,
with their happy and noisy ones.
15 So the common people and the great people will be brought down;
those who are proud will be humbled.
16 The LORD All-Powerful will receive glory by judging fairly;
the holy God will show himself holy by doing what is right.
17 Then the sheep will go anywhere they want,
and lambs will feed on the land that rich people once owned.

18 How terrible it will be for those people!
They pull their guilt and sins behind them
as people pull wagons with ropes.
19 They say, "Let God hurry;
let him do his work soon
so we may see it.
Let the plan of the Holy One of Israel happen soon
so that we will know what it is."

20 How terrible it will be for people who call good things bad
and bad things good,
who think darkness is light
and light is darkness,
who think sour is sweet
and sweet is sour.

21 How terrible it will be for people who think they are wise
and believe they are clever.

22 How terrible it will be for people who are famous for drinking wine
and are champions at mixing drinks.
23 They take money to set the guilty free
and don't allow good people to be judged fairly.
24 They will be destroyed
just as fire burns straw or dry grass.
They will be destroyed
like a plant whose roots rot
and whose flower dies and blows away like dust.
They have refused to obey the teachings of the LORD All-Powerful
and have hated the message from the Holy God of Israel.
25 So the LORD has become very angry with his people,
and he has raised his hand to punish them.
Even the mountains are frightened.
Dead bodies lie in the streets like garbage.

But the LORD is still angry;
his hand is still raised to strike down the people.

26 He raises a banner for the nations far away.
He whistles to call those people from the ends of the earth.
Look! The enemy comes quickly!
27 Not one of them becomes tired or falls down.
Not one of them gets sleepy and falls asleep.
Their weapons are close at hand,
and their sandal straps are not broken.
28 Their arrows are sharp,
and all of their bows are ready to shoot.
The horses' hoofs are hard as rocks,
and their chariot wheels move like a whirlwind.
29 Their shout is like the roar of a lion;
it is loud like a young lion.
They growl as they grab their captives.
There is no one to stop them from taking their captives away.
30 On that day they will roar
like the waves of the sea.
And when people look at the land,

they will see only darkness and
pain;
all light will become dark in this
thick cloud.

Isaiah Becomes a Prophet

6 In the year that King Uzziah died, I
saw the Lord sitting on a very high
throne. His long robe filled the Temple.
2Heavenly creatures of fire stood above
him. Each creature had six wings: It used
two wings to cover
its face, two wings
to cover its feet, and
two wings for flying.
3Each creature was
calling to the others:

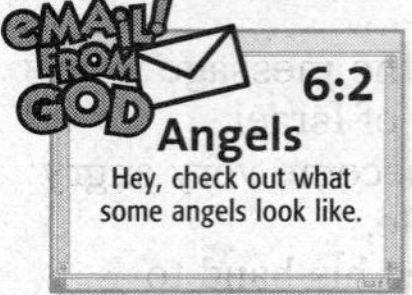

EMAIL! FROM GOD
6:2
Angels
Hey, check out what some angels look like.

"Holy, holy, holy is the LORD All-
Powerful.
His glory fills the whole earth."
4Their calling caused the frame around
the door to shake, as the Temple filled
with smoke.
5I said, "Oh, no! I will be destroyed. I
am not pure, and I live among people who
are not pure, but I have seen the King,
the LORD All-Powerful."
6One of the heavenly creatures used a
pair of tongs to take a hot coal from the
altar. Then he flew to me with the hot
coal in his hand. 7The creature touched
my mouth with the hot coal and said,
"Look, your guilt is taken away, because
this hot coal has touched your lips. Your
sin is taken away."
8Then I heard the Lord's voice, saying,
"Whom can I send? Who will go for us?"
So I said, "Here I am. Send me!"
9Then the Lord said, "Go and tell this
to the people:
'You will listen and listen, but you
will not understand.
You will look and look, but you will
not learn.'
10 Make the minds of these people
dumb.
Shut their ears. Cover their eyes.
Otherwise, they might really
understand
what they see with their eyes
and hear with their ears.
They might really understand in their
minds
and come back to me and be
healed."
11Then I asked, "Lord, how long
should I do this?"

FAITH links

DIRTY INSIDE

ISAIAH 6:1-7

If Jesus were to suddenly walk into your room right now, what would you think? How would you act? The prophet Isaiah saw a vision of God in the Temple. Angels surrounded God's throne. In such a holy place, Isaiah couldn't help but realize his own sin. Instead of trying to sweep it under the rug, he cried out his need to be made clean.

When you sin, it's as if you went outside and rolled around in the mud. Instead of being dirty on the outside, sin makes you dirty inside. Only God can remove the dirt and make you clean once more.

Need a sin "cleaning"? Check out these Faithlinks:

Facing the Consequences, Deuteronomy 3:21–29, p. 232

Real Repentance, Jeremiah 4:1–4, p. 993

The Watchman, Ezekiel 3:16–22, p. 1088

A Model of Forgiveness, Ezekiel 16:59–63, p. 1103

Clean Inside and Out, Luke 11:39–40, p. 1392

The Gift, John 3:16–18, p. 1427

He answered,
"Until the cities are destroyed
and the people are gone,
until there are no people left in the
houses,
until the land is destroyed and left
empty.
12 The LORD will send the people far
away,
and the land will be left empty.
13 One-tenth of the people will be left in
the land,
but it will be destroyed again.
These people will be like an oak tree
whose stump is left when the tree
is chopped down.
The people who remain will be
like a stump that will sprout
again."

Trouble with Aram

7 Now Ahaz was the son of Jotham, who
was the son of Uzziah. When Ahaz
was king of Judah, Rezin king of Aram
and Pekah son of Remaliah, the king of
Israel, went up to Jerusalem to fight
against it. But they were not able to defeat the city.
2Ahaz king of Judah
received a message say-
ing, "The armies of Aram
and Israel[n] have joined together."
When Ahaz heard this,
he and the people were
frightened. They shook
with fear like trees of the
forest blown by the wind.
3Then the LORD told
Isaiah, "You and your son
Shear-Jashub[n] should go and meet Ahaz
at the place where the water flows into
the upper pool, on the road where people
do their laundry. 4Tell Ahaz, 'Be careful.
Be calm and don't worry. Don't let those
two men, Rezin and Pekah son of Remaliah, scare you. Don't be afraid of their anger or Aram's anger, because they are
like two barely burning sticks that are
ready to go out. 5They have made plans
against you, saying, 6"Let's fight against
Judah and tear it apart. We will divide the
land for ourselves and make the son of
Tabeel the new king of Judah." 7But I,
the Lord GOD, say,
" 'Their plan will not succeed;
it will not happen,
8 because Aram is led by the city of
Damascus,
and Damascus is led by its weak
king, Rezin.
Within sixty-five years Israel will no
longer be a nation.
9 Israel is led by the city of Samaria,
and Samaria is led by its weak
king, the son of Remaliah.
If your faith is not strong,
you will not have strength enough
to last.' "

Immanuel—God Is with Us

10Then the LORD spoke to Ahaz
again, saying, 11"Ask for a sign from the
LORD your God to prove to yourself that
these things are true. It may be a sign
from as deep as the place of the dead or as
high as the heavens."
12But Ahaz said, "I will not ask for a
sign or test the LORD."
13Then Isaiah said, "Ahaz, descendant
of David, listen carefully! Isn't it bad
enough that you wear out
the patience of people?
Do you also have to wear
out the patience of my
God? 14The Lord himself
will give you a sign: The
virgin[n] will be pregnant.
She will have a son, and
she will name him
Immanuel.[n] 15He will be
eating milk curds and
honey when he learns to
reject what is evil and to choose what is
good. 16You are afraid of the kings of Israel and Aram now. But before the child

> The Lord himself will give you a sign: The virgin will be pregnant. She will have a son, and she will name him Immanuel.
> —Isaiah 7:14

7:2 Israel Literally, "Ephraim." Isaiah often uses "Ephraim" to mean all of Israel.

7:3 Shear-Jashub This name means "a part of the people will come back."

7:14 virgin The Hebrew word means "a young woman." Often this meant a girl who was not married and had not yet had sexual relations with anyone.

7:14 Immanuel This name means "God is with us."

learns to choose good and reject evil, the
lands of Israel and Aram will be empty.
17The LORD will bring troubled times to
you, your people, and to the people of
your father's family. They will be worse
than anything that has happened since
Israel separated from Judah. The LORD
will bring the king of Assyria to fight
against you.

18"At that time the LORD will whistle
for the Egyptians, and they will come like
flies from Egypt's faraway streams. He
will call for the Assyrians, and they will
come like bees. 19These enemies will
camp in the deep ravines and in the cliffs,
by the thornbushes and watering holes.
20The Lord will hire Assyria and use it
like a razor to punish Judah. It will be as if
the Lord is shaving the hair from Judah's
head and legs and removing Judah's beard.

21"At that time a person will be able to
keep only one young cow and two sheep
alive. 22There will be only enough milk
for that person to eat milk curds. All who
remain in the land will go back to eating
just milk curds and honey. 23In this land
there are now vineyards that have a thousand grapevines, which are worth about
twenty-five pounds of silver. But these
fields will become full of weeds and
thorns. 24The land will become wild and
useful only as a hunting ground. 25People
once worked and grew food on these
hills, but at that time people will not go
there, because the land will be filled with
weeds and thorns. Only sheep and cattle
will go to those places."

Assyria Will Come Soon

8 The LORD told me, "Take a large
scroll and write on it with an ordinary
pen: 'Maher-Shalal-Hash-Baz.' 2I will
gather some men to be reliable witnesses: Uriah the priest and Zechariah
son of Jeberekiah."

3Then I went to the prophetess, and
she became pregnant and had a son. The
LORD told me, "Name the boy Maher-
Shalal-Hash-Baz," 4because the king of
Assyria will take away all the wealth and
possessions of Damascus and Samaria
before the boy learns to say 'my father' or
'my mother.' "

5Again the LORD spoke to me, saying,
6"These people refuse to accept
the slow-moving waters of the pool
of Shiloah
and are terrified of Rezin
and Pekah son of Remaliah.
7So I, the Lord, will bring
the king of Assyria and all his
power against them,
like a powerful flood of water from
the Euphrates River.
The Assyrians will be like water
rising over the banks of the
river,
flowing over the land.
8That water will flow into Judah and
pass through it,
rising to Judah's throat.
Immanuel, this army will spread its
wings like a bird
until it covers your whole country."

9Be broken, all you nations,
and be smashed to pieces.
Listen, all you faraway countries.
Prepare for battle and be smashed
to pieces!
Prepare for battle and be smashed
to pieces!
10Make your plans for the fight,
but they will be defeated.
Give orders to your armies,
but they will be useless,
because God is with us.

Warnings to Isaiah

11The LORD spoke to me with his
great power and warned me not to follow
the lead of the rest of the people. He said,
12"People are saying that others make
plans against them,
but you should not believe them.
Don't be afraid of what they fear;
do not dread those things.
13But remember that the LORD All-
Powerful is holy.
He is the one you should fear;
he is the one you should dread.
14Then he will be a place of safety for
you.

8:3 Maher-Shalal-Hash-Baz This name means "there will soon be looting and stealing."

But for the two families of Israel,
he will be like a stone that causes
people to stumble,
like a rock that makes them fall.
He will be like a trap for the people
of Jerusalem,
and he will catch them in his
trap.
15 Many people will fall over this rock.
They will fall and be broken;
they will be trapped and caught."

16 Make an agreement.
Seal up the teaching while my
followers are watching.
17 I will wait for the LORD to help us,
the LORD who is ashamed of the
family of Israel.
I will wait for him.

18 I am here, and with me are the children the LORD has given me. We are
signs and proofs for the people of Israel
from the LORD All-Powerful, who lives on
Mount Zion.

19 Some people say, "Ask the mediums and fortune-tellers, who whisper
and mutter, what to do." But I tell you
that people should ask their God for help.
Why should people who are still alive
ask something from the dead? 20 You
should follow the teachings and the
agreement with the LORD. The mediums and fortune-tellers do not speak
the word of the LORD, so their words
are worth nothing.

21 People will wander through the
land troubled and hungry. When they become hungry, they will become angry and
will look up and curse their king and their
God. 22 They will look around them at
their land and see only trouble, darkness,
and awful gloom. And they will be forced
into the darkness.

A New Day Is Coming

9 But suddenly there will be no more
gloom for the land that suffered. In
the past God made the lands of Zebulun
and Naphtali hang their heads in shame,
but in the future those lands will be made
great. They will stretch from the road
along the Mediterranean Sea to the land
beyond the Jordan River and north to
Galilee, the land of people who are not
Israelites.

2 Before those people lived in
darkness,
but now they have seen a great
light.
They lived in a dark land,
but a light has shined on them.
3 God, you have caused the nation to
grow
and made the people happy.
And they have shown their happiness
to you,
like the joy during harvest time,
like the joy of people
taking what they have won in war.
4 Like the time you defeated Midian,
you have taken away their heavy
load
and the heavy pole from their backs
and the rod the enemy used to
punish them.
5 Every boot that marched in battle
and every uniform stained with
blood
has been thrown into the fire.
6 A child has been born to us;
God has given a son to us.
He will be responsible for leading
the people.
His name will be Wonderful
Counselor, Powerful God,
Father Who Lives Forever, Prince
of Peace.
7 Power and peace will be in his
kingdom
and will continue to grow forever.
He will rule as king on David's throne
and over David's kingdom.
He will make it strong
by ruling with justice and
goodness
from now on and forever.
The LORD All-Powerful will do this
because of his strong love for his
people.

God Will Punish Israel

8 The Lord sent a message against the
people of Jacob;
it says that God will judge Israel.
9 Then everyone in Israel, even the
leaders in Samaria,

WHAT'S IN A NAME?

ISAIAH 9:6

How many names do you have? If you have a middle name, you have three names—a first, middle, and last name. A nickname adds a fourth to your list. Speaking of names, have you ever heard Handel's *Messiah,* or at least part of that piece of music? It describes the names of the Messiah, which are included in this verse. In Isaiah's time, the people looked forward to the coming of the Messiah. Who was that Messiah? Jesus. These names are a way to describe his character. After reading these names, wouldn't you like to add another one to the list? How about *My Savior?*

Surf on to these Faithlinks about the importance of names:

The Name of the Lord, Exodus 33:19–23; 34:5–8, p. 120

A Hopeful Name, Hosea 1:3–11, p. 1172

Uprooted by Change, Amos 9:15, p. 1205

Name with a Purpose, Matthew 1:21, p. 1274

A Family Meal, Mark 14:23–26, p. 1356

Our Gift to God, Romans 12:1–2, p. 1536

will know that God has sent it.
Those people are proud and brag by saying,
10 "These bricks have fallen,
but we will build again with cut stones.
These small trees have been chopped down,
but we will put great cedars there."
11 But the LORD has brought the enemies of Rezin against them;
he has stirred up their enemies against them.
12 The Arameans came from the east
and the Philistines from the west,
and they ate up Israel with their armies.

But the LORD was still angry;
his hand was still raised to punish the people.

13 But the people did not return to the one who had struck them;
they did not follow the LORD All-Powerful.
14 So the LORD cut off Israel's head and tail,
taking away both the branch and stalk in one day.
15 The older leaders and important men were the head,
and the prophets who speak lies were the tail.
16 Those who led the people led them in the wrong direction,
and those who followed them were destroyed.
17 So the Lord is not happy with the young people,
nor will he show mercy to the orphans and widows.
All the people are separated from God and are very evil;
they all speak lies.

But the LORD is still angry;
his hand is still raised to strike down the people.

18 Evil is like a small fire.
First, it burns weeds and thorns.

Next, it burns the larger bushes in the forest,
and they all go up in a column of smoke.
19 The LORD All-Powerful is angry,
so the land will be burned.
The people are like fuel for the fire;
no one will try to save his brother or sister.
20 People will grab something on the right,
but they will still be hungry.
They will eat something on the left,
but they will not be filled.
Then they will each turn and eat their own children.
21 The people of Manasseh will fight against the people of Ephraim,
and Ephraim will fight against Manasseh.
Then both of them will turn against Judah.

But the LORD is still angry;
his hand is still raised to strike down the people.

10 How terrible it will be for those who make unfair laws,
and those who write laws that make life hard for people.
2 They are not fair to the poor,
and they rob my people of their rights.
They allow people to steal from widows
and to take from orphans what really belongs to them.
3 How will you explain the things you have done?
What will you do when your destruction comes from far away?
Where will you run for help?
Where will you hide your riches then?
4 You will have to bow down among the captives
or fall down among the dead bodies.
But the LORD is still angry;
his hand is still raised to strike down the people.

God Will Punish Assyria

5 God says, "How terrible it will be for the king of Assyria.
I use him like a rod to show my anger;
in anger I use Assyria like a club.
6 I send it to fight against a nation that is separated from God.
I am angry with those people,
so I command Assyria to fight against them,
to take their wealth from them,
to trample them down like dirt in the streets.
7 But Assyria's king doesn't understand that I am using him;
he doesn't know he is a tool for me.
He only wants to destroy other people
and to defeat many nations.
8 The king of Assyria says to himself,
'All of my commanders are like kings.
9 The city Calno is like the city Carchemish.
The city Hamath is like the city Arpad.
The city Samaria is like the city Damascus.
10 I defeated those kingdoms that worship idols,
and those idols were more than the idols of Jerusalem and Samaria.
11 As I defeated Samaria and her idols,
I will also defeat Jerusalem and her idols.' "

12 When the Lord finishes doing what
he planned to Mount Zion and Jerusalem,
he will punish Assyria. The king of Assyria is very proud, and his pride has
made him do these evil things, so God
will punish him. 13 The king of Assyria
says this:
"By my own power I have done these things;
by my wisdom I have defeated many nations.
I have taken their wealth,
and, like a mighty one, I have taken their people.
14 I have taken the riches of all these people,

like a person reaching into a bird's
nest.
I have taken these nations,
like a person taking eggs.
Not one raised a hand
or opened its mouth to stop me."

15 An ax is not better than the person
who swings it.
A saw is not
better than
the one who
uses it.

EMAIL! FROM GOD
10:15–16
Pride
Why should you
not boast?

A stick cannot
control the
person who
picks it up.
A club cannot pick up the person!
16 So the Lord GOD All-Powerful
will send a terrible disease upon
Assyria's soldiers.
The strength of Assyria will be
burned up
like a fire burning until everything
is gone.
17 God, the Light of Israel, will be like a
fire;
the Holy One will be like a flame.
He will be like a fire
that suddenly burns the weeds and
thorns.
18 The fire burns away the great trees
and rich farmlands,
destroying everything.
It will be like a sick person who
wastes away.
19 The trees left standing will be so
few
that even a child could count
them.

20 At that time some people will be left
alive in Israel
from the family of Jacob.
They will not continue to depend
on the person who defeated them.
They will learn truly to depend on
the LORD,
the Holy One of Israel.
21 Those who are left alive in Jacob's
family
will again follow the powerful God.
22 Israel, your people are many,
like the grains of sand by the sea.
But only a few of them will be left
alive to return to the LORD.
God has announced that he will
destroy the land
completely and fairly.
23 The Lord GOD All-Powerful will
certainly destroy this land,
as he has announced.

24 This is what the Lord GOD All-
Powerful says:
"My people living in Jerusalem,
don't be afraid of the Assyrians,
who beat you with a rod
and raise a stick against you, as
Egypt did.
25 After a short time my anger against
you will stop,
and then I will turn my anger to
destroying them."
26 Then the LORD All-Powerful will beat
the Assyrians with a whip
as he defeated Midian at the rock
of Oreb.
He will raise his stick over the
waters
as he did in Egypt.
27 Then the troubles that Assyria puts
on you
will be removed,
and the load they make you carry
will be taken away.

Assyria Invades Israel

28 The army of Assyria will enter near
Aiath.
Its soldiers will walk through
Migron.
They will store their food in
Micmash.
29 The army will go over the pass.
The soldiers will sleep at Geba.
The people of Ramah will be afraid,
and the people at Gibeah of Saul
will run away.
30 Cry out, Bath Gallim!
Laishah, listen!
Poor Anathoth!
31 The people of Madmenah are running
away;
the people of Gebim are hiding.
32 This day the army will stop at Nob.

They will shake their fist at Mount Zion,
at the hill of Jerusalem.

33 Watch! The Lord GOD All-Powerful
with his great power will chop them down like a great tree.
Those who are great will be cut down;
those who are important will fall to the ground.
34 He will cut them down
as a forest is cut down with an ax.
And the great trees of Lebanon
will fall by the power of the Mighty One.

The King of Peace Is Coming

11 A new branch will grow
from a stump of a tree;
so a new king will come
from the family of Jesse.[n]
2 The Spirit of the LORD will rest upon that king.
The Spirit will give him wisdom and understanding, guidance and power.
The Spirit will teach him to know and respect the LORD.
3 This king will be glad to obey the LORD.
He will not judge by the way things look
or decide by what he hears.
4 But he will judge the poor honestly;
he will be fair in his decisions for the poor people of the land.
At his command evil people will be punished,
and by his words the wicked will be put to death.
5 Goodness and fairness will give him strength,
like a belt around his waist.

> The Spirit will give him wisdom and understanding, guidance and power.
> —Isaiah 11:2

6 Then wolves will live in peace with lambs,
and leopards will lie down to rest with goats.
Calves, lions, and young bulls will eat together,
and a little child will lead them.
7 Cows and bears will eat together in peace.
Their young will lie down to rest together.
Lions will eat hay as oxen do.
8 A baby will be able to play near a cobra's hole,
and a child will be able to put his hand into the nest of a poisonous snake.
9 They will not hurt or destroy each other
on all my holy mountain,
because the earth will be full of the knowledge of the LORD,
as the sea is full of water.
10 At that time the new king from the
family of Jesse will stand as a banner for
all peoples. The nations
will come together around
him, and the place where
he lives will be filled
with glory. 11 At that time
the Lord will again reach
out and take his people
who are left alive in Assyria, North Egypt, South
Egypt, Cush, Elam, Babylonia, Hamath, and all
the islands of the sea.
12 God will raise a banner as a sign for all nations,
and he will gather the people of Israel who were forced from their country.
He will gather the scattered people of Judah
from all parts of the earth.
13 At that time Israel will not be jealous anymore,
and Judah will have no more enemies.
Israel will not be jealous of Judah,
and Judah will not hate Israel.
14 But Israel and Judah will attack the Philistines on the west.

11:1 Jesse King David's father.

Together they will take the riches
from the people of the east.
They will conquer Edom and Moab,
and the people of Ammon will be
under their control.
15 The LORD will dry up
the Red Sea of Egypt.
He will wave his arm over the
Euphrates River
and dry it up with a scorching wind.
He will divide it into seven small
rivers
so that people can walk across
them with their sandals on.
16 So God's people who are left alive
will have a way to leave Assyria,
just like the time the Israelites
came out of Egypt.

A Song of Praise to God

12 At that time you will say:
"I praise you, LORD!
You were angry with me,
but you are not angry with me now!
You have comforted me.
2 God is the one who saves me;
I will trust him
and not be
afraid.
The LORD, the
LORD gives
me strength
and makes
me sing.
He has saved me."
3 You will receive your salvation with
joy
as you would draw water from a
well.
4 At that time you will say,
"Praise the LORD and worship him.
Tell everyone what he has done
and how great he is.
5 Sing praise to the LORD, because he
has done great things.
Let all the world know what he has
done.
6 Shout and sing for joy, you people of
Jerusalem,
because the Holy One of Israel
does great things before your
eyes."

EMAIL FROM GOD
12:2
Courage
Where can you get
courage?

God's Message to Babylon

13 God showed Isaiah son of Amoz
this message about Babylon:
2 Raise a flag on the bare mountain.
Call out to the men.
Raise your hand to signal them
to enter through the gates for
important people.
3 I myself have commanded those
people
whom I have separated as mine.
I have called those warriors to carry
out my anger.
They rejoice and are glad to do my
will.

4 Listen to the loud noise in the
mountains,
the sound of many people.
Listen to the noise among the
kingdoms,
the sound of nations gathering
together.
The LORD All-Powerful is calling
his army together for battle.
5 This army is coming from a faraway
land,
from the edge of the horizon.
In anger the LORD is using this army
like a weapon
to destroy the whole country.

6 Cry, because the LORD's day of
judging is near;
the Almighty is sending
destruction.
7 People will be weak with fear,
and their courage will melt away.
8 Everyone will be afraid.
Pain and hurt will grab them;
they will hurt like a woman giving
birth to a baby.
They will look at each other in fear,
with their faces red like fire.

God's Judgment Against Babylon

9 Look, the LORD's day of judging is
coming—
a terrible day, a day of God's anger.
He will destroy the land
and the sinners who live in it.
10 The stars will not show their light;
the skies will be dark.

The sun will grow dark as it rises,
and the moon will not give its
light.
11 The LORD says, "I will punish the
world for its evil
and wicked people for their sins.
I will cause proud people to lose their
pride,
and I will destroy the pride of
those who are cruel to others.
12 People will be harder to find than
pure gold;
there will be fewer people than
there is fine gold in Ophir.
13 I will make the sky shake,
and the earth will be moved from
its place
by the anger of the LORD All-
Powerful
at the time of his burning anger.

14 "Then the people from Babylon will
run away like hunted deer
or like sheep who have no
shepherd.
Everyone will turn back to his own
people;
each will run back to his own land.
15 Everyone who is captured will be
killed;
everyone who is caught will be
killed with a sword.
16 Their little children will be beaten to
death in front of them.
Their houses will be robbed
and their wives raped.

17 "Look, I will cause the armies of
Media to attack Babylon.
They do not care about silver
or delight in gold.
18 Their soldiers will shoot the young
men with arrows;
they will show no mercy on
children,
nor will they feel sorry for little
ones.
19 Babylon is the most beautiful of all
kingdoms,
and the Babylonians are very
proud of it.
But God will destroy it
like Sodom and Gomorrah.
20 No one will ever live there
or settle there again.
No Arab will put a tent there;
no shepherd will bring sheep
there.
21 Only desert animals will live there,

FAITH links

WORLD NEWS

ISAIAH 13–19

If you've ever watched the news on TV, you know that a section of the news focuses on what's going on in the world. Isaiah's prophecies included a "world news" segment. Many important nations around the world did not obey God. God planned to punish them.

Many people view God as always angry, always ready to punish someone. Is that your view of God? God would prefer not to punish people. Instead, he offers mercy when we repent of our sin.

Out of Control?, Genesis 4, p. 8

Facing the Consequences, Deuteronomy 3:21–29, p. 232

Count on His Mercy, Judges 2:16–17; 3, p. 313

Don't Get Mad; Get Even?, Matthew 26:57–63; 27:11–14, p. 1323

That's Much Better!, Ephesians 2:4–5, p. 1599

It's Guaranteed!, 1 John 1:9–10, p. 1714

and their houses will be full of wild
dogs.
Owls will live there,
and wild goats will leap about in
the houses.
22 Wolves will howl within the strong
walls,
and wild dogs will bark in the
beautiful buildings.
The end of Babylon is near;
its time is almost over."

Israel Will Return Home

14 The LORD will show mercy to the
people of Jacob, and he will again
choose the people of Israel. He will settle
them in their own land. Then non-Israelite
people will join the Israelites and will
become a part of the family of Jacob.
2 Nations will take the Israelites back to
their land. Then those men and women
from the other nations will become
slaves to Israel in the LORD's land. In the
past the Israelites were their slaves, but
now the Israelites will defeat those nations and rule over them.

The King of Babylon Will Fall

3 The LORD will take away the Israelites' hard work and will comfort them.
They will no longer have to work hard as
slaves. 4 On that day Israel will sing this
song about the king of Babylon:
The cruel king who ruled us is
finished;
his angry rule is finished!
5 The LORD has broken the scepter of
evil rulers
and taken away their power.
6 The king of Babylon struck people in
anger
again and again.
He ruled nations
in anger
and continued
to hurt them.

EMAIL FROM GOD
14:5–6
Anger
Find out if God will punish anger.

7 But now, the
whole world rests and is quiet.
Now the people begin to sing.
8 Even the pine trees are happy,
and the cedar trees of Lebanon
rejoice.
They say, "The king has fallen,
so no one will ever cut us down
again."
9 The place of the dead is excited
to meet you when you come.
It wakes the spirits of the dead,
the leaders of the world.
It makes kings of all nations
stand up from their thrones to
greet you.
10 All these leaders will make fun of you
and will say,
"Now you are weak, as we are.
Now you are just like us."
11 Your pride has been sent down to the
place of the dead.
The music from your harps goes
with it.
Flies are spread out like your bed
beneath you,
and worms cover your body like a
blanket.
12 King of Babylon, morning star, you
have fallen from heaven,
even though you were as bright as
the rising sun!
In the past all the nations on earth
bowed down before you,
but now you have been cut down.
13 You told yourself,
"I will go up to heaven.
I will put my throne
above God's stars.
I will sit on the mountain of the
gods,
on the slopes of the sacred
mountain.
14 I will go up above the tops of the
clouds.
I will be like God Most High."
15 But you were brought down to the
grave,
to the deep places where the dead
are.

16 Those who see you stare at you.
They think about what has
happened to you
and say, "Is this the same man who
caused great fear on earth,
who shook the kingdoms,
17 who turned the world into a desert,
who destroyed its cities,

who captured people in war
and would not let them go home?"

18 Every king of the earth has been
buried with honor,
each in his own grave.
19 But you are thrown out of your
grave,
like an unwanted branch.
You are covered by bodies
that died in battle,
by bodies to be buried in a rocky pit.
You are like a dead body other
soldiers walk on.
20 You will not be buried with those
bodies,
because you ruined your own
country
and killed your own people.
The children of evil people
will never be mentioned again.

21 Prepare to kill his children,
because their father is guilty.
They will never again take control of
the earth;
they will never again fill the world
with their cities.

22 The LORD All-Powerful says this:
"I will fight against those people;
I will destroy Babylon and its people,
its children and their
descendants," says the LORD.
23 "I will make Babylon fit only for owls
and for swamps.
I will sweep Babylon as with a broom
of destruction,"
says the LORD All-Powerful.

God Will Punish Assyria

24 The LORD All-Powerful has made
this promise:
"These things will happen exactly as
I planned them;
they will happen exactly as I set
them up.
25 I will destroy the king of Assyria in
my country;
I will trample him on my
mountains.
He placed a heavy load on my people,
but that weight will be removed.

26 "This is what I plan to do for all the
earth.
And this is the hand that I have
raised over all nations."

27 When the LORD All-Powerful makes a
plan,
no one can stop it.
When the LORD raises his hand to
punish people,
no one can stop it.

God's Message to Philistia

28 This message was given in the year
that King Ahaz died:
29 Country of Philistia, don't be happy
that the king who struck you is
now dead.
He is like a snake that will give birth
to another dangerous snake.
The new king will be like a quick,
dangerous snake to bite you.
30 Even the poorest of my people will
be able to eat safely,
and people in need will be able to
lie down in safety.
But I will kill your family with hunger,
and all your people who are left
will die.

31 People near the city gates, cry out!
Philistines, be frightened,
because a cloud of dust comes from
the north.
It is an army, full of men ready to
fight.
32 What shall we tell the messengers
from Philistia?
Say that the LORD has made
Jerusalem strong
and that his poor people will go
there for safety.

God's Message to Moab

15 This is a message about Moab:
In one night armies took the
wealth from Ar in Moab,
and it was destroyed.
In one night armies took the wealth
from Kir in Moab,
and it was destroyed.
2 The people of Dibon go to the places
of worship to cry.

The people of Moab cry for the
cities of Nebo and Medeba.
Every head and beard has been
shaved to show how sad Moab
is.
3 In the streets they wear rough cloth
to show their sadness.
On the roofs[a] and in the public
squares,
they are crying loudly.
4 People in the cities Heshbon and
Elealeh cry out loud.
You can hear their voices far away
in the city Jahaz.
Even the soldiers are frightened;
they are shaking with fear.

5 My heart cries with sorrow for Moab.
Its people run away to Zoar for
safety;
they run to Eglath Shelishiyah.
People are going up the mountain
road to Luhith,
crying as they go.
People are going on the road to
Horonaim,
crying over their
destruction.
6 But the water of
Nimrim has
dried up.
The grass has dried
up,
and all the plants are
dead;
nothing green is
left.
7 So the people gather
up what they have saved
and carry it across the Ravine of
the Poplars.
8 Crying is heard everywhere in Moab.
Their crying is heard as far away
as the city Eglaim;
it is heard as far away as Beer
Elim.
9 The water of the city Dibon is full of
blood,
and I, the LORD, will bring even
more troubles to Dibon.
A few people living in Moab have
escaped the enemy,
but I will send lions to kill them.

16 Send the king of the land
the payment he demands.
Send a lamb from Sela through the
desert
to the mountain of Jerusalem.
2 The women of Moab
try to cross the river Arnon
like little birds
that have fallen from their nest.

3 They say: "Help us.
Tell us what to do.
Protect us from our enemies
as shade protects us from the noon
sun.
Hide us, because we are running for
safety!
Don't give us to our enemies.
4 Let those of us who were forced out
of Moab live in your land.
Hide us from our enemies."

The robbing of Moab will stop.
The enemy will be defeated;
those who hurt others will
disappear from the land.
5 Then a new loyal king
will come;
this faithful king will
be from the family
of David.
He will judge fairly
and do what is right.

This faithful king will be from the family of David. He will judge fairly and do what is right.
—Isaiah 16:5

6 We have heard that
the people of Moab
are proud and very
conceited.
They are very proud and angry,
but their bragging means nothing.
7 So the people of Moab will cry;
they will all be sad.
They will moan and groan
for the raisin cakes they had in Kir
Hareseth.
8 But the fields of Heshbon and the
vines of Sibmah cannot grow
grapes;

15:3 roofs In Bible times houses were built with flat roofs. The roof was used for drying things such as flax and fruit. And it was used as an extra room, as a place for worship, and as a cool place to sleep in the summer.

foreign rulers have destroyed the grapevines.
The grapevines once spread as far as the city of Jazer and into the desert;
they had spread as far as the sea.
9 I cry with the people of Jazer
for the grapevines of Sibmah.
I will cry with the people of Heshbon and Elealeh.
There will be no shouts of joy,
because there will be no harvest or ripe fruit.
10 There will be no joy and happiness in the orchards
and no songs or shouts of joy in the vineyards.
No one makes wine in the winepresses,
because I have put an end to shouts of joy.
11 My heart cries for Moab like a harp playing a funeral song;
I am very sad for Kir Hareseth.
12 The people of Moab will go to their places of worship
and will try to pray.
But when they go to their temple to pray,
they will not be able.

13 Earlier the LORD said these things
about Moab. 14 Now the LORD says, "In
three years all those people and what
they take pride in will be hated. (This is
three years as a hired helper would count
time.) There will be a few people left, but
they will be weak."

God's Message to Aram

17 This is a message about Damascus:
"The city of Damascus will be destroyed;
only ruins will remain.
2 People will leave the cities of Aroer.
Flocks will wander freely in those empty towns,
and there will be no one to bother them.
3 The strong, walled cities of Israel will be destroyed.
The government in Damascus will end.
Those left alive of Aram will be like the glory of Israel," says the LORD All-Powerful.

4 "At that time Israel's wealth will all be gone.
Israel will be like someone who has lost much weight from sickness.
5 That time will be like the grain harvest in the Valley of Rephaim.
The workers cut the wheat.
Then they cut the heads of grain from the plants
and collect the grain.
6 That time will also be like the olive harvest,
when a few olives are left.
Two or three olives are left in the top branches.
Four or five olives are left on full branches," says the LORD, the God of Israel.

7 At that time people will look to God, their Maker;
their eyes will see the Holy One of Israel.
8 They will not trust the altars they have made,
nor will they trust what their hands have made,
not even the Asherah idols and altars.

9 In that day all their strong cities will
be empty. They will be like the cities the
Hivites and the Amorites left when the
Israelites came to take the land. Everything will be ruined.
10 You have forgotten the God who saves you;
you have not remembered that God is your place of safety.
You plant the finest grapevines
and grapevines from faraway places.

eMAiL! FROM GOD
17:10
Money
What can all your stuff distract you from?

11 You plant your grapevines one day
and try to make them grow,
and the next day you make them
blossom.
But at harvest time everything will
be dead;
a sickness will kill all the
plants.

12 Listen to the many people!
Their crying is like the noise from
the sea.
Listen to the nations!
Their crying is like the crashing of
great waves.
13 The people roar like the waves,
but when God speaks harshly to
them, they will
run away.
They will be like chaff
on the hills being
blown by the
wind,
or like
tumbleweeds
blown away by a
storm.
14 At night the people
will be very
frightened.
Before morning, no one will be
left.
So our enemies will come to our
land,
but they will become nothing.

The idols of Egypt will tremble before him, and Egypt's courage will melt away.
—Isaiah 19:1

God's Message to Cush

18 How terrible it will be for the
land beyond the rivers of
Cush.
It is filled with the sound of wings.
2 That land sends messengers across
the sea;
they go on the water in boats made
of reeds.

Go, quick messengers,
to a people who are tall and
smooth-skinned,
who are feared everywhere.
They are a powerful nation that
defeats other nations.
Their land is divided by rivers.

3 All you people of the world, look!
Everyone who lives in the world,
look!
You will see a banner raised on a
mountain.
You will hear a trumpet sound.
4 The LORD said to me,
"I will quietly watch from where I
live,
like heat in the sunshine,
like the dew in the heat of harvest
time."
5 The time will come, after the flowers
have bloomed and before the
harvest,
when new grapes will be budding
and growing.
The enemy will cut
the plants with
knives;
he will cut down the
vines and take
them away.
6 They will be left for
the birds of the
mountains
and for the wild
animals.
Birds will feed on
them all
summer,
and wild animals will eat them that
winter."

7 At that time a gift will be brought to
the LORD All-Powerful
from the people who are tall and
smooth-skinned,
who are feared everywhere.
They are a powerful nation that
defeats other nations.
Their land is divided by rivers.
These gifts will be brought to the
place of the LORD All-Powerful,
to Mount Zion.

God's Message to Egypt

19 This is a message about Egypt:
Look, the LORD is coming on a
fast cloud
to enter Egypt.
The idols of Egypt will tremble
before him,

and Egypt's courage will melt
away.

2 The LORD says, "I will cause the
Egyptians to fight against
themselves.
People will fight with their
relatives;
neighbors will fight neighbors;
cities will fight cities;
kingdoms will fight kingdoms.
3 The Egyptians will be afraid,
and I will ruin their plans.
They will ask advice from their idols
and spirits of the dead,
from their mediums and fortune-
tellers."
4 The Lord GOD All-Powerful says,
"I will hand Egypt over to a hard
master,
and a powerful king will rule over
them."

5 The sea will become dry,
and the water will disappear from
the Nile River.
6 The canals will stink;
the streams of Egypt will decrease
and dry up.
All the water plants will rot;
7 all the plants along the banks of
the Nile will die.
Even the planted fields by the Nile
will dry up, blow away, and
disappear.
8 The fishermen, all those who catch
fish from the Nile,
will groan and cry;
those who fish in the Nile will be sad.
9 All the people who make cloth from
flax will be sad,
and those who weave linen will
lose hope.
10 Those who weave cloth will be
broken.
All those who work for money will
be sad.

11 The officers of the city of Zoan are
fools;
the wise men who advise the king
of Egypt give wrong advice.
How can you say to him, 'I am wise'?
How can you say, 'I am from the
old family of the kings'?
12 Egypt, where are your wise men?
Let them show you
what the LORD All-Powerful has
planned for Egypt.
13 The officers of Zoan have been
fooled;
the leaders of Memphis have
believed false things.
So the leaders of Egypt
lead that nation the wrong way.
14 The LORD has made the leaders
confused.
They have led Egypt to wander in
the wrong ways,
like drunk people stumbling in
their own vomit.
15 There is nothing Egypt can do;
no one there can help.

16 In that day the Egyptians will be
like women. They will be afraid of the
LORD All-Powerful, because he will raise
his hand to strike them down. 17 The land
of Judah will bring fear to Egypt. Anyone
there who hears the name Judah will be
afraid, because the LORD All-Powerful
has planned terrible things for them.
18 At that time five cities in Egypt will
speak Hebrew, the language of Canaan,
and they will promise to be loyal to the
LORD All-Powerful. One of these cities
will be named the City of Destruction.
19 At that time there will be an altar for
the LORD in the middle of Egypt and a
monument to the LORD at the border of
Egypt. 20 This will be a sign and a witness
to the LORD All-Powerful in the land of
Egypt. When the people cry to the LORD
for help, he will send someone to save
and defend them. He will rescue them
from those who hurt them.

21 So the LORD will show himself to
the Egyptians, and then they will know
he is the LORD. They will worship God
and offer many sacrifices. They will make
promises to the LORD and will keep
them. 22 The LORD will punish the Egyptians, but then he will heal them. They
will come back to the LORD, and he will
listen to their prayers and heal them.

23 At that time there will be a highway

from Egypt to Assyria, and the Assyrians
will go to Egypt, and the Egyptians will
go to Assyria. The Egyptians and Assyrians will worship God together. **24**At that
time Israel, Assyria, and Egypt will join
together, which will be a blessing for the
earth. **25**The LORD All-Powerful will
bless them, saying, "Egypt, you are my
people. Assyria, I made you. Israel, I own
you. You are all blessed!"

Assyria Will Defeat Egypt and Cush

20 Sargon king of Assyria sent a military commander to Ashdod to attack that city. So the commander attacked
and captured it. **2**Then the LORD spoke
through Isaiah son of Amoz, saying,
"Take the rough cloth off your body, and
take your sandals off your feet." So Isaiah
obeyed and walked around naked and
barefoot.

3Then the LORD said, "Isaiah my servant has walked around naked and barefoot for three years as a sign against
Egypt and Cush. **4**The king of Assyria
will carry away prisoners from Egypt and
Cush. Old people and young people will
be led away naked and
barefoot, with their but-
tocks bare. So the Egyp-
tians will be shamed.
5People who looked to
Cush for help will be
afraid, and those who
were amazed by Egypt's
glory will be shamed.
6People who live near
the sea will say, 'Look at
those countries. We trust-
ed them to help us. We ran to them so
they would save us from the king of
Assyria. So how will we be able to escape?' "

Disaster is coming from the desert like wind blowing in the south.
—Isaiah 21:1

God's Message to Babylon

21 This is a message about the Desert
by the Sea:*

Disaster is coming from the desert
like wind blowing in the south.
It is coming from a terrible
country.

2I have seen a terrible vision.
I see traitors turning against you
and people taking your wealth.

Elam, attack the people!
Media, surround the city and
attack it!
I will bring an end to the pain the
city causes.

3I saw those terrible things, and now I
am in pain;
my pains are like the pains of
giving birth.
What I hear makes me very afraid;
what I see causes me to shake
with fear.
4I am worried,
and I am shaking with fear.
My pleasant evening
has become a night of fear.

5They set the table;
they spread the rugs;
they eat and drink.
Leaders, stand up.
Prepare the shields for battle!

6The Lord said to me,
"Go, place a lookout
for the city
and have him report
what he sees.
7If he sees chariots and
teams of horses,
donkeys, or camels,
he should pay very
close attention."

8Then the lookout
called out,
"My master, each day I stand in the
watchtower watching;
every night I have been on guard.
9Look, I see a man coming in a chariot
with a team of horses."
The man gives back the answer,
"Babylon has fallen. It has fallen!
All the statues of her gods
lie broken on the ground."
10My people are crushed like grain on
the threshing floor.

21:1 Desert by the Sea Probably Babylon.

My people, I tell you what I have
heard
from the LORD All-Powerful,
from the God of Israel.

God's Message to Edom

11 This is a message about Dumah:[n]
Someone calls to me from Edom,
"Watchman, how much of the night
is left?
Watchman, how much longer will it
be night?"
12 The watchman answers,
"Morning is coming, but then night
will come again.
If you have something to ask,
then come back and ask."

God's Message to Arabia

13 This is a message about Arabia:
A group of traders from Dedan
spent the night near some trees in
Arabia.
14 They gave water to thirsty
travelers;
the people of Tema gave food
to those who were escaping.
15 They were running from swords,
from swords ready to kill,
from bows ready to shoot,
from a hard battle.
16 This is what the Lord said to me:
"In one year all the glory of the country
of Kedar will be gone. (This is a year as a
hired helper counts time.) 17 At that time
only a few of the archers, the soldiers of
Kedar, will be left alive." The LORD, the
God of Israel, has spoken.

God's Message to Jerusalem

22 This is a message about the Valley
of Vision:[n]
What is wrong with you people?
Why are you on your roofs?[n]
2 This city was a very busy city,
full of noise and wild parties.
Now your people have been killed,
but not with swords,
nor did they die in battle.
3 All your leaders ran away together,
but they have been captured
without using a bow.
All you who were captured
tried to run away before the enemy
came.
4 So I say, "Don't look at me.
Let me cry loudly.
Don't hurry to comfort me
about the destruction of
Jerusalem."
5 The Lord GOD All-Powerful has
chosen a special day
of riots and confusion.
People will trample each other in
the Valley of Vision.
The city walls will be knocked down,
and the people will cry out to the
mountain.
6 The soldiers from Elam will gather
their arrows
and their chariots and men on
horses.
Kir will prepare their shields.
7 Your nicest valleys will be filled with
chariots.
Horsemen will be ordered to guard
the gates of the city.
8 The walls protecting Judah will fall.

At that time the people of Jerusalem
depended on
the weapons kept at the Palace of
the Forest.
9 You saw that the walls of Jerusalem
had many cracks that needed
repairing.
You stored up water in the lower
pool.
10 You counted the houses of
Jerusalem,
and you tore down houses to repair
the walls with their stones.
11 You made a pool between the two
walls
to save water from the old pool,
but you did not trust the God who
made these things;

21:11 Dumah Another name for Edom.
22:1 Valley of Vision This probably means a valley near Jerusalem.
22:1 roofs In Bible times houses were built with flat roofs. The roof was used for drying things such as flax and fruit. And it was used as an extra room, as a place for worship, and as a cool place to sleep in the summer.

you did not respect the One who
planned them long ago.

12 The Lord GOD All-Powerful told the
people
to cry and be sad,
to shave their heads and wear
rough cloth.
13 But look, the people are happy
and are having wild
parties.
They kill the cattle
and the sheep;
they eat the food
and drink the
wine.
They say, "Let us eat
and drink,
because tomorrow
we will die."

They say, "Let us eat and drink, because tomorrow we will die."
—Isaiah 22:13

14 The LORD All-Powerful said to me:
"You people will die before this guilt is
forgiven." The Lord GOD All-Powerful
said this.

God's Message to Shebna

15 This is what the Lord GOD All-
Powerful says:
"Go to this servant Shebna,
the manager of the palace.
16 Say to him, 'What are you doing here?
Who said you could cut out a tomb
for your self here?
Why are you preparing your tomb in
a high place?
Why are you carving out a tomb
from the rock?
17 Look, mighty one! The LORD will
throw you away.
He will take firm hold of you
18 and roll you tightly into a ball
and throw you into another
country.
There you will die,
and there your fine chariots will
remain.
You are a disgrace to your master's
house.
19 I will force you out of your important
job,
and you will be thrown down from
your important place.'

20 "At that time I will call for my servant Eliakim son of Hilkiah. 21 I will take
your robe and put it on him and give him
your belt. I will hand over to him the important job you have, and he will be like a
father to the people of Jerusalem and the
family of Judah. 22 I will put the key to the
house of David around his neck. If he
opens a door, no one will be able to close
it; if he closes a door, no
one will be able to open it.
23 He will be like an honored chair in his father's
house. I will make him
strong like a peg that is
hammered into a strong
board. 24 All the honored
and important things of
his family will depend on
him; all the adults and little children will depend
on him. They will be like bowls and jars
hanging on him.

25 "At that time," says the LORD All-
Powerful, "the peg hammered into the
strong board will weaken. It will break
and fall, and everything hanging on it will
be destroyed." The LORD says this.

God's Message to Lebanon

23 This is a message about Tyre:
You trading ships, cry!
The houses and harbor of Tyre are
destroyed.
This news came to the ships
from the land of Cyprus.
2 Be silent, you who live on the island
of Tyre;
you merchants of Sidon, be silent.
Sailors have made you rich.
3 They traveled the sea to bring grain
from Egypt;
the sailors of Tyre brought grain
from the Nile Valley
and sold it to other nations.

4 Sidon, be ashamed.
Strong city of the sea, be ashamed,
because the sea says:
"I have not felt the pain of giving
birth;
I have not reared young men or
women."

5 Egypt will hear the news about Tyre,
and it will make Egypt hurt with
sorrow.

6 You ships should return to
Tarshish.
You people living near the sea
should be sad.
7 Look at your once happy city!
Look at your old, old city!
People from that city have traveled
far away to live.
8 Who planned Tyre's destruction?
Tyre made others rich.
Its merchants were treated like
princes,
and its traders were greatly
respected.
9 It was the LORD All-Powerful who
planned this.
He decided to make these proud
people unimportant;
he decided to disgrace those who
were greatly respected.
10 Go through your land, people of
Tarshish,
like the Nile goes through Egypt.
There is no harbor for you now!
11 The LORD has stretched his hand
over the sea
and made its kingdoms tremble.
He commands that Canaan's

CONNECT 2-YOU

A GOOD KIND OF SUFFERING

Tagg and I are talking about letting people know that you're a Christian. We have a friend who can share her own experience in this area. Let's welcome Sue, age 12, to Connect 2-You.

Hi, Sue. Tell us what happened.

Sue

Well, in science class we were talking about how the world was created. The teacher explained evolution; then he asked if any of us believed anything different. I raised my hand and told him that I believe God created the world like the Bible says. Now some kids are calling me names like Bible Girl and Jesus Freak. What should I do?

Take it as a compliment. You may think I'm joking, but I'm not. The Bible says that when people insult you for following Jesus, you are blessed. That means God likes what he sees in you. You might want to check out the tips on the Livin' It page on handling bad times, 1 Peter 4:12–19, p. 1704.

You may not enjoy being teased, Sue, but just think! Kids who may have never considered where life comes from may start wondering about the possibility of a Creator. Other Christian kids who were too insecure to share their faith might learn from your example. Aren't you glad you took a risk?

strong, walled cities be destroyed.
12 He said, "Sidon, you will not rejoice
any longer,
because you are destroyed.
Even if you cross the sea to Cyprus,
you will not find a place to rest."
13 Look at the land of the Babylonians;
it is not a country now.
Assyria has made it a place for wild
animals.
Assyria built towers to attack it;
the soldiers took all the treasures
from its cities,
and they turned it into ruins.
14 So be sad, you trading ships,
because your strong city is
destroyed.

15 At that time people will forget about
Tyre for seventy years, which is the
length of a king's life. After seventy
years, Tyre will be like the prostitute in
this song:

16 "Oh woman, you are forgotten.
Take your harp and walk through
the city.
Play your harp well. Sing your song
often.
Then people will remember
you."

17 After seventy years the LORD will
deal with Tyre, and it will again have
trade. It will be like a
prostitute for all the nations of the earth. 18 The
profits will be saved for
the LORD. Tyre will not
keep the money she
earns but will give them
to the people who serve
the LORD, so they will
have plenty of food and
nice clothes.

Look! The LORD will destroy the earth and leave it empty.
—Isaiah 24:1

The Lord Will Punish the World

24 Look! The LORD will destroy the
earth and leave it empty;
he will ruin the surface of the land
and scatter its people.
2 At that time the same thing will
happen to everyone:
to common people and priests,
to slaves and masters,
to women slaves and their women
masters,
to buyers and sellers,
to those who borrow and those
who lend,
to bankers and those who owe the
bank.
3 The earth will be completely empty.
The wealth will all be taken,
because the LORD has commanded
it.
4 The earth will dry up and die;
the world will grow weak and die;
the great leaders in this land will
become weak.
5 The people of the earth have ruined
it,
because they do not follow God's
teachings
or obey God's laws
or keep their agreement with God
that was to last forever.
6 So a curse will destroy the earth.
The people of the world are guilty,
so they will be burned up;
only a few will be left.
7 The new wine will be bad, and the
grapevines will die.
People who were happy will be
sad.
8 The happy music of the tambourines
will end.
The happy soundsof
wild parties will
stop.
The joyful music
from the harps
will end.
9 People will no longer
sing while they
drink their wine.
The beer will taste
bitter to those
who drink it.
10 The ruined city will be empty,
and people will hide behind closed
doors.
11 People in the streets will ask for
wine,
but joy will have turned to
sadness;
all the happiness will have left.
12 The city will be left in ruins,

and its gates will be smashed to pieces.
13 This is what will happen all over the earth
and to all the nations.
The earth will be like an olive tree after the harvest
or like the few grapes left on a vine after harvest.

14 The people shout for joy.
From the west they praise the greatness of the LORD.
15 People in the east, praise the LORD.
People in the islands of the sea, praise the name of the LORD, the God of Israel.
16 We hear songs from every part of the earth
praising God, the Righteous One.

But I said, "I am dying! I am dying!
How terrible it will be for me!
Traitors turn against people;
with their dishonesty, they turn against people."
17 There are terrors, holes, and traps
for the people of the earth.
18 Anyone who tries to escape from the sound of terror
will fall into a hole.
Anyone who climbs out of the hole
will be caught in a trap.
The clouds in the sky will pour out rain,
and the foundations of the earth will shake.
19 The earth will be broken up;
the earth will split open;
the earth will shake violently.
20 The earth will stumble around like someone who is drunk;
it will shake like a hut in a storm.
Its sin is like a heavy weight on its back;
it will fall and never rise again.

21 At that time the LORD will punish
the powers in the sky above
and the rulers on earth below.
22 They will be gathered together
like prisoners thrown into a dungeon;
they will be shut up in prison.
After much time they will be punished.
23 The moon will be embarrassed,
and the sun will be ashamed,
because the LORD All-Powerful will rule as king
on Mount Zion in Jerusalem.
Jerusalem's leaders will see his greatness.

A Song of Praise to God

25 LORD, you are my God.
I honor you and praise you,
because you have done amazing things.
You have always done what you said you would do;
you have done what you planned long ago.
2 You have made the city a pile of rocks
and have destroyed her walls.
The city our enemies built with strong walls is gone;
it will never be built again.
3 People from powerful nations will honor you;
cruel people from strong cities will fear you.
4 You protect the poor;
you protect the helpless when they are in danger.
You are like a shelter from storms,
like shade that protects them from the heat.
The cruel people attack
like a rainstorm beating against the wall,
5 like the heat in the desert.
But you, God, stop their violent attack.
As a cloud cools a hot day,
you silence the songs of those who have no mercy.

God's Banquet for His Servants

6 The LORD All-Powerful will prepare a feast
on this mountain for all people.
It will be a feast with all the best food and wine,
the finest meat and wine.

7 On this mountain God will destroy
the veil that covers all nations,
the veil that stretches over all
peoples;
8 he will destroy
death forever.
The Lord GOD
will wipe
away every
tear from
every face.
He will take away the shame of his
people from the earth.
The LORD has spoken.

25:8
Heaven
What will be missing in heaven?

9 At that time people will say,
"Our God is doing this!
We have waited for him, and he has
come to save us.
This is the LORD. We waited for
him,
so we will rejoice and be happy when
he saves us."
10 The LORD will protect Jerusalem,
but he will crush our enemy Moab
like straw that is trampled down in
the manure.
11 They will spread their arms in it
like a person who is swimming.
But God will bring down their pride,
and all the clever things they have
made will mean nothing.
12 Moab's high walls protect them,
but God will destroy these walls.
He will throw them down to the
ground,
even to the dust.

A Song of Praise to God

26 At that time people will sing this
song in Judah:
We have a strong city.
God protects us with its strong
walls and defenses.
2 Open the gates,
and the good people will enter,
those who follow God.
3 You, LORD, give true peace
to those who depend on you,
because they trust you.
4 So, trust the LORD always,
because he is our Rock forever.
5 He will destroy the proud city,
and he will punish the people
living there.
He will bring
that high
city down to
the ground
and throw it
down into
the dust.

26:4
Trust
Who is your Rock?

FAITH links
THINK ABOUT HIM
ISAIAH 26:3

Quick! Don't think of elephants, starting . . . now. Can't stop thinking of elephants, huh? Whenever you're told to stop thinking about something, your mind instantly focuses on that something. That's why Isaiah said that those who depend on God will be given true peace. By this he meant that those whose thoughts are often on God will experience his peace. God is the only source of true peace.

Feel like things are out of control? Check out these Faithlinks for help:

A Life of Thanksgiving, 1 Kings 1:47–48, p. 435

A Need to Change, Ecclesiastes 1:1–11, p. 873

Like a Tree, Jeremiah 17:5–8, p. 1016

Faith God Notices, Luke 18:35–43, p. 1406

A Different Kind of Fruit, Galatians 5:22–23, p. 1592

The "Quality" of Life, 2 Peter 1:5–8, p. 1708

6 Then those who were hurt by the
city will walk on its ruins;
those who were made poor by the
city will trample it under their
feet.

7 The path of life is level for those who
are right with God;
LORD, you make the way of life
smooth for those people.
8 But, LORD, we are waiting
for your way of justice.
Our souls want to remember
you and your name.
9 My soul wants to be with you at
night,
and my spirit wants to be with you
at the dawn of every day.
When your way of justice comes to
the land,
people of the world will learn the
right way of living.
10 Evil people will not learn to do good
even if you show them kindness.
They will continue doing evil, even if
they live in a good world;
they never see the LORD's
greatness.
11 LORD, you are ready to punish those
people,
but they do not see that.
Show them your strong love for your
people.
Then those who are evil will be
ashamed.
Burn them in the fire
you have prepared for your
enemies.
12 LORD, all our success is because of
what you have done,
so give us peace.
13 LORD, our God, other masters
besides you have ruled us,
but we honor only you.
14 Those masters are now dead;
their ghosts will not rise from
death.
You punished and destroyed them
and erased any memory of them.
15 LORD, you multiplied the number of
your people;
you multiplied them and brought
honor to yourself.
You made the borders of the land
wide.
16 LORD, people remember you when
they are in trouble;
they say quiet prayers to you when
you punish them.
17 LORD, when we are with you,
we are like a woman giving birth to
a baby;
she cries and has pain from the
birth.
18 In the same way, we had pain.
We gave birth, but only to wind.
We don't bring salvation to the land
or make new people for the world.
19 Your people have died, but they will
live again;
their bodies will rise from death.
You who lie in the ground,
wake up and be happy!
The dew covering you is like the dew
of a new day;
the ground will give birth to the
dead.

Judgment: Reward or Punishment

20 My people, go into your rooms
and shut your doors behind you.
Hide in your rooms for a short time
until God's anger is finished.
21 The LORD will leave his place
to punish the people of the world
for their sins.
The earth will show the blood of the
people who have been killed;
it will not cover the dead any
longer.

27 At that time the LORD will punish
Leviathan, the gliding snake.
He will punish Leviathan, the
coiled snake,
with his great and hard and
powerful sword.
He will kill the monster in the sea.

2 At that time
people will sing about the pleasant
vineyard.
3 "I, the LORD, will care for that
vineyard;
I will water it at the right time.
No one will hurt it,

because I will guard it day and
night.
4 I am not angry.
If anyone builds a wall of
thornbushes in war,
I will march to it
and burn it.
5 But if anyone comes
to me for safety
and wants to make
peace with me,
he should come and
make peace with
me."
6 In the days to come,
the people of
Jacob will be like
a plant with good roots;
Israel will grow like a plant
beginning to bloom.
Then the world will be filled with
their children.

But if anyone comes to me for safety and wants to make peace with me, he should come and make peace with me.
—Isaiah 27:5

The Lord Will Send Israel Away

7 The LORD has not hurt his people as
he hurt their enemies;
his people have not been killed like
those who tried to kill them.
8 He will settle his argument with
Israel by sending it far away.
Like a hot desert wind, he will
drive it away.
9 This is how Israel's guilt will be
forgiven;
this is how its sins will be taken
away:
Israel will crush the rocks of the altar
to dust,
and no statues or altars will be
left standing for the Asherah
idols.
10 At that time the strong, walled city
will be empty
like a desert.
Calves will eat grass there.
They will lie down there
and eat leaves from the branches.
11 The limbs will become dry and break
off,
so women will use them for
firewood.
The people refuse to understand,
so God will not comfort them;
their Maker will not be kind to
them.
12 At that time the LORD will begin
gathering his people one by one from the
Euphrates River to the brook of Egypt.
He will separate them
from others as grain is
separated from chaff.
13 Many of my people are
now lost in Assyria. Some
have run away to Egypt.
But at that time a great
trumpet will be blown,
and all those people will
come and worship the
LORD on that holy moun-
tain in Jerusalem.

Warnings to Israel

28 How terrible it will be for
Samaria, the pride of Israel's
drunken people!
That beautiful crown of flowers is
just a dying plant
set on a hill above a rich valley where
drunkards live.
2 Look, the Lord has someone who is
strong and powerful.
Like a storm of hail and strong
wind,
like a sudden flood of water pouring
over the country,
he will throw Samaria down to the
ground.
3 That city, the pride of Israel's
drunken people,
will be trampled underfoot.
4 That beautiful crown of flowers is
just a dying plant
set on a hill above a rich valley.
That city will be like the first fig of
summer.
Anyone who sees it
quickly picks it and eats it.

5 At that time the LORD All-Powerful
will be like a beautiful crown,
like a wonderful crown of flowers
for his people who are left alive.
6 Then he will give wisdom to the
judges who must decide cases
and strength to those who battle at
the city gate.

7 But now those leaders are drunk
with wine;
they stumble from drinking too
much beer.
The priests and prophets are drunk
with beer
and are filled with wine.
They stumble from too much beer.
The prophets are drunk when they
see their visions;
the judges stumble when they
make their decisions.
8 Every table is covered with vomit,
so there is not a clean place
anywhere.

9 The LORD is trying to
teach the people
a lesson;
he is trying to make
them understand
his teachings.
But the people are
like babies too
old for breast
milk,
like those who no longer nurse at
their mother's breast.
10 So they make fun of the LORD's
prophet and say:
"A command here, a command
there.
A rule here, a rule there.
A little lesson here, a little lesson
there."
11 So the LORD will use strange words
and foreign languages
to speak to these people.
12 God said to them,
"Here is a place of rest;
let the tired people come and rest.
This is the place of peace."
But the people would not listen.
13 So the words of the LORD will be,
"A command here, a command there.
A rule here, a rule there.
A little lesson here, a little lesson
there."
They will fall back and be defeated;
they will be trapped and captured.

14 So listen to the LORD's message, you
who brag,
you leaders in Jerusalem.
15 You say, "We have made an
agreement with death;
we have a contract with death.
When terrible punishment passes
by,
it won't hurt us.
Our lies will keep us safe,
and our tricks will hide us."
16 Because of these things, this is
what the Lord GOD says:
"I will put a stone in the ground in
Jerusalem,
a tested stone.
Everything will be
built on this
important and
precious rock.
Anyone who trusts
in it will never be
disappointed.
17 I will use justice as a
measuring line
and goodness as
the standard.
The lies you hide
behind will be
destroyed as if
by hail.
They will be washed away as if in a
flood.
18 Your agreement with death will be
erased;
your contract with death will not
help you.
When terrible punishment comes,
you will be crushed by it.
19 Whenever punishment comes, it will
take you away.
It will come morning after
morning;
it will defeat you by day and by
night.
Those who understand this
punishment will be terrified."
20 You will be like the person who tried
to sleep
on a bed that was too short
and with a blanket that was too
narrow
to wrap around himself.
21 The LORD will fight as he did at
Mount Perazim.

The LORD is trying to teach the people a lesson; he is trying to make them understand his teachings. —Isaiah 28:9

He will be angry as he was in the Valley of Gibeon.
He will do his work, his strange work.
He will finish his job, his strange job.
22 Now, you must not make fun of these things,
or the ropes around you will become tighter.
The Lord GOD All-Powerful has told me
how the whole earth will be destroyed.

The Lord Punishes Fairly

23 Listen closely to what I tell you;
listen carefully to what I say.
24 A farmer does not plow his field all the time;
he does not go on working the soil.
25 He makes the ground flat and smooth.
Then he plants the dill and scatters the cumin.
He plants the wheat in rows,
the barley in its special place,
and other wheat as a border around the field.
26 His God teaches him
and shows him the right way.
27 A farmer doesn't use heavy boards to crush dill;
he doesn't use a wagon wheel to crush cumin.
He uses a small stick to break open the dill,
and with a stick he opens the cumin.
28 The grain is ground to make bread.
People do not ruin it by crushing it forever.
The farmer separates the wheat from the chaff with his cart,
but he does not let his horses grind it.
29 This lesson also comes from the LORD All-Powerful,
who gives wonderful advice, who is very wise.

Warnings to Jerusalem

29 How terrible it will be for you, Jerusalem,
the city where David camped.
Your festivals have continued year after year.
2 I will attack Jerusalem,
and that city will be filled with sadness and crying.
It will be like an altar to me.
3 I will put armies all around you, Jerusalem;
I will surround you with towers
and with devices to attack you.
4 You will be pulled down and will speak from the ground;
I will hear your voice rising from the ground.
It will sound like the voice of a ghost;
your words will come like a whisper from the dirt.

5 Your many enemies will become like fine dust;
the many cruel people will be like chaff that is blown away.
Everything will happen very quickly.
6 The LORD All-Powerful will come
with thunder, earthquakes, and great noises,
with storms, strong winds, and a fire that destroys.
7 Then all the nations that fight against Jerusalem
will be like a dream;
all the nations that attack her
will be like a vision in the night.
8 They will be like a hungry man who dreams he is eating,
but when he awakens, he is still hungry.
They will be like a thirsty man who dreams he is drinking,
but when he awakens, he is still weak and thirsty.
It will be the same way with all the nations
who fight against Mount Zion.

9 Be surprised and amazed.
Blind yourselves so that you cannot see.
Become drunk, but not from wine.
Trip and fall, but not from beer.
10 The LORD has made you go into a deep sleep.

He has closed your eyes. (The
prophets are your eyes.)
He has covered your heads. (The
seers are your heads.)
11This vision is like the words of a
book that is closed and sealed. You may
give the book to someone who can read
and tell that person to read it. But he will
say, "I can't read the book, because it is
sealed." 12Or you may give the book to
someone who cannot read and tell him to
read it. But he will say, "I don't know how
to read."
13The Lord says:
"These people
say they love
me;
they show
honor to me
with words,
but their hearts
are far from me.
The honor they show me
is nothing but human rules.

EMAIL FROM GOD 29:13
Honoring God
What is hypocrisy?

14So I will continue to amaze these
people
by doing more and more miracles.
Their wise men will lose their
wisdom;
their wise men will not be able to
understand."

Warnings About Other Nations

15How terrible it will be for those who
try
to hide things from the LORD
and who do their work in darkness.
They think no one will see them or
know what they do.
16You are confused.
You think the clay is equal to the
potter.
You think that an object can tell the
one who made it,
"You didn't make me."
This is like a pot telling its maker,
"You don't know anything."

A Better Time Is Coming

17In a very short time, Lebanon will
become rich farmland,
and the rich farmland will seem
like a forest.
18At that time the deaf will hear the
words in a book.
Instead of having darkness and
gloom, the blind will see.
19The LORD will make the poor people
happy;
they will rejoice in the Holy One of
Israel.
20Then the people without mercy will
come to an end;
those who do not respect God will
disappear.
Those who enjoy doing evil will be
gone:
21those who lie about others in court,
those who trap people in court,
those who lie and take justice from
innocent people in court.
22This is what the LORD who set
Abraham free says to the family of Jacob:
"Now the people of Jacob will not be
ashamed
or disgraced any longer.
23When they see all their children,
the children I made with my hands,
they will say my name is holy.
They will agree that the Holy One
of Jacob is holy,
and they will respect the God of
Israel.
24People who do wrong will now
understand.
Those who complain will accept
being taught."

Warnings to the Stubborn Nation

30 The LORD said,
"How terrible it will be for these
stubborn children.
They make plans, but they don't ask
me to help them.
They make agreements with other
nations, without asking my
Spirit.
They are adding more and more
sins to themselves.
2They go down to Egypt for help
without asking me about it first.
They hope they will be saved by the
king of Egypt;

WHO ARE THE EGYPTIANS? Isaiah 30:2–5

The Egyptians were from the country founded by Mizraim, one of Noah's grandsons. Egyptians worshiped different parts of nature, like the sun, as if those parts were gods. They even worshiped the Nile River, which ran through their country.

It was in Egypt that the Israelites grew to be a nation. One man, Israel, and his sons moved to Egypt because there was no food in their land. After about 400 years, Israel's descendants had become a whole nation within Egypt, but they were a nation of slaves. (Look at Exodus 12:40, p. 92.) When they decided they wanted to leave, the king of Egypt wouldn't let them. He didn't want to lose all those hard workers. Finally, using a man named Moses, God convinced the king to let them go. Their leaving was called the "Exodus." After the Exodus, Egypt became a much weaker nation.

they want Egypt to protect them.
3 But hiding in Egypt will bring you
only shame;
Egypt's protection will only
disappoint you.
4 Your officers have gone to Zoan,
and your messengers have gone to
Hanes,
5 but they will be put to shame,
because Egypt is useless to them.
It will give no help and will be of no
use;
it will cause them only shame and
embarrassment."

God's Message to Judah

6 This is a message about the animals
in southern Judah:
Southern Judah is a dangerous place
full of lions and lionesses,
poisonous snakes and darting
snakes.
The messengers travel through there
with their wealth on the backs of
donkeys
and their treasure on the backs of
camels.
They carry them to a nation that
cannot help them,
7 to Egypt whose help is useless.
So I call that country Rahab the Do-
Nothing.

8 Now write this on a sign for the
people,
write this on a scroll,
so that for the days to come
this will be a witness forever.
9 These people are like children who
lie and refuse to obey;
they refuse to listen to the LORD's
teachings.
10 They tell the seers,
"Don't see any more visions!"
They say to the prophets,
"Don't tell us the truth!
Say things that will make us feel
good;
see only good things for us.
11 Stop blocking our path.
Get out of our way.
Stop telling us
about God, the Holy One of
Israel."
12 So this is what the Holy One of Israel says:
"You people have refused to accept
this message

and have depended on cruelty and
lies to help you.
13 You are guilty of these things.
So you will be like a high wall with
cracks in it
that falls suddenly and breaks into
small pieces.
14 You will be like a clay jar that breaks,
smashed into many pieces.
Those pieces will be too small
to take coals from the fire
or to get water from a well."

15This is what
the Lord GOD, the
Holy One of Israel,
says:
"If you come back
to me and
trust me, you will be saved.
If you will be calm and trust me,
you will be strong."
But you don't want to do that.

EMAIL FROM GOD
30:15
Courage
Check out where to go to find courage.

16 You say, "No, we need horses to run
away on."
So you will run away on horses.
You say, "We will ride away on fast
horses."
So those who chase you will be
fast.
17 One enemy will make threats,
and a thousand of your men will
run away.
Five enemies will make threats,
and all of you will run from them.
You will be left alone like a flagpole
on a hilltop,
like a banner on a hill.
18 The LORD wants to show his mercy
to you.
He wants to rise and comfort you.
The LORD is a fair God,
and everyone who waits for his
help will be happy.

The Lord Will Help His People

19You people who live on Mount Zion
in Jerusalem will not cry anymore. The
LORD will hear your crying, and he will
comfort you. When he hears you, he
will help you. **20**The Lord has given you
sorrow and hurt like the bread and water
you ate every day. He is your teacher; he
will not continue to hide from you, but
you will see your teacher with your own
eyes. **21**If you go the wrong way—to the
right or to the left—you will hear a voice
behind you saying, "This is the right way.
You should go this way." **22**You have statues covered with silver and gold, but you
will ruin them for further use. You will
throw them away like filthy rags and say,
"Go away!"

23At that time the LORD will send rain
for the seeds you plant in the ground, and
the ground will grow food for you. The
harvest will be rich and great, and you
will have plenty of food in the fields for
your animals. **24**Your oxen and donkeys
that work the soil will have all the food
they need. You will have to use shovels
and pitchforks to spread all their food.
25Every mountain and hill will have
streams filled with water. These things
will happen after many people are killed
and the towers are pulled down. **26**At that
time the light from the moon will be
bright like the sun, and the light from the
sun will be seven times brighter than
now, like the light of seven days. These
things will happen when the LORD bandages his broken people and heals the
hurts he gave them.

27 Look! The LORD comes from far
away.
His anger is like a fire with thick
clouds of smoke.
His mouth is filled with anger,
and his tongue is like a burning
fire.
28 His breath is like a rushing river,
which rises to the throat.
He will judge the nations as if he is
sifting them through the strainer
of destruction.
He will place in their mouths a bit
that will lead them the wrong
way.
29 You will sing happy songs
as on the nights you begin a
festival.
You will be happy like people
listening to flutes
as they come to the mountain of
the LORD,

to the Rock of Israel.
30 The LORD will cause all people to
hear his great voice
and to see his powerful arm come
down with anger,
like a great fire that burns
everything,
like a great storm with much rain
and hail.
31 Assyria will be afraid when it hears
the voice of the LORD,
because he will strike Assyria with
a rod.
32 When the LORD punishes Assyria
with a rod,
he will beat them to the music of
tambourines and harps;
he will fight against them with his
mighty weapons.
33 Topheth[n] has been made ready for a
long time;
it is ready for the king.
It was made deep and wide
with much wood and fire.
And the LORD's breath will come
like a stream of burning sulfur and
set it on fire.

Warnings About Relying on Egypt

31 How terrible it will be for those
people who go down to
Egypt for help.
They think horses will save them.
They think their many chariots
and strong horsemen will save
them.
But they don't trust God, the Holy
One of Israel,
or ask the LORD for help.
2 But he is wise and can bring them
disaster.
He does not change his warnings.
He will rise up and fight against the
evil people
and against those who try to help
evil people.
3 The Egyptians are only people and
are not God.
Their horses are only animals and
are not spirit.
The LORD will stretch out his arm,

FAITH links

THE FOUNDATION OF OUR HOPE

ISAIAH 31:1-8

Did you ever strongly believe something was true that turned out not to be true? When a person's belief crumbles, we usually say that his belief had no foundation. It's like trying to build a house without including a foundation. Sooner or later, the house will fall apart, because it has nothing to stand on.

Isaiah warned the Israelites against trusting the Egyptians for help. He knew that their hope in Egypt would soon crumble. Trusting God to defend them was the only hope with a solid foundation. What is your hope based on? Some people trust in money or power. Neither will last forever. Only God is all-powerful and everlasting.

Following the Crowd, Numbers 13; 14, p. 193

Down on Discipline?, Proverbs 29:15, p. 867

Long-lasting Hope, Hosea 14, p. 1184

Set for Life?, Obadiah 2–4, p. 1208

Put God First, Acts 5:27–32, p. 1472

More Money?, 1 Timothy 6:10, p. 1649

30:33 Topheth Gehenna; the Valley of Hinnom. Here people burned the bodies of criminals and animals, along with garbage.

and the one who helps will
stumble,
and the people who wanted help
will fall.
All of them will be destroyed
together.

4The LORD says this to me:
"When a lion or a lion's cub kills an
animal to eat,
it stands over the dead animal and
roars.
A band of shepherds
may be assembled against it,
but the lion will not be afraid of their
yelling
or upset by their noise.
So the LORD All-Powerful will come
down
to fight on Mount Zion and on its
hill.
5The LORD All-Powerful will defend
Jerusalem
like birds flying over their nests.
He will defend and save it;
he will 'pass over' and save
Jerusalem."

6You children of Israel, come back to
the God you fought
against. 7The time is
coming when each of
you will stop wor-
shiping idols of gold
and silver, which you
sinned by making.

eMAIL! FROM GOD
31:6–7
Money
What is more lasting than your things?

8"Assyria will be defeated by a
sword, but not the sword of a
person;
Assyria will be destroyed, but not
by a person's sword.
Assyria will run away from the sword
of God,
but its young men will be caught
and made slaves.
9They will panic, and their protection
will be destroyed.
Their commanders will be terrified
when they see God's battle
flag,"
says the LORD,
whose fire is in Jerusalem
and whose furnace is in
Jerusalem.

A Good Kingdom Is Coming

32 A king will rule in a way that
brings justice,
and leaders will make fair
decisions.
2Then each ruler will be like a shelter
from the wind,
like a safe place in a storm,
like streams of water in a dry land,
like a cool shadow from a large
rock in a hot land.

3People will look to the king for help,
and they will truly listen to what
he says.
4People who are now worried will be
able to understand.
Those who cannot speak clearly
now will then be able to speak
clearly and quickly.
5Fools will not be called great,
and people will not respect the
wicked.
6A fool says foolish things,
and in his mind he plans evil.
A fool does things that are wicked,
and he says wrong things about the
LORD.
A fool does not feed the hungry
or let thirsty people drink water.
7The wicked person uses evil like a
tool.
He plans ways to take everything
from the poor.
He destroys the poor with lies,
even when the poor person is in
the right.
8But a good leader plans to do good,
and those good things make him a
good leader.

Hard Times Are Coming

9You women who are calm now,
stand up and listen to me.
You women who feel safe now,
hear what I say.
10You women feel safe now,
but after one year you will be
afraid.
There will be no grape harvest
and no summer fruit to gather.
11Women, you are calm now, but you
should shake with fear.

Women, you feel safe now, but you should tremble.
Take off your nice clothes
and put rough cloth around your waist to show your sadness.
12 Beat your breasts in grief, because the fields that were pleasant are now empty.
Cry, because the vines that once had fruit now have no more grapes.
13 Cry for the land of my people,
in which only thorns and weeds now grow.
Cry for the city that once was happy
and for all the houses that once were filled with joy.
14 The palace will be empty;
people will leave the noisy city.
Strong cities and towers will be empty.
Wild donkeys will love to live there, and sheep will go there to eat.

Things Will Get Better

15 This will continue until God pours his Spirit from above upon us.
Then the desert will be like a fertile field
and the fertile field like a forest.
16 Justice will be found even in the desert,
and fairness will be found in the fertile fields.
17 That fairness will bring peace,
and it will bring calm and safety forever.
18 My people will live in peaceful places
and in safe homes
and in calm places of rest.
19 Hail will destroy the forest,
and the city will be completely destroyed.
20 But you will be happy as you plant seeds near every stream
and as you let your cattle and donkeys wander freely.

Justice will be found even in the desert, and fairness will be found in the fertile fields.
—Isaiah 32:16

Warnings to Assyria and Promises to God's People

33 How terrible it will be for you who destroy others
but have not been destroyed yet.
How terrible it will be for you, traitor,
whom no one has turned against yet.
When you stop destroying,
others will destroy you.
When you stop turning against others,
they will turn against you.

2 LORD, be kind to us.
We have waited for your help.
Give us strength every morning.
Save us when we are in trouble.
3 Your powerful voice makes people run away in fear;
your greatness causes the nations to run away.
4 Like locusts, your enemies will take away the things you stole in war.
Like locusts rushing about, they will take your wealth.
5 The LORD is very great, and he lives in a high place.
He fills Jerusalem with fairness and justice.
6 He will be your safety.
He is full of salvation, wisdom, and knowledge.
Respect for the LORD is the greatest treasure.

7 See, brave men are crying out in the streets;
those who tried to bring peace are crying loudly.
8 There is no one on the roads,
no one walking in the paths.
People have broken the agreements they made.
They refuse to believe the proof from witnesses.
No one respects other people.
9 The land is sick and dying;

Livin' it

TEMPTATIONS

Isaiah 33:15–16

Go Ahead; Try It Is there something that you would like to do, even though you know it's wrong? What tempts you? Maybe it's playing a computer game at your friend's house—one that your parents consider too violent. Or maybe it's copying test answers from the kid in front of you. How do you keep from giving in to these temptations—or do you?

Are you sometimes tempted to do something wrong because everyone else is doing it and you don't want to look like a nerd? God wants us to follow his laws even though it may be the unpopular thing to do. (Read Esther 3:2–4, p. 650.) Are you willing to stand for what's right, even when no one else does?

MORE FAITH links

"Hey, who are the chocolate cookies for? They look awfully good!"

"Those are for our new friends who are coming over to surf the 'net with us. Better not let them tempt you. Why don't you connect to these Faithlinks instead?"

Can't Live Without It?, Genesis 3, p. 7

- Is there anything you want that you would do *anything* to get? Link here to discover the disastrous results of giving in to temptation.

A Real Crowd-pleaser?, Micah 2:6–11, p. 1222

- Have you ever been tempted to tell someone something you thought that person wanted to hear? Why? Did you want him to like you? Did it work?
- Are you a people-pleaser or a God-pleaser? Being a God-pleaser takes courage. God gives you the courage to go against the crowd if necessary.

The Temptation Fighter, Matthew 4:1–11, p. 1278

- How do you handle the temptation to do something wrong? Do you walk away? Blame your parents for not letting you do it? Or get busy doing something else? This Faithlink tells you what Jesus did when he was tempted by the devil. Following his example is the best defense against temptations.

my FAVORITE links

Lebanon is ashamed and dying.
The Plain of Sharon is dry like the desert,
and the trees of Bashan and Carmel are dying.

10 The LORD says, "Now, I will stand up
and show my greatness.
Now, I will become important to the people.
11 You people do useless things
that are like hay and straw.
A destructive wind will burn you like fire.
12 People will be burned until their bones become like lime;
they will burn quickly like dry thornbushes."

13 You people in faraway lands, hear what I have done.
You people who are near me, learn about my power.
14 The sinners in Jerusalem are afraid;
those who are separated from God shake with fear.
They say, "Can any of us live through this fire that destroys?
Who can live near this fire that burns on and on?"
15 A person who does what is right
and speaks what is right,
who refuses to take money unfairly,
who refuses to take money to hurt others,
who does not listen to plans of murder,
who refuses to think about evil—
16 this is the kind of person who will be safe.
He will be protected as he would be in a high, walled city.
He will always have bread,
and he will not run out of water.
17 Your eyes will see the king in his beauty.
You will see the land that stretches far away.
18 You will think about the terror of the past:
"Where is that officer?
Where is the one who collected the taxes?
Where is the officer in charge of our defense towers?"
19 No longer will you see those proud people from other countries,
whose strange language you couldn't understand.

EMAIL FROM GOD
33:15–16
Honesty
Read how you should act.

God Will Protect Jerusalem

20 Look at Jerusalem, the city of our festivals.
Look at Jerusalem, that beautiful place of rest.
It is like a tent that will never be moved;
the pegs that hold her in place will never be pulled up,
and her ropes will never be broken.
21 There the LORD will be our Mighty One.
That land is a place with streams and wide rivers,
but there will be no enemy boats on those rivers;
no powerful ship will sail on them.
22 This is because the LORD is our judge.
The LORD makes our laws.
The LORD is our king.
He will save us.
23 You sailors from other lands, hear:
The ropes on your boats hang loose.
The mast is not held firm.
The sails are not spread open.
Then your great wealth will be divided.
There will be so much wealth that even the crippled people will carry off a share.
24 No one living in Jerusalem will say, "I am sick."
The people who live there will have their sins forgiven.

God Will Punish His Enemies

34 All you nations, come near and listen.
Pay attention, you peoples!

The earth and all the people in it
should listen,
the world and everything in it.
2 The LORD is angry with all the
nations;
he is angry with their armies.
He will destroy them and kill them
all.
3 Their bodies will be thrown outside.
The stink will rise from the bodies,
and the blood will flow down the
mountains.
4 The sun, moon, and stars will
dissolve,
and the sky will be rolled up like a
scroll.
The stars will fall
like dead leaves from a vine
or dried-up figs from a fig tree.
5 The LORD's sword in the sky is
covered with blood.
It will cut through Edom
and destroy those people as an
offering to the LORD.
6 The LORD's sword will be covered
with blood;
it will be covered with fat,
with the blood from lambs and goats,
with the fat from the kidneys of
sheep.
This is because the LORD decided
there will be a sacrifice in
Bozrah
and much killing in Edom.
7 The oxen will be
killed,
and the cattle and
the strong bulls.
The land will be filled
with their blood,
and the dirt will be
covered with
their fat.

The LORD has chosen a time for punishment.
—Isaiah 34:8

8 The LORD has chosen
a time for
punishment.
He has chosen a year when people
must pay for the wrongs they
did to Jerusalem.
9 Edom's rivers will be like hot tar.
Its dirt will be like burning sulfur.
Its land will be like burning tar.
10 The fires will burn night and day;
the smoke will rise from Edom
forever.
Year after year that land will be
empty;
no one will ever travel through
that land again.
11 Birds and small animals will own that
land,
and owls and ravens will live
there.
God will make it an empty wasteland;
it will have nothing left in it.
12 The important people will have no
one left to rule them;
the leaders will all be gone.
13 Thorns will take over the strong
towers,
and wild bushes will grow in the
walled cities.
It will be a home for wild dogs
and a place for owls to live.
14 Desert animals will live with the
hyenas,
and wild goats will call to their
friends.
Night animals will live there
and find a place of rest.
15 Owls will nest there and lay eggs.
When they hatch open, the owls
will gather their young under
their wings.
Hawks will gather
with their own kind.
16 Look at the LORD's
scroll and read what is
written there:
None of these will be
missing;
none will be
without its mate.
God has given the
command,
so his Spirit will
gather them
together.
17 God has divided the
land among
them,
and he has given them each their
portion.
So they will own that land forever
and will live there year after year.

God Will Comfort His People

35 The desert and dry land will become happy;
the desert will be glad and will produce flowers.
Like a flower, 2it will have many blooms.
It will show its happiness, as if it were shouting with joy.
It will be beautiful like the forest of Lebanon,
as beautiful as the hill of Carmel and the Plain of Sharon.
Everyone will see the glory of the LORD
and the splendor of our God.
3 Make the weak hands strong
and the weak knees steady.
4 Say to people who are frightened,
"Be strong. Don't be afraid.
Look, your God will come,
and he will punish your enemies.
He will make them pay for the wrongs they did,
but he will save you."

5 Then the blind people will see again,
and the deaf will hear.
6 Crippled people will jump like deer,
and those who can't talk now will shout with joy.
Water will flow in the desert,
and streams will flow in the dry land.
7 The burning desert will have pools of water,
and the dry ground will have springs.
Where wild dogs once lived,
grass and water plants will grow.
8 A road will be there;
this highway will be called "The Road to Being Holy."
Evil people will not be allowed to walk on that road;
only good people will walk on it.
No fools will go on it.
9 No lions will be there,
nor will dangerous animals be on that road.
They will not be found there.
That road will be for the people God saves;

FAITH links

JUSTICE SERVED

ISAIAH 35:3-4

In television shows and movies, one of the most satisfying things is to see a villain brought to justice. Isaiah wrote of a future time, when God would return. Finally the enemies of his people would be brought to justice. Isaiah did not say that God's people would be the ones to get even with their enemies. God would do the punishing.

Has someone made you angry recently? Feel like getting even? God claims revenge as part of his territory. That means only he can do it. When someone treats you unkindly, tell God all about it. Let him handle it.

Want to know how to handle that kid who always teases you? Check out these Faithlinks:

Can't Live Without It?, Genesis 3, p. 7

The Cover-up, Psalm 32:1–2, p. 733

Anger: Quick or Slow?, Psalm 86:15, p. 776

Quick to Forgive?, Mark 11:25, p. 1349

Say What?!, Ephesians 4:22–29, p. 1603

As Strong as Superman?, Philippians 4:13, p. 1615

10 the people the LORD has freed will
return there.
They will enter
Jerusalem
with joy,
and their
happiness
will last
forever.
Their gladness and joy will fill them
completely,
and sorrow and sadness will go far
away.

EMAIL FROM GOD
35:10
Following God
Where will following God lead you?

The Assyrians Invade Judah

36 During Hezekiah's fourteenth year
as king, Sennacherib king of Assyria attacked all the strong, walled cities
of Judah and captured them. 2The king of
Assyria sent out his field commander
with a large army from Lachish to King
Hezekiah in Jerusalem. When the commander came near the waterway from
the upper pool on the road where people
do their laundry, he stopped. 3Eliakim,
Shebna, and Joah went out to meet him.
Eliakim son of Hilkiah was the palace
manager, Shebna was the royal secretary,
and Joah son of Asaph was the recorder.
4The field commander said to them,
"Tell Hezekiah this:
" 'The great king, the king of Assyria,
says: What can you trust in now? 5You
say you have battle plans and power for
war, but your words mean nothing.
Whom are you trusting for help so that
you turn against me? 6Look, you are depending on Egypt to help you, but Egypt
is like a splintered walking stick. If you
lean on it for help, it will stab your hand
and hurt you. The king of Egypt will hurt
all those who depend on him. 7You might
say, "We are depending on the LORD our
God," but Hezekiah destroyed the LORD's
altars and the places of worship. Hezekiah
told Judah and Jerusalem, "You must worship only at this one altar."
8" 'Now make an agreement with my
master, the king of Assyria: I will give
you two thousand horses if you can find
enough men to ride them. 9You cannot
defeat one of my master's least important
officers, so why do you depend on Egypt
to give you chariots and horsemen? 10I
have not come to attack and destroy this
country without an order from the LORD.
The LORD himself told me to come to this
country and destroy it.' "
11Then Eliakim, Shebna, and Joah
said to the field commander, "Please
speak to us in the Aramaic language. We
understand it. Don't speak to us in Hebrew, because the people on the city wall
can hear you."
12But the commander said, "My master did not send me to tell these things
only to you and your king. He sent me to
speak also to those people sitting on the
wall who will have to eat their own dung
and drink their own urine like you."
13Then the commander stood and
shouted loudly in the Hebrew language,
"Listen to what the great king, the king
of Assyria says, 14The king says you
should not let Hezekiah fool you, because
he can't save you. 15Don't let Hezekiah
talk you into trusting the LORD by saying,
'The LORD will surely save us. This city
won't be handed over to the king of Assyria.'
16"Don't listen to Hezekiah. The king
of Assyria says, 'Make peace with me,
and come out of the city to me. Then
everyone will be free to eat the fruit from
his own grapevine and fig tree and to
drink water from his own well. 17After
that I will come and take you to a land like
your own—a land with grain and new
wine, bread and vineyards.'
18"Don't let Hezekiah fool you, saying, 'The LORD will save us.' Has a god of
any other nation saved his people from
the power of the king of Assyria?
19Where are the gods of Hamath and Arpad? Where are the gods of Sepharvaim?
They did not save Samaria from my
power. 20Not one of all the gods of these
countries has saved his people from me.
Neither can the LORD save Jerusalem
from my power."
21The people were silent. They didn't
answer the commander at all, because
King Hezekiah had ordered, "Don't answer him."
22Then Eliakim, Shebna, and Joah
tore their clothes to show how upset they

were. (Eliakim son of Hilkiah was the
palace manager, Shebna was the royal
secretary, and Joah son of Asaph was the
recorder.) The three men went to Hezekiah and told him what the field commander had said.

Hezekiah Asks God to Help

37 When King Hezekiah heard the
message, he tore his clothes and
put on rough cloth to show how sad he
was. Then he went into the Temple of the
LORD. 2Hezekiah sent Eliakim, the palace manager, and Shebna, the royal secretary, and the older priests to Isaiah.
They were all wearing rough cloth when
they came to Isaiah the prophet, the son
of Amoz. 3They told Isaiah, "This is what
Hezekiah says: Today is a day of sorrow
and punishment and disgrace, as when a
child should be born, but the mother is
not strong enough to give birth to it.
4The king of Assyria sent his field commander to make fun of the living God.
Maybe the LORD your God will hear what
the commander said and will punish him
for it. So pray for the few of us who are
left alive."

5When Hezekiah's officers came to
Isaiah, 6he said to them, "Tell your master this: The LORD says, 'Don't be afraid
of what you have heard. Don't be frightened by the words the servants of the
king of Assyria have spoken against me.
7Listen! I am going to put a spirit in the
king of Assyria. He will hear a report that
will make him return to his own country,
and I will cause him to die by the sword
there.' "

8The field commander heard that the
king of Assyria had left Lachish. When he
went back, he found the king fighting
against the city of Libnah.

9The king received a report that Tir-
hakah, the Cushite king of Egypt, was
coming to attack him. When the king of
Assyria heard this, he sent messengers
to Hezekiah, saying, 10"Tell Hezekiah
king of Judah: Don't be fooled by the god
you trust. Don't believe him when he
says Jerusalem will not be handed over to
the king of Assyria. 11You have heard
what the kings of Assyria have done.
They have completely defeated every
country, so do not think you will be
saved. 12Did the gods of those people
save them? My ancestors destroyed
them, defeating the cities of Gozan, Haran, and Rezeph, and the people of Eden
living in Tel Assar. 13Where are the kings
of Hamath and Arpad? Where are the
kings of Sepharvaim, Hena, and Ivvah?"

Hezekiah Prays to the Lord

14When Hezekiah received the letter
from the messengers and read it, he went
up to the Temple of the LORD. He spread
the letter out before the LORD 15and
prayed to the LORD: 16"LORD All-Powerful, you are the God of Israel, whose
throne is between the gold creatures
with wings, only you are God of all the
kingdoms of the earth. You made the
heavens and the earth. 17Hear, LORD,
and listen. Open your eyes, LORD, and
see. Listen to all the words Sennacherib
has said to insult the living God.

18"It is true, LORD, that the kings of
Assyria have destroyed all these countries and their lands. 19They have
thrown the gods of these nations into the
fire, but they were only wood and rock
statues that people made. So the kings
have destroyed them. 20Now, LORD our
God, save us from the
king's power so that
all the kingdoms of
the earth will know
that you, LORD, are
the only God."

EMAIL FROM GOD
37:20
Troubles
Who will help you overcome problems?

The Lord Answers Hezekiah

21Then Isaiah son of Amoz sent a
message to Hezekiah that said, "This is
what the LORD, the God of Israel, says:
'You prayed to me about Sennacherib
king of Assyria. 22So this is what the
LORD has said against Sennacherib:

The people of Jerusalem
hate you and make fun of you;
the people of Jerusalem
laugh at you as you run away.
23 You have insulted me and spoken
against me;
you have raised your voice
against me.

You have a proud look on your face,
which is against me, the Holy One of Israel!
24 You have sent your messengers to insult the Lord.
You have said, "With my many chariots
I have gone to the tops of the mountains,
to the highest mountains of Lebanon.
I have cut down its tallest cedars
and its best pine trees.
I have gone to its greatest heights
and its best forests.
25 I have dug wells in foreign countries
and drunk water there.
By the soles of my feet,
I have dried up all the rivers of Egypt."

26 " 'King of Assyria, surely you have heard.
Long ago I, the LORD, planned these things.
Long ago I designed them,
and now I have made them happen.
I allowed you to turn those strong, walled cities
into piles of rocks.
27 The people in those cities were weak;
they were frightened and put to shame.
They were like grass in the field,
like tender, young grass,
like grass on the housetop
that is burned by the wind before it can grow.

28 " 'I know when you rest,
when you come and go,
and how you rage against me.
29 Because you rage against me,
and because I have heard your proud words,
I will put my hook in your nose
and my bit in your mouth.
Then I will force you to leave my country
the same way you came.'

30 "Then the LORD said, 'Hezekiah, I
will give you this sign:
This year you will eat the grain that grows wild,
and the second year you will eat what grows wild from that.
But in the third year, plant grain and harvest it.
Plant vineyards and eat their fruit.
31 Some of the people in the family of Judah
will escape.
Like plants that take root,
they will grow strong and have many children.
32 A few people will come out of Jerusalem alive;
a few from Mount Zion will live.
The strong love of the LORD All-Powerful
will make this happen.'

33 "So this is what the LORD says
about the king of Assyria:
'He will not enter this city
or even shoot an arrow here.
He will not fight against it with shields
or build a ramp to attack the city walls.
34 He will return to his country the same way he came,
and he will not enter this city,'
says the LORD.
35 'I will defend and save this city
for my sake and for David, my servant.' "

36 Then the angel of the LORD went
out and killed one hundred eighty-five
thousand men in the Assyrian camp.
When the people got up early the next
morning, they saw all the dead bodies.
37 So Sennacherib king of Assyria left and
went back to Nineveh and stayed there.
38 One day as Sennacherib was worshiping in the temple of his god Nisroch,
his sons Adrammelech and Sharezer
killed him with a sword. Then they escaped to the land of Ararat. So Sennacherib's son Esarhaddon became king of
Assyria.

Hezekiah's Illness

38 At that time Hezekiah became
very sick; he was almost dead. The

prophet Isaiah son of Amoz went to see
him and told him, "This is what the LORD
says: Make arrangements, because you
are not going to live, but die."

2Hezekiah turned toward the wall and
prayed to the LORD, 3"LORD, please remember that I have always obeyed you. I
have given myself completely to you and
have done what you said was right."
Then Hezekiah cried loudly.

4Then the LORD spoke his word to
Isaiah: 5"Go to Hezekiah and tell him:
'This is what the LORD, the
God of your ancestor
David, says: I have
heard your prayer
and seen your tears.
So I will add fifteen
years to your life. 6I
will save you and
this city from the king of Assyria; I will
defend this city.

38:1–6
Prayer
Check out this example of answered prayer.

7" 'The LORD will do what he says.
This is the sign from the LORD to show
you: 8The sun has made a shadow go
down the stairway of Ahaz, but I will make
it go back ten steps.' " So the shadow
made by the sun went back up the ten
steps it had gone down.

9After Hezekiah king of Judah got
well, he wrote this song:

10I said, "I am in the middle of my life.
Do I have to go through the gates
of death?
Will I have the rest of my life taken
away from me?"
11I said, "I will not see the LORD
in the land of the living again.
I will not again see the people
who live on the earth.
12Like a shepherd's tent,
my home has been pulled down
and taken from me.
I am finished
like the cloth a weaver rolls up and
cuts from the loom.*
In one day you brought me to this
end.
13All night I cried loudly.
Like a lion, he crushed all my
bones.
In one day you brought me to this
end.
14I cried like a bird
and moaned like a dove.
My eyes became tired as I looked to
the heavens.
Lord, I have troubles. Please help
me."

15What can I say?
The Lord told me what would
happen and then made it happen.
I have had these troubles in my soul,
so now I will be humble all my life.
16Lord, because of you, people live.
Because of you, my spirit also
lives;
you made me well and let me live.
17It was for my own good
that I had such troubles.
Because you love me very much,
you did not let me die
but threw my sins
far away.
18People in the place of the dead
cannot praise you;
those who have died cannot sing
praises to you;
those who die don't trust you
to help them.
19The people who are alive are the
ones who praise you.
They praise you as I praise you
today.
A father should tell his children
that you provide help.
20The LORD saved me,
so we will play songs on stringed
instruments
in the Temple of the LORD
all the days of our lives.

21Then Isaiah said, "Make a paste
from figs and put it on Hezekiah's boil.
Then he will get well." 22Hezekiah then
asked Isaiah, "What will be the sign?
What will show that I will go up to the
Temple of the LORD?"

Messengers from Babylon

39 At that time Merodach-Baladan
son of Baladan was king of Babylon. He sent letters and a gift to Heze-

38:12 loom A machine for making cloth from
thread.

kiah, because he had heard that Hezekiah
had been sick and was now well. 2Heze-
kiah was pleased and showed the messengers what was in his storehouses: the
silver, gold, spices, expensive perfumes,
his swords and shields, and all his wealth.
He showed them everything in his palace
and in his kingdom.
3Then Isaiah the prophet went to
King Hezekiah and asked him, "What did
these men say? Where did they come
from?"
Hezekiah said, "They came from a faraway country—from Babylon."
4So Isaiah asked him, "What did they
see in your palace?"
Hezekiah said, "They saw everything
in my palace. I showed them all my
wealth."
5Then Isaiah said to Hezekiah: "Listen to the words of the LORD All-Powerful: 6'In the future everything in your
palace and everything your ancestors
have stored up until this day will be taken
away to Babylon. Nothing
will be left,' says the
LORD. 7Some of your own
children, those who will
be born to you, will be
taken away, and they will
become servants in the
palace of the king of Babylon."
8Hezekiah told Isaiah,
"These words from the
LORD are good." He said
this because he thought, "There will be
peace and security in my lifetime."

> The grass dies and the flowers fall, but the word of our God will live forever.
> —Isaiah 40:8

Israel's Punishment Will End

40 Your God says,
"Comfort, comfort my people.
2 Speak kindly to the people of
Jerusalem
and tell them
that their time of service is finished,
that they have paid for their sins,
that the LORD has punished
Jerusalem
twice for every sin they did."
3 This is the voice of one who calls out:
"Prepare in the desert
the way for the LORD.
Make a straight road in the dry lands
for our God.
4 Every valley should be raised up,
and every mountain and hill should
be made flat.
The rough ground should be made
level,
and the rugged ground should be
made smooth.
5 Then the glory of the LORD will be
shown,
and all people together will see it.
The LORD himself said these things."

6 A voice says, "Cry out!"
Then I said, "What shall I cry
out?"

"Say all people are like the grass,
and all their glory is like the
flowers of the field.
7 The grass dies and the flowers fall
when the breath of the LORD blows
on them.
Surely the people are
like grass.
8 The grass dies and the
flowers fall,
but the word of our
God will live
forever."
9 Jerusalem, you have
good news to tell.
Go up on a high
mountain.
Jerusalem, you have good news to
tell.
Shout out loud the good news.
Shout it out and don't be afraid.
Say to the towns of Judah,
"Here is your God."
10 Look, the Lord GOD is coming with
power
to rule all the people.
Look, he will bring reward for his
people;
he will have their payment with
him.
11 He takes care of his people like a
shepherd.
He gathers them like lambs in his
arms

and carries them close to him.
He gently leads the mothers of the lambs.

God Is Supreme

12 Who has measured the oceans in the palm of his hand?
Who has used his hand to measure the sky?
Who has used a bowl to measure all the dust of the earth
and scales to weigh the mountains and hills?
13 Who has known the mind of the LORD
or been able to give him advice?
14 Whom did he ask for help?
Who taught him the right way?
Who taught him knowledge
and showed him the way to understanding?

15 The nations are like one small drop in a bucket;
they are no more than the dust on his measuring scales.
To him the islands are no more than fine dust on his scales.
16 All the trees in Lebanon are not enough for the altar fires,
and all the animals in Lebanon are not enough for burnt offerings.
17 Compared to the LORD all the nations are worth nothing;
to him they are less than nothing.

18 Can you compare God to anything?
Can you compare him to an image of anything?
19 An idol is formed by a craftsman,
and a goldsmith covers it with gold
and makes silver chains for it.
20 A poor person cannot buy those expensive statues,
so he finds a tree that will not rot.
Then he finds a skilled craftsman
to make it into an idol that will not fall over.

21 Surely you know. Surely you have heard.
Surely from the beginning someone told you.
Surely you understand how the earth was created.
22 God sits on his throne above the circle of the earth,
and compared to him, people are like grasshoppers.
He stretches out the skies like a piece of cloth
and spreads them out like a tent to sit under.
23 He makes rulers unimportant
and the judges of this world worth nothing.
24 They are like plants that are placed in the ground,
like seeds that are planted.
As soon as they begin to grow strong,
he blows on them and they die,
and the wind blows them away like chaff.

25 God, the Holy One, says,
"Can you compare me to anyone?
Is anyone equal to me?"

EMAIL FROM GOD
40:25–28
Trust
Why can you trust God?

26 Look up to the skies.
Who created all these stars?
He leads out the army of heaven one by one
and calls all the stars by name.
Because he is strong and powerful,
not one of them is missing.

27 People of Jacob, why do you complain?
People of Israel, why do you say,
"The LORD does not see what happens to me;
he does not care if I am treated fairly"?
28 Surely you know.
Surely you have heard.
The LORD is the God who lives forever,
who created all the world.
He does not become tired or need to rest.
No one can understand how great his wisdom is.

FAITH links

FLY LIKE AN EAGLE

ISAIAH 40:28-31

Could you run two miles and not get tired? If you're not sure, try it and see. If you were an eagle, you could easily go two miles—above the ground that is. An eagle glides along on currents of warm air. Gliding keeps it from having to constantly flap its wings and grow tired. That's why Isaiah mentioned eagles when he shared God's message of comfort. Whenever we try to work for God in our own strength, we grow tired. But trusting in God allows us to build up strength. His strength is like a current of warm air that causes us to soar.

Here are some more links to keep you going:

God's Pep Talk, Joshua 1:5–9, p. 276

Keep On Praying, 1 Samuel 1, p. 354

Standing for What's Right, Esther 3:2–4, p. 651

When the Going Gets Tough, Lamentations 3:22–27, p. 1079

Small Beginnings, Zechariah 4:10, p. 1255

Facing Your Fears, Matthew 8:23–27, p. 1288

29 He gives strength to those who are tired
and more power to those who are weak.
30 Even children become tired and need to rest,
and young people trip and fall.
31 But the people who trust the LORD will become strong again.
They will rise up as an eagle in the sky;
they will run and not need rest;
they will walk and not become tired.

The Lord Will Help Israel

41 The LORD says, "Faraway countries, listen to me.
Let the nations become strong.
Come to me and speak;
we will meet together to decide who is right.

2 "Who caused the one to come from the east?
Who gives him victories everywhere he goes?
The one who brought him gives nations over to him
and defeats kings.
He uses his sword, and kings become like dust.
He uses his bow, and they are blown away like chaff.
3 He chases them and is never hurt,
going places he has never been before.
4 Who caused this to happen?
Who has controlled history since the beginning?
I, the LORD, am the one. I was here at the beginning,
and I will be here when all things are finished."

EMAIL FROM GOD 41:4
God
How long has God been around?

5 All you faraway places, look and be afraid;
all you places far away on the earth, shake with fear.
Come close and listen to me.
6 The workers help each other
and say to each other, "Be strong!"
7 The craftsman encourages the goldsmith,

and the workman who smooths the
metal with a hammer
encourages the one who shapes
the metal.
He says, "This metal work is good."
He nails the statue to a base so it
can't fall over.

Only the Lord Can Save Us

8 The LORD says, "People of Israel,
you are my servants.
People of Jacob, I chose you.
You are from the family of my
friend Abraham.
9 I took you from places far away on
the earth
and called you from a faraway
country.
I said, 'You are my servants.'
I have chosen you and have not
turned against you.
10 So don't worry, because I am with
you.
Don't be afraid, because I am your
God.
I will make you strong and will help
you;
I will support you with my right
hand that saves you.

11 "All those people who are angry with
you
will be ashamed and disgraced.
Those who are against you
will disappear and be lost.
12 You will look for your enemies,
but you will not find them.
Those who fought against you
will vanish completely.
13 I am the LORD your God,
who holds your right hand,
and I tell you, 'Don't be afraid.
I will help you.'
14 You few people of Israel who are left,
do not be afraid even though you
are weak as a worm.
I myself will help you," says the
LORD.
"The one who saves you is the
Holy One of Israel.
15 Look, I have made you like a new
threshing board
with many sharp teeth.
So you will walk on mountains and
crush them;
you will make the hills like chaff.
16 You will throw them into the air, and
the wind will carry them away;
a windstorm will scatter them.
Then you will be happy in the LORD;
you will be proud of the Holy One
of Israel.

17 "The poor and needy people look for
water,
but they can't find any.
Their tongues are dry with thirst.
But I, the LORD, will answer their
prayers;
I, the God of Israel, will not leave
them to die.
18 I will make rivers flow on the dry
hills
and springs flow through the
valleys.
I will change the desert into a lake of
water
and the dry land into fountains of
water.
19 I will make trees grow in the desert—
cedars, acacia, myrtle, and olive
trees.
I will put pine, fir, and cypress trees
growing together in the desert.
20 People will see these things and
understand;
they will think carefully about
these things and learn
that the LORD's power did this,
that the Holy One of Israel made
these things."

The Lord Challenges False Gods

21 The LORD says, "Present your case."
The King of Jacob says, "Tell me
your arguments.
22 Bring in your idols to tell us
what is going to happen.
Have them tell us what happened in
the beginning.
Then we will think about these
things,
and we will know how they will
turn out.
Or tell us what will happen in the
future.

23 Tell us what is coming next
so we will believe that you are gods.
Do something, whether it is good or bad,
and make us afraid.
24 You gods are less than nothing;
you can't do anything.
Those who worship you should be hated.

25 "I have brought someone to come out of the north."
I have called by name a man from the east, and he knows me.
He walks on kings as if they were mud,
just as a potter walks on the clay.
26 Who told us about this before it happened?
Who told us ahead of time so we could say, 'He was right'?
None of you told us anything;
none of you told us before it happened;
no one heard you tell about it.
27 I, the LORD, was the first one to tell Jerusalem that the people were coming home.
I sent a messenger to Jerusalem with the good news.
28 I look at the idols, but there is not one that can answer.
None of them can give advice;
none of them can answer my questions.
29 Look, all these idols are false.
They cannot do anything;
they are worth nothing.

The Lord's Special Servant

42 "Here is my servant, the one I support.
He is the one I chose, and I am pleased with him.
I have put my Spirit upon him,
and he will bring justice to all nations.
2 He will not cry out or yell
or speak loudly in the streets.
3 He will not break a crushed blade of grass
or put out even a weak flame.
He will truly bring justice;
4 he will not lose hope or give up
until he brings justice to the world.
And people far away will trust his teachings."

5 God, the LORD, said these things.
He created the skies and stretched them out.
He spread out the earth and everything on it.
He gives life to all people on earth,
to everyone who walks on the earth.
6 The LORD says, "I, the LORD, called you to do right,
and I will hold your hand
and protect you.
You will be the sign of my agreement with the people,
a light to shine for all people.
7 You will help the blind to see.
You will free those who are in prison,
and you will lead those who live in darkness out of their prison.

8 "I am the LORD. That is my name.
I will not give my glory to another;
I will not let idols take the praise that should be mine.
9 The things I said would happen have happened,
and now I tell you about new things.
Before those things happen,
I tell you about them."

A Song of Praise to the Lord

10 Sing a new song to the LORD;
sing his praise everywhere on the earth.
Praise him, you people who sail on the seas and you animals who live in them.
Praise him, you people living in faraway places.
11 The deserts and their cities should praise him.

41:25 someone . . . north This probably means Cyrus, a king of Persia.

The settlements of Kedar should
praise him.
The people living in Sela should sing
for joy;
they should shout from the
mountaintops.
12 They should give glory to the LORD.
People in faraway lands should
praise him.
13 The LORD will march out like a
strong soldier;
he will be excited like a man ready
to fight a war.
He will shout out the battle cry
and defeat his enemies.

14 The LORD says, "For a long time I
have said nothing;
I have been quiet and held myself
back.
But now I will cry out
and strain like a woman giving
birth to a child.
15 I will destroy the hills and
mountains
and dry up all their plants.
I will make the rivers become dry
land
and dry up the pools of water.
16 Then I will lead the blind along a way
they never knew;
I will guide them along paths they
have not known.
I will make the darkness become
light for them,
and the rough ground smooth.
These are the things I will do;
I will not leave my people.
17 But those who trust in idols,
who say to their statues,
'You are our gods'
will be rejected in disgrace.

Israel Refused to Listen to the Lord

18 "You who are deaf, hear me.
You who are blind, look and see.
19 No one is more blind than my servant
Israel
or more deaf than the messenger I
send.
No one is more blind than the person
I own
or more blind than the servant of
the LORD.
20 Israel, you have seen much, but you
have not obeyed.
You hear, but you refuse to listen."
21 The LORD made his teachings
wonderful,
because he is good.
22 These people have been defeated and
robbed.
They are trapped in pits
or locked up in prison.
Like robbers, enemies have taken
them away,
and there is no one to save them.
Enemies carried them off,
and no one said, "Bring them
back."

23 Will any of you listen to this?
Will you listen carefully in the
future?
24 Who let the people of Jacob be
carried off?
Who let robbers take Israel away?
The LORD allowed this to happen,
because we sinned against him.
We did not live the way he wanted us
to live
and did not obey his teaching.
25 So he became very angry with us
and brought terrible wars against
us.
It was as if the people of Israel had
fire all around them,
but they didn't know what was
happening.
It was as if they were burning,
but they didn't pay any attention.

God Is Always with His People

43 Now this is what the LORD says.
He created you, people of Jacob;
he formed you, people of Israel.
He says, "Don't
be afraid,
because I
have saved
you.
I have called
you by name,
and you are
mine.

43:1–2
Fears
Check to see if God is always with you.

FEARS

Isaiah 43:1–2

Livin' it

Scared to Death! What makes you break out in a cold sweat or want to run away and hide? Creepy, crawly things? The biggest bully in school? Or giving a speech in front of your class? What do you do when you're so afraid your stomach is turning cartwheels? Do you try to stop thinking about it? That's pretty hard to do, isn't it?

Isaiah had a better solution to overcoming fears. He said to focus on God and what he does for you. Then you will experience true peace. (Check out Isaiah 26:3.) How can you trust God to chase out the fear monsters?

Deborah, a leader of Israel, trusted God to handle a very scary situation. The commander of her army, Barak, didn't however. Find out what happened by linking to Judges 4, p. 315. When you face something scary, are you a Barak or a Deborah?

"Boy, Skweek, there's a lot that scares me—thunderstorms, scary movies, snakes. Do you think that God can help chase those fear monsters away?"

"No problem! Read on to find out how God can help you fight those fears!"

Big Lack Attack, 2 Kings 4:1–7, p. 480

- Link here to discover why you don't need to worry about running out of what you need.

Who Ya' Gonna Call?, Psalm 3:4, p. 711

- What's the most scared you've ever been? What did you do? Did you call someone?
- David's life was in danger, and he was really scared. Link here to find out how his solution can help you when you're scared.

A Word About Worry, Matthew 6:25–34, p. 1284

- Fears and worry usually go together. What do you worry about? How much does worrying help you? Link here to discover what Jesus has to say about worries.

Facing Your Fears, Matthew 8:23–27, p. 1288

- Imagine you are in a small boat in the middle of a large lake. Suddenly a fierce storm threatens to sink the boat—and you can't swim! How would you feel? Tell Jesus about your fears. He can handle any "storms" that come into your life.

my FAVORITE links

2 When you pass through the waters, I will be with you.
When you cross rivers, you will not drown.
When you walk through fire, you will not be burned,
nor will the flames hurt you.
3 This is because I, the LORD, am your God,
the Holy One of Israel, your Savior.
I gave Egypt to pay for you,
and I gave Cush and Seba to make you mine.
4 Because you are precious to me,
because I give you honor and love you,
I will give other people in your place;
I will give other nations to save your life.
5 Don't be afraid, because I am with you.
I will bring your children from the east
and gather you from the west.
6 I will tell the north: Give my people to me.
I will tell the south: Don't keep my people in prison.
Bring my sons from far away
and my daughters from faraway places.
7 Bring to me all the people who are mine,
whom I made for my glory,
whom I formed and made."

Judah Is God's Witness

8 Bring out the people who have eyes but don't see
and those who have ears but don't hear.
9 All the nations gather together,
and all the people come together.
Which of their gods said this would happen?
Which of their gods can tell what happened in the beginning?
Let them bring their witnesses to prove they were right.
Then others will say, "It is true."
10 The LORD says, "You are my witnesses
and the servant I chose.
I chose you so you would know and believe me,
so you would understand that I am the true God.
There was no God before me,
and there will be no God after me.
11 I myself am the LORD;
I am the only Savior.
12 I myself have spoken to you, saved you, and told you these things.
It was not some foreign god among you.
You are my witnesses, and I am God,"
says the LORD.
13 "I have always been God.
No one can save people from my power;
when I do something, no one can change it."

14 This is what the LORD, who saves you,
the Holy One of Israel, says:
"I will send armies to Babylon for you,
and I will knock down all its locked gates.
The Babylonians will shout their cries of sorrow.
15 I am the LORD, your Holy One,
the Creator of Israel, your King."

God Will Save His People Again

16 This is what the LORD says.
He is the one who made a road through the sea
and a path through rough waters.
17 He is the one who defeated the chariots and horses
and the mighty armies.
They fell together and will never rise again.
They were destroyed as a flame is put out.
18 The LORD says, "Forget what happened before,
and do not think about the past.
19 Look at the new thing I am going to do.
It is already happening. Don't you see it?

I will make a road in the desert
and rivers in the dry land.
20 Even the wild animals will be
thankful to me—
the wild dogs and owls.
They will honor me when I put water
in the desert
and rivers in the dry land
to give water to my people, the ones
I chose.
21 The people I made
will sing songs to praise me.

22 "People of Jacob, you have not called
to me;
people of Israel, you have become
tired of me.
23 You have not brought me your
sacrifices of sheep
nor honored me with your
sacrifices.
I did not weigh you down with
sacrifices to offer
or make you tired with incense to
burn.
24 So you did not buy incense for me;
you did not freely bring me fat
from your sacrifices.
Instead you have weighed me down
with your many sins;
you have made me tired of your
many wrongs.

25 "I, I am the One who forgives all
your sins, for my sake;
I will not remember your sins.
26 But you should remind me.
Let's meet and decide what is right.
Tell what you have done and show
you are right.
27 Your first father sinned,
and your leaders have turned
against me.
28 So I will make your holy rulers
unholy.
I will bring destruction on the
people of Jacob,
and I will let Israel be insulted."

The Lord Is the Only God

44 The LORD says, "People of Jacob,
you are my servants. Listen
to me!
People of Israel, I chose you."
2 This is what the LORD says, who
made you,
who formed you in your mother's
body,
who will help you:
"People of Jacob, my servants, don't
be afraid.
Israel, I chose you.
3 I will pour out water for the thirsty
land
and make streams flow on dry land.
I will pour out my Spirit into your
children
and my blessing on your
descendants.
4 Your children will grow like a tree in
the grass,
like poplar trees growing beside
streams of water.
5 One person will say, 'I belong to the
LORD,'
and another will use the name
Jacob.
Another will sign his name 'I am the
LORD's,'
and another will use the name
Israel."

6 The LORD, the king of Israel,
is the LORD All-Powerful, who
saves Israel.
This is what he says: "I am the
beginning and the end.
I am the only God.
7 Who is a god like me?
That god should come and prove it.
Let him tell and explain all that has
happened since I set up my
ancient people.
He should also tell what will
happen in the future.
8 Don't be afraid! Don't worry!
I have always told you what will
happen.
You are my witnesses.
There is no other God but me.
I know of no other Rock; I am the
only One."

Idols Are Useless

9 Some people make idols, but they are
worth nothing.

FAITH links

A USELESS THING

ISAIAH 44:9, 18-20

Would you expect a telephone pole to offer you comfort when you're feeling sad? A telephone pole is only useful for holding up phone lines. Yet the Israelites worshiped man-made wooden objects. Isaiah warned them against worshiping false gods. The false gods had replaced God in their hearts.

Worshiping a block of wood may seem silly. However, there are things in *our* lives that can seem more important to us than God. For example, we might think of money, popularity, and possessions more than we think about God. To God, these things are just as useless as a block of wood. God wants us to worship only him.

What You Value, Genesis 25:21–34, p. 34

Idol Talk, Exodus 32, p. 118

The Fence Riders, 1 Kings 18, p. 464

How Big Is God?, Job 38—41, p. 703

Braggin' Rights, Jeremiah 9:23–24, p. 1005

That's False!, 2 John 7–11, p. 1722

People treasure them, but they are
useless.
Those people are witnesses for the
statues, but those people cannot
see.
They know nothing, so they will be
ashamed.
10 Who made these gods?
Who made these useless idols?
11 The workmen who made them will
be ashamed,
because they are only human.
If they all would come together,
they would all be ashamed and
afraid.

12 One workman uses tools to heat
iron,
and he works over hot coals.
With his hammer he beats the metal
and makes a statue,
using his powerful arms.
But when he becomes hungry, he
loses his power.
If he does not drink water, he
becomes tired.

13 Another workman uses a line and a
compass
to draw on the wood.
Then he uses his chisels to cut a
statue
and his calipers to measure the
statue.
In this way, the workman makes the
wood look exactly like a person,
and this statue of a person sits in
the house.
14 He cuts down cedars
or cypress or oak trees.
Those trees grew by their own
power in the forest.
Or he plants a pine tree, and the
rain makes it grow.
15 Then he burns the tree.
He uses some of the wood for a
fire to keep himself warm.
He also starts a fire to bake his
bread.
But he uses part of the wood to make
a god, and then he worships it!
He makes the idol and bows down
to it!
16 The man burns half of the wood in
the fire.
He uses the fire to cook his meat,
and he eats the meat until he is
full.

He also burns the wood to keep himself warm. He says,
"Good! Now I am warm. I can see because of the fire's light."
17 But he makes a statue from the wood that is left and calls it his god.
He bows down to it and worships it.
He prays to it and says,
"You are my god. Save me!"
18 Those people don't know what they are doing. They don't understand!
It is as if their eyes are covered so they can't see.
Their minds don't understand.
19 They have not thought about these things;
they don't understand.
They have never thought to themselves,
"I burned half of the wood in the fire
and used the hot coals to bake my bread.
I cooked and ate my meat.
And I used the wood that was left to make this hateful thing.
I am worshiping a block of wood!"
20 He doesn't know what he is doing;
his confused mind leads him the wrong way.
He cannot save himself
or say, "This statue I am holding is a false god."

The Lord Is the True God

21 "People of Jacob, remember these things!
People of Israel, remember you are my servants.
I made you, and you are my servants.
So Israel, I will not forget you.
22 I have swept away your sins like a big cloud;
I have removed your sins like a cloud that disappears into the air.
Come back to me because I saved you."

23 Skies, sing for joy because the LORD did great things!
Earth, shout for joy, even in your deepest parts!
Sing, you mountains, with thanks to God.
Sing, too, you trees in the forest!
The LORD saved the people of Jacob!
He showed his glory when he saved Israel.
24 This is what the LORD says, who saved you,
who formed you in your mother's body:
"I, the LORD, made everything,
stretching out the skies by myself
and spreading out the earth all alone.
25 I show that the lying prophets' signs are false;
I make fools of those who do magic.
I confuse even wise men;
they think they know much, but I make them look foolish.
26 I make the messages of my servants come true;
I make the advice of my messengers come true.
I say to Jerusalem,
'People will live in you again!'
I say to the towns of Judah,
'You will be built again!'
I say to Jerusalem's ruins,
'I will repair you.'
27 I tell the deep waters, 'Become dry!
I will make your streams become dry!'
28 I say of Cyrus,* 'He is my shepherd
and will do all that I want him to do.
He will say to Jerusalem, "You will be built again!"
He will tell the Temple, "Your foundations will be rebuilt."' "

God Chooses Cyrus to Free Israel

45 This is what the LORD says to Cyrus, his appointed king:
"I hold your right hand
and will help you defeat nations
and take away other kings' power.

44:28 Cyrus A king of Persia who ruled from about 550-530 B.C.

I will open doors for you
so city gates will not stop you.
2 I will go before you
and make the mountains flat.
I will break down the bronze gates of the cities
and cut through their iron bars.
3 I will give you the wealth that is stored away
and the hidden riches
so you will know I am the LORD,
the God of Israel, who calls you by name.
4 I do these things for my servants, the people of Jacob,
and for my chosen people, the Israelites.
Cyrus, I call you by name,
and I give you a title of honor even though you don't know me.
5 I am the LORD. There is no other God;
I am the only God.
I will make you strong,
even though you don't know me,
6 so that everyone will know
there is no other God.
From the east to the west they will know
I alone am the LORD.
7 I made the light and the darkness.
I bring peace, and I cause troubles.
I, the LORD, do all these things.

8 "Sky above, make victory fall like rain;
clouds, pour down victory.
Let the earth receive it,
and let salvation grow,
and let victory grow with it.
I, the LORD, have created it.

9 "How terrible it will be for those who argue with the God who made them.
They are like a piece of broken pottery among many pieces.
The clay does not ask the potter,
'What are you doing?'
The thing that is made doesn't say to its maker,
'You have no hands.'
10 How terrible it will be for the child who says to his father,
'Why are you giving me life?'
How terrible it will be for the child who says to his mother,
'Why are you giving birth to me?' "

11 This is what the LORD,
the Holy One of Israel, and its Maker, says:
"You ask me about what will happen.
You question me about my children.
You give me orders about what I have made.
12 I made the earth
and all the people living on it.
With my own hands I stretched out the skies,
and I commanded all the armies in the sky.
13 I will bring Cyrus to do good things,
and I will make his work easy.
He will rebuild my city
and set my people free
without any payment or reward.
The LORD All-Powerful says this."

I am the LORD. There is no other God; I am the only God.
—Isaiah 45:5

14 The LORD says,
"The goods made in Egypt and Cush
and the tall people of Seba
will come to you
and will become yours.
The Sabeans will walk behind you,
coming along in chains.
They will bow down before you
and pray to you, saying,
'God is with you,
and there is no other God.' "

15 God and Savior of Israel,
you are a God that people cannot see.
16 All the people who make idols will be put to great shame;

they will go off together in
disgrace.
17 But Israel will be saved by the LORD,
and that salvation will continue
forever.
Never again will Israel be put to
shame.

18 The LORD created the heavens.
He is the God who formed the
earth and made it.
He did not want it to be empty,
but he wanted life on the earth.
This is what the LORD says:
"I am the LORD. There is no other
God.
19 I did not speak in secret
or hide my words in some dark
place.
I did not tell the family of Jacob
to look for me in empty places.
I am the LORD, and I speak the truth;
I say what is right.

20 "You people who have escaped from
other nations,
gather together and come before
me;
come near together.
People who carry idols of wood don't
know what they are doing.
They pray to a god who cannot
save them.
21 Tell these people to
come to me.
Let them talk about
these things
together.
Who told you long ago
that this would
happen?
Who told about it
long ago?
I, the LORD, said
these things.
There is no other God besides me.
I am the only good God. I am the
Savior.
There is no other God.

22 "All people everywhere,
follow me and be saved.
I am God. There is no other God.

I made you and will
take care of you.
I will carry you and
save you.
—Isaiah 46:4

23 I will make a promise by my own
power,
and my promise is true;
what I say will not be changed.
I promise that everyone will bow
before me
and will promise to follow me.
24 People will say about me, 'Goodness
and power
come only from the LORD.' "
Everyone who has been angry with
him
will come to him and be ashamed.
25 But with the LORD's help, the people
of Israel
will be found to be good,
and they will praise him.

False Gods Are Useless

46 Bel and Nebo bow down.
Their idols are carried by
animals.
The statues are only heavy loads that
must be carried;
they only make people tired.
2 These gods will all bow down.
They cannot save themselves
but will all be carried away like
prisoners.

3 "Family of Jacob, listen to me!
All you people from Israel who are
still alive, listen!
I have carried you
since you were
born;
I have taken care of
you from your
birth.
4 Even when you are
old, I will be the
same.
Even when your
hair has turned
gray, I will take
care of you.
I made you and will take care of you.
I will carry you and save you.

5 "Can you compare me to anyone?
No one is equal to me or like me.
6 Some people are rich with gold
and weigh their silver on the scales.

They hire a goldsmith, and he makes
it into a god.
Then they bow down and worship it.
7 They put it on their shoulders and
carry it.
They set it in its place, and there it
stands;
it cannot move from its place.
People may yell at it, but it cannot
answer.
It cannot save them from their
troubles.

8 "Remember this, and do not forget it!
Think about these things, you who
turn against God.
9 Remember what happened long ago.
Remember that I am God, and
there is no other God.
I am God, and there is no one like
me.
10 From the beginning I told you what
would happen in the end.
A long time ago I told you things
that have not yet happened.
When I plan something, it happens.
What I want to do, I will do.
11 I am calling a man from the east to
carry out my plan;
he will come like a hawk from a
country far away.
I will make what I have said come
true;
I will do what I have planned.
12 Listen to me, you stubborn people,
who are far from what is right.
13 I will soon do the things that are
right.
I will bring salvation soon.
I will save Jerusalem
and bring glory to Israel."

God Will Destroy Babylon

47 The LORD says, "City of Babylon,
go down and sit in the dirt.
People of Babylon, sit on the ground.
You are no longer the ruler.
You will no longer be called
tender or beautiful.
2 You must use large stones to grind
grain into flour.
Remove your veil and your nice
skirts.
Uncover your legs and cross the
rivers.
3 People will see your nakedness;
they will see your shame.
I will punish you;
I will punish every one of you."

4 Our Savior is named the LORD All-
Powerful;
he is the Holy One of Israel.

5 "Babylon, sit in darkness and say
nothing.
You will no longer be called the
queen of kingdoms.
6 I was angry with my people,
so I rejected those who belonged
to me.
I gave them to you,
but you showed them no mercy.
You even made the old people
work very hard.
7 You said, 'I will live forever
as the queen.'
But you did not think about these
things
or consider what would happen.

8 "Now, listen, you lover of pleasure.
You think you are safe.
You tell yourself,
'I am the only important person.
I will never be a widow
or lose my children.'
9 Two things will happen to you
suddenly, in a single day.
You will lose your children and
your husband.
These things will truly happen to
you,
in spite of all your magic,
in spite of your powerful tricks.
10 You do evil things, but you feel safe
and say, 'No one sees what I do.'
Your wisdom and knowledge
have fooled you.
You say to yourself,
'I am God, and no one is equal to
me.'
11 But troubles will come to you,
and you will not know how to stop
them.
Disaster will fall on you,

and you will not be able to keep it
away.
You will be destroyed quickly;
you will not even see it coming.

12 "Keep on using your tricks
and doing all your magic
that you have used since you were
young.
Maybe they will help you;
maybe you will be able to scare
someone.
13 You are tired of the advice you have
received.
So let those who study the sky—
those who tell the future by looking at
the stars and the new moons—
let them save you from what is
about to happen to you.
14 But they are like straw;
fire will quickly burn them up.
They cannot save themselves
from the power of the fire.
They are not like coals that give
warmth
nor like a fire that you may sit
beside.
15 You have worked with these people,
and they have been with you since
you were young,
but they will not be able to help
you.
Everyone will go his own way,
and there will be no one left to
save you."

God Controls the Future

48 The LORD says, "Family of Jacob,
listen to me.
You are called Israel,
and you come from the family of
Judah.
You swear by the LORD's name
and praise the God of Israel,
but you are not honest or sincere.
2 You call yourselves people of the holy
city,
and you depend on the God of
Israel,
who is named the LORD All-
Powerful.
3 Long ago I told you what would
happen.
I said these things and made them
known;
suddenly I acted, and these things
happened.
4 I knew you were stubborn;
your neck was like an iron
muscle,
and your head was like bronze.
5 So a long time ago I told you about
these things;
I told you about them before they
happened
so you couldn't say, 'My idols did
this,
and my wooden and metal statues
made these things happen.'

6 "You heard and saw everything that
happened,
so you should tell this news to
others.
Now I will tell you about new things,
hidden things that you don't know
yet.
7 These things are happening now, not
long ago;
you have not heard about them
before today.
So you cannot say, 'We already knew
about that.'
8 But you have not heard me; you have
not understood.
Even long ago you did not listen to
me.
I knew you would surely turn against
me;
you have fought against me since
you were born.
9 But for my own sake I will be
patient.
People will praise me for not
becoming angry
and destroying you.
10 I have made you pure, but not by fire,
as silver is made pure.
I have purified you by giving you
troubles.
11 I do this for myself, for my own
sake.
I will not let people speak evil
against me,
and I will not let some god take my
glory.

Israel Will Be Free

12 "People of Jacob, listen to me.
People of Israel, I have called you to be my people.
I am God;
I am the beginning and the end.
13 I made the earth with my own hands.
With my right hand I spread out the skies.
When I call them,
they come together before me."

14 All of you, come together and listen.
None of the gods said these things would happen.
The LORD has chosen someone
to attack the Babylonians;
he will carry out his wishes against Babylon.

15 "I have spoken; I have called him.[a]
I have brought him, and I will make him successful.
16 Come to me and listen to this.
From the beginning I have spoken openly.
From the time it began, I was there."

Now, the Lord GOD
has sent me with his Spirit.

17 This is what the LORD, who saves you,
the Holy One of Israel, says:
"I am the LORD your God,
who teaches you to do what is good,
who leads you in the way you should go.
18 If you had obeyed me,
you would have had peace like a full-flowing river.
Good things would have flowed to you like the waves of the sea.
19 You would have had many children,
as many as the grains of sand.
They would never have died out
nor been destroyed."

20 My people, leave Babylon!
Run from the Babylonians!
Tell this news with shouts of joy to the people;
spread it everywhere on earth.
Say, "The LORD has saved his servants, the people of Jacob."
21 They did not become thirsty when he led them through the deserts.
He made water flow from a rock for them.
He split the rock, and water flowed out.

"There is no peace for evil people," says the LORD.
—Isaiah 48:22

22 "There is no peace for evil people,"
says the LORD.

God Calls His Special Servant

49 All of you people in faraway places, listen to me.
Listen, all you nations far away.
Before I was born, the LORD called me to serve him.
The LORD named me while I was still in my mother's body.
2 He made my tongue like a sharp sword.
He hid me in the shadow of his hand.
He made me like a sharp arrow.
He hid me in the holder for his arrows.
3 He told me, "Israel, you are my servant.
I will show my glory through you."
4 But I said, "I have worked hard for nothing;
I have used all my power, but I did nothing useful.
But the LORD will decide what my work is worth;
God will decide my reward."
5 The LORD made me in the body of my mother

48:15 him This probably refers to Cyrus king of Persia.

to be his servant,
to lead the people of Jacob back to him
so that Israel might be gathered to him.
The LORD will honor me,
and I will get my strength from my God.
6 Now he told me,
"You are an important servant to me
to bring back the tribes of Jacob,
to bring back the people of Israel
who are left alive.
But, more importantly, I will make
you a light for all nations
to show people all over the world
the way to be saved."

7 The LORD who saves you
is the Holy One of Israel.
He speaks to the one who is hated by
the people,
to the servant of rulers.
This is what he says: "Kings will see
you and stand to honor you;
great leaders will bow down before
you,
because the LORD can be trusted.
He is the Holy One of Israel, who
has chosen you."

The Day of Salvation

8 This is what the LORD says:
"At the right time I will hear your
prayers.
On the day of salvation I will help
you.
I will protect you,
and you will be the sign of my
agreement with the people.
You will bring back the people to the
land
and give the land that is now
ruined back to its owners.
9 You will tell the prisoners, 'Come out
of your prison.'
You will tell those in darkness,
'Come into the light.'
The people will eat beside the roads,
and they will find food even on
bare hills.
10 They will not be hungry or thirsty.
Neither the hot sun nor the desert
wind will hurt them.

FAITH links

A MOTHER'S LOVE

ISAIAH 49:13-16

Do you ever have to remind your mother or stepmother of your name? Not likely. Even if you come from a family of many children and your mother slips and calls you by your brother's name, you know that your mother knows who you are. She could never forget you.

Isaiah explained that God's love for his people is like a mother's love. To him you are as unforgettable as you are to your mother. God says that even *if* a mother could forget her children (not likely!), he would never forget his people. So, on Mother's Day, give God a thought, too.

Surf on to see how much God loves you:

The Perfect Sacrifice, Leviticus 1—7, p. 135

Your Heavenly Dad, Psalm 103:13, p. 786

What's in a Name?, Isaiah 9:6, p. 908

A Hopeful Name, Hosea 1:3–11, p. 1172

Prove It!, Matthew 16:1–4, p. 1302

The Doubt Remover, Romans 10:8–10, p. 1533

The God who comforts them will
lead them
and guide them by springs of
water.

11 I will make my mountains into roads,
and the roads will be raised up.
12 Look, people are coming to me from far away,
from the north and from the west,
from Aswan in southern Egypt."

13 Heavens and earth, be happy.
Mountains, shout with joy,
because the LORD comforts his people
and will have pity on those who suffer.

Jerusalem and Her Children

14 But Jerusalem said, "The LORD has left me;
the Lord has forgotten me."

15 The LORD answers, "Can a woman forget the baby she nurses?
Can she feel no kindness for the child to which she gave birth?
Even if she could forget her children,
I will not forget you.
16 See, I have written your name on my hand.
Jerusalem, I always think about your walls.
17 Your children will soon return to you,
and the people who defeated you and destroyed you will leave.
18 Look up and look around you.
All your children are gathering to return to you."
The LORD says, "As surely as I live,
your children will be like jewels that a bride wears proudly.

19 "You were destroyed and defeated,
and your land was made useless.
But now you will have more people than the land can hold,
and those people who destroyed you will be far away.
20 Children were born to you while you were sad,
but they will say to you,
'This place is too small for us.
Give us a bigger place to live.'
21 Then you will say to yourself,
'Who gave me all these children?
I was sad and lonely,
defeated and separated from my people.
So who reared these children?
I was left all alone.
Where did all these children come from?' "

22 This is what the Lord GOD says:
"See, I will lift my hand to signal the nations;
I will raise my banner for all the people to see.
Then they will bring your sons back to you in their arms,
and they will carry your daughters on their shoulders.
23 Kings will teach your children,
and daughters of kings will take care of them.
They will bow down before you
and kiss the dirt at your feet.
Then you will know I am the LORD.
Anyone who trusts in me will not be disappointed."

24 Can the wealth a soldier wins in war be taken away from him?
Can a prisoner be freed from a powerful soldier?
25 This is what the LORD says:
"The prisoners will be taken from the strong soldiers.
What the soldiers have taken will be saved.
I will fight your enemies,
and I will save your children.
26 I will force those who trouble you to eat their own flesh.
Their own blood will be the wine that makes them drunk.
Then everyone will know
I, the LORD, am the One who saves you;
I am the Powerful One of Jacob who saves you."

Israel Was Punished for Its Sin

50 This is what the LORD says:
"People of Israel, you say I divorced your mother.
Then where is the paper that proves it?
Or do you think I sold you

to pay a debt?
Because of the evil things you did, I sold you.
Because of the times she turned against me, your mother was sent away.
2 I came home and found no one there;
I called, but no one answered.
Do you think I am not able to save you?
Do I not have the power to save you?
Look, I need only to shout and the sea becomes dry.
I change rivers into a desert,
and their fish rot because there is no water;
they die of thirst.
3 I can make the skies dark;
I can make them black like clothes of sadness."

God's Servant Obeys

4 The Lord GOD gave me the ability to teach
so that I know what to say to make the weak strong.
Every morning he wakes me.
He teaches me to listen like a student.
5 The Lord GOD helps me learn,
and I have not turned against him
nor stopped following him.
6 I offered my back to those who beat me.
I offered my cheeks to those who pulled my beard.
I won't hide my face from them
when they make fun of me and spit at me.
7 The Lord GOD helps me,
so I will not be ashamed.
I will be determined,
and I know I will not be disgraced.
8 He shows that I am innocent, and he is close to me.
So who can accuse me?
If there is someone, let us go to court together.
If someone wants to prove I have done wrong,
he should come and tell me.
9 Look! It is the Lord GOD who helps me.
So who can prove me guilty?
Look! All those who try will become useless like old clothes;
moths will eat them.

10 Who among you fears the LORD
and obeys his servant?
That person may walk in the dark
and have no light.
Then let him trust in the LORD
and depend on his God.

EMAIL! FROM GOD
50:10
Trust
Find out how to rely on God.

11 But instead, some of you want to light your own fires
and make your own light.
So, go, walk in the light of your fires,
and trust your own light to guide you.
But this is what you will receive from me:
You will lie down in a place of pain.

Jerusalem Will Be Saved

51 The LORD says, "Listen to me,
those of you who try to live right
and follow the LORD.
Look at the rock from which you were cut;
look at the stone quarry from which you were dug.
2 Look at Abraham, your ancestor,
and Sarah, who gave birth to your ancestors.
Abraham had no children when I called him,
but I blessed him and gave him many descendants.
3 So the LORD will comfort Jerusalem;
he will show mercy to those who live in her ruins.
He will change her deserts into a garden like Eden;
he will make her empty lands like the garden of the LORD.
People there will be very happy;
they will give thanks and sing songs.

4 "My people, listen to me;
my nation, pay attention to me.
I will give the people my teachings,
and my decisions will be like a
light to all people.
5 I will soon show that I do what is
right.
I will soon save you.
I will use my power and judge all
nations.
All the faraway places are waiting for
me;
they wait for my power to help
them.
6 Look up to the heavens.
Look around you at the earth
below.
The skies will disappear like clouds
of smoke.
The earth will become useless like
old clothes,
and its people will die like flies.
But my salvation will continue
forever,
and my goodness will never end.

7 "You people who know what is right
should listen to me;
you people who follow my
teachings should hear what I
say.
Don't be afraid of the evil things
people say,
and don't be upset by their insults.
8 Moths will eat those people as if they
were clothes,
and worms will eat them as if they
were wool.
But my goodness will continue
forever,
and my salvation will continue
from now on."

9 Wake up, wake up, and use your
strength,
powerful LORD.
Wake up as you did in the old times,
as you did a long time ago.
With your own power, you cut Rahab
into pieces
and killed that sea monster.
10 You dried up the sea
and the waters of the deep ocean.
You made the deepest parts of the
sea into a road
for your people to cross over and
be saved.
11 The people the LORD has freed will
return
and enter Jerusalem with joy.
Their happiness will last forever.
They will have joy and gladness,
and all sadness and sorrow will be
gone far away.

12 The LORD says, "I am the one who
comforts you.
So why should you be afraid of
people, who die?
Why should you fear people who
die like the grass?
13 Have you forgotten the LORD who
made you,
who stretched
out the skies
and made the
earth?
Why are you
always afraid
of those angry people who trouble
you
and who want to destroy?
But where are those angry people
now?
14 People in prison will soon be set free;
they will not die in prison,
and they will have enough food.
15 I am the LORD your God,
who stirs the sea and makes the
waves roar.
My name is the LORD All-
Powerful.
16 I will give you the words I want you
to say.
I will cover you with my hands and
protect you.
I made the heavens and the earth,
and I say to Jerusalem, 'You are my
people.' "

EMAIL! FROM GOD
51:12–13
Fears
Why should you not fear people?

God Punished Israel

17 Awake! Awake!
Get up, Jerusalem.
The LORD was very angry with you;
your punishment was like wine in
a cup.

The LORD made you drink that wine;
you drank the whole cup until you stumbled.
18 Jerusalem had many people,
but there was not one to lead her.
Of all the people who grew up there,
no one was there to guide her.
19 Troubles came to you two by two,
but no one will feel sorry for you.
There was ruin and disaster, great hunger and fighting.
No one can comfort you.
20 Your people have become weak.
They fall down and lie on every street corner,
like animals caught in a net.
They have felt the full anger of the LORD
and have heard God's angry shout.

21 So listen to me, poor Jerusalem,
you who are drunk but not from wine.
22 Your God will defend his people.
This is what the LORD your God says:
"The punishment I gave you is like a cup of wine.
You drank it and could not walk straight.
But I am taking that cup of my anger away from you,
and you will never be punished by my anger again.
23 I will now give that cup of punishment to those who gave you pain,
who told you,
'Bow down so we can walk over you.'
They made your back like dirt for them to walk on;
you were like a street for them to travel on."

Jerusalem Will Be Saved

52 Wake up, wake up, Jerusalem!
Become strong!
Be beautiful again,
holy city of Jerusalem.
The people who do not worship God
and who are not pure
will not enter you again.
2 Jerusalem, you once were a prisoner.
Now shake off the dust and stand up.
Jerusalem, you once were a prisoner.
Now free yourself from the chains around your neck.
3 This is what the LORD says:
"You were not sold for a price,
so you will be saved without cost."
4 This is what the Lord GOD says:
"First my people went down to Egypt to live.
Later Assyria made them slaves.

5 "Now see what has happened," says the LORD.
"Another nation has taken away my people for nothing.
This nation who rules them makes fun of me," says the LORD.
"All day long they speak against me.
6 This has happened so my people will know who I am,
and so, on that future day, they will know
that I am the one speaking to them.
It will really be me."

> How beautiful is the person who comes over the mountains to bring good news.
> —Isaiah 52:7

7 How beautiful is the person
who comes over the mountains to bring good news,
who announces peace and brings good news,
who announces salvation
and says to Jerusalem,
"Your God is King."
8 Listen! Your guards are shouting.
They are all shouting for joy!
They all will see with their own eyes
when the LORD returns to Jerusalem.
9 Jerusalem, your buildings are destroyed now,
but shout and rejoice together,

because the LORD has comforted his
people.
He has saved Jerusalem.
10 The LORD will show his holy power
to all the nations.
Then everyone on earth
will see the salvation of our God.

11 You people, leave, leave; get out of
Babylon!
Touch nothing that is unclean.
You men who carry the LORD's
things used in worship,
leave there and make yourselves
pure.
12 You will not be forced to leave
Babylon quickly;
you will not be forced to run away,
because the LORD will go before you,
and the God of Israel will guard
you from behind.

The Lord's Suffering Servant

13 The LORD says, "See, my servant
will act wisely.
People will greatly honor and
respect him.
14 Many people were shocked when
they saw him.
His appearance was so changed he
did not look like a man;
his form was changed so much
they could barely tell he was
human.
15 But now he will surprise many
nations.
Kings will be amazed and shut
their mouths.
They will see things they had not
been told about him,
and they will understand things
they had not heard."

53 Who would have believed what
we heard?
Who saw the LORD's power in this?
2 He grew up like a small plant before
the LORD,
like a root growing in a dry land.
He had no special beauty or form to
make us notice him;
there was nothing in his appearance
to make us desire him.

FAITH links

THE ONE WHO SUFFERED

ISAIAH 53

No one likes to suffer. If you get even the tiniest splinter in your finger, your whole body seems to react to the pain. Now imagine having a splinter in your finger for every person who ever lived. That would hurt a lot more than the one splinter! Isaiah wrote about someone whose whole life would be one of suffering. He would die for the sins of everyone who ever lived. Isaiah was talking about Jesus, who was born hundreds of years after this was written.

God loved us so much that "he gave his one and only Son" (John 3:16) to suffer for us. Now that's amazing love!

The Sign of His Presence, Exodus 40:34–38, p. 130

Approaching God, Numbers 3:10, p. 180

Plans for a Son, 1 Chronicles 22:5–19, p. 548

Believe the Impossible?, Ezekiel 37, p. 1131

Clean Inside and Out, Luke 11:39–40, p. 1392

The Gift, John 3:16–18, p. 1427

3 He was hated and rejected by people.
He had much pain and suffering.
People would not even look at him.
He was hated, and we didn't even
notice him.

4 But he took our suffering on him
and felt our pain for us.
We saw his suffering
and thought God was punishing
him.
5 But he was wounded for the wrong
we did;
he was crushed for the evil we did.
The punishment, which made us
well, was given to him,
and we are healed because of his
wounds.
6 We all have
wandered
away like
sheep;
each of us has
gone his own
way.
But the LORD has put on him the
punishment
for all the evil we have done.

EMAIL FROM GOD 53:6
Sin
Does everyone have a sin problem?

7 He was beaten down and punished,
but he didn't say a word.
He was like a lamb being led to be
killed.
He was quiet, as a sheep is quiet
while its wool is being cut;
he never opened his mouth.
8 Men took him away roughly and
unfairly.
He died without children to
continue his family.
He was put to death;
he was punished for
the sins of my
people.
9 He was buried with
wicked men,
and he died with
the rich.
He had done nothing
wrong,
and he had never
lied.

10 But it was the LORD who decided
to crush him and make him suffer.
The LORD made his life a penalty
offering,
but he will still see his descendants
and live a long life.
He will complete the things the
LORD wants him to do.
11 "After his soul suffers many things,
he will see life and be satisfied.
My good servant will make many
people right with God;
he will carry away their sins.
12 For this reason I will make him a
great man among people,
and he will share in all things with
those who are strong.
He willingly gave his life
and was treated like a criminal.
But he carried away the sins of many
people
and asked forgiveness for those
who sinned."

My good servant will make many people right with God; he will carry away their sins.
—Isaiah 53:11

People Will Return to Jerusalem

54 The LORD says, "Sing, Jerusalem.
You are like a woman who never
gave birth to children.
Start singing and shout for joy.
You never felt the pain of giving
birth,
but you will have more children
than the woman who has a
husband.
2 Make your tent bigger;
stretch it out and make it wider.
Do not hold back.
Make the ropes longer
and its stakes stronger,
3 because you will spread out to the
right and to the left.
Your children will
take over other
nations,
and they will again
live in cities that
once were
destroyed.

4 "Don't be afraid,
because you will
not be ashamed.
Don't be
embarrassed,
because you will
not be disgraced.
You will forget the shame you felt
earlier;
you will not remember the shame

you felt when you lost your
husband.
5 The God who made you is like your
husband.
His name is the LORD All-Powerful.
The Holy One of Israel is the one
who saves you.
He is called the God of all the
earth.
6 You were like a woman whose
husband left her,
and you were very sad.
You were like a wife who married
young
and then her husband left her.
But the LORD called you to be his,"
says your God.
7 God says, "I left you for a short time,
but with great kindness I will bring
you back again.
8 I became very angry
and hid from you for a time,
but I will show you mercy with
kindness forever,"
says the LORD who saves you.

9 The LORD says, "This day is like the
time of Noah to me.
I promised then that I would never
flood the world again.
In the same way, I promise I will not
be angry with you
or punish you again.
10 The mountains may disappear,
and the hills may come to an end,
but my love will never disappear;
my promise of peace will not come
to an end,"
says the LORD who shows mercy
to you.

11 "You poor city. Storms have hurt you,
and you have not been comforted.
But I will rebuild you with turquoise
stones,
and I will build your foundations
with sapphires.
12 I will use rubies to build your walls
and shining jewels for the gates
and precious jewels for all your
outer walls.
13 All your children will be taught by
the LORD,
and they will have much peace.
14 I will build you using fairness.
You will be safe from those who
would hurt you,
so you will have nothing to fear.
Nothing will come to make you
afraid.
15 I will not send anyone to attack you,
and you will defeat those who do
attack you.
16 "See, I made the blacksmith.
He fans the fire to make it hotter,
and he makes the kind of tool he
wants.
In the same way I have made the
destroyer to destroy.
17 So no weapon that is used against
you will defeat you.
You will show that those who
speak against you are wrong.
These are the good things my
servants receive.
Their victory comes from me,"
says the LORD.

God Gives What Is Good

55 The LORD says, "All you who are
thirsty,
come and drink.
Those of you who do not have
money,
come, buy and eat!
Come buy wine and milk
without money and without cost.
2 Why spend your money on
something that is not real food?
Why work for something that
doesn't really satisfy you?
Listen closely to me, and you will eat
what is good;
your soul will enjoy the rich food
that satisfies.
3 Come to me and listen;
listen to me so you may live.
I will make an agreement with you
that will last forever.
I will give you the blessings I
promised to David.
4 I made David a witness of my power
for all nations,
a ruler and commander of many
nations.

5 You will call for nations that you don't
yet know.
And these nations that do not
know you will run to you
because of the LORD your God,
because of the Holy One of Israel
who honors you."

6 So you should look for the LORD
before it is too late;
you should call to him while he is
near.
7 The wicked should stop doing
wrong,
and they should stop their evil
thoughts.
They should return to the LORD so
he may have mercy on them.
They should come to our God,
because he will freely forgive
them.

8 The LORD says, "My thoughts are
not like your thoughts.
Your ways are not like my ways.
9 Just as the heavens are higher than
the earth,
so are my ways higher than your
ways
and my thoughts higher than your
thoughts.
10 Rain and snow fall from the sky
and don't return without watering
the ground.
They cause the plants to sprout and
grow,
making seeds for the farmer
and bread for the people.
11 The same thing is true of the words I
speak.
They will not return to me empty.
They make the things happen that I
want to happen,
and they succeed in doing what I
send them to do.

12 "So you will go
out with joy
and be led out
in peace.
The mountains
and hills will
burst into song before you,

55:12
Joy
A picture of joy

FAITH links

WHAT GOD THINKS

ISAIAH 55:8-9

Do you know what your father or stepfather is thinking right now? Probably not, because you can't read minds. But sometimes, you *might* know how he will react to something. How is this possible? It's simple. You know how he reacted in the past. Your relationship with him causes you to know a lot about his likes and dislikes. Many times, we think we can figure God out that easily. We think we know what he thinks and how he will react. According to Isaiah, God doesn't think the way that we think. His thoughts and plans are far more superior. Don't try to second-guess God. Rather, trust that God knows what is best for you.

Here are some more links on putting your trust in God:

What He's Really Like, Deuteronomy 4:15–20, p. 233

An Admirable Quality, 1 Kings 10:1–13, p. 451

Plan for Success, 1 Chronicles 14:8–17, p. 538

How God Speaks, Job 33:14–17, p. 696

Future Hope, Joel 3:17–21, p. 1191

The Finished Product, Philippians 1:6, p. 1609

and all the trees in the fields will
clap their hands.
13 Large cypress trees will grow where
thornbushes
were.
Myrtle trees will
grow where
weeds were.
These things will be a
reminder of the
LORD's promise,
and this reminder
will never be
destroyed."

All Nations Will Obey the Lord

56 This is what the LORD says:
"Give justice to all people,
and do what is right,
because my salvation will come to
you soon.
Soon everyone will know that I do
what is right.
2 The person who obeys the law about
the Sabbath
will be blessed,
and the person who does no evil
will be blessed."

3 Foreigners who have joined the LORD
should not say,
"The LORD will not accept me with
his people."
The eunuch should not say,
"Because I cannot have
children, the LORD will not
accept me."
4 This is what the LORD says:
"The eunuchs should obey the law
about the Sabbath
and do what I want
and keep my agreement.
5 If they do, I will make their names
remembered
within my Temple and its walls.
It will be better for them than
children.
I will give them a name that will last
forever,
that will never be forgotten.
6 Foreigners will join the LORD
to worship him and love him,
to serve him,
to obey the law about the Sabbath,
and to keep my agreement.
7 I will bring these
people to my holy
mountain
and give them joy in
my house of
prayer.
The offerings and
sacrifices
they place on my
altar will please
me,
because my Temple
will be called
a house for prayer
for people from all nations."
8 The Lord GOD says—
he who gathers the Israelites that
were forced to leave their
country:
"I will bring together other people
to join those who are already
gathered."

My Temple will be called a house for prayer for people from all nations.
—Isaiah 56:7

Israel's Leaders Are Evil

9 All you animals of the field,
all you animals of the forest, come
to eat.
10 The leaders who are to guard the
people are blind;
they don't know what they are
doing.
All of them are like quiet dogs
that don't know how to bark.
They lie down and dream
and love to sleep.
11 They are like hungry dogs
that are never satisfied.
They are like shepherds
who don't know what they are
doing.
They all have gone their own
way;
all they want to do is satisfy
themselves.
12 They say, "Come, let's drink some
wine;
let's drink all the beer we want.
And tomorrow we will do this
again,
or, maybe we will have an even
better time."

Israel Does Not Follow God

57 Those who are right with God
may die,
but no one pays attention.
Good people are taken away,
but no one understands.
Those who do right are being taken
away from evil
2 and are given peace.
Those who live as God wants
find rest in death.

3 "Come here, you magicians!
Come here, you sons of prostitutes
and those who take part in
adultery!
4 Of whom are you making fun?
Whom are you insulting?
At whom do you stick out your
tongue?
You turn against God,
and you are liars.
5 You have sexual relations under
every green tree
to worship your gods.
You kill children in the ravines
and sacrifice them in the rocky
places.
6 You take the smooth rocks from the
ravines
as your portion.
You pour drink offerings on them to
worship them,
and you give grain offerings to
them.
Do you think this makes me want
to show you mercy?
7 You make your bed on every hill and
mountain,
and there you offer sacrifices.
8 You have hidden your idols
behind your doors and
doorposts.
You have left me, and you have
uncovered yourself.
You have pulled back the covers
and climbed into bed.
You have made an agreement with
those whose beds you love,
and you have looked at their
nakedness.
9 You use your oils and perfumes
to look nice for Molech.
You have sent your messengers to
faraway lands;
you even tried to send them to the
place of the dead.
10 You were tired from doing these
things,
but you never gave up.
You found new strength,
so you did not quit.

11 "Whom were you so afraid of
that you lied to me?
You have not remembered me
or even thought about me.
I have been quiet for a long time.
Is that why you are not afraid of me?
12 I will tell about your 'goodness' and
what you do,
and those things will do you no
good.
13 When you cry out for help,
let the gods you have gathered
help you.
The wind will blow them all away;
just a puff of wind will take them
away.
But the person who depends on me
will receive the land
and own my holy mountain."

The Lord Will Save His People

14 Someone will say, "Build a road!
Build a road! Prepare the way!
Make the way clear for my
people."
15 And this is the
reason: God
lives forever
and is holy.
He is high and
lifted up.
He says, "I live in
a high and holy place,
but I also live with people who are
sad and humble.
I give new life to those who are
humble
and to those whose hearts are
broken.
16 I will not accuse forever,
nor will I always be angry,
because then human life would grow
weak.

EMAIL FROM GOD
57:15
Humbleness
Who does God give new life to?

Human beings, whom I created,
would die.
17 I was angry because they were
dishonest in order to make money.
I punished them and turned away
from them in anger,
but they continued to do evil.
18 I have seen what they have done, but
I will heal them.
I will guide them and comfort them
and those who felt sad for them.
They will all praise me.
19 I will give peace, real peace, to those
far and near,
and I will heal them," says the
LORD.
20 But evil people are like the angry sea,
which cannot rest,
whose waves toss up waste and
mud.
21 "There is no peace for evil people,"
says my God.

How to Honor God

58 The LORD says, "Shout out loud.
Don't hold back.
Shout out loud like a trumpet.
Tell my people what they have done
against their God;
tell the family of Jacob about their
sins.
2 They still come every day looking for
me
and want to learn my ways.
They act just like a nation that does
what is right,
that obeys the commands of its
God.
They ask me to judge them fairly.
They want God to be near them.
3 They say, 'To honor you we had
special days when we gave up
eating,
but you didn't see.
We humbled ourselves to honor you,
but you didn't notice.' "
But the LORD says, "You do what
pleases yourselves on these
special days,
and you are unfair to your workers.
4 On these special days when you do
not eat, you argue and fight
and hit each other with your fists.

FAITH links

HOW TO WORSHIP GOD

ISAIAH 58

What do you think worshiping God means? Does it just involve going to church every Sunday? Isaiah would say a big no to that. True worship means taking care of the poor and homeless. It means giving clothes to those in need, feeding the hungry, and helping friends and relatives. In short it means caring for others. That's the way that God wants to be honored. If you truly worship God, treat others with kindness.

Want to worship God? Here are some ways to show it:

The MLP, Ruth 1:16–17, p. 345

The Way to Serve God, 1 Kings 9:4, p. 450

Helpful Advice, Job 12:4–5, p. 673

Kindness First, Matthew 9:35–36, p. 1290

The Number One Rule, Mark 12:28–31, p. 1351

The Worst Chore, John 13:3–17, p. 1447

You cannot do these things as you do
now
and believe your prayers are heard
in heaven.
5 This kind of special day is not what I
want.
This is not the way I want people

to be sorry for what they have
done.
I don't want people just to bow their
heads like a plant
and wear rough cloth and lie in
ashes to show their sadness.
This is what you do on your special
days when you do not eat,
but do you
think this is
what the
LORD wants?

58:5–7
Honoring God
How is God honored?

6 "I will tell you the
kind of
special day I want:
Free the people you have put in
prison unfairly
and undo their chains.
Free those to whom you are unfair
and stop their hard labor.
7 Share your food with the hungry
and bring poor, homeless people
into your own homes.
When you see someone who has no
clothes, give him yours,
and don't refuse to help your own
relatives.
8 Then your light will shine like the
dawn,
and your wounds will quickly heal.
Your God will walk before you,
and the glory of the LORD will
protect you from behind.
9 Then you will call out, and the LORD
will answer.
You will cry out, and he will say,
'Here I am.'

"If you stop making trouble for
others,
if you stop using cruel words and
pointing your finger at others,
10 if you feed those who are hungry
and take care of the needs of those
who are troubled,
then your light will shine in the
darkness,
and you will be bright like
sunshine at noon.
11 The LORD will always lead you.
He will satisfy your needs in dry
lands
and give strength to your bones.
You will be like a garden that has
much water,
like a spring that never runs dry.
12 Your people will rebuild the old cities
that are now in ruins;
you will rebuild their foundations.
You will be known for repairing the
broken places
and for rebuilding the roads and
houses.

13 "You must obey God's law about the
Sabbath
and not do what pleases
yourselves on that holy day.
You should call the Sabbath a joyful
day
and honor it as the LORD's holy day.
You should honor it by not doing
whatever you please
nor saying whatever you please on
that day.
14 Then you will find joy in the LORD,
and I will carry you to the high
places above the earth.
I will let you eat the crops of the
land your ancestor Jacob had."
The LORD has said these things.

The Evil That People Do

59 Surely the LORD's power is
enough to save you.
He can hear you when you ask him
for help.
2 It is your evil that has separated
you from your God.
Your sins cause him to turn away
from you,
so he does not hear you.
3 With your hands you have killed
others,
and with your fingers you have
done wrong.
With your lips you have lied,
and with your tongue you say evil
things.
4 People take each other to court
unfairly,
and no one tells the truth in
arguing his case.
They accuse each other falsely and
tell lies.

Livin' it

SIN

Isaiah 59:12–13

Covered with Mud! Ever fallen into the mud? It's very hard to get rid of it all. Even after you scrub yourself, you still may find bits of dirt under your fingernails or between your toes. Mud and dirt have a way of messing up everything. Even just a speck of dirt on a clean pair of pants can make you look pretty bad.

God often talks about sin as being dirty. When you sin, it's as if you went outside and rolled around in that mud on purpose. But instead of being dirty on the outside, sin makes you dirty inside. (Look at Isaiah 6.) How can God make you "clean" again?

Red to White, p. 896

Dirty Inside, p. 904

Real Repentance, p. 993

Clean Inside and Out, p. 1392

Keeping Clean, p. 1576

"Skweek, do you think a little bit of dirt is OK with God? I mean, I'm not really *that* bad!"

"I think you'd better read some of these other Faithlinks, Tagg. God hates sin, but he's got the best cleaner in the world for that! Read on!"

The Cover-up, Psalm 32:1–2, p. 733

- How long do you think you could hide a bag of smelly garbage—old food, that sort of thing—in your room? Not very long, right? The smell would give it away. Sin is like that garbage. How long do you think you can hide a sin from God? What is the only way to get rid of the garbage of sin?

What God "Hates," Proverbs 6:16–19, p. 835

- Link here to read about things that God hates.

The Sin Habit, Romans 7:15–20, p. 1527

- Ever had a habit you just couldn't break, no matter what you did? Paul had a habit like that—sin. What good things do you find hard to do?
- Connect here to find out how Jesus makes it possible for you to develop a habit of pleasing God.

my FAVORITE links

________________ ________________

________________ ________________

________________ ________________

They cause trouble and create
more evil.
5 They hatch evil like eggs from
poisonous snakes.
If you eat one of those eggs, you
will die,
and if you break one open, a
poisonous snake comes out.
People tell lies as they would spin a
spider's web.
6 The webs they make cannot be
used for clothes;
you can't cover yourself with those
webs.
The things they do are evil,
and they use their hands to hurt
others.
7 They eagerly run to do evil,
and they are always ready to kill
innocent people.
They think evil thoughts.
Everywhere they go they cause
ruin and destruction.
8 They don't know how to live in
peace,
and there is no fairness in their
lives.
They are dishonest.
Anyone who lives as they live will
never have peace.

Israel's Sin Brings Trouble

9 Fairness has gone far away;
goodness is nowhere to be
found.
We wait for the light, but there is
only darkness now.
We hope for a bright light, but all
we have is darkness.
10 We are like the blind feeling our way
along a wall.
We feel our way as if we had no
eyes.
In the brightness of day we trip as if
it were night.
We are like dead men among the
strong.
11 All of us growl like the bears.
We call out sadly like the doves.
We look for justice, but there isn't
any.
We want to be saved, but salvation
is far away.
12 We have done many wrong things
against our God;
our sins show we are wrong.
We know we have turned against
God;
we know the evil things we have
done:
13 sinning and
rejecting the
LORD,
turning away
from our God,
planning to hurt
others and to disobey God,
planning and speaking lies.

eMAIL! FROM GOD
59:12–13
Sin
Read about your sinful state.

14 So we have driven away justice,
and we have kept away from what
is right.
Truth is not spoken in the streets;
what is honest is not allowed to
enter the city.
15 Truth cannot be found anywhere,
and people who refuse to do evil
are attacked.

The LORD looked and could not find
any justice,
and he was displeased.
16 He could not find anyone to help the
people,
and he was surprised that there
was no one to help.
So he used his own power to save
the people;
his own goodness gave him
strength.
17 He covered himself with goodness
like armor.
He put the helmet of salvation on
his head.
He put on the clothes of punishment
and wrapped himself in the coat of
his strong love.
18 The LORD will pay back his enemies
for what they have done.
He will show his anger to those
who were against him;
he will punish the people in
faraway places as they deserve.
19 Then people from the west will fear
the LORD,
and people from the east will fear
his glory.

The LORD will come quickly like a
fast-flowing river,
driven by the breath of the LORD.

20 "Then a Savior will come to
Jerusalem
and to the people of Jacob who
have turned from sin,"
says the LORD.
21 The LORD says, "This is my agreement with these people: My Spirit and
my words that I give you will never leave
you or your children or your grandchildren, now and forever."

Jerusalem Will Be Great

60 "Jerusalem, get up and shine,
because your light has come,
and the glory of the LORD shines
on you.
2 Darkness now covers
the earth;
deep darkness
covers her
people.
But the LORD shines
on you,
and people see his
glory around you.
3 Nations will come to
your light;
kings will come to
the brightness of your sunrise.

> Jerusalem, get up and shine, because your light has come, and the glory of the LORD shines on you.
> —Isaiah 60:1

4 "Look around you.
People are gathering and coming to
you.
Your sons are coming from far away,
and your daughters are coming
with them.
5 When you see them, you will shine
with happiness;
you will be excited and full of joy,
because the wealth of the nations
across the seas will be given to
you;
the riches of the nations will come
to you.
6 Herds of camels will cover your land,
young camels from Midian and
Ephah.
People will come from Sheba
bringing gold and incense,
and they will sing praises to the
LORD.
7 All the sheep from Kedar will be
given to you;
the sheep from Nebaioth will be
brought to you.
They will be pleasing sacrifices on
my altar,
and I will make my beautiful
Temple more beautiful.

8 "The people are returning to you like
clouds,
like doves flying to their nests.
9 People in faraway lands are waiting
for me.
The great trading ships will come
first,
bringing your children from faraway
lands,
and with them
silver and gold.
This will honor the
LORD your God,
the Holy One of
Israel,
who does
wonderful things
for you.

10 "Jerusalem,
foreigners will
rebuild your
walls,
and their kings will serve you.
When I was angry, I hurt you,
but now I want to be kind to you
and comfort you.
11 Your gates will always be open;
they will not be closed day or night
so the nations can bring their wealth
to you,
and their kings will be led to you.
12 The nation or kingdom that doesn't
serve you will be destroyed;
it will be completely ruined.

13 "The great trees of Lebanon will be
given to you:
its pine, fir, and cypress trees
together.
You will use them to make my
Temple beautiful,

and I will give much honor to this
place where I rest my feet.
14 The people who have hurt you will
bow down to you;
those who hated you will bow
down at your feet.
They will call you The City of the
LORD,
Jerusalem, city of the Holy One of
Israel.

15 "You have been hated and left empty
with no one passing through.
But I will make you great from now
on;
you will be a place of happiness
forever and ever.
16 You will be given what you need from
the nations,
like a child drinking milk from its
mother.
Then you will know that it is I, the
LORD, who saves you.
You will know that the Powerful
One of Jacob protects you.
17 I will bring you gold in place of
bronze,
silver in place of iron,
bronze in place of wood,
iron in place of rocks.
I will change your punishment into
peace,
and you will be ruled by what is
right.
18 There will be no more violence in
your country;
it will not be ruined or destroyed.
You will name your walls Salvation
and your gates Praise.
19 The sun will no longer be your light
during the day
nor will the brightness from the
moon be your light,
because the LORD will be your light
forever,
and your God will be your glory.
20 Your sun will never set again,
and your moon will never be dark,
because the LORD will be your light
forever,
and your time of sadness will end.
21 All of your people will do what is
right.
They will receive the earth forever.
They are the plant I have planted,
the work of my own hands
to show my greatness.
22 The smallest family will grow to a
thousand.
The least important of you will
become a powerful nation.
I am the LORD,
and when it is time, I will make
these things happen quickly."

The Lord's Message of Freedom

61 The Lord GOD has put his Spirit
in me,
because the LORD has appointed
me to tell the good news to the
poor.
He has sent me to comfort those
whose hearts are broken,
to tell the captives they are free,
and to tell the prisoners they are
released.
2 He has sent me to announce the time
when the LORD will show his
kindness
and the time when our God will
punish evil people.
He has sent me to comfort all those
who are sad
3 and to help the sorrowing people of
Jerusalem.
I will give them a crown to replace
their ashes,
and the oil of gladness to replace
their sorrow,
and clothes of praise to replace
their spirit of sadness.
Then they will be called Trees of
Goodness,
trees planted by the LORD to show
his greatness.

4 They will rebuild the old ruins
and restore the places destroyed
long ago.
They will repair the ruined cities
that were destroyed for so long.

5 My people, foreigners will come to
tend your sheep.
People from other countries will
tend your fields and vineyards.

FAITH links

JESUS' MISSION AND YOURS

ISAIAH 61:1-2

When Jesus lived on earth, he stood up in the synagogue one day and read this passage from Isaiah. (See Luke 4:16–20, p. 1374.) He knew that his mission was to spread the good news of God's kingdom. If you're a Christian, that's your mission, too. God doesn't send you out blindly, not knowing how or when to do it. As Isaiah explained, the Holy Spirit is the One who helps you to serve God in the name of the Lord.

A Different Kind of People, Leviticus 11, p. 146

A Picture of the Past, Psalm 105, p. 789

A Bad Reaction, Jeremiah 36, p. 1043

Empty Words, Ezekiel 33:30–33, p. 1127

Love Him? Show It!, Amos 2:6–7, p. 1196

People of Faith, Hebrews 11, p. 1679

6 You will be called priests of the
LORD;
you will be named the servants of
our God.
You will have riches from all the
nations on earth,
and you will take pride in them.
7 Instead of being ashamed, my people
will receive twice as much
wealth.
Instead of being disgraced, they
will be happy because of what
they receive.
They will receive a double share of
the land,
so their happiness will continue
forever.
8 "I, the LORD, love justice.
I hate stealing and everything that
is wrong.
I will be fair and give my people what
they should have,
and I will make an agreement with
them that will continue forever.
9 Everyone in all nations will know the
children of my people,
and their children will be known
among the nations.
Anyone who sees them will know
that they are people the LORD has
blessed."
10 The LORD makes
me very
happy;
all that I am
rejoices in
my God.
He has covered me with clothes of
salvation
and wrapped me with a coat of
goodness,
like a bridegroom dressed for his
wedding,
like a bride dressed in jewels.
11 The earth causes plants to grow,
and a garden causes the seeds
planted in it to grow.
In the same way the Lord GOD will
make goodness and praise
come from all the nations.

EMAIL FROM GOD **61:10** **Joy** Reasons to be joyful

New Jerusalem

62 Because I love Jerusalem, I will
continue to speak for her;
for Jerusalem's sake I will not stop
speaking
until her goodness shines like a
bright light,
until her salvation burns bright like
a flame.
2 Jerusalem, the nations will see your
goodness,

and all kings will see your glory.
Then you will have a new name,
which the LORD himself will give you.
3 You will be like a beautiful crown in the LORD's hand,
like a king's crown in your God's hand.
4 You will never again be called the People that God Left,
nor your land the Land that God Destroyed.
You will be called the People God Loves,
and your land will be called the Bride of God,
because the LORD loves you.
And your land will belong to him as a bride belongs to her husband.
5 As a young man marries a woman,
so your children will marry your land.
As a man rejoices over his new wife,
so your God will rejoice over you.

EMAIL FROM GOD 62:5
Thankfulness
Is God thankful for you?

6 Jerusalem, I have put guards on the walls to watch.
They must not be silent day or night.
You people who remind the LORD of your needs in prayer
should never be quiet.
7 You should not stop praying to him
until he builds up Jerusalem
and makes it a city all people will praise.

8 The LORD has made a promise,
and by his power he will keep his promise.
He said, "I will never again give your grain
as food to your enemies.
I will not let your enemies drink the new wine
that you have worked to make.
9 The person who gathers food will eat it,
and he will praise the LORD.
The person who gathers the grapes will drink the wine
in the courts of my Temple."
10 Go through, go through the gates!
Make the way ready for the people.
Build up, build up the road!
Move all the stones off the road.
Raise the banner as a sign for the people.

11 The LORD is speaking
to all the faraway lands:
"Tell the people of Jerusalem,
'Look, your Savior is coming.
He is bringing your reward to you;
he is bringing his payment with him.' "
12 His people will be called the Holy People,
the Saved People of the LORD,
and Jerusalem will be called the City God Wants,
the City God Has Not Rejected.

The Lord Judges His People

63 Who is this coming from Edom,
from the city of Bozrah, dressed in red?
Who is this dressed in fine clothes
and marching forward with his great power?

He says, "I, the LORD, speak what is right.
I have the power to save you."

2 Someone asks, "Why are your clothes bright red
as if you had walked on the grapes to make wine?"

3 The LORD answers, "I have walked in the winepress alone,
and no one among the nations helped me.
I was angry and walked on the nations
and crushed them because of my anger.
Blood splashed on my clothes,
and I stained all my clothing.
4 I chose a time to punish people,

and the time has come for me to
save.
5 I looked around, but I saw no one to
help me.
I was surprised that no one
supported me.
So I used my own power to save my
people;
my own anger supported me.
6 While I was angry, I walked on the
nations.
In my anger I punished them
and poured their blood on the
ground."

The Lord's Kindness to His People

7 I will tell about the LORD's kindness
and praise him for everything he
has done.
I will praise the
LORD for the
many good
things he has
given us
and for his
goodness to the people of Israel.

63:7
Kindness
What kind of limits are on God's mercy?

He has shown great mercy to us
and has been very kind to us.
8 He said, "These are my people;
my children will not lie to me."
So he saved them.
9 When they suffered, he suffered also.
He sent his own angel to save
them.
Because of his love and kindness, he
saved them.
Since long ago he has picked them
up and carried them.
10 But they turned against him
and made his Holy Spirit very sad.
So he became their enemy,
and he fought against them.

11 But then his people remembered
what happened long ago,
in the days of Moses and the
Israelites with him.
Where is the LORD who brought the
people through the sea,
with the leaders of his people?
Where is the one
who put his Holy Spirit among
them,
12 who led Moses by the right hand
with his wonderful power,
who divided the water before them
to make his name famous forever,
13 who led the people through the deep
waters?
Like a horse walking through a
desert,
the people did not stumble.
14 Like cattle that go down to the valley,
the Spirit of the LORD gave the
people a place to rest.
LORD, that is the way you led your
people,
and by this you won for yourself
wonderful fame.

A Prayer for Help

15 LORD, look down from the heavens
and see;
look at us from your wonderful and
holy home in heaven.
Where is your strong love and
power?
Why are you keeping your love and
mercy from us?
16 You are our father.
Abraham doesn't know we are his
children,
and Israel doesn't recognize us.
LORD, you are our father.
You are called "the one who has
always saved us."
17 LORD, why are you making us
wander from your ways?
Why do you make us stubborn so
that we don't honor you?
For our sake come back to us,
your servants, who belong to you.
18 Your people had your Temple for a
while,
but now our enemies have walked
on your holy place and crushed
it.
19 We have become like people you
never ruled over,
like those who have never worn
your name.

64 Tear open the skies and come
down to earth
so that the mountains will tremble
before you.
2 Like a fire that burns twigs,

like a fire that makes water boil,
let your enemies know who you are.
Then all nations will shake with
fear when they see you.
3 You have done amazing things we did
not expect.
You came down, and the mountains
trembled before you.
4 From long ago no one has ever heard
of a God like you.
No one has ever seen a God
besides you,
who helps the people who trust
you.
5 You help those who enjoy doing good,
who remember how you want
them to live.
But you were angry because we
sinned.
For a long time we disobeyed,
so how can we be saved?
6 All of us are dirty with sin.
All the right things we have done
are like filthy pieces of cloth.
All of us are like
dead leaves,
and our sins,
like the wind,
have carried
us away.
7 No one worships
you
or even asks you to help us.
That is because you have turned
away from us
and have let our sins destroy us.

EMAIL FROM GOD 64:6
Sin
Is anyone free from sin?

8 But LORD, you are our father.
We are like clay, and you are the
potter;
your hands made us all.
9 LORD, don't continue to be angry
with us;
don't remember our sins forever.
Please, look at us,
because we are your people.
10 Your holy cities are empty like the
desert.
Jerusalem is like a desert;
it is destroyed.
11 Our ancestors worshiped you
in our holy and wonderful Temple,
but now it has been burned with fire,
and all our precious things have
been destroyed.
12 When you see these things, will you
hold yourself back from helping
us, LORD?
Will you be silent and punish us
beyond what we can stand?

FAITH CHALLENGE

Got another challenge for you. Read 64:8 to find out why you were created in a certain way. Knowing God is the potter, what does this mean to you? How does this affect how you should treat others?

TESTING IT

Isaiah 64:8
But LORD, you are our father. We are like clay, and you are the potter; your hands made us all.

____
____
____
____
____
____
____

All People Will Learn About God

65 The LORD says, "I made myself
known to people who were
not looking for me.
I was found by those who were not
asking me for help.
I said, 'Here I am. Here I am,'

to a nation that was not praying to
me.
2 All day long I stood ready to accept
people who turned against me,
but the way they continue to live is
not good;
they do anything they want to do.
3 Right in front of me
they continue to do things that
make me angry.
They offer sacrifices to their gods
in their gardens,
and they burn incense on altars of
brick.
4 They sit among the graves
and spend their nights waiting to
get messages from the dead.
They eat the meat of pigs,
and their pots are full of soup made
from meat that is wrong to eat.
5 But they tell others, 'Stay away, and
don't come near me.
I am too holy for you.'
These people are like smoke in my
nose.
Like a fire that burns all the time,
they continue to make me
angry.

6 "Look, it is written here before me.
I will not be quiet; instead, I will
repay you in full.
I will punish you for what you have
done.
7 I will punish you for your sins and
your ancestors' sins,"
says the LORD.
"They burned incense to gods on the
mountains
and shamed me on those hills.
So I will punish them as they should
be punished
for what they did."

8 This is what the LORD says:
"When there is juice left in the
grapes,
people do not destroy them,
because they know there is good
left in them.
So I will do the same thing to my
servants—
I will not completely destroy them.

9 I will leave some of the children of
Jacob,
and some of the people of Judah
will receive my mountain.
I will choose the people who will live
there;
my servants will live there.
10 Then the Plain of Sharon will be a
field for flocks,
and the Valley of Achor will be a
place for herds to rest.
They will be for the people who
want to follow me.

11 "But as for you who left the LORD,
who forgot about my holy
mountain,
who worship the god Luck,
who hold religious feasts for the
god Fate,
12 I decide your fate, and I will punish
you with my sword.
You will all be killed,
because I called you, but you refused
to answer.
I spoke to you, but you wouldn't
listen.
You did the things I said were evil
and chose to do things that
displease me."

13 So this is what the Lord GOD says:
"My servants will eat,
but you evil people will be hungry.
My servants will drink,
but you evil people will be thirsty.
My servants will be happy,
but you evil people will be shamed.
14 My servants will shout for joy
because of the goodness of their
hearts,
but you evil people will cry,
because you will be sad.
You will cry loudly, because your
spirits will be broken.
15 Your names will be like curses to my
servants,
and the Lord GOD will put you to
death.
But he will call his servants by
another name.
16 People in the land who ask for
blessings

will ask for them from the faithful
God.
And people in the land who make a
promise
will promise in the name of the
faithful God,
because the troubles of the past will
be forgotten.
I will make those troubles go away.

A New Time Is Coming

17 "Look, I will make new heavens and
a new earth,
and people will not remember the
past
or think about those things.
18 My people will be happy forever
because of the things I will make.
I will make a Jerusalem that is full of
joy,
and I will make her people a
delight.
19 Then I will
rejoice over
Jerusalem
and be
delighted
with my
people.
There will never again be heard in
that city
the sounds of crying and sadness.
20 There will never be a baby from that
city
who lives only a few days.
And there will never be an older
person
who doesn't have a long life.
A person who lives a hundred years
will be called young,
and a person who dies before he is
a hundred will be thought of as a
sinner.
21 In that city those who build houses
will live there.
Those who plant vineyards will get
to eat their grapes.
22 No more will one person build a
house and someone else live
there.
One person will not plant a garden
and someone else eat its fruit.
My people will live a long time,
as trees live long.
My chosen people will live there
and enjoy the things they make.
23 They will never again work for
nothing.
They will never again give birth to
children who die young.
All my people will be blessed by the
LORD;
they and their children will be
blessed.
24 I will provide for their needs before
they ask,
and I will help them while they are
still asking for help.
25 Wolves and lambs will eat together in
peace.
Lions will eat hay like oxen,
and a snake on the ground will not
hurt anyone.
They will not hurt or destroy each
other
on all my holy mountain,"
says the LORD.

eMAIL! FROM GOD
65:17–25
Future
Check out what your future holds.

The Lord Will Judge All Nations

66 This is what the LORD says:
"Heaven is my throne,
and the earth is my footstool.
So do you think you can build a house
for me?
Do I need a place to rest?
2 My hand made
all things.
All things are
here because
I made
them,"
says the LORD.

eMAIL! FROM GOD
66:2
Worship
How should you respond to God?

"These are the people I am pleased
with:
those who are not proud or
stubborn
and who fear my word.
3 But those people who kill bulls as a
sacrifice to me
are like those who kill people.
Those who kill sheep as a
sacrifice
are like those who break the necks
of dogs.
Those who give me grain offerings

are like those who offer me the
blood of pigs."
Those who burn incense
are like those who worship idols.
These people choose their own ways,
not mine,
and they love the terrible things
they do.
4 So I will choose their punishments,
and I will punish them with what
they fear most.
This is because I called to them, but
they did not listen.
I spoke to them, but they did not
hear me.
They did things I said were evil;
they chose to do things I did not
like."
5 You people who obey the words of
the LORD,
listen to what he says:
"Your brothers hated you
and turned against you because
you followed me.
Your brothers said, 'Let the LORD be
honored
so we may see you rejoice,'
but they will be punished.
6 Listen to the loud noise coming from
the city;
hear the noise from the Temple.
It is the LORD punishing his
enemies,
giving them the punishment they
should have.
7 "A woman does not give birth before
she feels the pain;
she does not give birth to a son
before the pain starts.
8 No one has ever heard of that
happening;
no one has ever seen that happen.
In the same way no one ever saw a
country begin in one day;
no one has ever heard of a new
nation beginning in one moment.
But Jerusalem will give birth to her
children
just as soon as she feels the birth
pains.
9 In the same way I will not cause pain
without allowing something new to
be born," says the LORD.
"If I cause you the pain,
I will not stop you from giving
birth to your new nation," says
your God.
10 "Jerusalem, rejoice.
All you people who love Jerusalem,
be happy.
Those of you who felt sad for
Jerusalem
should now feel happy with her.
11 You will take comfort from her and be
satisfied,
as a child is nursed by its mother.
You will receive her good things
and enjoy her wealth."
12 This is what the LORD says:
"I will give her peace that will flow to
her like a river.
The wealth of the nations will
come to her like a river
overflowing its banks.
Like babies you will be nursed and
held in my arms
and bounced on my knees.
13 I will comfort you
as a mother comforts her child.
You will be comforted in
Jerusalem."

14 When you see these things, you will
be happy,
and you will grow like the grass.
The LORD's servants will see his
power,
but his enemies will see his anger.
15 Look, the LORD is coming with fire
and his armies with clouds of
dust.
He will punish those people with his
anger;
he will punish them with flames of
fire.
16 The LORD will judge the people with
fire,
and he will destroy many people
with his sword;
he will kill many people.

66:3 dogs . . . pigs God did not want his people to offer dogs and pigs as sacrifices because they were unclean animals.

17"These people make themselves
holy and pure to go to worship their gods
in their gardens. Following each other
into their special gardens, they eat the
meat of pigs and rats and other hateful
things. But they will all be destroyed together," says the LORD.
18"I know they have evil thoughts
and do evil things, so I am coming to punish them. I will gather all nations and all
people, and they will come together and
see my glory.
19"I will put a mark on some of the
people, and I will send some of these
saved people to the nations: to Tarshish,
Libya, Lud (the land of archers), Tubal,
Greece, and all the faraway lands. These
people have never heard about what I
have done nor seen my glory. So the
saved people will tell the nations about
my glory. **20**And they will bring all your
fellow Israelites from all nations to my
holy mountain in Jerusalem. Your fellow
Israelites will come on horses, donkeys,
and camels and in chariots and wagons.
They will be like the grain offerings that
the people bring in clean containers to
the Temple," says the LORD. **21**"And I
will choose even some of these people to
be priests and Levites," says the LORD.
22"I will make new heavens and the
new earth, which will last forever," says
the LORD. "In the same way, your names
and your children will always be with me.
23All people will come to worship me
every Sabbath and every New Moon,"
says the LORD. **24**"They will go out and
see the dead bodies of the people who
sinned against me. The worms that eat
them will never die, and the fires that
burn them will never stop, and everyone
will hate to see those bodies."

Jeremiah

THE WEEPING PROPHET

Welcome, newbie! My name is Jeremiah. It was my sad job to tell God's people that they would soon be conquered by their enemies. I wept when the people refused to be sorry for their sins and turn back to God. In fact, I wept so much that people called me the weeping prophet. All my talk of sin and defeat got me into big trouble. Some people were so angry with me that they threw me down a well and left me to die. You'll have to check out Jeremiah 38:1–13 to find out how I survived.

I wrote this book basically because God told me to write it. I spoke God's words, and my friend Baruch wrote them all down. I sent Baruch to the Temple to read the book out loud. I hoped that the people would stop doing bad things and ask God to forgive them. When the king heard God's words, he cut the book into strips and burned it! Baruch and I had to write the book again.

JESUS WATCH

A message of hope is found in Jeremiah 23. The Lord promised to raise up a "good branch" in David's family tree. This "good branch" is Jesus, a descendant of King David. Jesus is a king who rules wisely and always does what is fair and just. Jeremiah gave us another name for Jesus: The Lord Does What Is Right. Jesus brings a new agreement with God. It is not like the old agreement that God made with Moses. In that agreement, God promised to bless his people if they obeyed his law. The people broke the old agreement by worshiping idols. In the new agreement, God promises to forgive our sins when we believe in Jesus. He sends the Holy Spirit to help us be holy and be more like Jesus.

my FAVORITE links

OTHER CONNECTIONS

Livin' it How carefully do you watch your words? Do you think that's important? God does, and the Bible has a lot to say about the way we use our words. Find out why it's best to think first and then speak when you download Loose lips?, Jeremiah 9:3.

Get the INFO The Israelites were surrounded by people who worshiped fake gods. Unfortunately for the Israelites, they quickly forgot about God and chased after these fake gods. Check out some of the gods that were worshiped back in Old Testament times at True or False Gods?, Jeremiah 48:7, 13.

MORE STUFF...

Object Lessons God gave Jeremiah these symbols to help him get his message through:

- Pot of boiling water tipping from the north is a symbol of the Babylonians who attacked Israel from the north (Jeremiah 1:13).
- Ruined linen belt represents the people of Israel who refused to listen to God (Jeremiah 13:1–13).
- Potter's clay is an image of God's ability to do whatever he wants with whomever he wants (Jeremiah 18:1–6).

"Who's a rotten fig?"

"I've heard of rotten eggs, but a rotten fig? Got me on that one. Maybe we should plug into Jeremiah 24 to find out."

MORE STUFF ON THE JEREMIAH SURFWATCH

A born-prophet, Jeremiah 1:4–10
Worthless idols, Jeremiah 10:1–5
A ruined belt, Jeremiah 13:1–11
The broken jar, Jeremiah 19
Stolen treasure, Jeremiah 52

- Too Young to Serve, **Jeremiah 1:4–9**
- A Broken Promise, **Jeremiah 2:1–8**
- All Talk, No Action, **Jeremiah 5:1–2**
- Braggin' Rights, **Jeremiah 9:23–24**
- A Hometown Hurt, **Jeremiah 11:8—12:6**
- Stand!, **Jeremiah 19:14—20:6**
- A Hopeful Future, **Jeremiah 29:11**
- What's Wrong About Rumors, **Jeremiah 29:24–32**
- A Promise from the Heart, **Jeremiah 31:31–33**
- Fear God or People?, **Jeremiah 38:14–21**

1 These are the words of Jeremiah son
of Hilkiah. He belonged to the family
of priests who lived in the town of Anathoth in the land of Benjamin. 2The LORD
spoke his word to Jeremiah during the
thirteenth year that Josiah son of Amon
was king of Judah. 3The LORD also spoke
to Jeremiah while Jehoiakim son of Josiah
was king of Judah and during the eleven
years that Zedekiah son of Josiah was
king of Judah. In the fifth month of his
last year, the people of Jerusalem were
taken away as captives.

The Lord Calls Jeremiah

4The LORD spoke his word to me, saying:
5"Before I made you in your mother's
womb, I chose you.
Before you were born, I set you
apart for a special work.
I appointed you as a prophet to the
nations."
6Then I said, "But Lord GOD, I don't
know how to speak. I am only a boy."
7But the LORD said to me, "Don't say,
'I am only a boy.' You must go everywhere I send you, and you must say everything I tell you to say. 8Don't be afraid
of anyone, because I am with you to protect you," says the LORD.
9Then the LORD reached out his hand
and touched my mouth. He said to me,
"See, I am putting my words in your
mouth. 10Today I have put you in charge
of nations and kingdoms. You will pull up
and tear down, destroy and overthrow,
build up and plant."

Jeremiah Sees Two Visions

11The LORD spoke his word to me,
saying: "Jeremiah, what do you see?"
I answered, "I see a stick of almond
wood."
12The LORD said to me, "You have
seen correctly, because I am watching to
make sure my words come true."
13The LORD spoke his word to me
again: "What do you see?"
I answered, "I see a pot of boiling water, tipping over from the north."
14The LORD said to me, "Disaster will
come from the north and strike all the
people who live in this country. 15In a
short time I will call all of the people in
the northern kingdoms," said the LORD.
"Those kings will come and set up
their thrones
near the entrance of the gates of
Jerusalem.

FAITH links

TOO YOUNG TO SERVE

JEREMIAH 1:4-9

"You're too young!" Have you heard those words recently in connection with an activity you can't do? Maybe you're too young to drive a car or vote right now, but there's one thing you're not too young for: serving God. Jeremiah thought that he was too young to speak for God. But God assured Jeremiah that he would help him. God would give him the words to say.

God has a purpose for everyone. God can use anyone to do his will—so let him use you.

Think God can't use you? Link here:

Everyone Can Help, Numbers 4, p. 181

Your Best Work, 1 Kings 6, p. 443

Said It? Do It!, Lamentations 2:17, p. 1077

Love Him? Show It!, Amos 2:6–7, p. 1196

Just Say Yes!, Matthew 9:9–13, p. 1289

My Best Serve, Acts 6:1–6, p. 1473

They will attack all the city walls
around Jerusalem
and all the cities in Judah.
16 And I will announce my judgments
against my people
because of their evil in turning
away from me.
They offered sacrifices to other gods
and worshiped idols they had made
with their own hands.

17"Jeremiah, get ready. Stand up and
tell them everything I command you to
say. Don't be afraid of the people, or I will
give you good reason to be afraid of them.
18 Today I am going to make you a strong
city, an iron pillar, a bronze wall. You will
be able to stand against everyone in the
land: Judah's kings, officers, priests, and
the people of the land. 19 They will fight
against you, but they will not defeat you,
because I am with you to protect you!"
says the LORD.

Israel Turns from God

2 The LORD spoke his word to me, saying: 2"Go and speak to the people of
Jerusalem, saying: This is what the LORD
says:

'I remember how faithful you were to
me when you were a young
nation.
You loved me like a young bride.
You followed me through the desert,
a land that had never been planted.
3 The people of Israel were holy to the
LORD,
like the first fruits from his
harvest.
Those who tried to hurt Israel were
judged guilty.
Disasters struck them,' " says the
LORD.

4 Hear the word of the LORD, family of
Jacob,
all you family groups of Israel.
5 This is what the LORD says:
"I was fair to your ancestors,
so why did they turn away from
me?
Your ancestors worshiped useless
idols
and became useless themselves.
6 Your ancestors didn't say,
'Where is the LORD who brought
us out of Egypt?
He led us through the desert,

FAITH links

A BROKEN PROMISE

JEREMIAH 2:1-8

Did someone ever promise you that he would be your friend forever, but later wound up breaking that promise? God told Jeremiah to tell the Israelites that they had been unfaithful to him. They had promised to be committed to him, but failed. A commitment is a promise to be faithful. Even though the people were unfaithful to God, God remained faithful to them.

When you make a commitment to a friend, that friend expects you to be loyal. If Jesus is your Savior, you've made a commitment to follow his commands. God wants you to honor your commitment to him.

A Serious Promise, Deuteronomy 23:21–23, p. 257

Loyal to a Friend, 2 Samuel 9, p. 409

The Salt Promise, 2 Chronicles 13:5, p. 576

You Are What You Do, Proverbs 20:11, p. 854

A Christian's Responsibility, Acts 11:26, p. 1484

Hot, Cold, or In Between?, Revelation 3:15, p. 1735

through a dry and rocky land,
through a dark and dangerous land.
He led us where no one travels or lives.'
7 I brought you into a fertile land
so you could eat its fruit and produce.
But you came and made my land unclean;
you made it a hateful place.
8 The priests didn't ask,
'Where is the LORD?'
The people who know the teachings didn't know me.
The leaders turned against me.
The prophets prophesied in the name of Baal
and worshiped useless idols.

9 "So now I will again tell what I have against you," says the LORD.
"And I will tell what I have against your grandchildren.
10 Go across the sea to the island of Cyprus and see.
Send someone to the land of Kedar to look closely.
See if there has ever been anything like this.
11 Has a nation ever exchanged its gods?
(Of course, its gods are not really gods at all.)
But my people have exchanged their glorious God
for idols worth nothing.
12 Skies, be shocked at the things that have happened
and shake with great fear!" says the LORD.
13 "My people have done two evils:
They have turned away from me,
the spring of living water.
And they have dug their own wells,
which are broken wells that cannot hold water.
14 Have the people of Israel become slaves?
Have they become like someone who was born a slave?
Why were they taken captive?
15 Enemies have roared like lions at Israel;
they have growled at Israel.
They have destroyed the land of Israel.
The cities of Israel lie in ruins,
and all the people have left.
16 The men from the cities of Memphis and Tahpanhes
have disgraced you by shaving the top of your head.
17 Haven't you brought this on yourselves
by turning away from the LORD your God
when he was leading you in the right way?
18 It did not help to go to Egypt
and drink from the Shihor River.
It did not help to go to Assyria
and drink from the Euphrates River.
19 Your evil will bring punishment to you,
and the wrong you have done will teach you a lesson.
Think about it and understand
that it is a terrible evil to turn away from the LORD your God.
It is wrong not to fear me,"
says the Lord GOD All-Powerful.

20 "Long ago you refused to obey me as an ox breaks its yoke.
You broke the ropes I used to hold you
and said, 'I will not serve you!'
In fact, on every high hill
and under every green tree
you lay down as a prostitute.
21 But I planted you as a special vine,
as a very good seed.
How then did you turn
into a wild vine that grows bad fruit?
22 Although you wash yourself with cleanser
and use much soap,
I can still see the stain of your guilt," says the Lord GOD.
23 "How can you say to me, 'I am not guilty.
I have not worshiped the Baal idols'?
Look at the things you did in the valley.

Think about what you have done.
You are like a she-camel in mating season
that runs from place to place.
24 You are like a wild donkey that lives in the desert
and sniffs the wind at mating time.
At that time who can hold her back?
Any male who chases her will easily catch her;
at mating time, it is easy to find her.
25 Don't run until your feet are bare
or until your throat is dry.
But you say, 'It's no use!
I love those other gods,
and I must chase them!'

26 "A thief is ashamed when someone catches him stealing.
In the same way, the family of Israel is ashamed—
they, their kings, their officers,
their priests, and their prophets.
27 They say to things of wood, 'You are my father,'
and to idols of stone, 'You gave birth to me.'
Those people won't look at me;
they have turned their backs to me.
But when they get into trouble, they say,
'Come and save us!'
28 Where are the idols you made for yourselves?
Let them come and save you
when you are in trouble!
People of Judah, you have as many idols
as you have towns!

29 "Why do you complain to me?
All of you have turned against me," says the LORD.
30 "I punished your people, but it did not help.
They didn't come back when they were punished.
With your swords you killed your prophets
like a hungry lion.

31 "People of Judah, pay attention to
the word of the LORD:
Have I been like a desert to the people of Israel
or like a dark and dangerous land?
Why do my people say, 'We are free to wander.
We won't come to you anymore'?
32 A young woman does not forget her jewelry,
and a bride does not forget the decorations for her dress.
But my people have forgotten me
for more days than can be counted.
33 You really know how to chase after love.
Even the worst women can learn evil ways from you.
34 Even on your clothes you have the blood
of poor and innocent people,
but they weren't thieves you caught breaking in.
You do all these things,
35 but you say, 'I am innocent.
God is not angry with me.'
But I will judge you guilty of lying,
because you say, 'I have not sinned.'
36 It is so easy for you to change your mind.
Even Egypt will let you down,
as Assyria let you down.
37 You will eventually leave that place
with your hands on your head, like captives.
You trusted those countries,
but you will not be helped by them,
because the LORD has rejected them.

Judah Is Unfaithful

3 "If a man divorces his wife
and she leaves him and marries another man,
should her first husband come back to her again?
If he went back to her, wouldn't the land become completely unclean?
But you have acted like a prostitute with many lovers,
and now you want to come back to me?" says the LORD.

2 "Look up to the bare hilltops, Judah.
Is there any place where you have not been a prostitute?
You have sat by the road waiting for lovers,
like an Arab in the desert.
You made the land unclean,
because you did evil and were like a prostitute.
3 So the rain has not come,
and there have not been any spring rains.
But your face still looks like the face of a prostitute.
You refuse even to be ashamed of what you did.
4 Now you are calling to me,
'My father, you have been my friend since I was young.
5 Will you always be angry at me?
Will your anger last forever?'
Judah, you said this,
but you did as much evil as you could!"

Judah and Israel Are like Sisters

6When King Josiah
was ruling Judah, the
LORD said to me, "Did you
see what unfaithful Israel
did? She was like a prostitute with her
idols on every hill and under every green
tree. 7I said to myself, 'Israel will come
back to me after she does this evil,' but
she didn't come back. And Israel's wicked sister Judah saw what she did. 8Judah
saw that I divorced unfaithful Israel because of her adultery, but that didn't
make Israel's wicked sister Judah afraid.
She also went out and acted like a prostitute! 9And she didn't care that she was
acting like a prostitute. So she made her
country unclean and was guilty of adultery, because she worshiped idols made
of stone and wood. 10Israel's wicked sister didn't even come back to me with her
whole heart, but only pretended," says
the Lord.
11The LORD said to me, "Unfaithful
Israel had a better excuse than wicked
Judah. 12Go and speak this message toward the north:

'Come back, unfaithful people of Israel,' says the LORD.
'I will stop being angry at you,
because I am full of mercy,' says the LORD.
'I will not be angry with you forever.
13 All you have to do is admit your sin—
that you turned against the LORD your God
and worshiped gods under every green tree
and didn't obey me,' " says the LORD.

14"Come back to me, you unfaithful
children," says the LORD, "because I am
your master. I will take one person from
every city and two from
every family group, and I
will bring you to Jerusa-
lem. 15Then I will give
you new rulers who will
be faithful to me, who will
lead you with knowledge
and understanding. 16In
those days there will be
many of you in the land,"
says the LORD. "At that
time people will no long-
er say, 'I remember the
Ark of the Agreement.' They won't think
about it anymore or remember it or miss
it or make another one. 17At that time
people will call Jerusalem The Throne of
the LORD, and all nations will come together in Jerusalem to show respect to
the LORD. They will not follow their stubborn, evil hearts anymore. 18In those
days the family of Judah will join the family of Israel. They will come together
from a land in the north to the land I gave
their ancestors.

19"I, the LORD, said,
'How happy I would be to treat you as my own children
and give you a pleasant land,
a land more beautiful than that of any other nation.'
I thought you would call me 'My Father'

Then I will give you new rulers who will be faithful to me, who will lead you with knowledge and understanding.
—Jeremiah 3:15

and not turn away from me.
20 But like a woman who is unfaithful to
her husband,
family of Israel, you have been
unfaithful to me," says the
LORD.

21 You can hear crying on the bare
hilltops.
It is the people of Israel crying and
praying for mercy.
They have become very evil
and have forgotten the LORD their
God.
22 "Come back to me, you unfaithful
children,
and I will forgive you for being
unfaithful."

"Yes, we will come to you,
because you are the LORD our
God.
23 It was foolish to worship idols on the
hills
and on the mountains.
Surely the salvation of Israel
comes from the LORD our God.
24 Since our youth, shameful gods have
eaten up in sacrifice
everything our ancestors worked
for—
their flocks and herds,
their sons and daughters.
25 Let us lie down in our shame,
and let our disgrace cover us like a
blanket.
We have sinned against the LORD our
God,
both we and our ancestors.
From our youth until now,
we have not obeyed the LORD our
God."

4 "If you will return, Israel,
then return to me," says the
LORD.
"If you will throw away your idols
that I hate,
then don't wander away from me.
2 If you say when you make a promise,
'As surely as the LORD lives,'
and you can say it in a truthful,
honest, and right way,
then the nations will be blessed by
him,
and they will praise him for what
he has done."

FAITH links

REAL REPENTANCE

JEREMIAH 4:1-4

When a person says, "Sorry!" but doesn't look or act sorry, would you believe her apology? Not likely! Her apology would seem pretty phony if her behavior remained the same. After Israel had sinned, God told them how to return to him. He wanted to see some real repentance. They had to get rid of their idols and keep the law that Moses had given them.

Repentance is a part of forgiveness. Although God offers forgiveness, he expects us to "turn away" from the things we do or say that displease him. That's real repentance.

Link here to see what God has to say about being really sorry:

Own Up to It, 2 Samuel 12:1–13, p. 412

This Hurts Me More?, 2 Chronicles 36:17–22, p. 606

Learning from Mistakes, Psalm 51:12–13, p. 748

Red to White, Isaiah 1:18, p. 896

The Watchman, Ezekiel 3:16–22, p. 1088

The Temptation Fighter, Matthew 4:1–11, p. 1278

3This is what the LORD says to the
people of Judah and to Jerusalem:
"Plow your unplowed fields,
and don't plant seeds among
thorns.
4Give yourselves to the service of the
LORD,
and decide to obey him,
people of Judah and people of
Jerusalem.
If you don't, my anger will spread
among you like a fire,
and no one will be able to put it
out,
because of the evil you have done.

Trouble from the North

5"Announce this message in Judah and
say it in Jerusalem:
'Blow the trumpet throughout the
country!'
Shout out loud and say,
'Come together!
Let's all escape to the strong,
walled cities!'
6Raise the signal flag toward
Jerusalem!
Run for your lives, and don't wait,
because I am bringing disaster from
the north
There will be terrible destruction."

7A lion has come out of his den;
a destroyer of nations has begun to
march.
He has left his home
to destroy your land.
Your towns will be destroyed
with no one left to live in them.
8So put on rough cloth,
show how sad you are, and cry
loudly.
The terrible anger of the LORD
has not turned away from us.

9"When this happens," says the LORD,
"the king and officers will lose
their courage.
The priests will be terribly afraid,
and the prophets will be shocked!"
10Then I said, "Lord GOD, you have
tricked the people of Judah and Jerusalem. You said, 'You will have peace,' but
now the sword is pointing at our
throats!"
11At that time this message will be
given to Judah and Jerusalem: "A hot
wind blows from the bare hilltops of the
desert toward the LORD's people. It is not
a gentle wind to separate grain from
chaff. 12I feel a stronger wind than that.
Now even I will announce judgments
against the people of Judah."
13Look! The enemy rises up like a
cloud,
and his chariots come like a
tornado.
His horses are faster than eagles.
How terrible it will be for us! We
are ruined!
14People of Jerusalem, clean the evil
from your hearts so that you can
be saved.
Don't continue making evil plans.
15A voice from Dan makes an
announcement
and brings bad news from the
mountains of Ephraim.
16"Report this to the nations.
Spread this news in Jerusalem:
'Invaders are coming from a faraway
country,
shouting words of war against the
cities of Judah.
17The enemy has surrounded
Jerusalem as men guard a field,
because Judah turned against
me,' " says the LORD.
18"The way you have lived and acted
has brought this trouble to you.
This is your punishment.
How terrible it is!
The pain stabs your heart!"

Jeremiah's Cry

19Oh, how I hurt! How I hurt!
I am bent over in pain.
Oh, the torture in my heart!
My heart is pounding inside me.
I cannot keep quiet,
because I have heard the sound of
the trumpet.
I have heard the shouts of war.
20Disaster follows disaster;

the whole country has been
destroyed.
My tents are destroyed in only a
moment.
My curtains are torn down quickly.
21 How long must I look at the war
flag?
How long must I listen to the war
trumpet?

22 The LORD says, "My people are
foolish.
They do not know me.
They are stupid children;
they don't understand.
They are skillful at doing evil,
but they don't know how to do
good."

Disaster Is Coming

23 I looked at the earth,
and it was empty and had no shape.
I looked at the sky,
and its light was gone.
24 I looked at the mountains,
and they were shaking.
All the hills were trembling.
25 I looked, and there were no people.
Every bird in the sky had flown
away.
26 I looked, and the good, rich land had
become a desert.
All its towns had been destroyed
by the LORD and his great anger.
27 This is what the LORD says:
"All the land will be ruined,
but I will not completely destroy it.
28 So the people in the land will cry
loudly,
and the sky will grow dark,
because I have spoken and will not
change my mind.
I have made a decision, and I will
not change it."

29 At the sound of the horsemen and
the archers,
all the people in the towns run
away.
They hide in the thick bushes
and climb up into the rocks.
All of the cities of Judah are empty;
no one lives in them.

30 Judah, you destroyed nation, what are
you doing?
Why do you put on your finest
dress
and decorate yourself with gold
jewelry?
Why do you put color around your
eyes?
You make yourself beautiful, but it
is all useless.
Your lovers hate you;
they want to kill you.

31 I hear a cry like a woman having a
baby,
distress like a woman having her
first child.
It is the sound of Jerusalem gasping
for breath.
She lifts her hands in prayer and
says,
"Oh! I am about to faint
before my murderers!"

No One Is Right

5 The LORD says, "Walk up and down
the streets of Jerusalem.
Look around and discover these
things.
Search the public squares of the city.
If you can find one person who does
honest things,
who searches for the truth,
I will forgive this city.
2 Although the people say, 'As surely as
the LORD lives!'
they don't really mean it."

3 LORD, don't you look for truth in
people?
You struck the people of Judah,
but they didn't feel any pain.
You crushed them,
but they refused to learn what is
right.
They became more stubborn than a
rock;
they refused to turn back to God.
4 But I thought,
"These are only the poor, foolish
people.
They have not learned the way of the
LORD

FAITH links

ALL TALK, NO ACTION

JEREMIAH 5:1-2

The story is told of a Greek philosopher named Diogenes (die-AH-juh-knees) who went around Athens in search of an honest man. He claimed not to have found one. God sent Jeremiah in a similar search around Jerusalem. Unlike Diogenes, God already knew that everyone was dishonest. They claimed to worship God, but their actions didn't match their words. They were spiritual phonies—all talk and no action!

God doesn't like spiritual phoniness! He expects his people to be honest. If we tell others that we worship God, but don't really do it, we might fool them. We never fool God, however.

Serious About the Sabbath, Exodus 31:15, p. 117

Always Truthful, Numbers 23:19, p. 208

No Middle Ground, Joshua 24:14–15, p. 307

Empty Words, Ezekiel 33:30–33, p. 1127

Perfectly Pleasing?, Matthew 5:1–12, p. 1280

One Thing to Do, Romans 4:1–5, p. 1523

and what their God wants them to
do.
5 So I will go to the leaders of Judah
and talk to them.
Surely they understand the way of
the LORD
and know what God wants them to
do."
But even the leaders had all joined
together to break away from the
LORD;
they had broken their ties with
him.
6 So a lion from the forest will attack
them.
A wolf from the desert will kill
them.
A leopard is waiting for them near
their towns.
It will tear to pieces anyone who
comes out of the city,
because the people of Judah have
sinned greatly.
They have wandered away from
the LORD many times.
7 The LORD said, "Tell me why I
should forgive you.
Your children have left me
and have made promises to idols
that are not gods at all.
I gave your children everything they
needed,
but they still were like an
unfaithful wife to me.
They spent much time in houses of
prostitutes.
8 They are like well-fed horses filled
with sexual desire;
each one wants another man's wife.
9 Shouldn't I punish the people of
Judah for doing these things?"
says the LORD.
"Shouldn't I give a nation such as
this the punishment it deserves?

10 "Go along and cut down Judah's
vineyards,
but do not completely destroy
them.
Cut off all her people as if they were
branches,
because they do not belong to the
LORD.
11 The families of Israel and Judah
have been completely unfaithful to
me," says the LORD.

12 Those people have lied about the
LORD
and said, "He will not do anything
to us!
Nothing bad will happen to us!
We will never see war or hunger!
13 The prophets are like an empty
wind;
the word of God is not in them.
Let the bad things they say happen
to them."
14 So this is what the LORD God All-
Powerful says:
"The people said I would not punish
them.
So, the words I give you will be
like fire,
and these people will be like wood
that it burns up.
15 Listen, family of Israel," says the
LORD,
"I will soon bring a nation from far
away to attack you.
It is an old nation that has lasted a
long time.
The people there speak a language
you do not know;
you cannot understand what they
say.
16 Their arrows bring death.
All their people are strong
warriors.
17 They will eat your crops and your
food.
They will eat your sons and
daughters.
They will eat your flocks and herds.
They will eat your grapes and
figs.
They will destroy with their swords
the strong, walled cities you
trust.
18 "Yet even then," says the LORD, "I
will not destroy you completely. 19 When
the people of Judah ask, 'Why has the
LORD our God done all these terrible
things to us?' then give them this answer: 'You have left the LORD and served
foreign idols in your own land. So now
you will serve foreigners in a land that
does not belong to you.'
20 "Announce this message to the
family of Jacob,
and tell it to the nation of Judah:
21 Hear this message, you foolish
people who have no sense.
They have eyes, but they don't
really see.
They have ears, but they don't
really listen.
22 Surely you are afraid of me," says the
LORD.
"You should shake with fear in my
presence.
I am the one who made the beaches
to be a border for the sea,
a border the water can never go
past.
The waves may pound the beach, but
they can't win over it.
They may roar, but they cannot go
beyond it.
23 But the people of Judah are stubborn
and have turned against me.
They have turned aside and gone
away from me.
24 They do not say to themselves,
'We should fear the LORD our God,
who gives us autumn and spring
rains in their seasons,
who makes sure we have the
harvest at the right time.'
25 But your evil has kept away both rain
and harvest.
Your sins have kept you from
enjoying good things.
26 There are wicked men among my
people.
Like those who make nets for
catching birds,
they set their traps to catch
people.
27 Like cages full of birds,
their houses are full of lies.
They have become rich and powerful.
28 They have grown big and fat.
There is no end to the evil things
they do.
They won't plead the case of the
orphan
or help the poor be judged fairly.
29 Shouldn't I punish the people of
Judah for doing these things?"
says the LORD.
"Shouldn't I give a nation such as
this the punishment it deserves?

30 "A terrible and shocking thing
has happened in the land of Judah:
31 The prophets speak lies,
and the priests take power into
their own hands,
and my people love it this way.
But what will you do when the end
comes?

Jerusalem Is Surrounded

6 "Run for your lives, people of
Benjamin!
Run away from Jerusalem!
Blow the war trumpet in the town of
Tekoa!
Raise the warning flag over the
town of Beth Hakkerem!
Disaster is coming from the north;
terrible destruction is coming to
you.
2 Jerusalem, I will destroy you,
you who are fragile and gentle.
3 Shepherds with their flocks will
come against Jerusalem.
They will set up their tents all
around her,
each shepherd taking care of his
own section."
4 They say, "Get ready to fight against
Jerusalem!
Get up! We will attack at noon!
But it is already getting late;
the evening shadows are growing
long.
5 So get up! We will attack at night.
We will destroy the strong towers
of Jerusalem!"
6 This is what the LORD All-Powerful
says:
"Cut down the trees around
Jerusalem,
and build an attack ramp to the top
of its walls.
This city must be punished.
Inside it is nothing but slavery.
7 Jerusalem pours out her evil
as a well pours out its water.
The sounds of violence and
destruction are heard within her.
I can see the sickness and hurts of
Jerusalem.
8 Listen to this warning, Jerusalem,
or I will turn my back on you
and make your land an empty desert
where no one can live."
9 This is what the LORD All-Powerful
says:
"Gather the few people of Israel who
are left alive,
as you would gather the last
grapes on a grapevine.
Check each vine again,
like someone who gathers grapes."
10 To whom can I speak? Whom can I
warn?
Who will listen to me?
The people of Israel have closed
ears,
so they cannot hear my warnings.
They don't like the word of the
LORD;
they don't want to listen to it!
11 But I am full of the anger of the
LORD,
and I am tired of holding it in.

"Pour out my anger on the children
who play in the street
and on the young men gathered
together.
A husband and his wife will both be
caught in his anger,
as will the very old.
12 Their houses will be turned over to
others,
along with their fields and wives,
because I will raise my hand
and punish the people of Judah,"
says the LORD.
13 "Everyone, from the least important
to the greatest,
is greedy for money.
Even the prophets and priests
all tell lies.
14 They tried to heal my people's
serious injuries
as if they were small wounds.
They said, 'It's all right, it's all right.'
But really, it is not all right.
15 They should be ashamed of the
terrible way they act,
but they are not ashamed at all.
They don't even know how to
blush about their sins.

So they will fall, along with everyone else.
They will be thrown to the ground when I punish them," says the LORD.
16 This is what the LORD says:
"Stand where the roads cross and look.
Ask where the old way is,
where the good way is, and walk on it.
If you do, you will find rest for yourselves.
But they have said, 'We will not walk on the good way.'
17 I set watchmen over you
and told you, 'Listen for the sound of the war trumpet!'
But they said, 'We will not listen.'
18 So listen, all you nations,
and pay attention, you witnesses.
Watch what I will do to the people of Judah.
19 Hear this, people of the earth:
I am going to bring disaster to the people of Judah
because of the evil they plan.
They have not listened to my messages
and have rejected my teachings.
20 Why do you bring me offerings of incense from the land of Sheba?
Why do you bring me sweet-smelling cane from a faraway land?
Your burnt offerings will not be accepted;
your sacrifices do not please me."
21 So this is what the LORD says:
"I will put problems in front of Judah.
Fathers and sons will stumble over them together.
Neighbors and friends will die."
22 This is what the LORD says:
"Look, an army is coming
from the land of the north;
a great nation is coming
from the far sides of the earth.
23 The soldiers carry bows and spears.
They are cruel and show no mercy.
They sound like the roaring ocean
when they ride their horses.
That army is coming lined up for battle,
ready to attack you, Jerusalem."

Ask where the old way is, where the good way is, and walk on it.
—Jeremiah 6:16

24 We have heard the news about that army
and are helpless from fear.
We are gripped by our pain,
like a woman having a baby.
25 Don't go out into the fields
or walk down the roads,
because the enemy has swords.
There is terror on every side.
26 My people, put on rough cloth
and roll in the ashes to show how sad you are.
Cry loudly for those who are dead,
as if your only son were dead,
because the destroyer
will soon come against us.
27 "Jeremiah, I have made you like a worker who tests metal,
and my people are like the ore.
You must observe their ways
and test them.
28 All my people have turned against me and are stubborn.
They go around telling lies about others.
They are like bronze and iron
that became covered with rust.
They all act dishonestly.
29 The fire is fanned to make it hotter,
but the lead does not melt.
The pure metal does not come out;
the evil is not removed from my people.
30 My people will be called rejected silver,
because the LORD has rejected them."

Jeremiah's Temple Message

7 This is the word that the LORD spoke
to Jeremiah: 2"Stand at the gate of
the Temple and preach this message
there:
" 'Hear the word of the LORD, all you
people of the nation of Judah! All you who
come through these gates to worship the
LORD, listen to this message! 3This is
what the LORD All-Powerful, the God of
Israel, says: Change your lives and do
what is right! Then I will let you live in
this place. 4Don't trust the lies of people
who say, "This is the Temple of the LORD.
This is the Temple of the LORD. This is
the Temple of the LORD!" 5You must
change your lives and do what is right. Be
fair to each other. 6You must not be hard
on strangers, orphans, and
widows. Don't kill
innocent people in
this place! Don't fol-
low other gods, or
they will ruin your
lives. 7If you do
these things, I will
let you live in this land that I gave to your
ancestors to keep forever.

EMAIL FROM GOD
7:5–7
Character
Find out how God wants you to treat others.

8" 'But look, you are trusting lies,
which is useless. 9Will you steal and
murder and be guilty of adultery? Will
you falsely accuse other people? Will you
burn incense to the god Baal and follow
other gods you have not known? 10If you
do that, do you think you can come before
me and stand in this place where I have
chosen to be worshiped? Do you think
you can say, "We are safe!" when you do
all these hateful things? 11This place
where I have chosen to be worshiped is
nothing more to you than a hideout for
robbers. I have been watching you, says
the LORD.
12" 'You people of Judah, go now to
the town of Shiloh, where I first made a
place to be worshiped. See what I did to it
because of the evil things the people of
Israel had done. 13You people of Judah
have done all these evil things too, says
the LORD. I spoke to you again and again,
but you did not listen to me. I called you,
but you did not answer. 14So I will destroy the place where I have chosen to be
worshiped in Jerusalem. You trust in that
place, which I gave to you and your ancestors, but I will destroy it just as I destroyed Shiloh. 15I will push you away
from me just as I pushed away your relatives, the people of Israel!'
16"As for you, Jeremiah, don't pray for
these people. Don't cry out for them or
ask anything for them or beg me to help
them, because I will not listen to you.
17Don't you see what they are doing in
the towns of Judah and in the streets of
Jerusalem? 18The children gather wood,
and the fathers use the wood to make a
fire. The women make the dough for
cakes of bread, and they offer them to the
Queen Goddess. They pour out drink offerings to other gods to make me angry.
19But I am not the one the people of Judah are really hurting, says the LORD.
They are only hurting themselves and
bringing shame upon themselves.
20" 'So this is what the Lord GOD
says: I will pour out my anger on this
place, on people and animals, on the trees
in the field and the crops in the ground.
My anger will be like a hot fire that no
one can put out.

Obedience Is More than Sacrifice

21" 'This is what the LORD All-Powerful, the God of Israel, says: Offer burnt
offerings along with your other sacrifices, and eat the meat yourselves!
22When I brought your ancestors out of
Egypt, I did not speak to them and give
them commands only about burnt offerings and sacrifices. 23I also gave them
this command: Obey me, and I will be
your God and you will be my people. Do
all that I command so that good things
will happen to you. 24But your ancestors
did not listen or pay attention to me.
They were stubborn and did whatever
their evil hearts wanted. They went
backward, not forward. 25Since the day
your ancestors left Egypt, I have sent my
servants, the prophets, again and again to
you. 26But your ancestors did not listen
or pay attention to me. They were very
stubborn and did more evil than their ancestors.'
27"Jeremiah, you will tell all these

things to the people of Judah, but they
will not listen to you. You will call to
them, but they will not answer you. 28So
say to them, 'This is the nation that has
not obeyed the LORD its God. These people do nothing when I correct them. They
do not tell the truth; it has disappeared
from their lips.

The Valley of Killing

29" 'Cut off your hair and throw it
away. Go up to the bare hilltop and cry
out, because the LORD has rejected these
people. He has turned his back on them,
and in his anger will punish them. 30The
people of Judah have done what I said
was evil, says the LORD. They have set
up their hateful idols in the place where I
have chosen to be worshiped and have
made it unclean. 31The people of Judah
have built places of worship at Topheth in
the Valley of Ben Hinnom. There they
burned their own sons and daughters as
sacrifices, something I never commanded. It never even entered my mind.
32So, I warn you. The days are coming,
says the LORD, when people will not call
this place Topheth or the Valley of Ben
Hinnom anymore. They will call it the
Valley of Killing. They will bury the dead
in Topheth until there is no room to bury
anyone else. 33Then the bodies of the
dead will become food for the birds of the
sky and for the wild animals. There will
be no one left alive to chase them away.
34I will end the happy sounds of the bride
and bridegroom. There will be no happy
sounds in the cities of Judah or in the
streets of Jerusalem, because the land
will become an empty desert!

8 " 'The LORD says: At that time they
will remove from their tombs the
bones of Judah's kings and officers,
priests and prophets, and the people of
Jerusalem. 2The bones will be spread on
the ground under the sun, moon, and
stars that the people loved and served
and went after and searched for and worshiped. No one will gather up the bones
and bury them. So they will be like dung
thrown on the ground. 3I will force the
people of Judah to leave their homes and
their land. Those of this evil family who
are not dead will wish they were, says the
LORD All-Powerful.'

Sin and Punishment

4"Say to the people of Judah: 'This is
what the LORD says:
When people fall down, don't they get up again?
And when someone goes the wrong way, doesn't he turn back?
5 Why, then, have the people of Jerusalem gone the wrong way
and not turned back?
They believe their own lies
and refuse to turn around and come back.
6 I have listened to them very carefully,
but they do not say what is right.
They do not feel sorry about their wicked ways,
saying, "What have I done?"
Each person goes his own way,
like a horse charging into a battle.
7 Even the birds in the sky
know the right times to do things.
The storks, doves, swifts, and thrushes
know when it is time to migrate.
But my people don't know
what the LORD wants them to do.

8" 'You keep saying, "We are wise,
because we have the teachings of the LORD."
But actually, those who explain the Scriptures
have written lies with their pens.
9 These wise men refused to listen to the word of the LORD,
so they are not really wise at all.
They will be ashamed.
They will be shocked and trapped.
10 So I will give their wives to other men
and their fields to new owners.
Everyone, from the least important to the greatest,
is greedy for money.

eMAIL! FROM GOD
8:10
Greed
Check out God's view of greed.

Even the prophets and priests
all tell lies.
11 They tried to heal my people's
serious injuries
as if they were small wounds.
They said, "It's all right, it's all
right."
But really, it is not all right.
12 They should be ashamed of the
terrible way they act,
but they are not ashamed at all.
They don't even know how to
blush about their sins.
So they will fall, along with everyone
else.
They will be thrown to the ground
when I punish them, says the
LORD.
13 " 'I will take away their crops, says
the LORD.
There will be no grapes on the
vine
and no figs on the fig tree.
Even the leaves will dry up and
die.
I will take away what I gave them.' "

14 "Why are we just sitting here?
Let's get together!
We have sinned against the LORD,
so he has given us poisoned water
to drink.
Come, let's run to the strong, walled
cities.
The LORD our God has decided
that we must die,
so let's die there.
15 We hoped to have peace,
but nothing good has come.
We hoped for a time when he would
heal us,
but only terror has come.
16 From the land of Dan,
the snorting of the enemy's horses
is heard.
The ground shakes from the
neighing of their large horses.
They have come and destroyed
the land and everything in it,
the city and all who live there."

17 "Look! I am sending poisonous
snakes to attack you.
These snakes cannot be charmed,
and they will bite you," says the
LORD.

Jeremiah's Sadness

18 God, you are my comfort when I am
very sad
and when I am afraid.
19 Listen to the sound of my people.
They cry from a faraway land:
"Isn't the LORD still in Jerusalem?
Isn't Jerusalem's king still there?"

But God says, "Why did the people
make me angry by worshiping
idols,
useless foreign idols?"

20 And the people say, "Harvest time is
over;
summer has ended,
and we have not been saved."

21 Because my people are crushed, I am
crushed.
I cry loudly and am afraid for them.
22 Isn't there balm in the land of Gilead?
Isn't there a doctor there?
So why aren't the hurts of my people
healed?
9 I wish my head were like a spring of
water
and my eyes like a fountain of
tears!
Then I could cry day and night
for my people who have been
killed.
2 I wish I had a place in the desert—
a house where travelers spend the
night—
so I could leave my people.
I could go away from them,
because they are all unfaithful to God;
they are all turning against him.

Judah's Failures

3 "They use their
tongues like
a bow,
shooting lies
from their
mouths like
arrows.

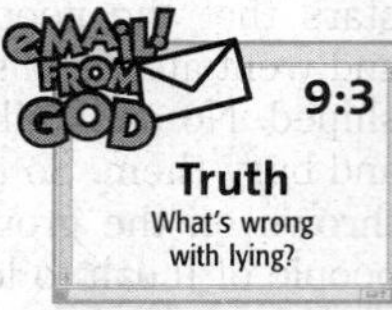

EMAIL! FROM GOD
9:3
Truth
What's wrong with lying?

CONTROLLING WHAT I SAY

Jeremiah 9:3

Livin' it

Loose Lips? What do you do when someone tells you a really important secret? Or tells you the latest rumor about that "bad kid" in school? Do you look for the first person you can tell, or do you refuse to pass on gossip? Do you have "loose lips"—telling secrets and spreading juicy stories? Or are your lips sealed?

Rumors and gossip can be very harmful to friendships or reputations if they are believed. God is very displeased with rumors and the people who spread them. (Check out Jeremiah 29:24–32.) What can you do when someone passes on a rumor to you? Try to find out the truth, or do the next best thing: Ignore it.

MORE FAITH links

A Special Promise, p. 217

A Gentle Answer, p. 847

What's Wrong About Rumors, p. 1032

The Peril of Poisonous Plans, p. 1221

The Whole Truth, p. 1438

Say What?!, p. 1603

"Hey, Skweek, did you hear the one about . . ."

"Whoa! Hold on a minute. I think you'd better check out these links before you say anything more!"

Just Kidding?, Genesis 21:8–10, p. 28

- Has anyone ever said something mean to you, then added, "I'm just kidding"? Have you ever done that to someone? How do you feel when someone teases you? To avoid hurting someone with your words, think how you would feel.

The Problem with Gossip, Proverbs 11:12–13, p. 840

- Gossip doesn't always mean passing on a rumor about someone. Link here to discover what rumors and gossip can lead to.

Trouble with the Tongue, James 3:3–12, p. 1692

- Have you ever said something nice to a friend, then turned around and called your brother or sister a mean name? This Faithlink has a lot to say about what comes out of our mouths!

my FAVORITE links

Lies, not truth,
have grown strong in the land.
They go from one evil thing to another.
They do not know who I am," says the LORD.
4 "Watch out for your friends,
and don't trust your own relatives,
because every relative is a cheater,
and every friend tells lies about you.
5 Everyone lies to his friend,
and no one speaks the truth.
The people of Judah have taught their tongues to lie.
They have become tired from sinning.
6 Jeremiah, you live in the middle of lies.
With their lies the people refuse to know me," says the LORD.

7 So this is what the LORD All-Powerful says:
"I will test the people of Judah as a person tests metal in a fire.
I have no other choice,
because my people have sinned.
8 Their tongues are like sharp arrows.
Their mouths speak lies.
Everyone speaks nicely to his neighbor,
but he is secretly planning to attack him.
9 Shouldn't I punish the people for doing this?" says the LORD.
"Shouldn't I give a nation like this the punishment it deserves?"

10 I, Jeremiah, will cry loudly for the mountains
and sing a funeral song for the empty fields.
They are empty, and no one passes through.
The mooing of cattle cannot be heard.
The birds have flown away,
and the animals are gone.

11 "I, the LORD, will make the city of Jerusalem a heap of ruins,
a home for wild dogs.
I will destroy the cities of Judah
so no one can live there."

12 What person is wise enough to understand these things? Is there someone
who has been taught by the LORD who
can explain them? Why was the land ruined? Why has it been made like an empty desert where no one goes?
13 The LORD answered, "It is because
Judah quit following my teachings that I
gave them. They have not obeyed me or
done what I told them to do. 14 Instead,
they were stubborn and followed the Baals, as their ancestors taught them to do.
15 So this is what the LORD All-Powerful,
the God of Israel, says: "I will soon make
the people of Judah eat bitter food and
drink poisoned water. 16 I will scatter
them through other nations that they and
their ancestors never knew about. I will
chase the people of Judah with the sword
until they are all killed."
17 This is what the LORD All-Powerful
says:
"Now, think about these things!
Call for the women who cry at funerals to come.
Send for those women who are good at that job.
18 Let them come quickly
and cry loudly for us.
Then our eyes will fill with tears,
and streams of water will flow from our eyelids.
19 The sound of loud crying is heard from Jerusalem:
'We are truly ruined!
We are truly ashamed!
We must leave our land,
because our houses are in ruins.' "

20 Now, women of Judah, listen to the word of the LORD;
open your ears to hear the words of his mouth.
Teach your daughters how to cry loudly.
Teach one another a funeral song.
21 Death has climbed in through our windows
and has entered our strong cities.

BRAGGIN' RIGHTS

JEREMIAH 9:23-24

What qualities or possessions do you admire? Some people admire those with great personalities, money, cool toys, high video game scores, or popularity. People with these qualities or possessions might even brag about having them. Bragging about something you have is also known as touting. Jeremiah told the Israelites about one quality that's worth touting: how much a person understands about God and what God wants them to do.

God is kind and fair toward others. Knowing him helps us to be kind and fair, too. That's worth bragging about.

Want to brag about something? Connect here:

From Zero to Hero, Judges 6; 7, p. 319

Plans for a Son, 1 Chronicles 22:5–19, p. 548

More Precious Than Gold, Psalm 19:7–10, p. 723

A Useless Thing, Isaiah 44:9, 18–20, p. 954

God's New Temple, Ezekiel 40–44, p. 1135

The Gift, John 3:16–18, p. 1427

Death has taken away our children
who play in the streets
and the young men who meet in
the city squares.

22 Say, "This is what the LORD says:
'The dead bodies of people will lie
in the open field like dung.
They will lie like grain a farmer has
cut,
but there will be no one to gather
them.' "
23 This is what the LORD says:
"The wise must not brag about their
wisdom.
The strong must not brag about
their strength.
The rich must not brag about their
money.
24 But if someone wants to brag, let him
brag
that he understands and knows me.
Let him brag that I am the LORD,
and that I am kind and fair,
and that I do things that are right
on earth.
This kind of bragging pleases me,"
says the LORD.

25 The LORD says, "The time is coming when I will punish all those who are
circumcised only in the flesh: 26 the people of Egypt, Judah, Edom, Ammon,
Moab, and the desert people who cut
their hair short. The men in all those
countries are not circumcised. And the
whole family of Israel does not give itself
to serving me."

The Lord and the Idols

10 Family of Israel, listen to what the
LORD says to you. 2 This is what
he says:
"Don't live like the people from other
nations,
and don't be afraid of special signs
in the sky,
even though the other nations are
afraid of them.
3 The customs of other people are
worth nothing.
Their idols are just wood cut from
the forest,
shaped by a worker with his chisel.
4 They decorate their idols with silver
and gold.
With hammers and nails they
fasten them down

so they won't fall over.
5 Their idols are like scarecrows in melon fields;
they cannot talk.
Since they cannot walk,
they must be carried.
Do not be afraid of those idols,
because they can't hurt you,
and they can't help you either."

6 LORD, there is no one like you.
You are great,
and your name is great and powerful.
7 Everyone should respect you, King of the nations;
you deserve respect.
Of all the wise people among the nations
and in all the kingdoms,
none of them is as wise as you.
8 Those wise people are stupid and foolish.
Their teachings come from worthless wooden idols.
9 Hammered silver is brought from Tarshish
and gold from Uphaz,
so the idols are made by craftsmen and goldsmiths.
They put blue and purple clothes on the idols.
All these things are made by skilled workers.
10 But the LORD is the only true God.
He is the only living God, the King forever.
The earth shakes when he is angry,
and the nations cannot stand up to his anger.

11 "Tell them this message: 'These
gods did not make heaven and earth; they
will be destroyed and disappear from
heaven and earth.'"

12 God made the earth by his power.
He used his wisdom to build the world
and his understanding to stretch out the skies.
13 When he thunders, the waters in the skies roar.
He makes clouds rise in the sky all over the earth.
He sends lightning with the rain
and brings out the wind from his storehouses.

Of all the wise people among the nations and in all the kingdoms, none of them is as wise as you.
—Jeremiah 10:7

14 People are so stupid and know so little.
Goldsmiths are made ashamed by their idols,
because those statues are only false gods.
They have no breath in them.
15 They are worth nothing; people make fun of them.
When they are judged, they will be destroyed.
16 But God, who is Jacob's Portion, is not like the idols.
He made everything,
and he chose Israel to be his special people.
The LORD All-Powerful is his name.

Destruction Is Coming

17 Get everything you own and prepare to leave,
you people who are trapped by your enemies.
18 This is what the LORD says:
"At this time I will throw out the people who live in this land.
I will bring trouble to them
so that they may be captured."

19 How terrible it will be for me
because of my injury.
My wound cannot be healed.
Yet I told myself,
"This is my sickness; I must suffer through it."
20 My tent is ruined,

and all its ropes are broken.
My children have gone away and left
me.
No one is left to put up my tent
again
or to set up a shelter for me.
21 The shepherds are stupid
and don't ask the LORD for advice.
So they do not have success,
and all their flocks are scattered
and lost.
22 Listen! The news is coming.
A loud noise comes from the north
to make the towns of Judah an empty
desert
and a home for wild dogs!

Jeremiah's Prayer

23 LORD, I know that a person's life
doesn't really belong to him.
No one can control his own life.
24 LORD, correct me, but be fair.
Don't punish me in your anger,
or you will destroy me.
25 Pour out your anger on other nations
that do not know you
and do not pray to you.
Those nations have destroyed Jacob's
family.
They have eaten him up
completely
and destroyed his homeland.

The Agreement Is Broken

11 These are the words that the LORD
spoke to Jeremiah: 2"Listen to the
words of this agreement and tell them to
the people of Judah and those living in Jerusalem. 3Tell them this is what the
LORD, the God of Israel, says: 'Cursed is
the person who does not obey the words
of this agreement 4that I made with your
ancestors when I brought them out of
Egypt. Egypt was like a furnace for melting iron!' I told them, 'Obey me and do
everything I command you. Then you
will be my people, and I will be your God.
5Then I will keep the promise I made to
your ancestors to give them a fertile
land.' And you are living in that country
today."
I answered, "Amen, LORD."

6The LORD said to me, "Announce
this message in the towns of Judah and in
the streets of Jerusalem: 'Listen to the
words of this agreement and obey them.
7I warned your ancestors to obey me
when I brought them out of Egypt. I have
warned them again and again to
this very day: "Obey
me!" 8But your an-
cestors did not lis-
ten to me. They
were stubborn and
did what their own
evil hearts wanted. So I made all the
curses of this agreement come upon
them. I commanded them to obey the
agreement, but they did not.' "

eMAIL! FROM GOD
11:7–8
Obedience
What happens when you disobey?

9Then the LORD said to me, "I know
the people of Judah and those living in Jerusalem have made secret plans. 10They
have gone back to the same sins their ancestors did. Their ancestors refused to
listen to my message and followed and
worshiped other gods instead. The families of Israel and Judah have broken the
agreement I made with their ancestors.
11So this is what the LORD says: 'I will
soon bring a disaster on the people of Judah which they will not be able to escape.
They will cry to me for help, but I will not
listen to them. 12The people living in the
towns of Judah and the city of Jerusalem
will pray to their idols to whom they burn
incense. But those idols will not be able
to help when disaster comes. 13Look,
people of Judah, you have as many idols
as there are towns in Judah. You have
built as many altars to burn incense to
that shameful god Baal as there are
streets in Jerusalem.'

14"As for you, Jeremiah, don't pray for
these people or cry out for them or ask
anything for them. I will not listen when
they call to me in the time of their trouble.
15 "What is my beloved Judah doing in
my Temple
when she makes many evil
plans?
Do you think animal sacrifices will
stop your punishment?
When you do your evil, then you are
happy."

A HOMETOWN HURT

JEREMIAH 11:8—12:6

How would you feel if neighbors plotted to hurt you in some way because of your belief about God? A group of people in Jeremiah's hometown plotted to kill him because he spoke for God. They didn't like what he had to say. God wanted Jeremiah to trust him, even if his own family turned against him. God assured Jeremiah that he would take care of him.

If you're the only Christian in your family, you might feel almost as if your family *had* turned against you. Even through this, God wants you to trust in him.

Sometimes it's hard to be a follower of Jesus. Surf here for some encouragement:

The Sacrifice, Genesis 22, p. 29

What Will You Risk?, Joshua 2, p. 278

What's Out Becomes In, Judges 11, p. 327

Wronged for What's Right, Ezra 4:4–5, p. 612

The Unpopular Choice, Mark 15:42–43, p. 1360

An Energy Boost, Acts 4:31, p. 1469

16 The LORD called you "a leafy olive tree,
with beautiful fruit and shape."
But with the roar of a strong storm
he will set that tree on fire,
and its branches will be burned up.

17The LORD All-Powerful, who planted you, has announced that disaster will
come to you. This is because the families
of Israel and Judah have done evil and
have made him angry by burning incense
to Baal.

Evil Plans Against Jeremiah

18The LORD showed me that men
were making plans against me. Because
he showed me what they were doing, I
knew they were against me. 19Before
this, I was like a gentle lamb waiting to be
butchered. I did not know they had made
plans against me, saying:

"Let us destroy the tree and its fruit.
Let's kill him so people will forget him."

20 But, LORD All-Powerful, you are a fair judge.
You know how to test peoples' hearts and minds.
I have told you what I have against them.
So let me see you give them the punishment they deserve.

21So the LORD speaks about the men
from Anathoth who plan to kill Jeremiah
and say, "Don't prophesy in the name of
the LORD, or we will kill you!" 22So this
is what the LORD All-Powerful says: "I
will soon punish the men from Anathoth.
Their young men will die in war. Their
sons and daughters will die from hunger.
23No one from the city of Anathoth will
be left alive, because I will cause a disaster to happen to them that year."

Jeremiah's First Complaint

12 LORD, when I bring my case to you,
you are always right.
But I want to ask you about the justice you give.
Why are evil people successful?
Why do dishonest people have such easy lives?

2 You have put the evil people here
like plants with strong roots.
They grow and produce fruit.
With their mouths they speak well of
you,
but their hearts are really far away
from you.
3 But you know my heart, LORD.
You see me and test my thoughts
about you.
Drag the evil people away like sheep
to be butchered.
Set them aside for the day of
killing.
4 How much longer will the land stay
dried up
and the grass in every field be
dead?
The animals and birds in the land
have died,
because the people are evil.
Yes, they are even saying,
"God does not see what happens
to us."

The Lord's Answer to Jeremiah

5 "If you get tired while racing against
people,
how can you race against horses?
If you stumble in a country that is
safe,
what will you do in the thick
thornbushes along the Jordan
River?
6 Even your own brothers and
members of your own family
are making plans against you.
They are crying out against you.
Don't trust them,
even when they say nice things to
you!

7 "I have left Israel;
I have left my people.
I have given the people I love
over to their enemies.
8 My people have become to me
like a lion in the forest.
They roar at me,
so I hate them.
9 My people have become to me
like a speckled bird attacked on all
sides by hawks.
Go, gather the wild animals.
Bring them to get something to
eat.
10 Many shepherds have ruined my
vineyards
and trampled the plants in my
field.
They have turned my beautiful field
into an empty desert.
11 They have turned my field into a
desert
that is wilted and dead.
The whole country is an empty
desert,
because no one who lives there
cares.
12 Many soldiers have marched over
those barren hills.
The LORD is using the armies to
punish that land
from one end to the other.
No one is safe.
13 The people have planted wheat,
but they have harvested only
thorns.
They have worked hard until they
were very tired,
but they have nothing for all their
work.
They are ashamed of their poor
harvest,
because the LORD's terrible anger
has caused this."

14 This is what the LORD said to me:
"Here is what I will do to all my wicked
neighbors who take the land I gave my
people Israel. I will pull them up and
throw them out of their land. And I will
pull up the people of Judah from among
them. 15 But after I pull them up, I will
feel sorry for them again. I will bring
each person back to his own property and
to his own land. 16 I want them to learn
their lessons well. In the past they taught
my people to swear by Baal's name. But
if they will now learn to swear by my
name, saying, 'As surely as the LORD
lives . . .' I will allow them to rebuild
among my people. 17 But if a nation will
not listen to my message, I will pull it up
completely and destroy it," says the
LORD.

Jeremiah's Linen Belt

13 This is what the LORD said to me:
"Go and buy a linen belt and put it
around your waist. Don't let the belt get
wet."
2So I bought a linen belt, just as the
LORD told me, and put it around my
waist. 3Then the LORD spoke his word to
me a second time: 4"Take the belt you
bought and are wearing, and go to Perath.
Hide the belt there in a crack in the
rocks." 5So I went to Perath and hid the
belt there, just as the LORD told me.
6Many days later the LORD said to me,
"Now go to Perath and get the belt I told
you to hide there." 7So I went to Perath
and dug up the belt and took it from
where I had hidden it. But now it was ruined; it was good for nothing.
8Then the LORD spoke his word to me.
9This is what the LORD said: "In the same
way I will ruin the pride of the people of
Judah and the great pride of Jerusalem.
10These evil people refuse to listen to my
warnings. They stubbornly do only what
they want to do, and they follow other
gods to serve and worship them. So they
will become like this linen belt—good
for nothing. 11As a belt is wrapped tightly
around a person's waist, I wrapped the
families of Israel and Judah around me,"
says the LORD. "I did that so they would
be my people and bring fame, praise, and
honor to me. But my people would not
listen.

Warnings About Leather Wine Bags

12"Say to them: 'This is what the
LORD, the God of Israel, says: All leather
bags for holding wine should be filled
with wine.' People will say to you: 'Of
course, we know all wine bags should be
filled with wine.' 13Then you will say to
them, 'This is what the LORD says: I will
make everyone in this land like a
drunken person—the kings who sit on
David's throne, the priests and the
prophets, and all the people who live in
Jerusalem. 14I will make them smash
against one another, fathers and sons
alike, says the LORD. I will not feel sorry
or have pity on them or show mercy that
would stop me from destroying them.' "

Threat of Slavery

15 Listen and pay attention.
Don't be too proud,
because the LORD has spoken to
you.
16 Give glory to the LORD your God
before he brings darkness
and before you slip and fall
on the dark hills.
You hope for light,
but he will turn it into thick
darkness;
he will change it into deep gloom.
17 If you don't listen to him,
I will cry secretly
because of your pride.
I will cry painfully,
and my eyes will overflow with
tears,
because the LORD's people will be
captured.

18 Tell this to the king and the queen
mother:
"Come down from your thrones,
because your beautiful crowns
have fallen from your heads."
19 The cities of southern Judah are
locked up,
and no one can open them.
All Judah will be taken as captives to
a foreign land;
they will be carried away
completely.

20 Jerusalem, look up and see
the people coming from the north.
Where is the flock God gave you to
care for,
the flock you bragged about?
21 What will you say when they appoint
as your heads
those you had thought were your
friends?
Won't you have much pain and
trouble,
like a woman giving birth to a
baby?
22 You might ask yourself,
"Why has this happened to me?"

It happened because of your many sins.
Because of your sins, your skirt was torn off
and your body has been treated badly.
23 Can a person from Cush change the color of his skin?
Can a leopard change his spots?
In the same way, Jerusalem, you cannot change and do good,
because you are accustomed to doing evil.

> Can a person from Cush change the color of his skin? Can a leopard change his spots?
> —Jeremiah 13:23

24 "I will scatter you like chaff that is blown away by the desert wind.
25 This is what will happen to you;
this is your part in my plans," says the LORD.
"Because you forgot me
and trusted in false gods,
26 I will pull your skirts up over your face
so everyone will see your shame.
27 I have seen the terrible things you have done:
your acts of adultery and your snorting,
your prostitution,
your hateful acts
on the hills and in the fields.
How terrible it will be for you, Jerusalem.
How long will you continue being unclean?"

A Time Without Rain

14 These are the words that the LORD spoke to Jeremiah about the time when there was no rain:
2 "The nation of Judah cries as if someone has died,
and her cities are very sad.
They are distressed over the land.
A cry goes up to God from Jerusalem.
3 The important men send their servants to get water.
They go to the wells,
but they find no water.
So they return with empty jars.
They are ashamed and embarrassed
and cover their heads in shame.
4 The ground is dry and cracked open,
because no rain falls on the land.
The farmers are upset and sad,
so they cover their heads in shame.
5 Even the mother deer in the field
leaves her newborn fawn to die,
because there is no grass.
6 Wild donkeys stand on the bare hills
and sniff the wind like wild dogs.
But their eyes go blind,
because there is no food."

7 We know that we suffer because of our sins.
LORD, do something to help us for the good of your name.
We have left you many times;
we have sinned against you.
8 God, the Hope of Israel,
you have saved Israel in times of trouble.
Why are you like a stranger in the land,
or like a traveler who only stays one night?
9 Why are you like someone who has been attacked by surprise,
like a warrior who is not able to save anyone?
But you are among us, LORD,
and we are called by your name
so don't leave us without help!
10 This is what the LORD says about the people of Judah:
"They really love to wander from me;
they don't stop themselves from leaving me.
So now the LORD will not accept them.

He will now remember the evil
they do
and will punish them for their
sins."

11Then the LORD said, "Don't pray
for good things to happen to the people
of Judah. 12Even if they give up eating,
I will not listen to their prayers. Even
if they offer burnt offerings and grain offerings to me, I will not accept them.
Instead, I will destroy the people of
Judah with war, hunger, and terrible diseases."

13But I said, "Oh, Lord GOD, the
prophets keep telling the people, 'You
will not suffer from an enemy's sword or
from hunger. I, the LORD, will give you
peace in this land.' "

14Then the LORD said to me, "Those
prophets are prophesying lies in my
name. I did not send them or appoint
them or speak to them. They have been
prophesying false visions, idolatries,
worthless magic, and their own wishful
thinking. 15So this is what
I say about the prophets
who are prophesying in
my name. I did not send
them. They say, 'No ene-
my will attack this coun-
try with swords. There
will never be hunger in
this land.' So those prophets will die from hunger
and from an enemy's
sword. 16And the people
to whom the prophets speak will be
thrown into the streets of Jerusalem.
There they will die from hunger and from
an enemy's sword. And no one will be
there to bury them, or their wives, or
their sons, or their daughters. I will punish them.

> Do foreign idols have the power to bring rain? Does the sky itself have the power to send down showers?
> —Jeremiah 14:22

17"Jeremiah, speak this message to
the people of Judah:

'Let my eyes be filled with tears
night and day, without stopping.
My people have received a terrible
blow;
they have been hurt badly.
18If I go into the country,
I see people killed by swords.
If I go into the city,
I see much sickness, because the
people have no food.
Both the priests and the prophets
have been taken to a foreign
land.' "

19LORD, have you completely rejected
the nation of Judah?
Do you hate Jerusalem?
Why have you hurt us so badly
that we cannot be made well
again?
We hoped for peace,
but nothing good has come.
We looked for a time of healing,
but only terror came.
20LORD, we admit that we are wicked
and that our ancestors did evil
things.
We have sinned against you.
21For your sake, do not hate us.
Do not take away the honor from
your glorious throne.
Remember your agreement with us,
and do not break it.
22Do foreign idols have
the power to
bring rain?
Does the sky itself
have the
power to
send down
showers?
No, it is you, LORD
our God.
You are our only
hope,
because you are the one who made
all these things.

15 Then the LORD said to me: "I
would not feel sorry for the people
of Judah even if Moses and Samuel
prayed for them. Send them away from
me! Tell them to go! 2When they ask
you, 'Where will we go?' tell them: 'This
is what the LORD says:

Those who are meant to die
will die.
Those who are meant to die in war
will die in war.
Those who are meant to die from
hunger
will die from hunger.

Those who are meant to be taken
captive
will be taken captive.'
3"I will send four kinds of destroyers
against them," says the LORD. "I will
send war to kill, dogs to drag the bodies
away, and the birds of the air and wild animals to eat and destroy the bodies. 4I
will make the people of Judah hated by
everyone on earth because of what
Manasseh did in Jerusalem. (Manasseh
son of Hezekiah was king of the nation of
Judah.)

5"Who will feel sorry for you,
Jerusalem?
Who will be sad and cry for you?
Who will go out of his way to ask
how you are?
6Jerusalem, you have left me," says
the LORD.
"You keep going farther and
farther away,
so I have taken hold of you and
destroyed you.
I was tired of holding back my
anger.
7I have separated the people of Judah
with my pitchfork
and scattered them at the city
gates of the land.
My people haven't changed their
ways.
So I have destroyed them
and taken away their children.
8There are more widows than grains
of sand in the sea.
I brought a destroyer at noontime
against the mothers
of the young men
of Judah.
I suddenly brought
pain and fear
on the people of
Judah.
9When the enemy
attacked, a
woman with
seven sons felt
faint because
they would
all die.
She became weak and unable to
breathe.
Her bright day became dark from
sadness.
She felt shame and disgrace.
And everyone else left alive in Judah
I will hand over to the enemies,
too!" says the LORD.

Jeremiah's Second Complaint

10Mother, I am sorry that you gave
birth to me
since I must accuse and criticize
the whole land.
I have not loaned or borrowed
anything,
but everyone curses me.
11The LORD said,
"I have saved you for a good
reason.
I have made your enemies beg you
in times of disaster and trouble.
12No one can smash a piece of iron or
bronze
that comes from the north.
13Your wealth and treasures
I will give to others free of charge,
because the people of Judah have
sinned
throughout the country.
14I will make you slaves to your
enemies
in a land you have never known.
My anger is like a hot fire,
and it will burn against you."

15LORD, you understand.
Remember me and take care
of me.
Punish for me
those who are
hurting me.
Don't destroy me
while you remain
patient with
them.
Think about the
shame I suffer
for you.
16Your words came to
me, and I
listened carefully
to them.
Your words made me very happy,
because I am called by your name,

Your words came to me, and I listened carefully to them. Your words made me very happy.
—Jeremiah 15:16

LORD God All-Powerful.
17 I never sat with the crowd
as they laughed and had fun.
I sat by myself, because you were there,
and you filled me with anger at the evil around me.
18 I don't understand why my pain has no end.
I don't understand why my injury is not cured or healed.
Will you be like a brook that goes dry?
Will you be like a spring that stops flowing?
19 So this is what the LORD says:
"If you change your heart and return to me, I will take you back.
Then you may serve me.
And if you speak things that have worth,
not useless words,
then you may speak for me.
Let the people of Judah turn to you,
but you must not change and be like them.
20 I will make you as strong as a wall to this people,
as strong as a wall of bronze.
They will fight against you,
but they will not defeat you,
because I am with you.
I will rescue you and save you,"
says the LORD.
21 "I will save you from these wicked people
and rescue you from these cruel people."

The Day of Disaster

16 Then the LORD spoke his word to
me: 2"You must not get married
or have sons or daughters in this place."
3The LORD says this about the sons
and daughters born in this land and their
mothers and fathers: 4"They will die of
terrible diseases, and no one will cry for
them or bury them. Their bodies will lie
on the ground like dung. They will die in
war, or they will starve to death. Their
bodies will be food for the birds of the sky
and for the wild animals."
5So this is what the LORD says: "Jeremiah, do not go into a house where there
is a funeral meal. Do not go there to cry
for the dead or to show your sorrow for
them," because I have taken back my
blessing, my love, and my pity from these
people," says the LORD. 6"Important
people and common people will die in the
land of Judah. No one will bury them or
cry for them or cut himself or shave his
head to show sorrow for them. 7No one
will bring food to comfort those who are
crying for the dead. No one will offer a
drink to comfort someone whose mother
or father has died.
8"Do not go into a house where the
people are having a feast to sit down to
eat and drink, 9because this is what the
LORD All-Powerful, the God of Israel,
says: I will soon stop the sounds of joy
and gladness and the happy sounds of
brides and bridegrooms in this place.
This will happen during your lifetime.
10"When you tell the people of Judah
these things, they will ask you, 'Why has
the LORD said these terrible things to us?
What have we done wrong? What sin
have we done against the LORD our God?'
11"Then say to them: 'This is because
your ancestors quit following me,' says
the LORD. 'And they followed other gods
and served and worshiped them. Your ancestors left me and quit obeying my
teaching. 12But you have done even
more evil than your ancestors. You are
very stubborn and do only what you want
to do; you have not obeyed me. 13So I
will throw you out of this country and
send you into a land that you and your ancestors never knew. There you can serve
other gods day and night, because I will
not help you or show you any favors.'
14"People say, 'As surely as the LORD
lives, who brought the people of Israel
out of Egypt . . . ' But the time is coming," says the LORD, "when people will
not say this anymore. 15They will say instead, 'As surely as the LORD lives, who
brought the Israelites from the northern
land and from all the countries where he
had sent them . . . ' And I will bring them
back to the land I gave to their ancestors.
16"I will soon send for many fisher-

men to come to this land," says the LORD.
"And they will catch the people of Judah.
After that, I will send for many hunters to
come to this land. And they will hunt the
people of Judah on every mountain and
hill and in the cracks
of the rocks. 17I see
everything they do.
They cannot hide
from me the things
they do; their sin is
not hidden from my
eyes. 18I will pay back the people of Judah
twice for every one of their sins, because
they have made my land unclean. They
have filled my country with their hateful
idols."

16:17
Sin
Can you hide sin from God?

19 LORD, you are my strength and my
protection,
my safe place in times of trouble.
The nations will come to you from all
over the world
and say, "Our ancestors had only
false gods,
useless idols that didn't help them.
20 Can people make gods for themselves?
They will not really be gods!"
21 The LORD says, "So I will teach
those who make idols.
This time I will teach them
about my power and my strength.
Then they will know
that my name is the LORD.

Judah's Guilty Heart

17 "The sin of the people of Judah is
written with an iron tool.
Their sins were cut with a hard
point into the stone that is their
hearts.
Their sins were cut into the
corners of their altars.
2 Even their children remember
their altars to idols and their
Asherah idols
beside the green trees
and on the high hills.
3 My mountain in the open country
and your wealth and treasures
I will give away to other people.
I will give away the places of
worship in your country,
because you sinned by worshiping
there.
4 You will lose the land I gave you,
and it is your own fault.
I will let your enemies take you as
their slaves
to a land you have never known.
This is because you have made my
anger burn like a hot fire,
and it will burn forever."

Trusting in Humans or God

5 This is what the LORD says:
"A curse is placed on those who trust
other people,
who depend on humans for strength,
who have stopped trusting the
LORD.
6 They are like a bush in a desert
that grows in a land where no one
lives,
a hot and dry land with bad soil.
They don't know about the good
things God can give.

7 "But the person who trusts in the
LORD will be blessed.
The LORD will show him that he
can be trusted.
8 He will be strong, like a tree planted
near water
that sends its roots by a stream.
It is not afraid when the days are hot;
its leaves are always green.
It does not worry in a year when no
rain comes;
it always produces fruit.
9 "More than anything else, a person's
mind is evil
and cannot be healed.
No one truly understands it.
10 But I, the LORD, look into a person's
heart
and test the mind.
So I can decide what each one
deserves;
I can give each one the right
payment for what he does."

11 Like a bird hatching an egg it did not
lay,
so are the people who get rich by
cheating.

LIKE A TREE

JEREMIAH 17:5-8

What is the biggest tree you have ever seen? Some redwood trees can grow as tall as 350 feet! Can you imagine being as tall as that? A tree like that needs plenty of sunlight and water in order to grow. According to Jeremiah, trusting God makes you like a well-watered tree with strong, deep roots. Those who trust in people only are like scorched desert bushes—stumpy, dry, and crackly. Which would you rather be?

The Cloud Guide, Numbers 9:15–23, p. 188

Listen Up!, 1 Kings 19:11–13, p. 467

A Look for the Book, 2 Chronicles 34:14–18, p. 603

How God Speaks, Job 33:14–17, p. 696

What God Thinks, Isaiah 55:8–9, p. 969

Our Heavenly Connection, Matthew 6:9–13, p. 1283

When their lives are half finished,
they will lose their riches.
At the end of their lives, it will be
clear they were fools.

12 From the beginning, our Temple has
been honored
as a glorious throne for God.
13 LORD, hope of Israel,
those who leave you will be
shamed.
People who quit following the LORD
will be like a name written in the
dust,
because they have left the LORD,
the spring of living water.

Jeremiah's Third Complaint

14 LORD, heal me, and I will truly be
healed.
Save me, and I will truly be saved.
You are the one I praise.
15 The people of Judah keep asking me,
"Where is the word from the
LORD?
Let's see that message come
true!"

16 LORD, I didn't run away from being
the shepherd you wanted.
I didn't want the terrible day to
come.
You know everything I have said;
you see all that is happening.
17 Don't be a terror to me.
I run to you for safety in times of
trouble.
18 Make those who are hurting me be
ashamed,
but don't bring shame to me.
Let them be terrified,
but keep me from terror.
Bring the day of disaster on my
enemies.
Destroy them, and destroy them
again.

Keeping the Sabbath Holy

19 This is what the LORD said to me:
"Go and stand at the People's Gate of Jerusalem, where the kings of Judah go in
and out. And then go to all the other gates
of Jerusalem. 20 Say to them there: 'Hear
the word of the LORD, kings of Judah, all
you people of Judah, and all who live in
Jerusalem, who come through these
gates into the city. 21 This is what the
LORD says: Be careful not to carry a load
on the Sabbath day or bring it through the
gates of Jerusalem. 22 Don't take a load
out of your houses on the Sabbath or do
any work on that day. But keep the Sabbath as a holy day, as I commanded your
ancestors. 23 But your ancestors did not

listen or pay attention to me. They were
very stubborn and did not listen. I punished them, but it didn't do any good.
24But you must be careful to obey me,
says the LORD. You must not bring a load
through the gates of Jerusalem on the
Sabbath, but you must keep the Sabbath
as a holy day and not do any work on that
day.

25" 'If you obey this command, kings
who sit on David's throne will come
through the gates of Jerusalem with their
officers. They will come riding in chariots
and on horses, along with the people of
Judah and Jerusalem. And the city of Jerusalem will have people living in it forever. **26**People will come to Jerusalem
from the villages around it, from the
towns of Judah, from the land of Benjamin, from the western hills, from the
mountains, and from southern Judah.
They will all bring to the Temple of the
LORD burnt offerings, sacrifices, grain offerings, incense, and offerings to show
thanks to God. **27**But you must obey me
and keep the Sabbath day as a holy day.
You must not carry any loads into Jerusalem on the Sabbath. If you don't obey me,
I will start a fire at the gates of Jerusalem, and it will burn until it burns even
the strong towers. And it will not be put
out.' "

The Potter and the Clay

18 This is the word the LORD spoke to
Jeremiah: **2**"Go down to the potter's
house, and I will give you my message
there." **3**So I went down to the potter's
house and saw him working at the
potter's wheel. **4**He was using his hands
to make a pot from clay, but something
went wrong with it. So he used that clay
to make another pot the way he wanted it
to be.

5Then the LORD spoke his word to
me: **6**"Family of Israel, can't I do the
same thing with you?" says the LORD.
"You are in my hands like the clay in the
potter's hands. **7**There may come a time
when I will speak about a nation or a
kingdom that I will pull up by its roots or
that I will pull down to destroy it. **8**But if
the people of that nation stop doing the
evil they have done, I will change my
mind and not carry out my plans to bring
disaster to them. **9**There may come another time when I will speak about a nation that I will build up and plant. **10**But if
I see it doing evil by not obeying me, I
will change my mind and not carry out
my plans to do good for them.

11"So, say this to the people of Judah
and those who live in Jerusalem: 'This is
what the LORD says: I am preparing disaster for you
and making plans
against you. So stop
doing evil. Change
your ways and do
what is right.' **12**But
the people of Judah
will answer, 'It won't do any good to try!
We will continue to do what we want.
Each of us will do what his stubborn, evil
heart wants!' "

> EMAIL FROM GOD **18:11**
> **Future**
> What's the future for someone who continues to sin?

13So this is what the LORD says:

"Ask the people in other nations this
question:
'Have you ever heard anything like
this?'
The people of Israel have done a
horrible thing.

14 The snow on the mountains of
Lebanon
never melts from the rocks.
Its cool, flowing streams
do not dry up.

15 But my people have forgotten me.
They burn incense to worthless
idols
and have stumbled in what they do
and in the old ways of their
ancestors.
They walk along back roads
and on poor highways.

16 So Judah's country will become an
empty desert.
People will not stop making fun
of it.
They will shake their heads as they
pass by;
they will be shocked at how the
country was destroyed.

17 Like a strong east wind,
I will scatter them before their
enemies.

At that awful time they will not see
me coming to help them;
they will see me leaving."

Jeremiah's Fourth Complaint

18Then the people said, "Come, let's
make plans against Jeremiah. Surely the
teaching of the law by the priest will not
be lost. We will still have the advice from
the wise men and the words of the prophets. So let's ruin him by telling lies about
him. We won't pay attention to anything
he says."

19 LORD, listen to me.
Listen to what my accusers are
saying!
20 Good should not be paid back with
evil,
but they have dug a pit in order to
kill me.
Remember that I stood before you
and asked you to do good things for
these people
and to turn your anger away from
them.
21 So now, let their children starve,
and let their enemies kill them
with swords.
Let their wives lose their children
and husbands.
Let the men from Judah be put to
death
and the young men be killed with
swords in battle.
22 Let them cry out in their houses
when you bring an enemy against
them suddenly.
Let all this happen, because my
enemies have dug
a pit to capture me and have
hidden traps for my feet.
23 LORD, you know
about all their plans to kill me.
Don't forgive their crimes
or erase their sins from your mind.
Make them fall from their places;
punish them while you are angry.

Judah Is like a Broken Jar

19 This is what the LORD said to me:
"Go and buy a clay jar from a potter. 2Take some of the older leaders of
the people and the priests, and go out to
the Valley of Ben Hinnom, near the front
of the Potsherd Gate. There speak the
words I tell you. 3Say, 'Kings of Judah and
people of Jerusalem, listen to this message from the LORD. This is what the
LORD All-Powerful, the God of Israel,
says: I will soon bring a disaster on this
place that will amaze and frighten everyone who hears about it. 4The people of
Judah have quit following me. They have
made this a place for foreign gods. They
have burned sacrifices to other gods that
neither they, nor their ancestors, nor the
kings of Judah had ever known before.
They filled this place with the blood of innocent people. 5They have built places
on hilltops to worship Baal, where they
burn their children in the fire to Baal.
That is something I did not command or
speak about; it never even entered my
mind. 6Now people call this place the Valley of Ben Hinnom or Topheth, but the
days are coming, says the LORD, when
people will call it the Valley of Killing.

7" 'At this place I will ruin the plans of
the people of Judah and Jerusalem. The
enemy will chase them, and I will have
them killed with swords. I will make their
dead bodies food for the birds and wild
animals. 8I will completely destroy this
city. People will make fun of it and shake
their heads when they pass by. They will
be shocked when they see how the city
was destroyed. 9An enemy army will surround the city and will not let anyone go
out to get food. I will make the people so
hungry that they will eat the bodies of
their own sons and daughters, and then
they will begin to eat each other.'

10"While the people with you are
watching, break that jar. 11Then say this:
'The LORD All-Powerful says: I will break
this nation and this city just as someone
breaks a clay jar that cannot be put back
together again. The dead people will be
buried here in Topheth, because there is
no other place for them. 12This is what I
will do to these people and to this place,
says the LORD. I will make this city like
Topheth. 13The houses in Jerusalem and
the king's palaces will become as unclean
as this place, Topheth, because the peo-

FAITH links

STAND!

JEREMIAH 19:14–20:6

Have you ever been afraid to stand up for something you knew was right? Many people hesitate to take a stand. They think about being made fun of or hurt by others. Jeremiah told the Jewish leaders that God would punish them because of their sin. Because he spoke God's truth, he was arrested. But that didn't stop Jeremiah from speaking the truth!

Taking a stand for the truth can be risky. God can give you the courage to stand for him, just as Jeremiah did.

Here are some more Faithlinks on taking a stand:

Fearful Service?, Exodus 4:1–17, p. 80

His OK to Obey, Deuteronomy 2:24–36, p. 230

Give In or Take a Stand?, 1 Kings 22:13–14, p. 472

A Memorial for Two Thieves, 1 Chronicles 7:21, p. 530

When Bad Things Happen, Ecclesiastes 3:16–17, p. 876

A Word About Worry, Matthew 6:25–34, p. 1284

ple worshiped gods on the roofs[n] of their
houses. They worshiped the stars and
burned incense to honor them and gave
drink offerings to gods.' "
14When Jeremiah left Topheth where
the LORD had sent him to prophesy, he
went to the LORD's Temple, stood in the
courtyard, and said to all the people:
15"This is what the LORD All-Powerful,
the God of Israel, says: 'I will soon bring
disaster to Jerusalem and the villages
around it, as I said I would. This will happen because the people are very stubborn and do not listen at all to what I
say.' "

Pashhur Will Be Captured

20 Pashhur son of Immer was a priest
and the highest officer in the Temple of the LORD. When he heard Jeremiah
prophesying in the Temple courtyard,
2he had Jeremiah the prophet beaten.
And he locked Jeremiah's hands and feet
between large blocks of wood at the Upper Gate of Benjamin of the LORD's Temple. **3**The next day when Pashhur took
Jeremiah out of the blocks of wood, Jeremiah said to him, "The LORD's name for
you is not Pashhur. Now his name for you
is Terror on Every Side. **4**This is what
the LORD says: 'I will soon make you a
terror to yourself and to all your friends.
You will watch enemies killing your
friends with swords. And I will give all
the people of Judah to the king of Babylon, who will take them away as captives
to Babylon and then will kill them with
swords. **5**I will give all the wealth of this
city to its enemies—its goods, its valuables, and the treasures of the kings of
Judah. The enemies will carry all those
valuables off to Babylon. **6**And Pashhur,
you and everyone in your house will be
taken captive. You will be forced to go to
Babylon, where you will die and be buried, you and your friends to whom you
have prophesied lies.' "

Jeremiah's Fifth Complaint

7LORD, you tricked me, and I was
fooled.
You are stronger than I am, so you
won.

19:13 roofs In Bible times houses were built with flat roofs. The roof was used for drying things such as flax and fruit. And it was used as an extra room, as a place for worship, and as a cool place to sleep in the summer.

I have become a joke;
everyone makes fun of me all day long.
8 Every time I speak, I shout.
I am always shouting about violence and destruction.
I tell the people about the message I received from the LORD,
but this only brings me insults.
The people make fun of me all day long.
9 Sometimes I say to myself,
"I will forget about the LORD.
I will not speak anymore in his name."
But then his message becomes like a burning fire inside me,
deep within my bones.
I get tired of trying to hold it inside of me,
and finally, I cannot hold it in.
10 I hear many people whispering about me:
"Terror on every side!
Tell on him! Let's tell the rulers about him."
My friends are all just waiting for me to make some mistake.
They are saying,
"Maybe we can trick him
so we can defeat him
and pay him back."
11 But the LORD is with me like a strong warrior,
so those who are chasing me will trip and fall;
they will not defeat me.
They will be ashamed because they have failed,
and their shame will never be forgotten.

12 LORD All-Powerful, you test good people;
you look deeply into the heart and mind of a person.
I have told you my arguments against these people,

EMAIL! FROM GOD 20:12
Judgment
Does God know your thoughts?

so let me see you give them the punishment they deserve.

13 Sing to the LORD!
Praise the LORD!
He saves the life of the poor
from the power of the wicked.

Jeremiah's Sixth Complaint

14 Let there be a curse on the day I was born;
let there be no blessing on the day when my mother gave birth to me.
15 Let there be a curse on the man who brought my father the news:
"You have a son!"
This made my father very glad.
16 Let that man be like the towns the LORD destroyed without pity.
Let him hear loud crying in the morning
and battle cries at noon,
17 because he did not kill me before I was born.
Then my mother would have been my grave;
she would have stayed pregnant forever.
18 Why did I have to come out of my mother's body?
All I have known is trouble and sorrow,
and my life will end in shame.

God Rejects King Zedekiah's Request

21 This is the word that the LORD
spoke to Jeremiah. It came when
Zedekiah king of Judah sent Pashhur son
of Malkijah and the priest Zephaniah son
of Maaseiah to Jeremiah. 2They said,
"Ask the LORD for us what will happen,
because Nebuchadnezzar king of Babylon
is attacking us. Maybe the LORD will do
miracles for us as he did in the past so
Nebuchadnezzar will stop attacking us
and leave."
3But Jeremiah answered them, "Tell
King Zedekiah this: 4'Here is what the
LORD, the God of Israel, says: You have
weapons of war in your hands to defend
yourselves against the king of Babylon

and the Babylonians, who are all around
the city wall. But I will make those weapons useless. Soon I will bring them into
the center of this city. **5**In my anger, my
very great anger, I myself will fight
against you with my great power and
strength. **6**I will kill everything living in
Jerusalem—both people and animals.
They will die from terrible diseases.
7Then, says the LORD, I'll hand over Zedekiah king of Judah, his officers, and the
people in Jerusalem who do not die from
the terrible diseases or battle or hunger,
to Nebuchadnezzar king of Babylon. I will
let those win who want to kill the people
of Judah, so the people of Judah and Jerusalem will be killed in war. Nebuchadnezzar will not show any mercy or pity or
feel sorry for them!'

8"Also tell this to the people of Jerusalem: 'This is what the LORD says: I will
let you choose to live or die. **9**Anyone
who stays in Jerusalem will die in war or
from hunger or from a terrible disease.
But anyone who goes out of Jerusalem
and surrenders to the Babylonians who
are attacking you will live. Anyone who
leaves the city will save his life as if it
were a prize won in war. **10**I have decided
to make trouble for this city and not to
help it, says the LORD. I will give it to the
king of Babylon, and he will burn it with
fire.'

11"Say to Judah's royal family: 'Hear
the word of the LORD. **12**Family of David,
this is what the LORD says:

You must judge people fairly every
morning.
Save the person who has been
robbed
from the power of his attacker.
If you don't, I will become very
angry.
My anger will be like a fire that no
one can put out,
because you have done evil things.

13" 'Jerusalem, I am against you,
you who live on top of the
mountain
over this valley, says the LORD.
You say, "No one can attack us
or come into our strong city."

14But I will give you the punishment
you deserve, says the LORD.
I will start a fire in your forests
that will burn up everything
around you!' "

Judgment Against Evil Kings

22 This is what the LORD says: "Go
down to the palace of the king of
Judah and prophesy this message there:
2'Hear the word of the LORD, king of Judah, who rules from David's throne. You
and your officers, and your people who
come through these gates, listen! **3**This
is what the LORD says: Do what is fair
and right. Save the one who has been
robbed from the power of his
attacker. Don't mis-
treat or hurt the
foreigners, orphans,
or widows. Don't
kill innocent people
here. **4**If you care-
fully obey these commands, kings who
sit on David's throne will come through
the gates of this palace with their officers
and people, riding in chariots and on
horses. **5**But if you don't obey these commands, says the LORD, I swear by my
own name that this king's palace will become a ruin.' "

> eMAIL FROM GOD
> **22:3–5**
> **Truth**
> Learn how to show justice.

6This is what the LORD says about the
palace where the king of Judah lives:

"You are tall like the forests of
Gilead,
like the mountaintops of Lebanon.
But I will truly make you into a
desert,
into towns where no one lives.
7I will send men to destroy the
palace,
each with his weapons.
They will cut up your strong,
beautiful cedar beams
and throw them into the fire.

8"People from many nations will pass
by this city and ask each other, 'Why has
the LORD done such a terrible thing to
Jerusalem, this great city?' **9**And the answer will be: 'Because the people of Judah quit following the agreement with
the LORD their God. They worshiped and
served other gods.' "

Judgment Against Jehoahaz

10 Don't cry for the dead king or be sad
about him.
But cry painfully for the king who
is being taken away,
because he will never return
or see his homeland again.

11 This is what the LORD says about
Jehoahaz son of Josiah who became king
of Judah after his father died and who has
left this place: "He will never return.
12 He will die where he has been taken captive, and he will not see this land again."

Judgment Against Jehoiakim

13 "How terrible it will be for one who
builds his palace by doing evil,
who cheats people so he can build
its upper rooms.
He makes his own people work for
nothing
and does not pay them.
14 He says, 'I will build a great palace
for myself
with large upper rooms.'
So he builds it with large windows
and uses cedar wood for the walls,
which he paints red.

15 "Does having a lot of cedar in your
house
make you a great king?
Your father was satisfied to have food
and drink.
He did what was right and fair,
so everything went well for him.
16 He helped those who were poor and
needy,
so everything went well for him.
That is what it means to know God,"
says the LORD.
17 "But you only look for and think
about
what you can get dishonestly.
You are even willing to kill innocent
people to get it.
You feel free to hurt people and to
steal from them."

18 So this is what the LORD says to Jehoiakim son of Josiah king of Judah:
"The people of Judah will not cry
when Jehoiakim dies,
saying: 'Oh, my brother,' or 'Oh,
my sister.'
They will not cry for him, saying:
'Oh, master,' or 'Oh, my king.'
19 They will bury him like a donkey,
dragging his body away
and throwing it outside the gates
of Jerusalem.

20 "Judah, go up to Lebanon and cry
out.
Let your voice be heard in Bashan.
Cry out from Abarim,
because all your friends are
destroyed!
21 Judah, when you were successful, I
warned you,
but you said, 'I won't listen.'
You have acted like this since you
were young;
you have not obeyed me.
22 Like a storm, my punishment will
blow all your shepherds away
and send your friends into
captivity.
Then you will really be ashamed and
disgraced
because of all the wicked things
you did.
23 King, you live in your palace,
cozy in your rooms of cedar.
But when your punishment comes,
how you will groan
like a woman giving birth to a
baby!

Judgment upon Jehoiachin

24 "As surely as I live," says the LORD,
"Jehoiachin son of Jehoiakim king of Judah, even if you were a signet ring on my
right hand, I would still pull you off. 25 I
will hand you over to Nebuchadnezzar
king of Babylon and to the Babylonians—
those people you fear because they want
to kill you. 26 I will throw you and your
mother into another country. Neither of
you was born there, but both of you will
die there. 27 They will want to come
back, but they will never be able to return."

28 Jehoiachin is like a broken pot
someone threw away;

he is like something no one wants.
Why will Jehoiachin and his children
be thrown out
and sent into a foreign land?
29 Land, land, land of Judah,
hear the word of the LORD!
30 This is what the LORD says:
"Write this down in the record about
Jehoiachin:
He is a man without children,
a man who will not be successful in
his lifetime.
And none of his descendants will be
successful;
none will sit on the throne of David
or rule in Judah."

FAITH links

YOUR FULL TRUST

JEREMIAH 22:20-22

The Israelites trusted the nations around them for protection. They made agreements with these nations to help each other. Unfortunately, these nations did things that God hated. Israel followed their example. God told Israel that their faith was in the wrong place. Instead of trusting God, they had trusted others.

We may not depend on other nations to help us each day, but we sometimes trust the wrong people. Maybe you've put all of your hope in a friendship that wound up being disappointing. God wants your full trust in him.

Obey? No Way!, Exodus 1:15–21, p. 76

When God Says No, 2 Samuel 7, p. 407

Give In or Take a Stand?, 1 Kings 22:13–14, p. 472

Two Kinds of People, Psalm 1, p. 710

A Fair-weather Friend, Obadiah 7, p. 1209

The Way to Be Wise, James 1:5, p. 1689

The Evil Leaders of Judah

23 "How terrible it will be for the
leaders of Judah, who are scatter-
ing and destroying my people," says the
LORD.
2 They are responsible for the people,
so the LORD, the God of Israel, says to
them: "You have scattered my people and
forced them away and not taken care of
them. So I will punish you for the evil
things you have done," says the LORD.
3 "I sent my people to other countries,
but I will gather those who are left alive
and bring them back to their own country.
Then they will have many children and
grow in number. 4 I will place new leaders
over my people, who will take care of
them. And my people will not be afraid or
terrified again, and none of them will be
lost," says the LORD.

The Good Branch Will Come

5 "The days are coming," says the LORD,
"when I will raise up a good branch
in David's family.
He will be a king who will rule in a
wise way;
he will do what is fair and right in
the land.
6 In his time Judah will be saved,
and Israel will live in safety.
This will be his name:
The LORD Does What Is Right.
7 "So the days are coming," says the
LORD, "when people will not say again:
'As surely as the LORD lives, who brought
Israel out of Egypt . . .' 8 But people will
say something new: 'As surely as the
LORD lives, who brought the descendants
of Israel from the land of the north and
from all the countries where he had sent
them away . . .' Then the people of Israel
will live in their own land."

False Prophets Will Be Punished

9A message to the prophets:
My heart is broken.
All my bones shake.
I'm like someone who is drunk,
like someone who has been
overcome with wine.
This is because of the LORD
and his holy words.
10 The land of Judah is full of people
who are guilty of adultery.
Because of this, the LORD cursed
the land.
It has become a very sad place,
and the pastures have dried up.
The people are evil
and use their power in the wrong
way.

11 "Both the prophets and the priests
live as if there were no God.
I have found them doing evil things
even in my own Temple," says
the LORD.
12 "So they will be in danger.
They will be forced into darkness
where they will be defeated.
I will bring disaster on them
in the year I punish them," says
the LORD.

13 "I saw the prophets of Samaria
do something wrong.
Those prophets prophesied by Baal
and led my people Israel away.
14 And I have seen the prophets of
Jerusalem
do terrible things.
They are guilty of adultery
and live by lies.
They encourage evil people to keep
on doing evil,
so the people don't stop sinning.
All of those people are like the city of
Sodom.
The people of Jerusalem are like
the city of Gomorrah to me!"
15So this is what the LORD All-Powerful says about the prophets:
"I will make those prophets eat bitter
food
and drink poisoned water,
because the prophets of Jerusalem
spread wickedness
through the whole country."
16This is what the LORD All-Powerful says:
"Don't pay
attention to
what those
prophets are
saying to
you.
They are trying
to fool you.
They talk about visions their own
minds made up,
not about visions from me.
17 They say to those who hate me:
'The LORD says: You will have
peace.'
They say to all those who are
stubborn and do as they please:
'Nothing bad will happen to you.'
18 But none of these prophets has stood
in the meeting of angels
to see or hear the message of the
LORD.
None of them has paid close
attention to his message.
19 Look, the punishment from the LORD
will come like a storm.
His anger will be like a hurricane.
It will come swirling down on the
heads of those wicked people.
20 The LORD's anger will not stop
until he finishes what he plans to
do.
When that day is over,
you will understand this clearly.
21 I did not send those prophets,
but they ran to tell their message.
I did not speak to them,
but they prophesied anyway.
22 But if they had stood in the meeting
of angels,
they would have told my message
to my people.
They would have turned the people
from their evil ways
and from doing evil.

23 "I am a God who is near," says the
LORD.
"I am also a God who is far away."

EMAIL! FROM GOD 23:16
Hope
Does it matter what you hope in?

FAITH CHALLENGE

Try this challenge. Read 23:24 to see what the Lord says about people who try to hide from him. What would make you want to hide from God? What are you hiding from God now? What do you plan to do about it?

TESTING IT

Jeremiah 23:24
"No one can hide where I cannot see him," says the LORD. "I fill all of heaven and earth," says the LORD.

24"No one can hide
where I cannot see him," says the
LORD.
"I fill all of heaven and earth," says
the LORD.
25"I have heard the prophets who
prophesy lies in my name. They say, 'I
have had a dream! I have had a dream!'
26How long will this continue in the
minds of these lying prophets? They
prophesy from their own wishful thinking. 27They are trying to make the people of Judah forget me by telling each
other these dreams. In the same way,
their ancestors forgot me and worshiped
Baal. 28Is straw the same thing as
wheat?" says the LORD. "If a prophet
wants to tell about his dreams, let him!
But let the person who hears my message speak it truthfully! 29Isn't my message like a fire?" says the LORD. "Isn't it
like a hammer that smashes a rock?
30"So I am against the false prophets," says the LORD. "They keep stealing
words from each other and say they are
from me. 31I am against the false prophets," says the LORD. "They use their own
words and pretend it is a message from
me. 32I am against the prophets who
prophesy false dreams," says the LORD.
"They mislead my people with their lies
and false teachings! I did not send them
or command them to do anything for me.
They can't help the people of Judah at
all," says the LORD.

The Sad Message from the Lord

33"Suppose the people of Judah, a
prophet, or a priest asks you: 'Jeremiah,
what is the message from the LORD?' You
will answer them and say, 'You are a
heavy load to the LORD, and I will throw
you down, says the LORD.' 34A prophet
or a priest or one of the people might say,
'This is a message from the LORD.' That
person has lied, so I will punish him and
his whole family. 35This is what you will
say to each other: 'What did the LORD answer?' or 'What did the LORD say?' 36But
you will never again say, 'The message of
the LORD,' because the only message you
speak is your own words. You have
changed the words of our God, the living
God, the LORD All-Powerful. 37This is
how you should speak to the prophets:
'What answer did the LORD give you?' or
'What did the LORD say?' 38But don't say,
'The message from the LORD.' If you use
these words, this is what the LORD says:
Because you called it a 'message from
the LORD,' though I told you not to use
those words, 39I will pick you up and
throw you away from me, along with Jerusalem, which I gave to your ancestors
and to you. 40And I will make a disgrace
of you forever; your shame will never be
forgotten."

The Good and Bad Figs

24 Nebuchadnezzar king of Babylon
captured Jehoiachin son of Jehoiakim and king of Judah, his officers, and all
the craftsmen and metalworkers of Judah. He took them away from Jerusalem
and brought them to Babylon. It was then
that the LORD showed me two baskets of
figs arranged in front of the Temple of the
LORD. **2**One of the baskets had very good
figs in it, like figs that ripen early in the
season. But the other basket had figs too
rotten to eat.

3The LORD said to me, "What do you
see, Jeremiah?"

I answered, "I see figs.
The good figs are very
good, but the rotten figs
are too rotten to eat."

4Then the LORD spoke
his word to me: **5**"This is
what the LORD, the God of
Israel, says: 'I sent the
people of Judah out of
their country to live in
the country of Babylon. I
think of those people as
good, like these good figs. **6**I will look
after them and bring them back to the
land of Judah. I will not tear them down,
but I will build them up. I will not pull
them up, but I will plant them so they can
grow. **7**I will make them want to know
me, that I am the LORD. They will be my
people, and I will be their God, because
they will return to me with their whole
hearts.

8" 'But the bad figs are too rotten to
eat.' So this is what the LORD says: 'Zedekiah king of Judah, his officers, and all
the people from Jerusalem who are left
alive, even those who live in Egypt, will
be like those rotten figs. **9**I will make
those people hated as an evil people by all
the kingdoms of the earth. People will
make fun of them and tell jokes about
them and point fingers at them and curse
them everywhere I scatter them. **10**I will
send war, hunger, and disease against
them. I will attack them until they have
all been killed. Then they will no longer
be in the land I gave to them and their
ancestors.' "

> The LORD has sent all his servants the prophets to you . . . but you have not listened or paid any attention to them.
> —Jeremiah 25:4

A Summary of Jeremiah's Preaching

25 This is the message that came to
Jeremiah concerning all the people of Judah. It came in the fourth year
that Jehoiakim son of Josiah was king of
Judah and the first year Nebuchadnezzar
was king of Babylon. **2**This is the message Jeremiah the prophet spoke to all
the people of Judah and Jerusalem:

3The LORD has spoken his word to me
again and again for these past twenty-
three years. I have been a prophet since
the thirteenth year of Josiah son of Amon
king of Judah. I have spo-
ken messages from the
LORD to you from that
time until today, but you
have not listened.

4The LORD has sent all
his servants the prophets
to you over and over
again, but you have not
listened or paid any attention to them. **5**Those
prophets have said, "Stop
your evil ways. Stop do-
ing what is wrong so you can stay in the
land that the LORD gave to you and your
ancestors to live in forever. **6**Don't follow
other gods to serve them or to worship
them. Don't make me, the LORD, angry
by worshiping idols that are the work of
your own hands, or I will punish you."

7"But you people of Judah did not listen to me," says the LORD. "You made me
angry by worshiping idols that were the
work of your own hands, so I punished
you."

8So this is what the LORD All-
Powerful says: "Since you have not listened to my messages, **9**I will send for all
the peoples of the north," says the LORD,
"along with my servant Nebuchadnezzar
king of Babylon. I will bring them all
against Judah, those who live there, and
all the nations around you, too. I will
completely destroy all those countries
and leave them in ruins forever. People
will be shocked when they see how badly
I have destroyed those countries. **10**I will
bring an end to the sounds of joy and happiness, the sounds of brides and bride-

grooms, and the sound of people grinding
meal. And I will take away the light of the
lamp. **11**That whole area will be an empty
desert, and these nations will be slaves of
the king of Babylon for seventy years.
12"But when the seventy years have
passed, I will punish the king of Babylon
and his entire nation for their evil," says
the LORD. "I will make that land a desert
forever. **13**I will make happen all the terrible things I said about Babylonia—
everything Jeremiah prophesied about all
those foreign nations, the warnings written in this book. **14**Even the Babylonians
will have to serve many nations and
many great kings. I will give them the
punishment they deserve for all their
own hands have done."

Judgment on the Nations

15The LORD, the God of Israel, said
this to me: "My anger is like the wine in a
cup. Take it from my hand and make all
the nations, to whom I am sending you,
drink all of my anger from this cup.
16They will drink my anger and stumble
about and act like madmen because of the
war I am going to send among them."
17So I took the cup from the LORD's
hand and went to those nations and made
them drink from it. **18**I served this wine
to the people of Jerusalem and the towns
of Judah, and the kings and officers of Judah, so they would become a ruin. Then
people would be shocked and would insult them and speak evil of them. And so
it has been to this day. **19**I also made
these people drink of the LORD's anger:
the king of Egypt, his servants, his officers, all his people, **20**and all the foreigners there; all the kings of the land of Uz;
all the kings of the Philistines (the kings
of the cities of Ashkelon, Gaza, Ekron,
and the people left at Ashdod); **21**the
people of Edom, Moab, and Ammon; **22**all
the kings of Tyre and Sidon; all the kings
of the coastal countries to the west;
23the people of Dedan and Tema and
Buz; all who cut their hair short; **24**all the
kings of Arabia; and the kings of the people who live in the desert; **25**all the kings
of Zimri, Elam, and Media; **26**and all the
kings of the north, near and far, one after
the other. I made all the kingdoms on
earth drink from the cup of the LORD's
anger, but the king of Babylon will drink
from this cup after all the others.
27"Then say to them, 'This is what
the LORD All-Powerful, the God of Israel,
says: Drink this cup of my anger. Get
drunk from it and vomit. Fall down and
don't get up because of the war I am
sending among you!'
28"If they refuse to take the cup from
your hand and drink, say to them, 'The
LORD All-Powerful says this: You must
drink from this cup. **29**Look! I am already
bringing disaster on Jerusalem, the city
that is called by my name. Do you think
you will not be punished? You will be
punished! I am sending war on all the
people of the earth, says the LORD All-
Powerful.'
30"You, Jeremiah, will prophesy against
them with all these words. Say to them:

'The LORD will roar from heaven
and will shout from his Holy
Temple.
He will roar loudly against his
land.
He will shout like people who walk
on grapes to make wine;
he will shout against all who live
on the earth.
31The noise will spread all over the
earth,
because the LORD will accuse all
the nations.
He will judge and tell what is wrong
with all people,
and he will kill the evil people with
a sword,' " says the LORD.

32This is what the LORD All-Powerful
says:

"Disasters will soon spread
from nation to nation.
They will come like a powerful
storm
from the faraway places on
earth."

33At that time those killed by the LORD
will reach from one end of the earth to
the other. No one will cry for them or
gather up their bodies and bury them.
They will be left lying on the ground like
dung.

34 Cry, you leaders! Cry out loud!
Roll around in the dust, leaders of
the people!
It is now time for you to be killed.
You will fall and be scattered,
like pieces of a broken jar.
35 There will be no place for the leaders
to hide;
they will not escape.
36 I hear the sound of the leaders
shouting.
I hear the leaders of the people
crying loudly,
because the LORD is destroying
their land.
37 Those peaceful pastures will be like
an empty desert,
because the LORD is very angry.
38 Like a lion, he has left his den.
Their land has been destroyed
because of the terrible war he
brought,
because of his fierce anger.

Jeremiah's Lesson at the Temple

26 This message came from the LORD
soon after Jehoiakim son of Josiah
became king of Judah. **2**This is what the
LORD said: "Jeremiah, stand in the courtyard of the Temple of the LORD. Give this
message to all the people of the towns of
Judah who are coming to worship at the
Temple of the LORD. Tell them everything I tell you to say; don't leave out a
word. **3**Maybe they will listen and stop
their evil ways. If they will, I will change
my mind about bringing on them the disaster that I am planning because of the
evil they have done. **4**Say to them: 'This
is what the LORD says: You must obey me
and follow my teachings that I gave you.
5You must listen to what my servants the
prophets say to you. I have sent them to
you again and again, but you did not listen. **6**If you don't obey me, I will destroy
my Temple in Jerusalem as I destroyed
my Holy Tent at Shiloh. When I do, people all over the world will curse Jerusalem.' "

7The priests, the prophets, and all the
people heard Jeremiah speaking these
words in the Temple of the LORD. **8**When
Jeremiah finished speaking everything
the LORD had commanded him to say, the
priests, prophets, and all the people
grabbed Jeremiah. They said, "You must
die! **9**How dare you prophesy in the name
of the LORD that this Temple will be destroyed like the one at Shiloh! How dare
you say that Jerusalem will become a
desert without anyone to live in it!" And
all the people crowded around Jeremiah
in the Temple of the LORD.

10Now when the officers of Judah
heard about what was happening, they
came out of the king's palace and went up
to the Temple of the LORD and took their
places at the entrance of the New Gate.
11Then the priests and prophets said to
the officers and all the other people, "Jeremiah should be killed. He prophesied
against Jerusalem, and you heard him
yourselves."

12Then Jeremiah spoke these words
to all the officers of Judah and all the
other people: "The LORD sent me to say
everything you have heard about this
Temple and this city. **13**Now change your
lives and start doing good and obey the
LORD your God. Then he will change his
mind and not bring on you the disaster he
has told you about. **14**As for me, I am in
your power. Do to me what you think is
good and right. **15**But be sure of one
thing. If you kill me, you will be guilty of
killing an innocent person. You will make
this city and everyone who lives in it
guilty, too! The LORD truly sent me to
you to give you this message."

16Then the officers and all the people
said to the priests and the prophets, "Jeremiah must not be killed. What he told us
comes from the LORD our God."

17Then some of the older leaders of
Judah stood up and said to all the people,
18"Micah, from the city of Moresheth,
was a prophet during the time Hezekiah
was king of Judah. Micah said to all the
people of Judah, 'This is what the LORD
All-Powerful says:

Jerusalem will be plowed like a field.
It will become a pile of rocks,
and the hill where the Temple
stands will be covered with
bushes.'

19"Hezekiah king of Judah and the

people of Judah did not kill Micah. You
know that Hezekiah feared the LORD and
tried to please the LORD. So the LORD
changed his mind and did not bring on Judah the disaster he had promised. If we
hurt Jeremiah, we will bring a terrible disaster on ourselves!"

20(Now there was another man who
prophesied in the name of the LORD. His
name was Uriah son of Shemaiah from
the city of Kiriath Jearim. He preached
the same things against Jerusalem and
the land of Judah that Jeremiah did.
21When King Jehoiakim, all his army officers, and all the leaders of Judah heard
Uriah preach, King Jehoiakim wanted to
kill Uriah. But Uriah heard about it and
was afraid. So he escaped to Egypt.
22Then King Jehoiakim sent Elnathan
son of Acbor and some other men to
Egypt, **23**and they brought Uriah back
from Egypt. Then they took him to King
Jehoiakim, who had Uriah killed with
a sword. His body was thrown into the
burial place where poor people are
buried.)

EMAIL FROM GOD
26:24
Friendship
Can standing up for a friend make a difference?

24Ahikam son of
Shaphan supported
Jeremiah. So Ahi-
kam did not hand
Jeremiah over to be
killed by the people.

Nebuchadnezzar Is Made Ruler

27 The LORD spoke his word to Jeremiah soon after Zedekiah son of
Josiah was made king of
Judah. **2**This is what the
LORD said to me: "Make a
yoke out of straps and
poles, and put it on the
back of your neck. **3**Then
send messages to the
kings of Edom, Moab, Am-
mon, Tyre, and Sidon by
their messengers who
have come to Jerusalem
to see Zedekiah king of
Judah. **4**Tell them to give this message to
their masters: 'The LORD All-Powerful,
the God of Israel, says: "Tell your masters: **5**I made the earth, its people, and all
its animals with my great power and
strength. I can give the earth to anyone I
want. **6**Now I have given all these lands
to Nebuchadnezzar king of Babylon, my
servant. I will make even the wild animals obey him. **7**All nations will serve
Nebuchadnezzar and his son and grandson. Then the time will come for Babylon
to be defeated, and many nations and
great kings will make Babylon their servant.

8" ' "But if some nations or kingdoms
refuse to serve Nebuchadnezzar king of
Babylon and refuse to be under his control, I will punish them with war, hunger,
and terrible diseases, says the LORD. I
will use Nebuchadnezzar to destroy
them. **9**So don't listen to your false
prophets, those who use magic to tell the
future, those who explain dreams, the
mediums, or magicians. They all tell you,
'You will not be slaves to the king of Babylon.' **10**They are telling you lies that will
cause you to be taken far from your
homeland. I will force you to leave your
homes, and you will die in another land.
11But the nations who put themselves
under the control of the king of Babylon
and serve him I will let stay in their own
country, says the LORD. The people from
those nations will live in their own land
and farm it." ' "

12I gave the same message to Zedekiah king of Judah. I said, "Put yourself
under the control of the king of Babylon
and serve him, and you will live. **13**Why
should you and your people die from war,
hunger, or disease, as the
LORD said would happen
to those who do not
serve the king of Bab-
ylon? **14**But the false
prophets are saying, 'You
will never be slaves to
the king of Babylon.'
Don't listen to them be-
cause they are prophesy-
ing lies to you! **15**'I did
not send them,' says the
LORD. 'They are prophesying lies and
saying the message is from me. So I will
send you away, Judah. And you and those
prophets who prophesy to you will die.' "

16Then I, Jeremiah, said to the priests

> I made the earth, its people, and all its animals with my great power and strength.
> —Jeremiah 27:5

and all the people, "This is what the LORD says: Those false prophets are saying, 'The Babylonians will soon return what they took from the Temple of the LORD.' Don't listen to them! They are prophesying lies to you. **17**Don't listen to those prophets. But serve the king of Babylon, and you will live. There is no reason for you to cause Jerusalem to become a ruin. **18**If they are prophets and have the message from the LORD, let them pray to the LORD All-Powerful. Let them ask that the items which are still in the Temple of the LORD and in the king's palace and in Jerusalem not be taken away to Babylon.

19"This is what the LORD All-Powerful says about those items left in Jerusalem: the pillars, the large bronze bowl, which is called the Sea, the stands that can be moved, and other things. **20**Nebuchadnezzar king of Babylon did not take these away when he took as captives Jehoiachin son of Jehoiakim king of Judah and all the other important people from Judah and Jerusalem to Babylon. **21**This is what the LORD All-Powerful, the God of Israel, says about the items left in the Temple of the LORD and in the king's palace and in Jerusalem: **22**'All of them will also be taken to Babylon. And they will stay there until the day I go to get them,' says the LORD. 'Then I will bring them back and return them to this place.' "

The False Prophet Hananiah

28 It was in that same year, in the fifth month of Zedekiah's fourth year as king of Judah, soon after he began to rule. The prophet Hananiah son of Azzur, from the town of Gibeon, spoke to me in the Temple of the LORD in front of the priests and all the people. He said: **2**"The LORD All-Powerful, the God of Israel, says: 'I have broken the yoke the king of Babylon has put on Judah. **3**Before two years are over, I will bring back everything that Nebuchadnezzar king of Babylon took to Babylon from the LORD's Temple. **4**I will also bring back Jehoiachin son of Jehoiakim king of Judah and all the other captives from Judah who went to Babylon,' says the LORD. 'So I will break the yoke the king of Babylon put on Judah.' "

5Then the prophet Jeremiah spoke to the prophet Hananiah in front of the priests and all the people who were standing in the Temple of the LORD. **6**He said, "Amen! Let the LORD really do that! May the LORD make the message you prophesy come true. May he bring back here everything from the LORD's Temple and all the people who were taken as captives to Babylon.

7"But listen to what I am going to say to you and all the people. **8**There were prophets long before we became prophets, Hananiah. They prophesied that war, hunger, and terrible diseases would come to many countries and great kingdoms. **9**But if a prophet prophesies that we will have peace and that message comes true, he can be recognized as one truly sent by the LORD."

10Then the prophet Hananiah took the yoke off Jeremiah's neck and broke it. **11**Hananiah said in front of all the people, "This is what the LORD says: 'In the same way I will break the yoke of Nebuchadnezzar king of Babylon. He put that yoke on all the nations of the world, but I will break it before two years are over.' " After Hananiah had said that, Jeremiah left the Temple.

12The LORD spoke his word to Jeremiah after the prophet Hananiah had broken the yoke off of the prophet Jeremiah's neck. **13**The LORD said, "Go and tell Hananiah, 'This is what the LORD says: You have broken a wooden yoke, but I will make a yoke of iron in its place! **14**The LORD All-Powerful, the God of Israel, says: I will put a yoke of iron on the necks of all these nations to make them serve Nebuchadnezzar king of Babylon, and they will be slaves to him. I will even give Nebuchadnezzar control over the wild animals.' "

15Then the prophet Jeremiah said to the prophet Hananiah, "Listen, Hananiah! The LORD did not send you, and you have made the people of Judah trust in lies. **16**So this is what the LORD says: 'Soon I will remove you from the earth. You will die this year, because you

taught the people to turn against the
LORD.' "
17Hananiah died in the seventh
month of that same year.

A Letter to the Captives in Babylon

29 This is the letter that Jeremiah
the prophet sent from Jerusalem
to the older leaders who were among the
captives, the priests, and the prophets.
He sent it to all the other people Nebuchadnezzar had taken as captives from
Jerusalem to Babylon. 2(This letter was
sent after all these people were taken
away: Jehoiachin the king and the queen
mother; the officers and leaders of Judah
and Jerusalem; and the craftsmen and
metalworkers from Jerusalem.) 3Zede-
kiah king of Judah sent Elasah son of Shaphan and Gemariah son of Hilkiah to
Babylon to Nebuchadnezzar king of Babylon. So Jeremiah gave them this letter to
carry to Babylon:
4This is what the LORD All-Powerful,
the God of Israel, says to all those people
I sent away from Jerusalem as captives to
Babylon: 5"Build houses and settle in the
land. Plant gardens and eat the food they
grow. 6Get married and have sons and
daughters. Find wives for your sons, and
let your daughters be married so they
also may have sons and daughters. Have
many children in Babylon; don't become
fewer in number. 7Also do good things for
the city where I sent
you as captives.
Pray to the LORD for
the city where you
are living, because if
good things happen
in the city, good
things will happen to you also." 8The
LORD All-Powerful, the God of Israel,
says: "Don't let the prophets among you
and the people who do magic fool you.
Don't listen to their dreams. 9They are
prophesying lies to you, saying that their
message is from me. But I did not send
them," says the LORD.
10This is what the LORD says: "Babylon will be powerful for seventy years.
After that time I will come to you, and I
will keep my promise to bring you back to
Jerusalem. 11I say this because I know
what I am planning for you," says the
LORD. "I have good plans for you, not
plans to hurt you. I will give you hope and
a good future. 12Then you will call my
name. You will come to me and pray to

EMAIL FROM GOD

29:7

Prayer

Why should you pray for people or places you don't like?

FAITH links

A HOPEFUL FUTURE

JEREMIAH 29:11

What are some of the plans you and your parents have made concerning your future? Maybe your parents have set aside a savings account to help pay for college. Or maybe you've told them about a career that you'd like to try. Whatever the plans are, you know that they were made to make sure that you have a hopeful future. God's plans are like that as well. As Jeremiah explained, God's plans for his people are good, not harmful.

Planning for the future? Connect here first:

Good Advice?, Leviticus 20:6, p. 162

The Green Light, 2 Samuel 2:1, p. 401

A Parent's Advice, Proverbs 1:8–9, p. 825

First Place, Haggai 1:7–11, p. 1248

The Choices of a Choice, Luke 5:1–11, p. 1375

Heavenly Treasure, Luke 12:32–34, p. 1394

me, and I will listen to you. 13You will
search for me. And when you search for
me with all your heart, you will find me!
14I will let you find me," says the LORD.
"And I will bring you back from your captivity. I forced you to leave this place, but
I will gather you from all the nations,
from the places I have sent you as captives," says the LORD. "And I will bring
you back to this place."
15You might say, "The LORD has
given us prophets here in Babylon."
16But the LORD says this about the
king who is sitting on David's throne now
and all the other people still in Jerusalem,
your relatives who did not go as captives
to Babylon with you. 17The LORD All-
Powerful says: "I will soon send war,
hunger, and terrible diseases against
those still in Jerusalem. I will make them
like bad figs that are too rotten to eat. 18I
will chase them with war, hunger, and
terrible diseases. I will make them hated
by all the kingdoms of the earth. People
will curse them and be shocked and will
use them as a shameful example wherever I make them go. 19This is because
they have not listened to my message,"
says the LORD. "I sent my message to
them again and again through my servants, the prophets, but they did not listen," says the LORD.
20You captives, whom I forced to
leave Jerusalem and go to Babylon, listen
to the message from the LORD. 21The
LORD All-Powerful, the God of Israel,
says this about Ahab son of Kolaiah and
Zedekiah son of Maaseiah: "These two
men have been prophesying lies to you,
saying that their message is from me.
But soon I will hand over those two
prophets to Nebuchadnezzar king of Babylon, and he will kill them in front of you.
22Because of them, all the captives from
Judah in Babylon will use this curse:
'May the LORD treat you like Zedekiah
and Ahab, whom the king of Babylon
burned in the fire.' 23They have done
evil things among the people of Israel.
They are guilty of adultery with their
neighbors' wives. They have also spoken
lies and said those lies were a message
from me. I did not tell them to do that. I

FAITH links

WHAT'S WRONG ABOUT RUMORS

JEREMIAH 29:24-32

Has anyone ever started a rumor about you or one of your friends that wasn't true? Rumors can be very harmful to friendships or reputations if they are believed. God had a message for Shemaiah, a man who spread a rumor about Jeremiah. He told people that Jeremiah was not a true prophet of God. God was very displeased with Shemaiah and promised to punish him.

When a rumor comes your way, you don't have to instantly believe it or pass it on. Instead, try to find out the truth for yourself, or do the next best thing: Ignore it.

What do you do when you hear the latest gossip? Link here for some good advice:

The Trouble with Jealousy, Genesis 37, p. 53

The Salt Promise, 2 Chronicles 13:5, p. 576

An Honest Reputation, Nehemiah 13:13, p. 644

Who Do You Prefer?, Proverbs 3:32, p. 830

The Verdict Is In?, Matthew 7:1–2, p. 1285

The Whole Truth, John 8:31–32, 45, p. 1438

know what they have done; I am a witness to it," says the LORD.
24Also give a message to Shemaiah
from the Nehelamite family. 25The LORD
All-Powerful, the God of Israel, says:
"Shemaiah, you sent letters in your name
to all the people in Jerusalem, to the
priest Zephaniah son of Maaseiah, and to
all the priests. 26You said to Zephaniah,
'The LORD has made you priest in place
of Jehoiada. You are to be in charge of the
Temple of the LORD. You should arrest
any madman who acts like a prophet.
Lock his hands and feet between wooden
blocks, and put iron rings around his
neck. 27Now Jeremiah from Anathoth is
acting like a prophet. So why haven't you
arrested him? 28Jeremiah has sent this
message to us in Babylon: You will be
there for a long time, so build houses and
settle down. Plant gardens and eat what
they grow.' "
29Zephaniah the priest read the letter
to Jeremiah the prophet. 30Then the
LORD spoke his word to Jeremiah:
31"Send this message to all the captives
in Babylon: 'This is what the LORD says
about Shemaiah the Nehelamite: Shemaiah has prophesied to you, but I did not
send him. He has made you believe a lie.
32So the LORD says, I will soon punish
Shemaiah the Nehelamite and his family.
He will not see the good things I will do
for my people, says the LORD. None of his
family will be left alive among the people,
because he has taught the people to turn
against me.' "

Promises of Hope

30 These are the words that the
LORD spoke to Jeremiah. 2The
LORD, the God of Israel, said: "Jeremiah,
write in a book all the words I have spoken to you. 3The days will come when I
will bring Israel and Judah back from captivity," says the LORD. "I will return them
to the land I gave their ancestors, and
they will own it!" says the LORD.
4The LORD spoke this message about
the people of Israel and Judah: 5This is
what the LORD said:
"We hear people crying from fear.
They are afraid; there is no peace.
6 Ask this question, and consider it:
A man cannot have a baby.
So why do I see every strong man
holding his stomach in pain like a
woman having a baby?
Why is everyone's face turning
white like a dead man's face?
7 This will be a terrible day!
There will never be another time
like this.
This is a time of great trouble for the
people of Jacob,
but they will be saved from it."

8 The LORD All-Powerful says, "At that
time
I will break the yoke from their
necks
and tear off the ropes that hold them.
Foreign people will never again
make my people slaves.
9 They will serve the LORD their God
and David their king,
whom I will send to them.

10 "So people of Jacob, my servants,
don't be afraid.
Israel, don't be frightened," says
the LORD.
"I will soon save you from that
faraway place where you are
captives.
I will save your family from that
land.
The people of Jacob will be safe and
have peace again;
there will be no enemy to frighten
them.
11 I am with you and will save you,"
says the LORD.
"I will completely destroy all those
nations
where I scattered you,
but I will not completely destroy
you.
I will punish you fairly,
but I will still punish you."
12This is what the LORD said:
"You people have a wound that
cannot be cured;
your injury will not heal.
13 There is no one to argue your case

and no cure for your sores.
So you will not be healed.
14 All those nations who were your friends have forgotten you.
They don't care about you.
I have hurt you as an enemy would.
I punished you very hard,
because your guilt was so great
and your sins were so many.
15 Why are you crying out about your injury?
There is no cure for your pain.
I did these things to you because of your great guilt,
because of your many sins.
16 But all those nations that destroyed you will now be destroyed.
All your enemies will become captives in other lands.
Those who stole from you will have their own things stolen.
Those who took things from you in war will have their own things taken.
17 I will bring back your health
and heal your injuries," says the LORD,
"because other people forced you away.
They said about you, 'No one cares about Jerusalem!' "
18 This is what the LORD said:
"I will soon make the tents of Jacob's people as they used to be,
and I will have pity on Israel's houses.
The city will be rebuilt on its hill of ruins,
and the king's palace will stand in its proper place.
19 People in those places will sing songs of praise.
There will be the sound of laughter.
I will give them many children
so their number will not be small.
I will bring honor to them
so no one will look down on them.
20 Their descendants will be as they were in the old days.
I will set them up as a strong people before me,
and I will punish the nations who have hurt them.
21 One of their own people will lead them;
their ruler will come from among them.
He will come near to me when I invite him.
Who would dare to come to me uninvited?" says the LORD.
22 "So you will be my people,
and I will be your God."
23 Look! It is a storm from the LORD!
He is angry and has gone out to punish the people.
Punishment will come like a storm crashing down on the evil people.
24 The LORD will stay angry
until he finishes punishing the people.
He will stay angry
until he finishes the punishment he planned.
When that day comes,
you will understand this.

The New Israel

31 The LORD says, "At that time I will
be God of all Israel's family groups,
and they will be my people."
2 This is what the LORD says:
"The people who were not killed by the enemy's sword
found help in the desert.
I came to give rest to Israel."
3 And from far away the LORD appeared to his people and said,
"I love you people
with a love that will last forever.
That is why I have continued showing you kindness.
4 People of Israel, I will build you up again,
and you will be rebuilt.
You will pick up your tambourines again
and dance with those who are joyful.
5 You will plant vineyards again
on the hills around Samaria.
The farmers will plant them
and enjoy their fruit.

FAITH links

HIS VALENTINE

JEREMIAH 31:3

You hear a lot about love when Valentine's Day rolls around. Many people talk about it as they hand out chocolates and valentine cards. But come February 15, it's like love has ended. The cards stop. The candy is gone. But here's some good news. Jeremiah has a valentine from God that you can read any day of the year. God promises to love you forever. Can anyone else make that claim?

The Rainbow Promise, Genesis 9:1–17, p. 14

A Thanksgiving Reminder, Exodus 12, p. 91

A Holiday Letter, Esther 9:20–23, p. 657

A Love Song, Zephaniah 3:17, p. 1246

How Do I Love You?, Malachi 1:1–5, p. 1267

The Gift of Worship, Matthew 2:10–12, p. 1275

6 There will be a time when watchmen
in the mountains of Ephraim
shout this message:
'Come, let's go up to Jerusalem to
worship the
LORD our
God!' "

31:6
Future
What's the future for believers?

7 This is what the
LORD says:
"Be happy and
sing for the people of Jacob.
Shout for Israel, the greatest of the
nations.
Sing your praises and shout this:
'LORD, save your people,
those who are left alive from the
nation of Israel!'
8 Look, I will soon bring Israel from
the country in the north,
and I will gather them from the
faraway places on earth.
Some of the people are blind and
crippled.
Some of the women are pregnant,
and some are ready to give birth.
A great many people will come
back.
9 They will be crying as they come,
but they will pray as I bring them
back.
I will lead those people by streams of
water
on an even road where they will
not stumble.
I am Israel's father,
and Israel is my firstborn son.

10 "Nations, listen to the message from
the LORD.
Tell this message in the faraway
lands by the sea:
'The one who scattered the people of
Israel will bring them back,
and he will watch over his people
like a shepherd.'
11 The LORD will pay for the people of
Jacob
and will buy them back from
people stronger than they were.
12 The people of Israel will come to the
high points of Jerusalem
and shout for joy.
Their faces will shine with happiness
about all the good things from
the LORD:
the grain, new wine, oil, young
sheep, and young cows.
They will be like a garden that has
plenty of water,
and they will not be troubled
anymore.
13 Then young women of Israel will be
happy and dance,
the young men and old men also.

I will change their sadness into
happiness;
I will give them comfort and joy
instead of sadness.
14 The priests will have more than
enough sacrifices,
and my people will be filled with
the good things I give them!"
says the LORD.

15 This is what the LORD says:
"A voice was heard in Ramah
of painful crying and deep
sadness:
Rachel crying for her children.
She refused to be comforted,
because her children are dead!"

16 But this is what the LORD says:
"Stop crying;
don't let your eyes fill with tears.
You will be rewarded for your work!"
says the LORD.
"The people will return from their
enemy's land.
17 So there is hope for you in the
future," says the LORD.
"Your children will return to their
own land.

18 "I have heard Israel moaning:
'LORD, you punished me, and I
have learned my lesson.
I was like a calf that had never
been trained.
Take me back so that I may come
back.
You truly are the LORD my God.
19 LORD, after I wandered away from
you,
I changed my heart and life.
After I understood,
I beat my breast with sorrow.
I was ashamed and disgraced,
because I suffered for the foolish
things I did when I was young.'

20 "You know that Israel is my dear
son,
The child I love.
Yes, I often speak against Israel,
but I still remember him.
I love him very much,
and I want to comfort him," says
the LORD.

21 "People of Israel, fix the road signs.
Put up signs to show you the way
home.
Watch the road.
Pay attention to the road on which
you travel.
People of Israel, come home,
come back to your towns.
22 You are an unfaithful daughter.
How long will you wander before
you come home?
The LORD has made something new
happen in the land:
A woman will go seeking a man."

23 The LORD All-Powerful, the God of
Israel, says: "I will again do good things
for the people of Judah. At that time the
people in the land of Judah and its towns
will again use these words: 'May the
LORD bless you, home of what is good,
holy mountain.' 24 People in all the towns
of Judah will live together in peace.
Farmers and those who move around
with their flocks will live together in
peace. 25 I will give rest and strength to
those who are weak and tired."

26 After hearing that, I, Jeremiah,
woke up and looked around. My sleep had
been very pleasant.

27 The LORD says, "The time is coming when I will help the families of Israel
and Judah and their children and animals
to grow. 28 In the past I watched over Israel and Judah, to pull them up and tear
them down, to destroy them and bring
them disaster. But now I will watch over
them to build them up and make them
strong," says the LORD.

29 "At that time people will no longer
say:
'The parents have eaten sour grapes,
and that caused the children to
grind their teeth from the sour
taste.'
30 Instead, each person will die for his
own sin; the person who eats sour grapes
will grind his own teeth.

The New Agreement

31 "Look, the time is coming," says the
LORD,
"when I will make a new agreement

with the people of Israel
and the people of Judah.
32 It will not be like the agreement
I made with their ancestors
when I took them by the hand
to bring them out of Egypt.
I was a husband to them,
but they broke that agreement,"
says the LORD.
33 "This is the agreement I will make
with the people of Israel at that
time," says the LORD:
"I will put my teachings in their
minds
and write them on their hearts.
I will be their God,
and they will be my people.
34 People will no longer have to teach
their neighbors and relatives
to know the LORD,
because all people will know me,
from the least to the most
important," says the LORD.
"I will forgive them for the wicked
things they did,
and I will not remember their sins
anymore."

The Lord Will Never Leave Israel

35 The LORD makes the sun shine in the
day
and the moon and stars to shine at
night.
He stirs up the sea so that its waves
crash on the shore.
The LORD All-Powerful is his
name.
This is what the LORD says:
36 "Only if these laws should ever
fail,"
says the LORD,
"will Israel's descendants ever stop
being a nation before me."
37 This is what the LORD says:
"Only if people can measure the sky
above
and learn the secrets of the earth
below,
will I reject all the descendants of
Israel
because of what they have done,"
says the LORD.

FAITH links

A PROMISE FROM THE HEART

JEREMIAH 31:31-33

When something is said to be written in stone, that means it's permanent. When God gave Moses the Ten Commandments, God wrote them on tablets of stone. God used the prophet Jeremiah to make a new promise with the people of Israel. In a future time, God said he would write his teachings on their hearts. That meant he would help them to be obedient. They would want to obey his laws because they loved him.

The heart is the center of obedience. It is there that we decide whether we will obey God. Believing from the heart is more permanent than stone.

How's your heart condition? Link here to see what God wants your heart to be like:

Lights, Camera, . . . Actions!, Genesis 12:1–3, p. 17

Do What You Want?, Judges 21:25, p. 341

The Wisdom of Obeying God, 1 Kings 11:1–13, p. 453

Like Silver, Psalm 12:6–8, p. 717

The Power of *If*, Mark 9:14–24, p. 1344

Out of Your Mind?, 1 Corinthians 2:16, p. 1547

The New Jerusalem

38The LORD says, "The time is coming when Jerusalem will be rebuilt for me—everything from the Tower of Hananel to the Corner Gate. **39**The measuring line will stretch from the Corner Gate straight to the hill of Gareb. Then it will turn to the place named Goah. **40**The whole valley where dead bodies and ashes are thrown, and all the terraces out to the Kidron Valley on the east as far as the corner of the Horse Gate—all that area will be holy to the LORD. The city of Jerusalem will never again be torn down or destroyed."

Jeremiah Buys a Field

32 This is the word the LORD spoke to Jeremiah in the tenth year Zedekiah was king of Judah, which was the eighteenth year of Nebuchadnezzar. **2**At that time the army of the king of Babylon was surrounding Jerusalem. Jeremiah the prophet was under arrest in the courtyard of the guard, which was at the palace of the king of Judah.

3Zedekiah king of Judah had put Jeremiah in prison there. Zedekiah had asked, "Why have you prophesied the things you have?" (Jeremiah had said, "This is what the LORD says: 'I will soon hand the city of Jerusalem over to the king of Babylon, and he will capture it. **4**Zedekiah king of Judah will not escape from the Babylonian army, but he will surely be handed over to the king of Babylon. And he will speak to the king of Babylon face to face and see him with his own eyes. **5**The king will take Zedekiah to Babylon, where he will stay until I have punished him,' says the LORD. 'If you fight against the Babylonians, you will not succeed.' ")

6While Jeremiah was in prison, he said, "The LORD spoke this word to me: **7**Your cousin Hanamel, son of your uncle Shallum, will come to you soon. Hanamel will say to you, 'Jeremiah, you are my nearest relative, so buy my field near the town of Anathoth. It is your right and your duty to buy that field.'

8"Then it happened just as the LORD had said. My cousin Hanamel came to me in the courtyard of the guard and said to me, 'Buy for yourself my field near Anathoth in the land of Benjamin. It is your right and duty to buy it and own it.' So I knew this was a message from the LORD.

9"I bought the field at Anathoth from my cousin Hanamel, weighing out seven ounces of silver for him. **10**I signed the record and sealed it and had some people witness it. I also weighed out the silver on the scales. **11**Then I took both copies of the record of ownership—the one that was sealed that had the demands and limits of ownership, and the one that was not sealed. **12**And I gave them to Baruch son of Neriah, the son of Mahseiah. My cousin Hanamel, the other witnesses who signed the record of ownership, and many Jews sitting in the courtyard of the guard saw me give the record of ownership to Baruch.

13"With all the people watching, I told Baruch, **14**'This is what the LORD All-Powerful, the God of Israel, says: Take both copies of the record of ownership—the sealed copy and the copy that was not sealed—and put them in a clay jar so they will last a long time. **15**This is what the LORD All-Powerful, the God of Israel, says: In the future my people will once again buy houses and fields for grain and vineyards in the land of Israel.'

16"After I gave the record of ownership to Baruch son of Neriah, I prayed to the LORD, **17**Oh, Lord GOD, you made the skies and the earth with your very great power. There is nothing too hard for you to do. **18**You show love and kindness to thousands of people, but you also bring punishment to children for their parents' sins. Great and powerful God, your name is the LORD All-Powerful. **19**You plan and do great things. You see everything that people do, and you reward people for the way they live and for what they do. **20**You did miracles and wonderful things in the land of Egypt. You have continued doing them in Israel and among the other nations even until today. So you have become well known. **21**You brought your people, the Israelites, out of Egypt using signs and miracles and your great power and strength. You brought great terror on everyone. **22**You gave them this land that

you promised to their ancestors long ago,
a fertile land. **23**They came into this land
and took it for their own, but they did not
obey you or follow your teachings. They
did not do everything you commanded.
So you made all these terrible things happen to them.

24"Look! The enemy has surrounded
the city and has built roads to the top of
the walls to capture it. Because of war,
hunger, and terrible diseases, the city
will be handed over to the Babylonians
who are attacking it. You said this would
happen, and now you see it is happening.
25But now, Lord GOD, you tell me, 'Buy
the field with silver and call in witnesses.' You tell me this while the Babylonian army is ready to capture the city."

26Then the LORD spoke this word to
Jeremiah: **27**"I am the LORD, the God of
every person on the earth. Nothing is impossible for me. **28**So this is what the
LORD says: I will soon hand over the city
of Jerusalem to the Babylonian army and
to Nebuchadnezzar king of Babylon, who
will capture it. **29**The Babylonian army is
already attacking the city of Jerusalem.
They will soon enter it and start a fire to
burn down the city and its houses. The
people of Jerusalem offered sacrifices to
Baal on the roofs[n] of those same houses
and poured out drink offerings to other
idols to make me angry. **30**From their
youth, the people of Israel and Judah
have done only the things I said were
wrong. They have made me angry by
worshiping idols made with their own
hands," says the LORD. **31**"From the day
Jerusalem was built until now, this city
has made me angry, so angry that I must
remove it from my sight. **32**I will destroy
it, because of all the evil the people of Israel and Judah have done. The people,
their kings and officers, their priests and
prophets, all the people of Judah, and the
people of Jerusalem have made me angry.
33They turned their backs to me, not
their faces. I tried to teach them again
and again, but they wouldn't listen or
learn. **34**They put their hateful idols in
the place where I have chosen to be worshiped, so they made it unclean. **35**In the
Valley of Ben Hinnom they built places to
worship Baal so they could burn their
sons and daughters as sacrifices to Molech. But I never commanded them to do
such a hateful thing. It never entered my
mind that they would do such a thing and
cause Judah to sin.

36"You are saying, 'Because of war,
hunger, and terrible diseases, the city
will be handed over to the king of Babylon.' But the LORD, the God of Israel,
says about Jerusalem: **37**I forced the people of Israel and Judah to leave their land,
because I was furious and very angry
with them. But soon I will gather them
from all the lands where I forced them to
go, and I will bring them back to this
place, where they may live in safety.
38The people of Israel and Judah will be
my people, and I will be their God. **39**I
will make them truly want to be one people with one goal. They will truly want to
worship me all their lives, for their own
good and for the good of their children after them.

40"I will make an agreement with
them that will last forever. I will never
turn away from them; I will always do
good to them. I will
make them want to
respect me so they
will never turn away
from me. **41**I will en-
joy doing good to
them. And with my
whole being I will
surely plant them in this land and make
them grow."

eMAIL! FROM GOD
32:40–41
God's Promises
How long do God's promises last?

42This is what the LORD says: "I have
brought this great disaster to the people
of Israel and Judah. In the same way I will
bring the good things that I promise to do
for them. **43**You are saying, 'This land is
an empty desert, without people or animals. It has been handed over to the Babylonians.' But in the future, people will
again buy fields in this land. **44**They will
use their money to buy fields. They

32:29 roofs In Bible times houses were built with flat roofs. The roof was used for drying things such as flax and fruit. And it was used as an extra room, as a place for worship, and as a cool place to sleep in the summer.

will sign and seal their agreements and
call in witnesses. They will again buy
fields in the land of Benjamin, in the area
around Jerusalem, in the towns of Judah
and in the mountains, in the western hills,
and in southern Judah. I will make everything as good for them as it once was,"
says the LORD.

The Promise of the Lord

33 While Jeremiah was still locked
up in the courtyard of the guards,
the LORD spoke his word
to him a second time:
2"These are the words of
the LORD, who made the
earth, shaped it, and gave
it order, whose name is
the LORD: **3**'Judah, pray to
me, and I will answer you.
I will tell you important
secrets you have never
heard before.' **4**This is
what the LORD, the God of
Israel, says about the houses in Jerusalem
and the royal palaces of Judah that have
been torn down to be used in defense of
the attack by the Babylonian army:
5'Some people will come to fight against
the Babylonians. They will fill these
houses with the bodies of people I killed in
my hot anger. I have turned away from
this city because of all the evil its people
have done.

6" 'But then I will bring health and
healing to the people there. I will heal
them and let them enjoy great peace and
safety. **7**I will bring Judah and Israel back
from captivity and make them strong
countries as in the past. **8**They sinned
against me, but I will wash away that sin.
They did evil and turned away from me,
but I will forgive them. **9**Then "Jerusalem" will be to me a name that brings joy!
And people from all nations of the earth
will praise it when they hear about the
good things I am doing there. They will
be surprised and shocked at all the good
things and the peace I will bring to Jerusalem.'

10"You are saying, 'Our country is an
empty desert, without people or animals.' But this is what the LORD says: It
is now quiet in the streets of Jerusalem
and in the towns of Judah, without people
or animals, but it will be noisy there
soon! **11**There will be sounds of joy and
gladness and the happy sounds of brides
and bridegrooms. There will be the
sounds of people bringing to the Temple
of the LORD their offerings of thanks to
the LORD. They will say,

'Praise the LORD All-Powerful,
because the LORD is good!
His love continues forever!'

They will say this be-
cause I will again do good
things for Judah, as I did
in the beginning," says
the LORD.

12This is what the
LORD All-Powerful says:
"This place is empty now,
without people or animals.
But there will be shep-
herds in all the towns of
Judah and pastures where
they let their flocks rest. **13**Shepherds
will again count their sheep as the sheep
walk in front of them. They will count
them in the mountains and in the western hills, in southern Judah and the land
of Benjamin, and around Jerusalem and
the other towns of Judah!" says the
LORD.

> Praise the LORD All-Powerful, because the LORD is good! His love continues forever!
> —Jeremiah 33:11

The Good Branch

14The LORD says, "The time is coming when I will do the good thing I promised to the people of Israel and Judah.

15In those days and at that time,
I will make a good branch sprout
from David's family.
He will do what is fair and right in
the land.
16At that time Judah will be saved,
and the people of Jerusalem will
live in safety.
The branch will be named:
The LORD Does What Is Right."

17This is what the LORD says: "Someone from David's family will always sit
on the throne of the family of Israel.
18And there will always be priests from
the family of Levi. They will always
stand before me to offer burnt offerings

and grain offerings and sacrifices to
me."
19The LORD spoke his word to Jeremiah, saying: 20"This is what the LORD
says: I have an agreement
with day and night that
they will always come at
the right times. If you
could change that agree-
ment, 21only then could
you change my agreement
with David and Levi. Only
then would my servant
David not have a descen-
dant ruling as king on
David's throne. And only
then would the family of Levi not be
priests serving me in the Temple. 22But I
will give many descendants to my servant
David and to the family group of Levi who
serve me in the Temple. They will be as
many as the stars in the sky that no one
can count. They will be as many as the
grains of sand on the seashore that no one
can measure."

> I will soon hand the city of Jerusalem over to the king of Babylon, and he will burn it down!
> —Jeremiah 34:2

23The LORD spoke his word to Jeremiah, saying: 24"Jeremiah, have you heard
what the people are saying? They say:
'The LORD turned away from the two
families of Israel and Judah that he
chose.' Now they don't think of my people as a nation anymore!"
25This is what the LORD says: "If I
had not made my agreement with day and
night, and if I had not made the laws for
the sky and earth, 26only then would I
turn away from Jacob's descendants. And
only then would I not let the descendants
of David my servant rule over the descendants of Abraham, Isaac, and Jacob.
But I will be kind to them and cause good
things to happen to them again."

A Warning to Zedekiah

34 The LORD spoke his word to
Jeremiah when Nebuchadnezzar
king of Babylon was fighting against Jerusalem and all the towns around it. Nebuchadnezzar had with him all his army and
the armies of all the kingdoms and peoples he ruled. 2This is what the LORD,
the God of Israel, said: "Jeremiah, go to
Zedekiah king of Judah and tell him: 'This
is what the LORD says: I will soon hand
the city of Jerusalem over to the king of
Babylon, and he will burn it down! 3You
will not escape from the king of Babylon;
you will surely be cap-
tured and handed over to
him. You will see the king
of Babylon with your own
eyes, and he will talk to
you face to face. And you
will go to Babylon. 4But,
Zedekiah king of Judah,
listen to the promise of
the LORD. This is what
the LORD says about you:
You will not be killed with
a sword. 5You will die in a peaceful way.
As people made funeral fires to honor
your ancestors, the kings who ruled before you, so people will make a funeral
fire to honor you. They will cry for you
and sadly say, "Ah, master!" I myself
make this promise to you, says the
LORD.' "
6So Jeremiah the prophet gave this
message to Zedekiah in Jerusalem. 7This
was while the army of the king of Babylon was fighting against Jerusalem and
the cities of Judah that had not yet been
taken—Lachish and Azekah. These were
the only strong, walled cities left in the
land of Judah.

Slaves Are Mistreated

8The LORD spoke his word to Jeremiah. This was after King Zedekiah had
made an agreement with all the people in
Jerusalem to free all the Hebrew slaves.
9Everyone was supposed to free his Hebrew slaves, both male and female. No
one was to keep a fellow Jew as a slave.
10All the officers and all the people accepted this agreement; they agreed to
free their male and female slaves and no
longer keep them as slaves. So all the
slaves were set free. 11But after that, the
people who had slaves changed their
minds. So they took back the people they
had set free and made them slaves again.
12Then the LORD spoke his word to
Jeremiah: 13"This is what the LORD, the
God of Israel, says: I brought your ancestors out of Egypt where they were slaves

and made an agreement with them. **14**I
said to your ancestors: 'At the end of
every seven years, each one of you must
set his Hebrew slaves free. If a fellow
Hebrew has sold himself to you, you
must let him go free after he has served
you for six years.' But your ancestors did
not listen or pay attention to me. **15**A
short time ago you changed your hearts
and did what I say is right. Each of you
gave freedom to his fellow Hebrews who
were slaves. And you even made an
agreement before me in the place where I
have chosen to be worshiped. **16**But now
you have changed your minds. You have
shown you do not honor me. Each of
you has taken back the male and female
slaves you had set free, and you have
forced them to become your slaves
again.

17"So this is what the LORD says: You
have not obeyed me. You have not given
freedom to your fellow Hebrews, neither
relatives nor friends. But now I will give
freedom, says the LORD, to war, to terrible diseases, and to hunger. I will make
you hated by all the kingdoms of the
earth. **18**I will hand over the men who
broke my agreement, who have not kept
the promises they made before me. They
cut a calf into two pieces before me and
walked between the pieces.[n] **19**These
people made the agreement before me by
walking between the pieces of the calf:
the leaders of Judah and Jerusalem, the
officers of the court, the priests, and all
the people of the land. **20**So I will hand
them over to their enemies and to everyone who wants to kill them. Their
bodies will become food for the birds of
the air and for the wild animals of the
earth. **21**I will hand Zedekiah king of
Judah and his officers over to their enemies, and to everyone who wants to kill
them, and to the army of the king of
Babylon, even though they have left
Jerusalem. **22**I will give the order, says
the LORD, to bring the Babylonian army
back to Jerusalem. It will fight against Jerusalem, capture it, set it on fire, and
burn it down. I will destroy the towns in
Judah so that they become ruins where
no one lives!"

The Recabite Family Obeys God

35 When Jehoiakim son of Josiah was
king of Judah, the LORD spoke his
word to Jeremiah, saying: **2** "Go to the
family of Recab. Invite them to come to
one of the side rooms of the Temple of
the LORD, and offer them wine to drink."

3So I went to get Jaazaniah son of
Jeremiah,[n] the son of Habazziniah. And I
gathered all of Jaazaniah's brothers and
sons and the whole family of the Recabites together. **4**Then I brought them into
the Temple of the LORD. We went into
the room of the sons of Hanan son of Ig-
daliah, who was a man of God. The room
was next to the one where the officers
stay and above the room of Maaseiah son
of Shallum, the doorkeeper in the Temple. **5**Then I put some bowls full of wine
and some cups before the men of the
Recabite family. And I said to them,
"Drink some wine."

6But the Recabite men answered,
"We never drink wine. Our ancestor Jonadab son of Recab gave us this command:
'You and your descendants must never
drink wine. **7**Also you must never build
houses, plant seeds, or plant vineyards,
or do any of those things. You must live
only in tents. Then you will live a long
time in the land where you are wander-
ers.' **8**So we Recabites have obeyed
everything Jonadab our ancestor commanded us. Neither we nor our wives,
sons, or daughters ever drink wine. **9**We
never build houses in which to live, or
own fields or vineyards, or plant crops.
10We have lived in tents and have obeyed
everything our ancestor Jonadab commanded us. **11**But when Nebuchadnezzar
king of Babylon attacked Judah, we said
to each other, 'Come, we must enter Jerusalem so we can escape the Babylonian
army and the Aramean army.' So we have
stayed in Jerusalem."

12Then the LORD spoke his word to
Jeremiah: **13**"This is what the LORD All-

34:18 They . . . pieces. This showed that the men were willing to be killed, like this animal, if they did not keep their agreement.

35:3 Jeremiah Not the prophet Jeremiah, but a different man with the same name.

Powerful, the God of Israel, says: Jeremiah, go and tell the men of Judah and the
people of Jerusalem: 'You should learn a
lesson and obey my message,' says the
LORD. **14**'Jonadab son of Recab ordered
his descendants not to drink wine, and
that command has been obeyed. Until today they have obeyed their ancestor's
command; they do not drink wine. But I,
the LORD, have given you messages
again and again, but you did not obey me.
15I sent all my servants the prophets to
you again and again, saying, "Each of you
must stop doing evil. You must change
and be good. Do not follow other gods to
serve them. If you obey me, you will live
in the land I have given to you and your
ancestors." But you have not listened to
me or paid attention to my message.
16The descendants of Jonadab son of Recab obeyed the commands their ancestor
gave them, but the people of Judah have
not obeyed me.'

17"So the LORD God All-Powerful,
the God of Israel, says: 'I will soon bring
every disaster I said would come to Judah
and to everyone living in Jerusalem. I
spoke to those people, but they refused
to listen. I called out to them, but they did
not answer me.' "

18Then Jeremiah said to the Recabites, "This is what the LORD All-Powerful, the God of Israel, says: 'You have
obeyed the commands of your ancestor
Jonadab and have followed all of his
teachings; you have done everything he
commanded.' **19**So this is what the LORD
All-Powerful, the God of Israel, says:
'There will always be a descendant of
Jonadab son of Recab to serve me.' "

Jehoiakim Burns Jeremiah's Scroll

36 The LORD spoke this word to Jeremiah during the fourth year that
Jehoiakim son of Josiah was king of Judah: **2**"Get a scroll. Write on it all the
words I have spoken to you about Israel
and Judah and all the nations. Write
everything from when I first spoke to
you, when Josiah was king, until now.
3Maybe the family of Judah will hear
what disasters I am planning to bring on
them and will stop doing wicked things.
Then I would forgive them for the sins
and the evil things they have done."

4So Jeremiah called for Baruch son of
Neriah. Jeremiah spoke the messages
the LORD had given him, and Baruch
wrote those messages on the scroll.
5Then Jeremiah commanded Baruch, "I
cannot go to the Temple of the LORD. I
must stay here. **6**So I want you to go to
the Temple of the LORD on a day when
the people are giving up eating. Read

A BAD REACTION

JEREMIAH 36

Have you ever shared your faith with someone, only to have him or her have a bad reaction? Jeremiah dictated the words God gave him to his secretary Baruch, who wrote them on a scroll. After King Jehoiakim read the scroll, he cut it apart and tossed it into the fire. He didn't like the truth.

Some people you talk to may not want to hear the truth about God. But don't let that stop you from sharing his truth with others.

Care for the Lost, Deuteronomy 22:1–3, p. 255

On the Wrong Foot, 2 Kings 21:1–2, 16, p. 509

A Picture of the Past, Psalm 105, p. 789

Go! No!, Jonah 1, p. 1213

The Greatest Commandment, Matthew 22:36–40, p. 1313

A Friend of Jesus, John 15:9–17, p. 1450

from the scroll to all the people of Judah
who come into Jerusalem from their
towns. Read the messages from the
LORD, which are the words you wrote on
the scroll as I spoke them to you. **7**Perhaps they will ask the LORD to help them.
Perhaps each one will stop doing wicked
things, because the LORD has announced
that he is very angry with them." **8**So
Baruch son of Neriah did everything
Jeremiah the prophet told him to do. In
the LORD's Temple he read aloud the
scroll that had the LORD's messages written on it.

9In the ninth month of the fifth year
that Jehoiakim son of Josiah was king, a
special time to give up eating was announced. All the people of Jerusalem and
everyone who had come into Jerusalem
from the towns of Judah were supposed
to give up eating to honor the LORD. **10**At
that time Baruch read to all the people
there the scroll containing Jeremiah's
words. He read the scroll in the Temple
of the LORD in the room of Gemariah son
of Shaphan, a royal secretary. That room
was in the upper courtyard at the entrance of the New Gate of the Temple.

11Micaiah son of Gemariah, the son of
Shaphan, heard all the messages from the
LORD that were on the scroll. **12**Micaiah
went down to the royal secretary's room
in the king's palace where all of the officers were sitting: Elishama the royal secretary; Delaiah son of Shemaiah; Elnathan
son of Acbor; Gemariah son of Shaphan;
Zedekiah son of Hananiah; and all the
other officers. **13**Micaiah told those officers everything he had heard Baruch read
to the people from the scroll.

14Then the officers sent a man named
Jehudi son of Nethaniah to Baruch.
(Nethaniah was the son of Shelemiah,
who was the son of Cushi.) Jehudi said
to Baruch, "Bring the scroll that you read
to the people and come with me."

So Baruch son of Neriah took the
scroll and went with Jehudi to the officers. **15**Then the officers said to Baruch, "Please sit down and read the scroll
to us."

So Baruch read the scroll to them.
16When the officers heard all the words,
they became afraid and looked at each
other. They said to Baruch, "We must
certainly tell the king about these
words." **17**Then the officers asked Baruch, "Tell us, please, where did you get
all these words you wrote on the scroll?
Did you write down what Jeremiah said
to you?"

18"Yes," Baruch answered. "Jeremiah
spoke them all to me, and I wrote them
down with ink on this scroll."

19Then the officers said to Baruch,
"You and Jeremiah must go and hide, and
don't tell anyone where you are."

20The officers put the scroll in the
room of Elishama the royal secretary.
Then they went to the king in the courtyard and told him all about the scroll.
21So King Jehoiakim sent Jehudi to get
the scroll. Jehudi brought the scroll from
the room of Elishama the royal secretary
and read it to the king and to all the officers who stood around the king. **22**It was
the ninth month of the year, so King Jehoiakim was sitting in the winter apart-
ment. There was a fire burning in a small
firepot in front of him. **23**After Jehudi had
read three or four columns, the king cut
those columns off of the scroll with a pen-
knife and threw them into the firepot. Finally, the whole scroll was burned in the
fire. **24**King Jehoiakim and his servants
heard everything that was said, but they
were not frightened! They did not tear
their clothes to show their sorrow. **25**Elnathan, Delaiah, and Gemariah even tried
to talk King Jehoiakim out of burning the
scroll, but he would not listen to them.
26Instead, the king ordered Jerahmeel
son of the king, Seraiah son of Azriel, and
Shelemiah son of Abdeel to arrest Baruch the secretary and Jeremiah the
prophet. But the LORD had hidden them.

27So King Jehoiakim burned the
scroll where Baruch had written all the
words Jeremiah had spoken to him. Then
the LORD spoke his word to Jeremiah:
28"Get another scroll. Write all the
words on it that were on the first scroll
that Jehoiakim king of Judah burned up.
29Also say this to Jehoiakim king of Judah: 'This is what the LORD says: You
burned up that scroll and said, "Why, Jer-

emiah, did you write on it 'the king of
Babylon will surely come and destroy
this land and the people and animals in
it'?" **30**So this is what the LORD says
about Jehoiakim king of Judah: Jehoiakim's descendants will not sit on
David's throne. When Jehoiakim dies, his
body will be thrown out on the ground. It
will be left out in the heat of the day and
in the cold frost of the night. **31**I will punish Jehoiakim and his children and his
servants, because they have done evil
things. I will bring disasters upon them
and upon all the people in Jerusalem and
Judah—everything I promised but which
they refused to hear.' "

32So Jeremiah took another scroll and
gave it to Baruch son of Neriah, his secretary. As Jeremiah spoke, Baruch wrote
on the scroll the same words that were
on the scroll Jehoiakim king of Judah had
burned in the fire. And many similar
words were added to the second scroll.

Jeremiah in Prison

37 Nebuchadnezzar king of Babylon
had appointed Zedekiah son of Josiah to be king of Judah. Zedekiah took
the place of Jehoiachin son of Jehoiakim.
2But Zedekiah, his servants, and the people of Judah did not listen to the words
the LORD had spoken through Jeremiah
the prophet.

3Now King Zedekiah sent Jehucal son
of Shelemiah and the priest Zephaniah
son of Maaseiah with a message to Jeremiah the prophet. This was the message:
"Jeremiah, please pray to
the LORD our God for us."

4At that time Jeremiah
had not yet been put into
prison. So he was free to
go anywhere he wanted.
5The army of the king of
Egypt had marched from
Egypt toward Judah. Now
the Babylonian army had
surrounded the city of
Jerusalem. When they
heard about the Egyptian army marching
toward them, the Babylonian army left
Jerusalem.

6The LORD spoke his word to Jere-
miah the prophet: **7**"This is what the
LORD, the God of Israel, says: Jehucal and
Zephaniah, I know Zedekiah king of Ju-
dah sent you to seek my help. Tell this to
King Zedekiah: 'The army of the king of
Egypt came here to help you, but they
will go back to Egypt. **8**After that, the
Babylonian army will return and attack
Jerusalem and capture it and burn it
down.'

9"This is what the LORD says: People
of Jerusalem, do not fool yourselves.
Don't say, 'The Babylonian army will
surely leave us alone.' They will not!
10Even if you defeated all of the Babylonian army that is attacking you and there
were only a few injured men left in their
tents, they would come from their tents
and burn down Jerusalem!"

11So the Babylonian army left Jerusalem to fight the army of the king of Egypt.
12Now Jeremiah tried to travel from Jerusalem to the land of Benjamin to get his
share of the property that belonged to his
family. **13**When Jeremiah got to the Benjamin Gate of Jerusalem, the captain in
charge of the guards arrested him. The
captain's name was Irijah son of Shelemiah son of Hananiah. Irijah said, "You
are leaving us to join the Babylonians!"

14But Jeremiah said to Irijah, "That's
not true! I am not leaving to join the Babylonians." Irijah refused to listen to Jeremiah, so he arrested Jeremiah and took
him to the officers of Jerusalem. **15**Those
rulers were very angry with Jeremiah
and beat him. Then they put him in jail in
the house of Jonathan the
royal secretary, which had
been made into a prison.
16So those people put
Jeremiah into a cell in a
dungeon, and Jeremiah
was there for a long time.

17Then King Zedekiah
sent for Jeremiah and had
him brought to the pal-
ace. Zedekiah asked him
in private, "Is there any
message from the LORD?"

Jeremiah answered, "Yes, there is.
Zedekiah, you will be handed over to the
king of Babylon." **18**Then Jeremiah said

What crime have I done against you or your officers or the people of Jerusalem?
—Jeremiah 37:18

to King Zedekiah, "What crime have I
done against you or your officers or the
people of Jerusalem? Why have you
thrown me into prison? **19**Where are
your prophets that prophesied this message to you: 'The king of Babylon will not
attack you or this land of Judah?' **20**But
now, my master, king of Judah, please listen to me, and please do what I ask of
you. Do not send me back to the house of
Jonathan the royal secretary, or I will die
there!"

21So King Zedekiah gave orders for
Jeremiah to be put under guard in the
courtyard of the guard and to be given
bread each day from the street of the bak-
ers until there was no more bread in the
city. So he stayed under guard in the
courtyard of the guard.

Jeremiah Is Thrown into a Well

38 Shephatiah son of Mattan, Gedaliah son of Pashhur, Jehucal son of
Shelemiah, and Pashhur son of Malkijah
heard what Jeremiah was telling all the
people. He said: **2**"This is what the LORD
says: 'Everyone who stays in Jerusalem
will die from war, or hunger, or terrible
diseases. But everyone who surrenders
to the Babylonian army will live; they will
escape with their lives and live.' **3**And
this is what the LORD says: 'This city of
Jerusalem will surely be handed over to
the army of the king of Babylon. He will
capture this city!' "

4Then the officers said to the king,
"Jeremiah must be put to death! He is
discouraging the soldiers who are still in
the city, and all the people, by what he is
saying to them. He does not want good to
happen to us; he wants to ruin us."

5King Zedekiah said to them, "Jeremiah is in your control. I cannot do anything to stop you."

6So the officers took Jeremiah and put
him into the well of Malkijah, the king's
son, which was in the courtyard of the
guards. The officers used ropes to lower
Jeremiah into the well, which did not
have any water in it, only mud. And Jeremiah sank down into the mud.

7But Ebed-Melech, a Cushite and a
servant in the palace, heard that the officers had put Jeremiah into the well. As
King Zedekiah was sitting at the Benjamin Gate, **8**Ebed-Melech left the palace
and went to the king. Ebed-Melech said
to him, **9**"My master and king, these rulers have acted in an evil way. They have
treated Jeremiah the prophet badly. They
have thrown him into a well and left him
there to die! When there is no more
bread in the city, he will starve to death."

10Then King Zedekiah commanded
Ebed-Melech the Cushite, "Take thirty
men from the palace and lift Jeremiah the
prophet out of the well before he dies."

11So Ebed-Melech took the men with
him and went to a room under the storeroom in the palace. He took some old
rags and worn-out clothes from that
room. Then he let those rags down with
some ropes to Jeremiah in the well.
12Ebed-Melech the Cushite said to Jeremiah, "Put these old rags and worn-out
clothes under your arms to be pads for
the ropes." So Jeremiah did as Ebed-
Melech said. **13**The men pulled Jeremiah
up with the ropes and lifted him out of
the well. And Jeremiah stayed under
guard in the courtyard of the guard.

Zedekiah Questions Jeremiah

14Then King Zedekiah sent someone
to get Jeremiah the prophet and bring
him to the third entrance to the Temple
of the LORD. The king said to Jeremiah, "I
am going to ask you something. Do not
hide anything from me, but tell me everything honestly."

15Jeremiah said to Zedekiah, "If I give
you an answer, you will surely kill me.
And even if I give you advice, you will not
listen to me."

16But King Zedekiah made a secret
promise to Jeremiah, "As surely as the
LORD lives who has given us breath and
life, I will not kill you. And I promise not
to hand you over to the officers who want
to kill you."

17Then Jeremiah said to Zedekiah,
"This is what the LORD God All-Powerful, the God of Israel, says: 'If you surrender to the officers of the king of Babylon,
your life will be saved. Jerusalem will not
be burned down, and you and your family

FAITH links

FEAR GOD OR PEOPLE?

JEREMIAH 38:14-21

King Zedekiah told Jeremiah that he wanted to know what God had to say to him. When Zedekiah heard that God wanted him to surrender to the Babylonians, he refused to obey. He was more afraid of the people around him than he was of God.

Who do you fear more: God or people? Being obedient to God can be hard when those around you do not believe in God. God wants you to fear him, rather than man. That means he wants you to be more concerned about what he thinks than about what others might think.

Connect to these Faithlinks on following the right leader:

Following the Crowd, Numbers 13; 14, p. 193

The Heart of the Matter, 1 Samuel 16, p. 375

A Wise Wish, 1 Kings 3:5–9, p. 439

Choosing a Friend, Proverbs 28:7, p. 865

Stand!, Jeremiah 19:14—20:6, p. 1019

The Unpopular Choice, Mark 15:42–43, p. 1360

will live. **18**But if you refuse to surrender
to the officers of the king of Babylon,
Jerusalem will be handed over to the
Babylonian army, and they will burn it
down. And you yourself will not escape
from them.' "

19Then King Zedekiah said to Jeremiah, "I'm afraid of some Jews who have
already gone over to the side of the Babylonian army. If the Babylonians hand me
over to them, they will treat me badly."

20But Jeremiah answered, "The Babylonians will not hand you over to the
Jews. Obey the LORD by doing what I tell
you. Then things will go well for you, and
your life will be saved. **21**But if you refuse to surrender to the Babylonians, the
LORD has shown me what will happen.
22All the women left in the palace of the
king of Judah will be brought out and tak-
en to the important officers of the king of
Babylon. Your women will make fun of
you with this song:

'Your good friends misled you
    and were stronger than you.
While your feet were stuck in the
        mud,
    they left you.'

23"All your wives and children will be
brought out and given to the Babylonian
army. You yourself will not even escape
from them. You will be taken prisoner by
the king of Babylon, and Jerusalem will
be burned down."

24Then Zedekiah said to Jeremiah,
"Do not tell anyone that I have been talking to you, or you will die. **25**If the officers find out I talked to you, they will
come to you and say, 'Tell us what you
said to King Zedekiah and what he said to
you. Don't keep any secrets from us. If
you don't tell us everything, we will kill
you.' **26**If they ask you, tell them, 'I was
begging the king not to send me back to
Jonathan's house to die.' "

27All the officers did come to question Jeremiah. So he told them everything the king had ordered him to say.
Then the officers said no more to Jeremiah, because no one had heard what Jeremiah and the king had discussed.

28So Jeremiah stayed under guard in
the courtyard of the guard until the day
Jerusalem was captured.

The Fall of Jerusalem

39 This is how Jerusalem was captured: Nebuchadnezzar king of
Babylon marched against Jerusalem with

his whole army and surrounded the city to attack it. This was during the tenth month of the ninth year Zedekiah was king of Judah. **2**This lasted until the ninth day of the fourth month in Zedekiah's eleventh year. Then the city wall was broken through. **3**And all these officers of the king of Babylon came into Jerusalem and sat down at the Middle Gate: Nergal-Sharezer of the district of Samgar; Nebo-Sarsekim, a chief officer; Nergal-Sharezer, an important leader; and all the other important officers.

> Find Jeremiah and take care of him. Do not hurt him, but do for him whatever he asks you.
> —Jeremiah 39:12

4When Zedekiah king of Judah and all his soldiers saw them, they ran away. They left Jerusalem at night and went out from the king's garden. They went through the gate that was between the two walls and then headed toward the Jordan Valley. **5**But the Babylonian army chased them and caught up with Zedekiah in the plains of Jericho. They captured him and took him to Nebuchadnezzar king of Babylon, who was at the town of Riblah in the land of Hamath. There Nebuchadnezzar passed his sentence on Zedekiah. **6**At Riblah the king of Babylon killed Zedekiah's sons and all the important officers of Judah as Zedekiah watched. **7**Then he put out Zedekiah's eyes. He put bronze chains on Zedekiah and took him to Babylon.

8The Babylonians set fire to the palace and to the houses of the people, and they broke down the walls around Jerusalem. **9**Nebuzaradan, commander of the king's special guards, took the people left in Jerusalem, those captives who had surrendered to him earlier, and the rest of the people of Jerusalem, and he took them all away to Babylon. **10**But Nebuzaradan, commander of the guard, left some of the poorest people of Judah behind. They owned nothing, but that day he gave them vineyards and fields.

11Nebuchadnezzar king of Babylon had given these orders about Jeremiah through Nebuzaradan, commander of the guard: **12**"Find Jeremiah and take care of him. Do not hurt him, but do for him whatever he asks you." **13**So Nebuchadnezzar sent these men for Jeremiah: Nebuzaradan, commander of the guards; Nebushazban, a chief officer; Nergal-Sharezer, an important leader; and all the other officers of the king of Babylon. **14**They had Jeremiah taken out of the courtyard of the guard. Then they turned him over to Gedaliah son of Ahikam son of Shaphan, who had orders to take Jeremiah back home. So they took him home, and he stayed among the people left in Judah.

15While Jeremiah was guarded in the courtyard, the LORD spoke his word to him: **16**"Jeremiah, go and tell Ebed-Melech the Cushite this message: 'This is what the LORD All-Powerful, the God of Israel, says: Very soon I will make my words about Jerusalem come true through disaster, not through good times. You will see everything come true with your own eyes. **17**But I will save you on that day, Ebed-Melech, says the LORD. You will not be handed over to the people you fear. **18**I will surely save you, Ebed-Melech. You will not die from a sword, but you will escape and live. This will happen because you have trusted in me, says the LORD.' "

Jeremiah Is Set Free

40 The LORD spoke his word to Jeremiah after Nebuzaradan, commander of the guards, had set Jeremiah free at the city of Ramah. He had found Jeremiah in Ramah bound in chains with all the captives from Jerusalem and Judah who were being taken away to Babylon. **2**When commander Nebuzaradan found Jeremiah, Nebuzaradan said to him, "The LORD your God announced this disaster would come to this place. **3**And now the LORD has done everything he said he would do. This disaster happened because the people of Judah sinned against the LORD and did not obey him. **4**But to-

day I am freeing you from the chains on
your wrists. If you want to, come with me
to Babylon, and I will take good care of
you. But if you don't want to come, then
don't. Look, the whole country is open to
you. Go wherever you wish." 5Before
Jeremiah turned to leave, Nebuzaradan
said, "Or go back to Gedaliah son of Ahikam, the son of Shaphan. The king of
Babylon has chosen him to be governor
over the towns of Judah. Go and live with
Gedaliah among the people, or go anywhere you want."

Then Nebuzaradan gave Jeremiah
some food and a present and let him go.
6So Jeremiah went to Gedaliah son of
Ahikam at Mizpah and stayed with him
there. He lived among the people who
were left behind in Judah.

The Short Rule of Gedaliah

7Some officers and their men from the
army of Judah were still out in the open
country. They heard that the king of Babylon had put Gedaliah son of Ahikam in
charge of the people who were left in the
land: the men, women, and children who
were the poorest. They were the ones
who were not taken to Babylon as captives. 8So these soldiers came to Gedaliah
at Mizpah: Ishmael son of Nethaniah,
Johanan and Jonathan sons of Kareah,

CONNECT 2-YOU

SMALL COMFORTS

When one of your friends is going through a bad time, how do you comfort him or her? We have a friend who has a problem in this area. Let's welcome Steve, age 10, to Connect 2-You.

Steve

Well, my best friend's mother died a few weeks ago, and I'm afraid to talk to him about it. I went to the funeral, but I haven't called or seen him since then. I just don't know what to say to him. I'm afraid that if I say the wrong thing, he's going to break down and start crying—and I don't think I could handle that. I know I'm being a terrible friend. What should I do?

Hi, Steve.
What's your problem?

The Bible is full of instructions for Christians to encourage one another, support one another, and comfort one another. The best thing you can do is to be honest with your friend. Tell him exactly how you're feeling. Ask him to tell you how he's feeling. Take a look at the Livin' It page on loving God's way, Mark 12:28-34, p. 1352, to get some tips on what the Bible says about comforting others.

Jesus says to love your neighbor as you love yourself. Try putting yourself in your friend's position. If it was your mom who had just died, what would you want people to say to you? How would you want your friend to show his love for you?

Seraiah son of Tanhumeth, the sons of Ephai the Netophathite, Jaazaniah son of the Maacathite, and their men.

9Gedaliah son of Ahikam, the son of Shaphan, made a promise to them, saying, "Do not be afraid to serve the Babylonians. Stay in the land and serve the king of Babylon. Then everything will go well for you. **10**I myself will live in Mizpah and will speak for you before the Babylonians who come to us here. Harvest the wine, the summer fruit, and the oil, and put what you harvest in your storage jars. Live in the towns you control."

11The Jews in Moab, Ammon, Edom, and other countries also heard that the king of Babylon had left a few Jews alive in the land. And they heard the king of Babylon had chosen Gedaliah as governor over them. (Gedaliah was the son of Ahikam, the son of Shaphan.) **12**When the people of Judah heard this news, they came back to Judah from all the countries where they had been scattered. They came to Gedaliah at Mizpah and gathered a large harvest of wine and summer fruit.

13Johanan son of Kareah and all the army officers of Judah still in the open country came to Gedaliah at Mizpah. **14**They said to him, "Don't you know that Baalis king of the Ammonite people wants you dead? He has sent Ishmael son of Nethaniah to kill you." But Gedaliah son of Ahikam did not believe them.

15Then Johanan son of Kareah spoke to Gedaliah in private at Mizpah. He said, "Let me go and kill Ishmael son of Nethaniah. No one will know anything about it. We should not let Ishmael kill you. Then all the Jews gathered around you would be scattered to different countries again, and the few people of Judah who are left alive would be lost."

16But Gedaliah son of Ahikam said to Johanan son of Kareah, "Do not kill Ishmael! The things you are saying about Ishmael are not true."

41 In the seventh month Ishmael son of Nethaniah and ten of his men came to Gedaliah son of Ahikam at Mizpah. (Nethaniah was the son of Elishama.) Now Ishmael was a member of the king's family and had been one of the officers of the king of Judah. While they were eating a meal with Gedaliah at Mizpah, **2**Ishmael and his ten men got up and killed Gedaliah son of Ahikam, the son of Shaphan, with a sword. (Gedaliah was the man the king of Babylon had chosen as governor over Judah.) **3**Ishmael also killed all the Jews and the Babylonian soldiers who were there with Gedaliah at Mizpah.

4The day after Gedaliah was murdered, before anyone knew about it, **5**eighty men came to Mizpah bringing grain offerings and incense to the Temple of the LORD. Those men from Shechem, Shiloh, and Samaria had shaved off their beards, torn their clothes, and cut themselves.[n] **6**Ishmael son of Nethaniah went out from Mizpah to meet them, crying as he walked. When he met them, he said, "Come with me to meet Gedaliah son of Ahikam." **7**So they went into Mizpah. Then Ishmael son of Nethaniah and his men killed seventy of them and threw the bodies into a deep well. **8**But the ten men who were left alive said to Ishmael, "Don't kill us! We have wheat and barley and oil and honey that we have hidden in a field." So Ishmael let them live and did not kill them with the others. **9**Now the well where he had thrown all the bodies had been made by King Asa as a part of his defenses against Baasha king of Israel. But Ishmael son of Nethaniah put dead bodies in it until it was full.

10Ishmael captured all the other people in Mizpah: the king's daughters and all the other people who were left there. They were the ones whom Nebuzaradan commander of the guard had chosen Gedaliah son of Ahikam to take care of. So Ishmael son of Nethaniah captured those people, and he started to cross over to the country of the Ammonites.

11Johanan son of Kareah and all his army officers with him heard about all the evil things Ishmael son of Nethaniah had done. **12**So they took their men and went

---

41:5 shaved . . . themselves The men did this to show they were sad about the Temple in Jerusalem being destroyed.

to fight Ishmael son of Nethaniah and caught him near the big pool of water at Gibeon. **13**When the captives Ishmael had taken saw Johanan and the army officers, they were glad. **14**So all the people Ishmael had taken captive from Mizpah turned around and ran to Johanan son of Kareah. **15**But Ishmael son of Nethaniah and eight of his men escaped from Johanan and ran away to the Ammonites.

16So Johanan son of Kareah and all his army officers saved the captives that Ishmael son of Nethaniah had taken from Mizpah after he murdered Gedaliah son of Ahikam. Among those left alive were soldiers, women, children, and palace officers. And Johanan brought them back from the town of Gibeon.

The Escape to Egypt

17-18 Johanan and the other army officers were afraid of the Babylonians. Since the king of Babylon had chosen Gedaliah son of Ahikam to be governor of Judah but Ishmael son of Nethaniah had murdered him, Johanan was afraid that the Babylonians would be angry. So they decided to run away to Egypt. On the way they stayed at Geruth Kimham, near the town of Bethlehem.

42 While there, Johanan son of Kareah and Jezaniah son of Hoshaiah went to Jeremiah the prophet. All the army officers and all the people, from the least important to the greatest, went along, too. **2**They said to him, "Jeremiah, please listen to what we ask. Pray to the LORD your God for all the people left alive from the family of Judah. At one time there were many of us, but you can see that there are few of us now. **3**So pray that the LORD your God will tell us where we should go and what we should do."

4Then Jeremiah the prophet answered, "I understand what you want me to do. I will pray to the LORD your God as you have asked. I will tell you everything he says and not hide anything from you."

5Then the people said to Jeremiah, "May the LORD be a true and loyal witness against us if we don't do everything the LORD your God sends you to tell us. **6**It does not matter if we like the message or not. We will obey the LORD our God, to whom we are sending you. We will obey what he says so good things will happen to us."

Obedience
Read this to see what happens when you obey.

7Ten days later the LORD spoke his word to Jeremiah. **8**Then Jeremiah called for Johanan son of Kareah, the army officers with him, and all the other people, from the least important to the greatest. **9**Jeremiah said to them, "You sent me to ask the LORD for what you wanted. This is what the God of Israel says: **10**'If you will stay in Judah, I will build you up and not tear you down. I will plant you and not pull you up, because I am sad about the disaster I brought on you. **11**Now you fear the king of Babylon, but don't be afraid of him. Don't be afraid of him,' says the LORD, 'because I am with you. I will save you and rescue you from his power. **12**I will be kind to you, and he will also treat you with mercy and let you stay in your land.'

13"But if you say, 'We will not stay in Judah,' you will disobey the LORD your God. **14**Or you might say, 'No, we will go and live in Egypt. There we will not see war, or hear the trumpets of war, or be hungry.' **15**If you say that, listen to the message of the LORD, you who are left alive from Judah. This is what the LORD All-Powerful, the God of Israel, says: 'If you make up your mind to go and live in Egypt, these things will happen: **16**You are afraid of war, but it will find you in the land of Egypt. And you are worried about hunger, but it will follow you into Egypt, and you will die there. **17**Everyone who goes to live in Egypt will die in war or from hunger or terrible disease. No one who goes to Egypt will live; no one will escape the terrible things I will bring to them.'

18"This is what the LORD All-Powerful, the God of Israel, says: 'I showed my anger against the people of Jerusalem. In the same way I will show my anger against you when you go to Egypt. Other nations will speak evil of you. People will be shocked by what will happen to you.

You will become a curse word, and people
will insult you. And you will never see
Judah again.'
19"You who are left alive in Judah, the
LORD has told you, 'Don't go to Egypt.'
Be sure you understand this; I warn you
today **20**that you are making a mistake
that will cause your deaths. You sent me
to the LORD your God, saying, 'Pray to
the LORD our God for us. Tell us everything the LORD our God says, and we will
do it.' **21**So today I have told you, but you
have not obeyed the LORD your God in all
that he sent me to tell you. **22**So now be
sure you understand this: You want to go
to live in Egypt, but you will die there by
war, hunger, or terrible diseases."

43 So Jeremiah finished telling the
people the message from the
LORD their God; he told them everything
the LORD their God had sent him to tell
them.
2Azariah son of Hoshaiah, Johanan
son of Kareah, and some other men were
too proud. They said to Jeremiah, "You
are lying! The LORD our God did not send
you to say, 'You must not go to Egypt to
live there.' **3**Baruch son of Neriah is
causing you to be against us. He wants
you to hand us over to the Babylonians so
they can kill us or capture us and take us
to Babylon."
4So Johanan, the army officers, and
all the people disobeyed the LORD's
command to stay in Ju-
dah. **5**But Johanan son of
Kareah and the army of-
ficers led away those
who were left alive from
Judah. They were the
people who had run
away from the Babyloni-
ans to other countries
but then had come back
to live in Judah. **6**They
led away the men, wom-
en, and children, and the king's daughters. Nebuzaradan commander of the
guard had put Gedaliah son of Ahikam
son of Shaphan in charge of those people.
Johanan also took Jeremiah the prophet
and Baruch son of Neriah. **7**These people
did not listen to the LORD. So they all
went to Egypt to the city of Tahpanhes.
8In Tahpanhes the LORD spoke his
word to Jeremiah: **9**"Take some large
stones. Bury them in the clay in the brick
pavement in front of the king of Egypt's
palace in Tahpanhes. Do this while the
Jews are watching you. **10**Then say to
them, 'This is what the LORD All-Powerful, the God of Israel, says: I will soon
send for my servant, Nebuchadnezzar
king of Babylon. I will set his throne over
these stones I have buried, and he will
spread his covering for shade above
them. **11**He will come here and attack
Egypt. He will bring death to those who
are supposed to die. He will make prisoners of those who are to be taken captive,
and he will bring war to those who are to
be killed with a sword. **12**Nebuchadnezzar will set fire to the temples of the gods
of Egypt and burn them. And he will take
the idols away as captives. As a shepherd
wraps himself in his clothes, so Nebuchadnezzar will wrap Egypt around him.
Then he will safely leave Egypt. **13**He
will destroy the stone pillars in the temple of the sun god in Egypt, and he will
burn down the temples of the gods of
Egypt.'"

Disaster in Egypt

44 Jeremiah received a message from
the LORD for all the Jews living in
Egypt—in the cities of Migdol, Tahpanhes, Memphis, and
in southern Egypt. This
was the message: **2**"The
LORD All-Powerful, the
God of Israel, says: You
saw all the terrible things
I brought on Jerusalem
and the towns of Judah,
which are ruins today
with no one living in
them. **3**It is because the
people who lived there
did evil. They made me angry by burning
incense and worshiping other gods that
neither they nor you nor your ancestors
ever knew. **4**I sent all my servants, the
prophets, to you again and again. By
them I said to you, 'Don't do this terrible
thing that I hate.' **5**But they did not listen

They made me angry by burning incense and worshiping other gods that neither they nor you nor your ancestors ever knew.
—Jeremiah 44:3

or pay attention. They did not stop doing
evil things and burning incense to other
gods. **6**So I showed my great anger
against them. I poured out my anger in
the towns of Judah and the streets of Jerusalem so they are only ruins and piles
of stones today.
7"Now the LORD All-Powerful, the
God of Israel, says: Why are you doing
such great harm to yourselves? You are
cutting off the men and women, children
and babies from the family of Judah, leaving yourselves without anyone from the
family of Judah. **8**Why do you want to
make me angry by making idols? Why do
you burn incense to the gods of Egypt,
where you have come to live? You will
destroy yourselves. Other nations will
speak evil of you and make fun of you.
9Have you forgotten about the evil things
your ancestors did? And have you forgotten the evil the kings and queens of Judah
did? Have you forgotten about the evil
you and your wives did? These things
were done in the country of Judah and in
the streets of Jerusalem. **10**Even to this
day the people of Judah are still too
proud. They have not learned to respect
me or to follow my teachings. They have
not obeyed the laws I gave you and your
ancestors.
11"So this is what the LORD All-
Powerful, the God of Israel, says: I am
determined to bring disasters on you. I
will destroy the whole family of Judah.
12The few who were left alive from Judah
were determined to go to Egypt and settle there, but they will all die in Egypt.
They will be killed in war or die from
hunger. From the least important to the
greatest, they will be killed in war or die
from hunger. Other nations will speak
evil about them. People will be shocked
by what has happened to them. They will
become a curse word, and people will insult them. **13**I will punish those people
who have gone to live in Egypt, just as I
punished Jerusalem, using swords, hunger, and terrible diseases. **14**Of the people of Judah who were left alive and have
gone to live in Egypt, none will escape
my punishment. They want to return to
Judah and live there, but none of them
will live to return to Judah, except a few
people who will escape."
15A large group of the people of Judah
who lived in southern Egypt were meeting together. Among them were many
women of Judah who were burning incense to other gods, and their husbands
knew it. All these people said to Jeremiah,
16"We will not listen to the message
from the LORD that you spoke to us.
17We promised to make sacrifices to the
Queen Goddess, and we will certainly do
everything we promised. We will burn incense and pour out drink offerings to
worship her, just as we, our ancestors,
kings, and officers did in the past. All of
us did these things in the towns of Judah
and in the streets of Jerusalem. At that
time we had plenty of food and were
successful, and nothing bad happened to
us. **18**But since we stopped making sacrifices to the Queen Goddess and stopped
pouring out drink offerings to her, we
have had great problems. Our people have
also been killed in war and by hunger."
19The women said, "Our husbands
knew what we were doing. We had their
permission to burn incense to the Queen
Goddess and to pour out drink offerings
to her. Our husbands knew we were making cakes that looked like her and were
pouring out drink offerings to her."
20Then Jeremiah spoke to all the people—men and women—who answered
him. **21**He said to them, "The LORD remembered that you and your ancestors,
kings and officers, and the people of the
land burned incense in the towns of Judah
and in the streets of Jerusalem. He remembered and thought about it. **22**Then
he could not be patient with you any longer. He hated the terrible things you did.
So he made your country an empty
desert, where no one lives. Other people
curse that country. And so it is today.
23All this happened because you burned
incense to other gods. You sinned against
the LORD. You did not obey him or follow
his teachings or the laws he gave you.
You did not keep your part of the agreement with him. So this disaster has happened to you. It is there for you to see."
24Then Jeremiah said to all those men

and women, "People of Judah who are
now in Egypt, hear the word of the LORD:
25The LORD All-Powerful, the God of Israel, says: You and your wives did what
you said you would do. You said, 'We will
certainly keep the promises we made. We
promised to make sacrifices to the Queen
Goddess and to pour out drink offerings
to her.' So, go ahead. Do the things you
promised, and keep your promises.
26But hear the word of the LORD. Listen,
all you Jews living in Egypt. The LORD
says, 'I have sworn by my great name:
The people of Judah now living in Egypt
will never again use my name to make
promises. They will never again say in
Egypt, "As surely as the Lord GOD
lives . . ." **27**I am watching over them,
not to take care of them, but to hurt
them. The Jews who live in Egypt will die
from swords or hunger until they are all
destroyed. **28**A few will escape being
killed by the sword and will come back to
Judah from Egypt. Then, of the people of
Judah who came to live in Egypt, those
who are left alive will know if my word or
their word came true. **29**I will give you a
sign that I will punish you here in Egypt,'
says the LORD. 'When you see it happen,
you will know that my promises to hurt
you will really happen.' **30**This is what
the LORD says: 'Hophra king of Egypt has
enemies who want to kill him. Soon I will
hand him over to his enemies just as I
handed Zedekiah king of Judah over to
Nebuchadnezzar king of Babylon, who
wanted to kill him.' "

A Message to Baruch

45 It was the fourth
year that Jehoia-
kim son of Josiah was
king of Judah. Jeremiah
the prophet told these
things to Baruch son of
Neriah, and Baruch wrote
them on a scroll: **2**"This
is what the LORD, the
God of Israel, says to you,
Baruch: **3**You have said, 'How terrible it
is for me! The LORD has given me sorrow
along with my pain. I am tired because of
my suffering and cannot rest.' "

> The LORD has given me sorrow along with my pain. I am tired because of my suffering and cannot rest.
> —Jeremiah 45:3

4The LORD said, "Say this to Baruch:
'This is what the LORD says: I will soon
tear down what I have built, and I will pull
up what I have planted everywhere in Judah. **5**Baruch, you are looking for great
things for yourself. Don't look for them,
because I will bring disaster on all the
people, says the LORD. You will have to
go many places, but I will let you escape
alive wherever you go.' "

Messages to the Nations

46 The LORD spoke this word to Jeremiah the prophet about the nations:
2This message is to Egypt. It is about
the army of Neco king of Egypt, which
was defeated at the city of Carchemish on
the Euphrates River by Nebuchadnezzar
king of Babylon. This was in the fourth
year that Jehoiakim son of Josiah was
king of Judah. This is the LORD's message to Egypt:

3"Prepare your shields, large and
small,
and march out for battle!
4Harness the horses
and get on them!
Go to your places for battle
and put on your helmets!
Polish your spears.
Put on your armor!
5What do I see?
That army is terrified,
and the soldiers are running away.
Their warriors are defeated.
They run away quickly
without looking
back.
There is terror on
every side!" says
the LORD.
6"The fast runners
cannot run away;
the strong soldiers
cannot escape.
They stumble and fall
in the north, by the
Euphrates River.
7Who is this, rising up like the Nile
River,
like strong, fast rivers?
8Egypt rises up like the Nile River,

like strong, fast rivers.
Egypt says, 'I will rise up and cover
the earth.
I will destroy cities and the people
in them!'
9 Horsemen, charge into battle!
Chariot drivers, drive hard!
March on, brave soldiers—
soldiers from the countries of
Cush and Put who carry shields,
soldiers from Lydia who use
bows.
10 "But that day belongs to the Lord
GOD All-Powerful.
At that time he will give those
people the punishment they
deserve.
The sword will kill until it is finished,
until it satisfies its thirst for their
blood.
The Lord GOD All-Powerful will offer
a sacrifice
in the land of the north, by the
Euphrates River.

11 "Go up to Gilead and get some balm,
people of Egypt!
You have prepared many medicines,
but they will not work;
you will not be healed.
12 The nations have heard of your
shame,
and your cries fill all the earth.
One warrior has run into another;
both of them have fallen down
together!"
13 This is the message the LORD
spoke to Jeremiah the prophet about
Nebuchadnezzar king of Babylon's coming to attack Egypt:
14 "Announce this message in Egypt,
and preach it in Migdol.
Preach it also in the cities of
Memphis and Tahpanhes:
'Get ready for war,
because the battle is all around
you.'
15 Egypt, why were your warriors
killed?
They could not stand because the
LORD pushed them down.
16 They stumbled again and again
and fell over each other.
They said, 'Get up. Let's go back
to our own people and our
homeland.
We must get away from our
enemy's sword!'
17 In their homelands those soldiers
called out,
'The king of Egypt is only a lot of
noise.
He missed his chance for glory!' "
18 The King's name is the LORD All-
Powerful.
He says, "As surely as I live,
a powerful leader will come.
He will be like Mount Tabor among
the mountains,
like Mount Carmel by the sea.
19 People of Egypt, pack your things
to be taken away as captives,
because Memphis will be destroyed.
It will be a ruin, and no one will
live there.

20 "Egypt is like a beautiful young cow,
but a horsefly is coming
from the north to attack her.
21 The hired soldiers in Egypt's army
are like fat calves,
because even they all turn and run
away together;
they do not stand strong against
the attack.
Their time of destruction is coming;
they will soon be punished.
22 Egypt is like a hissing snake that is
trying to escape.
The enemy comes closer and
closer.
They come against Egypt with axes
like men who cut down trees.
23 They will chop down Egypt's army
as if it were a great forest," says
the LORD.
"There are more enemy soldiers
than locusts;
there are too many to count.
24 The people of Egypt will be
ashamed.
They will be handed over to the
enemy from the north."
25 The LORD All-Powerful, the God
of Israel, says: "Very soon I will punish

Amon, the god of the city of Thebes. And
I will punish Egypt, her kings, her gods,
and the people who depend on the king.
26I will hand those people over to their
enemies, who want to kill them. I will
give them to Nebuchadnezzar king of
Babylon and his officers. But in the future, Egypt will live in peace as it once
did," says the LORD.

A Message to Israel

27"People of Jacob, my servants, don't
be afraid;
don't be
frightened,
Israel.
I will surely save
you from
those
faraway places
and your children from the lands
where they are captives.
The people of Jacob will have peace
and safety again,
and no one will make them afraid.
28People of Jacob, my servants, do not
be afraid,
because I am with you," says the
LORD.
"I will completely destroy the many
different nations
where I scattered you.
But I will not completely destroy
you.
I will punish you fairly,
but I will not let you escape your
punishment."

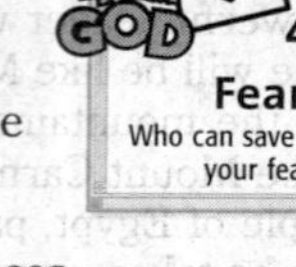

46:27
Fears
Who can save you from your fears?

A Message to the Philistines

47 Before the king of Egypt attacked
the city of Gaza, the LORD spoke
his word to Jeremiah the prophet. This
message is to the Philistine people.
2This is what the LORD says:
"See, the enemy is gathering in the
north like rising waters.
They will become like an
overflowing stream
and will cover the whole country like
a flood,
even the towns and the people
living in them.
Everyone living in that country
will cry for help;
the people will cry painfully.
3They will hear the sound of the
running horses
and the noisy chariots
and the rumbling chariot wheels.
Parents will not help their children to
safety,
because they will be too weak to
help.
4The time has come
to destroy all the Philistines.
It is time to destroy all who are left
alive
who could help the cities of Tyre
and Sidon.
The LORD will soon destroy the
Philistines,
those left alive from the island of
Crete.
5The people from the city of Gaza will
be sad and shave their heads.
The people from the city of
Ashkelon will be made silent.
Those left alive from the valley,
how long will you cut
yourselves?"

6"You cry, 'Sword of the LORD,
how long will you keep fighting?
Return to your holder.
Stop and be still.'
7But how can his sword rest
when the LORD has given it a
command?
He has ordered it
to attack Ashkelon and the
seacoast."

A Message to Moab

48 This message is to the country of
Moab.

This is what the LORD All-Powerful,
the God of Israel, says:
"How terrible it will be for the city of
Nebo,
because it will be ruined.
The town of Kiriathaim will be
disgraced and captured;

47:5 sad and . . . yourselves The people did these things to show their sadness.

TRUE OR FALSE GODS? Jeremiah 48:7, 13

The Israelites were surrounded by people who worshiped fake gods. Sometimes the Israelites made the mistake of paying attention to these fake gods as if they were real. There was one in particular, Baal, that the Israelites sometimes worshiped. Baal was a god who was supposed to help produce good crops and livestock. (Read Judges 2:10–11, p. 313.)

Each time God's children worshiped these fake gods, God himself had to point out their sin and bring them back to reality. Here are a few of the frequently mentioned fake gods in the Old Testament.

Ashtoreth	Baal's wife	Judges 2:13, p. 313
Bel	Babylonian god	Isaiah 46:1, p. 957
Chemosh	God of the Moabites and Ammonites	Jeremiah 48:7, 13, p. 1057
Dagon	Philistine god	1 Samuel 5:2–7, p. 360
Molech	Ammonite god	Leviticus 18:21, p. 159
Nebo	Babylonian god of wisdom and the arts	Isaiah 46:1, p. 957
Rimmon	Syrian god of rain	2 Kings 5:18, p. 483

the strong city will be disgraced
and shattered.
2 Moab will not be praised again.
Men in the town of Heshbon plan
Moab's defeat.
They say, 'Come, let us put an end
to that nation!'
Town of Madmen,* you will also be
silenced.
The sword will chase you.
3 Listen to the cries from the town of
Horonaim,
cries of much confusion and
destruction.
4 Moab will be broken up.
Her little children will cry for help.
5 Moab's people go up the path to the
town of Luhith,
crying loudly as they go.
On the road down to Horonaim,
cries of pain and suffering can be
heard.
6 Run! Run for your lives!
Go like a bush being blown
through the desert.
7 You trust in the things you do and in
your wealth,
so you also will be captured.
The god Chemosh will go into
captivity
and his priests and officers with
him.
8 The destroyer will come against
every town;
not one town will escape.

48:2 Madmen This name sounds like the Hebrew word for "be silenced."

The valley will be ruined,
and the high plain will be destroyed,
as the LORD has said.
9 Give wings to Moab,
because she will surely leave her land.
Moab's towns will become empty,
with no one to live in them.

10 A curse will be on anyone who doesn't do what the LORD says,
and a curse will be on anyone who holds back his sword from killing.

11 "The people of Moab have never known trouble.
They are like wine left to settle;
they have never been poured from one jar to another.
They have not been taken into captivity.
So they taste as they did before,
and their smell has not changed.
12 A time is coming," says the LORD,
"When I will send people to pour you from your jars.
They will empty Moab's jars
and smash her jugs.
13 The people of Israel trusted that god in the town of Bethel,
and they were ashamed when there was no help.
In the same way Moab will be ashamed of their god Chemosh.

14 "You cannot say, 'We are warriors!
We are brave men in battle!'
15 The destroyer of Moab and her towns has arrived.
Her best young men will be killed!" says the King,
whose name is the LORD All-Powerful.
16 "The end of Moab is near,
and she will soon be destroyed.
17 All you who live around Moab,
all you who know her, cry for her.
Say, 'The ruler's power is broken;
Moab's power and glory are gone.'

18 "You people living in the town of Dibon, come down from your place of honor
and sit on the dry ground,
because the destroyer of Moab has come against you.
And he has destroyed your strong, walled cities.
19 You people living in the town of Aroer,
stand next to the road and watch.
See the man running away and the woman escaping.
Ask them, 'What happened?'
20 Moab is filled with shame, because she is ruined.
Cry, Moab, cry out!
Announce at the Arnon River
that Moab is destroyed.
21 People on the high plain have been punished.
Judgment has come to these towns:
Holon, Jahzah, and Mephaath;
22 Dibon, Nebo, and Beth Diblathaim;
23 Kiriathaim, Beth Gamul, and Beth Meon;
24 Kerioth and Bozrah.
Judgment has come to all the towns of Moab, far and near.
25 Moab's strength has been cut off,
and its arm broken!" says the LORD.

26 "The people of Moab thought they were greater than the LORD,
so punish them until they act as if they are drunk.
Moab will fall and roll around in its own vomit,
and people will even make fun of it.
27 Moab, you made fun of Israel.
Israel was caught in the middle of a gang of thieves.
When you spoke about Israel,
you shook your head and acted as if you were better than it.
28 People in Moab, leave your towns empty
and go live among the rocks.
Be like a dove that makes its nest
at the entrance of a cave.

29 "We have heard that the people of Moab are proud,
very proud.

They are proud, very proud,
and in their hearts they think they are important."
30 The LORD says,
"I know Moab's great pride, but it is useless.
Moab's bragging accomplishes nothing.
31 So I cry sadly for Moab,
for everyone in Moab.
I moan for the people from the town of Kir Hareseth.
32 I cry with the people of the town of Jazer
for you, the grapevines of the town of Sibmah.
In the past your vines spread all the way to the sea,
as far as the sea of Jazer.
But the destroyer has taken over your fruit and grapes.
33 Joy and happiness are gone
from the large, rich fields of Moab.
I have stopped the flow of wine from the winepresses.
No one walks on the grapes with shouts of joy.
There are shouts,
but not shouts of joy.

34 "Their crying can be heard from Moabite towns,
from Heshbon to Elealeh and Jahaz.
It can be heard from Zoar as far away as Horonaim and Eglath Shelishiyah.
Even the waters of Nimrim are dried up.
35 I will stop Moab
from making burnt offerings at the places of worship
and from burning incense to their gods," says the LORD.

36 "My heart cries sadly for Moab like a flute playing a funeral song.
It cries like a flute for the people from Kir Hareseth.
The money they made has all been taken away.
37 Every head has been shaved
and every beard cut off.

FAITH CHALLENGE

Try this one. Read 48:30 to find out how the Lord feels about people who like to brag about themselves or what they have. How do you feel when you hear people bragging about things they've done? Is there some area in your life where you may be tempted to brag?

TESTING IT

Jeremiah 48:30
The LORD says, "I know Moab's great pride, but it is useless. Moab's bragging accomplishes nothing."

Everyone's hands are cut,
and everyone wears rough cloth around his waist.[n]
38 People are crying on every roof[n] in Moab
and in every public square.
There is nothing but sadness,

48:37 Every head . . . waist. The people did these things to show their sadness for those who had died.
48:38 roof In Bible times houses were built with flat roofs. The roof was used for drying things such as flax and fruit. And it was used as an extra room, as a place for worship, and as a cool place to sleep in the summer.

because I have broken Moab
like a jar no one wants," says the
LORD.
39 "Moab is shattered! The people are
crying!
Moab turns away in shame!
People all around her make fun of her.
The things that happened fill them
with great fear."

40 This is what the LORD says:
"Look! Someone is coming, like an
eagle diving down from the sky
and spreading its wings over Moab.
41 The towns of Moab will be captured,
and the strong, walled cities will be
defeated.
At that time Moab's warriors will be
frightened,
like a woman who is having a baby.
42 The nation of Moab will be
destroyed,
because they thought they were
greater than the LORD.
43 Fear, deep pits, and traps wait for
you,
people of Moab," says the LORD.
44 "People will run from fear,
but they will fall into the pits.
Anyone who climbs out of the pits
will be caught in the traps.
I will bring the year of punishment to
Moab," says the LORD.

45 "People have run from the powerful
enemy
and have gone to Heshbon for
safety.
But fire started in Heshbon;
a blaze has spread from the
hometown of Sihon king of
Moab.
It burned up the leaders of Moab
and destroyed those proud people.
46 How terrible it is for you, Moab!
The people who worship Chemosh
have been destroyed.
Your sons have been taken captive,
and your daughters have been
taken away.
47 "But in days to come,
I will make good things happen
again to Moab," says the LORD.

This ends the judgment on Moab.

A Message to Ammon

49 This message is to the Ammonite
people.

This is what the LORD says:
"Do you think that Israel has no
children?
Do you think there is no one to
take the land when the parents
die?
If that were true, why did Molech
take Gad's land
and why did Molech's people settle
in Gad's towns?"
2 The LORD says,
"The time will come when I will
make Rabbah,
the capital city of the Ammonites,
hear the battle cry.
It will become a hill covered with
ruins,
and the towns around it will be
burned.
Those people forced Israel out of that
land,
but now Israel will force them
out!" says the LORD.
3 "People in the town of Heshbon, cry
sadly because the town of Ai is
destroyed!
Those who live in Rabbah, cry
out!
Put on your rough cloth to show your
sadness, and cry loudly.
Run here and there for safety
inside the walls,
because Molech will be taken captive
and his priests and officers with
him.
4 You brag about your valleys
and about the fruit in your valleys.
You are like an unfaithful child
who believes his treasures will
save him.
You think, 'Who would attack me?'
5 I will soon bring terror on you
from everyone around you,"
says the Lord GOD All-Powerful.
"You will all be forced to run away,
and no one will be able to gather
you.

6 "But the time will come
when I will make good things
happen to the Ammonites again,"
says the LORD.

A Message to Edom

7 This message is to Edom. This is
what the LORD All-Powerful says:
"Is there no more wisdom in the
town of Teman?
Can the wise men of Edom no
longer give good advice?
Have they lost their wisdom?
8 You people living in the town of
Dedan,
run away and hide in deep caves,
because I will bring disaster on the
people of Esau.
It is time for me to punish them.
9 If workers came and picked the
grapes from your vines,
they would leave a few grapes
behind.
If robbers came at night,
they would steal only enough for
themselves.
10 But I will strip Edom bare.
I will find all their hiding places,
so they will not be able to hide
from me.
The children, relatives, and
neighbors will die,
and Edom will be no more.
11 Leave the orphans, and I will take
care of them.
Your widows also can trust in
me."
12 This is what the LORD says: "Some
people did not deserve to be punished,
but they had to drink from the cup of suffering anyway. People of Edom, you deserve to be punished, so you will not
escape punishment. You must certainly
drink from the cup of suffering." 13 The
LORD says, "I swear by my own name
that the city of Bozrah will become a pile
of ruins! People will be shocked by what
happened there. They will insult that city
and speak evil of it. And all the towns
around it will become ruins forever."
14 I have heard a message from the
LORD.
A messenger has been sent among
the nations, saying,
"Gather your armies to attack it!
Get ready for battle!"

15 "Soon I will make you the smallest of
nations,
and you will be greatly hated by
everyone.
16 Edom, you frightened other nations,
but your pride has fooled you.
You live in the hollow places of the
cliff
and control the high places of the
hills.
Even if you build your home as high
as an eagle's nest,
I will bring you down from there,"
says the LORD.
17 "Edom will be destroyed.
People who pass by will be
shocked to see the destroyed
cities,
and they will be amazed at all her
injuries.
18 Edom will be destroyed like the
cities of Sodom and Gomorrah
and the towns around them," says
the LORD.
"No one will live there!
No one will stay in Edom."

19 "Like a lion coming up from the thick
bushes near the Jordan River
to attack a strong pen for sheep,
I will suddenly chase Edom from its
land.
Who is the one I have chosen to do
this?
There is no one like me,
no one who can take me to court.
None of their leaders can stand up
against me."

20 So listen to what the LORD has
planned to do against Edom.
Listen to what he has decided to
do to the people in the town of
Teman.
He will surely drag away the young
ones of Edom.
Their hometowns will surely be
shocked at what happens to them.

21 At the sound of Edom's fall, the earth
will shake.
Their cry will be heard all the way
to the Red Sea.
22 The LORD is like an eagle swooping
down
and spreading its wings over the
city of Bozrah.
At that time Edom's soldiers will
become very frightened,
like a woman having a baby.

A Message to Damascus

23 This message is to the city of Damascus:
"The towns of Hamath and Arpad are
put to shame,
because they have heard bad news.
They are discouraged.
They are troubled like the tossing
sea.
24 The city of Damascus has become
weak.
The people want to run away;
they are ready to panic.
The people feel pain and suffering,
like a woman giving birth to a
baby.
25 Damascus was a city of my joy.
Why have the people not left that
famous city yet?
26 Surely the young men will die in the
city squares,
and all her soldiers will be killed at
that time," says the LORD All-
Powerful.
27 "I will set fire to the walls of
Damascus,
and it will completely burn the
strong cities of King Ben-
Hadad."

A Message to Kedar and Hazor

28 This message is to the tribe of Kedar and the kingdoms of Hazor, which
Nebuchadnezzar king of Babylon defeated. This is what the LORD says:
"Go and attack the people of Kedar,
and destroy the people of the East.
29 Their tents and flocks will be taken
away.
Their belongings will be carried
off—
their tents, all their goods, and
their camels.
Men will shout to them,
'Terror on every side!'

30 "Run away quickly!
People in Hazor, find a good place
to hide!" says the LORD.
"Nebuchadnezzar king of Babylon
has made plans against you
and wants to defeat you.

31 "Get up! Attack the nation that is
comfortable,
that is sure no one will defeat it,"
says the LORD.
"It does not have gates or fences to
protect it.
Its people live alone.
32 The enemy will steal their camels
and their large herds of cattle as
war prizes.
I will scatter the people who cut their
hair short to every part of the
earth,
and I will bring disaster on them
from everywhere," says the
LORD.
33 "The city of Hazor will become a
home for wild dogs;
it will be an empty desert forever.
No one will live there,
and no one will stay in it."

A Message to Elam

34 Soon after Zedekiah became king of
Judah, the LORD spoke this word to Jeremiah the prophet. This message is to the
nation of Elam.
35 This is what the LORD All-Powerful
says:
"I will soon break Elam's bow,
its greatest strength.
36 I will bring the four winds against
Elam
from the four corners of the skies.
I will scatter its people everywhere
the four winds blow;
its captives will go to every nation.
37 I will terrify Elam in front of their
enemies,
who want to destroy them.
I will bring disaster to Elam

http://www.KidsBible.com

ESTHER
MARY
JESUS
PAUL

1

Would you enter a contest knowing that it could totally change your life? What if winning the contest meant that you would have to leave your family and your neighborhood and go live somewhere else?

2

Would you risk your life to save the life of someone else? Would it depend on whether you knew that person? Would you take that risk for someone you didn't know at all? Esther had to make that very choice and decide whether she wanted to risk her life for a lot of people she had never met.

ESTHER

The Courage to Conquer Fear

Ever feel scared? Maybe you were afraid to try something new. Or maybe you were afraid that something bad could happen. Did you know that Bible queens like Esther felt scared, too? When you're feeling like the "Cowardly Lion," courage can help you to face your fears. Having courage doesn't mean facing your fears only once. You might have to face them again and again. See how God helped Esther overcome her fears by checking out

on the following page. The numbers match the question numbers on this page. Although God isn't mentioned in the Book of Esther, you can know that he was at work behind the scenes.

3

Think of the one person in your life that you try to avoid at all costs. Maybe it's an older boy at school who likes to tease you or a neighborhood girl who is bossy. Would you have the courage to meet that person face-to-face?

4

Everyone probably could face a scary situation, like having an operation, one time. But would you have to courage to go through the same scary situation more than once?

If someone started a holiday in honor of you, what would it be for—your soccer-playing skills, your ability to disappear when there's work to be done, or your courage? What would you like your holiday to honor about you?

Here's the Scoop

1

Entering a contest might not sound scary. But for Esther this was no ordinary contest. Esther's story was like Cinderella's in a way. The king of the land searched for a new wife. So, he set up a "beauty contest." Esther wasn't a "mayor's daughter" or someone with high connections. She was a Jewish orphan. Competing in the contest took courage. Out of all of the women, Esther was chosen. (Check out Esther 2:1–18, p. 649.)

2

Esther's cousin Mordecai gave Esther some bad news. A man named Haman had an evil plan to kill all of the Jews. Esther knew that the king could stop Haman. When Esther found out about Haman's evil plan, she risked her life to go before the king. Requesting to see the king without permission meant death. So Esther decided to fast and pray. She knew that God could give her the courage to face the king. (Read about it in Esther 4:1—5:3, p. 651.)

3

Esther knew all about needing courage to face an enemy. The second part of her plan involved inviting the king and Haman to dinner, not once but twice. Esther didn't blow her cool by screaming at Haman at the first dinner. She knew that she had to wait and plan. God gave her the courage to be patient. Finally, she was able to tell her story to the king. He believed her and took action. (Look up Esther 5:4–8; 7:1–7, p. 653.)

4

Trouble wasn't over for Esther and her people. Even though Haman had been caught, the Jewish people were still in danger. The king's law ordering all the Jewish people in the land to be killed still was in effect. Once again Esther had to risk her life and go before the king, suggesting another plan. Thanks to God, the king said yes to Esther's plan. Esther and her people were saved! (See Esther 8:1–8, p. 655.)

5

Because of Esther's courage, the Jews were saved from destruction. That's why Purim, a new holiday, was celebrated. Esther wrote a letter telling the Jews about the new holiday. Each year the Jewish people were to gather together and remember the courage of one orphan. (Check out Esther 9:26–32, p. 658.) Courage may not earn you a holiday with your name on it. But people will remember the courage God gives you to overcome a fear. Don't believe it? Trust God for courage and see what happens.

answers page

ESTHER
MARY
JESUS
PAUL

MARY

Totally Trusting

To *trust* means to have confidence in someone. The wise person puts his or her trust in someone dependable. God is someone you can always count on. Would you agree? Mary, the mother of Jesus, would. Mary wasn't perfect. She did not have all of the answers to the problems she faced throughout her life. At times, she was tempted to doubt. Check out the HERE'S THE SCOOP section on the next page to find out how Mary's trust in God deepened with each experience. The numbers match the question numbers on this page. Trusting God doesn't make a person perfect. It just means that you know where to go for help!

Are you willing to trust God even when he wants you to do something hard? What if it meant that, if you obeyed God, people might reject you or think bad things about you? That would be hard to do, wouldn't it? Yet Mary was asked to do just that. She knew if she said yes to God, it would mean certain rejection and ridicule.

2 If you knew that someone you loved was in danger, would you trust God to keep him or her safe? Would you be able to let God handle your fears and concerns?

3 Being a parent isn't always easy. (You might ask your parents if they would agree!) Ask your parents about what things they trust God for in raising you. Even though Mary was raising God's own son, it wasn't always easy for her, either.

4 Do you believe that God can do impossible things? What are some of the things that you trust God to do in your own life? Do you trust God can do the "impossible" for you?

5 Are you willing to trust God to bring good out of a bad situation? Suppose a grandparent gets sick, or a parent has just lost a job. Those are difficult situations for any family. How does trusting God help you and your family through these times?

Here's the Scoop

1 An angel announced that God would give Mary a son—the Son of God! Mary was probably just a teen at the time. Also, she wasn't married—only engaged to be married! If she had a son, others would think bad things about her. But Mary didn't grumble and say, "No way! Not me!" Instead, she said, "I am the servant of the Lord. Let this happen to me as you say!" (Luke 1:38). (Read about it in Luke 1:26–55, p. 1365.)

2 When Jesus was a young child, a jealous king wanted to kill him. This king was afraid that Jesus would one day take over his throne. But Mary's husband Joseph was warned in a dream to take the family to Egypt. Even though it meant that Mary and Joseph would have to leave their families and live in a foreign land, Mary trusted God to keep her son safe. (Look up Matthew 2:13–18, p. 1276.)

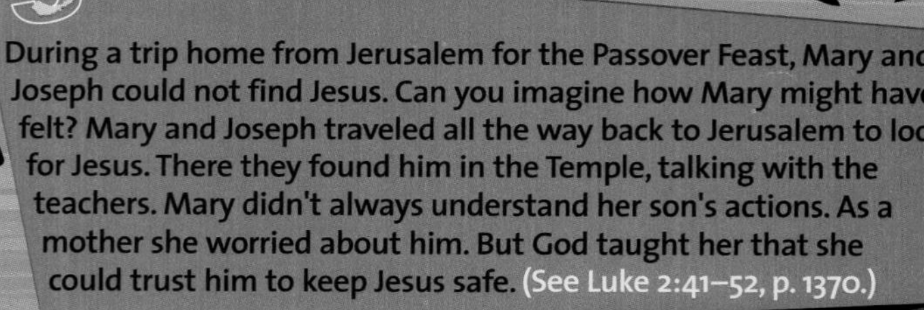

3 During a trip home from Jerusalem for the Passover Feast, Mary and Joseph could not find Jesus. Can you imagine how Mary might have felt? Mary and Joseph traveled all the way back to Jerusalem to look for Jesus. There they found him in the Temple, talking with the teachers. Mary didn't always understand her son's actions. As a mother she worried about him. But God taught her that she could trust him to keep Jesus safe. (See Luke 2:41–52, p. 1370.)

4 At a wedding in Cana, the host ran out of wine. That was embarrassing to the bride and groom. But Mary knew that one of the other wedding guests could help. Who was that guest? Her son Jesus, who was now an adult. She trusted him to do the impossible. And he did! He turned water into wine. Jesus did many more "impossible" things, like making the blind see, and forgiving people's sins, to demonstrate God's love and forgiveness. (Read John 2:1–11, p. 1424.)

5 One of the worst things that can happen to a parent is to watch his or her child suffer—and be unable to do anything about it. Mary stood near the cross where Jesus was crucified. She couldn't stop him from suffering. She couldn't take his place. She couldn't prevent him from dying. Yet Mary knew that Jesus died to pay the price for the sins of everyone—including her own. Mary was willing to trust him—her own son—as her Savior. Are you willing? (See John 19:25–26, p, 1457.)

answers page

and show them how angry I am!"
says the LORD.
"I will send a sword
to chase Elam
until I have killed
them all.
38 I will set up my
throne in Elam to
show that I am
king,
and I will destroy
its king and its
officers!" says
the LORD.

> My people have been like lost sheep. Their leaders have led them in the wrong way.
> —Jeremiah 50:6

39 "But I will make good things happen
to Elam again
in the future," says the LORD.

A Message to Babylon

50 This is the message the LORD
spoke to Babylon and the Babylonian people through Jeremiah the
prophet.
2 "Announce this to the nations.
Lift up a banner and tell them.
Speak the whole message and say:
'Babylon will be captured.
The god Bel will be put to shame,
and the god Marduk will be afraid.
Babylon's gods will be put to
shame,
and her idols will be afraid!'
3 A nation from the north will attack
Babylon
and make it like an empty desert.
No one will live there;
both people and animals will run
away."

4 The LORD says, "At that time
the people of Israel and Judah will
come together.
They will cry and look for the
LORD their God.
5 Those people will ask how to go to
Jerusalem
and will start in that direction.
They will come and join themselves
to the LORD.
They will make an agreement with
him that will last forever,
an agreement that will never be
forgotten.

6 "My people have been
like lost sheep.
Their leaders have
led them in the
wrong way
and made them
wander around in
the mountains
and hills.
They forgot where
their resting place
was.
7 Whoever saw my people hurt them.
And those enemies said, 'We did
nothing wrong.
Those people sinned against the
LORD, their true resting place,
the God their fathers trusted.'

8 "Run away from Babylon,
and leave the land of the
Babylonians.
Be like the goats that lead the
flock.
9 I will soon bring against Babylon
many great nations from the north.
They will take their places for war
against it,
and it will be captured by people
from the north.
Their arrows are like trained soldiers
who do not return from war with
empty hands.
10 The enemy will take all the wealth
from the Babylonians.
Those enemy soldiers will get all
they want," says the LORD.

11 "Babylon, you are excited and happy,
because you took my land.
You dance around like a young cow in
the grain.
Your laughter is like the neighing
of male horses.
12 Your mother will be very ashamed;
the woman who gave birth to you
will be disgraced.
Soon Babylonia will be the least
important of all the nations.
She will be an empty, dry desert.

13 Because of the LORD's anger,
no one will live there.
She will be completely empty.
Everyone who passes by Babylon
will be shocked.
They will shake their heads when
they see all her injuries.

14 "Take your positions for war against
Babylon,
all you soldiers with bows.
Shoot your arrows at Babylon! Do
not save any of them,
because Babylon has sinned
against the LORD.
15 Soldiers around Babylon, shout the
war cry!
Babylon has surrendered, her
towers have fallen,
and her walls have been torn
down.
The LORD is giving her people the
punishment they deserve.
You nations should give her what
she deserves;
do to her what she has done to
others.
16 Don't let the people from Babylon
plant their crops
or gather the harvest.
The soldiers treated their captives
cruelly.
Now, let everyone go back home.
Let everyone run to his own
country.

17 "The people of Israel are like a flock
of sheep that are scattered
from being chased by lions.
The first lion to eat them up
was the king of Assyria.
The last lion to crush their bones
was Nebuchadnezzar king of
Babylon."
18 So this is what the LORD All-
Powerful, the God of Israel, says:
"I will punish the king of Babylon and
his country
as I punished the king of Assyria.
19 But I will bring the people of Israel
back to their own pasture.
They will eat on Mount Carmel
and in Bashan.
They will eat and be full
on the hills of Ephraim and
Gilead."
20 The LORD says,
"At that time people will try to find
Israel's guilt,
but there will be no guilt.
People will try to find Judah's sins,
but no sins will be found,
because I will leave a few people
alive from Israel and Judah,
and I will forgive their sins.

21 "Attack the land of Merathaim.
Attack the people who live in
Pekod.
Chase them, kill them, and
completely destroy them.
Do everything I commanded you!"
says the LORD.

22 "The noise of battle can be heard all
over the country;
it is the noise of much
destruction.
23 Babylon was the hammer of the
whole earth,
but how broken and shattered that
hammer is now.
It is truly the most ruined
of all the nations.
24 Babylon, I set a trap for you,
and you were caught before you
knew it.
You fought against the LORD,
so you were found and taken
prisoner.
25 The LORD has opened up his
storeroom
and brought out the weapons of his
anger,
because the Lord GOD All-Powerful
has work to do
in the land of the Babylonians.
26 Come against Babylon from far away.
Break open her storehouses of
grain.
Pile up her dead bodies like heaps
of grain.
Completely destroy Babylon
and do not leave anyone alive.
27 Kill all the young men in Babylon;
let them be killed like animals.

How terrible it will be for them,
because the time has come for their defeat;
it is time for them to be punished.
28 Listen to the people running to escape the country of Babylon!
They are telling Jerusalem
how the LORD our God is punishing Babylon as it deserves
for destroying his Temple.

29 "Call for the archers
to come against Babylon.
Tell them to surround the city,
and let no one escape.
Pay her back for what she has done;
do to her what she has done to other nations.
Babylon acted with pride against the LORD,
the Holy One of Israel.
30 So her young men will be killed in her streets.
All her soldiers will die on that day," says the LORD.
31 "Babylon, you are too proud, and I am against you,"
says the Lord GOD All-Powerful.
"The time has come
for you to be punished.
32 Proud Babylon will stumble and fall,
and no one will help her get up.
I will start a fire in her towns,
and it will burn up everything around her."

33 This is what the LORD All-Powerful says:
"The people of Israel
and Judah are slaves.
The enemy took them as prisoners
and won't let them go.
34 But God is strong and will buy them back.
His name is the LORD All-Powerful.
He will surely defend them with power
so he can give rest to their land.
But he will not give rest to those living in Babylon."
35 The LORD says,
"Let a sword kill the people living in Babylon
and her officers and wise men!
36 Let a sword kill her false prophets,
and they will become fools.
Let a sword kill her warriors,
and they will be full of terror.
37 Let a sword kill her horses and chariots
and all the soldiers hired from other countries!
Then they will be like frightened women.
Let a sword attack her treasures,
so they will be taken away.
38 Let a sword attack her waters
so they will be dried up.
She is a land of idols,
and the people go crazy with fear over them.

39 "Desert animals and hyenas will live there,
and owls will live there,
but no people will ever live there again.
She will never be filled with people again.
40 God completely destroyed the cities of Sodom and Gomorrah
and the towns around them," says the LORD.
"In the same way no people will live in Babylon,
and no human being will stay there.

41 "Look! An army is coming from the north.
A powerful nation and many kings
are coming together from all around the world.
42 Their armies have bows and spears.
The soldiers are cruel and have no mercy.
As the soldiers come riding on their horses,
the sound is loud like the roaring sea.
They stand in their places, ready for battle.
They are ready to attack you, city of Babylon.

43 The king of Babylon heard about
those armies,
and he became helpless with fear.
Distress has gripped him.
His pain is like that of a woman
giving birth to a baby.

44 "Like a lion coming up from the thick
bushes near the Jordan River
to attack a strong pen for sheep,
I will suddenly chase the people of
Babylon from their land.
Who is the one I have chosen to do
this?
There is no one like me,
no one who can take me to court.
None of their leaders can stand up
against me."

45 So listen to what the LORD has
planned to do against Babylon.
Listen to what he has decided to
do to the people in the city of
Babylon.
He will surely drag away the young
ones of Babylon.
Their hometowns will surely be
shocked at what happens to
them.
46 At the sound of Babylon's capture,
the earth will shake.
People in all nations will hear
Babylon's cry of distress.

51 This is what the LORD says:
"I will soon cause a destroying
wind to blow
against Babylon
and the
Babylonian
people.
2 I will send foreign
people to destroy
Babylon
like a wind that
blows chaff away.
They will destroy
the land.
Armies will surround
the city
when the day of disaster comes
upon her.
3 Don't let the Babylonian soldiers
prepare their bows to shoot.
Don't even let them put on their
armor.
Don't feel sorry for the young men of
Babylon,
but completely destroy her army.
4 They will be killed in the land of the
Babylonians
and will die in her streets.
5 The Lord GOD All-Powerful
did not leave Israel and Judah,
even though they were completely
guilty
in the presence of the Holy One of
Israel.
6 "Run away from Babylon
and save your lives!
Don't stay and be killed because of
Babylon's sins.
It is time for the LORD to punish
Babylon;
he will give Babylon the
punishment she deserves.
7 Babylon was like a gold cup in the
LORD's hand
that made the whole earth
drunk.
The nations drank Babylon's wine,
so they went crazy.
8 Babylon has suddenly fallen and been
broken.
Cry for her!
Get balm for her pain,
and maybe she can be healed.

9 "Foreigners in Babylon say, 'We tried
to heal Babylon,
but she cannot be
healed.
So let us leave her
and each go to
his own country.
Babylon's
punishment is as
high as the sky;
it reaches to the
clouds.'

10 "The people of Judah
say, 'The LORD
has shown us to
be right.
Come, let us tell in Jerusalem
what the LORD our God has done.'

> The LORD has shown us to be right. Come, let us tell in Jerusalem what the LORD our God has done.
> —Jeremiah 51:10

11 "Sharpen the arrows!
Pick up your shields!
The LORD has stirred up the kings of the Medes,
because he wants to destroy Babylon.
The LORD will punish them as they deserve
for destroying his Temple.
12 Lift up a banner against the walls of Babylon!
Bring more guards.
Put the watchmen in their places,
and get ready for a secret attack!
The LORD will certainly do what he has planned
and what he said he would do against the people of Babylon.
13 People of Babylon, you live near much water
and are rich with many treasures,
but your end as a nation has come.
It is time to stop you from robbing other nations.
14 The LORD All-Powerful has promised in his own name:
'Babylon, I will surely fill you with so many enemy soldiers they will be like a swarm of locusts.
They will stand over you and shout their victory.'

15 "The LORD made the earth by his power.
He used his wisdom to build the world
and his understanding to stretch out the skies.
16 When he thunders, the waters in the skies roar.
He makes clouds rise in the sky all over the earth.
He sends lightning with the rain
and brings out the wind from his storehouses.

17 "People are so stupid and know so little.
Goldsmiths are made ashamed by their idols,
because those statues are only false gods.
They have no breath in them.
18 They are worth nothing; people make fun of them.
When they are judged, they will be destroyed.
19 But God, who is Jacob's Portion, is not like the idols.
He made everything,
and he chose Israel to be his special people.
The LORD All-Powerful is his name.

20 "You are my war club,
my battle weapon.
I use you to smash nations.
I use you to destroy kingdoms.
21 I use you to smash horses and riders.
I use you to smash chariots and drivers.
22 I use you to smash men and women.
I use you to smash old people and young people.
I use you to smash young men and young women.
23 I use you to smash shepherds and flocks.
I use you to smash farmers and oxen.
I use you to smash governors and officers.
24 "But I will pay back Babylon and all
the Babylonians for all the evil things
they did to Jerusalem in your sight," says
the LORD.
25 The LORD says,
"Babylon, you are a destroying mountain,
and I am against you.
You have destroyed the whole land.
I will put my hand out against you.
I will roll you off the cliffs,
and I will make you a burned-out mountain.
26 People will not find any rocks in Babylon big enough for cornerstones.
People will not take any rocks from Babylon to use for the foundation of a building,
because your city will be just a pile of ruins forever," says the LORD.

27 "Lift up a banner in the land!
Blow the trumpet among the nations!
Get the nations ready for battle against Babylon.
Call these kingdoms of Ararat, Minni, and Ashkenaz to fight against her.
Choose a commander to lead the army against Babylon.
Send so many horses that they are like a swarm of locusts.
28 Get the nations ready for battle against Babylon—
the kings of the Medes,
their governors and all their officers,
and all the countries they rule.
29 The land shakes and moves in pain,
because the LORD will do what he has planned to Babylon.
He will make Babylon an empty desert,
where no one will live.
30 Babylon's warriors have stopped fighting.
They stay in their protected cities.
Their strength is gone,
and they have become like frightened women.
Babylon's houses are burning.
The bars of her gates are broken.
31 One messenger follows another;
messenger follows messenger.
They announce to the king of Babylon
that his whole city has been captured.
32 The river crossings have been captured,
and the swamplands are burning.
All of Babylon's soldiers are terribly afraid."

33 This is what the LORD All-Powerful, the God of Israel, says:
"The city of Babylon is like a threshing floor,
where people crush the grain at harvest time.
The time to harvest Babylon is coming soon."

34 "Nebuchadnezzar king of Babylon has defeated and destroyed us.
In the past he took our people away,
and we became like an empty jar.
He was like a giant snake that swallowed us.
He filled his stomach with our best things.
Then he spit us out.
35 Babylon did terrible things to hurt us.
Now let those things happen to Babylon,"
say the people of Jerusalem.
"The people of Babylon killed our people.
Now let them be punished for what they did," says Jerusalem.

36 So this is what the LORD says:
"I will soon defend you, Judah,
and make sure that Babylon is punished.
I will dry up Babylon's sea
and make her springs become dry.
37 Babylon will become a pile of ruins,
a home for wild dogs.
People will be shocked by what happened there.
No one will live there anymore.
38 Babylon's people roar like young lions;
they growl like baby lions.
39 While they are stirred up,
I will give a feast for them
and make them drunk.
They will shout and laugh.
And they will sleep forever and never wake up!" says the LORD.
40 "I will take the people of Babylon to be killed.
They will be like lambs,
like sheep and goats waiting to be killed.

41 "How Babylon has been defeated!
The pride of the whole earth has been taken captive.
People from other nations are shocked at what happened to Babylon,
and the things they see make them afraid.
42 The sea has risen over Babylon;

its roaring waves cover her.
43 Babylon's towns are ruined and
empty.
It has become a dry, desert land,
a land where no one lives.
People do not even travel through
Babylon.
44 I will punish the god Bel in Babylon.
I will make him spit out what he
has swallowed.
Nations will no longer come to
Babylon;
even the wall around the city will
fall.

45 "Come out of Babylon, my people!
Run for your lives!
Run from the LORD's great anger.
46 Don't lose courage;
rumors will spread through the
land, but don't be afraid.
One rumor comes this year, and
another comes the next year.
There will be rumors of terrible
fighting in the country,
of rulers fighting against rulers.
47 The time will surely come
when I will punish the idols of
Babylon,
and the whole land will be disgraced.
There will be many dead people
lying all around.
48 Then heaven and earth and all that is
in them
will shout for joy about Babylon.
They will shout because the army
comes from the north
to destroy Babylon," says the
LORD.

49 "Babylon must fall, because she
killed people from Israel.
She killed people from everywhere
on earth.
50 You who have escaped being killed
with swords,
leave Babylon! Don't wait!
Remember the LORD in the
faraway land
and think about Jerusalem."

51 "We people of Judah are disgraced,
because we have been insulted.
We have been shamed,
because strangers have gone into
the holy places of the LORD's
Temple!"

52 So the LORD says, "The time is
coming soon
when I will punish the idols of
Babylon.
Wounded people will cry with pain
all over that land.
53 Even if Babylon grows until she
touches the sky,
and even if she makes her highest
cities strong,
I will send people to destroy her,"
says the LORD.

54 "Sounds of people crying are heard in
Babylon.
Sounds of people destroying things
are heard in the land of the
Babylonians.
55 The LORD is destroying Babylon
and making the loud sounds of the
city become silent.
Enemies come roaring in like ocean
waves.
The roar of their voices is heard all
around.
56 The army has come to destroy
Babylon.
Her soldiers have been captured,
and their bows are broken,
because the LORD is a God who
punishes people for the evil they
do.
He gives them the full punishment
they deserve.
57 I will make Babylon's rulers and wise
men drunk,
and her governors, officers, and
soldiers, too.
Then they will sleep forever and
never wake up," says the King,
whose name is the LORD All-
Powerful.

58 This is what the LORD All-Powerful
says:
"Babylon's thick wall will be
completely pulled down
and her high gates burned.
The people will work hard, but it
won't help;

their work will only become fuel
for the flames!"

A Message to Babylon

59This is the message that Jeremiah the prophet gave to the officer Seraiah son of Neriah, who was the son of Mahseiah. Seraiah went to Babylon with Zedekiah king of Judah in the fourth year Zedekiah was king of Judah. His duty was to arrange the king's food and housing on the trip. **60**Jeremiah had written on a scroll all the terrible things that would happen to Babylon, all these words about Babylon. **61**Jeremiah said to Seraiah, "As soon as you come to Babylon, be sure to read this message so all the people can hear you. **62**Then say, 'LORD, you have said that you will destroy this place so that no people or animals will live in it. It will be an empty ruin forever.' **63**After you finish reading this scroll, tie a stone to it and throw it into the Euphrates River. **64**Then say, 'In the same way Babylon will sink and will not rise again because of the terrible things I will make happen here. Her people will fall.' "

The words of Jeremiah end here.

The Fall of Jerusalem

52 Zedekiah was twenty-one years old when he became king, and he was king in Jerusalem for eleven years. His mother's name was Hamutal daughter of Jeremiah,[n] and she was from Libnah. **2**Zedekiah did what the LORD said was wrong, just as Jehoiakim had done. **3**All this happened in Jerusalem and Judah because the LORD was angry with them. Finally, he threw them out of his presence.

Zedekiah turned against the king of Babylon. **4**Then Nebuchadnezzar king of Babylon marched against Jerusalem with his whole army. They made a camp around the city and built devices all around the city walls to attack it. This happened on Zedekiah's ninth year, tenth month, and tenth day as king. **5**And the city was under attack until Zedekiah's eleventh year as king.

6By the ninth day of the fourth month, the hunger was terrible in the city; there was no food for the people to eat. **7**Then the city wall was broken through, and the whole army of Judah ran away at night. They left the city through the gate between the two walls by the king's garden. Even though the Babylonians were surrounding the city, Zedekiah and his men headed toward the Jordan Valley.

8But the Babylonian army chased King Zedekiah and caught him in the plains of Jericho. All of his army was scattered from him. **9**So the Babylonians captured Zedekiah and took him to the king of Babylon at the town of Riblah in the land of Hamath. There he passed sentence on Zedekiah. **10**At Riblah the king of Babylon killed Zedekiah's sons as he watched. The king also killed all the officers of Judah. **11**Then he put out Zedekiah's eyes, and put bronze chains on him, and took him to Babylon. And the king kept Zedekiah in prison there until the day he died.

12Nebuzaradan, commander of the king's special guards and servant of the king of Babylon, came to Jerusalem on the tenth day of the fifth month. This was in Nebuchadnezzar's nineteenth year as king of Babylon. **13**Nebuzaradan set fire to the Temple of the LORD, the palace, and all the houses of Jerusalem; every important building was burned. **14**The whole Babylonian army, led by the commander of the king's special guards, broke down all the walls around Jerusalem. **15**Nebuzaradan, the commander of the king's special guards, took captive some of the poorest people, those who were left in Jerusalem, those who had surrendered to the king of Babylon, and the skilled craftsmen who were left in Jerusalem. **16**But Nebuzaradan left behind some of the poorest people of the land to take care of the vineyards and fields.

17The Babylonians broke into pieces the bronze pillars, the bronze stands, and the large bronze bowl, called the Sea, which were in the Temple of the LORD. Then they carried all the bronze pieces to Babylon. **18**They also took the pots,

52:1 Jeremiah This is not the prophet Jeremiah but a different man with the same name.

shovels, wick trimmers, bowls, dishes, and all the bronze objects used to serve in the Temple. **19**The commander of the king's special guards took away bowls, pans for carrying hot coals, large bowls, pots, lampstands, pans, and bowls used for drink offerings. He took everything that was made of pure gold or silver.

20There was so much bronze that it could not be weighed: two pillars, the large bronze bowl called the Sea with the twelve bronze bulls under it, and the movable stands, which King Solomon had made for the Temple of the LORD.

21Each of the pillars was about twenty-seven feet high, eighteen feet around, and hollow inside. The wall of each pillar was three inches thick. **22**The bronze capital on top of the one pillar was about seven and one-half feet high. It was decorated with a net design and bronze pomegranates all around it. The other pillar also had pomegranates and was like the first pillar. **23**There were ninety-six pomegranates on the sides of the pillars. There was a total of a hundred pomegranates above the net design.

24The commander of the king's special guards took as prisoners Seraiah the chief priest, Zephaniah the priest next in rank, and the three doorkeepers. **25**He also took from the city the officer in charge of the soldiers, seven people who advised the king, the royal secretary who selected people for the army, and sixty other men from Judah who were in the city when it fell. **26**Nebuzaradan, the commander, took these people and brought them to the king of Babylon at the town of Riblah. **27**There at Riblah, in the land of Hamath, the king had them killed.

So the people of Judah were led away from their country as captives. **28**This is the number of the people Nebuchadnezzar took away as captives: in the seventh year, 3,023 Jews; **29**in Nebuchadnezzar's eighteenth year, 832 people from Jerusalem; **30**in Nebuchadnezzar's twenty-third year, Nebuzaradan, commander of the king's special guards, took 745 Jews as captives.

In all 4,600 people were taken captive.

Jehoiachin Is Set Free

31Jehoiachin king of Judah was in prison in Babylon for thirty-seven years. The year Evil-Merodach became king of Babylon he let Jehoiachin king of Judah out of prison. He set Jehoiachin free on the twenty-fifth day of the twelfth month. **32**Evil-Merodach spoke kindly to Jehoiachin and gave him a seat of honor above the seats of the other kings who were with him in Babylon. **33**So Jehoiachin put away his prison clothes, and for the rest of his life, he ate at the king's table. **34**Every day the king of Babylon gave Jehoiachin an allowance. This lasted as long as he lived, until the day Jehoiachin died.

Lamentations

FIVE SAD SONGS

Hi! Jeremiah the prophet, here. Have you ever cried a river of tears? Back when I was carrying God's message to his people, I cried so much I could have filled a river. The city of Jerusalem was in ruins. The walls were broken down, the houses burned, and most of the people were dead or sent away to a foreign land. The few people who remained were starving. Worst of all, the beautiful Temple of the Lord was destroyed and its treasures stolen by our enemies.

I wrote this book to tell people that God himself destroyed Jerusalem and the Temple as punishment for sin. This book is really five laments, or "sad songs," about our suffering. With the Temple destroyed, we had no place to worship. Had God abandoned us? No, his love never ends. Soon the time of punishment would be over and we would be allowed to return to our land. God would restore our nation.

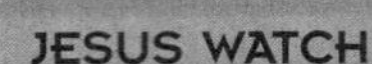

JESUS WATCH

In many ways, Jeremiah reminds us of Jesus. Both men were set apart for special work before they were even born. Jeremiah was chosen to be a prophet. Jesus was chosen to be our savior and king. Both men suffered rejection by the people around them. For 40 years Jeremiah warned the people that God would punish them for their sins, but people wouldn't listen. They continued to do just as they pleased. Jesus declared that he was the promised Messiah, but only a few people believed him. Some people even picked up rocks to hurl at him. Both wept over Jerusalem. Jeremiah was present when the city was destroyed by the Babylonians and was overcome with sadness. Many years after Jerusalem was rebuilt, Jesus wept because he knew that it would soon be destroyed again. Both men were arrested and left to suffer painful deaths. Jeremiah was thrown into a well where he was meant to sink down into the mud until he suffocated. The king sent soldiers to rescue him. Jesus was nailed to a cross and left to die. On the third day he rose from the dead.

OTHER CONNECTIONS

Livin' it Stop and really listen—listen to all the different noises around you, to the different voices telling you what to do. Stop to listen, and you quickly realize that the world is a pretty noisy place. Now try to hear God's voice above the din. Kinda hard, isn't it. Connect to Listen Up!, Lamentations 3:24–27, for some practical ways you can learn to listen to God's voice.

____

____

____

____

"When will the Lord's love end?"

"I know the answer to that one! Never! Check it out in Lamentations 3:22-23."

SOME OTHER SAD STUFF:

Looking for bread, Lamentations 1:11
God rejects the Temple, Lamentations 2:6–7
Return to the Lord, Lamentations 3:40–42

FAITH links

- Sow It and Reap, Lamentations 1:18
- Said It? Do It!, Lamentations 2:17
- When the Going Gets Tough, Lamentations 3:22–27

Jerusalem Cries over Her Loss

1 Jerusalem once was full of people,
but now the city is empty.
Jerusalem once was a great city
among the nations,
but now she[a] is like a widow.
She was like a queen of all the other
cities,
but now she is a slave.

2 She cries loudly at night,
and tears are on her cheeks.
There is no one to comfort her;
all who loved her are gone.
All her friends have turned against
her
and are now her enemies.

3 Judah has gone into captivity
where she suffers and works hard.
She lives among other nations,
but she has found no rest.
Those who chased her caught her
when she was in trouble.

4 The roads to Jerusalem are sad,
because no one comes for the
feasts.
No one passes through her gates.
Her priests groan,
her young women are suffering,
and Jerusalem suffers terribly.

5 Her foes are now her masters.
Her enemies enjoy the wealth they
have taken.
The LORD is punishing her
for her many sins.
Her children have gone away
as captives of the enemy.

6 The beauty of Jerusalem
has gone away.
Her rulers are like deer
that cannot find food.
They are weak
and run from the hunters.

7 Jerusalem is suffering and homeless.
She remembers all the good things
from the past.
But her people were defeated by the
enemy,
and there was no one to help her.
When her enemies saw her,
they laughed to see her ruined.

8 Jerusalem sinned terribly,
so she has become unclean.
Those who honored her now hate her,
because they have seen her
nakedness.
She groans
and turns away.

9 She made herself dirty by her sins
and did not think about what would
happen to her.
Her defeat was surprising,
and no one could comfort her.
She says, "LORD, see how I suffer,
because the enemy has won."

10 The enemy reached out and took
all her precious things.
She even saw foreigners
enter her Temple.
The LORD had commanded
foreigners
never to enter the meeting place of
his people.

11 All of Jerusalem's people groan,
looking for bread.
They are trading their precious
things for food
so they can stay alive.
The city says, "Look, LORD, and see.
I am hated."

12 Jerusalem says, "You who pass by on
the road don't seem to care.
Come, look at me and see:
Is there any pain like mine?
Is there any pain like that he has
caused me?
The LORD has punished me
on the day of his great anger.

13 "He sent fire from above
that went down into my bones.
He stretched out a net for my feet
and turned me back.

1:1 she In this poem the city of Jerusalem is described as a woman.

FAITH links

SOW IT AND REAP

LAMENTATIONS 1:18

Ever hear someone say, "You reap what you sow"? Sowing has to do with planting seed. If you plant corn, you expect corn to grow, rather than pumpkins. A person's actions are like the seed that is planted. If a person does bad things, bad things will happen to her. The Israelites disobeyed and reaped the consequences of their sin. Captivity in a strange land was the consequence.

When you choose to ignore a rule of your parents or of God, a punishment may result. Being punished is never pleasant. Yet correction can help you know right from wrong. Knowing the difference will help you make right choices in your life.

Need help in making the right decision? Link here:

This Hurts Me More?, 2 Chronicles 36:17–22, p. 606

Mind Guard, Proverbs 4:23, p. 831

Down on Discipline?, Proverbs 29:15, p. 867

A Blueprint for Living, Amos 5:14–15, p. 1200

Faith Workout, Acts 16:4–5, p. 1493

Cut to the Quick, Hebrews 4:12, p. 1670

He made me so sad and lonely
that I am weak all day.

14 "He has noticed my sins;
they are tied together by his hands;
they hang around my neck.
He has turned my strength into weakness.
The Lord has handed me over
to those who are stronger than I.

15 "The Lord has rejected
all my mighty men inside my walls.
He brought an army against me
to destroy my young men.
As if in a winepress, the Lord has crushed
the capital city of Judah.

16 "I cry about these things;
my eyes overflow with tears.
There is no one near to comfort me,
no one who can give me strength again.
My children are left sad and lonely,
because the enemy has won."

17 Jerusalem reaches out her hands,
but there is no one to comfort her.
The LORD commanded the people of Jacob
to be surrounded by their enemies.
Jerusalem is now unclean
like those around her.

18 Jerusalem says, "The LORD is right,
but I refused to obey him.
Listen, all you people,
and look at my pain.
My young women and men
have gone into captivity.

19 "I called out to my friends,
but they turned against me.
My priests and my older leaders
have died in the city
while looking for food
to stay alive.

20 "Look at me, LORD. I am upset
and greatly troubled.
My heart is troubled,

because I have been so stubborn.
Out in the streets, the sword kills;
inside the houses, death destroys.

21 "People have heard my groaning,
and there is no one to comfort me.
All my enemies have heard of my trouble,
and they are happy you have done this to me.
Now bring that day you have announced
so that my enemies will be like me.

22 "Look at all their evil.
Do to them what you have done to me
because of all my sins.
I groan over and over again,
and I am afraid."

The Lord Destroyed Jerusalem

2 Look how the Lord in his anger
has brought Jerusalem to shame.
He has thrown down the greatness of Israel
from the sky to the earth;
he did not remember the Temple, his footstool,
on the day of his anger.

2 The Lord swallowed up without mercy
all the houses of the people of Jacob;
in his anger he pulled down
the strong places of Judah.
He threw her kingdom and its rulers
down to the ground in dishonor.

3 In his anger he has removed
all the strength of Israel;
he took away his power from Israel
when the enemy came.
He burned against the people of Jacob like a flaming fire
that burns up everything around it.

4 Like an enemy, he prepared to shoot his bow,
and his hand was against us.
Like an enemy, he killed
all the good-looking people;
he poured out his anger like fire
on the tents of Jerusalem.

5 The Lord was like an enemy;
he swallowed up Israel.
He swallowed up all her palaces
and destroyed all her strongholds.
He has caused more moaning and groaning
for Judah.

6 He cut down his Temple like a garden;
he destroyed the meeting place.
The LORD has made Jerusalem forget
the set feasts and Sabbath days.
He has rejected the king and the priest
in his great anger.

7 The Lord has rejected his altar
and abandoned his Temple.
He has handed over to the enemy
the walls of Jerusalem's palaces.
Their uproar in the LORD's Temple
was like that of a feast day.

8 The LORD planned to destroy
the wall around Jerusalem.
He measured the wall
and did not stop himself from destroying it.
He made the walls and defenses sad;
together they have fallen.

9 Jerusalem's gates have fallen to the ground;
he destroyed and smashed the bars of the gates.
Her king and her princes are among the nations.
The teaching of the LORD has stopped,
and the prophets do not have
visions from the LORD.

10 The older leaders of Jerusalem
sit on the ground in silence.
They throw dust on their heads
and put on rough cloth to show their sadness.
The young women of Jerusalem

bow their heads to the ground in
sorrow.

11 My eyes have no more tears,
and I am sick to my stomach.
I feel empty inside,
because my people have been
destroyed.
Children and babies are fainting
in the streets of the city.

12 They ask their mothers,
"Where is the grain and wine?"
They faint like wounded soldiers
in the streets of the city
and die in their mothers' arms.

13 What can I say about you, Jerusalem?
What can I compare you to?
What can I say you are like?
How can I comfort you, Jerusalem?
Your ruin is as deep as the sea.
No one can heal you.

14 Your prophets saw visions,
but they were false and worth
nothing.
They did not point out your sins
to keep you from being captured.
They preached what was false
and led you wrongly.

15 All who pass by on the road
clap their hands at you;
they make fun of Jerusalem
and shake their heads.
They ask, "Is this the city that
people called
the most beautiful city,
the happiest place on earth?"

16 All your enemies open their mouths
to speak against you.
They make fun and grind their teeth
in anger.
They say, "We have swallowed you
up.
This is the day we were waiting for!
We have finally seen it happen."

17 The LORD has done what he planned;
he has kept his word
that he commanded long ago.
He has destroyed without mercy,
and he has let your enemies laugh
at you.
He has strengthened your
enemies.

FAITH links

SAID IT? DO IT!

LAMENTATIONS 2:17

If your mom or dad says, "Act up one more time and you're in for it!" you know he or she means what he/she says. God had told the Israelites that he would punish them if they disobeyed him. God followed through on what he said. Even though the consequence was a hard one for Israel, they learned that God was faithful to his word.

Following words with actions shows that you're a person who keeps your word. You may know someone who is all talk and no action. That person may say he'll do something, but does not follow through. Be a doer, not just a "sayer" of your words.

Ten Ways to Obey, Exodus 20, p. 103

Take My Advice, 1 Kings 2:2–4, p. 436

Mind Guard, Proverbs 4:23, p. 831

Too Young to Serve, Jeremiah 1:4–9, p. 988

Get Ready!, Mark 13:26–27, p. 1354

Attention, Please!, Luke 8:11–15, p. 1383

18 The people cry out to the Lord.
Wall of Jerusalem,
let your tears flow
like a river day and night.
Do not stop
or let your eyes rest.

19 Get up, cry out in the night,
even as the night begins.
Pour out your heart like water
in prayer to the Lord.
Lift up your hands in prayer to him
for the life of your children
who are fainting with hunger
on every street corner.

20 Jerusalem says: "Look, LORD, and see
to whom you have done this.
Women eat their own babies,
the children they have cared for.
Priests and prophets are killed
in the Temple of the Lord.

21 "People young and old
lie outside on the ground.
My young women and young men
have been killed by the sword.
You killed them on the day of your anger;
you killed them without mercy.

22 "You invited terrors to come against me on every side,
as if you were inviting them to a feast.
No one escaped or remained alive
on the day of the LORD's anger.
My enemy has killed
those I cared for and brought up."

The Meaning of Suffering

3 I am a man who has seen the suffering
that comes from the rod of the LORD's anger.
2 He led me
into darkness, not light.
3 He turned his hand against me
again and again, all day long.

4 He wore out my flesh and skin
and broke my bones.
5 He surrounded me with sadness
and attacked me with grief.
6 He made me sit in the dark,
like those who have been dead a long time.

7 He shut me in so I could not get out;
he put heavy chains on me.
8 I cry out and beg for help,
but he ignores my prayer.
9 He blocked my way with a stone wall
and led me in the wrong direction.

10 He is like a bear ready to attack me,
like a lion in hiding.
11 He led me the wrong way and let me stray
and left me without help.
12 He prepared to shoot his bow
and made me the target for his arrows.

13 He shot me in the kidneys
with the arrows from his bag.
14 I was a joke to all my people,
who make fun of me with songs all day long.
15 The LORD filled me with misery;
he made me drunk with suffering.

16 He broke my teeth with gravel
and trampled me into the dirt.
17 I have no more peace.
I have forgotten what happiness is.
18 I said, "My strength is gone,
and I have no hope in the LORD."

19 LORD, remember my suffering and my misery,
my sorrow and trouble.
20 Please remember me
and think about me.
21 But I have hope
when I think
of this:

22 The LORD's love
never ends;
his mercies never stop.
23 They are new every morning;
LORD, your loyalty is great.
24 I say to myself, "The LORD is mine,
so I hope in him."

EMAIL FROM GOD
3:21–22
Hope
Can you have hope in bad situations?

25 The LORD is good to those who hope
in him,
to those who seek him.
26 It is good to wait quietly
for the LORD to save.
27 It is good for someone to work hard
while he is young.

28 He should sit alone and be quiet;
the LORD has given him hard work
to do.
29 He should bow down to the ground;
maybe there is still hope.
30 He should let anyone slap his cheek;
he should be filled with shame.

31 The Lord will not reject
his people forever.
32 Although he brings sorrow,
he also has mercy and great love.
33 He does not like to punish people
or make them sad.

34 He sees if any prisoner of the earth
is crushed under his feet;
35 he sees if someone is treated
unfairly
before the Most High God;
36 the Lord sees
if someone is cheated in his case in
court.

37 Nobody can speak and have it happen
unless the Lord commands it.
38 Both bad and good things
come by the command of the Most
High God.
39 No one should complain
when he is punished for his sins.

40 Let us examine and see what we
have done
and then return to the LORD.
41 Let us lift up our hands and pray
from our hearts
to God in heaven:
42 "We have sinned and turned against
you,
and you have not forgiven us.

43 "You wrapped yourself in anger and
chased us;
you killed us without mercy.
44 You wrapped yourself in a cloud,
and no prayer could get through.
45 You made us like scum and trash
among the other nations.

WHEN THE GOING GETS TOUGH

LAMENTATIONS 3:22-27

Hard times can make life seem dark and hopeless. Jeremiah witnessed the invasion of Israel and the capture of his people because of God's judgment on their disobedience. Although things looked very bad, Jeremiah knew that God was good. He encouraged the people to put their hope in him. God was faithful. Someday he would help his people.

Whenever things go wrong in your life, you can trust that God is always faithful to his people. He won't forget about you.

Got a big problem? Connect here for some help:

Big Lack Attack, 2 Kings 4:1–7, p. 480

Happiness or Joy?, Job 29:18–19, p. 691

Fly Like an Eagle, Isaiah 40:28–31, p. 947

Your Feet on High Places, Habakkuk 3:18–19, p. 1239

Mission Impossible?, Mark 5:21–24, 35–43, p. 1337

Keep On Keepin' On, Revelation 13:10, p. 1744

LISTENING TO GOD

Lamentations 3:24–27

Livin' it

Listen Up! Stop sometime and count all the different people who want you to listen to them. Parents, brothers and sisters, teachers, friends, coaches, club leaders, and TV announcers are some of them. And they don't just want you to hear them—they want you to really listen. It's enough to make your ears and brain tired! How do you decide who to listen to and who to ignore?

God wants us to listen to him, too. Ever wonder how God speaks to a person? (Check out Job 33:14–17, p. 696.) God *does* speak to you through the Bible, through the Holy Spirit, and through people in your life. Are you quiet enough to hear him and *really* listen?

MORE FAITH links

Learning to Listen, p. 358

Listen Up!, p. 467

How God Speaks, p. 696

Hold On!, p. 1639

Pay Attention!, p. 1668

"Hey, Tagg, turn down that MIDI file! How can you hear yourself think?"

"I like to play my tunes good and loud. I don't need to hear myself think."

"Well, sometimes we need a bit of quiet, too, so we can hear what God has to say to us. Check it out in these Faithlinks!"

An Attention-Getter, Numbers 22, p. 207

- What would you do if your pet suddenly talked to you one morning, instead of barking, squeaking, or meowing? It would get your attention, wouldn't it? Link here to find out what God did to get someone's attention.

Prayer Priority, Luke 5:15–16, p. 1376

- What do you take time for each day? Things that are important and you take time for are *priorities.* For Jesus, prayer was a priority—is it for you?

You're a Fake!, 2 Peter 2:1, p. 1709

- Two sides of the story? Who do you listen to? This Faithlink helps you answer that question!

That's False!, 2 John 7–11, p. 1722

- Everyday your brain is filled with information—from school, from your friends, from the Internet, from TV. Do you know what's true and what's false? How much of the false do you allow in your brain? How do you know if you're listening to what God wants you to hear? If you're not sure, talk to your parents.

my FAVORITE links

46 "All of our enemies
open their mouths and speak
against us.
47 We have been frightened and fearful,
ruined and destroyed."
48 Streams of tears flow from my eyes,
because my people are destroyed.

49 My tears flow continually,
without stopping,
50 until the LORD looks down
and sees from heaven.
51 I am sad when I see
what has happened to all the
women of my city.

52 Those who are my enemies for no
reason
hunted me like a bird.
53 They tried to kill me in a pit;
they threw stones at me.
54 Water came up over my head,
and I said, "I am going to die."
55 I called out to you, LORD,
from the bottom of the pit.
56 You heard me calling, "Do not close
your ears
and ignore my gasps and shouts."
57 You came near when I called to you;
you said, "Don't be afraid."

58 Lord, you have taken my case
and given me back my life.
59 LORD, you have seen how I have
been wronged.
Now judge my case for me.
60 You have seen how my enemies took
revenge on me
and made evil plans against me.

61 LORD, you have heard their insults
and all their evil plans against me.
62 The words and thoughts of my
enemies
are against me all the time.
63 Look! In everything they do
they make fun of me with songs.

64 Pay them back, LORD,
for what they have done.
65 Make them stubborn,
and put your curse on them.
66 Chase them in anger, LORD,
and destroy them from under your
heavens.

The Attack on Jerusalem

4 See how the gold has lost its shine,
how the pure gold has dulled!
The stones of the Temple are
scattered
at every street corner.

2 The precious people of Jerusalem
were more valuable than gold,
but now they are thought of as clay
jars
made by the hands of a potter.

3 Even wild dogs give their milk
to feed their young,
but my people are cruel
like ostriches in the desert.

4 The babies are so thirsty
their tongues stick to the roofs of
their mouths.
Children beg for bread,
but no one gives them any.

5 Those who once ate fine foods
are now starving in the streets.
People who grew up wearing nice
clothes
now pick through trash piles.

6 My people have been punished
more than Sodom was.
Sodom was destroyed suddenly,
and no hands reached out to help
her.

7 Our princes were purer than snow,
and whiter than milk.
Their bodies were redder than
rubies;
they looked like sapphires.

8 But now they are blacker than coal,
and no one recognizes them in the
streets.
Their skin hangs on their bones;
it is as dry as wood.

9 Those who were killed in the war
were better off

than those killed by hunger.
They starve in pain and die,
because there is no food from the field.

10 With their own hands kind women
cook their own children.
They became food
when my people
were destroyed.

11 The LORD turned
loose all of his
anger;
he poured out his
strong anger.
He set fire to
Jerusalem,
burning it down to
the foundations.

The LORD turned loose all of his anger; he poured out his strong anger.
—Lamentations 4:11

12 Kings of the earth and people of the world
could not believe
that enemies and foes
could enter the gates of
Jerusalem.

13 It happened because her prophets
sinned
and her priests did evil.
They killed in the city
those who did what was right.

14 They wandered in the streets
as if they were blind.
They were dirty with blood,
so no one would touch their
clothes.

15 "Go away! You are unclean," people
shouted at them.
"Get away! Get away! Don't touch
us!"
So they ran away and wandered.
Even the other nations said,
"Don't stay here."

16 The LORD himself scattered them
and did not look after them
anymore.
No one respects the priests
or honors the older leaders.

17 Also, our eyes grew tired,
looking for help that never came.
We kept watch from our towers
for a nation to save us.

18 Our enemies hunted us,
so we could not even walk in the
streets.
Our end is near. Our
time is up.
Our end has come.

19 Those who chased us
were faster than
eagles in the sky.
They ran us into the
mountains
and ambushed us in
the desert.

20 The LORD's appointed king, who was
our very breath,
was caught in their traps.
We had said about him, "We will be
protected by him
among the nations."

21 Be happy and glad, people of Edom,
you who live in the land of Uz.
The cup of God's anger will come to
you;
then you will get drunk and go
naked.

22 Your punishment is complete,
Jerusalem.
He will not send you into captivity
again.
But the LORD will punish the sins of
Edom;
he will uncover your evil.

A Prayer to the Lord

5 Remember, LORD, what happened
to us.
Look and see our disgrace.
2 Our land has been turned over to
strangers;
our houses have been given to
foreigners.
3 We are like orphans with no father;
our mothers are like widows.
4 We have to buy the water we drink;

OTHER CONNECTIONS

GET THE INFO

Here are a few interesting places to stop and surf while reading through the Book of Ezekiel:

- When God told the Israelites to enter the land he promised them, it wasn't an easy task of just walking in and settling down. The Israelites had to wage a "holy war" to conquer the people already living there. Learn more about the different weapons both the Israelites and their enemies used in battle by logging onto Ancient War and Weapons, Ezekiel 23:24.
- Let's Visit Damascus, Ezekiel 27:18. Find out more about one of the oldest cities still existing in the world, which today is the capital of Syria.
- The Kings of Egypt, Ezekiel 29:1–16. The king of Egypt, also known as Pharaoh, had a lot of power. In fact, during those times, the king owned everything in the land. There were 30 different generations of pharaohs in Egyptian history. Link here to find out which Bible people had a "pharaoh encounter."

"Did you ever hear of dry bones coming to life?"

"Wow! That sounds pretty weird to me. Let's download Ezekiel 37 to find out."

CHECK THESE OUT:

Ezekiel's new hairstyle, Ezekiel 5
Wheels with eyes, Ezekiel 10
The useless vine, Ezekiel 15
A river that gives life, Ezekiel 47:1–12

FAITH links

- Our Awesome God, Ezekiel 1:26–28
- The Watchman, Ezekiel 3:16–22
- God's Instructions, Ezekiel 4:1–15
- Good Enough?, Ezekiel 8
- The Dead-end of the Occult, Ezekiel 13:17–23
- A Model of Forgiveness, Ezekiel 16:59–63
- A Hard Place, Ezekiel 28:25–26
- Empty Words, Ezekiel 33:30–33
- Believe the Impossible?, Ezekiel 37
- God's New Temple, Ezekiel 40—44

Ezekiel's Vision of Living Creatures

1 It was the thirtieth year, on the fifth
day of the fourth month of our captivity. I was by the Kebar River among the
people who had been carried away as captives. The sky opened, and I saw visions
of God.

2It was the fifth day of the month of
the fifth year that King Jehoiachin had
been a prisoner. **3**The LORD spoke his
word to Ezekiel son of Buzi in the land of
the Babylonians by the Kebar River.
There he felt the power of the LORD.

4When I looked, I saw a stormy wind
coming from the north. There was a great
cloud with a bright light around it and fire
flashing out of it. Something that looked
like glowing metal was in the center of
the fire. **5**Inside the cloud was what
looked like four living creatures, who
were shaped like humans, **6**but each of
them had four faces and four wings.
7Their legs were straight. Their feet
were like a calf's hoofs and sparkled like
polished bronze. **8**The living creatures
had human hands under their wings on
their four sides. All four of them had
faces and wings, **9**and their wings
touched each other. The living creatures
did not turn when they moved, but each
went straight ahead.

10Their faces looked like this: Each
living creature had a human face and the
face of a lion on the right side and the face
of an ox on the left side. And each one
also had the face of an eagle. **11**That was
what their faces looked like. Their wings
were spread out above. Each had two
wings that touched one of the other living
creatures and two wings that covered its
body. **12**Each went straight ahead. Wherever the spirit would go, the living creatures would also go, without turning.
13The living creatures looked like burning coals of fire or like torches. Fire went
back and forth among the living creatures. It was bright, and lightning flashed
from it. **14**The living creatures ran back
and forth like bolts of lightning.

15Now as I looked at the living creatures, I saw a wheel on the ground by
each of the living creatures with its four
faces. **16**The wheels and the way they
were made were like this: They looked
like sparkling chrysolite. All four of them
looked the same, like one wheel cross-
ways inside another wheel. **17**When they
moved, they went in any one of the four
directions, without turning as they went.
18The rims of the wheels were high and
frightening and were full of eyes all
around.

19When the living creatures moved,
the wheels moved beside them. When the
living creatures were lifted up from the
ground, the wheels also were lifted up.
20Wherever the spirit would go, the living
creatures would go. And the wheels were
lifted up beside them, because the spirit of
the living creatures was in the wheels.
21When the living creatures moved, the
wheels moved. When the living creatures
stopped, the wheels stopped. And when
the living creatures were lifted from the
ground, the wheels were lifted beside
them, because the spirit of the living creatures was in the wheels.

22Now, over the heads of the living
creatures was something like a dome that
sparkled like ice and was frightening.
23And under the dome the wings of the
living creatures were stretched out straight
toward one another. Each living creature
also had two wings covering its body. **24**I
heard the sound of their wings, like the
roaring sound of the sea, as they moved. It
was like the voice of God Almighty, a roaring sound like a noisy army. When the living creatures stopped, they lowered their
wings.

25A voice came from above the dome
over the heads of the living creatures.
When the living creatures stopped, they
lowered their wings. **26**Now above the
dome there was something that looked
like a throne. It looked like a sapphire
gem. And on the throne was a shape like
a human. **27**Then I noticed that from the
waist up the shape looked like glowing
metal with fire inside. From the waist
down it looked like fire, and a bright light
was all around. **28**The surrounding glow
looked like the rainbow in the clouds on a
rainy day. It seemed to look like the glory
of the LORD. So when I saw it, I bowed

FAITH links

OUR AWESOME GOD

EZEKIEL 1:26-28

You've heard a lot about the love of God and how you can have a relationship with him. Maybe you even think of him as the best friend you've ever had. That's great. But there's one other thing to consider about him: his holiness. The prophet Ezekiel had a vision of the glory of God. When he saw it, he fell facedown. Ezekiel was amazed at the presence of God.

God's holiness deserves our respect. How do you show what God's holiness means to you?

A Holiday Every Week, Leviticus 23:1–3, p. 166

A Song of Thanks, 1 Samuel 2, p. 356

Love That Will Last, Psalm 136, p. 813

What God "Hates," Proverbs 6:16–19, p. 835

Your Spiritual Roots, Zechariah 1:1–6, p. 1253

The Gift, John 3:16–18, p. 1427

facedown on the ground and heard a voice
speaking.

The Lord Speaks to Ezekiel

2 He said to me, "Human, stand up on
your feet so I may speak with you."
2While he spoke to me, the Spirit entered
me and put me on my feet. Then I heard
the LORD speaking to me.
3He said, "Human, I am sending you
to the people of Israel. That nation has
turned against me and broken away from
me. They and their ancestors have
sinned against me until this very day. **4**I
am sending you to people who are stubborn and who do not obey. You will say to
them, 'This is what the Lord GOD says.'
5They may listen, or they may not, since
they are a people who have turned
against me. But they will know that a
prophet has been among them. **6**You, human, don't be afraid of the people or their
words. Even though they may be like
thorny branches and stickers all around
you, and though you may feel like you
live with poisonous insects, don't be
afraid. Don't be afraid of their words or
their looks, because they are a people
who turn against me. **7**But speak my
words to them. They may listen, or they
may not, because they turn against me.
8But you, human, listen to what I say to
you. Don't turn against me as those people do. Open your mouth and eat what I
am giving you."
9Then I looked and saw a hand
stretched out to me, and a scroll was in it.
10He opened the scroll in front of me.
Funeral songs, sad writings, and words
about troubles were written on the front
and back.

3 Then the LORD said to me, "Human,
eat what you find; eat this scroll.
Then go and speak to the people of Israel." **2**So I opened my mouth, and he
gave me the scroll to eat.
3He said to me, "Human, eat this
scroll which I am giving you, and fill your
stomach with it." Then I ate it, and it was
as sweet as honey in my mouth.
4Then he said to me, "Human, go to
the people of Israel, and speak my words
to them. **5**You are not being sent to people whose speech you can't understand,
whose language is difficult. You are being
sent to Israel. **6**You are not being sent to
many nations whose speech you can't understand, whose language is difficult,
whose words you cannot understand. If I
had sent you to them, they would have
listened to you. **7**But the people of Israel
will not be willing to listen to you, because they are not willing to listen to me.
Yes, all the people of Israel are stubborn

and will not obey. 8See, I now make you
as stubborn and as hard as they are. 9I am
making you as hard as a diamond, harder
than stone. Don't be afraid of them or be
frightened by them, though they are a
people who turn against me."
10Also, he said to me, "Human, believe all the words I will speak to you, and
listen carefully to them. 11Then go to the
captives, your own people, and say to
them, 'The Lord GOD says this.' Tell
them this whether they listen or not."
12Then the Spirit lifted me up, and I
heard a loud rumbling sound behind me,
saying, "Praise the glory of the LORD in
heaven." 13I heard the wings of the living
creatures touching each other and the
sound of the wheels by them. It was a
loud rumbling sound. 14So the Spirit
lifted me up and took me away. I was unhappy and angry, and I felt the great
power of the LORD. 15I came to the captives from Judah, who lived by the Kebar
River at Tel Abib. I sat there seven days
where these people lived, feeling
shocked.

Israel's Warning

16After seven days the LORD spoke
his word to me again. He said, 17"Human, I now make you a watchman for Israel. Any time you hear a word from my
mouth, warn them for me. 18When I say
to the wicked, 'You will surely die,' you
must warn them so they may live. If you
don't speak out to warn the wicked to
stop their evil ways, they will die in their
sin. But I will hold you responsible for
their death. 19If you warn the wicked and
they do not turn from their wickedness
or their evil ways, they will die because
of their sin. But you will have saved your
life.
20"Again, those who do right may
turn away from doing good and do evil. If
I make something bad happen to them,
they will die. Because you have not
warned them, they will die because of
their sin, and the good they did will not
be remembered. But I will hold you responsible for their deaths. 21But if you
have warned those good people not to
sin, and they do not sin, they will surely

FAITH links

THE WATCHMAN 

EZEKIEL 3:16-22

The job of the keeper of a lighthouse is to warn ships of upcoming dangers. In the Old Testament, a watchman on a city wall had a similar job with some differences. A watchman had the responsibility of watching for the approaching enemy. Ezekiel had a similar responsibility. His job was to watch the people of Israel and warn them about God's coming judgment because of their sin. God warned Ezekiel to be faithful.

As Christians, we're to be faithful at telling others about Jesus to help them escape the coming judgment. Jesus' death has already made it possible for anyone to be found "not guilty."

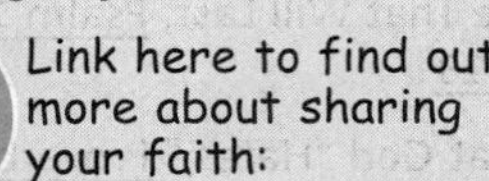

Link here to find out more about sharing your faith:

Can't Live Without It?, Genesis 3, p. 7

When Bad Turns to Worse, Exodus 5:6–12, p. 82

You're Out!, 2 Kings 17:5–7, p. 501

Red to White, Isaiah 1:18, p. 896

Tell All About Him!, Matthew 28:19, p. 1326

Just a Test, Luke 4:1–13, p. 1373

live, because they believed the warning.
And you will have saved your life."
22Then I felt the power of the LORD
there. He said to me, "Get up and go out
to the plain. There I will speak to you."
23So I got up and went out to the plain. I
saw the glory of the LORD standing there,
like the glory I saw by the Kebar River,
and I bowed facedown on the ground.
24Then the Spirit entered me and
made me stand on my feet. He spoke to
me and said, "Go, shut yourself up in
your house. 25As for you, human, the
people will tie you up with ropes so that
you will not be able to go out among
them. 26Also, I will make your tongue
stick to the roof of your mouth so you will
be silent. You will not be able to argue
with the people, even though they turn
against me. 27But when I speak to you, I
will open your mouth, and you will say to
them, 'The Lord GOD says this.' Those
who will listen, let them listen. Those
who refuse, let them refuse, because
they are a people who turn against me.

The Map of Jerusalem

4 "Now, human, get yourself a brick,
put it in front of you, and draw a map
of Jerusalem on it. 2Then surround it
with an army. Build battle works against
the city and a dirt road to the top of the
city walls. Set up camps around it, and
put heavy logs in place to break down the
walls. 3Then get yourself an iron plate
and set it up like an iron wall between
you and the city. Turn your face toward
the city as if to attack it and then attack.
This is a sign to Israel.
4"Then lie down on your left side, and
take the guilt of Israel on yourself. Their
guilt will be on you for the number of
days you lie on your left side. 5I have
given you the same number of days as
the years of the people's sin. So you will
have the guilt of Israel's sin on you for
three hundred ninety days.
6"After you have finished these three
hundred ninety days, lie down a second
time, on your right side. You will then
have the guilt of Judah on you. I will give
it to you for forty days, a day for each year
of their sin. 7Then you will look toward
Jerusalem, which is being attacked. With
your arm bare, you will prophesy against
Jerusalem. 8I will put ropes on you so
you cannot turn from one side to the
other until you have finished the days of
your attack on Jerusalem.
9"Take wheat, barley, beans, small
peas, and millet seeds, and put them in
one bowl, and make them into bread for
yourself. You will eat it the three hundred
ninety days you lie on your side. 10You

FAITH links

GOD'S INSTRUCTIONS 

EZEKIEL 4:1-15

Have you ever seen a stage play performed? The actors can make a scene come alive. Ezekiel had to act out the coming judgment on Israel. God told him exactly what to do and expected Ezekiel to follow his instructions to the letter.

God wants you to follow his instructions, too. You can find them in the Bible. As you live out these instructions, others will pay attention. Maybe someday, someone will ask you about Jesus.

See the Heart Behind It, Nehemiah 8; 9, p. 636

You're Invited!, Psalm 100, p. 784

Jesus' Mission and Yours, Isaiah 61:1–2, p. 978

God's New Temple, Ezekiel 40—44, p. 1135

Pass It On!, Joel 1:2–3, p. 1187

Believe It or Not, Luke 1:20, 38, p. 1366

will eat eight ounces of food every day at
set times. **11**You will drink about two-
thirds of a quart of water every day at set
times. **12**Eat your food as you would eat a
barley cake, baking it over human dung
where the people can see." **13**Then the
LORD said, "In the same
way Israel will eat un-
clean food among the na-
tions where I force them
to go."

14But I said, "No,
Lord GOD! I have never
been made unclean. From
the time I was young un-
til now I've never eaten
anything that died by it-
self or was torn by ani-
mals. Unclean meat has never entered
my mouth."

15"Very well," he said. "Then I will
give you cow's dung instead of human
dung to use for your fire to bake your
bread."

16He also said to me, "Human, I am
going to cut off the supply of bread to Jerusalem. They will eat the bread that is
measured out to them, and they will worry as they eat. They will drink water that
is measured out to them, and they will be
in shock as they drink it. **17**This is because bread and water will be hard to
find. The people will be shocked at the
sight of each other, and they will become
weak because of their sin.

Ezekiel Cuts His Hair

5 "Now, human, take a sharp sword, and
use it like a barber's razor to shave
your head and beard. Then take scales
and weigh and divide the hair. **2**Burn one-
third with fire in the middle of the city
when the days of the attack on Jerusalem
are over. Then take one-third and cut it
up with the knife all around the city. And
scatter one-third to the wind. This is how
I will chase them with a sword. **3**Also
take a few of these hairs and tie them in
the folds of your clothes. **4**Take a few
more and throw them into the fire and
burn them up. From there a fire will
spread to all the people of Israel.

5"This is what the Lord GOD says:
This is Jerusalem. I have put her at the
center of the nations with countries all
around her. **6**But she has refused to obey
my laws and has been more evil than the
nations. She has refused to obey my
rules, even more than nations around
her. The people of Jerusa-
lem have rejected my
laws and have not lived
by my rules.

7"So this is what the
Lord GOD says: You have
caused more trouble than
the nations around you.
You have not followed my
rules or obeyed my laws.
You have not even obeyed
the laws of the nations
around you.

8"So this is what the Lord GOD says: I
myself am against you, and I will punish
you as the nations watch. **9**I will do things
among you that I have not done before and
that I will never do anything like again,
because you do the things I hate. **10**So
parents among you will eat their children,
and children will eat their parents. I will
punish you and will scatter to the winds all
who are left alive. **11**So the Lord GOD
says: You have made my Temple unclean
with all your evil idols and the hateful
things you do. Because of this, as surely
as I live, I will cut you off. I will have no
pity, and I will show no mercy. **12**A third of
you will die by disease or be destroyed by
hunger inside your walls. A third will fall
dead by the sword outside your walls. And
a third I will scatter in every direction as I
chase them with a sword. **13**Then my anger will come to an end. I will use it up
against them, and then I will be satisfied.
Then they will know that I, the LORD,
have spoken. After I have carried out my
anger against them, they will know how
strongly I felt.

14"I will make you a ruin and a shame
among the nations around you, to be seen
by all who pass by. **15**Then the nations
around you will shame you and make fun
of you. You will be a warning and a terror
to them. This will happen when I punish
you in my great anger. I, the LORD, have
spoken. **16**I will send a time of hunger to

This is Jerusalem. I have put her at the center of the nations with countries all around her.
—Ezekiel 5:5

ish them for the way they have lived. The way they have judged others is the way I will judge them. Then they will know that I am the LORD."

Ezekiel's Vision of Jerusalem

8 It was the sixth year, on the fifth day of
the sixth month of our captivity. I was
sitting in my house with the older leaders
of Judah in front of me. There I felt the
power of the Lord GOD. 2I looked and
saw something that looked like a human.
From the waist down it looked like fire,
and from the waist up it looked like bright
glowing metal. 3It stretched out the
shape of a hand and caught me by the hair
on my head. The Spirit lifted me up between the earth and the sky. He took me
in visions of God to Jerusalem, to the entrance to the north gate of the inner
courtyard of the Temple. In the courtyard
was the idol that caused God to be jealous. 4I saw the glory of the God of Israel
there, as I had seen on the plain.
5Then he said to me, "Human, now
look toward the north." So I looked up
toward the north, and in the entrance
north of the gate of the altar was the idol
that caused God to be jealous.
6He said to me, "Human, do you see
what they are doing? Do you see how
many hateful things the people of Israel
are doing here that drive me far away
from my Temple? But you will see things
more hateful than these."
7Then he brought me to the entry of
the courtyard. When I looked, I saw a
hole in the wall. 8He said to me, "Human,
dig through the wall." So I dug through
the wall and saw an entrance.
9Then he said to me, "Go in and see
the hateful, evil things they are doing
here." 10So I entered and looked, and I
saw every kind of crawling thing and
hateful beast and all the idols of the people of Israel, carved on the wall all
around. 11Standing in front of these carvings and idols were seventy of the older
leaders of Israel and Jaazaniah son of Shaphan. Each man had his pan for burning
incense in his hand, and a sweet-smelling
cloud of incense was rising.
12Then he said to me, "Human, have
you seen what the older leaders of Israel
are doing in the dark? Have you seen
each man in the room of his own idol?
They say, 'The LORD doesn't see us. The

FAITH links

GOOD ENOUGH?

EZEKIEL 8

Most of us, if we're honest, think our behavior is good for the most part. We can easily think that someone else is capable of great evil, but not us! God showed Ezekiel a vision of the things that many leaders in Israel did—things God hated. These leaders thought that God did not notice their sin. But God saw everything. He knew that the people of Israel only pretended to worship him. He wanted them to be faithful to him once more.

God knows our hearts. We were all born with a desire to sin. Only Jesus gives us the freedom to choose to do right.

Here are some more Faithlinks on being faithful to Jesus:

Above the Law, 1 Kings 21, p. 470

A Memorial for Two Thieves, 1 Chronicles 7:21, p. 530

Let's Make a Deal, Daniel 1:8–21, p. 1150

A Fake Apology, Hosea 6:1–7, p. 1177

Perfectly Pleasing?, Matthew 5:1–12, p. 1280

A High Price, Romans 6:23, p. 1526

LORD has left the land.' " 13He also said
to me, "You will see even more hateful
things that they are doing."

14Then he brought me to the entrance of the north gate of the Temple of
the LORD, where I saw women sitting and
crying for Tammuz.[n] 15He said to me,
"Do you see, human? You will see things
even more hateful than these."

16Then he brought me into the inner
courtyard of the Temple. There I saw
about twenty-five men at the entrance to
the Temple of the LORD, between the
porch and the altar. With
their backs turned to the
Temple of the LORD, they
faced east and were wor-
shiping the sun in the
east.

17He said to me, "Do
you see, human? Is it un-
important that the people
of Judah are doing the
hateful things they have
done here? They have
filled the land with violence and made me
continually angry. Look, they are insulting me every way they can. 18So I will act
in anger. I will have no pity, nor will I
show mercy. Even if they shout in my
ears, I won't listen to them."

> The Temple was filled with the cloud, and the courtyard was full of the brightness from the glory of the LORD.
> —Ezekiel 10:4

Vision of the Angels

9 Then he shouted with a loud voice in
my ears, "You who are chosen to punish this city, come near with your weapon
in your hand." 2Then six men came from
the direction of the upper gate, which
faces north, each with his powerful weapon in his hand. Among them was a man
dressed in linen with a writing case at his
side. The men went in and stood by the
bronze altar.

3Then the glory of the God of Israel
went up from above the creatures with
wings, where it had been, to the place in
the Temple where the door opened. He
called to the man dressed in linen who
had the writing case at his side. 4He said
to the man, "Go through Jerusalem and
put a mark on the foreheads of the people
who groan and cry about all the hateful
things being done among them."

5As I listened, he said to the other
men, "Go through the city behind the
man dressed in linen and kill. Don't pity
anyone, and don't show mercy. 6Kill and
destroy old men, young men and women,
little children, and older women, but
don't touch any who have the mark on
them. Start at my Temple." So they
started with the older leaders who were
in front of the Temple.

7Then he said to the men, "Make the
Temple unclean, and fill the courtyards
with those who have been killed. Go
out!" So the men went
out and killed the people
in the city. 8While the
men were killing the peo-
ple, I was left alone. I
bowed facedown on the
ground and I cried out,
"Oh, Lord GOD! Will you
destroy everyone left
alive in Israel when you
turn loose your anger on
Jerusalem?"

9Then he said to me, "The sin of the
people of Israel and Judah is very great.
The land is filled with people who murder, and the city is full of people who are
not fair. The people say, 'The LORD has
left the land, and the LORD does not see.'
10But I will have no pity, nor will I show
mercy. I will bring their evil back on their
heads."

11Then the man dressed in linen with
the writing case at his side reported, "I
have done just as you commanded me."

The Coals of Fire

10 Then I looked and saw in the dome
above the heads of the living creatures something like a sapphire gem
which looked like a throne. 2The LORD
said to the man dressed in linen, "Go in
between the wheels under the living
creatures, fill your hands with coals of
fire from between the living creatures,
and scatter the coals over the city."

8:14 Tammuz Tammuz was a god in Babylon. Every year people thought this god died when the plants died. After they cried for him, they believed he came back to life, and the plants lived again.

captive. Then in the evening I dug
through the wall with my hands. I brought
my things out in the dark and carried
them on my shoulders as the people
watched.
8Then in the morning the LORD spoke
his word to me, saying: **9**"Human, didn't
Israel, who refuses to obey, ask you,
'What are you doing?'
10"Say to them, 'This is what the
Lord GOD says: This message is about
the king in Jerusalem and all the people
of Israel who live there.' **11**Say, 'I am a
sign to you.'
"The same things I have done will be
done to the people in Jerusalem. They
will be taken away from their country as
captives. **12**The king among them will
put his things on his shoulder in the dark
and will leave. The people will dig a hole
through the wall to bring him out. He will
cover his face so he cannot see the
ground. **13**But I will spread my net over
him, and he will be caught in my trap.
Then I will bring him to Babylon in the
land of the Babylonians. He will not see
that land, but he will die there. **14**All
who are around the king—his helpers
and all his army—I will scatter in every
direction, and I will chase them with a
sword.
15"They will know that I am the LORD
when I scatter them among the nations
and spread them among the countries.
16But I will save a few of them from the
sword and from hunger and disease.
Then they can tell about their hateful actions among the nations where they go.
Then they will know that I am the LORD."

The Lesson of Ezekiel's Shaking

17The LORD spoke his word to me,
saying: **18**"Human, tremble as you eat
your food, and shake with fear as you
drink your water. **19**Then say to the people of the land: 'This is what the Lord
GOD says about the people who live in
Jerusalem in the land of Israel: They will
eat their food with fear and drink their
water in shock, because their land will be
stripped bare because of the violence of
the people who live in it. **20**The cities
where people live will become ruins, and
the land will become empty. Then you
will know that I am the LORD.' "

The Visions Will Come True

21The LORD spoke his word to me,
saying: **22**"Human, what is this saying
you have in the land of Israel: 'The days
go by and every vision comes to nothing'? **23**So say to them, 'This is what the
Lord GOD says: I will make them stop
saying this, and nobody in Israel will use
this saying anymore.' But tell them, 'The
time is near when every vi-
sion will come true.
24There will be no
more false visions
or pleasing prophe-
cies inside the na-
tion of Israel, **25**but
I, the LORD, will speak. What I say will be
done, and it will not be delayed. You refuse to obey, but in your time I will say
the word and do it, says the Lord GOD.' "

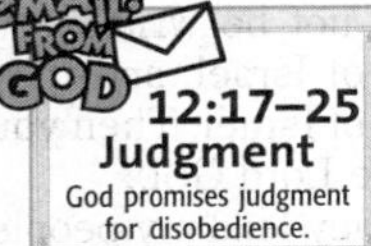
eMAIL! FROM GOD
12:17–25
Judgment
God promises judgment for disobedience.

26The LORD spoke his word to me,
saying: **27**"Human, the people of Israel
are saying, 'The vision that Ezekiel sees
is for a time many years from now. He is
prophesying about times far away.'
28"So say to them: 'The Lord GOD
says this: None of my words will be delayed anymore. What I have said will be
done, says the Lord GOD.' "

Ezekiel Speaks Against False Prophets

13 The LORD spoke his word to me,
saying: **2**"Human, prophesy against
the prophets of Israel. Say to those who
make up their own prophecies: 'Listen to
the word of the LORD. **3**This is what the
Lord GOD says: How terrible it will be for
the foolish prophets who follow their own
ideas and have not seen a vision from me!
4People of Israel, your prophets have
been like wild dogs hunting to kill and eat
among ruins. **5**Israel is like a house in
ruins, but you have not gone up into the
broken places or repaired the wall. So how
can Israel hold back the enemy in the battle on the LORD's day of judging? **6**Your
prophets see false visions and prophesy
lies. They say, "This is the message of the

LORD," when the LORD has not sent
them. But they still hope their words will
come true. 7You said, "This is the message of the LORD," but that is a false vision. Your prophecies are lies, because I
have not spoken.
8" 'So this is what the Lord GOD says:
Because you prophets spoke things that
are false and saw visions that do not
come true, I am against you, says the
Lord GOD. 9I will punish the prophets
who see false visions and prophesy lies.
They will have no place among my people. Their names will not be written on
the list of the people of Israel, and they
will not enter the land of Israel. Then you
will know that I am the Lord GOD.
10" 'It is because they lead my people
the wrong way by saying, "Peace!" when
there is no peace. When the people build
a weak wall, the prophets cover it with
whitewash to make it look strong. 11So
tell those who cover a weak wall with
whitewash that it will fall down. Rain will
pour down, hailstones will fall, and a
stormy wind will break the wall down.
12When the wall has fallen, people will
ask you, "Where is the whitewash you
used on the wall?"
13" 'So this is what the Lord GOD
says: I will break the wall with a stormy
wind. In my anger rain will pour down,
and hailstones will destroy the wall. 14I
will tear down the wall on which you put
whitewash. I will level it to the ground so
that people will see the wall's foundation.
And when the wall falls, you will be destroyed under it. Then you will know that
I am the LORD. 15So I will carry out my
anger on the wall and against those who
covered it with whitewash. Then I will
tell you, "The wall is gone, and those who
covered it with whitewash are gone.
16The prophets of Israel who prophesy
to Jerusalem and who see visions of
peace for the city, when there is no peace,
will be gone, says the Lord GOD." '

False Women Prophets

17"Now, human, look toward the
women among your people who make up
their own prophecies. Prophesy against
them. 18Say, 'This is what the Lord GOD

FAITH links

THE DEAD END OF THE OCCULT

EZEKIEL 13:17-23

Ouija boards. Séances. Psychics. They're all just simple party entertainment, right? If you think that, think again. God told Ezekiel to speak out against a group of women who called themselves prophets. They used so-called magic charms and encouraged people to sin. God wanted his people to be free from their lies and to listen only to his truth.

Many people today call psychics, hoping to catch a glimpse of the future. Others may seek those who claim to practice witchcraft, hoping to gain power. God is against these practices. Instead of being an avenue to truth, they're really a dead end. They allow the enemy of Christians—Satan—to control a person. Don't go there!

Don't get caught in a dead end! Connect here for God's wisdom:

What You Value, Genesis 25:21–34, p. 34

What He's Really Like, Deuteronomy 4:15–20, p. 233

The Fence Riders, 1 Kings 18, p. 464

A Hopeful Future, Jeremiah 29:11, p. 1031

Obeying God or Man?, Daniel 3:8–30, p. 1154

Long-lasting Hope, Hosea 14, p. 1184

says: How terrible it will be for women
who sew magic charms on their wrists
and make veils of every length to trap
people! You ruin the lives of my people
but try to save your own lives. **19**For
handfuls of barley and pieces of bread, you
have dishonored me among my people. By
lying to my people, who listen to lies, you
have killed people who
should not die, and you
have kept alive those who
should not live.

20" 'So this is what the
Lord GOD says: I am against
your magic charms, by
which you trap people as if
they were birds. I will tear
those charms off your
arms, and I will free those
people you have trapped
like birds. **21**I will also tear off your veils
and save my people from your hands.
They will no longer be trapped by your
power. Then you will know that I am the
LORD. **22**By your lies you have caused
those who did right to be sad, when I did
not make them sad. And you have encouraged the wicked not to stop being wicked,
which would have saved their lives. **23**So
you will not see false visions or prophesy
anymore, and I will save my people from
your power so you will know that I am the
LORD.' "

Stop Worshiping Idols

14 Some of the older leaders of Israel
came to me and sat down in front
of me. **2**Then the LORD spoke his word to
me, saying: **3**"Human, these men want to
worship idols. They put up evil things
that cause people to sin. Should I allow
them to ask me for help? **4**So speak to
them and tell them, 'This is what the
Lord GOD says: When any of the people
of Israel want to worship idols and put up
evil things that cause people to sin and
then come to the prophet, I, the LORD,
will answer them myself for worshiping
idols. **5**Then I will win back my people
Israel, who have left me because of all
their idols.'

6"So say to the people of Israel, 'This
is what the Lord GOD says: Change your
hearts and lives, and stop worshiping
idols. Stop doing all the things I hate.
7Any of the Israelites or foreigners in Israel can separate themselves from me by
wanting to worship idols or by putting up
the things that cause people to sin. Then
if they come to the prophet to ask me
questions, I, the LORD,
will answer them myself.
8I will reject them. I will
make them a sign and an
example, and I will sepa-
rate them from my peo-
ple. Then you will know
that I am the LORD.

9" 'But if the prophet
is tricked into giving a
prophecy, it is because I,
the LORD, have tricked
that prophet to speak. Then I will use my
power against him and destroy him from
among my people Israel. **10**The prophet
will be as guilty as the one who asks him
for help; both will be responsible for their
guilt. **11**Then the nation of Israel will not
leave me anymore or make themselves
unclean anymore with all their sins. They
will be my people, and I will be their GOD,
says the Lord GOD.' "

> This is what the Lord GOD says: Change your hearts and lives, and stop worshiping idols. Stop doing all the things I hate.
> —Ezekiel 14:6

Jerusalem Will Not Be Spared

12The LORD spoke his word to me,
saying: **13**"Human, if the people of a
country sin against me by not being loyal,
I will use my power against them. I will
cut off their supply of food and send a
time of hunger, destroying both people
and animals. **14**Even if three great men
like Noah, Daniel, and Job were in that
country, their goodness could save only
themselves, says the Lord GOD.

15"Or I might send wild animals into
that land, leaving the land empty and
without children. Then no one would
pass through it because of the animals.
16As surely as I live, says the Lord GOD,
even if Noah, Daniel, and Job were in the
land, they could not save their own sons
or daughters. They could save only
themselves, but that country would become empty.

17"Or I might bring a war against that

country. I might say, 'Let a war be fought in that land,' in this way destroying its people and its animals. **18**As surely as I live, says the Lord GOD, even if those three men were in the land, they could not save their sons or daughters. They could save only themselves.

19"Or I might cause a disease to spread in that country. I might pour out my anger against it, destroying and killing people and animals. **20**As surely as I live, says the Lord GOD, even if Noah, Daniel, and Job were in the land, they could not save their son or daughter. They could save only themselves because they did what was right.

21"This is what the Lord GOD says: My plans for Jerusalem are much worse! I will send my four terrible punishments against it—war, hunger, wild animals, and disease—to destroy its people and animals. **22**But some people will escape; some sons and daughters will be led out. They will come out to you, and you will see what happens to people who live as they did. Then you will be comforted after the disasters I have brought against Jerusalem, after all the things I have brought against it. **23**You will be comforted when you see what happens to them for living as they did, because you will know there was a good reason for what I did to Jerusalem, says the Lord GOD."

Story of the Vine

15 The LORD spoke his word to me, saying: **2**"Human, is the wood of the vine better than the wood of any tree in the forest? **3**Can wood be taken from the vine to make anything? Can you use it to make a peg on which to hang something? **4**If the vine is thrown into the fire for fuel, and the fire burns up both ends and starts to burn the middle, is it useful for anything? **5**When the vine was whole, it couldn't be made into anything. When the fire has burned it completely, it certainly cannot be made into anything."

6So this is what the Lord GOD says: "Out of all the trees in the forest, I have given the wood of the vine as fuel for fire. In the same way I have given up the people who live in Jerusalem **7**and will turn against them. Although they came through one fire, fire will still destroy them. When I turn against them, you will know that I am the LORD. **8**So I will make the land empty, because the people have not been loyal, says the Lord GOD."

The Lord's Kindness to Jerusalem

16 The LORD spoke his word to me, saying: **2**"Human, tell Jerusalem about her hateful actions. **3**Say, 'This is what the Lord GOD says to Jerusalem: Your beginnings and your ancestors were in the land of the Canaanites. Your father was an Amorite, and your mother was a Hittite. **4**On the day you were born, your cord[n] was not cut. You were not washed with water to clean you. You were not rubbed with salt or wrapped in cloths. **5**No one felt sorry enough for you to do any of these things for you. No, you were thrown out into the open field, because you were hated on the day you were born.

6" 'When I passed by and saw you kicking about in your blood, I said to you, "Live!" **7**I made you grow like a plant in the field. You grew up and became tall and became like a beautiful jewel. Your breasts formed, and your hair grew, but you were naked and without clothes.

8" 'Later when I passed by you and looked at you, I saw that you were old enough for love. So I spread my robe over you and covered your nakedness. I also made a promise to you and entered into an agreement with you so that you became mine, says the Lord GOD.

9" 'Then I bathed you with water, washed all the blood off of you, and put oil on you. **10**I put beautiful clothes made with needlework on you and put sandals of fine leather on your feet. I wrapped you in fine linen and covered you with silk. **11**I put jewelry on you: bracelets on your arms, a necklace around your neck, **12**a ring in your nose, earrings in your ears, and a beautiful crown on your head. **13**So you wore gold and silver. Your clothes were made of fine linen, silk, and

16:4 cord The umbilical cord that gives the unborn baby food and air from its mother.

beautiful needlework. You ate fine flour,
honey, and olive oil. You were very beautiful and became a queen. **14**Then you became famous among the nations, because
you were so beautiful. Your beauty was
perfect, because of the glory I gave you,
says the Lord GOD.

Jerusalem Becomes a Prostitute

15" 'But you trusted in your beauty.
You became a prostitute, because you
were so famous. You had sexual relations
with anyone who passed by. **16**You took
some of your clothes and made your
places of worship colorful. There you carried on your prostitution. These things
should not happen; they should never oc-
cur. **17**You also took your beautiful jewelry, made from my gold and silver I had
given you, and you made for yourselves
male idols so you could be a prostitute
with them. **18**Then you took your clothes
with beautiful needlework and covered
the idols. You gave my oil and incense as
an offering to them. **19**Also, you took the
bread I gave you, the fine flour, oil, and
honey I gave you to eat, and you offered
them before the gods as a pleasing smell.
This is what happened, says the Lord
GOD.

20" 'But your sexual sins were not
enough for you. You also took your sons
and daughters who were my children,
and you sacrificed them to the idols as
food. **21**You killed my children and offered them up in fire to the idols. **22**While
you did all your hateful acts and sexual
sins, you did not remember when you
were young, when you were naked and
had no clothes and were left in your
blood.

23" 'How terrible! How terrible it will
be for you, says the Lord GOD. After you
did all these evil things, **24**you built yourself a place to worship gods. You made for
yourself a place of worship in every city
square. **25**You built a place of worship at
the beginning of every street. You made
your beauty hateful, offering your body
for sex to anyone who passed by, so your
sexual sins became worse and worse.
26You also had sexual relations with the
Egyptians, who were your neighbors and
partners in sexual sin. Your sexual sins
became even worse, and they caused me
to be angry. **27**So then, I used my power
against you and took away some of your
land. I let you be defeated by those who
hate you, the Philistine women, who
were ashamed of your evil ways. **28**Also,
you had sexual relations with the Assyrians, because you could not be satisfied.
Even though you had sexual relations
with them, you still were not satisfied.
29You did many more sexual sins in Babylonia, the land of traders, but even this
did not satisfy you.

30" 'Truly your will is weak, says the
Lord GOD. You do all the things a stubborn prostitute does. **31**You built your
place to worship gods at the beginning of
every street, and you made places of
worship in every city square. But you
were not like a prostitute when you refused to accept payment.

32" 'You are a wife who is guilty of
adultery. You desire strangers instead of
your husband. **33**Men pay prostitutes,
but you pay all your lovers to come to
you. And they come from all around for
sexual relations. **34**So you are different
from other prostitutes. No man asks you
to be a prostitute, and you pay money instead of having money paid to you. Yes,
you are different.

The Prostitute Is Judged

35" 'So, prostitute, hear the word of
the LORD. **36**This is what the Lord GOD
says: You showed your nakedness to
other countries. You uncovered your
body in your sexual sins with them as
your lovers and with all your hateful
idols. You killed your children and offered
their blood to your idols. **37**So I will gather all your lovers with whom you found
pleasure. Yes, I will gather all those you
loved and those you hated. I will gather
them against you from all around, and I
will strip you naked in front of them so
they can see your nakedness. **38**I will
punish you as women guilty of adultery
or as murderers are punished. I will put
you to death because I am angry and jealous. **39**I will also hand you over to your
lovers. They will tear down your places

of worship and destroy other places where you worship gods. They will tear off your clothes and take away your jewelry, leaving you naked and bare. **40**They will bring a crowd against you to throw stones at you and to cut you into pieces with their swords. **41**They will burn down your houses and will punish you in front of many women. I will put an end to your sexual sins, and you will no longer pay your lovers. **42**Then I will rest from my anger against you, and I will stop being jealous. I will be quiet and not angry anymore.

43" 'Because you didn't remember when you were young, but have made me angry in all these ways, I will repay you for what you have done, says the Lord GOD. Didn't you add sexual sins to all your other acts which I hate?

44" 'Everyone who uses wise sayings will say this about you: "The daughter is like her mother." **45**You are like your mother, who hated her husband and children. You are also like your sisters, who hated their husbands and children. Your mother was a Hittite, and your father was an Amorite. **46**Your older sister is Samaria, who lived north of you with her daughters; your younger sister is Sodom, who lived south of you with her daughters. **47**You not only followed their ways and did the hateful things they did, but you were soon worse than they were in all your ways. **48**As surely as I live, says the Lord GOD, this is true. Your sister Sodom and her daughters never did what you and your daughters have done.

49" 'This was the sin of your sister Sodom: She and her daughters were proud and had plenty of food and lived in great comfort, but she did not help the poor and needy. **50**So Sodom and her daughters were proud and did things I hate in front of me. So I got rid of them when I saw what they did. **51**Also, Samaria did not do half the sins you do; you have done more hateful things than they did. So you make your sisters look good because of all the hateful things you have done. **52**You will suffer disgrace, because you have provided an excuse for your sisters. They are better than you are. Your sins were even more terrible than theirs. Feel ashamed and suffer disgrace, because you made your sisters look good.

53" 'But I will give back to Sodom and her daughters the good things they once had. I will give back to Samaria and her daughters the good things they once had. And with them I will also give back the good things you once had **54**so you may suffer disgrace and feel ashamed for all the things you have done. You even gave comfort to your sisters in their sins. **55**Your sisters, Sodom with her daughters and Samaria with her daughters, will return to what they were before. You and your daughters will also return to what you were before. **56**You humiliated your sister Sodom when you were proud, **57**before your evil was uncovered. And now the Edomite women and their neighbors humiliate you. Even the Philistine women humiliate you. Those around you hate you. **58**This is your punishment for your terrible sins and for actions that I hate, says the LORD.

God Keeps His Promises

59" 'This is what the Lord GOD says: I will do to you what you have done. You hated and broke the agreement you promised to keep. **60**But I will remember my agreement I made with you when you were young, and I will make an agreement that will continue forever with you. **61**Then you will remember what you have done and feel ashamed when you receive your sisters—both your older and your younger sisters. I will give them to you like daughters, but not because they share in my agreement with you. **62**I will set up my agreement with you, and you will know that I am the LORD. **63**You will remember what you did and feel ashamed. You will not open your mouth again because of your shame, when I forgive you for all the things you have done, says the Lord GOD.' "

The Eagle and the Vine

17 The LORD spoke his word to me, saying: **2**"Human, give a riddle and tell a story to the people of Israel. **3**Say, 'This is what the Lord GOD says: A

A MODEL OF FORGIVENESS

EZEKIEL 16:59-63

In order to learn some things, you need a model. If you wanted to draw a bowl of fruit, seeing one in front of you would help. If you wanted to improve your serve in tennis, watching someone else helps. God has always been the model for faithfulness and forgiveness. That's why God told Ezekiel that he would keep his promise to the people of Israel. He would forgive their sins, and do even more than he had ever promised them.

Even though we do wrong, and sin against God, he is always ready and willing to forgive us. He models forgiveness, so that we can forgive others.

Here are some more Faithlinks on why we need to forgive others:

Dirty Inside, Isaiah 6:1–7, p. 904

The God of Second Chances, Jonah 3, p. 1215

The Temptation Fighter, Matthew 4:1–11, p. 1278

Quick to Forgive?, Mark 11:25, p. 1349

Forgive Again?, Luke 17:3–4, p. 1402

A Happy Ending, Revelation 22:16–21, p. 1754

giant eagle with big wings and long feathers of many different colors came to Lebanon and took hold of the top of a cedar
tree. **4**He pulled off the top branch and
brought it to a land of traders, where he
planted it in a city of traders.

5" 'The eagle took some seed from
the land and planted it in a good field near
plenty of water. He planted it to grow like
a willow tree. **6**It sprouted and became a
low vine that spread over the ground.
The branches turned toward the eagle,
but the roots were under the eagle. So
the seed became a vine, and its branches
grew, sending out leaves.

7" 'But there was another giant eagle
with big wings and many feathers. The
vine then bent its roots toward this eagle.
It sent out its branches from the area
where it was planted toward the eagle so
he could water it. **8**It had been planted in
a good field by plenty of water so it could
grow branches and give fruit. It could
have become a fine vine.'

9"Say to them, 'This is what the Lord
GOD says: The vine will not continue to
grow. The first eagle will pull up the
vine's roots and strip off its fruit. Then
the vine and all its new leaves will dry up
and die. It will not take a strong arm or
many people to pull the vine up by its
roots. **10**Even if it is planted again, it will
not continue to grow. It will completely
dry up and die when the east wind hits it
in the area where it grew.' "

Zedekiah Against Nebuchadnezzar

11Then the LORD spoke his word to
me, saying: **12**"Say now to the people
who refuse to obey: 'Do you know what
these things mean?' Say: 'The king of
Babylon came to Jerusalem and took the
king and important men of Jerusalem and
brought them to Babylon. **13**Then he
took a member of the family of the king of
Judah and made an agreement with him,
forcing him to take an oath. The king also
took away the leaders of Judah **14**to make
the kingdom weak so it would not be
strong again. Then the kingdom of Judah
could continue only by keeping its agreement with the king of Babylon. **15**But the

king of Judah turned against the king of
Babylon by sending his messengers to
Egypt and asking them for horses and
many soldiers. Will the king of Judah succeed? Will the one who does such things
escape? He cannot break the agreement
and escape.
16" 'As surely as I live, says the Lord
GOD, he will die in Babylon, in the land of
the king who made him king of Judah.
The king of Judah hated his promise to
the king of Babylon and broke his agreement with him. **17**The king of Egypt with
his mighty army and many people will not
help the king of Judah in the war. The
Babylonians will build devices to attack
the cities and to kill many people. **18**The
king of Judah showed that he hated the
promise by breaking the
agreement. He promised
to support Babylon, but
he did all these things. So
he will not escape.
19" 'So this is what
the Lord GOD says: As
surely as I live, this is
true: I will pay back the
king of Judah for hating
my promise and breaking
my agreement. **20**I will
spread my net over him, and he will be
caught in my trap. Then I will bring him
to Babylon, where I will punish him for
the unfaithful acts he did against me.
21All the best of his soldiers who escape
will die by the sword, and those who live
will be scattered to every wind. Then you
will know that I, the LORD, have spoken.
22" 'This is what the Lord GOD says: I
myself will also take a young branch from
the top of a cedar tree, and I will plant it.
I will cut off a small twig from the top of
the tree's young branches, and I will plant
it on a very high mountain. **23**I will plant it
on the high mountain of Israel. Then it
will grow branches and give fruit and become a great cedar tree. Birds of every
kind will build nests in it and live in the
shelter of the tree's branches. **24**Then all
the trees in the countryside will know
that I am the LORD. I bring down the high
tree and make the low tree tall. I dry up
the green tree and make the dry tree
grow. I am the LORD. I have spoken, and I
will do it.' "

> As surely as I live, this is true: I will pay back the king of Judah for hating my promise and breaking my agreement.
> —Ezekiel 17:19

God Is Fair

18 The LORD spoke his word to me,
saying: **2**"What do you mean by
using this saying about the land of Israel:
'The parents have eaten sour grapes,
and that caused the children to
grind their teeth from the sour
taste'?
3"As surely as I live, says the Lord
GOD, this is true: You will not use this
saying in Israel anymore. **4**Every living
thing belongs to me. The life of the parent is mine, and the life of the child is
mine. The person who sins is the one
who will die.
5"Suppose a person is
good and does what is fair
and right. **6**He does not
eat at the mountain places
of worship. He does not
look to the idols of Israel
for help. He does not have
sexual relations with his
neighbor's wife or with a
woman during her time of
monthly bleeding. **7**He
does not mistreat anyone but returns
what was given as a promise for a loan. He
does not rob other people. He gives bread
to the hungry and clothes to those who
have none. **8**He does not lend money to
get too much interest or profit. He keeps
his hand from doing wrong. He judges
fairly between one person and another.
9He lives by my rules and obeys my laws
faithfully. Whoever does these things is
good and will surely live, says the Lord
GOD.
10"But suppose this person has a wild
son who murders people and who does
any of these other things. **11**(But the father himself has not done any of these
things.) This son eats at the mountain
places of worship. He has sexual relations with his neighbor's wife. **12**He mistreats the poor and needy. He steals and
refuses to return what was promised for
a loan. He looks to idols for help. He does
things which I hate. **13**He lends money

for too much interest and profit. Will this
son live? No, he will not live! He has
done all these hateful things, so he will
surely be put to death. He will be responsible for his own death.
14"Now suppose this son has a son
who has seen all his father's sins, but after seeing them does not do those things.
15He does not eat at the mountain places
of worship. He does not look to the idols
of Israel for help. He does not have sexual relations with his neighbor's wife.
16He does not mistreat anyone or keep
something promised for a loan or steal.
He gives bread to the hungry and clothes
to those who have none. **17**He keeps his
hand from doing wrong. He does not take
too much interest or profit when he lends
money. He obeys my laws and lives by
my rules. He will not die for his father's
sin; he will surely live. **18**But his father
took other people's money unfairly and
robbed his brother and did what was
wrong among his people. So he will die
for his own sin.
19"But you ask, 'Why is the son not
punished for the father's sin?' The son
has done what is fair and
right. He obeys all
my rules, so he will
surely live. **20**The
person who sins is
the one who will die.
A child will not be
punished for a par-
ent's sin, and a parent will not be punished for a child's sin. Those who do right
will enjoy the results of their own goodness; evil people will suffer the results of
their own evil.

EMAIL FROM GOD
18:19–20
Family
Will children be punished for the family's sin?

21"But suppose the wicked stop doing
all the sins they have done and obey all
my rules and do what is fair and right.
Then they will surely live; they will not
die. **22**Their sins will be forgotten. Because they have done what is right, they
will live. **23**I do not really want the wicked to die, says the Lord GOD. I want them
to stop their bad ways and live.
24"But suppose good people stop doing good and do wrong and do the same
hateful things the wicked do. Will they
live? All their good acts will be forgotten,
because they became unfaithful. They
have sinned, so they will die because of
their sins.
25"But you say, 'What the Lord does
isn't fair.' Listen, people of Israel. I am
fair. It is what you do that is not fair!
26When good people stop doing good and
do wrong, they will die because of it.
They will die, because they did wrong.
27When the wicked stop being wicked
and do what is fair and right, they will
save their lives. **28**Because they thought
about it and stopped doing all the sins
they had done, they will surely live; they
will not die. **29**But the people of Israel
still say, 'What the Lord does isn't fair.'
People of Israel, I am fair. It is what you
do that is not fair.
30"So I will judge you, people of Israel; I will judge each of you by what you
do, says the Lord GOD. Change your
hearts and stop all your sinning so sin
will not bring your ruin. **31**Get rid of all
the sins you have done, and get for yourselves a new heart and a new way of
thinking. Why do you want to die, people
of Israel? **32**I do not want anyone to die,
says the Lord GOD, so change your
hearts and lives so you may live.

A Sad Song for Israel

19 "Sing a funeral song for the leaders
of Israel. **2**Say:
'Your mother was like a female lion.
She lay down among the young lions.
She had many cubs.
3 When she brought up one of her
cubs,
he became a strong lion.
He learned to tear the animals he
hunted,
and he ate people.
4 The nations heard about him.
He was trapped in their pit,
and they brought him with hooks
to the land of Egypt.

5 " 'The mother lion waited and saw
that there was no hope for her cub.
So she took another one of her cubs
and made him a strong lion.
6 This cub roamed among the lions.
He was now a strong lion.

He learned to tear the animals he
hunted,
and he ate people.
7 He tore down their strong places
and destroyed their cities.
The land and everything in it
were terrified by the sound of his
roar.
8 Then the nations came against him
from areas all around,
and they spread their net over him.
He was trapped in their pit.
9 Then they put him into a cage with
chains
and brought him to the king of
Babylon.
They put him into prison
so his roar could not be heard
again
on the mountains of Israel.

10 " 'Your mother was like a vine in
your vineyard,
planted beside the water.
The vine had many branches and
gave much fruit,
because there was plenty of
water.
11 The vine had strong branches,
good enough for a king's
scepter.
The vine became tall
among the thick branches.
And it was seen, because it was tall
with many branches.
12 But it was pulled up by its roots in
anger
and thrown down to the ground.
The east wind dried it up.
Its fruit was torn off.
Its strong branches were broken off
and burned up.
13 Now the vine is planted in the desert,
in a dry and thirsty land.
14 Fire spread from the vine's main
branch,
destroying its fruit.
There is not a strong branch left on it
that could become a scepter for a
king.'

This is a funeral song; it is to be used as a funeral song."

Israel Has Refused God

20 It was the seventh year of our
captivity, in the fifth month, on the
tenth day of the month. Some of the older
leaders of Israel came to ask about the
LORD and sat down in front of me.

2 The LORD spoke his word to me, saying: 3 "Human, speak to the older leaders
of Israel and say to them: 'This is what
the Lord GOD says: Did you come to ask
me questions? As surely as I live, I will
not let you ask me questions.'

4 "Will you judge them? Will you judge
them, human? Let them know the hateful
things their ancestors did. 5 Say to them:
'This is what the Lord GOD says: When I
chose Israel, I made a promise to the descendants of Jacob. I made myself known
to them in Egypt, and I promised them, "I
am the LORD your God." 6 At that time I
promised them I would bring them out of
Egypt into a land I had found for them, a
fertile land, the best land in the world. 7 I
said to them, "Each one of you must
throw away the hateful idols you have
seen and liked. Don't make yourselves
unclean with the idols of Egypt. I am the
LORD your God."

8 " 'But they turned against me and
refused to listen to me. They did not
throw away the hateful idols which they
saw and liked; they did not give up the
idols of Egypt. Then I decided to pour out
my anger against them while they were
still in Egypt. 9 But I acted for the sake of
my name so it would not be dishonored in
full view of the nations where the Israelites lived. I made myself known to the Israelites with a promise to bring them out
of Egypt while the nations were watching. 10 So I took them out of Egypt and
brought them into the desert. 11 I gave
them my rules and told them about my
laws, by which people will live if they
obey them. 12 I also gave them my Sabbaths to be a sign between us so they
would know that I am the LORD who
made them holy.

13 " 'But in the desert Israel turned
against me. They did not follow my rules,
and they rejected my laws, by which people will live if they obey them. They dishonored my Sabbaths. Then I decided to

pour out my anger against them and destroy them in the desert. **14**But I acted for the sake of my name so it would not be dishonored in full view of the nations who watched as I had brought the Israelites out of Egypt. **15**And in the desert I swore to the Israelites that I would not bring them into the land I had given them. It is a fertile land, the best land in the world. **16**This was because they rejected my laws and did not follow my rules. They dishonored my Sabbaths and wanted to worship their idols. **17**But I had pity on them. I did not destroy them or put an end to them in the desert. **18**I said to their children in the desert, "Don't live by the rules of your parents, or obey their laws. Don't make yourselves unclean with their idols. **19**I am the LORD your God. Live by my rules, obey my laws, and follow them. **20**Keep my Sabbaths holy, and they will be a sign between me and you. Then you will know that I am the LORD your God."

> I am the LORD your God. Live by my rules, obey my laws, and follow them.
> —Ezekiel 20:19

21" 'But the children turned against me. They did not live by my rules, nor were they careful to obey my laws, by which people will live if they obey them. They dishonored my Sabbaths. So I decided to pour out my anger against them in the desert. **22**But I held back my anger. I acted for the sake of my name so it would not be dishonored in full view of the nations who watched as I brought the Israelites out. **23**And in the desert I swore to the Israelites that I would scatter them among the nations and spread them among the countries, **24**because they had not obeyed my laws. They had rejected my rules and dishonored my Sabbaths and worshiped the idols of their parents. **25**I also allowed them to follow rules that were not good and laws by which they could not live. **26**I let the Israelites make themselves unclean by the gifts they brought to their gods when they sacrificed their first children in the fire. I wanted to terrify them so they would know that I am the LORD.'

27"So, human, speak to the people of Israel. Say to them, 'This is what the Lord GOD says: Your ancestors spoke against me by being unfaithful to me in another way. **28**When I had brought them into the land I promised to give them, they saw every high hill and every leafy tree. There they offered their sacrifices to gods. They brought offerings that made me angry and burned their incense and poured out their drink offerings. **29**Then I said to them: What is this high place where you go to worship?' " (It is still called High Place today.)

30"So say to the people of Israel: 'This is what the Lord GOD says: Are you going to make yourselves unclean as your ancestors did? Are you going to be unfaithful and desire their hateful idols? **31**When you offer your children as gifts and sacrifice them in the fire, you are making yourselves unclean with all your idols even today. So, people of Israel, should I let you ask me questions? As surely as I live, says the Lord GOD, I will not accept questions from you.

32" 'What you want will not come true. You say, "We want to be like the other nations, like the people in other lands. We want to worship idols made of wood and stone." **33**As surely as I live, says the Lord GOD, I will use my great power and strength and anger to rule over you. **34**I will bring you out from the foreign nations. With my great power and strength and anger I will gather you from the lands where you are scattered. **35**I will bring you among the nations as I brought your ancestors into the desert with Moses. There I will judge you face to face. **36**I will judge you the same way I judged your ancestors in the desert of the land of Egypt, says the Lord GOD. **37**I will count you like sheep and will bring you into line with my agreement. **38**I will get rid of those who refuse to obey me and who turn against me. I will bring them out of the land where they are now

living, but they will never enter the land
of Israel. Then you will know that I am
the LORD.
39" 'This is what the Lord GOD says:
People of Israel, go serve your idols for
now. But later you will listen to me; you
will not continue to dishonor my holy
name with your gifts and gods. 40On my
holy mountain, the high mountain of Israel, all Israel will serve me in the land,
says the Lord GOD. There I will accept
you. There I will expect your offerings,
the first harvest of your offerings, and all
your holy gifts. 41I will accept you like
the pleasing smell of sacrifices when I
bring you out from the foreign nations
and gather you from the lands where you
are scattered. Then through you I will
show how holy I am so the nations will
see. 42When I bring you into the land of
Israel, the land I promised your ancestors, you will know that I am the LORD.
43There you will remember everything
you did that made you unclean, and then
you will hate yourselves for all the evil
things you have done. 44I will deal with
you for the sake of my name, not because
of your evil ways or unclean actions.
Then you will know I am the LORD, people of Israel, says the Lord GOD.' "

Babylon, the Lord's Sword

45Now the LORD spoke his word to
me, saying: 46"Human, look toward the
south. Prophesy against the south and
against the forest of the southern area.
47Say to that forest: 'Hear the word of
the LORD. This is what the Lord GOD
says: I am ready to start a fire in you that
will destroy all your green trees and all
your dry trees. The flames that burn will
not be put out. Every face from south to
north will feel their heat. 48Then all the
people will see that I, the LORD, have
started the fire. It will not be put out.' "
49Then I said, "Ah, Lord GOD! The
people are saying about me, 'He is only
telling stories.' "

21 Then the LORD spoke his word to
me, saying: 2"Human, look toward Jerusalem and speak against the
holy place. Prophesy against the land of
Israel. 3Say to Israel: 'This is what the
LORD says: I am against you. I will pull
my sword out of its holder, and I will cut
off from you both the wicked and those
who do right. 4Because I am going to cut
off the wicked and those who do right, my
sword will come out from its holder and
attack all people from south to north.
5Then all people will know that I, the
LORD, have pulled my sword out from its
holder. My sword will not go back in
again.'
6"So, human, groan with breaking
heart and great sadness. Groan in front of
the people. 7When they ask you, 'Why
are you groaning?' you will say, 'Because
of what I have heard is going to happen.
When it happens, every heart will melt
with fear, and all hands will become weak.
Everyone will be afraid; all knees will
become weak as water. Look, it is coming, and it will happen, says the Lord
GOD.' "
8The LORD spoke his word to me, saying: 9"Human, prophesy and say, 'This is
what the Lord says:
A sword, a sword,
made sharp and polished.
10It is made sharp for the killing.
It is polished to flash like lightning.
" 'You are not happy about this horrible punishment by the sword. But my son
Judah, you did not change when you were
only beaten with a rod.
11The sword should be polished.
It is meant to be held in the hand.
It is made sharp and polished,
ready for the hand of a killer.
12Shout and yell, human,
because the sword is meant for my
people,
for all the rulers of Israel.
They will be killed by the sword,
along with my people.
So beat your chest in sadness.
13" 'The test will come. And Judah,
who is hated by the armies of Babylon,
will not last, says the Lord GOD.'
14"So, human, prophesy
and clap your hands.
Let the sword strike
two or three times.
It is a sword meant for killing,

a sword meant for much killing.
This sword surrounds the people
to be killed.
15 Their hearts will melt with fear,
and many people will die.
I have placed the
killing sword
at all their city
gates.
Oh! The sword is
made to flash like
lightning.
It is held, ready for
killing.
16 Sword, cut on the
right side;
then cut on the left
side.
Cut anywhere your blade is
turned.
17 I will also clap my hands
and use up my anger.
I, the LORD, have spoken."

> Those who are important now will be made unimportant, and those who are unimportant now will be made important.
> —Ezekiel 21:26

Jerusalem to Be Destroyed

18The LORD spoke his word to me,
saying: 19"Human, mark two roads that
the king of Babylon and his sword can follow. Both of these roads will start from
the same country. And make signs where
the road divides and one way goes toward
the city. 20Mark one sign to show the
road he can take with his sword to Rabbah in the land of the Ammonites. Mark
the other sign to show the road to Judah
and Jerusalem, which is protected with
strong walls. 21The king of Babylon has
come to where the road divides, and he is
using magic. He throws lots with arrows
and asks questions of his family idols. He
looks at the liver of a sacrificed animal to
learn where he should go. 22The lot in
his right hand tells him to go to Jerusalem. It tells him to use logs to break
down the city gates, to shout the battle
cry and give the order to kill, and to build
a dirt road to the top of the walls and devices to attack the walls. 23The people of
Jerusalem have made agreements with
other nations to help them fight Babylon.
So they will think this prediction is
wrong, but it is really proof of their sin,
and they will be captured.

24"So this is what the Lord GOD says:
'You have shown how sinful you are by
turning against the LORD. Your sins are
seen in all the things you do. Because of
this proof against you, you will be taken
captive by the enemy.
25" 'You unclean and
evil leader of Israel, you
will be killed! The time of
your final punishment has
come. 26This is what the
Lord GOD says: Take off
the royal turban, and re-
move the crown. Things
will change. Those who
are important now will be
made unimportant, and
those who are unimportant now will be
made important. 27A ruin! A ruin! I will
make it a ruin! This place will not be rebuilt until the one comes who has a right
to be king. Then I will give him that right.'

The Punishment of Ammon

28"And you, human, prophesy and
say: 'This is what the Lord GOD says
about the people of Ammon and their insults:
A sword, a sword
is pulled out of its holder.
It is polished to kill and destroy,
to flash like lightning!
29 Prophets see false visions about you
and prophesy lies about you.
The sword will be put on the necks
of these unclean and evil people.
Their day of judging has come;
the time of final punishment has
come.
30 Put the sword back in its holder.
I will judge you
in the place where you were created,
in the land where you were born.
31 I will pour out my anger against you
and blast you with the fire of my
anger.
I will hand you over to cruel men,
experts in destruction.
32 You will be like fuel for the fire;
you will die in the land.
You will not be remembered,
because I, the LORD, have
spoken.' "

The Sins of Jerusalem

22 The LORD spoke his word to me,
saying: 2"And you, human, will
you judge? Will you judge the city of murderers? Then tell her about all her hateful acts. 3You are to say: 'This is what the
Lord GOD says: You are a city that kills
those who come to live there. You make
yourself unclean by making idols. 4You
have become guilty of murder and have
become unclean by your idols which you
have made. So you have brought your
time of punishment near; you have come
to the end of your years. That is why I
have made you a shame to the nations
and why all lands laugh at you. 5Those
near and those far away laugh at you with
your bad name, you city full of confusion.
6" 'Jerusalem, see how each ruler of
Israel in you has been trying to kill people. 7The
people in you hate their
fathers and mothers. They
mistreat the foreigners in
you and wrong the or-
phans and widows in you.
8You hate my holy things
and dishonor my Sab-
baths. 9The men in you
tell lies to cause the death
of others. The people in
you eat food offered to idols at the mountain places of worship, and they take part
in sexual sins. 10The men in you have
sexual relations with their fathers' wives
and with women who are unclean, during
their time of monthly bleeding. 11One
man in you does a hateful act with his
neighbor's wife, while another has shame-
fully made his daughter-in-law unclean
sexually. And another forces his half sister
to have sexual relations with him. 12The
people in you take money to kill others.
You take unfair interest and profits and
make profits by mistreating your neighbor. And you have forgotten me, says the
Lord GOD.
13" 'So, Jerusalem, I will shake my
fist at you for stealing money and for
murdering people. 14Will you still be
brave and strong when I punish you? I,
the LORD, have spoken, and I will act. 15I
will scatter you among the nations and
spread you through the countries. That is
how I will get rid of your uncleanness.
16But you, yourself, will be dishonored in
the sight of the nations. Then you will
know that I am the LORD.' "

> I will put you together and make you feel the heat of my anger. You will be melted down inside Jerusalem.
>
> —Ezekiel 22:21

Israel Is Worthless

17The LORD spoke his word to me,
saying: 18"Human, the people of Israel
have become useless like scum to me.
They are like the copper, tin, iron, and
lead left in the furnace when silver is purified. 19So this is what the Lord GOD
says: 'Because you have become useless
like scum, I am going to put you together
inside Jerusalem. 20People put silver,
copper, iron, lead, and tin together inside
a furnace to melt them down in a blazing
fire. In the same way I will gather you in
my hot anger and put you
together in Jerusalem and
melt you down. 21I will
put you together and
make you feel the heat of
my anger. You will be
melted down inside Je-
rusalem. 22As silver is
melted in a furnace, you
will be melted inside the
city. Then you will know
that I, the LORD, have
poured out my anger on you.' "

Sins of the People

23The LORD spoke his word to me,
saying: 24"Human, say to the land, 'You
are a land that has not had rain or showers when God is angry.' 25Like a roaring
lion that tears the animal it has caught,
Israel's rulers make evil plans. They
have destroyed lives and have taken treasure and valuable things. They have
caused many women to become widows.
26Israel's priests do cruel things to my
teachings and do not honor my holy
things. They make no difference between
holy and unholy things, and they teach
there is no difference between clean and
unclean things. They do not remember
my Sabbaths, so I am dishonored by
them. 27Like wolves tearing a dead animal, Jerusalem's leaders have killed people for profit. 28And the prophets try to

cover this up by false visions and by lying
messages. They say, 'This is what the
Lord GOD says' when the LORD has not
spoken. **29**The people cheat others and
steal. They hurt people who are poor and
needy. They cheat foreigners and do not
treat them fairly.

30"I looked for someone to build up
the walls and to stand before me where
the walls are broken to defend these people so I would not have to destroy them.
But I could not find anyone. **31**So I let
them see my anger. I destroyed them
with an anger that was like fire because of
all the things they have done, says the
Lord GOD."

Samaria and Jerusalem

23 The LORD spoke his word to me,
saying: **2**"Human, a woman had
two daughters. **3**While they were young,
they went to Egypt and became prostitutes. They let men touch and hold their
breasts. **4**The older girl was named Oholah, and her sister was named Oholibah.
They became my wives and had sons and
daughters. Oholah is Samaria, and Oholibah is Jerusalem.*

5"While still my wife, Samaria had
sexual relations with other men. She had
great sexual desire for her lovers, men
from Assyria. The Assyrians were warriors and **6**wore blue uniforms. They
were all handsome young captains and
lieutenants riding on horseback. **7**Samaria became a prostitute for all the important men in Assyria and made herself
unclean with all the idols of everyone she
desired. **8**She continued the prostitution
she began in Egypt. When she was
young, she had slept with men, and they
touched her breasts and had sexual relations with her.

9"So I handed her over to her lovers,
the Assyrians, that she wanted so badly.
10They stripped her naked and took
away her sons and daughters. Then they
killed her with a sword. Women everywhere began talking about how she had
been punished.

11"Her sister Jerusalem saw what
happened, but she became worse than
her sister in her sexual desire and prostitution. **12**She also desired the Assyrians,
who were all soldiers in beautiful uniforms—handsome young captains and
lieutenants riding horses. **13**I saw that
both girls were alike; both were prostitutes.

14"But Jerusalem went even further.
She saw carvings of Babylonian men on a
wall. They wore red **15**and had belts
around their waists and turbans on their
heads. They all looked like chariot officers born in Babylonia. **16**When she saw
them, she wanted to have sexual relations with them and sent messengers to
them in Babylonia. **17**So these Babylonian men came and had sexual relations
with her and made her unclean. After
that, she became sick of them. **18**But she
continued her prostitution so openly that
everyone knew about it. And I finally became sick of her, as I had her sister.
19But she remembered how she was a
young prostitute in Egypt, so she took
part in even more prostitution. **20**She
wanted men who behaved like animals in
their sexual desire. **21**In the same way
you desired to do the sinful things you
had done in Egypt. There men touched
and held your young breasts.

God's Judgment on Jerusalem

22"So, Jerusalem, this is what the
Lord GOD says: You are tired of your lovers. So now I will make them angry with
you and have them attack you from all
sides. **23**Men from Babylon and all Babylonia and men from Pekod, Shoa, and
Koa will attack you. All the Assyrians will
attack you: handsome young captains and
lieutenants, all of them important men
and all riding horses. **24**Those men will
attack with great armies and with their
weapons, chariots, and wagons. They will
surround you with large and small
shields and with helmets. And I will give
them the right to punish you, and they
will give you their own kind of punishment. **25**Then you will see how strong
my anger can be when they punish you in

23:4 Oholah . . . Jerusalem Throughout this chapter Samaria is used in place of Oholah, and Jerusalem is used in place of Oholibah.

ANCIENT WAR AND WEAPONS Ezekiel 23:24

In Old Testament times, there were a lot of wars over land. The Israelites fought in many of these kinds of wars as they moved into the land that God had promised them. One of the most famous is the war that Joshua led the people in at Jericho. To the Israelites, this was a "holy war" that God called them to fight in. In fact, Joshua told the priests and soldiers that the Lord had given them the city of Jericho. (See Joshua 6:16, p. 283.)

The Old Testament weapons used for wars were simple: the bow and arrow, the sling, the sword, the spear or lance, the battle-ax, and some protective armor. By the time Solomon became king, armies also used horses for battle, as well as chariots to make their attacks more swift. (Read 1 Kings 10:26, p. 452.)

As the Israelites became a stronger nation and more able to protect themselves, they sometimes trusted more in their own strength than in God's strength. Many of the Old Testament prophets preached to the Israelites about placing their trust in their swords rather than in the word of God. (Look at Jeremiah 39:18, p. 1048.)

their anger. They will cut off your noses
and ears. They will take away your sons
and daughters, and those who are left will
be burned. **26**They will take off your
clothes and steal your jewelry. **27**I will
put a stop to the sinful life you began
when you were in Egypt so that you will
not desire it or remember Egypt anymore.

28"This is what the Lord GOD says:
You became tired of your lovers, but I am
going to hand you over to those men you
now hate. **29**They will treat you with hate
and take away everything you worked for,
leaving you empty and naked. Everyone
will know about the sinful things you did.
Your sexual sins **30**have brought this on
you. You have had sexual relations with
the nations and made yourselves unclean
by worshiping their idols. **31**You did the
same things your sister did, so you will
get the same punishment, like a bitter
cup to drink.

32"This is what the Lord GOD says:

You will drink the same cup your
sister did,
and that cup is deep and wide.
Everyone will make fun of you,
because the cup is full.
33It will make you miserable and
drunk.
It is the cup of fear and ruin.
It is the cup of your sister Samaria.
34You will drink everything in it,
and then you will smash it
and tear at your breasts.
I have spoken, says the Lord GOD.

35"So this is what the Lord GOD says:
You have forgotten me and turned your
back on me. So you will be punished for
your sexual sins."

Judgment on Samaria and Jerusalem

36The LORD said to me: "Human, will
you judge Samaria and Jerusalem, showing them their hateful acts? **37**They are
guilty of adultery and murder. They have

taken part in adultery with their idols.
They even offered our children as sacrifices in the fire to be food for these idols.
38They have also done this to me: They
made my Temple unclean at the same
time they dishonored my Sabbaths.
39They sacrificed their children to their
idols. Then they entered my Temple at
that very time to dishonor it. That is what
they did inside my Temple!

40"They even sent for men from far
away, who came after a messenger was
sent to them. The two sisters bathed
themselves for them, painted their eyes,
and put on jewelry. **41**They sat on a fine
bed with a table set before it, on which
they put my incense and my oil.

42"There was the noise of a reckless
crowd in the city. Common people gathered, and drunkards were brought from
the desert. They put bracelets on the
wrists of the two sisters and beautiful
crowns on their heads. **43**Then I said
about the one who was worn out by her
acts of adultery, 'Let them continue their
sexual sins with her. She is nothing but a
prostitute.' **44**They kept going to her as
they would go to a prostitute. So they
continued to go to Samaria and Jerusalem, these shameful women. **45**But men
who do right will punish them as they
punish women who take part in adultery
and who murder people, because they are
guilty of adultery and murder.

46"This is what the Lord GOD says:
Bring together a mob against Samaria
and Jerusalem, and hand them over to be
frightened and robbed. **47**Let the mob kill
them by throwing stones at them, and let
them cut them down with their swords.
Let them kill their sons and daughters
and burn their houses down.

48"So I will put an end to sexual sins
in the land. Then all women will be
warned, and they will not do the sexual
sins you have done. **49**You will be punished for your sexual sins and the sin of
worshiping idols. Then you will know
that I am the Lord GOD."

The Pot and the Meat

24 The LORD spoke his word to me in
the ninth year of our captivity, in
the tenth month, on the tenth day of the
month. He said: **2**"Human, write down
today's date, this very date. The king of
Babylon has surrounded Jerusalem this
very day. **3**And tell a story to the people
who refuse to obey me. Say to them:
'This is what the Lord GOD says:

Put on the pot; put it on
and pour water in it.
4 Put in the pieces of meat,
the best pieces—the legs and the shoulders.
Fill it with the best bones.
5 Take the best of the flock,
and pile wood under the pot.
Boil the pieces of meat
until even the bones are cooked.

6" 'This is what the Lord GOD says:
How terrible it will be for the city of murderers!
How terrible it will be for the rusty pot
whose rust will not come off!
Take the meat out of it, piece by piece.
Don't choose any special piece.

7" 'The blood from her killings is still in the city.
She poured the blood on the bare rock.
She did not pour it on the ground
where dust would cover it.
8 To stir up my anger and revenge,
I put the blood she spilled on the bare rock
so it will not be covered.

9" 'So this is what the Lord GOD says:
How terrible it will be for the city of murderers!
I myself will pile the wood high for burning.
10 Pile up the wood
and light the fire.
Finish cooking the meat.
Mix in the spices,
and let the bones burn.
11 Then set the empty pot on the coals
so it may become hot and its copper sides glow.
The dirty scum stuck inside it may then melt

and its rust burn away.
12 But efforts to clean the pot have failed.
Its heavy rust cannot be removed, even in the fire.
13" 'By your sinful action you have
become unclean. I wanted to cleanse you,
but you are still unclean. You will never
be cleansed from your sin
until my anger against
you is carried out.
14" 'I, the LORD, have
spoken. The time has
come for me to act. I will
not hold back punishment
or feel pity or change my
mind. I will judge you by
your ways and actions,
says the Lord GOD.' "

> I will judge you by your ways and actions, says the Lord GOD.
> —Ezekiel 24:14

The Death of Ezekiel's Wife

15Then the LORD spoke his word to
me, saying: 16"Human, I am going to
take your wife from you, the woman you
look at with love. She will die suddenly,
but you must not be sad or cry loudly for
her or shed any tears. 17Groan silently;
do not cry loudly for the dead. Tie on your
turban, and put your sandals on your feet.
Do not cover your face, and do not eat the
food people eat when they are sad about a
death."
18So I spoke to the people in the
morning, and my wife died in the evening. The next morning I did as I had
been commanded.
19Then the people asked me, "Tell us,
what do the things you are doing mean
for us?"
20Then I said to them, "The LORD
spoke his word to me. He said, 21'Say to
the people of Israel, This is what the
Lord GOD says: I am going to dishonor
my Temple. You think it gives you
strength. You are proud of it, and you look
at it with love and tenderness. But your
sons and daughters that you left behind
in Jerusalem will fall dead by the sword.
22When that happens, you are to act as I
have: you are not to cover your face, and
you are not to eat the food people eat
when they are sad about a death. 23Your
turbans must stay on your heads, and
your sandals on your feet. You must not
cry loudly, but you must rot away in your
sins and groan to each other. 24So Ezekiel is to be an example for you. You must
do all the same things he did. When all
this happens, you will know that I am the
Lord GOD.'
25"And as for you, human, this is how it will
be. I will take away the
Temple that gives them
strength and joy, that
makes them proud. They
look at it with love, and it
makes them happy. And I
will take away their sons
and daughters also. 26At
that time a person who escapes will come to you
with information for you to hear. 27At that
very time your mouth will be opened. You
will speak and be silent no more. So you
will be a sign for them, and they will know
that I am the LORD."

Prophecy Against Ammon

25 The LORD spoke his word to me,
saying: 2"Human, look toward the
people of Ammon and prophesy against
them. 3Say to them, 'Hear the word of
the Lord GOD. This is what the Lord GOD
says: You were glad when my Temple
was dishonored, when the land of Israel
was ruined, and when the people of Judah
were taken away as captives. 4So I am
going to give you to the people of the
East to be theirs. They will set up their
camps among you and make their homes
among you. They will eat your fruit and
drink your milk. 5I will make the city of
Rabbah a pasture for camels and the land
of Ammon a resting place for sheep.
Then you will know that I am the LORD.
6This is what the Lord GOD says: You
have clapped your hands and stamped
your feet; you have laughed about all the
insults you made against the land of Israel. 7So I will use my power against you.
I will give you to the nations as if you
were treasures taken in war. I will wipe
you out of the lands so you will no longer

be a nation, and I will destroy you. Then you will know that I am the LORD.'

Prophecy Against Moab and Edom

8"This is what the Lord GOD says: 'Moab and Edom say, "The people of Judah are like all the other nations." **9**So I am going to take away the cities that protect Moab's borders, the best cities in that land: Beth Jeshimoth, Baal Meon, and Kiriathaim. **10**Then I will give Moab, along with the Ammonites, to the people of the East as their possession. Then, along with the Ammonites, Moab will not be a nation anymore. **11**So I will punish the people of Moab, and they will know that I am the LORD.'

> So I will use my power against you. I will give you to the nations as if you were treasures taken in war.
>
> —Ezekiel 25:7

Prophecy Against Edom

12"This is what the Lord GOD says: 'Edom took revenge on the people of Judah, and the Edomites became guilty because of it. **13**So this is what the Lord GOD says: I will use my power against Edom, killing every human and animal in it. And I will destroy Edom all the way from Teman to Dedan as they die in battle. **14**I will use my people Israel to take revenge on Edom. So the Israelites will do to Edom what my hot anger demands. Then the Edomites will know what my revenge feels like, says the Lord GOD.'

Prophecy Against Philistia

15"This is what the Lord GOD says: 'The Philistines have taken revenge with hateful hearts. Because of their strong hatred, they have tried to destroy Judah. **16**So this is what the Lord GOD says: I will use my power against the Philistines. I will kill the Kerethites, and I will destroy those people still alive on the coast of the Mediterranean Sea. **17**I will punish them in my anger and do great acts of revenge to them. They will know that I am the LORD when I take revenge on them.' "

Prophecy Against Tyre

26 It was the eleventh year of our captivity, on the first day of the month. The LORD spoke his word to me, saying: **2**"Human, the city of Tyre has spoken against Jerusalem: 'The city that traded with the nations is destroyed. Now we can be the trading center. Since the city of Jerusalem is ruined, we can make money.' **3**So this is what the Lord GOD says: I am against you, Tyre. I will bring many nations against you, like the sea beating its waves on your island shores. **4**They will destroy the walls of Tyre and pull down her towers. I will also scrape away her ruins and make her a bare rock. **5**Tyre will be an island where fishermen dry their nets. I have spoken, says the Lord GOD. The nations will steal treasures from Tyre. **6**Also, her villages on the shore across from the island will be destroyed by war. Then they will know that I am the LORD.

Nebuchadnezzar to Attack Tyre

7"This is what the Lord GOD says: I will bring a king from the north against Tyre. He is Nebuchadnezzar king of Babylon, the greatest king, with his horses, chariots, horsemen, and a great army. **8**He will fight a battle and destroy your villages on the shore across from the island. He will set up devices to attack you. He will build a road of earth to the top of the walls. He will raise his shields against you. **9**He will bring logs to pound through your city walls, and he will break down your towers with his iron bars. **10**His horses will be so many that they will cover you with their dust. Your walls will shake at the noise of horsemen, wagons, and chariots. The king of Babylon will enter your city gates as men enter a city where the walls are broken through. **11**The hoofs of his horses will run over your streets. He will kill your army with the sword, and your strong pillars will fall down to the ground. **12**Also, his men will

take away your riches and will steal the
things you sell. They will break down
your walls and destroy your nice houses.
They will throw your stones, wood, and
trash into the sea. **13**So I will stop your
songs; the music of your harps will not be
heard anymore. **14**I will make you a bare
rock, and you will be a place for drying
fishing nets. You will not be built again,
because I, the LORD, have spoken, says
the Lord GOD.

15"This is what the Lord GOD says to
Tyre: The people who live along the seacoast will shake with fear when they hear
about your defeat. Those of you who are
injured and dying will groan. **16**Then all
the leaders of the seacoast will get down
from their thrones, take off their beautiful needlework clothes, and show how
afraid they are. They will sit on the
ground and tremble all the time. When
they see you, they will be shocked.
17They will begin singing a funeral song
about you and will say to you:

'Tyre, you famous city, you have been
destroyed!
You have lost your sea power!
You and your people
had great power on the seas.
You made everyone around you
afraid of you.
18Now the people who live by the coast
tremble,
now that you have fallen.
The islands of the sea
are afraid because you have been
defeated.'

19"This is what the Lord GOD says: I
will make you an empty city, like cities
that have no people living in them. I will
bring the deep ocean waters over you,
and the Mediterranean Sea will cover
you. **20**At that time I will send you down
to the place of the dead to join those who
died long ago. I will make you live with
the dead below the earth in places that
are like old ruins. You will not come back
from there or have any place in the world
of the living again. **21**Other people will be
afraid of what happened to you, and it will
be the end of you. People will look for
you, but they will never find you again,
says the Lord GOD."

A Funeral Song for Tyre

27 The LORD spoke his word to me,
saying: **2**"Human, sing a funeral
song for the city of Tyre. **3**Speak to Tyre,
which has ports for the Mediterranean
Sea and is a place for trade for the people
of many lands along the seacoast. 'This is
what the Lord GOD says:

Tyre, you have said,
"I am like a beautiful ship."
4You were at home on the high seas.
Your builders made your beauty
perfect.
5They made all your boards
of fir trees from Mount Hermon.
They took a cedar tree from Lebanon
to make a ship's mast for you.
6They made your oars
from oak trees from Bashan.
They made your deck
from cypress trees from the coast
of Cyprus
and set ivory into it.
7Your sail of linen with designs sewed
on it came from Egypt
and became like a flag for you.
Your cloth shades over the deck were
blue and purple
and came from the island of
Cyprus.
8Men from Sidon and Arvad used oars
to row you.
Tyre, your skilled men were the
sailors on your deck.
9Workers of Byblos were with you,
putting caulk[n] in your ship's
seams.
All the ships of the sea and their
sailors
came alongside to trade with you.

10" 'Men of Persia, Lydia, and Put
were warriors in your navy
and hung their shields and helmets
on your sides.
They made you look beautiful.
11Men of Arvad and Cilicia
guarded your city walls all around.
Men of Gammad
were in your watchtowers

27:9 caulk Something like tar put between the boards of a ship to make it waterproof.

LET'S VISIT DAMASCUS

Ezekiel 27:18

Damascus, the current capital of Syria, is one of the oldest cities still existing in the world. A man named Uz (his great granddad was Noah) founded the city of Damascus. Damascus is near a lot of main highways, and so it is called a "trade center." That means people come there to buy and sell things. Damask was the most important item sold there in Old Testament times. (See Ezekiel 27:18–19.) That might be where Damascus got its name.

Whenever Damascus is mentioned in the New Testament, it has to do with the apostle Paul. He was on his way to Damascus to persecute Christians. Suddenly, the Lord was revealed to him in a bright flash of light that left him blind. Once he got to Damascus, God used a man named Ananias to heal him of the blindness. Paul became a Christian because of this experience; and instead of tormenting the Christians, he preached to them. (Check out the story in Acts 9:1–24, p. 1478.)

and hung their shields around your
walls.
They made your beauty perfect.
12" 'People of Tarshish became traders for you because of your great wealth.
They traded your goods for silver, iron,
tin, and lead.
13" 'People of Greece, Tubal, and Meshech became merchants for you. They
traded your goods for slaves and items of
bronze.
14" 'People of Beth Togarmah traded
your goods for work horses, war horses,
and mules.
15" 'People of Rhodes became merchants for you, selling your goods on
many coastlands. They brought back ivory tusks and valuable black wood as your
payment.
16" 'People of Aram became traders
for you, because you had so many good
things to sell. They traded your goods for
turquoise, purple cloth, cloth with designs sewed on, fine linen, coral, and rubies.
17" 'People of Judah and Israel became merchants for you. They traded
your goods for wheat from Minnith, and
for honey, olive oil, and balm.
18-19" 'People of Damascus became
traders for you because you have many
good things and great wealth. They traded your goods for wine from Helbon,
wool from Zahar, and barrels of wine from
Izal. They received wrought iron, cassia,
and sugar cane in payment for your good
things.
20" 'People of Dedan became merchants for you, trading saddle blankets
for riding.
21" 'People of Arabia and all the rulers of Kedar became traders for you.
They received lambs, male sheep, and
goats in payment for you.
22" 'The merchants of Sheba and Raamah became merchants for you. They
traded your goods for all the best spices,
valuable gems, and gold.
23" 'People of Haran, Canneh, Eden,
and the traders of Sheba, Asshur, and

Kilmad became merchants for you.
24They were paid with the best clothes,
blue cloth, cloth with designs sewed on,
carpets of many colors, and tightly wound
ropes.

25" 'Trading ships
carried the things you sold.
You were like a ship full of heavy
cargo
in the middle of the sea.
26The men who rowed you
brought you out into the high seas,
but the east wind broke you to pieces
in the middle of the sea.
27Your wealth, your trade, your goods,
your seamen, your sailors, your
workers,
your traders, your warriors,
and everyone else on board
sank into the sea
on the day your ship was wrecked.
28The people on the shore shake with
fear
when your sailors cry out.
29All the men who row
leave their ships;
the seamen and the sailors of other
ships
stand on the shore.
30They cry loudly about you;
they cry very much.
They throw dust on their heads
and roll in ashes to show they are
sad.
31They shave their heads for you,
and they put on rough cloth to
show they are upset.
They cry and sob for you;
they cry loudly.
32And in their loud crying
they sing a funeral song for you:
"No one was ever destroyed like
Tyre,
surrounded by the sea."
33When the goods you traded went out
over the seas,
you met the needs of many nations.
With your great wealth and goods,
you made kings of the earth rich.
34But now you are broken by the sea
and have sunk to the bottom.
Your goods and all the people on
board
have gone down with you.
35All those who live along the shore
are shocked by what happened to
you.
Their kings are terribly afraid,
and their faces show their fear.
36The traders among the nations hiss
at you.
You have come to a terrible end,
and you are gone forever.' "

Prophecy Against the King of Tyre

28 The LORD spoke his word to me,
saying: 2"Human, say to the ruler
of Tyre: 'This is what the Lord GOD says:
Because you are proud,
you say, "I am a god.
I sit on the throne of a god
in the middle of the seas."
You think you are as wise as a god,
but you are a human, not a god.
3You think you are wiser than Daniel.
You think you can find out all
secrets.
4Through your wisdom and
understanding
you have made yourself rich.
You have gained gold and silver
and have saved it in your
storerooms.
5Through your
great skill in
trading,
you have made
your riches
grow.
You are too proud
because of your
riches.

EMAIL FROM GOD
28:5
Talents
Beware of the talent trap.

6" 'So this is what the Lord GOD says:
You think you are wise
like a god,
7but I will bring foreign people against
you,
the cruelest nation.
They will pull out their swords
and destroy all that your wisdom
has built,
and they will dishonor your
greatness.
8They will kill you;
you will die a terrible death

THE KINGS OF EGYPT — Ezekiel 29:1–16

Another name for the kings of Egypt was *Pharaoh*. *Pharaoh* really means "great house" and was originally used to describe the king's palace, but as people used it, it came to mean something like "his honor" or "his majesty." The king of Egypt had a lot of power. By the rules of Egyptian government, the king owned everything in the land. The Egyptians believed that the kings would go on to rule the underworld after their deaths. That's part of the reason why the Egyptians took so much trouble to bury kings a certain way. Mummies were often kings who were buried in fancy, beautifully decorated graves along with their belongings.

In all, there were 30 different generations of pharaohs in Egypt. Many people from the Bible dealt with a king of Egypt. Abraham's wife was called to the king's palace. (See Genesis 12:14–20, p. 18.) Solomon married the daughter of a king of Egypt. (Look at 1 Kings 3:1, p. 438.) Probably the most famous is the king of Egypt who wouldn't let Moses take the Israelites out of Egypt until he and his countrymen had suffered ten plagues. (Check out Exodus 12:29–33, p. 92.)

ern Egypt, to the land they came from.
They will become a weak kingdom there.
15It will be the weakest kingdom, and it
will never again rule other nations. I will
make it so weak it will never again rule
over the nations. **16**The Israelites will
never again depend on Egypt. Instead,
Egypt's punishment will remind the Israelites of their sin in turning to Egypt for
help. Then they will know that I am the
Lord GOD.' "

Egypt Is Given to Babylon

17It was the twenty-seventh year of
our captivity, in the first month, on the
first day of the month. The LORD spoke
his word to me, saying: **18**"Human, Nebuchadnezzar king of Babylon made his
army fight hard against Tyre. Every
soldier's head was rubbed bare, and
every shoulder was rubbed raw. But Nebuchadnezzar and his army gained nothing
from fighting Tyre. **19**So this is what the
Lord GOD says: I will give the land of
Egypt to Nebuchadnezzar king of Babylon. He will take away Egypt's people
and its wealth and its treasures as pay for
his army. **20**I am giving Nebuchadnezzar
the land of Egypt as a reward for working
hard for me, says the Lord GOD.

21"At that time I will make Israel grow
strong again, and I will let you, Ezekiel,
speak to them. Then they will know that
I am the LORD."

Egypt Will Be Punished

30 The LORD spoke his word to me,
saying: **2**"Human, prophesy and
say, 'This is what the Lord GOD says:

Cry and say,
"The terrible day is coming."
3 The day is near;
the LORD's day of judging is near.
It is a cloudy day
and a time when the nations will
be judged.
4 An enemy will attack Egypt,
and Cush will tremble with fear.

When the killing begins in Egypt,
her wealth will be taken away,
and her foundations will be torn down.
5Cush, Put, Lydia, Arabia, Libya, and
some of my people who had made an
agreement with Egypt
will fall dead in war.
6" 'This is what the
LORD says:
Those who fight on Egypt's side will fall.
The power she is proud of will be lost.
The people in Egypt will fall dead in war
from Migdol in the north to Aswan in the south,
says the Lord GOD.
7They will be the most deserted lands.
Egypt's cities will be the worst of cities that lie in ruins.
8Then they will know that I am the LORD
when I set fire to Egypt
and when all those nations on her side are crushed.
9" 'At that time I will send messen-
gers in ships to frighten Cush, which now
feels safe. The people of Cush will tremble with fear when Egypt is punished.
And that time is sure to come.
10" 'This is what the Lord GOD
says:
I will destroy great numbers of people in Egypt
through the power of Nebuchadnezzar king of Babylon.
11Nebuchadnezzar and his army,
the cruelest army of any nation,
will be brought in to destroy the land.
They will pull out their swords against Egypt
and will fill the land with those they kill.
12I will make the streams of the Nile River become dry land,
and then I will sell the land to evil people.
I will destroy the land and everything in it
through the power of foreigners.
I, the LORD, have spoken.

This is what the LORD says: Those who fight on Egypt's side will fall. The power she is proud of will be lost.
—Ezekiel 30:6

Egypt's Idols Are Destroyed

13" 'This is what the
Lord GOD says:
I will destroy the idols
and take away the statues of gods from the city of Memphis.
There will no longer be a leader in Egypt,
and I will spread fear through the land of Egypt.
14I will make southern Egypt empty
and start a fire in Zoan
and punish Thebes.
15And I will pour out my anger against Pelusium,
the strong place of Egypt.
I will destroy great numbers of people in Thebes.
16I will set fire to Egypt.
Pelusium will be in great pain.
The walls of Thebes will be broken open,
and Memphis will have troubles every day.
17The young men of Heliopolis and Bubastis
will fall dead in war,
and the people will be taken away as captives.
18In Tahpanhes the day will be dark
when I break Egypt's power.
Then she will no longer be proud of her power.
A cloud will cover Egypt,
and her villages will be captured and taken away.
19So I will punish Egypt,
and they will know I am the LORD.' "

Egypt Becomes Weak

20It was in the eleventh year of our
captivity, in the first month, on the seventh day of the month. The LORD spoke
his word to me, saying: **21**"Human, I have
broken the powerful arm of the king of
Egypt. It has not been tied up, so it will
not get well. It has not been wrapped with
a bandage, so it will not be strong enough
to hold a sword in war. **22**So this is what
the Lord GOD says: I am against the king
of Egypt. I will break his arms, both the
strong arm and the broken arm, and I will
make the sword fall from his hand. **23**I will
scatter the Egyptians among the nations,
spreading them among the countries. **24**I
will make the arms of the king of Babylon
strong and put my sword in his hand. But
I will break the arms of the king of Egypt.
Then when he faces the king of Babylon,
he will cry out in pain like a dying person.
25So I will make the arms of the king of
Babylon strong, but the arms of the king
of Egypt will fall. Then people will know
that I am the LORD when I put my sword
into the hand of the king of Babylon and
he uses it in war against Egypt. **26**Then I
will scatter the Egyptians among the nations, spreading them among the countries. Then they will know that I am the
LORD."

A Cedar Tree

31 It was in the eleventh year of our
captivity, in the third month, on
the first day of the month. The LORD
spoke his word to me, saying: **2**"Human,
say to the king of Egypt and his people:

'No one is like you in your greatness.
3Assyria was once like a cedar tree in
Lebanon
with beautiful branches that
shaded the forest.
It was very tall;
its top was among the clouds.
4Much water made the tree grow;
the deep springs made it tall.
Rivers flowed
around the bottom of the tree
and sent their streams
to all other trees in the
countryside.
5So the tree was taller
than all the other trees in the
countryside.
Its limbs became long and big
because of so much water.
6All the birds of the sky
made their nests in the tree's
limbs.
And all the wild animals
gave birth under its branches.
All great nations
lived in the tree's shade.
7So the tree was great and beautiful,
with its long branches,
because its roots reached down to
much water.
8The cedar trees in the garden of God
were not as great as it was.
The pine trees
did not have such great limbs.
The plane trees
did not have such branches.
No tree in the garden of God
was as beautiful as this tree.
9I made it beautiful
with many branches,
and all the trees of Eden in the
garden of God
wanted to be like it.

10" 'So this is what the Lord GOD says:
The tree grew tall. Its top reached the
clouds, and it became proud of its height.
11So I handed it over to a mighty ruler of
the nations for him to punish it. Because it
was evil, I got rid of it. **12**The cruelest foreign nation cut it down and left it. The
tree's branches fell on the mountains and
in all the valleys, and its broken limbs
were in all the ravines of the land. All the
nations of the earth left the shade of that
tree. **13**The birds of the sky live on the
fallen tree. The wild animals live among
the tree's fallen branches. **14**So the trees
that grow by the water will not be proud to
be tall; they will not put their tops among
the clouds. None of the trees that are watered well will grow that tall, because they
all are meant to die and go under the
ground. They will be with people who
have died and have gone down to the place
of the dead.

15" 'This is what the Lord GOD says:
On the day when the tree went down to

the place of the dead, I made the deep
springs cry loudly. I covered them and
held back their rivers, and the great waters stopped flowing. I dressed Lebanon
in black to show her sadness about the
great tree, and all the trees in the countryside were sad about it. **16**I made the
nations shake with fear at the sound of
the tree falling when I brought it down to
the place of the dead. It went to join those
who have gone down to the grave. Then
all the trees of Eden and the best trees of
Lebanon, all the well-watered trees,
were comforted in the place of the dead
below the earth. **17**These trees had also
gone down with the great tree to the
place of the dead. They joined those who
were killed in war and those among the
nations who had lived under the great
tree's shade.

18" 'So no tree in Eden is equal to
you, Egypt, in greatness and honor, but
you will go down to join
the trees of Eden in the
place below the earth.
You will lie among un-
clean people, with those
who were killed in war.

" 'This is about the
king of Egypt and all his
people, says the Lord
GOD.' "

I will cause many people to be afraid when I bring you as a captive into other nations, to lands you have not known.
—Ezekiel 32:9

A Funeral Song

32 It was in the twelfth year of our
captivity, in the twelfth month, on
the first day of the month. The LORD
spoke his word to me, saying: **2**"Human,
sing a funeral song about the king of
Egypt. Say to him:

'You are like a young lion among the
nations.
You are like a crocodile in the seas.
You splash around in your streams
and stir up the water with your
feet,
making the rivers muddy.

3" 'This is what the Lord GOD says:
I will spread my net over you,
and I will use a large group of
people
to pull you up in my net.
4Then I will throw you on the land
dropping you onto the ground.
I will let the birds of the sky rest on
you
and all the animals of the earth eat
you until they are full.
5I will scatter your flesh on the
mountains
and fill the valleys with what is left
of you.
6I will drench the land with your
flowing blood
as far as the mountains,
and the ravines will be full of your
flesh.
7When I make you disappear,
I will cover the sky and make the
stars dark.
I will cover the sun with a cloud,
and the moon will not shine.
8I will make all the shining lights in
the sky
become dark over
you;
I will bring darkness
over your land,
says the Lord
GOD.
9I will cause many
people to be
afraid
when I bring you as
a captive into
other nations,
to lands you have not known.
10I will cause many people to be
shocked about you.
Their kings will tremble with fear
because of you
when I swing my sword in front of
them.
They will shake every moment
on the day you fall;
each king will be afraid for his own
life.

11" 'So this is what the Lord GOD
says:
The sword of the king of Babylon
will attack you.
12I will cause your people to fall
by the swords of mighty
soldiers,
the most terrible in the world.

They will destroy the pride of Egypt
and all its people.
13 I will also destroy all Egypt's cattle
which live alongside much water.
The foot of a human will not stir the
water,
and the hoofs of cattle will not
muddy it anymore.
14 So I will let the Egyptians' water
become clear.
I will cause their rivers to run as
smoothly as olive oil,
says the Lord GOD.
15 When I make the land of Egypt
empty
and take everything that is in the
land,
when I destroy all those who live in
Egypt,
then they will know that I am the
LORD.'

16"This is the funeral song people
will sing for Egypt. The women of the nations will sing it; they will sing a funeral
song for Egypt and all its people, says the
Lord GOD."

Egypt to Be Destroyed

17It was in the twelfth year of our captivity, on the fifteenth day of the month.
The LORD spoke his word to me, saying:
18"Human, cry for the people of Egypt.
Bring down Egypt, together with the
women of the powerful nations; bring
them down to the place of the dead below
the earth to join those who go to the
place of the dead. 19Say to them: 'Are you
more beautiful than others? Go lie down
in death with those who are unclean.'
20The Egyptians will fall among those
killed in war. The sword is ready; the enemy will drag Egypt and all her people
away. 21From the place of the dead the
leaders of the mighty ones will speak
about the king of Egypt and the nations
which help him: 'The unclean, those
killed in war, have come down here and
lie dead.'

22"Assyria and all its army lie dead
there. The graves of their soldiers are all
around. All were killed in war, 23and their
graves were put in the deepest parts of
the place of the dead. Assyria's army lies
around its grave. When they lived on
earth, they frightened people, but now all
of them have been killed in war.

24"The nation of Elam is there with
all its army around its grave. All of them
were killed in war. They had frightened
people on earth and were unclean, so
they went down to the lowest parts of the
place of the dead. They must carry their
shame with those who have gone down to
the place of the dead. 25A bed has been
made for Elam with all those killed in
war. The graves of her soldiers are all
around her. All Elam's people are unclean, killed in war. They frightened people when they lived on earth, but now
they must carry their shame with those
who have gone down to the place of the
dead. Their graves are with the rest who
were killed.

26"Meshech and Tubal are there with
the graves of all their soldiers around
them. All of them are unclean and have
been killed in war. They also frightened
people when they lived on earth. 27But
they are not buried with the other soldiers who were killed in battle long ago,
those who went with their weapons of
war to the place of the dead. These soldiers had their swords laid under their
heads and their shields on their bodies.
These mighty soldiers used to frighten
people when they lived on earth.

28"You, king of Egypt, will be broken
and lie among those who are unclean,
who were killed in war.

29"Edom is there also, with its kings
and all its leaders. They were mighty, but
now they lie in death with those killed in
war, with those who are unclean, with
those who have gone down to the place of
the dead.

30"All the rulers of the north and all
the Sidonians are there. Their strength
frightened people, but they have gone
down in shame with those who were
killed. They are unclean, lying with those
killed in war. They carry their shame
with those who have gone down to the
place of the dead.

31"The king of Egypt and his army
will see these who have been killed in

war. Then he will be comforted for all his soldiers killed in war, says the Lord GOD. **32**I made people afraid of the king of Egypt while he lived on earth. But he and all his people will lie among those who are unclean, who were killed in war, says the Lord GOD."

Ezekiel Is Watchman for Israel

33 The LORD spoke his word to me, saying: **2**"Human, speak to your people and say to them: 'Suppose I bring a war against a land. The people of the land may choose one of their men and make him their watchman. **3**When he sees the enemy coming to attack the land, he will blow the trumpet and warn the people. **4**If they hear the sound of the trumpet but do nothing, the enemy will come and kill them. They will be responsible for their own deaths. **5**They heard the sound of the trumpet but didn't do anything. So they are to blame for their own deaths. If they had done something, they would have saved their own lives. **6**But if the watchman sees the enemy coming to attack and does not blow the trumpet, the people will not be warned. Then if the enemy comes and kills any of them, they have died because of their own sin. But I will punish the watchman for their deaths.'

> EMAIL FROM GOD
> **33:1–6**
> **Responsibility**
> Are you responsible to help others?

7"You, human, are the one I have made a watchman for Israel. If you hear a word from my mouth, you must warn them for me. **8**Suppose I say to the wicked: 'Wicked people, you will surely die,' but you don't speak to warn the wicked to stop doing evil. Then they will die because they were sinners, but I will punish you for their deaths. **9**But if you warn the wicked to stop doing evil and they do not stop, they will die because they were sinners. But you have saved your life.

10"So you, human, say to Israel: 'You have said: Surely our law-breaking and sins are hurting us. They will kill us. What can we do so we will live?' **11**Say to them: 'The Lord GOD says: As surely as I live, I do not want any who are wicked to die. I want them to stop doing evil and live. Stop! Stop your wicked ways! You don't want to die, do you, people of Israel?'

12"Human, say to your people: 'The goodness of those who do right will not save them when they sin. The evil of wicked people will not cause them to be punished if they stop doing it. If good people sin, they will not be able to live by the good they did earlier.' **13**If I tell good people, 'You will surely live,' they might think they have done enough good and then do evil. Then none of the good things they did will be remembered. They will die because of the evil they have done. **14**Or, if I say to the wicked people, 'You will surely die,' they may stop sinning and do what is right and honest. **15**For example, they may return what somebody gave them as a promise to repay a loan, or pay back what they stole. If they live by the rules that give life and do not sin, then they will surely live, and they will not die. **16**They will not be punished for any of their sins. They now do what is right and fair, so they will surely live.

17"Your people say: 'The way of the Lord is not fair.' But it is their own ways that are not fair. **18**When the good people stop doing good and do evil, they will die for their evil. **19**But when the wicked stop doing evil and do what is right and fair, they will live. **20**You still say: 'The way of the Lord is not fair.' Israel, I will judge all of you by your own ways."

The Fall of Jerusalem Explained

21It was in the twelfth year of our captivity, on the fifth day of the tenth month. A person who had escaped from Jerusalem came to me and said, "Jerusalem has been captured." **22**Now I had felt the power of the LORD on me the evening before. He had made me able to talk again before this person came to me. I could speak; I was not without speech anymore.

23Then the LORD spoke his word to me, saying: **24**"Human, people who live in the ruins in the land of Israel are saying: 'Abraham was only one person, yet

he was given the land as his own. Surely
the land has been given to us, who are
many, as our very own.' 25So say to
them: 'This is what the Lord GOD says:
You eat meat with the blood still in it, you
ask your idols for help, and you murder
people. Should you then have the land as
your very own? 26You depend on your
sword and do terrible things which I hate.
Each of you has sexual relations with his
neighbor's wife. So should you have the
land?'

27"Say to them: 'This is what the
Lord GOD says: As surely as I live, those
who are among the city ruins in Israel
will be killed in war. I will cause those
who live in the country to be eaten by
wild animals. People hiding in the strongholds and caves will die of disease. 28I
will make the land an empty desert. The
people's pride in the land's power will
end. The mountains of Israel will become
empty so that no one will pass through
them. 29They will know that I am the
LORD when I make the land an empty
desert because of the things they have
done that I hate.'

30"But as for you, human, your people
are talking about you by the walls and in
the doorways of houses. They say to each
other: 'Come now, and hear the message
from the LORD.' 31So they come to you in
crowds as if they were really ready to listen. They sit in front of you as if they
were my people and hear your words, but
they will not obey them. With their
mouths they tell me they love me, but
their hearts desire their selfish profits.
32To your people you are nothing more
than a singer who sings love songs and
has a beautiful voice and plays a musical
instrument well. They hear your words,
but they will not obey them.

33"When this comes true, and it surely will happen, then the people will know
that a prophet has been among them."

FAITH links

EMPTY WORDS

EZEKIEL 33:30-33

Has anyone ever said he wanted to be your friend, but acted as if he didn't? God told Ezekiel that the Israelites claimed to listen to Ezekiel, but never planned to change the way they acted. Their words were empty. There was nothing behind them.

Actions should always follow words. If you tell God you want to follow his way, your actions should speak louder than your words. Don't just claim it; do it!

Are you a big talker, but don't back up your words with action? Link here:

A Use for Your Abilities, Genesis 41, p. 59

A Different Kind of People, Leviticus 11, p. 146

Your Stats, 1 Kings 15; 16, p. 460

Love Him? Show It!, Amos 2:6–7, p. 1196

A Reminder to Do What Is Right and True, Zechariah 7:8–10, p. 1257

Obey or Disobey?, Luke 20:20–26, p. 1409

The Leaders Are like Shepherds

34 The LORD spoke his word to me,
saying: 2"Human, prophesy against
the leaders of Israel, who are like shepherds. Prophesy and say to them: 'This is
what the Lord GOD says: How terrible it
will be for the shepherds of Israel who
feed only themselves! Why don't the
shepherds feed the flock? 3You eat the
milk curds, and you clothe yourselves
with the wool. You kill the fat sheep, but
you do not feed the flock. 4You have not

made the weak strong. You have not healed the sick or put bandages on those that were hurt. You have not brought back those who strayed away or searched for the lost. But you have ruled the sheep with cruel force. **5**The sheep were scattered, because there was no shepherd, and they became food for every wild animal. **6**My flock wandered over all the mountains and on every high hill. They were scattered all over the face of the earth, and no one searched or looked for them.

7" 'So, you shepherds, hear the word of the LORD. This is what the Lord GOD says: **8**As surely as I live, my flock has been caught and eaten by all the wild animals, because the flock has no shepherd. The shepherds did not search for my flock. No, they fed themselves instead of my flock. **9**So, you shepherds, hear the word of the LORD. **10**This is what the Lord GOD says: I am against the shepherds. I will blame them for what has happened to my sheep and will not let them tend the flock anymore. Then the shepherds will stop feeding themselves, and I will take my flock from their mouths so they will no longer be their food.

11" 'This is what the Lord GOD says: I, myself, will search for my sheep and take care of them. **12**As a shepherd takes care of his scattered flock when it is found, I will take care of my sheep. I will save them from all the places where they were scattered on a cloudy and dark day. **13**I will bring them out from the nations and gather them from the countries. I will bring them to their own land and pasture them on the mountains of Israel, in the ravines, and in all the places where people live in the land. **14**I will feed them in a good pasture, and they will eat grass on the high mountains of Israel. They will lie down on good ground where they eat grass, and they will eat in rich grassland on the mountains of Israel. **15**I will feed my flock and lead them to rest, says the Lord GOD. **16**I will search for the lost, bring back those that strayed away, put bandages on those that were hurt, and make the weak strong. But I will destroy those sheep that are fat and strong. I will tend the sheep with fairness.

> As a shepherd takes care of his scattered flock when it is found, I will take care of my sheep.
> —Ezekiel 34:12

17" 'This is what the Lord GOD says: As for you, my flock, I will judge between one sheep and another, between the male sheep and the male goats. **18**Is it not enough for you to eat grass in the good land? Must you crush the rest of the grass with your feet? Is it not enough for you to drink clear water? Must you make the rest of the water muddy with your feet? **19**Must my flock eat what you crush, and must they drink what you make muddy with your feet?

20" 'So this is what the Lord GOD says to them: I, myself, will judge between the fat sheep and the thin sheep. **21**You push with your side and with your shoulder, and you knock down all the weak sheep with your horns until you have forced them away. **22**So I will save my flock; they will not be hurt anymore. I will judge between one sheep and another. **23**Then I will put over them one shepherd, my servant David. He will feed them and tend them and be their shepherd. **24**Then I, the LORD, will be their God, and my servant David will be a ruler among them. I, the LORD, have spoken.

25" 'I will make an agreement of peace with my sheep and will remove harmful animals from the land. Then the sheep will live safely in the desert and sleep in the woods. **26**I will bless them and let them live around my hill. I will cause the rains to come when it is time; there will be showers to bless them. **27**Also the trees in the countryside will give their fruit, and the land will give its harvest. And the sheep will be safe on their land. Then they will know that I am the LORD when I break the bars of their captivity and save them from the power of those

who made them slaves. **28**They will not
be led captive by the nations again. The
wild animals will not eat them, but they
will live safely, and no one will make
them afraid. **29**I will give them a place famous for its good crops, so they will no
longer suffer from hunger in the land.
They will not suffer the insults of other
nations anymore. **30**Then they will know
that I, the LORD their God, am with them.
The nation of Israel will know that they
are my people, says the Lord GOD.
31You, my human sheep, are the sheep I
care for, and I am your God, says the Lord
GOD.' "

Prophecy Against Edom

35 The LORD spoke his word to me,
saying: **2**"Human, look toward
Edom and prophesy against it. **3**Say to it:
'This is what the Lord GOD says: I am
against you, Edom. I will stretch out my
hand against you and make you an empty
desert. **4**I will destroy your cities, and
you will become empty. Then you will
know that I am the LORD.

5" 'You have always been an enemy of
Israel. You let them be defeated in war
when they were in trouble at the time of
their final punishment. **6**So the Lord GOD
says, as surely as I live, I will let you be
murdered. Murder will chase you. Since
you did not hate murdering people, murder will chase you. **7**I will make Edom an
empty ruin and destroy everyone who
goes in or comes out of it. **8**I will fill its
mountains with those who are killed.
Those killed in war will fall on your hills,
in your valleys, and in all your ravines. **9**I
will make you a ruin forever; no one will
live in your cities. Then you will know
that I am the LORD.

10" 'You said, "These two nations, Israel and Judah, and these two lands will
be ours. We will take them for our own."
But the LORD was there. **11**So
this is what the
Lord GOD says: As
surely as I live, I
will treat you just as
you treated them.
You were angry and
jealous because you hated them. So I will

eMAIL FROM GOD
35:11–12
Hate
Will people hate you because you love God?

punish you and show the Israelites who I
am. **12**Then you will know that I, the
LORD, have heard all your insults against
the mountains of Israel. You said, "They
have been ruined. They have been given
to us to eat." **13**You have not stopped
your proud talk against me. I have heard
you. **14**This is what the Lord GOD says:
All the earth will be happy when I make
you an empty ruin. **15**You were happy
when the land of Israel was ruined, but I
will do the same thing to you. Mount Seir
and all Edom, you will become an empty
ruin. Then you will know that I am the
LORD.' "

Israel to Come Home

36 "Human, prophesy to the mountains of Israel and say: 'Mountains
of Israel, hear the word of the LORD.
2This is what the Lord GOD says: The
enemy has said about you, "Now the old
places to worship gods have become
ours." ' **3**So prophesy and say: 'This is
what the Lord GOD says: They have
made you an empty ruin and have
crushed you from all around. So you became a possession of the other nations.
People have talked and whispered against
you. **4**So, mountains of Israel, hear the
word of the Lord GOD. The Lord GOD
speaks to the mountains, hills, ravines,
and valleys, to the empty ruins and abandoned cities that have been robbed and
laughed at by the other nations. **5**This is
what the Lord GOD says: I speak in hot
anger against the other nations. I speak
against the people of Edom, who took my
land for themselves with joy and with
hate in their hearts. They forced out the
people and took their pastureland.' **6**So
prophesy about the land of Israel and say
to the mountains, hills, ravines, and valleys: 'This is what the Lord GOD says: I
speak in my jealous anger, because you
have suffered the insults of the nations.
7So this is what the Lord GOD says: I
promise that the nations around you will
also have to suffer insults.

8" 'But you, mountains of Israel, will
grow branches and fruit for my people,
who will soon come home. **9**I am concerned about you; I am on your side. You

will be plowed, and seed will be planted in you. **10**I will increase the number of people who live on you, all the people of Israel. The cities will have people living in them, and the ruins will be rebuilt. **11**I will increase the number of people and animals living on you. They will grow and have many young. You will have people living on you as you did before, and I will make you better off than at the beginning. Then you will know that I am the LORD. **12**I will cause my people Israel to walk on you and own you, and you will belong to them. You will never again take their children away from them.

13" 'This is what the Lord GOD says: People say about you, "You eat people and take children from your nation." **14**But you will not eat people anymore or take away the children, says the Lord GOD. **15**I will not make you listen to insults from the nations anymore; you will not suffer shame from them anymore. You will not cause your nation to fall anymore, says the Lord GOD.' "

The Lord Acts for Himself

16The LORD spoke his word to me again, saying: **17**"Human, when the nation of Israel was living in their own land, they made it unclean by their ways and the things they did. Their ways were like a woman's uncleanness in her time of monthly bleeding. **18**So I poured out my anger against them, because they murdered in the land and because they made the land unclean with their idols. **19**I scattered them among the nations, and they were spread through the countries. I punished them for how they lived and what they did. **20**They dishonored my holy name in the nations where they went. The nations said about them 'These are the people of the LORD, but they had to leave the land which he gave them.' **21**But I had concern for my holy name, which the nation of Israel had dishonored among the nations where they went.

eMAIL! FROM GOD
36:20–21
Following God
Does God care about his name?

22"So say to the people of Israel, 'This is what the Lord GOD says: Israel, I am going to act, but not for your sake. I will do something to help my holy name, which you have dishonored among the nations where you went. **23**I will prove the holiness of my great name, which has been dishonored among the nations. You have dishonored it among these nations, but the nations will know that I am the LORD when I prove myself holy before their eyes, says the Lord GOD.

24" 'I will take you from the nations and gather you out of all the lands and bring you back into your own land. **25**Then I will sprinkle clean water on you, and you will be clean. I will cleanse you from all your uncleanness and your idols. **26**Also, I will teach you to respect me completely, and I will put a new way of thinking inside you. I will take out the stubborn hearts of stone from your bodies, and I will give you obedient hearts of flesh. **27**I will put my Spirit inside you and help you live by my rules and carefully obey my laws. **28**You will live in the land I gave to your ancestors, and you will be my people, and I will be your God. **29**So I will save you from all your uncleanness. I will command the grain to come and grow; I will not allow a time of hunger to hurt you. **30**I will increase the harvest of the field so you will never again suffer shame among the nations because of hunger. **31**Then you will remember your evil ways and actions that were not good, and you will hate yourselves because of your sins and your terrible acts that I hate. **32**I want you to know that I am not going to do this for your sake, says the Lord GOD. Be ashamed and embarrassed about your ways, Israel.

33" 'This is what the Lord GOD says: This is what will happen on the day I cleanse you from all your sins: I will cause the cities to have people living in them again, and the destroyed places will be rebuilt. **34**The empty land will be plowed so it will no longer be a ruin for everyone who passes by to see. **35**They will say, "This land was ruined, but now it has become like the garden of Eden. The cities were destroyed, empty, and ruined,

but now they are protected and have people living in them." 36Then those nations
still around you will
know that I, the
LORD, have rebuilt
what was destroyed
and have planted
what was empty. I,
the LORD, have spo-
ken, and I will do it.'

EMAIL FROM GOD
36:36
Belief
Find out if God means what he says.

37"This is what the Lord GOD says: I
will let myself be asked by the people of
Israel to do this for them again: I will
make their people grow in number like a
flock. 38They will be as many as the
flocks brought to Jerusalem during her
holy feasts. Her ruined cities will be filled
with flocks of people. Then they will
know that I am the LORD."

The Vision of Dry Bones

37 I felt the power of the LORD on me,
and he brought me out by the Spirit of the LORD and put me down in the
middle of a valley. It was full of bones.
2He led me around among the bones, and
I saw that there were many bones in the
valley and that they were very dry. 3Then
he asked me, "Human, can these bones
live?"

I answered, "Lord GOD, only you
know."

4He said to me, "Prophesy to these
bones and say to them, 'Dry bones, hear
the word of the LORD. 5This is what the
Lord GOD says to the bones: I will cause
breath to enter you so you will come to
life. 6I will put muscles on you and flesh
on you and cover you with skin. Then I
will put breath in you so you will come to
life. Then you will know that I am the
LORD.'"

7So I prophesied as I was commanded. While I prophesied, there was a noise
and a rattling. The bones came together,
bone to bone. 8I looked and saw muscles
come on the bones, and flesh grew, and
skin covered the bones. But there was no
breath in them.

9Then he said to me, "Prophesy to
the wind." Prophesy, human, and say to
the wind, 'This is what the Lord GOD
says: Wind, come from the four winds,

FAITH links

BELIEVE THE IMPOSSIBLE?

EZEKIEL 37

In *Through the Looking Glass*, the sequel to *Alice in Wonderland*, the White Queen told Alice that she sometimes believed six impossible things before breakfast. Sounds silly? Yet Ezekiel was called to believe the impossible when he saw a vision of a valley full of bones. These bones represented the people of Israel. In God's eyes, they were spiritually dead. That meant they had no power to do anything for God. Even though they had sinned against God, God promised to give them life once more by forgiving them.

Sin makes a person "lifeless." Thanks to Jesus, new life is possible.

The Perfect Sacrifice, Leviticus 1—7, p. 135

Depend on Him!, 2 Chronicles 16:1–9, p. 579

Go for the Gold, Job 23:10, p. 685

Dirty Inside, Isaiah 6:1–7, p. 904

Inside the Heart of God, Micah 7:18–20, p. 1228

The Way to Heaven, John 14:1–6, p. 1448

37:9 wind This Hebrew word could also mean "breath" or "spirit."

and breathe on these people who were
killed so they can come back to life.' "
10So I prophesied as the LORD commanded me. And the breath came into them,
and they came to life and stood on their
feet, a very large army.

11Then he said to me, "Human, these
bones are like all the people of Israel.
They say, 'Our bones are dried up, and
our hope has gone. We are destroyed.'
12So, prophesy and say to them, 'This is
what the Lord GOD says: My people, I
will open your graves and cause you to
come up out of your graves. Then I will
bring you into the land of Israel. 13My
people, you will know that I am the LORD
when I open your graves and cause you
to come up from them. 14And I will put
my Spirit inside you, and you will come to
life. Then I will put you in your own land.
And you will know that I, the LORD, have
spoken and done it, says the LORD.' "

Judah and Israel Back Together

15The LORD spoke his word to me,
saying, 16"Human, take a stick and write
on it, 'For Judah and all the Israelites with
him.' Then take another stick and write
on it, 'The stick of Ephraim, for Joseph
and all the Israelites with him.' 17Then
join them together into one stick so they
will be one in your hand.

18"When your people say to you, 'Explain to us what you mean by this,' 19say
to them, 'This is what the Lord GOD says:
I will take the stick for Joseph and the
tribes of Israel with him, which is in the
hand of Ephraim, and I will put it with
the stick of Judah. I will make them into
one stick, and they will be one in my
hand.' 20Hold the sticks on which you
wrote these names in your hand so the
people can see them. 21Say to the people, 'This is what the Lord GOD says: I
am going to take the people of Israel from
among the nations where they have
gone. I will gather them from all around
and bring them into their own land. 22I
will make them one nation in the land, on
the mountains of Israel. One king will
rule all of them. They will never again be
two nations; they will not be divided into
two kingdoms anymore. 23They will not
continue to make themselves unclean by
their idols, their statues of gods
which I hate, or by
their sins. I will save
them from all the
ways they sin and
turn against me, and
I will make them
clean. Then they will be my people, and I
will be their God.

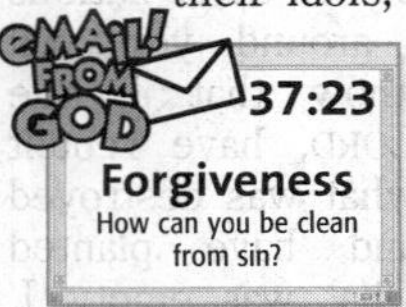

eMAIL! FROM GOD
37:23
Forgiveness
How can you be clean from sin?

24" 'My servant David will be their
king, and they will all have one shepherd.
They will live by my rules and obey my
laws. 25They will live on the land I gave
to my servant Jacob, the land in which
your ancestors lived. They will all live on
the land forever: they, their children, and
their grandchildren. David my servant
will be their king forever. 26I will make
an agreement of peace with them, an
agreement that continues forever. I will
put them in their land and make them
grow in number. Then I will put my Temple among them forever. 27The place
where I live will be with them. I will be
their God, and they will be my people.
28When my Temple is among them forever, the nations will know that I, the
LORD, make Israel holy.' "

Prophecy Against Gog

38 The LORD spoke his word to me,
saying, 2"Human, look toward
Gog of the land of Magog, the chief ruler
of the nations of Meshech and Tubal.
Prophesy against him 3and say, 'The
Lord GOD says this: I am against you,
Gog, chief ruler of Meshech and Tubal. 4I
will turn you around and put hooks in
your jaws. And I will bring you out with
all your army, horses, and horsemen, all
of whom will be dressed in beautiful uniforms. They will be a large army with
large and small shields and all having
swords. 5Persia, Cush, and Put will be
with them, all of them having shields and
helmets. 6There will also be Gomer with
all its troops and the nation of Togarmah
from the far north with all its troops—
many nations with you.

7" 'Be prepared. Be prepared, you and
all the armies that have come together to
make you their commander. 8After a long

time you will be called for service. After
those years you will come into a land that
has been rebuilt from war. The people in
the land will have been gathered from
many nations to the mountains of Israel,
which were empty for a long time. These
people were brought out from the nations, and they will all be living in safety.
9You will come like a storm. You, all your
troops, and the many nations with you
will be like a cloud covering the land.

10" 'This is what the Lord GOD says:
At that time ideas will come into your
mind, and you will think up an evil plan.
11You will say, "I will march against a
land of towns without walls. I will attack
those who are at rest and live in safety.
All of them live without city walls or gate
bars or gates. **12**I will capture treasures
and take loot. I will turn my power
against the rebuilt ruins that now have
people living in them. I will attack these
people who have been gathered from the
nations, who have become rich with farm
animals and property, who live at the center of the world." **13**Sheba, Dedan, and
the traders of Tarshish, with all its villages, will say to you, "Did you come to
capture treasure? Did you bring your
troops together to take loot? Did you
bring them to carry away silver and gold
and to take away farm animals and property?" '

14"So prophesy, human, and say to
Gog, 'This is what the Lord GOD says:
Now that my people Israel are living in
safety, you will know about it. **15**You will
come with many people from your place
in the far north. You will have a large
group with you, a mighty army, all riding
on horses. **16**You will attack my people
Israel like a cloud that covers the land.
This will happen in the days to come
when I bring you against my land. Gog,
then the nations will know me when they
see me prove how holy I am in what I do
through you.

17" 'This is what the Lord GOD says:
You are the one about whom I spoke in
past days. I spoke through my servants,
the prophets of Israel, who prophesied
for many years that I would bring you
against them. **18**This is what will happen:
On the day Gog attacks the land of Israel,
I will become very angry, says the Lord
GOD. **19**With jealousy and great anger I
tell you that at that time there will surely
be a great earthquake in Israel. **20**The
fish of the sea, the birds of the sky, the
wild animals, everything that crawls on
the ground, and all the people on the
earth will shake with fear before me. Also
the mountains will be thrown down, the
cliffs will fall, and every wall will fall to
the ground. **21**Then I will call for a war
against Gog on all my mountains, says
the Lord GOD. Everyone's sword will attack the soldier next to him. **22**I will punish Gog with disease and death. I will
send a heavy rain with hailstones and
burning sulfur on Gog, his army, and the
many nations with him.
23Then I will show
how great I am. I
will show my holi-
ness, and I will
make myself known
to the many nations
that watch. Then they will know that I am
the LORD.'

eMail from GOD **38:23**
God
Will the world ever see God's greatness?

The Death of Gog and His Army

39 "Human, prophesy against Gog
and say, 'This is what the Lord
GOD says: I am against you, Gog, chief
ruler of Meshech and Tubal. **2**I will turn
you around and lead you. I will bring you
from the far north and send you to attack
the mountains of Israel. **3**I will knock
your bow out of your left hand and throw
down your arrows from your right hand.
4You, all your troops, and the nations
with you will fall dead on the mountains
of Israel. I will let you be food for every
bird that eats meat and for every wild animal. **5**You will lie fallen on the ground,
because I have spoken, says the Lord
GOD. **6**I will send fire on Magog and
those who live in safety on the coastlands. Then they will know that I am
the LORD.

7" 'I will make myself known among
my people Israel, and I will not let myself
be dishonored anymore. Then the nations will know that I am the LORD, the
Holy One in Israel. **8**It is coming! It will

happen, says the Lord GOD. The time I
talked about is coming.
9" 'Then those who live in the cities
of Israel will come out and make fires
with the enemy's weapons. They will
burn them, both large and small shields,
bows and arrows, war clubs, and spears.
They will use the weap-
ons to burn in their fires
for seven years. 10They
will not need to take
wood from the field or
chop firewood from the
forests, because they will
make fires with the weap-
ons. In this way they will
take the treasures of those
who took their treasures;
they will take the loot of
those who took their loot, says the
Lord GOD.
11" 'At that time I will give Gog a burial place in Israel, in the Valley of the
Travelers, east of the Dead Sea. It will
block the road for travelers. Gog and all
his army will be buried there, so people
will call it The Valley of Gog's Army.
12" 'The people of Israel will be burying them for seven months to make the
land clean again. 13All the people in the
land will bury them, and they will be honored on the day of my victory, says the
Lord GOD.
14" 'The people of Israel will choose
men to work through the land to make it
clean. Along with others, they will bury
Gog's soldiers still lying dead on the
ground. After the seven months are finished, they will still search. 15As they go
through the land, anyone who sees a human bone is to put a marker by it. The
sign will stay there until the grave-
diggers bury the bone in The Valley of
Gog's Army. 16A city will be there named
Hamonah. So they will make the land
clean again.'
17"Human, this is what the Lord GOD
says: Speak to every kind of bird and wild
animal: 'Come together, come! Come together from all around to my sacrifice, a
great sacrifice which I will prepare for
you on the mountains of Israel. Eat flesh
and drink blood! 18You are to eat the
flesh of the mighty and drink the blood of
the rulers of the earth as if they were fat
animals from Bashan: male sheep, lambs,
goats, and bulls. 19You are to eat and
drink from my sacrifice which I have
prepared for you, eating fat until you are
full and drinking blood until you are
drunk. 20At my table you
are to eat until you are
full of horses and riders,
mighty men and all kinds
of soldiers,' says the Lord
GOD.
21"I will show my
glory among the nations.
All the nations will see
my power when I punish
them. 22From that time
onward the people of Isra-
el will know that I am the LORD their God.
23The nations will know Israel was taken
away captive because they turned against
me. So I turned away from them and handed them over to their enemies until all of
them died in war. 24Because of their uncleanness and their sins, I punished them
and turned away from them.
25"So this is what the Lord GOD says:
Now I will bring the people of Jacob back
from captivity, and I will have mercy on
the whole nation of Israel. I will not let
them dishonor me. 26The people will forget their shame and how they rejected
me when they live again in safety on their
own land with no one to make them
afraid. 27I will bring the people back from
other lands and gather them from the
lands of their enemies. So I will use my
people to show many nations that I am
holy. 28Then my people will know that I
am the LORD their God, because I sent
them into captivity among the nations,
but then I brought them back to their
own land, leaving no one behind. 29I will
not turn away from them anymore, because I will put my Spirit into the people
of Israel, says the Lord GOD."

> I will show my glory among the nations. All the nations will see my power when I punish them.
> —Ezekiel 39:21

The New Temple

40 It was the twenty-fifth year of our
captivity, at the beginning of the
year, on the tenth day of the month. It
was in the fourteenth year after Jerusa-

lem was captured. On that same day I felt
the power of the LORD, and he brought
me to Jerusalem. **2**In the visions of God
he brought me to the land of Israel and
put me down on a very high mountain.
On the south of the mountain there were
some buildings that looked like a city.
3He took me closer to the buildings, and I
saw a man who looked as if he were made
of bronze, standing in the gateway. He
had a cord made of linen and a stick in his
hand, both for measuring. **4**The man said
to me, "Human, look with your eyes and
hear with your ears. Pay attention to all
that I will show you, because that's why
you have been brought here. Tell the people of Israel all that you see."

The East Gateway

5I saw a wall that surrounded the
Temple area. The measuring stick in the
man's hand was ten and one-half feet
long. So the man measured the wall,
which was ten and one-half feet thick and
ten and one-half feet high.

6Then the man went to the east gateway. He went up its steps and measured
the opening of the gateway. It was ten and
one-half feet deep. **7**The rooms for the
guards were ten and one-half feet long
and ten and one-half feet wide. The walls
that came out between the guards' rooms
were about nine feet thick. The opening
of the gateway next to the porch that
faced the Temple was ten and one-half
feet deep.

8Then the man measured the porch of
the gateway. **9**It was about fourteen feet
deep, and its side walls were three and
one-half feet thick. The porch of the gateway faced the Temple.

10On each side of the east gateway
were three rooms, which measured the
same on each side. The walls between
each room were the same thickness.
11The man measured the width of the
entrance to the gateway, which was seventeen and one-half feet wide. The width
of the gate was about twenty-three feet.
12And there was a low wall about twenty-
one inches high in front of each room.
The rooms were ten and one-half feet on
each side. **13**The man measured the
gateway from the roof of one room to the
roof of the opposite room. It was about
forty-four feet from one door to the opposite door. **14**The man also measured the
porch, which was about thirty-five feet
wide. The courtyard was around the

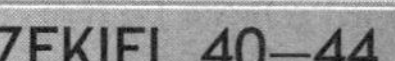

GOD'S NEW TEMPLE

EZEKIEL 40–44

Ezekiel saw a vision of a new Temple of God. The old Temple had been destroyed before the Israelites were taken in captivity to Babylon. But God showed Ezekiel how wonderful he would make the new Temple. More than that, the people of God would truly worship him with their whole hearts.

If you're a Christian, you provide a new temple for God within your own body. That's where the Holy Spirit lives. God wants you to worship him with your whole heart.

Connect to these links on worshiping God:

The Name of the Lord, Exodus 33:19–23; 34:5–8, p. 120

A Life of Thanksgiving, 1 Kings 1:47–48, p. 435

What's in a Name?, Isaiah 9:6, p. 908

Your Spiritual Roots, Zechariah 1:1–6, p. 1253

How Do I Love You?, Malachi 1:1–5, p. 1267

One Thing to Do, Romans 4:1–5, p. 1523

porch. **15**From the front of the outer side of the gateway to the front of the porch of the inner side of the gateway was eighty-seven and one-half feet. **16**The rooms and porch had small windows on both sides. The windows were narrower on the side facing the gateway. Carvings of palm trees were on each side wall of the rooms.

The Outer Courtyard

17Then the man brought me into the outer courtyard where I saw rooms and a pavement of stones all around the court. Thirty rooms were along the edge of the paved walkway. **18**The pavement ran alongside the gates and was as deep as the gates were wide. This was the lower pavement. **19**Then the man measured from the outer wall to the inner wall. The outer court between these two walls was one hundred seventy-five feet on the east and on the north.

The North Gateway

20The man measured the length and width of the north gateway leading to the outer courtyard. **21**Its three rooms on each side, its inner walls, and its porch measured the same as the first gateway. It was eighty-seven and one-half feet long and forty-four feet wide. **22**Its windows, porch, and carvings of palm trees measured the same as the east gateway. Seven steps went up to the gateway, and the gateway's porch was at the inner end. **23**The inner courtyard had a gateway across from the northern gateway like the one on the east. The man measured it and found it was one hundred seventy-five feet from inner gateway to outer gateway.

The South Gateway

24Then the man led me south where I saw a gateway facing south. He measured its inner walls and its porch, and they measured the same as the other gateways. **25**The gateway and its porch had windows all around like the other gateways. It was eighty-seven and one-half feet long and forty-four feet wide. **26**Seven steps went up to this gateway. Its porch was at the inner end, and it had carvings of palm trees on its inner walls. **27**The inner courtyard had a gateway on its south side. The man measured from gate to gate on the south side, which was one hundred seventy-five feet.

The Inner Courtyard

28Then the man brought me through the south gateway into the inner courtyard. The inner south gateway measured the same as the gateways in the outer wall. **29**The inner south gateway's rooms, inner walls, and porch measured the same as the gateways in the outer wall. There were windows all around the gateway and its porch. The gateway was eighty-seven and one-half feet long and forty-four feet wide. **30**Each porch of each inner gateway was about forty-four feet long and about nine feet wide. **31**The inner south gateway's porch faced the outer courtyard. Carvings of palm trees were on its side walls, and its stairway had eight steps.

32The man brought me into the inner courtyard on the east side. He measured the inner east gateway, and it was the same as the other gateways. **33**The inner east gateway's rooms, inside walls, and porch measured the same as the other gateways. Windows were all around the gateway and its porch. The inner east gateway was eighty-seven and one-half feet long and forty-four feet wide. **34**Its porch faced the outer courtyard. Carvings of palm trees were on its inner walls on each side, and its stairway had eight steps.

35Then the man brought me to the inner north gateway. He measured it, and it was the same as the other gateways. **36**Its rooms, inner walls, and porch measured the same as the other gateways. There were windows all around the gateway, which was eighty-seven and one-half feet long and forty-four feet wide. **37**Its porch faced the outer courtyard. Carvings of palm trees were on its inner walls on each side, and its stairway had eight steps.

Rooms for Preparing Sacrifices

38There was a room with a door that opened onto the porch of the inner north

gateway. In this room the priests washed
animals for the burnt offerings. **39**There
were two tables on each side of the
porch, on which animals for burnt offerings, sin offerings, and penalty offerings
were killed. **40**Outside, by each side wall
of the porch, at the entrance to the north
gateway, were two more tables. **41**So
there were four tables inside the gateway, and four tables outside. In all there
were eight tables on which the priests
killed animals for sacrifices. **42**There
were four tables made of cut stone for the
burnt offering. These tables were about
three feet long, three feet wide, and
about two feet high. On these tables the
priests put their tools which they used to
kill animals for burnt offerings and the
other sacrifices. **43**Double shelves three
inches wide were put up on all the walls.
The flesh for the offering was put on the
tables.

The Priests' Rooms

44There were two rooms in the inner
courtyard. One was beside the north
gateway and faced south. The other room
was beside the south gateway and faced
north. **45**The man said to me, "The room
which faces south is for the priests who
serve in the Temple area, **46**while the
room that faces north is for the priests
who serve at the altar. This second group
of priests are descendants of Zadok, the
only descendants of Levi who can come
near the LORD to serve him."

47The man measured the inner courtyard. It was a square—one hundred
seventy-five feet long and one hundred
seventy-five feet wide. The altar was in
front of the Temple.

The Temple Porch

48The man brought me to the porch of
the Temple and measured each side wall
of the porch. Each was about nine feet
thick. The doorway was twenty-four and
one-half feet wide. The side walls of the
doorway were each about five feet wide.
49The porch was thirty-five feet long and
twenty-one feet wide, with ten steps
leading up to it. Pillars were by the side
walls, one on each side of the entrance.

The Holy Place of the Temple

41 The man brought me to the Holy
Place and measured its side walls,
which were each ten and one-half feet
thick. **2**The entrance was seventeen and
one-half feet wide. The walls alongside
the entrance were each about nine feet
wide. The man measured the Holy Place,
which was seventy feet long and thirty-
five feet wide.

3Then the man went inside and measured the side walls of the next doorway.
Each was three and one-half feet thick.
The doorway was ten and one-half feet
wide, and the walls next to it were each
more than twelve feet thick. **4**Then the
man measured the room at the end of the
Holy Place. It was thirty-five feet long
and thirty-five feet wide. The man said to
me, "This is the Most Holy Place."

5Then the man measured the wall of
the Temple, which was ten and one-half
feet thick. There were side rooms seven
feet wide all around the Temple. **6**The
side rooms were on three different stories, each above the other, with thirty
rooms on each story. All around the Temple walls there were ledges for the side
rooms. The upper rooms rested on the
ledges but were not attached to the Temple walls. **7**The side rooms around the
Temple were wider on each higher story,
so rooms were wider on the top story. A
stairway went up from the lowest story
to the highest through the middle story.

8I also saw that the Temple had a
raised base all around. Its edge was the
foundation for the side rooms, and it was
ten and one-half feet thick. **9**The outer
wall of the side rooms was about nine feet
thick. There was an open area between
the side rooms of the Temple **10**and some
other rooms. It was thirty-five feet wide
and went all around the Temple. **11**The
side rooms had doors which led to the
open area around the outside of the Temple. One door faced north, and the other
faced south. The open area was about
nine feet wide all around.

12The building facing the private area
at the west side was one hundred twenty-
two and one-half feet wide. The wall
around the building was about nine feet

thick and one hundred fifty-seven and one-half feet long.

13Then the man measured the Temple. It was one hundred seventy-five feet long. The private area, including the building and its walls, was in all one hundred seventy-five feet long. 14Also the front of the Temple and the private area on its east side were one hundred seventy-five feet wide.

15The man measured the length of the building facing the private area on the west side, and it was one hundred seventy-five feet from one wall to the other.

The Holy Place, the Most Holy Place, and the outer porch 16had wood panels on the walls. By the doorway, the Temple had wood panels on the walls. The wood covered all the walls from the floor up to the windows, 17up to the part of the wall above the entrance.

All the walls inside the Most Holy Place and the Holy Place, and on the outside, in the porch, 18had carvings of creatures with wings and palm trees. A palm tree was between each carved creature, and every creature had two faces. 19One was a human face looking toward the palm tree on one side. The other was a lion's face looking toward the palm tree on the other side. They were carved all

CONNECT 2-YOU

ALL IN THE FAMILY

Tagg and I are talking with a friend who's having problems with her family. She wants to share some of those problems with us. So let's welcome Brittany, age 11, to Connect 2-You.

Welcome, Brittany. What's going on?

Brittany

My family is driving me crazy! Dad works all the time, and even when he's home, you can tell he's still thinking about things at the office. Mom loves to nag me about every little thing I do—the way I eat, the way I dress, the things I watch on TV, you name it. And my brother is completely wacko. He painted his whole room black and sits in there all the time listening to weird music. I can't move out for another eight years! How am I going to survive?

God tells us to honor our mother and father, but he doesn't say it will be easy. Living together under one roof takes a lot of patience and a lot of work. If you would like some tips on how to live with your parents and siblings in peace, check out the Livin' It page on living with your family, Exodus 20:12, p. 102.

Maybe the best thing you can do, Brittany, is to ask God to help you find some common ground with each member of your family. What can you talk about or do together that won't drive either of you crazy? If you'll make the effort to find some common ground, you'll probably find that the things that irritate you about each person don't bother you as much anymore.

around the Temple walls. 20From the
floor to above the entrance, palm trees
and creatures with wings were carved.
The walls of the Holy Place 21had square
doorposts. In front of the Most Holy
Place was something that looked like
22an altar of wood. It was more than five
feet high and three feet wide. Its corners,
base, and sides were wood. The man said
to me, "This is the table that is in the
presence of the LORD." 23Both the Holy
Place and the Most Holy Place had double doors. 24Each of the doors had two
pieces that would swing open. 25Carved
on the doors of the Holy Place were palm
trees and creatures with wings, like
those carved on the walls. And there was
a wood roof over the front Temple porch.
26There were windows and palm trees
on both side walls of the porch. The side
rooms of the Temple were also covered
by a roof over the stairway.

The Priests' Rooms

42 Then the man led me north out
into the outer courtyard and to the
rooms across from the private area and
the building. 2These rooms on the north
side were one hundred seventy-five feet
long and eighty-seven and one-half feet
wide. 3There was thirty-five feet of the
inner courtyard between them and the
Temple. On the other side, they faced
the stone pavement of the outer courtyard. The rooms were built in three stories like steps and had balconies. 4There
was a path on the north side of the rooms,
which was seventeen and one-half feet
wide and one hundred seventy-five feet
long. Doors led into the rooms from this
path. 5The top rooms were narrower, because the balconies took more space
from them. The rooms on the first and
second stories of the building were wider.
6The rooms were on three stories. They
did not have pillars like the pillars of the
courtyards. So the top rooms were farther back than those on the first and second stories. 7There was a wall outside
parallel to the rooms and to the outer
courtyard. It ran in front of the rooms for
eighty-seven and one-half feet. 8The row
of rooms along the outer courtyard was
eighty-seven and one-half feet long, and
the rooms that faced the Temple were
about one hundred seventy-five feet
long. 9The lower rooms had an entrance
on the east side so a person could enter
them from the outer courtyard, 10at the
start of the wall beside the courtyard.

There were rooms on the south side,
which were across from the private area
and the building. 11These rooms had a
path in front of them. They were like the
rooms on the north with the same length
and width and the same doors. 12The
doors of the south rooms were like the
doors of the north rooms. There was an
entrance at the open end of a path beside
the wall, so a person could enter at the
east end.

13The man said to me, "The north
and south rooms across from the private
area are holy rooms. There the priests
who go near the LORD will eat the most
holy offerings. There they will put the
most holy offerings: the grain offerings,
sin offerings, and the penalty offerings,
because the place is holy. 14The priests
who enter the Holy Place must leave
their serving clothes there before they
go into the outer courtyard, because
these clothes are holy. After they put
on other clothes, they may go to the
part of the Temple area which is for the
people."

Outside the Temple Area

15When the man finished measuring
inside the Temple area, he brought me
out through the east gateway. He measured the area all around. 16The man
measured the east side with the measuring stick; it was eight hundred seventy-
five feet by the measuring stick. 17He
measured the north side; it was eight
hundred seventy-five feet by the measuring stick. 18He measured the south side;
it was eight hundred seventy-five feet by
the measuring stick. 19He went around
to the west side; it measured eight hundred seventy-five feet by the measuring
stick. 20So he measured the Temple area
on all four sides. The Temple area had a
wall all around it that was eight hundred
seventy-five feet long and eight hundred

seventy-five feet wide. It separated what
was holy from that which was not holy.

The Lord Among His People

43 Then the man led me to the outer
east gateway, **2**and I saw the glory
of the God of Israel coming from the east.
It sounded like the roar of rushing water,
and its brightness made the earth shine.
3The vision I saw was like the vision I
had seen when the LORD came to destroy
the city and also like the vision I had seen
by the Kebar River. I bowed facedown on
the ground. **4**The glory of the LORD came
into the Temple area through the east
gateway.
5Then the Spirit picked
me up and brought me
into the inner courtyard.
There I saw the LORD's
glory filling the Temple.
6As the man stood at my
side, I heard someone
speaking to me from in-
side the Temple. **7**The
voice from the Temple
said to me, "Human, this
is my throne and the place where my feet
rest. I will live here among the Israelites
forever. The people of Israel will not
make my holy name unclean again. Neither the people nor their kings will make
it unclean with their sexual sins or with
the dead bodies of their kings. **8**The
kings made my name unclean by putting
their doorway next to my doorway, and
their doorpost next to my doorpost so
only a wall separated me from them.
When they did their acts that I hate, they
made my holy name unclean, and so I destroyed them in my anger. **9**Now let them
stop their sexual sins and take the dead
bodies of their kings far away from me.
Then I will live among them forever.
10"Human, tell the people of Israel
about the Temple so they will be
ashamed of their sins. Let them think
about the plan of the Temple. **11**If they
are ashamed of all they have done, let
them know the design of the Temple and
how it is built. Show them its exits and
entrances, all its designs, and also all its
rules and teachings. Write the rules as
they watch so they will obey all the
teachings and rules about the Temple.
12This is the teaching about the Temple:
All the area around the top of the mountain is most holy. This is the teaching
about the Temple.

> Then the Spirit picked me up and brought me into the inner courtyard. There I saw the LORD's glory filling the Temple.
> —Ezekiel 43:5

The Altar

13"These are the measurements of
the altar, using the measuring stick. The
altar's gutter is twenty-one inches high
and twenty-one inches wide, and its rim
is about nine inches around its edge. And
the altar is this tall: **14**From the ground
up to the lower ledge, it measures three
and one-half feet. It is
twenty-one inches wide.
It measures seven feet
from the smaller ledge to
the larger ledge and is
twenty-one inches wide.
15The place where the
sacrifice is burned on the
altar is seven feet high,
with its four corners
shaped like horns and
reaching up above it. **16**It
is square, twenty-one feet long and
twenty-one feet wide. **17**The upper ledge
is also square, twenty-four and one-half
feet long and twenty-four and one-half
feet wide. The rim around the altar is ten
and one-half inches wide, and its gutter is
twenty-one inches wide all around. Its
steps are on the east side."
18Then the man said to me, "Human,
this is what the Lord GOD says: These
are the rules for the altar. When it is built,
use these rules to offer burnt offerings
and to sprinkle blood on it. **19**You must
give a young bull as a sin offering to the
priests, the Levites who are from the
family of Zadok and who come near me to
serve me, says the Lord GOD. **20**Take
some of the bull's blood and put it on the
four corners of the altar, on the four corners of the ledge, and all around the rim.
This is how you will make the altar pure
and ready for God's service. **21**Then take
the bull for the sin offering and burn it in
the proper place in the Temple area, outside the Temple building.
22"On the second day offer a male

goat that has nothing wrong with it for a
sin offering. The priests will make the altar pure and ready for God's service as
they did with the young bull. **23**When you
finish making the altar pure and ready, offer a young bull and a male sheep from
the flock, which have nothing wrong with
them. **24**You must offer them in the presence of the LORD, and the priests are to
throw salt on them and offer them as a
burnt offering to the LORD.

25"You must prepare a goat every day
for seven days as a sin offering. Also, the
priests must prepare a young bull and
male sheep from the flock, which have
nothing wrong with them. **26**For seven
days the priests are to make the altar
pure and ready for God's service. Then
they will give the altar to God. **27**After
these seven days, on the eighth day, the
priests must offer your burnt offerings
and your fellowship offerings on the altar.
Then I will accept you, says the Lord
GOD."

The Outer East Gate

44 Then the man brought me back to
the outer east gateway of the
Temple area, but the gate was shut. **2**The
LORD said to me, "This gate will stay
shut; it will not be opened. No one may
enter through it, because the LORD God
of Israel has entered through it. So it
must stay shut. **3**Only the ruler himself
may sit in the gateway to eat a meal in the
presence of the LORD. He must enter
through the porch of the gateway and go
out the same way."

4Then the man brought me through
the outer north gate to
the front of the Temple.
As I looked, I saw the glory of the LORD filling the
Temple of the LORD, and I
bowed facedown on the
ground.

5The LORD said to me,
"Human, pay attention.
Use your eyes to see, and
your ears to hear. See and
hear everything I tell you
about all the rules and teachings of the
Temple of the LORD. Pay attention to the
entrance to the Temple and to all the exits from the Temple area. **6**Then speak to
those who refuse to obey. Say to the people of Israel, 'This is what the Lord GOD
says: Stop doing all your acts that I hate,
Israel! **7**You brought foreigners into my
Holy Place who were not circumcised in
the flesh and had not given themselves to
serving me. You dishonored my Temple
when you offered me food, fat, and blood.
You broke my agreement by all the things
you did that I hate. **8**You did not take care
of my holy things yourselves but put foreigners in charge of my Temple. **9**This is
what the Lord GOD says: Foreigners who
are not circumcised in flesh and who do
not give themselves to serving me may
not enter my Temple. Not even a foreigner living among the people of Israel may
enter.

10" 'But the Levites who stopped
obeying me when Israel left me and who
followed their idols must be punished for
their sin. **11**These Levites are to be servants in my Holy Place. They may guard
the gates of the Temple and serve in the
Temple area. They may kill the animals
for the burnt offering and the sacrifices
for the people. They may stand before
the people to serve them. **12**But these
Levites helped the people worship their
idols and caused the people of Israel to
fall, so I make this promise: They will be
punished for their sin, says the Lord
GOD. **13**They will not come near me to
serve as priests, nor will they come near
any of my holy things or the most holy
offerings. But they will be made ashamed
of the things they did that I hate. **14**I will
put them in charge of tak-
ing care of the Temple
area, all the work that
must be done in it.

15" 'But the priests
who are Levites and de-
scendants of Zadok took
care of my Holy Place
when Israel left me, so
they may come near to
serve me. They may
stand in my presence to
offer me the fat and blood of the animals
they sacrifice, says the Lord GOD. **16**They

See and hear everything I tell you about all the rules and teachings of the Temple of the LORD.
—Ezekiel 44:5

are the only ones who may enter my Holy
Place. Only they may come near my table
to serve me and take care of the things I
gave them to do.
17" 'When they enter the gates of the
inner courtyard, they must wear linen
robes. They must not wear wool to serve
at the gates of the inner courtyard or in
the Temple. **18**They will wear linen turbans on their heads and linen underclothes. They will not wear anything that
makes them perspire. **19**When they go
out into the outer courtyard to the people, they must take off their serving
clothes before they go. They must leave
these clothes in the holy rooms and put
on other clothes. Then they will not let
their holy clothes hurt the people.
20" 'They must not shave their heads
or let their hair grow long but must keep
the hair of their heads trimmed. **21**None
of the priests may drink wine when they
enter the inner courtyard. **22**The priests
must not marry widows or divorced
women. They may marry only virgins
from the people of Israel or widows of
priests. **23**They must teach my people
the difference between what is holy and
what is not holy. They must help my people know what is unclean and what is
clean.
24" 'In court they will act as judges.
When they judge, they will follow my
teachings. They must obey my laws and
my rules at all my special feasts and keep
my Sabbaths holy.
25" 'They must not go near a dead
person, making themselves unclean. But
they are allowed to make themselves unclean if the dead person is their father,
mother, son, daughter, brother, or a sister
who has not married. **26**After a priest has
been made clean again, he must wait
seven days. **27**Then he may go into the
inner courtyard to serve in the Temple,
but he must offer a sin offering for himself, says the Lord GOD.
28" 'These are the rules about the
priests and their property: They will
have me instead of property. You will not
give them any land to own in Israel; I am
what they will own. **29**They will eat the
grain offerings, sin offerings, and penalty
offerings. Everything Israel gives to me
will be theirs. **30**The best fruits of all the
first harvests and all the special gifts offered to me will belong to the priests. You
will also give to the priests the first part
of your grain that you grind and so bring a
blessing on your family. **31**The priests
must not eat any bird or animal that died
a natural death or one that has been torn
by wild animals.

The Land Is Divided

45 " 'When you divide the land for the
Israelite tribes by throwing lots,
you must give a part of the land to belong
to the LORD. It will be about seven miles
long and about six miles wide; all of this
land will be holy. **2**From this land, an area
eight hundred seventy-five feet square
will be for the Temple. There will be an
open space around the Temple that is
eighty-seven and one-half feet wide. **3**In
the holy area you will measure a part
about seven miles long and three miles
wide, and in it will be the Most Holy
Place. **4**This holy part of the land will be
for the priests who serve in the Temple,
who come near to the LORD to serve him.
It will be a place for the priests' houses
and for the Temple. **5**Another area about
seven miles long and more than three
miles wide will be for the Levites, who
serve in the Temple area. It will belong
to them so they will have cities in which
to live.
6" 'You must give the city an area that
is about one and one-half miles wide and
about seven miles long, along the side of
the holy area. It will belong to all the people of Israel.
7" 'The ruler will have land on both
sides of the holy area and the city. On the
west of the holy area, his land will reach
to the Mediterranean Sea. On the east of
the holy area, his land will reach to the
eastern border. It will be as long as the
land given to each tribe. **8**Only this land
will be the ruler's property in Israel. So
my rulers will not be cruel to my people
anymore, but they will let each tribe in
the nation of Israel have its share of the
land.
9" 'This is what the Lord GOD says:

You have gone far enough, you rulers of Israel! Stop being cruel and hurting people, and do what is right and fair. Stop forcing my people out of their homes, says the Lord GOD. **10**You must have honest scales, an honest dry measurement and an honest liquid measurement. **11**The dry measure and the liquid measure will be the same: The liquid measure will always be a tenth of a homer,[n] and the ephah will always be a tenth of a homer. The measurement they follow will be the homer. **12**The shekel[n] will be worth twenty gerahs, and a mina will be worth sixty shekels.

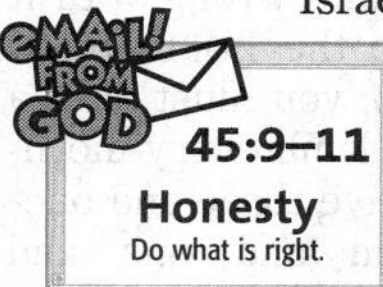
EMAIL FROM GOD
45:9–11
Honesty
Do what is right.

Offerings and Holy Days

13" 'This is the gift you should offer: a sixth of an ephah from every homer of wheat, and a sixth of an ephah from every homer of barley. **14**The amount of oil you are to offer is a tenth of a bath from each cor. (Ten baths make a homer and also make a cor.) **15**You should give one sheep from each flock of two hundred from the watering places of Israel. All these are to be offered for the grain offerings, burnt offerings, and fellowship offerings to remove sins so you will belong to God, says the Lord GOD. **16**All people in the land will give this special offering to the ruler of Israel. **17**It will be the ruler's responsibility to supply the burnt offerings, grain offerings, and drink offerings. These offerings will be given at the feasts, at the New Moons, on the Sabbaths, and at all the other feasts of Israel. The ruler will supply the sin offerings, grain offerings, and fellowship offerings to pay for the sins of Israel.

18" 'This is what the Lord GOD says: On the first day of the first month take a young bull that has nothing wrong with it. Use it to make the Temple pure and ready for God's service. **19**The priest will take some of the blood from this sin offering and put it on the doorposts of the Temple, on the four corners of the ledge of the altar, and on the posts of the gate to the inner courtyard. **20**You will do the same thing on the seventh day of the month for anyone who has sinned by accident or without knowing it. This is how you make the Temple pure and ready for God's service.

Passover Feast Offerings

21" 'On the fourteenth day of the first month you will celebrate the Feast of Passover. It will be a feast of seven days when you eat bread made without yeast. **22**On that day the ruler must offer a bull for himself and for all the people of the land as a sin offering. **23**During the seven days of the feast he must offer seven bulls and seven male sheep that have nothing wrong with them. They will be burnt offerings to the LORD, which the ruler will offer every day of the seven days of the feast. He must also offer a male goat every day as a sin offering. **24**The ruler must give as a grain offering one-half bushel for each bull and one-half bushel for each sheep. He must give a gallon of olive oil for each half bushel.

25" 'Beginning on the fifteenth day of the seventh month, when you celebrate the Feast of Shelters, the ruler will supply the same things for seven days: the sin offerings, burnt offerings, grain offerings, and the olive oil.

Rules for Worship

46 " 'This is what the Lord GOD says: The east gate of the inner courtyard will stay shut on the six working days, but it will be opened on the Sabbath day and on the day of the New Moon. **2**The ruler will enter from outside through the porch of the gateway and stand by the gatepost, while the priests offer the ruler's burnt offering and fellowship offering. The ruler will worship at the entrance of the gateway, and then he will go out. But the gate will not be shut until

45:11 homer The Hebrew word means "donkey-load." It measured about five dry bushels or one hundred seventy-five liquid quarts. So an ephah was about one-half bushel, and a bath was about eighteen quarts.

45:12 shekel In Ezekiel's time a shekel weighed about two-fifths of an ounce.

evening. **3**The people of the land will worship at the entrance of that gateway in the
presence of the LORD on the Sabbaths and
New Moons. **4**This is the burnt offering
the ruler will offer to the LORD on the Sabbath day: six male lambs that have nothing
wrong with them and a male sheep that
has nothing wrong with it. **5**He must give
a half-bushel grain offering with the male
sheep, but he may give as much grain offering with the lambs as he pleases. He
must also give a gallon of olive oil for
each half bushel of grain. **6**On the day of
the New Moon he must offer a young bull
that has nothing wrong with it. He must
also offer six lambs and a male sheep that
have nothing wrong with them. **7**The ruler
must give a half-bushel grain offering with
the bull and one-half bushel with the male
sheep. With the lambs, he may give as
much grain as he pleases. But he must give
a gallon of olive oil for each half bushel of
grain. **8**When the ruler enters, he must go
in through the porch of the gateway, and
he must go out the same way.

9" 'When the people of the land come
into the LORD's presence at the special
feasts, those who enter through the north
gate to worship must go out through the
south gate. Those who enter through the
south gate must go out through the north
gate. They must not return the same way
they entered; everyone must go out the
opposite way. **10**The ruler will go in with
the people when they go in and go out
with them when they go out.

11" 'At the feasts and regular times of
worship one-half bushel of grain must be
offered with a young bull, and one-half
bushel of grain must be offered with a
male sheep. But with an offering of
lambs, the ruler may give as much grain
as he pleases. He should give a gallon of
olive oil for each half bushel of grain.
12The ruler may give an offering as a
special gift to the LORD; it may be a burnt
offering or fellowship offering. When he
gives it to the LORD, the inner east gate
is to be opened for him. He must offer his
burnt offering or his fellowship offering
as he does on the Sabbath day. Then he
will go out, and the gate will be shut after
he has left.

13" 'Every day you will give a year-
old lamb that has nothing wrong with it
for a burnt offering to the LORD. Do it
every morning. **14**Also, you must offer a
grain offering with the lamb every morning. For this you will give three and one-
third quarts of grain and one and
one-third quarts of olive oil, to make the
fine flour moist, as a grain offering to the
LORD. This is a rule that must be kept
from now on. **15**So you must always give
the lamb, together with the grain offering
and the olive oil, every morning as a
burnt offering.

Rules for the Ruler

16" 'This is what the Lord GOD says:
If the ruler gives a gift from his land to
any of his sons, that land will belong to
the son and then to the son's children. It
is their property passed down from their
family. **17**But if the ruler gives a gift from
his land to any of his servants, that land
will belong to the servant only until the
year of freedom. Then the land will go
back to the ruler. Only the ruler's sons
may keep a gift of land from the ruler.
18The ruler must not take any of the
people's land, forcing them out of their
land. He must give his sons some of his
own land so my people will not be scattered out of their own land.' "

The Special Kitchens

19The man led me through the entrance at the side of the gateway to the
priests' holy rooms that face north.
There I saw a place at the west end.
20The man said to me, "This is where
the priests will boil the meat of the penalty offering and sin offering and bake the
grain offering. Then they will not need to
bring these holy offerings into the outer
courtyard, because that would hurt the
people."

21Then the man brought me out into
the outer courtyard and led me to its four
corners. In each corner of the courtyard
was a smaller courtyard. **22**Small courtyards were in the four corners of the
courtyard. Each small courtyard was the
same size, seventy feet long and fifty-two
and one-half feet wide. **23**A stone wall

was around each of the four small courtyards, and places for cooking were built
in each of the stone walls. 24The man
said to me, "These are the kitchens
where those who work in the Temple will
boil the sacrifices offered by the people."

The River from the Temple

47 The man led me back to the door
of the Temple, and I saw water
coming out from under the doorway and
flowing east. (The Temple faced east.)
The water flowed down from the south
side wall of the Temple and then south of
the altar. 2The man brought me out
through the outer north gate and led me
around outside to the outer east gate. I
found the water coming out on the south
side of the gate.

3The man went toward the east with a
line in his hand and measured about one-
third of a mile. Then he led me through
water that came up to my ankles. 4The
man measured about one-third of a mile
again and led me through water that
came up to my knees. Then he measured
about one-third of a mile again and led me
through water up to my waist. 5The man
measured about one-third of a mile again,
but it was now a river that I could not
cross. The water had risen too high; it
was deep enough for swimming; it was a
river that no one could cross. 6The man
asked me, "Human, do you see this?"

Then the man led me back to the bank
of the river. 7As I went back, I saw many
trees on both sides of the river. 8The man
said to me, "This water will flow toward
the eastern areas and go down into the
Jordan Valley. When it enters the Dead
Sea, it will become fresh. 9Everywhere
the river goes, there will be many fish.
Wherever this water goes the Dead Sea
will become fresh, and so where the river
goes there will be many living things.
10Fishermen will stand by the Dead Sea.
From En Gedi all the way to En Eglaim
there will be places to spread fishing
nets. There will be many kinds of fish in
the Dead Sea, as many as in the Mediterranean Sea. 11But its swamps and
marshes will not become fresh; they will
be left for salt. 12All kinds of fruit trees
will grow on both banks of the river, and
their leaves will not dry and die. The
trees will have fruit every month, because the water for them comes from the
Temple. The fruit from the trees will be
used for food, and their leaves for medicine."

Borders of the Land

13This is what the Lord GOD says:
"These are the borders of the land to be
divided among the twelve tribes of Israel.
Joseph will have two parts of land. 14You
will divide the land equally. I promised to
give it to your ancestors, so this land will
belong to you as family property.

15"This will be the border line of the
land: "On the north side it will start at the
Mediterranean Sea. It will go through
Hethlon, toward Lebo Hamath and on to
the towns of Zedad, 16Berothah, and Sib-
raim on the border between Damascus
and Hamath. Then it will go on to the
town of Hazer Hatticon on the border of
the country of Hauran. 17So the border
line will go from the Mediterranean Sea
east to the town of Hazar Enan, where
the land belonging to Damascus and Hamath lies on the north side. This will be
the north side of the land.

18"On the east side the border runs
south from a point between Hauran and
Damascus. It will go along the Jordan between Gilead and the land of Israel and
will continue to the town of Tamar on the
Dead Sea. This will be the east side of the
land.

19"On the south side the border line
will go east from Tamar all the way to the
waters of Meribah Kadesh. Then it will
run along the brook of Egypt to the Mediterranean Sea. This will be the south side
of the land.

20"On the west side the Mediterranean Sea will be the border line up to a
place across from Lebo Hamath. This will
be the west side of your land.

21"You will divide this land among the
tribes of Israel. 22You will divide it as
family property for yourselves and for
the foreigners who live and have children
among you. You are to treat these
foreigners the same as people born in

Israel; they are to share the land with the
tribes of Israel. **23**In whatever tribe the
foreigner lives, you will give him some
land," says the Lord GOD.

Dividing the Land

48 "These are the areas of the tribes
named here: Dan will have one
share at the northern
border. It will go from the
sea through Hethlon to
Lebo Hamath, all the way
to Hazar Enan, where
Damascus lies to the
north. It will stop there
next to Hamath. This will
be Dan's northern border
from the east side to the
Mediterranean Sea on
the west side.

2"South of Dan's border, Asher will
have one share. It will go from the east
side to the west side.

3"South of Asher's border, Naphtali
will have one share. It will go from the
east side to the west side.

4"South of Naphtali's border, Manasseh will have one share. It will go from
the east side to the west side.

5"South of Manasseh's border, Ephraim will have one share. It will go from
the east side to the west side.

6"South of Ephraim's border, Reuben
will have one share. It will go from the
east side to the west side.

7"South of Reuben's border, Judah
will have one share. It will go from the
east side to the west side.

8"South of Judah's border will be the
holy area which you are to give. It will be
about seven miles wide and as long and
wide as one of the tribes' shares. It will
run from the east side to the west side.
The Temple will be in the middle of this
area.

9"The share which you will give the
LORD will be about seven miles long and
three miles wide. **10**The holy area will be
divided among these people. The priests
will have land about seven miles long on
the north and south sides, and three
miles wide on the west and east sides.
The Temple of the LORD will be in the
middle of it. **11**This land is for the priests
who are given the holy duty of serving
the LORD. They are the descendants of
Zadok who did my work and did not leave
me when Israel and the Levites left me.
12They will have as their share a very
holy part of the holy portion of the land. It
will be next to the land of the Levites.

13"Alongside the land
for the priests, the Le-
vites will have a share
about seven miles long
and three miles wide; its
full length will be about
seven miles and its full
width about three miles.
14The Levites are not to
sell or trade any of this
land. They are not to let
anyone else own any of
this best part of the land, because it belongs to the LORD.

You are to treat these foreigners the same as people born in Israel; they are to share the land with the tribes of Israel.
—Ezekiel 47:22

City Property

15"The rest of the area will be about
one and one-half miles wide and seven
miles long. It will not be holy but will belong to the city and be used for homes
and pastures. The city will be in the middle of it. **16**These are the city's measurements: the north side will be about one
mile, the south side about one mile, the
east side about one mile, and the west
side about one mile. **17**The city's land for
pastures will be about four hundred
thirty-seven feet on the north, four hundred thirty-seven feet on the south, four
hundred thirty-seven feet on the east,
and four hundred thirty-seven feet on the
west. **18**Along the long side of the holy
area there will be left three miles on the
east and three miles on the west. It will
be used to grow food for the city workers.
19The city workers from all the tribes of
Israel will farm this land. **20**This whole
area will be square, seven miles by seven
miles. You shall give to the LORD the holy
share along with the city property.

21"Land that is left over on both sides
of the holy area and city property will belong to the ruler. That land will extend
east of the holy area to the eastern border and west of it to the Mediterranean

Sea. Both of these areas run the length of
the lands of the tribes, and they belong to
the ruler. The holy area with the Holy
Place of the Temple will be in the middle.
22The Levites' land and the city property
will be in the middle of the lands belonging to the ruler. Those lands will be between Judah's border and Benjamin's
border.

The Other Tribes' Land

23"Here is what the rest of the tribes
will receive: Benjamin will have one
share. It will go from the east side to the
Mediterranean Sea on the west side.
24"South of Benjamin's land, Simeon
will have one share. It will go from the
east side to the west side.
25"South of Simeon's land, Issachar
will have one share. It will go from the
east side to the west side.
26"South of Issachar's land, Zebulun
will have one share. It will go from the
east side to the west side.
27"South of Zebulun's land, Gad will
have one share. It will go from the east
side to the west side.
28"The southern border of Gad's land
will go east from Tamar on the Dead Sea
to the waters of Meribah Kadesh. Then it
will run along the brook of Egypt to the
Mediterranean Sea.
29"This is the land you will divide
among the tribes of Israel to be their
shares," says the Lord GOD.

The Gates of the City

30"These will be the outside borders
of the city: The north side will measure
more than one mile. **31**There will be
three gates facing north: Reuben's Gate,
Judah's Gate, and Levi's Gate, named for
the tribes of Israel.
32"The east side will measure more
than one mile. There will be three gates
facing east: Joseph's Gate, Benjamin's
Gate, and Dan's Gate.
33"The south side will measure more
than one mile. There will be three gates
facing south: Simeon's Gate, Issachar's
Gate, and Zebulun's Gate.
34"The west side will measure more
than one mile. There will be three gates
facing west: Gad's Gate, Asher's Gate,
and Naphtali's Gate.
35"The city will measure about six
miles around. From then on the name of
the city will be The LORD Is There."

ADVENTURES IN BABYLON

Hi! Daniel here. You have probably heard a few stories about me. I'm the one who survived a night in the lions' den. When I was a young man, my three friends and I were captured by our enemies and taken to live in the king's palace in Babylon. The king wanted us to be his servants, so we learned the language and the customs of Babylon. We were even given Babylonian names. Only one problem: the food. It had been offered to idols! It was against God's law to eat this food, but how could we refuse the food without insulting the king? Plug into Daniel 1 for the answer.

I wrote this book to encourage people to follow God even when times are difficult. One time my three friends had to make a choice: worship a 90-foot gold statue or be thrown into a blazing furnace. What would you do? Because they refused to worship the statue, they were tied up and thrown into the furnace. Imagine the king's surprise when he saw a fourth person in the fire. Who was it? Surf over to Daniel 3:25–30 to find out.

JESUS WATCH

God gave Daniel the ability to explain dreams. One time King Nebuchadnezzar had a strange dream and asked Daniel to explain it to him. In his dream the king saw a huge, frightening statue with a head of pure gold. The rest of the body was made of bronze, silver, iron, and clay. A rock hit the statue, and the statue crumbled. The rock became a large mountain that filled the earth.

Daniel explained that the statue stood for the kingdoms of the world that will come to an end someday. The rock stands for Jesus who will come and establish a kingdom that will never end.

God also gave Daniel dreams and visions about heaven. He saw Jesus coming into heaven on clouds. Jesus came near God's throne and was given the authority, glory, and strength of a king. People from every nation will serve him and his kingdom will last forever.

OTHER CONNECTIONS

GET THE INFO Connect to these information bulletin boards about people and places found in the Book of Daniel:

- Let's Visit Babylon, Daniel 2; 7. Find out more about one of the most powerful cities in the world during Bible times and the place where Daniel lived and served under three different kings.
- Who Are the Greeks?, Daniel 11:3–35. When Daniel predicted the Greeks would one day be a world power, they were a little known people. Yet Daniel's prediction, given to him in a vision by God, came true. Find out what importance the Greeks and their language were to play in the spread of the gospel throughout the world.

- Let's Make a Deal, Daniel 1:8–21
- Obeying God or Man?, Daniel 3:8–30
- The Writing's on the Wall, Daniel 5
- In the Lions' Den, Daniel 6
- Concern for All, Daniel 9

my FAVORITE links

____

____

____

____

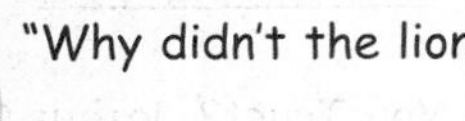
"Why didn't the lions eat Daniel?"

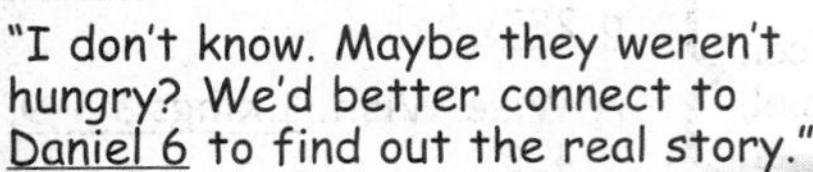
"I don't know. Maybe they weren't hungry? We'd better connect to Daniel 6 to find out the real story."

OTHER COOL STORIES IN DANIEL:

Eat your veggies!, Daniel 1
The heat is on!, Daniel 3
A grass-eating king, Daniel 4:28–37
Writing on the wall, Daniel 5:22–31

did you know?

Daniel Taken to Babylon

1 During the third year that Jehoiakim
was king of Judah, Nebuchadnezzar
king of Babylon came to Jerusalem and
surrounded it with his army. 2The Lord
allowed Nebuchadnezzar to capture Jehoiakim king of Judah. Nebuchadnezzar
also took some of the things from the
Temple of God, which he carried to Babylonia and put in the temple of his gods.
3Then King Nebuchadnezzar ordered
Ashpenaz, his chief officer, to bring some
of the Israelite men into his palace. He
wanted them to be from important families, including the family of the king of Judah. 4King Nebuchadnezzar wanted only
young Israelite men who had nothing
wrong with them. They were to be handsome and well educated, capable of learning and understanding, and able to serve
in his palace. Ashpenaz was to teach them
the language and writings of the Babylonians. 5The king gave the young men a certain amount of food and wine every day,
just like the food he ate. The young men
were to be trained for three years, and
then they would become servants of the
king of Babylon. 6Among those young
men were Daniel, Hananiah, Mishael, and
Azariah from the people of Judah.
7Ashpenaz, the chief officer, gave
them Babylonian names. Daniel's new
name was Belteshazzar, Hananiah's was
Shadrach, Mishael's was Meshach, and
Azariah's was Abednego.
8Daniel decided not to eat the king's
food or drink his wine because that would
make him unclean. So he asked Ashpenaz
for permission not to make himself unclean in this way.
9God made Ashpenaz, the chief officer,
want to be kind and merciful to Daniel,
10but Ashpenaz said to Daniel, "I am
afraid of my master, the king. He ordered
me to give you this food and drink. If you
begin to look worse than other young men
your age, the king will see this. Then he
will cut off my head because of you."
11Ashpenaz had ordered a guard to
watch Daniel, Hananiah, Mishael, and
Azariah. 12Daniel said to the guard,
"Please give us this test for ten days:
Don't give us anything but vegetables to

FAITH links

LET'S MAKE A DEAL

DANIEL 1:8-21

Suppose your schoolteacher involved your class in an activity that you and your parents agreed was wrong for you. Should you go along with the activity in order to be obedient? Daniel faced a similar situation. He was a servant to the king of Babylon, but he wanted to obey God. The king wanted him to eat the foods all his servants ate. Daniel wanted to eat the healthier food that he thought God would want him to eat. So Daniel suggested a test to see which foods made him healthier.

You may need to bargain with others sometimes. God can give you the wisdom to suggest other choices and to do what is right.

Here are some more Faithlinks on making smart choices:

Take Me to Your Leader, Numbers 27:12–23, p. 214

Who Do You Trust?, Joshua 9, p. 287

A Wise Wish, 1 Kings 3:5–9, p. 439

If You Want My Advice . . . , Proverbs 13:1, p. 843

That's False!, 2 John 7–11, p. 1722

Helpful Hints, 3 John 11, p. 1724

eat and water to drink. **13**After ten days compare how we look with how the other young men look who eat the king's food. See for yourself and then decide how you want to treat us, your servants."

14So the guard agreed to test them for ten days. **15**After ten days they looked healthier and better fed than all the young men who ate the king's food. **16**So the guard took away the king's special food and wine, feeding them vegetables instead.

EMAIL FROM GOD
1:17
Talents
Who gives you your talents?

17God gave these four young men wisdom and the ability to learn many things that people had written and studied. Daniel could also understand visions and dreams.

18At the end of the time set for them by the king, Ashpenaz brought all the young men to King Nebuchadnezzar. **19**The king talked to them and found that none of the young men were as good as Daniel, Hananiah, Mishael, and Azariah. So those four young men became the king's servants. **20**Every time the king asked them about something important, they showed much wisdom and understanding. They were ten times better than all the fortune-tellers and magicians in his kingdom! **21**So Daniel continued to be the king's servant until the first year Cyrus was king.

Nebuchadnezzar's Dream

2 During Nebuchadnezzar's second year as king, he had dreams that bothered him and kept him awake at night. **2**So the king called for his fortune-tellers, magicians, wizards, and wise men, because he wanted them to tell him what he had dreamed. They came in and stood in front of the king.

3Then the king said to them, "I had a dream that bothers me, and I want to know what it means."

4The wise men answered the king in the Aramaic language, "O king, live forever! Please tell us, your servants, your dream. Then we will tell you what it means."

5King Nebuchadnezzar said to them, "I meant what I said. You must tell me the dream and what it means. If you don't, I will have you torn apart, and I will turn your houses into piles of stones. **6**But if you tell me my dream and its meaning, I will reward you with gifts and great honor. So tell me the dream and what it means."

7Again the wise men said to the king, "Tell us, your servants, the dream, and we will tell you what it means."

8King Nebuchadnezzar answered, "I know you are trying to get more time, because you know that I meant what I said. **9**If you don't tell me my dream, you will be punished. You have all agreed to tell me lies and wicked things, hoping things will change. Now, tell me the dream so that I will know you can tell me what it really means!"

10The wise men answered the king, saying, "No one on earth can do what the king asks! No great and powerful king has ever asked the fortune-tellers, magicians, or wise men to do this; **11**the king is asking something that is too hard. Only the gods could tell the king this, but the gods do not live among people."

12When the king heard their answer, he became very angry. He ordered that all the wise men of Babylon be killed. **13**So King Nebuchadnezzar's order to kill the wise men was announced, and men were sent to look for Daniel and his friends to kill them.

14Arioch, the commander of the king's guards, was going to kill the wise men of Babylon. But Daniel spoke to him with wisdom and skill, **15**saying, "Why did the king order such a terrible punishment?" Then Arioch explained everything to Daniel. **16**So Daniel went to King Nebuchadnezzar and asked for an appointment so that he could tell the king what his dream meant.

17Then Daniel went to his house and explained the whole story to his friends Hananiah, Mishael, and Azariah. **18**Daniel asked his friends to pray that the God of heaven would show them mercy and help them understand this secret so he and his friends would

LET'S VISIT BABYLON

Daniel 2; 7

Babylon was the capital of the Babylonian Empire. It was located between two famous rivers, the Tigris and the Euphrates. Babylon was at its richest and finest when King Nebuchadnezzar II was king. Most important cities at that time had walls for protection. Babylon had a *double* wall and eight major gates into the city. The walls were decorated with colored bricks that had drawings of lions, dragons, and bulls. One of the most famous sights in Babylon was King Nebuchadnezzar's Hanging Gardens, one of the seven wonders of the ancient world.

At one time, God's people in Judah were taken as captives to Babylon. The stories that you have heard about Daniel in the lions' den and Daniel's friends in the fiery furnace happened in Babylon. Daniel predicted the destruction of Babylon, and today the whole city remains in ruins.

not be killed with the other wise men of
Babylon.
19During the night God explained the
secret to Daniel in a vision. Then Daniel
praised the God of heaven. **20**Daniel said:

"Praise God forever and ever,
because he has wisdom and
power.
21 He changes the times and seasons of
the year.
He takes away the power of kings
and gives their power to new
kings.
He gives wisdom to those who are
wise
and knowledge to those who
understand.
22 He makes known secrets that are
deep and hidden;
he knows what is hidden in
darkness,
and light is all around him.
23 I thank you and praise you, God of
my ancestors,
because you have given me
wisdom and power.
You told me what we asked of you;
you told us about the king's
dream."

The Meaning of the Dream

24Then Daniel went to Arioch, the
man King Nebuchadnezzar had chosen to
kill the wise men of Babylon. Daniel said
to him, "Don't put the wise men of Babylon to death. Take me to the king, and I
will tell him what his dream means."
25Very quickly Arioch took Daniel to
the king and said, "I have found a man
among the captives from Judah who can
tell the king what his dream means."
26The king asked Daniel, who was
also called Belteshazzar, "Are you able to
tell me what I dreamed and what it
means?"
27Daniel answered, "No wise man,
magician, or fortune-teller can explain to
the king the secret he has asked about.
28But there is a God in heaven who explains secret things, and he has shown
King Nebuchadnezzar what will happen
at a later time. This is your dream, the
vision you saw while lying on your bed:
29O king, as you were lying there, you
thought about things to come. God, who
can tell people about secret things,
showed you what is going to happen.
30God also told this secret to me, not because I have greater wisdom than any

other living person, but so that you may
know what it means. In that way you will
understand what went through your
mind.
31"O king, in your dream you saw a
huge, shiny, and frightening statue in
front of you. **32**The head of the statue
was made of pure gold. Its chest and arms
were made of silver. Its stomach and the
upper part of its legs were made of
bronze. **33**The lower part of the legs
were made of iron, while its feet were
made partly of iron and partly of baked
clay. **34**While you were looking at the
statue, you saw a rock cut free, but no
human being touched the rock. It hit the
statue on its feet of iron and clay and
smashed them. **35**Then the iron, clay,
bronze, silver, and gold broke to pieces at
the same time. They became like chaff on
a threshing floor in the summertime; the
wind blew them away, and there was
nothing left. Then the rock that hit the
statue became a very large mountain that
filled the whole earth.
36"That was your dream. Now we will
tell the king what it means. **37**O king, you
are the greatest king. God of heaven has
given you a kingdom, power, strength,
and glory. **38**Wherever people, wild animals, and birds live, God made you ruler
over them. King Nebuchadnezzar, you
are the head of gold on that statue.
39"Another kingdom will come after
you, but it will not be as great as yours.
Next a third kingdom, the bronze part,
will rule over the earth. **40**Then there
will be a fourth kingdom, strong as iron.
In the same way that iron crushes and
smashes things to pieces, the fourth
kingdom will smash and crush all the
other kingdoms.
41"You saw that the statue's feet and
toes were partly baked clay and partly
iron. That means the fourth kingdom will
be a divided kingdom. It will have some
of the strength of iron in it, just as you
saw iron was mixed with clay. **42**The toes
of the statue were partly iron and partly
clay. So the fourth kingdom will be partly
strong like iron and partly breakable like
clay. **43**You saw the iron mixed with clay,
but iron and clay do not hold together. In
the same way the people of the fourth
kingdom will be a mixture, but they will
not be united as one people.
44"During the time of those kings,
the God of heaven will set up another
kingdom that will never be destroyed or
given to another group of people. This
kingdom will crush all the other kingdoms and bring them to an end, but it will
continue forever.
45"King Nebuchadnezzar, you saw a
rock cut from a mountain, but no human
being touched it. The rock broke the iron,
bronze, clay, silver, and gold to pieces. In
this way the great God showed you what
will happen. The dream is true, and you
can trust this explanation."
46Then King Nebuchadnezzar fell
facedown on the ground in front of Daniel.
The king honored him and commanded
that an offering and incense be presented
to him. **47**Then the king said to Daniel,
"Truly I know your God is the greatest of
all gods, the Lord of all the kings. He tells
people about things they cannot know. I
know this is true, because you were able
to tell these secret things to me."
48Then the king gave Daniel many
gifts plus an important position in his
kingdom. Nebuchadnezzar made him
ruler over the whole area of Babylon and
put him in charge of all the wise men of
Babylon. **49**Daniel asked the king to
make Shadrach, Meshach, and Abednego
leaders over the area of Babylon, so the
king did as Daniel asked. Daniel himself
became one of the people who stayed at
the royal court.

The Gold Idol and Blazing Furnace

3 King Nebuchadnezzar made a gold
statue ninety feet high and nine feet
wide and set it up on the plain of Dura in
the area of Babylon. **2**Then he called for
the leaders: the governors, assistant governors, captains of the soldiers, people
who advised the king, keepers of the treasury, judges, rulers, and all other officers
in his kingdom. He wanted them to come
to the special service for the statue he had
set up. **3**So they all came for the special
service and stood in front of the statue

that King Nebuchadnezzar had set up.
4Then the man who made announce-
ments for the king said in a loud voice,
"People, nations, and those of every language, this is what you are commanded to
do: 5When you hear the sound of the
horns, flutes, lyres, zithers,* harps, pipes,
and all the other musical instruments, you
must bow down and worship the gold
statue that King Nebuchadnezzar has set
up. 6Anyone who doesn't bow down and
worship will immediately be thrown into a
blazing furnace."

7Now people, nations, and those who
spoke every language were there. When
they heard the sound of the horns, flutes,
lyres, zithers, pipes, and all the other musical instruments, they bowed down and
worshiped the gold statue King Nebuchadnezzar had set up.

8Then some Babylonians came up to
the king and began speaking against the
men of Judah. 9They said to King Nebuchadnezzar, "O king, live forever! 10O
king, you gave a command that everyone
who heard the horns, lyres, zithers,
harps, pipes, and all the other musical instruments would have to bow down and
worship the gold statue. 11Anyone who
wouldn't do this was to be thrown into a
blazing furnace. 12O king, there are some
men of Judah whom you made officers in
the area of Babylon that did not pay attention to your order. Their names are Shadrach, Meshach, and Abednego. They do
not serve your gods and do not worship
the gold statue you have set up."

13Nebuchadnezzar became very angry and called for Shadrach, Meshach,
and Abednego. When they were brought
to the king, 14Nebuchadnezzar said,
"Shadrach, Meshach, and Abednego, is it
true that you do not serve my gods nor
worship the gold statue I have set up?
15In a moment you will again hear the
sound of the horns, flutes, lyres, zithers,
harps, pipes, and all the other musical instruments. If you bow down and worship
the statue I made, that will be good. But if
you do not worship it, you will immediately be thrown into the blazing furnace.
What god will be able to save you from
my power then?"

FAITH links

OBEYING GOD OR MAN?

DANIEL 3:8-30

Imagine being told that you had to bow before a statue of the governor of your state. If you didn't bow, you'd be thrown in jail. What would you do? Shadrach, Meshach, and Abednego had been told to bow down to a statue of King Nebuchadnezzar. They had to decide if they would obey God or the king.

God wants us to obey the people that are in our government, except when obeying them causes us to disobey God. God honors our obedience to him, even if it means disobeying those in authority.

Who do you obey? Check out these links:

The Sacrifice, Genesis 22, p. 29

The Fence Riders, 1 Kings 18, p. 464

A Promise from the Heart, Jeremiah 31:31–33, p. 1037

The Greatest Commandment, Matthew 22:36–40, p. 1313

Believe It or Not, Luke 1:20, 38, p. 1366

A Christian's Responsibility, Acts 11:26, p. 1484

16Shadrach, Meshach, and Abednego
answered the king, saying, "Nebuchadnezzar, we do not need to defend our-

3:5 zithers Musical instruments with thirty to forty strings.

selves to you. **17**If you throw us into the
blazing furnace, the God we serve is able
to save us from the furnace. He will save
us from your power, O king. **18**But even
if God does not save us, we want you,
O king, to know this: We will not serve
your gods or worship the gold statue you
have set up."

19Then Nebuchadnezzar was furious
with Shadrach, Meshach, and Abednego,
and he changed his mind. He ordered
the furnace to be heated seven times hotter than usual. **20**Then he commanded
some of the strongest soldiers in his
army to tie up Shadrach, Meshach, and
Abednego and throw them into the blazing furnace.

21So Shadrach, Meshach, and Abednego were tied up and thrown into the
blazing furnace while still wearing their
robes, trousers, turbans, and other clothes.
22The king's command was very strict,
and the furnace was made so hot that the
flames killed the strong soldiers who
threw Shadrach, Meshach, and Abednego
into the furnace. **23**Firmly tied, Shadrach,
Meshach, and Abednego fell into the blazing furnace.

24Then King Nebuchadnezzar was so
surprised that he jumped to his feet. He
asked the men who advised him, "Didn't
we tie up only three men and throw them
into the fire?"

They answered, "Yes, O king."

25The king said, "Look! I see four
men walking around in the fire. They are
not tied up, and they are not burned. The
fourth man looks like a son of the gods."

26Then Nebuchadnezzar went to the
opening of the blazing furnace and shouted, "Shadrach, Meshach, and Abednego,
come out! Servants of the Most High
God, come here!"

So Shadrach, Meshach, and Abednego
came out of the fire. **27**When they came
out, the governors, assistant governors,
captains of the soldiers, and royal advisers crowded around them and saw that
the fire had not harmed their bodies.
Their hair was not burned, their robes
were not burned, and they didn't even
smell like smoke!

28Then Nebuchadnezzar said, "Praise
the God of Shadrach, Meshach, and
Abednego. Their God has sent his angel
and saved his servants from the fire!
These three men trusted their God and
refused to obey my command. They were
willing to die rather than serve or worship any god other than their own. **29**So I
now give this command: Anyone from
any nation or language who says anything
against the God of Shadrach, Meshach,
and Abednego will be torn apart and have
his house turned into a pile of stones. No
other god can save his people like this."
30Then the king promoted Shadrach,
Meshach, and Abednego in the area of
Babylon.

Nebuchadnezzar's Dream of a Tree

4 King Nebuchadnezzar sent this letter
to the people, nations, and those who
speak every language in all the world:

I wish you peace and great wealth!

2The Most High God has done
miracles and wonderful things for
me that I am happy to tell you
about.

3His wonderful acts are great,
and his miracles are mighty.
His kingdom goes on forever,
and his rule continues from
now on.

4I, Nebuchadnezzar, was happy
and successful at my palace, **5**but I
had a dream that made me afraid.
As I was lying on my bed, I saw pictures and visions in my mind that
alarmed me. **6**So I ordered all the
wise men of Babylon to come to
me and tell me what my dream
meant. **7**The fortune-tellers, magicians, and wise men came, and I
told them about the dream. But
they could not tell me what it
meant.

8Finally, Daniel came to me. (I
called him Belteshazzar to honor
my god, because the spirit of the
holy gods is in him.) I told my dream
to him. **9**I said, "Belteshazzar, you

are the most important of all the
fortune-tellers. I know that the
spirit of the holy gods is in you, so
there is no secret that is too hard
for you to understand. This was
what I dreamed; tell me what it
means. **10**These are the visions
I saw while I was lying in my bed: I
looked, and there in front of me
was a tree standing in the middle of
the earth. And it was very tall.
11The tree grew large and strong.
The top of the tree touched the sky
and could be seen from anywhere
on earth. **12**The leaves of the tree
were beautiful. It had plenty of
good fruit on it, enough food for
everyone. The wild animals found
shelter under the tree, and the
birds lived in its branches. Every
animal ate from it.

13"As I was looking at those
things in the vision while lying on
my bed, I saw an observer, a holy
angel coming down from heaven.
14He spoke very loudly and said,
'Cut down the tree and cut off its
branches. Strip off its leaves and
scatter its fruit. Let the animals
under the tree run away, and let
the birds in its branches fly away.
15But leave the stump and its
roots in the ground with a band of
iron and bronze around it; let it
stay in the field with the grass
around it.

" 'Let the man become wet
with dew, and let him live among
the animals and plants of the earth.
16Let him not think like a human
any longer, but let him have the
mind of an animal for seven years.

17" 'The observers gave this
command; the holy ones declared
the sentence. This is so all people
may know that the Most High God
rules over every kingdom on
earth. God gives those kingdoms
to anyone he wants, and he
chooses people to rule them who
are not proud.'

18"That is what I, King Nebuchadnezzar, dreamed. Now Belteshazzar,* tell me what the dream
means. None of the wise men in
my kingdom can explain it to me,
but you can, because the spirit of
the holy gods is in you."

FAITH links

EATING HUMBLE PIE

DANIEL 4

Who is the most powerful person you know? The mayor? A rich uncle? At one time, King Nebuchadnezzar was the most powerful ruler on earth. His palace was one of the wonders of the known world. All of that success went to his head. After Nebuchadnezzar expressed pride in his own "mighty power," God humbled Nebuchadnezzar in an unusual way.

Pride causes a person to think, *Look what I have done.* Humility keeps a person's sight on God. As Nebuchadnezzar learned, "He [God] is able to make proud people humble."

The Trouble with Jealousy, Genesis 37, p. 53

Put Pride Aside, Exodus 2:11–15, p. 78

What I've Got, 2 Kings 20:12–17, p. 508

Just a Test, Luke 4:1–13, p. 1373

Best Seat in the House, Luke 14:7–11, p. 1398

Most Wanted?, 2 Corinthians 10:1, p. 1580

4:18 Belteshazzar Another name for Daniel.

Daniel Explains the Dream

19Then Daniel, who was called Belteshazzar, was very quiet for a while, because his understanding of the dream frightened him. So the king said, "Belteshazzar, do not let the dream or its meaning make you afraid."

Then Belteshazzar answered, "My master, I wish the dream were about your enemies, and I wish its meaning were for those who are against you! **20**You saw a tree in your dream that grew large and strong. Its top touched the sky, and it could be seen from all over the earth. **21**Its leaves were beautiful, and it had plenty of fruit for everyone to eat. It was a home for the wild animals, and its branches were nesting places for the birds. **22**O king, you are that tree! You have become great and powerful, like the tall tree that touched the sky. Your power reaches to the far parts of the earth.

23"O king, you saw an observer, a holy angel, coming down from heaven who said, 'Cut down the tree and destroy it. But leave the stump and its roots in the ground with a band of iron and bronze around it; leave it in the field with the grass. Let him become wet with dew and live like a wild animal for seven years.'

24"This is the meaning of the dream, O king. The Most High God has commanded these things to happen to my master the king: **25**You will be forced away from people to live among the wild animals. People will feed you grass like an ox, and dew from the sky will make you wet. Seven years will pass, and then you will learn this lesson: The Most High God is ruler over every kingdom on earth, and he gives those kingdoms to anyone he chooses.

26"Since the stump of the tree and its roots were left in the ground, your kingdom will be given back to you when you learn that one in heaven rules your kingdom. **27**So, O king, please accept my advice. Stop sinning and do what is right. Stop doing wicked things and be kind to the poor. Then you might continue to be successful."

The King's Dream Comes True

28All these things happened to King Nebuchadnezzar. **29**Twelve months later as he was walking on the roof[n] of his palace in Babylon, **30**he said, "I have built this great Babylon as my royal home. I built it by my power to show my glory and my majesty."

31The words were still in his mouth when a voice from heaven said, "King Nebuchadnezzar, these things will happen to you: Your royal power has been taken away from you. **32**You will be forced away from people. You will live with the wild animals and will be fed grass like an ox. Seven years will pass before you learn this lesson: The Most High God rules over every kingdom on earth and gives those kingdoms to anyone he chooses."

33Immediately the words came true. Nebuchadnezzar was forced to go away from people, and he began eating grass like an ox. He became wet from dew. His hair grew long like the feathers of an eagle, and his nails grew like the claws of a bird.

34At the end of that time, I, Nebuchadnezzar, looked up toward heaven, and I could think normally again! Then I gave praise to the Most High God; I gave honor and glory to him who lives forever.

4:29 roof In Bible times houses were built with flat roofs. The roof was used for drying things such as flax and fruit. And it was used as an extra room, as a place for worship, and as a cool place to sleep in the summer.

God's rule is forever,
and his kingdom continues for
all time.
35 People on earth
are not truly important.
God does what he wants
with the powers of heaven
and the people on earth.
No one can stop his powerful hand
or question what he does.
36At that time I could think
normally again, and God gave back
my great honor and power and returned the glory to my kingdom.
The people who advised me and
the royal family came to me for
help again. I became king again and
was even greater and more powerful than before. **37**Now I, Nebuchadnezzar, give praise and honor
and glory to the King of heaven.
Everything he does is right and
fair, and he is able to make proud
people humble.

The Writing on the Wall

5 King Belshazzar gave a big banquet
for a thousand royal guests and drank
wine with them. **2**As Belshazzar was
drinking his wine, he gave orders to bring
the gold and silver cups that his ancestor
Nebuchadnezzar had taken from the
Temple in Jerusalem. This was so the
king, his royal guests, his wives, and his
slave women could drink from those
cups. **3**So they brought the gold cups that
had been taken from the Temple of God in
Jerusalem. And the king and his royal
guests, his wives, and his slave women
drank from them. **4**As they were drinking, they praised their gods, which were
made from gold, silver, bronze, iron,
wood, and stone.
5Suddenly the fingers of a person's
hand appeared and began writing on the
plaster of the wall, near the lampstand in
the royal palace. The king watched the
hand as it wrote.
6King Belshazzar was very frightened. His face turned white, his knees
knocked together, and he could not stand
up because his legs were too weak. **7**The
king called for the magicians, wise men,
and wizards of Babylon and said to them,
"Anyone who can read this writing and
explain it will receive purple clothes fit
for a king and a gold chain around his
neck. And I will make that person the
third highest ruler in the kingdom."
8Then all the king's wise men came
in, but they could not read the writing or
tell the king what it meant. **9**King Belshazzar became even more afraid, and his
face became even whiter. His royal
guests were confused.
10Then the king's mother, who had
heard the voices of the king and his royal
guests, came into the banquet room. She
said, "O king, live forever! Don't be
afraid or let your face be white with fear!
11There is a man in your kingdom who
has the spirit of the holy gods. In the days
of your father, this man showed understanding, knowledge, and wisdom like
the gods. Your father, King Nebuchadnezzar, put this man in charge of all the wise
men, fortune-tellers, magicians, and wizards. **12**The man I am talking about is
named Daniel, whom the king named
Belteshazzar. He was very smart and had
knowledge and understanding. He could
explain dreams and secrets and could answer very hard problems. Call for Daniel.
He will tell you what the writing on the
wall means."
13So they brought Daniel to the king,
and the king asked, "Is your name Daniel?
Are you one of the captives my father the
king brought from Judah? **14**I have heard
that the spirit of the gods is in you, and
that you are very smart and have knowledge and extraordinary understanding.
15The wise men and magicians were
brought to me to read this writing and to
explain what it means, but they could not
explain it. **16**I have heard that you are
able to explain what things mean and can
find the answers to hard problems. Read
this writing on the wall and explain it to
me. If you can, I will give you purple
clothes fit for a king and a gold chain to
wear around your neck. And you will become the third highest ruler in the kingdom."
17Then Daniel answered the king, "You

may keep your gifts for yourself, or
you may give those rewards to someone
else. But I will read the writing on the
wall for you and will explain to you what
it means.
18"O king, the Most High God made
your father Nebuchadnezzar a great, important, and powerful king. 19Because
God made him important, all the people,
nations, and those who spoke every language were very frightened of Nebuchadnezzar. If he wanted someone to die, he
killed that person. If he wanted someone
to live, he let that person live. Those he
wanted to promote, he promoted. Those
he wanted to be less important, he made
less important.
20"But Nebuchadnezzar became too
proud and stubborn, so he was taken off
his royal throne. His glory was taken
away. 21He was forced away from people,
and his mind became like the mind of an
animal. He lived with the wild donkeys
and was fed grass like an ox and became
wet with dew. These things happened to
him until he learned his lesson: The
Most High God rules over every kingdom on earth, and he sets anyone he
chooses over those kingdoms.
22"Belshazzar, you already knew
these things, because you are a descendant of Nebuchadnezzar. Still you have
not been sorry for what you have done.
23Instead, you have set yourself against
the Lord of heaven. You ordered the
drinking cups from the Temple of the
Lord to be brought to you. Then you and
your royal guests, your wives, and your
slave women drank wine from them. You
praised the gods of silver, gold, bronze,
iron, wood, and stone that are not really
gods; they cannot see or hear or understand anything. You did not honor God,
who has power over your life and everything you do. 24So God sent the hand that
wrote on the wall.
25"These are the words that were
written on the wall: 'Mene, mene, tekel,
and parsin.'
26"This is what the words mean:
Mene: God has counted the days until
your kingdom will end. 27Tekel: You have
been weighed on the scales and found not
good enough. 28Parsin: Your kingdom is
being divided and will be given to the
Medes and the Persians."

FAITH links

THE WRITING'S ON THE WALL

DANIEL 5

What is the most unusual way you've heard of for a message to be delivered? God delivered a message to Belshazzar in a unique way. He allowed the fingers of a hand to suddenly appear and write a message on a wall!

God has ways of getting his messages across. He doesn't always use a large handwritten note on a wall to get a person's attention. One of the most unique ways he's used was to send his Son to earth to become a human. Unlike the message delivered to Belshazzar, God's Son brought good news. God wants everyone to pay attention to that message. Are you paying attention?

Ten Ways to Obey, Exodus 20, p. 103

An Admirable Quality, 1 Kings 10:1–13, p. 451

More Precious Than Gold, Psalm 19:7–10, p. 723

Going My Way?, Hosea 8:1–6, p. 1179

Prove It!, Matthew 16:1–4, p. 1302

Want to Know? Ask!, Luke 9:45, p. 1386

29Then Belshazzar gave an order for
Daniel to be dressed in purple clothes
and to have a gold chain put around his
neck. And it was announced that Daniel
was the third highest ruler in the kingdom. 30That very same night Belshazzar,
king of the Babylonian people, was killed.
31So Darius the Mede became the new
king when he was sixty-two years old.

Daniel and the Lions

6 Darius thought it would be a good idea
to choose one hundred twenty governors who would rule his kingdom. 2He
chose three men as supervisors over
those governors, and Daniel was one of
the supervisors. The supervisors were to
ensure that the governors did not try to
cheat the king. 3Daniel showed that he
could do the work better than the other
supervisors and governors, so the king
planned to put Daniel in charge of the
whole kingdom. 4Because of this, the
other supervisors and governors tried to
find reasons to accuse Daniel about his
work in the government. But
they could not find
anything wrong with
him or any reason to
accuse him, because
he was trustworthy
and not lazy or dis-
honest. 5Finally these men said, "We will
never find any reason to accuse Daniel
unless it is about the law of his God."
6So the supervisors and governors
went as a group to the king and said:
"King Darius, live forever! 7The supervisors, assistant governors, governors,
the people who advise you, and the captains of the soldiers have all agreed that
you should make a new law for everyone
to obey: For the next thirty days no one
should pray to any god or human except
to you, O king. Anyone who doesn't obey
will be thrown into the lions' den. 8Now,
O king, make the law and sign your name
to it so that it cannot be changed, because
then it will be a law of the Medes and Persians and cannot be canceled." 9So King
Darius signed the law.
10Even though Daniel knew that the
new law had been written, he went to
pray in an upstairs room in his house,
which had windows that opened toward
Jerusalem. Three times each day Daniel
would kneel down to pray and thank God,
just as he always had done.

EMAIL FROM GOD 6:4–5
Character
An example of good character

IN THE LIONS' DEN

DANIEL 6

If you've ever been made fun of because you're smart or do all of your homework, you can relate to Daniel's experience. You've probably heard his story many times before. Jealous men came up with a law to trap Daniel. Because of the law, the king had Daniel thrown into the lions' den. But God prevented Daniel from being hurt.

People might try to make trouble for you because of your good work or because you follow God. When that happens, don't think that God has given up on you. He protected Daniel. He'll protect you, too.

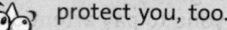

Feel like you're up against lions sometimes? Surf on for help:

Moses' Champion, Numbers 12, p. 192

Play Fair or Play Favorites?, Deuteronomy 1:16–18, p. 227

Wronged for What's Right, Ezra 4:4–5, p. 612

Go! No!, Jonah 1, p. 1213

Keep Up the Good Work!, Galatians 6:9–10, p. 1593

The Gentle Way, Titus 3:1–5, p. 1661

11Then those men went as a group
and found Daniel praying and asking God
for help. **12**So they went to the king and
talked to him about the law he had made.
They said, "Didn't you sign a law that
says no one may pray to any god or human except you, O king? Doesn't it say
that anyone who disobeys during the
next thirty days will be thrown into the
lions' den?"

The king answered, "Yes, that is the
law, and the laws of the Medes and Persians cannot be canceled."

13Then they said to the king, "Daniel,
one of the captives from Judah, is not paying attention to you, O king, or to the law
you signed. Daniel still prays to his God
three times every day." **14**The king became very upset when he heard this. He
wanted to save Daniel, and he worked
hard until sunset trying to think of a way
to save him.

15Then those men went as a group to
the king. They said, "Remember, O king,
the law of the Medes and Persians says
that no law or command given by the king
can be changed."

16So King Darius gave the order, and
Daniel was brought in and thrown into
the lions' den. The king said to Daniel,
"May the God you serve all the time save
you!" **17**A big stone was brought and
placed over the opening of the lions' den.
Then the king used his signet ring and
the rings of his royal officers to put special seals on the rock. This ensured
that no one would move the rock and
bring Daniel out. **18**Then King Darius
went back to his palace. He did not eat
that night, he did not have any entertainment brought to him, and he could
not sleep.

19The next morning King Darius got
up at dawn and hurried to the lions' den.
20As he came near the den, he was worried. He called out to Daniel, "Daniel,
servant of the living God! Has your God
that you always worship been able to
save you from the lions?"

21Daniel answered, "O king, live forever! **22**My God sent his angel to close
the lions' mouths. They have not hurt
me, because my God knows I am innocent. I never did anything wrong to you,
O king."

23King Darius was very happy and
told his servants to lift Daniel out of the
lions' den. So they lifted him out and did
not find any injury on him, because Daniel had trusted in his God.

24Then the king commanded that the
men who had accused Daniel be brought
to the lions' den. They, their wives, and
their children were thrown into the den.
The lions grabbed them before they hit
the floor of the den and crushed their
bones.

25Then King Darius wrote a letter to
all people and all nations, to those who
spoke every language in the world:

> I wish you great peace and
> wealth.
>
> **26**I am making a new law for
> people in every part of my king-
> dom. All of you must fear and re-
> spect the God of Daniel.
>
> Daniel's God is the living God;
> he lives forever.
> His kingdom will never be
> destroyed,
> and his rule will never end.
> **27**God rescues and saves people
> and does mighty miracles
> in heaven and on earth.
> He is the one who saved Daniel
> from the power of the lions.

28So Daniel was successful during the
time Darius was king and when Cyrus
the Persian was king.

Daniel's Dream about Four Animals

7 In Belshazzar's first year as king of
Babylon, Daniel had a dream. He saw
visions as he was lying on his bed, and he
wrote down what he had dreamed.

2"Daniel said: "I saw my vision at
night. In the vision the wind was blowing
from all four directions, which made the
sea very rough. **3**I saw four huge animals
come up from the sea, and each animal
was different from the others.

4"The first animal looked like a lion,

but had wings like an eagle. I watched
this animal until its wings were torn off.
It was lifted from the ground so that it
stood up on two feet like a human, and it
was given the mind of a human.
5"Then I saw a second animal before
me that looked like a bear. It was raised
up on one of its sides and had three ribs
in its mouth between its
teeth. It was told, 'Get up
and eat all the meat you
want!'
6"After that, I looked,
and there before me was
another animal. This ani-
mal looked like a leopard
with four wings on its
back that looked like a
bird's wings. This animal
had four heads and was
given power to rule.
7"After that, in my vision at night I
saw in front of me a fourth animal that
was cruel, terrible, and very strong. It
had large iron teeth. It crushed and ate
what it killed, and then it walked on whatever was left. This fourth animal was different from any animal I had seen before,
and it had ten horns.
8"While I was thinking about the
horns, another horn grew up among
them. It was a little horn with eyes like a
human's eyes. It also had a mouth, and
the mouth was bragging. The little horn
pulled out three of the other horns.

9"As I looked,
thrones were put in their places,
and God, who has been alive
forever, sat on his throne.
His clothes were white like snow,
and the hair on his head was white
like wool.
His throne was made from fire,
and the wheels of his throne were
blazing with fire.
10 A river of fire was flowing
from in front of him.
Many thousands of angels were
serving him,
and millions of angels stood before
him.
Court was ready to begin,
and the books were opened.

11"I kept on looking because the little
horn was bragging. I kept watching until
finally the fourth animal was killed. Its
body was destroyed, and it was thrown
into the burning fire. **12**(The power and
rule of the other animals had been taken
from them, but they were permitted to
live for a certain period of time.)
13"In my vision at
night I saw in front of me
someone who looked like
a human being coming on
the clouds in the sky. He
came near God, who has
been alive forever, and he
was led to God. **14**He was
given authority, glory, and
the strength of a king.
People of every tribe, nation, and language will
serve him. His rule will last forever, and
his kingdom will never be destroyed.

He was given authority, glory, and the strength of a king.
—Daniel 7:14

The Meaning of the Dream

15"I, Daniel, was worried. The visions that went through my mind frightened me. **16**I came near one of those
standing there and asked what all this
meant.
"So he told me and explained to me
what these things meant: **17**'The four
great animals are four kingdoms that will
come from the earth. **18**But the holy
people who belong to the Most High God
will receive the power to rule and will
have the power to rule forever, from
now on.'
19"Then I wanted to know what the
fourth animal meant, because it was different from all the others. It was very terrible and had iron teeth and bronze claws.
It was the animal that crushed and ate
what it killed and then walked on whatever was left. **20**I also wanted to know
about the ten horns on its head and about
the little horn that grew there. It had
pulled out three of the other ten horns
and looked greater than the others. It had
eyes and a mouth that kept bragging.
21As I watched, the little horn began
making war against God's holy people
and was defeating them **22**until God, who
has been alive forever, came. He judged

in favor of the holy people who belong to
the Most High God; then the time came
for them to receive the power to rule.
23"And he explained this to me: 'The
fourth animal is a fourth kingdom that will
come on the earth. It will be different from
all the other kingdoms and will destroy
people all over the world. It will walk on
and crush the whole earth. **24**The ten
horns are ten kings who will come from
this fourth kingdom. After those ten kings
are gone, another king will come. He will
be different from the kings who ruled before him, and he will defeat three of the
other kings. **25**This king will speak
against the Most High God, and he will
hurt and kill God's holy people. He will try
to change times and laws that have already been set. The holy people that belong to God will be in that king's power for
three and one-half years.
26" 'But the court will decide what
should happen. The power of the king
will be taken away, and his kingdom will
be completely destroyed. **27**Then the
holy people who belong to the Most High
God will have the power to rule. They
will rule over all the kingdoms under
heaven with power and greatness, and
their power to rule will last forever. People from all the other kingdoms will respect and serve them.'
28"That was the end of the dream. I,
Daniel, was very afraid. My face became
white from fear, but I kept everything to
myself."

Daniel's Vision

8 During the third year of King Belshazzar's rule, I, Daniel, saw another
vision, which was like the first one. **2**In
this vision I saw myself in the capital city
of Susa, in the area of Elam. I was standing by the Ulai Canal **3**when I looked up
and saw a male sheep standing beside the
canal. It had two long horns, but one horn
was longer and newer than the other. **4**I
watched the sheep charge to the west,
the north, and the south. No animal could
stand before him, and none could save
another animal from his power. He did
whatever he wanted and became very
powerful.
5While I was watching this, I saw a
male goat come from the west. This goat
had one large horn between his eyes that
was easy to see. He crossed over the
whole earth so fast that his feet hardly
touched the ground.
6In his anger the goat charged the
sheep with the two horns that I had seen
standing by the canal. **7**I watched the
angry goat attack the sheep and break
the sheep's two horns. The sheep was
not strong enough to stop it. The goat
knocked the sheep to the ground and
then walked all over him. No one was
able to save the sheep from the goat, **8**so
the male goat became very great. But
when he was strong, his big horn broke
off and four horns grew in place of the
one big horn. Those four horns pointed
in four different directions and were easy
to see.
9Then a little horn grew from one of
those four horns, and it became very big.
It grew to the south, the east, and toward
the beautiful land of Judah. **10**That little
horn grew until it reached to the sky. It
even threw some of the army of heaven
to the ground and walked on them!
11That little horn set itself up as equal to
God, the Commander of heaven's armies.
It stopped the daily sacrifices that were
offered to him, and the Temple, the place
where people worshiped him, was pulled
down. **12**Because there was a turning
away from God, the people stopped the
daily sacrifices. Truth was thrown down
to the ground, and the horn was successful in everything it did.
13Then I heard a holy angel speaking.
Another holy angel asked the first one,
"How long will the things in this vision
last—the daily sacrifices, the turning
away from God that brings destruction,
the Temple being pulled down, and the
army of heaven being walked on?"
14The angel said to me, "This will
happen for twenty-three hundred evenings and mornings. Then the holy place
will be repaired."
15I, Daniel, saw this vision and tried
to understand what it meant. In it I saw
someone who looked like a man standing
near me. **16**And I heard a man's voice

calling from the Ulai Canal: "Gabriel, explain the vision to this man."
17Gabriel came to where I was standing. When he came close to me, I was
very afraid and bowed facedown on the
ground. But Gabriel said to me, "Human
being, understand that this vision is
about the time of the end."
18While Gabriel was speaking, I fell
into a deep sleep with my face on the
ground. Then he touched me and lifted
me to my feet. **19**He said, "Now, I will
explain to you what will happen in the
time of God's anger. Your vision was
about the set time of the end.
20"You saw a male sheep with two
horns, which are the kings of Media and
Persia. **21**The male goat is the king of
Greece, and the big horn between its
eyes is the first king. **22**The four horns
that grew in the place of the broken horn
are four kingdoms. Those four kingdoms
will come from the nation of the first
king, but they will not be as strong as the
first king.
23"When the end comes near for
those kingdoms, a bold and cruel king
who tells lies will come. This will happen
when many people have turned against
God. **24**This king will be very powerful,
but his power will not come from himself.
He will cause terrible destruction and will be successful in everything he
does. He will destroy
powerful people and even
God's holy people. **25**This
king will succeed by using
lies and force. He will
think that he is very im-
portant. He will destroy
many people without
warning; he will try to
fight even the Prince of princes! But that
cruel king will be destroyed, and not by
human power.
26"The vision that has been shown to
you about these evenings and mornings
is true. But seal up the vision, because
those things won't happen for a long
time."
27I, Daniel, became very weak and
was sick for several days after that vision. Then I got up and went back to
work for the king, but I was very upset
about the vision. I didn't understand what
it meant.

> Then I got up and went back to work for the king, but I was very upset about the vision.
> —Daniel 8:27

Daniel's Prayer

9 These things happened during the
first year Darius son of Xerxes was
king over Babylon. He was a descendant
of the Medes. **2**During Darius' first year
as king, I, Daniel, was reading the Scriptures. I saw that the LORD told Jeremiah
that Jerusalem would be empty ruins for
seventy years.
3Then I turned to the Lord God and
prayed and asked him for help. I did not
eat any food. To show my sadness, I put on rough
cloth and sat in
ashes. **4**I prayed to
the LORD my God
and told him about
all of our sins. I said,
"Lord, you are a great God who causes
fear and wonder. You keep your agreement of love with all who love you and
obey your commands.

9:4–8
Sin
Seek forgiveness for your sins.

5"But we have sinned and done
wrong. We have been wicked and turned
against you, your commands, and your
laws. **6**We did not listen to your servants,
the prophets, who spoke
for you to our kings, our
leaders, our ancestors,
and all the people of the
land.
7"Lord, you are good
and right, but we are full
of shame today—the peo-
ple of Judah and Jeru-
salem, all the people of
Israel, those near and
far whom you scattered
among many nations because they were
not loyal to you. **8**LORD, we are all
ashamed. Our kings and leaders and our
fathers are ashamed, because we have
sinned against you.
9"But, Lord our God, you show us
mercy and forgive us even though we
have turned against you. **10**We have not
obeyed the LORD our God or the teachings he gave us through his servants, the

prophets. **11**All the people of Israel have disobeyed your teachings and have turned away, refusing to obey you. So you brought on us the curses and promises of punishment written in the Teachings of Moses, the servant of God, because we sinned against you.

12"You said these things would happen to us and our leaders, and you made them happen; you brought on us a great disaster. Nothing has ever been done on earth like what was done to Jerusalem. **13**All this disaster came to us just as it is written in the Teachings of Moses. But we have not pleaded with the LORD our God. We have not stopped sinning. We have not paid attention to your truth. **14**The LORD was ready to bring the disaster on us, and he did it because the LORD our God is right in everything he does. But we still did not obey him.

15"Lord our God, you used your power and brought us out of Egypt. Because of that, your name is known even today. But we have sinned and have done wrong. **16**Lord, you do what is right, but please do not be angry with Jerusalem, your city on your holy hill. Because of our sins and the evil things done by our ancestors, people all around insult and make fun of Jerusalem and your people.

17"Now, our God, hear the prayers of your servant. Listen to my prayer for help, and for your sake do good things for your holy place that is in ruins. **18**My God, pay attention and hear me. Open your eyes and see all the terrible things that have happened to us. See how our lives have been ruined and what has happened to the city that is called by your name. We do not ask these things because we are good; instead, we ask because of your mercy. **19**Lord, listen! Lord, forgive! Lord, hear us and do something! For your sake, don't wait, because your city and your people are called by your name."

Gabriel's Explanation

20While I was saying these things in my prayer to the LORD, my God, confessing my sins and the sins of the people of Israel and praying for God's holy hill, **21**Gabriel came to me. (I had seen him in my last vision.) He came flying quickly to me about the time of the evening sacrifice, while I was still praying. **22**He taught me and said to me, "Daniel, I have come to give you wisdom and to help you understand. **23**When you first started praying, an answer was given, and I came

FAITH links

CONCERN FOR ALL

DANIEL 9

How would you show concern for a large group of people? Would you buy everyone ice cream, if you could? Daniel prayed for a large group of people—the Israelites. He told God that he was sorry for his own sins and for theirs. He also asked God to be merciful.

Praying for others is one way to show your concern for them. You might start a prayer journal, listing the needs of others in one column and the answers you receive in another. As you receive an answer, don't forget to thank God.

Just a Little Respect, 1 Chronicles 11:10–19, p. 534

Seeing the Needs, Nehemiah 1, p. 625

Help for a Friend, Mark 2:1–5, p. 1332

Jesus' Prayer, John 17, p. 1453

An Encouraging Word, 1 Corinthians 1:3–5, p. 1545

The Sacrifice of Service, Philippians 2:17, 25–30, p. 1612

to tell you, because God loves you very
much. So think about the message and
understand the vision.

24"God has ordered four hundred
ninety years for your people and your
holy city for these reasons: to stop people from turning against God; to put an
end to sin; to take away evil; to bring in
goodness that continues forever; to bring
about the vision and prophecy; and to appoint a most holy place.

25"Learn and understand these
things. A command will come to rebuild
Jerusalem. The time from this command
until the appointed leader comes will be
forty-nine years and four hundred thirty-
four years. Jerusalem will be rebuilt with
streets and a trench filled with water
around it, but it will be built in times of
trouble. **26**After the four hundred thirty-
four years the appointed leader will be
killed; he will have nothing. The people
of the leader who is to come will destroy
the city and the holy place. The end of the
city will come like a flood, and war will
continue until the end. God has ordered
that place to be completely destroyed.
27That leader will make firm an agreement with many people for seven years.
He will stop the offerings and sacrifices
after three and one-half years. A destroyer will do terrible things until the
ordered end comes to the destroyed
city."

Daniel's Vision of a Man

10 During Cyrus' third year as king
of Persia, Daniel, whose name was
Belteshazzar, received a vision about a
great war. It was a true message that
Daniel understood.

2At that time I, Daniel, had been very
sad for three weeks. **3**I did not eat any
fancy food or meat, or drink any wine, or
use any perfumed oil for
three weeks.

4On the twenty-
fourth day of the
first month, I was
standing beside the
great Tigris River.
5While standing there, I looked up and
saw a man dressed in linen clothes with a
belt of fine gold wrapped around his waist.
6His body was like shiny yellow quartz.
His face was bright like lightning, and his
eyes were like fire. His arms and legs
were shiny like polished bronze, and his
voice sounded like the roar of a crowd.

7I, Daniel, was the only person who
saw the vision. The men with me did not
see it, because they were so frightened
that they ran away and hid. **8**So I was left
alone, watching this great vision. I lost
my strength, my face turned white like a
dead person, and I was helpless. **9**Then I
heard the man in the vision speaking. As
I listened, I fell into a deep sleep with my
face on the ground.

10Then a hand touched me and set me
on my hands and knees. I was so afraid
that I was shaking. **11**The man in the vision said to me, "Daniel, God loves you
very much. Think carefully about the
words I will speak to you, and stand up,
because I have been sent to you." When
he said this, I stood up, but I was still
shaking.

12Then the man said to me, "Daniel,
do not be afraid. Some time ago you decided to get understanding and to humble
yourself before your God. Since that time
God has listened to you, and I have come
because of your prayers. **13**But the
prince of Persia has been fighting against
me for twenty-one days. Then Michael,
one of the most important angels, came
to help me, because I had been left there
with the king of Persia. **14**Now I have
come to explain to you what will happen
to your people, because the vision is
about a time in the future."

15While he was speaking to me, I
bowed facedown and could not speak.
16Then one who looked like a man
touched my lips, so I opened my mouth
and started to speak. I said to the one
standing in front of me, "Master, I am upset and afraid because of what I saw in
the vision. I feel helpless. **17**Master, how
can I, your servant, talk with you? My
strength is gone, and it is hard for me to
breathe."

18The one who looked like a man
touched me again and gave me strength.
19He said, "Daniel, don't be afraid. God

> eMAIL FROM GOD **10:5–6**
> **Angels**
> Meet an amazing angel!

WHO ARE THE GREEKS? Daniel 11:3–35

The prophet Daniel predicted that Greece would become a great world power. (Read Daniel 11:3–35.) Sure enough, near the end of the Old Testament era, Greece did become a world power under the leadership of Alexander the Great. Alexander's goal was to spread Greek culture and ideas throughout the world. That's why you can still find Greek things almost everywhere, like the columns in some architecture and art.

The other great thing about Greece being a world power was that, during New Testament days, it was much easier to spread the gospel since one government ruled so much of the world. Also, since Greek was the universal language at that time, it was easy for people like the apostle Paul to preach in a lot of different places and still be understood.

loves you very much. Peace be with you. Be strong now; be courageous."

When he spoke to me, I became stronger and said, "Master, speak, since you have given me strength."

20Then he said, "Daniel, do you know why I have come to you? Soon I must go back to fight against the prince of Persia. When I go, the prince of Greece will
come, 21but I must first tell you what is written in the Book of Truth. No one stands with me against these enemies except Michael, the angel ruling over your people.

11 In the first year that Darius the Mede was king, I stood up to support Michael in his fight against the prince of Persia.

Kingdoms of the South and North

2"Now then, Daniel, I tell you the truth: Three more kings will rule in Persia, and then a fourth king will come. He will be much richer than all the kings of Persia before him and will use his riches to get power. He will stir up everyone
against the kingdom of Greece. 3Then a
mighty king will come, who will rule with great power and will do anything he
wants. 4After that king has come, his kingdom will be broken up and divided out toward the four parts of the world. His kingdom will not go to his descendants, and it will not have the power that he had, because his kingdom will be pulled up and given to other people.

5"The king of the South will become strong, but one of his commanders will become even stronger. He will begin to rule his own kingdom with great power.
6Then after a few years, a new friendship will develop. The daughter of the king of the South will marry the king of the North in order to bring peace. But she will not keep her power, and his family will not last. She, her husband, her child, and those who brought her to that country will be killed.

7"But a person from her family will become king of the South and will attack the armies of the king of the North. He will go into that king's strong, walled city
and will fight and win. 8He will take their gods, their metal idols, and their valuable things made of silver and gold back to Egypt. Then he will not bother the king
of the North for a few years. 9Next, the

king of the North will attack the king of
the South, but he will be beaten back to
his own country.

10"The sons of the king of the North
will prepare for war. They will get a large
army together that will move through the
land very quickly, like a powerful flood.
Later, that army will come back and fight
all the way to the strong, walled city of
the king of the South. **11**Then the king of
the South will become very angry and
will march out to fight against the king of
the North. The king of the North will
have a large army, but he will lose the
battle, **12**and the soldiers will be carried
away. The king of the South will then be
very proud and will kill thousands of soldiers from the northern army, but he will
not continue to be successful. **13**The king
of the North will gather another army,
larger than the first one. After several
years he will attack with a large army and
many weapons.

14"In those times many people will be
against the king of the South. Some of
your own people who love to fight will
turn against the king of the South, thinking it is time for God's promises to come
true. But they will fail. **15**Then the king
of the North will come. He will build
ramps to the tops of the city walls and
will capture a strong, walled city. The
southern army will not have the power to
fight back; even their best soldiers will
not be strong enough to stop the northern army. **16**So the king of the North will
do whatever he wants; no one will be able
to stand against him. He will gain power
and control in the beautiful land of Israel
and will have the power to destroy it.
17The king of the North will decide to
use all his power to fight against the king
of the South, but he will make a peace
agreement with the king of the South.
The king of the North will give one of his
daughters as a wife to the king of the
South so that he can defeat him. But
those plans will not succeed or help him.
18Then the king of the North will turn
his attention to cities along the coast of
the Mediterranean Sea and will capture
them. But a commander will put an end to
the pride of the king of the North, turning
his pride back on him. **19**After that happens the king of the North will go back to
the strong, walled cities of his own country, but he will lose his power. That will
be the end of him.

20"The next king of the North will
send out a tax collector so he will have
plenty of money. In a few years that ruler
will be killed, although he will not die in
anger or in a battle.

21"That ruler will be followed by a
very cruel and hated man, who will not
have the honor of being from a king's
family. He will attack the kingdom when
the people feel safe, and he will take
power by lying to the people. **22**He will
sweep away in defeat large and powerful
armies and even a prince who made an
agreement. **23**Many nations will make
agreements with that cruel and hated
ruler, but he will lie to them. He will gain
much power, but only a few people will
support him. **24**The richest areas will
feel safe, but that cruel and hated ruler
will attack them. He will succeed where
his ancestors did not. He will rob the
countries he defeats and will give those
things to his followers. He will plan to
defeat and destroy strong cities, but he
will be successful for only a short time.

25"That very cruel and hated ruler
will have a large army that he will use to
stir up his strength and courage. He will
attack the king of the South. The king of
the South will gather a large and very
powerful army and prepare for war. But
the people who are against him will make
secret plans, and the king of the South
will be defeated. **26**People who were supposed to be his good friends will try to
destroy him. His army will be swept
away in defeat; many of his soldiers will
be killed in battle. **27**Those two kings will
want to hurt each other. They will sit at
the same table and lie to each other, but it
will not do either one any good, because
God has set a time for their end to come.
28The king of the North will go back to
his own country with much wealth. Then
he will decide to go against the holy
agreement. He will take action and then
return to his own country.

29"At the right time the king of the

North will attack the king of the South
again, but this time he will not be successful as he was before. **30**Ships from
the west will come and fight against the
king of the North, so he will be afraid.
Then he will return and show his anger
against the holy agreement. He will be
good to those who have stopped obeying
the holy agreement.

31"The king of the North will send his
army to make the Temple in Jerusalem
unclean. They will stop the people from
offering the daily sacrifice, and then they
will set up the destroying terror. **32**The
king of the North will tell lies and cause
those who have not obeyed God to be ruined. But those who know God and obey
him will be strong and fight back.

33"Those who are wise will help the
others understand what is happening.
But they will be killed with swords, or
burned, or taken captive, or robbed of
their homes and possessions. These
things will continue for many days.
34When the wise ones are suffering, they
will get a little help, but many who join
the wise ones will not help them in their
time of need. **35**Some of the wise ones
will be killed. But the hard times must
come so they can be made stronger and
purer and without faults until the time of
the end comes. Then, at the right time,
the end will come.

The King Who Praises Himself

36"The king of the North will do
whatever he wants. He will brag about
himself and praise himself and think he is
even better than a god. He will say things
against the God of gods that no one has
ever heard. And he will be successful until all the bad things have happened. Then
what God has planned to happen will happen. **37**The king of the North will not
care about the gods his ancestors worshiped or the god that women worship.
He won't care about any god. Instead, he
will make himself more important than
any god. **38**The king of the North will
worship power and strength, which his
ancestors did not worship. He will honor
the god of power with gold and silver, expensive jewels and gifts. **39**That king will
attack strong, walled cities with the help
of a foreign god. He will give much honor
to the people who join him, making them
rulers in charge of many other people.
And he will make them pay him for the
land they rule.

40"At the time of the end, the king of
the South will fight a battle against the
king of the North. The king of the North
will attack with chariots, soldiers on
horses, and many large ships. He will invade many countries and sweep through
their lands like a flood. **41**The king of the
North will attack the beautiful land of Judah. He will defeat many countries, but
Edom, Moab, and the leaders of Ammon
will be saved from him. **42**The king of the
North will show his power in many countries; Egypt will not escape. **43**The king
will get treasures of gold and silver and
all the riches of Egypt. The Libyan and
Nubian people will obey him. **44**But the
king of the North will hear news from the
east and the north that will make him
afraid and angry. He will go to destroy
completely many nations. **45**He will set
up his royal tents between the sea and
the beautiful mountain where the holy
Temple is built. But, finally, his end will
come, and no one will help him.

The Time of the End

12 "At that time Michael, the great
prince who protects your people,
will stand up. There will be a time of
much trouble, the worst time since nations have been on earth, but your people
will be saved. Everyone whose name is
written in God's book will be saved.
2Many people who have already died will
live again. Some of them will wake up to
have life forever, but some will wake up
to find shame and disgrace forever. **3**The
wise people will shine like the brightness
of the sky. Those who teach others to live
right will shine like stars forever and
ever.

4"But you, Daniel, close up the book
and seal it. These things will happen at
the time of the end. Many people will go
here and there to find true knowledge."

5Then I, Daniel, looked, and saw two
other men. One was standing on my side

of the river, and the other was standing on
the far side. **6**The man who was dressed in
linen was standing over the water in the
river. One of the two men spoke to him
and asked, "How long will it be before
these amazing things come true?"
7The man dressed in linen, who stood
over the water, raised his
hands toward heaven.
And I heard him swear by
the name of God who
lives forever, "It will be
for three and one-half
years. The power of the
holy people will finally be
broken, and then all these
things will come true."
8I heard the answer,
but I did not really under-
stand, so I asked, "Master, what will happen after all these things come true?"

> As for you, Daniel, go your way until the end. You will get your rest, and at the end you will rise to receive your reward.
> —Daniel 12:13

9He answered, "Go your way, Daniel.
The message is closed up and sealed until the time of the end. **10**Many people
will be made clean, pure, and spotless,
but the wicked will continue to be
wicked. Those wicked people will not understand these things, but the wise will
understand them.
11"The daily sacrifice
will be stopped. Then,
after 1,290 days from
that time, the destroying
terror will be set up.
12Those who wait for the
end of the 1,335 days will
be happy.
13"As for you, Daniel,
go your way until the end.
You will get your rest,
and at the end you will rise to receive
your reward."

A CALL TO COME HOME

Hi, there. I am Hosea, a prophet of God. Have you ever had a really good friend? A friend you cared for deeply? What if that friend promised to go to the movies with you but at the last minute chose to go to a party with someone else? What if your friend refused to see you or even to talk with you on the phone? You would be sad, but probably not as sad as I was about my wife, Gomer. I loved her with all my heart, but she was not faithful to me. Gomer left me and our children, but one day I brought her home again.

I wrote this book to warn the people of Israel about their unfaithfulness to God. My life with Gomer was a picture of God and the unfaithful nation of Israel. God loved Israel even more than I loved Gomer and wanted Israel to worship him alone. The people of Israel continued to worship false gods, so God allowed them to be conquered by their enemies. But God, like Gomer and me, promised to bring Israel home one day to be his chosen people again.

JESUS WATCH

Gomer, in her unfaithfulness, was eventually held as a slave. Hosea loved her so much that he was willing to pay the price to buy her back. He paid six ounces of silver and ten bushels of barley to save her from a life of slavery. Before we believe in Jesus, we are slaves, too. Jesus said, "Everyone who lives in sin is a slave to sin" (John 8:34). Jesus loves us so much that he paid the price for our sins. He gave his life as a sacrifice and saved us from a life of sin. Now we are children of God and live to please our Father. God sends us the Holy Spirit who helps us become holy and more like Jesus.

"Why did the merchants use dishonest scales?"

"Sounds like they were a bunch of cheaters. Let's download Hosea 12:7–8 to find out."

FAITH links

- A Hopeful Name, Hosea 1:3–11
- A Fake Apology, Hosea 6:1–7
- Going My Way?, Hosea 8:1–6
- Long-lasting Hope, Hosea 14

1 The LORD spoke his word to Hosea
son of Beeri during the time that Uzziah, Jotham, Ahaz, and Hezekiah were
kings of Judah and Jeroboam son of Jehoash was king of Israel.

Hosea's Wife and Children

2When the LORD began speaking
through Hosea, the LORD said to him,
"Go, and marry an unfaithful woman and
have unfaithful children, because the
people in this country have been completely unfaithful to the LORD." 3So Hosea married Gomer daughter of Diblaim,
and she became pregnant and gave birth
to Hosea's son.
4The LORD said to Hosea, "Name him
Jezreel, because soon I will punish the
family of Jehu for the people they killed at
Jezreel. In the future I will put an end to
the kingdom of Israel 5and break the
power of Israel's army in the Valley of
Jezreel."
6Gomer became pregnant again and
gave birth to a daughter. The LORD said
to Hosea, "Name her Lo-Ruhamah,[n] because I will not pity Israel anymore, nor
will I forgive them. 7But I will show pity
to the people of Judah. I will save them,
but not by using bows or swords, horses
or horsemen, or weapons of war. I, the
LORD their God, will save them."
8After Gomer had stopped nursing
Lo-Ruhamah, she became pregnant again
and gave birth to another son. 9The
LORD said, "Name him Lo-Ammi,[n] because you are not my people, and I am not
your God.

God's Promise to Israel

10"But the number of the Israelites
will become like the grains of sand of the
sea, which no one can measure or count.
They were called, 'You are not my people,' but later they will be called 'children
of the living God.' 11The people of Judah
and Israel will join together again and will
choose one leader for themselves. They
will come up from the land, because the
day of Jezreel[n] will be truly great.
2 "You are to call your brothers, 'my
people,' and your sisters, 'you have
been shown pity.'

A HOPEFUL NAME

HOSEA 1:3-11

Suppose that instead of giving you the name you have, your parents had decided to name you after a characteristic of theirs. For example, "laughs a lot." Ridiculous, you say? Not to the prophet Hosea. The Israelites weren't faithful to God. So God told Hosea to choose names for his children that reflected the people's lack of faithfulness. God later provided hope by giving the people a new name: "children of the living God."

We sometimes choose hopeless names for ourselves when we do wrong things. For example, we might call ourselves "loser" or "hopeless." If you're a Christian, you can claim the name "child of the living God." That is a name to restore hope.

The Rainbow Promise, Genesis 9:1–17, p. 14

The God of Big Things, Joshua 10, p. 289

A Mother's Love, Isaiah 49:13–16, p. 961

Name with a Purpose, Matthew 1:21, p. 1274

Two Birthdays, John 3:1–7, p. 1426

Never Alone, Hebrews 13:5–6, p. 1684

1:6 Lo-Ruhamah This name in Hebrew means "not pitied."

1:9 Lo-Ammi This name in Hebrew means "not my people."

1:11 Jezreel This name in Hebrew means "God plants."

God Speaks About Israel

2 "Plead with your mother.[a]
Accuse her, because she is no
longer my wife,
and I am no longer her husband.
Tell her to stop acting like a
prostitute,
to stop behaving like an unfaithful
wife.
3 If she refuses, I will strip her naked
and leave her bare like the day she
was born.
I will make her dry like a desert,
like a land without water,
and I will kill her with thirst.
4 I will not take pity on her children,
because they are the children of a
prostitute.
5 Their mother has acted like a
prostitute;
the one who became pregnant with
them has acted disgracefully.
She said, 'I will chase after my
lovers,[a]
who give me my food and water,
wool and flax, wine and olive oil.'
6 So I will block her road with
thornbushes;
I will build a wall around her
so she cannot find her way.
7 She will run after her lovers,
but she won't catch them.
She will look for them,
but she won't find them.
Then she will say, 'I will go back to
my first husband,[a]
because life was better then for me
than it is now.'
8 But she does not know that I was the
one
who gave her grain, new wine, and
oil.
I gave her much silver and gold,
but she used it for Baal.

9 "So I will come back and take away
my grain at harvest time
and my new wine when it is ready.
I will take back my wool and linen
that covered her nakedness.
10 So I will show her nakedness to her
lovers,
and no one will save her from me.
11 I will put an end to all her celebrations:
her yearly festivals, her New
Moon festivals, and her
Sabbaths.
I will stop all of her special feasts.
12 I will destroy her vines and fig trees,
which she said were her pay from
her lovers.
I will turn them into a forest,
and wild animals will eat them.
13 I will punish her for all the times
she burned incense to the Baals.
She put on her rings and jewelry
and went chasing after her lovers,
but she forgot me!"
says the LORD.

14 "So I am going to attract her;
I will lead her into the desert
and speak tenderly to her.
15 There I will give her back her
vineyards,
and I will make the Valley of
Trouble a door of hope.
There she will respond as when she
was young,
as when she came out of Egypt."

16 The LORD says, "In the future she
will call me 'my husband;'
no longer will she call me 'my
baal.'[a]
17 I will never let her say the names of
Baal again;
people won't use their names
anymore.
18 At that time I will make an
agreement for them
with the wild animals, the birds,
and the crawling things.
I will smash from the land
the bow and the sword and the
weapons of war,
so my people will live in safety.
19 And I will make you my promised
bride forever.

2:2 mother Refers to the nation of Israel here.
2:5 lovers Refers to the nations surrounding Israel, who led Israel to worship false gods.
2:7 husband Refers to God here.
2:16 baal Another Hebrew word for husband, but it was the same word as the false god Baal.

I will be good and fair;
I will show you my love and mercy.
20 I will be true to you as my promised bride,
and you will know the LORD.

21 "At that time I will speak to you,"
says the LORD.
"I will speak to the skies,
and they will give rain to the earth.
22 The earth will produce grain, new wine, and oil;
much will grow because my people are called Jezreel."
23 I will plant my people in the land,
and I will show pity to the one I had called 'not shown pity.'
I will say, 'You are my people'
to those I had called 'not my people.'
And they will say to me, 'You are our God.' "

> I will be true to you as my promised bride, and you will know the LORD.
> —Hosea 2:20

Hosea Buys a Wife

3 The LORD said to me again, "Go, show
your love to a woman loved by someone else, who has been unfaithful to you.
In the same way the LORD loves the people of Israel, even though they worship
other gods and love to eat the raisin
cakes."[n]
2 So I bought her for six ounces of silver and ten bushels of barley. 3 Then I
told her, "You must wait for me for many
days. You must not be a prostitute, and
you must not have sexual relations with
any other man. I will act the same way
toward you."
4 In the same way Israel will live many
days without a king or leader, without
sacrifices or holy stone pillars, and without the holy vest or an idol. 5 After this,
the people of Israel will return to the
LORD their God and follow him and the
king from David's family. In the last days
they will turn in fear to the LORD, and he
will bless them.

The Lord's Word Against Israel

4 People of Israel, listen to the LORD's message.
The LORD has this against you who live in the land:
"The people are not true, not loyal to God,
nor do those who live in the land even know him.
2 Cursing, lying, killing, stealing and adultery are everywhere.
One murder follows another.
3 Because of this the land dries up,
and all its people are dying.
Even the wild animals and the birds of the air
and the fish of the sea are dying.

God's Case Against the Priests

4 "No one should accuse
or blame another person.
Don't blame the people, you priests,
when they quarrel with you.
5 You will be ruined in the day,
and your prophets will be ruined with you in the night.
I will also destroy your mother."[n]
6 My people will be destroyed,
because they have no knowledge.
You have refused to learn,
so I will refuse to let you be priests to me.
You have forgotten the teachings of your God,
so I will forget your children.
7 The more priests there are,
the more they sin against me.
I will take away their honor
and give them shame.
8 Since the priests live off the sin
offerings of the people,

2:22 Jezreel This name in Hebrew means "God plants."
3:1 raisin cakes This food was eaten in the feasts that honored false gods.
4:5 mother Refers to the nation of Israel here.

they want the people to sin more
and more.
9 The priests are as wrong as the
people,
and I will punish them both for
what they have done.
I will repay them for the wrong
they have done.

10 "They will eat
but not have enough;
they will have sexual relations with
the prostitutes,
but they will not have children,
because they have left the LORD
to give themselves to
11 prostitution,
to old and new wine,
which take away their ability to
understand.

God's Case Against the People

12 "My people ask wooden idols for
advice;
they ask those sticks of wood to
advise them!
Like prostitutes, they have chased
after other gods
and have left their own God.
13 They make sacrifices on the tops of
the mountains.
They burn offerings on the hills,
under oaks, poplars, and other trees,
because their shade is nice.
So your daughters become
prostitutes,
and your daughters-in-law are
guilty of adultery.

14 "But I will not punish your daughters
for becoming prostitutes,
nor your daughters-in-law
for their sins of adultery.
I will not punish them,
because the men have sexual
relations with prostitutes
and offer sacrifices with the temple
prostitutes.
A foolish people will be ruined.

15 "Israel, you act like a prostitute,
but do not be guilty toward the
LORD.
Don't go to Gilgal
or go up to Beth Aven.[n]
Don't make promises,
saying, 'As surely as the LORD
lives . . .'
16 The people of Israel are stubborn
like a stubborn young cow.
Now the LORD will feed them
like lambs in the open country.
17 The Israelites have chosen to
worship idols,
so leave them alone.
18 When they finish their drinking,
they completely give themselves
to being prostitutes;
they love these disgraceful ways.
19 They will be swept away as if by a
whirlwind,
and their sacrifices will bring them
only shame.

God's Word Against the Leaders

5 "Listen, you priests.
Pay attention, people of Israel.
Listen, royal family,
because you will all be judged.
You have been like a trap at Mizpah
and like a net spread out at Mount
Tabor.
2 You have done many evil things,
so I will punish you all.
3 I know all about the people of Israel;
what they have done is not hidden
from me.
Now that Israel acts like a prostitute,
it has made itself unclean.

4 "They will not give up their deeds
and return to their God.
They are determined to be unfaithful
to me;
they do not know the LORD.
5 Israel's pride testifies against them.
The people of Israel will stumble
because of their sin,
and the people of Judah will
stumble with them.
6 They will come to worship the LORD,
bringing their flocks and herds,
but they will not be able to find him,

4:15 Gilgal . . . Beth Aven Cities in Israel where people worshiped false gods.

because he has left them.
7 They have not been true to the
LORD;
they are children who do not
belong to him.
So their false worship
will destroy them and their land.

8 "Blow the horn in Gibeah
and the trumpet in Ramah.
Give the warning at Beth Aven,
and be first into battle, people of
Benjamin.
9 Israel will be ruined
on the day of punishment.
To the tribes of Israel
I tell the truth.
10 The leaders of Judah are like those
who steal other people's land.
I will pour my punishment over them
like a flood of water.
11 Israel is crushed by the punishment,
because it decided to follow idols.
12 I am like a moth to Israel,
like a rot to the people of Judah.

13 "When Israel saw its illness
and Judah saw its wounds,
Israel went to Assyria for help
and sent to the great king of
Assyria.
But he cannot heal
you
or cure your
wounds.
14 I will be like a lion to
Israel,
like a young lion to
Judah.
I will attack them
and tear them to
pieces.
I will drag them off,
and no one will be able to save them.
15 Then I will go back to my place
until they suffer for their guilt and
turn back to me.
In their trouble they will look for
me."

In their trouble they will look for me.
—Hosea 5:15

The People Are Not Faithful

6 "Come, let's go back to the LORD.
He has hurt us, but he will heal us.
He has wounded us, but he will
bandage our wounds.
2 In two days he will put new life in us;
on the third day he will raise us up
so that we may live in his presence
3 and know him.
Let's try to learn about the LORD;
he will come to us as surely as the
dawn comes.
He will come to us like rain,
like the spring rain that waters the
ground."

4 The LORD says, "Israel, what should
I do with you?
Judah, what should I do with you?
Your faithfulness is like a morning
mist,
like the dew that goes away early
in the day.
5 I have warned you by my prophets
that I will kill you and destroy you.
My justice comes out like bright
light.
6 I want faithful love
more than I want animal sacrifices.
I want people to know me
more than I want burnt offerings.
7 But they have broken the agreement
as Adam did;
they have been
unfaithful to me.
8 Gilead is a city of
people who do
evil;
their footprints are
bloody.
9 The priests are like
robbers waiting to
attack people;
they murder people
on the road to
Shechem*
and do wicked things.
10 I have seen horrible things in Israel.
Look at Israel's prostitution;
Israel has become unclean.

11 "Judah, I have set a harvest time for
you

6:9 Shechem A city of safety where people could go for protection.

FAITH links

A FAKE APOLOGY

HOSEA 6:1-7

Have you ever said you were sorry for something you did wrong only because you were caught? God told Hosea to speak out against the repentance of the Israelites. God knew that they were phony when they said that they wanted to learn about him. He also knew that they would soon go back to doing the same sins he caught them doing in the first place.

God is always willing to forgive you when you say you're sorry. But he wants more than just an apology. He wants you to mean what you say. How can you do this? Let your actions show that you're sorry.

Sorry about something you did? Link here on what to do about it:

Facing the Consequences, Deuteronomy 3:21–29, p. 232

A Hidden Sin, Joshua 7, p. 285

Above the Law, 1 Kings 21, p. 470

You Are What You Do, Proverbs 20:11, p. 854

Stand!, Jeremiah 19:14—20:6, p. 1019

From Useless to Useful, Philemon 11, p. 1663

when I will make the lives of my
people good again.

7 When I heal Israel,
Israel's sin will go away,
and so will Samaria's evil.

"They cheat a lot!
Thieves break into houses,
and robbers are in the streets.
2 It never enters their minds
that I remember all their evil
deeds.
The bad things they do are all around
them;
they are right in front of me.

Israel's Evil Kings

3 "They make the king happy with
their wickedness;
their rulers are glad with their lies.
4 But all of them are traitors.
They are like an oven heated by a
baker.
While he mixes the dough,
he does not need to stir up the fire.
5 The kings get so drunk they get sick
every day.
The rulers become crazy with
wine;
they make agreements with those
who do not know the true God.
6 They burn like an oven;
their hearts burn inside them.
All night long their anger is low,
but when morning comes, it
becomes a roaring fire.
7 All these people are as hot as an
oven;
they burn up their rulers.
All their kings fall,
and no one calls on me.

Israel and the Other Nations

8 "Israel mixes with other nations;
he is like a pancake cooked only on
one side.
9 Foreign nations have eaten up his
strength,
but he doesn't know it.
Israel is weak and feeble, like an old
man,
but he doesn't know it.

10 Israel's pride will cause their defeat;
they will not turn back to the LORD
their God
or look to him for help in all this.
11 Israel has become like a pigeon—
easy to fool and stupid.
First they call to Egypt for help.
Then they run to Assyria.
12 When they go, I will catch them in a
net,
I will bring them down like birds
from the sky;
I will punish them countless times
for their evil.
13 How terrible for
them
because they
left me!
They will be
destroyed,
because they
turned against me.
I want to save them,
but they have spoken lies against
me.
14 They do not call to me from their
hearts.
They just lie on their beds and
cry.
They come together to ask for grain
and new wine,
but they really turn away from me.
15 Though I trained them and gave
them strength,
they have made evil plans against
me.
16 They did not turn to the Most High
God.
They are like a loose bow that
can't shoot.
Because their leaders brag about
their strength,
they will be killed with swords,
and the people in Egypt
will laugh at them.

EMAIL! FROM GOD **7:13**
Sin
What does God think of your sin?

Israel Has Trusted Wrong Things

8 "Put the trumpet to your lips and
give the warning!
The enemy swoops down on the
LORD's people like an eagle.
The Israelites have broken my
agreement
and have turned against my
teachings.
2 They cry out to me,
'Our God, we in Israel know you!'
3 But Israel has rejected what is good,
so the enemy will chase them.
4 They chose their own kings
without asking my permission.
They chose their own leaders,
people I did not know.
They made their silver and gold into
idols,
and for all this they will be
destroyed.
5 I hate the calf-shaped idol of Israel!
I am very angry with the people.
How long will they remain unclean?
6 The idol is something a craftsman
made;
it is not God.
Israel's calf-shaped idol
will surely be smashed to pieces.

7 "Israel's foolish plans are like
planting the wind,
but they will harvest a storm.
Like a stalk with no head of grain,
it produces nothing.
Even if it produced something,
other nations would eat it.
8 Israel is eaten up;
the people are mixed among the
other nations
and have become useless to me.
9 Israel is like a wild donkey all by
itself.
They have run to Assyria;
They have hired other nations to
protect them.
10 Although Israel is mixed among the
nations,
I will gather them together.
They will become weaker and
weaker
as they suffer under the great king
of Assyria.

11 "Although Israel built more altars to
remove sin,
they have become altars for
sinning.
12 I have written many teachings for
them,

GOING MY WAY?

HOSEA 8:1-6

Have you ever made a decision on your own without asking a parent first? Maybe you told a friend you could sleep over at his house before you asked your mom. Some decisions don't require permission, of course. For example, you can pick out your own socks. But major decisions need a parent's approval. Hosea told the Israelites that the plans they made were without God's approval. They had rejected God's plans in favor of their own. Because of that, he wouldn't help them when trouble came.

If we claim to be children of God, he wants some say in what we do. When we reject God's plans and follow our own, we can't expect God to help us.

If you want God to help you, then check out these links:

Following the Crowd, Numbers 13; 14, p. 193

Facts About Following, Joshua 6, p. 283

Do What You Want?, Judges 21:25, p. 341

A Parent's Advice, Proverbs 1:8–9, p. 825

Faith Workout, Acts 16:4–5, p. 1493

Helpful Hints, 3 John 12, p. 1724

but they think the teachings are
strange and foreign.
13 The Israelites offer sacrifices to me
as gifts
and eat the meat,
but the LORD is not pleased with
them.
He remembers the evil they have
done,
and he will punish them for their
sins.
They will be slaves again as they
were in Egypt.
14 Israel has forgotten their Maker and
has built palaces;
Judah has built many strong,
walled cities.
But I will send fire on their cities
and destroy their strong
buildings."

Israel's Punishment

9 Israel, do not rejoice;
don't shout for joy as the other
nations do.
You have been like a prostitute
against your God.
You love the pay of prostitutes on
every threshing floor.
2 But the threshing floor and the
winepress will not feed the
people,
and there won't be enough new
wine.
3 The people will not stay in the
LORD's land.
Israel will return to being captives
as they were in Egypt,
and in Assyria they will eat food
that they are not allowed to eat.
4 The Israelites will not give offerings
of wine to the LORD;
they will not give him sacrifices.
Their sacrifices will be like food that
is eaten at a funeral;
it is unclean, and everyone who
eats it becomes unclean.
Their food will only satisfy their
hunger;
they cannot sacrifice it in the
Temple.
5 What will you do then on the day of
feasts

and on the day of the LORD's
festival?
6 Even if the people are not destroyed,
Egypt will capture them;
Memphis* will bury them.
Weeds will grow over their silver
treasures,
and thorns will drive them out of
their tents.
7 The time of punishment has come,
the time to pay for sins.
Let Israel know this:
You think the prophet
is a fool,
and you say the
spiritual person
is crazy.
You have sinned very
much,
and your hatred is
great.
8 Is Israel a watchman?
Are God's people
prophets?
Everywhere Israel goes, traps are
set for him.
He is an enemy in God's house.
9 The people of Israel have gone deep
into sin
as the people of Gibeah* did.
The Lord will remember the evil
things they have done,
and he will punish their sins.

10 "When I found Israel,
it was like finding grapes in the
desert.
Your ancestors were like
finding the first figs on the fig tree.
But when they came to Baal Peor,
they began worshiping an idol,
and they became as hateful as the
thing they worshiped.
11 Israel's glory will fly away like a bird;
there will be no more pregnancy,
no more births, no more getting
pregnant.
12 But even if the Israelites bring up
children,
I will take them all away.
How terrible it will be for them
when I go away from them!
13 I have seen Israel, like Tyre,
given a pleasant place.
But the people of Israel will soon
bring out
their children to be killed."
14 LORD, give them what they should
have.
What will you give them?
Make their women unable to have
children;
give them dried-up breasts that
cannot feed their babies.

> The Israelites were very wicked in Gilgal, so I have hated them there.
> —Hosea 9:15

15 "The Israelites were
very wicked in
Gilgal,
so I have hated
them there.
Because of the sinful
things they have
done,
I will force them to
leave my land.
I will no longer love
them;
their leaders have turned against
me.
16 Israel is beaten down;
its root is dying, and it has no fruit.
If they have more children,
I will kill the children they love."

17 God will reject them,
because they have not obeyed
him;
they will wander among the
nations.

Israel Will Pay for Sin

10 Israel is like a large vine
that produced plenty of fruit.
As the people became richer,
they built more altars for idols.
As their land became better,
they put up better stone pillars to
honor gods.
2 Their heart was false,
and now they must pay for their
guilt.

9:6 Memphis A city in Egypt famous for its tombs.

9:9 Gibeah The sins of the people of Gibeah caused a civil war. See Judges 19-21.

The LORD will break down their
altars;
he will destroy their holy stone
pillars.

3 Then they will say, "We have no king,
because we didn't honor the LORD.
As for the king,
he couldn't do anything for us."
4 They make many false promises
and agreements which they don't
keep.
So people sue each
other in court;
they are like
poisonous weeds
growing in a
plowed field.
5 The people from
Israel are
worried about
the calf-shaped idol
at Beth Aven.
The people will cry
about it,
and the priests will cry about it.
They used to shout for joy about
its glory,
6 but it will be carried off to Assyria
as a gift to the great king.
Israel will be disgraced,
and the people will be ashamed for
not obeying.
7 Israel will be destroyed;
its king will be like a chip of wood
floating on the water.
8 The places of false worship will be
destroyed,
the places where Israel sins.
Thorns and weeds will grow up
and cover their altars.
Then they will say to the mountains,
"Cover us!"
and to the hills, "Fall on us!"

9 "Israel, you have sinned since the
time of Gibeah,[n]
and the people there have
continued sinning.
But war will surely overwhelm them
in Gibeah,
because of the evil they have done
there.

Plant goodness, harvest the fruit of loyalty, plow the new ground of knowledge.
—Hosea 10:12

10 When I am ready,
I will come to punish them.
Nations will come together against
them,
and they will be punished for their
double sins.
11 Israel is like a well-trained young
cow
that likes to thresh grain.
I will put a yoke on her neck
and make her work hard in the
field.
Israel will plow,
and Judah will
break up the
ground.
12 I said, 'Plant
goodness,
harvest the fruit
of loyalty,
plow the new
ground of
knowledge.
Look for the LORD
until he comes
and pours goodness on you like
water.'
13 But you have plowed evil
and harvested trouble;
you have eaten the fruit of your lies.
Because you have trusted in your
own power
and your many soldiers,
14 your people will hear the noise of
battle,
and all your strong, walled cities
will be destroyed.
It will be like the time King Shalman
destroyed Beth Arbel in battle,
when mothers and their children
were bashed to death.
15 The same will happen to you, people
of Bethel,
because you did so much evil.
When the sun comes up,
the king of Israel will die.

God's Love for Israel

11 "When Israel was a child, I loved
him,

10:9 Gibeah The sins of the people of Gibeah caused a civil war. See Judges 19-21.

and I called my son out of Egypt.
2 But when I called the people of Israel,
they went away from me.
They offered sacrifices to the Baals
and burned incense to the idols.
3 It was I who taught Israel to walk,
and I took them by the arms,
but they did not understand
that I had healed them.
4 I led them with cords of human kindness,
with ropes of love.
I lifted the yoke from their neck
and bent down and fed them.

EMAIL FROM GOD 11:1
God
Does God love his people?

5 "The Israelites will become captives again, as they were in Egypt,
and Assyria will become their king,
because they refuse to turn back to God.
6 War will sweep through their cities
and will destroy them
and kill them because of their wicked plans.
7 My people have made up their minds
to turn away from me.
The prophets call them to turn to me,
but none of them honors me at all.

8 "Israel, how can I give you up?
How can I give you away, Israel?
I don't want to make you like Admah
or treat you like Zeboiim."
My heart beats for you,
and my love for you stirs up my pity.
9 I won't punish you in my anger,
and I won't destroy Israel again.
I am God and not a human;
I am the Holy One, and I am among you.
I will not come against you in anger.
10 They will go after the LORD,
and he will roar like a lion.
When he roars,
his children will hurry to him from the west.
11 They will come swiftly
like birds from Egypt
and like doves from Assyria.
I will settle them again in their homes,"
says the LORD.

You must return to your God; love him, do what is just, and always trust in him as your God.
—Hosea 12:6

The Lord Is Against Israel

12 Israel has surrounded me with lies;
the people have made evil plans.
And Judah turns against God,
the faithful Holy One.
12 What Israel does is as useless as chasing the wind;
he chases the east wind all day.
They tell more and more lies
and do more and more violence.
They make agreements with Assyria,
and they send a gift of olive oil to Egypt.
2 The LORD also has some things against Judah.
He will punish Israel for what they have done;
he will give them what they deserve.
3 Their ancestor Jacob held on to his brother's heel
while the two of them were being born.
When he grew to be a man,
he wrestled with God.
4 When Jacob wrestled with the angel and won,
he cried and asked for his blessing.
Later, God met with him at Bethel
and spoke with him there.

11:8 Admah . . . Zeboiim Two other cities destroyed when God destroyed Sodom and Gomorrah.

5 It was the LORD God All-Powerful;
the LORD is his great name.
6 You must return to your God;
love him, do what is just,
and always trust in him as your
God.

7 The merchants use dishonest scales;
they like to cheat people.
8 Israel said, "I am rich! I am someone
with power!"
All their money will do them no
good
because of the sins they have
done.

9 "But I am the LORD your God,
who brought you out of Egypt.
I will make you live in tents again
as you used to do on worship days.
10 I spoke to the prophets
and gave them many visions;
through them, I
taught my
lessons to you."

11 The people of Gilead
are evil,
worth nothing.
Though people
sacrifice bulls at
Gilgal,
their altars will
become like piles
of stone
in a plowed field.
12 Your ancestor Jacob fled to
Northwest Mesopotamia
where he worked to get a wife;
he tended sheep to pay for her.
13 Later the LORD used a prophet
to bring Jacob's descendants out of
Egypt;
he used a prophet
to take care of the Israelites.
14 But the Israelites made the Lord
angry when they killed other
people,
and they deserve to die for their
crimes.
The Lord will make them pay
for the disgraceful things they
have done.

The Final Word Against Israel

13 People used to fear the tribe of
Ephraim;
they were important people in
Israel.
But they sinned by worshiping Baal,
so they must die.
2 But they still keep on sinning more
and more.
They make idols of their silver,
idols that are cleverly made,
the work of a craftsman.
Yet the people of Israel say to each
other,
"Kiss those calf idols and sacrifice
to them."
3 So those people will be like the
morning mist;
they will disappear like the
morning dew.
They will be like chaff blown from
the threshing floor,
like smoke going
out a window.

You should have known no other God except me. I am the only one who saves.
—Hosea 13:4

4 "I, the LORD, have
been your God
since you were in
the land of Egypt.
You should have
known no other
God except me.
I am the only one
who saves.
5 I cared for them in the desert
where it was hot and dry.
6 I gave them food, and they became
full and satisfied.
But then they became too proud
and forgot me.
7 That is why I will be like a lion to
them,
like a leopard waiting by the road.
8 I will attack like a bear robbed of her
cubs,
ripping their bodies open.
I will devour them like a lion
and tear them apart like a wild
animal.

9 "Israel, I will destroy you.
Who will be your helper then?
10 What good is your king?

Can he save you in any of your
towns?
What good are your leaders?
You said, 'Give us a king and
leaders.'
11 So I gave you a king, but only in
anger,
and I took him away in my great
anger.
12 The sins of Israel are on record,
stored away, waiting for
punishment.
13 The pain of birth will come for him,
but he is like a foolish baby
who won't come out of its
mother's womb.
14 Will I save them from the place of the
dead?
Will I rescue them from death?
Where is your sickness, death?
Where is your pain, place of death?
I will show them no mercy.
15 Israel is doing well among the
nations,
but the LORD will send a wind from
the east,
coming from the desert,
that will dry up his springs and
wells of water.
He will destroy from their treasure
houses everything of value.
16 The nation of Israel will be ruined,
because it fought against God.
The people of Israel will die in war;
their children will be torn to
pieces,
and their pregnant women will be
ripped open."

Israel Returns to God

14 Israel, return to the LORD your
God,
because your sins have made you
fall.
2 Come back to the LORD
and say these words to him:
"Take away all our sin
and kindly receive us,
and we will keep the promises we
made to you.
3 Assyria cannot save us,
nor will we trust in our horses.
We will not say again, 'Our gods,'
to the things our hands have made.
You show mercy to orphans."
4 The LORD says,

FAITH links

LONG-LASTING HOPE

HOSEA 14

When you were a little kid, you might have counted on your mother's voice or a pacifier to make everything better when you were upset. What are the things that comfort you now? Hosea warned the Israelites against the false comfort of the idols and heroes that they had chosen. They looked to wooden gods they made or to other nations to make everything better. But only God could bring them real comfort.

Some things in life will only bring comfort for a short time. Many people trust money, the compliments of others, looks, and fame for comfort. When you need long-lasting hope, trust God.

Alone and Forgotten?, Genesis 40:23, p. 57

The Wisdom of Obeying God, 1 Kings 11:1–13, p. 453

Like Silver, Psalm 12:6–8, p. 717

The Foundation of Our Hope, Isaiah 31:1–8, p. 934

The Winner's Crown, 1 Corinthians 9:24–27, p. 1555

A Heavenly Sight, Revelation 21:1–4, p. 1753

"I will forgive them for leaving me
and will love them freely,
because I am not angry with them
anymore.
5 I will be like the dew to Israel,
and they will blossom like a lily.
Like the cedar trees in Lebanon,
their roots will be firm.
6 They will be like spreading
branches,
like the beautiful olive trees
and the sweet-smelling cedars in
Lebanon.
7 The people of Israel will again live
under my protection.
They will grow like the grain,
they will bloom like a vine,
and they will be as famous as the
wine of Lebanon.
8 Israel, have nothing to do with idols.
I, the LORD, am the one who
answers your prayers and
watches over you.
I am like a green pine tree;
your blessings come from me."

9 A wise person will know these things,
and an understanding person will
take them to heart.
The LORD's ways are right.
Good people live by following
them,
but those who turn against God die
because of them.

Joel

HUNGRY LOCUSTS

Welcome, newbie! My name is Joel, which means "the Lord is God." God gave me a message for his people right after swarms of locusts had destroyed all our crops. What's a locust? It's a large grasshopper with a huge appetite. Imagine millions of these insects munching on every plant in sight! The sheep and cattle could find nothing to eat. People were starving. I told the people this terrible destruction was from God. He sent the locusts as a punishment for sin.

I wrote this book to tell the people to turn back to God before it was too late. Another more terrible punishment—worse than locusts—might come if they did not repent and turn away from their sins. God said, "Come back to me with all your heart. Go without food, and cry and be sad" (Joel 2:12). God promises to punish those who sin, but he will richly bless those who follow his laws.

JESUS WATCH

On the night before he died, Jesus promised to send the Holy Spirit, his Helper, to guide us. The Holy Spirit helps us understand God's Word. Joel predicted that one day the Lord would give his Holy Spirit to all kinds of people. On that day, miracles in the sky and on the earth will take place. Then people will know that the Day of the Lord has come. It will be a terrible day of punishment, but anyone who calls on the name of the Lord will be saved. In the Book of Joel, we see Jesus as a judge. He will come on the Day of the Lord and punish those nations who conquered Israel and forced the people to live in foreign lands. Jesus will live on Mount Zion, and Jerusalem will be a holy place.

"Have you ever heard of milk flowing from the hills?"

"That's a new one on me. Let's surf over to Joel 3:18–21 to find out about it."

- Pass It On!, Joel 1:2–3
- Future Hope, Joel 3:17–21
-  A Swarm of Trouble, Joel 2:25–27

Locusts Destroy the Crops

1 The LORD spoke his word to Joel son
of Pethuel:
2 Older leaders, listen to this message.
Listen to me, all you who live in
the land.
Nothing like this has ever happened
during your lifetime
or during your ancestors' lifetimes.
3 Tell your children about these things,
let your children tell their children,
and let your grandchildren tell
their children.
4 What the cutting locusts have left,
the swarming locusts have eaten;
what the swarming locusts have left,
the hopping locusts have eaten,
and what the hopping locusts have
left,
the destroying locusts[n] have eaten.

5 Drunks, wake up and cry!
All you people who drink wine,
cry!
Cry because your wine
has been taken away from your
mouths.
6 A powerful nation has come into my
land
with too many soldiers to count.
It has teeth like a lion,
jaws like a female lion.
7 It has made my grapevine a waste
and made my fig tree a stump.
It has stripped all the bark off my
trees
and left the branches white.

8 Cry as a young woman cries
when the man she was going to
marry has died.
9 There will be no more grain or drink
offerings
to offer in the Temple of the LORD.
Because of this, the priests,
the servants of the LORD, are sad.
10 The fields are ruined;
the ground is dried up.
The grain is destroyed,
the new wine is dried up,
and the olive oil runs out.
11 Be sad, farmers.
Cry loudly, you who grow grapes.
Cry for the wheat and the barley.
Cry because the harvest of the
field is lost.
12 The vines have become dry,
and the fig trees are dried up.

FAITH links

PASS IT ON!

JOEL 1:2-3

Many people pass stories of their faith to their kids. They want their kids to love God as much as they do. God told the Israelites to pass on the stories of what God had done for them to their children. That way, their children would learn the importance of knowing God and obeying him. You can pass on stories of faith, too! How? You can tell other people what God has done in your life.

Faith of Our Fathers, Joshua 4:4–9, p. 280

A Picture of the Past, Psalm 105, p. 789

A Bad Reaction, Jeremiah 36, p. 1043

The Watchman, Ezekiel 3:16–22, p. 1088

Love for Free, Romans 5:8, p. 1524

People of Faith, Hebrews 11, p. 1679

1:4 cutting . . . locusts These are different names for an insect like a large grasshopper. The locust can quickly destroy trees, plants, and crops, and in this destruction Joel sees a warning. God will cause this type of destruction when he punishes his people.

The pomegranate trees, the date
palm trees, the apple trees—
all the trees in the field have died.
And the happiness of the people has
died, too.
13 Priests, put on your rough cloth and
cry to show your sadness.
Servants of the altar, cry out loud.
Servants of my God,
keep your rough cloth on all night
to show your sadness.
Cry because there will be no more
grain or drink offerings
to offer in the Temple of your God.
14 Call for a day when no one eats food!
Tell everyone to stop work!
Bring the older leaders
and everyone who lives in the
land
to the Temple of the LORD your God,
and cry out to the LORD.
15 What a terrible day it will be!
The LORD's day of judging is near,
when punishment will come
like a destroying attack from the
Almighty.

16 Our food is taken away
while we watch.
Joy and happiness are gone
from the Temple of our God.
17 Though we planted fig seeds,
they lie dry and dead in the dirt.
The barns are empty and falling
down.
The storerooms for grain have
been broken down,
because the grain has dried up.
18 The animals are groaning!
The herds of cattle wander around
confused,
because they have no grass to eat;
even the flocks of sheep suffer.
19 LORD, I am calling to you for help,
because fire has burned up the
open pastures,
and flames have burned all the
trees in the field.
20 Wild animals also need your help.
The streams of water have dried
up,
and fire has burned up the open
pastures.

The Coming Day of Judgment

2 Blow the trumpet in Jerusalem;
shout a warning on my holy
mountain.
Let all the people who live in the
land shake with fear,
because the LORD's day of judging
is coming;
it is near.
2 It will be a dark, gloomy day,
cloudy and black.
Like the light at sunrise,
a great and powerful army will
spread over the mountains.
There has never been anything like it
before,
and there will never be anything
like it again.

3 In front of them a fire destroys;
in back of them a flame burns.
The land in front of them is like the
garden of Eden;
the land behind them is like an
empty desert.
Nothing will escape from them.
4 They look like horses,
and they run like war horses.
5 It is like the noise of chariots
rumbling over the tops of the
mountains,
like the noise of a roaring fire
burning dry stalks.
They are like a powerful army lined
up for battle.
6 When they see them, nations shake
with fear,
and everyone's face becomes
pale.

7 They charge like soldiers;
they climb over the wall like
warriors.
They all march straight ahead
and do not move off their path.
8 They do not run into each other,
because each walks in line.
They break through all efforts to stop
them
and keep coming.
9 They run into the city.
They run at the wall
and climb into the houses,

entering through windows like
thieves.

10 Before them, earth and sky shake.
The sun and the moon become dark,
and the stars stop shining.
11 The LORD shouts out orders
to his army.
His army is very large!
Those who obey him are very
strong!
The LORD's day of judging
is an overwhelming and terrible
day.
No one can stand up against it!

Change Your Hearts

12 The LORD says, "Even now, come
back to me with all your heart.
Go without food, and cry and be
sad."

13 Tearing your clothes is not enough to
show you are sad;
let your heart be broken.
Come back to the LORD your God,
because he is kind and shows
mercy.
He doesn't become angry quickly,
and he has great love.
He can change his mind about
doing harm.
14 Who knows? Maybe he will turn back
to you
and leave behind a blessing for
you.
Grain and drink offerings belong to
the LORD your God.

15 Blow the trumpet in Jerusalem;
call for a day when no one eats
food.
Tell everyone to stop work.
16 Bring the people together
and make the meeting holy for the
LORD.
Bring together the older leaders,
as well as the children,
and even babies that still feed at
their mothers' breasts.
The bridegroom should come from
his room,
the bride from her bedroom.
17 The priests, the LORD's servants,
should cry
between the altar and the entrance
to the Temple.
They should say, "LORD, have mercy
on your people.
Don't let them be put to shame;
don't let other nations make fun of
them.
Don't let people in other nations ask,
'Where is their God?'"

The Lord Restores the Land

18 Then the LORD became concerned
about his land
and felt sorry for his people.
19 He said to them:
"I will send you grain, new wine,
and olive oil,
so that you will have plenty.
No more will I shame you
among the nations.
20 I will force the army from the north
to leave your land
and go into a dry, empty land.
Their soldiers in front will be forced
into the Dead Sea,
and those in the rear into the
Mediterranean Sea.
Their bodies will rot and stink.
The LORD has surely done a
wonderful thing!"

21 Land, don't be afraid;
be happy and full of joy,
because the LORD has done a
wonderful thing.
22 Wild animals, don't be afraid,
because the open pastures have
grown grass.
The trees have given fruit;
the fig trees and the grapevines
have grown much fruit.
23 So be happy, people of Jerusalem;
be joyful in the LORD your God.
Because he does what is right,
he has brought you rain;
he has sent the fall rain
and the spring rain for you, as
before.
24 And the threshing floors will be full
of grain;

FAITH links

A SWARM OF TROUBLE

JOEL 2:25-27

How much can you eat in one day? A swarm of locusts can eat tons of plants in one day. That would destroy a town's food supply! The prophet Joel used locusts as a symbol of destruction when he talked to the people about the punishment for their sins. But God promised to restore all that they had lost when their land was invaded.

Some events may happen that can cause you to feel as if your life is over. But God offers hope, even after something awful has happened.

Here are some more Faithlinks on hope:

Can't Live Without It?, Genesis 3, p. 7

When Bad Turns to Worse, Exodus 5:6–12, p. 82

A Hard Place, Ezekiel 28:25–26, p. 1120

Rock Solid, Habakkuk 1:12, p. 1236

That's Much Better!, Ephesians 2:4–5, p. 1599

A Happy Ending, Revelation 22:16–21, p. 1754

the barrels will overflow with new
wine and olive oil.

The Lord Speaks

25 "Though I sent my great army
against you—
those swarming locusts and
hopping locusts,
the destroying locusts and the
cutting locusts[*] that ate your
crops—
I will pay you back
for those years of trouble.
26 Then you will have plenty to eat
and be full.
You will praise the name of the LORD
your God,
who has done miracles for you.
My people will never again be
shamed.
27 Then you will know that I am among
the people of Israel,
that I am the LORD your God,
and there is no other God.
My people will never be shamed
again.

28 "After this,
I will pour out my Spirit on all
kinds of people.
Your sons and daughters will
prophesy,
your old men will dream dreams,
and your young men will see
visions.
29 At that time I will pour out my
Spirit
also on male slaves and female
slaves.
30 I will show miracles
in the sky and on the earth:
blood, fire, and thick smoke.
31 The sun will become dark,
the moon red as blood,
before the overwhelming and
terrible day of the LORD comes.
32 Then anyone who calls on the LORD
will be saved,
because on
Mount Zion
and in
Jerusalem
there will be
people who
will be saved,

2:32 Salvation
Who can be saved?

2:25 swarming . . . locusts These are different names for an insect like a large grasshopper. The locust can quickly destroy trees, plants, and crops, and in this destruction, Joel sees a warning. God will cause this type of destruction when he punishes his people.

just as the LORD has said.
Those left alive after the day of punishment
are the people whom the LORD called.

Punishment for Judah's Enemies

3 "In those days and at that time,
when I will make things better for Judah and Jerusalem,
2 I will gather all the nations together
and bring them down into the Valley Where the LORD Judges.
There I will judge them,
because those nations scattered my own people Israel
and forced them to live in other nations.
They divided up my land
3 and threw lots for my people.
They traded boys for prostitutes,
and they sold girls to buy wine to drink.

4 "Tyre and Sidon and all of you regions of Philistia! What did you have
against me? Were you punishing me for
something I did, or were you doing something to hurt me? I will very quickly do to
you what you have done to me. 5 You took
my silver and gold, and you put my precious treasures in your temples. 6 You
sold the people of Judah and Jerusalem to
the Greeks so that you could send them
far from their land.

7 "You sent my people to that faraway
place, but I will get them and bring them
back, and I will do to you what you have
done to them. 8 I will sell your sons and
daughters to the people of Judah, and
they will sell them to the Sabean people
far away." The LORD said this.

God Judges the Nations

9 Announce this among the nations:
Prepare for war!
Wake up the soldiers!
Let all the men of war come near and attack.
10 Make swords from your plows,
and make spears from your hooks for trimming trees.
Let even the weak person say,
"I am a soldier."
11 All of you nations, hurry,
and come together in that place.
LORD, send your soldiers
to gather the nations.
12 "Wake up, nations,
and come to attack in the Valley
Where the LORD Judges.

FAITH links

FUTURE HOPE

JOEL 3:17-21

Do you ever feel fearful about the future? Maybe you're worried about what will happen when you get to a certain grade or school. Joel preached a message to the Israelites about hope for the future. Even though they had gone through hard times because of the consequences of their sins, one day God would restore their land.

You don't have to fear what lies ahead. God promised to always be with you. He won't forget his promise.

Worrying got you down? Here are some helpful links:

A Major Problem, Genesis 15:6, p. 20

Who Ya' Gonna Call?, Psalm 3:4, p. 711

In Deep Water, Psalm 69, p. 760

A Tight Spot, Jonah 2, p. 1215

A Word About Worry, Matthew 6:25–34, p. 1284

Hope That Doesn't Fail, Acts 26:4–7, p. 1510

There I will sit to judge
all the nations on every side.
13 Swing the cutting tool,
because the harvest is ripe.
Come, walk on them as you would
walk on grapes to get their juice,
because the winepress is full
and the barrels are spilling over,
because these people are so evil!"

14 There are huge numbers of people
in the Valley of Decision,[*]
because the LORD's day of judging is
near
in the Valley of Decision.
15 The sun and the moon will become
dark,
and the stars will stop shining.
16 The LORD will roar like a lion from
Jerusalem;
his loud voice will thunder from
that city,
and the sky and the earth will
shake.
But the LORD will be a safe place for
his people,
a strong place of safety for the
people of Israel.

17 "Then you will know that I, the LORD
your God,
live on my holy Mount Zion.
Jerusalem will be a holy place,
and strangers will never even go
through it again.

A New Life Promised for Judah

18 "On that day wine will drip from the
mountains,
milk will flow from the hills,
and water will run through all the
ravines of Judah.
A fountain will flow from the Temple
of the LORD
and give water to the valley of
acacia trees.
19 But Egypt will become empty,
and Edom an empty desert,
because they were cruel to the
people of Judah.
They killed innocent people in that
land.
20 But there will always be people living
in Judah,
and people will live in Jerusalem
from now on.
21 Egypt and Edom killed my people,
so I will definitely punish them."

The LORD lives in Jerusalem!

3:14 Valley of Decision This is like the name "Valley Where the LORD Judges" in 3:2 and 3:12.

A CROOKED NATION

Hi; my name is Amos. I was a shepherd living near Jerusalem when God called me to be a prophet to the nation of Israel. Do you know what a plumb line is? It is a strong cord with a heavy weight at one end. It's a tool used by builders to see if a wall is really straight. God showed me in a dream that he held a plumb line up to the nation of Israel and found it to be very crooked. The people were not following God's laws.

I wrote this book to tell people to stop sinning and turn back to God. Not only did the people worship idols instead of the true God, but they also did not lead good lives. The nation of Israel was very rich at this time, but the wealthy people did not treat the poor fairly. "They walk on poor people as if they were dirt, and they refuse to be fair to those who are suffering" (Amos 2:7). I warned the people that Israel would be destroyed if they did not turn back to God and stop their evil practices.

JESUS WATCH

The nation of Israel was destroyed because of its sins, but God promised to restore it. Amos described the kingdom of David as a fallen tent that God will set up again. Jesus is the Son of David who will set up a kingdom that will never end. Someday Jesus will come back to judge the nations of the earth. The Day of the Lord will be a terrible day of punishment for people who sinned against God. God is patient and kind, but he will punish all who deserve it. Amos 5:18 says, "Why do you want that day to come? It will bring darkness for you, not light." Christians do not need to fear the Day of the Lord because Jesus promises to reward all who believe in him and follow his commandments.

my FAVORITE links

OTHER CONNECTIONS

Stop at Let's Visit Samaria, Amos 3:11–15, to find out about one of the oldest cities founded and built entirely by the Israelites. King Omri built Samaria to be the capital of the Northern Kingdom when Israel was divided into two nations. Check out the different roles Samaria played throughout the Bible.

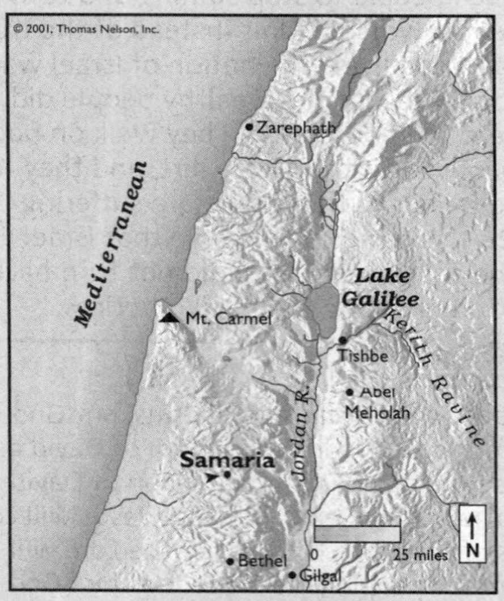

"Who made the stars?"

"I have a good guess, but let's check it out in Amos 5:8."

OTHER STUFF TO SURF:

Justice flowing like a river, Amos 5:24
Go home, Amos, Amos 7:10–17
God's promise, Amos 9:11–15

FAITH links

Love Him? Show It!, Amos 2:6–7

A Blueprint for Living, Amos 5:14–15

The "Ruler" of Our Lives, Amos 7:7–9

1 These are the words of Amos, one of the shepherds from the town of Tekoa. He saw this vision about Israel two years before the earthquake. It was at the time Uzziah was king of Judah and Jeroboam son of Jehoash was king of Israel.
2 Amos said,
"The LORD will roar from Jerusalem;
he will send his voice from Jerusalem.
The pastures of the shepherds will become dry,
and even the top of Mount Carmel will dry up."

Israel's Neighbors Are Punished

The People of Aram

3 This is what the LORD says:
"For the many crimes of Damascus,
I will punish them.
They drove over the people of Gilead
with threshing boards that had iron teeth.
4 So I will send fire upon the house of Hazael
that will destroy the strong towers of Ben-Hadad.
5 I will break down the bar of the gate to Damascus
and destroy the king who is in the Valley of Aven,
as well as the leader of Beth Eden.
The people of Aram will be taken captive to the country of Kir,"
says the LORD.

The People of Philistia

6 This is what the LORD says:
"For the many crimes of Gaza,
I will punish them.
They sold all the people of one area
as slaves to Edom.
7 So I will send a fire on the walls of Gaza
that will destroy the city's strong buildings.
8 I will destroy the king of the city of Ashdod,
as well as the leader of Ashkelon.
Then I will turn against the people of the city of Ekron,
and the last of the Philistines will die," says the Lord GOD.

The People of Phoenicia

9 This is what the LORD says:
"For the many crimes of Tyre,
I will punish them.
They sold all the people of one area
as slaves to Edom,
and they forgot the agreement
among relatives they had made with Israel.
10 So I will send fire on the walls of Tyre
that will destroy the city's strong buildings."

The LORD will roar from Jerusalem; he will send his voice from Jerusalem.
—Amos 1:2

The People of Edom

11 This is what the LORD says:
"For the many crimes of Edom,
I will punish them.
They hunted down their relatives,
the Israelites,
with the sword,
showing them no mercy.
They were angry all the time
and kept on being very angry.
12 So I will send fire on the city of Teman
that will even destroy the strong buildings of Bozrah."*

The People of Ammon

13 This is what the LORD says:
"For the many crimes of Ammon,
I will punish them.
They ripped open the pregnant women in Gilead
so they could take over that land
and make their own country larger.
14 So I will send fire on the city wall of Rabbah

1:12 Teman . . . Bozrah Since Teman was in northern Edom and Bozrah was in southern Edom, this means the whole country will be destroyed.

that will destroy its strong
buildings.
It will come during a day of battle,
during a stormy day with strong
winds.
15 Then their king and leaders will be
taken captive;
they will all be taken away
together," says the LORD.

The People of Moab

2 This is what the LORD says:
"For the many crimes of Moab,
I will punish them.
They burned the bones of the king
of Edom into lime.
2 So I will send fire on Moab
that will destroy the strong
buildings of the city of Kerioth.
The people of Moab will die in a
great noise,
in the middle of the sounds of war
and trumpets.
3 So I will bring an end to the king of
Moab,
and I will kill all its leaders with
him," says the LORD.

The People of Judah

4 This is what the LORD says:
"For the many crimes of Judah,
I will punish them.
They rejected the teachings of the
LORD
and did not keep his commands;
they followed the same gods
as their ancestors had followed.
5 So I will send fire on Judah,
and it will destroy the strong
buildings of Jerusalem."

Israel Is Punished

6 This is what the LORD says:
"For the many crimes of Israel,
I will punish them.
For silver, they sell people who have
done nothing wrong;
they sell the poor to buy a pair of
sandals.
7 They walk on poor people as if they
were dirt,
and they refuse to be fair to those
who are suffering.

FAITH links

LOVE HIM? SHOW IT!

AMOS 2:6-7

Suppose you lost your money to buy lunch at school. What if someone agreed to loan you money, but only if you agreed to pay him back double the amount? How would you feel? The poor Israelites found themselves in a worse situation. Amos warned the rich people that God saw how they cheated the poor people. Although the rich people talked about serving God, they treated others miserably.

God wants us to respond to the needs of those around us, not just give lip service. Helping others is the way to show real love for God.

Want to know how to best serve God? Surf here:

Give What You Can, Numbers 7:1–11, p. 186

Yours, Mine, and Ours?, 1 Samuel 25, p. 389

Jesus' Mission and Yours, Isaiah 61:1–2, p. 978

Concern for All, Daniel 9, p. 1165

That Thing You Do, Matthew 25:14–30, p. 1319

My Best Serve, Acts 6:1–6, p. 1473

Fathers and sons have sexual
relations with the same woman,
and so they ruin my holy name.

8 As they worship at their altars,
they lie down on clothes taken
from the poor.
They fine people,
and with that money they buy wine
to drink in the house of their god.

9 "But it was I who destroyed the
Amorites before them,
who were tall like cedar trees and
as strong as oaks—
I destroyed them completely.
10 It was I who brought you from the
land of Egypt
and led you for forty years through
the desert
so I could give you the land of the
Amorites.
11 I made some of your children to be
prophets
and some of your young people to
be Nazirites.
People of Israel, isn't this true?" says
the LORD.
12 "But you made the Nazirites drink
wine
and told the prophets not to
prophesy.
13 Now I will make you get stuck,
as a wagon loaded with grain gets
stuck.
14 No one will escape, not even the
fastest runner.
Strong people will not be strong
enough;
warriors will not be able to save
themselves.
15 Soldiers with bows and arrows will
not stand and fight,
and even fast runners will not get
away;
soldiers on horses will not escape
alive.
16 At that time even the bravest
warriors
will run away without their armor,"
says the LORD.

Warning to Israel

3 Listen to this word that the LORD has spoken against you, people of Israel, against the whole family he brought out of Egypt.

2 "I have chosen only you
out of all the families of the earth,
so I will punish you
for all your sins."

3 Two people will not walk together
unless they have agreed to do so.
4 A lion in the forest does not roar
unless it has caught an animal;
it does not growl in its den
when it has caught nothing.
5 A bird will not fall into a trap
where there is no bait;
the trap will not spring shut
if there is nothing to catch.
6 When a trumpet blows a warning in a
city,
the people tremble.
When trouble comes to a city,
the LORD has caused it.
7 Before the Lord GOD does anything,
he tells his plans to his servants
the prophets.
8 The lion has roared!
Who wouldn't be afraid?
The Lord GOD has spoken.
Who will not prophesy?

9 Announce this to the strong buildings
of Ashdod
and to the strong buildings of
Egypt:
"Come to the mountains of Samaria,
where you will see great confusion
and people hurting others."

10 "The people don't know how to do
what is right," says the LORD.
"Their strong buildings are filled
with treasures they took by
force from others."
11 So this is what the Lord GOD says:
"An enemy will take over the land
and pull down your strongholds;
he will take the treasures out of
your strong buildings."
12 This is what the LORD says:
"A shepherd might save from a lion's
mouth
only two leg bones or a scrap of an
ear of his sheep.
In the same way only a few Israelites
in Samaria will be saved—

LET'S VISIT SAMARIA **Amos 3:11–15**

Back in the Old Testament days Israel was divided into the Northern Kingdom and the Southern Kingdom. King Omri built Samaria to be the capital of the Northern Kingdom.

Samaria probably is best known as the place where Jesus had a conversation with a woman beside a well. (See John 4:5–42, p. 1428.) But Samaria was an important city to Israel even before Jesus' life on earth. There are only two other cities that the Bible mentions more than Samaria. Samaria was one of the few major cities founded and built entirely by the Israelites.

Samaria has been taken over by several different nations: Assyria, Babylonia, Persia, Greece, and Rome. When Herod the Great took over Samaria, he named it Sebaste—the Greek term for *Augustus*—in honor of the emperor of Rome.

people who now sit on their beds
and on their couches."
13"Listen and be witnesses against
the family of Jacob," says the Lord GOD,
the God All-Powerful.
14"When I punish Israel for their sins,
I will also destroy the altars at Bethel.
The corners of the altar will be cut off,
and they will fall to the ground.
15I will tear down the winter house,
together with the summer house.
The houses decorated with ivory will be destroyed,
and the great houses will come to an end," says the LORD.

Israel Will Not Return

4 Listen to this message, you cows of Bashan[n] on the Mountain of Samaria.
You take things from the poor
and crush people who are in need.
Then you command your husbands,
"Bring us something to drink!"
2The Lord GOD has promised this:
"Just as surely as I am a holy God,
the time will come
when you will be taken away by hooks,
and what is left of you with fishhooks.
3You will go straight out of the city
through holes in the walls,
and you will be thrown on the garbage dump," says the LORD.

4"Come to the city of Bethel and sin;
come to Gilgal and sin even more.
Offer your sacrifices every morning,
and bring one-tenth of your crops every three days.
5Offer bread made with yeast as a sacrifice to show your thanks,
and brag about the special offerings you bring,
because this is what you love to do, Israelites," says the Lord GOD.

4:1 Bashan Amos compares the rich, lazy women of Samaria to well-fed cows from Bashan, a place known for its rich animal pastures.

6 "I did not give you any food in your
cities,
and there was not
enough to eat in
any of your
towns,
but you did not
come back to
me," says the
LORD.
7 "I held back the rain
from you
three months
before harvest
time.
Then I let it rain on one city
but not on another.
Rain fell on one field,
but another field got none and
dried up.
8 People weak from thirst went from
town to town for water,
but they could not get enough to
drink.
Still you did not come back to me,"
says the LORD.
9 "I made your crops die from disease
and mildew.
When your gardens and your
vineyards got larger,
locusts ate your fig and olive trees.
But still you did not come back to
me," says the LORD.
10 "I sent disasters against you,
as I did to Egypt.
I killed your young men with swords,
and your horses were taken from
you.
I made you smell the stink from all
the dead bodies,
but still you did not come back to
me," says the LORD.
11 "I destroyed some of you
as I destroyed Sodom and
Gomorrah.
You were like a burning stick pulled
from a fire,
but still you did not come back to
me," says the LORD.

12 "So this is what I will do to you,
Israel;
because I will do this to you,
get ready to meet your God,
Israel."

He is the one who makes the mountains and creates the wind and makes his thoughts known to people.
—Amos 4:13

13 He is the one who
makes the
mountains
and creates the
wind
and makes his
thoughts known
to people.
He changes the dawn
into darkness
and walks over the
mountains of the
earth.
His name is the LORD God All-
Powerful.

Israel Needs to Repent

5 Listen to this funeral song that I sing
about you, people of Israel.
2 "The young girl Israel has fallen,
and she will not rise up again.
She was left alone in her own land,
and there is no one to help her
up."

3 This is what the Lord GOD says:
"If a thousand soldiers leave a city,
only a hundred will return;
if a hundred soldiers leave a city,
only ten will return."
4 This is what the LORD says to the
nation of Israel:
"Come to me and live.
5 But do not look in Bethel
or go to Gilgal,
and do not go down to
Beersheba.
The people of Gilgal will be taken
away as captives,
and Bethel will become nothing."
6 Come to the LORD and live,
or he will move like fire against
the descendants of Joseph.
The fire will burn Bethel,
and there will be no one to put it
out.
7 You turn justice upside down,
and you throw on the ground what
is right.

8 God is the one who made the star
groups Pleiades and Orion;
he changes darkness into the
morning light,
and the day into dark night.
He calls for the waters of the sea
to pour out on the earth.
The LORD is his name.
9 He destroys the protected city;
he ruins the strong, walled city.

10 You hate those who speak in court
against evil,
and you can't stand those who tell
the truth.
11 You walk on poor people,
forcing them to give you grain.
You have built fancy houses of cut
stone,
but you will not live in them.
You have planted beautiful
vineyards,
but you will not drink the wine
from them.
12 I know your many crimes,
your terrible sins.
You hurt people who do right,
you take money to do wrong,
and you keep the poor from getting
justice in court.
13 In such times the wise person will
keep quiet,
because it is a bad time.

14 Try to do good, not evil,
so that you will live,
and the LORD God All-Powerful will
be with you
just as you say he is.
15 Hate evil and love good;
be fair in the courts.
Maybe the LORD God All-Powerful
will be kind
to the people of Joseph who are
left alive.
16 This is what the Lord, the LORD
God All-Powerful, says:
"People will be crying in all the
streets;
they will be saying, 'Oh, no!' in the
public places.
They will call the farmers to come
and weep

FAITH links

A BLUEPRINT FOR LIVING

AMOS 5:14-15

A blueprint is a plan of action for a builder. By following the blueprint, the builder can successfully do his or her work. Many people say they want to do the right thing, but aren't quite sure how. Amos provides a blueprint for living a life that is pleasing to God. Do good; hate evil. As you follow this blueprint, God offers his help and guarantees your success at completing it.

I'll Never Forget What's-His-Name, Deuteronomy 8, p. 239

What's Out Becomes In, Judges 11, p. 327

A Wise Wish, 1 Kings 3:5–9, p. 439

Mind Guard, Proverbs 4:23, p. 831

Put God First, Acts 5:27–32, p. 1472

What's Good About You?, Philemon 4–7, p. 1663

and will pay people to cry out loud
for them.
17 People will be crying in all the
vineyards,
because I will pass among you to
punish you," says the LORD.

The Lord's Day of Judging

18 How terrible it will be for you who
want
the LORD's day of judging to come.

Why do you want that day to come?
It will bring darkness for you, not light.
19 It will be like someone who runs from a lion
and meets a bear,
or like someone who goes into his house
and puts his hand on the wall,
and then is bitten by a snake.
20 So the LORD's day of judging will bring darkness, not light;
it will be very dark, not light at all.

21 The LORD says, "I completely hate your feasts;
I cannot stand your religious meetings.
22 If you offer me burnt offerings and grain offerings,
I won't accept them.
You bring your best fellowship offerings of fattened cattle,
but I will ignore them.
23 Take the noise of your songs away from me!
I won't listen to the music of your harps.
24 But let justice flow like a river,
and let goodness flow like a stream that never stops.

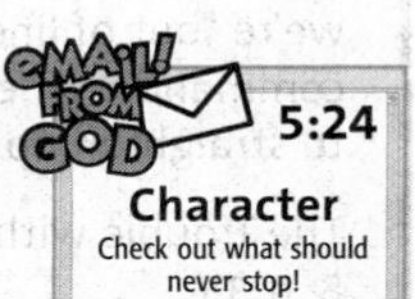

EMAIL! FROM GOD
5:24
Character
Check out what should never stop!

25 "People of Israel, you did not bring me sacrifices and offerings
while you traveled in the desert for forty years.
26 You have carried with you
your king, the god Sakkuth,
and Kaiwan your idol,
and the star gods you have made.
27 So I will send you away as captives beyond Damascus,"
says the LORD, whose name is the God All-Powerful.

Israel Will Be Destroyed

6 How terrible it will be for those who have an easy life in Jerusalem,
for those who feel safe living on Mount Samaria.
You think you are the important people of the best nation in the world;
the Israelites come to you for help.
2 Go look at the city of Calneh,
and from there go to the great city Hamath;
then go down to Gath of the Philistines.
You are no better than these kingdoms.
Your land is no larger than theirs.
3 You put off the day of punishment,
but you bring near the day when you can do evil to others.
4 You lie on beds decorated with ivory
and stretch out on your couches.
You eat tender lambs
and fattened calves.
5 You make up songs on your harps,
and, like David, you compose songs on musical instruments.
6 You drink wine by the bowlful
and use the best perfumed lotions.
But you are not sad over the ruin of Israel,
7 so you will be some of the first ones taken as slaves.
Your feasting and lying around will come to an end.

8 The Lord GOD made this promise;
the LORD God All-Powerful says:
"I hate the pride of the Israelites,
and I hate their strong buildings,
so I will let the enemy take the city
and everything in it."

9 At that time there might be only ten
people left alive in just one house, but
they will also die. 10 When the relatives
come to get the bodies to take them outside, one of them will call to the other and ask, "Are there any other dead bodies with you?"

That person will answer, "No."

Then the one who asked will say, "Hush! We must not say the name of the LORD."

11 The LORD has given the command;
the large house will be broken into pieces,
and the small house into bits.
12 Horses do not run on rocks,

and people do not plow rocks with
oxen.
But you have changed fairness into
poison;
you have changed what is right
into a bitter taste.
13 You are happy that the town of Lo
Debar was captured,
and you say, "We have taken
Karnaim" by our own strength."
14 The LORD God All-Powerful says,
"Israel, I will bring a nation against
you
that will make your people suffer
from Lebo Hamath in the north
to the valley south of the Dead
Sea."

The Vision of Locusts

7 This is what the Lord GOD showed
me: He was forming a swarm of locusts, after the king had taken his share
of the first crop and the second crop had
just begun growing. 2When the locusts
ate all the crops in the country, I said,
"Lord GOD, forgive us. How could Israel
live through this? It is too small already!"
3So the LORD changed his mind about
this. "It will not happen," said the LORD.

The Vision of Fire

4This is what the Lord GOD showed
me: The Lord GOD was calling for fire to
come down like rain. It burned up the
deep water and was going to burn up the
land. 5Then I cried out, "Lord GOD, stop!
How could Israel live through this? It is
too small already."
6So the LORD changed his mind about
this too. "It will not happen," said the
Lord GOD.

The Vision of the Plumb Line

7This is what he showed me: The
Lord stood by a straight wall, with a
plumb line in his hand. 8The LORD said to
me, "Amos, what do you see?"

I said, "A plumb line."

Then the Lord said, "See, I will put a
plumb line among my people Israel to
show how crooked they are. I will not
look the other way any longer.

THE "RULER" OF OUR LIVES

AMOS 7:7-9

Ever try to hang a picture on a wall? You could tell whether the picture was straight by measuring with a ruler. If you didn't use a ruler or tape measure, the picture would hang crookedly. Amos saw a vision of a plumb line. A plumb line was used to measure how straight a wall was. God used the plumb line to measure how "straight" the Israelites were. That meant he wanted to know how willing they were to get rid of their sin.

The Bible is used to measure how "straight" our lives are. It can show us the places where we're "out of line" with God's commands. Where do you need to straighten up?

The Trouble with Sin, Genesis 6—8, p. 11

Try to Remember, Deuteronomy 11:18–21, p. 243

A Look for the Book, 2 Chronicles 34:14–18, p. 603

Our Thirst Quencher, Psalm 42:1–3, p. 741

Life's Rule Book, 2 Timothy 3:15–17, p. 1655

The Sin "Braker," Jude 24–25, p. 1727

6:13 Lo Debar . . . Karnaim These were two not especially significant cities that the Israelites had captured in war.

9 "The places where Isaac's
descendants worship will be
destroyed,
Israel's holy places will be turned
into ruins,
and I will attack King Jeroboam's
family with the sword."

Amaziah Speaks Against Amos

10 Amaziah, a priest at Bethel, sent
this message to Jeroboam king of Israel:
"Amos is making evil plans against you
with the people of Israel. He has been
speaking so much that this land can't hold
all his words. 11 This is what Amos has
said:
'Jeroboam will die by the sword,
and the people of Israel will be
taken as captives
out of their own country.' "
12 Then Amaziah said to Amos, "Seer,
go back right now to Judah. Do your
prophesying and earn your living there,
13 but don't prophesy anymore here at
Bethel. This is the king's holy place, and
it is the nation's temple."
14 Then Amos answered Amaziah, "I
do not make my living as a prophet, nor
am I a member of a group of prophets. I
make my living as a shepherd, and I take
care of sycamore trees. 15 But the LORD
took me away from tending the flock and
said to me, 'Go, prophesy to my people
Israel.' 16 So listen to the LORD's word.
You tell me,
'Don't prophesy against Israel,
and stop prophesying against the
descendants of Isaac.'
17 "Because you have said this, the
LORD says:
'Your wife will become a prostitute in
the city,
and your sons and daughters will
be killed with swords.
Other people will measure your land
and divide it among
themselves,
and you will die in a foreign
country.
The people of Israel will definitely be
taken
from their own land as captives.' "

The Vision of Ripe Fruit

8 This is what the Lord GOD showed
me: a basket of summer fruit. 2 He
said to me, "Amos, what do you see?"
I said, "A basket of summer fruit."
Then the LORD said to me, "An end[n]
has come for my people Israel, because I
will not overlook their sins anymore.
3 "On that day the palace songs will
become funeral songs," says the Lord
GOD. "There will be dead bodies thrown
everywhere! Silence!"
4 Listen to me, you who walk on
helpless people,
you who are trying to destroy the
poor people of this country,
saying,
5 "When will the New Moon festival be
over
so we can sell grain?
When will the Sabbath be over
so we can bring out wheat to sell?
We can charge them more
and give them less,
and we can change the scales to
cheat the people.
6 We will buy poor people for silver,
and needy people for the price of a
pair of sandals.
We will even sell the wheat that
was swept up from the floor."
7 The LORD has sworn by his name,
the Pride of Jacob, "I will never forget
everything that these people did.
8 The whole land will shake because of
it,
and everyone who lives in the land
will cry for those who died.
The whole land will rise like the
Nile;
it will be shaken, and then it will
fall
like the Nile River in Egypt."
9 The Lord GOD says:
"At that time I will cause the sun to
go down at noon
and make the earth dark on a
bright day.
10 I will change your festivals into days
of crying for the dead,

8:2 end The Hebrew word for "end" sounds like the Hebrew word for "summer fruit."

and all your songs will become
songs of sadness.
I will make all of you wear rough
cloth to show your sadness;
I will make you shave your heads
as well.
I will make it like a time of crying for
the death of an only son,
and its end like the end of an awful
day."

11 The Lord GOD says:
"The days are
coming
when I will cause a
time of hunger in
the land.
The people will not be
hungry for bread
or thirsty for
water,
but they will be
hungry for words from the
LORD.

> The people will not be hungry for bread or thirsty for water, but they will be hungry for words from the LORD.
> —Amos 8:11

12 They will wander from the
Mediterranean Sea to the Dead
Sea,
from the north to the east.
They will search for the word of the
LORD,
but they won't find it.
13 At that time the beautiful young
women and the young men
will become weak from thirst.
14 They make promises by the idol in
Samaria
and say, 'As surely as the god of
Dan lives . . . '
and, 'As surely as the god of
Beersheba[*] lives, we promise . . . '
So they will fall
and never get up again."

Israel Will Be Destroyed

9 I saw the Lord standing by the altar,
and he said:
"Smash the top of the pillars
so that even the bottom of the
doors will shake.
Make the pillars fall on the people's
heads;
anyone left alive I will kill with a
sword.
Not one person will get away;
no one will escape.
2 If they dig down as deep as the place
of the dead,
I will pull them up from there.
If they climb up into heaven,
I will bring them down from there.
3 If they hide at the top of Mount
Carmel,
I will find them and take them
away.
If they try to hide from
me at the bottom
of the sea,
I will command a
snake to bite
them.
4 If they are captured
and taken away by
their enemies,
I will command the
sword to kill
them.
I will keep watch over them,
but I will keep watch to give them
trouble, not to do them good."

5 The Lord GOD All-Powerful touches
the land,
and the land shakes.
Then everyone who lives in the
land cries for the dead.
The whole land rises like the Nile
River
and falls like the river of Egypt.
6 The LORD builds his upper rooms
above the skies;
he sets their foundations on the
earth.
He calls for the waters of the sea
and pours them out on the land.
The LORD is his name.
7 The LORD says,
"Israel, you are no different to me
than the people of Cush.
I brought Israel out of the land of
Egypt,
and the Philistines from Crete,
and the Arameans from Kir.

8:14 Dan . . . Beersheba Dan was the city farthest north in Israel, and Beersheba was the city farthest south.

8 I, the Lord GOD, am watching the
sinful kingdom Israel.
I will destroy it
from off the earth,
but I will not completely destroy
Jacob's descendants," says the
LORD.
9 "I am giving the command
to scatter the nation of Israel
among all nations.
It will be like someone shaking grain
through a strainer,
but not even a tiny stone falls
through.
10 All the sinners among my people
will die by the sword—
those who say,
'Nothing bad will happen to us.'

The Lord Promises to Restore Israel

11 "The kingdom of David is like a fallen
tent,
but in that day I will set it up
again
and mend its broken places.
I will rebuild its ruins
as it was before.
12 Then Israel will take over what is left
of Edom
and the other nations that belong
to me,"
says the LORD,
who will make it happen.

13 The LORD says, "The time is coming
when there will be all kinds of
food.
People will still be harvesting
crops
when it's time to plow again.
People will still be taking the juice
from grapes
when it's time to plant again.
Wine will drip from the mountains
and pour from the hills.
14 I will bring my people Israel back
from captivity;
they will build the ruined cities
again,
and they will live in them.

FAITH links

UPROOTED BY CHANGE

AMOS 9:15

If you've ever seen someone move a plant from one location to the next, you know how unsettling that can be. Some plants don't thrive after being uprooted. Some events in life can cause you to feel uprooted. Going to a new school, moving to a new house, or a change in your family situation due to divorce can be pretty scary. The Israelites had been uprooted, their lives completely changed. Amos's book ends with the message of hope for them. There would come a time when they would not have to fear being uprooted again.

Change can be hard, sometimes. When you're feeling uprooted by change, God's presence can bring you stability.

Here are some Faithlinks on how to handle those big changes in your life:

Real Faith or Really Scared?, Judges 4, p. 315

Problem Solved, 2 Kings 20:1–11, p. 507

Lower Than Low, Job 19:13–25, p. 680

Future Hope, Joel 3:17–21, p. 1191

A Safe Place, Nahum 1:7, p. 1231

An Energy Boost, Acts 4:31, p. 1469

They will plant vineyards and drink
the wine from them;
they will plant gardens and eat
their fruit.
15 I will plant my people on their land,
and they will not be pulled out
again
from the land which I have given
them,"
says the LORD your God.

DESTROY EDOM

It's Obadiah the prophet here. I served God by telling the nation of Edom about God's plan to punish them. Do you remember the story of Jacob and Esau, the twin brothers who started fighting before they were even born? Esau sold his rights as a firstborn son to Jacob for a bowl of soup. Jacob then tricked his father Isaac into giving him the blessing that should have been given to Esau. When he found out that Jacob had stolen his inheritance, Esau was so angry he wanted to kill his brother. (Surf on over to Genesis 25—27, p. 33, for that exciting story.) Esau eventually forgave Jacob; but his descendants, the nation of Edom, were always enemies of Israel.

I wrote this book to tell people that Edom would be destroyed because it was an enemy of God's people. As our relatives, the Edomites should have helped defend Jerusalem from our enemies, but instead they laughed at our trouble. They were happy when Jerusalem was invaded and came to steal our treasures. The Edomites even captured people trying to escape and turned them over to the enemy. God said, "The same evil things you did to other people will happen to you" (Obadiah 15).

JESUS WATCH

The people of Edom were proud of their nation and did not think it could ever be destroyed. Their capital city of Sela was perched on a high cliff and could only be approached through a narrow gorge. How could anyone conquer Sela? Years later Edom was conquered and forced out of its mountain strongholds. The people moved to southern Israel and eventually were completely destroyed by the Romans. Edom was punished for its sins. Obadiah also talks about the day that Jesus will come to judge all the nations. It will be a day of terrible punishment for nations who were enemies of Israel. Jesus will restore the nation of Israel and rule as a king from Mount Zion in Jerusalem.

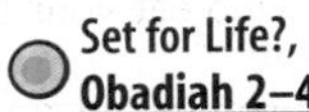

"What will Edom lose?"

"That's easy! Everything! Check out Obadiah 6-7."

WHAT ABOUT THIS?

Don't laugh at Israel, Obadiah 12–14

The holy mountain, Obadiah 17

Set for Life?, Obadiah 2–4

A Fair-weather Friend, Obadiah 7

The Lord Will Punish the Edomites

1 This is the vision of Obadiah.

This is what the Lord GOD says about Edom:[*]

We have heard a message from the
LORD.
A messenger has been sent among
the nations, saying,
"Attack! Let's go attack Edom!"

The Lord Speaks to the Edomites

2 "Soon I will make you the smallest of
nations.
You will be greatly hated by
everyone.
3 Your pride has fooled you,
you who live in the hollow places
of the cliff.
Your home is up high,
you who say to yourself,
'No one can bring me down to the
ground.'
4 Even if you fly high like the eagle
and make your nest among the
stars,
I will bring you down from there,"
says the LORD.
5 "You will really be ruined!
If thieves came to you,
if robbers came by night,
they would steal only enough for
themselves.
If workers came and picked the
grapes from your vines,
they would leave a few behind.
6 But you, Edom, will really lose
everything!
People will find all your hidden
treasures!
7 All the people who are your friends
will force you out of the land.
The people who are at peace with you
will trick you and defeat you.
Those who eat your bread with you
now
are planning a trap for you,
and you will not notice it."
8 The LORD says, "On that day
I will surely destroy the wise
people from Edom,
and those with understanding from
the mountains of Edom.
9 Then, city of Teman, your best
warriors will be afraid,

FAITH links

SET FOR LIFE?

OBADIAH 2-4

Do you think that money, fame, sports achievements, or power can make a person secure for life? The Edomites in Obadiah's day believed that their possessions made them secure. They felt proud because their city was like a fortress. No enemies could harm them, or so they thought. But Obadiah warned them that God would humble them.

Many prideful people boast that they "have it all" (money, fame, power) and are secure in themselves. But God can humble anyone.

Think money will solve your problems? Connect here:

Put Pride Aside, Exodus 2:11–15, p. 78

What I've Got, 2 Kings 20:12–17, p. 508

Wisdom About Wealth, Ecclesiastes 5:10–12, p. 878

A Robbery in Progress, Malachi 3:8–10, p. 1270

Your Heart's Desire, Luke 16:13–15, p. 1401

Share and Share Alike?, Acts 2:43–47, p. 1466

1 Edom The Edomites were the people who came from Esau, Jacob's twin brother. They were enemies of the Israelites.

FAITH links

A FAIR-WEATHER FRIEND

OBADIAH 7

What do you call a friend who is only around some of the time? No, that's not a riddle. Some friends are fair-weather friends. They only hang around when you have something they want. Obadiah warned the Israelites about their "fair-weather allies." These were the nations who claimed to help Israel. But Obadiah warned that one day these same nations would force Israel out of the land.

Fair-weather friends can hurt your feelings by their lack of loyalty. God is a friend who will never be disloyal. You can always depend on God.

Lights, Camera, . . . Actions!, Genesis 12:1–3, p. 17

The Gift of Friendship, 1 Samuel 18:1–3; 19, p. 381

Some Friendly Advice, Proverbs 17:9, 14, 17, p. 851

A Hopeful Name, Hosea 1:3–11, p. 1172

The Way to Heaven, John 14:1–6, p. 1448

Thanks for a Friend, 1 Thessalonians 1:1–3, p. 1630

and everyone from the mountains
of Edom will be killed.
10 You did violence to your relatives,
the Israelites,
so you will be covered with shame
and destroyed forever.
11 You stood aside without helping
while strangers carried Israel's
treasures away.
When foreigners entered Israel's city
gate
and threw lots to decide what part
of Jerusalem they would take,
you were like one of them.

Commands That Edom Broke

12 "Edom, do not laugh at your brother
Israel in his time of trouble
or be happy about the people of Judah
when they are destroyed.
Do not brag when cruel things are
done to them.
13 Do not enter the city gate of my
people
in their time of trouble
or laugh at their problems
in their time of trouble.
Do not take their treasures
in their time of trouble.
14 Do not stand at the crossroads
to destroy those who are trying to
escape.
Do not capture those who escape
alive and turn them over to their
enemy
in their time of trouble.

The Nations Will Be Judged

15 "The LORD's day of judging is coming
soon
to all the
nations.
The same evil
things you
did to other
people
will happen to
you;
they will come back upon your
own head.
16 Because you drank in my Temple,
all the nations will drink on and on.
They will drink and drink
until they disappear.
17 But on Mount Zion some will escape
the judgment,
and it will be a holy place.

eMAIL! FROM GOD
15
Judgment
What happens on the day of judgment?

The people of Jacob will take back
their land
from those who took it from them.
18 The people of Jacob will be like a fire
and the people of Joseph[n] like a
flame.
But the people of Esau[n] will be like
dry stalks.
The people of Jacob will set them
on fire and burn them up.
There will be no one left of the
people of Esau."
This will happen because the LORD
has said it.

19 Then God's people will regain
southern Judah from Edom;
they will take back the mountains
of Edom.
They will take back the western hills
from the Philistines.
They will regain the lands of
Ephraim and Samaria,
and Benjamin will take over
Gilead.
20 People from Israel who once were
forced to leave their homes
will take the land of the
Canaanites,
all the way to Zarephath.
People from Judah who once were
forced to leave Jerusalem and
live in Sepharad
will take back the cities of
southern Judah.
21 Powerful warriors will go up on
Mount Zion,
where they will rule the people
living on Edom's mountains.
And the kingdom will belong to the
LORD.

---

18 people of Jacob . . . Joseph The people who came from Jacob and Joseph, or the Israelites.
18 people of Esau The people who came from Esau, or the Edomites.

FISH BAIT!

Hi! I'm Jonah. I'll bet you've heard of me. I'm the one who spent three days and three nights inside a fish. When God told me to go preach to the people of Nineveh, I was shocked. Nineveh was the capital of Assyria, our greatest enemy. Assyrians skinned their enemies while they were still alive and dragged their captives away with giant fishhooks. I didn't want God to forgive Nineveh; I wanted him to destroy it! Instead of going to Nineveh, I got on a boat sailing the other direction. So, how did I end up in a fish? You'll have to turn to Jonah 1 for the whole fish story!

I wrote this book so that people would know that God wants all people to be sorry for their sins and follow his laws. I eventually did go to Nineveh to tell the people that God would destroy their city if they did not stop doing evil things. To my disgust, they listened! The people of Nineveh stopped eating for a while and wore rough clothes to show sadness for their sins. God is kind and merciful to people who are sorry for their sins, even when we aren't.

JESUS WATCH

Jesus worked many miracles, but the teachers of the law asked for a sign that would prove that he was the Son of God. Jesus said that the only sign would be the sign of Jonah. Just as Jonah was in the big fish for three days and nights, Jesus was in his grave for three days and nights. Jonah's experience with the fish reminds us of the death, burial, and resurrection of Jesus. When Jesus rose from the dead, he proved that he truly was the Son of God. Jonah's message for the Ninevites shows that God is concerned for all people, not just the people of Israel. God loves the people of the world so much that he sent Jesus to die for their sins. Anyone who believes in Jesus has eternal life. No one is excluded. People from all nations are invited.

my FAVORITE links

________________ ________________

________________ ________________

________________ ________________

________________ ________________

OTHER CONNECTIONS

GET THE INFO

- Let's Visit Nineveh, Jonah 1—4. Connect here to find out more about the capital of Assyria, one of the most powerful and evil empires during Old Testament times. Today, nothing remains of this ancient capital, fulfilling Bible prophecy.

MORE STUFF...

More Miracles The story of Jonah is filled with miracles that God sent to convince the reluctant prophet Jonah to take his message to the people of Nineveh. Check out what God did to give Jonah a "gentle" push.

- God sent a great storm that threatened the safety of the ship and its crew, including Jonah (Jonah 1:4–5).
- When Jonah was thrown overboard by the crew to save the ship, God provided a great fish to swallow Jonah. Jonah was kept safe inside the fish for three days and three nights (Jonah 1:14–17).
- God caused the fish to throw up Jonah on dry land. This time when God said to go, Jonah obeyed (Jonah 2:10—3:3).

"How long did it take to walk around the city of Nineveh?"

"Probably too long. Check it out in Jonah 3:3."

CHECK THESE OUT ON THE JONAH SURFWATCH:

A fishy prayer, Jonah 2
Ninevites stop eating, Jonah 3:5–10
The worm turns, Jonah 4

- Go! No!, Jonah 1
- A Tight Spot, Jonah 2
- The God of Second Chances, Jonah 3
- Mercy for an Enemy, Jonah 4

God Calls and Jonah Runs

1 The LORD spoke his word to Jonah son
of Amittai: 2"Get up, go to the great
city of Nineveh, and preach against it, because I see the evil things they do."
3But Jonah got up to run away from
the LORD by going to Tarshish. He went
to the city of Joppa, where he found a ship
that was going to the city of Tarshish. Jonah paid for the trip and went aboard,
planning to go to Tarshish to run away
from the LORD.
4But the LORD sent a great wind on
the sea, which made the sea so stormy
that the ship was in danger of breaking
apart. 5The sailors were afraid, and each
man cried to his own god. They began
throwing the cargo from the ship into the
sea to make the ship lighter.

But Jonah had gone down far inside
the ship to lie down, and he fell fast
asleep. 6The captain of the ship came and
said, "Why are you sleeping? Get up and
pray to your god! Maybe your god will
pay attention to us, and we won't die!"
7Then the men said to each other,
"Let's throw lots to see who caused
these troubles to happen to us."

When they threw lots, the lot showed
that the trouble had happened because of
Jonah. 8Then they said to him, "Tell us,
who caused our trouble? What is your
job? Where do you come from? What is
your country? Who are your people?"
9Then Jonah said to them, "I am a Hebrew. I fear the LORD, the God of heaven,
who made the sea and the land."
10The men were very afraid, and they
asked Jonah, "What terrible thing did you
do?" (They knew he was running away
from the LORD because he had told them.)
11Since the wind and the waves of the
sea were becoming much stronger, they
said to him, "What should we do to you to
make the sea calm down for us?"
12Jonah said to them, "Pick me up,
and throw me into the sea, and then it
will calm down. I know it is my fault that
this great storm has come on you."
13Instead, the men tried to row the
ship back to the land, but they could not,
because the sea was becoming more
stormy.

FAITH links

GO! NO!

JONAH 1

Suppose God told you to go to your worst enemy and tell him God loved him. Would you go? Jonah didn't! The Ninevites were cruel enemies of Israel. So Jonah set off for a city in the opposite direction. But God didn't let Jonah get away with being disobedient.

Sometimes we promise to serve God, but wind up running in the opposite direction when an opportunity to serve comes up that doesn't fit what we had in mind. God doesn't take no for an answer. When he says, "Go," what will you say?

Fearful Service?, Exodus 4:1–17, p. 80

Help for the Poor, Leviticus 5:7, p. 138

A Reminder to Be Fair, 2 Chronicles 19:5–11, p. 583

Too Young to Serve, Jeremiah 1:4–9, p. 988

The Most Fun, Acts 20:35, p. 1502

As Strong as Superman?, Philippians 4:13, p. 1615

Jonah's Punishment

14So the men cried to the LORD,
"LORD, please don't let us die because of
this man's life; please don't think we are
guilty of killing an innocent person.
LORD, you have caused all this to happen;
you wanted it this way." 15So they picked

LET'S VISIT NINEVEH

Jonah 1—4

Nineveh was founded by Nimrod, a descendant of Noah. (Check out Genesis 10:1–12, p. 14.) For many years Nineveh was the capital city of Assyria, a powerful and evil empire. Whenever most people talk about Nineveh, they think about the prophet Jonah. God asked Jonah to go and preach to the people of Nineveh, but Jonah didn't want to go. Jonah wanted God to punish them for their wickedness! When Jonah finally did preach to them, they repented of their sins . . . at least for a while. (Look at Jonah 3:10.)

About 150 years after Jonah's visit, Nineveh was completely destroyed. The Medes, Babylonians, and Scythians attacked the city after a flood that weakened the city wall and dissolved some of the bricks in the buildings. This fulfilled the prophecy of Nahum. (Read Nahum 2:1–6, p. 1232.)

up Jonah and threw him into the sea, and
the sea became calm. 16Then they began
to fear the LORD very much; they offered
a sacrifice to the LORD and made promises to him.

17The LORD caused a big fish to swallow Jonah, and Jonah was inside the fish
three days and three nights.

2 While Jonah was inside the fish, he
prayed to the LORD his God and said,

2 "When I was in danger,
I called to the LORD,
and he answered me.
I was about to die,
so I cried to you,
and you heard my voice.

EMAIL! FROM GOD 2:1
Prayer
Can God always hear your prayer?

3 You threw me into the sea,
down, down into the deep sea.
The water was all around me,
and your powerful waves flowed over me.

4 I said, 'I was driven out of your presence,
but I hope to see your Holy Temple again.'

5 The waters of the sea closed around my throat.
The deep sea was all around me;
seaweed was wrapped around my head.

6 When I went down to where the mountains of the sea start to rise,
I thought I was locked in this prison forever,
but you saved me from the pit of death,
LORD my God.

7 "When my life had almost gone,
I remembered the LORD.
I prayed to you,
and you heard my prayers in your Holy Temple.

8 "People who worship useless idols
give up their loyalty to you.

9 But I will praise and thank you
while I give sacrifices to you,
and I will keep my promises to you.
Salvation comes from the LORD!"

FAITH links

A TIGHT SPOT

JONAH 2

When you're in a tight spot, what do you do? Jonah was in big trouble. He had disobeyed God and wound up as a fish sandwich—hold the bread—as a result. So, what did he do? He prayed!

When you're in a jam, pray. You can pray wherever you are: outside, in your room, inside a fish. God will always listen to you.

Here are some more Faithlinks on what to do in a jam:

When You're Afraid, Genesis 32:9–12, p. 45

Your Best Defense, 2 Chronicles 20:1–12, p. 584

911, Psalm 28:6, p. 730

Small Beginnings, Zechariah 4:10, p. 1255

The Best Protection Plan, Matthew 2:13–18, p. 1276

Prayer Anywhere, Mark 1:35, p. 1331

FAITH links

THE GOD OF SECOND CHANCES

JONAH 3

Do you do what your parents tell you to do the first time they mention it? Or, do you wait until they ask you again? Jonah didn't obey the first time that God told him to go to Nineveh. After a little persuasion (being fish food!), Jonah was ready to listen.

When you blow it, God offers a second chance for obedience. Peter, one of Jesus' followers, also needed a second chance. (You can read about this in John 18 and 21, p. 1454.) Jesus willingly gave it to him. Do you need a second chance? Just ask God. He *is* the God of second chances.

The Perfect Leader?, Numbers 20:1–13, p. 203

Two Enemies, Nehemiah 6, p. 631

A Pity Party, Job 10, p. 671

A Model of Forgiveness, Ezekiel 16:59–63, p. 1103

Blessed Are the Weak?, 2 Corinthians 12:7–10, p. 1582

A Friendly Welcome, Philemon 18, p. 1664

10Then the LORD spoke to the fish, and the fish threw up Jonah onto the dry land.

God Calls and Jonah Obeys

3 The LORD spoke his word to Jonah again and said, **2**"Get up, go to the great city Nineveh, and preach to it what I tell you to say."

3So Jonah obeyed the LORD and got up and went to Nineveh. It was a very large city; just to walk across it took a person three days. **4**After Jonah had entered the city and walked for one day, he preached to the people, saying, "After forty days, Nineveh will be destroyed!"

5The people of Nineveh believed God.

FAITH links

MERCY FOR AN ENEMY

JONAH 4

Ever wonder how God could show love or forgiveness to someone who doesn't deserve it? Jonah did not want God to show love to his enemies, the Ninevites. But that's what God did. The Ninevites told God they were sorry for their sins. Instead of destroying them, he showed compassion by forgiving their sins.

God has mercy on anyone who turns away from his sin. Because he has not treated us the way we deserve, he wants us to show his mercy to our enemies as well.

How do you treat your enemies? Need help? Connect here:

Forgive Instead, Genesis 33, p. 47

Putting an Enemy in Check, 2 Kings 6:8–23, p. 486

Concern for All, Daniel 9, p. 1165

Justice Desserts, Habakkuk 2:4–8, p. 1237

The Number One Rule, Mark 12:28–31, p. 1351

Who Needs Love?, Luke 6:27–36, p. 1379

They announced that they would stop eating for a while, and they put on rough cloth to show their sadness. All the people in the city did this, from the most important to the least important.

6When the king of Nineveh heard this news, he got up from his throne, took off his robe, and covered himself with rough cloth and sat in ashes to show how upset he was.

7He sent this announcement through Nineveh:

> By command of the king and his important men: No person or animal, herd or flock, will be allowed to taste anything. Do not let them eat food or drink water. 8But every person and animal should be covered with rough cloth, and people should cry loudly to God. Everyone must turn away from evil living and stop doing harm all the time. 9Who knows? Maybe God will change his mind. Maybe he will stop being angry, and then we will not die.

10When God saw what the people did, that they stopped doing evil, he changed his mind and did not do what he had warned. He did not punish them.

God's Mercy Makes Jonah Angry

4 But this made Jonah very unhappy, and he became angry. 2He prayed to the LORD, "When I was still in my own country this is what I said would happen, and that is why I quickly ran away to Tarshish. I knew that you are a God who is kind and shows mercy. You don't become angry quickly, and you have great love. I knew you would choose not to cause harm. 3So now I ask you, LORD, please kill me. It is better for me to die than to live."

4Then the LORD said, "Do you think it is right for you to be angry?"

5Jonah went out and sat down east of the city. There he made a shelter for himself and sat in the shade, waiting to see what would happen to the city. 6The LORD made a plant grow quickly up over Jonah, which gave him shade and helped him to be more comfortable. Jonah was very pleased to have the plant. 7But the next day when the sun rose, God sent a worm to attack the plant so that it died.

8As the sun rose higher in the sky, God sent a very hot east wind to blow, and the sun became so hot on Jonah's head that he became very weak and wished he were dead. He said, "It is better for me to die than to live."

9But God said to Jonah, "Do you think it is right for you to be angry about the plant?"

Jonah answered, "It is right for me to be angry! I am so angry I could die!"

10And the LORD said, "You are so concerned for that plant even though you did nothing to make it grow. It appeared one day, and the next day it died. 11Then shouldn't I show concern for the great city Nineveh, which has more than one hundred twenty thousand people who do not know right from wrong, and many animals, too?"

Micah

MAKE GOOD PLANS

Hey, it's Micah here. Welcome to my homepage! I was a prophet of God, who lived about the same time as Isaiah and Hosea. Have you ever made plans to do good things, like play with a friend, plant a garden, or work on a school project? The people of Israel made plans, too, but their plans were bad! Rich people cheated the poor out of their property. Judges took money to decide who would win in court. People worshiped fake gods instead of the real thing—the true God of Israel. They thought nothing bad would happen to them because they were God's chosen people, but boy, were they wrong! God made some plans, too—to punish them for all their wickedness!

I wrote this book to tell people to stop doing evil things and ask God to forgive them. God told us what he wants: "to do what is right to other people, love being kind to others, and live humbly, obeying your God" (Micah 6:8). God expects us to follow his laws and to be honest in all we do. Why not make some plans today to show kindness to other people?

JESUS WATCH

In Micah 5, we read about God's most important plan. God planned to send a ruler who would take care of his people and bring them peace. The ruler would be born in Bethlehem, but come from very old times. His strength would be from God, and his power would be in the name of the Lord his God. Seven hundred years after Micah wrote these words, God sent Jesus, the long-awaited Messiah, to live among us as a man. Jesus was born in Bethlehem, just as Micah predicted. Jesus is also the Son of God, so he is eternal and comes from very old times. Like a shepherd, Jesus takes care of his people. We have peace with God because Jesus died to take the punishment for our sins. Jesus rules forever in heaven with the power God gave him. God gave Jesus a name that is above all names. One day everyone will know that Jesus is Lord of all.

my FAVORITE links

_______________ _______________

_______________ _______________

_______________ _______________

_______________ _______________

OTHER CONNECTIONS

Stop by Let's Visit Bethlehem, Micah 5:2, to find out more about this tiny hamlet nearly five miles south of Jerusalem. Although it probably is best known as the birthplace of Jesus, Bethlehem has played an important role in many Bible events. Check it out!

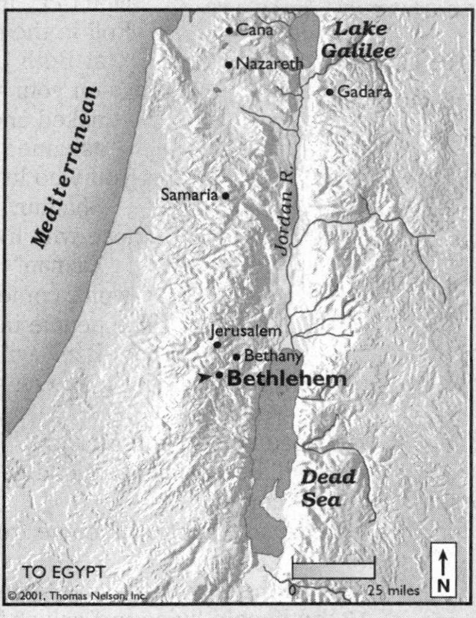

© 2001, Thomas Nelson, Inc.

"Do you think all the people of Israel were doing bad things?"

"It sure sounds like it. Better check out Micah 7:1-6. It doesn't sound like you would want to hang out with this crowd!"

DON'T MISS THESE GREAT STORIES:

Evil planners, Micah 2:1–2
No more bad news!, Micah 2:6–11
A new ruler, Micah 5:2–5
Micah's prayer, Micah 7:14–20

FAITH links

The Peril of Poisonous Plans, Micah 2:1–3

A Real Crowd-pleaser?, Micah 2:6–11

The Right Ingredients, Micah 6:8

Inside the Heart of God, Micah 7:18–20

Samaria and Israel to Be Punished

1 During the time that Jotham, Ahaz, and Hezekiah were kings of Judah, the word of the LORD came to Micah, who was from Moresheth. He saw these visions about Samaria and Jerusalem.

2 Hear this, all you nations;
listen, earth and all you who live on it.
The Lord GOD will be a witness against you,
the Lord from his Holy Temple.
3 See, the LORD is coming out of his place;
he is coming down to walk on the tops of the mountains.
4 The mountains will melt under him,
and the valleys will crack open,
like wax near a fire,
like water running down a hillside.
5 All this is because of Jacob's sin,
because of the sins of the nation of Israel.
What is the place of Jacob's sin?
Isn't it Samaria?
What is Judah's place of idol worship?
Isn't it Jerusalem?

> See, the LORD is coming out of his place; he is coming down to walk on the tops of the mountains.
> —Micah 1:3

The Lord Speaks

6 "So I will make Samaria a pile of ruins in the open country,
a place for planting vineyards.
I will pour her stones down into the valley
and strip her down to her foundations.
7 All her idols will be broken into pieces;
all the gifts to her idols will be burned with fire.
I will destroy all her idols,
and because Samaria earned her money by being unfaithful to me,
this money will be carried off by others who are not faithful to me."

Micah's Great Sadness

8 I will moan and cry because of this evil,
going around barefoot and naked.
I will cry loudly like the wild dogs
and make sad sounds like the owls do,
9 because Samaria's wound cannot be healed.
It will spread to Judah;
it will reach the city gate of my people,
all the way to Jerusalem.
10 Don't tell it in Gath.*
Don't cry in Acco.*
Roll in the dust at Beth Ophrah.*
11 Pass on your way, naked and ashamed,
you who live in Shaphir.*
Those who live in Zaanan*
won't come out.
The people in Beth Ezel* will cry,
but they will not give you any support.
12 Those who live in Maroth*
will be anxious for good news to come,
because trouble will come from the LORD,
all the way to the gate of Jerusalem.
13 You people living in Lachish,*
harness the fastest horse to the chariot.

1:10 Gath This name sounds like the Hebrew word for "tell."

1:10 Acco This name sounds like the Hebrew word for "cry."

1:10 Beth Ophrah This name means "house of dust."

1:11 Shaphir This name means "beautiful."

1:11 Zaanan This name sounds like the Hebrew word for "come out."

1:11 Beth Ezel This name means "house by the side of another," suggesting help or support.

1:12 Maroth This name sounds like the Hebrew word for "sad" or "miserable."

1:13 Lachish This name sounds like the Hebrew word for "horses."

Jerusalem's sins started in you;
yes, Israel's sins were found in you.
14 So you must give farewell gifts
to Moresheth* in Gath.
The houses in Aczib* will be false help
to the kings of Israel.
15 I will bring against you people who will take your land,
you who live in Mareshah.*
The glory of Israel
will go in to Adullam.
16 Cut off your hair to show you are sad
for the children you love.
Make yourself bald like the eagle,
because your children will be taken away to a foreign land.

The Evil Plans of People

2 How terrible it will be for people who plan wickedness,
who lie on their beds and make evil plans.
When the morning light comes, they do what they planned,
because they have the power to do so.
2 They want fields, so they take them;
they want houses, so they take them away.
They cheat people to get their houses;
they rob them even of their property.
3 That is why the LORD says:
"Look, I am planning trouble against such people,
and you won't be able to save yourselves.
You will no longer walk proudly,
because it will be a terrible time.
4 At that time people will make fun of you
and sing this sad song about you:
'We are completely ruined;

1:14 Moresheth This may be a play on the word "engaged," referring to a farewell gift to a bride.
1:14 Aczib This name means "lie" or "trick."
1:15 Mareshah This name sounds like the Hebrew word for a person who captures other cities and lands.

FAITH links

THE PERIL OF POISONOUS PLANS

MICAH 2:1-3

Micah had a message for the Israelites. The wealthy people cheated the poor out of their homes and land. But God saw what they did. So Micah told them that bad things would happen to those who planned to hurt others.

When you sow evil, you will reap it. Thoughts of getting even with others or plans to cause trouble for someone can sometimes backfire. When "poisonous plans" present themselves to you, put them where they belong—out of your mind.

Check out these Faithlinks on getting even:

More Powerful Than Revenge, Genesis 50:14–21, p. 71

Just a Little Respect, 1 Chronicles 11:10–19, p. 534

A Life-Saving Message, Esther 2:19–22, p. 650

A Gentle Answer, Proverbs 15:1, p. 847

Forgive and Forget, Ephesians 4:32, p. 1604

The Gentle Way, Titus 3:1–5, p. 1661

the LORD has taken away my
people's land.
Yes, he has taken it away from me
and divided our fields among our
enemies!' "
5 So you will have no one from the
LORD's people
to throw lots to divide the land.

Micah Is Asked Not to Prophesy

6 The prophets say, "Don't prophesy to
us!
Don't prophesy about these things!
Nothing to make us feel bad will
happen!"
7 But I must say this, people of Jacob:
The LORD is becoming angry about
what you have done.
My words are welcome
to the person who does what is
right.
8 But you are fighting against my
people like an enemy.
You take the coats from people
who pass by;
you rob them of their safety;
you plan war.
9 You've forced the women of my
people
from their nice houses;
you've taken my glory
from their children forever.
10 Get up and leave.
This is not your place of rest
anymore.
You have made this place unclean,
and it is doomed to destruction.
11 But you people want a false prophet
who will tell you nothing but lies.
You want one who promises to
prophesy good things for you
if you give him wine and beer.
He's just the prophet for you.

The Lord Promises to Rescue His People

12 "Yes, people of Jacob, I will bring all
of you together;
I will bring together all those left
alive in Israel.
I will put them together like sheep in
a pen,
like a flock in its pasture;

FAITH links

A REAL CROWD-PLEASER?

MICAH 2:6-11

Have you ever told someone something you thought that person wanted to hear? The Israelites tried to get Micah to say only what they wanted to hear. Micah refused to change the message God had given him just to please the people.

Are you a crowd-pleaser or a God-pleaser? A crowd-pleaser cares more about what others think than about what God thinks. Being a God-pleaser takes courage. God willingly supplies the courage you need to live for him.

Like to please others? Connect to these links:

What Will You Risk?, Joshua 2, p. 278

Give In or Take a Stand?, 1 Kings 22:13–14, p. 472

Fear God or People?, Jeremiah 38:14–21, p. 1047

When the Going Gets Tough, Lamentations 3:22–27, p. 1079

Facing Your Fears, Matthew 8:23–27, p. 1288

The Unpopular Choice, Mark 15:42–43, p. 1360

the place will be filled with many
people.
13 Someone will open the way and lead
the people out.

The people will break through the
gate and leave the city where
they were held captive.
Their king will go out in front of
them,
and the LORD will lead them."

The Leaders of Israel Are Guilty of Evil

3 Then I said,
"Listen, leaders of the people of
Jacob;
listen, you rulers of the nation of
Israel.
You should know how to decide cases
fairly,
2 but you hate good and love evil.
You skin my people alive
and tear the flesh off their bones.
3 You eat my people's flesh
and skin them and
break their
bones;
you chop them up like
meat for the pot,
like meat in a
cooking pan.
4 They will cry to the
LORD,
but he won't
answer them.
At that time he will
hide his face from them,
because what they have done is
evil."

They will cry to the LORD, but he won't answer them.
—Micah 3:4

5 The LORD says this about the prophets who teach his people the wrong way
of living:
"If these prophets are given food to
eat,
they shout, 'Peace!'
But if someone doesn't give them
what they ask for,
they call for a holy war against that
person.
6 So it will become like night for them,
without visions.
It will become dark for them,
without any way to tell the
future.
The sun is about to set for the
prophets;
their day will become dark.
7 The seers will be ashamed;
the people who see the future will
be embarrassed.
Yes, all of them will cover their
mouths,
because there will be no answer
from God."

Micah Is an Honest Prophet of God

8 But I am filled with power,
with the Spirit of the LORD,
and with justice and strength,
to tell the people of Jacob how they
have turned against God,
and the people of Israel how they
have sinned.
9 Leaders of Jacob and rulers of Israel,
listen to me,
you who hate fairness
and twist what is
right.
10 You build Jerusalem
by murdering
people;
you build it with
evil.
11 Its judges take money
to decide who
wins in court.
Its priests only teach
for pay,
and its prophets only look into the
future when they get paid.
But they lean on the LORD and say,
"The LORD is here with us,
so nothing bad will happen to us."
12 Because of you,
Jerusalem will be plowed like a
field.
The city will become a pile of
rocks,
and the hill on which the Temple
stands will be covered with
bushes.

The Mountain of the Lord

4 In the last days
the mountain on which the LORD's
Temple stands
will become the most important of
all mountains.
It will be raised above the hills,

and people from other nations will
come streaming to it.
2 Many nations will come and say,
"Come, let us go up to the
mountain of the LORD,
to the Temple of the God of Jacob,
so that he can teach us his ways,
and we can obey his teachings."
His teachings will go out from
Jerusalem,
the word of the LORD from that
city.
3 The Lord will judge many nations;
he will make decisions about
strong nations that are far away.
They will hammer their swords into
plow blades
and their spears into hooks for
trimming trees.
Nations will no longer raise swords
against other nations;
they will not train for war
anymore.
4 Everyone will sit under his own vine
and fig tree,
and no one will make them afraid,
because the LORD All-Powerful has
said it.
5 All other nations
may follow
their own
gods,
but we will
follow the
LORD our
God forever and ever.

eMAIL! FROM GOD 4:4
Fears
Should anyone make you afraid?

6 The LORD says, "At that time,
I will gather the crippled;
I will bring together those who
were sent away,
those whom I caused to have
trouble.
7 I will keep alive those who were
crippled,
and I will make a strong nation of
those who were sent away.
The LORD will be their king in
Mount Zion from now on and
forever.
8 And you, watchtower of the flocks,"
hill of Jerusalem,
to you will come the kingdom as in
the past.
Jerusalem, the right to rule will
come again to you."

Why the Israelites Must Go to Babylon

9 Now, why do you cry so loudly?
Is your king gone?
Have you lost your helper,
so that you are in pain, like a
woman trying to give birth?
10 People of Jerusalem, strain and be in
pain.
Be like a woman trying to give
birth,
because now you must leave the city
and live in the field.
You will go to Babylon,
but you will be saved from that
place.
The LORD will go there
and buy you back from your
enemies.
11 But now many nations
have come to fight against you,
saying, "Let's destroy Jerusalem.
We will look at her and be glad we
have defeated her."
12 But they don't know
what the LORD is thinking;
they don't understand his plan.
He has gathered them like bundles
of grain to the threshing floor.

13 "Get up and beat them, people of
Jerusalem.
I will make you strong as if you had
horns of iron
and hoofs of bronze.
You will beat many nations into
small pieces
and give their wealth to the LORD,
their treasure to the Lord of all the
earth."

5 So, strong city, gather your soldiers
together,
because we are surrounded and
attacked.
They will hit the leader of Israel
in the face with a club.

4:8 watchtower . . . flocks This probably means a part of Jerusalem. The leaders would be like shepherds in a tower watching their sheep.

LET'S VISIT BETHLEHEM Micah 5:2

Bethlehem is most famous as the home of King David and the place where Jesus was born. It is located five miles south of Jerusalem.

A lot of people visit Bethlehem on vacation. The main attraction is the Church of the Nativity. This church is supposed to be built over the place where Jesus was born, so tourists visit it a *lot* around Christmas. Some other places to sightsee in Bethlehem are the fields of Boaz, where Ruth gathered grain and met her husband (Read Ruth, p. 345.), and the Shepherds' Field, where the angels announced the birth of Jesus to the shepherds. (Check out Luke 2:8–18, p. 1368.)

The name *Bethlehem* means "House of Bread." Probably that is because in the Old Testament Bethlehem was known for producing grain. Later, Jesus called himself the "Bread of Life."

The Ruler to Be Born in Bethlehem

2 "But you, Bethlehem Ephrathah,
though you are too small to be among the army groups from Judah,
from you will come one who will rule Israel for me.
He comes from very old times,
from days long ago."

3 The LORD will give up his people
until the one who is having a baby gives birth;
then the rest of his relatives will return
to the people of Israel.
4 At that time the ruler of Israel will stand
and take care of his people
with the LORD's strength
and with the power of the name of the LORD his God.
The Israelites will live in safety,
because his greatness will reach all over the earth.
5 He will bring peace.

Rescue and Punishment

Assyria will surely come into our country
and walk over our large buildings.
We will set up seven shepherds,
eight leaders of the people.
6 They will destroy the Assyrians with their swords;
they will conquer the land of Assyria with their swords drawn.
They will rescue us from the Assyrians when they come into our land,
when they walk over our borders.

7 Then the people of Jacob who are left alive
will be to other people
like dew from the LORD
or rain on the grass—
it does not wait for human beings;
it does not pause for any person.
8 Those of Jacob's people who are left alive
will be scattered among many nations and peoples.

They will be like a lion among the
animals of the forest,
like a young lion in a flock of
sheep:
As it goes, it jumps on them
and tears them to pieces,
and no one can save them.
9 So you will raise your fist in victory
over your enemies,
and all your enemies will be
destroyed.

10 The LORD says, "At that time,
I will take your horses from you
and destroy your chariots.
11 I will destroy the cities in your
country
and tear down all your defenses.
12 I will take away the magic charms
you use
so you will have no more fortune-
tellers.
13 I will destroy your statues of gods
and the stone pillars you worship
so that you will no longer worship
what your hands have made.
14 I will tear down Asherah idols from
you
and destroy your cities.
15 In my anger and rage,
I will pay back the nations that
have not listened."

The Lord's Case

6 Now hear what the LORD says:
"Get up; plead your case in front of
the mountains;
let the hills hear your story.
2 Mountains, listen to the LORD's legal
case.
Foundations of the earth, listen.
The LORD has a legal case against his
people,
and he will accuse Israel."

3 He says, "My people, what did I do to
you?
How did I make you tired of me?
Tell me.
4 I brought you from the land of Egypt
and freed you from slavery;
I sent Moses, Aaron, and Miriam
to you.
5 My people, remember
the evil plans of Balak king of
Moab
and what Balaam son of Beor told
Balak.
Remember what happened from
Acacia to Gilgal
so that you will know the LORD
does what is right!"

6 You say, "What can I bring with me
when I come before the LORD,
when I bow before God on high?
Should I come before him with burnt
offerings,
with year-old calves?
7 Will the LORD be pleased with a
thousand male sheep?
Will he be pleased with ten
thousand rivers of oil?
Should I give my first child for the
evil I have done?
Should I give my very own child
for my sin?"
8 The LORD has told you, human, what
is good;
he has told you what he wants
from you:
to do what is right to other people,
love being kind to others,
and live humbly, obeying your
God.

9 The voice of the LORD calls to the
city,
and the wise person honors him.
So pay attention to the rod of
punishment;
pay attention to the One who
threatens to punish.
10 Are there still in the wicked house
wicked treasures
and the cursed false measure?
11 Can I forgive people who cheat
others
with wrong weights and scales?
12 The rich people of the city
do cruel things.
Its people tell lies;
they do not tell the truth.
13 As for me, I will make you sick.
I will attack you, ruining you
because of your sins.

THE RIGHT INGREDIENTS

MICAH 6:8

Have you ever used a recipe to cook something? If so, you know that whatever you're making is most likely to turn out good if you follow the recipe. Micah provides a "recipe" for right living. By following it, your life can be pleasing to God. Doing what is right, showing mercy, and being humble are the ingredients of a life that is deliciously pleasing to God.

Show Some Respect, Leviticus 19:32, p. 161

Patience, Please, Psalm 145:8–9, p. 819

Get Hot or Keep Cool?, Proverbs 12:16, p. 842

Welcome!, Matthew 19:13–15, p. 1307

The Worst Chore, John 13:3–17, p. 1447

Another Lazy Day?, 2 Thessalonians 3:6–13, p. 1640

14 You will eat, but you won't become full;
you will still be hungry and empty.
You will store up, but save nothing,
and what you store up, the sword will destroy.
15 You will plant,
but you won't harvest.
You will step on your olives,
but you won't get any oil from them.
You will crush the grapes,
but you will not drink the new wine.
16 This is because you obey the laws of King Omri
and do all the things that Ahab's family does;
you follow their advice.
So I will let you be destroyed.
The people in your city will be laughed at,
and other nations will make fun of you.

The Evil That People Do

7 Poor me! I am like a hungry man,
and all the summer fruit has been picked—
there are no grapes left to eat,
none of the early figs I love.
2 All of the faithful people are gone;
there is not one good person left in this country.
Everyone is waiting to kill someone;
everyone is trying to trap someone else.
3 With both hands they are doing evil.
Rulers ask for money,
and judges' decisions are bought for a price.
Rich people tell what they want,
and they get it.
4 Even the best of them is like a thornbush;
the most honest of them is worse than a prickly plant.
The day that your watchmen[n] warned you about has come.
Now they will be confused.
5 Don't believe your neighbor
or trust a friend.
Don't say anything,
even to your wife.
6 A son will not honor his father,
a daughter will turn against her mother,
and a daughter-in-law will be against her mother-in-law;

7:4 watchmen Another name for prophets. The prophets were like guards who stood on a city's wall and watched for trouble coming from far away.

a person's enemies will be
members of his own family.

The Lord's Kindness

7 Israel says, "I will look to the LORD
for help.
I will wait for God to save me;
my God will hear me.
8 Enemy, don't laugh at me.
I have fallen, but I will get up
again.
I sit in the shadow of trouble now,
but the LORD will be a light for me.
9 I sinned against the LORD,
so he was angry with me,
but he will defend my case in court.
He will bring about what is right
for me.
Then he will bring me out into the
light,
and I will see him set things right.
10 Then my enemies will see this,
and they will be ashamed,
those who said to me,
'Where is the LORD your God?'
I will look down on them.
They will get walked on, like mud
in the street."

Israel Will Return

11 The time will come when your walls
will be built again,
when your country will grow.
12 At that time your people will come
back to you
from Assyria and the cities of
Egypt,
and from Egypt to the Euphrates
River,
and from sea to sea and mountain
to mountain.
13 The earth will be ruined for the
people who live in it
because of their deeds.

A Prayer to God

14 So shepherd your people with your
stick;
tend the flock of people who
belong to you.
That flock now lives alone in the
forest
in the middle of a garden land.

FAITH links

INSIDE THE HEART OF GOD

MICAH 7:18-20

Ever watch a science show on TV that showed the inside of something? Maybe the program featured a look at the heart or eye, using the latest technology. This passage in Micah takes you inside of a heart without using technology. Whose heart is it? God's. The descriptions of what God loves to do can help you know what God is like. He is forgiving, merciful, loving, patient, and faithful. Is your heart like God's?

Check out these Faithlinks on having a heart like God's:

A Thanksgiving Reminder, Exodus 12, p. 91

How Big Is God?, Job 38—41, p. 703

Your Heavenly Dad, Psalm 103:13, p. 786

World News, Isaiah 13—19, p. 913

Remembering Jesus, Matthew 26:26–29, p. 1321

A Family Meal, Mark 14:23–26, p. 1356

Let them feed in Bashan and Gilead
as in days long ago.

15 "As in the days when I brought you
out of Egypt,
I will show them miracles."

16 When the nations see those miracles,
they will no longer brag about their
power.
They will put their hands over their
mouths,
refusing to listen.
17 They will crawl in the dust like a
snake,
like insects crawling on the ground.
They will come trembling from their
holes to the LORD our God
and will turn in fear before you.
18 There is no God like you.
You forgive those who are guilty of
sin;
you don't look at the sins of your
people
who are left alive.
You will not stay angry forever,
because you enjoy being kind.
19 You will have mercy on us again;
you will conquer our sins.
You will throw away all our sins
into the deepest part of the sea.
20 You will be true to the people of
Jacob,
and you will be kind to the people
of Abraham
as you promised to our ancestors
long ago.

DOWN WITH NINEVEH!

Hi, there! I'm Nahum the prophet. My message was for the great city of Nineveh, the capital of Assyria. Do you remember Jonah, the prophet who spent three days in the big fish? God sent Jonah to Nineveh to tell the people to stop doing evil things and ask God to forgive them. To Jonah's surprise, the people listened to his message and turned to God. Years passed, and the people of Nineveh forgot all about God. They did unspeakably cruel things to their enemies, especially to God's people. The Assyrians conquered Israel and dragged the people away with giant fishhooks.

I wrote this book to tell everyone that God would destroy the city of Nineveh for its wickedness. Many thought Nineveh was the mightiest city on earth. Its walls were 100 feet high and wide enough for three chariots to ride side by side around the city. Defeat seemed impossible, but God said he would completely destroy Nineveh. Turn to Nahum 2:1–10 to see how the city was attacked. (By the way, can you find Nineveh on any geography map today? What God says, he does!)

JESUS WATCH

Soon after Nahum spoke his prophecy, the Tigris River flooded and destroyed a part of the wall that surrounded Nineveh. The Babylonian army entered Nineveh through the damaged wall and carried off its treasure before setting the city on fire. God used the Babylonians to carry out his judgment. Someday Jesus will return to judge the nations. The Day of the Lord will be a terrible time of punishment for those nations who have not followed God's laws. The Lord will not let the guilty go unpunished. The earth will tremble when he comes to judge people for their sins. But people who believe in Jesus and follow God's laws have no need to fear the Day of the Lord. It will be a great time of joy and celebration! Just like Jesus promised, we will live in heaven with Jesus forever.

"What happens to people who make plans against the Lord?"

"Nothing but trouble. Connect to Nahum 1:9-10 and find out what God has in store for them."

A Safe Place, Nahum 1:7

DOWNLOAD THESE MESSAGES:

A jealous God, Nahum 1:2–6
Like an army of locusts, Nahum 3:15–17

1 This is the message for the city of Nineveh.ⁿ This is the book of the vision of Nahum, who was from the town of Elkosh.

The Lord Is Angry with Nineveh

2 The LORD is a jealous God who
punishes;
the LORD punishes and is filled
with anger.
The LORD punishes those who are
against him,
and he stays angry with his
enemies.
3 The LORD does not become angry
quickly,
and his power is great.
The LORD will not let the guilty go
unpunished.
Where the LORD goes, there are
whirlwinds and storms,
and the clouds are the dust
beneath his feet.
4 He speaks to the sea and makes it
dry;
he dries up all the rivers.
The areas of Bashan and Carmel dry
up,
and the flowers of Lebanon dry up.
5 The mountains shake in front of him,
and the hills melt.
The earth trembles when he comes;
the world and all who live in it
shake with fear.
6 No one can stay alive when he is
angry;
no one can survive his strong
anger.
His anger is poured out like fire;
the rocks are smashed by him.

7 The LORD is good,
giving protection in times of
trouble.
He knows who trusts in him.
8 But like a rushing flood,
he will completely destroy
Nineveh;
he will chase his enemies until he
kills them.

9 The LORD will completely destroy
anyone making plans against him.

FAITH links

A SAFE PLACE

NAHUM 1:7

When emergencies hit, everyone looks for a place of protection. If a tornado threatens your town, the best place to go for safety is a basement or a bathroom on the lowest floor of your house. If you're lost in a forest, a ranger's station can be a refuge. According to the prophet Nahum, God is a "place" of protection in times of trouble. God watches over you. Whenever you're afraid, talk to God. No matter what happens in your life, you can turn to God when trouble comes.

Here are some Faithlinks on dealing with those bad days:

When You're Afraid, Genesis 32:9–12, p. 45

Good Times and Bad, 1 Kings 17, p. 462

A Really Bad Day, Job 1:20–22; 2:10, p. 661

When the Going Gets Tough, Lamentations 3:22–27, p. 1079

It's Under Control, Romans 8:28, p. 1529

Hard Times, 2 Corinthians 1:8–10, p. 1570

Trouble will not come a second
time.
10 Those people will be like tangled
thorns

1:1 Nineveh The capital city of the country of Assyria. Nahum uses Nineveh to stand for all of Assyria.

or like people drunk from their
wine;
they will be burned up quickly like
dry weeds.
11 Someone has come from Nineveh
who makes evil plans against the
LORD
and gives wicked advice.
12 This is what the LORD says:
"Although Assyria is
strong and has
many people,
it will be defeated
and brought to an
end.
Although I have made
you suffer, Judah,
I will make you
suffer no more.
13 Now I will free you
from their
control
and tear away your chains."

14 The LORD has given you this
command, Nineveh:
"You will not have descendants to
carry on your name.
I will destroy the idols and metal
images
that are in the temple of your gods.
I will make a grave for you,
because you are wicked."

15 Look, there on the hills,
someone is bringing good news!
He is announcing peace!
Celebrate your feasts, people of
Judah,
and give your promised sacrifices
to God.
The wicked will not come to attack
you again;
they have been completely
destroyed.

Nineveh Will Be Defeated

2 The destroyer[a] is coming to attack
you, Nineveh.
Guard the defenses.
Watch the road.
Get ready.
Gather all your strength!

2 Destroyers have destroyed God's
people
and ruined their vines,
but the LORD will bring back Jacob's
greatness
like Israel's greatness.

3 The shields of his soldiers are red;
the army is dressed in red.
The metal on the
chariots flashes
like fire
when they are ready
to attack;
their horses are
excited.
4 The chariots race
through the
streets
and rush back and
forth through the
city squares.
They look like torches;
they run like lightning.

Destroyers have destroyed God's people and ruined their vines.
—Nahum 2:2

5 He[b] calls his officers,
but they stumble on the way.
They hurry to the city wall,
and the shield is put into place.
6 The river gates are thrown open,
and the palace is destroyed.
7 It has been announced that the
people of Nineveh
will be captured and carried away.
The slave girls moan like doves
and beat their breasts, because
they are sad.
8 Nineveh is like a pool,
and now its water is draining away.
"Stop! Stop!" the people yell,
but no one turns back.
9 Take the silver!
Take the gold!
There is no end to the treasure—
piles of wealth of every kind.
10 Nineveh is robbed, ruined, and
destroyed.
The people lose their courage, and
their knees knock.

2:1 destroyer The Babylonians, the Scythians, and the Medes destroyed Nineveh.
2:5 He This probably means the king of Assyria.

Stomachs ache, and everyone's
face grows pale.

11 Where is the lions'[n] den
and the place where they feed
their young?
Where did the lion, lioness, and cubs
go
without being afraid?
12 The lion killed enough for his cubs,
enough for his mate.
He filled his cave with the animals he
caught;
he filled his den
with meat he had
killed.

13 "I am against you,
Nineveh,"
says the LORD All-
Powerful.
"I will burn up your
chariots in
smoke,
and the sword will
kill your young lions.
I will stop you from hunting down
others on the earth,
and your messengers' voices
will no longer be heard."

Everyone who sees you will run away and say, "Nineveh is in ruins. Who will cry for her?"
—Nahum 3:7

It Will Be Terrible for Nineveh

3 How terrible it will be for the city
that has killed so many.
It is full of lies
and goods stolen from other
countries.
It is always killing somebody.
2 Hear the sound of whips
and the noise of the wheels.
Hear horses galloping
and chariots bouncing along!
3 Horses are charging,
swords are shining,
spears are gleaming!
Many are dead;
their bodies are piled up—
too many to count.
People stumble over the dead
bodies.
4 The city was like a prostitute;
she was charming and a lover of
magic.
She made nations slaves with her
prostitution
and her witchcraft.

5 "I am against you, Nineveh," says
the LORD All-Powerful.
"I will pull your dress up over your
face
and show the nations your nakedness
and the kingdoms your shame.
6 I will throw filthy garbage on you
and make a fool of you.
I will make people stare at you.
7 Everyone who sees
you will run away
and say,
'Nineveh is in ruins.
Who will cry for
her?'
Nineveh, where will
I find anyone to
comfort you?"

8 You are no better than
Thebes,[n]
who sits by the Nile
River
with water all around her.
The river was her defense;
the waters were like a wall around
her.
9 Cush and Egypt gave her endless
strength;
Put and Libya supported her.
10 But Thebes was captured
and went into captivity.
Her small children were beaten to
death
at every street corner.
Lots were thrown for her important
men,
and all of her leaders were put in
chains.

11 Nineveh, you will be drunk, too.
You will hide;
you will look for a place safe from
the enemy.
12 All your defenses are like fig trees
with ripe fruit.

2:11 lions' The symbol of Assyria was the lion.
3:8 Thebes A great city in Egypt.

When the tree is shaken, the figs
fall into the mouth of the eater.
13 Look at your soldiers.
They are all women!
The gates of your land
are wide open for your enemies;
fire has burned the bars of your
gates.

14 Get enough water before the long
war begins.
Make your defenses strong!
Get mud,
mix clay,
make bricks!
15 There the fire will burn you up.
The sword will kill you;
like grasshoppers eating crops, the
battle will completely destroy
you.
Grow in number like hopping locusts;
grow in number like swarming
locusts!
16 Your traders are more than the stars
in the sky,
but like locusts, they strip the land
and then fly away.
17 Your guards are like locusts.
Your officers are like swarms of
locusts
that hang on the walls on a cold
day.
When the sun comes up, they fly
away,
and no one knows where they have
gone.
18 King of Assyria, your rulers are
asleep;
your important men lie down to
rest.
Your people have been scattered on
the mountains,
and there is no one to bring them
back.
19 Nothing can heal your wound;
your injury will not heal.
Everyone who hears about you
applauds,
because everyone has felt your
endless cruelty.

Habakkuk

LOTS OF QUESTIONS

Hi, there! My name is Habakkuk. I'm the prophet who asked God a lot of questions. Have you ever noticed that some kids never get into trouble no matter how many bad things they do? Sometimes, it's the same thing with grown-ups. I asked God why he did not punish the people of Judah for their many sins. These people were bad! They worshiped idols, the rich cheated the poor, and judges no longer made fair decisions. God replied that he would send the Babylonians to punish the nation of Judah. I was shocked. The Babylonians? Those wicked, cruel people who did not even worship the true God?

I wrote this book to tell people to trust God. God is patient and wants everyone to stop doing evil and turn back to him. He may be slow to become angry, but eventually all those who sin will be punished. God *is* in control. "Those who are right with God will live by trusting in him" (Habakkuk 2:4).

JESUS WATCH

Someday Jesus will come to judge the nations for their sins. The Day of the Lord will be a terrible time of punishment for those people who have not followed God's laws. For people who believe in Jesus, though, the Day of the Lord will be glorious. Habakkuk wrote, "Then, just as water covers the sea, people everywhere will know the LORD's glory" (Habakkuk 2:14). God will make all things new. A new heaven and a new earth will appear. God's presence will be with his people always and the new city of Jerusalem will come down from heaven. The city will not need the sun to shine because God's glory will be its light and Jesus will be its lamp. God's people will live with him forever in heaven. (Check out what John has to say about this new heaven and earth in Revelation 21 and 22, p. 1752.)

"What was Habakkuk waiting for?"

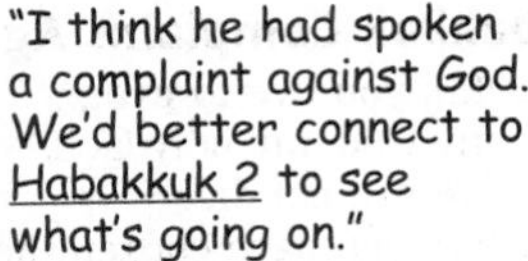

"I think he had spoken a complaint against God. We'd better connect to Habakkuk 2 to see what's going on."

FAITH links

- Rock Solid, **Habakkuk 1:12**
- Justice Desserts, **Habakkuk 2:4–8**
- Your Feet on High Places, **Habakkuk 3:18–19**

1 This is the message Habakkuk the prophet received.

Habakkuk Complains

2 LORD, how long must I ask for help
and you ignore me?
I cry out to you about violence,
but you do not save us!
3 Why do you make me see wrong
things
and make me look at trouble?
People are destroying things and
hurting others in front of me;
they are arguing and fighting.
4 So the teachings are weak,
and justice never comes.
Evil people gain while good people
lose;
the judges no longer make fair
decisions.

The Lord Answers

5 "Look at the nations!
Watch them and be amazed and
shocked.
I will do something in your lifetime
that you won't believe even when
you are told about it.
6 I will use the Babylonians,
those cruel and wild people
who march across the earth
and take lands that don't belong to
them.
7 They scare and frighten people.
They do what they want to do
and are good only to themselves.
8 Their horses are faster than
leopards
and quicker than wolves at sunset.
Their horse soldiers attack quickly;
they come from places far away.
They attack quickly, like an eagle
swooping down for food.
9 They all come to fight.
Nothing can stop them.
Their prisoners are as many as the
grains of sand.
10 They laugh at kings
and make fun of rulers.
They laugh at all the strong, walled
cities
and build dirt piles to the top of the
walls to capture them.

FAITH links

ROCK SOLID

HABAKKUK 1:12

A rock is one of the hardest substances on earth. A rock is pretty solid. Special tools are needed to dig through rock. If you stand on a large rock, you know it won't break under your weight. It also won't shift or slide and cause you to fall. To Habakkuk, God was a rock. He was solid and dependable. That meant he could put his whole trust in God. So can you.

Want to know who to trust? Connect here:

From Hopeless to Hopeful, Exodus 6:9, p. 83

Who Ya' Gonna Call?, Psalm 3:4, p. 711

Future Hope, Joel 3:17–21, p. 1191

Mission Impossible?, Mark 5:21–24, 35–43, p. 1337

Fully God, Fully Human, John 11:35, p. 1444

Never Alone, Hebrews 13:5–6, p. 1684

11 Then they leave like the wind and
move on.
They are guilty of worshiping their
own strength."

Habakkuk Complains Again

12 LORD, you live forever,
my God, my holy God.
We will not die.
LORD, you have chosen the
Babylonians to punish people;

our Rock, you picked them to
punish.
13 Your eyes are too good to look at
evil;
you cannot stand to see those who
do wrong.
So how can you put up with those
evil people?
How can you be quiet when the
wicked swallow up people who
are better than they are?
14 You treat people like fish in the sea,
like sea animals without a leader.
15 The enemy brings them in with
hooks.
He catches them in his net
and drags them in his fishnet.
So he rejoices and sings for joy.
16 The enemy offers sacrifices to his
net
and burns incense to worship it,
because it lets him live like the rich
and enjoy the best food.
17 Will he keep on taking riches with his
net?
Will he go on destroying people
without showing mercy?

2 I will stand like a guard to watch
and place myself at the tower.
I will wait to see what he will say to
me;
I will wait to learn how God will
answer my complaint.

The Lord Answers

2 The LORD answered me:
"Write down the vision;
write it clearly on clay tablets
so whoever reads it can run to tell
others.
3 It is not yet time for the message to
come true,
but that time is coming soon;
the message will come true.
It may seem like a long time,
but be patient and wait for it,
because it will surely come;
it will not be delayed.
4 The evil nation is very proud of itself;
it is not living as it should.
But those who are right with God
will live by trusting in him.

FAITH links

JUSTICE DESSERTS

HABAKKUK 2:4-8

"There's no justice in the world!" Have you heard anyone say that? Have *you* ever said that? Some people feel hopeless because of the cruelties of others. Watching people who seem to get away with doing wrong things causes them to wonder if God really cares. Habakkuk told the Israelites about what happens to bullies in the end. They get what their actions deserve. Habakkuk did not spread this message so that the people could gloat over the downfall of their enemies. He said this because of God's faithfulness in caring for those who are wronged by others. When others wrong you, you can trust that justice will be served.

Forgive Instead, Genesis 33, p. 47

Moses' Champion, Numbers 12, p. 192

A Giant Problem, 1 Samuel 17:32–51, p. 377

God's Sure Protection, Psalm 18, p. 721

The Gentle Way, Titus 3:1–5, p. 1661

Keep On Keepin' On, Revelation 13:10, p. 1744

5 "Just as wine can trick a person,
those who are too proud will not
last,
because their desire is like a grave's
desire for death,

and like death they always want
more.
They gather other nations for
themselves
and collect for themselves all the
countries.
6 But all the nations the Babylonians
have hurt will laugh at them.
They will make fun of the
Babylonians
and say, 'How terrible it will be for
the one that steals many things.
How long will that nation get rich
by forcing others to pay them?'

7 "One day the people from whom you
have taken money will turn
against you.
They will realize what is
happening and make you shake
with fear.
Then they will take everything you
have.
8 Because you have stolen from many
nations,
those who are left will take much
from you.
This is because you have killed many
people,
destroying countries and cities and
everyone in them.

9 "How terrible it will be for the nation
that becomes rich by doing
wrong,
thinking they will live in a safe
place
and escape harm.
10 Because you have made plans to
destroy many people,
you have made your own houses
ashamed of you.
Because of it, you will lose your
lives.
11 The stones of the walls will cry out
against you,
and the boards that support the
roof will agree that you are
wrong.

12 "How terrible it will be for the nation
that kills people to build a city,
that wrongs others to start a town.
13 The LORD All-Powerful will send fire
to destroy what those people have
built;
all the nations' work will be for
nothing.
14 Then, just as water covers the sea,
people everywhere will know the
LORD's glory.

15 "How terrible for the nation that
makes its neighbors drink,
pouring from the jug of wine until
they are drunk
so that it can look at their naked
bodies.
16 You Babylonians will be filled with
disgrace, not respect.
It's your turn to drink and fall to
the ground like a drunk person.
The cup of anger from the LORD's
right hand is coming around to
you.
You will receive disgrace, not
respect.
17 You hurt many people in Lebanon,
but now you will be hurt.
You killed many animals there,
and now you must be afraid
because of what you did
to that land, those cities, and the
people who lived in them.

The Message About Idols

18 "An idol does no good, because a
human made it;
it is only a statue that teaches lies.
The one who made it expects his
own work to help him,
but he makes idols that can't even
speak!
19 How terrible it will be for the one
who says to a wooden statue,
'Come to life!'
How terrible it will be for the one
who says to a silent stone, 'Get
up!'
It cannot tell you what to do.
It is only a statue covered with
gold and silver;
there is no life in it.
20 The LORD is in his Holy Temple;
all the earth should be silent in his
presence."

Habakkuk's Prayer

3 This is the prayer of Habakkuk the prophet, on shigionoth.
2 LORD, I have heard the news about
you;
I am amazed at what you have
done.
LORD, do great things once again in
our time;
make those things happen again in
our own days.
Even when you are angry,
remember to be kind.

3 God is coming from Teman;
the Holy One comes from Mount
Paran.[n] *Selah*
His glory covers the skies,
and his praise fills the earth.
4 He is like a bright light.
Rays of light shine from his hand,
and there he hides his power.
5 Sickness goes before him,
and disease follows behind him.
6 He stands and shakes the earth.
He looks, and the nations shake
with fear.
The mountains, which stood for ages,
break into pieces;
the old hills fall down.
God has always done this.

7 I saw that the tents of Cushan were
in trouble
and that the tents of Midian
trembled.
8 LORD, were you angry at the rivers,
or were you angry at the
streams?
Were you angry with the sea
when you rode your horses and
chariots of victory?[n]
9 You uncovered your bow
and commanded many arrows to be
brought to you. *Selah*
You split the earth with rivers.
10 The mountains saw you and shook
with fear.
The rushing water flowed.
The sea made a loud noise,
and its waves rose high.
11 The sun and moon stood still in the
sky;

FAITH links

YOUR FEET ON HIGH PLACES

HABAKKUK 3:18-19

A mountain goat doesn't worry about whether it will fall off a mountain. Its padded, "gripper" hooves give it the confidence it needs to skip nimbly up and down a mountain. Habakkuk assures you that you can have this sort of confidence in God. He gives you the confidence to serve him and the confidence to face whatever "mountains" (good times) or "valleys" (hard times) come your way in life. You can't get this kind of confidence on your own. It only comes from God.

Lacking confidence? Connect here for some help:

Good Plans, Genesis 45:7–8, p. 64

The Weak Link, Judges 16, p. 334

Weak? Great!, 2 Chronicles 14:11, p. 577

Too Young to Serve, Jeremiah 1:4–9, p. 988

A Model of Forgiveness, Ezekiel 16:59–63, p. 1103

The Power of *If*, Mark 9:14–24, p. 1344

3:3 Teman . . . Paran God is seen as again coming from the direction of Mount Sinai. He came from Sinai when he rescued his people from Egypt.
3:8 sea . . . victory This is probably talking about the Israelites crossing the Red Sea.

they stopped when they saw the
flash of your flying arrows
and the gleam of your shining
spear.
12 In anger you marched on the earth;
in anger you punished the nations.
13 You came out to save your people,
to save your chosen one.
You crushed the leader of the wicked
ones
and took everything he had, from
head to toe. *Selah*
14 With the enemy's own spear you
stabbed the leader of his army.
His soldiers rushed out like a
storm to scatter us.
They were happy
as they were robbing the poor
people in secret.
15 But you marched through the sea
with your horses,
stirring the great waters.

16 I hear these things, and my body
trembles;
my lips tremble when I hear the
sound.
My bones feel weak,
and my legs shake.

But I will wait patiently for the day of
disaster
that will come to the people who
attack us.
17 Fig trees may not grow figs,
and there may be no grapes on the
vines.
There may be no olives growing
and no food growing in the fields.
There may be no sheep in the pens
and no cattle in the barns.
18 But I will still be glad in the LORD;
I will rejoice in God my Savior.
19 The Lord GOD is my strength.
He makes
me like a
deer that
does not
stumble
so I can walk on
the steep
mountains.

For the director of music. On my stringed instruments.

EMAIL FROM GOD
3:17–19
Encouragement
Who helps you be strong?

Zephaniah

OBEY NOW!

Welcome to my homepage! My name is Zephaniah, and I was called by God to be a prophet to King Josiah. Maybe you've heard about Josiah. He was crowned king of Judah when he was only eight years old. Imagine one of your classmates as president! Pretty weird, huh? Even though Josiah was young, he realized what was important. Josiah loved God, so he told people to stop worshiping idols. He sent workmen to repair the Temple of the Lord, so that the people could worship the true God. Was Josiah surprised when the Book of the Teachings was found and read aloud! No one had been following God's laws for years!

I wrote this book to tell people to obey God before it was too late. The Lord's day of judging people and nations was coming soon. The nations who did not follow God would be punished. I told the people, "Do what is right. Learn to be humble. Maybe you will escape on the day the LORD shows his anger" (Zephaniah 2:3). Do you think they listened?

JESUS WATCH

Zephaniah told people to fear the Lord's day of judging. Someday Jesus will come on a cloud from heaven with great power and glory to judge everyone on earth. It will be a terrible time of punishment for those who have not obeyed God, but a day of rejoicing for all who believe in Jesus. Jesus will use a loud trumpet to send his angels all around the earth to gather up his chosen people. He will give his people honor and praise. The people will rejoice with all their hearts, for all sadness will be taken away. Jesus the King will be with them always.

"When do you think the day of the Lord's judging will be?"

"I don't think anyone knows for sure, but check out Zephaniah 1:14–18 for some details."

FAITH links

A Love Song, Zephaniah 3:17

CHECK THESE OUT:

One last chance, Zephaniah 2:1–3
Total destruction, Zephaniah 3:1–8
A new song!, Zephaniah 3:14–17

1 This is the word of the LORD that
came through Zephaniah while Josiah
son of Amon was king of Judah. Zephaniah was the son of Cushi, who was the
son of Gedaliah. Gedaliah was the son of
Amariah, who was the son of Hezekiah.

The Lord's Judgment

2 "I will sweep away everything
from the earth," says the LORD.
3 "I will sweep away the people and
animals;
I will destroy the birds in the air
and the fish of the sea.
I will ruin the evil people,
and I will remove
human beings
from the earth,"
says the LORD.

The Future of Judah

4 "I will punish Judah
and all the people
living in
Jerusalem.
I will remove from
this place
all signs of Baal, the false priests,
and the other priests.
5 I will destroy those who worship
the stars from the roofs,[n]
and those who worship and make
promises
by both the LORD and the god
Molech,
6 and those who turned away from the
LORD,
and those who quit following the
LORD and praying to him for
direction.
7 Be silent before the Lord GOD,
because the LORD's day for judging
people is coming soon.
The LORD has prepared a sacrifice;
he has made holy his invited
guests.
8 On the day of the LORD's sacrifice,
I, the LORD, will punish the princes
and the king's sons
and all those who wear foreign
clothes.
9 On that day I will punish those who
worship Dagon,
those who hurt others and tell lies
in the temples of their gods.

10 "On that day," says the LORD,
"a cry will be heard at the Fish Gate.
A wail will come from the new area
of the city,
and a loud crash will echo from the
hills.
11 Cry, you people living in the market
area,
because all the merchants will be
dead;
all the silver traders will be gone.
12 At that time I, the
LORD, will search
Jerusalem with
lamps.
I will punish those
who are satisfied
with themselves,
who think, 'The
LORD won't help
us or punish us.'
13 Their wealth will be
stolen
and their houses
destroyed.
They may build houses,
but they will not live in them.
They may plant vineyards,
but they will not drink any wine
from them.

At that time I, the LORD, will search Jerusalem with lamps. I will punish those who are satisfied with themselves.
—Zephaniah 1:12

The Lord's Day of Judging

14 "The LORD's day of judging is coming
soon;
it is near and coming fast.
The cry will be very sad on the day of
the LORD;
even soldiers will cry.
15 That day will be a day of anger,
a day of terror and trouble,
a day of destruction and ruin,
a day of darkness and gloom,
a day of clouds and blackness,
16 a day of alarms and battle cries.

1:5 roofs In Bible times houses were built with flat roofs. The roof was used for drying things such as flax and fruit. And it was used as an extra room, as a place for worship, and as a cool place to sleep in the summer.

'Attack the strong, walled cities!
Attack the corner towers!'
17 I will make life hard on the people;
they will walk around like the blind,
because they have sinned against the LORD.
Their blood will be poured out like dust,
and their insides will be dumped like trash.
18 On the day that God will show his anger,
neither their silver nor gold will save them.
The LORD's anger will be like a fire
that will burn up the whole world;
suddenly he will bring an end, yes, an end
to everyone on earth."

The Lord Asks People to Change

2 Gather together, gather,
you unwanted people.
2 Do it before it's too late,
before you are blown away like chaff,
before the LORD's terrible anger reaches you,
before the day of the LORD's anger comes to you.
3 Come to the LORD, all you who are not proud,
who obey his laws.
Do what is right.
Learn to be humble.
Maybe you will escape
on the day the LORD shows his anger.

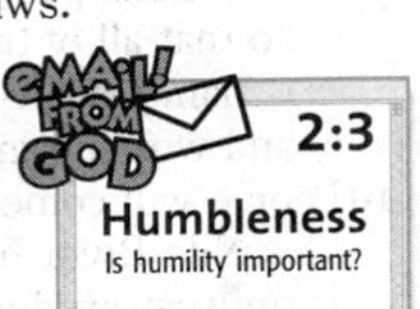
EMAIL! FROM GOD
2:3
Humbleness
Is humility important?

Philistia Will Be Punished

4 No one will be left in the city of Gaza,
and the city of Ashkelon will be destroyed.
Ashdod will be empty by noon,
and the people of Ekron will be chased away.
5 How terrible it will be for you who
live by the Mediterranean Sea,
you Philistines!
The word of the LORD is against you,
Canaan, land of the Philistines.

"I will destroy you
so that no one will be left."
6 The land by the Mediterranean Sea,
in which you live,
will become pastures, fields for shepherds, and pens for sheep.
7 It will belong to the descendants of Judah who are left alive.
There they will let their sheep eat grass.
At night they will sleep
in the houses of Ashkelon.
The LORD their God will pay attention to them
and will make their life good again.

Moab and Ammon Will Be Punished

8 "I have heard the insults of the country of Moab
and the threats of the people of Ammon.
They have insulted my people
and have taken their land."
9 So the LORD All-Powerful, the God of Israel, says,
"As surely as I live,
Moab will be destroyed like Sodom,
and Ammon will be destroyed like Gomorrah"—
a heap of weeds, a pit of salt,
and a ruin forever.
Those of my people who are left alive
will take whatever they want from them;
those who are left from my nation
will take their land."

10 This is what Moab and Ammon get
for being proud,
because they insulted and made fun of the people of the LORD All-Powerful.
11 The LORD will frighten them,
because he will destroy all the gods of the earth.
Then everyone in faraway places

2:9 Sodom . . . Gomorrah Two cities God destroyed because the people were so evil.

will worship him wherever they
are.

Cush and Assyria Will Be Destroyed

12 "You Cushites also
will be killed by my sword."
13 Then the LORD will turn against the
north
and destroy Assyria.
He will make Nineveh
a ruin as dry as a desert.
14 Flocks and herds will lie down there,
and all wild animals.
The owls and crows will sit
on the stone pillars.
The owl will hoot through the
windows,
trash will be in the doorways,
and the wooden boards of the
buildings will be gone.
15 This is the happy and safe city
that thinks there is no one else as
strong as it is.
But what a ruin it will be,
a place where wild animals live.
All those who pass by will make fun
and shake their fists.

Jerusalem Will Be Punished

3 How terrible for the wicked,
stubborn city of Jerusalem,
which hurts its own people.
2 It obeys no voice;
it can't be taught to do right.
It doesn't trust the LORD;
it doesn't worship its God.
3 Its officers are like roaring lions.
Its rulers are like hungry wolves
that attack in the evening,
and in the morning nothing is left
of those they attacked.
4 Its prophets are proud;
they are people who cannot be
trusted.
Its priests don't respect holy things;
they break God's teachings.
5 But the LORD is good, and he is there
in that city.
He does no wrong.
Every morning he governs the
people fairly;
every day he can be trusted.
But evil people are not ashamed of
what they do.

6 "I have destroyed nations;
their towers were ruined.
I made their streets empty
so no one goes there anymore.
Their cities are ruined;
no one lives there at all.
7 I said, 'Surely now Jerusalem will
respect me
and will accept my teaching.'
Then the place where they lived
would not be destroyed,
and I would not have to punish
them.
But they were still eager
to do evil in everything they did.
8 Just wait," says the LORD.
"Some day I will stand up as a
witness.
I have decided that I will gather
nations
and assemble kingdoms.
I will pour out my anger on them,
all my strong anger.
My anger will be like fire
that will burn up the whole world.

A New Day for God's People

9 "Then I will give the people of all
nations pure speech
so that all of them will speak the
name of the LORD
and worship me together.
10 People will come from where the
Nile River begins;
my scattered people will come
with gifts for me.
11 Then Jerusalem will not be ashamed
of the wrongs done against me,
because I will remove from this city
those who like to brag;
there will never be any more proud
people
on my holy mountain in
Jerusalem.
12 But I will leave in the city
the humble and those who are not
proud,
and they will trust in the LORD.

GOD'S LOVE FOR ME

Zephaniah 3:17

Livin' it

God's Love Note Suppose your mom stuck a note in your lunch or backpack that said she loved you and was thinking of you. How would that make you feel? How could it help if you were having a rough day?

God loves us and sends us love notes all the time. We can see them in the things around us and read them in the Bible. (Check out Zephaniah 3:17.) Can you imagine God singing with happiness just because of you? But you can believe it because God tells us he does. God's love for you never changes and never ends. That should make you feel like singing, too!

MORE FAITH links

Love That Will Last, p. 813

A Mother's Love, p. 961

The One Who Suffered, p. 966

His Valentine, p. 1035

A Love Song, p. 1246

The Love Magnet, p. 1694

"You know, Skweek, sometimes I get down when I make a real mess out of things—like when I yell at my brother or fight with my friend. I feel downright unlovable."

"I think we all have times when we feel like that, Tagg. That's the time to read one of God's love notes to you. Read on to find out more about God's amazing love for you!"

The Rainbow Promise, Genesis 9:1–17, p. 14

- Link here to find the true meaning of the rainbow and why it is one of God's love notes.

Our Heavenly Shepherd, Psalm 23, p. 726

- Psalm 23 compares God to a shepherd and his people to his sheep. How is God like a good shepherd? How are you like one of his sheep? Why do you need a shepherd? This Faithlink tells you what a wonderful shepherd we have.

Love for Free, Romans 5:8, p. 1524

- If you broke something that belonged to your parents, do you think they would stop loving you? Multiply your parents' love by a thousand and you can begin to understand the kind of love God has for you. You can't earn God's love—it's a gift! That's why God sent his Son, Jesus, to die for us. With whom can you share the good news of God's love?

my FAVORITE links

A LOVE SONG

ZEPHANIAH 3:17

Do you ever sing when you're happy? Can you imagine God singing with happiness? Zephaniah explained that in a future time, God would rejoice over his people with songs that showed his gladness because of them.

God sings because of you. That means he's glad to be around you. You can be assured of his love for you. Once you're confident of that love, you might feel like singing, too.

Check out God's love song for you:

A Time to Celebrate, Exodus 15:1–21, p. 95

Gratitude Attitude, Ezra 3, p. 611

Love That Will Last, Psalm 136, p. 813

What's in a Name?, Isaiah 9:6, p. 908

Too Busy to Worship?, Luke 2:8–20, p. 1368

Always Do This!, 1 Thessalonians 5:16–18, p. 1636

13 Those who are left alive in Israel
won't do wrong or tell lies;
they won't trick people with their
words.
They will eat and lie down
with no one to make them afraid."

A Happy Song

14 Sing, Jerusalem.
Israel, shout for joy!
Jerusalem, be happy
and rejoice with all your heart.
15 The LORD has stopped punishing
you;
he has sent your enemies away.
The King of Israel, the LORD, is with
you;
you will never again be afraid of
being harmed.
16 On that day Jerusalem will be told,
"Don't be afraid, city of Jerusalem.
Don't give up.
17 The LORD your God is with you;
the mighty One will save you.
He will rejoice over you.
You will rest in his love;
he will sing and be joyful about
you."

18 "I will take away the sadness planned
for you,
which would have made you very
ashamed.
19 At that time I will punish
all those who harmed you.
I will save my people who cannot
walk
and gather my people who have
been thrown out.
I will give them praise and honor
in every place where they were
shamed.
20 At that time I will gather you;
at that time I will bring you back
home.
I will give you honor and praise
from people everywhere
when I make things go well again for
you,
as you will see with your own
eyes," says the LORD.

GET BUSY!

Hi, there! My name is Haggai, and God sent me with a message to the governor and the high priest of Judah. Have you ever started a project but never taken the time to finish it? In my time, the Temple of the Lord was an unfinished project. God's people returned to their land from a long time of exile in a foreign land. At first, the people began rebuilding the Temple with a lot of enthusiasm and energy. But soon the project came to a screeching halt. Neighbors complained; and all the work on the Temple stopped. People found time to work on their own houses, but never had time to work on the Temple.

I wrote this book to remind people to put God first in their lives. Everyone has lots of things to do, but God's work should always come first. The people listened to my message, and work on the Temple started again. God promises to richly bless those who love him and follow his commands. How can you put God first in your life?

JESUS WATCH

God made a promise to Zerubbabel, the governor of Judah, that he would be as important as God's signet ring. A signet ring was pressed into the wax that sealed an important document. It guaranteed that the document was from the owner of the ring. God honored Zerubbabel for his work on the Temple by making him an ancestor of Jesus. Zerubbabel was a guarantee that God would send the Messiah. God also promised that the new Temple would be greater than the old Temple built by Solomon. Years later Herod the Great spent a fortune improving the Temple. However great the Temple of the Lord was, though, Jesus is greater.

"Hey, Tagg, what's wrong with living in a fancy house?"

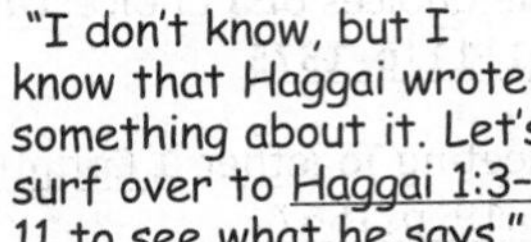

"I don't know, but I know that Haggai wrote something about it. Let's surf over to Haggai 1:3-11 to see what he says."

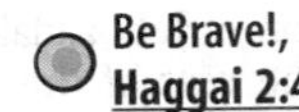

First Place, Haggai 1:7–11

Be Brave!, Haggai 2:4

DOWNLOAD THESE VERSES:

A better Temple, Haggai 2:6–9
Before and after, Haggai 2:15–19
Zerubbabel's reward, Haggai 2:20–23

It Is Time to Build the Temple

1 The prophet Haggai spoke the word of
the LORD to Zerubbabel son of Shealtiel, the governor of Judah, and to Joshua
son of Jehozadak, the high priest. This
message came in the second year that
Darius was king, on the first day of the
sixth month:
2“This is what the LORD All-Powerful
says: ‘The people say the right time has
not come to rebuild the Temple of the
LORD.’”
3Then Haggai the prophet spoke the
word of the LORD: 4“Is it right for you to
be living in fancy houses while the Temple is still in ruins?”
5This is what the LORD All-Powerful
says: “Think about what you have done.
6You have planted much, but you harvest
little. You eat, but you do not become full.
You drink, but you are still thirsty. You
put on clothes, but you are not warm
enough. You earn money, but then you
lose it all as if you had put it into a purse
full of holes.”
7This is what the LORD All-Powerful
says: “Think about what you have done.
8Go up to the mountains, bring back
wood, and build the Temple. Then I will
be pleased with it and be honored,” says
the LORD. 9“You look for much, but you
find little. When you bring it home, I destroy it. Why?” asks the LORD All-Powerful. “Because you all work hard for
your own houses while my house is
still in ruins! 10Because of what you
have done, the sky holds back its rain
and the ground holds back its crops. 11I
have called for a time without rain on the
land, and on the mountains, and on the
grain, the new wine, the olive oil, the
plants which the earth produces, the people, the farm animals, and all the work of
your hands.”
12Zerubbabel son of Shealtiel and
Joshua son of Jehozadak, the high priest,
and all the rest of the people who were
left alive obeyed the LORD their God and
the message from Haggai the prophet,
because the LORD their God had sent
him. And the people feared the LORD.
13Haggai, the LORD’s messenger,
gave the LORD’s message to the people,

FAITH links

FIRST PLACE

HAGGAI 1:7-11

Suppose your parents remodeled every room in your home except yours. You’d feel pretty neglected, wouldn’t you? The Israelites had returned to their land after being in Babylon for several years. After their return, the prophet Haggai warned them about their neglect in rebuilding God’s Temple. They had rebuilt their own homes, but they had forgotten about God’s. God wasn’t saying that they couldn’t fix their houses. He just wanted them to show how important he was to them.

When life gets busy, it’s easy to forget about God. We put all other activities first, ahead of doing things for God. But God wants his work to also be important to us. How important is it to you?

Reward for Obedience, Leviticus 26:3–13, p. 171

Plans for a Son, 1 Chronicles 22:5–19, p. 548

A Hopeful Future, Jeremiah 29:11, p. 1031

God’s New Temple, Ezekiel 40—44, p. 1135

The Choices of a Choice, Luke 5:1–11, p. 1375

Meeting Together, 1 Corinthians 16:19, p. 1567

saying, "The LORD says, 'I am with
you.'" 14The LORD stirred up Zerubbabel son of Shealtiel, the governor of
Judah, and Joshua son of Jehozadak, the
high priest, and all the rest of the people
who were left alive. So they came and
worked on the Temple of their God, the
LORD All-Powerful. 15They began on the
twenty-fourth day of the sixth month in
the second year Darius was king.

The Beauty of the Temple

2 On the twenty-first day of the seventh
month, the LORD spoke his word
through Haggai the prophet, saying,
2"Speak to Zerubbabel son of Shealtiel,
governor of Judah, and to Joshua son of
Jehozadak, the high priest, and to the rest
of the people who are left alive. Say, 3'Do
any of you remember how great the Temple was before it was destroyed? What
does it look like now? Doesn't it seem
like nothing to you?' 4But the LORD says,
'Zerubbabel, be brave. Also, Joshua son
of Jehozadak, the high priest, be brave.
And all you people who live in the land,
be brave,' says the LORD. 'Work, because
I am with you,' says the LORD All-Powerful. 5'I made a promise to you when you
came out of Egypt, and my Spirit is still
with you. So don't be afraid.'

6"This is what the LORD All-Powerful
says: 'In a short time I will once again
shake the heavens and the earth, the sea
and the dry land. 7I will shake all the nations, and they will bring their wealth.
Then I will fill this Temple with glory,'
says the LORD All-Powerful. 8'The silver
is mine, and the gold is mine,' says the
LORD All-Powerful. 9'The new Temple
will be greater than the one before,' says
the LORD All-Powerful. 'And in this place
I will give peace,' says the LORD All-
Powerful."

10On the twenty-fourth day of the
ninth month in the second year Darius
was king, the LORD spoke his word to
Haggai the prophet, saying, 11"This is
what the LORD All-Powerful says: 'Ask
the priests for a teaching. 12Suppose a
person carries in the fold of his clothes
some meat made holy for the LORD. If
that fold touches bread, cooked food,
wine, olive oil, or some other food, will
that be made holy?'"

The priests answered, "No."

FAITH links

BE BRAVE!

HAGGAI 2:4

God's people had a big job ahead of them when they prepared to rebuild the Temple. God had sent the prophet Haggai to encourage Zerubbabel, the governor of Judah, to begin the work without fear.

What fears, if any, are stopping you from serving God? A fearful situation does not always mean someone is making fun of you for what you believe. The fear of failure and discouragement can also stop you from serving God or doing what is right. God can help you take courage and do whatever he has called you to do.

Link here to find out how you can have courage:

A Message of Courage and Hope, 2 Kings 19:4–10, p. 505

The Big Risk, Esther 4:11—5:2, p. 652

When Bad Things Happen, Ecclesiastes 3:16–17, p. 876

The God of Second Chances, Jonah 3, p. 1215

Blessed Are the Weak?, 2 Corinthians 12:7–10, p. 1582

While You Wait, Jude 21, p. 1726

13Then Haggai said, "A person who
touches a dead body will become unclean. If he touches any of these foods,
will it become unclean, too?"

The priests answered, "Yes, it would
become unclean."

14Then Haggai answered, "The LORD
says, 'This is also true for the people of
this nation. They are unclean, and everything they do with their hands is unclean
to me. Whatever they offer at the altar is
also unclean.

15" 'Think about this from now on!
Think about how it was before you
started laying stones on top of stones to
build the Temple of the LORD. **16**A person used to come to a pile of grain expecting to find twenty basketfuls, but
there were only ten. And a person used
to come to the wine vat to take out fifty
jarfuls, but only twenty were there. **17**I
destroyed your work with diseases, mildew, and hail, but you still did not come
back to me,' says the LORD. **18**'It is the
twenty-fourth day of the ninth month,
the day in which the people finished
working on the foundation of the Temple
of the LORD. From now on, think about
these things: **19**Do you have seeds for
crops still in the barn? Your vines, fig
trees, pomegranates, and olive trees
have not given fruit yet. But from now on
I will bless you!'"

The Lord Makes a Promise to Zerubbabel

20Then the LORD spoke his word a
second time to Haggai on the twenty-
fourth day of the month. He said, **21**"Tell
Zerubbabel, the governor of Judah, 'I am
going to shake the heavens and the earth.
22I will destroy the foreign kingdoms and
take away the power of the kingdoms of
the nations. I will destroy the chariots
and their riders. The horses will fall with
their riders, as people kill each other
with swords.' **23**The LORD All-Powerful
says, 'On that day I will take you, Zerubbabel son of Shealtiel, my servant,' says
the LORD, 'and I will make you important
like my signet ring, because I have chosen you!' says the LORD All-Powerful."

Zechariah

UNDER CONSTRUCTION

Hey, it's Zechariah the prophet here. I was part of the first group of people who returned to Jerusalem after spending many years in a foreign country as captives. The big thing going on when I got back to Jerusalem was a major remodeling project. Has your family ever remodeled a room in your house? Ripped out the old carpeting, painted the walls, bought new furniture? It's a lot of hard work, but when you're finished the room is beautiful. It was the same with our city. Our enemies had destroyed the city, and now God had plans to bless his people and to make the city of Jerusalem beautiful again.

I wrote this book to encourage God's people to rebuild the Temple of the Lord. Building the Temple was a way to love and honor God. The Temple was the center of worship for our entire nation, and it was where God himself lived in a special way. God promised to make Jerusalem his chosen city again, if we would obey him and rebuild the Temple. With a new Temple, God said people would come from all over to worship him and Jerusalem would be peaceful and prosperous again.

JESUS WATCH

Many parts of the Book of Zechariah give us snapshots of Jesus. In Zechariah 9, he describes a king coming into Jerusalem on a donkey. In Bible times, a king who rode a horse was ready for war; but a king on a donkey came in peace. A few days before he died, Jesus rode into Jerusalem on a donkey. The people praised him and waved palm branches in his honor. He came to bring people peace with God. Zechariah also described a good shepherd who was rejected and sold for 30 pieces of silver. Jesus called himself the good shepherd. He was betrayed by Judas, one of his own disciples, and handed over to the soldiers for 30 pieces of silver. Another picture of Jesus was a stone with the message "And in one day I will take away the sin of this land" (Zechariah 3:9). On the day he died on the cross, Jesus took away the sin of the whole world. Jesus is the Branch who will build the Temple of the Lord. He will be a priest and a king. As a priest, Jesus asks God to forgive our sins. As a king, he rules forever from heaven.

OTHER CONNECTIONS

Livin' it What do you do when you see the needs of others around you? Ignore them and walk away? Offer to help? God wants us to care for others as he cares for us. Find out more about it by linking to Can I Help You?, Zechariah 7:8–9.

GET THE INFO

- Where Is God's Kingdom?, Zechariah 9:9–10. Ever wonder where exactly is the kingdom of God? Are you, like the Israelites, expecting a king with a palace and the whole works? Surf here to check out what the Bible means when it refers to God's kingdom.

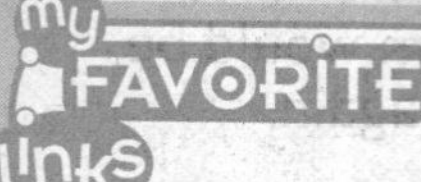

my FAVORITE links

____

____

____

____

"Why did the high priest need new clothes?"

"Maybe his clothes were dirty? Let's find out in Zechariah 3."

MORE ON THE ZECHARIAH SURFWATCH:

A flying scroll, Zechariah 5:1–4
Sins in a basket, Zechariah 5:5–11
Blessings for Jerusalem, Zechariah 8
The king is coming!, Zechariah 9:9–17

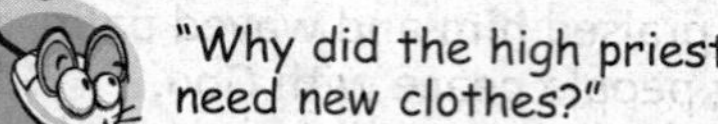

FAITH links

- **Your Spiritual Roots, Zechariah 1:1–6**
- **Small Beginnings, Zechariah 4:10**
- **A Reminder to Do What Is Right and True, Zechariah 7:8–10**
- **The Best Advice, Zechariah 10:2**

The Lord Calls His People Back

1 In the eighth month of the second
year Darius was king, the LORD spoke
his word to the prophet Zechariah son of
Berekiah, who was the son of Iddo. The
LORD said, 2"The LORD was very angry
with your ancestors. 3So tell the people:
This is what the LORD All-Powerful says:
'Return to me, and I will return to you,'
says the LORD All-Powerful. 4Don't be
like your ancestors. In the past the prophets said to them: This is what the LORD
All-Powerful says: 'Stop your evil ways
and evil actions.' But they wouldn't listen
or pay attention to me, says the LORD.
5Your ancestors are dead, and those
prophets didn't live forever. 6I commanded my words and laws to my servants the prophets, and they preached to
your ancestors, who returned to me. They
said, 'The LORD All-Powerful did as he
said he would. He punished us for the way
we lived and for what we did.' "

The Vision of the Horses

7It was on the twenty-fourth day of
the eleventh month, which is the month
of Shebat, in Darius's second year as
king. The LORD spoke his word to the
prophet Zechariah son of Berekiah, who
was the son of Iddo.

8During the night I had a vision. I saw
a man riding a red horse. He was standing
among some myrtle trees in a ravine,
with red, brown, and white horses behind
him.

9I asked, "What are these, sir?"

The angel who was talking with me
answered, "I'll show you what they are."

10Then the man standing among the
myrtle trees explained, "They are the
ones the LORD sent through all the
earth."

11Then they spoke to the LORD's angel, who was standing among the myrtle
trees. They said, "We have gone through
all the earth, and everything is calm and
quiet."

12Then the LORD's angel asked,
"LORD All-Powerful, how long will it be
before you show mercy to Jerusalem and
the cities of Judah? You have been angry
with them for seventy years now." 13So
the LORD answered the angel who was
talking with me, and his words were comforting and good.

14Then the angel who was talking to
me said to me, "Announce this: This is
what the LORD All-Powerful says: 'I have

FAITH links

YOUR SPIRITUAL ROOTS

ZECHARIAH 1:1-6

How far back can you trace your roots? The Israelites could trace their roots all the way back to Abraham. Some of their ancestors did not follow God. Through Zechariah, God called his people to stop sinning and return to him. God didn't want them to follow the bad examples of their ancestors, who had turned away from him.

God wants you to follow him, even if you're the first to become a Christian in your family. As a Christian, you're part of the spiritual heritage described in the Bible. (Check out Hebrews 11, p. 1679.)

A Direct Path, Proverbs 3:5–6, p. 829

His Valentine, Jeremiah 31:3, p. 1035

Empty Words, Ezekiel 33:30–33, p. 1127

Inside the Heart of God, Micah 7:18–20, p. 1228

When We Agree, Matthew 18:19–20, p. 1306

One Big, Happy Family, John 1:12, p. 1422

a strong love for Jerusalem. 15And I am very angry with the nations that feel so safe. I was only a little angry at them, but they made things worse.'

16"So this is what the LORD says: 'I will return to Jerusalem with mercy. My Temple will be rebuilt,' says the LORD All-Powerful, 'and the measuring line will be used to rebuild Jerusalem.'

17"Also announce: This is what the LORD All-Powerful says: 'My towns will be rich again. The LORD will comfort Jerusalem again, and I will again choose Jerusalem.' "

The Vision of the Horns

18Then I looked up and saw four animal horns. 19I asked the angel who was talking with me, "What are these?"

He said, "These are the horns that scattered the people of Judah, Israel, and Jerusalem."

20Then the LORD showed me four craftsmen. 21I asked, "What are they coming to do?"

He answered, "They have come to scare and throw down the horns. These horns scattered the people of Judah so that no one could even lift up his head. These horns stand for the nations that attacked the people of Judah and scattered them."

The Vision of the Measuring Line

2 Then I looked up and saw a man holding a line for measuring things. 2I asked him, "Where are you going?"

He said to me, "I am going to measure Jerusalem, to see how wide and how long it is."

3Then the angel who was talking with me left, and another angel came out to meet him. 4The second angel said to him, "Run and tell that young man, 'Jerusalem will become a city without walls, because there will be so many people and cattle in it. 5I will be a wall of fire around it,' says the LORD. 'And I will be the glory within it.'

6"Oh no! Oh no! Run away from Babylon, because I have scattered you like the four winds of heaven," says the LORD.

7"Oh no, Jerusalem! Escape, you who live right in Babylon." 8This is what the LORD All-Powerful says: "After he has honored me and sent me against the nations who took your possessions—because whoever touches you hurts what is precious to me—9I will shake my hand against them so that their slaves will rob them."

Then you will know that the LORD All-Powerful sent me.

10"Shout and be glad, Jerusalem. I am coming, and I will live among you," says the LORD. 11"At that time people from many nations will join with the LORD and will become my people. Then I will live among you, and you will know that the LORD All-Powerful has sent me to you. 12The LORD will take Judah as his own part of the holy land, and Jerusalem will be his chosen city again. 13Be silent, everyone, in the presence of the LORD. He is coming out of the holy place where he lives."

The Vision of the High Priest

3 Then he showed me Joshua, the high priest, standing in front of the LORD's angel. And Satan was standing by Joshua's right side to accuse him. 2The LORD said to Satan, "The LORD says no to you, Satan! The LORD who has chosen Jerusalem says no to you! This man was like a burning stick pulled from the fire."

3Joshua was wearing dirty clothes and was standing in front of the angel. 4The angel said to those standing in front of him, "Take off those dirty clothes."

Then the angel said to Joshua, "Look, I have taken away your sin from you, and I am giving you beautiful, fine clothes."

5Then I said, "Put a clean turban on his head." So they put a clean turban on his head and dressed him while the LORD's angel stood there.

6Then the LORD's angel said to Joshua, 7"This is what the LORD All-Powerful says: 'If you do as I tell you and serve me, you will be in charge of my Temple and my courtyards. And I will let you be with these angels who are standing here.

8" 'Listen, Joshua, the high priest, and your friends who are sitting in front of you. They are symbols of what will happen. I am going to bring my servant called the Branch. 9Look, I put this stone in front of Joshua, a stone with seven sides. I will carve a message on it,' says the LORD All-Powerful. 'And in one day I will take away the sin of this land.'

10"The LORD All-Powerful says, 'In that day, each of you will invite your neighbor to sit under your own grapevine and under your own fig tree.' "

The Vision of the Lampstand

4 Then the angel who was talking with me returned and woke me up as if I had been asleep. 2He asked me, "What do you see?"

I said, "I see a solid gold lampstand with a bowl at the top. And there are seven lamps and also seven places for wicks. 3There are two olive trees by it, one on the right of the bowl and the other on the left."

4I asked the angel who talked with me, "Sir, what are these?"

5The angel said, "Don't you know what they are?"

"No, sir," I said.

6Then he told me, "This is the word of the LORD to Zerubbabel: 'You will not succeed by your own strength or power, but by my Spirit,' says the LORD All-Powerful.

7"Who are you, big mountain? In front of Zerubbabel you will become flat land, and he will bring out the topmost stone, shouting, 'It's beautiful! It's beautiful!' "

8Then the LORD spoke his word to me again, saying, 9"Zerubbabel has laid the foundation of this Temple, and he will complete it. Then you will know that the LORD All-Powerful has sent me to you.

10"The people should not think that small beginnings are unimportant. They will be happy when they see Zerubbabel with tools, building the Temple.

"(These are the seven eyes of the LORD, which look back and forth across the earth.)"

FAITH links

SMALL BEGINNINGS

ZECHARIAH 4:10

Have you ever felt discouraged over a project that seemed to take forever? Maybe you've been feeling as if you've hardly made a dent in what you have to do. Or maybe you've witnessed to someone, but that person has barely responded. Although Zerubbabel and the Israelites had laid the foundation of the new Temple, it seemed like a small beginning. They had a long way to go to complete the Temple.

Small beginnings can still bring a rich harvest. Don't allow discouragement over small beginnings to keep you from doing other work for God. When in doubt, remember the story of the mustard seed (plug into Matthew 13:31–32, p. 1297; Mark 4:30–32, p. 1336; or Luke 13:18–19, p. 1395, for that story). That tiny seed was the beginning of a large tree.

Here are some Faithlinks on taking that first, tiny step.

Keep On Praying, 1 Samuel 1, p. 354

Depend on Him!, 2 Chronicles 16:1–9, p. 579

911, Psalm 28:6, p. 730

In the Lions' Den, Daniel 6, p. 1160

Your Feet on High Places, Habakkuk 3:18–19, p. 1239

Keep On Keepin' On, Revelation 13:10, p. 1744

11Then I asked the angel, "What are the two olive trees on the right and left of the lampstand?"

12I also asked him, "What are the two olive branches beside the two gold pipes, from which the olive oil flows to the lamps?"

13He answered, "Don't you know what they are?"

"No, sir," I said.

14So he said, "They are symbols of the two who have been appointed to serve the LORD of all the earth."

The Vision of the Flying Scroll

5 I looked up again and saw a flying scroll.

2The angel asked me, "What do you see?"

I answered, "I see a flying scroll, thirty feet long and fifteen feet wide."

3And he said to me, "This is the curse that will go all over the land. One side says every thief will be taken away. The other side says everyone who makes false promises will be taken away. 4The
LORD All-Powerful says, 'I will send it to the houses of thieves and to those who use my name to make false promises. The scroll will stay in that person's house and destroy it with its wood and stones.' "

The Vision of the Woman

5Then the angel who was talking with me came forward and said to me, "Look up and see what is going out."

6"What is it?" I asked.

He answered, "It is a measuring basket going out." He also said, "It is a symbol of the people's sins in all the land."

7Then the lid made of lead was raised, and there was a woman sitting inside the basket. 8The angel said, "The woman stands for wickedness." Then he pushed her back into the basket and put the lid back down.

9Then I looked up and saw two women going out with the wind in their wings. Their wings were like those of a stork, and they lifted up the basket between earth and the sky.

10I asked the angel who was talking with me, "Where are they taking the basket?"

11"They are going to Babylonia to build a temple for it," he answered. "When the temple is ready, they will set the basket there in its place."

The Vision of the Four Chariots

6 I looked up again and saw four chariots going out between two mountains,
mountains of bronze. 2Red horses pulled
the first chariot. Black horses pulled the
second chariot. 3White horses pulled the
third chariot, and strong, spotted horses
pulled the fourth chariot. 4I asked the angel who was talking with me, "What are these, sir?"

5He said, "These are the four spirits of heaven. They have just come from the presence of the Lord of the whole world.
6The chariot pulled by the black horses will go to the land of the north. The white horses will go to the land of the west, and the spotted horses will go to the land of the south."

7When the powerful horses went out, they were eager to go through all the earth. So he said, "Go through all the earth," and they did.

8Then he called to me, "Look, the horses that went north have caused my spirit to rest in the land of the north."

> A man whose name is the Branch will branch out from where he is, and he will build the Temple of the LORD.
> —Zechariah 6:12

A Crown for Joshua

9The LORD spoke his word to me, saying,
10"Take silver and gold from Heldai, Tobijah, and Jedaiah, who were captives in Babylon. Go that same day to the house of Josiah son of Zephaniah, who came from Babylon.
11Make the silver and gold into a crown, and put it on the head of Joshua son of Jehozadak, the high
priest. 12Tell him this is what the LORD
All-Powerful says: 'A man whose name is the Branch will branch out from where he

is, and he will build the Temple of the
LORD. 13One man[n] will build the Temple
of the LORD, and the other[n] will receive
honor. One man will sit on his throne and
rule, and the other will be a priest on his
throne. And these two men will work together in peace.' 14The crown will be
kept in the Temple of the LORD to remind
Heldai, Tobijah, Jedaiah, and Josiah son of
Zephaniah. 15People living far away will
come and build the Temple of the LORD.
Then you will know the LORD All-
Powerful has sent me to you. This will
happen if you completely obey the LORD
your God."

The People Should Show Mercy

7 In the fourth year Darius was king, on
the fourth day of the ninth month,
which is called Kislev, the LORD spoke
his word to Zechariah. 2The city of
Bethel sent Sharezer, Regem-Melech,
and their men to ask the LORD a question. 3They went to the prophets and
priests who were at the Temple of the
LORD All-Powerful. The men said, "For
years in the fifth month of each year we
have shown our sadness and gone without food. Should we continue to do this?"
4The LORD All-Powerful spoke his
word to me, saying, 5"Tell the priests and
the people in the land: 'For seventy years
you went without food and cried in the
fifth and seventh months, but that was
not really for me. 6And when you ate and
drank, it was really for yourselves. 7The
LORD used the earlier prophets to say the
same thing, when Jerusalem and the surrounding towns were at peace and
wealthy, and people lived in the southern
area and the western hills.' "
8And the LORD spoke his word to
Zechariah again, saying, 9"This is what
the LORD All-Powerful
says: 'Do what is
right and true. Be
kind and merciful to
each other. 10Don't
hurt widows and or-
phans, foreigners or
the poor; don't even think of doing evil to
somebody else.'
11"But they refused to pay attention;

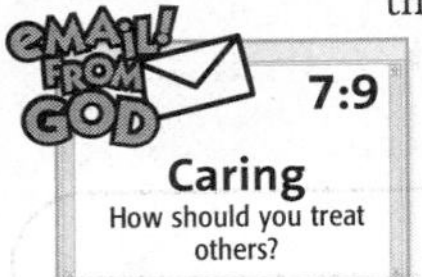
eMAIL! FROM GOD
7:9
Caring
How should you treat others?

FAITH links

A REMINDER TO DO WHAT IS RIGHT AND TRUE

ZECHARIAH 7:8-10

Do you ever complain that your parents are nagging, because they say the same things all the time? "Clean your room." "Do your homework." "Don't poke your brother." They say the same things because they want you to remember to do them.

Some messages are the same throughout the Bible. Love God. Love others. Don't seek to harm others. Be fair and honest. Show mercy. This was Zechariah's message to the Israelites. Why these same messages? People often need reminders about how God wants us to live and reminders to *do* what he tells us!

Need a reminder? Connect here:

Yours, Mine, and Ours?, 1 Samuel 25, p. 389

Take My Advice, 1 Kings 2:2–4, p. 436

See the Heart Behind It, Nehemiah 8; 9, p. 636

A Blueprint for Living, Amos 5:14–15, p. 1200

How to Make God Glad, Ephesians 6:1–2, p. 1605

The True Test, 1 John 3:18, p. 1718

6:13 One man This probably refers to Zerubbabel.
6:13 other This probably refers to Joshua.

Caring for Others

Zechariah 7:8–9

Livin' it

Can I Help You? Have you ever been in a large store and gotten lost? Panic starts to set in, and then you hear a salesman say, "Can I help you?" Whew! Those words are just what you need! It feels good to be on the receiving end of someone's concern and care, doesn't it? But how do you feel when someone needs your help? What do you do then?

God wants us to respond to the needs of those around us. Helping others is the way to show real love for God. (Read Amos 2:6–7, p. 1196.) How do your words and actions show concern for others?

When three strangers showed up at Abraham's tent, he did everything possible to welcome them. (Check out Genesis 18:1–8, p. 23.) How can you make people feel welcome—anywhere, anytime?

MORE FAITH links

Show You Care, p. 481
Seeing the Needs, p. 625
Help for the Hurting, p. 666
Meaningless Words, p. 684
Kindness Counts, p. 1489
You're Welcomed!, p. 1494

"Well, Skweek, how do you show you care for others?"

"Good question! Maybe when I lead someone to the right place on the computer? Does that count?"

Care for the Lost, Deuteronomy 22:1–3, p. 255

- Have you ever found a lost dog or cat? What did you do with it?
- God gave Adam the job of caring for the animals. We're still caretakers of the earth. How do you do your part in being a caretaker?

Kindness First, Matthew 9:35–36, p. 1290

- When you approach a crowd of kids, what's the first thing you think of? Are you thinking of someone that you want to avoid? Or why that girl doesn't wear cooler clothes? Jesus' first thought was a kind, caring one. How can you help someone who can use a kind word or act?

Don't Play Favorites, James 2:1–7, p. 1691

- Link here to see how God wants us to treat all people.

my FAVORITE links

they were stubborn and did not want to
listen anymore. **12**They made their
hearts as hard as rock and would not listen to the teachings of the LORD All-
Powerful. And they would not hear the
words he sent by his Spirit through the
earlier prophets. So the LORD All-
Powerful became very angry.
13" 'When I called to them, they
would not listen. So when they called to
me, I would not listen,' says the LORD
All-Powerful. **14**'I scattered them like a
hurricane to other countries they did not
know. This good land was left so ruined
behind them that no one could live
there. They had made the desired land
a ruin.' "

The Lord Will Bless Jerusalem

8 The LORD All-Powerful spoke his
word, saying, **2**This is what the LORD
All-Powerful says: "I have a very strong
love for Jerusalem. My strong love for
her is like a fire burning in me."
3This is what the LORD says: "I will
return to Jerusalem and live in it. Then it
will be called the City of Truth, and the
mountain of the LORD All-Powerful will
be called the Holy Mountain."
4This is what the LORD All-Powerful
says: "Old men and old women will again
sit along Jerusalem's streets, each carrying a cane because of age. **5**And the
streets will be filled with boys and girls
playing."
6This is what the LORD All-Powerful
says: "Those who are left alive then may
think it is too difficult to happen, but it is
not too difficult for me," says the LORD
All-Powerful. **7**This is what the LORD All-
Powerful says: "I will save my people
from countries in the east and west. **8**I
will bring them back, and they will live in
Jerusalem. They will be my people, and I
will be their good and loyal God."
9This is what the LORD All-Powerful
says: "Work hard, you who are hearing
these words today. The prophets spoke
these words when the foundation was
laid for the house of the LORD All-
Powerful, for the building of the Temple.
10Before that time there was no money
to hire people or animals. People could
not safely come and go because of the
enemies; I had turned everyone against
his neighbor. **11**But I will not do to these
people who are left what I did in the
past," says the LORD All-Powerful.
12"They will plant their seeds in
peace, their grapevines will have fruit,
the ground will give good crops, and the
sky will send rain. I will give all this to
the people who are left alive. **13**Judah and
Israel, your names have been used as
curses in other nations. But I will save
you, and you will become a blessing. So
don't be afraid; work hard."
14This is what the LORD All-Powerful
says: "When your ancestors made me angry, I planned to punish you. I did not
change my mind," says the LORD All-
Powerful. **15**"But now I will do something different. I am planning to do good
to Jerusalem and Judah. So don't be
afraid. **16**These are the things you should
do: Tell each other the truth. In the
courts judge with truth and complete
fairness. **17**Do not make plans to hurt
your neighbors, and don't love false
promises. I hate all these things," says
the LORD.
18The LORD All-Powerful spoke his
word to me again. **19**This is what the
LORD All-Powerful says: "The special
days when you give up eating in the
fourth, fifth, seventh, and tenth months
will become good, joyful, happy feasts in
Judah. But you must love truth and
peace."
20This is what the LORD All-Powerful
says: "Many people from many cities will
still come to Jerusalem. **21**People from
one city will go and say to those from another city, 'We are going to pray to the
LORD and to ask the LORD All-Powerful
for help. Come and go with us.' **22**Many
people and powerful nations will come
to worship the LORD All-Powerful in Jerusalem and to pray to the LORD for
help."
23This is what the LORD All-Powerful
says: "At that time, ten men from different countries will come and take hold of a
Judean by his coat. They will say to him,
'Let us go with you, because we have
heard that God is with you.' "

WHERE IS GOD'S KINGDOM? Zechariah 9:9–10

In Old Testament days, the Israelites looked forward to the coming of the Messiah. They thought the kingdom of God would be like a new king taking over a country. They thought there would be battles, and God would get back at their enemies.

The kingdom of God did begin when Jesus came, but it was not a kingdom of war and conquest. It was a kingdom of God's love, mercy, and forgiveness. Jesus brought about God's kingdom by dying for us and forgiving us instead of fighting our enemies for us.

Jesus said, though, that the kingdom of God would be shown in a different way when he comes the next time. Then it will be more like what the Old Testament Israelites had imagined.

Punishment on Israel's Enemies

9 This message is the word of the LORD.
The message is against the land of Hadrach
and the city of Damascus.
The tribes of Israel and all people
belong to the LORD.
2 The message is also against the city of Hamath, on the border,
and against Tyre and Sidon, with their skill.
3 Tyre has built a strong wall for herself.
She has piled up silver like dust
and gold like the mud in the streets.
4 But the Lord will take away all she has
and destroy her power on the sea.
That city will be destroyed by fire.
5 The city of Ashkelon will see it and be afraid.
The people of Gaza will shake with fear,
and the people of Ekron will lose hope.
No king will be left in Gaza,
and no one will live in Ashkelon anymore.
6 Foreigners will live in Ashdod,
and I will destroy the pride of the Philistines.
7 I will stop them from drinking blood
and from eating forbidden food.
Those left alive will belong to God.
They will be leaders in Judah,
and Ekron will become like the Jebusites.
8 I will protect my Temple
from armies who would come or go.
No one will hurt my people again,
because now I am watching them.

The King Is Coming

9 Rejoice greatly, people of Jerusalem!
Shout for joy, people of Jerusalem!
Your king is coming to you.
He does what is right, and he saves.
He is gentle and riding on a donkey,
on the colt of a donkey.
10 I will take away the chariots from Ephraim
and the horses from Jerusalem.
The bows used in war will be broken.
The king will talk to the nations about peace.

His kingdom will go from sea to
sea,
and from the Euphrates River to
the ends of the earth.

11 As for you, because of the blood of
the agreement with you
I will set your prisoners free from
the waterless pit.
12 You prisoners who have hope,
return to your place of safety.
Today I am telling you
that I will give you back twice as
much as before.
13 I will use Judah like a bow
and Ephraim like the arrows.
Jerusalem, I will use your men
to fight the men of Greece.
I will use you like a warrior's
sword.

14 Then the LORD will appear above
them,
and his arrows will shoot like
lightning.
The Lord GOD will blow the trumpet,
and he will march in the storms of
the south.
15 The LORD All-Powerful will protect
them;
they will destroy the enemy with
slingshots.
They will drink and shout like drunk
men.
They will be filled like a bowl
used for sprinkling blood at the
corners of the altar.
16 On that day the LORD their God will
save them
as if his people were sheep.
They will shine in his land
like jewels in a crown.
17 They will be so pretty and beautiful.
The young men will grow strong
on the grain
and the young women on new
wine.

The Lord's Promises

10 Ask the LORD for rain during the
springtime rains.
The LORD is the one who makes
the clouds.
He sends the showers
and gives everyone green fields.
2 Idols tell lies;

FAITH links

THE BEST ADVICE

ZECHARIAH 10:2

What people or places do you consider "in the know" as far as advice is concerned? Newspaper or magazine articles that answer personal questions? The Internet? The horoscopes? Zechariah warned the Israelites against seeking answers through idols or fortune-tellers. Neither provided the truth. Sound familiar? Many people today look for answers from psychics, horoscopes, fortune cookies, and other people, places, and things. They look everywhere for truth, except to God.

Truth can only be found by listening to God. God provides answers through his word, prayer, and the advice of other Christians. Need answers? Seek God's advice.

Who Do You Trust?, Joshua 9, p. 287

Prayer + Action = Success, Nehemiah 2:4–9, p. 626

The Prayer Habit, Psalm 5:1–3, p. 712

If You Want My Advice . . . , Proverbs 13:1, p. 843

Believe It or Not, Luke 1:20, 38, p. 1366

Pay Attention!, Hebrews 2:1, p. 1668

fortune-tellers see false visions
and tell about false dreams.
The comfort they give is worth nothing.
So the people are like lost sheep.
They are abused, because there is no shepherd.

3 The LORD says, "I am angry at my shepherds,
and I will punish the leaders.
I, the LORD All-Powerful, care
for my flock, the people of Judah.
I will make them like my proud war horses.
4 From Judah will come the cornerstone,
and the tent peg,
the battle bow,
and every ruler.
5 Together they will be like soldiers
marching to battle through muddy streets.
The LORD is with them,
so they will fight and defeat the horsemen.

6 "I will strengthen the people of Judah
and save the people of Joseph.
I will bring them back,
because I care about them.
It will be as though
I had never left them,
because I am the LORD their God,
and I will answer them.
7 The people of Ephraim will be strong like soldiers;
they will be glad as when they have drunk wine.
Their children will see it and rejoice;
they will be happy in the LORD.
8 I will call my people
and gather them together.
I will save them,
and they will grow in number as they grew in number before.
9 I have scattered them among the nations,
but in those faraway places, they will remember me.
They and their children will live and return.
10 I will bring them back from the land of Egypt
and gather them from Assyria.
I will bring them to Gilead and Lebanon
until there isn't enough room for them all.
11 They will come through the sea of trouble.
The waves of the sea will be calm,
and the Nile River will dry up.
I will defeat Assyria's pride
and destroy Egypt's power over other countries.
12 I will make my people strong,
and they will live as I say," says the LORD.

11 Lebanon, open your gates
so fire may burn your cedar trees.[a]
2 Cry, pine trees, because the cedar has fallen,
because the tall trees are ruined.
Cry, oaks in Bashan,
because the mighty forest has been cut down.
3 Listen to the shepherds crying
because their rich pastures are destroyed.
Listen to the lions roaring
because the lovely land of the Jordan River is ruined.

The Two Shepherds

4 This is what the LORD my God says:
"Feed the flock that are about to be
killed. 5 Their buyers kill them and are
not punished. Those who sell them say,
'Praise the LORD, I am rich.' Even the
shepherds don't feel sorry for their
sheep. 6 I don't feel sorry anymore for the
people of this country," says the LORD. "I
will let everyone be under the power of
his neighbor and king. They will bring
trouble to the country, and I will not save
anyone from them."

7 So I fed the flock about to be killed,
particularly the weakest ones. Then I
took two sticks; I called one Pleasant and
the other Union, and I fed the flock. 8 In
one month I got rid of three shepherds.

11:1 trees In this poem, trees, bushes, and animals stand for leaders of countries around Judah.

The flock did not pay attention to me, and
I got impatient with them. **9**I said, "I will
no longer take care of you like a shepherd. Let those that are dying die, and let
those that are to be destroyed be destroyed. Let those that are left eat each
other."

10Then I broke the stick named Pleasant to break the agreement God made
with all the nations. **11**That day it was broken. The weak ones in the flock who were
watching me knew this message was from
the LORD.

12Then I said, "If you want to pay me,
pay me. If not, then don't." So they paid
me thirty pieces of silver.

13The LORD said to me, "Throw the
money to the potter." That is how little
they thought I was worth.* So I took the
thirty pieces of silver and threw them to
the potter in the Temple of the LORD.

14Then I broke the second stick,
named Union, to break the brotherhood
between Judah and Israel.

15Then the LORD said to me, "Get the
things used by a foolish shepherd again,
16because I am going to get a new shepherd for the country. He will not care for
the dying sheep, or look for the young
ones, or heal the injured ones, or feed the
healthy. But he will eat the best sheep
and tear off their hoofs.

17"How terrible it will
be for the
useless shepherd
who abandoned the
flock.
A sword will strike
his arm and his
right eye.
His arm will lose all
its strength,
and his right eye
will go blind."

> How terrible it will be for the useless shepherd who abandoned the flock.
> —Zechariah 11:17

Jerusalem Will Be Saved

12 This message is the word of the
LORD to Israel. This is what the
LORD says, who stretched out the skies,
and laid the foundations of the earth, and
put the human spirit within: **2**"I will
make Jerusalem like a cup of poison to
the nations around her. They will come
and attack Jerusalem and Judah. **3**One
day all the nations on earth will come together to attack Jerusalem, but I will
make it like a heavy rock; anyone who
tries to move it will get hurt. **4**At that
time I will confuse every horse and cause
its rider to go crazy," says the LORD. "I
will watch over Judah, but I will blind all
the horses of the enemies. **5**Then the
leaders of Judah will say to themselves,
'The people of Jerusalem are strong, because the LORD All-Powerful is their
God.'

6"At that time I will make the leaders
of Judah like a fire burning a stack of
wood or like a fire burning straw. They
will destroy all the people around them
left and right. But the people of Jerusalem will remain safe.

7"The LORD will save the homes of
Judah first so that the honor given to
David's family and to the people of Jerusalem won't be greater than the honor
given to Judah. **8**At that time the LORD
will protect the people in Jerusalem.
Then even the weakest of them will be
strong like David. And the family of David will be like God, like an angel of the
LORD in front of them. **9**At that time I will
go to destroy all the nations that attack
Jerusalem.

Crying for the One They Stabbed

10"I will pour out on
David's family and the
people in Jerusalem a
spirit of kindness and
mercy. They will look at
me, the one they have
stabbed, and they will cry
like someone crying over
the death of an only child.
They will be as sad as
someone who has lost a firstborn son.
11At that time there will be much crying
in Jerusalem, like the crying for Hadad
Rimmon in the plain of Megiddo. **12**The
land will cry, each family by itself: the

11:13 worth This was a small amount. It was about the price paid for a slave.

family of David by itself and their wives by
themselves, the family of Nathan by itself
and their wives by themselves, 13the
family of Levi by itself and their wives by
themselves, the family of Shimei by itself
and their wives by themselves, 14and all
the rest of the families by themselves
and their wives by themselves.

13 "At that time a fountain will be
open for David's descendants and
for the people of Jerusalem to cleanse
them of their sin and uncleanness."

EMAIL FROM GOD
13:1
Guilt
How can you be made guilt-free?

2The LORD All-
Powerful says, "At
that time I will get
rid of the names of
the idols from the
land; no one will remember them anymore. I will also remove the prophets and
unclean spirits from the land. 3If a person
continues to prophesy, his own father and
mother, the ones who gave birth to him,
will tell him, 'You have told lies using the
LORD's name, so you must die.' When he
prophesies, his own father and mother
who gave birth to him will stab him.

4"At that time the prophets will be
ashamed of their visions and prophecies.
They won't wear the prophet's clothes
made of hair to trick people. 5Each of
them will say, 'I am not a prophet. I am a
farmer and have been a farmer since I
was young.' 6But someone will ask,
'What are the deep cuts on your body?'
And each will answer, 'I was hurt at my
friend's house.'

The Shepherd Is Killed

7 "Sword, hit the shepherd.
Attack the man who is my friend,"
says the LORD All-Powerful.
"Kill the shepherd,
and the sheep will scatter,
and I will punish the little ones."
8 The LORD says, "Two-thirds of the
people
through all the land will die. They
will be gone,
and one-third will be left.
9 The third that is left I will test with
fire,
purifying them like silver,
testing them like gold.
Then they will call on me,
and I will answer them.
I will say, 'You are my people,'
and they will say, 'The LORD is our
God.' "

The Day of Punishment

14 The LORD's day of judging is coming when the wealth you have
taken will be divided among you.

2I will bring all the nations together to
fight Jerusalem. They will capture the
city and rob the houses and attack the
women. Half the people will be taken
away as captives, but the rest of the people won't be taken from the city.

3Then the LORD will go to war against
those nations; he will fight as in a day of
battle. 4On that day he will stand on the
Mount of Olives, east of Jerusalem. The
Mount of Olives will split in two, forming
a deep valley that runs east and west.
Half the mountain will move toward the
north, and half will move toward the
south. 5You will run through this mountain valley to the other side, just as you
ran from the earthquake when Uzziah
was king of Judah. Then the LORD my
God will come and all the holy ones with
him.

6On that day there will be no light,
cold, or frost. 7There will be no other day
like it, and the LORD knows when it will
come. There will be no day or night; even
at evening it will still be light.

8At that time fresh water will flow
from Jerusalem. Half of it will flow east to
the Dead Sea, and half will flow west to
the Mediterranean Sea. It will flow summer and winter.

9Then the LORD will be king over the
whole world. At that time there will be
only one LORD, and his name will be the
only name.

10All the land south of Jerusalem from
Geba to Rimmon will be turned into a
plain. Jerusalem will be raised up, but it
will stay in the same place. The city will
reach from the Benjamin Gate and to the
First Gate to the Corner Gate, and from
the Tower of Hananel to the king's wine-

FAITH CHALLENGE

Got another challenge for you. Read 14:9 to find out what kind of government the world can expect in the future. How would the world be different today if the leaders of all countries gave up control to God?

TESTING IT

Zechariah 14:9
Then the LORD will be king over the whole world. At that time there will be only one LORD, and his name will be the only name.

presses. 11People will live there, and it
will never be destroyed again. Jerusalem
will be safe.

12But the LORD will bring a terrible
disease on the nations that fought against
Jerusalem. Their flesh will rot away while
they are still standing up. Their eyes will
rot in their sockets, and their tongues will
rot in their mouths. 13At that time the
LORD will cause panic. Everybody will
grab his neighbor, and they will attack
each other. 14The people of Judah will
fight in Jerusalem. And the wealth of the
nations around them will be collected—
much gold, silver, and clothes. 15A similar
disease will strike the horses, mules,
camels, donkeys, and all the animals in the
camps.

16All of those left alive of the people
who came to fight Jerusalem will come
back to Jerusalem year after year to worship the King, the LORD All-Powerful,
and to celebrate the Feast of Shelters.
17Anyone from the nations who does not
go to Jerusalem to worship the King, the
LORD All-Powerful, will not have rain fall
on his land. 18If the Egyptians do not go
to Jerusalem, they will not have rain.
Then the LORD will send them the same
terrible disease he sent the other nations
that did not celebrate the Feast of Shelters. 19This will be the punishment for
Egypt and any nation which does not go
to celebrate the Feast of Shelters.

20At that time the horses' bells will
have written on them: HOLY TO THE
LORD. The cooking pots in the Temple of
the Lord will be like the holy altar bowls.
21Every pot in Jerusalem and Judah will
be holy to the LORD All-Powerful, and
everyone who offers sacrifices will be
able to take food from them and cook in
them. At that time there will not be any
buyers or sellers in the Temple of the
LORD All-Powerful.

ONLY THE BEST!

Hi! I'm Malachi the prophet with a message for God's people. Imagine you are at a big party and you're the guest of honor. A pile of beautifully wrapped presents awaits you. You open the first one and find a beautiful coat with a big rip down the side. You open the second present and find a puzzle with several pieces missing. The next present is a toy car with a broken wheel. You are so hurt. Why would anyone give you presents like this? In my time, these were the kind of gifts people were offering to God. God's law required that offerings made at the Temple be absolutely perfect, but the priests made offerings that were second-rate at best. This did not please God at all.

I wrote this book to remind everyone that God deserves the best we can give him—not whatever is left over. Worship God with your whole heart. Obey his commandments with joy. Give generously to God's work. What does God promise for those who honor him? "I will open the windows of heaven for you and pour out all the blessings you need" (Malachi 3:10).

JESUS WATCH

In Malachi 4, God promised to send Elijah the prophet before the terrifying day of the Lord's judging. The "new Elijah" was John the Baptist, who came to prepare people for the Messiah. John told the people to turn away from their sins for the kingdom of heaven was coming soon. People came from all around to hear him preach. When they confessed their sins, John baptized them in the Jordan River. John told the people about the Messiah who was coming, one whose sandals he was not good enough to carry. Who is the Messiah? Jesus, of course! Jesus will return on the day of the Lord's judging to punish those who have refused to obey him. But those who honor and respect God will have their names written in a book to be remembered. Goodness will shine on them like the sun, and they will dance around like well-fed calves. Read about it in Malachi 4!

"What was so bad about the things the people were giving to God?"

"I think it has something to do with respect. Why don't we surf over to Malachi 1:6-14 to check it out."

- How Do I Love You?, Malachi 1:1–5
- A Halfhearted Offering, Malachi 1:6–14
- A Robbery in Progress, Malachi 3:8–10

1 This message is the word of the LORD
given to Israel through Malachi.

God Loves Israel

2The LORD said, "I have loved you."
But you ask, "How have you loved
us?"
The LORD said, "Esau and Jacob were
brothers. I loved Jacob, 3but I hated
Esau. I destroyed his mountain country
and left his land to the wild dogs of the
desert."
4The people of Edom might say, "We
were destroyed, but we will go back and
rebuild the ruins."
But the LORD All-Powerful says, "If
they rebuild them, I will destroy them.
People will say, 'Edom is a wicked country. The LORD is always angry with the
Edomites.' 5You will see these things
with your own eyes. And you will say,
'The LORD is great, even outside the borders of Israel!' "

The Priests Don't Respect God

6The LORD All-Powerful says, "A
child honors his father, and a servant
honors his master. I am a father, so why
don't you honor me? I am a master, so
why don't you respect me? You priests do
not respect me.
"But you ask, 'How have we shown
you disrespect?'
7"You have shown it by bringing unclean food to my altar.
"But you ask, 'What makes it unclean?'
"It is unclean because you don't respect the altar of the LORD. 8When you
bring blind animals as sacrifices, that is
wrong. When you bring crippled and sick
animals, that is wrong. Try giving them to
your governor. Would he be pleased with
you? He wouldn't accept you," says the
LORD All-Powerful.
9"Now ask God to be kind to you, but
he won't accept you with such offerings," says the LORD All-Powerful.
10"I wish one of you would close
the Temple doors so that you would not
light useless fires on my altar! I am
not pleased with you and will not accept
your gifts," says the LORD All-Powerful.
11"From the east to the west I will be
honored among the nations. Everywhere they will
bring incense and
clean offerings to
me, because I will
be honored among
the nations," says
the LORD All-Powerful.
12"But you don't honor me. You say
about the Lord's altar, 'It is unclean, and
the food has no worth.' 13You say, 'We are
tired of doing this,' and you sniff at it in
disgust," says the LORD All-Powerful.

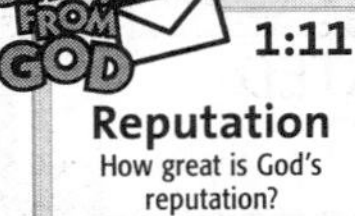

1:11
Reputation
How great is God's reputation?

HOW DO I LOVE YOU?

MALACHI 1:1-5

What do your parents or guardians do to show their love for you? You could probably come up with a list, couldn't you? The Israelites doubted God's love. So God told Malachi to remind them of his love.

There are times when we doubt God's love for us. Sometimes we need to be reminded of that love. Want a reminder of God's love? Here it is: Jesus.

The Sign of His Presence, Exodus 40:34–38, p. 130

Go for the Gold, Job 23:10, p. 685

Our Heavenly Shepherd, Psalm 23, p. 726

The "Ruler" of Our Lives, Amos 7:7–9, p. 1202

Too Busy to Worship?, Luke 2:8–20, p. 1368

MVFM?, Galatians 3:26–27, p. 1589

A HALFHEARTED OFFERING

MALACHI 1:6-14

Suppose you asked a friend for a piece of gum and he offered you one he had already chewed. What would you think of that offering? More than likely, you would feel that you deserved better. Malachi spoke out against the halfhearted offerings the Israelites gave. In the time of Moses, God had commanded the people to offer perfectly formed animals. Now some of the people halfheartedly offered whatever animals they felt like giving. God hated those offerings. As a king, he deserved better.

Many times, we may halfheartedly offer God our service or our money. He deserves better.

Here are some more links on giving God our best:

Everyone Can Help, Numbers 4, p. 181

Your Best Work, 1 Kings 6, p. 443

Service with a Smile, 1 Chronicles 6:31–49, p. 527

Set for Life?, Obadiah 2–4, p. 1208

Your Heart's Desire, Luke 16:13–15, p. 1401

Give Till It Hurts?, 2 Corinthians 8:6–9; 9:6–9, p. 1578

"And you bring hurt, crippled, and sick animals as gifts. You bring them as gifts, but I won't accept them from you," says the LORD.
14"The person who cheats will be cursed. He has a male animal in his flock and promises to offer it, but then he offers to the Lord an animal that has something wrong with it. I am a great king," says the LORD All-Powerful, "and I am feared by all the nations.

Rules for Priests

2 "Priests, this command is for you.
2Listen to me. Pay attention to what I say. Honor my name," says the LORD All-Powerful. "If you don't, I will send a curse on you and on your blessings. I have already cursed them, because you don't pay attention to what I say.
3"I will punish your descendants. I will smear your faces with the animal insides left from your feasts, and you will be thrown away with it.
4Then you will know that I am giving you this command so my agreement with Levi will continue," says the LORD All-Powerful.
5"My agreement for priests was with the tribe of Levi. I promised them life and peace so they would honor me. And they did honor me and fear me.
6They taught the true teachings and spoke no lies. With peace and honesty they did what I said they should do, and they kept many people from sinning.
7"A priest should teach what he knows, and people should learn the teachings from him, because he is the messenger of the LORD All-Powerful.
8But you priests have stopped obeying me. With your teachings you have caused many people to do wrong. You have broken the agreement with the tribe of Levi!" says the LORD All-Powerful.
9"You have not been careful to do what I say, but instead you take sides in court cases. So I have caused you to be hated and disgraced in front of everybody."

Judah Was Not Loyal to God

10We all have the same father; the same God made us. So why do people break their promises to each other and show no respect for the agreement our ancestors made with God? 11The people of Judah have broken their promises. They have done something God hates in Israel and Jerusalem: The people of Judah did not respect the Temple that the LORD loves, and the men of Judah married women who worship foreign gods. 12Whoever does this might bring offerings to the LORD All-Powerful, but the LORD will still cut that person off from the community of Israel.

13This is another thing you do. You cover the LORD's altar with your tears. You cry and moan, because he does not accept your offerings and is not pleased with what you bring. 14You ask, "Why?" It is because the LORD sees how you treated the wife you married when you were young. You broke your promise to her, even though she was your partner and you had an agreement with her. 15God made husbands and wives to become one body and one spirit for his purpose—so they would have children who are true to God.

So be careful, and do not break your promise to the wife you married when you were young.

16The LORD God of Israel says, "I hate divorce. And I hate people who do cruel things as easily as they put on clothes," says the LORD All-Powerful.

So be careful. And do not break your trust.

The Special Day of Judging

17You have tired the LORD with your words.

You ask, "How have we tired him?"

You did it by saying, "The LORD thinks anyone who does evil is good, and he is pleased with them." Or you asked, "Where is the God who is fair?"

3 The LORD All-Powerful says, "I will send my messenger, who will prepare the way for me. Suddenly, the Lord you are looking for will come to his Temple; the messenger of the agreement, whom you want, will come." 2No one can live through that time; no one can survive when he comes. He will be like a purifying fire and like laundry soap. 3Like someone who heats and purifies silver, he will purify the Levites and make them pure like gold and silver. Then they will bring offerings to the LORD in the right way. 4And the LORD will accept the offerings from Judah and Jerusalem, as it was in the past. 5The LORD All-Powerful says, "Then I will come to you and judge you. I will be quick to testify against those who take part in evil magic, adultery, and lying under oath, those who cheat workers of their pay and who cheat widows and orphans, those who are unfair to foreigners, and those who do not respect me.

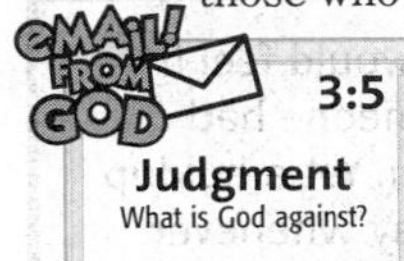
EMAIL! FROM GOD
3:5
Judgment
What is God against?

Stealing from God

6"I the LORD do not change. So you descendants of Jacob have not been destroyed. 7Since the time of your ancestors, you have disobeyed my rules and have not kept them. Return to me, and I will return to you," says the LORD All-Powerful.

"But you ask, 'How can we return?'

8"Should a person rob God? But you are robbing me.

"You ask, 'How have we robbed you?'

"You have robbed me in your offerings and the tenth of your crops. 9So a curse is on you, because the whole nation has robbed me. 10Bring to the storehouse a full tenth of what you earn so there will be food in my house. Test me in this," says the LORD All-Powerful. "I will open the windows of heaven for you and pour out all the blessings you need. 11I will stop the insects so they won't eat your crops. The grapes won't fall from your vines before they are ready to pick," says the LORD All-Powerful. 12"All the nations will call you blessed, because you will have a pleasant country," says the LORD All-Powerful.

The Lord's Promise of Mercy

13The LORD says, "You have said terrible things about me.

"But you ask, 'What have we said about you?'

14"You have said, 'It is useless to

A ROBBERY IN PROGRESS

MALACHI 3:8-10

Imagine how you would feel if you heard that someone had robbed your church. Yet a holdup occurs every Sunday whenever people refuse to give either their time or their money. Malachi delivered a message to the Israelites about giving. God had commanded the people to give a tithe of their harvest to him. A tithe was 10 percent. When the people forgot to give, God felt "robbed."

Giving to God is not a requirement because God needs what we give. God wants us to give to show the value of sharing what we have with others.

Connect here for more on sharing:

Share What You Have, Exodus 35:5–18, p. 123

Give What You Can, Numbers 7:1–11, p. 186

What's the Use?, 2 Kings 12:6–12, p. 495

Wisdom About Wealth, Ecclesiastes 5:10–12, p. 878

My Favorite!, Mark 10:17–23, p. 1347

Give from the Heart, Luke 21:1–4, p. 1410

serve God. It did no good to obey his laws and to show the LORD All-Powerful that we were sorry for what we did. 15So we say that proud people are happy. Evil people succeed. They challenge God and get away with it.' "

16Then those who honored the LORD spoke with each other, and the LORD listened and heard them. The names of those who honored the LORD and respected him were written in his presence in a book to be remembered.

3:14–18 Following God
Does God care if you follow him?

17The LORD All-Powerful says, "They belong to me; on that day they will be my very own. As a parent shows mercy to his child who serves him, I will show mercy to my people. 18You will again see the difference between good and evil people, between those who serve God and those who don't.

The Day of the Lord's Judging

4 "There is a day coming that will burn like a hot furnace, and all the proud and evil people will be like straw. On that day they will be completely burned up so that not a root or branch will be left," says the LORD All-Powerful. 2"But for you who honor me, goodness will shine on you like the sun, with healing in its rays. You will jump around, like well-fed calves. 3Then you will crush the wicked like ashes under your feet on the day I will do this," says the LORD All-Powerful.

4"Remember the teaching of Moses my servant, those laws and rules I gave to him on Mount Sinai for all the Israelites.

5"But I will send you Elijah the prophet before that great and terrifying day of the LORD's judging. 6Elijah will help parents love their children and children love their parents. Otherwise, I will come and put a curse on the land."

THE NEW TESTAMENT

A NEW KING

Hi, everyone. You might not know a lot about me. Before I met Jesus, I was a tax collector. If you know anything about tax collectors in my time, you know that we weren't exactly the nicest guys around. Some of us (myself included) often charged people more taxes than we should—and we kept the change. Let's just say I wasn't a real popular guy in town. When I began following Jesus, though, things changed! I became one of Jesus' 12 followers and later became a leader in the early church.

I wrote this book because I was a Jew who had become a follower of Jesus, or a Christian, as we were later called. I had a lot of Jewish friends who had become Christians, and I wanted them to understand that Jesus gave new meaning to God's rules. (Want a clue about my focus? Take a look at chapters 5—7 of my book, and you'll see me writing about Jesus' new spin on the Old Testament teachings.) I wanted all of my Jewish friends to know that the Messiah had indeed come to save his people. Hallelujah!

JESUS WATCH

Matthew gives us a beautiful picture of the Messiah promised in the Old Testament. To prove that Jesus is the promised Messiah, Matthew reaches back into the Old Testament for some words that help his readers understand who Jesus is. He often calls Jesus the "Son of David" to help his Jewish readers understand Jesus' relationship to their history, belonging to the family tree of King David. This phrase is used nine times in Matthew's book (and that's a lot, considering that same phrase is mentioned only six times in all the other Gospels). He's also called the "Servant of the Lord," connecting him with the God of the Old Testament. Matthew carefully selects stories and quotes from the Old Testament to help his Jewish readers understand just who Jesus is.

my FAVORITE links

______________________ ______________________

______________________ ______________________

______________________ ______________________

______________________ ______________________

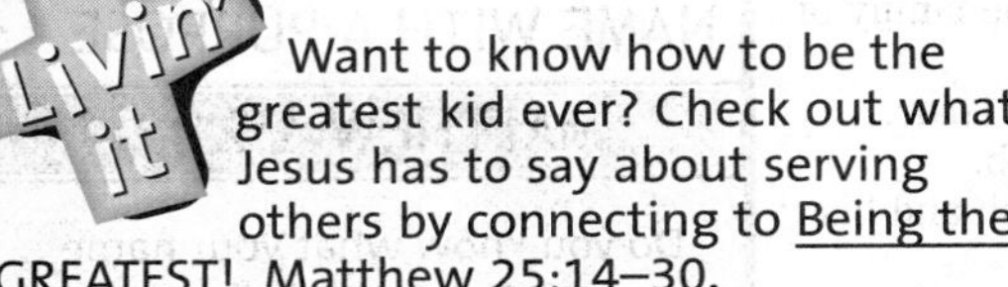

Livin' it Want to know how to be the greatest kid ever? Check out what Jesus has to say about serving others by connecting to Being the GREATEST!, Matthew 25:14–30.

GET THE INFO

Find out more about some important people and events in Jesus' ministry by downloading these sites:

- Jesus' Sermon Notes, Matthew 5:40. Link here for more information about Jesus' most famous sermon. It's all about how to live your life God's way.
- The Chosen Dozen, Matthew 10:1–29. Who were the men Jesus called to be his first followers? You probably can name a few, but do you know all of them? Find a list of their names by logging on here.

"Did the religious rulers really hate Jesus?"

"They sure did. Connect to Matthew 12 to find out what they said and wanted to do about Jesus."

CHECK OUT THESE OTHER COOL STORIES:

A get-away trip to Egypt, Matthew 2:13–15
Jesus' first sermon, Matthew 5—7
A faith that grows, Matthew 13:31–35
A deadly plot, Matthew 26:1–5

FAITH links

- **Name with a Purpose, Matthew 1:21**
- **The Best Protection Plan, Matthew 2:13–18**
- **Perfectly Pleasing?, Matthew 5:1–12**
- **A Word About Worry, Matthew 6:25–34**
- **Just Say Yes!, Matthew 9:9–13**
- **Your Choice of Fruit, Matthew 12:33–35**
- **Prove It!, Matthew 16:1–4**
- **Welcome!, Matthew 19:13–15**
- **The Greatest Commandment, Matthew 22:36–40**
- **That Thing You Do, Matthew 25:14–30**
- **Don't Get Mad; Get Even?, Matthew 26:57–63; 27:11–14**
- **Tell All About Him!, Matthew 28:19**

The Family History of Jesus

1 This is the family history of Jesus Christ. He came from the family of David, and David came from the family of Abraham.

2 Abraham was the father[a] of Isaac.
Isaac was the father of Jacob.
Jacob was the father of Judah and his brothers.
3 Judah was the father of Perez and Zerah.
(Their mother was Tamar.)
Perez was the father of Hezron.
Hezron was the father of Ram.
4 Ram was the father of Amminadab.
Amminadab was the father of Nahshon.
Nahshon was the father of Salmon.
5 Salmon was the father of Boaz.
(Boaz's mother was Rahab.)
Boaz was the father of Obed.
(Obed's mother was Ruth.)
Obed was the father of Jesse.
6 Jesse was the father of King David.
David was the father of Solomon.
(Solomon's mother had been Uriah's wife.)
7 Solomon was the father of Rehoboam.
Rehoboam was the father of Abijah.
Abijah was the father of Asa.
8 Asa was the father of Jehoshaphat.
Jehoshaphat was the father of Jehoram.
Jehoram was the ancestor of Uzziah.
9 Uzziah was the father of Jotham.
Jotham was the father of Ahaz.
Ahaz was the father of Hezekiah.
10 Hezekiah was the father of Manasseh.
Manasseh was the father of Amon.
Amon was the father of Josiah.
11 Josiah was the grandfather of Jehoiachin and his brothers.
(This was at the time that the people were taken to Babylon.)
12 After they were taken to Babylon:
Jehoiachin was the father of Shealtiel.
Shealtiel was the grandfather of Zerubbabel.
13 Zerubbabel was the father of Abiud.
Abiud was the father of Eliakim.
Eliakim was the father of Azor.

FAITH links

NAME WITH A PURPOSE

MATTHEW 1:21

Do you know what your name means? If you think about it, you might ask your parents to tell you what your name means and why they chose that name for you. Names were very important to people in Bible times. Jesus' name, which means "salvation," points to his purpose for coming to earth: to save people from sin.

If you believe in Jesus, you have a name and a purpose that is shared by millions of other believers. That name is *Christian*, which means "Christ-followers." (See Acts 11:26, p. 1484.) Since you bear the name, you can live up to it by living like Jesus.

Check out these Faithlinks to see what it means to belong to God:

The Perfect Sacrifice, Leviticus 1—7, p. 135

A Different Kind of People, Leviticus 11, p. 146

What's in a Name?, Isaiah 9:6, p. 908

A Fake Apology, Hosea 6:1–7, p. 1177

Your Civic Duty, Matthew 17:24–27, p. 1304

It's Free!, Ephesians 2:8–9, p. 1600

[a] **1:2 father** "Father" in Jewish lists of ancestors can sometimes mean grandfather or more distant relative.

14 Azor was the father of Zadok.
Zadok was the father of Akim.
Akim was the father of Eliud.
15 Eliud was the father of Eleazar.
Eleazar was the father of Matthan.
Matthan was the father of Jacob.
16 Jacob was the father of Joseph.
Joseph was the husband of Mary,
and Mary was the mother of Jesus.
Jesus is called the Christ.

17 So there were fourteen generations
from Abraham to David. And there were
fourteen generations from David until
the people were taken to Babylon. And
there were fourteen generations from
the time when the people were taken to
Babylon until Christ was born.

The Birth of Jesus Christ

18 This is how the birth of Jesus
Christ came about. His mother Mary was
engaged[n] to marry Joseph, but before
they married, she learned she was pregnant by the power of the Holy Spirit.
19 Because Mary's husband, Joseph, was
a good man, he did not want to disgrace
her in public, so he planned to divorce
her secretly.

20 While Joseph thought about these
things, an angel of the Lord came to him
in a dream. The angel said, "Joseph, descendant of David, don't be afraid to take
Mary as your wife, because the baby in
her is from the Holy Spirit. 21 She will
give birth to a son, and you will name him
Jesus,[n] because he will save his people
from their sins."

22 All this happened to bring about
what the Lord had said through the
prophet: 23 "The virgin will be pregnant.
She will have a son, and they will name
him Immanuel,"[n] which means "God is
with us."

24 When Joseph woke up, he did what
the Lord's angel had told him to do. Joseph took Mary as his wife, 25 but he did
not have sexual relations with her until
she gave birth to the son. And Joseph
named him Jesus.

Wise Men Come to Visit Jesus

2 Jesus was born in the town of Bethlehem in Judea during the time when

FAITH links

THE GIFT OF WORSHIP

MATTHEW 2:10-12

How far do you have to go to worship God? More than likely, the church you attend isn't very far away. The wise men traveled hundreds of miles from their homeland in the east to worship the newborn king, Jesus. They had followed a star in the night sky, which foretold the birth of a great king. They honored him by giving him gifts worthy of a king.

Like the wise men, we can offer Jesus the gift of worship. This gift can be offered anytime, anywhere. Worship is a gift that is more valuable than gold. What are some ways you worship Jesus?

My Worship Place, Genesis 35:1–14, p. 49

A Thanksgiving Reminder, Exodus 12, p. 91

A Reminder to Be Fair, 2 Chronicles 19:5–11, p. 583

You're Invited!, Psalm 100, p. 784

A Friend of Jesus, John 15:9–17, p. 1450

One of the Faithful, Acts 10:1–34, p. 1482

1:18 engaged For the Jewish people an engagement was a lasting agreement, which could only be broken by a divorce. If a bride-to-be was unfaithful, it was considered adultery, and she could be put to death.
1:21 Jesus The name "Jesus" means "salvation."
1:23 "The virgin . . . Immanuel" Quotation from Isaiah 7:14.

Herod was king. When Jesus was born,
some wise men from the east came to Jerusalem. 2They asked, "Where is the
baby who was born to be the king of the
Jews? We saw his star in the east and
have come to worship him."
3When King Herod heard this, he was
troubled, as well as all the people in Jerusalem. 4Herod called a meeting of all the
leading priests and teachers of the law
and asked them where the Christ would
be born. 5They answered, "In the town of
Bethlehem in Judea. The prophet wrote
about this in the Scriptures:

6'But you, Bethlehem, in the land of
Judah,
are important among the tribes of
Judah.
A ruler will come from you
who will be like a shepherd for my
people Israel.' " *Micah 5:2*

7Then Herod had a secret meeting
with the wise men and learned from them
the exact time they first saw the star.
8He sent the wise men to Bethlehem,
saying, "Look carefully for the child.
When you find him, come tell me so I can
worship him too."
9After the wise men heard the king,
they left. The star that they had seen in
the east went before them until it stopped
above the place where the child was.
10When the wise men saw the star, they
were filled with joy. 11They came to the
house where the child was and saw him
with his mother, Mary, and they bowed
down and worshiped him. They opened
their gifts and gave him treasures of gold,
frankincense, and myrrh. 12But God
warned the wise men in a dream not to go
back to Herod, so they returned to their
own country by a different way.

Jesus' Parents Take Him to Egypt

13After they left, an angel of the Lord
came to Joseph in a dream and said, "Get
up! Take the child and his mother and
escape to Egypt, because Herod is
starting to look for the child so he can
kill him. Stay in Egypt until I tell you to
return."
14So Joseph got up and left for Egypt
during the night with the child and his
mother. 15And Joseph stayed in Egypt
until Herod died. This happened to bring
about what the Lord had said through

FAITH links

THE BEST PROTECTION PLAN

MATTHEW 2:13-18

Who do you trust for protection when you're scared? A parent or guardian? A big brother or sister? When Jesus was a child, a jealous king wanted to have him killed. This king, Herod, didn't like the fact that the wise men called Jesus the "king of the Jews" (Look at Matthew 2:2). Herod wanted that title all to himself! But God wouldn't let anything happen to the One he had sent to save the world. In a series of dreams, God let Joseph know where to take Jesus to keep him safe. That's the kind of protection you can count on.

Surf on over here to find out how God cares for you:

A Major Problem, Genesis 15:6, p. 20

Forgive Instead, Genesis 33, p. 47

God's Pep Talk, Joshua 1:5–9, p. 276

A Hopeful Name, Hosea 1:3–11, p. 1172

Justice Desserts, Habakkuk 2:4–8, p. 1237

Hard Times, 2 Corinthians 1:8–10, p. 1570

the prophet: "I called my son out of
Egypt."'ⁿ

Herod Kills the Baby Boys

16When Herod saw that the wise men
had tricked him, he was furious. So he
gave an order to kill all the baby boys in
Bethlehem and in the surrounding area
who were two years old or younger. This
was in keeping with the time he learned
from the wise men. 17So what God had
said through the prophet Jeremiah came
true:

18 "A voice was heard in Ramah
of painful crying and deep sadness:
Rachel crying for her children.
She refused to be comforted,
because her children are dead."

Jeremiah 31:15

Joseph and Mary Return

19After Herod died, an angel of the
Lord spoke to Joseph in a dream while he
was in Egypt. 20The angel said, "Get up!
Take the child and his mother and go to
the land of Israel, because the people
who were trying to kill the child are now
dead."
21So Joseph took the child and his
mother and went to Israel. 22But he
heard that Archelaus was now king in Judea since his father Herod had died. So
Joseph was afraid to go there. After being
warned in a dream, he went to the area of
Galilee, 23to a town called Nazareth, and
lived there. And so what God had said
through the prophets came true: "He will
be called a Nazarene."'ⁿ

The Work of John the Baptist

3 About that time John the Baptist began preaching in the desert area of Judea. 2John said, "Change your hearts and
lives because the kingdom of heaven is
near." 3John the Baptist is the one Isaiah
the prophet was talking about when he
said:

"This is a voice of one
who calls out in the desert:
'Prepare the way for the Lord.
Make the road straight for him.' "

Isaiah 40:3

4John's clothes were made from
camel's hair, and he wore a leather belt
around his waist. For food, he ate locusts
and wild honey. 5Many people came from

FAITH links

A CHANGE OF HEART

MATTHEW 3:1-12

"I'm sorry." Have you said that lately? When we do wrong, many of us are quick to say it, but slow to really mean it.

When John the Baptist told the Israelites to "change your hearts and lives," he meant one thing: repent. To *repent* means more than just saying you're sorry for something you did wrong. It also involves making a decision to avoid doing what you did wrong. That takes action! But you're not in it alone. When you want to make a change, just ask God. He's always glad to help!

Can't Live Without It?, Genesis 3, p. 7

Alone and Forgotten?, Genesis 40:23, p. 57

The Weak Link, Judges 16, p. 334

A Life-Saving Message, Esther 2:19–22, p. 650

Red to White, Isaiah 1:18, p. 896

The Sin Habit, Romans 7:15–20, p. 1527

2:15 "I called . . . Egypt." Quotation from Hosea 11:1.

2:23 Nazarene A person from the city of Nazareth, a name probably meaning "branch" (see Isaiah 11:1).

Jerusalem and Judea and all the area
around the Jordan River to hear John.
6They confessed their sins, and he baptized them in the Jordan River.

7Many of the Pharisees and Sadducees came to the place where John was
baptizing people. When John saw them,
he said, "You are all snakes! Who warned
you to run away from God's coming punishment? **8**Do the things that show you
really have changed your hearts and
lives. **9**And don't think you can say to
yourselves, 'Abraham is our father.' I tell
you that God could make children for
Abraham from these rocks. **10**The ax is
now ready to cut down the trees, and every tree that does not produce good fruit
will be cut down and thrown into the fire."

11"I baptize you with water to show
that your hearts and lives have changed.
But there is one coming after me who is
greater than I am, whose sandals I am not
good enough to carry. He will baptize you
with the Holy Spirit and fire. **12**He will
come ready to clean the grain, separating
the good grain from the chaff. He will put
the good part of the grain into his barn,
but he will burn the chaff with a fire that
cannot be put out.""

Jesus Is Baptized by John

13At that time Jesus came from Galilee to the Jordan River and wanted John
to baptize him. **14**But John tried to stop
him, saying, "Why do you come to me to
be baptized? I need to be baptized by
you!"

15Jesus answered, "Let it be this way
for now. We should do all things that are
God's will." So John agreed to baptize
Jesus.

16As soon as Jesus was baptized, he
came up out of the water. Then heaven
opened, and he saw God's Spirit coming
down on him like a dove. **17**And a voice
from heaven said, "This is my Son, whom
I love, and I am very pleased with him."

3:10 The ax . . . fire. This means that God is ready to punish his people who do not obey him.

3:12 He will . . . out. This means that Jesus will come to separate good people from bad people, saving the good and punishing the bad.

FAITH links

THE TEMPTATION FIGHTER

MATTHEW 4:1-11

How do you handle the temptation to do something wrong? When Jesus was tempted, he used the Scriptures for strength. Every time the devil tried to tempt him, Jesus would say, "It is written." Jesus relied on what God said to help him fight the devil's temptations.

Food helps our bodies grow and stay healthy. But there is another kind of food that can help us when we're tempted. That food is "spiritual food." That's what the Bible provides. It teaches us about God and helps us grow stronger in our faith. So, next time you're facing a tough temptation, remember what's written in the Bible!

Need help resisting that urge to do something wrong? Click here:

The Cloud Guide, Numbers 9:15–23, p. 188

In Deep Water, Psalm 69, p. 760

What God "Hates," Proverbs 6:16–19, p. 835

Eating Humble Pie, Daniel 4, p. 1156

The "Ruler" of Our Lives, Amos 7:7–9, p. 1202

Cut to the Quick, Hebrews 4:12, p. 1670

The Temptation of Jesus

4 Then the Spirit led Jesus into the
desert to be tempted by the devil.
2Jesus ate nothing for forty days and
nights. After this, he was very hungry.
3The devil came to Jesus to tempt him,
saying, "If you are the Son of God, tell
these rocks to become bread."

4Jesus answered, "It is written in the
Scriptures, 'A person does not live by eating only bread, but by everything God
says.' "[n]

5Then the devil led Jesus to the holy
city of Jerusalem and put him on a high
place of the Temple. 6The devil said, "If
you are the Son of God, jump down, because it is written in the Scriptures:

'He has put his angels in charge of
you.
They will catch you in their hands
so that you will not hit your foot on a
rock.' " *Psalm 91:11-12*

7Jesus answered him, "It also says in
the Scriptures, 'Do not test the Lord your
God.' "[n]

8Then the devil led Jesus to the top of
a very high mountain and showed him all
the kingdoms of the world and all their
splendor. 9The devil said, "If you will
bow down and worship me, I will give you
all these things."

10Jesus said to the devil, "Go away
from me, Satan! It is written in the Scriptures, 'You must worship the
Lord your God and
serve only him.' "[n]

11So the devil
left Jesus, and an-
gels came and took
care of him.

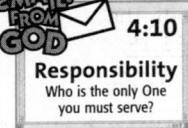

EMAIL FROM GOD 4:10
Responsibility
Who is the only One you must serve?

Jesus Begins Work in Galilee

12When Jesus heard that John had
been put in prison, he went back to Galilee. 13He left Nazareth and went to live
in Capernaum, a town near Lake Galilee,
in the area near Zebulun and Naphtali.
14Jesus did this to bring about what the
prophet Isaiah had said:

15 "Land of Zebulun and land of
Naphtali
along the sea,
beyond the Jordan River.
This is Galilee where the non-
Jewish people live.
16 These people who live in darkness
will see a great light.
They live in a place covered with the
shadows of death,
but a light will shine on them."
Isaiah 9:1-2

Jesus Chooses Some Followers

17From that time Jesus began to
preach, saying, "Change your hearts and
lives, because the kingdom of heaven is
near."

18As Jesus was walking by Lake Galilee, he saw two brothers, Simon (called
Peter) and his brother Andrew. They
were throwing a net into the lake because
they were fishermen. 19Jesus said,
"Come follow me, and I will make you
fish for people." 20So Simon and Andrew
immediately left their nets and followed
him.

21As Jesus continued walking by
Lake Galilee, he saw two other brothers,
James and John, the sons of Zebedee.
They were in a boat with their father
Zebedee, mending their nets. Jesus told
them to come with him. 22Immediately
they left the boat and their father, and
they followed Jesus.

Jesus Teaches and Heals People

23Jesus went everywhere in Galilee,
teaching in the synagogues, preaching
the Good News about the kingdom of
heaven, and healing all the people's diseases and sicknesses. 24The news about
Jesus spread all over Syria, and people
brought all the sick to him. They were
suffering from different kinds of diseases.
Some were in great pain, some had demons, some were epileptics,[n] and some
were paralyzed. Jesus healed all of them.

4:4 'A person . . . says.' Quotation from Deuteronomy 8:3.

4:7 'Do . . . God.' Quotation from Deuteronomy 6:16.

4:10 'You . . . him.' Quotation from Deuteronomy 6:13.

4:24 epileptics People with a disease that causes them sometimes to lose control of their bodies and maybe faint, shake strongly, or not be able to move.

25Many people from Galilee, the Ten
Towns,[a] Jerusalem, Judea, and the land
across the Jordan River followed him.

Jesus Teaches the People

5 When Jesus saw the crowds, he went
up on a hill and sat down. His followers came to him, 2and he began to teach
them, saying:

3"Those people who know they have
great spiritual needs are happy,
because the kingdom of heaven
belongs to them.
4Those who are sad now are happy,
because God will comfort them.
5Those who are humble are happy,
because the earth will belong to
them.
6Those who want to do right more
than anything else are happy,
because God will fully satisfy
them.
7Those who show mercy to others are
happy,
because God will show mercy to
them.
8Those who are pure in their thinking
are happy,
because they will be with God.
9Those who work to bring peace are
happy,
because God will call them his
children.
10Those who are treated badly for
doing good are happy,
because the kingdom of heaven
belongs to them.

11"People will insult you and hurt
you. They will lie and say all kinds of evil
things about you because you follow me.
But when they do, you will be happy.
12Rejoice and be glad, because you have
a great reward waiting for you in heaven.
People did the same evil things to the
prophets who lived before you.

You Are like Salt and Light

13"You are the salt of the earth. But if
the salt loses its salty taste, it cannot be

4:25 Ten Towns In Greek, called "Decapolis." It was an area east of Lake Galilee that once had ten main towns.

FAITH links

PERFECTLY PLEASING?

MATTHEW 5:1-12

Parents have their own way of letting kids know what pleases them. Some of these ways are called "rules." Think of the ones you have at home. When the rules are followed, everybody's happy, right? Not always!

Jesus once preached a sermon on a hilltop (See The Sermon on the Mount, p. 1280) to let people know how to please God. The people who are the most happy are those who trust God and want to please him. Pleasing God doesn't mean that life automatically becomes perfect. Also, God isn't expecting everyone to be perfect at pleasing him. He just wants people to be willing.

Link here to find out what else pleases God:

Serious About the Sabbath, Exodus 31:15, p. 117

The Wisdom of Obeying God, 1 Kings 11:1–13, p. 453

Good Enough?, Ezekiel 8, p. 1093

A Family Meal, Mark 14:23–26, p. 1356

Helpful Hints, 3 John 11, p. 1724

made salty again. It is good for nothing, except to be thrown out and walked on.

14"You are the light that gives light to the world. A city that is built on a hill cannot be hidden.15And people don't hide a light under a bowl. They put it on a lampstand so the light shines for all the people in the house. 16In the same way, you should be a light for other people. Live so that they will see the good things you do and will praise your Father in heaven.

The Importance of the Law

17"Don't think that I have come to destroy the law of Moses or the teaching of the prophets. I have not come to destroy them but to bring about what they said. 18I tell you the truth, nothing will disappear from the law until heaven and earth are gone. Not even the smallest letter or the smallest part of a letter will be lost until everything has happened. 19Whoever refuses to obey any command and teaches other people not to obey that command will be the least important in the kingdom of heaven. But whoever obeys the commands and teaches other people to obey them will be great in the kingdom of heaven. 20I tell you that if you are no more obedient than the teachers of the law and the Pharisees, you will never enter the kingdom of heaven.

Jesus Teaches About Anger

21"You have heard that it was said to our people long ago, 'You must not murder anyone.[n] Anyone who murders another will be judged.' 22But I tell you, if you are angry with a brother or sister,[n] you will be judged. If you say bad things to a brother or sister, you will be judged by the council. And if you call someone a fool, you will be in danger of the fire of hell.

23"So when you offer your gift to God at the altar, and you remember that your brother or sister has something against you, 24leave your gift there at the altar. Go and make peace with that person, and then come and offer your gift.

25"If your enemy is taking you to court, become friends quickly, before you go to court. Otherwise, your enemy might turn you over to the judge, and the judge might give you to a guard to put you in jail. 26I tell you the truth, you will not leave there until you have paid everything you owe.

Jesus Teaches About Sexual Sin

27"You have heard that it was said, 'You must not be guilty of adultery.'[n] 28But I tell you that if anyone looks at a woman and wants to sin sexually with her, in his mind he has already done that sin with the woman. 29If your right eye causes you to sin, take it out and throw it away. It is better to lose one part of your body than to have your whole body thrown into hell. 30If your right hand causes you to sin, cut it off and throw it away. It is better to lose one part of your body than for your whole body to go into hell.

Jesus Teaches About Divorce

31"It was also said, 'Anyone who divorces his wife must give her a written divorce paper.'[n] 32But I tell you that anyone who divorces his wife forces her to be guilty of adultery. The only reason for a man to divorce his wife is if she has sexual relations with another man. And anyone who marries that divorced woman is guilty of adultery.

Make Promises Carefully

33"You have heard that it was said to our people long ago, 'Don't break your promises, but keep the promises you make to the Lord.'[n] 34But I tell you, never swear an oath. Don't swear an oath using

---

5:21 You . . . anyone. Quotation from Exodus 20:13; Deuteronomy 5:17.

5:22 brother . . . sister Although the Greek text reads "brother" here and throughout this book, Jesus' words were meant for the entire church, including men and women.

5:27 'You . . . adultery.' Quotation from Exodus 20:14; Deuteronomy 5:18.

5:31 'Anyone . . . divorce paper.' Quotation from Deuteronomy 24:1.

5:33 'Don't . . . Lord.' This refers to Leviticus 19:12; Numbers 30:2; Deuteronomy 23:21.

JESUS' SERMON NOTES

Matthew 5—7

One of Jesus' most famous sermons is called the "Sermon on the Mount." (Look at Matthew 5—7.) It's called that because Jesus taught from the side of a mountain. The place where this sermon might have been given is marked today by a beautiful little church called the "Chapel on the Mount of Beatitudes." The sermon is all about how to live life God's way.

Here are some things you might have heard of from this famous sermon:

The beatitudes, or blessings, that come by living God's way (5:1–12)
Jesus' followers are "the salt of the earth" (5:13–16)
Don't fight back (5:38–42)
Jesus' model prayer (6:9–13)
God is more important than money (6:19–24)
The most important rule (7:12)

the name of heaven, because heaven is
God's throne. 35Don't swear an oath using the name of the earth, because the
earth belongs to God. Don't swear an
oath using the name of Jerusalem, because that is the city of the great King.
36Don't even swear by your own head,
because you cannot make one hair on
your head become white or black. 37Say
only yes if you mean yes, and no if you
mean no. If you say more than yes or no,
it is from the Evil One.

Don't Fight Back

38"You have heard that it was said,
'An eye for an eye, and a tooth for a
tooth.'" 39But I tell you, don't stand up
against an evil person. If someone slaps
you on the right cheek, turn to him the
other cheek also. 40If someone wants to
sue you in court and take your shirt, let
him have your coat also. 41If someone
forces you to go with him one mile, go
with him two miles. 42If a person asks
you for something, give it to him. Don't
refuse to give to someone who wants to
borrow from you.

Love All People

43"You have heard that it was said,
'Love your neighbor" and
hate your enemies.'
44But I say to you,
love your enemies.
Pray for those who
hurt you. 45If you do
this, you will be true
children of your Father in heaven. He
causes the sun to rise on good people and
on evil people, and he sends rain to those
who do right and to those who do wrong.
46If you love only the people who love
you, you will get no reward. Even the tax
collectors do that. 47And if you are nice
only to your friends, you are no better
than other people. Even those who don't
know God are nice to their friends. 48So
you must be perfect, just as your Father
in heaven is perfect.

EMAIL! FROM GOD
5:43–44
Love
Love your enemies.

5:38 'An eye . . . tooth.' Quotation from Exodus 21:24; Leviticus 24:20; Deuteronomy 19:21.
5:43 'Love your neighbor' Quotation from Leviticus 19:18.

Jesus Teaches About Giving

6 “Be careful! When you do good
things, don’t do them in front of people to be seen by them. If you do that, you
will have no reward from your Father in
heaven.
2“When you give to the poor, don’t be
like the hypocrites. They blow trumpets
in the synagogues and on the streets so
that people will see them and honor
them. I tell you the truth, those hypocrites already have their full reward. 3So
when you give to the poor, don’t let anyone know what you are doing. 4Your giving should be done in secret. Your Father
can see what is done in secret, and he will
reward you.

Jesus Teaches About Prayer

5“When you pray, don’t be like the
hypocrites. They love to stand in the synagogues and on the street corners and
pray so people will see them. I tell you
the truth, they already have their full reward. 6When you pray, you should go into
your room and close the door and pray to
your Father who cannot be seen. Your
Father can see what is done in secret, and
he will reward you.
7“And when you pray, don’t be like
those people who don’t know God. They
continue saying things that mean nothing, thinking that God will hear them because of their many words. 8Don’t be like
them, because your Father knows the
things you need before you ask him. 9So
when you pray, you should pray like this:
‘Our Father in heaven,
may your name always be kept holy.
10 May your kingdom come
and what you want be done,
here on earth as it is in heaven.
11 Give us the food we need for each day.
12 Forgive us for our sins,
just as we have forgiven those who
sinned against us.
13 And do not cause us to be tempted,
but save us from the Evil One.’
14Yes, if you forgive others for their sins,
your Father in heaven will also forgive
you for your sins. 15But if you don’t forgive others, your Father in heaven will
not forgive your sins.

FAITH links

OUR HEAVENLY CONNECTION

MATTHEW 6:9-13

A baby is not born with a complete understanding of how to speak. As they develop, they learn to make sounds by listening to others. When you were a baby, your parents talked to you to help you learn to communicate with them.

That’s how it is with prayer. We can talk to God through prayer. When Jesus preached on the hillside (Check out The Sermon on the Mount, p. 1280), he taught his followers how to pray. You can talk to God at any time and tell him whatever is on your mind. When you pray, trust that he cares and will answer.

When You’re Afraid, Genesis 32:9–12, p. 45

Help to Understand, 2 Samuel 14, p. 416

A Promise from the Heart, Jeremiah 31:31–33, p. 1037

God’s New Temple, Ezekiel 40—44, p. 1135

Prayer Anywhere, Mark 1:35, p. 1331

An Energy Boost, Acts 4:31, p. 1469

Jesus Teaches About Worship

16"When you give up eating," don't put on a sad face like the hypocrites. They make their faces look sad to show people they are giving up eating. I tell you the truth, those hypocrites already have their full reward. 17So when you give up eating, comb your hair and wash your face. 18Then people will not know that you are giving up eating, but your Father, whom you cannot see, will see you. Your Father sees what is done in secret, and he will reward you.

God Is More Important than Money

19"Don't store treasures for yourselves here on earth where moths and rust will destroy them and thieves can break in and steal them. 20But store your treasures in heaven where they cannot be destroyed by moths or rust and where thieves cannot break in and steal them. 21Your heart will be where your treasure is.

6:19–20
Money
Check out the treasures in heaven.

22"The eye is a light for the body. If your eyes are good, your whole body will be full of light. 23But if your eyes are evil, your whole body will be full of darkness. And if the only light you have is really darkness, then you have the worst darkness.

24"No one can serve two masters. The person will hate one master and love the other, or will follow one master and refuse to follow the other. You cannot serve both God and worldly riches.

Don't Worry

25"So I tell you, don't worry about the food or drink you need to live, or about the clothes you need for your body. Life is more than food, and the body is more than clothes. 26Look at the birds in the air. They don't plant or harvest or store

6:16 give up eating This is called "fasting." The people would give up eating for a special time of prayer and worship to God. It was also done to show sadness and disappointment.

FAITH links

A WORD ABOUT WORRY

MATTHEW 6:25-34

What do you worry about? Do you spend time thinking about things like who your friends are, who will sit with you at lunch, or whether you'll do well on the big math test? When Jesus preached on the hillside (Read about it in The Sermon on the Mount, p. 1280), he talked about worry. God wants us to stop worrying. Why? Because God promises to take care of us each day. That doesn't mean that bad things will never happen to you. It means that when they do, you will know that God cares about them and that you can talk to him about whatever happens.

Got some major worries? Connect here to find out how to be worry-free:

A Major Problem, Genesis 15:6, p. 20

God's Pep Talk, Joshua 1:5–9, p. 276

Listen Up!, 1 Kings 19:11–13, p. 467

Future Hope, Joel 3:17–21, p. 1191

Blessed Are the Weak?, 2 Corinthians 12:7–10, p. 1582

A Soldier's Story, 2 Timothy 2:3, p. 1653

food in barns, but your heavenly Father
feeds them. And you know that you are
worth much more than the birds. 27You
cannot add any time to your life by worrying about it.
28"And why do you worry about
clothes? Look at how the lilies in the field
grow. They don't work or make clothes
for themselves. 29But I tell you that even
Solomon with his riches was not dressed
as beautifully as one of these flowers.
30God clothes the grass in the field,
which is alive today but tomorrow is
thrown into the fire. So you can be even
more sure that God will clothe you. Don't
have so little faith! 31Don't worry and
say, 'What will we eat?' or 'What will we
drink?' or 'What will we wear?' 32The
people who don't know God keep trying
to get these things, and your Father in
heaven knows you need them. 33The
thing you should want most is God's
kingdom and doing what God wants.
Then all these other things you need will
be given to you. 34So don't worry about
tomorrow, because tomorrow will have
its own worries. Each day has enough
trouble of its own.

Be Careful About Judging Others

7 "Don't judge other people, or you will
be judged. 2You will be judged in the
same way that you judge others, and the
amount you give to others will be given
to you.
3"Why do you notice the little piece of
dust in your friend's eye, but you don't notice the big piece of wood in your own eye?
4How can you say to your friend,
'Let me take that little piece of dust out of your eye'? Look at yourself! You still have that big piece of wood in your own
eye. 5You hypocrite!
First, take the wood out of your own eye.
Then you will see clearly to take the dust
out of your friend's eye.
6"Don't give holy things to dogs, and
don't throw your pearls before pigs. Pigs
will only trample on them, and dogs will
turn to attack you.

eMAIL! FROM GOD

7:3–5

Decisions

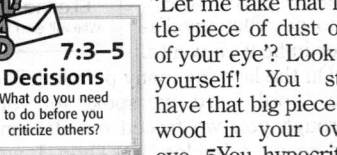

What do you need to do before you criticize others?

Ask God for What You Need

7"Ask, and God will give to you.
Search, and you will find. Knock, and the

THE VERDICT IS IN? 

MATTHEW 7:1-2

"You're a loser!" Have you ever heard words like that? Have you ever said words like that? Many times, we find it easy to make a judgment about someone. We're not always right in our opinions about a person.

Jesus warns us not to judge others. Judging others means seeing something bad in another person. When we judge others, we will be judged. Jesus said that because he knows that we're not God. We don't have God's perfect judgment. So the next time you're tempted to judge someone, keep this word in mind: DON'T.

Download these Faithlinks to find out more about caring for others:

Family Feud, Genesis 27, p. 37

A Special Promise, Numbers 30:1–2, p. 217

Care for the Lost, Deuteronomy 22:1–3, p. 255

A Gentle Answer, Proverbs 15:1, p. 847

You Are What You Do, Proverbs 20:11, p. 854

Ya' Gotta Love It?, 1 John 2:15, p. 1715

door will open for you. **8**Yes, everyone who asks will receive. Everyone who searches will find. And everyone who knocks will have the door opened.

9"If your children ask for bread, which of you would give them a stone? **10**Or if your children ask for a fish, would you give them a snake? **11**Even though you are bad, you know how to give good gifts to your children. How much more your heavenly Father will give good things to those who ask him!

The Most Important Rule

12"Do to others what you want them to do to you. This is the meaning of the law of Moses and the teaching of the prophets.

The Way to Heaven Is Hard

13"Enter through the narrow gate. The gate is wide and the road is wide that leads to hell, and many people enter through that gate. **14**But the gate is small and the road is narrow that leads to true life. Only a few people find that road.

People Know You by Your Actions

15"Be careful of false prophets. They come to you looking gentle like sheep, but they are really dangerous like wolves. **16**You will know these people by what they do. Grapes don't come from thornbushes, and figs don't come from thorny weeds. **17**In the same way, every good tree produces good fruit, but a bad tree produces bad fruit. **18**A good tree cannot produce bad fruit, and a bad tree cannot produce good fruit. **19**Every tree that does not produce good fruit is cut down and thrown into the fire. **20**In the same way, you will know these false prophets by what they do.

21"Not all those who say that I am their Lord will enter the kingdom of heaven. The only people who will enter the kingdom of heaven are those who do what my Father in heaven wants.

EMAIL! FROM GOD
7:21
Eternal Life
Who will enter heaven?

22On the last day many people will say to me, 'Lord, Lord, we spoke for you, and through you we forced out demons and did many miracles.' **23**Then I will tell them clearly, 'Get away from me, you who do evil. I never knew you.'

Two Kinds of People

24"Everyone who hears my words and obeys them is like a wise man who built his house on rock. **25**It rained hard,

FAITH links

ASK, SEARCH, KNOCK

MATTHEW 7:7-10

Have you ever wanted to ask for something, but weren't sure what to ask? Jesus knew that people don't always know what to ask God for. That's why he told his followers to "Ask, search, and knock." This means to keep on asking for what you need.

Does this mean that God will automatically give us what we ask for if we keep asking him? No. God knows what we need. He answers prayer three ways: "Yes," "No," and "Wait." The final decision is always up to him. He just wants us to keep on asking!

Approaching God, Numbers 3:10, p. 180

Who Do You Trust?, Joshua 9, p. 287

Keep On Praying, 1 Samuel 1, p. 354

Plan for Success, 1 Chronicles 14:8–17, p. 538

Think About Him, Isaiah 26:3, p. 926

When We Agree, Matthew 18:19–20, p. 1306

the floods came, and the winds blew and
hit that house. But it did not fall, because
it was built on rock. **26**Everyone who
hears my words and does not obey them
is like a foolish man who built his house
on sand. **27**It rained hard, the floods
came, and the winds blew and hit that
house, and it fell with a big crash."

28When Jesus finished saying these
things, the people were amazed at his
teaching, **29**because he did not teach like
their teachers of the law. He taught like a
person who had authority.

Jesus Heals a Sick Man

8 When Jesus came down from the hill,
great crowds followed him. **2**Then a
man with a skin disease came to Jesus.
The man bowed down before him and
said, "Lord, you can heal me if you will."

3Jesus reached out his hand and
touched the man and said, "I will. Be
healed!" And immediately the man was
healed from his disease. **4**Then Jesus
said to him, "Don't tell anyone about this.
But go and show yourself to the priest[n]
and offer the gift Moses commanded[n] for
people who are made well. This will show
the people what I have done."

Jesus Heals a Soldier's Servant

5When Jesus entered the city of Capernaum, an army officer came to him,
begging for help. **6**The officer said,
"Lord, my servant is at home in bed. He
can't move his body and is in much pain."

7Jesus said to the officer, "I will go
and heal him."

8The officer answered, "Lord, I am
not worthy for you to come into my
house. You only need to command it, and
my servant will be healed. **9**I, too, am a
man under the authority of others, and I
have soldiers under my command. I tell
one soldier, 'Go,' and he goes. I tell another soldier, 'Come,' and he comes. I
say to my servant, 'Do this,' and my servant does it.

10When Jesus heard this, he was
amazed. He said to those who were following him, "I tell you the truth, this is
the greatest faith I have found, even in
Israel. **11**Many people will come from the
east and from the west and will sit and eat
with Abraham, Isaac, and Jacob in the
kingdom of heaven. **12**But those people
who should be in
the kingdom will be
thrown outside into
the darkness, where
people will cry and
grind their teeth
with pain."

EMAIL FROM GOD
8:12
Hell
What will the people in hell be doing?

13Then Jesus said to the officer, "Go
home. Your servant will be healed just as
you believed he would." And his servant
was healed that same hour.

Jesus Heals Many People

14When Jesus went to Peter's house,
he saw that Peter's mother-in-law was
sick in bed with a fever. **15**Jesus touched
her hand, and the fever left her. Then she
stood up and began to serve Jesus.

16That evening people brought to
Jesus many who had demons. Jesus
spoke and the demons left them, and he
healed all the sick. **17**He did these things
to bring about what Isaiah the prophet
had said:

"He took our suffering on him
and carried our diseases." *Isaiah 53:4*

People Want to Follow Jesus

18When Jesus saw the crowd around
him, he told his followers to go to the
other side of the lake. **19**Then a teacher
of the law came to Jesus and said, "Teacher, I will follow you any place you go."

20Jesus said to him, "The foxes have
holes to live in, and the birds have nests,
but the Son of Man has no place to rest
his head."

21Another man, one of Jesus' followers, said to him, "Lord, first let me go and
bury my father."

22But Jesus told him, "Follow me, and
let the people who are dead bury their
own dead."

8:4 show . . . priest The Law of Moses said a priest must say when a Jewish person with a skin disease was well.

8:4 Moses commanded Read about this in Leviticus 14:1-32.

Jesus Calms a Storm

23Jesus got into a boat, and his followers went with him. 24A great storm arose
on the lake so that waves covered the
boat, but Jesus was sleeping. 25His followers went to him and woke him, saying, "Lord, save us! We will drown!"
26Jesus answered, "Why are you
afraid? You don't have enough faith."
Then Jesus got up and gave a command
to the wind and the waves, and it became
completely calm.
27The men were amazed and said,
"What kind of man is this? Even the wind
and the waves obey him!"

Jesus Heals Two Men with Demons

28When Jesus arrived at the other
side of the lake in the area of the Gadarene[n] people, two men who had demons
in them met him. These men lived in the
burial caves and were so dangerous that
people could not use the road by those
caves. 29They shouted, "What do you
want with us, Son of God? Did you come
here to torture us before the right time?"
30Near that place there was a large
herd of pigs feeding. 31The demons
begged Jesus, "If you make us leave
these men, please send us into that herd
of pigs."
32Jesus said to them, "Go!" So the
demons left the men and went into the
pigs. Then the whole herd rushed down
the hill into the lake and were drowned.
33The herdsmen ran away and went into
town, where they told about all of this
and what had happened to the men who
had demons. 34Then the whole town
went out to see Jesus. When they saw
him, they begged him to leave their area.

Jesus Heals a Paralyzed Man

9 Jesus got into a boat and went back
across the lake to his own town.
2Some people brought to Jesus a man
who was paralyzed and lying on a mat.
When Jesus saw the faith of these people,
he said to the paralyzed man, "Be encouraged, young man. Your sins are forgiven."
3Some of the teachers of the law said

FACING YOUR FEARS

MATTHEW 8:23-27

Suppose you were in a small boat in the middle of a large lake. Now suppose you faced the worst storm you've ever seen. How would you feel? Jesus' followers were used to fishing on Lake Galilee. But a sudden huge storm terrified them. Where was Jesus when this happened? In the boat, asleep! After his followers expressed their fears, Jesus stopped the storm.

Jesus will help you with any fear that you may have. When you are afraid, don't be afraid to tell him all about it. He can handle any "storm" your life can dish out.

Jesus can chase those fears away! Check it out:

The Rainbow Promise, Genesis 9:1–17, p. 14

Moses' Champion, Numbers 12, p. 192

A Really Bad Day, Job 1:20–22; 2:10, p. 661

Go for the Gold, Job 23:10, p. 685

The Unpopular Choice, Mark 15:42–43, p. 1360

Keep On Keepin' On, Revelation 13:10, p. 1744

8:28 **Gadarene** From Gadara, an area southeast of Lake Galilee.

JUST SAY YES!

MATTHEW 9:9-13

Imagine Jesus coming up to you on the school playground and asking you to work with him. What would you say? Jesus often did that in the Bible. He approached people where they were working and living and asked them to come and work with him.

Jesus didn't look for those people who were rich or important. He looked for people who would be faithful to him. When you are asked to do something for Jesus, you should always be ready to respond and help. A willing heart that is ready to work for Jesus is very pleasing to him.

The Sacrifice, Genesis 22, p. 29

Play Fair or Play Favorites?, Deuteronomy 1:16–18, p. 227

Peace in the Family, Psalm 133, p. 811

Best Seat in the House, Luke 14:7–11, p. 1398

Glad to Help!, Romans 15:17–20, p. 1541

Hot, Cold, or In Between?, Revelation 3:15, p. 1735

to themselves, "This man speaks as if he
were God. That is blasphemy!"[n]
4Knowing their thoughts, Jesus said,
"Why are you thinking evil thoughts?
5Which is easier: to say, 'Your sins are
forgiven,' or to tell him, 'Stand up and
walk'? 6But I will prove to you that the
Son of Man has authority on earth to forgive sins." Then Jesus said to the paralyzed man, "Stand up, take your mat, and
go home." 7And the man stood up and
went home. 8When the people saw this,
they were amazed and praised God for
giving power like this to human beings.

Jesus Chooses Matthew

9When Jesus was leaving, he saw a
man named Matthew sitting in the tax
collector's booth. Jesus said to him, "Follow me," and he stood up and followed
Jesus.
10As Jesus was having dinner at
Matthew's house, many tax collectors
and "sinners" came and ate with Jesus
and his followers. 11When the Pharisees
saw this, they asked Jesus' followers,
"Why does your teacher eat with tax collectors and sinners?"
12When Jesus heard them, he said, "It
is not the healthy people who need a doctor, but the sick. 13Go and learn what this
means: 'I want kindness more than I
want animal sacrifices.'[n] I did not come to
invite good people but to invite sinners."

Jesus' Followers Are Criticized

14Then the followers of John[n] came to
Jesus and said, "Why do we and the Pharisees often give up eating for a certain
time,[n] but your followers don't?"
15Jesus answered, "The friends of the
bridegroom are not sad while he is with
them. But the time will come when the
bridegroom will be taken from them, and
then they will give up eating.
16"No one sews a patch of unshrunk
cloth over a hole in an old coat. If he does,
the patch will shrink and pull away from

9:3 blasphemy Saying things against God or not showing respect for God.
9:13 'I want . . . sacrifices.' Quotation from Hosea 6:6.
9:14 John John the Baptist, who preached to people about Christ's coming (Matthew 3, Luke 3).
9:14 give up . . . time This is called "fasting." The people would give up eating for a special time of prayer and worship to God. It was also done to show sadness and disappointment.

the coat, making the hole worse. 17Also,
people never pour new wine into old
leather bags. Otherwise, the bags will
break, the wine will spill, and the wine
bags will be ruined. But people always
pour new wine into new wine bags. Then
both will continue to be good."

Jesus Gives Life to a Dead Girl and Heals a Sick Woman

18While Jesus was saying these
things, a leader of the synagogue came to
him. He bowed down before Jesus and
said, "My daughter has just died. But if
you come and lay your hand on her, she
will live again." 19So Jesus and his followers stood up and went with the leader.
20Then a woman who had been bleeding for twelve years came behind Jesus
and touched the edge of his coat. 21She
was thinking, "If I can just touch his
clothes, I will be healed."
22Jesus turned and saw the woman
and said, "Be encouraged, dear woman.
You are made well because you believed." And the woman was healed from
that moment on.
23Jesus continued along with the
leader and went into his house. There he
saw the funeral musicians and many people crying. 24Jesus said, "Go away. The
girl is not dead, only asleep." But the
people laughed at him. 25After the crowd
had been thrown out of the house, Jesus
went into the girl's room and took hold of
her hand, and she stood up. 26The news
about this spread all around the area.

Jesus Heals More People

27When Jesus was leaving there, two
blind men followed him. They cried out,
"Have mercy on us, Son of David!"
28After Jesus went inside, the blind
men went with him. He asked the men,
"Do you believe that I can make you see
again?"

They answered, "Yes, Lord."
29Then Jesus touched their eyes and
said, "Because you believe I can make
you see again, it will happen." 30Then
the men were able to see. But Jesus
warned them strongly, saying, "Don't tell
anyone about this." 31But the blind men
left and spread the news about Jesus all
around that area.
32When the two men were leaving,
some people brought another man to
Jesus. This man could not talk because

FAITH links

KINDNESS FIRST

MATTHEW 9:35-36

When you approach a crowd of kids at the park or in the hall at school, what's the first thing you think of? Are you thinking about the kid you want to avoid because he made fun of you the other day? Or why that girl doesn't dress nicer? Jesus' first thought was usually a kind one. He could not move through a crowd without helping someone.

Can you think of someone who could use a kind word or a kind act? Let Jesus' example inspire you to move out in kindness.

Connect to these other links on being the "kind" of kid that pleases God:

Fairness for All, Deuteronomy 24:17, p. 258

Helpful Advice, Job 12:4–5, p. 673

The Problem with Gossip, Proverbs 11:12–13, p. 840

Jesus' Mission and Yours, Isaiah 61:1–2, p. 978

Love Him? Show It!, Amos 2:6–7, p. 1196

Welcome!, Matthew 19:13–15, p. 1307

THE CHOSEN DOZEN — Matthew 10:1–29

Jesus chose 12 men to work closely with him in his ministry. Some people think he picked 12 because that's how many tribes there were in Israel. Jesus had many more people that helped him in his ministry, but these 12 were his inner circle. Of his 12 followers, 3 were Jesus' closest friends: Peter, James, and John.

These 12 men are sometimes called "followers" and sometimes called "apostles." A follower is a person who is learning from someone else. An apostle is someone with a special message or commission. (Check out John 13:16, p. 1447.) These men were both. They followed Jesus and learned from him. Then when he was gone, they carried on his work. The 12 were Simon Peter, Andrew, James the son of Zebedee, John, Philip, Bartholomew, Matthew, Thomas, Simon, James the son of Alphaeus, Thaddaeus, and Judas, who betrayed Jesus. (See Matthew 10:1–4.) Matthias was chosen by the apostles to replace Judas after Jesus left earth and went back to heaven. (Read Acts 1:26, p. 1464.)

he had a demon in him.
33After Jesus forced the demon to leave the man, he was able to speak. The crowd was amazed and said, "We have never seen anything like this in Israel."

34But the Pharisees said, "The prince of demons is the one that gives him power to force demons out."

35Jesus traveled through all the towns and villages, teaching in their synagogues, preaching the Good News about the kingdom, and healing all kinds of diseases and sicknesses.
36When he saw the crowds, he felt sorry for them because they were hurting and helpless, like sheep without a shepherd.
37Jesus said to his followers, "There are many people to harvest but only a few workers to help harvest them.
38Pray to the Lord, who owns the harvest, that he will send more workers to gather his harvest."[n]

Jesus Sends Out His Apostles

10 Jesus called his twelve followers together and gave them authority to drive out evil spirits and to heal every kind of disease and sickness.
2These are the names of the twelve apostles: Simon (also called Peter) and his brother Andrew; James son of Zebedee, and his brother John;
3Philip and Bartholomew; Thomas and Matthew, the tax collector; James son of Alphaeus, and Thaddaeus;
4Simon the Zealot and Judas Iscariot, who turned against Jesus.

5Jesus sent out these twelve men with the following order: "Don't go to the non-Jewish people or to any town where the Samaritans live.
6But go to the people of Israel, who are like lost sheep.
7When you go, preach this: 'The kingdom of heaven is near.'
8Heal the sick, raise the dead to life again, heal those who have skin diseases, and force demons out of people. I give you these powers freely, so help other people freely.

9:37-38 "There are . . . harvest." As a farmer sends workers to harvest the grain, Jesus sends his followers to bring people to God.

9Don't carry any money with you—gold
or silver or copper. 10Don't carry a bag or
extra clothes or sandals or a walking
stick. Workers should be given what they
need.

11"When you enter a city or town,
find some worthy person there and stay
in that home until you leave. 12When you
enter that home, say, 'Peace be with you.'
13If the people there welcome you, let
your peace stay there. But if they don't
welcome you, take back the peace you
wished for them. 14And if a home or town
refuses to welcome you or listen to you,
leave that place and shake its dust off
your feet." 15I tell you the truth, on the
Judgment Day it will be better for the
towns of Sodom and Gomorrah" than for
the people of that town.

Jesus Warns His Apostles

16"Listen, I am sending you out like
sheep among wolves. So be as smart as
snakes and as innocent as doves. 17Be
careful of people, because they will arrest
you and take you to court and whip you in
their synagogues. 18Because of me you
will be taken to stand before governors
and kings, and you will tell them and the
non-Jewish people about me. 19When
you are arrested, don't worry about what
to say or how to say it. At that time you
will be given the things to say. 20It will
not really be you speaking but the Spirit
of your Father speaking through you.

21"Brothers will give their own
brothers to be killed, and fathers will give
their own children to be killed. Children
will fight against their own parents and
have them put to death. 22All people will
hate you because you follow me, but
those people who
keep their faith until
the end will be
saved. 23When you
are treated badly in
one city, run to another
city. I tell you
the truth, you will not finish going
through all the cities of Israel before the
Son of Man comes.

eMAIL! FROM GOD
10:22
Perseverance
What will you get for keeping on despite rejection?

24"A student is not better than his
teacher, and a servant is not better than
his master. 25A student should be satisfied
to become like his teacher; a servant
should be satisfied to become like his
master. If the head of the family is called
Beelzebul, then the other members of
the family will be called worse names!

Fear God, Not People

26"So don't be afraid of those people,
because everything that is hidden will be
shown. Everything that is secret will be
made known. 27I tell you these things
in the dark, but I want you to tell them in
the light. What you hear whispered in
your ear you should shout from the
housetops. 28Don't be afraid of people,
who can kill the body but cannot kill the
soul. The only one you should fear is the
one who can destroy the soul and the body
in hell. 29Two sparrows cost only a penny,
but not even one of them can die without
your Father's knowing it. 30God even
knows how many hairs are on your head.
31So don't be afraid. You are worth much
more than many sparrows.

Tell People About Your Faith

32"All those who stand before others
and say they believe in me, I will say before
my Father in heaven that they belong
to me. 33But all who stand before
others and say they do not believe in me,
I will say before my Father in heaven that
they do not belong to me.

34"Don't think that I came to bring
peace to the earth. I did not come to bring
peace, but a sword. 35I have come so that

'a son will be against his father,
a daughter will be against her
mother,
a daughter-in-law will be against her
mother-in-law.
36 A person's enemies will be
members of his own family.'

Micah 7:6

37"Those who love their father or
mother more than they love me are not
worthy to be my followers. Those who

10:14 shake . . . feet. A warning. It showed that they had rejected these people.

10:15 Sodom and Gomorrah Two cities that God destroyed because the people were so evil.

love their son or daughter more than
they love me are not worthy to be my followers. **38**Whoever is not willing to carry
the cross and follow me is not worthy of
me. **39**Those who try to hold on to their
lives will give up true life. Those who
give up their lives for me will hold on to
true life. **40**Whoever accepts you also accepts me, and whoever accepts me also
accepts the One who sent me. **41**Whoever meets a prophet and accepts him
will receive the reward of a prophet. And
whoever accepts a good person because
that person is good will receive the reward of a good person. **42**Those who give
one of these little ones a cup of cold water because they are my followers will
truly get their reward."

Jesus and John the Baptist

11 After Jesus finished telling these
things to his twelve followers, he
left there and went to the towns in Galilee to teach and preach.

2John the Baptist was in prison, but
he heard about what Christ was doing. So
John sent some of his followers to Jesus.
3They asked him, "Are you the One who
is to come, or should we wait for someone else?"

4Jesus answered them, "Go tell John
what you hear and see: **5**The blind can
see, the crippled can walk, and people
with skin diseases are healed. The deaf
can hear, the dead are raised to life, and
the Good News is preached to the poor.
6Those who do not stumble in their faith
because of me are blessed."

7As John's followers were leaving,
Jesus began talking to the people about
John. Jesus said, "What did you go out
into the desert to see? A reed[n] blown by
the wind? **8**What did you go out to see? A
man dressed in fine clothes? No, those
who wear fine clothes live in kings' palaces. **9**So why did you go out? To see a
prophet? Yes, and I tell you, John is more
than a prophet. **10**This was written about
him:

'I will send my messenger ahead of
you,
who will prepare the way for you.'

Malachi 3:1

11I tell you the truth, John the Baptist is
greater than any other person ever born,
but even the least important person in the
kingdom of heaven is greater than John.
12Since the time John the Baptist came
until now, the kingdom of heaven has
been going forward in strength, and people have been trying to take it by force.
13All the prophets and the law of Moses
told about what would happen until the
time John came. **14**And if you will believe
what they said, you will believe that John
is Elijah, whom they said would come.
15You people who can hear me, listen!

16"What can I say about the people of
this time? What are they like? They are
like children sitting in the marketplace,
who call out to each other,

17'We played music for you, but you did
not dance;
we sang a sad song, but you did not
cry.'

18John came and did not eat or drink like
other people. So people say, 'He has a demon.' **19**The Son of Man came, eating
and drinking, and people say, 'Look at
him! He eats too much and drinks too
much wine, and he is a friend of tax collectors and sinners.' But wisdom is
proved to be right by what it does."

Jesus Warns Unbelievers

20Then Jesus criticized the cities
where he did most of his miracles, because the people did not change their
lives and stop sinning. **21**He said, "How
terrible for you, Korazin! How terrible
for you, Bethsaida! If the same miracles I
did in you had happened in Tyre and
Sidon,[n] those people would have changed
their lives a long time ago. They would
have worn rough cloth and put ashes on
themselves to show they had changed.
22But I tell you, on the Judgment Day it
will be better for Tyre and Sidon than for
you. **23**And you, Capernaum,[n] will you be

11:7 reed It means that John was not ordinary or weak like grass blown by the wind.

11:21 Tyre and Sidon Towns where wicked people lived.

11:21, 23 Korazin . . . Bethsaida . . . Capernaum Towns by Lake Galilee where Jesus preached to the people.

lifted up to heaven? No, you will be thrown down to the depths. If the miracles I did in you had happened in Sodom,[n] its people would have stopped sinning, and it would still be a city today. 24But I tell you, on the Judgment Day it will be better for Sodom than for you."

Jesus Offers Rest to People

25At that time Jesus said, "I praise you, Father, Lord of heaven and earth, because you have hidden these things from the people who are wise and smart. But you have shown them to those who are like little children. 26Yes, Father, this is what you really wanted.

27"My Father has given me all things. No one knows the Son, except the Father. And no one knows the Father, except the Son and those whom the Son chooses to tell.

28"Come to me, all of you who are tired and have heavy loads, and I will give you rest. 29Accept my teachings and learn from me, because I am gentle and humble in spirit, and you will find rest for your lives. 30The teaching that I ask you to accept is easy; the load I give you to carry is light."

EMAIL! FROM GOD
11:30
Troubles
How can Jesus help with your problems?

Jesus Is Lord of the Sabbath

12 At that time Jesus was walking through some fields of grain on a Sabbath day. His followers were hungry, so they began to pick the grain and eat it. 2When the Pharisees saw this, they said to Jesus, "Look! Your followers are doing what is unlawful to do on the Sabbath day."

3Jesus answered, "Have you not read what David did when he and the people with him were hungry? 4He went into God's house, and he and those with him ate the holy bread, which was lawful only for priests to eat. 5And have you not read in the law of Moses that on every Sabbath day the priests in the Temple break this law about the Sabbath day? But the priests are not wrong for doing that. 6I tell you that there is something here that is greater than the Temple. 7The Scripture says, 'I want kindness more than I want animal sacrifices.'[n] You don't really know what those words mean. If you understood them, you would not judge those who have done nothing wrong.

8"So the Son of Man is Lord of the Sabbath day."

Jesus Heals a Man's Hand

9Jesus left there and went into their synagogue, 10where there was a man with a crippled hand. They were looking for a reason to accuse Jesus, so they asked him, "Is it right to heal on the Sabbath day?"[n]

11Jesus answered, "If any of you has a sheep, and it falls into a ditch on the Sabbath day, you will help it out of the ditch. 12Surely a human being is more important than a sheep. So it is lawful to do good things on the Sabbath day."

13Then Jesus said to the man with the crippled hand, "Hold out your hand." The man held out his hand, and it became well again, like the other hand. 14But the Pharisees left and made plans to kill Jesus.

Jesus Is God's Chosen Servant

15Jesus knew what the Pharisees were doing, so he left that place. Many people followed him, and he healed all who were sick. 16But Jesus warned the people not to tell who he was. 17He did these things to bring about what Isaiah the prophet had said:

18"Here is my servant whom I have
chosen.
I love him, and I am pleased with
him.
I will put my Spirit upon him,
and he will tell of my justice to all
people.
19He will not argue or cry out;
no one will hear his voice in the
streets.

11:23 Sodom A city that God destroyed because the people were so evil.
12:7 'I . . . sacrifices.' Quotation from Hosea 6:6.
12:10 "Is it right . . . day?" It was against Jewish Law to work on the Sabbath day.

20 He will not break a crushed blade of
grass
or put out even a weak flame
until he makes justice win the victory.
21 In him will the non-Jewish people
find hope." *Isaiah 42:1-4*

Jesus' Power Is from God

22Then some people brought to Jesus
a man who was blind and could not talk,
because he had a demon. Jesus healed
the man so that he could talk and see.
23All the people were amazed and said,
"Perhaps this man is the Son of David!"
24When the Pharisees heard this,
they said, "Jesus uses the power of
Beelzebul, the ruler of demons, to force
demons out of people."
25Jesus knew what the Pharisees
were thinking, so he said to them,
"Every kingdom that is divided against
itself will be destroyed. And any city or
family that is divided against itself will
not continue. **26**And if Satan forces out
himself, then Satan is divided against
himself, and his kingdom will not continue. **27**You say that I use the power of
Beelzebul to force out demons. If that is
true, then what power do your people use
to force out demons? So they will be your
judges. **28**But if I use the power of God's
Spirit to force out demons, then the kingdom of God has come to you.
29"If anyone wants to enter a strong
person's house and steal his things, he
must first tie up the strong person. Then
he can steal the things from the house.
30"Whoever is not with me is against
me. Whoever does not work with me is
working against me. **31**So I tell you, people can be forgiven for every sin and everything they say against God. But
whoever speaks against the Holy Spirit
will not be forgiven. **32**Anyone who
speaks against the Son of Man can be forgiven, but anyone who speaks against the
Holy Spirit will not be forgiven, now or in
the future.

People Know You by Your Words

33"If you want good fruit, you must
make the tree good. If your tree is not
good, it will have bad fruit. A tree is
known by the kind of fruit it produces.
34You snakes! You are evil people, so
how can you say anything good? The
mouth speaks the things that are in the
heart. **35**Good people have good things in
their hearts, and so they say good things.
But evil people have evil in their hearts,
so they say evil things. **36**And I tell you
that on the Judgment Day people will be

FAITH links

YOUR CHOICE OF FRUIT

MATTHEW 12:33-35

Would you expect a fruit tree that has been lovingly cared for to produce rotten fruit? Probably not, right? A good tree produces good fruit. A bad tree . . . well, you get the idea. Jesus used that story to talk about our words. A heart full of love will cause a person to say kind and loving things. A heart full of hate or evil will cause a person to say mean and hateful things. Anyone who hangs around you will know the kind of "tree" you are. So, what kind of fruit are you producing?

Who Do You Prefer?, Proverbs 3:32, p. 830

The Right Ingredients, Micah 6:8, p. 1227

How Do I Love You?, Malachi 1:1–5, p. 1267

Welcome!, Matthew 19:13–15, p. 1307

Who Needs Love?, Luke 6:27–36, p. 1379

Full of Faith, 1 Thessalonians 4:1, p. 1633

eMAIL! FROM GOD
12:36
Judgment
Will God judge the words you speak?

responsible for every careless thing they have said. **37**The words you have said will be used to judge you. Some of your words will prove you right, but some of your words will prove you guilty."

The People Ask for a Miracle

38Then some of the Pharisees and teachers of the law answered Jesus, saying, "Teacher, we want to see you work a miracle as a sign."

39Jesus answered, "Evil and sinful people are the ones who want to see a miracle for a sign. But no sign will be given to them, except the sign of the prophet Jonah. **40**Jonah was in the stomach of the big fish for three days and three nights. In the same way, the Son of Man will be in the grave three days and three nights. **41**On the Judgment Day the people from Nineveh[n] will stand up with you people who live now, and they will show that you are guilty. When Jonah preached to them, they were sorry and changed their lives. And I tell you that someone greater than Jonah is here. **42**On the Judgment Day, the Queen of the South[n] will stand up with you people who live today. She will show that you are guilty, because she came from far away to listen to Solomon's wise teaching. And I tell you that someone greater than Solomon is here.

People Today Are Full of Evil

43"When an evil spirit comes out of a person, it travels through dry places, looking for a place to rest, but it doesn't find it. **44**So the spirit says, 'I will go back to the house I left.' When the spirit comes back, it finds the house still empty, swept clean, and made neat. **45**Then the evil spirit goes out and brings seven other spirits even more evil than it is, and they go in and live there. So the person has even more trouble than before. It is the same way with the evil people who live today."

Jesus' True Family

46While Jesus was talking to the people, his mother and brothers stood outside, trying to find a way to talk to him. **47**Someone told Jesus, "Your mother and brothers are standing outside, and they want to talk to you."

48He answered, "Who is my mother? Who are my brothers?" **49**Then he pointed to his followers and said, "Here are my mother and my brothers. **50**My true brother and sister and mother are those who do what my Father in heaven wants."

eMAIL! FROM GOD
12:50
God's Family
Who are Jesus' true siblings?

A Story About Planting Seed

13 That same day Jesus went out of the house and sat by the lake. **2**Large crowds gathered around him, so he got into a boat and sat down, while the people stood on the shore. **3**Then Jesus used stories to teach them many things. He said: "A farmer went out to plant his seed. **4**While he was planting, some seed fell by the road, and the birds came and ate it all up. **5**Some seed fell on rocky ground, where there wasn't much dirt. That seed grew very fast, because the ground was not deep. **6**But when the sun rose, the plants dried up, because they did not have deep roots. **7**Some other seed fell among thorny weeds, which grew and choked the good plants. **8**Some other seed fell on good ground where it grew and produced a crop. Some plants made a hundred times more, some made sixty times more, and some made thirty times more. **9**You people who can hear me, listen."

Why Jesus Used Stories to Teach

10The followers came to Jesus and asked, "Why do you use stories to teach the people?"

12:41 Nineveh The city where Jonah preached to warn the people. Read Jonah 3.

12:42 Queen of the South The Queen of Sheba. She traveled a thousand miles to learn God's wisdom from Solomon. Read 1 Kings 10:1-13.

11Jesus answered, "You have been
chosen to know the secrets about the
kingdom of heaven, but others cannot
know these secrets. **12**Those who have
understanding will be given more, and
they will have all they need. But those
who do not have understanding, even
what they have will be taken away from
them. **13**This is why I use stories to
teach the people: They see, but they
don't really see. They hear, but they don't
really hear or understand. **14**So they
show that the things Isaiah said about
them are true:

'You will listen and listen, but you
will not understand.
You will look and look, but you will
not learn.
15 For the minds of these people have
become stubborn.
They do not hear with their ears,
and they have closed their eyes.
Otherwise they might really
understand
what they see with their eyes
and hear with their ears.
They might really understand in their
minds
and come back to me and be
healed.' *Isaiah 6:9-10*

16But you are blessed, because you see
with your eyes and hear with your ears.
17I tell you the truth, many prophets and
good people wanted to see the things that
you now see, but they did not see them.
And they wanted to hear the things that
you now hear, but they did not hear them.

Jesus Explains the Seed Story

18"So listen to the meaning of that
story about the farmer. **19**What is the
seed that fell by the road? That seed is
like the person who hears the message
about the kingdom but does not understand it. The Evil One comes and takes
away what was planted in that person's
heart. **20**And what is the seed that fell on
rocky ground? That seed is like the person who hears the teaching and quickly
accepts it with joy. **21**But he does not let
the teaching go deep into his life, so he
keeps it only a short time. When trouble
or persecution comes because of the
teaching he accepted, he quickly gives
up. **22**And what is the seed that fell
among the thorny weeds? That seed is
like the person who hears the teaching
but lets worries about this life and the
temptation of wealth stop that teaching
from growing. So the teaching does not
produce fruit[n] in that person's life. **23**But
what is the seed that fell on the good
ground? That seed is
like the person who
hears the teaching
and understands it.
That person grows
and produces fruit,
sometimes a hun-
dred times more, sometimes sixty times
more, and sometimes thirty times more."

EMAIL! FROM GOD
13:23
Witnessing
Find out how some hear God's word.

A Story About Wheat and Weeds

24Then Jesus told them another
story: "The kingdom of heaven is like a
man who planted good seed in his field.
25That night, when everyone was asleep,
his enemy came and planted weeds
among the wheat and then left. **26**Later,
the wheat sprouted and the heads of
grain grew, but the weeds also grew.
27Then the man's servants came to him
and said, 'You planted good seed in your
field. Where did the weeds come from?'
28The man answered, 'An enemy planted
weeds.' The servants asked, 'Do you
want us to pull up the weeds?' **29**The
man answered, 'No, because when you
pull up the weeds, you might also pull up
the wheat. **30**Let the weeds and the
wheat grow together until the harvest
time. At harvest time I will tell the workers, "First gather the weeds and tie them
together to be burned. Then gather the
wheat and bring it to my barn."'"

Stories of Mustard Seed and Yeast

31Then Jesus told another story:
"The kingdom of heaven is like a mustard
seed that a man planted in his field.
32That seed is the smallest of all seeds,
but when it grows, it is one of the largest

13:22 produce fruit To produce fruit means to have in your life the good things God wants.

garden plants. It becomes big enough for
the wild birds to come and build nests in
its branches."
33Then Jesus told another story:
"The kingdom of heaven is like yeast that
a woman took and hid in a large tub of
flour until it made all the dough rise."
34Jesus used stories to tell all these
things to the people; he always used stories to teach them. **35**This is as the
prophet said:

"I will speak using stories;
I will tell things that have been
secret since the world was
made." *Psalm 78:2*

Jesus Explains About the Weeds

36Then Jesus left the crowd and went
into the house. His followers came to him
and said, "Explain to us the meaning of
the story about the weeds in the field."
37Jesus answered, "The man who
planted the good seed in the field is the
Son of Man. **38**The field is the world, and
the good seed are all of God's children
who belong to the kingdom. The weeds
are those people who belong to the Evil
One. **39**And the enemy who planted the
bad seed is the devil. The harvest time is
the end of the world, and the workers
who gather are God's angels.
40"Just as the weeds are pulled up
and burned in the fire, so it will be at the
end of the world. **41**The Son of Man will
send out his angels, and they will gather
out of his kingdom all who cause sin and
all who do evil. **42**The angels will throw
them into the blazing furnace, where the
people will cry and grind their teeth with
pain. **43**Then the good people will shine
like the sun in the kingdom of their
Father. You people who can hear me,
listen.

Stories of a Treasure and a Pearl

44"The kingdom of heaven is like a
treasure hidden in a field. One day a man
found the treasure, and then he hid it in
the field again. He was so happy that he
went and sold everything he owned to
buy that field.
45"Also, the kingdom of heaven is like
a man looking for fine pearls. **46**When he
found a very valuable pearl, he went and
sold everything he had and bought it.

A Story of a Fishing Net

47"Also, the kingdom of heaven is like
a net that was put into the lake and
caught many different kinds of fish.
48When it was full, the fishermen pulled
the net to the shore. They sat down and
put all the good fish in baskets and threw
away the bad fish. **49**It will be this way at
the end of the world. The angels will
come and separate the evil people from
the good people. **50**The angels will throw
the evil people into the blazing furnace,
where people will cry and grind their
teeth with pain."
51Jesus asked his followers, "Do you
understand all these things?"
They answered, "Yes, we understand."
52Then Jesus said to them, "So every
teacher of the law who has been taught
about the kingdom of heaven is like the
owner of a house. He brings out both new
things and old things he has saved."

Jesus Goes to His Hometown

53When Jesus finished teaching with
these stories, he left there. **54**He went to
his hometown and taught the people in
the synagogue, and they were amazed.
They said, "Where did this man get this
wisdom and this power to do miracles?
55He is just the son of a carpenter. His
mother is Mary, and his brothers are
James, Joseph, Simon, and Judas. **56**And
all his sisters are here with us. Where
then does this man get all these things?"
57So the people were upset with Jesus.
But Jesus said to them, "A prophet is
honored everywhere except in his hometown and in his own home."
58So he did not do many miracles
there because they had no faith.

How John the Baptist Was Killed

14 At that time Herod, the ruler of
Galilee, heard the reports about
Jesus. **2**So he said to his servants, "Jesus
is John the Baptist, who has risen from
the dead. That is why he can work these
miracles."

3Sometime before this, Herod had arrested John, tied him up, and put him into
prison. Herod did this because of Herodias, who had been the wife of Philip,
Herod's brother. **4**John had been telling
Herod, "It is not lawful for you to be married to Herodias." **5**Herod wanted to kill
John, but he was afraid of the people, because they believed John was a prophet.
6On Herod's birthday, the daughter of
Herodias danced for Herod and his
guests, and she pleased him. **7**So he
promised with an oath to give her anything she wanted. **8**Herodias told her
daughter what to ask for, so she said to
Herod, "Give me the head of John the
Baptist here on a platter." **9**Although King
Herod was very sad, he had made a promise, and his dinner guests had heard him.
So Herod ordered that what she asked for
be done. **10**He sent soldiers to the prison
to cut off John's head. **11**And they brought
it on a platter and gave it to the girl, and
she took it to her mother. **12**John's followers came and got his body and buried it.
Then they went and told Jesus.

More than Five Thousand Fed

13When Jesus heard what had happened to John, he left in a boat and went
to a lonely place by himself. But the
crowds heard about it and followed him
on foot from the towns. **14**When he arrived, he saw a great crowd waiting. He
felt sorry for them and healed those who
were sick.
15When it was evening, his followers
came to him and said, "No one lives in
this place, and it is already late. Send the
people away so they can go to the towns
and buy food for themselves."
16But Jesus answered, "They don't
need to go away. You give them something to eat."
17They said to him, "But we have
only five loaves of bread and two fish."
18Jesus said, "Bring the bread and the
fish to me." **19**Then he told the people to
sit down on the grass. He took the five
loaves and the two fish and, looking to
heaven, he thanked God for the food.
Jesus divided the bread and gave it to his
followers, who gave it to the people.
20All the people ate and were satisfied.
Then the followers filled twelve baskets
with the leftover pieces of food. **21**There
were about five thousand men there who
ate, not counting women and children.

FAITH links

SAD TIMES

MATTHEW 14:13-14

Some things in life are hard. One of the hardest things to deal with is when someone you love dies. When Jesus heard that John the Baptist had been killed, he went off by himself for a while. Still the crowds followed him. Even though he probably wanted to be by himself, he took the time to heal the sick and help those around him.

When you lose someone you love, you're going to feel sad. Just know that you have a Savior who understands what you're going through. He is always with you.

Jesus does care when you are feeling sad. Check it out:

A Message of Courage and Hope, 2 Kings 19:4–10, p. 505

Problem Solved, 2 Kings 20:1–11, p. 507

Full Circle, Job 42, p. 706

Remembering Jesus, Matthew 26:26–29, p. 1321

Mission Impossible?, Mark 5:21–24, 35–43, p. 1337

Who Needs Love?, Luke 6:27–36, p. 1379

Jesus Walks on the Water

22Immediately Jesus told his followers to get into the boat and go ahead of
him across the lake. He stayed there to
send the people home. **23**After he had
sent them away, he went by himself up
into the hills to pray. It was late, and
Jesus was there alone. **24**By this time,
the boat was already far away from land.
It was being hit by waves, because the
wind was blowing against it.

25Between three and six o'clock in
the morning, Jesus came to them, walking on the water. **26**When his followers
saw him walking on the water, they were
afraid. They said, "It's a ghost!" and cried
out in fear.

27But Jesus quickly spoke to them,
"Have courage! It is I. Do not be afraid."

28Peter said, "Lord, if it is really you,
then command me to come to you on the
water."

29Jesus said, "Come."

And Peter left the boat and walked on
the water to Jesus. **30**But when Peter
saw the wind and the waves, he became
afraid and began to sink. He shouted,
"Lord, save me!"

31Immediately Jesus reached out his
hand and caught Peter. Jesus said, "Your
faith is small. Why did you doubt?"

32After they got into the boat, the
wind became calm. **33**Then those who
were in the boat worshiped Jesus and
said, "Truly you are the Son of God!"

34When they had crossed the lake,
they came to shore at Gennesaret.
35When the people there recognized
Jesus, they told people all around there
that Jesus had come, and they brought all
their sick to him. **36**They begged Jesus to
let them touch just the edge of his coat,
and all who touched it were healed.

Obey God's Law

15 Then some Pharisees and teachers of the law came to Jesus from
Jerusalem. They asked him, **2**"Why don't
your followers obey the unwritten laws
which have been handed down to us?
They don't wash their hands before they
eat."

3Jesus answered, "And why do you refuse to obey God's command so that you
can follow your own teachings? **4**God
said, 'Honor your father and your
mother,'[n] and 'Anyone who says cruel
things to his father or mother must be put
to death.'[n] **5**But you say a person can tell
his father or mother, 'I have something I
could use to help you, but I have given it
to God already.' **6**You teach that person
not to honor his father or his mother. You
rejected what God said for the sake of
your own rules. **7**You are hypocrites! Isaiah was right when he said about you:

8'These people show honor to me
with words,
but their hearts are far from me.
9Their worship of me is worthless.
The things they teach are nothing
but human rules.' " *Isaiah 29:13*

10After Jesus called the crowd to him,
he said, "Listen and understand what I am
saying. **11**It is not what people put into
their mouths that makes them unclean. It
is what comes out of their mouths that
makes them unclean."

12Then his followers came to him and
asked, "Do you know that the Pharisees
are angry because of what you said?"

13Jesus answered, "Every plant that
my Father in heaven has not planted himself will be pulled up by the roots. **14**Stay
away from the Pharisees; they are blind
leaders. And if a blind person leads a
blind person, both will fall into a ditch."

15Peter said, "Explain the example to
us."

16Jesus said, "Do you still not understand? **17**Surely you know that all the
food that enters the mouth goes into
the stomach and then goes out of the
body. **18**But what people say with their
mouths comes from
the way they think;
these are the things
that make people
unclean. **19**Out of
the mind come evil
thoughts, murder,

eMAIL FROM GOD
15:18
Honesty
Check out what your thoughts and speech should be like.

15:4 'Honor . . . mother.' Quotation from Exodus 20:12; Deuteronomy 5:16.

15:4 'Anyone . . . death.' Quotation from Exodus 21:17.

FAITH CHALLENGE

Here's a challenge for you. Read 15:11 to discover what Jesus has to say about what comes out of our mouths. How do you respond when your friends use bad language or talk about things they shouldn't?

TESTING IT

Matthew 15:11
It is not what people put into their mouths that makes them unclean. It is what comes out of their mouths that makes them unclean.

adultery, sexual sins, stealing, lying, and
speaking evil of others. **20**These things
make people unclean; eating with un-
washed hands does not make them unclean."

Jesus Helps a Non-Jewish Woman

21Jesus left that place and went to the
area of Tyre and Sidon. **22**A Canaanite
woman from that area came to Jesus and
cried out, "Lord, Son of David, have mercy
on me! My daughter has a demon, and she
is suffering very much."
23But Jesus did not answer the woman.
So his followers came to Jesus and
begged him, "Tell the woman to go away.
She is following us and shouting."
24Jesus answered, "God sent me only
to the lost sheep, the people of Israel."
25Then the woman came to Jesus
again and bowed before him and said,
"Lord, help me!"
26Jesus answered, "It is not right to
take the children's bread and give it to
the dogs."
27The woman said, "Yes, Lord, but
even the dogs eat the crumbs that fall
from their masters' table."
28Then Jesus answered, "Woman,
you have great faith! I will do what you
asked." And at that moment the woman's
daughter was healed.

Jesus Heals Many People

29After leaving there, Jesus went
along the shore of Lake Galilee. He went
up on a hill and sat there.
30Great crowds came to Jesus, bringing with them the lame, the blind, the
crippled, those who could not speak, and
many others. They put them at Jesus'
feet, and he healed them. **31**The crowd
was amazed when they saw that people
who could not speak before were now
able to speak. The crippled were made
strong. The lame could walk, and the
blind could see. And they praised the God
of Israel for this.

More than Four Thousand Fed

32Jesus called his followers to him
and said, "I feel sorry for these people,
because they have already been with me
three days, and they have nothing to eat.
I don't want to send them away hungry.
They might faint while going home."
33His followers asked him, "How can
we get enough bread to feed all these
people? We are far away from any town."
34Jesus asked, "How many loaves of
bread do you have?"
They answered, "Seven, and a few
small fish."
35Jesus told the people to sit on the
ground. **36**He took the seven loaves of
bread and the fish and gave thanks to
God. Then he divided the food and gave it

to his followers, and they gave it to the people. **37**All the people ate and were satisfied. Then his followers filled seven baskets with the leftover pieces of food. **38**There were about four thousand men there who ate, besides women and children. **39**After sending the people home, Jesus got into the boat and went to the area of Magadan.

The Leaders Ask for a Miracle

16 The Pharisees and Sadducees came to Jesus, wanting to trick him. So they asked him to show them a miracle from God.

2Jesus answered, "At sunset you say we will have good weather, because the sky is red. **3**And in the morning you say that it will be a rainy day, because the sky is dark and red. You see these signs in the sky and know what they mean. In the same way, you see the things that I am doing now, but you don't know their meaning. **4**Evil and sinful people ask for a miracle as a sign, but they will not be given any sign, except the sign of Jonah."[n] Then Jesus left them and went away.

Guard Against Wrong Teachings

5Jesus' followers went across the lake, but they had forgotten to bring bread. **6**Jesus said to them, "Be careful! Beware of the yeast of the Pharisees and the Sadducees."

7His followers discussed the meaning of this, saying, "He said this because we forgot to bring bread."

8Knowing what they were talking about, Jesus asked them, "Why are you talking about not having bread? Your faith is small. **9**Do you still not understand? Remember the five loaves of bread that fed the five thousand? And remember that you filled many baskets with the leftovers? **10**Or the seven loaves of bread that fed the four thousand and the many baskets you filled then also? **11**I was not talking to you about bread. Why don't you understand that? I am telling you to beware of the yeast of the Pharisees and the Sadducees." **12**Then the followers understood that Jesus was not telling them to beware of the yeast used in bread but to beware of the teaching of the Pharisees and the Sadducees.

FAITH links

PROVE IT!

MATTHEW 16:1-4

Are you the kind of person who has to "see it" to believe it? In Jesus' day, the religious leaders—the Pharisees and the Sadducees—wanted proof that Jesus was who he said he was. They wanted a sign from heaven.

The Bible provides proof that Jesus is the Savior. The Gospels—Matthew, Mark, Luke, and John—provide eyewitness proof that Jesus died for your sins, rose from the dead, returned to heaven, and plans to return to earth someday. That's all the proof you need!

When Bad Turns to Worse, Exodus 5:6–12, p. 82

From Zero to Hero, Judges 6; 7, p. 319

Hurry Up and Wait, 2 Samuel 5, p. 405

On the Wrong Foot, 2 Kings 21:1–2, 16, p. 509

Two Ways to Grow, Luke 2:46–52, p. 1370

Life's Rule Book, 2 Timothy 3:15–17, p. 1655

16:4 sign of Jonah Jonah's three days in the fish are like Jesus' three days in the tomb. The story about Jonah is in the Book of Jonah.

Peter Says Jesus Is the Christ

13When Jesus came to the area of
Caesarea Philippi, he asked his followers,
"Who do people say the Son of Man is?"
14They answered, "Some say you are
John the Baptist. Others say you are Elijah, and still others say you are Jeremiah
or one of the prophets."
15Then Jesus asked them, "And who
do you say I am?"
16Simon Peter answered, "You are
the Christ, the Son of the living God."
17Jesus answered, "You are blessed,
Simon son of Jonah, because no person
taught you that. My Father in heaven
showed you who I am. 18So I tell you,
you are Peter.[n] On this rock I will build
my church, and the power of death will
not be able to defeat it. 19I will give you
the keys of the kingdom of heaven; the
things you don't allow on earth will be
the things that God does not allow, and
the things you allow on earth will be the
things that God allows." 20Then Jesus
warned his followers not to tell anyone
he was the Christ.

Jesus Says that He Must Die

21From that time on Jesus began telling his followers that he must go to Jerusalem, where the older Jewish leaders,
the leading priests, and the teachers of
the law would make him suffer many
things. He told them he must be killed
and then be raised from the dead on the
third day.
22Peter took Jesus aside and told him
not to talk like that. He said, "God save
you from those things, Lord! Those
things will never happen to you!"
23Then Jesus said to Peter, "Go away
from me, Satan![n] You are not helping me!
You don't care about the things of God,
but only about the things people think are
important."
24Then Jesus said to his
followers, "If people
want to follow me,
they must give up
the things they want.
They must be willing
even to give up their
lives to follow me.

eMAIL! FROM GOD
16:24
Following God
What must you do to follow Jesus?

25Those who want to save their lives will
give up true life, and those who give up
their lives for me will have true life. 26It is
worth nothing for them to have the whole
world if they lose their souls. They could
never pay enough to buy back their souls.
27The Son of Man will come again with his
Father's glory and with his angels. At that
time, he will reward them for what they
have done. 28I tell you the truth, some people standing here will see the Son of Man
coming with his kingdom before they die."

Jesus Talks with Moses and Elijah

17 Six days later, Jesus took Peter,
James, and John, the brother of
James, up on a high mountain by themselves. 2While they watched, Jesus' appearance was changed; his face became
bright like the sun, and his clothes became white as light. 3Then Moses and
Elijah[n] appeared to them, talking with
Jesus.
4Peter said to Jesus, "Lord, it is good
that we are here. If you want, I will put up
three tents here—one for you, one for
Moses, and one for Elijah."
5While Peter was talking, a bright
cloud covered them. A voice came from
the cloud and said, "This is my Son,
whom I love, and I am very pleased with
him. Listen to him!"
6When his followers heard the voice,
they were so frightened they fell to the
ground. 7But Jesus went to them and
touched them and said, "Stand up. Don't
be afraid." 8When they looked up, they
saw Jesus was now alone.
9As they were coming down the
mountain, Jesus commanded them not to
tell anyone about what they had seen until the Son of Man had risen from the
dead.
10Then his followers asked him, "Why

16:18 Peter The Greek name "Peter," like the Aramaic name "Cephas," means "rock."
16:23 Satan Name for the devil, meaning "the enemy." Jesus means that Peter was talking like Satan.
17:3 Moses and Elijah Two of the most important Jewish leaders in the past. God had given Moses the Law, and Elijah was an important prophet.

do the teachers of the law say that Elijah
must come first?"
11Jesus answered, "They are right to
say that Elijah is coming and that he will
make everything the way it should be.
12But I tell you that Elijah has already
come, and they did not recognize him.
They did to him whatever they wanted to
do. It will be the same with the Son of
Man; those same people will make the
Son of Man suffer." 13Then the followers
understood that Jesus was talking about
John the Baptist.

Jesus Heals a Sick Boy

14When Jesus and his followers came
back to the crowd, a man came to Jesus
and bowed before him. 15The man said,
"Lord, have mercy on my son. He has
epilepsy[n] and is suffering very much, because he often falls into the fire or into
the water. 16I brought him to your followers, but they could not cure him."
17Jesus answered, "You people have
no faith, and your lives are all wrong.
How long must I put up with you? How
long must I continue to be patient with
you? Bring the boy here." 18Jesus commanded the demon inside the boy. Then
the demon came out, and the boy was
healed from that time on.
19The followers came to Jesus when
he was alone and asked, "Why couldn't
we force the demon out?"
20Jesus answered, "Because your
faith is too small. I tell you the truth, if
your faith is as big as a mustard seed, you
can say to this mountain, 'Move from
here to there,' and it will move. All
things will be possible for you." 21[n]

Jesus Talks About His Death

22While Jesus' followers were gathering in Galilee, he said to them, "The Son
of Man will be handed over to people,
23and they will kill him. But on the third
day he will be raised from the dead." And
the followers were filled with sadness.

Jesus Talks About Paying Taxes

24When Jesus and his followers came
to Capernaum, the men who collected
the Temple tax came to Peter. They

FAITH links

YOUR CIVIC DUTY

MATTHEW 17:24-27

Being a Christian makes you an honorary citizen of heaven. But being a Christian doesn't mean you can stop obeying the laws of the land. After all, Jesus willingly paid the required temple tax for himself and for Peter.

This story reminds us to respect and obey our leaders (for example, teachers, principals, and the mayor). That way, we can be good citizens of heaven and of earth!

Want the good citizen award? Download these links:

A Use for Your Abilities, Genesis 41, p. 59

A Memorial for Two Thieves, 1 Chronicles 7:21, p. 530

A Reminder to Do What Is Right and True, Zechariah 7:8–10, p. 1257

Too Busy to Worship?, Luke 2:8–20, p. 1368

Calling Anyone!, Acts 23:12–22, p. 1506

Who's on First?, 3 John 9–10, p. 1723

17:15 epilepsy A disease that causes a person sometimes to lose control of his body and maybe faint, shake strongly, or not be able to move.
17:21 Verse 21 Some Greek copies add verse 21: "That kind of spirit comes out only if you use prayer and give up eating."

asked, "Does your teacher pay the Temple tax?"
25Peter answered, "Yes, Jesus pays
the tax."
Peter went into the house, but before
he could speak, Jesus said to him, "What
do you think? The kings of the earth collect different kinds of taxes. But who
pays the taxes—the king's children or
others?"
26Peter answered, "Other people pay
the taxes."
Jesus said to Peter, "Then the children of the king don't have to pay taxes.
27But we don't want to upset these tax
collectors. So go to the lake and fish. After you catch the first fish, open its
mouth and you will find a coin. Take that
coin and give it to the tax collectors for
you and me."

Who Is the Greatest?

18 At that time the followers came to
Jesus and asked, "Who is greatest
in the kingdom of heaven?"
2Jesus called a little child to him and
stood the child before his followers.
3Then he said, "I tell you the truth, you
must change and become like little children. Otherwise, you will never enter the
kingdom of heaven. 4The greatest person in the kingdom of heaven is the one
who makes himself humble like this
child.
5"Whoever accepts a child in my
name accepts me. 6If one of these little
children believes in me, and someone
causes that child to sin, it would be better
for that person to have a large stone tied
around the neck and be drowned in the
sea. 7How terrible for the people of the
world because of the things that cause
them to sin. Such things will happen, but
how terrible for the one who causes them
to happen! 8If your hand or your foot
causes you to sin, cut it off and throw it
away. It is better for you to lose part of
your body and live forever than to have
two hands and two feet and be thrown
into the fire that burns forever. 9If your
eye causes you to sin, take it out and
throw it away. It is better for you to have
only one eye and live forever than to have
two eyes and be thrown into the fire of
hell.

A Lost Sheep

10"Be careful. Don't think these little
children are worth nothing. I tell you that
they have angels in heaven who are always with my Father in heaven. 11*n*
12"If a man has a hundred sheep but
one of the sheep gets lost, he will leave
the other ninety-nine on the hill and go to
look for the lost sheep. 13I tell you the
truth, he is happier about that one sheep
than about the ninety-nine that were
never lost. 14In the same way, your Father in heaven does not want any of these
little children to be lost.

When a Person Sins Against You

15"If your fellow believer sins against
you, go and tell him in private what he did
wrong. If he listens to you, you have
helped that person to be your brother or
sister again. 16But if he refuses to listen,
go to him again and take one or two other
people with you. 'Every case may be
proved by two or three witnesses.'*n* 17If
he refuses to listen to them, tell the
church. If he refuses to listen to the
church, then treat him like a person who
does not believe in God or like a tax collector.
18"I tell you the truth, the things you
don't allow on earth will be the things
God does not allow. And the things you
allow on earth will be the things that God
allows.
19"Also, I tell you that if two of you on
earth agree about something and pray for
it, it will be done for you by my Father in
heaven. 20This is true because if two or
three people come together in my name,
I am there with them."

An Unforgiving Servant

21Then Peter came to Jesus and
asked, "Lord, when my fellow believer
sins against me, how many times must I

18:11 Verse 11 Some Greek copies add verse 11: "The Son of Man came to save lost people."
18:16 'Every . . . witnesses.' Quotation from Deuteronomy 19:15.

FAITH links

WHEN WE AGREE

MATTHEW 18:19-20

You know that 1 + 1 = 2, right? But did you also know that 1 + 1 = 3? Want to know how? Jesus once said that when two or more believers agree about something in prayer, he promised to be with them.

Need some power behind that prayer? Check out these Faithlinks:

The Name of the Lord, Exodus 33:19–23; 34:5–8, p. 120

Deciding Wisely, 1 Kings 3:16–28, p. 440

Fly Like an Eagle, Isaiah 40:28–31, p. 947

A Useless Thing, Isaiah 44:9, 18–20, p. 954

Pass It On!, Joel 1:2–3, p. 1187

You've Got the Power!, Acts 1:1–8; 2:1–4, p. 1463

forgive him? Should I forgive him as many as seven times?"

22Jesus answered, "I tell you, you must forgive him more than seven times. You must forgive him even if he wrongs you seventy times seven.

23"The kingdom of heaven is like a king who decided to collect the money his servants owed him. **24**When the king began to collect his money, a servant who owed him several million dollars was brought to him. **25**But the servant did not have enough money to pay his master, the king. So the master ordered that everything the servant owned should be sold, even the servant's wife and children. Then the money would be used to pay the king what the servant owed.

EMAIL! FROM GOD
18:21–35
Forgiveness
How many times do you need to forgive?

26"But the servant fell on his knees and begged, 'Be patient with me, and I will pay you everything I owe.' **27**The master felt sorry for his servant and told him he did not have to pay it back. Then he let the servant go free.

28"Later, that same servant found another servant who owed him a few dollars. The servant grabbed him around the neck and said, 'Pay me the money you owe me!'

29"The other servant fell on his knees and begged him, 'Be patient with me, and I will pay you everything I owe.'

30"But the first servant refused to be patient. He threw the other servant into prison until he could pay everything he owed. **31**When the other servants saw what had happened, they were very sorry. So they went and told their master all that had happened.

32"Then the master called his servant in and said, 'You evil servant! Because you begged me to forget what you owed, I told you that you did not have to pay anything. **33**You should have showed mercy to that other servant, just as I showed mercy to you.' **34**The master was very angry and put the servant in prison to be punished until he could pay everything he owed.

35"This king did what my heavenly Father will do to you if you do not forgive your brother or sister from your heart."

Jesus Teaches About Divorce

19 After Jesus said all these things, he left Galilee and went into the area of Judea on the other side of the Jordan River. **2**Large crowds followed him, and he healed them there.

3Some Pharisees came to Jesus and tried to trick him. They asked, "Is it right for a man to divorce his wife for any reason he chooses?"

4Jesus answered, "Surely you have
read in the Scriptures: When God made
the world, 'he made them male and
female.'[n] 5And God said, 'So a man will
leave his father and mother and be united
with his wife, and the two will become
one body.'[n] 6So there are not two, but
one. God has joined the two together, so
no one should separate them."
7The Pharisees asked, "Why then did
Moses give a command for a man to divorce his wife by giving her divorce papers?"
8Jesus answered, "Moses allowed
you to divorce your wives because you
refused to accept God's teaching, but divorce was not allowed in the beginning.
9I tell you that anyone who divorces his
wife and marries another woman is guilty
of adultery. The only reason for a man to
divorce his wife is if his wife has sexual
relations with another man."
10The followers said to him, "If that is
the only reason a man can divorce his
wife, it is better not to marry."
11Jesus answered, "Not everyone can
accept this teaching, but God has made
some able to accept it. 12There are different reasons why some men cannot
marry. Some men were born without the
ability to become fathers. Others were
made that way later in life by other people. And some men have given up marriage because of the kingdom of heaven.
But the person who can marry should accept this teaching about marriage."[n]

Jesus Welcomes Children

13Then the people brought their little
children to Jesus so he could put his
hands on them[n] and pray for them. His
followers told them to stop, 14but Jesus
said, "Let the little children come to me.
Don't stop them, because the kingdom of
heaven belongs to people who are like
these children." 15After Jesus put his
hands on the children, he left there.

A Rich Young Man's Question

16A man came to Jesus and asked,
"Teacher, what good thing must I do to
have life forever?"
17Jesus answered, "Why do you ask

FAITH links

WELCOME!

MATTHEW 19:13-15

Quick! Think of a time when someone made you feel welcome. Jesus took time to make children feel welcome, even though his followers felt that he was "too busy" or important to do so. Jesus even used children to teach a lesson to adults. First, he said that a person needed the faith of a child in order to enter heaven. Then he promised that when a person accepts a child in his name, they accept him as well. So, what will you do this week to welcome others like Jesus?

Roll Out the Welcome Wagon, Genesis 18:2–8, p. 24

Kind or Fair?, 1 Samuel 30, p. 395

A Traveling Bible Study, 2 Chronicles 17:9, p. 580

How to Worship God, Isaiah 58, p. 972

A Broken Promise, Jeremiah 2:1–8, p. 989

Get Ready!, Mark 13:26–27, p. 1354

19:4 'he made . . . female.' Quotation from Genesis 1:27 or 5:2.
19:5 'So . . . body.' Quotation from Genesis 2:24.
19:12 But . . . marriage. This may also mean, "The person who can accept this teaching about not marrying should accept it."
19:13 put his hands on them Showing that Jesus gave special blessings to these children.

me about what is good? Only God is good.
But if you want to have life forever, obey
the commands."
18The man asked, "Which commands?"
Jesus answered, " 'You must not murder anyone; you must not be guilty of
adultery; you must not steal; you must
not tell lies about your neighbor; 19honor
your father and mother;[n] and love your
neighbor as you love yourself.' "[n]
20The young man said, "I have
obeyed all these things. What else do I
need to do?"
21Jesus answered, "If you want to be
perfect, then go and sell your possessions and give the money to the poor. If
you do this, you will have treasure in
heaven. Then come
and follow me."
22But when the
young man heard
this, he left sorrow-
fully, because he
was rich.

EMAIL! FROM GOD
19:21–22
Money
Jesus is more important than your stuff.

23Then Jesus said to his followers, "I
tell you the truth, it will be hard for a rich
person to enter the kingdom of heaven.
24Yes, I tell you that it is easier for a
camel to go through the eye of a needle
than for a rich person to enter the kingdom of God."
25When Jesus' followers heard this,
they were very surprised and asked,
"Then who can be saved?"
26Jesus looked at them and said,
"This is something people cannot do, but
God can do all things."
27Peter said to Jesus, "Look, we have
left everything and followed you. So what
will we have?"
28Jesus said to them, "I tell you the
truth, when the age to come has arrived,
the Son of Man will sit on his great
throne. All of you who followed me will
also sit on twelve thrones, judging the
twelve tribes of Israel. 29And all those
who have left houses, brothers, sisters,
father, mother, children, or farms to follow me will get much more than they left,
and they will have life forever. 30Many
who have the highest place now will have
the lowest place in the future. And many
who have the lowest place now will have
the highest place in the future.

A Story About Workers

20 "The kingdom of heaven is like a
person who owned some land.
One morning, he went out very early to
hire some people to work in his vineyard.
2The man agreed to pay the workers one
coin[n] for working that day. Then he sent
them into the vineyard to work. 3About
nine o'clock the man went to the marketplace and saw some other people standing there, doing nothing. 4So he said to
them, 'If you go and work in my vineyard,
I will pay you what your work is worth.'
5So they went to work in the vineyard.
The man went out again about twelve
o'clock and three o'clock and did the
same thing. 6About five o'clock the man
went to the marketplace again and saw
others standing there. He asked them,
'Why did you stand here all day doing
nothing?' 7They answered, 'No one gave
us a job.' The man said to them, 'Then
you can go and work in my vineyard.'
8"At the end of the day, the owner of
the vineyard said to the boss of all the
workers, 'Call the workers and pay them.
Start with the last people I hired and end
with those I hired first.'
9"When the workers who were hired
at five o'clock came to get their pay, each
received one coin. 10When the workers
who were hired first came to get their
pay, they thought they would be paid
more than the others. But each one of
them also received one coin. 11When
they got their coin, they complained to
the man who owned the land. 12They
said, 'Those people were hired last and
worked only one hour. But you paid them
the same as you paid us who worked hard
all day in the hot sun.' 13But the man
who owned the vineyard said to one of
those workers, 'Friend, I am being fair to

19:19 'You . . . mother.' Quotation from Exodus 20:12-16; Deuteronomy 5:16-20.
19:19 'love . . . yourself.' Quotation from Leviticus 19:18.
20:2 coin A Roman denarius. One coin was the average pay for one day's work.

you. You agreed to work for one coin.
14So take your pay and go. I want to give
the man who was hired last the same pay
that I gave you. 15I can do what I want
with my own money. Are you jealous because I am good to those people?'
16"So those who have the last place
now will have the first place in the future,
and those who have the first place now
will have the last place in the future."

Jesus Talks About His Own Death

17While Jesus was going to Jerusalem, he took his twelve followers aside
privately and said to them, 18"Look, we
are going to Jerusalem. The Son of Man
will be turned over to the leading priests
and the teachers of the law, and they will
say that he must die. 19They will give the
Son of Man to the non-Jewish people to
laugh at him and beat him with whips and
crucify him. But on the third day, he will
be raised to life again."

A Mother Asks Jesus a Favor

20Then the wife of Zebedee came to
Jesus with her sons. She bowed before
him and asked him to do something for
her.
21Jesus asked, "What do you want?"
She said, "Promise that one of my
sons will sit at your right side and the
other will sit at your left side in your
kingdom."
22But Jesus said, "You don't understand what you are asking. Can you drink
the cup that I am about to drink?"[n]
The sons answered, "Yes, we can."
23Jesus said to them, "You will drink
from my cup. But I cannot choose who
will sit at my right or my left; those
places belong to those for whom my Father has prepared them."
24When the other ten followers heard
this, they were angry with the two brothers.
25Jesus called all
the followers to-
gether and said,
"You know that the
rulers of the non-
Jewish people love
to show their power
over the people. And their important leaders love to use all their authority. 26But it
should not be that way among you. Whoever wants to become great among you
must serve the rest of you like a servant.
27Whoever wants to become first among
you must serve the rest of you like a

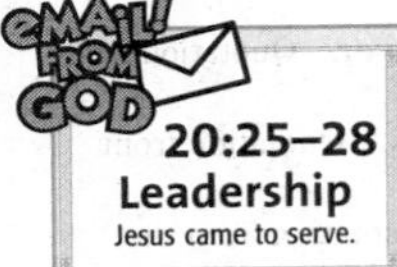

20:25–28
Leadership
Jesus came to serve.

FAITH links

THE WAY TO GREATNESS

MATTHEW 20:20-28

If you wanted others to think you were important, what would you do? The mother of two of Jesus' followers wanted her sons to have important positions in the kingdom of God. Jesus gave his followers some advice about greatness that can be said in two words: "Serve others." You can start by putting others first. That's the way to true greatness.

Download these links for more on true greatness:

Fearful Service?, Exodus 4:1–17, p. 80

The Way to Serve God, 1 Kings 9:4, p. 450

Prayer + Action = Success, Nehemiah 2:4–9, p. 626

The Verdict Is In?, Matthew 7:1–2, p. 1285

Better Than Some?, Luke 18:9–14, p. 1405

A Different Kind of Fruit, Galatians 5:22–23, p. 1592

20:22 drink . . . drink Jesus used the idea of drinking from a cup to ask if they could accept the same terrible things that would happen to him.

slave. **28**In the same way, the Son of Man
did not come to be served. He came to
serve others and to give his life as a ransom for many people."

Jesus Heals Two Blind Men

29When Jesus and his followers were
leaving Jericho, a great many people followed him. **30**Two blind men sitting by
the road heard that Jesus was going by, so
they shouted, "Lord, Son of David, have
mercy on us!"
31The people warned the blind men
to be quiet, but they shouted even more,
"Lord, Son of David, have mercy on us!"
32Jesus stopped and said to the blind
men, "What do you want me to do for
you?"
33They answered, "Lord, we want to
see."
34Jesus felt sorry for the blind men
and touched their eyes, and at once they
could see. Then they followed Jesus.

Jesus Enters Jerusalem as a King

21 As Jesus and his followers were
coming closer to Jerusalem, they
stopped at Bethphage at the hill called
the Mount of Olives. From there Jesus
sent two of his followers **2**and said to
them, "Go to the town you can see there.
When you enter it, you will quickly find a
donkey tied there with its colt. Untie
them and bring them to me. **3**If anyone
asks you why you are taking the donkeys,
say that the Master needs them, and he
will send them at once."
4This was to bring about what the
prophet had said:

5 "Tell the people of Jerusalem,
'Your king is coming to you.
He is gentle and riding on a donkey,
on the colt of a donkey.' "
Isaiah 62:11; Zechariah 9:9

6The followers went and did what
Jesus told them to do. **7**They brought the
donkey and the colt to Jesus and laid their
coats on them, and Jesus sat on them.
8Many people spread their coats on the
road. Others cut branches from the trees
and spread them on the road. **9**The people were walking ahead of Jesus and behind him, shouting,

"Praise[n] to the Son of David!
God bless the One who comes in the
name of the Lord! *Psalm 118:26*
Praise to God in heaven!"

10When Jesus entered Jerusalem, all
the city was filled with excitement. The
people asked, "Who is this man?"
11The crowd said, "This man is Jesus,
the prophet from the town of Nazareth in
Galilee."

Jesus Goes to the Temple

12Jesus went into the Temple and
threw out all the people who were buying
and selling there. He turned over the tables of those who were exchanging different kinds of money, and he upset the
benches of those who were selling doves.
13Jesus said to all the people there, "It is
written in the Scriptures, 'My Temple
will be called a house for prayer.'[n] But
you are changing it into a 'hideout for
robbers.' "[n]
14The blind and crippled people came
to Jesus in the Temple, and he healed
them. **15**The leading priests and the
teachers of the law saw that Jesus was
doing wonderful things and that the children were praising him in the Temple,
saying, "Praise[n] to the Son of David." All
these things made the priests and the
teachers of the law very angry.
16They asked Jesus, "Do you hear the
things these children are saying?"
Jesus answered, "Yes. Haven't you
read in the Scriptures, 'You have taught
children and babies to sing praises'?"[n]
17Then Jesus left and went out of the
city to Bethany, where he spent the
night.

21:9, 15 Praise Literally, "Hosanna," a Hebrew word used at first in praying to God for help. At this time it was probably a shout of joy used in praising God or his Messiah.

21:13 'My Temple . . . prayer.' Quotation from Isaiah 56:7.

21:13 'hideout for robbers.' Quotation from Jeremiah 7:11.

21:16 'You . . . praises' Quotation from the Septuagint (Greek) version of Psalm 8:2.

The Power of Faith

18Early the next morning, as Jesus
was going back to the city, he became hungry. 19Seeing a fig tree beside the road,
Jesus went to it, but there were no figs on
the tree, only leaves. So Jesus said to the
tree, "You will never again have fruit."
The tree immediately dried up.

20When his followers saw this, they
were amazed. They asked, "How did the
fig tree dry up so quickly?"

21Jesus answered, "I tell you the
truth, if you have faith and do not doubt,
you will be able to do what I did to this
tree and even more. You will be able to say
to this mountain, 'Go, fall into the sea.'
And if you have faith, it will happen. 22If
you believe, you will get anything you ask
for in prayer."

Leaders Doubt Jesus' Authority

23Jesus went to the Temple, and
while he was teaching there, the leading
priests and the older leaders of the people came to him. They said, "What authority do you have to do these things?
Who gave you this authority?"

24Jesus answered, "I also will ask you
a question. If you answer me, then I will
tell you what authority I have to do these
things. 25Tell me: When John baptized
people, did that come from God or just
from other people?"

They argued about Jesus' question,
saying, "If we answer, 'John's baptism
was from God,' Jesus will say, 'Then why
didn't you believe him?' 26But if we say,
'It was from people,' we are afraid of
what the crowd will do because they all
believe that John was a prophet."

27So they answered Jesus, "We don't
know."

Jesus said to them, "Then I won't tell
you what authority I have to do these
things.

A Story About Two Sons

28"Tell me what you think about this:
A man had two sons. He went to the first
son and said, 'Son, go and work today in
my vineyard.' 29The son answered, 'I
will not go.' But later the son changed his
mind and went. 30Then the father went
to the other son and said, 'Son, go and
work today in my vineyard.' The son answered, 'Yes, sir, I will go and work,' but
he did not go. 31Which of the two sons
obeyed his father?"

The priests and leaders answered,
"The first son."

Jesus said to them, "I tell you the
truth, the tax collectors and the prostitutes will enter the kingdom of God before you do. 32John came to show you the
right way to live. You did not believe him,
but the tax collectors and prostitutes believed him. Even after seeing this, you
still refused to change your ways and believe him.

A Story About God's Son

33"Listen to this story: There was a
man who owned a vineyard. He put a wall
around it and dug a hole for a winepress
and built a tower. Then he leased the land
to some farmers and left for a trip.
34When it was time for the grapes to be
picked, he sent his servants to the farmers to get his share of the grapes. 35But
the farmers grabbed the servants, beat
one, killed another, and then killed a third
servant with stones. 36So the man sent
some other servants to the farmers, even
more than he sent the first time. But the
farmers did the same thing to the servants that they had done before. 37So the
man decided to send his son to the farmers. He said, 'They will respect my son.'
38But when the farmers saw the son,
they said to each other, 'This son will inherit the vineyard. If we kill him, it will
be ours!' 39Then the farmers grabbed
the son, threw him out of the vineyard,
and killed him. 40So what will the owner
of the vineyard do to these farmers when
he comes?"

41The priests and leaders said, "He
will surely kill those evil men. Then he
will lease the vineyard to some other
farmers who will give him his share of
the crop at harvest time."

42Jesus said to them, "Surely you
have read this in the Scriptures:

'The stone that the builders rejected
became the cornerstone.

The Lord did this,
and it is wonderful to us.'

Psalm 118:22-23

43"So I tell you that the kingdom of God will be taken away from you and given to people who do the things God wants in his kingdom. **44**The person who falls on this stone will be broken, and on whomever that stone falls, that person will be crushed."*

45When the leading priests and the Pharisees heard these stories, they knew Jesus was talking about them. **46**They wanted to arrest him, but they were afraid of the people, because the people believed that Jesus was a prophet.

A Story About a Wedding Feast

22 Jesus again used stories to teach the people. He said, **2**"The kingdom of heaven is like a king who prepared a wedding feast for his son. **3**The king invited some people to the feast. When the feast was ready, the king sent his servants to tell the people, but they refused to come.

4"Then the king sent other servants, saying, 'Tell those who have been invited that my feast is ready. I have killed my best bulls and calves for the dinner, and everything is ready. Come to the wedding feast.'

5"But the people refused to listen to the servants and left to do other things. One went to work in his field, and another went to his business. **6**Some of the other people grabbed the servants, beat them, and killed them. **7**The king was furious and sent his army to kill the murderers and burn their city.

8"After that, the king said to his servants, 'The wedding feast is ready. I invited those people, but they were not worthy to come. **9**So go to the street corners and invite everyone you find to come to my feast.' **10**So the servants went into the streets and gathered all the people they could find, both good and bad. And the wedding hall was filled with guests.

11"When the king came in to see the guests, he saw a man who was not dressed for a wedding. **12**The king said, 'Friend, how were you allowed to come in here? You are not dressed for a wedding.' But the man said nothing. **13**So the king told some servants, 'Tie this man's hands and feet. Throw him out into the darkness, where people will cry and grind their teeth with pain.'

14"Yes, many people are invited, but only a few are chosen."

Is It Right to Pay Taxes or Not?

15Then the Pharisees left that place and made plans to trap Jesus in saying something wrong. **16**They sent some of their own followers and some people from the group called Herodians.* They said, "Teacher, we know that you are an honest man and that you teach the truth about God's way. You are not afraid of what other people think about you, because you pay no attention to who they are. **17**So tell us what you think. Is it right to pay taxes to Caesar or not?"

18But knowing that these leaders were trying to trick him, Jesus said, "You hypocrites! Why are you trying to trap me? **19**Show me a coin used for paying the tax." So the men showed him a coin.* **20**Then Jesus asked, "Whose image and name are on the coin?"

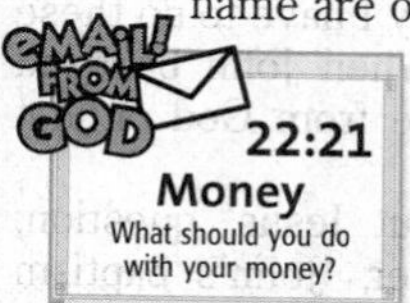

EMAIL! FROM GOD
22:21
Money
What should you do with your money?

21The men answered, "Caesar's."

Then Jesus said to them, "Give to Caesar the things that are Caesar's, and give to God the things that are God's."

22When the men heard what Jesus said, they were amazed and left him and went away.

Some Sadducees Try to Trick Jesus

23That same day some Sadducees came to Jesus and asked him a question. (Sadducees believed that people would not rise from the dead.) **24**They said,

---

21:44 Verse 44 Some copies do not have verse 44.
22:16 Herodians A political group that followed Herod and his family.
22:19 coin A Roman denarius. One coin was the average pay for one day's work.

"Teacher, Moses said if a married man dies without having children, his brother must marry the widow and have children for him. 25Once there were seven brothers among us. The first one married and died. Since he had no children, his brother married the widow. 26Then the second brother also died. The same thing happened to the third brother and all the other brothers. 27Finally, the woman died. 28Since all seven men had married her, when people rise from the dead, whose wife will she be?"

29Jesus answered, "You don't understand, because you don't know what the Scriptures say, and you don't know about the power of God. 30When people rise from the dead, they will not marry, nor will they be given to someone to marry. They will be like the angels in heaven. 31Surely you have read what God said to you about rising from the dead. 32God said, 'I am the God of Abraham, the God of Isaac, and the God of Jacob.'* God is the God of the living, not the dead."

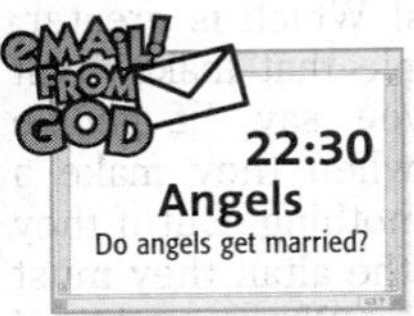

22:30
Angels
Do angels get married?

33When the people heard this, they were amazed at Jesus' teaching.

The Most Important Command

34When the Pharisees learned that the Sadducees could not argue with Jesus' answers to them, the Pharisees met together. 35One Pharisee, who was an expert on the law of Moses, asked Jesus this question to test him: 36"Teacher, which command in the law is the most important?"

37Jesus answered, " 'Love the Lord your God with all your heart, all your soul, and all your mind.'* 38This is the first and most important command. 39And the second command is like the first: 'Love your neighbor as you love yourself.'* 40All the law and the writings of the prophets depend on these two commands."

Jesus Questions the Pharisees

41While the Pharisees were together, Jesus asked them, 42"What do you think about the Christ? Whose son is he?"

FAITH links

THE GREATEST COMMANDMENT

MATTHEW 22:36-40

You've read the Ten Commandments, right? (If not, do not pass "Go" until you read Exodus 20:1–17, p. 101.) Of all the commandments, which do you think is the most important? Keep the Sabbath holy? Do not steal? According to Jesus, the most important commandment is to love God with all of your heart, soul, and mind. That means loving him with your whole being. The second commandment is to love others as much as you love yourself. Two commandments, one purpose: love. Now, that's not so hard to remember, is it?

Made in His Image, Genesis 1:26–27, p. 4

Help for the Poor, Leviticus 5:7, p. 138

Too Young to Serve, Jeremiah 1:4–9, p. 988

Your Full Trust, Jeremiah 22:20–22, p. 1023

Help for a Friend, Mark 2:1–5, p. 1332

From Useless to Useful, Philemon 11, p. 1663

22:32 'I am . . . Jacob.' Quotation from Exodus 3:6.
22:37 'Love . . . mind.' Quotation from Deuteronomy 6:5.
22:39 'Love . . . yourself.' Quotation from Leviticus 19:18.

They answered, "The Christ is the
Son of David."
43Then Jesus said to them, "Then why
did David call him 'Lord'? David, speaking
by the power of the Holy Spirit, said,

44'The Lord said to my Lord:
Sit by me at my right side,
until I put your enemies under
your control.' *Psalm 110:1*

45David calls the Christ 'Lord,' so how
can the Christ be his son?"
46None of the Pharisees could answer
Jesus' question, and after that day no one
was brave enough to ask him any more
questions.

Jesus Accuses Some Leaders

23 Then Jesus said to the crowds and
to his followers, 2"The teachers of
the law and the Pharisees have the authority to tell you what the law of Moses
says. 3So you should obey and follow
whatever they tell you, but their lives are
not good examples for you to follow. They
tell you to do things, but they themselves
don't do them. 4They make strict rules
and try to force people to obey them, but
they are unwilling to help those who
struggle under the weight of their rules.
5"They do good things so that other
people will see them. They make the
boxes[n] of Scriptures that they wear bigger, and they make their special prayer
clothes very long. 6Those Pharisees and
teachers of the law love to have the most
important seats at feasts and in the synagogues. 7They love people to greet them
with respect in the marketplaces, and they
love to have people call them 'Teacher.'
8"But you must not be called
'Teacher,' because you have only one
Teacher, and you are all brothers and sisters together. 9And don't call any person
on earth 'Father,' because you have one
Father, who is in heaven. 10And you
should not be called 'Master,' because
you have only one Master, the Christ.
11Whoever is your servant is the greatest among you. 12Whoever makes himself great will be made humble. Whoever
makes himself humble will be made
great.
13"How terrible for you, teachers of
the law and Pharisees! You are hypocrites! You close the door for people to
enter the kingdom of heaven. You yourselves don't enter, and you stop others
who are trying to enter. 14[n]
15"How terrible for you, teachers of
the law and Pharisees! You are hypocrites! You travel across land and sea to
find one person who will change to your
ways. When you find that person, you
make him more fit for hell than you are.
16"How terrible for you! You guide
the people, but you are blind. You say, 'If
people swear by the Temple when they
make a promise, that means nothing. But
if they swear by the gold that is in the
Temple, they must keep that promise.'
17You are blind fools! Which is greater:
the gold or the Temple that makes that
gold holy? 18And you say, 'If people
swear by the altar when they make a
promise, that means nothing. But if they
swear by the gift on the altar, they must
keep that promise.' 19You are blind!
Which is greater: the gift or the altar that
makes the gift holy? 20The person who
swears by the altar is really using the altar and also everything on the altar.
21And the person who swears by the
Temple is really using the Temple and
also everything in the Temple. 22The
person who swears by heaven is also using God's throne and the One who sits on
that throne.
23"How terrible for you, teachers of
the law and Pharisees! You are hypocrites! You give to God one-tenth of
everything you earn—even your mint,
dill, and cumin.[n] But you don't obey the

23:5 boxes Small leather boxes containing four important Scriptures. Some Jews tied these to their foreheads and left arms, probably to show they were very religious.

23:14 Verse 14 Some Greek copies add verse 14: "How terrible for you, teachers of the law and Pharisees. You are hypocrites. You take away widows' houses, and you say long prayers so that people will notice you. So you will have a worse punishment."

23:23 mint, dill, and cumin Small plants grown in gardens and used for spices. Only very religious people would be careful enough to give a tenth of these plants.

really important teachings of the law—
justice, mercy, and being loyal. These are
the things you should do, as well as those
other things. **24**You guide the people, but
you are blind! You are like a person who
picks a fly out of a drink and then swallows a camel![n]

25"How terrible for you, teachers of
the law and Pharisees! You are hypocrites! You wash the outside of your cups
and dishes, but inside they are full of
things you got by cheating others and by
pleasing only yourselves. **26**Pharisees,
you are blind! First make the inside of the
cup clean, and then the outside of the cup
can be truly clean.

27"How terrible for you, teachers of
the law and Pharisees! You are hypocrites! You are like
tombs that are
painted white. Out-
side, those tombs
look fine, but inside,
they are full of the
bones of dead peo-
ple and all kinds of unclean things. **28**It is
the same with you. People look at you
and think you are good, but on the inside
you are full of hypocrisy and evil.

eMAIL! FROM GOD
23:27–28
Being Pure
It's what's on the inside that counts.

29"How terrible for you, teachers of
the law and Pharisees! You are hypocrites! You build tombs for the prophets,
and you show honor to the graves of
those who lived good lives. **30**You say, 'If
we had lived during the time of our ancestors, we would not have helped them
kill the prophets.' **31**But you give proof
that you are children of those who murdered the prophets. **32**And you will complete the sin that your ancestors started.

33"You are snakes! A family of poisonous snakes! How are you going to escape
God's judgment? **34**So I tell you this: I am
sending to you prophets and wise men
and teachers. Some of them you will kill
and crucify. Some of them you will beat in
your synagogues and chase from town to
town. **35**So you will be guilty for the
death of all the good people who have
been killed on earth—from the murder of
that good man Abel to the murder of
Zechariah[n] son of Berakiah, whom you
murdered between the Temple and the
altar. **36**I tell you the truth, all of these
things will happen to you people who are
living now.

Jesus Feels Sorry for Jerusalem

37"Jerusalem, Jerusalem! You kill the
prophets and stone to death those who are
sent to you. Many times I wanted to
gather your people as a hen gathers her
chicks under her wings, but you did not
let me. **38**Now your house will be left
completely empty. **39**I tell you, you will
not see me again until that time when
you will say, 'God bless the One who
comes in the name of the Lord.' "[n]

The Temple Will Be Destroyed

24 As Jesus left the Temple and was
walking away, his followers came
up to show him the Temple's buildings.
2Jesus asked, "Do you see all these
buildings? I tell you the truth, not one
stone will be left on another. Every stone
will be thrown down to the ground."

3Later, as Jesus was sitting on the
Mount of Olives, his followers came to be
alone with him. They said, "Tell us, when
will these things happen? And what will
be the sign that it is time for you to come
again and for this age to end?"

4Jesus answered, "Be careful that no
one fools you. **5**Many will come in my
name, saying, 'I am the Christ,' and they
will fool many people. **6**You will hear
about wars and stories of wars that are
coming, but don't be afraid. These things
must happen before the end comes. **7**Nations will fight against other nations;
kingdoms will fight against other kingdoms. There will be times when there is
no food for people to eat, and there will
be earthquakes in different places.
8These things are like the first pains
when something new is about to be born.

9"Then people will arrest you, hand
you over to be hurt, and kill you. They

23:24 You . . . camel! Meaning, "You worry about the smallest mistakes but commit the biggest sin."
23:35 Abel . . . Zechariah In the order of the books of the Hebrew Old Testament, the first and last men to be murdered.
23:39 'God . . . Lord.' Quotation from Psalm 118:26.

will hate you because you believe in me.
10At that time, many will lose their faith,
and they will turn against each other and
hate each other. **11**Many false prophets
will come and cause many people to believe lies. **12**There will be more and more
evil in the world, so most people will stop
showing their love for each other. **13**But
those people who keep their faith until
the end will be saved. **14**The Good News
about God's kingdom will be preached in
all the world, to every nation. Then the
end will come.

15"Daniel the prophet
spoke about 'the destroy-
ing terror.'[n] You will see
this standing in the holy
place." (You who read this
should understand what it
means.) **16**"At that time,
the people in Judea should
run away to the moun-
tains. **17**If people are on
the roofs[n] of their houses,
they must not go down to
get anything out of their
houses. **18**If people are in the fields, they
must not go back to get their coats. **19**At
that time, how terrible it will be for wom-
en who are pregnant or have nursing babies! **20**Pray that it will not be winter or a
Sabbath day when these things happen
and you have to run away, **21**because at
that time there will be much trouble.
There will be more trouble than there
has ever been since the beginning of the
world until now, and nothing as bad will
ever happen again. **22**God has decided to
make that terrible time short. Otherwise,
no one would go on living. But God will
make that time short to help the people
he has chosen. **23**At that time, someone
might say to you, 'Look, there is the
Christ!' Or another person might say,
'There he is!' But don't believe them.
24False Christs and false prophets will
come and perform great wonders and
miracles. They will try to fool even the
people God has chosen, if that is possible.
25Now I have warned you about this before it happens.

26"If people tell you, 'The Christ is in
the desert,' don't go there. If they say,
'The Christ is in the inner room,' don't
believe it. **27**When the Son of Man
comes, he will be seen by everyone, like
lightning flashing from the east to the
west. **28**Wherever the dead body is,
there the vultures will gather.

29"Soon after the trouble of those days,
'the sun will grow dark,
and the moon will not give its
light.
The stars will fall from the sky.
And the powers of the heavens will
be shaken.' *Isaiah 13:10; 34:4*

30"At that time, the
sign of the Son of Man
will appear in the sky.
Then all the peoples of
the world will cry. They
will see the Son of Man
coming on clouds in the
sky with great power and
glory. **31**He will use a loud
trumpet to send his an-
gels all around the earth,
and they will gather his
chosen people from every
part of the world.

> But those people who keep their faith until the end will be saved.
> —Matthew 24:13

32"Learn a lesson from the fig tree:
When its branches become green and soft
and new leaves appear, you know summer is near. **33**In the same way, when you
see all these things happening, you will
know that the time is near, ready to
come. **34**I tell you the truth, all these
things will happen while the people of
this time are still living. **35**Earth and sky
will be destroyed, but the words I have
said will never be destroyed.

When Will Jesus Come Again?

36"No one knows when that day or
time will be, not the angels in heaven, not
even the Son. Only the Father knows.
37When the Son of Man comes, it will be
like what happened during Noah's time.
38In those days before the flood, people

24:15 'the destroying terror' Mentioned in Daniel 9:27; 12:11 (see also Daniel 11:31).

24:17 roofs In Bible times houses were built with flat roofs. The roof was used for drying things such as flax and fruit. And it was used as an extra room, as a place for worship, and as a cool place to sleep in the summer.

were eating and drinking, marrying and
giving their children to be married, until
the day Noah entered the boat. **39**They
knew nothing about what was happening
until the flood came and destroyed them.
It will be the same when the Son of Man
comes. **40**Two men will be in the field.
One will be taken, and the other will be
left. **41**Two women will be grinding grain
with a mill.[n] One will be taken, and the
other will be left.

42"So always be ready, because you
don't know the day your Lord will come.
43Remember this: If the owner of the
house knew what time of night a thief
was coming, the owner would watch and
not let the thief break in. **44**So you also
must be ready, because the Son of Man
will come at a time you don't expect him.

45"Who is the wise and loyal servant
that the master trusts to give the other
servants their food at the right time?
46When the master comes and finds the
servant doing his work, the servant will
be blessed. **47**I tell you the truth, the
master will choose that servant to take
care of everything he owns. **48**But suppose that evil servant thinks to himself,
'My master will not come back soon,'
49and he begins to beat the other servants and eat and get drunk with others
like him? **50**The master will come when
that servant is not ready and is not expecting him. **51**Then the master will cut
him in pieces and send him away to be
with the hypocrites, where people will
cry and grind their teeth with pain.

A Story About Ten Bridesmaids

25 "At that time the kingdom of heaven
will be like ten bridesmaids who
took their lamps and went to wait for the
bridegroom. **2**Five of them were foolish
and five were wise. **3**The five foolish
bridesmaids took their lamps, but they
did not take more oil for the lamps to
burn. **4**The wise bridesmaids took their
lamps and more oil in jars. **5**Because the
bridegroom was late, they became sleepy
and went to sleep.

6"At midnight someone cried out,
'The bridegroom is coming! Come and
meet him!' **7**Then all the bridesmaids
woke up and got their lamps ready. **8**But
the foolish ones said to the wise, 'Give us
some of your oil, because our lamps are
going out.' **9**The wise bridesmaids answered, 'No, the oil we have might not be
enough for all of us. Go to the people who
sell oil and buy some for yourselves.'

10"So while the five foolish bridesmaids went to buy oil, the bridegroom
came. The bridesmaids who were ready
went in with the bridegroom to the wedding feast. Then the door was closed and
locked.

11"Later the others came back and
said, 'Sir, sir, open the door to let us in.'
12But the bridegroom answered, 'I tell
you the truth, I don't want to know you.'

13"So always be ready, because you
don't know the day or the hour the Son of
Man will come.

A Story About Three Servants

14"The kingdom of heaven is like a
man who was going to another place for a
visit. Before he left, he called for his servants and told them to take care

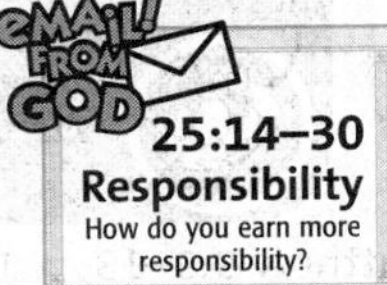
EMAIL! FROM GOD
25:14–30
Responsibility
How do you earn more responsibility?

of his things while
he was gone. **15**He
gave one servant
five bags of gold, an-
other servant two
bags of gold, and a
third servant one
bag of gold, to each one as much as he
could handle. Then he left. **16**The servant who got five bags went quickly to invest the money and earned five more
bags. **17**In the same way, the servant who
had two bags invested them and earned
two more. **18**But the servant who got one
bag went out and dug a hole in the ground
and hid the master's money.

19"After a long time the master came
home and asked the servants what they
did with his money. **20**The servant who
was given five bags of gold brought five
more bags to the master and said, 'Master, you trusted me to care for five bags of
gold, so I used your five bags to earn five
more.' **21**The master answered, 'You did

24:41 mill Two large, round, flat rocks used for grinding grain to make flour.

SERVING

Matthew 25:14–30

Livin' it

Being the GREATEST! Would you like to be really great—you know, the kid everyone looks up to? How can you get that way? Some people think it's how much money you have or how famous you are. Other people think it's how good someone is at a particular sport or if he or she looks cool.

But Jesus has a different idea of what makes a person great. Jesus said true greatness comes from helping and caring for others. (Check out Matthew 23:11.)

Serving others helps us pay attention to other people and their needs and not just think about ourselves. Jesus himself said that he came to serve others, not to have people serve him. (See Mark 10:45, p. 1348.) Who could be a better example of "greatness" than Jesus? Whose idea of greatness do you plan to follow—Jesus' example or the world's?

MORE FAITH links

The Way to Serve God, p. 450
Service with a Smile, p. 527
The Worst Chore, p. 1447
My Best Serve, p. 1473

"I'm not sure I get this—Jesus says that if we want to be first, we should serve others? How does that work?"

"I'm not exactly sure. Better download some of these other links on serving. Maybe we'll get a clue!"

Just Say Yes!, Matthew 9:9–13, p. 1289

- What do you say when your mom or dad asks you to do something for them?
- How about your brother or sister? What about a friend? What if it's Jesus asking you to do something?

Calling Anyone!, Acts 23:12–22, p. 1506

- We all like to feel important. But there are many people who do great things without anyone knowing about it. Find out about one of these people and what he did by linking here!

Help for the Body, Romans 12:3–8, p. 1536

- Everybody is good at doing something. What are you good at doing? Making people smile? Singing, or helping around the house? How do you use your talents and abilities?

Your Faith Example, 1 Timothy 4:12, p. 1646

- Link here to discover how you can serve God!

my FAVORITE links

FAITH links

THAT THING YOU DO

MATTHEW 25:14-30

Think about something you do well. Can you draw? Laugh? Tell a joke? Jesus once told a story about a man who gave each of his three servants a different number of bags of gold. He told them "to take care of his things" while he was gone. Two of the servants used the bags of gold to make more gold for their master. The other servant took his one bag of gold and did nothing with it. Jesus told his disciples that the master was pleased with the two servants, but angry with the one who did nothing with what he was given.

God wants each of us to use the gifts he has given us—whether it's a special talent or ability, our money or our time—to serve others. He doesn't give them to us to forget about them or to use for ourselves. When we use our talents and abilities, we sometimes gain more responsibilities, like two of the men did in the story. Just think: when you use your talents to help others, God feels glad. You will, too!

Share What You Have, Exodus 35:5–18, p. 123

Show Some Respect, Leviticus 19:32, p. 161

Take Me to Your Leader, Numbers 27:12–23, p. 214

A Bad Reaction, Jeremiah 36, p. 1043

Too Busy to Worship?, Luke 2:8–20, p. 1368

well. You are a good and loyal servant. Because you were loyal with small things, I will let you care for much greater things. Come and share my joy with me.'

22"Then the servant who had been given two bags of gold came to the master and said, 'Master, you gave me two bags of gold to care for, so I used your two bags to earn two more.'
23The master answered, 'You did well. You are a good and loyal servant. Because you were loyal with small things, I will let you care for much greater things. Come and share my joy with me.'

24"Then the servant who had been given one bag of gold came to the master and said, 'Master, I knew that you were a hard man. You harvest things you did not plant. You gather crops where you did not sow any seed.
25So I was afraid and went and hid your money in the ground. Here is your bag of gold.'
26The master answered, 'You are a wicked and lazy servant! You say you knew that I harvest things I did not plant and that I gather crops where I did not sow any seed.
27So you should have put my gold in the bank. Then, when I came home, I would have received my gold back with interest.'

28"So the master told his other servants, 'Take the bag of gold from that servant and give it to the servant who has ten bags of gold.
29Those who have much will get more, and they will have much more than they need. But those who do not have much will have everything taken away from them.'
30Then the master said, 'Throw that useless servant outside, into the darkness where people will cry and grind their teeth with pain.'

The King Will Judge All People

31"The Son of Man will come again in his great glory, with all his angels. He will be King and sit on his great throne.
32All the nations of the world will be gathered before him, and he will separate them into two groups as a shepherd separates the sheep from the goats.
33The Son of Man will put the sheep on his right and the goats on his left.

34"Then the King will say to the

people on his right, 'Come, my Father has given you his blessing. Receive the kingdom God has prepared for you since the world was made. **35**I was hungry, and you gave me food. I was thirsty, and you gave me something to drink. I was alone and away from home, and you invited me into your house. **36**I was without clothes, and you gave me something to wear. I was sick, and you cared for me. I was in prison, and you visited me.'

eMAIL! FROM GOD
25:34–40
Sickness
Who should you care for?

37"Then the good people will answer, 'Lord, when did we see you hungry and give you food, or thirsty and give you something to drink? **38**When did we see you alone and away from home and invite you into our house? When did we see you without clothes and give you something to wear? **39**When did we see you sick or in prison and care for you?'

40"Then the King will answer, 'I tell you the truth, anything you did for even the least of my people here, you also did for me.'

41"Then the King will say to those on his left, 'Go away from me. You will be punished. Go into the fire that burns forever that was prepared for the devil and his angels. **42**I was hungry, and you gave me nothing to eat. I was thirsty, and you gave me nothing to drink. **43**I was alone and away from home, and you did not invite me into your house. I was without clothes, and you gave me nothing to wear. I was sick and in prison, and you did not care for me.'

44"Then those people will answer, 'Lord, when did we see you hungry or thirsty or alone and away from home or without clothes or sick or in prison? When did we see these things and not help you?'

45"Then the King will answer, 'I tell you the truth, anything you refused to do for even the least of my people here, you refused to do for me.'

46"These people will go off to be punished forever, but the good people will go to live forever."

The Plan to Kill Jesus

26 After Jesus finished saying all these things, he told his followers, **2**"You know that the day after tomorrow is the day of the Passover Feast. On that day the Son of Man will be given to his enemies to be crucified."

3Then the leading priests and the older leaders had a meeting at the palace of the high priest, named Caiaphas. **4**At the meeting, they planned to set a trap to arrest Jesus and kill him. **5**But they said, "We must not do it during the feast, because the people might cause a riot."

Perfume for Jesus' Burial

6Jesus was in Bethany at the house of Simon, who had a skin disease. **7**While Jesus was there, a woman approached him with an alabaster jar filled with expensive perfume. She poured this perfume on Jesus' head while he was eating.

8His followers were upset when they saw the woman do this. They asked, "Why waste that perfume? **9**It could have been sold for a great deal of money and the money given to the poor."

10Knowing what had happened, Jesus said, "Why are you troubling this woman? She did an excellent thing for me. **11**You will always have the poor with you, but you will not always have me. **12**This woman poured perfume on my body to prepare me for burial. **13**I tell you the truth, wherever the Good News is preached in all the world, what this woman has done will be told, and people will remember her."

Judas Becomes an Enemy of Jesus

14Then one of the twelve apostles, Judas Iscariot, went to talk to the leading priests. **15**He said, "What will you pay me for giving Jesus to you?" And they gave him thirty silver coins. **16**After that, Judas watched for the best time to turn Jesus in.

Jesus Eats the Passover Meal

17On the first day of the Feast of Unleavened Bread, the followers came to

Jesus. They said, "Where do you want us
to prepare for you to eat the Passover
meal?"

18Jesus answered, "Go into the city to
a certain man and tell him, 'The Teacher
says: The chosen time is near. I will have
the Passover with my followers at your
house.'" **19**The followers did what Jesus
told them to do, and they prepared the
Passover meal.

20In the evening Jesus was sitting at
the table with his twelve followers. **21**As
they were eating, Jesus said, "I tell you the
truth, one of you will turn against me."

22This made the followers very sad.
Each one began to say to Jesus, "Surely,
Lord, I am not the one who will turn
against you, am I?"

23Jesus answered, "The man who has
dipped his hand with me into the bowl is
the one who will turn against me. **24**The
Son of Man will die, just as the Scriptures
say. But how terrible it will be for the person who hands the Son of Man over to be
killed. It would be better for him if he had
never been born."

25Then Judas, who would give Jesus
to his enemies, said to Jesus, "Teacher,
surely I am not the one, am I?"

Jesus answered, "Yes, it is you."

The Lord's Supper

26While they were eating, Jesus took
some bread and thanked God for it and
broke it. Then he gave it to his followers
and said, "Take this bread and eat it; this
is my body."

27Then Jesus took a cup and thanked
God for it and gave it to the followers. He
said, "Every one of you drink this. **28**This
is my blood which is the new agreement
that God makes with his people. This
blood is poured out for many to forgive
their sins. **29**I tell you this: I will not
drink of this fruit of the vine[n] again until
that day when I drink it new with you in
my Father's kingdom."

30After singing a hymn, they went out
to the Mount of Olives.

Jesus' Followers Will Leave Him

31Jesus told his followers, "Tonight
you will all stumble in your faith on

FAITH links

REMEMBERING JESUS 

MATTHEW 26:26-29

Facing the death of a friend or relative is hard. You can't help remembering how much he or she meant to you. Before Jesus went to the cross, he had one last meal with his 12 followers. During the meal, he gave a piece of bread to each of his followers. The bread represented his body. He passed around a cup, which represented his blood. He did this to teach his followers how to remember him after he was gone.

Today, we call the bread and cup the Lord's Supper or Communion. The Lord's Supper reminds us of how Jesus gave his life for us.

Link here to see what else Jesus does for us:

Reward for Obedience, Leviticus 26:3–13, p. 171

Our Heavenly Shepherd, Psalm 23, p. 726

The Bible: Good for Your Faith, Psalm 119, p. 802

Your Spiritual Roots, Zechariah 1:1–6, p. 1253

Name with a Purpose, Matthew 1:21, p. 1274

Life After Death?, 1 Corinthians 15:12–13, p. 1563

26:29 fruit of the vine Product of the grapevine; this may also be translated "wine."

account of me, because it is written in the
Scriptures:

'I will kill the shepherd,
and the sheep will scatter.'

Zechariah 13:7

32But after I rise from the dead, I will go
ahead of you into Galilee."

33Peter said, "Everyone else may
stumble in their faith because of you, but
I will not."

34Jesus said, "I tell you the truth, tonight before the rooster crows you will
say three times that you don't know me."

35But Peter said, "I will never say
that I don't know you! I will even die with
you!" And all the other followers said the
same thing.

Jesus Prays Alone

36Then Jesus went with his followers
to a place called Gethsemane. He said to
them, "Sit here while I go over there and
pray." **37**He took Peter and the two sons
of Zebedee with him, and he began to be
very sad and troubled. **38**He said to them,
"My heart is full of sorrow, to the point of
death. Stay here and watch with me."

39After walking a little farther away
from them, Jesus fell to the ground and
prayed, "My Father, if it is possible, do
not give me this cup[n] of suffering. But do
what you want, not what I want." **40**Then
Jesus went back to his followers and
found them asleep. He said to Peter, "You
men could not stay awake with me for
one hour? **41**Stay awake and pray for
strength against temptation. The spirit
wants to do what is right, but the body is
weak."

42Then Jesus went away a second
time and prayed, "My Father, if it is not
possible for this painful thing to be taken
from me, and if I must do it, I pray that
what you want will be done."

43Then he went back to his followers,
and again he found them asleep, because
their eyes were heavy. **44**So Jesus left
them and went away and prayed a third
time, saying the same thing.

45Then Jesus went back to his followers and said, "Are you still sleeping and
resting? The time has come for the Son of
Man to be handed over to sinful people.
46Get up, we must go. Look, here comes
the man who has turned against me."

Jesus Is Arrested

47While Jesus was still speaking, Judas, one of the twelve apostles, came up.
With him were many people carrying
swords and clubs who had been sent from
the leading priests and the older Jewish
leaders of the people. **48**Judas had
planned to give them a signal, saying,
"The man I kiss is Jesus. Arrest him."
49At once Judas went to Jesus and said,
"Greetings, Teacher!" and kissed him.

50Jesus answered, "Friend, do what
you came to do."

Then the people came and grabbed
Jesus and arrested him. **51**When that
happened, one of Jesus' followers reached
for his sword and pulled it out. He struck
the servant of the high priest and cut off
his ear.

52Jesus said to the man, "Put your
sword back in its place. All who use
swords will be killed with swords. **53**Surely you know I could ask my Father, and
he would give me more than twelve
armies of angels. **54**But it must happen
this way to bring about what the Scriptures say."

55Then Jesus said to the crowd, "You
came to get me with swords and clubs as
if I were a criminal. Every day I sat in the
Temple teaching, and you did not arrest
me there. **56**But all these things have
happened so that it will come about as the
prophets wrote." Then all of Jesus' followers left him and ran away.

Jesus Before the Leaders

57Those people who arrested Jesus
led him to the house of Caiaphas, the high
priest, where the teachers of the law and
the older Jewish leaders were gathered.
58Peter followed far behind to the courtyard of the high priest's house, and he sat
down with the guards to see what would
happen to Jesus.

26:39 cup Jesus is talking about the terrible things that will happen to him. Accepting these things will be very hard, like drinking a cup of something bitter.

FAITH links

DON'T GET MAD; GET EVEN?

MATTHEW 26:57-63; 27:11-14

When someone treats you unkindly, what do you do? Do you get mad or think about getting even? (Be honest!) After Jesus was arrested and put on trial, people made fun of him and called him names. He didn't get mad or say mean things. Instead, he remained silent for the most part. He refused to treat them the way they treated him.

When we're mistreated, many of us are tempted to get even. When those times come, think about what Jesus would do. Don't let others cause you to do wrong. Two wrongs never make a right!

Got someone bugging you? Link here for help:

Out of Control?, Genesis 4, p. 8

Give Revenge a Rest, Leviticus 19:18, p. 160

The MLP, Ruth 1:16–17, p. 345

Mind Guard, Proverbs 4:23, p. 831

Get Hot or Keep Cool?, Proverbs 12:16, p. 842

Forgive Again?, Luke 17:3–4, p. 1402

59The leading priests and the whole
Jewish council tried to find something
false against Jesus so they could kill him.
60Many people came and told lies about
him, but the council could find no real
reason to kill him. Then two people came
and said, **61**"This man said, 'I can destroy
the Temple of God and build it again in
three days.' "

62Then the high priest stood up and
said to Jesus, "Aren't you going to answer?
Don't you have something to say
about their charges against you?" **63**But
Jesus said nothing.

Again the high priest said to Jesus, "I
command you by the power of the living
God: Tell us if you are the Christ, the Son
of God."

64Jesus answered, "Those are your
words. But I tell you, in the future you
will see the Son of Man sitting at the
right hand of God, the Powerful One, and
coming on clouds in the sky."

65When the high priest heard this, he
tore his clothes and said, "This man has
said things that are against God! We don't
need any more witnesses; you all heard
him say these things against God.
66What do you think?"

The people answered, "He should
die."

67Then the people there spat in
Jesus' face and beat him with their fists.
Others slapped him. **68**They said, "Prove
to us that you are a prophet, you Christ!
Tell us who hit you!"

Peter Says He Doesn't Know Jesus

69At that time, as Peter was sitting in
the courtyard, a servant girl came to him
and said, "You also were with Jesus of
Galilee."

70But Peter said to all the people
there that he was never with Jesus. He
said, "I don't know what you are talking
about."

71When he left the courtyard and was
at the gate, another girl saw him. She said
to the people there, "This man was with
Jesus of Nazareth."

72Again, Peter said he was never with
him, saying, "I swear I don't know this
man Jesus!"

73A short time later, some people standing there went to Peter and said, "Surely you are one of those who followed Jesus. The way you talk shows it."

74Then Peter began to place a curse on himself and swear, "I don't know the man." At once, a rooster crowed. 75And Peter remembered what Jesus had told him: "Before the rooster crows, you will say three times that you don't know me." Then Peter went outside and cried painfully.

Jesus Is Taken to Pilate

27 Early the next morning, all the leading priests and older leaders of the people decided that Jesus should die. 2They tied him, led him away, and turned him over to Pilate, the governor.

Judas Kills Himself

3Judas, the one who had given Jesus to his enemies, saw that they had decided to kill Jesus. Then he was very sorry for what he had done. So he took the thirty silver coins back to the priests and the leaders, 4saying, "I sinned; I handed over to you an innocent man."

The leaders answered, "What is that to us? That's your problem, not ours."

5So Judas threw the money into the Temple. Then he went off and hanged himself.

6The leading priests picked up the silver coins in the Temple and said, "Our law does not allow us to keep this money with the Temple money, because it has paid for a man's death." 7So they decided to use the coins to buy Potter's Field as a place to bury strangers who died in Jerusalem. 8That is why that field is still called the Field of Blood. 9So what Jeremiah the prophet had said came true: "They took thirty silver coins. That is how little the Israelites thought he was worth. 10They used those thirty silver coins to buy the potter's field, as the Lord commanded me."[n]

Pilate Questions Jesus

11Jesus stood before Pilate the governor, and Pilate asked him, "Are you the king of the Jews?"

Jesus answered, "Those are your words."

12When the leading priests and the older leaders accused Jesus, he said nothing.

13So Pilate said to Jesus, "Don't you hear them accusing you of all these things?"

14But Jesus said nothing in answer to Pilate, and Pilate was very surprised at this.

Pilate Tries to Free Jesus

15Every year at the time of Passover the governor would free one prisoner whom the people chose. 16At that time there was a man in prison, named Barabbas, who was known to be very bad. 17When the people gathered at Pilate's house, Pilate said, "Whom do you want me to set free: Barabbas or Jesus who is called the Christ?" 18Pilate knew that the people turned Jesus in to him because they were jealous.

19While Pilate was sitting there on the judge's seat, his wife sent this message to him: "Don't do anything to that man, because he is innocent. Today I had a dream about him, and it troubled me very much."

20But the leading priests and older leaders convinced the crowd to ask for Barabbas to be freed and for Jesus to be killed.

21Pilate said, "I have Barabbas and Jesus. Which do you want me to set free for you?"

The people answered, "Barabbas."

22Pilate asked, "So what should I do with Jesus, the one called the Christ?"

They all answered, "Crucify him!"

23Pilate asked, "Why? What wrong has he done?"

But they shouted louder, "Crucify him!"

24When Pilate saw that he could do nothing about this and that a riot was starting, he took some water and washed his hands[n] in front of the crowd. Then he

27:9–10 "They . . . commanded me." See Zechariah 11:12-13 and Jeremiah 32:6-9.

27:24 washed his hands He did this as a sign to show that he wanted no part in what the people did.

said, "I am not guilty of this man's death.
You are the ones who are causing it!"
25All the people answered, "We and
our children will be responsible for his
death."
26Then he set Barabbas free. But
Jesus was beaten with whips and handed
over to the soldiers to be crucified.
27The governor's soldiers took Jesus
into the governor's palace, and they all
gathered around him. **28**They took off his
clothes and put a red robe on him. **29**Using thorny branches, they made a crown,
put it on his head, and put a stick in his
right hand. Then the soldiers bowed before Jesus and made fun of him, saying,
"Hail, King of the Jews!" **30**They spat on
Jesus. Then they took his stick and began
to beat him on the head. **31**After they finished, the soldiers took off the robe and
put his own clothes on him again. Then
they led him away to be crucified.

Jesus Is Crucified

32As the soldiers were going out of
the city with Jesus, they forced a man
from Cyrene, named Simon, to carry the
cross for Jesus. **33**They all came to the
place called Golgotha, which means the
Place of the Skull. **34**The soldiers gave
Jesus wine mixed with gall[n] to drink. He
tasted the wine but refused to drink it.
35When the soldiers had crucified him,
they threw lots to decide who would get
his clothes. **36**The soldiers sat there and
continued watching him. **37**They put a
sign above Jesus' head with a charge
against him. It said: THIS IS JESUS, THE
KING OF THE JEWS. **38**Two robbers were
crucified beside Jesus, one on the right
and the other on the left. **39**People
walked by and insulted Jesus and shook
their heads, **40**saying, "You said you
could destroy the Temple and build it
again in three days. So save yourself!
Come down from that cross if you are
really the Son of God!"
41The leading priests, the teachers of
the law, and the older Jewish leaders
were also making fun of Jesus. **42**They
said, "He saved others, but he can't save
himself! He says he is the king of Israel!
If he is the king, let him come down now
from the cross. Then we will believe in
him. **43**He trusts in God, so let God save
him now, if God really wants him. He
himself said, 'I am the Son of God.' "
44And in the same way, the robbers who
were being crucified beside Jesus also insulted him.

Jesus Dies

45At noon the whole country became
dark, and the darkness lasted for three
hours. **46**About three o'clock Jesus cried
out in a loud voice, "Eli, Eli, lama sabach-
thani?" This means, "My God, my God,
why have you rejected me?"
47Some of the people standing there
who heard this said, "He is calling Elijah."
48Quickly one of them ran and got a
sponge and filled it with vinegar and tied
it to a stick and gave it to Jesus to drink.
49But the others said, "Don't bother him.
We want to see if Elijah will come to save
him."
50But Jesus cried out again in a loud
voice and died.
51Then the curtain in the Temple[n]
was torn into two pieces, from the top to
the bottom. Also, the earth shook and
rocks broke apart. **52**The graves opened,
and many of God's people who had died
were raised from the dead. **53**They came
out of the graves after Jesus was raised
from the dead and went into the holy city,
where they appeared to many people.
54When the army officer and the soldiers guarding Jesus saw this earthquake
and everything else that happened, they
were very frightened and said, "He really
was the Son of God!"
55Many women who had followed
Jesus from Galilee to help him were
standing at a distance from the cross,
watching. **56**Mary Magdalene, and Mary
the mother of James and Joseph, and the
mother of James and John were there.

27:34 gall Probably a drink of wine mixed with drugs to help a person feel less pain.

27:51 curtain in the Temple A curtain divided the Most Holy Place from the other part of the Temple. That was the special building in Jerusalem where God commanded the Jewish people to worship him.

Jesus Is Buried

57That evening a rich man named Joseph, a follower of Jesus from the town of
Arimathea, came to Jerusalem. 58Joseph
went to Pilate and asked to have Jesus'
body. So Pilate gave orders for the soldiers to give it to Joseph. 59Then Joseph
took the body and wrapped it in a clean
linen cloth. 60He put Jesus' body in a new
tomb that he had cut out of a wall of rock,
and he rolled a very large stone to block
the entrance of the tomb. Then Joseph
went away. 61Mary Magdalene and the
other woman named Mary were sitting
near the tomb.

The Tomb of Jesus Is Guarded

62The next day, the day after Preparation Day, the leading priests and the
Pharisees went to Pilate. 63They said,
"Sir, we remember that while that liar
was still alive he said, 'After three days I
will rise from the dead.' 64So give the
order for the tomb to be guarded closely
till the third day. Otherwise, his followers
might come and steal the body and tell
people that he has risen from the dead.
That lie would be even worse than the
first one."

65Pilate said, "Take some soldiers
and go guard the tomb the best way you
know." 66So they all went to the tomb
and made it safe from thieves by sealing
the stone in the entrance and putting soldiers there to guard it.

Jesus Rises from the Dead

28 The day after the Sabbath day was
the first day of the week. At dawn
on the first day, Mary Magdalene and another woman named Mary went to look
at the tomb.

2At that time there was a strong
earthquake. An angel of the Lord came
down from heaven, went to the tomb, and
rolled the stone away from the entrance.
Then he sat on the stone. 3He was shining as bright as lightning, and his clothes
were white as snow. 4The soldiers guarding the tomb shook with fear because of
the angel, and they became like dead
men.

5The angel said to the women, "Don't
be afraid. I know that you are looking for
Jesus, who has been crucified. 6He is not
here. He has risen from the dead as he
said he would. Come and see the place
where his body was. 7And go quickly and

FAITH links

TELL ALL ABOUT HIM!

MATTHEW 28:19

Think about someone you admire. If a friend asked you about that person, what would you say about him or her? Before Jesus returned to heaven, his followers were given the job of telling the world about their best friend, Jesus. He was someone *they* admired. If you're a follower of Jesus, that's your job, too. Does this mean you have to immediately get on a plane to Australia in order to talk about Jesus? No, unless you and your folks just happen to be going there. It *does* mean, though, being willing to tell people about Jesus wherever you happen to be.

Faith of Our Fathers, Joshua 4:4–9, p. 280

See the Heart Behind It, Nehemiah 8; 9, p. 636

A Picture of the Past, Psalm 105, p. 789

Remember Your Creator, Ecclesiastes 12:1, 13, p. 885

Inside the Heart of God, Micah 7:18–20, p. 1228

The Number One Rule, Mark 12:28–31, p. 1351

tell his followers, 'Jesus has risen from
the dead. He is going into Galilee ahead
of you, and you will see him there.' "
Then the angel said, "Now I have told
you."
8The women left the tomb quickly.
They were afraid, but they were also
very happy. They ran to tell Jesus' followers what had happened. **9**Suddenly, Jesus
met them and said, "Greetings." The
women came up to him, took hold of his
feet, and worshiped him. **10**Then Jesus
said to them, "Don't be afraid. Go and tell
my followers to go on to Galilee, and they
will see me there."

The Soldiers Report to the Leaders

11While the women went to tell
Jesus' followers, some of the soldiers
who had been guarding the tomb went
into the city to tell the leading priests
everything that had happened. **12**Then
the priests met with the older leaders
and made a plan. They paid the soldiers a
large amount of money **13**and said to
them, "Tell the people that Jesus' followers came during the night and stole the
body while you were asleep. **14**If the governor hears about this, we will satisfy
him and save you from trouble." **15**So the
soldiers kept the money and did as they
were told. And that story is still spread
among the people even today.

Jesus Talks to His Followers

16The eleven followers went to Galilee to the mountain where Jesus had told
them to go. **17**On the mountain they saw
Jesus and worshiped him, but some of
them did not believe it was really Jesus.
18Then Jesus came to them and said, "All
power in heaven and on earth is
given to me. **19**So
go and make follow-
ers of all people in
the world. Baptize
them in the name of
the Father and the
Son and the Holy
Spirit. **20**Teach them to obey everything
that I have taught you, and I will be with
you always, even until the end of this
age."

eMAIL FROM GOD
28:19–20
Witnessing
Check out Jesus' final command.

JESUS ON THE MOVE

Hi, there. I'm Mark. I'm glad you're reading my book. I was just a little older than you when I experienced the things in this book. Even though I wasn't one of *the* disciples, I *was* an early follower of Jesus. I spent a lot of time with Jesus, went with Paul on some of his missionary journeys, and I worked with Barnabas (another early missionary) to spread the gospel. In later years, I knew Peter pretty well, and he told me plenty!

So, why did I write this book? I wrote it for a group of non-Jews who formed a church in Rome. I wanted them to know the same Jesus I did. So I wrote this to tell them about him. But I didn't want to give them looonnnnggg, boring stories. I filled my book with a lot of action-packed short stories about Jesus serving everyone he met. A lot of people say this was the first Gospel written. I guess I was in a hurry!

JESUS WATCH

Mark's Gospel gives us snapshots of Jesus' ministry with lots of details. Before the first chapter is over, Mark describes Jesus' baptism, his temptation in the desert, calling the disciples, casting out demons, and healing people. Whew! And that's just the first chapter! Jesus' personality in this book can best be described as "immediately." You see Jesus going somewhere "immediately" or doing something "immediately." Jesus was always moving forward to reach his goal.

Mark's way of showing us Jesus in this book is really simple. He offers us a picture of Jesus as the servant-king. Chapters 1—10 portray Jesus on a mission to serve many, in a variety of ways and places. Chapters 11—16 portray Jesus as the perfect servant, giving his life for the sins of the people that he loves.

my FAVORITE links

__________ __________

__________ __________

__________ __________

__________ __________

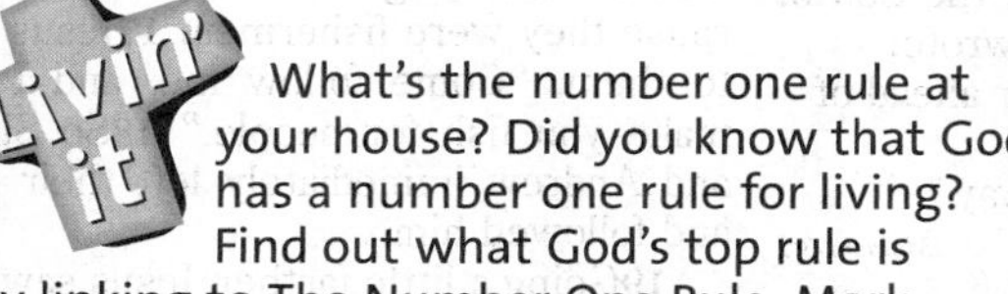

Livin' it What's the number one rule at your house? Did you know that God has a number one rule for living? Find out what God's top rule is by linking to The Number One Rule, Mark 12:28–34. See if it's one you can live by.

Visit these information bulletin boards to find out more about important places and people you'll find in the Book of Mark:

- A Place to Worship, Mark 6:2. Jesus did not worship in a church like the one you may attend. Instead, Jesus and his family would gather at the local synagogue. Link here for more about this important meeting place.
- Connect to Saints, Sinners, or Religious Leaders?, Mark 7:1–13, to learn more about the group of men who were most opposed to Jesus and his teachings. Decide for yourself how you would describe these men!
- Jesus—God With Us, Mark 16. Download this map for a look at the key places in Jesus' childhood, his early ministry, and his later ministry.

"Hey, Tagg, does Mark's book talk about the end times when Jesus will return again?"

"Sure does, Skweek. Surf through Mark 13, and you'll find out a lot. Then take a look at these other really cool stories."

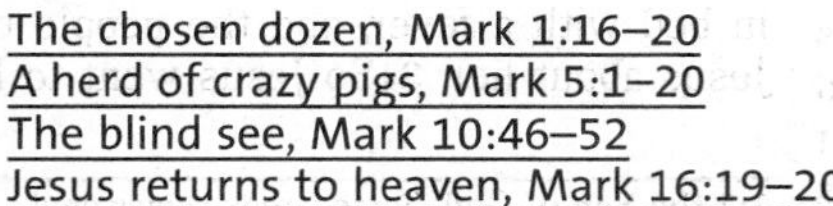

The chosen dozen, Mark 1:16–20
A herd of crazy pigs, Mark 5:1–20
The blind see, Mark 10:46–52
Jesus returns to heaven, Mark 16:19–20

FAITH links

- Prayer Anywhere, Mark 1:35
- Help for a Friend, Mark 2:1–5
- Mission Impossible?, Mark 5:21–24, 35–43
- The Power of *If*, Mark 9:14–24
- My Favorite!, Mark 10:17–23
- Quick to Forgive?, Mark 11:25
- The Number One Rule, Mark 12:28–31
- Get Ready!, Mark 13:26–27
- A Family Meal, Mark 14:23–26
- The Unpopular Choice, Mark 15:42–43

John Prepares for Jesus

1 This is the beginning of the Good News about Jesus Christ, the Son of God,[n] **2**as the prophet Isaiah wrote:

"I will send my messenger ahead of
you,
who will prepare your way."

Malachi 3:1

3"This is a voice of one
who calls out in the desert:
'Prepare the way for the Lord.
Make the road straight for him.' "

Isaiah 40:3

4John was baptizing people in the desert and preaching a baptism of changed hearts and lives for the forgiveness of sins. **5**All the people from Judea and Jerusalem were going out to him. They confessed their sins and were baptized by him in the Jordan River. **6**John wore clothes made from camel's hair, had a leather belt around his waist, and ate locusts and wild honey. **7**This is what John preached to the people: "There is one coming after me who is greater than I; I am not good enough even to kneel down and untie his sandals. **8**I baptize you with water, but he will baptize you with the Holy Spirit."

Jesus Is Baptized

9At that time Jesus came from the town of Nazareth in Galilee and was baptized by John in the Jordan River. **10**Immediately, as Jesus was coming up out of the water, he saw heaven open. The Holy Spirit came down on him like a dove, **11**and a voice came from heaven: "You are my Son, whom I love, and I am very pleased with you."

12Then the Spirit sent Jesus into the desert. **13**He was in the desert forty days and was tempted by Satan. He was with the wild animals, and the angels came and took care of him.

Jesus Chooses Some Followers

14After John was put in prison, Jesus went into Galilee, preaching the Good News from God. **15**He said, "The right time has come. The kingdom of God is near. Change your hearts and lives and believe the Good News!"

16When Jesus was walking by Lake Galilee, he saw Simon[n] and his brother Andrew throwing a net into the lake because they were fishermen. **17**Jesus said to them, "Come follow me, and I will make you fish for people." **18**So Simon and Andrew immediately left their nets and followed him.

19Going a little farther, Jesus saw two more brothers, James and John, the sons of Zebedee. They were in a boat, mending their nets. **20**Jesus immediately called them, and they left their father in the boat with the hired workers and followed Jesus.

Jesus Forces Out an Evil Spirit

21Jesus and his followers went to Capernaum. On the Sabbath day He went to the synagogue and began to teach. **22**The people were amazed at his teaching, because he taught like a person who had authority, not like their teachers of the law.**23**Just then, a man was there in the synagogue who had an evil spirit in him. He shouted, **24**"Jesus of Nazareth! What do you want with us? Did you come to destroy us? I know who you are—God's Holy One!"

25Jesus commanded the evil spirit, "Be quiet! Come out of the man!" **26**The evil spirit shook the man violently, gave a loud cry, and then came out of him.

27The people were so amazed they asked each other, "What is happening here? This man is teaching something new, and with authority. He even gives commands to evil spirits, and they obey him." **28**And the news about Jesus spread quickly everywhere in the area of Galilee.

Jesus Heals Many People

29As soon as Jesus and his followers left the synagogue, they went with James and John to the home of Simon[n] and Andrew. **30**Simon's mother-in-law was sick in bed with a fever, and the people told Jesus about her. **31**So Jesus went to her

---

1:1 the Son of God Some Greek copies omit these words.

1:16, 29 Simon Simon's other name was Peter.

FAITH links

PRAYER ANYWHERE

MARK 1:35

Suppose someone told you that you could talk to your mom or dad only on Sundays and only while sitting at the dining room table. Sounds pretty silly? Well, God is your heavenly Father. Some people believe that they can only talk to God at certain times and at one certain place—church. What do you believe?

Jesus often woke up early and went off by himself to pray. Prayer can take place anywhere. You can talk to God on your way to school, in the car, or on the playground. God is always ready to listen to you—anytime, anywhere!

Need to talk to God? Connect here:

From Hopeless to Hopeful, Exodus 6:9, p. 83

What Will You Risk?, Joshua 2, p. 278

Real Faith or Really Scared?, Judges 4, p. 315

No Doubt About It, Job 36:5, p. 699

Hope That Doesn't Fail, Acts 26:4–7, p. 1510

Thoughts on Thoughts, Philippians 4:8–9, p. 1614

bed, took her hand, and helped her up. The fever left her, and she began serving them.

32That evening, after the sun went
down, the people brought to Jesus all who
were sick and had demons in them.
33The whole town gathered at the door.
34Jesus healed many who had different
kinds of sicknesses, and he forced many
demons to leave people. But he would
not allow the demons to speak, because
they knew who he was.

35Early the next morning, while it
was still dark, Jesus woke and left the
house. He went to a lonely place, where
he prayed. 36Simon and his friends went
to look for Jesus. 37When they found
him, they said, "Everyone is looking for
you!"

38Jesus answered, "We should go to
other towns around here so I can preach
there too. That is the reason I came."
39So he went everywhere in Galilee,
preaching in the synagogues and forcing
out demons.

Jesus Heals a Sick Man

40A man with a skin disease came to
Jesus. He fell to his knees and begged
Jesus, "You can heal me if you will."

41Jesus felt sorry for the man, so he
reached out his hand and touched him
and said, "I will. Be healed!" 42Immedi-
ately the disease left the man, and he was
healed.

43Jesus told the man to go away at
once, but he warned him strongly,
44"Don't tell anyone about this. But go
and show yourself to the priest. And offer
the gift Moses commanded for people
who are made well.[n] This will show the
people what I have done." 45The man left
there, but he began to tell everyone that
Jesus had healed him, and so he spread
the news about Jesus. As a result, Jesus
could not enter a town if people saw him.
He stayed in places where nobody lived,
but people came to him from everywhere.

Jesus Heals a Paralyzed Man

2 A few days later, when Jesus came
back to Capernaum, the news spread

1:44 Moses . . . well Read about this in Leviticus 14:1-32.

FAITH links

HELP FOR A FRIEND

MARK 2:1-5

Would you go out of your way to help a friend? Four people wanted to take their paralyzed friend to Jesus. Since Jesus was in a crowded house, they made a hole in the roof and lowered him down, bed and all.

Jesus wants you to have the same kind of concern for your friends. You don't have to tear up a roof to help a friend, however. You can tell her about Jesus, pray for him, say kind words to her when she's feeling sad, or just be willing to listen to him. Your friend will be glad you care!

Here are some more Faithlinks on caring for your friends:

Giving Your Part, Leviticus 27:30, p. 173

An Unsung Hero, Ruth 2:12, 15–16, p. 347

The Heart of the Matter, 1 Samuel 16, p. 375

Lower Than Low, Job 19:13–25, p. 680

God's Instructions, Ezekiel 4:1–15, p. 1089

Kindness First, Matthew 9:35–36, p. 1290

that he was at home. **2**Many people gathered together so that there was no room
in the house, not even outside the door.
And Jesus was teaching them God's message. **3**Four people came, carrying a paralyzed man. **4**Since they could not get to
Jesus because of the crowd, they dug a
hole in the roof right above where he was
speaking. When they got through, they
lowered the mat with the paralyzed man
on it. **5**When Jesus saw the faith of these
people, he said to the paralyzed man,
"Young man, your sins are forgiven."

6Some of the teachers of the law were
sitting there, thinking to themselves,
7"Why does this man say things like
that? He is speaking as if he were God.
Only God can forgive sins."

8Jesus knew immediately what these
teachers of the law were thinking. So he
said to them, "Why are you thinking
these things? **9**Which is easier: to tell
this paralyzed man, 'Your sins are forgiven,' or to tell him, 'Stand up. Take
your mat and walk'? **10**But I will prove to
you that the Son of Man has authority on
earth to forgive sins." So Jesus said to
the paralyzed man, **11**"I tell you, stand
up, take your mat, and go home." **12**Immediately the paralyzed man stood up,
took his mat, and walked out while everyone was watching him.

The people were amazed and praised God. They said, "We have never seen anything like this!"

13Jesus went to the lake again. The
whole crowd followed him there, and he
taught them. **14**While he was walking
along, he saw a man named Levi son of
Alphaeus, sitting in the tax collector's
booth. Jesus said to him, "Follow me,"
and he stood up and followed Jesus.

15Later, as Jesus was having dinner at
Levi's house, many tax collectors and
"sinners" were eating there with Jesus
and his followers. Many people like this
followed Jesus. **16**When the teachers of
the law who were Pharisees saw Jesus
eating with the tax collectors and "sinners," they asked his followers, "Why
does he eat with tax collectors and sinners?"

17Jesus heard this and said to them,
"It is not the healthy people who need
a doctor, but the sick. I did not come
to invite good people but to invite sinners."

Jesus' Followers Are Criticized

18Now the followers of John[n] and the Pharisees often gave up eating for a certain time.[n] Some people came to Jesus and said, "Why do John's followers and the followers of the Pharisees often give up eating, but your followers don't?"

19Jesus answered, "The friends of the bridegroom do not give up eating while the bridegroom is still with them. As long as the bridegroom is with them, they cannot give up eating. **20**But the time will come when the bridegroom will be taken from them, and then they will give up eating.

21"No one sews a patch of unshrunk cloth over a hole in an old coat. Otherwise, the patch will shrink and pull away—the new patch will pull away from the old coat. Then the hole will be worse. **22**Also, no one ever pours new wine into old leather bags. Otherwise, the new wine will break the bags, and the wine will be ruined along with the bags. But new wine should be put into new leather bags."

Jesus Is Lord of the Sabbath

23One Sabbath day, as Jesus was walking through some fields of grain, his followers began to pick some grain to eat. **24**The Pharisees said to Jesus, "Why are your followers doing what is not lawful on the Sabbath day?"

25Jesus answered, "Have you never read what David did when he and those with him were hungry and needed food? **26**During the time of Abiathar the high priest, David went into God's house and ate the holy bread, which is lawful only for priests to eat. And David also gave some of the bread to those who were with him."

27Then Jesus said to the Pharisees, "The Sabbath day was made to help people; they were not made to be ruled by the Sabbath day. **28**So then, the Son of Man is Lord even of the Sabbath day."

Jesus Heals a Man's Hand

3 Another time when Jesus went into a synagogue, a man with a crippled hand was there. **2**Some people watched Jesus closely to see if he would heal the man on the Sabbath day so they could accuse him.

3Jesus said to the man with the crippled hand, "Stand up here in the middle of everyone."

4Then Jesus asked the people, "Which is lawful on the Sabbath day: to do good or to do evil, to save a life or to kill?" But they said nothing to answer him.

5Jesus was angry as he looked at the people, and he felt very sad because they were stubborn. Then he said to the man, "Hold out your hand." The man held out his hand and it was healed. **6**Then the Pharisees left and began making plans with the Herodians[n] about a way to kill Jesus.

Many People Follow Jesus

7Jesus left with his followers for the lake, and a large crowd from Galilee followed him. **8**Also many people came from Judea, from Jerusalem, from Idumea, from the lands across the Jordan River, and from the area of Tyre and Sidon. When they heard what Jesus was doing, many people came to him. **9**When Jesus saw the crowds, he told his followers to get a boat ready for him to keep people from crowding against him. **10**He had healed many people, so all the sick were pushing toward him to touch him. **11**When evil spirits saw Jesus, they fell down before him and shouted, "You are the Son of God!" **12**But Jesus strongly warned them not to tell who he was.

Jesus Chooses His Twelve Apostles

13Then Jesus went up on a mountain and called to him the men he wanted, and they came to him. **14**Jesus chose twelve men and called them apostles. He wanted them to be with him, and he wanted to

---

2:18 John John the Baptist, who preached to the Jewish people about Christ's coming (Mark 1:4-8).
2:18 gave . . . time This is called "fasting." The people would give up eating for a special time of prayer and worship to God. It was also done to show sadness and disappointment.
3:6 Herodians A political group that followed Herod and his family.

send them out to preach 15and to have
the authority to force demons out of people. 16These are the twelve men he
chose: Simon (Jesus named him Peter),
17James and John, the sons of Zebedee
(Jesus named them Boanerges, which
means "Sons of Thunder"), 18Andrew,
Philip, Bartholomew, Matthew, Thomas,
James the son of Alphaeus, Thaddaeus,
Simon the Zealot, 19and Judas Iscariot,
who later turned against Jesus.

Some People Say Jesus Has a Devil

20Then Jesus went home, but again a
crowd gathered. There were so many
people that Jesus and his followers could
not eat. 21When his family heard this,
they went to get him because they
thought he was out of his mind. 22But the
teachers of the law from Jerusalem were
saying, "Beelzebul is living inside him!
He uses power from the ruler of demons
to force demons out of people."

23So Jesus called the people together
and taught them with stories. He said,
"Satan will not force himself out of people.
24A kingdom that is divided cannot continue, 25and a family that is divided cannot
continue. 26And if Satan is against himself
and fights against his own people, he cannot continue; that is the end of Satan.

CONTROL YOURSELF

Ever stop to think about the things you are thankful for? We have a friend who is having some problems in this area. Let's welcome Max, age 9, to Connect 2-You.

Max

My mom says I spend too much time wishing for things I don't have instead of appreciating what I do have. She says I'm not grateful for the things God has given me. What does that mean? Should I go around saying thank-you for every little thing that happens?

Hi, Max. What's the problem?

Sometimes it's easy to forget how much God does for us, Max. But when you take time to stop and really think about it, you'll be amazed at what comes to mind. If you'd like some tips on how to do this, check out the Livin' It page on being thankful, Colossians 2:6–7, p. 1623. It may help you develop a "thanksgiving" attitude year-round!

It also helps to put yourself in God's position, Max. How would you feel if you did something really nice for someone and that person never said thank-you or even noticed what you had done? Just as we like to be thanked for things we do, so does God! Remember that next time you catch the grumblings.

27No one can enter a strong person's
house and steal his things unless he first
ties up the strong person. Then he can
steal things from the house. **28**I tell you
the truth, all sins that people do and all the
things people say against God can be forgiven. **29**But anyone who speaks against
the Holy Spirit will never be forgiven; he
is guilty of a sin that continues forever."
30Jesus said this because the teachers of the law said that he had an evil
spirit inside him.

Jesus' True Family

31Then Jesus' mother and brothers arrived. Standing outside, they sent someone in to tell him to come out. **32**Many
people were sitting around Jesus, and
they said to him, "Your mother and brothers are waiting for you outside."
33Jesus asked, "Who are my mother
and my brothers?" **34**Then he looked at
those sitting around him and said, "Here
are my mother and my brothers! **35**My
true brother and sister and mother are
those who do what God wants."

A Story About Planting Seed

4 Again Jesus began teaching by the
lake. A great crowd gathered around
him, so he sat down in a boat near the
shore. All the people stayed on the shore
close to the water. **2**Jesus taught them
many things, using stories. He said,
3"Listen! A farmer went out to plant his
seed. **4**While he was planting, some seed
fell by the road, and the birds came and
ate it up. **5**Some seed fell on rocky
ground where there wasn't much dirt.
That seed grew very fast, because the
ground was not deep. **6**But when the sun
rose, the plants dried up because they did
not have deep roots. **7**Some other seed
fell among thorny weeds, which grew and
choked the good plants. So those plants
did not produce a crop. **8**Some other seed
fell on good ground and began to grow. It
got taller and produced a crop. Some
plants made thirty times more, some
made sixty times more, and some made a
hundred times more."
9Then Jesus said, "You people who
can hear me, listen!"

Jesus Tells Why He Used Stories

10Later, when Jesus was alone, the
twelve apostles and others around him
asked him about the stories.
11Jesus said, "You can know the secret about the kingdom of God. But to
other people I tell everything by using
stories **12**so that:

'They will look and look, but they
will not learn.
They will listen and listen, but
they will not understand.
If they did learn and understand,
they would come back to me and
be forgiven.' " *Isaiah 6:9-10*

Jesus Explains the Seed Story

13Then Jesus said to his followers,
"Don't you understand this story? If you
don't, how will you understand any story?
14The farmer is like a person who plants
God's message in people. **15**Sometimes
the teaching falls on the road. This is like
the people who hear the teaching of God,
but Satan quickly comes and takes away
the teaching that was planted in them.
16Others are like the seed planted on
rocky ground. They hear the teaching and
quickly accept it with joy. **17**But since
they don't allow the teaching to go deep
into their lives, they keep it only a short
time. When trouble or persecution comes
because of the teaching they accepted,
they quickly give up. **18**Others are like the
seed planted among the thorny weeds.
They hear the teaching, **19**but the worries
of this life, the temptation of wealth, and
many other evil desires keep the teaching
from growing and producing fruit[n] in their
lives. **20**Others are like the seed planted
in the good ground. They hear the teaching and accept it. Then they grow and produce fruit—sometimes thirty times more,
sometimes sixty times more, and sometimes a hundred times more."

Use What You Have

21Then Jesus said to them, "Do you
hide a lamp under a bowl or under a bed?
No! You put the lamp on a lampstand.

4:19 producing fruit To produce fruit means to have in your life the good things God wants.

22Everything that is hidden will be made
clear and every secret thing will be made
known. 23You people who can hear me,
listen!

24"Think carefully about what you
hear. The way you give to others is the
way God will give to you, but God will give
you even more. 25Those who have understanding will be given more. But those
who do not have understanding, even
what they have will be taken away from
them."

Jesus Uses a Story About Seed

26Then Jesus said, "The kingdom of
God is like someone who plants seed in
the ground. 27Night and day, whether the
person is asleep or awake, the seed still
grows, but the person does not know how
it grows. 28By itself the earth produces
grain. First the plant grows, then the
head, and then all the grain in the head.
29When the grain is ready, the farmer
cuts it, because this is the harvest time."

A Story About Mustard Seed

30Then Jesus said, "How can I show
you what the kingdom of God is like?
What story can I use to explain it? 31The
kingdom of God is like
a mustard seed, the smallest seed you plant in the
ground. 32But when plant-
ed, this seed grows and becomes the largest of all
garden plants. It produces
large branches, and the
wild birds can make nests
in its shade."

> The kingdom of God is like a mustard seed, the smallest seed you plant in the ground.
>
> —Mark 4:31

33Jesus used many
stories like these to teach
the crowd God's message—as much as
they could understand. 34He always used
stories to teach them. But when he and
his followers were alone, Jesus explained
everything to them.

Jesus Calms a Storm

35That evening, Jesus said to his followers, "Let's go across the lake."
36Leaving the crowd behind, they took
him in the boat just as he was. There
were also other boats with them. 37A
very strong wind came up on the lake.
The waves came over the sides and into
the boat so that it was already full of water. 38Jesus was at the back of the boat,
sleeping with his head on a cushion. His
followers woke him and said, "Teacher,
don't you care that we are drowning!"

39Jesus stood up and commanded the
wind and said to the waves, "Quiet! Be
still!" Then the wind stopped, and it became completely calm.

40Jesus said to his followers, "Why
are you afraid? Do you still have no
faith?"

41The followers were very afraid and
asked each other, "Who is this? Even the
wind and the waves obey him!"

A Man with Demons Inside Him

5 Jesus and his followers went to the
other side of the lake to the area of
the Gerasene people. 2When Jesus got
out of the boat, instantly a man with an
evil spirit came to him from the burial
caves. 3This man lived in the caves, and
no one could tie him up, not even with a
chain. 4Many times people had used
chains to tie the man's hands and feet,
but he always broke them off. No one was
strong enough to control
him. 5Day and night he
would wander around the
burial caves and on the
hills, screaming and cut-
ting himself with stones.
6While Jesus was still far
away, the man saw him,
ran to him, and fell down
before him.

7The man shouted in
a loud voice, "What do
you want with me, Jesus, Son of the Most
High God? I command you in God's name
not to torture me!" 8He said this because
Jesus was saying to him, "You evil spirit,
come out of the man."

9Then Jesus asked him, "What is your
name?"

He answered, "My name is Legion,"
because we are many spirits." 10He

5:9 Legion Means very many. A legion was about five thousand men in the Roman army.

FAITH links

MISSION IMPOSSIBLE?

MARK 5:21-24, 35-43

Got a hard problem in your life? Maybe you, like Jairus the synagogue leader, are wondering what Jesus can do for you. Jairus didn't have a hard problem. He had an *impossible* problem. His daughter was dying. He knew that only Jesus could help her. By the time Jesus arrived, she had died. But Jesus did the impossible by bringing her back to life.

Hard problems help us learn to trust God. Through them, we learn that Jesus has the power to do anything. When you're faced with the impossible, put your trust in the God of impossibilities.

Good Plans, Genesis 45:7–8, p. 64

A Holiday Letter, Esther 9:20–23, p. 657

Happiness or Joy?, Job 29:18–19, p. 691

Prove It!, Matthew 16:1–4, p. 1302

Just for the Asking, Romans 3:23–28, p. 1522

Fear-Fighters, 2 Timothy 1:7, p. 1652

begged Jesus again and again not to send
them out of that area.
11A large herd of pigs was feeding on
a hill near there. 12The demons begged
Jesus, "Send us into the pigs; let us go
into them." 13So Jesus allowed them to
do this. The evil spirits left the man and
went into the pigs. Then the herd of
pigs—about two thousand of them—
rushed down the hill into the lake and
were drowned.
14The herdsmen ran away and went
to the town and to the countryside, telling everyone about this. So people went
out to see what had happened. 15They
came to Jesus and saw the man who used
to have the many evil spirits, sitting,
clothed, and in his right mind. And they
were frightened. 16The people who saw
this told the others what had happened to
the man who had the demons living in
him, and they told about the pigs. 17Then
the people began to beg Jesus to leave
their area.
18As Jesus was getting back into the
boat, the man who was freed from the demons begged to go with him.
19But Jesus would not let him. He
said, "Go home to your family and tell
them how much the Lord has done for
you and how he has had mercy on you."
20So the man left and began to tell the
people in the Ten Towns[n] about what
Jesus had done for him. And everyone
was amazed.

Jesus Gives Life to a Dead Girl and Heals a Sick Woman

21When Jesus went in the boat back
to the other side of the lake, a large
crowd gathered around him there. 22A
leader of the synagogue, named Jairus,
came there, saw Jesus, and fell at his feet.
23He begged Jesus, saying again and
again, "My daughter is dying. Please
come and put your hands on her so she
will be healed and will live." 24So Jesus
went with him.
A large crowd followed Jesus and
pushed very close around him. 25Among
them was a woman who had been bleeding for twelve years. 26She had suffered
very much from many doctors and had
spent all the money she had, but instead

5:20 Ten Towns In Greek, called "Decapolis." It was an area east of Lake Galilee that once had ten main towns.

of improving, she was getting worse.
27When the woman heard about Jesus,
she came up behind him in the crowd and
touched his coat. **28**She thought, "If I can
just touch his clothes, I will be healed."
29Instantly her bleeding stopped, and
she felt in her body that she was healed
from her disease.

30At once Jesus felt power go out
from him. So he turned around in the
crowd and asked, "Who touched my
clothes?"

31His followers said, "Look at how
many people are pushing against you! And
you ask, 'Who touched me?' "

32But Jesus continued looking around
to see who had touched him. **33**The
woman, knowing that she was healed,
came and fell at Jesus' feet. Shaking with
fear, she told him the whole truth. **34**Jesus
said to her, "Dear woman, you are made
well because you believed. Go in peace;
be healed of your disease."

35While Jesus was still speaking,
some people came from the house of the
synagogue leader. They said, "Your
daughter is dead. There is no need to
bother the teacher anymore."

36But Jesus paid no attention to what
they said. He told the synagogue leader,
"Don't be afraid; just believe."

37Jesus let only Peter, James, and
John the brother of James go with him.
38When they came to the house of the
synagogue leader, Jesus found many people there making lots of noise and crying
loudly. **39**Jesus entered the house and
said to them, "Why are you crying and
making so much noise? The child is not
dead, only asleep." **40**But they laughed at
him. So, after throwing them out of the
house, Jesus took the child's father and
mother and his three followers into the
room where the child was. **41**Taking hold
of the girl's hand, he said to her, "Talitha,
koum!" (This means, "Young girl, I tell
you to stand up!") **42**At once the girl
stood right up and began walking. (She
was twelve years old.) Everyone was
completely amazed. **43**Jesus gave them
strict orders not to tell people about this.
Then he told them to give the girl something to eat.

Jesus Goes to His Hometown

6 Jesus left there and went to his hometown, and his followers went with
him. **2**On the Sabbath day he taught in
the synagogue. Many people heard him
and were amazed, saying, "Where did
this man get these teachings? What is
this wisdom that has been given to him?
And where did he get the power to do
miracles? **3**He is just the carpenter, the
son of Mary and the brother of James, Joseph, Judas, and Simon. And his sisters
are here with us." So the people were
upset with Jesus.

4Jesus said to them, "A prophet is
honored everywhere except in his hometown and with his own people and in his
own home." **5**So Jesus was not able to
work any miracles there except to heal a
few sick people by putting his hands on
them. **6**He was amazed at how many people had no faith.

Then Jesus went to other villages in
that area and taught. **7**He called his
twelve followers together and got ready
to send them out two by two and gave
them authority over evil spirits. **8**This is
what Jesus commanded them: "Take
nothing for your trip except a walking
stick. Take no bread, no bag, and no
money in your pockets. **9**Wear sandals,
but take only the clothes you are wearing. **10**When you enter a house, stay
there until you leave that town. **11**If the
people in a certain place refuse to welcome you or listen to you, leave that
place. Shake its dust off your feet[n] as a
warning to them."

12So the followers went out and
preached that people should change their
hearts and lives. **13**They forced many demons out and put olive oil on many sick
people and healed them.

How John the Baptist Was Killed

14King Herod heard about Jesus, because he was now well known. Some
people said, "He is John the Baptist, who
has risen from the dead. That is why he
can work these miracles."

6:11 Shake . . . feet A warning. It showed that
they were rejecting these people.

A PLACE TO WORSHIP

Mark 6:2

The synagogue was a local gathering place where Jews of all ages met to pray and study the teachings of Moses. There were many synagogues in Jerusalem, because a new one could be started every time ten or more men committed to studying together. There were no sacrifices offered at the synagogue like there were at the Temple. When people went to the synagogue, they would read from books of the Bible, pray, and listen to someone teach. Different men taught at different times. Jesus read the Scriptures in the synagogue in Nazareth (See Luke 4:16–30, p. 1374.), and he often taught in synagogues. (Look up Matthew 4:23, p. 1279.)

Synagogue buildings usually were rectangular with a large sitting area, like many church sanctuaries today. The congregation sat on stone benches along the walls or cross-legged on the floor. The main piece of furniture in a synagogue was the place where the sacred scrolls (like our Bible) were kept. The apostle Paul preached at synagogues on his missionary journeys. (Check out Acts 13:5, p. 1486; 14:1, p. 1489.)

15Others said, "He is Elijah."[n]

Other people said, "Jesus is a prophet, like the prophets who lived long ago."
16When Herod heard this, he said, "I killed John by cutting off his head. Now he has risen from the dead!"

17Herod himself had ordered his soldiers to arrest John and put him in prison in order to please his wife, Herodias. She had been the wife of Philip, Herod's brother, but then Herod had married her.
18John had been telling Herod, "It is not lawful for you to be married to your brother's wife."
19So Herodias hated John and wanted to kill him. But she couldn't,
20because Herod was afraid of John and protected him. He knew John was a good and holy man. Also, though John's preaching always bothered him, he enjoyed listening to John.

21Then the perfect time came for Herodias to cause John's death. On Herod's birthday, he gave a dinner party for the most important government leaders, the commanders of his army, and the most important people in Galilee.
22When the daughter of Herodias came in and danced, she pleased Herod and the people eating with him.

So King Herod said to the girl, "Ask me for anything you want, and I will give it to you."
23He promised her, "Anything you ask for I will give to you—up to half of my kingdom."

24The girl went to her mother and asked, "What should I ask for?"

Her mother answered, "Ask for the head of John the Baptist."

25At once the girl went back to the king and said to him, "I want the head of John the Baptist right now on a platter."

26Although the king was very sad, he had made a promise, and his dinner guests had heard it. So he did not want to

---

6:15 Elijah A great prophet who spoke for God and who lived hundreds of years before Christ. See 1 Kings 17.

refuse what she asked. 27Immediately
the king sent a soldier to bring John's
head. The soldier went and cut off John's
head in the prison 28and brought it back
on a platter. He gave it to the girl, and the
girl gave it to her mother. 29When John's
followers heard this, they came and got
John's body and put it in a tomb.

More than Five Thousand Fed

30The apostles gathered around Jesus
and told him about all the things they had
done and taught. 31Crowds of people
were coming and going so that Jesus and
his followers did not even have time to
eat. He said to them, "Come away by
yourselves, and we will go to a lonely
place to get some rest."

32So they went in a boat by themselves to a lonely place. 33But many people saw them leave and recognized them.
So from all the towns they ran to the
place where Jesus was going, and they
got there before him. 34When he arrived,
he saw a great crowd waiting. He felt
sorry for them, because they were like
sheep without a shepherd. So he began to
teach them many things.

35When it was late in the day, his
followers came to him and said, "No
one lives in this place, and it is already
very late. 36Send the people away so they
can go to the countryside and towns
around here to buy themselves something
to eat."

37But Jesus answered, "You give
them something to eat."

They said to him, "We would all have to work a month to earn enough money to buy that much bread!"

38Jesus asked them, "How many
loaves of bread do you have? Go and see."

When they found out, they said, "Five loaves and two fish."

39Then Jesus told his followers to
have the people sit in groups on the
green grass. 40So they sat in groups of
fifty or a hundred. 41Jesus took the five
loaves and two fish and, looking up to
heaven, he thanked God for the food. He
divided the bread and gave it to his followers for them to give to the people.
Then he divided the two fish among them
all. 42All the people ate and were satisfied. 43The followers filled twelve baskets with the leftover pieces of bread and
fish. 44There were five thousand men
who ate.

Jesus Walks on the Water

45Immediately Jesus told his followers to get into the boat and go ahead of
him to Bethsaida across the lake. He
stayed there to send the people home.
46After sending them away, he went into
the hills to pray.

47That night, the boat was in the middle of the lake, and Jesus was alone on
the land. 48He saw his followers struggling hard to row the boat, because the
wind was blowing against them. Between
three and six o'clock in the morning,
Jesus came to them, walking on the water, and he wanted to walk past the boat.
49But when they saw him walking on the
water, they thought he was a ghost and
cried out. 50They all saw him and were
afraid. But quickly Jesus spoke to them
and said, "Have courage! It is I. Do not be
afraid." 51Then he got into the boat with
them, and the wind became calm. The
followers were greatly amazed. 52They
did not understand about the miracle of
the five loaves, because their minds were
closed.

53When they had crossed the lake,
they came to shore at Gennesaret and tied
the boat there. 54When they got out of the
boat, people immediately recognized
Jesus. 55They ran everywhere in that
area and began to bring sick people on
mats wherever they heard he was. 56And
everywhere he went—into towns, cities,
or countryside—the people brought the
sick to the marketplaces. They begged
him to let them touch just the edge of his
coat, and all who touched it were healed.

Obey God's Law

7 When some Pharisees and some
teachers of the law came from Jerusalem, they gathered around Jesus. 2They
saw that some of Jesus' followers ate
food with hands that were not clean, that
is, they hadn't washed them. 3(The Pharisees and all the Jews never eat before

SAINTS, SINNERS, OR RELIGIOUS LEADERS?

Mark 7:1–13

The Pharisees and Sadducees were two groups of Jewish religious leaders. Jesus had disagreements with both groups during his life on earth.

The word *Pharisee* means "separated." The Pharisees concentrated on keeping themselves separate from people who did not observe certain religious laws. The Pharisees made up some of these laws. Like if God gave one law, "Keep the Sabbath holy," the Pharisees would interpret that into a lot of rules and regulations about what it meant to keep the Sabbath holy. Jesus didn't ever disagree with God's laws, but he often disagreed with all the rules and regulations that the Pharisees made up and added to God's laws.

The Sadducees were priests, merchants, and aristocrats. They stuck to God's original laws, but they did not believe in the resurrection of the dead. You can see how Jesus would disagree with that! (Check out Mark 12:18–27.)

washing their hands in a special way according to their unwritten laws. 4And
when they buy something in the market,
they never eat it until they wash themselves in a special way. They also follow
many other unwritten laws, such as the
washing of cups, pitchers, and pots.)
5The Pharisees and the teachers of
the law said to Jesus, "Why don't your
followers obey the unwritten laws which
have been handed down to us? Why do
your followers eat their food with hands
that are not clean?"
6Jesus answered, "Isaiah was right
when he spoke about you hypocrites. He
wrote,

'These people show honor to me
with words,
but their hearts are far from me.
7 Their worship of me is worthless.
The things they teach are nothing
but human rules.' *Isaiah 29:13*

8You have stopped following the commands of God, and you follow only human
teachings."
9Then Jesus said to them, "You cleverly ignore the commands of God so you
can follow your own teachings. 10Moses
said, 'Honor your father and your
mother,'[n] and 'Anyone who says cruel
things to his father or mother must be
put to death.'[n] 11But you say a person
can tell his father or mother, 'I have
something I could use to help you, but it
is Corban—a gift to God.' 12You no
longer let that person use that money for
his father or his mother. 13By your own
rules, which you teach people, you are
rejecting what God said. And you do
many things like that."
14After Jesus called the crowd to him
again, he said, "Every person should listen to me and understand what I am saying. 15There is nothing people put into
their bodies that makes them unclean.

7:10 'Honor . . . mother' Quotation from Exodus 20:12; Deuteronomy 5:16.

7:10 'Anyone . . . death.' Quotation from Exodus 21:17.

People are made unclean by the things
that come out of them."**16**[n]

17When Jesus left the people and
went into the house, his followers asked
him about this story. **18**Jesus said, "Do
you still not understand? Surely you
know that nothing that enters someone
from the outside can make that person
unclean. **19**It does not go into the mind,
but into the stomach. Then it goes out of
the body." (When Jesus said this, he
meant that no longer was any food unclean for people to eat.)

20And Jesus said, "The things that
come out of people are the things that
make them unclean. **21**All these evil
things begin inside people, in the mind:
evil thoughts, sexual sins, stealing, murder, adultery, **22**greed, evil actions, lying,
doing sinful things, jealousy, speaking
evil of others, pride, and foolish living.
23All these evil things come from inside
and make people unclean."

Jesus Helps a Non-Jewish Woman

24Jesus left that place and went to the
area around Tyre. When he went into a
house, he did not want anyone to know
he was there, but he could not stay hidden. **25**A woman whose daughter had an
evil spirit in her heard that he was there.
So she quickly came to Jesus and fell at
his feet. **26**She was Greek, born in Phoenicia, in Syria. She begged Jesus to force
the demon out of her daughter.

27Jesus told the woman, "It is not
right to take the children's bread and give
it to the dogs. First let the children eat all
they want."

28But she answered, "Yes, Lord, but
even the dogs under the table can eat the
children's crumbs."

29Then Jesus said, "Because of your
answer, you may go. The demon has left
your daughter."

30The woman went home and found
her daughter lying in bed; the demon was
gone.

Jesus Heals a Deaf Man

31Then Jesus left the area around Tyre
and went through Sidon to Lake Galilee,
to the area of the Ten Towns.[n] **32**While
he was there, some people brought a man
to him who was deaf and could not talk
plainly. The people begged Jesus to put his
hand on the man to heal him.

33Jesus led the man away from the
crowd, by himself. He put his fingers in
the man's ears and then spit and touched
the man's tongue. **34**Looking up to
heaven, he sighed and said to the man,
"Ephphatha!" (This means, "Be opened.")
35Instantly the man was able to hear and
to use his tongue so that he spoke clearly.

36Jesus commanded the people not to
tell anyone about what happened. But the
more he commanded them, the more
they told about it. **37**They were completely amazed and said, "Jesus does
everything well. He makes the deaf hear!
And those who can't talk he makes able
to speak."

More than Four Thousand People Fed

8 Another time there was a great crowd
with Jesus that had nothing to eat. So
Jesus called his followers and said, **2**"I
feel sorry for these people, because they
have already been with me for three
days, and they have nothing to eat. **3**If I
send them home hungry, they will faint
on the way. Some of them live a long way
from here."

4Jesus' followers answered, "How
can we get enough bread to feed all these
people? We are far away from any town."

5Jesus asked, "How many loaves of
bread do you have?"

They answered, "Seven."

6Jesus told the people to sit on the
ground. Then he took the seven loaves,
gave thanks to God, and divided the
bread. He gave the pieces to his followers to give to the people, and they did so.
7The followers also had a few small fish.
After Jesus gave thanks for the fish, he
told his followers to give them to the peo-

7:16 Verse 16 Some Greek copies add verse 16: "You people who can hear me, listen!"

7:31 Ten Towns In Greek, called "Decapolis." It was an area east of Lake Galilee that once had ten main towns.

ple also. **8**All the people ate and were satisfied. Then his followers filled seven
baskets with the leftover pieces of food.
9There were about four thousand people
who ate. After they had eaten, Jesus sent
them home. **10**Then right away he got
into a boat with his followers and went to
the area of Dalmanutha.

The Leaders Ask for a Miracle

11The Pharisees came to Jesus and
began to ask him questions. Hoping to
trap him, they asked Jesus for a miracle
from God. **12**Jesus sighed deeply and
said, "Why do you people ask for a miracle as a sign? I tell you the truth, no sign
will be given to you." **13**Then Jesus left
the Pharisees and went in the boat to the
other side of the lake.

Guard Against Wrong Teachings

14His followers had only one loaf of
bread with them in the boat; they had forgotten to bring more. **15**Jesus warned
them, "Be careful! Beware of the yeast of
the Pharisees and the yeast of Herod."

16His followers discussed the meaning of this, saying, "He said this because
we have no bread."

17Knowing what they were talking
about, Jesus asked them, "Why are you
talking about not having bread? Do you
still not see or understand? Are your
minds closed? **18**You have eyes, but you
don't really see. You have ears, but you
don't really listen. Remember when **19**I
divided five loaves of bread for the five
thousand? How many baskets did you fill
with leftover pieces of food?"

They answered, "Twelve."

20"And when I divided seven loaves of
bread for the four thousand, how many
baskets did you fill with leftover pieces of
food?"

They answered, "Seven."

21Then Jesus said to them, "Don't
you understand yet?"

Jesus Heals a Blind Man

22Jesus and his followers came to
Bethsaida. There some people brought a
blind man to Jesus and begged him to
touch the man. **23**So Jesus took the blind
man's hand and led him out of the village.
Then he spit on the man's eyes and put
his hands on the man and asked, "Can
you see now?"

24The man looked up and said, "Yes, I
see people, but they look like trees walking around."

25Again Jesus put his hands on the
man's eyes. Then the man opened his
eyes wide and they were healed, and he
was able to see everything clearly.
26Jesus told him to go home, saying,
"Don't go into the town."

Peter Says Jesus Is the Christ

27Jesus and his followers went to the
towns around Caesarea Philippi. While
they were traveling, Jesus asked them,
"Who do people say I am?"

28They answered, "Some say you are
John the Baptist. Others say you are
Elijah,[n] and others say you are one of the
prophets."

29Then Jesus asked, "But who do you
say I am?"

Peter answered, "You are the Christ."

30Jesus warned his followers not to
tell anyone who he was.

31Then Jesus began to teach them
that the Son of Man must suffer many
things and that he would be rejected by
the older Jewish leaders, the leading
priests, and the teachers of the law. He
told them that the Son of Man must be
killed and then rise from the dead after
three days. **32**Jesus told them plainly
what would happen. Then Peter took
Jesus aside and began to tell him not to
talk like that. **33**But Jesus turned and
looked at his followers. Then he told
Peter not to talk that way. He said, "Go
away from me, Satan![n] You don't care
about the things of God, but only about
things people think are important."

34Then Jesus called the crowd to him,
along with his followers. He said, "If people want to follow me, they must give up

---

8:28 Elijah A man who spoke for God and who lived hundreds of years before Christ. See 1 Kings 17.

8:33 Satan Name for the devil meaning "the enemy." Jesus means that Peter was talking like Satan.

the things they want. They must be willing even to give up their lives to follow
me. 35Those who want
to save their lives
will give up true life.
But those who give
up their lives for me
and for the Good
News will have true
life. 36It is worth nothing for them to
have the whole world if they lose their
souls. 37They could never pay enough to
buy back their souls. 38The people who
live now are living in a sinful and evil
time. If people are ashamed of me and my
teaching, the Son of Man will be ashamed
of them when he comes with his Father's
glory and with the holy angels."

EMAIL! FROM GOD
8:34–36
Money
What it means to follow Jesus

9 Then Jesus said to the people, "I tell
you the truth, some people standing
here will see the kingdom of God come
with power before they die."

Jesus Talks with Moses and Elijah

2Six days later, Jesus took Peter,
James, and John up on a high mountain by
themselves. While they watched, Jesus'
appearance was changed. 3His clothes
became shining white, whiter than any
person could make them. 4Then Elijah
and Moses[n] appeared to them, talking
with Jesus.

5Peter said to Jesus, "Teacher, it is
good that we are here. Let us make three
tents—one for you, one for Moses, and
one for Elijah." 6Peter did not know what
to say, because he and the others were so
frightened.

7Then a cloud came and covered
them, and a voice came from the cloud,
saying, "This is my Son, whom I love.
Listen to him!"

8Suddenly Peter, James, and John
looked around, but they saw only Jesus
there alone with them.

9As they were coming down the
mountain, Jesus commanded them not to
tell anyone about what they had seen until the Son of Man had risen from the
dead.

10So the followers obeyed Jesus, but
they discussed what he meant about rising from the dead.

FAITH links

THE POWER OF *IF*

MARK 9:14-24

One of the most powerful words in the English language is the word *if.* That tiny word can mean the difference between belief and unbelief. A father asked Jesus for help for his son. When the father said, "If you can do anything," Jesus knew that he had trouble believing.

Part of learning to trust God is learning to admit when you have a problem believing in him. God is never fooled when we claim to have faith that we really don't have. If you don't have it, admit it! Then, like the father, ask Jesus to help you have faith.

Download these links for more on faith:

Lights, Camera, . . . Actions!, Genesis 12:1–3, p. 17

Complaints, Complaints!, Exodus 16:1–3, p. 97

A Serious Promise, Deuteronomy 23:21–23, p. 257

Wisdom in Store, Proverbs 2:6–7, p. 828

A Word About Worry, Matthew 6:25–34, p. 1284

Heavenly Treasure, Luke 12:32–34, p. 1394

9:4 Elijah and Moses Two of the most important Jewish leaders in the past. God had given Moses the Law, and Elijah was an important prophet.

11Then they asked Jesus, "Why do
the teachers of the law say that Elijah
must come first?"

12Jesus answered, "They are right to
say that Elijah must come first and make
everything the way it should be. But why
does the Scripture say that the Son of
Man will suffer much and that people will
treat him as if he were nothing? **13**I tell
you that Elijah has already come. And
people did to him whatever they wanted
to do, just as the Scriptures said it would
happen."

Jesus Heals a Sick Boy

14When Jesus, Peter, James, and John
came back to the other followers, they
saw a great crowd around them and the
teachers of the law arguing with them.
15But as soon as the crowd saw Jesus,
the people were surprised and ran to welcome him.

16Jesus asked, "What are you arguing
about?"

17A man answered, "Teacher, I
brought my son to you. He has an evil
spirit in him that stops him from talking.
18When the spirit attacks him, it throws
him on the ground. Then my son foams at
the mouth, grinds his teeth, and becomes
very stiff. I asked your followers to force
the evil spirit out, but they couldn't."

19Jesus answered, "You people have
no faith. How long must I stay with you?
How long must I put up with you? Bring
the boy to me."

20So the followers brought him to
Jesus. As soon as the evil spirit saw
Jesus, it made the boy lose control of
himself, and he fell down and rolled on
the ground, foaming at the mouth.

21Jesus asked the boy's father, "How
long has this been happening?"

The father answered, "Since he was
very young. **22**The spirit often throws
him into a fire or into water to kill him. If
you can do anything for him, please have
pity on us and help us."

23Jesus said to the father, "You said,
'If you can!' All things are possible for the
one who believes."

24Immediately the father cried out, "I
do believe! Help me to believe more!"

25When Jesus saw that a crowd was
quickly gathering, he ordered the evil
spirit, saying, "You spirit that makes people unable to hear or speak, I command
you to come out of this boy and never enter him again!"

26The evil spirit screamed and caused
the boy to fall on the ground again. Then
the spirit came out. The boy looked as if
he were dead, and many people said, "He
is dead!" **27**But Jesus took hold of the
boy's hand and helped him to stand up.

28When Jesus went into the house,
his followers began asking him privately,
"Why couldn't we force that evil spirit
out?"

29Jesus answered, "That kind of spirit
can only be forced out by prayer."

Jesus Talks About His Death

30Then Jesus and his followers left
that place and went through Galilee. He
didn't want anyone to know where he
was, **31**because he was teaching his followers. He said to them, "The Son of
Man will be handed over to people, and
they will kill him. After three days, he
will rise from the dead." **32**But the followers did not understand what Jesus
meant, and they were afraid to ask him.

Who Is the Greatest?

33Jesus and his followers went to Capernaum. When they went into a house
there, he asked them, "What were you
arguing about on the road?" **34**But the
followers did not answer, because their
argument on the road was about which
one of them was the greatest.

35Jesus sat down and called the
twelve apostles to him. He said, "Whoever wants to be the most important
must be last of all and servant of all."

36Then Jesus took a small child and
had him stand among them. Taking the
child in his arms, he said, **37**"Whoever
accepts a child like this in my name accepts me. And whoever accepts me accepts the One who sent me."

Anyone Not Against Us Is for Us

38Then John said, "Teacher, we saw
someone using your name to force demons

out of a person. We told him to stop, because he does not belong to our group."
39But Jesus said, "Don't stop him, because anyone who uses my name to do
powerful things will not easily say evil
things about me. 40Whoever is not
against us is with us. 41I tell you the
truth, whoever gives you a drink of
water because you
belong to the Christ
will truly get his re-
ward.
42"If one of
these little children
believes in me, and someone causes that
child to sin, it would be better for that
person to have a large stone tied around
his neck and be drowned in the sea. 43If
your hand causes you to sin, cut it off. It
is better for you to lose part of your body
and live forever than to have two hands
and go to hell, where the fire never goes
out. 44[n] 45If your foot causes you to sin,
cut it off. It is better for you to lose part of
your body and to live forever than to have
two feet and be thrown into hell. 46[n] 47If
your eye causes you to sin, take it out. It
is better for you to enter the kingdom of
God with only one eye than to have two
eyes and be thrown into hell. 48In hell
the worm does not die; the fire is never
put out. 49Every person will be salted
with fire.
50"Salt is good, but if the salt loses its
salty taste, you cannot make it salty
again. So, be full of salt, and have peace
with each other."

EMAIL FROM GOD
9:41
Giving
What is your reward for giving to others?

Jesus Teaches About Divorce

10 Then Jesus left that place and
went into the area of Judea and
across the Jordan River. Again, crowds
came to him, and he taught them as he
usually did.
2Some Pharisees came to Jesus and
tried to trick him. They asked, "Is it right
for a man to divorce his wife?"
3Jesus answered, "What did Moses
command you to do?"
4They said, "Moses allowed a man to
write out divorce papers and send her
away."[n]
5Jesus said, "Moses wrote that command for you because you were stubborn. 6But when God made the world,
'he made them male and female.'[n] 7'So a
man will leave his father and mother and
be united with his wife, 8and the two will
become one body.'[n] So there are not two,
but one. 9God has joined the two together,
so no one should separate them."
10Later, in the house, his followers
asked Jesus again about the question of
divorce. 11He answered, "Anyone who
divorces his wife and marries another
woman is guilty of adultery against her.
12And the woman who divorces her husband and marries another man is also
guilty of adultery."

Jesus Accepts Children

13Some people brought their little
children to Jesus so he could touch them,
but his followers told them to stop.
14When Jesus saw this, he was upset and
said to them, "Let the little children
come to me. Don't stop them, because
the kingdom of God belongs to people
who are like these children. 15I tell you
the truth, you must accept the kingdom
of God as if you were a little child, or you
will never enter it." 16Then Jesus took
the children in his arms, put his hands on
them, and blessed them.

A Rich Young Man's Question

17As Jesus started to leave, a man ran
to him and fell on his knees before Jesus.
The man asked, "Good teacher, what
must I do to have life forever?"
18Jesus answered, "Why do you call
me good? Only God is good. 19You know
the commands: 'You must not murder
anyone. You must not be guilty of adultery. You must not steal. You must not tell

9:44 Verse 44 Some Greek copies of Mark add verse 44, which is the same as verse 48.

9:46 Verse 46 Some Greek copies of Mark add verse 46, which is the same as verse 48.

10:4 "Moses . . . away." Quotation from Deuteronomy 24:1.

10:6 'he made . . . female.' Quotation from Genesis 1:27.

10:7-8 'So . . . body.' Quotation from Genesis 2:24.

MY FAVORITE!

MARK 10:17-23

Suppose someone were to ask you to give up your most cherished possession to prove your love for God. How willing would you be to give it up?

Jesus once talked to a young man who had a lot of possessions. He knew that the young man loved his possessions more than he loved God. God wants people to love him more than they love things. He's not against your having possessions. He just wants to have first place in your life. So . . . does he?

What You Value, Genesis 25:21–34, p. 34

Obey? No Way!, Exodus 1:15–21, p. 76

Care to Be Fair?, Joshua 18:1–8, p. 299

A Parent's Advice, Proverbs 1:8–9, p. 825

A Halfhearted Offering, Malachi 1:6–14, p. 1268

A Robbery in Progress, Malachi 3:8–10, p. 1270

lies about your neighbor. You must not
cheat. Honor your father and mother.' "[n]
20The man said, "Teacher, I have
obeyed all these things since I was a boy."
21Jesus, looking at the man, loved
him and said, "There is one more thing
you need to do. Go and sell everything
you have, and give the money to the poor,
and you will have treasure in heaven.
Then come and follow me."
22He was very sad to hear Jesus say
this, and he left sorrowfully, because he
was rich.
23Then Jesus looked at his followers
and said, "How hard it will be for the rich
to enter the kingdom of God!"
24The followers were amazed at what
Jesus said. But he said again, "My children, it is very hard to enter the kingdom
of God! 25It is easier for a camel to go
through the eye of a needle than for a rich
person to enter the kingdom of God."
26The followers were even more surprised and said to each other, "Then who
can be saved?"
27Jesus looked at them and said,
"This is something people cannot do, but
God can. God can do all things."
28Peter said to Jesus, "Look, we have
left everything and followed you."
29Jesus said, "I tell you the truth, all
those who have left houses, brothers,
sisters, mother, father, children, or farms
for me and for the Good News 30will get
more than they left. Here in this world
they will have a hundred times more
homes, brothers, sisters, mothers, children, and fields. And with those things,
they will also suffer for their belief. But
in the age that is coming they will have
life forever. 31Many who have the highest place now will have the lowest place
in the future. And many who have the
lowest place now will have the highest
place in the future."

Jesus Talks About His Death

32As Jesus and the people with him
were on the road to Jerusalem, he was
leading the way. His followers were
amazed, but others in the crowd who followed were afraid. Again Jesus took the
twelve apostles aside and began to tell
them what was about to happen in Jerusalem. 33He said, "Look, we are going to
Jerusalem. The Son of Man will be turned
over to the leading priests and the teachers of the law. They will say that he must
die, and they will turn him over to the
non-Jewish people, 34who will laugh at

10:19 'You . . . mother.' Quotation from Exodus 20:12-16; Deuteronomy 5:16-20.

him and spit on him. They will beat him
with whips and crucify him. But on the
third day, he will rise to life again."

Two Followers Ask Jesus a Favor

35Then James and John, sons of Zebedee, came to Jesus and said, "Teacher, we
want to ask you to do something for us."
36Jesus asked, "What do you want me
to do for you?"
37They answered, "Let one of us sit
at your right side and one of us sit at your
left side in your glory in your kingdom."
38Jesus said, "You don't understand
what you are asking. Can you drink the
cup that I must drink? And can you be
baptized with the same kind of baptism
that I must go through?"[n]
39They answered, "Yes, we can."
Jesus said to them, "You will drink the
same cup that I will drink, and you will be
baptized with the same baptism that I
must go through. **40**But I cannot choose
who will sit at my right or my left; those
places belong to those for whom they
have been prepared."
41When the other ten followers heard
this, they began to be angry with James
and John.
42Jesus called them together and
said, "The other nations have rulers. You
know that those rulers love to show their
power over the people, and their important leaders love to use all their authority.
43But it should not be that way among
you. Whoever wants to become great
among you must serve the rest of you
like a servant. **44**Whoever wants to become the first among you must serve all
of you like a slave. **45**In the same way, the
Son of Man did not come to be served. He
came to serve others and to give his life
as a ransom for many people."

Jesus Heals a Blind Man

46Then they came to the town of Jericho. As Jesus was leaving there with his
followers and a great many people, a
blind beggar named Bartimaeus son of
Timaeus was sitting by the road. **47**When
he heard that Jesus from Nazareth was
walking by, he began to shout, "Jesus,
Son of David, have mercy on me!"
48Many people warned the blind man
to be quiet, but he shouted even more,
"Son of David, have mercy on me!"
49Jesus stopped and said, "Tell the
man to come here."
So they called the blind man, saying,
"Cheer up! Get to your feet. Jesus is calling you." **50**The blind man jumped up,
left his coat there, and went to Jesus.
51Jesus asked him, "What do you
want me to do for you?"
The blind man answered, "Teacher, I
want to see."
52Jesus said, "Go, you are healed because you believed." At once the man
could see, and he followed Jesus on the
road.

Jesus Enters Jerusalem as a King

11 As Jesus and his followers were
coming closer to Jerusalem, they
came to the towns of Bethphage and
Bethany near the Mount of Olives. From
there Jesus sent two of his followers
2and said to them, "Go to the town you
can see there. When you enter it, you will
quickly find a colt tied, which no one has
ever ridden. Untie it and bring it here to
me. **3**If anyone asks you why you are doing this, tell him its Master needs the
colt, and he will send it at once. "
4The followers went into the town,
found a colt tied in the street near the
door of a house, and untied it. **5**Some
people were standing there and asked,
"What are you doing? Why are you untying that colt?" **6**The followers answered
the way Jesus told them to answer, and
the people let them take the colt.
7They brought the colt to Jesus and
put their coats on it, and Jesus sat on it.
8Many people spread their coats on the
road. Others cut branches in the fields
and spread them on the road. **9**The people were walking ahead of Jesus and behind him, shouting,

"Praise God!
God bless the One who comes in the
name of the Lord! *Psalm 118:26*

10:38 Can you . . . through? Jesus was asking if they could suffer the same terrible things that would happen to him.

FAITH links

QUICK TO FORGIVE?

MARK 11:25

More than likely, you can easily think of something someone did to make you mad. But how quick are you to forgive the person who hurt you? Are you as fast as a cheetah, quick to forgive? Or, are you a turtle, slow in forgiving others?

Jesus talked often about forgiveness. God wants you to forgive others for whatever they have done to you. Forgiveness is not something to offer only if you feel like it. It's something God wants you to give, no matter what. When you forgive others, God will forgive you.

Where do you rate on forgiving others? Check it out here:

More Powerful Than Revenge, Genesis 50:14–21, p. 71

What's Out Becomes In, Judges 11, p. 327

Some Friendly Advice, Proverbs 17:9, 14, 17, p. 851

A Model of Forgiveness, Ezekiel 16:59–63, p. 1103

The Choices of a Choice, Luke 5:1–11, p. 1375

The Whole Truth, John 8:31–32, 45, p. 1438

10 God bless the kingdom of our father
David!
That kingdom is coming!
Praise[n] to God in heaven!"
11 Jesus entered Jerusalem and went
into the Temple. After he had looked at
everything, since it was already late, he
went out to Bethany with the twelve
apostles.
12 The next day as Jesus was leaving
Bethany, he became hungry. **13** Seeing a
fig tree in leaf from far away, he went to
see if it had any figs on it. But he found no
figs, only leaves, because it was not the
right season for figs. **14** So Jesus said to
the tree, "May no one ever eat fruit from
you again." And Jesus' followers heard
him say this.

Jesus Goes to the Temple

15 When Jesus returned to Jerusalem,
he went into the Temple and began to
throw out those who were buying and
selling there. He turned over the tables
of those who were exchanging different
kinds of money, and he upset the benches
of those who were selling doves. **16** Jesus
refused to allow anyone to carry goods
through the Temple courts. **17** Then he
taught the people, saying, "It is written in
the Scriptures, 'My Temple will be called
a house for prayer for people from all
nations.'[n] But you are changing God's
house into a 'hideout for robbers.' "[n]
18 The leading priests and the teachers of the law heard all this and began trying to find a way to kill Jesus. They were
afraid of him, because all the people were
amazed at his teaching. **19** That evening,
Jesus and his followers left the city.

The Power of Faith

20 The next morning as Jesus was
passing by with his followers, they saw
the fig tree dry and dead, even to the

11:10 Praise Literally, "Hosanna," a Hebrew word used at first in praying to God for help, but at this time it was probably a shout of joy used in praising God or his Messiah.
11:17 'My Temple . . . nations.' Quotation from Isaiah 56:7.
11:17 'hideout for robbers.' Quotation from Jeremiah 7:11.

roots. 21Peter remembered the tree and
said to Jesus, "Teacher, look! The fig tree
you cursed is dry and dead!"

22Jesus answered, "Have faith in
God. 23I tell you the truth, you can say to
this mountain, 'Go, fall into the sea.' And
if you have no doubts in your mind and
believe that what you say will happen,
God will do it for you. 24So I tell you to
believe that you have received the things
you ask for in prayer, and God will give
them to you. 25When you are praying, if
you are angry with someone, forgive him
so that your Father in heaven will also
forgive your sins." 26[n]

Leaders Doubt Jesus' Authority

27Jesus and his followers went again
to Jerusalem. As Jesus was walking in
the Temple, the leading priests, the
teachers of the law, and the older leaders
came to him. 28They said to him, "What
authority do you have to do these things?
Who gave you this authority?"

29Jesus answered, "I will ask you one
question. If you answer me, I will tell you
what authority I have to do these things.
30Tell me: When John baptized people,
was that authority from God or just from
other people?"

31They argued about Jesus' question,
saying, "If we answer, 'John's baptism
was from God,' Jesus will say, 'Then why
didn't you believe him?' 32But if we say,
'It was from other people,' the crowd will
be against us." (These leaders were
afraid of the people, because all the people believed that John was a prophet.)

33So they answered Jesus, "We don't
know."

Jesus said to them, "Then I won't tell
you what authority I have to do these
things."

A Story About God's Son

12 Jesus began to use stories to teach
the people. He said, "A man
planted a vineyard. He put a wall around
it and dug a hole for a winepress and built
a tower. Then he leased the land to some
farmers and left for a trip. 2When it was
time for the grapes to be picked, he sent a
servant to the farmers to get his share of
the grapes. 3But the farmers grabbed the
servant and beat him and sent him away
empty-handed. 4Then the man sent another servant. They hit him on the head
and showed no respect for him. 5So the
man sent another servant, whom they
killed. The man sent many other servants; the farmers beat some of them and
killed others.

6"The man had one person left to
send, his son whom he loved. He sent
him last of all, saying, 'They will respect
my son.'

7"But the farmers said to each other,
'This son will inherit the vineyard. If we
kill him, it will be ours.' 8So they took the
son, killed him, and threw him out of the
vineyard.

9"So what will the owner of the vineyard do? He will come and kill those
farmers and will give the vineyard to
other farmers. 10Surely you have read
this Scripture:

'The stone that the builders rejected
became the cornerstone.
11 The Lord did this,
and it is wonderful to us.' "

Psalm 118:22-23

12The Jewish leaders knew that the
story was about them. So they wanted to
find a way to arrest Jesus, but they were
afraid of the people. So the leaders left
him and went away.

Is It Right to Pay Taxes or Not?

13Later, the Jewish leaders sent some
Pharisees and Herodians[n] to Jesus to trap
him in saying something wrong. 14They
came to him and said, "Teacher, we know
that you are an honest man. You are not
afraid of what other people think about
you, because you pay no attention to who
they are. And you teach the truth about
God's way. Tell us: Is it right to pay taxes
to Caesar or not? 15Should we pay them,
or not?"

11:26 Verse 26 Some early Greek copies add verse 26: "But if you don't forgive other people, then your Father in heaven will not forgive your sins."

12:13 Herodians A political group that followed Herod and his family.

But knowing what these men were
really trying to do, Jesus said to them,
"Why are you trying to trap me? Bring
me a coin to look at." 16They gave Jesus
a coin, and he asked, "Whose image and
name are on the coin?"
They answered, "Caesar's."
17Then Jesus said to them, "Give to
Caesar the things that are Caesar's, and
give to God the things that are God's."
The men were amazed at what Jesus
said.

Some Sadducees Try to Trick Jesus

18Then some Sadducees came to
Jesus and asked him a question. (Sadducees believed that people would not rise
from the dead.) 19They said, "Teacher,
Moses wrote that if a man's brother dies,
leaving a wife but no children, then that
man must marry the widow and have
children for his brother. 20Once there
were seven brothers. The first brother
married and died, leaving no children.
21So the second brother married the
widow, but he also died and had no children. The same thing happened with the
third brother. 22All seven brothers married her and died, and none of the brothers had any children. Finally the woman
died too. 23Since all seven brothers had
married her, when people rise from the
dead, whose wife will she be?"
24Jesus answered, "Why don't you
understand? Don't you know what the
Scriptures say, and don't you know about
the power of God? 25When people rise
from the dead, they will not marry, nor
will they be given to someone to marry.
They will be like the angels in heaven.
26Surely you have read what God said
about people rising from the dead. In the
book in which Moses wrote about the
burning bush,[n] it says that God told Moses, 'I am the God of Abraham, the God of
Isaac, and the God of Jacob.'[n] 27God is
the God of the living, not the dead. You
Sadducees are wrong!"

The Most Important Command

28One of the teachers of the law
came and heard Jesus arguing with the

FAITH links

THE NUMBER ONE RULE

MARK 12:28-31

Throughout your life, you'll hear a lot of rules. What do you think is the most important rule you can follow? Wash behind your ears? Clean your room? Don't talk with your mouth full? The people of Israel had hundreds of rules to follow to show their obedience to God. The religious leaders made up many of these rules.

A man once asked Jesus to name the most important rule of all. Jesus told him that the most important rule was to love God, and the second was to love others. Love is more important than any sacrifice we can make.

Link here for more on loving your enemies:

Your Worst Enemy, Exodus 7—11, p. 85

No Thanksgiving?, 2 Kings 23:21–23, p. 512

Meaningless Words, Job 21:34, p. 684

Two Are Better, Ecclesiastes 4:9–12, p. 877

Obey or Disobey?, Luke 20:20–26, p. 1409

Kindness Counts, Acts 14:3, p. 1489

12:26 burning bush Read Exodus 3:1-12 in the Old Testament.
12:26 'I am . . . Jacob.' Quotation from Exodus 3:6.

LOVING GOD'S WAY
Mark 12:28–34

Livin' it

The Number One Rule Lists, lists, and more lists. Everyone loves to look at lists! We have lists of the Top 10 songs, the Top 10 businesses, or the Top 10 basketball teams. On all Top 10 lists, the most important is number one. Do you have a list of rules in your classroom or at home? Is the most important one at the top of the list?

A man once asked Jesus to name the most important rule of all—number one on Jesus' list. Jesus told him that the most important rules were to love God and others. (Look at Mark 12:28–31.) How can you make loving God number one on your Top 10 list of things to do?

MORE FAITH links

What God Wants, p. 242
Go! No!, p. 1213
The Best Choice, p. 1560
Don't Play Favorites, p. 1691
The True Test, p. 1718

"Hey, Tagg, what's the top rule on your list?"

"That's easy. Don't surf on to any unsupervised websites."

"That's a good safety rule. But how about downloading these Faithlinks to find out God's number one rule?"

Kind or Fair?, 1 Samuel 30, p. 395
- Suppose you and a friend did a project together to win a prize, but a third friend chose not to help you. Would it be fair to let the third friend share in the prize? Even though some of his soldiers grumbled, David agreed to share and share alike. When you have to choose between kindness and your idea of fairness, what will you do?

The Worst Chore, John 13:3–17, p. 1447
- What's the worst chore you can think of doing? How would you feel if you had to do it? Link here to see how the disciples felt about Jesus' doing the worst chore anyone could do.

Kindness Counts, Acts 14:3, p. 1489
- What's the coolest ability you wish you had? To play a sport or musical instrument better than anyone else? To write a best-seller or paint a masterpiece? What would you do with your ability? How can you use the abilities you *do* have to help others and show love to God?
- Being kind is an ability God gives you. When you're kind to others, they see God's love for them. Remember—kindness counts!

Sadducees. Seeing that Jesus gave good
answers to their questions, he asked
Jesus, "Which of the commands is most
important?"
29Jesus answered, "The most important command is this: 'Listen, people of
Israel! The Lord our God is the only
Lord. 30Love the Lord your
God with all your
heart, all your soul,
all your mind, and
all your strength.'[n]
31The second com-
mand is this: 'Love
your neighbor as
you love yourself.'[n] There are no commands more important than these."

EMAIL FROM GOD
12:29–30
Love
What is the most important command that God has given you?

32The man answered, "That was a
good answer, Teacher. You were right
when you said God is the only Lord and
there is no other God besides him. 33One
must love God with all his heart, all his
mind, and all his strength. And one must
love his neighbor as he loves himself.
These commands are more important
than all the animals and sacrifices we offer to God."
34When Jesus saw that the man answered him wisely, Jesus said to him,
"You are close to the kingdom of God."
And after that, no one was brave enough
to ask Jesus any more questions.
35As Jesus was teaching in the Temple, he asked, "Why do the teachers of
the law say that the Christ is the son of
David? 36David himself, speaking by the
Holy Spirit, said:

'The Lord said to my Lord:
Sit by me at my right side,
until I put your enemies under
your control.' *Psalm 110:1*

37David himself calls the Christ 'Lord,' so
how can the Christ be his son?" The large
crowd listened to Jesus with pleasure.
38Jesus continued teaching and said,
"Beware of the teachers of the law. They
like to walk around wearing fancy
clothes, and they love for people to greet
them with respect in the marketplaces.
39They love to have the most important
seats in the synagogues and at feasts.
40But they cheat widows and steal their
houses and then try to make themselves
look good by saying long prayers. They
will receive a greater punishment."

True Giving

41Jesus sat near the Temple money
box and watched the people put in their
money. Many rich people gave large
sums of money. 42Then a poor widow
came and put in two small copper coins,
which were only worth a few cents.
43Calling his followers to him, Jesus
said, "I tell you the truth, this poor widow
gave more than all those rich people.
44They gave only what they did not
need. This woman is very poor, but she
gave all she had; she gave all she had to
live on."

The Temple Will Be Destroyed

13 As Jesus was leaving the Temple,
one of his followers said to him,
"Look, Teacher! How beautiful the buildings are! How big the stones are!"
2Jesus said, "Do you see all these
great buildings? Not one stone will be left
on another. Every stone will be thrown
down to the ground."
3Later, as Jesus was sitting on the
Mount of Olives, opposite the Temple, he
was alone with Peter, James, John, and
Andrew. They asked Jesus, 4"Tell us,
when will these things happen? And what
will be the sign that they are going to
happen?"
5Jesus began to answer them, "Be
careful that no one fools you. 6Many people will come in my name, saying, 'I am
the One,' and they will fool many people.
7When you hear about wars and stories
of wars that are coming, don't be afraid.
These things must happen before the end
comes. 8Nations will fight against other
nations, and kingdoms against other
kingdoms. There will be earthquakes in
different places, and there will be times
when there is no food for people to eat.
These things are like the first pains when
something new is about to be born.

12:30 'Listen . . . strength.' Quotation from Deuteronomy 6:4-5.

12:31 'Love . . . yourself.' Quotation from Leviticus 19:18.

9"You must be careful. People will arrest you and take you to court and beat
you in their synagogues. You will be
forced to stand before kings and governors, to tell them about me. This will happen to you because you follow me. 10But
before these things happen, the Good
News must be told to all people. 11When
you are arrested and judged, don't worry
ahead of time about what you should say.
Say whatever is given you to say at that
time, because it will not really be you
speaking; it will be the Holy Spirit.

12"Brothers will give their own
brothers to be killed, and fathers will give
their own children to be killed. Children
will fight against their own parents and
cause them to be put to death. 13All people will hate you because you follow me,
but those people who keep their faith until the end will be saved.

14"You will see 'the destroying
terror'[n] standing where it should not be."
(You who read this should understand
what it means.) "At that time, the people
in Judea should run away to the mountains. 15If people are on the roofs[n] of
their houses, they must not go down or
go inside to get anything out of their
houses. 16If people are in the fields, they
must not go back to get their coats. 17At
that time, how terrible it will be for
women who are pregnant or have nursing
babies! 18Pray that these things will not
happen in winter, 19because those days
will be full of trouble. There will be more
trouble than there has ever been since
the beginning, when God made the
world, until now, and nothing as bad will
ever happen again. 20God has decided to
make that terrible time short. Otherwise,
no one would go on living. But God will
make that time short to help the people
he has chosen. 21At that time, someone
might say to you, 'Look, there is the
Christ!' Or another person might say,
'There he is!' But don't believe them.
22False Christs and false prophets will
come and perform great wonders and
miracles. They will try to fool even the
people God has chosen, if that is possible.
23So be careful. I have warned you about
all this before it happens.

FAITH links

GET READY!

MARK 13:26-27

You know that a new school year starts every fall. No one has to convince you that you need to get ready for that event at the end of the summer. You just do what you need to do to get ready, right? (Even if you don't *want* to!)

Jesus told his followers that he would return to earth someday. Although no one knows when that will happen, it *will* happen. We need to be ready for him to return. How do you get ready? Here are some ways: read the Bible, pray, and do what God says.

Here are some other links on ways to get ready:

Ten Ways to Obey, Exodus 20, p. 103

The Perfect Sacrifice, Leviticus 1—7, p. 135

The Perfect Leader?, Numbers 20:1–13, p. 203

A Tight Spot, Jonah 2, p. 1215

Our Heavenly Connection, Matthew 6:9–13, p. 1283

Prayer Priority, Luke 5:15–16, p. 1376

13:14 'the destroying terror' Mentioned in Daniel 9:27; 12:11 (cf. Daniel 11:31).

13:15 roofs In Bible times houses were built with flat roofs. The roof was used for drying things such as flax and fruit. And it was used as an extra room, as a place for worship, and as a cool place to sleep in the summer.

24“During the days after this trouble
comes,
‘the sun will grow dark,
and the moon will not give its light.
25 The stars will fall from the sky.
And the powers of the heavens will
be shaken.’ *Isaiah 13:10; 34:4*
26“Then people will see the Son of
Man coming in clouds with great power
and glory. 27Then he will send his angels
all around the earth to gather his chosen
people from every part of the earth and
from every part of heaven.
28“Learn a lesson from the fig tree:
When its branches become green and
soft and new leaves appear, you know
summer is near. 29In the same way, when
you see these things happening, you will
know that the time is near, ready to
come. 30I tell you the truth, all these
things will happen while the people of
this time are still living. 31Earth and sky
will be destroyed, but the words I have
said will never be destroyed.
32“No one knows when that day or
time will be, not the angels in heaven, not
even the Son. Only the Father knows.
33Be careful! Always be ready, because
you don’t know when that time will be.
34It is like a man who goes on a trip. He
leaves his house and lets his servants take
care of it, giving each one a special job to
do. The man tells the servant guarding
the door always to be watchful. 35So always be ready, because you don’t know
when the owner of the house will come
back. It might be in the evening, or at midnight, or in the morning while it is still
dark, or when the sun rises. 36Always be
ready. Otherwise he might come back
suddenly and find you sleeping. 37I tell
you this, and I say this to everyone: ‘Be
ready!’ ”

The Plan to Kill Jesus

14 It was now only two days before
the Passover and the Feast of Unleavened Bread. The leading priests and
teachers of the law were trying to find a
trick to arrest Jesus and kill him. 2But
they said, “We must not do it during the
feast, because the people might cause a
riot.”

A Woman with Perfume for Jesus

3Jesus was in Bethany at the house of
Simon, who had a skin disease. While
Jesus was eating there, a woman approached him with an alabaster jar filled
with very expensive perfume, made of
pure nard. She opened the jar and poured
the perfume on Jesus’ head.
4Some who were there became upset
and said to each other, “Why waste that
perfume? 5It was worth a full year’s
work. It could have been sold and the
money given to the poor.” And they got
very angry with the woman.
6Jesus said, “Leave her alone. Why

EMAIL FROM GOD
14:6–9
Giving
Check out this example of giving.

are you troubling
her? She did an ex-
cellent thing for me.
7You will always
have the poor with
you, and you can
help them anytime
you want. But you will not always have
me. 8This woman did the only thing she
could do for me; she poured perfume on
my body to prepare me for burial. 9I tell
you the truth, wherever the Good News
is preached in all the world, what this
woman has done will be told, and people
will remember her.”

Judas Becomes an Enemy of Jesus

10One of the twelve apostles, Judas
Iscariot, went to talk to the leading
priests to offer to hand Jesus over to
them. 11These priests were pleased
about this and promised to pay Judas
money. So he watched for the best time
to turn Jesus in.

Jesus Eats the Passover Meal

12It was now the first day of the Feast
of Unleavened Bread when the Passover
lamb was sacrificed. Jesus’ followers said
to him, “Where do you want us to go
and prepare for you to eat the Passover
meal?”
13Jesus sent two of his followers and
said to them, “Go into the city and a man
carrying a jar of water will meet you. Follow him. 14When he goes into a house,
tell the owner of the house, ‘The Teacher

says: Where is my guest room in which I
can eat the Passover meal with my followers?' 15The owner will show you a
large room upstairs that is furnished and
ready. Prepare the food for us there."
16So the followers left and went into
the city. Everything happened as Jesus
had said, so they prepared the Passover
meal.
17In the evening, Jesus went to that
house with the twelve. 18While they
were all eating, Jesus said, "I tell you the
truth, one of you will turn against me—
one of you eating with me now."
19The followers were very sad to
hear this. Each one began to say to Jesus,
"I am not the one, am I?"
20Jesus answered, "It is one of the
twelve—the one who dips his bread into
the bowl with me. 21The Son of Man will
die, just as the Scriptures say. But how
terrible it will be for the person who
hands the Son of Man over to be killed. It
would be better for him if he had never
been born."

The Lord's Supper

22While they were eating, Jesus took
some bread and thanked God for it and
broke it. Then he gave it to his followers
and said, "Take it; this is my body."
23Then Jesus took a cup and thanked
God for it and gave it to the followers, and
they all drank from the cup.
24Then Jesus said, "This is my blood
which is the new agreement that God
makes with his people. This blood is
poured out for many. 25I tell you the
truth, I will not drink of this fruit of the
vine[n] again until that day when I drink it
new in the kingdom of God."
26After singing a hymn, they went out
to the Mount of Olives.

Jesus' Followers Will Leave Him

27Then Jesus told the followers, "You
will all stumble in your faith, because it is
written in the Scriptures:

'I will kill the shepherd,
and the sheep will scatter.'

Zechariah 13:7

28But after I rise from the dead, I will go
ahead of you into Galilee."

FAITH links

A FAMILY MEAL

MARK 14:23-26

Mealtimes are times for families to be together. Jesus and his followers were like a family. On the night before Jesus' death, they shared a special meal together. Jesus knew how important it was for them to be together.

As Christians, we're all part of God's family. Although all of us can't fit in one room together, there is a special meal that we can all share no matter where we are in the world. This meal is called the Lord's Supper. The bread and the cup are what we share to remember the most important member of our family—Jesus.

The Fence Riders, 1 Kings 18, p. 464

Give In or Take a Stand?, 1 Kings 22:13–14, p. 472

Plans for a Son, 1 Chronicles 22:5–19, p. 548

A Fair-Weather Friend, Obadiah 7, p. 1209

Ask, Search, Knock, Matthew 7:7–10, p. 1286

One Big, Happy Family, John 1:12, p. 1422

29Peter said, "Everyone else may
stumble in their faith, but I will not."
30Jesus answered, "I tell you the

14:25 fruit of the vine Product of the grapevine; this may also be translated "wine."

truth, tonight before the rooster crows
twice you will say three times you don't
know me."
31But Peter insisted, "I will never say
that I don't know you! I will even die with
you!" And all the other followers said the
same thing.

Jesus Prays Alone

32Jesus and his followers went to a
place called Gethsemane. He said to
them, "Sit here while I pray." 33Jesus
took Peter, James, and John with him, and
he began to be very sad and troubled.
34He said to them, "My heart is full of
sorrow, to the point of death. Stay here
and watch."
35After walking a little farther away
from them, Jesus fell to the ground and
prayed that, if possible, he would not
have this time of suffering. 36He prayed,
"Abba,[n] Father! You can do all things.
Take away this cup[n] of suffering. But do
what you want, not what I want."
37Then Jesus went back to his followers and found them asleep. He said to Peter, "Simon, are you sleeping? Couldn't
you stay awake with me for one hour?
38Stay awake and pray for strength
against temptation. The spirit wants to
do what is right, but the body is weak."
39Again Jesus went away and prayed
the same thing. 40Then he went back to
his followers, and again he found them
asleep, because their eyes were very
heavy. And they did not know what to say
to him.
41After Jesus prayed a third time, he
went back to his followers and said to
them, "Are you still sleeping and resting?
That's enough. The time has come for
the Son of Man to be handed over to sinful people. 42Get up, we must go. Look,
here comes the man who has turned
against me."

Jesus Is Arrested

43At once, while Jesus was still
speaking, Judas, one of the twelve apostles, came up. With him were many people carrying swords and clubs who had
been sent from the leading priests, the
teachers of the law, and the older Jewish
leaders.
44Judas had planned a signal for them,
saying, "The man I kiss is Jesus. Arrest
him and guard him while you lead him
away." 45So Judas went straight to Jesus
and said, "Teacher!" and kissed him.
46Then the people grabbed Jesus and arrested him. 47One of his followers standing nearby pulled out his sword and
struck the servant of the high priest and
cut off his ear.
48Then Jesus said, "You came to get
me with swords and clubs as if I were a
criminal. 49Every day I was with you
teaching in the Temple, and you did not
arrest me there. But all these things have
happened to make the Scriptures come
true." 50Then all of Jesus' followers left
him and ran away.
51A young man, wearing only a linen
cloth, was following Jesus, and the people
also grabbed him. 52But the cloth he was
wearing came off, and he ran away naked.

Jesus Before the Leaders

53The people who arrested Jesus led
him to the house of the high priest,
where all the leading priests, the older
Jewish leaders, and the teachers of the
law were gathered. 54Peter followed far
behind and entered the courtyard of the
high priest's house. There he sat with
the guards, warming himself by the fire.
55The leading priests and the whole
Jewish council tried to find something
that Jesus had done wrong so they could
kill him. But the council could find no
proof of anything. 56Many people came
and told false things about him, but all
said different things—none of them
agreed.
57Then some people stood up and lied
about Jesus, saying, 58"We heard this man
say, 'I will destroy this Temple that people
made. And three days later, I will build
another Temple not made by people.' "

14:36 Abba Name that a Jewish child called his father.

14:36 cup Jesus is talking about the terrible things that will happen to him. Accepting these things will be very hard, like drinking a cup of something bitter.

59But even the things these people said did not agree.

60Then the high priest stood before them and asked Jesus, "Aren't you going to answer? Don't you have something to say about their charges against you?" 61But Jesus said nothing; he did not answer.

eMAIL! FROM GOD
14:61–62
Jesus
Will the Messiah come again?

The high priest asked Jesus another question: "Are you the Christ, the Son of the blessed God?"

62Jesus answered, "I am. And in the future you will see the Son of Man sitting at the right hand of God, the Powerful One, and coming on clouds in the sky."

63When the high priest heard this, he tore his clothes and said, "We don't need any more witnesses! 64You all heard him say these things against God. What do you think?"

They all said that Jesus was guilty and should die. 65Some of the people there began to spit at Jesus. They blindfolded him and beat him with their fists and said, "Prove you are a prophet!" Then the guards led Jesus away and beat him.

Peter Says He Doesn't Know Jesus

66While Peter was in the courtyard, a servant girl of the high priest came there. 67She saw Peter warming himself at the fire and looked closely at him.

Then she said, "You also were with Jesus, that man from Nazareth."

68But Peter said that he was never with Jesus. He said, "I don't know or understand what you are talking about." Then Peter left and went toward the entrance of the courtyard. And the rooster crowed.*

69The servant girl saw Peter there, and again she said to the people who were standing nearby, "This man is one of those who followed Jesus." 70Again Peter said that it was not true.

A short time later, some people were standing near Peter saying, "Surely you are one of those who followed Jesus, because you are from Galilee, too."

71Then Peter began to place a curse on himself and swear, "I don't know this man you're talking about!"

72At once, the rooster crowed the second time. Then Peter remembered what Jesus had told him: "Before the rooster crows twice, you will say three times that you don't know me." Then Peter lost control of himself and began to cry.

Pilate Questions Jesus

15 Very early in the morning, the leading priests, the older leaders, the teachers of the law, and all the Jewish council decided what to do with Jesus. They tied him, led him away, and turned him over to Pilate, the governor.

2Pilate asked Jesus, "Are you the king of the Jews?"

Jesus answered, "Those are your words."

3The leading priests accused Jesus of many things. 4So Pilate asked Jesus another question, "You can see that they are accusing you of many things. Aren't you going to answer?"

5But Jesus still said nothing, so Pilate was very surprised.

Pilate Tries to Free Jesus

6Every year at the time of the Passover the governor would free one prisoner whom the people chose. 7At that time, there was a man named Barabbas in prison who was a rebel and had committed murder during a riot. 8The crowd came to Pilate and began to ask him to free a prisoner as he always did.

9So Pilate asked them, "Do you want me to free the king of the Jews?" 10Pilate knew that the leading priests had turned Jesus in to him because they were jealous. 11But the leading priests had persuaded the people to ask Pilate to free Barabbas, not Jesus.

12Then Pilate asked the crowd again, "So what should I do with this man you call the king of the Jews?"

14:68 And . . . crowed. A few, early Greek copies leave out this phrase.

13They shouted, "Crucify him!"
14Pilate asked, "Why? What wrong
has he done?"
But they shouted even louder, "Crucify him!"
15Pilate wanted to please the crowd,
so he freed Barabbas for them. After having Jesus beaten with whips, he handed
Jesus over to the soldiers to be crucified.
16The soldiers took Jesus into the
governor's palace (called the Praeto-
rium) and called all the other soldiers together. 17They put a purple robe on
Jesus and used thorny branches to make
a crown for his head. 18They began to
call out to him, "Hail, King of the Jews!"
19The soldiers beat Jesus on the head
many times with a stick. They spit on
him and made fun of him by bowing on
their knees and worshiping him. 20After
they finished, the soldiers took off the
purple robe and put his own clothes on
him again. Then they led him out of the
palace to be crucified.

Jesus Is Crucified

21A man named Simon from Cyrene,
the father of Alexander and Rufus, was
coming from the fields to the city. The
soldiers forced Simon to carry the cross
for Jesus. 22They led Jesus to the place
called Golgotha, which means the Place
of the Skull. 23The soldiers tried to give
Jesus wine mixed with myrrh to drink,
but he refused. 24The soldiers crucified
Jesus and divided his clothes among
themselves, throwing lots to decide what
each soldier would get.
25It was nine o'clock in the morning
when they crucified Jesus. 26There was a
sign with this charge against Jesus written on it: THE KING OF THE JEWS. 27They
also put two robbers on crosses beside
Jesus, one on the right, and the other on
the left. 28[n] 29People walked by and insulted Jesus and shook their heads, saying, "You said you could destroy the
Temple and build it again in three days.
30So save yourself! Come down from
that cross!"
31The leading priests and the teachers of the law were also making fun of
Jesus. They said to each other, "He saved
other people, but he can't save himself.
32If he is really the Christ, the king of Israel, let him come down now from the
cross. When we see this, we will believe
in him." The robbers who were being
crucified beside Jesus also insulted him.

Jesus Dies

33At noon the whole country became
dark, and the darkness lasted for three
hours. 34At three o'clock Jesus cried in a
loud voice, "Eloi, Eloi, lama sabach-
thani." This means, "My God, my God,
why have you rejected me?"
35When some of the people standing
there heard this, they said, "Listen! He is
calling Elijah."
36Someone there ran and got a
sponge, filled it with vinegar, tied it to a
stick, and gave it to Jesus to drink. He
said, "We want to see if Elijah will come
to take him down from the cross."
37Then Jesus cried in a loud voice and
died.
38The curtain in the Temple[n] was
torn into two pieces, from the top to the
bottom. 39When the army officer who
was standing in front of the cross saw
what happened when Jesus died, he said,
"This man really was the Son of God!"
40Some women were standing at a
distance from the cross, watching; among
them were Mary Magdalene, Salome,
and Mary the mother of James and Joseph. (James was her youngest son.)
41These women had followed Jesus in
Galilee and helped him. Many other
women were also there who had come
with Jesus to Jerusalem.

Jesus Is Buried

42This was Preparation Day. (That
means the day before the Sabbath day.)

15:28 Verse 28 Some Greek copies add verse 28: "And the Scripture came true that says, 'They put him with criminals.' "

15:38 curtain in the Temple A curtain divided the Most Holy Place from the other part of the Temple. That was the special building in Jerusalem where God commanded the Jewish people to worship him.

THE UNPOPULAR CHOICE

MARK 15:42-43

How important is popularity to you? Would you be willing to admit you believed in something if doing so made you look unpopular? Joseph was an important Jewish leader who believed in Jesus. But Jesus had just been put to death. Many who followed Jesus were afraid they would be treated badly, too. Believing in Jesus as Savior was not the popular choice! Yet Joseph was brave enough to ask Pontius Pilate, the Roman governor, for Jesus' body in order to bury it.

Serving Jesus takes courage. It involves standing up for what you believe in, even if your beliefs are not the most popular.

Looking to win a popularity contest? Check out these Faithlinks first:

An Example Not to Follow, Leviticus 18:1–3, p. 157

Trailblazers of Faith, 2 Kings 22:1–2, p. 510

Wronged for What's Right, Ezra 4:4–5, p. 612

Go! No!, Jonah 1, p. 1213

Be Brave!, Haggai 2:4, p. 1249

Faith That Pleases God, Luke 7:1–9, p. 1380

That evening, **43**Joseph from Arimathea
was brave enough to go to Pilate and ask
for Jesus' body. Joseph, an important
member of the Jewish council, was one of
the people who was waiting for the kingdom of God to come. **44**Pilate was amazed
that Jesus would have already died, so he
called the army officer who had guarded
Jesus and asked him if Jesus had already
died. **45**The officer told Pilate that he was
dead, so Pilate told Joseph he could have
the body. **46**Joseph bought some linen
cloth, took the body down from the cross,
and wrapped it in the linen. He put the
body in a tomb that was cut out of a wall of
rock. Then he rolled a very large stone to
block the entrance of the tomb. **47**And
Mary Magdalene and Mary the mother of
Joseph saw the place where Jesus was
laid.

Jesus Rises from the Dead

16 The day after the Sabbath day,
Mary Magdalene, Mary the mother
of James, and Salome bought some
sweet-smelling spices to put on Jesus'
body. **2**Very early on that day, the first day
of the week, soon after sunrise, the
women were on their way to the tomb.
3They said to each other, "Who will roll
away for us the stone that covers the entrance of the tomb?"

4Then the women looked and saw
that the stone had already been rolled
away, even though it was very large.
5The women entered the tomb and saw a
young man wearing a white robe and sitting on the right side, and they were
afraid.

6But the man said, "Don't be afraid.
You are looking for Jesus from Nazareth,
who has been crucified. He has risen
from the dead; he is not here. Look, here
is the place they laid him. **7**Now go and
tell his followers and Peter, 'Jesus is going into Galilee ahead of you, and you will
see him there as he told you before.' "

8The women were confused and
shaking with fear, so they left the tomb
and ran away. They did not tell anyone
about what happened, because they were
afraid.

GET THE INFO

JESUS—GOD WITH US

Mark 16

1. Childhood.
Jesus was born in Bethlehem. (Look up Luke 2:1–7, p. 1367.) While he was still a young child, his parents took him to Egypt to escape King Herod's threat to kill all the boy babies in Bethlehem. (Check out Matthew 2:13–15, p. 1276.) Jesus grew up at Nazareth. (Read Matthew 2:19–23, p. 1277.)

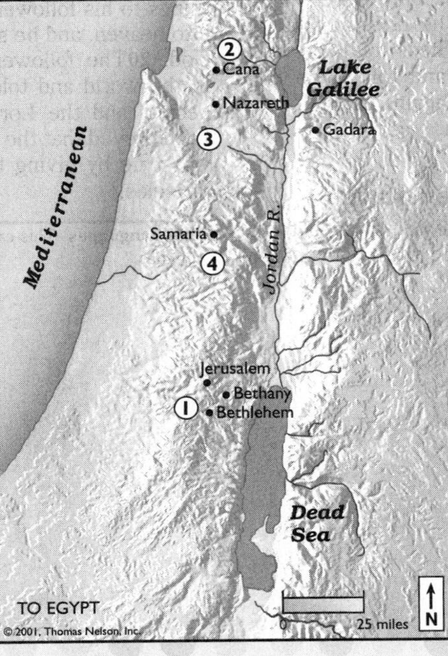

2. Beginnings.
Jesus' ministry began when his cousin John baptized him in the Jordan River. Jesus then spent 40 days alone in the desert where he was tempted by Satan. (Check out Mark 1:9–13.) Jesus performed his first miracle at a wedding in Cana when he turned water into wine for the guests. (Read John 2:1–12, p. 1424.)

3. Early Ministry.
Jesus preached his famous Sermon on the Mount. (Check out Matthew 5–7, p. 1280.) He demonstrated his power from God by bringing a young man back to life (Read Luke 7:11–17, p. 1380) and getting demons out of a man in Gadara. (Look at Luke 8:26–39, p. 1383.) Jesus' reputation grew, as did opposition from religious leaders to his ministry.

4. Later ministry.
Jesus did even more amazing things. He healed ten lepers in Samaria. (See Luke 17:11–19, p. 1402.) He raised his friend Lazarus from the dead in Bethany. (Look up John 11:38–44, p. 1443.) As God planned, Jesus was arrested, crucified, and raised from the dead in Jerusalem. (Check out Mark 14—16.)

Verses 9-20 are not included in two of the best and oldest Greek manuscripts of Mark.

Some Followers See Jesus

[**9**After Jesus rose from the dead early
on the first day of the week, he showed
himself first to Mary Magdalene. One
time in the past, he had forced seven demons out of her. **10**After Mary saw Jesus,
she went and told his followers, who
were very sad and were crying. **11**But
Mary told them that Jesus was alive. She
said that she had seen him, but the followers did not believe her.

12Later, Jesus showed himself to two
of his followers while they were walking
in the country, but he did not look the
same as before. **13**These followers went
back to the others and told them what
had happened, but again, the followers
did not believe them.

Jesus Talks to the Apostles

14Later Jesus showed himself to the
eleven apostles while they were eating,
and he criticized them because they had
no faith. They were stubborn and refused
to believe those who had seen him after
he had risen from the dead.

15Jesus said to his followers, "Go
everywhere in the world, and tell the
Good News to everyone. **16**Anyone who
believes and is baptized will be saved, but
anyone who does not believe will be punished. **17**And those who believe will be
able to do these things as proof: They will
use my name to force out demons. They
will speak in new languages.* **18**They will
pick up snakes and drink poison without
being hurt. They will touch the sick, and
the sick will be healed."

19After the Lord Jesus said these
things to his followers, he was carried up
into heaven, and he sat at the right side of
God. **20**The followers went everywhere
in the world and told the Good News to
people, and the Lord helped them. The
Lord proved that the Good News they told
was true by giving them power to work
miracles.]

16:17 languages This can also be translated "tongues."

THE TRUE HEALER

Hi. Luke here. I'm the only non-Jewish writer in the New Testament, but I was one of the first people to accept that Jesus is God's Son. Most people know that I am a doctor, but did you also know that I was also a constant companion of Paul, one of the leaders of the early church? Because I was with Paul, I also ended up in prison with him. (You can check out that story in Colossians 4:14, p. 1627.)

I wrote this book because my friend Theophilus hadn't heard about Jesus, and I wanted to tell him everything that I knew. But that's not all. I also wanted to give a very organized and detailed account of what Jesus had done. There were a lot of stories floating around about Jesus. So I wrote this to set the record straight. I made sure that all of my facts were correct, and I double-checked them before I wrote this book.

JESUS WATCH

Luke focuses on two important elements about Jesus in this book—his humanity and his compassion. Luke goes to a lot of trouble to write down a complete history of Jesus' relatives in chapter 3. It traces Jesus' family history all the way back to Adam! This was an important list because it helped the people understand that Jesus was God's Son. Luke also helps us understand Jesus' humanity through a detailed description of the physical things that happened to Jesus at his crucifixion. And he shares a lot about Jesus' compassion for people through telling stories about Jesus healing the sick and caring for hurting people.

More than anything, Luke combines the historical facts about Jesus with the truth of what he did while he walked the earth to paint an amazingly accurate picture of the Messiah.

my FAVORITE links

_______________ _______________

_______________ _______________

_______________ _______________

_______________ _______________

OTHER CONNECTIONS

Livin' it

How much is too much stuff? For God's take on that subject click on Such a Lot of Stuff!, Luke 12; 13, and see if you may need to downsize your closet a bit!

What's the one thing that you do especially well? Is it easy for you to share that ability or talent with others? Find out how God wants you to use the gifts and abilities he has given you by logging on to Attitude Check, Luke 17:7–10.

Ever mess up big time? Did you feel like running away to the farthest point on the globe? Or like giving up? Before you pack your bags or quit, check out how God views our weaknesses and failures by connecting to Oh No! Not Again!, Luke 22:54–62.

You won't want to miss these info bulletin boards:

- A Model Prayer, Luke 11:1. Is it hard sometimes to find the right words when you're praying? Jesus' disciples thought so. In fact, they asked Jesus for advice on how to pray. Link here to find out Jesus' answer.
- Log on to Jesus' Last Week, Luke 22, for an overview of the events that occurred from the time Jesus entered Jerusalem to a cheering crowd to the darkest hour when he was nailed to a cross.
- One of the key places in Jesus' life and ministry is the small town of Nazareth. Find out more about this town by downloading Let's Visit Nazareth, Luke 24:19.

"Hey, Skweek, did Luke actually *see* any of the things that he writes about in this book?"

"Probably not. But plug into Luke 1:1-4, and tell me what you think!"

HEY, CHECK OUT THESE AMAZING STORIES FROM LUKE'S GOSPEL:

Birth of a king, Luke 2:1–20
Growing up, Luke 2:39–52
A huge lunch, Luke 9:10–17
The risen Lord, Luke 24

FAITH links

- Believe It or Not, Luke 1:20, 38
- Exercising Patience, Luke 2:25–28, 36–37
- Two Ways to Grow, Luke 2:46–52
- The Choices of a Choice, Luke 5:1–11
- Who Needs Love?, Luke 6:27–36
- Faith That Pleases God, Luke 7:1–9
- Want to Know? Ask!, Luke 9:45
- Best Seat in the House, Luke 14:7–11
- Your Heart's Desire, Luke 16:13–15
- Better Than Some?, Luke 18:9–14
- Faith God Notices, Luke 18:35–43
- Give from the Heart, Luke 21:1–4

Luke Writes About Jesus' Life

1 Many have tried to report on the things that happened among us. **2**They have written the same things that we learned from others—the people who saw those things from the beginning and served God by telling people his message. **3**Since I myself have studied everything carefully from the beginning, most excellent[n] Theophilus, it seemed good for me to write it out for you. I arranged it in order **4**to help you know that what you have been taught is true.

Zechariah and Elizabeth

5During the time Herod ruled Judea, there was a priest named Zechariah who belonged to Abijah's group.[n] Zechariah's wife, Elizabeth, came from the family of Aaron. **6**Zechariah and Elizabeth truly did what God said was good. They did everything the Lord commanded and were without fault in keeping his law. **7**But they had no children, because Elizabeth could not have a baby, and both of them were very old.

8One day Zechariah was serving as a priest before God, because his group was on duty. **9**According to the custom of the priests, he was chosen by lot to go into the Temple of the Lord and burn incense. **10**There were a great many people outside praying at the time the incense was offered. **11**Then an angel of the Lord appeared to Zechariah, standing on the right side of the incense table. **12**When he saw the angel, Zechariah was startled and frightened. **13**But the angel said to him, "Zechariah, don't be afraid. God has heard your prayer. Your wife, Elizabeth, will give birth to a son, and you will name him John. **14**He will bring you joy and gladness, and many people will be happy because of his birth. **15**John will be a great man for the Lord. He will never drink wine or beer, and even from birth, he will be filled with the Holy Spirit. **16**He will help many people of Israel return to the Lord their God. **17**He will go before the Lord in spirit and power like Elijah. He will make peace between parents and their children and will bring those who are not obeying God back to the right way of thinking, to make a people ready for the coming of the Lord."

18Zechariah said to the angel, "How can I know that what you say is true? I am an old man, and my wife is old, too."

19The angel answered him, "I am Gabriel. I stand before God, who sent me to talk to you and to tell you this good news. **20**Now, listen! You will not be able to speak until the day these things happen, because you did not believe what I told you. But they will really happen."

21Outside, the people were still waiting for Zechariah and were surprised that he was staying so long in the Temple. **22**When Zechariah came outside, he could not speak to them, and they knew he had seen a vision in the Temple. He could only make signs to them and remained unable to speak. **23**When his time of service at the Temple was finished, he went home.

24Later, Zechariah's wife, Elizabeth, became pregnant and did not go out of her house for five months. Elizabeth said, **25**"Look what the Lord has done for me! My people were ashamed[n] of me, but now the Lord has taken away that shame."

An Angel Appears to Mary

26During Elizabeth's sixth month of pregnancy, God sent the angel Gabriel to Nazareth, a town in Galilee, **27**to a virgin. She was engaged to marry a man named Joseph from the family of David. Her name was Mary. **28**The angel came to her and said, "Greetings! The Lord has blessed you and is with you."

29But Mary was very startled by what the angel said and wondered what this greeting might mean.

30The angel said to her, "Don't be afraid, Mary; God has shown you his grace. **31**Listen! You will become pregnant and give birth to a son, and you will name him Jesus. **32**He will be great and

---

1:3 excellent This word was used to show respect to an important person like a king or ruler.

1:5 Abijah's group The Jewish priests were divided into twenty-four groups. See 1 Chronicles 24.

1:25 ashamed The Jewish people thought it was a disgrace for women not to have children.

FAITH links

BELIEVE IT OR NOT

LUKE 1:20, 38

Did you know that you could choose to believe something if you wanted to believe? An angel brought good news to Zechariah, a priest of Israel, and Mary, the future wife of Joseph the carpenter. Mary chose to believe the angel's news that she would have a son. Zechariah heard similar news—his wife would have a son. He was doubtful, however.

God wants us to have faith that he can do the impossible if he chooses to do so. Having faith means choosing to believe, even though you can't see any proof. Choose to believe in God!

What do you believe? Check it out here:

Idol Talk, Exodus 32, p. 118

Our Thorough God, Leviticus 13, p. 149

A Direct Path, Proverbs 3:5–6, p. 829

Believe the Impossible?, Ezekiel 37, p. 1131

The Power of *If*, Mark 9:14–24, p. 1344

Attention, Please!, Luke 8:11–15, p. 1383

will be called the Son of the Most High.
The Lord God will give him the throne of
King David, his ancestor. **33**He will rule
over the people of Jacob forever, and his
kingdom will never end."

34Mary said to the angel, "How will
this happen since I am a virgin?"

35The angel said to Mary, "The Holy
Spirit will come upon you, and the power
of the Most High
will cover you. For
this reason the baby
will be holy and will
be called the Son of
God. **36**Now Eliza-
beth, your relative, is
also pregnant with a son though she is
very old. Everyone thought she could not
have a baby, but she has been pregnant
for six months. **37**God can do anything!"

38Mary said, "I am the servant of the
Lord. Let this happen to me as you say!"
Then the angel went away.

1:35 **Jesus**
Check out Jesus' role in the Trinity.

Mary Visits Elizabeth

39Mary got up and went quickly to a
town in the hills of Judea. **40**She came to
Zechariah's house and greeted Elizabeth.
41When Elizabeth heard Mary's greeting,
the unborn baby inside her jumped, and
Elizabeth was filled with the Holy Spirit.
42She cried out in a loud voice, "God has
blessed you more than any other woman,
and he has blessed the baby to which you
will give birth. **43**Why has this good thing
happened to me, that the mother of my
Lord comes to me? **44**When I heard your
voice, the baby inside me jumped with joy.
45You are blessed because you believed
that what the Lord said to you would
really happen."

Mary Praises God

46Then Mary said,
"My soul praises the Lord;
47 my heart rejoices in God my
Savior,
48 because he has shown his concern
for his humble servant girl.
From now on, all people will say that
I am blessed,
49 because the Powerful One has
done great things for me.
His name is holy.
50 God will show his mercy forever and
ever

to those who worship and serve
him.
51 He has done mighty deeds by his
power.
He has scattered the people who
are proud
and think great things about
themselves.
52 He has brought down rulers from
their thrones
and raised up the humble.
53 He has filled the hungry with good
things
and sent the rich away with
nothing.
54 He has helped his servant, the
people of Israel,
remembering to show them
mercy
55 as he promised to our ancestors,
to Abraham and to his children
forever."

56 Mary stayed with Elizabeth for
about three months and then returned
home.

The Birth of John

57 When it was time for Elizabeth to
give birth, she had a boy. 58 Her neighbors and relatives heard how good the
Lord was to her, and they rejoiced with
her.

59 When the baby was eight days old,
they came to circumcise him. They wanted to name him Zechariah because this
was his father's name, 60 but his mother
said, "No! He will be named John."

61 The people said to Elizabeth, "But
no one in your family has this name."
62 Then they made signs to his father to
find out what he would like to name
him.

63 Zechariah asked for a writing tablet
and wrote, "His name is John," and
everyone was surprised. 64 Immediately
Zechariah could talk again, and he began
praising God. 65 All their neighbors became alarmed, and in all the mountains of
Judea people continued talking about all
these things. 66 The people who heard
about them wondered, saying, "What will
this child be?" because the Lord was with
him.

Zechariah Praises God

67 Then Zechariah, John's father, was
filled with the Holy Spirit and prophesied:

68 "Let us praise the Lord, the God of
Israel,
because he has come to help his
people and has given them
freedom.
69 He has given us a powerful Savior
from the family of God's servant
David.
70 He said that he would do this
through his holy prophets who
lived long ago:
71 He promised he would save us from
our enemies
and from the power of all those
who hate us.
72 He said he would give mercy to our
fathers
and that he would remember his
holy promise.
73 God promised Abraham, our father,
74 that he would save us from the
power of our enemies
so we could serve him without
fear,
75 being holy and good before God as
long as we live.

76 "Now you, child, will be called a
prophet of the Most High God.
You will go before the Lord to
prepare his way.
77 You will make his people know that
they will be saved
by having their sins forgiven.
78 With the loving mercy of our God,
a new day from heaven will dawn
upon us.
79 It will shine on those who live in
darkness,
in the shadow of death.
It will guide us into the path of peace."

80 And so the child grew up and became strong in spirit. John lived in the
desert until the time when he came out
to preach to Israel.

The Birth of Jesus

2 At that time, Augustus Caesar sent an
order that all people in the countries

under Roman rule must list their names
in a register. 2This was the first registration;[n] it was taken while Quirinius was
governor of Syria. 3And all went to their
own towns to be registered.
4So Joseph left Nazareth, a town in
Galilee, and went to the town of Bethlehem in Judea, known as the town of David.
Joseph went there because he was from
the family of David. 5Joseph registered
with Mary, to whom he was engaged[n] and
who was now pregnant. 6While they were
in Bethlehem, the time came for Mary to
have the baby, 7and she gave birth to her
first son. Because there were no rooms
left in the inn, she wrapped the baby with
pieces of cloth and laid him in a box where
animals are fed.

Shepherds Hear About Jesus

8That night, some shepherds were in
the fields nearby watching their sheep.
9Then an angel of the Lord stood before
them. The glory of the Lord was shining
around them, and they became very
frightened. 10The angel said to them,
"Do not be afraid. I am bringing you good
news that will be a great joy to all the
people. 11Today your Savior was born in
the town of David. He is Christ, the Lord.
12This is how you will know him: You
will find a baby wrapped in pieces of cloth
and lying in a feeding box."
13Then a very large group of angels
from heaven joined the first angel, praising God and saying:
14"Give glory to God in heaven,
and on earth let there be peace
among the people who please
God."
15When the angels left them and went
back to heaven, the shepherds said to
each other, "Let's go to Bethlehem. Let's
see this thing that has happened which
the Lord has told us about."
16So the shepherds went quickly and
found Mary and Joseph and the baby, who
was lying in a feeding box. 17When they
had seen him, they told what the angels
had said about this child. 18Everyone
was amazed at what the shepherds said
to them. 19But Mary treasured these
things and continued to think about

FAITH links

TOO BUSY TO WORSHIP?

LUKE 2:8-20

Imagine yourself as a busy shepherd, watching a herd of frisky sheep. Suddenly the night sky becomes alive with first one angel, then a very large group of angels. How would you feel? The shepherds who witnessed this event "became very frightened" (Luke 2:9). But when the angels announced the birth of the Savior, their fear turned to excitement. They left their herds and went to worship him.

God looks for people who aren't too busy to worship him. He wants you to make worship an important part of your life.

My Worship Place, Genesis 35:1–14, p. 49

A Song of Thanks, 1 Samuel 2, p. 356

Your Heavenly Dad, Psalm 103:13, p. 786

God's Valuable Gift: You, Psalm 127:3–5, p. 809

Faith Workout, Acts 16:4–5, p. 1493

Meeting Together, 1 Corinthians 16:19, p. 1567

2:2 registration Census. A counting of all the people and the things they own.
2:5 engaged For the Jewish people, an engagement was a lasting agreement. It could only be broken by divorce.

them. 20Then the shepherds went back to their sheep, praising God and thanking him for everything they had seen and heard. It had been just as the angel had told them.

21When the baby was eight days old, he was circumcised and was named Jesus, the name given by the angel before the baby began to grow inside Mary.

Jesus Is Presented in the Temple

22When the time came for Mary and
Joseph to do what the law of Moses
taught about being made pure,* they took
Jesus to Jerusalem to present him to the
Lord. 23(It is written in the law of the
Lord: "Every firstborn male shall be
given to the Lord.")* 24Mary and Joseph
also went to offer a sacrifice, as the law of
the Lord says: "You must sacrifice two
doves or two young pigeons."*

Simeon Sees Jesus

25In Jerusalem lived a man named
Simeon who was a good man and godly.
He was waiting for the time when God
would take away Israel's sorrow, and the
Holy Spirit was in him. 26Simeon had
been told by the Holy Spirit that he would
not die before he saw the Christ promised by the Lord. 27The Spirit led Simeon
to the Temple. When Mary and Joseph
brought the baby Jesus to the Temple to
do what the law said they must do,
28Simeon took the baby in his arms and
thanked God:

29 "Now, Lord, you can let me, your servant,
die in peace as you said.
30 With my own eyes I have seen your salvation,
31 which you prepared before all people.
32 It is a light for the non-Jewish people to see
and an honor for your people, the Israelites."

33Jesus' father and mother were
amazed at what Simeon had said about
him. 34Then Simeon blessed them and
said to Mary, "God has chosen this child
to cause the fall and rise of many in Israel. He will be a sign from God that

FAITH links

EXERCISING PATIENCE

LUKE 2:25-28, 36-37

What is the longest amount of time you've ever waited for something? Simeon and Anna were two people of Israel who waited a long time for God to send the Savior. God told Simeon that he would not die until he saw the promised Savior. Anna, too, had grown old waiting.

The birth of the Savior had been announced over seven hundred years before it actually took place. That's a long time to wait! Sometimes God allows us to wait before he makes things happen. Waiting helps to develop patience within you. Patience doesn't come automatically. It takes . . . patience to develop.

Need some patience? Download these links:

An Attention-Getter, Numbers 22, p. 207

A Long Wait, Joshua 14:6–15, p. 294

Fly Like an Eagle, Isaiah 40:28–31, p. 947

Stand!, Jeremiah 19:14—20:6, p. 1019

Ask, Search, Knock, Matthew 7:7–10, p. 1286

Just a Test, Luke 4:1–13, p. 1373

2:22 pure The Law of Moses said that forty days after a Jewish woman gave birth to a son, she must be cleansed by a ceremony at the Temple. Read Leviticus 12:2-8.

2:23 "Every . . . Lord." Quotation from Exodus 13:2.

2:24 "You . . . pigeons." Quotation from Leviticus 12:8.

many people will not accept **35**so that the
thoughts of many will be made known.
And the things that will happen will make
your heart sad, too."

Anna Sees Jesus

36There was a prophetess, Anna,
from the family of Phanuel in the tribe of
Asher. Anna was very old. She had once
been married for seven years. **37**Then
her husband died, and she was a widow
for eighty-four years. Anna never left the
Temple but worshiped God, going without food and praying day and night.
38Standing there at that time, she
thanked God and spoke about Jesus to all
who were waiting for God to free Jerusalem.

Joseph and Mary Return Home

39When Joseph and Mary had done
everything the law of the Lord commanded, they went home to Nazareth,
their own town in Galilee. **40**The little
child grew and became strong. He was
filled with wisdom, and God's goodness
was upon him.

Jesus As a Boy

41Every year Jesus' parents went to
Jerusalem for the Passover Feast. **42**When
he was twelve years old, they went to the
feast as they always did. **43**After the feast
days were over, they started home. The
boy Jesus stayed behind in Jerusalem,
but his parents did not know it. **44**Thinking that Jesus was with them in the
group, they traveled for a whole day.
Then they began to look for him among
their family and friends. **45**When they did
not find him, they went back to Jerusalem to look for him there. **46**After three
days they found Jesus sitting in the Temple with the teachers, listening to them
and asking them questions. **47**All who
heard him were amazed at his understanding and answers. **48**When Jesus'
parents saw him, they were astonished.
His mother said to him, "Son, why did
you do this to us? Your father and I were
very worried about you and have been
looking for you."
49Jesus said to them, "Why were you
looking for me? Didn't you know that I
must be in my Father's house?" **50**But
they did not understand the meaning of
what he said.

FAITH links

TWO WAYS TO GROW

LUKE 2:46-52

Did you know there's more than one way to grow? There's the usual way: eat the right foods, exercise, and so on to become strong and healthy. But there's another way to grow—in faith. To grow in faith you also need the right kind of food—"spiritual food." That comes from reading the Bible, going to church, and learning from other Christians about God.

Once, when Jesus was 12, he was found in the Temple, listening to the religious leaders and asking them questions. Asking questions is one way to grow in faith. If you have questions, you can talk to your parents, your Sunday school teacher, or your pastor.

A Time to Celebrate, Exodus 15:1–21, p. 95

Our Thirst Quencher, Psalm 42:1–3, p. 741

Jesus' Mission and Yours, Isaiah 61:1–2, p. 978

Said It? Do It!, Lamentations 2:17, p. 1077

Pass It On!, Joel 1:2–3, p. 1187

The Choices of a Choice, Luke 5:1–11, p. 1375

51Jesus went with them to Nazareth
and was obedient to them. But his mother
kept in her mind all that had happened.
52Jesus became wiser and grew physically. People liked him, and he pleased
God.

The Preaching of John

3 It was the fifteenth year of the rule of
Tiberius Caesar. These men were under Caesar: Pontius Pilate, the ruler of
Judea; Herod, the ruler of Galilee; Philip,
Herod's brother, the ruler of Iturea and
Traconitis; and Lysanias, the ruler of Ab-
ilene. 2Annas and Caiaphas were the high
priests. At this time, the word of God
came to John son of Zechariah in the
desert. 3He went all over the area around
the Jordan River preaching a baptism of
changed hearts and lives for the forgiveness of sins. 4As it is written in the book
of Isaiah the prophet:

"This is a voice of one
  who calls out in the desert:
'Prepare the way for the Lord.
  Make the road straight for him.
5 Every valley should be filled in,
  and every mountain and hill should
    be made flat.
Roads with turns should be made
    straight,
  and rough roads should be made
    smooth.
6 And all people will know about the
  salvation of God!' " *Isaiah 40:3-5*

7To the crowds of people who came to
be baptized by John, he said, "You are all
snakes! Who warned you to run away
from God's coming punishment? 8Do the
things that show you really have changed
your hearts and lives. Don't
begin to say to your-
selves, 'Abraham is
our father.' I tell you
that God could make
children for Abra-
ham from these
rocks. 9The ax is now ready to cut down
the trees, and every tree that does not
produce good fruit will be cut down and
thrown into the fire."[n]

10The people asked John, "Then what
should we do?"

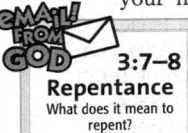

EMAIL FROM GOD
3:7–8
Repentance
What does it mean to repent?

FAITH CHALLENGE

Try this challenge. Read 3:8 to discover how we should act in front of other people. How long would it take for someone who doesn't know you to figure out that you're a Christian?

TESTING IT

Luke 3:8
Do the things that show you really have changed your hearts and lives.

11John answered, "If you have two
shirts, share with the person who does
not have one. If you have food, share that
also."

12Even tax collectors came to John to
be baptized. They said to him, "Teacher,
what should we do?"

13John said to them, "Don't take more
taxes from people than you have been ordered to take."

14The soldiers asked John, "What
about us? What should we do?"

3:9 The ax . . . fire. This means that God is ready to punish his people who do not obey him.

John said to them, "Don't force people
to give you money, and don't lie about
them. Be satisfied with the pay you get."
15Since the people were hoping for
the Christ to come, they wondered if
John might be the one.
16John answered everyone, "I baptize
you with water, but there is one coming
who is greater than I am. I am not good
enough to untie his sandals. He will baptize you with the Holy Spirit and fire.
17He will come ready to clean the grain,
separating the good grain from the chaff.
He will put the good part of the grain into
his barn, but he will burn the chaff with a
fire that cannot be put out."[n] 18And John
continued to preach the Good News, saying many other things to encourage the
people.
19But John spoke against Herod, the
governor, because of his sin with Herodias, the wife of Herod's brother, and because of the many other evil things
Herod did. 20So Herod did something
even worse: He put John in prison.

Jesus Is Baptized by John

21When all the people were being
baptized by John, Jesus also was baptized.
While Jesus was praying, heaven opened
22and the Holy Spirit came down on him
in the form of a dove. Then a voice came
from heaven, saying, "You are my Son,
whom I love, and I am very pleased with
you."

The Family History of Jesus

23When Jesus began his ministry, he
was about thirty years old. People
thought that Jesus was Joseph's son.
Joseph was the son[n] of Heli.
24 Heli was the son of Matthat.
Matthat was the son of Levi.
Levi was the son of Melki.
Melki was the son of Jannai.
Jannai was the son of Joseph.
25 Joseph was the son of Mattathias.
Mattathias was the son of Amos.
Amos was the son of Nahum.
Nahum was the son of Esli.
Esli was the son of Naggai.
26 Naggai was the son of Maath.
Maath was the son of Mattathias.
Mattathias was the son of Semein.
Semein was the son of Josech.
Josech was the son of Joda.
27 Joda was the son of Joanan.
Joanan was the son of Rhesa.
Rhesa was the son of Zerubbabel.
Zerubbabel was the grandson of
Shealtiel.
Shealtiel was the son of Neri.
28 Neri was the son of Melki.
Melki was the son of Addi.
Addi was the son of Cosam.
Cosam was the son of Elmadam.
Elmadam was the son of Er.
29 Er was the son of Joshua.
Joshua was the son of Eliezer.
Eliezer was the son of Jorim.
Jorim was the son of Matthat.
Matthat was the son of Levi.
30 Levi was the son of Simeon.
Simeon was the son of Judah.
Judah was the son of Joseph.
Joseph was the son of Jonam.
Jonam was the son of Eliakim.
31 Eliakim was the son of Melea.
Melea was the son of Menna.
Menna was the son of Mattatha.
Mattatha was the son of Nathan.
Nathan was the son of David.
32 David was the son of Jesse.
Jesse was the son of Obed.
Obed was the son of Boaz.
Boaz was the son of Salmon.
Salmon was the son of Nahshon.
33 Nahshon was the son of Amminadab.
Amminadab was the son of Admin.
Admin was the son of Arni.
Arni was the son of Hezron.
Hezron was the son of Perez.
Perez was the son of Judah.
34 Judah was the son of Jacob.
Jacob was the son of Isaac.
Isaac was the son of Abraham.
Abraham was the son of Terah.
Terah was the son of Nahor.
35 Nahor was the son of Serug.
Serug was the son of Reu.

3:17 He will . . . out. This means that Jesus will come to separate good people from bad people, saving the good and punishing the bad.

3:23 son "Son" in Jewish lists of ancestors can sometimes mean grandson or more distant relative.

Reu was the son of Peleg.
Peleg was the son of Eber.
Eber was the son of Shelah.
36 Shelah was the son of Cainan.
Cainan was the son of Arphaxad.
Arphaxad was the son of Shem.
Shem was the son of Noah.
Noah was the son of Lamech.
37 Lamech was the son of Methuselah.
Methuselah was the son of Enoch.
Enoch was the son of Jared.
Jared was the son of Mahalalel.
Mahalalel was the son of Kenan.
38 Kenan was the son of Enosh.
Enosh was the son of Seth.
Seth was the son of Adam.
Adam was the son of God.

Jesus Is Tempted by the Devil

4 Jesus, filled with the Holy Spirit, returned from the Jordan River. The Spirit led Jesus into the desert
2 where
the devil tempted Jesus for forty days. Jesus ate nothing during that time, and when those days were ended, he was very hungry.
3 The devil said to Jesus, "If you are the Son of God, tell this rock to become bread."
4 Jesus answered, "It is written in the Scriptures: 'A person does not live by eating only bread.' "[n]
5 Then the devil took Jesus and showed him all the kingdoms of the world
in an instant. 6 The devil said to Jesus, "I
will give you all these kingdoms and all their power and glory. It has all been given to me, and I can give it to anyone I
wish. 7 If you worship me, then it will all
be yours."
8 Jesus answered, "It is written in the Scriptures: 'You must worship the Lord your God and serve only him.' "[n]
9 Then the devil led Jesus to Jerusalem and put him on a high place of the Temple. He said to Jesus, "If you are the
Son of God, jump down. 10 It is written in
the Scriptures:

'He has put his angels in charge of
you
to watch over you.' *Psalm 91:11*

11 It is also written:
'They will catch you in their hands

FAITH links

JUST A TEST

LUKE 4:1-13

What tempts you the most? The devil tried to tempt Jesus with food, power, and pride. Since Jesus had been in the wilderness for 40 days without food, Satan knew that Jesus would be very hungry. He wanted Jesus to help himself for the wrong reason.

Temptation itself is not a sin. Giving in to temptation is what causes sin. God allows temptation in our lives to help us grow stronger in faith. When temptation comes, think of it as a test that you need to pass. With God on your side, you can pass with flying colors!

Download these links for more help in passing the test!

Facing the Consequences, Deuteronomy 3:21–29, p. 232

Real Repentance, Jeremiah 4:1–4, p. 993

Sow It and Reap, Lamentations 1:18, p. 1075

Forgive Again?, Luke 17:3–4, p. 1402

A High Price, Romans 6:23, p. 1526

Lost Love?, Revelation 2:4, p. 1733

4:4 'A person . . . bread.' Quotation from Deuteronomy 8:3.
4:8 'You . . . him.' Quotation from Deuteronomy 6:13.

so that you will not hit your foot on
a rock.' " *Psalm 91:12*
12Jesus answered, "But it also says in
the Scriptures: 'Do not test the Lord
your God.' "[n]
13After the devil had tempted Jesus in
every way, he left him to wait until a better time.

Jesus Teaches the People

14Jesus returned to Galilee in the
power of the Holy Spirit, and stories
about him spread all through the area.
15He began to teach in their synagogues,
and everyone praised him.
16Jesus traveled to Nazareth, where
he had grown up. On the Sabbath day he
went to the synagogue, as he always did,
and stood up to read. **17**The book of Isaiah the prophet was given to him. He
opened the book and found the place
where this is written:

18 "The Lord has put his Spirit in me,
because he appointed me to tell
the Good News to the poor.
He has sent me to tell the captives
they are free
and to tell the blind that they can
see again. *Isaiah 61:1*
God sent me to free those who have
been treated unfairly *Isaiah 58:6*
19 and to announce the time when the
Lord will show his kindness."
Isaiah 61:2

20Jesus closed the book, gave it back
to the assistant, and sat down. Everyone
in the synagogue was watching Jesus
closely. **21**He began to say to them,
"While you heard these words just now,
they were coming true!"
22All the people spoke well of Jesus
and were amazed at the words of grace he
spoke. They asked, "Isn't this Joseph's
son?"
23Jesus said to them, "I know that
you will tell me the old saying: 'Doctor,
heal yourself.' You want to say, 'We heard
about the things you did in Capernaum.
Do those things here in your own
town!' " **24**Then Jesus said, "I tell you
the truth, a prophet is not accepted in his
hometown. **25**But I tell you the truth,
there were many widows in Israel during
the time of Elijah. It did not rain in Israel
for three and one-half years, and there
was no food anywhere in the whole country. **26**But Elijah was sent to none of
those widows, only to a widow in Zarephath, a town in Sidon. **27**And there were
many with skin diseases living in Israel
during the time of the prophet Elisha.
But none of them were healed, only Naaman, who was from the country of Syria."
28When all the people in the synagogue heard these things, they became
very angry. **29**They got up, forced Jesus
out of town, and took him to the edge of
the cliff on which the town was built.
They planned to throw him off the edge,
30but Jesus walked through the crowd
and went on his way.

Jesus Forces Out an Evil Spirit

31Jesus went to Capernaum, a city in
Galilee, and on the Sabbath day, he taught
the people. **32**They were amazed at his
teaching, because he spoke with authority.
33In the synagogue a man who had within
him an evil spirit shouted in a loud voice,
34"Jesus of Nazareth! What do you want
with us? Did you come to destroy us? I
know who you are—God's Holy One!"
35Jesus commanded the evil spirit,
"Be quiet! Come out of the man!" The
evil spirit threw the man down to the
ground before all the people and then left
the man without hurting him.
36The people were amazed and said
to each other, "What does this mean?
With authority and power he commands
evil spirits, and they come out." **37**And
so the news about Jesus spread to every
place in the whole area.

Jesus Heals Many People

38Jesus left the synagogue and went
to the home of Simon.[n] Simon's mother-
in-law was sick with a high fever, and
they asked Jesus to help her. **39**He came
to her side and commanded the fever to
leave. It left her, and immediately she got
up and began serving them.

4:12 'Do . . . God.' Quotation from Deuteronomy 6:16.

4:38 Simon Simon's other name was Peter.

40When the sun went down, the people brought those who were sick to Jesus.
Putting his hands on each sick person, he
healed every one of them. 41Demons
came out of many people, shouting, "You
are the Son of God." But Jesus commanded the demons and would not allow
them to speak, because they knew Jesus
was the Christ.
42At daybreak, Jesus went to a lonely
place, but the people looked for him.
When they found him, they tried to keep
him from leaving. 43But Jesus said to
them, "I must preach about God's kingdom to other towns, too. This is why I
was sent."
44Then he kept on preaching in the
synagogues of Judea.

Jesus' First Followers

5 One day while Jesus was standing beside Lake Galilee, many people were
pressing all around him to hear the word
of God. 2Jesus saw two boats at the shore
of the lake. The fishermen had left them
and were washing their nets. 3Jesus got
into one of the boats, the one that belonged to Simon,* and asked him to push
off a little from the land. Then Jesus sat
down and continued to teach the people
from the boat.
4When Jesus had finished speaking,
he said to Simon, "Take the boat into
deep water, and put your nets in the water to catch some fish."
5Simon answered, "Master, we worked
hard all night trying to catch fish, and we
caught nothing. But you say to put the
nets in the water, so I will." 6When the
fishermen did as Jesus told them, they
caught so many fish that the nets began to
break. 7They called to their partners in
the other boat to come and help them.
They came and filled both boats so full
that they were almost sinking.
8When Simon Peter saw what had
happened, he bowed down before Jesus
and said, "Go away from me, Lord. I am a
sinful man!" 9He and the other fishermen were amazed at the many fish they

5:3 **Simon** Simon's other name was Peter.

FAITH links

THE CHOICES OF A CHOICE

LUKE 5:1-11

You have plans for your life, right? Maybe you've thought about going to college someday and having a fabulous career. Now suppose you met someone who could do amazing things. Would you give up your life plans just to work with that person?

Being a Christian is a choice that leads to other choices. For Jesus' followers, this choice involved giving up their fishing business to be with Jesus full time. Many people say no to Christianity because they think that God wants them to be miserable. But that's not true. A loving God has loving plans for his people. The choice to follow him is up to you.

What's your choice? Connect here to know what choice is best for you:

What You Value, Genesis 25:21–34, p. 34

The Green Light, 2 Samuel 2:1, p. 401

Does Crime Pay?, Psalm 37:1–7, p. 736

Choosing a Friend, Proverbs 28:7, p. 865

You've Got the Power!, Acts 1:1–8; 2:1–4, p. 1463

Just Say No!, Titus 2:11–12, p. 1660

caught, as were 10James and John, the
sons of Zebedee, Simon's partners.
Jesus said to Simon, "Don't be afraid.
From now on you will fish for people."
11When the men brought their boats to
the shore, they left everything and followed Jesus.

Jesus Heals a Sick Man

12When Jesus was in one of the
towns, there was a man covered with a
skin disease. When he saw Jesus, he
bowed before him and begged him,
"Lord, you can heal me if you will."
13Jesus reached out his hand and
touched the man and said, "I will. Be
healed!" Immediately the disease disappeared. 14Then Jesus said, "Don't tell
anyone about this, but go and show yourself to the priest[n] and offer a gift for your
healing, as Moses commanded.[n] This will
show the people what I have done."
15But the news about Jesus spread
even more. Many people came to hear
Jesus and to be healed of their sicknesses, 16but Jesus often slipped away to
be alone so he could pray.

Jesus Heals a Paralyzed Man

17One day as Jesus was teaching the
people, the Pharisees and teachers of the
law from every town in Galilee and Judea
and from Jerusalem were there. The
Lord was giving Jesus the power to heal
people. 18Just then, some men were
carrying on a mat a man who was paralyzed. They tried to bring him in and put
him down before Jesus. 19But because
there were so many people there, they
could not find a way in. So they went up
on the roof and lowered the man on his
mat through the ceiling into the middle of
the crowd right before Jesus. 20Seeing
their faith, Jesus said, "Friend, your sins
are forgiven."
21The Jewish teachers of the law and
the Pharisees thought to themselves,
"Who is this man who is speaking as if he
were God? Only God can forgive sins."
22But Jesus knew what they were
thinking and said, "Why are you thinking
these things? 23Which is easier: to say,
'Your sins are forgiven,' or to say, 'Stand
up and walk'? 24But I will prove to you
that the Son of Man has authority on
earth to forgive sins." So Jesus said to

FAITH links

PRAYER PRIORITY

LUKE 5:15-16

What do you make time for each day? The things you make time for are called *priorities*. That's another word to describe the things that are important to you.

For Jesus, prayer was a priority each day. He often went to a place where he could be alone to pray. Jesus knew how important it was to talk with his Father, without being interrupted. On your list of priorities, make sure to add prayer. If it were important enough for Jesus, it should be important enough for you!

I'll Never Forget What's-His-Name, Deuteronomy 8, p. 239

Your Heavenly Dad, Psalm 103:13, p. 786

The Writing's on the Wall, Daniel 5, p. 1159

Going My Way?, Hosea 8:1–6, p. 1179

Heavenly Treasure, Luke 12:32–34, p. 1394

A Good Habit, Ephesians 6:18, p. 1606

5:14 show . . . priest The Law of Moses said a priest must say when a Jewish person with a skin disease was well.

5:14 Moses commanded Read about this in Leviticus 14:1-32.

the paralyzed man, "I tell you, stand up, take your mat, and go home."

25At once the man stood up before them, picked up his mat, and went home, praising God. **26**All the people were fully amazed and began to praise God. They were filled with much respect and said, "Today we have seen amazing things!"

Levi Follows Jesus

27After this, Jesus went out and saw a tax collector named Levi sitting in the tax collector's booth. Jesus said to him, "Follow me!" **28**So Levi got up, left everything, and followed him.

29Then Levi gave a big dinner for Jesus at his house. Many tax collectors and other people were eating there, too. **30**But the Pharisees and the men who taught the law for the Pharisees began to complain to Jesus' followers, "Why do you eat and drink with tax collectors and sinners?"

31Jesus answered them, "It is not the healthy people who need a doctor, but the sick. **32**I have not come to invite good people but sinners to change their hearts and lives."

Jesus Answers a Question

33They said to Jesus, "John's followers often give up eating[n] for a certain time and pray, just as the Pharisees do. But your followers eat and drink all the time."

34Jesus said to them, "You cannot make the friends of the bridegroom give up eating while he is still with them. **35**But the time will come when the bridegroom will be taken away from them, and then they will give up eating."

36Jesus told them this story: "No one takes cloth off a new coat to cover a hole in an old coat. Otherwise, he ruins the new coat, and the cloth from the new coat will not be the same as the old cloth. **37**Also, no one ever pours new wine into old leather bags. Otherwise, the new wine will break the bags, the wine will spill out, and the leather bags will be ruined. **38**New wine must be put into new leather bags. **39**No one after drinking old wine wants new wine, because he says, 'The old wine is better.' "

Jesus Is Lord over the Sabbath

6 One Sabbath day Jesus was walking through some fields of grain. His followers picked the heads of grain, rubbed them in their hands, and ate them. **2**Some Pharisees said, "Why do you do what is not lawful on the Sabbath day?"

3Jesus answered, "Have you not read what David did when he and those with him were hungry? **4**He went into God's house and took and ate the holy bread, which is lawful only for priests to eat. And he gave some to the people who were with him." **5**Then Jesus said to the Pharisees, "The Son of Man is Lord of the Sabbath day."

Jesus Heals a Man's Hand

6On another Sabbath day Jesus went into the synagogue and was teaching, and a man with a crippled right hand was there. **7**The teachers of the law and the Pharisees were watching closely to see if Jesus would heal on the Sabbath day so they could accuse him. **8**But he knew what they were thinking, and he said to the man with the crippled hand, "Stand up here in the middle of everyone." The man got up and stood there. **9**Then Jesus said to them, "I ask you, which is lawful on the Sabbath day: to do good or to do evil, to save a life or to destroy it?" **10**Jesus looked around at all of them and said to the man, "Hold out your hand." The man held out his hand, and it was healed.

11But the Pharisees and the teachers of the law were very angry and discussed with each other what they could do to Jesus.

Jesus Chooses His Apostles

12At that time Jesus went off to a mountain to pray, and he spent the night praying to God. **13**The next morning, Jesus called his followers to him and chose twelve of them, whom he named apostles: **14**Simon (Jesus named him

---

5:33 give up eating This is called "fasting." The people would give up eating for a special time of prayer and worship to God. It was also done to show sadness and disappointment.

Peter), his brother Andrew, James, John,
Philip, Bartholomew, 15Matthew, Thomas, James son of Alphaeus, Simon (called
the Zealot), 16Judas son of James, and Judas Iscariot, who later turned Jesus over
to his enemies.

Jesus Teaches and Heals

17Jesus and the apostles came down
from the mountain, and he stood on level
ground. A large group of his followers
was there, as well as many people from
all around Judea, Jerusalem, and the seacoast cities of Tyre and Sidon. 18They all
came to hear Jesus teach and to be healed
of their sicknesses, and he healed those
who were troubled by evil spirits. 19All
the people were trying to touch Jesus,
because power was coming from him and
healing them all.

20Jesus looked at his followers and
said,

"You people who are poor are happy,
because the kingdom of God
belongs to you.
21You people who are now hungry are
happy,
because you will be satisfied.
You people who are now crying are
happy,
because you will laugh with joy.

22"People will hate you, shut you out,
insult you, and say you are evil because
you follow the Son of Man. But when
they do, you will be happy. 23Be full of joy
at that time, because you have a great reward waiting for you in heaven. Their ancestors did the same things to the
prophets.

24"But how terrible it will be for you
who are rich,
because you have had your easy
life.
25How terrible it will be for you who
are full now,
because you will be hungry.
How terrible it will be for you who
are laughing now,
because you will be sad and cry.

26"How terrible when everyone says
only good things about you, because their
ancestors said the same things about the
false prophets.

Love Your Enemies

27"But I say to you who are listening,
love your enemies. Do good to those who
hate you, 28bless those who curse you,
pray for those who are cruel to you. 29If
anyone slaps you on one

eMAIL! FROM GOD
6:27
Caring
Are you really supposed
to love your enemies?

cheek, offer him the
other cheek, too. If
someone takes your
coat, do not stop
him from taking
your shirt. 30Give
to everyone who asks you, and when
someone takes something that is yours,
don't ask for it back. 31Do to others what
you would want them to do to you. 32If
you love only the people who love you,
what praise should you get? Even sinners love the people who love them. 33If
you do good only to those who do good to
you, what praise should you get? Even
sinners do that! 34If you lend things to
people, always hoping to get something
back, what praise should you get? Even
sinners lend to other sinners so that they
can get back the same amount! 35But
love your enemies, do good to them, and
lend to them without hoping to get anything back. Then you will have a great reward, and you will be children of the Most
High God, because he is kind even to
people who are ungrateful and full of sin.
36Show mercy, just as your Father shows
mercy.

Look at Yourselves

37"Don't judge other people, and you
will not be judged. Don't accuse others of
being guilty, and you will not be accused
of being guilty. Forgive, and you will be
forgiven. 38Give, and you will receive.
You will be given much. Pressed down,
shaken together, and running over, it will
spill into your lap. The way you give to
others is the way God will give to you."

39Jesus told them this story: "Can a
blind person lead another blind person?
No! Both of them will fall into a ditch.
40A student is not better than the teacher, but the student who has been fully
trained will be like the teacher.

41"Why do you notice the little piece
of dust in your friend's eye, but you don't

WHO NEEDS LOVE?

LUKE 6:27-36

Loving friends and family is pretty simple, right? Those who love us and take care of us deserve our love in return.

When Jesus preached his Sermon on the Mount (See the info site on The Sermon on the Mount, p. 1280), He talked about a group that needs love even more. Who are these people? Enemies. In other words, we're to show love to those who treat us badly. This is the kind of love that God has. God's love is given freely. No one has to earn it. Next time you meet an enemy, instead of thinking about getting even, think about praying for him. That's the way to show love.

Here are some more Faithlinks on showing love:

Forgive Instead, Genesis 33, p. 47

More Powerful Than Revenge, Genesis 50:14–21, p. 71

Own Up to It, 2 Samuel 12:1–13, p. 412

Listen Up!, 1 Kings 19:11–13, p. 467

Your Choice of Fruit, Matthew 12:33–35, p. 1295

As Strong as Superman?, Philippians 4:13, p. 1615

notice the big piece of wood in your own
eye? 42How can you say to your friend,
'Friend, let me take that little piece of
dust out of your eye' when you cannot
see that big piece of wood in your own
eye! You hypocrite! First, take the wood
out of your own eye. Then you will see
clearly to take the dust out of your
friend's eye.

Two Kinds of Fruit

43"A good tree does not produce bad
fruit, nor does a bad tree produce good
fruit. 44Each tree is known by its own
fruit. People don't gather figs from thornbushes, and they don't get grapes from
bushes. 45Good people bring good things
out of the good they stored in their
hearts. But evil people bring evil things
out of the evil they stored in their hearts.
People speak the things that are in their
hearts.

Two Kinds of People

46"Why do you call me, 'Lord, Lord,'
but do not do what I say? 47I will show
you what everyone is like who comes to
me and hears my words and obeys.
48That person is like a man building a
house who dug deep and laid the foundation on rock. When the floods came, the
water tried to wash the house away, but it
could not shake it, because the house was
built well. 49But the one who hears my
words and does not obey is like a man
who built his house on the ground without a foundation. When the floods came,
the house quickly fell and was completely
destroyed."

Jesus Heals a Soldier's Servant

7 When Jesus finished saying all these
things to the people, he went to Capernaum. 2There was an army officer
who had a servant who was very important to him. The servant was so sick he
was nearly dead. 3When the officer heard
about Jesus, he sent some older Jewish
leaders to him to ask Jesus to come and
heal his servant. 4The men went to Jesus
and begged him, saying, "This officer is
worthy of your help. 5He loves our people, and he built us a synagogue."

6So Jesus went with the men. He was
getting near the officer's house when the
officer sent friends to say, "Lord, don't
trouble yourself, because I am not worthy to have you come into my house.
7That is why I did not come to you myself. But you only need to command it,
and my servant will be healed. 8I, too, am
a man under the authority of others, and I
have soldiers under my command. I tell
one soldier, 'Go,' and he goes. I tell another soldier, 'Come,' and he comes. I say
to my servant, 'Do this,' and my servant
does it."
9When Jesus heard this, he was
amazed. Turning to the crowd that was
following him, he said, "I tell you, this is
the greatest faith I have found anywhere,
even in Israel."
10Those who had been sent to Jesus
went back to the house where they found
the servant in good health.

Jesus Brings a Man Back to Life

11Soon afterwards Jesus went to a
town called Nain, and his followers and a
large crowd traveled with him. 12When
he came near the town gate, he saw a funeral. A mother, who was a widow, had
lost her only son. A large crowd from the
town was with the mother while her son
was being carried out. 13When the Lord
saw her, he felt very sorry for her and
said, "Don't cry." 14He went up and
touched the coffin, and the people who
were carrying it stopped. Jesus said,
"Young man, I tell you, get up!" 15And
the son sat up and began to talk. Then
Jesus gave him back to his mother.
16All the people were amazed and began praising God, saying, "A great prophet
has come to us! God has come to help his
people."
17This news about Jesus spread
through all Judea and into all the places
around there.

John Asks a Question

18John's followers told him about all
these things. He called for two of his followers 19and sent them to the Lord to
ask, "Are you the One who is to come, or
should we wait for someone else?"
20When the men came to Jesus, they
said, "John the Baptist sent us to you
with this question: 'Are you the One who

FAITH links

FAITH THAT PLEASES GOD

LUKE 7:1-9

Have you even been amazed by something someone has said? That's what happened to Jesus. An army officer went to him, hoping that he would heal his servant. But he didn't expect Jesus to come to his house and do it. He knew that Jesus only had to say the word and his servant would be healed. Jesus was "amazed" when he heard that (Luke 7:9).

That's the kind of faith that pleases God. This is not a wishy-washy, gee-I-hope-he-can-do-it kind of faith. This is the kind of faith that moves mountains.

Here are some other links on pleasing God:

Lights, Camera, . . . Actions!, Genesis 12:1–3, p. 17

An Attention-Getter, Numbers 22, p. 207

The Fence Riders, 1 Kings 18, p. 464

Remember Your Creator, Ecclesiastes 12:1, 13, p. 885

Heavenly Treasure, Luke 12:32–34, p. 1394

The Doubt Remover, Romans 10:8–10, p. 1533

is to come, or should we wait for someone else?' "
21At that time, Jesus healed many
people of their sicknesses, diseases, and
evil spirits, and he gave sight to many
blind people. **22**Then Jesus answered
John's followers, "Go tell John what you
saw and heard here. The blind can see,
the crippled can walk, and people with
skin diseases are healed. The deaf can
hear, the dead are raised to life, and the
Good News is preached to the poor.
23Those who do not stumble in their
faith because of me are blessed!"
24When John's followers left, Jesus
began talking to the people about John:
"What did you go out into the desert to
see? A reed[n] blown by the wind? **25**What
did you go out to see? A man dressed in
fine clothes? No, people who have fine
clothes and much wealth live in kings'
palaces. **26**But what did you go out to
see? A prophet? Yes, and I tell you, John
is more than a prophet. **27**This was written about him:

'I will send my messenger ahead of
you,
who will prepare the way for you.'
Malachi 3:1

28I tell you, John is greater than any
other person ever born, but even the
least important person in the kingdom of
God is greater than John."
29(When the people, including the tax
collectors, heard this, they all agreed that
God's teaching was good, because they
had been baptized by John. **30**But the
Pharisees and experts on the law refused
to accept God's plan for themselves; they
did not let John baptize them.)
31Then Jesus said, "What shall I say
about the people of this time? What are
they like? **32**They are like children sitting in the marketplace, calling to one another and saying,

'We played music for you, but you did
not dance;
we sang a sad song, but you did not
cry.'

33John the Baptist came and did not eat
bread or drink wine, and you say, 'He has
a demon in him.' **34**The Son of Man came
eating and drinking, and you say, 'Look at
him! He eats too much and drinks too
much wine, and he is a friend of tax collectors and sinners!' **35**But wisdom is
proved to be right by what it does."

A Woman Washes Jesus' Feet

36One of the Pharisees asked Jesus to
eat with him, so Jesus went into the
Pharisee's house and sat at the table. **37**A
sinful woman in the town learned that
Jesus was eating at the Pharisee's house.
So she brought an alabaster jar of perfume **38**and stood behind Jesus at his
feet, crying. She began to wash his feet
with her tears, and she dried them with
her hair, kissing them many times and
rubbing them with the perfume. **39**When
the Pharisee who asked Jesus to come to
his house saw this, he thought to himself,
"If Jesus were a prophet, he would know
that the woman touching him is a sinner!"
40Jesus said to the Pharisee, "Simon,
I have something to say to you."

Simon said, "Teacher, tell me."

41Jesus said, "Two people owed money
to the same banker. One owed five hundred coins[n] and the other owed fifty.
42They had no money to pay what they
owed, but the banker told both of them
they did not have to pay him. Which person will love the banker more?"
43Simon, the Pharisee, answered, "I
think it would be the one who owed him
the most money."

Jesus said to Simon, "You are right."
44Then Jesus turned toward the woman
and said to Simon, "Do you see this woman? When I came into your house, you
gave me no water for my feet, but she
washed my feet with her tears and dried
them with her hair. **45**You gave me no
kiss of greeting, but she has been kissing
my feet since I came in. **46**You did not put
oil on my head, but she poured perfume
on my feet. **47**I tell you that her many
sins are forgiven, so she showed great
love. But the person who is forgiven only
a little will love only a little."

7:24 reed It means that John was not ordinary or weak like grass blown by the wind.

7:41 coins Roman denarii. One coin was the average pay for one day's work.

48Then Jesus said to her, "Your sins
are forgiven."
49The people sitting at the table began to say among themselves, "Who is
this who even forgives sins?"
50Jesus said to the woman, "Because
you believed, you are saved from your
sins. Go in peace."

The Group with Jesus

8 After this, while Jesus was traveling
through some cities and small towns,
he preached and told the Good News
about God's kingdom. The twelve apostles were with him, **2**and also some
women who had been healed of sicknesses and evil spirits: Mary, called Magdalene, from whom seven demons had
gone out; **3**Joanna, the wife of Cuza (the
manager of Herod's house); Susanna; and
many others. These women used their
own money to help Jesus and his apostles.

A Story About Planting Seed

4When a great crowd was gathered,
and people were coming to Jesus from
every town, he told them this story:
5"A farmer went out to plant his seed.
While he was planting, some seed fell by
the road. People walked on the seed, and
the birds ate it up. **6**Some seed fell on
rock, and when it began to grow, it died
because it had no water. **7**Some seed fell
among thorny weeds, but the weeds
grew up with it and choked the good
plants. **8**And some seed fell on good
ground and grew and made a hundred
times more."

As Jesus finished the story, he called
out, "You people who can hear me, listen!"
9Jesus' followers asked him what this
story meant.
10Jesus said, "You have been chosen
to know the secrets about the kingdom of
God. But I use stories to speak to other
people so that:

'They will look, but they may not
see.
They will listen, but they may not
understand.' *Isaiah 6:9*

11"This is what the story means: The
seed is God's message. **12**The seed that
fell beside the road is like the people who
hear God's teaching, but the devil comes
and takes it away from them so they cannot believe it and be saved. **13**The seed
that fell on rock is like those who hear
God's teaching and accept it gladly, but
they don't allow the teaching to go deep
into their lives. They believe for a while,
but when trouble comes, they give up.
14The seed that fell among the thorny
weeds is like those who hear God's
teaching, but they let the worries, riches,
and pleasures of this life keep them from
growing and producing good fruit. **15**And
the seed that fell on the good ground is
like those who hear God's teaching with
good, honest hearts and obey it and patiently produce good fruit.

Use What You Have

16"No one after lighting a lamp covers it with a bowl or hides it under a bed.
Instead, the person puts it on a lampstand so those who come in will see the
light. **17**Everything that is hidden will become clear, and every secret thing will be
made known. **18**So be careful how you
listen. Those who have understanding
will be given more. But those who do not
have understanding, even what they
think they have will be taken away from
them."

Jesus' True Family

19Jesus' mother and brothers came to
see him, but there was such a crowd they
could not get to him. **20**Someone said to
Jesus, "Your mother and your brothers
are standing outside, wanting to see
you."
21Jesus answered them, "My mother
and my brothers are those who listen to
God's teaching and obey it!"

Jesus Calms a Storm

22One day Jesus and his followers got
into a boat, and he said to them, "Let's go
across the lake." And so they started
across. **23**While they were sailing, Jesus
fell asleep. A very strong wind blew up on
the lake, causing the boat to fill with water, and they were in danger.

FAITH links

ATTENTION, PLEASE!

LUKE 8:11-15

A person's actions tell you how much he or she is paying attention to what is said. For example, if your teacher told you, "Open your book to page 9," not doing so would show your lack of attention. Jesus once told a story about a person who planted seeds in different types of soil. The story points to the need to pay attention to God's message. The seed represented God's message. The soil represented the way people respond to that news. Often, people hear the news of Jesus, but don't do anything about it. Are you paying attention? What kind of seed are you?

Good Advice?, Leviticus 20:6, p. 162

Do What You Want?, Judges 21:25, p. 341

This Hurts Me More?, 2 Chronicles 36:17–22, p. 606

You Are What You Do, Proverbs 20:11, p. 854

Prayer Priority, Luke 5:15–16, p. 1376

Hold On!, 2 Thessalonians 2:15–17, p. 1639

24The followers went to Jesus and
woke him, saying, "Master! Master! We
will drown!"
Jesus got up and gave a command to
the wind and the waves. They stopped,
and it became calm. 25Jesus said to his
followers, "Where is your faith?"
The followers were afraid and amazed
and said to each other, "Who is this that
commands even the wind and the water,
and they obey him?"

A Man with Demons Inside Him

26Jesus and his followers sailed
across the lake from Galilee to the area of
the Gerasene people. 27When Jesus got
out on the land, a man from the town who
had demons inside him came to Jesus.
For a long time he had worn no clothes
and had lived in the burial caves, not in a
house. 28When he saw Jesus, he cried
out and fell down before him. He said
with a loud voice, "What do you want
with me, Jesus, Son of the Most High
God? I beg you, don't torture me!" 29He
said this because Jesus was commanding
the evil spirit to come out of the man.
Many times it had taken hold of him.
Though he had been kept under guard
and chained hand and foot, he had broken
his chains and had been forced by the demon out into a lonely place.
30Jesus asked him, "What is your
name?"
He answered, "Legion,"* because many
demons were in him. 31The demons
begged Jesus not to send them into eternal darkness.* 32A large herd of pigs was
feeding on a hill, and the demons begged
Jesus to allow them to go into the pigs. So
Jesus allowed them to do this. 33When
the demons came out of the man, they
went into the pigs, and the herd ran down
the hill into the lake and was drowned.
34When the herdsmen saw what had
happened, they ran away and told about
this in the town and the countryside.
35And people went to see what had happened. When they came to Jesus, they
found the man sitting at Jesus' feet,
clothed and in his right mind, because the
demons were gone. But the people were

8:30 "Legion" Means very many. A legion was about five thousand men in the Roman army.
8:31 eternal darkness Literally, "the abyss," something like a pit or a hole that has no end.

frightened. **36**The people who saw this happen told the others how Jesus had made the man well. **37**All the people of the Gerasene country asked Jesus to leave, because they were all very afraid. So Jesus got into the boat and went back to Galilee.

38The man whom Jesus had healed begged to go with him, but Jesus sent him away, saying, **39**"Go back home and tell people how much God has done for you." So the man went all over town telling how much Jesus had done for him.

Jesus Gives Life to a Dead Girl and Heals a Sick Woman

40When Jesus got back to Galilee, a crowd welcomed him, because everyone was waiting for him. **41**A man named Jairus, a leader of the synagogue, came to Jesus and fell at his feet, begging him to come to his house. **42**Jairus' only daughter, about twelve years old, was dying.

While Jesus was on his way to Jairus' house, the people were crowding all around him. **43**A woman was in the crowd who had been bleeding for twelve years, but no one was able to heal her. **44**She came up behind Jesus and touched the edge of his coat, and instantly her bleeding stopped. **45**Then Jesus said, "Who touched me?"

When all the people said they had not touched him, Peter said, "Master, the people are all around you and are pushing against you."

46But Jesus said, "Someone did touch me, because I felt power go out from me." **47**When the woman saw she could not hide, she came forward, shaking, and fell down before Jesus. While all the people listened, she told why she had touched him and how she had been instantly healed. **48**Jesus said to her, "Dear woman, you are made well because you believed. Go in peace."

49While Jesus was still speaking, someone came from the house of the synagogue leader and said to him, "Your daughter is dead. Don't bother the teacher anymore."

50When Jesus heard this, he said to Jairus, "Don't be afraid. Just believe, and your daughter will be well."

51When Jesus went to the house, he let only Peter, John, James, and the girl's father and mother go inside with him. **52**All the people were crying and feeling sad because the girl was dead, but Jesus said, "Stop crying. She is not dead, only asleep."

53The people laughed at Jesus because they knew the girl was dead. **54**But Jesus took hold of her hand and called to her, "My child, stand up!" **55**Her spirit came back into her, and she stood up at once. Then Jesus ordered that she be given something to eat. **56**The girl's parents were amazed, but Jesus told them not to tell anyone what had happened.

Jesus Sends Out the Apostles

9 Jesus called the twelve apostles together and gave them power and authority over all demons and the ability to heal sicknesses. **2**He sent the apostles out to tell about God's kingdom and to heal the sick. **3**He said to them, "Take nothing for your trip, neither a walking stick, bag, bread, money, or extra clothes. **4**When you enter a house, stay there until it is time to leave. **5**If people do not welcome you, shake the dust off of your feet[n] as you leave the town, as a warning to them."

6So the apostles went out and traveled through all the towns, preaching the Good News and healing people everywhere.

Herod Is Confused About Jesus

7Herod, the governor, heard about all the things that were happening and was confused, because some people said, "John the Baptist has risen from the dead." **8**Others said, "Elijah has come to us." And still others said, "One of the prophets who lived long ago has risen from the dead." **9**Herod said, "I cut off John's head, so who is this man I hear such things about?" And Herod kept trying to see Jesus.

9:5 shake . . . feet A warning. It showed that they had rejected these people.

More than Five Thousand Fed

10When the apostles returned, they told Jesus everything they had done. Then Jesus took them with him to a town called Bethsaida where they could be alone together. **11**But the people learned where Jesus went and followed him. He welcomed them and talked with them about God's kingdom and healed those who needed to be healed.

12Late in the afternoon, the twelve apostles came to Jesus and said, "Send the people away. They need to go to the towns and countryside around here and find places to sleep and something to eat, because no one lives in this place."

13But Jesus said to them, "You give them something to eat."

They said, "We have only five loaves of bread and two fish, unless we go buy food for all these people." **14**(There were about five thousand men there.)

Jesus said to his followers, "Tell the people to sit in groups of about fifty people."

15So the followers did this, and all the people sat down. **16**Then Jesus took the five loaves of bread and two fish, and looking up to heaven, he thanked God for the food. Then he divided the food and gave it to the followers to give to the people. **17**They all ate and were satisfied, and what was left over was gathered up, filling twelve baskets.

Jesus Is the Christ

18One time when Jesus was praying alone, his followers were with him, and he asked them, "Who do the people say I am?"

19They answered, "Some say you are John the Baptist. Others say you are Elijah.[n] And others say you are one of the prophets from long ago who has come back to life."

20Then Jesus asked, "But who do you say I am?"

Peter answered, "You are the Christ from God."

21Jesus warned them not to tell anyone, saying, **22**"The Son of Man must suffer many things. He will be rejected by the older Jewish leaders, the leading priests, and the teachers of the law. He will be killed and after three days will be raised from the dead."

23Jesus said to all of them, "If people want to follow me, they must give up the things they want. They must be willing to give up their lives daily to follow me. **24**Those who want to save their lives will give up true life. But those who give up their lives for me will have true life. **25**It is worth nothing for them to have the whole world if they themselves are destroyed or lost. **26**If people are ashamed of me and my teaching, then the Son of Man will be ashamed of them when he comes in his glory and with the glory of the Father and the holy angels. **27**I tell you the truth, some people standing here will see the kingdom of God before they die."

EMAIL FROM GOD 9:24
Life
Jesus offers true life.

Jesus Talks with Moses and Elijah

28About eight days after Jesus said these things, he took Peter, John, and James and went up on a mountain to pray. **29**While Jesus was praying, the appearance of his face changed, and his clothes became shining white. **30**Then two men, Moses and Elijah,[n] were talking with Jesus. **31**They appeared in heavenly glory, talking about his departure which he would soon bring about in Jerusalem. **32**Peter and the others were very sleepy, but when they awoke fully, they saw the glory of Jesus and the two men standing with him. **33**When Moses and Elijah were about to leave, Peter said to Jesus, "Master, it is good that we are here. Let us make three tents—one for you, one for Moses, and one for Elijah." (Peter did not know what he was talking about.)

34While he was saying these things, a cloud came and covered them, and they

---

9:19 Elijah A man who spoke for God and who lived hundreds of years before Christ. See 1 Kings 17.

9:30 Moses and Elijah Two of the most important Jewish leaders in the past. God had given Moses the Law, and Elijah was an important prophet.

became afraid as the cloud covered them.
35A voice came from the cloud, saying, "This is my Son, whom I have chosen. Listen to him!"

36When the voice finished speaking, only Jesus was there. Peter, John, and James said nothing and told no one at that time what they had seen.

Jesus Heals a Sick Boy

37The next day, when they came
down from the mountain, a large crowd
met Jesus. 38A man in the crowd shouted
to him, "Teacher, please come and look at
my son, because he is my only child.
39An evil spirit seizes my son, and suddenly he screams. It causes him to lose control of himself and foam at the mouth. The evil spirit keeps on hurting him and
almost never leaves him. 40I begged
your followers to force the evil spirit out, but they could not do it."

41Jesus answered, "You people have no faith, and your lives are all wrong. How long must I stay with you and put up with you? Bring your son here."

42While the boy was coming, the demon threw him on the ground and made him lose control of himself. But Jesus gave a strong command to the evil spirit and healed the boy and gave him back to
his father. 43All the people were amazed
at the great power of God.

Jesus Talks About His Death

While everyone was wondering about all that Jesus did, he said to his followers,
44"Don't forget what I tell you now: The Son of Man will be handed over to peo-
ple." 45But the followers did not understand what this meant; the meaning was hidden from them so they could not understand. But they were afraid to ask Jesus about it.

FAITH links

WANT TO KNOW? ASK!

LUKE 9:45

When you don't understand something you've heard or studied, what do you do? If you want to be wise, the best thing to do is to ask questions. When Jesus' followers didn't understand what Jesus said, they were afraid to ask him about it. Many times, people are afraid to ask questions because they're afraid of looking stupid. Whenever you have questions about God, or your Bible, don't be afraid to ask someone to help you. God wants you to know all about him!

Download these links on getting wisdom:

An Example Not to Follow, Leviticus 18:1–3, p. 157

Learning to Listen, 1 Samuel 3, p. 358

Braggin' Rights, Jeremiah 9:23–24, p. 1005

The Dead End of the Occult, Ezekiel 13:17–23, p. 1098

The Power of Prayer, Acts 12:5, p. 1485

One Thing to Do, Romans 4:1–5, p. 1523

Who Is the Greatest?

46Jesus' followers began to have an
argument about which one of them was
the greatest. 47Jesus knew what they
were thinking, so he took a little child
and stood the child beside him. 48Then
Jesus said, "Whoever accepts this little child in my name accepts me. And whoever accepts me accepts the One who sent me, because whoever is least among you all is really the greatest."

Anyone Not Against Us Is for Us

49John answered, "Master, we saw someone using your name to force demons out

of people. We told him to stop, because
he does not belong to our group."
50But Jesus said to him, "Don't stop
him, because whoever is not against you
is for you."

A Town Rejects Jesus

51When the time was coming near for
Jesus to depart, he was determined to go
to Jerusalem. **52**He sent some men ahead
of him, who went into a town in Samaria
to make everything ready for him. **53**But
the people there would not welcome him,
because he was set on going to Jerusalem. **54**When James and John, followers
of Jesus, saw this, they said, "Lord, do
you want us to call fire down from heaven
and destroy those people?"[n]
55But Jesus turned and scolded them.
56Then[n] they went to another town.

Following Jesus

57As they were going along the road,
someone said to Jesus, "I will follow you
any place you go."
58Jesus said to them, "The foxes have
holes to live in, and the birds have nests,
but the Son of Man has no place to rest
his head."
59Jesus said to another man, "Follow
me!"
But he said, "Lord, first let me go and
bury my father."
60But Jesus said to him, "Let the people who are dead bury their own dead.
You must go and tell about the kingdom
of God."
61Another man said, "I will follow
you, Lord, but first let me go and say
good-bye to my family."
62Jesus said, "Anyone who begins to
plow a field but keeps looking back is of
no use in the kingdom of God."

Jesus Sends Out the Seventy-Two

10 After this, the Lord chose seventy-
two[n] others and sent them out in
pairs ahead of him into every town and
place where he planned to go. **2**He said to
them, "There are a great many people to
harvest, but there are only a few workers. So pray to God, who owns the harvest, that he will send more workers to
help gather his harvest. **3**Go now, but listen! I am sending you out like sheep
among wolves. **4**Don't carry a purse, a
bag, or sandals, and don't waste time talking with people on the road. **5**Before you
go into a house, say, 'Peace be with this
house.' **6**If peaceful people live there,
your blessing of peace will stay with them,
but if not, then your blessing will come
back to you. **7**Stay in the peaceful house,
eating and drinking what the people there
give you. A worker should be given his
pay. Don't move from house to house. **8**If
you go into a town and the people welcome you, eat what they give you. **9**Heal
the sick who live there, and tell them,
'The kingdom of God is near you.' **10**But if
you go into a town, and the people don't
welcome you, then go into the streets and
say, **11**'Even the dirt from your town that
sticks to our feet we wipe off against you.[n]
But remember that the kingdom of God is
near.' **12**I tell you, on the Judgment Day it
will be better for the people of Sodom[n]
than for the people of that town.

Jesus Warns Unbelievers

13"How terrible for you, Korazin!
How terrible for you, Bethsaida! If the
miracles I did in you had happened in Tyre
and Sidon,[n] those people would have
changed their lives long ago. They would
have worn rough cloth and put ashes on
themselves to show they had changed.
14But on the Judgment Day it will be
better for Tyre and Sidon than for you.
15And you, Capernaum,[n] will you be lifted

9:54 Verse 54 Here, some Greek copies add: ". . . as Elijah did."

9:55-56 Verses 55-56 Some copies read: "But Jesus turned and scolded them. And Jesus said, 'You don't know what kind of spirit you belong to. [56]The Son of Man did not come to destroy the souls of people but to save them.' Then . . . ."

10:1 seventy-two Many Greek copies read seventy.

10:11 dirt . . . you A warning. It showed that they had rejected these people.

10:12 Sodom City that God destroyed because the people were so evil.

10:13 Tyre and Sidon Towns where wicked people lived.

10:13, 15 Korazin, Bethsaida, Capernaum Towns by Lake Galilee where Jesus preached to the people.

up to heaven? No! You will be thrown down to the depths!

16"Whoever listens to you listens to me, and whoever refuses to accept you refuses to accept me. And whoever refuses to accept me refuses to accept the One who sent me."

Satan Falls

17When the seventy-two[n] came back, they were very happy and said, "Lord, even the demons obeyed us when we used your name!"

10:17
Demons
Find out who the demons obey.

18Jesus said, "I saw Satan fall like lightning from heaven. **19**Listen, I have given you power to walk on snakes and scorpions, power that is greater than the enemy has. So nothing will hurt you. **20**But you should not be happy because the spirits obey you but because your names are written in heaven."

Jesus Prays to the Father

21Then Jesus rejoiced in the Holy Spirit and said, "I praise you, Father, Lord of heaven and earth, because you have hidden these things from the people who are wise and smart. But you have shown them to those who are like little children. Yes, Father, this is what you really wanted.

22"My Father has given me all things. No one knows who the Son is, except the Father. And no one knows who the Father is, except the Son and those whom the Son chooses to tell."

23Then Jesus turned to his followers and said privately, "You are blessed to see what you now see. **24**I tell you, many prophets and kings wanted to see what you now see, but they did not, and they wanted to hear what you now hear, but they did not."

The Good Samaritan

25Then an expert on the law stood up to test Jesus, saying, "Teacher, what must I do to get life forever?"

26Jesus said, "What is written in the law? What do you read there?"

27The man answered, "Love the Lord your God with all your heart, all your soul, all your strength, and all your mind."[n] Also, "Love your neighbor as you love yourself."[n]

28Jesus said to him, "Your answer is right. Do this and you will live."

29But the man, wanting to show the importance of his question, said to Jesus, "And who is my neighbor?"

30Jesus answered, "As a man was going down from Jerusalem to Jericho, some robbers attacked him. They tore off his clothes, beat him, and left him lying there, almost dead. **31**It happened that a priest was going down that road. When he saw the man, he walked by on the other side. **32**Next, a Levite[n] came there, and after he went over and looked at the man, he walked by on the other side of the road. **33**Then a Samaritan[n] traveling down the road came to where the hurt man was. When he saw the man, he felt very sorry for him. **34**The Samaritan went to him, poured olive oil and wine[n] on his wounds, and bandaged them. Then he put the hurt man on his own donkey and took him to an inn where he cared for him. **35**The next day, the Samaritan brought out two coins,[n] gave them to the innkeeper, and said, 'Take care of this man. If you spend more money on him, I will pay it back to you when I come again.' "

36Then Jesus said, "Which one of these three men do you think was a neighbor to the man who was attacked by the robbers?"

37The expert on the law answered,

10:17 seventy-two Many Greek copies read seventy.

10:27 "Love . . . mind." Quotation from Deuteronomy 6:5.

10:27 "Love . . . yourself." Quotation from Leviticus 19:18.

10:32 Levite Levites were members of the tribe of Levi who helped the Jewish priests with their work in the Temple. Read 1 Chronicles 23:24-32.

10:33 Samaritan Samaritans were people from Samaria. These people were part Jewish, but the Jews did not accept them as true Jews. Samaritans and Jews disliked each other.

10:34 olive oil and wine Oil and wine were used like medicine to soften and clean wounds.

10:35 coins Roman denarii. One coin was the average pay for one day's work.

FAITH CHALLENGE

Try this one. Read 10:29 to find out what important question a religious leader wanted Jesus to answer. According to Jesus' definition, who are *your* neighbors? How do you need to change your definition of a neighbor?

TESTING IT

Luke 10:29

But the man, wanting to show the importance of his question, said to Jesus, "And who is my neighbor?"

"The one who showed him mercy."

Jesus said to him, "Then go and do what he did."

Mary and Martha

38While Jesus and his followers were traveling, Jesus went into a town. A woman named Martha let Jesus stay at her house. 39Martha had a sister named Mary, who was sitting at Jesus' feet and listening to him teach. 40But Martha was busy with all the work to be done. She went in and said, "Lord, don't you care that my sister has left me alone to do all the work? Tell her to help me."

41But the Lord answered her, "Martha, Martha, you are worried and upset about many things. 42Only one thing is important. Mary has chosen the better thing, and it will never be taken away from her."

Jesus Teaches About Prayer

11 One time Jesus was praying in a certain place. When he finished, one of his followers said to him, "Lord, teach us to pray as John taught his followers."

2Jesus said to them, "When you pray, say:

'Father, may your name always be
kept holy.
May your kingdom come.
3 Give us the food we need for each day.
4 Forgive us for our sins,
because we forgive everyone who
has done wrong to us.
And do not cause us to be tempted.' "

Continue to Ask

5Then Jesus said to them, "Suppose one of you went to your friend's house at midnight and said to him, 'Friend, loan me three loaves of bread. 6A friend of mine has come into town to visit me, but I have nothing for him to eat.' 7Your friend inside the house answers, 'Don't bother me! The door is already locked, and my children and I are in bed. I cannot get up and give you anything.' 8I tell you, if friendship is not enough to make him get up to give you the bread, your boldness will make him get up and give you whatever you need. 9So I tell you, ask, and God will give to you. Search, and you will find. Knock, and the door will open for you. 10Yes, everyone who asks will receive. The one who searches will find. And everyone who knocks will have the door opened. 11If your children ask for a fish, which of you would give them a snake instead? 12Or, if your children ask for an egg, would you give them a scorpion? 13Even though you are bad, you know how to give good things to your children. How much more your heavenly Father will give the Holy Spirit to those who ask him!"

A MODEL PRAYER

Luke 11:1

Jesus said that we should pray with faith and simplicity. He gave us a model prayer to follow. This prayer is sometimes called "The Lord's Prayer." The prayer is in the Bible in the Gospels of Matthew and Luke. In Matthew, the prayer appears in Jesus' famous sermon called "The Sermon on the Mount." (Read Matthew 6:9–13, p. 1283.) In Luke, it appears after the disciples asked Jesus to teach them how to pray. (See Luke 11:1–4.) Here's what the different parts of the prayer mean:

"Our Father in heaven, may your name always be kept holy" (Matthew 6:9).

We can worship and respect God when we pray.

"May your kingdom come and what you want be done, here on earth as it is in heaven" (6:10). We should want what God wants when we pray.

"Give us the food we need for each day" (6:11).

We can ask God for what we need when we pray.

"Forgive us for our sins, just as we have forgiven those who sinned against us" (6:12).

We can ask God for forgiveness when we pray.

"And do not cause us to be tempted, but save us from the Evil One" (6:13).

We can ask God to protect us from sin and evil when we pray.

Jesus' Power Is from God

14One time Jesus was sending out a demon that could not talk. When the demon
came out, the man who had been unable to
speak, then spoke. The people were
amazed. **15**But some of them said, "Jesus
uses the power of Beelzebul, the ruler of
demons, to force demons out of people."

16Other people, wanting to test Jesus,
asked him to give them a sign from
heaven. **17**But knowing their thoughts,
he said to them, "Every kingdom that is
divided against itself will be destroyed.
And a family that is divided against itself
will not continue. **18**So if Satan is divided
against himself, his kingdom will not continue. You say that I use the power of
Beelzebul to force out demons. **19**But if I
use the power of Beelzebul to force out
demons, what power do your people use
to force demons out? So they will be your
judges. **20**But if I use the power of God to
force out demons, then the kingdom of
God has come to you.

21"When a strong person with many
weapons guards his own house, his possessions are safe. **22**But when someone
stronger comes and defeats him, the
stronger one will take away the weapons
the first man trusted and will give away
the possessions.

23"Anyone who is not with me is
against me, and anyone who does not
work with me is working against me.

The Empty Person

24"When an evil spirit comes out of a
person, it travels through dry places,

looking for a place to rest. But when it
finds no place, it says, 'I will go back to
the house I left.' **25**And when it comes
back, it finds that house swept clean and
made neat. **26**Then the evil spirit goes
out and brings seven other spirits more
evil than it is, and they go in and live
there. So the person has even more trouble than before."

People Who Are Truly Happy

27As Jesus was saying these things, a
woman in the crowd called out to Jesus,
"Happy is the mother who gave
birth to you and
nursed you."

EMAIL! FROM GOD
11:28
Obedience
What will make you really happy?

28But Jesus said,
"No, happy are those
who hear the teach-
ing of God and obey
it."

The People Want a Miracle

29As the crowd grew larger, Jesus
said, "The people who live today are evil.
They want to see a miracle for a sign, but
no sign will be given them, except the
sign of Jonah.[n] **30**As Jonah was a sign for
those people who lived in Nineveh, the
Son of Man will be a sign for the people of
this time. **31**On the Judgment Day the
Queen of the South[n] will stand up with
the people who live now. She will show
they are guilty, because she came from
far away to listen to Solomon's wise
teaching. And I tell you that someone
greater than Solomon is here. **32**On the
Judgment Day the people of Nineveh will
stand up with the people who live now,
and they will show that you are guilty.
When Jonah preached to them, they were
sorry and changed their lives. And I tell
you that someone greater than Jonah is
here.

Be a Light for the World

33"No one lights a lamp and puts it in
a secret place or under a bowl, but on a
lampstand so the people who come in can
see. **34**Your eye is a light for the body.
When your eyes are good, your whole
body will be full of light. But when your
eyes are evil, your whole body will be full
of darkness. **35**So be careful not to let the
light in you become darkness. **36**If your
whole body is full of light, and none of it is
dark, then you will shine bright, as when
a lamp shines on you."

Jesus Accuses the Pharisees

37After Jesus had finished speaking, a
Pharisee asked Jesus to eat with him. So
Jesus went in and sat at the table. **38**But
the Pharisee was surprised when he saw
that Jesus did not wash his hands[n] before
the meal. **39**The Lord said to him, "You
Pharisees clean the outside of the cup
and the dish, but inside you are full of
greed and evil. **40**You foolish people! The
same one who made what is outside also
made what is inside. **41**So give what is in
your dishes to the poor, and then you will
be fully clean. **42**How terrible for you
Pharisees! You give God one-tenth of
even your mint, your rue, and every
other plant in your garden. But you fail to
be fair to others and to love God. These
are the things you should do while continuing to do those other things. **43**How
terrible for you Pharisees, because you
love to have the most important seats in
the synagogues, and you love to be
greeted with respect in the marketplaces. **44**How terrible for you, because
you are like hidden graves, which people
walk on without knowing."

Jesus Talks to Experts on the Law

45One of the experts on the law said
to Jesus, "Teacher, when you say these
things, you are insulting us, too."

46Jesus answered, "How terrible for
you, you experts on the law! You make
strict rules that are very hard for people
to obey, but you yourselves don't even
try to follow those rules. **47**How terrible
for you, because you build tombs for the

11:29 sign of Jonah Jonah's three days in the fish are like Jesus' three days in the tomb. See Matthew 12:40.

11:31 Queen of the South The Queen of Sheba. She traveled a thousand miles to learn God's wisdom from Solomon. Read 1 Kings 10:1-3.

11:38 wash his hands This was a Jewish religious custom that the Pharisees thought was very important.

FAITH links

CLEAN INSIDE AND OUT

LUKE 11:39-40

Would you drink out of a cup that was clean on the outside but dirty on the inside? The answer is obvious, wouldn't you say? You'd want the inside to match the outside.

Jesus told the Pharisees that they were clean on the outside, but dirty on the inside. By this he meant they had sinful thoughts and actions. Yet they tried to make themselves look good in public. God wants us to be clean outside and in. He doesn't want us to pretend that we have no sin. Being quick to admit that we've done wrong and to ask God to forgive us keeps us clean on the inside.

A Holiday Every Week, Leviticus 23:1–3, p. 166

Does Crime Pay?, Psalm 37:1–7, p. 736

Red to White, Isaiah 1:18, p. 896

Real Repentance, Jeremiah 4:1–4, p. 993

The "Ruler" of Our Lives, Amos 7:7–9, p. 1202

Obey or Disobey?, Luke 20:20–26, p. 1409

prophets whom your ancestors killed!
48And now you show that you approve of
what your ancestors did. They killed the
prophets, and you build tombs for them!
49This is why in his wisdom God said, 'I
will send prophets and apostles to them.
They will kill some, and they will treat
others cruelly.' **50**So you who live now
will be punished for the deaths of all the
prophets who were killed since the beginning of the world—**51**from the killing
of Abel to the killing of Zechariah,* who
died between the altar and the Temple.
Yes, I tell you that you who are alive now
will be punished for them all.

52"How terrible for you, you experts
on the law. You have taken away the key
to learning about God. You yourselves
would not learn, and you stopped others
from learning, too."

53When Jesus left, the teachers of the
law and the Pharisees began to give him
trouble, asking him questions about
many things, **54**trying to catch him saying something wrong.

Don't Be Like the Pharisees

12 So many thousands of people had
gathered that they were stepping
on each other. Jesus spoke first to his followers, saying, "Beware of the yeast of
the Pharisees, because they are hypocrites. **2**Everything that is hidden will be
shown, and everything that is secret will
be made known. **3**What you have said in
the dark will be heard in the light, and
what you have whispered in an inner
room will be shouted from the housetops.

4"I tell you, my friends, don't be afraid
of people who can kill the body but after
that can do nothing more to hurt you. **5**I
will show you the one to fear. Fear the
one who has the power to kill you and
also to throw you into hell. Yes, this is the
one you should fear.

6"Five sparrows are sold for only two
pennies, and God does not forget any of
them. **7**But God even knows how many
hairs you have on your head. Don't be
afraid. You are worth much more than
many sparrows.

Don't Be Ashamed of Jesus

8"I tell you, all those who stand before
others and say they believe in me, I, the

11:51 Abel . . . Zechariah In the Hebrew Old Testament, the first and last men to be murdered.

Son of Man, will say before the angels of
God that they belong to me. **9**But all who
stand before others and say they do not
believe in me, I will say before the angels
of God that they do not belong to me.

10"Anyone who speaks against the
Son of Man can be forgiven, but anyone
who speaks against the Holy Spirit will
not be forgiven.

11"When you are brought into the
synagogues before the leaders and other
powerful people, don't worry about how
to defend yourself or what to say. **12**At
that time the Holy Spirit will teach you
what you must say."

Jesus Warns Against Selfishness

13Someone in the crowd said to Jesus,
"Teacher, tell my brother to divide with
me the property our father left us."

14But Jesus said to him, "Who said I
should judge or decide between you?"
15Then Jesus said to them, "Be careful
and guard against all kinds of greed. Life
is not measured by how much one owns."

16Then Jesus told this story: "There
was a rich man who had some land, which
grew a good crop. **17**He thought to himself, 'What will I do? I have no place to
keep all my crops.' **18**Then he said, 'This
is what I will do: I will tear down my
barns and build bigger ones, and there I
will store all my grain and other goods.
19Then I can say to myself, "I have
enough good things stored to last for
many years. Rest, eat, drink, and enjoy
life!" '

20"But God said to him, 'Foolish man!
Tonight your life will be taken from you.
So who will get those things you have
prepared for yourself?'

21"This is how it will be for those who
store up things for themselves and are
not rich toward God."

Don't Worry

22Jesus said to his followers, "So I tell
you, don't worry about the food you need
to live, or about the clothes you need for
your body. **23**Life is more than food, and
the body is more than clothes. **24**Look at
the birds. They don't plant or harvest,
they don't have storerooms or barns, but
God feeds them. And you are worth much
more than birds. **25**You cannot add any
time to your life by worrying about it.
26If you cannot do even the little things,
then why worry about the big things?
27Consider how the lilies grow; they
don't work or make clothes for themselves. But I tell you that even Solomon
with his riches was not dressed as beautifully as one of these flowers. **28**God
clothes the grass in the field, which is
alive today but tomorrow is thrown into
the fire. So how much more will God
clothe you? Don't have so little faith!
29Don't always think about what you will
eat or what you will drink, and don't keep
worrying. **30**All the people in the world
are trying to get these things, and your
Father knows you need them. **31**But
seek God's kingdom, and all the other
things you need will be given to you.

Don't Trust in Money

32"Don't fear, little flock, because
your Father wants to give you the kingdom. **33**Sell your possessions and give to
the poor. Get for yourselves purses that
will not wear out, the treasure in heaven
that never runs out, where thieves can't
steal and moths can't destroy. **34**Your
heart will be where your treasure is.

Always Be Ready

35"Be dressed, ready for service, and
have your lamps shining. **36**Be like servants who are waiting for their master to
come home from a wedding party. When
he comes and knocks, the servants immediately open the door for him. **37**They will
be blessed when their master comes
home, because he sees that they were
watching for him. I tell you the truth, the
master will dress himself to serve and tell
the servants to sit at the table, and he will
serve them. **38**Those servants will be
happy when he comes in and finds them
still waiting, even if it is midnight or later.

39"Remember this: If the owner of
the house knew what time a thief was
coming, he would not allow the thief to
enter his house. **40**So you also must be
ready, because the Son of Man will come
at a time when you don't expect him!"

FAITH links

HEAVENLY TREASURE

LUKE 12:32-34

Think about what you value most. This might be something you spend most of your time thinking about. This could also be a goal that you have for your life. What you value is what you treasure. Jesus preached a sermon to teach people about God's kingdom. He talked about storing treasure in heaven. If you treasure learning about God and helping others, you'll store up treasure in heaven.

What's important to you? Check out these Faithlinks:

What You Value, Genesis 25:21–34, p. 34

Remembering What He Said, Deuteronomy 6:4–9, p. 236

What God Thinks, Isaiah 55:8–9, p. 969

Empty Words, Ezekiel 33:30–33, p. 1127

The Choices of a Choice, Luke 5:1–11, p. 1375

You're a Fake!, 2 Peter 2:1, p. 1709

Who Is the Trusted Servant?

41Peter said, "Lord, did you tell this
story to us or to all people?"
42The Lord said, "Who is the wise
and trusted servant that the master
trusts to give the other servants their
food at the right time? 43When the master comes and finds the servant doing his
work, the servant will be blessed. 44I tell
you the truth, the master will choose that
servant to take care of everything he
owns. 45But suppose the servant thinks
to himself, 'My master will not come
back soon,' and he begins to beat the
other servants, men and women, and to
eat and drink and get drunk. 46The master will come when that servant is not
ready and is not expecting him. Then the
master will cut him in pieces and send
him away to be with the others who don't
obey.
47"The servant who knows what his
master wants but is not ready, or who
does not do what the master wants, will
be beaten with many blows! 48But the
servant who does not know what his
master wants and does things that should
be punished will be beaten with few
blows. From everyone who has been
given much, much will be demanded. And
from the one trusted with much, much
more will be expected.

Jesus Causes Division

49"I came to set fire to the world, and
I wish it were already burning! 50I have a
baptism* to suffer through, and I feel very
troubled until it is over. 51Do you think I
came to give peace to
the earth? No, I tell
you, I came to di-
vide it. 52From now
on, a family with five
people will be divided,
three against two, and
two against three.
53They will be divid-
ed: father against son and son against
father, mother against daughter and
daughter against mother, mother-in-law
against daughter-in-law and daughter-in-
law against mother-in-law."

EMAIL FROM GOD

12:51–53
Family
Is there anything that is more important than the family?

Understanding the Times

54Then Jesus said to the people,
"When you see clouds coming up in the
west, you say, 'It's going to rain,' and it
happens. 55When you feel the wind begin
to blow from the south, you say, 'It will be

12:50 I . . . baptism Jesus was talking about the suffering he would soon go through.

a hot day,' and it happens. 56Hypocrites!
You know how to understand the appearance of the earth and sky. Why don't you
understand what is happening now?

Settle Your Problems

57"Why can't you decide for yourselves what is right? 58If your enemy is
taking you to court, try hard to settle it
on the way. If you don't, your enemy
might take you to the judge, and the
judge might turn you over to the officer,
and the officer might throw you into jail.
59I tell you, you will not get out of there
until you have paid everything you owe."

Change Your Hearts

13 At that time some people were
there who told Jesus that Pilate[*]
had killed some people from Galilee
while they were worshiping. He mixed
their blood with the blood of the animals
they were sacrificing to God. 2Jesus answered, "Do you think this happened to
them because they were more sinful than
all others from Galilee? 3No, I

EMAIL! FROM GOD
13:3–5
Repentance
Change your heart–
or else!

tell you. But unless
you change your
hearts and lives, you
will be destroyed as
they were! 4What
about those eigh-
teen people who died when the tower of
Siloam fell on them? Do you think they
were more sinful than all the others who
live in Jerusalem? 5No, I tell you. But unless you change your hearts and lives, you
will all be destroyed too!"

The Useless Tree

6Jesus told this story: "A man had a fig
tree planted in his vineyard. He came
looking for some fruit on the tree, but he
found none. 7So the man said to his gardener, 'I have been looking for fruit on
this tree for three years, but I never find
any. Cut it down. Why should it waste the
ground?' 8But the servant answered,
'Master, let the tree have one more year
to produce fruit. Let me dig up the dirt
around it and put on some fertilizer. 9If
the tree produces fruit next year, good.
But if not, you can cut it down.' "

Jesus Heals on the Sabbath

10Jesus was teaching in one of the
synagogues on the Sabbath day. 11A
woman was there who, for eighteen
years, had an evil spirit in her that made
her crippled. Her back was always bent;
she could not stand up straight. 12When
Jesus saw her, he called her over and
said, "Woman, you are free from your
sickness." 13Jesus put his hands on her,
and immediately she was able to stand up
straight and began praising God.

14The synagogue leader was angry
because Jesus healed on the Sabbath day.
He said to the people, "There are six
days when one has to work. So come to
be healed on one of those days, and not
on the Sabbath day."

15The Lord answered, "You hypocrites! Doesn't each of you untie your
work animals and lead them to drink water every day—even on the Sabbath day?
16This woman that I healed, a daughter
of Abraham, has been held by Satan for
eighteen years. Surely it is not wrong for
her to be freed from her sickness on a
Sabbath day!" 17When Jesus said this, all
of those who were criticizing him were
ashamed, but the entire crowd rejoiced at
all the wonderful things Jesus was doing.

Stories of Mustard Seed and Yeast

18Then Jesus said, "What is God's
kingdom like? What can I compare it
with? 19It is like a mustard seed that a
man plants in his garden. The seed grows
and becomes a tree, and the wild birds
build nests in its branches."

20Jesus said again, "What can I compare God's kingdom with? 21It is like
yeast that a woman took and hid in a large
tub of flour until it made all the dough
rise."

The Narrow Door

22Jesus was teaching in every town
and village as he traveled toward Jerusalem. 23Someone said to Jesus, "Lord,
will only a few people be saved?"

13:1 Pilate Pontius Pilate was the Roman governor of Judea from A.D. 26 to A.D. 36.

Livin' it

HANDLING MY STUFF

Luke 12; 13

Such a Lot of Stuff! Do you need to move stuffed animals to get in bed? Are CDs and books overflowing the shelves? Do your clothes get squashed into your closet and dresser drawers? How important is "your stuff" to you? How often do you use what you have? Can you even find it when you want it?

Jesus preached a sermon to help his listeners understand that loving God and loving money or possessions don't mix. (Check Luke 16:13–15.) You can't love God and possessions. Whichever is loved more—God or money— is the heart's desire. What is *your* heart's desire?

MORE FAITH links

"Help! I'm being buried with too much stuff!"

"Hang on, Tagg. These Faithlinks will help you handle all that stuff."

What I've Got, 2 Kings 20:12–17, p. 508

- Are you ever tempted to brag about the cool stuff you have? What would you do if you no longer had those things? There's nothing wrong in having nice things. But the stuff you have doesn't make you special. God gives you everything, and he makes you special. Now that's something to brag about!

My Favorite!, Mark 10:17–23, p. 1347

- Suppose someone asked you to give up your favorite possession to prove you loved God. How willing would you be to give it up? Link here to see how a man reacted to such a suggestion.

Share and Share Alike?, Acts 2:43–47, p. 1466

- How willing are you to share what you have with others? Would it make a difference in what you were being asked to share? Early Christians shared everything they had because of their love of God. How can you share some of God's love and some of your possessions with someone today?

my FAVORITE links

Jesus said, **24**"Try hard to enter
through the narrow door, because many
people will try to enter there, but they
will not be able. **25**When the owner of the
house gets up and closes the door, you
can stand outside and knock on the door
and say, 'Sir, open the door for us.' But he
will answer, 'I don't know you or where
you come from.' **26**Then you will say, 'We
ate and drank with you, and you taught in
the streets of our town.' **27**But he will
say to you, 'I don't know you or where
you come from. Go away from me, all you
who do evil!' **28**You will cry and grind
your teeth with pain when you see Abraham, Isaac, Jacob, and all the prophets in
God's kingdom, but you yourselves
thrown outside. **29**People will come from
the east, west, north, and south and will
sit down at the table in the kingdom of
God. **30**There are those who have the
lowest place in life now who will have the
highest place in the future. And there are
those who have the highest place now
who will have the lowest place in the future."

Jesus Will Die in Jerusalem

31At that time some Pharisees came
to Jesus and said, "Go away from here!
Herod wants to kill you!"

32Jesus said to them, "Go tell that fox
Herod, 'Today and tomorrow I am forcing
demons out and healing people. Then, on
the third day, I will reach my goal.' **33**Yet I
must be on my way today and tomorrow
and the next day. Surely it cannot be right
for a prophet to be killed anywhere except in Jerusalem.

34"Jerusalem, Jerusalem! You kill the
prophets and stone to death those who
are sent to you. Many times I wanted to
gather your people as a hen gathers her
chicks under her wings, but you would
not let me. **35**Now your house is left
completely empty. I tell you, you will not
see me until that time when you will say,
'God bless the One who comes in the
name of the Lord.' "[n]

Healing on the Sabbath

14 On a Sabbath day, when Jesus
went to eat at the home of a leading Pharisee, the people were watching
Jesus very closely. **2**And in front of him
was a man with dropsy.[n] **3**Jesus said to
the Pharisees and experts on the law, "Is
it right or wrong to heal on the Sabbath
day?" **4**But they would not answer his
question. So Jesus took the man, healed
him, and sent him away. **5**Jesus said to
the Pharisees and teachers of the law, "If
your child or ox falls into a well on the
Sabbath day, will you not pull him out
quickly?" **6**And they could not answer
him.

Don't Make Yourself Important

7When Jesus noticed that some of the
guests were choosing the best places to
sit, he told this story: **8**"When someone
invites you to a wedding feast, don't take
the most important seat, because someone more important than you may have
been invited. **9**The host, who invited
both of you, will come to you and say,
'Give this person your seat.' Then you
will be embarrassed and will have to
move to the last place. **10**So when you
are invited, go sit in a seat that is not important. When the host comes to you, he
may say, 'Friend, move up here to a more
important place.' Then all the other
guests will respect you. **11**All who make
themselves great will be made humble,
but those who make themselves humble
will be made great."

You Will Be Rewarded

12Then Jesus said to the man who had
invited him, "When you give a lunch or a
dinner, don't invite only your friends,
your family, your other relatives, and
your rich neighbors. At another
time they will invite
you to eat with
them, and you will
be repaid. **13**Instead,
when you give a
feast, invite the poor,
the crippled, the

EMAIL! FROM GOD
14:13–14
Caring
Find out the kind of people you should care for.

13:35 'God . . . Lord.' Quotation from Psalm 118:26.

14:2 dropsy A sickness that causes the body to swell larger and larger.

FAITH links

BEST SEAT IN THE HOUSE

LUKE 14:7-11

Suppose you and a friend were invited to a party to meet someone famous. Now, let's say there was only one seat next to the famous person. Would you take it or would you let your friend have it?

Jesus once told a story about taking the best seats at a party. The people who wanted others to think they were important would take the best seats. Jesus used this story to teach people to be humble. Humble people don't try to make themselves look important. They don't have to. God says he will make the humble great!

Here are some more links on being humble:

Fairness for All, Deuteronomy 24:17, p. 258

The Way to Serve God, 1 Kings 9:4, p. 450

Seeing the Needs, Nehemiah 1, p. 625

Set for Life?, Obadiah 2–4, p. 1208

Glad to Help!, Romans 15:17–20, p. 1541

Brag on Him!, 1 Corinthians 3:18–23, p. 1548

lame, and the blind. **14**Then you will be
blessed, because they have nothing and
cannot pay you back. But you will be repaid when the good people rise from the
dead."

A Story About a Big Banquet

15One of those at the table with Jesus
heard these things and said to him, "Happy are the people who will share in the
meal in God's kingdom."

16Jesus said to him, "A man gave a
big banquet and invited many people.
17When it was time to eat, the man sent
his servant to tell the guests, 'Come.
Everything is ready.'

18"But all the guests made excuses.
The first one said, 'I have just bought a
field, and I must go look at it. Please excuse me.' **19**Another said, 'I have just
bought five pairs of oxen; I must go and
try them. Please excuse me.' **20**A third
person said, 'I just got married; I can't
come.' **21**So the servant returned and
told his master what had happened. Then
the master became angry and said, 'Go at
once into the streets and alleys of the
town, and bring in the poor, the crippled,
the blind, and the lame.' **22**Later the servant said to him, 'Master, I did what you
commanded, but we still have room.'
23The master said to the servant, 'Go out
to the roads and country lanes, and urge
the people there to come so my house
will be full. **24**I tell you, none of those
whom I invited first will eat with me.' "

The Cost of Being Jesus' Follower

25Large crowds were traveling with
Jesus, and he turned and said to them,
26"If anyone comes to me but loves his
father, mother, wife, children, brothers,
or sisters—or even life—more than me,
he cannot be my follower. **27**Whoever is
not willing to carry the cross and follow
me cannot be my follower. **28**If you want
to build a tower, you first sit down and
decide how much it will cost, to see if you
have enough money to finish the job. **29**If
you don't, you might lay the foundation,
but you would not be able to finish. Then
all who would see it would make fun of
you, **30**saying, 'This person began to
build but was not able to finish.'

31"If a king is going to fight another
king, first he will sit down and plan. He will

decide if he and his ten thousand soldiers can defeat the other king who has twenty thousand soldiers. **32**If he can't, then while the other king is still far away, he will send some people to speak to him and ask for peace. **33**In the same way, you must give up everything you have to be my follower.

Don't Lose Your Influence

34"Salt is good, but if it loses its salty taste, you cannot make it salty again. **35**It is no good for the soil or for manure; it is thrown away.

"You people who can hear me, listen."

A Lost Sheep, a Lost Coin

15 The tax collectors and sinners all came to listen to Jesus. **2**But the Pharisees and the teachers of the law began to complain: "Look, this man welcomes sinners and even eats with them."

3Then Jesus told them this story: **4**"Suppose one of you has a hundred sheep but loses one of them. Then he will leave the other ninety-nine sheep in the open field and go out and look for the lost sheep until he finds it. **5**And when he finds it, he happily puts it on his shoulders **6**and goes home. He calls to his friends and neighbors and says, 'Be happy with me because I found my lost sheep.' **7**In the same way, I tell you there is more joy in heaven over one sinner who changes his heart and life, than over ninety-nine good people who don't need to change.

eMAIL! FROM GOD
15:7
Repentance
What gives heaven joy?

8"Suppose a woman has ten silver coins,[n] but loses one. She will light a lamp, sweep the house, and look carefully for the coin until she finds it. **9**And when she finds it, she will call her friends and neighbors and say, 'Be happy with me because I have found the coin that I lost.' **10**In the same way, there is joy in the presence of the angels of God when one sinner changes his heart and life."

The Son Who Left Home

11Then Jesus said, "A man had two sons. **12**The younger son said to his father, 'Give me my share of the property.' So the father divided the property between his two sons. **13**Then the younger son gathered up all that was his and traveled far away to another country. There he wasted his money in foolish living. **14**After he had spent everything, a time came when there was no food anywhere in the country, and the son was poor and hungry. **15**So he got a job with one of the citizens there who sent the son into the fields to feed pigs. **16**The son was so hungry that he wanted to eat the pods the pigs were eating, but no one gave him anything. **17**When he realized what he was doing, he thought, 'All of my father's servants have plenty of food. But I am here, almost dying with hunger. **18**I will leave and return to my father and say to him, "Father, I have sinned against God and have done wrong to you. **19**I am no longer worthy to be called your son, but let me be like one of your servants." ' **20**So the son left and went to his father.

"While the son was still a long way off, his father saw him and felt sorry for his son. So the father ran to him and hugged and kissed him. **21**The son said, 'Father, I have sinned against God and have done wrong to you. I am no longer worthy to be called your son.' **22**But the father said to his servants, 'Hurry! Bring the best clothes and put them on him. Also, put a ring on his finger and sandals on his feet. **23**And get our fat calf and kill it so we can have a feast and celebrate. **24**My son was dead, but now he is alive again! He was lost, but now he is found!' So they began to celebrate.

25"The older son was in the field, and as he came closer to the house, he heard the sound of music and dancing. **26**So he called to one of the servants and asked what all this meant. **27**The servant said, 'Your brother has come back, and your father killed the fat calf, because your brother came home safely.' **28**The older son was angry and would not go in to the feast. So his father went out and begged him to come in. **29**But the older son said

15:8 silver coins Roman denarii. One coin was the average pay for one day's work.

to his father, 'I have served you like a slave for many years and have always obeyed your commands. But you never gave me even a young goat to have at a feast with my friends. **30**But your other son, who wasted all your money on prostitutes, comes home, and you kill the fat calf for him!' **31**The father said to him, 'Son, you are always with me, and all that I have is yours. **32**We had to celebrate and be happy because your brother was dead, but now he is alive. He was lost, but now he is found.' "

EMAIL FROM GOD 15:32
Salvation
Check out a time to celebrate.

True Wealth

16 Jesus also said to his followers, "Once there was a rich man who had a manager to take care of his business. This manager was accused of cheating him. **2**So he called the manager in and said to him, 'What is this I hear about you? Give me a report of what you have done with my money, because you can't be my manager any longer.' **3**The manager thought to himself, 'What will I do since my master is taking my job away from me? I am not strong enough to dig ditches, and I am ashamed to beg. **4**I know what I'll do so that when I lose my job people will welcome me into their homes.'

5"So the manager called in everyone who owed the master any money. He asked the first one, 'How much do you owe?' **6**He answered, 'Eight hundred gallons of olive oil.' The manager said to him, 'Take your bill, sit down quickly, and write four hundred gallons.' **7**Then the manager asked another one, 'How much do you owe?' He answered, 'One thousand bushels of wheat.' Then the manager said to him, 'Take your bill and write eight hundred bushels.' **8**So, the master praised the dishonest manager for being smart. Yes, worldly people are smarter with their own kind than spiritual people are.

9"I tell you, make friends for yourselves using worldly riches so that when those riches are gone, you will be welcomed in those homes that continue forever. **10**Whoever can be trusted with a little can also be trusted with a lot, and whoever is dishonest with a little is dishonest with a lot. **11**If you cannot be trusted with worldly riches, then who will trust you with true riches? **12**And if you cannot be trusted with things that belong to someone else, who will give you things of your own?

13"No servant can serve two masters. The servant will hate one master and love the other, or will follow one master and refuse to follow the other. You cannot serve both God and worldly riches."

EMAIL FROM GOD 16:13
Money
Can Christians serve both God and money?

God's Law Cannot Be Changed

14The Pharisees, who loved money, were listening to all these things and made fun of Jesus. **15**He said to them, "You make yourselves look good in front of people, but God knows what is really in your hearts. What is important to people is hateful in God's sight.

16"The law of Moses and the writings of the prophets were preached until John[*] came. Since then the Good News about the kingdom of God is being told, and everyone tries to enter it by force. **17**It would be easier for heaven and earth to pass away than for the smallest part of a letter in the law to be changed.

Divorce and Remarriage

18"If a man divorces his wife and marries another woman, he is guilty of adultery, and the man who marries a divorced woman is also guilty of adultery."

The Rich Man and Lazarus

19Jesus said, "There was a rich man who always dressed in the finest clothes and lived in luxury every day. **20**And a very poor man named Lazarus, whose body was covered with sores, was laid at the rich man's gate. **21**He wanted to eat

16:16 John John the Baptist, who preached to people about Christ's coming (Matthew 3, Luke 3).

FAITH links

YOUR HEART'S DESIRE

LUKE 16:13-15

What do you love? Some people, if they're honest, will say that they love their possessions. Maybe they have some great video games, or the latest super-fast computer. Some just seem to love the money it takes to buy those possessions.

One day Jesus preached a sermon to help his listeners understand how to please God. (Check out The Sermon on the Mount, p. 1280.) He wanted them to know that loving God and loving worldly riches don't mix. You can't love one if you love the other. Loving one or the other means having it as your heart's desire. What is *your* heart's desire?

The Sacrifice, Genesis 22, p. 29

Ten Ways to Obey, Exodus 20, p. 103

When God Says No, 2 Samuel 7, p. 407

A Look for the Book, 2 Chronicles 34:14–18, p. 603

A Robbery in Progress, Malachi 3:8–10, p. 1270

More Money?, 1 Timothy 6:10, p. 1649

only the small pieces of food that fell from
the rich man's table. And the dogs would
come and lick his sores. 22Later, Lazarus
died, and the angels carried him to the
arms of Abraham. The rich man died, too,
and was buried. 23In the place of the
dead, he was in much pain. The rich man
saw Abraham far away with Lazarus at
his side. 24He called, 'Father Abraham,
have mercy on me! Send Lazarus to dip
his finger in water and cool my tongue,
because I am suffering in this fire!' 25But
Abraham said, 'Child, remember when
you were alive you had the good things in
life, but bad things happened to Lazarus.
Now he is comforted here, and you are
suffering. 26Besides, there is a big pit between you and us, so no one can cross
over to you, and no one can leave there
and come here.' 27The rich man said, 'Father, then please send Lazarus to my
father's house. 28I have five brothers,
and Lazarus could warn them so that
they will not come to this place of pain.'
29But Abraham said, 'They have the law
of Moses and the writings of the prophets; let them learn from them.' 30The
rich man said, 'No, father Abraham! If
someone goes to them from the dead,
they would believe and change their
hearts and lives.' 31But Abraham said to
him, 'If they will not listen to Moses and
the prophets, they will not listen to
someone who comes back from the
dead.' "

Sin and Forgiveness

17 Jesus said to his followers, "Things
that cause people to sin will happen, but how terrible for the person who
causes them to happen! 2It would be better for you to be thrown into the sea with
a large stone around your neck than to
cause one of these little ones to sin. 3So
be careful!

"If another follower sins, warn him,
and if he is sorry and stops sinning, forgive him. 4If he sins against you seven
times in one day and says that he is sorry
each time, forgive him."

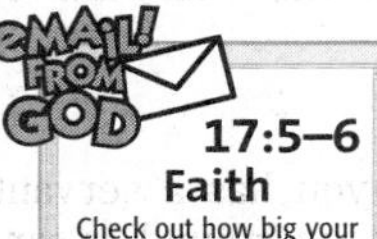

17:5–6
Faith
Check out how big your faith should be.

How Big Is Your Faith?

5The apostles said
to the Lord, "Give us
more faith!"

FAITH links

FORGIVE AGAIN?

LUKE 17:3-4

How many times do you think a person should be forgiven for the same offense? Let's say that a friend said something mean to you. Could you forgive her if she said the same thing to you over and over again? Jesus said that we should always be ready to forgive someone, no matter how many times that person asks for forgiveness. Don't worry if you think you can't forgive from the heart. God just wants you to be willing. He's willing to help you when you find it hard to forgive.

Made in His Image, Genesis 1:26–27, p. 4

Yours, Mine, and Ours?, 1 Samuel 25, p. 389

A Memorial for Two Thieves, 1 Chronicles 7:21, p. 530

Teaching Others, Ezra 7:8–10, p. 617

Help for a Friend, Mark 2:1–5, p. 1332

Give from the Heart, Luke 21:1–4, p. 1410

6The Lord said, "If your faith were
the size of a mustard seed, you could say
to this mulberry tree, 'Dig yourself up
and plant yourself in the sea,' and it
would obey you.

Be Good Servants

7"Suppose one of you has a servant
who has been plowing the ground or caring for the sheep. When the servant
comes in from working in the field, would
you say, 'Come in and sit down to eat'?
8No, you would say to him, 'Prepare
something for me to eat. Then get yourself ready and serve me. After I finish
eating and drinking, you can eat.' **9**The
servant does not get any special thanks
for doing what his master commanded.
10It is the same with you. When you have
done everything you are told to do, you
should say, 'We are unworthy servants;
we have only done the work we should
do.' "

Be Thankful

11While Jesus was on his way to Jerusalem, he was going through the area between Samaria and Galilee. **12**As he
came into a small town, ten men who had
a skin disease met him there. They did
not come close to Jesus **13**but called to
him, "Jesus! Master! Have mercy on us!"
14When Jesus saw the men, he said,
"Go and show yourselves to the priests."[n]
As the ten men were going, they were
healed. **15**When one of them saw that he
was healed, he went back to Jesus, praising God in a loud voice. **16**Then he bowed
down at Jesus' feet and thanked him.
(And this man was a Samaritan.) **17**Jesus
said, "Weren't ten men healed? Where
are the other nine? **18**Is this Samaritan
the only one who came back to thank
God?" **19**Then Jesus said to him, "Stand
up and go on your way. You were healed
because you believed."

God's Kingdom Is Within You

20Some of the Pharisees asked Jesus,
"When will the kingdom of God come?"
Jesus answered, "God's kingdom is
coming, but not in a way that you will be
able to see with your eyes. **21**People will
not say, 'Look, here it is!' or, 'There it is!'
because God's kingdom is within[n] you."
22Then Jesus said to his followers,
"The time will come when you will want

17:14 show . . . priests The Law of Moses said a priest must say when a person with a skin disease became well.

17:21 within Or "among."

Being Responsible

Luke 17:7–10

Livin' it

Attitude Check Think about something you can do really well. Can you draw? Tell a joke? Sing? Play sports? Listen? Do these talents and abilities help make you popular and everybody's friend?

Of all the things others notice about you, is being *responsible* one of them? Ruth was responsible. She had an attitude of helping others rather than thinking of ways others could help her. (Check Ruth 2:1–7, p. 346.) Do others think of you as a responsible kid?

Jesus once told a story about showing responsibility. In it he shared what God wants us to do with the special gifts, talents, and abilities he gives us. (Read about it in Matthew 25:14–30, p. 1317.) How can you use your talents in a way that makes God happy and shows you are responsible?

"So God wants us to use our talents and abilities in a responsible way—not just waste them. Hmm! Think I need to do a talent check."

"I know what I'm good at—I'm fast! I know I have a responsibility to help people find things in a hurry! How'm I doing so far?"

MORE FAITH links

Read My Lips?, p. 260
Your Response to Responsibility, p. 346
You Are What You Do, p. 854
That Thing You Do, p. 1319

Promises, Promises, Judges 2:1–3, p. 312
- Have you ever made a promise you didn't keep? What happened?
- Being a responsible person means keeping your promises. How can you do that even when it's hard?

A Christian's Responsibility, Acts 11:26, p. 1484
- As a citizen of a country, you have certain responsibilities. What are some of those responsibilities?
- One of the responsibilities of being a Christian is to grow in faith. How do the people in your church help you grow?

Say What?!, Ephesians 4:22–29, p. 1603
- Do you ever hurt people by what you say? Being responsible for the words that come out of our mouths is important, too!

Trouble with the Tongue, James 3:3–12, p. 1692
- Link here to discover how a small tongue can cause BIG trouble. How can you be responsible for what you say?

my FAVORITE links

very much to see one of the days of the
Son of Man. But you will not see it.
23People will say to you, 'Look, there he
is!' or, 'Look, here he is!' Stay where you
are; don't go away and search.

When Jesus Comes Again

24"When the Son of Man comes
again, he will shine like lightning, which
flashes across the sky and lights it up
from one side to the other. **25**But first he
must suffer many things and be rejected
by the people of this time. **26**When the
Son of Man comes again, it will be as it
was when Noah lived. **27**People were eating, drinking, marrying, and giving their
children to be married until the day Noah
entered the boat. Then the flood came
and killed them all. **28**It will be the same
as during the time of Lot. People were
eating, drinking, buying, selling, planting,
and building. **29**But the day Lot left
Sodom,[n] fire and sulfur rained down from
the sky and killed them all. **30**This is how
it will be when the Son of Man comes
again.

31"On that day, a person who is on the
roof and whose belongings are in the
house should not go inside to get them. A
person who is in the field should not go
back home. **32**Remember Lot's wife.[n]
33Those who try to keep their lives will
lose them. But those who give up their
lives will save them. **34**I tell you, on that
night two people will be sleeping in one
bed; one will be taken and the other will
be left. **35**There will be two women
grinding grain together; one will be
taken, and the other will be left." **36**[n]

37The followers asked Jesus, "Where
will this be, Lord?"

Jesus answered, "Where there is a
dead body, there the vultures will gather."

God Will Answer His People

18 Then Jesus used this story to teach
his followers that they should always pray and never lose hope. **2**"In a
certain town there was a judge who did
not respect God or care about people. **3**In
that same town there was a widow who
kept coming to this judge, saying, 'Give
me my rights against my enemy.' **4**For a
while the judge refused to help her. But
afterwards, he thought to himself, 'Even
though I don't respect God or care about
people, **5**I will see that she gets her
rights. Otherwise she will continue to
bother me until I am worn out.' "

6The Lord said, "Listen to what the
unfair judge said. **7**God will always give
what is right to his people who cry to him
night and day, and he will not be slow to
answer them. **8**I tell you, God will help
his people quickly. But when the Son of
Man comes again, will he find those on
earth who believe in him?"

Being Right with God

9Jesus told this story to some people
who thought they were very good and
looked down on everyone else: **10**"A
Pharisee and a tax collector both went to
the Temple to pray. **11**The Pharisee stood
alone and prayed, 'God, I thank you that I
am not like other people who steal, cheat,
or take part in adultery, or even like this
tax collector. **12**I give up eating[n] twice a
week, and I give one-tenth of everything
I get!'

13"The tax collector, standing at a distance, would not even look up to heaven.
But he beat on his chest because he was
so sad. He said, 'God, have mercy on me,
a sinner.' **14**I tell you, when this man
went home, he was right with God, but
the Pharisee was not. All who make
themselves great will be made humble,
but all who make themselves humble will
be made great."

Who Will Enter God's Kingdom?

15Some people brought even their babies to Jesus so he could touch them.

17:29 Sodom City that God destroyed because the people were so evil.

17:32 Lot's wife A story about what happened to Lot's wife is found in Genesis 19:15-17, 26.

17:36 Verse 36 A few Greek copies add verse 36: "Two people will be in the field. One will be taken, and the other will be left."

18:12 give up eating This is called "fasting." The people would give up eating for a special time of prayer and worship to God. It was also done to show sadness and disappointment.

FAITH links

BETTER THAN SOME?

LUKE 18:9-14

You probably feel pretty good about yourself, right? Most of us, if we're honest, feel that we're pretty good or at least better than some people we might know. Jesus told a story about a Pharisee and a tax collector. The Pharisee thought that he was better than the tax collector. Jesus told the story as a warning about pride. Since God can see what we're *really* like, he's not impressed when we brag about ourselves. So, instead of bragging, remember the tax collector's prayer. The humble way is always the best way.

Check out these links for something to really brag about:

Just Kidding?, Genesis 21:8–10, p. 28

Put Pride Aside, Exodus 2:11–15, p. 78

Giving Your Part, Leviticus 27:30, p. 173

Help for the Outsiders, Nehemiah 5:9–10, p. 630

Jesus' Prayer, John 17, p. 1453

The "Eyes" Have It?, 1 Corinthians 12, p. 1559

When the followers saw this, they told
them to stop. **16**But Jesus called for the
children, saying, "Let the little children
come to me. Don't stop them, because
the kingdom of God belongs to people
who are like these children. **17**I tell you
the truth, you must accept the kingdom
of God as if you were a child, or you will
never enter it."

A Rich Man's Question

18A certain leader asked Jesus, "Good
Teacher, what must I do to have life forever?"

19Jesus said to him, "Why do you call
me good? Only God is good. **20**You know
the commands: 'You must not be guilty of
adultery. You must not murder anyone.
You must not steal. You must not tell lies
about your neighbor. Honor your father
and mother.' "[n]

21But the leader said, "I have obeyed
all these commands since I was a boy."

22When Jesus heard this, he said to
him, "There is still one more thing you
need to do. Sell everything you have and
give it to the poor, and you will have treasure in heaven. Then come and follow
me." **23**But when the man heard this, he
became very sad, because he was very
rich.

24Jesus looked at him and said, "It is
very hard for rich people to enter the
kingdom of God. **25**It is easier for a camel
to go through the eye of a needle than for
a rich person to enter the kingdom of
God."

Who Can Be Saved?

26When the people heard this, they
asked, "Then who can be saved?"

27Jesus answered, "God can do things
that are not possible for people to do."

28Peter said, "Look, we have left
everything and followed you."

29Jesus said, "I tell you the truth, all
those who have left houses, wives, brothers, parents, or children for the kingdom
of God **30**will get much more in this life.
And in the age that is coming, they will
have life forever."

Jesus Will Rise from the Dead

31Then Jesus took the twelve apostles aside and said to them, "We are going

18:20 'You . . . mother.' Quotation from Exodus 20:12-16; Deuteronomy 5:16-20.

to Jerusalem. Everything the prophets
wrote about the Son of Man will happen.
32He will be turned over to those who are
evil. They will laugh at him, insult him, spit
on him, 33beat him with whips, and kill
him. But on the third day, he will rise to life
again." 34The apostles did not understand
this; the meaning was hidden from them,
and they did not realize what was said.

Jesus Heals a Blind Man

35As Jesus came near the city of Jericho, a blind man was sitting beside the
road, begging. 36When he heard the people coming down the road, he asked,
"What is happening?"

37They told him, "Jesus, from Nazareth, is going by."

38The blind man cried out, "Jesus,
Son of David, have mercy on me!"

39The people leading the group
warned the blind man to be quiet. But the
blind man shouted even more, "Son of
David, have mercy on me!"

40Jesus stopped and ordered the blind
man to be brought to him. When he came
near, Jesus asked him, 41"What do you
want me to do for you?"

He said, "Lord, I want to see."

42Jesus said to him, "Then see. You
are healed because you believed."

43At once the man was able to see,
and he followed Jesus, thanking God. All
the people who saw this praised God.

Zacchaeus Meets Jesus

19 Jesus was going through the city
of Jericho. 2A man was there
named Zacchaeus, who was a very important tax collector, and he was wealthy.
3He wanted to see who Jesus was, but he
was not able because he was too short to
see above the crowd. 4He ran ahead to a
place where Jesus would come, and he
climbed a sycamore tree so he could see
him. 5When Jesus came to that place, he
looked up and said to him, "Zacchaeus,
hurry and come down! I must stay at
your house today."

6Zacchaeus came down quickly and
welcomed him gladly. 7All the people saw
this and began to complain, "Jesus is
staying with a sinner!"

FAITH links

FAITH GOD NOTICES

LUKE 18:35-43

When you need help, how quick are you to ask for it? When you ask for help how much faith do you have that you'll receive what you ask for? A blind man by the road was quick to yell for help when he heard that Jesus was near. He knew that Jesus could give him sight. The people around him tried to silence him, but he would not be silent. His enthusiastic cry for help showed his faith. Jesus couldn't help but take notice. That's the kind of faith that always pleases God. Do you have that kind of faith?

A Different Kind of People, Leviticus 11, p. 146

Building Tools, Ezra 6:15, p. 615

How God Speaks, Job 33:14–17, p. 696

Hope That Doesn't Fail, Acts 26:4–7, p. 1510

Our Interpreter, Romans 8:26, p. 1528

While You Wait, Jude 21, p. 1726

8But Zacchaeus stood and said to the
Lord, "I will give half of my possessions
to the poor. And if I have cheated anyone,
I will pay back four times more."

9Jesus said to him, "Salvation has
come to this house today, because this man also
belongs to the family
of Abraham. 10The
Son of Man came to
find lost people and
save them."

EMAIL! FROM GOD
19:10
Jesus
Why did Jesus come to earth?

A Story About Three Servants

11As the people were listening to
this, Jesus told them a story because he
was near Jerusalem and they thought
God's kingdom would appear immediately. **12**He said: "A very important man
went to a country far away to be made a
king and then to return home. **13**So he
called ten of his servants and gave a coin[n]
to each servant. He said, 'Do business
with this money until I get back.' **14**But
the people in the kingdom hated the man.
So they sent a group to follow him and
say, 'We don't want this man to be our
king.'

15"But the man became king. When
he returned home, he said, 'Call those
servants who have my money so I can
know how much they earned with it.'

16"The first servant came and said,
'Sir, I earned ten coins with the one you
gave me.' **17**The king said to the servant,
'Excellent! You are a good servant. Since
I can trust you with small things, I will let
you rule over ten of my cities.'

18"The second servant said, 'Sir, I
earned five coins with your one.' **19**The
king said to this servant, 'You can rule
over five cities.'

20"Then another servant came in and
said to the king, 'Sir, here is your coin
which I wrapped in a piece of cloth and
hid. **21**I was afraid of you, because you
are a hard man. You even take money that
you didn't earn and gather food that you
didn't plant.' **22**Then the king said to the
servant, 'I will condemn you by your own
words, you evil servant. You knew that I
am a hard man, taking money that I didn't
earn and gathering food that I didn't
plant. **23**Why then didn't you put my
money in the bank? Then when I came
back, my money would have earned some
interest.'

24"The king said to the men who
were standing by, 'Take the coin away
from this servant and give it to the servant who earned ten coins.' **25**They said,
'But sir, that servant already has ten
coins.' **26**The king said, 'Those who have
will be given more, but those who do not
have anything will have everything taken
away from them. **27**Now where are my
enemies who didn't want me to be king?
Bring them here and kill them before
me.' "

Jesus Enters Jerusalem as a King

28After Jesus said this, he went on toward Jerusalem. **29**As Jesus came near
Bethphage and Bethany, towns near the
hill called the Mount of Olives, he sent
out two of his followers. **30**He said, "Go
to the town you can see there. When you
enter it, you will find a colt tied there,
which no one has ever ridden. Untie it
and bring it here to me. **31**If anyone asks
you why you are untying it, say that the
Master needs it."

32The two followers went into town
and found the colt just as Jesus had told
them. **33**As they were untying it, its owners came out and asked the followers,
"Why are you untying our colt?"

34The followers answered, "The
Master needs it." **35**So they brought it to
Jesus, threw their coats on the colt's
back, and put Jesus on it. **36**As Jesus rode
toward Jerusalem, others spread their
coats on the road before him.

37As he was coming close to Jerusalem, on the way down the Mount of Olives, the whole crowd of followers began
joyfully shouting praise to God for all the
miracles they had seen. **38**They said,

"God bless the king who comes in
the name of the Lord! *Psalm 118:26*
There is peace in heaven and glory to
God!"

39Some of the Pharisees in the crowd
said to Jesus, "Teacher, tell your followers not to say these things."

40But Jesus answered, "I tell you, if
my followers didn't say these things,
then the stones would cry out."

Jesus Cries for Jerusalem

41As Jesus came near Jerusalem, he
saw the city and cried for it, **42**saying, "I
wish you knew today what would bring
you peace. But now it is hidden from
you. **43**The time is coming when your

19:13 coin A Greek "mina." One mina was enough money to pay a person for working three months.

enemies will build a wall around you and
will hold you in on all sides. **44**They will
destroy you and all your people, and not
one stone will be left on another. All this
will happen because you did not recognize the time when God came to save
you."

Jesus Goes to the Temple

45Jesus went into the Temple and began to throw out the people who were
selling things there. **46**He said, "It is
written in the Scriptures, 'My Temple
will be a house for prayer.'[n] But you have
changed it into a 'hideout for robbers'!'"[n]

47Jesus taught in the Temple every
day. The leading priests, the experts on
the law, and some of the leaders of the
people wanted to kill Jesus. **48**But they
did not know how they could do it, because all the people were listening
closely to him.

Jewish Leaders Question Jesus

20 One day Jesus was in the Temple,
teaching the people and telling
them the Good News. The leading
priests, teachers of the law, and older
leaders came up to talk with him, **2**saying, "Tell us what authority you have to
do these things? Who gave you this authority?"

3Jesus answered, "I will also ask you a
question. Tell me: **4**When John baptized
people, was that authority from God or
just from other people?"

5They argued about this, saying, "If
we answer, 'John's baptism was from
God,' Jesus will say, 'Then why did you
not believe him?' **6**But if we say, 'It was
from other people,' all the people will
stone us to death, because they believe
John was a prophet." **7**So they answered
that they didn't know where it came
from.

8Jesus said to them, "Then I won't tell
you what authority I have to do these
things."

A Story About God's Son

9Then Jesus told the people this story:
"A man planted a vineyard and leased it to
some farmers. Then he went away for a
long time. **10**When it was time for the
grapes to be picked, he sent a servant to
the farmers to get some of the grapes.
But they beat the servant and sent him
away empty-handed. **11**Then he sent another servant. They beat this servant
also, and showed no respect for him, and
sent him away empty-handed. **12**So the
man sent a third servant. The farmers
wounded him and threw him out. **13**The
owner of the vineyard said, 'What will I
do now? I will send my son whom I love.
Maybe they will respect him.' **14**But
when the farmers saw the son, they said
to each other, 'This son will inherit the
vineyard. If we kill him, it will be ours.'
15So the farmers threw the son out of the
vineyard and killed him.

"What will the owner of this vineyard
do to them? **16**He will come and kill
those farmers and will give the vineyard
to other farmers."

When the people heard this story,
they said, "Let this never happen!"

17But Jesus looked at them and said,
"Then what does this verse mean:

> 'The stone that the builders rejected
> became the cornerstone'?
>
> *Psalm 118:22*

18Everyone who falls on that stone will
be broken, and the person on whom it
falls, that person will be crushed!"

19The teachers of the law and the
leading priests wanted to arrest Jesus at
once, because they knew the story was
about them. But they were afraid of what
the people would do.

Is It Right to Pay Taxes or Not?

20So they watched Jesus and sent
some spies who acted as if they were sincere. They wanted to trap Jesus in saying
something wrong so they could hand him
over to the authority and power of the
governor. **21**So the spies asked Jesus,
"Teacher, we know that what you say and
teach is true. You pay no attention to who
people are, and you always teach the

19:46 'My Temple . . . prayer.' Quotation from Isaiah 56:7.

19:46 'hideout for robbers' Quotation from Jeremiah 7:11.

OBEY OR DISOBEY?

LUKE 20:20-26

Do you think that disobeying a law just because you're a Christian is ever right? Jesus was once asked whether paying taxes to the Romans was the right thing to do. Jesus' answer shows the importance of obeying our leaders. This does not mean doing something that you know is wrong. It does mean showing respect for the leaders in authority.

Download these links on showing respect:

Obey? No Way!, Exodus 1:15–21, p. 76

Play Fair or Play Favorites?, Deuteronomy 1:16–18, p. 227

Your Best Work, 1 Kings 6, p. 443

Depend on Him!, 2 Chronicles 16:1–9, p. 579

Welcome!, Matthew 19:13–15, p. 1307

Help for the Body, Romans 12:3–8, p. 1536

truth about God's way. **22**Tell us, is it
right for us to pay taxes to Caesar or
not?"

23But Jesus, knowing they were trying to trick him, said, **24**"Show me a coin.
Whose image and name are on it?"

They said, "Caesar's."

25Jesus said to them, "Then give to
Caesar the things that are Caesar's, and
give to God the things that are God's."

26So they were not able to trap Jesus
in anything he said in the presence of the
people. And being amazed at his answer,
they became silent.

Some Sadducees Try to Trick Jesus

27Some Sadducees, who believed
people would not rise from the dead,
came to Jesus. **28**They asked, "Teacher,
Moses wrote that if a man's brother dies
and leaves a wife but no children, then
that man must marry the widow and have
children for his brother. **29**Once there
were seven brothers. The first brother
married and died, but had no children.
30Then the second brother married the
widow, and he died. **31**And the third
brother married the widow, and he died.
The same thing happened with all seven
brothers; they died and had no children.
32Finally, the woman died also. **33**Since
all seven brothers had married her,
whose wife will she be when people rise
from the dead?"

34Jesus said to them, "On earth, people marry and are given to someone to
marry. **35**But those who will be worthy to
be raised from the dead and live again will
not marry, nor will they be given to someone to marry. **36**In that life
they are like angels
and cannot die. They
are children of God,
because they have
been raised from the
dead. **37**Even Moses
clearly showed that the dead are raised to
life. When he wrote about the burning
bush,ⁿ he said that the Lord is 'the God of
Abraham, the God of Isaac, and the God
of Jacob.'ⁿ **38**God is the God of the living,
not the dead, because all people are alive
to him."

EMAIL FROM GOD 20:36 **Angels** Can angels die?

39Some of the teachers of the law
said, "Teacher, your answer was good."
40No one was brave enough to ask him
another question.

20:37 burning bush Read Exodus 3:1-12 in the Old Testament.

20:37 'the God of . . . Jacob' These words are taken from Exodus 3:6.

Is the Christ the Son of David?

41Then Jesus said, "Why do people
say that the Christ is the Son of David?
42In the book of Psalms, David himself
says:

'The Lord said to my Lord:
Sit by me at my right side,
43 until I put your enemies under
your control.'[n] *Psalm 110:1*

44David calls the Christ 'Lord,' so how
can the Christ be his son?"

Jesus Accuses Some Leaders

45While all the people were listening,
Jesus said to his followers, 46"Beware of
the teachers of the law. They like to walk
around wearing fancy clothes, and they
love for people to greet them with respect in the marketplaces. They love to
have the most important seats in the synagogues and at feasts. 47But they cheat
widows and steal their houses and then
try to make themselves look good by saying long prayers. They will receive a
greater punishment."

True Giving

21 As Jesus looked up, he saw some
rich people putting their gifts into
the Temple money box.[n] 2Then he saw a
poor widow putting two small copper
coins into the box. 3He said, "I tell you
the truth, this poor widow gave more
than all those rich people. 4They gave
only what they did not need. This woman
is very poor, but she gave all she had to
live on."

The Temple Will Be Destroyed

5Some people were talking about the
Temple and how it was decorated with
beautiful stones and gifts offered to God.

But Jesus said, 6"As for these things
you are looking at, the time will come
when not one stone will be left on another. Every stone will be thrown down."

7They asked Jesus, "Teacher, when
will these things happen? What will be
the sign that they are about to take
place?"

8Jesus said, "Be careful so you are not
fooled. Many people will come in my
name, saying, 'I am the One' and, 'The
time has come!' But don't follow them.
9When you hear about wars and riots,
don't be afraid, because these things
must happen first, but the end will come
later."

10Then he said to them, "Nations will
fight against other nations, and kingdoms

FAITH links

GIVE FROM THE HEART

LUKE 21:1-4

What do you suppose is enough money to give in an offering at church? Jesus was more impressed with a widow who gave two copper coins in the Temple than he was with a rich man who gave a lot of money. Why? Because the widow was very poor and gave all that she had. God wants all of your heart to be in what you give. So, next time you give, think about giving a gift from the heart.

Help for the Poor, Leviticus 5:7, p. 138

His OK to Obey, Deuteronomy 2:24–36, p. 230

What I've Got, 2 Kings 20:12–17, p. 508

Some Friendly Advice, Proverbs 17:9, 14, 17, p. 851

Your Civic Duty, Matthew 17:24–27, p. 1304

The Most Fun, Acts 20:35, p. 1502

20:43 until . . . control Literally, "until I make your enemies a footstool for your feet."

21:1 money box A special box in the Jewish place of worship where people put their gifts to God.

against other kingdoms. **11**In various places there will be great earthquakes, sicknesses, and a lack of food. Fearful events and great signs will come from heaven.

12"But before all these things happen, people will arrest you and treat you cruelly. They will judge you in their synagogues and put you in jail and force you to stand before kings and governors, because you follow me. **13**But this will give you an opportunity to tell about me. **14**Make up your minds not to worry ahead of time about what you will say. **15**I will give you the wisdom to say things that none of your enemies will be able to stand against or prove wrong. **16**Even your parents, brothers, relatives, and friends will turn against you, and they will kill some of you. **17**All people will hate you because you follow me. **18**But none of these things can really harm you. **19**By continuing to have faith you will save your lives.

Jerusalem Will Be Destroyed

20"When you see armies all around Jerusalem, you will know it will soon be destroyed. **21**At that time, the people in Judea should run away to the mountains. The people in Jerusalem must get out, and those who are near the city should not go in. **22**These are the days of punishment to bring about all that is written in the Scriptures. **23**How terrible it will be for women who are pregnant or have nursing babies! Great trouble will come upon this land, and God will be angry with these people. **24**They will be killed by the sword and taken as prisoners to all nations. Jerusalem will be crushed by non-Jewish people until their time is over.

Don't Fear

25"There will be signs in the sun, moon, and stars. On earth, nations will be afraid and confused because of the roar and fury of the sea. **26**People will be so afraid they will faint, wondering what is happening to the world, because the powers of the heavens will be shaken. **27**Then people will see the Son of Man coming in a cloud with power and great glory. **28**When these things begin to happen, look up and hold your heads high, because the time when God will free you is near!"

Jesus' Words Will Live Forever

29Then Jesus told this story: "Look at the fig tree and all the other trees. **30**When their leaves appear, you know that summer is near. **31**In the same way, when you see these things happening, you will know that God's kingdom is near.

32"I tell you the truth, all these things will happen while the people of this time are still living. **33**Earth and sky will be destroyed, but the words I have spoken will never be destroyed.

Be Ready All the Time

34"Be careful not to spend your time feasting, drinking, or worrying about worldly things. If you do, that day might come on you suddenly, **35**like a trap on all people on earth. **36**So be ready all the time. Pray that you will be strong enough to escape all these things that will happen and that you will be able to stand before the Son of Man."

37During the day, Jesus taught the people in the Temple, and at night he went out of the city and stayed on the Mount of Olives. **38**Every morning all the people got up early to go to the Temple to listen to him.

Judas Becomes an Enemy of Jesus

22 It was almost time for the Feast of Unleavened Bread, called the Passover Feast. **2**The leading priests and teachers of the law were trying to find a way to kill Jesus, because they were afraid of the people.

3Satan entered Judas Iscariot, one of Jesus' twelve apostles. **4**Judas went to the leading priests and some of the soldiers who guarded the Temple and talked to them about a way to hand Jesus over to them. **5**They were pleased and agreed to give Judas money. **6**He agreed and watched for the best time to hand Jesus

JESUS' LAST WEEK Luke 22

When people talk about Holy Week, they are talking about the last week of Jesus' life before his death and resurrection. The week began when Jesus rode into Jerusalem on a colt to cheering crowds. That is called the "triumphal entry."

Sunday	Jesus enters Jerusalem as a King	Mark 11:1–11, p. 1348
Monday	Jesus kicks merchants out of the Temple	Mark 11:15–19, p. 1349
Tuesday	The leading priests, teachers of the Law, and older teachers pick a fight with Jesus	Luke 20:1–8, p. 1408
	Jesus talks about his death and return	Matthew 24; 25, p. 1315
	Judas becomes an enemy of Jesus	Luke 22:3–6, p. 1411
Thursday	Jesus celebrates the Passover	John 13:1–30, p. 1446
	Jesus begins the Lord's Supper tradition	Mark 14:22–26, p. 1356
	Jesus prays for his followers and for us	John 17, p. 1453
Friday	Jesus is arrested	Mark 14:43–50, p. 1357
	Peter says he doesn't know Jesus	John 18:15–27, p. 1455
	Jesus is crucified between two thieves	Mark 15:16–27, p. 1359
Sunday	Jesus is raised from the dead!	Luke 24:1–9, p. 1417

over to them when he was away from the crowd.

Jesus Eats the Passover Meal

7The Day of Unleavened Bread came
when the Passover lambs had to be sacrificed. **8**Jesus said to Peter and John, "Go
and prepare the Passover meal for us to eat."

9They asked, "Where do you want us
to prepare it?" **10**Jesus said to them, "After you go into the city, a man carrying a jar of water will meet you. Follow him into the house that he enters, **11**and tell
the owner of the house, 'The Teacher says: Where is the guest room in which I may eat the Passover meal with my followers?' **12**Then he will show you a large, furnished room upstairs. Prepare the Passover meal there."

13So Peter and John left and found everything as Jesus had said. And they prepared the Passover meal.

The Lord's Supper

14When the time came, Jesus and the apostles were sitting at the table. **15**He
said to them, "I wanted very much to eat

this Passover meal with you before I suffer. **16**I will not eat another Passover
meal until it is given its true meaning in
the kingdom of God."
17Then Jesus took a cup, gave thanks,
and said, "Take this cup and share it
among yourselves. **18**I will not drink
again from the fruit of the vine[n] until
God's kingdom comes."
19Then Jesus took some bread, gave
thanks, broke it, and gave it to the apostles, saying, "This is my body, which I am
giving for you. Do this to remember me."
20In the same way, after supper, Jesus
took the cup and said, "This cup is the
new agreement that God makes with his
people. This new agreement begins with
my blood which is poured out for you.

Who Will Turn Against Jesus?

21"But one of you will turn against
me, and his hand is with mine on the table. **22**What God has planned for the Son
of Man will happen, but how terrible it
will be for that one who turns against the
Son of Man."
23Then the apostles asked each other
which one of them would do that.

Be Like a Servant

24The apostles also began to argue
about which one of them was the most
important. **25**But Jesus said to them,
"The kings of the non-Jewish people rule
over them, and those who have authority
over others like to be called 'friends of
the people.' **26**But you must not be like
that. Instead, the greatest among you
should be like the youngest, and the
leader should be like the servant. **27**Who
is more important: the one sit-
ting at the table or
the one serving?
You think the one at
the table is more im-
portant, but I am
like a servant among
you.

28"You have stayed with me through
my struggles. **29**Just as my Father has
given me a kingdom, I also give you a
kingdom **30**so you may eat and drink at
my table in my kingdom. And you will sit
on thrones, judging the twelve tribes of
Israel.

Don't Lose Your Faith!

31"Simon, Simon, Satan has asked to
test all of you as a farmer sifts his wheat.
32I have prayed that you will not lose
your faith! Help your brothers be stronger when you come back to me."
33But Peter said to Jesus, "Lord, I am
ready to go with you to prison and even
to die with you!"
34But Jesus said, "Peter, before the
rooster crows this day, you will say three
times that you don't know me."

Be Ready for Trouble

35Then Jesus said to the apostles,
"When I sent you out without a purse, a
bag, or sandals, did you need anything?"
They said, "No."
36He said to them, "But now if you
have a purse or a bag, carry that with you.
If you don't have a sword, sell your coat
and buy one. **37**The Scripture says, 'He
was treated like a criminal,'[n] and I tell you
this scripture must have its full meaning.
It was written about me, and it is happening now."
38His followers said, "Look, Lord,
here are two swords."
He said to them, "That is enough."

Jesus Prays Alone

39Jesus left the city and went to the
Mount of Olives, as he often did, and his
followers went with him. **40**When he
reached the place, he said to them, "Pray
for strength against temptation."
41Then Jesus went about a stone's
throw away from them. He kneeled down
and prayed, **42**"Father, if you are willing,
take away this cup[n] of suffering. But do
what you want, not what I want." **43**Then
an angel from heaven appeared to him to
strengthen him. **44**Being full of pain,

22:18 fruit of the vine Product of the grapevine; this may also be translated "wine."

22:37 'He . . . criminal' Quotation from Isaiah 53:12.

22:42 cup Jesus is talking about the painful things that will happen to him. Accepting these things will be hard, like drinking a cup of something bitter.

Failures and Weaknesses

Luke 22:54–62

Livin' it

Oh No! Not Again! Ever had one of those days that no matter how hard you try, everything seems to go wrong? Maybe you've been working on controlling your temper. But then you disagree with a call in the baseball game and forget about staying calm. The bat is thrown to the ground and angry words come spouting out of your mouth! How do you feel when you fail at something? Do you feel it's not worth trying anymore because you'll only goof up again?

Timothy had failed in something, and then he was afraid to try something new. Paul had some advice for Timothy. He reminded Timothy that God had given him the gifts of power, love, and self-control. These could help him when he was afraid of failure. (Read 2 Timothy 1:7, p. 1650.) How can God help you to deal with failure?

"I sure am glad to know that God is there for us—even when we mess up!"

"Me, too! Because I really make a mess of things sometimes! Do you remember the time I clicked on the delete button at the wrong time? That was a huge goof-up!"

MORE FAITH links

The Perfect Leader?, p. 203

A Hard Place, p. 1120

Blessed Are the Weak?, p. 1582

You're Correct!, p. 1683

Toss Those Troubles!, p. 1706

Weak? Great!, 2 Chronicles 14:11, p. 577
- Link here to discover what's so great about being weak.

Learning from Mistakes, Psalm 51:12–13, p. 748
- If you saw a friend about to do something you just got grounded for, would you try to stop him? That's what is known as learning from your mistakes. Think of some mistakes you've been corrected for. What did you learn from those mistakes?

The God of Second Chances, Jonah 3, p. 1215
- Do you do what your parents tell you to do the first time they ask? Or, do you wait until they ask again? What happens if they need to ask you several times?
- When you "blow it," God offers a second chance to obey him. What do you need a second (or third) chance for?

my FAVORITE links

Jesus prayed even harder. His sweat was like drops of blood falling to the ground.
45When he finished praying, he went to his followers and found them asleep because of their sadness. 46Jesus said to
them, "Why are you sleeping? Get up and pray for strength against temptation."

Jesus Is Arrested

47While Jesus was speaking, a crowd came up, and Judas, one of the twelve apostles, was leading them. He came close to Jesus so he could kiss him.

48But Jesus said to him, "Judas, are you using the kiss to give the Son of Man to his enemies?"

49When those who were standing around him saw what was happening, they said, "Lord, should we strike them
with our swords?" 50And one of them struck the servant of the high priest and cut off his right ear.

51Jesus said, "Stop! No more of this." Then he touched the servant's ear and healed him.

52Those who came to arrest Jesus were the leading priests, the soldiers who guarded the Temple, and the older leaders. Jesus said to them, "You came out here with swords and clubs as though
I were a criminal. 53I was with you every day in the Temple, and you didn't arrest me there. But this is your time—the time when darkness rules."

Peter Says He Doesn't Know Jesus

54They arrested Jesus, and led him away, and brought him into the house of the high priest. Peter followed far behind
them. 55After the soldiers started a fire in the middle of the courtyard and sat together, Peter sat with them.
56A servant girl saw Peter sitting there in the firelight, and looking closely at him, she said, "This man was also with him."

57But Peter said this was not true; he said, "Woman, I don't know him."

58A short time later, another person saw Peter and said, "You are also one of them."

But Peter said, "Man, I am not!"

59About an hour later, another man insisted, "Certainly this man was with him, because he is from Galilee, too."

60But Peter said, "Man, I don't know what you are talking about!"

At once, while Peter was still speaking, a rooster crowed.
61Then the Lord turned and looked straight at Peter. And Peter remembered what the Lord had said: "Before the rooster crows this day, you will say three times that you don't
know me." 62Then Peter went outside and cried painfully.

The People Make Fun of Jesus

63The men who were guarding Jesus began making fun of him and beating him.

64They blindfolded him and said, "Prove that you are a prophet, and tell us
who hit you." 65They said many cruel things to Jesus.

Jesus Before the Leaders

66When day came, the council of the older leaders of the people, both the leading priests and the teachers of the law, came together and led Jesus to their
highest court. 67They said, "If you are the Christ, tell us."

Jesus said to them, "If I tell you, you
will not believe me. 68And if I ask you,
you will not answer. 69But from now on, the Son of Man will sit at the right hand of the powerful God."

70They all said, "Then are you the Son of God?"

Jesus said to them, "You say that I am."

71They said, "Why do we need witnesses now? We ourselves heard him say this."

Pilate Questions Jesus

23 Then the whole group stood up and led Jesus to Pilate.[n]
2They began to accuse Jesus, saying, "We caught this man telling things that mislead our people. He says that we should not pay taxes to Caesar, and he calls himself the Christ, a king."

3Pilate asked Jesus, "Are you the king of the Jews?"

23:1 Pilate Pontius Pilate was the Roman governor of Judea from A.D. 26 to A.D. 36.

Jesus answered, "Those are your
words."
4Pilate said to the leading priests and
the people, "I find nothing against this
man."
5They were insisting, saying, "But
Jesus makes trouble with the people,
teaching all around Judea. He began in
Galilee, and now he is here."

Pilate Sends Jesus to Herod

6Pilate heard this and asked if Jesus
was from Galilee. 7Since Jesus was under
Herod's authority, Pilate sent Jesus to
Herod, who was in Jerusalem at that
time. 8When Herod saw Jesus, he was
very glad, because he had heard about
Jesus and had wanted to meet him for a
long time. He was hoping to see Jesus
work a miracle. 9Herod asked Jesus
many questions, but Jesus said nothing.
10The leading priests and teachers of the
law were standing there, strongly accusing Jesus. 11After Herod and his soldiers
had made fun of Jesus, they dressed him
in a kingly robe and sent him back to Pilate. 12In the past, Pilate and Herod had
always been enemies, but on that day
they became friends.

Jesus Must Die

13Pilate called the people together
with the leading priests and the rulers.
14He said to them, "You brought this
man to me, saying he makes trouble
among the people. But I have questioned
him before you all, and I have not found
him guilty of what you say. 15Also, Herod
found nothing wrong with him; he sent
him back to us. Look, he has done nothing for which he should die. 16So, after I
punish him, I will let him go free." 17[n]
18But the people shouted together,
"Take this man away! Let Barabbas go
free!" 19(Barabbas was a man who was in
prison for his part in a riot in the city and
for murder.)
20Pilate wanted to let Jesus go free
and told this to the crowd. 21But they
shouted again, "Crucify him! Crucify
him!"
22A third time Pilate said to them,
"Why? What wrong has he done? I can
find no reason to kill him. So I will have
him punished and set him free."
23But they continued to shout, demanding that Jesus be crucified. Their
yelling became so loud that 24Pilate decided to give them what they wanted.
25He set free the man who was in jail for
rioting and murder, and he handed Jesus
over to them to do with him as they
wished.

Jesus Is Crucified

26As they led Jesus away, Simon, a
man from Cyrene, was coming in from
the fields. They forced him to carry
Jesus' cross and to walk behind him.
27A large crowd of people was following Jesus, including some women who
were sad and crying for him. 28But Jesus
turned and said to them, "Women of Jerusalem, don't cry for me. Cry for yourselves and for your children. 29The time
is coming when people will say, 'Happy
are the women who cannot have children
and who have no babies to nurse.'
30Then people will say to the mountains,
'Fall on us!' And they will say to the hills,
'Cover us!' 31If they act like this now
when life is good, what will happen when
bad times come?"[n]
32There were also two criminals led
out with Jesus to be put to death. 33When
they came to a place called the Skull, the
soldiers crucified Jesus and the criminals—one on his right and the other on
his left. 34Jesus said, "Father, forgive
them, because they don't know what
they are doing."[n]
The soldiers threw lots to decide who
would get his clothes. 35The people
stood there watching. And the leaders
made fun of Jesus, saying, "He saved others. Let him save himself if he is God's
Chosen One, the Christ."
36The soldiers also made fun of him,

23:17 Verse 17 A few Greek copies add verse 17: "Every year at the Passover Feast, Pilate had to release one prisoner to the people."

23:31 If . . . come? Literally, "If they do these things in the green tree, what will happen in the dry?"

23:34 Verse 34 Some early Greek copies do not have this first part of the verse.

coming to Jesus and offering him some
vinegar. 37They said, "If you are the king
of the Jews, save yourself!" 38At the top
of the cross these words were written:
THIS IS THE KING OF THE JEWS.

39One of the criminals on a cross began to shout insults at Jesus: "Aren't you
the Christ? Then save yourself and us."

40But the other criminal stopped him
and said, "You should fear God! You are
getting the same punishment he is. 41We
are punished justly, getting what we deserve for what we did. But this man has
done nothing wrong." 42Then he said,
"Jesus, remember me when you come
into your kingdom."

43Jesus said to him, "I tell you the
truth, today you will be with me in
paradise."[n]

Jesus Dies

44It was about noon, and the whole
land became dark until three o'clock in
the afternoon, 45because the sun did not
shine. The curtain in the
Temple[n] was torn in two.
46Jesus cried out in a
loud voice, "Father, I give
you my life." After Jesus
said this, he died.

47When the army offi-
cer there saw what hap-
pened, he praised God,
saying, "Surely this was a
good man!"

48When all the people
who had gathered there to watch saw
what happened, they returned home,
beating their chests because they were
so sad. 49But those who were close
friends of Jesus, including the women
who had followed him from Galilee, stood
at a distance and watched.

> When the army officer there saw what happened, he praised God, saying, "Surely this was a good man!"
> —Luke 23:47

Joseph Takes Jesus' Body

50There was a good and religious man
named Joseph who was a member of the
council. 51But he had not agreed to the
other leaders' plans and actions against
Jesus. He was from the town of Arimathea and was waiting for the kingdom of
God to come. 52Joseph went to Pilate to
ask for the body of Jesus. 53He took the
body down from the cross, wrapped it in
cloth, and put it in a tomb that was cut out
of a wall of rock. This tomb had never
been used before. 54This was late on
Preparation Day, and when the sun went
down, the Sabbath day would begin.

55The women who had come from
Galilee with Jesus followed Joseph and
saw the tomb and how Jesus' body was
laid. 56Then the women left to prepare
spices and perfumes.

On the Sabbath day they rested, as the
law of Moses commanded.

Jesus Rises from the Dead

24 Very early on the first day of the
week, at dawn, the women came
to the tomb, bringing the spices they had
prepared. 2They found the stone rolled
away from the entrance of the tomb, 3but
when they went in, they did not find the
body of the Lord Jesus. 4While they were
wondering about this, two men in shining
clothes suddenly stood beside them.
5The women were very
afraid and bowed their
heads to the ground. The
men said to them, "Why
are you looking for a living person in this place
for the dead? 6He is not
here; he has risen from
the dead. Do you remem-
ber what he told you in
Galilee? 7He said the Son
of Man must be handed
over to sinful people, be crucified, and
rise from the dead on the third day."
8Then the women remembered what
Jesus had said.

9The women left the tomb and told all
these things to the eleven apostles and
the other followers. 10It was Mary Magdalene, Joanna, Mary the mother of
James, and some other women who told
the apostles everything that had happened at the tomb. 11But they did not

---

23:43 paradise Another word for heaven.
23:45 curtain in the Temple A curtain divided the Most Holy Place from the other part of the Temple, the special building in Jerusalem where God commanded the Jewish people to worship him.

LET'S VISIT NAZARETH Luke 24:19

Nazareth is in southern Galilee about 30 miles from the Mediterranean Sea. It doesn't get really hot or really cold there, making it a great place to live. Nazareth is not mentioned in the Old Testament, but we know that it existed at least 1,500 years before Jesus was born.

It was in Nazareth that the angel appeared to Mary and told her that Jesus would be born. (Read Luke 1:26–38.) After Jesus' family traveled to Egypt, they came back to Nazareth, and Jesus grew up there. (Check out Matthew 2:23, p. 1277; Luke 3:23.) In fact, Jesus was closely associated with Nazareth. (Check out John 1:45, p. 1423.)

Today Nazareth is called En-Nasira. About 30,000 people live there.

believe the women, because it sounded
like nonsense. 12But Peter got up and
ran to the tomb. Bending down and looking in, he saw only the cloth that Jesus' body had been wrapped in. Peter went away to his home, wondering about what had happened.

Jesus on the Road to Emmaus

13That same day two of Jesus' followers were going to a town named Emmaus, about seven miles from Jerusalem.
14They were talking about everything
that had happened. 15While they were
talking and discussing, Jesus himself came near and began walking with them,
16but they were kept from recognizing
him. 17Then he said, "What are these things you are talking about while you walk?"

The two followers stopped, looking
very sad. 18The one named Cleopas answered, "Are you the only visitor in Jerusalem who does not know what just happened there?"

19Jesus said to them, "What are you talking about?"

They said, "About Jesus of Nazareth. He was a prophet who said and did many powerful things before God and all the
people. 20Our leaders and the leading priests handed him over to be sentenced
to death, and they crucified him. 21But
we were hoping that he would free Israel. Besides this, it is now the third day since
this happened. 22And today some women among us amazed us. Early this morning
they went to the tomb, 23but they did not find his body there. They came and told us that they had seen a vision of angels
who said that Jesus was alive! 24So some
of our group went to the tomb, too. They found it just as the women said, but they did not see Jesus."

25Then Jesus said to them, "You are foolish and slow to believe everything
the prophets said. 26They said that the Christ must suffer these things before he
enters his glory." 27Then starting with what Moses and all the prophets had said about him, Jesus began to explain everything that had been written about himself in the Scriptures.

28They came near the town of Emmaus, and Jesus acted as if he were going
farther. 29But they begged him, "Stay with us, because it is late; it is almost night." So he went in to stay with them.

30When Jesus was at the table with them, he took some bread, gave thanks, divided it, and gave it to them. 31And
then, they were allowed to recognize

Jesus. But when they saw who he was, he disappeared. **32**They said to each other, "It felt like a fire burning in us when Jesus talked to us on the road and explained the Scriptures to us."

33So the two followers got up at once and went back to Jerusalem. There they found the eleven apostles and others gathered. **34**They were saying, "The Lord really has risen from the dead! He showed himself to Simon."

35Then the two followers told what had happened on the road and how they recognized Jesus when he divided the bread.

Jesus Appears to His Followers

36While the two followers were telling this, Jesus himself stood right in the middle of them and said, "Peace be with you."

37They were fearful and terrified and thought they were seeing a ghost. **38**But Jesus said, "Why are you troubled? Why do you doubt what you see? **39**Look at my hands and my feet. It is I myself! Touch me and see, because a ghost does not have a living body as you see I have."

40After Jesus said this, he showed them his hands and feet. **41**While they still could not believe it because they were amazed and happy, Jesus said to them, "Do you have any food here?" **42**They gave him a piece of broiled fish. **43**While the followers watched, Jesus took the fish and ate it.

44He said to them, "Remember when I was with you before? I said that everything written about me must happen—everything in the law of Moses, the books of the prophets, and the Psalms."

45Then Jesus opened their minds so they could understand the Scriptures. **46**He said to them, "It is written that the Christ would suffer and rise from the dead on the third day **47**and that a change of hearts and lives and forgiveness of sins would be preached in his name to all nations, starting at Jerusalem. **48**You are witnesses of these things. **49**I will send you what my Father has promised, but you must stay in Jerusalem until you have received that power from heaven."

eMail FROM GOD
24:46–47
Good News
Who is the Good News for?

Jesus Goes Back to Heaven

50Jesus led his followers as far as Bethany, and he raised his hands and blessed them. **51**While he was blessing them, he was separated from them and carried into heaven. **52**They worshiped him and returned to Jerusalem very happy. **53**They stayed in the Temple all the time, praising God.

GOD WITH US

Hi! I'm John. Want to know more about me? Well, I was a fisherman who left his fishing nets behind to follow Jesus. A lot of people get me confused with John the Baptist, but we're two different people. My brother James and I were part of Jesus' original 12 followers. In fact, I was the one called "the follower Jesus loved." (Check it out in John 13:23.) This isn't the only book I wrote either. I wrote three letters (known as 1, 2, and 3 John) and the Book of Revelation. I lived a very long life, and even served the church in Ephesus for many years before my death.

You're probably wondering why I wrote this book. Just read John 20:31 to see why. I wrote this book to let people know that Jesus was truly the Son of God. Since I was both an eyewitness to the things I wrote about and a follower of Jesus, I wanted everyone who read my book to get a clear picture that Jesus was God's own Son.

JESUS WATCH

John's Gospel helps us understand Jesus as God. How does he do this? First, he does this through seven "I Am" statements that Jesus made. Jesus said things like, "I am the bread that gives life" and "I am the way, and the truth, and the life." By presenting these statements, John helps his readers understand Jesus' connection with God. (Remember God's conversation with Moses in Exodus 3, p. 79? God uses the words *I Am* there, too. Take a moment to read that now.) Second, John helps us understand Jesus as a man by allowing us to see Jesus' human side. He lets us see Jesus when he's tired, thirsty, upset, troubled, and in anguish.

my FAVORITE links

OTHER CONNECTIONS

Livin' it

Ever play "Follow the Leader"? The game can be fun. But when it comes down to real life, following the *right* leader is important. Connect to Follow the Right Leader, John 2, to find out how important it is.

Which would you rather be—full of joy, or full of happiness? Do you know the difference? Download what God has to say about it at I Got the Joy, Joy, Joy, Joy, John 16:24.

GET THE INFO

Here are some interesting facts you'll find in the Book of John:

- Let's Visit Capernaum, John 4:46–54. Stop by this info bulletin board to find out more about this small town where Jesus spent a lot of time during his ministry on earth.
- Jesus referred to himself with many different names. Find out what some of those titles are by logging on to The Names of Jesus, John 6:35.
- Ever wonder why there are four books about Jesus' life and ministry? Stop by Biographies from Every View, John 19, to find out why.
- Let's Visit Lake Galilee, John 21. You may have heard people refer to Lake Galilee as the Sea of Galilee. But if you connect here, you'll find out that this body of fresh water is really a lake.

"Hey, Tagg, I don't understand. How can a man become a word? No, wait a minute. How can a word become a man?"

"It's easy if you're God. Read about what Jesus did in John 1:1-14."

WANT TO READ SOME OTHER AWESOME STORIES IN JOHN'S GOSPEL? SURF OVER TO THESE EXCITING STORIES:

John the Baptist, John 1:15–34
Water into wine, John 2:1–10
A prayer for all followers, John 13; 14
The darkest hour, John 19:17–37

did you know?

FAITH links

- One Big, Happy Family, John 1:12
- Two Birthdays, John 3:1–7
- The Gift, John 3:6–18
- The Whole Truth, John 8:31–32, 45
- Our Good Shepherd, John 10:11–15
- Fully God, Fully Human, John 11:35
- The Worst Chore, John 13:3–17
- The Way to Heaven, John 14:1–6
- A Friend of Jesus, John 15:9–17
- Jesus' Prayer, John 17

Christ Comes to the World

1 In the beginning there was the Word.[n]
The Word was with God, and the Word
was God. 2He was with God in

the beginning. 3All
things were made by
him, and nothing was
made without him.
4In him there was
life, and that life was
the light of all people.
5The Light shines in the darkness, and the
darkness has not overpowered it.
6There was a man named John[n] who
was sent by God. 7He came to tell people
the truth about the Light so that through
him all people could hear about the Light
and believe. 8John was not the Light, but
he came to tell people the truth about the
Light. 9The true Light that gives light to
all was coming into the world!
10The Word was in the world, and the
world was made by him, but the world did
not know him. 11He came to the world
that was his own, but his own people did
not accept him. 12But to all who did accept him and believe in him he gave the
right to become children of God. 13They
did not become his children in any human
way—by any human parents or human
desire. They were born of God.
14The Word became a human and
lived among us. We saw his glory—the
glory that belongs to the only Son of the
Father—and he was full of grace and
truth. 15John tells the truth about him
and cries out, saying, "This is the One I
told you about: 'The One who comes after me is greater than I am, because he
was living before me.' "
16Because he was full of grace and
truth, from him we all received one gift
after another. 17The law was given
through Moses, but grace and truth came
through Jesus Christ. 18No one has ever
seen God. But God the only Son is very
close to the Father,[n] and he has shown us
what God is like.

John Tells People About Jesus

19Here is the truth John[n] told when
the leaders in Jerusalem sent priests and
Levites to ask him, "Who are you?"

FAITH links

ONE BIG, HAPPY FAMILY

JOHN 1:12

Who are some of the people in your family? What's the best thing about being part of your family? If you're a Christian, you also belong to another family—the family of God. Because of Jesus, we "have the right to become children of God" That makes God our heavenly Father! Knowing Jesus is the best thing about being part of this family!

Download these links for more benefits on being part of God's family:

The Name of the Lord, Exodus 33:19–23; 34:5–8, p. 120

A Different Kind of People, Leviticus 11, p. 146

Real Repentance, Jeremiah 4:1–4, p. 993

Name with a Purpose, Matthew 1:21, p. 1274

You've Got the Power!, Acts 1:1–8; 2:1–4, p. 1463

Always Do This!, 1 Thessalonians 5:16–18, p. 1636

1:1 Word The Greek word is "logos," meaning any kind of communication; it could be translated "message." Here, it means Christ, because Christ was the way God told people about himself.

1:6, 19 John John the Baptist, who preached to people about Christ's coming (Matthew 3, Luke 3).

1:18 But . . . Father This could be translated, "But the only God is very close to the Father." Also, some Greek copies say, "But the only Son is very close to the Father."

20John spoke freely and did not refuse
to answer. He said, "I am not the Christ."
21So they asked him, "Then who are
you? Are you Elijah?"[n]
He answered, "No, I am not."
"Are you the Prophet?"[n] they asked.
He answered, "No."
22Then they said, "Who are you?
Give us an answer to tell those who sent
us. What do you say about yourself?"
23John told them in the words of the
prophet Isaiah:
"I am the voice of one
calling out in the desert:
'Make the road straight for the
Lord.' " *Isaiah 40:3*
24Some Pharisees who had been sent
asked John: 25"If you are not the Christ
or Elijah or the Prophet, why do you baptize people?"
26John answered, "I baptize with water, but there is one here with you that
you don't know about. 27He is the One
who comes after me. I am not good
enough to untie the strings of his sandals."
28This all happened at Bethany on the
other side of the Jordan River, where
John was baptizing people.
29The next day John saw Jesus coming toward him. John said, "Look, the
Lamb of God,[n] who takes away the sin of
the world! 30This is the One I was talking about when I said, 'A man will come
after me, but he is greater than I am, because he was living before me.' 31Even I
did not know who he was, although I
came baptizing with water so that the
people of Israel would know who he is."
32-33Then John said, "I saw the Spirit
come down from heaven in the form of a
dove and rest on him. Until then I did not
know who the Christ was. But the God
who sent me to baptize with water told
me, 'You will see the Spirit come down
and rest on a man; he is the One who will
baptize with the Holy Spirit.' 34I have
seen this happen, and I tell you the truth:
This man is the Son of God."

The First Followers of Jesus

35The next day John[n] was there again
with two of his followers. 36When he saw
Jesus walking by, he said, "Look, the
Lamb of God!"[n]
37The two followers heard John say
this, so they followed Jesus. 38When
Jesus turned and saw them following
him, he asked, "What are you looking
for?"
They said, "Rabbi, where are you
staying?" ("Rabbi" means "Teacher.")
39He answered, "Come and see." So
the two men went with Jesus and saw
where he was staying and stayed there
with him that day. It was about four
o'clock in the afternoon.
40One of the two men who followed
Jesus after they heard John speak about
him was Andrew, Simon Peter's brother.
41The first thing Andrew did was to find
his brother Simon and say to him, "We
have found the Messiah." ("Messiah"
means "Christ.")
42Then Andrew took Simon to Jesus.
Jesus looked at him and said, "You are Simon son of John. You will be called Cephas." ("Cephas" means "Peter."[n])
43The next day Jesus decided to go to
Galilee. He found Philip and said to him,
"Follow me."
44Philip was from the town of Bethsaida, where Andrew and Peter lived.
45Philip found Nathanael and told him,
"We have found the man that Moses
wrote about in the law, and the prophets
also wrote about him. He is Jesus, the
son of Joseph, from Nazareth."
46But Nathanael said to Philip, "Can
anything good come from Nazareth?"
Philip answered, "Come and see."
47As Jesus saw Nathanael coming

1:21 Elijah A prophet who spoke for God. He lived hundreds of years before Christ and was expected to return before Christ (Malachi 4:5-6).
1:21 Prophet They probably meant the prophet that God told Moses he would send (Deuteronomy 18:15-19).
1:29, 36 Lamb of God Name for Jesus. Jesus is like the lambs that were offered for a sacrifice to God.
1:35 John John the Baptist, who preached to people about Christ's coming (Matthew 3, Luke 3).
1:42 Peter The Greek name "Peter," like the Aramaic name "Cephas," means "rock."

toward him, he said, "Here is truly an Israelite. There is nothing false in him."

48Nathanael asked, "How do you know me?"

Jesus answered, "I saw you when you were under the fig tree, before Philip told you about me."

49Then Nathanael said to Jesus, "Teacher, you are the Son of God; you are the King of Israel."

50Jesus said to Nathanael, "Do you believe simply because I told you I saw you under the fig tree? You will see greater things than that." 51And Jesus said to them, "I tell you the truth, you will all see heaven open and 'angels of God going up and coming down'[n] on the Son of Man."

The Wedding at Cana

2 Two days later there was a wedding in the town of Cana in Galilee. Jesus' mother was there, 2and Jesus and his followers were also invited to the wedding. 3When all the wine was gone, Jesus' mother said to him, "They have no more wine."

4Jesus answered, "Dear woman, why come to me? My time has not yet come."

5His mother said to the servants, "Do whatever he tells you to do."

6In that place there were six stone water jars that the Jews used in their washing ceremony.[n] Each jar held about twenty or thirty gallons.

7Jesus said to the servants, "Fill the jars with water." So they filled the jars to the top.

8Then he said to them, "Now take some out and give it to the master of the feast."

So they took the water to the master. 9When he tasted it, the water had become wine. He did not know where the wine came from, but the servants who had brought the water knew. The master of the wedding called the bridegroom 10and said to him, "People always serve the best wine first. Later, after the guests have been drinking awhile, they serve the cheaper wine. But you have saved the best wine till now."

11So in Cana of Galilee Jesus did his first miracle. There he showed his glory, and his followers believed in him.

Jesus in the Temple

12After this, Jesus went to the town of Capernaum with his mother, brothers, and followers. They stayed there for just a few days. 13When it was almost time for the Jewish Passover Feast, Jesus went to Jerusalem.

eMAIL! FROM GOD
2:13–17
Anger
Hey, do you know what made Jesus angry?

14In the Temple he found people selling cattle, sheep, and doves. He saw others sitting at tables, exchanging different kinds of money. 15Jesus made a whip out of cords and forced all of them, both the sheep and cattle, to leave the Temple. He turned over the tables and scattered the money of those who were exchanging it. 16Then he said to those who were selling pigeons, "Take these things out of here! Don't make my Father's house a place for buying and selling!"

17When this happened, the followers remembered what was written in the Scriptures: "My strong love for your Temple completely controls me."[n]

18Some of his people said to Jesus, "Show us a miracle to prove you have the right to do these things."

19Jesus answered them, "Destroy this temple, and I will build it again in three days."

20They answered, "It took forty-six years to build this Temple! Do you really believe you can build it again in three days?"

21(But the temple Jesus meant was his own body. 22After Jesus was raised from the dead, his followers remembered that Jesus had said this. Then they believed the Scripture and the words Jesus had said.)

1:51 'angels . . . down' These words are from Genesis 28:12.

2:6 washing ceremony The Jewish people washed themselves in special ways before eating, before worshiping in the Temple, and at other special times.

2:17 "My . . . me." Quotation from Psalm 69:9.

FOLLOWING JESUS

John 2

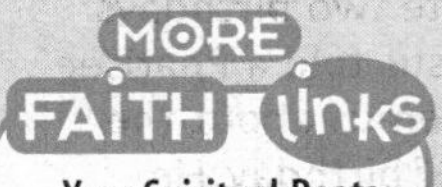

Follow the Right Leader Do you like to play the games "Follow the Leader" or "Simon Says"? What happens in these games if you don't do exactly what the leaders do or say? Now think of some situations in real life where it's really important to follow the leader's directions. What could happen if you went your own way?

How do you know you will go to heaven when you die? Jesus answered that question by telling us that the *only* way to heaven is through him. Following Jesus will take you to your heavenly home someday—nothing else will get you there. (Look at John 14:1–6.) How can you follow Jesus?

MORE FAITH links

Your Spiritual Roots, p. 1253

Two Birthdays, p. 1426

The Way to Heaven, p. 1448

The Winner's Crown, p. 1555

An Unselfish Example, p. 1611

The Coming Attraction, p. 1634

"Hey, Skweek, want to play 'follow Tagg'? I know lots of awe-some places we could link up to."

"Depends. Are you a good leader? I don't want to get lost or anything. Maybe we ought to learn more about what makes a good leader. Try surfing to these Faithlinks first!"

A Memorial for Two Thieves, 1 Chronicles 7:21, p. 530

- Do you know anything about your family history? Are there any interesting or embarrassing facts about any of your ancestors? If someone wrote about your life, what would your actions say about you? Would it say you followed Jesus—or someone else?

One Big, Happy Family, John 1:12, p. 1422

- What's the best thing about belonging to your family? Link here to find out about another family you belong to.

Hope That Doesn't Fail, Acts 26:4–7, p. 1510

- Imagine being dragged into court and told to defend yourself for being a follower of Jesus. What would you do? What would you say?
- How can following Jesus give you hope? What do you hope for?

my FAVORITE links

23When Jesus was in Jerusalem for
the Passover Feast, many people believed in him because they saw the miracles he did. **24**But Jesus did not trust
himself to them because he knew them
all. **25**He did not need anyone to tell him
about people, because he knew what was
in people's minds.

Nicodemus Comes to Jesus

3 There was a man named Nicodemus
who was one of the Pharisees and an
important Jewish leader. **2**One night Nicodemus came to Jesus and said, "Teacher,
we know you are a teacher sent from
God, because no one can do the miracles
you do unless God is with him."
3Jesus answered, "I tell you the truth,
unless one is born again, he cannot be in
God's kingdom."
4Nicodemus said, "But if a person is
already old, how can he be born again?
He cannot enter his mother's body again.
So how can a person be born a second
time?"
5But Jesus answered, "I tell you the
truth, unless one is born from water and
the Spirit, he cannot enter God's kingdom. **6**Human life comes from human
parents, but spiritual life comes from the
Spirit. **7**Don't be surprised when I tell
you, 'You must all be born again.' **8**The
wind blows where it wants to and you
hear the sound of it, but you don't know
where the wind comes from or where it is
going. It is the same with every person
who is born from the Spirit."
9Nicodemus asked, "How can this
happen?"
10Jesus said, "You are an important
teacher in Israel, and you don't understand these things? **11**I tell you the truth,
we talk about what we know, and we tell
about what we have seen, but you don't
accept what we tell you. **12**I have told you
about things here on earth, and you do
not believe me. So you will not believe
me if I tell you about things of heaven.
13The only one who has ever gone up to
heaven is the One who came down from
heaven—the Son of Man.
14"Just as Moses lifted up the snake
in the desert," the Son of Man must also
be lifted up. **15**So that everyone who believes can have eternal life in him.
16"God loved the world so
much that he gave
his one and only Son
so that whoever be-
lieves in him may
not be lost, but have
eternal life. **17**God

FAITH links

TWO BIRTHDAYS

JOHN 3:1-7

Celebrating a birthday is exciting! Did you know that you could celebrate two birthdays each year? Jesus told a Pharisee named Nicodemus about the second kind of birthday. He called this being "born again." People who accept Jesus become new people, thanks to the Holy Spirit. That's something to celebrate!

The Perfect Sacrifice, Leviticus 1—7, p. 135

The God of Big Things, Joshua 10, p. 289

A Given, 1 Chronicles 5:18–20, p. 526

What's in a Name?, Isaiah 9:6, p. 908

A Family Meal, Mark 14:23–26, p. 1356

A Family Resemblance, Galatians 3:6–9, p. 1588

eMAIL! FROM GOD
3:15–16
Eternal Life
What is needed for eternal life?

3:14 Moses . . . desert When the Israelites were dying from snake bites, God told Moses to put a brass snake on a pole. The people who looked at the snake were healed (Numbers 21:4-9).

did not send his Son into the world to
judge the world guilty, but to save the
world through him. 18People who believe
in God's Son are not judged guilty. Those
who do not believe have already been
judged guilty, because they have not believed in God's one and only Son. 19They
are judged by this fact: The Light has
come into the world, but they did not
want light. They wanted darkness, because they were doing evil things. 20All
who do evil hate the light and will not
come to the light, because it will show all
the evil things they do. 21But those who
follow the true way come to the light, and
it shows that the things they do were
done through God."

Jesus and John the Baptist

22After this, Jesus and his followers
went into the area of Judea, where he
stayed with his followers and baptized
people. 23John was also baptizing in Ae-
non, near Salim, because there was plenty of water there. People were going
there to be baptized. 24(This was before
John was put into prison.)

25Some of John's followers had an argument with a Jew about religious
washing.[n] 26So they came to John and
said, "Teacher, remember the man who
was with you on the other side of the Jordan River, the one you spoke about so
much? He is baptizing, and everyone is
going to him."

27John answered, "A man can get only
what God gives him. 28You yourselves
heard me say, 'I am not the Christ, but I
am the one sent to prepare the way for
him.' 29The bride belongs only to the
bridegroom. But the friend who helps the
bridegroom stands by and listens to him.
He is thrilled that he gets to hear the
bridegroom's voice. In the same way, I
am really happy. 30He must become
greater, and I must become less important.

The One Who Comes from Heaven

31"The One who comes from above is
greater than all. The one who is from the
earth belongs to the earth and talks about
things on the earth. But the One who
comes from heaven is greater than all.
32He tells what he has seen and heard,

FAITH links

THE GIFT

JOHN 3:16-18

Have you ever given a gift that helped a whole group of people? Maybe you gave a gift to your family that everyone could use. God gave a gift to the whole world. He sent his Son to die for the sins of everyone—including you! How do you receive this gift? All you have to do is to believe that Jesus died for your sins, not just everyone else's. Now you have eternal life. That's quite a gift, isn't it?

Here are some more Faithlinks on God's gift to us:

When Bad Turns to Worse, Exodus 5:6–12, p. 82

Our Heavenly Shepherd, Psalm 23, p. 726

A Direct Path, Proverbs 3:5–6, p. 829

A Love Song, Zephaniah 3:17, p. 1246

A Change of Heart, Matthew 3:1–12, p. 1277

Too Busy to Worship?, Luke 2:8–20, p. 1368

3:25 religious washing The Jewish people washed themselves in special ways before eating, before worshiping in the Temple, and at other special times.

but no one accepts what he says. **33**Whoever accepts what he says has proven
that God is true. **34**The One whom God
sent speaks the words of God, because
God gives him the Spirit fully. **35**The Father loves the Son and has given him
power over everything. **36**Those who believe in the Son have eternal life, but
those who do not obey the Son will never
have life. God's anger stays on them."

Jesus and a Samaritan Woman

4 The Pharisees heard that Jesus was
making and baptizing more followers than John, **2**although Jesus himself
did not baptize people, but his followers
did. **3**Jesus knew that the Pharisees had
heard about him, so he left Judea and
went back to Galilee. **4**But on the way
he had to go through the country of Samaria.

5In Samaria Jesus came to the town
called Sychar, which is near the field Jacob gave to his son Joseph. **6**Jacob's well
was there. Jesus was tired from his long
trip, so he sat down beside the well. It
was about twelve o'clock noon. **7**When a
Samaritan woman came to the well to get
some water, Jesus said to her, "Please
give me a drink." **8**(This happened while
Jesus' followers were in town buying
some food.)

9The woman said, "I am surprised
that you ask me for a drink, since you are
a Jewish man and I am a Samaritan woman." (Jewish people are not friends with
Samaritans.)

10Jesus said, "If you only knew the
free gift of God and who it is that is asking you for water, you would have asked
him, and he would have given you living
water."

11The woman said, "Sir, where will
you get this living water? The well is
very deep, and you have nothing to get
water with. **12**Are you greater than Jacob, our father, who gave us this well and
drank from it himself along with his sons
and flocks?"

13Jesus answered, "Everyone who
drinks this water will be thirsty again,
14but whoever drinks the water I give
will never be thirsty. The water I give
will become a spring of water gushing up
inside that person, giving eternal life."

15The woman said to him, "Sir, give
me this water so I will never be thirsty
again and will not have to come back here
to get more water."

16Jesus told her, "Go get your husband and come back here."

17The woman answered, "I have no
husband."

Jesus said to her, "You are right to say
you have no husband. **18**Really you have
had five husbands, and the man you live
with now is not your husband. You told
the truth."

19The woman said, "Sir, I can see that
you are a prophet. **20**Our ancestors worshiped on this mountain, but you say that
Jerusalem is the place where people
must worship."

21Jesus said, "Believe me, woman.
The time is coming when neither in Jerusalem nor on this mountain will you actually worship the Father. **22**You Samaritans
worship something you don't understand.
We understand what we worship, because
salvation comes from the Jews.

> EMAIL FROM GOD
> **4:21–26**
> **Jesus**
> Jesus is the Messiah.

23The time is com-
ing when the true
worshipers will wor-
ship the Father in
spirit and truth, and
that time is here al-
ready. You see, the Father too is actively
seeking such people to worship him.
24God is spirit, and those who worship
him must worship in spirit and truth."

25The woman said, "I know that the
Messiah is coming." (Messiah is the One
called Christ.) "When the Messiah comes,
he will explain everything to us."

26Then Jesus said, "I am he—I, the
one talking to you."

27Just then his followers came back
from town and were surprised to see him
talking with a woman. But none of them
asked, "What do you want?" or "Why are
you talking with her?"

28Then the woman left her water jar

4:9 Jewish people . . . Samaritans This can also be translated "Jewish people don't use things that Samaritans have used."

and went back to town. She said to the
people, 29"Come and see a man who told
me everything I ever did. Do you think
he might be the Christ?" 30So the people
left the town and went to see Jesus.
31Meanwhile, his followers were begging him, "Teacher, eat something."
32But Jesus answered, "I have food to
eat that you know nothing about."
33So the followers asked themselves,
"Did somebody already bring him food?"
34Jesus said, "My food is to do what
the One who sent me wants me to do and
to finish his work. 35You have a saying,
'Four more months till harvest.' But I tell
you, open your eyes and look at the fields
ready for harvest now. 36Al-
ready, the one who
harvests is being
paid and is gather-
ing crops for eternal
life. So the one who
plants and the one
who harvests celebrate at the same time.
37Here the saying is true, 'One person
plants, and another harvests.' 38I sent
you to harvest a crop that you did not
work on. Others did the work, and you
get to finish up their work."[n]

EMAIL FROM GOD
4:34–38
Witnessing
Check out the real harvest.

39Many of the Samaritans in that
town believed in Jesus because of what
the woman said: "He told me everything
I ever did." 40When the Samaritans came
to Jesus, they begged him to stay with
them, so he stayed there two more days.
41And many more believed because of
the things he said.
42They said to the woman, "First we
believed in Jesus because of your speech,
but now we believe because we heard
him ourselves. We know that this man
really is the Savior of the world."

Jesus Heals an Officer's Son

43Two days later, Jesus left and went
to Galilee. 44(Jesus had said before that a
prophet is not respected in his own country.) 45When Jesus arrived in Galilee, the
people there welcomed him. They had
seen all the things he did at the Passover
Feast in Jerusalem, because they had
been there, too.
46Jesus went again to visit Cana in
Galilee where he had changed the water
into wine. One of the king's important officers lived in the city of Capernaum, and
his son was sick. 47When he heard that
Jesus had come from Judea to Galilee, he
went to Jesus and begged him to come to
Capernaum and heal his son, because his
son was almost dead. 48Jesus said to him,
"You people must see signs and miracles
before you will believe in me."
49The officer said, "Sir, come before
my child dies."
50Jesus answered, "Go. Your son will
live."
The man believed what Jesus told him
and went home. 51On the way the man's
servants came and met him and told him,
"Your son is alive."
52The man asked, "What time did my
son begin to get well?"
They answered, "Yesterday at one
o'clock the fever left him."
53The father knew that one o'clock
was the exact time that Jesus had said,
"Your son will live." So the man and all
the people who lived in his house believed in Jesus.
54That was the second miracle Jesus
did after coming from Judea to Galilee.

Jesus Heals a Man at a Pool

5 Later Jesus went to Jerusalem for a
special feast. 2In Jerusalem there is a
pool with five covered porches, which is
called Bethzatha[n] in the Hebrew language.[n]
This pool is near the Sheep Gate. 3Many
sick people were lying on the porches beside the pool. Some were blind, some were
crippled, and some were paralyzed.[n] 5A

4:38 I . . . their work. As a farmer sends workers to harvest grain, Jesus sends his followers out to bring people to God.

5:2 Bethzatha Also called Bethsaida or Bethesda, it is a pool of water north of the Temple in Jerusalem.

5:2 Hebrew language Hebrew or Aramaic, the languages of many people in this region in the first century.

5:3 Verse 3 Some Greek copies add "and they waited for the water to move." A few later copies add verse 4: "Sometimes an angel of the Lord came down to the pool and stirred up the water. After the angel did this, the first person to go into the pool was healed from any sickness he had."

LET'S VISIT CAPERNAUM

John 4:46–54

Capernaum was a fishing town on the shores of Lake Galilee. The name *Capernaum* means "Village of Nahum." It was probably named for the man who owned the land where the village was built. (This is not the Old Testament prophet, Nahum.)

Jesus spent a lot of time around Capernaum. He healed many people, including an army officer's servant (Check out Matthew 8:5–13, p. 1287.), a paralyzed man (See Mark 2:1–12, p. 1331.), and an important officer of the king's son. (Look at John 4:46–54.) It was also near Capernaum, that Jesus called several of his disciples. (Check out Mark 1:16–21, p. 1330; Mark 2:1, 13–14, p. 1331.) Before Jesus died, he cursed this city because of its unbelief (Look at Matthew 11:23–24, p. 1293.) and predicted its ruin. (See Luke 10:15, p. 1387.) Today there is nothing left of Capernaum but the ruins.

man was lying there who had been sick
for thirty-eight years. **6**When Jesus saw
the man and knew that he had been sick
for such a long time, Jesus asked him,
"Do you want to be well?"

7The sick man answered, "Sir, there
is no one to help me get into the pool
when the water starts moving. While I
am coming to the water, someone else always gets in before me."

8Then Jesus said, "Stand up. Pick up
your mat and walk." **9**And immediately
the man was well; he picked up his mat
and began to walk.

The day this happened was a Sabbath
day. **10**So the Jews said to the man who
had been healed, "Today is the Sabbath.
It is against our law for you to carry your
mat on the Sabbath day."

11But he answered, "The man who
made me well told me, 'Pick up your mat
and walk.' "

12Then they asked him, "Who is the
man who told you to pick up your mat and
walk?"

13But the man who had been healed
did not know who it was, because there
were many people in that place, and
Jesus had left.

14Later, Jesus found the man at the
Temple and said to him, "See, you are
well now. Stop sinning so that something
worse does not happen to you."

15Then the man left and told his people that Jesus was the one who had made
him well.

16Because Jesus was doing this on
the Sabbath day, some evil people began
to persecute him. **17**But Jesus said to
them, "My Father never stops working,
and so I keep working, too."

18This made them try still harder to
kill him. They said, "First Jesus was
breaking the law about the Sabbath day.
Now he says that God is his own Father,
making himself equal with God!"

Jesus Has God's Authority

19But Jesus said, "I tell you the truth,
the Son can do nothing alone. The Son
does only what he sees the Father doing,
because the Son does whatever the Father does. **20**The Father loves the Son
and shows the Son all the things he himself does. But the Father will show the
Son even greater things than this so that
you can all be amazed. **21**Just as the Father raises the dead and gives them life,

so also the Son gives life to those he
wants to. 22In fact, the Father judges no
one, but he has given the Son power to do
all the judging 23so that all people will
honor the Son as much as they honor the
Father. Anyone who does not honor the
Son does not honor the Father who sent
him.
24"I tell you the truth, whoever hears
what I say and believes in the

eMAIL! FROM GOD
5:24
God's Promises
Check out God's promise to all believers.

One who sent me
has eternal life. That
person will not be
judged guilty but has
already left death
and entered life. 25I
tell you the truth, the time is coming and
is already here when the dead will hear
the voice of the Son of God, and those who
hear will have life. 26Life comes from the
Father himself, and he has allowed the
Son to have life in himself as well. 27And
the Father has given the Son the power to
judge, because he is the Son of Man.
28Don't be surprised at

eMAIL! FROM GOD
5:28–29
Eternal Life
Who will receive eternal punishment?

this: A time is com-
ing when all who are
dead and in their
graves will hear his
voice. 29Then they
will come out of
their graves. Those who did good will rise
and have life forever, but those who did
evil will rise to be judged guilty.

Jesus Is God's Son

30"I can do nothing alone. I judge only
the way I am told, so my judgment is fair.
I don't try to please myself, but I try to
please the One who sent me.
31"If only I tell people about myself,
what I say is not true. 32But there is another who tells about me, and I know that
the things he says about me are true.
33"You have sent people to John, and
he has told you the truth. 34It is not that I
accept such human telling; I tell you this
so you can be saved. 35John was like a
burning and shining lamp, and you were
happy to enjoy his light for a while.
36"But I have a proof about myself
that is greater than that of John. The
things I do, which are the things my Father gave me to do, prove that the Father
sent me. 37And the Father himself who
sent me has given proof about me. You
have never heard his voice or seen what
he looks like. 38His teaching does not
live in you, because you don't believe in
the One the Father sent. 39You carefully
study the Scriptures because you think
they give you eternal life. They do in fact
tell about me, 40but you refuse to come
to me to have that life.
41"I don't need praise from people.
42But I know you—I know that you don't
have God's love in you. 43I have come

FAITH CHALLENGE

Hey there! Read 5:30 to find out whom Jesus cared about pleasing. If you decided to spend a whole day doing things to please God instead of pleasing yourself, where would you go and what would you do?

TESTING IT

John 5:30
I can do nothing alone. I judge only the way I am told, so my judgment is fair. I don't try to please myself, but I try to please the One who sent me.

from my Father and speak for him, but
you don't accept me. But when another
person comes, speaking only for himself,
you will accept him. **44**You try to get
praise from each other, but you do not try
to get the praise that comes from the
only God. So how can you believe?
45Don't think that I will stand before the
Father and say you are wrong. The one
who says you are wrong is Moses, the
one you hoped would save you. **46**If you
really believed Moses, you would believe me, because Moses wrote about
me. **47**But if you don't believe what
Moses wrote, how can you believe what
I say?"

More than Five Thousand Fed

6 After this, Jesus went across Lake
Galilee (or, Lake Tiberias). **2**Many
people followed him because they saw
the miracles he did to heal the sick.
3Jesus went up on a hill and sat down
there with his followers. **4**It was almost
the time for the Jewish Passover Feast.

5When Jesus looked up and saw a
large crowd coming toward him, he said
to Philip, "Where can we buy enough
bread for all these people to eat?"
6(Jesus asked Philip this question to test
him, because Jesus already knew what he
planned to do.)

7Philip answered, "We would all have
to work a month to buy enough bread for
each person to have only a little piece."

8Another one of his followers, Andrew,
Simon Peter's brother, said, **9**"Here is a
boy with five loaves of barley bread and
two little fish, but that is not enough for so
many people."

10Jesus said, "Tell the people to sit
down." This was a very grassy place, and
about five thousand men sat down there.
11Then Jesus took the loaves of bread,
thanked God for them, and gave them to
the people who were sitting there. He did
the same with the fish, giving as much as
the people wanted.

12When they had all had enough to
eat, Jesus said to his followers, "Gather
the leftover pieces of fish and bread so
that nothing is wasted." **13**So they gathered up the pieces and filled twelve baskets with the pieces left from the five
barley loaves.

14When the people saw this miracle
that Jesus did, they said, "He must truly
be the Prophet[n] who is coming into the
world."

15Jesus knew that the people planned
to come and take him by force and make
him their king, so he left and went into
the hills alone.

Jesus Walks on the Water

16That evening Jesus' followers went
down to Lake Galilee. **17**It was dark now,
and Jesus had not yet come to them. The
followers got into a boat and started
across the lake to Capernaum. **18**By now
a strong wind was blowing, and the
waves on the lake were getting bigger.
19When they had rowed the boat about
three or four miles, they saw Jesus walking on the water, coming toward the boat.
The followers were afraid, **20**but Jesus
said to them, "It is I. Do not be afraid."
21Then they were glad to take him into
the boat. At once the boat came to land at
the place where they wanted to go.

The People Seek Jesus

22The next day the people who had
stayed on the other side of the lake knew
that Jesus had not gone in the boat with
his followers but that they had left without him. And they knew that only one
boat had been there. **23**But then some
boats came from Tiberias and landed near
the place where the people had eaten the
bread after the Lord had given thanks.
24When the people saw that Jesus and
his followers were not there now, they
got into boats and went to Capernaum to
find Jesus.

Jesus, the Bread of Life

25When the people found Jesus on the
other side of the lake, they asked him,
"Teacher, when did you come here?"

26Jesus answered, "I tell you the
truth, you aren't looking for me because

6:14 Prophet They probably meant the prophet that God told Moses he would send (Deuteronomy 18:15-19).

THE NAMES OF JESUS

John 6:35

The two names Christians use the most for God's Son are *Jesus* and *Christ*. *Jesus* is a form of the Hebrew word for *Joshua*. It means "God is salvation." The name *Christ* came from a Greek term that means "Messiah." Here are some other names for Jesus used in the New Testament.

Alpha and Omega	He is the Beginning and the End	Revelation 21:6, p. 1753
Bread of Life	He is the one essential food	John 6:35, p. 1434
Most Important Stone	He is our sure foundation	Ephesians 2:20, p. 1600
Good Shepherd	He takes care of us	John 10:11, p. 1441
High Priest	He offered the perfect sacrifice for our sins	Hebrews 3:1, p. 1669
Immanuel	This name means "God is with us"	Matthew 1:23, p. 1275
King of Kings	The almighty ruler	Revelation 19:16, p. 1751
Lamb of God	Gave his life as a sacrifice for us	John 1:29, p. 1423
Light of the World	Jesus brings hope in the darkness	John 9:5, p. 1440
Son of Man	Jesus is all human and all God	Matthew 24:30, p. 1316

you saw me do miracles. You are looking
for me because you ate the bread and
were satisfied. **27**Don't work for the food
that spoils. Work for the food that stays
good always and gives eternal life. The
Son of Man will give you this food, because on him God the Father has put his
power."

28The people asked Jesus, "What are
the things God wants us to do?"

29Jesus answered, "The work God
wants you to do is this: Believe the One
he sent."

30So the people asked, "What miracle
will you do? If we see a miracle, we will
believe you. What will you do? **31**Our fathers ate the manna in the desert. This is
written in the Scriptures: 'He gave them
bread from heaven to eat.' "[n]

6:31 'He gave . . . eat.' Quotation from Psalm 78:24.

32Jesus said, "I tell you the truth, it was not Moses who gave you bread from heaven; it is my Father who is giving you the true bread from heaven. **33**God's bread is the One who comes down from heaven and gives life to the world."

34The people said, "Sir, give us this bread always."

35Then Jesus said, "I am the bread that gives life. Whoever comes to me will never be hungry, and whoever believes in me will never be thirsty. **36**But as I told you before, you have seen me and still don't believe. **37**The Father gives me my people. Every one of them will come to me, and I will always accept them. **38**I came down from heaven to do what God wants me to do, not what I want to do. **39**Here is what the One who sent me wants me to do: I must not lose even one whom God gave me, but I must raise them all on the last day. **40**Those who see the Son and believe in him have eternal life, and I will raise them on the last day. This is what my Father wants."

EMAIL FROM GOD
6:38–40
Resurrection
Who did Jesus promise to raise?

41Some people began to complain about Jesus because he said, "I am the bread that comes down from heaven." **42**They said, "This is Jesus, the son of Joseph. We know his father and mother. How can he say, 'I came down from heaven'?"

43But Jesus answered, "Stop complaining to each other. **44**The Father is the One who sent me. No one can come to me unless the Father draws him to me, and I will raise that person up on the last day. **45**It is written in the prophets, 'They will all be taught by God.'[n] Everyone who listens to the Father and learns from him comes to me. **46**No one has seen the Father except the One who is from God; only he has seen the Father. **47**I tell you the truth, whoever believes has eternal life. **48**I am the bread that gives life. **49**Your ancestors ate the manna in the desert, but still they died. **50**Here is the bread that comes down from heaven. Anyone who eats this bread will never die. **51**I am the living bread that came down from heaven. Anyone who eats this bread will live forever. This bread is my flesh, which I will give up so that the world may have life."

52Then the evil people began to argue among themselves, saying, "How can this man give us his flesh to eat?"

53Jesus said, "I tell you the truth, you must eat the flesh of the Son of Man and drink his blood. Otherwise, you won't have real life in you. **54**Those who eat my flesh and drink my blood have eternal life, and I will raise them up on the last day. **55**My flesh is true food, and my blood is true drink. **56**Those who eat my flesh and drink my blood live in me, and I live in them. **57**The living Father sent me, and I live because of the Father. So whoever eats me will live because of me. **58**I am not like the bread your ancestors ate. They ate that bread and still died. I am the bread that came down from heaven, and whoever eats this bread will live forever." **59**Jesus said all these things while he was teaching in the synagogue in Capernaum.

The Words of Eternal Life

60When the followers of Jesus heard this, many of them said, "This teaching is hard. Who can accept it?"

61Knowing that his followers were complaining about this, Jesus said, "Does this teaching bother you? **62**Then will it also bother you to see the Son of Man going back to the place where he came from? **63**It is the Spirit that gives life. The flesh doesn't give life. The words I told you are spirit, and they give life. **64**But some of you don't believe." (Jesus knew from the beginning who did not believe and who would turn against him.) **65**Jesus said, "That is the reason I said, 'If the Father does not bring a person to me, that one cannot come.' "

66After Jesus said this, many of his followers left him and stopped following him.

67Jesus asked the twelve followers, "Do you want to leave, too?"

6:45 'They. . . God.' Quotation from Isaiah 54:13.

68Simon Peter answered him, "Lord,
where would we go? You have the words
that give eternal life. 69We believe and
know that you are the Holy One from
God."
70Then Jesus answered, "I chose all
twelve of you, but one of you is a devil."
71Jesus was talking about Judas, the
son of Simon Iscariot. Judas was one of
the twelve, but later he was going to turn
against Jesus.

Jesus' Brothers Don't Believe

7 After this, Jesus traveled around Galilee. He did not want to travel in Judea, because some evil people there
wanted to kill him. 2It was time for the
Feast of Shelters. 3So Jesus' brothers
said to him, "You should leave here and
go to Judea so your followers there can
see the miracles you do. 4Anyone who
wants to be well known does not hide
what he does. If you are doing these
things, show yourself to the world."
5(Even Jesus' brothers did not believe in
him.)
6Jesus said to his brothers, "The right
time for me has not yet come, but any
time is right for you. 7The world cannot
hate you, but it hates me, because I tell it
the evil things it does. 8So you go to the
feast. I will not go yet to this feast, because the right time for me has not yet
come." 9After saying this, Jesus stayed
in Galilee.
10But after Jesus' brothers had gone
to the feast, Jesus went also. But he did
not let people see him. 11At the feast
some people were looking for him and
saying, "Where is that man?"
12Within the large crowd there, many
people were whispering to each other
about Jesus. Some said, "He is a good
man."
Others said, "No, he fools the people." 13But no one was brave enough to
talk about Jesus openly, because they
were afraid of the older leaders.

Jesus Teaches at the Feast

14When the feast was about half over,
Jesus went to the Temple and began to
teach. 15The people were amazed and
said, "This man has never studied in
school. How did he learn so much?"
16Jesus answered, "The things I
teach are not my own, but they come
from him who sent me. 17If people
choose to do what God wants, they will
know that my teaching comes from God
and not from me. 18Those who teach
their own ideas are trying to get honor
for themselves. But those who try to
bring honor to the one who sent him
speak the truth, and there is nothing false
in them. 19Moses gave you the law,* but
none of you obeys that law. Why are you
trying to kill me?"
20The people answered, "A demon
has come into you. We are not trying to
kill you."
21Jesus said to them, "I did one miracle, and you are all amazed. 22Moses
gave you the law about circumcision.
(But really Moses did not give you circumcision; it came from our ancestors.)
And yet you circumcise a baby on a Sabbath day. 23If a baby can be circumcised
on a Sabbath day to obey the law
of Moses, why are
you angry at me for
healing a person's
whole body on the
Sabbath day? 24Stop
judging by the way
things look, but judge by what is really
right."

eMAIL! FROM GOD
7:24
Judgment
Don't judge by appearances.

Is Jesus the Christ?

25Then some of the people who lived
in Jerusalem said, "This is the man they
are trying to kill. 26But he is teaching
where everyone can see and hear him,
and no one is trying to stop him. Maybe
the leaders have decided he really is the
Christ. 27But we know where this man is
from. And when the real Christ comes,
no one will know where he comes from."
28Jesus, teaching in the Temple, cried
out, "Yes, you know me, and you know
where I am from. But I have not come by
my own authority. I was sent by the One
who is true, whom you don't know. 29But

7:19 law Moses gave God's people the Law that God gave him on Mount Sinai (Exodus 34:29-32).

I know him, because I am from him, and
he sent me."
30When Jesus said this, the people
tried to take him. But no one was able to
touch him, because it was not yet the
right time. **31**But many of the people believed in Jesus. They said, "When the
Christ comes, will he do more miracles
than this man has done?"

The Leaders Try to Arrest Jesus

32The Pharisees heard the crowd
whispering these things about Jesus. So
the leading priests and the Pharisees
sent some Temple guards to arrest him.
33Jesus said, "I will be with you a little
while longer. Then I will go back to the
One who sent me. **34**You will look for me,
but you will not find me. And you cannot
come where I am."
35Some people said to each other,
"Where will this man go so we cannot
find him? Will he go to the Greek cities
where our people live and teach the
Greek people there? **36**What did he mean
when he said, 'You will look for me, but
you will not find me,' and 'You cannot
come where I am'?"

Jesus Talks About the Spirit

37On the last and most important day
of the feast Jesus stood up and said in a
loud voice, "Let anyone who is thirsty
come to me and drink. **38**If anyone believes in me, rivers of living water will
flow out from that person's heart, as the
Scripture says." **39**Jesus was talking
about the Holy Spirit. The Spirit had not
yet been given, because Jesus had not yet
been raised to glory. But later, those who
believed in Jesus would receive the
Spirit.

The People Argue About Jesus

40When the people heard Jesus'
words, some of them said, "This man
really is the Prophet."[n]
41Others said, "He is the Christ."
Still others said, "The Christ will not
come from Galilee. **42**The Scripture says
that the Christ will come from David's
family and from Bethlehem, the town
where David lived." **43**So the people did
not agree with each other about Jesus.
44Some of them wanted to arrest him,
but no one was able to touch him.

Some Leaders Won't Believe

45The Temple guards went back to
the leading priests and the Pharisees,
who asked, "Why didn't you bring
Jesus?"
46The guards answered, "The words
he says are greater than the words of any
other person who has ever spoken!"
47The Pharisees answered, "So Jesus
has fooled you also! **48**Have any of the
leaders or the Pharisees believed in him?
No! **49**But these people, who know nothing about the law, are under God's
curse."
50Nicodemus, who had gone to see
Jesus before, was in that group.[n] He said,
51"Our law does not judge a man without
hearing him and knowing what he has
done."
52They answered, "Are you from Galilee, too? Study the Scriptures, and you
will learn that no prophet comes from
Galilee."

Some early Greek manuscripts do not contain 7:53—8:11.

[**53**And everyone left and went home.

The Woman Caught in Adultery

8 Jesus went to the Mount of Olives.
2But early in the morning he went
back to the Temple, and all the people
came to him, and he sat and taught them.
3The teachers of the law and the Pharisees brought a woman who had been
caught in adultery. They forced her to
stand before the people. **4**They said to
Jesus, "Teacher, this woman was caught
having sexual relations with a man who is
not her husband. **5**The law of Moses
commands that we stone to death every

7:40 Prophet They probably meant the prophet God told Moses he would send (Deuteronomy 18:15-19).

7:50 Nicodemus . . . group. The story about Nicodemus going and talking to Jesus is in John 3:1-21.

woman who does this. What do you say
we should do?" **6**They were asking this
to trick Jesus so that they could have
some charge against him.

But Jesus bent over and started writing on the ground with his finger. **7**When
they continued to ask Jesus their question, he raised up and said, "Anyone here
who has never sinned can throw the first
stone at her." **8**Then Jesus bent over
again and wrote on the ground.

9Those who heard Jesus began to
leave one by one, first the older men and
then the others. Jesus was left there
alone with the woman standing before
him. **10**Jesus raised up again and asked
her, "Woman, where are they? Has no
one judged you guilty?"

11She answered, "No one, sir."

Then Jesus said, "I also don't judge
you guilty. You may go now, but don't sin
anymore."]

Jesus Is the Light of the World

12Later, Jesus talked to the people
again, saying, "I am
the light of the world.
The person who fol-
lows me will never
live in darkness but
will have the light
that gives life."

EMAIL FROM GOD 8:12
Following God
Read to see what you should follow.

13The Pharisees said to Jesus, "When
you talk about yourself, you are the only
one to say these things are true. We cannot accept what you say."

14Jesus answered, "Yes, I am saying
these things about myself, but they are
true. I know where I came from and
where I am going. But you don't know
where I came from or where I am going.
15You judge by human standards. I am not
judging anyone. **16**But when I do judge,
my judging is true, because I am not
alone. The Father who sent me is with
me. **17**Your own law says that when two
witnesses say the same thing, you must
accept what they say. **18**I am one of the
witnesses who speaks about myself, and
the Father who sent me is the other witness."

19They asked, "Where is your father?"

Jesus answered, "You don't know me
or my Father. If you knew me, you would
know my Father, too." **20**Jesus said these
things while he was teaching in the Temple, near where the money is kept. But
no one arrested him, because the right
time for him had not yet come.

The People Misunderstand Jesus

21Again, Jesus said to the people, "I
will leave you, and you will look for me,
but you will die in your sins. You cannot
come where I am going."

22So the Jews asked, "Will Jesus kill
himself? Is that why he said, 'You cannot
come where I am going'?"

23Jesus said, "You people are from
here below, but I am from above. You belong to this world, but I don't belong to
this world. **24**So I told you that you would
die in your sins. Yes, you will die in your
sins if you don't believe that I am he."

25They asked, "Then who are you?"

Jesus answered, "I am what I have
told you from the beginning. **26**I have
many things to say and decide about you.
But I tell people only the things I have
heard from the One who sent me, and he
speaks the truth."

27The people did not understand that
he was talking to them about the Father.
28So Jesus said to them, "When you lift
up the Son of Man, you will know that I am
he. You will know that these things I do
are not by my own authority but that I
say only what the Father has taught me.
29The One who sent me is with me. I always do what is pleasing to him, so he
has not left me alone." **30**While Jesus
was saying these things, many people believed in him.

Freedom from Sin

31So Jesus said to the Jews who believed in him, "If you continue to obey
my teaching, you are truly my followers.
32Then you will know the truth, and the
truth will make you free."

33They answered, "We are Abraham's children, and we have never been
anyone's slaves. So why do you say we
will be free?"

FAITH links

THE WHOLE TRUTH

JOHN 8:31-32, 45

Has anyone ever lied to you? The next time he or she tells you something, believing that person becomes harder doesn't it? Sometimes people lie because they're afraid that others won't like the truth. Jesus always told the truth, even though doing so often caused trouble for him with the religious leaders of Israel. They didn't like to hear him tell the truth about God or about their sin.

Jesus called himself the truth. Because he *is* the truth, that's what we ought to always tell if we believe in him.

Jesus takes what we say very seriously. So should we! Check it out:

The Best Policy, Genesis 29:16–29, p. 41

Who Do You Prefer?, Proverbs 3:32, p. 830

A Broken Promise, Jeremiah 2:1–8, p. 989

The Verdict Is In?, Matthew 7:1–2, p. 1285

The Deadliest Lie, Acts 5:1–11, p. 1471

Say What?!, Ephesians 4:22–29, p. 1603

34Jesus answered, "I tell you the
truth, everyone who lives in sin is a slave
to sin. **35**A slave does not stay with a
family forever, but a son belongs to the
family forever. **36**So if the Son makes you
free, you will be truly free. **37**I know you
are Abraham's children, but you want to
kill me because you don't accept my
teaching. **38**I am telling you what my Father has shown me, but you do what your
father has told you."

39They answered, "Our father is
Abraham."

Jesus said, "If you were really
Abraham's children, you would do the
things Abraham did. **40**I am a man who
has told you the truth which I heard from
God, but you are trying to kill me. Abraham did nothing like that. **41**So you are
doing the things your own father did."

But they said, "We are not like children who never knew who their father
was. God is our Father; he is the only Father we have."

42Jesus said to them, "If God were
really your Father, you would love me,
because I came from God and now I am
here. I did not come by my own authority;
God sent me. **43**You don't understand
what I say, because you cannot accept my
teaching. **44**You belong to your
father the devil, and
you want to do what
he wants. He was a
murderer from the
beginning and was
against the truth,
because there is no truth in him. When
he tells a lie, he shows what he is really
like, because he is a liar and the father of
lies. **45**But because I speak the truth, you
don't believe me. **46**Can any of you prove
that I am guilty of sin? If I am telling the
truth, why don't you believe me? **47**The
person who belongs to God accepts what
God says. But you don't accept what God
says, because you don't belong to God."

EMAIL! FROM GOD 8:44
Satan
Is the devil completely evil?

Jesus Is Greater than Abraham

48They answered, "We say you are a
Samaritan and have a demon in you. Are
we not right?"

49Jesus answered, "I have no demon
in me. I give honor to my Father, but
you dishonor me. **50**I am not trying to
get honor for myself. There is One
who wants this honor for me, and he
is the judge. **51**I tell you the truth, who-

ever obeys my teaching will never die."
52They said to Jesus, "Now we know
that you have a demon in you! Even
Abraham and the prophets died. But you
say, 'Whoever obeys my teaching will
never die.' **53**Do you think you are greater than our father Abraham, who died?
And the prophets died, too. Who do you
think you are?"
54Jesus answered, "If I give honor to
myself, that honor is worth nothing. The
One who gives me honor is my Father,
and you say he is your God. **55**You don't
really know him, but I know him. If I said
I did not know him, I would be a liar like
you. But I do know him, and I obey what
he says. **56**Your father Abraham was very
happy that he would see my day. He saw
that day and was glad."
57They said to him, "You have never
seen Abraham! You are not even fifty
years old."
58Jesus answered, "I tell you the
truth, before Abraham was even born, I
am!" **59**When Jesus said this, the people
picked up stones to throw at him. But
Jesus hid himself, and then he left the
Temple.

Jesus Heals a Man Born Blind

9 As Jesus was walking along, he saw a
man who had been born blind. **2**His

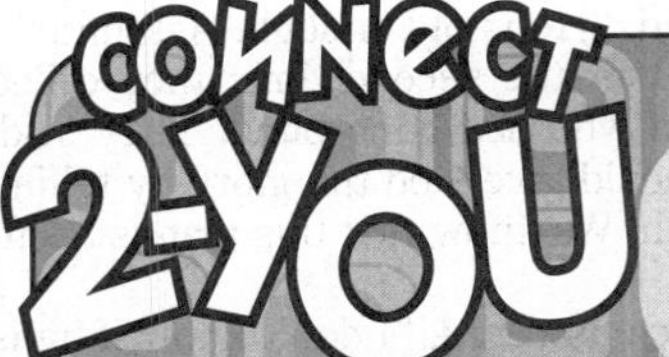
CONNECT
2-YOU

DID YOU HEAR ABOUT . . . ?

Hi, everybody. Tagg and I are talking about gossip. We have a friend who is struggling with this problem. Let's welcome Juli, age 11, to Connect 2-You.

Hi, Juli.
What's your problem?

Juli

My friends call me a gossip, and I guess they're right. I love to talk about what other people are doing. It drives me crazy if there are things going on in my friend's lives that I don't know about. And when someone tells me something, I can't wait to tell other people about it. All my friends are the same way. What do you think?

Gossip can be pretty tempting, Juli. But the Bible says we should control our tongues and not let our tongues control us. For some tips on how to get rid of gossip in your life, take a look at the Livin' It page on controlling what you say, Jeremiah 9:3, p. 1003.

When you learn to control your tongue, Juli, you may be surprised at what happens with your friends. When people start to realize that they can trust you not to tell their secrets, you will find that your friendships get deeper and stronger. Think of it as a reward for obeying God's commands.

followers asked him, "Teacher, whose sin
caused this man to be born blind—his
own sin or his parents' sin?"
3Jesus answered, "It is not this man's
sin or his parents' sin that made him be
blind. This man was born blind so that
God's power could be shown in him.
4While it is daytime, we must continue
doing the work of the One who sent me.
Night is coming, when no one can work.
5While I am in the world, I am the light of
the world."

6After Jesus said this, he spit on the
ground and made some mud with it and
put the mud on the man's eyes. 7Then he
told the man, "Go and wash in the Pool of
Siloam." (Siloam means Sent.) So the man
went, washed, and came back seeing.

8The neighbors and some people who
had earlier seen this man begging said,
"Isn't this the same man who used to sit
and beg?"

9Some said, "He is the one," but others said, "No, he only looks like him."

The man himself said, "I am the man."

10They asked, "How did you get your
sight?"

11He answered, "The man named
Jesus made some mud and put it on my
eyes. Then he told me to go to Siloam and
wash. So I went and washed, and then I
could see."

12They asked him, "Where is this man?"
"I don't know," he answered.

Pharisees Question the Healing

13Then the people took to the Pharisees the man who had been blind. 14The
day Jesus had made mud and healed his
eyes was a Sabbath day. 15So now the
Pharisees asked the man, "How did you
get your sight?"

He answered, "He put mud on my
eyes, I washed, and now I see."

16So some of the Pharisees were saying, "This man does not keep the Sabbath
day, so he is not from God."

But others said, "A man who is a sinner can't do miracles like these." So they
could not agree with each other.

17They asked the man again, "What
do you say about him since it was your
eyes he opened?"

The man answered, "He is a prophet."
18These leaders did not believe that
he had been blind and could now see
again. So they sent for the man's parents
19and asked them, "Is this your son who
you say was born blind? Then how does
he now see?"

20His parents answered, "We know
that this is our son and that he was born
blind. 21But we don't know how he can
now see. We don't know who opened his
eyes. Ask him. He is old enough to speak
for himself." 22His parents said this because they were afraid of the older
leaders, who had already decided that
anyone who said Jesus was the Christ
would be avoided. 23That is why his parents said, "He is old enough. Ask him."

24So for the second time, they called
the man who had been blind. They said,
"You should give God the glory by telling
the truth. We know that this man is a sinner."

25He answered, "I don't know if he is
a sinner. One thing I do know: I was blind,
and now I see."

26They asked, "What did he do to
you? How did he make you see again?"

27He answered, "I already told you,
and you didn't listen. Why do you want to
hear it again? Do you want to become his
followers, too?"

28Then they insulted him and said,
"You are his follower, but we are followers of Moses. 29We know that God spoke
to Moses, but we don't even know where
this man comes from."

30The man answered, "This is a very
strange thing. You don't know where he
comes from, and yet he opened my eyes.
31We all know that God does not listen to
sinners, but he listens to anyone who
worships and obeys him. 32Nobody has
ever heard of anyone giving sight to a
man born blind. 33If this man were not
from God, he could do nothing."

34They answered, "You were born
full of sin! Are you trying to teach us?"
And they threw him out.

Spiritual Blindness

35When Jesus heard that they had
thrown him out, Jesus found him and

said, "Do you believe in the Son of Man?"
36He asked, "Who is the Son of Man,
sir, so that I can believe in him?"
37Jesus said to him, "You have seen
him. The Son of Man is the one talking
with you."
38He said, "Lord, I believe!" Then
the man worshiped Jesus.
39Jesus said, "I came into this world
so that the world could be judged. I came
so that the blind[n] would see and so that
those who see will become blind."
40Some of the Pharisees who were
nearby heard Jesus say this and asked,
"Are you saying we are blind, too?"
41Jesus said, "If you were blind, you
would not be guilty of sin. But since you
keep saying you see, your guilt remains."

The Shepherd and His Sheep

10 Jesus said, "I tell you the truth,
the person who does not enter the
sheepfold by the door, but climbs in some
other way, is a thief and a robber. 2The
one who enters by the door is the shepherd of the sheep. 3The one who guards
the door opens it for him. And the sheep
listen to the voice of the shepherd. He
calls his own sheep by name and leads
them out. 4When he brings all his sheep
out, he goes ahead of them, and they follow him because they know his voice.
5But they will never follow a stranger.
They will run away from him because
they don't know his voice." 6Jesus told
the people this story, but they did not understand what it meant.

Jesus Is the Good Shepherd

7So Jesus said again, "I tell you the
truth, I am the door for the sheep. 8All
the people who came before me
were thieves and
robbers. The sheep
did not listen to
them. 9I am the
door, and the person
who enters through
me will be saved and will be able to come
in and go out and find pasture. 10A thief
comes to steal and kill and destroy, but I
came to give life—life in all its fullness.
11"I am the good shepherd. The good
shepherd gives his life for the sheep.
12The worker who is paid to keep the
sheep is different from the shepherd who
owns them. When the worker sees a wolf
coming, he runs away and leaves the
sheep alone. Then the wolf attacks the
sheep and scatters them. 13The man
runs away because he is only a paid

EMAIL FROM GOD
10:10
Life
What did Jesus come to give?

FAITH links

OUR GOOD SHEPHERD

JOHN 10:11-15

If you've ever been around sheep, you know how helpless they are. A shepherd has to help them do just about everything. They also depend on him or her for protection.

Guess what? Jesus says that we're like sheep, and he is our shepherd. That means he takes care of us. He even gave his life for us. Now that's good news!

God has the best protection plan! Link here for more:

Fearful Service?, Exodus 4:1–17, p. 80

What's in a Name?, Isaiah 9:6, p. 908

His Valentine, Jeremiah 31:3, p. 1035

A Word About Worry, Matthew 6:25–34, p. 1284

Prove It!, Matthew 16:1–4, p. 1302

Most Wanted?, 2 Corinthians 10:1, p. 1580

9:39 blind Jesus is talking about people who are spiritually blind, not physically blind.

worker and does not really care about the sheep.

14-15"I am the good shepherd. I know my sheep, as the Father knows me. And my sheep know me, as I know the Father. I give my life for the sheep. **16**I have other sheep that are not in this flock, and I must bring them also. They will listen to my voice, and there will be one flock and one shepherd. **17**The Father loves me because I give my life so that I can take it back again. **18**No one takes it away from me; I give my own life freely. I have the right to give my life, and I have the right to take it back. This is what my Father commanded me to do."

19Again the leaders did not agree with each other because of these words of Jesus. **20**Many of them said, "A demon has come into him and made him crazy. Why listen to him?"

21But others said, "A man who is crazy with a demon does not say things like this. Can a demon open the eyes of the blind?"

Jesus Is Rejected

22The time came for the Feast of Dedication at Jerusalem. It was winter, **23**and Jesus was walking in the Temple in Solomon's Porch. **24**Some people gathered around him and said, "How long will you make us wonder about you? If you are the Christ, tell us plainly."

25Jesus answered, "I told you already, but you did not believe. The miracles I do in my Father's name show who I am. **26**But you don't believe, because you are not my sheep. **27**My sheep listen to my voice; I know them, and they follow me. **28**I give them eternal life, and they will never die, and no one can steal them out of my hand. **29**My Father gave my sheep to me. He is greater than all, and no person can steal my sheep out of my Father's hand. **30**The Father and I are one."

eMAIL! FROM GOD
10:25–27
Following God
How can you know Jesus?

31Again some of the people picked up stones to kill Jesus. **32**But he said to them, "I have done many good works from the Father. Which of these good works are you killing me for?"

33They answered, "We are not killing you because of any good work you did, but because you speak against God. You are only a human, but you say you are the same as God!"

34Jesus answered, "It is written in your law that God said, 'I said, you are gods.'[n] **35**This Scripture called those people gods who received God's message, and Scripture is always true. **36**So why do you say that I speak against God because I said, 'I am God's Son'? I am the one God chose and sent into the world. **37**If I don't do what my Father does, then don't believe me. **38**But if I do what my Father does, even though you don't believe in me, believe what I do. Then you will know and understand that the Father is in me and I am in the Father."

39They tried to take Jesus again, but he escaped from them.

40Then he went back across the Jordan River to the place where John had first baptized. Jesus stayed there, **41**and many people came to him and said, "John never did a miracle, but everything John said about this man is true." **42**And in that place many believed in Jesus.

The Death of Lazarus

11 A man named Lazarus was sick. He lived in the town of Bethany, where Mary and her sister Martha lived. **2**Mary was the woman who later put perfume on the Lord and wiped his feet with her hair. Mary's brother was Lazarus, the man who was now sick. **3**So Mary and Martha sent someone to tell Jesus, "Lord, the one you love is sick."

4When Jesus heard this, he said, "This sickness will not end in death. It is for the glory of God, to bring glory to the Son of God." **5**Jesus loved Martha and her sister and Lazarus. **6**But when he heard that Lazarus was sick, he stayed where he was for two more days. **7**Then Jesus said to his followers, "Let's go back to Judea."

10:34 'I . . . gods.' Quotation from Psalm 82:6.

8The followers said, "But Teacher, some people there tried to stone you to death only a short time ago. Now you want to go back there?"

9Jesus answered, "Are there not twelve hours in the day? If anyone walks in the daylight, he will not stumble, because he can see by this world's light. **10**But if anyone walks at night, he stumbles because there is no light to help him see."

11After Jesus said this, he added, "Our friend Lazarus has fallen asleep, but I am going there to wake him."

12The followers said, "But Lord, if he is only asleep, he will be all right."

13Jesus meant that Lazarus was dead, but his followers thought he meant Lazarus was really sleeping. **14**So then Jesus said plainly, "Lazarus is dead. **15**And I am glad for your sakes I was not there so that you may believe. But let's go to him now."

16Then Thomas (the one called Didymus) said to the other followers, "Let us also go so that we can die with him."

Jesus in Bethany

17When Jesus arrived, he learned that Lazarus had already been dead and in the tomb for four days. **18**Bethany was about two miles from Jerusalem. **19**Many of the Jews had come there to comfort Martha and Mary about their brother.

20When Martha heard that Jesus was coming, she went out to meet him, but Mary stayed home. **21**Martha said to Jesus, "Lord, if you had been here, my brother would not have died. **22**But I know that even now God will give you anything you ask."

23Jesus said, "Your brother will rise and live again."

24Martha answered, "I know that he will rise and live again in the resurrection* on the last day."

eMAiL FROM GOD
11:25
Eternal Life
What does Jesus give?

25Jesus said to her, "I am the resurrection and the life. Those who believe in me will have life even if they die. **26**And everyone who lives and believes in me will never die. Martha, do you believe this?"

27Martha answered, "Yes, Lord. I believe that you are the Christ, the Son of God, the One coming to the world."

Jesus Cries

28After Martha said this, she went back and talked to her sister Mary alone. Martha said, "The Teacher is here and he is asking for you." **29**When Mary heard this, she got up quickly and went to Jesus. **30**Jesus had not yet come into the town but was still at the place where Martha had met him. **31**The Jews were with Mary in the house, comforting her. When they saw her stand and leave quickly, they followed her, thinking she was going to the tomb to cry there.

32But Mary went to the place where Jesus was. When she saw him, she fell at his feet and said, "Lord, if you had been here, my brother would not have died."

33When Jesus saw Mary crying and the Jews who came with her also crying, he was upset and was deeply troubled. **34**He asked, "Where did you bury him?"

"Come and see, Lord," they said.

35Jesus cried.

36So the Jews said, "See how much he loved him."

37But some of them said, "If Jesus opened the eyes of the blind man, why couldn't he keep Lazarus from dying?"

Jesus Raises Lazarus

38Again feeling very upset, Jesus came to the tomb. It was a cave with a large stone covering the entrance. **39**Jesus said, "Move the stone away."

Martha, the sister of the dead man, said, "But, Lord, it has been four days since he died. There will be a bad smell."

40Then Jesus said to her, "Didn't I tell you that if you believed you would see the glory of God?"

41So they moved the stone away from the entrance. Then Jesus looked up and said, "Father, I thank you that you heard me. **42**I know that you always hear me,

---

11:24 resurrection Being raised from the dead to live again.

FAITH links

FULLY GOD, FULLY HUMAN

JOHN 11:35

When a friend feels sad, you feel sad, too, don't you? Jesus felt exactly the same way. The shortest verse in the Bible tells us that when a friend of his died, Jesus cried. Jesus is God, but he is also human. He has feelings just like you do. That means he can understand when you're feeling sad about something. You can trust that he cares.

Download these links for more about God's care for you:

Your Heavenly Parent, Exodus 2:1–10, p. 77

Depend on Him!, 2 Chronicles 16:1–9, p. 579

A Safe Place, Nahum 1:7, p. 1231

It's Under Control, Romans 8:28, p. 1529

Life After Death?, 1 Corinthians 15:12–13, p. 1563

Go for It!, Hebrews 12:1–4, p. 1682

but I said these things because of the
people here around me. I want them to
believe that you sent me." 43After Jesus
said this, he cried out in a loud voice,
"Lazarus, come out!" 44The dead man
came out, his hands and feet wrapped
with pieces of cloth, and a cloth around
his face.

Jesus said to them, "Take the cloth off
of him and let him go."

The Plan to Kill Jesus

45Many of the people, who had come
to visit Mary and saw what Jesus did, believed in him. 46But some of them went
to the Pharisees and told them what
Jesus had done. 47Then the leading
priests and Pharisees called a meeting of
the council. They asked, "What should
we do? This man is doing many miracles.
48If we let him continue doing these
things, everyone will believe in him.
Then the Romans will come and take
away our Temple and our nation."

49One of the men there was Caiaphas,
the high priest that year. He said, "You
people know nothing! 50You don't realize
that it is better for one man to die for the
people than for the whole nation to be
destroyed."

51Caiaphas did not think of this himself. As high priest that year, he was
really prophesying that Jesus would die
for their nation 52and for God's scattered
children to bring them all together and
make them one.

53That day they started planning to
kill Jesus. 54So Jesus no longer traveled
openly among the people. He left there
and went to a place near the desert, to a
town called Ephraim and stayed there
with his followers.

55It was almost time for the Passover
Feast. Many from the country went up to
Jerusalem before the Passover to do the
special things to make themselves pure.
56The people looked for Jesus and stood
in the Temple asking each other, "Is he
coming to the Feast? What do you
think?" 57But the leading priests and the
Pharisees had given orders that if anyone
knew where Jesus was, he must tell
them. Then they could arrest him.

Jesus with Friends in Bethany

12 Six days before the Passover Feast,
Jesus went to Bethany, where
Lazarus lived. (Lazarus is the man Jesus
raised from the dead.) 2There they had a
dinner for Jesus. Martha served the food,
and Lazarus was one of the people eating
with Jesus. 3Mary brought in a pint of
very expensive perfume made from pure
nard. She poured the perfume on Jesus'

feet, and then she wiped his feet with her
hair. And the sweet smell from the perfume filled the whole house.
4Judas Iscariot, one of Jesus' followers who would later turn against him,
was there. Judas said, **5**"This perfume
was worth three hundred coins.[n] Why
wasn't it sold and the money given to
the poor?" **6**But Judas did not really
care about the poor; he said this because he was a thief. He was the one who
kept the money box, and he often stole
from it.
7Jesus answered, "Leave her alone. It
was right for her to save this perfume for
today, the day for me to be prepared for
burial. **8**You will always have the poor
with you, but you will not always have
me."

The Plot Against Lazarus

9A large crowd of people heard that
Jesus was in Bethany. So they went there
to see not only Jesus but Lazarus, whom
Jesus raised from the dead. **10**So the
leading priests made plans to kill Lazarus, too. **11**Because of Lazarus many of
the Jews were leaving them and believing in Jesus.

Jesus Enters Jerusalem

12The next day a great crowd who had
come to Jerusalem for the Passover Feast
heard that Jesus was coming there. **13**So
they took branches of palm trees and
went out to meet Jesus, shouting,

"Praise[n] God!
God bless the One who comes in the
name of the Lord!
God bless the King of Israel!"

Psalm 118:25-26

14Jesus found a colt and sat on it. This
was as the Scripture says,
15"Don't be afraid, people of
Jerusalem!
Your king is coming,
sitting on the colt of a donkey."

Zechariah 9:9

16The followers of Jesus did not understand this at first. But after Jesus was
raised to glory, they remembered that
this had been written about him and that
they had done these things to him.

People Tell About Jesus

17There had been many people with
Jesus when he raised Lazarus from the
dead and told him to come out of the
tomb. Now they were telling others
about what Jesus did. **18**Many people
went out to meet Jesus, because they had
heard about this miracle. **19**So the Pharisees said to each other, "You can see that
nothing is going right for us. Look! The
whole world is following him."

Jesus Talks About His Death

20There were some Greek people,
too, who came to Jerusalem to worship
at the Passover Feast. **21**They went to
Philip, who was from Bethsaida in Galilee, and said, "Sir, we would like to see
Jesus." **22**Philip told Andrew, and then
Andrew and Philip told Jesus.
23Jesus said to them, "The time has
come for the Son of Man to receive his
glory. **24**I tell you the truth, a grain of
wheat must fall to the ground and die to
make many seeds. But if it never dies, it
remains only a single seed. **25**Those who
love their lives will lose them, but
those who hate their lives in
this world will keep
true life forever.
26Whoever serves
me must follow me.
Then my servant will
be with me every-
where I am. My Fa-
ther will honor anyone who serves me.

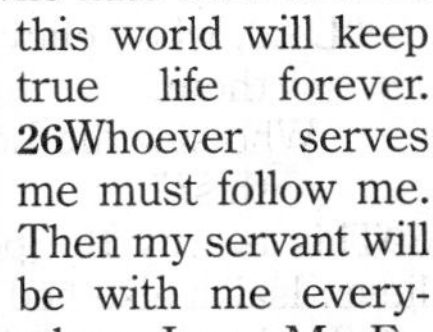

12:26 Following God
How can you know Jesus is near?

27"Now I am very troubled. Should I
say, 'Father, save me from this time'? No,
I came to this time so I could suffer. **28**Father, bring glory to your name!"
Then a voice came from heaven, "I
have brought glory to it, and I will do it
again."
29The crowd standing there, who
heard the voice, said it was thunder.
But others said, "An angel has spoken
to him."

12:5 coins One coin, a denarius, was the average pay for one day's work.

12:13 Praise Literally, "Hosanna," a Hebrew word used at first in praying to God for help, but at this time it was probably a shout of joy used in praising God or his Messiah.

30Jesus said, "That voice was for your
sake, not mine. 31Now is the time for the
world to be judged; now the ruler of this
world will be thrown down. 32If I am lifted up from the earth, I will draw all people toward me." 33Jesus said this to show
how he would die.

34The crowd said, "We have heard
from the law that the Christ will live forever. So why do you say, 'The Son of Man
must be lifted up'? Who is this 'Son of
Man'?"

35Then Jesus said, "The light will be
with you for a little longer, so walk while
you have the light. Then the darkness
will not catch you. If you walk in the darkness, you will not know where you are
going. 36Believe in the light while you
still have it so that you will become children of light." When Jesus had said this,
he left and hid himself from them.

Some People Won't Believe in Jesus

37Though Jesus had done many miracles in front of the people, they still did
not believe in him. 38This was to bring
about what Isaiah the prophet had said:

"Lord, who believed what we told
them?
Who saw the Lord's power in
this?" *Isaiah 53:1*

39This is why the people could not believe: Isaiah also had said,

40"He has blinded their eyes,
and he has closed their minds.
Otherwise they would see with their
eyes
and understand in their minds
and come back to me and be
healed." *Isaiah 6:10*

41Isaiah said this because he saw Jesus'
glory and spoke about him.

42But many believed in Jesus, even
many of the leaders. But because of the
Pharisees, they did not say they believed
in him for fear they would be put out of
the synagogue. 43They loved praise from
people more than praise from God.

44Then Jesus cried out, "Whoever believes in me is really believing in the One
who sent me. 45Whoever sees me sees
the One who sent me. 46I have come as
light into the world so that whoever believes in me would not stay in darkness.

47"Anyone who hears my words and
does not obey them, I do not judge, because I did not come to judge the world,
but to save the world. 48There is a judge
for those who refuse to believe in me and
do not accept my words. The word I have
taught will be their judge on the last day.
49The things I taught were not from myself. The Father who sent me told me
what to say and what to teach. 50And I
know that eternal life comes from what
the Father commands. So whatever I say
is what the Father told me to say."

Jesus Washes His Followers' Feet

13 It was almost time for the Passover
Feast. Jesus knew that it was time
for him to leave this world and go back to
the Father. He had always loved those
who were his own in the world, and he
loved them all the way to the end.

2Jesus and his followers were at the
evening meal. The devil had already persuaded Judas Iscariot, the son of Simon,
to turn against Jesus. 3Jesus knew that
the Father had given him power over
everything and that he had come from
God and was going back to God. 4So during the meal Jesus stood up and took off
his outer clothing. Taking a towel, he
wrapped it around his waist. 5Then he
poured water into a bowl and began to
wash the followers' feet, drying them
with the towel that was wrapped around
him.

6Jesus came to Simon Peter, who said
to him, "Lord, are you going to wash my
feet?"

7Jesus answered, "You don't understand now what I am doing, but you will
understand later."

8Peter said, "No, you will never wash
my feet."

Jesus answered, "If I don't wash your
feet, you are not one of my people."

9Simon Peter answered, "Lord, then
wash not only my feet, but wash my
hands and my head, too!"

10Jesus said, "After a person has had a
bath, his whole body is clean. He needs
only to wash his feet. And you men are

ESTHER
MARY
JESUS
PAUL

1

Suppose your mom told you not to eat anything before dinner. Now suppose someone offered you a candy bar, your favorite chips, or a yummy cupcake. Would you eat it?

2

What are you good at? Skating? Soccer? Are you ever tempted to show off in front of others? (Be honest!) If someone popular dared you to do something dangerous in order to prove how "good" you really are, would you do it? What if you knew, deep down, that it was wrong?

Jesus

Taking the Temptation Test

Those terrible, troublesome temptations! When you least expect it, one will pop into your life—a temptation to eat the last piece of cake; a temptation to cheat on a test; or a temptation to disobey your parents. One thing's for sure: everyone faces temptations of some kind. Even Jesus was tempted during his time on earth. But Jesus knew how to handle temptations. Want to find out how Jesus was tempted and what he did? Turn the page to check out the

HERE'S THE SCOOP

section whose number matches the number for the question on this page. And take a lesson from the Master in how to pass the temptation test!

3

What would you do if you were told you could have anything you wanted—even a trillion dollars? Sounds good so far, doesn't it? But suppose you were told that you had to take a "shortcut," like cheating on a test or obeying someone who does wrong things. Would you do it?

4

If you had the power to get back at someone who hurt you, even if doing it was wrong, would you use that power? Think about a situation where you would be tempted the most to use this power.

5

Suppose you were asked to make a sacrifice that would save someone else. For example, giving blood or bone marrow. Now suppose you were told that this sacrifice would be really, really painful. Would you still make that sacrifice?

Here's the Scoop

1

Jesus once fasted for 40 days out of obedience to God the Father. He was really hungry. But when the devil told him to make bread out of stones, Jesus used the Scriptures to tell him "NO!" Jesus knew that the devil wanted him to do something selfish to show off his power. He also knew that the Word of God gave a person the power to resist temptation. It will help you to resist temptation, too. (See Matthew 4:3–4, p. 1279.)

2

The devil wanted Jesus to throw himself off the Temple to prove that God would help him. This was another way for Jesus to show off in front of others. The devil tried to tempt Jesus by quoting from the Scriptures. Jesus knew that he didn't have to prove who he was. He also didn't have to prove that the Father would take care of him. So he used the Word of God to tell Satan to back off. When was the last time you did that? (Check out Luke 4:9–12, p. 1373.)

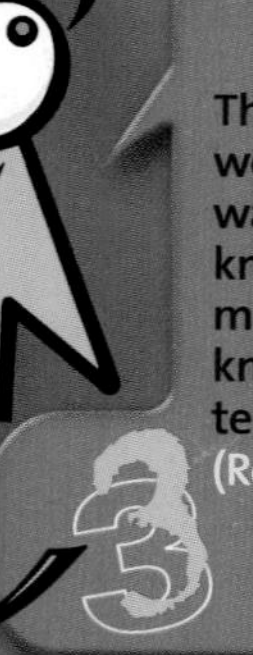

3

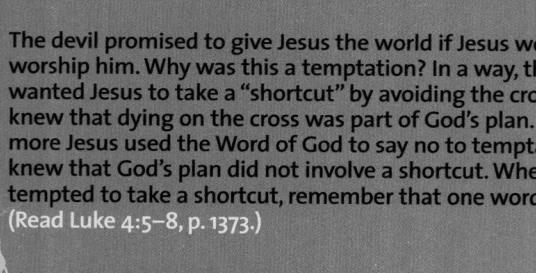

The devil promised to give Jesus the world if Jesus would only worship him. Why was this a temptation? In a way, the devil wanted Jesus to take a "shortcut" by avoiding the cross. Jesus knew that dying on the cross was part of God's plan. Once more Jesus used the Word of God to say no to temptation. He knew that God's plan did not involve a shortcut. When you're tempted to take a shortcut, remember that one word: NO! (Read Luke 4:5–8, p. 1373.)

4

A crowd of people charged toward Jesus to arrest him in the garden of Gethsemane. Jesus knew that he would be treated badly and would later be put to death. Peter, one of Jesus' disciples, tried to use violence to stop the crowd. But even though Jesus had the power to stop them from taking him, he didn't. Instead, he reminded everyone of what the Word of God said. Guess what he did next. He obeyed it. (Read about it in John 18:1–11, p. 1454.)

5

While Jesus was on the cross, people around him made fun of him. They told him that he could save himself if he wanted to. Jesus had the power to save himself or to call angels to rescue him from the cross. But Jesus went to the cross to die for the sins of everyone. If Jesus had given in to the temptation to free himself, we would all be lost! He chose to say no to temptation and yes to obedience. You can, too. (Check out Mark 15:21–32, p. 1359.)

answers page

ESTHER

MARY

JESUS

PAUL

PAUL

Hope for Hard Times

Everyone goes through bad times at some point in life. What are bad times? Failing a test. Having a pet die. Going through an illness. Being badly treated by others. How do you usually respond when bad times come your way? The way a person acts during hard times shows whether or not he or she has faith in God. Bad times can strengthen a person's faith, but they can also cause someone weak in faith to turn away from God. Paul experienced bad times as a missionary and apostle for God. Go to HERE'S THE SCOOP on the following page to find out what happened to his faith. The numbers match the question numbers on this page.

1 If someone spread false rumors about you to others, how would you feel? What would you do? Would you defend yourself or try to get back at that person by spreading rumors about them? Paul constantly faced situations where people said things about him that weren't true.

2 Suppose you were treated badly, even though you tried to do good. Would you try to get even? Or would you continue to do good? Paul faced major opposition even as he was trying to do good.

3 How would you respond if you were accused of something that you didn't do? Imagine your teacher walks into the classroom and accuses you of cheating when you haven't. What would you say in defense of yourself?

4 A life-threatening circumstance can be discouraging. Many are tempted to give up or be angry with God. How willing are you to trust God through the difficult times?

5 How do you react when the weather wrecks your plans? Do you cry "no fair," or do you try to be flexible? Some storms can throw a ship—or a life—off course. How can you stay on course?

Here's the Scoop

1 Paul and another missionary named Barnabas went to a town called Iconium to tell people about Jesus. But some of the Jewish people tried to make trouble for them. They said bad things about Paul and Barnabas. But they refused to stop preaching about Jesus. Instead, Paul and Barnabas trusted God. He gave them hope to make it through the hard times. (Read Acts 14:1–7, p. 1489.)

2 Paul and Silas used God's power to help a servant girl. But instead of being thanked for their good deed, they were arrested, beaten and thrown in prison! Amazingly, Paul didn't try to get even, and he didn't complain about being treated unfairly. Instead, he sang praise songs with Silas! Later, when God sent an earthquake to shake the walls of the jail down, they stayed to help the jailer! Because of them, the jailer and his family were baptized as believers. (Check out Acts 16:16–40, p. 1494.)

3 A group of men accused Paul of making the Jewish Temple unclean. They told the people that what Paul was teaching was against the Law of Moses. The men stirred the crowd up so that they tried to kill him. Roman soldiers finally arrested Paul just to get him safely away from the mob. Even though the men told lies about him, Paul didn't say bad things in return. He continued to tell the Good News of Jesus. (Look up Acts 21:27–36, p. 1503.)

4 Over 40 men came up with a plan to kill Paul. Paul's nephew overheard the whole thing and was able to tell the Roman guards about it. During this time while Paul was in jail based on false accusations, Paul didn't get angry with God because he was treated unfairly. He didn't complain, and he didn't question what God was doing. Paul continued to pray and trust God to protect him. He chose to keep his eyes on God, instead of on his circumstances. (Read Acts 23:11–22, p. 1506.)

5 While on his way to stand trial in Rome, Paul's ship was sunk in a storm. How did Paul handle this? Paul prayed. During the storm, God sent an angel to tell Paul that no one's life would be lost. Everyone would make it to shore safely. God took care of Paul. Months later, he sailed on another ship to Rome. So there you have it. Prayer, praise, and the power of God helped Paul through the hard times. Are these part of your strategy for getting through bad times? (Check out Acts 27:13—28:10–11, p. 1511.)

answers page

FAITH links

THE WORST CHORE

JOHN 13:3-17

Think of the worst chore that you hope you never have to do. That will give you some idea of how Jesus' followers felt when he began to wash their feet. In Jesus' time, washing a person's feet was considered the worst chore anyone could do. Only servants washed feet. So why did Jesus get up and do it? He wanted to provide an example of service. He wants us to be willing to serve others just as he did. So . . . what will you do?

A Use for Your Abilities, Genesis 41, p. 59

Yours, Mine, and Ours?, 1 Samuel 25, p. 389

The Way to Serve God, 1 Kings 9:4, p. 450

That Thing You Do, Matthew 25:14–30, p. 1319

You're Welcomed!, Acts 16:14–15, p. 1494

The Sacrifice of Service, Philippians 2:17, 25–30, p. 1612

clean, but not all of you." **11**Jesus knew
who would turn against him, and that is
why he said, "Not all of you are clean."
12When he had finished washing their
feet, he put on his clothes and sat down
again. He asked, "Do you understand
what I have just done for you? **13**You call
me 'Teacher' and 'Lord,' and you are
right, because that is what I am. **14**If I,
your Lord and Teacher, have washed your
feet, you also should wash each other's
feet. **15**I did this as an example so that
you should do as I have done for you. **16**I
tell you the truth, a servant is not greater
than his master. A messenger is not
greater than the one who sent him. **17**If
you know these things, you will be happy
if you do them.
18"I am not talking about all of you. I
know those I have chosen. But this is to
bring about what the Scripture said: 'The
man who ate at my table has turned
against me.'"[n] **19**I am telling you this now
before it happens so that when it happens, you will believe that I am he. **20**I
tell you the truth, whoever accepts anyone I send also accepts me. And whoever
accepts me also accepts the One who
sent me."

Jesus Talks About His Death

21After Jesus said this, he was very
troubled. He said openly, "I tell you the
truth, one of you will turn against me."
22The followers all looked at each
other, because they did not know whom
Jesus was talking about. **23**One of the followers sitting[n] next to Jesus was the follower Jesus loved. **24**Simon Peter
motioned to him to ask Jesus whom he
was talking about.
25That follower leaned closer to Jesus
and asked, "Lord, who is it?"
26Jesus answered, "I will dip this
bread into the dish. The man I give it to is
the man who will turn against me." So
Jesus took a piece of bread, dipped it, and
gave it to Judas Iscariot, the son of Simon. **27**As soon as Judas took the bread,
Satan entered him. Jesus said to him,
"The thing that you will do—do it
quickly." **28**No one at the table understood why Jesus said this to Judas.
29Since he was the one who kept the
money box, some of the followers
thought Jesus was telling him to buy
what was needed for the feast or to give
something to the poor.
30Judas took the bread Jesus gave

13:18 'The man . . . me.' Quotation from Psalm 41:9.

13:23 sitting Literally, "lying." The people of that time ate lying down and leaning on one arm.

him and immediately went out. It was
night.
31When Judas was gone, Jesus said,
"Now the Son of Man receives his glory,
and God receives glory through him. 32If
God receives glory through him, then
God will give glory to the Son through
himself. And God will give him glory
quickly."
33Jesus said, "My children, I will be
with you only a little longer. You will look
for me, and what I told the Jews, I tell you
now: Where I am going you cannot come.
34"I give you a new command: Love
each other. You must
love each other as
I have loved you.
35All people will
know that you are
my followers if you
love each other."

13:34–35
Love
You must love each other.

Peter Will Say He Doesn't Know Jesus

36Simon Peter asked Jesus, "Lord,
where are you going?"
Jesus answered, "Where I am going
you cannot follow now, but you will follow
later."
37Peter asked, "Lord, why can't I follow you now? I am ready to die for you!"
38Jesus answered, "Are you ready to
die for me? I tell you the truth, before the
rooster crows, you will say three times
that you don't know me."

Jesus Comforts His Followers

14 Jesus said, "Don't let your hearts
be troubled. Trust in God, and
trust in me. 2There are many rooms in
my Father's house; I would not tell you
this if it were not true. I am going there
to prepare a place for you. 3After I go and
prepare a place for you, I will come back
and take you to be with me so that you
may be where I am. 4You know the way
to the place where I am going."
5Thomas said to Jesus, "Lord, we
don't know where you are going. So how
can we know the way?"
6Jesus answered, "I am the way, and
the truth, and the life. The only way to
the Father is through me. 7If you really
knew me, you would know my Father,
too. But now you do know him, and you
have seen him."
8Philip said to him, "Lord, show us
the Father. That is all we need."
9Jesus answered, "I have been with
you a long time now. Do you still not
know me, Philip? Whoever has seen me
has seen the Father. So why do you say,
'Show us the Father'? 10Don't you be-

FAITH links

THE WAY TO HEAVEN

JOHN 14:1-6

How do you know you'll go to heaven after you die? Many people often wonder about that question. There's only one sure way to get to heaven: through Jesus. He is the way, the truth, and the life. Because Jesus willingly went to the cross for our sins, anyone who trusts him will have a heavenly home someday. That's a promise you can count on!

Here are some more Faithlinks about God's amazing promise to us:

God's New Home, 2 Chronicles 7:11–22, p. 570

How Big Is God?, Job 38—41, p. 703

Clean Inside and Out, Luke 11:39–40, p. 1392

Life After Death?, 1 Corinthians 15:12–13, p. 1563

The Coming Attraction, 1 Thessalonians 4:13–18, p. 1634

A Heavenly Sight, Revelation 21:1–4, p. 1753

lieve that I am in the Father and the Father is in me? The words I say to you don't come from me, but the Father lives in me and does his own work. **11**Believe me when I say that I am in the Father and the Father is in me. Or believe because of the miracles I have done. **12**I tell you the truth, whoever believes in me will do the same things that I do. Those who believe will do even greater things than these, because I am going to the Father. **13**And if you ask for anything in my name, I will do it for you so that the Father's glory will be shown through the Son. **14**If you ask me for anything in my name, I will do it.

The Promise of the Holy Spirit

15"If you love me, you will obey my commands. **16**I will ask the Father, and he will give you another Helper* to be with you forever—**17**the Spirit of truth. The world cannot accept him, because it does not see him or know him. But you know him, because he lives with you and he will be in you.

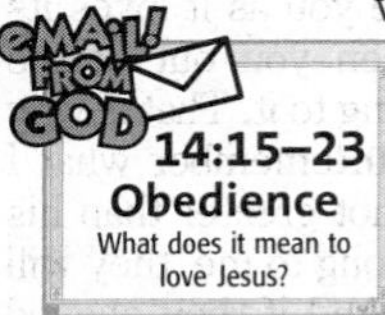

EMAIL FROM GOD
Who has power over death?
14:15–23
Obedience
What does it mean to love Jesus?

18"I will not leave you all alone like orphans; I will come back to you. **19**In a little while the world will not see me anymore, but you will see me. Because I live, you will live, too. **20**On that day you will know that I am in my Father, and that you are in me and I am in you. **21**Those who know my commands and obey them are the ones who love me, and my Father will love those who love me. I will love them and will show myself to them."

22Then Judas (not Judas Iscariot) said, "But, Lord, why do you plan to show yourself to us and not to the rest of the world?"

23Jesus answered, "If people love me, they will obey my teaching. My Father will love them, and we will come to them and make our home with them. **24**Those who do not love me do not obey my teaching. This teaching that you hear is not really mine; it is from my Father, who sent me.

25"I have told you all these things while I am with you. **26**But the Helper will teach you everything and will cause you to remember all that I told you. This Helper is the Holy Spirit whom the Father will send in my name.

27"I leave you peace; my peace I give you. I do not give it to you as the world does. So don't let your hearts be troubled or afraid. **28**You heard me say to you, 'I am going, but I am coming back to you.' If you loved me, you should be happy that I am going back to the Father, because he is greater than I am. **29**I have told you this now, before it happens, so that when it happens, you will believe. **30**I will not talk with you much longer, because the ruler of this world is coming. He has no power over me, **31**but the world must know that I love the Father, so I do exactly what the Father told me to do.

"Come now, let us go.

Jesus Is Like a Vine

15 "I am the true vine; my Father is the gardener. **2**He cuts off every branch of mine that does not produce fruit. And he trims and cleans every branch that produces fruit so that it will produce even more fruit. **3**You are already clean because of the words I have spoken to you. **4**Remain in me, and I will remain in you. A branch cannot produce fruit alone but must remain in the vine. In the same way, you cannot produce fruit alone but must remain in me.

5"I am the vine, and you are the branches. If any remain in me and I remain in them, they produce much fruit. But without me they can do nothing. **6**If any do not remain in me, they are like a branch that is thrown away and then dies. People pick up dead branches, throw them into the fire, and burn them. **7**If you remain in me and follow my teachings, you can ask anything you want, and it will be given to you. **8**You should produce

14:16 Helper "Counselor" or "Comforter." Jesus is talking about the Holy Spirit.

much fruit and show that you are my followers, which brings glory to my Father.
9I loved you as the Father loved me. Now
remain in my love. 10I have obeyed my
Father's commands, and I remain in his
love. In the same way, if you obey my
commands, you will remain in my love.
11I have told you these things so that you
can have the same joy I have and so that
your joy will be the fullest possible joy.
12"This is my command: Love each other
as I have loved you. 13The greatest love
a person can show is to die for his friends.
14You are my friends if you do what I command you. 15I no longer call you servants,
because a servant does not know what his
master is doing. But I call you friends,
because I have made known
to you everything I
heard from my Father.
16You did not choose
me; I chose you. And
I gave you this work:
to go and produce
fruit, fruit that will last. Then the Father
will give you anything you ask for in my
name. 17This is my command: Love each
other.

eMAIL! FROM GOD
15:13–15
Friendship
Check out what makes a true friend.

Jesus Warns His Followers

18"If the world hates you, remember
that it hated me first. 19If you belonged to
the world, it would love you as it loves its
own. But I have chosen you out of the
world, so you don't belong to it. That is why
the world hates you. 20Remember what I
told you: A servant is not greater than his
master. If people did wrong to me, they will
do wrong to you, too. And if they obeyed
my teaching, they will obey yours, too.
21They will do all this to you on account of
me, because they do not know the One
who sent me. 22If I had not come and spoken to them, they would not be guilty of
sin, but now they have no excuse for their
sin. 23Whoever hates me also hates my
Father. 24I did works among them that no
one else has ever done. If I had not done
these works, they would not be guilty of
sin. But now they have seen what I have
done, and yet they have hated both me
and my Father. 25But this happened so
that what is written in their law would be
true: 'They hated me for no reason.'"[n]
26"I will send you the Helper[n] from
the Father; he is the Spirit of truth who
comes from the Father. When he comes,
he will tell about me, 27and you also must
tell people about me, because you have
been with me from the beginning.

FAITH links

A FRIEND OF JESUS

JOHN 15:9-17

Want to know how to be a friend of Jesus? Jesus himself tells you how. First, love others. Second, do what he says. In fact, loving others is one of Jesus' commands. How do you do that? By being willing to serve others. Jesus gave his life for us. More than likely, none of us will be called on to give our lives to help a friend. But we can still do whatever it takes to serve and help others.

Give What You Can, Numbers 7:1–11, p. 186

Care for the Lost, Deuteronomy 22:1–3, p. 255

Loyal to a Friend, 2 Samuel 9, p. 409

Just Say Yes!, Matthew 9:9–13, p. 1289

An Encouraging Word, 1 Corinthians 1:3–5, p. 1545

Come On In!, 1 Peter 4:9–10, p. 1705

15:25 'They . . . reason.' These words could be from Psalm 35:19 or Psalm 69:4.

15:26 Helper "Counselor" or "Comforter." Jesus is talking about the Holy Spirit.

16 "I have told you these things to
keep you from giving up. **2**People
will put you out of their synagogues. Yes,
the time is coming when those who kill
you will think they are offering service to
God. **3**They will do this because they
have not known the Father and they have
not known me. **4**I have told you these
things now so that when the time comes
you will remember that I warned you.

The Work of the Holy Spirit

"I did not tell you these things at the
beginning, because I was with you then.
5Now I am going back to the One who
sent me. But none of you asks me,
'Where are you going?' **6**Your hearts are
filled with sadness because I have told
you these things. **7**But I tell you the
truth, it is better for you that I go away.
When I go away, I will send the Helper[n] to
you. If I do not go away, the Helper will
not come. **8**When the Helper comes, he
will prove to the people of the world the
truth about sin, about being right with
God, and about judgment. **9**He will prove
to them that sin is not believing in me.
10He will prove to them that being right
with God comes from my going to the Father and not being seen anymore. **11**And
the Helper will prove to them that judgment happened when the ruler of this
world was judged.

12"I have many more things to say to
you, but they are too much for you now.
13But when the Spirit of truth comes, he
will lead you into all truth. He will not
speak his own words, but he will speak
only what he hears, and he will tell you
what is to come. **14**The Spirit of truth will
bring glory to me, because he will take
what I have to say and tell it to you. **15**All
that the Father has is mine. That is why I
said that the Spirit will take what I have
to say and tell it to you.

Sadness Will Become Happiness

16"After a little while you will not see
me, and then after a little while you will
see me again."

17Some of the followers said to each
other, "What does Jesus mean when he
says, 'After a little while you will not see
me, and then after a little while you will
see me again'? And what does he mean
when he says, 'Because I am going to the
Father'?" **18**They also asked, "What does
he mean by 'a little while'? We don't understand what he is saying."

19Jesus saw that the followers wanted
to ask him about this, so he said to them,
"Are you asking each other what I meant
when I said, 'After a little while you will
not see me, and then after a little while
you will see me again'? **20**I tell you the
truth, you will cry and be sad, but the
world will be happy. You will be sad, but
your sadness will become joy. **21**When a
woman gives birth to a baby, she has pain,
because her time has come. But when
her baby is born, she forgets the pain, because she is so happy that a child has
been born into the world. **22**It is the same
with you. Now you are sad, but I will see
you again and you will be happy, and no
one will take away your joy. **23**In that day
you will not ask me for any-
thing. I tell you the
truth, my Father
will give you any-
thing you ask for in
my name. **24**Until
now you have not
asked for anything
in my name. Ask and you will receive, so
that your joy will be the fullest possible
joy.

eMail FROM GOD
16:23–24
Prayer
In whose name should you pray?

Victory over the World

25"I have told you these things, using
stories that hide the meaning. But the
time will come when I will not use stories
like that to tell you things; I will speak to
you in plain words about the Father. **26**In
that day you will ask the Father for things
in my name. I mean, I will not need to ask
the Father for you. **27**The Father himself
loves you. He loves you because you
loved me and believed that I came from
God. **28**I came from the Father into the
world. Now I am leaving the world and
going back to the Father."

29Then the followers of Jesus said,

16:7 Helper "Counselor" or "Comforter." Jesus is talking about the Holy Spirit.

HAVING JOY
John 16:24

Livin' it

I Got the Joy, Joy, Joy, Joy Did you ever sing the song "I Got the Joy, Joy, Joy, Joy Down in My Heart"? What kind of joy is that? Where does it come from?

God gives you the joy that never goes away no matter what. This is the joy that we have, knowing God loves us. (Look at Acts 3:1–16, p. 1466.) Imagine how you'd feel if someone suddenly solved a problem you've had all of your life—like curing a life-threatening disease or helping you become a math whiz overnight. Jesus' death solved the humongous problem of sin in your life by forgiving those sins. Now that's pure joy! How does that make you feel "down in your heart"?

MORE FAITH links

A Life of Thanksgiving, p. 435
A Need to Change, p. 873
Think About Him, p. 926
A Different Kind of Fruit, p. 1592
The "Quality" of Life, p. 1708

"Hey, Skweek, did you know you can be joyful even when things are kinda' rotten?"

"Really? Bet that's what these Faithlinks are talking about."

Happiness or Joy?, Job 29:18–19, p. 691
- Do you know the difference between happiness and joy? Happiness depends on circumstances. When everything is going great, you feel happy. But happiness doesn't last forever. Joy comes from God and is always there—in bad times or good times. Which would you rather have: joy or happiness?

Blessed Are the Weak?, 2 Corinthians 12:7–10, p. 1582
- No one likes to be thought of as weak—in our bodies or in the way we do things. God helps us when we're weak. Link here to learn where Paul found joy and strength when he was weak.

Always Do This!, 1 Thessalonians 5:16–18, p. 1636
- What are some things you always do, besides breathing? Do you laugh a lot? Sing? Complain? Blow milk out of your nose? Some actions probably depend on what's happening in your life. This Faithlink lists three activities to *always* do. How can you include them in your personal "always do" list?

my FAVORITE links

"You are speaking clearly to us now and
are not using stories that are hard to
understand. 30We can see now that you
know all things. You can answer a
person's question even before it is asked.
This makes us believe you came from
God."
31Jesus answered, "So now you believe? 32Listen to me; a time is coming
when you will be scattered, each to his
own home. That time is now here. You
will leave me alone, but I am never really
alone, because the Fa-
ther is with me.
33"I told you
these things so that
you can have peace
in me. In this world
you will have trou-
ble, but be brave! I have defeated the
world."

> **E-MAIL FROM GOD**
> **16:33**
> **Comfort**
> Having troubles? Take comfort in this.

Jesus Prays for His Followers

17 After Jesus said these things, he
looked toward heaven and prayed,
"Father, the time has come. Give glory to
your Son so that the Son can give glory to
you. 2You gave the Son power over all
people so that the Son could give eternal
life to all those you gave him. 3And this is
eternal life: that people know you, the
only true God, and that they know Jesus
Christ, the One you sent. 4Having finished the work you gave me to do, I
brought you glory on earth. 5And now,
Father, give me glory with you; give me
the glory I had with you before the world
was made.
6"I showed what you are like to those
you gave me from the world. They belonged to you, and you gave them to me,
and they have obeyed your teaching.
7Now they know that everything you
gave me comes from you. 8I gave them
the teachings you gave me, and they accepted them. They knew that I truly
came from you, and they believed that
you sent me. 9I am praying for them. I am
not praying for people in the world but for
those you gave me, because they are
yours. 10All I have is yours, and all you
have is mine. And my glory is shown
through them. 11I am coming to you; I
will not stay in the world any longer. But
they are still in the world. Holy Father,
keep them safe by the power of your
name, the name you gave me, so that
they will be one, just as you and I are one.

> **FAITH links**
> **JESUS' PRAYER**
> **JOHN 17**
>
> Suppose you were having the worst day of your life. Would you immediately think about helping someone else? Jesus faced one of the worst days of his life. He knew that he would soon be arrested and put to death. Before he went to the cross, he prayed for his followers. Jesus knew that they would need God's help in all that they did. He also prayed that his followers would get along with each other.
>
> Praying for someone is one way to show concern for that person. Let Jesus' prayer be a reminder to you to pray for the needs of others. Let it remind you, too, of how much Jesus cares for you!
>
> What God Wants, Deuteronomy 10:12–13, p. 242
>
> Just a Little Respect, 1 Chronicles 11:10–19, p. 534
>
> Your Heavenly Dad, Psalm 103:13, p. 786
>
> Concern for All, Daniel 9, p. 1165
>
> Prayer Priority, Luke 5:15–16, p. 1376
>
> Prayer for a Friend, Colossians 1:9–12, p. 1620

12While I was with them, I kept them safe by the power of your name, the name you gave me. I protected them, and only one of them, the one worthy of destruction, was lost so that the Scripture would come true.

13"I am coming to you now. But I pray these things while I am still in the world so that these followers can have all of my joy in them. **14**I have given them your teaching. And the world has hated them, because they don't belong to the world, just as I don't belong to the world. **15**I am not asking you to take them out of the world but to keep them safe from the Evil One. **16**They don't belong to the world, just as I don't belong to the world. **17**Make them ready for your service through your truth; your teaching is truth. **18**I have sent them into the world, just as you sent me into the world. **19**For their sake, I am making myself ready to serve so that they can be ready for their service of the truth.

eMAiL! FROM GOD
17:17
Truth
Is God's Word the truth?

20"I pray for these followers, but I am also praying for all those who will believe in me because of their teaching. **21**Father, I pray that they can be one. As you are in me and I am in you, I pray that they can also be one in us. Then the world will believe that you sent me. **22**I have given these people the glory that you gave me so that they can be one, just as you and I are one. **23**I will be in them and you will be in me so that they will be completely one. Then the world will know that you sent me and that you loved them just as much as you loved me.

eMAiL! FROM GOD
17:23
Salvation
What happens when you are saved?

24"Father, I want these people that you gave me to be with me where I am. I want them to see my glory, which you gave me because you loved me before the world was made. **25**Father, you are the One who is good. The world does not know you, but I know you, and these people know you sent me. **26**I showed them what you are like, and I will show them again. Then they will have the same love that you have for me, and I will live in them."

Jesus Is Arrested

18 When Jesus finished praying, he went with his followers across the Kidron Valley. On the other side there was a garden, and Jesus and his followers went into it.

2Judas knew where this place was, because Jesus met there often with his followers. Judas was the one who turned against Jesus. **3**So Judas came there with a group of soldiers and some guards from the leading priests and the Pharisees. They were carrying torches, lanterns, and weapons.

4Knowing everything that would happen to him, Jesus went out and asked, "Who is it you are looking for?"

5They answered, "Jesus from Nazareth."

"I am he," Jesus said. (Judas, the one who turned against Jesus, was standing there with them.) **6**When Jesus said, "I am he," they moved back and fell to the ground.

7Jesus asked them again, "Who is it you are looking for?"

They said, "Jesus of Nazareth."

8"I told you that I am he," Jesus said. "So if you are looking for me, let the others go." **9**This happened so that the words Jesus said before would come true: "I have not lost any of the ones you gave me."

10Simon Peter, who had a sword, pulled it out and struck the servant of the high priest, cutting off his right ear. (The servant's name was Malchus.) **11**Jesus said to Peter, "Put your sword back. Shouldn't I drink the cup[n] the Father gave me?"

Jesus Is Brought Before Annas

12Then the soldiers with their commander and the guards arrested Jesus. They tied him **13**and led him first to An-

18:11 cup Jesus is talking about the painful things that will happen to him. Accepting these things will be very hard, like drinking a cup of something bitter.

nas, the father-in-law of Caiaphas, the
high priest that year. **14**Caiaphas was the
one who told the Jews that it would be
better if one man died for all the people.

Peter Says He Doesn't Know Jesus

15Simon Peter and another one of
Jesus' followers went along after Jesus.
This follower knew the high priest, so he
went with Jesus into the high priest's
courtyard. **16**But Peter waited outside
near the door. The follower who knew
the high priest came back outside, spoke
to the girl at the door, and brought Peter
inside. **17**The girl at the door said to Peter, "Aren't you also one of that man's followers?"

Peter answered, "No, I am not!"

18It was cold, so the servants and
guards had built a fire and were standing
around it, warming themselves. Peter
also was standing with them, warming
himself.

The High Priest Questions Jesus

19The high priest asked Jesus questions about his followers and his teaching. **20**Jesus answered, "I have spoken
openly to everyone. I have always taught
in synagogues and in the Temple, where
all the Jews come together. I never said
anything in secret. **21**So why do you
question me? Ask the people who heard
my teaching. They know what I said."

22When Jesus said this, one of the
guards standing there hit him. The guard
said, "Is that the way you answer the
high priest?"

23Jesus answered him, "If I said
something wrong, then show what it was.
But if what I said is true, why do you hit
me?"

24Then Annas sent Jesus, who was
still tied, to Caiaphas the high priest.

Peter Says Again He Doesn't Know Jesus

25As Simon Peter was standing and
warming himself, they said to him,
"Aren't you one of that man's followers?"

Peter said it was not true; he said,
"No, I am not."

26One of the servants of the high
priest was there. This servant was a relative of the man whose ear Peter had cut
off. The servant said, "Didn't I see you
with him in the garden?"

27Again Peter said it wasn't true. At
once a rooster crowed.

Jesus Is Brought Before Pilate

28Early in the morning they led Jesus
from Caiaphas's house to the Roman
governor's palace. They would not go inside the palace, because they did not
want to make themselves unclean;[n] they
wanted to eat the Passover meal. **29**So
Pilate went outside to them and asked,
"What charges do you bring against this
man?"

30They answered, "If he were not a
criminal, we wouldn't have brought him
to you."

31Pilate said to them, "Take him
yourselves and judge him by your own
law."

"But we are not allowed to put anyone
to death," the Jews answered. **32**(This
happened so that what Jesus said about
how he would die would come true.)

33Then Pilate went back inside the
palace and called Jesus to him and asked,
"Are you the king of the Jews?"

34Jesus said, "Is that your own question, or did others tell you about me?"

35Pilate answered, "I am not one of
you. It was your own people and their
leading priests who handed you over to
me. What have you done wrong?"

36Jesus answered, "My kingdom does
not belong to this world. If it belonged to
this world, my servants would fight so
that I would not be given over to the
Jews. But my kingdom is from another
place."

37Pilate said, "So you are a king!"

Jesus answered, "You are the one saying I am a king. This is why I was born
and came into the world: to tell people
the truth. And everyone who belongs to
the truth listens to me."

18:28 unclean Going into the Roman palace would make them unfit to eat the Passover Feast, according to their Law.

BIOGRAPHIES FROM EVERY VIEW John 19

If they all tell about the life of Jesus, why are there four Gospels instead of just one? Maybe because each Gospel writer wrote to a different kind of person and for a different reason so they explained Jesus' story a different way. Together, the four Gospels give us a better picture of who Jesus was than only one Gospel could have done.

Matthew wrote to the Jews to show them that Jesus was the Messiah promised in the Old Testament. Mark focused on Jesus as a servant who helped people. Luke wrote to Gentiles (non-Jewish people) to give the full story of Jesus' life, from his birth to the birth of the church. John emphasized who Jesus was, rather than what he did. John wanted his readers to understand that Jesus was God himself. (Read John 20:31.)

38Pilate said, "What is truth?" After
he said this, he went out to the crowd
again and said to them, "I find nothing
against this man. 39But it is your custom
that I free one prisoner to you at Passover time. Do you want me to free the
'king of the Jews'?"
40They shouted back, "No, not him!
Let Barabbas go free!" (Barabbas was a
robber.)

19 Then Pilate ordered that Jesus be
taken away and whipped. 2The
soldiers made a crown from some thorny
branches and put it on Jesus' head and
put a purple robe around him. 3Then they
came to him many times and said, "Hail,
King of the Jews!" and hit him in the face.
4Again Pilate came out and said to
them, "Look, I am bringing Jesus out to
you. I want you to know that I find nothing
against him." 5So Jesus came out, wearing
the crown of thorns and the purple robe.
Pilate said to them, "Here is the man!"
6When the leading priests and the
guards saw Jesus, they shouted, "Crucify
him! Crucify him!"

But Pilate answered, "Crucify him
yourselves, because I find nothing
against him."
7The leaders answered, "We have a
law that says he should die, because he
said he is the Son of God."
8When Pilate heard this, he was even
more afraid. 9He went back inside the palace and asked Jesus, "Where do you come
from?" But Jesus did not answer him.
10Pilate said, "You refuse to speak to me?
Don't you know I have power to set you
free and power to have you crucified?"
11Jesus answered, "The only power
you have over me is the power given to
you by God. The man who turned me in
to you is guilty of a greater sin."
12After this, Pilate tried to let Jesus
go. But some in the crowd cried out,
"Anyone who makes himself king is
against Caesar. If you let this man go, you
are no friend of Caesar."
13When Pilate heard what they were
saying, he brought Jesus out and sat
down on the judge's seat at the place
called The Stone Pavement. (In the Hebrew language[n] the name is Gabbatha.)
14It was about noon on Preparation Day
of Passover week. Pilate said to the
crowd, "Here is your king!"

19:13 Hebrew language Hebrew or Aramaic, the languages of many people in this region in the first century.

15They shouted, "Take him away! Take him away! Crucify him!"

Pilate asked them, "Do you want me to crucify your king?"

The leading priests answered, "The only king we have is Caesar."

16So Pilate handed Jesus over to them to be crucified.

Jesus Is Crucified

The soldiers took charge of Jesus. **17**Carrying his own cross, Jesus went out to a place called The Place of the Skull, which in the Hebrew language[n] is called Golgotha. **18**There they crucified Jesus. They also crucified two other men, one on each side, with Jesus in the middle. **19**Pilate wrote a sign and put it on the cross. It read: JESUS OF NAZARETH, THE KING OF THE JEWS. **20**The sign was written in Hebrew, in Latin, and in Greek. Many of the people read the sign, because the place where Jesus was crucified was near the city. **21**The leading priests said to Pilate, "Don't write, 'The King of the Jews.' But write, 'This man said, "I am the King of the Jews." ' "

22Pilate answered, "What I have written, I have written."

23After the soldiers crucified Jesus, they took his clothes and divided them into four parts, with each soldier getting one part. They also took his long shirt, which was all one piece of cloth, woven from top to bottom. **24**So the soldiers said to each other, "We should not tear this into parts. Let's throw lots to see who will get it." This happened so that this Scripture would come true:

"They divided my clothes among them,
and they threw lots for my
clothing." *Psalm 22:18*

So the soldiers did this.

25Standing near his cross were Jesus' mother, his mother's sister, Mary the wife of Clopas, and Mary Magdalene. **26**When Jesus saw his mother and the follower he loved standing nearby, he said to his mother, "Dear woman, here is your son." **27**Then he said to the follower, "Here is your mother." From that time on, the follower took her to live in his home.

Jesus Dies

28After this, Jesus knew that everything had been done. So that the Scripture would come true, he said, "I am thirsty."[n] **29**There was a jar full of vinegar there, so the soldiers soaked a sponge in it, put the sponge on a branch of a hyssop plant, and lifted it to Jesus' mouth. **30**When Jesus tasted the vinegar, he said, "It is finished." Then he bowed his head and died.

31This day was Preparation Day, and the next day was a special Sabbath day. Since the religious leaders did not want the bodies to stay on the cross on the Sabbath day, they asked Pilate to order that the legs of the men be broken[n] and the bodies be taken away. **32**So the soldiers came and broke the legs of the first man on the cross beside Jesus. Then they broke the legs of the man on the other cross beside Jesus. **33**But when the soldiers came to Jesus and saw that he was already dead, they did not break his legs. **34**But one of the soldiers stuck his spear into Jesus' side, and at once blood and water came out. **35**(The one who saw this happen is the one who told us this, and whatever he says is true. And he knows that he tells the truth, and he tells it so that you might believe.) **36**These things happened to make the Scripture come true: "Not one of his bones will be broken."[n] **37**And another Scripture says, "They will look at the one they stabbed."[n]

Jesus Is Buried

38Later, Joseph from Arimathea asked Pilate if he could take the body of Jesus. (Joseph was a secret follower of Jesus, because he was afraid of some of

---

19:17 Hebrew language Hebrew or Aramaic, the languages of many people in this region in the first century.

19:28 "I am thirsty." Read Psalms 22:15; 69:21.

19:31 broken The breaking of their bones would make them die sooner.

19:36 "Not one . . . broken." Quotation from Psalm 34:20. The idea is from Exodus 12:46; Numbers 9:12.

19:37 "They . . . stabbed." Quotation from Zechariah 12:10.

the leaders.) Pilate gave his permission,
so Joseph came and took Jesus' body
away. 39Nicodemus, who earlier had
come to Jesus at night, went with Joseph.
He brought about seventy-five pounds of
myrrh and aloes. 40These two men took
Jesus' body and wrapped it with the
spices in pieces of linen cloth, which is
how they bury the dead. 41In the place
where Jesus was crucified, there was a
garden. In the garden was a new tomb
that had never been used before. 42The
men laid Jesus in that tomb because it
was nearby, and they were preparing to
start their Sabbath day.

Jesus' Tomb Is Empty

20 Early on the first day of the week,
Mary Magdalene went to the tomb
while it was still dark. When she saw that
the large stone had been moved away
from the tomb, 2she ran to Simon Peter
and the follower whom Jesus loved. Mary
said, "They have taken the Lord out of
the tomb, and we don't know where they
have put him."

3So Peter and the other follower
started for the tomb. 4They were both
running, but the other follower ran faster
than Peter and reached the tomb first.
5He bent down and looked in and saw the
strips of linen cloth lying there, but he did
not go in. 6Then following him, Simon
Peter arrived and went into the tomb and
saw the strips of linen lying there. 7He
also saw the cloth that had been around
Jesus' head, which was folded up and laid
in a different place from the strips of lin-
en. 8Then the other follower, who had
reached the tomb first, also went in. He
saw and believed. 9(They did not yet understand from the Scriptures that Jesus
must rise from the dead.)

Jesus Appears to Mary Magdalene

10Then the followers went back
home. 11But Mary stood outside the
tomb, crying. As she was crying, she bent
down and looked inside the tomb. 12She
saw two angels dressed in white, sitting
where Jesus' body had been, one at the
head and one at the feet.

13They asked her, "Woman, why are
you crying?"

She answered, "They have taken
away my Lord, and I don't know where
they have put him." 14When Mary said
this, she turned around and saw Jesus
standing there, but she did not know it
was Jesus.

15Jesus asked her, "Woman, why are
you crying? Whom are you looking for?"

Thinking he was the gardener, she
said to him, "Did you take him away, sir?
Tell me where you put him, and I will get
him."

16Jesus said to her, "Mary."

Mary turned toward Jesus and said in
Hebrew,[n] "Rabboni." (This means Teacher.)

17Jesus said to her, "Don't hold on to
me, because I have not yet gone up to the
Father. But go to my brothers and tell
them, 'I am going back to my Father and
your Father, to my God and your God.' "

18Mary Magdalene went and said to
the followers, "I saw the Lord!" And she
told them what Jesus had said to her.

Jesus Appears to His Followers

19When it was evening on the first
day of the week, the followers were together. The doors were locked, because
they were afraid of the older leaders.
Then Jesus came and stood right in the
middle of them and said, "Peace be with
you." 20After he said this, he showed
them his hands and his side. The followers were thrilled when they saw the
Lord.

21Then Jesus said again, "Peace be
with you. As the Father sent me, I now
send you." 22After he said this, he
breathed on them and said, "Receive the
Holy Spirit. 23If you forgive anyone his
sins, they are forgiven. If you don't forgive them, they are not forgiven."

Jesus Appears to Thomas

24Thomas (called Didymus), who was
one of the twelve, was not with them

20:16 Hebrew language Hebrew or Aramaic, the languages of many people in this region in the first century.

when Jesus came. **25**The other followers
kept telling Thomas, "We saw the Lord."
But Thomas said, "I will not believe it
until I see the nail marks in his hands and
put my finger where the nails were and
put my hand into his side."
26A week later the followers were in
the house again, and Thomas was with
them. The doors were locked, but Jesus
came in and stood right in
the middle of them. He
said, "Peace be with
you." **27**Then he said to
Thomas, "Put your finger
here, and look at my
hands. Put your hand
here in my side. Stop be-
ing an unbeliever and be-
lieve."
28Thomas said to him,
"My Lord and my God!"
29Then Jesus told him, "You believe
because you see me. Those who believe
without seeing me will be truly happy."

Those who believe without seeing me will be truly happy.
—John 20:29

Why John Wrote This Book

30Jesus did many other miracles in
the presence of his followers that are not
written in this book. **31**But these are
written so that you may believe that
Jesus is the Christ, the Son of God. Then,
by believing, you may have life through
his name.

Jesus Appears to Seven Followers

21 Later, Jesus showed himself to his
followers again—this time at Lake
Galilee.[a] This is how he showed himself:
2Some of the followers were together:
Simon Peter, Thomas (called Didymus),
Nathanael from Cana in Galilee, the two
sons of Zebedee, and two other followers.
3Simon Peter said, "I am going out to
fish."
The others said, "We will go with
you." So they went out and got into the
boat. They fished that night but caught
nothing.
4Early the next morning Jesus stood
on the shore, but the followers did not
know it was Jesus. **5**Then he said to
them, "Friends, did you catch any fish?"
They answered, "No."
6He said, "Throw your net on the
right side of the boat, and you will find
some." So they did, and they caught so
many fish they could not pull the net back
into the boat.
7The follower whom Jesus loved said
to Peter, "It is the Lord!" When Peter
heard him say this, he wrapped his coat
around himself. (Peter
had taken his clothes off.)
Then he jumped into the
water. **8**The other followers went to shore in the
boat, dragging the net
full of fish. They were
not very far from shore,
only about a hundred
yards. **9**When the followers stepped out of the
boat and onto the shore,
they saw a fire of hot coals. There were
fish on the fire, and there was bread.
10Then Jesus said, "Bring some of the
fish you just caught."
11Simon Peter went into the boat and
pulled the net to the shore. It was full of
big fish, one hundred fifty-three in all, but
even though there were so many, the net
did not tear. **12**Jesus said to them, "Come
and eat." None of the followers dared ask
him, "Who are you?" because they knew
it was the Lord. **13**Jesus came and took
the bread and gave it to them, along with
the fish.
14This was now the third time Jesus
showed himself to his followers after he
was raised from the dead.

Jesus Talks to Peter

15When they finished eating, Jesus
said to Simon Peter, "Simon son of John
do you love me more than these?"
He answered, "Yes, Lord, you know
that I love you."
Jesus said, "Feed my lambs."
16Again Jesus said, "Simon son of
John do you love me?"
He answered, "Yes, Lord, you know
that I love you."
Jesus said, "Take care of my sheep."

21:1 Lake Galilee Literally, "Sea of Tiberias."

LET'S VISIT LAKE GALILEE

John 21

Lake Galilee is almost 13 miles long and about 8 miles wide. The water in it is fresh water, not salt water like in the ocean. Because it is so large, sometimes it is referred to as the Sea of Galilee.

Jesus recruited 11 of his disciples from this area. Many of them were fishermen who worked in Lake Galilee. Because of where the lake is located, terrible storms can sweep down from the mountains creating sudden, violent storms. This is probably the type of storm that Jesus miraculously calmed for his disciples. (Check out Matthew 8:27, p. 1288.)

17A third time he said, "Simon son of
John do you love me?"
Peter was hurt because Jesus asked
him the third time, "Do you love me?"
Peter said, "Lord, you know everything;
you know that I love you!"
He said to him, "Feed my sheep.
18I tell you the truth, when you were
younger, you tied your own belt and went
where you wanted. But when you are old,
you will put out your hands and someone
else will tie you and take you where you
don't want to go." 19(Jesus said this to
show how Peter would die to give glory
to God.) Then Jesus said to Peter, "Follow me!"
20Peter turned and saw that the follower Jesus loved was walking behind
them. (This was the follower who had
leaned against Jesus at the supper and had
said, "Lord, who will turn against you?")
21When Peter saw him behind them, he
asked Jesus, "Lord, what about him?"
22Jesus answered, "If I want him to
live until I come back, that is not your
business. You follow me."
23So a story spread among the followers that this one would not die. But Jesus
did not say he would not die. He only
said, "If I want him to live until I come
back, that is not your business."
24That follower is the one who is telling these things and who has now written
them down. We know that what he says is
true.
25There are many other things Jesus
did. If every one of them were written
down, I suppose the whole world would
not be big enough for all the books that
would be written.

THE GOOD NEWS SPREADS

Hi; it's Luke again. You remember me, right? I wrote the Gospel of Luke. Here's a little secret that I'll let you in on now. I wrote the Gospel of Luke to tell my friend about what Jesus did. Well, I wrote Acts as part two of the story, to tell people what happened in the lives of Jesus' followers after he returned to heaven. Since I was Paul's traveling companion, I actually saw much of what I wrote about in this book. You'll notice that I use the word *we* when I joined Paul. (Check out Acts 16:10 to see when I joined Paul.)

I wrote this book because I wanted to record the happenings in the lives of Jesus' followers, who became known as Christians. (You can read up on that in Acts 11:19–26.) A lot of people title my book "The Acts of the Holy Spirit" because a lot of what happens in this book is the Holy Spirit working in the lives of Jesus' followers. What's really great about this book is that it's not finished. The acts of his followers are still happening today. Isn't that cool? This book is still being written!

JESUS WATCH

The living Savior is the theme of this book. Jesus is alive and well, living in the lives of the early believers, working and struggling with their relationship with him without being able to actually see him. Jesus is presented as both Lord and Savior through the lives of his followers who do miracles, are persecuted, and preach and travel searching for others who haven't heard about Jesus.

my FAVORITE links

OTHER CONNECTIONS

Livin' it

What do you do with the money you have? For some sound advice on how to use your money, connect to Being Wise About Money, Acts 5:1–5.

Quick! Think of a person in your life who really bugs you. How do you handle that kind of person in your life? Download What *Am* I Going to Do?, Acts 15:1–29, for some thoughts on this subject.

Check out these exciting people and places you'll find in the Book of Acts:

- Angels Watching Over Us, Acts 8. Find out about God's special messengers.
- Let's Visit Antioch, Acts 13:1–3. Stop here to find out what made this ancient city important to the early church.
- Let's Visit Athens, Acts 17:15—18:1. Find out more about this famous Greek capital when you link here.
- Let's Visit Philippi, Acts 20. Download the info here about the first European city to have a church.
- Did you know that Paul was a Roman citizen as well as an Israelite? Learn more about A Man of Two Countries, Acts 22.
- Trace the many journeys of Paul when you link to The Life of Paul, Acts 27; 28.

"Hey, Tagg, did you hear about the man who fell asleep during one of Paul's sermons?"

"Wow! That must have been one long sermon! Did you hear that he fell out of the window? Connect to Acts 20:6-12 to get the flash on that story!"

did YOU know?

HEY, CHECK OUT THESE OTHER AMAZING THINGS THAT ARE RECORDED IN THIS BOOK:

Fire falls from the sky, Acts 2:1–13
Paul escapes in a basket, Acts 9:19–25
Peter's miraculous jailbreak, Acts 12:3–19
Shipwrecked!, Acts 27

FAITH links

- You've Got the Power!, **Acts 1:1–8; 2:1–4**
- Flex Your Faith, **Acts 3:1–16**
- The Deadliest Lie, **Acts 5:1–11**
- Put God First, **Acts 5:27–32**
- My Best Serve, **Acts 6:1–6**
- The Person Most Likely to Give?, **Acts 9:36–42**
- The Power of Prayer, **Acts 12:5**
- Kindness Counts, **Acts 14:3**
- You're Welcomed!, **Acts 16:14–15**
- Hope That Doesn't Fail, **Acts 26:4–7**

Luke Writes Another Book

1 To Theophilus.
The first book I wrote was about
everything Jesus began to do and teach
2until the day he was taken up into
heaven. Before this, with the help of the
Holy Spirit, Jesus told the apostles he
had chosen what they should do. 3After
his death, he showed himself to them and
proved in many ways that he was alive.
The apostles saw Jesus during the forty
days after he was raised from the dead,
and he spoke to them about the kingdom
of God. 4Once when he was eating with
them, he told them not to leave Jerusalem. He said, "Wait here to receive the
promise from the Father which I told you
about. 5John baptized people with water,
but in a few days you will be baptized
with the Holy Spirit."

Jesus Is Taken Up Into Heaven

6When the apostles were all together,
they asked Jesus, "Lord, are you now going to give the kingdom back to Israel?"
7Jesus said to them, "The Father is the
only One who has the authority to decide
dates and times. These things are not
for you to know. 8But
when the Holy Spirit
comes to you, you
will receive power.
You will be my wit-
nesses—in Jerusa-
lem, in all of Judea,
in Samaria, and in every part of the
world."

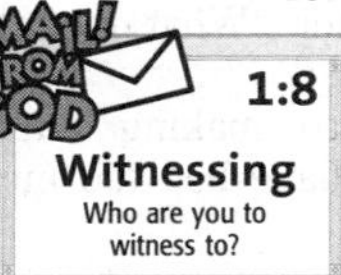

eMAIL! FROM GOD
1:8
Witnessing
Who are you to witness to?

9After he said this, as they were
watching, he was lifted up, and a cloud
hid him from their sight. 10As he was going, they were looking into the sky. Suddenly, two men wearing white clothes
stood beside them. 11They said, "Men of
Galilee, why are you standing here looking into the sky? Jesus, whom you saw
taken up from you into heaven, will come
back in the same way you saw him go."

A New Apostle Is Chosen

12Then they went back to Jerusalem
from the Mount of Olives. (This mountain is about half a mile from Jerusalem.)
13When they entered the city, they went
to the upstairs room where they were
staying. Peter, John, James, Andrew,
Philip, Thomas, Bartholomew, Matthew,

FAITH links

YOU'VE GOT THE POWER!

ACTS 1:1-8; 2:1-4

Could you lift a bus with your bare hands? Probably not. Yet you could lift one if you were behind the controls of a crane or a large tow truck. That would give you the power to do it.

Jesus told followers to wait in Jerusalem for the Holy Spirit to come. He knew that the Holy Spirit would give them the power to do the work that Jesus did. They couldn't do this work on their own. Neither can we. If you know Jesus, you've got the power—the Holy Spirit. He provides the strength you need to do what God wants you to do.

Download these links for more on the Holy Spirit:

The Sign of His Presence, Exodus 40:34–38, p. 130

Keep On Praying, 1 Samuel 1, p. 354

Empty Words, Ezekiel 33:30–33, p. 1127

Ask, Search, Knock, Matthew 7:7–10, p. 1286

Two Birthdays, John 3:1–7, p. 1426

Our Interpreter, Romans 8:26, p. 1528

James son of Alphaeus, Simon (known as
the Zealot), and Judas son of James were
there. **14**They all continued praying together with some women, including
Mary the mother of Jesus, and Jesus'
brothers.

15During this time there was a meeting of the believers (about one hundred
twenty of them). Peter stood up and said,
16-17"Brothers and sisters,[n] in the Scriptures the Holy Spirit said through David
something that must happen involving
Judas. He was one of our own group and
served together with us. He led those
who arrested Jesus." **18**(Judas bought a
field with the money he got for his evil
act. But he fell to his death, his body
burst open, and all his intestines poured
out. **19**Everyone in Jerusalem learned
about this so they named this place
Akeldama. In their language Akeldama
means "Field of Blood.") **20**"In the Book
of Psalms," Peter said, "this is written:

'May his place be empty;
leave no one to live in it.' *Psalm 69:25*

And it is also written:

'Let another man replace him as
leader.' *Psalm 109:8*

21-22"So now a man must become a
witness with us of Jesus' being raised
from the dead. He must be one of the
men who were part of our group during
all the time the Lord Jesus was among
us—from the time John was baptizing
people until the day Jesus was taken up
from us to heaven."

23They put the names of two men before the group. One was Joseph Barsabbas, who was also called Justus. The
other was Matthias. **24-25**The apostles
prayed, "Lord, you know the thoughts of
everyone. Show us which one of these
two you have chosen to do this work.
Show us who should be an apostle in
place of Judas, who turned away and went
where he belongs." **26**Then they used
lots to choose between them, and the lots
showed that Matthias was the one. So he
became an apostle with the other eleven.

The Coming of the Holy Spirit

2 When the day of Pentecost came, they
were all together in one place. **2**Suddenly a noise like a strong, blowing wind
came from heaven and filled the whole
house where they were sitting. **3**They
saw something like flames of fire that
were separated and stood over each person there. **4**They were all filled with the
Holy Spirit, and they began to speak different languages[n] by the power the Holy
Spirit was giving them.

5There were some religious Jews
staying in Jerusalem who were from
every country in the world. **6**When they
heard this noise, a crowd came together.
They were all surprised, because each
one heard them speaking in his own language. **7**They were completely amazed at
this. They said, "Look! Aren't all these
people that we hear speaking from Galilee? **8**Then how is it possible that we
each hear them in our own languages?
We are from different places: **9**Parthia,
Media, Elam, Mesopotamia, Judea, Cappadocia, Pontus, Asia, **10**Phrygia, Pamphylia, Egypt, the areas of Libya near
Cyrene, Rome **11**(both Jews and those
who had become Jews), Crete, and Arabia. But we hear them telling in our own
languages about the great things God has
done!" **12**They were all amazed and confused, asking each other, "What does this
mean?"

13But others were making fun of
them, saying, "They have had too much
wine."

Peter Speaks to the People

14But Peter stood up with the eleven
apostles, and in a loud voice he spoke to
the crowd: "My fellow Jews, and all of
you who are in Jerusalem, listen to me.
Pay attention to what I have to say.
15These people are not drunk, as you
think; it is only nine o'clock in the morning! **16**But Joel the prophet wrote about
what is happening here today:

17'God says: In the last days

1:16–17 Brothers and sisters Although the Greek text says "Brothers" here and throughout this book, the words of the speakers were meant for the entire church, including men and women.
2:4 languages This can also be translated "tongues."

I will pour out my Spirit on all
kinds of people.
Your sons and daughters will
prophesy.
Your young men will see visions,
and your old men will dream
dreams.
18 At that time I will pour out my
Spirit
also on my male slaves and female
slaves,
and they will prophesy.
19 I will show miracles
in the sky and on the earth:
blood, fire, and thick smoke.
20 The sun will become dark,
the moon red as blood,
before the overwhelming and
glorious day of the Lord will
come.
21 Then anyone who calls on the Lord
will be saved.' *Joel 2:28-32*

22"People of Israel, listen to these
words: Jesus from Nazareth was a very
special man. God clearly showed this to
you by the miracles, wonders, and signs
he did through Jesus. You all know this,
because it happened right here among
you. **23**Jesus was given to you, and with
the help of those who don't know the law,
you put him to death by nailing him to a
cross. But this was God's plan which he
had made long ago; he knew all this
would happen. **24**God raised Jesus from
the dead and set him free from the pain of
death, because death could not hold him.
25For David said this about him:

'I keep the Lord before me always.
Because he is close by my side,
I will not be hurt.
26 So I am glad, and I rejoice.
Even my body has hope,
27 because you will not leave me in the
grave.
You will not let your Holy One rot.
28 You will teach me how to live a holy
life.
Being with you will fill me with
joy.' *Psalm 16:8-11*

29"Brothers and sisters, I can tell you
truly that David, our ancestor, died and
was buried. His grave is still here with us
today. **30**He was a prophet and knew God
had promised him that he would make a
person from David's family a king just as
he was.[n] **31**Knowing this before it happened, David talked about the Christ rising from the dead. He said:

'He was not left in the grave.
His body did not rot.'

32So Jesus is the One whom God raised
from the dead. And we are all witnesses
to this. **33**Jesus was lifted up to heaven
and is now at God's right side. The Father has given the Holy Spirit to Jesus
as he promised. So Jesus has poured
out that Spirit, and this is what you now
see and hear. **34**David was not the one
who was lifted up to heaven, but he
said:

'The Lord said to my Lord,
"Sit by me at my right side,
35 until I put your enemies under your
control." '[n] *Psalm 110:1*

36"So, all the people of Israel should
know this truly: God has made Jesus—
the man you nailed to the cross—both
Lord and Christ."

37When the people heard this, they
felt guilty and asked Peter
and the other apos-
tles, "What shall we
do?"

> eMAIL! FROM GOD
> **2:37–38**
> **Salvation**
> What to do when you are saved

38Peter said to
them, "Change your
hearts and lives and
be baptized, each one of you, in the name
of Jesus Christ for the forgiveness of
your sins. And you will receive the gift of
the Holy Spirit. **39**This promise is for
you, for your children, and for all who are
far away. It is for everyone the Lord our
God calls to himself."

40Peter warned them with many
other words. He begged them, "Save
yourselves from the evil of today's people!" **41**Then those people who accepted
what Peter said were baptized. About
three thousand people were added to the
number of believers that day. **42**They
spent their time learning the apostles'

2:30 God . . . was See 2 Samuel 7:13; Psalm 132:11.

2:35 until . . . control Literally, "until I make your enemies a footstool for your feet."

teaching, sharing, breaking bread,* and praying together.

The Believers Share

43The apostles were doing many miracles and signs, and everyone felt great respect for God. **44**All the believers were together and shared everything.

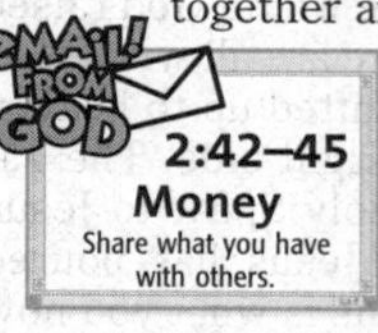

45They would sell their land and the things they owned and then divide the money and give it to anyone who needed it. **46**The believers met together in the Temple every day. They ate together in their homes, happy to share their food with joyful hearts. **47**They praised God and were liked by all the people. Every day the Lord added those who were being saved to the group of believers.

Peter Heals a Crippled Man

3 One day Peter and John went to the Temple at three o'clock, the time set each day for the afternoon prayer service. **2**There, at the Temple gate called Beautiful Gate, was a man who had been crippled all his life. Every day he was carried to this gate to beg for money from the people going into the Temple. **3**The man saw Peter and John going into the Temple and asked them for money. **4**Peter and John looked straight at him and said, "Look at us!" **5**The man looked at them, thinking they were going to give him some money. **6**But Peter said, "I don't have any silver or gold, but I do have something else I can give you. By the power of Jesus Christ from Nazareth, stand up and walk!" **7**Then Peter took the man's right hand and lifted him up. Immediately the man's feet and ankles became strong. **8**He jumped up, stood on his feet, and began to walk. He went into the Temple with them, walking and jumping and praising God. **9-10**All the people recognized him as the crippled man who always sat by the Beautiful Gate begging for money. Now they saw this same man walking and praising God, and they were amazed. They wondered how this could happen.

FAITH links

SHARE AND SHARE ALIKE?

ACTS 2:43-47

On a scale of 1 to 10 (10 being very willing), how willing are you to share what you have with others? Would you rank yourself at 8? 9? Or are you a 3? If we're honest, most of us would say that we have moments when we don't feel like sharing. The first-century Christians believed in sharing everything they had. They shared food, money, and other possessions with each other. What made them feel like sharing? God's love. Why not share some of God's love with someone today?

What do you have to give? Link here for more on giving:

Share What You Have, Exodus 35:5–18, p. 123

Give What You Can, Numbers 7:1–11, p. 186

A Small Percent, Deuteronomy 14:22–23, p. 247

Wisdom About Wealth, Ecclesiastes 5:10–12, p. 878

Your Heart's Desire, Luke 16:13–15, p. 1401

Give to Give, 1 Corinthians 16:1–4, p. 1566

2:42 breaking bread This may mean a meal as in verse 46, or the Lord's Supper, the special meal Jesus told his followers to eat to remember him (Luke 22:14-20).

Peter Speaks to the People

11While the man was holding on to
Peter and John, all the people were
amazed and ran to them at Solomon's
Porch. 12When Peter saw this, he said to
them, "People of Israel, why are you surprised? You are looking at us as if it were
our own power or goodness that made
this man walk. 13The God of Abraham,
Isaac, and Jacob, the God of our ancestors, gave glory to Jesus, his servant. But
you handed him over to be killed. Pilate
decided to let him go free, but you told
Pilate you did not want Jesus. 14You did
not want the One who is holy and good
but asked Pilate to give you a
murderer[n] instead.
15And so you killed
the One who gives
life, but God raised
him from the dead.
We are witnesses to
this. 16It was faith in Jesus that made this
crippled man well. You can see this man,
and you know him. He was made completely well because of trust in Jesus, and
you all saw it happen!
17"Brothers and sisters, I know you
did those things to Jesus because neither
you nor your leaders understood what
you were doing. 18God said through the
prophets that his Christ would suffer and
die. And now God has made these things
come true in this way. 19So you must
change your hearts and lives! Come back
to God, and he will forgive your sins.
Then the Lord will send the time of rest.
20And he will send Jesus, the One he
chose to be the Christ. 21But Jesus must
stay in heaven until the time comes when
all things will be made right again. God
told about this time long ago when he
spoke through his holy prophets. 22Mo-
ses said, 'The Lord your God will give
you a prophet like me, who is one of your
own people. You must listen to everything he tells you. 23Anyone who does
not listen to that prophet will die, cut off
from God's people.'[n] 24Samuel, and all
the other prophets who spoke for God after Samuel, told about this time now.
25You are descendants of the prophets.
You have received the agreement God

eMAIL FROM GOD 3:15
Jesus
What does Jesus give?

FAITH links

FLEX YOUR FAITH

ACTS 3:1-16

Imagine how you'd feel if someone suddenly solved a problem you've had all of your life. That's what happened to a lame man who begged for money outside of the Temple gate. Meeting Peter and John, two of Jesus' followers, changed his life. Through the power of the Holy Spirit, the lame man was healed. He had asked for money, but received something better.

Sometimes, God uses problems in our lives to help us grow in faith. Learning about the way God helps others also helps our faith to grow.

Learning to Trust, Psalm 25:4–5, p. 727

The Watchman, Ezekiel 3:16–22, p. 1088

Your Feet on High Places, Habakkuk 3:18–19, p. 1239

Tell All About Him!, Matthew 28:19, p. 1326

The Way to Heaven, John 14:1–6, p. 1448

Out of Your Mind?, 1 Corinthians 2:16, p. 1547

3:14 murderer Barabbas, the man the crowd asked Pilate to set free instead of Jesus (Luke 23:18).

3:22–23 'The Lord . . . people.' Quotation from Deuteronomy 18:15, 19.

made with your ancestors. He said to
your father Abraham, 'Through your descendants all the nations on the earth will
be blessed.'[n] **26**God has raised up his servant Jesus and sent him to you first to
bless you by turning each of you away
from doing evil."

Peter and John at the Council

4 While Peter and John were speaking
to the people, priests, the captain of
the soldiers that guarded the Temple, and
Sadducees came up to them. **2**They were
upset because the two apostles were
teaching the people and were preaching
that people will rise from the dead
through the power of Jesus. **3**The older
leaders grabbed Peter and John and put
them in jail. Since it was already night,
they kept them in jail until the next day.
4But many of those who had heard Peter
and John preach believed the things they
said. There were now about five thousand in the group of believers.

5The next day the rulers, the older
leaders, and the teachers of the law met
in Jerusalem. **6**Annas the high priest, Caiaphas, John, and Alexander were there,
as well as everyone from the high
priest's family. **7**They made Peter and
John stand before them and then asked
them, "By what power or authority did
you do this?"

8Then Peter, filled with the Holy Spirit, said to them, "Rulers of the people and
you older leaders, **9**are you questioning
us about a good thing that was done to a
crippled man? Are you asking us who
made him well? **10**We want all of you and
all the people to know that this man was
made well by the power of Jesus Christ
from Nazareth. You crucified him, but
God raised him from the dead. This man
was crippled, but he is now well and able
to stand here before you because of the
power of Jesus. **11**Jesus is

> 'the stone'[n] that you builders rejected,
> which has become the
> cornerstone.' *Psalm 118:22*

12Jesus is the only One who can save
people. His name is the only power in the
world that has been given to save people.
We must be saved through him."

13The leaders saw that Peter and
John were not afraid to speak, and they
understood that these men had no special
training or education. So they were
amazed. Then they realized that Peter
and John had been with Jesus. **14**Because
they saw the healed man standing there
beside the two apostles, they could say
nothing against them. **15**After the leaders ordered them to leave the meeting,
they began to talk to each other. **16**They
said, "What shall we do with these men?
Everyone in Jerusalem knows they have
done a great miracle, and we cannot say it
is not true. **17**But to keep it from spreading among the people, we must warn
them not to talk to people anymore using
that name."

18So they called Peter and John in
again and told them not to speak or to
teach at all in the name of Jesus. **19**But
Peter and John an-
swered them, "You
decide what God
would want. Should
we obey you or
God? **20**We cannot
keep quiet. We must
speak about what we have seen and
heard." **21**The leaders warned the apostles again and let them go free. They
could not find a way to punish them, because all the people were praising God
for what had been done. **22**The man who
received the miracle of healing was more
than forty years old.

EMAIL FROM GOD
4:19–20
Responsibility
What are you responsible for?

The Believers Pray

23After Peter and John left the meeting of leaders, they went to their own
group and told them everything the leading priests and the older leaders had said
to them. **24**When the believers heard
this, they prayed to God together, "Lord,
you are the One who made the sky, the
earth, the sea, and everything in them.
25By the Holy Spirit, through our father
David your servant, you said:

> 'Why are the nations so angry?

3:25 'Through . . . blessed.' Quotation from Genesis 22:18; 26:4.

4:11 stone A symbol meaning Jesus.

Why are the people making
useless plans?
26 The kings of the earth prepare to
fight,
and their leaders make plans
together
against the Lord
and his Christ.' *Psalm 2:1-2*
27These things really happened when
Herod, Pontius Pilate, and some of the
people all came together against Jesus
here in Jerusalem. Jesus is your holy servant, the One you made to be the Christ.
28These people made your plan happen
because of your power and your will.
29And now, Lord, listen to their threats.
Lord, help us, your servants, to speak
your word without fear. 30Help us to be
brave by showing us your power to heal.
Give proofs and make miracles happen by
the power of Jesus, your holy servant."
31After they had prayed, the place
where they were meeting was shaken.
They were all filled with the Holy Spirit,
and they spoke God's word without fear.

The Believers Share

32The group of believers were united
in their hearts and spirit. All those in the
group acted as though their private property belonged to everyone in the group.
In fact, they shared everything. 33With
great power the apostles were telling
people that the Lord Jesus was truly
raised from the dead. And God blessed all
the believers very much. 34No one in the
group needed anything. From time to
time those who owned fields or houses
sold them, brought the money, 35and
gave it to the apostles. Then the money
was given to anyone who needed it.
36One of the believers was named Joseph, a Levite born in Cyprus. The apostles called him Barnabas (which means
"one who encourages"). 37Joseph owned
a field, sold it, brought the money, and
gave it to the apostles.

FAITH links

AN ENERGY BOOST

ACTS 4:31

Some cartoon superheroes have to put on a special ring or costume in order to gain their super powers. If they didn't have access to those items, they couldn't save the world!

The apostles had access to an amazing power far greater than any made-up superhero's. When the apostles asked God to show his power to them, he made the building shake and filled them with the Holy Spirit. That same power is available to us. God may not cause a building to shake when you pray. But the Holy Spirit can fill you with courage when you're afraid. Now, *that's* power!

Need a power boost? Connect here:

What Will You Risk?, Joshua 2, p. 278

Good Times and Bad, 1 Kings 17, p. 462

A Message of Courage and Hope, 2 Kings 19:4–10, p. 505

911, Psalm 28:6, p. 730

Facing Your Fears, Matthew 8:23–27, p. 1288

Prayer Anywhere, Mark 1:35, p. 1331

Ananias and Sapphira Die

5 But a man named Ananias and his wife
Sapphira sold some land. 2He kept
back part of the money for himself; his
wife knew about this and agreed to it. But
he brought the rest of the money and
gave it to the apostles. 3Peter said, "Ananias, why did you let Satan rule your
thoughts to lie to the Holy Spirit and to
keep for yourself part of the money you

Livin' it

HANDLING MY MONEY

Acts 5:1–5

Being Wise About Money Imagine entering a contest and winning the grand prize of $1,000. Or maybe you received $500 for your birthday—from a rich relative you didn't know you had! What would you do with that money—spend it right away or save some of it? Would you give some of it away?

Just like everything else you have, your money is a blessing from God. God wants you to use your money wisely and think of it as another way to serve him and other people. (Check Ecclesiastes 5:10–12, p. 878.) Want to be wise about money? Don't make it the center of your life.

MORE FAITH links

"Tagg, what are you going to do with that big check you got for your birthday?"

"Well, I could buy an awful lot of ice cream cones with it. What flavor do you like?"

"Maybe you better plan first how to spend your money. Check out these Faithlinks for some help."

Give What You Can, Numbers 7:1–11, p. 186

- Do you give some of your money as a church offering? What are some of the things that the offering money is used for? What if you don't have much money to give? We all have the responsibility to give what we can, whether it's money, time, or help.

A Halfhearted Offering, Malachi 1:6–14, p. 1268

- How would you react if you asked your friend for a piece of gum and he offered you one he had already chewed? Yuck! This Faithlink tells how God feels about halfhearted offerings.

More Money?, 1 Timothy 6:10, p. 1649

- What would you do if you won a million dollars? How do you think it would change your life? Can money make a person happy? Paul said that loving money leads to all kinds of evil. He didn't say *money* is sinful—but the love of it can make a person greedy. Money should be used wisely. How will you use your money?

my FAVORITE links

__________ __________

__________ __________

__________ __________

received for the land? **4**Before you sold
the land, it belonged to you. And even after you sold it, you could have used the
money any way you wanted. Why did you
think of doing this? You lied to God, not
to us!" **5-6**When Ananias heard this, he
fell down and died. Some young men
came in, wrapped up his body, carried it
out, and buried it. And everyone who
heard about this was filled with fear.
7About three hours later his wife
came in, but she did not know what had
happened. **8**Peter said to her, "Tell me,
was the money you got for your field this
much?"

Sapphira answered, "Yes, that was the
price."

9Peter said to her, "Why did you and
your husband agree to test the Spirit of
the Lord? Look! The men who buried
your husband are at the door, and they
will carry you out." **10**At that moment
Sapphira fell down by his feet and died.
When the young men came in and saw
that she was dead, they carried her out
and buried her beside her husband.
11The whole church and all the others
who heard about these things were filled
with fear.

The Apostles Heal Many

12The apostles did many signs and
miracles among the people. And they
would all meet together on Solomon's
Porch. **13**None of the others dared to join
them, but all the people respected them.
14More and more men and women believed in the Lord and were added to the
group of believers. **15**The people placed
their sick on beds and mats in the streets,
hoping that when Peter passed by at least
his shadow might fall on them. **16**Crowds
came from all the towns around Jerusalem, bringing their sick and those who
were bothered by evil spirits, and all of
them were healed.

Leaders Try to Stop the Apostles

17The high priest and all his friends (a
group called the Sadducees) became very
jealous. **18**They took the apostles and put
them in jail. **19**But during the night, an
angel of the Lord opened the doors of the
jail and led the apostles outside. The angel said, **20**"Go stand in the Temple and
tell the people everything about this new
life." **21**When the apostles heard this,
they obeyed and went into the Temple
early in the morning and continued
teaching.

When the high priest and his friends
arrived, they called a meeting of the leaders and all the important older men. They
sent some men to the jail to bring the
apostles to them. **22**But, upon arriving,

THE DEADLIEST LIE

ACTS 5:1-11

One of the scariest stories in the Bible has to be the story of Ananias and Sapphira. Both lied to the apostle Peter about the price of some land that they sold. As the result of that lie, both died on the spot! That scared everyone!

God hates lying. (See Proverbs 6:17, p. 833.) He wants his followers to feel the same way. Do you hate it enough not to do it?

An Honest Reputation, Nehemiah 13:13, p. 644

Who Do You Prefer?, Proverbs 3:32, p. 830

What's Wrong About Rumors, Jeremiah 29:24–32, p. 1032

The Whole Truth, John 8:31–32, 45, p. 1438

The Worst Chore, John 13:3–17, p. 1447

With All Your Heart, Colossians 3:23, p. 1626

the officers could not find the apostles. So they went back and reported to the leaders. **23**They said, "The jail was closed and locked, and the guards were standing at the doors. But when we opened the doors, the jail was empty!" **24**Hearing this, the captain of the Temple guards and the leading priests were confused and wondered what was happening.

25Then someone came and told them, "Listen! The men you put in jail are standing in the Temple teaching the people." **26**Then the captain and his men went out and brought the apostles back. But the soldiers did not use force, because they were afraid the people would stone them to death.

27The soldiers brought the apostles to the meeting and made them stand before the leaders. The high priest questioned them, **28**saying, "We gave you strict orders not to continue teaching in that name. But look, you have filled Jerusalem with your teaching and are trying to make us responsible for this man's death."

29Peter and the other apostles answered, "We must obey God, not human authority! **30**You killed Jesus by hanging him on a cross. But God, the God of our ancestors, raised Jesus up from the dead! **31**Jesus is the One whom God raised to be on his right side, as Leader and Savior. Through him, all people could change their hearts and lives and have their sins forgiven. **32**We saw all these things happen. The Holy Spirit, whom God has given to all who obey him, also proves these things are true."

EMAIL! FROM GOD 5:29

Obedience

Check out who you should obey.

33When the leaders heard this, they became angry and wanted to kill them. **34**But a Pharisee named Gamaliel stood up in the meeting. He was a teacher of the law, and all the people respected him. He ordered the apostles to leave the meeting for a little while. **35**Then he said, "People of Israel, be careful what you are planning to do to these men. **36**Remember when Theudas appeared? He said he was a great man, and about four hundred men joined him. But he was killed, and all his followers were scattered; they were

FAITH links

PUT GOD FIRST

ACTS 5:27-32

Sometimes you can get into trouble for doing the right thing. Peter and John, two followers of Jesus, were thrown into prison for healing a man at the Temple. The religious leaders demanded to know by whose authority they healed the man. After hearing that Jesus helped them, Peter and John were told not to talk to people in Jesus' name. They chose to obey God, rather than do what the leaders told them to do.

God wants you to obey people in authority. But he wants you to obey him first of all. Put God first!

God wants to be No. 1 in your life. Link here to find out more:

Following the Crowd, Numbers 13; 14, p. 193

I'll Never Forget What's-His-Name, Deuteronomy 8, p. 239

A Hopeful Future, Jeremiah 29:11, p. 1031

A Blueprint for Living, Amos 5:14–15, p. 1200

The Choices of a Choice, Luke 5:1–11, p. 1375

Keeping Clean, 2 Corinthians 7:1, p. 1576

able to do nothing. 37Later, a man named
Judas came from Galilee at the time of
the registration.[n] He also led a group of
followers and was killed, and all his followers were scattered. 38And so now I
tell you: Stay away from these men, and
leave them alone. If their plan comes
from human authority, it will fail. 39But if
it is from God, you will not be able to stop
them. You might even be fighting against
God himself!"
The leaders agreed with what Gamaliel said. 40They called the apostles in,
beat them, and told them not to speak in
the name of Jesus again. Then they let
them go free. 41The apostles left the
meeting full of joy because they were
given the honor of suffering disgrace for
Jesus. 42Every day in the Temple and in
people's homes they continued teaching
the people and telling the Good News—
that Jesus is the Christ.

Seven Leaders Are Chosen

6 The number of followers was growing. But during this same time, the
Greek-speaking followers had an argument with the other followers. The
Greek-speaking widows were not getting
their share of the food that was given out
every day. 2The twelve apostles called
the whole group of followers together
and said, "It is not right for us to stop our
work of teaching God's word in order to
serve tables. 3So, brothers and sisters,
choose seven of your own men who are
good, full of the Spirit and full of wisdom.
We will put them in charge of this work.
4Then we can continue to pray and to
teach the word of God."
5The whole group liked the idea, so
they chose these seven men: Stephen (a
man with great faith and full of the Holy
Spirit), Philip,[n] Procorus, Nicanor, Ti-
mon, Parmenas, and Nicolas (a man from
Antioch who had become a follower of
the Jewish religion). 6Then they put
these men before the apostles, who
prayed and laid their hands[n] on them.
7The word of God was continuing to
spread. The group of followers in Jerusalem increased, and a great number of the
Jewish priests believed and obeyed.

FAITH links

MY BEST SERVE 

ACTS 6:1-6

Christians in the first century had a problem. The poor weren't being helped. But the apostles had too much work to do. They wanted to be able to preach and teach. So, how did they solve the problem? They chose other believers to help with the work.

God wants his people to work together. One person should not be expected to do everything. Each person in the church is good at something and is important to the church. What are you good at? How can you help out in your church?

Everyone Can Help, Numbers 4, p. 181

Your Response to Responsibility, Ruth 2:1–7, p. 346

Your Best Work, 1 Kings 6, p. 443

Operation Cooperation, Ezra 1:5, p. 609

The Way to Greatness, Matthew 20:20–28, p. 1309

Help for the Body, Romans 12:3–8, p. 1536

5:37 registration Census. A counting of all the people and the things they own.
6:5 Philip Not the apostle named Philip.
6:6 laid their hands The laying on of hands had many purposes, including the giving of a blessing, power, or authority.

Stephen Is Accused

8Stephen was richly blessed by God
who gave him the power to do great miracles and signs among the people. **9**But
some people were against him. They belonged to the synagogue of Free Men* (as
it was called), which included people
from Cyrene, Alexandria, Cilicia, and
Asia. They all came and argued with Stephen.

10But the Spirit was helping him to
speak with wisdom, and his words were
so strong that they could not argue with
him. **11**So they secretly urged some men
to say, "We heard Stephen speak against
Moses and against God."

12This upset the people, the older
leaders, and the teachers of the law. They
came and grabbed Stephen and brought
him to a meeting of the leaders. **13**They
brought in some people to tell lies about
Stephen, saying, "This man is always
speaking against this holy place and the
law of Moses. **14**We heard him say that
Jesus from Nazareth will destroy this
place and that Jesus will change the customs Moses gave us." **15**All the people in
the meeting were watching Stephen
closely and saw that his face looked like
the face of an angel.

Stephen's Speech

7 The high priest said to Stephen, "Are
these things true?"

2Stephen answered, "Brothers and
fathers, listen to me. Our glorious God
appeared to Abraham, our ancestor, in
Mesopotamia before he lived in Haran.
3God said to Abraham, 'Leave your country and your relatives, and go to the land I
will show you.'* **4**So Abraham left the
country of Chaldea and went to live in
Haran. After Abraham's father died, God
sent him to this place where you now
live. **5**God did not give Abraham any of
this land, not even a foot of it. But God
promised that he would give this land to
him and his descendants, even before
Abraham had a child. **6**This is what God
said to him: 'Your descendants will be
strangers in a land they don't own. The
people there will make them slaves and
will mistreat them for four hundred
years. **7**But I will punish the nation
where they are slaves. Then your descendants will leave that land and will
worship me in this place.'* **8**God made an
agreement with Abraham, the sign of
which was circumcision. And so when
Abraham had his son Isaac, Abraham circumcised him when he was eight days
old. Isaac also circumcised his son Jacob,
and Jacob did the same for his sons, the
twelve ancestors* of our people.

9"Jacob's sons became jealous of Joseph and sold him to be a slave
in Egypt. But God
was with him **10**and
saved him from all
his troubles. The
king of Egypt liked
Joseph and respect-
ed him because of the wisdom God gave
him. The king made him governor of
Egypt and put him in charge of all the
people in his palace.

EMAIL! FROM GOD
7:9
Jealousy
What can jealousy cause?

11"Then all the land of Egypt and Canaan became so dry that nothing would
grow, and the people suffered very much.
Jacob's sons, our ancestors, could not
find anything to eat. **12**But when Jacob
heard there was grain in Egypt, he sent
his sons there. This was their first trip to
Egypt. **13**When they went there a second
time, Joseph told his brothers who he
was, and the king learned about Joseph's
family. **14**Then Joseph sent messengers
to invite Jacob, his father, to come to
Egypt along with all his relatives
(seventy-five persons altogether). **15**So
Jacob went down to Egypt, where he and
his sons died. **16**Later their bodies were
moved to Shechem and put in a grave
there. (It was the same grave Abraham
had bought for a sum of money from the
sons of Hamor in Shechem.)

6:9 Free Men Jewish people who had been slaves or whose fathers had been slaves, but were now free.

7:3 'Leave . . . you.' Quotation from Genesis 12:1.

7:7 'Your descendants . . . place.' Quotation from Genesis 15:13-14 and Exodus 3:12.

7:8 twelve ancestors Important ancestors of the people of Israel; the leaders of the twelve tribes of Israel.

17"The promise God made to Abraham was soon to come true, and the number of people in Egypt grew large.
18Then a new king, who did not know
who Joseph was, began to rule Egypt.
19This king tricked our people and was
cruel to our ancestors, forcing them to
leave their babies outside to die. **20**At
this time Moses was born, and he was
very beautiful. For three months Moses
was cared for in his father's house.
21When they put Moses outside, the
king's daughter adopted him and raised
him as if he were her own son. **22**The
Egyptians taught Moses everything they
knew, and he was a powerful man in what
he said and did.

23"When Moses was about forty
years old, he thought it would be good to
visit his own people, the people of Israel.
24Moses saw an Egyptian mistreating
one of his people, so he defended the Israelite and punished the Egyptian by killing him. **25**Moses thought his own people
would understand that God was using
him to save them, but they did not.
26The next day when Moses saw two
men of Israel fighting, he tried to make
peace between them. He said, 'Men, you
are brothers. Why are you hurting each
other?' **27**The man who was hurting the
other pushed Moses away and said, 'Who
made you our ruler and judge? **28**Are you
going to kill me as you killed the Egyptian yesterday?'[n] **29**When Moses heard
him say this, he left Egypt and went to
live in the land of Midian where he was a
stranger. While Moses lived in Midian, he
had two sons.

30"Forty years later an angel appeared to Moses in the flames of a burning bush as he was in the desert near
Mount Sinai. **31**When Moses saw this, he
was amazed and went near to look closer.
Moses heard the Lord's voice say, **32**'I
am the God of your ancestors, the God of
Abraham, Isaac, and Jacob.'[n] Moses began to shake with fear and was afraid to
look. **33**The Lord said to him, 'Take off
your sandals, because you are standing
on holy ground. **34**I have seen the troubles my people have suffered in Egypt. I
have heard their cries and have come
down to save them. And now, Moses, I
am sending you back to Egypt.'[n]

35"This Moses was the same man the
two men of Israel rejected, saying, 'Who
made you a ruler and judge?'[n] Moses is
the same man God sent to be a ruler and
savior, with the help of the angel that
Moses saw in the burning bush. **36**So
Moses led the people out of Egypt. He
worked miracles and signs in Egypt, at
the Red Sea, and then in the desert for
forty years. **37**This is the same Moses
that said to the people of Israel, 'God will
give you a prophet like me, who is one of
your own people.'[n] **38**This is the Moses
who was with the gathering of the Israelites in the desert. He was with the angel
that spoke to him at Mount Sinai, and he
was with our ancestors. He received
commands from God that give life, and he
gave those commands to us.

39"But our ancestors did not want to
obey Moses. They rejected him and
wanted to go back to Egypt. **40**They said
to Aaron, 'Make us gods who will lead us.
Moses led us out of Egypt, but we don't
know what has happened to him.'[n] **41**So
the people made an idol that looked like a
calf. Then they brought sacrifices to it
and were proud of what they had made
with their own hands. **42**But God turned
against them and did not try to stop them
from worshiping the sun, moon, and
stars. This is what is written in the book
of the prophets: God says,

'People of Israel, you did not bring
me sacrifices and offerings
while you traveled in the desert
for forty years.
43You have carried with you
the tent to worship Molech

7:27–28 'Who . . . yesterday?' Quotation from Exodus 2:14.

7:32 'I am . . . Jacob.' Quotation from Exodus 3:6.

7:33–34 'Take . . . Egypt.' Quotation from Exodus 3:5-10.

7:35 'Who . . . judge?' Quotation from Exodus 2:14.

7:37 'God . . . people.' Quotation from Deuteronomy 18:15.

7:40 'Make . . . him.' Quotation from Exodus 32:1.

and the idols of the star god
Rephan that you made to
worship.
So I will send you away beyond
Babylon.' *Amos 5:25-27*
44"The Holy Tent where God spoke
to our ancestors was with them in the
desert. God told Moses how to make this
Tent, and he made it like the plan God
showed him. **45**Later, Joshua led our ancestors to capture the lands of the other
nations. Our people went in, and God
forced the other people out. When our
people went into this new land, they took
with them this same Tent they had received from their ancestors. They kept it
until the time of David, **46**who pleased
God and asked God to let him build a
house for him, the God of Jacob. **47**But
Solomon was the one who built the Temple.
48"But the Most High does not live in
houses that people build with their
hands. As the prophet says:
49'Heaven is my throne,
and the earth is my footstool.
So do you think you can build a house
for me? says the Lord.
Do I need a place to rest?
50Remember, my hand made all these
things!'" *Isaiah 66:1-2*
51Stephen continued speaking: "You
stubborn people! You have not given your
hearts to God, nor will you listen to him!
You are always against what the Holy
Spirit is trying to tell you, just as your
ancestors were. **52**Your ancestors tried
to hurt every prophet who ever lived.
Those prophets said long ago that the
One who is good would come, but your
ancestors killed them. And now you have
turned against and killed the One who is
good. **53**You received the law of Moses,
which God gave you through his angels,
but you haven't obeyed it."

Stephen Is Killed

54When the leaders heard this, they
became furious. They were so mad they
were grinding their teeth at Stephen.
55But Stephen was full of the Holy Spirit.
He looked up to heaven and saw the glory
of God and Jesus standing at God's right
side. **56**He said, "Look! I see heaven
open and the Son of Man standing at
God's right side."
57Then they shouted loudly and covered their ears and all ran at Stephen.
58They took him out of the city and began to throw stones at him to kill him.
And those who told lies against Stephen
left their coats with a young man named
Saul. **59**While they were throwing
stones, Stephen prayed, "Lord Jesus, receive my spirit." **60**He fell on his knees
and cried in a loud voice, "Lord, do not
hold this sin against them." After Stephen said this, he died.
8 Saul agreed that the killing of Stephen
was good.

Troubles for the Believers

On that day the church of Jerusalem
began to be persecuted, and all the believers, except the apostles, were scattered throughout Judea and Samaria.
2And some religious people buried
Stephen and cried loudly for him. **3**Saul
was also trying to destroy the church, going from house to house, dragging out
men and women and putting them in jail.
4And wherever they were scattered,
they told people the Good News.

Philip Preaches in Samaria

5Philip went to the city of Samaria and
preached about the Christ. **6**When the
people there heard Philip and saw the
miracles he was doing, they all listened
carefully to what he said. **7**Many of these
people had evil spirits in them, but Philip
made the evil spirits leave. The spirits
made a loud noise when they came out.
Philip also healed many weak and crippled people there. **8**So the people in that
city were very happy.
9But there was a man named Simon in
that city. Before Philip came there, Simon
had practiced magic and amazed all the
people of Samaria. He bragged and called
himself a great man. **10**All the people—
the least important and the most important—paid attention to Simon, saying,
"This man has the power of God, called
'the Great Power'!" **11**Simon had amazed
them with his magic so long that the peo-

ANGELS WATCHING OVER US

Acts 8

In the New Testament, angels are special messengers for God. (See Hebrews 1:14, p. 1668.) An angel named Gabriel brought the news to Mary that she would give birth to Jesus, the Messiah. (Look at Luke 1:26–38, p. 1365.) Besides passing along messages, angels were also used by God to guide and protect his children. On several occasions, angels assisted Jesus during his ministry on earth. For example, angels helped Jesus while he was in the desert (Matthew 4:11, p. 1279) and helped roll away the stone from the tomb. (Look up Matthew 28:2–6, p. 1326.) Angels still exist today and still do God's work. We don't always see them, but they are there.

Here are some New Testament events that involved angels:

An angel told Zechariah about the birth of his son	Luke 1:11–20, p. 1365
An angel warned Joseph about Herod's plan to kill Jesus; told Joseph about Herod's death	Matthew 2:13, 19–20, p. 1276
Angels announced Jesus' birth to shepherds	Luke 2:8–15, p. 1368
Angels helped Jesus during his temptation	Matthew 4:11, p. 1279
Angels opened the grave and announced Jesus' resurrection	Matthew 28:2–7, p. 1326
An angel sent Philip into the desert to meet the eunuch	Acts 8:26–27, p. 1478
An angel instructed Cornelius to send for Peter	Acts 10:3–8, p. 1481
An angel released Peter from prison	Acts 12:7, p. 1485
An angel made Herod sick	Acts 12:23, p. 1486
An angel reassured Paul in a storm	Acts 27:23–24, p. 1512

ple became his followers. **12**But when
Philip told them the Good News about
the kingdom of God and the power of
Jesus Christ, men and women believed
Philip and were baptized. **13**Simon himself believed, and after he was baptized,
he stayed very close to Philip. When he
saw the miracles and the powerful things
Philip did, Simon was amazed.

14When the apostles who were still in

Jerusalem heard that the people of Samaria had accepted the word of God, they
sent Peter and John to them. **15**When Peter and John arrived, they prayed that the
Samaritan believers might receive the
Holy Spirit. **16**These people had been
baptized in the name of the Lord Jesus,
but the Holy Spirit had not yet come
upon any of them. **17**Then, when the two
apostles began laying their hands on the
people, they received the Holy Spirit.

18Simon saw that the Spirit was given
to people when the apostles laid their
hands on them. So he offered the apostles
money, **19**saying, "Give me also this power so that anyone on whom I lay my
hands will receive the Holy Spirit."

20Peter said to him, "You and your
money should both be destroyed, because you thought you could buy God's
gift with money. **21**You cannot share with
us in this work since your heart is not
right before God. **22**Change your heart!
Turn away from this evil thing you have
done, and pray to the Lord. Maybe he will
forgive you for thinking this. **23**I see that
you are full of bitter jealousy and ruled by
sin."

24Simon answered, "Both of you pray
for me to the Lord so the things you have
said will not happen to me."

25After Peter and John told the people
what they had seen Jesus do and after
they had spoken the message of the Lord,
they went back to Jerusalem. On the way,
they went through many Samaritan
towns and preached the Good News to
the people.

Philip Teaches an Ethiopian

26An angel of the Lord said to Philip,
"Get ready and go south to the road that
leads down to Gaza from Jerusalem—the
desert road." **27**So Philip got ready and
went. On the road he saw a man from
Ethiopia, a eunuch. He was an important
officer in the service of Candace, the
queen of the Ethiopians; he was responsible for taking care of all her money. He
had gone to Jerusalem to worship.
28Now, as he was on his way home, he
was sitting in his chariot reading from the
Book of Isaiah, the prophet. **29**The Spirit
said to Philip, "Go to that chariot and stay
near it."

30So when Philip ran toward the chariot, he heard the man reading from Isaiah
the prophet. Philip asked, "Do you understand what you are reading?"

31He answered, "How can I understand unless someone explains it to me?"
Then he invited Philip to climb in and sit
with him. **32**The portion of Scripture he
was reading was this:

"He was like a sheep being led to be
killed.
He was quiet, as a lamb is quiet
while its wool is being cut;
he never opened his mouth.
33 He was shamed and was treated
unfairly.
He died without children to continue
his family.
His life on earth has ended."

Isaiah 53:7-8

34The officer said to Philip, "Please
tell me, who is the prophet talking about—
himself or someone else?" **35**Philip began
to speak, and starting with this same
Scripture, he told the man the Good News
about Jesus.

36While they were traveling down the
road, they came to some water. The officer said, "Look, here is water. What is
stopping me from being baptized?"
37[n] **38**Then the officer commanded the
chariot to stop. Both Philip and the officer went down into the water, and Philip
baptized him. **39**When they came up out
of the water, the Spirit of the Lord took
Philip away; the officer never saw him
again. And the officer continued on his
way home, full of joy. **40**But Philip appeared in a city called Azotus and
preached the Good News in all the towns
on the way from Azotus to Caesarea.

Saul Is Converted

9 In Jerusalem Saul was still threatening the followers of the Lord by saying he would kill them. So he went to the

8:37 Verse 37 Some late copies of Acts add verse 37: "Philip answered, 'If you believe with all your heart, you can.' The officer said, 'I believe that Jesus Christ is the Son of God.' "

high priest 2and asked him to write letters to the synagogues in the city of Damascus. Then if Saul found any followers
of Christ's Way, men or women, he would
arrest them and bring them back to Jerusalem.

3So Saul headed toward Damascus.
As he came near the city, a bright light
from heaven suddenly flashed around
him. 4Saul fell to the ground and heard a
voice saying to him, "Saul, Saul! Why are
you persecuting me?"

5Saul said, "Who are you, Lord?"

The voice answered, "I am Jesus,
whom you are persecuting. 6Get up now
and go into the city. Someone there will
tell you what you must do."

7The people traveling with Saul stood
there but said nothing. They heard the
voice, but they saw no one. 8Saul got up
from the ground and opened his eyes, but
he could not see. So those with Saul took
his hand and led him into Damascus. 9For
three days Saul could not see and did not
eat or drink.

10There was a follower of Jesus in
Damascus named Ananias. The Lord
spoke to Ananias in a vision, "Ananias!"

Ananias answered, "Here I am, Lord."

11The Lord said to him, "Get up and
go to Straight Street. Find the house of
Judas,[n] and ask for a man named Saul
from the city of Tarsus. He is there now,
praying. 12Saul has seen a vision in
which a man named Ananias comes to
him and lays his hands on him. Then he is
able to see again."

13But Ananias answered, "Lord, many
people have told me about this man and
the terrible things he did to your holy people in Jerusalem. 14Now he has come
here to Damascus, and the leading priests
have given him the power to arrest everyone who worships you."

15But the Lord said to Ananias, "Go! I
have chosen Saul for an important work.
He must tell about me to those who are
not Jews, to kings, and to the people of
Israel. 16I will show him how much he
must suffer for my name."

17So Ananias went to the house of Judas. He laid his hands on Saul and said,
"Brother Saul, the Lord Jesus sent me.
He is the one you saw on the road on
your way here. He sent me so that you
can see again and be filled with the Holy
Spirit." 18Immediately, something that
looked like fish scales fell from Saul's
eyes, and he was able to see again! Then
Saul got up and was baptized. 19After he
ate some food, his strength returned.

Saul Preaches in Damascus

Saul stayed with the followers of
Jesus in Damascus for a few days. 20Soon
he began to preach about Jesus in the
synagogues, saying, "Jesus is the Son of
God."

21All the people who heard him were
amazed. They said, "This is the man who
was in Jerusalem trying to destroy those
who trust in this name! He came here to
arrest the followers of Jesus and take
them back to the leading priests."

22But Saul grew more powerful. His
proofs that Jesus is the Christ were so
strong that his own people in Damascus
could not argue with him.

23After many days, they made plans
to kill Saul. 24They were watching the
city gates day and night, but Saul learned
about their plan. 25One night some followers of Saul helped him leave the city
by lowering him in a basket through an
opening in the city wall.

Saul Preaches in Jerusalem

26When Saul went to Jerusalem, he
tried to join the group of followers, but
they were all afraid of him. They did not
believe he was really a follower. 27But
Barnabas accepted Saul and took him to
the apostles. Barnabas explained to them
that Saul had seen the Lord on the road
and the Lord had spoken to Saul. Then he
told them how boldly Saul had preached
in the name of Jesus in Damascus.

28And so Saul stayed with the followers, going everywhere in Jerusalem,
preaching boldly in the name of the Lord.
29He would often talk and argue with the
Jewish people who spoke Greek, but they
were trying to kill him. 30When the

9:11 Judas This is not either of the apostles named Judas.

A FRIEND IN NEED

ACTS 9:27

How would you react if the meanest person you know suddenly became nice? Saul, who later became known as the apostle Paul, used to be an enemy of Christians. But one day, he became a follower of Jesus. He needed a friend to teach him more about Jesus and to show the other believers that he could be trusted. Barnabas was that friend. God looks for people who are willing to befriend those who need Jesus. Are you willing?

Link here to find out more about sharing Jesus with your friends:

The Gift of Friendship, 1 Samuel 18:1–3; 19, p. 381

A Life-Saving Message, Esther 2:19–22, p. 650

Jesus' Mission and Yours, Isaiah 61:1–2, p. 978

Tell All About Him!, Matthew 28:19, p. 1326

Quick to Forgive?, Mark 11:25, p. 1349

As Strong as Superman?, Philippians 4:13, p. 1615

followers learned about this, they took
Saul to Caesarea and from there sent him
to Tarsus.
31The church everywhere in Judea,
Galilee, and Samaria had a time of peace

9:31 **Encouragement**
Who is your source of encouragement?

and became stronger. Respecting the Lord by the way they lived, and being encouraged by the Holy Spirit, the group of believers continued to grow.

Peter Heals Aeneas

32As Peter was traveling through all
the area, he visited God's people who
lived in Lydda. 33There he met a man
named Aeneas, who was paralyzed and
had not been able to leave his bed for the
past eight years. 34Peter said to him,
"Aeneas, Jesus Christ heals you. Stand up
and make your bed." Aeneas stood up immediately. 35All the people living in Lydda and on the Plain of Sharon saw him and
turned to the Lord.

Peter Heals Tabitha

36In the city of Joppa there was a follower named Tabitha (whose Greek
name was Dorcas). She was always doing
good deeds and kind acts. 37While Peter
was in Lydda, Tabitha became sick and
died. Her body was washed and put in a
room upstairs. 38Since Lydda is near
Joppa and the followers in Joppa heard
that Peter was in Lydda, they sent two
messengers to Peter. They begged him,
"Hurry, please come to us!" 39So Peter
got ready and went with them. When he
arrived, they took him to the upstairs
room where all the widows stood around
Peter, crying. They showed him the
shirts and coats Tabitha had made when
she was still alive. 40Peter sent everyone
out of the room and kneeled and prayed.
Then he turned to the body and said,
"Tabitha, stand up." She opened her
eyes, and when she saw Peter, she sat up.
41He gave her his hand and helped her
up. Then he called the saints and the widows into the room and showed them that
Tabitha was alive. 42People everywhere
in Joppa learned about this, and many believed in the Lord. 43Peter stayed in Joppa for many days with a man named
Simon who was a tanner.

FAITH links

THE PERSON MOST LIKELY TO GIVE?

ACTS 9:36-42

Who is the kindest, most giving person you know? If the Christians in Joppa were asked this question, they would say Tabitha. Tabitha, also called Dorcas, used her sewing ability to give to others. Because she was so loving to her community, the people in the town made a special request of the apostle Peter. When she died, he brought her back to life through the Holy Spirit!

Tabitha's selfless giving is an example for any Christian. Even if you don't know how to sew a button, you can still use your abilities to help someone. Ready, set, serve!

Giving Your Part, Leviticus 27:30, p. 173

Show You Care, 2 Kings 4:10, p. 481

Service with a Smile, 1 Chronicles 6:31–49, p. 527

My Favorite!, Mark 10:17–23, p. 1347

Share and Share Alike?, Acts 2:43–47, p. 1466

Give to Give, 1 Corinthians 16:1–4, p. 1566

Peter Teaches Cornelius

10 At Caesarea there was a man
named Cornelius, an officer in the
Italian group of the Roman army. 2Cor-
nelius was a religious man. He and all the
other people who lived in his house worshiped the true God. He gave much of his
money to the poor and prayed to God often. 3One afternoon about three o'clock,
Cornelius clearly saw a vision. An angel
of God came to him and said, "Cornelius!"
4Cornelius stared at the angel. He became afraid and said, "What do you want,
Lord?"
The angel said, "God has heard your
prayers. He has seen that you give to the
poor, and he remembers you. 5Send
some men now to Joppa to bring back a
man named Simon who is also called Peter. 6He is staying with a man, also
named Simon, who is a tanner and has a
house beside the sea." 7When the angel
who spoke to Cornelius left, Cornelius
called two of his servants and a soldier, a
religious man who worked for him. 8Cor-
nelius explained everything to them and
sent them to Joppa.
9About noon the next day as they
came near Joppa, Peter was going up to
the roof[n] to pray. 10He was hungry and
wanted to eat, but while the food was being prepared, he had a vision. 11He saw
heaven opened and something coming
down that looked like a big sheet being
lowered to earth by its four corners. 12In
it were all kinds of animals, reptiles, and
birds. 13Then a voice said to Peter, "Get
up, Peter; kill and eat."
14But Peter said, "No, Lord! I have
never eaten food that is unholy or unclean."
15But the voice said to him again,
"God has made these things clean so
don't call them 'unholy'!" 16This happened three times, and at once the sheet
was taken back to heaven.
17While Peter was wondering what
this vision meant, the men Cornelius
sent had found Simon's house and were

10:9 roof In Bible times houses were built with flat roofs. The roof was used for drying things such as flax and fruit. And it was used as an extra room, as a place for worship, and as a cool place to sleep in the summer.

FAITH links

ONE OF THE FAITHFUL

ACTS 10:1-34

Cornelius was a Roman army officer who served God by his faithfulness in giving generously to the poor and in prayer. Faithfulness is a quality that few may acknowledge. Yet everyone benefits from a faithful giver. God rewarded Cornelius's faithfulness by using him to help Peter understand that God loves *all* people, not just the Jews.

How faithful are you in giving? Connect to these links for help:

Giving Your Part, Leviticus 27:30, p. 173

Give What You Can, Numbers 7:1–11, p. 186

Too Young to Serve, Jeremiah 1:4–9, p. 988

Go! No!, Jonah 1, p. 1213

Give from the Heart, Luke 21:1–4, p. 1410

Give Till It Hurts?, 2 Corinthians 8:6–9; 9:6–9, p. 1578

standing at the gate. **18**They asked, "Is
Simon Peter staying here?"
19While Peter was still thinking about
the vision, the Spirit said to him, "Listen,
three men are looking for you. **20**Get up
and go downstairs. Go with them without
doubting, because I have sent them to
you."
21So Peter went down to the men and
said, "I am the one you are looking for.
Why did you come here?"
22They said, "A holy angel spoke to
Cornelius, an army officer and a good
man; he worships God. All the people respect him. The angel told Cornelius to
ask you to come to his house so that he
can hear what you have to say." **23**So Peter asked the men to come in and spend
the night.
The next day Peter got ready and
went with them, and some of the followers from Joppa joined him. **24**On the following day they came to Caesarea.
Cornelius was waiting for them and had
called together his relatives and close
friends. **25**When Peter entered, Cornelius met him, fell at his feet, and worshiped
him. **26**But Peter helped him up, saying,
"Stand up. I too am only a human." **27**As
he talked with Cornelius, Peter went inside where he saw many people gathered. **28**He said,
"You people under-
stand that it is
against our law for
Jewish people to as-
sociate with or visit
anyone who is not
Jewish. But God has shown me that I
should not call any person 'unholy' or
'unclean.' **29**That is why I did not argue
when I was asked to come here. Now,
please tell me why you sent for me."

eMAIL! FROM GOD
10:28
Respect
How should you regard others?

30Cornelius said, "Four days ago, I
was praying in my house at this same
time—three o'clock in the afternoon.
Suddenly, there was a man standing before me wearing shining clothes. **31**He
said, 'Cornelius, God has heard your
prayer and has seen that you give to the
poor and remembers you. **32**So send
some men to Joppa and ask Simon Peter
to come. Peter is staying in the house of a
man, also named Simon, who is a tanner
and has a house beside the sea.' **33**So I
sent for you immediately, and it was very
good of you to come. Now we are all here
before God to hear everything the Lord
has commanded you to tell us."
34Peter began to speak: "I really understand now that to God every person is
the same. **35**In every country God accepts anyone who worships him and does
what is right. **36**You know the message

that God has sent to the people of Israel
is the Good News that peace has come
through Jesus Christ. Jesus is the Lord of
all people! **37**You know what has happened all over Judea, beginning in Galilee
after John[n] preached to the people about
baptism. **38**You know about Jesus from
Nazareth, that God gave him the Holy
Spirit and power. You know how Jesus
went everywhere doing good and healing
those who were ruled by the devil, because God was with him. **39**We saw what
Jesus did in Judea and in Jerusalem, but
the Jews in Jerusalem killed him by hanging him on a cross. **40**Yet, on the third
day, God raised Jesus to life and caused
him to be seen, **41**not by all the people,
but only by the witnesses God had already chosen. And we are those witnesses who ate and drank with him after
he was raised from the dead. **42**He told
us to preach to the people and to tell
them that he is the one whom God chose
to be the judge of the living and the dead.
43All the prophets say it is true that all
who believe in Jesus will be forgiven of
their sins through Jesus' name."

44While Peter was still saying this,
the Holy Spirit came down on all those
who were listening. **45**The Jewish believers who came with Peter were amazed
that the gift of the Holy Spirit had been
given even to the nations. **46**These believers heard them speaking in different
languages[n] and praising God. Then Peter
said, **47**"Can anyone keep these people
from being baptized with water? They
have received the Holy Spirit just as we
did!" **48**So Peter ordered that they be
baptized in the name of Jesus Christ.
Then they asked Peter to stay with them
for a few days.

Peter Returns to Jerusalem

11 The apostles and the believers in
Judea heard that some who were
not Jewish had accepted God's
teaching too. **2**But
when Peter came to
Jerusalem, some
people argued with
him. **3**They said,
"You went into the

EMAIL! FROM GOD
11:2–18
Obedience
Read this example of obedience.

homes of people who are not circumcised
and ate with them!"

4So Peter explained the whole story
to them. **5**He said, "I was in the city of
Joppa, and while I was praying, I had a vision. I saw something that looked like a
big sheet being lowered from heaven by
its four corners. It came very close to
me. **6**I looked inside it and saw animals,
wild beasts, reptiles, and birds. **7**I heard a
voice say to me, 'Get up, Peter. Kill and
eat.' **8**But I said, 'No, Lord! I have never
eaten anything that is unholy or unclean.'
9But the voice from heaven spoke again,
'God has made these things clean, so
don't call them unholy.' **10**This happened
three times. Then the whole thing was
taken back to heaven. **11**Right then three
men who were sent to me from Caesarea
came to the house where I was staying.
12The Spirit told me to go with them
without doubting. These six believers
here also went with me, and we entered
the house of Cornelius. **13**He told us
about the angel he saw standing in his
house. The angel said to him, 'Send some
men to Joppa and invite Simon Peter to
come. **14**By the words he will say to you,
you and all your family will be saved.'
15When I began my speech, the Holy
Spirit came on them just as he came on
us at the beginning. **16**Then I remembered the words of the Lord. He said,
'John baptized with water, but you will be
baptized with the Holy Spirit.' **17**Since
God gave them the same gift he gave us
who believed in the Lord Jesus Christ,
how could I stop the work of God?"

18When the believers heard this, they
stopped arguing. They praised God and
said, "So God is allowing even other nations to turn to him and live."

The Good News Comes to Antioch

19Many of the believers were scattered when they were persecuted after
Stephen was killed. Some of them went

10:37 John John the Baptist, who preached to people about Christ's coming (Luke 3).

10:46 languages This can also be translated "tongues."

as far as Phoenicia, Cyprus, and Antioch
telling the message to others, but only to
Jews. 20Some of these believers were
people from Cyprus and Cyrene. When
they came to Antioch, they spoke also to
Greeks, telling them the Good News
about the Lord Jesus. 21The Lord was
helping the believers, and a large group
of people believed and turned to the
Lord.

22The church in Jerusalem heard
about all of this, so they sent Barnabas to
Antioch. 23-24Barnabas was a good man,
full of the Holy Spirit and full of faith.
When he reached Antioch and saw how
God had blessed the people, he was glad.
He encouraged all the believers in Antioch always to obey the Lord with all their
hearts, and many people became followers of the Lord.

25Then Barnabas went to the city of
Tarsus to look for Saul, 26and when he
found Saul, he brought him to Antioch.
For a whole year Saul and Barnabas met
with the church and taught many people
there. In Antioch the followers were
called Christians for the first time.

27About that time some prophets
came from Jerusalem to Antioch. 28One
of them, named Agabus, stood up and
spoke with the help of the Holy Spirit. He
said, "A very hard time is coming to the
whole world. There will be no food to
eat." (This happened when Claudius
ruled.) 29The believers all decided to
help the followers who lived in Judea, as
much as each one could. 30They gathered the money and gave it to Barnabas
and Saul, who brought it to the elders in
Judea.

Herod Agrippa Hurts the Church

12 During that same time King Herod
began to mistreat some who belonged to the church. 2He ordered James,
the brother of John, to be killed by the
sword. 3Herod saw that some of the people liked this, so he decided to arrest Peter, too. (This happened during the time
of the Feast of Unleavened Bread.)

4After Herod arrested Peter, he put
him in jail and handed him over to
be guarded by sixteen soldiers. Herod

FAITH links

A CHRISTIAN'S RESPONSIBILITY

ACTS 11:26

If you're a citizen of the United States, you're called an American. As an American, you have certain rights and responsibilities. One of those responsibilities is to obey the laws of the land.

In Antioch during the first century, believers of Jesus were called Christians for the first time. That word means "a follower of Christ (Jesus)." There are rights and responsibilities attached to being a Christian. One of those responsibilities is to grow in faith. Saul (Paul) and Barnabas helped the believers in Antioch to grow in their faith. How do the people in your church help you to grow?

Download these Faithlinks for some tips on growing in faith:

A Serious Promise, Deuteronomy 23:21–23, p. 257

Promises, Promises, Judges 2:1–3, p. 312

Obeying God or Man?, Daniel 3:8–30, p. 1154

Your Civic Duty, Matthew 17:24–27, p. 1304

Faith That Pleases God, Luke 7:1–9, p. 1380

Meeting Together, 1 Corinthians 16:19, p. 1567

planned to bring Peter before the people
for trial after the Passover Feast. 5So Peter was kept in jail, but the church prayed
earnestly to God for him.

Peter Leaves the Jail

6The night before Herod was to bring
him to trial, Peter was sleeping between
two soldiers, bound with two chains.
Other soldiers were guarding the door of
the jail. 7Suddenly, an angel of the Lord
stood there, and a light shined in the cell.
The angel struck Peter on the side and
woke him up. "Hurry! Get up!" the angel
said. And the chains fell off Peter's hands.
8Then the angel told him, "Get dressed
and put on your sandals." And Peter did.
Then the angel said, "Put on your coat
and follow me." 9So Peter followed him
out, but he did not know if what the angel
was doing was real; he thought he might
be seeing a vision. 10They went past the
first and second guards and came to the
iron gate that separated them from the
city. The gate opened by itself for them,
and they went through it. When they had
walked down one street, the angel suddenly left him.
11Then Peter realized what had happened. He thought, "Now I know that the
Lord really sent his angel to me. He rescued me from Herod and from all the
things the people thought would happen."
12When he considered this, he went
to the home of Mary, the mother of John
Mark. Many people were gathered there,
praying. 13Peter knocked on the outside
door, and a servant girl named Rhoda
came to answer it. 14When she recognized Peter's voice, she was so happy she
forgot to open the door. Instead, she ran
inside and told the group, "Peter is at the
door!"
15They said to her, "You are crazy!"
But she kept on saying it was true, so
they said, "It must be Peter's angel."
16Peter continued to knock, and when
they opened the door, they saw him and
were amazed. 17Peter made a sign with
his hand to tell them to be quiet. He explained how the Lord led him out of the
jail, and he said, "Tell James and the
other believers what happened." Then
he left to go to another place.
18The next day the soldiers were
very upset and wondered what had happened to Peter. 19Herod looked everywhere for him but could not find him. So
he questioned the guards and ordered
that they be killed.

FAITH links

THE POWER OF PRAYER

ACTS 12:5

Peter's friends made a big difference in his life while he was in prison. No, they didn't send him a file in a cake. They prayed for him. Because of their faithfulness in prayer, God rescued Peter from prison.

Prayer can be powerful. How powerful? The God who created the universe listens to and answers your prayer. Is that powerful enough for you?

Here are some more Faithlinks on the power of prayer:

Just a Little Respect, 1 Chronicles 11:10–19, p. 534

The Prayer Habit, Psalm 5:1–3, p. 712

When We Agree, Matthew 18:19–20, p. 1306

Prayer Priority, Luke 5:15–16, p. 1376

Jesus' Prayer, John 17, p. 1453

A Good Habit, Ephesians 6:18, p. 1606

LET'S VISIT ANTIOCH

Acts 13:1–3

A man named Seleucus started the city of Antioch. He named it after his dad, Antiochus. He built it about 300 miles north of Jerusalem on the bank of a river called Orontes. Antioch was the capital of Syria during New Testament times. It was the third largest city in the whole Roman Empire.

Antioch was built on a trade route. That meant many people traveled by on their way to trade and do business. Because of that, Antioch became an important place for sharing the Good News. People could hear the Good News, then go home and tell all their friends. In fact, it was in Antioch that Jesus' followers were first called "Christians." (Check out Acts 11:26.) Antioch also became the birthplace of foreign missions, because Paul used the Antioch church as a base of operations for some of his missionary tours.

The Death of Herod Agrippa

Later Herod moved from Judea and
went to the city of Caesarea, where he
stayed. **20**Herod was very angry with the
people of Tyre and Sidon, but the people
of those cities all came in a group to him.
After convincing Blastus, the king's personal servant, to be on their side, they
asked Herod for peace, because their
country got its food from his country.
21On a chosen day Herod put on his
royal robes, sat on his throne, and made a
speech to the people. **22**They shouted,
"This is the voice of a god, not a human!"
23Because Herod did not give the glory
to God, an angel of the Lord immediately
caused him to become sick, and he was
eaten by worms and died.
24God's message continued to spread
and reach people.
25After Barnabas and Saul finished
their task in Jerusalem, they returned to
Antioch, taking John Mark with them.

Barnabas and Saul Are Chosen

13 In the church at Antioch there
were these prophets and teachers:
Barnabas, Simeon (also called Niger),
Lucius (from the city of Cyrene), Manaen
(who had grown up with Herod, the ruler), and Saul. **2**They were all worshiping
the Lord and giving up eating for a
certain time.ⁿ During this time the Holy
Spirit said to them, "Set apart for me Barnabas and Saul to do a special work for
which I have chosen them."
3So after they gave up eating and
prayed, they laid their hands onⁿ Barnabas and Saul and sent them out.

Barnabas and Saul in Cyprus

4Barnabas and Saul, sent out by the
Holy Spirit, went to the city of Seleucia.
From there they sailed to the island of
Cyprus. **5**When they came to Salamis,
they preached the Good News of God in
the synagogues. John Mark was with
them to help.
6They went across the whole island to
Paphos where they met a magician

13:2 giving up . . . time This is called "fasting." The people would give up eating for a special time of prayer and worship to God. It was also done sometimes to show sadness and disappointment.

13:3 laid their hands on The laying on of hands had many purposes, including the giving of a blessing, power, or authority.

named Bar-Jesus. He was a false prophet
7who always stayed close to Sergius Pau-
lus, the governor and a smart man. He
asked Barnabas and Saul to come to him,
because he wanted to hear the message
of God. **8**But Elymas, the magician, was
against them. (Elymas is the name for
Bar-Jesus in the Greek language.) He
tried to stop the governor from believing
in Jesus. **9**But Saul, who was also called
Paul, was filled with the Holy Spirit. He
looked straight at Elymas **10**and said,
"You son of the devil! You are an enemy
of everything that is right! You are full of
evil tricks and lies, always trying to
change the Lord's truths into lies. **11**Now
the Lord will touch you, and you will be
blind. For a time you will not be able to
see anything—not even the light from
the sun."

Then everything became dark for Elymas, and he walked around, trying to find
someone to lead him by the hand.
12When the governor saw this, he believed because he was amazed at the
teaching about the Lord.

Paul and Barnabas Leave Cyprus

13Paul and those with him sailed from
Paphos and came to Perga, in Pamphylia.
There John Mark left them to return to
Jerusalem. **14**They continued their trip
from Perga and went to Antioch, a city in
Pisidia. On the Sabbath day they went
into the synagogue and sat down. **15**After
the law of Moses and the writings of the
prophets were read, the leaders of the
synagogue sent a message to Paul and
Barnabas: "Brothers, if you have any
message that will encourage the people,
please speak."

16Paul stood up, raised his hand, and
said, "You Israelites and you who worship God, please listen! **17**The God of the
Israelites chose our ancestors. He made
the people great during the time they
lived in Egypt, and he brought them out
of that country with great power. **18**And
he was patient with them for forty years
in the desert. **19**God destroyed seven nations in the land of Canaan and gave the
land to his people. **20**All this happened in
about four hundred fifty years.

"After this, God gave them judges until the time of Samuel the prophet.
21Then the people asked for a king, so
God gave them Saul son of Kish. Saul was
from the tribe of Benjamin and was king
for forty years. **22**After God took him
away, God made David their king. God
said about him: 'I have found in David son
of Jesse the kind of man I want. He will
do all I want him to do.' **23**So God has
brought Jesus, one of David's descendants, to Israel to be its Savior, as he
promised. **24**Before Jesus came, John[n]
preached to all the people of Israel about
a baptism of changed hearts and lives.
25When he was finishing his work, he
said, 'Who do you think I am? I am not the
Christ. He is coming later, and I am not
worthy to untie his sandals.'

26"Brothers, sons of the family of
Abraham, and others who worship God,
listen! The news about this salvation has
been sent to us. **27**Those who live in Jerusalem and their leaders did not realize
that Jesus was the Savior. They did not
understand the words that the prophets
wrote, which are read every Sabbath day.
But they made them come true when
they said Jesus was guilty. **28**They could
not find any real reason for Jesus to be
put to death, but they asked Pilate to
have him killed. **29**When they had done
to him all that the Scriptures had said,
they took him down from the cross and
laid him in a tomb. **30**But God raised him
up from the dead! **31**After this, for many
days, those who had gone with Jesus from
Galilee to Jerusalem saw him. They are
now his witnesses to the people. **32**We
tell you the Good News about the promise
God made to our ancestors. **33**God has
made this promise come true for us, his
children, by raising Jesus from the dead.
We read about this also in Psalm 2:

'You are my Son.
    Today I have become your Father.'

Psalm 2:7

34God raised Jesus from the dead, and he
will never go back to the grave and
become dust. So God said:

13:24 John John the Baptist, who preached to people about Christ's coming (Luke 3).

'I will give you the holy and sure
blessings
that I promised to David.' *Isaiah 55:3*
35But in another place God says:
'You will not let your Holy One rot.'
Psalm 16:10
36David did God's will during his lifetime. Then he died and was buried beside his ancestors, and his body did rot
in the grave. 37But the One God raised
from the dead did not rot in the grave.
38-39Brothers, understand what we
are telling you: You can
have forgiveness of
your sins through
Jesus. The law of
Moses could not
free you from your
sins. But through
Jesus everyone who
believes is free from all sins. 40Be careful! Don't let what the prophets said happen to you:
41'Listen, you people who doubt!
You can wonder, and then die.
I will do something in your lifetime
that you won't believe even when
you are told about it!'" *Habakkuk 1:5*
42While Paul and Barnabas were leaving the synagogue, the people asked
them to tell them more about these
things on the next Sabbath. 43When the
meeting was over, many people with
those who had changed to worship God
followed Paul and Barnabas from that
place. Paul and Barnabas were persuading them to continue trusting in God's
grace.
44On the next Sabbath day, almost
everyone in the city came to hear the
word of the Lord. 45Seeing the crowd,
the Jewish people became very jealous
and said insulting things and argued
against what Paul said. 46But Paul and
Barnabas spoke very boldly, saying, "We
must speak the message of God to you
first. But you refuse to listen. You are
judging yourselves not worthy of having
eternal life! So we will now go to the people of other nations. 47This is what the
Lord told us to do, saying:
'I have made you a light for the
nations;

EMAIL! FROM GOD
13:38–39
Forgiveness
Who can be forgiven?

FAITH CHALLENGE

Here's one for you. Read 13:47 to find out what the Lord has in mind for his people. How can you be a light to the people around you? What are some ways you already are a light?

TESTING IT

Acts 13:47
This is what the Lord told us to do, saying: "I have made you a light for the nations; you will show people all over the world the way to be saved."

you will show people all over the
world the way to be saved.'"
Isaiah 49:6
48When those who were not Jewish
heard Paul say this, they were happy and
gave honor to the message of the Lord.
And the people who were chosen to have
life forever believed the message.
49So the message of the Lord was
spreading through the whole country.
50But the Jewish people stirred up some
of the important religious women and the
leaders of the city. They started trouble
against Paul and Barnabas and forced
them out of their area. 51So Paul and Bar-

nabas shook the dust off their feet[n] and went to Iconium. 52But the followers were filled with joy and the Holy Spirit.

Paul and Barnabas in Iconium

14 In Iconium, Paul and Barnabas went as usual to the synagogue. They spoke so well that a great many Jews and Greeks believed. 2But some people who did not believe excited the others and turned them against the believers. 3Paul and Barnabas stayed in Iconium a long time and spoke bravely for the Lord. He showed that their message about his grace was true by giving them the power to work miracles and signs. 4But the city was divided. Some of the people agreed with the Jews, and others believed the apostles.

5Some who were not Jews, some Jews, and some of their rulers wanted to mistreat Paul and Barnabas and to stone them to death. 6When Paul and Barnabas learned about this, they ran away to Lystra and Derbe, cities in Lycaonia, and to the areas around those cities. 7They announced the Good News there, too.

Paul in Lystra and Derbe

8In Lystra there sat a man who had been born crippled; he had never walked. 9As this man was listening to Paul speak, Paul looked straight at him and saw that he believed God could heal him. 10So he cried out, "Stand up on your feet!" The man jumped up and began walking around. 11When the crowds saw what Paul did, they shouted in the Lycaonian language, "The gods have become like humans and have come down to us!" 12Then the people began to call Barnabas "Zeus"[n] and Paul "Hermes,"[n] because he was the main speaker. 13The priest in the temple of Zeus, which was near the city, brought some bulls and flowers to the city gates. He and the people wanted to offer a sacrifice to Paul and Barnabas. 14But when the apostles, Barnabas and Paul, heard about it, they tore their clothes. They ran in among the people, shouting, 15"Friends, why are you doing these things? We are only human

FAITH links

KINDNESS COUNTS

ACTS 14:3

What is the coolest ability you wish you had? To leap tall buildings at a single bound? To play a sport or musical instrument better than anyone? Paul and Barnabas, two apostles of Jesus, were able to perform miracles. That's pretty cool! They did these not for show but to demonstrate God's kindness.

When you are kind to others, they can see God's love for them. So, remember: kindness counts!

Download these links on how you can make kindness count:

Help for the Poor, Leviticus 5:7, p. 138

Yours, Mine, and Ours?, 1 Samuel 25, p. 389

Seeing the Needs, Nehemiah 1, p. 625

Your Choice of Fruit, Matthew 12:33–35, p. 1295

The Greatest Commandment, Matthew 22:36–40, p. 1313

Share and Share Alike?, Acts 2:43–47, p. 1466

13:51 shook . . . feet A warning. It showed that they had rejected these people.
14:12 "Zeus" The Greeks believed in many false gods, of whom Zeus was most important.
14:12 "Hermes" The Greeks believed he was a messenger for the other gods.

beings like you. We are bringing you the
Good News and are telling you to turn
away from these worthless things and
turn to the living God. He is the One who
made the sky, the earth, the sea, and
everything in them. **16**In the past, God
let all the nations do what they wanted.
17Yet he proved he is real by showing
kindness, by giving you rain from heaven
and crops at the right times, by giving
you food and filling your hearts with joy."
18Even with these words, they were
barely able to keep the crowd from offering sacrifices to them.

19Then some evil people came from
Antioch and Iconium and persuaded the
people to turn against Paul. So they
threw stones at him and dragged him out
of town, thinking they had killed him.
20But the followers gathered around
him, and he got up and went back into the
town. The next day he and Barnabas left
and went to the city of Derbe.

The Return to Antioch in Syria

21Paul and Barnabas told the Good
News in Derbe, and many became followers. Paul and Barnabas returned to Lystra, Iconium, and Antioch, **22**making the
followers of Jesus stronger and helping
them stay in the faith. They said, "We
must suffer many things to enter God's
kingdom." **23**They chose elders for each
church, by praying and giving up eating
for a certain time.[a] These elders had
trusted the Lord, so Paul and Barnabas
put them in the Lord's care.

24Then they went through Pisidia and
came to Pamphylia. **25**When they had
preached the message in Perga, they
went down to Attalia. **26**And from there
they sailed away to Antioch where the
believers had put them into God's care
and had sent them out to do this work.
Now they had finished.

27When they arrived in Antioch, Paul
and Barnabas gathered the church together. They told the church all about
what God had done with them and how
God had made it possible for those who
were not Jewish to believe. **28**And they
stayed there a long time with the followers.

The Meeting at Jerusalem

15 Then some people came to Antioch from Judea and began teaching
the non-Jewish believers: "You cannot be
saved if you are not circumcised as Moses taught us." **2**Paul and Barnabas were
against this teaching and argued with
them about it. So the church decided to
send Paul, Barnabas, and some others to
Jerusalem where they could talk more
about this with the apostles and elders.

3The church helped them leave on the
trip, and they went through the countries
of Phoenicia and Samaria, telling all about
how the other nations had turned to God.
This made all the believers very happy.
4When they arrived in Jerusalem, they
were welcomed by the apostles, the elders, and the church. Paul, Barnabas, and
the others told about everything God had
done with them. **5**But some of the believers who belonged to the Pharisee group
came forward and said, "The non-Jewish
believers must be circumcised. They
must be told to obey the law of Moses."

6The apostles and the elders gathered
to consider this problem. **7**After a long
debate, Peter stood up and said to them,
"Brothers, you know that in the early
days God chose me from among you to
preach the Good News to the nations.
They heard the Good News from me, and
they believed. **8**God, who knows the
thoughts of everyone, accepted them. He
showed this to us by giving them the
Holy Spirit, just as he did to us. **9**To God,
those people are not different from us.
When they believed, he made their
hearts pure. **10**So now why are you testing God by putting a heavy load around
the necks of the non-Jewish believers? It
is a load that neither we nor our ancestors were able to carry. **11**But we believe
that we and they too will be saved by the
grace of the Lord Jesus."

12Then the whole group became quiet. They listened to Paul and Barnabas
tell about all the miracles and signs that

14:23 giving . . . time This is called "fasting." The people would give up eating for a special time of prayer and worship to God. It was also done sometimes to show sadness and disappointment.

HANDLING CONFLICTS

Acts 15:1–29

Livin' it

What *Am* I Going to Do? Is there someone that is always "bugging" you? Maybe someone who always calls you names or makes fun of you? When these things happen, it can make you feel angry, scared, or ready to get even. What do you do? Do you ask someone for help? Who?

Jesus tells us how to handle people who cause us problems and sometimes make our life miserable. His way of dealing with those hard to love people is very different from what most people would tell you. (Check out Matthew 5:38–48, p. 1282.) Are you willing to be friends with people who act like your enemies? This will not be easy, but with Jesus' help you can do it. You may even turn an "enemy" into a friend!

MORE FAITH links

The Trouble with Jealousy, p. 53
Give Revenge a Rest, p. 160
Play Fair or Play Favorites?, p. 227
Wronged for What's Right, p. 612
The Peril of Poisonous Plans, p. 1221
Winning a Friend, p. 1654

"What's the fastest way to turn an 'enemy' into a friend?"

"Got me. Maybe pay him $10?"

"Nope! Log on to these Faithlinks to find out how!"

Does Crime Pay?, Psalm 37:1–7, p. 736

- This Faithlink tells you to trust God to handle problems and conflicts in your life.

In Deep Water, Psalm 69, p. 760

- Conflicts (problems and troubles) in your life can make you feel like you're in deep water or even mud. Do you think you will never have conflicts in your life? Not likely! What are some conflicts you are dealing with? Link here to learn about David's way of dealing with conflict.

Forgive and Forget, Ephesians 4:32, p. 1604

- When someone is really giving you a hard time, what do you feel like doing? Do you easily forget about that person's bad behavior toward you? If not, you are holding a grudge.
- What's the opposite of holding a grudge? Forgiving someone. That isn't always easy to do. But since God always forgives us, that's what we ought to do for anyone who hurts us. Know anyone who needs your forgiveness?

my FAVORITE links

God did through them among the people.
13After they finished speaking, James
said, "Brothers, listen to me. **14**Simon
has told us how God showed his love for
those people. For the first time he is accepting from among them a people to be
his own. **15**The words of the prophets
agree with this too:

16'After these things I will return.
The kingdom of David is like a
fallen tent.
But I will rebuild its ruins,
and I will set it up.
17Then those people who are left alive
may ask the Lord for help,
and the other nations that belong
to me,
says the Lord,
who will make it happen.
18And these things have been known
for a long time.' *Amos 9:11-12*

19"So I think we should not bother the
other people who are turning to God.
20Instead, we should write a letter to
them telling them these things: Stay away
from food that has been offered to idols
(which makes it unclean), any kind of
sexual sin, eating animals that have been
strangled, and blood. **21**They should do
these things, because for a long time in
every city the law of Moses has been
taught. And it is still read in the synagogue every Sabbath day."

Letter to Non-Jewish Believers

22The apostles, the elders, and the
whole church decided to send some of
their men with Paul and Barnabas to Antioch. They chose Judas Barsabbas and
Silas, who were respected by the believers. **23**They sent the following letter
with them:

From the apostles and elders,
your brothers.

To all the non-Jewish believers
in Antioch, Syria, and Cilicia:

Greetings!

24We have heard that some of
our group have come to you and
said things that trouble and upset
you. But we did not tell them to do
this. **25**We have all agreed to
choose some messengers and send
them to you with our dear friends
Barnabas and Paul—**26**people who
have given their lives to serve our
Lord Jesus Christ. **27**So we are
sending Judas and Silas, who will
tell you the same things. **28**It has
pleased the Holy Spirit that you
should not have a heavy load to
carry, and we agree. You need to do
only these things: **29**Stay away
from any food that has been offered
to idols, eating any animals that
have been strangled, and blood,
and any kind of sexual sin. If you
stay away from these things, you
will do well.

Good-bye.

30So they left Jerusalem and went to
Antioch where they gathered the church
and gave them the letter. **31**When they
read it, they were very happy because of
the encouraging message. **32**Judas and
Silas, who were also prophets, said many
things to encourage the believers and
make them stronger. **33**After some time
Judas and Silas were sent off in peace by
the believers, and they went back to
those who had sent them. **34**"

35But Paul and Barnabas stayed in
Antioch and, along with many others,
preached the Good News and taught the
people the message of the Lord.

Paul and Barnabas Separate

36After some time, Paul said to Barnabas, "We should go back to all those
towns where we preached the message
of the Lord. Let's visit the believers and
see how they are doing."

37Barnabas wanted to take John Mark
with them, **38**but he had left them at
Pamphylia; he did not continue with them
in the work. So Paul did not think it was a
good idea to take him. **39**Paul and Barnabas had such a serious argument about
this that they separated and went different ways. Barnabas took Mark and sailed
to Cyprus, **40**but Paul chose Silas and

15:34 Verse 34 Some Greek copies add verse 34: ". . . but Silas decided to remain there."

left. The believers in Antioch put Paul
into the Lord's care, 41and he went
through Syria and Cilicia, giving strength
to the churches.

Timothy Goes with Paul

16 Paul came to Derbe and Lystra,
where a follower named Timothy
lived. Timothy's mother was Jewish and a
believer, but his father was a Greek.
2The believers in Lystra and Iconium
respected Timothy and said good things
about him. 3Paul wanted Timothy to
travel with him, but all the people living
in that area knew that Timothy's father
was Greek. So Paul circumcised Timothy
to please his mother's people. 4Paul and
those with him traveled from town to
town and gave the decisions made by the
apostles and elders in Jerusalem for the
people to obey. 5So the churches became
stronger in the faith and grew larger
every day.

Paul Is Called Out of Asia

6Paul and those with him went
through the areas of
Phrygia and Galatia
since the Holy Spir-
it did not let them
preach the Good
News in the country
of Asia. 7When they
came near the country of Mysia, they
tried to go into Bithynia, but the Spirit of
Jesus did not let them. 8So they passed
by Mysia and went to Troas. 9That night
Paul saw in a vision a man from Macedonia. The man stood and begged, "Come
over to Macedonia and help us." 10After
Paul had seen the vision, we immediately
prepared to leave for Macedonia, understanding that God had called us to tell the
Good News to those people.

EMAIL! FROM GOD
16:6–7
God's Will
Read this to see who will lead you.

Lydia Becomes a Christian

11We left Troas and sailed straight to
the island of Samothrace. The next day
we sailed to Neapolis.[n] 12Then we went
by land to Philippi, a Roman colony[n] and
the leading city in that part of Macedonia.
We stayed there for several days.
13On the Sabbath day we went outside

FAITH links

FAITH WORKOUT

ACTS 16:4-5

Paul, Silas, and Timothy traveled from place to place helping other Christians to grow in faith. When the Christians they met learned about God and his plans for them, their faith grew stronger.

You know what a personal trainer is, right? That's a person who helps someone else get in good physical shape. Other Christians can be like "spiritual personal trainers" in our lives. One of the ways other Christians help us is to explain the Scriptures to us. Think about how your pastor, a parent, or your Sunday school teacher helps you to understand God's Word. When we help each other, we're helped as well.

Try to Remember, Deuteronomy 11:18–21, p. 243

Learning to Listen, 1 Samuel 3, p. 358

Plan for Success, 1 Chronicles 14:8–17, p. 538

Our Thirst Quencher, Psalm 42:1–3, p. 741

Two Ways to Grow, Luke 2:46–52, p. 1370

Out with the Old!, Colossians 3:1–14, p. 1625

16:11 Neapolis City in Macedonia. It was the first city Paul visited on the continent of Europe.
16:12 Roman colony A town begun by Romans with Roman laws, customs, and privileges.

the city gate to the river where we
thought we would find a special place for
prayer. Some women had gathered there,
so we sat down and talked with them.
14One of the listeners was a woman
named Lydia from the city of Thyatira
whose job was selling purple cloth. She
worshiped God, and he opened her mind
to pay attention to what Paul was saying.
15She and all the people in her house
were baptized. Then she invited us to her
home, saying, "If you think I am truly a
believer in the Lord, then come stay in my
house." And she persuaded us to stay
with her.

Paul and Silas in Jail

16Once, while we were going to the
place for prayer, a servant girl
met us. She had a
special spirit* in her,
and she earned a lot
of money for her
owners by telling
fortunes. **17**This girl
followed Paul and
us, shouting, "These men are servants of
the Most High God. They are telling you
how you can be saved."

EMAIL FROM GOD
16:16–18
Demons
Who can drive out evil spirits?

18She kept this up for many days.
This bothered Paul, so he turned and said
to the spirit, "By the power of Jesus
Christ, I command you to come out of
her!" Immediately, the spirit came out.
19When the owners of the servant
girl saw this, they knew that now they
could not use her to make money. So they
grabbed Paul and Silas and dragged them
before the city rulers in the marketplace.
20They brought Paul and Silas to the Roman rulers and said, "These men are
Jews and are making trouble in our city.
21They are teaching things that are not
right for us as Romans to do."
22The crowd joined the attack against
them. The Roman officers tore the
clothes of Paul and Silas and had them
beaten with rods. **23**Then Paul and Silas
were thrown into jail, and the jailer was
ordered to guard them carefully. **24**When
he heard this order, he put them far inside the jail and pinned their feet down
between large blocks of wood.

FAITH links

YOU'RE WELCOMED!

ACTS 16:14-15

Hospitality is another way to say making someone feel welcome. That's what Lydia did for Paul and the other missionaries with whom he traveled. After becoming a believer herself, Lydia invited Paul to stay at her home.

Showing hospitality is one way to care for others. You don't have to own a home or even *be* at home to be hospitable. Hospitality starts with an attitude of welcome. No matter where you are, you can help someone feel welcome.

Know how to make others feel welcomed? Click here to find out:

Care for the Lost, Deuteronomy 22:1–3, p. 255

Show You Care, 2 Kings 4:10, p. 481

Service with a Smile, 1 Chronicles 6:31–49, p. 527

Love Him? Show It!, Amos 2:6–7, p. 1196

The Worst Chore, John 13:3–17, p. 1447

Come On In!, 1 Peter 4:9–10, p. 1705

25About midnight Paul and Silas were
praying and singing songs to God as the
other prisoners listened. **26**Suddenly,

16:16 spirit This was a spirit from the devil, which caused her to say she had special knowledge.

there was a strong earthquake that shook
the foundation of the jail. Then all the
doors of the jail broke open, and all the
prisoners were freed from their chains.
27The jailer woke up and saw that the jail
doors were open. Thinking that the prisoners had already escaped, he got his
sword and was about to kill himself.
28But Paul shouted, "Don't hurt yourself!
We are all here."

29The jailer told someone to bring a
light. Then he ran inside and, shaking
with fear, fell down before Paul and Silas.
30He brought them outside and said,
"Men, what must I do to be saved?"

31They said to him, "Believe in the
Lord Jesus and you will be saved—you
and all the people in your house." **32**So
Paul and Silas told the message of the
Lord to the jailer and all the people in his
house. **33**At that hour of the night the
jailer took Paul and Silas and washed their
wounds. Then he and all his people were
baptized immediately. **34**After this the
jailer took Paul and Silas home and gave
them food. He and his family were very
happy because they now believed in God.

35The next morning, the Roman officers sent the police to tell the jailer, "Let
these men go free."

36The jailer said to Paul, "The officers
have sent an order to let you go free. You
can leave now. Go in peace."

37But Paul said to the police, "They
beat us in public without a trial, even
though we are Roman citizens. And they
threw us in jail. Now they want to make
us go away quietly. No! Let them come
themselves and bring us out."

38The police told the Roman officers
what Paul said. When the officers heard
that Paul and Silas were Roman citizens,
they were afraid. **39**So they came and told
Paul and Silas they were sorry and took
them out of jail and asked them to leave
the city. **40**So when they came out of the
jail, they went to Lydia's house where
they saw some of the believers and encouraged them. Then they left.

Paul and Silas in Thessalonica

17 Paul and Silas traveled through
Amphipolis and Apollonia and
came to Thessalonica where there was a
synagogue. **2**Paul went into the synagogue as he always did, and on each Sabbath day for three weeks, he talked with
his fellow Jews about the Scriptures. **3**He
explained and proved that the Christ
must die and then rise from the dead. He
said, "This Jesus I am telling you about is
the Christ." **4**Some of them were convinced and joined Paul and Silas, along
with many of the Greeks who worshiped
God and many of the important women.

5But some others became jealous. So
they got some evil men from the marketplace, formed a mob, and started a riot.
They ran to Jason's house, looking for
Paul and Silas, wanting to bring them out
to the people. **6**But when they did not
find them, they dragged Jason and some
other believers to the leaders of the city.
The people were yelling, "These people
have made trouble everywhere in the
world, and now they have come here too!
7Jason is keeping them in his house. All
of them do things against the laws of Caesar, saying there is another king, called
Jesus."

8When the people and the leaders of
the city heard these things, they became
very upset. **9**They made Jason and the
others put up a sum of money. Then they
let the believers go free.

Paul and Silas Go to Berea

10That same night the believers sent
Paul and Silas to Berea where they went
to the synagogue. **11**These people were
more willing to listen than the people in
Thessalonica. The Bereans were eager
to hear what Paul and Silas said and studied the Scriptures every
day to find out if
these things were
true. **12**So, many of
them believed, as
well as many impor-
tant Greek women

EMAIL FROM GOD
17:11–12
Bible
Find out why reading the Bible is important.

16:27 kill himself He thought the leaders would kill him for letting the prisoners escape.

16:37 Roman citizens Roman law said that Roman citizens must not be beaten before they had a trial.

LET'S VISIT ATHENS

Acts 17:15—18:1

Athens was the capital of a state in Greece called Attica. Athens was the center of art, architecture, literature, and politics during the Golden Age of the Greeks (fifth century B.C.). Some people call it the birthplace of western civilization and culture.

When people visit Athens, one of the most famous sights they go to see is called the Parthenon. The Parthenon is actually the ruins that are left of an ancient Greek building. Another famous spot is Mars' Hill, which was like a courtroom for ancient Greeks.

The apostle Paul visited Athens during his second missionary journey. (Read Acts 17:15—18:1.) He spent some time sightseeing and found a statue built to honor "A GOD WHO IS NOT KNOWN." (See Acts 17:23.) Paul used that statue to teach the people about the one true God.

and men. 13But the people in Thessalonica learned that Paul was preaching the
word of God in Berea, too. So they came
there, upsetting the people and making
trouble. 14The believers quickly sent
Paul away to the coast, but Silas and Timothy stayed in Berea. 15The people leading Paul went with him to Athens. Then
they carried a message from Paul back to
Silas and Timothy for them to come to
him as soon as they could.

Paul Preaches in Athens

16While Paul was waiting for Silas and
Timothy in Athens, he was troubled because he saw that the city was full of
idols. 17In the synagogue, he talked with
the Jews and the Greeks who worshiped
God. He also talked every day with people in the marketplace.

18Some of the Epicurean and Stoic
philosophers* argued with him, saying,
"This man doesn't know what he is talking about. What is he trying to say?" Others said, "He seems to be telling us about
some other gods," because Paul was telling them about Jesus and his rising from
the dead. 19They got Paul and took him
to a meeting of the Areopagus,* where
they said, "Please explain to us this new
idea you have been teaching. 20The
things you are saying are new to us, and
we want to know what this teaching
means." 21(All the people of Athens and
those from other countries who lived
there always used their time to talk about
the newest ideas.)

22Then Paul stood before the meeting
of the Areopagus and said, "People of
Athens, I can see you are very religious
in all things. 23As I was going through
your city, I saw the objects you worship. I
found an altar that had these words written on it: TO A GOD WHO IS NOT KNOWN.
You worship a god that you don't know,
and this is the God I am telling you about!
24The God who made the whole world
and everything in it is the Lord of the
land and the sky. He does not live in tem-

17:18 Epicurean and Stoic philosophers Philosophers were those who searched for truth. Epicureans believed that pleasure, especially pleasures of the mind, were the goal of life. Stoics believed that life should be without feelings of joy or grief.

17:19 Areopagus A council or group of important leaders in Athens. They were like judges.

ples built by human hands. **25**This God is
the One who gives life, breath, and
everything else to people. He does not
need any help from them; he has everything he needs. **26**God began by making
one person, and from him came all the
different people who live everywhere in
the world. God decided exactly when and
where they must live. **27**God wanted
them to look for him and perhaps search
all around for him and find him, though he
is not far from any of us: **28**'We live in
him. We walk in him. We are in him.'
Some of your own poets have said: 'For
we are his children.' **29**Since we are
God's children, you must not think that
God is like something that people imagine or make from gold, silver, or rock.
30In the past, people did not understand
God, and he ignored this. But now, God
tells all people in the world to change
their hearts and lives. **31**God has set a
day that he will judge all the world with
fairness, by the man he chose long ago.
And God has proved this to everyone by
raising that man from the dead!"

32When the people heard about Jesus
being raised from the dead, some of them
laughed. But others said, "We will hear
more about this from you later." **33**So
Paul went away from them. **34**But some
of the people believed Paul and joined
him. Among those who believed was
Dionysius, a member of the Areopagus,
a woman named Damaris, and some
others.

Paul in Corinth

18 Later Paul left Athens and went to
Corinth. **2**Here he met a Jew
named Aquila who had been born in the
country of Pontus. But Aquila and his
wife, Priscilla, had recently moved to
Corinth from Italy, because Claudius[n]
commanded that all Jews must leave
Rome. Paul went to visit Aquila and Priscilla. **3**Because they were tentmakers,
just as he was, he stayed with them and
worked with them. **4**Every Sabbath day
he talked with the Jews and Greeks in the
synagogue, trying to persuade them to
believe in Jesus.

5Silas and Timothy came from Macedonia and joined Paul in Corinth. After
this, Paul spent all his time telling people
the Good News, showing them that Jesus
is the Christ. **6**But they would not accept
Paul's teaching and said some evil things.
So he shook off the dust from his clothes[n]
and said to them, "If you are not saved, it
will be your own fault! I have done all I
can do! After this, I will go only to other
nations." **7**Paul left the synagogue and
moved into the home of Titius Justus,
next to the synagogue. This man worshiped God. **8**Crispus was the leader of
that synagogue, and he and all the people
living in his house believed in the Lord.
Many others in Corinth also listened to
Paul and believed and were baptized.

9During the night, the Lord told Paul
in a vision: "Don't be afraid.
Continue talking to
people and don't be
quiet. **10**I am with
you, and no one will
hurt you because
many of my people
are in this city." **11**Paul stayed there for a
year and a half, teaching God's word to
the people.

eMAIL FROM GOD **18:9**
Witnessing
Are you afraid to share your faith?

Paul Is Brought Before Gallio

12When Gallio was the governor of
the country of Southern Greece, some
people came together against Paul and
took him to the court. **13**They said, "This
man is teaching people to worship God in
a way that is against our law."

14Paul was about to say something,
but Gallio spoke, saying, "I would listen
to you if you were complaining about a
crime or some wrong. **15**But the things
you are saying are only questions about
words and names—arguments about
your own law. So you must solve this
problem yourselves. I don't want to be a
judge of these things." **16**And Gallio
made them leave the court.

17Then they all grabbed Sosthenes,

18:2 Claudius The emperor (ruler) of Rome, A.D. 41–54.

18:6 shook . . . clothes This was a warning to show that Paul was finished talking to the people in that city.

the leader of the synagogue, and beat him
there before the court. But this did not
bother Gallio.

Paul Returns to Antioch

18Paul stayed with the believers for
many more days. Then he left and sailed
for Syria, with Priscilla and Aquila. At
Cenchrea Paul cut off his hair,[n] because
he had made a promise to God. **19**Then
they went to Ephesus, where Paul left
Priscilla and Aquila. While Paul was
there, he went into the synagogue and
talked with the people. **20**When they
asked him to stay with them longer, he
refused. **21**But as he left, he said, "I will
come back to you again if God wants me
to." And so he sailed away from Ephesus.
22When Paul landed at Caesarea, he
went and gave greetings to the church in
Jerusalem. After that, Paul went to Antioch. **23**He stayed there for a while and
then left and went through the regions of
Galatia and Phrygia. He traveled from
town to town in these regions, giving
strength to all the followers.

Apollos in Ephesus and Corinth

24A Jew named Apollos came to Ephesus. He was born in the city of Alexandria and was a good speaker who knew the
Scriptures well. **25**He had been taught
about the way of the Lord and was always
very excited when he spoke and taught
the truth about Jesus. But the only baptism Apollos knew about was the baptism
that John[n] taught. **26**Apollos began to
speak very boldly in the synagogue, and
when Priscilla and Aquila heard him, they
took him to their home and helped him
better understand the way of God. **27**Now
Apollos wanted to go to the country of
Southern Greece. So the believers helped
him and wrote a letter to the followers
there, asking them to accept him. These
followers had believed in Jesus because of
God's grace, and when
Apollos arrived, he
helped them very
much. **28**He argued
very strongly with
the Jews before all
the people, clearly
proving with the Scriptures that Jesus is
the Christ.

EMAIL! FROM GOD
18:28
Bible
What do the Scriptures prove?

Paul in Ephesus

19 While Apollos was in Corinth, Paul
was visiting some places on the
way to Ephesus. There he found some
followers **2**and asked them, "Did you receive the Holy Spirit when you believed?"
They said, "We have never even
heard of a Holy Spirit."
3So he asked, "What kind of baptism
did you have?"
They said, "It was the baptism that
John taught."
4Paul said, "John's baptism was a baptism of changed hearts and lives. He told
people to believe in the one who would
come after him, and that one is Jesus."
5When they heard this, they were
baptized in the name of the Lord Jesus.
6Then Paul laid his hands on them,[n] and
the Holy Spirit came upon them. They
began speaking different languages[n] and
prophesying. **7**There were about twelve
people in this group.
8Paul went into the synagogue and
spoke out boldly for three months. He
talked with the people and persuaded
them to accept the things he said about
the kingdom of God. **9**But some of them
became stubborn. They refused to believe and said evil things about the Way of
Jesus before all the people. So Paul left
them, and taking the followers with him,
he went to the school of a man named
Tyrannus. There Paul talked with people
every day **10**for two years. Because of his
work, every Jew and Greek in the country of Asia heard the word of the Lord.

The Sons of Sceva

11God used Paul to do some very special miracles. **12**Some people took hand-

---

18:18 cut . . . hair Jews did this to show that the time of a special promise to God was finished.

18:25 John John the Baptist, who preached to people about Christ's coming (Luke 3).

19:6 laid his hands on them The laying on of hands had many purposes, including the giving of a blessing, power, or authority.

19:6 languages This can also be translated "tongues."

kerchiefs and clothes that Paul had used
and put them on the sick. When they did
this, the sick were healed and evil spirits
left them.
13But some people also were traveling around and making evil
spirits go out of peo-
ple. They tried to
use the name of the
Lord Jesus to force
the evil spirits out.
They would say, "By
the same Jesus that Paul talks about, I
order you to come out!" 14Seven sons of
Sceva, a leading priest, were doing this.
15But one time an evil spirit said to
them, "I know Jesus, and I know about
Paul, but who are you?"
16Then the man who had the evil spirit jumped on them. Because he was so
much stronger than all of them, they ran
away from the house naked and hurt.
17All the people in Ephesus—Jews and
Greeks—learned about this and were
filled with fear and gave great honor to
the Lord Jesus. 18Many of the believers
began to confess openly and tell all the
evil things they had done. 19Some of
them who had used magic brought their
magic books and burned them before
everyone. Those books were worth
about fifty thousand silver coins.[n]
20So in a powerful way the word of
the Lord kept spreading and growing.
21After these things, Paul decided to
go to Jerusalem, planning to go through
the countries of Macedonia and Southern
Greece and then on to Jerusalem. He
said, "After I have been to Jerusalem, I
must also visit Rome." 22Paul sent Timothy and Erastus, two of his helpers,
ahead to Macedonia, but he himself
stayed in Asia for a while.

EMAIL FROM GOD
19:13–16
Demons
Do evil spirits have power?

Trouble in Ephesus

23And during that time, there was
some serious trouble in Ephesus about
the Way of Jesus. 24A man named Demetrius, who worked with silver, made little
silver models that looked like the temple
of the goddess Artemis.[n] Those who did
this work made much money. 25Deme-
trius had a meeting with them and some
others who did the same kind of work. He
told them, "Men, you know that we make
a lot of money from our business. 26But
look at what this man Paul is doing. He
has convinced and turned away many
people in Ephesus and in almost all of
Asia! He says the gods made by human
hands are not real. 27There is a danger
that our business will lose its good name,
but there is also another danger: People
will begin to think that the temple of the
great goddess Artemis is not important.
Her greatness will be destroyed, and Artemis is the goddess that everyone in
Asia and the whole world worships."
28When the others heard this, they
became very angry and shouted, "Artemis, the goddess of Ephesus, is great!"
29The whole city became confused. The
people grabbed Gaius and Aristarchus,
who were from Macedonia and were traveling with Paul, and ran to the theater.
30Paul wanted to go in and talk to the
crowd, but the followers did not let him.
31Also, some leaders of Asia who were
friends of Paul sent him a message, begging him not to go into the theater.
32Some people were shouting one thing,
and some were shouting another. The
meeting was completely confused; most
of them did not know why they had come
together. 33They put a man named Alexander in front of the people, and some of
them told him what to do. Alexander
waved his hand so he could explain
things to the people. 34But when they
saw that Alexander was a Jew, they all
shouted the same thing for two hours:
"Great is Artemis of Ephesus!"
35Then the city clerk made the crowd
be quiet. He said, "People of Ephesus,
everyone knows that Ephesus is the city
that keeps the temple of the great goddess Artemis and her holy stone[n] that fell
from heaven. 36Since no one can say this
is not true, you should be quiet. Stop and

19:19 fifty thousand silver coins Probably drachmas. One coin was enough to pay a worker for one day's labor.

19:24 Artemis A Greek goddess that the people of Asia Minor worshiped.

19:35 holy stone Probably a meteorite or stone that the people thought looked like Artemis.

think before you do anything. 37You
brought these men here, but they have
not said anything evil against our goddess or stolen anything from her temple.
38If Demetrius and those who work with
him have a charge against anyone they
should go to the courts and judges where
they can argue with each other. 39If there
is something else you want to talk about,
it can be decided at the regular town
meeting of the people. 40I say this because some people might see this trouble
today and say that we are rioting. We
could not explain this, because there is
no real reason for this meeting." 41After
the city clerk said these things, he told
the people to go home.

Paul in Macedonia and Greece

20 When the trouble stopped, Paul
sent for the followers to come to
him. After he encouraged them and then
told them good-bye, he left and went to
the country of Macedonia. 2He said many
things to strengthen the followers in the
different places on his way through Macedonia. Then he went to Greece, 3where
he stayed for three months. He was
ready to sail for Syria, but some evil people were planning something against
him. So Paul decided to go back through
Macedonia to Syria. 4The men who went
with him were Sopater son of Pyrrhus,
from the city of Berea; Aristarchus and
Secundus, from the city of Thessalonica;
Gaius, from Derbe; Timothy; and Tychicus and Trophimus, two men from the
country of Asia. 5These men went on
ahead and waited for us at Troas. 6We
sailed from Philippi after the Feast of Unleavened Bread. Five days later we met
them in Troas, where we stayed for
seven days.

Paul's Last Visit to Troas

7On the first day of the week,* we all
met together to break bread,* and Paul
spoke to the group. Because he was planning to leave the next day, he kept on
talking until midnight. 8We were all together in a room upstairs, and there were
many lamps in the room. 9A young man
named Eutychus was sitting in the window. As Paul continued talking, Eutychus
was falling into a deep sleep. Finally, he
went sound asleep and fell to the ground
from the third floor. When they picked
him up, he was dead. 10Paul went down
to Eutychus, knelt down, and put his
arms around him. He said, "Don't worry.
He is alive now." 11Then Paul went upstairs again, broke bread, and ate. He
spoke to them a long time, until it was
early morning, and then he left. 12They
took the young man home alive and were
greatly comforted.

The Trip from Troas to Miletus

13We went on ahead of Paul and sailed
for the city of Assos, where he wanted to
join us on the ship. Paul planned it this
way because he wanted to go to Assos by
land. 14When he met us there, we took
him aboard and went to Mitylene. 15We
sailed from Mitylene and the next day
came to a place near Kios. The following
day we sailed to Samos, and the next day
we reached Miletus. 16Paul had already
decided not to stop at Ephesus, because
he did not want to stay too long in the
country of Asia. He was hurrying to be in
Jerusalem on the day of Pentecost, if that
were possible.

The Elders from Ephesus

17Now from Miletus Paul sent to Ephesus and called for the elders of the
church. 18When they came to him, he
said, "You know about my life from
the first day I came to Asia. You know the
way I lived all the time I was with you.
19The evil people made plans against
me, which troubled me very much. But
you know I always served the Lord un-
selfishly, and I often cried. 20You know I
preached to you and did not hold back
anything that would help you. You know
that I taught you in public and in your

20:7 first day of the week Sunday, which for Jews began at sunset on our Saturday. But if in this part of Asia a different system of time was used, then the meeting was on our Sunday night.

20:7 break bread Probably the Lord's Supper, the special meal that Jesus told his followers to eat to remember him (Luke 22:14-20).

LET'S VISIT PHILIPPI

Acts 20

Philippi is a European city. At first, Philippi was called Krenides, which means "wells" or "springs." Later, it was renamed after Philip II. (Philip was the father of Alexander the Great, the Greek conqueror.)

From the ruins of the city we know that it had a market (like an outdoor shopping mall). We also know there was a gate. (Read about it in Acts 16:12–13.) There was a seat of judgment (like a courtroom), a library, and a jail. This jail might have been the place where Paul and Silas were in prison together. (Look at Acts 16:23–40.) You might remember that they prayed and sang until an earthquake shook the jail during the night. The church at Philippi was the first European church. Paul and Silas founded the church by meeting with a women's prayer group. Lydia, a businesswoman, became the first Christian there. (Read Acts 16:12–15, 40.)

homes. **21**I warned both Jews and Greeks
to change their lives and turn to God and
believe in our Lord Jesus. **22**But now I
must obey the Holy Spirit and go to Jerusalem. I don't know what will happen to
me there. **23**I know only that in every
city the Holy Spirit tells me that troubles
and even jail wait for me. **24**I don't care
about my own life. The most important
thing is that I complete my mission, the
work that the Lord Jesus gave me—to
tell people the Good News about God's
grace.

25"And now, I know that none of you
among whom I was preaching the kingdom of God will ever see me again. **26**So
today I tell you that if any of you should
be lost, I am not responsible, **27**because I
have told you everything God wants you
to know. **28**Be careful for yourselves and
for all the people the Holy Spirit has
given to you to care for. You must be like
shepherds to the church of God,[n] which
he bought with the death of his own son.
29I know that after I leave, some people
will come like wild wolves and try to destroy the flock. **30**Also, some from your
own group will rise up and twist the truth
and will lead away followers after them.
31So be careful! Always remember that
for three years, day and night, I never
stopped warning each of you, and I often
cried over you.

32"Now I am putting you in the care of
God and the message about his grace. It
is able to give you strength, and it will
give you the blessings God has for all his
holy people. **33**When I was with you, I
never wanted anyone's money or fine
clothes. **34**You know I always worked to
take care of my own needs and the needs
of those who were with me. **35**I showed
you in all things that you should work as I
did and help the weak. I taught you to remember the words Jesus said: 'It is more
blessed to give than to receive.' "

36When Paul had said this, he knelt
down with all of them and prayed.
37-38 And they all cried because Paul had
said they would never see him again.
They put their arms around him and
kissed him. Then they went with him to
the ship.

20:28 of God Some Greek copies say, "of the Lord."

THE MOST FUN

ACTS 20:35

Which do you think is the most fun: giving a gift or receiving a gift? Let's face it—we like to receive. It's fun to get things and to have people serve us. So, receiving is more fun, right? Jesus and the apostle Paul would disagree. Jesus once said, "It is more blessed to give than to receive." Don't believe that? Try it and see!

Download these links to find out the most fun of all:

Share What You Have, Exodus 35:5–18, p. 123

A Small Percent, Deuteronomy 14:22–23, p. 247

Gifts from the Heart, 1 Chronicles 29, p. 557

Happiness or Joy?, Job 29:18–19, p. 691

The Person Most Likely to Give?, Acts 9:36–42, p. 1481

Give to Give, 1 Corinthians 16:1–4, p. 1566

Paul Goes to Jerusalem

21 After we all said good-bye to them,
we sailed straight to the island of
Cos. The next day we reached Rhodes,
and from there we went to Patara.
2There we found a ship going to Phoenicia, so we went aboard and sailed away.
3We sailed near the island of Cyprus,
seeing it to the north, but we sailed on to
Syria. We stopped at Tyre because the
ship needed to unload its cargo there.
4We found some followers in Tyre and
stayed with them for seven days.
Through the Holy Spirit they warned
Paul not to go to Jerusalem. 5When we
finished our visit, we left and continued
our trip. All the followers, even the wom-
en and children, came outside the city
with us. After we all knelt on the beach
and prayed, 6we said good-bye and got on
the ship, and the followers went back
home.

7We continued our trip from Tyre and
arrived at Ptolemais, where we greeted
the believers and stayed with them for
a day. 8The next day we left Ptolemais
and went to the city of Caesarea. There
we went into the home of Philip the
preacher, one of the seven helpers,* and
stayed with him. 9He had four unmarried
daughters who had the gift of prophesying. 10After we had been there for some
time, a prophet named Agabus arrived
from Judea. 11He came to us and borrowed Paul's belt and used it to tie his
own hands and feet. He said, "The Holy
Spirit says, 'This is how evil people in Jerusalem will tie up the man who wears
this belt. Then they will give him to the
older leaders.' "

12When we all heard this, we and the
people there begged Paul not to go to Jerusalem. 13But he said, "Why are you
crying and making me so sad? I am not
only ready to be tied up in Jerusalem, I
am ready to die for the Lord Jesus!"

14We could not persuade him to stay
away from Jerusalem. So we stopped
begging him and said, "We pray that what
the Lord wants will be done."

15After this, we got ready and started
on our way to Jerusalem. 16Some of the
followers from Caesarea went with us
and took us to the home of Mnason,
where we would stay. He was from Cyprus and was one of the first followers.

Paul Visits James

17In Jerusalem the believers were
glad to see us. 18The next day Paul went

21:8 helpers The seven men chosen for a special work described in Acts 6:1-6. Sometimes they are called "deacons."

with us to visit James, and all the elders were there. **19**Paul greeted them and told them everything God had done among the other nations through him. **20**When they heard this, they praised God. Then they said to Paul, "Brother, you can see that many thousands of our people have become believers. And they think it is very important to obey the law of Moses. **21**They have heard about your teaching, that you tell our people who live among the nations to leave the law of Moses. They have heard that you tell them not to circumcise their children and not to obey customs. **22**What should we do? They will learn that you have come. **23**So we will tell you what to do: Four of our men have made a promise to God. **24**Take these men with you and share in their cleansing ceremony.[n] Pay their expenses so they can shave their heads.[n] Then it will prove to everyone that what they have heard about you is not true and that you follow the law of Moses in your own life. **25**We have already sent a letter to the non-Jewish believers. The letter said: 'Do not eat food that has been offered to idols, or blood, or animals that have been strangled. Do not take part in sexual sin.' "

26The next day Paul took the four men and shared in the cleansing ceremony with them. Then he went to the Temple and announced the time when the days of the cleansing ceremony would be finished. On the last day an offering would be given for each of the men.

27When the seven days were almost over, some of his people from Asia saw Paul at the Temple. They caused all the people to be upset and grabbed Paul. **28**They shouted, "People of Israel, help us! This is the man who goes everywhere teaching against the law of Moses, against our people, and against this Temple. Now he has brought some Greeks into the Temple and has made this holy place unclean!" **29**(They said this because they had seen Trophimus, a man from Ephesus, with Paul in Jerusalem. They thought that Paul had brought him into the Temple.)

30All the people in Jerusalem became upset. Together they ran, took Paul, and dragged him out of the Temple. The Temple doors were closed immediately. **31**While they were trying to kill Paul, the commander of the Roman army in Jerusalem learned that there was trouble in the whole city. **32**Immediately he took some officers and soldiers and ran to the place where the crowd was gathered. When the people saw them, they stopped beating Paul. **33**The commander went to Paul and arrested him. He told his soldiers to tie Paul with two chains. Then he asked who he was and what he had done wrong. **34**Some in the crowd were yelling one thing, and some were yelling another. Because of all this confusion and shouting, the commander could not learn what had happened. So he ordered the soldiers to take Paul to the army building. **35**When Paul came to the steps, the soldiers had to carry him because the people were ready to hurt him. **36**The whole mob was following them, shouting, "Kill him!"

37As the soldiers were about to take Paul into the army building, he spoke to the commander, "May I say something to you?"

The commander said, "Do you speak Greek? **38**I thought you were the Egyptian who started some trouble against the government not long ago and led four thousand killers out to the desert."

39Paul said, "No, I am a Jew from Tarsus in the country of Cilicia. I am a citizen of that important city. Please, let me speak to the people."

40The commander gave permission, so Paul stood on the steps and waved his hand to quiet the people. When there was silence, he spoke to them in the Hebrew language.

Paul Speaks to the People

22 Paul said, "Friends, fellow Jews, listen to my defense to you."

21:24 cleansing ceremony The special things Jews did to end the Nazirite promise.

21:24 shave their heads Jews did this to show that their promise was finished.

A MAN OF TWO COUNTRIES

Acts 22

Paul was a Jewish man, yet he was born in a town that was ruled by Rome. Because of that, he was an Israelite, but he also was a Roman citizen. (Check out Acts 22:28.) A Roman citizen could not be tied up or put into prison without a trial. A Roman citizen also wasn't supposed to be beaten or whipped. Another law said that if a Roman citizen felt he was not receiving a fair trial under local authorities, he could appeal his cause to Rome.

Sometimes being a Roman citizen really helped Paul out. Once he and his partner Silas were bound, beaten, and imprisoned by Roman authorities at Philippi. When Paul told the authorities that they were Roman citizens, the authorities let them go immediately. (Read Acts 16:16–40.) Another time in Jerusalem, Paul was taken into custody by Roman soldiers. Because he was a Roman citizen, he was not beaten and was able to get a hearing that eventually led him to Rome. (See Acts 22:24–29.)

2When they heard him speaking the Hebrew language,* they became very quiet.
Paul said, **3**"I am a Jew, born in Tarsus in
the country of Cilicia, but I grew up in
this city. I was a student of Gamaliel,*
who carefully taught me everything
about the law of our ancestors. I was very
serious about serving God, just as are all
of you here today. **4**I persecuted the people who followed the Way of Jesus, and
some of them were even killed. I arrested men and women and put them in jail.
5The high priest and the whole council of
older leaders can tell you this is true.
They gave me letters to the brothers in
Damascus. So I was going there to arrest
these people and bring them back to Jerusalem to be punished.

6"About noon when I came near Damascus, a bright light from heaven suddenly flashed all around me. **7**I fell to the
ground and heard a voice saying, 'Saul,
Saul, why are you persecuting me?' **8**I
asked, 'Who are you, Lord?' The voice
said, 'I am Jesus from Nazareth whom
you are persecuting.' **9**Those who were
with me did not hear the voice, but they
saw the light. **10**I said, 'What shall I do,
Lord?' The Lord answered, 'Get up and
go to Damascus. There you will be told
about all the things I have planned for you
to do.' **11**I could not see, because the
bright light had made me blind. So my
companions led me into Damascus.

12"There a man named Ananias came
to me. He was a religious man; he obeyed
the law of Moses, and all the Jews who
lived there respected him. **13**He stood by
me and said, 'Brother Saul, see again!'
Immediately I was able to see him. **14**He
said, 'The God of our ancestors chose you
long ago to know his plan, to see the Righteous One, and to hear words from him.
15You will be his witness to all people,
telling them about what you have seen
and heard. **16**Now, why wait any longer?
Get up, be baptized, and wash your sins
away, trusting in him to save you.'

17"Later, when I returned to Jerusa-

22:2 Hebrew language Hebrew or Aramaic, the languages of many people in this region in the first century.

22:3 Gamaliel A very important teacher of the Pharisees, a Jewish religious group (Acts 5:34).

lem, I was praying in the Temple, and I
saw a vision. **18**I saw the Lord saying to
me, 'Hurry! Leave Jerusalem now! The
people here will not accept the truth
about me.' **19**But I said, 'Lord, they know
that in every synagogue I put the believers in jail and beat them. **20**They also
know I was there when Stephen, your
witness, was killed. I stood there agreeing and holding the coats of those who
were killing him!' **21**But the Lord said to
me, 'Leave now. I will send you far away
to the other nations.' "

22The crowd listened to Paul until he
said this. Then they began shouting, "Kill
him! Get him out of the world! He should
not be allowed to live!" **23**They shouted,
threw off their coats,[n] and threw dust into
the air.[n]

24Then the commander ordered the
soldiers to take Paul into the army building and beat him. He wanted to make
Paul tell why the people were shouting
against him like this. **25**But as the soldiers were tying him up, preparing to
beat him, Paul said to an officer nearby,
"Do you have the right to beat a Roman
citizen[n] who has not been proven guilty?"

26When the officer heard this, he
went to the commander and reported it.
The officer said, "Do you know what you
are doing? This man is a Roman citizen."

27The commander came to Paul and
said, "Tell me, are you really a Roman citizen?"

He answered, "Yes."

28The commander said, "I paid a lot of
money to become a Roman citizen."

But Paul said, "I was born a citizen."

29The men who were preparing to
question Paul moved away from him immediately. The commander was frightened because he had already tied Paul,
and Paul was a Roman citizen.

Paul Speaks to Leaders

30The next day the commander decided to learn why the Jews were accusing Paul. So he ordered the leading
priests and the council to meet. The commander took Paul's chains off. Then he
brought Paul out and stood him before
their meeting.

23 Paul looked at the council and
said, "Brothers, I have lived my
life without guilt feelings before God up to
this day." **2**Ananias,[n] the high priest, heard
this and told the men who were standing
near Paul to hit him on the mouth. **3**Paul
said to Ananias, "God will hit you, too!
You are like a wall that has been painted
white. You sit there and judge me, using
the law of Moses, but you are telling them
to hit me, and that is against the law."

4The men standing near Paul said to
him, "You cannot insult God's high priest
like that!"

5Paul said, "Brothers, I did not know
this man was the high priest. It is written
in the Scriptures, 'You must not curse a
leader of your people.' "[n]

6Some of the men in the meeting
were Sadducees, and others were Pharisees. Knowing this, Paul shouted to
them, "My brothers, I am a Pharisee, and
my father was a Pharisee. I am on trial
here because I believe that people will
rise from the dead."

7When Paul said this, there was an argument between the Pharisees and the
Sadducees, and the group was divided.
8(The Sadducees do not believe in angels
or spirits or that people will rise from the
dead. But the Pharisees believe in them
all.) **9**So there was a great uproar. Some
of the teachers of the law, who were
Pharisees, stood up and argued, "We find
nothing wrong with this man. Maybe an
angel or a spirit did speak to him."

10The argument was beginning to
turn into such a fight that the commander
was afraid some evil people would tear
Paul to pieces. So he told the soldiers to
go down and take Paul away and put him
in the army building.

11The next night the Lord came and

22:23 threw off their coats This showed that the people were very angry with Paul.

22:23 threw dust into the air This showed even greater anger.

22:25 Roman citizen Roman law said that Roman citizens must not be beaten before they had a trial.

23:2 Ananias This is not the same man named Ananias in Acts 22:12.

23:5 'You . . . people.' Quotation from Exodus 22:28.

stood by Paul. He said, "Be brave! You have told people in Jerusalem about me. You must do the same in Rome."

FAITH links

CALLING ANYONE!

ACTS 23:12-22

There are many unsung heroes in life. Paul's nephew learned about an evil plot to kill Paul. He told Paul about the plot and saved his life. Quick! For a chance to be known as the smartest person in the world, what was Paul's nephew's name? Give up? The answer is: no one knows! The Bible doesn't list his name. But we know that what he did for Paul was very important.

Sometimes God causes unknown people to do important things for him. God can use anyone to serve him. You don't have to be brave or have super strength. You just have to be willing.

Check out these links for more on serving God:

A Use for Your Abilities, Genesis 41, p. 59

His OK to Obey, Deuteronomy 2:24–36, p. 230

Your Stats, 1 Kings 15; 16, p. 460

Just Say Yes!, Matthew 9:9–13, p. 1289

That Thing You Do, Matthew 25:14–30, p. 1319

The "Eyes" Have It?, 1 Corinthians 12, p. 1559

12In the morning some evil people
made a plan to kill Paul, and they took an
oath not to eat or drink anything until
they had killed him. 13There were more
than forty men who made this plan.
14They went to the leading priests and
the older leaders and said, "We have
taken an oath not to eat or drink until we
have killed Paul. 15So this is what we
want you to do: Send a message to the
commander to bring Paul out to you as
though you want to ask him more questions. We will be waiting to kill him while
he is on the way here."
16But Paul's nephew heard about this
plan and went to the army building and
told Paul. 17Then Paul called one of the
officers and said, "Take this young man to
the commander. He has a message for
him."
18So the officer brought Paul's nephew
to the commander and said, "The prisoner, Paul, asked me to bring this young
man to you. He wants to tell you something."
19The commander took the young
man's hand and led him to a place where
they could be alone. He asked, "What do
you want to tell me?"
20The young man said, "The Jews
have decided to ask you to bring Paul
down to their council meeting tomorrow.
They want you to think they are going to
ask him more questions. 21But don't believe them! More than forty men are hiding and waiting to kill Paul. They have all
taken an oath not to eat or drink until
they have killed him. Now they are waiting for you to agree."
22The commander sent the young
man away, ordering him, "Don't tell anyone that you have told me about their
plan."

Paul Is Sent to Caesarea

23Then the commander called two officers and said, "I need some men to go to
Caesarea. Get two hundred soldiers, seventy horsemen, and two hundred men
with spears ready to leave at nine o'clock
tonight. 24Get some horses for Paul to
ride so he can be taken to Governor Felix
safely." 25And he wrote a letter that said:

26From Claudius Lysias.
To the Most Excellent Governor Felix:
Greetings.
27Some of the Jews had taken
this man and planned to kill him.
But I learned that he is a Roman
citizen, so I went with my soldiers
and saved him. **28**I wanted to know
why they were accusing him, so I
brought him before their council
meeting. **29**I learned that these
people said Paul did some things
that were wrong by their own laws,
but no charge was worthy of jail or
death. **30**When I was told that
some of them were planning to kill
Paul, I sent him to you at once. I
also told them to tell you what they
have against him.

31So the soldiers did what they were
told and took Paul and brought him to the
city of Antipatris that night. **32**The next
day the horsemen went with Paul to
Caesarea, but the other soldiers went
back to the army building in Jerusalem.
33When the horsemen came to Caesarea
and gave the letter to the governor, they
turned Paul over to him. **34**The governor
read the letter and asked Paul, "What
area are you from?" When he learned
that Paul was from Cilicia, **35**he said, "I
will hear your case when those who are
against you come here, too." Then the
governor gave orders for Paul to be kept
under guard in Herod's palace.

Paul Is Accused

24 Five days later Ananias, the high
priest, went to the city of Caesarea with some of the older leaders and a
lawyer named Tertullus. They had come
to make charges against Paul before the
governor. **2**Paul was called into the meeting, and Tertullus began to accuse him,
saying, "Most Excellent Felix! Our people enjoy much peace because of you, and
many wrong things in our country are being made right through your wise help.
3We accept these things always and in
every place, and we are thankful for
them. **4**But not wanting to take any more
of your time, I beg you to be kind and listen to our few words. **5**We have found
this man to be a troublemaker, stirring up
his people everywhere in the world. He
is a leader of the Nazarene group. **6**Also,
he was trying to make the Temple unclean, but we stopped him." **8**By asking
him questions yourself, you can decide if
all these things are true." **9**The others
agreed and said that all of this was true.
10When the governor made a sign for
Paul to speak, Paul said, "Governor Felix,
I know you have been a judge over this
nation for a long time. So I am happy to
defend myself before you. **11**You can
learn for yourself that I went to worship
in Jerusalem only twelve days ago.
12Those who are accusing me did not
find me arguing with anyone in the Temple or stirring up the people in the synagogues or in the city. **13**They cannot
prove the things they are saying against
me now. **14**But I will tell you this: I worship the God of our ancestors as a follower of the Way of Jesus. The others say
that the Way of Jesus is not the right way.
But I believe everything that is taught in
the law of Moses and that is written in
the books of the Prophets. **15**I have the
same hope in God that they have—the
hope that all people, good and bad, will
surely be raised from the dead. **16**This is
why I always try to do what I believe is
right before God and people.
17"After being away from Jerusalem
for several years, I went back to bring
money to my people and to offer sacrifices. **18**I was doing this when they found
me in the Temple. I had finished the
cleansing ceremony and had not made
any trouble; no people were gathering
around me. **19**But there were some people from the country of Asia who should
be here, standing before you. If I have
really done anything wrong, they are the
ones who should accuse me. **20**Or ask
these people here if they found any

24:6 Verse 6 Some Greek copies add 6b-8a: "And we wanted to judge him by our own law. [7]But the officer Lysias came and used much force to take him from us. [8]And Lysias commanded those who wanted to accuse Paul to come to you."

wrong in me when I stood before the
council in Jerusalem. 21But I did shout
one thing when I stood before them: 'You
are judging me today because I believe
that people will rise from the dead!' "
22Felix already understood much
about the Way of Jesus. He stopped the
trial and said, "When commander Lysias
comes here, I will decide your case."
23Felix told the officer to keep Paul
guarded but to give him some freedom
and to let his friends bring what he
needed.

Paul Speaks to Felix and His Wife

24After some days Felix came with
his wife, Drusilla, who was Jewish, and
asked for Paul to be brought to him. He
listened to Paul talk about believing in
Christ Jesus. 25But Felix became afraid
when Paul spoke about living right, self-
control, and the time when God will
judge the world. He said, "Go away now.
When I have more time, I will call for
you." 26At the same time Felix hoped
that Paul would give him some money, so
he often sent for Paul and talked with
him.

27But after two years, Felix was replaced by Porcius Festus as governor.
But Felix had left Paul in prison to please
the Jews.

Paul Asks to See Caesar

25 Three days after Festus became
governor, he went from Caesarea
to Jerusalem. 2There the leading priests
and the important leaders made charges
against Paul before Festus. 3They asked
Festus to do them a favor. They wanted
him to send Paul back to Jerusalem, because they had a plan to kill him on the
way. 4But Festus answered that Paul
would be kept in Caesarea and that he
himself was returning there soon. 5He
said, "Some of your leaders should go
with me. They can accuse the man there
in Caesarea, if he has really done something wrong."

6Festus stayed in Jerusalem another
eight or ten days and then went back to
Caesarea. The next day he told the soldiers to bring Paul before him. Festus
was seated on the judge's seat 7when
Paul came into the room. The people who
had come from Jerusalem stood around
him, making serious charges against him,
which they could not prove. 8This is what
Paul said to defend himself: "I have done
nothing wrong against the law, against
the Temple, or against Caesar."

9But Festus wanted to please the people. So he asked Paul, "Do you want to go
to Jerusalem for me to judge you there on
these charges?"

10Paul said, "I am standing at Caesar's judgment seat now, where I should
be judged. I have done nothing wrong to

FAITH CHALLENGE

Hey there! Read 24:25 to see what one Roman leader said about becoming a Christian. Why do you think some people are afraid to hear about becoming a Christian? What would you tell them about the need to know Jesus?

TESTING IT

Acts 24:25
But Felix became afraid when Paul spoke about living right, self-control, and the time when God will judge the world. He said, "Go away now. When I have more time, I will call for you."

them; you know this is true. 11If I have
done something wrong and the law says I
must die, I do not ask to be saved from
death. But if these charges are not true,
then no one can give me to them. I want
Caesar to hear my case!"
12Festus talked about this with his advisers. Then he said, "You have asked to
see Caesar, so you will go
to Caesar!"

> If I have done something wrong and the law says I must die, I do not ask to be saved from death.
> —Acts 25:11

Paul Before King Agrippa

13A few days later
King Agrippa and Bernice
came to Caesarea to visit
Festus. 14They stayed
there for some time, and
Festus told the king about
Paul's case. Festus said,
"There is a man that Felix left in prison.
15When I went to Jerusalem, the leading
priests and the older leaders there made
charges against him, asking me to sentence him to death. 16But I answered,
'When a man is accused of a crime, Romans do not hand him over until he has
been allowed to face his accusers and defend himself against their charges.' 17So
when these people came here to Caesarea for the trial, I did not waste time. The
next day I sat on the judge's seat and
commanded that the man be brought in.
18They stood up and accused him, but
not of any serious crime as I thought they
would. 19The things they said were
about their own religion and about a man
named Jesus who died. But Paul said that
he is still alive. 20Not knowing how to
find out about these questions, I asked
Paul, 'Do you want to go to Jerusalem and
be judged there?' 21But he asked to be
kept in Caesarea. He wants a decision
from the emperor.[n] So I ordered that he
be held until I could send him to Caesar."
22Agrippa said to Festus, "I would
also like to hear this man myself."
Festus said, "Tomorrow you will hear
him."
23The next day Agrippa and Bernice
appeared with great show, acting like
very important people. They went into
the judgment room with the army leaders
and the important men of Caesarea. Then
Festus ordered the soldiers to bring Paul
in. 24Festus said, "King Agrippa and all
who are gathered here with us, you see
this man. All the people, here and in Jerusalem, have complained to me about him,
shouting that he should not live any
longer. 25When I judged him, I found no
reason to order his death.
But since he asked to be
judged by Caesar, I de-
cided to send him. 26But
I have nothing definite
to write the emperor
about him. So I have
brought him before all of
you—especially you, King
Agrippa. I hope you can
question him and give me
something to write. 27I
think it is foolish to send a prisoner to
Caesar without telling what charges are
against him."

Paul Defends Himself

26 Agrippa said to Paul, "You may
now speak to defend yourself."
Then Paul raised his hand and began
to speak. 2He said, "King Agrippa, I am
very happy to stand before you and will
answer all the charges the evil people
make against me. 3You know so much
about all the customs and the things they
argue about, so please listen to me patiently.
4"All my people know about my whole
life, how I lived from the beginning in my
own country and later in Jerusalem.
5They have known me for a long time. If
they want to, they can tell you that I was
a good Pharisee. And the Pharisees obey
the laws of my tradition more carefully
than any other group. 6Now I am on trial
because I hope for the promise that God
made to our ancestors. 7This is the
promise that the twelve tribes of our people hope to receive as they serve God day
and night. My king, they have accused
me because I hope for this same promise!
8Why do any of you people think it is

25:21 emperor The ruler of the Roman Empire, which was almost all the known world.

FAITH links

HOPE THAT DOESN'T FAIL

ACTS 26:4-7

Imagine being dragged into court and told to defend yourself for being a Christian. This was Paul's situation. After being arrested and taken before the Jewish king, Agrippa, Paul stated his defense. His explanation can be summed up in three words: hope in Jesus. This is the kind of hope that won't fail in a crisis. This hope is eternal!

When you believe in Jesus, you have hope because you know that he keeps his promises. He promised to always be with you, no matter what. That's the kind of hope the world needs!

A Message of Courage and Hope, 2 Kings 19:4–10, p. 505

Comfort from the Word, Job 26:3–4, p. 688

A Hopeful Name, Hosea 1:3–11, p. 1172

A Safe Place, Nahum 1:7, p. 1231

Mission Impossible?, Mark 5:21–24, 35–43, p. 1337

Our Good Shepherd, John 10:11–15, p. 1441

impossible for God to raise people from
the dead?
9"I, too, thought I ought to do many
things against Jesus from Nazareth.
10And that is what I did in Jerusalem.
The leading priests gave me the power to
put many of God's people in jail, and
when they were being killed, I agreed it
was a good thing. 11In every synagogue,
I often punished them and tried to make
them speak against Jesus. I was so angry
against them I even went to other cities
to find them and punish them.
12"One time the leading priests gave
me permission and the power to go to
Damascus. 13On the way there, at noon, I
saw a light from heaven. It was brighter
than the sun and flashed all around me
and those who were traveling with me.
14We all fell to the ground. Then I heard a
voice speaking to me in the Hebrew
language,[n] saying, 'Saul, Saul, why are
you persecuting me? You are only hurting yourself by fighting me.' 15I said,
'Who are you, Lord?' The Lord said, 'I am
Jesus, the one you are persecuting.
16Stand up! I have chosen you to be my
servant and my witness—you will tell
people the things that you have seen and
the things that I will show you. This is
why I have come to you today. 17I will
keep you safe from your own people and
also from the others. I am sending you to
them 18to open their eyes so that they
may turn away from darkness to the
light, away from the power of Satan and
to God. Then their sins can be forgiven,
and they can have a place with those people who have been made holy by believing in me.'
19"King Agrippa, after I had this vision
from heaven, I obeyed it. 20I began telling people that they should change their
hearts and lives and turn to God and do
things to show they really had changed. I
told this first to those in Damascus, then
in Jerusalem, and in every part of Judea,
and also to the other people. 21This is
why the Jews took me and were trying to
kill me in the Temple. 22But God has
helped me, and so I stand here today, telling all people, small and great, what I
have seen. But I am saying only what
Moses and the prophets said would happen—23that the Christ would die, and as
the first to rise from the dead, he would
bring light to all people."

26:14 Hebrew language Hebrew or Aramaic, the languages of many people in this region in the first century.

Paul Tries to Persuade Agrippa

24While Paul was saying these things
to defend himself, Festus said loudly,
"Paul, you are out of your mind! Too
much study has driven you crazy!"
25Paul said, "Most excellent Festus, I
am not crazy. My words are true and sensible. 26King Agrippa knows about these
things, and I can speak freely to him. I
know he has heard about all of these
things, because they did not happen off in
a corner. 27King Agrippa, do you believe
what the prophets wrote? I know you believe."
28King Agrippa said to Paul, "Do you
think you can persuade me to become a
Christian in such a short time?"
29Paul said, "Whether it is a short or a
long time, I pray to God that not only you
but every person listening to me today
would be saved and be like me—except
for these chains I have."
30Then King Agrippa, Governor Festus, Bernice, and all the people sitting
with them stood up 31and left the room.
Talking to each other, they said, "There
is no reason why this man should die or
be put in jail." 32And Agrippa said to Festus, "We could let this man go free, but he
has asked Caesar to hear his case."

Paul Sails for Rome

27 It was decided that we would sail
for Italy. An officer named Julius,
who served in the emperor's[n] army,
guarded Paul and some other prisoners.
2We got on a ship that was from the city
of Adramyttium and was about to sail to
different ports in the country of Asia. Aristarchus, a man from the city of Thessalonica in Macedonia, went with us. 3The
next day we came to Sidon. Julius was
very good to Paul and gave him freedom
to go visit his friends, who took care of
his needs. 4We left Sidon and sailed close
to the island of Cyprus, because the wind
was blowing against us. 5We went across
the sea by Cilicia and Pamphylia and landed at the city of Myra, in Lycia. 6There
the officer found a ship from Alexandria
that was going to Italy, so he put us on it.
7We sailed slowly for many days. We
had a hard time reaching Cnidus because
the wind was blowing against us, and we
could not go any farther. So we sailed by
the south side of the island of Crete near
Salmone. 8Sailing past it was hard. Then
we came to a place called Fair Havens,
near the city of Lasea.
9We had lost much time, and it was
now dangerous to sail, because it was already after the Day of Cleansing.[n] So Paul
warned them, 10"Men, I can see there
will be a lot of trouble on this trip. The
ship, the cargo, and even our lives may be
lost." 11But the captain and the owner of
the ship did not agree with Paul, and the
officer believed what the captain and
owner of the ship said. 12Since that harbor was not a good place for the ship to
stay for the winter, most of the men decided that the ship should leave. They
hoped we could go to Phoenix and stay
there for the winter. Phoenix, a city on
the island of Crete, had a harbor which
faced southwest and northwest.

The Storm

13When a good wind began to blow
from the south, the men on the ship
thought, "This is the wind we wanted, and
now we have it." So they pulled up the
anchor, and we sailed very close to the
island of Crete. 14But then a very strong
wind named the "northeaster" came
from the island. 15The ship was caught in
it and could not sail against it. So we
stopped trying and let the wind carry us.
16When we went below a small island
named Cauda, we were barely able to
bring in the lifeboat. 17After the men
took the lifeboat in, they tied ropes
around the ship to hold it together. The
men were afraid that the ship would hit
the sandbanks of Syrtis,[n] so they lowered
the sail and let the wind carry the ship.
18The next day the storm was blowing us
so hard that the men threw out some of

27:1 emperor The ruler of the Roman Empire, which was almost all the known world.

27:9 Day of Cleansing An important Jewish holy day in the fall of the year. This was the time of year that bad storms arose on the sea.

27:17 Syrtis Shallow area in the sea near the Libyan coast.

the cargo. **19**A day later with their own hands they threw out the ship's equipment. **20**When we could not see the sun or the stars for many days, and the storm was very bad, we lost all hope of being saved.

21After the men had gone without food for a long time, Paul stood up before them and said, "Men, you should have listened to me. You should not have sailed from Crete. Then you would not have all this trouble and loss. **22**But now I tell you to cheer up because none of you will die. Only the ship will be lost. **23**Last night an angel came to me from the God I belong to and worship. **24**The angel said, 'Paul, do not be afraid. You must stand before Caesar. And God has promised you that he will save the lives of everyone sailing with you.' **25**So men, have courage. I trust in God that everything will happen as his angel told me. **26**But we will crash on an island."

27On the fourteenth night we were still being carried around in the Adriatic Sea.[n] About midnight the sailors thought we were close to land, **28**so they lowered a rope with a weight on the end of it into the water. They found that the water was one hundred twenty feet deep. They went a little farther and lowered the rope again. It was ninety feet deep. **29**The sailors were afraid that we would hit the rocks, so they threw four anchors into the water and prayed for daylight to come. **30**Some of the sailors wanted to leave the ship, and they lowered the lifeboat, pretending they were throwing more anchors from the front of the ship. **31**But Paul told the officer and the other soldiers, "If these men do not stay in the ship, your lives cannot be saved." **32**So the soldiers cut the ropes and let the lifeboat fall into the water.

33Just before dawn Paul began persuading all the people to eat something. He said, "For the past fourteen days you have been waiting and watching and not eating. **34**Now I beg you to eat something. You need it to stay alive. None of you will lose even one hair off your heads." **35**After he said this, Paul took some bread and thanked God for it before all of them. He broke off a piece and began eating. **36**They all felt better and started eating, too. **37**There were two hundred seventy-six people on the ship. **38**When they had eaten all they wanted, they began making the ship lighter by throwing the grain into the sea.

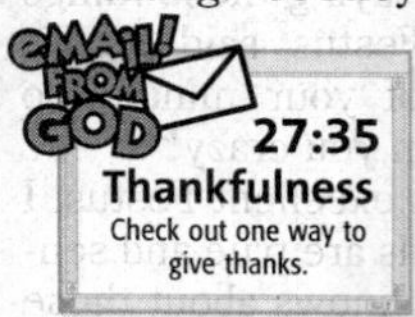

EMAIL! FROM GOD
27:35
Thankfulness
Check out one way to give thanks.

The Ship Is Destroyed

39When daylight came, the sailors saw land. They did not know what land it was, but they saw a bay with a beach and wanted to sail the ship to the beach if they could. **40**So they cut the ropes to the anchors and left the anchors in the sea. At the same time, they untied the ropes that were holding the rudders. Then they raised the front sail into the wind and sailed toward the beach. **41**But the ship hit a sandbank. The front of the ship stuck there and could not move, but the back of the ship began to break up from the big waves.

42The soldiers decided to kill the prisoners so none of them could swim away and escape. **43**But Julius, the officer, wanted to let Paul live and did not allow the soldiers to kill the prisoners. Instead he ordered everyone who could swim to jump into the water first and swim to land. **44**The rest were to follow using wooden boards or pieces of the ship. And this is how all the people made it safely to land.

Paul on the Island of Malta

28 When we were safe on land, we learned that the island was called Malta. **2**The people who lived there were very good to us. Because it was raining and very cold, they made a fire and welcomed all of us. **3**Paul gathered a pile of sticks and was putting them on the fire when a poisonous snake came out because of the heat and bit him on the hand. **4**The people living on the island saw the

---

27:27 Adriatic Sea The sea between Greece and Italy, including the central Mediterranean.

THE LIFE OF PAUL

Acts

1. Early life. Saul was born in Tarsus, both a Jew *and* a Roman citizen. (Read Acts 22:3.) He studied with a famous Jewish teacher named Gamaliel and became a well-respected religious leader. Saul hunted down Christians and punished them for their faith. (Look at Acts 8:3.) Later, Saul met Jesus on his way to Damascus and became a leader of Christ-followers, known as Christians. (See Acts 9:1–9.)

2. Preparation. Paul began working at first with the Christians in Damascus (Look up Acts 9:22.), Arabia (Check out Galatians 1:17, p. 1587.), and Jerusalem. Then he went to Tarsus for about ten years because the Jewish leaders were against him. (Read Acts 9:26–30.)

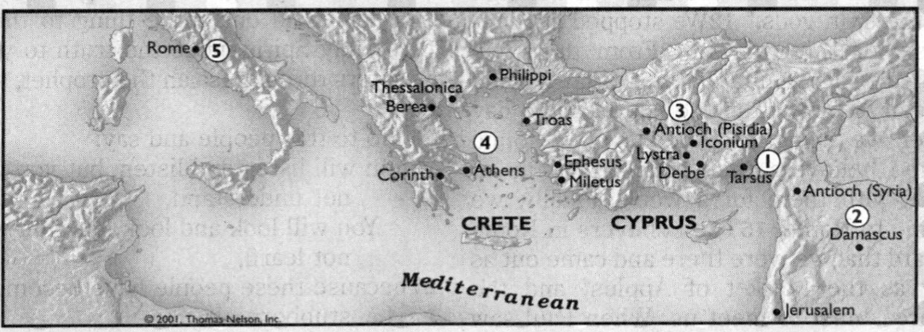

3. Early missionary work. Paul traveled to Cyprus, Antioch, Iconium, Lystra, and Derbe with his good friend Barnabas. They took the message of the gospel to non-Jewish people. (Look at Acts 11:19–26. See also Acts 13 and 14 for more information about their travels.)

4. Later trips. On Paul's second missionary trip, he traveled to Macedonia, Philippi, Thessalonica, Berea, Athens, and Corinth. (Look up Acts 16:1—18:23.) On his third missionary trip, he worked with the churches at Ephesus, Troas, and Miletus. (Check out Acts 19 and 20.)

5. After he was put in jail for his preaching, Paul appealed his case to Rome. (Read Acts 25.) He traveled by ship to Rome for a trial. (Look up Acts 27.) Even as a prisoner in Rome he continued to preach about Jesus. (See Acts 28:17–31.) It's possible that Paul was executed around A.D. 68.

snake hanging from Paul's hand and said
to each other, "This man must be a murderer! He did not die in the sea, but
Justice[n] does not want him to live." 5But
Paul shook the snake off into the fire and
was not hurt. 6The people thought that
Paul would swell up or fall down dead.
They waited and watched him for a long
time, but nothing bad happened to him.
So they changed their minds and said,
"He is a god!"
7There were some fields around there
owned by Publius, an important man on
the island. He welcomed us into his
home and was very good to us for three

28:4 Justice The people thought there was a god named Justice who would punish bad people.

days. 8Publius' father was sick with a fever and dysentery.[n] Paul went to him,
prayed, and put his hands on the man and
healed him. 9After this, all the other sick
people on the island came to Paul, and he
healed them, too. 10-11The
people on the island
gave us many hon-
ors. When we were
ready to leave, three
months later, they
gave us the things
we needed.

EMAIL! FROM GOD
28:10–11
Giving
How can you help God's workers?

Paul Goes to Rome

We got on a ship from Alexandria that
had stayed on the island during the winter. On the front of the ship was the sign
of the twin gods.[n] 12We stopped at Syra-
cuse for three days. 13From there we
sailed to Rhegium. The next day a wind
began to blow from the south, and a day
later we came to Puteoli. 14We found
some believers there who asked us to
stay with them for a week. Finally, we
came to Rome. 15The believers in Rome
heard that we were there and came out as
far as the Market of Appius[n] and the
Three Inns[n] to meet us. When Paul saw
them, he was encouraged and thanked
God.

Paul in Rome

16When we arrived at Rome, Paul was
allowed to live alone, with the soldier
who guarded him.

17Three days later Paul sent for the
leaders there. When they came together,
he said, "Brothers, I have done nothing
against our people or the customs of our
ancestors. But I was arrested in Jerusalem and given to the Romans. 18After
they asked me many questions, they
could find no reason why I should be
killed. They wanted to let me go free,
19but the evil people there argued
against that. So I had to ask to come to
Rome to have my trial before Caesar. But
I have no charge to bring against my own
people. 20That is why I wanted to see
you and talk with you. I am bound with
this chain because I believe in the hope of
Israel."

21They answered Paul, "We have received no letters from Judea about you.
None of our Jewish brothers who have
come from there brought news or told us
anything bad about you. 22But we want
to hear your ideas, because we know that
people everywhere are speaking against
this religious group."

23Paul and the people chose a day for a
meeting and on that day many more of the
Jews met with Paul at the place he was
staying. He spoke to them all day long.
Using the law of Moses and the prophets'
writings, he explained the kingdom of
God, and he tried to persuade them to believe these things about Jesus. 24Some
believed what Paul said, but others did
not. 25So they argued and began leaving
after Paul said one more thing to them:
"The Holy Spirit spoke the truth to your
ancestors through Isaiah the prophet, saying,

26'Go to this people and say:
You will listen and listen, but you will
not understand.
You will look and look, but you will
not learn,
27because these people have become
stubborn.
They don't hear with their ears,
and they have closed their eyes.
Otherwise, they might really
understand
what they see with their eyes
and hear with their ears.
They might really understand in their
minds
and come back to me and be
healed.' *Isaiah 6:9-10*

28"I want you to know that God has
also sent his salvation to all nations, and
they will listen!" 29[n]

28:8 dysentery A sickness like diarrhea.
28:10–11 twin gods Statues of Castor and Pollux, gods in old Greek tales.
28:15 Market of Appius A town about twenty-seven miles from Rome.
28:15 Three Inns A town about thirty miles from Rome.
28:29 Verse 29 Some late Greek copies add verse 29: "After Paul said this, the Jews left. They were arguing very much with each other."

30Paul stayed two full years in his own rented house and welcomed all people who came to visit him. 31He boldly
preached about the kingdom of God and taught about the Lord Jesus Christ, and no one tried to stop him.

BACK TO THE BASICS

Hi; Paul here. You might have read about me in Luke's book, Acts. I was a Jewish religious leader who had a life-changing encounter with the living Jesus. As a result, instead of killing Jesus' followers, I became a leader in the early church! You can guess I caused quite a stir when I began telling others about Jesus! Some say this letter I wrote to my friends in Rome was one of my most important books. Read my other books, and you decide!

I wrote this book to help this young church understand the basics about my teachings on Jesus, God, the church, and differences between Jews and non-Jews. The church in Rome was full of all sorts of controversies over what to believe. So, I wrote this letter to them to set the record straight. And in the process I ended up writing what has become a lesson on the Christian faith that is important to all followers at all times.

JESUS WATCH

The significance of Jesus fills this book. What significance? Well, Paul takes time in this book to help believers understand who we are without Jesus and what effect Jesus has on our lives—and ultimately on our eternity.

In Romans, Paul explains that Jesus is the giver of eternal life. It's a gift that's not only free, but also one that frees us from the punishment we would face if we didn't know him. As Paul explains, without Jesus, we would be totally lost. When Jesus died on the cross, he totally defeated death for all those who believe in him. That's a powerful message, and Paul wanted *everyone* to know it and understand it.

my FAVORITE links

OTHER CONNECTIONS

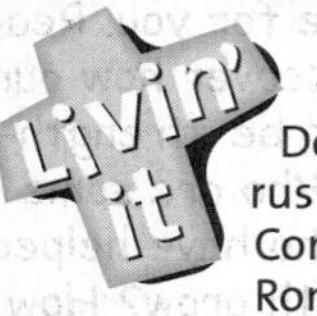

What's the first thing you want to do when you get some wonderful news? Do you keep it to yourself or do you rush right out to tell someone else? Connect to Have I Got News for You!, Romans 10:14–17, to see what God wants us to do with *his* good news!

Find out what God has to say about keeping the peace in your home, or among your friends, when you download Peace and Quiet?, Romans 14:19.

Link to Let's Visit Rome, Romans 1:15, to learn more about the largest and most famous city in New Testament times.

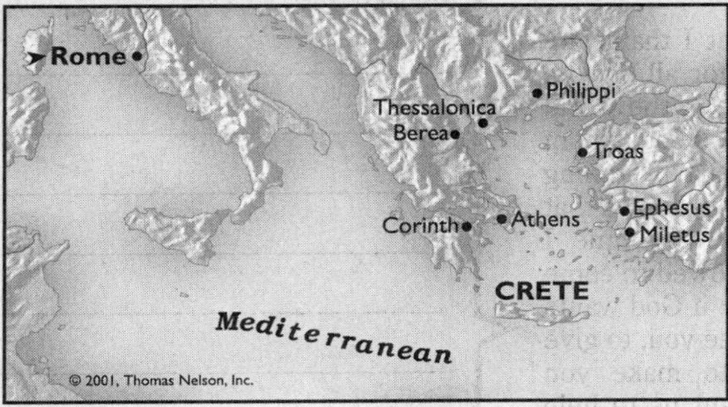

FAITH links

- Just for the Asking, Romans 3:23–28
- Love for Free, Romans 5:8
- A High Price, Romans 6:23
- The Sin Habit, Romans 7:15–20
- It's Under Control, Romans 8:28
- The Doubt Remover, Romans 10:8–10
- Our Gift to God, Romans 12:1–2
- Glad to Help!, Romans 15:17–20

"Hey, Skweek, quick question here. Does God ever stop loving us?"

"No way! Check out Romans 8:38–39 to see what Paul has to say about that."

did you know?

THE BOOK OF ROMANS HAS A LOT OF OTHER REALLY FANTASTIC TRUTHS. CHECK OUT THESE:

Everyone needs Jesus!, Romans 3:9–20
The father of our faith, Romans 4
God's Spirit rules!, Romans 8
Live by God's rules, Romans 12; 13

1 From Paul, a servant of Christ Jesus.
God called me to be an apostle and
chose me to tell the Good News.
2God promised this Good News long
ago through his prophets, as it is written
in the Holy Scriptures. **3-4**The Good
News is about God's Son, Jesus Christ
our Lord. As a man, he was born from the
family of David. But through the Spirit of
holiness he was appointed to be God's
Son with great power by rising from the
dead. **5**Through Christ, God gave me the
special work of an apostle, which was to
lead people of all nations to believe and
obey. I do this work for him. **6**And you
who are in Rome are also called to belong
to Jesus Christ.
7To all of you in Rome whom God
loves and has called to be his holy people:
Grace and peace to you from God our
Father and the Lord Jesus Christ.

A Prayer of Thanks

8First I want to say that I thank my
God through Jesus Christ for all of you,
because people everywhere in the world
are talking about your faith. **9**God, whom
I serve with my whole heart by telling
the Good News about his Son, knows that
I always mention you **10**every time I
pray. I pray that I will be allowed to come
to you, and this will happen if God wants
it. **11**I want very much to see you, to give
you some spiritual gift to make you
strong. **12**I mean that I want us to help
each other with the faith we have. Your
faith will help me, and my faith will help
you. **13**Brothers and sisters,[n] I want you
to know that I planned many times to
come to you, but this has not been possible. I wanted to come so that I could help
you grow spiritually as I have helped the
other non-Jewish people.
14I have a duty to all people—Greeks
and those who are not Greeks, the wise
and the foolish. **15**That is why I want so
much to preach the Good News to you in
Rome.
16I am proud of the Good News, because it is the power God uses to save
everyone who believes—to save the
Jews first, and also to save those who are
not Jews. **17**The Good News shows how

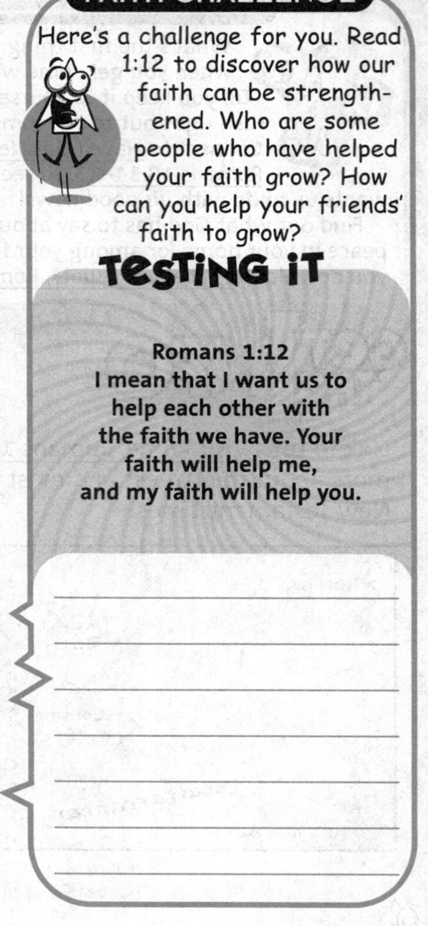

God makes people right with himself—
that it begins and ends with faith. As the
Scripture says, "But those who are right
with God will live by trusting in him."[n]

All People Have Done Wrong

18God's anger is shown from heaven
against all the evil and wrong things peo-

1:13 Brothers and sisters Although the Greek text says "Brothers" here and throughout this book, Paul's words were meant for the entire church, including men and women.
1:17 "But those . . . him." Quotation from Habakkuk 2:4.

LET'S VISIT ROME

Romans 1:15

During New Testament times, Rome was the largest and most famous city of its day. (Have you heard the phrase, "All roads lead to Rome"?) Over a million people lived there. It was the center of the whole Roman Empire. Sometimes it was called *Urbs Septicollis* ("City of the Seven Hills"), because it was literally built on seven hills.

Some famous sights in Rome are the Forum, the center of the city with roads in all directions, and the Colosseum, where games like the Olympics were held. Rome also had many temples for worshiping false gods, public baths, aqueducts, and arches. The apostle Paul was a prisoner in Rome when he wrote letters to churches that are part of the New Testament.

ple do. By their own evil lives they hide
the truth. **19**God shows his anger because some knowledge of him has been
made clear to them. Yes, God has shown
himself to them. **20**There are things
about him that people cannot see—his
eternal power and all
the things that make
him God. But since
the beginning of the
world those things
have been easy to
understand by what
God has made. So

1:20
Following God
Has God shown himself to people?

people have no excuse for the bad things
they do. **21**They knew God, but they did
not give glory to God or thank him. Their
thinking became useless. Their foolish
minds were filled with darkness. **22**They
said they were wise, but they became
fools. **23**They traded the glory of God
who lives forever for the worship of idols
made to look like earthly people, birds,
animals, and snakes.

24Because they did these things, God
left them and let them go their sinful way,
wanting only to do evil. As a result, they
became full of sexual sin, using their
bodies wrongly with each other. **25**They
traded the truth of God for a lie. They
worshiped and served what had been created instead of the God who created
those things, who should be praised forever. Amen.

26Because people did those things,
God left them and let them do the shameful things they wanted to do. Women
stopped having natural sex and started
having sex with other women. **27**In the
same way, men stopped having natural
sex and began wanting each other. Men
did shameful things with other men, and
in their bodies they received the punishment for those wrongs.

28People did not think it was important to have a true knowledge of God. So
God left them and allowed them to have
their own worthless thinking and to do
things they should not do. **29**They are
filled with every kind of sin, evil, selfishness, and hatred. They are full of jealousy, murder, fighting, lying, and thinking
the worst about each other. They gossip
30and say evil things about each other.
They hate God. They are rude and conceited and brag about themselves. They
invent ways of doing evil. They do not
obey their parents. **31**They are foolish,
they do not keep their promises, and they
show no kindness or mercy to others.

32They know God's law says that those who live like this should die. But they themselves not only continue to do these evil things, they applaud others who do them.

You People Also Are Sinful

2 If you think you can judge others, you are wrong. When you judge them, you are really judging yourself guilty, because you do the same things they do. **2**God judges those who do wrong things, and we know that his judging is right. **3**You judge those who do wrong, but you do wrong yourselves. Do you think you will be able to escape the judgment of God? **4**He has been very kind and patient, waiting for you to change, but you think nothing of his kindness. Perhaps you do not understand that God is kind to you so you will change your hearts and lives. **5**But you are stubborn and refuse to change, so you are making your own punishment even greater on the day he shows his anger. On that day everyone will see God's right judgments. **6**God will reward or punish every person for what that person has done. **7**Some people, by always continuing to do good, live for God's glory, for honor, and for life that has no end. God will give them life forever. **8**But other people are selfish. They refuse to follow truth and, instead, follow evil. God will give them his punishment and anger. **9**He will give trouble and suffering to everyone who does evil—to the Jews first and also to those who are not Jews. **10**But he will give glory, honor, and peace to everyone who does good—to the Jews first and also to those who are not Jews. **11**For God judges all people in the same way.

2:4
Kindness
God has been kind to you.

12People who do not have the law and who are sinners will be lost, although they do not have the law. And, in the same way, those who have the law and are sinners will be judged by the law. **13**Hearing the law does not make people right with God. It is those who obey the law who will be right with him. **14**(Those who are not Jews do not have the law, but when they freely do what the law commands, they are the law for themselves. This is true even though they do not have the law. **15**They show that in their hearts they know what is right and wrong, just as the law commands. And they show this by their consciences. Sometimes their thoughts tell them they did wrong, and sometimes their thoughts tell them they did right.) **16**All these things will happen on the day when God, through Christ Jesus, will judge people's secret thoughts. The Good News that I preach says this.

The Jews and the Law

17What about you? You call yourself a Jew. You trust in the law of Moses and brag that you are close to God. **18**You know what he wants you to do and what is important, because you have learned the law. **19**You think you are a guide for the blind and a light for those who are in darkness. **20**You think you can show foolish people what is right and teach those who know nothing. You have the law; so you think you know everything and have all truth. **21**You teach others, so why don't you teach yourself? You tell others not to steal, but you steal. **22**You say that others must not take part in adultery, but you are guilty of that sin. You hate idols, but you steal from temples. **23**You brag about having God's law, but you bring shame to God by breaking his law, **24**just as the Scriptures say: "Those who are not Jews speak against God's name because of you."[n]

25If you follow the law, your circumcision has meaning. But if you break the law, it is as if you were never circumcised. **26**People who are not Jews are not circumcised, but if they do what the law says, it is as if they were circumcised. **27**You Jews have the written law and circumcision, but you break the law. So those who are not circumcised in their bodies, but still obey the law, will show that you are guilty. **28**They can do this be-

2:24 "Those . . . you." Quotation from Isaiah 52:5; Ezekiel 36:20.

cause a person is not a true Jew if he is
only a Jew in his physical body; true circumcision is not only on the outside of
the body. 29A person is a Jew only if he is
a Jew inside; true circumcision is done in
the heart by the Spirit, not by the written
law. Such a person gets praise from God
rather than from people.

3 So, do Jews have anything that other
people do not have? Is there anything
special about being circumcised? 2Yes, of
course, there is in every way. The most
important thing is this: God trusted the
Jews with his teachings. 3If some Jews
were not faithful to him, will that stop
God from doing what he promised? 4No!
God will continue to be true even when
every person is false. As the Scriptures
say:

"So you will be shown to be right
when you speak,
and you will win your case."
Psalm 51:4

5When we do wrong, that shows more
clearly that God is right. So can we say
that God is wrong to punish us? (I am
talking as people might talk.) 6No! If God
could not punish us, he could not judge
the world.

7A person might say, "When I lie, it
really gives him glory, because my lie
shows God's truth. So why am I judged a
sinner?" 8It would be the same to say,
"We should do evil so that good will
come." Some people find fault with us and
say we teach this, but they are wrong and
deserve the punishment they will receive.

All People Are Guilty

9So are we Jews
better than others?
No! We have al-
ready said that Jews
and those who are
not Jews are all guilty
of sin. 10As the Scrip-
tures say:

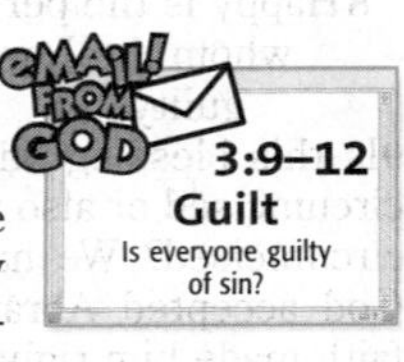

"There is no one who always does
what is right,
not even one.
11 There is no one who understands.
There is no one who looks to God
for help.
12 All have turned away.
Together, everyone has become
useless.
There is no one who does anything
good;
there is not even one." *Psalm 14:1-3*
13 "Their throats are like open graves;
they use their tongues for telling
lies." *Psalm 5:9*
"Their words are like snake poison."
Psalm 140:3
14 "Their mouths are full of cursing and
hate." *Psalm 10:7*
15 "They are always ready to kill
people.
16 Everywhere they go they cause ruin
and misery.
17 They don't know how to live in
peace." *Isaiah 59:7-8*
18 "They have no fear of God." *Psalm 36:1*

19We know that the law's commands
are for those who have the law. This
stops all excuses and brings the whole
world under God's judgment, 20because
no one can be made right with God by following the law. The law only shows us
our sin.

How God Makes People Right

21But God has a way to make people
right with him without the law, and he has
now shown us that way which the law and
the prophets told us about. 22God makes
people right with himself through their
faith in Jesus Christ. This is true for all
who believe in Christ, because all people
are the same: 23All
have sinned and are
not good enough for
God's glory, 24and all
need to be made right
with God by his
grace, which is a free

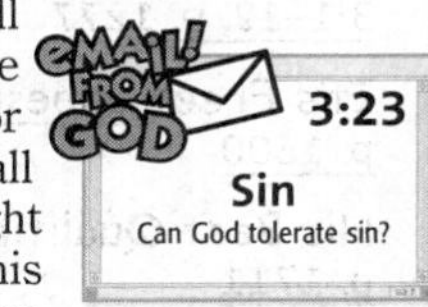

gift. They need to be made free from sin
through Jesus Christ. 25God gave him as
a way to forgive sin through faith in the
blood of Jesus' death. This showed that
God always does what is right and fair, as
in the past when he was patient and did
not punish people for their sins. 26And
God gave Jesus to show today that he
does what is right. God did this so he

JUST FOR THE ASKING

ROMANS 3:23-28

Got time for some good news and bad news about sin? Let's start with the bad news first. The bad news is that everyone has sinned. *Everyone.* The good news is that we have hope because of Jesus. He's the only One "good enough" to free us from sin. Why? Because he never sinned.

Knowing this helps us to face up to our sin. God knows that we blow it from time to time. He just wants us to own up to it. Because of Jesus, forgiveness is ours for the asking.

Here are some more Faithlinks on forgiveness. Check them out!

The Perfect Sacrifice, Leviticus 1—7, p. 135

The One Who Suffered, Isaiah 53, p. 966

Believe the Impossible?, Ezekiel 37, p. 1131

A Change of Heart, Matthew 3:1–12, p. 1277

It's Free!, Ephesians 2:8–9, p. 1600

His Best Qualities, 2 Peter 3:9, p. 1711

could judge rightly and so he could make
right any person who has faith in Jesus.
27So do we have a reason to brag
about ourselves? No! And why not? It is
the way of faith that stops all bragging,
not the way of trying to obey the law. **28**A
person is made right with God through
faith, not through obeying the law. **29**Is
God only the God of the Jews? Is he not
also the God of those who are not Jews?
30Of course he is, because there is only
one God. He will make Jews right with
him by their faith, and he will also make
those who are not Jews right with him
through their faith. **31**So do we destroy
the law by following the way of faith? No!
Faith causes us to be what the law truly
wants.

The Example of Abraham

4 So what can we say that Abraham,[n]
the father of our people, learned about
faith? **2**If Abraham was made right by the
things he did, he had a reason to brag. But
this is not God's view, **3**because the Scripture says, "Abraham believed God, and
God accepted Abraham's faith, and that
faith made him right with God."[n]
4When people work, their pay is not
given as a gift, but as something earned.
5But people cannot do any
work that will make
them right with God.
So they must trust in
him, who makes even
evil people right in
his sight. Then God
accepts their faith, and that makes them
right with him. **6**David said the same
thing. He said that people are truly
blessed when God, without paying attention to good deeds, makes people right
with himself.

7"Happy are they
whose sins are forgiven,
whose wrongs are pardoned.
8Happy is the person
whom the Lord does not consider
guilty." *Psalm 32:1-2*

9Is this blessing only for those who are
circumcised or also for those who are not
circumcised? We have already said that
God accepted Abraham's faith and that
faith made him right with God. **10**So how
did this happen? Did God accept Abra-

EMAIL FROM GOD 4:5
Trust
Trusting in God pays off.

4:1 Abraham Most respected ancestor of the Jews. Every Jew hoped to see Abraham.

4:3 "Abraham . . . God." Quotation from Genesis 15:6.

FAITH links

ONE THING TO DO

ROMANS 4:1-5

Abraham, one of the founding fathers of the Jewish nation, was a man of faith. He trusted God to save him. He knew that he could not earn God's favor or mercy by something he did.

Many times we think we have to do things to earn God's mercy. If that's something you believe, take a lesson from Abraham. Have faith in God. That's all you have to do!

The Wisdom of Obeying God, 1 Kings 11:1–13, p. 453

Remember Your Creator, Ecclesiastes 12:1, 13, p. 885

Let's Make a Deal, Daniel 1:8–21, p. 1150

Perfectly Pleasing?, Matthew 5:1–12, p. 1280

The Greatest Commandment, Matthew 22:36–40, p. 1313

Our Gift to God, Romans 12:1–2, p. 1536

ham before or after he was circumcised? It was before his circumcision. **11**Abraham was circumcised to show that he was right with God through faith before he was circumcised. So Abraham is the father of all those who believe but are not circumcised; he is the father of all believers who are accepted as being right with God. **12**And Abraham is also the father of those who have been circumcised and who live following the faith that our father Abraham had before he was circumcised.

God Keeps His Promise

13Abraham[n] and his descendants received the promise that they would get the whole world. He did not receive that promise through the law, but through being right with God by his faith. **14**If people could receive what God promised by following the law, then faith is worthless. And God's promise to Abraham is worthless, **15**because the law can only bring God's anger. But if there is no law, there is nothing to disobey.

16So people receive God's promise by having faith. This happens so the promise can be a free gift. Then all of Abraham's children can have that promise. It is not only for those who live under the law of Moses but for anyone who lives with faith like that of Abraham, who is the father of us all. **17**As it is written in the Scriptures: "I am making you a father of many nations."[n] This is true before God, the God Abraham believed, the God who gives life to the dead and who creates something out of nothing.

18There was no hope that Abraham would have children. But Abraham believed God and continued hoping, and so he became the father of many nations. As God told him, "Your descendants also will be too many to count."[n] **19**Abraham was almost a hundred years old, much past the age for having children, and Sarah could not have children. Abraham thought about all this, but his faith in God did not become weak. **20**He never doubted that God would keep his promise, and he never stopped believing. He grew stronger in his faith and gave praise to God. **21**Abraham felt sure that God was able to do what he had promised. **22**So, "God accepted Abraham's faith, and that faith made him right with God."[n] **23**Those words ("God accepted Abraham's faith") were written

---

4:13 Abraham Most respected ancestor of the Jews. Every Jew hoped to see Abraham.

4:17 "I . . . nations." Quotation from Genesis 17:5.

4:18 "Your . . . count." Quotation from Genesis 15:5.

4:22 "God . . . God." Quotation from Genesis 15:6.

not only for Abraham 24but also for us.
God will accept us also because we believe in the One who raised Jesus our
Lord from the dead. 25Jesus was given to
die for our sins, and he was raised from
the dead to make us right with God.

Right with God

5 Since we have been made right with
God by our faith, we have peace with
God. This happened through our Lord
Jesus Christ, 2who has brought us into
that blessing of God's grace that we now
enjoy. And we are happy because of the
hope we have of sharing God's glory. 3We
also have joy with
our troubles, be-
cause we know that
these troubles pro-
duce patience. 4And
patience produces
character, and char-
acter produces hope. 5And this hope will
never disappoint us, because God has
poured out his love to fill our hearts. He
gave us his love through the Holy Spirit,
whom God has given to us.

EMAIL FROM GOD
5:3
Perseverance
What will hard times produce?

6When we were unable to help ourselves, at the moment of our need, Christ
died for us, although we were living
against God. 7Very few people will die to
save the life of someone else. Although
perhaps for a good person someone
might possibly die. 8But God shows his
great love for us in this way: Christ died
for us while we were still sinners.

9So through Christ we will surely be
saved from God's anger, because we have
been made right with God by the blood of
Christ's death. 10While we were God's
enemies, he made friends with us
through the death of his Son. Surely, now
that we are his friends, he will save us
through his Son's life. 11And not only
that, but now we are also very happy in
God through our Lord Jesus Christ.
Through him we are now God's friends
again.

Adam and Christ Compared

12Sin came into the world because of
what one man did, and with sin came
death. This is why everyone must die—
because everyone sinned. 13Sin was in
the world before the law of Moses, but
sin is not counted against us as breaking
a command when there is no law. 14But

FAITH links

LOVE FOR FREE

ROMANS 5:8

If you broke something that belonged to your mom or dad, do you think he or she would stop loving you? No, right? (Don't break something to try to prove this.) Your mom or dad would love you no matter what. That's the kind of love God has for us. We call this kind of love *unconditional*. That's another way to say love freely given, with no strings attached. You can't earn this love. It's a gift! That's why God sent his Son to die for us. That's what the Good News of the gospel is all about. Why not share it with someone?

Connect here to find out how to share the Good News with others:

The Sign of His Presence, Exodus 40:34–38, p. 130

A Priest Without Sin, Leviticus 4:3–7, p. 136

God's Sure Protection, Psalm 18, p. 721

One Big, Happy Family, John 1:12, p. 1422

Two Birthdays, John 3:1–7, p. 1426

The Doubt Remover, Romans 10:8–10, p. 1533

from the time of Adam to the time of Moses, everyone had to die, even those who had not sinned by breaking a command, as Adam had.

Adam was like the One who was coming in the future. **15**But God's free gift is not like Adam's sin. Many people died because of the sin of that one man. But the grace from God was much greater; many people received God's gift of life by the grace of the one man, Jesus Christ. **16**After Adam sinned once, he was judged guilty. But the gift of God is different. God's free gift came after many sins, and it makes people right with God. **17**One man sinned, and so death ruled all people because of that one man. But now those people who accept God's full grace and the great gift of being made right with him will surely have true life and rule through the one man, Jesus Christ.

18So as one sin of Adam brought the punishment of death to all people, one good act that Christ did makes all people right with God. And that brings true life for all. **19**One man disobeyed God, and many became sinners. In the same way, one man obeyed God, and many will be made right. **20**The law came to make sin worse. But when sin grew worse, God's grace increased. **21**Sin once used death to rule us, but God gave people more of his grace so that grace could rule by making people right with him. And this brings life forever through Jesus Christ our Lord.

Dead to Sin but Alive in Christ

6 So do you think we should continue sinning so that God will give us even more grace? **2**No! We died to our old sinful lives, so how can we continue living with sin? **3**Did you forget that all of us became part of Christ when we were baptized? We shared his death in our baptism. **4**When we were baptized, we were buried with Christ and shared his death. So, just as Christ was raised from the dead by the wonderful power of the Father, we also can live a new life.

5Christ died, and we have been joined with him by dying too. So we will also be joined with him by rising from the dead as he did. **6**We know that our old life died with Christ on the cross so that our sinful selves would have no power over us and we would not be slaves to sin. **7**Anyone who has died is made free from sin's control.

8If we died with Christ, we know we will also live with him. **9**Christ was raised from the dead, and we know that he cannot die again. Death has no power over him now. **10**Yes, when Christ died, he died to defeat the power of sin one time—enough for all time. He now has a new life, and his new life is with God. **11**In the same way, you should see yourselves as being dead to the power of sin and alive with God through Christ Jesus.

12So, do not let sin control your life here on earth so that you do what your sinful self wants to do. **13**Do not offer the parts of your body to serve sin, as things to be used in doing evil. Instead, offer yourselves to God as people who have died and now live. Offer the parts of your body to God to be used in doing good. **14**Sin will not be your master, because you are not under law but under God's grace.

Be Slaves of Righteousness

15So what should we do? Should we sin because we are under grace and not under law? No! **16**Surely you know that when you give yourselves like slaves to obey someone, then you are really slaves of that person. The person you obey is your master. You can follow sin, which brings spiritual death, or you can obey God, which makes you right with him. **17**In the past you were slaves to sin—sin controlled you. But thank God, you fully obeyed the things that you were taught. **18**You were made free from sin, and now you are slaves to goodness. **19**I use this example because this is hard for you to understand. In the past you offered the parts of your body to be slaves to sin and evil; you lived only for evil. In the same way now you must give yourselves to be slaves of goodness. Then you will live only for God.

20In the past you were slaves to sin, and goodness did not control you. **21**You

did evil things, and now you are ashamed
of them. Those things only bring death.
22But now you are free from sin and have
become slaves of God. This brings you a
life that is only for God, and this gives
you life forever. **23**When people sin, they
earn what sin pays—death. But God
gives us a free gift—life forever in Christ
Jesus our Lord.

An Example from Marriage

7 Brothers and sisters, all of you understand the law of Moses. So surely you
know that the law rules over people only
while they are alive. **2**For example, a
woman must stay married to her husband
as long as he is alive. But if her husband
dies, she is free from the law of marriage.
3But if she marries another man while
her husband is still alive, the law says she
is guilty of adultery. But if her husband
dies, she is free from the law of marriage.
Then if she marries another man, she is
not guilty of adultery.
4In the same way, my brothers and
sisters, your old selves died, and you became free from the law through the body
of Christ. This happened so that you
might belong to someone else—the One
who was raised from the dead—and so
that we might be used in service to God.
5In the past, we were ruled by our sinful
selves. The law made us want to do sinful
things that controlled our bodies, so the
things we did were bringing us death. **6**In
the past, the law held us like prisoners,
but our old selves died, and we were
made free from the law. So now we serve
God in a new way with the Spirit, and not
in the old way with written rules.

Our Fight Against Sin

7You might think I am saying that sin
and the law are the same thing. That is
not true. But the law was the only way I
could learn what sin meant. I would
never have known what it means to want
to take something belonging to someone
else if the law had not said, "You must not
want to take your neighbor's things."[n]
8And sin found a way to use that command and cause me to want all kinds of
things I should not want. But without the
law, sin has no power. **9**I was alive before
I knew the law. But when the law's com-

7:7 "You . . . things." Quotation from Exodus 20:17.

FAITH links

A HIGH PRICE

ROMANS 6:23

If you told someone a lie, would you expect the police to suddenly arrest you and a judge to sentence you to death? Chances are you wouldn't, but guess what. According to God's law, any sin we commit earns us the death penalty. That's what Paul means when he says, "When people sin, they earn what sin pays—death." The silver lining in that dark cloud is that Jesus has already paid the price. His sacrifice on the cross makes it possible for you to be pronounced "not guilty" by God—the ultimate judge. God doesn't force you to accept this free gift, however. The choice is yours.

Own Up to It, 2 Samuel 12:1–13, p. 412

Dirty Inside, Isaiah 6:1–7, p. 904

The Watchman, Ezekiel 3:16–22, p. 1088

A Hard Place, Ezekiel 28:25–26, p. 1120

Lost Love?, Revelation 2:4, p. 1733

A Happy Ending, Revelation 22:16–21, p. 1754

mand came to me, then sin began to live,
10and I died. The command was meant to
bring life, but for me it brought death.
11Sin found a way to fool me by using the
command to make me die.

12So the law is holy, and the command
is holy and right and good. **13**Does this
mean that something that is good
brought death to me? No! Sin used something that is good to bring death to me.
This happened so that I could see what
sin is really like; the command was used
to show that sin is very evil.

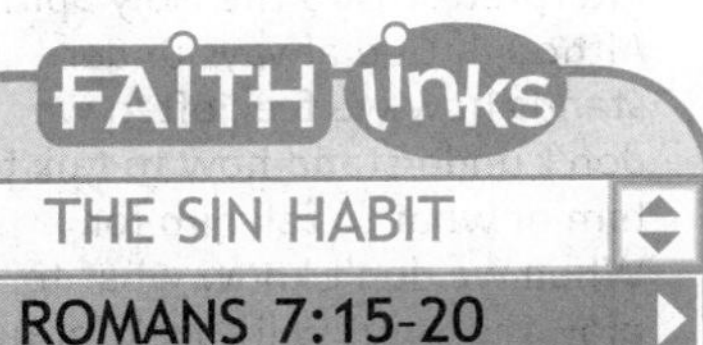

FAITH links
THE SIN HABIT
ROMANS 7:15-20

Ever had a habit you just couldn't break, no matter what you did? The apostle Paul knew what that was like. In fact, his habit is our habit—sin. As Paul said, "I want to do the things that are good, but I do not do them." But this story has a happy ending. Thanks to Jesus' death on the cross, we can develop a new habit. It's called "pleasing God." As you think about doing that, the sin habit is broken.

The Trouble with Sin, Genesis 6–8, p. 11

Facing the Consequences, Deuteronomy 3:21–29, p. 232

Above the Law, 1 Kings 21, p. 470

A Swarm of Trouble, Joel 2:25–27, p. 1190

Clean Inside and Out, Luke 11:39–40, p. 1392

The Gift, John 3:16–18, p. 1427

The War Within Us

14We know that the law is spiritual,
but I am not spiritual since sin rules me as
if I were its slave. **15**I do not understand
the things I do. I do not do what I want to
do, and I do the things I hate. **16**And if I do
not want to do the hated things I do, that
means I agree that the law is good. **17**But I
am not really the one who is doing these
hated things; it is sin living in me that
does them. **18**Yes, I know that nothing
good lives in me—I mean nothing good
lives in the part of me that is earthly and
sinful. I want to do the things that are
good, but I do not do them. **19**I do not do
the good things I want to do, but I do the
bad things I do not want to do. **20**So if I do
things I do not want to do, then I am not
the one doing them. It is sin living in me
that does those things.

21So I have learned this rule: When I
want to do good, evil is there with me.
22In my mind, I am happy with God's law.
23But I see another law working in my
body, which makes war against the law
that my mind accepts. That other law
working in my body is the law of sin, and
it makes me its prisoner. **24**What a miserable man I am! Who will save me from
this body that brings me death? **25**I thank
God for saving me through Jesus Christ
our Lord!

So in my mind I am a slave to God's
law, but in my sinful self I am a slave to
the law of sin.

Be Ruled by the Spirit

8 So now, those who are in Christ Jesus
are not judged guilty. **2**Through
Christ Jesus the law of the Spirit that
brings life made me free from the law
that brings sin and death. **3**The law was
without power, because the law was
made weak by our sinful selves. But God
did what the law could not do. He sent his
own Son to earth with the same human
life that others use for sin. By sending his
Son to be an offering for sin, God used a
human life to destroy sin. **4**He did this so
that we could be the kind of people the
law correctly wants us to be. Now we do
not live following our sinful selves, but
we live following the Spirit.

5Those who live following their sinful
selves think only about things that their
sinful selves want. But those who live
following the Spirit are thinking about
the things the Spirit wants them to do. 6If
people's thinking is controlled by the sinful self, there is death. But if their thinking is controlled by the Spirit, there is life
and peace. 7When people's thinking is
controlled by the sinful self, they are
against God, because they refuse to obey
God's law and really are not even able to
obey God's law. 8Those people who are
ruled by their sinful selves cannot please
God.

9But you are not ruled by your sinful
selves. You are ruled by the Spirit, if
that Spirit of God really lives in you.
But the person who does not have the
Spirit of Christ does not belong to
Christ. 10Your body will always be dead
because of sin. But if Christ is in you,
then the Spirit gives you life, because
Christ made you right with God. 11God
raised Jesus from the dead, and if God's
Spirit is living in you, he will also give life
to your bodies that die. God is the One
who raised Christ from the dead, and he
will give life through his Spirit that lives
in you.

12So, my brothers and sisters, we
must not be ruled by our sinful selves or
live the way our sinful selves want. 13If
you use your lives to do the wrong things
your sinful selves want, you will die spiritually. But if you use the Spirit's help to
stop doing the wrong things you do with
your body, you will have true life.

14The true children of God are those
who let God's Spirit lead them. 15The
Spirit we received does not make us
slaves again to fear; it makes us children
of God. With that Spirit we cry out,
"Father."* 16And the Spirit himself joins
with our spirits to say we are
God's children. 17If
we are God's chil-
dren, we will receive
blessings from God
together with Christ.
But we must suffer
as Christ suffered so that we will have
glory as Christ has glory.

EMAIL! FROM GOD

8:17–18
Troubles
Here's some hope in bad times.

FAITH links

OUR INTERPRETER

ROMANS 8:26

If you've seen an interpreter work, you know that he or she translates for two parties who can't understand each other. Did you know that we have an interpreter? He's the Holy Spirit. Although God always understands how we feel, often we don't understand how to talk to him or what to ask him for. When we don't know what to pray, the Spirit will speak for us. All we have to do is trust that God knows best!

Connect here to find out how the Holy Spirit helps you pray:

Keep On Praying, 1 Samuel 1, p. 354

Learning to Trust, Psalm 25:4–5, p. 727

When We Agree, Matthew 18:19–20, p. 1306

Flex Your Faith, Acts 3:1–16, p. 1467

An Energy Boost, Acts 4:31, p. 1469

A Good Habit, Ephesians 6:18, p. 1606

Our Future Glory

18The sufferings we have now are
nothing compared to the great glory that
will be shown to us. 19Everything God
made is waiting with excitement for God

8:15 "Father" Literally, "Abba, Father." Jewish children called their fathers "Abba."

FAITH links

IT'S UNDER CONTROL

ROMANS 8:28

Ever feel that you've blown it so badly that life seems like it's over? At times like that, it's easy to believe that nothing good can ever happen again. That's why it's great to know that God has everything under control. He can make something good happen out of a bad situation. That's what Paul, the writer of the letter to the Romans, wants Christians to know. Why is that important? Knowing this can help us not to worry when things go wrong.

Here are some Faithlinks to help you when you think things are getting out of control:

When Bad Turns to Worse, Exodus 5:6–12, p. 82

Full Circle, Job 42, p. 706

When Bad Things Happen, Ecclesiastes 3:16–17, p. 876

When the Going Gets Tough, Lamentations 3:22–27, p. 1079

Rock Solid, Habakkuk 1:12, p. 1236

Thoughts on Thoughts, Philippians 4:8–9, p. 1614

to show his children's glory completely.
20Everything God made was changed to
become useless, not by its own wish but
because God wanted it and because all
along there was this hope: **21**that everything God made would be set free from
ruin to have the freedom and glory that
belong to God's children.
22We know that everything God made
has been waiting until now in pain, like a
woman ready to give birth. **23**Not only
the world, but we also have been waiting
with pain inside us. We have the Spirit as
the first part of God's promise. So we are
waiting for God to finish making us his
own children, which means our bodies
will be made free. **24**We were saved, and
we have this hope. If we see what we are
waiting for, that is not really hope. People
do not hope for something they already
have. **25**But we are hoping for something
we do not have yet, and we are waiting
for it patiently.
26Also, the Spirit helps us with our
weakness. We do not know how to pray
as we should. But the Spirit himself
speaks to God for us, even begs God for
us with deep feelings that words cannot
explain. **27**God can see what is in
people's hearts. And he knows what is in
the mind of the Spirit, because the Spirit
speaks to God for his people in the way
God wants.
28We know that in everything God
works for the good of those who love
him. They are the people he called, because that was his plan. **29**God knew
them before he made the world, and he
decided that they would be like his Son so
that Jesus would be the firstborn[n] of
many brothers. **30**God planned for them
to be like his Son; and those he planned
to be like his Son, he also called; and
those he called, he also made right with
him; and those he made right, he also glo-
rified.

God's Love in Christ Jesus

31So what should we say about this? If
God is with us, no one can defeat us.
32He did not spare his own Son but gave
him for us all. So with Jesus, God will
surely give us all things. **33**Who can accuse the people God has chosen? No one,
because God is the One who makes them

8:29 firstborn Here this probably means that Christ was the first in God's family to share God's glory.

right. **34**Who can say God's people are
guilty? No one, because Christ Jesus
died, but he was also raised from the
dead, and now he is on God's right side,
begging God for us. **35**Can anything separate us from the love Christ has for us?
Can troubles or problems or sufferings or
hunger or nakedness or danger or violent
death? **36**As it is written in the Scriptures:

"For you we are in danger of death all
the time.
People think we are worth no more
than sheep to be killed."

Psalm 44:22

37But in all these things we have full
victory through God who showed his love
for us. **38**Yes, I am sure that neither
death, nor life, nor angels, nor ruling
spirits, nothing now, nothing in the future, no powers, **39**nothing above us,
nothing below us, nor anything else in
the whole world will ever be able to separate us from the love of God that is in
Christ Jesus our Lord.

God and the Jewish People

9 I am in Christ, and I am telling you the
truth; I do not lie. My conscience is
ruled by the Holy Spirit, and it tells me I
am not lying. **2**I have great sorrow and always feel much sadness. **3**I wish I could
help my Jewish brothers and sisters, my
people. I would even wish that I were
cursed and cut off from Christ if that
would help them. **4**They are the people of
Israel, God's chosen children. They have
seen the glory of God, and they have the
agreements that God made between himself and his people. God gave them the
law of Moses and the right way of worship and his promises. **5**They are the descendants of our great ancestors, and
they are the earthly family into which
Christ was born, who is God over all.
Praise him forever![n] Amen.

6It is not that God failed to keep his
promise to them. But only some of the
people of Israel are truly God's people,[n]
7and only some of Abraham's[n] descendants are true children of Abraham. But
God said to Abraham: "The descendants
I promised you will be from Isaac."[n]
8This means that not all of Abraham's
descendants are God's true children.
Abraham's true children are those who
become God's children because of the
promise God made to Abraham. **9**God's
promise to Abraham was this: "At the
right time I will return, and Sarah will
have a son."[n] **10**And that is not all. Rebekah's sons had the same father, our father Isaac. **11-12**But before the two boys
were born, God told Rebekah, "The older
will serve the younger."[n] This was before
the boys had done anything good or bad.
God said this so that the one chosen
would be chosen because of God's own
plan. He was chosen because he was the
one God wanted to call, not because of
anything he did. **13**As the Scripture says,
"I loved Jacob, but I hated Esau."[n]

14So what should we say about this?
Is God unfair? In no way. **15**God said to
Moses, "I will show kindness to anyone
to whom I want to show kindness, and I
will show mercy to anyone to whom I
want to show mercy."[n] **16**So God will
choose the one to whom he decides to
show mercy; his choice does not depend
on what people want or try to do. **17**The
Scripture says to the king of Egypt: "I
made you king for this reason: to show
my power in you so that my name will be
talked about in all the earth."[n] **18**So God
shows mercy where he wants to show
mercy, and he makes stubborn the people
he wants to make stubborn.

19So one of you will ask me: "Then
why does God blame us for our sins? Who
can fight his will?" **20**You are only human,

9:5 born . . . forever! This can also mean "born. May God, who rules over all things, be praised forever!"

9:6 God's people Literally, "Israel," the people God chose to bring his blessings to the world.

9:7 Abraham Most respected ancestor of the Jews. Every Jew hoped to see Abraham.

9:7 "The descendants . . . Isaac." Quotation from Genesis 21:12.

9:9 "At . . . son." Quotation from Genesis 18:10, 14.

9:11-12 "The older . . . younger." Quotation from Genesis 25:23.

9:13 "I . . . Esau." Quotation from Malachi 1:2-3.

9:15 "I . . . mercy." Quotation from Exodus 33:19.

9:17 "I . . . earth." Quotation from Exodus 9:16.

and human beings have no right to question God. An object should not ask the
person who made it, "Why did you make
me like this?" **21**The potter can make
anything he wants to make. He can use
the same clay to make one thing for special use and another thing for daily use.
22It is the same way with God. He
wanted to show his anger and to let people see his power. But he patiently stayed
with those people he was angry with—
people who were made ready to be destroyed. **23**He waited with patience so
that he could make known his rich glory
to the people who receive his mercy. He
has prepared these people to have his
glory, **24**and we are those people whom
God called. He called us not from the
Jews only but also from those who are not
Jews. **25**As the Scripture says in Hosea:

"I will say, 'You are my people'
to those I had called 'not my
people.'
And I will show my love
to those people I did not love."
Hosea 2:1, 23

26 "They were called,
'You are not my people,'
but later they will be called
'children of the living God.' "
Hosea 1:10

27And Isaiah cries out about Israel:
"The people of Israel are many,
like the grains of sand by the sea.
But only a few of them will be saved,
28 because the Lord will quickly and
completely punish the people on
the earth." *Isaiah 10:22-23*

29 It is as Isaiah said:
"The Lord All-Powerful
allowed a few of our descendants
to live.
Otherwise we would have been
completely destroyed
like the cities of Sodom and
Gomorrah."[n] *Isaiah 1:9*

30So what does all this mean? Those
who are not Jews were not trying to make
themselves right with God, but they
were made right with God because of
their faith. **31**The people of Israel tried to
follow a law to make themselves right
with God. But they did not succeed,
32because they tried to make themselves
right by the things they did instead of
trusting in God to make them right. They
stumbled over the stone that causes people to stumble. **33**As it is written in the
Scripture:

"I will put in Jerusalem a stone that
causes people to stumble,
a rock that makes them fall.
Anyone who trusts in him will never
be disappointed." *Isaiah 8:14; 28:16*

10 Brothers and sisters, the thing I
want most is for all the Jews to be
saved. That is my prayer to God. **2**I can
say this about them: They really try to
follow God, but they do not know the
right way. **3**Because they did not know
the way that God makes people right with
him, they tried to make themselves right
in their own way. So they did not accept
God's way of making people right.
4Christ ended the law so that everyone
who believes in him may be right with
God.
5Moses writes about being made right
by following the law. He says, "A person
who obeys these things will live because
of them."[n] **6**But this is what the Scripture
says about being made right through
faith: "Don't say to yourself, 'Who will go
up into heaven?' " (That means, "Who
will go up to heaven and bring Christ
down to earth?") **7**"And do not say, 'Who
will go down into the world below?' "
(That means, "Who will go down and
bring Christ up from the dead?") **8**This is
what the Scripture says: "The word is
near you; it is in your mouth and in your
heart."[n] That is the teaching of
faith that we are
telling. **9**If you use
your mouth to say,
"Jesus is Lord," and
if you believe in
your heart that God
raised Jesus from the dead, you will be

EMAIL! FROM GOD
10:8–10
Salvation
Check out how to be saved.

9:29 Sodom and Gomorrah Two cities that God destroyed because the people were so evil.
10:5 "A person . . . them." Quotation from Leviticus 18:5.
10:6-8 Verses 6-8 Quotations from Deuteronomy 9:4; 30:12-14; Psalm 107:26.

Livin' it

SHARING MY FAITH

Romans 10:14–17

Have I Got News for You! Imagine that you just heard some wonderful news—you "aced" a really tough test. Or your mom doesn't have cancer. Or your family's going to Hawaii for a whole month. What's the first thing you want to do? You probably want to spread the news. Who would you tell? Why would you tell them?

God wants you to spread his good news—that because Jesus died on the cross and took the punishment for our sins, we can live forever with him in heaven. That's the best news ever! In fact, did you know that Jesus' final words to his followers instructed them to do just that—to tell everyone about him! (Check out Matthew 28:19, p. 1327.) Do you have family, friends, and acquaintances who need to hear about God's great love for them? Make sure to tell them today!

MORE FAITH links

Learning from Mistakes p. 748

Jesus' Mission and Yours, p. 978

Pass It On!, p. 1187

Tell All About Him!, p. 1326

Your Faith Story, p. 1650

What's Good About You?, p. 1663

"Hey, Tagg, want to hear some great news?"

"What? Did we just win a prize or something?"

"Oh, it's better than that. Just surf over to some of these Faithlinks, and you'll find out!"

A Life-Saving Message, Esther 2:19–22, p. 650

- Mordecai heard about a plan to kill the king and reported it. The king's life was saved. God has given you an important life-saving message to tell others. Who will you share it with?

A Bad Reaction, Jeremiah 36, p. 1043

- Have you ever shared your faith with someone, only to have him or her have a bad reaction? How did you handle it? What do you do when people don't want to hear about God? How can you keep on sharing your faith?

Attention, Please!, Luke 8:11–15, p. 1383

- How much are you paying attention to what God has to say to you? Link here to find out what kind of soil you are for God.

my FAVORITE links

FAITH links

THE DOUBT REMOVER

ROMANS 10:8-10

Want to know, really know, without the shadow of a doubt that you're going to heaven? The apostle Paul provides the answer: Believe in Jesus and say it! That's all you have to do. Believe that Jesus died for your sins and that God raised Jesus from the dead. Do you believe that Jesus rose from the dead? Do you have faith in God? Have you told someone about what you believe? Then you're going to heaven someday! There's no doubt about it!

Approaching God, Numbers 3:10, p. 180

The God of Big Things, Joshua 10, p. 289

A Picture of the Past, Psalm 105, p. 789

Two Birthdays, John 3:1–7, p. 1426

Flex Your Faith, Acts 3:1–16, p. 1467

People of Faith, Hebrews 11, p. 1679

saved. **10**We believe with our hearts, and
so we are made right with God. And we
use our mouths to say that we believe,
and so we are saved. **11**As the Scripture
says, "Anyone who trusts in him will never be disappointed."ⁿ **12**That Scripture
says "anyone" because there is no difference between those who are Jews and
those who are not. The same Lord is the
Lord of all and gives many blessings to all
who trust in him, **13**as the Scripture says,
"Anyone who calls on the Lord will be
saved."ⁿ

14But before people can ask the Lord
for help, they must believe in him; and
before they can believe in him, they must
hear about him; and for them to hear
about the Lord, someone must
tell them; **15**and be-
fore someone can go
and tell them, that
person must be sent.
It is written, "How
beautiful is the per-
son who comes to
bring good news."ⁿ **16**But not all the Jews
accepted the good news. Isaiah said, "Lord,
who believed what we told them?"ⁿ **17**So
faith comes from hearing the Good News,
and people hear the Good News when
someone tells them about Christ.

EMAIL FROM GOD

10:14–15
Witnessing
How will people hear the Good News?

18But I ask: Didn't people hear the
Good News? Yes, they heard—as the
Scripture says:

> "Their message went out through all
> the world;
> their words go everywhere on
> earth." *Psalm 19:4*

19Again I ask: Didn't the people of Israel
understand? Yes, they did understand.
First, Moses says:

> "I will use those who are not a nation
> to make you jealous.
> I will use a nation that does not
> understand to make you angry."
> *Deuteronomy 32:21*

20Then Isaiah is bold enough to say:

> "I was found by those who were not
> asking me for help.
> I made myself known to people
> who were not looking for me."
> *Isaiah 65:1*

21But about Israel God says,

> "All day long I stood ready to accept

10:11 "Anyone . . . disappointed." Quotation from Isaiah 28:16.

10:13 "Anyone . . . saved." Quotation from Joel 2:32.

10:15 "How . . . news." Quotation from Isaiah 52:7.

10:16 "Lord, . . . them?" Quotation from Isaiah 53:1.

people who disobey and are
stubborn." *Isaiah 65:2*

God Shows Mercy to All People

11 So I ask: Did God throw out his
people? No! I myself am an Israelite from the family of Abraham, from the
tribe of Benjamin. **2**God chose the Israelites to be his people before they were
born, and he has not thrown his people
out. Surely you know what the Scripture
says about Elijah, how he prayed to God
against the people of Israel. **3**"Lord," he
said, "they have killed your prophets, and
they have destroyed your altars. I am the
only prophet left, and now they are trying
to kill me, too."[n] **4**But what answer did
God give Elijah? He said, "But I have left
seven thousand people in Israel who
have never bowed down before Baal."[n]
5It is the same now. There are a few people that God has chosen by his grace.
6And if he chose them by grace, it is not
for the things they have done. If they
could be made God's people by what they
did, God's gift of grace would not really
be a gift.

7So this is what has happened: Although the Israelites tried to be right
with God, they did not succeed, but the
ones God chose did become right with
him. The others were made stubborn and
refused to listen to God. **8**As it is written
in the Scriptures:

"God gave the people a dull mind so
they could not understand."
Isaiah 29:10

"He closed their eyes so they could
not see
and their ears so they could not
hear.
This continues until today."
Deuteronomy 29:4

9And David says:

"Let their own feasts trap them and
cause their ruin;
let their feasts cause them to
stumble and be paid back.
10Let their eyes be closed so they
cannot see
and their backs be forever weak
from troubles." *Psalm 69:22-23*

11So I ask: When the Jews fell, did
that fall destroy them? No! But their mistake brought salvation to those who are
not Jews, in order to make the Jews jealous. **12**The Jews' mistake brought rich
blessings for the world, and the Jews'
loss brought rich blessings for the non-
Jewish people. So surely the world will
receive much richer blessings when
enough Jews become the kind of people
God wants.

13Now I am speaking to you who are
not Jews. I am an apostle to those who
are not Jews, and since I have that work, I
will make the most of it. **14**I hope I can
make my own people jealous and, in that
way, help some of them to be saved.
15When God turned away from the Jews,
he became friends with other people in
the world. So when God accepts the
Jews, surely that will bring them life after
death.

16If the first piece of bread is offered
to God, then the whole loaf is made holy.
If the roots of a tree are holy, then the
tree's branches are holy too.

17It is as if some of the branches from
an olive tree have been broken off. You
non-Jewish people are like the branch of
a wild olive tree that has been joined to
that first tree. You now share the
strength and life of the first tree, the
Jews. **18**So do not brag about those
branches that were broken off. If you
brag, remember that you do not support
the root, but the root supports you. **19**You
will say, "Branches were broken off so
that I could be joined to their tree."
20That is true. But those branches were
broken off because they did not believe,
and you continue to be part of the tree
only because you believe. Do not be
proud, but be afraid. **21**If God did not let
the natural branches of that tree stay,
then he will not let you stay if you don't
believe.

22So you see that God is kind and also
very strict. He punishes those who stop
following him. But God is kind to you, if

11:3 "They . . . too." Quotation from 1 Kings 19:10, 14.

11:4 "But . . . Baal." Quotation from 1 Kings 19:18.

you continue following in his kindness. If
you do not, you will be cut off from the
tree. 23And if the Jews will believe in
God again, he will accept
them back. God is able to
put them back where they
were. 24It is not natural
for a wild branch to be
part of a good tree. And
you who are not Jews are
like a branch cut from a
wild olive tree and joined
to a good olive tree. But
since those Jews are like
a branch that grew from
the good tree, surely they can be joined
to their own tree again.

> But God is kind to you, if you continue following in his kindness. If you do not, you will be cut off from the tree.
> —Romans 11:22

25I want you to understand this secret, brothers and sisters, so you will
understand that you do not know everything: Part of Israel has been made stubborn, but that will change when many
who are not Jews have come to God.
26And that is how all Israel will be saved.
It is written in the Scriptures:

"The Savior will come from Jerusalem;
he will take away all evil from the
family of Jacob."
27And I will make this agreement with
those people
when I take away their sins."
Isaiah 59:20-21; 27:9

28The Jews refuse to accept the Good
News, so they are God's enemies. This
has happened to help you who are not
Jews. But the Jews are still God's chosen
people, and he loves them very much because of the promises he made to their
ancestors. 29God never changes his
mind about the people he calls and the
things he gives them. 30At one time you
refused to obey God. But now you have
received mercy, because those people refused to obey. 31And now the Jews refuse
to obey, because God showed mercy to
you. But this happened so that they also
can receive mercy from him. 32God has
given all people over to their stubborn
ways so that he can show mercy to all.

Praise to God

33Yes, God's riches are very great,
and his wisdom and knowledge have no
end! No one can explain the things God
decides or understand his ways. 34As the
Scripture says,

"Who has known the
mind of the
Lord,
or who has been
able to give him
advice?"
Isaiah 40:13

35 "No one has ever
given God
anything
that he must pay
back." *Job 41:11*

36Yes, God made all things, and
everything continues through him and
for him. To him be the glory forever!
Amen.

Give Your Lives to God

12 So brothers and sisters, since God
has shown us great mercy, I beg
you to offer your lives as a living sacrifice
to him. Your offering must be only for
God and pleasing to him, which is the
spiritual way for you to worship. 2Do not
change yourselves to be
like the people of
this world, but be
changed within by a
new way of think-
ing. Then you will
be able to decide
what God wants for you; you will know
what is good and pleasing to him and
what is perfect. 3Because God has given
me a special gift, I have something to say
to everyone among you. Do not think you
are better than you are. You must decide
what you really are by the amount of faith
God has given you. 4Each one of us has a
body with many parts, and these parts all
have different uses. 5In the same way, we
are many, but in Christ we are all one
body. Each one is a part of that body, and
each part belongs to all the other parts.
6We all have different gifts, each of which
came because of the grace God gave us.
The person who has the gift of prophecy

EMAIL! FROM GOD
12:2
God
Find out what is pleasing to God.

11:26 Jacob Father of the twelve family groups of Israel, the people God chose to be his people.

FAITH links

OUR GIFT TO GOD

ROMANS 12:1-2

If you have a good friend, you know what a gift friendship can be. You offer yourself to your friend wholeheartedly. God offers us a gift through his Son Jesus. The least we can do is offer him a gift in return. Know what gift would really please God? You. He wants you to be willing to lay aside your own plans for your life in favor of his plans. He also wants you to be willing to lay aside the desire to do wrong things and do what's right. That's what being "a living sacrifice" is all about.

Connect here to find out more about being a "living sacrifice":

Fearful Service?, Exodus 4:1–17, p. 80

Your Best Work, 1 Kings 6, p. 443

Your Stats, 1 Kings 15; 16, p. 460

Too Young to Serve, Jeremiah 1:4–9, p. 988

Your Feet on High Places, Habakkuk 3:18–19, p. 1239

That Thing You Do, Matthew 25:14–30, p. 1319

FAITH links

HELP FOR THE BODY

ROMANS 12:3-8

Your body is made of many parts. Each one is important. A church is made of many people. Each one is important, also. That's why the church is known as "the body of Christ." God gave each person in the church a gift or ability to do something. Some people have a gift of serving; some have a gift of being generous. What is your gift? Whatever it is, you can use it to help the body!

Check out these links on being responsible:

Everyone Can Help, Numbers 4, p. 181

Your Response to Responsibility, Ruth 2:1–7, p. 346

A Big Responsibility, 2 Kings 11, p. 494

Building Together, Nehemiah 3, p. 627

Love Him? Show It!, Amos 2:6–7, p. 1196

A Christian's Responsibility, Acts 11:26, p. 1484

should use that gift in agreement with
the faith. 7Anyone who has the gift of
serving should serve. Anyone who has
the gift of teaching should teach. 8Who-
ever has the gift of encouraging others
should encourage. Whoever has the gift
of giving to others should give freely.
Anyone who has the gift of being a leader
should try hard when he leads. Whoever
has the gift of showing mercy
to others should do
so with joy.

EMAIL FROM GOD 12:9

Hate

What should you hate?

9Your love must
be real. Hate what
is evil, and hold on
to what is good.

10Love each other like brothers and sisters. Give each other more honor than
you want for yourselves. 11Do not be
lazy but work hard, serving the Lord with
all your heart. 12Be joyful because you
have hope. Be patient when trouble
comes, and pray at all times. 13Share
with God's people who need help. Bring
strangers in need into your homes.

14Wish good for those who harm you;
wish them well and do not curse them.
15Be happy with those who are happy,
and be sad with those who are sad.
16Live in peace with each other. Do not
be proud, but make friends with those
who seem unimportant. Do not think
how smart you are.

17If someone does wrong to you, do
not pay him back by doing wrong to him.
Try to do what everyone thinks is right.
18Do your best to live in peace with everyone. 19My friends, do not try to punish others when they wrong you, but wait
for God to punish them with his anger. It
is written: "I will punish those who do
wrong; I will repay them,"[n] says the
Lord. 20But you should do this:

"If your enemy is hungry, feed him;
if he is thirsty, give him a drink.
Doing this will be like pouring
burning coals on his head."

Proverbs 25:21-22

21Do not let evil defeat you, but defeat
evil by doing good.

Christians Should Obey the Law

13 All of you must yield to the government rulers. No one rules unless
God has given him the power to rule, and
no one rules now
without that power
from God. 2So those
who are against the
government are really
against what God has
commanded. And they
will bring punishment on themselves.
3Those who do right do not have to fear
the rulers; only those who do wrong fear
them. Do you want to be unafraid of the
rulers? Then do what is right, and they
will praise you. 4The ruler is God's servant to help you. But if you do wrong,
then be afraid. He has the power to punish; he is God's servant to punish those
who do wrong. 5So you must yield to the
government, not only because you might
be punished, but because you know it is
right.

6This is also why you pay taxes. Rulers are working for God and give their
time to their work. 7Pay everyone, then,
what you owe. If you owe any kind of tax,
pay it. Show respect and honor to them
all.

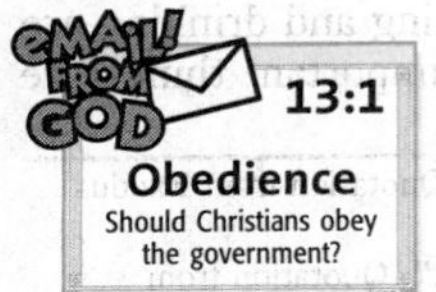

Obedience
Should Christians obey the government?

FAITH CHALLENGE

I've got another one for you. Read 13:7 to discover what we owe each other and how we are to pay it. What is the best way to show respect and honor to your teacher? Your principal? A police officer? Your parents?

TESTING IT

Romans 13:7
Pay everyone, then, what you owe. If you owe any kind of tax, pay it. Show respect and honor to them all.

12:19 **"I . . . them"** Quotation from Deuteronomy 32:35.

Loving Others

8Do not owe people anything, except
always owe love to each other, because
the person who loves others has obeyed
all the law. 9The law says, "You must not
be guilty of adultery. You must not murder
anyone. You must not steal. You must not
want to take your neighbor's things."[n] All
these commands and all others are really
only one rule: "Love your neighbor as you
love yourself."[n] 10Love never hurts a
neighbor, so loving is obeying all the law.

11Do this because we live in an important time. It is now time for you to
wake up from your sleep, because our
salvation is nearer now than when we
first believed. 12The "night"[n] is almost
finished, and the "day"[n] is almost here.
So we should stop doing things that belong to darkness and take up the weapons
used for fighting in the light. 13Let us
live in a right way, like people who belong
to the day. We should not have wild parties or get drunk. There should be no
sexual sins of any kind, no fighting or
jealousy. 14But clothe yourselves with
the Lord Jesus Christ and forget about
satisfying your sinful self.

Do Not Criticize Other People

14 Accept into your group someone
who is weak in faith, and do not
argue about opinions. 2One person believes it is right to eat all kinds of food.[n]
But another, who is weak, believes it is
right to eat only vegetables. 3The one
who knows that it is right to eat any kind
of food must not reject the one who eats
only vegetables. And the person who
eats only vegetables must not think that
the one who eats all foods is wrong, because God has accepted that person.
4You cannot judge another person's servant. The master decides if the servant is
doing well or not. And the Lord's servant
will do well because the Lord helps him
do well.

5Some think that one day is more important than another, and others think
that every day is the same. Let all be sure
in their own mind. 6Those who think one
day is more important than other days
are doing that for the Lord. And those
who eat all kinds of food are doing that for
the Lord, and they give thanks to God.
Others who refuse to eat some foods do
that for the Lord, and they give thanks to
God. 7We do not live or die for ourselves.
8If we live, we are living for the Lord, and
if we die, we are dying for the Lord. So
living or dying, we belong to the Lord.

9The reason Christ died and rose
from the dead to live again was so he
would be Lord over both the dead and the
living. 10So why do you judge your brothers or sisters in Christ? And why do you
think you are better than they are? We
will all stand before God to be judged,
11because it is written in the Scriptures:

" 'As surely as I live,' says the Lord,
'Everyone will bow before me;
everyone will say that I am God.' "

Isaiah 45:23

12So each of us will have to answer to
God.

Do Not Cause Others to Sin

13For that reason we should stop
judging each other. We must make up our
minds not to do anything that will make
another Christian sin. 14I am in the Lord
Jesus, and I know that there is no food
that is wrong to eat. But if a person believes something is wrong, that thing
is wrong for him. 15If you hurt your
brother's or sister's faith because of
something you eat, you are not really following the way of love. Do not destroy
someone's faith by eating food he thinks
is wrong, because Christ died for him.
16Do not allow what you think is good to
become what others say is evil. 17In the
kingdom of God, eating and drinking are
not important. The important things are

13:9 "You . . . things." Quotation from Exodus 20:13-15, 17.

13:9 "Love . . . yourself." Quotation from Leviticus 19:18.

13:12 "night" This is used as a symbol of the sinful world we live in. This world will soon end.

13:12 "day" This is used as a symbol of the good time that is coming, when we will be with God.

14:2 all . . . food The Jewish law said there were some foods Jews should not eat. When Jews became Christians, some of them did not understand they could now eat all foods.

Being a Peacemaker

Romans 14:19

Livin' it

Peace and Quiet? Is your house always peaceful and quiet? Or are there arguments and disagreements between parents and kids, and among the kids themselves? How do you react in these situations? Do you try to be a peacemaker or do you stir things up a bit and become a peacebreaker?

A peacemaker tries to make peace between two people who aren't getting along. A peacebreaker starts trouble wherever he or she goes. God wants his followers to be peacemakers. (Look at James 3:18, p. 1693.) Which would you rather have—the reward of the peacemaker or the trouble of the peacebreaker? How can you be a peacemaker where you are today?

More Faith Links

"What's the matter, Tagg? You're looking a bit unhappy."

"It's my two friends. They're mad at each other and won't talk to each other. I don't know what to do!"

"That sure sounds like a big problem. Why don't you download these Faithlinks and see how you can be a peacemaker in this situation?"

Peace in the Family, Psalm 133, p. 811

- Ever wish you and other members of your family could get along all the time? How about you and your friends? What can you do to make this happen?
- God's love makes it possible for people to "live together in peace." Even brothers and sisters!

Winning a Friend, 2 Timothy 2:23–24, p. 1654

- Have you ever argued with someone about something that wasn't really important? Link up here to hear Paul's advice about "foolish and stupid arguments."

The Way to Get Along, 1 Peter 3:8–9, p. 1703

- What was the last thing you argued about with your brother or sister? When you and your brother or sister fight, how do you feel? How does that compare with the way you feel when you get along? This Faithlink gives some great advice for getting along with family and friends. Give it a go!

my FAVORITE links

living right with God, peace, and joy in
the Holy Spirit. **18**Anyone who serves
Christ by living this way is pleasing God
and will be accepted by other people.
19So let us try to do what makes
peace and helps one another.

eMAIL! FROM GOD
14:19
Peace
How can you be a peacemaker?

20Do not let the
eating of food de-
stroy the work of
God. All foods are
all right to eat, but it
is wrong to eat food
that causes someone else to sin. **21**It is
better not to eat meat or drink wine or do
anything that will cause your brother or
sister to sin.
22Your beliefs about these things
should be kept secret between you and
God. People are happy if they can do what
they think is right without feeling guilty.
23But those who eat something without
being sure it is right are wrong because
they did not believe it was right. Anything that is done without believing it is
right is a sin.

15 We who are strong in faith should
help the weak with their weaknesses, and not please only ourselves.
2Let each of us please our neighbors for
their good, to help them be stronger in
faith. **3**Even Christ did not live to please
himself. It was as the Scriptures said:
"When people insult you, it hurts me."*n*
4Everything that was written in the past
was written to teach us. The Scriptures
give us patience and encouragement so
that we can have hope. **5**Patience and encouragement come from God. And I pray
that God will help you all agree with each
other the way Christ Jesus wants. **6**Then
you will all be joined together, and you
will give glory to God the Father of our
Lord Jesus Christ. **7**Christ accepted you,
so you should accept each other, which
will bring glory to God. **8**I tell you that
Christ became a servant of the Jews to
show that God's promises to the Jewish
ancestors are true. **9**And he also did this
so that those who are not Jews could give
glory to God for the mercy he gives to
them. It is written in the Scriptures:

"So I will praise you among the non-
Jewish people.
I will sing praises to your name."

Psalm 18:49

10The Scripture also says,

"Be happy, you who are not Jews,
together with his people."

Deuteronomy 32:43

11Again the Scripture says,

"All you who are not Jews, praise the
Lord.
All you people, sing praises to
him."

Psalm 117:1

12And Isaiah says,

"A new king will come from the
family of Jesse.*n*
He will come to rule over the non-
Jewish people,
and they will have hope because of
him."

Isaiah 11:10

13I pray that the God who gives hope
will fill you with much joy and peace
while you trust in him. Then your hope
will overflow by the power of the Holy
Spirit.

Paul Talks About His Work

14My brothers and sisters, I am sure
that you are full of goodness. I know that
you have all the knowledge you

eMAIL! FROM GOD
15:14
Kindness
What should you be filled with?

need and that you
are able to teach
each other. **15**But I
have written to you
very openly about
some things I want-
ed you to remember.
I did this because God gave me this special gift: **16**to be a minister of Christ
Jesus to those who are not Jews. I served
God by teaching his Good News, so that
the non-Jewish people could be an offering that God would accept—an offering
made holy by the Holy Spirit.
17So I am proud of what I have done
for God in Christ Jesus. **18**I will not talk
about anything except what Christ has
done through me in leading those who
are not Jews to obey God. They have
obeyed God because of what I have said
and done, **19**because of the power of mir-

15:3 "When . . . me." Quotation from Psalm 69:9.
15:12 Jesse Jesse was the father of David, king of Israel. Jesus was from their family.

FAITH links

GLAD TO HELP!

ROMANS 15:17-20

Paul was proud of his work for God because of Jesus. He could be proud because he knew that Jesus helped him in everything that he did. His eagerness to serve showed his worship of God.

There are many ways to serve God. When you're glad, like Paul, to serve God, God is pleased. Pride in doing the work of the Lord through the help of Jesus is the best kind of pride.

Gratitude Attitude, Ezra 3, p. 611

All Talk, No Action, Jeremiah 5:1–2, p. 996

A Halfhearted Offering, Malachi 1:6–14, p. 1268

The Way to Greatness, Matthew 20:20–28, p. 1309

Best Seat in the House, Luke 14:7–11, p. 1398

The "Eyes" Have It?, 1 Corinthians 12, p. 1559

acles and the great things they saw, and
because of the power of the Holy Spirit. I
preached the Good News from Jerusalem
all the way around to Illyricum, and so I
have finished that part of my work. **20**I
always want to preach the Good News in
places where people have never heard of
Christ, because I do not want to build on
the work someone else has already started. **21**But it is written in the Scriptures:

"Those who were not told about him
will see,
and those who have not heard
about him will understand."

Isaiah 52:15

Paul's Plan to Visit Rome

22This is the reason I was stopped
many times from coming to you. **23**Now I
have finished my work here. Since for
many years I have wanted to come to
you, **24**I hope to visit you on my way to
Spain. After I enjoy being with you for a
while, I hope you can help me on my trip.
25Now I am going to Jerusalem to help
God's people. **26**The believers in Macedonia and Southern Greece were happy
to give their money to help the poor
among God's people at Jerusalem.
27They were happy to do this, and really
they owe it to them. These who are not
Jews have shared in the Jews' spiritual
blessings, so they should use their material possessions to help the Jews. **28**After I am sure the poor in Jerusalem get
the money that has been given for them, I
will leave for Spain and stop and visit you.
29I know that when I come to you I will
bring Christ's full blessing.

30Brothers and sisters, I beg you to
help me in my work by praying to God for
me. Do this because of our Lord Jesus
and the love that the Holy Spirit gives us.
31Pray that I will be saved from the non-
believers in Judea and that this help I
bring to Jerusalem will please God's people there. **32**Then, if God wants me to, I
will come to you with joy, and together
you and I will have a time of rest. **33**The
God who gives peace be with you all.
Amen.

Greetings to the Christians

16 I recommend to you our sister
Phoebe, who is a helper[n] in the
church in Cenchrea. **2**I ask you to accept
her in the Lord in the way God's people
should. Help her with anything she
needs, because she has helped me and
many other people also.

3Give my greetings to Priscilla and

16:1 helper Literally, "deaconess." This might mean the same as one of the special women helpers in 1 Timothy 3:11.

Aquila, who work together with me in Christ Jesus **4**and who risked their own lives to save my life. I am thankful to them, and all the non-Jewish churches are thankful as well. **5**Also, greet for me the church that meets at their house.

Greetings to my dear friend Epenetus, who was the first person in the country of Asia to follow Christ. **6**Greetings to Mary, who worked very hard for you. **7**Greetings to Andronicus and Junia, my relatives, who were in prison with me. They are very important apostles. They were believers in Christ before I was. **8**Greetings to Ampliatus, my dear friend in the Lord. **9**Greetings to Urbanus, a worker together with me for Christ. And greetings to my dear friend Stachys. **10**Greetings to Apelles, who was tested and proved that he truly loves Christ. Greetings to all those who are in the family of Aristobulus. **11**Greetings to Herodion, my fellow citizen. Greetings to all those in the family of Narcissus who belong to the Lord. **12**Greetings to Tryphena and Tryphosa, women who work very hard for the Lord. Greetings to my dear friend Persis, who also has worked very hard for the Lord. **13**Greetings to Rufus, who is a special person in the Lord, and to his mother, who has been like a mother to me also. **14**Greetings to Asyncritus, Phlegon, Hermes, Patrobas, Hermas, and all the brothers who are with them. **15**Greetings to Philologus and Julia, Nereus and his sister, and Olympas, and to all God's people with them. **16**Greet each other with a holy kiss. All of Christ's churches send greetings to you.

17Brothers and sisters, I ask you to look out for those who cause people to be against each other and who upset other people's faith. They are against the true teaching you learned, so stay away from them. **18**Such people are not serving our Lord Christ but are only doing what pleases themselves. They use fancy talk and fine words to fool the minds of those who do not know about evil. **19**All the believers have heard that you obey, so I am very happy because of you. But I want you to be wise in what is good and innocent in what is evil.

EMAIL! FROM GOD
16:19
Obedience
Does it matter if you obey?

20The God who brings peace will soon defeat Satan and give you power over him.

The grace of our Lord Jesus be with you.

21Timothy, a worker together with me, sends greetings, as well as Lucius, Jason, and Sosipater, my relatives.

22I am Tertius, and I am writing this letter from Paul. I send greetings to you in the Lord.

23Gaius is letting me and the whole church here use his home. He also sends greetings to you, as do Erastus, the city treasurer, and our brother Quartus. **24**[n]

25Glory to God who can make you strong in faith by the Good News that I tell people and by the message about Jesus Christ. The message about Christ is the secret that was hidden for long ages past but is now made known. **26**It has been made clear through the writings of the prophets. And by the command of the eternal God it is made known to all nations that they might believe and obey.

27To the only wise God be glory forever through Jesus Christ! Amen.

16:24 Verse 24 Some Greek copies add verse 24: "The grace of our Lord Jesus Christ be with all of you. Amen."

1 Corinthians

GROWING PAINS

Hi, guys! It's me, Paul. You may know that I was a key figure in spreading the gospel about Jesus and starting churches. In fact, did you know that I helped start the church in Corinth? I wanted a church in Corinth because it was such a busy city filled with people going from Corinth to all parts of the world. (At the time, Corinth was the second most important city, next to Rome.) Hey, I figured if I could plant a church there, I knew I could reach the whole world!

I wrote this letter because the church in Corinth was having a lot of problems. Since it was a major city, it had people from all over visiting it. These people brought with them all sorts of different beliefs and practices. So, I wrote to the church there to help them answer questions about false gods, marriage, worship, gifts of the Holy Spirit, and other issues . . . you know, the type of stuff normal people in a normal church might struggle with.

JESUS WATCH

You can find Jesus all over this book, because Jesus was the focus of Paul's life. Paul writes about the effect that believing in Jesus has on a follower's life. Paul wanted to tell his Corinthian friends to understand that Jesus and his teachings should be at the very center of their lives. In other words, he wanted Christians both then and today to know that believing in Jesus impacts every area of life.

Paul says that Jesus "has become for us wisdom from God" (1 Corinthians 1:30). Paul wanted believers to know that Jesus was for everyone. You didn't have to be really smart, or really rich, or really pretty to believe in Jesus. Jesus is someone anyone can approach and have a relationship with.

my FAVORITE links

_______________ _______________

_______________ _______________

_______________ _______________

_______________ _______________

OTHER CONNECTIONS

Livin' it What kind of effort do you put into a school project? What about playing your favorite sport? How about dusting your room? Connect to Good, Better, Best, 1 Corinthians 9:24–27, to see what kind of effort God wants from you—no matter what you do.

Everyone on earth will someday die. But as believers in Jesus, Christians don't have to fear death. Link to The Final End?, 1 Corinthians 15:50–57, to find out why.

MORE STUFF...

Love Notes Jesus' kind of love goes beyond a feeling you have for someone or something. Jesus' love is a choice. In 1 Corinthians 13, Paul gives a list of all the things love is and love is not. Take a look:

- Love is patient, kind, and trusting.
- It does not keep track of wrongs that have been done, and it does not get upset with others.
- It is not jealous, rude, or selfish.
- Love does not like evil, but is happy with truth.

"Yo, Tagg, what was the deal with the Corinthians taking each other to court?"

"I dunno. Read it in 1 Corinthians 6:1-8, and tell me what you think."

did you know?

CHECK OUT THESE OTHER REALLY COOL THINGS IN 1 CORINTHIANS:

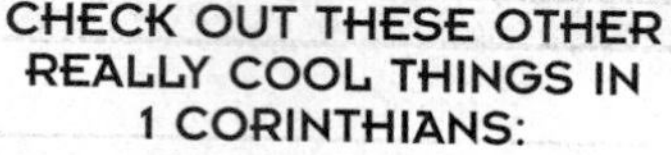

The Lord's Supper, 1 Corinthians 10:17–33
Our spiritual gifts, 1 Corinthians 12—14
The book on love, 1 Corinthians 13
Jesus is alive: It's a fact, 1 Corinthians 15

- Out of Your Mind?, 1 Corinthians 2:16
- Brag on Him!, 1 Corinthians 3:18–23
- I'll Be the Judge!, 1 Corinthians 4:4–5
- The Winner's Crown, 1 Corinthians 9:24–27
- A Family Celebration, 1 Corinthians 11:23–29
- The "Eyes" Have It?, 1 Corinthians 12
- The Best Choice, 1 Corinthians 13
- Life After Death?, 1 Corinthians 15:12–13
- Give to Give, 1 Corinthians 16:1–4
- Meeting Together, 1 Corinthians 16:19

1 From Paul. God called me to be an
apostle of Christ Jesus because that
is what God wanted. Also from Sosthenes, our brother in Christ.
2To the church of God in Corinth, to
you who have been made holy in Christ
Jesus. You were called to be God's holy
people with all people everywhere who
pray in the name of the Lord Jesus
Christ—their Lord and ours:
3Grace and peace to you from God our
Father and the Lord Jesus Christ.

Paul Gives Thanks to God

4I always thank my God for you because of the grace God has given you in
Christ Jesus. 5I thank God because in
Christ you have been made rich in every
way, in all your speaking and in all your
knowledge. 6Just as our witness about
Christ has been guaranteed to you, 7so
you have every gift from God while you
wait for our Lord Jesus Christ to come
again. 8Jesus will keep you strong until
the end so that there will be no wrong in
you on the day our Lord
Jesus Christ comes
again. 9God, who has
called you to share
everything with his
Son, Jesus Christ
our Lord, is faithful.

eMAIL! FROM GOD
1:8
Perseverance
Who will keep you strong?

Problems in the Church

10I beg you, brothers and sisters,* by
the name of our Lord Jesus Christ that all
of you agree with each other and not be
split into groups. I beg that you be completely joined together by having the
same kind of thinking and the same purpose. 11My brothers and sisters, some
people from Chloe's family have told me
quite plainly that there are quarrels
among you. 12This is what I mean: One
of you says, "I follow Paul"; another says,
"I follow Apollos"; another says, "I follow
Peter"; and another says, "I follow
Christ." 13Christ has been divided up
into different groups! Did Paul die on the
cross for you? No! Were you baptized in
the name of Paul? No! 14I thank God I did
not baptize any of you except Crispus and
Gaius 15so that now no one can say you

FAITH links

AN ENCOURAGING WORD

1 CORINTHIANS 1:3-5

If you're searching for a good way to help a friend, here is one way: encourage him and pray for him. The apostle Paul was concerned about the church he helped to start in Corinth. So he wrote them a letter. He told them how he thanked God for them. He also encouraged them to rely on God for help.

We may not always know what our friends need. God, however, always knows. So, the next time you have a spare minute, why not pray for a friend? Then, send your friend a note or e-mail message to let him know that you care.

Here are some more Faithlinks on being a good friend:

Show Some Respect, Leviticus 19:32, p. 161

Give What You Can, Numbers 7:1–11, p. 186

The MLP, Ruth 1:16–17, p. 345

The Salt Promise, 2 Chronicles 13:5, p. 576

You Are What You Do, Proverbs 20:11, p. 854

Get Ready!, Mark 13:26–27, p. 1354

1:10 brothers and sisters Although the Greek text says "brothers" here and throughout this book, Paul's words were meant for the entire church, including men and women.

were baptized in my name. **16**(I also baptized the family of Stephanas, but I do not remember that I baptized anyone else.) **17**Christ did not send me to baptize people but to preach the Good News. And he sent me to preach the Good News without using words of human wisdom so that the cross[n] of Christ would not lose its power.

Christ Is God's Power and Wisdom

18The teaching about the cross is foolishness to those who are being lost, but to us who are being saved it is the power of God. **19**It is written in the Scriptures:

> "I will cause the wise men to lose
> their wisdom;
> I will make the wise men unable to
> understand." *Isaiah 29:14*

20Where is the wise person? Where is the educated person? Where is the skilled talker of this world? God has made the wisdom of the world foolish. **21**In the wisdom of God the world did not know God through its own wisdom. So God chose to use the message that sounds foolish to save those who believe. **22**The Jews ask for miracles, and the Greeks want wisdom. **23**But we preach a crucified Christ. This is a big problem to the Jews, and it is foolishness to those who are not Jews. **24**But Christ is the power of God and the wisdom of God to those people God has called—Jews and Greeks. **25**Even the foolishness of God is wiser than human wisdom, and the weakness of God is stronger than human strength.

26Brothers and sisters, look at what you were when God called you. Not many of you were wise in the way the world judges wisdom. Not many of you had great influence. Not many of you came from important families. **27**But God chose the foolish things of the world to shame the wise, and he chose the weak things of the world to shame the strong. **28**He chose what the world thinks is unimportant and what the world looks down on and thinks is nothing in order to destroy what the world thinks is important. **29**God did this so that no one can brag in his presence. **30**Because of God you are in Christ Jesus, who has become for us wisdom from God. In Christ we are put right with God, and have been made holy, and have been set free from sin. **31**So, as the Scripture says, "If someone wants to brag, he should brag only about the Lord."[n]

eMAIL! FROM GOD
1:28
Pride
What has God chosen?

The Message of Christ's Death

2 Dear brothers and sisters, when I came to you, I did not come preaching God's secret with fancy words or a show of human wisdom. **2**I decided that while I was with you I would forget about everything except Jesus Christ and his death on the cross. **3**So when I came to you, I was weak and fearful and trembling. **4**My teaching and preaching were not with words of human wisdom that persuade people but with proof of the power that the Spirit gives. **5**This was so that your faith would be in God's power and not in human wisdom.

God's Wisdom

6However, I speak a wisdom to those who are mature. But this wisdom is not from this world or from the rulers of this world, who are losing their power. **7**I speak God's secret wisdom, which he has kept hidden. Before the world began, God planned this wisdom for our glory. **8**None of the rulers of this world understood it. If they had, they would not have crucified the Lord of glory. **9**But as it is written in the Scriptures:

> "No one has ever seen this,
> and no one has ever heard about it.

eMAIL! FROM GOD
2:6–8
Wisdom
Check out the difference between God's wisdom and human wisdom.

1:17 cross Paul uses the cross as a picture of the Good News, the story of Christ's death and rising from the dead for people's sins. The cross, or Christ's death, was God's way to save people.
1:31 "If . . . Lord." Quotation from Jeremiah 9:24.

FAITH links

OUT OF YOUR MIND?

1 CORINTHIANS 2:16

If you could be anyone else in the world, who would you want to be? Why? Do you ever wish you could be the smartest person in the world or the richest? Many people wish they were someone else, at least for a day. Although you can't really be someone else, there is a way that you can *think* like someone else. No fooling! The apostle Paul tells us that we have the mind of Christ. That means we can think like Jesus. Thinking like Jesus means letting the Holy Spirit show us how to live. It means wanting what God wants.

Fatherly Advice, Exodus 18, p. 99

A Different Kind of People, Leviticus 11, p. 146

Our Thirst Quencher, Psalm 42:1–3, p. 741

Love Him? Show It!, Amos 2:6–7, p. 1196

A Family Meal, Mark 14:23–26, p. 1356

Most Wanted?, 2 Corinthians 10:1, p. 1580

No one has ever imagined
what God has prepared for those
who love him." *Isaiah 64:4*
10But God has shown us these things
through the Spirit.
The Spirit searches out all things,
even the deep secrets of God. 11Who
knows the thoughts that another person
has? Only a person's spirit that lives
within him knows his thoughts. It is the
same with God. No one knows the
thoughts of God except the Spirit of God.
12Now we did not receive the spirit of
the world, but we received the Spirit that
is from God so that we can know all that
God has given us. 13And we speak about
these things, not with words taught us by
human wisdom but with words taught us
by the Spirit. And so we explain spiritual
truths to spiritual people. 14A person
who does not have the Spirit does not accept the truths that come from the Spirit
of God. That person thinks they are foolish and cannot understand them, because
they can only be judged to be true by the
Spirit. 15The spiritual person is able to
judge all things, but no one can judge
him. The Scripture says:
16"Who has known the mind of the Lord?
Who has been able to teach him?"
Isaiah 40:13
But we have the mind of Christ.

Following People Is Wrong

3 Brothers and sisters, in the past I
could not talk to you as I talk to spiritual people. I had to talk to you as I would
to people without the Spirit—babies in
Christ. 2The teaching I gave you was like
milk, not solid food, because you were
not able to take solid food. And even now
you are not ready. 3You are still not spiritual, because there is jealousy and quarreling among you, and this shows that
you are not spiritual. You are acting like
people of the world. 4One of you says, "I
belong to Paul," and another says, "I belong to Apollos." When you say things
like this, you are acting like people of the
world.

5Is Apollos important? No! Is Paul
important? No! We are only servants of
God who helped you believe. Each one of
us did the work God gave us to

EMAIL FROM GOD
3:5–9
Witnessing
How can you help others grow in faith?

do. 6I planted the
seed, and Apollos
watered it. But God
is the One who made
it grow. 7So the one
who plants is not

important, and the one who waters is not
important. Only God, who makes things
grow, is important. **8**The one who plants
and the one who waters have the same
purpose, and each will be rewarded for
his own work. **9**We are God's workers,
working together; you are like God's
farm, God's house.
10Using the gift God gave me, I laid
the foundation of that house like an expert builder. Others are building on that
foundation, but all people should be careful how they build on it. **11**The foundation
that has already been laid is Jesus Christ,
and no one can lay down any other foundation. **12**But if people build on that foundation, using gold, silver, jewels, wood,
grass, or straw, **13**their work will be
clearly seen, because the Day of Judgment[n] will make it visible. That Day will
appear with fire, and the fire will test
everyone's work to show what sort of
work it was. **14**If the building that has
been put on the foundation still stands,
the builder will get a reward. **15**But if the
building is burned up, the builder will suffer loss. The builder will be saved, but it
will be as one who escaped from a fire.
16Don't you know that you are God's
temple and that God's Spirit lives in you?
17If anyone destroys God's temple, God
will destroy that person, because God's
temple is holy and you are that temple.
18Do not fool yourselves. If you think
you are wise in this world, you should become a fool so that you can become truly
wise, **19**because the wisdom of this world
is foolishness with God. It is written in
the Scriptures, "He catches those who
are wise in their own clever traps."[n] **20**It
is also written in the Scriptures, "The
Lord knows what wise people think. He
knows their thoughts are just a puff of
wind."[n] **21**So you should not brag about
human leaders. All things belong to you:
22Paul, Apollos, and Peter; the world,
life, death, the present, and the future—
all these belong to you. **23**And you belong
to Christ, and Christ belongs to God.

Apostles Are Servants of Christ

4 People should think of us as servants
of Christ, the ones God has trusted

FAITH links

BRAG ON HIM!

1 CORINTHIANS 3:18-23

Ever brag about who you know? Many people brag to others about famous people they know. That's called "name dropping." For example, "My third cousin is a friend of ________ (fill in the name of someone you admire)." They think that knowing these people makes them cool.

Paul wrote to the Christians in Corinth to warn them to stop bragging. They bragged about the leaders they knew. Instead, Paul encouraged them to brag about belonging to Jesus. That's good advice! Knowing him gives us plenty to brag about!

Connect here to find out more about getting rid of pride in your life:

Good Advice?, Leviticus 20:6, p. 162

The Weak Link, Judges 16, p. 334

A Right to Get Even?, 1 Samuel 24, p. 388

The Problem with Pride, Isaiah 2:11, p. 898

All Talk, No Action, Jeremiah 5:1–2, p. 996

Say What?!, Ephesians 4:22–29, p. 1603

3:13 Day of Judgment The day Christ will come to judge all people and take his people home to live with him.

3:19 "He . . . traps." Quotation from Job 5:13.

3:20 "The Lord . . . wind." Quotation from Psalm 94:11.

with his secrets. 2Now in this way those
who are trusted with something valuable
must show they are worthy of that trust.
3As for myself, I do not care if I am
judged by you or by any human court. I do
not even judge myself. 4I know of no
wrong I have done, but this does not
make me right before the Lord. The Lord
is the One who judges me. 5So do not
judge before the right time; wait until the
Lord comes. He will bring to light things
that are now hidden in darkness, and will
make known the secret purposes of
people's hearts. Then God will praise
each one of them.

6Brothers and sisters, I have used
Apollos and myself as examples so you
could learn through us the meaning of
the saying, "Follow only what is written
in the Scriptures." Then you will not be
more proud of one person than another.
7Who says you are better than others?
What do you have that was not given to
you? And if it was given to you, why do
you brag as if you did not receive it as a
gift?

8You think you already have everything you need. You think you are rich.
You think you have become kings without us. I wish you really were kings so we
could be kings together with you. 9But it
seems to me that God has put us apostles
in last place, like those sentenced to die.
We are like a show for the whole world to
see—angels and people. 10We are fools
for Christ's sake, but you are very wise in
Christ. We are weak, but you are strong.
You receive honor, but we are shamed.
11Even to this very hour we do not have
enough to eat or drink or to wear. We are
often beaten, and we have no homes in
which to live. 12We work hard with our
own hands for our food. When people
curse us, we bless them. When they hurt
us, we put up with it. 13When they tell
evil lies about us, we speak nice words
about them. Even today, we are treated
as though we were the garbage of the
world—the filth of the earth.

14I am not trying to make you feel
ashamed. I am writing this to give you a
warning as my own dear children. 15For
though you may have ten thousand
teachers in Christ, you do not have many
fathers. Through the Good News I became your father in Christ Jesus, 16so I
beg you, please follow my example.
17That is why I am sending to you Timothy, my son in the Lord. I love Timothy,

FAITH links

I'LL BE THE JUDGE!

1 CORINTHIANS 4:4-5

Has someone ever said something about you that weren't true? Or made a hurtful comment about something you said or did without knowing why? Being misjudged or misunderstood by someone hurts.

The Christians in Corinth believed something that was untrue about Paul. So he wrote to set the record straight. His warning to them is also a warning to us not to judge other Christians. Only God knows a person's heart. He alone judges perfectly.

Want to know who is the perfect judge? Link here:

Learning to Listen, 1 Samuel 3, p. 358

Help for the Hurting, Job 6:29–30, p. 666

Learning from Mistakes, Psalm 51:12–13, p. 748

Eating Humble Pie, Daniel 4, p. 1156

Better Than Some?, Luke 18:9–14, p. 1405

A Family Celebration, 1 Corinthians 11:23–29, p. 1558

and he is faithful. He will help you remember my way of life in Christ Jesus, just as I teach it in all the churches everywhere.

18Some of you have become proud, thinking that I will not come to you again. 19But I will come to you very soon if the Lord wishes. Then I will know what the proud ones do, not what they say, 20because the kingdom of God is present not in talk but in power. 21Which do you want: that I come to you with punishment or with love and gentleness?

> It is not my business to judge those who are not part of the church. God will judge them.
> —1 Corinthians 5:12–13

Wickedness in the Church

5 It is actually being said that there is sexual sin among you. And it is a kind that does not happen even among people who do not know God. A man there has his father's wife. 2And you are proud! You should have been filled with sadness so that the man who did this should be put out of your group. 3I am not there with you in person, but I am with you in spirit. And I have already judged the man who did that sin as if I were really there. 4When you meet together in the name of our Lord Jesus, and I meet with you in spirit with the power of our Lord Jesus, 5then hand this man over to Satan. So his sinful self[n] will be destroyed, and his spirit will be saved on the day of the Lord.

6Your bragging is not good. You know the saying, "Just a little yeast makes the whole batch of dough rise." 7Take out all the old yeast so that you will be a new batch of dough without yeast, which you really are. For Christ, our Passover lamb, has been sacrificed. 8So let us celebrate this feast, but not with the bread that has the old yeast—the yeast of sin and wickedness. Let us celebrate this feast with the bread that has no yeast—the bread of goodness and truth.

9I wrote you in my earlier letter not to associate with those who sin sexually. 10But I did not mean you should not associate with those of this world who sin sexually, or with the greedy, or robbers, or those who worship idols. To get away from them you would have to leave this world. 11I am writing to tell you that you must not associate with those who call themselves believers in Christ but who sin sexually, or are greedy, or worship idols, or abuse others with words, or get drunk, or cheat people. Do not even eat with people like that.

12-13It is not my business to judge those who are not part of the church. God will judge them. But you must judge the people who are part of the church. The Scripture says, "You must get rid of the evil person among you."[n]

Judging Problems Among Christians

6 When you have something against another Christian, how can you bring yourself to go before judges who are not right with God? Why do you not let God's people decide who is right? 2Surely you know that God's people will judge the world. So if you are to judge the world, are you not able to judge small cases as well? 3You know that in the future we will judge angels, so surely we can judge the ordinary things of this life. 4If you have ordinary cases that must be judged, are you going to appoint people as judges who mean nothing to the church? 5I say this to shame you. Surely there is someone among you wise enough to judge a complaint between believers. 6But now one believer goes to court against another believer—and you do this in front of unbelievers!

eMAIL! FROM GOD
6:3
Angels
Find out who you will judge someday.

5:5 sinful self Literally, "flesh." This could also mean his body.

5:12-13 "You . . . you." Quotation from Deuteronomy 17:7; 19:19; 22:21, 24; 24:7.

7The fact that you have lawsuits against each other shows that you are already defeated. Why not let yourselves be wronged? Why not let yourselves be cheated? **8**But you yourselves do wrong and cheat, and you do this to other believers!

9-10 Surely you know that the people who do wrong will not inherit God's kingdom. Do not be fooled. Those who sin sexually, worship idols, take part in adultery, those who are male prostitutes, or men who have sexual relations with other men, those who steal, are greedy, get drunk, lie about others, or rob—these people will not inherit God's kingdom. **11**In the past, some of you were like that, but you were washed clean. You were made holy, and you were made right with God in the name of the Lord Jesus Christ and in the Spirit of our God.

Use Your Bodies for God's Glory

12"I am allowed to do all things," but all things are not good for me to do. "I am allowed to do all things," but I will not let anything make me its slave. **13**"Food is for the stomach, and the stomach for food," but God will destroy them both. The body is not for sexual sin but for the Lord, and the Lord is for the body. **14**By his power God has raised the Lord from the dead and will also raise us from the dead. **15**Surely you know that your bodies are parts of Christ himself. So I must never take the parts of Christ and join them to a prostitute! **16**It is written in the Scriptures, "The two will become one body."[n] So you should know that anyone who joins with a prostitute becomes one body with the prostitute. **17**But the one who joins with the Lord is one spirit with the Lord.

18So run away from sexual sin. Every other sin people do is outside their bodies, but those who sin sexually sin against their own bodies. **19**You should know that your body is a temple for the Holy Spirit who is in you. You have received the Holy Spirit from God. So you do not belong to yourselves, **20**because you were bought by God for a price. So honor God with your bodies.

About Marriage

7 Now I will discuss the things you wrote me about. It is good for a man not to have sexual relations with a woman. **2**But because sexual sin is a danger, each man should have his own wife, and each woman should have her own husband. **3**The husband should give his wife all that he owes her as his wife. And the wife should give her husband all that she owes him as her husband. **4**The wife does not have full rights over her own body; her husband shares them. And the husband does not have full rights over his own body; his wife shares them. **5**Do not refuse to give your bodies to each other, unless you both agree to stay away from sexual relations for a time so you can give your time to prayer. Then come together again so Satan cannot tempt you because of a lack of self-control. **6**I say this to give you permission to stay away from sexual relations for a time. It is not a command to do so. **7**I wish that everyone were like me, but each person has his own gift from God. One has one gift, another has another gift.

8Now for those who are not married and for the widows I say this: It is good for them to stay unmarried as I am. **9**But if they cannot control themselves, they should marry. It is better to marry than to burn with sexual desire.

10Now I give this command for the married people. (The command is not from me; it is from the Lord.) A wife should not leave her husband. **11**But if she does leave, she must not marry again, or she should make up with her husband. Also the husband should not divorce his wife.

12For all the others I say this (I am saying this, not the Lord): If a Christian man has a wife who is not a believer, and she is happy to live with him, he must not divorce her. **13**And if a Christian woman has a husband who is not a believer, and he is happy to live with her, she must not divorce him. **14**The husband who is not a believer is made holy through his

---

6:16 "The two . . . body." Quotation from Genesis 2:24.

believing wife. And the wife who is not a
believer is made holy through her believing husband. If this were not true, your
children would not be clean, but now
your children are holy.
15But if those who are not believers
decide to leave, let them leave. When
this happens, the Christian man or woman is free. But God called us to live in
peace. 16Wife, you don't know; maybe
you will save your husband. And husband, you don't know; maybe you will
save your wife.

Live as God Called You

17But in any case each one of you
should continue to live the way God has
given you to live—the way you were
when God called you. This is a rule I
make in all the churches. 18If a man was
already circumcised when he was called,
he should not undo his circumcision. If a
man was without circumcision when he
was called, he should not be circumcised.
19It is not important if a man is circumcised or not. The important thing is obeying God's commands. 20Each one of you
should stay the way you were when God
called you. 21If you were a slave when
God called you, do not let that bother
you. But if you can be free, then make
good use of your freedom. 22Those who
were slaves when the
Lord called them are free
persons who belong to
the Lord. In the same
way, those who were free
when they were called
are now Christ's slaves.
23You all were bought at a
great price, so do not become slaves of people.
24Brothers and sisters,
each of you should stay as
you were when you were called, and stay
there with God.

Questions About Getting Married

25Now I write about people who are
not married. I have no command from the
Lord about this; I give my opinion. But I
can be trusted, because the Lord has
shown me mercy. 26The present time is a
time of trouble, so I think it is good for
you to stay the way you are. 27If you have
a wife, do not try to become free from her.
If you are not married, do not try to find a
wife. 28But if you decide to marry, you
have not sinned. And if a girl who has
never married decides to marry, she has
not sinned. But those who marry will
have trouble in this life, and I want you to
be free from trouble.
29Brothers and sisters, this is what I
mean: We do not have much time left. So
starting now, those who have wives
should live as if they had no wives.
30Those who are crying should live as if
they were not crying. Those who are
happy should live as if they were not happy. Those who buy things should live as if
they own nothing. 31Those who use the
things of the world should live as if they
were not using them, because this world
in its present form will soon be gone.
32I want you to be free from worry. A
man who is not married is busy with the
Lord's work, trying to please the Lord.
33But a man who is married is busy with
things of the world, trying to please his
wife. 34He must think about two
things—pleasing his wife and pleasing
the Lord. A woman who is not married or
a girl who has never married is busy with
the Lord's work. She wants to be holy in
body and spirit. But a
married woman is busy
with things of the world,
as to how she can please
her husband. 35I am say-
ing this to help you, not
to limit you. But I want
you to live in the right
way, to give yourselves
fully to the Lord without
concern for other things.
36If a man thinks he is
not doing the right thing with the girl he
is engaged to, if she is almost past the
best age to marry and he feels he should
marry her, he should do what he wants.
They should get married. It is no sin.
37But if a man is sure in his mind that
there is no need for marriage, and has his
own desires under control, and has decided not to marry the one to whom he is

You all were bought at a great price, so do not become slaves of people.
—1 Corinthians 7:23

engaged, he is doing the right thing. **38**So the man who marries his girl does right, but the man who does not marry will do better.

39A woman must stay with her husband as long as he lives. But if her husband dies, she is free to marry any man she wants, but she must marry in the Lord. **40**The woman is happier if she does not marry again. This is my opinion, but I believe I also have God's Spirit.

About Food Offered to Idols

8 Now I will write about meat that is sacrificed to idols. We know that "we all have knowledge." Knowledge puffs you up with pride, but love builds up. **2**If you think you know something, you do not yet know anything as you should. **3**But if any person loves God, that person is known by God.

eMAIL FROM GOD
8:1–3
Wisdom
What is true knowledge?

4So this is what I say about eating meat sacrificed to idols: We know that an idol is really nothing in the world, and we know there is only one God. **5**Even though there are things called gods, in heaven or on earth (and there are many "gods" and "lords"), **6**for us there is only one God—our Father. All things came from him, and we live for him. And there is only one Lord—Jesus Christ. All things were made through him, and we also were made through him.

7But not all people know this. Some people are still so used to idols that when they eat meat, they still think of it as being sacrificed to an idol. Because their conscience is weak, when they eat it, they feel guilty. **8**But food will not bring us closer to God. Refusing to eat does not make us less pleasing to God, and eating does not make us better in God's sight.

9But be careful that your freedom does not cause those who are weak in faith to fall into sin. **10**You have "knowledge," so you eat in an idol's temple.[n] But someone who is weak in faith might see you eating there and be encouraged to eat meat sacrificed to idols while thinking it is wrong to do so. **11**This weak believer for whom Christ died is ruined because of your "knowledge." **12**When you sin against your brothers and sisters in Christ like this and cause them to do what they feel is wrong, you are also sinning against Christ. **13**So if the food I eat causes them to fall into sin, I will never eat meat again so that I will not cause any of them to sin.

Paul Is like the Other Apostles

9 I am a free man. I am an apostle. I have seen Jesus our Lord. You people are all an example of my work in the Lord. **2**If others do not accept me as an apostle, surely you do, because you are proof that I am an apostle in the Lord.

3This is the answer I give people who want to judge me: **4**Do we not have the right to eat and drink? **5**Do we not have the right to bring a believing wife with us when we travel as do the other apostles and the Lord's brothers and Peter? **6**Are Barnabas and I the only ones who must work to earn our living? **7**No soldier ever serves in the army and pays his own salary. No one ever plants a vineyard without eating some of the grapes. No person takes care of a flock without drinking some of the milk.

8I do not say this by human authority; God's law also says the same thing. **9**It is written in the law of Moses: "When an ox is working in the grain, do not cover its mouth to keep it from eating."[n] When God said this, was he thinking only about oxen? No. **10**He was really talking about us. Yes, that Scripture was written for us, because it goes on to say: "The one who plows and the one who works in the grain should hope to get some of the grain for their work." **11**Since we planted spiritual seed among you, is it too much if we should harvest from you some things for this life? **12**If others have the right to get something from you, surely we have this right, too. But we do not use it. No, we put up with everything ourselves so that

8:10 idol's temple Building where a god is worshiped.

9:9 "When an ox . . . eating." Quotation from Deuteronomy 25:4.

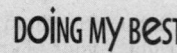

Livin' it

DOING MY BEST

1 Corinthians 9:24–27

Good, Better, Best Ever go to buy a bike and have three choices: the basic model, the better model, and then the top-of-the-line model? You buy the one that best fits your needs and budget. If you were being rated on how you do things, what rating would you usually get? Would your rating depend on what you were doing? For example, maybe you would do your top-of-the-line work on an important test, but barely make the grade in room cleaning!

God wants you to do *everything* with your best effort, no matter what you do. (Read Colossians 3:23, p. 1626.) Keeping Jesus in mind as you work will help you give it your all. Try to do your best—whether it's taking out the garbage or trying out for the soccer team!

MORE FAITH links

A Big Responsibility, p. 494

Building Tools, p. 615

Building Together, p. 627

My Best Serve, p. 1473

With All Your Heart, p. 1626

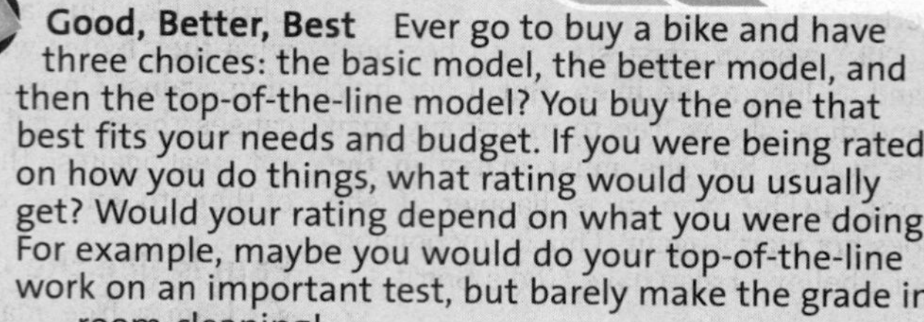

"Tagg! Where have you been? I've been looking all over the web for you!"
"I was hiding. I had some chores to do, and I didn't feel like doing them. Do you think it's safe to come back now?"
"Tagg, that's not the way to handle a hard chore. Better surf over to these Faithlinks right now for good advice on doing your best—no matter what the chore is!"

An Unsung Hero, Ruth 2:12, 15–16, p. 347
- Have you ever felt unappreciated in what you do to help others? What do you do when you feel that way? Remember, God sees everything. He wants you to do your best even if no one else notices.

Your Best Work, 1 Kings 6, p. 443
- What are the activities you put the most effort into? Only the things you like to do? Everything you do? Link here to see how King Solomon would have answered these questions.

Small Beginnings, Zechariah 4:10, p. 1255
- Read this Faithlink for encouragement about small beginnings.

Another Lazy Day?, 2 Thessalonians 3:6–13, p. 1640
- Ever wish there were no chores for you to do or homework or . . . anything else for that matter? We all wish that sometimes. But that's not God's plan—he wants us to be willing to work hard and do our best. How can keeping busy help keep you out of trouble?

my FAVORITE links

we will not keep anyone from believing
the Good News of Christ. 13Surely you
know that those who work at the Temple
get their food from the Temple, and those
who serve at the altar get part of what is
offered at the altar. 14In the same way,
the Lord has commanded that those who
tell the Good News should get their living from this work.
15But I have not used any of these
rights. And I am not writing this now to
get anything from you. I would rather die
than to have my reason for bragging tak-
en away. 16Telling the Good News does
not give me any reason for bragging. Telling the Good News is my duty—something I must do. And how terrible it will
be for me if I do not tell the Good News.
17If I preach because it is my own choice,
I have a reward. But if I preach and it is
not my choice to do so, I am only doing
the duty that was given to me. 18So what
reward do I get? This is my reward: that
when I tell the Good News I can offer it
freely. I do not use my full rights in my
work of preaching the Good News.
19I am free and belong to no one. But I
make myself a slave to all people to win
as many as I can. 20To the Jews I became
like a Jew to win the Jews. I myself am
not ruled by the law. But to those who are
ruled by the law I became like a person
who is ruled by the law. I did this to win
those who are ruled by the law. 21To
those who are without the law I became
like a person who is without the law. I did
this to win those people who are without
the law. (But really, I am not without
God's law—I am ruled by Christ's law.)
22To those who are weak, I became weak
so I could win the weak. I have become
all things to all people so I could save
some of them in any way possible. 23I do
all this because of the Good News and so
I can share in its blessings.
24You know that in a race all the runners run, but only one gets the prize. So
run to win! 25All those who compete in
the games use self-control so they can
win a crown. That crown is an earthly
thing that lasts only a short time, but our
crown will never be destroyed. 26So I do
not run without a goal. I fight like a boxer

FAITH links

THE WINNER'S CROWN

1 CORINTHIANS 9:24-27

Have you ever won a race? Winning can be very exciting, especially if you have something to show for it, like a trophy or a medal.

The apostle Paul compared living the Christian life to running a race. No one easily wins a race. You have to work hard to be good enough to finish a race, let alone win it. Living as a Christian takes work, too. Instead of being handed a trophy that could tarnish or become lost, we have the promise of a crown that "will never be destroyed" (1 Corinthians 9:25). This is the eternal life that God promised.

Download these Faithlinks to find out what it takes to be a true winner:

The Rainbow Promise, Genesis 9:1–17, p. 14

Trailblazers of Faith, 2 Kings 22:1–2, p. 510

Your Best Defense, 2 Chronicles 20:1–12, p. 584

More Precious Than Gold, Psalm 19:7–10, p. 723

The Power of *If*, Mark 9:14–24, p. 1344

Praise Him!, Revelation 5:12, p. 1736

who is hitting something—not just the
air. **27**I treat my body hard and make it my
slave so that I myself will not be disquali-
fied after I have preached to others.

Warnings from Israel's Past

10 Brothers and sisters, I want you to
know what happened to our ancestors who followed Moses. They were
all under the cloud and all went through
the sea. **2**They were all baptized as followers of Moses in the cloud and in the
sea. **3**They all ate the same spiritual food,
4and all drank the same spiritual drink.
They drank from that spiritual rock that
followed them, and that rock was Christ.
5But God was not pleased with most of
them, so they died in the desert.

6And these things happened as examples for us, to stop us from wanting evil
things as those people did. **7**Do not worship idols, as some of them did. Just as it
is written in the Scriptures: "They sat
down to eat and drink, and then they got
up and sinned sexually."[n] **8**We must not
take part in sexual sins, as some of them
did. In one day twenty-three thousand of
them died because of their sins. **9**We
must not test Christ as some of them did;
they were killed by snakes. **10**Do not
complain as some of them did; they were
killed by the angel that destroys.

11The things that happened to those
people are examples. They were written
down to teach us, because we live in a
time when all these things of the past
have reached their goal. **12**If you think
you are strong, you should be careful not
to fall. **13**The only temptation that has
come to you is that which everyone has.
But you can trust God, who will not per-
mit you to be tempted more than you can
stand. But when you are tempted, he will
also give you a way to escape so that you
will be able to stand it.

14So, my dear friends, run away from
the worship of idols. **15**I am speaking to
you as to intelligent people; judge for
yourselves what I say. **16**We give thanks
for the cup of blessing,[n] which is a sharing in the blood of Christ. And the bread
that we break is a sharing in the body of
Christ. **17**Because there is one loaf of
bread, we who are many are one body,
because we all share that one loaf.

18Think about the Israelites: Do not
those who eat the sacrifices share in the
altar? **19**I do not mean that the food sacrificed to an idol is important. I do not
mean that an idol is anything at all. **20**But
I say that what is sacrificed to idols is offered to demons, not to God. And I do not
want you to share anything with demons.
21You cannot drink the cup of the Lord
and the cup of demons also. You cannot
share in the Lord's table and the table of
demons. **22**Are we trying to make the
Lord jealous? We are not stronger than
he is, are we?

How to Use Christian Freedom

23"We are allowed to do all things,"
but all things are not good for us to do.
"We are allowed to do all things," but not
all things help others grow stronger.
24Do not look out only for yourselves.
Look out for the good of others also.

25Eat any meat that is sold in the
meat market. Do not ask questions to see
if it is meat you think is wrong to eat.
26You may eat it, "because the earth belongs to the Lord, and everything in it."[n]

27Those who are not believers may
invite you to eat with them. If you want to
go, eat anything that is put before you.
Do not ask questions to see if you think it
might be wrong to eat. **28**But if anyone
says to you, "That food was offered to
idols," do not eat it. Do not eat it because
of that person who told you and because
eating it might be thought to be wrong.
29I don't mean you think it is wrong, but
the other person might. But why, you
ask, should my freedom be judged by
someone else's conscience? **30**If I eat the
meal with thankfulness, why am I criticized because of something for which I
thank God?

10:7 "They . . . sexually." Quotation from Exodus 32:6.

10:16 cup of blessing The cup of the fruit of the vine that Christians thank God for and drink at the Lord's Supper.

10:26 "because . . . it" Quotation from Psalms 24:1; 50:12; 89:11.

31The answer is, if you eat or drink, or if you do anything, do it all for the glory of God. **32**Never do anything that might hurt others—Jews, Greeks, or God's church—**33**just as I, also, try to please everybody in every way. I am not trying to do what is good for me but what is good for most people so they can be saved.

The answer is, if you eat or drink, or if you do anything, do it all for the glory of God.
—1 Corinthians 10:31

11 Follow my example, as I follow the example of Christ.

Being Under Authority

2I praise you because you remember me in everything, and you follow closely the teachings just as I gave them to you. **3**But I want you to understand this: The head of every man is Christ, the head of a woman is the man,[n] and the head of Christ is God. **4**Every man who prays or prophesies with his head covered brings shame to his head. **5**But every woman who prays or prophesies with her head uncovered brings shame to her head. She is the same as a woman who has her head shaved. **6**If a woman does not cover her head, she should have her hair cut off. But since it is shameful for a woman to cut off her hair or to shave her head, she should cover her head. **7**But a man should not cover his head, because he is the likeness and glory of God. But woman is man's glory. **8**Man did not come from woman, but woman came from man. **9**And man was not made for woman, but woman was made for man. **10**So that is why a woman should have a symbol of authority on her head, because of the angels.

11But in the Lord women are not independent of men, and men are not independent of women. **12**This is true because woman came from man, but also man is born from woman. But everything comes from God. **13**Decide this for yourselves: Is it right for a woman to pray to God with her head uncovered? **14**Even nature itself teaches you that wearing long hair is shameful for a man. **15**But long hair is a woman's glory. Long hair is given to her as a covering. **16**Some people may still want to argue about this, but I would add that neither we nor the churches of God have any other practice.

The Lord's Supper

17In the things I tell you now I do not praise you, because when you come together you do more harm than good. **18**First, I hear that when you meet together as a church you are divided, and I believe some of this. **19**(It is necessary to have differences among you so that it may be clear which of you really have God's approval.) **20**When you come together, you are not really eating the Lord's Supper.[n] **21**This is because when you eat, each person eats without waiting for the others. Some people do not get enough to eat, while others have too much to drink. **22**You can eat and drink in your own homes! You seem to think God's church is not important, and you embarrass those who are poor. What should I tell you? Should I praise you? I do not praise you for doing this.

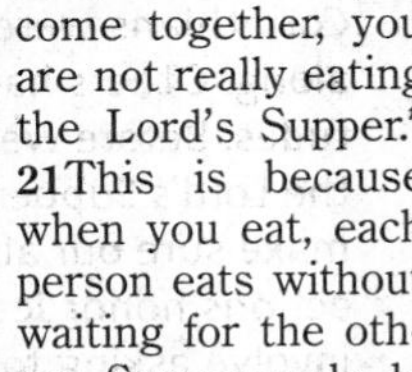

eMAIL! FROM GOD
11:17–22
Following God
How can you identify followers of God?

23The teaching I gave you is the same teaching I received from the Lord: On the night when the Lord Jesus was handed over to be killed, he took bread **24**and gave thanks for it. Then he broke the bread and said, "This is my body; it is for you. Do this to remember me." **25**In the same way, after they ate, Jesus took the cup. He said, "This cup is the new agreement that is sealed with the blood of my death. When you drink this, do it to remember me." **26**Every time you eat this

11:3 the man This could also mean "her husband."

11:20 Lord's Supper The meal Jesus told his followers to eat to remember him (Luke 22:14-20).

A FAMILY CELEBRATION

1 CORINTHIANS 11:23-29

If you've ever been to a family party where two family members weren't getting along, you know how uncomfortable that can be. Their disagreement brings a dark cloud to an otherwise joyful celebration.

Paul wrote to the Christians of Corinth about the Lord's Supper. The Lord's Supper is a family celebration in honor of Jesus. Unfortunately, some of the Corinthians weren't getting along. Others had sinful attitudes. Before we participate in the Lord's Supper, we need to make sure our attitudes and actions honor Jesus. That might involve asking for forgiveness from God or from some other person we've hurt. When we do this, the whole "family" will be able to honor Jesus.

What God Wants, Deuteronomy 10:12–13, p. 242

Mourning for an Enemy, 2 Samuel 1, p. 399

God's New Home, 2 Chronicles 7:11–22, p. 570

The Watchman, Ezekiel 3:16–22, p. 1088

The Number One Rule, Mark 12:28–31, p. 1351

Family Time, Hebrews 10:25, p. 1678

bread and drink this cup you are telling
others about the Lord's death until he
comes.

27So a person who eats the bread or
drinks the cup of the Lord in a way that is
not worthy of it will be guilty of sinning
against the body and the blood of the
Lord. **28**Look into your own hearts before you eat the bread and drink the cup,
29because all who eat the bread and drink
the cup without recognizing the body eat
and drink judgment against themselves.
30That is why many in your group are
sick and weak, and many have died.
31But if we judged ourselves in the right
way, God would not judge us. **32**But when
the Lord judges us, he punishes us so
that we will not be destroyed along with
the world.

33So my brothers and sisters, when
you come together to eat, wait for each
other. **34**Anyone who is too hungry
should eat at home so that in meeting together you will not bring God's judgment
on yourselves. I will tell you what to do
about the other things when I come.

Gifts from the Holy Spirit

12 Now, brothers and sisters, I want
you to understand about spiritual
gifts. **2**You know the way you lived before
you were believers. You let yourselves
be influenced and led away to worship
idols—things that could not speak. **3**So I
want you to understand that no one who
is speaking with the help of God's Spirit
says, "Jesus be cursed." And no one can
say, "Jesus is Lord," without the help of
the Holy Spirit.

4There are different kinds of gifts, but
they are all from the same Spirit. **5**There
are different ways to serve but the same
Lord to serve. **6**And there are different
ways that God works through people but
the same God. God works in all of us in
everything we do. **7**Something from the
Spirit can be seen in each person, for the
common good. **8**The Spirit gives one person the ability to speak with wisdom, and
the same Spirit gives another the ability
to speak with knowledge. **9**The same
Spirit gives faith to one person. And, to
another, that one Spirit gives gifts of

healing. 10The Spirit gives to another
person the power to do miracles, to another the ability to prophesy. And he gives to another the ability to know the difference between good and evil spirits. The Spirit gives one person the ability to speak in different kinds of languages[n] and to another the ability to interpret those
languages. 11One Spirit, the same Spirit, does all these things, and the Spirit decides what to give each person.

The Body of Christ Works Together

12A person's body is only one thing, but it has many parts. Though there are many parts to a body, all those parts make only one body. Christ is like that also.
13Some of us are Jews, and some are Greeks. Some of us are slaves, and some are free. But we were all baptized into one body through one Spirit. And we were all made to share in the one Spirit.
14The human body has many parts.
15The foot might say, "Because I am not a hand, I am not part of the body." But saying this would not stop the foot from being a part of the body.
16The ear might say, "Because I am not an eye, I am not part of the body." But saying this would not stop the ear from being a part of the body.
17If the whole body were an eye, it would not be able to hear. If the whole body were an ear, it would not be able to smell.
18-19If each part of the body were the same part, there would be no body. But truly God put all the parts, each one of them, in the body as he wanted them.
20So then there are many parts, but only one body.
21The eye cannot say to the hand, "I don't need you!" And the head cannot say to the foot, "I don't need you!"
22No! Those parts of the body that seem to be the weaker are really necessary.
23And the parts of the body we think are less deserving are the parts to which we give the most honor. We give special respect to the parts we want to hide.
24The more respectable parts of our body need no special care. But God put the body together and gave more honor to the parts that need it
25so our body would not be

FAITH links

THE "EYES" HAVE IT?

1 CORINTHIANS 12

Suppose your whole body was made up of only one eye. What would happen? Well, for one thing, you'd have trouble walking, breathing, and eating.

In a physical body, every part is important. That's the way the church—Jesus' "body"—is, too! The Spirit has given each member a special ability. Some teach, some encourage others, and still others preach. Sometimes, however, we start to wish we had someone else's ability. Or, we might think our ability is better than someone else's. When that happens, we stop working together. God wants us to be thankful for the gifts he has given us and to respect the gifts of others.

Want to know how to use your gifts? Connect here:

Serious About the Sabbath, Exodus 31:15, p. 117

Loyal to a Friend, 2 Samuel 9, p. 409

The Problem with Pride, Isaiah 2:11, p. 898

The Right Ingredients, Micah 6:8, p. 1227

Jesus' Prayer, John 17, p. 1453

The Sacrifice of Service, Philippians 2:17, 25–30, p. 1612

12:10 languages This can also be translated "tongues."

divided. God wanted the different parts
to care the same for each other. **26**If one
part of the body suffers, all the other
parts suffer with it. Or if one part of our
body is honored, all the other parts share
its honor.

27Together you are the body of
Christ, and each one of you is a part of
that body. **28**In the church God has given a
place first to apostles, second to prophets, and third to teachers. Then God has
given a place to those who do miracles,
those who have gifts of healing, those
who can help others, those who are able
to govern, and those who can speak in
different languages.[n] **29**Not all are apostles. Not all are prophets. Not all are
teachers. Not all do miracles. **30**Not all
have gifts of healing. Not all speak in different languages. Not all interpret those
languages. **31**But you should truly want
to have the greater gifts.

Love Is the Greatest Gift

And now I will show you the best way
of all.

13 I may speak in different languages[n]
of people or even angels. But if I
do not have love, I am only a noisy bell or
a crashing cymbal. **2**I may have the gift of
prophecy. I may understand all the secret
things of God and have all knowledge,
and I may have faith so great I can move
mountains. But even with all these
things, if I do not have love, then I am
nothing. **3**I may give away everything I
have, and I may even give my body as an
offering to be burned.[n] But I gain nothing
if I do not have love.

4Love is patient and kind. Love is not
jealous, it does not brag, and it
is not proud. **5**Love
is not rude, is not
selfish, and does not
get upset with oth-
ers. Love does not
count up wrongs
that have been done. **6**Love is not happy
with evil but is happy with the truth.
7Love patiently accepts all things. It always trusts, always hopes, and always
remains strong.

8Love never ends. There are gifts of

FAITH links

THE BEST CHOICE

1 CORINTHIANS 13

Who or what do you love? Many people think they know what love is, but their actions prove otherwise! This chapter in 1 Corinthians is sometimes called the "love chapter." It explains what love is and what it is not. Love is not a feeling. It is an act of the will, or a choice you make. You can choose to love someone by not being rude to him or her, or letting him or her go first. In fact, God commands us to love others, including our enemies. Love is the greatest gift we can have or offer. Choose love today!

Click here to find out more about loving others God's way:

Roll Out the Welcome Wagon, Genesis 18:2–8, p. 24

Anger: Quick or Slow?, Psalm 86:15, p. 776

Who Do You Prefer?, Proverbs 3:32, p. 830

Sow It and Reap, Lamentations 1:18, p. 1075

Just Say Yes!, Matthew 9:9–13, p. 1289

The True Test, 1 John 3:18, p. 1718

12:28; 13:1 languages This can also be translated "tongues."

13:3 Verse 3 Other Greek copies read: "hand over my body in order that I may brag."

prophecy, but they will be ended. There
are gifts of speaking in different languages, but those gifts will stop. There is
the gift of knowledge, but it will come to
an end. **9**The reason is that our knowledge and our ability to prophesy are not
perfect. **10**But when perfection comes,
the things that are not perfect will end.
11When I was a child, I talked like a child,
I thought like a child, I reasoned like a
child. When I became a man, I stopped
those childish ways. **12**It is the same with
us. Now we see a dim reflection, as if we
were looking into a mirror, but then we
shall see clearly. Now I know only a part,
but then I will know fully, as God has
known me. **13**So these three things continue forever: faith, hope, and love. And
the greatest of these is love.

Desire Spiritual Gifts

14 You should seek after love, and
you should truly want to have the
spiritual gifts, especially the gift of
prophecy. **2**I will explain why. Those who
have the gift of speaking in different
languages[n] are not speaking to people;
they are speaking to God. No one understands them; they are speaking secret
things through the Spirit. **3**But those who
prophesy are speaking to people to give
them strength, encouragement, and comfort. **4**The ones who speak in different
languages are helping only themselves,
but those who prophesy are helping the
whole church. **5**I wish all of you had the
gift of speaking in different kinds of languages, but more, I wish you would
prophesy. Those who prophesy are greater than those who can only speak in different languages—unless someone is
there who can explain what is said so that
the whole church can be helped.

6Brothers and sisters, will it help you
if I come to you speaking in different languages? No! It will help you only if I bring
you a new truth or some new knowledge,
or prophecy, or teaching. **7**It is the same
as with lifeless things that make sounds—
like a flute or a harp. If they do not make
clear musical notes, you will not know
what is being played. **8**And in a war, if the
trumpet does not give a clear sound, who
will prepare for battle? **9**It is the same
with you. Unless you speak clearly with
your tongue, no one can understand what
you are saying. You will be talking into
the air! **10**It may be true that there are
all kinds of sounds in the world, and none
is without meaning. **11**But unless I understand the meaning of what someone
says to me, I will be a foreigner to him,
and he will be a foreigner to me. **12**It is
the same with you. Since you want spiritual gifts very much, seek most of all to
have the gifts that help the church grow
stronger.

13The one who has the gift of speaking in a different language should pray for
the gift to interpret what is spoken. **14**If I
pray in a different language, my spirit is
praying, but my mind does nothing. **15**So
what should I do? I will pray with my
spirit, but I will also pray with my mind. I
will sing with my spirit, but I will also
sing with my mind. **16**If you praise God
with your spirit, those persons there
without understanding cannot say amen[n]
to your prayer of thanks, because they do
not know what you are saying. **17**You may
be thanking God in a good way, but the
other person is not helped.

18I thank God that I speak in different
kinds of languages more than all of you.
19But in the church meetings I would
rather speak five words I understand in
order to teach others than thousands of
words in a different language.

20Brothers and sisters, do not think
like children. In evil things be like babies,
but in your thinking you should be like
adults. **21**It is written in the Scriptures:

> "With people who use strange words
> and foreign languages
> I will speak to these people.
> But even then they will not listen to
> me," *Isaiah 28:11-12*

says the Lord.

22So the gift of speaking in different
kinds of languages is a proof for those
who do not believe, not for those who do

14:2 languages This can also be translated "tongues."

14:16 amen To say amen means to agree with the things that were said.

believe. And prophecy is for people who
believe, not for those who do not believe.
23Suppose the whole church meets together and everyone speaks in different
languages. If some people come in who
do not understand or do not believe, they
will say you are crazy. **24**But suppose
everyone is prophesying and some people come in who do not believe or do not
understand. If everyone is prophesying,
their sin will be shown to them, and they
will be judged by all that they hear. **25**The
secret things in their hearts will be made
known. So they will bow down and worship God saying, "Truly, God is with
you."

Meetings Should Help the Church

26So, brothers and sisters, what
should you do? When you meet together,
one person has a song, and another has a
teaching. Another has a new truth from
God. Another speaks in a different
language,* and another person interprets
that language. The purpose of all these
things should be to help the church grow
strong. **27**When you meet together, if
anyone speaks in a different language, it
should be only two, or not more than
three, who speak. They should speak one
after the other, and someone else should
interpret. **28**But if there is no interpreter,
then those who speak in a different language should be quiet in the church
meeting. They should
speak only to themselves
and to God.

29Only two or three
prophets should speak,
and the others should
judge what they say. **30**If
a message from God
comes to another person
who is sitting, the first
speaker should stop.
31You can all prophesy
one after the other. In this way all the
people can be taught and encouraged.
32The spirits of prophets are under the
control of the prophets themselves.
33God is not a God of confusion but a God
of peace.

As is true in all the churches of God's
people, **34**women should keep quiet in
the church meetings. They are not allowed to speak, but they must yield to
this rule as the law says. **35**If they want
to learn something, they should ask their
own husbands at home. It is shameful for
a woman to speak in the church meeting.
36Did God's teaching come from you? Or
are you the only ones to whom it has
come?

37Those who think they are prophets
or spiritual persons should understand
that what I am writing to you is the
Lord's command. **38**Those who ignore
this will be ignored by God.

39So my brothers and sisters, you
should truly want to prophesy. But do not
stop people from using the gift of speaking in different kinds of languages. **40**But
let everything be done in a right and or-
derly way.

God is not a God of confusion but a God of peace.
—1 Corinthians 14:33

The Good News About Christ

15 Now, brothers and sisters, I want
you to remember the Good News I
brought to you. You received this Good
News and continue strong in it. **2**And you
are being saved by it if you continue believing what I told you. If you do not, then
you believed for nothing.

3I passed on to you what I received, of
which this was most important: that
Christ died for our sins, as the Scriptures
say; **4**that he was buried and was raised to
life on the third day as the
Scriptures say; **5**and that
he was seen by Peter and
then by the twelve apos-
tles. **6**After that, Jesus
was seen by more than
five hundred of the believers at the same time.
Most of them are still living today, but some have
died. **7**Then he was seen
by James and later by all
the apostles. **8**Last of all he was seen by
me—as by a person not born at the normal time. **9**All the other apostles are
greater than I am. I am not even good

14:26 language This can also be translated "tongue."

enough to be called an apostle, because I
persecuted the church of God. 10But
God's grace has made me what I am, and
his grace to me was not wasted. I worked
harder than all the other apostles. (But it
was not I really; it was God's grace that
was with me.) 11So if I preached to you or
the other apostles preached to you, we all
preach the same thing, and this is what
you believed.

We Will Be Raised from the Dead

12Now since we preached that Christ
was raised from the dead, why do some of
you say that people will not be raised
from the dead? 13If no one is ever raised
from the dead, then Christ has not been
raised. 14And if Christ has not been
raised, then our preaching is worth nothing, and your faith is worth nothing.
15And also, we are guilty of lying about
God, because we tes-
tified of him that he
raised Christ from
the dead. But if peo-
ple are not raised
from the dead, then
God never raised
Christ. 16If the dead are not raised,
Christ has not been raised either. 17And
if Christ has not been raised, then your
faith has nothing to it; you are still guilty
of your sins. 18And those in Christ who
have already died are lost. 19If our hope
in Christ is for this life only, we should be
pitied more than anyone else in the
world.

20But Christ has truly been raised
from the dead—the first one and proof
that those who sleep in death will also be
raised. 21Death has come because of
what one man did, but the rising from
death also comes because of one man.
22In Adam all of us die. In the same way,
in Christ all of us will be made alive again.
23But everyone will be raised to life in
the right order. Christ was first to be
raised. When Christ comes again, those
who belong to him will be raised to life,
24and then the end will come. At that
time Christ will destroy all rulers, authorities, and powers, and he will hand
over the kingdom to God the Father.

eMAIL! FROM GOD
15:12–21
Resurrection
The bottom line of Christian faith

FAITH links

LIFE AFTER DEATH?

1 CORINTHIANS 15:12-13

Ever hear someone talk about life after death? Some people believe that after a person dies, nothing happens. He or she just doesn't exist anymore. So, what do you believe will happen after you die? Is the thought too scary to think about?

If you're a Christian, you don't have to be scared to think about death. You know that your life will go on, even after you die! That's what Paul wanted the Christians in Corinth to know and believe. A Christian's hope is in Jesus. Since he was raised from the dead, that means you will be, too, someday. There is life after death: eternal life!

Link here to find out more about why Christians shouldn't fear death:

A Friend in Deed, Job 2:13, p. 662

Who Ya' Gonna Call?, Psalm 3:4, p. 711

Love That Will Last, Psalm 136, p. 813

Sad Times, Matthew 14:13–14, p. 1299

The Coming Attraction, 1 Thessalonians 4:13–18, p. 1634

Never Alone, Hebrews 13:5–6, p. 1684

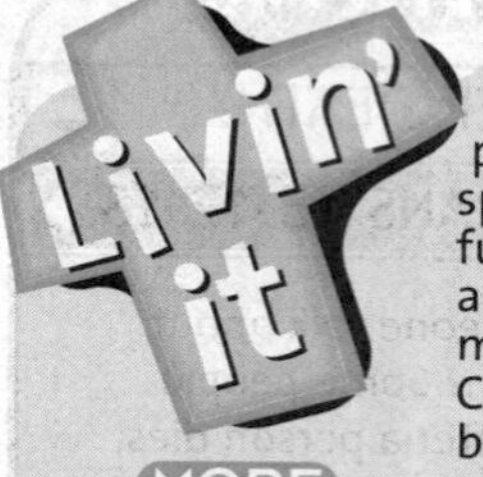

Death

1 Corinthians 15:50–57

The Final End? If someone close to you died, you probably felt an overwhelming sadness and may have spent a lot of time crying. If you have ever been to a funeral, you know that is how people react to the loss of a loved one. People feel sad because they know they will miss seeing that person and talking to him or her. But Christians, even in their sadness, can feel happiness because they know that they *will* see the person again someday—in heaven. How can knowing that comfort you and help you comfort others?

Some people believe that after someone dies, that's the end—he or she just doesn't exist anymore. Paul wanted Christians not to fear death, but to know the truth. (Read 1 Corinthians 15:12–13.) If you're a Christian, you know that there is life after death: eternal life through Jesus.

MORE FAITH links

Sad Times, p. 1299

Remembering Jesus, p. 1321

Mission Impossible?, p. 1337

Life After Death?, p. 1563

The Coming Attraction, p. 1634

"Skweek, do you ever think about death? It's such a scary topic; I don't like to think about it."

"I know it can be scary to think about, but if you connect to these links you'll find out that believers in Jesus have another way of thinking about death."

Love That Will Last, Psalm 136, p. 813
- Is there anything you know that lasts forever? Some bad things may seem to last forever but eventually they go away. How about people, do they last forever? Christians don't live on earth forever, but where *do* they last forever? This Faithlink tells about another thing that you can count on to last forever.

Fully God, Fully Human, John 11:35, p. 1444
- When a friend feels sad, you feel sad, too, don't you? And when someone you love dies, you feel very sad. Link here to find out how Jesus felt about a sad situation.

A Heavenly Sight, Revelation 21:1–4, p. 1753
- What is the most beautiful place you have ever seen? What did you like best about that place?
- What do you think heaven will be like? If you fear what the future may hold, think about this description of heaven, and be glad!

my FAVORITE links

25Christ must rule until he puts all enemies under his control. **26**The last enemy
to be destroyed will be death. **27**The
Scripture says that God put all things under his control."[n] When it says "all things"
are under him, it is clear this does not include God himself. God is the One who
put everything under his control. **28**After
everything has been put under the Son,
then he will put himself under God, who
had put all things under him. Then God
will be the complete ruler over everything.

29If the dead are never raised, what
will people do who are being baptized for
the dead? If the dead are not raised at all,
why are people being baptized for them?

30And what about us? Why do we put
ourselves in danger every hour? **31**I die
every day. That is true, brothers and sisters, just as it is true that I brag about you
in Christ Jesus our Lord. **32**If I fought
wild animals in Ephesus only with human
hopes, I have gained nothing. If the dead
are not raised, "Let us eat and drink, because tomorrow we will die."[n]

33Do not be fooled: "Bad friends will
ruin good habits." **34**Come back to your
right way of thinking and stop sinning.
Some of you do not know God—I say this
to shame you.

What Kind of Body Will We Have?

35But someone may ask, "How are
the dead raised? What kind of body will
they have?" **36**Foolish person! When you
sow a seed, it must die in the ground before it can live and grow. **37**And when you
sow it, it does not have the same "body"
it will have later. What you sow is only a
bare seed, maybe wheat or something
else. **38**But God gives it a body that he
has planned for it, and God gives each
kind of seed its own body. **39**All things
made of flesh are not the same: People
have one kind of flesh, animals have
another, birds have another, and fish
have another. **40**Also there are heavenly
bodies and earthly bodies. But the beauty
of the heavenly bodies is one kind, and the
beauty of the earthly bodies is another.
41The sun has one kind of beauty, the
moon has another beauty, and the stars
have another. And each star is different in
its beauty.

42It is the same with the dead who are
raised to life. The body that is "planted"
will ruin and decay, but it is raised to a life
that cannot be destroyed. **43**When the
body is "planted," it is without honor,
but it is raised in glory. When the body
is "planted," it is weak, but when it is
raised, it is powerful. **44**The body that
is "planted" is a physical body. When it is
raised, it is a spiritual body.

There is a physical body, and there is
also a spiritual body. **45**It is written in the
Scriptures: "The first man, Adam, became a living person."[n] But the last
Adam became a spirit that gives life.
46The spiritual did not come first, but the
physical and then the spiritual. **47**The
first man came from the dust of the earth.
The second man came from heaven.
48People who belong to the earth are like
the first man of earth. But those people
who belong to heaven are like the man of
heaven. **49**Just as we were made like the
man of earth, so we will also be made like
the man of heaven.

50I tell you this, brothers and sisters:
Flesh and blood cannot have a part in the
kingdom of God. Something that will ruin
cannot have a part in something that
never ruins. **51**But look! I tell you this
secret: We will not all sleep in death, but
we will all be changed. **52**It will take only
a second—as quickly as an eye blinks—
when the last trumpet sounds. The trumpet will sound, and those who have died
will be raised to live forever, and we will
all be changed. **53**This body that can be
destroyed must clothe itself with something that can never be destroyed. And
this body that dies must clothe itself with
something that can never die. **54**So this
body that can be destroyed will clothe itself with that which can never be destroyed, and this body that dies will

---

15:27 God put . . . control. From Psalm 8:6.
15:32 "Let us . . . die." Quotation from Isaiah 22:13; 56:12.
15:45 "The first . . . person." Quotation from Genesis 2:7.

clothe itself with that which can never
die. When this happens, this Scripture
will be made true:

"Death is destroyed forever in
victory." *Isaiah 25:8*

55"Death, where is your victory?
Death, where is your pain?" *Hosea 13:14*

56Death's power to hurt is sin, and the
power of sin is the law. 57But we thank
God! He gives us the victory through our
Lord Jesus Christ.

58So my dear brothers and sisters,
stand strong. Do not let anything change
you. Always give yourselves fully to the
work of the Lord, because you know that
your work in the Lord is never wasted.

The Gift for Other Believers

16 Now I will write about the collection of money for God's people. Do
the same thing I told the Galatian
churches to do: 2On the first day of every
week, each one of you should put aside
money as you have been blessed. Save it
up so you will not have to collect money
after I come. 3When I arrive, I will send
whomever you approve to take your gift
to Jerusalem. I will send them with letters of introduction, 4and if it seems
good for me to go also, they will go along
with me.

Paul's Plans

5I plan to go through Macedonia, so I
will come to you after I go through there.
6Perhaps I will stay with you for a time or
even all winter. Then you can help me on
my trip, wherever I go. 7I do not want to
see you now just in passing. I hope to
stay a longer time with you if the Lord
allows it. 8But I will stay at Ephesus until
Pentecost, 9because a good opportunity
for a great and growing work has been
given to me now. And there are many
people working against me.

10If Timothy comes to you, see to it
that he has nothing to fear with you, because he is working for the Lord just as I
am. 11So none of you should treat Timothy as unimportant, but help him on his
trip in peace so that he can come back to
me. I am expecting him to come with the
brothers.

12Now about our brother Apollos: I
strongly encouraged him to visit you with
the other brothers. He did not at all want
to come now; he will come when he has
the opportunity.

FAITH links

GIVE TO GIVE

1 CORINTHIANS 16:1-4

Paul wrote to remind the Corinthian Christians to give money to help poor Christians in Jerusalem. Giving is something we do to help one another. Most churches use the offerings received each week to pay the salaries of church workers, to help people in need, and to support missionaries. When members of a church family give what they can, that allows the church to do what it does best—help people learn about Jesus.

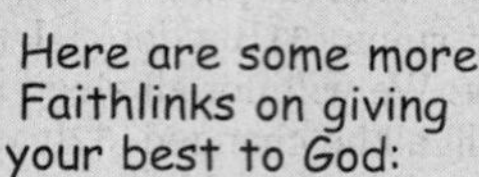

Here are some more Faithlinks on giving your best to God:

Giving Your Part, Leviticus 27:30, p. 173

Give What You Can, Numbers 7:1–11, p. 186

The Way to Serve God, 1 Kings 9:4, p. 450

Love Him? Show It!, Amos 2:6–7, p. 1196

Give Till It Hurts?, 2 Corinthians 8:6–9; 9:6–9, p. 1578

Hot, Cold, or In Between?, Revelation 3:15, p. 1735

Paul Ends His Letter

13Be alert. Continue strong in the
faith. Have courage, and be strong. 14Do
everything in love.
15You know that
the family of Stephanas were the first
believers in Southern Greece and that
they have given
themselves to the service of God's people. I ask you, brothers and sisters, 16to
follow the leading of people like these
and anyone else who works and serves
with them.
17I am happy that Stephanas, Fortunatus, and Achaicus have come. You are
not here, but they have filled your place.
18They have refreshed my spirit and
yours. You should recognize the value of
people like these.
19The churches in the country of Asia
send greetings to you. Aquila and Priscilla greet you in the Lord, as does the
church that meets in their house. 20All
the brothers and sisters here send greetings. Give each other a holy kiss when
you meet.
21I, Paul, am writing this greeting
with my own hand.
22If anyone does not love the Lord, let
him be separated from God—lost forever!
Come, O Lord!
23The grace of the Lord Jesus be with
you.
24My love be with all of you in Christ
Jesus.

eMAIL! FROM GOD

16:13 Courage

What should you do when you're afraid?

FAITH links

MEETING TOGETHER

1 CORINTHIANS 16:19

Do you remember the finger-play game, "This is the church, this is the steeple; open the door, and see all the people"? In that game, the fingers represent the people in the church. It shows that the church is not a building, but a living "body" of people who meet together regularly.

The apostle Paul ended his letter with a greeting from a married couple named Aquila and Priscilla. They were part of a church group that met in their home. Whether Christians meet in homes, schools, or other types of buildings, God is pleased when his people meet together to worship him. Is attending church regularly part of your weekly routine?

A Thanksgiving Reminder, Exodus 12, p. 91

Serious About the Sabbath, Exodus 31:15, p. 117

Facts About Following, Joshua 6, p. 283

Inside the Heart of God, Micah 7:18–20, p. 1228

Heavenly Treasure, Luke 12:32–34, p. 1394

Two Birthdays, John 3:1–7, p. 1426

2 Corinthians

A CASE FOR THE DEFENSE

It's me—Paul again. This is my second letter to my friends in Corinth. And, in case you're wondering, this book *is* different from 1 Corinthians. That first book was all about the problems that the church in Corinth was having. But this one is entirely different. I'm not complaining here, but serving God can be really hard. It's not always real fun being poor and hungry and tired and in constant danger. It wasn't always fun, but I wanted my friends to understand that I would go through *anything* to tell people about Jesus!

I wrote this letter to set the record straight. You see, a lot of the Jewish leaders didn't like my message or me. So they started telling lies about me. (They even accused me of being a false teacher!) I wanted my friends to understand that the Christian life is not all about success, power, and fame, like they were saying. It's about following and obeying Jesus—even if it means suffering and being misunderstood!

JESUS WATCH

Paul's ministry was all about telling people about Jesus, and this letter is no exception. In this letter, Paul focuses on helping us understand Jesus as our comforter in the bad times. And Paul promises that for all followers, bad times happen. Throughout the book, Paul talks about Jesus as our comforter (1:5), our victory (2:14), our Lord (4:5), our light (4:6), and our gift (9:15). Paul faced many tough times, but he was able to continue in spite of his difficulties because he knew the truth—Jesus is always with us. We can be encouraged by that same truth today!

my FAVORITE links

OTHER CONNECTIONS

Livin' it Do you mind sharing your stuff with other kids? Or do you worry about your stuff getting lost, or ruined? What's more important—your stuff or your friends? Find out what the Bible has to say about the things we own by linking to Sharing Your Stuff, 2 Corinthians 8:1–9.

- Let's Visit Corinth, 2 Corinthians 6. Connect here to find out why Corinth was such a perfect place for Paul to preach about the Good News.

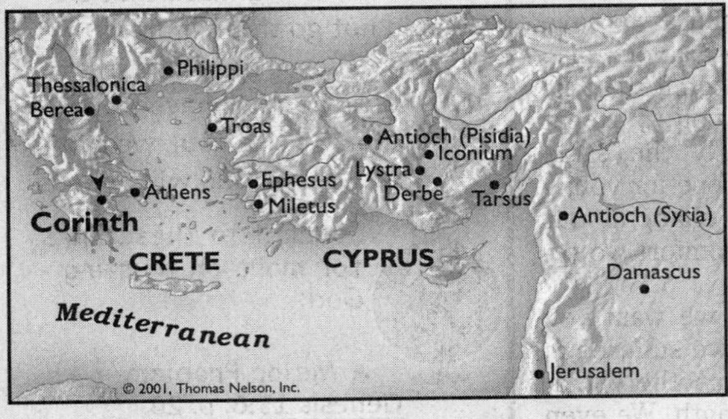

"Hey, Tagg. Does Paul really talk about giving to the church in this letter?"

"He sure does. Paul writes about that in 2 Corinthians 8:7-15."

OTHER COOL STUFF IN THIS BOOK:

Victory!, 2 Corinthians 2:14–17
Becoming God's friend, 2 Corinthians 5:11–21
Paul's defense, 2 Corinthians 10

FAITH links

- **Hard Times, 2 Corinthians 1:8–10**
- **Keeping Clean, 2 Corinthians 7:1**
- **Give Till It Hurts?, 2 Corinthians 8:6–9; 9:6–9**
- **Most Wanted?, 2 Corinthians 10:1**
- **Blessed Are the Weak?, 2 Corinthians 12:7–10**

1 From Paul, an apostle of Christ Jesus.
I am an apostle because that is what
God wanted. Also from Timothy our
brother in Christ.
To the church of God in Corinth, and
to all of God's people everywhere in
Southern Greece:
2Grace and peace to you from God our
Father and the Lord Jesus Christ.

Paul Gives Thanks to God

3Praise be to the God and Father of
our Lord Jesus Christ. God is the Father
who is full of mercy and all comfort. 4He
comforts us every time we have trouble,
so when others have trouble, we can
comfort them with the same comfort God
gives us. 5We share in the many sufferings of Christ. In the same way, much
comfort comes to us through Christ. 6If
we have troubles, it is for your
comfort and salva-
tion, and if we have
comfort, you also
have comfort. This
helps you to accept
patiently the same
sufferings we have. 7Our hope for you is
strong, knowing that you share in our
sufferings and also in the comfort we receive.
8Brothers and sisters,[n] we want you
to know about the trouble we suffered in
Asia. We had great burdens there that
were beyond our own strength. We even
gave up hope of living. 9Truly, in our own
hearts we believed we would die. But
this happened so we would not trust in
ourselves but in God, who raises people
from the dead. 10God saved us from
these great dangers of death, and he will
continue to save us. We have put our
hope in him, and he will save us again.
11And you can help us with your prayers.
Then many people will give thanks for
us—that God blessed us because of their
many prayers.

EMAIL FROM GOD
1:3–11
Comfort
Are sad people important to God?

1:8 Brothers and sisters Although the Greek text says "Brothers" here and throughout this book, Paul's words were meant for the entire church, including men and women.

FAITH links

HARD TIMES

2 CORINTHIANS 1:8-10

What is your first reaction when hard times come? Many people tend to panic or get angry with God. They think, *Why is this happening to me? Why did God allow this to happen? Does God still care about me?*

The apostle Paul faced many tough situations as a missionary. At times, he even thought he would die! But the hard times helped him to trust God for help.

God never promised that we would not go through hard times. As Jesus once said, "In this world you will have trouble" (John 16:33). Like Paul, we can trust that God will help us.

Connect to these links for more on trusting God:

A Major Problem, Genesis 15:6, p. 20

Moses' Champion, Numbers 12, p. 192

A Pity Party, Job 10, p. 671

Dirty Inside, Isaiah 6:1–7, p. 904

Facing Your Fears, Matthew 8:23–27, p. 1288

Keep On Keepin' On, Revelation 13:10, p. 1744

The Change in Paul's Plans

12This is what we are proud of, and I
can say it with a clear conscience: In
everything we have done in the world,
and especially with you, we have had an
honest and sincere heart from God. We
did this by God's grace, not by the kind of
wisdom the world has. **13-14**We write to
you only what you can read and understand. And I hope that as you have understood some things about us, you may
come to know everything about us. Then
you can be proud of us, as we will be
proud of you on the day our Lord Jesus
Christ comes again.

15I was so sure of all this that I made
plans to visit you first so you could be
blessed twice. **16**I planned to visit you on
my way to Macedonia and again on my
way back. I wanted to get help from you
for my trip to Judea. **17**Do you think that I
made these plans without really meaning
it? Or maybe you think I make plans as
the world does, so that I say yes, yes and
at the same time no, no.

18But if you can believe God, you can
believe that what we tell you is never
both yes and no. **19**The Son of God, Jesus
Christ, that Silas and Timothy and I
preached to you, was not yes and no. In
Christ it has always been yes. **20**The yes
to all of God's promises is in Christ, and
through Christ we say yes to the glory of
God. **21**Remember, God is the One who
makes you and us strong in Christ. God
made us his chosen people. **22**He put his
mark on us to show that we are his, and
he put his Spirit in our hearts to be a
guarantee for all he has promised.

23I tell you this, and I ask God to be
my witness that this is true: The reason I
did not come back to Corinth was to keep
you from being punished or hurt. **24**We
are not trying to control your faith. You
are strong in faith. But we are workers
with you for your own joy.

2 So I decided that my next visit to you
would not be another one to make
you sad. **2**If I make you sad, who will
make me glad? Only you can make me
glad—particularly the person whom I
made sad. **3**I wrote you a letter for this
reason: that when I came to you I would
not be made sad by the people who
should make me happy. I felt sure of all of
you, that you would share my joy. **4**When
I wrote to you before, I was very troubled
and unhappy in my heart, and I wrote
with many tears. I did not write to make
you sad, but to let you know how much I
love you.

Forgive the Sinner

5Someone there among you has
caused sadness, not to me, but to all of
you. I mean he caused sadness to all in
some way. (I do not want to make it sound
worse than it really is.) **6**The punishment
that most of you gave him is enough for
him. **7**But now you should forgive him
and comfort him to keep him from having
too much sadness and giving up completely. **8**So I beg you to show that you
love him. **9**I wrote you to test you and to
see if you obey in everything. **10**If you
forgive someone, I also forgive him. And
what I have forgiven—if I had anything to
forgive—I forgave it for you, as if Christ
were with me. **11**I did this so that Satan
would not win anything from us, because
we know very well what Satan's plans
are.

Paul's Concern in Troas

12When I came to Troas to preach the
Good News of Christ, the Lord gave me a
good opportunity there. **13**But I had no
peace, because I did not find my brother
Titus. So I said good-bye to them at Troas
and went to Macedonia.

Victory Through Christ

14But thanks be to God, who always
leads us in victory through Christ. God
uses us to spread his knowledge everywhere like a sweet-smelling perfume.
15Our offering to God is this: We are the
sweet smell of Christ among those who
are being saved and among those who are
being lost. **16**To those who are lost, we
are the smell of death that brings death,
but to those who are being saved, we are
the smell of life that brings life. So who
is able to do this work? **17**We do not
sell the word of God for a profit as many
other people do. But in Christ we speak

the truth before God, as messengers of
God.

Servants of the New Agreement

3 Are we starting to brag about ourselves again? Do we need letters of
introduction to you or from you, like
some other people? 2You yourselves are
our letter, written on our hearts, known
and read by everyone. 3You show that
you are a letter from Christ sent through
us. This letter is not written with ink but
with the Spirit of the living God. It is not
written on stone tablets[n] but on human
hearts.
4We can say this, because through
Christ we feel certain before God. 5We
are not saying that we can do this work
ourselves. It is God who makes us able to
do all that we do. 6He made us able to be
servants of a new agreement from himself to his people. This new agreement is
not a written law, but it is of the Spirit.
The written law brings death, but the
Spirit gives life.
7The law that brought death was written in words on stone. It came with God's
glory, which made Moses' face so bright
that the Israelites could not continue to
look at it. But that glory later disappeared. 8So surely the new way that
brings the Spirit has even more glory. 9If
the law that judged people guilty of sin
had glory, surely the new way that makes
people right with God has much greater
glory. 10That old law had glory, but it
really loses its glory when it is compared
to the much greater glory of this new
way. 11If that law which disappeared
came with glory, then this new way which
continues forever has much greater
glory.
12We have this hope, so we are very
bold. 13We are not like Moses, who put a
covering over his face so the Israelites
would not see it. The glory was dis-
appearing, and Moses did not want them
to see it end. 14But their minds were
closed, and even today that same covering hides the meaning when they read
the old agreement. That covering is tak-
en away only through Christ. 15Even today, when they read the law of Moses,
there is a covering over their minds.
16But when a person changes and follows the Lord, that covering is taken
away. 17The Lord is the Spirit, and where the
Spirit of the Lord is,
there is freedom.
18Our faces, then,
are not covered. We
all show the Lord's
glory, and we are being changed to be like
him. This change in us brings ever greater glory, which comes from the Lord, who
is the Spirit.

eMAIL! FROM GOD 3:18
Faith
What will change you?

Preaching the Good News

4 God, with his mercy, gave us this
work to do, so we don't give up. 2But
we have turned away from secret and
shameful ways. We use no trickery, and
we do not change the teaching of God. We
teach the truth plainly, showing everyone
who we are. Then they can know in their
hearts what kind of people we are in
God's sight. 3If the Good News that we
preach is hidden, it is hidden only to
those who are lost. 4The devil who rules
this world has blinded the minds of those
who do not believe. They cannot see the
light of the Good News—the Good News
about the glory of Christ, who is exactly
like God. 5We do not preach about ourselves, but we preach that Jesus Christ is
Lord and that we are your servants for
Jesus. 6God once said, "Let the light
shine out of the darkness!" This is the
same God who made his light shine in our
hearts by letting us know the glory of
God that is in the face of Christ.

Spiritual Treasure in Clay Jars

7We have this treasure from God, but
we are like clay jars that hold the treasure. This shows that the great power is
from God, not from us. 8We have troubles
all around us, but we are not defeated. We
do not know what to do, but we do not
give up the hope of living. 9We are persecuted, but God does not leave us. We
are hurt sometimes, but we are not de-

3:3 stone tablets Meaning the Law of Moses that was written on stone tablets (Exodus 24:12; 25:16).

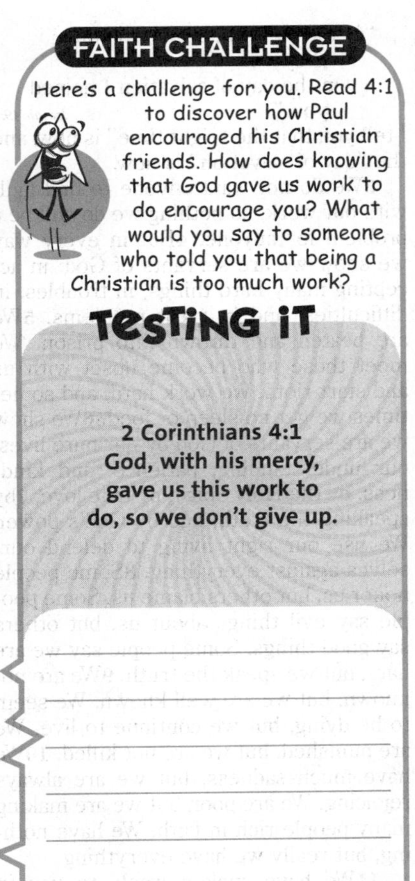

Here's a challenge for you. Read 4:1 to discover how Paul encouraged his Christian friends. How does knowing that God gave us work to do encourage you? What would you say to someone who told you that being a Christian is too much work?

stroyed. 10We carry the death of Jesus in
our own bodies so that the life of Jesus
can also be seen in our bodies. 11We are
alive, but for Jesus we are always in danger of death so that the life of
Jesus can be seen in
our bodies that die.
12So death is work-
ing in us, but life is
working in you.

eMAIL! FROM GOD 4:8–12
Worry
Does God care about your worries?

13It is written in
the Scriptures, "I believed, so I spoke."[n]
Our faith is like this, too. We believe, and
so we speak. 14God raised the Lord
Jesus from the dead, and we know that
God will also raise us with Jesus. God will
bring us together with you, and we will
stand before him. 15All these things are
for you. And so the grace of God that is
being given to more and more people will
bring increasing thanks to God for his
glory.

Living by Faith

16So we do not give up. Our physical
body is becoming older and weaker, but
our spirit inside us is made new every
day. 17We have small troubles for a while
now, but they are helping us gain an eternal glory that is much greater than the
troubles. 18We set our eyes not on what
we see but on what we cannot see. What
we see will last only a short time, but
what we cannot see will last forever.

5 We know that our body—the tent we
live in here on earth—will be destroyed. But when that happens, God will
have a house for us. It will not be a house
made by human hands; instead, it will be
a home in heaven that will last forever.
2But now we groan in this tent. We want
God to give us our heavenly home, 3be-
cause it will clothe us so we will not be
naked. 4While we live in this body, we
have burdens, and we groan. We do not
want to be naked, but we want to be
clothed with our heavenly home. Then
this body that dies will be fully covered
with life. 5This is what God made us for,
and he has given us the Spirit to be a
guarantee for this new life.

6So we always have courage. We
know that while we live in this body, we
are away from the Lord. 7We
live by what we be-
lieve, not by what
we can see. 8So I
say that we have
courage. We really
want to be away
from this body and be at home with the
Lord. 9Our only goal is to please God
whether we live here or there, 10because
we must all stand before Christ to be
judged. Each of us will receive what we

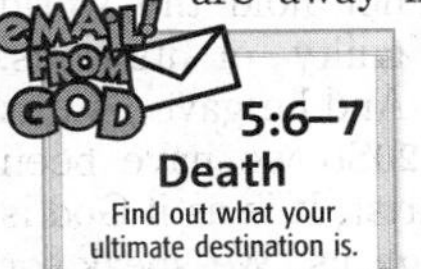

eMAIL! FROM GOD
5:6–7
Death
Find out what your ultimate destination is.

4:13 "I . . . spoke." Quotation from Psalm 116:10.

should get—good or bad—for the things
we did in the earthly body.

Becoming Friends with God

11Since we know what it means to
fear the Lord, we try to help people accept the truth about us. God knows what
we really are, and I hope that in your
hearts you know, too. 12We are not trying
to prove ourselves to you again, but we
are telling you about ourselves so you
will be proud of us. Then you will have an
answer for those who are proud about
things that can be seen rather than what
is in the heart. 13If we are out of our
minds, it is for God. If we have our right
minds, it is for you. 14The love of Christ
controls us, because we know that One
died for all, so all have died. 15Christ died
for all so that those who live would not
continue to live for themselves. He died
for them and was raised from the dead so
that they would live for him.
16From this time on we do not think
of anyone as the world does. In the past
we thought of Christ as the world thinks,
but we no longer think of him in that way.
17If anyone belongs to Christ, there is a
new creation. The old things have gone;
everything is made new! 18All this is
from God. Through Christ, God made
peace between us and himself, and God
gave us the work of telling everyone
about the peace we can have with him.
19God was in Christ, making
peace between the
world and himself.
In Christ, God did
not hold the world
guilty of its sins.
And he gave us this
message of peace. 20So we have been
sent to speak for Christ. It is as if God is
calling to you through us. We speak for
Christ when we beg you to be at peace
with God. 21Christ had no sin, but God
made him become sin so that in Christ
we could become right with God.

EMAIL FROM GOD
5:18–21
Witnessing
What does God want you to share?

6 We are workers together with God,
so we beg you: Do not let the grace
that you received from God be for nothing. 2God says,

"At the right time I heard your
prayers.
On the day of salvation I helped
you." *Isaiah 49:8*

I tell you that the "right time" is now, and
the "day of salvation" is now.
3We do not want anyone to find fault
with our work, so nothing we do will be a
problem for anyone. 4But in every way
we show we are servants of God: in accepting many hard things, in troubles, in
difficulties, and in great problems. 5We
are beaten and thrown into prison. We
meet those who become upset with us
and start riots. We work hard, and sometimes we get no sleep or food. 6We show
we are servants of God by our pure lives,
our understanding, patience, and kindness, by the Holy Spirit, by true love, 7by
speaking the truth, and by God's power.
We use our right living to defend ourselves against everything. 8Some people
honor us, but others blame us. Some people say evil things about us, but others
say good things. Some people say we are
liars, but we speak the truth. 9We are not
known, but we are well known. We seem
to be dying, but we continue to live. We
are punished, but we are not killed. 10We
have much sadness, but we are always
rejoicing. We are poor, but we are making
many people rich in faith. We have nothing, but really we have everything.
11We have spoken freely to you in
Corinth and have opened our hearts to
you. 12Our feelings of love for you have
not stopped, but you have stopped your
feelings of love for us. 13I speak to you as
if you were my children. Do to us as we
have done—open your hearts to us.

Warning About Non-Christians

14You are not the same as those who
do not believe. So do not join yourselves
to them. Good and bad do not belong together. Light and darkness cannot share
together. 15How can Christ and Belial,
the devil, have any agreement? What can
a believer have together with a nonbe-
liever? 16The temple of God cannot have
any agreement with idols, and we are the
temple of the living God. As God said: "I
will live with them and walk with them.

LET'S VISIT CORINTH **2 Corinthians 6**

Today Corinth is a small town; but when the apostle Paul was alive, it was a busy city full of industry and sales. It was on a narrow strip of land in Greece with water on both sides, making it a convenient port for ships. That was one reason why it was a good place for Paul to preach. He knew that his listeners would go from there to many other places, and then they could share the Good News.

Corinth also had many temples to false gods. When people in Corinth became Christians, they had to learn a lot about living holy lives. Paul wrote two letters to the church there, which we know as 1 and 2 Corinthians. Both of those books contain instructions on living for Christ in an evil environment.

And I will be their God, and they will be
my people."[n]
17 "Leave those people,
and be separate, says the Lord.
Touch nothing that is unclean,
and I will accept you."
Isaiah 52:11; Ezekiel 20:34, 41

18 "I will be your father,
and you will be my sons and
daughters,
says the Lord Almighty."
2 Samuel 7:14; 7:8

7 Dear friends, we have these promises
from God, so we should make ourselves pure—free from anything that
makes body or soul unclean. We should
try to become holy in the way we live,
because we respect God.

Paul's Joy

2Open your hearts to us. We have not
done wrong to anyone, we have not ruined the faith of anyone, and we have not
cheated anyone. 3I do not say this to
blame you. I told you before that we love
you so much we would live or die with
you. 4I feel very sure of you and am very
proud of you. You give me much comfort,
and in all of our troubles I have great joy.
5When we came into Macedonia, we
had no rest. We found trouble all around
us. We had fighting on the outside and
fear on the inside. 6But God, who comforts those who are troubled, comforted
us when Titus came. 7We were comforted, not only by his coming but also by the
comfort you gave him. Titus told us about
your wish to see me and that you are
very sorry for what you did. He also told
me about your great care for me, and
when I heard this, I was much happier.
8Even if my letter made you sad, I am
not sorry I wrote it. At first I was sorry,
because it made you sad, but you were
sad only for a short time. 9Now I am happy, not because you were made sad, but
because your sorrow made you change
your lives. You became sad in the way
God wanted you to, so you were not hurt
by us in any way. 10The kind of sorrow
God wants makes people change their
hearts and lives. This leads to salvation,
and you cannot be sorry for that. But the

6:16 "I . . . people." Quotation from Leviticus 26:11-12; Jeremiah 32:38; Ezekiel 37:27.

FAITH links

KEEPING CLEAN

2 CORINTHIANS 7:1

Let's say you just put on some new clothes, clothes you really like. Would you immediately go outside and leap into the nearest mud puddle? You probably wouldn't. You'd want to keep as clean as possible to avoid messing up your new clothes. God wants his people to be as clean as possible on the inside. Keeping clean and pure means avoiding people or things that could harm you spiritually. These include television shows or movies that your parents don't want you to watch, kids who try to influence you to do things you know are wrong, and so on.

Keeping clean honors God.

Download these Faithlinks for ways to keep clean for God:

Can't Live Without It, Genesis 3, p. 7

A Choice to Make, Deuteronomy 30:15–20, p. 265

In Your Best Interests, Ruth 3, p. 349

Down on the Ant Farm, Proverbs 6:6–11, p. 833

Prayer for a Friend, Colossians 1:9–12, p. 1620

The Way to Be Wise, James 1:5, p. 1689

kind of sorrow the world has brings
death. **11**See what this sorrow—the sorrow God wanted you to have—has done
to you: It has made you very serious. It
made you want to prove you were not
wrong. It made you angry and afraid. It
made you want to see me. It made you
care. It made you want the right thing to
be done. You proved you were innocent in
the problem. **12**I wrote that letter, not because of the one who did the wrong or
because of the person who was hurt. I
wrote the letter so you could see, before
God, the great care you have for us.
13That is why we were comforted.

Not only were we very comforted, we
were even happier to see that Titus was
so happy. All of you made him feel much
better. **14**I bragged to Titus about you,
and you showed that I was right. Everything we said to you was true, and you
have proved that what we bragged about
to Titus is true. **15**And his love for you is
stronger when he remembers that you
were all ready to obey. You welcomed him
with respect and fear. **16**I am very happy
that I can trust you fully.

Christian Giving

8 And now, brothers and sisters, we
want you to know about the grace
God gave the churches in Macedonia.
2They have been tested by great troubles, and they are very poor. But they
gave much because of their great joy. **3**I
can tell you that they gave as much as
they were able and even more than they
could afford. No one told them to do it.
4But they begged and pleaded with us to
let them share in this service for God's
people. **5**And they gave in a way we did
not expect: They first gave themselves
to the Lord and to us. This is what God
wants. **6**So we asked Titus to help you
finish this special work of grace since he
is the one who started it. **7**You are rich in
everything—in faith, in speaking, in
knowledge, in truly wanting to help, and
in the love you learned from us. In the
same way, be strong also in the grace of
giving.

8I am not commanding you to give.
But I want to see if your love is true by
comparing you with others that really
want to help. **9**You know the grace of our
Lord Jesus Christ. You know that Christ

SHARING

2 Corinthians 8:1–9

Livin' it

Sharing Your Stuff Sharing your stuff with someone can be hard. Maybe it'll get ruined, or lost, or never returned. And how about sharing your money? The money you get for gifts, for allowance, or for doing jobs should be yours to use any way you want, right? Maybe you feel like you *have* to give some of your money to church or Sunday school but you'd really like that new computer game instead. Paul talked a lot about giving and sharing—and it doesn't always involve things or money. (Look at 2 Corinthians 8:6–9; 9:6–9.)

Jesus doesn't say you have to share or give away everything. What he does want, though, is for you to give willingly and cheerfully. (Check out Luke 21:1–4, p. 1410.) How do you share what you have—because you want to, or because you *have* to?

MORE FAITH links

"Hey, Tagg, how about sharing your candy bar with me?"

"Do I have to? I'm really feeling hungry!"

"Haven't you been paying attention? You better check out what God has to say about sharing!"

Share What You Have, Exodus 35:5–18, p. 123
- God wants us to share what we have with others. How do you share your money, time, and talents to do the work of God?

Care to Be Fair?, Joshua 18:1–8, p. 299
- When you need to share with someone, what do you do to be fair?
- God wants us to care about being fair. What is one way you've come up with to share what God gives you?

What's the Use?, 2 Kings 12:6–12, p. 495
- Do you know what your offering money is used for? If you're not sure, ask someone who knows (like your pastor).

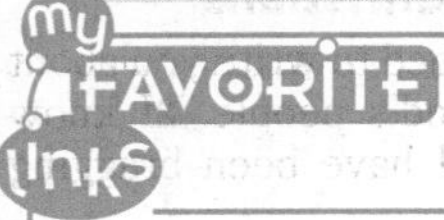

GIVE TILL IT HURTS?

2 CORINTHIANS 8:6-9; 9:6-9

Many people give out of obligation. They feel they have to give, especially to the church. In his letter to the Corinthian Christians, Paul talked a lot about giving. He wanted them to know that they were not forced to give. In fact, God wants people to be "glad givers." As Paul said, a person should give what his or her heart tells him/her to give. Giving doesn't always involve money. You can "give" your time to help someone. You can also donate clothes or toys to people in need. You'll be glad you did!

Fairness for All, Deuteronomy 24:17, p. 258

A Reminder to Be Fair, 2 Chronicles 19:5–11, p. 583

Set for Life?, Obadiah 2–4, p. 1208

Go! No!, Jonah 1, p. 1213

The Gift of Worship, Matthew 2:10–12, p. 1275

The Way to Greatness, Matthew 20:20–28, p. 1309

was rich, but for you he became poor so
that by his becoming poor you might become rich.
10This is what I think you should do:
Last year you were the first to want to
give, and you were the first who gave.
11So now finish the work you started.
Then your "doing" will be equal to your
"wanting to do." Give from what you
have. **12**If you want to give, your gift will
be accepted. It will be judged by what you
have, not by what you do not have. **13**We
do not want you to have troubles while
other people are at ease, but we want
everything to be equal. **14**At this time
you have plenty. What you have can help
others who are in need. Then later, when
they have plenty, they can help you when
you are in need, and all will be equal.
15As it is written in the Scriptures, "The
person who gathered more did not have
too much, nor did the person who gathered less have too little."[n]

Titus and His Companions Help

16I thank God because he gave Titus
the same love for you that I have. **17**Titus
accepted what we asked him to do. He
wanted very much to go to you, and this
was his own idea. **18**We are sending with
him the brother who is praised by all the
churches because of his service in
preaching the Good News. **19**Also, this
brother was chosen by the churches to
go with us when we deliver this gift of
money. We are doing this service to bring
glory to the Lord and to show that we
really want to help.
20We are being careful so that no one
will criticize us for the way we are handling this large gift. **21**We are trying hard
to do what the Lord accepts as right and
also what people think is right.
22Also, we are sending with them our
brother, who is always ready to help. He
has proved this to us in many ways, and
he wants to help even more now, because
he has much faith in you.
23Now about Titus—he is my partner
who is working with me to help you. And
about the other brothers—they are sent
from the churches, and they bring glory
to Christ. **24**So show these men the proof
of your love and the reason we are proud
of you. Then all the churches can see it.

Help for Fellow Christians

9 I really do not need to write you about
this help for God's people. **2**I know
you want to help. I have been bragging

8:15 "The person . . . little." Quotation from Exodus 16:18.

about this to the people in Macedonia,
telling them that you in Southern Greece
have been ready to give since last year.
And your desire to give has made most of
them ready to give also. **3**But I am sending the brothers to you so that our bragging about you in this will not be empty
words. I want you to be ready, as I said
you would be. **4**If any of the people from
Macedonia come with me and find that
you are not ready, we will be ashamed
that we were so sure of you. (And you
will be ashamed, too!) **5**So I thought I
should ask these brothers to go to you
before we do. They will finish getting in
order the generous gift you promised so
it will be ready when we come. And it will
be a generous gift—not one that you did
not want to give.

6Remember this: The person who
plants a little will have a small harvest,
but the person who
plants a lot will have
a big harvest. **7**Each
one should give as
you have decided in
your heart to give.
You should not be
sad when you give, and you should not
give because you feel forced to give. God
loves the person who gives happily. **8**And
God can give you more blessings than
you need. Then you will always have
plenty of everything—enough to give to
every good work. **9**It is written in the
Scriptures:

"He gives freely to the poor.
The things he does are right and
will continue forever." *Psalm 112:9*

10God is the One who gives seed to the
farmer and bread for food. He will give
you all the seed you need and make it
grow so there will be a great harvest from
your goodness. **11**He will make you rich
in every way so that you can always give
freely. And your giving through us will
cause many to give thanks to God.
12This service you do not only helps the
needs of God's people, it also brings
many more thanks to God. **13**It is a proof
of your faith. Many people will praise God
because you obey the Good News of
Christ—the gospel you say you believe—and because you freely share with
them and with all others. **14**And when
they pray, they will wish they could be
with you because of the great grace that
God has given you. **15**Thanks be to God
for his gift that is too wonderful for
words.

eMAIL! FROM GOD
9:6–8
Giving
What kind of giver does God love?

Paul Defends His Ministry

10 I, Paul, am begging you with the
gentleness and the kindness of
Christ. Some people say that I am easy
on you when I am with you and bold when
I am away. **2**They think we live in a
worldly way, and I plan to be very bold
with them when I come. I beg you that
when I come I will not need to use that
same boldness with you. **3**We do live in
the world, but we do not fight in the same
way the world fights. **4**We fight with
weapons that are different from those the
world uses. Our weapons have power
from God that can destroy the enemy's
strong places. We destroy people's arguments **5**and every proud thing that raises
itself against the knowledge of God. We
capture every thought and make it give
up and obey Christ. **6**We are ready to
punish anyone there who does not obey,
but first we want you to obey fully.

7You must look at the facts before
you. If you feel sure that you belong to
Christ, you must remember that we belong to Christ just as you do. **8**It is true
that we brag freely about the authority
the Lord gave us. But this authority is to
build you up, not to tear you down. So I
will not be ashamed. **9**I do not want you
to think I am trying to scare you with my
letters. **10**Some people say, "Paul's letters are powerful and sound important,
but when he is with us, he is weak. And
his speaking is nothing." **11**They should
know this: We are not there with you
now, so we say these things in letters.
But when we are there with you, we will
show the same authority that we
show in our letters.

12We do not dare
to compare our-
selves with those
who think they are
very important. They

eMAIL! FROM GOD
10:12–13
Pride
Check out how to measure your value.

FAITH links

MOST WANTED?

2 CORINTHIANS 10:1

What are the qualities that you admire most in a person? Some admire people with strong personalities. Others like people who have a sense of humor. Humbleness and gentleness are not usually in the top five "most admired" qualities! The apostle Paul appealed to the Corinthian believers "with the gentleness and the kindness of Christ." These qualities require that we lay aside our pride as they develop. Sounds hard? It is. That's why the Holy Spirit has to do the work for us!

Connect here to find out about the qualities God admires:

The Cloud Guide, Numbers 9:15–23, p. 188

A Friend in Deed, Job 2:13, p. 662

Mind Guard, Proverbs 4:23, p. 831

What God "Hates," Proverbs 6:16–19, p. 835

Believe It or Not, Luke 1:20, 38, p. 1366

Don't Play Favorites, James 2:1–7, p. 1691

use themselves to measure themselves,
and they judge themselves by what they
themselves are. This shows that they
know nothing. 13But we will not brag
about things outside the work that was
given us to do. We will limit our bragging
to the work that God gave us, and this includes our work with you. 14We are not
bragging too much, as we would be if we
had not already come to you. But we have
come to you with the Good News of
Christ. 15We limit our bragging to the
work that is ours, not what others have
done. We hope that as your faith continues to grow, you will help our work to
grow much larger. 16We want to tell the
Good News in the areas beyond your city.
We do not want to brag about work that
has already been done in another
person's area. 17But, "If someone wants
to brag, he should brag only about the
Lord."[n] 18It is not those who say they are
good who are accepted but those who the
Lord thinks are good.

Paul and the False Apostles

11 I wish you would be patient with
me even when I am a little foolish,
but you are already doing that. 2I am jealous over you with a jealousy that comes
from God. I promised to give you to
Christ, as your only husband. I want to
give you as his pure bride. 3But I am
afraid that your minds will be led away
from your true and pure following of
Christ just as Eve was tricked by the
snake with his evil ways. 4You are very
patient with anyone who comes to you
and preaches a different Jesus from the
one we preached. You are very willing to
accept a spirit or gospel that is different
from the Spirit and Good News you received from us.

5I do not think that those "great apostles" are any better than I am. 6I may not
be a trained speaker, but I do have knowledge. We have shown this to you clearly
in every way.

7I preached God's Good News to you
without pay. I made myself unimportant
to make you important. Do you think that
was wrong? 8I accepted pay from other
churches, taking their money so I could
serve you. 9If I needed something when I
was with you, I did not trouble any of you.

10:17 "If . . . Lord." Quotation from Jeremiah 9:24.

The brothers who came from Macedonia
gave me all that I needed. I did not allow
myself to depend on you in any way, and I
will never depend on you. **10**No one in
Southern Greece will stop me from bragging about that. I say this with the truth
of Christ in me. **11**And why do I not depend on you? Do you think it is because I
do not love you? God knows that I love
you.

12And I will continue doing what I am
doing now, because I want to stop those
people from having a reason to brag.
They would like to say that the work they
brag about is the same as ours. **13**Such
men are not true apostles but are workers who lie. They change themselves to look like
apostles of Christ.
14This does not sur-
prise us. Even Satan
changes himself to
look like an angel of
light.[n] **15**So it does not surprise us if
Satan's servants also make themselves
look like servants who work for what is
right. But in the end they will be punished for what they do.

EMAIL FROM GOD
11:14
Satan
Satan disguises himself.

Paul Tells About His Sufferings

16I tell you again: No one should think
I am a fool. But if you think so, accept me
as you would accept a fool. Then I can
brag a little, too. **17**When I brag because I
feel sure of myself, I am not talking as the
Lord would talk but as a fool. **18**Many
people are bragging about their lives in
the world. So I will brag too. **19**You are
wise, so you will gladly be patient with
fools! **20**You are even patient with those
who order you around, or use you, or
trick you, or think they are better than
you, or hit you in the face. **21**It is shameful to me to say this, but we were too
"weak" to do those things to you!

But if anyone else is brave enough to
brag, then I also will be brave and brag.
(I am talking as a fool.) **22**Are they
Hebrews?[n] So am I. Are they Israelites?
So am I. Are they from Abraham's family? So am I. **23**Are they serving Christ? I
am serving him more. (I am crazy to talk
like this.) I have worked much harder
than they. I have been in prison more often. I have been hurt more in beatings. I
have been near death many times. **24**Five
times the Jews have given me their punishment of thirty-nine lashes with a whip.
25Three different times I was beaten
with rods. One time I was almost stoned
to death. Three times I was in ships that
wrecked, and one of those times I spent a
night and a day in the sea. **26**I have gone
on many travels and have been in danger
from rivers, thieves, my own people, the
Jews, and those who are not Jews. I have
been in danger in cities, in places where
no one lives, and on the sea. And I have
been in danger with false Christians. **27**I
have done hard and tiring work, and
many times I did not sleep. I have been
hungry and thirsty, and many times I
have been without food. I have been cold
and without clothes. **28**Besides all this,
there is on me every day the load of my
concern for all the churches. **29**I feel
weak every time someone is weak, and I
feel upset every time someone is led into
sin.

30If I must brag, I will brag about the
things that show I am weak. **31**God
knows I am not lying. He is the God and
Father of the Lord Jesus Christ, and he is
to be praised forever. **32**When I was in
Damascus, the governor under King Are-
tas wanted to arrest me, so he put guards
around the city. **33**But my friends lowered me in a basket through a hole in the
city wall. So I escaped from the governor.

A Special Blessing in Paul's Life

12 I must continue to brag. It will do
no good, but I will talk now about
visions and revelations[n] from the Lord. **2**I
know a man in Christ who was taken up
to the third heaven fourteen years ago. I
do not know whether the man was in his
body or out of his body, but God knows.
3-4 And I know that this man was taken up

11:14 angel of light Messenger from God. The devil fools people so that they think he is from God.

11:22 Hebrews A name for the Jews that some Jews were very proud of.

12:1 revelations Revelation is making known a truth that was hidden.

to paradise.[n] I don't know if he was in his
body or away from his body, but God
knows. He heard things he is not able to
explain, things that no human is allowed
to tell. 5I will brag about a man like that,
but I will not brag about myself, except
about my weaknesses. 6But if I wanted to
brag about myself, I would not
be a fool, because I
would be telling the
truth. But I will not
brag about myself. I
do not want people
to think more of me
than what they see me do or hear me say.

EMAIL! FROM GOD
12:6 Reputation
Should you worry about what you do and say?

7So that I would not become too proud
of the wonderful things that were shown
to me, a painful physical problem[n] was
given to me. This problem was a messenger from Satan, sent to beat me and keep
me from being too proud. 8I begged the
Lord three times to take this problem
away from me. 9But he said to me, "My
grace is enough for you. When you are
weak, my power is made perfect in you."
So I am very happy to brag about my
weaknesses. Then Christ's power can
live in me. 10For this reason I am happy
when I have weaknesses, insults, hard
times, sufferings, and all kinds of troubles for Christ. Because when I am weak,
then I am truly strong.

Paul's Love for the Christians

11I have been talking like a fool, but
you made me do it. You are the ones who
should say good things about me. I am
worth nothing, but those "great apostles" are not worth any more than I am!
12When I was with you, I patiently did
the things that prove I am an apostle—
signs, wonders, and miracles. 13So you
received everything that the other
churches have received. Only one thing
was different: I was not a burden to you.
Forgive me for this!
14I am now ready to visit you the third
time, and I will not be a burden to you. I
want nothing from you, except you. Chil-

12:3-4 paradise Another word for heaven.
12:7 painful physical problem Literally, "thorn in the flesh."

FAITH links

BLESSED ARE THE WEAK?

2 CORINTHIANS 12:7-10

No one likes to be thought of as weak. The old saying "Only the strong survive" shows how society views weakness. Yet everyone has a weakness of some sort. Paul wrote about a physical weakness that he asked God to remove. But God said no. Instead, he told Paul that he was strong when Paul was weak.

God helps us when we're weak. What is a weakness? Fear is, for one thing. Our weaknesses remind us to rely on God. When we're weak, he's strong. Next time you're feeling weak, ask God to lend you some of his strength. He'll be glad to do it.

Want to be strong? Better be weak first! Check it out:

When You're Afraid, Genesis 32:9–12, p. 45

The Perfect Leader?, Numbers 20:1–13, p. 203

The God of Big Things, Joshua 10, p. 289

What God Thinks, Isaiah 55:8–9, p. 969

Facing Your Fears, Matthew 8:23–27, p. 1288

Thoughts on Thoughts, Philippians 4:8–9, p. 1614

dren should not have to save up to give to
their parents. Parents should save to give
to their children. **15**So I am happy to give
everything I have for you, even myself. If
I love you more, will you love me less?

16It is clear I was not a burden to you,
but you think I was tricky and lied to
catch you. **17**Did I cheat
you by using any of the
messengers I sent to
you? No, you know I did
not. **18**I asked Titus to go
to you, and I sent our
brother with him. Titus
did not cheat you, did he?
No, you know that Titus
and I did the same thing
and with the same spirit.

19Do you think we
have been defending ourselves to you all
this time? We have been speaking in
Christ and before God. You are our dear
friends, and everything we do is to make
you stronger. **20**I am afraid that when I
come, you will not be what I want you to
be, and I will not be what you want me to
be. I am afraid that among you there may
be arguing, jealousy, anger, selfish fighting, evil talk, gossip, pride, and confusion. **21**I am afraid that when I come to
you again, my God will make me ashamed
before you. I may be saddened by many of
those who have sinned because they
have not changed their hearts or turned
from their sexual sins and the shameful
things they have done.

> It is true that we are weak in Christ, but for you we will be alive in Christ by God's power.
> —2 Corinthians 13:4

Final Warnings and Greetings

13 I will come to you for the third
time. "Every case must be proved
by two or three witnesses."[n] **2**When I
was with you the second time, I gave a
warning to those who had sinned. Now I
am away from you, and I give a warning
to all the others. When I come to you
again, I will not be easy with them. **3**You
want proof that Christ is speaking
through me. My proof is that he is not
weak among you, but he is powerful. **4**It
is true that he was weak when he was
killed on the cross, but he lives now by
God's power. It is true that we are weak
in Christ, but for you we will be alive in
Christ by God's power.

5Look closely at yourselves. Test yourselves
to see if you are living in
the faith. You know that
Jesus Christ is in you—
unless you fail the test.
6But I hope you will see
that we ourselves have
not failed the test. **7**We
pray to God that you will
not do anything wrong. It
is not important to see that we have
passed the test, but it is important that
you do what is right, even if it seems we
have failed. **8**We cannot do anything
against the truth, but only for the truth.
9We are happy to be weak, if you are
strong, and we pray that you will become
complete. **10**I am writing this while I am
away from you so that when I come I will
not have to be harsh in my use of authority. The Lord gave me this authority to
build you up, not to tear you down.

11Now, brothers and sisters, I say
good-bye. Try to be complete. Do what I
have asked you to do. Agree with each
other, and live in peace. Then the God of
love and peace will be with you.

12Greet each other with a holy kiss.
13All of God's holy people send greetings
to you.

14The grace of the Lord Jesus Christ,
the love of God, and the fellowship of the
Holy Spirit be with you all.

13:1 "Every . . . witnesses." Quotation from Deuteronomy 19:15.

REAL FREEDOM

Hi, people! It's me, Paul. You probably remember me through a few other books I've written. I was a really good Pharisee—a well-known and popular religious leader, who hated those followers of a man called Jesus. But then I met Jesus on a dusty road while on my way to kill even more Christians. That wonderful moment changed the direction of my life forever; and since then, I have spent hours and hours telling everyone about what Jesus has done in my life.

I wrote this letter to the church in a place called Galatia because my friends there were hearing two different messages about what Jesus had done for them. One message was true: that Jesus died for them . . . and that was all they needed. The other message was wrong: that Jesus died for them, but that they also needed to keep a bunch of ancient rules. So, to clear things up, I wrote this letter to them to remind them about who Jesus was and what he had done.

JESUS WATCH

In this book, Jesus is portrayed as someone who frees people who are slaves to obeying every single rule in the law. These people believed that by obeying *all* the rules, they could be saved from their sin. Paul tells his readers that Jesus' death on the cross is all a person needs to be saved and freed from sin. This message was true for believers then, and it's true for believers now. The really cool thing is that all God wants from us is our complete faith in the work done by his Son. Nothing more, nothing less.

my FAVORITE links

OTHER CONNECTIONS

Livin' it What are some "good" things that you do? Ever consider why you do good things? Link to That (Good) Thing You Do, Galatians 6:9–10, to discover why God wants us to do good things.

MORE STUFF...

Good, Bad Fruit In Galatians 5:16–26, Paul outlined two types of behavior: behaving according to our human nature and behaving according to our Spirit nature. Check out the differences in the type of "fruit," or our actions, each produce:

- Human nature: Worshiping gods; making trouble; hating; being jealous; being angry; being selfish; making people angry with each other; and feeling envy.
- Spirit nature: Love; joy; peace; patience; kindness; goodness; faithfulness; gentleness; and self-control.

What kind of fruit do you produce?

"Hey, Tagg. Are we really supposed to serve other people?"

"You bet. And we're supposed to do it with love. Check out Galatians 5:13 to see what it says."

MORE COOL STUFF TO SURF:

Peter is wrong!, Galatians 2:11–21
Real faith, Galatians 3:6–9
Fruit for the soul, Galatians 5:22–26
A good harvest, Galatians 6:7–10

FAITH links

- A Family Resemblance, Galatians 3:6–9
- MVFM?, Galatians 3:26–27
- At the Right Time, Galatians 4:4
- A Different Kind of Fruit, Galatians 5:22–23
- Keep Up the Good Work!, Galatians 6:9–10

1 From Paul, an apostle. I was not chosen to be an apostle by human beings,
nor was I sent from human beings. I was
made an apostle through Jesus Christ and
God the Father who raised Jesus from the
dead. 2This letter is also from all those of
God's family[n] who are with me.
To the churches in Galatia:[n]
3Grace and peace to you from God our
Father and the Lord Jesus Christ. 4Jesus
gave himself for our sins to free us from
this evil world we live in, as God the Father planned. 5The glory belongs to God
forever and ever. Amen.

The Only Good News

6God, by his grace through Christ,
called you to become his people. So I am
amazed that you are turning away so
quickly and believing something different
than the Good News. 7Really, there is no
other Good News. But some people are
confusing you; they want to change the
Good News of Christ. 8We preached to
you the Good News. So if we ourselves,
or even an angel from heaven, should
preach to you something different, we
should be judged guilty! 9I said this before, and now I say it again: You have already accepted the Good News. If anyone
is preaching something different to you,
he should be judged guilty!
10Do you think I am trying to make
people accept me? No, God is the One I
am trying to please. Am I trying to please
people? If I still wanted to please people,
I would not be a servant of Christ.

Paul's Authority Is from God

11Brothers and sisters,[n] I want you to
know that the Good News I preached to
you was not made up by human beings.
12I did not get it from humans, nor did
anyone teach it to me, but Jesus Christ
showed it to me.
13You have heard about my past life in
the Jewish religion. I attacked the church
of God and tried to destroy it. 14I was becoming a leader in the Jewish religion,
doing better than most other Jews of my
age. I tried harder than anyone else to
follow the teachings handed down by our
ancestors.

FAITH CHALLENGE

Got another challenge for you. Read 1:10 to discover what Paul said to those who accused him of trying to please people. What's wrong with trying to please other people? How would you describe yourself—as a people-pleaser or a God-pleaser? What do you need to change?

TESTING IT

Galatians 1:10
Do you think I am trying to make people accept me? No, God is the One I am trying to please. Am I trying to please people? If I still wanted to please people, I would not be a servant of Christ.

15But God had special plans for me
and set me apart for his work even before
I was born. He called me through his
grace 16and showed his son to me so that
I might tell the Good News about him to

1:2 those . . . family The Greek text says "brothers."

1:2 Galatia Probably the same country where Paul preached and began churches on his first missionary trip. Read the Book of Acts, chapters 13 and 14.

1:11 Brothers and sisters Although the Greek text says "Brothers" here and throughout this book, Paul's words were meant for the entire church, including men and women.

those who are not Jewish. When God
called me, I did not get advice or help
from any person. **17**I did not go to Jerusalem to see those who were apostles before I was. But, without waiting, I went
away to Arabia and later went back to Damascus.

18After three years I went to Jerusalem to meet Peter and stayed with him
for fifteen days. **19**I met no other apostles, except James, the brother of the
Lord. **20**God knows that these things I
write are not lies. **21**Later, I went to the
areas of Syria and Cilicia.

22In Judea the churches in Christ had
never met me. **23**They had only heard it
said, "This man who was attacking us is
now preaching the same faith that he
once tried to destroy." **24**And these believers praised God because of me.

Other Apostles Accepted Paul

2 After fourteen years I went to Jerusalem again, this time with Barnabas. I
also took Titus with me. **2**I went because
God showed me I should go. I met with
the believers there, and in private I told
their leaders the Good News that I
preach to the non-Jewish people. I did not
want my past work and the work I am
now doing to be wasted. **3**Titus was with
me, but he was not forced to be circumcised, even though he was a Greek. **4**We
talked about this problem because some
false believers had come into our group
secretly. They came in like spies to over-
turn the freedom we have in Christ
Jesus. They wanted to make us slaves.
5But we did not give in to those false believers for a minute. We wanted the truth
of the Good News to continue for you.

6Those leaders who seemed to be important did not change the
Good News that I
preach. (It doesn't
matter to me if they
were "important" or
not. To God every-
one is the same.)
7But these leaders saw that I had been
given the work of telling the Good News
to those who are not Jewish, just as Peter
had the work of telling the Jews. **8**God
gave Peter the power to work as an apostle for the Jewish people. But he also gave
me the power to work as an apostle for
those who are not Jews. **9**James, Peter,
and John, who seemed to be the leaders,
understood that God had given me this
special grace, so they accepted Barnabas
and me. They agreed that they would go
to the Jewish people and that we should
go to those who are not Jewish. **10**The
only thing they asked us was to remember
to help the poor—something I really
wanted to do.

eMail! FROM GOD **2:6**
Jealousy
Should you envy other Christians?

Paul Shows that Peter Was Wrong

11When Peter came to Antioch, I
challenged him to his face, because he
was wrong. **12**Peter ate with the non-
Jewish people until some Jewish people
sent from James came to Antioch. When
they arrived, Peter stopped eating with
those who weren't Jewish, and he separated himself from them. He was afraid of
the Jews. **13**So Peter was a hypocrite, as
were the other Jewish believers who
joined with him. Even Barnabas was influenced by what these Jewish believers
did. **14**When I saw they were not following the truth of the Good News, I spoke
to Peter in front of them all. I said, "Peter,
you are a Jew, but you are not living like a
Jew. You are living like those who are not
Jewish. So why do you now try to force
those who are not Jewish to live like
Jews?"

15We were not born as non-Jewish
"sinners," but as Jews. **16**Yet we know
that a person is made right with God not
by following the law, but by trusting in
Jesus Christ. So we, too, have put our
faith in Christ Jesus, that we might be
made right with God because we trusted
in Christ. It is not because we followed
the law, because no one can be made right
with God by following the law.

17We Jews came to Christ, trying to
be made right with God, and it became
clear that we are sinners, too. Does this
mean that Christ encourages sin? No!
18But I would really be wrong to begin
teaching again those things that I gave
up. **19**It was the law that put me to death,

and I died to the law so that I can now live
for God. 20I was put to death on the cross
with Christ, and I do not live anymore—it
is Christ who lives in me. I still live in my
body, but I live by faith in the Son of God
who loved me and gave himself to save
me. 21By saying these things I am not
going against God's grace. Just the opposite, if the law could make us right with
God, then Christ's death would be useless.

Blessing Comes Through Faith

3 You people in Galatia were told very
clearly about the death of Jesus
Christ on the cross. But you were foolish;
you let someone trick you. 2Tell me this
one thing: How did you receive the Holy
Spirit? Did you receive the Spirit by following the law? No, you received the
Spirit because you heard the Good News
and believed it. 3You began your life in
Christ by the Spirit. Now are you trying
to make it complete by your own power?
That is foolish. 4Were all your experiences wasted? I hope not! 5Does God
give you the Spirit and work miracles
among you because you follow the law?
No, he does these things because you
heard the Good News and believed it.
6The Scriptures say the same thing
about Abraham: "Abraham believed God,
and God accepted Abraham's faith, and
that faith made him right with God."[n] 7So
you should know that the true children of
Abraham are those who have faith. 8The
Scriptures, telling what would happen in
the future, said that God would make the
non-Jewish people right through their
faith. This Good News was told to Abraham beforehand, as the Scripture says:
"All nations will be blessed through
you."[n] 9So all who believe as Abraham
believed are blessed just as Abraham
was. 10But those who depend on following the law to make them right are under
a curse, because the Scriptures say,
"Anyone will be cursed who does not always obey what is written in the Book of
the Law."[n] 11Now it is clear that no one
can be made right with God by the law,
because the Scriptures say, "Those who
are right with God will live by trusting in

A FAMILY RESEMBLANCE

GALATIANS 3:6-9

Has anyone ever told you that you look like your mom or dad? You can't help but share a family resemblance. If you're a Christian, you also look like Abraham, one of Israel's founding fathers. You don't have to run to a mirror to check. The resemblance is not physical. As Christians, we share the same faith as Abraham. He believed that God would save him, and so do we. Because of this faith, we are Abraham's children, and we will be blessed like Abraham was.

Download these Faithlinks to find out more about being part of God's family:

On the Wrong Foot, 2 Kings 21:1–2, 16, p. 509

Trailblazers of Faith, 2 Kings 22:1–2, p. 510

Jesus' Mission and Yours, Isaiah 61:1–2, p. 978

Name with a Purpose, Matthew 1:21, p. 1274

Remembering Jesus, Matthew 26:26–29, p. 1321

A Christian's Responsibility, Acts 11:26, p. 1484

3:6 "Abraham . . . God." Quotation from Genesis 15:6.

3:8 "All . . . you." Quotation from Genesis 12:3 and 18:18.

3:10 "Anyone . . . Law." Quotation from Deuteronomy 27:26.

him."[n] 12The law is not based on faith. It
says, "A person who obeys these things
will live because of them."[n] 13Christ
took away the curse the law put on us. He
changed places with us and put himself
under that curse. It is written in the
Scriptures, "Anyone whose body is displayed on a tree[n] is cursed." 14Christ did
this so that God's blessing promised to
Abraham might come through Jesus
Christ to those who are not Jews. Jesus
died so that by our believing we could receive the Spirit that God promised.

The Law and the Promise

15Brothers and sisters, let us think in
human terms: Even an agreement made
between two persons is firm. After that
agreement is accepted by both people, no
one can stop it or add anything to it.
16God made promises both to Abraham
and to his descendant. God did not say,
"and to your descendants." That would
mean many people. But God said, "and to
your descendant." That means only one
person; that person is Christ. 17This is
what I mean: God had an agreement with
Abraham and promised to keep it. The
law, which came four hundred thirty
years later, cannot change that agreement and so destroy God's promise to
Abraham. 18If the law could give us
Abraham's blessing, then the promise
would not be necessary. But that is not
possible, because God freely gave his
blessings to Abraham through the promise he had made.
19So what was the law for? It was
given to show that the wrong things people do are against God's will. And it continued until the special descendant, who
had been promised, came. The law was
given through angels who used Moses
for a mediator[n] to give the law to people.
20But a mediator is not needed when
there is only one side, and God is only
one.

The Purpose of the Law of Moses

21Does this mean that the law is
against God's promises? Never! That
would be true only if the law could make
us right. But God did not give a law that

FAITH links

MVFM?

GALATIANS 3:26-27

A birth certificate lets the world know whose child you are. Your last name is also an indication of where you belong. You're a valuable member of your family. As a Christian, you also belong to God because of your faith in Jesus. You're a valuable member of that family, too! Consider yourself an MVFM: Most Valuable Family Member!

Find out more about how valuable you are to God:

The Rainbow Promise, Genesis 9:1–17, p. 14

Approaching God, Numbers 3:10, p. 180

How Big Is God?, Job 38—41, p. 703

Perfectly Pleasing?, Matthew 5:1–12, p. 1280

A Family Celebration, 1 Corinthians 11:23–29, p. 1558

The Finished Product, Philippians 1:6, p. 1609

3:11 "Those . . . him." Quotation from Habakkuk 2:4.

3:12 "A person . . . them." Quotation from Leviticus 18:5.

3:13 displayed on a tree Deuteronomy 21:22-23 says that when a person was killed for doing wrong, the body was hung on a tree to show shame. Paul means that the cross of Jesus was like that.

3:19 mediator A person who helps one person talk to or give something to another person.

can bring life. 22Instead, the Scriptures
showed that the whole world is bound by
sin. This was so the promise would be
given through faith to people who believe
in Jesus Christ.
23Before this faith came, we were all
held prisoners by the law. We had no freedom until God showed us the way of faith
that was coming. 24In other words, the
law was our guardian leading us to Christ
so that we could be made right with God
through faith. 25Now the way of faith has
come, and we no longer live under a
guardian.
26-27You were all baptized into
Christ, and so you were all clothed with
Christ. This means that you are all children of God through faith in Christ Jesus.
28In Christ, there is no difference between Jew and Greek, slave and free person, male and female. You are all
the same in Christ
Jesus. 29You belong
to Christ, so you are
Abraham's descen-
dants. You will in-
herit all of God's
blessings because of
the promise God made to Abraham.

eMAIL! FROM GOD
3:28–29
Respect
Are some people better than others?

4 I want to tell you this: While those
who will inherit their fathers' property are still children, they are no different from slaves. It does not matter that
the children own everything. 2While
they are children, they must obey those
who are chosen to care for them. But
when the children reach the age set by
their fathers, they are free. 3It is the
same for us. We were once like children,
slaves to the useless rules of this world.
4But when the right time came, God sent
his Son who was born of a woman and
lived under the law. 5God did this so he
could buy freedom for those who were
under the law and so we could become
his children.
6Since you are God's children, God
sent the Spirit of his Son into your
hearts, and the Spirit cries out, "Father."* 7So now you are not a slave; you
are God's child, and God will give you the
blessing he promised, because you are
his child.

FAITH links

AT THE RIGHT TIME

GALATIANS 4:4

Ever wish that time would speed up or slow down? Maybe you waited for something wonderful to happen. Or, maybe you waited for something that you dreaded. Sometimes we wish that time would speed up when we're waiting for God to answer our prayers. God wants us to trust his timing. He knows just when to make things happen. He waited for the perfect time to send his Son to earth. Since God is perfect, his timing is also perfect. He's always on time!

If you have trouble waiting, check out these links:

Can't Live Without It?, Genesis 3, p. 7

From Hopeless to Hopeful, Exodus 6:9, p. 83

Learning to Trust, Psalm 25:4–5, p. 727

911, Psalm 28:6, p. 730

Exercising Patience, Luke 2:25–28, 36–37, p. 1369

His Best Qualities, 2 Peter 3:9, p. 1711

Paul's Love for the Christians

8In the past you did not know God.
You were slaves to gods that were not
real. 9But now you know the true God.
Really, it is God who knows you. So why

4:6 "Father" Literally, "Abba, Father." Jewish children called their fathers "Abba."

do you turn back to those weak and useless rules you followed before? Do you
want to be slaves to those things again?
10You still follow teachings about special
days, months, seasons, and years. **11**I am
afraid for you, that my work for you has
been wasted.

12Brothers and sisters, I became like
you, so I beg you to become like me. You
were very good to me before. **13**You remember that it was because of an illness
that I came to you the first time, preaching the Good News. **14**Though my sickness was a trouble for you, you did not
hate me or make me leave. But you welcomed me as an angel from God, as if I
were Jesus Christ himself! **15**You were
very happy then, but where is that joy
now? I am ready to testify that you would
have taken out your eyes and given them
to me if that were possible. **16**Now am I
your enemy because I tell you the truth?

17Those people[n] are working hard to
persuade you, but this is not good for
you. They want to persuade you to turn
against us and follow only them. **18**It is
good for people to show interest in you,
but only if their purpose is good. This is
always true, not just when I am with you.
19My little children, again I feel the pain
of childbirth for you until you truly become like Christ. **20**I wish I could be with
you now and could change the way I am
talking to you, because I do not know
what to think about you.

The Example of Hagar and Sarah

21Some of you still want to be under
the law. Tell me, do you know what the
law says? **22**The Scriptures say that
Abraham had two sons. The mother of
one son was a slave woman, and the
mother of the other son was a free woman. **23**Abraham's son from the slave
woman was born in the normal human
way. But the son from the free woman
was born because of the promise God
made to Abraham.

24This story teaches something else:
The two women are like the two agreements between God and his people. One
agreement is the law that God made on
Mount Sinai,[n] and the people who are under this agreement are like slaves. The
mother named Hagar is like that agreement. **25**She is like Mount Sinai in Arabia
and is a picture of the earthly Jewish city
of Jerusalem. This city and its people, the
Jews, are slaves to the law. **26**But the
heavenly Jerusalem, which is above, is
like the free woman. She is our mother.
27It is written in the Scriptures:

"Be happy, Jerusalem.
You are like a woman who never
gave birth to children.
Start singing and shout for joy.
You never felt the pain of giving
birth,
but you will have more children
than the woman who has a
husband." *Isaiah 54:1*

28My brothers and sisters, you are
God's children because of his promise, as
Isaac was then. **29**The son who was born
in the normal way treated the other son
badly. It is the same today. **30**But what
does the Scripture say? "Throw out the
slave woman and her son. The son of the
slave woman should not inherit anything.
The son of the free woman should receive it all."[n] **31**So, my brothers and sisters, we are not children of the slave
woman, but of the free woman.

Keep Your Freedom

5 We have freedom now, because Christ
made us free. So stand strong. Do not
change and go back into the slavery of
the law. **2**Listen, I Paul tell you that if you
go back to the law by being circumcised,
Christ does you no good. **3**Again, I warn
every man: If you allow yourselves to be
circumcised, you must follow all the law.
4If you try to be made right with God
through the law, your life with Christ is
over—you have left God's grace. **5**But
we have the true hope that comes from
being made right with God, and by the

4:17 Those people They are the false teachers who were bothering the believers in Galatia (Galatians 1:7).

4:24 Mount Sinai Mountain in Arabia where God gave his Law to Moses (Exodus 19 and 20).

4:30 "Throw . . . all." Quotation from Genesis 21:10.

Spirit we wait eagerly for this hope.
6When we are in Christ Jesus, it is not
important if we are circumcised or not.
The important thing is faith—the kind of
faith that works through love.
7You were running a good race. Who
stopped you from following the true way?
8This change did not come from the One
who chose you. 9Be careful! "Just a little
yeast makes the whole batch of dough
rise." 10But I trust in the Lord that you
will not believe those different ideas.
Whoever is confusing you with such
ideas will be punished.
11My brothers and sisters, I do not
teach that a man must be circumcised. If I
teach circumcision, why am I still being
attacked? If I still taught circumcision,
my preaching about the cross would not
be a problem. 12I wish the people who
are bothering you would castrate[n] themselves!
13My brothers and sisters, God called
you to be free, but do not use your freedom as an excuse to do what pleases your
sinful self. Serve each other with love.
14The whole law is made complete in
this one command: "Love your neighbor
as you love yourself."[n] 15If you go on
hurting each other and tearing each other
apart, be careful, or you will completely
destroy each other.

The Spirit and Human Nature

16So I tell you: Live by following the
Spirit. Then you will not do what your
sinful selves want. 17Our sinful selves
want what is against the Spirit, and the
Spirit wants what is against our sinful
selves. The two are against each other, so
you cannot do just what you please.
18But if the Spirit is leading you, you are
not under the law.
19The wrong things the sinful self
does are clear: being sexually unfaithful,
not being pure, taking part in sexual sins,
20worshiping gods, doing witchcraft, hating, making trouble, being jealous, being
angry, being selfish, making people angry
with each other, causing divisions among
people, 21feeling envy, being drunk, having wild and wasteful parties, and doing
other things like these. I warn you now

FAITH links

A DIFFERENT KIND OF FRUIT

GALATIANS 5:22-23

What's your favorite fruit? Did you know that the Spirit has some fruit that are his favorites? They're not the kind you might be thinking about. He prefers fruit like love, joy, peace, patience, kindness, goodness, faithfulness, gentleness, and self-control. In fact, this "fruit" is called the fruit of the Spirit. Why is it called that? Because it helps us grow in faith. As we trust God, love, joy, peace, and so on are the fruit that the Holy Spirit develops within us. What "fruit" do you need more of in your life?

I Want It *Now!*, Judges 14:1–3, p. 332

Fair All the Time?, 2 Samuel 8:15, p. 408

The Way to Serve God, 1 Kings 9:4, p. 450

One Big, Happy Family, John 1:12, p. 1422

Always Do This!, 1 Thessalonians 5:16–18, p. 1636

The "Quality" of Life, 2 Peter 1:5–8, p. 1708

5:12 castrate To cut off part of the male sex organ. Paul uses this word because it is similar to "circumcision." Paul wanted to show that he is very upset with the false teachers.

5:14 "Love . . . yourself." Quotation from Leviticus 19:18.

as I warned you before: Those who do
these things will not inherit God's kingdom. 22But the Spirit produces the fruit
of love, joy, peace, patience, kindness,
goodness, faithfulness, 23gentleness,
self-control. There is no law that says
these things are wrong. 24Those who belong to Christ Jesus have crucified their
own sinful selves. They have given up
their old selfish feelings and the evil
things they wanted to do. 25We get our
new life from the Spirit, so we should follow the Spirit. 26We must not be proud or
make trouble with each other or be jealous of each other.

Help Each Other

6 Brothers and sisters, if someone in
your group does something wrong,
you who are spiritual should go to that
person and gently help make him right
again. But be careful, because you might
be tempted to sin, too. 2By helping each
other with your troubles, you truly obey
the law of Christ. 3If anyone thinks he is
important when he really is not, he is only
fooling himself. 4Each person should
judge his own actions and not compare
himself with others. Then he can be proud
for what he himself has done. 5Each person must be responsible for himself.

6Anyone who is learning the teaching
of God should share all the good things
he has with his teacher.

Life Is like Planting a Field

7Do not be fooled: You cannot cheat
God. People harvest only what they
plant. 8If they plant to satisfy their sinful
selves, their sinful selves will bring them
ruin. But if they plant to please the Spirit,
they will receive eternal life from the
Spirit. 9We must not become tired of doing good. We will receive our harvest of
eternal life at the right time if we do not
give up. 10When we have the opportunity to help anyone, we should do it. But we
should give special attention to those
who are in the family of believers.

Paul Ends His Letter

11See what large letters I use to write
this myself. 12Some people are trying to

KEEP UP THE GOOD WORK!

GALATIANS 6:9-10

Who has the most fun in movies or on TV: the good guy or the villain? The good guy, you say? Nope! Usually, the bad guy looks like he's having fun destroying everything. The good guy has a hard time saving the world and is rarely thanked by anyone.

Movies and TV show what the world values. What's bad is sometimes seen as good. God still wants his people to do good things. Unfortunately, we can easily become discouraged. That's why the apostle Paul said to not give up doing good works. The good things we can do include saying kind things to each other, telling people about Jesus, and praying for one another. Don't miss out on an opportunity to do something good today!

Here are some more Faithlinks on being a good guy:

Lights, Camera, . . . Actions!, Genesis 12:1–3, p. 17

Roll Out the Welcome Wagon, Genesis 18:2–8, p. 24

The Green Light, 2 Samuel 2:1, p. 401

Small Beginnings, Zechariah 4:10, p. 1255

You're Welcomed!, Acts 16:14–15, p. 1494

Your Faith Example, 1 Timothy 4:12, p. 1646

DOING GOOD

Galatians 6:9–10

Livin' it

That (Good) Thing You Do Some people do "random acts of kindness." That means that they do something good for someone because that person needs help. Sometimes the person receiving the help often doesn't even know who has helped him or her. Why do *you* do good things? Do you expect to receive something from doing good? What?

God wants his people to do good things. Sometimes we can become discouraged when we see others doing anything they please, without giving a thought to anyone else. Paul said never to give up doing good. (Read Galatians 6:9–10.) What good thing can you do for someone today?

MORE FAITH links

"Look, Skweek, if I do one more good deed today, I'm going to get this cool merit badge. Then everyone will know I do lots of good things!"

"It's good to do good things, but maybe you ought to surf over to these links to see *why* God wants us to do good things."

A Blueprint for Living, Amos 5:14–15, p. 1200
- A blueprint is a plan of action for a builder. Link here to find out about God's blueprint for your life. Following it carefully can lead to success in your life!

A Reminder to Do What Is Right and True, Zechariah 7:8–10, p. 1257
- Do you ever complain that your parents are nagging, because they say the same things all the time? Why do they need to say the same things? What might happen if they never reminded you of what you are to do? Some messages are repeated over and over in the Bible. Can you think of some of those messages? Why do they need to be repeated?

The True Test, 1 John 3:18, p. 1718
- If someone said they loved you but never said anything nice about you or did nice things for you, would you believe him? Love is more than just words; it's showing that love in the good things we do. What good thing can you do for someone today to show that you love him or her?

force you to be circumcised so the Jews
will accept them. They are afraid they
will be attacked if they follow only the
cross of Christ."[n] **13**Those who are circumcised do not obey the law themselves, but they want you to be
circumcised so they can brag about what
they forced you to do. **14**I hope I will
never brag about things like that. The
cross of our Lord Jesus Christ is my only
reason for bragging. Through the cross of
Jesus my world was crucified, and I died
to the world. **15**It is not important if a
man is circumcised or uncircumcised.
The important thing is being the new people God has made. **16**Peace and mercy to
those who follow this rule—and to all of
God's people.

17So do not give me any more trouble.
I have scars on my body that show[n] I belong to Christ Jesus.

18My brothers and sisters, the grace
of our Lord Jesus Christ be with your
spirit. Amen.

6:12 cross of Christ Paul uses the cross as a picture of the Good News, the story of Christ's death and rising from the dead to pay for our sins. The cross, or Christ's death, was God's way to save us.
6:17 that show Many times Paul was beaten and whipped by people who were against him because he was teaching about Christ. The scars were from these beatings.

NOTHING BUT CHRISTIAN

Welcome, newbie! I'm glad you're reading this letter. I'm Paul, and I hope you remember who I am. I was a well-known Jewish leader who spent a lot of time arresting and hassling followers of Jesus, known as Christians. After I met Jesus, though, I became the champion of the church—teaching new believers and telling others about Jesus. (You can check out that incredible story by downloading Acts 9, p. 1478.) I wrote this letter from jail. I spent a lot of time in jail because the Jewish leaders and others did not like my message. (Kind of like how I was before I met Jesus!)

My friends at the church in Ephesus were facing a critical issue. Those who had been Jews before they met Jesus claimed that if you wanted to become a Christian, you had to become a Jew first and obey all the laws of Moses. Ridiculous! So, I wrote this letter to tell my friends at Ephesus that there's no such thing as a Jewish Christian or a non-Jewish Christian. We're all just Christians!

JESUS WATCH

Through his writings, Paul became known for the phrase "in Christ." That phrase appears several times in this book. In fact, Paul covers just about every important issue for believers in this book and answers it with the assurance that we are "in Jesus." For example, Paul says that we were adopted through Christ (Ephesians 1:5). We are made alive together through Jesus (Ephesians 2:5). And, as followers, we share in the promise that God made in Jesus (Ephesians 3:6). Paul takes great care to help the believers in Ephesus, and even us, understand that Jesus is our key for everyday living, as well as for eternal living. Without Jesus, we'd be lost!

my FAVORITE links

______________ ______________

______________ ______________

______________ ______________

______________ ______________

OTHER CONNECTIONS

GET THE INFO

- Let's Visit Ephesus, Ephesians 3. Today there's nothing left but ruins of this ancient Greek city, but during New Testament times Ephesus was a thriving, important center. Download the info here to find out more.

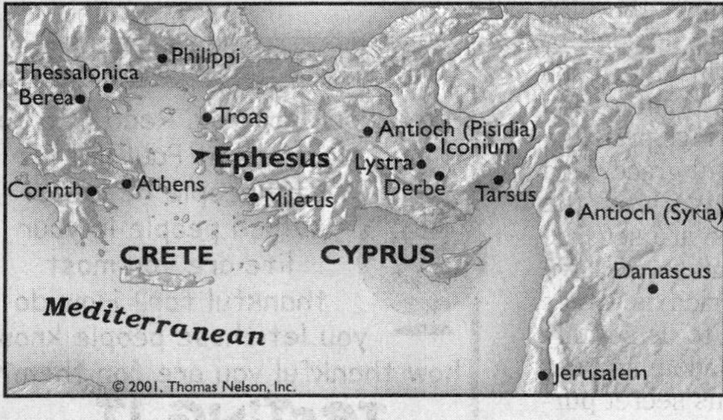

- That's Much Better!, Ephesians 2:4–5
- It's Free!, Ephesians 2:8–9
- Say What?!, Ephesians 4:22–29
- Forgive and Forget, Ephesians 4:32
- How to Make God Glad, Ephesians 6:1–2
- A Good Habit, Ephesians 6:18

"Hey, Skweek! What's the deal about children obeying their parents?"

"Paul had a lot to say about that! Let's connect to Ephesians 6:1-4 and look at it together."

did you know?

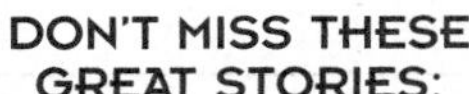

DON'T MISS THESE GREAT STORIES:

Paul's special prayer, Ephesians 1:15–23
Don't be a baby!, Ephesians 4:11–16
Living in light, Ephesians 5:1–14
Get ready for battle!, Ephesians 6:10–18

1 From Paul, an apostle of Christ Jesus.
I am an apostle because that is what
God wanted.

To God's holy people living in Ephesus, believers in Christ Jesus:
2Grace and peace to you from God our
Father and the Lord Jesus Christ.

Spiritual Blessings in Christ

3Praise be to the God and Father of
our Lord Jesus Christ. In Christ, God has
given us every spiritual blessing in the
heavenly world. 4That is, in Christ, he
chose us before the world was made so
that we would be his holy people—people without blame before him. 5Because
of his love, God had already decided to
make us his own children through Jesus
Christ. That was what he wanted and
what pleased him, 6and it brings praise to
God because of his wonderful grace. God
gave that grace to us freely, in Christ, the
One he loves. 7In Christ we are set free
by the blood of his death, and so we have
forgiveness of sins. How rich is God's
grace, 8which he has given to us so fully
and freely. God, with full wisdom and understanding, 9let us know his secret purpose. This was what God wanted, and he
planned to do it through Christ. 10His
goal was to carry out his plan, when the
right time came, that all things in heaven
and on earth would be joined together in
Christ as the head.

11In Christ we were chosen to be
God's people, because from the very beginning God had decided this in keeping
with his plan. And he is the One who
makes everything agree with what he decides and wants. 12We are the first people who hoped in Christ, and we were
chosen so that we would bring praise to
God's glory. 13So it is with you. When
you heard the true teaching—the Good
News about your salvation—you believed in Christ. And in Christ, God put
his special mark of ownership on you by
giving you the Holy Spirit that he had
promised. 14That Holy Spirit is the guarantee that we will receive what God
promised for his people until God gives
full freedom to those who are his—to
bring praise to God's glory.

Paul's Prayer

15That is why since I heard about
your faith in the Lord Jesus and your love
for all God's people, 16I have not stopped
giving thanks to God for you. I always
remember you in
my prayers, 17ask-
ing the God of our
Lord Jesus Christ,
the glorious Father,
to give you a spirit
of wisdom and reve-
lation so that you will know him better.
18I pray also that you will have greater
understanding in your heart so you will

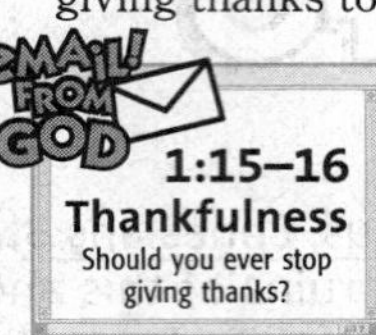

1:15–16
Thankfulness
Should you ever stop giving thanks?

FAITH CHALLENGE

Here's one for you. Read 1:16 to learn what Paul did for the people he loved. Which people in your life are you most thankful for? How do you let those people know how thankful you are for them?

TESTING IT

Ephesians 1:16
I have not stopped giving thanks to God for you. I always remember you in my prayers.

FAITH links

THAT'S MUCH BETTER! 

EPHESIANS 2:4-5

Let's suppose you did something wrong, like telling a lie. After admitting that you told a lie, suppose you were given a hug instead of being punished. How would you feel? That's what mercy is all about. *Mercy* means not giving someone the punishment that he deserves. As sinners, we deserve punishment. God treats us much better than we deserve. Since he's merciful to us, shouldn't we treat other people much better than they deserve, too?

Download these links for more on how to treat others:

The Trouble with Jealousy, Genesis 37, p. 53

World News, Isaiah 13—19, p. 913

A Model of Forgiveness, Ezekiel 16:59–63, p. 1103

Inside the Heart of God, Micah 7:18–20, p. 1228

Forgive and Forget, Ephesians 4:32, p. 1604

It's Guaranteed!, 1 John 1:9–10, p. 1714

know the hope to which he has called us
and that you will know how rich and glorious are the blessings God has promised
his holy people. **19**And you will know that
God's power is very great for us who believe. That power is the same as the great
strength **20**God used to raise Christ from
the dead and put him at his right side in
the heavenly world. **21**God has put Christ
over all rulers, authorities, powers, and
kings, not only in this world but also in the
next. **22**God put everything under his
power and made him the head over everything for the church, **23**which is Christ's
body. The church is filled with Christ, and
Christ fills everything in every way.

We Now Have Life

2 In the past you were spiritually dead
because of your sins and the things
you did against God. **2**Yes, in the past you
lived the way the world lives, following
the ruler of the evil powers that are
above the earth. That same spirit is now
working in those who refuse to obey God.
3In the past all of us lived like them, trying to please our sinful selves and doing
all the things our bodies and minds wanted. We should have suffered God's anger
because of the way we were. We were the
same as all other people.

4But God's mercy is great, and he loved
us very much. **5**Though we were spiritually
dead because of the things we did against
God, he gave us new life with Christ. You
have been saved by God's grace. **6**And he
raised us up with Christ and gave us a seat
with him in the heavens. He did this for
those in Christ Jesus **7**so that for all future
time he could show the very great riches of
his grace by being kind to us in Christ
Jesus. **8**I mean that you have been saved
by grace through believing. You did not
save yourselves; it was a gift from God. **9**It
was not the result of your own efforts, so
you cannot brag about it. **10**God has made
us what we are. In Christ Jesus, God made
us to do good works, which God planned
in advance for us to live our lives doing.

One in Christ

11You were not born Jewish. You are
the people the Jews call "uncircumcised."'ⁿ Those who call you "uncircumcised" call themselves "circumcised."
(Their circumcision is only something
they themselves do on their bodies.)

2:11 uncircumcised People not having the mark of circumcision as the Jews had.

FAITH links

IT'S FREE!

EPHESIANS 2:8-9

What did you do to earn your family's love this week? Did you do everything right? Did you get along with everyone? What's that you say? You did absolutely nothing to earn their love? Not one teensy, weensy little thing? The fact is, you can't earn their love. God's grace is the same way. We can't earn it—it's a gift. You could no more earn it than you could fly to the moon on your own power. God sent his Son to die for us. Because of that, we are saved from the punishment for our sins. That's a free gift!

Made in His Image, Genesis 1:26–27, p. 4

Big Lack Attack, 2 Kings 4:1–7, p. 480

Dirty Inside, Isaiah 6:1–7, p. 904

A Hard Place, Ezekiel 28:25–26, p. 1120

A Family Celebration, 1 Corinthians 11:23–29, p. 1558

From Useless to Useful, Philemon 11, p. 1663

12Remember that in the past you were
without Christ. You were not citizens of
Israel, and you had no part in the
agreements[n] with the promise that God
made to his people. You had no hope, and
you did not know God. 13But now in
Christ Jesus, you who were far away from
God are brought near through the blood
of Christ's death. 14Christ himself is our
peace. He made both Jewish people and
those who are not Jews
one people. They
were separated as
if there were a wall
between them, but
Christ broke down
that wall of hate by
giving his own body. 15The Jewish law
had many commands and rules, but Christ
ended that law. His purpose was to make
the two groups of people become one
new people in him and in this way make
peace. 16It was also Christ's purpose to
end the hatred between the two groups,
to make them into one body, and to bring
them back to God. Christ did all this with
his death on the cross. 17Christ came and
preached peace to you who were far away
from God, and to those who were near to
God. 18Yes, it is through Christ we all
have the right to come to the Father in
one Spirit.

EMAIL FROM GOD 2:14

Peace

Who is your peace?

19Now you who are not Jewish are not
foreigners or strangers any longer, but
are citizens together with God's holy
people. You belong to God's family. 20You
are like a building that was built on the
foundation of the apostles and prophets.
Christ Jesus himself is the most important stone[n] in that building, 21and that
whole building is joined together in
Christ. He makes it grow and become a
holy temple in the Lord. 22And in Christ
you, too, are being built together with the
Jews into a place where God lives
through the Spirit.

Paul's Work in Telling the Good News

3 So I, Paul, am a prisoner of Christ
Jesus for you who are not Jews.
2Surely you have heard that God gave me
this work through his grace to help you.

2:12 agreements The agreements that God gave to his people in the Old Testament.

2:20 most important stone Literally, "cornerstone." The first and most important stone in a building.

LET'S VISIT EPHESUS

Ephesians 3

Today the city of Ephesus is in ruins; but in New Testament days, it was an important city with a huge auditorium that held 25,000 people. It had gymnasiums and impressive public buildings. One of the Seven Wonders of the Ancient World, the temple of Diana, can be found in Ephesus.

The church at Ephesus may have been started by Priscilla and Aquila. (Check out Acts 18:18–21, p. 1498.) The church was about two years old when Paul came to town. Later, the apostle John, one of Jesus' disciples, settled at Ephesus and ministered there after Paul. John was exiled on the Isle of Patmos just off the coast. While he was there, God used him to write the Book of Revelation. In it, he wrote to seven churches; and one of them was the church at Ephesus. (See Revelation 1:11; 2:1–7, p. 1732.)

3He let me know his secret by showing it
to me. I have already written a little about
this. **4**If you read what I wrote then, you
can see that I truly understand the secret
about the Christ. **5**People who lived in
other times were not told that secret. But
now, through the Spirit, God has shown
that secret to his holy apostles and
prophets. **6**This is that secret: that
through the Good News those who are
not Jews will share with the Jews in
God's blessing. They belong to the same
body, and they share together in the
promise that God made in Christ Jesus.

7By God's special gift of grace given
to me through his power, I became a servant to tell that Good News. **8**I am the
least important of all God's people, but
God gave me this gift—to tell those who
are not Jews the Good News about the
riches of Christ, which are too great to
understand fully. **9**And God gave me the
work of telling all people about the plan
for his secret, which has been hidden in
him since the beginning of time. He is the
One who created everything. **10**His purpose was that through the church all the
rulers and powers in the heavenly world
will now know God's wisdom, which has
so many forms. **11**This agrees with the
purpose God had since the beginning of
time, and he carried out his plan through
Christ Jesus our Lord. **12**In Christ we can
come before God with freedom and without fear. We can do this through faith in
Christ. **13**So I ask you not to become discouraged because of the sufferings I am
having for you. My sufferings are for your
glory.

The Love of Christ

14So I bow in prayer before the Father
15from whom every family in heaven and
on earth gets its true name. **16**I ask the
Father in his great glory to give you the
power to be strong inwardly through his
Spirit. **17**I pray that Christ will live in
your hearts by faith and that your life will
be strong in love and be built on love.
18And I pray that you and all God's holy
people will have the power to understand
the greatness of Christ's love—how wide
and how long and how high and how deep
that love is. **19**Christ's love is greater
than anyone can ever know, but I pray
that you will be able to know that love.
Then you can be filled with the fullness
of God.

20With God's power working in us,
God can do much, much more than anything we can ask or imagine. 21To him be
glory in the church and in Christ Jesus for
all time, forever and ever. Amen.

The Unity of the Body

4 I am in prison because I belong to the
Lord. God chose you to be his people,
so I urge you now to live the life to which
God called you. 2Always be humble, gentle, and patient, accepting each

eMAIL! FROM GOD
4:2
Love
How can you love other people?

other in love. 3You
are joined together
with peace through
the Spirit, so make
every effort to con-
tinue together in
this way. 4There is one body and one
Spirit, and God called you to have one
hope. 5There is one Lord, one faith, and
one baptism. 6There is one God and Father of everything. He rules everything
and is everywhere and is in everything.
7Christ gave each one of us the special gift of grace, showing how generous
he is. 8That is why it says in the Scriptures,

"When he went up to the heights,
he led a parade of captives,
and he gave gifts to people."

Psalm 68:18

9When it says, "He went up," what
does it mean? It means that he first came
down to the earth. 10So Jesus came
down, and he is the same One who went
up above all the heaven. Christ did that to
fill everything with his presence. 11And
Christ gave gifts to people—he made
some to be apostles, some to be prophets, some to go and tell the Good News,
and some to have the work of caring for
and teaching God's people. 12Christ gave
those gifts to prepare God's holy people
for the work of serving, to make the body
of Christ stronger. 13This work must
continue until we are all joined together
in the same faith and in the same knowledge of the Son of God. We must become
like a mature person, growing until we
become like Christ and have his perfection.
14Then we will no longer be babies.
We will not be tossed about like a ship
that the waves carry one way and

eMAIL! FROM GOD
4:13–14
Learning
When should you stop learning about God?

then another. We
will not be influ-
enced by every new
teaching we hear
from people who are
trying to fool us.
They make plans
and try any kind of trick to fool people
into following the wrong path. 15No!
Speaking the truth with love, we will
grow up in every way into Christ, who is
the head. 16The whole body depends on
Christ, and all the parts of the body are
joined and held together. Each part does
its own work to make the whole body
grow and be strong with love.

The Way You Should Live

17In the Lord's name, I tell you this.
Do not continue living like those who do
not believe. Their thoughts are worth
nothing. 18They do not understand, and
they know nothing, because they refuse
to listen. So they cannot have the life that
God gives. 19They have lost all feeling of
shame, and they use their lives for doing
evil. They continually want to do all kinds
of evil. 20But what you learned in Christ
was not like this. 21I know that you heard
about him, and you are in him, so you
were taught the truth that is in Jesus.
22You were taught to leave your old
self—to stop living the evil way you lived
before. That old self becomes worse, because people are fooled by the evil things
they want to do. 23But you were taught
to be made new in your hearts, 24to become a new person. That new person is
made to be like God—made to be truly
good and holy.
25So you must stop telling lies. Tell
each other the truth, because we

eMAIL! FROM GOD
4:26–27
Anger
Check out this good advice on anger.

all belong to each
other in the same
body."* 26When you
are angry, do not
sin, and be sure to
stop being angry be-

4:25 Tell . . . body. Quotation from Zechariah 8:16.

SAY WHAT?!

EPHESIANS 4:22-29

Words can hurt. Think about the last time someone said something mean to you. Those words hurt, didn't they? Name-calling, telling lies, gossip, and bad language are ways we use words to hurt others and ourselves. Paul, the writer of Ephesians, warned the Ephesian Christians to watch their words. Instead of putting others down, they were told to build others up with their words. Kind words are the way to "help others become stronger." Be a builder, not a destroyer, with your words!

Here are some more links on choosing your words carefully:

Just Kidding?, Genesis 21:8–10, p. 28

The Best Policy, Genesis 29:16–29, p. 41

A Special Promise, Numbers 30:1–2, p. 217

Peace in the Family, Psalm 133, p. 811

I'll Be the Judge!, 1 Corinthians 4:4–5, p. 1549

The Gentle Way, Titus 3:1–5, p. 1661

fore the end of the day. **27**Do not give the
devil a way to defeat you. **28**Those who are
stealing must stop stealing and start working. They should earn an honest living for
themselves. Then they will have something to share with those who are poor.

29When you talk, do not say harmful
things, but say what people need—words
that will help others become stronger.
Then what you say will do good to those
who listen to you. **30**And do not make the
Holy Spirit sad. The Spirit is God's proof
that you belong to him. God gave you
the Spirit to show that God will make
you free when the final day comes. **31**Do
not be bitter or angry or mad. Never
shout angrily or say things to hurt others.
Never do anything evil. **32**Be kind and
loving to each other, and forgive each
other just as God forgave you in Christ.

Living in the Light

5 You are God's children whom he
loves, so try to be like him. **2**Live a
life of love just as Christ loved us and
gave himself for us as a sweet-smelling
offering and sacrifice to God.

3But there must be no sexual sin
among you, or any kind of evil or greed.
Those things are not right for God's holy
people. **4**Also, there must be no evil talk
among you, and you must not speak foolishly or tell evil jokes. These things are
not right for you. Instead, you should be
giving thanks to God. **5**You can be sure of
this: No one will have a place in the kingdom of Christ and of God who sins sexually, or does evil things, or is greedy.
Anyone who is greedy is serving a false
god.

6Do not let anyone fool you by telling
you things that are not true, because
these things will bring God's anger on
those who do not obey him. **7**So have
nothing to do with them. **8**In the past you
were full of darkness, but now you are full
of light in the Lord. So live like children
who belong to the light. **9**Light brings
every kind of goodness, right living, and
truth. **10**Try to learn what pleases the
Lord. **11**Have nothing to do with the
things done in darkness, which are not
worth anything. But show that they are
wrong. **12**It is shameful even to talk about
what those people do in secret. **13**But the
light makes all things easy to see, **14**and
everything that is made easy to see can
become light. This is why it is said:

"Wake up, sleeper!

FORGIVE AND FORGET

EPHESIANS 4:32

What's the opposite of holding a grudge? Forgiving someone. Although that question was easy to answer, the answer itself is not always easy to do. Or so we think. The apostle Paul encouraged the Christians in the city of Ephesus to forgive others. Since God always forgives us, that's what we ought to do for anyone who hurts us.

Here is more on what God has to say about forgiveness:

More Powerful Than Revenge, Genesis 50:14–21, p. 71

Putting an Enemy in Check, 2 Kings 6:8–23, p. 486

Does Crime Pay?, Psalm 37:1–7, p. 736

Mercy for an Enemy, Jonah 4, p. 1216

The Best Protection Plan, Matthew 2:13–18, p. 1276

Who Needs Love?, Luke 6:27–36, p. 1379

Rise from death,
and Christ will shine on you."

15So be very careful how you live. Do
not live like those who are not wise, but
live wisely. 16Use every chance you have
for doing good, because these are evil
times. 17So do not be foolish but learn
what the Lord wants you to do. 18Do not
be drunk with wine, which will ruin you,
but be filled with the Spirit. 19Speak to
each other with psalms, hymns, and spiritual songs, singing and making music in
your hearts to the
Lord. 20Always give
thanks to God the Father for everything,
in the name of our
Lord Jesus Christ.

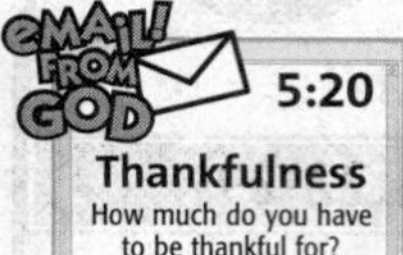

5:20
Thankfulness
How much do you have to be thankful for?

Wives and Husbands

21Yield to obey each other because
you respect Christ.

22Wives, yield to your husbands, as
you do to the Lord, 23because the husband is the head of the wife, as Christ is
the head of the church. And he is the Savior of the body, which is the church. 24As
the church yields to Christ, so you wives
should yield to your husbands in everything.

25Husbands, love your wives as Christ
loved the church and gave himself for it
26to make it belong to God. Christ used
the word to make the church clean by
washing it with water. 27He died so that
he could give the church to himself like a
bride in all her beauty. He died so that the
church could be pure and without fault,
with no evil or sin or any other wrong
thing in it. 28In the same way, husbands
should love their wives as they love
their own bodies. The man who loves
his wife loves himself. 29No one ever
hates his own body, but feeds and takes
care of it. And that is what Christ does
for the church, 30because we are parts
of his body. 31The Scripture says, "So a
man will leave his father and mother
and be united with his wife, and the two
will become one body."[n] 32That secret
is very important—I am talking about
Christ and the church. 33But each one
of you must love his wife as he loves
himself, and a wife must respect her
husband.

Children and Parents

6 Children, obey your parents as the
Lord wants, because this is the right
thing to do. 2The command says, "Honor

5:31 "So . . . body." Quotation from Genesis 2:24.

FAITH links

HOW TO MAKE GOD GLAD

EPHESIANS 6:1-2

Want to make God glad? Do you really want to please him? Then read the three words at the end of this sentence carefully: Obey your parents. Before you roll your eyes, think about it for a minute. Your parents love you and want what's best for you. If you really want to show respect for your parents (see verse 2), then listen to what they say and do it!

Want advice on handling your parents? Connect here:

Fatherly Advice, Exodus 18, p. 99

Care for the Lost, Deuteronomy 22:1–3, p. 255

In Your Best Interests, Ruth 3, p. 349

When I Need Advice, 1 Kings 12:1–17, p. 455

If You Want My Advice . . . , Proverbs 13:1, p. 843

Your Civic Duty, Matthew 17:24–27, p. 1304

your father and mother."[n] This is the first
command that has a prom-
ise with it—3"Then
everything will be
well with you, and
you will have a long
life on the earth."[n]
4Fathers, do not
make your children angry, but raise them
with the training and teaching of the Lord.

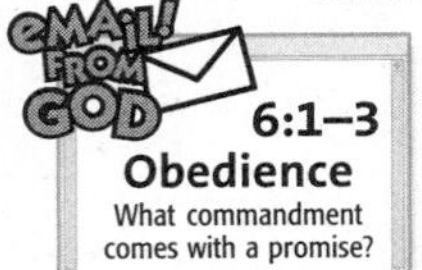

6:1–3
Obedience
What commandment comes with a promise?

Slaves and Masters

5Slaves, obey your masters here on
earth with fear and respect and from a
sincere heart, just as you obey Christ.
6You must do this not only while they are
watching you, to please them. With all
your heart you must do what God wants
as people who are obeying Christ. 7Do
your work with enthusiasm. Work as if
you were serving the Lord, not as if you
were serving only men and women. 8Re-
member that the Lord will give a reward
to everyone, slave or free, for doing good.
9Masters, in the same way, be good to
your slaves. Do not threaten them. Remember that the One who is your Master
and their Master is in heaven, and he
treats everyone alike.

Wear the Full Armor of God

10Finally, be strong in the Lord and in
his great power. 11Put on the full armor
of God so that you can fight against the
devil's evil tricks. 12Our fight is not
against people on earth but against the
rulers and authorities and the powers of
this world's darkness, against the spiritual powers of evil in the heavenly world.
13That is why you need to put on God's
full armor. Then on the day of evil you
will be able to stand strong. And when
you have finished the whole
fight, you will still
be standing. 14So
stand strong, with
the belt of truth tied
around your waist
and the protection
of right living on your chest. 15On your
feet wear the Good News of peace to help
you stand strong. 16And also use the
shield of faith with which you can stop all
the burning arrows of the Evil One.
17Accept God's salvation as your helmet,
and take the sword of the Spirit, which is
the word of God. 18Pray in the Spirit at
all times with all kinds of prayers, asking
for everything you need. To do this you

6:13
Perseverance
What do you need to keep standing?

6:2 "Honor . . . mother." Quotation from Exodus 20:12; Deuteronomy 5:16.

6:3 "Then . . . earth." Quotation from Exodus 20:12; Deuteronomy 5:16.

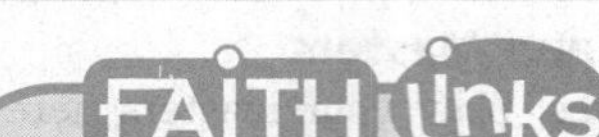

A GOOD HABIT

EPHESIANS 6:18

What are some of your habits? Some habits are good; some are bad. It is said that a habit takes 21 days to develop. So, for the next 21 days, why not make daily prayer a habit? You'll find that once you start, this is one habit you won't want to break. God tells us to never stop praying for each other. Does this mean you have to mutter a prayer for 24 hours straight? No. It just means to be prepared to pray.

Link here for more about good habits for a healthy faith:

When God Says No, 2 Samuel 7, p. 407

Building Together, Nehemiah 3, p. 627

The Bible: Good for Your Faith, Psalm 119, p. 802

Wisdom in Store, Proverbs 2:6–7, p. 828

Tell All About Him!, Matthew 28:19, p. 1326

Faith Workout, Acts 16:4–5, p. 1493

must always be ready and never give up.
Always pray for all God's people.
19Also pray for me that when I speak,
God will give me words so that I can tell
the secret of the Good News without fear.
20I have been sent to preach this Good
News, and I am doing that now, here in
prison. Pray that when I preach the Good
News I will speak without fear, as I
should.

Final Greetings

21I am sending to you Tychicus, our
brother whom we love and a faithful
servant of the Lord's work. He will tell
you everything that is happening with
me. Then you will know how I am and
what I am doing. **22**I am sending him to
you for this reason—so that you will
know how we are, and he can encourage you.
23Peace and love with faith to you
from God the Father and the Lord Jesus
Christ. **24**Grace to all of you who love our
Lord Jesus Christ with love that never
ends.

Philippians

NUMERAL UNO!

Okay, you know who this is, right? It's me, Paul. Remember who I was before I met Jesus? I was a powerful Jewish leader, who arrested and killed Jesus' followers. I was convinced that Jesus was nothing more than a rebellious troublemaker. Until Jesus met me on the road to Damascus, that is. After he changed my life, Jesus became the most important person in my life. My mission became telling others about Jesus and serving them. It was important to me that believers should work together and help each other. My friends at Philippi often helped me. (Check out Philippians 4:14–16.) In fact, the church at Philippi was one of my favorite churches. Which is why I wrote this letter.

The church in Philippi was having trouble, and I wanted to help them. Some people were telling them that they had to follow Jesus' teaching *and* Moses' teaching in order to be a true Christian. But that wasn't the truth—they only needed to follow Jesus' teachings. I wanted my friends in Philippi to understand that Jesus should be the most important person in their lives. A lot of us know people who are very important to us—our friends, our parents, our teachers. But for Christians, Jesus needs to be Numeral Uno!

JESUS WATCH

Paul gives us several snapshots of Jesus in this letter. Paul calls Jesus his life (Philippians 1:21); he is the picture of true unselfishness (Philippians 2:5); and Jesus is Paul's power source (Philippians 4:13). Paul talks a lot about Jesus in this book. He helps us understand that a life lived for Jesus isn't always easy, but it *is* one that is exciting and always changing. Paul shows us how his belief in Jesus has affected his life. Then he encourages his friends (and us!) to give their lives to Jesus—the only way they'll ever be really happy.

my FAVORITE links

OTHER CONNECTIONS

Livin' it Each school year you "grow" in the amount of knowledge you have learned. Each year, you grow physically. But how do you "grow" in faith? Find out by downloading How Are You Growing?, Philippians 1:1–11.

How do you feel when your best friend gets a better bike than you? How about when the kid down the street beats you out for the baseball team? Link to The Perfect Life!, Philippians 4:10–13, to learn how to be content with whatever you have.

MORE STUFF...

Joy Philippians is sometimes called the "joy letter." The word "joy" is mentioned more than 15 times. But did you know that Paul wrote this letter while he was in jail? Not a very joyful place, yet Paul found plenty of reasons to be joyful. Here are a few things he said about joy:

- Pray with joy. (Philippians 1:4)
- Joy each other with joy. (Philippians 2:17–18)
- Welcome those who work for Jesus with joy. (Philippians 2:25–30)
- Enjoy your faith in the Lord. (Philippians 3:1)
- Enjoy being with other Christians. (Philippians 4:1)
- Always be joyful. (Philippians 4:4)

"Hey, Tagg, want to hear the true secret of happiness?"

"Does it involve getting lots of cool stuff?"

"I don't think so. Better plug into Philippians 4:10-13."

did you know?

MORE ON THE PHILIPPIANS SURFWATCH:

No grumbling allowed, Philippians 2:14–18
Getting first prize, Philippians 3:12–14
What, me worry?, Philippians 4:5–9

The Finished Product, Philippians 1:6

An Unselfish Example, Philippians 2:5–8

The Sacrifice of Service, Philippians 2:17, 25–30

Thoughts on Thoughts, Philippians 4:8–9

As Strong as Superman?, Philippians 4:13

But I Want It?, Philippians 4:19

1 From Paul and Timothy, servants of
Christ Jesus.
To all of God's holy people in Christ
Jesus who live in Philippi, including your
elders and deacons:
2Grace and peace to you from God our
Father and the Lord Jesus Christ.

Paul's Prayer

3I thank my God every time I remember you, 4always praying with joy for all
of you. 5I thank God for the help you gave
me while I preached the Good News—
help you gave from the first day you believed until now. 6God began doing a
good work in you, and I am sure he will
continue it until it is finished when Jesus
Christ comes again.
7And I know that I am right to think
like this about all of you, because I have
you in my heart. All of you share in God's
grace with me while I am in prison and
while I am defending and proving the
truth of the Good News. 8God knows
that I want to see you very much, because I love all of you with the love of
Christ Jesus.
9This is my prayer for you: that your
love will grow more and more; that you
will have knowledge and understanding
with your love; 10that you will see the
difference between good and bad and will
choose the good; that you will be pure
and without wrong for the coming of
Christ; 11that you will do many good
things with the help of Christ to bring
glory and praise to God.

FAITH links

THE FINISHED PRODUCT

PHILIPPIANS 1:6

When you start a project, you like to see it through, don't you? Just think: you are a project for God. First, God helped you trust Jesus as your Savior. Because of that, God will keep working in you throughout your life to help you grow in faith. He won't give up on you. You can count on God to finish the "job"!

Here are some Faithlinks to encourage you to keep on going:

Good Plans, Genesis 45:7–8, p. 64

Always Truthful, Numbers 23:19, p. 208

The Prayer Habit, Psalm 5:1–3, p. 712

Your Full Trust, Jeremiah 22:20–22, p. 1023

Empty Words, Ezekiel 33:30–33, p. 1127

A Friend of Jesus, John 15:9–17, p. 1450

Paul's Troubles Help the Work

12I want you brothers and sisters[n] to
know that what has happened to me has
helped to spread the Good News. 13All
the palace guards and everyone else
knows that I am in prison because I am a
believer in Christ. 14Because I am in
prison, most of the believers have become more bold in Christ and are not
afraid to speak the word of God.
15It is true that some preach about
Christ because they are jealous and am-
bitious, but others preach about Christ
because they want to help. 16They
preach because they have love, and they
know that God gave me the work of defending the Good News. 17But the others
preach about Christ for selfish and wrong
reasons, wanting to make trouble for me
in prison.
18But it doesn't matter. The important thing is that in every way, whether

1:12 brothers and sisters Although the Greek text says "brothers" here and throughout this book, Paul's words were meant for the entire church, including men and women.

Livin' it

GROWING IN FAITH

Philippians 1:1–11

How Are You Growing? You've probably heard from someone (like a grandma or an aunt), "Look how big you are! You are growing like a weed!" There are other ways to grow, too, besides physically. You can grow in the amount of knowledge you learn at school. You can grow socially in learning how to get along with others. You also can grow in faith. Growing in faith means learning more about God and what's important to him, as you read the Bible, attend Sunday school, and trust God more.

Most of your physical growth takes place before you're an adult. But growing in faith should never stop, even if you live to be 100. (Check out Philippians 1:6.) God will keep working in you to help you grow in faith. He never gives up—count on him to finish the "job"! How is your faith growing?

MORE FAITH links

Trailblazers of Faith, p. 510
Two Ways to Grow, p. 1370
Faith Workout, p. 1493
Full of Faith, p. 1633
How Do You Grow?, p. 1659

"Hey, Skweek, have you noticed how big I've gotten in the last month or so?"

"I sure have, Tagg. But did you know that you can grow spiritually, too? Download these Faithlinks to find out how!"

The "Ruler" of Our Lives, Amos 7:7–9, p. 1202
- Ever try to hang a picture? Did it hang straight? You can tell if it's straight by using a ruler. The Bible is used to measure how "straight" our lives are. It can show us where we are crooked or "out of line" with how God wants us to live. Where do you need to straighten up?

Inside the Heart of God, Micah 7:18–20, p. 1228
- This Faithlink helps you to know what God is like.

Prove It!, Matthew 16:1–4, p. 1302
- Are you the kind of person who doesn't believe something unless it can be proven? Do you think "seeing is believing"? Many people in Jesus' day and today want proof that Jesus is the Savior. Where can you find that proof? Why can you believe every bit of it?

A Different Kind of Fruit, Galatians 5:22–23, p. 1592
- What's your favorite fruit? The Holy Spirit has some fruits that are his favorites, too. They're not the kind you might be thinking about, though. Link here to discover the kind of "fruits" that help you grow in faith.

my FAVORITE links

for right or wrong reasons, they are
preaching about Christ. So I am happy,
and I will continue to be happy. 19Be-
cause you are praying for me and the
Spirit of Jesus Christ is helping me, I
know this trouble will bring my freedom.
20I expect and hope that I will not fail
Christ in anything but that I will have the
courage now, as always, to show the
greatness of Christ in my life here on
earth, whether I live or die. 21To me the
only important thing about living is
Christ, and dying would be profit for
me. 22If I continue living in my body, I
will be able to work for the Lord.

EMAIL FROM GOD 1:23
Heaven
Is heaven better than earth?

I do not know what
to choose—living or
dying. 23It is hard to
choose between the
two. I want to leave
this life and be with
Christ, which is much better, 24but you
need me here in my body. 25Since I am
sure of this, I know I will stay with you to
help you grow and have joy in your faith.
26You will be very happy in Christ Jesus
when I am with you again.

27Only one thing concerns me: Be
sure that you live in a way that brings
honor to the Good News of Christ. Then
whether I come and visit you or am away
from you, I will hear that you are standing
strong with one purpose, that you work
together as one for the faith of the Good
News, 28and that you are not afraid of
those who are against you. All of this is
proof that your enemies will be destroyed but that you will be saved by
God. 29God gave you the honor not only
of believing in Christ but also of suffering
for him, both of which bring glory to
Christ. 30When I was with you, you saw
the struggles I had, and you hear about
the struggles I am having now. You yourselves are having the same kind of struggles.

2 Does your life in Christ give you
strength? Does his love comfort you?
Do we share together in the spirit? Do
you have mercy and kindness? 2If so,
make me very happy by having the same
thoughts, sharing the same love, and having one mind and purpose. 3When you

EMAIL FROM GOD
2:3
Humbleness
How should you think of others?

do things, do not
let selfishness or
pride be your guide.
Instead, be humble
and give more honor
to others than to

FAITH links

AN UNSELFISH EXAMPLE

PHILIPPIANS 2:5-8

Have you ever seen a mold that's used to make copies of something? For example, a mold, or model, is used to make plastic statues and other things. In much the same way, Jesus is our mold. He is the model for unselfishness. First, he left heaven to become a human on earth. He willingly gave his life so that we could have God's forgiveness for our sins.

The Holy Spirit uses the "mold" of Jesus to shape your life as a Christian. This does not mean that you lose everything that is uniquely you. It just means that you become more and more like Jesus.

The Perfect Leader?, Numbers 20:1–13, p. 203

Help to Understand, 2 Samuel 14, p. 416

Help for the Outsiders, Nehemiah 5:9–10, p. 630

Mind Guard, Proverbs 4:23, p. 831

Just Say Yes!, Matthew 9:9–13, p. 1289

A Different Kind of Fruit, Galatians 5:22–23, p. 1592

yourselves. 4Do not be interested only in
your own life, but be interested in the lives
of others.

Be Unselfish Like Christ

5In your lives you must think and act
like Christ Jesus.
6 Christ himself was like God in everything.
But he did not think that being equal with God was something to be used for his own benefit.
7 But he gave up his place with God and made himself nothing.
He was born to be a man and became like a servant.
8 And when he was living as a man, he humbled himself and was fully obedient to God,
even when that caused his death— death on a cross.
9 So God raised him to the highest place.
God made his name greater than every other name
10 so that every knee will bow to the name of Jesus—
everyone in heaven, on earth, and under the earth.
11 And everyone will confess that Jesus Christ is Lord
and bring glory to God the Father.

Be the People God Wants You to Be

12My dear friends, you have always
obeyed God when I was with you. It is
even more important that you obey now
while I am away from you. Keep on working to complete your salvation with fear
and trembling, 13because God is working
in you to help you want to do and be able
to do what pleases him.
14Do everything without complaining
or arguing. 15Then you will be innocent
and without any wrong. You will be God's
children without fault. But you are living
with crooked and mean people all around
you, among whom you shine like stars in
the dark world. 16You offer the teaching
that gives life. So when Christ comes
again, I can be happy because my work
was not wasted. I ran the race and won.

FAITH links

THE SACRIFICE OF SERVICE

PHILIPPIANS 2:17, 25-30

If you've read some of the Old Testament books, you know about the animal sacrifices the people of Israel gave to God. Sacrifices were the only way that people could be forgiven of their sins. When Jesus died on the cross, he was the once-and-for-all sacrifice for sins. Animal sacrifices were no longer required. Instead, we give service as a sacrifice to God. Think about the missionaries you've read about or the ones your church sponsors. Many missionaries have given their lives to serve God. That's the ultimate sacrifice. What will you do to serve God?

Download these Faithlinks on serving others:

Made in His Image, Genesis 1:26–27, p. 4

What God Wants, Deuteronomy 10:12–13, p. 242

From Zero to Hero, Judges 6; 7, p. 319

You Are What You Do, Proverbs 20:11, p. 854

Obey or Disobey?, Luke 20:20–26, p. 1409

The Worst Chore, John 13:3–17, p. 1447

17Your faith makes you offer your lives as a sacrifice in serving God. If I have to offer my own blood with your sacrifice, I will be happy and full of joy with all of you. **18**You also should be happy and full of joy with me.

Timothy and Epaphroditus

19I hope in the Lord Jesus to send Timothy to you soon. I will be happy to learn how you are. **20**I have no one else like Timothy, who truly cares for you. **21**Other people are interested only in their own lives, not in the work of Jesus Christ. **22**You know the kind of person Timothy is. You know he has served with me in telling the Good News, as a son serves his father. **23**I plan to send him to you quickly when I know what will happen to me. **24**I am sure that the Lord will help me to come to you soon.

25Epaphroditus, my brother in Christ, works and serves with me in the army of Christ. When I needed help, you sent him to me. I think now that I must send him back to you, **26**because he wants very much to see all of you. He is worried because you heard that he was sick. **27**Yes, he was sick, and nearly died, but God had mercy on him and me too so that I would not have more sadness. **28**I want very much to send him to you so that when you see him you can be happy, and I can stop worrying about you. **29**Welcome him in the Lord with much joy. Give honor to people like him, **30**because he almost died for the work of Christ. He risked his life to give me the help you could not give in your service to me.

The Importance of Christ

3 My brothers and sisters, be full of joy in the Lord. It is no trouble for me to write the same things to you again, and it will help you to be more ready. **2**Watch out for those who do evil, who are like dogs, who demand to cut[a] the body. **3**We are the ones who are truly circumcised. We worship God through his Spirit, and our pride is in Christ Jesus. We do not put trust in ourselves or anything we can do, **4**although I might be able to put trust in myself. If anyone thinks he has a reason to trust in himself, he should know that I have greater reason for trusting in myself. **5**I was circumcised eight days after my birth. I am from the people of Israel and the tribe of Benjamin. I am a Hebrew, and my parents were Hebrews. I had a strict view of the law, which is why I became a Pharisee. **6**I was so enthusiastic I tried to hurt the church. No one could find fault with the way I obeyed the law of Moses. **7**Those things were important to me, but now I think they are worth nothing because of Christ. **8**Not only those things, but I think that all things are worth nothing compared with the greatness of knowing Christ Jesus my Lord. Because of him, I have lost all those things, and now I know they are worthless trash. This allows me to have Christ **9**and to belong to him. Now I am right with God, not because I followed the law, but because I believed in Christ. God uses my faith to make me right with him. **10**I want to know Christ and the power that raised him from the dead. I want to share in his sufferings and become like him in his death. **11**Then I have hope that I myself will be raised from the dead.

Continuing Toward Our Goal

12I do not mean that I am already as God wants me to be. I have not yet reached that goal, but I continue trying to reach it and to make it mine. Christ wants me to do that, which is the reason he made me his. **13**Brothers and sisters, I know that I have not yet reached that goal, but there is one thing I always do. Forgetting the past and straining toward what is ahead, **14**I keep trying to reach the goal and get the prize for which God called me through Christ to the life above.

> EMAIL FROM GOD
> **3:12–14**
> **Faith**
> What is your ultimate goal?

15All of us who are spiritually mature should think this way, too. And if there are things you do not agree with, God will make them clear to you. **16**But we should

3:2 cut The word in Greek is like the word "circumcise," but it means "to cut completely off."

continue following the truth we already
have.
17Brothers and sisters, all of you
should try to follow my example and to
copy those who live the way we showed
you. 18Many people live like enemies of
the cross of Christ. I have often told you
about them, and it makes me cry to tell
you about them now. 19In the end, they
will be destroyed. They do whatever
their bodies want, they are proud of their
shameful acts, and they think only about
earthly things. 20But our homeland is in
heaven, and we are waiting for our Savior,
the Lord Jesus Christ, to come from
heaven. 21By his power to rule all things,
he will change our simple bodies and
make them like his own glorious body.

What the Christians Are to Do

4 My dear brothers and sisters, I love
you and want to see you. You bring
me joy and make me proud of you, so
stand strong in the Lord as I have told
you.
2I ask Euodia and Syntyche to agree
in the Lord. 3And I ask you, my faithful
friend, to help these women. They
served with me in telling the Good News,
together with Clement and others who
worked with me, whose names are written in the book of life.*
4Be full of joy in the Lord always. I
will say again, be full of joy.
5Let everyone see that you are gentle
and kind. The Lord is coming soon. 6Do
not worry about anything, but pray and
ask God for everything you need, always
giving thanks. 7And God's peace, which
is so great we cannot understand it, will
keep your hearts and minds in Christ
Jesus.
8Brothers and sisters, think about the
things that are good and worthy of praise. Think
about the things that
are true and honor-
able and right and
pure and beautiful
and respected. 9Do

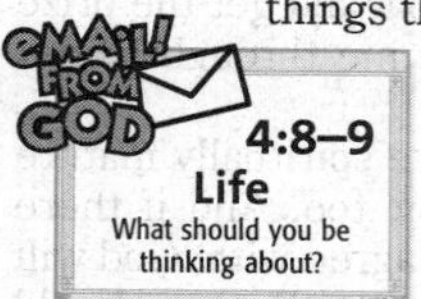

eMAIL FROM GOD
4:8–9
Life
What should you be thinking about?

4:3 book of life God's book that has the names of all God's chosen people (Revelation 3:5; 21:27).

FAITH links

THOUGHTS ON THOUGHTS

PHILIPPIANS 4:8-9

Which is easier: to think good thoughts or bad thoughts? Sadly, thinking bad thoughts is easier. What are bad thoughts? Some include worrying over a problem, thoughts of revenge and other angry thoughts, and the ever-popular "what-ifs?" What-if thoughts are usually fears over what might be. For example, *What if I fail the math test? What if no one likes me?* Thoughts like those can make you miserable. That's why the apostle Paul suggested that we think of what's true, honorable, right, pure, beautiful, and respected. Thoughts like those can bring you peace.

Need help in controlling those thoughts? Connect here:

When You're Afraid, Genesis 32:9–12, p. 45

What's Out Becomes In, Judges 11, p. 327

Who Ya' Gonna Call?, Psalm 3:4, p. 711

When Bad Things Happen, Ecclesiastes 3:16–17, p. 876

Who Needs Love?, Luke 6:27–36, p. 1379

Keep On Keepin' On, Revelation 13:10, p. 1744

FAITH links

AS STRONG AS SUPERMAN?

PHILIPPIANS 4:13

If you've ever worried about what you can't do, here is some good news. You have the strength to do anything! How is that possible? If you trust Jesus as your Savior, you can "do all things." Although this does not mean you'll be able to lift a train, it does mean you can do things you didn't think were possible. What kinds of things? Well, you can forgive someone who hurt you. You can overcome your fears. You can even show love to an enemy. With Jesus, you can do it!

Want to do the impossible? Anything is possible with God. Check it out!

Alone and Forgotten?, Genesis 40:23, p. 57

Moses' Champion, Numbers 12, p. 192

Get Hot or Keep Cool?, Proverbs 12:16, p. 842

Don't Get Mad; Get Even?, Matthew 26:57–63; 27:11–14, p. 1323

Mission Impossible?, Mark 5:21–24, 35–43, p. 1337

A Friendly Welcome, Philemon 18, p. 1664

what you learned and received from me, what I told you, and what you saw me do. And the God who gives peace will be with you.

FAITH links

BUT I WANT IT?

PHILIPPIANS 4:19

Want to stop worrying over what you have or don't have? Then read what Paul says in this verse. God will give you everything you need. Before you head to the nearest mall to buy, buy, buy, consider this. God will give you what you need, but those needs may not include your *wants.* Needs include food, clothing, shelter, and so on. As for wants, well, you know what those are. You can trust that God will provide what you need.

Connect here to find out how God takes care of your needs:

Your Heavenly Parent, Exodus 2:1–10, p. 77

Listen Up!, 1 Kings 19:11–13, p. 467

Lower Than Low, Job 19:13–25, p. 680

911, Psalm 28:6, p. 730

A Tight Spot, Jonah 2, p. 1215

Love for Free, Romans 5:8, p. 1524

Paul Thanks the Christians

10I am very happy in the Lord that
you have shown your care for me again.
You continued to care about me, but there
was no way for you to show it. **11**I am not
telling you this because I need anything. I
have learned to be satisfied with the
things I have and with everything that
happens. **12**I know how to live when I am

Being Content

Philippians 4:10–13

Livin' it

The Perfect Life! What would make your life perfect? Would it be having more things? Would it be living somewhere else or maybe having your brother or sister live somewhere else for a while? What keeps you from feeling satisfied (being content) with what you have?

Paul tells you how to be content with what you *do* have. You can do this by trusting God to give you everything you need. (Look at Philippians 4:19.) What is the difference between what you *want* and what you *need*?

MORE FAITH links

Complaints, Complaints!, p. 97

A Life of Thanksgiving, p. 435

Wisdom About Wealth, p. 878

Think About Him, p. 926

More Money?, p. 1649

"Boy, if only I had a million dollars! Then I could buy whatever I wanted—and I'd get you something, too, Skweek!"

"Well, that's real nice of you, Tagg, but maybe you'd better surf over to these Faithlinks to find out the difference between wanting more and being content with what you have."

When the Green-eyed Monster Strikes, 1 Samuel 18:6–9, p. 379

- Has someone ever compared you with someone else? Did the comparison make you feel good or bother you? Why?
- Jealousy is called the "green-eyed monster" because it can make us act like one. Have you ever been jealous? What did you do about it? You can always tell God how you feel, and he can help you be content.

A Need to Change, Ecclesiastes 1:1–11, p. 873

- What makes you bored and not content with your life? How do you act when you are bored? The next time you find life "Boooorrring!" think of how you can change the situation. What can you do to be more content?

Mission Impossible?, Mark 5:21–24, 35–43, p. 1337

- Link here to discover how God handles hard problems and brings contentment.

poor, and I know how to live when I have
plenty. I have learned the secret of being
happy at any time in everything that happens, when I have enough to eat and
when I go hungry, when I have more than
I need and when I do not have enough.
13I can do all things through Christ, because he gives me strength.

14But it was good that you helped me
when I needed it. **15**You Philippians remember when I first preached the Good
News there. When I left Macedonia, you
were the only church that gave me help.
16Several times you sent me things I
needed when I was in Thessalonica.
17Really, it is not that I want to receive
gifts from you, but I want you to have the
good that comes from giving. **18**And now
I have everything, and more. I have all I
need, because Epaphroditus brought
your gift to me. It is like a sweet-smelling
sacrifice offered to God, who accepts that
sacrifice and is pleased with it. **19**My God
will use his wonderful riches in Christ
Jesus to give you everything you need.
20Glory to our God and Father forever
and ever! Amen.

21Greet each of God's people in
Christ. Those who are with me send
greetings to you. **22**All of God's people
greet you, particularly those from the
palace of Caesar.

23The grace of the Lord Jesus Christ
be with you all.

ONLY JESUS

Let's take a test to see if you know who I am. I was a well-known religious leader who hated Christians. One day, I met Jesus. After that, I became *the* spokesman for Jesus. Because of my message, I made a lot of people mad and spent a lot of time in jail. You got it! It's me, Paul. In fact, I wrote this letter from jail. (My friend Timothy helped me. Check out Colossians 1:1.) I never visited the church at Colossae, but I worked in Ephesus, about 100 miles away. Most likely, a young man named Epaphras heard the truth about Jesus and told others in Colossae. That's how news spread in those days.

The church in Colossae was having problems that were similar to those many other young churches were having—false teachings. In fact, the city was full of people teaching wrong things. Some taught that the human body was evil. Others were teaching that Christians should worship angels! So, I wrote this letter to my fellow believers to help them understand that the body isn't an evil thing, and that we're supposed to worship only Jesus.

JESUS WATCH

In this book, Paul portrays Jesus as the ruler who is "over all rulers and powers." Paul presents Jesus as a "cosmic Christ" (in other words, he explains how Jesus is in charge of everything in the universe). How does he do this? He explains that Jesus existed before anything else (Colossians 1:17); he is the head of the church (Colossians 1:18); and he is the risen Lord (Colossians 3:1). Paul's portrayal of Jesus as an all-powerful leader isn't so people would fear Jesus. Instead, Paul was out to prove to people that Jesus was everything they ever dreamed that he could be. We can trust Jesus because he was everything he said he was!

my FAVORITE links

OTHER CONNECTIONS

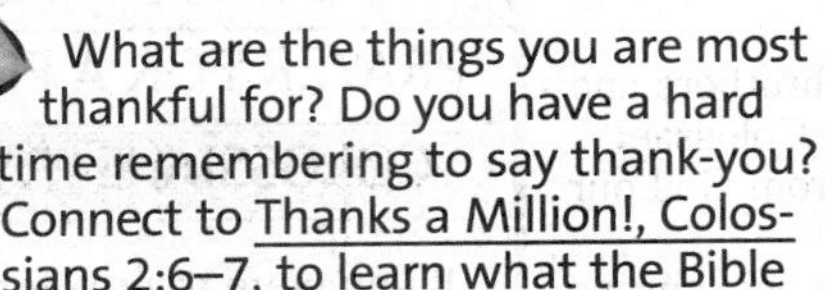

Livin' it What are the things you are most thankful for? Do you have a hard time remembering to say thank-you? Connect to Thanks a Million!, Colossians 2:6–7, to learn what the Bible has to say about having a gratitude attitude.

If you were to make a list of the top qualities you would like to develop, what would those be? Being smarter or more athletic? Being strong or being kind? When you become a Christian, God begins to work from the inside out to change you into the person He wants you to become. Check it out by linking to Out with the Old!, Colossians 3:1–14.

MORE STUFF...

The New You Ever heard the expression "get a life"? In one sense that's what happens when you believe in Jesus—you get a *new* life and become a new person in Jesus. That means you need to get rid of the old way of doing things and do things that God wants you to do. Here are a few examples from Colossians 3:1–14:

- Get rid of being greedy and doing evil things.
- Get rid of bad tempers, doing or saying things to hurt others, and using bad words when you speak.
- Do be kind, gentle, humble, and patient with others. Love each other!

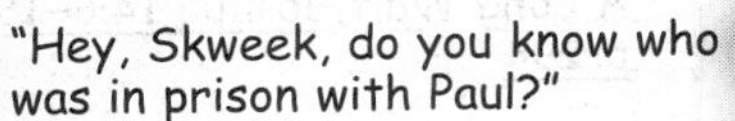

"Hey, Skweek, do you know who was in prison with Paul?"

"Nope. But you can check out the prisoner list in Colossians 4:10-14 and find out."

did you know?

DOWNLOAD THESE AWESOME STORIES:

God's enemies, Colossians 1:21–23
By Jesus' rules, Colossians 2:16–23
A new life, Colossians 3:1–11

FAITH links

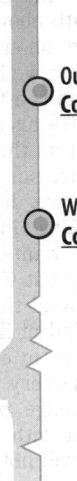

- **Prayer for a Friend, Colossians 1:9–12**
- **Just Like a Tree, Colossians 1:23**
- **Out with the Old!, Colossians 3:1–14**
- **With All Your Heart, Colossians 3:23**

1 From Paul, an apostle of Christ Jesus.
I am an apostle because that is what
God wanted. Also from Timothy, our
brother.
2To the holy and faithful brothers and
sisters[n] in Christ that live in Colossae:
Grace and peace to you from God our
Father.
3In our prayers for you we always
thank God, the Father of our Lord Jesus
Christ, 4because we have heard about
the faith you have in Christ Jesus and the
love you have for all of God's people.
5You have this faith and love because of
your hope, and what you hope for is kept
safe for you in heaven. You learned about
this hope when you heard the message
about the truth, the Good News 6that
was told to you. Everywhere in the world
that Good News is bringing blessings and
is growing. This has happened with you,
too, since you heard the Good News and
understood the truth about the grace of
God. 7You learned about God's grace
from Epaphras, whom we love. He works
together with us and is a faithful servant
of Christ for us. 8He also told us about
the love you have from the Holy Spirit.
9Because of this, since the day we
heard about you, we have continued
praying for you, asking God that you will
know fully what he wants. We pray that
you will also have great wisdom and understanding in spiritual things 10so that
you will live the kind of life that honors
and pleases the Lord in every way. You
will produce fruit in every good work and
grow in the knowledge of God. 11God
will strengthen you with his own great
power so that you will not give up when
troubles come, but you will be patient.
12And you will joyfully give thanks to the
Father who has made you able to have a
share in all that he has prepared for his
people in the kingdom of light. 13God has
freed us from the power of darkness, and
he brought us into the kingdom of his
dear Son. 14The Son paid for our sins,
and in him we have forgiveness.

1:2 brothers and sisters Although the Greek text says "brothers" here and throughout this book, Paul's words were meant for the entire church, including men and women.

FAITH links

PRAYER FOR A FRIEND

COLOSSIANS 1:9-12

If you were to pray for a friend, what would you ask God for? In his letter to the Christians in the city of Colossae, Paul prayed that they would have God's best. What was God's best? He prayed that they would have wisdom and understanding. He also prayed that they would know what God wanted them to do for him.

Paul was glad to pray for the Colossian Christians since he could not be with them. He knew that God would always take care of them. The best thing you can do for a friend is to pray for her and ask for God's wisdom and strength for her.

God really wants to help your friends. Connect here to find out more:

What He's Really Like, Deuteronomy 4:15–20, p. 233

A Long Wait, Joshua 14:6–15, p. 294

Learning from Mistakes, Psalm 51:12–13, p. 748

You've Got the Power!, Acts 1:1–8; 2:1–4, p. 1463

The Finished Product, Philippians 1:6, p. 1609

Pay Attention!, Hebrews 2:1, p. 1668

The Importance of Christ

15No one can see God, but Jesus
Christ is exactly like him. He ranks higher
than everything that has been made.
16Through his power all things were
made—things in heaven
and on earth, things
seen and unseen, all
powers, authorities,
lords, and rulers. All
things were made
through Christ and
for Christ. 17He was
there before anything was made, and all
things continue because of him. 18He is
the head of the body, which is the church.
Everything comes from him. He is the
first one who was raised from the dead.
So in all things Jesus has first place.
19God was pleased for all of himself to
live in Christ. 20And through Christ, God
has brought all things back to himself
again—things on earth and things in
heaven. God made peace through the
blood of Christ's death on the cross.

EMAIL! FROM GOD
1:15–16
Jesus
Did Jesus create the world?

21At one time you were separated
from God. You were his enemies in your
minds, and the evil things you did were
against God. 22But now God has made
you his friends again. He did this through
Christ's death in the body so that he
might bring you into God's presence as
people who are holy, with no wrong, and
with nothing of which God can judge you
guilty. 23This will happen if you continue
strong and sure in your faith. You must
not be moved away from the hope
brought to you by the Good News that
you heard. That same Good News has
been told to everyone in the world, and I,
Paul, help in preaching that Good News.

Paul's Work for the Church

24I am happy in my sufferings for you.
There are things that Christ must still
suffer through his body, the church. I am
accepting, in my body, my part of these
things that must be suffered. 25I became
a servant of the church because God gave
me a special work to do that helps you,
and that work is to tell fully the message
of God. 26This message is the secret that
was hidden from everyone since the beginning of time, but now it is made known
to God's holy people. 27God decided to
let his people know this rich and glorious

FAITH links

JUST LIKE A TREE

COLOSSIANS 1:23

A seed or plant needs to be placed deeply enough in the ground to allow it to take root and grow. Shallow soil won't let the roots grow deeply enough, resulting in a weak plant. A tree with strong, healthy roots is hard to move.

Paul wanted the Christians in the city of Colossae to have strong, deeply rooted faith. How can you have that kind of faith? Reading the Bible, praying, and learning from other Christians can help. As you grow older, your faith will be stronger. Pray that God will continue to grow your faith deep and strong.

Here are more Faithlinks on growing faith as strong as a tree:

A Life of Thanksgiving, 1 Kings 1:47–48, p. 435

An Admirable Quality, 1 Kings 10:1–13, p. 451

Braggin' Rights, Jeremiah 9:23–24, p. 1005

The Best Advice, Zechariah 10:2, p. 1261

Best Seat in the House, Luke 14:7–11, p. 1398

How Do You Grow?, Titus 1:1, p. 1659

secret which he has for all people. This
secret is Christ himself, who is in you.
He is our only hope for glory. 28So we
continue to preach Christ to each person,
using all wisdom to warn and to teach
everyone, in order to bring each one into
God's presence as a mature person in
Christ. 29To do this, I work and struggle,
using Christ's great strength that works
so powerfully in me.

2 I want you to know how hard I work
for you, those in Laodicea, and others
who have never seen me. 2I want them
to be strengthened and joined together
with love so that they may be rich in their
understanding. This leads to their knowing fully God's secret, that is, Christ himself. 3In him all the treasures of wisdom
and knowledge are safely kept.

4I say this so that no one can fool you
by arguments that seem good, but are
false. 5Though I am absent from you in
my body, my heart is with you, and I am
happy to see your good lives and your
strong faith in Christ.

Continue to Live in Christ

6As you received Christ Jesus the
Lord, so continue to live in him. 7Keep
your roots deep in him and
have your lives built
on him. Be strong in
the faith, just as you
were taught, and al-
ways be thankful.

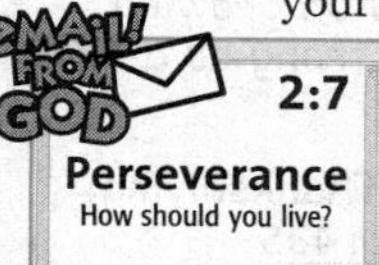
eMAIL! FROM GOD
2:7
Perseverance
How should you live?

8Be sure that no
one leads you away with false and empty
teaching that is only human, which
comes from the ruling spirits of this
world, and not from Christ. 9All of God
lives in Christ fully (even when Christ
was on earth), 10and you have a full and
true life in Christ, who is ruler over all
rulers and powers.

11Also in Christ you had a different
kind of circumcision, a circumcision not
done by hands. It was through Christ's
circumcision, that is, his death, that you
were made free from the power of your
sinful self. 12When you were baptized,
you were buried with Christ, and you
were raised up with him through your
faith in God's power that was shown
when he raised Christ from the dead.
13When you were spiritually dead because of your sins and because you were
not free from the power of your sinful
self, God made you alive with Christ, and
he forgave all our sins. 14He canceled the
debt, which listed all the rules we failed
to follow. He took away that record with
its rules and nailed it to the cross. 15God
stripped the spiritual rulers and powers
of their authority. With the cross, he won
the victory and showed the world that
they were powerless.

Don't Follow People's Rules

16So do not let anyone make rules for
you about eating and drinking or about a
religious feast, a New Moon Festival, or
a Sabbath day. 17These things were like a
shadow of what was to come. But what is
true and real has come and is found in
Christ. 18Do not let anyone disqualify
you by making you humiliate yourself
and worship angels. Such people enter
into visions, which fill them with foolish
pride because of their human way of
thinking. 19They do not hold tightly to
Christ, the head. It is from him that all
the parts of the body are cared for and
held together. So it grows in the way God
wants it to grow.

20Since you died with Christ and
were made free from the ruling spirits of
the world, why do you act as if you still
belong to this world by following rules
like these: 21"Don't eat this," "Don't
taste that," "Don't even touch that
thing"? 22These rules refer to earthly
things that are gone as soon as they are
used. They are only man-made commands and teachings. 23They seem to be
wise, but they are only part of a man-
made religion. They make people pretend not to be proud and make them
punish their bodies, but they do not really
control the evil desires of the sinful self.

Your New Life in Christ

3 Since you were raised from the dead
with Christ, aim at what is in heaven,
where Christ is sitting at the right hand
of God. 2Think only about the things in
heaven, not the things on earth. 3Your

Being Thankful

Colossians 2:6–7

Livin' it

Thanks a Million! How do you feel about writing thank-you notes? On a scale of 1 to 10, does it rate a 10? When your mom reminds you to thank Aunt Lisa for that lovely sweater, do you suddenly develop a permanently cramped writing hand? Paul tells us to be thankful always—for everything and not just the stuff that we like.

Things aren't the only items we should be thankful for. God also wants us to be thankful for the people in our lives who love and help us. (Read 1 Thessalonians 1:1–3, p. 1630.) Who are the people in your life you are thankful for? Why are you thankful for them? Tell them how you feel—how about saying, "Thanks a million!"

More Faith Links

A Thanksgiving Reminder, p. 91
A Life of Thanksgiving, p. 435
Gratitude Attitude, p. 611
A Holiday Letter, p. 657
Thanks for a Friend, p. 1630

"Who are you most thankful for, Tagg?"

"Well, I'm thankful for you and for all our friends who come and visit us."

"Those are good things to be thankful for, Tagg. Here are some other thoughts on things to be thankful for. Check them out!"

A Song of Thanks, 1 Samuel 2, p. 356
- When you're feeling thankful, how do you show it? What are you thankful to God for? Link here to join Hannah in a song of thanks.

No Thanksgiving?, 2 Kings 23:21–23, p. 512
- Can you imagine what it would be like if everyone in the United States stopped celebrating Thanksgiving? You probably would miss it, but you don't really need a Thanksgiving Day and some turkey to be thankful. What are some ways you show thankfulness to God every day—365 days a year?

Ten Things I Like About You, 2 Thessalonians 1:3–4, p. 1638
- Have you ever bragged to someone else about what a friend could do? What did you tell them about your friend? Why did you do it?
- How has God helped someone you know? How will you thank God for his help? How will you let that person know that you're proud of him or her?

My Favorite Links

______________ ______________
______________ ______________
______________ ______________

GENTLENESS

Colossians 3:1–14

Livin' it

Out with the Old! How about a makeover? If you get a cool new haircut or start wearing the latest styles, others will probably notice. But how about a makeover on the inside, where people can't see it by looking at you? The only way others can tell that you've changed your attitude is by the way you act.

When we become Christians, God begins to change us, starting from the inside out. We need to get rid of stuff like anger, jealousy, and bad attitudes. God helps make us over with better stuff—like patience, kindness, and gentleness. (Check out Colossians 3:1–14.) What kind of an inside makeover do you need? What new attitudes and actions will take the place of the old ones?

MORE FAITH links

Just Kidding?, p. 28
Help for the Hurting, p. 666
A Gentle Answer, p. 847
The Right Ingredients, p. 1227
Kindness First, p. 1290
I'll Be the Judge!, p. 1549

"Hey, Skweek, I love those stylin' colors of yours!"

"Thanks, Tagg, but have you noticed I've been a lot more patient lately? That's what really counts. Check it out on these Faithlinks."

Who Needs Love?, Luke 6:27–36, p. 1379
- Who needs your love, kindness, and gentleness the most? Link here to find out how Jesus answers that question.

Most Wanted?, 2 Corinthians 10:1, p. 1580
- What are the Top 10 qualities you admire most in a person? What makes you really like someone? Is it someone who is a leader or someone who is always funny? Link here to discover which qualities made Paul's Top 10 list. You may be surprised!

The Gentle Way, Titus 3:1–5, p. 1661
- What's the first thing you think of doing when your brother or sister says something mean to you? Do you ever think of being kind and gentle? Showing kindness instead of getting back at someone isn't always easy. How can you do this the next time someone bugs you?

my FAVORITE links

old sinful self has died, and your new life
is kept with Christ in God. 4Christ is our
life, and when he comes again, you will
share in his glory.
5So put all evil things out of your life:
sexual sinning, doing evil, letting evil
thoughts control you, wanting things that
are evil, and greed. This is really serving
a false god. 6These things make God
angry.[n] 7In your past, evil life you also did
these things.
8But now also put these things out of
your life: anger, bad temper, doing or saying things to hurt others,
and using evil words
when you talk. 9Do
not lie to each other.
You have left your
old sinful life and the
things you did be-
fore. 10You have begun to live the new
life, in which you are being made new and
are becoming like the One who made
you. This new life brings you the true
knowledge of God. 11In the new life
there is no difference between Greeks
and Jews, those who are circumcised and
those who are not circumcised, or people
who are foreigners, or Scythians.[n] There
is no difference between slaves and free
people. But Christ is in all believers, and
Christ is all that is important.
12God has chosen you and made you
his holy people. He loves you. So always
do these things: Show mercy to others,
be kind, humble, gentle, and patient.
13Get along with each other, and forgive
each other. If someone does wrong to
you, forgive that person because the
Lord forgave you. 14Do all these things;
but most important, love each other.
Love is what holds you all together in
perfect unity. 15Let the peace that Christ
gives control your thinking, because you
were all called together in one body[n] to
have peace. Always be thankful. 16Let
the teaching of Christ live in you
richly. Use all wis-
dom to teach and in-
struct each other
by singing psalms,
hymns, and spiritual
songs with thankful-
ness in your hearts to God. 17Everything
you do or say should be done to obey
Jesus your Lord. And in all you do, give
thanks to God the Father through Jesus.

E-MAIL FROM GOD 3:8–9
Life
Check out some things you shouldn't do.

E-MAIL FROM GOD 3:16
Music
Why should you make music?

FAITH links

OUT WITH THE OLD!

COLOSSIANS 3:1-14

When we become Christians, God begins to change us, starting from the inside out. There are certain things we have to get rid of—like anger and jealousy and bad attitudes. When we get rid of those things, God can begin to make us new and help us do the right things—like being patient and kind with others; getting along, and above all else, loving others as Jesus loves us.

What attitudes do you need to get rid of? Connect here:

A Shortcut, 1 Samuel 13:1–14, p. 369

Give In or Take a Stand?, 1 Kings 22:13–14, p. 472

A Memorial for Two Thieves, 1 Chronicles 7:21, p. 530

Patience, Please, Psalm 145:8–9, p. 819

A Direct Path, Proverbs 3:5–6, p. 829

Kindness First, Matthew 9:35–36, p. 1290

3:6 These . . . angry Some Greek copies add: "against the people who do not obey God."
3:11 Scythians The Scythians were known as very wild and cruel people.
3:15 body The spiritual body of Christ, meaning the church or his people.

FAITH links

WITH ALL YOUR HEART

COLOSSIANS 3:23

What are some tasks that you find hardest to do? Homework? Chores? When you're faced with a task you don't particularly like, what do you do? Some of us tend to work halfheartedly, just trying to get through the chore. Sometimes we even complain about having to do the work in the first place. Are you ever tempted to do that?

God wants you to do everything with your best effort, no matter what you do. Keeping Jesus in mind as you work will help you put your whole heart into what you do. That was Paul's advice to the Colossian Christians—and for you.

Need an attitude adjustment on doing your best? Link here:

Everyone Can Help, Numbers 4, p. 181

Operation Cooperation, Ezra 1:5, p. 609

Down on the Ant Farm, Proverbs 6:6–11, p. 833

Love for a Lifetime, Song of Solomon 6:8–9, p. 891

The Gift of Worship, Matthew 2:10–12, p. 1275

Better Than Some?, Luke 18:9–14, p. 1405

Your New Life with Other People

18Wives, yield to the authority of your husbands, because this is the right thing to do in the Lord.

19Husbands, love your wives and be gentle with them.

20Children, obey your parents in all things, because this pleases the Lord.

21Fathers, do not nag your children. If you are too hard to please, they may want to stop trying.

22Slaves, obey your masters in all things. Do not obey just when they are watching you, to gain their favor, but serve them honestly, because you respect the Lord. 23In all the work you are doing, work the best you can. Work as if you were doing it for the Lord, not for
people. 24Remember that you will re-
ceive your reward from the Lord, which he promised to his people. You are serving the Lord Christ. 25But remember
that anyone who does wrong will be punished for that wrong, and the Lord treats everyone the same.

4 Masters, give what is good and fair to your slaves. Remember that you have a Master in heaven.

What the Christians Are to Do

2Continue praying, keeping alert, and
always thanking God. 3Also pray for us that God will give us an opportunity to tell people his message. Pray that we can preach the secret that God has made known about Christ. This is
why I am in prison. 4Pray that I can speak in a way that will make it clear, as I should.

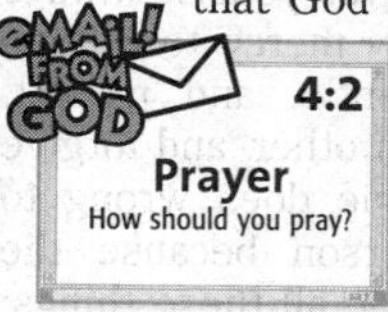
eMAIL! FROM GOD
4:2
Prayer
How should you pray?

5Be wise in the way you act with people who are not believers, making the most of every opportunity.
6When you talk, you should always be kind and pleasant so you will be able to answer everyone in the way you should.

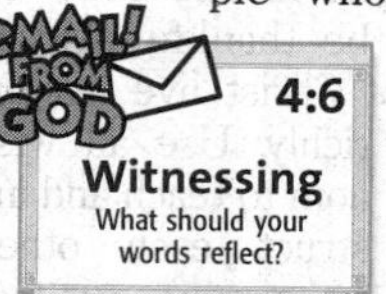
eMAIL! FROM GOD
4:6
Witnessing
What should your words reflect?

News About the People with Paul

7Tychicus is my dear brother in Christ
and a faithful minister and servant with
me in the Lord. He will tell you all the
things that are happening to me. **8**This is
why I am sending him: so you may know
how we are and he may encourage you. **9**I
send him with Onesimus, a faithful and
dear brother in Christ, and one of your
group. They will tell you all that has happened here.

10Aristarchus, a prisoner with me,
and Mark, the cousin of Barnabas, greet
you. (I have already told you what to do
about Mark. If he comes, welcome him.)
11Jesus, who is called Justus, also greets
you. These are the only Jewish believers
who work with me for the kingdom of
God, and they have been a comfort to me.
12Epaphras, a servant of Jesus Christ,
from your group, also greets you. He always prays for you that you will grow to
be spiritually mature and have everything
God wants for you. **13**I know he has
worked hard for you and the people in
Laodicea and in Hierapolis. **14**Demas and
our dear friend Luke, the doctor, greet you.

15Greet the brothers in Laodicea.
And greet Nympha and the church that
meets in her house. **16**After this letter is
read to you, be sure it is also read to the
church in Laodicea. And you read the letter that I wrote to Laodicea. **17**Tell Archippus, "Be sure to finish the work the
Lord gave you."

18I, Paul, greet you and write this
with my own hand. Remember me in
prison. Grace be with you.

1 Thessalonians

JESUS WILL RETURN!

Hi; it's Paul again. You're about to read one of the first letters I wrote after I became a follower of Jesus. I actually began the church in Thessalonica (a city that's located in what is called Europe today). I spent three Sabbath days preaching in the Jewish place of worship, called a synagogue. (For more on synagogue, connect to Mark 6, p. 1338.) When the Jewish people wouldn't believe what I was saying, I went to the non-Jewish people and preached to them. I did this a lot. I told everybody I could about the change that Jesus had made in my life.

Thessalonica was a seaport city with nearly 200,000 people in it. That is one big city! You can imagine all of the different types of beliefs that were circulating through that city. I wrote this letter to help believers there understand one key truth—the promised return of Jesus. You see, some people were spreading rumors that Jesus had *already* returned. So I wrote to them to give them all of the facts that I could about Jesus' return. Hey, Jesus *is* coming, but he hasn't come yet!

JESUS WATCH

Guess what. You can count on Jesus returning. He promised it. The Old Testament even promised it. Much of the portrayal of Jesus in this book focuses on the fact that Jesus is coming back. He's presented as the believer's hope and our deliverer (1 Thessalonians 1:10). Paul spends most of his time in this book helping the Thessalonians understand that Jesus *is* returning. And when Jesus comes back, all who believe in him will experience the most incredible homecoming ever! We *will* see Jesus again!

my FAVORITE links

_______________ _______________

_______________ _______________

_______________ _______________

_______________ _______________

OTHER CONNECTIONS

Livin' it

How good are you at waiting for things? Can you sit quietly or do you get antsy? Download Let Me Do It!, 1 Thessalonians 5, to find out how good you are at waiting for things—and what it takes to be good at the waiting game.

GET THE INFO

- Let's Visit Thessalonica, 1 Thessalonians 3. Do you know who the city of Thessalonica was named after? Connect here to find out the answer and more about this ancient Greek city that still exists today.

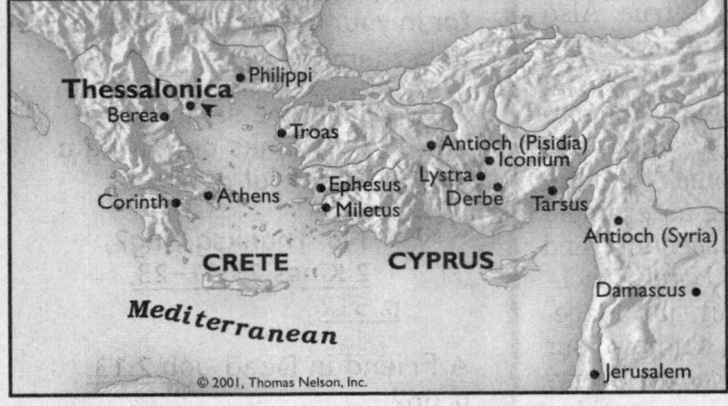

"Hey, Tagg, do you think we'll know when Jesus comes back?"

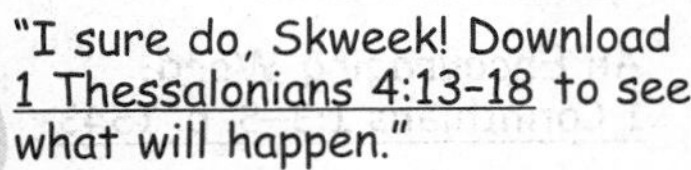

"I sure do, Skweek! Download 1 Thessalonians 4:13-18 to see what will happen."

MORE COOL SITES TO CHECK OUT:

Paul's pride and joy, 1 Thessalonians 2:17–20
A life that pleases God, 1 Thessalonians 4:1–12
Get ready for Jesus, 1 Thessalonians 5:1–11

FAITH links

Thanks for a Friend, 1 Thessalonians 1:1–3

Full of Faith, 1 Thessalonians 4:1

The Coming Attraction, 1 Thessalonians 4:13–18

Always Do This!, 1 Thessalonians 5:16–18

1 From Paul, Silas, and Timothy.
To the church in Thessalonica, the church in God the Father and the Lord Jesus Christ:

Grace and peace to you.

The Faith of the Thessalonians

2We always thank God for all of you
and mention you when we pray. 3We con-
tinually recall before God our Father the things you have done because of your faith and the work you have done because of your love. And we thank him that you continue to be strong because of your hope in our Lord Jesus Christ.
4Brothers and sisters,* God loves you, and we know he has chosen you, 5because
the Good News we brought to you came not only with words, but with power, with the Holy Spirit, and with sure knowledge that it is true. Also you know how we lived when we were with you in order to help you. 6And you
became like us and like the Lord. You suffered much, but still you accepted the teaching with the joy that comes from the Holy Spirit. 7So you became an example
to all the believers in Macedonia and Southern Greece. 8And the Lord's teach-
ing spread from you not only into Macedonia and Southern Greece, but now your faith in God has become known everywhere. So we do not need to say anything about it. 9People everywhere are telling
about the way you accepted us when we were there with you. They tell how you stopped worshiping idols and began serving the living and true God. 10And you
wait for God's Son, whom God raised from the dead, to come from heaven. He is Jesus, who saves us from God's angry judgment that is sure to come.

1:4–5
Good News
Does believing in the Good News help you?

Paul's Work in Thessalonica

2 Brothers and sisters, you know our visit to you was not a failure. 2Before
we came to you, we suffered in Philippi. People there insulted us, as you know, and many people were against us. But our God helped us to be brave and to tell

FAITH links

THANKS FOR A FRIEND

1 THESSALONIANS 1:1-3

For whom are you thankful? Each time Paul wrote a letter to a group of Christians, he mentioned how thankful he was for them. In this letter to Christians in Thessalonica, Paul spoke for Silas and Timothy, two missionaries who traveled with him. Not only were they thankful, they also prayed for the Thessalonian Christians.

It's great to be thankful to God for the people in our lives. Think of the people you are thankful for in your life and ask God to help them.

Here are some more Faithlinks on having a thankful attitude:

No Thanksgiving?, 2 Kings 23:21–23, p. 512

A Friend in Deed, Job 2:13, p. 662

911, Psalm 28:6, p. 730

A Fair-weather Friend, Obadiah 7, p. 1209

An Encouraging Word, 1 Corinthians 1:3–5, p. 1545

Always Do This!, 1 Thessalonians 5:16–18, p. 1636

1:4 Brothers and sisters Although the Greek text says "Brothers" here and throughout this book, Paul's words were meant for the entire church, including men and women.

FAITH CHALLENGE

Try this challenge. Read 2:2 to find out what happened to Paul in Philippi. What would you do if you saw kids making fun of one of your Christian friends at school?

TESTING IT

1 Thessalonians 2:2
Before we came to you, we suffered in Philippi. People there insulted us, as you know, and many people were against us. But our God helped us to be brave and to tell you his Good News.

you his Good News. **3**Our appeal does not
come from lies or wrong reasons, nor
were we trying to trick you. **4**But we
speak the Good News because God tested
us and trusted us to do it. When we
speak, we are not trying to please people,
but God, who tests our hearts. **5**You
know that we never tried to influence
you by saying nice things about you. We
were not trying to get your money; we
had no selfishness to hide from you. God
knows that this is true. **6**We were not
looking for human praise, from you or
anyone else, **7**even though as apostles of
Christ we could have used our authority
over you.

But we were very gentle with you,
like a mother caring for her little children. **8**Because we loved you, we were
happy to share not only God's Good
News with you, but even our own lives.
You had become so dear to us! **9**Brothers
and sisters, I know you remember our
hard work and difficulties. We worked
night and day so we would not burden any
of you while we preached God's Good
News to you.

10When we were with you, we lived
in a holy and honest way, without fault.
You know this is true, and so does God.
11You know that we treated each of you
as a father treats his own children. **12**We
encouraged you, we urged you, and we
insisted that you live good lives for God,
who calls you to his glorious kingdom.

13Also, we always thank God because
when you heard his message from us,
you accepted it as the word of
God, not the words
of humans. And it
really is God's mes-
sage which works in
you who believe.
14Brothers and sis-
ters, your experiences have been like
those of God's churches in Christ that are
in Judea.[n] You suffered from the people of
your own country, as they suffered from
the Jews, **15**who killed both the Lord
Jesus and the prophets and forced us to
leave that country. They do not please
God and are against all people. **16**They
try to stop us from teaching those who
are not Jews so they may be saved. By
doing this, they are increasing their sins
to the limit. The anger of God has come
to them at last.

EMAIL FROM GOD **2:13**
Belief
How is God able to work through you?

Paul Wants to Visit Them Again

17Brothers and sisters, though we
were separated from you for a short time,
our thoughts were still with you. We
wanted very much to see you and tried
hard to do so. **18**We wanted to come to
you. I, Paul, tried to come more than
once, but Satan stopped us. **19**You are our

2:14 Judea The Jewish land where Jesus lived and taught and where the church first began.

LET'S VISIT THESSALONICA

1 Thessalonians 3

Thessalonica was founded by the Macedonian king Cassander in 315 B.C. He named the city after his wife. (She was the sister of the Greek military conqueror, Alexander the Great.) The apostle Paul worked for several months in Thessalonica and later wrote two letters, which we now call 1 and 2 Thessalonians, to the church there. Paul visited Thessalonica during his second missionary journey through Macedonia. (Check out Acts 17:1–9, p. 1495.) He loved the Thessalonian church. (See 1 Thessalonians 2:1–12.)

An important road in Thessalonica was called the Egnatian Way. It was a Roman military highway. Today Thessalonica is called Salonika. The Egnatian Way is still one of the main roads.

hope, our joy, and the crown we will take pride in when our Lord Jesus Christ
comes. 20Truly you are our glory and our joy.

3 When we could not wait any longer, we decided it was best to stay in Athens alone
2and send Timothy to you. Timothy, our brother, works with us for God and helps us tell people the Good News about Christ. We sent him to strengthen and encourage you in your
faith 3so none of you would be upset by these troubles. You yourselves know that we must face these troubles.
4Even when we were with you, we told you we all would have to suffer, and you know it
has happened. 5Because of this, when I could wait no longer, I sent Timothy to you so I could learn about your faith. I was afraid the devil had tempted you, and then our hard work would have been wasted.

6But Timothy now has come back to us from you and has brought us good news about your faith and love. He told us that you always remember us in a good way and that you want to see us just
as much as we want to see you. 7So, brothers and sisters, while we have much trouble and suffering, we are encouraged
about you because of your faith. 8Our life is really full if you stand strong in the
Lord. 9We have so much joy before our God because of you. We cannot thank him enough for all the joy we feel.
10Night and day we continue praying with all our heart that we can see you again and give you all the things you need to make your faith strong.

11Now may our God and Father himself and our Lord Jesus prepare the way
for us to come to you. 12May the Lord make your love grow more and multiply for each other and for all people so that you will love others as we love you.
13May your hearts be made strong so that you will be holy and without fault before our God and Father when our Lord Jesus comes with all his holy ones.

A Life that Pleases God

4 Brothers and sisters, we taught you how to live in a way that will please God, and you are living that way. Now we ask and encourage you in the Lord Jesus
to live that way even more. 2You know what we told you to do by the authority of
the Lord Jesus. 3God wants you to be holy and to stay away from sexual sins.

FAITH links

FULL OF FAITH

1 THESSALONIANS 4:1

Who is your favorite teacher? Many people have said that their most favorite teacher happened to be the one who was the hardest. Why? Because that teacher knew what her student could do. She wanted the best for that student and made sure he lived up to his potential.

Paul had taught the Christians in Thessalonica about God and how to please him. He knew that they were capable of doing great things for God. He wanted them to live up to that potential. That's what the people at your church want for you. Your pastor or your Sunday school teacher wants you to grow in faith and reach your full faith potential.

Help for the Poor, Leviticus 5:7, p. 138

Plans for a Son, 1 Chronicles 22:5–19, p. 548

How Big Is God?, Job 38—41, p. 703

What's in a Name?, Isaiah 9:6, p. 908

Help for a Friend, Mark 2:1–5, p. 1332

You're Correct!, Hebrews 12:5–7, p. 1683

4He wants each of you to learn to control
your own body[n] in a way that is holy and
honorable. 5Don't use your body for sexual sin like the people who do not know
God. 6Also, do not wrong or cheat another Christian in this way. The Lord will
punish people who do those things as we
have already told you and warned you.
7God called us to be holy and does not
want us to live in sin. 8So the person who
refuses to obey this teaching is disobeying God, not simply a human teaching.
And God is the One who gives us his
Holy Spirit.

9We do not need to write you about
having love for your Christian family, because God has already taught you to love
each other. 10And truly you do love the
Christians in all of Macedonia. Brothers
and sisters, now we encourage you to
love them even more.

11Do all you can to live a peaceful life.
Take care of your own business,
and do your own
work as we have al-
ready told you. 12If
you do, then people
who are not believ-
ers will respect you,
and you will not have to depend on others
for what you need.

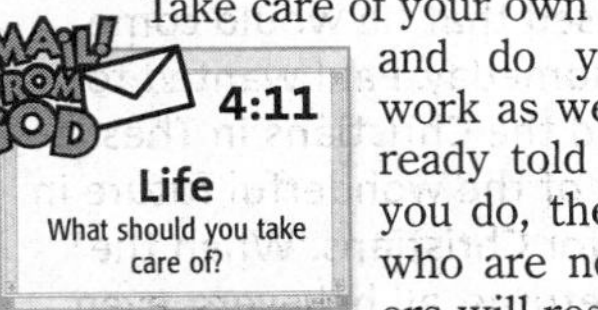

eMAIL FROM GOD
4:11
Life
What should you take care of?

The Lord's Coming

13Brothers and sisters, we want you
to know about those Christians who have
died so you will not be sad, as others who
have no hope. 14We believe that Jesus
died and that he rose again. So, because
of him, God will raise with Jesus those
who have died. 15What we tell you now is
the Lord's own message. We who are living when the Lord comes again will not
go before those who have already died.
16The Lord himself will come down from
heaven with a loud command, with the
voice of the archangel,[n] and with the
trumpet call of God. And those who have
died believing in Christ will rise first.
17After that, we who are still alive will be
gathered up with them in the clouds to
meet the Lord in the air. And we will be

4:4 learn . . . body This might also mean "learn to live with your own wife."

4:16 archangel The leader among God's angels or messengers.

with the Lord for-
ever. 18So encour-
age each other with
these words.

EMAIL FROM GOD
4:13–18
Pain
Check out how to treat each other in times of pain.

Be Ready for the Lord's Coming

5 Now, brothers and sisters, we do not
need to write you about times and
dates. 2You know very well that the day
the Lord comes again will be a surprise,
like a thief that comes in the night.
3While people are saying, "We have
peace and we are safe," they will be destroyed quickly. It is like pains that come
quickly to a woman having a baby. Those
people will not escape. 4But you, brothers and sisters, are not living in darkness, and so that day will not surprise
you like a thief. 5You are all people who
belong to the light and to the day. We do
not belong to the night or to darkness.
6So we should not be like other people
who are sleeping, but we should be alert
and have self-control. 7Those who sleep,
sleep at night. Those who get drunk, get
drunk at night. 8But we belong to the day,
so we should control ourselves. We
should wear faith and love to protect us,
and the hope of salvation should be our
helmet. 9God did not choose us to suffer
his anger but to have salvation through
our Lord Jesus Christ. 10Jesus died for
us so that we can live together with him,
whether we are alive or dead when he
comes. 11So encourage each other and
give each other strength, just as you are
doing now.

Final Instructions and Greetings

12Now, brothers and sisters, we ask
you to appreciate those who work hard
among you, who lead you in the
Lord and teach you.
13Respect them with
a very special love
because of the work
they do.
Live in peace with
each other. 14We ask you, brothers and
sisters, to warn those who do not work.
Encourage the people who are afraid.
Help those who are weak. Be patient

EMAIL FROM GOD
5:12–14
Laziness
Who should you encourage to work?

FAITH links

THE COMING ATTRACTION

1 THESSALONIANS 4:13-18

You've seen movie trailers, right? They're those mini-movies that are shown right before the main feature. They pump up your excitement about a movie that "is coming to a theater near you soon!" This passage is like a "trailer" for Jesus' return to earth. Before he left, Jesus promised that he would come back someday. Paul wanted to remind the Christians in Thessalonica of the wonderful future in store for Christians. When the Lord returns, all believers, even those who have died, will be with Jesus. That was encouraging news then and now.

Download these Faithlinks on your wonderful future:

His Valentine, Jeremiah 31:3, p. 1035

God's New Temple, Ezekiel 40—44, p. 1135

A Hopeful Name, Hosea 1:3–11, p. 1172

A Word About Worry, Matthew 6:25–34, p. 1284

Fully God, Fully Human, John 11:35, p. 1444

Hope That Doesn't Fail, Acts 26:4–7, p. 1510

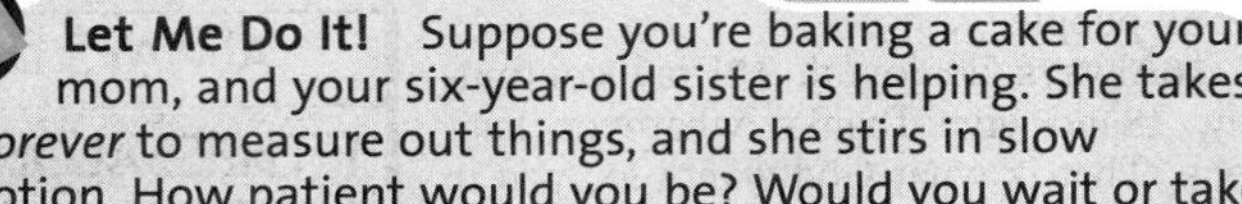

Patience

1 Thessalonians 5

Livin' it

Let Me Do It! Suppose you're baking a cake for your mom, and your six-year-old sister is helping. She takes *forever* to measure out things, and she stirs in slow motion. How patient would you be? Would you wait or take over? What things or people make you the most impatient? When are you the most patient?

Fortunately for us, God is very patient. Even when we make the same mistakes over and over, God patiently loves us and forgives us. He wants us to be patient, too. Sometimes that means waiting a long, long time. (Look at Luke 2:25–28, 36–37, p. 1369.) How do you feel about waiting for something? Does it drive you nuts? Waiting helps to develop patience within you—and that doesn't just happen overnight.

MORE FAITH links

"Boy, Tagg, you sure are jumpy today. You're all over the computer screen. What's up?"

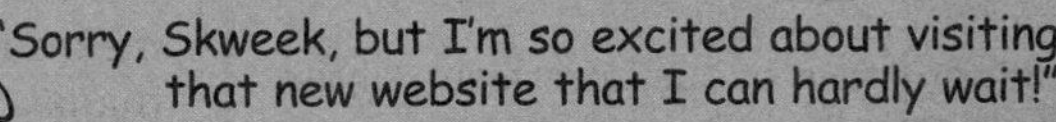

"Sorry, Skweek, but I'm so excited about visiting that new website that I can hardly wait!"

"Sounds like you could use a bit of patience. Surf over to these Faithlinks while you're waiting! It may just help."

A Long Wait, Joshua 14:6–15, p. 294
- How do you feel when you have to wait 40 minutes for something? How about 40 days? Or 40 weeks? Now imagine having to wait 40 years to get something you were promised? Would you wait or give up? Link here to find out that God always keeps his promises—even though you may have to wait.

Hurry Up and Wait, 2 Samuel 5, p. 405
- How would you rate yourself on the patience scale (1=not at all patient; 10= very patient)? One way to become more patient is to not try to predict when something is going to happen. How can trusting in God's timing help you?

A Happy Ending, Revelation 22:16–21, p. 1754
- Do you like stories with happy endings? Want to know a real-life story that has a guaranteed happy ending? It's your story if you trust Jesus as your Savior. Christians patiently wait for the day when their life story will have a happy ending as they live with Jesus in heaven. Do you look forward to Jesus' return?

my FAVORITE links

with everyone. 15Be sure that no one
pays back wrong for wrong, but always
try to do what is good for each other and
for all people.
16Always be joyful. 17Pray continually, 18and give thanks whatever happens. That is what God wants for you in
Christ Jesus.
19Do not hold back the work of the
Holy Spirit. 20Do not treat prophecy as if
it were unimportant. 21But test everything. Keep what is good, 22and stay
away from everything that is evil.
23Now may God himself, the God of
peace, make you pure, belonging only to
him. May your whole self—spirit, soul,
and body—be kept safe and without fault
when our Lord Jesus Christ comes.
24You can trust the One who calls you to
do that for you.
25Brothers and sisters, pray for us.
26Give each other a holy kiss when
you meet. 27I tell you by the authority of
the Lord to read this letter to all the believers.
28The grace of our Lord Jesus Christ
be with you.

FAITH links

ALWAYS DO THIS!

1 THESSALONIANS 5:16-18

What are some things you always do, besides breathing? Do you laugh a lot? Sing? Complain? Blow milk out of your nose? Some actions probably depend on what's happening in your life. If you're feeling sick, you may not feel like laughing.

Paul gave the Christians in Thessalonica three activities to always do: be joyful, pray, give thanks. That's good advice for us, too. Does this mean you have to be joyful or thank God if someone steals your bike? No. It means having an attitude of thanks. It means being joyful that God is with you always. That's something to always be thankful for!

Check out all you have to be thankful for:

A Thanksgiving Reminder, Exodus 12, p. 91

A Life of Thanksgiving, 1 Kings 1:47–48, p. 435

A Wise Wish, 1 Kings 3:5–9, p. 439

Love That Will Last, Psalm 136, p. 813

Our Gift to God, Romans 12:1–2, p. 1536

A Different Kind of Fruit, Galatians 5:22–23, p. 1592

2 Thessalonians

JESUS' RETURN—PART TWO

It's Paul here. This is my second letter to my friends at Thessalonica (a city that's located in what we now call Europe), written about six months after the first letter. I loved the church at Thessalonica. I started this church as part of my desire to tell everyone about who I used to be—a Jewish religious leader who hated Christians. (To find out how the church got started, surf over to 1 Thessalonians, p. 1628.) After Jesus had changed my life, I wanted everyone to know that he could do the same for them.

My pals in Thessalonica were *still* having trouble understanding when Jesus would return. In my first letter to them (check it out if you haven't read it yet), I tried to help them understand that Jesus had *not* returned yet ('cause they were being told that he *had* returned). Well, now they were believing that Jesus would return soon, and they didn't have to do anything . . . just sit around and wait! Imagine, believers in the city weren't going to work or anything. Not a cool scene! So, I wrote this letter to help them understand (again) when Jesus would return.

JESUS WATCH

Seeing Jesus in this letter is a lot like seeing Jesus in Paul's first letter to the Thessalonians. Jesus' return is portrayed as something that believers can trust in and look forward to. But Paul also helps his readers understand the other side of Jesus' return. Those who haven't received Jesus as savior have an entirely different event awaiting them. People who don't know Jesus can expect terrifying things to happen to them. (Check out 2 Thessalonians 1:6–10 and 2:8–12 for the details on this.)

Jesus is presented as someone believers can trust. Unbelievers must surrender to him or prepare for an unpleasant awakening at his return. But Paul's aim isn't to strike depression in the lives of unbelievers. He does all of this, hoping that those who haven't trusted Jesus yet will give their lives to him.

"Hey, Tagg! Guess what Paul said to do about people who refused to listen to him?"

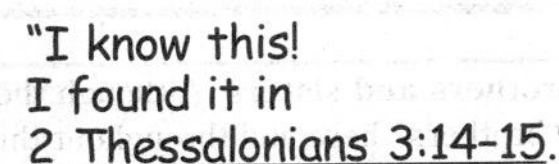

"I know this! I found it in 2 Thessalonians 3:14-15."

FAITH links

- Ten Things I Like About You, 2 Thessalonians 1:3–4
- Hold On!, 2 Thessalonians 2:15–17
- Another Lazy Day?, 2 Thessalonians 3:6–13

1 From Paul, Silas, and Timothy.
To the church in Thessalonica in God
our Father and the Lord Jesus Christ:
2Grace and peace to you from God the
Father and the Lord Jesus Christ.

Paul Talks About God's Judgment

3We must always thank God for you,
brothers and sisters.[n] This is only right,
because your faith is growing more and
more, and the love that every one of you
has for each other is increasing. 4So we
brag about you to the other churches of
God. We tell them about the way you continue to be strong and have faith even
though you are being treated badly and
are suffering many troubles.
5This is proof that God is right in his
judgment. He wants you to be counted
worthy of his kingdom for which you are
suffering. 6God will do what is right. He
will give trouble to those who trouble
you. 7And he will give rest to you who
are troubled and to us also when the Lord
Jesus appears with burning fire from
heaven with his powerful angels. 8Then
he will punish those who do not know
God and who do not obey the Good News
about our Lord Jesus Christ. 9Those people will be punished with a destruction
that continues forever. They will be kept
away from the Lord and from his great
power. 10This will happen on the day
when the Lord Jesus comes to receive
glory because of his holy people. And all
the people who have believed will be
amazed at Jesus. You will be in that group,
because you believed what we told you.
11That is why we always pray for you,
asking our God to help you live the kind
of life he called you to live. We pray that
with his power God will help you do the
good things you want and perform the
works that come from your faith. 12We
pray all this so that the name of our Lord
Jesus Christ will have glory in you, and
you will have glory in him. That glory
comes from the grace of our God and the
Lord Jesus Christ.

Evil Things Will Happen

2 Brothers and sisters, we have something to say about the coming of our

FAITH links

TEN THINGS I LIKE ABOUT YOU

2 THESSALONIANS 1:3-4

Have you ever bragged to someone else about what a friend could do? Maybe you were happy when a friend learned to ski or made an A on a test. That's news worth sharing.

Paul was thankful for the way God helped the Christians in Thessalonica. He was proud of how their faith had grown. He told Christians in other cities about the Thessalonian Christians. How has God helped someone you know? How will you let that person know that you're proud of him or her?

Here are some more Faithlinks on learning to be thankful:

Time to Celebrate, Exodus 15:1–21, p. 95

A Holiday Every Week, Leviticus 23:1–3, p. 166

Uniquely You, Psalm 139:13–14, p. 815

Think About Him, Isaiah 26:3, p. 926

Perfectly Pleasing?, Matthew 5:1–12, p. 1280

The Power of *If*, Mark 9:14–24, p. 1344

1:3 brothers and sisters Although the Greek text says "brothers" here and throughout this book, Paul's words were meant for the entire church, including men and women.

Lord Jesus Christ and the time when we
will meet together with him. 2Do not become easily upset in your thinking or
afraid if you hear that the day of the Lord
has already come. Someone may say this
in a prophecy or in a message or in a letter as if it came from us. 3Do not let anyone fool you in any way. That day of the
Lord will not come until the turning
away[n] from God happens and the Man of
Evil, who is on his way to hell, appears.
4He will be against and put himself above
anything called God or anything that people worship. And that Man of Evil will
even go into God's Temple and sit there
and say that he is God.
5I told you when I was with you that
all this would happen. Do you not remember? 6And now you know what is
stopping that Man of Evil so he will appear at the right time. 7The secret power
of evil is already working in the world,
but there is one who is stopping that
power. And he will continue to stop it until he is taken out of the way. 8Then that
Man of Evil will appear, and the Lord
Jesus will kill him with the breath that
comes from his mouth and will destroy
him with the glory of his coming. 9The
Man of Evil will come by the power of
Satan. He will have great power, and he
will do many different false miracles,
signs, and wonders. 10He will use every
kind of evil to trick those who are lost.
They will die, because they refused to
love the truth. (If they loved the truth,
they would be saved.) 11For this reason
God sends them something powerful that
leads them away from the truth so they
will believe a lie. 12So all those will be
judged guilty who did not believe the
truth, but enjoyed doing evil.

You Are Chosen for Salvation

13Brothers and sisters, whom the
Lord loves, God chose you from the beginning to be saved. So we must always
thank God for you. You are saved by the
Spirit that makes you holy and by your
faith in the truth. 14God used the Good
News that we preached to call you to be
saved so you can share in the glory of our
Lord Jesus Christ. 15So, brothers and
sisters, stand strong and continue to believe the teachings we gave you in our
speaking and in our letter.

FAITH links

HOLD ON!

2 THESSALONIANS 2:15-17

What information do you find yourself holding on to? Maybe a commercial jingle is going around in your head right now. Or maybe you know exactly how many nose hairs a rhinoceros has, if any.

Paul wrote two letters to the Christians in Thessalonica. In this second letter, he told them to hold on to what they had been taught about Jesus. That information was worth holding on to.

What have you been taught about God? Listening to your pastor, thinking about Scriptures, and praying are three ways to help you to hold on to what you know about God.

Alone and Forgotten?, Genesis 40:23, p. 57

Good Times and Bad, 1 Kings 17, p. 462

What God "Hates," Proverbs 6:16–19, p. 835

A Bad Reaction, Jeremiah 36, p. 1043

Faith Workout, Acts 16:4–5, p. 1493

One Thing to Do, Romans 4:1–5, p. 1523

2:3 turning away Or "the rebellion."

16-17May our Lord Jesus Christ himself and God our Father encourage you and strengthen you in every good thing you do and say. God loved us, and through his grace he gave us a good hope and encouragement that continues forever.

Pray for Us

3And now, brothers and sisters, pray for us that the Lord's teaching will continue to spread quickly and that people will give honor to that teaching, just as happened with you.
2And pray that we will be protected from stubborn and evil people, because not all people believe.
3But the Lord is faithful and will give you strength and will protect you from the Evil One.
4The Lord makes us feel sure that you are doing and will continue to do the things we told you.
5May the Lord lead your hearts into God's love and Christ's patience.

The Duty to Work

6Brothers and sisters, by the authority of our Lord Jesus Christ we command you to stay away from any believer who refuses to work and does not follow the teaching we gave you.
7You yourselves know that you should live as we live. We were not lazy when we were with you.
8And when we ate another person's food, we always paid for it. We worked very hard night and day so we would not be an expense to any of you.
9We had the right to ask you to help us, but we worked to take care of ourselves so we would be an example for you to follow.
10When we were with you, we gave you this rule: "Anyone who refuses to work should not eat."
11We hear that some people in your group refuse to work. They do nothing but busy themselves in other people's lives.
12We command those people and beg them in the Lord Jesus Christ to work quietly and earn their own food.
13But you, brothers and sisters, never become tired of doing good.
14If some people do not obey what we tell you in this letter, then take note of them. Have nothing to do with them so they will feel ashamed.
15But do not treat them as enemies. Warn them as fellow believers.

FAITH links

ANOTHER LAZY DAY?

2 THESSALONIANS 3:6-13

Ever wish there were no chores for you to do or homework or . . . anything else for that matter? If so, you're not the only one to wish that. Some of the Christians in Thessalonica didn't want to work. But Paul had a warning for them. Those who didn't work shouldn't eat. He didn't want the Christians to be lazy.

God wants us to be willing to work hard. When we spend a lot of time doing nothing, that can lead us to do the wrong thing. Some people begin to gossip about others or cause trouble in other ways. Keeping busy helps us to keep out of trouble.

Don't like to work too hard? Think again and download these links:

A Use for Your Abilities, Genesis 41, p. 59

Fearful Service?, Exodus 4:1–17, p. 80

Your Response to Responsibility, Ruth 2:1–7, p. 346

Meaningless Words, Job 21:34, p. 684

Exercising Patience, Luke 2:25–28, 36–37, p. 1369

Trouble with the Tongue, James 3:3–12, p. 1692

Final Words

16Now may the Lord of peace give
you peace at all times and in every way.
The Lord be with all of you.
17I, Paul, end this letter now in my
own handwriting. All my letters have this
to show they are from me. This is the
way I write.
18The grace of our Lord Jesus Christ
be with you all.

1 & 2 Timothy

GOOD ADVICE

It's Paul again. I hope you remember who I am! On top of all that happened to me (like persecuting believers, being persecuted when Jesus changed my life, and traveling all over to train believers), I also had a select group of people that I spent extra time with to help them with the ministry that God had given them. These are really my last letters to Timothy. I wrote this letter while in prison in Rome, awaiting execution for my faith.

Timothy was a young pastor who was a good friend. I loved him like a son. A while back, I spent a lot of time with Timothy. I wrote this letter as sort of a review guide—to remind him of the things I taught him. But that's not all. Timothy was also dealing with a lot of false teachings. So I wanted to give him advice about how to deal with that. I also wanted to advise him on how he ought to live his life—pastors should be role models for their congregations! Both 1 and 2 Timothy are about how church leaders should act and what it takes to be a leader in the church. I hope you learn as much from these letters as Timothy did!

JESUS WATCH

Jesus is presented in both 1 and 2 Timothy as someone who stands in the gap between humans and God, to help make us right before our holy Father. In 1 Timothy, Jesus is presented as the "one way humans can reach God" (1 Timothy 2:5) and the source of our spiritual strength, faith, and love (1 Timothy 1:12–14). Paul also helps us understand that Jesus came to give himself as a "payment to free all people" (1 Timothy 2:6). Paul wants us to know that Jesus came for us. And when he did, whatever barrier existed between us and God was torn down.

In 2 Timothy, Paul gives us snapshots of Jesus' ability to conquer death and offer eternal life to everyone who believes in Jesus. For example, Paul says that Jesus offers us a salvation that comes with a glory that doesn't end (2 Timothy 2:10). Those who believe in Jesus will also get a crown for waiting "with love for him to come again" (2 Timothy 4:8).

my FAVORITE links

OTHER CONNECTIONS

Livin' it

If things don't go your way, what do you usually do? Throw a fit? Walk away? Go up to your room and slam the door shut? Take a few tips from the Bible on learning how to increase your self-control by logging on to In Control, 2 Timothy 1:7.

GET THE INFO

- Powerful Women of Faith, 2 Timothy 4. Connect here to discover where you can find some of the most powerful women in the New Testament—women like Jesus' mother Mary, Elizabeth, Priscilla, and others.

MORE STUFF...

Good Workers It takes a lot of work and self-control to be a faithful follower of Jesus. Paul uses several examples in telling us how to "keep the faith." Check it out:

- Be a good servant and use our faith. (1 Timothy 4:6–10)
- Be a good soldier who wants to please Jesus. (2 Timothy 2:3–4)
- Be an athlete who trains hard and follows all the rules. (2 Timothy 2:5)

"Hey, Skweek? I heard that Paul explains in one of his letters to Timothy how to get rich quick!"

"Not exactly, Tagg. Check out 1 Timothy 6:6–10 to see what Paul is really talking about."

MORE ON THE TIMOTHY SURFWATCH:

The secret to worship, 1 Timothy 2; 3
The good fight, 1 Timothy 6:12–16
A loyal soldier, 2 Timothy 2:1–13
Key to wisdom, 2 Timothy 3:14–17

FAITH links

- The Leaders in Your Life, 1 Timothy 2:1–4
- Your Faith Example, 1 Timothy 4:12
- More Money?, 1 Timothy 6:10
- Your Faith Story, 2 Timothy 1:5
- Fear-Fighters, 2 Timothy 1:7
- A Soldier's Story, 2 Timothy 2:3
- Winning a Friend, 2 Timothy 2:23–24
- Life's Rule Book, 2 Timothy 3:15–17

1 From Paul, an apostle of Christ Jesus, by the command of God our Savior and Christ Jesus our hope.

2To Timothy, a true child to me because you believe:

Grace, mercy, and peace from God the Father and Christ Jesus our Lord.

Warning Against False Teaching

3I asked you to stay longer in Ephesus when I went into Macedonia so you could command some people there to stop teaching false things. 4Tell them not to spend their time on stories that are not true and on long lists of names in family histories. These things only bring arguments; they do not help God's work, which is done in faith. 5The purpose of this command is for people to have love, a love that comes from a pure heart and a good conscience and a true faith. 6Some people have missed these things and turned to useless talk. 7They want to be teachers of the law, but they do not understand either what they are talking about or what they are sure about.

8But we know that the law is good if someone uses it lawfully. 9We also know that the law is not made for good people but for those who are against the law and for those who refuse to follow it. It is for people who are against God and are sinful, who are not holy and have no religion, who kill their fathers and mothers, who murder, 10who take part in sexual sins, who have sexual relations with people of the same sex, who sell slaves, who tell lies, who speak falsely, and who do anything against the true teaching of God. 11That teaching is part of the Good News of the blessed God that he gave me to tell.

Thanks for God's Mercy

12I thank Christ Jesus our Lord, who gave me strength, because he trusted me and gave me this work of serving him. 13In the past I spoke against Christ and persecuted him and did all kinds of things to hurt him. But God showed me mercy, because I did not know what I was doing. I did not believe. 14But the grace of our Lord was fully given to me, and with that grace came the faith and love that are in Christ Jesus.

15What I say is true, and you should fully accept it: Christ Jesus came into the world to save sinners, of whom I am the worst. 16But I was given mercy so that in me, the worst of all sinners, Christ Jesus could show that he has patience without limit. His patience with me made me an example for those who would believe in him and have life forever. 17To the King that rules forever, who will never die, who cannot be seen, the only God, be honor and glory forever and ever. Amen.

18Timothy, my child, I am giving you a command that agrees with the prophecies that were given about you in the past. I tell you this so you can follow them and fight the good fight. 19Continue to have faith and do what you know is right. Some people have rejected this, and their faith has been shipwrecked. 20Hymenaeus and Alexander have done that, and I have given them to Satan so they will learn not to speak against God.

eMAIL! FROM GOD
1:18–19
Following God
How can you live a godly life?

Some Rules for Men and Women

2 First, I tell you to pray for all people, asking God for what they need and being thankful to him. 2Pray for rulers and for all who have authority so that we can have quiet and peaceful lives full of worship and respect for God. 3This is good, and it pleases God our Savior, 4who wants all people to be saved and to know the truth. 5There is one God and one way human beings can reach God. That way is through Christ Jesus, who is himself human. 6He gave himself as a payment to free all people. He is proof that came at the right time. 7That is why I was chosen to tell the Good News and to be an apostle. (I am telling the truth; I am not lying.) I was chosen to teach those who are not Jews to believe and to know the truth.

FAITH links

THE LEADERS IN YOUR LIFE

1 TIMOTHY 2:1-4

Who are the leaders in your life? These may include teachers, police officers, the principal of your school, the mayor of your town, and the governor of your state. When Paul wrote a letter to Timothy, a young pastor, he told Timothy to pray for the people in authority. God wants us to pray for our leaders. If we do, God tells us that we will have a "quiet and peaceful" life. What could you pray for? You can pray that these leaders will make wise and fair decisions. You can also ask God to protect each leader from harm.

Check out these Faithlinks on how to show respect to others:

Fatherly Advice, Exodus 18, p. 99

Big Lack Attack, 2 Kings 4:1–7, p. 480

Prayer + Action = Success, Nehemiah 2:4–9, p. 626

Like Silver, Psalm 12:6–8, p. 717

Our Heavenly Connection, Matthew 6:9–13, p. 1283

I'll Be the Judge!, 1 Corinthians 4:4–5, p. 1549

8So, I want the men everywhere to
pray, lifting up their hands in a holy manner, without anger and arguments.
9Also, women should wear proper
clothes that show respect and self-control, not using braided hair or gold or
pearls or expensive clothes. 10Instead,
they should do good deeds, which is right for women who say they worship God.
11Let a woman learn by listening quietly and being ready to cooperate in
everything. 12But I do not allow a woman
to teach or to have authority over a man, but to listen quietly, 13because Adam was
formed first and then Eve. 14And Adam
was not tricked, but the woman was
tricked and became a sinner. 15But she
will be saved through having children if they continue in faith, love, and holiness, with self-control.

Elders in the Church

3 What I say is true: Anyone wanting to become an elder desires a good work.
2An elder must not give people a reason
to criticize him, and he must have only one wife. He must be self-controlled, wise, respected by others, ready to welcome guests, and able to teach. 3He must
not drink too much wine or like to fight, but rather be gentle and peaceable, not
loving money. 4He must be a good family
leader, having children who cooperate with full respect. 5(If someone does not
know how to lead the family, how can that person take care of God's church?) 6But
an elder must not be a new believer, or he might be too proud of himself and be judged guilty just as the devil was. 7An
elder must also have the respect of people who are not in the church so he will not be criticized by others and caught in the devil's trap.

Deacons in the Church

8In the same way, deacons must be
respected by others, not saying things they do not mean. They must not drink too much wine or try to get rich by cheating others. 9With a clear conscience they
must follow the secret of the faith that God made known to us. 10Test them
first. Then let them serve as deacons if

you find nothing wrong in them. 11In the
same way, women* must be respected by
others. They must not speak evil of others. They must be self-controlled and
trustworthy in everything. 12Deacons
must have only one wife and be good
leaders of their children and their own
families. 13Those who serve well as deacons are making an honorable place for
themselves, and they will be very bold in
their faith in Christ Jesus.

The Secret of Our Life

14Although I hope I can come to
you soon, I am writing these things to you
now. 15Then, even if I am delayed, you
will know how to live in the family of God.
That family is the church of the
living God, the sup-
port and foundation
of the truth. 16With-
out doubt, the secret
of our life of worship
is great:

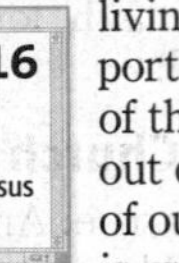

eMAIL! FROM GOD 3:16
Jesus
Why you worship Jesus

He was shown to us in a human body,
proved right in spirit,
and seen by angels.
He was preached to those who are
not Jews,
believed in by the world,
and taken up in glory.

A Warning About False Teachers

4 Now the Holy Spirit clearly says that
in the later times some people will
stop believing the faith. They will follow
spirits that lie and teachings of demons. 2Such teach-
ings come from the
false words of liars
whose consciences
are destroyed as if
by a hot iron. 3They
forbid people to
marry and tell them not to eat certain
foods which God created to be eaten with
thanks by people who believe and know
the truth. 4Everything God made is good,
and nothing should be refused if it is ac-

4:1
Satan
Who are on Satan's team?

3:11 **women** This might mean the wives of the deacons, or it might mean women who serve in the same way as deacons.

FAITH links

YOUR FAITH EXAMPLE

1 TIMOTHY 4:12

In Paul's letter to his friend Timothy, Paul gave Timothy some good advice. Timothy was the pastor of a church. Paul told Timothy not to let others put him down because he was young. He also reminded Timothy that he could set an example for the people in his church family.

Did you ever think that you could be an example for others? You can! The same God who helped Timothy will help you, too. You can start by getting involved at church. Ask your parents, pastor, or Sunday school teacher what you can do to help out. You are never too young to serve God!

Download these Faithlinks to find out how you can be a good example:

Share What You Have, Exodus 35:5–18, p. 123

The Heart of the Matter, 1 Samuel 16, p. 375

Learning from Mistakes, Psalm 51:12–13, p. 748

Your Spiritual Roots, Zechariah 1:1–6, p. 1253

Exercising Patience, Luke 2:25–28, 36–37, p. 1369

Your Faith Story, 2 Timothy 1:5, p. 1650

cepted with thanks, 5because it is made
holy by what God has said and by prayer.

Be a Good Servant of Christ

6By telling these things to the brothers and sisters,[n] you will be a good servant of Christ Jesus. You will be made strong by the words of the faith and the good teaching which you have been following. 7But do not follow foolish stories that disagree with God's truth, but train yourself to serve God. 8Training your body helps you in some ways, but serving God helps you in every way by bringing you blessings in this life and in the future life, too. 9What I say is true, and you should fully accept it. 10This is why we work and struggle: We hope in the living God who is the Savior of all people, especially of those who believe.

11Command and teach these things. 12Do not let anyone treat you as if you are unimportant because you are young. Instead, be an example to the believers with your words, your actions, your love, your faith, and your pure life. 13Until I come, continue to read the Scriptures to the people, strengthen them, and teach them. 14Use the gift you have, which was given to you through prophecy when the group of elders laid their hands on[n] you. 15Continue to do those things; give your life to doing them so your progress may be seen by everyone. 16Be careful in your life and in your teaching. If you continue to live and teach rightly, you will save both yourself and those who listen to you.

Rules for Living with Others

5 Do not speak angrily to an older man, but plead with him as if he were your father. Treat younger men like brothers, 2older women like mothers, and younger women like sisters. Always treat them in a pure way.

3Take care of widows who are truly widows. 4But if a widow has children or grandchildren, let them first learn to do their duty to their own family and to repay their parents or grandparents. That pleases God. 5The true widow, who is all alone, puts her hope in God and continues to pray night and day for God's help. 6But the widow who uses her life to please herself is really dead while she is alive. 7Tell the believers to do these things so that no one can criticize them. 8Whoever does not care for his own relatives, especially his own family members, has turned against the faith and is

FAITH CHALLENGE

Hey there! Read 5:4 to learn what God expects from children. How do you typically react when your parents ask you to do things around the house? What can you do about your attitude at home?

TESTING IT

1 Timothy 5:4
But if a widow has children or grandchildren, let them first learn to do their duty to their own family and to repay their parents or grandparents. That pleases God.

4:6 brothers and sisters Although the Greek text says "brothers" here and throughout this book, Paul's words refer to the entire church, including men and women.

4:14 laid their hands on The laying on of hands had many purposes, including the giving of a blessing, power, or authority.

worse than someone who does not believe in God.

9To be on the list of widows, a woman must be at least sixty years old. She must have been faithful to her husband. **10**She must be known for her good works—works such as raising her children, welcoming strangers, washing the feet of God's people, helping those in trouble, and giving her life to do all kinds of good deeds.

11But do not put younger widows on that list. After they give themselves to Christ, they are pulled away from him by their physical needs, and then they want to marry again. **12**They will be judged for not doing what they first promised to do. **13**Besides that, they learn to waste their time, going from house to house. And they not only waste their time but also begin to gossip and busy themselves with other people's lives, saying things they should not say. **14**So I want the younger widows to marry, have children, and manage their homes. Then no enemy will have any reason to criticize them. **15**But some have already turned away to follow Satan.

16If any woman who is a believer has widows in her family, she should care for them herself. The church should not have to care for them. Then it will be able to take care of those who are truly widows.

17The elders who lead the church well should receive double honor, especially those who work hard by speaking and teaching, **18**because the Scripture says: "When an ox is working in the grain, do not cover its mouth to keep it from eating,"[n] and "A worker should be given his pay."[n]

19Do not listen to someone who accuses an elder, without two or three witnesses. **20**Tell those who continue sinning that they are wrong. Do this in front of the whole church so that the others will have a warning.

21Before God and Christ Jesus and the chosen angels, I command you to do these things without showing favor of any kind to anyone.

22Think carefully before you lay your hands on[n] anyone, and don't share in the sins of others. Keep yourself pure.

23Stop drinking only water, but drink a little wine to help your stomach and your frequent sicknesses.

24The sins of some people are easy to see even before they are judged, but the sins of others are seen only later. **25**So also good deeds are easy to see, but even those that are not easily seen cannot stay hidden.

6 All who are slaves under a yoke should show full respect to their masters so no one will speak against God's name and our teaching. **2**The slaves whose masters are believers should not show their masters any less respect because they are believers. They should serve their masters even better, because they are helping believers they love.

You must teach and preach these things.

False Teaching and True Riches

3Anyone who has a different teaching does not agree with the true teaching of our Lord Jesus Christ and the teaching that shows the true way to serve God. **4**This person is full of pride and understands nothing, but is sick with a love for arguing and fighting about words. This brings jealousy, fighting, speaking against others, evil mistrust, **5**and constant quarrels from those who have evil minds and have lost the truth. They think that serving God is a way to get rich.

6Serving God does make us very rich, if we are satisfied with what we have. **7**We brought nothing into the world, so we can take nothing out. **8**But, if we have food and clothes, we will be satisfied with that. **9**Those who want to become rich bring temptation to themselves and are caught in a trap. They want many foolish and harmful things that ruin and destroy

5:18 "When . . . eating," Quotation from Deuteronomy 25:4.

5:18 "A worker . . . pay." Quotation from Luke 10:7.

5:22 lay your hands on The laying on of hands had many purposes, including the giving of a blessing, power, or authority.

FAITH links

MORE MONEY?

1 TIMOTHY 6:10

Can money make a person happy? Some people would say yes. The apostle Paul would say no. In his first letter to his friend Timothy, Paul told him that loving money leads to "all kinds of evil." Paul did not say that *money* is sinful. What he meant was that the desire for riches makes a person greedy. It also leads to other problems.

Money is one of the resources that are available to us. Like any resource, money should be used wisely. How will you use your money?

Here are some links on being content with what you have:

A Small Percent, Deuteronomy 14:22–23, p. 247

Take My Advice, 1 Kings 2:2–4, p. 436

Uniquely You, Psalm 139:13–14, p. 815

First Place, Haggai 1:7–11, p. 1248

Give to Give, 1 Corinthians 16:1–4, p. 1566

The "Quality" of Life, 2 Peter 1:5–8, p. 1708

people. 10The love of money causes all
kinds of evil. Some people have left the
faith, because they wanted to get more
money, but they have caused themselves
much sorrow.

Some Things to Remember

11But you, man of God, run away from
all those things. Instead, live in the right
way, serve God, have faith, love,
patience, and gentleness. 12Fight the
good fight of faith,
grabbing hold of the
life that continues
forever. You were
called to have that
life when you confessed the good confession
before many witnesses. 13In the
sight of God, who gives life to everything,
and of Christ Jesus, I give you a
command. Christ Jesus made the good
confession when he stood before Pontius
Pilate. 14Do what you were commanded
to do without wrong or blame until our
Lord Jesus Christ comes again. 15God
will make that happen at the right time.
He is the blessed and only Ruler, the
King of all kings and the Lord of all lords.
16He is the only One who never dies. He
lives in light so bright no one can go near
it. No one has ever seen God, or can see
him. May honor and power belong to God
forever. Amen.

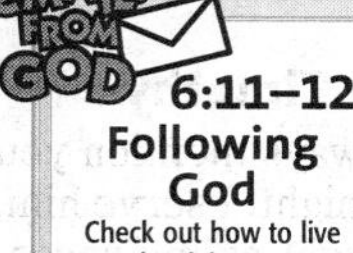

eMAiL! FROM GOD
6:11–12
Following God
Check out how to live the right way.

17Command those who are rich with
things of this world not to be proud. Tell
them to hope in God, not
in their uncertain
riches. God richly
gives us everything
to enjoy. 18Tell the
rich people to do
good, to be rich in
doing good deeds, to
be generous and ready to share. 19By doing
that, they will be saving a treasure for
themselves as a strong foundation for the
future. Then they will be able to have the
life that is true life.

eMAiL! FROM GOD
6:18
Giving
Check out how the rich should live.

20Timothy, guard what God has trusted
to you. Stay away from foolish, useless
talk and from the arguments of what is
falsely called "knowledge." 21By saying
they have that "knowledge," some have
missed the true faith.

Grace be with you.

1 From Paul, an apostle of Christ Jesus
by the will of God. God sent me to tell
about the promise of life that is in Christ
Jesus.
2To Timothy, a dear child to me:
Grace, mercy, and peace to you from
God the Father and Christ Jesus our
Lord.

Encouragement for Timothy

3I thank God as I always mention you
in my prayers, day and night. I serve him,
doing what I know is right as my ancestors did. **4**Remembering that you cried
for me, I want very much to see you so I
can be filled with joy. **5**I remember your
true faith. That faith first lived in your
grandmother Lois and in your mother
Eunice, and I know you now have that
same faith. **6**This is why I remind you to
keep using the gift God gave you when I
laid my hands on[n] you. Now let it grow, as
a small flame grows into a fire. **7**God did
not give us a spirit that makes us afraid
but a spirit of power and love and self-
control.
8So do not be ashamed to tell people
about our Lord Jesus, and do not be
ashamed of me, in prison for the Lord.
But suffer with me for the Good News.
God, who gives us the strength to do
that, **9**saved us and made us his holy people. That was not because of anything we
did ourselves but because of God's purpose and grace. That grace was given to
us through Christ Jesus before time began, **10**but it is now shown to us by the
coming of our Savior Christ Jesus. He
destroyed death, and through the Good
News he showed us the way to have
life that cannot be de-
stroyed. **11**I was cho-
sen to tell that Good
News and to be an
apostle and a teacher.
12I am suffering now
because I tell the
Good News, but I am not ashamed, because I know Jesus, the One in whom I

EMAIL FROM GOD 1:12
God's Promises
Find out what Jesus promises to those who trust him.

1:6 laid my hands on The laying on of hands had many purposes, including the giving of a blessing, power, or authority.

FAITH links

YOUR FAITH STORY

2 TIMOTHY 1:5

Think about something you've learned from a parent or grandparent. Maybe your mom taught you a recipe that was passed down from generation to generation. Maybe your grandpa taught you how to whistle.

In Paul's letter to his friend Timothy, Paul reminded Timothy about what he learned from his mother and grandmother. They taught Timothy about God. Parents and grandparents today can "pass down" their faith by telling their children about God and how they lived their lives as Christians. What have your parents or grandparents taught you about God? Pass it on!

Download these Faithlinks about sharing your faith:

A Use for Your Abilities, Genesis 41, p. 59

On the Wrong Foot, 2 Kings 21:1–2, 16, p. 509

Love for a Lifetime, Song of Solomon 6:8–9, p. 891

Two Ways to Grow, Luke 2:46–52, p. 1370

The Finished Product, Philippians 1:6, p. 1609

What's Good About You?, Philemon 4–7, p. 1663

Livin' it

SELF-CONTROL

2 Timothy 1:7

In Control When little kids don't get their way, they sometimes scream and stomp their feet. They may even throw themselves on the floor and yell. They haven't learned to control their emotions and actions. How about you? Have you developed self-control, or do you still do a bit of foot-stomping, screaming, and door-slamming?

Which is easier—to think good thoughts or bad thoughts? To be calm and controlled or to lose it? Paul has some suggestions for gaining self-control. (Look at Philippians 4:8–9, p. 1614.) How can good thoughts help you be more in control of your life?

MORE FAITH links

A Gentle Answer, p. 847

The Right Ingredients, p. 1227

Fear-Fighters, p. 1652

Just Say No!, p. 1660

The "Quality" of Life, p. 1708

"Will you look at this, Skweek? My teacher is making me do my lesson all over again because my paper got a bit messy."

"I'd say your paper was more than a bit messy, Tagg. Besides learning some discipline is good for you—it helps develop self-control. Check it out!

I Want It *Now!*, Judges 14:1–3, p. 332

- Do you find it hard to wait for something you really want? How do you react when you can't have something immediately? Do you pout? Whine? Beg? Do those methods usually work?
- Part of self-control means learning to control your need to have something *right now!* A person with self-control takes time to make wise choices about his or her wants. Can't stand to wait? God can help—just ask him.

Get Hot or Keep Cool?, Proverbs 12:16, p. 842

- If someone called you a name, what would you do? Get mad and call the person the same name—or worse? Sulk about it? Keep your cool and ignore it? Link here to see what God has to say about it.

Down on Discipline?, Proverbs 29:15, p. 867

- Wish your parents would never nag you about things you do wrong? Why do parents and others who care about you correct you? How does their correction make you feel? This Faithlink gives some very good reasons for discipline. How can discipline help *you* develop self-control?

my FAVORITE links

FAITH links

FEAR-FIGHTERS

2 TIMOTHY 1:7

Have you ever been afraid that you couldn't do something? Maybe a recent failure has caused you to be afraid to try something new. Paul's friend Timothy felt that way. In his letter to Timothy, Paul had some advice. He told Timothy that God gave him gifts to help him. What were these gifts? Power, love, and self-control. If you're a Christian, you have these gifts, too. Whenever you fear that you can't do something, think about what you can do: trust God to help you.

Next time you're afraid, think about these Faithlinks:

Your Heavenly Parent, Exodus 2:1–10, p. 77

Always Truthful, Numbers 23:19, p. 208

Stand!, Jeremiah 19:14—20:6, p. 1019

In the Lions' Den, Daniel 6, p. 1160

A Different Kind of Fruit, Galatians 5:22–23, p. 1592

The "Quality" of Life, 2 Peter 1:5–8, p. 1708

have believed. And I am sure he is able to
protect what he has trusted me with until
that day.* 13Follow the pattern of true
teachings that you heard from me in faith
and love, which are in Christ Jesus.
14Protect the truth that you were given;
protect it with the help of the Holy Spirit
who lives in us.
15You know that everyone in the
country of Asia has left me, even Phyge-
lus and Hermogenes. 16May the Lord
show mercy to the family of Onesiphorus, who has often helped me and was not
ashamed that I was in prison. 17When he
came to Rome, he looked eagerly for me
until he found me. 18May the Lord allow
him to find mercy from the Lord on that
day. You know how many ways he helped
me in Ephesus.

A Loyal Soldier of Christ Jesus

2 You then, Timothy, my child, be strong
in the grace we have in Christ Jesus.
2You should teach people whom you can
trust the things you and many others
have heard me say. Then they will be able
to teach others. 3Share in the troubles
we have like a good soldier of Christ
Jesus. 4A soldier wants to please the en-
listing officer, so no one serving in the
army wastes time with everyday matters. 5Also an athlete who takes part in a
contest must obey all the rules in order
to win. 6The farmer who works hard
should be the first person to get some of
the food that was grown. 7Think about
what I am saying, because the Lord will
give you the ability to understand everything.
8Remember Jesus Christ, who was
raised from the dead, who is from the
family of David. This is the Good News I
preach, 9and I am suffering because of it
to the point of being bound with chains
like a criminal. But God's teaching is not
in chains. 10So I patiently accept all these
troubles so that those whom God has
chosen can have the salvation that is in
Christ Jesus. With that salvation comes
glory that never ends.
11This teaching is true:

If we died with him, we will also live
with him.
12 If we accept suffering, we will also
rule with him.

1:12 day The day Christ will come to judge all people and take his people to live with him.

FAITH links

A SOLDIER'S STORY

2 TIMOTHY 2:3

Think a soldier's life is easy? No way. A soldier has to perform hard duties, obey commanding officers, and march, march, march. A soldier's life is one of endurance. He or she is trained to do his/her job without complaining.

Paul encouraged Timothy to endure suffering like a soldier would. How can you do that? Persevere, which is another way of saying, don't give up! Instead of looking for the easy way out, keep on going.

Need some encouragement? Download here:

When You're Afraid, Genesis 32:9–12, p. 45

Two Enemies, Nehemiah 6, p. 631

A Really Bad Day, Job 1:20–22; 2:10, p. 661

Future Hope, Joel 3:17–21, p. 1191

The Power of Prayer, Acts 12:5, p. 1485

Keep Going!, James 1:2–3, p. 1688

If we refuse to accept him, he will
refuse to accept us.
13 If we are not faithful, he will still be
faithful,
because he cannot be false to
himself.

A Worker Pleasing to God

14Continue teaching these things,
warning people in God's presence not to
argue about words. It does not help anyone, and it ruins those who listen. 15Make
every effort to give yourself to God as the
kind of person he will accept. Be a worker
who is not ashamed and who uses the true
teaching in the right way. 16Stay away
from foolish, useless talk, because that
will lead people further away from God.
17Their evil teaching will spread like a
sickness inside the body. Hymenaeus and
Philetus are like that. 18They have left
the true teaching, saying that the rising
from the dead has already taken place, and
so they are destroying the faith of some
people. 19But God's strong foundation
continues to stand. These words are written on the seal: "The Lord knows those
who belong to him,"[n] and "Everyone who
wants to belong to the Lord must stop doing wrong."

20In a large house there are not only
things made of gold and silver, but also
things made of wood and clay. Some things
are used for special purposes, and others
are made for ordinary jobs. 21All who
make themselves clean from evil will be
used for special purposes. They will be
made holy, useful to the Master, ready to
do any good work.

22But run away from the evil young
people like to do. Try hard to live right
and to have faith, love, and
peace, together with
those who trust in
the Lord from pure
hearts. 23Stay away
from foolish and stu-
pid arguments, be-
cause you know they grow into quarrels.
24And a servant of the Lord must not
quarrel but must be kind to everyone, a
good teacher, and patient. 25The Lord's
servant must gently teach those who disagree. Then maybe God will let them
change their minds so they can accept
the truth. 26And they may wake up and

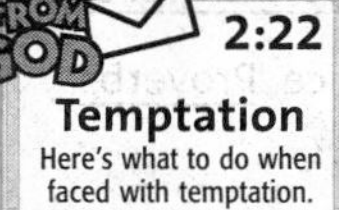

2:22 **Temptation**
Here's what to do when faced with temptation.

2:19 "The Lord . . . him" Quotation from Numbers 16:5.

WINNING A FRIEND

2 TIMOTHY 2:23-24

Have you ever argued with someone about something that was not really important? Paul had advice for his friend Timothy about "foolish and stupid arguments." What was his advice? Avoid them! Instead, be kind to everyone.

Next time you find yourself in an argument ask yourself these questions: Is this worth arguing about? Is it important for me to be right or to win this argument? If you find that it is not important, you can stop the argument by giving in to your friend. Let him know that your friendship is more important than the argument. You will win him over with your kindness!

Family Feud, Genesis 27, p. 37

Care to Be Fair?, Joshua 18:1–8, p. 299

A Friend in Deed, Job 2:13, p. 662

Some Friendly Advice, Proverbs 17:9, 14, 17, p. 851

Welcome!, Matthew 19:13–15, p. 1307

Trouble with the Tongue, James 3:3–12, p. 1692

escape from the trap of the devil, who
catches them to do what he wants.

The Last Days

3 Remember this! In the last days there
will be many troubles, 2because people will love themselves, love money,
brag, and be proud. They will say evil
things against others and will not obey
their parents or be thankful or be the
kind of people God wants. 3They will not
love others, will refuse to forgive, will
gossip, and will not control themselves.
They will be cruel, will hate what is good,
4will turn against their friends, and will
do foolish things without thinking. They
will be conceited, will love pleasure instead of God, 5and will act as if they
serve God but will not have his power.
Stay away from those people. 6Some of
them go into homes and get control of
silly women who are full of sin and are led
by many evil desires. 7These women are
always learning new teachings, but they
are never able to understand the truth
fully. 8Just as Jannes and Jambres were
against Moses, these people are against
the truth. Their thinking has been ruined, and they have failed in trying to follow the faith. 9But they will not be
successful in what they do, because as
with Jannes and Jambres, everyone will
see that they are foolish.

Obey the Teachings

10But you have followed what I teach,
the way I live, my goal, faith, patience,
and love. You know I never give up.
11You know how I have been hurt and
have suffered, as in Antioch, Iconium,
and Lystra. I have suffered, but the Lord
saved me from all those troubles.
12Everyone who wants to live as God desires, in Christ Jesus, will be hurt. 13But
people who are evil and cheat others will
go from bad to worse. They will fool others, but they will also be fooling themselves.

14But you should continue following
the teachings you learned. You know
they are true, because you trust those
who taught you. 15Since you were a child
you have known the Holy Scriptures
which are able to
make you wise. And
that wisdom leads
to salvation through
faith in Christ Jesus.
16All Scripture is

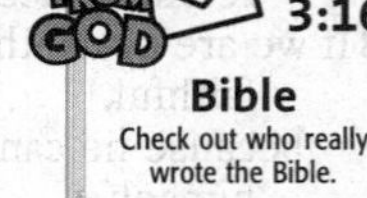

3:16

Bible

Check out who really wrote the Bible.

FAITH links

LIFE'S RULE BOOK

2 TIMOTHY 3:15-17

Have you ever tried to learn a new sport? What did you do to learn it? Many people try to watch videos or read books about the sport. These videos and books explain the rules and provide tips on how a person can get better at the sport. If a person didn't know the rules of the sport, he or she would not be able to play the game well.

In the second letter to Timothy, Paul encouraged Timothy to study the Bible. The Bible is our "rule book" for life. It teaches us about God and helps us to grow stronger in our faith. It's all we need to know about how to live in a way that honors God.

Here are some more Faithlinks about playing by the rules:

What He's Really Like, Deuteronomy 4:15–20, p. 233

Read My Lips?, Deuteronomy 26:16–19, p. 260

The Problem with Gossip, Proverbs 11:12–13, p. 840

The Foundation of Our Hope, Isaiah 31:1–8, p. 934

Our Heavenly Connection, Matthew 6:9–13, p. 1283

How Do You Grow?, Titus 1:1, p. 1659

given by God and is useful for teaching,
for showing people what is wrong in their
lives, for correcting faults, and for teaching how to live right. **17**Using the Scriptures, the person who serves God will be
capable, having all that is needed to do
every good work.

4 I give you a command in the presence
of God and Christ Jesus, the One who
will judge the living and the dead, and by
his coming and his kingdom: **2**Preach the
Good News. Be ready at all times, and tell
people what they
need to do. Tell them
when they are wrong.
Encourage them with
great patience and
careful teaching, **3**because the time will
come when people will not listen to the
true teaching but will find many more
teachers who please them by saying the
things they want to hear. **4**They will stop
listening to the truth and will begin to
follow false stories. **5**But you should control yourself at all times, accept troubles,
do the work of telling the Good News,
and complete all the duties of a servant
of God.

6My life is being given as an offering
to God, and the time has come for me to
leave this life. **7**I have fought the good
fight, I have finished the race, I have kept
the faith. **8**Now, a crown is being held for
me—a crown for being right with God.
The Lord, the judge who judges rightly,
will give the crown to me on that day[n]—
not only to me but to all those who have
waited with love for him to come again.

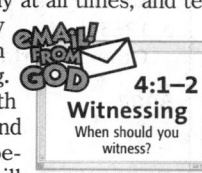

> **EMAIL FROM GOD** 4:1–2
> **Witnessing**
> When should you witness?

Personal Words

9Do your best to come to me as soon
as you can, **10**because Demas, who loved
this world, left me and went to Thessalonica. Crescens went to Galatia, and Titus went to Dalmatia. **11**Luke is the only
one still with me. Get Mark and bring
him with you when you come, because he
can help me in my work here. **12**I sent
Tychicus to Ephesus. **13**When I was in

4:8 day The day Christ will come to judge all people and take his people to live with him.

POWERFUL WOMEN OF FAITH

2 Timothy 4

Mary, the mother of Jesus, is perhaps the most famous woman of the New Testament. Think about it . . . she was the very first person to believe in Jesus. She is an example of faith, humility, and service. (Read Luke 1:26–56, p. 1365.)

Other important women in the New Testament include:

Anna	Recognized baby Jesus as the Messiah	Luke 2:36–38, p. 1370
Elizabeth	Mother of John the Baptist	Luke 1:5, 13, p. 1365
Eunice	Timothy's mom, who passed on her faith to him	2 Timothy 1:5, p. 1650
Lois	Timothy's grandma, who passed on her faith to him	2 Timothy 1:5, p. 1650
Lydia	Was converted by Paul during his ministry in Philippi	Acts 16:14, p. 1494
Martha and Mary	Sisters of Lazarus and friends of Jesus	Luke 10:38–42, p. 1389
Mary Magdalene	Jesus cast demons out of this woman; a follower of Jesus	Matthew 27:56–61, p. 1325; Mark 16:9, p. 1362
Priscilla	Worked with Paul at Corinth and Ephesus	Acts 18:2, 18, 19, p. 1497
Salome	Mother of Jesus' disciples, James and John	Matthew 20:20–24, p. 1309; Matthew 27:56, p. 1325; Mark 15:40, p. 1359
Tabitha (Dorcas)	Peter raised her from the dead	Acts 9:36–41, p. 1480

Troas, I left my coat there with Carpus.
So when you come, bring it to me, along
with my books, particularly the ones
written on parchment.[n] **14**Alexander the
metalworker did many harmful things
against me. The Lord will punish him for
what he did. **15**You also should be careful
that he does not hurt you, because he
fought strongly against our teaching.

16The first time I defended myself, no
one helped me; everyone left me. May
they be forgiven. **17**But the Lord stayed
with me and gave me strength so I could
fully tell the Good News to all those who
are not Jews. So I was saved from the
lion's mouth. **18**The Lord will save me
when anyone tries to hurt me, and he will
bring me safely to his heavenly kingdom.
Glory forever and ever be the Lord's.
Amen.

Final Greetings

19Greet Priscilla and Aquila and the
family of Onesiphorus. **20**Erastus stayed
in Corinth, and I left Trophimus sick in
Miletus. **21**Try as hard as you can to
come to me before winter.

Eubulus sends greetings to you. Also
Pudens, Linus, Claudia, and all the brothers and sisters in Christ greet you.

22The Lord be with your spirit. Grace
be with you.

4:13 parchment A writing paper made from the skins of sheep.

ADVICE FOR A PASTOR

Hi! It's me again, Paul. You remember me, right? Well, in case you've forgotten, let me clue you in on my background. I used to persecute Christians. Then, one day, I met Jesus and he changed my life. After that moment, I spent my life encouraging believers in the faith and telling others about the change Jesus made in my life.

I wrote this letter to my friend Titus—a non-Jew (sometimes called a Gentile) who was a Christian and had become a pastor. My friend really needed some advice about the inner workings of the church. I advised him about how he could create order in the church so it would run smoothly. I also gave him some advice about how to elect elders and other church officials. That's not all. I also instructed Titus to teach the truth and gave him advice about how believers in the church should treat each other. I think this letter still is helping pastors and ministers today!

JESUS WATCH

While Paul spends much of his time writing about the basics of church management, he also takes time to paint a rich portrait of Jesus. In just a few words, Paul presents Jesus as both God and our savior, who paid the price for our sins. Paul urges Titus to wait for "our great hope and the coming of the glory of our great God and Savior Jesus Christ" (Titus 2:13). Paul wants believers to be patient and wait for Jesus, the promise and hope of their salvation. Paul's other purpose in writing this letter is to help people who are called to serve in the church to know they're not alone. Serving Jesus won't always be easy, but Jesus promises that he'll be present with us to comfort us and help us when things get out of control. God will never give us more than we can handle. Awesome!

FAITH links

"Do you know what the people of Crete were like, Tagg?"

"Were they like Crete-tures? Just a little joke, Skweek!"

"Very funny. But if you really want to know about them, connect to Titus 1:10–16 for Paul's description."

- How Do You Grow?, **Titus 1:1**
- Just Say No!, **Titus 2:11–12**
- The Gentle Way, **Titus 3:1–5**

1 From Paul, a servant of God and an
apostle of Jesus Christ. I was sent to
help the faith of God's chosen people and
to help them know the truth that shows
people how to serve God. 2That faith and
that knowledge come from the hope for
life forever, which God promised to us
before time began. And God cannot lie.
3At the right time God let the world
know about that life through preaching.
He trusted me with that work, and I
preached by the command of God our
Savior.

4To Titus, my true child in the faith
we share:

Grace and peace from God the Father
and Christ Jesus our Savior.

Titus' Work in Crete

5I left you in Crete so you could finish
doing the things that still needed to be
done and so you could appoint elders in
every town, as I directed you. 6An elder
must not be guilty of doing wrong, must
have only one wife, and must have believing children. They must not be
known as children who are wild and do
not cooperate. 7As God's manager, an elder must not be guilty of doing wrong,
being selfish, or becoming angry quickly.
He must not drink too much wine, like to
fight, or try to get rich by cheating others. 8An elder must be ready to welcome
guests, love what is good, be wise, live
right, and be holy and self-controlled.
9By holding on to the trustworthy word
just as we teach it, an elder can help people by using true teaching, and he can
show those who are against the true
teaching that they are wrong.

10There are many people who refuse
to cooperate, who talk about worthless
things and lead others into the wrong
way—mainly those who say all who are
not Jews must be circumcised. 11These
people must be stopped, because they
are upsetting whole families by teaching
things they should not teach, which they
do to get rich by cheating people. 12Even
one of their own prophets said, "Cretans
are always liars, evil animals, and lazy
people who do nothing but eat." 13The
words that prophet said are true. So
firmly tell those people they are wrong so
they may become strong in the faith,
14not accepting Jewish false stories and

FAITH links

HOW DO YOU GROW?

TITUS 1:1

If you've heard the nursery rhyme "Mary, Mary, quite contrary," you know how her garden grows. Gardens aren't the only things capable of growth. Paul described his purpose for writing a letter to a church leader named Titus. He wanted to help Titus grow in faith. He also described how that faith would grow.

Your faith can grow, too. How does your faith grow? It grows as you read the Bible, pray, and talk to other Christians about God. When you learn more about God, your faith in him becomes stronger.

Here are some more Faithlinks on giving your faith a workout:

A Given, 1 Chronicles 5:18–20, p. 526

Peace in the Family, Psalm 133, p. 811

Like a Tree, Jeremiah 17:5–8, p. 1016

God's Instructions, Ezekiel 4:1–15, p. 1089

The Temptation Fighter, Matthew 4:1–11, p. 1278

Faith God Notices, Luke 18:35–43, p. 1406

the commands of people who reject the
truth. **15**To those who are pure, all things
are pure, but to those who are full of sin
and do not believe, nothing is pure. Both
their minds and their consciences have
been ruined. **16**They say they know God,
but their actions show they do not accept
him. They are hateful people, they refuse
to obey, and they are useless for doing
anything good.

Following the True Teaching

2 But you must tell everyone what to do
to follow the true teaching. **2**Teach
older men to be self-controlled, serious,
wise, strong in faith, in love, and in patience.
3In the same way, teach older women
to be holy in their behavior, not speaking
against others or enslaved to too much
wine, but teaching what is good. **4**Then
they can teach the young women to love
their husbands, to love their children, **5**to
be wise and pure, to be good workers at
home, to be kind, and to yield to their
husbands. Then no one will be able to
criticize the teaching God gave us.
6In the same way, encourage young
men to be wise. **7**In every way be an example of doing good deeds. When you
teach, do it with honesty and serious-
ness. **8**Speak the truth so that you cannot
be criticized. Then those who are against
you will be ashamed because there is
nothing bad to say about us.
9Slaves should yield to their own
masters at all times, trying to please
them and not arguing with them. **10**They
should not steal from them but should
show their masters they can be fully
trusted so that in everything they do
they will make the teaching of God our
Savior attractive.
11That is the way we should live, because God's grace that can save everyone has come. **12**It teaches us not to live
against God nor to do the evil things the
world wants to do. Instead, that grace
teaches us to live now in a wise and right
way and in a way that shows we serve
God. **13**We should live like that while we
wait for our great hope and the coming of
the glory of our great God and Savior
Jesus Christ. **14**He gave himself for us so
he might pay the price to free us from all
evil and to make us pure people who belong only to him—people who are always
wanting to do good deeds.

FAITH links

JUST SAY NO!

TITUS 2:11-12

What's a two-letter word that begins with *N* and is the opposite of yes? *No.* Yet when it comes to not giving in to temptation, we sometimes forget that simple little word.

Paul wrote to Titus with advice on how to live. He told Titus to say no to doing wrong things and say yes to what's right. Each day you'll be faced with making similar choices. Think about some of the choices you're faced with right now. When you're tempted to do something that you know is wrong, remember that simple little word, and just say no!

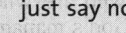

Download these links on saying ***NO*** to temptations:

Complaints, Complaints!, Exodus 16:1–3, p. 97

I Want It *Now!,* Judges 14:1–3, p. 332

The Prayer Habit, Psalm 5:1–3, p. 712

What's Wrong About Rumors, Jeremiah 29:24–32, p. 1032

The Right Ingredients, Micah 6:8, p. 1227

A Friend of Jesus, John 15:9–17, p. 1450

15Say these things and encourage the
people and tell them what is wrong in
their lives, with all authority. Do not let
anyone treat you as if you were unimportant.

The Right Way to Live

3 Remind the believers to yield to the
authority of rulers and government
leaders, to obey them, to be ready to do
good, 2to speak no evil about anyone, to
live in peace, and to be gentle and polite
to all people.

3In the past we also were foolish. We
did not obey, we were wrong, and we
were slaves to many things our bodies
wanted and enjoyed. We spent our lives
doing evil and being jealous. People hated
us, and we hated each other. 4But when
the kindness and love of God our Savior
was shown, 5he saved us because of his
mercy. It was not because of good deeds
we did to be right with him. He saved us
through the washing that made us new
people through the Holy Spirit. 6God
poured out richly upon us that Holy Spirit
through Jesus Christ our Savior. 7Being
made right with God by his grace,
we could have the
hope of receiving the
life that never ends.

EMAIL FROM GOD 3:7
Eternal Life
What is your hope?

8This teaching is
true, and I want you
to be sure the peo-
ple understand these things. Then those
who believe in God will be careful to use
their lives for doing good. These things
are good and will help everyone.

9But stay away from those who have
foolish arguments and talk about useless
family histories and argue and quarrel
about the law. Those things are worth
nothing and will not help anyone. 10After
a first and second warning, avoid someone who causes arguments. 11You can
know that such people are evil and sinful;
their own sins prove them wrong.

Some Things to Remember

12When I send Artemas or Tychicus
to you, make every effort to come to me
at Nicopolis, because I have decided to
stay there this winter. 13Do all you can to
help Zenas the lawyer and Apollos on
their journey so that they have everything they need. 14Our people must
learn to use their lives for doing good
deeds to provide what is necessary so
that their lives will not be useless.

15All who are with me greet you.
Greet those who love us in the faith.

Grace be with you all.

THE GENTLE WAY

TITUS 3:1-5

What's the first thing you think about doing when a brother or sister says something mean to you? Did you ever think about being kind and gentle? That was Paul's advice to Titus. Paul knew that Titus would have to teach other Christians. That was one of his duties as a church leader. So Paul told Titus to remind Christians how to live. Paul's advice to Titus is for you today. Showing kindness instead of getting back at someone is not always easy. But since God is kind to us, we can be kind toward others—even those who treat us unkindly.

Family Feud, Genesis 27, p. 37

Give Revenge a Rest, Leviticus 19:18, p. 160

Patience, Please, Psalm 145:8–9, p. 819

A Gentle Answer, Proverbs 15:1, p. 847

Quick to Forgive?, Mark 11:25, p. 1349

That's Much Better!, Ephesians 2:4–5, p. 1599

FREE AT LAST!

Hello, everybody. It's me, Paul again. This very short letter is one of the last letters written by me in the Bible. It's also one of my most personal letters. While many of my other letters were written to churches, this one is written to my good friend Philemon, who was a Christian living in Colossae. I was in prison in Rome when I wrote this letter. While in prison, I met Onesimus, Philemon's slave who had run away. He came to Rome looking for his freedom from physical slavery, but he received much more when he found and became a follower of Jesus.

I wrote this letter to Philemon on Onesimus's behalf. I wanted Philemon (and the others who were members of Philemon's house church) to understand that Onesimus was now a brother in Christ and to accept him as a fellow believer. So, I asked Philemon to release Onesimus from slavery. It was a bold request, but do you know what happened? Philemon did set Onesimus free, and it's possible that Onesimus became a leader in the church. Praise God!

JESUS WATCH

Sin and forgiveness are painted in an incredible picture through the retelling of the story of Onesimus—the runaway slave. Paul feels compelled to encourage Philemon to forgive Onesimus and then agrees to take on whatever debt Onesimus owes Philemon. In a very practical way, Paul's efforts demonstrate what Jesus does for us.

Many people have a lot of stuff to say about our sins. Some people want us to believe that we'll never get rid of our sin. Others want us to believe that Jesus forgives our sins, but he never forgets them. But Paul's letter to Philemon completely blows those ideas out of the water. Through Jesus' saving work on the cross, our debt of sin is forgiven, and we can enter into a relationship with God.

"Hey, Tagg, does Paul *really* say that he'll repay Onesimus's debt?"

"He sure does! You can read about that in Philemon 18-19."

FAITH links

What's Good About You?, Philemon 4–7

From Useless to Useful, Philemon 11

A Friendly Welcome, Philemon 18

1From Paul, a prisoner of Christ
Jesus, and from Timothy, our brother.
To Philemon, our dear friend and
worker with us; 2to Apphia, our sister; to
Archippus, a worker with us; and to the
church that meets in your home:
3Grace and peace to you from God our
Father and the Lord Jesus Christ.

Philemon's Love and Faith

4I always thank my God when I mention you in my prayers, 5because I hear
about the love you have for all God's holy
people and the faith you have in the Lord
Jesus. 6I pray that the faith you share
may make you understand every blessing
we have in Christ. 7I have great joy and

FAITH links

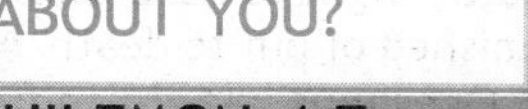

WHAT'S GOOD ABOUT YOU?

PHILEMON 4-7

Think of a time when someone said something nice about you. Maybe he or she told you about a quality you have that he/she liked. Paul complimented his friend Philemon on how he shared his faith with others. The work Philemon did for the Lord made Paul feel glad. Would you like someone to think that of you? There's one way you can be sure that someone does: tell someone about Jesus.

Want to help out a friend? Tell them about Jesus!

From Zero to Hero, Judges 6; 7, p. 319

Operation Cooperation, Ezra 1:5, p. 609

Jesus' Mission and Yours, Isaiah 61:1–2, p. 978

Stand!, Jeremiah 19:14—20:6, p. 1019

Help for a Friend, Mark 2:1–5, p. 1332

Calling Anyone!, Acts 23:12–22, p. 1506

FAITH links

FROM USELESS TO USEFUL

PHILEMON 11

Have you ever messed up so badly that you felt useless? Onesimus's story can help you take heart. Although the name *Onesimus* meant "useful," he made himself useless by stealing from his master Philemon. He then ran away to avoid being punished. Yet, something happened when Onesimus met Paul. He became a Christian and was very helpful to Paul.

Feeling useless? God is always willing to give you a second chance. When you accept his forgiveness, you're on your way to becoming useful once more.

Facing the Consequences, Deuteronomy 3:21–29, p. 232

You're Out!, 2 Kings 17:5–7, p. 501

Justice Served, Isaiah 35:3–4, p. 940

A Change of Heart, Matthew 3:1–12, p. 1277

Your Choice of Fruit, Matthew 12:33–35, p. 1295

Your Faith Example, 1 Timothy 4:12, p. 1646

comfort, my brother, because the love
you have shown to God's people has refreshed them.

Accept Onesimus as a Brother

8So, in Christ, I could be bold and order you to do what is right. 9But because I
love you, I am pleading with you instead.
I, Paul, an old man now and also a prisoner
for Christ Jesus, 10am pleading with you
for my child Onesimus, who became my
child while I was in prison. 11In the past
he was useless to you, but now he has become useful for both you and me.

12I am sending him back to you, and
with him I am sending my own heart. 13I
wanted to keep him with me so that in
your place he might help me while I am in
prison for the Good News. 14But I did not
want to do anything without asking you
first so that any good you do for me will
be because you want to do it, not because
I forced you. 15Maybe Onesimus was
separated from you for a short time so
you could have him back forever— 16no
longer as a slave, but better than a slave,
as a loved brother. I love him very much,
but you will love him even more, both as
a person and as a believer in the Lord.

17So if you consider me your partner,
welcome Onesimus as you would welcome me. 18If he has done anything
wrong to you or if he owes you anything,
charge that to me. 19I, Paul, am writing
this with my own hand. I will pay it back,
and I will say nothing about what you owe
me for your own life. 20So, my brother, I
ask that you do this for me in the Lord:
Refresh my heart in Christ. 21I write this
letter, knowing that you will do what I ask
you and even more.

22One more thing—prepare a room
for me in which to stay, because I hope
God will answer your prayers and I will
be able to come to you.

Final Greetings

23Epaphras, a prisoner with me for
Christ Jesus, sends greetings to you.
24And also Mark, Aristarchus, Demas,
and Luke, workers together with me,
send greetings.
25The grace of our Lord Jesus Christ
be with your spirit.

FAITH links

A FRIENDLY WELCOME

PHILEMON 18

Paul wanted Philemon to forgive his runaway slave Onesimus. Not only that, Paul wanted Philemon to treat Onesimus like a Christian brother. Legally, Philemon had the right to have Onesimus punished or put to death. After all, Onesimus had stolen from his master and had run away. Running away was enough to earn Onesimus a severe punishment. Paul wanted Philemon to treat Onesimus the way Jesus once treated Philemon.

Jesus always welcomes us back no matter what we do. Since he's willing to do that, he wants us to be willing to forgive those who wrong us. Has someone hurt you recently? Ask God to help you forgive that person.

Is there someone you need to forgive? God can help. Connect here to find out more:

The Perfect Leader?, Numbers 20:1–13, p. 203

Count on His Mercy, Judges 2:16–17; 3, p. 313

A Mother's Love, Isaiah 49:13–16, p. 961

Name with a Purpose, Matthew 1:21, p. 1274

Forgive Again?, Luke 17:3–4, p. 1402

The Finished Product, Philippians 1:6, p. 1609

NEVER GO BACK!

Hi, everyone. No one really knows who wrote this letter, but I (Paul again!) will tell you about it. Some people think I wrote it anyway because the way it was written looks a lot like the other stuff I've written. Others think that it was written by Apollos (check out Acts 18:24 and 19:1, p. 1498) or another one of my traveling companions. It doesn't really matter who wrote Hebrews because the most important thing is it's full of unbelievable truth.

The letter was written to a church that met in a home in the Jewish section of Rome. The church was experiencing a lot of problems. The writer wanted to tell the people two things: First, they needed to pay attention to the things that God was saying; and second, they needed to *do* what God was telling them. You see, these people were tempted to go back to the old way of doing things and follow the old Jewish traditions. But the message in Hebrews is clear for those people struggling in their faith and for you, too: "Never, never, never go back." Life in Christ, and eventually eternal life, is far, far better than anything else around. It's worth the struggle and worth the wait.

JESUS WATCH

The writer of Hebrews makes one of the strongest cases in the New Testament for Jesus' divine (or godly) nature. The writer describes Jesus as our divine, yet human, prophet, priest, and king. Whew! That's a tall order! But not for Jesus—he's God! The writer of Hebrews takes on Jesus' humanity and his deity and describes, explains, and praises both aspects. In fact, the writer of this book uses over 20 different words to describe Jesus' attributes and accomplishments. The bottom-line conclusion that Hebrews makes is that Jesus is the best! There is no better than Jesus. He's all-powerful. He's the highest king. He's the perfect savior. And he lived just like we did. Now that's an awesome God!

my FAVORITE links

______________________ ______________________

______________________ ______________________

______________________ ______________________

______________________ ______________________

OTHER CONNECTIONS

Livin' it When you hear the word "faithful," what do you think of? A dog? Your best friend? How about God? What about you? Learn what it means to be faithful from the wonderful examples of faith you'll find by connecting to True Blue, Hebrews 11.

GET THE INFO

- Death on a Cross, Hebrews 6:6. Most everyone knows that Jesus died on a cross, but did you know that crucifixion—to be killed on a cross—was the worst form of punishment the Romans used? Find out more by linking here.

MORE STUFF...

It Takes Faith. What does it mean to have faith? The writer of Hebrews defines faith in Hebrews 11 by saying it is being sure of what God will do even if you can't touch it, see it, or even feel it. Check out the list of people who pleased God because of their faith and have made it into the Hall of Faith: Abel, Enoch, Noah, Abraham, Isaac, Jacob, Moses, Rahab, and others.

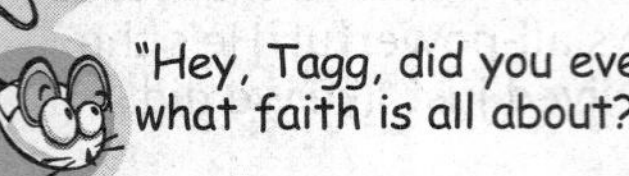

"Hey, Tagg, did you ever wonder what faith is all about?"

"Yeah, sometimes it can be hard to understand exactly what people mean by faith. But if you download Hebrews 11, I think you'll learn a lot."

did you know?

MORE ON THE HEBREWS SURFWATCH:

Better than angels, Hebrews 1
The greatest of all, Hebrews 3
Grow up!, Hebrews 6:1–12

FAITH links

- Touched by an Angel?, **Hebrews 1:3–4**
- Pay Attention!, **Hebrews 2:1**
- Cut to the Quick, **Hebrews 4:12**
- Family Time, **Hebrews 10:25**
- People of Faith, **Hebrews 11**
- Go for It!, **Hebrews 12:1–4**
- You're Correct!, **Hebrews 12:5–7**
- Never Alone, **Hebrews 13:5–6**

God Spoke Through His Son

1 In the past God spoke to our ancestors
through the prophets many times and
in many different ways. 2But now in
these last days God has spoken to us
through his Son. God has chosen his Son
to own all things, and through him he
made the world. 3The Son reflects the
glory of God and shows exactly what God
is like. He holds everything together
with his powerful word. When the Son
made people clean from their sins, he sat
down at the right side of God, the Great
One in heaven. 4The Son became much
greater than the angels, and God gave
him a name that is much greater than
theirs.

5This is because God never said to
any of the angels,

"You are my Son.
Today I have become your Father."
Psalm 2:7

Nor did God say of any angel,

"I will be his Father,
and he will be my Son." *2 Samuel 7:14*

6And when God brings his firstborn Son
into the world, he says,

"Let all God's angels worship him."[n]
Psalm 97:7

7This is what God said about the angels:

"God makes his angels become like
winds.
He makes his servants become
like flames of fire." *Psalm 104:4*

8But God said this about his Son:

"God, your throne will last forever
and ever.
You will rule your kingdom with
fairness.
9 You love right and hate evil,
so God has chosen you from
among your friends;
he has set you apart with much
joy." *Psalm 45:6-7*

10God also says,

"Lord, in the beginning you made the
earth,
and your hands made the skies.

1:6 "Let . . . him." These words are found in Deuteronomy 32:43 in the Septuagint, the Greek version of the Old Testament, and in a Hebrew copy among the Dead Sea Scrolls.

FAITH links

TOUCHED BY AN ANGEL?

HEBREWS 1:3-4

Have you ever wondered about angels? Maybe you've seen television shows or read books about angels. They're powerful messengers God created to serve him. Some spend all their time praising him. Although angels are important and powerful, there is someone who is greater than they are. Who is that? Jesus. That's what the writer of Hebrews wanted Christians to know. Some first-century Christians believed that angels were to be worshiped. The Bible tells us that Jesus has been given authority over everyone—including angels. That means only he deserves to be worshiped.

Download these links for more reasons to praise God:

The Name of the Lord, Exodus 33:19–23; 34:5–8, p. 120

You're Invited!, Psalm 100, p. 784

Concern for All, Daniel 9, p. 1165

A Family Meal, Mark 14:23–26, p. 1356

An Unselfish Example, Philippians 2:5–8, p. 1611

Fear-Fighters, 2 Timothy 1:7, p. 1652

11 They will be destroyed, but you will
remain.
They will all wear out like clothes.
12 You will fold them like a coat.
And, like clothes, you will change
them.
But you never change,
and your life will never end."
Psalm 102:25-27
13 And God never said this to an angel:
"Sit by me at my right side
until I put your enemies under your
control."[n] *Psalm 110:1*
14 All the angels
are spirits who serve
God and are sent to
help those who will
receive salvation.

EMAIL! FROM GOD
1:14
Help
How do angels help Christians?

Our Salvation Is Great

2 So we must be more careful to follow
what we were taught. Then we will
not stray away from the truth. 2The
teaching God spoke through angels was
shown to be true, and anyone who did not
follow it or obey it received the punishment that was earned. 3So surely we also
will be punished if we ignore this great
salvation. The Lord himself first told
about this salvation, and it was proven
true to us by those who heard him. 4God
also proved it by using wonders, great
signs, many kinds of miracles, and by giving people gifts through the Holy Spirit,
just as he wanted.

Christ Became like Humans

5God did not choose angels to be the
rulers of the new world that was coming,
which is what we have been talking
about. 6It is written in the Scriptures,
"Why are people important to you?
Why do you take care of human
beings?
7 You made them a little lower than the
angels
and crowned them with glory and
honor.
8 You put all things under their
control." *Psalm 8:4-6*
When God put everything under their
control, there was nothing left that they

FAITH links

PAY ATTENTION!

HEBREWS 2:1

What are the things you pay attention to easily? Your favorite TV show or video? A computer game? We usually pay attention to whatever we're interested in.

The writer of Hebrews wanted to remind Christians to pay attention to God's Word. Why was that important? There were many teachers who claimed to know about God, but did not tell the truth about him. Knowing the truth of God's Word would keep the Christians from believing lies. That was true then and now. So, how can you pay attention to God's Word? The best way is to read it and do what it says.

Here are some more Faithlinks on knowing God's Word:

Ten Ways to Obey, Exodus 20, p. 103

Learning to Listen, 1 Samuel 3, p. 358

Wronged for What's Right, Ezra 4:4–5, p. 612

A Promise from the Heart, Jeremiah 31:31–33, p. 1037

The Way to Be Wise, James 1:5, p. 1689

You're a Fake!, 2 Peter 2:1, p. 1709

1:13 until . . . control Literally, "until I make your enemies a footstool for your feet."

did not rule. Still, we do not yet see them
ruling over everything. **9**But we see
Jesus, who for a short
time was made lower
than the angels. And now
he is wearing a crown of
glory and honor because
he suffered and died. And
by God's grace, he died
for everyone.

10God is the One who
made all things, and all
things are for his glory.
He wanted to have many
children share his glory, so he made the
One who leads people to salvation perfect through suffering.

11Jesus, who makes people holy, and
those who are made holy are from the
same family. So he is not ashamed to call
them his brothers and sisters.[n] **12**He
says,

"Then, I will tell my fellow Israelites
about you;
I will praise you in the public
meeting." *Psalm 22:22*

13He also says,

"I will trust in God." *Isaiah 8:17*

And he also says,

"I am here, and with me are the
children God has given me."
Isaiah 8:18

14Since these children are people
with physical bodies, Jesus himself became like them. He did this so that, by
dying, he could destroy the one who has
the power of death—the devil—**15**and
free those who were like slaves all their
lives because of their fear of death.
16Clearly, it is not angels that Jesus
helps, but the people who are from
Abraham.[n] **17**For this reason Jesus had to
be made like his brothers in every way so
he could be their merciful and faithful
high priest in service to God. Then Jesus
could bring forgiveness for their sins.
18And now he can help those who are
tempted, because he himself suffered and
was tempted.

Jesus Is Greater than Moses

3 So all of you holy brothers and sisters,
who were called by God, think about
Jesus, who was sent to us and is the high
priest of our faith. **2**Jesus was faithful to
God as Moses was in
God's family. **3**Jesus has
more honor than Moses,
just as the builder of a
house has more honor
than the house itself.
4Every house is built by
someone, but the builder
of everything is God him-
self. **5**Moses was faithful
in God's family as a ser-
vant, and he told what
God would say in the future. **6**But Christ
is faithful as a Son over God's house. And
we are God's house if we keep on being
very sure about our great hope.

> Every house is built by someone, but the builder of everything is God himself.
> —Hebrews 3:4

We Must Continue to Follow God

7So it is as the Holy Spirit says:

"Today listen to what he says.
8 Do not be stubborn as in the past
when you turned against God,
when you tested God in the desert.
9 There your ancestors tried me and
tested me
and saw the things I did for forty
years.
10 I was angry with them.
I said, 'They are not loyal to me
and have not understood my
ways.'
11 I was angry and made a promise,
'They will never enter my rest.' "[n]
Psalm 95:7-11

12So brothers and sisters, be careful
that none of you has an evil, unbelieving
heart that will turn you away from the living God. **13**But encourage each other
every day while it is "today."[n] Help each
other so none of you will become hard-
ened because sin has tricked you. **14**We

2:11 brothers and sisters Although the Greek text says "brothers" here and throughout this book, the writer's words were meant for the entire church, including men and women.

2:16 Abraham Most respected ancestor of the Jews. Every Jew hoped to see Abraham.

3:11 rest A place of rest God promised to give his people.

3:13 "today" This word is taken from verse 7. It means that it is important to do these things now.

all share in Christ if we keep till the end
the sure faith we had in the beginning.
15This is what the Scripture says:

"Today listen to what he says.
Do not be stubborn as in the past
when you turned against God."

Psalm 95:7-8

16Who heard God's voice and was
against him? It was all those people Moses led out of Egypt. **17**And with whom
was God angry for forty years? He was
angry with those who sinned, who died in
the desert. **18**And to whom was God talking when he promised that they would
never enter his rest? He was talking to
those who did not obey him. **19**So we see
they were not allowed to enter and have
God's rest, because they did not believe.
4 Now, since God has left us the promise that we may enter his rest, let us
be very careful so none of you will fail to
enter. **2**The Good News was preached to
us just as it was to them. But the teaching
they heard did not help them, because
they heard it but did not accept it with
faith. **3**We who have believed are able to
enter and have God's rest. As God has
said,

"I was angry and made a promise,
'They will never enter my rest.'"

Psalm 95:11

But God's work was finished from the
time he made the world. **4**In the Scriptures he talked about the seventh day of
the week: "And on the seventh day God
rested from all his works."[n] **5**And again
in the Scripture God said, "They will
never enter my rest."

6It is still true that some people will
enter God's rest, but those who first
heard the way to be saved did not enter,
because they did not obey. **7**So God
planned another day, called "today." He
spoke about that day through David a
long time later in the same Scripture
used before:

"Today listen to what he says.
Do not be stubborn." *Psalm 95:7-8*

8We know that Joshua[n] did not lead the
people into that rest, because God spoke
later about another day. **9**This shows that
the rest[n] for God's people is still coming.
10Anyone who enters God's rest will rest

FAITH links

CUT TO THE QUICK

HEBREWS 4:12

If you've ever seen a sword or seen someone use one on TV, you know that it is sharp enough to cut through a lot of things. The writer of Hebrews compared God's Word—the Bible—to a double-edged sword. Why? When you hear it, it acts as a sword on your heart. That means it reveals your hidden attitudes and causes you to want to do better. The truth can hurt sometimes. When we follow the truth, however, we feel better. Let God's Word cut out the bad attitudes and thoughts in your life.

The Trouble with Sin, Genesis 6—8, p. 11

A Holiday Every Week, Leviticus 23:1–3, p. 166

Your Stats, 1 Kings 15; 16, p. 460

How Do I Love You?, Malachi 1:1–5, p. 1267

Too Busy to Worship?, Luke 2:8–20, p. 1368

Hold On!, 2 Thessalonians 2:15–17, p. 1639

4:4 "And . . . works." Quotation from Genesis 2:2.

4:8 Joshua After Moses died, Joshua became leader of the Jewish people and led them into the land that God promised to give them.

4:9 rest Literally, "sabbath rest," meaning a sharing in the rest that God began after he created the world.

from his work as God did. 11Let us try as
hard as we can to enter God's rest so that
no one will fail by following the example
of those who refused to obey.

12God's word is alive and working and
is sharper than a double-edged sword. It
cuts all the way into us, where the soul
and the spirit are joined,
to the center of our joints
and bones. And it judges
the thoughts and feelings
in our hearts. 13Nothing
in all the world can be
hidden from God. Every-
thing is clear and lies
open before him, and to
him we must explain the
way we have lived.

> Even though Jesus was the Son of God, he learned obedience by what he suffered.
> —Hebrews 5:8

Jesus Is Our High Priest

14Since we have a great high priest,
Jesus the Son of God, who has gone into
heaven, let us hold on to the faith we
have. 15For our high priest is able to understand our weaknesses. When he lived
on earth, he was tempted in every way
that we are, but he did not sin.
16Let us, then, feel
very sure that we can
come before God's
throne where there is
grace. There we can
receive mercy and
grace to help us when we need it.

> EMAIL FROM GOD 4:16
> **Courage**
> Where can you find help when you need it?

5 Every high priest is chosen from
among other people. He is given the
work of going before God for them to offer gifts and sacrifices for sins. 2Since he
himself is weak, he is able to be gentle
with those who do not understand and
who are doing wrong things. 3Because he
is weak, the high priest must offer sacrifices for his own sins and also for the sins
of the people.

4To be a high priest is an honor, but no
one chooses himself for this work. He
must be called by God as Aaron[n] was. 5So
also Christ did not choose himself to
have the honor of being a high priest, but
God chose him. God said to him,

"You are my Son.
Today I have become your Father."

Psalm 2:7

6And in another Scripture God says,
"You are a priest forever,
a priest like Melchizedek."[n]

Psalm 110:4

7While Jesus lived on earth, he prayed
to God and asked God for help. He prayed
with loud cries and tears to the One who
could save him from
death, and his prayer was
heard because he trusted
God. 8Even though Jesus
was the Son of God, he
learned obedience by
what he suffered. 9And
because his obedience
was perfect, he was able
to give eternal salvation
to all who obey him. 10In
this way God made Jesus
a high priest, a priest like Melchizedek.

Warning Against Falling Away

11We have much to say about this, but
it is hard to explain because you are so
slow to understand. 12By now you
should be teachers, but you need someone to teach you again the first lessons of
God's message. You still need the teaching that is like milk. You are not ready for
solid food. 13Anyone who lives on milk is
still a baby and knows nothing about right
teaching. 14But solid food is for those
who are grown up. They have practiced
in order to know the difference between
good and evil.

6 So let us go on to grown-up teaching.
Let us not go back over the beginning
lessons we learned about Christ. We
should not again start teaching about faith
in God and about turning away from those
acts that lead to death. 2We should not
return to the teaching about baptisms,[n]
about laying on of hands,[n] about the

5:4 Aaron Aaron was Moses' brother and the first Jewish high priest.

5:6 Melchizedek A priest and king who lived in the time of Abraham. (Read Genesis 14:17-24.)

6:2 baptisms The word here may refer to Christian baptism, or it may refer to the Jewish ceremonial washings.

6:2 laying on of hands The laying on of hands had many purposes, including the giving of a blessing, power, or authority.

DEATH ON A CROSS

Hebrews 6:6

The Romans used crucifixion—to be killed on a cross—as their worst form of the death penalty. It was used only for criminals and slaves. Sometimes when a person was killed on a cross, their wrists were tied to a crossbeam of wood. Other times their wrists were actually nailed to the wood. Then the crossbeam would be attached to a tall stake. Their feet might also be nailed to the tall stake.

When people were hung on a cross like this, they had a hard time holding themselves up so they could breathe. Eventually, they died because they got too tired to hold themselves up. It was a horrible way to die. In fact, it was so horrible that the Israelites wouldn't even talk about it in an everyday conversation. Some people wondered how Jesus could be the Messiah and yet die such a shameful death. Paul said, though, that Jesus' death on a cross was the power of God for all of us. (Check out 1 Corinthians 1:23–24, p. 1546.)

raising of the dead and eternal judgment.
3And we will go on to grown-up teaching
if God allows.

4Some people cannot be brought back
again to a changed life. They were once
in God's light, and enjoyed heaven's gift,
and shared in the Holy Spirit. **5**They
found out how good God's word is, and
they received the powers of his new
world. **6**But they fell away from Christ. It
is impossible to bring them back to a
changed life again, because they are nailing the Son of God to a cross again and
are shaming him in front of others.

7Some people are like land that gets
plenty of rain. The land produces a good
crop for those who work it, and it receives
God's blessings. **8**Other people are like
land that grows thorns and weeds and is
worthless. It is in danger of being cursed
by God and will be destroyed by fire.

9Dear friends, we are saying this to
you, but we really expect better things
from you that will lead to your salvation.
10God is fair; he will not forget the work
you did and the love you showed for him
by helping his people. And he will remember that you are still helping them.
11We want each of you to go on with the
same hard work all your lives so you will
surely get what you hope for. **12**We do not
want you to become lazy. Be like those
who through faith and patience will receive what God has promised.

13God made a promise to Abraham.
And as there is no one greater than God,
he used himself when he swore to Abraham, **14**saying, "I will surely bless you and
give you many descendants."ⁿ **15**Abraham waited patiently for this to happen,
and he received what God promised.

16People always use the name of
someone greater than themselves when
they swear. The oath proves that what
they say is true, and this ends all arguing.
17God wanted to prove that his promise
was true to those who would get what he
promised. And he wanted them to understand clearly that his purposes never

6:14 "I . . . descendants." Quotation from Genesis 22:17.

change, so he made an oath. **18**These two
things cannot change: God cannot lie
when he makes a promise,
and he cannot lie
when he makes an
oath. These things
encourage us who
came to God for
safety. They give us
strength to hold on to the hope we have
been given. **19**We have this hope as an
anchor for the soul, sure and strong. It
enters behind the curtain in the Most
Holy Place in heaven, **20**where Jesus has
gone ahead of us and for us. He has become the high priest forever, a priest like
Melchizedek.[n]

eMAIL! FROM GOD **6:18**
Truth
Can God lie?

The Priest Melchizedek

7 Melchizedek[n] was the king of Salem
and a priest for God Most High. He
met Abraham when Abraham was coming
back after defeating the kings. When
they met, Melchizedek blessed Abraham,
2and Abraham gave him a tenth of everything he had brought back from the battle. First, Melchizedek's name means
"king of goodness," and he is king of Salem, which means "king of peace." **3**No
one knows who Melchizedek's father or
mother was,[n] where he came from, when
he was born, or when he died. Melchizedek is like the Son of God; he continues
being a priest forever.

4You can see how great Melchizedek
was. Abraham, the great father, gave him
a tenth of everything that he won in battle. **5**Now the law says that those in the
tribe of Levi who become priests must
collect a tenth from the people—their
own people—even though the priests
and the people are from the family of
Abraham. **6**Melchizedek was not from
the tribe of Levi, but he collected a tenth
from Abraham. And he blessed Abraham,
the man who had God's promises. **7**Now
everyone knows that the more important
person blesses the less important person. **8**Priests receive a tenth, even
though they are only men who live and
then die. But Melchizedek, who received
a tenth from Abraham, continues living,
as the Scripture says. **9**We might even
say that Levi, who receives a tenth, also
paid it when Abraham paid Melchizedek a
tenth. **10**Levi was not yet born, but he
was in the body of his ancestor when
Melchizedek met Abraham.

11The people were given the law[n]
based on a system of priests from the
tribe of Levi, but they could not be made

FAITH CHALLENGE

Here's a challenge for you. Read 6:12 to find out what kind of people we should look up to. What person has had the biggest impact on your life? What areas of your life are you most tempted to be "lazy" in? School work? Chores at home? Bible study?

TESTING IT

Hebrews 6:12
We do not want you to become lazy. Be like those who through faith and patience will receive what God has promised.

6:20; 7:1 Melchizedek A priest and king who lived in the time of Abraham. (Read Genesis 14:17-24.)

7:3 No . . . was Literally, "Melchizedek was without father, without mother, without genealogy."

7:11 The . . . law This refers to the people of Israel who were given the Law of Moses.

perfect through that system. So there
was a need for another priest to come, a
priest like Melchizedek, not Aaron.
12And when a different kind of priest
comes, the law must be changed, too.
13We are saying these things about
Christ, who belonged to a different tribe.
No one from that tribe ever served as a
priest at the altar. **14**It is clear that our
Lord came from the tribe of Judah, and
Moses said nothing about priests belonging to that tribe.

Jesus Is like Melchizedek

15And this becomes even more clear
when we see that another priest comes
who is like Melchizedek.* **16**He was not
made a priest by human rules and laws
but through the power of his life, which
continues forever. **17**It is said about him,

> "You are a priest forever,
> a priest like Melchizedek."
>
> *Psalm 110:4*

18The old rule is now set aside, because it was weak and useless. **19**The
law of Moses could not make anything
perfect. But now a better hope has been
given to us, and with this hope we can
come near to God. **20**It is important that

7:15 Melchizedek A priest and king who lived in the time of Abraham. (Read Genesis 14:17-24.)

DOING YOUR BEST

Hi, everybody. How important is it to you to do your best? Sometimes? All the time? We have a friend who's having some problems in this area. Let's welcome Zachary, age 9, to Connect 2-You.

Hello, Zachary. What's your problem?

My problem is school. I must be dumb or something because I have to work twice as hard as everyone else just to get C's. It's not fair. My teacher says she wishes she had a whole class of students just like me, but I think she's just saying that. Is it really worth it to work so hard just to be average?

Good question, Zachary. The Bible has some interesting things to say about this topic. You won't find any verses that tell us to make straight A's or to be the best at something. What the Bible does tell us is to run the race that is set before us. That means to do our best in every situation. That's all God asks from us—our best, whether our best earns us an "A" or a "C." If you would like some tips in this area, check out the Livin' It page on doing your best, 1 Corinthians 9:24-27, p. 1554.

God doesn't judge us based on how well we do compared to other people, Zachary. He judges us based on what we do with the talents and abilities he has given us. Keep doing your best, Zachary. You won't find it a waste of time.

God did this with an oath. Others became
priests without an oath, **21**but Christ became a priest with God's oath. God said:

"The Lord has made a promise
and will not change his mind.
'You are a priest forever.' "

Psalm 110:4

22This means that Jesus is the guarantee
of a better agreement[n] from God to his
people.

23When one of the other priests died,
he could not continue being a priest. So
there were many priests. **24**But because
Jesus lives forever, he will never stop
serving as priest. **25**So he is able always
to save those who come to God through
him because he always lives, asking God
to help them.

26Jesus is the kind of high priest we
need. He is holy, sinless, pure, not influenced by sinners, and he is raised above
the heavens. **27**He is not like the other
priests who had to offer sacrifices every
day, first for their own sins, and then for
the sins of the people. Christ offered his
sacrifice only once and for all time when
he offered himself. **28**The law chooses
high priests who are people with weaknesses, but the word of God's oath came
later than the law. It made God's Son to
be the high priest, and that Son has been
made perfect forever.

Jesus Is Our High Priest

8 Here is the point of what we are saying: We have a high priest who sits on
the right side of God's throne in heaven.
2Our high priest serves in the Most Holy
Place, the true place of worship that was
made by God, not by humans.

3Every high priest has the work of offering gifts and sacrifices to God. So our
high priest must also offer something to
God. **4**If our high priest were now living
on earth, he would not be a priest, because there are already priests here who
follow the law by offering gifts to God.
5The work they do as priests is only a
copy and a shadow of what is in heaven.
This is why God warned Moses when he
was ready to build the Holy Tent: "Be
very careful to make everything by the
plan I showed you on the mountain."[n]

6But the priestly work that has been
given to Jesus is much

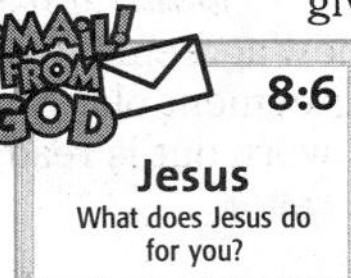

eMAIL! FROM GOD
8:6
Jesus
What does Jesus do for you?

greater than the
work that was given
to the other priests.
In the same way, the
new agreement that
Jesus brought from
God to his people is much greater than
the old one. And the new agreement is
based on promises of better things.

7If there had been nothing wrong with
the first agreement,[n] there would have
been no need for a second agreement.
8But God found something wrong with
his people. He says:

"Look, the time is coming, says the
Lord,
when I will make a new agreement
with the people of Israel
and the people of Judah.
9 It will not be like the agreement
I made with their ancestors
when I took them by the hand
to bring them out of Egypt.
But they broke that agreement,
and I turned away from them, says
the Lord.
10 This is the agreement I will make
with the people of Israel at that
time, says the Lord.
I will put my teachings in their minds
and write them on their hearts.
I will be their God,
and they will be my people.
11 People will no longer have to teach
their neighbors and relatives
to know the Lord,
because all people will know me,
from the least to the most
important.
12 I will forgive them for the wicked
things they did,

7:22 agreement God gives a contract or agreement to his people. For the Jews, this agreement was the Law of Moses. But now God has given a better agreement to his people through Christ.

8:5 "Be . . . mountain." Quotation from Exodus 25:40.

8:7 first agreement The contract God gave the Jewish people when he gave them the Law of Moses.

and I will not remember their sins
anymore." *Jeremiah 31:31-34*

13God called this a new agreement, so he has made the first agreement old. And anything that is old and worn out is ready to disappear.

The Old Agreement

9 The first agreement[n] had rules for worship and a man-made place for worship. **2**The Holy Tent was set up for this. The first area in the Tent was called the Holy Place. In it were the lamp and the table with the bread that was made holy for God. **3**Behind the second curtain was a room called the Most Holy Place. **4**In it was a golden altar for burning incense and the Ark covered with gold that held the old agreement. Inside this Ark was a golden jar of manna, Aaron's rod that once grew leaves, and the stone tablets of the old agreement. **5**Above the Ark were the creatures that showed God's glory, whose wings reached over the lid. But we cannot tell everything about these things now.

6When everything in the Tent was made ready in this way, the priests went into the first room every day to worship. **7**But only the high priest could go into the second room, and he did that only once a year. He could never enter the inner room without taking blood with him, which he offered to God for himself and for sins the people did without knowing they did them. **8**The Holy Spirit uses this to show that the way into the Most Holy Place was not open while the system of the old Holy Tent was still being used. **9**This is an example for the present time. It shows that the gifts and sacrifices offered cannot make the conscience of the worshiper perfect. **10**These gifts and sacrifices were only about food and drink and special washings. They were rules for the body, to be followed until the time of God's new way.

The New Agreement

11But when Christ came as the high priest of the good things we now have, he entered the greater and more perfect tent. It is not made by humans and does not belong to this world. **12**Christ entered the Most Holy Place only once—and for all time. He did not take with him the blood of goats and calves. His sacrifice was his own blood, and by it he set us free from sin forever. **13**The blood of goats and bulls and the ashes of a cow are sprinkled on the people who are unclean, and this makes their bodies clean again. **14**How much more is done by the blood of Christ. He offered himself through the eternal Spirit[n] as a perfect sacrifice to God. His blood will make our consciences pure from useless acts so we may serve the living God.

15For this reason Christ brings a new agreement from God to his people. Those who are called by God can now receive the blessings he has promised, blessings that will last forever. They can have those things because Christ died so that the people who lived under the first agreement could be set free from sin.

16When there is a will,[n] it must be proven that the one who wrote that will is dead. **17**A will means nothing while the person is alive; it can be used only after the person dies. **18**This is why even the first agreement could not begin without blood to show death. **19**First, Moses told all the people every command in the law. Next he took the blood of calves and mixed it with water. Then he used red wool and a branch of the hyssop plant to sprinkle it on the book of the law and on all the people. **20**He said, "This is the blood that begins the Agreement that God commanded you to obey."[n] **21**In the same way, Moses sprinkled the blood on the Holy Tent and over all the things used in worship. **22**The law says that al-

---

9:1 first agreement The contract God gave the Jewish people when he gave them the Law of Moses.

9:14 Spirit This refers to the Holy Spirit, to Christ's own spirit, or to the spiritual and eternal nature of his sacrifice.

9:16 will A legal document that shows how a person's money and property are to be distributed at the time of death. This is the same word in Greek as "agreement" in verse 15.

9:20 "This . . . obey." Quotation from Exodus 24:8.

most everything must be made clean by
blood, and sins cannot be forgiven without blood to show death.

Christ's Death Takes Away Sins

23So the copies of the real things in
heaven had to be made clean by animal
sacrifices. But the real things in heaven
need much better sacrifices. 24Christ did
not go into the Most Holy Place made by
humans, which is only a copy of the real
one. He went into heaven itself and is
there now before God to help us. 25The
high priest enters the Most Holy Place
once every year with blood that is not his
own. But Christ did not offer himself
many times. 26Then he would have had
to suffer many times since the world was
made. But Christ came only once and for
all time at just the right time to take away
all sin by sacrificing himself.

EMAIL FROM GOD
9:27–28
Salvation
What Jesus will bring at his second coming

27Just as everyone
must die once and be
judged, 28so Christ
was offered as a sac-
rifice one time to
take away the sins of
many people. And he will come a second
time, not to offer himself for sin, but to
bring salvation to those who are waiting
for him.

10 The law is only an unclear picture
of the good things coming in the
future; it is not the real thing. The people
under the law offer the same sacrifices
every year, but these sacrifices can never
make perfect those who come near to
worship God. 2If the law could make
them perfect, the sacrifices would have
already stopped. The worshipers would
be made clean, and they would no longer
have a sense of sin. 3But these sacrifices
remind them of their sins every year,
4because it is impossible for the blood of
bulls and goats to take away sins.

5So when Christ came into the world,
he said:

"You do not want sacrifices and
offerings,
but you have prepared a body for
me.
6You do not ask for burnt offerings
and offerings to take away sins.
7Then I said, 'Look, I have come.
It is written about me in the book.
God, I have come to do what you
want.' " *Psalm 40:6-8*

8In this Scripture he first said, "You do
not want sacrifices and offerings. You do
not ask for burnt offerings and offerings
to take away sins." (These are all sacrifices that the law commands.) 9Then he
said, "Look, I have come to do what you
want." God ends the first system of sacrifices so he can set up the new system.
10And because of this, we are made holy
through the sacrifice Christ made in his
body once and for all time.

11Every day the priests stand and do
their religious service, often offering the
same sacrifices. Those sacrifices can
never take away sins. 12But after Christ
offered one sacrifice for sins, forever, he
sat down at the right side of God. 13And
now Christ waits there for his enemies to
be put under his power. 14With one sacrifice he made perfect forever those who
are being made holy.

15The Holy Spirit also tells us about
this. First he says:

16"This is the agreement[n] I will make
with them at that time, says the
Lord.
I will put my teachings in their hearts
and write them on their minds."
Jeremiah 31:33

17Then he says:

"Their sins and the evil things they
do—
I will not remember anymore."
Jeremiah 31:34

18Now when these have been forgiven,
there is no more need for a sacrifice for
sins.

Continue to Trust God

19So, brothers and sisters, we are
completely free to enter the Most Holy
Place without fear because of the blood of
Jesus' death. 20We can enter through a
new and living way that Jesus opened for

10:16 agreement God gives a contract or agreement to his people. For the Jews, this agreement was the Law of Moses. But now God has given a better agreement to his people through Christ.

us. It leads through the curtain—Christ's
body. 21And since we have a great priest
over God's house, 22let us come near to
God with a sincere heart and a sure faith,
because we have been made free from a
guilty conscience, and our bodies have
been washed with pure water. 23Let us
hold firmly to the hope that we have confessed, because we can trust God to do
what he promised.
24Let us think about each other and
help each other to show love and do good
deeds. 25You should not stay away from
the church meetings, as some are doing,
but you should meet together and encourage each other. Do this even more as
you see the day[n] coming.
26If we decide to go on sinning after
we have learned the truth, there is no
longer any sacrifice for sins. 27There is
nothing but fear in waiting for the judgment and the terrible fire that will destroy all those who live against God.
28Anyone who refused to obey the law of
Moses was found guilty from the proof
given by two or three witnesses. He was
put to death without mercy. 29So what do
you think should be done to those who do
not respect the Son of God, who look at
the blood of the agreement that made
them holy as no different from others'
blood, who insult the Spirit of God's
grace? Surely they should have a much
worse punishment. 30We know that God
said, "I will punish those who do wrong; I
will repay them."[n] And he also said, "The
Lord will judge his people."[n] 31It is a terrible thing to fall into the hands of the living God.
32Remember those days in the past
when you first learned the truth. You had
a hard struggle with many sufferings, but
you continued strong. 33Sometimes you
were hurt and attacked before crowds of
people, and sometimes you shared with
those who were being treated that way.
34You helped the prisoners. You even had
joy when all that you owned was taken
from you, because you knew you had
something better and more lasting.
35So do not lose the courage you had
in the past, which has a great reward.
36You must hold on, so you can do what

FAITH links

FAMILY TIME

HEBREWS 10:25

Think about how life would change if you and your family only met together once every two or three months. You would hardly know each other, wouldn't you? Even though they may bug you at times, you've got to admit that your family is pretty cool. (C'mon, admit it.)

God wants his family to be close. That's why the writer of Hebrews encouraged Christians to meet together often. That's why church involvement is important. When we're together as a church family, we can encourage each other. We can show love to one another. Who can you encourage today in your family? How about in your church family?

Family Feud, Genesis 27, p. 37

Approaching God, Numbers 3:10, p. 180

The MLP, Ruth 1:16–17, p. 345

Peace in the Family, Psalm 133, p. 811

Faith Workout, Acts 16:4–5, p. 1493

MVFM?, Galatians 3:26–27, p. 1589

10:25 day The day Christ will come to judge all people and take his people to live with him.
10:30 "I . . . them." Quotation from Deuteronomy 32:35.
10:30 "The Lord . . . people." Quotation from Deuteronomy 32:36; Psalm 135:14.

God wants and receive what he has
promised. 37For in a very short time,
"The One who is coming will come
and will not be delayed.
38 The person who is right with me
will live by trusting in me.
But if he turns back with fear,
I will not be pleased with him."

Habakkuk 2:3-4

39But we are not those who turn back
and are lost. We are people who have
faith and are saved.

What Is Faith?

11 Faith means being sure of the
things we hope for and knowing
that something is real even if we
do not see it. 2Faith
is the reason we re-
member great peo-
ple who lived in the
past.

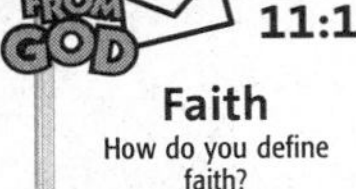

11:1

Faith

How do you define faith?

3It is by faith we
understand that the whole world was
made by God's command so what we see
was made by something that cannot be
seen.
4It was by faith that Abel offered God
a better sacrifice than Cain did. God said
he was pleased with the gifts Abel offered and called Abel a good man because
of his faith. Abel died, but through his
faith he is still speaking.
5It was by faith that Enoch was taken
to heaven so he would not die. He could
not be found, because God had taken him
away. Before he was taken, the Scripture
says that he was a man who truly pleased
God. 6Without faith no one can please
God. Anyone who comes to God must believe that he is real and that he rewards
those who truly want to find him.
7It was by faith that Noah heard God's
warnings about things he could not yet
see. He obeyed God and built a large boat
to save his family. By his faith, Noah
showed that the world was wrong, and he
became one of those who are made right
with God through faith.
8It was by faith Abraham obeyed
God's call to go to another place God
promised to give him. He left his own
country, not knowing where he was to go.

FAITH links

PEOPLE OF FAITH

HEBREWS 11

Who is one of your heroes? Maybe this is a person you've read about in a story. Chapter 11 of Hebrews describes some real-life heroes. They're "heroes of the faith." Why are their lives so special? They had great faith. That's why this chapter is called the "faith" chapter of the Bible. You've probably heard some of these stories in Sunday school. Abraham and Sarah, Jacob, Joseph, Moses, and others show us what having faith in God is like.

You can be a hero of faith to someone. How? You can start by sharing your faith with someone. Let that person know what God has done in your life. You'll be a true hero!

Download these Faithlinks on telling others what God has done for you:

A Bad Reaction, Jeremiah 36, p. 1043

How Do I Love You?, Malachi 1:1–5, p. 1267

Just Say Yes!, Matthew 9:9–13, p. 1289

The Unpopular Choice, Mark 15:42–43, p. 1360

Prayer Priority, Luke 5:15–16, p. 1376

The Gift, John 3:16–18, p. 1427

BEING FAITHFUL

Hebrews 11

Livin' it

True Blue Have you ever heard someone say, "He's a true-blue friend"? What do you think that means—a friend who fell into a tub of blue paint? Or someone who went out in mid-winter with no coat? 'Fraid not. It's describing someone who is loyal and sticks with you, no matter what. Do you have a friend like that? Are you that kind of friend?

The writer of Hebrews tells about some people who were "heroes of the faith." They were loyal and faithful to God. They showed this great faith in their lives. (Look at Hebrews 11.) How can you be a hero of faith? You can start by letting others know what God has done in your life! Then you can be "true blue" to God!

MORE FAITH links

An Unsung Hero, p. 347
Loyal to a Friend, p. 409
The Salt Promise, p. 576
Love for a Lifetime, p. 891
A Broken Promise, p. 989
One of the Faithful, p. 1482

"Who are some of your heroes, Tagg?"

"Well, I'm really into Captain Computer and Super Surfman. How about you?"

"Those guys are cool, but check out these real heroes when you download these links."

Lights, Camera, . . . Actions!, Genesis 12:1–3, p. 17
- Imagine being asked to pack your things and move to a foreign country—one you know nothing about. Would you go? Check out this link to see what Abraham did.
- Being faithful to God involves actions, not just words. What do your actions tell about you?

Read My Lips?, Deuteronomy 26:16–19, p. 260
- Suppose you told your mother you would take out the garbage, but didn't do it. Would she believe that you really meant what you said? God wants us to do what we say. Do you mean what you say? Then act like it!

Believe It or Not, Luke 1:20, 38, p. 1366
- Did you know that you could choose to believe something if you wanted to believe? Link here to learn about faithful people who believed God could do the impossible.

my FAVORITE links

9It was by faith that he lived like a foreigner in the country God promised to
give him. He lived in tents with Isaac and
Jacob, who had received that same promise from God. **10**Abraham was waiting
for the city[n] that has real foundations—
the city planned and built by God.

11He was too old to have children, and
Sarah could not have children. It was by
faith that Abraham was made able to become a father, because he trusted God to
do what he had promised. **12**This man
was so old he was almost dead, but from
him came as many descendants as there
are stars in the sky. Like the sand on the
seashore, they could not be counted.

13All these great people died in faith.
They did not get the things that God
promised his people, but they saw them
coming far in the future and were glad.
They said they were like visitors and
strangers on earth. **14**When people say
such things, they show they are looking
for a country that will be their own. **15**If
they had been thinking about the country
they had left, they could have gone back.
16But they were waiting for a better
country—a heavenly country. So God is
not ashamed to be called their God, because he has prepared a city for them.

17It was by faith that Abraham, when
God tested him, offered his son Isaac as a
sacrifice. God made the promises to
Abraham, but Abraham was ready to offer
his own son as a sacrifice. **18**God had
said, "The descendants I promised you
will be from Isaac."[n] **19**Abraham believed
that God could raise the dead, and really,
it was as if Abraham got Isaac back from
death.

20It was by faith that Isaac blessed the
future of Jacob and Esau. **21**It was by faith
that Jacob, as he was dying, blessed each
one of Joseph's sons. Then he worshiped
as he leaned on the top of his walking
stick.

22It was by faith that Joseph, while he
was dying, spoke about the Israelites
leaving Egypt and gave instructions
about what to do with his body.

23It was by faith that Moses' parents
hid him for three months after he was
born. They saw that Moses was a beautiful baby, and they were not afraid to disobey the king's order.

24It was by faith that Moses, when he
grew up, refused to be called the son of
the king of Egypt's daughter. **25**He chose
to suffer with God's people instead of enjoying sin for a short time. **26**He thought
it was better to suffer for the Christ than
to have all the treasures of Egypt, because he was looking for God's reward.
27It was by faith that Moses left Egypt
and was not afraid of the king's anger.
Moses continued strong as if he could
see the God that no one can see. **28**It was
by faith that Moses prepared the Passover and spread the blood on the doors so
the one who brings death would not kill
the firstborn sons of Israel.

29It was by faith that the people
crossed the Red Sea as if it were dry land.
But when the Egyptians tried it, they
were drowned.

30It was by faith that the walls of Jericho fell after the people had marched
around them for seven days.

31It was by faith that Rahab, the prostitute, welcomed the spies and was not
killed with those who refused to obey
God.

32Do I need to give more examples? I
do not have time to tell you about Gideon,
Barak, Samson, Jephthah, David, Samuel,
and the prophets. **33**Through their faith
they defeated kingdoms. They did what
was right, received God's promises, and
shut the mouths of lions. **34**They stopped
great fires and were saved from being
killed with swords. They were weak, and
yet were made strong. They were powerful in battle and defeated other armies.
35Women received their dead relatives
raised back to life. Others were tortured
and refused to accept their freedom so
they could be raised from the dead to a
better life. **36**Some were laughed at and
beaten. Others were put in chains and
thrown into prison. **37**They were stoned

11:10 city The spiritual "city" where God's people live with him. Also called "the heavenly Jerusalem." (See Hebrews 12:22.)

11:18 "The descendants . . . Isaac." Quotation from Genesis 21:12.

to death, they were cut in half, and they
were killed with swords. Some wore the
skins of sheep and goats. They were poor,
abused, and treated badly. 38The world
was not good enough for them! They wandered in deserts and mountains, living in
caves and holes in the earth.
39All these people are known for their
faith, but none of them received what God
had promised. 40God planned to give us
something better so that they would be
made perfect, but only together with us.

Follow Jesus' Example

12 We have around us many people
whose lives tell us what faith
means. So let us run the race that is before us and never give up. We should remove from our lives anything that would
get in the way and the sin that so easily
holds us back. 2Let us look only to Jesus,
the One who began our faith and who
makes it perfect. He suffered death on
the cross. But he accepted the shame as
if it were nothing because of the joy that
God put before him. And now he is sitting
at the right side of God's throne. 3Think
about Jesus' example. He held on while
wicked people were doing evil things to
him. So do not get tired and stop trying.

God Is like a Father

4You are struggling against sin, but
your struggles have not yet caused you
to be killed. 5You have forgotten the encouraging words that call you his children:

"My child, don't think the Lord's
discipline is worth nothing,
and don't stop trying when he
corrects you.
6 The Lord disciplines those he loves,
and he punishes everyone he
accepts as his child." *Proverbs 3:11-12*

7So hold on through your sufferings,
because they are like a father's discipline. God is treating you as
children. All chil-
dren are disciplined
by their fathers. 8If
you are never disci-
plined (and every
child must be disci-
plined), you are not true children. 9We
have all had fathers here on earth who
disciplined us, and we respected them.

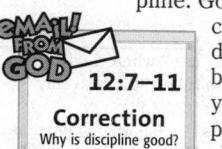

eMail! FROM GOD
12:7–11
Correction
Why is discipline good?

GO FOR IT!

HEBREWS 12:1-4

Have you ever seen a marathon runner competing in a race? Running a marathon takes endurance. You can't stop at the first mile and still call yourself a marathon runner. You have to make it all 26 miles to cross the finish line.

The writer of Hebrews compared the Christian life to a race. Being a Christian requires endurance, just like being a marathon runner does. You have to endure hard times, disappointments, and other struggles. But God promises his presence and his help. He's with you all the way, cheering you on!

Link here to find out about your biggest cheerleader:

From Hopeless to Hopeful, Exodus 6:9, p. 83

Your Worst Enemy, Exodus 7—11, p. 85

Faith of Our Fathers, Joshua 4:4–9, p. 280

A Given, 1 Chronicles 5:18–20, p. 526

Attention, Please! Luke 8:11–15, p. 1383

The Sacrifice of Service, Philippians 2:17, 25–30, p. 1612

FAITH links

YOU'RE CORRECT!

HEBREWS 12:5-7

Not many of us like to be disciplined, even when we do wrong. What does discipline mean? It means to correct someone. Why do parents discipline their children? They do it because they love them and want the best for their children. The writer of Hebrews wrote advice for Christians about discipline. Like any parent, God disciplines his children when they do wrong. God's discipline shows his love for us.

From Hopeless to Hopeful, Exodus 6:9, p. 83

The Weak Link, Judges 16, p. 334

A Shortcut, 1 Samuel 13:1–14, p. 369

A Model of Forgiveness, Ezekiel 16:59–63, p. 1103

Believe It or Not, Luke 1:20, 38, p. 1366

Don't Play Favorites, James 2:1–7, p. 1691

So it is even more important that we accept discipline from the Father of our
spirits so we will have life. 10Our fathers
on earth disciplined us for a short time in
the way they thought was best. But God
disciplines us to help us, so we can become holy as he is. 11We do not enjoy
being disciplined. It is painful, but later,
after we have learned from it, we have
peace, because we start living in the right
way.

Be Careful How You Live

12You have become weak, so make
yourselves strong again. 13Live in the
right way so that you will be saved and
your weakness will not cause you to be
lost.

14Try to live in peace with all people,
and try to live free from sin. Anyone
whose life is not holy will never see the
Lord. 15Be careful that no one fails to receive God's grace and begins to cause
trouble among you. A person like that can
ruin many of you. 16Be careful that no
one takes part in sexual sin or is like
Esau and never thinks about God. As the
oldest son, Esau would have received
everything from his father, but he sold all
that for a single meal. 17You remember
that after Esau did this, he wanted to
get his father's blessing, but his father
refused. Esau could find no way to
change what he had done, even though
he wanted the blessing so much that he
cried.

18You have not come to a mountain
that can be touched and that is burning
with fire. You have not come to darkness,
sadness, and storms. 19You have not
come to the noise of a trumpet or to the
sound of a voice like the one the people of
Israel heard and begged not to hear another word. 20They did not want to hear
the command: "If anything, even an animal, touches the mountain, it must be put
to death with stones."[n] 21What they saw
was so terrible that Moses said, "I am
shaking with fear."[n]

22But you have come to Mount Zion,[n]
to the city of the living God, the heavenly
Jerusalem. You have come to thousands
of angels gathered together with joy.
23You have come to the meeting of God's
firstborn[n] children whose names are

12:20 "If . . . stones." Quotation from Exodus 19:12-13.

12:21 "I . . . fear." Quotation from Deuteronomy 9:19.

12:22 Mount Zion Another name for Jerusalem, here meaning the spiritual city of God's people.

12:23 firstborn The first son born in a Jewish family was given the most important place in the family and received special blessings. All of God's children are like that.

written in heaven. You have come to God,
the judge of all people, and to the spirits
of good people who have been made perfect. 24You have come to Jesus, the One
who brought the new agreement from
God to his people, and you have come to
the sprinkled blood* that has a better
message than the blood of Abel.*
25So be careful and do not refuse to
listen when God speaks. Others refused
to listen to him when he warned them on
earth, and they did not escape. So it will
be worse for us if we refuse to listen to
God who warns us from heaven. 26When
he spoke before, his voice shook the
earth, but now he has promised, "Once
again I will shake not only the earth but
also the heavens."* 27The words "once
again" clearly show us that everything
that was made—things that can be shak-
en—will be destroyed. Only the things
that cannot be shaken will remain.
28So let us be thankful, because we
have a kingdom that cannot be shaken.
We should worship God in a way that
pleases him with respect and fear, 29be-
cause our God is like a fire that burns
things up.

13 Keep on loving each other as
brothers and sisters. 2Remember
to welcome strangers, because some
who have done this have welcomed angels without knowing it. 3Remember
those who are in prison as if you were in
prison with them. Remember those who
are suffering as if you were suffering with
them.
4Marriage should be honored by everyone, and husband and wife should keep
their marriage pure. God will judge as
guilty those who take part in sexual sins.
5Keep your lives free from the love of
money, and be satisfied with what you
have. God has said,

"I will never leave you;
I will never forget you."

Deuteronomy 31:6

6So we can be sure when we say,

"I will not be afraid, because the Lord
is my helper.
People can't do anything to me."

Psalm 118:6

7Remember your leaders who taught

FAITH links

NEVER ALONE 

HEBREWS 13:5-6

Quick! Name someone who is always with you—not just some of the time, but always. Can't think of anyone? God is with you 24/7. Know what else? He will never forget about you. N-E-V-E-R. Can anyone else make that claim?

That's why the writer of Hebrews quoted God's promise from the Book of Deuteronomy. God promised his people in Old Testament times that he wouldn't leave them or forget about them. That promise is for you, too. He also promises to help you. You don't have to be afraid of anything. Isn't that good news?

Connect here for more good news:

Good Plans, Genesis 45:7–8, p. 64

The Perfect Sacrifice, Leviticus 1—7, p. 135

Real Faith or Really Scared?, Judges 4 , p. 315

Long-lasting Hope, Hosea 14, p. 1184

Mission Impossible?, Mark 5:21–24, 35–43, p. 1337

Hard Times, 2 Corinthians 1:8–10, p. 1570

12:24 sprinkled blood The blood of Jesus' death.
12:24 Abel The son of Adam and Eve, who was killed by his brother Cain (Genesis 4:8).
12:26 "Once . . . heavens." Quotation from Haggai 2:6, 21.

God's message to you. Remember how
they lived and died, and copy their faith.
8Jesus Christ is the same yesterday, today, and forever.

9Do not let all kinds of strange teachings lead you into the wrong way. Your
hearts should be strengthened by God's
grace, not by obeying rules about foods,
which do not help those who obey them.

10We have a sacrifice, but the priests
who serve in the Holy Tent cannot eat
from it. 11The high priest carries the
blood of animals into the Most Holy Place
where he offers this blood for sins. But
the bodies of the animals are burned outside the camp. 12So Jesus also suffered
outside the city to make his people holy
with his own blood. 13So let us go to
Jesus outside the camp, holding on as he
did when we are abused.

14Here on earth we do not have a city
that lasts forever, but we are looking for
the city that we will
have in the future.
15So through Jesus
let us always offer to
God our sacrifice of
praise, coming from
lips that speak his
name. 16Do not forget to do good to others, and share with them, because such
sacrifices please God.

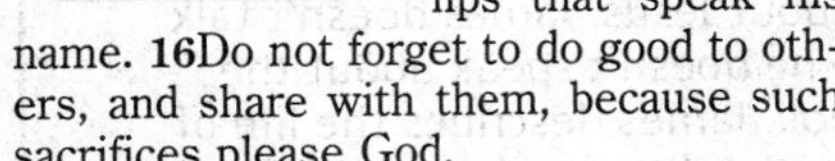

13:15
Thankfulness
What can you offer God?

17Obey your leaders and act under
their authority. They are watching over
you, because they are responsible for
your souls. Obey them so that they will
do this work with joy, not sadness. It will
not help you to make their work hard.

18Pray for us. We are sure that we
have a clear conscience, because we always want to do the right thing. 19I especially beg you to pray so that God will
send me back to you soon.

20-21I pray that the God of peace will
give you every good thing you need so
you can do what he wants. God raised
from the dead our Lord Jesus, the Great
Shepherd of the sheep, because of the
blood of his death. His blood began the
eternal agreement that God made with his
people. I pray that God will do in us what
pleases him, through Jesus Christ, and to
him be glory forever and ever. Amen.

22My brothers and sisters, I beg you
to listen patiently to this message I have
written to encourage you, because it is
not very long. 23I want you to know that
our brother Timothy has been let out of
prison. If he arrives soon, we will both
come to see you.

24Greet all your leaders and all of
God's people. Those from Italy send
greetings to you.

25Grace be with you all.

FAITH IN ACTION

Hi, newbies! I'm James, and I'm glad you're reading this book. You're probably wondering who I am. I was the half brother of Jesus. And I also was the leader of the church in Jerusalem. If you connect to Acts 15:12–21, p. 1490, you'll see that I was really the head of the whole church. I often worked together with Paul. Even though we didn't always agree on everything, we made major decisions for the church.

I wrote this book to Christians who were having trouble living out their faith. You know, believing in Jesus is much more than just knowing about him. To be a true follower of Jesus it's important that we not only say that we are Christians, but we also have to show it by doing good things. We've got to behave ourselves like Jesus is with us all of the time. And, we've got to treat other people the same. That's a lot, huh. But Jesus helps us do it!

JESUS WATCH

The Book of James doesn't say much about Jesus. James doesn't talk specifically about the life of Jesus, and he doesn't speak about the return of Jesus. But, throughout his book, James describes the life of someone who's been invaded by Jesus. He talks about people who have turned their lives over to Jesus and how that should affect their lives. His book also describes many of the teachings of Jesus and makes many references to the Sermon on the Mount (check out Matthew 5:10–12, p. 1280, and Matthew 6:19, p. 1284.).

James wants to give us a picture of Jesus as the role model for our own lives. We can't just know a lot about Jesus and his teachings. We've got to take what we know and apply it to our lives. Um, I think it's called, "Walking the walk *and* talking the talk." You can do it!

my FAVORITE links

OTHER CONNECTIONS

Livin' it Does it take a lot to make you angry? Or does the littlest thing set you off? Find out what God has to say about anger and some advice on how to handle your fuse—whether it's short or long—by downloading You Make Me Sooo Mad!, James 1:19–21.

MORE STUFF...

Growing Close to God James gives five keys to growing closer to God. Take a look at these five ways from James 4:7–10:

- Be willing to follow God no matter what (v. 7).
- Don't give in to the devil's temptations to do things you know are wrong (v. 7).
- Stop doing those things that displease God; focus instead on things that please God (v. 8).
- When you do something wrong, don't be *sorry*; be *sorrowful* over how you have disappointed God (v. 9).
- Remember who God is—He is the One who gives you your worth and value (v. 10). Depend on him!

FAITH links

- Keep Going!, James 1:2–3
- The Way to Be Wise, James 1:5
- Don't Play Favorites, James 2:1–7
- Trouble with the Tongue, James 3:3–12
- A Peacemaker or a Peacebreaker?, James 3:18
- The Love Magnet, James 4:7–8

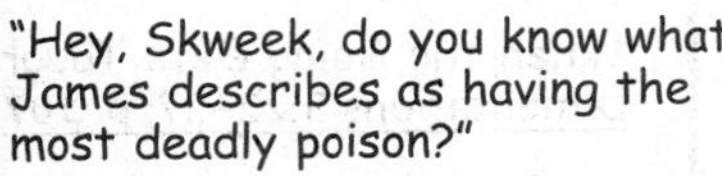

"Hey, Skweek, do you know what James describes as having the most deadly poison?"

"I don't know. It must be some kind of snake."

"Nope, you're wrong. Better check out James 3:7-10 to find out. I think you'll be surprised!"

DON'T MISS WHAT JAMES HAS TO SAY ABOUT . . .

Bad times, James 1:1–8
Faith that's dead, James 2:14–26
Real wisdom, James 3:13–18
The power of prayer, James 5:13–18

1 From James, a servant of God and of
the Lord Jesus Christ.
To all of God's people who are scattered everywhere in the world:

Greetings.

Faith and Wisdom

2My brothers and sisters,* when you
have many kinds of troubles, you should
be full of joy, 3because you know that
these troubles test your faith, and this
will give you patience. 4Let your patience show itself perfectly in what you
do. Then you will be perfect and complete and will have everything you need.
5But if any of you needs wisdom, you
should ask God for it. He is generous and
enjoys giving to all people, so he will give
you wisdom. 6But when you ask God,
you must believe and not doubt. Anyone
who doubts is like a wave in the sea,
blown up and down by the wind. 7-8Such
doubters are thinking two different
things at the same time, and they cannot
decide about anything they do. They
should not think they will receive anything from the Lord.

True Riches

9Believers who are poor should be
proud, because God has made them spiritually rich. 10Those who are rich should
be proud, because God has shown them
that they are spiritually poor. The rich
will die like a wild flower in the grass.
11The sun rises with burning heat and
dries up the plants. The flower falls off,
and its beauty is gone. In the same way
the rich will die while they are still taking
care of business.

Temptation Is Not from God

12When people are tempted and still
continue strong, they should be happy.
After they have proved their faith, God
will reward them with life forever. God
promised this to all those who love him.
13When people are tempted, they should
not say, "God is tempting me." Evil cannot tempt God, and God himself does not
tempt anyone. 14But people are tempted

FAITH links

KEEP GOING!

JAMES 1:2-3

Your mom or dad gets sick. A bigger kid picks on you at school. Sometimes bad things happen. How do you respond to hard times? Some people are tempted to give up. Others become angry with God. They may say, "If God loved me, this wouldn't happen."

When hard times come, James says, "Don't give up. Instead, keep going!" Hard times help to produce patience in your life. Patience helps you not to give up. Having faith in hard times is difficult. But when the hard times are over, your faith will be stronger!

Here is some more hope for hard times:

Meaningless Words, Job 21:34, p. 684

When the Going Gets Tough, Lamentations 3:22–27, p. 1079

The God of Second Chances, Jonah 3, p. 1215

Ask, Search, Knock, Matthew 7:7–10, p. 1286

Just a Test, Luke 4:1–13, p. 1373

Hard Times, 2 Corinthians 1:8–10, p. 1570

1:2 brothers and sisters Although the Greek text says "brothers" here and throughout this book, James's words were meant for the entire church, including men and women.

when their own evil desire leads them
away and traps them. 15This desire leads
to sin, and then the sin grows and brings
death.

16My dear brothers and sisters, do not
be fooled about this. 17Every good action
and every perfect gift is from God. These
good gifts come down from the Creator of
the sun, moon, and stars, who does not
change like their shifting shadows. 18God
decided to give us life through the word of
truth so we might be the most important
of all the things he made.

Listening and Obeying

19My dear brothers and sisters, always be willing to listen and slow to
speak. Do not become angry easily, 20be-
cause anger will not help you live the
right kind of life God wants. 21So put out
of your life every evil thing and every
kind of wrong. Then in gentleness accept
God's teaching that is planted in your
hearts, which can save you.

22Do what God's teaching says; when
you only listen and do nothing, you are
fooling yourselves. 23Those who hear
God's teaching and do nothing are like
people who look at themselves in a mirror. 24They see their faces and then go
away and quickly forget what they looked
like. 25But the truly
happy people are
those who carefully
study God's perfect
law that makes peo-
ple free, and they
continue to study it.
They do not forget what they heard, but
they obey what God's teaching says.
Those who do this will be made happy.

1:25
Blessings
What brings you real happiness?

The True Way to Worship God

26People who think they are religious
but say things they should not say are
just fooling themselves. Their "religion"
is worth nothing. 27Religion that God accepts as pure and without fault is this:
caring for orphans or widows who need
help, and keeping yourself free from the
world's evil influence.

FAITH links

THE WAY TO BE WISE

JAMES 1:5

Psst. Come closer. Closer. That's close enough. Want to know the secret to being wise? Two words: Ask God. That's James's advice for wisdom seekers. God is the source of wisdom. Having wisdom does not mean you become a know-it-all. It means you're willing to learn to do what's right.

What do you need wisdom for? For those hard situations where you have to make a choice between doing what's right and doing what's wrong. Wisdom helps you know when to ask for help. The best thing about having wisdom is this: God helps you to use it.

Check out these Faithlinks on wising up:

The Cloud Guide, Numbers 9:15–23, p. 188

Plan for Success, 1 Chronicles 14:8–17, p. 538

Seeing the Needs, Nehemiah 1, p. 625

Wisdom in Store, Proverbs 2:6–7, p. 828

Prayer Priority, Luke 5:15–16, p. 1376

Keeping Clean, 2 Corinthians 7:1, p. 1576

ANGER
James 1:19–21

Livin' it

You Make Me Sooo Mad! What things or people drive you up a wall and make you so angry that you just want to scream? Is it your little brother getting into your things? Or the big kid always picking on you? Or maybe a computer that crashes when you're winning a game? How do you handle your anger?

Instead of spouting off and really letting someone have it when you're angry with them, God has a better idea. Be willing to forgive others for the mean things they do. (Read Luke 17:3–4, p. 1401.) How do you think forgiving someone might make you less angry?

Is it ever OK to be angry? Yes, when you are angry about disobedience to God and his Word. Jesus became angry when he saw what was happening in the Temple. (Look at Matthew 21:12–13, p. 1310.) Do you ever become angry at situations where God is being ignored? How do you handle a situation like that?

MORE FAITH links

Patience, Please, p. 819
What God "Hates," p. 835
Justice Served, p. 940
Don't Get Mad; Get Even?, p. 1323
Out with the Old!, p. 1625

"Arrrgghh! I can't stand it when my computer gets all jammed up and crashes! It makes me soooooo angry I can hardly move straight!"

"Boy, Tagg, it sounds like you have a problem with your temper. Why don't you count to 10 and then download these Faithlinks. They'll help you cool down!"

Out of Control?, Genesis 4, p. 8
- Link here to see how terrible anger can become when it is out of control.

Anger: Quick or Slow?, Psalm 86:15, p. 776
- Which are you quick to do—get angry at someone or show kindness to people? When someone really bugs you, what's the easiest thing to do? Get angry, right? Which do you think God does the quickest: become angry or show kindness to you? What do you need to do to be more like that?

A Gentle Answer, Proverbs 15:1, p. 847
- Have you ever noticed that when someone makes you mad and you say something mean back to that person, you both feel angrier? What usually happens if you are sarcastic or start shouting? Does anything get settled? Link here to find a better way to handle that situation.

my FAVORITE links

Love All People

2 My dear brothers and sisters, as believers in our glorious Lord Jesus
Christ, never think some people are more
important than others. 2Suppose someone comes into your church meeting
wearing nice clothes and a gold ring. At
the same time a poor person comes in
wearing old, dirty clothes. 3You show special attention to the one wearing nice
clothes and say, "Please, sit here in this
good seat." But you say to the poor person, "Stand over there," or, "Sit on the
floor by my feet." 4What are you doing?
You are making some people more important than others, and with evil thoughts
you are deciding that one person is better.
5Listen, my dear brothers and sisters!
God chose the poor in the world to be
rich with faith and to receive the kingdom
God promised to those who love him.
6But you show no respect to the poor.
The rich are always trying to control your
lives. They are the ones who take you to
court. 7And they are the ones who speak
against Jesus, who owns you.
8This royal law is found in the Scriptures: "Love your neighbor as you love
yourself."[n] If you obey this law, you are
doing right. 9But if you treat one person
as being more important than another,
you are sinning. You are guilty of breaking God's law. 10A person who follows all
of God's law but fails to obey even one
command is guilty of breaking all the
commands in that law. 11The same God
who said, "You must not be guilty of
adultery,"[n] also said, "You must not murder anyone."[n] So if you do not take part in
adultery but you murder someone, you
are guilty of breaking all of God's law.
12In everything you say and do, remember that you will be judged by the law that
makes people free. 13So you must show
mercy to others, or God will not show
mercy to you when he judges you. But
the person who shows mercy can stand
without fear at the judgment.

Faith and Good Works

14My brothers and sisters, if people
say they have faith, but do nothing, their
faith is worth nothing. Can faith like that

FAITH links

DON'T PLAY FAVORITES 

JAMES 2:1-7

How would you feel if your teacher only gave good grades to students who could buy her nice things? You'd probably feel terrible if you weren't one of the students who could do that. Besides, your teacher wouldn't be a very good teacher if she did that! That's why God does not want us to play favorites. Playing favorites means only being nice to certain people. In James's day, some Christians were nice to the rich but ignored the poor. That's not the way God wants us to be! We're to treat all people the same—with kindness.

Just Kidding?, Genesis 21:8–10, p. 28

A Small Percent, Deuteronomy 14:22–23, p. 247

Your Best Work, 1 Kings 6, p. 443

The Problem with Pride, Isaiah 2:11, p. 898

The Way to Greatness, Matthew 20:20–28, p. 1309

Who's on First?, 3 John 9–10, p. 1723

2:8 "Love . . . yourself." Quotation from Leviticus 19:18.
2:11 "You . . . adultery." Quotation from Exodus 20:14 and Deuteronomy 5:18.
2:11 "You . . . anyone." Quotation from Exodus 20:13 and Deuteronomy 5:17.

save them? 15A brother or sister in
Christ might need clothes or food. 16If
you say to that person, “God be with you!
I hope you stay warm and get plenty to
eat,” but you do not give what that person needs, your words are worth nothing.
17In the same way, faith that is alone—
that does nothing—is dead.
18Someone might say, “You have
faith, but I have deeds.” Show me your
faith without doing anything, and I will
show you my faith by what I do. 19You
believe there is one God. Good! But the
demons believe that, too, and they tremble with fear.
20You foolish person! Must you be
shown that faith that does nothing is
worth nothing? 21Abraham, our ancestor,
was made right with God by what he did
when he offered his son Isaac on the altar.
22So you see that Abraham’s faith and
the things he did worked together. His
faith was made perfect by what he did.
23This shows the full meaning of the
Scripture that says: “Abraham believed
God, and God accepted Abraham’s faith,
and that faith made him right with God.”[n]
And Abraham was called God’s friend.[n]
24So you see that people are made right
with God by what they do, not by faith
only.
25Another example is Rahab, a prostitute, who was made right with God by
something she did. She welcomed the
spies into her home and helped them escape by a different road.
26Just as a person’s body that does
not have a spirit is dead, so faith that does
nothing is dead!

Controlling the Things We Say

3 My brothers and sisters, not many of
you should become teachers, because
you know that we who teach will be
judged more strictly. 2We all make many
mistakes. If people never said anything
wrong, they would be perfect and able to
control their entire selves, too. 3When
we put bits into the mouths of horses to
make them obey us, we can control their
whole bodies. 4Also a ship is very big,
and it is pushed by strong winds. But a
very small rudder controls that big ship,

FAITH links

TROUBLE WITH THE TONGUE

JAMES 3:3-12

Have you ever said something nice to someone? Think about how that person felt. Have you ever said something that you wished you hadn’t said? Maybe it was something that hurt someone. How do you think *that* person felt? How did you feel after saying it? Just think—both statements came out of the same mouth. James tells us to watch what we say. The same mouth should not be used for good *and* for evil. God wants us to use our words for good!

Need help controlling your words? Connect here:

More Powerful Than Revenge, Genesis 50:14–21, p. 71

A Right to Get Even?, 1 Samuel 24, p. 388

The Peril of Poisonous Plans, Micah 2:1–3, p. 1221

Kindness First, Matthew 9:35–36, p. 1290

The Whole Truth, John 8:31–32, 45, p. 1438

Another Lazy Day?, 2 Thessalonians 3:6–13, p. 1640

2:23 “Abraham . . . God.” Quotation from Genesis 15:6.

2:23 God’s friend These words about Abraham are found in 2 Chronicles 20:7 and Isaiah 41:8.

FAITH links

A PEACEMAKER OR A PEACEBREAKER?

JAMES 3:18

Are you a peacemaker or a peacebreaker? A peacemaker tries his or her best to make peace between two people who aren't getting along. A peacemaker also tries to get along with others. A peacebreaker starts trouble wherever he or she goes. Maybe he doesn't like the game the other kids are playing and demands that another be played. Maybe she tries to start a rumor about another girl.

James reminds us that peacemakers will be rewarded. Peacebreakers don't receive anything but trouble. Which would you rather have?

Download these links on keeping the peace:

Forgive Instead, Genesis 33, p. 47

Kind or Fair?, 1 Samuel 30, p. 395

Peace in the Family, Psalm 133, p. 811

The Verdict Is In?, Matthew 7:1–2, p. 1285

I'll Be the Judge!, 1 Corinthians 4:4–5, p. 1549

The Way to Get Along, 1 Peter 3:8–9, p. 1703

making it go wherever the pilot wants.
5It is the same with the tongue. It is a
small part of the body, but it brags about
great things.

A big forest fire can be started with
only a little flame. 6And the tongue is like
a fire. It is a whole world of evil among
the parts of our bodies. The tongue
spreads its evil through the whole body.
The tongue is set on fire by hell, and it
starts a fire that influences all of life.
7People can tame every kind of wild animal, bird, reptile, and fish, and they have
tamed them, 8but no one can tame the
tongue. It is wild and evil and full of
deadly poison. 9We use our tongues to
praise our Lord and Father, but then we
curse people, whom God made like himself. 10Praises and curses come from the
same mouth! My brothers and sisters,
this should not happen. 11Do good and
bad water flow from the same spring?
12My brothers and sisters, can a fig tree
make olives, or can a grapevine make
figs? No! And a well full of salty water
cannot give good water.

True Wisdom

13Are there those among you who are
truly wise and understanding? Then they
should show it by living right and doing
good things with a gentleness that comes
from wisdom. 14But if you are selfish and
have bitter jealousy in your hearts, do
not brag. Your bragging is a lie that hides
the truth. 15That kind of "wisdom" does
not come from God but from the world. It
is not spiritual; it is from the devil.
16Where jealousy and selfishness are,
there will be confusion and every kind of
evil. 17But the wisdom that comes from
God is first of all pure, then peaceful,
gentle, and easy to please. This wisdom
is always ready to help those who are
troubled and to do good for others. It is
always fair and honest. 18People who
work for peace in a peaceful way plant a
good crop of right-living.

Give Yourselves to God

4 Do you know where your fights and
arguments come from? They come
from the selfish desires that war within
you. 2You want things, but you do not
have them. So you are ready to kill and
are jealous of other people, but you still
cannot get what you want. So you argue

and fight. You do not get what you want,
because you do not ask God. 3Or when
you ask, you do not receive because the
reason you ask is wrong. You want things
so you can use them for your own pleasures.
4So, you are not loyal to God! You
should know that loving the world is the
same as hating God. Anyone who wants
to be a friend of the world becomes God's
enemy. 5Do you think the Scripture
means nothing that says, "The Spirit that
God made to live in us wants us for himself alone"?" 6But God gives us even
more grace, as the Scripture says,

"God is against the proud,
but he gives grace to the humble."

Proverbs 3:34

7So give yourselves completely to
God. Stand against the devil, and the
devil will run from you. 8Come near to
God, and God will come near to
you. You sinners,
clean sin out of your
lives. You who are
trying to follow God
and the world at the
same time, make
your thinking pure. 9Be sad, cry, and
weep! Change your laughter into crying
and your joy into sadness. 10Don't be too
proud in the Lord's presence, and he will
make you great.

> **EMAIL! FROM GOD** 4:8
> **Worship**
> How can God come closer to you?

You Are Not the Judge

11Brothers and sisters, do not tell evil
lies about each other. If you speak against
your fellow believers or judge them, you
are judging and speaking against the law
they follow. And when you are judging
the law, you are no longer a follower of
the law. You have become a judge. 12God
is the only Lawmaker and Judge. He is
the only One who can save and destroy.
So it is not right for you to judge your
neighbor.

Let God Plan Your Life

13Some of you say, "Today or tomorrow we will go to some city. We will stay
there a year, do business, and make
money." 14But you do not know what will
happen tomorrow! Your life is like a mist.
You can see it for a short time, but then it
goes away. 15So you should say, "If the
Lord wants, we will live and do this or
that." 16But now you are proud and you
brag. All of this bragging is wrong.

> **FAITH links**
>
> **THE LOVE MAGNET**
>
> **JAMES 4:7-8**
>
> Think of a magnet, one of those horseshoe-shaped ones. Now think of a piece of metal. How long would it take for the metal to be pulled close to the magnet? No time at all, right? Now think of God as the magnet and yourself as the piece of metal. Unlike the magnet, God doesn't snatch you to him. He waits for you to come. That's why James tells us to come near to God. As we come near to God, he comes near to us. God's love is what attracts us to him. It's more powerful than any magnet!
>
> Time to Celebrate, Exodus 15:1–21, p. 95
>
> Your Total Trust, Deuteronomy 1:32, p. 229
>
> Happiness or Joy?, Job 29:18–19, p. 691
>
> A Direct Path, Proverbs 3:5–6, p. 829
>
> The Best Protection Plan, Matthew 2:13–18, p. 1276
>
> Faith That Pleases God, Luke 7:1–9, p. 1380

4:5 "The Spirit . . . alone." These words may be from Exodus 20:5.

17Anyone who knows the right thing to
do, but does not do it, is sinning.

A Warning to the Rich

5 You rich people, listen! Cry and be
very sad because of the troubles that
are coming to you. **2**Your riches have rotted, and your clothes have been eaten by
moths. **3**Your gold and silver have rusted,
and that rust will be a proof that you were
wrong. It will eat your bodies like fire.
You saved your treasure for the last days.
4The pay you did not give the workers
who mowed your fields cries out against
you, and the cries of the workers have
been heard by the Lord All-Powerful.
5Your life on earth was full of rich living
and pleasing yourselves with everything
you wanted. You made yourselves fat,
like an animal ready to be killed. **6**You
have judged guilty and then murdered innocent people, who were not against you.

Be Patient

7Brothers and sisters, be patient until
the Lord comes again. A farmer
patiently waits for
his valuable crop to
grow from the earth
and for it to receive
the autumn and
spring rains. **8**You,
too, must be patient. Do not give up hope,
because the Lord is coming soon.
9Brothers and sisters, do not complain
against each other or you will be judged
guilty. And the Judge is ready to come!
10Brothers and sisters, follow the example of the prophets who spoke for the
Lord. They suffered many hard things,
but they were patient. **11**We say they are
happy because they did not give up. You
have heard about Job's patience, and you
know the Lord's purpose for him in the
end. You know the Lord is full of mercy
and is kind.

EMAIL! FROM GOD
5:7–8
Perseverance
Don't give up!

Be Careful What You Say

12My brothers and sisters, above all,
do not use an oath when you make a
promise. Don't use the name of heaven,
earth, or anything else to prove what you
say. When you mean yes, say only yes,
and when you mean no, say only no so
you will not be judged guilty.

The Power of Prayer

13Anyone who is having troubles
should pray. Anyone who is happy should
sing praises. **14**Anyone who is sick
should call the church's elders. They
should pray for and pour oil on the
person[n] in the name of the Lord. **15**And
the prayer that is said with faith will
make the sick person well; the Lord will

5:14 pour oil on the person Oil was used in the name of the Lord as a sign that the person was now set apart for God's special attention and care.

FAITH CHALLENGE

Got another one for you. Read 5:13 for some important instructions. If you prayed more often, what effect do you think it would have on your life? What are some things in your life for which you can "sing praises"?

TESTING IT

James 5:13
Anyone who is having troubles should pray. Anyone who is happy should sing praises.

heal that person. And if the person has
sinned, the sins will be forgiven.

EMAIL! FROM GOD
5:16
Courage
Find out why prayer is important.

16Confess your sins
to each other and
pray for each other
so God can heal you.
When a believing
person prays, great
things happen. 17Elijah was a human being just like us. He prayed that it would
not rain, and it did not rain on the land for
three and a half years! 18Then Elijah
prayed again, and the rain came down
from the sky, and the land produced crops
again.

Saving a Soul

19My brothers and sisters, if one of
you wanders away from the truth, and
someone helps that person come back,
20remember this: Anyone who brings a
sinner back from the wrong way will save
that sinner's soul from death and will
cause many sins to be forgiven.

1 & 2 Peter

ADVICE TO LIVE ON

Hello! I'm Peter, and I hope that you like these two books. I certainly knew a lot about being a follower of Jesus. I was one of the first 12 disciples and one of Jesus' three closest friends. Before I was a disciple, I was a fisherman. I followed Jesus during all of his ministry. And I was with him just before he was killed. I wasn't always the best follower, though. I made *a lot* of mistakes. In fact, when Jesus was facing *his* greatest trial, I told people I didn't even know him. It was one of the worst moments of my life. But the good news for me—and for you—is that Jesus forgives and loves us.

I wrote these two letters to give believers advice on how to live their lives for Jesus. So, I give advice to husbands and wives, teachers and church leaders. I also warn believers about false teachers and some untrue things they were saying. And, a lot was also being said about the return of Jesus, so I try to clear up some of the things believers were hearing.

JESUS WATCH

The world we live in can be cruel and unforgiving. It's not easy to live out the beliefs that Jesus calls us to. But, 1 Peter addresses this by presenting Jesus as the example we're to follow when we're facing rejection, troubles, or suffering because of what we believe. Jesus is our hope! And he's the source of our strength and unbelievable joy—even when we're going through some bad times.

Second Peter takes a similar approach, but applies it in a new way. In 1 Peter, Jesus is our strength when we're suffering. In 2 Peter, Jesus is our source for knowledge and power. In other words, if we're ever going to grow up in our faith, we've got to rely on Jesus to help us grow.

my FAVORITE links

_______________ _______________

_______________ _______________

_______________ _______________

_______________ _______________

OTHER CONNECTIONS

Livin' it Ever have one of those days when everything seemed to go wrong? God not only offers to help carry the load for you when things go bad, but God also can guide you through the tough times. Check it out by logging on to Help!, 1 Peter 4:12–19.

GET THE INFO

- A Fisher of People, 1 Peter 1. If you think you've had times when you disappointed God, you'll be glad to meet Peter. Peter went through some low points in his walk with Jesus before becoming a bold leader in the early church. Find out more about Peter's life by linking here.

MORE STUFF...

Service, Please! How do you describe Christian service? Peter describes different ways you can serve others. You can read more about it in 1 Peter 4:7–11:

- Love each other deeply
- Forgive each other's sins.
- Welcome guests into your home.

"What do you think will happen to people who teach false things, Tagg?"

"I know one thing—they'll be in big trouble. Surf over to 2 Peter 2, and tell me what you think."

HEY! LOOK AT THESE OTHER COOL STORIES:

The "living stone," 1 Peter 2:4–10
Passing the test, 1 Peter 4:12–19
Like a thief, 2 Peter 3:8–13

FAITH links

- **The Way to Get Along, 1 Peter 3:8–9**
- **Come On In!, 1 Peter 4:9–10**
- **Toss Those Troubles!, 1 Peter 5:7**
- **The "Quality" of Life, 2 Peter 1:5–8**
- **You're a Fake!, 2 Peter 2:1**
- **His Best Qualities, 2 Peter 3:9**

GET THE INFO

A FISHER OF PEOPLE

1 Peter 1

1. Simon Peter was born at Bethsaida. He was a fisherman until Jesus called him to "fish for people." (Check out Luke 5:1–11, p. 1375.)

2. In Caesarea Philippi, Jesus changed Simon's name to Peter, which means "rock," after Peter recognized Jesus as the Son of the living God. (Read Matthew 16:13–16, p. 1303.)

3. Peter, along with James and John, went with Jesus on a high mountain. They watched as Jesus' appearance changed and Jesus' face became as bright as the sun. (See Matthew 17:1–9, p. 1303.)

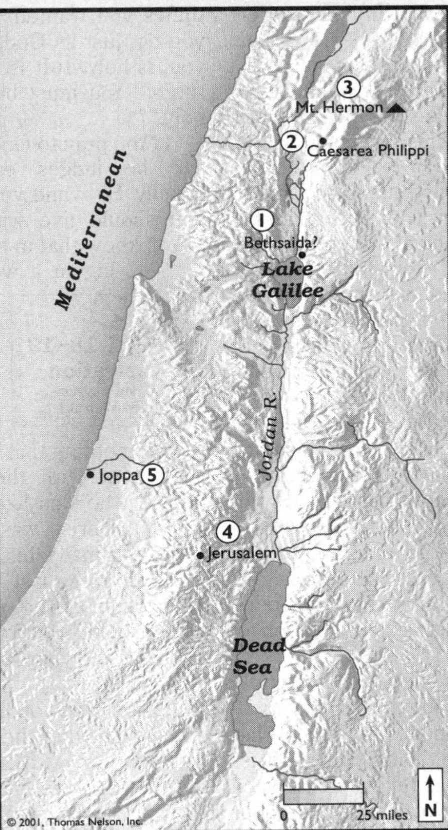

4. Peter hit his lowest point the night before Jesus was crucified when he said three times he didn't even know Jesus. (See Matthew 26:69–75, p. 1323.) After Jesus was raised from the dead, he appeared to Peter and the other disciples in Jerusalem. (Look at Luke 24:33–49, p. 1419.)

5. Peter became a bold leader in the early church at Jerusalem. (Check out Acts 2:14–41, p. 1464.) He also preached to non-Jewish people after God gave him a vision in Joppa. (Read Acts 10:9–23, p. 1481.)

1 From Peter, an apostle of Jesus Christ.
To God's chosen people who are away
from their homes and are scattered
all around the countries of Pontus, Galatia, Cappadocia, Asia, and Bithynia. 2God

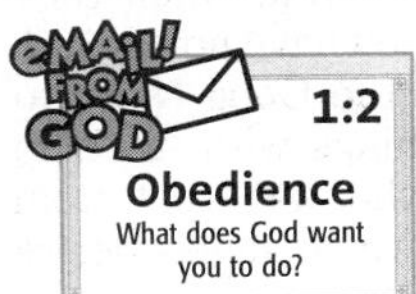

1:2
Obedience
What does God want you to do?

planned long ago to
choose you by mak-
ing you his holy
people, which is the
Spirit's work. God

wanted you to obey him and to be made
clean by the blood of the death of Jesus
Christ.

Grace and peace be yours more and
more.

We Have a Living Hope

3Praise be to the God and Father of
our Lord Jesus Christ. In God's great
mercy he has caused us to be born again
into a living hope, because Jesus Christ
rose from the dead. **4**Now we hope for
the blessings God has for his children.
These blessings, which cannot be destroyed or be spoiled or lose their beauty,
are kept in heaven for you. **5**God's power
protects you through your faith until salvation is shown to you at the end of time.
6This makes you very happy, even
though now for a short time different
kinds of troubles may make you sad.
7These troubles come to prove that your
faith is pure. This purity of faith is worth
more than gold, which can be proved to
be pure by fire but will ruin. But the purity of your faith will bring you praise and
glory and honor when Jesus Christ is
shown to you. **8**You have not seen Christ,
but still you love him. You cannot see him
now, but you believe in him. So you are
filled with a joy that cannot be explained,
a joy full of glory. **9**And you are receiving
the goal of your faith—the salvation of
your souls.

10The prophets searched carefully
and tried to learn about this salvation.
They prophesied about the grace that
was coming to you. **11**The Spirit of Christ
was in the prophets, telling in advance
about the sufferings of Christ and about
the glory that would follow those sufferings. The prophets tried to learn about
what the Spirit was showing them, when
those things would happen, and what the
world would be like at that time. **12**It was
shown them that their service was not
for themselves but for you, when they
told about the truths you have now heard.
Those who preached the Good News to
you told you those things with the help
of the Holy Spirit who was sent from
heaven—things into which angels desire
to look.

A Call to Holy Living

13So prepare your minds for service
and have self-control. All your hope
should be for the gift of grace that will be
yours when Jesus Christ is shown to you.
14Now that you are obedient children of
God do not live as you did in the past. You
did not understand, so you did the evil
things you wanted. **15**But be holy in all
you do, just as God, the One who called
you, is holy. **16**It is written in the Scriptures: "You must be holy, because I am
holy."[n]

17You pray to God and call him Father,
and he judges each person's work
equally. So while you are here on earth,
you should live with respect for God.
18You know that in the past you were living in a worthless way, a way
passed down from
the people who lived
before you. But you
were saved from
that useless life. You
were bought, not
with something that ruins like gold or silver, **19**but with the precious blood of
Christ, who was like a pure and perfect
lamb. **20**Christ was chosen before the
world was made, but he was shown to the
world in these last times for your sake.
21Through Christ you believe in God,
who raised Christ from the dead and gave
him glory. So your faith and your hope are
in God.

E-MAIL FROM GOD
1:18–19
Salvation
How was your salvation bought?

22Now that you have made your souls
pure by obeying the truth, you can have
true love for your Christian brothers and
sisters.[n] So love each other deeply with
all your heart. **23**You have been born
again, and this new life did not come from
something that dies, but from something
that cannot die. You were born again
through God's living message that continues forever. **24**The Scripture says,

"All people are like the grass,

1:16 "You must be . . . holy." Quotation from Leviticus 11:45; 19:2; 20:7.

1:22 brothers and sisters Although the Greek text says "brothers" here and throughout this book, Peter's words were meant for the entire church, including men and women.

and all their glory is like the
flowers of the field.
The grass dies and the flowers fall,
25 but the word of the Lord will live
forever." *Isaiah 40:6-8*

And this is the word that was preached to
you.

Jesus Is the Living Stone

2 So then, rid yourselves of all evil, all
lying, hypocrisy, jealousy, and evil
speech. 2As newborn babies want milk,
you should want the pure and simple
teaching. By it you can grow up and be
saved, 3because you have already examined and seen how good the Lord is.
4Come to the Lord Jesus, the "stone"[n]
that lives. The people of the world did not
want this stone, but he was the stone
God chose, and he was precious. 5You
also are like living stones, so let yourselves be used to build a spiritual temple—to be holy priests who offer spiritual
sacrifices to God. He will accept those
sacrifices through Jesus Christ. 6The
Scripture says:

"I will put a stone in the ground in
Jerusalem.
Everything will be built on this
important and precious rock.
Anyone who trusts in him
will never be disappointed." *Isaiah 28:16*

7This stone is worth much to you who
believe. But to the people who do not believe,

"the stone that the builders rejected
has become the cornerstone." *Psalm 118:22*

8Also, he is

"a stone that causes people to
stumble,
a rock that makes them fall." *Isaiah 8:14*

They stumble because they do not obey
what God says, which is what God
planned to happen to them.
9But you are a chosen people, royal
priests, a holy nation, a people for God's
own possession. You were chosen to tell
about the wonderful acts of God, who
called you out of darkness into his wonderful light. 10At one time you were not a
people, but now you are God's people.
In the past you had never received
mercy, but now you have received
God's mercy.

Live for God

11Dear friends, you are like foreigners and strangers in this world. I beg you
to avoid the evil things your bodies want
to do that fight against your soul. 12Peo-
ple who do not believe are living all
around you and might say that you are
doing wrong. Live such good lives that
they will see the good things you do and
will give glory to God on the day when
Christ comes again.

Yield to Every Human Authority

13For the Lord's sake, yield to the
people who have authority in this world:
the king, who is the highest authority,
14and the leaders who are sent
by him to punish
those who do wrong
and to praise those
who do right. 15It
is God's desire that
by doing good you
should stop foolish people from saying stupid things about you. 16Live as free people, but do not use your freedom as an
excuse to do evil. Live as servants of
God. 17Show respect for all people: Love
the brothers and sisters of God's family,
respect God, honor the king.

> eMAIL FROM GOD 2:15
> **Respect**
> Why should you do good things?

Follow Christ's Example

18Slaves, yield to the authority of
your masters with all respect, not only
those who are good and kind, but also
those who are dishonest. 19A person
might have to suffer even when it is unfair, but if he thinks of God and stands the
pain, God is pleased. 20If you are beaten
for doing wrong, there is no reason to
praise you for being patient in your punishment. But if you suffer for doing good,
and you are patient, then God is pleased.
21This is what you were called to do, because Christ suffered for you and gave

---

2:4 "stone" The most important stone in God's spiritual temple or house (his people).

FAITH CHALLENGE

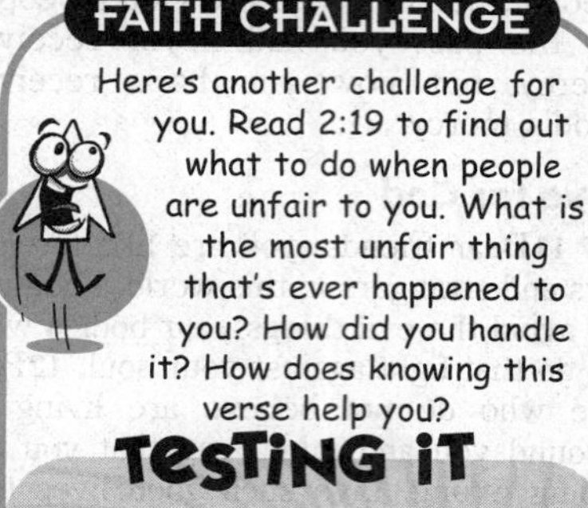

Here's another challenge for you. Read 2:19 to find out what to do when people are unfair to you. What is the most unfair thing that's ever happened to you? How did you handle it? How does knowing this verse help you?

TESTING IT

1 Peter 2:19
A person might have to suffer even when it is unfair, but if he thinks of God and stands the pain, God is pleased.

____

____

____

____

____

____

____

you an example to follow. So you should
do as he did.
22 "He had never sinned,
and he had never lied." *Isaiah 53:9*
23People insulted Christ, but he

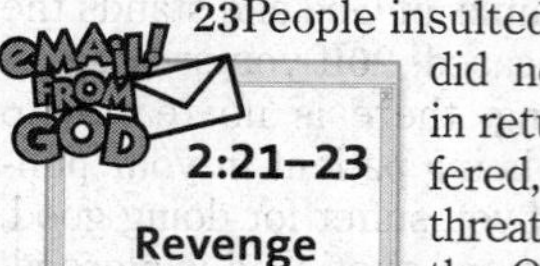
EMAIL! FROM GOD
2:21–23
Revenge
Follow Jesus' example.

did not insult them
in return. Christ suf-
fered, but he did not
threaten. He let God,
the One who judges
rightly, take care of
him. 24Christ carried our sins in his body
on the cross so we would stop living for
sin and start living for what is right. And
you are healed because of his wounds.
25You were like sheep that wandered
away, but now you have come back to the
Shepherd and Protector of your souls.

Wives and Husbands

3 In the same way, you wives should
yield to your husbands. Then, if some
husbands do not obey God's teaching,
they will be persuaded to believe without
anyone's saying a word to them. They
will be persuaded by the way their wives
live. 2Your husbands will see the pure
lives you live with your respect for God.
3It is not fancy hair, gold jewelry, or fine
clothes that should make you beautiful.
4No, your beauty should come from within you—the beauty of a gentle and quiet
spirit that will never be destroyed and is
very precious to God. 5In this same way
the holy women who lived long ago and
followed God made themselves beautiful,
yielding to their own husbands. 6Sarah
obeyed Abraham, her husband, and called
him her master. And you women are true
children of Sarah if you always do what is
right and are not afraid.
7In the same way, you husbands
should live with your wives in an understanding way, since they are weaker than
you. But show them respect, because
God gives them the same blessing he
gives you—the grace that gives true life.
Do this so that nothing will stop your
prayers.

Suffering for Doing Right

8Finally, all of you should be in agreement, understanding each other, loving
each other as family, being kind and humble. 9Do not do wrong to repay a

EMAIL! FROM GOD
3:9
Enemies
Check out how to repay an insult.

wrong, and do not
insult to repay an in-
sult. But repay with
a blessing, because
you yourselves were
called to do this so
that you might receive a blessing. 10The
Scripture says,
"A person must do these things
to enjoy life and have many happy
days.
He must not say evil things,
and he must not tell lies.

FAITH links

THE WAY TO GET ALONG

1 PETER 3:8-9

What was the last thing you argued about with your brother or sister? Sometimes people argue because they don't understand something about another person. When you and your brother or sister fight, how do you feel? Compare that feeling to the way you feel when you do get along.

Peter, one of Jesus' 12 followers, wrote a letter to help Christians learn about God. He gave advice to help them get along with each other. He told them to try to understand each other, love each other, and be kind. That's the way to get along. Try it sometime with a family member or a friend, and see what happens.

Here are some more Faithlinks about getting along with others:

Family Feud, Genesis 27, p. 37

Give Revenge a Rest, Leviticus 19:18, p. 160

A Parent's Advice, Proverbs 1:8–9, p. 825

Justice Desserts, Habakkuk 2:4–8, p. 1237

Best Seat in the House, Luke 14:7–11, p. 1398

Winning a Friend, 2 Timothy 2:23–24, p. 1654

11 He must stop doing evil and do good.
He must look for peace and work
for it.
12 The Lord sees the good people
and listens to their prayers.
But the Lord is against
those who do evil." *Psalm 34:12-16*
13 If you are trying hard to do good, no
one can really hurt you. **14** But even if you
suffer for doing right, you are blessed.
"Don't be afraid of what they fear;
do not dread those things."
Isaiah 8:12-13
15 But respect Christ as the holy Lord in
your hearts. Always be ready to answer
everyone who asks you to explain about
the hope you have, **16** but answer in a
gentle way and with respect. Keep a clear
conscience so that those who speak evil
of your good life in Christ will be made
ashamed. **17** It is better to suffer for doing
good than for doing wrong if that is what
God wants. **18** Christ himself suffered for
sins once. He was not guilty, but he suffered for those who are guilty to bring
you to God. His body was killed, but he
was made alive in the spirit. **19** And in the
spirit he went and preached to the spirits
in prison **20** who refused to obey God long
ago in the time of Noah. God was waiting
patiently for them while Noah was building the boat. Only a few people—eight in
all—were saved by water. **21** And that water is like baptism that now saves you—
not the washing of dirt from the body, but
the promise made to God from a good
conscience. And this is because Jesus
Christ was raised from the dead. **22** Now
Jesus has gone into heaven and is at
God's right side ruling over angels, authorities, and powers.

Change Your Lives

4 Since Christ suffered while he was in
his body, strengthen yourselves with
the same way of thinking Christ had. The
person who has suffered in the body is
finished with sin. **2** Strengthen yourselves so that you will live here on earth
doing what God wants, not the evil things
people want. **3** In the past you wasted too
much time doing what nonbelievers enjoy. You were guilty of sexual sins, evil

Livin' it

HANDLING BAD TIMES

1 Peter 4:12–19

Help! Do you lug a backpack full of books and papers to school each day? Does it ever get heavy? Imagine carrying twice the heaviest load you've ever carried all day, everywhere you go. Pretty soon you would feel bent over and dragging along. What if someone offered to take the heavy load from you? How would you feel then?

The things you worry about and the bad times you have can cause you to feel loaded down. But God offers to take that heavy load from you. (Read 1 Peter 5:7.) God takes on your load because he loves you. So, go ahead. Toss God those troubles!

MORE FAITH links

- When Bad Turns to Worse, p. 82
- Good Times and Bad, p. 462
- A Really Bad Day, p. 661
- When the Going Gets Tough, p. 1079
- A Soldier's Story, p. 1653

"What's up with you today, Tagg? You're not acting like you usually do."

"I'm really worried. My friend has been sick for a long time."

"Sorry to hear that, Tagg. When something bad happens to someone you care about, that can get you down. But I know someone who can help! Connect to these Faithlinks to learn more."

A Giant Problem, 1 Samuel 17:32–51, p. 377
- Do you ever feel small and worthless—like an ant meeting up with the bottom of a giant shoe? Sometimes problems can make us feel that way. What are some giant problems in your life? Talk to God about them. He can cut those problems down to size.

Lower Than Low, Job 19:13–25, p. 680
- Job had terrible problems and he felt miserable. Link here to discover what Job did when he hit "rock bottom."

Sad Times, Matthew 14:13–14, p. 1299
- Have you ever had someone you loved die? How did you feel? What was the hardest part? One of Jesus' friends died, and he felt sad about it. He went off by himself for a while. When you feel sad about someone dying, remember that Jesus understands and is with you. How can that help you?

Hard Times, 2 Corinthians 1:8–10, p. 1570
- What is your first reaction when hard times come? Do you panic or get angry with God? Paul went through lots of hard times—he even thought he would die. Link here to see how Paul reacted to these bad times.

my FAVORITE links

desires, drunkenness, wild and drunken parties, and hateful idol worship. 4Nonbelievers think it is strange that you do not do the many wild and wasteful things they do, so they insult you. 5But they will have to explain this to God, who is ready to judge the living and the dead. 6For this reason the Good News was preached to those who are now dead. Even though they were judged like all people, the Good News was preached to them so they could live in the spirit as God lives.

FAITH links

COME ON IN!

1 PETER 4:9-10

Who do you like to invite to your house? Your best friend? Any friend? Only certain ones? In his first letter, Peter encouraged the Christians to be hospitable to *any* believers who showed up at their house. Being hospitable means being kind to the people who visit you. In Bible times, there were no hotels and motels like the ones we enjoy today. Travelers generally depended on the kindness of others.

You can be hospitable to anyone, anywhere you are. Being hospitable doesn't mean being choosy about whom you welcome. It means welcoming anyone who comes.

Care for the Lost, Deuteronomy 22:1–3, p. 255

The MLP, Ruth 1:16–17, p. 345

Kind or Fair?, 1 Samuel 30, p. 395

Jesus' Mission and Yours, Isaiah 61:1–2, p. 978

The Right Ingredients, Micah 6:8, p. 1227

The Worst Chore, John 13:3–17, p. 1447

Use God's Gifts Wisely

7The time is near when all things will end. So think clearly and control yourselves so you will be able to pray. 8Most importantly, love each other deeply, because love will cause many sins to be forgiven. 9Open your homes to each other, without complaining. 10Each of you has received a gift to use to serve others. Be good servants of God's various gifts of grace. 11Anyone who speaks should speak words from God. Anyone who serves should serve with the strength God gives so that in everything God will be praised through Jesus Christ. Power and glory belong to him forever and ever. Amen.

Suffering as a Christian

12My friends, do not be surprised at the terrible trouble which now comes to test you. Do not think that something strange is happening to you. 13But be happy that you are sharing in Christ's sufferings so that you will be happy and full of joy when Christ comes again in glory.

eMAIL! FROM GOD
4:12–19
Troubles
Find the joy in your troubles.

14When people insult you because you follow Christ, you are blessed, because the glorious Spirit, the Spirit of God, is with you.
15Do not suffer for murder, theft, or any other crime, nor because you trouble other people. 16But if you suffer because you are a Christian, do not be ashamed. Praise God because you wear that name.
17It is time for judgment to begin with God's family. And if that judging begins with us, what will happen to those people who do not obey the Good News of God?
18"If it is very hard for a good person to
be saved,

the wicked person and the sinner
will surely be lost!'"[a]

19So those who suffer as God wants
should trust their souls to the faithful
Creator as they continue to do what is
right.

The Flock of God

5 Now I have something to say to the
elders in your group. I also am an elder. I have seen Christ's sufferings, and I
will share in the glory that will be shown
to us. I beg you to 2shepherd God's flock,
for whom you are responsible. Watch
over them because you want to, not because you are forced. That is how God
wants it. Do it because you are happy to
serve, not because you want money. 3Do
not be like a ruler over people you are responsible for, but be good examples to
them. 4Then when Christ, the Chief
Shepherd, comes, you will get a glorious
crown that will never lose its beauty.

5In the same way, younger people
should be willing to be under older people. And all of you should be very humble
with each other.

"God is against the proud,
but he gives grace to the humble."

Proverbs 3:34

6Be humble under God's powerful
hand so he will lift you up when the right
time comes. 7Give all your worries to
him, because he cares about you.

8Control yourselves and be careful!
The devil, your enemy, goes around like
a roaring lion looking
for someone to eat.
9Refuse to give in to
him, by standing
strong in your faith.
You know that your
Christian family all
over the world is having the same kinds
of suffering.

EMAIL! FROM GOD
5:8
Satan
Who is the devil's enemy?

10And after you suffer for a short
time, God, who gives all grace, will make
everything right. He will make you
strong and support you and keep you
from falling. He called you to share in his
glory in Christ, a glory that will continue
forever. 11All power is his forever and
ever. Amen.

FAITH links

TOSS THOSE TROUBLES!

1 PETER 5:7

What is the heaviest load you have ever carried? Imagine carrying twice that load all day, everywhere you went. (If you have trouble imagining that, grab about five or six heavy books and lug them around.) Now imagine someone offering to take that heavy load from you. Imagine how much lighter you would feel! That's what Peter says God does for you. The things that worry you can cause you to feel loaded down. God promises you can toss your load of worries onto him. Why? Because he loves you. So, go ahead. Toss those troubles. He can handle 'em!

Don't worry! Connect here to see how God can take care of those fears:

The Trouble with Sin, Genesis 6—8, p. 11

Your Worst Enemy, Exodus 7—11, p. 85

A Pity Party, Job 10, p. 671

911, Psalm 28:6, p. 730

Future Hope, Joel 3:17–21, p. 1191

The God of Second Chances, Jonah 3, p. 1215

[a] **4:18 "If . . . lost!"** Quotation from Proverbs 11:31 in the Septuagint, the Greek version of the Old Testament.

Final Greetings

12I wrote this short letter with the
help of Silas, who I know is a faithful
brother in Christ. I wrote to encourage
you and to tell you that this is the true
grace of God. Stand strong in that grace.

13The church in Babylon, who was
chosen like you, sends you greetings.
Mark, my son in Christ, also greets you.
14Give each other a kiss of Christian love
when you meet.

Peace to all of you who are in Christ.

1 From Simon Peter, a servant and
apostle of Jesus Christ.
To you who have received a faith as
valuable as ours, because our God and
Savior Jesus Christ does what is right.
2Grace and peace be given to you
more and more, because you truly know
God and Jesus our Lord.

God Has Given Us Blessings

3Jesus has the power of God, by which
he has given us everything we need to
live and to serve God. We have these
things because we know him. Jesus
called us by his glory and goodness.
4Through these he gave us the very
great and precious promises. With these
gifts you can share in being like God, and
the world will not ruin you with its evil
desires.
5Because you have these blessings,
do your best to add
these things to your
lives: to your faith,
add goodness; and to
your goodness, add
knowledge; 6and to
your knowledge, add
self-control; and to your self-control, add
patience; and to your patience, add service for God; 7and to your service for God,
add kindness for your brothers and sisters
in Christ; and to this kindness, add love.
8If all these things are in you and are
growing, they will help you to be useful
and productive in your knowledge of our
Lord Jesus Christ. 9But anyone who does
not have these things cannot see clearly.
He is blind and has forgotten that he was
made clean from his past sins.
10My brothers and sisters,[*] try hard
to be certain that you really are called and
chosen by God. If you do all these things,
you will never fall. 11And you will be
given a very great welcome into the eternal kingdom of our Lord and Savior Jesus
Christ.
12You know these things, and you are

eMAIL! FROM GOD
1:5–8
Perseverance
Check out how to grow in faith.

1:10 brothers and sisters Although the Greek text reads "brothers" here and throughout this book, Peter's words were meant for the entire church, including men and women.

FAITH links

THE "QUALITY" OF LIFE

2 PETER 1:5-8

Ever hear people talk about what they need to make life better? Some might feel they need more money to improve their quality of life. Others might feel they need something meaningful to do.

Peter, one of Jesus' followers, has some advice for making life better. In the second letter that he wrote, he talked about some spiritual qualities Christians could add to their lives to make life better *for others*. What are these qualities? Goodness, knowledge, self-control, patience, service, kindness, and love. These are also the fruit of the Spirit. (See Galatians 5:22–23, p. 1592.) Don't leave home without 'em!

Check out what qualities you should be taking along each day:

Learning to Listen, 1 Samuel 3, p. 358

The Green Light, 2 Samuel 2:1, p. 401

Our Thirst Quencher, Psalm 42:1–3, p. 741

Down on the Ant Farm, Proverbs 6:6–11, p. 833

Want to Know? Ask!, Luke 9:45, p. 1386

A Different Kind of Fruit, Galatians 5:22–23, p. 1592

very strong in the truth, but I will always
help you remember them. 13I think it is
right for me to help you remember as
long as I am in this body. 14I know I must
soon leave this body, as our Lord Jesus
Christ has shown me. 15I will try my best
so that you may be able to remember
these things even after I am gone.

We Saw Christ's Glory

16When we told you about the powerful coming of our Lord Jesus Christ, we
were not telling just smart stories that
someone invented. But we saw the greatness of Jesus with our own eyes. 17Jesus
heard the voice of God, the Greatest
Glory, when he received honor and glory
from God the Father. The voice said,
"This is my Son, whom I love, and I am
very pleased with him." 18We heard that
voice from heaven while we were with
Jesus on the holy mountain.

19This makes us more sure about the
message the prophets gave. It is good for
you to follow closely what they said as
you would follow a light shining in a dark
place, until the day begins and the morning star rises in your hearts. 20Most of
all, you must understand this: No prophecy in the Scriptures ever comes from
the prophet's own interpretation. 21No
prophecy ever came from what a person
wanted to say, but people led by the Holy
Spirit spoke words from God.

False Teachers

2 There used to be false prophets
among God's people, just as you will
have some false teachers in your group.
They will secretly teach things that are
wrong—teachings that will cause people
to be lost. They will even refuse to accept
the Master, Jesus, who bought their freedom. So they will bring quick ruin on
themselves. 2Many will follow their evil
ways and say evil things about the way of
truth. 3Those false teachers only want
your money, so they will use you by telling
you lies. Their judgment spoken against
them long ago is still coming, and their
ruin is certain.

FAITH links

YOU'RE A FAKE!

2 PETER 2:1

Imagine how you'd feel if someone suddenly walked into your classroom at school and announced that your teacher was a fake and taught you stuff that was wrong. You'd be pretty amazed, wouldn't you? Peter made a similar announcement when he talked about a group of teachers in the area. He called them false teachers. These teachers did not tell the truth about God. Peter warned the Christians about them so that they would continue believing what was true.

When people talk to you about God, you might wonder how you can know what's true and what's false. The Bible can help. It will always tell you what's true!

Download these Faithlinks to get the real truth:

Good Advice?, Leviticus 20:6, p. 162

Remembering What He Said, Deuteronomy 6:4–9, p. 236

The Prayer Habit, Psalm 5:1–3, p. 712

Long-lasting Hope, Hosea 14, p. 1184

Hope That Doesn't Fail, Acts 26:4–7, p. 1510

That's False!, 2 John 7–11, p. 1722

EMAIL FROM GOD 2:4
Angels
What happened to the angels who sinned?

4When angels sinned, God did not let
them go free without punishment. He sent them
to hell and put them
in caves of darkness
where they are being
held for judgment.
5And God punished
the world long ago when he brought a
flood to the world that was full of people
who were against him. But God saved
Noah, who preached about being right
with God, and seven other people with
him. 6And God also destroyed the evil
cities of Sodom and Gomorrah[n] by burning them until they were ashes. He made
those cities an example of what will happen to those who are against God. 7But
he saved Lot from those cities. Lot, a
good man, was troubled because of the
filthy lives of evil people. 8(Lot was a
good man, but because he lived with evil
people every day, his good heart was hurt
by the evil things he saw and heard.) 9So
the Lord knows how to save those who
serve him when troubles come. He will
hold evil people and punish them, while
waiting for the Judgment Day. 10That
punishment is especially for those who
live by doing the evil things their sinful
selves want and who hate authority.

These false teachers are bold and do
anything they want. They are not afraid
to speak against the angels. 11But even
the angels, who are much stronger and
more powerful than false teachers, do not
accuse them with insults before the Lord.
12But these people speak against things
they do not understand. They are like animals that act without thinking, animals
born to be caught and killed. And, like
animals, these false teachers will be destroyed. 13They have caused many people to suffer, so they themselves will
suffer. That is their pay for what they
have done. They take pleasure in openly
doing evil, so they are like dirty spots and
stains among you. They delight in trickery while eating meals with you. 14Every
time they look at a woman they want her,
and their desire for sin is never satisfied.
They lead weak people into the trap of
sin, and they have taught their hearts
to be greedy. God will punish them!
15These false teachers left the right road
and lost their way, following the way Balaam went. Balaam was the son of Beor,
who loved being paid for doing wrong.
16But a donkey, which cannot talk, told
Balaam he was sinning. It spoke with a
man's voice and stopped the prophet's
crazy thinking.

17Those false teachers are like springs
without water and clouds blown by a
storm. A place in the blackest darkness
has been kept for them. 18They brag with
words that mean nothing. By their evil
desires they lead people into the trap of
sin—people who are just beginning to escape from others who live in error.
19They promise them freedom, but they
themselves are not free. They are slaves
of things that will be destroyed. For people are slaves of anything that controls
them. 20They were made free from the
evil in the world by knowing our Lord and
Savior Jesus Christ. But if they return to
evil things and those things control them,
then it is worse for them than it was before. 21Yes, it would be better for them to
have never known the right way than to
know it and to turn away from the holy
teaching that was given to them. 22What
they did is like this true saying: "A dog
goes back to what it has thrown up,"[n] and,
"After a pig is washed, it goes back and
rolls in the mud."

Jesus Will Come Again

3 My friends, this is the second letter I
have written you to help your honest
minds remember. 2I want you to think
about the words the holy prophets spoke
in the past, and remember the command
our Lord and Savior gave us through your
apostles. 3It is most important for you to
understand what will happen in the last
days. People will laugh at you. They will
live doing the evil things they want to do.
4They will say, "Jesus promised to come
again. Where is he? Our fathers have

2:6 Sodom and Gomorrah Two cities God destroyed because the people were so evil.

2:22 "A dog . . . up" Quotation from Proverbs 26:11.

FAITH links

HIS BEST QUALITIES

2 PETER 3:9

What do you think is your best quality? Your winning personality? Your smile? Your kindness? All of God's qualities are his best ones. But Peter talked about two in particular: his faithfulness and patience. Some of the Christians in Peter's day wondered what was taking Jesus so long to return. Peter wanted them to know that God was faithful in keeping his promises. He patiently allows everyone the opportunity to ask for his forgiveness. If you haven't done that yet, what are you waiting for?

The Perfect Sacrifice, Leviticus 1–7, p. 135

A Shortcut, 1 Samuel 13:1–14, p. 369

Hurry Up and Wait, 2 Samuel 5, p. 405

A Hard Place, Ezekiel 28:25–26, p. 1120

A High Price, Romans 6:23, p. 1526

It's Guaranteed!, 1 John 1:9–10, p. 1714

died, but the world continues the way it
has been since it was made." **5**But they
do not want to remember what happened
long ago. By the word of God heaven was
made, and the earth was made from water and with water. **6**Then the world was
flooded and destroyed with water. **7**And
that same word of God is keeping heaven
and earth that we now have in order to be
destroyed by fire. They are being kept for
the Judgment Day and the destruction of
all who are against God.

8But do not forget this one thing, dear
friends: To the Lord one day is as a thousand years, and a thousand years is as
one day. **9**The Lord is not slow in doing
what he promised—the way some people
understand slowness. But God is being
patient with you. He does not want anyone to be lost, but he wants all people to
change their hearts and lives.

10But the day of the Lord will come
like a thief. The skies will disappear with
a loud noise. Everything in them will be
destroyed by fire, and the earth and
everything in it will be burned up.[a] **11**In
that way everything will be destroyed. So
what kind of people should you be? You
should live holy lives and serve God,
12as you wait for and look forward to the
coming of the day of God. When that day
comes, the skies will be destroyed with
fire, and everything in them will melt
with heat. **13**But God made a promise to
us, and we are waiting for a new heaven
and a new earth where goodness lives.

14Dear friends, since you are waiting
for this to happen, do your best to be
without sin and without fault. Try to be at
peace with God. **15**Remember that we
are saved because our Lord is patient.
Our dear brother Paul told you the same
thing when he wrote to you with the wisdom that God gave him. **16**He writes
about this in all his letters. Some things
in Paul's letters are hard to understand,
and people who are ignorant and weak in
faith explain these things falsely. They
also falsely explain the other Scriptures,
but they are destroying themselves by
doing this.

17Dear friends, since you already
know about this, be careful. Do not let
those evil people lead you away by the
wrong they do. Be careful so you will not
fall from your strong faith. **18**But grow in
the grace and knowledge of our Lord and
Savior Jesus Christ. Glory be to him now
and forever! Amen.

3:10 will be burned up Many Greek copies say, "will be found." One copy says, "will disappear."

1, 2, & 3 John

REAL JESUS

Hi, guys! It's me again, John. I'm glad you're reading these short letters I wrote. You may remember that I wrote another book about Jesus to let people know that he truly was the Son of God. Just in case you *don't* remember all of that stuff about me, let me fill you in. I was Jesus' favorite disciple. In fact, I was an eyewitness to everything that Jesus did. In other words, I was with Jesus all of the time. Imagine, being that close to God—every day! It was awesome!

I wrote these letters to believers about three different topics. So you won't get confused, let me give you one quick idea about each letter. I wrote 1 John because there were some people who were saying that Jesus looked like a human but really wasn't. Well, I lived and ate and walked with Jesus. I *knew* this wasn't true. I wrote 2 John to remind Christians to stay away from people who say that Jesus wasn't really human. And I wrote 3 John to my good friend Gaius to encourage him to continue to seek the truth and help those who were teaching the truth. Remember what the truth is? (Hint: Download John 14:6, p. 1448.)

JESUS WATCH

John's three letters remind believers that Jesus is a real person—and he's really God. John's portrayal through these three letters is built on a firm foundation that Jesus walked with believers as fully God and completely human (a super tough thing to understand!). These three books help both John's first readers and us to realize that Jesus isn't someone who doesn't understand our daily lives and needs. He loves us, and he loves being with us—even today!

my FAVORITE links

OTHER CONNECTIONS

Livin' it What would you consider the hardest thing about being a kid? Is close to the top of your list trying to obey all the rules that you are given—rules at home, rules at school, rules at Sunday school? What about obeying God's rules? Download Loving to Obey, 1 John 2:3–6, to learn how important it is to follow God's rules.

MORE STUFF...

Good and Bad Teachers How can you tell the difference between a good teacher and a false teacher? In his letters, John gives some important differences. Check it out below:

- Good teachers believe that Jesus came to earth as a human (1 John 4:2).
- False teachers refuse to admit that Jesus came to earth (1 John 4:3).
- Those who don't believe in God listen to false teachers; God's people listen to good teachers (1 John 4:5–6).
- False teachers don't follow only Jesus' teachings, but add other teachings (2 John 9–11).
- False teachers do evil things; good teachers obey God (3 John 11).

FAITH links

- It's Guaranteed!, 1 John 1:9–10
- Ya' Gotta Love It?, 1 John 2:15
- The True Test, 1 John 3:18
- Love and Obey, 2 John 6
- That's False!, 2 John 7–11
- What Any Parent Wants, 3 John 3–4
- Who's on First?, 3 John 9–10
- Helpful Hints, 3 John 11

"Hey, Tagg, do you know who John calls a liar?"

"I think I know the answer to that one. Let's surf over to 1 John 2:22-23 to make sure."

CHECK OUT SOME OTHER COOL STUFF IN JOHN'S BOOKS:

Source of love, 1 John 4:7–21
Ask anything!, 1 John 5:13–15
False teachers not wanted, 2 John 7–11
The greatest joy, 3 John 4

1 We write you now about what has always existed, which we have heard,
we have seen with our own eyes, we
have looked at, and we have touched with
our hands. We write to you about the
Word[n] that gives life. 2He who gives life
was shown to us. We saw him and can
give proof about it. And now we announce to you that he has life that continues forever. He was with God the Father
and was shown to us. 3We announce to
you what we have seen and heard, because we want you also to have fellowship with us. Our fellowship is with God
the Father and with his Son, Jesus Christ.
4We write this to you so you can be full of
joy with us.

God Forgives Our Sins

5Here is the message we have heard
from Christ and now announce to you:
God is light,[n] and in him there is no darkness at all. 6So if we say we have fellowship with God, but we continue living
in darkness, we are liars and do not follow the truth. 7But if we live in the light,
as God is in the light, we can share fellowship with each other. Then the blood
of Jesus, God's Son, cleanses us from
every sin.

8If we say we have no sin, we are fooling ourselves, and the truth is not in us.
9But if we confess our sins, he will forgive
our sins, because we can trust God to do
what is right. He will cleanse us from all
the wrongs we have done. 10If we say we
have not sinned, we make God a liar, and
we do not accept God's teaching.

Jesus Is Our Helper

2 My dear children, I write this letter to
you so you will not sin. But if anyone
does sin, we have a helper in the presence of the Father—Jesus Christ, the
One who does what is right. 2He is
the way our sins are
taken away, and not
only our sins but the
sins of all people.
3We can be sure
that we know God if

EMAIL FROM GOD
2:3
Obedience
What is a sign that you know God?

FAITH links

IT'S GUARANTEED!

1 JOHN 1:9-10

Some items you buy may come with a money-back guarantee. A guarantee is a promise. If you're not completely satisfied with what you bought, you can return it to the manufacturer and receive a full refund. It's great to have a guarantee, especially one with no strings attached. But having one is no good unless the manufacturer honors that guarantee.

In his first letter, John, one of Jesus' 12 followers, wrote about a guarantee that God will honor. If you do something wrong and confess what you've done, God promises to forgive you. Why? Because he's faithful. You have his word on it.

Download these links to find out how God deals with your sin:

A Priest Without Sin, Leviticus 4:3–7, p. 136

A Hidden Sin, Joshua 7, p. 285

A Pity Party, Job 10, p. 671

Believe the Impossible?, Ezekiel 37, p. 1131

One Big, Happy Family, John 1:12, p. 1422

It's Free!, Ephesians 2:8–9, p. 1600

1:1 Word The Greek word is "logos," meaning any kind of communication. Here, it means Christ, who was the way God told people about himself.
1:5 light Here, this word is used as a symbol of God's goodness or truth.

FAITH links

YA' GOTTA LOVE IT?

1 JOHN 2:15

You probably get lots of advice from your mom or dad, right? He or she wants to make sure you know what's right and what's wrong. The apostle John wrote a letter to Christians to help them know what was right and what was wrong. That's why he warned them to avoid loving the things of the world. What is the world? It includes the people and ideas that are opposed to God. Loving the things of the world means wanting or doing the wrong things, like being greedy or selfish. These attitudes make us unable to love people the way that God loves.

An Example Not to Follow, Leviticus 18:1–3, p. 157

Fairness for All, Deuteronomy 24:17, p. 258

Comfort from the Word, Job 26:3–4, p. 688

The Verdict Is In?, Matthew 7:1–2, p. 1285

Best Seat in the House, Luke 14:7–11, p. 1398

You've Got the Power!, Acts 1:1–8; 2:1–4, p. 1463

we obey his commands. **4**Anyone who
says, "I know God," but does not obey
God's commands is a liar, and the truth is
not in that person. **5**But if someone obeys
God's teaching, then in that person God's
love has truly reached its goal. This is
how we can be sure we are living in God:
6Whoever says that he lives in God must
live as Jesus lived.

The Command to Love Others

7My dear friends, I am not writing a
new command to you but an old command you have had from the beginning. It
is the teaching you have already heard.
8But also I am writing a new command to
you, and you can see its truth in Jesus
and in you, because the darkness is passing away, and the true light is already
shining.

9Anyone who says, "I am in the light,"[n]
but hates a brother or sister,[n] is still in
the darkness. **10**Whoever loves a brother
or sister lives in the light and will not
cause anyone to stumble in his faith.
11But whoever hates a brother or sister
is in darkness, lives in darkness, and
does not know where to go, because the
darkness has made that person blind.

12I write to you, dear children,
because your sins are forgiven
through Christ.
13I write to you, parents,
because you know the One who
existed from the beginning.
I write to you, young people,
because you have defeated the Evil
One.
14I write to you, children,
because you know the Father.
I write to you, parents,
because you know the One who
existed from the beginning.
I write to you, young people,
because you are strong;
the teaching of God lives in you,
and you have defeated the Evil
One.

15Do not love the world or the things
in the world. If you love the world, the
love of the Father is not in you. **16**These
are the ways of the world: wanting to
please our sinful selves, wanting the

2:9 light Here, this word is used as a symbol of God's goodness or truth.

2:9 brother or sister Although the Greek text says "brother" here and throughout this book, the writer's words were meant for the entire church, including men and women.

OBEYING GOD

1 John 2:3–6

Loving to Obey Yada, yada, yada—same old warning over and over again? Why do things need repeating a zillion times? Maybe it's because lots of people do what *they* think is right, rather than what God says. God wants us to be obedient to him and not follow what *we* think is right and wrong. (Check out Judges 21:25, p. 342.)

God gives us advice about right and wrong. He tells us to stay away from people and ideas that go against God. If we love the things of the world, it means we can't love God. You can't love the world *and* God at the same time. (Look up 1 John 2:15.) Which will you choose—loving the world, or loving God?

MORE FAITH links

Obeying God or Man?, p. 1154

A Reminder to Do What Is Right and True, p. 1257

The Number One Rule, p. 1351

Your Heart's Desire, p. 1401

Obey or Disobey?, p. 1409

Love and Obey, p. 1721

"You know, Tagg, obeying God is one of the most important things you can do."

"I guess so! Just download some of these Faithlinks to see what else God has to say about obeying him."

Ten Ways to Obey, Exodus 20, p. 103
- Who makes the rules at home or at school? How do you feel about rules?
- God gave us a set of rules called the Ten Commandments. Which one of the commandments is the hardest for you to obey?

I Insist!, 1 Samuel 8; 9, p. 363
- Have you ever begged your parents for something that you later wished you hadn't?
- How about insisting on having your own way? What happens if your way isn't God's way? Are you still going to do it?

The Greatest Commandment, Matthew 22:36–40, p. 1313
- What do you think is the No. 1 rule to obey? Link here to find out what Jesus has to say about it.

Put God First, Acts 5:27–32, p. 1472
- Did you ever get in trouble for doing the right thing? What happened?
- What if someone in authority asked you to do something that God says is wrong? What would you do?

sinful things we see, and being too proud
of what we have. None of

these come from the
Father, but all of
them come from the
world. 17The world
and everything that
people want in it are
passing away, but the person who does
what God wants lives forever.

Reject the Enemies of Christ

18My dear children, these are the last
days. You have heard that the enemy of
Christ is coming, and now many enemies
of Christ are already here. This is how we
know that these are the last days.
19These enemies of Christ were in our
fellowship, but they left us. They never
really belonged to us; if they had been a
part of us, they would have stayed with
us. But they left, and this shows that
none of them really belonged to us.

20You have the gift[n] that the Holy One
gave you, so you all know the truth. 21I
do not write to you because you do not
know the truth but because you do know
the truth. And you know that no lie
comes from the truth.

22Who is the liar? It is the person who
does not accept Jesus as the Christ. This
is the enemy of Christ: the person who
does not accept the Father and his Son.
23Whoever does not accept the Son does
not have the Father. But whoever confesses the Son has the Father, too.

24Be sure you continue to follow the
teaching you heard from the beginning. If
you continue to follow what you heard
from the beginning, you will stay in the
Son and in the Father. 25And this is what
the Son promised to us—life forever.

26I am writing this letter about those
people who are trying to lead you the
wrong way. 27Christ gave you a special
gift that is still in you, so you do not need
any other teacher. His gift teaches you
about everything, and it is true, not false.
So continue to live in Christ, as his gift
taught you.

28Yes, my dear children, live in him so
that when Christ comes back, we can be
without fear and not be ashamed in his
presence. 29If you know that Christ is all
that is right, you know that all who do
right are God's children.

We Are God's Children

3 The Father has loved us so much that
we are called children of God. And we
really are his children. The reason the
people in the world do not know us is that
they have not known him. 2Dear friends,
now we are children of God, and we have
not yet been shown what we will be in the
future. But we know that when Christ
comes again, we will be like him, because
we will see him as he really is. 3Christ is
pure, and all who have this hope in Christ
keep themselves pure like Christ.

4The person who sins breaks God's
law. Yes, sin is living against God's law.
5You know that Christ came to take away
sins and that there is no sin in Christ. 6So
anyone who lives in Christ does not go on
sinning. Anyone who goes on sinning has
never really understood Christ and has
never known him.

7Dear children, do not let anyone lead
you the wrong way. Christ is

eMAIL! FROM GOD
3:7–8
Satan
Who destroys the devil's work?

all that is right. So
to be like Christ a
person must do what
is right. 8The devil
has been sinning
since the beginning,
so anyone who continues to sin belongs to
the devil. The Son of God came for this
purpose: to destroy the devil's work.

9Those who are God's children do not
continue sinning, because the new life
from God remains in them. They are not
able to go on sinning, because they have
become children of God. 10So we can see
who God's children are and who the
devil's children are: Those who do not do
what is right are not God's children, and
those who do not love their brothers and
sisters are not God's children.

We Must Love Each Other

11This is the teaching you have heard
from the beginning: We must love each

2:20 gift This might mean the Holy Spirit, or it might mean teaching or truth as in verse 24.

FAITH links

THE TRUE TEST

1 JOHN 3:18

If someone said that he loved you, but acted as if he didn't want to be around you, would you believe that he loved you? You wouldn't, would you? You'd want to see some proof of that love. John, one of Jesus' 12 followers, had a lot to say about love in his letter. Love is more than just words. Love involves action. Don't just say you love someone, John says. Show it!

Here's some help on how to pass the "love" test:

Show Some Respect, Leviticus 19:32, p. 161

Choosing Sides, 1 Samuel 20, p. 382

Building Together, Nehemiah 3, p. 627

A Friend of Jesus, John 15:9–17, p. 1450

The Best Choice, 1 Corinthians 13, p. 1560

Who's on First?, 3 John 9–10, p. 1723

other. **12**Do not be like Cain who belonged to the Evil One and killed his
brother. And why did he kill him? Because the things Cain did were evil, and
the things his brother did were good.
13Brothers and sisters, do not be surprised when the people of the world hate
you. **14**We know we have left death and
have come into life because we love each
other. Whoever does not love is still
dead. **15**Everyone who hates a brother or
sister is a murderer,ⁿ and you know that
no murderers have eternal life in them.
16This is how we know what real love is:
Jesus gave his life for us. So we should
give our lives for our brothers and sisters. **17**Suppose someone has enough
to live and sees a brother or sister in
need, but does not help. Then God's love
is not living in that person. **18**My children, we should love people not only with
words and talk, but by our actions and
true caring.

19-20 This is the way we know that we
belong to the way of truth. When our
hearts make us feel guilty, we can still
have peace before God. God is greater
than our hearts, and he knows everything.
21My dear friends, if our hearts do not
make us feel guilty, we can come without
fear into God's presence. **22**And God
gives us what we ask for because we obey
God's commands and do what pleases
him. **23**This is what God commands: that
we believe in his Son, Jesus Christ, and
that we love each other, just as he commanded. **24**The people who obey God's
commands live in God, and God lives in
them. We know that God lives in us because of the Spirit God gave us.

Warning Against False Teachers

4 My dear friends, many false prophets
have gone out into the world. So do
not believe every spirit, but test the spirits to see if they are from God. **2**This is
how you can know God's Spirit: Every
spirit who confesses that Jesus Christ
came to earth as a human is from God.
3And every spirit who refuses to say this
about Jesus is not from God. It is the spirit of the enemy of Christ, which you have
heard is coming, and now he is already in
the world.

4My dear children, you belong to God
and have defeated them; because God's
Spirit, who is in you, is greater than the

3:15 Everyone . . . murderer If one person hates a brother or sister, then in the heart that person has killed that brother or sister. Jesus taught about this sin to his followers (Matthew 5:21-26).

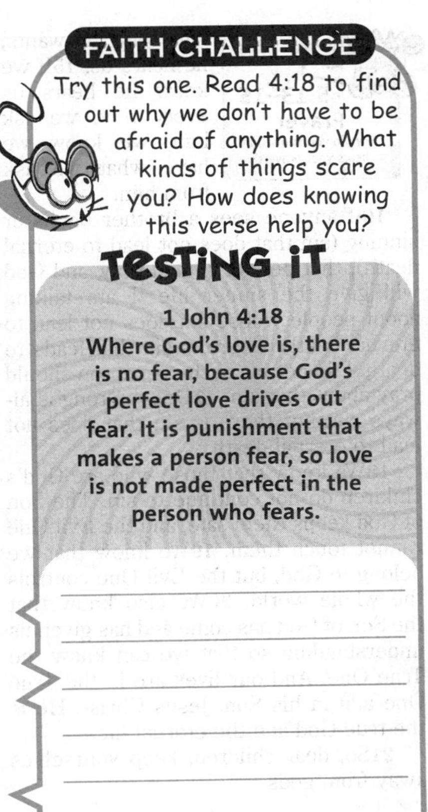

devil, who is in the world. 5And they belong to the world, so what they say is
from the world, and the world listens to
them. 6But we belong to God, and those
who know God listen to us. But those
who are not from God do not listen to us.
That is how we know the Spirit that is
true and the spirit that is false.

FAITH CHALLENGE
Try this one. Read 4:18 to find out why we don't have to be afraid of anything. What kinds of things scare you? How does knowing this verse help you?
TESTING IT
1 John 4:18
Where God's love is, there is no fear, because God's perfect love drives out fear. It is punishment that makes a person fear, so love is not made perfect in the person who fears.

Love Comes from God

7Dear friends, we should love each
other, because love comes from God.
Everyone who loves has become God's
child and knows God. 8Whoever does not
love does not know God, because God is
love. 9This is how God showed his love
to us: He sent his one and only Son into
the world so that we could have life
through him. 10This is what real love is:
It is not our love for God; it is God's love
for us in sending his Son to be the way to
take away our sins.
11Dear friends, if God loved us that
much we also should love each other.
12No one has ever seen God, but if we
love each other, God lives in us, and his
love is made perfect in us.
13We know that we live in God and he
lives in us, because he gave us his Spirit.
14We have seen and can testify that the
Father sent his Son to be the Savior of
the world. 15Whoever confesses that
Jesus is the Son of God has God living inside, and that person lives in God. 16And
so we know the love that God has for us,
and we trust that love.

God is love. Those who live in love
live in God, and God lives in them.
17This is how love is made perfect in us:
that we can be without fear on the day
God judges us, because in this world we
are like him. 18Where God's
love is, there is no
fear, because God's
perfect love drives
out fear. It is punish-
ment that makes a
person fear, so love
is not made perfect in the person who
fears.

> EMAIL FROM GOD **4:18**
> **Fears**
> What can drive away your fears?

19We love because God first loved us.
20If people say, "I love God," but hate
their brothers or sisters, they are liars.
Those who do not love their brothers and
sisters, whom they have seen, cannot
love God, whom they have never seen.
21And God gave us this command: Those
who love God must also love their brothers and sisters.

Faith in the Son of God

5 Everyone who believes that Jesus is
the Christ is God's child, and whoever
loves the Father also loves the Father's
children. 2This is how we know
we love God's chil-
dren: when we love
God and obey his
commands. 3Loving
God means obeying
his commands. And

> EMAIL FROM GOD **5:1–3**
> **Obedience**
> How can you show love for others?

God's commands are not too hard for us,
4because everyone who is a child of God
conquers the world. And this is the victory that conquers the world—our faith.
5So the one who wins against the world is
the person who believes that Jesus is the
Son of God.

6Jesus Christ is the One who came by
water[n] and blood.[n] He did not come by
water only, but by water and blood. And
the Spirit says that this is true, because
the Spirit is the truth. **7**So there are three
witnesses that tell us about Jesus: **8**the
Spirit, the water, and the blood; and these
three witnesses agree. **9**We believe people when they say something is true. But
what God says is more important, and he
has told us the truth about his own Son.
10Anyone who believes in the Son of God
has the truth that God told us. Anyone
who does not believe makes God a liar,
because that person does not believe
what God told us about his Son. **11**This is
what God told us: God has given us eternal life, and this life is in his Son. **12**Whoever has the Son has life, but whoever
does not have the Son of God does not
have life.

We Have Eternal Life Now

13I write this letter to you who believe in the Son of God so you will know
you have eternal life. **14**And this is the
boldness we have in God's presence: that
if we ask God for anything that agrees

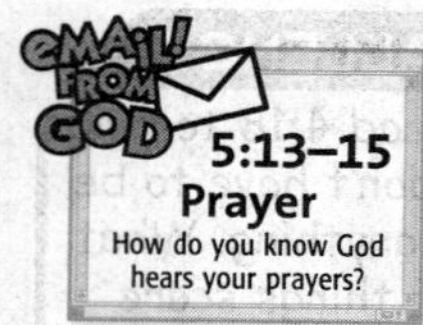

5:13–15
Prayer
How do you know God hears your prayers?

with what he wants,
he hears us. **15**If we
know he hears us
every time we ask
him, we know we
have what we ask
from him.

16If anyone sees a brother or sister
sinning (sin that does not lead to eternal
death), that person should pray, and God
will give the sinner life. I am talking
about people whose sin does not lead to
eternal death. There is sin that leads to
death. I do not mean that a person should
pray about that sin. **17**Doing wrong is always sin, but there is sin that does not
lead to eternal death.

18We know that those who are God's
children do not continue to sin. The Son
of God keeps them safe, and the Evil One
cannot touch them. **19**We know that we
belong to God, but the Evil One controls
the whole world. **20**We also know that
the Son of God has come and has given us
understanding so that we can know the
True One. And our lives are in the True
One and in his Son, Jesus Christ. He is
the true God and the eternal life.

21So, dear children, keep yourselves
away from gods.

5:6 water This probably means the water of Jesus' baptism.

5:6 blood This probably means the blood of Jesus' death.

From the Elder.[n]
To the chosen lady[n] and her children:
I love all of you in the truth,[n] and all
those who know the truth love you. **2**We
love you because of the truth that lives in
us and will be with us forever.
3Grace, mercy, and peace from God
the Father and his Son, Jesus Christ, will
be with us in truth and love.

4I was very happy to learn that some
of your children are following the way of
truth, as the Father commanded

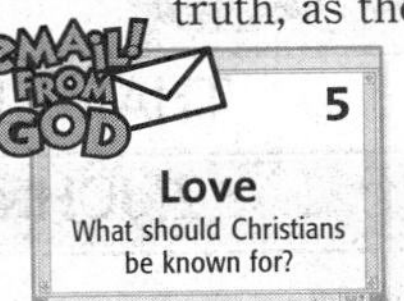

us. **5**And now, dear
lady, this is not a new
command but is the
same command we
have had from the
beginning. I ask you
that we all love each other. **6**And love
means living the way God commanded us
to live. As you have heard from the beginning, his command is this: Live a life of
love.
7Many false teachers are in the world
now who do not confess that Jesus Christ
came to earth as a human. Anyone who
does not confess this is a false teacher
and an enemy of Christ. **8**Be careful yourselves that you do not lose everything
you have worked for, but that you receive
your full reward.
9Anyone who goes beyond Christ's
teaching and does not continue to follow
only his teaching does not have God. But
whoever continues to follow the teaching
of Christ has both the Father and the Son.
10If someone comes to you and does not
bring this teaching, do not welcome or
accept that person into your house. **11**If
you welcome such a person, you share in
the evil work.
12I have many things to write to you,
but I do not want to use paper and ink.
Instead, I hope to come to you and talk
face to face so we can be full of joy. **13**The
children of your chosen sister[n] greet you.

LOVE AND OBEY

2 JOHN 6

What's the connection between love and obedience? One goes with the other. If you love your parents, you do what they tell you to do. If you love God, you do what he tells you to do.

That's what John, one of Jesus' followers, wrote about in his second letter. Jesus once told his followers that those who loved him obeyed his commands. (See John 15:14, p. 1450. John wrote that book, too!) Know what one of his commands is? Love others. So . . . how will you obey that command this week?

Give Revenge a Rest, Leviticus 19:18, p. 160

The Gift of Friendship, 1 Samuel 18:1–3; 19, p. 381

Help for the Outsiders, Nehemiah 5:9–10, p. 630

A Friend in Deed, Job 2:13, p. 662

Your Choice of Fruit, Matthew 12:33–35, p. 1295

Forgive Again?, Luke 17:3–4, p. 1402

1 Elder "Elder" means an older person. It can also mean a special leader in the church (as in Titus 1:5).
1 lady This might mean a woman, or in this letter it might mean a church. If it is a church, then "her children" would be the people of the church.
1 truth The truth or "Good News" about Jesus Christ that joins all believers together.
13 sister Sister of the "lady" in verse 1. This might be another woman or another church.

THAT'S FALSE!

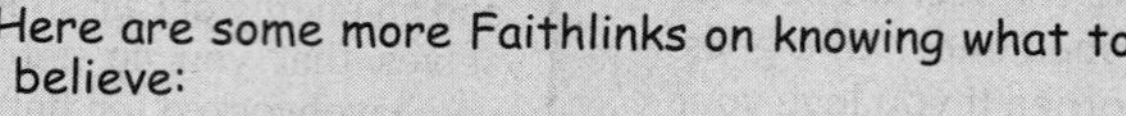

Has anyone ever tried to make you believe something that was not true? The apostle John warned Christians about false teachers in the area. These teachers did not believe that Jesus was God. John told the Christians not to even allow these teachers to enter their homes.

You may not have people coming to your door with false information. But you receive a lot of information each day at school, in the neighborhood, on the Internet, and on TV. Do you know what's true and what's false? How much of what's false do you allow in your brain? If you're not sure about what you're hearing or reading, talk to a parent or your pastor.

Here are some more Faithlinks on knowing what to believe:

The Sacrifice, Genesis 22, p. 29

Take Me to Your Leader, Numbers 27:12–23, p. 214

A Look for the Book, 2 Chronicles 34:14–18, p. 603

The One Who Suffered, Isaiah 53, p. 966

Faith Workout, Acts 16:4–5, p. 1493

The Way to Be Wise, James 1:5, p. 1689

FAITH links

WHAT ANY PARENT WANTS

3 JOHN 3-4

What do you think your parents want for your life? Most parents or guardians want their children to grow up to be respected members of society—fully mature and wise. John was like a father to the Christians he wrote letters to. He had hopes and dreams for them, just like any parent. One dream was for them to live in a way that would please God. He wanted them to keep believing what was true about God. Guess what? That's what *your* parents want for you, too.

Check out God's plans and hopes for you:

Forgive Instead, Genesis 33, p. 47

Obey? No Way!, Exodus 1:15–21, p. 76

More Precious Than Gold, Psalm 19:7–10, p. 723

Pass It On!, Joel 1:2–3, p. 1187

Quick to Forgive?, Mark 11:25, p. 1349

How to Make God Glad, Ephesians 6:1–2, p. 1605

FAITH links

WHO'S ON FIRST?

3 JOHN 9-10

Is there a Diotrephes in your life? No, that's not a new kind of video game. Diotrephes was a church leader who made trouble for visiting church leaders sent by John. Instead of welcoming them, Diotrephes ignored them and tried to stop anyone else in the church from helping them. He wanted to be seen as the most important person in his church community.

All Christians are part of a team. There are no MVPs (Most Valuable Players). Part of the team's duty includes respecting church leaders and welcoming those who visit. That duty takes humility and a willingness to serve others. Are you willing?

Play Fair or Play Favorites?, Deuteronomy 1:16–18, p. 227

Your Response to Responsibility, Ruth 2:1–7, p. 346

Building Together, Nehemiah 3, p. 627

Best Seat in the House, Luke 14:7–11, p. 1398

An Unselfish Example, Philippians 2:5–8, p. 1611

The True Test, 1 John 3:18, p. 1718

From the Elder.[n]
To my dear friend Gaius, whom I love
in the truth:[n]
2My dear friend, I know your soul is
doing fine, and I pray that you are doing
well in every way and that your health is
good. 3I was very happy when some

1 Elder "Elder" means an older person. It can also mean a special leader in the church (as in Titus 1:5).

1 truth The truth or "Good News" about Jesus Christ that joins all believers together.

brothers and sisters[n] came and told me
about the truth in your life and how you
are following the way of truth. 4Nothing
gives me greater joy than to hear that my
children are following the way of truth.
5My dear friend, it is good that you
help the brothers and sisters, even those
you do not know. 6They told the church
about your love. Please help them to continue their trip in a way worthy of God.
7They started out in service to Christ,
and they have been accepting nothing
from nonbelievers. 8So we should help
such people; when we do, we share in
their work for the truth.
9I wrote something to the church, but
Diotrephes, who loves to be their leader,
will not listen to us. 10So if I come, I will
talk about what Diotrephes is doing,
about how he lies and says evil things
about us. But more than that, he refuses
to accept the other brothers and sisters;
he even stops those who do want to accept them and puts them out of the
church.
11My dear friend, do not follow what
is bad; follow what is good.
The one who does
good belongs to
God. But the one
who does evil has
never known God.
12Everyone says
good things about Demetrius, and the
truth agrees with what they say. We also
speak well of him, and you know what we
say is true.
13I have many things I want to write
you, but I do not want to use pen and ink.
14I hope to see you soon and talk face to
face. 15Peace to you. The friends here
greet you. Please greet each friend there
by name.

Life
Read about following what is good.

3 brothers and sisters Although the Greek text says "brothers" here and throughout this book, the writer's words were meant for the entire church, including men and women.

FAITH links

HELPFUL HINTS

3 JOHN 11

Did your mother ever say, "If so-and-so jumped off a bridge, would you do that?" That's an answer many parents give in response to their children's desire to do something everyone else does. Usually, that "something" is an activity the parent isn't crazy about.

In his letter, the apostle John didn't mention any bridges. Instead, he told the Christians not to follow a bad example. Instead, they should do what was right. Want to do what's right? You'll need a model for right behavior. The Bible mentions the perfect model: Jesus. Follow him, and you can't go wrong!

Connect here to find out more about the perfect role model:

What's Out Becomes In, Judges 11, p. 327

I Insist!, 1 Samuel 8; 9, p. 363

Mind Guard, Proverbs 4:23, p. 831

Small Beginnings, Zechariah 4:10, p. 1255

Two Ways to Grow, Luke 2:46–52, p. 1370

Out with the Old!, Colossians 3:1–14, p. 1625

Jude

FIGHT FOR THE FAITH!

Hi; I'm Jude. You probably don't know who I am. Here's the 411 on me—I'm the older brother of James (he wrote James and was the leader of the church in Jerusalem) and Jesus' half brother. It's hard to imagine, but I didn't actually believe in Jesus until *after* he rose from the dead. I had a lot to learn about Jesus when I finally believed. The Bible doesn't talk a lot about me, but I probably served in the Jerusalem church with James and was certainly around very important biblical people.

I wrote this book to let the first believers know that it was important to understand what they believed. A lot of Christians were running around saying they were believers, but they weren't really thinking about what that meant; and a lot of the teachings floating around about Jesus were really wrong. There were also many rebellious people in the church—and I wanted these people to stop being rebellious.

JESUS WATCH

Jude gives us two very distinct pictures of Jesus. On the one hand, believers are told to fight for their faith they know is true and to keep themselves in the love of God. Jude calls them (and us) to look for God's mercy and seek eternal life, because those who don't will be punished. At the same time, Jude reminds us that Jesus protects us and keeps us from stumbling in our walk with him.

If we'll "keep ourselves in Jesus" and trust in God's ability to guard every step we take, Jude promises that we'll enter into a type of friendship with God that is wonderful. Knowing God can feel impossible, and following what God commands can be unbelievably difficult. But Jude reassures us that God is strong and able to keep us from falling.

FAITH links

"Tagg, do you know what God did to those angels who rebelled against him?"

"Rebelling angels? I'd better check this out, Skweek! Where do I go?"

"Try connecting to Jude 6, and tell me what you find out."

While You Wait, Jude 21

The Sin "Braker," Jude 24–25

1From Jude, a servant of Jesus Christ
and a brother of James.
To all who have been called by God.
God the Father loves you, and you have
been kept safe in Jesus Christ:
2Mercy, peace, and love be yours
richly.

God Will Punish Sinners

3Dear friends, I wanted very much to
write you about the salvation we all
share. But I felt the need to write you
about something else: I want to encourage you to fight hard for the faith that was
given the holy people of God once and for
all time. 4Some people have secretly entered your group. Long ago the prophets
wrote about these people who will be
judged guilty. They are against God and
have changed the grace of our God into a
reason for sexual sin. They also refuse to
accept Jesus Christ, our only Master and
Lord.
5I want to remind you of some things
you already know: Remember that the
Lord saved his people by bringing them
out of the land of Egypt. But later he destroyed all those who did not believe.
6And remember the
angels who did not
keep their place of
power but left their
proper home. The
Lord has kept these
angels in darkness,
bound with everlasting chains, to be
judged on the great day. 7Also remember
the cities of Sodom and Gomorrah[n] and
the other towns around them. In the
same way they were full of sexual sin and
people who desired sexual relations that
God does not allow. They suffer the punishment of eternal fire, as an example for
all to see.
8It is the same with these people who
have entered your group. They are guided
by dreams and make themselves filthy
with sin. They reject God's authority and
speak against the angels. 9Not even the

eMAIL! FROM GOD
6
Hell
What happened to angels who rebelled?

7 Sodom and Gomorrah Two cities God destroyed because they were so evil.

FAITH links

WHILE YOU WAIT

JUDE 21

What events do you find the hardest to wait for? Your birthday? Christmas? Many Christians have a hard time waiting for Jesus' return to earth. Jude, the half brother of Jesus, wrote a letter to encourage Christians to stay in God's love while they waited for Jesus to return. Staying in God's love means living for him and obeying what he says.

Jude knew that false teachers would try to lure the Christians that he wrote to away from God. That's why he told them to stick with God. We should, too. How do you stick with God? You can pray, read your Bible, and get involved at church.

Check out these Faithlinks on the best way to stick with God:

Our Thorough God, Leviticus 13, p. 149

Patience, Please, Psalm 145:8–9, p. 819

The Gift of Worship, Matthew 2:10–12, p. 1275

Faith God Notices, Luke 18:35–43, p. 1406

Keeping Clean, 2 Corinthians 7:1, p. 1576

A Heavenly Sight, Revelation 21:1–4, p. 1753

FAITH links

THE SIN "BRAKER"

JUDE 24-25

If you've ever been on inline skates, you know what falling is like. As you learned to skate better, you learned how to brake and keep your knees bent to avoid falling.

Jude, the half brother of Jesus, wrote about another type of falling. To fall means to sin. Trusting in God's strength helps to keep you from giving in to the temptation to sin. These verses are a prayer that many churches use at the end of a service. Next time you're out skating, think about how God puts the brakes on sin in your life.

The Trouble with Jealousy, Genesis 37, p. 53

A Long Wait, Joshua 14:6–15, p. 294

World News, Isaiah 13—19, p. 913

Facing Your Fears, Matthew 8:23–27, p. 1288

The Way to Be Wise, James 1:5, p. 1689

A Happy Ending, Revelation 22:16–21, p. 1754

archangel[n] Michael, when he argued with
the devil about who would have the body
of Moses, dared to judge the devil guilty.
Instead, he said, "The Lord punish you."
10But these people speak against things
they do not understand. And what they do
know, by feeling, as dumb animals know
things, are the very things that destroy
them. **11**It will be terrible for them. They
have followed the way of Cain, and for
money they have given themselves to doing the wrong that Balaam did. They have
fought against God as Korah did, and like
Korah, they surely will be destroyed.
12They are like dirty spots in your special
Christian meals you share. They eat with
you and have no fear, caring only for themselves. They are clouds without rain,
which the wind blows around. They are
autumn trees without fruit that are pulled
out of the ground. So they are twice dead.
13They are like wild waves of the sea,
tossing up their own shameful actions like
foam. They are like stars that wander in
the sky. A place in the blackest darkness
has been kept for them forever.

14Enoch, the seventh descendant
from Adam, said about these people:
"Look, the Lord is coming with many
thousands of his holy angels to **15**judge
every person. He is coming to punish
all who are against God for all the evil
they have done against him. And he will
punish the sinners who are against God
for all the evil they have said against
him."

16These people complain and blame
others, doing the evil things they want
to do. They brag about themselves, and
they flatter others to get what they want.

A Warning and Things to Do

17Dear friends, remember what the
apostles of our Lord Jesus Christ said before. **18**They said to you, "In the last
times there will be people who laugh
about God, following their own evil desires which are against God." **19**These
are the people who divide you, people
whose thoughts are only of this
world, who do not
have the Spirit.

20But dear friends,
use your most holy
faith to build your-
selves up, praying in

EMAIL FROM GOD 20
Prayer
What's the best way to build faith?

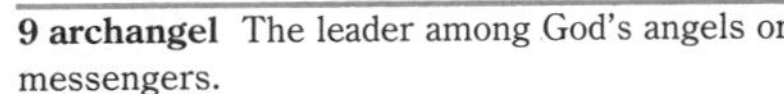

9 archangel The leader among God's angels or messengers.

the Holy Spirit. 21Keep yourselves in
God's love as you wait for the Lord Jesus
Christ with his mercy to give you life for-
ever.

22Show mercy to some people who
have doubts. 23Take others out of the
fire, and save them. Show mercy mixed
with fear to others, hating even their
clothes which are dirty from sin.

Praise God

24God is strong and can help you not
to fall. He can bring you before his glory
without any wrong in you and can give
you great joy. 25He is the only God, the
One who saves us. To him be glory, greatness, power, and authority through Jesus
Christ our Lord for all time past, now, and
forever. Amen.

A NEW BEGINNING

Hi, everyone! It's John here. Hey, do you remember what other books I wrote? That's right. I wrote the Gospel of John and three letters (1, 2, and 3 John). I was known as the disciple Jesus loved the most. But being a disciple of Jesus wasn't always easy. Because I was a leader of a church, the Roman emperor Domitian sent me away to the island of Patmos, which was really like a prison. (Do you know that the enemies of the faith wanted to do me harm? Praise God that he protected me!) I wrote this letter (my last one) while I was there.

Why did I write this book? I wanted to give my friends and fellow believers hope by letting them know that Jesus was in control of *everything*—even when they were facing some pretty tough times. But I didn't want the Roman officials to understand what I was saying. (I'm sure they would try to get rid of more Christians.) So I used a lot of symbols in my book that only believers would understand. Kind of like writing to your friends in a secret code! Pretty sneaky, huh?

JESUS WATCH

John's book gives a dramatic and powerful glimpse—or revelation—into what will happen when Jesus returns to earth. John portrays Jesus as the conquering king, the judge over all the earth, and the loving redeemer. The book begins with a picture of Jesus' breathtaking glory and shows his power over the entire church. Want some quick snapshots of Jesus in Revelation? Jesus is: ruler of the kings of the earth (Revelation 1:5); the First and the Last (Revelation 1:17); the One who sits on the throne (Revelation 5:13); the Word of God (Revelation 19:13); the King of Kings and Lord of Lords (Revelation 19:16); and the Alpha and the Omega (Revelation 22:13). We worship an awesome God!

Through these pictures, believers are offered hope. God's message throughout this book, and through the life of Jesus, is clear—trusting Jesus for eternal life is essential. We could live apart from Jesus—but we'd lack so much. Power, wisdom, blessings. The list is long. Choosing to live for Jesus might not offer us an easy life, but it does mean that we get to spend eternity with the conquering, loving, and redeeming Lamb of God. What will you choose to do?

OTHER CONNECTIONS

- The Follower Jesus Loved, Revelation 1. Along with Peter and his brother James, John was one of the followers closest to Jesus. In fact, John refers to himself as "the follower Jesus loved." Find out more about John's life and ministry by connecting here.
- What Do You Call the Devil?, Revelation 12:9. Some people think of the devil as that cute character in the red suit with the horns and pitchfork. But the Bible tells us that the devil is the very enemy of God. Download this info bulletin board to find out the various names used for Satan in the Scripture.

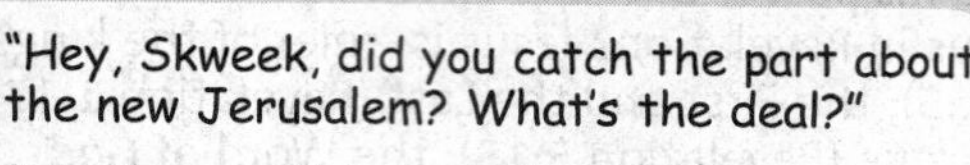

"Hey, Skweek, did you catch the part about the new Jerusalem? What's the deal?"

"That's not all! John tells us about a new heaven and a new earth! You'd better surf over to Revelation 21 right now. This is too good to miss!"

CHECK OUT THESE OTHER COOL STORIES:

A heavenly sight, Revelation 4
Bowls of anger, Revelation 15; 16
Satan's last stand, Revelation 20:1–15
The river of life, Revelation 22:1–2
Final words, Revelation 22:18–21

- Lost Love?, Revelation 2:4
- Hot, Cold, or In Between?, Revelation 3:15
- Praise Him!, Revelation 5:12
- Keep On Keepin' On, Revelation 13:10
- A Heavenly Sight, Revelation 21:1–4
- A Happy Ending, Revelation 22:16–21

THE FOLLOWER JESUS LOVED

Revelation 1

1. John was a fisherman along Lake Galilee with his brother James, when Jesus called them to be his followers. (Look up Matthew 4:21–22, p. 1279.) He and his brother were nicknamed "Sons of Thunder."

2. Along with Peter and James, John was one of the followers closest to Jesus throughout his ministry. He also went with Jesus to a high mountain, where he saw Jesus' appearance change. (Read Matthew 17:1–9, p. 1303.)

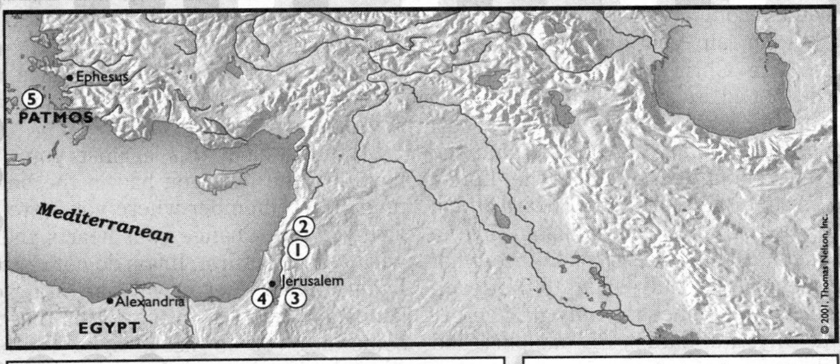

3. John stayed close to Jesus during his final week. He was there at the Lord's Supper, Jesus' prayer time in Gethsemane, Jesus' trial, and even his death on the cross. (Look up John 19:25–27, p. 1457.)

4. John worked with Peter as leader of the early church in Jerusalem. (See Acts 3 and 4, p. 1466.)

5. John was sent to live alone on the island called Patmos as punishment for preaching the word of God. That's probably where he wrote his message about Jesus and his letters that are a part of the New Testament. That's also where he wrote the Book of Revelation, the last book in the New Testament. (Check out Revelation 1:1–11.)

John Tells About This Book

1 This is the revelation* of Jesus Christ,
which God gave to him, to show his
servants what must soon happen. And
Jesus sent his angel to show it to his servant John, 2who has told everything he has
seen. It is the word of God; it is the message from Jesus Christ. 3Happy is the one
who reads the words of God's message,
and happy are the people who hear this
message and do what is written in it. The
time is near when all of this will happen.

Jesus' Message to the Churches

4From John.

To the seven churches in the country of Asia:

Grace and peace to you from the One
who is and was and is coming, and from
the seven spirits before his throne, 5and
from Jesus Christ. Jesus is the faithful
witness, the first among those raised

1:1 revelation Making known truth that has been hidden.

from the dead. He is the ruler of the
kings of the earth.
He is the One who loves us, who
made us free from our sins with the blood
of his death. 6He made us to be a kingdom of priests who serve God his Father.
To Jesus Christ be glory and power forever and ever! Amen.
7Look, Jesus is coming with the
clouds, and everyone will see him, even
those who stabbed him. And all peoples
of the earth will cry loudly because of
him. Yes, this will happen! Amen.
8The Lord God says, “I am the Alpha
and the Omega.”[n] I am the One who is and
was and is coming. I am the Almighty.”
9I, John, am your brother. All of us
share with Christ in suffering, in the
kingdom, and in patience to continue. I
was on the island of Patmos,[n] because I
had preached the word of God and the
message about Jesus. 10On the Lord’s
day I was in the Spirit, and I heard a loud
voice behind me that sounded like a
trumpet. 11The voice said, “Write what
you see in a book and send it to the seven
churches: to Ephesus, Smyrna, Pergamum, Thyatira, Sardis, Philadelphia, and
Laodicea.”
12I turned to see who was talking to
me. When I turned, I saw seven golden
lampstands 13and someone among the
lampstands who was “like a Son of
Man.”[n] He was dressed in a long robe
and had a gold band around his chest.
14His head and hair were white like
wool, as white as snow, and his eyes were
like flames of fire. 15His feet were like
bronze that glows hot in a furnace, and
his voice was like the noise of flooding
water. 16He held seven stars in his right
hand, and a sharp double-edged sword
came out of his mouth. He looked like the
sun shining at its brightest time.
17When I saw him, I fell down at his
feet like a dead man. He put his right
hand on me and said, “Do not be afraid. I
am the First and the Last. 18I am the One
who lives; I was dead, but look, I am alive
forever and ever! And I hold the keys to
death and to the place of the dead. 19So
write the things you see, what is now and
what will happen later. 20Here is the secret of the seven stars that you saw in my
right hand and the seven golden lampstands: The seven lampstands are the
seven churches, and the seven stars are
the angels of the seven churches.

To the Church in Ephesus

2 “Write this to the angel of the church
in Ephesus:
“The One who holds the seven stars
in his right hand and walks among the
seven golden lampstands says this: 2I
know what you do, how you work hard
and never give up. I know you do not put
up with the false teachings of evil people.
You have tested those who say they are
apostles but really are not, and you found
they are liars. 3You have patience and
have suffered troubles for my name and
have not given up.
4“But I have this against you: You
have left the love you had in the beginning. 5So remember where you were before you fell. Change your hearts and do
what you did at first. If you do not change,
I will come to you and will take away your
lampstand from its place. 6But there is
something you do that is right: You hate
what the Nicolaitans[n] do, as much as I.
7“Every person who has ears should
listen to what the Spirit says to the
churches. To those who win the victory I
will give the right to eat the fruit from the
tree of life, which is in the garden of God.

To the Church in Smyrna

8“Write this to the angel of the church
in Smyrna:
“The One who is the First and the
Last, who died and came to life again,
says this: 9I know your troubles and that
you are poor, but really you are rich! I
know the bad things some people say
about you. They say they are Jews, but

1:8 Alpha and the Omega The first and last letters of the Greek alphabet. This means “the beginning and the end.”
1:9 Patmos A small island in the Aegean Sea, near the coast of Asia Minor (modern Turkey).
1:13 “like . . . Man” “Son of Man” is a name Jesus called himself.
2:6 Nicolaitans This is the name of a religious group that followed false beliefs and ideas.

FAITH links

LOST LOVE?

REVELATION 2:4

Have you ever stopped being friends with someone? Maybe this was a friend you used to play with all the time, but no longer do so. Some relationships change over time. That's because our feelings sometimes change. But there are some relationships we have that we hope will never change.

In Ephesians 1:15, Paul complimented the Ephesians on how much love they had for Jesus. Here, Jesus told them that they didn't have as much love as they used to have. They had lost the enthusiasm they had had for Jesus. Jesus wanted them to confess any sins in their lives and ask for his forgiveness. Is that what you need to do? Don't wait!

Count on His Mercy, Judges 2:16–17; 3, p. 313

A Memorial for Two Thieves, 1 Chronicles 7:21, p. 530

Anger: Quick or Slow?, Psalm 86:15, p. 776

Concern for All, Daniel 9, p. 1165

Remembering Jesus, Matthew 26:26–29, p. 1321

A Christian's Responsibility, Acts 11:26, p. 1484

they are not true Jews. They are a synagogue that belongs to Satan. **10**Do not be
afraid of what you are about to suffer. I
tell you, the devil will put some of you in
prison to test you, and you will suffer for
ten days. But be faithful, even if you have
to die, and I will give you the crown of
life.

11"Everyone who has ears should
listen to what the Spirit says to the
churches. Those who win the victory will
not be hurt by the second death.

To the Church in Pergamum

12"Write this to the angel of the
church in Pergamum:

"The One who has the sharp, double-
edged sword says this: **13**I know where
you live. It is where Satan has his throne.
But you are true to me. You did not refuse
to tell about your faith in me even during
the time of Antipas, my faithful witness
who was killed in your city, where Satan
lives.

14"But I have a few things against
you: You have some there who follow the
teaching of Balaam. He taught Balak how
to cause the people of Israel to sin by eating food offered to idols and by taking
part in sexual sins. **15**You also have some
who follow the teaching of the Nicolaitans.[n] **16**So change your hearts and lives.
If you do not, I will come to you quickly
and fight against them with the sword
that comes out of my mouth.

17"Everyone who has ears should listen to what the Spirit says to the
churches.

"I will give some of the hidden manna
to everyone who wins the victory. I will
also give to each one who wins the victory a white stone with a new name written on it. No one knows this new name
except the one who receives it.

To the Church in Thyatira

18"Write this to the angel of the
church in Thyatira:

"The Son of God, who has eyes that
blaze like fire and feet like shining bronze,
says this: **19**I know what you do. I know
about your love, your faith, your service,
and your patience. I know that you are doing more now than you did at first.

2:15 Nicolaitans This is the name of a religious group that followed false beliefs and ideas.

20"But I have this against you: You let
that woman Jezebel spread false teachings. She says she is a prophetess, but by
her teaching she leads my people to take
part in sexual sins and to eat food that is
offered to idols. 21I have given her time
to change her heart and turn away from
her sin, but she does not want to change.
22So I will throw her on a bed of suffering. And all those who take part in adultery with her will suffer greatly if they do
not turn away from the wrongs she does.
23I will also kill her followers. Then all
the churches will know I am the One who
searches hearts and minds, and I will repay each of you for what you have done.
24"But others of you in Thyatira have
not followed her teaching and have not
learned what some call Satan's deep secrets. I say to you that I will not put any
other load on you. 25Only continue in
your loyalty until I come.
26"I will give power over the nations
to everyone who wins the victory and
continues to be obedient to me until
the end.
27 'You will rule over them with an iron
rod,
as when pottery is broken into
pieces.' *Psalm 2:9*
28This is the same power I received from
my Father. I will also give him the morning star. 29Everyone who has ears should
listen to what the Spirit says to the
churches.

To the Church in Sardis

3 "Write this to the angel of the church
in Sardis:
"The One who has the seven spirits
and the seven stars says this: I know
what you do. People say that you are
alive, but really you are dead. 2Wake up!
Make yourselves stronger before what
you have left dies completely. I have
found that what you are doing is less than
what my God wants. 3So do not forget
what you have received and heard. Obey
it, and change your hearts and lives. So
you must wake up, or I will come like a
thief, and you will not know when I will
come to you. 4But you have a few there
in Sardis who have kept their clothes un-
stained, so they will walk with me and
will wear white clothes, because they are
worthy. 5Those who win the victory will
be dressed in white clothes like them.
And I will not erase their names from the
book of life, but I will say they belong to
me before my Father and before his angels. 6Everyone who has ears should listen to what the Spirit says to the
churches.

To the Church in Philadelphia

7"Write this to the angel of the church
in Philadelphia:
"This is what the One who is holy and
true, who holds the key of David, says.
When he opens a door, no one can close
it. And when he closes it, no one can open
it. 8I know what you do. I have put an
open door before you, which no one can
close. I know you have a little strength,
but you have obeyed my teaching and
were not afraid to speak my name.
9Those in the synagogue that belongs to
Satan say they are Jews, but they are not
true Jews; they are liars. I will make
them come before you and bow at your
feet, and they will know that I have loved
you. 10You have obeyed my teaching
about not giving up your faith. So I will
keep you from the time of trouble that
will come to the whole world to test
those who live on earth.
11"I am coming soon. Continue
strong in your faith so no one will take
away your crown. 12I will make those
who win the victory pillars in the temple
of my God, and they will never have to
leave it. I will write on them the name of
my God and the name of the city of my
God, the new Jerusalem,[n] that comes
down out of heaven from my God. I will
also write on them my new name.
13Everyone who has ears should listen
to what the Spirit says to the churches.

To the Church in Laodicea

14"Write this to the angel of the
church in Laodicea:

3:12 Jerusalem This name is used to mean the spiritual city God built for his people. See Revelation 21-22.

FAITH links

HOT, COLD, OR IN BETWEEN?

REVELATION 3:15

Cold, hot, and lukewarm are three different temperatures. We like cocoa to be hot and soft drinks to be cold. Not many people like anything lukewarm. Jesus feels the same way.

One day, the apostle John saw a vision of the risen Jesus. Jesus had a message for Christians in the city of Laodicea. He didn't like the fact that they were lukewarm. That meant they were halfhearted about God. When you have faith in God and do what he says, you're "on fire" for God. If you don't believe in God, that means you're cold. Jesus wants you to be hot or cold, not in between! Go for hot!

Check out these Faithlinks on having a faith that is "hot":

Always Truthful, Numbers 23:19, p. 208

A Reminder to Be Fair, 2 Chronicles 19:5–11, p. 583

A Picture of the Past, Psalm 105, p. 789

Dirty Inside, Isaiah 6:1–7, p. 904

Tell All About Him!, Matthew 28:19, p. 1326

Attention, Please!, Luke 8:11–15, p. 1383

"The Amen," the faithful and true witness, the beginning of all God has made,
says this: 15I know what you do, that you
are not hot or cold. I wish that you were
hot or cold! 16But because you are lukewarm—neither hot, nor cold—I am ready
to spit you out of my mouth. 17You say, 'I
am rich, and I have become wealthy and do not need anything.' But you do not know that you are really miserable, pitiful, poor, blind, and
naked. 18I advise you to buy from me gold made pure in fire so you can be truly rich. Buy from me white clothes so you can be clothed and so you can cover your shameful nakedness. Buy from me medicine to put on your eyes so you can truly see.

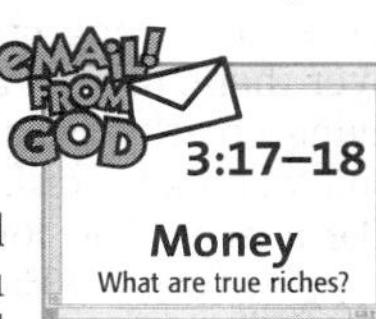
EMAIL FROM GOD
3:17–18
Money
What are true riches?

19"I correct and punish those whom I
love. So be eager to do right, and change
your hearts and lives. 20Here I am! I
stand at the door and knock. If you hear my voice and open the door, I will come in and eat with you, and you will eat with me.
21"Those who win the victory will sit
with me on my throne in the same way that I won the victory and sat down with
my Father on his throne. 22Everyone
who has ears should listen to what the Spirit says to the churches."

John Sees Heaven

4 After the vision of these things I looked, and there before me was an open door in heaven. And the same voice that spoke to me before, that sounded like a trumpet, said, "Come up here, and I will show you what must happen after
this." 2Immediately I was in the Spirit,
and before me was a throne in heaven,
and someone was sitting on it. 3The One
who sat on the throne looked like precious stones, like jasper and carnelian. All around the throne was a rainbow the
color of an emerald. 4Around the throne
there were twenty-four other thrones with twenty-four elders sitting on them. They were dressed in white and had

3:14 Amen Used here as a name for Jesus; it means to agree fully that something is true.

golden crowns on their heads. 5Lightning
flashes and noises and thundering came
from the throne. Before the throne seven
lamps were burning, which are the seven
spirits of God. 6Also before the throne
there was something that looked like a
sea of glass, clear like crystal.

In the center and around the throne
were four living creatures with eyes all
over them, in front and in back. 7The first
living creature was like a lion. The second was like a calf. The third had a face
like a man. The fourth was like a flying
eagle. 8Each of these four living
creatures had six
wings and was cov-
ered all over with
eyes, inside and out.
Day and night they
never stop saying:

EMAIL FROM GOD
4:8
Heaven
What will you see in heaven?

"Holy, holy, holy is the Lord God
Almighty.
He was, he is, and he is coming."

9These living creatures give glory,
honor, and thanks to the One who sits on
the throne, who lives forever and ever.
10Then the twenty-four elders bow down
before the One who sits on the throne,
and they worship him who lives forever
and ever. They put their crowns down before the throne and say:

11 "You are worthy, our Lord and God,
to receive glory and honor and
power,
because you made all things.
Everything existed and was made,
because you wanted it."

5 Then I saw a scroll in the right hand of
the One sitting on the throne. The
scroll had writing on both sides and was
kept closed with seven seals. 2And I saw
a powerful angel calling in a loud voice,
"Who is worthy to break the seals and
open the scroll?" 3But there was no one
in heaven or on earth or under the earth
who could open the scroll or look inside
it. 4I cried hard because there was no one
who was worthy to open the scroll or
look inside. 5But one of the elders said to
me, "Do not cry! The Lion[n] from the tribe
of Judah, David's descendant, has won
the victory so that he is able to open the
scroll and its seven seals."

FAITH links

PRAISE HIM!

REVELATION 5:12

Do you like to sing at church? What songs do you like to sing? Songs about Jesus help us praise him and express our love for him. Have you ever seen a large group of people singing the chorus to Handel's *Messiah?* Imagine seeing not people, but *angels* singing praises to God—more angels than you ever thought you would see and hear. In a vision of heaven, the apostle John saw and heard thousands and thousands of angels praising Jesus. Since God is so awesome, they couldn't help *but* praise him. Do you feel the same way? If so, give him some praise!

Want to tell God you love him? Connect here:

Idol Talk, Exodus 32, p. 118

Do What You Want?, Judges 21:25, p. 341

How Big Is God?, Job 38—41, p. 703

Our Awesome God, Ezekiel 1:26–28, p. 1087

Two Birthdays, John 3:1–7, p. 1426

The Sin Habit, Roman 7:15–20, p. 1527

6Then I saw a Lamb standing in the
center of the throne and in the middle of

5:5 Lion Here refers to Christ.

the four living creatures and the elders. The Lamb looked as if he had been killed. He had seven horns and seven eyes, which are the seven spirits of God that
were sent into all the world. 7The Lamb
came and took the scroll from the right hand of the One sitting on the throne.
8When he took the scroll, the four living creatures and the twenty-four elders bowed down before the Lamb. Each one of them had a harp and golden bowls full of incense, which are the prayers of
God's holy people. 9And they all sang a
new song to the Lamb:

"You are worthy to take the scroll
and to open its seals,
because you were killed,
and with the blood of your death
you bought people for God
from every tribe, language, people,
and nation.
10 You made them to be a kingdom of
priests for our God,
and they will rule on the earth."

11Then I looked, and I heard the voices of many angels around the throne, and the four living creatures, and the elders. There were thousands and thousands of angels, 12saying in a loud voice:

"The Lamb who was killed is worthy
to receive power, wealth, wisdom,
and strength,
honor, glory, and praise!"

13Then I heard all creatures in heaven and on earth and under the earth and in the sea saying:

"To the One who sits
on the throne
and to the Lamb
be praise and honor
and glory and
power
forever and ever."

14The four living creatures said, "Amen," and the elders bowed down and worshiped.

6 Then I watched while the Lamb opened the first of the seven seals. I heard one of the four living creatures say
with a voice like thunder, "Come!" 2I
looked, and there before me was a white horse. The rider on the horse held a bow, and he was given a crown, and he rode out, determined to win the victory.

3When the Lamb opened the second seal, I heard the second living creature
say, "Come!" 4Then another horse came out, a red one. Its rider was given power to take away peace from the earth and to make people kill each other, and he was given a big sword.

5When the Lamb opened the third seal, I heard the third living creature say, "Come!" I looked, and there before me was a black horse, and its rider held a pair
of scales in his hand. 6Then I heard something that sounded like a voice coming from the middle of the four living creatures. The voice said, "A quart of wheat for a day's pay, and three quarts of barley for a day's pay, and do not damage the olive oil and wine!"

7When the Lamb opened the fourth seal, I heard the voice of the fourth living
creature say, "Come!" 8I looked, and there before me was a pale horse. Its rider was named death, and Hades[n] was following close behind him. They were given power over a fourth of the earth to kill people by war, by starvation, by disease, and by the wild animals of the earth.

9When the Lamb opened the fifth seal, I saw under the altar the souls of those who had been killed because they were faithful to the word of God and to the message they had received. 10These souls shouted in a loud voice, "Holy and true Lord, how long until you judge the people of the earth and punish them for killing
us?" 11Then each one of them was given a white robe and was told to wait a short time longer. There were still some of their fellow servants and brothers and sisters[n] in

> Holy and true Lord, how long until you judge the people of the earth and punish them for killing us?
> —Revelation 6:10

6:8 Hades The unseen world of the dead.
6:11 brothers and sisters Although the Greek text says "brothers" here and throughout this book, both men and women would have been included.

the service of Christ who must be killed
as they were. They had to wait until all of
this was finished.
12Then I watched while the Lamb
opened the sixth seal, and there was a
great earthquake. The sun became black
like rough black cloth, and the whole
moon became red like blood. **13**And the
stars in the sky fell to the earth like figs
falling from a fig tree when the wind
blows. **14**The sky disappeared as a scroll
when it is rolled up, and every mountain
and island was moved from its place.
15Then the kings of the earth, the rulers, the generals, the rich people, the
powerful people, the slaves, and the free
people hid themselves in caves and in the
rocks on the mountains. **16**They called to
the mountains and the rocks, "Fall on us.
Hide us from the face of the One who sits
on the throne and from the anger of the
Lamb! **17**The great day for their anger
has come, and who can stand against it?"

The 144,000 People of Israel

7 After the vision of these things I saw
four angels standing at the four corners of the earth. The angels were holding the four winds of the earth to keep
them from blowing on the land or on the
sea or on any tree. **2**Then I saw another
angel coming up from the east who had
the seal of the living God. And he called
out in a loud voice to the four angels to
whom God had given power to harm the
earth and the sea. **3**He said to them, "Do
not harm the land or the sea or the trees
until we mark with a sign the foreheads
of the people who serve our God." **4**Then
I heard how many people were marked
with the sign. There were one hundred
forty-four thousand from every tribe of
the people of Israel.

5From the tribe of Judah twelve
thousand were marked with
the sign,
from the tribe of Reuben twelve
thousand,
from the tribe of Gad twelve
thousand,
6from the tribe of Asher twelve
thousand,
from the tribe of Naphtali
twelve thousand,
from the tribe of Manasseh
twelve thousand,
7from the tribe of Simeon twelve
thousand,
from the tribe of Levi twelve
thousand,
from the tribe of Issachar
twelve thousand,
8from the tribe of Zebulun
twelve thousand,
from the tribe of Joseph twelve
thousand,
and from the tribe of Benjamin
twelve thousand were
marked with the sign.

The Great Crowd Worships God

9After the vision of these things I
looked, and there was a great number of
people, so many that no one could count
them. They were from every nation,
tribe, people, and language of the earth.
They were all standing before the throne
and before the Lamb, wearing white
robes and holding palm branches in their
hands. **10**They were shouting in a loud
voice, "Salvation belongs to our God,
who sits on the throne, and to the Lamb."
11All the angels were standing around
the throne and the elders and the four living creatures. They all bowed down on
their faces before the throne and worshiped God, **12**saying, "Amen! Praise,
glory, wisdom, thanks, honor, power, and
strength belong to our God forever and
ever. Amen!"
13Then one of the elders asked me,
"Who are these people dressed in white
robes? Where did they come from?"
14I answered, "You know, sir."
And the elder said to me, "These are
the people who have come out of the
great distress. They have washed their
robes[n] and made them white in the blood
of the Lamb. **15**Because of this, they are
before the throne of God. They worship
him day and night in his temple. And the
One who sits on the throne will be pres-

7:14 washed their robes This means they believed in Jesus so that their sins could be forgiven by Christ's blood.

ent with them. 16Those people will never be hungry again, and they will never be thirsty again. The sun will not hurt them, and no heat will burn them, 17because the Lamb at the center of the throne will be their shepherd. He will lead them to springs of water that give life. And God will wipe away every tear from their eyes."

> EMAIL FROM GOD **7:17**
> **Heaven**
> Check out who will be at the center of heaven.

The Seventh Seal

8 When the Lamb opened the seventh seal, there was silence in heaven for about half an hour. 2And I saw the seven angels who stand before God and to whom were given seven trumpets.

3Another angel came and stood at the altar, holding a golden pan for incense. He was given much incense to offer with the prayers of all God's holy people. The angel put this offering on the golden altar before the throne. 4The smoke from the incense went up from the angel's hand to God with the prayers of God's people. 5Then the angel filled the incense pan with fire from the altar and threw it on the earth, and there were flashes of lightning, thunder and loud noises, and an earthquake.

The Seven Angels and Trumpets

6Then the seven angels who had the seven trumpets prepared to blow them.

7The first angel blew his trumpet, and hail and fire mixed with blood were poured down on the earth. And a third of the earth, and all the green grass, and a third of the trees were burned up.

8Then the second angel blew his trumpet, and something that looked like a big mountain, burning with fire, was thrown into the sea. And a third of the sea became blood, 9a third of the living things in the sea died, and a third of the ships were destroyed.

10Then the third angel blew his trumpet, and a large star, burning like a torch, fell from the sky. It fell on a third of the rivers and on the springs of water. 11The name of the star is Wormwood.[n] And a third of all the water became bitter, and many people died from drinking the water that was bitter.

12Then the fourth angel blew his trumpet, and a third of the sun, and a third of the moon, and a third of the stars were struck. So a third of them became dark, and a third of the day was without light, and also the night.

13While I watched, I heard an eagle that was flying high in the air cry out in a loud voice, "Trouble! Trouble! Trouble for those who live on the earth because of the remaining sounds of the trumpets that the other three angels are about to blow!"

9 Then the fifth angel blew his trumpet, and I saw a star fall from the sky to the earth. The star was given the key to the deep hole that leads to the bottomless pit. 2Then it opened up the hole that leads to the bottomless pit, and smoke came up from the hole like smoke from a big furnace. Then the sun and sky became dark because of the smoke from the hole. 3Then locusts came down to the earth out of the smoke, and they were given the power to sting like scorpions.[n] 4They were told not to harm the grass on the earth or any plant or tree. They could harm only the people who did not have the sign of God on their foreheads. 5These locusts were not given the power to kill anyone, but to cause pain to the people for five months. And the pain they felt was like the pain a scorpion gives when it stings someone. 6During those days people will look for a way to die, but they will not find it. They will want to die, but death will run away from them.

7The locusts looked like horses prepared for battle. On their heads they wore what looked like crowns of gold, and their faces looked like human faces. 8Their hair was like women's hair, and their teeth were like lions' teeth. 9Their chests looked like iron breastplates, and

8:11 Wormwood Name of a very bitter plant; used here to give the idea of bitter sorrow.
9:3 scorpions A scorpion is an insect that stings with a bad poison.

the sound of their wings was like the
noise of many horses and chariots hurrying into battle. **10**The locusts had tails
with stingers like scorpions, and in their
tails was their power to hurt people for
five months. **11**The locusts had a king
who was the angel of the bottomless pit.
His name in the Hebrew language is
Abaddon and in the Greek language is
Apollyon."

12The first trouble is past; there are
still two other troubles that will come.

13Then the sixth angel blew his trumpet, and I heard a voice coming from the
horns on the golden altar that is before
God. **14**The voice said to the sixth angel
who had the trumpet, "Free the four angels who are tied at the great river Euphrates." **15**And they let loose the four
angels who had been kept ready for this
hour and day and month and year so they
could kill a third of all people on the
earth. **16**I heard how many troops on
horses were in their army—two hundred
million.

17The horses and their riders I saw in
the vision looked like this: They had
breastplates that were fiery red, dark
blue, and yellow like sulfur. The heads of

9:11 Abaddon, Apollyon Both names mean "Destroyer."

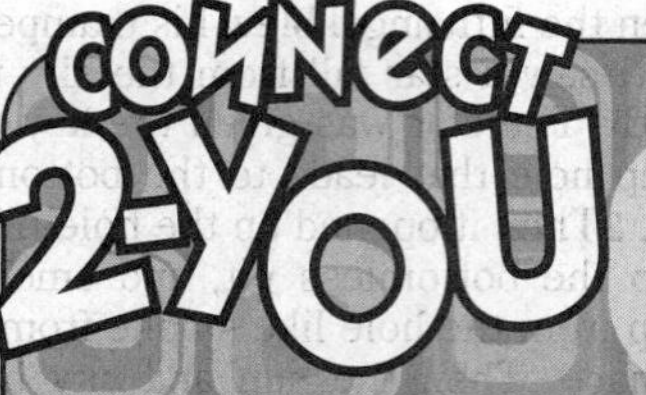

FORGIVE ME

Hey, everybody. Is there someone in your life that you need to forgive? Or that you need forgiveness from? We have a friend who's struggling in this area. Please welcome Joey, age 10, to Connect 2-You.

Hi, Joey. What's up?

Joey

A few weeks ago, my little sister destroyed my baseball card collection. She was mad at me, so she went into my room and started ripping

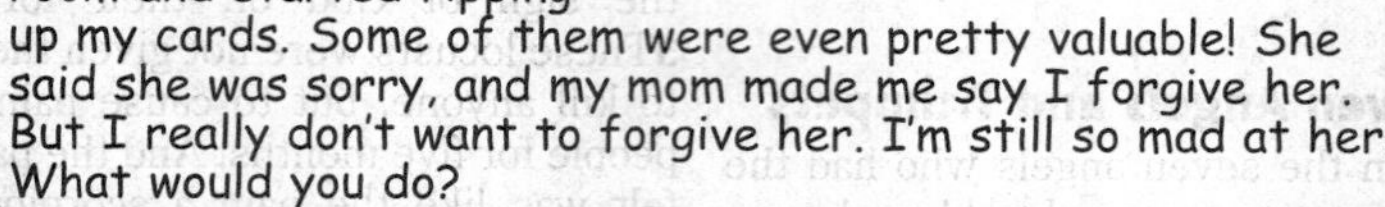

up my cards. Some of them were even pretty valuable! She said she was sorry, and my mom made me say I forgive her. But I really don't want to forgive her. I'm still so mad at her! What would you do?

I understand how you're feeling, Joey. It is hard to forgive someone when they do something mean to us. But think of it in this way: God forgives us for everything we do—no matter how bad it is—if we ask him to. And he wants us to do the same for people who ask us for forgiveness. If you would like some tips on how to accept your sister's apology, check out the Livin' It page on forgiveness, Genesis 50:14–21, p.71.

I know you're mad at your sister, Joey. But it's important for you to forgive her. It's pretty tough to ask God to forgive us if we're not willing to forgive others.

the horses looked like heads of lions, with fire, smoke, and sulfur coming out of their mouths. **18**A third of all the people on earth were killed by these three terrible disasters coming out of the horses' mouths: the fire, the smoke, and the sulfur. **19**The horses' power was in their mouths and in their tails; their tails were like snakes with heads, and with them they hurt people.

20The other people who were not killed by these terrible disasters still did not change their hearts and turn away from what they had made with their own hands. They did not stop worshiping demons and idols made of gold, silver, bronze, stone, and wood—things that cannot see or hear or walk. **21**These people did not change their hearts and turn away from murder or evil magic, from their sexual sins or stealing.

The Angel and the Small Scroll

10 Then I saw another powerful angel coming down from heaven dressed in a cloud with a rainbow over his head. His face was like the sun, and his legs were like pillars of fire. **2**The angel was holding a small scroll open in his hand. He put his right foot on the sea and his left foot on the land. **3**Then he shouted loudly like the roaring of a lion. And when he shouted, the voices of seven thunders spoke. **4**When the seven thunders spoke, I started to write. But I heard a voice from heaven say, "Keep hidden what the seven thunders said, and do not write them down."

> He is the One who made the skies and all that is in them, the earth and all that is in it.
> —Revelation 10:6

5Then the angel I saw standing on the sea and on the land raised his right hand to heaven, **6**and he made a promise by the power of the One who lives forever and ever. He is the One who made the skies and all that is in them, the earth and all that is in it, and the sea and all that is in it. The angel promised, "There will be no more waiting! **7**In the days when the seventh angel is ready to blow his trumpet, God's secret will be finished. This secret is the Good News God told to his servants, the prophets."

8Then I heard the same voice from heaven again, saying to me: "Go and take the open scroll that is in the hand of the angel that is standing on the sea and on the land."

9So I went to the angel and told him to give me the small scroll. And he said to me, "Take the scroll and eat it. It will be sour in your stomach, but in your mouth it will be sweet as honey." **10**So I took the small scroll from the angel's hand and ate it. In my mouth it tasted sweet as honey, but after I ate it, it was sour in my stomach. **11**Then I was told, "You must prophesy again about many peoples, nations, languages, and kings."

The Two Witnesses

11 I was given a measuring stick like a rod, and I was told, "Go and measure the temple of God and the altar, and count the people worshiping there. **2**But do not measure the yard outside the temple. Leave it alone, because it has been given to those who are not God's people. And they will trample on the holy city for forty-two months. **3**And I will give power to my two witnesses to prophesy for one thousand two hundred sixty days, and they will be dressed in rough cloth to show their sadness."

4These two witnesses are the two olive trees and the two lampstands that stand before the Lord of the earth. **5**And if anyone tries to hurt them, fire comes from their mouths and kills their enemies. And if anyone tries to hurt them in whatever way, in that same way that person will die. **6**These witnesses have the power to stop the sky from raining during the time they are prophesying. And they have power to make the waters become blood, and they have power to send every kind of trouble to the earth as many times as they want.

7When the two witnesses have finished

telling their message, the beast that
comes up from the bottomless pit will
fight a war against them. He will defeat
them and kill them. **8**The bodies of the
two witnesses will lie in the street of the
great city where the Lord was killed.
This city is named Sodom[n] and Egypt,
which has a spiritual meaning. **9**Those
from every race of people, tribe, language, and nation will look at the bodies
of the two witnesses for three and one-
half days, and they will refuse to bury
them. **10**People who live on the earth will
rejoice and be happy because these two
are dead. They will send each other gifts,
because these two prophets brought
much suffering to those who live on the
earth.

11But after three and one-half days,
God put the breath of life into the two
prophets again. They stood on their feet,
and everyone who saw them became
very afraid. **12**Then the two prophets
heard a loud voice from heaven saying,
"Come up here!" And they went up into
heaven in a cloud as their enemies
watched.

13In the same hour there was a great
earthquake, and a tenth of
the city was destroyed.
Seven thousand people
were killed in the earth-
quake, and those who did
not die were very afraid
and gave glory to the God
of heaven.

14The second trouble
is finished. Pay attention:
The third trouble is com-
ing soon.

> Then the seventh angel blew his trumpet.
> —Revelation 11:15

The Seventh Trumpet

15Then the seventh angel blew his
trumpet. And there were loud voices in
heaven, saying:

"The power to rule the world now
belongs to our Lord and his
Christ,
and he will rule forever and ever."

16Then the twenty-four elders, who
sit on their thrones before God, bowed
down on their faces and worshiped God.
17They said:

"We give thanks to you, Lord God
Almighty,
who is and who was,
because you have used your great
power
and have begun to rule!
18The people of the world were angry,
but your anger has come.
The time has come to judge the
dead,
and to reward your servants the
prophets
and your holy people,
all who respect you, great and
small.
The time has come to destroy those
who destroy the earth!"

19Then God's temple in heaven was
opened. The Ark that holds the agreement God gave to his people could be
seen in his temple. Then there were
flashes of lightning, noises, thunder, an
earthquake, and a great hailstorm.

The Woman and the Dragon

12 And then a great wonder appeared
in heaven: A woman was clothed
with the sun, and the moon was under
her feet, and a crown of
twelve stars was on her
head. **2**She was pregnant
and cried out with pain,
because she was about
to give birth. **3**Then another wonder appeared
in heaven: There was a
giant red dragon with
seven heads and seven
crowns on each head. He
also had ten horns. **4**His
tail swept a third of the stars out of the
sky and threw them down to the earth.
He stood in front of the woman who was
ready to give birth so he could eat her
baby as soon as it was born. **5**Then the
woman gave birth to a son who will rule all
the nations with an iron rod. And her child
was taken up to God and to his throne.
6The woman ran away into the desert to a
place God prepared for her where she

11:8 Sodom City that God destroyed because the people were so evil.

WHAT DO YOU CALL THE DEVIL? Revelation 12:9

Satan is the enemy of God, his people, and all that is good. He is evil. He is a liar. He constantly tempts people to sin. (Read 1 Thessalonians 3:5, p. 1632.) He fell from God's service and talked other angels into following him. (See Revelation 12:9.) When Jesus returns, Satan will be completely defeated and thrown into the lake of burning sulfur. (Look at Revelation 20:1–10.)

Here are some names for Satan used in the New Testament:

Beelzebul, ruler of demons	Matthew 12:24, p. 1295
The enemy	Matthew 13:39, p. 1298
A liar; the father of lies	John 8:44, p. 1438
Ruler of darkness	Ephesians 6:12, p. 1605
A roaring lion	1 Peter 5:8, p. 1706
Angel of the bottomless pit	Revelation 9:11, p. 1740
The dragon	Revelation 12:7, p. 1743
Old snake	Revelation 20:2, p. 1752

would be taken care of for one thousand two hundred sixty days.

7Then there was a war in heaven. Michael[n] and his angels fought against the dragon, and the dragon and his angels
fought back. **8**But the dragon was not strong enough, and he and his angels lost
their place in heaven. **9**The giant dragon was thrown down out of heaven. (He is that old snake called the devil or Satan, who tricks the whole world.) The dragon with his angels was thrown down to the earth.

10Then I heard a loud voice in heaven saying:

"The salvation and the power and the
kingdom of our God
and the authority of his Christ
have now come.
The accuser of our brothers and
sisters,
who accused them day and night
before our God,
has been thrown down.

11 And our brothers and sisters
defeated him
by the blood of the Lamb's death
and by the message they
preached.
They did not love their lives so much
that they were afraid of death.

12 So rejoice, you heavens
and all who live there!
But it will be terrible for the earth
and the sea,

12:7 Michael The archangel—leader among God's angels or messengers (Jude 9).

because the devil has come down
to you!
He is filled with anger,
because he knows he does not
have much time."

13When the dragon saw he had been
thrown down to the earth, he hunted for
the woman who had given birth to the
son. 14But the woman was given the two
wings of a great eagle so she could fly to
the place prepared for her in the desert.
There she would be taken care of for
three and one-half years, away from the
snake. 15Then the snake poured water
out of its mouth like a river toward the
woman so the flood would carry her away.
16But the earth helped the woman by
opening its mouth and swallowing the
river that came from the mouth of the
dragon. 17Then the dragon was very
angry at the woman, and he went off to
make war against all her other children—
those who obey God's commands and
who have the message Jesus taught.

18And the dragon stood on the seashore.

The Two Beasts

13 Then I saw a beast coming up out
of the sea. It had ten horns and
seven heads, and there was a crown on
each horn. A name against God was written on each head. 2This beast looked like
a leopard, with feet like a bear's feet and a
mouth like a lion's mouth. And the dragon gave the beast all of his power and
his throne and great authority. 3One of
the heads of the beast looked as if it had
been killed by a wound, but this death
wound was healed. Then the whole world
was amazed and followed the beast.
4People worshiped the dragon because
he had given his power to the beast. And
they also worshiped the beast, asking,
"Who is like the beast? Who can make
war against it?"

5The beast was allowed to say proud
words and words against God, and it was
allowed to use its power for forty-two
months. 6It used its mouth to speak
against God, against God's name, against
the place where God lives, and against all
those who live in heaven. 7It was given
power to make war against God's holy
people and to defeat them. It was given
power over every tribe, people, language, and nation. 8And all who live on
earth will worship the beast—all the people since the beginning of the world
whose names are not written in the

FAITH links

KEEP ON KEEPIN' ON

REVELATION 13:10

The apostle John had a vision of the future. He saw God's people going through a difficult time. They weren't going through hard times because they had done wrong. They were going through hard times because they were faithful to Jesus.

No one escapes hard times in this life. Hard times help develop perseverance. That's a long word meaning the determination to keep on going, no matter what. Those who endure to the end are rewarded. So, keep on being faithful to Jesus.

Here are some links to help you when the going gets tough:

Alone and Forgotten?, Genesis 40:23, p. 57

Who Ya' Gonna Call?, Psalm 3:4, p. 711

Be Brave!, Haggai 2:4, p. 1249

Our Good Shepherd, John 10:11–15, p. 1441

The Winner's Crown, 1 Corinthians 9:24–27, p. 1555

Keep Going!, James 1:2–3, p. 1688

Lamb's book of life. The Lamb is the One
who was killed.
9Anyone who has ears should listen:
10If you are to be a prisoner,
then you will be a prisoner.
If you are to be killed with the sword,
then you will be killed with the
sword.
This means that God's holy people must
have patience and faith.
11Then I saw another beast coming
up out of the earth. It had two horns like a
lamb, but it spoke like a dragon. **12**This
beast stands before the first beast and
uses the same power the first beast has.
By this power it makes everyone living
on earth worship the first beast, who had
the death wound that was healed. **13**And
the second beast does great miracles so
that it even makes fire come down from
heaven to earth while people are watching. **14**It fools those who live on earth by
the miracles it has been given the power
to do. It does these miracles to serve the
first beast. The second beast orders people to make an idol to honor the first
beast, the one that was wounded by the
deadly sword but sprang to life again.
15The second beast was given power to
give life to the idol of the first one so that
the idol could speak. And the second
beast was given power to command all
who will not worship the image of the
beast to be killed. **16**The second beast
also forced all people, small and great,
rich and poor, free and slave, to have a
mark on their right hand or on their forehead. **17**No one could buy or sell without
this mark, which is the name of the beast
or the number of its name. **18**This takes
wisdom. Let the one who has understanding find the meaning of the number,
which is the number of a person. Its number is six hundred sixty-six.

The Song of the Saved

14 Then I looked, and there before me
was the Lamb standing on Mount
Zion.[n] With him were one hundred forty-
four thousand people who had his name
and his Father's name written on their
foreheads. **2**And I heard a sound from
heaven like the noise of flooding water
and like the sound of loud thunder. The
sound I heard was like people playing
harps. **3**And they sang a new song before
the throne and before the four living
creatures and the elders. No one could
learn the new song except the one hundred forty-four thousand who had been
bought from the earth. **4**These are the
ones who did not do sinful things with
women, because they kept themselves
pure. They follow the Lamb every place
he goes. These one hundred forty-four

FAITH CHALLENGE

Hey there! Read 14:6-7 to get an idea of what God's judgment will be like. How do you feel when you hear that God will one day judge all people?

TESTING IT

Revelation 14:6–7

Then I saw another angel flying high in the air. He had the eternal Good News to preach to those who live on earth . . . "Fear God and give him praise, because the time has come for God to judge all people. So worship God who made the heavens, and the earth, and the sea, and the springs of water."

14:1 Mount Zion Another name for Jerusalem; here meaning the spiritual city of God's people.

thousand were bought from among the
people of the earth as people to be offered to God and the Lamb. 5They were
not guilty of telling lies; they are without
fault.

The Three Angels

6Then I saw another angel flying high
in the air. He had the eternal Good News
to preach to those who live on earth—to
every nation, tribe, language, and people.
7He preached in a loud voice, "Fear God
and give him praise, because the time has
come for God to judge all people. So worship God who made the heavens, and the
earth, and the sea, and the springs of
water."

8Then the second angel followed the
first angel and said, "Ruined, ruined is
the great city of Babylon! She made all
the nations drink the wine of the anger of
her adultery."

9Then a third angel followed the first
two angels, saying in a loud voice: "If
anyone worships the beast and his idol
and gets the beast's mark on the forehead or on the hand, 10that one also will
drink the wine of God's anger, which is
prepared with all its strength in the cup of
his anger. And that person will be put in
pain with burning sulfur before the holy
angels and the Lamb. 11And the smoke
from their burning pain will rise forever
and ever. There will be no rest, day or
night, for those who worship the beast
and his idol or who get the mark of his
name." 12This means God's holy people must be patient. They must obey
God's commands and keep their faith in
Jesus.

13Then I heard a voice from heaven
saying, "Write this: Happy are the dead
who die from now on in the Lord."

The Spirit says, "Yes, they will rest
from their hard work, and the reward of
all they have done stays with them."

The Earth Is Harvested

14Then I looked, and there before me
was a white cloud, and sitting on the
white cloud was One who looked like a
Son of Man.[n] He had a gold crown on his
head and a sharp sickle[n] in his hand.
15Then another angel came out of the
temple and called out in a loud voice to
the One who was sitting on the cloud,
"Take your sickle and harvest from the
earth, because the time to harvest has
come, and the fruit of the earth is ripe."
16So the One who was sitting on the
cloud swung his sickle over the earth,
and the earth was harvested.

17Then another angel came out of the
temple in heaven, and he also had a sharp
sickle. 18And then another angel, who
has power over the fire, came from the
altar. This angel called to the angel with
the sharp sickle, saying, "Take your
sharp sickle and gather the bunches of
grapes from the earth's vine, because
its grapes are ripe." 19Then the angel
swung his sickle over the earth. He gathered the earth's grapes and threw them
into the great winepress of God's anger.
20They were trampled in the winepress
outside the city, and blood flowed out of
the winepress as high as horses' bridles
for a distance of about one hundred
eighty miles.

The Last Troubles

15 Then I saw another wonder in
heaven that was great and amazing. There were seven angels bringing
seven disasters. These are the last disasters, because after them, God's anger is
finished.

2I saw what looked like a sea of glass
mixed with fire. All of those who had won
the victory over the beast and his idol and
over the number of his name
were standing by the
sea of glass. They
had harps that God
had given them.
3They sang the song
of Moses, the ser-
vant of God, and the song of the Lamb:

EMAIL FROM GOD
15:3–4
Worship
Will everyone worship
God someday?

"You do great and wonderful things,
Psalm 111:2
Lord God Almighty.
Amos 3:13

14:14 Son of Man "Son of Man" is a name Jesus called himself.

14:14 sickle A farming tool with a curved blade. It was used to harvest grain.

Everything the Lord does is right
and true, *Psalm 145:17*
King of the nations.
4 Everyone will respect you, Lord, *Jeremiah 10:7*
and will honor you.
Only you are holy.
All the nations will come
and worship you, *Psalm 86:9-10*
because the right things you have
done
are now made known." *Deuteronomy 32:4*
5After this I saw that the temple (the
Tent of the Agreement) in heaven was
opened. 6And the seven angels bringing
the seven disasters came out of the temple. They were dressed in clean, shining
linen and wore golden bands tied around
their chests. 7Then one of the four living
creatures gave to the seven angels seven
golden bowls filled with the anger of God,
who lives forever and ever. 8The temple
was filled with smoke from the glory and
the power of God, and no one could enter
the temple until the seven disasters of
the seven angels were finished.

The Bowls of God's Anger

16 Then I heard a loud voice from the
temple saying to the seven angels,
"Go and pour out the seven bowls of
God's anger on the earth."
2The first angel left and poured out
his bowl on the land. Then ugly and painful sores came upon all those who had the
mark of the beast and who worshiped his
idol.
3The second angel
poured out his bowl on the
sea, and it became blood
like that of a dead man,
and every living thing in
the sea died.
4The third angel
poured out his bowl on the
rivers and the springs of
water, and they became
blood. 5Then I heard the
angel of the waters saying:
"Holy One, you are the One who is
and who was.
You are right to decide to punish
these evil people.

> "Holy One, you are the One who is and who was. You are right to decide to punish these evil people."
> —Revelation 16:5

6 They have poured out the blood of
your holy people and your
prophets.
So now you have given them blood
to drink as they deserve."
7And I heard a voice coming from the altar saying:
"Yes, Lord God Almighty,
the way you punish evil people is
right and fair."
8The fourth angel poured out his bowl
on the sun, and he was given power to
burn the people with fire. 9They were
burned by the great heat, and they cursed
the name of God, who had control over
these disasters. But the people refused
to change their hearts and lives and give
glory to God.
10The fifth angel poured out his bowl
on the throne of the beast, and darkness
covered its kingdom. People gnawed
their tongues because of the pain.
11They also cursed the God of heaven
because of their pain and the sores they
had, but they refused to change their
hearts and turn away from the evil things
they did.
12The sixth angel poured out his bowl
on the great river Euphrates so that the
water in the river was dried up to prepare
the way for the kings from the east to
come. 13Then I saw three evil spirits
that looked like frogs coming out of the
mouth of the dragon, out of the mouth of
the beast, and out of the mouth of the
false prophet. 14These evil spirits are
the spirits of demons,
which have power to do
miracles. They go out to
the kings of the whole
world to gather them to-
gether for the battle on
the great day of God Al-
mighty.
15"Listen! I will come
as a thief comes! Happy
are those who stay awake
and keep their clothes on
so that they will not walk around naked
and have people see their shame."
16Then the evil spirits gathered the
kings together to the place that is called
Armageddon in the Hebrew language.

17The seventh angel poured out his bowl into the air. Then a loud voice came out of the temple from the throne, saying, "It is finished!" **18**Then there were flashes of lightning, noises, thunder, and a big earthquake—the worst earthquake that has ever happened since people have been on earth. **19**The great city split into three parts, and the cities of the nations were destroyed. And God remembered the sins of Babylon the Great, so he gave that city the cup filled with the wine of his terrible anger. **20**Then every island ran away, and mountains disappeared. **21**Giant hailstones, each weighing about a hundred pounds, fell from the sky upon people. People cursed God for the disaster of the hail, because this disaster was so terrible.

The Woman on the Animal

17 Then one of the seven angels who had the seven bowls came and spoke to me. He said, "Come, and I will show you the punishment that will be given to the great prostitute, the one sitting over many waters. **2**The kings of the earth sinned sexually with her, and the people of the earth became drunk from the wine of her sexual sin."

3Then the angel carried me away by the Spirit to the desert. There I saw a woman sitting on a red beast. It was covered with names against God written on it, and it had seven heads and ten horns. **4**The woman was dressed in purple and red and was shining with the gold, precious jewels, and pearls she was wearing. She had a golden cup in her hand, a cup filled with evil things and the uncleanness of her sexual sin. **5**On her forehead a title was written that was secret. This is what was written:

THE GREAT BABYLON
MOTHER OF PROSTITUTES
AND OF THE EVIL THINGS OF THE EARTH

6Then I saw that the woman was drunk with the blood of God's holy people and with the blood of those who were killed because of their faith in Jesus.

When I saw the woman, I was very amazed. **7**Then the angel said to me, "Why are you amazed? I will tell you the secret of this woman and the beast she rides—the one with seven heads and ten horns. **8**The beast you saw was once alive but is not alive now. But soon it will come up out of the bottomless pit and go away to be destroyed. There are people who live on earth whose names have not been written in the book of life since the beginning of the world. They will be amazed when they see the beast, because he was once alive, is not alive now, but will come again.

9"You need a wise mind to understand this. The seven heads on the beast are seven mountains where the woman sits. **10**And they are seven kings. Five of the kings have already been destroyed, one of the kings lives now, and another has not yet come. When he comes, he must stay a short time. **11**The beast that was once alive, but is not alive now, is also an eighth king. He belongs to the first seven kings, and he will go away to be destroyed.

12"The ten horns you saw are ten kings who have not yet begun to rule, but they will receive power to rule with the beast for one hour. **13**All ten of these kings have the same purpose, and they will give their power and authority to the beast. **14**They will make war against the Lamb, but the Lamb will defeat them, because he is Lord of lords and King of kings. He will defeat them with his called, chosen, and faithful followers."

He will defeat them with his called, chosen, and faithful followers.
—Revelation 17:14

15Then the angel said to me, "The waters that you saw, where the prostitute sits, are peoples, races, nations, and languages. **16**The ten horns and the beast you saw will hate the prostitute. They will take everything she has and leave her naked. They will eat her body and burn her with fire. **17**God made the ten horns want to

carry out his purpose by agreeing to give
the beast their power to rule, until what
God has said comes about. 18The woman
you saw is the great city that rules over
the kings of the earth."

Babylon Is Destroyed

18 After the vision of these things, I
saw another angel coming down
from heaven. This angel had great power,
and his glory made the earth bright. 2He
shouted in a powerful voice:

"Ruined, ruined is the great city of
Babylon!
She has become a home for
demons
and a prison for every evil spirit,
and a prison for every unclean bird
and unclean beast.
3She has been ruined, because all the
peoples of the earth
have drunk the wine of the desire
of her sexual sin.
She has been ruined also because the
kings of the earth
have sinned sexually with her,
and the merchants of the earth
have grown rich from the great
wealth of her luxury."

4Then I heard another voice from
heaven saying:

"Come out of that city, my people,

WISE WORDS

Hi, kids. Tagg and I are talking about listening to what other people say. We have a friend who's having a problem in this area. Let's let him tell you about it. Please welcome Danny, 10, to Connect 2-You.

Hello, Danny. What's your problem?

Danny

Well, I hate to call him a problem because I love him, but it's my grandfather. He's always trying to give me advice about what I should and shouldn't do. He always says it in a nice way, but it's still hard to listen to him. I mean, what does he know? He was a kid, like, 60 years ago.

I hear you, Danny. It can be frustrating to have people always tell you what's best for you. But the Bible says your grandfather's words are a valuable treasure. I hope you don't let them go to waste.

That's right, Danny. It's called wisdom, and it means knowing the right thing to do. Because your grandfather has been around for so long and has seen so much, he knows things that you may never learn—unless you listen to him. Remember, God has put him in your life for a reason. For more tips in this area, check out the Livin' It page on wisdom, Proverbs 2, p. 827.

so that you will not share in her
sins,
so that you will not receive the
disasters that will come to her.
5 Her sins have piled up as high as the
sky,
and God has not forgotten the
wrongs she has done.
6 Give that city the same as she gave
to others.
Pay her back twice as much as she
did.
Prepare wine for her that is twice as
strong
as the wine she prepared for
others.
7 She gave herself much glory and rich
living.
Give her that much suffering and
sadness.
She says to herself, 'I am a queen
sitting on my throne.
I am not a widow; I will never be
sad.'
8 So these disasters will come to her in
one day:
death, and crying, and great
hunger,
and she will be destroyed by
fire,
because the Lord God who judges
her is powerful."
9 The kings of the earth who sinned
sexually with her and shared her wealth
will see the smoke from her burning.
Then they will cry and be sad because of
her death. 10 They will be afraid of her
suffering and stand far away and say:
"Terrible! How terrible for you, great
city,
powerful city of Babylon,
because your punishment has come
in one hour!"
11 And the merchants of the earth will
cry and be sad about her, because now
there is no one to buy their cargoes—
12 cargoes of gold, silver, jewels, pearls,
fine linen, purple cloth, silk, red cloth; all
kinds of citron wood and all kinds of
things made from ivory, expensive wood,
bronze, iron, and marble; 13 cinnamon,
spice, incense, myrrh, frankincense,
wine, olive oil, fine flour, wheat, cattle,
sheep, horses, carriages, slaves, and human lives.
14 The merchants will say,
"Babylon, the good things you
wanted are gone from you.
All your rich and fancy things have
disappeared.
You will never have them again."
15 The merchants who became rich from
selling to her will be afraid of her suffering and will stand far away. They will cry
and be sad 16 and say:
"Terrible! How terrible for the great
city!
She was dressed in fine linen,
purple and red cloth,
and she was shining with gold,
precious jewels, and pearls!
17 All these riches have been destroyed
in one hour!"
Every sea captain, every passenger,
the sailors, and all those who earn their
living from the sea stood far away from
Babylon. 18 As they saw the smoke from
her burning, they cried out loudly, "There
was never a city like this great city!"
19 And they threw dust on their heads
and cried out, weeping and being sad.
They said:
"Terrible! How terrible for the great
city!
All the people who had ships on the
sea
became rich because of her wealth!
But she has been destroyed in one
hour!
20 Be happy because of this, heaven!
Be happy, God's holy people and
apostles and prophets!
God has punished her because of
what she did to you."
21 Then a powerful angel picked up a
large stone, like one used for grinding
grain, and threw it into the sea. He said:
"In the same way, the great city of
Babylon will be thrown down,
and it will never be found again.
22 The music of people playing harps
and other instruments, flutes,
and trumpets,
will never be heard in you again.
No workman doing any job
will ever be found in you again.

The sound of grinding grain
will never be heard in you again.
23 The light of a lamp
will never shine in you again,
and the voices of a bridegroom and bride
will never be heard in you again.
Your merchants were the world's great people,
and all the nations were tricked by your magic.
24 You are guilty of the death of the prophets and God's holy people
and all who have been killed on earth."

People in Heaven Praise God

19 After this vision and announcement I heard what sounded like a great many people in heaven saying:
"Hallelujah!ⁿ
Salvation, glory, and power belong to our God,
2 because his judgments are true and right.
He has punished the prostitute
who made the earth evil with her sexual sin.
He has paid her back for the death of his servants."
3 Again they said:
"Hallelujah!
She is burning, and her smoke will rise forever and ever."
4 Then the twenty-four elders and the four living creatures bowed down and worshiped God, who sits on the throne. They said:
"Amen, Hallelujah!"
5 Then a voice came from the throne, saying:
"Praise our God, all you who serve him
and all you who honor him, both small and great!"
6 Then I heard what sounded like a great many people, like the noise of flooding water, and like the noise of loud thunder. The people were saying:

> On his robe and on his upper leg was written this name:
> KING OF KINGS AND LORD OF LORDS.
> —Revelation 19:16

"Hallelujah!
Our Lord God, the Almighty, rules.
7 Let us rejoice and be happy
and give God glory,
because the wedding of the Lamb has come,
and the Lamb's bride has made herself ready.
8 Fine linen, bright and clean, was given to her to wear."
(The fine linen means the good things done by God's holy people.)
9 And the angel said to me, "Write
this: Happy are those who have been invited to the wedding meal of the Lamb!" And the angel said, "These are the true words of God."
10 Then I bowed down at the angel's
feet to worship him, but he said to me, "Do not worship me! I am a servant like you and your brothers and sisters who have the message of Jesus. Worship God, because the message about Jesus is the spirit that gives all prophecy."

The Rider on the White Horse

11 Then I saw heaven opened, and
there before me was a white horse. The rider on the horse is called Faithful and True, and he is right when he judges and
makes war. 12 His eyes are like burning
fire, and on his head are many crowns. He has a name written on him, which no one
but himself knows. 13 He is dressed in a
robe dipped in blood, and his name is the
Word of God. 14 The armies of heaven, dressed in fine linen, white and clean, were following him
on white horses. 15 Out of
the rider's mouth comes a sharp sword that he will use to defeat the nations, and he will rule them with a rod of iron. He will crush out the wine in the winepress of the terrible
anger of God the Almighty. 16 On his robe
and on his upper leg was written this name: KING OF KINGS AND LORD OF LORDS.

19:1 Hallelujah This means "praise God!"

17Then I saw an angel standing in the
sun, and he called with a loud voice to all
the birds flying in the sky: "Come and
gather together for the great feast of God
18so that you can eat the bodies of kings,
generals, mighty people, horses and their
riders, and the bodies of
all people—free, slave,
small, and great."
19Then I saw the
beast and the kings of
the earth. Their armies
were gathered together
to make war against the
rider on the horse and his
army. **20**But the beast
was captured and with
him the false prophet who
did the miracles for the beast. The false
prophet had used these miracles to trick
those who had the mark of the beast and
worshiped his idol. The false prophet and
the beast were thrown alive into the lake
of fire that burns with sulfur. **21**And their
armies were killed with the sword that
came out of the mouth of the rider on the
horse, and all the birds ate the bodies until they were full.

The Thousand Years

20 I saw an angel coming down from
heaven. He had the key to the bottomless pit and a large chain in his hand.
2The angel grabbed the dragon, that old
snake who is the devil and Satan, and tied
him up for a thousand years. **3**Then he
threw him into the bottomless pit, closed
it, and locked it over him. The angel did
this so he could not trick the people of
the earth anymore until the thousand
years were ended. After a thousand years
he must be set free for a short time.
4Then I saw some thrones and people
sitting on them who had been given the
power to judge. And I saw the souls of
those who had been killed because they
were faithful to the message of Jesus and
the message from God. They had not
worshiped the beast or his idol, and they
had not received the mark of the beast on
their foreheads or on their hands. They
came back to life and ruled with Christ
for a thousand years. **5**(The others that
were dead did not live again until the
thousand years were ended.) This is the
first raising of the dead. **6**Happy and holy
are those who share in this first raising of
the dead. The second death has no power
over them. They will be priests for God
and for Christ and will
rule with him for a thousand years.
7When the thousand
years are over, Satan will
be set free from his prison. **8**Then he will go out
to trick the nations in all
the earth—Gog and Magog—to gather them for
battle. There are so many
people they will be like
sand on the seashore. **9**And Satan's army
marched across the earth and gathered
around the camp of God's people and the
city God loves. But fire came down from
heaven and burned them up. **10**And
Satan, who tricked them, was thrown
into the lake of burning sulfur with the
beast and the false prophet. There they
will be punished day and night forever
and ever.

> Happy and holy are those who share in this first raising of the dead. The second death has no power over them.
> —Revelation 20:6

People of the World Are Judged

11Then I saw a great white throne and
the One who was sitting on it. Earth and
sky ran away from him and disappeared.
12And I saw the dead, great and small,
standing before the throne. Then books
were opened, and the book of life was
opened. The dead were judged by what
they had done, which was written in the
books. **13**The sea gave up the dead who
were in it, and Death and Hades[n] gave up
the dead who were in them. Each person
was judged by what he had done. **14**And
Death and Hades were thrown into the
lake of fire. The lake of fire is the second
death. **15**And anyone whose name was
not found written in the book of life was
thrown into the lake of fire.

The New Jerusalem

21 Then I saw a new heaven and a
new earth. The first heaven and

20:13 Hades The place of the dead.

the first earth had disappeared, and there
was no sea anymore. 2And I saw the holy
city, the new Jerusalem,* coming down
out of heaven from God. It was prepared
like a bride dressed for her husband.
3And I heard a loud voice from the
throne, saying, "Now God's presence is
with people, and he will live with them,
and they will be his people. God himself
will be with them and will be their God.
4He will wipe away every tear from their
eyes, and there will be no more death,

21:4

Heaven

Will you be sad in heaven?

sadness, crying, or
pain, because all the
old ways are gone."
5The One who
was sitting on the
throne said, "Look!
I am making every-
thing new!" Then he said, "Write this,
because these words are true and can be
trusted."
6The One on the throne said to me,
"It is finished. I am the Alpha and the
Omega,* the Beginning and the End. I
will give free water from the spring of the
water of life to anyone who is thirsty.
7Those who win the victory will receive
this, and I will be their God, and they will
be my children. 8But cowards, those who
refuse to believe, who do evil things, who
kill, who sin sexually, who do evil magic,
who worship idols, and who tell lies—all
these will have a place in the lake of burning sulfur. This is the second death."
9Then one of the seven angels who
had the seven bowls full of the seven last
troubles came to me, saying, "Come with
me, and I will show you the bride, the
wife of the Lamb." 10And the angel carried me away by the Spirit to a very large
and high mountain. He showed me the
holy city, Jerusalem, coming down out of
heaven from God. 11It was shining with
the glory of God and was bright like a
very expensive jewel, like a jasper, clear
as crystal. 12The city had a great high
wall with twelve gates with twelve angels at the gates, and on each gate was
written the name of one of the twelve
tribes of Israel. 13There were three
gates on the east, three on the north,
three on the south, and three on the
west. 14The walls of the city were built
on twelve foundation stones, and on the
stones were written the names of the
twelve apostles of the Lamb.
15The angel who talked with me had a
measuring rod made of gold to measure

21:2 new Jerusalem The spiritual city where God's people live with him.

21:6 Alpha and the Omega The first and last letters of the Greek alphabet. This means "the beginning and the end."

A HEAVENLY SIGHT

REVELATION 21:1-4

What is the most beautiful city you have ever seen? What did you like best about that place? The apostle John saw a vision of heaven. What an amazing place! God had created a new heaven and a new earth. No one would be sad or lonely or filled with hate ever again. This was a hopeful sight for John.

If you fear what the future may hold, think about John's vision of heaven. We have a bright future ahead!

Fearful Service?, Exodus 4:1–17, p. 80

Approaching God, Numbers 3:10, p. 180

All Talk, No Action, Jeremiah 5:1–2, p. 996

Uprooted by Change, Amos 9:15, p. 1205

Just a Test, Luke 4:1–13, p. 1373

The Way to Heaven, John 14:1–6, p. 1448

the city, its gates, and its wall. **16**The city
was built in a square, and its length was
equal to its width. The angel measured
the city with the rod. The city was twelve
thousand stadia[n] long, twelve thousand
stadia wide, and twelve thousand stadia
high. **17**The angel also measured the
wall. It was one hundred forty-four
cubits[n] high, by human measurements,
which the angel was using. **18**The wall
was made of jasper, and the city was
made of pure gold, as pure as glass.
19The foundation stones of the city walls
were decorated with every kind of jewel.
The first foundation was jasper, the second was sapphire, the third was chal-
cedony, the fourth was emerald, **20**the
fifth was onyx, the sixth was carnelian,
the seventh was chrysolite, the eighth
was beryl, the ninth was topaz, the tenth
was chrysoprase, the eleventh was jacinth, and the twelfth was amethyst.
21The twelve gates were twelve pearls,
each gate having been made from a single
pearl. And the street of the city was made
of pure gold as clear as glass.

22I did not see a temple in the city,
because the Lord God Almighty and the
Lamb are the city's temple. **23**The city
does not need the sun or the moon to
shine on it, because the glory of God is its
light, and the Lamb is the city's lamp.
24By its light the people of the world will
walk, and the kings of the earth will bring
their glory into it. **25**The city's gates will
never be shut on any day, because there
is no night there. **26**The glory and the
honor of the nations will be brought into
it. **27**Nothing unclean and no one who
does shameful things or tells lies will
ever go into it. Only those whose names
are written in the Lamb's book of life will
enter the city.

22 Then the angel showed me the
river of the water of life. It was
shining like crystal and was flowing from
the throne of God and of the Lamb **2**down

FAITH links

A HAPPY ENDING

REVELATION 22:16-21

What's your favorite story? Most people like a story with a happy ending. Want to know a real-life story that has a guaranteed happy ending? Your story. If you trust Jesus as your Savior, you have that hope of Jesus' return. He's already made it possible for you to be forgiven of sin. Now he's preparing a place for you to live in heaven with him forever.

In this passage, the apostle John looked forward to the second coming of Jesus. John was tired of hard times and the evil that never seemed to go away. The thought of Jesus' return gave him comfort. Do you look forward to Jesus' return? Then, join John and Christians throughout the ages in saying, "Amen. Come, Lord Jesus!"

Worried about the future? Download these links:

A Holiday Every Week, Leviticus 23:1–3, p. 166

The One Who Suffered, Isaiah 53, p. 966

A Fair-weather Friend, Obadiah 7, p. 1209

Rock Solid, Habakkuk 1:12, p. 1236

Prove It!, Matthew 16:1–4, p. 1302

Just for the Asking, Romans 3:23–28, p. 1522

21:16 stadia One stadion was a distance of about two hundred yards; about one-eighth of a Roman mile.

21:17 cubits A cubit is about half a yard, the length from the elbow to the tip of the little finger.

the middle of the street of the city. The
tree of life was on each side of the river. It
produces fruit twelve times a year, once
each month. The leaves of the tree are
for the healing of all the nations. **3**Nothing that God judges guilty will be in that
city. The throne of God and of the Lamb
will be there, and God's servants will
worship him. **4**They will see his face, and
his name will be written on their foreheads. **5**There will never be night again.
They will not need the light of a lamp or
the light of the sun, because the Lord
God will give them light. And they will
rule as kings forever and ever.

6The angel said to me, "These words
can be trusted and are true." The Lord,
the God of the spirits of the prophets,
sent his angel to show his servants the
things that must happen soon.

7"Listen! I am coming soon! Happy is
the one who obeys the words of prophecy
in this book."

8I, John, am the one who heard and
saw these things. When I heard and saw
them, I bowed down to worship
at the feet of the
angel who showed
these things to me.
9But the angel said
to me, "Do not wor-
ship me! I am a ser-
vant like you, your brothers the prophets,
and all those who obey the words in this
book. Worship God!"

EMAIL! FROM GOD
22:8–9
Heaven
Who had a vision of heaven?

10Then the angel told me, "Do not
keep secret the words of prophecy in this
book, because the time is near for all this
to happen. **11**Let whoever is doing evil
continue to do evil. Let whoever is unclean continue to be unclean. Let whoever is doing right continue to do right.
Let whoever is holy continue to be holy."

12"Listen! I am coming soon! I will
bring my reward with me, and I will
repay each one of you for what you have
done. **13**I am the Alpha and the Omega,"[n]
the First and the Last, the Beginning and
the End.

14"Happy are those who wash their
robes[n] so that they will receive the right
to eat the fruit from the tree of life and
may go through the gates into the city.
15Outside the city are the evil people,
those who do evil magic, who sin sexually, who murder, who worship idols, and
who love lies and tell lies.

16"I, Jesus, have sent my angel to tell
you these things for the churches. I am
the descendant from the family of David,
and I am the bright morning star."

17The Spirit and the bride say,
"Come!" Let the one who hears this say,
"Come!" Let whoever is thirsty come;
whoever wishes may have the water of
life as a free gift.

18I warn everyone who hears the
words of the prophecy of this book: If
anyone adds anything to these words,
God will add to that person the disasters
written about in this book. **19**And if anyone takes away from the words of this
book of prophecy, God will take away that
one's share of the tree of life and of the
holy city, which are written about in this
book.

20Jesus, the One who says these
things are true, says, "Yes, I am coming
soon."

Amen. Come, Lord Jesus!

21The grace of the Lord Jesus be with
all. Amen.

22:13 Alpha and the Omega The first and last letters of the Greek alphabet. This means "the beginning and the end."

22:14 wash their robes This means they believed and obeyed Jesus so that their sins could be forgiven by Christ's blood. The "washing" may refer to baptism (Acts 22:16).

SEARCH ENGINE

ACTIONS

ADVICE

ANGELS

ANGER

ANSWERS TO PRAYERS

ARGUING

AUTHORITY

BAD TIMES

BEHAVIOR

BELIEVING

BIBLE STUDY

BLESSINGS

BRAVERY

CARING FOR ANIMALS

CARING FOR OTHERS

CELEBRATING

CHANGE

CHOICES

CHRISTIAN(S)

CHURCH ATTENDANCE

CHURCH

COMFORTING OTHERS

COMPASSION

CONFESSING MY SINS

CONFLICTS

CONTENTMENT

CONTROLLING WHAT I SAY

COURAGE

DUTIES

ENCOURAGEMENT

ENCOURAGING OTHERS

ENDURANCE

ENEMIES

ENVY

ETERNAL LIFE

FAILURES

FAIRNESS

FAITH

FAMILY

FEARS

FIGHTING

FOLLOWING JESUS

FORGIVENESS

FORGIVING OTHERS

FRIENDSHIPS

GENTLENESS

GIFTS FROM GOD

GIVING

GOALS

GOD

GOOD DEEDS

GOSSIP

GRACE

GREED

GUILTY

HAPPINESS

HEAVEN

HOLY SPIRIT

HONESTY

HONORING PARENT(S)

HOPE

HOSPITALITY

HUMBLENESS

JEALOUSY

JOY

JUDGMENT

KINDNESS

LEADERS

LISTENING TO GOD

LISTENING TO OTHERS

LONELINESS

LOVE

LOVING LIKE GOD LOVES

NEED(S)

OBEYING GOD

OBEYING OTHERS

OBEYING THE LAW

OBLIGATIONS

PARENT(S)

PATIENCE

PEACE

PEACEMAKING

PEER PRESSURE

PERSEVERANCE (KEEP GOING)

POPULARITY

PRAISING GOD

PRAYING

PRIDE

PRIORITIES

PROBLEMS

PROMISES

PROTECTION

QUITTING

REPENTANCE

REPUTATION

RESPECTING MY ELDERS

RESPECTING OTHERS

RESPONSIBILITY

RESURRECTION

REVENGE

RULES

RUMORS

SADNESS

SALVATION

SELF-CONTROL

SELF-ESTEEM

SELFISHNESS

SERVING

SHARING

SHARING MY FAITH

SINS

STEWARDSHIP

SUFFERING

SUNDAY SCHOOL

SUPERSTITION

TALENTS

TEACHERS

TEMPTATION

TRUSTING IN OTHERS

TRUTHFULNESS

WEAKNESSES

WISDOM

SKWEEK & TAGG'S
TOP 50 BIBLE SITES

Want to know where to quickly find the Top 50 most visited sites in the Bible?

That's easy! Just stop here and you can quickly locate where to go to read about those well-known stories, like David and Goliath or the flood or when Jesus came into Jerusalem. When you're finished reading them, come back here, check it off the list, and go on to the next site. By the way, my favorite story is Jesus feeding all those hungry people with only two fish and five loaves of bread!

You got it, Tagg. This is an easy and quick way to read through the highlights in the Bible—all you have to do is pick where you want to start!

Check box after visiting each site ✔

A

Abraham and Isaac
Genesis 11:27—25:11, p. 17 ☐

Adam and Eve
Genesis 2:4—3:24, p. 5 ☐

B

Beatitudes
Matthew 5:1–12, p. 1280 ☐
Luke 6:20–23, p. 1378 ☐

C

Cain and Abel
Genesis 4:1–24, p. 8 ☐

Creation
Genesis 1:1—2:3, p. 1 ☐
Genesis 2:4–25, p. 5 ☐

D

Daniel
Daniel 1—6, p. 1150 ☐

Daniel and His Friends
Daniel 3, p. 1153 ☐

David, the King
1 Samuel 16—30, p. 374 ☐
2 Samuel 1—24, p. 399 ☐
1 Chronicles 11—22; 28; 29, p. 534 ☐

David and Goliath
1 Samuel 17, p. 375 ☐

E

Elijah the Prophet
1 Kings 17—19; 21, p. 462 ☐

F

Fruit of the Spirit
Galatians 5:22–23, p. 1593 ☐

G

Golden Rule
Matthew 7:12, p. 1286 ☐

Good Samaritan
Luke 10:25–37, p. 1388 ☐

Great Commandment
Matthew 22:34–40, p. 1313 ☐
Mark 12:28–34, p. 1351 ☐
Luke 10:25–28, p. 1388 ☐

Great Commission
Matthew 28:18–20, p. 1327 ☐

J

Jacob
Genesis 25:19—33:20; 35, p. 34 ☐

Jesus' Birth and Boyhood
Matthew 1:18—2:23, p. 1275 ☐
Luke 2, p. 1367 ☐

Jesus' Baptism
Matthew 3:13–17, p. 1278 ☐
Mark 1:9–11, p. 1330 ☐
Luke 3:21–22, p. 1372 ☐

Jesus' Temptation
Matthew 4:1–11, p. 1279 ☐
Mark 1:12–13, p. 1330 ☐
Luke 4:1–13, p. 1373 ☐

Jesus' Glory Revealed (Transfiguration)
Matthew 17:1–13, p. 1303 ☐
Mark 9:2–13, p. 1344 ☐
Luke 9:28–36, p. 1385 ☐

Jesus Entering Jerusalem
Matthew 21:1–11, p. 1310 ☐
Mark 11:1–11, p. 1348 ☐
Luke 19:28–40, p. 1407 ☐
John 12:12–19, p. 1445 ☐

Jesus' Last Supper (the Lord's Supper)
Matthew 26:26–30, p. 1321 ☐
Mark 14:22–26, p. 1356 ☐
Luke 22:14–38, p. 1412 ☐
1 Corinthians 11:23–25, p. 1557 ☐

Jesus' Arrest
Matthew 26:47–56, p. 1322 ☐
Mark 14:43–50, p. 1357 ☐
Luke 22:47–53, p. 1415 ☐
John 18:3–14, p. 1454 ☐

Jesus' Crucifixion (death)
Matthew 27:32–66, p. 1325 ☐
Mark 15:21–47, p. 1359 ☐
Luke 23:26–56, p. 1416 ☐

Jesus' Resurrection
Matthew 28:1–15, p. 1326 ☐
Mark 16:1–13, p. 1360 ☐
Luke 24:1–12, p. 1417 ☐
John 20:1–18, p. 1458 ☐

Jesus' Ascension (going to heaven)
Mark 16:19–20, p. 1362 ☐
Luke 24:50–53, p. 1419 ☐

JESUS' MIRACLES (SELECTED)

Calming the Storm
Matthew 8:23–27, p. 1288 ☐
Mark 4:35–41, p. 1336 ☐
Luke 8:22–25, p. 1382 ☐

Feeding the Crowds
Matthew 14:13–21, p. 1299 ☐
Matthew 15:32–39, p. 1301 ☐
Mark 6:30–44, p. 1340 ☐
Mark 8:1–10, p. 1342 ☐
Luke 9:10–17, p. 1385 ☐
John 6:5–15, p. 1432 ☐

Raising Lazarus from the Dead
John 11:1–44, p. 1442 ☐

John the Baptist
Matthew 3:1–12, p. 1277 ☐
Mark 1:1–8, p. 1330 ☐
Luke 3:1–20, p. 1371 ☐
John 1:19–28, p. 1422 ☐

Jonah
Jonah 1—4, p. 1213 ☐

Joseph, the Boy Sold by His Brothers
Genesis 37; 39—50, p. 51 ☐

Joshua
Joshua 1—12; 23; 24, p. 276 ☐

L

Lord's Prayer
Matthew 6:9–13, p. 1283 ☐
Luke 11:1–4, p. 1389 ☐

Love Chapter
1 Corinthians 13, p. 1560 ☐

M

Moses
Exodus 2—19; 32—34, p. 77 ❑

N

New Birth
John 3, p. 1426 ❑

Noah and the Flood
Genesis 6:9—8:22, p. 10 ❑

P

Passover
Exodus 12:1–30, p. 90 ❑

Paul
Acts 9—28, p. 1478 ❑

Pentecost
Acts 2:1–42, p. 1464 ❑

Prodigal Son
Luke 15:11–32, p. 1399 ❑

R

Ruth
Ruth 1—4, p. 345 ❑

S

Samson
Judges 13—16, p. 330 ❑

Samuel
1 Samuel 1—3; 7—16, p. 354 ❑

Saul, King of Israel
1 Samuel 8—11; 13; 15; 28; 31, p. 362 ❑

Sermon on the Mount
Matthew 5—7, p. 1280 ❑
Luke 6:20–49, p. 1378 ❑

Shepherd Psalm
Psalm 23, p. 726 ❑

Sower and the Seeds
Matthew 13:1–23, p. 1296 ❑
Mark 4:1–20, p. 1335 ❑
Luke 8:4–15, p. 1382 ❑

T

Ten Commandments
Exodus 20:1–17, p. 101 ❑
Deuteronomy 5:1–21, p. 235 ❑

Z

Zacchaeus
Luke 19:1–10, p. 1406 ❑

HOW TO READ YOUR

KIDSBIBLE.COM

Hey, Skweek, everybody knows that it's a good thing to read your Bible. But it's such a big book! I mean, how are you supposed to get started?

That's a good question, Tagg. And believe it or not, there are a lot of different ways to read through your Bible. When you think about it, the Bible is really a mini-library because it is one book that contains 66 different books.

Wow! I never thought about it that way before! That's a lot of reading to do!

Right! But we've got several different ways you can read *KidsBible.com* that break the Bible into easy-to-manage pieces. Take a look below at the different ways you can get started on this exciting, life-changing journey!

SKWEEK & TAGG'S

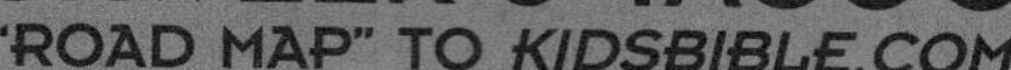

30 DAYS WITH JESUS

On this *KidsBible.com* journey, you will spend 30 days retracing the path Jesus took while he was here on earth. You'll read about his much-awaited birth, his boyhood, the beginning of his ministry, his key teachings, and about the ultimate sacrifice Jesus made so we can live with him in heaven for all eternity. You won't want to miss a day!

50 DAYS IN THE NEW TESTAMENT

These next 50 days will focus on what happened *after* Jesus returned to heaven. You'll meet many of the leaders of the early church—Peter, James, Stephen, John, and of course, Paul. You will follow Paul's adventures and struggles as he spreads the Good News of Jesus to the world, and you'll hear many of his key teachings to those early Christian communities.

You will read letters from James (Jesus' half brother), Peter, and John with teaching that is as important to us today as it was to those early believers. You'll complete your trek by reading about the final, yet-to-happen event—when Jesus will return and establish a new world and a new kingdom!

50 DAYS IN THE OLD TESTAMENT

In the beginning . . . those words are probably familiar to you, and you probably have heard many of the stories from the Old Testament. But have you ever followed the stories from the beginning to see where they fit into the history of Israel? Here's an opportunity to spend 50 days in the Old Testament, hitting the highlights of some familiar Bible heroes, like Abraham, Moses, David, Daniel, and others. You will discover that the Old Testament is really one story about God's love for his people and his ultimate plan to send a Savior for people then and today—his Son, Jesus Christ.

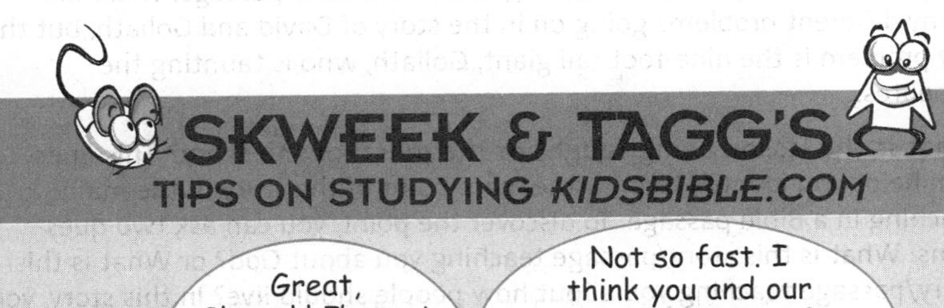
SKWEEK & TAGG'S
TIPS ON STUDYING *KIDSBIBLE.COM*

Great, Skweek! I've got my *KidsBible.com;* I've got my "road map" for reading the Bible; I'm all set to go!
Not so fast. I think you and our friend would benefit from knowing something about how to *study* the Bible.
What do you mean *study?* Are we taking a test or something?
Hold on, Tagg! We're not going to be testing anybody about anything! But remember, the Bible is God's Word. It's filled with lots of good instructions on how to live, how to handle those difficult situations in your life, and how to be a follower of Jesus. If you're just reading the stories and not really thinking about what these stories mean to you, then you probably will miss out on a lot of what God has to say to you!

I never thought about reading the Bible like that before! What do I have to do?

Well, there are many different ways to study the Bible. Here's one that just uses four questions. When you read a Bible passage or story, you can ask:

- **Who are the people in the story?** This helps you identify who's involved in the Bible passage or story. Take the story of David and Goliath, for example, 1 Samuel 17, p. 375. The main characters involved in this familiar story are the Israelites led by King Saul; their archenemies, the Philistines; the Philistines' champion fighter, Goliath; and a young shepherd boy named David.

  In a Bible passage, the people may not be as easy to identify. But remember, the people can be the ones hearing the story or teaching and/or the person telling the story or teaching.

- **What's the problem or the teaching in this story or passage?** This question is asking you to tell in your own words what is going on in the story or what the person is teaching about in a Bible passage. There are many different problems going on in the story of David and Goliath, but the ***big*** problem is the nine-foot tall giant, Goliath, who is taunting the Israelites.

- **What is the lesson being taught or the moral of the story?** This question helps you identify what is the main point of the story or the main teaching in a Bible passage. To discover the point, you can ask two questions: What is this story/passage teaching you about God? or What is this story/passage teaching you about how people should live? In this story, you learn that God can help you defeat the big problems in your life and that God wants his people to trust and depend on him.

- **What does God want me to do?** This is where God speaks to you! Maybe you decide that God wants you to face the "giants" in your life—whether it's tomorrow's math test or the boy down the street who calls you names. Or maybe God wants you to trust him to help you through the battles in your life.

One more thing. When you read your Bible, you might want to write down your answers to these four questions or to any others that you may have about the passage. You don't have to write a lot; just jot down a sentence or two. We've included a few lines with each Bible reading entry so you can write down what you have learned in your *KidsBible.com.*

OK, Skweek, now are we ready? Let the journey begin!

30 DAYS WITH JESUS

1. John 1:1–51 ❑
What I learned …

2. Luke 2:1–52 ❑
What I learned …

3. Mark 1:1–11 ❑
What I learned …

4. Luke 4:1–44 ❑
What I learned …

5. John 3:1–36 ❑
What I learned …

6. Luke 5:1–39 ❑
What I learned …

7. John 4:1–54 ❑
What I learned …

8. Luke 6:1–49 ❑
What I learned …

9. Luke 7:1–50 ❑
What I learned …

10. Luke 8:1–56 ❑
What I learned …

11. Mark 8:1–38 ❑
What I learned …

12. Luke 10:1–52 ❑
What I learned …

13. Matthew 5:1–48 ❑
What I learned …

14. Matthew 6:1–34 ❑
What I learned …

15. Matthew 7:1–29 ❑
What I learned …

16. Luke 14:1–35 ❑
What I learned …

17. Luke 15:1–32 ❑
What I learned …

18. Luke 16:1–31 ❑
What I learned …

19. John 8:1–59 ❑
What I learned …

20. Luke 17:1–37 ❑
What I learned …

21. Luke 18:1–43 ❑
What I learned …

22. John 9:1–41 ❑
What I learned …

23. Luke 19:1–48 ❑
What I learned …

24. Luke 20:1–47 ❑
What I learned …

25. John 10:1–42 ❑
What I learned …

26. John 11:1–57 ❑
What I learned …

27. Mark 13:1–37 ❑
What I learned …

28. Luke 22:1–71 ❑
What I learned …

29. Matthew 27:1–66 ❑
What I learned …

30. Luke 24:1–53 ❑
What I learned …

50 DAYS IN THE NEW TESTAMENT

1. Acts 1:1–11 ☐
What I learned ...

2. Acts 2:1–47 ☐
What I learned ...

3. Acts 8:26–40 ☐
What I learned ...

4. Acts 9:1–31 ☐
What I learned ...

5. Acts 11:1–18 ☐
What I learned ...

6. Acts 16:11–40 ☐
What I learned ...

7. Acts 17:16–33 ☐
What I learned ...

8. Acts 21:1–16, 27–40 ☐
What I learned ...

9. Acts 26:1–32 ☐
What I learned ...

10. Acts 27:13–44 ☐
What I learned ...

11. Acts 28:16–31 ☐
What I learned ...

12. Romans 3:1–31 ☐
What I learned ...

13. Romans 8:1–39 ☐
What I learned ...

14. Romans 12:1–21 ☐
What I learned ...

15. 1 Corinthians 13:1–13 ☐
What I learned ...

16. 1 Corinthians 15:1–58 ☐
What I learned ...

17. 2 Corinthians 1:15—2:11 ❑
What I learned ...

18. 2 Corinthians 4:1–18 ❑
What I learned ...

19. 2 Corinthians 8:1–15 ❑
What I learned ...

20. Galatians 2:11–21 ❑
What I learned ...

21. Galatians 5:1–26 ❑
What I learned ...

22. Galatians 6:1–10 ❑
What I learned ...

23. Ephesians 2:1–22 ❑
What I learned ...

24. Ephesians 5:1–21 ❑
What I learned ...

25. Ephesians 5:22—6:9 ❑
What I learned ...

26. Ephesians 6:10–20 ❑
What I learned ...

27. Philippians 1:3–26 ❑
What I learned ...

28. Philippians 2:5–18 ❑
What I learned ...

29. Philippians 3:1–16 ❑
What I learned ...

30. Philippians 4:1–13 ❑
What I learned ...

31. Colossians 1:15–29 ❑
What I learned ...

32. Colossians 3:1—4:1 ❑
What I learned ...

33. 1 Thessalonians 4:1–18 ❑
What I learned ...

34. 1 Thessalonians 5:1–11 ❑
What I learned ...

35. 2 Thessalonians 2:1–12 ❑
What I learned ...

36. 1 Timothy 6:1–19 ❑
What I learned ...

37. 2 Timothy 2:1–26 ❑
What I learned ...

38. Titus 3:1–11 ❑
What I learned ...

39. Philemon 8–20 ❑
What I learned ...

40. Hebrews 11:1–40 ❑
What I learned ...

41. Hebrews 12:1–11 ❑
What I learned ...

42. James 1:1–27 ❑
What I learned ...

43. James 2:1–19 ❑
What I learned ...

44. James 3:1–18 ❑
What I learned ...

45. James 5:1–18 ❑
What I learned ...

46. 1 Peter 1:3–25 ❑
What I learned ...

47. 2 Peter 1:3–21 ❑
What I learned ...

48. 1 John 1:1—2:17 ❑
What I learned ...

49. Revelation 4:1–11 ❑
What I learned ...

50. Revelation 21:1—22:21 ❑
What I learned ...

50 DAYS IN THE OLD TESTAMENT

1. Genesis 1:1—2:3 ☐
What I learned ...

2. Genesis 3:1–24 ☐
What I learned ...

3. Genesis 6:9—7:24 ☐
What I learned ...

4. Genesis 8:1—9:17 ☐
What I learned ...

5. Genesis 17:1–22 ☐
What I learned ...

6. Genesis 22:1–19 ☐
What I learned ...

7. Genesis 25:19–34 ☐
What I learned ...

8. Genesis 27:1—28:9 ☐
What I learned ...

9. Genesis 37:1–36 ☐
What I learned ...

10. Genesis 41:1–57 ☐
What I learned ...

11. Genesis 45:1–28 ☐
What I learned ...

12. Exodus 1:8—2:15 ☐
What I learned ...

13. Exodus 3:1—4:17 ☐
What I learned ...

14. Exodus 5:1—6:13 ☐
What I learned ...

15. Exodus 12:1–42 ☐
What I learned ...

16. Exodus 13:17—14:31 ☐
What I learned ...

17. Exodus 20:1–21 ❑
What I learned . . .

18. Numbers 13:1–33 ❑
What I learned . . .

19. Joshua 2:1–24 ❑
What I learned . . .

20. Joshua 6:1–27 ❑
What I learned . . .

21. Judges 16:4–31 ❑
What I learned . . .

22. 1 Samuel 1:1–28 ❑
What I learned . . .

23. 1 Samuel 3:1–21 ❑
What I learned . . .

24. 1 Samuel 10:1–27 ❑
What I learned . . .

25. 1 Samuel 16:1–13 ❑
What I learned . . .

26. 1 Samuel 17:1–58 ❑
What I learned . . .

27. 1 Samuel 24:1–22 ❑
What I learned . . .

28. 2 Samuel 11:1—12:25 ❑
What I learned . . .

29. 1 Kings 3:1–28 ❑
What I learned . . .

30. 1 Kings 17:8–24 ❑
What I learned . . .

31. 1 Kings 18:1–46 ❑
What I learned . . .

32. 2 Kings 2:1–18 ❑
What I learned . . .

33. 2 Kings 4:8–37 ❑
What I learned . . .

34. 2 Chronicles 35:20—36:23 ❑
What I learned . . .

35. Esther 2:1–23 ❑
What I learned ...

36. Esther 6:1—8:8 ❑
What I learned ...

37. Job 1:1—2:13 ❑
What I learned ...

38. Job 42:1–17 ❑
What I learned ...

39. Psalm 23 ❑
What I learned ...

40. Psalm 51 ❑
What I learned ...

41. Psalm 100 ❑
What I learned ...

42. Psalm 121 ❑
What I learned ...

43. Psalm 145 ❑
What I learned ...

44. Proverbs 4:1–27 ❑
What I learned ...

45. Ecclesiastes 11:9—12:14 ❑
What I learned ...

46. Isaiah 53:1–12 ❑
What I learned ...

47. Daniel 1:1–21 ❑
What I learned ...

48. Daniel 3:1–30 ❑
What I learned ...

49. Daniel 6:1–28 ❑
What I learned ...

50. Jonah 1:1—4:11 ❑
What I learned ...